The Dictionary of Art · volume twenty-two

The Dictionary of Art

22

Montald

TO

Neufforge

GROVE

The Dictionary of Art

edited by JANE TURNER, in thirty-four volumes, 1996

Reprinted with minor corrections, 1998

This edition is distributed within the United Kingdom and Europe
by Macmillan Publishers Limited, London, and within the United States and Canada by
Grove's Dictionaries Inc., New York.

Text keyboarded by Wearset Limited, Sunderland, England
Database management by Pindar plc, York, England
Imagesetting by William Clowes Limited, Suffolk, England
Printed and bound by China Translation and Printing Services Ltd, Hong Kong

British Library Cataloguing in Publication Data

The dictionary of art
  1. Art - Dictionaries 2. Art - History -
    Dictionaries
  I. Turner, Jane
  703

ISBN 1-884446-00-0

Library of Congress Cataloging in Publication Data

The dictionary of art / editor, Jane Turner.
  p. cm.
  Includes bibliographical references and index.
  Contents: 1. A to Anckerman
  ISBN 1-884446-00-0 (alk. paper)
  1. Art—Encyclopedias.
  I. Turner, Jane, 1956–
N31.D5   1996   96–13628
703—dc20   CIP

Contents

General Abbreviations

The abbreviations employed throughout this dictionary, most of which are listed below, do not vary, except for capitalization, regardless of the context in which they are used, including bibliographical citations and for locations of works of art. The principle used to arrive at these abbreviations is that their full form should be easily deducible, and for this reason acronyms have generally been avoided (e.g. Los Angeles Co. Mus. A. instead of LACMA). The same abbreviation is adopted for cognate forms in foreign languages and in most cases for plural and adjectival forms (e.g. A.= Art, Arts, Arte, Arti etc). Not all related forms are listed below. Occasionally, if a name, for instance of an artists' group or exhibiting society, is repeated within the text of one article, it is cited in an abbreviated form after its first mention in full (e.g. The Pre-Raphaelite Brotherhood (PRB) was founded...); the same is true of archaeological periods and eras, which are abbreviated to initial letters in small capitals (e.g. In the Early Minoan (EM) period...). Such abbreviations do not appear in this list. For the reader's convenience, separate full lists of abbreviations for locations, periodical titles and standard reference books and series are included as Appendices A–C in vol. 33.

A.	Art, Arts	Anthropol.	Anthropology	Azerbaij.	Azerbaijani
A.C.	Arts Council	Antiqua.	Antiquarian, Antiquaries	B.	Bartsch [catalogue of Old Master prints]
Acad.	Academy	app.	appendix		
AD	Anno Domini	approx.	approximately	b	born
Add.	Additional, Addendum	AR	Arkansas (USA)	BA	Bachelor of Arts
addn	addition	ARA	Associate of the Royal Academy	Balt.	Baltic
Admin.	Administration			bapt	baptized
Adv.	Advances, Advanced	Arab.	Arabic	BArch	Bachelor of Architecture
Aesth.	Aesthetic(s)	Archaeol.	Archaeology	Bart	Baronet
Afr.	African	Archit.	Architecture, Architectural	Bask.	Basketry
Afrik.	Afrikaans, Afrikaner	Archv, Archvs	Archive(s)	BBC	British Broadcasting Corporation
A.G.	Art Gallery				
Agrar.	Agrarian	Arg.	Argentine	BC	Before Christ
Agric.	Agriculture	ARHA	Associate of the Royal Hibernian Academy	BC	British Columbia (Canada)
Agron.	Agronomy			BE	Buddhist era
Agy	Agency	ARIBA	Associate of the Royal Institute of British Architects	Beds	Bedfordshire (GB)
AH	Anno Hegirae	Armen.	Armenian	Behav.	Behavioural
A. Inst.	Art Institute	ARSA	Associate of the Royal Scottish Academy	Belarus.	Belarusian
AK	Alaska (USA)			Belg.	Belgian
AL	Alabama (USA)	Asiat.	Asiatic	Berks	Berkshire (GB)
Alb.	Albanian	Assist.	Assistance	Berwicks	Berwickshire (GB; old)
Alg.	Algerian	Assoc.	Association	BFA	Bachelor of Fine Arts
Alta	Alberta (Canada)	Astron.	Astronomy	Bibl.	Bible, Biblical
Altern.	Alternative	AT&T	American Telephone & Telegraph Company	Bibliog.	Bibliography, Bibliographical
a.m.	ante meridiem [before noon]			Biblioph.	Bibliophile
Amat.	Amateur	attrib.	attribution, attributed to	Biog.	Biography, Biographical
Amer.	American	Aug	August	Biol.	Biology, Biological
An.	Annals	Aust.	Austrian	bk, bks	book(s)
Anatol.	Anatolian	Austral.	Australian	Bkbinder	Bookbinder
Anc.	Ancient	Auth.	Author(s)	Bklore	Booklore
Annu.	Annual	Auton.	Autonomous	Bkshop	Bookshop
Anon.	Anonymous(ly)	Aux.	Auxiliary	BL	British Library
Ant.	Antique	Ave.	Avenue	Bld	Build
Anthol.	Anthology	AZ	Arizona (USA)	Bldg	Building

Bldr	Builder	Chin.	Chinese	Cur.	Curator, Curatorial, Curatorship
BLitt	Bachelor of Letters/Literature	Christ.	Christian, Christianity	Curr.	Current(s)
BM	British Museum	Chron.	Chronicle	CVO	Commander of the [Royal] Victorian Order
Boh.	Bohemian	Cie	Compagnie [French]	Cyclad.	Cycladic
Boliv.	Bolivian	Cinema.	Cinematography	Cyp.	Cypriot
Botan.	Botany, Botanical	Circ.	Circle	Czech.	Czechoslovak
BP	Before present (1950)	Civ.	Civil, Civic	$	dollars
Braz.	Brazilian	Civiliz.	Civilization(s)	*d*	died
BRD	Bundesrepublik Deutschland [Federal Republic of Germany (West Germany)]	Class.	Classic, Classical	d.	denarius, denarii [penny, pence]
		Clin.	Clinical		
		CO	Colorado (USA)	Dalmat.	Dalmatian
Brecons	Breconshire (GB; old)	Co.	Company; County	Dan.	Danish
Brez.	Brezonek [lang. of Brittany]	Cod.	Codex, Codices	DBE	Dame Commander of the Order of the British Empire
Brit.	British	Col., Cols	Collection(s); Column(s)		
Bros	Brothers	Coll.	College	DC	District of Columbia (USA)
BSc	Bachelor of Science	collab.	in collaboration with, collaborated, collaborative	DDR	Deutsche Demokratische Republik [German Democratic Republic (East Germany)]
Bucks	Buckinghamshire (GB)				
Bulg.	Bulgarian	Collct.	Collecting		
Bull.	Bulletin	Colloq.	Colloquies	DE	Delaware (USA)
bur	buried	Colomb.	Colombian	Dec	December
Burm.	Burmese	Colon.	Colonies, Colonial	Dec.	Decorative
Byz.	Byzantine	Colr	Collector	ded.	dedication, dedicated to
C	Celsius	Comm.	Commission; Community	Democ.	Democracy, Democratic
C.	Century	Commerc.	Commercial	Demog.	Demography, Demographic
c.	*circa* [about]	Communic.	Communications	Denbs	Denbighshire (GB; old)
CA	California	Comp.	Comparative; compiled by, compiler	dep.	deposited at
Cab.	Cabinet			Dept	Department
Caerns	Caernarvonshire (GB; old)	Concent.	Concentration	Dept.	Departmental, Departments
C.A.G.	City Art Gallery	Concr.	Concrete	Derbys	Derbyshire (GB)
Cal.	Calendar	Confed.	Confederation	Des.	Design
Callig.	Calligraphy	Confer.	Conference	destr.	destroyed
Cam.	Camera	Congol.	Congolese	Dev.	Development
Cambs	Cambridgeshire (GB)	Congr.	Congress	Devon	Devonshire (GB)
can	canonized	Conserv.	Conservation; Conservatory	Dial.	Dialogue
Can.	Canadian	Constr.	Construction(al)	diam.	diameter
Cant.	Canton(s), Cantonal	cont.	continued	Diff.	Diffusion
Capt.	Captain	Contemp.	Contemporary	Dig.	Digest
Cards	Cardiganshire (GB; old)	Contrib.	Contributions, Contributor(s)	Dip. Eng.	Diploma in Engineering
Carib.	Caribbean	Convalesc.	Convalescence	Dir.	Direction, Directed
Carms	Carmarthenshire (GB; old)	Convent.	Convention	Directrt	Directorate
Cartog.	Cartography	Coop.	Cooperation	Disc.	Discussion
Cat.	Catalan	Coord.	Coordination	diss.	dissertation
cat.	catalogue	Copt.	Coptic	Distr.	District
Cath.	Catholic	Corp.	Corporation, Corpus	Div.	Division
CBE	Commander of the Order of the British Empire	Corr.	Correspondence	DLitt	Doctor of Letters/Literature
		Cors.	Corsican	DM	Deutsche Mark
Celeb.	Celebration	Cost.	Costume	Doc.	Document(s)
Celt.	Celtic	Cret.	Cretan	Doss.	Dossier
Cent.	Centre, Central	Crim.	Criminal	DPhil	Doctor of Philosophy
Centen.	Centennial	Crit.	Critical, Criticism	Dr	Doctor
Cer.	Ceramic	Croat.	Croatian	Drg, Drgs	Drawing(s)
cf.	confer [compare]	CT	Connecticut (USA)	DSc	Doctor of Science/Historical Sciences
Chap., Chaps	Chapter(s)	Cttee	Committee		
Chem.	Chemistry	Cub.	Cuban	Dut.	Dutch
Ches	Cheshire (GB)	Cult.	Cultural, Culture	Dwell.	Dwelling
Chil.	Chilean	Cumb.	Cumberland (GB; old)	E.	East(ern)

EC	European (Economic) Community	figs	figures	Heb.	Hebrew
Eccles.	Ecclesiastical	Filip.	Filipina(s), Filipino(s)	Hell.	Hellenic
Econ.	Economic, Economies	Fin.	Finnish	Her.	Heritage
Ecuad.	Ecuadorean	FL	Florida (USA)	Herald.	Heraldry, Heraldic
ed.	editor, edited (by)	*fl*	*floruit* [he/she flourished]	Hereford & Worcs	Hereford & Worcester (GB)
edn	edition	Flem.	Flemish		
eds	editors	Flints	Flintshire (GB; old)	Herts	Hertfordshire (GB)
Educ.	Education	Flk	Folk	HI	Hawaii (USA)
e.g.	*exempli gratia* [for example]	Flklore	Folklore	Hib.	Hibernia
Egyp.	Egyptian	fol., fols	folio(s)	Hisp.	Hispanic
Elem.	Element(s), Elementary	Found.	Foundation	Hist.	History, Historical
Emp.	Empirical	Fr.	French	HMS	His/Her Majesty's Ship
Emul.	Emulation	frag.	fragment	Hon.	Honorary, Honourable
Enc.	Encyclopedia	Fri.	Friday	Horiz.	Horizon
Encour.	Encouragement	FRIBA	Fellow of the Royal Institute of British Architects	Hort.	Horticulture
Eng.	English			Hosp.	Hospital(s)
Engin.	Engineer, Engineering	FRS	Fellow of the Royal Society, London	HRH	His/Her Royal Highness
Engr., Engrs	Engraving(s)			Human.	Humanities, Humanism
		ft	foot, feet	Hung.	Hungarian
Envmt	Environment	Furn.	Furniture	Hunts	Huntingdonshire (GB; old)
Epig.	Epigraphy	Futur.	Futurist, Futurism	IA	Iowa
Episc.	Episcopal	g	gram(s)	ibid.	*ibidem* [in the same place]
Esp.	Especially	GA	Georgia (USA)	ICA	Institute of Contemporary Arts
Ess.	Essays	Gael.	Gaelic		
est.	established	Gal., Gals	Gallery, Galleries	Ice.	Icelandic
etc	*etcetera* [and so on]	Gaz.	Gazette	Iconog.	Iconography
Ethnog.	Ethnography	GB	Great Britain	Iconol.	Iconology
Ethnol.	Ethnology	Gdn, Gdns	Garden(s)	ID	Idaho (USA)
Etrus.	Etruscan	Gdnr(s)	Gardener(s)	i.e.	*id est* [that is]
Eur.	European	Gen.	General	IL	Illinois (USA)
Evangel.	Evangelical	Geneal.	Genealogy, Genealogist	Illum.	Illumination
Exam.	Examination	Gent.	Gentleman, Gentlemen	illus.	illustrated, illustration
Excav.	Excavation, Excavated	Geog.	Geography	Imp.	Imperial
Exch.	Exchange	Geol.	Geology	IN	Indiana (USA)
Excurs.	Excursion	Geom.	Geometry	in., ins	inch(es)
exh.	exhibition	Georg.	Georgian	Inc.	Incorporated
Exp.	Exposition	Geosci.	Geoscience	inc.	incomplete
Expermntl	Experimental	Ger.	German, Germanic	incl.	includes, including, inclusive
Explor.	Exploration	G.I.	Government/General Issue (USA)	Incorp.	Incorporation
Expn	Expansion			Ind.	Indian
Ext.	External	Glams	Glamorganshire (GB; old)	Indep.	Independent
Extn	Extension	Glos	Gloucestershire (GB)	Indig.	Indigenous
f, ff	following page, following pages	Govt	Government	Indol.	Indology
		Gr.	Greek	Indon.	Indonesian
F.A.	Fine Art(s)	Grad.	Graduate	Indust.	Industrial
Fac.	Faculty	Graph.	Graphic	Inf.	Information
facs.	facsimile	Green.	Greenlandic	Inq.	Inquiry
Fam.	Family	Gr.-Roman	Greco-Roman	Inscr.	Inscribed, Inscription
fasc.	fascicle	Gt	Great	Inst.	Institute(s)
fd	feastday (of a saint)	Gtr	Greater	Inst. A.	Institute of Art
Feb	February	Guat.	Guatemalan	Instr.	Instrument, Instrumental
Fed.	Federation, Federal	Gym.	Gymnasium	Int.	International
Fem.	Feminist	h.	height	Intell.	Intelligence
Fest.	Festival	ha	hectare	Inter.	Interior(s), Internal
fig.	figure (illustration)	Hait.	Haitian	Interdiscip.	Interdisciplinary
Fig.	Figurative	Hants	Hampshire (GB)	intro.	introduced by, introduction
		Hb.	Handbook	inv.	inventory

Inven.	Invention	m	metre(s)	Moldov.	Moldovan
Invest.	Investigation(s)	m.	married	MOMA	Museum of Modern Art
Iran.	Iranian	M.	Monsieur	Mon.	Monday
irreg.	irregular(ly)	MA	Master of Arts; Massachusetts (USA)	Mongol.	Mongolian
Islam.	Islamic			Mons	Monmouthshire (GB; old)
Isr.	Israeli	Mag.	Magazine	Montgoms	Montgomeryshire (GB; old)
It.	Italian	Maint.	Maintenance	Mor.	Moral
J.	Journal	Malay.	Malaysian	Morav.	Moravian
Jam.	Jamaican	Man.	Manitoba (Canada); Manual	Moroc.	Moroccan
Jan	January	Manuf.	Manufactures	Movt	Movement
Jap.	Japanese	Mar.	Marine, Maritime	MP	Member of Parliament
Jav.	Javanese	Mason.	Masonic	MPhil	Master of Philosophy
Jew.	Jewish	Mat.	Material(s)	MS	Mississippi (USA)
Jewel.	Jewellery	Math.	Mathematic	MS., MSS	manuscript(s)
Jord.	Jordanian	MBE	Member of the Order of the British Empire	MSc	Master of Science
jr	junior			MT	Montana (USA)
Juris.	Jurisdiction	MD	Doctor of Medicine; Maryland (USA)	Mt	Mount
KBE	Knight Commander of the Order of the British Empire			Mthly	Monthly
		ME	Maine (USA)	Mun.	Municipal
KCVO	Knight Commander of the Royal Victorian Order	Mech.	Mechanical	Mus.	Museum(s)
		Med.	Medieval; Medium, Media	Mus. A.	Museum of Art
kg	kilogram(s)	Medic.	Medical, Medicine	Mus. F.A.	Museum of Fine Art(s)
kHz	kilohertz	Medit.	Mediterranean	Music.	Musicology
km	kilometre(s)	Mem.	Memorial(s); Memoir(s)	N.	North(ern); National
Knowl.	Knowledge	Merions	Merionethshire (GB; old)	n	refractive index of a medium
Kor.	Korean	Meso-Amer.	Meso-American		
KS	Kansas (USA)			n.	note
KY	Kentucky (USA)	Mesop.	Mesopotamian	N.A.G.	National Art Gallery
Kyrgyz.	Kyrgyzstani	Met.	Metropolitan	Nat.	Natural, Nature
£	libra, librae [pound, pounds sterling]	Metal.	Metallurgy	Naut.	Nautical
		Mex.	Mexican	NB	New Brunswick (Canada)
l.	length	MFA	Master of Fine Arts	NC	North Carolina (USA)
LA	Louisiana (USA)	mg	milligram(s)	ND	North Dakota (USA)
Lab.	Laboratory	Mgmt	Management	n.d.	no date
Lancs	Lancashire (GB)	Mgr	Monsignor	NE	Nebraska; Northeast(ern)
Lang.	Language(s)	MI	Michigan	Neth.	Netherlandish
Lat.	Latin	Micrones.	Micronesian	Newslett.	Newsletter
Latv.	Latvian	Mid. Amer.	Middle American	Nfld	Newfoundland (Canada)
lb, lbs	pound(s) weight	Middx	Middlesex (GB; old)	N.G.	National Gallery
Leb.	Lebanese	Mid. E.	Middle Eastern	N.G.A.	National Gallery of Art
Lect.	Lecture	Mid. Eng.	Middle English	NH	New Hampshire (USA)
Legis.	Legislative	Mid Glam.	Mid Glamorgan (GB)	Niger.	Nigerian
Leics	Leicestershire (GB)	Mil.	Military	NJ	New Jersey (USA)
Lex.	Lexicon	Mill.	Millennium	NM	New Mexico (USA)
Lg.	Large	Min.	Ministry; Minutes	nm	nanometre (10^{-9} metre)
Lib., Libs	Library, Libraries	Misc.	Miscellaneous	nn.	notes
Liber.	Liberian	Miss.	Mission(s)	no., nos	number(s)
Libsp	Librarianship	Mlle	Mademoiselle	Nord.	Nordic
Lincs	Lincolnshire (GB)	mm	millimetre(s)	Norm.	Normal
Lit.	Literature	Mme	Madame	Northants	Northamptonshire (GB)
Lith.	Lithuanian	MN	Minnesota	Northumb.	Northumberland (GB)
Liturg.	Liturgical	Mnmt, Mnmts	Monument(s)	Norw.	Norwegian
LLB	Bachelor of Laws			Notts	Nottinghamshire (GB)
LLD	Doctor of Laws	Mnmtl	Monumental	Nov	November
Lt	Lieutenant	MO	Missouri (USA)	n.p.	no place (of publication)
Lt-Col.	Lieutenant-Colonel	Mod.	Modern, Modernist	N.P.G.	National Portrait Gallery
Ltd	Limited	Moldav.	Moldavian	nr	near

Nr E.	Near Eastern	Per.	Period	Ptg(s)	Painting(s)
NS	New Style; Nova Scotia (Canada)	Percep.	Perceptions	Pub.	Public
n. s.	new series	Perf.	Performance, Performing, Performed	pubd	published
NSW	New South Wales (Australia)			Publ.	Publicity
NT	National Trust	Period.	Periodical(s)	pubn(s)	publication(s)
Ntbk	Notebook	Pers.	Persian	PVA	polyvinyl acetate
Numi.	Numismatic(s)	Persp.	Perspectives	PVC	polyvinyl chloride
NV	Nevada (USA)	Peru.	Peruvian	Q.	quarterly
NW	Northwest(ern)	PhD	Doctor of Philosophy	4to	quarto
NWT	Northwest Territories (Canada)	Philol.	Philology	Qué.	Québec (Canada)
		Philos.	Philosophy	R	reprint
NY	New York (USA)	Phoen.	Phoenician	r	recto
NZ	New Zealand	Phot.	Photograph, Photography, Photographic	RA	Royal Academician
OBE	Officer of the Order of the British Empire			Radnors	Radnorshire (GB; old)
		Phys.	Physician(s), Physics, Physique, Physical	RAF	Royal Air Force
Obj.	Object(s), Objective			Rec.	Record(s)
Occas.	Occasional	Physiog.	Physiognomy	red.	reduction, reduced for
Occident.	Occidental	Physiol.	Physiology	Ref.	Reference
Ocean.	Oceania	Pict.	Picture(s), Pictorial	Refurb.	Refurbishment
Oct	October	pl.	plate; plural	reg	regit [ruled]
8vo	octavo	Plan.	Planning	Reg.	Regional
OFM	Order of Friars Minor	Planet.	Planetarium	Relig.	Religion, Religious
OH	Ohio (USA)	Plast.	Plastic	remod.	remodelled
OK	Oklahoma (USA)	pls	plates	Ren.	Renaissance
Olymp.	Olympic	p.m.	post meridiem [after noon]	Rep.	Report(s)
OM	Order of Merit	Polit.	Political	repr.	reprint(ed); reproduced, reproduction
Ont.	Ontario (Canada)	Poly.	Polytechnic		
op.	opus	Polynes.	Polynesian	Represent.	Representation, Representative
opp.	opposite; opera [pl. of opus]	Pop.	Popular	Res.	Research
OR	Oregon (USA)	Port.	Portuguese	rest.	restored, restoration
Org.	Organization	Port.	Portfolio	Retro.	Retrospective
Orient.	Oriental	Posth.	Posthumous(ly)	rev.	revision, revised (by/for)
Orthdx	Orthodox	Pott.	Pottery	Rev.	Reverend; Review
OSB	Order of St Benedict	POW	prisoner of war	RHA	Royal Hibernian Academician
Ott.	Ottoman	PRA	President of the Royal Academy	RI	Rhode Island (USA)
Oxon	Oxfordshire (GB)			RIBA	Royal Institute of British Architects
oz.	ounce(s)	Pract.	Practical		
p	pence	Prefect.	Prefecture, Prefectural	RJ	Rio de Janeiro State
p., pp.	page(s)	Preserv.	Preservation	Rlwy	Railway
PA	Pennsylvania (USA)	prev.	previous(ly)	RSA	Royal Scottish Academy
p.a.	per annum	priv.	private	RSFSR	Russian Soviet Federated Socialist Republic
Pak.	Pakistani	PRO	Public Record Office		
Palaeontol.	Palaeontology, Palaeontological	Prob.	Problem(s)	Rt Hon.	Right Honourable
		Proc.	Proceedings	Rur.	Rural
Palest.	Palestinian	Prod.	Production	Rus.	Russian
Pap.	Paper(s)	Prog.	Progress	S	San, Santa, Santo, Sant', São [Saint]
para.	paragraph	Proj.	Project(s)		
Parag.	Paraguayan	Promot.	Promotion	S.	South(ern)
Parl.	Parliament	Prop.	Property, Properties	s.	solidus, solidi [shilling(s)]
Paroch.	Parochial	Prov.	Province(s), Provincial	Sask.	Saskatchewan (Canada)
Patriarch.	Patriarchate	Proven.	Provenance	Sat.	Saturday
Patriot.	Patriotic	Prt, Prts	Print(s)	SC	South Carolina (USA)
Patrm.	Patrimony	Prtg	Printing	Scand.	Scandinavian
Pav.	Pavilion	pseud.	pseudonym	Sch.	School
PEI	Prince Edward Island (Canada)	Psych.	Psychiatry, Psychiatric	Sci.	Science(s), Scientific
Pembs	Pembrokeshire (GB; old)	Psychol.	Psychology, Psychological	Scot.	Scottish
		pt	part	Sculp.	Sculpture

SD	South Dakota (USA)	suppl., suppls	supplement(s), supplementary	Urb.	Urban
SE	Southeast(ern)	Surv.	Survey	Urug.	Uruguayan
Sect.	Section	SW	Southwest(ern)	US	United States
Sel.	Selected	Swed.	Swedish	USA	United States of America
Semin.	Seminar(s), Seminary	Swi.	Swiss	USSR	Union of Soviet Socialist Republics
Semiot.	Semiotic	Symp.	Symposium		
Semit.	Semitic	Syr.	Syrian	UT	Utah
Sept	September	Tap.	Tapestry	*v*	*verso*
Ser.	Series	Tas.	Tasmanian	VA	Virginia (USA)
Serb.	Serbian	Tech.	Technical, Technique	V&A	Victoria and Albert Museum
Serv.	Service(s)	Technol.	Technology	Var.	Various
Sess.	Session, Sessional	Territ.	Territory	Venez.	Venezuelan
Settmt(s)	Settlement(s)	Theat.	Theatre	Vern.	Vernacular
S. Glam.	South Glamorgan (GB)	Theol.	Theology, Theological	Vict.	Victorian
Siber.	Siberian	Theor.	Theory, Theoretical	Vid.	Video
Sig.	Signature	Thurs.	Thursday	Viet.	Vietnamese
Sil.	Silesian	Tib.	Tibetan	viz.	*videlicet* [namely]
Sin.	Singhala	TN	Tennessee (USA)	vol., vols	volume(s)
sing.	singular	Top.	Topography	vs.	versus
SJ	Societas Jesu [Society of Jesus]	Trad.	Tradition(s), Traditional	VT	Vermont (USA)
Skt	Sanskrit	trans.	translation, translated by; transactions	Vulg.	Vulgarisation
Slav.	Slavic, Slavonic			W.	West(ern)
Slov.	Slovene, Slovenian	Transafr.	Transafrican	w.	width
Soc.	Society	Transatlant.	Transatlantic	WA	Washington (USA)
Social.	Socialism, Socialist	Transcarpath.	Transcarpathian	Warwicks	Warwickshire (GB)
Sociol.	Sociology	transcr.	transcribed by/for	Wed.	Wednesday
Sov.	Soviet	Triq.	Triquarterly	W. Glam.	West Glamorgan (GB)
SP	São Paulo State	Tropic.	Tropical	WI	Wisconsin (USA)
Sp.	Spanish	Tues.	Tuesday	Wilts	Wiltshire (GB)
sq.	square	Turk.	Turkish	Wkly	Weekly
sr	senior	Turkmen.	Turkmenistani	W. Midlands	West Midlands (GB)
Sri L.	Sri Lankan	TV	Television		
SS	Saints, Santi, Santissima, Santissimo, Santissimi; Steam ship	TX	Texas (USA)	Worcs	Worcestershire (GB; old)
		U.	University	Wtrcol.	Watercolour
SSR	Soviet Socialist Republic	UK	United Kingdom of Great Britain and Northern Ireland	WV	West Virginia (USA)
St	Saint, Sankt, Sint, Szent			WY	Wyoming (USA)
Staffs	Staffordshire (GB)	Ukrain.	Ukrainian	Yb., Y.-b.	Yearbook, Year-book
Ste	Sainte	Un.	Union	Yem.	Yemeni
Stud.	Study, Studies	Underwtr	Underwater	Yorks	Yorkshire (GB; old)
Subalp.	Subalpine	UNESCO	United Nations Educational, Scientific and Cultural Organization	Yug.	Yugoslavian
Sum.	Sumerian			Zamb.	Zambian
Sun.	Sunday	Univl	Universal	Zimb.	Zimbabwean
Sup.	Superior	unpubd	unpublished		

A Note on the Use of the Dictionary

This note is intended as a short guide to the basic editorial conventions adopted in this dictionary. For a fuller explanation, please refer to the Introduction, vol. 1, pp. xiii–xx.

Abbreviations in general use in the dictionary are listed on pp. vii–xii; those used in bibliographies and for locations of works of art or exhibition venues are listed in the Appendices in vol. 33.

Alphabetization of headings, which are distinguished in bold typeface, is letter by letter up to the first comma (ignoring spaces, hyphens, accents and any parenthesized or bracketed matter); the same principle applies thereafter. Abbreviations of 'Saint' and its foreign equivalents are alphabetized as if spelt out, and headings with the prefix 'Mc' appear under 'Mac'.

Authors' signatures appear at the end of the article or sequence of articles that the authors have contributed; in multipartite articles, any section that is unsigned is by the author of the next signed section. Where the article was compiled by the editors or in the few cases where an author has wished to remain anonymous, this is indicated by a square box (□) instead of a signature.

Bibliographies are arranged chronologically (within a section, where divided) by order of year of first publication and, within years, alphabetically by authors' names. Abbreviations have been used for some standard reference books; these are cited in full in Appendix C in vol. 33, as are abbreviations of periodical titles (Appendix B). Abbreviated references to alphabetically arranged dictionaries and encyclopedias appear at the beginning of the bibliography (or section).

Biographical dates when cited in parentheses in running text at the first mention of a personal name indicate that the individual does not have an entry in the dictionary. The presence of parenthesized regnal dates for rulers and popes, however, does not necessarily indicate the lack of a biography of that person. Where no dates are provided for an artist or patron, the reader may assume that there is a biography of that individual in the dictionary (or, more rarely, that the person is so obscure that dates are not readily available).

Cross-references are distinguished by the use of small capital letters, with a large capital to indicate the initial letter of the entry to which the reader is directed; for example, 'He commissioned LEONARDO DA VINCI . . .' means that the entry is alphabetized under 'L'.

M

[continued]

Montald, Constant (*b* Ghent, 4 Dec 1862; *d* Brussels, 1944). Belgian painter, illustrator and teacher. He studied at the Koninklijke Academie of Ghent, and first made his mark by winning the Prix de Rome in 1886 with *Diagorus Borne in Triumph*. This success allowed him to travel throughout Europe and the Near East. In 1896 he took part in the first Salon d'Art Idéaliste, organized by Jean Delville, and exhibited there regularly. In the same year he became professor of decorative art at the Académie Royale des Beaux-Arts in Brussels, a post he held for the next 37 years. He was a founder-member of L'Art Monumental in 1920. In 1928 he illustrated the *Legend of Uilenspiegel and Lamme Goedzak* (Brussels) by Charles de Coster.

Montald's early lyrical and dramatic compositions, such as the *Human Struggle* (1885–6; untraced), were succeeded by more weighty, meditative and idealist works. He produced a large number of monumental and decorative works (mostly untraced) in which he used allegory and symbolism; for example, *Under the Sacred Tree* (Brussels, Pal. Cinquantenaire) and *St Francis of Assisi* (Rougemont, Château). His style was imbued with a profound knowledge of the art of the past. He became a muralist after seeing the Sistine Chapel in Rome, and his persistent use of matt pigment derived from his admiration for Giotto, although he himself never painted directly on the wall. The high-key colours he chose were inspired by 14th- and 15th-century Italian primitives and by his memory of the interior of St Mark's in Venice, which encouraged him to introduce gold into his monumental works. He borrowed from Egypt the hieratic forms of his figures and from Pierre Puvis de Chavannes his lack of modelling, perspective and narrative. His decorative aesthetic emphasized physical immateriality and psychological distance. Montald was a specialist in the use of distemper. He produced numerous portraits, for example that of his close friend *Emile Verhaeren*.

BIBLIOGRAPHY
J. Delville: 'Constant Montald', *Annu. Acad. Royale Belgique/Jb. Kon. Acad. België* (1948)
G. van Herreweghe: *Le Peintre idéaliste Constant Montald* (Ghent, 1954)
Constant Montald (exh. cat., Brussels, La Médiatine, 1982)

BERNADETTE THOMAS

Monta Mozuna. *See* MOZUNA, KIKŌ.

Montaner, Bartolomé Maura y. *See* MAURA Y MONTANER, BARTOLOMÉ.

Montañés, Juan Martínez (*b* Alcalá la Real (Jaén), *bapt* 16 March 1568; *d* Seville, 18 June 1649). Spanish sculptor. He strove constantly for perfection, and, although he did not paint his own statues, he arranged for polychrome to be added by the most competent masters. Montañés was frequently sought for prestigious sculptural commissions in Seville, and he ran the most complete and organized workshop in the city, with an enormous production, similar to that run by Gregorio Fernández in Valladolid. The names of many of his collaborators are known, which implies that he was the director of a large enterprise. He planned and directed work and carried out the execution of appropriate parts or whole works as requested by his customers.

1. Early works, to 1603. 2. Middle period, 1603–27. 3. Late works, after 1627.

1. EARLY WORKS, TO 1603. According to Francisco Pacheco (1649), Montañés was trained in Granada. His master was probably PABLO DE ROJAS, whose influence on him is apparent. When Montañés arrived in Granada, around 1579, the high altar of the monastery of S Jerónimo was being completed by the Sevillian sculptor Juan Bautista Vázquez. Montañés returned to Seville *c*. 1587, and in that year he married Ana de Villegas.

The cosmopolitan city of Seville was the ideal setting for a sculptor to develop his talent. There was a constant flow of works of art, books and engravings through the city, and many foreign artists worked there. Seville also had close links with the American world. Montañés came into contact with the sculptors Gaspar Núñez Delgado, Bautista Vázquez and Andrés de Ocampo and was influenced by the works of Jerónimo Hernández. The stylized forms of Hernández's work, however, evolved into more realistic models in the hands of Montañés.

On 1 December 1588 Montañés was examined in sculpture by the sculptors Gaspar del Águila and Miguel Adán (*fl* 1593–8), appointed examiners by the city of Seville, and he was authorized to contract for sculpture and altarpieces. His usual medium was polychrome wood, and he used only the best masters, including Pacheco, to apply the polychrome. Montañés also designed and directed the construction of his altarpieces. His first work was a large wooden *St Christopher* (1597; Seville, El Salvador). The realistic anatomy and powerful rendering of muscles and blood vessels already show his abandonment of Mannerism. The very detailed folds of material, which are characteristic of his work, are already present. In 1597 the joiner Juan de Oviedo coordinated the construction of the altarpiece (destr.) for the convent of S Clara, Llerena, Badajoz, and chose Montañés to carve the statue of *St Jerome* (*in situ*). The figure has great muscular tension and conveys mysticism through gestures and facial expressions. Montañés began to receive commissions for America at an early date. In 1598 he signed contracts for 35 ciboria for various convents in the kingdom of Nueva Granada, a large commission, which indicates that he had already achieved a considerable reputation. In the same year he made several statues for the catafalque erected in Seville Cathedral for the funeral rites of Philip II. This occasion was planned by Juan de Oviedo and was recorded in verse by Miguel de Cervantes (1547–1616).

2. MIDDLE PERIOD, 1603–27. In 1603 Montañés carved the *Crucifix of the Chalices* (Seville Cathedral, Sacristía Cálices; see fig. 1), which was commissioned by Mateo Vázquez de Leca, Archdeacon of Carmona, for his private chapel. The Archdeacon had given up a dissolute life, and the *Crucifix* was intended as a work of expiation. Montañés received precise instructions dated 5 April 1603 from his patron (Martín González, 1983, p. 137). Christ was to appear as if in dialogue with the devotee and was to have his head inclined, as if he were talking to the faithful. The conversation was to appear to be one of persuasion, and the *Crucifix* should express Christ's suffering for the penitent. Montañés completed the sculpture with great care, as is indicated by his declaration that he wished the work to remain in Spain and not to go to the Indies, so that the fame of the master who had made it for the glory of God might be known. According to Pacheco (1649), Montañés followed a model by Michelangelo. This was probably a copy (untraced), then in Seville, that had been made in Rome in 1577 by Giacomo del Duca. Pacheco also states that Montañés followed a vision of the Crucifixion, narrated by St Bridget (*can* 1391) in her *Revelations*, in which Christ appeared crucified with four nails. In Montañés's carving the body of Christ is highly naturalistic and elegant, with careful attention paid to the modelling of the anatomy. Polychrome was applied by Pacheco in matt tones in order to make it appear lifelike. In 1617 Montañés carved a replica, though of lesser quality, the *Crucifix of the Abandoned* (Seville, S Ángel).

The life-size figure of *St Dominic* (1605; Seville, Mus. B.A.; *see* DOMINICAN ORDER, fig. 4) is the only remaining part of the high altar of the monastery of S Domingo de Portacoeli, which lay outside the walls of Seville. Pacheco again applied the polychrome. The tension of the earlier *St Jerome* at Llerena is less in evidence in the more ascetic figure of *St Dominic*, which is more naturalistic; the muscles appear to contract, while the folds of the draperies form a solid mass as a base. The *Infant Jesus* (1606; Seville

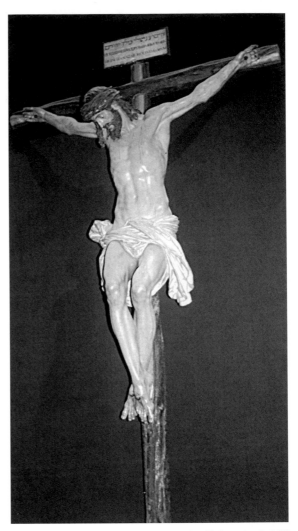

1. Juan Martínez Montañés: *Crucifix of the Chalices*, wood, 1603 (Seville Cathedral, Sacristía Cálices)

Cathedral), carved for the Cofradía del Santísimo Sacramento established in the cathedral, is highly naturalistic and was designed to appeal to popular taste. In contrast to contemporary ascetic tendencies Montañés's image is one of tenderness, which also conforms to Counter-Reformation ideals. The Infant Jesus was a favourite subject in Spanish convents, where the nuns liked to dress the Infant in various costumes. The softness of the modelling explains the nickname often given to Montañés of 'the Andalusian Lysippus'. The subject was frequently represented in Seville, but Montañés's treatment of it became widely followed.

In 1606 he carved the *Immaculate Conception* for the altar of S Maria de la Consolación, El Pedroso, Seville (*in situ*). He modelled the face on those of local Sevillian women and gave it fine and beautiful features. The voluminous folds of cloth provide stability and balance to the figure, and the half-moon and cherubim below act as solid support.

In 1607 Montañés was commissioned to make all the sculpture, but not the architecture, for the high altar of the convent of the Immaculate Conception, Lima, Peru (*in situ*). The series of small reliefs depicts episodes from the *Life of St John the Baptist*, with the burial of the saint in the centre of the predella in a composition inspired by representations of the entombment of Christ. The Crucifixion, in which the feet are joined by a single nail, is placed in the central niche, an unusual arrangement, for the customary position was in the upper section of the altarpiece. The whole work is blandly and elegantly modelled, prefiguring the type of image made by Alonso Cano.

In 1609, when he was at the height of his fame, Montañés received a demanding and detailed contract from the Hieronymite Order to design and carve the high altar of the convent of S Isidoro del Campo, Santiponce, Seville (*in situ*). The commission involved a considerable amount of work, and the participation of Montañés's workshop was authorized with the specification that the important parts, such as the statue of the titular saint, were to be executed entirely by Montañés. The architecture of the altar was probably influenced by Gaspar Becerra (Proske), and Montañés must have known the high altar of Astorga Cathedral, which Becerra began in 1558, at least through drawings. *St Jerome* (see fig. 2) occupies the

2. Juan Martínez Montañés: *St Jerome*, wood, detail of the high altarpiece, 1609 (Santiponce, S Isidoro del Campo)

central niche and is modelled fully in the round, as it was intended to be removed for processions. The saint is shown kneeling and appears intensely alive. The depiction of the powerful muscles, deep wrinkles and folds as well as the strong degree of tension are all highly realistic. Although Montañés was required to sculpt the *St Jerome* personally, it possesses a certain degree of drama, which may have been due to the influence of Juan de Mesa, who also worked on the altarpiece. Its reliefs are ordered and elegant. The angels in the *Adoration of the Shepherds* are idealized with such subtlety that they are reminiscent of Hellenistic models. The altarpiece has lateral funerary niches containing statues of the founders of the monastery, Alonso Pérez de Guzmán and his wife María Coronel, shown in prayer.

The statue of *St Ignatius Loyola* (1610; Seville, U. Chapel) was made to celebrate the Spanish saint's beatification (*can* 1622). It is clothed, and Montañés carved only the head and hands. For the head he used a copy of Ignatius's death-mask and the *Life of Father Ignatius of Loyola* (Madrid, 1595) by Pedro de Rivadeneira. Using these sources, he was able to convey the powerful inner life and moral character of the saint and portray his sad and tearful face. In 1624 he carved *St Francis of Borja* (Seville, U. Chapel), who is also shown deep in contemplation. The processional statue by Montañés of *Christ of the Passion* (*c*. 1619; Seville, El Salvador) is also a clothed and serene figure, modelled with perfection.

3. LATE WORKS, AFTER 1627. In 1628 Montañés was commissioned to design the architecture and make the statue of the *Virgin* for the Chapel of the Alabastros, Seville Cathedral, dedicated to the Immaculate Conception, a cult of great significance and popularity in Seville at the time. The contract stipulated that Montañés was not allowed to use assistants, and the price was to be calculated on completion. The patron also required that the face of the *Virgin of the Immaculate Conception* should express humility and modesty (see fig. 3).

In 1634 Montañés was commissioned by the Carthusians at the Cartuja de Las Cuevas to sculpt *St Bruno* (Seville, Mus. B.A.). The face suggests the natural qualities of soft skin, but the expression is one of exalted mysticism. The sculptor's fame reached the court in Madrid, and he was summoned there in 1635, probably on the advice of Caspar de Guzmán y Pimental, the Conde-Duque de Olivares, and Diego Velázquez, both of Sevillian origin. Montañés was asked to make a bust in clay of *Philip IV* (1635–6; untraced), which may have been sent to Italy and used as a model by Pietro Tacca for the equestrian statue (1636–40) he was making of the King for the gardens of the Buen Retiro, Madrid (now Madrid, Plaza de Oriente). Although some sources suggest that Tacca used a painting as a model, there are traces of Montañés's style in the completed statue (Proske, p. 10). The Sevillian sculptor was held in such esteem that Velázquez painted his portrait: *Juan Martínez Montañés* (1635–6; Madrid, Prado), which shows him sculpting the head of the King.

The high altar of S Miguel, Jerez de la Frontera, was one of Montañés's most ambitious works. Although it was commissioned in 1609, the architecture of the altarpiece was not completed until 1627, and the sculptures were not

3. Juan Martínez Montañés: *St Virgin of the Immaculate Conception*, wood, 1628 (Seville Cathedral, Chapel of the Alabastros)

'the god of wood' ('*el dios de la madera*'), and he was held in the highest esteem. He had created some of the finest and most moving sculpture of his time. His statues appear to be alive but simultaneously project a spiritual quality conveying a powerful mysticism, which makes them transcend their immediate surroundings. Christ is shown in dialogue; the Child tenderly stretches out his arms; and St Jerome is a figure of strength and passion. One of the qualities of Spanish art of the period is that in its attempt to achieve Realism it transcends reality.

Ceán Bermúdez

BIBLIOGRAPHY

F. Pacheco: *Arte* (1649); ed. F. Sánchez Cantón (1956)
C. López Martínez: *Documentos para la historia del arte en Andalucía*, 2 vols (Seville, 1927–8)
——: *Arquitectos, escultores y pintores vecinos de Sevilla* (Seville, 1928)
——: *Desde Jerónimo Hernández hasta Martínez Montañés* (Seville, 1929)
J. Hernández Díaz and H. Sancho Corbacho: *Arquitectos y escultores sevillanos* (Seville, 1931)
C. López Martínez: *Desde Martínez Montañés hasta Pedro Roldán* (Seville, 1932)
J. Pulido Rubio: 'Estudio documental de algunos sagrarios tallados por Juan Martínez Montañés con destino a unos conventos de América', *An. U. Hisp.*, vi (1943), pp. 91–125
D. Angulo Iñiguez: 'Martínez Montañés y su escuela en Honduras y Guatemala', *Archv Esp. A.*, xx (1947), pp. 285–91
J. Hernández Díaz: *Juan Martínez Montañés* (Seville, 1949)
J. J. Martín González: 'La influencia de Montañés en Tenerife', *Archv Esp. A.*, xxxii (1959), pp. 322–4
J. de Mesa and T. Gisbert: 'Una obra de Montañés en Bolivia', *Archv Hisp.*, xxxi (1959), pp. 37–42
E. Harth-Tere: 'Una obra de Montañés en Lima', *Cuad. Hisp. Amer.*, 152–3 (1962), pp. 261–71
J. Hernández Díaz: 'Martínez Montañés en Lima', *An. U. Hisp.*, xxv (1965), pp. 99–108
B. Gilman Proske: *Juan Martínez Montañés: Sevillian Sculptor* (New York, 1967)
Martínez Montañés (1568–1649) y la escultura andaluza de su tiempo (exh. cat. by J. Hernández Díaz, Madrid, Casón Buen Retiro, 1969)
J. Bernales: 'Escultura montañesina en el virreinato del Perú', *Archv Hisp.*, lvii (1974), pp. 9–120
J. Hernández Díaz: *Martínez Montañés: El Lisipo andaluz*, Arte Hispalense (Seville, 1976)
——: *La escultura del siglo XXII*, Summa A.: Hist. Gen. A., xxvi (Madrid, 1982)
J. J. Martín González: *Escultura barroca en España, 1600–1770* (Madrid, 1983)
J. Hernández Díaz: *Juan Martínez Montañés (1568–1649)* (Seville, 1987)

J. J. MARTÍN GONZÁLEZ

Montano, Benito Arias. *See* ARIAS MONTANO, BENITO.

Montano, Giovanni Battista (*b* Milan, 1534; *d* Rome, 1621). Italian wood-carver, sculptor and architect. He moved from Milan to Rome during the reign of Pope Gregory XIII and worked originally as a cabinetmaker. Only a few of his works survive, including, in particular, the crucifix in the Cappella del Sacramento of S Maria dell'Anima and the coffered ceilings in the oratory of the Arciconfraternità dei Convalescenti e Pelligrini and S Giuseppe dei Falegname, all in Rome. He also made the organ fronts for the north transept of S Giovanni in Laterano and for the churches of S Maria di Loreto (destr. 1852) and S Maria dei Monti (destr. 19th century), Rome. In addition, he prepared plans for the Capella de' Falconis in S Maria dei Monti and for the church of S Giuseppe dei Falegname, where he was architect from 1590. S Giuseppe, a church with a single aisle flanked by two longitudinal chapels, was the church of the Roman guild of joiners and cabinetmakers. The detailed treatment

finished until 1643 (all *in situ*). Successive changes were made, which increased its Baroque character. The statues are not placed in niches but stand in the foreground and project outwards in a striking manner. Montañés had to employ numerous collaborators and this, together with delays in payment, prolonged the completion of the work. He transferred part of this large commission to the sculptor José de Arce, the Flemish master who brought a powerful Baroque art to Seville. Montañés's hand can be recognized in the figures of *St Peter* and *St Paul*. He also worked on the reliefs depicting the *Transfiguration* and the *Archangel Michael* (both completed in 1643). The latter is carved in high relief and is his most Baroque work. It seems almost to have been conceived as a challenge to the large-scale altar paintings that were then usual in Seville. St Michael triumphs over Lucifer and the seething Inferno, and the flames below further dramatize this colossal relief.

When Montañés died in 1649, sculpture in Seville was imbued with his style. His contemporaries nicknamed him

of the façade (completed 1602), with its delicately silhouetted volutes and its unusual aediculae, reveals the hand of a man who had served a cabinetmaking apprenticeship and recalls his numerous designs for tabernacles, which were published posthumously. Montano's workshop also frequently constructed architectural models, including those for Ottaviano Mascherino's concept for the church of SS Luca e Martina, Rome, and Giacomo della Porta's for a burial chapel for the Medici in Florence.

As a member of the Accademia di S Luca, Montano lectured on architecture, but his most important works were his drawings based on ancient ruins in Rome and the surrounding area, some of which were later adapted by Sebastian Serlio, Andrea Palladio, Etienne Dupérac, Pirro Ligorio and Giovanni Salustio Peruzzi. The drawings were bequeathed to the Accademia di S Luca and are now in Milan (Castello Sforzesco), London (Soane Mus.; V&A), Oxford (Ashmolean), Edinburgh (N.G.) and Berlin (Kstbib.). Some of the drawings were published for the first time between 1624 and 1636 by Giovanni Battista Soria, Callisto Ferrante and Bartolomeo de' Rossi (*fl* 1621–5). In 1684 the seven single volumes were republished in a new five-volume edition. Although Montano is known sometimes to have climbed into caves and grottoes to get his views of buildings, he then embellished the ruins with elevations and sections based on his own ideas. His interest in them was not genuinely archaeological; he was much more concerned with providing a formal repertory of details, spaces, volumes and spatial relationships that could be removed from any context, which explains why he ignored exact measurements.

Giovanni Baglione named only Soria and Vincenzo della Greca as Montano's pupils, although his influence was much greater. His designs for tabernacles, groundplans and elevations, sometimes reconstructed along symmetrical lines in accordance with contemporary ideas, influenced the foremost architects of the next generation. Their effect can be seen in Pietro da Cortona's designs for SS Luca e Martina, Gianlorenzo Bernini's church of S Andrea al Quirinale and Guarino Guarini's altar designs. The most durable impact of Montano's study of antiquity, however, can be seen in the work of Francesco Borromini.

WRITINGS
G. B. Soria, ed.: *Scielta D. varii tempietta antichi* (Rome, 1624)
——: *Diversi ornamenti capricciosi per depositi o altari* (Rome, 1625)
C. Ferrante, ed.: *Architettura con diversi ornamenti cavati dall'antico* (Rome, 1628)
G. B. Soria, ed.: *Tabernacoli diversi* (Rome, 1628)
——: *Li cinque libri di architettura* (Rome, 1684)

BIBLIOGRAPHY
G. Baglione: *Vite* (1642); ed. V. Mariani (1935)
G. Zander: 'Le invenzione architettoniche di Giovanni Battista Montano, milanese', *Quad. Ist. Stor. Archit.*, 49–50 (1962), pp. 1–32
J. von Hennenberg: 'Emilio dei Cavalieri, Giacomo della Porta and G. B. Montano', *J. Soc. Archit. Hist.*, xxxvi (1977), pp. 252–5
A. Bedon: 'Architettura e archaeologia nella Roma del cinquecento: Giovan Battista Montano', *A. Lombarda*, n. s., lxv/2 (1983), pp. 111–26
B. Ringbeck: *Giovanni Battista Soria: Architekt Scipione Borgheses* (diss., U. Münster, 1987)

BIRGITTA RINGBECK

Montauti, Antonio (*b* Florence, *c.* 1685; *d* Rome, after 1740). Italian sculptor, medallist and possible architect. A pupil in Florence of Giuseppe Piamontini, he was first active as a medallist; one of his earliest and most exquisite medals celebrated the visit of King Frederick IV of Denmark and Norway to Florence in 1708. On the obverse is a portrait of the King; on the reverse, a view of the city with a reclining river god personifying the Arno (Florence, Bargello). A medal of *Conte Lorenzo Magalotti*, dated 1712 (version, London, BM), has Apollo on the reverse, whose exaggerated sway in the hips is reflected in two later small bronzes (Rome, Pal. Corsini). There are also two medals of the *Grand Duke Gian Gastone de' Medici* (before 1723 and 1731; both Florence, Bargello). Montauti's careful characterizations in the portrait medals are reflected in his marble portrait busts. One, of *Gian Gastone de' Medici* (*c.* 1724; Florence, Arcisp. S Maria Nuo.), emphasizes the ugly features of large nose, pouting lips and jutting chin by using a schematic treatment for the wig.

Small bronzes also formed an important part of Montauti's work. His masterpiece, the *Return of the Prodigal Son*, signed and dated 1724 (h. 631 mm; Detroit, MI, Inst. A.), is one of 12 bronze groups made for the Electress Palatine Anna Maria Luisa de' Medici. The *Prodigal Son* is a fine example of the new dramatic treatment of pictorial groups that was emerging in Florence in the 1720s. A second version of the group (h. 650 mm) is in the National Museum of Wales at Cardiff.

Montauti does not seem to have made life-size marble statues before the mid-1720s. In Florence his most interesting examples are *Innocence* and *Religion* in the Cappella Maggiore of S Maria Maddalena dei Pazzi. Their animated drapery folds are descriptive of the form beneath; that of *Innocence* forms a strong, serpentine curve. Montauti was commissioned to complete this series of Cardinal Virtues with *Faith* and *Penitence* opposite. However, these were executed later by Innocenzo Spinazzi. Montauti also contributed statues to the basilica of Mafra, Portugal, for which he carved *St Peter* and *St Paul* in 1732. St Peter's drapery still reveals the form beneath, whereas St Paul's heavy folds of drapery across the hips anticipate Montauti's Roman works.

In 1733 Montauti was called to Rome by the diplomat Cardinal Alamanno Salviati, for whom he may have made the second version of the *Prodigal Son*. Unfortunately, the contents of Montauti's Florentine studio were shipwrecked during the move. His principal Roman commissions were *St Benedict* (1735), one of the series of gigantic statues of the founders of religious orders in St Peter's; and the life-size *Pietà* for the crypt of the Corsini Chapel in S Giovanni in Laterano. The *Pietà*, completed before 1736, recalls the marble bas-relief of the same subject carved by Agostino Cornacchini for the crypt chapel in the basilica of Superga, Turin. Montauti's later works are characterized by a new, Roman monumentality, with more classical poses, full drapery and expressive faces. In the *Pietà* the expression on the Virgin's face recalls those of Bernini's ecstatic female figures, and the Instruments of the Passion are offset by heavy, cascading drapery. In 1735 Clement XII appointed Montauti Architect of St Peter's (but there is no evidence that he ever worked as an architect); after this he appears to have lost interest in his career as a sculptor.

BIBLIOGRAPHY

K. Lankheit: *Florentinische Barockplastik: Die Kunst am Hofe der letzten Medici, 1670–1743* (Munich, 1962), pp. 228–9 [incl. F. M. N. Gabburri's life of Montauti]

The Twilight of the Medici: Late Baroque Art in Florence, 1670–1743 (exh. cat., ed. S. F. Rossen; Detroit, MI, Inst. A., 1974), pp. 86–9

J. Montagu: 'Antonio Montauti's *Return of the Prodigal Son*', *Bull. Detroit Inst. A.*, liv/1 (1975), pp. 14–23

V. Johnson: 'La medaglia barocca in Toscana', *Medaglia*, v/10 (1975), pp. 40–44, 68

R. Enggass: *Early Eighteenth-century Sculpture in Rome*, 2 vols (University Park, PA, and London, 1976), pp. 189–92

FLAVIA ORMOND

Monte, del. Italian family of lawyers, ecclesiastics and patrons. The family, whose ancestral town was Monte San Savino, 20 km south-west of Arezzo, established itself in the 16th century under Antonio Maria Ciocchi del Monte (1462–1533). His nephew Giovanni Maria Ciocchi del Monte was the future Pope Julius III. During the reign of Julius III, the del Monte family continued to prosper, with numerous male and female relatives receiving the benefits of ecclesiastical incomes, titles and property. Baldovino del Monte (*d* 1556), created Conte di Monte San Savino, inherited from his brother Julius III the Villa Giulia in Rome and had a palazzo there (now the Palazzo Firenze) and the family palazzo in Monte San Savino extended and further embellished for his use.

(1) Pope Julius III [Giovanni Maria Ciocchi del Monte] (*b* Rome, 10 Sept 1487; elected 7 Feb 1550; *d* Rome, 23 March 1555). He studied law in Perugia and Bologna before undertaking theological studies under the direction of the Dominican Ambrosius Catharinus (*c.* 1484–1553). In his early career he benefited from the patronage of his uncle Antonio Maria Ciocchi del Monte, receiving a number of ecclesiastical preferments. After his uncle's death (1533) he continued to prosper and was appointed successively vice-legate to Bologna (1534), Cardinal Presbyter (1536), Cardinal Bishop (1543) and co-president of the Council of Trent (1545). During his pontificate Julius made continuous efforts towards Church reform, ordering the resumption of the Council of Trent and initiating a programme to control the conferment of benefices and to change the administration of the curia. He nevertheless ensured that his relatives were granted lucrative benefices, titles and properties.

A generous patron, Julius placed several eminent humanists in his chancery, appointed Marcello Cervini (1501–55, later Pope Marcellus II) as Vatican Librarian and reformed La Sapienza, the University of Rome. He was an important patron of the composer Palestrina who dedicated his *Missarum liber primus* (Rome, 1554) to him. He also took a lively and informed interest in architecture. As he tended to be difficult and exacting, his relationships with artists were often fraught. He appointed Giorgio Vasari in 1550 to design and oversee a decorative scheme (completed 1552) for the funerary chapel of his uncles, Antonio and Fabiano del Monte, in S Pietro in Montorio, Rome. It contains an altarpiece, the *Baptism of St Paul*, and, in the vault, scenes from the *Life of St Paul*, painted by Vasari and his assistants, and two tomb monuments by BARTOLOMEO AMMANATI, one with a statue of *Theology*, the other with a statue of *Justice*. Ammanati was probably also responsible for the marble balustrade and the fine stucco decoration in the vault of the chapel.

Julius had inherited from his uncle a property outside the Porta del Popolo, Rome, which as pope he expanded and rebuilt as the luxurious Villa Giulia (1551–3). As he changed his mind countless times in the course of construction, the chronology and attribution of the various phases of design and construction are both complex and insecure. Vasari claimed that he responded to the Pope's ideas and executed the original designs (which were shown to Michelangelo for comment, and which formed the basis for work done afterwards by himself, Ammanati and Jacopo Vignola; *see* VIGNOLA, JACOPO, fig. 3). In its present form, the architectural scheme unfolds in an orderly and ingeniously integrated sequence: the two-storey villa; the first semicircular courtyard; another loggia; and the second courtyard which encloses, on a lower level, the profusely decorated nymphaeum. The centrepiece of the nymphaeum is a fountain decorated by colossal statues of the *Tiber* and the *Arno*. Nearly all the rich interior decoration of the villa (on which Giovanni da Udine as stuccoist and Taddeo Zuccaro and Federico Zuccaro as painters collaborated) has now disappeared. The magnificent collection of antique sculptures housed there was removed to the Vatican in the late 16th century. In its scale, scenographic design and combination of artificial and natural features, the villa presented a grandiose emulation of the imperial villas of antiquity, consonant with Julius's aspirations. In the vicinity of the new villa, he also commissioned Vignola to erect (1550–*c.* 1553) the tiny votive church of S Andrea in Via Flaminia as thanksgiving for his escape from death during the Sack of Rome (1527). Its oval dome anticipates the first use of an oval plan for a church, in his S Anna degli Palafrenieri (1565) in the Vatican.

Under the auspices of Julius III, Girolamo da Carpi supervised the modifications of the Villa Belvedere at the Vatican Palace. Michelangelo replaced the circular staircase of DONATO BRAMANTE's Belvedere exedra with a double flight of stairs and conceived the idea of adding two upper storeys to it, subsequently carried out by Pirro Ligorio under Pope Pius IV. Julius also commissioned the decoration of the Stanza della Cleopatra (the present Atrio del Torso) with a scheme which embraced rich stuccowork and a series of murals on themes close to Julius's heart by Daniele da Volterra.

Shortly after his election, Julius III asked Vasari to prepare a new urban scheme for his family home-town, Monte San Savino. Although the scheme was never carried out, several smaller projects were, including the paving of the central portion of the city in brick, renovating the Palazzo Pretorio and the Porta Fiorentina, and adding a new loggia to the sanctuary of S Maria delle Vertighe outside the town's walls. Work also resumed on the Palazzo del Monte at Monte San Savino in order to furnish Baldovino del Monte with a suitable country residence. The architect was Nanni di Baccio Bigio who was apparently also responsible for building the garden loggia. The palazzo bears a striking resemblance to Michelangelo's rejected project of *c.* 1546–8 to link by bridge the Palazzo Farnese, Rome, to the grounds of the Villa Farnesina across the Tiber. It is possible that the Pope personally urged Nanni to complete the palazzo in this manner. Work was still being executed there in the 1560s.

BIBLIOGRAPHY

G. de Angelis d'Ossat: 'La vicenda architettonica del manierismo', *Atti del XIV congresso di storia dell'architettura: Brescia, Mantova, Cremona, 1965*, pp. 95–113
N. W. Canedy: 'The Decoration of the Stanza della Cleopatra', *Essays in the History of Art Presented to Rudolf Wittkower* (London, 1967), pp. 110–18
F. L. Moore: 'A Contribution to the Study of the Villa Giulia', *Röm. Jb. Kstgesch.*, xii (1969), pp. 171–94
T. Falk: 'Studien zur Topographie und Geschichte der Villa Giulia in Rom', *Röm. Jb. Kstgesch.*, xiii (1971), pp. 101–78
C. Davis: 'Ammanati, Michelangelo, and the Tomb of Francesco del Nero', *Burl. Mag.*, cxviii (1976), pp. 472–84
D. Coffin: *The Villa in the Life of Renaissance Rome* (Princeton, 1979)
B. F. Davidson: 'The Landscapes of the Vatican Logge from the Reign of Pope Julius III', *A. Bull.*, lxv (1983), pp. 587–602
A. Nova: 'Bartolomeo Ammanati e Prospero Fontana a Palazzo Firenze: Architettura e emblemi per Giulio III Del Monte', *Ric. Stor. A.*, 21 (1983), pp. 53–76
——: 'The Chronology of the Del Monte Chapel in S Pietro in Montorio in Rome', *A. Bull.*, lxvi (1984), pp. 150–54
L. Satkowski: 'The Palazzo del Monte in Monte San Savino and the Codex Geymüller', *Studies in Honour of Craig Hugh Smyth*, ii (Florence, 1985), pp. 653–60

DIANA NORMAN

Monte, Deodaat [Déodat; Deodatus] **del** [van der Mont] (*bapt* St Truiden, 24 Sept 1582; *d* Antwerp, 24 Nov 1644). Flemish painter. He is primarily important as the earliest known pupil and assistant of Peter Paul Rubens. From a certificate drawn up for him by Rubens in 1628, it is known that in 1600 he travelled to Italy in Rubens's service. Other documents confirm this: in 1608, for example, del Monte witnessed Rubens's contract with the Oratorians for the execution of a 'Nativity', intended for the high altar of S Filippo Neri in Fermo. In October 1608 he returned to Antwerp with Rubens. Immediately after this he enrolled as a member of the Guild of St Luke.

Little is known about del Monte's own commissions. In 1610 he made an altarpiece for the church at Mortsel, a village near Antwerp; in 1614 he painted a *Transfiguration* for Antwerp Cathedral (Antwerp, Kon. Mus. S. Kst.); in Onze-Lieve-Vrouw Hemelvaart, Munsterbilzen, there is a signed *Lamentation* (1623). His style can be judged from the last two surviving works: both paintings show that he followed the classical plasticity of work produced by Rubens between *c.* 1612 and 1618. The foreshortened body of Christ in the *Lamentation* is, moreover, clearly based on the figure of Christ in Rubens's *Holy Trinity* (*c.* 1613–15; Antwerp, Kon. Mus. S. Kst.).

Del Monte is documented as having made several other works for institutions in Antwerp, including an *Adoration of the Magi* for the Falcon monastery, another version of the same theme and a *Christ Carrying the Cross* for the Jesuit convent (all untraced). He is described as an 'engineer' in various commissions for prominent Catholic rulers, such as the Pfalzgraf von Neuburg, King Philip IV of Spain and the Archduke and Archduchess Albert and Isabella. He was also evidently active as an art dealer.

BIBLIOGRAPHY

N. Scheuer-Raps: *Deodat del Monte, son temps, sa vie, ses oeuvres* (Aalter, 1956)
G. Baeck: 'Deodatus van der Mont' *NBW*, 7 (1977), col. 603–611
M. L. Hairs: *Dans le sillage de Rubens: Les Peintres d'histoire anversois au XVIIe siècle* (Liège, 1977), pp. 46–8

HANS VLIEGHE

Monte, Francesco Maria Bourbon del. *See* BOURBON DEL MONTE, FRANCESCO MARIA.

Monte Albán. Site in Mexico, in the Valley of Oaxaca. It was an important Pre-Columbian ZAPOTEC city, later occupied by MIXTECS. At the convergence of the Valley of Oaxaca's three arms, on a small range of hills (*c.* 600 m), Monte Albán was founded by peoples from neighbouring villages *c.* 600 BC as a ceremonial centre. The site had probably long been sacred. By the time of Monte Albán's founding, the Zapotecs had established long-distance trading contacts with OLMEC centres in the Gulf Coast and had developed a calendrical system for recording dates and events on stone.

The ancient city grew by stages but apparently not at first with a long-term plan, except that a grand work of art was clearly intended. An enormous plaza, measuring 400 m (north–south) by 250 m (east–west), was laid out, and calendrical inscriptions were incorporated into a wall. As problems in construction and settlement arose, remedies were improvised, and the hilltops of the range were gradually modified as the urban centre grew. While major public buildings, monuments and élite residences were built around the hilltop plaza, *c.* 2600 residential terraces were constructed on the irregular slopes of the range. Erection and rebuilding of public buildings and monuments on the plaza continued for over 1000 years, mostly obliterating evidence of the first constructions.

The earliest surviving evidence of the city (Monte Albán I; *c.* 500–*c.* 200 BC) indicates that the Main Plaza was conceived from the beginning and maintained its shape and size throughout habitation. The plaza was created by levelling the principal hilltop and by incorporating obstructive rock outcrops into buildings. Near the south-west corner of the plaza a long wall incorporates stone slabs carved in low relief depicting figures traditionally called *danzantes* (see fig.). (Only 42 of the 320 complete and fragmentary *danzantes* found on the Main Plaza remain in place.) Most scholars concur that the figures represent captured and dead enemies, bearing some of the earliest complete hieroglyphic inscriptions in Mesoamerica (*see also* MESOAMERICA, PRE-COLUMBIAN, §V, 2). In the north-east corner of the plaza, at a right angle to the *danzantes* wall, another early wall fragment lies deeply buried under later buildings. It bears a large stucco relief thought to be a stylized serpentine creature. As the city population increased rapidly, neighbourhood clusters developed on the hilltops and slopes around the Main Plaza, and levelling of the plaza continued. A huge platform structure was begun at the north end, replacing a much smaller building. Towards the end of Monte Albán I, work had begun on an extensive defensive wall delimiting the northern, north-western and western boundaries of the city.

In Monte Albán II (*c.* 200 BC–*c.* AD 300) the inhabitants extended their interests beyond the Valley of Oaxaca, including the establishment of a garrison town at Cuicatlán 100 km to the north-east. The Main Plaza was further defined with enclosing buildings. Near the centre of the

Monte Albán, stone slab carved in low relief depicting a bearded *danzante*, Monte Albán I, *c.* 500–*c.* 200 BC

southern half, Structure J was built in an arrow-point plan and orientated differently from the principal plaza axis, apparently for astronomical observation and calculation. An early version of the ballcourt was built at the northeast corner of the plaza, and the élite were buried in rectangular tombs with roofs of stone slabs.

The ceramics of these periods included finely polished and slipped cream and brown wares for everyday use and featured bridged spouts, tetrapod bases and anthropomorphic and zoomorphic vessels. In period I a few vessels have Olmec-like 'tiger-mouth' features (e.g. Mexico City, Mus. N. Antropol.; Oaxaca, Mus. Reg.). Fine-paste grey wares were also made and became dominant in later periods.

Population continued to increase in Monte Albán IIIA (*c.* AD 300–*c.* 500). The Main Plaza continued to be levelled and paved and more structures were built to enclose it. The ballcourt was modified to its final form, the huge South Platform (h. 15 m) was constructed across the southern end of the plaza, and the Northern Platform and subsidiary structures, including a sunken court, were begun. Relief carvings now appeared on free-standing stelae rather than on mounted slabs. Elaborate tomb burials continued, including wall paintings (*see* MESOA-MERICA, PRE-COLUMBIAN, fig. 27).

Tripod vessels, jars with spouts and fine-paste engraved and incised grey wares of careful workmanship predominated. Thin Orange pottery, figurines and four stelae at the corners of the South Platform show clear signs of contact with TEOTIHUACÁN in the Basin of Mexico. The stelae depict Teotihuacán officials, identifiable by their tasselled headdresses, leaving Teotihuacán and being greeted in Monte Albán by Zapotec officials. A Zapotec enclave has also been identified at Teotihuacán. In Monte Albán IIIB (*c.* AD 500–*c.* 750) the valley population was further centralized around the city and reached its peak of *c.* 25,000. Buildings around the Main Plaza now completely enclosed it except for three narrow, easily defended passages. A set of three platforms supporting buildings was completed down the centre of the plaza along the long axis, and the Northern Platform and sunken court were completed. Around the city most of the 15 subdivisions were each dominated by a specific craft specialization, and clusters of élite residences were surrounded by more ordinary houses. Monte Albán IIIB was a period of prosperity, but towards its end technical quality declined in building and craftsmanship, and quantity and repetition replaced quality and invention. In Monte Albán IV (*c.* AD 750–*c.* 1000) the population declined severely in and around the Main Plaza, and the plaza itself was eventually abandoned. As the population dispersed into the valley, several smaller cities increased in size. The first Mixtec incursions into the Valley of Oaxaca occurred after *c.* AD 900. Although the Main Plaza and central city were deserted, élite families continued to reopen their tombs to bury their dead. In Monte Albán V (*c.* AD 1000–1521) the ceremonial centre remained a dead city, although the Mixtecs continued to reuse some of the Zapotec tombs and a few of the buildings for special ceremonies.

BIBLIOGRAPHY
A. Caso and I. Bernal: *Urnas de Oaxaca* (Mexico City, 1952)
M. Covarrubias: *Indian Art of Mexico and Central America* (New York, 1957)
R. Wauchope and G. Willey, eds: 'Archaeology of Southern Mesoamerica, Part Two', *HB. Mid. Amer. Ind.*, iii (1965), pp. 788–987
F. Boos: *The Ceramic Sculptures of Ancient Oaxaca* (New York, 1966)
J. Paddock, ed.: *Ancient Oaxaca: Discoveries in Mexican Archaeology and History* (Stanford, 1966)
A. Caso, I. Bernal and J. R. Acosta: *La cerámica de Monte Albán* (Mexico City, 1967)
R. E. Blanton: *Monte Albán: Settlement Patterns at the Ancient Zapotec Capital* (New York, 1978)
E. E. Blanton and others: *Ancient Mesoamerica: A Comparison of Three Regions* (Cambridge, 1981), pp. 43–109
K. V. Flannery and J. Marcus, eds: *The Cloud People: Divergent Evolution of the Zapotec and Mixtec Civilizations* (New York, 1983)
The Art of Ancient Mexico (exh. cat., ed. M. Ryan; London, Hayward Gal., 1992)

JOHN PADDOCK

Monte Alto. Site of Pre-Columbian MAYA culture, *c.* 20 km south-west of Escuintla, on the Pacific slopes of Guatemala. It was probably occupied from the 8th century BC to *c.* AD 200, with a florescence towards the end of that time, but by *c.* AD 200 it would have been surpassed in political importance by the Maya sites of KAMINALJUYÚ and IZAPA. The site layout at Monte Alto has parallel north–south oriented plazas flanked by platforms and mounds, a pattern typical of the Middle Pre-Classic period (*c.* 1000–*c.* 300 BC).

The sculpture of the Pacific slopes is relatively little known. Although much has been found, the pieces are almost always in the context of former ceremonial centres, but often smashed and reused. Boulder sculptures, plain stone stelae and plain round altars have all been found at Monte Alto. The boulder sculpture probably dates from the Late Pre-Classic period (*c.* 300 BC–*c.* AD 250). Lee A. Parsons, who worked with Edwin Shook at Monte Alto from 1968, believed that the plain sculpture at the site belongs to the Late Pre-Classic (or Izapan) period (*see* MESOAMERICA, PRE-COLUMBIAN, §IV, 2(iv)), while the boulder sculptures may have been carved at an earlier date and only reset in Late Pre-Classic times. There was some re-occupation of the site during the Late Classic period (*c.* AD 600–*c.* 900). The boulder sculptures are crude and simple, fashioned from volcanic basalt boulders of the type still found on the alluvial plain. Their low-relief carvings generally follow the form of the stone. There are two related types of boulder sculptures: large, fat-cheeked, 'colossal' human heads, and massive, full-figure human effigies; the latter generally have faces like those of the heads, with a diagonal cheekline framing either side of the mouth. The heads are unique to Monte Alto, but potbellied figures, related to the full-figure human effigies, are found at other sites in the region. The potbellied figures, which probably preceded the effigy boulders, may derive from the earlier plump, baby-faced ceramic figures of the Mesoamerican Central Highlands and Kaminaljuyú. One sculpture represents an elaborately carved human head with jaguar features and incorporates OLMEC iconographic elements. These pieces are more sophisticated in style than other Monte Alto sculpture. A small greenstone mask found at the site was probably a Pre-Classic period heirloom, hidden during the Late Classic period occupation.

It has been suggested that the Monte Alto heads may have preceded the colossal heads of the Olmec Gulf Coast heartland (*see* MESOAMERICA, PRE-COLUMBIAN, §IV, 2(i)), but they are now generally believed to be later. The Monte Alto heads are *c.* 1.5 m high and may represent decapitated heads; their closed eyes seem to indicate dead faces. Similar visages are seen on the neckless, big-shouldered boulder figures, which have their hands placed frontally at their waists and their legs carved in very low relief near the bottoms of the boulders, with the soles of the feet facing toward the centreline. They are not usually carved on the base or rear. They wear ear ornaments and collars, but their gender is not indicated. One figure sculpture (Monument 6) has open eyes and is slightly different in style from the rest; it may be somewhat earlier. Much of the Monte Alto sculpture is in the open-air archaeological display Parque Arqueológica in La Democracía.

BIBLIOGRAPHY
S. W. Miles: 'Sculpture of the Guatemala–Chiapas Highlands and Pacific Slopes, and Associated Hieroglyphs', *Hb. Mid. Amer. Ind.*, ii (1965), pp. 237–75
L. A. Parsons: 'Post-Olmec Stone Sculpture', *The Olmec and their Neighbors: Essays in Memory of Matthew W. Stirling*, ed. E. P. Benson (Washington, DC, 1981), pp. 257–88
——: *The Origins of Maya Art*, Studies in Pre-Columbian Art and Archaeology, xxviii (Washington, DC, 1986)
M. P. Hatch: 'A Seriation of Monte Alto Sculptures', *New Frontiers in the Archaeology of the Pacific Coast of Southern Mesoamerica*, ed. F. Bove and L. Heller, Anthropological Research Papers, xxxix (Tempe, AZ, 1989), pp. 25–41
ELIZABETH P. BENSON

Montebelo, Marquês de. *See* MACHADO DA SILVA CASTRO E VASCONCELOS, FÉLIX.

Montecassino. Benedictine abbey in Lazio, Italy. The birthplace of Western monasticism, it was founded *c.* AD 529 by St Benedict (*c.* AD 480–*c.* 547; *see* BENEDICTINE ORDER, §1) on the mountain overlooking the town of Casinum, on the site of a pagan temple. Benedict wrote the Rule here after 534, and he was buried alongside his sister, St Scholastica, in the chapel of St John the Baptist. The architectural history of the abbey (*see* §1 below) is closely linked with historical events. Montecassino was sacked by the Lombards *c.* 589, and it lay abandoned until *c.* 718, when a small community was founded there; it was reformed *c.* 729, and the monastery was rebuilt by Willibald, from Waltham Abbey. The abbey grew more powerful during the 8th century: Carloman, brother of Pepin the Short, was a monk there *c.* 746, and Paul the Deacon stayed for ten years until his death *c.* 799. When the church was destroyed by the Muslims in 883, the monks fled to Teano, and thence to Capua, from where Montecassino was refounded in 950 by Abbot Aligernus (*reg* 949–86). The abbey flourished under DESIDERIUS, abbot from 1058 until he became Pope Victor III in 1086, becoming an important centre of art and manuscript production (*see* §2 below). He rebuilt the monastery to house 200 monks, and his new church was consecrated in 1071 by Pope Alexander II. Montecassino was made a bishopric in 1322 by Pope John XXII. In 1349 the abbey suffered a violent earthquake; the rebuilding (1357–66) was financed by the Avignon pope, Urban V (*reg* 1362–70).

The strategic position of the abbey, dominating the plain of Cassino, made it a point of military importance, and it was caught up in successive wars during the 15th century. Following the victory of Gonsalvo de Cordova at Garigliano (1503), the monastery was restored, and there followed three centuries of relative tranquillity. In the mid-17th century Abbot Quesada (*reg* 1650–53) began rebuilding the church, which was completed in 1727, when the new basilica was consecrated by Pope Benedict XIII. It suffered at the hands of the French under General Championnet in 1798, but it was restored by Pope Pius VII. In 1806 it was secularized by Joseph Bonaparte but re-established in 1815. In World War II the site was reduced to ruins, but it has since been restored to its appearance after the 17th-century rebuilding.

BIBLIOGRAPHY
T. Leccisotti: *Montecassino* (Montecassino, 1946, rev. 10/1983)
G. Giovannoni: *L'abbazia di Montecassino*, I Monumenti Italiani e la Guerra, iii (Florence, 1947)
H. Bloch: *Montecassino in the Middle Ages*, 3 vols (Rome, 1986)
RONALD BAXTER

1. Architecture. 2. Centre of production. 3. Manuscripts.

1. ARCHITECTURE. The nucleus of the monastery was the oratory of St John the Baptist founded by St Benedict on top of a mountain, on the site of an altar dedicated to Apollo. According to the archaeological evidence, it was a small apsidal building, corresponding approximately to the area from the main altar to the first bay of the nave in the present basilica. Benedict also founded the nearby oratory of St Martin, which was also small. The monastic buildings were simple constructions, probably built of makeshift materials or rudimentary masonry, but St Benedict's lodgings were located in the two-storey entrance tower. The

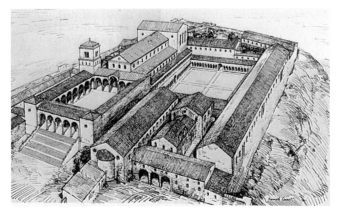

1. Montecassino Abbey as *c.* 1100, after its rebuilding by Abbot Desiderius (1066–71); reconstruction drawing by Kenneth Conant, 1935

chapel of St John the Baptist was enlarged and embellished under Abbot Gisulfo (*reg* 797–817) because—according to Leo of Ostia—it was considered by this time to be too small and unworthy to house the remains of the founder saint. The new church, which was almost as wide as the present building but considerably shorter, retained the choir of the original oratory, and it was divided by columns into a nave and two aisles, terminating in three eastern apses. A second church, dedicated to the Saviour, was built by Abbot Gisulfo on an identical plan at the foot of the mountain; it is described in minute detail in Leo's chronicle of Montecassino. In the course of successive restoration projects and improvements, Gisulfo's mountain-top basilica acquired a type of westwork on the façade and towers at the atrium entrance, a design that reflected those of Carolingian and Ottonian buildings in northern Europe (e.g. St Emmeram, Regensburg).

Under Abbot DESIDERIUS (*reg* 1058–87), Montecassino entered one of its most flourishing periods. The Abbot enlisted the services of the most skilled men of the day to rebuild the abbey church (now also dedicated to St Benedict): architects from Amalfi and Lombardy, mosaicists from Constantinople (now Istanbul). The materials (columns and marble) were brought specially from Rome, and the work was finished in only five years (1066–71). The carrying up of the first marble column by a group of pious people in 1066 was one of the first acts associated with the CULT OF CARTS. The basilica was considered one of the wonders of the world, comparable with the great mythical constructions of the East. The surviving bronze doors, which are still in use, fragments of the main portal, mosaic pavement and wall decoration, several capitals and other marble slabs, give some idea of the splendour and quality of the decoration.

The basilica, which measured 21.0×48.4 m externally, was in some respects similar to the previous building. It had an aisled nave with a ten-bay columnar arcade, a high, non-projecting transept and three equally projecting eastern apses, of which the central one was broader than the others. The entrance to the main apse was articulated by corner columns, a motif adopted from Islamic architecture. The building had no crypt, but the presbytery was raised above the floor level of the nave by about eight steps. The

church had an atrium in front of the façade and a campanile on the north. The church portico that formed part of the atrium reportedly had pointed arches, this being the first introduction of this arch type into western Europe. The whole arrangement can be seen in the early 16th-century drawings of the abbey by Antonio da Sangallo the younger and Battista da Sangallo (Florence, Uffizi) and from the survey carried out by the abbot and engineer Don Angelo Pantoni after World War II. Further details emerge from the precise description of Leo of Ostia. An overall impression of Desiderius's basilica can be formed from Salerno Cathedral, which is probably a direct derivation, as well as from the numerous churches in Campania that were modelled on Montecassino. Willard and Conant's reconstruction of Desiderius's church and convent (see fig. 1) made in 1935 is still substantially valid, although it was later partially corrected and improved by Conant.

On completion of the church, reconstruction of the earlier monastic buildings, including the ancient chapel of St Martin, was begun. New facilities were created for the monks and for pilgrims, a massive entrance tower was built with corner columns, and the entire abbey, which had become the target of numerous predators, was encircled by walls. No expense was spared for this rebuilding work. The chronicle records that, among other wonders, there was a huge bakery of such monumental beauty that many pilgrims often headed towards it, mistaking it for a church. The monastic complex remained practically unaltered until in 1349 a violent earthquake almost irretrievably destroyed the prestigious basilica and its decoration. The Benedictine Pope Urban V (*reg* 1362–70) provided for the rebuilding of the monastery and took over control himself for a period. The layout and the distribution of the columns of Desiderius's church were respected, as can be seen from the Sangallo drawings, which were executed before the building suffered any significant changes.

After the abbey became part of the Congregazione di S Giustina di Padua in 1504, the medieval buildings were progressively transformed. Antonio da Sangallo the younger probably built the cloister and steps leading up to the basilica, which are decidedly 15th century in taste, while Abbot Angelo de Faggis (*reg* 1559–64) instigated the building of the Chiostro del Priore, adjacent to the church, and the Loggia del Paradiso, so called because of the unique panoramic view that it affords. The loggia links the three cloisters or lower porticos, so creating a suggestive sequence that is seen as one crosses the threshold of the monastery. The church, to which a crypt was added in 1543, was given a Baroque facing of marble and stucco, later completed with paintings by various artists including those (1677; destr. World War II) by Luca Giordano. From 1649 the work of restructuring the abbey was directed by Cosimo Fanzago, who had remodelled the high altar in 1636. His definitive arrangement of the building complex remained virtually unchanged until the destruction of World War II, after which the abbey was faithfully rebuilt in the same manner.

BIBLIOGRAPHY

Leo of Ostia: *Chronica monasterii Casinensis* (MS.; late 11th century); ed. H. Hoffmann, Mnmt Ger. Hist., Scriptores, xxxiv (Hannover, 1980), pp. 358–457

G. Giovannoni: *Rilievi ed opere architettoniche del cinquecento a Montecassino* (Montecassino, 1929), pp. 305–35

A. Willard: 'A Project for the Graphic Reconstruction of the Romanesque Abbey at Monte Cassino', *Speculum*, x (1935), pp. 144–6 [with drgs by K. J. Conant]

E. Scaccia Scarafoni: 'Note su fabbriche ed opere medioevali a Montecassino', *Boll. A.*, xxx (1936), pp. 97–121

A. Pantoni: 'Problemi archeologici cassinesi: La basilica predesideriana', *Riv. Archeol. Crist.*, xvi (1939), pp. 271–88

E. Scaccia Scarafoni: 'La "torre di S Benedetto" e le fabbriche medievali di Montecassino', *Boll. Ist. Stor. It. Med. Evo & Archv Murator.*, lix (1944), pp. 137–83

K. J. Conant: *Carolingian and Romanesque Architecture, 800–1200*, Pelican Hist. A. (Harmondsworth, 1959, rev. 1974)

A. Pantoni: *Le vicende della basilica di Montecassino attraverso la documentazione archeologica*, Misc. Cassinese, xxxvi (Montecassino, 1973)

G. Urban: 'Die Klosterakademie von Montecassino und der Neubau der Abteikirche im 11 Jahrhundert', *Röm. Jb. Kstgesch.*, xv (1975), pp. 11–23

G. Carbonara: '*Iussu Desideri*': Montecassino e l'architettura campano-abruzzese nell'undicesimo secolo (Rome, 1979)

M. d'Onofrio and V. Pace: *La Campania*, Italia Romanica, iv (Milan, 1981)

MARIO D'ONOFRIO

2. CENTRE OF PRODUCTION.

(i) Manuscripts Nothing is known of manuscript painting at Montecassino before the 10th century because most of the books perished when the abbey was sacked by the Muslims in 883, and most of the remainder, taken to Teano by the fleeing monks, were destroyed in a fire there. A survival from the abbacy of Giovanni (*reg* 914–43), when the monks were moved from Teano to Capua, is a copy of Paul the Deacon's commentary on Benedict's Rule (Montecassino Abbey, Bib., MS. 175, fol. 2r), which contains a dedication miniature of *Abbot Giovanni before St Benedict*. After the community's return to Montecassino under Aligernus (*reg* 949–86), manuscript production began slowly to accelerate, and a form of interlace initial inhabited by small animals (deriving from English or Franco-Saxon models) became popular. Early examples appear in a book of *Homilies* (Montecassino Abbey, Bib., MS. 269) made during Aligernus's abbacy. The scriptorium became more active through contacts with the Ottonian court during the abbacy of Theobald (*reg* 1022–36). In this period Montecassino was given a lavish Gospel book (Rome, Vatican, Bib. Apostolica, MS. Ott. lat. 74) by Emperor Henry II, ostensibly a gift to express gratitude to St Benedict for a cure in 1022, but also containing a warning against an alliance with Byzantium. Initials copied from this manuscript did not appear in Cassinese illumination for another 50 years, but a copy of Gregory I's *Moralia in Job* (*c.* 1022–36; Montecassino Abbey, Bib., MS. 73, fol. 4r) contains a dedication picture of *Abbot Theobald with St Gregory*, which is indebted to Ottonian illumination, and a contemporary illustrated Rabanus Maurus manuscript (Montecassino Abbey, Bib., MS. 132) must have been derived ultimately from a Carolingian model.

Manuscripts provide the best evidence of a new phase in artistic production inaugurated by Abbot Desiderius (*see also* §(ii) below). Although much has been made of Leo of Ostia's account of Desiderius's employment of Byzantine craftsmen to produce works for the abbey and train local pupils, it should be stressed that the craftsmen from Constantinople were hired for specific tasks, which did not include painting of any kind. The similarities between Desiderian miniatures and near-contemporary

Byzantine works are the result of the foreign artists providing new models for indigenous painters. That the most striking parallels can be made between Cassinese manuscripts and Byzantine mosaics supports this view. The Exultet rolls produced at Montecassino continued the tradition of the Bari Exultet rolls produced *c.* 1000 (for discussion and illustration *see* EXULTET ROLLS). The finest of these is in London (*c.* 1070–80; BL, Add. MS. 30337; *see* ROMANESQUE, fig. 56). Its soft, chiffon-like drapery, drawn with a sketchy line and including large bare panels, compares with both the Bari Exultets and the early 11th-century mosaics of Hosios Loukas. This style persisted into the abbacy of Oderisius (*reg* 1087–1105) when it is seen in a Breviary (*c.* 1099; Paris, Bib. Mazarine, MS. 364).

In contrast, the *Lives of SS Benedict, Maurus and Scholastica* (1072–86; Rome, Bib. Apostolica, MS. Vat. lat. 1202; see fig. 2) includes among *c.* 100 miniatures a cycle of the *Life of St Benedict* with illustrations stylistically related to a contemporary Byzantine Psalter (London, BL, MS. Add. 40731). The angular, crystalline drapery is similar to the wall paintings at Sant'Angelo in Formis, with comb-like shading, possibly an attempt to copy the chrysography

2. *Desiderius Presenting Books and Churches to St Benedict*; miniature from the *Lives of SS Benedict, Maurus and Scholastica*, 1072–86 (Rome, Vatican, Biblioteca Apostolica, MS. Vat. lat. 1202, fol. 1r)

of such contemporary Byzantine mosaics as those at Dafni. It has been argued that this group can be associated with Desiderius's import of Byzantine artists (Garrison), but there are also striking resemblances in composition, background treatment, facial shading and drapery conventions between the Sant'Angelo wall paintings and Ottonian wall paintings at Reichenau, which indicate the importance of continuing artistic links with the Empire. These Byzantinizing characteristics are features associated with paint rather than line, and it is significant that the two Desiderian books of *Homilies* illustrated with drawings (Montecassino Abbey, Bib., MSS 98–9) combine the angular line of this second group with the bare drapery panels of the first. The angel in the drawing of the *Annunciation* (MS. 99, fol. 5*r*) is formally similar to mosaics in Vatopedi Monastery, Mt Athos, but the same drawing contains a survival of the Franco–Saxon interlace associated with the abbey since the 10th century.

BIBLIOGRAPHY

E. A. Lowe: *The Beneventan Script* (Oxford, 1914)

M. Avery: *The Exultet Rolls of South Italy* (Princeton, 1936)

E. B. Garrison: 'Contributions to the History of Twelfth-century Umbro-Roman Painting: I', *Studies in the History of Mediaeval Italian Painting*, ii (Florence, 1955–6), pp. 21–46 [32–8]

N. Acocella: *La decorazione pittorica di Montecassino dalle didascalie di Alfano I (sec. XI)* (Salerno, 1966)

F. Newton: 'The Desiderian Scriptorium at Monte Cassino: The *Chronicle* and Some Surviving Manuscripts', *Dumbarton Oaks Pap.*, xxx (1976), pp. 35–54

RONALD BAXTER

(ii) Craftsmen and artists. The height of Montecassino's artistic activity and influence coincided with the abbacy of Desiderius (*reg* 1058–87). He commissioned the bronze doors for his new basilica from artists in Constantinople and also, according to the later chronicle of Leo of Ostia, hired craftsmen there to provide mosaics at Montecassino and train the monks in mosaic, metalwork and carving. Of the Byzantine work at Montecassino, only the doors and fragments of the mosaic pavement survive. Thus knowledge of the figure style introduced by the Byzantine craftsmen is based largely on surviving manuscripts (*see* §(i) above) and on the wall paintings in the nearby church of SANT'ANGELO IN FORMIS, which were commissioned by Desiderius. Traditionally, therefore, Montecassino has been seen as the source of an 'Italo-Byzantine style', which spread throughout Europe and to Rome, in particular. Much that has been ascribed to the tradition inaugurated by Desiderius, however, may represent the remnant of earlier Byzantine incursions, incorporated into indigenous styles.

Perhaps the strongest case for Cassinese influence outside the immediate area can be made for the slightly later work at Salerno Cathedral, particularly in the light of the association of Alfanus, Archbishop of Salerno (*reg* 1058–85) with both monuments (*see* SALERNO, §1): originally a monk at Montecassino, Alfanus was a lifelong friend of Desiderius and attended the dedication of the new abbey church in 1071, in honour of which he wrote an ode. He was co-founder of the cathedral (begun 1080) at Salerno. Although nothing survives from Montecassino with which the fragments of figural mosaic at Salerno may be compared, points of similarity have been noted between drapery details at Salerno, those in Desiderian manuscripts, and in mosaics at Vatopedi Monastery on Mt Athos. The appearance of drapery motifs that were innovative in the East at Salerno and in the manuscripts indicates a common and recent Byzantine origin. Outside Italy the position is more complex: one cannot ignore the possibility that such Burgundian works as the Cluny Lectionary (*c*. 1100–10; Paris, Bib. N., MS. nouv. acq. lat. 2246) and the Cîteaux Jerome *Commentary on Prophets* (*c*. 1110–20; Dijon, Bib. Mun., MS. 132), which have been compared with Cassinese manuscripts (e.g. the Exultet roll, *c*. 1070–80; London, BL, Add. MS. 30337; *see* ROMANESQUE, fig. 56), relied on Byzantinizing models transmitted via Germany.

In the later work at the abbey there was a tendency to employ local artists where possible. The total transformation of the monastic buildings in the 16th century is well documented, and the records show that although successive abbots called on masters from all parts of Italy, only once was an artist of any great stature employed. This was for the design (1531) of the funerary chapel of Piero di Lorenzo de' Medici by Antonio da Sangallo the younger. Piero's burial in the abbey was a chance result of his drowning in the Garigliano River in battle in 1503. Sangallo was commissioned, not by the abbot, Agostino da Padova, but by the Medici pope, Clement VII. The presence of such local craftsmen as Zucca da Gaeta, author of the intaglio benches (1534–8) in the sacristy, and Marco Mazzaroppi di Cassino (1550–1620), who worked on the crypt paintings (1557–8), testifies to a continuing craft tradition in the area, but the recruitment of outside specialists such as Marco Pina da Brescia, who began the crypt paintings, or Cima Fiorentino, who was paid for unspecified work in the dormitory in 1519, indicates gaps in local expertise. The resulting work was high in quality but conservative in design.

BIBLIOGRAPHY

C. R. Dodwell: *Painting in Europe, 800–1200*, Pelican Hist. A. (Harmondsworth, 1971), pp. 129–38

E. Kitzinger: 'The First Mosaic Decoration of Salerno Cathedral', *Jb. Österreich. Byz.*, xxi (1972), pp. 149–62; also in *The Art of Byzantium and the Medieval West: Selected Studies*, ed. W. E. Kleinbauer (Bloomington and London, 1976), pp. 271–89

Monte Cassino, Giovanni da. *See* GIOVANNI DA MONTE CASSINO.

Monte di Giovanni del Fora. *See* FORA, DEL, (2).

Montefeltro. Italian dynasty of rulers and patrons. Buonconte, Lord of Montefeltro (*reg* 1213–41), gained control of Urbino in 1234, and for more than two centuries the family were important condottieri, often in the service of Siena or Arezzo. The wealth and lands gained by (1) Federigo II da Montefeltro financed the patronage of one of the most enlightened rulers of the early Renaissance. The power of the duchy declined under his only son, (2) Guidobaldo da Montefeltro.

(1) Federigo [Federico] **II da Montefeltro**, 1st Duke of Urbino (*b* Gubbio, 1422; *reg* 1444–82; *d* Ferrara, 10 Sept 1482). He was the illegitimate son of Guidantonio da Montefeltro, Count of Urbino (*reg* 1404–43). In his youth he spent two years at the Gonzaga court in Mantua, attended the humanist school of Vittorino da Feltre and served as a condottiere from 1437. He became Count of

Urbino after the assassination of his half-brother, Oddantonio (*reg* 1443–4). Federigo's mastery of warfare was renowned throughout Europe. In 1444 he served the Sforzas of Milan and was later employed by Florence and Naples (1451). He was infrequently engaged after the peace of Lodi (1454), although various city-states retained the promise of his service. In 1469 he headed the alliance of Naples, Milan and Florence against Pope Paul II (*reg* 1464–71). In 1474, however, he was created Duke of Urbino by Sixtus IV (*reg* 1471–84) and granted the rights to land in Romagna. He fought for the papacy against Florence in 1479.

The two facets of Federigo's life, the cunning warrior and the enlightened patron, were celebrated in biographies by VESPASIANO DA BISTICCI and GIOVANNI SANTI. They were also captured by JUSTUS OF GHENT in his portrait of *Federigo da Montefeltro and his Son Guidobaldo* (*c.* 1476; Urbino, Pal. Ducale; *see* URBINO, fig. 1), depicted examining a manuscript while dressed in armour. Especially during the later years of his reign, Federigo had a surplus of funds and time available for art and architectural patronage: from the late 1460s he may have invested more money in patronage than any other Italian ruler of his day. He built or refurbished residences throughout his lands, including the Palazzo Comunale (rebuilt 1463), Cagli, the Corte Alta (1464–70), Fossombrone, the Palazzo Ducale (from 1472), Urbania, and the Palazzo Ducale (from 1476; *see* FRANCESCO DI GIORGIO MARTINI, §1), Gubbio. The court at Urbino, however, remained the centre of his attentions (*see* URBINO, §2).

Baldassare Castiglione wrote that the commanding Palazzo Ducale at Urbino was 'thought by many the most beautiful to be found anywhere in all Italy and he furnished it so well with every suitable thing that it seemed not a palace but a city in the form of a palace'. It was built in several campaigns from the 1440s to the 1470s (*see* URBINO, §4 and fig. 3). Construction was directed successively by several architects, including the Florentine Maso di Bartolommeo, the Dalmatian Luciano Laurana (1466–72; for discussion and illustration *see* LAURANA, LUCIANO) and the Sienese Francesco di Giorgio Martini (from 1476). The three-storey, classically articulated façade facing the city was decorated with 72 stone reliefs by AMBROGIO BAROCCI showing ancient and modern instruments of war. The interior, however, was intended to display the achievements of the remarkable array of progressive artists, scholars and theoreticians who were drawn to the Duke's court, including Alberti (*see* ALBERTI, LEON BATTISTA; *see also* ARCHITECTURAL DRAWING, fig. 4). By 1482 the palace library contained some 1100 volumes, many purchased from Vespasiano, who also advised on acquisitions. Local artists were employed to provide illuminations for many of the manuscripts and decorate certain rooms in the palace.

According to Vespasiano, Federigo could not find Italian oil painters to his taste and brought Justus of Ghent to Urbino, where his work included the 28 portraits of *Famous Men* (*c.* 1473–6; Paris, Louvre; Urbino, Pal. Ducale) for the Duke's *studiolo*, a painting called *Federigo, Guidobaldo and Others Listening to a Discourse* (*c.* 1480; London, Hampton Court, Royal Col.) and a further seven paintings of the *Liberal Arts* (*Music* and *?Rhetoric* (London,

N.G.) for the *studiolo* in the Palazzo Ducale, Gubbio. Both *studioli* were decorated with some of the most elaborate surviving 15th-century intarsia designs (*see* STUDIOLO, fig. 1; Gubbio intarsia now in New York, Met.). The artist with the greatest hold on Federigo's patronage, however, would appear to have been Piero della Francesca, who dedicated *De prospectiva pingendi* (Parma, Bib. Palatina, MS. 1576) to the Duke (*see* PIERO DELLA FRANCESCA, §§I and III). Some scholars have suggested that he may have served as an artistic adviser, and others have even given him partial credit for the design of the Urbino palace. The extent and identity of Piero's work for Federigo remain uncertain, but it includes the double portrait of *Federigo da Montefeltro and Battista Sforza* (*c.* 1472; Florence, Uffizi), with their *Triumphs* shown on the reverse. Federigo's sense of loss on his wife's death in 1472 is poignantly illustrated in his lone presence kneeling before the Virgin and Child in the Brera Altarpiece (mid-1470s; Milan, Brera).

(2) Guidobaldo da Montefeltro, 2nd Duke of Urbino (*b* Urbino, 24 Jan 1472; *reg* 1482–1508; *d* Fossombrone, 23 April 1508). Son of (1) Federigo da Montefeltro. Guidobaldo was less successful as a condottiere than his father and seriously impoverished, reducing his opportunity for patronage. He completed the construction of the Palazzo Ducale, Gubbio, and added manuscripts and printed books to the ducal library. Piero della Francesca dedicated to the Duke his *Libellus de quinque corporibus regularibus* (after 1485; Rome, Vatican, Bib. Apostolica, Cod. Urb. 273), and Giovanni Santi had been appointed court painter by 1488. Guidobaldo seems to have been an early patron of Santi's son, Raphael (*see* RAPHAEL, §I, 1(i)). BALDASSARE CASTIGLIONE provided an idealized account of life at Urbino from 1504, although he complained that his stipends often went unpaid. Guidobaldo and his wife, Elisabetta Gonzaga, remained childless, and he adopted his nephew Francesco Maria I della Rovere as his heir in 1504 (*see* ROVERE, DELLA (i), (3)).

BIBLIOGRAPHY
Vespasiano da Bisticci: *Vite di uomini illustri* (1480s; Bologna, Bib. U., MS. 1452); ed. A. Greco (Florence, 1970); Eng. trans. by W. G. Waters and E. Waters as *Renaissance Princes, Popes and Prelates: The Vespasiano Memoirs* (London, 1926/*R* New York, 1963), pp. 83–114
G. Santi: *La vita e la gesta di Federico da Montefeltro duca d'Urbino: Cronaca* (1482–7; Rome, Vatican, Bib. Apostolica, MS. Vat. Ottob. lat. 1305); ed. L. Michelini Tocci (Rome, 1985)
B. Castiglione: *Il libro del cortegiano* (Venice, 1528); Eng. trans. by T. Hoby as *The Courtyer* (London, 1561) and by C. Singleton as *The Book of the Courtier by Baldesar Castiglione* (Garden City, NY, 1959)
P. Rotondi: *Il Palazzo Ducale di Urbino*, 2 vols (Urbino, 1950–51; Eng. trans., London, 1969)
C. H. Clough: *The Duchy of Urbino in the Renaissance* (London, 1981)
G. Cerboni Baiardi, G. Chittolini and P. Floriani, ed.: *Federico di Montefeltro: Lo stato/le arti/la cultura*, 3 vols (Rome, 1986)
L. Cheles: *The Studiolo of Urbino: An Iconographic Investigation* (Wiesbaden, 1986)

ROGER J. CRUM

Montefiore, Gentile da. *See* GENTILE DA MONTEFIORE.

Monteiro, José Luís (*b* Montelavar, nr Sintra, 25 Oct 1849; *d* Lisbon, 21 Jan 1942). Portuguese architect and teacher. After studying architecture at the Academia de Belas Artes, Lisbon, he went with a state scholarship to Paris (1874–8), where he was a pupil of Jean-Louis Pascal. He won several prizes there and collaborated in the reconstruction of the Hôtel de Ville, Paris. His training was completed in Rome (1878–80). On his return to Lisbon he took up an appointment as municipal architect, which he had won by competition while still in Rome. Working with Ressano Garcia, director of the city's Technical Department, Monteiro was one of the principal agents for the modernization of public works in Lisbon. He also designed several important buildings in Lisbon in the late 19th and early 20th centuries: the Rossio Central Railway Station (1886–7), with a neo-Manueline façade; the adjacent Hotel Palace (1890–92); the Liceu Central (1887); and the Church of the Angels (1908–11), which replaced the church demolished to make way for the new Avenida Almirante Reis. For each of these projects Monteiro used a different style: an academic neo-classicism, for the church; the style of French Second Empire façades for the Hotel Palace; and an eclectic style for the Rossio Station. Some of his designs for private houses show the same aesthetic variation; for example the designs of the Chalet Biester, Sintra, and Casa Faial, Cascais, were influenced by English models.

Monteiro was also aware of current technological innovations. Although the façade of the Rossio Station is a pastiche of 16th-century Manueline architecture, the interior contains one of the first iron vaults in Lisbon, a solution he used again in the design of the Sala de Portugal (1897) in the headquarters of Sociedade de Geografia, Lisbon. In other projects, such as the Liceu Central and the barracks (1891–2), Bombeiros, Monteiro used a functional approach that reduced the importance of the façade in favour of the practical requirements of the building. The artistic and academic element of his training remained evident in all his work, however, and in the many temporary structures he designed, including pavilions, allegorical floats and rostrums, he was able to embody a dream-like notion of architecture without the practical constraints of permanent reality. Monteiro also played an important role as teacher. From 1881 to 1920 he held the Chair of Architecture at the Escola de Belas Artes, Lisbon, and was one of the chief influences in the formation of later generations of Portuguese architects.

BIBLIOGRAPHY
J. A. Piloto: *Homenagem prestada ao insigne arquiteto José Luís Monteiro* (Lisbon, 1925)
J.-A. França: *A arte em Portugal no século XIX*, ii (Lisbon, 1966), pp. 17–19
N. Portas: 'A evolução da arquitetura moderna em Portugal: Uma interpretação', *História da arquitetura moderna*, ed. B. Zevi, ii (Lisbon, 1970)
RAQUEL HENRIQUES DA SILVA

Monteiro, (Porfírio) Pardal (*b* Feb 1897; *d* Dec 1957). Portuguese architect. He trained in the Escola de Belas Artes, Lisbon, and in the studio of Ventura Terra. His family was connected with the marble industry, and his early works consist of craftsmanlike buildings in the Art Deco style, for example houses at 207–15 Avenida 5 de Outubro (1929; Valmôr Prize), the Cais do Sodré railway station (1925–8), both in Lisbon, and the Caixa Geral de Depósitos bank (1930), Avenida dos Aliados, Oporto. Closer to Functionalism in style are his first public buildings: the Instituto Superior Técnico (1927–35), Alameda Afonso Henriques, where Monteiro taught engineering, and the adjacent Instituto Nacional de Estatística (1931–5), Lisbon. Monteiro was important as a designer of public buildings. His work, most of which involved collaboration with others, was based on a profound knowledge of construction technology; elegant but never daring in style, it used a restricted, easily comprehensible vocabulary. The conservatism of his later style, a synthesis of eclecticism, Art Deco and modernism, lent itself to adaptation according to the fluctuations of official taste in the 1940s and 1950s. Notable examples in Lisbon include the church of Rósario de Fátima (1934–8); the headquarters of the *Diário de Notícias* (1940); the Fluviais de Alcântara (1942) and Conde de Óbidos (1945) railway stations; Cidade Universitária (1940–57), Campo Grande; and LNEC laboratories (1952), Avenida do Brasil.

BIBLIOGRAPHY
J.-A. França: *A arte em Portugal no século XX* (Lisbon, 1974), pp. 250–51
Os anos 40 na arte portuguesa (exh. cat., ed. F. C. Gulbenkian; Lisbon, Fund. Gulbenkian, 1982), ii, pp. 130–32
JOSÉ MANUEL FERNANDES

Monteiro, Vicente do Rego. *See* REGO MONTEIRO, VICENTE DO.

Monteith. Type of large footed bowl with two drop-ring handles and a notched or scalloped rim. Made in silver, pewter, glass or ceramic, it was used for cooling wine-glasses, which were suspended by their feet in the water it contained. It could be converted into a punch-bowl by the provision of a detachable rim and was often made with a matching ladle and set of beakers. The monteith was popular in England, Ireland, Scotland, Germany and the USA between *c.* 1677 and *c.* 1720 (e.g. silver monteith by John Coney, *c.* 1700–10; New Haven, CT, Yale U. A.G.; *see* UNITED STATES OF AMERICA, fig. 48). Its fluted or panelled body is usually chased or embossed and the rim enriched with scrollwork, foliage and cherubs' heads. It was recorded in 1683 that it was named after a Scotsman called Monteigh, who wore a cloak with scalloped hem. A similar vessel in France was known as a *rafraîchissoir* or a *verrière*.

□

Montelatici, Francesco. *See* CECCO BRAVO.

Montelupo. Italian centre of maiolica production. This small town near Florence was an important centre of ceramics production from the mid-15th century. The potters of Montelupo, many of whom originally came from other Italian centres of maiolica production, must have found favourable working conditions, and from the end of the 15th century their pottery was held in such high regard that some of them were able to move their kilns to the countryside around Florence or even, as in the case of the family known as the Fattorini (*see* SCHIAVON), to the Cafaggiolo ceramic factory, which was under the patronage of the grand dukes of Tuscany. During the Renaissance the maiolica from Montelupo reflected typical Italian themes, including East-Asian and Gothic floral decoration and portraits. The colour range was very striking, particularly during the 16th and 17th centuries. An outstanding group of wares known as *arlecchini* were so called because they were decorated with a vivid, multi-coloured palette dominated by yellow. This technique was used for painting characters from the *commedia dell'arte*, Spanish soldiers and swashbuckling bullies (e.g. plate, *c.* 1600–60; London, BM; *see* ITALY, fig. 85). Brightly coloured wares continued to be produced during the 19th and 20th centuries.

BIBLIOGRAPHY
G. Cora and A. Fanfani: 'Vasai di Montelupo', *Faenza*, lxix (1983), pp. 289–306, 401–8; lxx (1984), pp. 58–113, 235–77, 507–55: lxxi (1985), pp. 129–71, 350–91
F. Berti: *La maiolica di Montelupo* (Milan, 1986)

CARMEN RAVANELLI GUIDOTTI

Montelupo, da [Sinibaldi]. Italian family of sculptors and architects. They were active in central and northern Italy from the end of the 15th century to the mid-16th.

(1) Baccio da Montelupo [Bartolomeo Sinibaldi] (*b* Montelupo, 1469; *d* Lucca, 1535). According to Vasari, he studied antique sculpture in the gardens of Lorenzo de' Medici in Florence with Michelangelo and others. His career was linked to Dominican patronage and the supporters of Girolamo Savonarola. His first documented work is a terracotta *Pietà* group (1495), from which four figures survive at S Domenico, Bologna. His wooden crucifix (*in situ*) for S Marco, Florence, dates from 1496. With other followers of Savonarola, Baccio fled in 1498 to Bologna and Venice. A wooden figure of *St Sebastian* (Bologna, S Maria del Baraccano) attributed to him may date from this period. He also carved a *Christ and the Twelve Apostles* (untraced; those in Ferrara Cathedral are not by Baccio). For S Lorenzo in Florence he carved a wooden crucifix (*c.* 1500; untraced; the cork crucifix in S Lorenzo is not by Baccio), and the figure of the *Christ Child* (*in situ*) for the tympanum of the marble tabernacle by DESIDERIO DA SETTIGNANO has been attributed to him (Verdier, 1983). In the following years Baccio's workshop specialized in the production of wooden crucifixes, including those in S Maria Novella, Florence, and SS Flora e Lucilla, Arezzo.

Between 1504 and 1510 Baccio made a number of works for S Godenzo, Val di Sieve, Mugello; a polychrome wood *St Sebastian* (1506) survives there. He often worked with Michelangelo and may have assisted him on figures for the Piccolomini Altar (Siena Cathedral). The carved frame of Michelangelo's Doni Tondo (*Holy Family*; *c.* 1505; Florence, Uffizi) has been convincingly attributed to him (Lisner, 1965). He supplied the marble figure of *Mars* (and possibly also *Neptune*) for the monument of *Benedetto Pesaro* (1506) in S Maria dei Frari, Venice. In 1515 he completed his finest sculpture, the bronze statue of *St John the Evangelist* for Orsanmichele, Florence, made in competition for the guild of silk merchants. In this period he began a long association with the city of Lucca, where Dominican influence was strong. Three enamelled busts, a *Virgin and Child*, *St Romano* and *St Pellegrino* (all Lucca, S Concordio in Contrada), are attributed to him. The influence of Savonarolan ideas may be felt in a marble altar with the figure of the *Redeemer* (1518; Lucca, Segromigno Monte, S Lorenzo). Michelangelo may have helped Baccio to win his most important commission, to design S Paolino, Lucca (begun 1518). An important commission

for the tomb of *Bishop Niccolò Pandolfini* (*d* 1519) in the Badia of Pistoia remained unfinished.

The last years of Baccio's life are not well documented. As he probably employed many assistants, it is difficult to gauge the stylistic range of his workshop. He has been identified with the Master of the David and St John Statuettes. While his art demonstrates an affinity to Donatello, it is even more closely related to that of the della Robbia workshop and of Benedetto da Maiano. His later style also shows an awareness of the work of Andrea Sansovino.

BIBLIOGRAPHY
F. Albertini: *Memoriale di molte statue e pitture della città di Firenze* (Florence, 1510); repr. in *Five Early Guides to Rome and Florence*, intro. P. Murray (Farnborough, 1972)
G. Vasari: *Vite* (1550, rev. 2/1568); ed. G. Milanesi (1878–85), iv, pp. 258, 539–62
F. Sansovino: *Venetia, città nobilissima et singolare* (Venice, 1581), p. 66a
C. de Fabriczy: 'Scultura in legno di Baccio da Montelupo', *Riv. A.*, i (1903), pp. 67–8
A. del Vita: 'Un crucifisso di Baccio da Montelupo ritrovato nella chiesa di S. Flora e Lucilla in Arezzo', *Riv. A.*, vii (1910), pp. 90–92
F. Filippino: 'Baccio da Montelupo in Bologna', *Dedalo*, iii (1927–8), pp. 527–42
M. Weinberger: 'A Bronze Statuette in the Frick Collection and its Connections with Michelangelo', *Gaz. B.-A.*, xxxix (1952), pp. 103–14
M. Lisner: 'Zum Rahmen von Michelangelos Madonna Doni', *Studien zur Geschichte der europäischen Plastik: Festschrift Theodor Müller* (Munich, 1965), pp. 167–78
J. Pope-Hennessy and A. Radcliffe: *Italian Sculpture* (New York, 1970), pp. 54–8; iii of *The Frick Collection*
P. Verdier: 'Il putto ignoto', *Bull. Cleveland Mus. A.*, lxx/7 (1983), pp. 303–11
F. Petrucci: 'Baccio da Montelupo a Lucca', *Paragone*, xxxv (1984), pp. 3–22

(2) Raffaello [Raffaele] **da Montelupo** [Sinibaldi] (*b* Florence, 9 July 1504; *d* Orvieto, before 26 Dec 1566). Son of (1) Baccio da Montelupo. Trained by his father and the goldsmith Michelangelo Viviani in Florence, he worked briefly in Carrara in 1521 and entered the workshop of Lorenzo Lotti in Rome in 1523. There he assisted on projects including the tomb of the poet *Bernardino Capella* (*c.* 1460–1524) in S Stefano Rotondo, the tomb of *Raphael* (Pantheon) and in the Cappella Chigi (S Maria del Popolo). It was probably through the circle of Raphael that he met influential supporters, such as Baldassare Turini and Antonio da Sangallo (ii). He also made drawings after the Antique (destr.) during this formative period, which ended in 1527 with the Sack of Rome. His first major commission was to assist in the execution of the marble decoration designed by Andrea Sansovino for the Santa Casa (1530–33) at Loreto, where he worked with Niccolò Tribolo, Giovan Francesco da Sangallo, Simone Mosca and others under the direction of Antonio da Sangallo (i). He carved the relief of the *Adoration of the Magi*, the left half of the *Birth of the Virgin*, the *Visitation* and some putti. In 1533–4 for Michelangelo he carved the statue of *St Damian* for the New Sacristy in S Lorenzo, Florence. Influence from his period in Loreto is apparent in his relief of the *Adoration of the Magi* (1538–41) for Simone Mosca's altar of the *Magi* in Orvieto Cathedral. In 1541–2 Raffaelo completed the seated figure of *Leo X*, left unfinished by Baccio Bandinelli, for the Pope's tomb (Rome, S Maria sopra Minerva). Between 1542 and 1545 for Michelangelo's tomb of *Julius II* (Rome, S Pietro in Vincoli) he worked on the over life-size statues of the

Virgin and Child, on the *Prophet* and *Sibyl* and possibly on *Leah* and *Rachel*.

In 1544 Raffaello executed the colossal marble statue of the *Archangel Michael* for the top of Castel Sant'Angelo, Rome, to replace one lost during the Sack of Rome; it in turn was replaced in 1753. Other works from the 1540s include the funerary monument to *Sigismondo Dondolo* (1543; Rome, S Maria della Consolazione) and the tomb of *Girolamo de' Giustini* (1548–9; Rome, S Maria della Pace). He also worked as an architect for Tiberio Crispi (1497–1566), papal castellan of Castel Sant'Angelo, where he built the Loggia of Paul III, the vestibule of the Sala Paolina and the new papal apartments (1542–5). During the same period he constructed Crispi's palace at Bolsena (begun by Mosca). In 1553 he completed the tomb of *Baldassare Turini*, begun by Pierino da Vinci, for Pescia Cathedral. In that year also he succeeded Mosca as *capomaestro* of the cathedral works at Orvieto, where his work included statues of the *Risen Christ*, *Adam* and *Eve* and the Apostle programmes for the nave and the façade; most of these were completed after his death. In the 1550s he supervised the construction of Crispi's palace and of S Lorenzo in Vineis, both in Orvieto. Raffaello often worked collaboratively and completed projects begun by others, which did not encourage the development of a distinctive personal style. His sculpture was influenced by the Raphaelesque style of Lotti and the classicism of Andrea Sansovino, his architecture by Antonio da Sangallo (ii).

BIBLIOGRAPHY

Thieme–Becker
G. Vasari: *Vite* (1550, rev. 2/1568); ed. G. Milanesi (1878–85), iv, pp. 539ff
R. Borghini: *Il riposo* (Florence, 1584), pp. 407ff
J. W. Gaye: *Carteggio*, iii (Florence, 1840), pp. 581ff [autobiographical fragments]
A. Venturi: *Storia* (1901–40), x
K. Weil-Garris: *The Santa Casa di Loreto: Problems in Cinquecento Sculpture* (New York and London, 1977)
T. R. Verellen: *Raffaello da Montelupo als Bildhauer und Architekt* (diss., U. Hamburg, 1981)

TILL R. VERELLEN

Montenegro [Crna Gora]. Republic of the former Yugoslavia in the Balkan peninsula, south-eastern Europe. It borders Bosnia and Herzegovina, Serbia and Albania, with the Adriatic Sea to the west (see fig. 1). It is mainly mountainous and covers an area of 13,812 sq. km. The population is *c.* 580,000, and the capital is Podgorica (known as Titograd, 1946–92). The area was part of SERBIA from the late 12th century until the mid-14th. By the end of the 15th century it had been incorporated into the Ottoman empire, but the Montenegrins retained a measure of autonomy and in 1838 were officially recognized by the Ottomans as independent. In 1918 Montenegro became part of the Kingdom of Serbs, Croats and Slovenes (Kingdom of Yugoslavia from 1929), and it was later a constituent republic of the Communist Republic of Yugoslavia (1945–92). Within modern Montenegro there is a clear distinction between the mountainous region, which rises steeply from the coast to 2000 m, and the narrow coastal strip, including the Dalmatian Boka Kotorska (Gulf of Kotor), which was given to Montenegro by the Communist government in 1945. This explains the stylistic and cultural differences between the coastal area, which has a mainly Roman Catholic Croat population, and the mountainous region, inhabited by Orthodox Montenegrins.

I. Architecture. II. Painting, graphic arts and sculpture. III. Decorative arts. IV. Museums.

I. Architecture.

The most prominent ecclesiastical building in Montenegro is the Romanesque Catholic cathedral of St Tryphon in Kotor (9th century; rebuilt 1166; see fig. 2). The two towers of the west front were added in the 17th century. Early proto-Romanesque forms are discernible in the Roman Catholic churches of St Paul (1266), St Mary (Collegiata; 1221) and St Luke (1195) in Kotor. These are simple spaces, each with a single nave. Gothic influences are apparent only in the decorative elements (portals, rosettes, window frames). In the coastal area, there are several surviving Renaissance palaces in Kotor (Pima, Gregorina, Bizanti) and in Perast (Bujević Palace). The jewel in the Gulf of Kotor is the Catholic church on the island of Gospa od Škrpjela (17th century), which has Baroque elements. The late Baroque is represented by the 18th-century church in Prčanj. The Orthodox churches in the mountainous region are usually aisleless, with vestibules on the north and south sides, simple domes and one or two spires at the west end. Stylistically, they are a mixture of Byzantine and Mediterranean influences, with Serbian influence in the later buildings (15th–17th centuries). Vernacular architecture in the mountainous areas consisted mainly of timber buildings with steep shingle roofs. There are significant Venetian towns and fortifications at Herceg-Novi (founded by Stephen Tvrtko I of Bosnia in 1382) and at Kotor, Bar and Ulcinj, all dating from the Middle Ages.

Austria occupied the Gulf of Kotor in 1814 and rebuilt its coastal fortifications. After World War II, owing to the prominence of Montenegrins among the Yugoslav partisan troops led by Marshal Tito, the republic benefited from a Socialist rebuilding programme that focused mainly on industrial and urban construction, particularly in Titograd (Podgorica). These buildings, however, with a few exceptions, have little architectural value.

BIBLIOGRAPHY

Enciklopedija likovnih umjetnosti [Encyclopedia of fine arts], i (Zagreb, 1959), pp. 675–7

PAUL TVRTKOVIĆ

II. Painting, graphic arts and sculpture.

The earliest surviving wall paintings in Montenegro are those depicting *Michael, King of Zeta*, in St Michael's Church near Ston, which have links with Carolingian art. The ornamentation of such illuminated manuscripts as the Miroslav Evangeliary (*c.* 1180; Belgrade, N. Mus.), however, reveals Romanesque influence, while the Byzantine tradition is evident in the Gospel of Vukan (*c.* 1200; St Petersburg, Rus. N. Lib., F. n. I. 82; see SERBIA, §III, 1(iii)). Among the finest wall paintings in Montenegro is the cycle of the *Life of St Elias* (1252) in Morača Monastery, which is important for the history of Serbian medieval art. One of the earliest documented printmakers was the monk Makarije, who in 1494–6 worked at the

1. Map of Montenegro

printing house of Pri Djordje Crnojević (*reg* 1490–96). The printing house was influenced both technically and artistically by Italy, as is evident in the woodcuts in the Cetinje Octateuch (Cetinje, 1494). In the 15th and 16th centuries, owing to the Turkish occupation of the Balkans, most Orthodox ecclesiastical books were produced in the printing house of Božidar Vuković-Podgoričanin and his son Vićenco, who were living in exile in Venice. Most of the woodcuts in Vuković's books were in Post-Byzantine style and were influenced by Italo-Cretan icon painting. The woodcuts also served as models for later icons.

Morača Monastery was the centre of icon painting at which Georgije Mitrofanović (*fl* 1615/16–22) from Chilandar Monastery on Mt Athos probably painted his first icons; his pupils and their followers continued to work there, among them Kir Kozma, Avesalom Vujičić and Zograf Radul (*see* POST-BYZANTINE ART, §III, 1(iii)). The

Baroque style is evident in the work of artists of the Kotor school, primarily TRIPO KOKOLJA (e.g. his paintings in the church at Gospa od Škrpjela) and Antun Mazarović (who painted royal portraits in Vienna and Warsaw in the 18th century). Montenegrin painters, notably the Rafajlović family, continued to execute wall paintings, icons and iconostases during the 19th century, but the second half of the century was characterized by the work of foreign artists: the French painter and lithographer Théodore Valério (1819–79), who produced prints of Montenegrin life for travel books, the Czech painter Jaroslav Čermak (1831–78), the Croats Ferdo Quiquerez (1845–93) and Vlaho Bukovac (1855–1922) and the Serb Paja Jovanović (1859–1957). Their work inspired many Montenegrin artists, including Anastas Bocarić (1864–1944) and Marko Gregović (1866–1941). The turn of the 20th century was marked by the abandonment of academicist realism in favour of a more modern style akin to Impressionism, as in the work of Petar Poček (1878–1963) and Djoko Popović (1887–1911).

There was also great interest in photography in the 19th century, inspired largely by the enthusiasm of the Montenegrin ruler, Petar Petrović Njegoš, who sent Duke Milorad Medaković from Cetinje to Dubrovnik to study the new medium. By the end of the century a number of professional portrait photography studios were operating. Montenegrin printmaking had ceased with the demise of Vuković's printing house at the end of the 16th century but was revived in the 19th century with the re-establishment of the printing house in Cetinje. In the early 20th century the painter and printmaker Ilija Šobajić (1876–1953) produced prints of figures and landscapes in which he showed interest in problems of form. The printmaker Mirko Kujačić (1901–87) executed genre studies of fishermen's lives, while Ivo Novaković (1913–41) created a series of linocuts on social themes.

Many Montenegrin artists, including Miloš Vušković (1900–75), Jovan Zonjić (1907–61), Mirko Kujačić, Mihajlo Vukotić (1904–44) and Milan Božović (1909–91), lived and worked in Belgrade in the inter-war years, finding a place in local artistic circles there. MILO MILUNOVIĆ and PETAR LUBARDA both had a significant impact on Serbian art, particularly after World War II. Milunović was influenced by Cézanne and Cubism, while Lubarda adopted the idiom of American Abstract Expressionism. Milunović was also a printmaker who played a prominent role in educating Montenegrin students of printmaking. DADO (Miodrag Djurić), an internationally acclaimed Surrealistic painter and printmaker, moved to Paris, but his works

2. Montenegro, cathedral of St Tryphon, Kotor, 1166; west front after 1667

continued to be informed by imagery reflecting his childhood experience of wartime Montenegro (see fig. 3). Vuko Radović (b 1911) and Savo Vujović (1900–73), who belonged to the older generation, as well as many younger painters, such as Aleksandar Prijić (1920–86), Vojo Stanić (b 1924), Cvetko Lainović (b 1931) and Ksenija Vulović (b 1930), were active in post-war Montenegro.

Photography continued to play an important role in Montenegrin art life in the 20th century. Such photographers as Savo Orović provided important documentation of World War II, and notable post-war photographers included Milan Pešić, Jovo Marić and Milan Raonić. Many museums and art schools also helped promote an interest in the form. Among printmakers, Milenko Žarković (b 1940) produced compositions with historical reminiscences, while Jakov Djuričić (b 1942) perfected colour techniques and produced diptychs with poetic titles, in which objects were given a new, precisely defined graphic expression charged with eroticism. The work of Dimitrije Popović (b 1951), with its use of dry-point technique, is notable for its linear qualities and its quasi-mannerist, Post-modern spirit. Anka Burić (b 1956) used various techniques to develop an original visual language of poetic intimacy and fantasy. A department of graphic art was opened at Cetinje University in 1988, providing opportunities for the development of such talented young printmakers as Mirko Toljić (b 1962), known for his use of a rare lithographic technique conveying broad expressive forms linked to the human figure. Sculpture was perhaps less popular, although notable exponents included Marko Brežanin (1883–1956), Risto Stjović (1894–1974) and Luka Tomanović (1909–92), who worked within the classical tradition.

BIBLIOGRAPHY

D. Radojčić: 'O štampariji Crnojević' [About the Crnojević printing house], *Glasnik skopskog naučnog društva* (Skopje, 1938), pp. 161–6

D. Medaković: *Grafika srpskih štampanih knjiga XV–XVII veka* [The graphic art of Serbian printed books of the 15th to 17th centuries] (Belgrade, 1958)

Slikari i vajari iz Crne Gore, 1900–1960 [Painters and sculptors of Montenegro, 1900–1960] (exh. cat. by V. Djurić, Cetinje, Crna Gora A.G., 1964)

Jugoslovenska grafika, 1900–1950 (exh. cat. by M. B. Protić and others, Belgrade, Mus. Contemp. A., 1977)

P. Mijović: *Umjetničko blago Crne Gore* [The art treasure of Montenegro] (Belgrade, 1980)

V. Kraut: *Istorija srpske grafike od XV do XX veka* [The history of Serbian graphic art from the 15th to the 20th century] (Gornji Milanovac, 1985)

S. Petković: *Morača* (Belgrade, 1986)

STANISLAV ŽIVKOVIĆ, with VANYA KRAUT

III. Decorative arts.

Montenegrin decorative arts show the influence of old Albanian and Slav traditions, with Byzantine and Turkish Islamic features also visible in the mountainous inland areas and ancient Roman influence evident along the coast. Such traditional crafts as wool weaving, wood carving and pottery continued to be practised in the inland areas until the 1930s and 1940s, but in the coastal zone, the commercial manufacture of home furnishings, dishes, dress, jewellery and weapons replaced domestic production. Montenegrins paid great attention to decorating their homes.

Wooden chests were one of the most important items of furniture, and through the study of these chests from around the 13th century to the mid-20th it is possible to trace the many influences on Montenegrin art. The most important workshops were in the Gulf of Kotor, where carpentry developed in the 13th century. Skadar chests were famous for their painted floral decorations, showing a strong Levantine–Baroque influence. The front, sides and inside of the lid were usually decorated with crude blue, green, yellow and red stylized tulips and poppies. A common motif was the six-pointed star, framed in white, symbolizing the sun. Until the late 20th century the chest was an integral part of a bridal dowry. Other carved wooden furnishings included cradles, usually painted with motifs designed to ward off the 'evil eye', three-legged chairs, spinning wheels, smoking equipment and musical instruments. The head of a horse or goat was carved on the end of the neck of the traditional stringed instrument (*gusla*) symbolizing strength, persistence and dignity. The bow was curved in the form of a snake. Dishes were of wood, earthenware or copper. Metal dishes were made by professional craftsmen and were highly decorated by hammering and engraving. Islamic influences were evident in such dishes as well as in coffeepots and cups, copper pans and washbowls etc. Some of the finest decoration on metal is on weapons, which were made out of iron, silver and gold, decorated with precious and semi-precious stones, and were an important part of a man's attire. Jewellery, often filigree, was made by craftsmen around the Gulf of Kotor. Black, hand-thrown pottery was typical of the mountain regions, where it was used for cooking. Around Lake Skadar, pottery was finer and partially glazed, used for storing honey and pickled foods.

Domestic interiors were decorated with such woollen and other textile furnishings as rugs, cradle covers, towels, tablecloths and wall hangings. The older rugs were made of thick wool, woven in dark blue, brown, green and blue with geometrical floral or animal motifs. Women's costumes varied according to the region, the most archaic form being a type of skirt called *dzupeleta*, of Illyrian origin and made of alternating oblique-cut, heavy cloth and woollen strips, which narrow at the waist, giving a bell-like look. This black garment was decorated with pearls and embroidered with plant and animal motifs—often cocks or eagles. Men's dress was also simple; the traditional jacket had long sleeves, which also widened in a bell-like shape and fell to the knees. Simple materials were replaced in the wealthier regions by velvet and silk embroidered and trimmed with silver and gold. This type of dress was in use until the early 20th century, when it was gradually replaced by more 'European' style dress.

BIBLIOGRAPHY
N. Pantelic: *L'Art populaire yougoslave* (Belgrade, 1980)
Folk Art of Montenegro (exh. cat., London, Horniman Mus. & Lib., 1983)
Z. Mrvaljevic: *Narodna nošnja Crna Gore* [Folk costume of Montenegro] (Zagreb, 1988)

DIANE WALLER

IV. Museums.

There are 20 museums and collections in Montenegro, the earliest of which, the State Museum in Cetinje, was founded in 1893. There followed the City Museum in

3. Dado: *Massacre of the Innocents*, oil on canvas, 1958–9 (Paris, Pompidou, Musée National d'Art Moderne)

Perast (1936), the Maritime Museum in Kotor (1938), the Orthodox Church Museum in Cetinje (1939), which houses religious works as well as examples of early printing from the Crnojević printing press, and the Ethnographical Museum (1951), also in Cetinje. There is an archaeological collection at the Roman Catholic church of St Mary in Budva, and the Njegoš Museum (1951) in Cetinje contains memorabilia of the former Montenegrin royal family. The Crna Gora Art Gallery was founded in Cetinje in 1950 and consists mainly of works by Montenegrin artists, but it also has a representative collection of paintings by the Croatian Vlaho Bukovac. Also on display there are copies of wall paintings (13th–18th centuries) from the monasteries at Morača, Praskvica and Reževic.

BIBLIOGRAPHY
Enciklopedija likovnih umjetnosti [Encyclopedia of fine arts], ii (Zagreb, 1962), p. 347; iii (1964), p. 517

PAUL TVRTKOVIĆ

Montenegro (Nervo), Roberto (*b* Guadalajara, 19 Feb 1887; *d* Mexico City, 13 Oct 1968). Mexican painter, printmaker, illustrator and stage designer. In 1903 he began studying painting in Guadalajara under Félix Bernardelli, an Italian who had established a school of painting and music there, and he produced his first illustrations for

Revista moderna, a magazine that promoted the Latin American modernist movement and for which his cousin, the poet Amado Nervo, wrote. In 1905 he enrolled at the Escuela Nacional de Arte in Mexico City, where Diego Rivera was also studying, and won a grant to study in Europe. After two years in Madrid, Montenegro moved in 1907 to Paris, where he continued his studies and had his first contact with Cubism, meeting Picasso, Braque and Gris.

After a short stay in Mexico, Montenegro returned to Paris. At the outbreak of World War I he moved to Barcelona and from there to Mallorca, where he lived as a fisherman for the next four years. During his stay in Europe he assimilated various influences, in particular from Symbolism, from Art Nouveau (especially Aubrey Beardsley) and from William Blake.

On his return to Mexico Montenegro worked closely with José Vasconcelos, Secretary of State for Public Education during the presidency of Alvaro Obregón in the early 1920s, faithfully following his innovative ideas on murals and accompanying him on journeys in Mexico and abroad. He was put in charge of the Departamento de Artes Plásticas in 1921 and was invited by Vasconcelos to 'decorate' the walls of the former convent, the Colegio Máximo de S Pedro y S Pablo in Mexico City. The first of these works, executed in 1922, consisted of the mural *Tree of Life* (*see* MURAL, fig. 4), relating the origin and destiny of man, and two designs for richly ornamented stained-glass windows influenced by popular art: *Guadalajara Tapdance* and *The Parakeet-seller*. They were followed by two further murals in the same building: the *Festival of the Holy Cross* (1923–4), representing the popular festival of 3 May celebrated by bricklayers and stonemasons, and *Resurrection* (1931–3), with a geometric composition bearing a slight Cubist influence. Further murals followed, including *Spanish America* (1924; Mexico City, Bib. Ibero-Amer. & B.A.), an allegory of the historical and spiritual union of Latin America in the form of a map, and *The Story*, also known as *Aladdin's Lamp* (1926; Mexico City, Cent. Escolar Benito Juárez), a formally designed painting with Oriental figures similar in style to a mural made for Vasconcelos's private offices.

Although Montenegro claimed to be a 'subrealist' rather than a Surrealist, in his easel paintings he mixed reality and fantasy; two such works, which fall well within the bounds of Surrealism, were shown in 1940 at the International Exhibition of Surrealism held at the Galería de Arte Mexicano in Mexico City. In his later work Montenegro evolved an abstract style, although he never lost his interest in popular, pre-Hispanic and colonial art. He was also a fine portrait painter, and from the 1940s to the 1960s he produced a splendid series of self-portraits in which he is shown reflected in a convex mirror, thus combining elements of Mannerism and popular art. He illustrated books, made incursions into stage design, working for both the ballet and the theatre, and in 1934 created the Museo de Arte Popular in the recently inaugurated Palacio de Bellas Artes in Mexico City, becoming its first director.

WRITINGS
Planos en el tiempo (Mexico City, 1962) [autobiography]

BIBLIOGRAPHY
J. Fernández: *Roberto Montenegro* (Mexico City, 1962)
I. Rodríguez Prampolini: *El surrealismo y el arte fantástico de México* (Mexico City, 1969)
E. Acevedo and others: *Guía de murales del centro histórico de la Ciudad de México* (Mexico City, 1984)
Roberto Montenegro, 1887–1968 (exh. cat., Mexico City, Mus. N.A., 1984)
L. Morales: *Las artes plásticas en México de 1920 a 1950* (Madrid, 1986)
LEONOR MORALES

Montepulciano, Pasquino da. *See* PASQUINO DA MONTEPULCIANO.

Montero, Luis (*b* Piura, 27 Oct 1827; *d* El Callao, 22 March 1869). Peruvian painter. He studied at the Academia de Dibujo y Pintura in Lima under Ignacio Merino. He won a Peruvian government travel grant to study in Europe and spent some time in Italy, where he entered the Accademia di Belle Arti in Florence. In 1851 he returned to Peru, where he replaced Merino as director of the Academia de Dibujo y Pintura. The State gave him another grant, which enabled him to live in Italy from 1852 to 1855 and to travel to Paris. From 1856 to 1859 he lived in Havana, Cuba, where he married. He returned to Peru before living again from 1861 to 1868 in Italy, where he painted the *Funeral of Atahualpa* (3.5×4.3 m, 1867; Lima, Mus. A.), a solemn and grandiloquent history painting, which he exhibited with great success in Brazil, Argentina and Chile; it was purchased by the Peruvian government and reproduced on the 500 Sol banknote. He was awarded the Medalla de Oro del Congreso and a pension for life.

BIBLIOGRAPHY
T. Núñez Ureta: *Pintura contemporánea peruana: Primera parte, 1820–1920* (Lima, 1975)
L. E. Tord: 'Historia de las artes plásticas en el Perú', *Historia del Perú*, ix (Lima, 1980)
LUIS ENRIQUE TORD

Monterrey [formerly Nuestra Señora de Monterrey]. Mexican city and capital of the state of Nuevo León, situated in the north-east of the country. The country's third largest city, it has a population of *c.* 2.5 million. Various attempts at colonization by the Spanish during the 16th century culminated in the founding in 1596 of Nuestra Señora de Monterrey by Diego de Montemayor. The limited economic interest that the area offered the Spanish, its northern location, the bellicosity of the local indigenous people and the belated establishment and Christianization of the settlement all explain the small number of architectural examples dating from the colonial period. The only significant works that remain are the former hacienda of S Pedro (1660) and the chapel of the former Palacio de Nuestra Señora de Guadalupe (1787; now Museo Regional El Obispado). The first signs of a regional architecture came after Mexican independence was achieved in 1821. The new rail connection between Monterrey and Mexico City, opened in 1887, fostered industrial development. Notable constructions from this period include the first buildings for the Cervecería Cuauhtémoc (1871; now Museo de Monterrey); those of the iron and steel foundry (1900); and the Vidriera Monterrey (1909). Also significant were the Palacio de Gobierno (1895), the Banco Mercantil (1900) and the Arco de la Independencia Nacional (1910) by A. Gilles, all examples of Neo-classical architecture.

Monterrey finally experienced a cultural boom in the 1970s. In 1974 the Centro de Arte Vitro was founded, followed in 1976 by the Casa de la Cultura de Nuevo León. In 1977 the Museo de Monterrey was established in the old brewery, and the following year the Centro Cultural Alfa was built by Fernando Garza Treviño, later incorporating the stained-glass window *The Universe* (1988) by Rufino Tamayo. Various monumental sculptural works were also erected, including *Homage to the Sun* (h. 27 m, 1979) by Tamayo, works by Manuel Felguérez (1981) and Luis Barragán (1983), and the *Gate of Monterrey* (1985) and *The Irises* (1989) by Enrique Carbajal Sebastián. Revolutionary urban design came to Monterrey in 1985 with the creation of the Gran Plaza, perhaps the largest in the world, by Oscar Bulnes and Benjamín Félix. Bulnes was also responsible for designing the Teatro de la Ciudad, the new Palacio Legislativo, the administrative tower of the Gobierno Estatal building and the INFONAVIT building, all built around the square. He also designed the Centro de Tecnología Avanzada (1989) at the Instituto Tecnológico de Monterrey, an apt symbol of the new era of prosperity being experienced by the city. Other products of this prosperity include the ambitious Parque Fundidora by Eduardo Terraza and the new Museo de Arte Contemporáneo (1991), the work of Ricardo Legorreta.

BIBLIOGRAPHY

I. Cavazos: *Diccionario biográfico de Nuevo León* (Monterrey, 1984)
R. Mendirichaga: *Los cuatro tiempos de un pueblo* (Monterrey, 1985)
I. Cavazos: *Síntesis histórica del estado de Nuevo León* (Monterrey, 1988)
X. Moyssén: *Catorce artistas contemporáneos de Monterrey* (Monterrey, 1991)

XAVIER MOYSSÉN LECHUGA

Monterrey, 6th Conde de [Acevedo y Zúñiga, Manuel de] (*b c.* 1590; *d* Madrid, 1653). Spanish patron and collector. He was brother-in-law to the powerful Conde-Duque de Olivares. He became Ambassador to Rome in 1628 and served from 1631 to 1637 as Viceroy of Naples, where he was an enlightened patron. An avid but discriminating collector of paintings in his own right, Don Manuel was also involved as agent in the transfer to Philip IV, either by purchase from or as a gift by Niccolò Ludovisi (*see* LUDOVISI), of *Bacchanal of the Andrians* (mid-1520s) and the *Worship of Venus* (1519; both Madrid, Prado), two paintings by TITIAN that were acquired for the Spanish royal collection before 1658. In 1633 Don Manuel helped provide paintings to decorate the palace of the Buen Retiro (*see* MADRID, §IV, 1) for Philip IV, sending to Spain 12 cartloads of works commissioned from Giovanni Lanfranco (various scenes from the *Life of Imperial Rome*, *c.* 1634; Madrid, Prado; Aranjuez, Pal. Real); Domenichino (*Exequies*, 1635; Madrid, Prado); Giovanni Francesco Romanelli; Aniello Falcone and Andrea di Lione (works with a Roman Imperial theme); and other Seicento masters.

From 1636 Don Manuel built the convent and church of the Agustinas Descalzas (Recoletas) in Salamanca, for whose altars he commissioned both architectural elements and images in Naples. Among the commissioned works were pictures by Jusepe de Ribera (*Immaculate Conception, Pietà, St Januarius*), Guido Reni and Lanfranco, and marble tomb sculptures of the *Conde* and his wife, *Dona Leonor Maria de Guzmán* (1591–1654), by Giuliano Finelli (all in *situ*), all shipped to Spain in 1638. These works form the best preserved example of an Italian Baroque ensemble in Spain; Ribera's *Immaculate Conception* was particularly influential in Spain. Don Manuel's palace on the Prado de San Geronimo, Madrid, was arranged like a museum; it included chalk drawings of swimmers (untraced; attributed to Michelangelo; Carducho writing before 1633), a *Holy Family* (untraced) attributed to Raphael and Venetian paintings, including a *St Catherine Adoring the Crucifix* (Boston, MA, Mus. F.A.) by Titian and his workshop.

After Don Manuel's death, the Monterrey estates were inherited by his niece, Dona Inés-Francisca de Zúñiga (*c.* 1635–1710), wife of Don Juan Domingo de Guzmán, the second son of the 6th Marqués del Carpio. The picture collection became part of the CARPIO (Haro y Guzmán) holdings in 1710, from which it passed into the ALBA estates in 1733.

BIBLIOGRAPHY

V. Carducho: *Diálogos de la pintura* (Madrid, 1633); *R* in F. J. Sánchez Cantón: *Fuentes literarias*, ii (Madrid, 1933), pp. 100–03
A. García Boiza: *Una fundación de Monterrey: La iglesia y convento de M. M. Agustinas de Salamanca* (Salamanca, 1945)
A. Madruga Real: 'Cosimo Fanzago en las Agustinas de Salamanca', *Goya*, cxxv (1975), pp. 291–7
A. E. Pérez Sánchez: 'Las colecciones de pintura del Conde de Monterrey (1653)', *Bol. Real Acad. Hist.*, clxxiv/3 (1977), pp. 417–59
M. Burke: *Private Collections of Italian Art in 17th-century Spain* (diss., New York U., 1984; microfilm, Ann Arbor, 1986), i, pp. 57–72; ii, docs 2.3–2.5

MARCUS BURKE

Monte sacro. *See* SACROMONTE.

Montesquieu, Baron de [Secondat, Charles-Louis de] (*b* Labrède, Gironde, 18 Jan 1689; *d* Paris, 10 Feb 1755). French jurist and writer. He was born into the Bordeaux nobility and was destined for a legal career. He was President of the Parlement of Bordeaux from 1716 to 1725, but from 1722 he mainly devoted himself to writing. He made frequent visits to Paris, where he was welcomed into all the literary circles; the Académie Française elected him a member in 1727. A year later Montesquieu set out on a long journey (1728–9) through Europe, particularly through England and Italy; his observations on the customs and institutions of the places he travelled through were recorded in copious notes that gave a prominent place to art. For a person whose interests had been chiefly literary, the fine arts were a novel experience. Montesquieu was a meticulous and highly observant tourist. In Italy he followed well-trodden itineraries: in Milan, he admired Leonardo da Vinci's *Last Supper* (S Maria delle Grazie) and enquired about the process for fixing oils on a mural base. In Florence, being a considerable scholar of Roman history, he first directed his attention to the chronologically arranged collection of busts of the ancient emperors in the Uffizi, attempting to read in them a progressive artistic decline. He admired the doors executed by Lorenzo Ghiberti for the Baptistery in Florence and wrote a long note on the historical significance of the Gothic style. In Rome he was greatly delighted by Raphael's *Transfiguration* (Rome, Pin. Vaticana) and by the works of Guido Reni and Domenichino.

In 1753, at the request of the writer and philosopher Jean le Rond d'Alembert, Montesquieu wrote the article on taste ('Goût') for the *Encyclopédie* (1751–65). He considered judgement in matters of taste to be relative, being the product both of humanity's limited capacity for perception and of people's individual education and culture; he tried, however, to justify the existence of classical canons in art. His historical writings and his methods had a profound influence on Johann Joachim Winckelmann.

WRITINGS

'Goût', *Encyclopédie*, ed. D. Diderot and J. d'Alembert, vii (Paris, 1757), pp. 762–7 [incomplete]

D. Oster, ed.: *Oeuvres complètes* (Paris, 1964), pp. 214–304 [*Voyage en Italie*], 853–1082 [*Mes Pensées*]

C. Beyer, ed.: *Essai sur le goût* (Geneva, 1967) [complete version of the text]

BIBLIOGRAPHY

E. P. Dargan: *The Aesthetic Doctrine of Montesquieu: Its Application in his Writings* (Baltimore, 1907)

J. Ehrard: *Montesquieu critique d'art* (Paris, 1965)

C. Rosso: 'I piaceri dell'arte e l'esperienza italiana di Montesquieu', *Illuminismo, felicità, dolore: Miti e ideologie francesi* (Naples, 1969), pp. 201–10

A. Becq: *Genèse de l'esthétique française moderne: De la raison classique à l'imagination créatrice, 1680–1814* (Pisa, 1984), i, pp. 344–51, 421–5

G. Van Den Abbele: 'Montesquieu *touriste*, or a View from the Top', *Espr. Créateur*, xxv/3 (1985), pp. 64–74

PASCAL GRIENER

Montesquiou(-Fezensac), Robert, Comte de (*b* Paris, 7 March 1855; *d* Menton, 11 Dec 1921). French writer, poet and collector. He was taught first by a private tutor, then at the Lycée Bonaparte (now Condorcet) in Paris, and finally by the Jesuits at Vaugirard in Paris, a tutelage he detested. At the age of about 20 he came into contact with the literary avant-garde in Paris, meeting such figures as Stéphane Mallarmé, Paul Bourget and José-Maria de Heredia, and first saw a painting by Gustave Moreau, an artist he came to admire greatly. Montesquiou's exotic tastes and lifestyle formed the model for Des Esseintes, the main protagonist in Joris-Karl Huysmans's novel *À rebours* (Paris, 1884), and this further enhanced his fame. He was also the model for a less flattering character—the Baron de Charlus—in Marcel Proust's *À la recherche du temps perdu* (Paris, 1913–27). Montesquiou's visual aesthetic was paradigmatic of the Symbolist movement and was best displayed in his interior design schemes for his appartements in the Quai d'Orsay and the Rue Franklin: in both he mixed the most incongruous objects and colours. The former, for example, had midnight-blue walls, violet carpets, glass cases containing ties and socks, along with designs by William Morris and engravings by Whistler. He shared the contemporary interest in Japanese art, and *kakemono* (hanging scrolls) and Japanese embroideries also featured.

Montesquiou was a staunch supporter and friend of the glass designers Emile Gallé and René Lalique, and his encouragement of their work helped to establish the Art Nouveau style in France. He also knew the artist Paul César Helleu, from whom he commissioned many portraits of his female friends. 'Women-flowers, flower-children, these are the true models of Helleu, master of elegance', he wrote in *Paul Helleu: Peintre et graveur* (Paris, 1919, p. 18). In 1884 he visited London, attracted by the work of the Pre-Raphaelites Edward Burne-Jones and William Morris, and made a second visit in 1890, accompanied by the painter Jacques-Emile Blanche. In London he became a close friend of Whistler, whose painting he came to prefer to Moreau's.

In addition to such volumes of poetry as *Les Chauves-souris* (Paris, 1892), Montesquiou wrote many essays and articles, some of which appeared in *Gazette des beaux-arts*, *Les Arts* and *Les Arts de la vie*. The collection *Autels privilégiés* (Paris, 1898) includes essays on Leonardo da Vinci, William Blake, described as 'the Fra Angelico of the strange and terrible' (p. 198), Burne-Jones, Arnold Böcklin and Théodore Chassériau. There is also a review of Tolstoy's *What Is Art?* (1898) in which he gives his own definition of the work of art as 'Love which has for its object nothing other than itself': a perfect expression of the art for art's sake aesthetic. *Altesses sérénissimes* (Paris, 1907) features a substantial essay on Moreau and pieces on Albert Besnard, Giovanni Boldini, John Singer Sargent and Auguste Rodin. His highly critical essay on Sargent earned Bernard Berenson's approval for attacking the artist Berenson called 'that idol of the Anglo-Saxons'. *Assemblée de notables* (Paris, 1908) contained a brief essay on Aubrey Beardsley in which he wrote (p. 27): 'This prodigious artist . . . had looked at Botticelli and Burne-Jones, Dürer and Whistler, Japanese albums and Greek vases and from this diverse, amalgamated contemplation, resulted a fantasmagoria, wild and serious, frightening and charming.' As much through his energy and tastes as through his writing, Montesquiou was one of the most characteristic and influential of the literary Symbolists. The portrait of him by Giovanni Boldini—*Comte Robert de Montesquiou* (1897; Paris, Mus. d'Orsay)—shows him in a typically dandyish pose.

WRITINGS

Autels privilégiés (Paris, 1898)

Altesses sérénissimes (Paris, 1907)

L'Inextricable graveur: Rodolphe Bresdin (Paris, 1913)

Paul Helleu: Peintre et graveur (Paris, 1919)

Diptyque de Flandre, triptyque de France (Paris, 1921)

BIBLIOGRAPHY

H. Tabart and J. Place: *Bibliographie des auteurs modernes de langue française* (Paris, 1928–)

L. A. G. M. Thomas: *L'Esprit de Montesquiou* (Paris, 1943)

P. Jullian: *Robert de Montesquiou* (Paris, 1965; Eng. trans., London, 1967)

Monteverde, Giulio (*b* Bistagno, nr Alessandria, 8 Oct 1837; *d* Rome, 3 Oct 1917). Italian sculptor. He attended the Accademia Ligustica (1862–5) in Genoa, studying under the guidance of Santo Varni (1807–85), while at the same time working for a cabinetmaker. He won the Pensionato Artistico Triennale and in 1865 went to Rome, where he had immediate success with groups and single figures that were sculpted in a Romantic–Realist style, while also following academic principles. In 1874 he began teaching at the Accademia di Belle Arti in Rome. His fame was established above all by two works: the *Youth of Christopher Columbus* (1870; Genoa, Gal. A. Mod.) and *Edward Jenner Injecting the Vaccine into his Son* (1873; Genoa, Gal. Pal. Bianco). In the latter work the rather static figure of the doctor is contrasted with the free and dynamic form of the child, thus creating a remarkable plastic effect that was often repeated. Monteverde's major work, however, was such celebratory sculpture as the *Genius of Benjamin Franklin* (1871; Rome, Piazza dell'Indipendenza), *Victor-Emanuel II* (1880; Bologna, Giardini Margherita) and *Vincenzo Bellini* (1893; Catania, Piazza Stesicoro). He also obtained numerous commissions from South American countries for monuments celebrating their national heroes and executed a remarkable series of groups and figures for funerary monuments in the cemeteries of Rome, Genoa and Turin. The sculptor also took part in the realization of the monument to *Victor-Emanuel II* (1885–1911) in Rome: he created the colossal group in gilded bronze depicting *Thought* (1910–11), placed at the foot of the great stairway. The symbolic theme of this work, however, was foreign to the artist's mentality and the result was weak, lacking expressive or allegorical force; it was criticized adversely, even at the time of its installation.

Thieme–Becker   BIBLIOGRAPHY

E. Lavagnino: *L'arte moderna*, ii (Turin, 1955), pp. 653–5
F. Sborgi: 'Giulio Monteverde', *La scultura a Genova e in Liguria*, iii (Genoa, 1989), pp. 380–86
M. de Micheli: *La scultura dell'ottocento* (Turin, 1992), pp. 240–44

VALERIO TERRAROLI

Montevideo [San Felipe y Santiago de Montevideo]. Capital of Uruguay and port situated on the north bank of the Río de la Plata estuary. Its population of *c.* 1.3 million is spread over an area of 400 sq. km. sq. It was founded by the Spanish on a narrow peninsula in 1724 as San Felipe y Santiago de Montevideo, a modest settlement and stronghold to detain the advance of Portuguese Brazil. Though not rich in natural resources, the region had abundant wild cattle that had bred in the 17th century.

The earliest urban layout of Montevideo (Ciudad Vieja, 1724–1830), which was in the usual grid-plan form of Hispano-American towns, has been fundamentally preserved, although, apart from the Cerro Fortress (1801–9) designed by the Colonel of the Royal Body of Engineers, José del Pozo y Marqui (1751–1814), only a few traces of its notable military constructions remain (e.g. Puerta Ciudadela, 1741, by Diego Cardoso). The city also lacks any outstanding examples of general colonial buildings. None pre-dates the last decades of the 18th century, by which time Baroque buildings had been almost entirely superseded by the severe academic Neo-classicism of the Cabildo (1804–11), designed by TOMAS TORIBIO, or had been replaced, as with the Matriz church (1792; later Cathedral), the exterior of which was eventually executed in an Italianate Neo-classical style. A Pompeian design was adopted in the ground-plan of one- and two-storey houses, with rooms distributed around two central patios. From the mid-18th century flat or terraced roofs, reflecting Andalusian influence, began to replace sloping roofs; the balcony also appeared, persisting in Montevidean architecture until the mid-20th century.

Following independence, in 1830 Montevideo became the Uruguayan capital, and its city walls were destroyed. Under the spur of increased European (principally Italian) immigration a new city was designed, also with a grid-plan layout, next to the earlier one. Growth continued with settlements along the routes that linked the city to the surrounding areas, and these too generally followed the grid-plan. Builders created a standard house-style that still

Montevideo, view of the skyline from the north-west, showing (centre) the Banco de la República (1938), by Giovanni Veltoni (1880–1942) and Raúl Lerena Acevedo (1888–1971), and (foreground) the Aduana (1920s) by Jorge Herron (1897–1969)

respected the Pompeian ground-plan but not its dimensions: house fronts became narrower (10–12 m), while depth was maintained (at 50 m). Rooms were constructed along one side only, the height of the roof was raised (5–6 m) and the semicircular arch was substituted by the pointed arch. Façades were faced with Florentine ashlar and incorporated dressed-stone window frames and carved wooden doors. Interiors were enriched with marble, stucco and ceramic tiles. Representative of standardized houses were those in the Rens districts in the north and south of the city, developed by the financier Emilio Rens c. 1890. Until well into the 20th century the standard ground-plan predominated in housing, acquiring eclectic, historicist features at times, including Palladian columns, Mudéjar and Gothic window frames and the latest innovations of Art Nouveau. Public buildings, such as tram and railway stations, factories, markets and shops, were often outstanding examples of eclecticism. The Italian engineer Luis Andreoni (1853–1936) was responsible for a number of notable buildings, including the Central Railway Station (1897).

Although Art Nouveau flourished in the early 20th century in such buildings as the house (1922) built by Juan Antonio Ruis (1893–1974) for himself, Italianate Neo-classicism persisted in the renowned Palacio Legislativo (1925) built in marble by the Italian GAETANO MORETTI. From the 1930s the combined influences of Art Deco, the Bauhaus, Frank Lloyd Wright and Le Corbusier transformed architecture in Montevideo (see fig.), notably in the work of JULIO VILAMAJO (e.g. Facultad de Ingeniería, 1937–8, Universidad de Montevideo). Further expansion also took place along the banks of the Río de la Plata, and curtain-wall buildings appeared here (for housing) and in the city (e.g. the Notariado building, 1962–7, by Studio Cinco). The dominant influence of Le Corbusier and Modernism gradually gave way, however, to buildings that expressed greater variety of form and colour, and the city remained broadly characterized by low-level construction (and unabated expansion). Its atmosphere is further enhanced by a profusion of tree-lined avenues and by its coastal avenue, the Rambla.

As with architecture the visual arts were unremarkable in Montevideo before the 19th century, when Neoclassicism was the dominant style. Two of the most notable figures active in the city between the late 19th century and mid-20th were PEDRO FIGARI (see URUGUAY, fig. 3) and JOAQUÍN TORRES GARCÍA, who introduced Neo-plasticism and Constructivism from Europe. The cultural life of the city is enhanced by various museums, the most notable being the Museo Nacional de Artes Plásticas, which has extensive collections of Uruguayan and European art.

For further discussion of the art and architecture of Montevideo see URUGUAY.

BIBLIOGRAPHY
J. Giuria: La arquitectura en el Uruguay, ii (Montevideo, 1955)
A. González and others: Iconografía de Montevideo, Consejo Departamental de Montevideo (Montevideo, 1955)
J. Abella Trías: Montevideo, la ciudad en que vivimos (Montevideo, 1960)
C. Altezor and others: Historia urbanística y edilicia de la ciudad de Montevideo (Montevideo, 1971)
M. Canessa de Sanguinetti: La ciudad vieja de Montevideo (Montevideo, 1976)

MARTA CANESSA DE SANGUINETTI

Montfaucon, Bernard de (b Château de Soulage [Soulatgé], Aude, 16 Jan 1655; d Paris, 21 Dec 1741). French monk and writer. After serving in Germany in the French army of Henri de La Tour d'Auvergne, Vicomte de Turenne, he entered the scholarly Maurist community of Benedictines, making his profession in 1676; he went on to specialize in studies of the Greek Fathers, pursuing these in various abbeys and in Paris. Among his many works in this field is an edition of the writings of St Athanasius (1698) and the Paleographia graeca (1708), an important catalogue of Greek manuscripts. Shortly after publication of the former he went to Rome. On his return he published Diarium italicum (1702), a journal of his travels, the popularity of which led to several translations.

About 1693 Montfaucon began patiently to gather together all available prints and drawings of antique and early medieval art and artefacts he could find. By the early 1720s he reckoned he had between 30,000 and 40,000 of them—the largest corpus by then ever assembled. His aim as an historian was to attempt for the 'Egyptian, Greek, Etruscan, Roman and Gallic nations and numerous others' what he had achieved, through examination of their manuscripts, for the world of the Greek Fathers. The eventual result was his L'Antiquité expliquée et représentée en figures, a voluminous pictorial encyclopedia. Montfaucon's subject-matter, illustrated by 1400 prints, was organized conceptually, and in the text he ranged from discussions of the Greek and Roman gods and heroes to religious customs and domestic and funerary rites. He selected the prints he used for their clarity of detail rather than for any intrinsic artistic merit (which few of them have); they give no sense of scale to the statues, reliefs and other objects they depict, and modern works and forgeries are innocently scattered among authentic examples. L'Antiquité expliquée immediately established itself as an unrivalled source-book for scholars and artists and remained so into the 19th century. It was eventually replaced by the thirteen-volume Musée de sculpture ancienne et moderne (1826–53) of Charles-Othon, Comte de Clarac.

Montfaucon's last major undertaking was Les Monumens de la monarchie française, in which numerous engravings of monarchs and their regalia from the Merovingians to the Bourbon Henry IV, as well as significant incidents from their reigns, determined the textual points of reference for his historical survey. The portraits were based on original examples provided by seals, miniatures, tapestries, tomb effigies and other sources; some engravings of the last-named proved invaluable during the restoration of fragments found in 1977 of effigies that had been in the cathedral of Notre-Dame, Paris, and had been smashed during the French Revolution.

WRITINGS
Diarium italicum, sive monumentorum veterum, bibliothecarum, musaeorum, etc. (Paris, 1702); It. trans. by F. de' Ficorini as Osservazioni . . . sopra l'antichità di Roma descritte nel 'Diario italico' dal B. de Montfaucon (1709); Eng. trans. as The Travels of Father Montfaucon from Paris thro' Italy in the Years 1698, 1699 and 1700 (London, 1712); rev. trans. by J. Henley of 1702 edn as The Antiquities of Italy . . . Being the Travels of B. de Montfaucon (London, 1725)

L'Antiquité expliquée et représentée en figures, 10 vols (Paris, 1719, rev. 1722–4), and *Supplément*, 5 vols (Paris, 1724); Eng. trans. by D. Humphreys as *Antiquity Explained and Represented in Sculptures*, 10 vols (London, 1721–5/R New York, 1976) [incl. trans. of *Supplément*]

Les Monumens de la monarchie française, qui comprennent l'histoire de France, avec les figures de chaque règne, que l'injure du tems a épargnées, 5 vols (Paris, 1729–33)

BIBLIOGRAPHY
Dom Tassin: *Histoire littéraire de la Congrégation de Saint-Maur* (Paris, 1770), pp. 585–616
E. de Broglie: *La Société de l'abbaye de Saint-Germain-des-Prés au XVIIIe siècle: B. de Montfaucon et les Bernardins*, 2 vols (Paris, 1891)
H. Wilhem, U. Berlière and A. Dubourg: *Nouveau Supplément à l'histoire littéraire de la Congrégation de Saint-Maur*, 3 vols (Paris, 1908–32)
H. Leclercq: 'Montfaucon', *Dictionnaire d'archéologie chrétienne et de liturgie* (Paris, 1934)
                                    JACQUES DUBOIS

Montferrand, (Henri Louis) August Ricard de [Monferran, Ogyust] (*b* Chaillot, Paris, 23 Jan 1786; *d* St Petersburg, 28 June 1858). Russian architect and writer of French birth. He studied architecture (1806–13) at the École Spéciale, Paris, and then worked in the office of Napoleon's chief architects Charles Percier and Pierre François Léonard Fontaine. He also worked with J. Molineau, the general inspector of architecture in Paris. In 1814 he presented an album of architectural designs to Alexander I, Tsar of Russia (*reg* 1801–25), and in the spring of 1816 he arrived in St Petersburg. That summer he was appointed senior draughtsman of the Committee for Construction and Hydraulic Works and he became head of the drawing office the following January, having been appointed court architect the previous month.

Montferrand's main structures in the classical style, the Lobanov-Rostovsky house (1817–20), St Isaac's Cathedral (1818–58) and the Alexander Column (1829–34), played an important role in the new layout of St Petersburg planned by Karl Rossi, reflecting the outburst of triumphalism following the defeat of Napoleon. The Lobanov-Rostovsky house occupies an entire trapezoid-shaped block facing Admiralteysky Prospect to the north and St Isaac's Cathedral to the west and has octastyle porticoes on arched bases. The cathedral (*see* ST PETERSBURG, fig. 4) has a symbolic role linked to the idea of Russia as the 'Third Rome'. Thus, despite the compact volume, the fact that the main façades are on the long north and south sides, and the five cupolas traditional on Russian cathedrals, there is a strong resemblance to St Peter's, Rome, and its descendants, including St Paul's Cathedral, London, and Les Invalides, Paris. The Alexander Column in Palace Square, a memorial to the victory over Napoleon, is also linked to such famous models as Pompey's Pillar in Alexandria, the Trajan and Antonine columns in Rome and the Column of the Great Army in the Place Vendôme, Paris. It is the tallest column in the world (47.5 m).

A tendency to eclecticism first appeared in Montferrand's preliminary designs for St Isaac's Cathedral, of which there are schemes in Roman, Gothic, Chinese, Indian, Moorish and Byzantine styles, and in his Moorish-Gothic designs for the Naryshkin dacha (1821 and 1829) in the Crimea. His first buildings in these styles followed the creation (1823) of the first public park in St Petersburg, at Yekateringof; they were in Gothic (the station, the lion house and the farm), Russian (the peasant izbas), Moorish and Chinese styles. Plans for Gothic structures in St Petersburg, for example police boxes, a foundry and his own house, were never executed, as non-classical designs for the façades of town houses in Russia were permitted only in the second half of the 19th century. From the mid-1820s, however, these exotic styles were widely used in interiors, for example in Montferrand's own house on the Moyka, his dacha and the Demidov and Gagarin houses (1830–40) on Bol'shaya Morskaya Street. The façades of the latter two houses derive from Baroque and Renaissance architecture and the Gagarin house is marked by the picturesqueness of the rhythmic asymmetrical composition. Montferrand worked a great deal on interiors, designing for the Winter Palace (1827–early 1830s) the Hall of Peter the Great, the Field Marshall's Hall and the Rotunda, as well as the private rooms of the Empresses Aleksandra Fyodorovna and Mariya Fyodorovna. His gifts as an interior designer were also used for the funeral decorations and catafalques in the Winter Palace, the Kazan' Cathedral (now the Museum of the History of Religion) and the cathedral of SS Peter and Paul, all in St Petersburg.

Montferrand published lavishly illustrated books on the construction of St Isaac's Cathedral and the Alexander Column, paying much attention not only to questions of construction and descriptions of the complex arrangements for raising the monolithic columns of the cathedral and the Alexander Column, but also to analysis and evaluation of architectural works dating from antiquity and the Renaissance and the expression of his own ideas on architecture.

WRITINGS
Plans et détails du monument consacré à la mémoire de l'empereur Alexandre (Paris, 1836)
L'Église cathédrale de St-Isaac: Description architectural, pittoresque et historique de ce monument par A. K. de Montferrand (Paris, 1845)

BIBLIOGRAPHY
N. P. Nikitin: *Ogyust Monferan: Proyektirovaniye i stroitel'stvo Isaakiyevskogo sobora i Aleksandrovskoy kolonny* [August Montferrand: the planning and construction of St Isaac's Cathedral and the Alexander Column] (Leningrad, 1939)
A. L. Rotach: *Isaakiyevskiy sobor: Vydayushchiysya pamyatnik russkoy arkhitektury* [St Isaac's Cathedral: an outstanding monument of Russian architecture] (Leningrad, 1962)
I. D. Karpovich and G. V. Yakirina: *Isaakiyevskiy sobor* [St Isaac's Cathedral] (Leningrad, 1972)
G. P. Butikov and G. A. Khvostova: *Isaakiyevskiy sobor* [St Isaac's Cathedral] (Lenizdat, 1979)
A. L. Rotach and O. A. Chekanova: *Monferran* (Lenizdat, 1979)
Ordena Lenina Akademiya Khudozhestr SSR: Nauchno-issledovatel'skiy muzey. Ogyust Monferan, 1786–1858 [The Order of Lenin Academy of Arts of the USSR: Scientific Research Museum. August Montferrand, 1786–1858] (exh. cat. by V. K. Shuysky, Leningrad, Acad. A. Sci. Res. Mus., 1986)
O. A. Chekanova and A. L. Rotach: *Ogyust Monferran*, Mastera Arkhitektury (Leningrad, 1990)
                                    YE. I. KIRICHENKO

Montfoort, Anthonie van. *See* BLOCKLANDT, ANTHONIE.

Montford, Paul Raphael (*b* Kentish Town, London, 1 Nov 1868; *d* Melbourne, 15 Jan 1938). English sculptor, active in Australia. The son of Horace Montford, Curator of Schools at the Royal Academy of Art, London, he learnt modelling from his father and drawing at the Lambeth School of Art. After studying on a Landseer and British Institute scholarship at the Royal Academy and winning a Gold Medal in 1891, he taught sculpture at the Chelsea

School of Art (South-West London Polytechnic) from 1898 to 1903. He also specialized in architectural decoration, completing, for example, reliefs (1892) for Battersea Town Hall and Polytechnic and bronze figure groups (1914) for the Kelvin-Way Bridge, Glasgow. In 1912 he married Marian Alice Dibden, a portrait- and miniature painter. In 1921, attracted by the light, which he believed conducive to monumental sculpture, they travelled to Australia. Montford became very influential in the Victorian Artists' Society, of which he was President 1930–31. He frequently used the daily press to air avant-garde opinions about the social and environmental role of sculpture in modern cities. He encouraged and assisted such emerging Australian sculptors as Lyndon Dadswell. Montford's flamboyance, theatrical personality and Bohemian lifestyle were talking points in Melbourne society and led to more than 70 sculptural commissions, including a controversial 1927 commission for the external sculptures of Melbourne's Shrine of Remembrance. Its classicizing architecture precluded the Australian subject-matter and historical authenticity he usually incorporated in his works and attracted criticism. His seated statue of the Australian poet *Adam Lindsay Gordon* (1930–31), a bronze that won the Gold Medal of the Royal Society of British Sculptors in 1934, and is located outside Parliament House, Spring Street, Melbourne, is a more popular example of his work. Montford died in Melbourne, but his ashes were scattered in woods at Leatherhead, England. When his family returned to London in 1939 they were granted a civil list pension for his services to sculpture.

AUDB

BIBLIOGRAPHY

K. W. Scarlett: *Australian Sculptors* (Melbourne, 1980)
G. Sturgeon: *The Development of Australian Sculpture 1788–1975* (London, 1980)
S. Beattie: *The New Sculpture* (New Haven, 1983)
J. Zimmer: 'Paul Raphael Montford', *A. & Australia*, xx/1 (1990), pp. 94–101

Montfort, Nicolas-Alexandre Salins de. *See* SALINS DE MONTFORT, NICOLAS-ALEXANDRE.

Montgomery, 1st Earl of. *See* HERBERT, (1).

Monthermer, Marquess of. *See under* BRUDENELL.

Monti, Cesare, Archbishop of Milan (*b* Milan, 1593; *d* Milan, 1650). Italian ecclesiastic, patron and collector. He was born into a noble family in Milan in 1593 and from an early age was destined for an ecclesiastical career. He studied law at the University of Pavia and afterwards held important offices in the Roman Inquisition and the Propaganda Fide under Popes Gregory XV and Urban VIII. In 1629 he was appointed papal nuncio to Naples and in 1630 became papal ambassador to Madrid. On the death of Cardinal Federico Borromeo (1631), the Pope appointed Monti Archbishop of Milan, and in 1633, the year in which he was made titular Cardinal of S Maria in Trasportina, he took possession of his diocese. Monti proved to be wise and zealous, making numerous pastoral visits throughout his territory and promulgating many decrees. Like Borromeo, who founded the Biblioteca Ambrosiana and Pinacoteca Ambrosiana, Monti was genuinely devoted to culture and the arts. He wrote orations,

poems and epithalamia. As Archbishop of Milan he initiated a series of artistic projects: he restored and enlarged the Palazzo Arcivescovile in Milan, promoted the construction of the shrine and convent of Concesa d'Adda, near Como, and completed the construction of the shrine to the Madonna del Bosco at Imbersago, also near Como. He arranged for the greatly venerated body of Carlo Borromeo to be laid in a magnificent casket made of crystal and silver, which had been given to him by King Philip IV of Spain. Monti's name is linked most closely with the exceptional picture gallery of 16th- and 17th-century paintings of the Lombard–Veneto school, which he collected with unflagging enthusiasm between 1630 and 1650. The pictures hung in the rooms of the Palazzo Arcivescovile in Milan and in the country residences of Magenta and Groppello d'Adda, both near Milan. The Cardinal, whose admiration for painting often led to profound meditations on their sacred subject-matter, surrounded himself with important canvases by Giulio Cesare Procaccini, Daniele Crespi, Morazzone and Cerano, the leading painters of the early 17th-century Lombard school. He also collected works by 16th-century Lombard masters (the Cremonese Campi family and the Milanese Andrea Solario, Marco d'Oggiono, Bernardino Luini and Gaudenzio Ferrari) and those of the Veneto (Paris Bordone, Bonifazio de'Pitati and others). When it was not possible for him to obtain original works by important painters he had copies made. This explains the significant number of copies after celebrated pictures by such artists as Correggio, Raphael and del Sarto that form part of the episcopal collection. In 1650, shortly before his death, Cardinal Monti drew up an 'Instrumentum Donationis', by which he designated the Archbishops of Milan, his successors, as perpetual heirs to his collection. The archbishop's gallery was written about with great enthusiasm in the Milanese sources of the 17th and 18th centuries. However, in the early 19th century it suffered grave losses when the Napoleonic government in occupation decreed that the most important part of the collection be transferred to the Accademia di Belle Arti di Brera. The collection is now divided between the Palazzo Arcivescovile and the Brera.

BIBLIOGRAPHY

E. Cazzani: *Vescovi e arcivescovi di Milano* (Milan, 1955), pp. 254–6
G. Melzi d'Eril: 'Federico Borromeo e Cesare Monti: Collezionisti milanesi', *Stor. A.*, xv–xvi (1972), pp. 73–81
P. Marani: 'La collezione Monti e la fortuna di Andrea del Sarto nella Milano del seicento', *Brera Notizie*, xiii (1986)
S. C. Colombo: 'La quadreria Arcivescovile di Milano', *A. Crist.*, dccxxx (1989), pp. 43–56

MARCO CARMINATI

Monti, Francesco (*b* Bologna, 1685; *d* Brescia, 14 April 1768). Italian painter and draughtsman. He was the son of a tailor who served the Este court in Modena during the 1690s. Monti studied with the foremost painter in Modena, Sigismondo Caula (*b* 1637), for three years from *c*. 1700. In 1703 he moved to Bologna and entered the studio of Giovanni Gioseffo dal Sole. Roli (1962) defined the formative influences on Monti's art as dal Sole and Donato Creti on the one hand, and Giuseppe Maria Crespi and Antonio Gionima on the other. Monti evolved a distinctive personal idiom, characterized by graceful figures reminiscent of the style of Parmigianino, but perhaps more directly inspired by the more extravagant late Mannerist idiom of such painters as Bartholomeus Spranger and Josef Heintz I of the court of Rudolf II at Prague. Monti may have known their work through prints by Aegidius Sadeler II, Jan Muller and others. This exotic figure style, with fluent, swaying forms and faces suggestively muted by half-shadow was accompanied by unusual shades of colour that glow richly in darkened settings. Monti's art contributed to a neo-Mannerist strain in 18th-century Emilian painting; he was perhaps its most sophisticated exponent.

Monti's career flourished in the 1720s, and he was commissioned to execute history paintings for an ever-widening patrician clientele, which included the senatorial Ranuzzi family of Bologna and the Genoese Durazzo family. Pictures such as the three large scenes from the *Life of Alexander* (1720s; Genoa, Pal. Durazzo Pallavicini), with their impressive *mise-en-scène* and complex arrangement of figures, reveal the artist's exceptional inventive and technical assurance. Monti's familiarity with Venetian painting of the earlier years of the century, especially with the art of Giovanni Battista Pittoni, is clearly reflected in his sophisticated taste and virtuosity. In 1723–30 the Irish impresario Owen McSwiny planned to commission from leading Bolognese and Venetian painters a series of 24 large paintings of allegorical tombs commemorating famous figures of British history; he intended specialists in landscape, architectural and figure painting to collaborate. He visited Bologna to promote the project, and in 1726, the same year that Monti was elected Principe of the Accademia Clementina, Bologna, he commissioned Monti to paint figures in four of the series (two in Milan, Alcidi Boccacci priv. col., see Roli, 1977, pls 229a, 229b; two in Bologna, Pin. N.); they were painted in collaboration with the landscape painter Nunzio Ferrajuoli and the specialist in architectural ruins Pietro Paltronieri (1673–1741). The *Allegorical Tomb of Archibald Campbell, Duke of Argyll* (after 1730; Bologna, Pin. N.) is the only nocturnal scene in the series. In addition to this commission Monti received ecclesiastical commissions from cities throughout Emilia-Romagna and Lombardy. The most impressive of these altarpieces is the huge and powerful *Death of St Peter Martyr* (mid-1730s; Modena, S Domenico).

Monti also painted decorative frescoes and after 1735 was chiefly occupied with large-scale fresco commissions in Lombardy, especially in Brescia, where he frescoed the Palazzo Martinengo with scenes from Roman history (1736; untraced) and painted decorations in grisaille in the church of S Maria della Pace (1737–43). He also decorated the church of S Bartolommeo at Bergamo and in 1743 the church of S Girolamo de' Giustiziati at Cremona. Here he decorated the cupola with an intensely dramatic *Resurrection* and frescoed an *Agony in the Garden* over the main entrance; he also painted an altarpiece, the *Virgin and Child Appearing to St Jerome*. Monti was a prolific draughtsman, making academic studies from the life model in black chalk (examples, Bologna, Pin N.) and compositional studies, such as the red chalk drawing *Christ Driving the Money-changers from the Temple* (1740s; Bergamo, Accad. Carrara B.A.), which are distinguished by their expressive freedom of handling.

BIBLIOGRAPHY

G. C. Zanotti: *Storia dell'Accademia Clementina di Bologna*, ii (Bologna, 1739), pp. 217–26

L. Crespi: *Felsina pittrice, vite de' pittori bolognesi*, iii (Rome, 1769), pp. 313–16

R. Roli: 'Traccia per Francesco Monte, bolognese', *A. Ant. & Mod.*, 17 (1962), pp. 86–98

D. Miller: 'Viani, Graziani and Monti: Contributions to the Bolognese Settecento', *A. Ant. & Mod.*, 25 (1964), pp. 97–100

——: 'Vittorio Bigari and Francesco Monti, Two Decorative Painters of the Bolognese Settecento', *A.Q.* [Detroit], xxxi (1968), pp. 421–32

U. Ruggieri: *Franceschini Monti, bolognese, 1685–1768* (Bergamo, 1968) [a study of the drgs]

M. Cazort: 'Some Drawings by Francesco Monti and the Soft Chalk Style', *Master Drgs*, ix/2 (1973), pp. 161–8

R. Roli: *Pittura bolognese, 1650–1800: Dal Cignani ai Gandolfi* (Bologna, 1977), pp. 62–5, 121–3

L'arte del settecento emiliano: La pittura dell'Accademia Clementina (exh. cat., Bologna, Pal. Podestà, 1979), pp. 69–75

Disegni di artisti bolognesi dal seicento all'ottocento delle collezioni Schloss Fachsenfeld e della Graphische Sammlung Staatsgalerie Stuttgart (exh. cat. by C. Thiem, Stuttgart, Staatsgal.; Bologna, Pin. N.; 1982–3), pp. 84–6

R. Roli: 'Una revisione dovuta: Da Francesco Monti a Giuseppe Varotti', *Mus. Ferrar.: Boll. Annu.*, 15 (1985–7), pp. 91–8 [attrib. to Varotti a group of ptgs previously attrib. to Monti]

The Settecento: Italian Rococo and Early Neo-classical Paintings (exh. cat., London, Matthiesen F.A., 1987), pp. 128–34

DWIGHT C. MILLER

Monti, Paolo (*b* Novara, 11 Aug 1908; *d* Milan, 29 Nov 1982). Italian photographer and teacher. A self-taught photographer, he took up the medium as an amateur in 1946. Feeling it to be the perfect medium for his aesthetic and creative needs, he dedicated himself to its study with increasing seriousness and enthusiasm. In December 1947 with Gino Bolognini (*b* 1908), Luciano Scattola (1902–79) and Andrea Bresciani he founded La Gondola, a club in Venice. It soon became a leading centre for photographic research, which in Italy at that time was mainly the preserve of amateur photographers, and among the first practitioners were Giuseppe Cavalli and his group, La Bussola. In 1953 Monti became a professional photographer, specializing mostly in architectural and design photography.

In 1970 Monti was commissioned by the Istituto Regionale to work on a photographic catalogue of the artistic patrimony of Emilia-Romagna, systematically documenting the historic centres of towns and villages throughout the region, including even those of minor artistic importance. This was a pioneering project in Italy. Monti's aesthetic research, especially in the post-war years, was influenced by Subjektive Fotografie (*see* STEINERT, OTTO). Between 1970 and 1974 Monti taught photographic technique at the University of Bologna. His many photographic surveys of architecture are often compared, for their range and scientific thoroughness, to the work carried out by the Alinari family in Italy in the previous century.

PHOTOGRAPHIC PUBLICATIONS

with E. Arslan: *Venezia gotica* (Milan, 1970)

BIBLIOGRAPHY

G. Turroni: *Nuova fotografia italiana* (Milan, 1959)

Paolo Monti: Trent'anni di fotografia, 1948–1978 (exh. cat. by G. Turroni, Reggio Emilia, Pal. Com., 1978)

R. Valtorta: *Paolo Monti: Laboratorio assolano* (Milan, 1985)

G. Chiaramonte: *Paolo Monti: Milano negli anni cinquanta* (Milan, 1986)

I. Zannier: 'Le astrazioni involontarie di Paolo Monti', *Fotologia*, v (Florence, 1986), pp. 52–69

ITALO ZANNIER

Monti, Raffaelle (*b* Iseo, Ticino, 1818; *d* London, 16 Oct 1881). Italian sculptor. Son of the sculptor Gaetano Monti

(1766–1847), who assisted in the decoration of the Milanese monuments initiated under Napoleon, such as the Arco della Pace. Raffaelle studied with his father and under Pompeo Marchesi at the Accademia di Belle Arti di Brera in Milan. His contemporaries, impressed by the individualism of Lorenzo Bartolini, deliberately sought out non-classical influences, including the Baroque. In Monti's case this experimentalism did not result in realism; instead, he developed a personal strain of precious and virtuoso fantasy.

Monti's initial successes were with the Classical subjects. His *Alexander and Bucephalus* (untraced) won him a gold medal at the Academy, and in 1838 his group *Ajax Defending the Body of Patroclus* (untraced) secured him an invitation to Vienna. The outstanding project of his four-year stay there was the pediment representing the *Apotheosis of Pannonia* for the National Museum in Budapest. Executed in collaboration with the Munich sculptor Ludwig Schaller (1804–65), it was cast in zinc for the sake of lightness. Monti was in Milan from 1842 to 1846, then travelled to London, and during this first stay in England executed for William Spencer, 6th Duke of Devonshire, a *Veiled Vestal* in marble (Eastbourne, Compton Pal.). Such veiled figures, deriving from an 18th-century tradition pioneered by Antonio Corradini, came to be recognized as Monti's speciality, though others soon capitalized on his revival of the theme. He returned briefly to Italy, where he fought in the abortive uprising of 1848, but fled back to London after the defeat of the insurgents at Custozza, and remained there for the rest of his life. A series of reviews of the English art scene that Monti later contributed to the *Gazette des Beaux-Arts* (1859) shows how deftly he felt the artistic pulse of his adopted country. When he entered the market for tomb sculpture, he encapsulated current High-Church leanings in his monument to *Barbara, Lady de Mauley* (Hatherop, Glos, St Nicholas), a neo-Gothic effigy flanked by symbolic angels. Sensuality and contrition are combined in his *Eve after the Fall* (ex-Grittleton House, Wilts; see Read, fig. 174), exhibited at the Great Exhibition of 1851, and the Victorian taste for idealized genre was catered to in his group *Sister Anglers* (1851; untraced).

Like many other immigrant sculptors, Monti saw in the expansion of the industrial arts, stimulated by the Great Exhibition, a chance to compete with indigenous talents. His productivity grew, though he was reduced briefly to bankruptcy during his involvement, from 1853, with the Crystal Palace Company at Sydenham. Here he participated in the historical reconstructions and executed decorative sculpture for the rebuilt palace and its grounds. In an ambitious relief for the Covent Garden Opera House 1858, representing Orpheus and Ossian as embodiments of Music and Poetry, he gave a nationalistic twist to artistic personification. In 1861, after experimenting for three years with electrotype with Elkingtons, the Birmingham metalworking firm, Monti executed the largest monument ever cast by this technique, the equestrian statue of *Charles Stewart, 3rd Marquess of Londonderry*, for the market-place in Durham. The following year, at the London International Exhibition, he showed his vision of resurgent Italy, a marble group of *A Sleep of Sorrow and a Dream of Joy* (London, V&A; see fig.). This neo-Baroque extravaganza

Raffaelle Monti: *A Sleep of Sorrow and a Dream of Joy*, marble, h. 1.7 m, 1861 or 1862 (London, Victoria and Albert Museum)

marked the climax of Monti's poetic and allegorical mode. In his remaining years he was preoccupied with the applied arts, modelling statuettes and busts for Copelands Statuary Porcelain and designing silverware for the firm of C. F. Hancock.

BIBLIOGRAPHY

Gunnis

Obituary, *A. J.* [London], (1881), p. 352

A. Radcliffe: 'Monti's Allegory of the Risorgimento', *V&A Mus. Bull.*, i/3 (1965), pp. 25–38

B. Read: *Victorian Sculpture* (New Haven and London, 1982), p. 143

PHILIP WARD-JACKSON

Monticelli, Adolphe(-Joseph-Thomas) (*b* Marseille, 14 Oct 1824; *d* Marseille, 29 June 1886). French painter. In 1846, after studying at the Ecole d'Art in Marseille, Monticelli left Provence to study in Paris with Paul Delaroche. Although he had been trained to work in a Neo-classical style by his teachers in Marseille, in Paris he admired the Troubadour pictures of such artists as Pierre Révoil and Fleury Richard and the bold colours and rich surface impasto of Delacroix's oil sketches. He also copied many of the Old Masters in the Louvre. When he returned to Marseille in 1847 Emile Loubon (1809–63), newly appointed director of the Ecole de Dessin in Marseille and a friend of many realist landscape painters in Paris, encouraged him and another local painter, Paul Guigou, to record the landscapes and traditional village scenes of Provence (e.g. *Rural Scene*, Marseille, Mus. Grobet-Labadié).

In 1855–6 Monticelli returned to Paris, where he met the Barbizon landscape painter Narcisse Diaz. They went on painting excursions to the Forest of Fontainebleau together; Monticelli often followed Diaz's example of including nudes and Watteau-inspired costumed figures in his landscapes, as in the *Island of Cythera* (1863–5; St Louis, MO, A. Mus.). Diaz, who was himself influenced by Delacroix's bright colours, encouraged Monticelli to use more spontaneous brushstrokes to achieve a sketch-like finish. Monticelli lived in Paris from 1863 to 1870, during the Second Empire, when interest in Rococo art and delight in the ballet, theatre and opera were at their height. He began to specialize in theatrical, brightly coloured *fêtes galantes* showing elegantly gowned women and gallant gentlemen relaxing in natural settings. Around 1869–70 Guigou introduced Monticelli to the Impressionists at the Café Guerbois, and Monticelli began to use small touches of paint in a landscape style close to that of Camille Pissarro, as in *Orchard in Flower* (c. 1871; Amsterdam, Rijksmus.).

After the outbreak of the Franco-Prussian War (1870–71) Monticelli returned to Marseille, where he remained for the rest of his life and developed his mature style. He and Cézanne, whom he had known since the 1860s, often painted together in the region around Aix and Marseille, between 1878 and 1884. Although Monticelli earned his living by painting portraits, still-lifes (e.g. *Still-life with White Jug*, c. 1878-80; Paris, Mus. d'Orsay; see fig.) and *fêtes galantes*, his Provençal landscape sketches began to

be more experimental (e.g. *Under the Trees*, c. 1883–5; New York, Lewyt priv. col.), their thicker textures and brighter colours giving them a quality of expressionistic abstraction. Their vigorous brushwork foreshadows later paintings executed by van Gogh in Saint-Rémy. Parts of the wooden support were left bare to act as a foil for the intensely coloured and thickly painted highlights. Monticelli's style was considered so unusual by local collectors and critics that he began to be described as insane. He took these reports with good humour, telling his friends that it would take 50 years for people to understand his experimentation with colour and impasto.

In 1886 van Gogh discovered some of Monticelli's mature works in the Galerie Delarebeyrette, Paris. He began to imitate Monticelli's flower-pieces, for example in *Hollyhocks in a One-eared Vase* (1886; Zurich, Ksthaus), and later bought six paintings for his personal collection. Van Gogh hoped that his paintings, such as *Seascape at Saintes-Maries* (1888; Moscow, Pushkin Mus. F. A.), would be understood as a continuation of Monticelli's later experimental pictures. In 1890 van Gogh and his brother Theo funded the publication of the first book about Monticelli; Guigou's text, which praises him as a genius of colour and refutes his insanity, is complemented by lithographs of Monticelli's work by A. M. Lauzet (1865–

Adolphe Monticelli: *Still-life with White Jug*, oil on panel, 490×630 mm, c. 1878–80 (Paris, Musée d'Orsay)

98), including several from the van Gogh brothers' collection. Most of Monticelli's experimental and stylistic innovations have been ascribed to van Gogh, although van Gogh readily acknowledged his indebtedness to the Marseille painter.

BIBLIOGRAPHY

P. Guigou: *Monticelli* (Paris, 1890) [with lithographs by A. M. Lauzet]
A. Gouirand: *Monticelli* (Paris, 1900)
L. Guinand: *La Vie et les oeuvres de Monticelli* (Marseille, 1931)
Monticelli et le baroque provençal (exh. cat. by G. Bazin, Paris, Mus. Orangerie, 1953)
A. Sheon: 'Monticelli and van Gogh', *Apollo*, lxxxv (1967), pp. 444–8
A. M. Alauzen: *Monticelli: Sa vie et son oeuvre* (Paris, 1969)
Monticelli: His Contemporaries, his Influence (exh. cat. by A. Sheon, Pittsburgh, Carnegie Mus. A., 1978)
A. Sheon: *Monticelli, 1824–1886* (Marseille, 1986)

AARON SHEON

Monticello. House at Shadwell, near Charlottesville, VA, designed and later remodelled by THOMAS JEFFERSON for his own use. Although Jefferson continued to work on the house for more than 40 years, there were two main building programmes, in 1770–82 and 1796–1809. Jefferson began designing the house in 1767, mainly using for his guide James Leoni's *The Architecture of A. Palladio* (London, 1715–20 or the edition of 1742 or both). This first version of the house had two-storey porticos to a five-bay central block on the entrance and garden fronts, with a Doric order under an Ionic order on the porticos. Around 1777 the first changes were made, with the addition of octagonal bows to the wings and garden front of the central block. Jefferson used his hilltop site to advantage to conceal the service wings (planned in the 1770s but built during the remodelling in modified form after 1800). He reversed the usual Palladian scheme, where the wings flank an entrance court, by placing the wings behind the house and setting them into the side of the hill. The roofs are transformed into terrace walkways connected to the main floor of the house and serve both as extensions for the house and as landscape elements.

In 1796, as a result of his first-hand experience of French architecture in Paris, Jefferson began remodelling and enlarging the house from eight to twenty-one rooms. He removed the upper storey and constructed a dome, the first on an American house, over the garden front. The additions reflected French architectural thinking on the division of space. Reception rooms were made the height of the main order on the exterior. Bedrooms were arranged in two tiers, with their windows positioned to suggest a single-storey house. Further bedrooms on the second floor were concealed under the roof and lighted by skylights. The interior had decorative schemes based on Classical and Palladian examples. The number, variety and placement of windows, as well as the proportions and contrast of red brick and white dressings, give the façade a restless quality, unusual in a Neo-classical building. It was also too personal and idiosyncratic to have any significant influence. Jefferson's great interest in horticulture and garden design is shown at Monticello, where the gardens would also have been full of buildings if Jefferson had been rich enough to construct them.

BIBLIOGRAPHY

F. Kimball: *Thomas Jefferson, Architect: Original Designs in the Collection of Thomas Jefferson Coolidge, Junior, with an Essay and Notes* (Boston, 1916/R New York, 1968)
E. M. Betts, ed.: *Thomas Jefferson's Garden Book, 1766–1824* (Philadelphia, 1944)
K. Lehman: *Thomas Jefferson, American Humanist* (New York, 1947)
F. D. Nichols: *Thomas Jefferson's Architectural Drawings* (Charlottesville, 1961, rev. Boston, 5/1984)
F. D. Nichols and J. A. Bear: *Monticello* (Charlottesville, 1967, rev. 1982)
W. B. O'Neal: 'A Bibliography of Publications about Thomas Jefferson as an Architect', *American Association of Architectural Bibliographers Papers*, vi (Charlottesville, 1969)
W. H. Pierson: *American Buildings and their Architects: The Colonial and Neoclassical Styles* (Garden City, NY, 1970)
The Eye of TH: Jefferson (exh. cat. by W. H. Adams; Washington, DC, N.G.A., 1976)
W. H. Adams: *Jefferson's Monticello* (New York, 1983)
F. Shuffelton: *Thomas Jefferson: A Comprehensive, Annotated Bibliography of Writings about him, 1822–1980* (New York, 1983)

WILLIAM L. BEISWANGER

Montiel, Ramona. *See under* BERNI, ANTONIO.

Montluçon [Molisson]**, de.** French family of painters and illuminators. Jean Raoul de Montluçon (*b* Montluçon, 1417; *d* Bourges, 1494) settled in Bourges *c.* 1460, when he married Louise Debrielle, the daughter of a local notary. Unusually for a painter, he owned three houses and a vineyard in Bourges, and in 1469 he was living in a house near that of the illuminator Jean Colombe. The Book of Hours belonging to the Bourbon Chappes family (Paris, Bib. Arsenal, MS. 438) bears his signature on the border of the chasuble worn by the high priest in the *Marriage of the Virgin* (JOHANNES DE MONTELUCIO ME PINXIT). Jean also signed himself phonetically as MOLUSON, as in the Monypenny Breviary (sold London, Sotheby's, 19 June 1989, lot 3031), which belonged to a member of a family of Scottish origin living in Berry.

Jean and his son Jacquelin Raoul (*b* Bourges, 1463; *d* Bourges, 1505) were held in high esteem in Bourges, where they executed wall paintings, produced designs for stained-glass windows, and painted sculptures and escutcheons. They regularly supplied the decorations for the annual Corpus Christi procession. They also collaborated with the workshop of Jean Colombe. (Compare, for example, the illuminations of the *Finding of the True Cross* in the Monypenny Breviary, fol. 525*v*, with that in the Book of Hours of Louis de Laval; Paris, Bib. N., MS. Lat. 920, fol. 311*v*.) The intensity of expression, the lighting and the atmosphere distinguish Jacquelin's style from that of his father, whom he succeeded in 1494. Jean tended to depict half-figures in close-up, often popular types, and his son further developed these interests. Their style has a particular, direct appeal, however, quite different from that of Jean Fouquet or Jean Colombe, and is more popular and violent, with picturesque narratives and numerous figures crowded into fantastic, ponderous architectural settings. Among their lesser known works is a Book of Hours (Grenoble, Bib. Mun., MS. 1011), which can be compared with that at Yale (New Haven, CT, Yale U. Lib., MS. 77); a signed but dismembered altarpiece (*Annunciation, Raising of Lazarus*; Lyon, Mus. B.-A.; *Martyrdom of St Catherine, Descent into Limbo*; Chambéry, Mus. B.-A.); and a large altarpiece in seven panels depicting the *Life of the Virgin*, in Notre-Dame, Montluçon, which was possibly executed by Jean Raoul before he settled in Bourges.

BIBLIOGRAPHY

R. Fournier-Sarlovèze: 'Quelques primitifs du centre de la France', *Rev. A. Anc. & Mod.* (1902–4), pp. 1–33

A. van de Put: 'The Monypenny Breviary', *Proc. Soc. Antiqua. Scotland*, vi (1922), pp. 72–114

J. Y. Ribault: 'Recherches sur deux points d'histoire de l'art à propos des relations artistiques entre le Berry et le Bourbonnais à la fin du Moyen Age', *Bull. Soc. Emul. Bourbon.*, lv (1967), pp. 313–22

C. Sterling: 'Etudes savoyardes, I: Au temps du duc Amédée', *L'Oeil*, 178 (1969), pp. 2–13; 195–6 (1971), pp. 14–19

——: 'Carnet savoyard' *Rev. Louvre*, xxviii (1978), pp. 333–42

C. Schaefer: 'Nouvelles Observations au sujet des Heures de Louis de Laval', *A. Ouest*, 1–2 (1980), pp. 33–68

——: 'Die Romuleon-Handschrift (78 D 10) des Berliner Kupferstichkabinetts', *Jb. Berlin. Mus.* (1981), pp. 125–78 (142)

D. Moulinet: 'Les Heures de Jean de Montluçon à la Bibliothèque de l'Arsenal', *Etud. Bourbon.*, n.s. 11, 234 (1985)

CLAUDE SCHAEFER

Montmorency, Anne, Duc de [Constable of France] (*b* Chantilly, 15 March 1493; *d* Paris, 12 Nov 1567). French patron and collector. From 1510 he served with the French army in Italy, and the accession of Francis I in 1515 marked the beginning of his ascendancy at court. The combination of inheritance and royal favour made him one of the richest noblemen in France, and despite his rough character and military and political ineptitude, he became a patron of the arts. He discovered the potter Bernard Palissy at Saintes and introduced him at court and also, despite his own intransigent Catholicism, intervened in Palissy's favour when he was imprisoned as a Huguenot.

He provided himself with magnificent residences, and filled them with works of art. From 1527 he had the château of Chantilly rebuilt by Pierre Chambiges. From 1536 to 1543 he rebuilt the château of Fère-en-Tardenois (Aisne), of which only the portal survives. The famous gallery of the château, by JEAN BULLANT, supported on a series of monumental arches, was not erected until 1552–62. It too survives. About 1537, the year before he was made Constable of France, de Montmorency began the rebuilding of the château of Ecouen, where he employed Jean Goujon around 1544, then Jean Bullant, who lived there from 1556 to 1578. The important art collection housed at Ecouen included two of Michelangelo's statues of *Slaves* (marble; Paris, Louvre; *see* MICHELANGELO, fig. 2) housed in the south portico of the courtyard, Rosso Fiorentino's *Pietà* (Paris, Louvre), a copy of Leonardo's *Last Supper* by Marco d'Oggiono, an enamelled altarpiece by Pierre Reymond in the chapel (*in situ*), ceramic paving tiles by Masséot Abaquesne, a series of stained-glass panels illustrating the *Life of Psyche* (Chantilly, Mus. Condé) and antique busts. (A rustic grotto by Palissy was added in 1556.)

In 1548 de Montmorency was involved in the protection of antique remains in Languedoc. In 1551 he was made Duc de Montmorency by Henry II. In 1552 he bought a house in Paris. He had it enlarged by Bullant; it already contained a gallery painted by Primaticcio. The inventory of this house reveals its riches, which included a library, large collections of arms and armour, antiquities and paintings, 15 sets of figural tapestries, painted enamels (especially portraits; *see* ENAMEL, colour pl. IV, fig. 1) and Palissy ware and pottery from Saint-Porchaire. In 1560 he added the Petit Château, built by Bullant, to his château in Chantilly.

Churches on de Montmorency's lands also benefited from his patronage: he commissioned Bullant to work at St Martin, Montmorency, and donated stained-glass windows representing him, his wife and children (*in situ*); at Taverny, near Pontoise, he donated to the church a sculpted stone altarpiece (*in situ*); at St Acceul, Ecouen, he rebuilt the choir and provided stained-glass windows of scenes from the *Life of the Virgin* and portraits of his family (*in situ*). Beyond the fragments of decoration surviving at the châteaux of Chantilly and Ecouen, many works bearing his coat of arms testify to de Montmorency's patronage. They include an enamelled basin decorated with the *Feast of the Gods* by Léonard Limosin (Paris, priv. col.); pieces of a maiolica service (London, BM; Oxford, Ashmolean; New York, Met.; Rouen, Mus. Cer.; Turin, Pal. Madama) made in Urbino in 1535 by Guido Durantino (*d* 1576); a suit of armour (Paris, Mus. Armée); as well as numerous illuminated manuscripts (Paris, Bib. N.). The Constable was mortally wounded at the Battle of St Denis and was commemorated at St Martin, Montmorency, by a tomb designed by Bullant with statuary by Barthélémy Prieur and Martin Lefort (marble, 1568; fragments Paris, Louvre), and by a monument containing his heart by the same artists in the church of the Celestines, Paris (marble and bronze, 1571–6; Paris, Louvre).

BIBLIOGRAPHY

F. de Lasteyrie: 'Un Grand Seigneur du XVIe siècle: Le Connétable de Montmorency', *Gaz. B.-A.* (1879)

F. Decrue: *A. de Montmorency, grand maître et connétable de France sous le règne de François 1er* (Paris, 1885)

——: *Anne duc de Montmorency* (Paris, 1889)

L. Mirot: *L'Hôtel et les collections du connétable de Montmorency* (Paris, 1920)

BERTRAND JESTAZ

Montor, Jean-Alexis-François Artaud de. *See* ARTAUD DE MONTOR, JEAN-ALEXIS-FRANÇOIS.

Montorfano. Italian family of painters. Paolino da Montorfano (*fl* Milan, 1402–30) worked in Milan Cathedral as a painter and as a painter of stained glass. Abramo (di Alberto) da Montorfano (*fl* Milan, 1430–38), in 1430 also employed in Milan Cathedral, apparently worked regularly for the Visconti and was a member of the painters' guild, as was his son Alberto (di Abraam) de Montorfano (*fl* Milan, *c*. 1450–81). Giovanni da Montorfano (*fl* 1452–70) worked in Milan Cathedral in 1452 and 1454, and in Genoa from 1457; a signed *St Martin and the Beggar* exists (Paris, Gal. Petit, Cernuschi Sale, 25–6 May 1900, no. 65). Giovanni Donato (di Alberto) da Montorfano (*b* Milan, *c*. 1460; *d* Milan, 1502/3), who may have been active from the late 1470s, is best known for his fresco of the *Crucifixion* (signed and dated 1495; Milan, S Maria delle Grazie). Several frescoes in S Pietro in Gessate, Milan, in the chapels of St Anthony, St John the Baptist and the Virgin, are attributed to him, but their dating and attribution are problematic; his hand is most plausibly seen in the St Anthony frescoes. Frescoes of scenes from the *Life of St Catherine* in S Maria delle Grazie, long attributed to him, have recently been tentatively reassigned to Cristoforo de Mottis (*fl* 1461; *d* 1493). Four fresco fragments of saints (ex-S Maria della Rosa, Milan; Milan, Pin.

Ambrosiana) are from around the same time as the *Crucifixion*. It is likely that Giovanni Donato's brother Vincenzo (di Alberto) da Montorfano (*d* after 1484) was also a painter and that the pair first worked with their father Alberto. One of Giovanni Donato's three sons, Alberto (di Giovanni Donato) da Montorfano (*b* Milan, 1491/2; *d* Milan, 1524) was also a painter, though none of his works has been identified. In 1513 Bernardino (or Bernardo) da Montorfano was a painter in Genoa.

BIBLIOGRAPHY

Thieme–Becker

Annali della Fabbrica del Duomo (Milan, 1877–85), i, ii, app. II, app. III [Paolino, Abramo and Giovanni da Montorfano]

F. Mazzini: *Affreschi lombardi del quattrocento* (Milan, 1965) [Giovanni Donato da Montorfano, illustrations, bibliography]

A. Frattini: 'Documenti per la committenza nella chiesa di S Pietro in Gessate', *A. Lombarda*, vi/65 (1983), pp. 27–48

G. Mulazzani: 'La decorazione pittorica: il quattrocento', *S Maria delle Grazie in Milano* (Milan, 1983), pp. 112–39 [Giovanni Donato da Montorfano, bibliography, illustrations]

J. Shell: *Painters in Milan, 1490–1530* (diss., U. New York, 1986), pp. 375, 381–7, 838–57 [Abramo, Alberto (di Abraam) and Alberto (di Giovanni Donato) da Montorfano]

JANICE SHELL

Montorsoli, Giovanni Angelo (*b* Montorsoli, nr Florence, ?1507; *d* Florence, 31 Aug 1563). Italian sculptor and architect. After a three-year apprenticeship with Andrea di Piero Ferrucci, he worked as an assistant in Rome (producing rosettes on the cornices of St Peter's), Perugia and Volterra. He then went to Florence to work on the New Sacristy (Medici Chapel) and the Biblioteca Laurenziana at S Lorenzo, probably from 1524; the influence of Michelangelo was to prove decisive. Work at S Lorenzo was suspended as a result of the expulsion of the Medici in 1527, and Montorsoli decided to enter a religious order; he was inducted into the Servite Order at SS Annunziata in 1530, taking his vows in 1531. For his monastery church he restored the wax portraits of the Medici family, which had been destroyed in 1527, and modelled new ones of *Leo X*, *Clement VII*, *Matthias Corvinus* and *Giacomo V d'Appiano, Duke of Piombino* (untraced). In 1532 Michelangelo recommended him to Clement VII to restore antique statues in the Vatican; his restorations of the *Laokoon* group (*see* LAOKOON and ROME ANCIENT, fig. 59) and the *Apollo Belvedere* (both Rome, Vatican, Mus. Pio-Clementino) ensured their enduring fame. In Rome Montorsoli also produced a marble portrait of *Clement VII* (untraced) and assisted Michelangelo on the tomb of *Julius II*.

From the end of 1533 Montorsoli again contributed to work on the Medici Chapel at S Lorenzo, producing a model for the statue of *St Cosmas*, which, after revision by Michelangelo, he carved in marble (completed 1536–7; see fig.). Late in 1534 he was again in Rome, working on the tomb of *Julius II*, and then briefly in Paris, working for Francis I. On his journey through northern Italy he studied the work of Giulio Romano in Mantua and Jacopo Sansovino in Venice.

Back in Florence, Montorsoli contributed to the ephemeral decorations for the entry of Charles V in 1536; he then completed the tomb of *Angelo Aretino* (Arezzo, S Pier Piccolo). In 1536 he probably also received the prestigious commission for the marble tomb of the poet *Jacopo Sannazaro*, which was erected in 1541 in the Servite

Giovanni Angelo Montorsoli: *St Cosmas*, marble, h. 2 m, 1533–6/7 (Florence, S Lorenzo)

church of S Maria del Parto, Naples. It consists of a portrait bust on an antique-style sarcophagus, beneath which is a finely worked relief flanked by smoothly polished seated statues of *Apollo* and *Minerva*; the niche sculpture of *St James* is based on a model by Jacopo Sansovino, indicating that Montorsoli was able to adapt his style according to the nature of the contract.

Shortly after receiving the Sannazaro commission, Montorsoli was asked by Cosimo I de' Medici to produce a marble statue of *Hercules and Antaeus* intended to surmount Niccolò Tribolo's Fountain of Hercules at his villa at Castello (the *bozzetto* was destroyed by Baccio Bandinelli in 1547). In 1538 Montorsoli was commissioned to complete Bandinelli's statue of *Andrea Doria* to stand in front of the Palazzo Ducale, Genoa. The marble statue, badly damaged in 1797, depicted the *pater patriae* in Roman armour standing above vanquished Turks. Further works in Genoa include a marble statue of *St John the Evangelist*

(1540–41) for one of the apse niches of the cathedral and the decoration (1541) of the Doria family church, S Matteo. There he furnished the apse with five niche figures and the presbytery walls with polychrome marble incrustation and reliefs of the Evangelists beside the tombs of saints; the ceiling and cupola were decorated with figural stuccowork. He also executed the marble tomb of *Andrea Doria* for the crypt. Two marble portrait busts of *Charles V* (Naples, Capodimonte; Madrid, Prado) date from the Emperor's visit to Genoa in 1541. After completing the decoration of S Matteo, Montorsoli produced plans for the garden behind the Palazzo Doria, rising in terraces to a colossal stucco statue of *Neptune*. All that survives of his work there is an antique-inspired marble fountain group of a triton and a dolphin; standing on an island in a pool, it is an early example of sculpture erected in close harmony with nature.

In September 1547 Montorsoli travelled to Messina to produce the Fountain of Orion in front of the cathedral. The elaborately carved marble basin supports four reclining river-gods, the first use of such a formula in Renaissance art and also the first example of an urban fountain whose symbolism is directly related to water; a statue of the city's founder, *Orion*, surmounts two further basins. Before the fountain could be erected in 1553, the church of S Lorenzo had to be demolished to make way for it. It was rebuilt elsewhere to plans by Montorsoli (destr. 1783). Montorsoli's second outstanding work in Messina is the marble Fountain of Neptune (1553–7) at the harbour. This consists of a colossal statue of *Neptune* on a high socle above a basin from which rise the fettered *Scylla* and *Charybdis*, the sea monsters of the Straits of Messina. Once again his work introduced a new fountain type, that with a single central figure. In 1550 he designed the interior of Messina Cathedral, which has 12 chapels with statues of the Apostles; he himself supplied the marble *St Peter* in 1555. That year he also designed his second architectural work, the lighthouse in the harbour. Fragments of the monument for *Andrea Sluiti*, once at Domenico, are now in the Museo Regionale in Messina.

Having remained in Messina for ten years, in 1557 Montorsoli went to Rome in response to Paul IV's appeal that all who had left the monastic life (Montorsoli had ceased wearing the habit in 1533) should return to their orders. His last important work was the free-standing marble high altar of S Maria dei Servi in Bologna (1558/9–61). Its many sculptures are set into a polychrome marble architectural setting with three niches separated by columns; Vasari particularly singled out for praise the central statue of the *Risen Christ*. At the end of his life Montorsoli's main interest was in the foundation of the Accademia del Disegno in Florence and the conversion of the former chapter house of his monastery church into a memorial chapel for artists, the chapel of S Luca.

BIBLIOGRAPHY
G. Vasari: *Vite* (1550, rev. 2/1568); ed. G. Milanesi, vi (1881), pp. 629–60
S. Boscarino: 'L'opera di Giovanni Angelo Montorsoli a Messina (1547–1557)', *Quad. Ist. Stor. Archit.*, xx–xxi (1957), pp. 1–12
C. Manara: *Montorsoli e la sua opera genovese* (Genoa, 1959)
M. Weinberger: 'Portrait Busts by Montorsoli', *Scritti di storia dell' arte in onore di Maria Salmi*, iii (Rome, 1963), pp. 39–48
S. Ffolliott: *Civic Sculpture in the Renaissance: Montorsoli's Fountains at Messina* (diss., University Park, PA State U., 1979; microfilm, Ann Arbor, 1984)
K. Möseneder: *Montorsoli: Die Brunnen* (Mittenwald, 1979)
C. Elam: 'The Mural Drawings in Michelangelo's New Sacristy', *Burl. Mag.*, cxxiii (1981), p. 601
P. Boccardo: *Andrea Doria e le arti: Committenza e mecendismo a Genova* (Rome, 1989)
B. Daschke: *Fra Giovan Angelo da Montorsoli: Ein Florentiner Bildhauer des 16. Jarhunderts* (Berlin, 1994)

KARL MÖSENEDER

Montoyer, Louis (Joseph) (*b* Mariemont, *c.* 1749; *d* Vienna, 5 June 1811). Flemish building contractor and architect. His early works, Pope Adrian VI College at Leuven (1776–8) and the boarding house of the Theresian college at Aalst (1779–82), were conceived according to strict classical principles and with a sense of monumentality. With Barnabé Guimard, Montoyer worked on the grandiose urban plan for the Place Royale and a pleasure garden in the upper part of Brussels. He also acted as contractor and supplier of building materials for Guimard's Council of Brabant building (1778–83; now the Belgian parliament building), and, after Laurent Benoît Dewez, he was the most important representative of classicism in the Austrian Netherlands at this time. He enjoyed the favour of Albrecht, Herzog von Saxe-Teschen, and his wife Marie-Christina, governors of the Austrian Netherlands, who commissioned him, with the Tournai architect Antoine-Marie Payen (1749–93/8), to build Schoonenberg Castle at Laeken (completed 1784; now the Royal Palace), which is particularly notable for its great rotunda. Twelve Corinthian columns and allegorical representations of the months of the year by the sculptor Gilles Lambert Godecharle decorate the high-domed vestibule. In 1785–6 Montoyer built the church of St-Jacques sur Coudenberg on the Place Royale, for which Guimard and Jean-Benoît-Vincent Barré had already made some designs. To Montoyer's utter humiliation, part of the dome collapsed on 28 March 1786; thereafter he withdrew from public life for a period. Due to the political situation, in 1795 he fled with Albrecht to Vienna where he had a flourishing career as court architect. The Albertina (1801–4), the Zeremoniensaal in the Hofburg (1804–7) and the Palais Rasumofsky (1805–11) were his most important achievements.

BIBLIOGRAPHY
BNB; Thieme–Becker
G. des Marcz: 'La Place Royale à Bruxelles: Genèse de l'oeuvre, sa conception et ses auteurs', *Mém. Acad. Royale Belgique: Cl. B.-A.*, n.s. 2, i (1923), pp. 69–73
R. Wagner-Rieger: *Wiens Architektur im 19. Jahrhundert* (Vienna, 1970)
A. van Ypersele de Strihou and P. van Ypersele de Strihou: *Laken: Een huis voor keizer en koning* (Brussels, 1970)
W. van den Steene: *Het Paleis der Natie* (Brussels, 1981)

J.-P. ESTHER

Montpellier. French city and capital of the Hérault *département*, with a population of *c.* 201,000. It is first recorded in AD 985 as two towns (Montpellier and Montpelliéret), both of which passed by marriage to the crown of Aragon in 1204 and were reunited with France by Philip IV in 1293. The city expanded greatly in the Middle Ages, and its medical school (incorporated *c.* 1220) drew students from across Europe. Montpellier became a thriving

Montpellier, Promenade du Peyrou with the water-tower, 1765–72

commercial centre; Jacques Coeur, the Bourges trader and patron, funded the decoration of the Loge des Marchands (1448; now Hôtel des Trésoriers de France) and established a branch of his business in the city. Little now remains of the medieval walls, except the Tour de la Babote (12th and 14th centuries) and the Tour des Pins (now housing the city archives). In 1367 Pope Urban V (*reg* 1362–70) founded a Benedictine monastery, the abbey church of which is now the cathedral (the choir and one of the four towers were rebuilt in the 19th century in the Gothic Revival style). The Jardin des Plantes was founded in 1593, the first BOTANIC GARDEN in France.

The 16th-century Wars of Religion destroyed the city's prosperity and reached their height in 1622 during the siege of the city by Louis XIII (who commissioned the building of the Citadel in 1624). During the later 17th century and the 18th the city's prosperity revived, and it became an important administrative centre, the supreme courts being established there. A number of religious communities returned to the city and built conventual buildings, including the Jesuits, whose Collège (1682) is now a museum. The aristocracy and middle class competed in the construction of hôtels, most of which still exist. The majority are in the 17th-century classical style, but the local Gothic tradition also greatly influenced their designs. The hôtels in Montpellier are arranged around closed courtyards, one side of which is occupied by a monumental outside staircase, which, as in the case of the Hôtel de Manse and the Hôtel des Trésoriers de France, is the

principal decorative feature. Among the principal architects, Simon Levesville (*fl* Montpellier, 1629–45) built the hôtels de Mirman, Sarret and Castries, while AUGUSTIN-CHARLES D'AVILER, a student of Jules Hardouin Mansart and a theorist, who worked in Montpellier from 1691 to 1701, engaged in more diverse activities, building the church of St Denis and the monumental city gates and supervising the building of the Porte du Peyrou, a triumphal arch. He was also largely responsible for the introduction of the C-shaped hôtel (e.g. the Hôtel Deydé), a design popular in Paris. Jean-Antoine GIRAL (from a local family of architects) built the anatomy theatre of St Côme (1752–7; now Chamber of Commerce) and the Promenade du Peyrou (1765–72). The latter was both a royal square intended for the equestrian statue of *Louis XIV* (destr. 1792; present statue 1838) by Pierre Mazeline and Simon Hurtrelle and the site of the water-tower (see fig.), the terminus of an aqueduct surmounted by a classical temple. Throughout the 18th century there spread a fashion for 'folies', rustic châteaux built on the periphery of the city. The finest are Flaugergues (*c.* 1700), La Mogère (1715) and, above all, La Mosson (1723), a sumptuous estate erected for the treasurer of the Bourse, Joseph Bonnier, the decoration of which is associated with Lambert-Sigisbert Adam and Jean Raoux.

Most of the painters born in Montpellier did not pursue their careers there, although, after his trips to Paris, Rome and then Stockholm, Sébastien Bourdon returned to Montpellier in 1656–7 with the intention of founding an academy. Although this plan was not realized, he did execute the *Fall of Simon Magus* (1656) for the high altar of the cathedral (*in situ*), as well as a number of portraits. The portrait painter Jean Ranc went to Spain in 1722, where he became the foremost painter in the court of Philip V, while his contemporary, Jean Raoux, came under the patronage of Philippe de Vendôme (1665–1727), Grand Prior of the Knights of Malta. Finally, Joseph-Marie Vien worked mainly in Paris and also in Rome, where he was director of the Académie de France from 1775. Having been originally based on medical requirements, the production of earthenware in Montpellier was developed under Estève and Favier in the 17th century and then in the 18th century under Ollivier, whose workshop became a royal manufactory in 1725.

The French Revolution (1789–95) did not greatly alter the appearance of the city, but under the new regimes Montpellier lost its administrative role in the area and therefore became of less importance. However, after the arrival of the railway in the early 19th century, the wine trade received a new impetus, and the city revived. A completely new district grew up in the area between the old town and the station; plans for redevelopment in the Parisian style of Baron Georges-Eugène Haussmann were drawn up but, because of insufficient funds, were never fully realized. Nevertheless, from the mid-19th century several major buildings were completed: the Neo-Attic law courts (1846–53), the Gothic Revival church of Ste Anne (1866–9), the neo-Byzantine Protestant church and the classicizing Préfecture (1865–70); the theatre (1888) imitated the Opéra in Paris. The major event of the 19th century was the foundation of the Musée Fabre by the Montpellier painter FRANÇOIS-XAVIER FABRE, whose success as a portrait painter enabled him to form a collection. This was centred on classical drawings, 17th-century French landscapes and Italian paintings, which are among the major works of the museum. His first donation was made in 1825, the museum opened in 1828, and he left the rest of the collection to the city on his death. Other donations were soon made, including a collection of sculptures by Jean-Antoine Houdon, a collection of northern paintings and, most importantly, the donation (1868) and bequest (1876) of ALFRED BRUYAS. Thereafter, the works of several Montpellier painters were also given to the museum, including that of Alexandre Cabanel and a fine collection of the paintings of Frédéric Bazille. In addition, Fabre promoted the foundation of the city's library and school of fine arts. Also in the city is the Musée Atger, comprising the collection of drawings assembled by Xavier Atger (1759–1833).

In the 20th century the Antigone urban centre (1979–83), designed by Ricardo Bofill, was built, which continued the local classicizing tradition in urban planning, and two artists from the city, Claude Viallat and Daniel Dezeuze (*b* 1942), were prominent members of the SUPPORTS-SURFACES group.

BIBLIOGRAPHY

C. d'Aigrefeuille: *Histoire de la ville de Montpellier* (Montpellier, 1737); ed. L. de La Cour de la Pijardière (Montpellier, 1876–83)

L. de Roque: *Biographie Montpelliéraine: Peintres, sculpteurs et architectes* (Montpellier, 1877)

G. Cholvy and others: *Histoire de Montpellier* (Toulouse, 1984)

G. Fabre and others: *Montpellier, 985–1985* (Montpellier, 1985)

T. Bajou and V. Bajou: *Chefs-d'oeuvres de la peinture/100 Masterpieces* (Montpellier, 1988) [bilingual text]

T. Bajou: 'The Musée Fabre and its Collectors', *Apollo*, cxxx (1989), pp. 3–11

THIERRY BAJOU

Montpensier, Duc de. *See* ORLÉANS, (11).

Montreal [Fr. Montréal]. Canadian city, the largest of the province of Québec and the second-largest in the country. It is also the second-largest French-speaking city in the world. It occupies an archipelago at the confluence of several major maritime routes, including the St Lawrence River, which links the Atlantic Ocean with the Great Lakes, the Ottawa River, which provides access to the north-west areas of the province of Québec, and the Richelieu River, which connects southern Québec with north-east USA. Mont Royal, a large volcanic hill 233 m high after which the city was named, rises from the centre of the principal island, Ile de Montréal. The presence of strong rapids originally made the St Lawrence River impassable at this point and forced travellers to stop there. Impressed with the favourable site, they established a settlement, developing the main island first as a fur-trading post and later as the fastest-growing town in the colony of Nouvelle-France. In 1760 Montreal, as part of Nouvelle-France, was ceded to Britain. Between 1844 and 1849 it was the capital of Canada and for a century was the country's chief commercial, financial and industrial centre. The city has continued to be pre-eminent in the fields of literature and the visual and performing arts.

1. History and urban development. 2. Art life and organization. 3. Centre of furniture production.

1. HISTORY AND URBAN DEVELOPMENT. Although there had been an Iroquois Indian village (Hochelaga) on the site for hundreds of years, in 1642, Paul de Chomedey, Sieur de Maisonneuve, founded the missionary colony of Ville-Marie from a private association of pious members called Messieurs et Dames de la Société de Notre-Dame pour la Conversion des Sauvages de la Nouvelle-France. Numerous religious orders were brought from France, principally to convert the various native tribes in the area and to establish a strong Roman Catholic presence in North America. Until the early 18th century, Montreal remained a town of a few thousand inhabitants. Real growth did not begin until the 1720s, when its strategic position at the head of fur-trading and exploration routes to the west and north opened up the town to an influx of French settlers. During the 18th century Montreal's fortifications were strengthened and extended, giving the appearance of a medieval French *bastide*, or fortress.

Some stone buildings survive from the 17th and 18th centuries, among them the seminary of St Sulpice (Vieux Séminaire), the central part of which was built by 1685, and the château de Ramezay, designed by Pierre Couturier (1705–6; destr.) as the governor's residence and rebuilt (1756–7) by master mason Paul Texier Lavigne. Both of these structures were designed in a form of French classicism that was adapted to suit local geographic and climatic conditions. The orthogonal layout of the streets of modern Montreal has its sources in the original subdivision of farmed hillside plots separated by lanes and paths. After 1760, the year in which Nouvelle-France was ceded to Great Britain, the British presence became stronger. Phillips, Victoria and Dominion squares were laid out in the British fashion, and the architecture of public buildings and monuments showed the influence of British models. The Neo-classical style was popular in the first half of the 19th century. Nelson's Monument (1809), modelled after Trajan's Column (AD 113) in Rome, was the first Neo-classical monument in Canada, pre-dating Nelson's Column (1839–42) by William Railton (c. 1801–77) in Trafalgar Square, London. The grey stone church of Notre-Dame (1823–9) by James O'Donnell (1774–1830) and Christ Church Cathedral (1856–9; preliminary design by Frank Wills, and following his death in 1857 work was continued by Thomas S. Scott) are impressive examples of the Gothic Revival style, while the Neo-classical Bank of Montreal building (1845–7) by John Wells recalls buildings of that style in English cities. The Marché Bonsecours (1844–7) by WILLIAM FOOTNER has a long horizontal format in imitation of the British designs of William Chambers and Robert Adam. The planning and development of the Parc Mont-Royal from 1876 to 1881 by Frederick Law Olmsted marked the beginning of an increasingly visible American influence in both architecture and urban development, as seen in Windsor Station (1887–8) and Viger Station (1897–8; now an administrative building), both by the American architect Bruce Price, in the extension (1901–4) to the Bank of Montreal by McKim, Mead & White, and in the development of the town of Maisonneuve (annexed by Montreal in 1918), the latter project inspired by the CITY BEAUTIFUL MOVEMENT.

Certain French-speaking architects designed buildings in the same fashionable styles. These included HENRI-MAURICE PERRAULT, whose Hôtel de Ville (1874–8), with its classical façade and mansard (gambrel) roof, was inspired by the Second Empire style, and Jean Omer Marchand, who built the mother house of the Soeurs de la Congrégation Notre-Dame (1905–8). However, others perpetuated a vernacular tradition appropriate to Québec. One of them was VICTOR BOURGEAU, who imaginatively used the local grey stone to execute such attractive buildings as the Hôtel-Dieu (1850–61), the mother house of the Soeurs Grises (1869–71) and the chapel (1878) of the monastery of the Bon Pasteur.

Growing industrial production and the new steam-driven means of transport were among the factors contributing to Montreal's first great wave of urbanization (1880–1920). During this time the population increased from 150,000 to over 600,000, and the municipality grew rapidly by annexing the neighbouring parishes and towns. The business centre grew up along Rue Saint-Jacques, giving rise to some remarkable proto-rationalist industrial architecture (e.g. the original stores and warehouses of the Religieuses hospitaliéres de Saint Joseph, which was built in many phases by different architects: 1861 (Victor Bourgeau), 1871–2 (Michel Laurent), 1873–4 (Albert Mesnard) and 1873–4 (Henri-Maurice Perrault); it is known now as the Les Cours Le Royer complex. The introduction of an electric tram system encouraged the decentralization of popular residential areas, which were developing as rows of two- and three-storey brick houses with curved openwork iron staircases on their exteriors leading to the upper floors. The wealthier residents, most of whom were English-speaking, lived in stone houses on the slopes of Mont Royal. Within the city, a division along language lines arose, with the French living mainly in the east and the English in the west, with the Boulevard Saint-Laurent serving as an unofficial frontier between them.

Urban development slowed during the first half of the 20th century, and only a few imposing buildings were constructed. Those in the Beaux-Arts style include the Sun Life building (begun 1914; Darling & Pearson), the first skyscraper in Montreal, and the Banque Royale (1922–8) by York & Sawyer. The main building (1928–42) of the Université de Montréal, the largest francophone university outside France, was designed by ERNEST CORMIER in the Art Deco style. It was not until the 1950s that the second wave of urbanization occurred, during which time the population doubled in 20 years from 1.5 million to 3 million. This resulted in an uncontrolled growth of building and the appearance of American-style suburbs. Because of the development of a network of motorways, the city's population for the first time spread to the south bank of the St Lawrence River and north to Ile Jésus. However, despite this spectacular development, it was at this time that Toronto replaced Montreal as Canada's largest and most important city.

The construction of Place Ville-Marie (1955–62), a multi-functional complex built by I. M. Pei, marked the transfer of the business centre to the north and west away from Rue Saint-Jacques towards the Boulevard Dorchester (now Boulevard René Lévesque), a street that had been widened for that purpose at the beginning of 1950 (see fig. 1). Other developments followed, including the Place Victoria (1965; Luigi Moretti), Place Bonaventure (1966) by RAY AFFLECK, the Complexe Desjardins (1976; towers: Blouin, Blouin, Guité & Roy; hotel: Quellet & Reeves; base: Longpré, Marchand & Goudreau) and the Place Guy Favreau (1983; Larose, Laliberté, Petrucci & Webb; and Zerafa, Menkes, Housden). These were connected by underground corridors to the métro and gave rise to a city whose system of subterranean links is considered the most highly developed in the world. The métro itself was begun in the early 1960s, and the architecture and interior design of several of its stations are notable. Perhaps the most striking building in the city is Habitat '67, a structure that was designed by MOSHE SAFDIE as part of the development for the international exhibition, Expo '67. These mass-produced, prefabricated concrete units were a daring attempt to solve the problem of urban housing (see CANADA, fig. 3). As the city developed from the 1950s to the 1970s—a period coinciding with the Révolution Tranquille (Quiet Revolution) that transformed French-Canadian society—little or no attention was paid to the existing fabric. In reaction to this, there was a strong concern for the preservation of Montreal's building heritage. This resulted in the gentrification of old neighbourhoods and in the construction, in the city centre, of the Maison Alcan (1980–83) by Affleck, a complex that is a sensitive blend of modern and traditional styles. Architecture of the late 1980s reflects the style of Post-modernism and tends to blend effectively with the environment; such examples include the Industrial Life Tower (1986) and La Maison

1. Montreal, view of the skyline looking south from the Belvédère, Mont Royal (Mount Royal), showing the city centre with Place Ville-Marie (1955–62) to left of centre and the St Lawrence River in the distance, 1987

des Coopérants (1988; Webb, Zerafa, Menkes & Housden). In 1987–91 the World Trade Center, Old Montreal, was built by ARCOP (Architects in cooperation) and Provencher Roy, with the same architectural approach as that for Maison Alcan.

BIBLIOGRAPHY
K. Jenkins: *Montreal, Island City of the St Lawrence* (New York, 1966)
J. I. Cooper: *Montreal: A Brief History* (Montreal, 1969)
R. Rumilly: *Histoire de Montréal*, 5 vols (Montreal, 1970–74)
J.-C. Marsan: *Montréal en évolution: Historique du développement de l'architecture et de l'environnement montréalais* (Montreal, 1974; Eng. trans., Kingston, 1981)
C. Grenier and J. Wolfe: *Guide Montréal: Un Guide architectural et historique* (Montreal, 1983)
L. Whiteson: *Modern Canadian Architecture* (Edmonton, 1983)
G. Pinard: *Montréal: Son histoire, son architecture*, 5 vols (Montreal, 1986–92)

JEAN-CLAUDE MARSAN

2. ART LIFE AND ORGANIZATION. Religious institutions were the dominant force in the cultural development of Montreal and other settlements in Nouvelle-France. François de Montmorency-Laval (1623–1708), the first Bishop of Québec, brought master craftsmen from France to establish a school of arts and crafts at Cap Tourmente, near Quebec City. There, wood-carving, panelling and decorating were part of an extensive programme of sculpting for the various churches and chapels, including several in and around Montreal. Paul Labrosse (*fl* 1720–50) and his family were some of several artisans who worked as wood-carvers near Montreal. Painting was a combination of the accomplished 17th-century French Baroque style transplanted to North America and its rather naive interpretation in a folk idiom. One of the best-known artists of this period was CLAUDE FRANÇOIS, a pupil of Simon Vouet, who, after joining the Recollect Order as Frère Luc, came to Nouvelle-France in 1670 to paint for the Church. EX-VOTO paintings were popular and were produced mainly by local artists to commemorate miraculous events and to give thanks to either St Anne or the Virgin. Most Canadian silver dates from about the beginning of the 18th century. Previously, any small and precious items were brought directly from France (*see* CANADA, §IX).

In 1760 Nouvelle-France was ceded to Great Britain, and Montreal became a British garrison post. British officers trained as topographers produced drawings and watercolour paintings, mainly of historical importance. However, some, such as James Duncan (1806–81), who worked in Montreal, painted works of artistic value. JAMES PATTISON COCKBURN, commander of the Royal Artillery, worked mainly in Quebec City but also sketched in Montreal, and GEORGE HERIOT included views of Montreal in his *Travels through the Canadas*, 2 vols (London, 1807). The French-speaking artists François Malepart de Beaucourt (1740–94) and Louis Dulongpré (1754–1843) were active in Montreal in the second half of the 18th century.

By the beginning of the 19th century, Montreal was becoming a significant inland port, and a wealthy English mercantile class was being established. In order to satisfy the demand by the upper classes for portraits, a local school developed. Some of the more accomplished painters were itinerant Americans; other were Canadians, such as THÉOPHILE HAMEL, who, although his studio was in Quebec City, painted several sitters from Montreal. By about 1850, painters from Montreal began to respond to the Canadian landscape and way of life. The German-born Otto Jacobi (1812–1901) was invited to Canada to paint a view of Shawinigan Falls to present as a gift to Edward, Prince of Wales (later Edward VII), during the latter's visit to Montreal in 1860. William Raphael (1833–1914) executed landscapes and genre scenes in a style similar to German Romantic painting. CORNELIUS KRIEGHOFF lived in Montreal and its environs from the early 1840s to 1853 and painted portraits of native peoples and scenes of habitant life, often for British army officers stationed there. Allan Edson (1846–88) and Adolphe Vogt (1842–71) were two other well-known landscape painters, the latter also known for his detailed studies of animals. The photographic firm of Notman Studios, run by WILLIAM NOTMAN, employed skilled artists, among them JOHN ARTHUR FRASER, to colour photographs and paint backdrops. Notman, Fraser and several businessmen helped to found the Art Association of Montreal in 1860, designed to hold annual exhibitions, build a collection, further art education and generally promote the arts. The Society of Canadian Artists (1867–72) was a group of professional painters that included Jacobi, Raphael, Edson and Vogt as charter members. Its founding president was the portrait painter John Bell-Smith (1810–83). Important collectors of art included GEORGE A. DRUMMOND and Sir WILLIAM VAN HORNE. Although some collectors tentatively accepted Impressionism, works by the traditional painters of the Barbizon and Hague schools were more popular.

WILLIAM BRYMNER, a portrait and genre painter, attended the Académie Julian in Paris in 1878, the first Canadian artist to go to Paris to study. Around 1900 other Canadians studying there brought back techniques of Impressionism to Montreal. MAURICE CULLEN adapted the style to the Canadian landscape. The expatriate JAMES WILSON MORRICE, a friend of Matisse, worked in a Post-Impressionist style. Morrice's decorative manner was taken up by several young painters in Montreal, including A. Y. JACKSON, who later became well known as a member of the Group of Seven, based in Toronto. JOHN LYMAN

2. Paul-Emile Borduas: *Sous le Vent de l'île (On the Leeward Side)*, oil on canvas, 1.1×1.5m, 1947 (Ottawa, National Gallery of Canada)

founded the Contemporary Arts Society (1939–48) to promote modern art and to counter the popularity of the Group of Seven, who relied heavily on the Canadian landscape for their subject-matter. The members of the Contemporary Arts Society had no particular common style, but rather shared a concern with the formal aspects of painting and were especially influenced by such artists as Picasso and Matisse. Paul-Emile Borduas and Marian Scott (1906–93) were two prominent members. The Beaver Hall Hill Group was a loosely based affiliation of figure painters, most of whom were women, English-speaking and former pupils of Brymner's at the Art Association of Montreal school. Three of the most talented were PRUDENCE HEWARD, EDWIN H. HOLGATE and Sarah Robertson (1891–1948).

During World War II and after, many French-speaking artists looked to Surrealism in Paris and Abstract Expressionism in New York for inspiration. Through his teaching, ALFRED PELLAN, who was influenced by Surrealism, precipitated a modern movement among a number of young painters in Montreal after his return to Quebec in 1940. PAUL-EMILE BORDUAS, whose style was based on Surrealist theories, was the leader of LES AUTOMATISTES (see fig. 2). Borduas influenced the Action painter JEAN-PAUL RIOPELLE, living in Paris, and the printmaker ALBERT DUMOUCHEL. GOODRIDGE ROBERTS, though remaining faithful to figure painting and the landscape, understood and assimilated modernist ideas, especially those of Cézanne. Abstract painting was more systematically explored by the next generation of artists, including CHARLES GAGNON. LES PLASTICIENS, a group who became known in the mid-1950s and who included GUIDO MOLINARI (see CANADA, fig. 6), CLAUDE TOUSIGNANT and YVES GAUCHER, painted hard-edge geometric works. In 1956 the Non-Figurative Artists' Association of Montreal was founded, which included Les Plasticiens and other abstract painters. During this time, the Galerie l'Actuelle was the premier venue for abstract art. In the 1960s and 1970s such artists as Molinari and Tousignant responded to Op art. From the 1970s there was a renewal of interest in the human figure, as seen, for example, in the photographic work of Sorel Cohen (b 1936) and the massive gestural drawings of BETTY GOODWIN. However, abstraction remained a motivating force for sculptors, particularly for those working in concrete, such as Roland Poulin (b 1940) and Claude Mongrain (b 1948). Many commercial and artist-run galleries have been established in Montreal, among them the artist-run Véhicule (founded 1971–2), the first of its kind in the city, and the Powerhouse Gallery (now Galerie Centrale), founded in 1973 and one of the first women's-run galleries in Canada. Parachute (1975–), Canada's only art magazine that is internationally distributed, is published in Montreal.

BIBLIOGRAPHY

The Arts of French Canada, 1613–1870 (exh. cat. by M. Barbeau, Detroit, MI, Inst. A.; Albany, NY, Inst. Hist. & A.; Montreal, A. Assoc. and elsewhere; 1946)
C. P. DeVolpi and P. S. Winkworth: Montreal: A Pictorial Record: Historical Prints and Illustrations of the City of Montreal, Province of Quebec, Canada, i (Montreal, 1963)
J. R. Harper: Painting in Canada: A History (Toronto, 1966)
——: Early Painters and Engravers in Canada (Toronto, 1970, 3/1981)
D. Reid: A Concise History of Canadian Painting (Toronto, 1973, rev. 2/1988)
T. Fenton and K. Wilkin: Modern Painting in Canada: Major Movements in Twentieth-century Canadian Art (Edmonton, 1978)
D. Reid: 'Our Own Country Canada': Being an Account of the National Aspirations of the Principal Landscape Artists in Montreal and Toronto, 1860–1890 (Ottawa, 1979)

FRANZISKA KRUSCHEN

3. CENTRE OF FURNITURE PRODUCTION. From the 17th century through to the mid-18th most furniture in French Canada was made by individual artisans in provincial versions of the Louis XIII, XIV and XV styles. In the closing years of the 18th century and the beginning of the 19th, however, a new class of British merchants in Montreal created the climate and the demand necessary for the development of a formal furniture industry in a taste that reflected directly mid-Georgian style untouched by either French or American influences. Formal furniture was purely English in character until c. 1830, after which it was influenced by the American use of Empire and revival styles. Between 1800 and 1850 in Montreal more than 120 employers or self-employed craftsmen, almost 90% of them of British origin, are documented as working in this tradition. Little of their considerable production has been specifically identified through surviving pieces, paper labels or other records. Some of these enterprises remained small, but others, such as Hilton & Baird (c. 1823–45) or Forster & Try (1817–24), grew large, often working 'from the most recent London patterns' (Can. Courant, 10 July 1819) in both local (black walnut, maple, cherry, birch) and imported woods. Mass-production methods were introduced c. 1850. Between 1850 and 1870 the number of cabinetmakers more than quadrupled as speciality carvers and gilders appeared, while such entrepreneurs as John Hilton (c. 1792–1866), with 92 employees in 1863, dominated the trade.

BIBLIOGRAPHY

E. Collard: 'Montreal Cabinetmakers and Chairmakers, 1800–1850: A Check List', Antiques, cv/5 (1974), pp. 1132–46
J. Minhinnick and P. Shackleton: 'Early Furniture of Canada: The English and American Influence, 1760–1840', Can. Colr, ix/1 (1974), pp. 25–9
L. Vermette: 'Ebéniste à meublier', Can. Colr, xx/3 (1985), pp. 45–50

JOHN A. FLEMING

Montréal. See KRAK DE MONREAL.

Montreuil, Pierre de. See PIERRE DE MONTREUIL.

Mont-Saint-Michel Abbey. Benedictine abbey on an island off the coast of Normandy, France (see fig.).

1. HISTORY. The first chapel on this site was founded in 708 by Aubert, Bishop of Avranches, after the Archangel Michael had appeared to him in a dream. The oratory, consecrated in 709, was served by a community of 12 canons. It apparently survived the Norman invasions, but the observance of the rule became very relaxed. In 966 Richard I, Duke of Normandy (reg 942–96), established there Benedictine monks from St Wandrille Abbey under the direction of Abbot Maynard (reg 966–91), who began the reconstruction of the church and other buildings. The church was burnt in 992 and rebuilt on a larger scale by Abbot Hildebert II (reg 1017–23) from 1023, at the time of the monastic reforms in Normandy carried out by Richard II (reg 996–1027) and William of Volpiano (962–

Mont-Saint-Michel Abbey, begun 1023, view from the north-west

1031). The Romanesque church was completed *c.* 1085, but the north side had to be restored after it collapsed in 1103 and after a fire in 1112, which also necessitated the reconstruction of the dormitory and gallery by Abbot Roger II (*reg* 1106–22). From 1154 Abbot Robert de Torigny (*reg* 1154–86) rebuilt the western façade block (destr. 1780) and the abbey entrance. New monastic buildings (the 'Merveille') were constructed after another fire during a siege in 1203. Begun under Abbot Jourdain (*reg c.* 1192–1212), they were mainly the work of Abbot Raoul de Iles (*reg* 1212–28).

During the Hundred Years War the fortifications of Mont-Saint-Michel were reinforced (1420–49), and the Romanesque choir collapsed (1421). Construction of the present chevet began in 1448. In 1622 the abbey became part of the Congregation of St Maur; the three western nave bays and the façade were destroyed and replaced with a large terrace. The abbey was dissolved at the Revolution (1789–95), and it was used as a prison in the 19th century. It was severely burnt in 1856, but thorough restorations were not undertaken until 1874. The architects

included Edouard Jules Corroyer, Victor Petitgrand, Paul Emile Antoine Gout (1852–1923) and Y. M. Froidevaux. The buildings of Mont-Saint-Michel are constructed of granite, but there is some limestone in the cloister.

2. ARCHITECTURE.

(i) Pre-Romanesque buildings. The excavations of 1908 revealed the existence of two pre-Romanesque churches built after 966. One of these, Notre-Dame-sous-terre at the west end of the nave, was a small church with twin aisles separated by an arcade carried on rectangular piers; it was extended towards the west during the 11th century. The narrow brick voussoirs of the arcades and the use of regular, square-shaped stones confirm that the building dates from Abbot Maynard's time; they are similar to techniques employed in contemporary buildings (e.g. Ouilly-le-Vicomte and Rugles). The remains of a church with a single-cell nave and a triangular chevet were discovered above this building under the floor of the Romanesque church in 1908; they probably belong to the

church built by Richard I and mentioned by some contemporaries including Ordericus Vitalis (*De moribus et actis primorum Normanniae ducum*, ed. J. Lair in *Mém. Soc. Antiqua. Normandie*, 3rd ser., iii, 1865, p. 290).

(ii) Romanesque buildings. The layout of the Romanesque choir, begun in 1023, is known from excavations (1964), and from an illumination in the Très Riches Heures of Jean, Duc de Berry (Chantilly, Mus. Condé, MS. 65), which dates from before the collapse of 1421. It had an ambulatory but apparently no radiating chapels. The transept, built over two crypts covered respectively with groin and barrel vaults, was completed by 1058 by Abbot Raoul du Mont (*reg* 1048–58). It has broad barrel vaults, which, like those of the crypt, counterbalance and buttress each other. The walls are articulated by tall arcades, enclosing two storeys. The south side of the nave dates from before 1085, but it was no doubt planned from 1023, since its construction corresponds to that of buildings dating from the first half of the 11th century such as Bernay Abbey and Coutances Cathedral. Similarly, the 'giant order' employed in the transept and the south elevation of the nave was also employed before 1060 at Speyer Cathedral. The sculptural decoration is sober, but some of the transept capitals illustrate the vogue in Normandy for Corinthian-derived capitals, which lasted until the 1060s.

The Romanesque buildings include the chapel of the Thirty Candles (the crypt under the north transept arm, which was altered in the 13th century), and the dormitory, most of which was rebuilt after 1112. It is a large rectangular room, the windows of which were altered in the 13th century; the western half was destroyed in 1780. The gallery remains from the old 11th-century cloister, built against the north wall of Notre-Dame-sous-terre and remodelled in the 12th century. It is a long rectangular room with two aisles divided by rows of columns supporting rib vaults. Supports and vaults were added *c.* 1135–40. The chaplaincy (Salle de l'Aquilon) beneath the gallery is divided into two aisles by a row of columns. Its waterleaf capitals, suggesting a date of *c.* 1135, and its groin vaults with pointed transverse arches show Cistercian influence. A wall passage links the gallery to other rooms in the Romanesque abbey. Traces also remain of the kitchen and the infirmary, which were later extensively remodelled, and of the ossuary and the guest-house.

(iii) Gothic buildings. Construction of the Merveille (so-called on account of its structural audacity) was begun in 1212 and was almost complete by 1228. It is a three-storey building supported by tall buttresses and has an almost military austerity and solidity, reflecting the difficult nature of the site. The basement level comprises the almonry and the storeroom; above are the guest hall and the knights' hall and on the third floor the monastic refectory, the cloister and the archive. A chapter house was intended to open off the west wall of the cloister, but it was never built. The architecture of the knights' hall is particularly interesting, with its three rows of tall columns and its rib vaults resting on capitals with finely carved foliate decoration, similar in style to those in the choirs of Hambye Abbey and Coutances Cathedral. The guest hall has two rib-vaulted aisles divided by tall columns; it is lit by tall

lancets and has two monumental fireplaces. The cloister (1225–8) is particularly lavish, with two sets of coloured shafts set in a syncopated rhythm, probably derived from English work (e.g. Lincoln Cathedral choir aisles), and supporting miniature vaults and arcades with richly carved spandrels. The columns with their moulded capitals have often been thought to be of Purbeck marble imported from England, but they are of Norman origin in a material termed 'granitelle' by Corroyer. The carved arcades are of limestone from Caen.

A vast crypt (1446–50) with massive round piers supports the choir, reflecting its layout. The choir, with its ambulatory and radiating chapels, is a good example of Late Gothic in Normandy; it has tall, pointed arcades, a glazed triforium, a very large clerestory and delicate tracery and flying buttresses, all of which recall the style of the 14th-century choir of St Ouen, Rouen.

The village that grew up around the abbey lies huddled within the fortifications and includes a Romanesque parish church, remodelled in the 15th century. The fortifications include crenellated ramparts, towers and a 14th-century barbican, which reinforce the abbey's own defences (the Tour Claudine protects the monastery entrance).

BIBLIOGRAPHY

Dom J. Huynes: *Histoire générale de l'abbaye du Mont-Saint-Michel* (1640), ed. E. de Robillard de Beaurepaire, 2 vols, Société de L'Histoire de Normandie (Rouen, 1877–8)
E. Corroyer: *Description de l'abbaye du Mont-Saint-Michel et de ses abords* (Paris, 1877)
Dom T. Le Roy: *Les Curieuses Recherches du Mont-Saint-Michel*, 2 vols, (Caen, 1877–8)
P. Gout: *Le Mont-Saint-Michel: Etude archéologique et architecturale des monuments*, 2 vols (Paris, 1910)
G. Bazin: *Le Mont-Saint-Michel* (Paris, 1933/R 1982)
C. Besnard: *Le Mont-Saint-Michel*, Petites Monographies Grands Edifices France (Paris, 1945)
Millénaire monastique du Mont (Paris, 1966–)
M. de Bouard: 'Notre-Dame-sous-terre: Essai de datation', *J. Sav.* (1961), pp. 10–27
Y. M. Froidevaux: 'L'Eglise Notre-Dame-sous-terre', *Mnmts Hist. France* (1961), pp. 145–66
——: 'La Terrasse de l'ouest du Mont-Saint-Michel', *Congr. Archéol. France*, cxxiv (1966), pp. 447–57
J. Vallery-Radot: 'Le Mont-Saint-Michel: Travaux et découvertes', *Congr. Archéol. France*, cxxiv (1966), pp. 413–46
H. Decaens: *Le Mont-Saint-Michel*, Nuit Temps (La Pierre-qui-Vire, 1979)
L. Grant: *Gothic Architecture in Normandy, 1150–1250* (diss., U. London, 1986)

MAYLIS BAYLÉ

Montserrat. *See under* ANTILLES, LESSER.

Monument, public. Object created to remind viewers of specific individuals or events, or an object regarded as representing a past civilization, even if its original purpose was different. This article discusses the first meaning—purpose-built, mainly sculptural monuments created for commemoration and addressed to the public and it is concerned primarily with the history and development of the public monument in the Western tradition. Further information on specific monuments can be found under the relevant city or site article, and information on types of monuments is given in the following art form articles: BRIDGE, BUST, CROSS, EQUESTRIAN MONUMENT, FOUNTAIN, MAUSOLEUM, OBELISK, PYRAMID, RELIQUARY, SARCOPHAGUS, STATUE, STELE, TOMB and TRIUMPHAL ARCH.

1. INTRODUCTION. The desire to commemorate human values through monuments is universal. Their form varies from sculptural monuments—the main emphasis in this article—to menhirs, mausoleums or entire cities honouring a ruler, for example Versailles in France or Karlsruhe in Germany. Treated as propaganda tools, monuments are often used to reinforce the political power of their patrons. To render their messages intelligible and effective they are often traditional in style and iconography. If abstract, they generally have a simple, geometric shape, such as Boullée's unexecuted spherical design for a cenotaph to *Isaac Newton* (1784; for illustration *see* BOULLÉE, ETIENNE-LOUIS). Even in modern revolutionary contexts, such novel forms as Vladimir Tatlin's model (1919–20; destr.) for a monument to the Third International, also known as Tatlin's Tower (*see* TATLIN, VLADIMIR, fig. 2), were rapidly forsaken for monumental statues of political leaders. Sometimes old forms and symbols have been superficially modified to consolidate a new ideology, for example the Vendôme Column in Paris (*see* §5 below).

The location of public monuments is also significant. In order to be accessible to the viewer they are usually in urban squares, streets or parks. Some squares have been specifically created to accommodate them, as with the Piazza Venezia in Rome for the monument to *Victor-Emanuel II, King of Italy* (1885–1911) by Giuseppe Sacconi. A more isolated location, however, can assist the visual impact of a monument: for example, the statue of *Liberty* (dedicated 1886) by Frédéric-Auguste Bartholdi is situated on Bedloe's Island in New York Harbor to be visible to the 'poor, huddled masses' migrating to the USA, as well as to provide a pilgrimage point for Americans. Likewise, the isolated but dramatically effective location of the Walhalla (1830–42), a German hall of fame, near Donaustauf by LEO VON KLENZE reinforces its role of commemorating German genius.

The ultimate success of a public monument is indicated by the extent to which it becomes synonymous with the civilization that created it: thus the Colosseum (AD 69/79–80) has come to symbolize the greatness of ancient Rome (*see* ROME, §V, 6 and ROME ANCIENT, fig. 28), while the statue of *Liberty* (for illustration *see* BARTHOLDI, FRÉDÉRIC-AUGUSTE) does the same for the USA and for the concept of liberty itself. So powerful and effective is such symbolism that monuments are sometimes interpreted as instruments of oppression as well as salvation. They are also subject to counter-propaganda, iconoclastic vandalism and destruction. These reactions transcend ideology and are almost as old as the monuments themselves. They range from the *damnatio memoriae* strictures of the Carthaginian theologian Tertullian (*c.* AD 160–220), who condemned Roman idolatry, to the dismantling of statues of Lenin in liberalized eastern European states in the late 20th century. It is possible, however, to overestimate the extent of iconoclastic destruction of monuments and underestimate the extent to which they have been 'recycled' or preserved: for example, the sarcophagus of the tomb of *Charlemagne* in the Palatine Chapel in Aachen Cathedral is probably the late Antonine Proserpina Sarcophagus. Almost every country has laws to preserve its public monuments, often for touristic and aesthetic reasons rather than commemorative ones.

2. ANTIQUITY. The ancient Egyptian word *men* means 'monument' and is often found in dedicatory inscriptions. Egyptian funerary monuments aimed to bring a closer union between the deceased and the gods. Other monuments, such as votive stelae, temples and obelisks, were often erected in propitiation of deities. Royal pyramids emphasized the Old Kingdom concept of kingship as the pivot of the cosmos; the immensity of the Great Pyramid of Cheops (*reg c.* 2551–*c.* 2528 BC) at Giza (for illustration *see* GIZA) also powerfully affirmed the king's temporal power. With the New Kingdom (*c.* 1540–*c.* 1075 BC) the latter was emphasized: the four colossal rock-cut statues (*c.* 1290 BC) of *Ramesses II* (*reg c.* 1279–*c.* 1213 BC) at Abu Simbel (for illustration *see* ABU SIMBEL) are a spectacular example of regal glorification. Similar motives explain the Achaemenian reliefs on the rock-cut tomb of *Darius I* (*reg c.* 521–486 BC) at Naqsh-i Rustam, near PERSEPOLIS.

The earliest Greek monumental art was greatly influenced by contact with the East as the Orientalizing period (720–*c.* 570 BC) label suggests. Public monuments in pre-Hellenistic Greece (before 323 BC) were, however, intended to honour the city state rather than glorify the individual. The most famous example of this is the Parthenon (447–432 BC; *see* ATHENS, fig. 11) in Athens, where Pheidias' statue of *Athena Parthenos* (446–438 BC; h. 13 m, destr.), the goddess of Athens, was displayed. The Panathenaic procession to Athena on the Parthenon frieze probably honoured victims of the Battle of Marathon (490 BC; *see* FRIEZE, fig. 1). Greek monuments proclaimed both human merit and religion; the humanist emphasis contrasts with the greater importance of the afterlife in Egyptian monuments. A new historical and archaeological consciousness of public monuments is found in the work of such Greek writers as Herodotus, Thucydides and most significantly PAUSANIAS, whose *Description of Greece* (AD 150–80) provides detailed discussions of the public monuments he saw on his travels. His fascination with their appearance, workmanship and scale emerges in the description of Pheidias' bronze *Athena Promachos* (470–446 BC; destr.) on the Acropolis. Pausanias recorded inscriptions on the monuments and gave an account of the ceremonial rites, history and myths surrounding them. He also distinguished between dignified, predominantly artistic monuments and such utilitarian monuments as porticos, agoras and theatres.

Hellenistic public monuments were richer and more elaborate than those of Classical Greece. Due to political changes there was a movement away from commemorating the experiences of the city state towards the Eastern tradition of grandiose glorification of individual rulers. The best-known example is the Mausoleum (370/65–*c.* 350 BC; destr.) at Halikarnassos (now Bodrum) in Turkey, which commemorated Mausolos, satrap (governor) of Caria in Asia Minor. The Mausoleum was rectangular in plan with sides measuring 38.4×32.0 m and is one of the Seven Wonders of the World (*see* HALIKARNASSOS, §2 and fig. 2-4).

While Roman public monuments are not noted for breaking new conceptual or artistic ground, they gave late Hellenistic artists an unprecedented opportunity to exploit their talents. The distinctive qualities of Roman art—realistic portraiture, continuous narrative and three-dimensionality—culminated in monuments of the 1st and 2nd centuries AD. The most distinctively Roman monument is the triumphal arch. These usually commemorated major events, such as the *Capture of Jerusalem* depicted in narrative reliefs on the Arch of Titus (*c*. AD 81) in Rome (*see* TRIUMPHAL ARCH, fig. 1). Monumental relief sculpture was also applied in other important contexts: the Ara Pacis Augustae (13 BC, dedicated 9 BC; *see* ROME, §V, 4 and fig. 22) commemorated, as its name suggests, the peace, stability and prosperity that Emperor Augustus attempted to establish. Trajan's Column (dedicated AD 113; *see* ROME, ANCIENT, fig. 76) in the Forum of Trajan, Rome, is more grandiose in its glorification, and Trajan, Emperor of Rome, is frequently depicted in the reliefs. The column was originally intended as a look-out post, although it was dedicated as a war memorial and became the tomb of Trajan in AD 117, surmounted with a colossal bronze statue of *Trajan* (*see* ROME, §V, 7). Portrait statues of emperors were also important public monuments, often, like that of Trajan, surmounting columns. The gilt-bronze equestrian statue of *Marcus Aurelius* (AD 166–80; Rome, Piazza del Campidoglio; *see* ROME, ANCIENT, fig. 61) typifies Roman realism and was the prototype for many later monuments.

3. EARLY CHRISTIAN, BYZANTINE AND MEDIEVAL. From AD 313, when the Edict of Milan was issued granting toleration to Christians, such monuments as temples, baths and theatres, which had been previously venerated, gradually decayed. Many of these buildings were, however, transformed and rededicated to Christian worship; others were pulled down to provide material for constructing new monuments. Early churches inherited the Roman function of being commemorative monuments, for example the basilican church of the Holy Sepulchre (AD 326–1099), Golgotha (*see* JERUSALEM, §II, 2). The church of the Holy Apostles (330s; destr. 1461), Constantinople, was built by Constantine the Great to serve as his mausoleum (*see* ISTANBUL, §III, 9(i)). Until the early 7th century emperors continued to be commemorated in the Roman tradition by monumental portrait statues surmounting columns (*see* EARLY CHRISTIAN AND BYZANTINE ART, §IV, 1). They were no longer portrayed as gods, however, but as leaders of Christians against the barbarians. Rulers and dignitaries were occasionally portrayed in monumental mosaics. Those at the church of S Vitale (consecrated 547 AD) in Ravenna commemorate the role of Justinian (*see* MOSAIC, fig. 6) and his wife Theodora (*see* EARLY CHRISTIAN AND BYZANTINE ART, fig. 39) in building the edifice. There is, however, no mistaking the overwhelmingly religious slant in Byzantine iconography.

Western Christian art during the Migration period and up to the Romanesque period retained a stronger cult of personality than that of the Byzantine Empire. Ancient public monuments were sometimes reused, as for example

the gilt-bronze equestrian statue (untraced) reportedly placed by Theodoric (*reg* 493–526) in his palace courtyard in Ravenna and later transported by Charlemagne to his capital at Aachen. The sculptural revival of the Ottonian period produced diverse public monuments, for example: Charlemagne's tomb in the Palatine Chapel in Aachen Cathedral, which was highly venerated in later centuries; such reliquaries as the gold statue of *St Faith* (late 9th century–early 10th; Conques, Trésor Ste-Foy; see fig. 1) and the Essen Virgin (*c*. 980; Essen Minster; *see* RELIQUARY, fig. 2); and the bronze Column of Christ (*c*. 1020; Hildesheim Cathedral; *see* CLASSICISM, fig. 1) with scenes from the *Life of Christ*, which was commissioned by

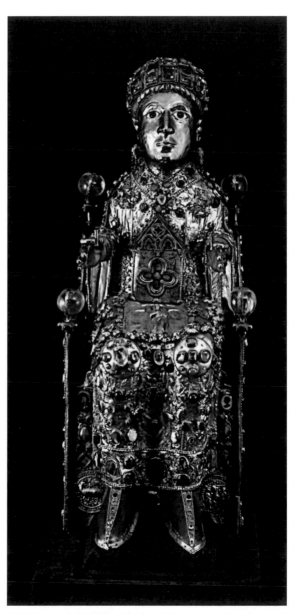

1. Reliquary of *St Faith*, gold, silver gilt, gems, pearls and enamel, h. 850 mm, late 9th century–early 10th (Conques, Trésor de l'Eglise Sainte-Foy)

BERNWARD, Bishop of Hildesheim. The Column of Christ revived the classicism of Trajan's Column, while its monumentality foreshadowed the Romanesque style. Funerary monuments reappeared from the 12th century either as a recumbent figure of the deceased surmounting a sarcophagus (e.g. tomb of *Richard Beauchamp, Earl of Warwick, c.* 1447; *see* ENGLAND, fig. 26) or as a slab set into the floor.

Reliquaries and crosses qualify as among the most important Gothic monuments. The Sainte-Chapelle (1239/43–8; *see* PARIS, §V, 2), was built to shelter the Grande Châsse, containing such relics as the Crown of Thorns and a fragment of the True Cross, while the Eleanor Crosses were erected by King Edward I of England to commemorate each stage where the coffin of his wife, Eleanor of Castile (1246–90), rested on its way to London (*see* CROSS, §II, 3 and fig. 2). Churches replaced ancient mausoleums as the burial places of ruling families, for example Westminster Abbey (*see* LONDON, §V, 2) for the English kings and SAINT-DENIS ABBEY near Paris for the French. In turn funerary monuments sometimes became pilgrimage shrines, for example that of St Thomas Becket, Archbishop of Canterbury (dedicated 1220; destr. 1538), in Canterbury Cathedral.

Increasing numbers of Romanesque and Gothic monuments commemorated secular themes, the temporal power of rulers and donors. In 1215 Emperor Frederick II reinterred the relics of Charlemagne in a shrine (1170–1215) in the Palatine Chapel in Aachen Cathedral, which was decorated on the roof with scenes from Charlemagne's life; and the Capua Gate (1234–40), a triumphal arch at the entrance to CAPUA in Italy that was built and possibly designed by Frederick, includes a life-size, enthroned togate figure of himself (Capua, Mus. Prov. Campano; for illustration *see* HOHENSTAUFEN, (2)). The identity of the life-size equestrian statue known as *The Rider* (mid-13th century; *see* BAMBERG, fig. 3) in Bamberg Cathedral is unknown but is thought to be a statue of a ruler, possibly representing Constantine the Great, Emperor Henry II, Frederick II, Stephen I of Hungary (*reg* 997–1038) or David. The figures of *Eckehard II* and his wife *Uta* (*c.* 1250; *see* NAUMBURG, fig. 1) in the west chancel of Naumburg Cathedral are early examples of Gothic sculpture honouring lay donors. Fountains, usually located in city centres, were common from the 13th century and often incorporated allegorical sculpture. Nicola Pisano's Great Fountain (1277–8; *see* FOUNTAIN, fig. 1) in Perugia between the cathedral and the Palazzo dei Priori fuses both Classical and Gothic iconography and styles.

4. RENAISSANCE, MANNERISM AND BAROQUE. Early 15th-century artists extended both intellectually and emotionally the admiration expressed by Plutarch regarding Classical monuments and culture, for example in Ghiberti's writings on Classical statuary in his *Commentaries* and Brunelleschi's archaeological research in Rome. The sculptural decoration of Florence Cathedral and the Orsanmichele by Ghiberti, Donatello and Nanni di Banco are civic monuments as much as religious sculptures. They reflect both the self-consciousness of Florence as the new Rome and, in the Orsanmichele figures, inter-guild rivalry. Overtly secular monuments rapidly followed. There was a

revival of the Roman concept of genius, illustrated by monuments celebrating the achievements of the figures commemorated and aimed at a grateful public. Examples include Paolo Uccello's monument to *Sir John Hawkwood* (1436; *see* UCCELLO, PAOLO, fig. 1) in Florence Cathedral and Donatello's influential equestrian monument to *Gattamelata* (1447–53; Padua, Piazza del Santo; *see* DONATELLO, fig. 4).

Michelangelo's *David* (1501–4; original, Florence, Accademia, *see* ITALY, fig. 54; copy, Florence, Piazza della Signoria) was originally intended for a buttress of Florence Cathedral, but when it was completed it was considered too important for that location and instead was placed in front of the Palazzo Vecchio, the seat of government, where it had a more public status. The democratic Commune government considered it an allegory of Florentine moral strength and the victory of Republicanism over tyranny. Other statues were erected around it, including *Hercules and Cacus* (1534) by Bandinelli (*see* BANDINELLI, BACCIO, fig. 2), *Perseus with Head of Medusa* (1545) by Cellini (*see* CELLINI, BENVENUTO, fig. 6) the figures on the Fountain of Neptune (*c.* 1560–75) by Bartolomeo Ammanati (*see* AMMANATI, BARTOLOMEO, fig. 2) and the *Rape of a Sabine Woman* (1580s) by Giambologna (*see* GIAMBOLOGNA, fig. 2), which was situated in the Loggia dei Lanzi. The stylistic evolution of these works is less relevant in this discussion than their functional continuity: they aimed both to assert Florence's status as the capital of Tuscany and to commemorate the patronage, good taste and glory of the Medici family. They therefore corresponded to the ideas propounded by the theorists FILARETE and FRANCESCO DI GIORGIO MARTINI in the 15th century. In his *Trattato di architettura* (1461–4) Filarete described how the prince's palace of his ideal city acquired monumentality through sculptural adornments, while in his *Trattati* Francesco advocated a spacious square surrounding the palace, filled with monuments to enhance aesthetic pleasure and princely prestige.

Baroque monuments carried the Renaissance concept of glorifying royal power much further and were the aesthetic and functional articulation of the centralized, absolutist state. The château of Versailles (first enlarged by Louis Le Vau in 1668; *see* VERSAILLES, §1) is the most spectacular absolutist monument. It not only provided accommodation for thousands but also functioned as the centre of government. In the gardens monumental sculptures by such artists as François Girardon and Antoine Coyzevox further contributed to the grandeur. Monuments also propagated faith in the Church, rendered with dramatic effect in the tombs of *Urban VIII* (1642–7; *see* SARCOPHAGUS, fig. 5) and *Alexander VII* (1671–8; both Rome, St Peter's) by Gianlorenzo Bernini (*see* BERNINI, (2)). Bernini's civic monuments in Rome, notably the Triton Fountain (1642–3; Rome, Piazza Barberini; *see* FOUNTAIN, fig. 5) and the Fountain of the Four Rivers Fountain (1648–51; Rome, Piazza Navona), carried similar messages. In the latter fountain (see fig. 2) the coat of arms and dove allude to papal rule over the world, as indicated by the marble personifications of the rivers *Danube, Nile, Ganges* and *Plate*. Bernini's influences on the public monuments of many other sculptors was enduring. His theatricality gave way to a lighter, almost

2. Fountain of the Four Rivers by Gianlorenzo Bernini, 1648–51, Piazza Navona, Rome

frivolous touch in the *Oceanus* group (1743–59) on the Trevi Fountain (1732–57) at the north end of the Via di San Vincenzo in Rome, designed by Nicola Salvi and Giovanni Battista Maini with the marble figures carved by Pietro Bracci (for illustration *see* SALVI, NICOLA). The particular style of Bernini's Baroque was adapted to the light and to the traditional sandstone materials used for the religious groups the *Vision of St Lutgard* (1710) by Matyáš Bernard Braun and *SS Vincent Ferrer and Procopius* (1712) by Ferdinand Maximilián Brokof on the Charles Bridge in Prague.

5. NEO-CLASSICISM. During the 18th century there was a gradual shift from monuments symbolic of absolutism to monuments of enlightened humanitarianism (*see* ENLIGHTENMENT, THE). Figures of genius as well as sovereigns were therefore commemorated, and the intention was to enlighten, not to overawe or indoctrinate. English monuments played a leading role in this. The tomb of *Sir Isaac Newton* (1731; see fig. 3) by Michael Rysbrack in the nave of Westminster Abbey, London, is much more than a church monument: its religious imagery is minimized, and its ambitiousness, scale and prominent position celebrate the modern 'culture' hero. Stylistically, however, Rysbrack's work remained essentially Baroque. The same applies to the marble statue of *George Frideric*

Handel (1738; London, V&A; *see* STATUE, fig. 7) by Louis-François Roubiliac. Janson (1985) described its content as 'novel and prophetic of the future; it is the first monument to a culture hero made within his own lifetime'. Its topicality was ensured by its original location in the Vauxhall Gardens in London, where Handel's music was sometimes performed (*see* LONDON, §V, 6). French counterparts to these monuments include the marble statues of *Voltaire Nude* (1776; Paris, Inst. France) by Jean-Baptiste Pigalle and *Voltaire Seated* (1781; Paris, Mus. Comédie-Fr.) by Jean-Antoine Houdon. Both illustrated the new vogue for antiquity and were modelled from life. The equestrian monument to *Peter the Great* (1766–82; St Petersburg, Decembrists' Square) by Etienne-Maurice Falconet attempted to commemorate an enlightened rather than an absolute monarch (for illustration *see* EQUESTRIAN MONUMENT). In a similar spirit the Directeur-Général des Bâtiments du Roi Charles-Claude Flahaut de La Billarderie commissioned, on behalf of Louis XVI, a series of four life-size statues of illustrious Frenchmen, called *grands hommes*, every two years between 1777 and 1789 to decorate the Grande Galerie in the Louvre, Paris, and to 'reawaken virtue and patriotism'.

During the French Revolution (1789–95) the call for 'virtue and patriotism' from radicals led to the legalized destruction of public monuments associated with the *ancien régime*. Many revolutionary monuments were

3. Tomb of *Sir Isaac Newton* by Michael Rysbrack, 1731, Westminster Abbey, London

commissioned, but few have survived. Others, such as the colossal plaster statue of *Liberty* (1794; destr.) by Charles-Louis Corbet, fell victim to political vicissitudes; it was originally built for the deconsecrated church of St Maurice in Lille, which had been converted into a Temple for the Eternal One, but it was destroyed following the Concordat (1801) between Napoleon and Pope Pius VII. The political impact of monumental sculpture was not lost on Napoleon, who reportedly stated, 'If I weren't a conqueror, I would wish to be a sculptor.'

Napoleon's Parisian monuments fused Neo-classicism with the absolutist glorification of soverign power. The Arc de Triomphe du Carrousel (1806–8) in the Place du Carrousel was designed by Charles Percier and Pierre François Léonard Fontaine and was based on the Arch of Septimius Severus in Rome; Napoleon crowned it with bronze horses taken from the church of S Marco in Venice. Others include the Vendôme (formerly Austerlitz or Colonne de la Grande Armée) Column (1806–10) in the Place Vendôme and the Arc de Triomphe (1806–36) in the Place Charles-de-Gaulle (formerly Place d'Etoile (*see* PARIS, fig. 8)). The last, a 50 m high triumphal arch by Jean-François-Thérèse Chalgrin, was the most ambitious and politically controversial. Napoleon intended it for his own glorification, and after the Restoration the Bourbon monarchy used it for their own ends. Louis-Philippe's government, which supervised its completion, considered it an opportunity to symbolize political reconciliation. The best known of the four huge reliefs flanking the monument is François Rude's the *Departure of the Volunteers of 1792*, generally known as La Marseillaise (1833–6; *see* RUDE, FRANÇOIS, fig. 1). The Vendôme Column (h. 43.5 m) by Vivant-Denon, Jacques Gondoin and Jean-Baptiste Lepère was based on Trajan's Column in Rome and perfectly illustrates the potent political symbolism that public monuments could assume. It was originally surmounted with a bronze figure of *Napoleon* (1810) as a Roman emperor by Denis-Antoine Chaudet, which was melted down in 1814 by royalists and replaced with a fleur-de-lis; a figure of a uniformed Napoleon was reinstated in 1831, and in 1863 Napoleon III replaced that with a replica of the original. In 1871 the Commune ordered the demolition of the column, which they regarded as a militarist symbol, but the Third Republic (1870–1940) reinstated the column in 1873–4.

These Napoleonic edifices influenced numerous counterparts outside France. The Constitution Arch (erected 1846) in London by Decimus Burton was temporarily topped by Matthew Cotes Wyatt's gigantic equestrian statue of the *Duke of Wellington* (completed 1846) and emulated the Napoleonic triumphal arch. Nelson's Column (h. 45.69 m; 1840–43) in Trafalgar Square, London, was designed by William Railton (*d* 1877), and Edward Hodges Baily made the granite figure of Horatio, Viscount Nelson (1844; 5 m), which was erected on the top. What was seen as the timeless dignity of antiquity made it the preferred mode for monumental architecture and sculpture. A sculptural example is Horatio Greenough's statue of *George Washington* (1832–41; Washington, DC, N. Mus. Amer. Hist.; *see* UNITED STATES OF AMERICA, fig. 20) for the Rotunda of the US Capitol, in which Washington is

portrayed as an Olympian Zeus, naked to the waist. Neoclassical idealism was tempered in the statue by specific allusions to North and South American politics and to the discoverer Christopher Columbus (Janson, p. 79). These, however, did not satisfy a public who would have preferred a realistic, more modern likeness.

6. REALISM, MODERNISM AND POST-MODERNISM. The eclecticism of 19th-century art was reflected in public monuments. Neo-classicism was complemented by the Gothic Revival, which was often chosen for nationalistic reasons. Examples include the Kreuzberg (designed 1817–18; completed 1821), a Gothic Revival monument in Berlin, which fused the neo-Gothic architecture of KARL FRIEDRICH SCHINKEL with Neo-classical figures by Christian Daniel Rauch, FRIEDRICH TIECK and LUDWIG WICHMANN; and the Albert Memorial (1863–76) in Kensington Gardens, London, which incorporates elements of Italianate Gothic architecture by George Gilbert Scott I and such realist sculptures as the bronze statue of *Prince Albert* by John Henry Foley (for illustration *see* FOLEY, JOHN HENRY). The spirit of Bertel Thorvaldsen's *Lion of Lucerne* (1819–21; Lucerne, Denkmalstrasse), a colossal monument to the faithful Swiss guards of Louis XVI, is clearly Romantic, having been hewn into a cliff face, but the style of the sculpture is Neo-classical.

In 19th-century monumental sculpture, Realism gradually supplanted idealism. Classical allegory, however, often continued to play an important role, and it is the dominant element in the most famous public monument of the century, the statue of *Liberty* (dedicated 1886) on Bedloe's Island, New York Harbor, by Frédéric-Auguste Bartholdi (for illustraion *see* BARTHOLDI, FRÉDÉRIC-AUGUSTE). The simple, idealized handling relates to Antonio Canova's Neo-classical figure of *Religion* on the funerary monument to *Clement XIII* (1783–92) in St Peter's, Rome. Popular involvement in its construction, through public subscription, distinguishes it from monuments of previous centuries. Since its erection it has been championed as embodying the ideal of liberty, whether by the conservative political leadership of the 1880s or by the student demonstrators who in 1989 erected a temporary replica in Tiananmen Square, Beijing.

Between 1870 and 1914 a large proportion of the monuments in the Western world, especially those incorporating statuary, were erected. Explanations for this 'statuemania' include the growth of industrial democracy, national self-consciousness and imperialism. The Italian Risorgimento inspired innumerable statues of Giuseppe Garibaldi; South American independence inspired statues of Simon Bolívar; and the rise of British imperialism inspired statues of Queen Victoria. Often monuments assumed an ambitious scale, producing what Janson called the 'Tower of Babel syndrome', as seen in the colossal Leipzig Battle Monument, also known as the *Volkerschachtdenkmal* (1896–1913), in Leipzig by Bruno Schmitz and in Rome the monument to *Victor-Emanuel II, King of Italy* (1885–1911; *see* ROME, fig. 10) by GIUSEPPE SACCONI. The artistic quality of such monuments has been berated: Janson claimed that mediocrity inevitably accompanies proliferation. There are, however, many exceptions, including Bartholdi's colossal *Lion of Belfort*

4. Royal Artillery Memorial by Sargeant Jagger, 1921–5, Hyde Park Corner, London

(1871–80), which was set in a cliff face in Belfort; Emmanuel Fremiet's *Joan of Arc* (bronze, 1874; Paris, Place des Pyramides), the popularity of which inspired replicas in such disparate locations as Portland, OR, and Melbourne in Australia; Alfred Gilbert's Shaftesbury Memorial (1885–93; London, Piccadilly Circus), whose allegorical figure of *Eros* (*see* GILBERT, ALFRED, fig. 1) was a rejection of what Gilbert dubbed 'coat-and-trousers' realism; and Augustus Saint-Gaudens's Sherman Monument (1892–1903; New York, Grand Army Plaza).

The beginning of the demise of the public monument is traditionally ascribed to the radical modernity of Auguste Rodin's *Burghers of Calais* (1884–95) in front of the Hôtel de Ville in Calais and his figure of *Honoré de Balzac* (1891–8; Paris, Mus. Rodin). This, however, ignores the fact that many conventional, Realist monuments continued to be erected at this time and were very well received: examples include Jules Dalou's *Triumph of the Republic* (1879–99) in the Place de la Nation, Paris (for illustration *see* DALOU, JULES), and Daniel Chester French's marble seated figure of *Abraham Lincoln* for the Lincoln Memorial (dedicated 1922; Washington, DC).

With few exceptions, such as ERNST BARLACH and WILHELM LEHMBRUCK, modernist sculptors were unwilling to produce monuments commemorating World War

I. The huge demand, together with conservative public opinion, however, brought traditional results. War memorials of World War I were similar to their 19th-century predecessors, although there was less overt heroicizing of war and more emphasis was laid on the ordinary soldier. This was movingly conveyed in Sargeant Jagger's Royal Artillery Memorial (1921–5; see fig. 4) in Hyde Park Corner, London. In general, however, sculpture was usually subsidiary to architectural memorials, and simple obelisks or crosses were preferred. The employment of traditional forms did not necessarily produce mediocrity: the Cenotaph (1920) in Whitehall, London, by EDWIN LUTYENS is clearly in the Classical tradition and is effective both as a war memorial and as a piece item of street architecture.

The ascendancy of modernism in North America and Europe by the mid-20th century led to what might be described as 'the death of the public monument'. Glorification of events or individuals using historical motifs, ornament or allegory was rejected. Form and function became the dominant aesthetic. Architecture was in the ascendant, sometimes assuming sculptural qualities, as with Eero Saarinen's Jefferson National Expansion memorial (1948–68) in St Louis, MO, which incorporates a stainless-steel arch. Military victims of World War II were usually commemorated through the addition of their names to existing monuments. The few major modern artists who designed war memorials emphasized horror, not glory: for example in the *Destroyed City* (1951–3) in the Leuvehaven Gardens, Rotterdam, by OSSIP ZADKINE a figure of a woman with arms outstretched commemorates the bombing of Rotterdam in World War II. The Pop art sculpture of Claes Oldenburg gave the public monument a new twist. His *Lipstick Ascending, on Caterpillar Tracks* (1969; New Haven, CT, Yale U. A.G.) wittily symbolized opposition to the Vietnam War. Official American commemoration of Vietnam came belatedly with the Veterans' Memorial (1982) in Washington, DC, a simple, V-shaped, black granite form by Maya Lin on which the names of the 58,132 American servicemen killed or lost in Vietnam are listed. The Arc de la Défense (designed 1981) in Paris by Paul Audreau and Jean-Pierre Buffi (*b* 1937) also returns to monumental first principles. The twin towers revive the triumphal arch concept and have been called Post-modern for their apparent links with the geometric simplicity of Boullée's monumental Neoclassicism. Economic rationalism interacts, however, with monumentality—each tower provides 40,000 sq. m of office space.

Public monuments of a more traditional, figurative nature continued to be erected in the 20th century: the Mount Rushmore National Memorial (1925–41) in South Dakota by Gutzon Borglum (1867–1941), which depicts the heads of four American presidents, is almost as familiar an image as the statue of *Liberty*. The Art Deco sculpture of Paul Manship seen in the Prometheus Fountain (1934) in the Rockefeller Center, New York, has always been popular with the public but has only recently been accorded art historical respect (for illustration *see* ROCKEFELLER). The reverse applies to Henry Moore's monumental sculpture, for example the *Reclining Figure* (1956–7; Paris, UNESCO Headquarters). After a lull of over 50 years, there was a revival in the 1980s of the portrait statue in Western cities. Modernism could not efface the desire, which seemed ever stronger, to commemorate human achievement through figurative monuments. This may take a traditional form of honouring military and political leaders, as in the statue in London of *Louis, 1st Earl Mountbatten* (1983; Whitehall) by Franta Belsky (*b* 1921). Alternatively, it may reflect more recent ideologies, such as the feminist-inspired Kate Sheppard National Memorial to Women's Suffrage (1993; Christchurch) by Margriet Windhavsen (*b* 1942). The work honours Sheppard's role in making New Zealand the world's first country to enfranchise women.

BIBLIOGRAPHY
E. Panofsky: *Tomb Sculpture* (New York, 1964)
C. Avery: *Florentine Renaissance Sculpture* (London, 1970)
R. Butler: *Western Sculpture: Definitions of Man* (Boston, 1975)
M. Trachtenberg: *The Statue of Liberty* (New York, 1977, rev. 2/1986)
M. Greenhalgh: *The Classical Tradition in Art* (London, 1978)
F. Haskell and N. Penny: *Taste and the Antique: The Lure of Classical Sculpture* (New Haven, 1981)
H. W. Janson: *Nineteenth-century Sculpture* (London, 1985)
M. Warner: *Monuments and Maidens: The Allegory of Female Form* (London, 1985)
A. Boime: *Hollow Icons: The Politics of Sculpture in 19th-century France* (Kent, OH, 1987)

J. Blackwood: *London's Immortals: The Complete Commemorative Outdoor Statues* (London, 1989)
J. Hargrove: *The Statues of Paris: An Open-air Pantheon* (Antwerp, 1989)
J. Montagu: *Roman Baroque Sculpture: The Industry of Art* (New Haven, 1990)
A. Borg: *War Memorials from Antiquity to the Present* (London, 1991)

MARK STOCKER

Monvel, Maurice Boutet de. *See* BOUTET DE MONVEL, MAURICE.

Monzo, Osvaldo (*b* Buenos Aires, 3 July 1950). Argentine painter. He was self-taught and came to prominence in the early 1980s as part of a current of Neo-expressionism and New Image painting that related to international developments emanating from Europe and the USA. He favoured schematic images presented as signs, their flatness counteracted only by the sensations of space induced by his use of colour and texture. He often incorporated written inscriptions into his pictures, as in a series entitled *Little Red Riding Hood and the Wolf*, in which he included quotations from the writings of Sigmund Freud to suggest the figures' subconscious desires.

BIBLIOGRAPHY
J. Glusberg: *Del Pop-art a la Nueva Imagen* (Buenos Aires, 1985), pp. 512–14

HORACIO SAFONS

Moody, Ronald (*b* Kingston, Jamaica, 1900; *d* London, 6 Feb 1984). Jamaican sculptor. He initially studied dentistry in London but began teaching himself the rudiments of sculpture, abandoning dentistry in 1933. As a sculptor he was strongly influenced by Egyptian, Chinese and Indian art and by Oriental philosophy. His best sculptures exhibit the hieratic qualities of Egyptian art and exude what he called the 'silence', the inner 'peace' that he associated with the best Egyptian and Buddhist art. He was deeply affected by the dropping of the atomic bomb on Japan in 1945 and in much of his subsequent work he dealt with man's potential for self-destruction, as in *Warrior* (1974; Kingston, Wallace Campbell col.), which depicts a figure with a stethoscope 'listening', Moody said, 'with all the care and attention to the bomb that the doctor spends on his patient'.

For an illustration of his work *see* CARIBBEAN ISLANDS, fig. 5

BIBLIOGRAPHY
P. Archer-Straw and K. Robinson: *Jamaican Art* (Kingston, 1990)

DAVID BOXER

Moor [Orlov], Dmitry (Stakhiyevich) (*b* Novocherkassk, 22 Oct 1883; *d* Moscow, 24 Oct 1946). Russian illustrator and poster artist. He had no formal training as an artist and started working as an amateur illustrator in 1908 for the satirical newspaper *Budil'nik*, to which he contributed regularly until 1917. Influenced by the *Jugendstil* caricatures of Thomas Heine and the Simplicissimus group, Moor quickly demonstrated his mastery of line and sense of subtle irony, as in the cartoons *Representative of the People* (1913) and *The Liberal* (1915; see Kozlov, p. [17]).

Moor's career as a caricaturist and poster artist began just after the October Revolution of 1917, when he produced numerous satires on the White Army, the

Capitalist blockade, the Church and other topics, many of which have become famous. Drawn in a crisp and simple style, sometimes in black and white, sometimes brightly coloured, Moor's posters are reminiscent of *lubki* (cheap, handcoloured broadsheets, *see* LUBOK) and, like them, communicate the message immediately and clearly (e.g. a *Red Gift for the White Pan*, *Have you Volunteered?* and *Vrangel is Still Alive: Beat him Down without Mercy* (all 1920; see Kozlov, pp. [29], [15] and [28]). Moor also focused attention on the domestic tragedies of the new republic: starvation in the Volga region (e.g. *Help!*, 1922; see Kozlov, p. [30]), disease (*Cholera in the Village*, 1924; see Kozlov, p. [34]), and speculation—a favourite theme of his drawings for the journal *Krokodil* beginning in 1922. Occasionally Moor experimented with rather abstract, even Suprematist approaches in his propaganda posters, as in the geometric composition in red, black and white for the *Power of the Attraction of the Treasures of the Earth* (1922).

Throughout the 1920s Moor contributed numerous cartoons to newspapers and magazines such as *Pravda* and *Bezbozhnik u Stanka*. Together with Aleksandr Deyneka, Viktor Deni (1893–1946) and Mikhail Cheremnykh, he established the foundations of the Soviet school of caricature and left a deep imprint on an entire generation of young graphic artists, especially the Kurkyniksy. Moor drew on his rich experience during World War II, producing a graphic series called the *History of Fritz* (1943; see Kozlov, pp. [44–50]) and a number of posters that shocked with their grotesque and bestial caricatures of Hitler and the German army. He also illustrated literary works, including Ivan Krylov's *Basni (Fables)* and works by Vladimir Mayakovsky and Mikhail Saltykov-Shchedrin, but they rarely carried the psychological force of his caricatures and posters.

WRITINGS
Yu. Khalaminsky, ed.: *Ya Bolshevik!* [I am a Bolshevik] (Moscow, 1967)

BIBLIOGRAPHY
A. Kozlov: *D. S. Moor* (Moscow, 1949)
Yu. Khalaminsky: *D. Moor* (Moscow, 1961)
M. Ioffe: 'Moor', *Desyat' ocherkov o khudozhnikakh-satirakh* [Ten essays on satirical artists] (Moscow, 1971), pp. 28–55
G. Piltz: *Dmitri Moor* (Berlin, 1973)

JOHN E. BOWLT

Moor, Karel de (*b* Leiden, 25 Feb 1655; *d* Leiden or Warmond, 16 Feb 1738). Dutch painter and printmaker. He is considered one of the most important Dutch portrait painters of the late 17th century and the early 18th. He studied in Leiden with Gerrit Dou, Abraham van den Tempel, Frans van Mieris (i) and Godfried Schalcken. In 1683 he became a member of the Leiden Guild of St Luke, of which he later occupied numerous administrative posts. In 1694, or shortly before, he founded the Leidse Tekenacademie together with Willem van Mieris and Jacob van Toorenvliet (*c.* 1635–1719) and, with van Mieris, was director until 1736. During his early career de Moor not only was active as a portrait painter but also produced genre and narrative pictures; in these latter he conformed closely to the LEIDEN 'FINE' PAINTERS of the preceding generation. The city governors of Leiden commissioned an overmantel (destr. by fire, 1929) from him for the Stadhuis. Despite his success as a genre and narrative

painter, he gradually devoted more and more of his output to portraiture, for which he acquired a considerable reputation during his lifetime. The influence of his teachers, particularly van den Tempel and Schalcken, can be seen in his portraits, but his best works show considerable originality, as can be seen from the group portrait of the *Governors of the Leiden Cloth Hall* (1692; Leiden, Stedel. Mus. Lakenhal). De Moor's reputation extended far beyond the borders of his native country; in 1714 he was knighted by Emperor Charles VI (*reg* 1711–40), and Peter the Great of Russia is also believed to have sat to him for a portrait. De Moor also produced a number of engravings and mezzotints (e.g. the *Self-portrait*, 1690; Hollstein, no. 16). His students included his son Karel Isaac de Moor (1696–1751), who was also active as a portrait painter.

BIBLIOGRAPHY
Hollstein: *Dut. & Flem.*; Thieme–Becker
R. E. O. Ekkart and others: *Leids kunst-legaat: Kunst en historie rondom 'Ars Aemula Naturae'* (Leiden, 1974), pp. 10–14
Leidse fijnschilders: Van Gerrit Dou tot Frans van Mieris de jonge, 1630–1760 (exh. cat. by E. J. Sluijter and others, Leiden, Stedel. Mus. Lakenhal, 1988), pp. 45, 182–5

RUDOLF EKKART

Moora, Harri (*b* Ehavere, nr Tartu, 2 March 1900; *d* Tallinn, 2 May 1968). Estonian archaeologist. He studied archaeology at Tartu University from 1920 to 1925 under A. M. Tallgren and B. Nerman. In 1930 he became acting professor of archaeology and head of the Archaeological Laboratory and Museum at Tartu University. He was made a permanent professor in 1938 and was head of the faculty of archaeology there from 1940 to 1950. In 1947 he was appointed head of the archaeological section at the Institute for the History of the Estonian SSR in Tallinn and became an academician of the Estonian SSR Academy of Sciences in 1957. He conducted research into the Early Iron Age in the south-eastern Baltic region and into the history and culture of the Baltic region as a whole, using a combined archaeological-ethnographical approach. He devoted special attention to the early decorative art of the south-eastern Baltic region, particularly the typology of ornament, notably in enamel brooches dating to the middle of the first century AD; he also studied ancient monuments of Estonian architecture and urban construction, for example the site of the settlement of Lõhavere.

BIBLIOGRAPHY
Studia archaeologica in memoriam Harri Moora (Tallinn, 1970)

V. YA. PETRUKHIN

Moorcroft, William (*b* Burslem, Staffs, 1872; *d* ?Cobridge, Staffs, 14 Oct 1945). English ceramics designer. He came from an artistic family and studied ceramics in Burslem, London and Paris, qualifying as an art teacher in 1897. From 1898 he worked for James Macintyre & Co. Ltd of Burslem, where he developed 'Florian' ware, an innovative line of tableware and ornamental ware in floral designs using slip trailing and coloured glazes. By 1913 Moorcroft had his own factory at Cobridge, where he produced his richly coloured pottery, with its simple shapes decorated with pomegranates, orchids, toadstools and other exotica, often on deep blue backgrounds (examples in London, V&A). In 1913 he introduced his distinctive 'Powder-blue' line of tableware, which was made until

1963. He was appointed potter to Queen Mary by royal warrant in 1928. He passed on the secret of his high-fired, flambé glazes to his son Walter Moorcroft (*b* 1917), who took over the Cobridge factory and generated his own designs, until his retirement in 1987.

BIBLIOGRAPHY

G. A. Godden: *British Pottery* (London, 1974)

P. Atterbury: *Moorcroft Pottery: A Guide to the Pottery of William and Walter Moorcroft, 1897–1986* (London, 1987)

□

Moore. English family of painters. William Moore (1790–1851) was a provincial portrait painter, and four of his fifteen sons and daughters, of whom (1) Albert Joseph Moore was the youngest, were also artists. Edwin Moore (1813–93) and William Moore jr (1817–1909) were topographical painters working mainly in watercolours. John Collingham Moore (1829–80) painted landscapes and child portraits and worked in Rome with the artistic group known as the ETRUSCAN SCHOOL. Next to Albert, the most talented of the Moore brothers was Henry Moore (1831–95), elected ARA in 1885 and RA in 1893. He had a high reputation in the 19th century for his marine paintings, typically studies of the open seas. Henry was precise in observation of atmosphere and wave form and his work became increasingly bold in execution and colour. *The Clearness after Rain* (1887; priv. col., see 1978 exh. cat., p. 61) gained him the Légion d'honneur at the Exposition Universelle of 1889 in Paris.

DNB

BIBLIOGRAPHY

F. Maclean: *Henry Moore*, The Makers of British Art (London, 1905)

Great Victorian Pictures (exh. cat., Leeds, C.A.G., 1978)

The Moore Family Pictures: Paintings, Watercolours and Drawings by Albert and Henry Moore, their Brothers William, John Collingham and Edwin and their Father William Moore Snr (exh. cat., ed. J. Harnoll; York, C.A.G., 1980) [essays on Henry Moore and rediscovered works by Albert Moore; works by all family members repr.]

(1) Albert Joseph Moore (*b* York, 4 Sept 1841; *d* London, 25 Sept 1893). He showed precocious artistic talent as a child and entered the Royal Academy Schools in London in 1858. His early work shows a Pre-Raphaelite influence common to his generation. The watercolour *Study of an Ash Trunk* (1857; Oxford, Ashmolean) is very Ruskinian in its precise handling of naturalistic detail. Moore made two visits abroad: in 1859 to France with the architect William Eden Nesfield and in the winter of 1862–3 to Rome with his brother John Collingham Moore. *Elijah's Sacrifice* (1863; exh. RA 1865; Bury St Edmunds, A.G.), one of Moore's earliest large-scale oil paintings, was executed while he was in Rome. Its biblical subject and sombre tone are typical of his output in the early 1860s and relate to the work of Ford Madox Brown and Edward Armitage. However, the picture is decorative rather than archaeological in mood and already reveals an interest in colour and drapery that characterized his mature style.

In the 1860s Moore designed illustrations, tiles, wallpaper and stained glass, most notably for Morris, Marshall, Faulkner & Co. He was also prominent as an ecclesiastical and domestic mural painter, initially in Nesfield's country houses such as Coombe Abbey, Warwicks. His classicism, which first became apparent in his domestic murals, was encouraged by intensive study of Classical sculpture, in particular the Elgin Marbles at the British Museum, London. Little of his mural work survives, but the life-size figures of *A Greek Play* (tempera on canvas, 1868; London, V&A) painted for the proscenium arch of the Queen's Theatre, London, show that he abandoned chiaroscuro for a flat, decorative treatment of colour. Perhaps they also betray an admiration for Japanese prints, which were first admired in Britain by architects such as Nesfield.

In 1865 Moore began to produce his first decorative easel paintings, for example *Pomegranates* (254×356 mm, 1866; London, Guildhall A.G.). The decorative qualities of the classically draped figures impressed James McNeill Whistler, whose work emulated Moore's between 1867 and 1870. Whistler may also have devised his butterfly signature after Moore began to use an anthemion (honeysuckle) device in 1867. Moore's aesthetic is comparable to that of Whistler, Swinburne and Walter Pater, all of whom, as advocates of ART FOR ART'S SAKE and contributors to the AESTHETIC MOVEMENT, believed that the beauty of form, composition and colour should be the sole end of art; Classical sculpture was its spiritual source, music its preferred metaphor. Moore's Academy exhibits of 1869 formed an Aesthetic manifesto. *The Quartette: A Painter's Tribute to the Art of Music, AD 1868* (priv. col., see 1975 exh. cat., no. 25) depicts a contemporary string quartet in Classical draperies. 'Anachronism is the soul of art', Moore later declared. *A Venus* (1869; York, C.A.G.; see fig.) is a nude derived from the *Venus de Milo*. The indefinite article implies that the painting is not a representation of the Greek goddess, but rather an ideal of female beauty with minimal reference to myth or story. She stands in front of a white azalea in a Chinese vase. The colour, in a high key, is an exquisite harmony of white, pink and blue. The canvas is coarse and reviewers noted a frescolike technique. Moore's Aestheticism was the most extreme type of formalism possible before the development of abstract art.

In his works of the 1870s the subject-matter became even less important, and titles of the paintings referred to still-lifes rather than to figures. In the 1880s, however, hints of situation and narrative returned, for example *Reading Aloud* (1884; Glasgow, A.G. & Mus.). Moore's last work, *Loves of the Winds and the Seasons* (1893; Blackburn, Mus. & A.G.), was a large and elaborate allegory of human relationships in a landscape setting. Baldry, his biographer, suggested that the changes in Moore's art were caused by the humanizing effect of a long illness, but changing taste and financial necessity probably played a larger part.

In the 1860s Moore won commissions from Dante Gabriel Rossetti's circle of patrons, particularly F. R. Leyland (who owned *A Venus*) and James Leathart. William Connal, who owned *Reading Aloud*, was his main patron in the 1880s. Moore probably had financial problems in his last decade, when he did some private teaching. He exhibited regularly at the Grosvenor Gallery, London, an important supporter of the Aesthetic Movement after it opened in 1877, and also at the Royal Academy. He was never elected ARA, however, probably because his intransigent Aestheticism made enemies. Moore was a reclusive figure. Among his few friends was Whistler, for whom he appeared in the artist's libel action against John Ruskin in 1878.

Moore's working method was elaborate. Drawn and painted studies and nude and draped cartoons preceded successive layers of work on the canvas itself. He frequently finished his studies as paintings, which accounts for the groups of related works from the 1870s and 1880s. *Beads* (1875; Edinburgh, N.G.), *A Sofa* (1875; priv. col., see Baldry, p. 76) and *Apples* (1875; priv. col., see 1961 exh. cat., no. 106) differ only in colour, trivial accessories and title. *Red Berries* (*c.* 1884; see 1978 exh. cat., p. 152)

Albert Joseph Moore: *A Venus*, oil on canvas, 1600×762 mm, 1869 (York, City Art Gallery)

repeats the reading girl from *Reading Aloud* in blue and green rather than pink and grey. It is Moore's innate sense of colour harmony and constant recourse to nature in his paintings of figures, draperies and flowers that raise his work above the level of decoration. From the 1880s pastel was a favourite medium.

BIBLIOGRAPHY
A. L. Baldry: *Albert Moore: His Life and Works* (London, 1894) [still the standard work; a good checklist and well illustrated]
R. Walker: 'Private Picture Collections in Glasgow and the West of Scotland: Mr William Connal's Collection of Works by Albert Moore', *Mag. A.*, xvii (1894), pp. 59–64
Victorian Paintings (exh. cat., London, Agnew's, 1961)
Albert Moore and his Contemporaries (exh. cat., ed. R. Green; Newcastle upon Tyne, Laing A.G., 1972)
Victorian Olympians (exh. cat., ed. R. Free; Sydney, A.G. NSW, 1975) [includes works by Moore]
Victorian High Renaissance (exh. cat., ed. G. Hedberg; Manchester, C.A.G., 1978) [includes a short biography of Moore and 22 works by the artist, including colour illustrations]
H. J. Morgan: *Theory and Practice in the Work of Watts, Leighton, Burne-Jones and Moore* (diss., U. London, 1982)
R. Green: *Albert Moore: Catalogue Raisonné* (in preparation)

HILARY MORGAN

Moore, Charles W(illard) (*b* Benton Harbor, MI, 31 Oct 1925). American architect and teacher. He studied architecture at the University of Michigan, Ann Arbor, from 1942 to 1947 (BArch, 1947). He then practised architecture in California (1947–9 and 1954–5), travelled in Europe and the Near East (1949–50), taught at the University of Utah in Salt Lake City (1950–52), and served in the US Army in Japan and Korea (1952–4). In 1956 Moore received the degree of MFA from Princeton University, NJ, and went on to earn a PhD (1957) there. After teaching for one year at Princeton (1958–9), he became an Associate Professor at the University of California at Berkeley (1959–62) and then chairman of its Department of Architecture (1962–5). In 1962, together with architects Richard Whitaker, Donlyn Lyndon (*b* 1936) and William Turnbull (1935–97), he founded the firm MLTW, within which he produced his best work in the 1960s and 1970s.

The most influential period of Moore's teaching career took place after 1965 when he accepted the chairmanship of the Department of Architecture at Yale University, New Haven, CT (1965–7), followed by a term as Dean (1969–70) and as Professor (1970–75). During his tenure at Yale Moore set up a new architectural practice, Charles W. Moore Associates, in Essex, CT (from 1969). Between 1975 and 1985 Moore was Professor of Architecture at the University of California at Los Angeles, while continuing also as visiting professor at Yale University. During this decade his architectural work was done in partnership with various associates, most notably the Urban Innovations Group in Los Angeles. After 1985 Moore held an endowed chair of architecture at the University of Texas in Austin. Moore was, with Robert Venturi and Colin Rowe, one of the most influential architectural teachers of his generation. In his lectures and publications, as well as in the buildings he designed, there was a strong sense of architectural history, and of the value of vernacular regional architecture. He was a skilful publicist, seeing architecture as a performing art with the architect as juggler.

Charles W. Moore: condominium, Sea Ranch development, San Francisco, CA, 1963–5

During his early years in California Moore designed a number of important structures, notably a condominium at the Sea Ranch development, San Francisco, CA (1963–5; *see* fig.), and Kresge College of the University of California at Santa Cruz (1964–74). The novelty of these buildings is in their animated sociability and in the distinctly regional style of their materials. Kresge College is in a highly simplified and geometric version of California stucco, and is laid out as a self-contained village of 600 students, while Sea Ranch draws upon the wood siding and single-pitch roofs of indigenous rural buildings. Both in California (Orinda, 1962) and in Connecticut (New Haven, 1967; Essex, 1973) Moore built houses for himself that can be interpreted as a manifesto of his own architectural philosophy for the private residence. He proposed the aedicule as the replacement for the traditional hearth, partly influenced by Louis Kahn, his teacher at Princeton. He also borrowed from the traditions of theatre design and stage setting, providing surprises and unexpected views. Other examples of his experiments in residential design are the Klotz house (1967–70) in Westerly, Rhode Island, CT, and the Koizim house (1970) in Westport, CT.

Moore's compositions for larger-scale buildings, for example the public housing estates in New Haven, CT, at Church Street South (1966–9), were not as successful, partly because he did not consider the public aspect of the whole. An exception is the Piazza d'Italia, New Orleans, LA (1977–8), where Moore demonstrated his interest in urban-scaled compositions (*see* FOUNTAIN, fig. 7). This work has been accused of frivolity and of trivializing the great monuments of Western architecture, but these architectural elements are used wittily, as comments on the vocabulary of classical buildings.

In the 1980s Moore's practice turned increasingly towards public buildings and commissions with a distinct urban scale. He designed a number of parks (e.g. Hermann Park, Houston, TX, 1982) and temporary pavilions for fairs (e.g. Indiana Landing project, Indianapolis, 1981–2). Moore worked in particular for colleges and universities (e.g. Williams College Museum of Art, Williamstown, MA, 1977–86), religious institutions (e.g. St Matthew's Episcopal Church, Pacific Palisades, CA, 1979–83), commercial buildings (e.g. Hancock Bank Plaza, Gulfport, MS, 1980) and hotels (e.g. Embassy Hotel, Los Angeles, CA, 1984).

WRITINGS
with G. Allen and D. Lyndon: *The Place of Houses* (New York, 1974)
with G. Allen: *Dimensions: Space, Shape and Scale in Architecture* (New York, 1976)
with W. J. Mitchell and W. Turnbull jr: *The Poetics of Gardens* (Cambridge, MA, 1988)

BIBLIOGRAPHY
'The Work of Charles W. Moore', *A & U* (May 1978) [whole issue]
G. Allen: *Charles Moore* (New York, 1980)
D. Littlejohn: *Architect: The Life and Work of Charles W. Moore* (New York, 1984)
F. Z. Louie de Malave: *Charles W. Moore: North American Architect* (Monticello, 1985)
E. J. Johnson, ed.: *Charles Moore, Buildings and Projects, 1949–1986* (New York, 1986)

MARTHA POLLAK

Moore, David (Murray) (*b* Sydney, 6 April 1927). Australian photographer. He was introduced to the creative possibilities of the camera when his father brought home a book on the work of Edward Weston. From 1948 until 1951 he worked in the studio of Max Dupain, where he learnt professional studio techniques during the week, walking the streets with a camera in his spare time. A rigorous apprenticeship refined an inherent aesthetic sensitivity. His growing interest in photojournalism then led Moore to London. He was commissioned by *Time, Life, Fortune, Look* and *The Observer* and was also included in the famous exhibition at MOMA, New York, the *Family of Man* (1955).

In 1958 Moore returned to Sydney, where he specialized in American magazine and industrial commissions, notably with Life Books, *National Geographic* and Exxon. As the public became sated by photojournalistic essays, and the magazines that published them were undermined by the popularity of television, Moore refined his work; instead of the dramatic situation and the climactic moment, he began, as he said, 'to look for the ordinary and show how extraordinary and meaningful it is'. In the 1970s, influenced by the coastal landscape of his Lobster Bay retreat, he began to explore form, sensuality and rhythm. Moore's work has a spontaneous freshness that can transform the otherwise straight picture. He had an unerring ability to capture the underlying forms within his subject and to be sensitive to the relationships of their shapes. Underpinning these strengths is a warmth of feeling for the world and the people that inhabit it, thereby avoiding a cerebral and analytical result.

WRITINGS

with R. Hall: *Australia: Image of Nation, 1850–1950* (Sydney, 1983)

BIBLIOGRAPHY

I. McKenzie: *David Moore*, Contemporary Photographers: Australia 1 (Melbourne, 1980)

DAVID P. MILLAR

Moore, George (Augustus) (*b* Moore Hall, Co. Mayo, 24 Feb 1852; *d* London, 21 Jan 1933). Irish writer, critic and painter. In 1861 he was sent to Oscott College in Birmingham, to prepare for a military career but subsequently moved to London, where he briefly enrolled in drawing classes at the South Kensington School of Art. After taking various other art classes of short duration, in 1873 he went to Paris, studying first under Alexandre Cabanel at the Ecole des Beaux-Arts and then at the Académie Julian, with Gustave Boulanger and Jules Lefebvre. After a brief stay in London (1874–5), from 1875 to 1879 he was again in Paris, where he was an habitué of the Café de la Nouvelle-Athènes and met Emile Zola and such painters as Manet, Degas and Renoir. Although at first he disliked Impressionist art, he soon began to champion the work of Degas and especially Manet. At this time Moore began to realize that his own talents lay not in painting but in writing. From 1879 to 1901 he divided his time between London and Ireland. In London he frequented literary and artistic circles, was a member of the Hogarth Club and promoted the paintings of the French Impressionists. His first novel, *A Modern Lover* (London, 1883), deals with the art world of the 1870s and 1880s in a style that is reminiscent of Zola in its clumsy realism yet nevertheless challenged the popular sentimental English novels of the time. He often chose to cast people from the art world in the guise of characters in his novels: for example Mr Bendish in *A Modern Lover* is based on the art dealer Paul Durand-Ruel.

Moore was an early contributor of art criticism to *The Hawk* and between 1891 and 1895 was art critic for *The Speaker*. In *Impressions and Opinions* (London, 1891) he attacked the French system of art education, criticizing the methods of instruction in the Ecole des Beaux-Arts and the Académie Julian, which he said destroyed an artist's individuality. He reinforced these ideas in *Modern Painting* (London, 1893, rev. New York, 1923), where he dealt critically with such issues as the dominance of public taste and the dictates of consumerism in art. He also denounced the eclecticism of Whistler and praised Manet and Degas, whom he felt pursued their own unique visions. His most successful novel, *Esther Waters*, was published in 1894. He spent the years 1901 to 1911 in Ireland, where he took part in the Irish literary renaissance, and then returned to London, where he lived until his death, writing essays, novels and a book of criticism, *Conversations in Ebury Street* (London, 1924). He owned works by his friends Manet, Monet, Degas, Berthe Morisot, Charles Conder and Ford Madox Brown and was painted by such artists as Walter Richard Sickert, Henry Tonks, Jack B. Yeats and Jacques-Emile Blanche. The best-known painting of him is by Manet (1879; New York, Met.).

WRITINGS

Confessions of a Young Man (London, 1888)
Impressions and Opinions (London, 1891)
Modern Painting (London, 1893, rev. New York, 1923)
Reminiscences of the Impressionist Painters (Dublin, 1906)

BIBLIOGRAPHY

J. Hone: *The Life of George Moore* (New York, 1936)
F. W. Seinfelt: *George Moore: Ireland's Unconventional Realist* (Philadelphia, 1975)
A. Farrow: *George Moore*, Twayne's English Authors (London, 1978) [good disc. of his ideas on art]
J. E. Dunleavy, ed.: *George Moore in Perspective*, Irish Literary Studies, xvi (Naas, Co. Kildare; Gerrards Cross, Bucks; and Totowa, NJ; 1984)

Moore, Henry (Spencer) (*b* Castleford, W. Yorks, 30 July 1898; *d* Perry Green, Much Hadham, Herts, 31 Aug 1986). English sculptor, draughtsman and printmaker. Generally acknowledged as the most important British sculptor of the 20th century, he took the human figure as his central subject-matter throughout his career. Although he witnessed revolutionary stylistic changes and the emergence of new sculptural materials during his working life, he borrowed from diverse cultural traditions and artists in order to give his work a profound resonance with the art of the past. His female figures, echoing the forms of mountains, valleys, cliffs and caves, extended and enriched the landscape tradition, which he embraced as part of his English artistic heritage.

1. Life and work. 2. Working methods and technique.

1. LIFE AND WORK.

(i) Before 1940. The seventh child of a miner, he was brought up in the small industrial town of Castleford. His father, a self-educated man, had great ambitions for his children and insisted that Henry should first qualify as a teacher (he worked as a student teacher at Temple Street Elementary School in 1915–16) and then pursue, if he wished, a career in art.

Moore joined the army in 1917 and was sent to France. He was gassed in the Battle of Cambrai and returned to England to convalesce. In 1919 he began the two-year course at Leeds School of Art. There he read Roger Fry's

Vision and Design (London, 1920), which introduced him to his most important formative influences: non-Western sculpture, with its three-dimensional realization of form and use of direct carving. In Leeds he had access to the art collection of Michael Sadler (1861–1943), then Vice-Chancellor of Leeds University, which included works by Cézanne and Gauguin. In 1921 Moore was awarded a scholarship to study sculpture at the Royal College of Art in London. His weekly visits to the British Museum were far more influential on his early development than his academic course work. In his effort to remove 'the Greek spectacles from the eyes of the modern sculptor' (Moore, 1966, p. 57), Moore focused on African and Oceanic work, but above all on Pre-Columbian art. A conflict soon arose between his academic studies and his interest in non-European sculptural traditions. He realized the value of drawing and modelling from life and reached a compromise—concentrating on academic course work during term and leaving weekends and holidays free to pursue his own sculptural interests. He received constant encouragement from Sir William Rothenstein, the newly appointed principal of the Royal College.

Throughout his life Moore's appetite for the history of world sculpture was insatiable. Drawings of sculptures in his early sketchbooks indicate that Palaeolithic fertility goddesses, Cycladic and early Greek art, Sumerian, Egyptian and Etruscan sculpture, African, Oceanic, Peruvian and Pre-Columbian sculpture particularly interested him. He noted in a 1926 sketchbook: 'Keep ever prominent the world tradition—the big view of Sculpture'.

Like Constantin Brancusi, Amedeo Modigliani, Jacob Epstein and Henri Gaudier-Brzeska, Moore believed passionately in direct carving and in 'truth to materials', respecting the inherent character of stone or wood. Almost all of his works from the 1920s and 1930s were carved sculptures, initially inspired by Pre-Columbian stone carving. One of Moore's earliest sculptures, the small marble *Snake* (1924; priv. col., see Read and Bowness, i, p. 5), almost paraphrases the rattlesnake carvings of the Aztecs. The larger Hornton stone *Mother and Child* (1924–5; Manchester, C.A.G.) established a lifelong theme. In this carving Moore was still struggling to make the material do what he wanted, to free the forms from the massive block of stone. The forms were buried inside each other and the heads given no necks 'simply because I was frightened to weaken the stone' (Moore, 1968, p. 45).

Moore made his first visit to Paris in 1923 and was overwhelmed by the work of Cézanne, which he saw in the private collection of Auguste Pellerin (1852–1929) in Neuilly. In 1924 Moore was appointed sculpture instructor at the Royal College. He spent six months in 1926 visiting museums and churches in France and Italy, where he greatly admired Giotto and Masaccio and the late work of Michelangelo. On his return to Britain he found that it took some time to rid himself of their influence, as he thought he should, in order to maintain his basis in non-Western work. In 1928 he had his first one-man exhibition at the Warren Gallery in London. He sold several sculptures and about 30 drawings, several to Jacob Epstein and Augustus John. He also received his first public commission, a relief carving of the *West Wind* in Portland stone

for the new headquarters of London Underground railway at St James's Park.

In 1929 Moore married Irina Radetsky, a student of painting at the Royal College. During the next six years she was the model for a series of life drawings such as *Seated Figure: Life Drawing* (1934; AC Eng). Moore also began work on his most important carving of the decade, the brown Hornton stone *Reclining Figure* (1929; Leeds, C.A.G.). This sculpture was inspired by the Toltec-Maya basalt reclining figure of the warrior priest *Chacmool* (Mexico City, Mus. N. Antropol.; *see* MESOAMERICA, PRE-COLUMBIAN, fig. 22), which Moore later cited as the one sculpture that most influenced his early work. The characteristics that Moore admired in the *Chacmool*—'its stillness and alertness, a sense of readiness, and the whole presence of it, and the legs coming down like columns' (personal communication)—could describe many of his own reclining figures, which echo its pose and massive form. There are numerous drawings for the Leeds carving. Throughout the 1920s and 1930s, when almost all his sculptures were carved in stone or wood, Moore's preparatory drawings enabled him to work out various poses and formal variations. The one that held his attention was then translated into sculpture. *Reclining Woman* (green Hornton stone, 1930; Ottawa, N.G.), the pendant of the Leeds *Reclining Figure*, was at one time entitled *Mountains*. It was the first of many sculptures in which the female figure became a metaphor for landscape.

Moore's sculpture of the 1930s was enriched by quite different influences. It reflects contemporary developments in Paris, particularly the work of Picasso, Hans Arp and Alberto Giacometti. *Composition* (blue Hornton stone, 1931; priv. col., see Read and Bowness, i, p. 75), in which a hole is pierced through the stone between the head and the arm, marks a radical change of direction in Moore's work: it was almost certainly inspired by Picasso's sculpture *Metamorphosis* (1928; Paris, Mus. Picasso). In 1934 Moore undertook a series of small two-, three-, and four-piece carvings that have much in common with Hans Arp's *Bell and Navels* (1931; New York, MOMA) and Alberto Giacometti's *Woman with Her Throat Cut* (1932; Edinburgh, N.G.). In *Four-Piece Composition: Reclining Figure* (1934; London, Tate) the dismembered anatomy of the head, legs and navel is quite apparent, anticipating, on a small scale, the great two- and three-piece reclining figures of 1959–65. The subject-matter of Moore's work of 1932–6 is, in some cases, no longer readily identifiable, although the human, psychological element informs even the seemingly abstract work of the 1930s. The enigmatic nature of a carving such as the Pynkado-wood *Two Forms* (1934; New York, MOMA) has much in common with the work of the Surrealists, whom Moore admired. Structurally, the sculpture is concerned with the relationship between the larger and smaller forms, but symbolically it represents a mother and child; the bigger, pelvic shape looming above and protecting the smaller embryonic form of a child. In 1933 Moore joined Unit One, a group of avant-garde painters, sculptors and architects. During the second half of the 1930s he lived and worked in Hampstead, London, in close proximity to members Barbara Hepworth and Ben Nicholson and also Naum Gabo and Piet Mondrian. Although he retained his independence,

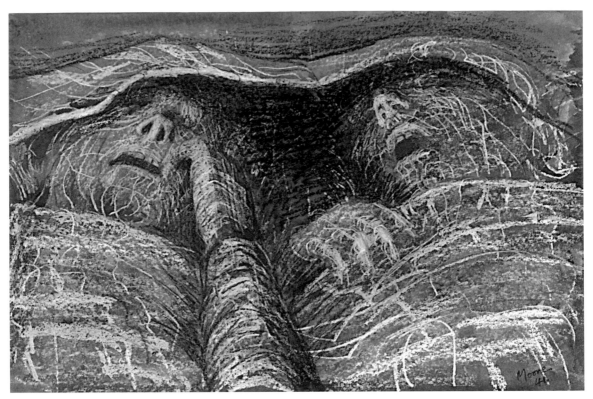

1. Henry Moore: *Two Sleepers*, chalk and gouache on coloured paper, 1941 (Chichester, Pallant House Gallery)

there was a good deal of cross-fertilization in the work of Moore, Hepworth and Nicholson.

(ii) 1940 and after. In 1940, when Moore's London studio was damaged in a bombing raid, he and Irina moved to Perry Green, Much Hadham, 50 km north of London. He was appointed an Official War Artist and began his famous series of shelter drawings of Londoners resting and sleeping on the Underground station platforms. The subject combined two of his favourite motifs: 'I saw hundreds of Henry Moore Reclining Figures stretched along the platforms' and 'even the train tunnels seemed to be like the holes in my sculpture' (Moore, 1966, pp. 212 and 216). His shelter drawings (e.g. *Two Sleepers*, wax crayon, chalk and watercolour, 1941; Chichester, Pallant House Gal.; see fig. 1), with their almost visionary intensity and sense of shared danger, are Moore's greatest achievement as a draughtsman. His approach to the human figure was more naturalistic than before because the situation brought out what he considered the humanist side of his work. Through exhibitions of these war-time drawings, Moore's work was at last beginning to be understood and appreciated by the general public. In the *Madonna and Child* (brown Hornton stone, 1943–4) in St Matthew's Church, Northampton, and in a series of family sculptures (1944–9), his more naturalistic treatment of the human figure and the use of drapery directly relates to the shelter drawings. For these projects, Moore made preliminary studies in clay and plaster, which were later cast in bronze. One of the few personal events of Moore's life that directly affected his work was the birth of his only child, Mary, in

1946. His drawings of Irina nursing the baby and his studies of domestic interiors reflect the intimacy of family life. In 1946 Moore had a major retrospective exhibition at the Museum of Modern Art, New York.

The bronze *Reclining Figure* (1951; London, Tate) commissioned by the Arts Council for the Festival of Britain (1951) was a landmark in Moore's development. Previously the holes in his sculptures were dominated by the solid forms surrounding them but here 'the space and the form are completely dependent on and inseparable from each other' (Moore, 1968, p. 188). His work became less frontal and more completely three-dimensional. The reclining figure and the mother and child remained the dominant subjects of his sculpture. *Working Model for Upright Interior and Exterior Forms* (bronze, 1951; Toronto, A.G. Ont.) represents, on a semi-abstract, symbolic level, the mother and child theme in which the outer shell of the sculpture protects the embryonic form within. Inspired by Malanggan carvings from New Ireland, it is one of Moore's few post-war sculptures based on non-Western art.

After the mid-1950s the sources for many of Moore's sculptures were natural forms such as bones, shells, pebbles and flint stones. The bronze *Warrior with Shield* (1953–4; Toronto, A.G. Ont.) was inspired by a pebble, which reminded Moore of the shape of a stump of a leg amputated at the hip. The bronze *Falling Warrior* (1956–7; Huddersfield, A.G.) and the bronze mutilated *Goslar Warrior* (1973–4; Santa Cruz, CA, City Mus.) continued the warrior theme.

During the 1960s and 1970s financial success made it possible for Moore to work on a larger scale. Between 1959 and 1964 he created a series of two- and three-piece reclining figures, culminating in his largest work of that time, the bronze *Reclining Figure* (1963–5) commissioned by Lincoln Center, New York. In earlier sculptures, the human figure echoed the forms of mountains, hills and valleys; in this series the metaphor is reversed: rugged cliffs, caves, rocks and dramatic sea-worn headlands become the human body.

Until the mid-1950s Moore made countless preparatory drawings for sculpture as well as pictorial studies of interiors and sculptures in landscape settings. He drew little between 1955 and 1970; but during the last 15 years of his life he increasingly devoted his time to drawing as an activity pleasurable in itself and independent of his sculpture. He first made prints in 1931, and he experimented with a process he called collograph (for illustration *see* COLLOTYPE). Printmaking did not, however, become a major part of his work until the late 1960s, when he produced series such as *Elephant Skull* (1969), *Stonehenge* (1973), *Illustrations to W. H. Auden's Poems* (1973) and the *Sheep Portfolios* (1972 and 1974). By the end of his life he had produced 719 prints.

In his late bronzes and carvings, Moore continued to explore the themes of the reclining figure and the mother and child. In addition, a number of semi-abstract symbolic sculptures show a concern for human relationships, for example the powerful sexual overtones of the bronze *Large Two Forms* (1966 and 1969; Toronto, A.G. Ont.) and the bronze *Sheep Piece* (1971–2; artist's col., see Read and Bowness, iv, pls 176–81). In the 1970s there were many major exhibitions of Moore's work, the finest being at Forte di Belvedere, overlooking Florence (1972). The Henry Moore Sculpture Centre in the Art Gallery of Ontario, Toronto, opened in 1974. It comprises the world's largest public collection of Moore's work, most of it donated by him between 1971 and 1974. In 1977 the Henry Moore Foundation was established at Much Hadham, and Moore presented 36 sculptures to the Tate Gallery in 1978.

2. WORKING METHODS AND TECHNIQUE. From 1921 to the late 1930s Moore's sculptures, almost without exception, were carved directly in stone or wood, and they were invariably based on preparatory drawings (*see* DRAWING, colour pl. II, fig. 2). His passion for direct carving included an interest in using the stone available in his own

2. Henry Moore: *Recumbent Figure*, green Hornton stone, 889×1327×737 mm, 1938 (London, Tate Gallery)

country: for *Recumbent Figure* (green Hornton stone, 1938; London, Tate; see fig. 2) he used stone from a quarry in Oxfordshire. Around 1938 Moore began a practice that remained an integral part of his working method for the rest of his life: making maquettes (small models) on which the larger sculptures were based, for example a small sketch model (140 mm long; see Read and Bowness, i, no. 184) for the 1938 *Recumbent Figure*. Preparatory maquettes proliferated in the 1940s with numerous studies in terracotta for the stone *Madonna and Child* in St Matthew's Church, Northampton. In the late 1930s Moore began having his work cast in lead or bronze from the terracotta or plaster originals. Although at this time he abandoned a doctrinaire belief in direct carving, Moore remained essentially a carver for the rest of his career. He continued to work in stone or wood and increasingly in plaster (to be cast in bronze), a material that can be carved once it has hardened. In the late 1930s Moore began hiring young sculptors to assist him with larger works. Among the many assistants who worked with Moore over the years were Bernard Meadows, Anthony Caro and Phillip King.

In the mid-1950s Moore's working method changed. As his sculptures became less frontal and began to have an organic completeness from many points of view, he found that working from a drawing of a sculptural idea of a single view was contrary to his aims. He preferred to work out his ideas directly in the form of small maquettes.

WRITINGS

Henry Moore on Sculpture, ed. P. James (London, 1966)
Henry Moore, photographs J. Hedgecoe (London, 1968)
Henry Moore: Sculpture and Environment, photographs D. Finn (New York, 1976)
Henry Moore at the British Museum, photographs D. Finn (London, 1981)
Henry Moore: My Ideas, Inspiration, and Life as an Artist, photographs J. Hedgecoe (London, 1986)

BIBLIOGRAPHY

H. Read: *Henry Moore* (London, 1934)
G. Grigson: *Henry Moore*, Penguin Modern Painters (Harmondsworth, 1943)
H. Read and A. Bowness, eds: *Henry Moore: Sculpture and Drawings*, 6 vols (London, 1944–88) [all sculp. illus. incl. some now untraced or destr.]
Henry Moore (exh. cat. by J. J. Sweeney, New York, MOMA, 1946)
Sculpture and Drawings by Henry Moore (exh. cat., ed. A. D. B. Sylvester; London, Tate, 1951)
E. Neumann: *The Archetypal World of Henry Moore*, trans. R. F. C. Hull (New York, 1959)
H. Read: *Henry Moore: A Study of His Life and Work* (London, 1965)
70 Years of Henry Moore (exh. cat., ed. D. Mitchinson Otterlo, Kröller-Müller, 1968) [pict. biog., incl. much hitherto unpub. mat.]
J. Russell: *Henry Moore* (Harmondsworth, 1968, rev. 2/1973)
Henry Moore (exh. cat. by D. Sylvester, London, Tate, 1968)
R. Melville: *Henry Moore: Sculptures and Drawings, 1929–1969* (London, 1970) [many illus.]
D. Mitchinson: *Henry Moore: Unpublished Drawings* (Turin, 1971)
H. J. Seldis: *Henry Moore in America* (New York, 1973)
G. Cramer, A. Grant and D. Mitchinson, eds: *Henry Moore: Catalogue of Graphic Work*, 4 vols (Geneva, 1973, 1986)
K. Clark: *Henry Moore Drawings* (London, 1974)
The Drawings of Henry Moore (exh. cat., ed. A. G. Wilkinson; London, Tate; Toronto, A.G. Ont. 1977) [first major retro. of Moore's drgs]
A. G. Wilkinson: *The Moore Collection in the Art Gallery of Ontario* (Toronto, 1977; rev. as *Henry Moore Remembered: The Collection at the Art Gallery of Ontario*, 1987)
G. Levine: *With Henry Moore: The Artist at Work* (London, 1978) [phot. portrait]
Gauguin to Moore: Primitivism in Modern Sculpture (exh. cat. by A. G. Wilkinson, Toronto, A.G. Ont., 1981)
Henry Moore: Early Carvings, 1920–1940 (exh. cat. by A. Garrould, T. Friedman and D. Mitchinson, Leeds, C.A.G., 1982)
Henry Moore: 60 Years of His Art (exh. cat. by W. S. Lieberman, New York, Met., 1983)
R. Berthaud: *The Life of Henry Moore* (London, 1987)

ALAN G. WILKINSON

Moore, Morris J. (*b* 1811; *d* Rome, 18 Dec 1885). English writer and collector. He took part in the Greek War of Independence in 1830 and then settled in Rome, though still keeping a residence in London. While in Italy he studied the work of the Renaissance masters, particularly Raphael, and built up a collection of paintings. He achieved notoriety in Britain, however, through a series of letters he wrote to *The Times* in 1846 and 1847 (which he subsequently collected and published), attacking the management of the National Gallery, then under the keepership of Sir Charles Locke Eastlake (*see* EASTLAKE, (3)). His outrage was first provoked by the new policy of cleaning works, which he thought had seriously damaged such paintings as Rubens's *War and Peace* and Titian's *Bacchus and Ariadne*. This view was shared by many and reflected the contemporary belief that Old Master paintings were characteristically subdued in colour. John Ruskin, who thought the general indignation exaggerated, became the object of further letters from Moore, who referred to Ruskin merely as 'the Oxford Graduate'. The outcry over the cleaning actually forced Eastlake to resign (1847). Moore also criticized the Gallery's purchasing policy, accusing Eastlake of buying inferior works at inflated prices. Towards the end of his life Moore had occasion to renew his attack when his offer to sell the National Gallery his *Apollo and Marsyas* (1509; Paris, Louvre), which he believed to be by Raphael, was turned down and the work's authenticity questioned. The Louvre bought it instead (1883) and it is now attributed to Pietro Vannucci Perugino (*c.* 1448–1523). Moore's support for the arts included a large contribution to help purchase Raphael's birthplace in Urbino in 1873 so it could be set up as a museum.

WRITINGS

The Abuses of the National Gallery (London, 1847)
Raphael's Apollo and Marsyas: A European Scandal (Edinburgh, 1883)

BIBLIOGRAPHY

Obituary, *The Times* (24 Dec 1885)
F. Haskell: 'Un martyr de l'attribution: Morris Moore et l'*Apollon et Marsyas* du Louvre', *Rev. A.*, 42 (1978), pp. 78–88

□

Moore, Temple (Lushington) (*b* Tullamore, Ireland, 7 June 1856; *d* London, 30 June 1920). English architect. He was articled to George Gilbert Scott II (*see* SCOTT (ii), (2)) from 1875 to 1878. He then set up in independent practice but continued to assist his former master and completed several of Scott's buildings after his mental breakdown. His early churches, such as All Saints (1885–1903), Peterborough, show the strong influence of Scott's work, but by the time he designed St Peter's (1893–1911), Barnsley, S Yorks, Moore had transcended the work of his master and shown great resourcefulness in planning to produce highly picturesque but thoroughly practical internal effects. His genius at fitting large churches on to awkward and confined urban sites was well demonstrated at St Columba's (1902–8), Middlesbrough, Cleveland, while in his late work, such as St James's (1911–14),

Clacton, Essex, Moore combined round with pointed arches and eliminated internal mouldings. His other notable churches include St Wilfrid's (1905–14), Harrogate, Yorks, and All Saints' (1904–6), Tooting, London. One of the leading church architects of Late Victorian and Edwardian England, Moore remained firmly in the tradition of the Gothic Revival, but he displayed remarkable originality in the planning and massing of his churches even while depending upon precedent for detail. Unlike such other church architects as G. F. Bodley, who reacted against the aggressive originality of High Victorian Gothic, Moore preferred English 13th-century precedents to Late Gothic for inspiration. Initially owing to his wife's family connections, Moore worked extensively in Yorkshire, but his office was always in London. His pupils included Giles and Adrian Gilbert Scott, and his practice was continued by his son-in-law Leslie T. Moore (1883–1957).

BIBLIOGRAPHY

H. S. Goodhart-Rendel: 'The Churches of Temple Moore', *Archit. Rev.* [London], lix (1926), pp. 12–17
——: 'The Work of Temple Moore', *J. RIBA*, xxxv (1928), pp. 470–92
M. T. Moore: 'A Biographical Note on Temple Moore, Esq., F.R.I.B.A.', *Temple Moore* (exh. cat., Barnsley, St Peter, 1963); review by J. Betjeman in *St Peter's Newspaper*, 128 (Jan 1964)
G. Stamp: 'Victorian Survival or Revival? The Case of H. S. Goodhart-Rendel', *AA Files*, 15 (1987), pp. 60–67

GAVIN STAMP

Moorish [Hindoo, Indo-Saracenic] **style.** Term used specifically in the 19th century to describe a Western style based on the architecture and decorative arts of the Muslim inhabitants (the Moors) of north-west Africa and (between 8th and 15th centuries) of southern Spain; it is often used imprecisely to include Arab and Indian influences. A similar revivalist style prevalent specifically in Spain around the same time is known as the MUDÉJAR REVIVAL. Although their rule in Spain finally ended in 1492, the Moors remained indispensably part of the European vision of the East. (*See also* ORIENTALISM.)

In the Renaissance *moreschi* were bandlike patterns allied to grotesques. The Swiss Johann Heinrich Müntz, who visited Spain in 1748 and drew unspecified Moorish buildings, designed a Moorish garden building (1750; London, RIBA) that may have formed the basis for the Alhambra (destr.), one of a series of exotic buildings designed by William Chambers after 1758 for the Royal Botanic Gardens at Kew, near London. Further early interest was shown by the painter William Hodges, who was in India between 1779 and 1784, in his *Travels in India* (1793), which incorporated much of a dissertation (prepared in 1787) on the prototypes of architecture, 'Hindoo, Moorish and Gothic'. He linked minarets with natural origins in pointed rocks. The style was acceptable to advocates of the Picturesque and was thus used at the Royal Pavilion in Brighton for the Indian Stables (1803–8) by WILLIAM PORDEN and the exterior reconstruction of the Pavilion itself (1815–22) by John Nash, with onion domes and minarets (for illustration *see* BRIGHTON).

While Romantic interest in an imaginary, dreamlike Orient, typified by Samuel Taylor Coleridge's poem *Kubla Khan* (1816), readily included the Moors, their history and particular contribution to Spanish and Western culture were reappraised after the Napoleonic Wars, as Spain and Morocco attracted writers, painters and travellers. The writers included Victor Hugo (his poem-cycle *Les Orientales* of 1829) and Washington Irving (*The Alhambra*, 1832). The artists included Eugène Delacroix (on a French diplomatic visit to Morocco in 1832), David Roberts (in Spain 1832–3) and John Frederick Lewis (in Spain 1832–4). The work of Roberts and Lewis was widely reproduced in popular publications. The best-known traveller was Richard Ford, whose *Handbook for Travellers in Spain and Readers at Home* (1845) reached nine editions by 1900. Literature about Spain tended to evoke the fantasy of the 14th-century courtyards and halls of the Alhambra, Granada, but encouraged an interest in Moorish gardens, particularly the Generalife, also in Granada (e.g. Frederic Leighton's oil painting of 1874, *Moorish Garden: A Dream of Granada*, Armidale, NSW, Teachers' Coll.).

At the same time detailed studies of Moorish art and architecture began to appear (e.g. James Cavanah Murphy's *Arabian Antiquities of Spain*, 1815). The colour-patterns of the Alhambra were recorded (1832–3) by JOSEPH-PHILIBERT GIRAULT DE PRANGEY and later by OWEN JONES, whose first-hand record, originally undertaken in 1834 with Jules Goury (1803–34) and continued in 1837, appeared in his monumental *Plans, Elevations and Sections of the Alhambra* (London, 1842–5). In his *Grammar of Ornament* (1856), Jones demonstrated his belief that the Moors were the authors of fundamental principles of pattern design and colour deployment. All his examples of 'Moresque' ornament came from the Alhambra, and he constructed an Alhambra Court (1854; destr. 1936) at the Sydenham Crystal Palace, London. As a result of his work, motifs derived from the Alhambra became a mainstay of manuals of ornament for over half a century.

The Moorish style proved a versatile resource. Ludwig von Zanth used it at the Villa Wilhelma (1842–64) at Stuttgart for King William I of Württemberg (*reg* 1816). William Burges played freely with it in his wildly eclectic interior schemes for Cardiff Castle (from 1865), which included in the dining-room a Saracenic ceiling with an eight-pointed star. Most archaeologically correct was the Arab Hall (1877–9) at Leighton House, London, designed by George Aitchison (1825–1910) for Frederic Leighton, with a marble pool and walls decorated with 14th- and 15th-century Islamic tiles and screens and glass from Cairo and Damascus. The style spread widely, from the Palais du Trocadéro (destr. 1936), designed for the Exposition Universelle in Paris of 1878 by Owen GABRIEL DAVIOUD and Jules Bourdais (*b* 1835), to hotels in Florida, USA.

Hispano-Moresque ceramics were collected (e.g. by Alfred Ducane Godman in the 1860s, now London, BM; and Charles Lang Freer in the early 20th century, now Washington, DC, Freer), and they also influenced contemporary designs. For the mass market, Owen Jones designed tiles in Moorish style for the Minton ceramic factory, and Islamic style tin-glazed earthenwares were made in the factories of Ulysse Cantagalli (*d* 1901) in Florence and Zsolnay in Pécs (e.g. plate by Zsolnay of polychrome, painted earthenware, *c.* 1878; London, V&A). At the same time William De Morgan in England and Joseph-Théodore Deck in Paris were producing handmade, lustred 'art pottery' in Isnik, Hispano-Moresque, Byzantine and Persian designs.

Moorish-style Billiard Room, Newhouse Park, St Albans, Hertfordshire, probably by the architect of the house, S. C. Capes (1826/7–1901), 1880s-1890s (destr. 1986)

Towards the end of the 19th century the Moorish style reinforced its popular appeal. It was considered particularly suitable for halls and such masculine retreats as smoking and billiard rooms (see fig.), of which few English examples survive. The Moorish Smoking Room (c. 1880) from John D. Rockefeller's house in New York (now in New York, Brooklyn Mus.) has a cornice of 'Arab' arches, richly patterned walls, ebony woodwork and tasselled and fringed chairs. In London Carlo Bugatti created a distinctive bedroom (c. 1890; destr.) for the town house of Cyril Flower, Baron Battersea, a commission probably earned from the display of his work at the Italian Exhibition at Earls Court, London, in 1888. The style was also used by design firms such as Liberty & Co., London, and S. Bing, Paris.

Paradoxically, Moorish ideas were also used in synagogue design as part of a movement to emphasize Judaism's non-European origins (see JEWISH ART, §II, 1(iii)(a)). For the interior of the Dresden synagogue (1838–40; destr.; see JEWISH ART, fig. 10), Gottfried Semper used 'Saracenic' forms deriving in part from a study of Islamic work in Sicily. The synagogue at Leipzig (1853–4) by Semper's pupil Otto Simonson (1829–after 1856) included the Moorish horseshoe arch, which was later used in

synagogues in Cologne, Berlin and Vienna and in Russia. In the USA the Isaac M. Wise Temple (1863–5) in Cincinnati by James Keys Wilson combined the style with Gothic, in a manner widely imitated (e.g. the Temple Emanu-El, New York, 1866–8; destr. 1901; by Leopold Eidlitz).

Association with places of entertainment and relaxation led to the Moorish style becoming widely used for theatres, restaurants, piers and bandstands. Examples in New York include the Central Park bandstand (begun 1859) by Owen Jones's pupil Jacob Wrey Mould, and the Casino Theatre (1880–82; destr. 1930) by FRANCIS H. KIMBALL, with 'Alhambresque' capitals and horseshoe arches. English examples include the Royal Panopticon of Science and Art (1854; interior reconstructed 1883; destr. 1936), Leicester Square, London, by Thomas Hayter Lewis (1818–89), an educational establishment that ironically became a music hall within two years; many theatres by Frank Matcham (e.g. the Empire Palace in Edinburgh, 1892; destr. 1911); and even cinemas (e.g. the Astoria [now the Academy], Brixton, London, 1929; by E. A. Stone, with an interior decorated to resemble the Generalife, Granada). The courtyard (1918–21) designed by Philip Tilden (1887–1956) at Port Lympne, Kent, was for a client, Sir Philip Sassoon, whose family was of Levantine origin. By the early 20th century, however, the distinctive historical associations and qualities of mood that had given the Moorish style its special resonance in the West became obscured, and the style was largely abandoned.

BIBLIOGRAPHY

G. Sheldon: *Artistic Houses*, 2 vols (New York, 1882–4/*R* as one vol., 1971)
'Moorish Decoration', *Decorator & Furnisher*, v/4 (Jan 1885), p. 141
A. van de Put: *Hispano-Moresque Ware of the XV Century* (London, 1904)
A. Adburgham: *Liberty's: A Biography of a Shop* (London, 1975)
O. Grabar: *The Alhambra* (Cambridge, MA, 1978)
B. M. Walker: *Frank Matcham: Theatre Architect* (Belfast, 1980)
P. Dejean: *Carlo, Rembrandt, Ettore-Jean Bugatti* (New York, 1982)
M. Darby: *The Islamic Perspective: An Aspect of British Architecture and Design in the 19th Century* (London, 1983)
R. Head: *The Indian Style* (London, 1986)
G. Dumur: *Delacroix et le Maroc* (Paris, 1988)
J. Sweetman: *The Oriental Obsession: Islamic Inspiration in British and American Art and Architecture, 1500–1920* (Cambridge, 1988)

JOHN SWEETMAN, with assistance from A. R. GARDNER

Moosbrugger, Caspar [Andreas] (*b* Au im Bregenzerwald, 15 May 1656; *d* Einsiedeln, 26 Aug 1723). German architect. He served his apprenticeship with Christian Thumb, completing it in 1673. In 1674 he began to work as a mason under Johann Georg Kuen (1642–91) on the construction of the new monks' choir at the Benedictine abbey church at Einsiedeln. In 1682 he was admitted as a lay brother there and assumed the religious name of Caspar. He attained the grade of building expert and abbey architect, working as an adviser or architect for Einsiedeln and many other Benedictine abbeys in Switzerland and south Germany. He was largely self-taught in architectural theory and history, but his designs, especially those for Einsiedeln Abbey, bear witness to his knowledge of French and Italian architectural treatises, such as Augustin-Charles d'Aviler's *Cours d'architecture* (Paris, 1693) and Andrea Pozzo's *Perspectiva pictorum et architectorum* (Rome, 1693–1700). Moreover, numerous drawings by Moosbrugger survive (Lucerne, Burgerbib.), copied from Italian architectural treatises and engravings, for example, Sebastiano Serlio's treatise on architecture, the *Chiese di Roma* by Giovanni Orlando (*c.* 1590–1648) and the *Varie bella inventioni de tempio e depositi, ornamenta di altari* (Paris, 1631) by Vallerien Regnard (*fl* 1630–50). He may also have co-authored the *Auer Lehrgang*, comprising two volumes of architectural designs and copies from engravings, intended as a training manual for architects and masons (the main parts were published in the catalogue of the 1973 Einsiedeln exhibition). For his work, Moosbrugger had at his disposal the extensive collection of architectural treatises and engravings in the library at Einsiedeln.

Moosbrugger's collaboration is documented in architectural work at such abbeys as Muri (1684–1719); Weingarten (1685, 1717); Fischingen (1685, 1706 and 1716); St Katharinenthal (1690); Ittingen (1698); Kalchrain (1697 and 1702); Rheinau (1702); Engelberg (1704); and the parish churches at Lachen (1703) and Solothurn, St Ursen (1711). Buildings executed to his plans include the abbey church at Disentis (1696–1712), a wall-pillar church with a four-bay nave, transept, presbytery widened to resemble a transept and chancel narrower than the nave; the Benedictine abbey of Seedorf (from 1695); and the Meinradskapelle at Etzel (1697–8). His main work, however, was the rebuilding of the abbey complex and church of Einsiedeln (*see* EINSIEDELN ABBEY), which he began planning after the death of Kuen in 1691. Construction of the new abbey was carried out from 1704, and the new

Caspar Moosbrugger: elevation, designed 1705-6, of the west façade of Einsiedeln Abbey and abbey church, partially executed from 1718 (Einsiedeln, Stiftsarchiv)

church was begun in 1719. Whether and how far Moosbrugger made use of plans by Kuen in this work has not been satisfactorily clarified. The plan of the complex, grouped around four courtyards and accentuated by corner pavilions, with the church on its central axis, shows the influence of schemes by the Weingarten Benedictine father Gabriel Buzelin (1599–1681) for Admont Abbey (1647), which were in turn influenced by designs by Domenico Allio and those by Domenico Sciassia for St Lambrecht in Styria, as well as by Franz Beer's plans for the Cistercian abbey at Salem (from 1697). By contrast, the façades at Einsiedeln, articulated by rusticated pilaster-strips, are, like the extensive series of designs for the church (see fig.), decisively influenced by the French and Italian treatises.

The combination or juxtaposition of centralized and longitudinal spaces is the main theme of Moosbrugger's designs for the church at Einsiedeln. These evolved from his first plans, compilations drawing on architectural motifs from the 16th century, to the building actually executed, with an octagonal first bay reflected in the convex west façade (see SWITZERLAND, fig. 2) and two square, centralized bays beyond. Until the end of the work, Moosbrugger continued to incorporate fresh ideas, for example those offered by the scientist Luigi Fernando Marsigli (1658–1730) of Bologna, to whom the abbot of Einsiedeln had sent one of Moosbrugger's plans for the abbey church, inviting him to comment. Moosbrugger also took ideas from contemporary plans, especially those of Franz Beer and Donato Frisoni, for the abbey church in Weingarten (see WEINGARTEN ABBEY). All this shows with rare clarity how the self-taught Moosbrugger, who scarcely advanced beyond the stage of dilettante monk, achieved, through his unconventional use of various plan forms, designs that were in some respects bizarre but in others ahead of their time. The realization of many such designs seems to have foundered precisely on his defective knowledge of building construction and organization and only a small number of his plans were executed. Most of his church designs are based on the wall-pillar system, which he used in both longitudinal and centralized structures. His experimental designs with oval spaces and with wide-span spaces with four supports, usually accompanied by a ring of chapels, anticipated spatial solutions later realized by such architects as Dominikus Zimmermann in the pilgrimage churches of Steinhausen (1728–31) and Die Wies (1744–57), or by Peter Thumb II in the abbey church of St Gall (1750s).

BIBLIOGRAPHY

L. Birchler: *Einsiedeln und sein Architekt Bruder Caspar Moosbrugger* (Augsburg, 1924)
——: 'Beiträge zur Kunstgeschichte des Klosters Muri', *Z. Schweiz. Archäol. & Kstgesch.*, vi (1944), pp. 85–99
A. Reinle: 'Ein Fund barocker Kirchen- und Klosterpläne', *Z. Schweiz. Archäol. & Kstgesch.*, xi (1950), pp. 216–47
H. J. Sauermost: 'Schema und Eigenbrödler: Eine Analyse der Vorarlberger-Forschung', *Unsere Kstdkml.*, xx (1969), pp. 310–21
Die Vorarlberger Barockbaumeister (exh. cat., ed. W. Oechslin; Einsiedeln, 1973), pp. 3–6, 22–78, 168–224, 257–84
N. Lieb and F. Dieth: *Die Vorarlberger Barockbaumeister*, 3 vols (Munich and Zurich, 1976), pp. 25–6, 47–52, 104–5

ULRICH KNAPP

Mootwingee. Site of Aboriginal culture, *c.* 100 km northeast of Broken Hill, in the arid country of western New South Wales, south-east Australia. It is known for its complex of pecked rock engravings; these are concentrated on an area of sloping sandstone pavements (*c.* 100×30 m), although others are more dispersed. Some are found along an ephemeral creek that leads to the base of the sandstone outcrop where there are several rock holes that provided the Aborigines with a permanent water-supply. The rock holes were discovered by Europeans in the mid-19th century and were visited by several exploring expeditions in the 1860s. Although the engravings are within sight of the water-holes, which were of great importance to European settlers and travellers in the region, they were not documented until the 1920s. The area containing the engravings and other Aboriginal relics was declared a reserve in 1927. It was subsequently incorporated into a larger National Park, and in 1986 the local Aboriginal community became involved in its management. Some locations around the engraving site, particularly some painted rock shelters, retain mythological significance, and access is therefore restricted.

The engravings at Mootwingee are mainly figurative, although non-figurative motifs also occur. Identifiable subject-matter includes many bird and animal tracks as well as some silhouettes of emu, macropod and unidentified animals pecked out as solid areas. Human figures are represented with what appear to be very large vertical headdresses, much taller than the figures themselves. Some are shown holding a spear or boomerang, but neither hunting nor any other activity is depicted. Non-figurative designs include circles, arcs, meandering lines, mazes and star-like patterns. The engravings are not very deep, and, as they have darkened to the colour of the rock surface, their visibility depends on light conditions.

Information provided in 1960 by one of the traditional Aboriginal custodians suggests that during the period of early European contact the Mootwingee site was a focus for rainmaking ceremonies, and some groups of figures were said to illustrate such rituals. Ancestral beings associated with the site include the 'eagle hawk' (wedge-tailed eagle), crow, spider, dingo, watersnake and kangaroo. Apart from the kangaroo, however, these creatures are not identifiable among the engravings. According to the informant, the Mootwingee site also had mythological links to other engraving sites further to the west, at Sturt's Meadow and Euriowie. The Sturt's Meadow site, rather different in character and probably older, contains engravings with carbonate coatings carbon-dated to *c.* 10,000 BP. Although the physical condition of the Mootwingee site suggests some antiquity, it is not yet possible to date the engravings. The pavements with engravings have spalled, and some have broken up and moved down the slope, resulting in some engraved motifs being split and their two sections separated.

See also ABORIGINAL AUSTRALIA, §II, 2(ii)(a).

BIBLIOGRAPHY

F. D. McCarthy and N. W. G. MacIntosh: 'The Archaeology of Mootwingee, New South Wales', *Rec. Austral. Mus.*, xxv (1962), pp. 249–98

DARRELL LEWIS

Mopope, Stephen (*b* near Redstone, OK, 28 Aug 1900; *d* Anadarko, OK, 14 Feb 1974). Native American Kiowa

Stephen Mopope: *Eagle Dancer*, casein on paper, 262×200 mm, *c.* 1930 (private collection)

painter. He was brought up with full opportunity to participate in Kiowa religious and cultural life. In his youth, the Feather Dance (the Kiowa version of the Ghost Dance) was still being practised, with symbolic imagery on clothing. The Peyote religion, with its strong designs and colour visions, was also important. Mopope's first art teachers were his great-uncles Ohettoint (Oheltoint, Charles O. Buffalo; 1852–1934), a former Fort Marion prisoner (*see* NATIVE NORTH AMERICAN ART, §IV, 2(i) and (ii)), and SILVERHORN. He helped Ohettoint, Silverhorn and others of the family in painting a new version of the 'Tipi with Battle Pictures' (1916–18; destr.; original tipi design, *c.* 1840; model of original by Ohettoint, 1890s, see Ewers), and was one of a group of young Kiowas encouraged to draw and paint by Suzie Peters (1873–1965), a government field matron. Years later, in 1927, she secured their admission to the University of Oklahoma as non-matriculated art students. Oscar B. Jacobson (1882–1966), head of the Art Department, became their mentor and sponsor. Mopope was the most prolific and versatile of the 'Six Kiowas'. His subject-matter includes genre scenes, portraits, lyrical and mystical themes, recollections of old ceremonies and, above all, depictions of contemporary dancers (see fig.). The latter, meticulously crafted, mirror the decorativeness of the colourful costumes while capturing the sense of motion in virtuoso Plains dancers. In the 1930s, Mopope painted several murals in public buildings in Oklahoma and one in the Department of Interior Building in Washington, DC.

BIBLIOGRAPHY

O. B. Jacobson: *Kiowa Indian Art* (Nice, 1929) [colour pls]

J. C. Ewers: *Murals in the Round: Painted Tipis of the Kiowa and Kiowa-Apache Indians* (Washington, DC, 1978)

One Hundred Years of Native American Painting (exh. cat. by A. Silberman, Oklahoma City, OK Mus. A., 1978)

ARTHUR SILBERMAN

MOPP. *See* OPPENHEIMER, MAX.

Mor (van Dashorst) [Moro], **Antonis** [Anthonis; Antonio] (*b* Utrecht, 1516–20; *d* Antwerp, ?1576). North Netherlandish painter, active also in the southern Netherlands, Italy, Spain, Portugal and England. As court painter to Philip II of Spain, he depicted members of the most powerful ruling élite in 16th-century Europe. He took elements from Titian and from the Netherlandish tradition of his master, Jan van Scorel, establishing a distinctive new style that combined austerity and a formality of pose with penetrating insights into his sitters' characters. He also depicted successful merchants in Antwerp and artists and intellectuals in the humanist circles in which he moved. His career bears witness to the competing and sometimes contradictory claims of material security, social prestige and an ideal of artistic and intellectual individuality.

1. Before mid-1550: Utrecht, Italy and the southern Netherlands. 2. 1550–?1553: Spain and Portugal. 3. 1554–5: England. 4. 1555–9: The southern Netherlands and Utrecht. 5. 1559–?1561: Spain. 6. ?1561–?1576: Utrecht and the southern Netherlands.

1. BEFORE MID-1550: UTRECHT, ITALY AND THE SOUTHERN NETHERLANDS. Mor was apprenticed to Jan van Scorel in Utrecht, where his father was almost certainly a dyer (*verwer*). He had become van Scorel's assistant by *c.* 1540, when he was probably involved in the production of van Scorel's three altarpieces for the abbey of Marchiennes, near Douai (Douai, Mus. Mun.). Van Mander claimed that Mor travelled to Italy in his youth, thus almost certainly before 1547, the year in which, aged about 30, he registered in the Antwerp Guild of St Luke. Evidence of his presence in Rome is provided by a legal record of an assault on him by a Flemish painter, who apparently stole a drawing from him in the Roman Forum. According to van Mander, Mor also visited other parts of Italy, and documents suggest that he may have had contact with Ferrante Gonzaga.

Mor could not have stayed abroad for more than about three years, as is known from two datable paintings executed in Utrecht. His first known signed work, *Two Canons* (Berlin, Gemäldegal.), is dated 1544. Both men were canons of Utrecht Cathedral and former pilgrims to Jerusalem, and their portrait is related to van Scorel's paintings of members of Jerusalem confraternities. However, Mor's signature on this picture and his (undated) registration in the Utrecht painters' guild suggest a degree of independence from his master. On 14 October 1546 Mor, described as 'painter and burgher in Utrecht', was paid for a *Resurrection* for the abbey of Marienweerd at Culemborg.

Nothing is known of Mor between his registration in the Antwerp guild in 1547 and 18 September 1549, when he was described as painter to Antoine Perrenot de Granvelle, Bishop of Arras, in a payment from Prince Philip of Spain, who was then in Antwerp. Mor's employment by Granvelle probably dates from after August 1548, when this statesman established himself at the Brussels court of Philip's father, the Holy Roman Emperor Charles V. A signed portrait of *Granvelle* (1549; Vienna, Ksthist. Mus.) and Mor's other court portraits from 1549–50 show standing three-quarter-length, three-quarter-view figures lit from the side, unlike the *Two Canons*, where a profile is employed and the figures are depicted in half-length and lit from the direction in which they move. These differences have been ascribed to the influence of Titian, and comparisons are often drawn between Mor's *Granvelle* and Titian's contemporary portrait of the same sitter (1548; Kansas City, MO, Nelson–Atkins Mus. A.). Granvelle, an admirer of Titian, may well have asked Mor to employ the Venetian's three-quarter-length format, although the suggestion that Mor accompanied Granvelle to Augsburg and met Titian there in 1548 is unproven. Mor could have seen portraits by Titian in Brussels by the end of 1548, but the sidelighting that is so characteristic of Mor's male portraits from 1549 is not especially associated with Titian. Mor's massive, imposing figures are reminiscent of Jan Vermeyen and south Netherlandish portraiture of the 1540s. In their combination of apparent naturalness with insistent monumentality they are also consistent with Mor's own *Two Canons* of 1544.

Mor's connection with Granvelle led to a successful career at the Habsburg court as a specialist in full-size portraits. In 1549–50 he needed several assistants to help him portray the royalty, nobles and notables gathered in Brussels to recognize Philip as heir to the Netherlands. Besides Granvelle, Mor's patrons at the court of Charles V and his sister Mary of Hungary included their sister Eleanor, dowager Queen of France, and noble families such as the Glymes of Bergen and the Lannoys of Molenbeek, as well as Philip himself.

2. 1550–?1553: SPAIN AND PORTUGAL. In the summer of 1550 Mor received an imperial Habsburg command to portray members of the royal family in Portugal. He travelled to Lisbon via Spain, where he painted the Regent *Maximilian of Austria* in late 1550 and Maximilian's wife *Mary* in 1551 (both Madrid, Prado). These full-length images apparently show the influence of Germanic portrait painters, particularly Jakob Seisnegger. Mor had evidently been in Portugal for some time by March 1552, when Prince Philip, by then back in Spain, asked him to come to his court. Mor probably left for Spain soon after 12 September 1552.

Mor's journey to Portugal had been instigated by Mary of Hungary, Regent of the Netherlands, who commissioned portraits of four of her Portuguese relatives. These paintings, together with portraits by Titian, may well have been displayed in a special gallery in Mary's palace at Binche and eventually formed the core of Philip II's portrait gallery at El Pardo, where they were destroyed by fire in 1604. In Portugal Queen Catherine ordered portraits from Mor that almost certainly duplicated the images owned by Mary, her sister. While abroad Mor also executed works for Granvelle and was probably employed by Philip. According to van Mander, he was also enthusiastically patronized by the Portuguese nobility.

3. 1554–5: ENGLAND. Mor is documented as living in Brussels in November 1553. After his return from Spain

he was variously described as Granvelle's painter, painter to Prince Philip and painter to the Imperial Majesty. In autumn 1554 he was commissioned, probably by Charles V, to portray the English queen Mary Tudor, who in July had become Philip's second wife. Mor apparently travelled to England in November, and the picture appears to have been completed by 20 December 1554. The portrait of *Mary Tudor* is among the most significant images of Mor's career and survives in two signed examples, of which the better is in the Prado, Madrid (see fig. 1), the other at Compton Wynyates, Warwicks. The composition of the painting is modelled on Titian's seated portraits of Charles V's wife, Isabella of Portugal, so that Mary Tudor, as wife of Charles's heir Philip, is made emphatically recognizable as the successor to Charles's own revered consort. Such reference to visual models as a means of characterizing sitters according to their role or status is typical of Mor. Equally powerful is his use of acutely observed volumes, surfaces and textures to create a convincing individual likeness. In counterpointing these two aspects of portraiture, *Mary Tudor* exemplifies Mor's approach to painting court sitters.

Mor was formally appointed Philip's painter in London on 20 December 1554, probably as a reward for the portrait of *Mary Tudor*. He was to receive an annual salary of 300 scudi in addition to payment for individual works. Philip may also have provided lodgings, materials, transport and expenses while Mor was executing his commissions. Since payment was conditional on attendance at court, subsequent salary records enable Mor's whereabouts

1. Antonis Mor: *Mary Tudor*, oil on panel, 1.09×0.84 m, 1554 (Madrid, Museo del Prado)

to be ascertained until 1 September 1561, when this salary ceased.

4. 1555–9: THE SOUTHERN NETHERLANDS AND UTRECHT. Mor had returned to Brussels by autumn 1555, when he portrayed *Willem of Orange* (Kassel, Schloss Wilhelmshöhe). A *Crucifixion* (untraced) was executed for the Chartreuse of Scheut near Brussels in 1555, and a *Resurrected Christ between SS Peter and Paul* (Chantilly, Mus. Condé) apparently dates from 1556. Few portraits from 1555–9 survive, but numerous copies and derivations indicate the nature of Mor's work from this period, during which Charles V abdicated in favour of Philip in 1555 and in 1556 retired to Spain with his two sisters, Mary of Hungary and Eleanor of France. The ceremonies marking these events brought nobles to court and were propitious for portraiture. A further occasion for commemoration was the Habsburg defeat of the French at Saint-Quentin in August 1557. Philip II did not participate in this battle, but Mor made it the King's personal triumph by a portrait of *Philip II at Saint-Quentin* (best example, Madrid, Escorial).

The verse pinned to the casel in Mor's *Self-portrait* (Florence, Uffizi) reveals that by 1558 Mor considered his relationship with Philip II analogous to that of the ancient Greek artist Apelles with Alexander the Great. Philip may have shared Mor's exalted view of his role; he was reportedly extremely fond of Mor and certainly accorded him several significant favours at this period. In July 1559 Mor returned to Utrecht, where he kept property and where his wife and children may well have lived. Around this time he must have painted the tondo bust portrait of *Jan van Scorel* (1559; London, Soc. Antiqua.), which was intended for van Scorel's tomb monument. Mor immortalized his master's art by making visual references to van Scorel's own portraiture and by an explicitly virtuoso execution that pays personal tribute to van Scorel's teaching.

5. 1559–?1561: SPAIN. In 1559 Mor travelled to Spain, probably accompanying Philip II when he sailed from the Netherlands on 29 August. While in Spain, he is likely to have been involved in planning Philip II's new portrait gallery at the palace of El Pardo, near Madrid. No dated works survive from this period, although *Joanna of Austria* (Madrid, Prado; *see* DRESS, fig. 27) must have been painted in Spain *c.* 1560. Mor's sensitivity to function and meaning is revealed by this portrait, in which the sitter, who had successfully governed Spain during her brother Philip II's absence, is visualized as a figure of authority. She is depicted in some respects as a timeless statue, inaccessible and motionless in empty space, but Mor's impeccable technique and precise observation also create a convincing illusion that the living Joanna directly confronts the viewer, as she would a visiting subordinate. Mor employed immense skill, not to assert but to conceal the intellectual and technical role of the artist, so that a highly contrived effect appears as an objective view of reality.

Mor apparently left Spain earlier than expected, probably soon after 25 October 1561, when he received an extraordinary payment for work in progress. According to van Mander, he impertinently touched Philip's shoulder with his mahlstick and fled because he feared retribution from those jealous of his influence. Although some such incident may have convinced Mor to abandon the lucrative patronage of the Spanish court, other reasons probably also influenced his decision not to return. The termination of his salary in September 1561 as part of an administrative reorganization perhaps aggrieved or worried him, and ill-health doubtless played its part—in 1563 and 1564 it was difficult to travel 'propter herniam'.

6. ?1561–?1576: UTRECHT AND THE SOUTHERN NETHERLANDS. Having left Spain, Mor apparently divided his time between Utrecht and the southern Netherlands. He was frequently in Utrecht and may have been based there, although in August and September 1563 he was in Brussels, where he was in touch with the court of Margaret of Parma. Continued contact with the Habsburgs is suggested by van Buchell's report (*c.* 1600) that Mor retained a modest pension from Philip II, by his production of a definitive image of Philip's fourth wife, *Anne of Austria*, in 1570 (Vienna, Ksthist. Mus.) and by the fact that he was still being called Philip's painter in 1573. Evidence that Mor knew intellectuals such as Dominicus Lampsonius and Hubertus Goltzius suggests, however, that the material profit and social prestige of the court artist had perhaps become less important to him than the honour of being the independent practitioner of a liberal art.

In 1564 Mor was in Antwerp 'making his profit from portraying the merchants'. The pendant portraits (both Amsterdam, Rijkmus.), probably of *Thomas Gresham* and his wife *Anne Fernely*, seem representative of such non-court portraits. Seated and interrelated compositions characterize the sitters as less aloof and self-contained than monarchs and nobles, and although the seated poses may derive ultimately from court portraits such as *Mary Tudor*, in painting merchants Mor did not define his sitters' roles with reference to particular visual exemplars. Rather he combined acute observation with a slightly informal conception to produce portraits that appear simultaneously objective and immediate (see fig. 2).

Mor is not known to have been in Utrecht after 24 July 1567. Van Mander alleged that he was called from Utrecht into the service of the Duque de Alba, the new Governor of the Netherlands, who arrived in Brussels at the end of August 1567. Mor is documented in Antwerp in 1567 and 1568 and was living there by 1573, but it is possible that he worked for Alba in Brussels from 1568 to 1572. Although no pictures survive that can be specifically linked with Alba's patronage, in 1572 the Duque appointed Mor's son-in-law Receiver of West Flanders, probably as a reward for the painter's services. Mor's reported delight at being employed by Alba and his definitive move south aged about 50 may have been prompted by financial insecurity, perhaps heightened by the political violence and iconoclasm in the Netherlands from 1566. Mor may also have been influenced to abandon Utrecht by difficulties with his family; he apparently quarrelled with his profligate only son, Philips, in July 1567.

Mor spent his last years in Antwerp. Having painted a *Venus and Adonis* for the new Antwerp Stadhuis (town hall) before 1571, he was working on a *Circumcision* for

2. Antonis Mor: *Portrait of a Nobleman Pointing to a Clock*, oil on panel, 996×795 mm, 1565 (Paris, Musée du Louvre)

Antwerp Cathedral when he died. His last known surviving work is a portrait of his friend the numismatist and painter *Hubertus Goltzius* (1573–4; Brussels, Mus. Royaux A. & Hist.; *see* PORTRAITURE, fig. 10). This intimate and penetrating image, said to have been rapidly executed after a couple of sittings over breakfast, bears witness to Mor's undiminished skill.

BIBLIOGRAPHY

EARLY SOURCES

L. Guicciardini: *Descrittione di tutti i Paesi Bassi* (Antwerp, 1576), p. 99
G. Argote de Molina: *Discurso sobre la Montería* (Seville, 1582/*R* Madrid, 1983), pp. 100–09
A. van Buchell: *'Res pictoriae': Aantekeningen over kunstenaars en kunstwerken* . . . (MS.; 1583–1639); ed. G. J. Hoogewerff and J. Q. van Regteren Altena (The Hague, 1928)
H. Junius: *Batavia: In qua praeter gentis et insulae antiquitatem originem* (Leiden, 1588), pp. 238–9
K. van Mander: *Schilder-boeck* ([1603]–1604), fols 226*v*, 230*v*–31*v*, 238*v*, 248*v*

GENERAL

C. Kramm: *Der levens en werken der Hollandsche en Vlaamsche kunstschilders* (Amsterdam, 1860), cols 1156–63
A. Bertolotti: *Artisti belgi e olandesi a Roma nei secoli XVI e XVII* (Florence, 1880), p. 46
G. J. Hoogewerff: 'Documenten betreffend Nederlandsche schilders te Rome omstreeks het midden der XVIe eeuw', *Meded. Ned. Hist. Inst. Rome*, n. s. 2, ii (1932), pp. 163–4
M. J. Friedländer: *Die altniederländische Malerei* (Berlin, 1924–37), xiii (1936) pp. 118–32; Eng. trans. as *Early Netherlandish Painting* (Leiden 1967–76), xiii (1975), pp. 63–9, 101–6, 115–16 [best plates and further bibliog.]
P. M. M. Geurts: *De Utrechtse Kannunik Philippus Morus Neolatijns dichter* (Nieuwkoop, 1977), pp. 13–34
Kunst voor de beeldenstorm (exh. cat., ed. J. P. Filedkok, W. Halsema-Kubes and W. T. Kloek; Amsterdam, Rijksmus., 1986), pp. 334–8 [entries on Mor by J. Woodall]

MONOGRAPHS

H. Hymans: *Antonio Moro, son oeuvre et son temps* (Brussels, 1910)
G. Marlier: *Anthonis Mor van Dashorst* (Brussels, 1934)
L. C. J. Frerichs: *Antonio Moro* (Amsterdam, [1947])

SPECIALIST STUDIES

R. Beer: 'Acten Regesten und Inventare aus dem Archivo general zu Simancas', *Jb. Ksthist. Samml. Wien*, xii (1891), p. 98
V. von Loga: 'Antonis Mor als Hofmaler Karls V und Philips II', *Jb. Ksthist. Samml. Wien*, xxvii (1907/9), pp. 92–123
F. J. Sánchez Cantón: 'La Crucifixion de Moro', *Archv Esp. A.*, xiv (1940–41), pp. 79–80
G. Marlier: 'Nieuwe gegevens omtrent Anthonis Mor', *Gentse Bijdr. Kstgesch.*, viii (1942), pp. 205–10
H. van Gelder: 'Moro's goudsmid', *Ned. Ksthist. Jb.*, i (1947), pp. 47–57
M. Piquard: 'Le Cardinal de Granvelle et les artistes et les écrivains d'après les documents de Besançon', *Rev. Belge Archéol. & Hist. A.*, xvii (1947–8), pp. 133–47 (141–2)
J. Puraye: 'Antonio Moro et Dominique Lampson', *Oud-Holland*, lxiv (1949), pp. 175–83
A. Staring: 'Vraagstukken der Oranje iconografie: Is Mor's Willem van Oranje te Kassel een origineel?', *Oud-Holland*, lxvi (1951), pp. 68–75
F. Zeri: 'Antonio Moro: Un "San Pietro Apostolo"', *Paragone*, xxxix (1953), pp. 44–6
R. F. P. de Beaufort: 'De abdij Marienweerd', *Bijdr. Meded. Ver. 'Gelre'*, lvi (1957), pp. 179–94
R. van Luttervelt: 'Een schilderij van Anna van Buren en andere portretten uit haar omgeving', *Oud-Holland*, lxxiv (1959), pp. 183–202
W. A. Wijburg: 'Antonie Mor van Dashorst "vermaard schilder van Utrecht" en zijn naaste familie', *Ned. Leeuw*, lxxvi (1959), cols 230–48
K. Langedijk: 'La Resurrection du Christ: Une Oeuvre exceptionnelle d'Antonio Moro retrouvée à Chantilly', *Gaz. B.-A.*, n. s. 6, lxviii (1966), pp. 233–8
J. G. van Gelder: 'Scorel, More, Bellegambe und Orley in Marchiennes', *Oud-Holland*, lxxxvii (1973), pp. 156–76
J. R. J. van Asperen de Boer and M. Faries: 'Research during the Jan van Scorel in Utrecht Exhibition: A Report', *Simiolus*, ix (1977), pp. 169–82 (177–81)
J. A. L. de Meyere: 'Utrechtse schilderkunst in de tweede helft van de 16de eeuw', *Jb. Oud-Utrecht* (1978), pp. 106–92 (129–50)
E. H. Groeneveld: 'Een herziene biografie van Anthonis Mor', *Jb.: Kon. Mus. S. Kst.* (1981), pp. 97–117

JOANNA WOODALL

Mora, de (i). Spanish family of architects. (1) Francisco de Mora was the chief disciple of Juan de Herrera and became his successor (from Sept 1598), while his nephew (2) Juan Gómez de Mora in turn became his uncle's most valued pupil and, after Francisco's death, inherited his various titles and posts.

(1) Francisco de Mora (*b* Cuenca, 15 Aug 1552; *d* Madrid, 10 Aug 1610). He trained with Juan de Herrera in royal construction works from 1579. In Lisbon, during the annexation of the Kingdom of Portugal (1580), he provided designs for the Carthusian monastery of Évora (1589). As architect to the Spanish kings Philip II and Philip III, he also received commissions from Duque Francisco Gómez de Sandoval y Rojas, Prime Minister and royal favourite. Mora remodelled the Palacio Real (1610) in Valladolid, designed the restoration of the palace of El Pardo (1604; destr.) and submitted designs for the archives of Simancas (1588) and the church of S María (1595) in the Alhambra, Granada. He also helped Herrera with his schemes at Segovia (the Alcázar), Uclés and above all at the Escorial (*see* ESCORIAL, §2). At the Escorial he built the Botica (the medical dispensary) and the Pasadizo (passageway), both with superimposed orders of pilasters arranged on the outside, the Casa de Compaña (the family quarters), the Cachicanía (gardener's cottage) and the

Estanque Grande (great pond; 1589), all functional structures that followed the guidelines recommending simplicity that Juan Bautista de Toledo had established in the Patio de los Mascarones (small courtyard) of the monastery. By the Estanque Grande, Mora built a staircase of fantastic and original design.

In the town of Escorial de Abajo, at the request of Philip II, Mora built the parish church of S Bernabé (1593) in a style strongly influenced by the classical precepts in evidence at the Escorial. The church, which has a nave with deep recesses between abutments, forms one continuous vaulted space without a transept. Spatial simplicity and structural precision are achieved by means of a diaphanous interplay of volumes allied to an uncompromising plainness. A similar layout was employed for his church of the Descalzas Reales in Valladolid (construction supervised by Diego de Praves; 1615). Mora gave precedence to the longitudinal aspect of the building by diminishing the transept and eliminating all the side chapels. His finest ecclesiastical work was the convent of S José (1607–10) in Ávila, founded by St Teresa in 1562. His freedom to manoeuvre was limited by the fact that work had already begun at the site. The church is flanked with chapels in vaulted recesses forming independent areas, while the nave is sectioned into vaults cut into four vertical planes with no transept. He laid the foundations for the façade in a new manner, which became a feature of court architecture throughout the 17th century: Mora created a narthex with a three-bay arcade on columns and arranged the rest of the façade on two levels to comply with the need for communication with the saint's old church.

Francisco de Mora had a decisive influence on civil architecture and urban planning in Spain, most notably at Lerma, where he designed a ducal palace (1618). Conceived as a kind of prism without towers, it was built around a large courtyard with its main façade facing on to the Plaza Ducal. The remainder of the palace, enclosed like the Escorial, overlooks the countryside. Mora continued work on urban planning in Madrid as Juan de Herrera's successor, building a large section of the Plaza Mayor (*see* MADRID, fig. 2) and the Panadería (bakery), a task completed by his nephew (2) Juan Gómez de Mora. In Valladolid Francisco designed the Plaza de S Pablo in the Palacio Real. These schemes followed the principles established by their initiators, Francisco de Salamanca (*d* 1573) at Valladolid (1561) and Herrera at Madrid (1585) and Toledo (1589), creating carefully arranged, airy spaces with views by laying out straight streets and rectangular porticoed squares lined with houses of equal height and uniform façades.

BIBLIOGRAPHY

E. Llaguno y Amírola: *Noticias*, iii (1829)

J. Martí y Monsó: *Estudios histórico–artísticos relativos principalmente a Valladolid* (Valladolid, 1898–1901)

E. García Chico: *Documentos para el estudio del arte en Castilla*, i (Valladolid, 1940)

L. Cervera Vera: 'La Iglesia del Monasterio de San José en Ávila', *Bol. Soc. Esp. Excurs.*, liv (1950), pp. 1–155

G. Kubler: *Arquitectura de los siglos XVII y XVIII*, A. Hisp., xiv (Madrid, 1957)

F. Chueca Goitia: 'Herrera y el herrerianismo', *Goya*, 56–7 (1963), pp. 98–115

J. de Sigüenza: *Fundación del Monasterio de El Escorial* (Madrid, 1963)

L. Cervera Vera: *El conjunto palacial de la villa de Lerma* (Valencia, 1967)

A. Bustamante García: *La arquitectura clasicista del foco vallisoletano, 1561–1640* (Valladolid, 1983)

A. Bustamante García and F. Marías: 'Francisco de Mora y la arquitectura portuguesa', *As relaçoes artísticas entre Portugal e Espanha na época dos descobrimentos* (Coimbra, 1987), pp. 277–318

——: 'De las Descalzas Reales a la Plaza Mayor: Dibujos madrileños de Windsor Castle de la colección de Cassiano dal Pozzo', *Terceras Jornadas de Arte* (Madrid, 1991), pp. 78–85

(2) Juan Gómez de Mora (*b* Cuenca, 26 May 1586; *d* Madrid, 22 Feb 1648). Nephew and pupil of (1) Francisco de Mora. He took over his uncle's posts after the latter's death in 1610, becoming royal architect (Feb 1611), architect to Francisco Gómez de Sandoval y Rojas, Duke of Lerma, and Maestro Mayor of the city of Madrid (1615). An early independent work of his is the church of the Encarnación (1611–16), which uses a narthex loggia, as introduced by his uncle at S José (1607–10), Ávila. The steep pediment rises 1 in 4, over twice the Vitruvian ratio. Juan Gómez worked for the Duke on his palace (destr.) in Madrid and completed the Ducal Palace (1616) at Lerma, which he also modified. He altered his uncle's plans for the roofs and added towers at the corners so that the original horizontal, prismatic proportions disappeared, making way for the development of a typical towered edifice influenced by the Alcázar, Madrid. Mora's links with the Duke of Lerma's circle led to his appointment as architect in charge of the plans for the Colegio Málaga (1614) and the principal courtyard of the Colegio Mayor de S Ildefonso (both in Alcalá de Henares). His most spectacular construction in Alcalá de Henares was the convent and church of Las Bernardas (1618). The church is particularly striking. It is a rectangular construction with an inscribed oval. The entrance bay, presbytery and choir all lie on the main axis. A pair of rectangular chapels on the cross axis and four oval chapels on the diagonals are carved out of the walling between the rectilinear periphery and the central ellipse, around which they form subsidiary spaces. The plan was a novelty for the court; it derives from Francesco da Volterra's project (1590) for S Giacomo degli Incurabili, Rome. In his articulation of the walls and design for the elevation, Juan Gómez followed his uncle's example in his recourse to planar surfaces and simplified classical elements, concealing the exterior of the dome under a polygonal roof culminating in a spire like that of the monastery at Uclés.

In Madrid, Juan Gómez continued working on the Plaza Mayor and developing the surrounding area (1617). He drew up new plans (following those of his uncle) and enclosed the great rectangle, ordering the streets and dwellings that provided access to this area. As an urban planner, Mora followed the tradition imposed by Philip II (stemming from the reconstruction of Valladolid in 1561 and adhered to by Juan Bautista de Herrera in Madrid and Toledo) in which a city was conceived as a living entity in which public well-being prevailed over private interests. The axes of activity were the streets and squares, designed on straight, regular lines, to which the façades of the buildings would conform, in a uniform manner in terms of height, articulation, external decoration and roof details. This notion of regularity and of an overall view in which only certain significant buildings would stand out, as, for example, the Panadería in the Plaza Mayor, is a distinctive characteristic of classical urban planning in Spain, followed without any deviation by Juan Gómez. He also designed the town hall (1629; altered) in Madrid, based on the models with corner towers built by Herrera at Valladolid and Toledo. Mora took his inspiration for the nine-bay façade from 16th-century palace architecture in Rome; a tall ground-floor in ashlar is succeeded by a brick *piano nobile* articulated by pilaster strips with windows, which are doubled at the end bays beneath the towers.

Juan Gómez's most important patrons were Philip III and Philip IV, despite the low esteem in which he was held by the Conde-Duque de Olivares (Gaspar de Guzmán y Pimentel Olivares) and the enmity of Giovanni Battista Crescenzi. In 1636 Juan Gómez lost his post as His Majesty's Chief Designer (Trazador Mayor), and he was succeeded by Francisco Praves (*fl* 1582–1620; *d* 1637), the royal architect. He regained his post in 1643, after the deaths of Crescenzi and Olivares. As a servant of the King, Juan Gómez had collaborated in work on the Pantheon at the monastery of S Lorenzo el Real in El Escorial. In 1617 Crescenzi, who was responsible for the plans as executed there, caused serious problems for Philip II's workshop. The enmity between Juan Gómez and Crescenzi lasted during the lifetime of both men and may have been linked to their different conceptions of architecture: Crescenzi preferred a richly decorated Roman Mannerism, while Juan Gómez favoured the *estilo desornamentado*, an extremely severe, unadorned classicism. The latter's contributions to the Royal Works were those of a pure classicist. He continued to work on the Alcázar (destr. 1734), Madrid, raising its great main façade (1612–30), which exhibited notable echoes of that executed by (1) Francisco de Mora for the Palacio Real in Valladolid. He also continued to work on the buildings of Aranjuez (1626), introducing modifications to Herrera's designs as regards the ground-plan. He designed the Cárcel de Corte (1629; now the Ministerio de Asuntos Exteriores), which resembled the Alcázar, Madrid, being a rectangle with corner towers, two courtyards and a dividing staircase. The façade was a schematic repetition of the one at the Alcázar.

Juan Gómez de Mora also built the small suburban palace of La Zarzuela (1634) in Madrid for the Cardinal Prince Fernando, which was completely rebuilt after the Spanish Civil War (1936–9). It forms a rectangular block, with a central courtyard, surrounded by gardens. Wings with porticos extend on both sides of the façade. It is a country seat, using the rustic Doric order, with very steep slate roofs and garrets utilized as bedrooms. By order of Philip IV, Juan Gómez modified the Torre de la Parada of the Zarzuela (1635), adding a structure that surrounds Luis de Vega's old tower like a crinoline. At the express wish of Philip III, Juan Gómez designed the Real Colegio de la Compañía de Jesús ('La Clerecía'; 1618) in Salamanca, but building was not completed until 1779. The immense edifice (7000 sq. m) is constructed in the form of a U and is rigorously functional. The church and sacristy, with the exception of the dome and façade, were built to Juan Gómez's designs, which followed the Jesuit tradition established in their 16th-century buildings at Valladolid. The church is in a pure classical style, formed by a sequence of arches with galleries between Doric pilasters; it was undoubtedly influenced by Herrera, not least in the siting of the choir behind the altar, as Herrera had done at S María in the Alhambra, Granada.

Juan Gómez de Mora was the most important classical architect in Spain during the first half of the 17th century. His style, inherited from Juan de Herrera and (1) Francisco de Mora, had to contend with the decorative innovations imported from Italy by Giovanni Battista Crescenzi and the wave of Andalusian classicism alien to Herrera, which was brought to the court by Pedro Sánchez (1568–1633).

BIBLIOGRAPHY

F. de los Santos: *Descripción breve del Monasterio de S Lorenzo el Real del Escorial, única maravilla del mundo* (Madrid, 1657/*R* 1984)
E. Llaguno y Amírola: *Noticias*, iii (1829)
M. del Saltillo: 'Al margen de la Exposición de Caza: Alonso Martínez de Espinar: La Casa Regia de la Zarzuela: Noticias de su construcción', *A. Esp.*, xviii (1950–51), pp. 115–34
J. J. Martín González: 'El Panteón de San Lorenzo de El Escorial', *Archv Esp. A.*, 122 (1958), pp. 198–213
——: 'Nuevos datos sobre la construcción del Panteón de El Escorial', *Bol. Semin. Estud. A. & Arqueol.*, xxvi (1960), pp. 230–35
A. Bonet Correa: *Iglesias madrileñas del siglo XVII* (Madrid, 1961)
J. J. Martín González: 'El Panteón de El Escorial', *Goya*, 56–57 (1963), pp. 140–47
L. Cervera Vera: *El conjunto palacial de la villa de Lerma* (Valencia, 1967)
A. Rodríguez G. de Ceballos: *Estudios del barroco salmantino: El Colegio Real de la Compañía de Jesús, 1617–1779* (Salamanca, 1969)
A. Bonet Correa: *Morfología y ciudad: Urbanismo y arquitectura durante el Antiguo Régimen en España* (Barcelona, 1978)
C. Román Pastor: *Sebastián de la Plaza: Alarife de la villa de Alcalá de Henares* (Alcalá de Henares, 1979)
J. J. Martín González: 'El Panteón de El Escorial y la arquitectura barroca', *Bol. Semin. Estud. A. & Arqueol.*, xlvii (1981), pp. 265–84
A. Rodríguez G. de Ceballos: 'Entre el Manierismo y el Barroco: Iglesias españolas de planta oval', *Goya*, 177 (1983), pp. 98–107
V. Tovar Martín: *Arquitectura madrileña del siglo XVII: Datos para su estudio* (Madrid, 1983)
Juan Gómez de Mora (1586–1648) (exh. cat., ed. M. Agulló y Cobo; Madrid, Ayuntamiento, 1986)
A. Bustamante García and F. Marías: 'De las Descalzas Reales a la Plaza Mayor: Dibujos madrileños de Windsor Castle de la colección de Cassiano dal Pozzo', *Terceras Jornadas de Arte* (Madrid, 1991), pp. 73–85

A. BUSTAMANTE GARCÍA

Mora, de (ii). Spanish family of sculptors. Bernardo de Mora (*bapt* Porreras, Mallorca, 13 Oct 1614; *d* Granada, Jan 1684) probably began his training in Baza (Granada) in the workshop of Cecilio López Criado, with whom he collaborated until he moved to Granada in 1650 to begin working with Pedro de Mena and to direct his workshop. When Alonso Cano arrived in Granada in 1652, both Mora and Mena became influenced by his work. Mora's earliest surviving sculpture is the *Ecce homo* (1659; Granada, Capilla Real), a half-length figure in polychromed wood of a type commonly used by Mena, to whom the piece has been attributed. Christ, crowned with thorns and with arms folded and bound against his chest, is depicted in a state of inner reflection. Mora's work is not documented again until 1665, when he collaborated with his son José de Mora (*bapt* Baza, Granada, 1 March 1642; *d* Granada, ?25 Oct 1724) in the execution of the grey marble sculptures on the façade of the Basilica de Nuestra Señora de las Angustias, Granada. After the departure of Pedro de Mena in 1658 and the death of Cano in 1667, Bernardo de Mora's workshop was the most important in Granada. In 1675 he executed his most significant work, the polychromed wooden figure of *St Michael* for the Ermita de S Miguel el Alto in the Albaycín district of

Granada. The influence of Cano is evident in the treatment of the face and in the general conception of the figure of the triumphant archangel, shown from the front. Cano's style is also seen in Mora's last works of *c.* 1679, such as *St John of God*, *St Raphael the Archangel* and the *Virgin as a Child*, all in S Juan de Dios, Granada; however, their immediate realism and the sumptuousness of their clothing gives them a certain banal quality. In general, his sculpture is modest and impersonal, qualities that often make his work difficult to identify.

José de Mora was a pupil of his father, Bernardo de Mora, and executed his first known work with him in 1665 (see above). More important was, again, the powerful influence of Cano, whose style left its mark on his work from the outset. This influence is obvious in the most important work of his first period in Granada, the *Immaculate Conception* in SS Justo y Pastor, which closely resembles a version of Cano's (1655–6; Granada Cathedral, Sacristy) but has a greater pictorial sense. In about 1666 Mora moved to Madrid to work with Sebastián de Herrera Barnuevo, a pupil of Cano, but he made frequent extended visits back to Granada. In 1671 he created one of his most important works, the *Mater dolorosa* for S Felipe Neri (now S Ana), Granada. The kneeling life-size figure, dressed in widow's garb, displays deep reflection and controlled pain. Contemporary with this work is his only crucifix, *Christ of Mercy*, in S Gregorio Bético (now S José), Granada. After the death of Herrera Barnuevo in 1671, he was nominated Escultor del Rey to Charles II the following year. Unfortunately, the works he executed for the King have been lost, and from his Madrid period there remains only a pair of busts, *Ecce homo* and *Mater dolorosa* (both Madrid, Las Maravillas), executed in the style of Pedro de Mena. During the 1670s his style became more original. His sculptures became melancholic, almost sickly looking, although they still remained restful. Hands and faces became the focus of expression as physical suffering was understated. He enhanced the realism of his sculptures by using real hair and rope and glass for tears. He applied his own polychromy, using cold, intense colours in brilliant and uniform hues. In 1680 he finally returned to his father's workshop in Granada. The nervous, morbid and stylized manner of his figures becomes stronger after 1704, following the death of his wife. His last sculptures (e.g. *St Joseph* and *St Bruno*, 1705–12; Granada, Monasterio de la Cartuja) show an influence of the Baroque style. In his last years he turned exclusively to drawing.

Diego de Mora (*bapt* Granada, 30 Nov 1658; *d* Granada, 16 Jan 1729) was also a son and pupil of Bernardo de Mora and, like his father and brother, was influenced by Cano. He collaborated with his brother until a family quarrel led him to open his own workshop and establish his career independently. He is significant for continuing the tradition of the 17th-century school of sculpture in Granada into the 18th century. Only two sculptures can be securely attributed to him, both of which reveal a sound apprenticeship and limited artistic personality. *St Gregory of Baetica* (1707; Granada Cathedral) and the seated *Madonna of Mercy* (1724; Granada, S Ildefonso) demonstrate the stylistic influence of his brother José in the treatment of folds and surfaces, although not in the grouping of figures, which are more robust and tranquil than his brother's. Neither do they convey the same sense of melancholy. Also attributed to him are a series of polychromed wooden panels, one of which is *Our Lady of Carmen* in the convent of the Carmelitas Calzadas, Granada.

BIBLIOGRAPHY
A. Gallego Burín: *José de Mora* (Granada, 1925/*R* 1988)
——: 'Tres familias de escultores: Los Menas, los Moras y los Roldanes', *Archv Esp. A. & Arqueol.*, i (1925), pp. 323–31
L. Magaña Bisbal: 'Una familia de escultores: Los Mora', *Archv Esp. A.*, xcviii (1952), pp. 143–57
M. E. Gómez Moreno: *Escultura del siglo XVII*, A. Hisp., xvi (Madrid, 1958), pp. 274–9
J. J. Martín González: *Escultura barroca en España, 1600–1700*, Manuales arte cátedra (Madrid, 1986/*R* 1991), pp. 232–4
NATIVIDAD SÁNCHEZ ESTEBAN

Mora (y Palomar), Enrique de la (*b* Guadalajara, 16 June 1907; *d* Mexico City, 9 May 1978). Mexican architect. He graduated from the Universidad Nacional Autónoma de Mexico in 1930 and then began working with José Villagrán. Here, from the late 1930s he experimented with shell structures as a means of transcending the straight lines and right-angles that dominated the architecture of the time. While such contemporaries as Carlos Obregón Santacilia and Enrique Yáñez at times shared this approach, de la Mora was exceptional in the persistence of his commitment to it. Such works as the church of the Purisima (1947), Monterrey, were among the very earliest shell concrete churches. All four arms of a conventional cruciform plan are formed in parabolic vaults that spring from ground level, as are four chapels of lower section on each side of the nave. The external surfaces of the vaults are completely smooth and contrast markedly with a free-standing brick campanile of simple tapered form.

In the early 1950s de la Mora became involved with the social building programme of the time: examples of his work from this period include the Guardaria Infantil (1952) for the Secretaría de Communicaciones and the Facultad de Filosofía (1953–4) in the Ciudad Universitaria, both in Mexico City. These were followed by a series of outstanding churches, designed in collaboration with FÉLIX CANDELA. S Antonio de las Huertas (1956), Mexico City, was the first of a number with centralized plans, made possible by the revision of the liturgy, and was an early example of the development of reinforced concrete shells with free edges. The chapel of Nuestra Señora de la Soledad (1956–8), Mexico City, is a minor masterpiece in which de la Mora (with Candela and Fernando López Carmona) took advantage of the compositional richness of a rhomboid plan, covered it with a single hyperbolic paraboloid shell (hypar) and set it astride massive rubble walls that dip to form a great curving crescent-shaped stained-glass window behind the altar. The chapel of S Vicente de Paul (1958–62), Coyoacán, Mexico City, and the almost contemporary chapel of S José Obrero (1957–62), Monterrey, are less impressive but still structurally adventurous in their treatment of the double curved vault, allowing de la Mora to create an architectural language quite different from that of the International Style.

De la Mora also undertook a number of public and commercial buildings, such as the Bolsa Mexicana (1956) and the headquarters building for the Compañía de Seguros Monterrey (1960–62; with Alberto González Pozo), both in Mexico City. The former boasts a trading floor spanned by hypar cross-vaults designed by Candela, while in the latter two 30-m high concrete columns rise to support a massive longitudinal beam that is used to anchor 15 double cantilevers on each side; the floor slabs are suspended from the latter, leaving most of the site area free at ground level. There were some later churches, for example the Santuario de Guadalupe (1965), Madrid, Spain, and Santa Cruz (1967) at San Luis Potosí, but de la Mora probably never surpassed the mastery of the Soledad.

BIBLIOGRAPHY

M. L. Cetto: *Modern Architecture in Mexico* (Stuttgart, 1961), pp. 36–40, 50–51, 72–3, 123–5, 138
F. Bullrich: *New Directions in Latin American Architecture* (London, 1969), pp. 54–62
A. G. Pozo: *Enrique de la Mora: Vida y obra* (Mexico City, 1981)

RAMÓN VARGAS

Moraglia, Giacomo (*b* Milan, 7 July 1791; *d* Milan, 1 Feb 1860). Italian architect. He studied at the Accademia di Brera, Milan, and after winning a scholarship went to Rome (1817–20), where he pursued advanced architectural studies. He then returned to Milan and in 1821 qualified as an architect. He was among the most active professional architects in Milan during the 19th century, working almost exclusively in Lombardy, but there is as yet no comprehensive record of his architecture apart from his work for the Church. An early civil commission was the triumphal arch originally dedicated to the Emperor Francis I (*reg* 1792–1835) at the Milanese customs barrier at Porta Comasina (1825–6; now the Porta Garibaldi), and completed with the signalmen's houses between 1834 and 1836. The scheme combined picturesque effects with a formal Neo-classicism that was typical of all his work. Moraglia also designed industrial architecture, notable examples being the Kramer Press (1825) in Milan and Count Calderara's sugar refinery, where he reconciled Neo-classicism with the functional demands of production. A similar commitment to functional considerations can be seen in the plans (1837) for the Ospedale Civile at Sondrio, in which he introduced technological and organizational refinements.

Moraglia was, however, primarily an architect of churches, and the plans of most of them are based on a Greek cross with the central space covered by a low spherical dome; examples include S Gerardo (1836) in Monza; S Vittore (1844) in Missaglia; the parish church of S Carlo (1846) in Magadino, Switzerland; and the Oratory (1855) of the Villa Carlotta in Tremezzo on Lake Como. The decorations were designed in the most academically classical style, almost untouched by the contemporary debate on eclecticism or the search for a new style. He sometimes used proto-Renaissance forms that in Milan were called 'Bramantesque', for example in the reconstruction of the nave (1836) of S Maria dei Miracoli at Cantù, but he was mainly faithful to Neo-classical formulae despite having clerical patrons with considerable importance in cultural matters. For Monsignor Luigi Biraghi he designed the Collegio delle Marcelline (1837–9) at Cernusco sul Naviglio and for Monsignor Antonio Rosmini

he built the Collegio dei Padri Rosminiani (1842–7) at Stresa. He was also the architect to the seminaries of the diocese of Milan, and in that capacity, from 1840, he supervised numerous alterations and restorations to the Seminario della Canonica in Milan and those of Seveso, Pollegio and Monza.

Moraglia planned numerous country villas and town houses, probably the most important being the Palazzo Melzi d'Eril in the Via Manin, Milan, built between 1841 and 1846 as an adaptation of existing buildings. Here Moraglia's austere language and ability to obtain pictorial effects with extreme economy of means reveal the client's desire to express himself and his social position. A similar language can be seen in the exterior design of the almost contemporary Palazzo Civico (1844–5) in Lugano, Switzerland, the imposing volume of which is divided into façades articulated by bands of ashlar. The palazzo is planned around a solemn court decorated with two orders, in which there is an echo of Palladio's classicism mediated through early 17th-century Milanese examples. In 1839 Moraglia became a Socio d'Arte at the Accademia and in 1841 a member of the Commissione d'Ornato di Milano. Of his numerous sons, only Pietro Moraglia (*b* 1829) followed his father's career, and he completed his unfinished works.

BIBLIOGRAPHY

Portoghesi
A. Negri: 'Inizi e sviluppi di un'architettura dell'industria a Milano', *Archeologia industriale in Lombardia: Milano e la bassa padana* (Milan, 1982), pp. 105–9
G. Melzi d'Eril: *Palazzo Melzi d'Eril alla Cavalchina in Milano* (Milan, 1987)
S. Della Torre and R. Bergossi: 'Moraglia, Giacomo', *Dizionario della chiesa ambrosiana*, iv (Milan, in preparation)

STEFANO DELLA TORRE

Moragues, Pere (*fl* 1358; *d* before 1388). Catalan sculptor and goldsmith. He is first documented in 1358 in Barcelona, where he executed some wooden sculptures (untraced). A wooden *Virgin and Child* in the church of La Merced, Barcelona, has been attributed to him and linked to a commission for this church in 1361. In 1366 Moragues received a royal commission to make seven stone crosses (destr.) for the monastery of Montserrat, near Barcelona; he was still working for Montserrat in 1373. In 1379 he was in Saragossa where he made his most important work in sculpture, the tomb of *Archbishop Lope Fernández de Luna* in the Capilla de S Miguel of the cathedral. Executed during the Archbishop's lifetime, the tomb was probably completed *c*. 1382, the year in which King Peter IV commissioned him to make tombs for several members of his family in S Francisco, Saragossa (destr.). The tombs of *Ramón Serra el Vell* in S María, Cervera, and *Juan Fernández de Heredia* in the parish church of Caspe (Saragossa) are also attributed to him. Moragues was first documented as a goldsmith in Saragossa. In 1383 he carved moulds for some royal seals, and in 1384, also by royal commission, he began work on one of the principal examples of medieval Catalan goldsmiths' work, the reliquary monstrance for the Capilla de los Corporales in the parish church of Daroca (Daroca, Mus. Santismo Misterio). In 1388 his widow received the final payments due to him for this work.

Pere Moragues was the most important Catalan sculptor of his period. He enjoyed royal patronage and revitalized the stylistic traditions of sculptors in the royal service of the second quarter of the 14th century. He attached crucial importance to gesture and to the individual characterization of his figures; in this he reflected tendencies in the international style of the period. His work shows minute attention to detail and a tendency to preciosity, characteristics that were a consequence of his activity as a goldsmith.

BIBLIOGRAPHY

A. M. Albareda: 'Pere Moragues: Escultor i orfebre', *Estud. U. Catalans*, xxii (1936), pp. 499–524

A. Duran Sanpere and J. Ainaud de Lasarte: *Escultura gótica*, A. Hisp., viii (Madrid, 1956)

N. de Dalmases and A. José Pitarch: *L'art gòtic s. XIV–XV*, Història de l'Art Català, iii (Barcelona, 1984)

N. de Dalmases and D. Giralt-Miracle: *Plateros y joyeros de Cataluña* (Barcelona, 1985)

JOSEP BRACONS I CLAPÉS

Morais, Cristóvão de (*fl* Lisbon, 1551–*c.* 1573). Portuguese painter. He was probably of Spanish origin but should not be confused with the artist of the same name active in Andalusia. Cristóvão de Morais may have trained in Flanders and was possibly the Christophele Moralys who was a pupil of Cornelis Buys in Antwerp in 1538. He was active in Portuguese court circles from 1551 to around 1573, and, although he was not appointed Royal Painter, he was Examiner of Painters in 1554 and attained nobility when he was made King-at-Arms. In 1551 he painted and gilded a royal litter and in 1554 a bed for Catherine, Queen of Portugal, wife of King John III Aviz; and in 1567 he painted the retable for the high altar in the Mosteiro da Conceição, Beja, for all of which he was highly paid (all works untraced).

Morais is first documented in 1571 as portraitist to King Sebastian (*reg* 1557–78); this refers to the magnificent portrait of the young *King Sebastian* (Lisbon, Mus. N. A. Ant.), for which Morais was paid in advance, and which, according to two letters of Queen Catherine, was made to be sent to Pope Pius V. Morais's portraits resemble those of Giovanni Battista Moroni, but he developed more deeply the allegorical and psychological significance of his sitters, especially in his portraits of King Sebastian, who is presented as Universal Defender and Restorer of Christianity in a way that can be seen as reviving a Dante myth.

An earlier portrait of *King Sebastian* (1565; Madrid, Convent of the Descalzas Reales) shows the King aged 11. In 1572 or 1573 Morais portrayed the King aged 18 (Granada, priv. col.), a picture which is almost a replica of the Lisbon portrait. Letters in the Arquivo de Finanças, Lisbon, refer to a portrait commissioned by Gabriel de Zayas and executed in 1573 and 1574, which may be the Granada painting.

BIBLIOGRAPHY

V. Serrão: *A pintura maneirista em Portugal* (Lisbon, 1982), pp. 48–81

F. A. Baptista Pereira: 'O retrato de D. Sebastião de M. N. A. A.: Uma leitura iconológica', *Prelo*, 11 (1986), pp. 53–66

F. A. BAPTISTA PEREIRA

Moral, Enrique del (*b* Irapuato, Guanajuato, 20 Jan 1906; *d* Mexico City, 11 June 1987). Mexican architect. He graduated in 1928 from the Escuela de Arquitectura at the Universidad Nacional Autónoma de México, where he belonged to the first generation of students under José Villagrán. Through his studies and through working in Villagrán's practice, del Moral encountered Functionalism, but in his subsequent works he tried to produce designs that were in keeping with both Mexican traditions and his own personal aesthetic ideals, transcending radical functionalism and seeking an approach that was sensitive to physical, socio-economic and cultural factors.

Del Moral's first works were carried out in collaboration with Marcial Gutiérrez Camarena (1902–54). These were almost exclusively private houses of an elemental simplicity and imbued with the spirit of Le Corbusier. Typical of this period are ten houses for workers, built in Irapuato, Guanajuato, in 1936, which show the influence of the International Style. He continued to work in this idiom into the 1940s, for example in several apartment buildings in the Cuauhtemoc area of Mexico City, such as those in Plaza Melchor Ocampo (1940–42). At the same time, however, he was beginning to develop a new form of expression. In his designs for private houses such as that of the Iturbe family in San Angel (1946) and his own house in Tacubaya (1949), he adopted a more openly emotional and regionalist approach, producing works that have affinities with the distinctive works of Luís Barragán. His movement in this direction was curtailed, however, by the commencement of an intermittent partnership with MARIO PANI, whose strong personality and commitment to a modified version of the International Style led del Moral to pursue a different approach. The principal works carried out in collaboration with Pani were the master plan and the Rectoría (1951–2) in the Ciudad Universitaria of the Universidad Nacional Autónoma de México (with mural decoration by David Alfaro Siqueiros), the Secretaría de Recursos Hidráulicos (1950–53), situated in the Paseo de la Reforma, a series of houses, hotels and the airport (1954–5) in Acapulco, Guerrero.

Del Moral also produced a number of important public buildings, beginning with the Casacuarán Primary School (1946), Guanajuato. This was followed in the 1950s by the Mercado de la Merced (1956–7) in Mexico City, in which he found a hygienic, economical solution for the retailing of perishable goods, without abandoning his aesthetic ideals. Then, in the 1960s he was responsible for the Procuraduría General de Justicia (1959–69) and the Tesorería del Distrito Federal (1962–3; both destr. in the 1985 earthquake) in Mexico City. Del Moral also established a reputation as the designer of numerous hospitals throughout the country, remarkable for the skill and care with which he allowed for clinical requirements while providing works well suited to their urban context. Perhaps the most representative are the Clínica hospital (1966–8) for the Instituto Mexicano de Seguro Social in Ciudad Obregón, Sonora, and the hospital in Cuautla, Morelos (1967). Del Moral was a professor of architecture in the Universidad de México from 1934 to 1950 and received numerous awards, including the Premio Nacional de Artes in 1978.

WRITINGS

El hombre y la arquitectura: Ensayos y testimonias (Mexico City, 1983)

BIBLIOGRAPHY

Contemp. Architects

'Enrique del Moral', *Arquit. México*, 100 (1968), pp. 42–7

'Enrique del Moral', *Testimonios vivos: 20 arquitectos* (Mexico City, 1981)

S. Pinoncelly: *La obra de Enrique del Moral* (Mexico City, 1983)

L. Noelle: 'Enrique del Moral', *Arquitectos contemporáneos de México* (Mexico City, 1988)

F. González Gortázar, ed.: *La arquitectura mexicana del siglo XX* (Mexico City, 1994)

LOUISE NOELLE

Morales, Armando (*b* Granada, Nicaragua, 15 Jan 1927). Nicaraguan painter. He studied at the Escuela Nacional de Bellas Artes, Managua, from 1941 to 1945 and 1948 to 1953 and at the Pratt Graphic Art Center, New York, from 1960 to 1964. He exhibited extensively internationally from 1953 and in 1957 made his first visit to New York through a Guggenheim Fellowship. His first paintings treated local landscapes, still-lifes and genre scenes in a realistic vein, but the work for which he is best known constitutes two distinct phases. From the mid-1950s until the late 1960s, in works such as *Ferry Boat* (1964; Managua, Banco Cent. de Nicaragua), he combined figurative elements with broad abstract forms, sombre colours and a thick impasto influenced by the work of Antoni Tàpies.

In the early 1970s Morales turned to a distinctive figurative style of Magic Realism in works such as *Seated Woman* (1971; Managua, Banco Cent. de Nicaragua), based to some extent on the Pittura Metafisica of Giorgio de Chirico but with a subtle tonal modulation of his own. From 1982 he made his main home in Paris, where he served in the revolutionary government of Nicaragua as a representative to UNESCO.

BIBLIOGRAPHY
G. Compton: 'A Word with Armando Morales', *Américas*, ix/6 (1957), p. 17

Pintura contemporánea de Nicaragua: Segundo aniversario del triunfo de la Revolución Popular Sandinista (exh. cat., Mexico City, Inst. N. B.A., 1981)

C. Martínez Rivas: 'Morales—una observación y cuatro preguntas', *Nicaráuac* 10 (Aug 1984), pp. 175–8

Pintura contemporánea de Nicaragua, Unión Nacional de Artistas Plásticos (Managua, 1986), pp. 42–5

Armando Morales: Recent Paintings (exh. cat. by D. Ashton, New York, Claude Bernard Gal., 1987)

DAVID CRAVEN

Morales, Ignacio Diaz. *See* DIAZ MORALES, IGNACIO.

Morales, Luis de [el Divino] (*b* ?Badajoz, *c.* 1520; *d* Badajoz, ?1586). Spanish painter. The origins of his highly individual style are complex. His meticulous technique and the prominent echoes of the style and forms of Leonardo da Vinci and Raphael indicate the formative influence of Italianizing Flemish painters. This accords with Palomino's statement that Morales was trained in Seville by the Flemish Mannerist painter Peeter de Kempeneer (known in Spain as Pedro de Campaña), who is recorded in Spain from 1537. It has been suggested that Morales visited Italy *c.* 1540, but this seems most unlikely. His contact with Portuguese painting, particularly that of Frei Carlos and the Évoran school, was important, and his knowledge of German and Flemish prints contributed to his repertory of forms.

Morales's earliest dated work, the *Virgin with the Little Bird* (1546; Madrid, Moret priv. col., see Gaya Nuño, pl. 2), executed for the parish church of La Concepción in Badajoz, shows an Italianate clarity of form and harmony of composition. Probably close in date to this painting is his only surviving signed work, the *Madonna of Purity* (Naples, S Pietro Maggiore), which, although much altered by Baroque additions, still preserves characteristics that recall Raphael. In 1554 Luis was paid for an altarpiece of four panels depicting the *Annunciation, Adoration of the Magi, Pietà* and *Stigmatization of St Francis* (now Badajoz, Mus. Dioc.–Catedralicio) for the Capilla del Sagrario in Badajoz Cathedral. The *Pietà*, with its sense of tragic drama, presages Morales's typical treatment of the theme in subsequent representations.

The epithet 'el Divino', which has been applied to Morales since at least the early 18th century, has been explained by the exclusively religious character of his oeuvre, but its appropriateness lies in his success in expressing the fervid and impassioned spirituality of Spanish society, an achievement that is equalled only by El Greco. The restricted iconographic range of his work concentrates on the imagery of the Passion, particularly on the *Ecce homo* (e.g. Madrid, Real Acad. S Fernando; New York, Hisp. Soc. America) and *Pietà* (Madrid, Pal. Episcopal; 1560–70; and Real. Acad. S Fernando; see fig.). His treatments of the *Virgin and Child* also often include intimations of death, as for example in the *Virgin and Child with Yarnwinder* (New York, Hisp. Soc. America; Berlin, Gemäldegal.). Morales's concentration on these themes is paralleled in the preferred subjects of meditation of contemporary Spanish mystics such as St Peter of Alcántara (1499–1562), Fray Luis de Granada (1504–88) and Juan de Avila (1500–69). The numerous replicas, versions and variants of these subjects, particularly of the

Luis de Morales: *Pietà*, oil on panel, 1.26×0.98 m, 1560–70 (Madrid, Real Academia de San Fernando)

Virgin and Child (e.g. London, N.G.; Madrid, Prado, 944; Mexico City, Acad. S Carlos), testify to their enormous popularity as devotional images.

The most intense period of activity in Morales's career was the 1560s. From 1563 to 1568 he painted 20 panels with scenes from the *Life of Christ* for the high altar of Nuestra Señora de la Asunción in Arroyo de la Luz, Cáceres (*in situ*). Stylistically a fusion of Flemish and Italian elements, the individual panels nonetheless betray a restricted understanding of perspective, and there are obvious problems with spatial organization. The altarpiece shows extensive workshop collaboration, but there are some fine passages in the *Presentation in the Temple* (of which there is an excellent version in the Prado, no. 943) and in the *Descent into Limbo*. In 1564 he received the commission for the high altar of the Dominican church of S Domingo in Évora, Portugal, and the two panels that survive, the *Virgin and Child* and *St John the Baptist* (both Lisbon, Mus. N. A. Ant.), display a perfectly understood sense of Italianate monumentality and form. Workshop participation is again apparent in the altarpiece commissioned in 1565 by Ginés Martínez for the church of Higuera La Real and in the six panels (1567–70) that Morales contributed to the high altar of S Martín in Plasencia.

In 1564 Morales painted a portrait of the Bishop of Badajoz, *Juan de Ribera* (Madrid, Prado), and from that year he effectively became his official painter. Ribera, who was later made Archbishop of Valencia (1569), was an ardent reformer and sought to implement the decrees of the Council of Trent in his own diocese. He commissioned numerous works from Morales including the triptych of the *Ecce homo, the Virgin and St John* (1564–9; Cadiz, Viuda de Bueno priv. col., see Gaya Nuño, pl. 24), in which the Archbishop himself is represented beside his namesake saint, and the religious allegory of the *Judgement of the Soul of Juan de Ribera* (Valencia, Colegio del Patriarca), which shows an angel presenting the soul of the dead patron to the Trinity. Ribera may also have commissioned the *Holy Family* (New York, Hisp. Soc. America), one of Morales's most interesting works, which includes a diagram of the horoscope of Christ taken from *De astrorum iudiciis* (Basle, 1554), an edition of Ptolemy's *Tetrabiblos* by Gerolamo Cardano (1501–76). The inscription *Turris Ader* above the tower in the background has been shown to derive from Erasmus's commentary on the Gospel of St Luke, in which it is stated that there was a tower of this name close to Bethlehem. Although these arcane references might indicate patronage by the cultivated Archbishop, Trapier has argued that the use of the Lombard *sfumato* technique suggests a date after 1574, when Bernardino Luini's *Holy Family* (Madrid, Prado) was installed in the Escorial. This might explain the typological similarities of the Virgin and female attendant in the two paintings. A work that is closer in treatment and composition to the painting by Luini is the *Holy Family with St John the Baptist* (?mid-1570s) in the treasury of the Augustinian collegiate church of Roncesvalles. A variant of this work with the Virgin shown full-length and without St Joseph is in the New Cathedral in Salamanca. With its meticulous finish and steely colouring it constitutes one of Morales's most striking and memorable works.

Palomino states that Morales was invited to paint in the Escorial by Philip II but that, after executing several devotional works for the King ('since his ability was not suited to other things, nor to works on a large scale'), he returned to Badajoz, albeit generously recompensed. Philip is reputed to have given a painting of *Christ Bearing the Cross with the Virgin and St John* by Morales to the monastery of S Jerónimo in Madrid; this may perhaps be identified with the one formerly in the Mayorga Collection, Madrid. The figure of Christ in the latter is heavily dependent on Sebastiano del Piombo's famous prototype (1520; Madrid, Prado, no. 345), which the Spaniard copied several times (e.g. Barcelona, Grases priv. col., see Gaya Nuño, pl. 12; Valencia, Colegio del Patriarca).

Since Morales's works show little evolution of style, the chronology of his undocumented works remains uncertain, but from the documents it appears that his later years were marked by a decline in quality, a falling-off of commissions and by financial difficulties. His last major commission was the high altar (1575–6) of S Salvador in Elvas, Portugal, for which he painted three panels, the *Visitation, Adoration of the Magi* and *Presentation in the Temple*. Their poor state of preservation makes it difficult to comment on their quality.

BIBLIOGRAPHY

A. A. Palomino de Castro y Velasco: *Museo pictórico* (1715–24), iii; Eng. trans. by N. Alaya Mallory as *Lives of the Eminent Spanish Painters and Sculptors* (Cambridge, 1987), pp. 38–9
A. Rodríguez-Moñino: 'El Divino Morales en Portugal, 1565 y 1576', *Bol. Museus N. A. Ant.*, iii (1944), pp. 5–19
——: 'El retablo de Morales en Higuera la Real', *Bol. Soc. Esp. Excurs.*, liii (1945), pp. 25–56
——: 'El Beato Juan de Ribera y no el Beato Juan de Villegas', *A. Esp.*, xvi (1946), p. 39
E. Du Gué Trapier: *Luis de Morales and Leonardesque Influences in Spain* (New York, 1953)
D. Angulo Iñíguez: *Pintura del renacimento*, A. Hisp., xii (Madrid, 1954), pp. 231–46
J. A. Gaya Nuño: *Luis de Morales* (Madrid, 1961)
A. Bäcksbacka: *Luis de Morales* (Helsinki, 1962)
A. E. Pérez Sánchez: *El retablo de Morales en Arroyo de la Luz* (Madrid, 1974)
C. Solis Rodríguez: 'Luis de Morales: Nuevas aportaciones documentales', *Rev. Estud. Extrem.*, xxxiii (1977), pp. 571–652; xxxiv (1978), pp. 49–137
A. Rodríguez and G. de Ceballos: 'El mundo espiritual del pintor Luis de Morales', *Goya*, 196 (1987), pp. 194–203

GABRIELE FINALDI

Morales de los Ríos (y García Pimentel), Adolfo (*b* Seville, 10 March 1858; *d* Rio de Janeiro, 3 Sept 1928). Spanish architect, writer and teacher, active in Brazil. He was educated by the Jesuits at Puerto de Santa María and the Real Seminario de Nobles, Vergara. After an original preference for studying engineering in Madrid, he attended the Ecole d'Architecture in Paris from 1877 to 1882. His teachers included Jules Merindole (*d* 1888) and Genepin, through whom he met Viollet-le-Duc. After finishing his studies he returned to Spain and took part in numerous competitions: for the Casino at San Sebastián, the Mercado Central, Valencia, the Banco de España, Madrid, the Gran Teatro, Cadiz, and others. He also became active in politics, in the Reformista party, but was unsuccessful as a candidate and left for South America in 1889, settling permanently in Brazil. Based in Rio de Janeiro, he established an architectural career and became one of the more prominent exponents there of late 19th-century eclecticism. He typically worked on large, monumental projects, with spacious ground-plans and façades divided (in the French style) by projecting bays. Outstanding among these are the Escola (now Museu) Nacional de Belas Artes (1908) and the Tribunal Supremo, both in Rio, as well as hotels, mausolea and numerous temporary exhibition spaces. He also designed several houses in the neo-Mudéjar style, for example the building that is now the Instituto des Pesquisas Oswaldo Cruz, on the outskirts of Rio. His other activities included painting and sculpture, and he wrote on a variety of subjects. He held the chair of stereotomy at the Escola Nacional de Belas Artes, Rio de Janeiro, where he also taught composition and the history of architecture.

BIBLIOGRAPHY

A. Morales de los Ríos: *Figura, vida e obra de Adolfo Morales de los Ríos* (Rio de Janeiro, 1959)

A. Villar: 'Modernismo en Cádiz', *Archv Hispal.* (1973)

ALBERTO VILLAR MOVELLÁN

Moralis, Yannis (*b* Arta, 23 April 1916). Greek painter, printmaker, illustrator, stage designer and decorative artist. From 1931 to 1936 he studied painting and printmaking at the Higher School of Fine Arts in Athens under Konstantinos Parthenis and Yannis Kefallinos (1893–1957). As soon as he graduated he participated in the exhibition of Greek printmakers that was organized in Czechoslovakia in 1936. The same year, on a scholarship from the Academy of Athens, he went to Rome and then to Paris to study at the Ecole Supérieure des Beaux-Arts and the Ecole des Arts et Métiers. He returned to Athens in 1940, when he participated in the last pre-war panhellenic exhibition, in which he was awarded the first prize. During the period of the German occupation (1941–4) he started painting portraits to earn his living. In these his restricted palette and the opposition of light and shadow with as little half-tone as possible reveal his concern with the flattening of form and space. His post-war canvases are painted with a directness of execution and solidly modelled forms. His concern with the structure of form led him gradually to geometrical compositions. In 1949 he was among the founder-members of the art group Armos, which aimed to develop a modern idiom under the influence of the Ecole de Paris. He had promoted this idea since becoming professor of painting at the Higher School of Fine Arts in Athens (1947–84). From 1958 to 1962 he designed the linear composition of an antique procession, executed on marble, for the façades of the Hilton Hotel, Athens. After the 1960s he painted monumental compositions with archaic forms inspired by Classical Attic gravestones. His leitmotif was the female figure represented with a strong frontal light within geometrical spaces with simple tonal contrasts. In his later works his concern for abstraction led him to the painting of monumental archaic forms and linear patterns. He was also actively involved in engraving, book illustration and stage design for over 30 dramas and ballets. He designed posters, building façades and interiors as well as a large number of compositions in stone, ceramic and wood for public buildings, and tapestries for which he received the gold medal at the Internationalen Handwerkersmesse in Munich in 1973. He participated in numerous panhellenic and international group exhibitions, including the Venice Biennale (1958), and had many one-man shows in Greece.

FANI-MARIA TSIGAKOU

Moran, Thomas (*b* Bolton, Lancs, 12 Jan 1837; *d* Santa Barbara, CA, 26 Aug 1926). American painter and printmaker of English birth. His brothers Edward (1829–1901), John (*fl* 1860–71) and Peter (1841–1914) were also active as artists. His family emigrated from England and in 1845 settled in Philadelphia where Moran began his career as an illustrator. He was guided by his brother Edward, an associate of the marine painter James Hamilton, whose successful career afforded an example for Moran. Between the ages of 16 and 19 Moran was apprenticed to the Philadelphia wood-engraving firm Scattergood & Telfer; he then began to paint more seriously in watercolour and expanded his work as an illustrator. In the 1860s he produced lithographs of the landscapes around the Great Lakes. While in London in 1861 (the first of many trips to England) he was introduced to the work of J. M. W. Turner, which remained a vital influence on him throughout his career. Moran owned a set of the *Liber studiorum* and was particularly impressed by Turner's colour and sublime conception of landscape. With his wife, Mary Nimmo Moran (1842–99), an etcher and landscape painter, he participated in the etching revival, scraping fresh and romantic landscapes and reproductive etchings (e.g. *Conway Castle, after J. M. W. Turner*, 1879). During the 1870s and 1880s his designs for wood-engraved illustrations appeared in most of the major magazines and in gift books, which brought him money and recognition.

Between 1871 and 1892 Moran travelled extensively in the western USA, visiting Yosemite, the Teton Mountains, New Mexico and Arizona, as well as Mexico. He achieved his first success as a painter in oil and watercolour after he had been commissioned to illustrate a *Scribner's* article on the Yellowstone area. During the summer of 1871 and in the company of the photographer WILLIAM HENRY JACKSON, Moran drew and painted in watercolour hundreds of sketches of the spectacular, and then virtually unknown, regions of Wyoming Territory. Moran kept these sketches (Yellowstone National Park) all his life. He used them as the basis for the many fully realized watercolours commissioned in the 1870s and for a very large painting, *Grand Canyon of the Yellowstone* (1872; Washington, DC, US Dept Interior, on loan to Washington, DC, N. Mus. Amer. A.). The reception of this picture as 'the finest historical landscape yet painted in this country' (*New York Tribune*) signalled Moran's emergence as a rival to Albert Bierstadt and assured him recognition in the final years of the popularity of landscape as grand, exotic spectacle. The sketches were used as part of the successful campaign to designate Yellowstone the first national park. His monumental canvas was the first landscape painting to be purchased by the US government (in 1872) and quickly became a symbol of territorial exploration and westward expansion. It was followed two years later by an equally ambitious painting, *Chasm of the Colorado* (1873–4; Washington, DC, US Dept Interior, on loan to Washington, DC, N. Mus. Amer. A.; see fig.), inspired by sketches

Thomas Moran: *Chasm of the Colorado*, oil on canvas, 2.14×3.68 m, 1873–4 (Washington, DC, US Department of the Interior, on loan to Washington, DC, National Museum of American Art)

made in the Grand Canyon region in 1873. Although the government purchased this painting as a pendant to *Grand Canyon of the Yellowstone*, critics greeted it much less enthusiastically and most recoiled at its overpowering and forbidding vista, which for them lacked necessary human reference and, therefore, meaning. Perhaps influenced by such criticism, Moran never again attempted such a daring composition or so large a canvas, and he returned to more acceptable landscapes, such as the *Mountain of the Holy Cross* (1875; priv. col.).

Moran also visited Italy twice (in 1886 and 1890) and began to spend more time in East Hampton, Long Island, NY. His most lyrical paintings explore the relation of architecture to water in Venice and East Hampton. By 1900 Moran's popularity had waned and many of his major canvases went unsold. Although he maintained his appeal with a broad public, he was out of favour with critics and artists. He spent his last years between East Hampton and Santa Barbara, CA, recreating his favourite subjects, especially the varied landscape of the Grand Canyon.

UNPUBLISHED SOURCES
East Hampton, NY, Lib. [MS] Tulsa, OK, Gilcrease Inst. Amer. Hist. & A. [MS]

BIBLIOGRAPHY
'Fine Arts: Mr. Thomas Moran's "Great Canon of the Yellowstone"', *New York Tribune* (4 May 1872), p. 2
T. Wilkins: *Thomas Moran: Artist of the Mountains* (Norman, OK, 1966)
The Drawings and Watercolors of Thomas Moran (1837–1926) (exh. cat. by T. S. Fern, South Bend, U. Notre Dame, 1976)
C. Clark: *Thomas Moran's Watercolors of the American West* (Austin, TX, 1980)
A. Morand and N. Friese: *The Prints of Thomas Moran in the Thomas Gilcrease Institute of American History and Art, Tulsa, Oklahoma* (Tulsa, 1986)
J. Kinsey: *Thomas Moran and the Surveying of the West* (Washington, DC, 1992)

CAROL CLARK

Morandi. *See* TERRIBILIA.

Morandi, Giorgio (*b* Bologna, 20 July 1890; *d* Bologna, 18 June 1964). Italian painter, draughtsman and printmaker. At the age of 17 he enrolled at the Accademia di Belle Arti in Bologna and discovered contemporary art in books on Impressionism, Paul Cézanne, Georges Seurat and Henri Rousseau. He read with interest the articles by Ardengo Soffici in *La voce* and saw the Venice Biennale of 1910, where he first came across the painting of Auguste Renoir. During this period he often went to Florence to study the works of Giotto, Masaccio and Paolo Uccello. Between 1911 and 1914, when he was in Rome, he was impressed by the work of Claude Monet and, especially, Paul Cézanne. At the Futurist exhibition *Lacerba*, held in the Libreria Gonnelli, Florence, in 1913–14, he met Umberto Boccioni. Shortly afterwards he showed his first paintings at the Albergo Baglioni in Bologna and the Galleria Sprovieri in Rome. When he was not painting, he taught drawing in primary schools. As an adolescent he associated with those most receptive to new ideas in Bologna, including the painter Osvaldo Licini and the writer Mario Bacchelli. In 1918–19 he worked with Bacchelli and Giuseppe Raimondi (1898–1976) on the Bologna magazine *La raccolta* and came into contact with Mario Broglio, editor of the Rome review *Valori plastici*. Morandi lived in Bologna throughout his life, except for a number of short stays during World War II in the neighbouring village of Grizzana, where he painted some landscapes.

Giorgio Morandi: *Still-life*, oil on canvas, 375×457 mm, 1946 (London, Tate Gallery)

Morandi worked in a figurative and increasingly symbolic mode and had a cautious and disciplined approach to his work. He tirelessly repainted the same subjects (mainly still-lifes in the studio) with an intellectually rigorous approach like that of Cézanne, in order to convey a personal sense of time and of the reach of memory and to bring out the unique qualities of the object, which he imbued with a sense of vulnerability and which he approached with awe. Morandi was neither isolated nor ascetic, but an artist conscious of the results of the figurative avant-garde movements and of the events of his time. The classical nature of his style is apparent in his craftsmanlike compositional rigour.

The few early landscapes by Morandi that have survived are constructed in units in the manner of Cézanne and show a considered understanding of tonal values, as in, for example, *Landscape* (1913; Rome, priv. col., see Vitali, 1970, pl. 4). While Italian art was shaken by Futurism, Morandi developed his pictorial researches in a highly personal direction, seeking to reconcile visual and cognitive experience. At this time he painted objects in thin colours, for example *Still-life* (1914; New York, MOMA), which depicts traditional Cubist subject-matter. Although, like those of Georges Braque and Picasso, these objects create

a rhythmic context, they are suffused with a lyricism not found in the work of the Cubists. In his progressive development of the theories of Cézanne, whose work he admired at the Rome Secession in 1914, Morandi captured forms in the fleeting essence of profile and imbued them with a transient quality. He produced refined compositions of flowers (e.g. *Flowers*, 1916; Rome, priv. col., see Vitali, 1970, pl. 25) in which the objects become central figures in an enchanted silent life and mirror the artist's aspirations to harmony and clarity in perception.

Around 1918 Morandi produced his own interpretation of Pittura Metafisica, not by exploring the allusive, as Carlo Carrà and Giorgio de Chirico did, but by concentrating on the more tangible: his compositions of objects and outlines as, for example, in the *Still-life* (1918; St Petersburg, Hermitage), with its dummy torso in a box-like construction, already have a vitality of their own in their calibrated and rigorous formal arrangements. Closely related to the formal strictness of these paintings, which were more metaphysical in atmosphere than in subject-matter, were the innovations in perspective of the 1920s, when Morandi rediscovered Paolo Uccello and Piero della Francesca. Rather than resurrecting their use of space or their luminosity, he was inspired by them in his use of spatial intervals, the interrelations of forms and the use of light brushing against the object to articulate the object and its essential nature. In his contact with his fellow contributors to the magazine *Valori plastici* in 1920–21, Morandi reflected on the increasing trend for the 'rappel à l'ordre' (a return to classical values) and also on the alternatives that the leading artists of the day were proposing in opposition to the fragmented figurative avant-garde. During these years Morandi's attitude to the work of Jean-Siméon Chardin and Jean-Baptiste-Camille Corot seems to have changed: what Morandi wanted from them was the possibility of giving immediacy to the mundane objects that fascinated him, which he wished to place in an unlimited space that was free from the chance element of impressionistic phenomena.

Even though Morandi exhibited with de Chirico and Carrà in Berlin and Florence in 1921 and in the first two *Novecento italiano* exhibitions (1926 and 1929), he did not ally himself with any group but continued to pursue his own idea of natural truth. He was given no official recognition at the time, but the most aware critics, including Ardengo Soffici, Roberto Longhi and Cesare Brandi, realised the great value of the intimacy of his objects and the emotional content of his work. Morandi's still-life subject matter became increasingly elaborate. The result of this, together with his extreme sensitivity in the use of light, was that the most ordinary shapes (such as pots, bottles and boxes) took on a further meaning: they became impressive either because of their potential monumentality, which gave them the mysterious and elusive aura of a cathedral, or because their allusions took the viewer by surprise or gradually became apparent, as can be seen in *Still-life* (1946; London, Tate; see fig.). Sometimes reality was as if spellbound, and the objects conveyed a sense of timelessness.

When Morandi took up landscape painting again at Grizzana after 1940 he eschewed any sort of descriptiveness and chose a more sustained substance in colour, based above all on sunlit or rotting shades of green, calcareous blues and a wide range of ochres as in, for example, *Landscape* (1943; Rome, priv. col., see Vitali, 1970, pl. 156). Here, the more fluid brushwork immobilizes the disquieting force of the material and gives the spectator a sense of the silent vibrations of the natural world.

Morandi achieved remarkable results in his drawings and prints. His use in his etchings of opposed and intersecting lines, cut at various levels and thicknesses, is further evidence of the dedicated manner in which he developed his compositions, for example in *Large Still-life with Fourteen Objects* (1934; see Basile, p. 143). As in his painting, the light impregnates the objects and radiates out from them in a series of pulsations, reflecting Morandi's personal emotional response; the chiaroscuros, graduated by line, evoke the quality of the materials, characterize the objects and suggest their aura. Even in the plainest drawings, which are never repetitive but intended to investigate the essence of the object, for example the late *Still-life* (1962; untraced, see E. Tavoni, ed., *Morandi: Disegni*, ii, no. 493), depicting only one object, it is possible to find the basis of Morandi's restrained and intense approach and his combination of intellect and emotion.

BIBLIOGRAPHY

F. Arcangeli: *12 opere di Giorgio Morandi* (Milan, 1950)
G. Gnudi: *Giorgio Morandi* (Florence, 1950)
G. Brandi: *Morandi* (Florence, 1953)
F. Arcangeli: *Giorgio Morandi* (Milan, 1964, R 1968)
A. Martini: *Giorgio Morandi* (Milan, 1964)
M. Carrà: 'Carrà e Morandi', *A. Mod.*, 75 (1967), pp. 81–112, 118–20, 343–8
J. Leymarie: *Gli acquarelli di Morandi* (Bologna, 1968)
F. Solmi: *Giorgio Morandi, storia e leggenda* (Bologna, 1968)
G. Marchiori: *Giorgio Morandi: Le incisioni* (Rome and Venice, 1969)
G. Raimondi: *Anni con Giorgio Morandi* (Milan, 1970)
L. Vitali: *Giorgio Morandi pittore* (Milan, 1970)
V. Zurlini: *50 acquarelli di Giorgio Morandi* (Turin, 1973)
L. Vitali: *Morandi: Catalogo generale*, 2 vols (Milan, 1977)
E. Tavoni, ed.: *Morandi: Disegni*, 2 vols (Rome, 1981 & 1984)
Giorgio Morandi (exh. cat., preface J. T. Demetrion, texts C. Magnani and J. M. Lukach; San Francisco, CA, MOMA; New York, Guggenheim; Des Moines, IA, A. Cent.; 1981)
Giorgio Morandi (exh. cat., Madrid, Paseo Castellana, 1984)
F. Basile: *Morandi incisore* (Bologna, 1985)
Giorgio Morandi (exh. cat. by P. G. Castagnoli and others, Leningrad, Hermitage; Bologna, Gal. Com. A. Mod.; Milan, Civ. Mus. A. Contemp.; 1989)
Giorgio Morandi, 1890–1990 (exh. cat. by M. Pasquali and others, Bologna, Gal. Com. A. Mod., 1990)
Morandi (exh. cat. by P. G. Castagnoli and S. Evangelisti, Budapest, Mus. F.A., 1991)
Giorgio Morandi, artista d'Europa (exh. cat. by M. Pasquali, Brussels, Le Botanique, 1992)

PIERO PACINI

Morandi, Riccardo (*b* Rome, 1 Sept 1902; *d* Rome, 25 Dec 1989). Italian engineer and teacher. Having graduated from the Scuola di Applicazione per Ingegneri in Rome in 1927, he began to specialize in structural calculation and technological experimentation, his research focusing on problems in the calculation, design and construction of large structures. He became chiefly concerned with the design and building of constructions in reinforced concrete, and he paid particular attention to the innovative aspects of this technology, especially the use of pre-stressed reinforced concrete. His work can be linked to the strain of constructional rationalism originating in 19th-century designs for bridges, viaducts, factories and large-span roofing, as well as to the 20th-century works of Pier Luigi Nervi, Robert Maillart, Félix Candela and Eduardo Torroja y Miret, with whom Morandi contributed to the transformation of reinforced concrete from a purely structural medium to an instrument of architectural expression. Morandi's works often appear as features within the landscape, characterizing the surrounding area. One of his most famous executed projects is the bridge (1957–62) on Lake Maracaibo, Venezuela, which is *c*. 9 km long, with five central spans of 235 m each and with trestles 100 m high. In Italy he built, among other projects, the terminal (1957–60; with Vincenzo Monaco and Amedeo Luccichenti) for the Leonardo da Vinci Airport, Fiumicino, Rome, and numerous bridges for the Autostrada del Sole, and the motorway viaduct (1960–65) over the River Polcevera near Genoa. He also collaborated with Gustavo Colonnetti and Piero Gazzola on the project (1961; unexecuted) for the raising of the temples at Abu Simbel in Egypt, and he taught at the universities of Florence, Rome and Florida.

WRITINGS
Forma e struttura dei ponti (Florence, 1959)

BIBLIOGRAPHY
G. Boaga, ed.: *Riccardo Morandi* (Bologna, 1984)
G. Imbesi, M. Morandi and F. Moschini, eds: *Riccardo Morandi* (Rome, 1991)

MATILDE BAFFA RIVOLTA

Morandini (da Poppi), Francesco. *See* POPPI.

Morando, Bernardo (*b* Padua, *c.* 1540; *d* Zamość, 1600–01). Italian architect, active in Poland. He is first mentioned in Poland in 1569 as the architect who continued the extension of the Royal Castle in Warsaw. He visited France between 1573 and *c.* 1575 and then entered the service of Chancellor Jan Zamoyski as designer and builder. In 1578 Zamoyski commissioned him to plan the new town of Zamość, which was founded on 3 April 1580, and which took some 20 years to complete. One of the finest Renaissance urban schemes in northern Europe, it was the forerunner of a number of Polish town centres that were laid out on a rectangular grid plan on the estates of noblemen in accordance with the principles expounded in such Italian treatises as Pietro Cataneo's *I quattro primi libri dell'architettura* (Venice, 1554; for further discussion of the urban planning *see* ZAMOŚĆ). Morando also designed many of the principal buildings at Zamość, including the collegiate church, university (the academy), town hall, standard tenement blocks and bastion fortification gateways (mostly rebuilt in the second quarter of the 17th century and first half of the 19th); he endowed these buildings with the forms of early classicizing Venetian Mannerism, current some 50 years previously and mainly derived from Giovanni Maria Falconetto and Michele Sanmicheli. He also borrowed ideas from Sebastiano Serlio's treatise. The most outstanding of his works in Zamość is the collegiate church (1587–98 and later; elevations altered *c.* 1820). It is an Italianate basilica with a five-bay nave (vaulted after 1613), aisles and side chapels. The lower, polygonal choir features a coffered vault. The Corinthian order is used to articulate the nave, with Doric in the aisles and pilasters in the chapels. Light and dark elements are alternated in a Mannerist way, while the regular articulation of the orders ensures a harmonious effect. Morando's work greatly influenced the Italian architects in Lwów (now Lviv), and through them the south-east regions of Poland (now the Ukraine).

PSB

BIBLIOGRAPHY
W. Tatarkiewicz: 'Bernardo Morando: Réalisateur de la ville idéale', *Atti del XVIII congresso internazionale di storia dell'arte: Venice, 1956*, pp. 297–9
A. Miłobędzki: *Zarys dziejów architektury w Polsce* [An outline of architecture in Poland] (Warsaw, 1963, rev. 3/1978), pp. 149–52, 164
W. Kalinowski: *City Development in Poland up to the Mid-19th Century* (Warsaw, 1966), p. 96
J. Kowalczyk: *Kolegiata w Zamościu* [The collegiate church in Zamość] (Warsaw, 1968)
——: *Zamość: Città ideale in Polonia: Il fondatore Jan Zamoyski e l'architetto Bernardo Morando* (Wrocław, 1986)

ADAM MIŁOBĘDZKI

Morando, Paolo. *See* CAVAZZOLA, PAOLO.

Morani, Vincenzo (*b* Polistena, nr Reggio Calabria, 12 July 1809; *d* Rome, 1870). Italian painter. The son of the engraver and painter Fortunato Morani (*d* 1844), he enrolled in the Accademia di Belle Arti in Naples in 1828, where he was a pupil of Costanzo Angelini and Camillo Guerra (1797–1852). In 1834 he went to Rome, having won a scholarship set up by the Bourbon court for the most deserving pupils of the Accademia. In Rome he was encouraged to work in the style established by Vincenzo Camuccini and was also introduced to the work of the German painter Friedrich Overbeck, which had a considerable influence on him. In 1831 Morani was commissioned to paint frescoes for the refectory of the Benedictine monastery of Santa Trinità at Cava de' Tirreni. He painted a large scene of the *Pilgrimage of Pope Urban II and Count Roger the Norman*. At Cava de' Tirreni he met the Scottish Romantic novelist Walter Scott, who entrusted him with the task of copying certain manuscripts in the monastery library at Cava, some of which were later published by the historian and palaeographer Scipione Volpicella. For the Bourbon court he painted a *Holy Family* (1846) and a *Crucifixion* (1847; both Naples, New Cemetery).

Between 1840 and 1850, after returning to Rome, Morani painted the frescoes in the chapel of the Palazzo Torlonia at Castelgandolfo and on the ceilings of the Palazzo Conti and Palazzo Torlonia. In 1854 he created a fresco for the Roman church of S Paolo fuori le Mura. During the same period he also sent a number of works to the abbey church of Santa Trinità at Cava de' Tirreni, a *Deposition* (1852), *St Benedict Sending his Disciple St Placidus to Sicily* (1853) and the *Martyrdom of St Felicity and her Seven Sons* (1856), all of which have a strongly naturalistic quality, even though in their composition and use of pose and gesture they are inspired by Classical prototypes. In 1857 Morani was again summoned to Cava, this time to paint frescoes for the vaults of the abbey church.

Thieme-Becker

BIBLIOGRAPHY
P. Guillaume: *Essai historique sur l'Abbaye de Cava* (1877)
A. Busiri Vici: *Accademia romana di San Luca* (1895)

ROSANNA CIOFFI

Mora Noli, José Guillermo (*b* Panama City, 24 Dec 1923; *d* Panama City, 4 Jan 1981). Panamanian sculptor and printmaker. He trained under the painters Humberto Ivaldi and Carlos Villalaz (1900–66). He held his first important one-man show in Panama in 1944 and left soon after to study at the Art Institute of Chicago and at the Art Students League in New York. He spent the rest of his life in Panama, where he taught art and produced numerous sculptures and murals for public buildings. Mora Noli invented *Cilindrismo*, which was a theory of Constructivist sculpture. He was the first Panamanian to create monumental sculptures, for example the statue to the heroine *Rufina Alfaro* (granite, 1947; Los Santos, Parque 10 de noviembre); because of his concern with historical and nationalist themes he also received numerous commissions for busts of illustrious Panamanian figures. In sculptures such as *Choco Indian* (mahogany, 1945; Panama City, Mus. Antropol. Reina Torres Araúz) he favoured rough surfaces rather than a polished finish in order to emphasize form and an expressive content.

BIBLIOGRAPHY
Encuentro de Escultura (exh. cat., ed. M. E. Kupfer; Panama City, Mus. A. Contemp., 1978), pp. 40–41

MONICA E. KUPFER

Morante, Pedro Diaz. *See* DIAZ MORANTE, PEDRO.

Morava. River valley near Niš in Serbia. Gabriel Millet first used the name Morava to distinguish the school of architecture and painting represented by the monastery churches built there between the reign of Prince Lazar (*reg* 1371–89) and 1459 when the castle of Smederevo was surrendered to the Turks.

1. ARCHITECTURE. The principal features of Morava church architecture are the trefoil plan and the rich sculptural ornament that decorates the articulated façades. Most churches were built in the Byzantine masonry style with alternating courses of brick and stone. The trefoil plan was derived from the churches on MT ATHOS, and it developed into two distinct types, represented by the churches at Kruševac (*c.* 1377–8) and Ravanica (*c.* 1375–7). The latter was founded by Prince Lazar, who was later buried there; it stands behind a long, white wall that formed part of the original monastery enclosure. Apses on the east, north and south sides create the church's trefoil plan; it is surmounted by five domes, the central one resting on four piers, while the smaller corner domes are raised on square pedestals. A similar design was used for the churches at Ljubostinja (*c.* 1385), Nova Pavlica (*c.* 1385), Drenča (1382) and at Resava (*c.* 1406–18; now Manasija), which was the principal foundation of Stephen Lazarević (*reg* 1389–1427). It is made almost entirely of ashlar stone and together with the remains of other conventual buildings is surrounded by high defensive walls reinforced by 11 towers. The Lazarica of Kruševac, Prince Lazar's court chapel, has a simpler plan. Its single main dome rests on a square base but has no internal supports; a massive belfry surmounts the narthex. Among the monastic churches that follow this design are those at Gornjak (*c.* 1380), Naupara (*c.* 1380), Kalenić (*c.* 1413) and Lipovac (1399).

A feature shared by all these churches is the ornamental carving of various tightly knit interlaces or rinceaux and fabulous animals that decorate the window and door arches, pilaster strips, rose windows and blind arches of the façades. Perhaps the most exuberant example of this kind of decoration is the church at Kalenić (1413–17). Occasionally, as in the church at Ljubostinja, the motifs used in Morava sculpture are also painted on to the building's exterior. The origin of these motifs is uncertain, with scholars tracing them to Russia, Armenia and Georgia (Korać), as well as to Western art.

2. PAINTINGS. The development of a Morava school of painting did not really begin until the 1380s, when it is probable that artists trained in Thessaloniki painted the wall paintings in the church at Ravanica. Above this church's west entrance is the *Assumption of the Virgin*, with Prince Lazar and his family depicted on the left. On the walls and vault of the nave are scenes from the *Life of Christ*, the *Passion* and *Twelve Great Feasts*. The central apse is filled with portraits of the saints, the *Communion of the Apostles* and in the vault the *Virgin and Child with Angels*. This iconographic programme with its emphasis on Christ's ministry and the use of medallion portraits of the saints to divide the zones and decorate the arches and columns was followed in the Morava's other churches. Other characteristic features include the presence of warrior saints in the side apses, the use of architectural backgrounds and the modelling of faces and figures in the Palaeologan idiom. The wall paintings in the churches at Ljubostinja, Nova Pavlica and Rudenica reveal a close association with the work of John the Painter from Prilep, some of whose finest paintings (1389) are in the monastery of St Andrew on the Treska River. Here and in the Morava churches flesh is portrayed with dark shadows and sharp reflections of light, while the elaborate folds of the clinging drapery convey the forms of the figures beneath.

In the early 15th century a new artistic style began to develop; it is reflected in the second layer of wall paintings in the church at Ljubostinja, which were painted by John's brother, Makarios the Painter. This was also the period when the churches at Sisojevac, Resava (built *c.* 1408–18) and Kalenić were painted, probably by artists who had trained at Thessaloniki; the wall paintings at Sisojevac and Resava have been likened to those in the chapel of the Anargyroi in the monastery of Vatopedi on Mt Athos (see

Morava, Resava (now Manasija) Church, south apse, wall painting of *SS Artemius and Jacob*, early 15th century

Djurić, 1960). As Stephen Lazarević's mausoleum, the church at Resava contains what are often considered to be the best examples of Serbian Orthodox painting. The wall paintings include the *Dormition of the Virgin* and a portrait of the founder with a model of the church on the west wall above and to the left of the entrance respectively; the *Life of the Virgin* and the *Passion* on the side walls of the nave; medallions of saints on the piers; *Parables* and full-length portraits of warrior and other saints in the central and side apses (see fig.). The figures are depicted wearing contemporary clothing and with recognizably individual features, and set against architectural backgrounds. Despite the inclusion of many details of everyday life, however, these wall paintings, unlike Western art, continue to be subordinated to the Byzantine ideas of the abstract and divine in which the use of gold for nimbi and drapery symbolizes the presence of the Holy Spirit. Although the wall paintings in the church at Kalenić are of a similar date, they have a more delicate and melancholy quality than those at Resava and may be the work of the miniature painter Radoslav. They include a portrait of the founder on the north wall of the narthex and the usual scenes from the *Life of Christ* and *Life of the Virgin* on the nave and narthex walls respectively. The miraculous atmosphere of these scenes is emphasized by the use of *sfumato* in the outlines of figures and buildings.

BIBLIOGRAPHY

V. J. Djurić: 'Solunsko poreklo resavskog živopisa' [The Thessalonican origins of the painting at Resava], *Zbornik Radova Vizant. Inst.*, vi (1960), pp. 119–24

——: 'Freske crkvice sv. Besrebrnika despota Jovana Uglješe u Vatopedu i njihov značaj za ispitivanje solunskog porekla resavskog živopisa [Wall paintings in the chapel of the Anargyroi at Vatopedi and their significance for the research into the Thessalonican origins of the painting at Resava], *Zbornik Radova Vizant. Inst.*, vii (1961), pp. 125–37

——: 'Nastanak graditeljskog stila Moravske škole' [The development of the architectural style of the Morava school], *Zbornik Likovne Umetnosti*, i (1965), pp. 33–60

——: *La Peinture murale de l'Ecole de la Morava* (Belgrade, 1968)

V. Korać: 'Les Origines de l'architecture de l'Ecole de la Morava', *L'Ecole de la Morava et son temps: Belgrade, 1968*, pp. 157–68

J. Maksimović: 'Moravska skulptura' [Moravian sculpture], *L'Ecole de la Morava et son temps: Belgrade, 1968*, pp. 181–8

V. J. Djurić: 'Srpski državni sabori u Peći i crkveno graditeljstvo [State councils in Peć and church architecture], *Le Prince Lazar*, ed. I. Božić and V. J. Djurić (Belgrade, 1975), pp. 105–21

SRDJAN DJURIĆ

Moravia. *See under* CZECH REPUBLIC.

Moravian Brethren [Herrnhuters; Renewed Church of the Brethren; Unitas Fratrum (Unity of Brethren); now officially the Moravian Church]. Protestant Episcopal church. Originating among followers of Jan Huss (*c.* 1372–1415), the Brethren regarded the Scriptures (interpreted by the community) as the sole rule for faith and conduct. Taking Christ's Sermon on the Mount as their model, they stressed personal piety while rejecting military service, the pursuit of wealth and the veneration of saints. During the Reformation the group formed alliances with both the German Lutherans and the Polish Calvinists, uniting with the Poles at the Synod of Kozminek (1555). They were among the first Protestant groups to emphasize the value of education, so that in 1609 Emperor Rudolf II handed over to their administration the University of Prague as part of his guarantee of Bohemian rights, and the influential educator Johannes Comenius (1592–1670) was a prominent Moravian clergyman. Vigorously suppressed after the Battle of White Mountain (1620), in 1722 remnants of the Brethren accepted the offer of sanctuary of Nikolaus Ludwig, Graf von Zinzendorf (1700–60), on one of his Saxon estates, and it is from this period that the sect dates its 'renewal'. Under the Zinzendorf patronage (the Count was both the Brethren's feudal lord and later bishop, while his countess, Erdmuth Dorothea von Zinzendorf, administered its finances), the Moravians began the evangelical projects for which they became widely known. Satellite communities were founded in Europe, and missions were sent to the Danish West Indies, Greenland, Africa and Asia, while settlements were established in North America as centres for both Native American and immigrant evangelization (e.g. Savannah, GA, 1735; Nazareth, PA, 1740; Bethlehem, PA, 1741; and Salem, NC, 1766). Reflecting the communal aspects of their belief and polity, Moravian settlements were planned communities, combining industrial, agricultural and domestic structures. Their 18th-century colonial architecture (which is richly documented) was based on a German vocabulary; such elements as herringbone-pattern doors and steeply pitched tile roofs (pierced by multi-storey dormers) contrasted with contemporary structures of the communities' English neighbours. Moravians excelled at handicrafts: a memorandum (1756) from Bethlehem, PA, lists 47 kinds of activity, including such technologically advanced trades as organ-building and clockmaking. Their work as gunsmiths, brassfounders and potters was particularly highly valued in North America.

In keeping with their general emphasis on inner spirituality, the Moravian cult tends towards simplicity. The liturgy (published in the *Hymn Book*) is similar to that of the Lutherans, while the 'lovefeast' is a Moravian innovation. Music, both hymns and highly developed concerted works, is of high importance, and the sect supports an agency, the Moravian Music Foundation, Inc., Winston-Salem, NC, for its preservation and study. Pictorial decoration is allowed, Moravians having no tradition of iconoclasm, but its purpose is didactic and not ornamental; the paintings by preacher–artist John Valentine Haydt (1700–80) of the *Life of Christ* in the Old Chapel, Bethlehem, were hung without frames 'so that it should not appear that they were placed there with a view to ornament the building'. Unique to Moravians, but largely abandoned by modern congregations, was their traditional practice of burial by 'choirs'. The dead were divided, not by family, but by sex, age and marital status, their graves marked by uniform monuments of simple, low, stone slabs (scrubbed annually by the congregation on Holy Saturday). Such cemeteries were precursors of modern military cemeteries and present an irenic view unique in necrological architecture. In 1988 the Moravian Church included 500,000 members (divided into 22 governing 'Provinces'), the largest number of which were in Africa.

BIBLIOGRAPHY

D. Cranz: *Alte und neue Brüder-Historie oder Kurzefasste Geschichte der evangelischen Brüder-Unität*, (Barby, 1771); Eng. trans as *The Ancient and Modern History of the Brethren: Or, a Succinct Narrative of the Protestant Church of the United Brethren* (London, 1780)

A. G. Spangenberg: *An Exposition of Christian Doctrine as Taught in the Protestant Church of the United Bretheren or the Unitas Fratrum* (London, 1784)

J. T. Müller: *Geschichte der böhmischen Brüder*, 3 vols (Herrnhut, 1922–31)

J. T. Hamilton and K. G. Hamilton: *History of the Moravian Church, 1722–1957* (Bethlehem, PA, 1967)

W. Murtagh: *Moravian Architecture and Town Planning* (Chapel Hill, 1967)

Hymnal and Liturgies of the Moravian Church (Elk Grove, IL, 1969)

C. Reed: *Henry Chapman and the Moravian Pottery and Tile Works* (Philadelphia, 1987)

MICHAEL LINTON

Morazzone, il [Mazzucchelli, Pier Francesco] (*b* Morazzone, 3 July 1573; *d* 1625/6). Italian painter and draughtsman. With Cerano, Giulio Cesare Procaccini and Tanzio da Varallo he was one of the principal Lombard painters of the early 17th century. Like many of his contemporaries, he was strongly affected by the piety and mysticism of the teaching of St Carlo Borromeo, yet his work is distinguished from theirs by a greater classicism, owing to his training in Rome. He is well known for his altarpieces, but his outstanding achievements are large decorative frescoes for the sacrimonti at Varallo and Varese (*see* SACROMONTE and VARALLO, SACRO MONTE, §2 and fig. 2). He was an original draughtsman, and the major collections of his drawings are in Milan (Bib. Ambrosiana) and Florence (Uffizi).

1. Training and early works, to 1611. 2. Later works, after 1611.

1. TRAINING AND EARLY WORKS, TO 1611. Morazzone was taken to Rome before 1592 by his father, a master mason. Borsieri (1619) claimed that he was taught there principally by the Sienese painter Ventura Salimbeni, whereas Baglione (1642) stated that he frequented the various academies of Rome. It is likely that he also gained experience in the workshop of the Cavaliere d'Arpino. In Rome, Morazzone worked in several important churches, including S Maria Maddalena delle Convertite, the courtyard of S Giovanni in Laterano and the sacristy of St Peter's. The only such works to have survived are two frescoes in the church of S Silvestro in Capite, a *Visitation* and an *Adoration of the Magi*. These works draw on a variety of stylistic sources and suggest a response to the art of Taddeo Zuccari and of Sienese followers of Federico Barocci such as Salimbeni.

Around 1597, for reasons that are not clear, Morazzone left Rome, and by 1598 he was in Varese. His first documented works there are vault frescoes of *Musician Angels* and the *Coronation of the Virgin* in the chapel of the Rosary in S Vittore. He soon established himself in Lombardy and in Piedmont. In 1602 he worked in Milan Cathedral, with Paolo Camillo Landriani ('il Duchino', 1560–1618) on the *Meeting of St Carlo Borromeo with Duke Emanuel-Philibert of Savoy*, and alone on *St Carlo Borromeo Refusing Ecclesiastical Benefices* (both *in situ*), parts of a cycle of paintings illustrating the saint's life. His frescoes in the chapel of S Giorgio in the Santuario at Rho, showing scenes from the *Life of St George* (probably commissioned prior to 1603), indicate that at this point he was moving away from Roman Mannerism and developing a more typically Lombard style, strongly influenced by the early 16th-century art of Gaudenzio Ferrari. There followed frescoes of scenes from the *Life of a Martyred Soldier* (1603–6) in the church of the Crocefisso at Tradate. Here

stylistic differences between the central and lateral scenes have led some to consider the fresco on the altar wall as the work of another artist.

In 1605–6 Morazzone worked for the first time on the sacromonte at Varallo, frescoing the chapel of the *Ascent to Calvary*. The contract for this work, which had been drawn up in 1602, stipulated that he model his work on Ferrari's frescoes (*c*. 1509) for the chapel of the *Crucifixion*. This influence shows in the realism of the soldiers riding through a broad landscape, which serves as a backdrop to sculpted figures by Jean de Wespin. In 1608 Morazzone was commissioned to paint 12 small scenes from the *Life of St Abbondio* to be set into the embroidery of the standard of the Compagnia del SS Sacramento of Como (Como Cathedral). He received payments in 1609 and 1610, which suggests that his work on these paintings alternated with work on frescoes of the *Passion* (completed May 1609) in the chapel of the Flagellation on another sacromonte, that at Varese. The putti in the frescoes at Varese reveal the lingering influence of the Cavaliere d'Arpino's method of composition (1962 exh. cat., p. 45).

On 25 July 1609 Morazzone was commissioned to execute the frescoes in the chapel of the Ecce homo on the sacromonte of Varallo (*see* VARALLO, SACRO MONTE, fig. 2). Here he worked (1610) with the sculptor Giovanni d'Enrico to create a *tour de force* of illusionism: d'Enrico's terracotta figures are surrounded by Morazzone's painted scenes, the frescoes fully integrating with the sculptures to give an impression of extended space. A fresco of *Vulcan's Forge* (Milan, Castello Sforzesco), originating from a house in Morazzone traditionally identified as the painter's own, also dates from this period. In the *Annunciation* (*c*. 1610; Lucca, Mus. & Pin. N.) the archaic setting conforms with the demands of the Counter-Reformation for simplicity and clarity and the figures indicate a familiarity with works by Camillo and Giulio Cesare Procaccini. *Jacob Wrestling with the Angel* (Milan, Pal. Arcivescovile) is usually dated to *c*. 1610.

2. LATER WORKS, AFTER 1610. The altarpiece *Mary Magdalene Borne to Heaven by Angels* (completed 1611; Varese, S Vittore; see fig. 1), capped with an image of God the Father and set with a predella beneath of a *Noli me tangere* in a vast landscape, is close in date to an elegant *Adoration of the Magi* (Milan, S Antonio Abate; see fig. 2), which makes use of a similar range of bright hues. To the same period belongs a *St Roch*, strongly reminiscent of Cerano, and a cycle of frescoes with scenes from the lives of *St Roch*, *St Lawrence 'dal Pozzo'* and *St Lawrence the Deacon* in S Bartolomeo, Borgomanero. The *Massacre of the Innocents* (Milan, Pal. Arcivescovile) dates from 1611–12, and the *Fall of the Rebel Angels* (Como, Mus. Civ. Archeol.) between 1609 and 1612.

Payments to Morazzone are recorded between May 1611 and August 1612 for the frescoes in the Sagrestia dei Mansionari in Como Cathedral. The ceiling fresco, which shows the *Coronation of the Virgin*, is close in style to the frescoes in the chapel of the Ecce homo in Varallo, both being indebted to Ferrari. Also in 1612 Morazzone was working in S Agostino in Como, where he executed four scenes from the *Life of the Virgin* for the Cappella della Cintura: the *Nativity*, the *Presentation of the Virgin*, the

1. Morazzone: *Mary Magdalene Borne to Heaven by Angels*, oil on canvas, completed 1611 (Varese, S Vittore)

Marriage at Cana and the *Pentecost*. The *Pentecost* is reminiscent of Barocci, whereas in the *Nativity* the example of Ferrari is again dominant, the arrangement of the scene on two levels being a direct borrowing from him. It is not clear whether the chapel's small frescoes of the *Life of the Virgin*, framed with stuccowork, are by Morazzone (1990 exh. cat.) or a follower (1961 exh. cat.). In 1613 the Canon of Como Cathedral, Quintilio Lucini Passalacqua, commissioned the decoration of a writing-desk (Milan, Castello Sforzesco), for which Morazzone painted five biblical scenes on copper, thematically linked to the moral proposed by the Canon himself: 'When Reason takes the senses as its guide, things go awry.'

In 1614 Morazzone was once more in Varallo to begin the decoration of the chapel of the Condemnation, which had been commissioned in 1610. The frescoes, completed in 1617, and in particular the angels, demonstrate the influence of the contemporary works of Giulio Cesare Procaccini, which characterizes all Morazzone's work of this decade. In 1615 he received the final payment for the *Pentecost* (Milan, Castello Sforzesco), which originally decorated the vault of the Sala delle Congregazioni, adjacent to the chapel of the Tribunale di Provvisione in Milan, and in which the daring foreshortening that dominates the composition recalls similar illusionistic experiments carried out in Lombardy by Giulio Campi and

Giovanni Paolo Lomazzo. In the same period he frescoed scenes from the *Life of the Virgin* (1615–17) and executed in oil the *Fifteen Mysteries of the Rosary* for the chapel of the Rosary, S Vittore, Varese.

In 1616 Morazzone helped fresco chapel X of the sacromonte at Orta with the *Vision of St Francis*, but his work there does not extend beyond the internal grille; the mediocre frescoes (1623) around the altar are by G. F. Monti. Between 1616 and 1619 Morazzone returned to S Bartolomeo, Borgomanero, to work in the chapel of S Carlo, painting an altarpiece with *St Carlo Borromeo in Glory* and frescoes of scenes from the *Life of St Carlo* drawn from the biography of the saint written in 1610 by G. P. Giussano. The altarpiece is conservative in format, but it is an intensely dramatic and harshly realistic work, which suggests awareness of work by Tanzio da Varallo, who had recently returned to Piedmont from Rome.

In 1617 Morazzone was paid for the altarpiece, showing the *Virgin of the Rosary with SS Dominic and Catherine of Siena*, for the Certosa di Pavia. Here his style draws closest to the dominant tendency in Milanese painting established by Cerano and Giulio Cerare Procaccini (Gregori). The artist's frenetic activity in these years includes a commission from the Tovagliari family for frescoes (1617) in the chapel of the *Assumption of the Virgin* in S Ambrogio, Varese. Between 1617 and 1619 he painted six canvases of scenes from the *Life of the Virgin* for the presbytery of S Maria Nascente, Arona (4 *in situ*; 2 untraced), all characterized by spectacular Caravaggesque chiaroscuro effects. The *St Roch* (Milan, Castello Sforzesco) executed for the side wall of the chapel of the Tribunale di Provvisione in Milan and the *Dream of Elijah* (Milan, S Raffaele) also date from this period. The small picture of *St Carlo Adoring the Crucifix* (1618; Milan, Pal. Arcivescovile) is an outstanding example of the profound pathos and religious mysticism of Morazzone's most powerful art.

The artist was in Novara towards 1620 to execute the frescoes, and the canvas of the *Last Judgement*, in the chapel of the Buona Morte in S Gaudenzio (1619–20). This dramatic cycle, with its macabre details, horrifying imagery and doom-laden atmosphere, is one of his outstanding works and epitomizes the morbid intensity of Lombard painting in the early 17th century. Almost contemporary are the *Marriage of the Virgin* (Gallarate, S Maria Assunta) and the *Virgin and Child with St Francis* now in S Carlo al Corso, Rome. Slightly later are the *Martyrdom of St Catherine* in S Maria, Oleggio, and *Christ and the Samaritan Woman* (Milan, Brera), which reveal the influence of contemporary Genoese painting. That Morazzone received commissions from Liguria is suggested by the altarpiece of *St Carlo Adoring the Virgin*, in the parish church of Sestri Levante, Genoa.

In this period Morazzone participated, together with Cerano and the Procaccini, in the execution of a series of canvases for Charles-Emanuel I, Duke of Savoy, which represent the territories ruled by the House of Savoy. The series was painted in Turin between 1618 and 1623; the only surviving work by Morazzone is the large *Allegory of the Province of Susa* (Turin, Gal. Sabauda). In the first half of the 1620s he collaborated with Cerano and Giulio Cesare Procaccini on the *Martyrdom of SS Rufina and*

These frescoes were begun in 1625 but never completed; indeed Morazzone executed only two figures of Prophets: *David* and *Isaiah*. On 12 May 1626 the Bishop of Piacenza and the cathedral authorities engaged the services of Guercino to complete the cycle, and it is probable that by that date Morazzone was dead.

BIBLIOGRAPHY

G. Borsieri: *Il supplimento delle nobiltà di Milano* (Milan, 1619)

Q. Lucino Passalacqua: *Quattro lettere istoriche* (Como, 1620)

G. Pasta: *Il quadro delle tre mani* (Milan, 1634)

G. Baglione: *Vite* (1642); ed. V. Mariani (1935)

G. Nicodemi: 'Lettere inedite di Pier Francesco Mazzucchelli detto il Morazzone', *Archv Stor. Lombardo*, (1925), pp. 369–82

——: *Pier Francesco Mazzucchelli detto 'il Morazzone'* (Varese, 1927)

——: '"L'artificiosissimo scrittoio" di Quintilio Lucini Passalacqua conservato nel Castello Sforzesco di Milano', *Aevum*, xv/19 (1941), pp. 281–315

Il manierismo piemontese e lombardo del seicento (exh. cat., Turin, Pal. Madama; Ivrea, Centr. Cult. Olivetti, 1955)

R. Ciardi: 'Documenti e commenti sul Morazzone', *Crit. A.*, vi (1959), pp. 145–65

M. Rosci: 'Contributi al Morazzone', *Boll. A.*, xliv (1959), pp. 151–7

Il Morazzone (exh. cat., ed. M. Gregori; Varese, 1962)

G. Rosa: 'Cinque dipinti del Morazzone al Castello Sforzesco di Milano', *A. Lombarda*, vii (1962), pp. 59–62

M. Valsecchi: 'Schede lombarde II: Un Morazzone che è un Cairo', *Paragone*, xiii/149 (1962), pp. 56–68

V. Pilon: 'Un impresa pittorica dimenticata del Morazzone', *A. Crist.*, lii (1964), pp. 327–35

M. Valsecchi: 'Schede lombarde per G. C. Procaccini (e il Morazzone)', *Paragone*, xxi/243 (1970), pp. 12–35

R. Longhi: 'Codicilli alle "schede lombarde" di Marco Valsecchi', *Paragone*, xxi/243 (1970), pp. 35–9

Il seicento lombardo (exh. cat., ed. G. A. dell'Acqua; Milan, Pal. Reale and Bib. Ambrosiana, 1973), pp. 26–8 [cat. of drawings, books and prints]; pp. 44–51 [essay by M. Valsecchi]

G. Young: 'Two Related Sketches by il Morazzone', *Burl. Mag.*, cxviii (1976), pp. 503–4

F. Viatte: 'Nouvelles acquisitions: A propos d'un nouveau dessin de Morazzone', *Rev. Louvre*, xxvii (1977), pp. 164–9

P. R. Pesenti: 'Il quadro delle tre mani a Brera: Tecnica e stile in G. C. Procaccini, Morazzone e Cerano', *Stud. Stor. A.* (1980), pp. 7–21

L. Rinaldi: 'Il Morazzone a Sant' Ambrogio Olona: Documenti per gli affreschi della cappella della Beata Vergine Assunta', *A. Lombarda* (1984), pp. 167–71

N. Turner: 'Some Unpublished Drawings by Morazzone', *Master Drgs*, xxii (1984), pp. 426–30

S. Coppa: 'Morazzone', *Pinacoteca di Brera: Scuole lombarda, ligure e piemontese, 1535–1796* (Milan, 1989), pp. 306–15

Il seicento a Como: Dipinti dai Musei Civici e dal territorio (exh. cat., ed. R. Taroito; Como, Mus. Civ. Archeol., 1989–90), pp. 11–77

ALBERTO BERTONI

2. Morazzone: *Adoration of the Magi*, oil on canvas, 4.05×1.77 m, c. 1611 (Milan, S Antonio Abate)

Secunda (Milan, Brera), a picture now celebrated as *il quadro delle tre mani*. Morazzone was responsible for the execution of the torturer in the centre of the picture, the angel above and the heads of the background figures.

Among Morazzone's last works are canvases commissioned by Ferdinando Gonzaga, 6th Duke of Mantua, in 1622 and 1623 (the *Marriage at Cana* in a private collection in Rome is perhaps an oil sketch for one of these), *SS Anthony Abbot and Paul the Hermit* (Milan, Brera), which almost certainly comes from the Archbishop's Palace in Milan, and frescoes in the dome of Piacenza Cathedral.

Morbelli, Angelo (*b* Alessandria, 18 July 1853; *d* Milan, 7 Nov 1919). Italian painter. He received his first lessons in drawing in Alessandria, and in 1867 he travelled on a local study grant to Milan, where he was based for the rest of his life. He enrolled at the Accademia di Brera and from 1867 to 1876 studied drawing and painting there under Raffaele Casnedi and Giuseppe Bertini, whose influence is seen in both the subject-matter and technique of his early works. These include perspective views, anecdotal genre scenes and history paintings. In the *Dying Goethe* (1880; Alessandria, Pin. Civ.) the theatrical setting, enriched by a sophisticated execution and a well-modulated use of colour, derives from the teaching of Casnedi and Bertini, while the historic–romantic quality of this painting also recalls the style of Francesco Hayez. In the years that followed, Morbelli began to concentrate more on themes such as labour and the life of the poor, influenced perhaps

Angelo Morbelli: *Christmas of Those Left Behind*, oil on canvas, 0.59×1.04 m, 1903 (Venice, Galleria Internazionale d'Arte Moderna di Ca' Pesaro)

by Realist painters of the 1880s such as Achille D'Orsi, Francesco Paolo Michetti and Teofilo Patini. Morbelli's *Return to the Stable* (1882; priv. col., see Scotti p. 24) shows him progressively adopting a lighter palette with bluish shadows and rougher, more fragmented brushwork.

An important step towards Realism is seen in *Last Days* (1883; Milan, Gal. A. Mod.), set in a room of the Pio Albergo Trivulzio, a rest home for the aged homeless and destitute of Milan. The figures of the old people are built up with thick brushstrokes of dominant browns, and these tones are linked to the dominant yellowish shades of the refectory, prompting an emotional response to the scene, for which Morbelli was much praised. Morbelli's respect for the real had already led him to use photography in order to study the framing and composition of his images; but he had also seen something of French, German, English and Dutch Realism (for example the work of Hubert von Herkomer and Max Liebermann), in reproduction if not directly when travelling in Germany and France. In *Asphyxia* (1884; part in Turin, Gal. Civ. A. Mod., part in priv. col.), showing a suicide couple, and *Sold* (1884; Milan, Gal. A. Mod.) Morbelli adopted a cruder Realism. However, these paintings were not well received by critics, and in response Morbelli again began to concentrate on scenes from the Pio Albergo Trivulzio, producing works such as *Last Sacrament* (1884; Rome, G.N.A. Mod.), in which the brushstroke is deliberately broken up and there is an increasing use of juxtaposed pure colours in the search for greater atmospheric truth. Such experiments are further documented by the two versions of *Milan Central Station* (1887; Rome, Ferrovie Stato and 1889; Milan, Gal. A. Mod.), in which the sharpness of the image is lost in the attempt to convey a sense of atmosphere. In *Dawn* (1891; Barcelona, Mus. Mun. B.A.), a calm scene of a woman and child at a farmyard pump, Morbelli accentuated the use of pure colours in accordance with the laws of complementarity, seeking to establish the mixture as a product of the observer's perception.

From this point onwards Morbelli was one of the leading exponents of Divisionism, and his experiments progressed with greater assurance: his brushstrokes became more deliberate and regular and his handling of light more secure. This phase culminated in the celebrated scene painted in the rice fields near Vercelli, *For Eighty Centesimi!* (1895; Vercelli, Mus. Civ. Borgogna). Morbelli then returned to some of his former themes, painting, for example, a Divisionist version of *Sold!* (1897; priv. col., see Scotti p. 24). However, he continued to study the old people in the Pio Albergo Trivulzio, where he had obtained a room of his own in which to carry out his work. The numerous canvases he painted there constitute a true 'poem of old age' in which Morbelli compared the human condition with natural scenes. In *A Map in Winter* (1903; Alessandria, Pin. Civ.) he juxtaposed the white hair of his elderly sitters as it is reflected in the few rays of light coming through the window of the home, with the whiteness coming from outside, from the roofs of the city under snow. Other works in this group are the *Christmas of Those Left Behind* (1903; Venice, Ca' Pesaro; see fig.) and *Winter in the Pio Albergo Trivulzio* (1909; Turin, Gal. Civ. A. Mod.). In the triptych *Dream and Reality* (1905) the Symbolist strain in these works comes to the fore: the interrelation of opposite principles is suggested by placing a symbol of young life and hope between images of age and memory. The centre of the triptych shows a young couple embracing on a balcony and turning to look upwards at the stars, while the side panels both show solitary old people. Morbelli also carried out a large number of Divisionist landscapes, especially during his summers in the family country house at Colma di Rosignano near Monferrato, for example *Sunday Dawn* (1915; Piacenza, Gal. A. Mod. Ricci Oddi). In some of these works a note of abandon and of solitude reveals a melancholic and symbolic interpretation of landscape, as in *'Era già l'ora che volge al desio'* (1913; priv. col., see Scotti p. 97).

BIBLIOGRAPHY

Mostra degli artisti alessandrini dell'ottocento (exh. cat., ed. A. Mensi and R. Scaglia; Alessandria, Pin. Civ., 1940)
Mostra commemorativa del pittore Angelo Morbelli (exh. cat., ed. A. Mensi; Alessandria, Pin. Civ., 1953)
T. Fiori, ed.: *Archivi del divisionismo*, 2 vols (Rome, 1968)
Mostra del divisionismo italiano (exh. cat., Milan, Pal. Permanente, 1970)
M. Poggialini Tominetti: *Angelo Morbelli: Il primo divisionismo nella sua opera e nelle lettere a Pellizza da Volpedo* (Milan, 1971)
A. P. Quinsac: *La Peinture divisioniste italienne, 1880–1895: Origines et premiers développements* (Paris, 1972)
Post-Impressionism (exh. cat., London, RA, 1979) [section on Italy by S. Berresford]
Angelo Morbelli (exh. cat., ed. L. Caramel; Alessandria, Pal. Cuttica, 1982)
Divisionismo italiano (exh. cat., Trent, Pal. Albere, 1990)
A. Scotti: *Angelo Morbelli* (Soncino, 1991)

AURORA SCOTTI TOSINI

Morbidezza [It.: 'softness']. Delicate rendering of flesh tones in a work of art, as in the paintings of Correggio.

Morceau de réception [Fr.: 'reception piece']. Name used by the French Académie Royale de Peinture et de Sculpture (*see* PARIS, §VI, 1) from its foundation in 1648 until its dissolution in 1793 for a presentation piece submitted as part of the requirement for membership. The institutional structure and many of the artistic practices of the Académie Royale were based on those of the Communauté des Maîtres Peintres et Sculpteurs de Paris (*see* PARIS, §III, 2). One such borrowing was the guild distinction between apprentice, journeyman and master, which the Académie translated into student, provisional member (*agréé*) and academician. The *morceau de réception*, to be accepted as proof of artistic competence before the *agréé* was permitted full membership of the Académie, was equivalent to the guild's requirement on the journeyman to produce a masterpiece.

From the first the Académie emphasized the probity of its selection procedure, designed to contrast with that of the guild, in which venality and nepotism were rife. Candidates were sponsored by two academicians and submitted one or more works to the members, who voted secretly. If accepted, the candidate took the title of *agréé*, recorded in a *lettre de provision*. The *agréé* was then required to execute the *morceau de réception*, the subject of which was indicated either by the Director or by the Chancellor of the Académie. This work was normally to be completed within three years. If accepted (*reçu*), the artist became an *académicien*. Although the pretensions of the Académie were in theory entirely based on history painting (*see* HISTORY PAINTING, §1), which stood at the pinnacle of the contemporary hierarchy of genres, in practice painters of less highly regarded genres were also accepted. As early as 1648 Louis, Antoine and Mathieu Le Nain had gained admittance as painters of *bambochades* (low-life scenes); in 1717 Antoine Watteau was accepted as a painter of *fêtes galantes*, a category specially invented to accommodate his otherwise unclassifiable pictures; the unfortunate Jean-Baptiste Greuze was rejected as a history painter by the Académie in 1769 when it received him only as a painter of genre scenes.

In practice, however, the *morceau de réception* was often neglected by Académie and *agréés* alike. As early as July 1648 the Académie noted the promise made by every academician to offer a *morceau de réception* for the decoration of the Académie; yet for most of the 1650s no new work was added to the collection. The statutes of 1651 waived an entrance fee for poor members but insisted, 'rich or poor, the candidate will present a painting, if he be painter, or a work of sculpture, if he be sculptor, and those who are already academicians will do the same' (Article VIII). In 1653 the Académie again insisted that all outstanding *morceaux de réception* should be presented within four months. With the arrival of Jean-Baptiste Colbert as Vice-protector in 1661 the Académie was expected to demonstrate its probity. Important revisions to the statutes of 1663, by which year the Académie still possessed only thirteen paintings and five sculptures, included the stipulation that the candidate would, if made *agréé*, present a reception piece that would remain the property of the Académie (Article XXIII). In 1664 Colbert once again ordered the Académie to adhere to the regulations and call in outstanding *morceaux de réception*, on pain of permanent exclusion for defaulters. Among those who still procrastinated was Philippe de Champaigne, a founder-member, who did not present his *morceau de réception*, a portrait of the Académie's first protector, *Pierre Séguier* (untraced), until 1671. Some *agréés* must have feared rejection: it was only in 1751 that the statutes, revised to enhance the objectivity of the selection procedure, introduced anonymity of the candidate to ensure that rejection would not be professionally damaging. Others could not afford the entrance fee, on average 100 livres and obligatory from 1660. Many of these artists never submitted their *morceaux de réception*, believing that they enjoyed all the advantages of the Académie—above all, protection from guild intimidation—as *agréés*. The lack of rigour with which the Académie prosecuted those in default of the regulations may have been due to the fear that the guild would attract academic defectors. However, with the suppression of the guild in 1776 the Directeur-Général des Bâtiments, Comte d'Angiviller, wrote in 1788 to J.-B.-M. Pierre, Director of the Académie, that now the King had 'liberated' the fine arts, there was no longer any reason for laxity.

The Académie also feared fraud: another party executing the reception piece. As early as 1657 candidates were required to produce the sketches or models for their *morceaux de réception* under supervision at the Académie; from 1703 this was stipulated for the finished work as well, although in 1711 it was conceded that sculptors should be allowed to produce the final work in their own studios. Even then the Académie remained cautious, and in 1778 Jean-Joseph Foucou, considered a weak candidate, was ordered to work in the Académie.

Unlike the post-Revolutionary Académie, the Académie Royale de Peinture and Sculpture included women members, among them Elisabeth Sophie Chéron, who submitted a *Self-portrait* (Versailles, Château, on dep. Paris,

Louvre) in 1672 for her reception, Rosalba Carriera (*Nymph of Apollo*, 1722; untraced) and Elisabeth Vigée-Lebrun (*Peace Bringing Abundance*, 1783; Paris, Louvre). The Revolution (1789–95) brought an end for the *morceau de réception*: in 1793 the Académie, as a royalist institution, was abolished and its collection irrevocably dispersed, most works, such as the Louvre's *Charles Le Brun* by Nicolas de Largillière of 1683–6, entering French public collections. On the reconstitution of the Académie two years later as a *classe* of the Institut de France, the *morceau de réception*, with its echoes of guild practice, was abandoned.

BIBLIOGRAPHY

M. Duvivier: 'Sujets des morceaux de réception des membres de l'ancienne Académie de peinture, sculpture et gravure (1648–1793)', *Archvs A. Fr.*, Documents, ii (1852–3), pp. 353–91

[Henri Testelin]: *Mémoires pour servir à l'histoire de l'Académie royale de peinture et de sculpture de 1648 jusqu'en 1664*, ed. A. de Montaiglon, 2 vols (Paris, 1853)

A. de Montaiglon, ed.: *Procès-verbaux de l'Académie royale de peinture et de sculpture, 1648–1792*, 10 vols (Paris, 1875–1909)

L. Vitet: *L'Académie royale de peinture et de sculpture: Etude historique* (Paris, 1880)

A. Fontaine: *Les Collections de l'Académie royale de peinture et de sculpture* (Paris, 1930)

PAUL DURO

Mordant (i). Term for the acidic solution in which the metal plate or object is immersed in the printing processes of etching and aquatint. The acid bites into the unprotected areas of the plate, creating the hollows that hold the ink during printing.

Mordant (ii). Term for the resin or oil layer used in gilding to stick the gold leaf on to the prepared surface of wood, sealed plaster or paint (*see* GILDING, §I, 1(i)).

RUPERT FEATHERSTONE

Mordant (iii). Term for the substance used to fix the colour in dyeing and printing textiles (*see* TEXTILE, §III, 1(ii)). □

Mordvinia [Mordovia]. *See under* RUSSIA, §XII, 3.

More, Jacob (*b* Edinburgh, 1740; *d* Rome, 1 Oct 1793). Scottish painter, active in Italy. The son of an Edinburgh merchant, he was first apprenticed to a goldsmith and then, from 1766, to the Norie family of house-painters. In the 1760s he produced numerous sketches of the Scottish Lowlands (examples Edinburgh, N.G.), and in 1769 he designed and executed stage sets at the Theatre Royal, Edinburgh, for the first productions after the legalizing of the theatre in Scotland. More's Edinburgh period culminated in a series of oil paintings of the *Falls of the River Clyde*, three of which are in public collections: *Corra Linn* (Edinburgh, N.G.), *Stonebyres Linn* (London, Tate) and *Bonnington Linn* (Cambridge, Fitzwilliam). These paintings are regarded as the first serious artistic interpretations of the Scottish landscape, depictions by previous artists having been essentially topographical in character. More took a set of three of them to the Society of Artists Exhibition in London in 1771, at which he gained widespread recognition and the personal encouragement of Sir Joshua Reynolds. He stayed in London for a couple of years, studying under Richard Wilson and (judging from his later style) working as a scene-painter.

By 1773 More was in Rome, producing increasingly large Italianate landscapes with an acknowledged debt to Richard Wilson and Claude Lorrain: a typical example is the *Tiber Estuary* (1784; Cambridge, St Catharine's Coll.). He excelled in depicting atmospheric effects in glowing colours (e.g. *View of Rome across the Tiber*, *c*. 1780; Adelaide, A.G. S. Australia) and the misty haze of waterfalls (e.g. *Landscape with Classical Figures*, 1780; Ickworth, Suffolk, NT), and he was soon one of the most fashionable painters in Rome. The vast, brilliantly lit skies that dominate his compositions (e.g. *Morning* and *Evening*, 1785; both Glasgow A.G. & Mus.) demonstrate clearly his theatrical training, as do the dramatic scenes of waterfalls and volcanic eruptions (e.g. *Mount Vesuvius in Eruption: The Last Days of Pompeii*, 1780; Edinburgh, N.G.). His numerous sketches reveal a light, rapid touch; his finished watercolours are competent but pedestrian (examples Edinburgh, N.G.; New Haven, CT, Yale Cent. Brit. A.). In the late 1770s More worked with Allan Ramsay, preparing sketches for Ramsay's projected treatise on Horace's Sabine Villa.

In 1781 More was elected to the Accademia di S Luca, Rome. Two years later he presented his *Self-portrait* to the Uffizi Gallery, Florence (*in situ*). During the 1780s he worked increasingly as an agent and dealer. His Letterbook (1786–7; Edinburgh, U. Lib.) contains details of transactions with his chief patron, Frederick Augustus Hervey, 4th Earl of Bristol, as well as advice on the techniques of landscape painting to such patrons as Sir George Beaumont. More also worked as a landscape gardener: during the 1780s he laid out a garden and lake in the grounds of the Villa Borghese, Rome, in the English Picturesque style. He died in Rome shortly before his planned return to Britain, and his *Panorama of Rome* (untraced), commissioned by Prince Augustus Frederick, Duke of Sussex (1773–1843), the sixth son of George III, was set up at Buckingham House in London soon after.

More's importance lies chiefly in his early achievements as a pioneer of landscape painting in Scotland, in which he paved the way for more prolific artists, such as Alexander Nasmyth. The highly polished and theatrical style of his later work was hugely popular in its day but became unfashionable in the 19th century; a period of neglect followed until the mid-20th century.

UNPUBLISHED SOURCES

Edinburgh, U. Lib. [Letterbook of 1786–7]

BIBLIOGRAPHY

D. Irwin and F. Irwin: *Scottish Painters at Home and Abroad, 1700–1900* (London, 1975)

J. Holloway: 'Two Projects to Illustrate Allan Ramsay's Treatise on Horace's Sabine Villa', *Master Drgs*, xiv (1976), pp. 280–86

The Discovery of Scotland (exh. cat., ed. J. Holloway and L. Errington; Edinburgh, N.G., 1978)

P. R. Andrew: *Jacob More, 1740–1793* (diss., U. Edinburgh, 1981)

——: 'An English Garden in Rome', *Country Life*, clxix (23 April 1981), pp. 1136–8

——: 'Jacob More and the Earl-Bishop of Derry', *Apollo*, cxxiv (1986), pp. 88–94

——: 'The Watercolours of Jacob More', *Old Wtrcol. Soc. Club*, lxi (1986), pp. 27–41

——: 'Jacob More's *Falls of Clyde* Paintings', *Burl. Mag.*, cxxix (1987), pp. 84–8

——: 'Rival Portraiture: Jacob More, the Roman Academician', *Apollo*, cxxx (1989), pp. 304–7
——: 'Jacob More: Biography and a Checklist of Works', *Walpole Soc.*, lv (1989/90), pp. 105–196

PATRICIA R. ANDREW

More, Sir **Thomas** (*b* London, 6 Feb 1478; *d* London, 6 July 1535). English statesman, writer and martyr. He was the son of a judge and was educated at Oxford and at the Inns of Court. He entered Parliament, where he rose rapidly, becoming Master of Requests (1517), Treasurer to the Exchequer (1521) and Speaker of the House of Commons (1523); finally he, reluctantly, succeeded Cardinal Wolsey as Lord Chancellor in 1529. Concerned at Henry VIII's increasing antagonism towards the Church of Rome, he resigned his post in 1532. Following his refusal to acknowledge Henry as the head of the English Church, More was imprisoned, tried for high treason and beheaded in 1535. He was canonized on the fourth centenary of his death. More's interest in the visual arts was limited, the clearest indication of his attitudes being found in his celebrated *Utopia* (1516). The Utopians' aesthetic was utilitarian: they avoided finery (as More himself did whenever possible) and lived in unadorned, solidly built houses. The tomb he commissioned for himself in Chelsea Old Church was Gothic rather than Renaissance in style, suggesting a lack of interest in the avant-garde. It is only by chance that, through his friend and fellow humanist Erasmus, he came in contact with Hans Holbein the younger, the foremost portrait painter of the period. Holbein painted a magnificent portrait of More (1527; New York, Frick; *see* PORTRAITURE, fig. 6) and also one of *Sir Thomas More and his Family*; the original of this is lost and is known only through copies and preparatory sketches (Windsor Castle, Berks, Royal Col.).

BIBLIOGRAPHY
R. W. Chambers: *Thomas More* (London, 1935)
S. Morison: *The Likeness of Thomas More: An Iconographical Survey of Three Centuries* (London, 1963)
J. B. Trapp: 'Thomas More and the Visual Arts', *Saggi sul rinascimento*, ed. S. Rossi (Milan, 1984)

RICHARD JOHN

Moreau. French family of artists. The brothers (1) Louis-Gabriel and (2) Jean-Michel Moreau were the sons of a Paris wigmaker. They both worked in the same media but achieved success in different fields, Louis-Gabriel working principally as an innovative landscape painter and Jean-Michel as a book illustrator and a recorder of contemporary manners and events. Horace Vernet was Jean-Michel's grandson, from the marriage of his daughter to Carle Vernet.

(1) Louis-Gabriel Moreau *[l'aîné]* (*b* Paris, before 24 April 1740; *d* Paris, 12 Oct 1805). Painter, draughtsman and etcher. He trained with the painter Pierre Antoine de Machy and exhibited for the first time in 1760 at the Exposition de la Jeunesse, showing views of ruins painted in gouache and watercolour over pencil, and employing a clear, bright palette. In 1764 he was received as a member of the Académie de St Luc, where he continued to exhibit landscapes with ruins and figures in various media until the Revolution (1789–95). In 1779 he exhibited in Montpellier, and it is possible that he travelled in the south of France, although most of his landscapes show subjects in Paris and its environs. In 1787 and 1788 he failed in attempts to become a member of the Académie Royale de Peinture et de Sculpture, but he was painter to the Comte d'Artois (later Charles X) and had lodgings in the Louvre. From 1791 he was able to exhibit at the open Salon at the Louvre, continuing to do so until 1804. In the years 1793–

Louis-Gabriel Moreau: *View of the Château de Madrid*, pen and ink with watercolour heightened with white gouache, 355×650 mm, 1774 (Rouen, Musée des Beaux Arts)

5 he also worked as a restorer and curator at the newly established Muséum National, Paris.

Moreau's sensitive and original landscape paintings reflect the taste for the 'natural' in late 18th-century France, found also in the writings of Salomon Gessner, Jean-Jacques Rousseau and James Thomson, in such aristocratic fancies as Mme de Pompadour's dairy at Crécy or Marie-Antoinette's rustic *hameau* at Versailles, and also in the growing popularity of the informal 'English' garden. In such apparently artlessly composed works as *View of the Château de Madrid* (1774; Rouen, Mus. B.-A.; see fig.), the *Demolition of the Abbey of Montmartre* (oil on paper laid down on canvas, exh. Salon 1804; Paris, Louvre) and *View of the Château of Saint-Cloud* (oil on canvas, 1804; Los Angeles, CA, Co. Mus. A.), as well as in such scenes as the *Torrent* (gouache and watercolour; Cambridge, Fitzwilliam), Moreau combined topographic and picturesque elements with delicate colouring and an attention to the effects of light at different times of day that seem to anticipate the fresh and unemphatic works of the early 19th-century English landscape painters and the artists of Barbizon. The same qualities can also be seen in his etched compositions (examples in Paris, Bib. N.).

(2) Jean-Michel Moreau [le jeune] (*b* Paris, 26 March 1741; *d* Paris, 30 Nov 1814). Draughtsman, engraver and painter, brother of (1) Louis-Gabriel Moreau. He was the pupil of the painter and engraver Louis-Joseph Le Lorrain, with whom he went to St Petersburg in 1758 on Le Lorrain's appointment as first director of the Academy of Fine Arts. Moreau was appointed a professor of drawing at the Academy. He executed a number of works in Russia, including a red-chalk portrait of the *Empress Elizabeth* (Paris, Bib. N.). In 1759 he returned to Paris and, virtually abandoning painting, entered the workshop of the engraver Jacques-Philippe Lebas, producing drawings for engravers to work from after such contemporary artists as François Boucher and Jean-Baptiste Greuze, as well as after Rembrandt and other Old Masters (*see* DRESS, fig. 46). During the 1760s he also provided drawings to be engraved for Caylus's *Recueil d'antiquités* and for Diderot and d'Alembert's *Encyclopédie* and collaborated as an engraver with Boucher, François Eisen, Hubert-François Gravelot and Charles Monnet (1732–1808) on the illustrations for an edition of Ovid's *Metamorphoses*. By 1770, the year in which he succeeded Charles-Nicolas Cochin (ii) as Dessinateur des Menus Plaisirs du Roi, his career was sufficiently well established for him to employ other engravers including Noël Le Mire, Nicolas and Robert De Launay and Elise Saugrain (*b* 1753) to reproduce his own designs. Popular and successful, he illustrated a large number of literary works including the *Chansons* of Laborde (1773), the collected works of Rousseau (1773–82) and the collected works of Voltaire (1782–9). In his role as draughtsman to the Menus Plaisirs, and from 1781 as Dessinateur et Graveur du Cabinet du Roi, he recorded many court festivities in drawings of great finesse, such as the pen and wash *Illumination of the Park at Versailles on the Occasion of the Marriage of the Dauphin* (1770; Paris, Louvre), which amply demonstrates his mastery of composition, detail and handling of light. His best-known works, which provide an incomparable record of the

fashionable dress and manners of the last years of the *ancien régime*, are the many illustrations that he contributed to the second and third series of the famous *Monument du costume physique et morale* (1777, 1783), published by his uncle by marriage, L.-F. Prault.

In 1785 Moreau travelled to Italy in the company of the architect Gabrielle-Pierre-Martin Dumont, and in 1789 he was received as a member of the Académie Royale on presentation of the pen-and-wash drawing *Tullia Driving her Chariot over the Body of her Father* (Paris, Louvre). He was receptive to new ideas and fared well under the French Revolution (1789–95), turning his talents to the illustration of Republican events (e.g. the pen-and-wash drawing *The Crowning of Bailly*) and a series of engraved portraits of Deputies at the Assemblée National (Paris, Bib. N.), as well as becoming a teacher at the Ecoles Centrales de la Ville in Paris, where among his many pupils was his grandson Horace Vernet. He continued to work as an illustrator, undertaking a series of 112 drawings for the New Testament (1791–8) and providing drawings for an edition of Gessner's *Idylls* (1795). In 1814 he was reappointed Dessinateur et Graveur du Roi by Louis XVIII.

In whatever medium he worked, Moreau was able to capture with great fluency and delicacy fine nuances of gesture, pose and light, a talent that made him one of the greatest book illustrators and most acute observers of fashionable life of the 18th century.

BIBLIOGRAPHY

F. Mahérault: *L'Oeuvre gravé de Jean-Michel Moreau le jeune* (Paris, 1880)
A. Moureau: *Les Moreau* (Paris, 1893)
P. Dorbec: 'Les Premiers Peintres du paysage parisien', *Gaz. B.-A.*, n. s. 2, xl (1908), pp. 441–70
C. Normand: *Moreau le jeune* (Paris, 1909)
A. M. Hind, ed.: *Fragonard, Moreau le jeune and French Engravers, Etchers and Illustrators of the Late XVIII Century* (London, 1913)
R. Bouyer: 'Le Paysage au XVIIIe siècle: Louis-Gabriel Moreau l'aîné, 1740–1706' [sic], *A. & Artistes*, xxii (1921), pp. 89–95
Hubert Robert et Louis Moreau (exh. cat., Paris, Gal. Charpentier, 1922)
G. Wildenstein: *Louis Moreau: Un Peintre de paysage au XVIIIe siècle* (Paris, 1923)
J. Cayeux: 'Un Précurseur, Louis Moreau, 1740–1806', *Conn. A.*, xxxvii (1955), pp. 32–7
P. Prouté: *Les Eaux-fortes de Louis Moreau l'aîné, essai de catalogue* (1956)
Hubert Robert et Louis Moreau (exh. cat., ed. J. Cailleux; Paris, Gal. Cailleux, 1957)
G. Wildenstein: 'Sur les Eaux-fortes de Moreau l'aîné', *Gaz. B.-A.*, n. s. 5, lii (1958), pp. 369–78
M. Cormack: 'An Italian Sketchbook by Moreau le Jeune', *Apollo*, lxxxvii (1968), pp. 124–8
C. Constans: 'Les Moreau, peintres français', *Petit Larousse de la peinture*, ii (Paris, 1979)

CELIA ALEGRET

Moreau, Gustave (*b* Paris, 6 April 1826; *d* Paris, 18 April 1898). French painter and teacher. He was a strongly individual artist whose highly wrought interpretations of mythical and religious scenes were widely admired during his lifetime.

1. EARLY LIFE AND WORK, TO 1870. A student of François-Edouard Picot at the Ecole des Beaux-Arts in Paris, Moreau competed unsuccessfully for the Prix de Rome in 1848 and 1849 but received several government commissions between 1849 and 1854. His earliest works,

apart from some family portraits and landscape drawings, are in a Romantic style indebted to Delacroix and Théodore Chassériau, whose studio was next door to Moreau's, and who became a good friend. The first painting he exhibited at the Salon was a *Pietà* (1851; untraced) strongly influenced by Delacroix. In 1853 he showed the *Song of Songs* (Dijon, Mus. B.-A.) and *Darius, Fleeing after the Battle of Arbela, Stops, Exhausted, to Drink in a Pond* (Paris, Mus. Moreau), which was influenced by Chassériau. Although he received favourable reviews, he was unsatisfied with his work, wishing to reconcile the dramatic language of Romanticism with academic ideals of order, balance and decorum based on Renaissance classicism. This can be seen in the *Young Athenians in the Labyrinth on Crete* (Bourg-en-Bresse, Mus. Ain), exhibited but unnoticed in the Exposition Universelle in Paris in 1855.

Moreau began a two-year stay in Italy in 1857, studying the Old Masters in Rome, Florence and Venice. During this period he was close to Degas as well as to other young artists such as Elie Delaunay, Léon Bonnat, Eugène Fromentin, Henri Léopold Lévy and Emile Lévy, all of whom became established painters in the following decades. His drawings, copies and notebooks reveal a profound immersion in Italian artistic culture. Italian painting formed him as an artist and inspired in him a fervent belief in the spiritual value of art. After creating an unimpressive *Road to Calvary* (1862; Decazeville, Notre-Dame), he synthesized his Italian experience into an original style. He spent several years in the early 1860s on a major work, *Oedipus and the Sphinx* (New York, Met.), for which he made numerous preparatory drawings and studies (Paris, Mus. Moreau). The painting, which won a medal at the Salon of 1864, was purchased by Prince Napoléon-Jérôme Bonaparte and marked the establishment of his reputation. The painting draws on classical art and the work of Mantegna, Giovanni Bellini and Ingres and exemplifies Moreau's desire to demonstrate an understanding of the Old Masters in an original way. Its harsh, linear contours and miniscule strokes create a hatched modelling derived from Renaissance art and his academic training. Over life-sized, the painting depicts a confrontation between Oedipus and the sphinx: the composition, despite its violence, is frozen, and the figures are expressionless and this contradictory stillness is both evocative and mysterious. Moreau's notes reveal that he was concerned with the oppositions between good and evil, male and female, physicality and spirituality, and the painting's power and complexity struck a responsive chord among both critics and the public, even prompting caricatures in the popular press.

Moreau explored the style and subject of *Oedipus* throughout the 1860s, producing large symbolic paintings often focused on contrasting concepts such as life versus death, the clash between love and ambition (e.g. *Jason and Medea*, 1865; Paris, Mus. d'Orsay) or the sacrifice required for art (e.g. *Young Man and Death*, 1865; Cambridge, MA, Fogg). *Diomedes Devoured by his Horses* (1865; Rouen, Mus. B.-A.) is exceptional for Moreau's work of this period in its classical theme of retribution, smaller figures and violent action.

2. LATER CAREER, 1870–96. By the late 1860s critics had become negative about Moreau's work: what had been provocative had become familiar. In response, he withdrew from exhibition and undertook a long and serious re-evaluation of his art during and after the Franco-Prussian War. His new style was indebted to Baroque art, especially that of Rembrandt, and to his use of small wax maquettes as preparatory models. *Salome Dancing before Herod* (1876; Los Angeles, CA, Armand Hammer Mus. A.; see fig. 1) heralded this phase of Moreau's art and elicited enthusiastic responses at the Salon of 1876. Moreau emphasized the contrast of light and dark, with small figures in an elaborate, eclectic setting containing a mixture of precise, linear passages and painterly, suggestive ones.

The subject of *Salome* is a variation on the theme of the *femme fatale*, which attracted many 19th-century artists. Moreau used symbolic details to reiterate meaning: Diana of Ephesus placed above Herod is a potent image of female power, and the images of a panther and a sphinx emphasize Salome's role as temptress and destroyer. *Hercules and the Hydra of Lerna* (1876; Chicago, IL, A. Inst.), exhibited at the same Salon as *Salome*, shares its exploration of colour and texture and its theme, a confrontation of good and evil.

Also in the 1870s Moreau began to exhibit watercolours showing a similar technical exploration and excitement as his oils, for example *Phaeton* (1878; Paris, Louvre) and *The Apparition* (1876; Paris, Louvre; see fig. 2). They attracted the attention of Antony Roux (*d* 1913), a collector fascinated by the fables of La Fontaine, who commissioned Moreau, among others, to work on this theme, eventually purchasing 63 of his watercolours. Moreau finished few large paintings after his last Salon exhibition in 1880 with *Galatea* (Paris, Robert Lebel Col.) and *Helen* (untraced). In 1882 he began to revise many of the paintings in his studio, some of which dated from the 1850s. He enlarged them, adding detail and texture, but few were ever completed. This process illustrated Moreau's belief that the artist should always try to balance inspiration and intellect. All the large unfinished paintings in the Musée Gustave Moreau indicate his inability to solve this dilemma.

Moreau continued to paint numerous small oils and watercolours, such as *Giotto* (*c*. 1882; Paris, Louvre, Cab. Dessins), and tried to combine a number of these in the ambitious, unfinished *Life of Humanity* (1879–86; Paris, Mus. Moreau), a large, multipartite work with individually titled panels dealing with themes of universal history. The deaths of his mother in 1884 and his mistress, Alexandrine Dureux, in 1890 did not prevent a continual output of small works, which sold well to a steady clientele, and official recognition continued. He was made Officier of the Légion d'honneur in 1883 and was elected to the Académie des Beaux-Arts of the Institut de France in 1888. His fame grew when Joris-Karl Huysmans wrote emotionally of his art in the novel *A Rebours* (1884).

One of the few large paintings finished in the last decade of Moreau's life, *Jupiter and Semele* (1889–95; Paris, Mus. Moreau), successfully synthesizes his aesthetic and thematic concerns. Ostensibly relating a Greek myth, the painting contains numerous symbolic figures and decorative details from wide-ranging sources, illustrating man's

1. Gustave Moreau: *Salome Dancing before Herod*, oil on canvas, 1.44×1.04 m, 1876 (Los Angeles, CA, Armand Hammer Museum of Art and Cultural Center)

2. Gustave Moreau: *The Apparition*, watercolour, 1.05×0.72 m, 1876 (Paris, Musée du Louvre)

aspiration to join with the divine. The Arcadian god Pan, accompanied by symbolic figures of Sadness and Death, refers to the work of the Pre-Raphaelite artist Edward Burne-Jones, which he admired, as well as to his own earlier paintings. Jupiter's traditional attributes are enhanced with symbols of sexual potency and eternal power from Indian, Egyptian and occult traditions. He also holds a lyre, classical symbol of creativity. While Jupiter's pose is based on Classical sources, the underlying artistic inspiration is derived from the Flemish Renaissance.

In his exploration of the mythological idea of union with the divine, Moreau joined Gauguin and Edvard Munch in seeking comprehensive answers to the basic dilemmas of life. He wrote two long commentaries explaining *Jupiter and Semele* but also suggested that the viewer approach it with an open mind. This Symbolist aesthetic (*see* SYMBOLISM) is based on ideas dating back to the neo-Platonic teachings of the eclectic philosophers Victor Cousin and Theodore Jouffroy (1796–1842), who had influenced him in his youth. However, he did not identify with the younger Symbolist painters and he refused to exhibit at the Salon de la Rose+Croix.

Moreau was appointed professor at the Ecole des Beaux-Arts in Paris in 1892. He was a popular and admired teacher; his students included Albert Marquet and Matisse. He especially favoured Rouault, and he strongly influenced Matisse's views on art, as well as those of many of the Fauves. Moreau was more open than other academic teachers: even when urging his students to copy the Old Masters, he directed them to a much broader range of art than was the norm and encouraged them to find their own direction.

Moreau's last commission was for a cartoon (*The Poet and the Siren*, 1895) for a tapestry woven at the Gobelins (1896–9; Paris, Mobilier N.). In the 1890s he began to work from photographs of his models posing. He began to think of posterity and in 1895 he remodelled his Paris house into a museum, containing the record of his entire working life. Finished in 1896, it became an official state museum in 1902; Rouault was its director. The Musée Gustave Moreau holds over 1000 paintings and oil sketches, 15,000 drawings, numerous sketchbooks, notebooks and letters, his library and his studio props, but only a few large finished paintings.

WRITINGS

B. Wright and P. Moisy, eds: *Moreau et Eugène Fromentin (Documents inédits)* (La Rochelle, 1972)
P. L. Mathieu, ed.: *L'Assembleur de rêves: Ecrits complets de Gustave Moreau* (Fontfroide, 1984)

BIBLIOGRAPHY

L. Thévenin: *L'Esthétique de Gustave Moreau* (Paris, 1897)
P. Flat: *Le Musée Gustave Moreau* (Paris, 1899)
A. Renan: *Gustave Moreau* (Paris, 1900)
G. Desvallières: *L'Oeuvre de Gustave Moreau* (Paris, 1913)
G. Bou: *Moreau à Decazeville* (Rodez, 1964)
R. von Holten: *Gustave Moreau: Symbolist* (Stockholm, 1965)
J. Kaplan: 'Gustave Moreau's *Jupiter and Semele*', *A.Q.* [Detroit], xxxiii (1970), pp. 393–414
H. Dorra: 'The Guesser Guessed: Gustave Moreau's *Oedipus*', *Gaz. B.-A.*, 6th ser., lxxxi (1973), pp. 129–40
Catalogue des peintures, dessins, cartons, aquarelles exposées dans les galeries du Musée Gustave Moreau, Paris, Mus. Moreau cat. (Paris, 1974)
J. Kaplan: *Gustave Moreau* (Los Angeles, 1974)
P.-L. Mathieu: *Gustave Moreau: Sa vie, son oeuvre* (Paris, 1976)
A. Perrig: 'Bemerkungen zu Gustave Moreau (1826–1898) *Salomé*', *Krit. Ber.*, v/4–5 (1977), pp. 5–25
O. P. Sebastiani: 'L'influence de Michel-Ange sur Gustave Moreau', *Rev. Louvre*, xxvii (1977), pp. 140–52
H. Hofstätter: *Gustave Moreau* (Cologne, 1978)
J. Kaplan: *The Art of Gustave Moreau: Theory, Style, and Content* (Ann Arbor, 1982)
P. Bittler and P.-L. Mathieu: *Catalogue des dessins de Gustave Moreau* (Paris, 1983)
P.-L. Mathieu: *Gustave Moreau: Aquarelles* (Fribourg, 1984)
Gustave Moreau Symbolist (exh. cat., ed. T. Stooss; Zurich, Ksthaus, 1986)
Maison d'artiste maison-musée: L'exemple de Gustave Moreau (exh. cat. by G. Lacambre, Paris, Mus. d'Orsay, 1987)

JULIUS KAPLAN

Moreau, Karl, Ritter von (*b* ?1758; *d* Vienna, 3 Nov 1840). French architect, active in Austria. He was trained at the Académie de l'Architecture in Paris and went to Vienna with Pierre-François-Léonard Fontaine in 1794 at the invitation of Prince Nicholas II Esterházy. Moreau belonged to a group of French architects that included Nicolas Jadot, Isidore Canevale and Louis Montoyer, who were active in Vienna in the late 18th century and who had a decisive influence on Vienna's architecture of the time without integrating with local production. Consequently, two parallel architectural streams influenced Neoclassicism in Vienna: the plain, unpretentious works of local artists and the strongly contrasting progressive trends of the French architects.

Moreau's personal attempts to introduce elements of French *architecture révolutionnaire* into Austrian architecture are most clearly seen in his design for the remodelling (1795–1805) of the Schloss Esterházy in Kismarton (now Eisenstadt). He envisioned a huge castle, with belvedere-like pavilions connected by long, low wings and with rich colonnades. Although only the garden front was actually executed, Moreau's grand design was greatly influential for further achievements in Viennese Neo-classical architecture (*see* KORNHÄUSEL, JOSEPH). His Viennese palaces—the Lubomirsky (1806), Pálffy (1809–13) and Esterházy-Erdödy (1810–12)—belong to the finest aristocratic architecture built in the city before the Congress of Vienna in 1814. After 1815 he concentrated on public buildings, including the National Bank (1819–23) in Vienna and the Frauenbad (1821), one of the numerous public baths in nearby Baden. In these designs Moreau used the more severe and purely cubic elements of the *architecture révolutionnaire*, thus participating in the new trend of Biedermeier architecture.

BIBLIOGRAPHY

Thieme–Becker

R. Kastner: 'Das Werk des Architekten Karl Moreau', *Alte & Mod. Kst*, xcii (1967), pp. 8–15

R. Wagner-Rieger: *Vom Klassizismus bis zur Secession*, Gesch. Stadt Wien, vii/3 (Vienna, 1973), pp. 106–8, 123–4

S. Kronbichler-Skacha: 'Architektur des Klassizismus in Wien', *Österreich. Z. Kst & Dkmlpf.*, xxxiii (1979), pp. 27–41

SUSANNE KRONBICHLER-SKACHA

Moreau, Luc-Albert (*b* Paris, 9 Dec 1882; *d* Paris, 25 April 1948). French painter and printmaker. Originally destined for a legal career, he studied law for some time before working as a solicitor's clerk. Uninterested in law, he then began to study Asian and African languages and obtained a diploma from the Ecole des Langues Orientales in Paris in 1906. Soon afterwards he began making infrequent visits to the Académie Julian in Paris, working in the studio of Jean-Paul Laurens, and there met and befriended Jean-Louis Boussingault and André Dunoyer de Segonzac. He then spent a short period at the Académie de la Palette where he received lessons from Charles Guérin, Georges-Olivier Desvallières and Pierre Laprade. In 1907 he worked with Boussingault and Dunoyer de Segonzac at a villa in St Tropez rented from Paul Signac. He first exhibited at the Salon d'Automne in 1908 and at the Salon des Indépendants in 1909.

Moreau's early works included landscapes and especially female nudes, such as *Hippolyte* (1910; see Allard, p. 23). Their rather melancholy appearance led critics such as Guillaume Apollinaire and André Salmon to link them to the poetry of Charles Baudelaire. From about 1912 he began to show the influence of Cubism, constructing his paintings with geometrical facets, as in *Landscape in Provence* (1913; see Allard, p. 37). He fought in World War I and was badly injured in 1918, though he resumed painting by 1919. His war experiences inspired most of his paintings of the early 1920s, such as *Soldiers in the Trench* (1923; Paris, Pompidou), and it is in these works that the influence of Cubism is most overt. Whereas previously it appeared only in a limited geometric treatment of objects, here this tendency is more extreme and is used to flatten the pictorial space, so blending foreground and background. Between 1919 and 1925 he was vice-president of the Société des Artistes Indépendants.

In 1925 Moreau went to live in St Tropez. By the late 1920s the traces of Cubism in his work had vanished and he developed into one of the chief exponents of NÉO-RÉALISME, a consciously anti-modern style that marked a return to the perceived spirit of the French tradition. Moreau's works, such as the *Bedroom of Neighbours* (1928; Paris, Pompidou), were thereafter characterized by a poetic, realist approach to interiors, landscapes and figure subjects. Moreau was also a keen printmaker specializing in etching and lithography (e.g. the *Temptation of St Anthony*, see Roger-Marx, p. 269), and it is perhaps this work that most sustained his posthumous reputation. His interest in boxing inspired various prints and led to the illustrations for *Physiologie de la Boxe* (Paris, 1930) by E. de Courrières, for which Henri de Montherlant wrote the preface. He also depicted the subject in paintings such as *Knock-out* (Paris, Pompidou). His numerous other illustrated books included François Bernouard's *Futile* (Paris, 1911), Jeanne Dortzal's *Sur les toits bleus du soir* (Paris, 1911), Roger Allard's *Les Feux de la Saint-Jean* (Paris, 1919) and Colette's *La Naissance du jour* (Paris, 1931), and he contributed illustrations to a number of journals including *Schekerazade* (1910–11), *Panurge* (1912), *Montjoie!* (1913–14) and *Le Crapouillot* (1915–19).

BIBLIOGRAPHY

R. Allard: *Luc-Albert Moreau* (Paris, 1920)

C. Roger-Marx: 'The Lithographs of Luc-Albert Moreau', *Prt Colr Q.*, xvii/8 (1930), pp. 260–78

J. R. Thomé: *Catalogue de l'oeuvre lithographié et gravé de Luc-Albert Moreau* (Paris, 1938)

□

Moreau, Mathurin (*b* Dijon, 18 Nov 1822; *d* Paris, 14 Feb 1912). French sculptor and entrepreneur. His father, Jean-Baptiste Moreau (1797–1855), a sculptor in Dijon, was best known for his restoration of the medieval tombs of the Dukes of Burgundy, which had been damaged during the French Revolution. In 1841 Mathurin entered the Ecole des Beaux-Arts, Paris, where he trained under Etienne-Jules Ramey and Augustin-Alexandre Dumont. He made his Salon début in 1848 with *Elegy* (plaster, Dijon, Mus. B.-A.). In 1852 his *Flower Fairy*, exhibited at the Salon in plaster, was commissioned by the State in bronze (Dijon, Mus. B.-A.). At the 1861 Salon, his marble *Spinner* was also bought by the State, for the Musée du Luxembourg, Paris (version, Dijon. Mus. B.-A.). Poetic and uncontentious works of this kind continued to earn Moreau medals and prizes at subsequent Salons and international exhibitions. Among his public works, he contributed decorative sculpture to the new Opéra and to the rebuilt Hôtel de Ville in Paris, and also produced some commemorative statues, such as that in Dijon to *Sadi Carnot*, President of the French Republic (marble and bronze, 1899; Dijon, Place de la République), which he executed in collaboration with Paul Gasq (*b* 1860; *fl* 1881–1909). However, it was probably the extent of his entrepreneurial activities that won for Moreau an influential position in public life. Having provided many sculpture models for commercial exploitation by the Val d'Osne foundry, he became one of the administrators of the Société du Val d'Osne. Together with his pupil and namesake, Auguste Moreau (1834–1917), he continued, well into the 20th century, to supply models for the manufacture of decorative bronze statuettes that were wholly untouched by more avant-garde endeavours. From 1878 Moreau was mayor of the 19th arrondissement in Paris. The *Civil Marriage*, a painting by Henri Gervex that hangs in the Salle des Mariages of the Mairie of that arrondissement, shows Moreau officiating at his son's civil marriage ceremony, before a distinguished audience.

BIBLIOGRAPHY

Lami
J.-C. Ancet: *Une famille de sculpteurs bourguignons: Les Moreau* (diss., U. Dijon, 1974)

PHILIP WARD-JACKSON

Moreau, Robert (*b* Paris; *fl* 1532–40). Netherlandish sculptor of French origin. He became a citizen of Antwerp in 1532–3 and in 1533 entered the Guild of St Luke, to which wood-carvers belonged. Evidently he also worked in stone, for on 2 July 1536 he received a contract from the emissary of the Bishop of Dunkeld, Scotland, to supply six pieces of black polished marble to frame the Bishop's copper tomb plaque (destr.). On 17 June 1537 he received a prestigious commission from the wealthy abbey of Gembloux to produce a large carved wooden altarpiece (destr. 1563) with ten scenes from the *Lives of SS Peter and Paul* and including a donor portrait of the abbot, Antoine Papin (*d* 1541), all to be carved within two years for a fee of 800 gold florins. Moreau is last documented in 1540, when he offered as surety for a debt a 'chaire seigneuriale du boys taillée à l'antique' (wooden pulpit in antique style).

The inscription *Morea* appears on the sleeve of a figure in the *Circumcision* scene in a carved and polychromed wooden altarpiece with painted wings from St Geneviève, Oplinter (Brussels, Mus. Royaux A. & Hist.). Formerly thought to be by the Leuven carver Willem Hessels, the altarpiece bears the Antwerp carvers' incised hand mark, certifying Antwerp craftsmanship. The corpulent, elongated figures in flamboyantly exaggerated poses show an idiosyncratic interpretation of Antwerp Mannerism also found in the carved altarpieces from the churches of Herbais-sous-Piétrain (Brussels, Mus. Royaux A. & Hist.), Ophoven, Neerhaeren and 's-Herenelderen. The association of this style with Moreau seems likely but is not proven.

BIBLIOGRAPHY

F. Donnet: 'Le Sculpteur Robert Moreau', *An. Acad. Royale Archéol. Belgique* (1899–1900), pp. 37–54
L. Crick: 'L'Auteur du retable d'Oplinter', *Bull. Mus. Royaux A. & Hist.*, vi/1 (1934), pp. 13–16

KIM W. WOODS

Moreau-Desproux, Pierre-Louis (*b* Paris, 1727; *d* Paris, 1793). French architect. Having failed to win the Prix de Rome for architecture, he accepted the offer of his more successful friend Charles de Wailly (1730–98) to share the prize. In Rome (1754–6) they were both involved, together with Marie-Joseph Peyre, in the archaeological excavations of the Baths of Diocletian. On his return to Paris, Moreau-Desproux's first commission was the Hôtel de Chavannes on the Boulevard du Temple (1758–60; destr.); it earned a critical analysis from the Abbé Laugier, who perceived in him a promising exponent of the early phase of a new style. His subsequent private commissions included the

Palladian Pavillon Carré de Beaudoin (1770) on the Butte Montmartre and the remodelling of the Hôtel de Luynes (*c.* 1775; destr.; reassembled stateroom, Paris, Louvre). From 1764 to 1770 he rebuilt the Opéra and its façade (destr. 1781) on the first court of the Palais-Royal.

In succession to his uncle Jean-Baptiste-Augustin Beausire (1702–?86), Moreau-Desproux held from 1764 to 1787 the post of Maître des Bâtiments de la Ville de Paris; his official functions included designing the decorations for ceremonies arranged by the City, including the firework display in celebration of the wedding in 1770 of the Dauphin (later Louis XVI) and Marie-Antoinette. The centrepiece of the display was a temple erected on the Place Louis XV (now the Place de la Concorde). Moreau-Desproux's talents were most evident in his temporary building framing the Place de Grève and his drawing (based on an original idea of Francesco Bettini's) for the firework display on the Seine (both 1782), to celebrate the birth of a Dauphin.

BIBLIOGRAPHY

M. Gallet: 'Dessins de Pierre-Louis Moreau-Desproux pour des édifices parisiens', *Bull. Mus. Carnavalet*, xiv (1961), pp. 6–15
——: *Demeures parisiennes: L'Epoque Louis XVI* (Paris, 1964)
A. C. Gruber: *Les Grandes Fêtes et leurs décors à l'époque de Louis XVI* (Geneva, 1972)
A. Braham: *The Architecture of the French Enlightenment* (London, 1980)
M. Heimbürger-Ravalli: 'Un Décorateur de fêtes italien en France et son projet pour le feu d'artifice de Paris en 1782 à l'occasion de la naissance du dauphin', *Gaz. B.-A.*, lxxxxvi (January 1980)
Le Faubourg Saint-Germain. La Rue Saint-Dominique, hôtels et amateurs (exh. cat., Paris, Mus. Rodin, 1984)
Le Palais Royal (exh. cat., ed. B. de Montgolfier; Paris, Carnavalet, 1988)

MARC-H. JORDAN

Moreau-Nélaton, Etienne (*b* Paris, 2 Dec 1859; *d* Paris, 25 April 1927). French historian, collector and painter. His grandfather Adolphe Moreau (1800–59), a stockbroker, was a collector of modern paintings and a friend and patron of Eugène Delacroix, Alexandre-Gabriel Decamps and other Romantic artists; his father Adolphe Moreau (1827–82), a Conseiller d'Etat and administrator of the Compagnie des Chemins de Fer de l'Est, married in 1856 the ceramicist Camille Nélaton (1840–97). After studying at the Ecole Normale Supérieure, Paris (1878–81), Moreau-Nélaton decided in 1882 to become an artist and studied informally with Henri-Joseph Harpignies and Albert Maignan, who were friends of the family. He subsequently pursued a career as a painter, exhibiting at the Salon from 1885. He painted in a variety of styles, and was accomplished, if not strikingly original; his best works, influenced by Manet and Berthe Morisot, are intimate scenes of family life from the period 1901–7, such as *Reading* (1903; Paris, Mus. d'Orsay), a portrait of his son.

Moreau-Nélaton was one of the most passionate collectors of his time, acquiring paintings, drawings and prints not for financial gain but as a historian and connoisseur. He consolidated the family holdings by buying works by Delacroix and by Corot (e.g. the *Pont de Narni*, 1826; Paris, Louvre), and it is appropriate that *c.* 1897–1900 he should have bought Henri Fantin-Latour's *Homage to Eugène Delacroix* (1864; Paris, Louvre). He was a strong supporter of contemporary painters and bought works by the Impressionists, including Monet, Pissarro and Sisley. He seems to have bought specifically with the intention of giving his collections to the French nation and in 1888–90 was one of the subscribers to the appeal for Manet's *Olympia* (1863; Paris, Mus. d'Orsay). His purchase of Manet's *Déjeuner sur l'herbe* (1862; Paris, Mus. d'Orsay) in 1900 was thus intended to ensure that Manet should be worthily represented in the Musée du Louvre. In 1906 he donated the greater part of his collection to the Louvre, which received further paintings on his death.

From around 1913 Moreau-Nélaton gradually abandoned painting to concentrate on compiling documentary histories of the greatest French artists of his generation: Delacroix, Corot, Manet, Jean-François Millet, Johan Barthold Jongkind and others. The series of works he produced remains of fundamental importance, relying not on theory but on a strictly empirical basis of documentary evidence, much of which the author himself owned and which he bequeathed to the Bibliothèque Nationale, Paris. He was also one of the first to study seriously the portraits by Jean Clouet and François Clouet and their followers at the French court, and his work in this notoriously dangerous minefield remains the standard authority.

WRITINGS

with A. Robaut: *L'Oeuvre de Corot*, 4 vols (Paris, 1905)
Delacroix raconté par lui-même, 2 vols (Paris, 1916)
Jongkind raconté par lui-même (Paris, 1918)
Millet raconté par lui-même, 3 vols (Paris, 1921)
Les Clouet et leurs émules, 3 vols (Paris, 1924)
Daubigny raconté par lui-même (Paris, 1925)
Manet raconté par lui-même, 2 vols (Paris, 1926)
Bonvin raconté par lui-même (Paris, 1927)

BIBLIOGRAPHY

V. Pomarède: *Etienne Moreau-Nélaton: Un Collectionneur peintre ou un peintre collectionneur* (Paris, 1988)
De Corot aux impressionnistes: Donations Moreau-Nélaton (exh. cat., Paris, Grand Pal., 1991)

Moreelse, Paulus (Jansz.) (*b* Utrecht, 1571; *d* Utrecht, 5 March 1638). Dutch painter, draughtsman, architect and urban planner. He was from a well-to-do family, which settled in Utrecht *c.* 1568. According to van Mander, Paulus studied with the Delft portrait painter Michiel van Mierevelt and was in Italy before 1596, the year he became an independent master in the saddlemakers' guild, to which Utrecht painters then belonged. On 8 June 1602 he married Antonia Wyntershoven, by whom he had at least ten children. The most famous of his many pupils was Dirck van Baburen, who studied with him in 1611, when the Utrecht artists set up their own Guild of St Luke. Moreelse was instrumental in this and became its first dean. In 1618, after a series of political disagreements, a number of citizens, including Moreelse and the painter Joachim Wtewael, petitioned the town council to resign. When that occurred, Moreelse became a member of the new council and continued to hold various public offices until his death. He was a strong supporter of plans to found a university in Utrecht and was closely involved in the preparations and in its opening in 1636, even designing the cap presented to graduating students.

Moreelse's most important architectural design (known from drawings and prints, Zeist, Rijksdienst Mnmtz.) was for the Catherijnepoort (1621–5; destr.), one of the town gates. With this impressive structure he introduced the Italianate style into Utrecht. In 1624 he presented plans for the town's expansion to the council, which rejected them. His son Hendrick Moreelse, law professor at Utrecht University and a burgomaster of the town, implemented them posthumously in 1663.

Moreelse's earliest dated portrait painting is a *Portrait of a Man* (1602; ex-E. Hahr priv. col., Stockholm; see de Jonge, fig. 18). In the following year he painted a *Militia Company* (1603; untraced) for the headquarters of the archers' company in Amsterdam and in 1616 another of the same title for the headquarters of the crossbowmen's civic guard company (Amsterdam, Rijksmus.). As a consequence of his political activities, he received important commissions from the start of his career. Many eminent figures had their portraits painted by him or owned work of his. On 6 April 1627 the States of Utrecht resolved to present Prince Frederick Henry and his bride Amalia van Solms with one painting by Cornelis van Poelenburch, one by Roelandt Savery and two by Moreelse, these being *A Shepherd* (1627; Schwerin, Staatl. Mus.) and *A Shepherdess* (untraced). According to an inventory drawn up in 1632–4, five of Frederick Henry's *c.* 100 paintings were by Moreelse, whose many commissions from court circles included portraits of *Herzog Christian von Brunswick-Lüneburg* (1619; Brunswick, Herzog Anton Ulrich-Mus.) and *Sophia Hedwig, Countess of Nassau Dietz, as Caritas, with her Children* ('Charity', 1621; Apeldoorn, Pal. Het Loo; *see* ALLEGORY, fig. 8). This striking painting, a good example of a *portrait historié* or combination of portrait and allegory, makes a remarkable contrast to the formal life-size portrait of the same woman, *Sophia Hedwig of Brunswick-Wolfenbüttel* (1611; London, Hampton Court, Royal Col.), that Moreelse had painted ten years previously. Apart from the court and nobility, he portrayed persons of his own circle, for example the Utrecht artist *Abraham Bloemaert* (1609) and the scholar and close friend *Arnhout van Buchell* (1610; both Utrecht, Cent. Mus.). Several of his surviving portraits are of fellow town councillors, such as *Philips Ram* (1625; Utrecht, Cent. Mus.) and *Anthonie van Mansfelt* (1636; Brussels, Mus. A. Anc.).

Moreelse's best paintings of mythological subjects include *Venus and Adonis* (1622; Stuttgart, Staatsgal.), *Venus and Cupid* (1630; St Petersburg, Hermitage), *Cimon and Pero* (1633; Edinburgh, N.G.) and *Paris Holding the Apple* (1638; Brussels, Mus. A. Anc.). Most notable among his religious paintings are the *Beheading of John the Baptist* (1618; Lisbon, Mus. N. A. Ant.) and *Allegorical Representation of Piety* (1619; ex-C. J. K. van Aalst priv. col., Hoevelaken; see de Jonge, fig. 157). He was one of the earliest painters of arcadian scenes, a genre that originated in Utrecht, producing his first shepherds and shepherdesses in 1622 and continuing to paint similar scenes throughout his career. Exceptionally attractive among the many that survive is the *Portrait of Two Children in Pastoral Dress* (1622; The Hague, Rijksdienst Beeld. Kst, on loan to Utrecht, Cent. Mus.; *see* fig.).

Moreelse also made a number of drawings, which date primarily to his early period (e.g. *Judgement of Solomon*, before 1600; Amsterdam, Rijksmus.). Only a few engravings made after works or designs by him survive; two chiaroscuro prints of 1612 are attributed to him: *Cupid and Two Women* (Berlin, Kupferstichkab.) and the *Death of Lucretia* (Utrecht, Cent. Mus.).

Paulus Moreelse: *Portrait of Two Children in Pastoral Dress*, oil on canvas, 1205×950 mm, 1622 (The Hague, Rijksdienst Beeldende Kunst, on loan to Utrecht, Centraal Museum)

Paulus's sister Maria married the sculptor Willem Colijn de Nole (*d* 1620), and three of his own children became artists—his sons Johannes (Pauwelsz.) Moreelse (after 1602–34) and Benjamin (Pauwelsz.) Moreelse (before 1629–49) and a daughter—as did his nephew Willem Moreelse (1618/23–66).

BIBLIOGRAPHY
K. van Mander: *Schilder-boeck* ([1603]–04), fol. 280*v*
P. T. A. Swillens: 'Paulus Moreelse—"Const-schilder en raedt in de vroedtschap"', *Jb. Oud-Utrecht* (1926), pp. 114–35
C. H. de Jonge: *Paulus Moreelse: Portret- en genreschilder te Utrecht, 1571–1638* (Assen, 1938) [with many incorrect attrib.]
J. Rosenberg, S. Slive and E. H. ter Kuile, eds: *Dutch Art and Architecture, 1600–1800*, Pelican Hist. A. (Harmondsworth, 1966, rev. 2/1977), pp. 391–2
E. Taverne: *In 't land van belofte: In de nieuwe stadt* (Maarssen, 1978), pp. 242–78
M. J. Bok: 'Paulus Jansz. Moreelse', *Nieuw licht op de Gouden Eeuw* (exh. cat., ed. A. Blankert and L. J. Slatkes; Utrecht, Cent. Mus.; Brunswick, Herzog Anton Ulrich-Mus.; 1986–7), pp. 317–27
J. A. L. DE MEYERE

Moreira, Jorge (Machado) (*b* Paris, 23 Feb 1904; *d* 1992). Brazilian architect. He graduated in 1932 from the Escola Nacional de Belas Artes, Rio de Janeiro, where he participated in the reforms (1930–31) of Lúcio Costa when Modernist teachers including Gregori Warchavchik were introduced. He then worked for a construction company in Rio and designed some houses and blocks of flats. In 1936 he entered private practice and joined the team that developed the design for the Ministry of Education and Health (1936–45; now the Palácio da Cultura; *see* BRAZIL, fig. 5) in Rio with Le Corbusier; led

by Lúcio Costa, it also included Carlos Leão (1906–82), Affonso Eduardo Reidy, Ernani Vasconcelos (1912–87) and Oscar Niemeyer. This building introduced Le Corbusier's rationalist principles of Modernism to Brazil, influencing the work of all its young architects thereafter. Moreira, however, was the only one who did not subsequently move away from Le Corbusier's original postulates, becoming perhaps their most representative exponent in Brazil. He continued to use simple, prismatic shapes, never accepting the free structural forms developed by Oscar Niemeyer at Pampulha (1942–4), and he advised his students to avoid originality for its own sake as this would lead to unfortunate results for the less experienced. From 1949 to 1962 Moreira was involved principally with work for the Cidade Universitária in Rio de Janeiro; completed buildings include the engineering school, medical centre, child care institute and architecture school. All the buildings have a common identity in their clarity of form, use of similar materials, simple rectangular and transverse blocks, pilotis, open screens or *brise-soleil* and high-quality execution often including glazed tile mosaics, yet each is differently designed according to its different functions. The latter two buildings won first prize at the São Paulo Biennale (1953 and 1957 respectively) and the group won a gold medal at the Exposition Universelle (1958) in Brussels. Two projects in Rio de Janeiro for the financier Antonio Ceppas, a block of flats (1952) with its façades articulated by lattice grilles and movable louvres for ventilation, and a house (1958), also show Moreira's attachment to rationalist principles, used with a strong artistic imagination and attention to detail to produce works of great architectural merit.

BIBLIOGRAPHY
H. R. Hitchcock: *Latin American Architecture since 1945* (New York, 1955)
H. E. Mindlin: *Modern Architecture in Brazil* (Amsterdam and Rio de Janeiro, 1956)
Y. Bruand: *Arquitetura contemporânea no Brasil* (São Paulo, 1981)
A. Xavier, A. Britto and A. L. Nobre: *Arquitetura moderna no Rio de Janeiro* (São Paulo, 1991)
CARLOS A. C. LEMOS

Morel [Maurel]. French family of sculptors and architects. Although the family were active in Lyon from the 14th century, its two most important members (1) Pierre Morel and his son (2) Jacques Morel did most of their work elsewhere in France.

(1) Pierre Morel (*fl* 1386; *d* 1402). He should probably be identified with a certain 'maistre Perrin l'ymageur' ('sculptor'), who is recorded in 1386 and 1388 in Lyon. By 1390 he had apparently left Lyon, and from then on he was active in Avignon in the service of the papal court. In 1393 Morel was sent to Annecy by the anti-pope, Clement VII (*reg* 1378–94), in order to investigate a proposed building of a Celestine monastery. There he is referred to as 'Peyrenius', or 'quarryman', but it is as architect and Master of the Works that he worked on Clement's major project, the construction of a church at the Celestine monastery in Avignon. The cornerstone was laid in 1395, the year after Clement's death, and Morel's name appears on a contract signed in 1396. In 1401 the work was sufficiently advanced for Clement's body to be transferred. Morel was evidently also responsible for the decoration of the church, which included architectural sculpture, as well as for the tomb itself, from which fragments of the *gisant* (Avignon, Mus. Petit Pal.) and three figures from the bier (Virgin and Child, Apostle, Avignon, Mus. Petit Pal.; St Simon, Marseilles, Mus. Grobet-Labadié) remain.

Stylistic evidence suggests that Morel also served as architect for the church of St Martial, Avignon. As at the Celestine church, the design and handling of Flamboyant detail at St Martial represents a new northern element in the architecture of papal Avignon. Morganstern has also attributed to Morel the well-known tomb of Cardinal JEAN DE LA GRANGE, originally located against the wall of the choir at St Martial. The tomb, probably unfinished at the deaths of both the Cardinal and Morel in 1402, was destroyed in the Revolution (1789–95). Fragments preserved in the Musée Lapidaire in Avignon reveal the work of several hands. Morganstern's attribution, based largely on observed similarities between the architecture of the building and architectural details of the tomb, as well as on comparisons with sculpture of the Celestine church, has nevertheless not been accepted by Baron, who considers the La Grange sculpture to be more closely related to Burgundian work.

BIBLIOGRAPHY

Lami; Thieme-Becker

A. M. Morganstern: 'Pierre Morel, Master of Works in Avignon', *A. Bull.*, lviii (1976), pp. 323–49

F. Baron: 'Collèges apostoliques . . . dans la sculpture avignonnaise des XIVe et XVe siècles', *Rev. Louvre*, xxix (1979), pp. 169–86

Les Fastes du gothique: Le Siècle de Charles V (exh. cat. by J. Favier and others, Paris, Grand Pal., 1981–2), no. 100 [entry by F. Baron]

M. Beaulieu and V. Beyer: *Dictionnaire des sculpteurs français du moyen âge* (Paris, 1992), pp. 297–8

DOROTHY GILLERMAN

(2) Jacques Morel (*b* ?Lyon; *fl* 1418; *d* Angers, 1459). Son of (1) Pierre Morel. He was a widely travelled and prolific artist. He was named Master of the Works of Lyon Cathedral in 1418 and was contracted to execute an elaborate tomb for *Cardinal Amédée de Saluces* there in 1420 (destr. 1562). After leaving Lyon in 1424 or 1425, Morel worked in the Rhône valley and elsewhere in southern and central France. He is cited as an inhabitant of Toulouse in a commission for a silver altarpiece for Avignon Cathedral (1429; apparently never completed), as active in Béziers (1433; work for St Aphrodise), and as collaborator of Simon de Beaujeu in Tarascon (*c.* 1433). This was followed by periods of residence in Avignon (1441–5), Montpellier (1445–8) and Rodez, where in 1448 he received a contract for the construction and sculptural decoration of the south portal of the cathedral (work left incomplete in 1456). In 1448 he was commissioned to carve the alabaster tomb of *Charles I, Duke of Bourbon* (*d* 1456) and his wife *Anne of Burgundy* for the Chapelle Neuve of St Pierre, Souvigny. Completed in 1453, this is his only documented work to survive. Morel spent his last years from 1453 in Angers, where he completed the tomb of *King René of Anjou* (*d* 1480) and his first wife *Isabelle of Lorraine* (*d* 1453) in Angers Cathedral (begun 1450 by Jean Pocet (*d* 1452) and his son; destr.).

The Bourbon tomb in Souvigny was based on that of *Philip the Bold* (Dijon, Mus. B.-A.) by CLAUS SLUTER and his nephew Claus de Werve (as prescribed in the preserved contract). In spite of its fragmentary state, it is one of the masterpieces of French 15th-century sculpture. The monumentality and vigour of the recumbent effigies reveal Morel as one of the few artists fully to grasp and assimilate Sluter's style. While the garments of these figures retain Sluter's dramatic sculptural contrasts, they are more crumpled, sharpened in detail and animated by a restless sense of movement. The damaged faces are notable for their expressive force, heightened in the head of Duke Charles by his windswept hair, which is composed of crisply cut, aerated serpentine curls. As in Philip the Bold's tomb, the rectangular base is articulated by delicate architectural forms into a miniature alabaster 'cloister' originally set with small angels with coats of arms of the deceased as well as 44 weepers now lost. Two weepers (Moulins, Mus. Moulins) that have at times been associated with the Souvigny tomb are of inferior quality and differ markedly from Morel's style. On the other hand, the energetic verve of the historiated consoles with prophets in the Chapelle Neuve housing the tomb clearly show Morel's hand. Other attributions to the sculptor remain problematic. Foremost among these is the heavily restored alabaster tomb effigy of *Agnès Sorel* (*d* 1450), mistress of Charles VII, in Loches Castle (Indre-et-Loire), probably the work of a more conservative assistant or follower. While the commission of 1429 for a silver altarpiece suggests that Morel may also have worked in precious metal, the attempt to ascribe to him the silver bust of *St John the Baptist* in the abbey church of Quarante (Hérault) remains unconvincing on stylistic grounds.

BIBLIOGRAPHY

L. Courajod: 'Jacques Morel', *Gaz. Archéol.* (1885), pp. 236–55

N. Rondot: 'Jacques Morel, sculpteur lyonnais', *Réun. Soc. B.-A. Dépt.*, xiii (1889), pp. 622–52

Abbé Requin: 'Le Sculpteur Jacques Morel', *Réun. Soc. B.-A. Dépt.*, xiv (1890), pp. 87–95

J. Denais: 'Le Tombeau du roi René à la cathédrale d'Angers', *Réun. Soc. B.-A. Dépt.*, xv (1891), pp. 133–54

H. Stein: 'Une Dynastie d'architectes: Les Morel', *Moyen Age* (1910), pp. 235–44

H. Drouot: 'Jacques Morel et l'école de Dijon', *An. Bourgogne*, ii (1930), pp. 254–79

E. Bonnet: 'Le Sculpteur Jacques Morel à Montpellier', *Monspeliensa*, ii (1937), pp. 127–36

G. Troescher: *Die burgundische Plastik des ausgehenden Mittelalters und ihre Wirkungen auf die europäische Kunst* (Frankfurt, 1940), pp. 124–7

J. Thuile: 'Une Oeuvre orfèvrée de Jacques Maurel, le Saint Jean-Baptiste du prieuré de Quarante', *Bull. Mnmtl*, lxiv (1956), pp. 181–206

F. Robin: *La Cour d'Anjou-Provence: La Vie artistique sous le règne de René* (Paris, 1985), pp. 240–44

J. STEYAERT

Morel, Carlos (*b* Buenos Aires, 12 Feb 1813; *d* Quilmes, nr Buenos Aires, 10 Sept 1894). Argentine painter and lithographer. He studied drawing with Josef Guth at the University of Buenos Aires from 1827 to 1830. He was the first Argentine artist to complete his training within the country and is considered the earliest to have produced noteworthy work. He began as a miniaturist, painting portraits in collaboration with another Argentine painter, Fernando García del Molino (1813–99), including a portrait of the married couple *Juan Manuel de Rosas and Encarnación Ezcurra* (1836; García Lawson col.) and one of *Encarnación Ezcurra* (1839; Buenos Aires, Mus. Hist. N.). In 1841 he published eight lithographs depicting regional customs and manners as part of a large series printed by the firm Ibarra. In 1842 he travelled to Rio de Janeiro; on his return in 1844 his album *Usos y costumbres del Rio de la Plata*, including prints such as *Washerwomen* and *Army Parade*, were published by the Litografía de las Artes, the lithographic workshop of Luis Aldao in Buenos Aires. These were later widely reproduced in publications about Argentina during that period. Among Morel's oil paintings, *Cavalry Battle during the Regime of Rosas* and *Charge of the Cavalry Division of the Federal Army*, together with the watercolour *Gaucho Cavalry* (all 1839–40; Buenos Aires, Mus. N. B.A.), testify to his ability as both a history painter and a painter of local customs; his genuine sympathy for such themes is expressed by his lively brushwork and dynamic compositions. The cruel persecution of Morel's family by the dictator Juan Manuel de Rosas probably contributed to the artist's mental instability, leading to his almost total seclusion during the last 50 years of his life. This factor, together with the disappearance of much of his work (documented by the painter and historian Alfredo González Garaño (1886–1969) and the historian and art critic Alejo González Garaño (1877–1946)), led to his later neglect, although his reputation has since been rehabilitated.

BIBLIOGRAPHY

Carlos Morel (exh. cat. by A. Gonzalez Garaño, Buenos Aires, Asoc. Amigos A., 1933)
J. L. Pagano: *El arte de los argentinos*, i (Buenos Aires, 1937)
A. Matienzo: *Carlos Morel: Precursor del arte argentino* (Buenos Aires, 1959)
A. L. Ribera: 'La pintura', *Historia general del arte en la Argentina*, iii (1984), pp. 111–347

NELLY PERAZZO

Morellet, François (*b* Cholet, Maine-et-Loire, 30 April 1926). French painter, sculptor and stage designer. A self-taught artist, he began his career in 1952, painting endless repetitions of *tirets* (Fr.: 'hyphens'), which formed optically vibrating patterns. In the late 1950s he began series of *trames*, grids of small squares, then of lines drawn on paper and finally of aluminium rods. In works such as *8 Grids* (1958; Paris, Pompidou) the vertical, horizontal and diagonal lines at times form circles, creating the sparkling effect of a galaxy. In more sculptural works such as *Sphere-grid* (1962; priv. col., see 1986 exh. cat., p. 83) straight metal rods form a sphere that revolves when hung.

Morellet was a founder-member of the Groupe de Recherche d'Art Visuel (GRAV) in 1960. Besides contributing experiments with lines and spaces, like other members of GRAV he worked with optical effects, light and movement, producing grids of randomly flashing light bulbs, and from 1965 of neon rods. The role of the after-image was important in these works. The line became important again in the late 1960s when he taped black lines, *Adhesives*, on walls and buildings; in 1973 he began a series of *Disestablished Pictures* in which rectilinear canvases were placed at odd angles on a wall but united by a straight line running through them.

By 1981 the line had disappeared and Morellet placed canvases, sometimes outlined by coloured neon, seemingly at random against the wall (see 1986 exh. cat., p. 149). He also used these forms as decor for ballet from 1977. After constructing linear pieces of wire and timber poles in 1982 (see 1986 exh. cat., p. 151), he developed *Complementary*

Forms in 1983, in which, for example, a circle on a wall is paired with a circular branch on the ground (e.g. *Arcs of Complementary Circles*; Toulouse, Mus. Jacobins), or branches and plant stems are complemented by rigorous geometric shapes.

BIBLIOGRAPHY

François Morellet (exh. cat. by S. Lemoine, Chambéry, Mus. Savois., 1982)
François Morellet: Systems (exh. cat. by C. Kotik and J. van der Marck, Buffalo, NY, Albright-Knox A.G., 1984)
S. Lemoine: *François Morellet* (Zurich, 1986)
Morellet (exh. cat., ed. B. Blistène; Paris, Pompidou, 1986)

D. C. BARRETT

Morelli [Soldiero]**, Domenico** (*b* Naples, 7 July 1823; *d* Naples, 13 Aug 1901). Italian painter and teacher. Unique among his Italian colleagues in enjoying an international reputation in his lifetime, he was, with Filippo Palizzi (*see* PALIZZI, (2)), the leading exponent of the Neapolitan school of painting in the second half of the 19th century and a major figure in the artistic and cultural life of Italy. His realistic treatment of Romantic subjects revitalized academic painting, and his bold rendering of light and dark and his use of colour influenced both academic artists and more innovative painters such as the *Macchiaioli*.

1. Early work, to 1865. 2. Mature work, after 1865.

1. EARLY WORK, TO 1865. Morelli trained at the Reale Istituto di Belle Arti in Naples (1836–55) under Costanzo Angelini, Camillo Guerra (1797–1874), Filippo Marsigli (1790–1867) and Giuseppe Mancinelli (1813–75). While there he met Palizzi, with whom he formed an enduring friendship; he later credited Palizzi with having taught him to observe nature and expressively convey its effects by means of colour tones and chiaroscuro. In 1845 Morelli won the Concorso Triennale, gaining a prize that enabled him briefly to visit Rome, to which he returned in subsequent years and where he admired the work of Raphael and Michelangelo and came in contact with the Nazarenes (1847).

Morelli took part in the political uprising of 1848, being wounded and (briefly) arrested. In the same year, with the *Angel Appearing to Goffredo* (Naples, Gal. Accad. B.A.), he gained a scholarship to study in Rome, but because the political situation made this impossible, he used the scholarship in Naples instead. In 1850 he visited Florence with his future brother-in-law Pasquale Villari (1826–1917), who suggested literary themes to him and inspired him to paint Christian subjects with patriotic overtones, among them *Christian Martyrs Carried to Heaven by Angels* (1855; Naples, Capodimonte). Morelli's interest in the history paintings of Paul Delaroche is apparent in several works of the 1850s, including *Cesare Borgia at Capua* (1852; ex-Tasca Lanza priv. col., Palermo, see Levi, p. 54), his first significant history painting. The subject was drawn from Francesco Guicciardini's *Storia d'Italia* (1561–4) and it contains a reference to an illustration of the Inquisition by Joseph Nicolas Robert-Fleury as well as architecture inspired by Raphael's *School of Athens* (Rome, Vatican, Stanza Segnatura). Under the influence of Delaroche, Morelli adapted Palizzi's realism to historical themes and subjects taken from Romantic literature, rendering them as episodes of real life in order to enhance their impact:

his theory was that 'the purpose of painting is to represent figures and things, not seen, but imagined yet real at the same time'.

Morelli's first and most significant work in the new style, *The Iconoclasts* (1855; Naples, Capodimonte), is characterized by bold structural definition, strong modelling in chiaroscuro, fiery colouring in the manner of 17th-century Neapolitan painting and lack of finish. With this realistic representation of the martyrdom of the Byzantine monk and painter St Lazarus (*d c.* 867), Morelli alluded to the persecution of liberal artists by the Bourbon government. Similarly, the simulated reality of *Christian Martyrs* evoked the factual reality of friends and patriots killed in the uprising in Naples. The emphatic diagonals linking the figures in this picture and the dramatic colouring illustrate Morelli's taste for theatricality. Both paintings were exhibited in 1855 at the Esposizione di Belle Arti, Naples, where *The Iconoclasts* received public acclaim that established Morelli's reputation and was seen as a significant step in the move away from Neo-classicism towards Romantic Realism in history painting in Naples. Despite its political innuendo, it was purchased by Ferdinand II, King of Naples and Sicily, who in 1857 commissioned from the artist a fresco cycle of the *Life of St Francis* (unexecuted; 2 *bozzetti* in Rome, G.N.A. Mod.) for S Francesco, Gaeta. It was in his portraits that Morelli's realistic vocabulary was most effective; for example, the portrait of *Bernardo Celentano* (1859; Rome, G.N.A. Mod.), with its penetrating characterization and strong physical presence, is regarded as a prime example of 19th-century Italian Realism.

In 1855–6 Morelli travelled extensively in Italy and in Germany, the Low Countries and England, visiting painters, museums, collections and, in Paris, the Exposition Universelle (1855). He met some of the leading painters of the time—including Jean-Léon Gérôme and Ernest Meissonier in France, Louis Gallait in Belgium and Lawrence Alma-Tadema in England—and greatly admired the work of Rembrandt and Delaroche, as well as examples of German decorative art. In Milan, Venice (where he was drawn to the work of Giambattista Tiepolo) and Florence he met painters who were reacting to the constraints of an academic training. This stimulated him to establish links with artists from other regions that were intended to lead to the formation—with the unification of Italy—of a national style.

In the 1850s Morelli became a friend of the collector Giovanni Vonwiller, with whom he travelled and from whom he received several commissions. In Florence Morelli executed for him *Florentine Aubade in the Time of Lorenzo de' Medici* (1856; ex-Sonzogno priv. col., Milan; oil sketch, Rome, G.N.A. Mod.), probably inspired by *Sunday in Florence in the Fifteenth Century* (1855; Fontainebleau, Château) by Auguste Gendron. Its bold tonal structure and modelling of forms in chiaroscuro, its brilliant colours, depiction of natural light and bravura brushwork was to influence such academic painters as Stefano Ussi but was also to make an impact on the development of the *macchia* aesthetic in Florence in the late 1850s (*see* MACCHIAIOLI). Morelli also retained enthusiastic followers in northern Italy, particularly in Milan. At the first Esposizione Nazionale in Florence, in 1861, where *The Iconoclasts* met with enormous public and critical success, Morelli was hailed as the national leader of the new school of *Verismo storico* (*see* VERISMO).

Morelli became increasingly interested in quick, loose renderings and nuances of colour. This resulted in a progressive softening of forms, as shown by *Tasso and Eleonora d'Este* (*c.* 1863; Rome, G.N.A. Mod.), one of his most accomplished and evocative paintings, which he retained in his studio during his lifetime. The more finished second version, *Tasso and the Eleonoras* (1865; Rome, G.N.A. Mod.), on account of the freedom of the brushwork, unusual and harmonious juxtaposition of lustrous colours and tonal gradations, appeared extremely 'modern' and earned him fame as a colourist, winning a prize at the Exposition Universelle of 1867 in Paris.

2. MATURE WORK, AFTER 1865. By the mid-1860s Morelli had become one of the most celebrated painters in Italy, enjoying also a certain international reputation. In 1864 he had been appointed Consulente Ufficiale per gli acquisti della Casa Reale for the new Capodimonte collection; in this capacity, and as adviser to Vonwiller, Morelli shaped the character of the major 19th-century Neapolitan art collections. In 1867 he was appointed a member of the jury at the Exposition Universelle in Paris. In 1868 he became Professore di Pittura and in 1876 Direttore della Scuola di Figura at the Istituto di Belli Arti in Naples. Together with Palizzi, he carried out a reform of teaching methods that encouraged the exchange of ideas and freedom of expression, which attracted students from other cities. He was known and respected throughout Italy, and his guidance was sought by art schools and academies across the country.

In the late 1860s Morelli's subject-matter changed. He abandoned historical subjects and began to concentrate on religious themes, finding inspiration in both the Bible and the Koran—for example *Muhammed's Paradise* (1866–7; untraced) or *Muhammed's Prayer* (?1882; Trieste, Mus. Civ. Revoltella). This cycle began with the large painting of the *Assumption* (1864–9; *in situ*), which was commissioned for the ceiling of the chapel in the Palazzo Reale in Naples. In his approach to these subjects Morelli broke away from traditional formulae, carefully reading the sacred texts which he supplemented by studying contemporary literature on Islam, the writings of Joseph-Ernest Renan (1823–92)—in particular *La Vie de Jésus* (1863), a map of Palestine and numerous photographs, and by making contact with the Rabbi of Naples. All this he undertook in an attempt to convey an authentic character and atmosphere in scenes represented as if he were a contemporary observer. Stylistically he found inspiration in the art of Donatello. Such pictures as the *Marys on Mt Calvary* (*c.* 1870–71; Naples, Mus. N. S Martino; see fig. 1) display his talent for evoking strong emotion and for endowing biblical events with a human dimension, using a new, simplified language. His taste for powerful 'effect' and 'expression' is present in several strongly Rembrandt-esque scenes, structured with a forceful pattern of light and dark (e.g. *Deposition*, *c.* 1867; Rome, G.N.A. Mod.). Many of his works from this period are characterized by the expressive lack of finish, already evident in 1863.

Morelli worked with equal enthusiasm on paintings depicting lofty themes and on such commissions as designs

1. Domenico Morelli: *Marys on Mt Calvary*, oil on canvas, 710×790 mm, *c.* 1870–71 (Naples, Museo Nazionale di San Martino)

(see Vertova, 1975, nos 26–7) for the crib (Caserta, Pal. Reale) of the Prince of Naples (later Victor-Emanuel III, King of Italy) in 1869. In 1870 he was commissioned to decorate the curtain (*in situ*) for the new Teatro Municipale (now Teatro Verdi), Salerno, with a depiction of the *Battle of the Lega Campana against the Saracens* ('*Expulsion of the Saracens from Salerno*'). The image has a striking border of complex linear interlacings, reminiscent of medieval illuminations, in the painting of which Morelli was assisted by Giuseppe Sciuti and Ignazio Perricci (1834–1907).

In the early to mid-1870s Morelli's brushwork became even broader and freer, his palette brighter and splashed with light, especially after the arrival in Naples in 1874 of Mariano Fortuny y Marsal. They formed a close friendship, sharing an enthusiasm for the light and colour of the Mediterranean. An interest in exotic and Orientalist subjects manifested itself in a series of erotic nudes and sensual female figures, among them *Lady with a Fan* (1874; Naples, Banco di Napoli) and such anecdotal scenes as *Turkish Cemetery* (1876–8; Florence, Pitti). Morelli is remembered principally in this period for the *Temptation of St Anthony* (1878–9; Rome, G.N.A. Mod.; see fig. 2), a highly charged image that expresses one of the preoccupations of the time in its depiction of woman as the embodiment of earthly temptation as well as his own concern with the dualistic opposition of matter and spirit. Like most of his religious paintings, this work was not meant to be hung in a church for the devotion of the faithful; rather, it is a personal expression of philosophical idealism and emotional conflict. He executed three or four versions and numerous preparatory drawings. Morelli was seldom satisfied with his pictures, which he reworked many times over periods of years, often to the frustration of his clients, among whom was the French art dealer Adolphe Goupil.

In the 1870s and 1880s Morelli stayed at different times in the country at Cava de' Tirreni, where he painted numerous landscapes on small wood panels and a few watercolours, which are free and spontaneous recordings of a poetic response to nature. He used these images in his late compositions, in which landscape settings are invested with transcendental significance. The sterile nature of the *Temptation* and *The Obsessed* (1873–6; Milan, Casa Riposo Musicisti), symbol of sin and suffering, gave way to the fertile, festive nature of *Pater Noster* (1885–90) and the melancholy hill in a melting sunset light of *Loves of the Angels* (*c.* 1885; both Rome, G.N.A. Mod.). Based on a poem by Thomas Moore, *Loves* represents a theme that fascinated Morelli for some 20 years (from *c.* 1874) and of which he executed several versions. In these late pictures his manner became more abstract, his juxtaposition of colour at times strident, the light intense and penetrating, the figures diaphanous; the paintings have philosophical overtones that go beyond the subject represented. Morelli had moved from a literary Romanticism

2. Domenico Morelli: *Temptation of St Anthony*, oil on canvas, 1.38×2.25 m, 1878–9 (Rome, Galleria Nazionale d'Arte Moderna)

towards a more expressive form, which, in its externalization of ideas and feelings, parallels the Symbolist fusion of art and idea.

In 1883 Morelli was commissioned to produce cartoons (1884–9; Amalfi, Mus. Stor. Mun.) for mosaics on the pediment (the *Apocalypse*), the arches of the upper order (the *Apostles*) and the portal of Amalfi Cathedral. Between 1895 and 1898 he was commissioned to produce seven of the 100 illustrations for the Illustrated Bible (Amsterdam, 1900). He executed numerous preparatory drawings, including *Herodiad* (1897) and the *Prodigal Son* (1898; both Rome, G.N.A. Mod.). Throughout his career he produced numerous drawings, mostly in preparation for his paintings: the early ones, in pencil, are characterized by solid lines, the use of chiaroscuro and attention to detail; in later years he worked almost exclusively in pen and ink, using very fine, rapid lines, at times intricate and agitated, and ink blotches for dramatic expressive effects. For the most part he seems to have been preoccupied with individual poses, but he also sketched whole compositions, rapidly and vividly rendered in tiny dimensions and framed with a firm line.

In 1897 Morelli became Direttore Artistico of the Museo Artistico Industriale in Naples, an arts and crafts school that he had collaborated in founding in 1880. In 1886–99 he was responsible, with Guglielmo Raimondi, for the decoration of the maiolica façade of the building. Having resigned from the Istituto di Belli Arti in 1881, he returned as Direttore delle Scuole di Pittura di Figura e d'Ornamentazione in 1891, took charge of its art gallery in 1892 and became Direttore in 1896, before succeeding Palizzi as Presidente in 1899. Praised by his contemporaries as the poet-philosopher of the Christian legend, in his very late works, predominantly on a small scale, Morelli celebrated biblical expressions of piety, love and repentance; such was the dream-like *Shulamite and the Shepherd (Song of Songs)* (1901; Rome, G.N.A. Mod.), one of his last, unfinished works. At his death the Italian State purchased all the works in his studio: 47 paintings and *bozzetti*, 90 wood panels with landscape sketches and over 800 drawings and watercolours (all Rome, G.N.A. Mod.).

WRITINGS

Ricordi della scuola napoletana di pittura dopo il '40 e Filippo Palizzi (Naples, 1901)

BIBLIOGRAPHY

A. R. Willard: *Morelli* (Boston, 1895)
P. Villari: 'Domenico Morelli', *Nuova Antol.*, 4th ser., xcviii (1902), pp. 385–407
S. di Giacomo: *Domenico Morelli pittore* (Rome, 1905)
P. Levi: *Domenico Morelli nella vita e nell'arte: Mezzo secolo di pittura italiana* (Rome, 1906) [the only comprehensive monograph to date]
V. Spinazzola: *Domenico Morelli* (Milan, 1925)
G. Moroncini: *Il genio di Domenico Morelli* (Naples, 1933)
E. Campana: *41 disegni di Morelli e gli autoritratti di Vetri, Palizzi, Fortuny* (Naples, 1940)
C. Maltese: 'Otto paesaggi di Domenico Morelli', *Boll. A.*, xxxvi/4 (1951), pp. 240–45
Filippo Palizzi e Domenico Morelli (exh. cat., Naples, Soc. Promot. B.A. 'Salvator Rosa', 1961)
L. Vertova: 'Aggiunte a Domenico Morelli', *Ant. Viva*, xiv/1 (1975), pp. 41–53
Domenico Morelli e la sua epoca (sale cat., intro. L. Vertova; Rome, Christie's, 10 June 1975)
I. Lapi Ballerini: '"Comme si c'eût été Jérusalem" ... (II)', *Ant. Viva*, xviii/5–6 (1979), pp. 59–70
R. Causa: 'La pittura napoletana dell'ottocento', *Catalogo dell'arte italiana dell'ottocento*, ed. P. Levi, xiii (Milan, 1984), pp. 13–119
Il secondo '800 italiano: Le poetiche del vero (exh. cat., ed. R. Barilli; Milan, Pal. Reale, 1988)
M. A. Fusco: 'Morelli, Domenico', *La pittura in Italia: L'ottocento*, ed. E. Castelnuovo, ii (Milan, 1991), p. 929

EFREM GISELLA CALINGAERT

Morelli [Morell], **Giovanni (Lorenzo)** [Lermolieff, Ivan [Iwan]; Schäffer, Nicholas [Nicolaus]] (*b* Verona, 25 Feb 1819; *d* Bergamo, 28 Feb 1891). Italian politician, writer, collector and art historian. He was by birth an Italian, by parentage and education a Swiss Protestant, having attended the Kantonschule at Aarau (1826–32), and by intellectual development a German, having studied medicine and comparative anatomy at the universities of Munich and Erlangen (1833–8). An anonymous watercolour (*c.* 1835; Bergamo, Zavaritt priv. col.; see fig.) depicts him in his undergraduate lodgings at Munich, surrounded by anatomical drawings, hung skeletons and shelves of books, including a first edition of Johann Wolfgang von Goethe's works and textbooks by the French comparative anatomist Georges Cuvier. Morelli qualified as a doctor with Ignatius Döllinger, an influential biologist, but never practised clinical medicine. His real scientific interest was in comparative anatomy. Other interests are demonstrated by his publication, under the pseudonym Nicholas Schäffer, of *Balvi Magnus* (Munich, 1836/*R* 1991), a parody of iconographical method as practised by the archaeological faculty at Munich, written to entertain an artists' beer-drinking society. At Munich he made lasting contacts with artists such as Wilhelm Kaulbach and Buonaventura Genelli. In November 1837 he moved to the Protestant university at Erlangen, where he wrote, again under the pseudonym Schäffer, *Das Miasma Diabolicum* (Strasbourg, 1839/*R* 1990), a parody of the anti-aesthetic beliefs of a religious sect known as Die Mystiker. By June 1838 he was in Berlin, where he frequented Bettina von Arnim's salon and met the scientist Alexander von Humboldt as well as such artists as Karl Blechen, Ludwig Tieck and Wilhelm Stier. In August 1838 he accompanied the geologist Louis Agassiz to Switzerland, where Agassiz applied Cuvierian principles of morphological comparison to geology and formulated his theory of a global ice age. From late 1838 to 1840 he studied in Paris at the Jardin des Plantes, after which, disillusioned with science, he began a career as a writer. In Paris he met the dealer and connoisseur Otto Mündler, who became his first artistic mentor.

Having italianized his name on his return to Italy in 1840, Morelli wrote plays in order to refamiliarize himself with the language and was introduced by the writer Alessandro Manzoni to a group of Florentine intellectuals who played a leading part in the Risorgimento: Gino Capponi, Giovanni Battista Giorgini, Giuseppe Giusti, Niccolò Antinori and Giovanni Battista Niccolini, with whom he corresponded for the rest of his life. He introduced these new friends to German aesthetics, translating Johann Pieter Eckermann's conversations with

German school: *Giovanni Morelli in his Study at the University of Munich*, watercolour, 210×300 mm, *c.* 1835 (Bergamo, Zavaritt private collection)

Goethe (unpublished) as well as Friedrich Schelling's lecture on Dante (published in *Opere di G.-B. Niccolini*, Florence, 1858) and that of 1807 on aesthetics ('Sopra la relazione tra l'arte belli e la natura', *Lo spettatore industriale*, Milan, 1845). In the 1840s he wrote anonymous articles for the *Allgemeine Zeitung* in an attempt to influence German opinion against the repressive Austro-Hungarian regime in northern Italy, a cause that he continued to champion thereafter.

In the 1850s Morelli frequented political and artistic circles in Milan and Turin, and he met a group of English collectors, notably Sir Charles Lock Eastlake (the first director of the National Gallery, London), Sir James Hudson (English ambassador at Turin) and Sir AUSTEN HENRY LAYARD, for whom he bought pictures and whom he instructed in his method of scientific connoisseurship. They all frequented the studio of Giuseppe Molteni at the Brera, Milan, where paintings were restored, examined and reattributed while awaiting export licences.

After the unification of Italy, Morelli was elected to the Camera dei Deputati as the representative for Bergamo (1860–70) and in 1873 became a senator. He directed his energy towards the urgent reform of Italian museums, which he managed to implement by serving on numerous commissions. He helped to formulate new legislation concerning the exportation of works of art from Italy, made recommendations about the reform of instruction in artistic academies and assisted in the development of a more enlightened programme of conservation in Italian museums, with the help of Luigi Cavenaghi and Giovanni Secco-Suardo.

On retiring from politics, Morelli dedicated himself to promoting his new scientific method of connoisseurship, whereby he revised the attributions of paintings in public and private collections in Italy and Germany. He began with a series of articles (1874–6) on the Galleria Borghese, Rome, under the pseudonym Iwan Lermolieff (almost an anagram of his real name, particularly with his more usual spelling Ivan). His approach was influenced by the theories of scientific classification that he had studied with Döllinger and developed into a method of connoisseurship based on the analysis of characters and inspired by Cuvier's theory of the correlation of the parts. He distinguished three sets of characters in the 'language' of form: the poses and movement of figures, folds of drapery and colour constitute the general impression and therefore the least important set; the most important consists of anatomical details (e.g. hands, ears), landscape background and the harmony of colour; a peripheral set of artists' habitual modes of expression is not always applicable. Schelling's belief in the existence of parallels between nature and the spirit informed Morelli's view that forms reflected the spirit of their creator. He also appropriated Goethe's term 'morphology' for the scientific study of external forms in painting. After Freud wrote (1914) about the Morellian method in his study of Michelangelo's *Moses*, the method was often paralleled with the way in which psychoanalysis explores personality; Wind (1963) and others have emphasized the third, peripheral, set of characters to the neglect of the other two, an interpretation

that has been challenged by Anderson (1987) and Pau (1987). In 1880 Morelli published an account of the principal German collections of Italian Old Master paintings at Munich, Dresden and Berlin, again under the pseudonym Lermolieff, with significant reattributions for hundreds of paintings. This was followed by a series of important articles on Raphael studies (1881–2). In his last years he produced a definitive version of his collected writings as *Kunstkritische Studien* (1890–93), the last volume of which was published posthumously. Among his immediate disciples were Gustavo Frizzoni, Jean Paul Richter and Jocelyn Ffoulkes, who translated his works into English. His method was followed by the English collectors mentioned above, by the Viennese school of art historians (e.g. Julius von Schlosser), by Bernard Berenson and by archaeologists (e.g. J. D. Beazley), who even more than art historians needed to classify numerous anonymous fragments.

WRITINGS

Morelli wrote under various pseudonyms, beginning with Nicholas (or Nicolaus) Schäffer and finally as Ivan (or Iwan) Lermolieff, which he used for the authorship of his art-historical writings. For foreign editions he adapted a translation of his Italian name, Johannes Schwarze.

Iwan Lermolieff: 'Die Galerien Roms: Ein kritischer Versuch von Iwan Lermolieff. I. Die Galerie Borghese: Aus dem Russischen übersetzt von Dr Johannes Schwarze, mit Illustrationen', *Z. Bild. Kst*, ix (1874), pp. 1–11, 73–81, 171–8, 249–53; x (1875), pp. 97–106, 207–11, 264–73, 329–34; xi (1876), pp. 132–7, 168–73; rev. as book (Leipzig, 1890; rev. Eng. trans., London, 1892; rev. It. trans., Milan, 1897; rev. 1991)

Ivan Lermolieff: *Die Werke italienischer Meister in den Galerien von München, Dresden und Berlin: Ein kritischer Versuch von Ivan Lermolieff, aus dem Russischen übersetzt von Dr Johannes Schwarze* (Leipzig, 1880, rev. 2/1891–3; rev. Eng. trans., London, 1883, 2/1893; rev. It. trans., Bologna, 1886)

Kunstkritische Studien über italienische Malerei, 3 vols (Leipzig, 1890–93) [collct. writings, incl. biog. mem. by G. Frizzoni, iii, pp. xi–lxii]; Eng. trans., ed. C. J. Ffoulkes as *Italian Painters: Critical Studies of their Works* (London, 1892–1900) [incl. biog. intro. by H. Layard, i, pp. 1–39]

I. Richter and J. Richter, eds: Italienische Malerei der Renaissance im Briefwechsel von Giovanni Morelli und Jean Paul Richter, 1876–1891 (Baden-Baden, 1960)

BIBLIOGRAPHY

S. Freud: 'Der Moses des Michelangelo', *Imago*, iii (1914), pp. 15–36
E. Wind: 'Critique of Connoisseurship', *Art and Anarchy* (London, 1963), pp. 32–51, 139–53
R. Wollheim: 'Giovanni Morelli and the Origins of Scientific Connoisseurship', *On Art and the Mind* (London, 1973)
J. Fleming: 'Art Dealing and the Risorgimento', *Burl. Mag.*, cxv (1973), pp. 4–16; cxxi (1979), pp. 492–508, 568–80
C. Ginzburg: 'Spie: Radici di un paradigma indiziario', *Riv. Stor. Contemp.*, vii (1978), pp. 1–14; rev. in *Miti, emblemi, spie* (Turin, 1986), pp. 197–276
H. Zerner: 'Giovanni Morelli et la science de l'art', *Rev. A.* [Paris], xl–xli (1978), pp. 209–15
J. Anderson: 'Morelli and Layard', *Austen Henry Layard tra l'Oriente e Venezia: Venezia, 1983*, pp. 109–37
M. Panzeri: 'La Raccolta Morelli nell'Accademia Carrara di Bergamo: Un'ipotesi ricostruttiva del primo allestimento (1892)', *Archv Stor. Bergam.*, viii (1985), pp. 55–105
G. Agosti: 'Giovanni Morelli corrispondente di Niccolò Antinori', *Studi e ricerche di collezionismo e museografia Firenze, 1820–1920* (Pisa, 1985), pp. 1–83
F. Zeri and F. Rossi: *La Raccolta Morelli nell'Accademia Carrara* (Bergamo, 1986)
J. Anderson: 'Giovanni Morelli et sa définition de la "scienza dell'arte"', *Rev. A.* [Paris], lxxxv (1987), pp. 49–55
M. Panzeri and G. O. Bravi: *La figura e l'opera di Giovanni Morelli: Materiali di ricerca, Bergomum*, i (1987) [with list of writings and bibliog.], pp. 349–57
R. Pau: 'Le origini scientifiche del metodo morelliano', *Giovanni Morelli e la cultura dei conoscitori: Atti del convegno internazionale: Bergamo, 1987*

J. Anderson, ed.: *Giovanni Morelli's erste pseudonyme Veröffentlichungen 'Balvi magnus' und 'Das Miasma diabolicum'* (Würzburg, 1991) [with intro. and full bibliog.]
Giovanni Morelli: Collezionista di disegni (exh. cat., ed. M. T. Fiorio; Milan, Castello Sforzesco, 1994–5)

JAYNIE ANDERSON

Morelli, Lazzaro (*b* Ascoli Piceno, 30 Oct 1608; *d* 8 Sept 1691, *bur* Rome). Italian sculptor. He was trained by and worked with his father, Fulgenzio Morelli (*d c.* 1639), a sculptor and architect in Florence. He then moved to Rome, where he worked first with François Du Quesnoy and, from 1643, with Gianlorenzo Bernini, whose assistant he remained until the master's death in 1680. Bernini clearly held him in esteem, for Morelli was given work on some of his most important studio projects. In St Peter's, Rome, Morelli's work included the decoration of the pilasters of the nave and aisles (1645–50); the two putti over the tomb of *Urban VIII* (1646–7); and the gigantic stucco figure of *Peace* that fills the left spandrel of the third arch on the right of the nave (1647). In S Maria del Popolo, Rome, he made the stucco figure of *St Pudenziana*, over an arch in the nave (1655); and he contributed decorative work in stucco and travertine for the attic story of the Porta del Popolo (1656). He worked on the *Cathedra Petri* (1657–66) in St Peter's and supervised the project in 1665 while Bernini was in France. He carved 47 of the 90 statues in travertine for the colonnades of St Peter's Square (1660–73); the *Angel Carrying the Scourge* for the Ponte S Angelo, Rome (1669); the statue of *Truth* and the shroud on the tomb of *Alexander VII* (1673–6; Rome, Vatican, St Peter's). Morelli executed the travertine statues of female saints for the façade of S Maria di Monte Santo and a statue for S Maria dei Miracoli (1674–6), both in Rome. He also produced the colossal statue of *Benignity* on Mattia de' Rossi's tomb of *Pope Clement X* (1676–86) in St Peter's. His best student was Giuseppe Giosafatti, who helped spread Bernini's style to the Marches.

BIBLIOGRAPHY
Thieme–Becker
L. Pascoli: *Vite* (1730–36), ii, pp. 445–50
R. Wittkower: *Bernini* (London, 1966), pp. 20, 34, nos 30, 47, 58, 61, 67
V. Martinelli: *Le statue berniniane del Colonnato di San Pietro* (Rome, 1987), pp. 219–21
J. Montagu: *Roman Baroque Sculpture* (London, 1989), pp. 1, 97, 113–14, 128, 146–7
ROBERT H. WESTIN

Morelli, Nicola [Niccolò] (*b* Rome, 12 Sep 1771; *d* Rome, Feb 1838). Italian gem-engraver. He was a member of the Congregazione dei Virtuosi del Pantheon and the Accademia di S Luca (1812). He was renowned for his cameo portraits, preferring the technique to that of intaglio. Particularly noteworthy are the portrait of *Francis I, Emperor of Austria* (Vienna, Ksthist. Mus.) and the numerous works commissioned by the Bonaparte family. These include a cameo portrait of *Marie-Letizia*, a cameo with facing portraits of Lucien Bonaparte's two wives, *Cristine Boyer* (1773–1800) and *Alexandrine Blechamps* (1778–1855), another cameo portrait of *Alexandrine Blechamps* (all Rome, Mus. Napoleonico) and two portrait cameos of *Napoleon* (Rome, Villa Giulia; ex-Liverpool Mus.), the latter example given by Napoleon and Empress Marie Louise to Marshal Ney and his wife. (For an illustration of another cameo portrait by Morelli of *Napoleon see* GEM-ENGRAVING, fig. 17.) Morelli created (1807) a well-known parure that was given by Cardinal Joseph Fesch to his half-sister Marie-Letizia Bonaparte: the necklace, brooch and earrings contained nine cameo portraits of the Bonaparte family: *Napoleon I, Cardinal Fesch, Louis, King of Holland, Joseph, King of Naples and Spain, Carlo Maria Bonaparte, Lucien, 1st Prince of Canino, Jérôme, King of Westphalia, Pauline Borghese* and *Caroline Murat*.

Morelli also made many copies of ancient gem-engravings and executed many pieces with mythological subjects. These included a bust of *Alexander the Great* (Vienna, Ksthist. Mus.), a bust, possibly of *Jove* (St Petersburg, Hermitage), *Medusa* (Vienna, Ksthist. Mus.), *Cupid and Psyche* (Vienna, Ksthist. Mus.), a Bacchic scene (Berlin, Pergamonmus.), a bust of *Minerva* (London, BM), a bust of *Cupid* (London, BM), two Bacchantes (New York, Met.) and a bust of Bacchus (London, BM). Three cameos signed by Morelli (*Bacchic Scene, Eros on a Goat, Eros on a Swan* are in a necklace (New York, priv. col.), and two cameos for Anatole Demidov, Prince of San Donato, depicting *Bacchus and Cupid* and a *Bacchic Dance*, are documented by engravings in Guattani (1807). A cameo of *St George and the Dragon*, possibly intended for a patron's Order of the Garter, is in an English private collection. Morelli's works are signed N. MORELLI or with the Greek form of his name. They typify the fashion for gems of different-coloured strata, a taste that later became more pronounced in the works of Giuseppe Girometti and Benedetto Pistrucci. The latter was Morelli's pupil in Rome before 1800. It is possible that some of Nicola's works may have been confused with those of Gioacchino Morelli (*b* 1784), who worked in Rome as a gem-engraver around the same time, although there is little documentation regarding the latter's work. There is an oil portrait of Morelli by his son Carlo Morelli in Rome at the Accademia di S Luca.

BIBLIOGRAPHY
Forrer; Thieme–Becker
G. A. Guattani: *Memorie Enciclopediche Romane*, ii (Rome, 1807), pp. 8–10; iv (Rome, 1809), p. 157
A. Furtwängler: *Beschreibung der geschnittenen Steine im Antiquarium* (Berlin, 1896), p. 355
O. M. Dalton: *Catalogue of the Engraved Gems of the Post-classical Periods. . .in the British Museum* (London, 1915), nos 71, 98
F. Eichler and E. Kris: *Die Kameen im Kunsthistorischen Museum in Wien* (Vienna, 1927), pp. 215–16, nos 607–10
E. Kris: *Catalogue of Postclassical Cameos in the Milton Weil Collection* (Vienna, 1932), p. 37, figs 89, 90
R. Righetti: *Incisori di gemme e cammei a Roma* (Rome, [1954]), pp. 50–51
——: *Gemme e cammei delle collezioni comunali* (Rome, 1955), pp. 82–4, nos 1–3
G. C. Bulgari: *Argentieri, gemmari e orafi d'Italia, Roma*, ii (Rome, 1959), p. 178
L. Pirzio Biroli Stefanelli: 'Nicola Morelli incisore in pietre dure, Accademico di merito di S Luca, virtuoso del Pantheon', *Bollettino dei Musei comunali di Roma*, vi (1992), pp. 63–76, figs 1–11
LUCIA PIRZIO BIROLI STEFANELLI

Moreno, Francisco de Paula Mendoza y. *See* MENDOZA Y MORENO, FRANCISCO DE PAULA.

Moreno, José (*b* Burgos, ?1642; *d* Burgos, ?1674). Spanish painter. His early training was in Burgos, and he then went to Madrid, where he was a pupil of Francisco de Solís.

According to Palomino, he returned to Burgos when he was 30 and died soon after. Palomino named only three of his works: the *Flight into Egypt*, *St Catherine* and *St Anthony*, without any indication of their location. Two signed canvases of the *Flight into Egypt* are known (Madrid, Prado; and Minneapolis, MN, Inst. A.). Other works by Moreno include a *Visitation* (1662; Madrid, Prado), an *Annunciation* (1668; Madrid, Convent of the Salesas Reales), *St Francis* and *St John the Baptist* (both 1669; Saragossa, Mus. Prov. B.A.). The composition of the *Visitation* is harmonious, with warm tonalities and the figures of the Virgin and St Anne standing in contrapposto, while the *Flight into Egypt* (Madrid, Prado) includes a fine landscape background. Of four paintings formerly in the Dominican convent of St Paul in Burgos, three are in the parish church of Quintanadueñas, near Burgos, where they were moved when the convent was dissolved in the 19th century. These are the *Immaculate Conception*, *St Michael Releasing Souls from Purgatory* and an *Allegory of the Gregorian Mass*; the fourth, portraying *St John the Evangelist*, remains untraced. Another documented work, a *Holy Family*, is also lost. Moreno was an accurate draughtsman and favoured soft colour tonalities.

BIBLIOGRAPHY

A. A. Palomino de Castro y Velasco: *Museo pictórico* (1715–24/R 1947), p. 976
D. Angulo Iñiguez: 'José Moreno', *Archv Esp. A.*, xxix (1956), p. 67
——: *Pintura del siglo XVII*, Ars Hispaniae (Madrid, 1971), p. 301
J. Ibáñez: 'Obras del pintor José Moreno en Quintanadueñas (Burgos)', *Bol. Semin. Estud. A. & Arqueol.*, xliii (1977), pp. 491–4
A. E. Pérez Sánchez: *Pintura barroca española* (Madrid, 1992), p. 303

ENRIQUE VALDIVIESO

Moreno Capdevila, Francisco (*b* Barcelona, 18 Jan 1926). Mexican printmaker and painter of Spanish birth. He emigrated to Mexico in 1938 and took Mexican nationality in 1939. He studied painting at the Escuela de Artes Plásticas in Mexico City and printmaking under Carlos Alvarado Lang. In his prolific production of murals and easel paintings he showed a preference for acrylics and for warm tones and strong colours contrasted with black, as in the mural the *Conquest and Destruction of Tenochtitlán, Mexico* (1964; Mexico City, Mus. Ciudad). Using a forceful Expressionist technique, he fluctuated between representational and abstract idioms, with an underlying current of social criticism.

Moreno Capdevilla earned a high reputation also as an illustrator and printmaker, producing woodcuts, etchings and lithographs. In 1968, for example, he exhibited a series of etchings entitled *Light and Darkness* (see 1987 exh. cat., fig. 172), a dramatic vision of existence in which black and white achieves its maximum expression. He trained several generations of artists at the Escuela Nacional de Artes Plásticas.

BIBLIOGRAPHY

H. Covantes: *El grabado mexicano en el siglo XX, 1922–1981* (Mexico City, 1982), pp. 167–8
Capdevila, visión múltiple (exh. cat. by A Rodríguez and M. E. Garmendia, Mexico City, Pal. B.A., 1987)

XAVIER MOYSSÉN

Moreno Villa, José (*b* Malaga, 16 Feb 1887; *d* Mexico, 25 April 1955). Spanish painter, poet, critic and art historian. He studied history of art at the university of Madrid and worked as a medievalist at the Centro de Estudios Históricos (1910–16). He was an archivist at the Instituto Jovellanos in Gijón (1921–2) and head of archives at the Palacio Real (1931–6); concurrently he was a tutor at the Residencia de Estudiantes (1917–36) and director of the journal *Arquitectura* (1927–33). Having been exiled from Madrid to Valencia with other artists and intellectuals in November 1936, he was sent in 1937 to the USA as part of a cultural propaganda visit. While there, he was invited by the Mexican government to base himself in Mexico, where he remained until 1955; he catalogued the works of art deposited in the Bienes Nacionales and worked for both Casa de España en México and the Colegio de México.

Self-taught as a painter, Moreno Villa produced works in a form of poetic Surrealism, which became more luminous, incorporating elements of a fantastic expressionism (e.g. the *Stone on one's Back*, oil on canvas, 1931; Madrid, Mus. N. Cent. A. Reina Sofía). He participated in numerous exhibitions, including the Primera Exposición de los Artistas Ibéricos in Madrid (1925) and the *Exposición internacional del surrealismo*, held at the Galería de Arte Mexicano in Mexico City (1940). In 1924 he translated Heinrich Wölfflin's *Kunstgeschichtliche Grundbegriffe* into Spanish. The subjects for his art historical writing and criticism included the art of Velázquez and Mexican Colonial sculpture. As a poet he broke with *modernismo* and proclaimed the new poetry of the Generación del 27 (including García Lorca and Rafael Alberti). Examples of his paintings are housed in the Museo Nacional Centro de Arte Reina Sofía and the Biblioteca Nacional in Madrid, and in the Museo Provincial de Bellas Artes in Málaga.

WRITINGS

Velázquez (Madrid, 1920, rev. 2/1961)
La escultura colonial mexicana (Mexico City, 1941, rev. 2/1986)
Lo mexicano en las artes plásticas (Mexico City, 1948, rev. 2/1986)

BIBLIOGRAPHY

José Moreno Villa, 1887–1955 (exh. cat., Málaga, Mus. Prov. B.A., 1977)
E. Carmona: *José Moreno Villa y los orígenes de las vanguardias artísticas en España, 1909–1936* (Malaga, 1985)
José Moreno Villa (1887–1955) (exh. cat., ed. J. Pérez de Ayala; Madrid, Bib. N., 1987)

JUAN PÉREZ DE AYALA

Moretti, Cristoforo (*fl* 1450–75). Italian painter. A minor but prolific Milanese artist, he first appears as a creditor of the Borromeo family in Milan in 1450 and 1451. The following year, several letters addressed to Duke Francesco Sforza (*reg* 1450–66) show him as painter primarily of pennants and horse trappings. Moretti continued to work for the Sforza family during the 1450s. In 1462, however, he was banished from Milan for writing a defamatory letter about the wife of the court physician Cristoforo da Soncino.

Documents after 1463 indicate that the artist then moved into the nearby region of Piedmont, where he painted coats of arms and the communal tower in Turin. In 1467 he decorated a chapel in Casale Monferrato for William VI, Margrave of Monferrat (*reg* 1464–83), and three years later he provided an altarpiece for S Marco, Vercelli. He left incomplete fresco decorations in this same church when he returned to Milan in 1469, after his banishment had been lifted. He rejoined the group of artists working for the Sforza court, and notarial deeds suggest that he became a wealthy man.

Moretti's only signed work is a triptych of the *Virgin and Child with SS Gervase and Lawrence* from S Aquilino, Milan (Milan, Mus. Poldi Pezzoli). On the basis of this work, which shows the strong influence of Michelino da Besozzo, numerous other pictures, miniatures and a painted glass reliquary have been attributed to Moretti. The most convincing attributions include the *Crucifixion* (Berlin, Gemäldegal.) and the *Virgin with Saints* (Munich, Alte Pin.).

BIBLIOGRAPHY
E. Motta: 'Una lettera di Cristoforo Moretti', *Boll. Svizzera It.*, vii (1885), p. 176
——: 'Ancora una supplica del pittore Cristoforo Moretti', *Boll. Svizzera It.*, vii (1885), p. 246
F. Malaguzzi-Valeri: *Pittori lombardi del quattrocento* (Milan, 1902), pp. 79–88
G. Biscaro: 'Note di storia dell'arte e della cultura a Milano dai libri mastri Borromeo, 1427–1478', *Archv. Stor. Lombardo*, xvi (1914), pp. 71, 108
R. Longhi: 'I resti del polittico di Cristoforo Moretti già in Sant' Aquilino di Milano', *Pinacotheca*, i (1928), pp. 75–9
M. Natale: *Museo Poldi-Pezzoli: Dipinti* (Milan, 1982), pp. 67–71

E. SAMUELS WELCH

Moretti, Gaetano (*b* Milan, 26 July 1860; *d* 30 Dec 1938). Italian architect and teacher. He was the son of a well-known Milanese furniture-maker, Luigi Gaetano (*b* 1828), from whom he learnt the craft of inlay work and modelling in wood. After attending technical school he went to the Accademia di Brera, where he studied under CAMILLO BOITO and obtained a diploma in architectural design (1883). In 1886 he became a professor of architecture at the Brera, and he was appointed to the Chair when Boito retired in 1908. Indeed, Boito's influence on Moretti's work was evident throughout the latter's career, particularly in his rigorous assembling of historical styles in a closely observed but never vulgar eclecticism, skilfully adapted to different building types and functions.

Moretti's career began brilliantly, with prize-winning entries in the competitions for the façade of Milan Cathedral (1888) and the Palazzo del Parlamento in Rome (1889). Despite its symmetrical plan, his first important commission, the new cemetery (1894) at Chiavari, near Genoa, had considerable emotional power, as a result of the theatrical nature of its hillside setting and a style enlivened by medieval and oriental motifs. The most productive period of his career as an architect, between 1896 and 1914, began with the Crespi Mausoleum and cemetery at Crespi d'Adda, near Capriate d'Adda. In the monumental mausoleum, although there are still references to Egyptian and central Asian architecture, by refining themes already found at Chiavari, he at last arrived at a coherent style that reflected the power of industrial patronage, and the building became a model for the funerary buildings of the time. His work at the Esposizione Internazionale d'Arte Decorativa at Turin in 1902 demonstrates that despite his attachment to the Stile Floreale, the Italian Art Nouveau style, he was basically loyal to the tradition of Boito's eclecticism. Moretti achieved his most convincing results with the restrained elegance of the residential buildings on the Via Legnano (1907) and Via Majno (1911) in Milan, which show an awareness of the Wagnerschule, and in the relaxed and unforced arrangement of the various blocks of the Kursaal buildings at Varese (1906; destr. 1944). In his most famous work, the hydroelectric power station at Trezzo d'Adda (1906), the allusion to a mock-medieval style is completely personal, sensitive to the symbolic importance of the theme and the character of the site.

Despite the elegance of his architectural solutions and of the decorative elements, which show his awareness of the most advanced European thinking, Moretti's work during this period remained faithful to the historicist tradition and reflected his concern with old buildings, particularly in Lombardy. He had been a friend and close collaborator of LUCA BELTRAMI from the time of the latter's restoration of the Castello Sforzesco (1893–1905) in Milan, and he applied his historical methods in the practice of conservation, succeeding Beltrami as Director (1895–1908) of the Ufficio Regionale per Conservazione dei Monumenti. Among other buildings, he worked on the restoration (1894, with Cesare Nava) of S Sepolcro in Milan and the reconstruction (1903–12) of the campanile of S Marco, Venice. He was also involved with numerous religious buildings and their furnishings (such as S Francesco, at Gallarate, Lombardy, in 1909).

After World War I Moretti was much less active. Appointed to chair many ministerial commissions to promote contemporary Italian art abroad, he made useful contacts in South America, where he had already established a reputation in 1909 with his winning design (unexecuted) for a competition for the monument to Argentinian independence in Buenos Aires. He did, however, design the eclectic Galleria di Belle Arti (1921), now the Museo de Arte Italiano in Lima, Peru, and the Neo-classical Legislative Palace (1913–25) in Montevideo, Uruguay, laying out the surrounding area with theatrical perspective axes in the 19th-century manner. His marginal position on the contemporary Italian architectural scene was confirmed by his dwindling commissions (such as an office block on the Piazza Duomo, Milan, in 1926, with Ambrogio Annoni (1882–1954)), but his belief in a rationally structured classicism remained, as did his authority as a teacher, and in 1934 he became head of the new Faculty of Architecture in Milan.

WRITINGS
Il nuovo cimitero per la città di Chiavari (Milan, 1894)
'La conservazione dei monumenti in Egitto e Grecia', *Boll. Ufficiale Min. Pub. Istr.*, xlviii (1902)
Sistemazione di piazza de Ferrari (Genoa, 1905)
La conservazione dei monumenti della Lombardia dal 1 luglio 1900 al 31 dicembre 1906 (Milan, 1908)
Costruzioni, concorsi, schizzi, intro. by L. Beltrami (Milan, 1912)
El monumento a la Revolución de Mayo y a la independiencia argentina, en Buenos Aires (Milan, 1914)
'Camillo Boito', *Atti Coll. Ingeg. & Architetti Milano* (1915)
'Criteri nei restauri dei monumenti sacri', *A. Crist.* (1921)

BIBLIOGRAPHY
A. Annoni: 'Un maestro dell'architettura tra l'ottocento e il novecento: Gaetano Moretti', *Politecnico di Milano: Inaugurazione dell'anno accademico 1951/52* (Milan, 1952)
M. Calzavara: 'L'architetto Gaetano Moretti', *Casabella*, 218 (1958)
M. Nicoletti: *L'architettura Liberty in Italia* (Rome and Bari, 1978)
L. Rinaldi: *Gaetano Moretti* (Milan, 1993)

LUCA RINALDI

Moretti, Luigi (*b* Rome, 2 Jan 1907; *d* Isola di Capraia, 14 July 1973). Italian architect, urban planner and writer. Trained as an architect in Rome, he graduated in 1930 and advanced rapidly through contacts within the Fascist party. His principal early works in Rome are the Casa della Gioventù (1933–40) in Trastevere, the planning of the Foro Italico (1934–40), the design of some individual buildings there—the Casa delle Armi (1934–6), a gymnasium for Mussolini and the Cella Commemorativa (1940)—and a competition entry (1938) for the Ministry of External Affairs Building (EUR), Rome. Already eclectic, his architecture of this period combined the Rationalism of the Milan–Como school with references to the monumental architecture of Imperial Rome. After the war he initially worked in Milan, building an apartment hotel in Via Corridoni and a residential and commercial complex at Via Rugabella. In Rome he designed two apartment buildings—Casa Astrea (1949) in Monteverde Nuovo and Casa Il Girasole (1950) in the Parioli district—and a sculptural, free-flowing villa, La Saracena (1954), at Santa Marinella.

The Casa Il Girasole is Moretti's best-known work. The building is on a rough-hewn stone plinth and presents to the street an extraordinary façade that oversails the corners to appear cardboard thin. This façade is shaped along the roofline to suggest an assymetrical classical pediment and is split down the middle to form a deep cleft that marks the entrance. While it alludes to traditional Roman apartment buildings in plan and to Classical architecture in elevation, at the same time form follows function in an entirely rational way. The building puzzled critics at the time; its gentle satire of Modernism cast early doubt on the integrity of the Modern Movement, and Robert Venturi cited it as an exemplar to Post-modernism (see R. Venturi: *Complexity and Contradiction in Architecture* (London, 2/1977), pp. 20, 22).

Moretti was a formidable theoretician, and in 1950 he founded the architectural magazine *Spazio*, which he edited until 1952. His own contributions included a discussion of the visual importance of surface modelling in Classical architecture and an analysis of spatial sequence in buildings. This was illustrated with negative models where the rooms and linking spaces were expressed as solid and the supporting structure as void. During World War II Moretti's contacts with mathematicians at Rome University working on military operational research led to his concept of 'parametric architecture'; this was a design method whereby architectural and urban-planning requirements could be quantified mathematically, then projected into built form. The objective was to create an architecture more truly functional than the stylistic Functionalism of the Modern Movement. This led to pioneering work with computers in architecture; in 1957 he formed the Istituto Nazionale per la Ricerca Matematica e Operativa per l'Urbanistica (IRMOU).

After 1960 Moretti designed a variety of large-scale commercial buildings in the USA, Canada, Algeria and the Middle East. The most important are the Watergate residential complex (1961–3), Washington, DC, an Italian–American development, and the Stock Exchange Tower (1961–7) at Place Victoria, Montreal, an elegant building structured in concrete, with engineer Pier Luigi Nervi. His work in Italy from this period includes residential buildings, such as the San Maurizio apartments (1962) in the Monte Mario district of Rome, office buildings in EUR for Esso and the Società Generale Immobiliare (1963–5), the thermal spa, Boniface VIII (1965), at Fiuggi, a bridge over the Tiber for the metro (1965–73) and office buildings (1972–4) in Via Morgagni and adjacent to Piazzale Flaminia (1971–4).

It is difficult to classify Moretti's work within modern Italian architectural history. Deeply rooted as he was in the Modern Movement, Moretti responded to the Roman context by introducing forms of historical imagery that avoid the Neo-realism of Mario Ridolfi's architecture, with its associated interest in provincial building construction. On a broader level, his work evades rigid classification into either historical eclecticism or orthodox Modernism as practised by the Rationalist architects of the Milanese school.

WRITINGS

ed.: *Spazio*, i–vii (1950–53) [incl. several articles by Moretti]
'Ricerca matematica in architettura e urbanistica', *Moebius*, iv/1 (1971–2)

BIBLIOGRAPHY

G. Ungaretti: *50 immagini di architettura di Luigi Moretti* (Rome, 1968)
R. Bonelli, ed.: *Moretti* (Rome, 1975) [with list of writings]

MICHAEL FORSYTH

Moretto (da Brescia) [Bonvicino, Alessandro] (*b* Brescia, *c.* 1498; *d* Brescia, between 9 Nov and 22 Dec 1554). Italian painter. Together with Romanino and Giovanni Girolamo Savoldo, he was one of the most distinguished painters of Brescia of the 16th century. Influenced by both Lombard verism and contemporary Venetian painters, Moretto created an individual style in which realism and Venetian light and colour were perfectly balanced. He was personally involved in the local movement of Roman Catholic reform, and this is reflected in his direct, solemn and often moving depictions of religious subjects. He was also an innovative portrait painter.

1. Before 1530. 2. 1530–54.

1. BEFORE 1530. Moretto's birthdate is calculated from a document of 1548 in which he declared that he was about 50 years old, but another document (Boselli, 1976), which names Moretto as early as 1514, suggests that the traditional date may not be strictly accurate. Moretto was born to a family of local artists originating in the town of Ardesio. His father, Pietro Bonvicino (*d* before Aug 1515), and his uncle Alessandro Bonvicino (*d* before Nov 1484) both worked on projects in the Loggia in Brescia and painted heraldic devices throughout the 1480s and 1490s. Although much of Moretto's later career is well documented, his development from 1516 to 1520 cannot be precisely charted.

Despite the attributional confusion outlined by Panazza (see 1965 exh. cat.), the organ shutters with *SS Faustino and Giovita* (Lovere, S Maria in Valvendra), commissioned for the Old Cathedral, Brescia, are securely dated early works. The shutters were begun in August 1515 by Floriano Ferramola (1480–1528), who painted the exterior scenes of the *Annunciation*, and Moretto received his first payment in November 1516 for the equestrian saints in fashionable contemporary dress. A lunette of the *Coronation of the Virgin with Saints* (Brescia, S Giovanni Evangelista) signed *Alexander. Brix.* is clearly by the same hand, although Morelli, followed by Nicodemi, thought it so close to Romanino that they attributed it, along with a small group of additional works, to Romanino's hypothetical 'brother or cousin' Alessandro. Boselli (1943) convincingly attributed it to Moretto and dated it *c.* 1516. The impressive *Christ Carrying the Cross with Donor* (Bergamo, Gal. Accad. Carrara) was once dated 1518. Three smaller paintings, *Christ and the Samaritan Woman* (Bergamo, Gal. Accad. Carrara), *Christ among the Animals* (New York, Met.) and *Christ Blessing St John the Baptist* (London, N.G.), the latter two possibly fragments, should also be dated *c.* 1518. Several other high-quality works have been attributed to the youthful Moretto: of these, the most interesting are the *St Roch with other Saints* (S Euphemia della Fonte, Parish Church; on dep. Brescia, Pin. Civ. Tosio-Martinengo), traditionally given to Romanino but probably by Moretto deeply under the influence of Romanino (A. Ballarin, unpublished lecture); and an attribution of a *Virgin between SS Gregory and Valentine* in S Gregorio delle Alpi, near Feltre (Fiocco, 1948).

Moretto's training and early travels are undocumented, but this body of work of *c.* 1515–20 demonstrates that he quickly outstripped his first collaborator, Ferramola. While Ridolfi's assertion (1648) that Moretto studied with Titian cannot be confirmed, his works of *c.* 1518 are so deeply influenced by Venetian art, above all that of Titian, that it is reasonable to assume he made a journey to Venice or at least to Padua. That Moretto was closely attentive to the work of Romanino is clear as early as 1516 in the organ shutters (A. Ballarin, unpublished lecture). Other Lombard artists, especially Vincenzo Foppa, also influenced him.

By 1517 Moretto was an important figure in Brescia; that year he attended a meeting of local artists in the church of S Luca, and after 1520 he played a leading role in such local organizations as the Scuola del Sacramento of the cathedral, where he was elected to the council, and received a string of important commissions. In March 1520 Mattia Ugoni, Bishop of Famagosta, requested money at a meeting of the city council for a *gonfalone* (processional banner) commemorating the relics of the True Cross housed in Brescia Cathedral. This banner, only one side of which is extant (Brescia, Pin. Civ. Tosio-Martinengo), shows the *Exaltation of the Reliquary of the Holy Cross between SS Faustino and Giovita*; the worshippers below include identifiable portraits. Although the cartellino is now blank, Ridolfi said that Moretto's signature was then legible. The connection with Ugoni was fruitful for Moretto, who later painted frescoes of *Moses and the Burning Bush* and the *Prophets* for the Bishop's private chapel in the family palazzo (Brescia, Pin. Civ. Tosio-Martinengo).

Perhaps Moretto's most important commission of the 1520s came from the deputies of the Confraternità del Sacramento and the prior of the Augustinian canons of S Giovanni Evangelista, Brescia, for the decoration of the Cappella del Sacramento in their church. The contract is dated 21 March 1521. The decorative scheme was shared with Romanino, and their canvases were arranged around Bernardo Zenale's pre-existent altarpiece of the *Deposition* (*c.* 1505), set in an elaborate framework carved by the local sculptor Stefano Lamberti in 1509. Moretto's contribution includes a lunette of the *Last Supper*, *Elias and the Angel*, the *Gathering of Manna*, the *Evangelist Luke*, the *Evangelist Mark* and a series of *Prophets*. The theme of the cycle is Christ as the food of life: it is a significant early example of a complex decorative scheme for a sacrament chapel of a type that became common in Italy only later in the 16th century.

A standard (untraced) for the guild of the Mercanzia was dated 1523, while the *Portrait of a Monk* (Verona, Castelvecchio), which, according to Guazzoni (1981), represents Girolamo Savonarola, and the contract for the *Assumption* for the high altar of the Old Cathedral of Brescia both date from 1524. Moretto's inventive approach to portraiture, already apparent in the intense posthumous portrait of Savonarola, is seen again in the full-length *Portrait of a Gentleman*, dated 1526 (London, N.G.), which may depict Gerolamo II Avogadro. The format and the presentation of the subject are similar to those made famous by Titian in his portrayal of *Charles V with his Dog* (1533; Madrid, Prado), but Moretto's painting antedates that work by some seven years. It is therefore seminal in the development in Italy of this type of portrait, possibly originating in Germany. In 1526 Moretto received an important commission from the Comune of Brescia for a fresco of the *Translation of the Remains of SS Faustino and Giovita* (destr.; copy by Pietro Maria Bagnadore, 1603; Brescia, Loggia). It was painted on an exterior wall of the Porta Brusata to mark the location of a miracle and typifies the emphasis Moretto's patrons placed on local religious themes.

By 1528 Moretto's reputation in Brescia was secure, and he began to make contacts in other Lombard towns. A letter of December 1528 from Lorenzo Lotto in Bergamo invited Moretto to continue Lotto's work decorating the choir of S Maria Maggiore for the society of the Misericordia of that city and demonstrated his admiration for Moretto's painting. Moretto went to Bergamo and was paid for his trip and for various drawings for intarsias on 26 January 1529, but any work he may have done there is unidentified.

2. 1530–54. Moretto continued to travel in the 1530s: on 23 December 1530 he wrote from Milan to Monsignor Savello in Salò about the work of G. G. Antegnati, the organ builder. In 1535 he joined the court of Isabella d'Este at Solarolo, and he was again in Milan in 1541. Correspondents included Pietro Aretino, who wrote thanking him for a portrait (untraced) in 1544. But above all Moretto continued to work in Brescia, buying a house in the S Clemente district in 1533 and becoming increasingly involved in local affairs.

A group of paintings from the 1530s exemplifies the various directions that Moretto's work was taking. The altarpiece of *St Margaret of Antioch with SS Jerome and Francis of Assisi* (Brescia, S Francesco) is dated 1530, and the *Massacre of the Innocents* (Brescia, S Giovanni Evangelista) was commissioned the same year, by two members of the Casari family in honour of their young nephew, and was consecrated in December 1532. The first documents for the decoration of the Cappella del Sacramento in the

1. Moretto: *Supper at Emmaus*, oil on canvas, 1.47×3.05 m, *c.* 1526 (Brescia, Pinacoteca Civica Tosio–Martinengo)

Old Cathedral date from 1531, and between then and 1534 Moretto probably produced four paintings for it, including the important lunette of the *Sacrifice of Isaac.* (The project was taken up again in the 1550s and continued after Moretto's death.) The altarpiece of the *Apparition of the Virgin to the Deaf-mute Filippo Viotti* for the sanctuary at Paitone (*in situ*), commemorating the appearance of the Virgin to a young peasant, is usually dated 1533–4, a convincing date stylistically and also tied to that of the miracle and the foundation of the church. According to Boselli (1954), the *Coronation of the Virgin with Saints* (Brescia, SS Nazaro e Celso) was executed in 1534, and in June 1536 a group of Bergamask patricians commissioned the altarpiece of the *Virgin and Child with SS Andrew, Eusebia, Domno and Domneone* (Bergamo, S Andrea). *St Nicholas of Bari Presenting Pupils of Galeazzo Rovelli to the Virgin and Child* (the Rovelli Altarpiece; Brescia, Pin. Civ. Tosio-Martinengo) was painted for the church of S Maria dei Miracoli in 1539; the cartouche includes the name of the patron, Galeazzo Rovelli, a Brescian schoolmaster.

Each of this impressive series of paintings illustrates a variation on Moretto's shifting combination of elements drawn both from the local tradition and from the Veneto and central Italy. In the *St Margaret* altar the forms are of an amplitude reminiscent of Palma Vecchio, while Moretto's reputation as the 'Raphael of Brescia' rests on the classicizing *Massacre of the Innocents.* His continuing strong interest in Venetian art is exemplified by the Rovelli Altarpiece, which evidently refers to Titian's Pesaro *Madonna* (Venice, S Maria Gloriosa dei Frari), and by the sumptuous *St Giustina with a Donor* (Vienna, Ksthist. Mus.), which is undated but related to various paintings of the 1530s. Such works as the *Virgin* at Paitone belong to a local, Lombard tradition and draw on the example of Vincenzo Foppa. In this painting, the strong colouring is softened by the silvery greys and rust colours found in Foppa's late works, and there is a subdued, even sombre mood derived from the same source. As in Moretto's

earlier works, those of the 1530s contain poetic depictions of landscape and a distinctive manipulation of light that exaggerates the surface qualities of textiles; both are evident in the *Coronation* in SS Nazaro e Celso. The naturalistic detail and rough figure types in such paintings as the altarpiece in S Andrea, Bergamo, or the earlier *Supper at Emmaus* (*c.* 1526; Brescia, Pin. Civ. Tosio-Martinengo; see fig. 1) led Longhi (1929) to see Moretto as a predecessor of Caravaggio.

By the end of the 1530s Moretto increasingly avoided narrative and showed a marked preference for static and iconic forms: ideological changes in the religious community of Brescia partially account for this shift to simple, legible and forceful images (Guazzoni, 1981). Altars of the Sacrament were in demand—four by Moretto date from the 1540s—commissioned for rural churches throughout the large diocese. These include two of Moretto's most striking works, *Christ with Symbols of the Passion and the Eucharist and SS Cosmas and Damian* (Marmentino, SS Cosma e Damiano) and *Christ with Symbols of the Passion and the Eucharist and SS Bartholomew and Roch* (Castenedolo, S Bartolomeo), in which figures, symbols and architecture are arranged with symmetry and geometric order in spare, but powerful compositions. The Sacrament altar of *Christ with Moses and Solomon* (1541; Brescia, SS Nazaro e Celso) is a good example of the imagery of this decade: Moses and Solomon lean on stelae carved with inscriptions below the resurrected Christ, whose blood flows into a chalice held by an angel with a tablet reading 'Hic est sangus novis testamentum'. This urge to illustrate Roman Catholic dogma reached its high point late in Moretto's career in a pair of organ shutters of *SS Peter and Paul Supporting the Church* (Brescia, Seminario di S Angelo). Here, behind raised red curtains, the two muscular apostles literally hoist a church on to their shoulders.

Works from Moretto's studio continued to be in great demand throughout the 1540s: altarpieces were sent to S

Giorgio in Braida at Verona (1540), the church of the Umiliati at Verona (1541; ex-Kaiser-Friedrich Mus., Berlin; destr.), S Maria presso S Celso in Milan (1540–41) and S Stefano in Bergamo (1544; Milan, Ambrosiana). Moretto continued to produce a remarkable series of portraits as well, culminating in the *Portrait of a Young Man* (London, N.G.; see fig. 2), probably painted to commemorate the wedding of Fortunato Martinengo in 1542 (Boselli, 1978). This depiction of a richly dressed, pensive gentleman, with a Greek inscription on his velvet hat, surrounded by inkwells and other accoutrements, is a significant contribution to a genre of portraiture started by Lorenzo Lotto. Unique in Moretto's oeuvre is his design for the decoration of a small room in the Palazzo Salvadego, Brescia, commissioned on the occasion of a marriage between a Martinengo and a Gonzaga in 1543. Although the poor state of preservation of the mixed-technique frescoes makes it difficult to discuss style or quality, this is a festive and unusual scheme, showing young women seated on balustrades set in landscapes with towns, hills and lakes.

There is an unmistakable decline in the execution of many works from the later 1540s, and many of the paintings produced in Moretto's studio are marred by the intervention of students. The series of altarpieces painted for St Clemente, Brescia, exhibit a certain awkwardness typical of many of these later canvases, while in the *Virgin and Child with St Bernardino and other Saints* (London, N.G.) all five male saints are adapted from earlier works. However, in these years Moretto also created some of his most profound and deeply felt images. In the *Christ with an Angel* (Brescia, Pin. Civ. Tosio-Martinengo) he banished all accessories and almost all colour, concentrating attention on the grief-stricken angel and tortured figure of

Christ. His last painting, the *Entombment* (New York, Met.), is dated October 1554.

Moretto seems to have been most comfortable working in oil or tempera on canvas, although a number of his works up to *c.* 1530 are on panel (e.g. *St Margaret of Antioch with SS Jerome and Francis of Assisi*). Several of his later paintings, particularly those in tempera, are extremely fragile and have lost paint layers; this should not obscure Moretto's move to a more muted palette later in his career. Only a handful of drawings can be attributed to him with any degree of certainty (see the list in 1988 exh. cat.). Many questions also remain regarding Moretto's studio: he took on a number of pupils, the most important of whom was Giovanni Battista Moroni.

BIBLIOGRAPHY

EARLY SOURCES

G. Vasari: *Vite* (1550, rev. 2/1568); ed. G. Milanesi (1878–85), vi, pp. 505–6

P. Aretino: *Lettere sull'arte di Pietro Aretino* (before 1556), ed. E. Camesasca (Milan, 1957), i, p. 231; ii, p. 24

B. Faino: *Catalogo delle chiese di Brescia: MSS E.VII.6 e E.I.10 della Biblioteca Queriniana di Brescia, 1630–1669*; ed. C. Boselli (Brescia, 1961)

C. Ridolfi: *Meraviglie* (1648), ed. D. von Hadeln (1914–24), i, pp. 147, 262–7, 415

F. Paglia: *Il giardino della pittura: MSS G.IV.9 e Di Rosa 8 della Biblioteca Queriniana di Brescia, c. 1667–1675*; ed. C. Boselli (Brescia, 1967)

G. A. Averoldi: *Le scelte pitture di Brescia additate al forestiere* (Brescia, 1700)

F. Maccarinelli: *Le glorie di Brescia: MS. della Biblioteca Queriniana di Brescia, 1747–1751*; ed. C. Boselli (Brescia, 1959)

G. B. Carboni: *Le pitture e le sculture di Brescia* (Brescia, 1760)

B. Zamboni: *Memorie intorno alle pubbliche fabbriche di Brescia* (1778)

P. Sgulmero: *Il Moretto a Verona: Per le nozze Boschetti–Musato* (Verona, 1899)

C. Boselli: 'Documenti inediti di storia d'arte bresciana', *Comment. Ateneo Brescia* (1946–7), pp. 1–15

L. Chiodi: 'Lettere inedite di Lorenzo Lotto', *Bergomum*, n. s. 2, lxii (1968), p. 137

C. Boselli: *Regesto artistico dei notai roganti in Brescia dall'anno 1500 all'anno 1560* (Brescia, 1976)

M. C. Rodeschini: 'Note sulle due pale del Moretto a Bergamo', *Not. Pal. Albani*, x (1981), pp. 23–35

S. Guerrini: 'Note e documenti per la storia dell'arte bresciana dal XVI al XVIII secolo', *Brixia Sacra*, xxi (1986), pp. 3–85

GENERAL

DBI: 'Bonvicino, Alessandro'; Thieme–Becker

S. Fenaroli: *Dizionario degli artisti bresciani* (Brescia, 1877)

I. Lermolieff [G. Morelli]: *Die Werke italienischer Meister in den Galerien von München, Dresden und Berlin* (Leipzig, 1880)

B. Berenson: *Central and North Italian Schools*, i (1968), pp. 274–9

S. Freedberg: *Painting in Italy, 1500–1600*, Pelican Hist. A. (Harmondsworth, 1971, 2/1983), pp. 367–72

M. Gregori: *Pittura del cinquecento a Brescia* (Milan, 1986)

G. Briganti, ed.: *La pittura in Italia: Il cinquecento* (Milan, 1987)

MONOGRAPHS

S. Feraroli: *Alessandro Bonvicino soprannominato il Moretto* (Brescia, 1875)

P. Molmenti: *Il Moretto da Brescia* (Brescia, 1898)

P. da Ponte: *L'opere del Moretto*, 2 vols (Brescia, 1898)

G. Gombosi: *Moretto da Brescia* (Basle, 1943) [standard monograph]

C. Boselli: *Moretto* (Brescia, 1954)

E. Cassa Salvi: *Moretto* (Milan, 1966)

V. Guazzoni: *Moretto: Il tema sacro* (Brescia, 1981) [excellent intro.]

P. V. Begni Redona: *Alessandro Bonvicino, il Moretto da Brescia* (Brescia, 1988)

Alessandro Bonvicino, il Moretto (exh. cat., Brescia, Monastero S Giulia, 1988)

SPECIALIST STUDIES

P. Guerrini: 'L'altare dei SS Innocenti in S Giovanni e la famiglia Casari', *Illus. Bresc.* (1 Jan 1907), pp. 7–9

2. Moretto: *Portrait of a Young Man*, oil on canvas, 1.14×0.94 m, *c.* 1542 (London, National Gallery)

R. Longhi: 'Cose bresciana del cinquecento', *L'Arte*, xx (1917), pp. 99–114; also in *Scritti giovanile* (Florence, 1961)

E. Lovarini: *Le sontuossime nozze di Hieronimo Martinengo: Pubblicate per le nozze Caponi–Benati* (Cividale del Friuli, 1922)

G. Nicodemi: 'Per un libro sul Romanino', *L'Arte*, xxix (1926), pp. 277–80

R. Longhi: 'Quesiti caravaggeschi: I precedenti', *Pinacotheca*, v–vi (1929), pp. 258–320; also in *Me pinxit e quesiti caravaggeschi* (Florence, 1968)

R. Eisler: 'Jesus among the Animals', *A. America*, xxiii (1935), pp. 137–9

A. Morassi: *Catalogo delle cose d'arte e d'antichità d'Italia: Brescia* (Rome, 1939)

La pittura bresciana del Rinascimento (exh. cat., ed. F. Lechi; Brescia, Pin. Civ. Tosio-Martinengo, 1939)

C. Boselli: 'Alexander Brixiensis', *L'Arte*, xiv (1943), pp. 95–129

Pittura in Brescia dal duecento all'ottocento (exh. cat., ed. G. Panazza and C. Boselli; Brescia, Ist. Cult., 1946)

C. Boselli: 'Asterischi morettiani', *A. Ven.*, ii (1948), pp. 85–98

G. Fiocco: 'Un'opera giovanile del Moretto', *Boll. A.*, xxxiii (1948), pp. 330–34

P. Guerrini: 'La scuola del duomo', *Mem. Stor. Dioc. Brescia*, xix (1952), pp. 29–52

C. Boselli: 'Il gonfalone delle SS Croci', *Comment. Ateneo Brescia* (1953), pp. 101–9

——: 'Noterella bresciana', *A. Ven.*, xi (1957), pp. 204–5

R. Bossaglia: 'La pittura bresciana del cinquecento', *Storia di Brescia*, ii (Brescia, 1963)

Mostra di Girolamo Romanino (exh. cat., ed. G. Panazza; Brescia, Duomo Vecchio, 1965)

C. Gould: *The Sixteenth-century Italian Schools*, London, N.G. cat. (London, 1975), pp. 155–65

G. Testori: *Romanino e Moretto alla cappella del Sacramento* (Brescia, 1975)

C. Boselli: 'Noterella morettiana: Il presunto Sciarra Martinengo di Londra e la sua datazione', *A. Lombarda*, il (1978), pp. 83–4

Bergamo per Lorenzo Lotto (exh. cat., ed. G. Mascherpa and others; Bergamo, Gall. Accad. Carrara, 1980)

ANDREA BAYER

Moretto da Bergamo [Moro di Martino]. *See* CODUSSI, MAURO.

Moreux, Jean-Charles (*b* Paris, 1889; *d* Paris, 1956). French architect. He studied architecture at the Ecole des Beaux-Arts in Paris and then took the course in Monuments Historiques. Influenced by his friendship with André Lurçat, he adhered to contemporary architectural theories throughout the 1920s. In 1926 he designed the Wanda Landowska Concert Hall as well as a number of private houses in which he used a metal framework as the basis of his structures. He also produced theoretical plans for workshop and studio buildings and for an overall reorganization of the architecture of Paris. He was one of the foremost members of the French group at CIAM. In the early 1930s Moreux began to express doubts about what he referred to as 'tubism' and to distance himself from the ideals of the day. Thereafter, Moreux rediscovered the attractions of traditional forms and materials, which he used in a number of houses in Paris (often reinterpreting the architecture of buildings designed in a functionalist spirit, such as the Hefferlin house belonging to Lurçat, which Moreux transformed into a Spanish-style caprice in 1937).

Moreux also devoted his attention to studying the history and design of museums and to interior architecture; he introduced a number of elements into the decoration of some of his domestic interior designs (such as stuffed animals or shells) and worked in order to reconstitute fantastical natural landscapes. Much of Moreux's work was dominated by garden design. In 1938 he executed the layouts and rocaille constructions for the Square des Gobelins in Paris, and he later directed work on a large number of other private and public gardens such as that of the French Embassy in London. He also restored a number of examples of 17th- and 18th-century landscaping. Moreux was also an active instigator behind the rediscovery of Claude-Nicolas Ledoux' architectural work, on whom he wrote a monograph.

WRITINGS
with M. Raval: *Claude-Nicolas Ledoux, 1736–1806* (Paris, 1945)

BIBLIOGRAPHY
A. Laprade: 'L'Oeuvre de Jean-Charles Moreux', *L'Architecture*, lii (July 1939), pp. 239–46

S. Day, M. Mosser and G. Ragot: *Jean-Charles Moreux* (Paris, 1993)

JEAN-LOUIS COHEN

Morey, Charles Rufus (*b* Hastings, Michigan, 20 Nov 1877; *d* Princeton, 28 Aug 1955). American art historian. He graduated from the University of Michigan in 1899 and received his MA in Classics there in 1900. After three years in Rome as a fellow in the American School of Classical Studies, he moved to Princeton University, joining the Department of Art and Archaeology in 1906 and quickly gaining an international reputation as America's leading scholar of Late Antique and medieval art. He was chairman of that department from 1925 to 1945, occupying the Marquand Professorship from 1938 until his retirement. During his tenure he founded the Princeton Index of Christian Art, organized the joint American–French excavations at Antioch, and was instrumental in the creation of the Firestone Library. His greatest contributions to scholarship were in the field of medieval figural art, particularly the origins of Christian art in the transformation of the classical heritage in the early Middle Ages. His eminent reputation as classicist, medievalist and administrator led to a number of important positions outside Princeton. He was invited by the Vatican Library to edit the scholarly catalogues of the Museo Sacro, contributing the volumes on ivory and gold glass. After World War II, he held several posts in Rome: Acting Director of the American School (1945–7), first President of the Union of Archaeological and Historical Institutes (1945), and cultural attaché to the American Embassy (1945–50). He was a founder and lifelong supporter of the College Art Association, a fellow of the Medieval Academy, and recipient of numerous honours in the USA, Italy, France and Belgium.

WRITINGS
Lost Mosaics and Frescoes of Rome of the Mediaeval Period (Princeton, 1915)

The Sarcophagus of Claudia Antonia Sabina and the Asiatic Sarcophagi (Princeton, 1924), i/5 of *Sardis*, 17 vols (1916–)

'The Sources of Mediaeval Style', *A. Bull.*, vii (1924), pp. 35–50

The Miniatures of the Manuscripts of Terence prior to the Thirteenth Century (Princeton, 1930)

Gli oggetti di avorio e di osso del Museo Sacro Vaticano (Rome, 1936)

The Mosaics of Antioch (London, 1938)

Early Christian Art (London, 1942, rev. Princeton, 1953)

Mediaeval Art (New York, 1942)

BIBLIOGRAPHY
A. Bull., xxxii [Festschrift and bibliography]

R. Lee: 'Charles Rufus Morey, 1877–1955', *A. Bull.*, xxxvii, pp. iii–vii

F. H. Taylor: 'Charles Rufus Morey, 1877–1955', *Sat. Rev.*, xxxviii (15 Oct 1955), pp. 11, 33–4

LAWRENCE E. BUTLER

Morgan, F(rederick) Cleveland (*b* Montreal, 1 Dec 1881; *d* Senneville, nr Montreal, 3 Oct 1962). Canadian collector. He was educated in Canada and England, receiving degrees from McGill University, Montreal and Cambridge University, England. In 1904 he joined the family-owned department store, Henry Morgan & Company. His influence in Montreal extended to the Arts Club (as a charter member), Canadian Handicraft Guild, McCord Museum, McGill Library and Montreal Museum of Fine Arts. Joining the Art Association of Montreal in 1907 (later Montreal Museum of Fine Arts) and serving on most committees, he was a member of the executive committee from 1940 until his death and president from 1948 to 1956. From 1952 he was a member of the board of trustees of the National Gallery of Canada until his resignation in 1959 as a protest 'against unwarranted government interference'.

Morgan's main interest was in the decorative arts and he assembled an important catalogued collection, purchased mainly in London and New York, most of which he gave to the Montreal Museum of Fine Arts. As a young man his enthusiasm for Japanese pottery and Chinese porcelain was encouraged by Sir William Cornelius Van Horne. In 1916 Morgan became the first Chairman of the Museum Committee of the Montreal Museum of Fine Arts (later the Decorative Arts Committee) and was entirely responsible for the department for the next 46 years. Under his influence the collection grew to over 7000 objects to include medieval Western art, Far Eastern pottery and porcelain, Islamic art, Luristan bronzes, Benin masks, Pre-Columbian gold and early traditional furniture of Quebec. Morgan also had a lasting interest in landscape gardening and horticulture and was Vice-president of the Royal Horticultural Society from 1944.

BIBLIOGRAPHY
Apollo, ciii/171 (1976) [issue ded. to Montreal Museum of Fine Arts col.]
N. Morgan: *F. Cleveland Morgan and the Decorative Arts Collection at the Montreal Museum of Fine Arts* (diss., Montreal, Concordia U., 1985)
NORMA MORGAN

Morgan, James (*d* Cheesequake, NJ, 26 Feb 1784). American potter. In 1750 he inherited property near the head of Cheesequake Creek, NJ, from his father and from about that time owned a tavern known as Cheesequake Hotel and Morgan House. From about 1754 he also operated in the same location a stoneware pottery, which may have been started in the early 1740s by members of the Dutch Staats family. Morgan's access to the rich clay resources in this vicinity gave rise to the designation of certain clays as 'Morgan's best'. The wares were not marked, but fragments of pots, jugs, jars, mugs, chamber pots, bowls, plates, cups, colanders and pitchers have been found (e.g. Trenton, NJ State Mus.). Grey salt-glazed stoneware in the Rhenish manner with incised and blue-filled decoration is characteristic. The pottery spawned others in the area, which became an important centre for stoneware production in the 19th century. James Morgan jr (1756–1822) operated the pottery from his father's death in 1784 until *c.* 1805, when he founded a pottery in nearby South River Bridge. Thomas Warne (1763–1813) may have been an apprentice or journeyman in Morgan's pottery. In 1786 Warne married Mary Morgan, daughter of James Morgan sr, and shortly thereafter established a pottery near by, which he later ran in association with his son-in-law Joshua Letts until *c.* 1813. It continued to be used by subsequent potters.

BIBLIOGRAPHY
M. L. Branin: *The Early Makers of Handcrafted Earthenware and Stoneware in Central and Southern New Jersey* (Rutherford, 1988)
ELLEN PAUL DENKER

Morgan, J(ohn) Pierpont (*b* Hartford, CT, 17 April 1837; *d* Rome, 31 March 1913). American collector and banker. He was the son of the merchant banker Junius P. Morgan, whose business he continued, and in the late 19th century and the early 20th he was one of the most powerful men in the USA. He did no significant collecting until after his father's death in 1890, when he began to acquire fine manuscripts, incunabula, autographs, first editions and rare books ranging from a copy of the Gutenberg Bible (*see* BIBLE, fig. 6), the Mainz Psalter of 1459 and the Lindau Gospels (9th century) to the original autograph manuscripts of John Keats's *Endymion* and Charles Dickens's *A Christmas Carol*. By 1900 this collection had grown to such proportions that Charles Follen McKim was commissioned to design an Italian Renaissance-style palazzo in New York to hold it (now the Pierpont Morgan Library), and in 1904 BELLE DA COSTA GREENE was appointed curator. He often purchased entire library collections, for example that of Richard Bennett, which included illuminated manuscripts, early books and part of the medieval library of William Morris and 32 items printed by William Caxton.

Morgan began collecting works of art in the early 1900s. By the time of his death his collection was vast and generally considered to be one of the best in the world, with an estimated value of some £160,000,000. His holdings ranged widely and included Byzantine ivories and enamels, Italian maiolica (e.g. plates by Giorgio Andreoli, dated 1525 and 1529), East Asian porcelain, enamel work (e.g. Stavelot Triptych, *c.* 1150; *see* ROMANESQUE, fig. 78), 18th-century snuffboxes, miniatures, French tapestries and furniture and Old Master drawings and paintings, among them Lucas Cranach the elder's portrait of *Martin Luther* (*c.* 1525). Most of the paintings he owned were 18th-century French and English works, including the series of panels painted by Jean-Honoré Fragonard for the pavilion of Marie-Jeanne Bécu, Comtesse Du Barry at Louveciennes in 1772 (now New York, Frick), and Thomas Gainsborough's *Georgiana, Duchess of Devonshire* (1785; Washington, DC, N.G.A.), with a small group of 16th- and 17th-century pieces, including a *Portrait of a Moor* (*c.* 1570), from the workshop of Tintoretto. The breadth of Morgan's collection resulted from his desire to acquire only the most highly prized works of all types, rather than a comprehensive selection of any one area. To this end he regularly purchased entire collections: among those he acquired were the Gréau collection of ancient glass, the Le Breton collection of faience, the collection of *boiseries* of Georges Hoentschel (1855–1915), and the collection of Old Master drawings assembled by Charles Fairfax Murray. To help him in his search for works, Morgan used a number of experts, such as the German museum curator

Wilhelm von Bode and the English dealers Thos Agnew and Sons.

In keeping with the mood of nascent national pride characteristic of America in the late 19th century, Morgan wished to build up a collection whose quality and range would make travel to Europe superfluous. However, although the Metropolitan Museum in New York (of which Morgan was first a Trustee and then President) was destined to receive his collection, until the early 1910s his holdings, for the most part acquired in Europe, remained housed in his European properties or were placed on loan at the Victoria and Albert Museum in London. This was because until 1910 duty had to be paid on the import of art into the USA. In 1912 Morgan's collection was shipped to New York. In 1913, a small selection of paintings was displayed at the Metropolitan Museum. Following his death in 1913, the bulk of the collection was exhibited there, for what was to be the only time. Although Morgan left his collection to his son, J. P. Morgan (1867–1943), with the proviso that it should be placed in the public domain, it was decided that Morgan's estate was not large enough to provide for the continuation of the family banking business, and about half the collection was sold. Eventually approximately 40% of Morgan's collection went to the Metropolitan Museum, *c.* 4000 works of art ranging from an altarpiece by Raphael, the *Virgin and Child Enthroned with Saints* (1504–5), to 18th-century jewellery. His collection of bronzes, Italian Renaissance objects, 17th-century silver and 18th-century porcelain is now in the Wadsworth Atheneum, Hartford, CT, while the illuminated manuscripts, incunabula, autograph manuscripts, rare books, Old Master drawings and prints remain in the Pierpont Morgan Library, where they are regularly exhibited to the public.

BIBLIOGRAPHY
W. Roberts: *Pictures in the Collection of J. P. Morgan at Prince's Gate* (London, 1907)
Guide to the Loan Exhibition of the J. Pierpont Morgan Collection (exh. cat., New York, Met., 1914)
F. H. Taylor: *Pierpont Morgan as Collector and Patron, 1837–1913* (New York, Pierpont Morgan Lib., 1957)
A. B. Saarinen: *The Proud Possessors* (London, 1959)
A. DEIRDRE ROBSON

Morgan, Julia (*b* San Francisco, CA, 26 Jan 1872; *d* San Francisco, 2 Feb 1957). American architect. She was probably the first woman to study in the architecture section of the Ecole des Beaux-Arts, having previously graduated in engineering from the University of California at Berkeley. Morgan was also one of the first women to sustain a long-standing and well-known practice in the USA. Working primarily in the suburbs of San Francisco and other northern California communities, she designed hundreds of residences and numerous schools, college buildings, churches and facilities for the Young Women's Christian Association (Y.W.C.A.) between 1904 and 1940. Women philanthropists and women's organizations comprised a major portion of her clientele. Morgan designed lavish schemes for newspaper owner William Randolph Hearst, especially the enormous compound at San Simeon (begun 1919) on the California coast. However, most of her work is modest in scale and unpretentious in character. Often these buildings possess the simple, rustic qualities associated with the American Arts and Crafts Movement, as seen at St John's Presbyterian Church, Berkeley (1908, 1910; now the Julia Morgan Center for the Performing Arts), or the Drexler house (1913), Woodside, CA. Sometimes inspiration was also drawn from the English Arts and Crafts Movement, as is evident at the Goodrich house (1919), Saratoga, CA. Many other examples are more formal in tone, with references to the classical tradition in England and Italy, for example the Chickering house (1912), Piedmont, CA, and the Y.W.C.A. (1913–14), Oakland, CA. After World War I Morgan's work became more consciously picturesque and even theatrical, such as the Berkeley City Women's Club (1929–30). In both plan and elevation, her buildings adhere to Beaux-Arts principles and are composed in a straightforward manner, demonstrating a clear, purposeful order in the arrangement of space, form and detail. While unusual in its diversity of expression, Morgan's oeuvre represents the mainstream of 20th-century American academic work at its best.

BIBLIOGRAPHY
W. T. Steilberg: 'Some Examples of the Work of Julia Morgan', *Architect & Engin. CA*, lv/2 (1918), pp. 39–107
R. Longstreth: 'Julia Morgan: Some Introductory Notes', *Perspecta*, 15 (1975), pp. 74–86; repr. as *Julia Morgan, Architect* (Berkeley, 1977, R 1986)
S. Boutelle: 'Women's Networks: Julia Morgan and her Clients', *Heresies*, xi/3 (1981), pp. 91–4
——: *Julia Morgan, Architect* (New York, 1988)
D. Favro: 'Sincere and good: The Architectural Practice of Julia Morgan', *J. Archit. & Planning Res.*, iv/2 (1992), pp. 112–28
RICHARD LONGSTRETH

Morgan, William De. *See* DE MORGAN, (1).

Morgenstern, Christian (Ernst Bernhard) (*b* Hamburg, 29 Sept 1805; *d* Munich, 26 Feb 1867). German painter. After training from 1824 with Siegfried Bendixen (1786–1864) in Hamburg, he studied at the Kunstakademi in Copenhagen in 1827 and made sketching trips to Sweden and Norway. He then settled permanently in Munich. He was influenced in particular by 17th-century Dutch painters, notably Jacob van Ruisdael, the Copenhagen *plein-air* painters, the emerging Norwegian landscape school and the early Realist painters working in Munich, such as Johann Georg von Dillis. Morgenstern explored objective, pure landscape painting with intimate motifs in such works as *Beech-tree Trunks in Fredericksdal near Copenhagen* (1828; Hamburg, Ksthalle). He also painted scenes combining closely rendered foreground details with extensive, light-filled backgrounds remarkable for their brilliant atmospheric colours, as in *Landscape at Lake Starnberg* (*c.* 1830–40; Munich, Lenbachhaus.).

Morgenstern was among the first German painters to concentrate on *plein-air* sketching in watercolour, depicting such relatively new subjects as desolate regions, unusual geological or floral phenomena and striking atmospheric conditions, especially mists, sunset or moonlight. He treated these in a proto-Impressionist technique that was generally free and bold, with visible brushwork. Gradually his landscape views encompassed ever larger panoramas while eliminating the immediate foreground, as in *Evening Mood in the Ammer Valley near Polling* (1853; Karlsruhe, Staatl. Ksthalle). As his vision became more subjective, his paintings drew closer to the earlier Romanticism of

Caspar David Friedrich, with an emphasis on the loneliness and spiritual transcendence of landscape, the insignificance of the human factor and the overwhelming totality embodied in the distant view. For Morgenstern the 'distant view' (*Fernshau*) became an expression of foreboding (*Fernshaudern*) or anguish as well as a dream of spiritual liberation.

BIBLIOGRAPHY

S. Wichmann: *Realismus und Impressionismus in Deutschland* (Stuttgart, 1964)
M. Mauss: *Christian E. B. Morgenstern* (diss., U. Marburg, 1969)
A. Zweite, ed.: *Münchner Landschaftsmalerei* (Munich, 1979)

RUDOLF M. BISANZ

Morgenthaler, Ernst (*b* Klein-Dietwil, nr Huttwil, 11 Dec 1887; *d* Höngg, nr Zurich, 7 Sept 1962). Swiss painter. His family moved to Berne in 1897, where he studied at various schools. After leaving school he worked for several years in the silk trade. At the same time he began to draw and paint in the evenings and also started to contribute caricatures to the *Nebelspalter*. After deciding to devote himself to art he studied in Berlin under the German painter Fritz Burger (1867–1927) and at the Ecole des Beaux-Arts in Zurich under the Swiss painter Eduard Stiefel (*b* 1875). In 1914 he met Cuno Amiet and spent some time with him at his studio in Oschwand, which not only improved his technique but also gave him greater confidence. In Munich in 1916 he worked with Klee and also at the school of the German painter Heinrich Knirr (1862–1944). Though Klee had a similar fantasising approach to reality his more abstract, avant-garde style did not suit Morgenthaler, who preferred to stay closer to the Post-Impressionist style. Typical of his work at this time was the poetic *Woodland Fairy Tale* (1916; Erlenbach, Dr Ulrich priv. col., see 1957 exh. cat., no. 3), which captured a fleeting and mysterious moonlit scene.

From 1918 to 1928 Morgenthaler lived successively at Oberhofen am Thunersee, Wollshofen and Küsnacht. His love for the fantastic had by this time become more subdued, lingering in his ability to effect touching transfigurations of everyday scenes, many of them revealing a great human sympathy, as in *The Family* (1925; Aarau, Aargau. Ksthaus). As well as figure and portrait works he also painted several town- and landscapes, such as *House in Küsnacht* (1927; Glarus, Ksthaus), though these were almost invariably animated by human or animal figures. From 1928 to 1931 he stayed in Meudon near Paris, during which time his palette brightened. Paintings such as *Veronika* (1932; Solothurn, J. Müller priv. col., see Wehrli) used bright colours and an economy of detail similar to that found in Matisse's work.

In 1932 Morgenthaler settled in Höngg, near Zurich, where he lived until his death; his painting style remained constant from that time. Since the 1920s he had intermittently painted scenes of working life and these reappeared in such paintings as *The Foundry* (1946; Zurich, Escher Wyss Col., see 1957 exh. cat., no. 63). Throughout his life he was a keen traveller, making trips to Italy, France, Morocco and Tunisia, and these provided the subject-matter for many watercolours and oils, such as the watercolour *Tunisians* (1949; priv. col., see 1962 exh. cat., no. 154). The imaginary subjects that had dominated his earliest work recurred occasionally in his mature period, as in *Moonlit Night with Three Angels* (*c.* 1940; Solothurn, J. Müller priv. col., see 1962 exh. cat., no. 49). His sensitive depictions of intimate, everyday scenes continued in various late works such as *In Maloja* (1955; Glarus, Ksthaus). He became a friend of many writers living in Switzerland, most notably Hermann Hesse, whose novels have much in common with Morgenthaler's work, incorporating a poetic mixture of reality and the fantastic.

BIBLIOGRAPHY

G. Jedlicka: *Ernst Morgenthaler* (Paris, 1933)
R. Wehrli: *Ernst Morgenthaler* (Neuchâtel, 1953)
Ernst Morgenthaler (exh. cat. by F. Meyer and E. Morgenthaler, Berne, Ksthalle, 1957)
Ernst Morgenthaler (exh. cat. by H. Theler, Berne, Ksthalle, 1962)

□

Morghen. Italian family of etchers and engravers. The best known was (1) Raphael Morghen, but his father Filippo Morghen (*b* 1730, *d* after 1807) and uncle Giovanni Elia Morghen (*b* 1721; *d* after 1789) also had successful careers as engravers, as did his brother Guglielmo Morghen (*fl* mid-18th century to *c.* 1825).

(1) Raphael [Raffaele] **Morghen** (*b* Naples, 19 June 1758; *d* Florence, 8 April 1833). Etcher and engraver. He trained in Naples with his father and uncle and worked there as an etcher of scenes, topographical views and reproductions until 1778, when he went to train in Rome with Giovanni Volpato, from whom he learnt the French method of line-engraving and whose daughter Domenica he married in 1781. Thus his early combination of etching followed by engraving was gradually replaced by the technically demanding method of line-engraving and reinforcing with drypoint. Precise line from his burin and controlled, graduated tone from his regular hatching distinguish his almost photographic engravings. His exhaustively precise style was perceived as the equivalent with the burin to the chalk and brush of the Raphaelesque ideal, and among the most admired of his prints were the engravings after Raphael's Madonnas and *Transfiguration* (Rome, Pin. Vaticana). Hind observed, however, that 'Morghenesque' came to stand for a technique that was highly proficient but expressively vacuous. In his day he was known as one of the leading reproductive engravers in Italy. Some 254 prints—of all categories of subject-matter and many reproductive engravings—were catalogued by Palmerini, and an extensive collection of impressions and trial proofs is preserved in the Gabinetto Disegni e Stampe of the Galleria degli Uffizi, Florence. He represented in engraving the Neo-classical ideals that inspired the paintings of Vincenzo Camuccini in Rome and Luigi Sabatelli and Pietro Benvenuti in Florence. His influence was extensive and enduring through his role as a teacher. In 1793 he was called to Florence to found a school of engraving by Grand Duke Ferdinando III de' Medici (*reg* 1790–1801) and was named as professor in the Accademia di Belle Arti in 1803. He also was a member of the Institut de France and named a Cavalier of the Légion d'honneur in 1816. Among his pupils was his son Antonio Morghen (1788–1853), who engraved his portrait.

BIBLIOGRAPHY

Thieme–Becker
N. Palmerini: *Opere d'int. del cav. Raffaelo Morghen* (Florence, 3/1824)

P. Kristeller: *Kupferstich und Holzschnitt in vier Jahrhunderten* (Berlin, 4/1922)
A. M. Hind: *A History of Engraving and Etching from the 15th Century to the Year 1914* (London, 3/1923)

MILES CHAPPELL

Morgner, Wilhelm (*b* Soest, Westphalia, 27 Jan 1891; *d* Langemarck, 12 Aug 1917). German painter. One of the youngest of the first-generation Expressionists, in 1908 he attended the school in Worpswede run by the German painter Georg Tappert (1880–1957). They became firm friends and Tappert provided the support and encouragement that Morgner needed after his return to Soest in 1910. Morgner's earliest work was influenced by Jean-François Millet and the German Impressionists, but by 1910 he had discovered the work of van Gogh, whose late style he subjected to a radical, Expressionist transformation. Pictures from 1911 such as *Brickworks, Blue Man with Trolley* (Münster, Westfäl. Landesmus.) combine a continued interest in the subject of peasants at work in the landscape with stylized, decorative composition and an anti-naturalistic use of colour. Despite spending much of his time in the isolation of Soest, Morgner's reputation was established early in modernist circles in Berlin and Munich. In 1911 he joined the Neue Sezession at Tappert's suggestion, and in 1912 took part in the second Blaue Reiter exhibition and the Cologne *Sonderbund*. In 1912 and 1913 Herwarth Walden's influential journal *Der Sturm* published wood- and linocuts by Morgner, and his drawing *The Brickmaker* (Soest, Städt. Kult.- & Verksamt) was included in the *Blaue Reiter Almanach*. The experience of the work of Kandinsky and Alexei Jawlenski caused Morgner to experiment with abstraction in works such as *Astral Composition XXII* (1912; Münster, Westfäl. Landesmus.). In 1913 he was called up for military service and he made only drawings and watercolours after this date. These last works witnessed a return to a more realistic style which contained none of the imaginary idealism of his pre-war Expressionist paintings.

BIBLIOGRAPHY
P. Selz: *German Expressionist Painting* (Berkeley, 1957)
E. G. Güse: *Wilhelm Morgner* (Münster, Westfäl. Landesmus., 1983)
L. Nerowski-Fisch: *Wilhelm Morgner: Ein Beitrag zum deutschen Expressionismus* (Soest, 1984)

COLIN RHODES

Morgues, Jacques Le Moyne de. *See* LE MOYNE DE MORGUES, JACQUES.

Mori, Camilo (*b* Valparaíso, 24 Sept 1896; *d* Santiago, 7 Dec 1973). Chilean painter. He studied from 1914 at the Escuela de Bellas Artes in Santiago, where he was taught by Juan Francisco González and others, and in 1920 he made his first trip to Europe, meeting Juan Gris and exhibiting at the Salon d'Automne in Paris. In 1928 he was sent to Paris as one of a group of the 26 best students from the Escuela de Bellas Artes; he remained there until 1931, when he returned to Chile.

Mori was one of the instigators of the Grupo Montparnasse, the Chilean group of painters formed in 1923 with Luis Vargas Rosas (1898–1977), who gave the group its name, and Henriette Petit (1894–1983). Influenced above all by Cézanne, they aimed to break with a traditional approach to representational painting and looked to contemporary French painting for support, taking as their name a district of Paris associated with avant-garde art. Their formation was marked by an exhibition organized by Vargas Rosas at the Rivas y Calvo auction house in Santiago; works by Vargas Rosas, Petit, Julio Ortiz de Zárate (1887–1946) and José Perotti were included. A second exhibition, *Salón de Junio*, was held at the same venue in June 1925, with Mori and Manuel Ortiz de Zárate (1887–1946) also participating; on this occasion they strengthened their links with Europe by including works by painters such as Picasso, Gris, Léger, Jacques Lipchitz and Louis Marcoussis.

Mori's early influences included not only Cézanne but also the work of Cubists, notably Braque and Picasso, for example in *L'Intransigeant* (1929; see Galaz and Ivelič, p. 213), a table-top still-life with a newspaper, fish and fruit. His figure paintings, such as *Boxer* (1923; see Galaz and Ivelič, p. 209), with a massive figure dominating an interior space, or the later portrait of his wife, *Maruja Vargas* (1943; see Galaz and Ivelič, p. 213), are more traditional in technique, the latter work resembling late 19th-century French naturalism. At the Salón Oficial in Santiago in 1928, a polemical exhibition for which he acted as commissioner, he exhibited *Traveller* (Santiago, Mus. N. B.A.), sombre in colouring and melancholic in mood.

In 1938 Mori travelled to New York to decorate the Chilean pavilion for the World's Fair held there in that year. Remaining in the USA until 1940, during this period he came under the influence of Pittura Metafisica. During his long life, however, he experimented with such a variety of styles that many other developments in 20th-century art, including Constructivism and Surrealism, were also reflected in his work. For example, *Interior* (1951; see exh. cat.), a formalized and decorative still-life of bottles and jugs viewed in silhouette, suggests an awareness of Purism, although by the 1960s, for example in *Valparaíso* (740×1000 mm, 1962; see exh. cat.), he was working in a style close to *Art informel*.

BIBLIOGRAPHY
Retrospectiva Camilo Mori: Su vida y su obra (exh. cat. by R. Bindis, Santiago, Mus. N. B.A., 1974)
G. Galaz and M. Ivelič: *La pintura en Chile desde la colonia hasta 1981* (Santiago, 1981), pp. 204, 209, 211–13, 255

CARLOS LASTARRIA HERMOSILLA

Mori, Yoshitoshi (*b* Tokyo, 31 October 1898; *d* 29 May 1992). Japanese printmaker and textile dyer. He graduated from the Kawabata School of Fine Arts in 1923 and later studied under MUNEYOSHI YANAGI and the textile dyer Keisuke Serizawa. After working on dyed textiles for 30 years, Yoshitoshi gradually shifted to the creation of stencil prints in the late 1950s. He developed a new and distinctive style that combined stencil printing (*kappazuri*), traditionally applied to textiles, and stencil dyeing (*katazome*). He entered one of his first prints, *Kure no ichi* ('Year End Market'; 1957) in the 1st International Biennale of Prints in Tokyo (1957). The final choice between Yōzō Hamaguchi and Yoshitoshi aroused a famous debate about Japanese versus Western values. Yoshitoshi's prints show a strong interest in *kabuki* theatre, which was probably due to his having been brought up by his aunt Kin Harada, who was a teacher of *kabuki* chanting. He also favoured folklore, village life and historical subjects, such as the Kamakura-period (1185–1333) *Heike monogatari* ('The Tale of the Heike'; 1970–76; Tokyo, N. Mus. Mod. A.).

See also JAPAN, §IX, 2(iii)(g).

BIBLIOGRAPHY
Mori Yoshitoshi Kappa Ban [Stencil prints of Mori Yoshitoshi]: *70th Anniversary of Artistic Achievement Mori Yoshitoshi Exhibition* (exh. cat., Leiden, Rijksmus. Vlkenknd., 1985) [bilingual text]
ARLETTE P. KOUWENHOVEN

Moria. *See under* LESBOS.

Morice, Sir **Humphry** (*b* 1723; *d* Naples, 18 Oct 1785). English collector and politician. In 1750 he inherited from a cousin, Sir William Morice, 3rd Baronet, the estate of Werrington and control of four parliamentary seats in Cornwall. From 1750 until 1780 he was MP for the boroughs of Launceston and Newport. He held a number of sinecures including the Lord Wardenship of the Stannaries from 1763 until 1783. His inheritance also contained the nucleus of a picture collection that William Morice had bought from Owen McSwiny, including most of the series of allegorical paintings (now widely dispersed) commemorating British worthies that McSwiny had commissioned from Giambattista Piazzetta, Marco Ricci and various other Venetian and Bolognese artists. He considerably expanded this collection. Landscapes were a particular interest, and works by Salvator Rosa, such as his pendants the *Preaching of the Baptist* (*c.* 1650; St Louis, MO, A. Mus.) and *Baptism of the Eunuch* (*c.* 1645; ex-Walter Chrysler priv. col., New York), Claude Lorrain, Nicolas Poussin, Gaspard Dughet, Jan Frans van Bloemen, Canaletto and others were kept at his villa, The Grove, near Chiswick, London. Persistent ill-health caused Morice to visit Italy in 1760–62, 1768–9 and after 1783. In 1762 he acquired Pompeo Batoni's *Diana and Cupid* (1761; New York, Met.) and that year sat to Batoni for a portrait of corresponding dimensions (priv. col., see Clark, 1985, no. 241): this is Batoni's only Grand Tour portrait of a sitter in a reclining pose. A year after Morice's death his collection was sold to John, 2nd Earl of Ashburnham.

BIBLIOGRAPHY
P. Toynbee, ed.: 'Horace Walpole's Journals of Visits to Country Seats, &c.', *Walpole Soc.*, xvi (1927–8), p. 77
L. Namier and J. Brooke: *The History of Parliament: The House of Commons, 1754–1790* (London, 1964), pp. 166–8
A. M. Clark: *Pompeo Batoni: A Complete Catalogue of his Works with an Introductory Text*, ed. E. P. Bowron, (Oxford, 1985), nos 235, 241–3
FRANCIS RUSSELL

Morienval, Notre-Dame. Former Benedictine abbey in the département de l'Oise, France. A double monastery existed at Morienval as early as the mid-9th century: an act of Charles III the Simple *c.* 920 confirms donations by his grandmother, Irmentraude (*d* 896). An early 12th-century act suggests that a translation of the relics of St Anobert occurred between 1070 and 1102. The former date coincides approximately with the demolition of the east end of the Carolingian church and the construction of a chevet flanked by lateral towers, together with the base and first two storeys of the tower porch to the west. Following this, the simple Carolingian nave was replaced

Morienval, Notre-Dame, capital from the north nave arcade, late 11th century

by a nave with aisles. In a third campaign, the third storey of the tower porch was completed, probably by 1105. Some 15 or 20 years later, the apse collapsed and was replaced by the present one with false ambulatory, which was thoroughly restored in the late 19th century.

These building phases are reflected in the capitals. Simplicity of form and decoration characterize those of the lateral towers, executed during the first campaign. A variety of geometric decorative motifs (stars, spirals etc) and stylized leaves are set in simple compositions, carved in low relief. In the second building phase, the decorative vocabulary is similar, but the north nave arcade capitals incorporate new motifs (masks and palmette leaves; see fig.). They are carved with greater freedom and introduce more complex compositions. The capitals of the third storey of the tower porch are characterized by deeper relief, transforming the angle masks, leaves and vines into full, undulating forms. In the 12th-century ambulatory capitals the trend towards greater plasticity is continued. They bear motifs such as masked birds and windswept leaves, which are typical of capitals in a few rural churches in the neighbouring region around Beauvais. The 11th-century capitals, on the other hand, form a cohesive group, which fits with capitals produced during the second half of the 11th century in the region centered on the Aisne and Oise rivers, north-east of Paris.

BIBLIOGRAPHY
E. Lefèvre-Pontalis: 'Le Plan primitif de l'église de Morienval', *Bull. Mnmt.*, lxxii (1908), pp. 477–83
D. V. Johnson: 'Architectural Sculpture of the Aisne and Oise Valleys during the Second Half of the 11th Century', *Cah. Archéol.*, 37 (1989), pp. 19–44
DANIELLE VALIN JOHNSON

Morikage. *See* KUSUMI MORIKAGE.

Morillon, Antoine (*b* Leuven, early 1520s; *d* Brussels, 11 Oct 1556). South Netherlandish medallist, epigrapher and scholar. His father, Guy Morillon, was associated with Erasmus in the period of the foundation of the Collegium Trilingue in Leuven and later became Secretary to Charles V, Holy Roman Emperor. Antoine trained in the Classical languages at the Collegium Trilingue and matriculated on 4 April 1532. The earliest medal attributed to him dates from 1543 and is a portrait of *D. Christo Abeuuszum* (Brussels, Bib. Royale Albert Ier, Cab. Médailles). He entered the service of Cardinal Granvelle (to whom his brother Maximilien was Secretary) and was one of the first artists from the Low Countries to be sent to Italy to undertake a programme of recording Classical inscriptions and works of art. His sketches (untraced) include the Mensa Isiaca (Turin, Mus. Egizio), a rectangular bronze tablet that formed one of the bases for Western knowledge of hieroglyphs until Napoleon invaded Egypt. In Rome, *c.* 1551–3, he moved in a circle that included the writer Stephanus Wijnants Pigge (1520–1604), Antonio Agustín and Rodolfo Pio da Carpi. He returned to the southern Netherlands some time after 5 September 1553. Four medals survive from his remaining years, *Seneca, Theophrastus, Socrates* (London, BM) and *Aristotle* (mentioned by Tourneur, 1913, p. 402), all apparently based directly on portrait sculptures seen in Italy. Towards the end of his life he began to organize his epigraphic material for publication, passing many texts to Martin de Smet (*fl* 1534–78) and Pigge, and what is perhaps this unfinished corpus still survives in the Universiteitsbibliotheek, Amsterdam, (MS. 111).

BIBLIOGRAPHY
Corpus inscriptionum latinarum, VI/i (Berlin, 1876), pp. liii–liv
J. Simonis: *L'Art du médailleur en Belgique*, i (Brussels, 1900), pp. 93–109
V. Tourneur: 'Extraits des procès-verbaux', *Rev. Belge Num.*, lxix (1913), pp. 392–402
H. de Vocht: *History of the Foundation and Rise of the Collegium Trilingue Lovaniense, 1517–50*, iii (Leuven, 1954), pp. 305–12
M. H. Crawford: 'Antoine Morillon', *J. Warb. & Court. Inst.* (in preparation)

MICHAEL H. CRAWFORD,
with MADELEINE VAN DE WINCKEL

Morin, Jean (*b* Paris, *c.* 1590; *d* Paris, 1650). French engraver. Very little is known of his life beyond what may be learnt from his prints. His work consists mainly of reproductive portraits after Philippe de Champaigne and van Dyck, and landscapes after Jacques Fouquier. He is said to have started his career as a painter, but no painting by him is known. Six of his landscape prints are his own compositions. He is chiefly remarkable for his technique, which, although it was developed out of that of the school of van Dyck, was largely his own invention. His plates were first etched and then finished in a mixture of line and stipple, with the latter dominating. This strikingly personal system produced very effective portraits in which the character of the sitter is well expressed. His best work was after Philippe de Champaigne, notably portraits of *François Potier, Marquis de Gèvres, Arnaud d'Andilly, René de Longueil, Marquis de Maisons, Henri de Lorraine, Comte d'Harcourt* and *Antoine Vitré*. His particular skill lay in producing contrasts of tone between the different parts of his plates, although this sometimes led to inharmonious

juxtapositions. He employed an unusual printing procedure, each *tirage* being on a separate quire of paper and the quires being used in the same sequence for each of his portraits.

BIBLIOGRAPHY
A. P. F. Robert-Dumesnil: *Le Peintre-graveur français* (Paris, 1835–71), ii, xi
M. Hornibrook and C. Petitjean: *Catalogue of the Engraved Portraits of Jean Morin* (Cambridge, 1945)
O. Barnard: 'Jean Morin's Etched Portraits', *Prt Q.*, ii (1985), p. 38

J. M. PINKERTON

Morinck, Hans (*b* Gorinchem, South Holland, *c.* 1555; *d* Konstanz, 1616). Dutch sculptor, active in Germany. He is first documented in September 1578 as working at Petershausen Abbey, near Konstanz, but stylistic evidence suggests that before going there, Morinck may have visited northern Italy, particularly Padua and Venice. In 1582 he became a citizen of Konstanz. Annual increases in income, documented in the city's tax records, attest to his commercial success. He was able to buy his own house in 1587 and was twice married and twice widowed.

Morinck's earliest projects reveal the strong influence of two other sculptors in the Konstanz area: the anonymous Netherlandish master who between 1575 and 1584 carved the decorations of the Rittersaal at Schloss Heiligenberg, north of Überlingen, and Master Michael (the Monogrammist MVDV) of Petershausen. Morinck adopted the Heiligenberg Master's restrained interpretation of the published designs for strapwork and architectural decoration by Cornelis Floris, as well as his taste for Italianate figures, in his own early works, such as the limestone epitaphs of *Gebhard von Schellenberg and his Wife* (1583–4) in SS Verena and Gallus, Hüfingen and of *Andreas vom Stain* (1589–90) in Konstanz Cathedral. Morinck's stocky *St Gebhard* and *St Barbara* from the Stain Epitaph, with their selfconscious contrapposto and the broad, diagonally cut drapery folds, are variations on the figure of *Justice* from the Heiligenberg chimney. From Master Michael, with whom he may have collaborated at Petershausen, Morinck borrowed the short, heavily built figure types, the shallow-relief carving technique and, most significantly, a lasting preference for Netherlandish prints as compositional models.

During the 1580s, Morinck worked in both wood and stone, although he increasingly preferred the fine-grain Öhninger limestone for the numerous epitaphs and religious reliefs that he carved for the cathedral and for St Stephan in Konstanz. His most important commission of the 1580s, the *Coronation of the Virgin* altar (1586; untraced) for the choir of the new abbey church of St Blasien, was probably of wood. The contemporary *Adoration of the Magi* group (Konstanz, former Jesuitenkirche) reveals how Morinck used lime-wood to create more animated figures and more varied drapery patterns. These beautifully polychromed statues demonstrate, however, that Morinck still conceived of the human body as the sum of its parts rather than as an organic, unified whole.

Most of Morinck's later works are stone-relief sculptures. In the epitaph of his first wife, *Effrasina Morinck*, which he carved and set on the exterior of the choir of St Stephan shortly after her death in 1591, he employed shallow relief, but with subtle spatial transitions from the

Hans Morinck: *Entombment*, limestone relief, 1.16×0.73 m, 1609–10 (Konstanz, St Stephan)

Entombment relief (1609–10; see fig.) in St Stephan, perhaps his most beautiful extant creation. Here the rhythmic motion of Christ's torso is repeated in the lines of the swooning Virgin. The poses of the other characters are subordinated, yet skilfully direct the viewer's gaze back to Christ or to the Virgin. Morinck subtly modulated the areas of high and low relief so that each section flows smoothly into the next; even the background landscape with a view of Jerusalem seems essential to the whole composition, rather than an afterthought, as in many of the artist's earlier carvings. The handling of figure and drapery cutting is much finer and more detailed than before.

At the end of his career Morinck had finally achieved a unity of composition and a level of quality that rivalled those of the best sculptors then active in Germany. Morinck's works had a strong influence on other sculptors in the Lake Constance region. Melchior Binder's *Mary and Christ with St Anne* (lime-wood, 1595; Ostrach, St Pankratius) borrows poses and the overall composition from Morinck's *St Anne* altar (1590) in Konstanz Cathedral, although Binder was probably never his pupil. The influence of Morinck's style and cutting technique may also be seen in the early sculptures of Jörg Zürn and of Virgil Moll (*fl c.* 1588–1606), both from Überlingen.

BIBLIOGRAPHY

H. Mahn: 'Hans Morinck und die Anfänge der Barockskulptur am Bodensee', *Z. Dt. Ver. Kstwiss.*, vi (1930), pp. 162–206

H. Rott: *Quellen und Forschungen zur südwestdeutschen und schweizerischen Kunstgeschichte im 15. und 16. Jahrhunderts* (Stuttgart, 1933), i, pp. 92–4

Barock am Bodensee (exh. cat., Bregenz, Kstlerhaus Pal. Thurn & Taxis, 1964), pp. xxi, xxiii, xxiv–xxv, xxix, xxx, xxxv, 35–6

C. Zoege von Manteuffel: *Die Bildhauerfamilie Zürn, 1606–1666* (Weissenhorn, 1969), pp. 28, 86–91, 131, 362 9

H. Ricke: *Hans Morinck: Ein Wegbereiter des Barockskulptur am Bodensee* (Sigmaringen, 1973) [crit. study with cat. rais.]

Die Renaissance im deutschen Südwesten, 2 vols (exh. cat., Heidelberg, Schloss, 1986), ii, pp. 558–61

JEFFREY CHIPPS SMITH

Morinobu. *See* KANŌ, (11).

Morison, Stanley (Arthur) (*b* Wanstead, Essex, 6 May 1889; *d* London, 11 Oct 1967). English typographic designer and writer. He began his career at 14 as a bank clerk in London. A keen interest in typography and type design led him to a job on *The Imprint* (1912–13), a short-lived periodical aimed at improving standards in printing. He then joined the publishing firm of Burns and Oates, where from 1913 to 1917 he learned editing and book design. He worked (1919–21) for the English book designer Sir Francis Meynell (1891–1975), founder of the Nonesuch Press, at Pelican Press, then for the Cloister Press in Manchester (1921–2). In 1922 he helped launch a new typographic magazine, *The Fleuron*, with the English typographic designer Oliver Simon (1895–1956), and in 1923 his criticism of the Monotype Corporation's range of typefaces led to him being appointed its typographic adviser, which enabled him to expand on his ideas; he remained Monotype Corporation's consultant until his death. He revived and adapted antique typefaces such as Garamond (1922), Baskerville (1923) and Bembo (1929), and commissioned new typeface designs from artists and craftsmen like Eric Gill (e.g. Gill Sans, 1928) and Berthold

---

barely raised cloak of the Virgin to the more fully rounded body of the dead Christ. For this, Morinck's simplest and most restrained sculpture, the artist based his grieving Virgin, with the dead Christ lying between her legs and the flanking angels supporting Christ's arms, on the composition of Michelangelo's drawing of the *Pietà* (1546; Boston, MA, Isabella Stewart Gardner Mus.), engraved by Nicolaus Beatrizet in 1547. More typical of Morinck's style during the 1590s are the monumental and raw-boned figures on the tomb of *Helene von Raitenau* (1595) in SS Petrus and Paulus, Örsingen. Morinck heightened the tension of the *Lamentation* and *Entombment* scenes by crowding his characters together and by exploiting light and dark contrasts through the use of a much higher relief. By making Christ much larger than the other holy figures, he disregarded proportional unity in favour of dramatic effect.

Morinck's finest stone carvings were made *c.* 1600. In them the squat and rather stiff figures of the early Schellenberg Epitaph gave way to highly elongated and complexly posed figures, such as Christ in the *Trinity* relief (*c.* 1600; Karlsruhe, Bad. Landesmus.) and the *Crucifixion* relief (1606) in Oberstadion. The anatomical awkwardness of the Christ in the epitaph of *Effrasina Morinck* sharply contrasts with the graceful harmony of Christ in the

Wolpe (Albertus, 1935–40). In addition he was adviser to the Cambridge University Press from 1924 to 1959.

In 1929, having offered to redesign it, Morison joined *The Times* and revolutionized its appearance with a new typeface, Times New Roman, designed by him and launched in 1932. He edited the *Times Literary Supplement* from 1945 to 1947, though his association with *The Times* was to continue until his retirement in 1960. As well as being a prolific writer on typography and calligraphy, his great contribution was to bring new clarity and creative possibilities to typography in its modern applications.

WRITINGS
Four Centuries of Fine Printing (London, 1924)
First Principles of Typography (London, 1936)

BIBLIOGRAPHY
J. W. Carter: *A Handlist of the Writings of Stanley Morison . . .*(London, 1950)
N. Barker: *Stanley Morison* (London, 1972)

□

Mori Sosen [Jokansai; Reibyōan; Reimyōan; Sosen] (*b* ?Nagasaki or Nishinomiya, 1747; *d* Osaka, 1821). Japanese painter. He probably began his training under his father, the Osaka painter Mori Jokansai [Hanaya Seibei] (*d* 1777). He is recorded as studying with Okamoto Yūkoku (*fl* 18th century), who also taught his father and his elder brother, Mori Shūhō (1738–1823), and with the KANŌ SCHOOL painter Yamamoto [Shobei] Joshunsai (1721–84). Sosen is also known to have associated with many prominent artists and scholars who lived in or passed through Osaka, including the Confucian scholar and patron Kimura Kenkadō and the literati painters Tani Bunchō and Tanomura Chikuden. His acquaintance with MARUYAMA ŌKYO can only be assumed because his adopted son Mori Tetsuzan [Tessan] (1775–1841) was one of Ōkyo's 'Ten Great Disciples', but Ōkyo's influence is evident in Sosen's work.

Sosen and his brothers comprised the first generation of the Osaka-based Mori school, which is generally viewed as an independent branch of the Maruyama–Shijō school (*see* JAPAN, §VI, 4(viii)). Like the Maruyama–Shijō school, the Mori school emphasized verisimilitude in the portrayal of objects from nature and favoured the depiction of landscapes, animals, plants and the human figure. Both groups were patronized by urban merchants, Buddhist temples and Shinto shrines. Sosen was not the oldest painter in the Mori family, but he was considered the best, and by 1790 he was the head of the school. He specialized in the depiction of animals and is considered the foremost Japanese painter of monkeys, which he is reputed to have observed in their natural habitat so as to be able to represent them accurately. So closely was he associated with paintings of monkeys that *c.* 1807 he changed part of the character *so* ('ancestor') in his name Sosen to its homonym meaning 'monkey'.

Sosen's work was enormously popular, and his output was prodigious, but dated paintings by him are rare, and a chronological development in his style is difficult to postulate. (This is further complicated by numerous forgeries, some produced before his death.) *Monkeys in Stone Lanterns in the Snow* (Ikeda, Itsuō A. Mus.; see fig.) represents a blend of various artistic traditions. The way in which he combined realistic detail with more abstract

Mori Sosen: *Monkeys in Stone Lanterns in the Snow*, hanging scroll, ink and colours on silk, 1046×383 mm, late 18th century or early 19th (Ikeda, Itsuō Art Museum)

elements produces a dramatic effect: landscape elements such as the foliage, rendered by means of dark, angular strokes (a conservative Kanō-school device), and the snow-covered stone lanterns defined by modulated washes (a technique pioneered by Maruyama Ōkyo) contrast with the meticulous manner of delineating the monkeys' fur. His gift for capturing the life-spirit of the monkeys is revealed in their carefully observed poses. Beyond his skill in portraying the animal's outward appearance, Sosen also imbued his monkeys with compellingly lifelike personalities, a characteristic that elevates his art above that of his contemporaries in this genre. Later Mori-school followers were principally trained by Sosen's adopted son Mori Tetsuzan and by the latter's adopted sons Mori Ippō (1798–1871) and Mori Kansai (1814–94) and pupil Wada Gesshin [Gozan] (1800–70).

BIBLIOGRAPHY

M. Kōno: 'Mori Sosen kenkyū jōsetsu' [Introduction to the study of Mori Sosen], *Kokka*, 950 (1972), pp. 5–25
J. Hillier: *The Uninhibited Brush: Japanese Art in the Shijō Style* (London, 1974)
S. Kimura: 'Sosen kō' [Study on Sosen], *Kobijutsu*, 49 (1975), pp. 57–70
Kinsei Osaka gadan [Eng. title: Osaka Painting Schools in the Edo Period] (exh. cat., Osaka, Mus. A., 1983)

PATRICIA J. GRAHAM

Morisot, Berthe(-Marie-Pauline) (*b* Bourges, Cher, 14 Jan 1841; *d* Paris, 2 March 1895). French painter and printmaker. As the child of upper middle-class parents, Marie-Joséphine-Cornélie and Edme Tiburce Morisot, she was expected to be a skilled amateur artist and was thus given appropriate schooling. In 1857 she attended drawing lessons with Geoffroy-Alphonse Chocarne (*fl* 1838–57), but in 1858 she and her sister Edma left to study under Joseph-Benoît Guichard, a pupil of Ingres and Delacroix. In the same year they registered as copyists in the Louvre, copying Veronese and Rubens. The sisters were introduced to Jean-Baptiste-Camille Corot in 1861 and took advice from him and subsequently from his pupil, Achille-François Oudinot (1820–91). Through these artists they became familiar with current debates on naturalism and began to work *en plein air*, painting at Pontoise, Normandy and Brittany (e.g. *Thatched Cottage in Normandy*, 1865; priv. col., see Angoulvent, no. 11).

Morisot exhibited in the Salon from 1864 to 1868 and received encouraging reviews. In late 1867 or 1868, Henri Fantin-Latour introduced her to Edouard Manet, for whom she modelled, and who became her close friend. In December 1874 she married his brother Eugène. Although Manet advised Morisot on her work, she was never his formal pupil, and their relationship was more reciprocal than is usually supposed. Morisot was not persuaded by Manet to remain within the official exhibiting forum and was instrumental in persuading him to lighten his palette in the 1870s.

Morisot was a central member of the group of artists who initiated the Impressionist exhibitions in the 1870s and 1880s. In 1874 she submitted nine works to the first Impressionist Exhibition; thereafter she resolved never to return to the Salon. She showed in seven of the eight exhibitions (1874, 1876, 1877, 1880, 1881, 1882 and 1886), missing only the exhibition of 1879 due to illness following the birth of her daughter Julie at the end of 1878. She was directly involved in the organization of some of these exhibitions and identified strongly with the aesthetic and political principles that led to the establishment of an exhibition forum outside the Salon. In March 1875 Morisot participated with Renoir, Camille Pissarro, Monet and Alfred Sisley in an auction at the Hôtel Drouot, her works fetching marginally higher prices than theirs. Her work was handled by the dealer Paul Durand-Ruel, although she was never financially dependent on sales. Her home was a meeting-place for intellectuals and artists, including Renoir, Degas, Mary Cassatt and Stéphane Mallarmé.

Morisot was regarded by critics such as Paul Mantz (1821–95) and Théodore Duret as a quintessential Impressionist. They believed that she was capable of achieving an 'impression' of nature that was unmediated and

Berthe Morisot: *Summer's Day*, oil on canvas, 457×752 mm, 1879 (London, National Gallery)

'sincere', and they asserted that such a proclivity was the product of the allegedly feminine characteristics of superficiality and innate sensitivity to surface appearances. However, Morisot's use of luminous tonalities, painterly brushmarks, sketchy surfaces and unprimed canvas, and her adherence to modern-life subject-matter (e.g. *Summer's Day*, 1879; London, N.G.; see fig.) are features shared with her Impressionist colleagues, male and female.

Morisot executed pastels and watercolours throughout her life, as well as lithographs and drypoints around 1888 to 1890. In her last years she favoured suggestive and mythic subjects and increased linearity in drawing, as seen in the *Cherry Tree* (1891; Paris, priv. col., see Adler and Garb, 1987, no. 56).

WRITINGS
D. Rouart, ed.: *Correspondance de Berthe Morisot* (Paris, 1950; Eng. trans., rev. by K. Adler and T. Garb, London, 1986)

BIBLIOGRAPHY
C. Roger-Marx: 'Les Femmes peintres et l'Impressionnisme: Berthe Morisot', *Gaz. B.-A.*, n.s. 2, xxxviii (1907), pp. 491–508
A. Forreau: *Berthe Morisot* (Paris, 1925)
M. Angoulvent: *Berthe Morisot* (Paris, 1933)
Berthe Morisot (exh. cat., intro. P. Valéry; Paris, Mus. Orangerie, 1941)
Berthe Morisot (exh. cat., intro. D. Rouart; ACGB, 1950)
E. Mongan: *Berthe Morisot: Drawings, Pastels, Watercolours* (New York, 1960)
M. L. Bataille and G. Wildenstein: *Berthe Morisot: Catalogue des peintures, pastels et aquarelles* (Paris, 1961; rev., 2 vols, 1988) [cat. rais.]
J. Bailly-Herzberg: 'Les Estampes de Berthe Morisot', *Gaz. B.-A.*, n.s. 5, xciii (1979), pp. 215–27
J. D. Rey: *Berthe Morisot* (Näfels, 1982)
A. Clairet: '*Le Cerisier* de Mézy', *L'Oeil*, 358 (1985), pp. 48–51
K. Adler and T. Garb: *Berthe Morisot* (Oxford, 1987)
Berthe Morisot (exh. cat. by C. Stuckey, Washington, DC, N.G.A.; Fort Worth, TX, Kimbell A. Mus.; South Hadley, MA, Mount Holyoke Coll. A. Mus.; 1987–8)
A. Higonnet: *Berthe Morisot's Images of Women* (Cambridge, MA, 1993)
For further bibliography see IMPRESSIONISM.

TAMAR GARB

Morisset, Gérard (*b* Cap Santé, Quebec, 11 Dec 1898; *d* Cap Santé, 28 Dec 1970). Canadian architectural historian, art historian and illustrator. Originally trained as a notary, in 1929 he went to Lyon for a year to study with the innovative architect and urban planner Tony Garnier. He then studied (1930–34) at the Ecole du Louvre, Paris, on a bursary provided by the Province of Quebec. In 1934 he returned to Canada to take up a post as Inspecteur de l'Enseignement du Dessin in the Provincial Department of Public Instruction under Athanase David. David encouraged him to begin compiling an Inventaire des Oeuvres d'Art de la Province de Québec (now part of Cent. Doc. Min. Affaires Cult., Quebec City), on the model of 19th-century French *inventaires* by Viollet-le-Duc or Prosper Mérimée (1803–70). In 1937 Morisset began his patient work of compiling documents and newspaper articles and copying from books; he also travelled all over the province every summer photographing architecture and artefacts. By the time he left the Inventaire in 1953 it was an institution unique in Canada for scale and scope and, as the work of a single individual, unique anywhere. It was soon used as a tool for scholarly writing by himself and by others, to whom he generously made it available. His own scholarly production includes seventeen books and nine major articles, covering the painting, sculpture, decorative arts (especially silver) and architecture of the French

tradition in Quebec. He was also an illustrator, notably of his own novels, for example *Novembre 1775* (1948). From 1953 to 1970 he was director of the Musée du Québec, where he was active in preservation and restoration.

WRITINGS
Le Cap Santé: Ses Eglises et son trésor (Quebec City, 1944, rev. 1980)
L'Architecture en Nouvelle-France (Quebec City, 1949, 2/1981)

BIBLIOGRAPHY
A la Découverte du patrimoine avec Gérard Morisset: Exposition présentée au Musée du Québec du 4 février au 1 mars 1981 (Quebec City, 1981)

ALAN GOWANS

Moriyama, Daido (*b* Osaka, 10 Oct 1938). Japanese photographer and writer. He studied photography at the studio of Takeji Iwamiya in Osaka, moving in 1961 to Tokyo to work as an assistant to Eikoh Hosoe. His collection of photographs *Nippon gekijō shashinchō* presented high-contrast, rough images in which he drew attention to the indigenous world that remained in the shadows of rapid economic growth. In the same year he became the focus of attention for young aggressive photographers through his participation in the group magazine *Provoke* with Kōji Tagi (*b* 1928), Takuma Nakahira (*b* 1938), Yutaka Takanashi (*b* 1935) and Takahiko Okada (*b* 1939) and through his energetic contributions to magazines such as *Asahi Camera*, *Camera Mainichi* and *Asahi Journal*. His collections of photographs include *Karyūdo*, *Shashinyo sayōnara*, *Hikari to Kage* and *Nakaji eno tabi*. His photography is characterized by a vivid physical sensibility. Typically, the gloomier parts of cities usually hidden from sight by the glittering artificial world are sniffed out, as if by an animal, and brought into the light. In Moriyama's photographs, familiar and often seen objects and scenes are viewed in a harsh brilliance.

WRITINGS
Inu no kioku [Memories of a dog] (Tokyo, 1984)
Shashin to no taiwa [Dialogues with photographs] (Tokyo, 1985)

PHOTOGRAPHIC PUBLICATIONS
Nippon gekijō shashinchō [Japan photo-theatre] (Tokyo, 1968)
Karyūdo [Hunter] (Tokyo, 1972)
Shashinyo sayōnara [Photographs, farewell] (Tokyo, 1972)
Hikari to Kage [Light and shade] (Tokyo, 1982)
Nakaji eno tabi [Trip to Nakaji] (Tokyo, 1987)
St Lou eno Tegami [Letters to St Lou] (Tokyo, 1990)
Daido, Hysteric (Tokyo, 1993–94)

BIBLIOGRAPHY
A. Hasegawa: *Shashin o miru me* [Eyes that see photographs] (Tokyo, 1985)
Black Sun: The Eyes of Four (exh. cat. by M. Holborn, Oxford, MOMA; London, Serpentine Gal.; Philadelphia, PA, Mus. A.; 1986)
Eleven Photographers in Japan, 1965–75 (exh. cat. by K. Iizawa and R. Kaneko, Yamaguchi, Prefect. Mus., 1989), pp. 33–44
M. Holborn; *Beyond Japan: A Photo Theatre* (London, 1991), pp. 126–43

KOHTARO IIZAWA

Moriyama, Raymond (*b* Vancouver, 11 Oct 1929). Canadian architect. He trained as an architect at the University of Toronto (1949–54) and at McGill University, Montreal (1954–7). He entered private practice in Toronto in 1958, operating a partnership from 1969 with Ted Teshima (*b* 1938). From the beginning of his career he undertook a wide range of work, from industrial design for Crothers Caterpillar (1959) to lavatory facilities for the Metropolitan Toronto Parks System (1960). His first large built commission, the Civic Garden Centre (1961) at North York, Ontario, was awarded a Massey Medal for Architecture. It marked the beginning of a constant concern with the ensemble of building and landscaping. This continued in such projects as a master-plan for the Ontario Science Centre (1964), North York, the Toronto Zoological Park (1966), Scarborough, Erindale campus of the University of Toronto (1967), and most notably North York City Centre (1983).

Moriyama's early and consistent concern for environmental and ecological issues was allied to this; he served as chairperson for the Mid-Canada Conference Task Force on Environmental and Ecological Factors (1969–70), and he undertook private research on waste regulation, dynamic structures and solar heating. His architectural reputation was enhanced by a succession of large commissions, predominantly for educational uses. Among the best-known buildings are Scarborough Civic Centre (1972–3), which is a series of relatively simple large masses, and the central branch of the Metropolitan Library in Toronto (1976–7; see LIBRARY fig. 5). The latter is one of several large open atrium libraries built worldwide in the 1970s and one of the most successful aesthetically. Its central open space is sufficiently large and uncluttered to be effectively dramatic, but each level and stairway is given its own formal identity within a coherent overall scheme. The library exemplifies Moriyama's aesthetic approach. In the 1980s Moriyama's office began to receive commissions outside Canada, especially in the USA (e.g. Place St Charles, New Orleans, LA, 1983–4).

WRITINGS
'Urban Renewal: Planning the Neighbourhood', *J. Royal Archit. Inst. Canada*, xxxv/1 (1958), pp. 21–4; 2, pp. 56–9
'Metropolitan Library, Toronto', *Can. Architect*, xxiii/1 (1978), pp. 20–29

BIBLIOGRAPHY
Contemp. Architects
J. M. Vastokas: 'Architecture, Meaning and Values: Raymond Moriyama and the New Metropolitan Toronto Library', *Artscanada* (Feb/March 1978), pp. 18–31
L. Whiteson: *Modern Canadian Architecture* (Edmonton, 1983), pp. 6–7, 168–79
R. WINDSOR LISCOMBE

Morlaiter, Giovan [Johann] **Maria** (*b* ?Venice, 1699; *d* Venice, 21 Feb 1781). Italian sculptor. His father, Gregorio, was a glassworker from the Alto Adige. Morlaiter's training as a sculptor may have taken place in Venice, and certainly his style has much in common with that of Venetian sculptors such as Filippo Parodi, Giuseppe Torretti and Francesco Cabianca; it also, however, has markedly Rococo characteristics that would have been more readily assimilated by an artist from outside the Venetian mainstream tradition.

Whatever Morlaiter's artistic origins, he soon established a high reputation in Venice with a dynamic and precious manner, demonstrated in the *Crucifix* (*c.* 1732) he sculpted for S Maria degli Scalzi, which coincided well with contemporary taste. Typical also of his work, with their dynamic outline and luminous, faceted surfaces, are the marble figures of *St Benedict* and *St Scholastica* (1735; Fratta Polesine, SS Pietro e Paolo). Between 1735 and 1737 Morlaiter sculpted a marble frame with a *Glory of Angels* for S Maria del Carmine at Brescia, and a marble

statue of *St Anthony Abbot* for the high altar and a bust of the *Patriarch Dionisio Dolfin* for the façade of S Antonio Abate at Udine.

Morlaiter's most renowned series of sculptures was produced between 1738 and *c.* 1755 for the church of the Gesuati in Venice, where his contribution includes all the marble statues in the niches, the low reliefs above the niches, the marble frame with two angels for the altar of St Dominic, the decoration of the high altar and the altar of the Saints. The sculpted frame for the altar of St Dominic was probably completed first and the statue of *Melchisedek* last in the series. The sculptures are executed with great liveliness and the shining outlines that are so characteristic of his style. Morlaiter probably collaborated again with Giorgio Massari, the architect of the church, on the decoration of two other of his Venetian churches: the Pietà and S Maria della Fava. For the church of the Pietà he executed the marble figures of the *Archangel Michael* and the *Archangel Gabriel* (1745) at the sides of the high altar and for S Maria della Fava, again for the high altar, a pair of marble angels holding a bunch of grapes and some ears of wheat. In 1746 he was commissioned to sculpt marble busts of the pope, *Benedict XIV*, and *Cardinal Carlo Rezzonico* for the choir of Padua Cathedral (*in situ*). These were followed by a monumental marble relief to honour *Marshal Johann Matthias von der Schulenburg* (1747, erected 1756; Venice, Arsenale) and a statue of *St Jerome Emiliani* for S Maria della Salute, Venice.

When the Venetian Accademia was founded in 1756, Morlaiter was one of the first council members, and he became an instructor in 1760. The works he produced in his later years are in much the same style as his earlier sculptures, although his final works perhaps lack some of the dynamism that characterized his maturity. The *Virgin and Child* (1761; Venice, Zitelle) is an interesting example of his late style, as are also the *Blessed Gregory Barbarigo* and the *Immaculate Virgin* (both Venice, S Maria del Giglio) and the *St Lawrence* (Rovigo, S Francesco). The reliefs for the chapel of the Rosary in SS Giovanni e Paolo, Venice, showing the *Rest on the Flight into Egypt* and *Christ among the Doctors* are more difficult to date precisely; they may be from his maturity.

Morlaiter, along with other sculptors, sent works to Russia. His marble group of *Aeneas Rescuing his Father from Burning Troy* is in the palace at Gatcina, near St Petersburg, and his marble figures of *Mars* and *Diana* are still in the palace park. These are the few secular works in a predominantly religious oeuvre. Morlaiter may have made garden statues; none has been identified, but there are numerous *bozzetti* for full-scale works, including some especially fine nudes, both in terracotta and in raw modelled clay (Venice, Ca' Rezzonico).

Morlaiter had a son, Gregorio (*b* Venice, 1738; *d* Venice, 1784), who was also a sculptor. Few of his works survive, and of these the most interesting is the *St Mark* on the high altar of S Francesco di Paola, Venice, which suggests that he was of more than average ability.

BIBLIOGRAPHY
L. Coletti: 'Marchiori or Morlaiter?', *A. Ven.*, xiii/xiv (1959–60), pp. 138–46

C. Semenzato: *La scultura veneta del seicento e del settecento* (Venice, 1966)
A. N. Cellini: *La scultura del settecento* (Turin, 1982)

CAMILLO SEMENZATO

Morland. English family of painters and draughtsmen. The father of (1) Henry Robert Morland has been supposed to be a George Henry Morland (*d* ?1789), whose epitome appears in the *DNB*; Davies, however, cast doubt on whether George Henry ever existed. There are works of 1675 and *c*. 1705, signed respectively *Henry Morland* and *Moreland*, which are difficult to attribute. Henry Robert Morland was a minor artist specializing in genre and fancy pictures in the second half of the 18th century. His sister Maria (*fl* 1780s) also painted genre pictures, exhibiting at the Royal Academy in 1785–6. Of Henry Robert's sons, (2) George Morland was an immensely prolific painter, chiefly of rustic and smuggling scenes, and another Henry was active as a dealer. In 1786 Maria married the engraver William Ward, while George married William's sister Anne; a close working relationship ensued, since there was an extensive market both in Britain and abroad for engravings after Morland's pictures. His colourful personality and racy life provided popular subject-matter for biographers for several years after his death.

(1) Henry Robert Morland (*b* ?London, ?6 Oct 1716; *d* London, 30 Nov 1797). He is first mentioned as a painter in 1754; in 1757 he married Jane Lacam, the daughter of a Huguenot jeweller. Despite this good match, in 1760 he was forced to sell his house in Leicester Square to Joshua Reynolds and accept charitable assistance from the Society of Artists. Two years later he was declared bankrupt. From 1760 Morland frequently exhibited works in both crayon and oil. He appears to have relied on a number of genre designs which he often repeated, re-exhibited and popularized through engravings. *Girl Opening Oysters* (Glasgow, A.G. & Mus.), for example, was exhibited at the Free Society in 1769 and the Society of Artists in 1783; it was also engraved. This work shows the influence of Dutch genre painting, but *Laundry Maid Ironing* (exh. 1768; London, Tate) is more French: the cool tonality and the tranquillity of this domestic scene is reminiscent of Philip Mercier's work. Morland's portraits, such as *Queen Charlotte* (1765; Oxford, Queen's Coll.), are less successful. Despite supplementing his earnings by working as a dealer, restorer and colourman, he continued to receive charitable help from the Royal Academy until his death.

BIBLIOGRAPHY

Waterhouse: *18th C.*
C. Farthing: 'George Morland's Father: A Neglected Painter', *Connoisseur*, cxiv (1944), pp. 101–4
M. Davies: *The British School*, London, N.G. cat. (London, 1946)

HUGH BELSEY

(2) George Morland (*b* London, 26 June ?1763; *d* London, 29 Oct 1804). Son of (1) Henry Robert Morland. He first exhibited chalk drawings in 1773 at the Royal Academy; his father recognized his precocious talent and bound him apprentice for seven years from 1777. Morland's chief employment during this period lay in copying and forging paintings, particularly 17th-century Dutch landscapes, although he also made a number of sea-pieces after Claude-Joseph Vernet. The excessive discipline imposed upon him during his apprenticeship may have inspired the libertarianism and disregard for social convention that characterized his later years. Although he entered the Royal Academy Schools, his attendance was sporadic; he preferred to frequent alehouses, such as the Cheshire Cheese in Russell Court.

In 1780, the year the engraver John Raphael Smith published prints after Morland's the *Angler's Repast* and a *Party Angling*, George Romney offered Morland a three-year apprenticeship, but this he refused. In 1781, without his father's knowledge, Morland began working for an Irish dealer in London, who paid him only enough to ensure his continued dependence. When Morland's apprenticeship ended in 1784, he moved from the family home; the following year he was living in Margate, Kent, having been taken up by a Mrs Hill, whom he also accompanied on a trip to France. By the spring or early summer of 1786 he was back in London, exhibiting at the Royal Academy that year. In September he married Anne, a sister of the engravers William and James Ward, both of whom had trained under Smith. At this period in his career Morland was producing sentimental genre pictures in the manner of Francis Wheatley; the moralizing thrust of many of them derived ultimately from William Hogarth as, for example, in the *Idle Mechanic* and the *Industrious Mechanic*, or the *Idle Laundress*, which William Blake engraved in 1788.

By 1787 Morland was displaying what was to become a characteristic restlessness, while selling his works to the dealers through a middle-man named Irwin. He preferred the independence of disposing of his finished pictures through dealers rather than seeking out commissions, even declining an invitation to supply Carlton House with 'a room of pictures' for the Prince of Wales (later George IV). According to Dawe (1807), 'the reasons Morland assigned for disliking to work for gentlemen were, his choosing not to accommodate himself to the whims of his employers'. By this time Morland was rapidly becoming a popular artist. In 1788 alone 33 of his paintings were engraved and published, worked on by no fewer than 11 engravers, but his continued profligacy was beginning to get him into serious debt. He engaged a lawyer to look after his interests and in 1789 is thought to have made the first of several trips to the Isle of Wight in order to evade his creditors. When in London he moved lodgings regularly, for a while living opposite an inn at Paddington, which supplied him with low-life subject-matter. He also began to take on pupils for financial reasons. One such student, David Brown, who at the age of 35 had sold his business in order to article himself to Morland, bought Morland's the *Farmer's Stable* (London, Tate) for 40 guineas, exhibited it at the Royal Academy in 1791 and then sold it for 100 guineas, receiving at the same time 120 guineas for Morland's the *Straw Yard*.

From *c*. 1790 Morland began working on larger canvases, producing the very large number of rustic and smuggling scenes with which he is particularly associated. His paintings of the early 1790s, generally considered his best, are designed and finished with some care; later works show signs of being hastily executed pot-boilers. When broke he could paint a saleable picture at phenomenal speed (two and a half hours has been recorded; see Gilbey and Cuming, pp. 215–16), and if he was pressed too hard by his creditors he simply disappeared into the country. This enforced familiarity with rural life informs such anecdotal pictures as the *Benevolent Sportsman* (exh. RA 1792; Cambridge, Fitzwilliam; see fig.), commissioned by a Colonel Stuart and engraved by Joseph Grozer (*b c.* 1755) in 1795. Other representative works from this period include *Gypsies around a Camp Fire in a Wooded Landscape* (Bristol, Mus. & A.G.), *Morning: Higglers Preparing for Market* (1791; London, Tate) and the *Tavern Door* (Edinburgh, N.G.). In 1792, while Morland was once again in hiding from creditors (possibly in the Lake District), the dealer Daniel Orme opened an extremely successful Morland Gallery in Bond Street, London, with over one hundred of Morland's works on sale. Morland, meanwhile, continued to paint, sending works to the capital with his servant. Around 1793 Smith also opened a temporary Morland Gallery in London, issuing *A Descriptive Catalogue of Thirty-six Pictures Painted by George Morland*, all of which he intended to engrave and publish by subscription.

Although Morland was back in London in 1793, by this time his marriage was in difficulties and he spent regular periods away, often in the company of gypsies. Various arrangements were made to help him meet his debts, but despite the ready market for his works, now often sold through Henry, his brother, Morland was eventually arrested for debt. He soon regained his freedom but for the rest of the decade his life was largely spent on the run, holed up in confined quarters. His work, nevertheless, was still popular with engravers and the public: 13 prints after his works were published in 1797, a year in which he sent seven pictures for exhibition at the Royal Academy. In April 1799 he and his wife went to the Isle of Wight in order to evade bailiffs, but he was back in London by November. In December he was arrested for debt and imprisoned, being freed by legal amnesty in 1801. Despite his chronic alcoholism Morland's output towards the end of his career was staggering—he is reputed to have painted some 800 pictures in the last eight years of his life. Friends continued to help him, but after his further arrest for debt in October 1804 he appears to have drunk himself into a terminal coma.

Morland's technique was assured; he painted in the light and fluid manner of such contemporaries as Wheatley and Julius Caesar Ibbetson, but stylistic reminiscences of Dutch masters and Thomas Gainsborough are also apparent. Although his work appears at first to fit comfortably within the idiom of sentimental rural genre, closer inspection reveals much of the class tension of the period and the subliminal propaganda that underlay the production and reception of rural imagery: the mounted figure in the *Benevolent Sportsman*, playing his allotted role, gives alms to gypsies who assert their domestic independence on common land at a time when much of it was being appropriated by landowners for their own agriculture or

George Morland: *Benevolent Sportsman*, oil on canvas, 1.02×1.37 m, 1792 (Cambridge, Fitzwilliam Museum)

sporting pursuits. In addition, Morland's celebration of alehouses disturbed more conservative tastes, and some of his female figures appeared to some to be too wanton, when compared with the usual, more stereotypical, rural nymphs. On occasion, engravers chose to make their prints more attractive to potential customers by transforming into willing and smiling faces the often expressionless features of Morland's rural proletariat. In 1793, for example, James Ward made just such adjustments when preparing his *Sunset: A View in Leicestershire*, a print he based on Morland's painting the *Door of a Village Inn* (London, Tate). Prints made after Morland's works, most of which were executed in mezzotint, were sold at prices ranging from 3s. 6d. to one guinea. The large market that existed for them in Britain, and in France and Germany as well, made his name everywhere known, and helped generate the rash of anecdotal biographies that swiftly appeared after his death.

BIBLIOGRAPHY

W. Collins: *Memoirs of a Painter* (London, 1805)
F. W. Blagdon: *Authentic Memoirs of the Late George Morland* (London, 1806)
J. Hassell: *Memoirs of the Life of the Late George Morland* (London, 1806)
G. Dawe: *The Life of George Morland* (London, 1807)
J. T. H. Baily: *George Morland: A Biographical Essay . . . with a Catalogue of the Engraved Pictures*, 3 vols (London, 1906)
W. Gilbey and E. D. Cuming: *George Morland: His Life and Works* (London, 1907)
George Morland (exh. cat. by D. Thomas, ACGB, 1954)
J. Burke: *English Art, 1714–1800* (London, 1976)
J. Barrell: 'George Morland', *The Dark Side of the Landscape: The Rural Poor in English Painting, 1730–1840* (Cambridge, 1982), pp. 89–129

MICHAEL ROSENTHAL

Morlanes. Spanish family of sculptors.

(1) Gil de Morlanes (i) [*el viejo*] (*b* Saragossa, *c.* 1450; *d* Saragossa, *c.* 1515). He was well known and successful, and he was assisted by his son, (2) Gil de Morlanes *el joven*. His work was executed at the time of the transition in Spain from Late Gothic to Renaissance art. He was particularly noted for his retables, into which in his later work he incorporated Renaissance elements, as is seen in the reliefs for the retable of Montearagón (1506; Huesca Cathedral). He also specialized in the carving of funerary monuments for leading families. The royal tombs that he carved for the Cistercian monastery of S Maria de Poblet, Tarragona, include those for *Ferdinand I* (*d* 1416), *John II* (*d* 1479), *Juana Enriquez* and the *Infanta Dona Marina*, all of which have been badly damaged and heavily restored. His most important work, however, is the façade for the Hieronymite monastery of S Engracia in Saragossa, on which he was engaged from 1512 to 1515. The work was continued from 1515 until 1519 by his son. The early Renaissance façade, partly destroyed in the Peninsular War (from 1808) and over-restored in 1891–8, has fine balustered columns on the lower tier and a pediment with pilasters, all covered with fine and abundant decoration. The Plateresque portal shows the kneeling figures of the founders, Ferdinand II of Aragón and Isabella I of Castile and León, praying to the Virgin and flanked by St Jerome and St Paula. Morlanes the elder's splendid mansion in Saragossa, the Casa de los Morlanes, was completed *c.* 1515.

(2) Gil de Morlanes (ii) [*el joven*] (*fl* Saragossa, 1515–47). Son of (1) Gil de Morlanes (i). Having continued the work started by his father on S Engracia, Saragossa, from 1515 to 1519, he worked with Gabriel Yolí (*fl* 1515; *d* 1538) on the retable (1520) for the chapel of S Augustín in Saragossa Cathedral, on a retable dedicated to Nuestra Señora del Portillo (1521; untraced) for the church of the same name and on the retable of the *Visitation* (Saragossa, Semin. Nue.) for the church of SS Juan y Pedro (destr. 1969). The courtyard of the Palacio de los Pardo (now Mus. Camón Aznar) in Saragossa is attributed to him, and he also collaborated on the Casa de los Morlanes. His most important and characteristic work, however, is the interior decoration of the Lonja of Saragossa (1541–51), which shows the exquisite refinement of his Plateresque ornamental carving.

BIBLIOGRAPHY

M. Serrano y Sanz: 'Gil Morlanes, escultor del siglo XV y principios del XVI', *Rev. Archvs, Bib. & Mus.* (May–June 1916)

GERMÁN RAMALLO ASENSIO

Morley, Malcolm (*b* London, 1931). English painter active in the USA. After attending the Camberwell School of Arts and Crafts in London from 1952 to 1953, he studied at the Royal College of Art, London, from 1954 to 1957. Deeply impressed by the Abstract Expressionist paintings in an exhibition of American art (London, Tate, 1956), he made a brief visit to the USA in 1957 and settled permanently in New York in 1958. While earning his living as a waiter he developed an abstract idiom influenced by Barnett Newman, limiting himself primarily to horizontal bands in black and white, as in *Battle of Hastings* (1964; see 1983–4 exh. cat., p. 75).

After trying in 1964 to paint a ship from real life Morley turned to photographs of ships, which he copied in a meticulous *trompe l'oeil* style with the aid of a grid, as in *Empire Monarch* (1965; Kansas City, KS, Larry and Cindy Meeker priv. col.; see 1983–4 exh. cat., p. 18). As a child Morley had made many detailed models of ships, which may help account for his choice of subject matter. These and the other pictures using ship imagery that followed, such as *On Deck* (1966; New York, Met.), marked the beginning of Photorealism in the USA, although Morley preferred the term Super Realism. He moved from these to all manner of photographic images, including travel brochures, reproductions of celebrated paintings (e.g. *Vermeer, Portrait of the Artist in his Studio*, 1968; Sweden, priv. col., see 1983–4 exh. cat., p. 25) and contemporary scenes. Often he would turn both the source material and canvas upside down so as to reproduce it as accurately as possible without stylizing it. Like the Pop artists who preceded him, by focusing on the repeatability of images he questioned the basis of artistic creativity. Replicating the original in an almost mechanical way and conceiving of the painting simply as a coloured surface, Morley undermined the distinction between the abstract and the figurative.

Although he abandoned Photorealism as a style in the early 1970s, Morley continued to examine the relationship between images and the objective reality they purported to portray. The Photorealist rendering of a telephone book in *St John's Yellow Pages* (1971; Cologne, Mus. Ludwig) is accompanied by a real electric bell that negates the illusion of the image by making its flatness apparent. In *Los Angeles Yellow Pages* (1971; Humlebæk, Louisiana Mus.) the front of a torn telephone book was painted in a mixture of acrylic and wax encaustic so that the tears could be represented in relief, but this very literalism draws attention to the image as a painted surface. In another work, *Kodak Castle* (1971; Utica, NY, Munson–Williams–Proctor Inst.), Morley reproduced the folded corner of his source material, paradoxically emphasizing the flatness of his painting by reference to another two-dimensional artefact. Throughout this period in particular Morley was influenced by the philosophy and ideas about perception of Maurice Merleau-Ponty. Even after adopting looser, more expressionist brushwork in the early 1970s, Morley remained committed to the conceptual approach to painting that had characterized his Photorealist works, with their focus on the process of painting.

In the early 1970s Morley's interest in the life and work of van Gogh as representative of the myth of the romantic artist led him to shoot 11 hours of film as part of a project called *The Discipline of Vincent, the Ballroom Dancer*. From 1975 to 1976 he produced a number of pictures depicting scenes of disaster, such as *Train Wreck* (1975; Vienna, Mus. 20. Jhts), in which he seemed to be destroying the remnants of his own previous style. While working in Tampa, FL, for 18 months from 1977 to 1979 he began using his own watercolours and drawings as models for his oil paintings, much as he had previously used found material, claiming that the method allowed him the freedom to incorporate abrupt changes of scale as a challenge to conventional hierarchies. A series of watercolours and drawings of the archaeology and landscape of Crete and Greece, which he visited in 1982, formed the basis of some of his later paintings, such as *Albatross* (1985; see 1986 exh. cat.), painted in an energetic style that invited comparison with the work of younger Neo-expressionist painters working in Europe and the USA. In 1984 Morley was the first recipient of the Turner Prize administered through the Tate Gallery in London.

BIBLIOGRAPHY

K. Levin: 'Malcolm Morley: Post-style Illusionism', *A. Mag.*, xlvii/4 (1973), pp. 60–63; repr. in *Super Realism: A Critical Anthology*, ed. G. Battcock (New York, 1975), pp. 170–88
Malcolm Morley: Paintings, 1965–82 (exh. cat. by M. Compton, Basle, Ksthalle; Rotterdam, Boymans–van Beuningen; London, Whitechapel A.G.; and elsewhere; 1983–4)
Malcolm Morley (exh. cat. by J. Yau, London, Fabian Carlsson Gal., 1985)
Malcolm Morley: New Paintings and Watercolours, 1984–1986 (exh. cat., New York, Xavier Fourcade, 1986)
Malcolm Morley (exh. cat., New York, Pace Gal., 1988)
Malcolm Morley (exh. cat., London, Anthony d'Offay Gal., 1990)

Morlon, Pierre-Alexandre (*b* Mâcon, Saône-et-Loire, 4 June 1878; *d* 1951). French sculptor and medallist. He was a pupil of Alexandre Falguière, Antonin Mercié and Jules-Clément Chaplain at the Ecole des Beaux-Arts, Paris, and exhibited at the Salon from 1900, winning a gold medal in 1920 and a medal of honour in 1926. He was responsible for numerous war memorials, including those at Charolles and La Clayette, Saône-et-Loire, and at Rambevilliers, Vosges, as well as for a large number of medals, including *To Arms* (1907), the *Allied Victory Medal*, the *Apple*

(1930) and the *Battle of Flanders* (1937). His style is typical of French decorative arts in the inter-war period, combining geometric decorative forms with a continuing commitment to representation.

BIBLIOGRAPHY

Dictionnaire des artistes contemporains, iii (Paris, 1934), pp. 58–9
Catalogue général des éditions de la Monnaie de Paris, iii (Paris, [1978]), pp. 267–77

MARK JONES

Morlotti, Ennio (*b* Lecco, 21 Sept 1910). Italian painter. He studied at the Accademia di Belle Arti in Florence with Felice Carena (1936–7). In 1937 he went to Paris, where he studied the works of Courbet, Cézanne and Picasso, whose *Guernica* (1937; Madrid, Cent. Reina Sofía) he saw at the Exposition Universelle. His landscapes and nudes of 1938–40, already displaying his characteristic impasto, were very obviously influenced by these three artists. In 1939 he moved to Milan, where he attended the Accademia di Belle Arti for three years. In 1940 he joined the Corrente movement and exhibited aggressive figure paintings indebted to Picasso in the movement's gallery (1944) together with Bruno Cassinari and E. Treccani. After World War II he was one of the signatories in Milan of the 'Manifesto del Realismo' (1946), which concentrated on contemporary social concerns. However, in Paris, where he went in 1947, he came into direct contact with such *Art informel* artists as Wols and Nicolas de Staël. This encounter was an important factor in directing him towards matter painting following the most advanced European trends. Among members of the Fronte Nuovo delle Arti, with whom he exhibited at the Venice Biennale of 1948, he represented a trend towards a progressive dissolution of form, which later became the distinctive stylistic feature of the Gruppo degli Otto Pittori Italiani, with whom he exhibited at the Biennale of 1952. At the Biennale of 1956 he had a room devoted to himself. The dominant motif of his painting, particularly after 1960, was landscape, particularly that of Lombardy, even though it may have lost any explicit narrative or descriptive references (e.g. *Landscape at Merate*, 1959; Lecco, Gal. Com. A.). His own individual naturalism has been defined as a transference, in terms of colour and substance, on to canvas of the biological rhythms of nature, its organic and inorganic stratification. In his work during the 1970s figures and nudes again reappeared in these landscapes. However, by the mid-1980s their lush vegetation was replaced by arid unpopulated images.

BIBLIOGRAPHY

G. Testori: *Morlotti* (Milan, 1951)
Morlotti: Figure, 1942–1975 (exh. cat. by R. Tassi, Parma, Pal. Pilotta, 1975)

ANTONELLO NEGRI

Mormons [Church of Jesus Christ of the Latter-day Saints]. Religious sect. It was founded in 1830 in a farmhouse near Fayette, NY, by Joseph Smith jr (1805–44), who declared that he had been called by God as a modern prophet to restore Christianity in its purity. The name was taken from the *Book of Mormon*, a companion scripture to the Bible, narrating the religious history of an ancient American people who were visited by the resurrected Christ; this was translated from golden plates and

Mormon temple, Kensington, MD, near Washington, DC, 1969–73

symbol of the Church, with its buttressed granite walls and six spires.

Early Utah meeting-houses were generally simple rectangular adobe structures with gabled roofs, but as settlements grew they became more elaborate, with entrances and towers in a variety of revival styles (e.g. the Gothic-style Brigham City Tabernacle, 1875–96). Between 1910 and 1925 Frank Lloyd Wright's influence resulted in imposing modern temples (e.g. in Cardston, Alberta, 1912–23), while the Idaho Falls Temple (1937–43) was impressive among many later Mormon buildings reflecting American Art Deco influence. After World War II, the Church accommodated its international growth through a centrally directed programme, producing hundreds of standardized meeting-houses, while temples built during this period, for example at Kensington, MD, near Washington, DC (1969–73; see fig.), often attempt to evoke the spired appearance of the Salt Lake Temple in contemporary style.

Although Mormon meeting-houses and tabernacles seldom included paintings and sculpture, the Church offered many commissions for portraits, public sculpture, and symbolic landscape murals in temples. Mormon art in the late 19th century was dominated by European convert immigrants, including the Scandinavian genre painter C. C. A. Christensen (1831–1912). Some, with Church sponsorship, studied in Paris, including the Impressionist painter John Hafen (1857–1910). Prominent Mormon artists in the 20th century include the painter Minerva Teichert (1889–1976) and the realist sculptor Avard Fairbanks (1897–1987). Folk arts and handicrafts also flourished in Utah, especially furniture-making and quilting; in the 20th century converts, particularly in Latin America, Polynesia and East Asia, translated Mormon concepts into the styles and media of local folk art traditions. The Museum of Church History and Art, opened in Salt Lake City in 1984, exhibits works of fine and folk arts by Mormons from around the world, and collections of Mormon art are also displayed at the Museum of Fine Arts at the University of Utah and at Utah State Historical Society, both in Salt Lake City.

See also TEMPLE, §VII.

BIBLIOGRAPHY
S. White: *The Mormons: The Church of Jesus Christ of Latter-day Saints* (Beaverton, OH, 1980)
G. B. Hinckley and others: *Temples of the Church of Jesus Christ of Latter-day Saints* (Salt Lake City, 1988)

PAUL L. ANDERSON

Morny, Charles-Auguste, Duc de (*b* Paris, ?21 Oct 1811; *d* Paris, 10 March 1865). French politician and collector. He was the natural son of Hortense de Beauharnais and Charles-Joseph, Comte de Flahaut, and thus half-brother to Louis-Napoleon Bonaparte, later Napoleon III. Known as the Comte de Morny, he was brought up by his paternal grandmother, Madame de Souza (1761–1836), who owned a fine collection of paintings (Titian, Adriaen van Ostade, Carlo Dolci), and her love of art descended to her grandson. In 1837 he abandoned his military career and in 1842 entered politics, becoming deputy for Clermont-Ferrand.

Morny's taste for art led him to collect paintings. However, in order to fund his financial speculations, he

published by Smith in 1830. A central teaching of the Church was that members should gather to the American frontier to build the City of Zion in preparation for Christ's millennial reign. Attempts to build latter-day Zion aroused violent opposition in Ohio, Missouri and Illinois, culminating in the assassination (1844) of Joseph Smith and his brother Hyrum Smith. In 1847 Brigham Young (1801–77), Smith's successor as president and prophet, founded Salt Lake City, UT, as a new headquarters, and over the next 30 years he established hundreds of settlements in the region. Between 1847 and 1900 more than 100,000 converts (mostly American, Canadian, British and Scandinavian) travelled to Utah, and in the 20th century an ambitious missionary programme increased international Church membership to 7 million by 1990.

From its early days, the Mormon Church sponsored and inspired architecture, urban planning, painting and sculpture. Mormon urban planning began with Smith's *Plat of the City of Zion* (Zion, MO, 1833), which called for cities housing 15,000 to 20,000 believers, laid out in a geometric plan of large square blocks and broad streets surrounding temples and storehouses. In all, *c.* 700 communities modelled on Smith's plan were founded throughout the western USA. The Church's emphasis on community building was particularly important. The first Mormon temple (1834–7) in Kirtland, OH, was an impressive Federal style structure with Gothic details. In Utah various functions of the early temples were divided among several building types: ward (neighbourhood) meeting-houses for congregational worship, tabernacles for regional conferences and other large gatherings, and temples for sacred ceremonies. The Salt Lake Temple (1853–93; for illustration *see* SALT LAKE CITY), designed by Truman O. Angell (1810–87), became the architectural

was obliged on several occasions to sell his collection, reconstituting it between sales; between 1841 and 1848 there were five sales. In 1841 he sold, among other paintings, the *Rape of Europa* by Boucher (London, Wallace). In 1848 *The Modiste* by Boucher (London, Wallace) and *Connoisseurs in a Room Hung with Pictures* attributed to Michiel van Mierevelt (London, N.G.) were sold in London along with 110 other Dutch and French paintings, at a sale that had to be suspended because the prices were so poor. In 1852 Morny once more sold part of his collection. The Musée du Louvre bought the two paintings: *Portrait of a Woman* by Balthasar Denner and *Village Crossed by a Road* by Aert van der Neer. Several other works were withdrawn from the sale: *David and Bathsheba* by Jan Massys, which he presented to the Louvre, and the *Halt during the Chase* by Watteau (London, Wallace), which appeared in the sale held after Morny's death.

In 1854 Napoleon III appointed Morny President of the Corps Législatif, the collection of paintings being transferred to the President's official residence, the Hôtel de Lassay. In 1856 Morny was sent as Special Emissary to Tsar Alexander II; during his stay in Russia he increased his collection, most notably with the *Rape of Europa* by Rembrandt (New York, priv. col.), and the *Head of a Young Girl* by Greuze (Paris, Mus. Jacquemart-André).

On his return to France Morny presided over the jury judging the paintings of the 1859 Salon, and later over the French section of the 1862 Universal Exposition in London, to which he sent paintings from his collection by contemporary artists such as Ernest Meissonier, Jean-Léon Gérôme and Joseph-Nicolas Robert-Fleury. In that same year Napoleon III created him Duc de Morny. He also collected sculptures, among them a bust of *Mme de Serilly* by Jean-Antoine Houdon (London, Wallace), and two antique red marble busts of satyrs, which he had acquired in Russia. He also set up an 'Oriental salon', filled with precious objects from India, Japan, Persia and from the sacking of the Summer Palace in Peking. The sale held after Morny's death lasted 11 days and included *The Gilder* (Portrait of Herman Doomer) by Rembrandt (New York, Met.); the *Bird-song Organ* by Chardin and the *Wool Winder* by Greuze (New York, Frick); *The Swing* and *The Souvenir* by Fragonard (London, Wallace) and *The Windmills* by Meindert Hobbema (Paris, Petit Pal.). Morny's six paintings by Meissonier fetched very high prices (115,750 francs in all); the Wallace collection has three, one of them being the *Hired Assassins*, while another, *Young Man Working* (1852), was later given to the Louvre.

BIBLIOGRAPHY

V. Vernier: *Les Joyaux de la peinture: La Galerie de M. le comte de Morny* (Paris, 1862)
L. Lagrange: 'La Galerie de M. le duc de Morny', *Gaz. B.-A.*, xiv (1863), pp. 289–306, 385–401
A. Jacquemart: 'Collection d'objets d'art de M. le duc de Morny', *Gaz. B.-A.*, xv (1863), pp. 393–419; xvi (1864), pp. 28–50
M. Parturier: *Morny et son temps* (Paris, 1969)

FRANÇOISE MAISON

Moro, Angolo del. *See* ANGOLO DEL MORO, DELL'.

Moro, Cristoforo, Doge of Venice (*b* Venice, *c.* 1390; *d* Venice, 9 Nov 1471). Italian ruler and patron. Born into a noble Venetian family, he studied at the University of Padua and then steadily climbed the conventional round of official positions: Captain of Brescia, then of Padua, Ambassador in Rome, *Savio del Consiglio*, Ducal Counsellor, Procurator of S Marco and finally Doge (elected 12 May 1462). His contemporaries considered him harsh and avaricious; nevertheless two Venetian churches owe important works to his generosity. He had three altars built by ANTONIO RIZZO at S Marco between 1465 and 1469; those of St James and St Paul still stand against the first piers of the south and north transepts, respectively; of the third there remains only a relief of the *Virgin and Child* set in the altarpiece of the chapel of St Clement. He also presented to the basilica two large silver-gilt candlesticks in Venetian Gothic style (Venice, Tesoro S Marco). He was patron to the new hospital of S Giobbe and actively promoted its construction; since he had no direct heir, he left all his possessions for the completion of the church, where he had had a tomb for himself and his wife, Cristina Sanudo, built below the sanctuary in 1470. He recommended that Antonio Gambello should be entrusted with the work, but Pietro Lombardo was employed instead. Only the doge's generosity, therefore, and not his taste, was responsible for the carved portal and the presbytery with a cupola supported on pendentives, which were influential in the development of Renaissance forms in Venice. Under his rule work continued on the Arco Foscari in the Doge's Palace (*see* VENICE, fig. 24): it incorporated his arms and his statue (destr. 1797), although it is not clear whether he was personally involved in the project. His face is known from a portrait (Venice, S Giobbe) painted by a member of the school of Gentile Bellini and a medal (see G. F. Hill: *Corpus*, 1930, no. 411) by Antonello della Moneta (*fl* 1454–84). He can thus be recognized as the doge adoring the infant Christ in a *Nativity* (Philadelphia, PA, Mus. A.) attributed to Lazzaro Bastiani, which he must have commissioned.

BIBLIOGRAPHY

P. Paoletti: *L'architettura e la scultura del rinascimento in Venezia* (Venice, 1893)
A. da Mosto: *I dogi di Venezia* (Milan, 1960), pp. 220–26
D. Pincus: *The Arco Foscari* (New York and London, 1976)

BERTRAND JESTAZ

Moro, il. *See* TORBIDO, FRANCESCO.

Morocco, Kingdom of [Arab. Al-Mamlaka al-Maghribiyya]. Country in North Africa with its capital at Rabat. Morocco has an area *c.* 458,700 sq. km with coastlines along the Mediterranean Sea to the north and Atlantic Ocean to the west, bounded in the east by Algeria and in the south by Western Sahara. Geographically Morocco is divided into distinct regions: the populous plains and plateaux of the west; the Rif Mountains along the Mediterranean coast; the Atlas Mountains, which cross the country from south-west to north-east; the pre-Sahara region in the south; and the high plateau in the east. The population of 23,000,000 (1987 estimate) consists of a mixture of Arabs and Berbers, the majority of which is Sunni Muslim; there is also a small Jewish community and some Christians. Arabic is the official language; about half the population speak Berber dialects, and French and Spanish are also spoken. The economy is based on

Michel Pinseau and the Royal Architectural Workshop: Great Mosque of Hassan II, Casablanca, Morocco, completed 1993

agriculture, fishing and minerals, particularly phosphates. Since the 1970s the tourist industry has been a major source of revenue. Morocco's Berber–Arab heritage (being the only Arab country that did not come under Ottoman rule), its historical ties with France and Spain (which possesses the enclaves of Ceuta and Melilla) and its situation in Africa have produced a distinct cultural character. This article covers the art produced in the country in the 20th century. For its earlier history *see* AFRICA, §VII, 1, ALMOHAD, ALMORAVID, BERBER, ID- RISID, ISLAMIC ART, MARINID, ROME, ANCIENT, and SA'DI.

Morocco is a constitutional monarchy under a dynasty (*see* 'ALAWI) founded in the 17th century, which traces its lineage back to the Prophet Muhammad. European inter- ests coupled with Moroccan instability led to the establish- ment of a French protectorate in 1912, which allowed Spain a small area mainly in the north with its capital at Tétouan, while Tangier was confirmed as an international city. Although the sultan was nominal ruler, power lay in the hands of the French resident-general, the first of whom was Hubert Lyautey (1854–1934). Large numbers of French and some Spanish settled in Morocco, and a modern educational system was introduced. After World War II the independence movement, led by Sultan Mu- hammad, gathered momentum. In 1956 Morocco was granted full independence, and Tangier's international regime was abolished. The Sultan became king as Muham- mad V (*reg* 1927–61; king from 1957) and was succeeded by Hassan II (*reg* 1961–). In 1975 Morocco claimed sovereignty over the then Spanish Sahara, from which Spain withdrew; war followed against the Polisario Front, fighting for self-determination (*see* WESTERN SAHARA).

As Resident-General from 1912 until 1925, Lyautey initiated urban, architectural and cultural development in French Morocco. In reaction to the destruction of build- ings by French forces in Algeria, Lyautey's policy was to preserve the old towns of Morocco as historic monuments and build the new colonial towns separately. HENRI PROST, Lyautey's principal urban planner, oversaw the creation of new suburbs at FEZ, MARRAKESH, MEKNÈS and RABAT,

the last of which became the capital. They were built according to the most innovative European ideas, but Lyautey also encouraged an Arabizing style, sympathetic to local culture. For example, the house of the resident- general (now the French embassy) in Rabat, built in 1918 by the architects ALBERT LAPRADE and Adrien Laforgue, used elements of traditional Moroccan house- and garden- plans, as well as local architectural forms and decoration. A group of architects under Prost built the major existing administrative buildings of French Morocco in this Arab- izing style, such as the Law Courts (1915) in Casablanca by Joseph Marrast (*b* 1881), the Post Office in Casablanca and the main railway station in Rabat (*c.* 1920) by Laforgue, and the Bank of Morocco buildings in Rabat and Casa- blanca (*c.* 1920) by Auguste-Alexandre Cadet (*b* 1881) and Edmond Charles Brion (*b* 1885). The French also built new towns that were modern versions of old walled towns, such as the New Medina (Quartier Habous; 1916) in Casablanca by Laprade, Cadet and Brion.

After independence, Hassan II commissioned major buildings such as the mausoleum of his father, Muhammad V, in Rabat (completed 1973), by the Vietnamese architect Vo Toan (*b* 1924). The mausoleum is in a neo-traditional style: highly conservative Moroccan architectural decora- tion is applied to modern construction materials and structures. This style is characteristic of King Hassan's programme of palace building in all the major towns. The Great Mosque of Hassan II (completed 1993; see fig.) in Casablanca is one of the largest mosques in the world. The work of the French architect Michel Pinseau and the Royal Architectural Workshop, it employed numerous Moroccan craftsmen. The mosque is the centre of a cultural complex and has a minaret rising to 175 m.

The neo-traditional style has also been used for hotels, although it is sometimes no more than a decorative pastiche. An interesting example is the Hotel Tichka (1986) in Marrakesh by CHARLES BOCCARA. Affluent Moroccan and foreign private patronage encouraged numerous ex- periments in this style, such as the Sijelmassi House (1981) in Casablanca by Abdelrahim Sijelmassi and the Abtan House (1984) in Marrakesh by Boccara.

The rapid population increase and migration from rural areas have led to the decay of many old towns and the proliferation of unplanned buildings and shanty towns. The Moroccan Ministry of Housing and Urban Planning organized some urban rehabilitation projects, and in 1980 UNESCO launched an appeal and gave technical assis- tance for the conservation of Fez, an enormous task. One government project to build low-income housing within a local tradition, the Dar Lamane Complex (1979–83) in Casablanca by Abderrahim Charai (*b* 1934) and Aziz Lazrak (*b* 1944), won the Aga Khan Award for Architec- ture in 1986. Also notable were the government housing projects of the Toubkal quarter and the suburb of Assif (1978) in Marrakesh by Boccara.

Modern Moroccan art reflects diverse cultural traditions: Berber, Arab–Islamic and Western. Figural and easel painting commenced after the creation of the French and Spanish protectorates in 1912, when several Moroccan artists, inspired by the presence of European painters, began to take up the new medium. The self-taught painter Muhammad ibn 'Ali Rabati (1861–1939), for example, worked on small naive paintings of Moroccan life. This trend continued in the work of the self-taught painter Moulay Ahmed Drissi (1923–73). Naive art was also pursued by such artists as Muhammad ibn Allal (Ben Allal; *b* 1924), Chaïbia (*b* 1929), Ahmed Yacoubi (1932–86) and Fatima Hassan (*b* 1945), continuing after independence.

The first school of fine art in Morocco, the Escuela Preparatoria de Bellas Artes, was established in Tétouan in 1945 by the Spanish painter Mario Bertuchi (1898–1985). Mohamed Serghini (*b* 1923) was the first Moroccan to join the Tétouan school, before going to Madrid to continue his training; he later became director of the Escuela Preparatoria de Bellas Artes. In 1950 the French founded the Ecole des Beaux-Arts in Casablanca. With the opening of these schools, Orientalist and naive painting began to lose their former popularity.

After independence several artists were given grants to train in Europe and the USA. Their return to Morocco in the 1960s in the intellectual ferment of political change stimulated a new direction in painting. The most significant was AHMED CHERKAOUI, who studied in Paris and Warsaw. He made a synthesis between modern abstract art and forms derived from Berber art. Other painters also adopted Western abstract, expressionist or neo-realist traditions and attempted to incorporate indigenous forms in their works. FARID BELKAHIA, for example, trained at the Ecole des Beaux-Arts in Paris (1954–9) and in theatrical design in Prague (1959–62), and then returned to Morocco, where he was appointed director of the Ecole des Beaux-Arts in Casablanca (1962–74). In 1964, together with two other painters who were teaching at the school, MOHAMMED MELEHI and Mohamed Chebaa (*b* 1935), he introduced Arabic calligraphy and local crafts into the curriculum. These artists became known as the 'Casablanca Group'. Belkahia used in his work such traditional Moroccan materials as copper and leather, treating them with dyes, modelling them into abstract forms and sometimes tattooing the surfaces (e.g. *Dawn II*, 1984; Paris, Inst. Monde Arab.).

In the 1970s contacts with other Arab artists developed in importance. The Moroccan Association of Plastic Arts, which was founded in 1972, encouraged these contacts, and participated in inter-Arab meetings in Baghdad (1972 and 1974), Algiers (1974), Tunis (1975) and other Arab capitals. In 1978 the annual cultural festival at Asilah was inaugurated, which has exhibitions of Arab art as well as being a festival of music and poetry. Brightly coloured murals decorate the white walls of the town.

The first Moroccan sculptors were also self-taught, such as Mubarak Brahim (1920–61), who worked with stone and had several followers, and Abdelhaq Sijelmassi (*b* 1938), who has used diverse material: wood, stone, ceramics, metal and cement, the latter for his works in Casablanca (e.g. *Monumental Sculpture*, 1983; gardens of Résidence Moulay Youssef). Boujemaa Lakhdar (*b* 1940), who was inspired by Berber and African traditions, worked with wood and metal. Hassan Slaoui (*b* 1946), who studied in Rabat and Paris, worked with wood after 1977, especially thuya-wood, sometimes inlaying it with bone or metal. Omar Youssufi (*b* 1950), who settled in France, has produced compositions of sand, ceramics and wood that

are meant to be touched or turned (e.g. *Sand Sculpture*; Amman, N.G. F.A.).

Morocco is rich in its decorative arts, and pottery, metalwork, carpets and leatherwork continue to be made following traditional practices. Glazed and wheel-turned ceramic production was traditionally located in the towns of Fez, Meknès, Tétouan and Rabat-Salé; today it is largely concentrated in Fez and Safi. The ceramics are fired in the traditional way, producing bright earthenware pots and plates with geometric patterns. Unglazed pottery, usually manufactured without a wheel, is still a rural craft, as practised, for example, among the Ghomara of the far north, or the Shluh of the south Atlas. Metalwork, particularly engraved brass and copper, is produced in many centres (*see* BRASS, fig. 9). The production of decorated arms such as daggers, swords, rifles and pistols has, however, largely ceased. Jewellery is one of Morocco's most distinctive decorative arts, with a rich variety of forms both in the rural tradition of silver jewellery and the gold jewellery of the cities.

Carpets from the tribal areas of the Rif or Middle and High Atlas mountains have an enormous variety of distinctive markings. The knotted carpets of the urban tradition, mostly of Rabat, are derived from Turkish prototypes. In embroidery there used to be a different style in each of the major towns, but in the late 20th century the most widely produced was the Fez embroidery, with its tiny cross-stitch. Leatherwork is much practised, producing traditional *babouches* (open backed footwear) as well as modern bags, jackets and belts. Marquetry work is produced in Essaouira, where cedar- and thuya-wood are made into boxes, chess sets and traditional furniture.

The survival of Morocco's decorative arts tradition was probably due to its relative isolation until the beginning of the 20th century, and the official encouragement given by the French; the art historian Prosper Ricard (1874–1952) directed the Service des Arts Indigènes during the first decades of the protectorate. Artisanal centres were created in all the major towns to ensure the continuity of the crafts and to serve as exhibition and sales rooms; the Moroccan Ministry of Crafts and Social Affairs has continued to open new centres.

The study of Moroccan art and archaeology began under the French protectorate and was conducted largely by the Institut des Hautes Etudes Marocaines in Rabat, which published the influential journals *Hespéris* (continued after independence as *Hespéris–Tamuda*) and *Archives marocaines*. Another important journal was *Mauritania*, published by the Spanish Franciscan mission in Tangier. The most important Roman sites in Morocco are VOLUBILIS and Lixus (nr Larache). Rock art is preserved in the south, for example at Foum al-Hassan and Oukaïmeden.

Prosper Ricard established three of Morocco's major museums with art collections: the Oudaïa Museum in Rabat, the Dar Batha Museum in Fez and the Dar Jamaï Museum in Meknès. There are also traditional crafts museums in various towns, sometimes with adjacent crafts schools. The main archaeological museum is in Rabat, which contains most of the finds from Volubilis. Modern Moroccan art is exhibited at the Musée d'Art Contemporain in Tangier, which opened in 1990, and in the 1990s a centre of contemporary art in Casablanca was planned (due to open in late 1996).

For further illustration *see* ISLAMIC ART, fig. 75.

BIBLIOGRAPHY

P. Ricard: *Corpus des tapis marocains*, 4 vols (Paris, 1923/*R* 1975)
J. Gallotti and A. Laprade: *Le Jardin et la maison arabe au Maroc* (Paris, 1924)
H. Terrasse and J. Hainaut: *Les Arts décoratifs au Maroc* (Paris, 1925)
M. Sijelmassi: *La Peinture marocaine* (Paris, 1972)
A. Boukobza: *La Poterie marocaine* (Casablanca, 1974)
M. Sijelmassi: *Les Arts traditionnels au Maroc* (Paris, 1974)
V. Toan: *Le Mausolée Mohammed V* (Casablanca, 1976)
A. Paccard: *Le Maroc et l'artisanat traditionnel islamique dans l'architecture* (Paris, 1979); Eng. trans. as *Traditional Islamic Crafts in Moroccan Architecture* (London, 1980)
M. Ben Bashir and N. Mohammedi: *La Politique culturelle au Maroc* (Paris, 1981)
F. Béguin: *Arabisances: Décor architectural et tracé urbain en Afrique du Nord, 1830–1950* (Paris, 1983)
A. Flamand: *Regard sur la peinture contemporaine au Maroc* (Casablanca, 1983)
Tunisia, Egypt, Morocco: Contemporary Houses, Traditional Values (exh. cat. by B. B. Taylor, London, Zamana Gal., 1985)
Mimar, 22 (1986) [issue on contemp. Moroc. archit.]
W. Ali, ed.: *Contemporary Art from the Islamic World* (London, 1989), pp. 211–18
T. Maraini: *Ecrits sur l'art: Choix de textes—Maroc, 1967–1989* (Rabat, 1989)
M. Sijelmassi: *L'Art contemporain au Maroc* (Paris, 1989)
L. Dennis and L. Dennis: *Living in Morocco: Design from Casablanca to Marrakesh* (London, 1992)
J. Hedgecoe and S. S. Damluji: *Zillij: The Art of Moroccan Ceramics* (Reading, 1992)

S. J. VERNOIT

Morone. Italian family of painters. (1) Domenico Morone was the leading early Renaissance painter of Verona, and his son (2) Francesco Morone was similarly important for Veronese High Renaissance painting.

(1) Domenico Morone (*b* Verona, *c.* 1442; *d* Verona, *c.* 1518). Vasari—exceptionally well informed on Veronese artists—asserted that Domenico was taught by students of the Gothic painter Stefano da Verona. His earliest signed work, a fine *Virgin and Child* dated 29 April 1483 (Berlin, Gemäldegal.), reveals his conversion to Andrea Mantegna's ideas, partly as filtered through Giovanni Bellini and Francesco Benaglio. His next, the signed and dated *Expulsion of the Bonacolsi from Mantua* (1494; Mantua, Pal. Ducale; *see* MANTUA, fig. 1), parallels the Venetian panoramic narratives of Gentile Bellini and Vittore Carpaccio and may owe much to Giovanni Bellini's lost battle paintings for the Doge's Palace in Venice. Though damaged and repainted (the distant landscape, for example, is new), this spirited narrative remains valuable both for its detailed description of 15th-century Mantua and as the most convincing large-scale Quattrocento battle-piece that survives.   Around 1500 Domenico's workshop executed major fresco cycles in Verona's churches: the crossing and lantern of S Maria in Organo (payments 1495–9), the Medici Chapel in S Bernadino and the upper zones of the chapel of S Biagio in SS Nazaro e Celso (with G. M. Falconetto, (2) Francesco Morone, Girolamo Mocetto and others). All are much damaged, and scholars differ as to which portions Domenico himself painted, but all display a large-scale mastery of Mantegnesque perspective and decorative effects. Unenterprising by comparison are Domenico's signed and dated frescoes from the oratory of S Nicola at Paladon (*Standing Saints*, 1502; Verona, Castelvecchio). Not so the workshop's best-preserved fresco cycle, dated 1503, in the monastery library of S Bernadino. It depicts Franciscan saints and doctors as lifesize friars on illusionistic pedestals and gives one whole wall to a panoramic, quasi-narrative *Virgin and Child with Saints and Donors in a Landscape*. The concept's originality and the figures' homely naturalism are both remarkable. The few paintings attributable to Domenico after this date show a decline in quality, and he seemingly painted little in his last years.   Domenico Morone is traditionally and rightly considered a pioneer of Renaissance painting in Verona. His personal contribution is difficult to appraise more precisely because so few documented works survive, most of them seriously damaged and many of them collaborative. They suggest a capable and versatile practitioner who infused a basically Mantegnesque style with a distinctively earthy realism. He established points of departure for the next generation of Veronese painters: his son Francesco, Michele da Verona, the brothers Caroto and Girolamo dai Libri.

(2) Francesco Morone (*b* Verona, 1471; *d* Verona, 16 May 1529). Son of (1) Domenico Morone. He was taught by his father, with whom he collaborated *c.* 1500–05. His imposing *Crucifixion* (1498; Verona, S Bernadino), however, owes more to Bartolommeo Montagna and Giovanni Buonconsiglio from nearby Vicenza in its dark, lofty sky and lyrical expressiveness. Dated altarpieces of 1502 (Milan, Brera) and 1503 (Verona, S Maria in Organo), both depicting the *Virgin and Child Enthroned with Saints*, show the geometric rounding off of figures and the symmetry of arrangement characteristic of Francesco's mature art, as well as a subtle interplay of lights and colours. They reflect a study both of Mantegna's high altarpiece for S Maria in Organo (1496) and of Venetian models. Mantegnesque too is the illusionistic cupola Francesco painted in fresco for S Maria in Organo's sacristy (payments 1505–7), lauded by Vasari and still startling in its perspectival virtuosity. Giovanni Bellini's predawn *Resurrection* (Berlin, Gemäldegal.) furnished a precedent for the marvellously observed and calibrated sunset skies that transfigure several of Francesco Morone's panels, for instance the *Stigmatization of St Francis* (Verona, Castelvecchio) or the *Virgin and Child* (Verona, Bib. Capitolare). Those skies, overarching dusky crags, fir trees and valleys inspired by Albrecht Dürer's prints produce effects unique to this artist in his time and curiously prophetic of Caspar David Friedrich.   Francesco Morone's style did not change radically during the three decades of his career. He was impervious to the innovations of Giorgione and Titian in Venice, but his later art does exhibit—in the idealized regularity of figures and faces, the symmetrical harmony of compositions and the usual tenor of dignified calm—a distant approach to some aspects of Raphaelesque classicism. This approach appears especially in his occasional collaborations with his close friend Girolamo dai Libri, notably the organ shutters for S Maria in Organo (1515; Marcellise, parish church). These depict paired *Saints*, paired *Prophets* and a *Nativity* set against deep, sub-alpine landscapes. Some modern scholars have considered Francesco Morone essentially a continuer of his father's presumed innovations. Vasari was more accurate: 'He was taught the principles of art by his father, but so exerted himself as shortly to become a much better artist.' Nothing in Domenico's surviving work foreshadows the subtle luminism, the understated monumentality or the poetic sensibility that make Francesco's a decidedly personal statement. Francesco's art moreover consolidated in the High Renaissance generation certain distinctively Veronese aesthetic preferences, for example for slightly phosphorescent colours in particular combinations and for firm, rounded forms. These determined the style of Francesco's pupil Paolo Cavazzola and can still be seen two generations later in that of Paolo Veronese.

BIBLIOGRAPHY

G. Vasari: *Vite* (1550, rev. 2/1568); ed. G. Milanesi (1878–85), v, pp. 307–14

V. Cipolla: 'Il testamento di Francesco Morone', *Archv Ven.*, xxiii (1882), pp. 213–16

G. Gerola: 'Questioni storiche d'arte veronese: 4. Per la biografia di Liberale da Verona; 7. Intorno a Domenico Morone', *Madonna Verona*, iii (1909), no. 1, pp. 24–34; no. 2, pp. 104–13

L. Simeoni: *Verona: Guida storico-artistica della città e della provincia* (Verona, 1909)

R. Wittkower: 'Studien zur Geschichte der Malerei in Verona', *Jb. Kstwiss.*, ii (1924–5), pp. 185–222, 269–89

R. Brenzoni: *Domenico Morone* (Florence, 1956)

C. del Bravo: 'Francesco Morone', *Paragone*, xiii/151 (1962), pp. 3–23

H. J. Eberhardt: 'Domenico Morone', *Maestri della pittura veronese*, ed. P. Brugnoli (Verona, 1974), pp. 91–100

M. T. Cuppini: 'Verona nel quattrocento: L'arte', *Verona e il suo territorio*, iv/1 (Verona, 1981), pp. 381–401

H. J. Eberhardt: 'Nuovi studi su Domenico Morone', *Miniatura veronese del rinascimento* (exh. cat., Verona, 1986), pp. 103–16, 144–6

M. Lucco: *La pittura in Italia: Il quattrocento*, ed. F. Zeri (Milan, 1987), i, pp. 148–50, 166; ii, p. 713

M. Lucco, ed.: *La pittura nel Veneto: Il quattrocento* (Milan, 1990) [esp. writings by S. Marinelli: ii, pp. 641–53, 760–61]

FRANCIS L. RICHARDSON

Morone Mola, Gasparo. *See* MOLA (ii), (2).

Moroni, Andrea (*b* Albino, Bergamo; *fl* 1532; *d* ?Padua, 1560). Italian architect. He was active mainly in and around Padua, where he became the leading architect of the generation after Giovanni Maria Falconetto and was a contemporary of Palladio. He is closely associated with several important buildings in the city after 1532, although in the past his identity has been confused with that of his protégé Andrea da Valle. In July 1532 Moroni was appointed *proto* (chief surveyor) to S Giustina, Padua, a post that he retained until his death. The church has a complex building history. Before 1532 several architects had been asked to submit designs and make models, and initially it seems that Alessandro Leopardi's proposals were to be followed. Leopardi's model formed the basis for the earliest work on site, but little had been achieved by the time of his death in 1522. In 1532 Moroni was asked to produce his own model and to comment on Leopardi's scheme. In 1532–3 work recommenced on the choir walls and sacristy; by 1536 it was possible to vault the chapels of S Massimo and S Giuliano; after 1541 the vaulting of the choir began, and the chapels of the Innocenti and S Arnaldo were completed. After 1550 the vault to the crossing was in place, but only after Moroni's death were the other chapels vaulted and the nave piers and vaults built. The façade was never completed. After

Moroni's death Andrea da Valle became *proto* and completed the nave, cupolas and the sanctuary. The church was completed only in 1580. Although da Valle's later contribution was important (he had assisted Moroni for many years), the basic plan and form are Moroni's; the imposing church has a rigorous and highly disciplined architectural language to the interior. The spatial arrangements of the east end are particularly complex, with many subsidiary chapels clustered around the chancel and sanctuary, but all is clearly articulated and ordered.

As Padua's leading architect, Moroni also had other commitments, and it is significant that because of these his original annual salary as *proto* of S Giustina was gradually reduced from 120 ducats to only 36 ducats. One such project was the Palazzo del Podestà (now Palazzo Municipale); this is almost exclusively his own work, and it was begun in 1539–40. Rapid early progress was made, and the large pilasters of the portico were erected up to the first-floor windows. However, completion took many years as a result of erratic funding by the Venetian government. The imposing façade on to Piazza delle Erbe is on four storeys and is rusticated. The strong ground-floor colonnade is reminiscent of Jacopo Sansovino's Palazzo Corner (from *c*.1545) in Venice. Above the colonnade is the *piano nobile*, and above that a continuous balcony to the second floor, above which is a low attic. The balcony thus divides the façade into two approximately equal parts, with the upper part unified by a giant order of pilasters. The colonnade in the main courtyard again has echoes of Sansovino, while the two upper *piani nobili* have fine windows in a disciplined, rather Palladian manner. The smaller courtyard is simpler, with minimal windows to the *piano nobile* and attic but with complex, rather heavy arcading to the ground floor. The interior has a particularly fine doorway on the first floor, perhaps influenced by Falconetto. The palace was nearly complete by Moroni's death, and a local builder completed the Doric courtyard to his design.

Moroni also made an important contribution to the main university building, the Palazzo del Bò, although other architects worked there both before and after him. The most notable feature by Moroni is the fine central courtyard (see fig.) with two superimposed colonnades, Doric below and Ionic above, with careful classical trabeation. This work has been variously ascribed to Palladio, Michele Sanmicheli and da Valle. However, Moroni had been city *proto* since 1540, and as the university was a public, city-owned building, it is now accepted as his work. The courtyard is perhaps the finest Renaissance work in Padua, and its three wings can be dated: north wing, 1546–7; east wing, 1555; west wing, 1558–9. The main façade is probably also Moroni's work, again with a rusticated ground-floor colonnade and two superimposed *piani nobili*, with large windows surmounted by triangular pediments on the first floor and segmental on the second. Moroni was also responsible for the establishment in 1545 of the university's Orto Botanico; founded by decree of the Venetian Senate, it was the first such scientific collection in Europe. It was not completed until after 1554 and still survives, but Moroni's rusticated gateway has been lost.

Andrea Moroni: central courtyard, Palazzo del Bò, Padua, 1546–59

Two further works in Padua, and another near by, deserve mention. The Palazzo Zacco on Prato della Valle is a substantial house with a ground-floor colonnade and a typically Venetian bay-structure. The façade is of a simple, stripped-down classical appearance, but the house has a complex roof-line, with a row of obelisks alternating with semicircular gables above the windows, and it has a central aedicula. The Loggia della Corte Capitaniato is another official work, in Moroni's capacity as city *proto*; it is a small, three-bay structure, noble and dignified in appearance, again with a strongly moulded, rusticated ground-floor. The fine *piano nobile* has large, well-proportioned windows with triangular pediments. The Certosa di Vigodarzere also contains work by Moroni, chiefly in the two cloisters. The larger is restrained and elegant, but the smaller—unusually—is fully rusticated, including the Doric columns. Moroni also probably designed the portal to the church façade. Moroni's style exhibits the early influence of Falconetto and, perhaps, Alvise Cornaro; some of his work shows a refined sense of proportion, particularly in colonnades and fenestration. His was a pure classicism, showing little of the Mannerism that followed. An architect of considerable local importance, he showed a sensitivity often lacking in such figures; this may be partly attributed to the refined taste of his Paduan patrons and to the influence of nearby Venice.

BIBLIOGRAPHY

J. Cavacci: *Historiarum Coenobii D. Justinae Patavinae*, 6 vols (Venice, 1606)
P. Selvatico: *Guida di Padova* (Padua, 1869)
N. Baldoria: 'Il Riccio e il Leopardi architetti della chiesa di S Giustina di Padova', *Stor. A.* (1891)
A. Venturi: *Storia* (1901–40)
G. Lorenzetti: 'Il cortile e la loggia dell' Università di Padova', *Boll. Mus. Civ. Padova*, xi (1908), pp. 124–56
E. Lovarini: 'Di Andrea da Valle, architetto', *Riv. Italia* (June 1910)
E. Rigoni: *L'architetto Andrea Moroni* (Padua, 1939)
R. Pepi: *L'abbazia di S Giustina* (Padua, 1966)
N. Gallimberti: *Il volto di Padova* (Padua, 1968)
G. Bresciani Alvarez: *La basilica di S Giustina* (Castelfranco Veneto, 1970)

RICHARD J. GOY

Moroni, Giovanni [Giovan] **Battista** (*b* Albino, ?1520–24; *d* Albino, ?after 5 March 1578). Italian painter. He was the most significant painter of the 16th-century school of Bergamo and is best known for his portraits, which feature a naturalistic rendering of both faces and costume and an objective approach to character.

1. EARLY CAREER, TO *c.* 1560. A document dated 6 March 1549 refers to Moroni as an administrative procurator, which implies that he was then at least 25 years old. He was trained in Brescia, in the workshop of Moretto. Moroni's religious paintings, particularly the early works,

are characterized by explicit borrowings from Moretto's pictures. Two drawings by Moroni (both 1543; Brescia, Pin. Civ. Tosio-Martinengo), his first securely dated works, show figures of saints copied from paintings by Moretto. It is likely that Moroni collaborated with the Brescian painter in some of his works: for instance, some scholars have identified his hand in Moretto's *St Roch and the Angel* (Budapest, Mus. F.A.) and the *Coronation of the Virgin* (Brescia, S Angelo). Others have attributed outright to Moroni paintings once given to Moretto, for example the two *Angels* (London, N.G.; see fig. 1) and the *Assumption of the Virgin* (Orzivecchi, SS Pietro e Paolo).

In the second half of the 1540s Moroni was working in Trent, contemporaneously with the first session of the Council. In 1548 he executed an *Annunciation* (Trent, Congregazione di Carità, on dep. Osp. Riuniti) and a *St Clare* (Trent, Mus. Dioc.; on dep.) for the church of S Chiara there. In 1549 he is documented in Brescia and his native Albino, and in that year, according to Tassi (1793), he also executed the frescoes (destr.) in the Palazzo Spini in Bergamo. The portraits of the poet *Isotta Brembati* (Bergamo, Gal. Accad. Carrara) and *Marco Antonio Savelli* (Lisbon, Mus. Gulbenkian), presumably early works, show Moroni's impressive qualities as a portrait painter. He was still in Trent in the early 1550s, and the portraits of *Ludovico Madruzzo* (Chicago, IL, A. Inst.) and *Gianfederico Madruzzo* (Washington, DC, N.G.A.), nephews of Cristoforo Madruzzo, Prince Bishop of Trent, can be dated to these years. According to Bartoli (1780), the altarpiece of the *Virgin in Glory with the Four Fathers of the Church and St John the Evangelist* (Trent, S Maria Maggiore) dates from 1551, and this is confirmed by stylistic considerations. The picture, which is modelled on Moretto's altarpiece of the same subject (Frankfurt am Main, Städel. Kstinst.), is exemplary in the severity of its formal arrangement, in its clear exposition of the doctrinal content and in the kind of image required by the Counter-Reformation, to which Moroni remained faithful in all his religious works.

For the rest of the 1550s Moroni's activity was concentrated in the Bergamo region. Two paintings of the *Assumption of the Virgin* (Cenate Sopra, parish church; Oneta, parish church) and the *Crucifixion with SS Francis and Anthony* (Bergamo, Suore della Beata Capitanio) probably date from this period. In these works Moroni's treatment of formulae derived from Moretto is more academic, characterized by colours of an enamel-like brightness and a greater clarity of design. Dated and datable portraits of these years include the *Portrait of a Young Nobleman* (1553; Honolulu, HI, Acad. A.), the *Portrait of ?Michel de l'Hôpital* (1554; Milan, Ambrosiana) and *Lucrezia Vertova* (1556–7; New York, Met.). It is probably in this period that he executed the full-length *Portrait of a Gentleman* (London, N.G.), which depicts a member of the Avogadro family; the unadorned setting and direct representation of the sitter testify to Moroni's divergence from the canons of portraiture as developed by Titian.

The date 1560 appears on the portraits of the *Duke of Albuquerque* (Berlin, Bodemus.), *The Poet* (Brescia, Pin. Civ. Tosio-Martinengo) and the celebrated 'Cavaliere in Rosa' (*Gian Girolamo Grumelli*; Bergamo, Moroni priv. col., see Pope-Hennessy, p. 223). The sharp colouring of

1. Giovanni Battista Moroni (attrib.): *An Angel*, oil on panel, 1.51×0.53 m, after 1543 (London, National Gallery)

the Cavaliere's costume indicates Moroni's rejection of Venetian tonal harmonies in favour of dazzling, metallic tones used by contemporary Brescian painters. The sitter is portrayed against a background of Classical ruins, a device Moroni used on several occasions, often (as in this case) with reliefs and inscriptions of a moralizing or celebratory tone.

2. MATURE WORK, *c.* 1561 AND AFTER. Numerous documents testify to Moroni's presence in Albino after 1561 and particularly in the 1570s, when he was employed in the town council's administration. During the 1560s he executed the *Crucifixion with SS Bernard and Anthony of Padua* (Albino, S Giuliano), the *Virgin and Child with SS Barbara and Catherine* (Bondo Petello, S Barbara) and *Christ Carrying the Cross* (Albino, Santuario della Madonna del Pianto). The unpretentious and melancholic tenor of these paintings and their engaging naturalistic immediacy make them among the artist's finest religious works.

Moroni's style became more austere during the 1560s, as is evident from the many dated works of the period. The standard he executed for the parish church of Pradalunga, with *St Christopher* on one side and the *Glory of the Eucharist* on the other, was valued on 1 July 1562, indicating that it had just been completed. The altarpiece of the *Assumption of the Virgin* (Palazzago, S Giovanni Battista) dates from 1564 according to Calvi (1676–7), and the date 1566 is inscribed on the *Deposition* (Bergamo, Gal. Accad. Carrara) from the church of the Zoccolanti in Gandino. The altarpiece of the *Virgin and Child with SS Peter, Paul and John the Evangelist* in S Pietro at Parre was completed in 1567. Compositionally it recalls Moretto's Rovelli Altarpiece (Brescia, Pin. Civ. Tosio-Martinengo), but its pale Mannerist inflections link it to works by the Cremonese painters Camillo Boccaccino and Bernardino Campi. The *Virgin and Child* (1567; Bergamo, Gal. Accad. Carrara) for the church of the Madonna della Ripa at Desenzano al Serio is a variant of Giovanni Bellini's panel of the same subject and date (Bergamo, Gal. Accad. Carrara), which once hung in the convent of the Monache di Alzano. The painting by Bellini was copied by Moroni, probably earlier, in another canvas (Brescia, priv. col.; see Rossi, 1977, p. 56). One of Moroni's most praised works, the *Last Supper* (Romano di Lombardia, S Maria Assunta), was commissioned in 1565 but delivered only in 1569.

Among the portraits of the early 1560s are those of *Giovanni Bressani* (1562; Edinburgh, N.G.) and *Pietro Secco Suardo* (1563; Florence, Uffizi). In 1565 Moroni executed the *Portrait of a Member of the Mosca Family* (Amsterdam, Rijksmus.) and *Antonio Navagero* (Milan, Brera), which in its directness and intimacy typifies Moroni's refusal to engage in the rhetoric of display. A similarly unconventional treatment of the sitter can be seen in the portrait of *Giovanni Antonio Pantera* (Florence, Uffizi), of uncertain date. The date 1567 has been uncovered on the *Portrait of a 29-year-old Nobleman* (Bergamo, Gal. Accad. Carrara), the intensity of which makes it one of Moroni's portrait masterpieces. The lively *Portrait of a Young Girl of the Redetti Family* (Bergamo, Gal. Accad. Carrara) and '*The Tailor*' (*c.*1570; London, N.G.; see fig. 2), aspects of which imitate the work of Caravaggio (Longhi), also belong to this period.

Among the most typical works in Moroni's vast oeuvre are devotional portraits, in which the sitter is depicted with a religious scene in the background. Examples of this genre are *Two Devotees of the Virgin and Child and St Michael* (Richmond, VA, Mus. F.A.) and the *Crucified Christ with SS John the Baptist and Sebastian with a Donor* (Bergamo, S Alessandro della Croce), which is later in date. Even in the late religious works Moroni displays an

2. Giovanni Battista Moroni: '*The Tailor*', oil on canvas, 970×740 mm, *c.* 1570 (London, National Gallery)

immunity to the formal complexities of the Mannerist style, preferring to present religious scenes in a simple, straightforward manner. This purposefully conservative attitude is most apparent in his continued use of the polyptych format into the 1560s (e.g. in S Bernardo in Roncola) and the 1570s (S Giorgio in Fiorano al Serio, begun 1575; S Vittore in Gaverina, dated 1576).

Moroni's late portraits, on the other hand, show a development in the direction of softer, more atmospheric effects, in which the objective and naturalistic rendering characteristic of the earlier works is replaced by a more full-bodied treatment, apparent, for example, in the pair of Spini portraits (Bergamo, Gal. Accad. Carrara), datable to the early 1570s on the basis of the sitters' ages. Similar stylistic characteristics are evident in the portraits of *Vincenzo Guarinoni* (1572; Cleveland, OH, Mus. A.), *Jacopo Foscarini* (1575; Budapest, Mus. F.A.), *Paolo Vidoni Cedrelli* (1576; Bergamo, Gal. Accad. Carrara) and in the *Portrait of ?Francesco Spini* (1576; Boston, MA, Isabella Stewart Gardner Mus.). Moroni's late religious works include the *Coronation of the Virgin* (Bergamo, S Alessandro alla Croce), the altarpiece of the *Virgin and Saints* in Bergamo Cathedral, both dated 1576, the altarpiece of the *Virgin and Child with SS Peter and Andrew* (1577) in S Andrea in Fino del Monte and the incomplete *Last Judgement* (Goriago, S Pancrazio), commissioned in 1577.

UNPUBLISHED SOURCES

Trent, Bib. Com., MS. 1207 [F. Bartoli: *I a pitture, sculture ed architetture che adornano le chiese ed altri pubblici luoghi della città di Trento*, 1780]

BIBLIOGRAPHY

D. Calvi: *Effemeride sacro profana di quanto di memorabile sia successo in Bergamo, sua diocese et territorio*, 3 vols (Milan, 1676–7)

F. M. Tassi: *Vite de' pittori, scultori e architetti bergamaschi* (Bergamo, 1793), i, pp. 162–72

C. von Lutzow: 'Giovanni Battista Moroni', *Graph. Kst.*, xiv (1891), pp. 21–6

G. Lafenestre: 'Les Portraits des Madruzzi par Titian et G. B. Moroni', *Rev. A. Anc. & Mod.*, xxi (1907), pp. 351–60

F. Frizzoni: 'Moretto und Moroni: Eine Charakterisierung auf Grund zweier massgebender Studienblätter', *Münch. Jb. Bild. Kst*, vii (1912), pp. 28–38

M. Biancale: 'Giovanni Battista Moroni e i pittori bresciani', *L'Arte*, xvii (1914), pp. 289–300, 321–2

A. Locatelli Milesi: 'Un grande ritrattista: G. B. Moroni', *Emporium*, xliv (1916), pp. 376–87

H. Merten: *Giovanni Battista Moroni: Des Meisters Gemälde und Zeichnungen* (Marburg, 1928)

R. Longhi: 'Quesiti caravaggeschi. II: I precedenti', *Pinacoteca*, v–vi (1929), pp. 258–320; also in *Me pinxit e quesiti cava vaggeschi* (Florence, 1968)

G. Lendorff: *G. B. Moroni der Porträt-Maler von Bergamo* (Winterthur, 1933)

D. Cugini: *Moroni pittore* (Bergamo, 1939)

G. Gombosi: *Il Moretto da Brescia* (Basle, 1943)

W. Suida: 'Aggiunte all'opera di Giovanni Battista Moroni', *Emporium*, cix (1949), pp. 51–7

I pittori della realtà in Lombardia (exh. cat. by R. Longhi, R. Cipriani and G. Testori, Milan, Pal. Reale, 1953)

J. Pope-Hennessy: *The Portrait in the Renaissance* (New York and London, 1966), pp. 205, 207, 223, 321

M. Gregori: 'Il ritratto di Alessandro Vittoria del Moroni a Vienna', *Paragone*, xxvii/317–19 (1976), pp. 91–100

F. Rossi: 'Giovan Battista Moroni nel quarto centenario della morte', *Not. Pal. Albani*, vi (1977), pp. 50–59

H. Brigstocke: 'A Moroni Portrait for Edinburgh', *Burl. Mag.*, cxx (1978), pp. 457–61

C. Gould: 'G B Moroni and the Genre Portrait in the Cinquecento', *Apollo*, cviii (1978), pp. 316–21

G. Testori and G. Frangi: *Moroni in Val Seriana* (Brescia, 1978)

Giovanni Battista Moroni: 400th Anniversary Exhibition (exh. cat. by A. Braham, London, N.G., 1978)

M. Gregori: 'Giovanni Battista Moroni', *I pittori bergamaschi: Il cinquecento* (Bergamo, 1979), iii, pp. 95–377 [with list of works and bibliog.]

M. Cali: '"Verità" e "Religione" nella pittura di Giovan Battista Moroni (a proposito della mostra di Bergamo)', *Prospettiva*, xxiii (1980), pp. 11–23

G. Previtali: 'Il bernoccolo del conoscitore (a proposito del presunto *Ritratto di Gian Girolamo Albani* attribuito al Moroni)', *Prospettiva*, xxiv (1981), pp. 24–31

The Genius of Venice, 1500–1600 (exh. cat., ed. C. Hope and J. Martineau; London, RA, 1983), pp. 186–92 [entries by M. Gregori]

Seicento a Bergamo (exh. cat., Bergamo, Pal. Ragione, 1987), pp. 47–50, 227–8 [entries by V. Guazzoni]

F. Rossi: 'Giovan Battista Moroni: Ritratti di famiglia', *Osservatorio A.*, iv (1990), pp. 68–73

FRANCESCO FRANGI

Moronobu. *See* HISHIKAWA MORONOBU.

Morow [Moreau], **John** (*b* Paris; *fl c.* 1400). ?French architect and mason, active in Scotland. He is recorded in two inserted inscriptions in the south transept of the Cistercian abbey church of Melrose (Borders). A framed tablet records that he was born 'in Parysse' and says that he was responsible for all mason-work at St Andrews, the high kirk of Glasgow, Melrose, Paisley, Nithsdale and Galloway. The other inscription, which is cut into the coursed masonry around the head of a doorway, includes a coat of arms with a mason's compasses and a number of fleurs-de-lis—the latter presumably emphasizing Morow's French origins.

On stylistic grounds the surviving works most likely to be attributable to Morow are: the first two chapels added along the south side of the nave of Melrose Abbey, and perhaps the completion of the shell of the south transept there; the eastern bays of the north nave aisle of Paisley Abbey (Strathclyde); the choir and south transept of the collegiate church of Lincluden, which is in Nithsdale (Dumfries and Galloway). Beyond this a number of corbels presumed to be from the demolished western towers of Glasgow Cathedral may be by a sculptor who worked at Melrose and Lincluden, while parts of the nave of St Andrews as remodelled after a fire of 1378 may also show some French traits. All of these works are probably datable to the end of the 14th century or the early decades of the 15th, a period when major church building in Scotland was again beginning to gain momentum after the devastating wars with England. At this period new ideas appear to have been sought from a range of sources, including France.

Melrose, Paisley and Lincluden all have window tracery and moulding types in common and reveal a striking elegance of proportion and detail. Particularly noteworthy are window-tracery designs that show something of the balance between restrained curvilinearity and 'spherical' forms to be found in some of the few French buildings of the late 14th century, and this would seem to confirm their designer's French origins.

BIBLIOGRAPHY

Inventory of Roxburgh, Royal Comm. Anc. & Hist. Mnmts Scotland, (Edinburgh, 1956), ii, pp. 279–80

R. Fawcett: 'Scottish Medieval Window Tracery', *Studies in Scottish Antiquity*, ed. D. J. Breeze (Edinburgh, 1984), pp. 155–7

RICHARD FAWCETT

Morozov [Morosov], **Ivan (Abramovich)** (*b* Moscow, 1871; *d* Karlsbad, 22 June 1921). Russian collector. Along with Sergey Shchukin, he was by far the most important Russian collector of modern French art in the early 20th century. He was born into a large family of wealthy Moscow industrialists, his father running a textile mill in Kalinin (now Tver'). As a boy he received art lessons from the young Konstantin Korovin and often visited the picture gallery of his great-uncle, Gerasim Khludov, which contained many works by the Wanderers. After graduating from the Eidgenössische Technische Hochschule in Zurich, he settled in Kalinin (now Tver') and took over the family business there. His elder brother Mikhail Morozov (1870–1903) was the first to start collecting, and he did so with considerable discernment and audacity. His collection, posthumously donated to the Tret'yakov Gallery in Moscow, included work by such leading Russian artists as Mikhail Vrubel', Valentin Serov, Konstantin Korovin and Leonid Pasternak, as well as works by the Barbizon school, Manet, Renoir, Degas, Monet, Toulouse-Lautrec, Denis, Bonnard, Munch, Gauguin and van Gogh. Ivan Morozov began to collect art seriously soon after moving to Moscow in 1900, when he came into contact with his brother's circles. Favouring Impressionist and Symbolist tendencies in Russian art, he bought works by Vrubel', Serov, Isaak Levitan, Aleksandr Golovin, Konstantin Somov, Alexandre Benois and Korovin, and was an early patron of Nikolay Sapunov, Mikhail Larionov, Natal'ya Goncharova, Pyotr Utkin (1877–1934), Pavel Kuznetsov and Marc

Chagall. By 1913 his collection included 430 Russian works.

Morozov's smaller collection of modern French art (including 149 paintings and sculptures by 1912) was to be of most significance and, though less accessible than Shchukin's, an inspiration to a generation of Russian artists. The collection began with the purchase of Alfred Sisley's *Frost in Louveciennes* (1873; Moscow, Pushkin Mus. F.A.) in 1903. Initially, Ivan took over his brother's enthusiasm for the Nabis, commissioning decorative panels for his Moscow mansion from both Denis (five panels of the *Story of Psyche*, 1908; St Petersburg, Hermitage) and Bonnard (*Morning in Paris* and *Evening in Paris*, both 1911; St Petersburg, Hermitage) and being advised by the former on his frequent visits to Paris. In 1907 he began to collect Gauguin and, together with Shchukin, was responsible for the flow of Gauguin's Tahitian paintings into Moscow. In addition, he bought *Café at Arles* (1888; Moscow, Pushkin Mus. F.A.) and van Gogh's companion piece the *Night Café* (1888; New Haven, CT, Yale U. A.G.) from Ambroise Vollard in 1908. The following year the dealer Druet persuaded him to buy several more major pieces of van Gogh's last period, for example the *Prisoners' Round* (1889–90; Moscow, Pushkin Mus. F.A.). His selection of Impressionist works was also highly diverse, including works by Monet, Camille Pissarro, Degas and Renoir (e.g. *Woman with a Fan*, 1881; St Petersburg, Hermitage). The French artist most extensively represented in Morozov's collection was Paul Cézanne. Starting in 1907 he amassed 18 Cézannes: while concentrating on landscapes, he also purchased such works as *A Smoker* (mid-1890s) and *Self-portrait in a Cap* (1873–5) (both St Petersburg, Hermitage). Although his selection of Cézannes was similar to Shchukin's, the two differed in their attitude to Henri Matisse and Pablo Picasso. Morozov was less enthusiastic: he owned only three Picassos, including the only Cubist work in his collection, the portrait of *Ambroise Vollard* (1910; Moscow, Pushkin Mus. F.A.); his Matisses included several Fauvist works and the Moroccan triptych (1912; Moscow, Pushkin Mus. F.A.). After the Revolution of 1917, Morozov's collection was nationalized and, like Shchukin's, opened to the public as the Museum of New Western Painting in Moscow; however, in 1948 they were divided between the State Hermitage Museum in St Petersburg and the Pushkin Museum of Fine Arts in Moscow. Briefly he acted as an assistant curator before leaving for short-lived exile in Germany.

BIBLIOGRAPHY

B. N. Ternovets: 'Le Musée d'Art Moderne de Moscou (anciennes collections Stzhoukine et Morossoff)', *Amour A.*, 12 (1925), pp. 455–88

M. Ginsburg: 'Art Collectors of Old Russia: The Morosovs and the Shchukins', *Apollo*, xcviii (1973), pp. 470–85

B. Whitney Kean: *All the Empty Palaces: The Merchant Patrons of Modern Art in Pre-revolutionary Russia* (London, 1983)

Morozov i Shcukin: Russikiye Kollektsionery. Ot Mone do Pikasso [Morozov and Shchukin: Russian Collectors. From Monet to Picasso] (exh. cat., ed. G. Kelch; Essen, Mus. Flkwang; Moscow, Pushkin Mus. F.A.; St Petersburg, Hermitage; 1993)

JEREMY HOWARD

Morphey, Garret (*b* Dublin, *fl* 1680; *d* Dublin, 1716). Irish painter. Described by Crookshank and Glin as 'the first Irish-born painter of any stature', he produced many portraits now owned by the National Gallery of Ireland, Dublin (on view at Malahide Castle, Co. Dublin), that show him to have been a highly professional artist, both in terms of his technical refinements and in his ability to maintain a steady flow of commissions over a period of some 30 years. He may have studied in France, almost certainly visited the Netherlands and was definitely in England in the second half of the 1680s. He painted portraits for a number of Yorkshire families and must have travelled south to Welbeck Abbey, Notts, to carry out a portrait commission of *Henry Cavendish, 2nd Duke of Newcastle* (1686; Welbeck Abbey, Notts).

Morphey was a Jacobite sympathizer; in the early 1680s, for example, he produced at least three portraits of *Archbishop Oliver Plunkett* (version, Dublin, N.G.). The most impressive of the many portraits of Jacobites produced after his return to Ireland *c*. 1690 is *Lady Neil O'Neill* (*c*. 1691; priv. col., see Crookshank and Glin, p. 25). One of the most sophisticated portraits painted in Ireland before the 18th century, it was possibly commissioned as a memorial to the sitter's late husband, Sir Neil O'Neill, who was mortally wounded at the Battle of the Boyne in 1690. Lady O'Neill leans against an urn decorated with a skull and bones. The painting shows Morphey's thorough knowledge of current English and continental portraiture, the former exemplified in the work of Sir Peter Lely and John Michael Wright, the latter by the Dutch artist Caspar Netscher.

See also IRELAND, fig. 8.

BIBLIOGRAPHY

Strickland; Waterhouse: *18th C.*

A. Crookshank and the Knight of Glin: *The Painters of Ireland, c. 1660–1920* (London, 1978), pp. 22–9

FINTAN CULLEN

Morrel [Morsel], Jakob. *See* MARELL, JAKOB.

Morren, George (*b* Ekeren, nr Antwerp, 27 July 1868; *d* Brussels, 21 Nov 1941). Belgian painter, sculptor and decorative artist. He came from a prosperous bourgeois family and was therefore able to devote himself exclusively to art without financial worries. Encouraged by Emile Claus, a family friend, he enrolled at the Koninklijke Academie voor Schone Kunsten in Antwerp; he left after a short time, however, disliking the conformist teaching methods. In 1888 he moved to Paris, where he frequented the studios of Alfred Roll, Pierre Puvis de Chavannes and Eugène Carrière. He began working in an Impressionist style, turning *c*. 1890 to a Neo-Impressionist style as a means of giving more solid form to light. He returned in February 1892 to Antwerp, where he took part in the activities of avant-garde groups, particularly Als ik Kan, L'Association pour l'Art, La Libre Esthétique and Eenigen, of which he was a founder-member in 1902. He exhibited regularly in these circles in the company of Neo-Impressionist painters such as Claus, Georges Lemmen, Théo Van Rysselberghe, Henry Van de Velde, Paul Signac and Seurat. In 1904 he and Claus became members of the group Vie et Lumière.

Morren's paintings, such as *Young Woman at her Toilet* (1903) and *Two Young Girls* (1907; both Brussels, Mus. A. Mod.), convey the vibration and iridescence of light.

Although he abandoned Neo-Impressionism in favour of more pronounced forms and brighter colours, he was not swayed by newer artistic currents such as Cubism, Expressionism or abstract art. In 1910 he acquired a property in Saint-Germain-en-Laye, near Paris, which became a meeting-place for his Impressionist and Neo-Impressionist friends. He returned to Belgium only around 1925. A vast retrospective of 141 of his works was held in 1926 at the Galerie Giroux in Brussels. In addition to paintings and drawings, he executed sculptures and ventured successfully into the decorative arts.

BNB

BIBLIOGRAPHY
C. Bernard: *George Morren* (Brussels, 1950)
S. Goyens de Hensch: *L'Impressionisme et le Fauvisme en Belgique* (Tielt, 1988)

GISÈLE OLLINGER-ZINQUE

Morrice, James Wilson (*b* Montreal, 10 Aug 1865; *d* Tunis, 23 Jan 1924). Canadian painter. From a wealthy Montreal family, he trained as a lawyer but went to Paris in late 1889 to devote himself entirely to painting. He spent a brief time at the Académie Julian and then studied with Henri-Joseph Harpignies. He soon became friends with several American artists including Maurice Prendergast and Robert Henri. Like other painters of his generation, Morrice was strongly influenced in the 1890s by the work of James McNeill Whistler and a friend of Walter Sickert.

By 1895 Morrice established what became a lifelong pattern of constant travel through Europe, especially France, Italy and the Netherlands, as well as annual visits to Montreal, where he painted such winter images as *Return from School* (*c*. 1900; Toronto, A.G. Ont.). The ports of southern France and the palaces of Venice, like the cafés and boulevards of Paris, were a source of sensual pleasure which he readily transformed into intimate evocations (e.g. *Venice at the Golden Hour*, *c*. 1901–2; Montreal, Mus. F.A.). Morrice's lengthy observation of and empathy for his subject-matter is evident in his delicate yet solid realizations. He exhibited regularly at the International Society of Sculptors, Painters and Gravers, London, and the Société Nationale des Beaux-Arts, Paris. In 1903 Morrice was the first Canadian to participate in the Venice Biennale and he exhibited at the Salon d'Automne from 1905. Despite the highly favourable comments he

James Wilson Morrice: *Landscape, Trinidad*, oil on canvas, 542×653 mm, *c*. 1921 (Ottawa, National Gallery of Canada)

received at his many European showings, the submissions he regularly made to Canadian exhibitions, such as the Canadian Art Club, went almost unnoticed.

By about 1905 Morrice abandoned his Whistlerian tonal harmonies in favour of the intense colour and decorative clarity of Post-Impressionism, probably as a result of his friendship with the Irish painter Roderic O'Conor, who introduced him to the work of Paul Gauguin. The intimist atmosphere of Nabi painting becomes increasingly evident in Morrice's images of the solitary figure such as *Nude with a Feather* (*c.* 1909–13; Montreal, Mus. F.A.) and his vignettes of Paris such as *Quai des Grands-Augustins* (*c.* 1904; Paris, Mus. d'Orsay). Long a member of the expatriate community, Morrice associated in Paris with several British writers including Somerset Maugham and Arnold Bennett, both of whom modelled fictional characters after this elusive, restless painter. Clive Bell commented on several occasions that it was Morrice who taught him to 'see'.

In search of bright light and colour, Morrice began to travel to North Africa and the West Indies; in 1912 he made two trips to Tangiers where he consolidated his relationship with Henri Matisse. Morrice, whom Matisse recalled in 1925 as 'the painter with the delicate eye', gained a new confidence and assurance from this contact. Works from subsequent travels to Cuba and Jamaica in 1915 and to Trinidad in 1921 suggest Matisse's influence in Morrice's use of light as a function of colour. His work is seen in its most progressive and resolved form in the increasingly cursive and rhythmic drawing of his late paintings, such as *Circus at Santiago, Cuba* (*c.* 1915; Montreal, Mus. F.A.) and *Landscape, Trinidad* (*c.* 1921; Ottawa, N.G.; see fig.).

In 1918 Morrice returned to watercolour, a medium he had not used for 20 years. Although he continued to travel in the last years of his life, he suffered increasingly from ill-health and died in Tunis at the age of 58. Morrice was long recognized in Europe, but his reputation was not secure in his own country until the emergence of Canadian modernism.

BIBLIOGRAPHY

D. Buchanan: *James Wilson Morrice: A Biography* (Toronto, 1936)
J. Lyman: *Morrice* (Montreal, 1945)
J. O'Brian: 'Morrice, O'Conor, Gauguin, Bonnard et Vuillard', *Rev. U. Moncton*, xv/2–3 (1982), pp. 9–34
L. Dorais: *J. W. Morrice*, Canadian Artists Series (Ottawa, 1985)
James Wilson Morrice, 1865–1924 (exh. cat., ed. N. Cloutier; Montreal, Mus. F.A., 1986)

SANDRA PAIKOWSKY

Morris. English family of architects. The precise family relationship between (1) Roger Morris and (2) Robert Morris is unclear; the latter, who was better known as an architectural theorist, is described as a 'kinsman' of the former.

(1) Roger Morris (*b* London, 19 April 1695; *d* 31 Jan 1749). He was one of the second generation of Palladian architects who developed and extended its already established forms. The son of a carpenter, in 1724 he was engaged on speculative house-building in the west end of London. He worked with Colen Campbell, initially as builder at Leicester House, London (1724; destr.), as a draughtsman for an unexecuted project for Goodwood House, W. Sussex (1725), and as an intermediary between the patron (John Aislabie) and the dying Campbell at Studley Royal, W. Yorks, in 1729. During the same period Morris worked even more closely with HENRY HERBERT, later 9th Earl of Pembroke, on building Marble Hill House, London (1724) (where Campbell might also have been involved), and at the White Lodge in Richmond New Park, Surrey (1727–9), which brought with it a minor appointment in the Office of Works, and they continued this partnership for several aristocratic commissions during the next decade. His own long apprenticeship concluded with a visit to Italy in 1731–2.

Morris's contribution to English Palladianism lies in the variety of his villa designs. In part this is due to the fact that his work on larger commissions did not fully materialize, has only partly survived and is weakened by uncertain attribution. His villas show an inventive variety of form, by which the conventional rectangular core was set off by subsidiary geometric blocks at the corners, as at Combe Bank, Sundridge, Kent (1727–8), or which serve as porches, as at Westcombe, Greenwich, Kent (*c.* 1730; destr.). More significant, Morris enlivened the back of Whitton Place, London (1732–9), with a three-sided bay which prefigured the way in which later Palladian architects, such as Isaac Ware, James Paine or Sir Robert Taylor, broke up the cubic rigidity of the villa prototypes of Campbell or Richard Boyle, 3rd Earl of Burlington. The elevational vocabulary of Morris's designs is also remarkable for a series of motifs, including circular windows or panels, and pyramidal roofs with small, usually octagonal caps, which distinguish his work from contemporaries. Both in the use of such motifs as circular, plain-moulded openings and in his interest in breaking up simple forms, he shows an awareness of the individual style of Sir John Vanbrugh unique at that time.

More remarkable than Morris's innovative Palladianism are his two Gothic buildings, Clearwell Castle, Glos (1727–8), and Inveraray, Strathclyde (from 1745). The former, one of the earliest English examples of a revived interest in medieval building, is far more sturdy and authentic than William Kent's contemporary work at Esher Place, Surrey (1733; destr.). At Inveraray, with its large scale and circular corner turrets, Morris initiated a model for the Scottish Baronial style of architecture (*see* GOTHIC REVIVAL, §I); its three-storey central tower recalls similar ideas by Vanbrugh, who had provided an early design (for further discussion *see* SCOTLAND, §II).

Despite holding a lucrative official appointment in the Royal Ordinance, Morris did not build up a career in the Office of Works unlike several of his contemporaries; nor did he, like James Gibbs or Ware, use publications to promote his reputation. His surviving letters do not suggest that he possessed a formal education comparable to that of his kinsman (2) Robert Morris. Instead Morris appears to have remained the constant architectural assistant of those aristocrats who had a serious personal interest in the subject, such as Lord Herbert, Charles Lennox, 2nd Duke of Richmond, and Archibald Campbell, 3rd Duke of Argyll. He may also have been involved in works built for John Fane, 7th Earl of Westmorland, most significantly the precociously Neo-classical church at Mereworth, Kent (1744–6).

For an example of Morris's work *see* VILLA, fig. 8.

BIBLIOGRAPHY

Colvin
M. P. G. Draper and W. A. Eden: *Marble Hill House* (London, 1970)
I. G. Lindsay and M. Cosh: *Inveraray and the Dukes of Argyll* (Edinburgh, 1973)
T. P. Connor: 'Bubo's House', *Archit. Hist.*, xxvii (1984), pp. 111–15
J. Harris: 'An English Neo-Palladian Episode and its Connections with Visentini in Venice', *Archit. Hist.*, xxvii (1984), pp. 231–40

T. P. CONNOR

(2) Robert Morris (*b* Twickenham, Surrey, *c*. 1701; *d* London, 12 Nov 1754). Throughout his career Morris was associated with the architectural practice of (1) Roger Morris. A design illustrated in *An Essay in Defence of Ancient Architecture* (pp. 84–5) closely resembles Marble Hill House (1724–9), built by Roger Morris. No details of professional collaboration are known; this reference illustrates critical approbation, however. The work that Robert Morris did on his own, however, was minor. He worked on the south front of Culverthorpe (*c*. 1730–35), Lincs, and made alterations to Inverary Castle (from 1745), Strathclyde. These projects are competent but show little innovation. He undertook various small interior alterations and designed fireplaces (all destr.), but his importance rests chiefly upon his writings on architecture.

His theoretical writings embody the ideas and principles of early and mid-18th-century architecture and gardening. He was the most prolific English writer on these subjects in his time and the principal theorist of English Palladianism. The principal arguments of his architectural theory were published as a series of *Lectures on Architecture*. His unique and significant contribution to architectural theory is summarized in his declaration that 'the first care in respect to [architectural] decoration is justly appropriating the design to the situation. . .so blending art and nature together' (*Lectures*, p. 86). This passage defines the principle of dependency of the form of a building on the form of its situation. Morris called the resulting blending together of art and nature 'harmony', and made it the standard against which the success and beauty of any work was to be measured.

Morris's idea of the situation differed from earlier ideas about the architectural site; convenience, suitability and salubriousness became less important than the image or the visual character of the setting: 'Let the spot direct [the architect] to the dress and ornaments' (*An Essay upon Harmony*, p. 35). His ideas about the harmony between the building and the situation derived also from concepts of nature articulated through the writings of Joseph Addison, Alexander Pope and Anthony Ashley Cooper, 3rd Earl of Shaftesbury. No other English architectural writer of the time, however, was able to translate so effectively ideas about nature into principles of architectural order.

While Morris's published designs exemplify Palladian compositional patterns and motifs, especially in the use of the architectural orders in the manner of his contemporaries Richard Boyle, 3rd Earl of Burlington, Colen Campbell, Roger Morris and James Leoni, he argued that the visual character of the location for each building should

furnish the designer with the proper ideas of its appearance. This argument explains why the architectural orders are absent from many of his designs. Elaborate and refined surface articulation was not deemed appropriate to some situations, such as those described as 'grave' or 'rugged', and Morris reached the novel conclusion that propriety and beauty in architecture could be achieved in some situations without the use of the orders. The basis for design then lay outside the canons of the classical tradition. Evidence of this attitude towards design can be seen in the architecture of contemporary English and French landscape gardens. Morris's writings were also influential in American architecture. Many designs by Thomas Jefferson, for example, derive from plates in Morris's books (for further discussion *see* JEFFERSON, THOMAS).

WRITINGS

An Essay in Defence of Ancient Architecture (London, 1728/*R* Amersham, Bucks, 1971)
Lectures on Architecture (London, 1734, 1736)
An Essay upon Harmony as it Relates Chiefly to Situation and Building (London, 1739)
The Art of Architecture: A Poem in Imitation of Horace's Art of Poetry (London. 1742)
Rural Architecture (London, 1750/*R* Amersham, Bucks, 1971) [reissued as *Select Architecture* (London, 1755, 1757/*R* 1975)]
The Architectural Remembrancer (London, 1751/*R* Amersham, Bucks, 1971) [reissued as *Architecture Improved* (London, 1755, 1757)]

BIBLIOGRAPHY

Colvin
W. Gibson: 'Literary Influences on Robert Morris's First Excursion in Architectural Theory', *Rendezvous*, vi (1971), pp. 1–14
D. Cruickshank: 'An English Reason', *Archit. J.*, iv (1983), pp. 49–58
J. Archer: *The Literature of British Domestic Architecture, 1715–1842* (Cambridge, MA, 1985), pp. 575–87
D. Leatherbarrow: 'Architecture and Situation: A Study of the Architectural Writings of Robert Morris', *J. Soc. Archit. Hist.*, xliv (1985), pp. 48–59

DAVID LEATHERBARROW

Morris, Sir Cedric (Lockwood), 9th Baronet of Clasemont (*b* Swansea, 11 Dec 1889; *d* Ipswich, 8 Feb 1982). Welsh painter and horticulturist. He was a self-taught painter but attended the *académies libres* in Paris as a young man. With his companion, the painter Arthur Lett-Haines (1894–1978), he was a member of the art communities of Newlyn in Cornwall (1919–20), Paris (1921–6) and London (1926–39). From 1926 to 1932 Morris took part in the Society (*see* <SEVEN & FIVE> SOCIETY). Although he had experimented with abstraction *c*. 1922, he resigned from the society when it moved away from representation. Between 1937 and *c*. 1975 Morris and Lett-Haines directed the distinctly non-academic East Anglian School of Painting and Drawing; in 1940 the school was moved to Morris's home at Benton End, Hadleigh, Suffolk, where he also cultivated a garden and bred irises.

Morris's paintings combine a strong sense of colour with pictorial economy, often with unusual tactility. Conveyed with great immediacy, a painting's principal motif is usually juxtaposed boldly with a contrasting background. His subjects include still-lifes and flower paintings, such as *Iris Seedlings* (1943; London, Tate); landscapes and townscapes, both local and from his wide travels; animals and birds, such as *Greenland Falcon* (1928; Belfast, Ulster Mus.). Some of his most arresting works are his penetrating portraits, for example that of his student *Lucian Freud*

(1940; London, Tate). The attitudes implied by his paintings range from tenderness to satire. Morris, averse to English tastefulness, seemed at times closer to the sensibility of the Neue Sachlichkeit. His paintings include protests against prudery, environmental pollution and also hypocrisy, as in the *Entry of Moral Turpitude into New York Harbour* (1926; priv. col., see exh. cat. 1984, no. 31).

BIBLIOGRAPHY
Cedric Morris (exh. cat. by R. Morphet, London, Tate, 1984)

RICHARD MORPHET

Morris, George. *See under* BONNIN & MORRIS.

Morris, Robert (*b* Kansas City, MO, 9 Feb 1931). American sculptor and painter. He studied (1948–50) at the University of Kansas City and then at the Kansas City Art Institute. By 1951 he was in San Francisco and attended the California School of Fine Arts, but he interrupted his studies after a year to serve in the Army Corps of Engineers. During his tour of duty he visited Arizona and Korea. In 1953 he moved to Reed College in Oregon, where he spent two years. He returned to San Francisco in 1955 and spent the rest of the decade engaged in experimental dance and improvisational theatre. His first one-man exhibition took place there in 1957. From 1961 to 1963 Morris studied art history at Hunter College in New York, where he settled.

Morris's early sculpture tended to emphasize a banal repertoire of form and subject-matter, while attempting to investigate the role of language in artistic representation. *Metered Bulb* (1963; Jasper Johns priv. col., see 1971 exh. cat., p. 57), in which a working lightbulb is displayed with an electric company meter monotonously recording its energy expenditure, is typical of his early work's use of unconventional expressive means. At the same time, however, Morris continued his involvement with performance art, for which he reunited with former collaborators Walter De Maria, Yvonne Rainer (*b* 1934) and La Monte Young (*b* 1935), who had also moved to New York. Through an influential series of articles that began to appear, irregularly, in the New York art press *c.* 1966, Morris assumed a highly visible position in determining both the objectives and the tenor of MINIMALISM in America, then in its early stages. Yet, while his impersonal and often doctrinaire manifestos were received favourably by a large number of young artists, he himself was frequently regarded as provocative and even flamboyant. This apparent schism posed some difficulties for critics who found his enigmatic behaviour hard to reconcile with the comparative reserve of other leading sculptors drawn to the movement. It led a number of critics to associate Morris's irreverence with the highly controversial activities of the FLUXUS group, despite the fact that his first New York gallery exhibitions consisted of large conceptually inspired pieces, such as *Untitled* (0.7 m cubes of plexiglass mirror on wood, 1965; see 1971 exh. cat., p. 22), whose scale and geometric simplicity had much in common with Minimalism. Indeed, this type of sculpture maintained a privileged place within his output during the 1970s, although his practice increasingly moved beyond the constraints of conventional media.

For the next ten years Morris's work was characterized by the use of ephemeral materials. He experimented with heavy felt, mirrors, textile waste products, steam and dirt in an effort to dematerialize the object, creating works that could be appreciated only briefly before they disappeared or were removed by the artist, for example *Untitled* (steam, 1968–9; see 1971 exh. cat., p. 122). The photographic documentation of these works was often the only material trace of these attempts to negate the very physicality of the artistic gesture.

In the light of this ambition, it is even more startling to consider Morris's work of the 1980s, for example *Untitled* (1983; New York, Robert and Nancy Kaye priv. col., see 1986 exh. cat., p. 49), part of the *Firestorm* series. Morris returned to drawing and painting at this time, producing works of a heroic scale. Through an integration of sculpture and two-dimensional images, he evoked an apocalyptic vision of the modern world. Using 'Hydrocal' and welded steel to create dark framing elements that bear skulls and other body parts in their relief panels, he set into these frames canvases whose lush landscapes are evocations of the apocalypse or holocausts. In abandoning issues of the phenomenology of the work of art, which had so deeply and consistently affected the first 20 years of his activity, Morris may have ultimately adopted a bleaker vision of the questions that surrounded artistic practice towards the end of the 20th century.

WRITINGS
'Anti-form', *Artforum*, vi/8 (1968), pp. 33–5
'Some Notes on the Phenomenology of Making: The Search for the Motivated', *Artforum*, viii/8 (1970), pp. 62–6

BIBLIOGRAPHY
M. Friedman: 'Robert Morris: Polemics and Cubes', *A. Int.*, x/10 (1966), pp. 23–7
Robert Morris (exh. cat. by J. Leering, Eindhoven, Stedel. Van Abbemus, 1968)
Robert Morris (exh. cat., ed. A. Michelson; Washington, DC, Corcoran Gal. A., 1969)
Robert Morris (exh. cat. by M. Compton and D. Sylvester, London, Tate, 1971)
J. Gilbert-Rolfe: 'Robert Morris: The Complication of Exhaustion', *Artforum*, xiii/1 (1974), pp. 44–9
Robert Morris: Selected Works, 1970–1980 (exh. cat., ed. M. Mayo; Houston, TX, Contemp. A. Mus., 1982)
Robert Morris: Works of the Eighties (exh. cat., ed. E. Fry; Newport Beach, CA, Harbor A. Mus.; Chicago, IL, Mus. Contemp. A.; 1986)

DERRICK R. CARTWRIGHT

Morris, Tim(othy William) (*b* Windsor, Berks, 14 March 1941; *d* Muldersdrif, 31 May 1990). South African potter of English birth. In 1959 he spent a year at the Brighton College of Art and then went to the St Martin's School of Art in London. After qualifying in 1963 for a teaching diploma at London University, where one of his lecturers encouraged him to further his training, in 1964 he went to study pottery at the Central School of Arts and Crafts, London. In 1965 he moved to South Africa. Initially he tried portrait painting as a living but abandoned it in favour of starting his own pottery studio. With Helen Martin (*b* 1942) he started a studio in Johannesburg, which lasted only two years. In 1967 he moved to Larsens Farm near Muldersdrif, where he opened a temporary studio. A one-man exhibition at the Goodman Gallery, Johannesburg, in 1969 marked a turning-point in his career, and he built a permanent studio at Muldersdrif. Until 1976 he produced stoneware sculpture that shows the influence of his training at the Central School, but he then changed to unglazed stoneware. In the 1980s he continued to work in stoneware (see SOUTH AFRICA, fig. 8) and also experimented with fine forms in porcelain, drawing his motifs from nature.

BIBLIOGRAPHY

L. Goodman: 'Timothy Morris', *Artlook*, 40 (March 1970), pp. 26–8

A. E. DUFFEY

Morris, William (*b* Walthamstow [now in London], 24 March 1834; *d* London, 3 Oct 1896). English designer, writer and activist. His importance as both a designer and propagandist for the arts cannot easily be overestimated, and his influence has continued to be felt throughout the 20th century. He was a committed Socialist whose aim was that, as in the Middle Ages, art should be for the people and by the people, a view expressed in several of his writings. After abandoning his training as an architect, he studied painting among members of the Pre-Raphaelites. In 1861 he founded his own firm, Morris, Marshall, Faulkner & Co. (from 1875 Morris & Co.), which produced stained glass, furniture, wallpaper and fabrics (see §3 below). Morris's interests constantly led him into new activities such as his last enterprise, the Kelmscott Press (see §5 below). In 1950 his home at Walthamstow became the William Morris Gallery. The William Morris Society was founded in 1956, and it publishes a biannual journal and quarterly newsletter.

1. Introduction. 2. Early life and influences. 3. Morris & Co. 4. Politics, art and labour. 5. The Kelmscott Press.

1. INTRODUCTION. There is a temptation to divide William Morris's life into separate compartments and to write of him as the poet, the designer, the businessman, the Socialist, the protector of ancient buildings and the printer; he was all of these, but his life was a coherent whole, and his eventual aim was to create a society that would value art and that would be totally infused with art. His position was paradoxical. He had an intense sense of the ambiguities of the modern world, feeling that it presented the opportunities of spreading the benefits of 'civilization' even as it raised considerable obstacles to their achievement. His conception of civilization was very different from the way in which the word was usually understood. He was less concerned with bringing the rewards of materialism to the many than with enriching their lives through Socialism. As a Marxist he believed in 'progress' and that the bourgeoisie was 'doomed', and he was deeply aware of the discontents of modern civilization. He also had an admiration for the earlier days of human history and for the values of the medieval world, particularly the sharing of work in the guilds and the tradition of craftsmen being involved in every aspect of production. Further, he had an affection for the powers of 'barbarism', in his regard for the life of the German tribes and in his abiding interest in Iceland, which he visited several times from 1871 onwards in connection with his fascination for ancient Norse sagas.

Although Morris dedicated his life to art, art in and of itself was not his highest value. As he remarked in a lecture to the Trades' Guild of Learning (*The Lesser Arts*, 1877), his first public talk (and the first of hundreds):

I do not want art for a few, any more than education for a few, or freedom for a few. No, rather than art should live this poor thin life among a few exceptional men, despising those beneath them for an ignorance for which they themselves are responsible, for a brutality that they will not struggle with—rather than this, I would that the world should indeed sweep away all art for a while, as I said before I thought it possible she might do: rather than the wheat should rot in the miser's granary, I would that the earth had it, that it might yet have a chance to quicken in the dark.

He was intensely concerned with the relationship between the maker and the user. 'To give people pleasure in the things they must perforce *use*, that is one great office of decoration; to give people pleasure in the things they must perforce *make*, that is the other use of it' (ibid.) But pleasure was only the beginning of what he envisaged in the relationship between maker and user.

It was Morris's wish to create a better art and a better world, each to be a function of the other. Eleven years before his death he was the subject of a cartoon in *Funny Folks* (11 Oct 1885) that became known as 'The Earthly Paradox' (an ironic reference to his long poem *The Earthly Paradise*, 1868–70). The particular point of the cartoon, which depicts a policeman polishing Morris's boots, was to mock the English class system (which Morris both used and hated) whereby the authorities treated him far more leniently (through no wish of his own) than ordinary workmen after their arrest for participating in a political demonstration. By this time Morris was a leading designer, businessman, poet and political figure. While primary attention is paid in this article to his role as an artist, it would be contrary to everything he stood for to treat his artistic life in isolation.

2. EARLY LIFE AND INFLUENCES. Originally from Wales, Morris's grandfather moved to Worcester, and his father became a successful stockbroker in London. The family fortune was made by speculation in a Devonshire copper mine. Morris was the third child and eldest surviving son. When he was six the family moved to its grandest residence, Woodford Hall, Essex, surrounded by Epping Forest and near to the Thames. There his imagination was filled with the past, particularly medievalism, inspired by his reading of Walter Scott and by the time he spent in the forest, through which he would walk or ride, at times dressed in a miniature suit of armour made for him. His father died in 1848, but the family was left very well-off: Morris had an annual income of £900 when he turned 21, and he was never in financial need. At 13 he was sent to the new public school Marlborough, designed for the sons of the affluent business classes. Despite a student rebellion while he was there, he received a fairly good Classical education, and his musical taste was developed. His greatest pleasure at this time was wandering in the Wiltshire countryside, on the Downs, in the Savernake Forest; his growing love of nature was to have a substantial effect on his work as a designer.

In January 1853 Morris entered Exeter College, Oxford. During his early years at Oxford his interests broadened. He assumed, as did his family, that he would become a clergyman; with the religious ferment at Oxford at the time, such a position might well be a reforming one, also fitting in with the upward mobility of the newly enriched members of the middle classes. But he and his greatest friend, Edward Burne-Jones, became infatuated with the world of the arts. They explored churches near Oxford on horseback, and during the summer of 1854 Morris travelled to France and saw for the first time the northern Gothic cathedrals. With Burne-Jones and others, he took a similar trip the following summer, and the two friends resolved that they would make their contribution to the world, carrying on their 'Holy Warfare against the age', not through becoming priests but rather through art, Burne-Jones to be a painter and Morris an architect. Morris became increasingly aware of the social implications of art through his reading of Thomas Carlyle and, most importantly, John Ruskin, which he acknowledged was 'a sort of revelation' (letter to Andreas Scheu, 5 Sept 1883). For Morris the most important chapter in Ruskin's *The Stones of Venice* (1851–3) was 'On the Nature of Gothic'; when the chapter was issued in 1892 as a separate publication of the Kelmscott Press, Morris wrote in his preface to it 'in future days it will be considered as one of the very few necessary utterances of this century'. From Ruskin, Morris learnt both a profound discontent with the society that was being created in 19th-century England and also a profound interest in the worker's relationship with work, the satisfactions to be derived from all types of work, particularly artistic. Perhaps most important of all, Ruskin made him regard art and society as intertwined. He also learnt to be suspicious of the perfections possible from machines and to recognize the evils of the division of labour, even if in his own business he had to make compromises. These beliefs had a continuing influence on his approach to design, although they created something of a paradox for him. Many of his designs proved to be best done by machines, and he was not automatically against their use. It was often difficult for him, and certainly it was for his followers, to draw the fine line between excessive dependence on machines and a willingness to use them to improve the quality of life.

During his time at Oxford, Morris was also beginning his literary career. In his own day his greatest artistic fame was probably as a poet; indeed, he might well have succeeded Tennyson as Poet Laureate if he had not been a Socialist. He has since become better known as a designer, political thinker and activist, while his poetry is of interest primarily to the specialist. Having graduated in the autumn of 1855, in January 1856 he articled himself in Oxford to the Gothic Revival architect G. E. Street, who influenced Morris not only in his style but also in his commitment to 'total' building, a belief that every aspect of a building is significant and must be understood by the architect. Morris came to believe that the greatest artistic achievements were the making of buildings and books. It is striking that both are necessarily cooperative enterprises, even if they have a guiding figure in their creation. He trained with Street for only nine months, and part of that time was spent with him on a summer tour of the Low Countries.

In 1856 Morris subsidized the 12 issues of the *Oxford and Cambridge Magazine* as a vehicle for the literary efforts of his friends and himself. Many of his early shorter poems, now held to be his best, were collected in *The Defence of Guenevere and Other Poems*, dedicated to Dante Gabriel Rossetti and published in 1858.

Morris's life exemplified his belief that the intelligent person could tackle almost every task, that it was a matter of talent rather than what he regarded as the dubious Renaissance notion of genius. He had boundless energy, but the breadth of his interests made it difficult for him to settle on the best means to serve his artistic skills. A period of artistic experimentation in the late 1850s helped him find his way: he concluded that he was not to be an architect, and he now became a student of his new friend, the leader of the Pre-Raphaelites, Dante Gabriel Rossetti. He moved to London where he shared rooms with Burne-Jones. The prelude to his finding his true artistic career was his dissatisfaction with the furniture available in the shops and his consequent determination to design his own. He continued learning to paint, first in London and then in Oxford during a joyful summer in 1857 when he, Rossetti, Burne-Jones and others—a second generation of the Pre-Raphaelites—painted murals from Arthurian themes in the Debating Chamber of the Oxford Union. Because of faulty technique, the murals rapidly faded and are no longer at all distinct. Also in Oxford that summer Rossetti met Jane Burden, then 17, the daughter of a local groom. She became one of Rossetti's most frequent models and his close companion. In 1858 Morris painted her in his only surviving easel painting, *La Belle Iseult*, formerly known as *Queen Guenevere* (London, Tate). In 1859 Morris married Jane. The marriage moved him closer to his most important contribution to the world of art: to be a designer and an entrepreneur of design. In 1859 he commissioned his friend Philip Webb, whom he had originally met in Street's office, to build a house for him in Bexleyheath, Kent. Called Red House, it was intended not only as a home for Jane and himself but also as a 'palace of art' for a community of like-minded artists. In the event, only the Morrises and their two daughters, Jenny and May, lived there and only until 1865. Then, in order to be closer to his business, he moved back to London.

The importance and originality of Red House have received widely differing assessment from scholars. There is no question that it was a successful building in itself, its simplified Gothic style having echoes of medievalism without being eclectic or historicist. The building and design of the house, and particularly its internal design by Morris himself, led to the founding of the design firm Morris, Marshall, Faulkner & Co. in 1861. Morris, after his period of apprenticeship, was now coming into his own.

3. MORRIS & CO. Despite the original name of the firm (in which Burne-Jones, Rossetti, Webb and Ford Madox Brown were also active), Morris was the dominant figure, as was acknowledged when it was reorganized in 1875, with a fair amount of recrimination and bitterness, as Morris & Co. In the early years of the firm, he continued to work happily with a group, which in theory at least was his ideal. But from now on there was a recurring cycle in his working life: he would start out with a group and a

1. 'Sussex' armchair designed by Philip Webb for Morris, Marshall, Faulkner & Co., ash, h. 845 mm, c. 1868 (London, William Morris Gallery and Brangwyn Gift)

purchaser, it was not always true to the material from which it was made, it was not faithful to Ruskin. Although to modern eyes many of Morris's designs appear elaborate, in their own time they represented a move towards simplicity, and he himself became increasingly adept at a whole range of design. Even before the founding of the firm, he had designed furniture and had done embroidery (*see* EMBROIDERY §2). He now began to design wallpaper, the first pattern being 'Daisy' (1862). He was perfectly happy to produce such traditional designs as that for Webb's plain, rush-seated 'Sussex' chair (see fig. 1), based on a vernacular prototype. The 'Morris' chair, a large, simple, rather box-like chair famous for its method of reclining, was in fact another traditional design adapted by Webb, at the suggestion of Warrington Taylor, the business manager who succeeded Faulkner.

The firm became well known for the making of stained glass, and it is now regarded as one of the finest stained-glass makers of the 19th century, with rich, ungarish colours (particularly Morris's accomplishment) and designs by Burne-Jones (*see* STAINED GLASS, fig. 11 and colour pl. VI, fig. 2), Rossetti and Morris himself (see fig. 2). Sewter (1974–5) argued that it was the best glass made since the 16th century. As he pointed out, the glass was modern and, despite Morris's interests in the medieval period, was not imitative, specifically in the choice of deep colours not found in medieval glass. The firm prospered owing to the spate of Gothic Revival church building and restorations taking place during the century. Later, when Morris became particularly concerned with the condition and restoration of older buildings, he refused to put new glass in old buildings.

Morris fulfilled his own belief that an individual was capable of many arts. But as he was both the designer and

hope of cooperation; when the group failed he would start out again, eventually operating on his own. The persistence of this ideal, of working in a group, is stated eloquently in *News from Nowhere* (1890), a picture of Utopia, which became his most famous prose work.

Rossetti, Burne-Jones and Madox Brown were still primarily committed to painting, and Webb would remain primarily an architect, but they all created designs, which Morris then executed. Peter Paul Marshall was a surveyor friend of Madox Brown; Charles Faulkner, an old Oxford friend of Morris and a mathematician, for a while provided business help, although the financing came mostly from Morris's mother. The firm's prospectus (see Mackail, i, pp. 150–52) had some of the arrogance of youth in its statement that design was now sufficiently important that

> Artists of reputation should devote their time to it. Although no doubt particular instances of success may be cited, still it must be generally felt that attempts of this kind hitherto have been crude and fragmentary.... Having among their number men of varied qualifications, they will be able to undertake any species of decoration, mural or otherwise, from pictures, properly so-called, down to the consideration of the smallest work susceptible of art beauty.

In Morris's view, with some but not too much exaggeration, design was in a degraded state. It was too fanciful, its purpose was frequently to demonstrate the wealth of the

2. William Morris: *Annunciation*, cartoon for stained glass at St Michael, Brighton, West Sussex, pencil, watercolour and ink, 780×880 mm, 1862 (London, William Morris Gallery and Brangwyn Gift)

the entrepreneur, the experience of his numerous work-men may have been more limited than his theory sug-gested. He was involved in the designing and the doings of all aspects of his firm. At the same time he wrote a great deal of poetry, which he regarded as similar in its requirements to the regularity and skill needed for weaving. When Morris started to produce tapestry in 1879, he would get up at 5 a.m. to weave and at the same time compose verse. As long as narrative poems were read as novels, these works were very popular; most of his longer poems, however, have come to be regarded as his least successful. As he remarked 'That talk of inspiration is sheer nonsense, I may tell you that flat, there is no such thing; it is a mere matter of craftsmanship' (Stansky, p. 46).

Perhaps Morris's greatest accomplishment was as a designer of the flat patterns to be found in the firm's wallpapers and fabrics and later in its carpets. He was a pattern maker of genius, his designs flowing from his love and observation of natural forms (see fig. 3). The wallpa-pers and textile designs have been the most enduring contributions and have once again become almost as popular as they were in their own time (see DYE, colour pl. IV, fig. 2). According to an article in *The Spectator* (anon., 24 Nov 1883, p. 1508), 'Morris has become a household word for all who wish their material surround-ings to be beautiful yet appropriate for homely use, "neat not gaudy"'. Ultimately the firm designed some 53 wall-papers and around 37 chintzes. Morris stated that his aim was 'to combine clearness of form and firmness of structure with the mystery which comes of abundance and richness of detail' (*Arts and Crafts Exhibition Society Catalogue of the First Exhibition*, London, New Gal., 1888, p. 27). His patterns drew on his familiarity with nature, and, later on, they were also based on his study of the textiles acquired by the Victoria and Albert Museum, London, many of them bought on his advice. As Fiona Clark (1973, p. 8) remarked, 'Within a Gothic-derived net of incredible complexity, he combines from two to five different plants without destroying the natural system of growth peculiar to each'. The revival of interest in Morris springs from the concurrent emphasis on 'naturalness', with substances being as true to themselves as possible. As Morris commented, he had tried 'to make woollen substances as woollen as possible, cotton as cottony as possible, and so on' (Morris to Emma Lazarus, 21 April 1884, Kelvin, ii, p. 276). His goods became increasingly popular, and he eventually had his works at Merton Abbey, Surrey, where the firm moved in 1881, and a shop on Oxford Street, London. All the firm's tapestry commis-sions were carried out at Merton Abbey, notable examples including *Angeli laudantes* (1894; London, V&A; *see* TAPESTRY, fig. 12). He continued to seek inspiration in the country, renting Kelmscott Manor on the border of Oxfordshire and Gloucestershire, near the source of the Thames.

4. POLITICS, ART AND LABOUR. Morris drove himself hard, continued to be a poet and from the 1870s on became more involved with public matters. At the same time, he continually explored other areas, including some that were not of particular interest for his design firm. For several years from 1869 he devoted his Sundays to calligraphy, creating approximately 1500 manuscript and decorated pages (*see* MANUSCRIPT, §II, 3 and fig. 8). His Sundays were later given over to preaching Socialism by Hammersmith Bridge near his last London home, Kelms-cott House on the Thames where he moved in 1878. (The house is now owned by the William Morris Society.) Politics became very important to him not only in itself but also for its implications for the relation of art and society, and it led him to found what later became part of the environmentalist movement. In 1876 he became a follower of William Gladstone in his campaign to evict the Turks from the Balkans, expressing his indignation over the issue in 'The Eastern Question' (from the manifesto *To the Workingmen of England*, 1877). Once he began to be publicly active, he became increasingly so. He wrote a letter to the press (*The Athenaeum*, 10 March 1877), protesting against the restoration of Tewkesbury Abbey by George Gilbert I Scott (ii):

> My eye just now caught the word 'restoration' in the morning paper, and, on looking closer, I saw that this time it is nothing less than the minster of Tewkesbury that is to be destroyed by Sir Gilbert Scott. Is it altogether too late to do something to save it—it and whatever else of beautiful or historical value is still left us on the sites of the ancient buildings we were once so famous for?

In April 1877 he founded the Society for the Protection of Ancient Buildings, or 'Anti-Scrape' as it was nicknamed. By the late 1990s it was still continuing as the advocate of the built world and was the first of (ultimately) numerous societies dedicated to an attempt to preserve the national heritage. His view was his own. Some who believed that they had the interest of a building at heart thought that its restoration, as Scott proposed to do, was a benign act. For Morris, such a step was no better or indeed worse than allowing the building to be destroyed and something else being put up in its place. He felt that a building was an organic being and that its evolution over the centuries should be preserved. As with a human being, if it could be preserved through patches and comparatively simple means, well and good. If not, it would be better for it to

3. William Morris: 'Tulip' pattern, cotton printed from woodblocks, 1875 (London, Victoria and Albert Museum)

be given a decent burial. Restoration was a lifeless way of proceeding. Morris's significance in this area for the history of art and architecture was substantial, leading to a new respect for and interest in older buildings. It was also significant as marking his opposition to building in historical styles, which he came to see as a meaningless re-creation of the past.

Through his public involvement, particularly in the realm of buildings, Morris became more aware of capitalists more interested in profits than preservation. Politically, he became more left-wing. His interest in design and the workers who created the objects brought into focus the relationship between art and labour. He saw that this was not merely a question for his own firm but a more public matter. He began to give public lectures. Many of them became the important essays that led such scholars as E. P. Thompson to regard him, along with Marx, as the greatest theoretician of the alienation of labour. In 1882 he published a collection of five of his talks, *Hopes and Fears for Art*. The title is characteristic of Morris, with its suggestion of advance and retreat, almost a verbal equivalent of his pattern designs. His political career moved in a similar fashion. In January 1883 he joined the Social Democratic Federation, a Marxist–Socialist political group, but he disapproved of its interest in using traditional parliamentary means; at the end of 1884 he and other dissidents formed the Socialist League, which he left in 1890 because it was too anarchist. He then formed his own small political group, the Hammersmith Socialist Society. Following the pattern of his political life in his artistic life, he was committed to the idea of groups and cooperation, yet found it hard to get along with others and needed to be the person in charge. As stated in his story about the 14th-century rebellion of Wat Tyler, *A Dream of John Ball* (1888), 'Fellowship is heaven, and lack of fellowship is hell: fellowship is life and the lack of fellowship is death'. Also in that text is his statement: 'how men fight and lose the battle, and the thing that they fought for comes about in spite of their defeat, and when it comes turns out not to be what they meant, and other men have to fight for what they meant under another name'. He yearned for fellowship, and in *News from Nowhere* he depicted the Utopia of the 21st century where life would be dominated by fellowship. Typically, the narrator of the tale, William Guest, representing Morris's own views, is not really part of the Utopia, being a visitor from the present to the future. The last line alludes to his hope that the society depicted 'may be called a vision rather than a dream', an echo of Morris's first lecture. The physical appearance of the world is as if it were furnished by Morris & Co.

Although Morris was impatient with followers and cooperated with them only reluctantly, his influence on other designers was considerable, particularly when he was at the height of his activities in the 1880s. It was formalized in such leading design organizations as the Century Guild (founded 1882), the Art Workers' Guild (1884) and C. R. Ashbee's Guild of Handicraft and the Arts and Crafts Exhibition Society (both 1888; *see* ARTS AND CRAFTS MOVEMENT). Of course, the many individuals who followed in Morris's footsteps varied greatly in how they followed his example; Ruskin was a considerable

influence as well. Morris was a dominating force who set the terms that those who came after followed, adapted or rebelled against.

5. THE KELMSCOTT PRESS. A lecture at the first exhibition of the Arts and Crafts Exhibition Society in 1888 impelled Morris into his last artistic adventure. There were lectures in connection with the exhibition, and Morris gave two of them, on tapestry and carpet weaving. Emery Walker (1851–1933) lectured on printing, reflecting the experience he and Morris had just had designing *The House of the Wolfings*, the first of Morris's nine prose romances. (When the lecture was printed in 1893, it was credited to both Morris and Walker.) Morris was particularly struck by the images of characters designed by the typographer Nicolas Jenson that Walker projected on the screen. Over the next few years Morris proceeded to establish the Kelmscott Press, which printed fifty-three books between 1891 and 1898, two years after Morris's death. In *A Note by William Morris on his Aims in Founding the Kelmscott Press* (1898) he wrote:

> I began printing books with the hope of producing some which would have a definite claim to beauty, while at the same time they should be easy to read and should not dazzle the eye, or trouble the intellect of the reader by eccentricity of form in the letters.

Some would argue that Morris's typefaces—Golden, Troy and Chaucer—were too elaborate, as were his books. To the modern eye, they can be a little difficult to read.

The masterpiece of the Kelmscott Press was the edition of *Chaucer*, for which Burne-Jones made the 87 woodcut illustrations and Morris the decorations (see fig. 4). It took four years to produce and was not finished until June 1896, shortly before his death. Morris focused attention on every aspect of the design of the book: he regarded the text, paper, ink and binding as equally important units within the design, each opening of the book also being a coherent whole. What he called his 'little typographical adventure' also served to sum up the nature of his influence (*see also* TYPOGRAPHY). He was the inspiration of the private press movement: Doves, Vale, Eragny, Essex House, Ashendene and others. It was a luxury trade that could be afforded only by the well-off. At the same time, as with the productions of Morris & Co., the design approach—the aim (not necessarily always achieved)—of truth to material, of simplicity, of forms and designs that might be produced less expensively—set examples not only for his contemporaries but also for later generations. At the least he had a considerable effect on how the modern world has looked, although his influence may have been exaggerated in Nikolaus Pevsner's controversial and influential study *Pioneers of the Modern Movement* (1936). Later scholars have concentrated on Morris's extraordinary skill as a designer, acknowledging that he reduced the fussiness of Victorian design and moved towards the fusion of beauty and function.

In the 1890s Morris was in declining health and could no longer be as politically active as he had been, even though he did not change his political commitments. He continued to collect early printed books and medieval illuminations, to work for the Kelmscott Press and to write prose romances until his death. He was buried at the

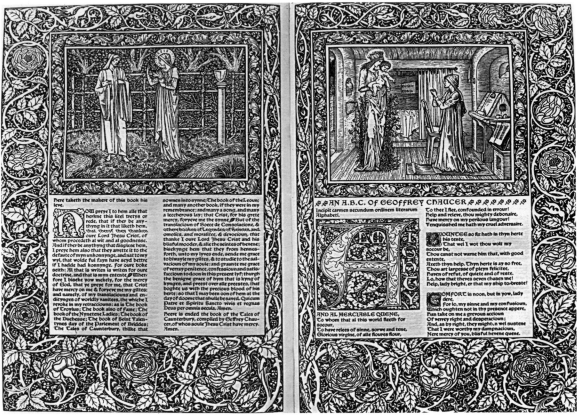

4. William Morris: decoration of a spread from the Kelmscott *Chaucer*, illustrated by Edward Burne-Jones, pp. 222–3, page size 423×285 mm, 1896 (London, William Morris Gallery and Brangwyn Gift)

village of Kelmscott under a tomb executed by Webb in an Icelandic style, raised from the ground on short stone stilts. Having aimed to create a better world in all its aspects, he had lived by his own maxim: 'Have nothing in your house that you do not know to be useful, or believe to be beautiful' (*The Beauty of Life*, lecture, 1880).

WRITINGS

M. Morris, ed.: *The Collected Works*, 24 vols (London, 1910–15)
——: *William Morris: Artist, Writer, Socialist*, 2 vols (Oxford, 1936) [incl. mat. not in *The Collected Works*]
A. Briggs, ed.: *William Morris: Selected Writings and Designs* (Harmondsworth, 1962); *R* as *William Morris: News from Nowhere and Selected Writings and Designs* (1984)
E. D. Le Mire, ed.: *The Unpublished Lectures of William Morris* (London and Detroit, 1969)
W. S. Peterson, ed.: *The Ideal Book* (Berkeley, 1982)
N. Kelvin, ed.: *The Collected Letters of William Morris*, 2 vols (Princeton, 1984–7) [vol. iii in preparation]

BIBLIOGRAPHY

H. B. Forman: *The Books of William Morris* (London, 1897)
A. Vallance: *William Morris: His Art, his Writings, his Public Life* (London, 1897/*R* 1986)
J. W. Mackail: *The Life of William Morris*, 2 vols (London, 1899)
H. H. Sparling: *The Kelmscott Press and William Morris* (London, 1924)
G. H. Crow: *William Morris Designer* (London, 1934)
N. Pevsner: *Pioneers of the Modern Movement* (London, 1936, New York, 2/1949), rev. as *Pioneers of Modern Design: From William Morris to Gropius* (London, 1960, rev. 1975/*R* 1984)
E. P. Thompson: *William Morris: Romantic to Revolutionary* (London, 1955, rev. New York, 1976)
P. Henderson: *William Morris* (London, 1967)
P. Thompson: *The Work of William Morris* (London, 1967, rev. 1977)
R. Watkinson: *William Morris as Designer* (London, 1967)
Catalogue of the Morris Collection: William Morris Gallery, Walthamstow (Walthamstow, 1969)
G. Naylor: *The Arts and Crafts Movement* (London, 1971)
F. Clark: *William Morris: Wallpaper and Chintzes* (London, 1973)
A. C. Sewter: *The Stained Glass of William Morris and his Circle*, 2 vols (New Haven, 1974–5)
J. Lindsay: *William Morris* (London, 1975)
William Morris and the Art of the Book (exh. cat., ed. P. Needham; New York, Pierpont Morgan Lib., 1976)
I. Bradley: *William Morris and his World* (New York, 1978)
Morris and Company (exh. cat. by C. Gene, London, F.A. Soc., 1979)
P. Faulkner: *Against the Age: An Introduction to William Morris* (London, 1980)
Morris & Company in Cambridge (exh. cat. by D. Robinson and S. Wildman, Cambridge, Fitzwilliam, 1980)
Textiles by William Morris and Morris & Co., 1861–1940 (exh. cat. by O. Fairclough and E. Leary, Birmingham, Mus. & A.G., 1981)
William Morris and Kelmscott (exh. cat., Farnham, W. Surrey Coll. A. & Des., 1981)
D. Robinson: *William Morris, Edward Burne-Jones and the Kelmscott Chaucer* (London, 1982)
L. Parry: *William Morris Textiles* (New York, 1983)
W. S. Peterson: *A Bibliography of the Kelmscott Press* (Oxford, 1984)
William Morris Today (exh. cat., London, ICA, 1984)
William Morris and the Middle Ages (exh. cat., ed. J. Banham and J. Harris; U. Manchester, Whitworth A.G., 1984)
P. Stansky: *Redesigning the World: William Morris, the 1880s, and the Arts and Crafts* (Princeton, 1985)
E. Boris: *Art and Labor: Ruskin, Morris and the Craftsman Ideal in America* (Philadelphia, 1986)
G. Naylor, ed.: *William Morris by Himself: Designs and Writings* (London, 1988)

C. Harvey and J. Press: *William Morris: Design and Enterprise in Victorian Britain* (Manchester, 1991)
W. Peterson: *The Kelmscott Press* (Berkeley, 1991)
F. MacCarthy: *William Morris* (London, 1994)
William Morris (exh. cat., ed. L. Parry; London, V&A, 1996)

PETER STANSKY

Morrison. Irish family of architects. (1) Richard Morrison was the son of John Morrison, an architect who practised in Munster in the second half of the 18th century, enjoying the patronage of the influential Charles Agar (1736–1809), Bishop of Cloyne, later Archbishop of Cashel and of Dublin. Richard Morrison trained his second son, (2) William Vitruvius Morrison, and was in partnership with him until 1825.

(1) Richard Morrison, Sir (*b* ?Midleton, Co. Cork, 1767; *d* Old Conna, Co. Dublin, 31 Oct 1849). In 1786 he entered the Dublin Society's school of architectural drawing under Henry Aaron Baker and subsequently set up practice (*c.* 1790) in Clonmel, Co. Tipperary. There he was commissioned by Agar, as Archbishop of Cashel, to design a spire for Cashel Protestant Cathedral (only partly executed). The most important building of his years in Clonmel was the late Palladian-style County Court-House (*c.* 1790–1801), the first, best (and most intact) of six county court-houses built to his plans. By 1793 he had moved to Dublin, where his only significant surviving buildings are Sir Patrick Dun's Hospital (1803–16), Grand Canal Street, and the north and east blocks of the Botany Bay court in Trinity College (1813–15). Most of his commissions were for building or enlarging country houses, of which the simple classical villas he designed in the first decade of the 19th century are particularly attractive: Bearforest (1807–8; burnt *c.* 1920, since rebuilt on a slightly different plan), Co. Cork; Kilpeacon, Co. Limerick; Cangort Park (1807), Co. Offaly; and Weston (*c.* 1807; destr.), Co. Galway. Although when enlarging an existing house (as was usually the case) he would often disguise it in a castle-style or Gothic skin, he was never fully at home with the principles of Picturesque irregularity and remained essentially an eclectic classical architect. The earliest of his castle-style conversions was at Shanganagh, Co. Dublin (1801); the most extensive at Thomastown Castle, Co. Tipperary (1812; in ruins). The mansions on which he collaborated with his son until 1825 are listed below. Following the dissolution of the father-and-son partnership in 1825, relatively little of his work is recorded, although his later work includes the completion of Baronscourt, Co. Tyrone, after his son William's death, additions to Tullynally (*c.* 1842), Co. W. Meath, and the stables (1840s) at Howth Castle, Co. Dublin. In 1839 he founded the Royal Institute of the Architects of Ireland, and in 1841 he was knighted. Although in his *Designs* Morrison proposes an innovative arrangement of entrance hall and inner vestibule, in other respects both his publications express a conservative taste and outlook.

WRITINGS
Useful and Ornamental Designs in Architecture Composed in the Manner of the Antique and Most Approved Taste of the Present Day (Dublin, 1793)
Architecture: Introductory Lecture Delivered at the Meeting of the Royal Institute of the Architects of Ireland, June 28th, 1844 (Dublin, 1844)

(2) William Vitruvius Morrison (*b* Clonmel, Co. Tipperary, 22 April 1794; *d* Old Conna, Co. Dublin, 16 Oct 1838). Son of (1) Richard Morrison. His precocious architectural talent had become evident as early as 1810. He received all his training from his father with whom, during the next decade, he collaborated on several castellated Tudor and Gothic Revival houses, including Ballyheigue Castle (burnt 1921; partly rest.), Co. Kerry; Borris House, Co. Carlow; and Shelton Abbey and Kilruddery (remodelled 1953–6; much of the Morrisons' work demolished as a result), both in Co. Wicklow. In 1821 he visited Rome, Paestum, Paris and England, manifesting a more seriously archaeological interest in ancient, medieval and Tudor architectural sources than his father ever showed. On his return home father and son continued to work at Kilruddery and collaborated on two large Neo-classical mansions: Ballyfin (1822), Co. Laois, and Fota (*c.* 1825), Co. Cork. Around 1825 William Morrison began to work independently. During the late 1820s and early 1830s he designed a series of Tudor Revival cottages and houses which were the earliest and most distinguished examples of the genre produced by an Irish architect. His masterpiece, Clontarf Castle (1836–7), Co. Dublin, is a Picturesque ensemble in the style of three different periods, with Norman and 14th-century towers abutting an Elizabethan manor house. In 1828 he designed two closely similar Neo-classical court-houses at Tralee (interior gutted and remodelled *c.* 1980), Co. Kerry, and at Carlow, Co. Carlow. Other Neo-classical work included the remodelling of Oak Park (1832), Co. Carlow, and of Baronscourt (remodelled 1946), Co. Tyrone, which was completed after his death by his father.

BIBLIOGRAPHY
J. Morrison: 'Life of the Late William Vitruvius Morrison, of Dublin, Architect', *Q. Pap. Archit.*, i (1844); also in *Dublin Bldr*, i (1 June 1859), pp. 72–3
E. McParland: 'Sir Richard Morrison's Country Houses: The Smaller Villas—I', 'Building in the Grand Manner: Sir Richard Morrison's Country Houses—II', *Country Life*, cliii (24 and 31 May 1973), pp. 1462–6, 1538–41
A. M. Rowan, ed.: *The Architecture of Richard Morrison and William Vitruvius Morrison* (Dublin, 1989)

☐

Morrison, James (*b* Middle Wallop, Hants, before 6 Sept 1789; *d* Basildon, Essex, 30 Oct 1857). English merchant and collector. The son of an innkeeper, he began work as a shopman for a firm of wholesale haberdashers in 1809; in 1814 he married his employer's daughter and took over sole direction of the firm, Todd & Co., increasing its turnover dramatically. He invested widely and his acumen was graphically illustrated by his success in cornering the market in black crêpe at the time of the death of Queen Charlotte in 1821. He was an MP from 1830 until 1847.

Morrison was one of the archetypal collectors of the second quarter of the 19th century in England, and his taste was remarkably consistent, though bound by the limits of prevailing fashion. His interest in the arts owed much to his long association with the architect John Papworth, who remodelled his four houses in turn at Balham Hill; 95 Upper Harley Street, London; Fonthill, Wilts; and Basildon. His first major purchase was Constable's *The Lock* (Madrid, Mus. Thyssen-Bornemisza), acquired at the Royal Academy in 1824 at the suggestion of H. W. Pickersgill. Shortly afterwards he wrote to Papworth: 'If I get very good things I shall become attached to the arts, if not I shall desert them for another hobby' (Gatty, p. 249). He proceeded to buy British pictures, including works by Wilkie, Eastlake and Turner, and in 1831 acquired his first Old Master, Claude Lorrain's *Landscape with the Adoration of the Golden Calf* (Manchester, C.A.G.). This was followed by a series of equally distinguished purchases, including a *Virgin and Child* by Parmigianino (Sudeley Castle, Glos, Walter Morrison priv. col.) and Poussin's *Triumph of Pan* (London, N.G.; *see* POUSSIN, NICOLAS, fig. 2). Morrison's commercial acumen found a new outlet in his association with William Buchanan, whose judgement of pictures was evidently less reliable than his own. Their outstanding joint venture was the acquisition *en bloc* of the collection of 17th-century Dutch and Flemish pictures formed by Edward Grey of Harringay, much of which Morrison himself retained, including Rembrandt's *Hendrickje Stoffels* (London, N.G.).

Morrison's second son, Alfred Morrison (1821–97), inherited Fonthill. Like his father he was keenly interested in pictures, owning the 15th-century anonymous Flemish triptych after which the Master of the Morrison Triptych is named (Toledo, OH, Mus. A.) and notable Italian and northern European 16th-century portraits. He also collected ceramics and autographs, while his wife, Mabel, daughter of the Rev. R. S. C. Chermside, was recognized by contemporaries as a pioneer in her taste for antique furniture and arrangement of period rooms at Fonthill.

BIBLIOGRAPHY
G. F. Waagen: *Galleries and Cabinets of Art in Great Britain* (London, 1857), pp. 105–13, 300–12
R. Gatty: *Portrait of a Merchant Prince: James Morrison, 1789–1857* (Northallerton, 1977)

FRANCIS RUSSELL

Morrison Irwin, Harriet. *See* IRWIN, HARRIET MORRISON.

Morrisseau, Norval (*b* Fort William, 14 March 1931). Native North American Indian Ojibwe painter. He was a member of the Royal Academy of Art in Canada and perhaps the most recognized native Canadian artist. Morrisseau's pictographic painting style is derived from the birchbark scrolls of the Ojibwe medicine society, from the rock art of the Great Lakes Woodland region and from Ojibwe oral traditions. His original ambition was to transcribe Ojibwe oral traditions into a visual form (then forbidden), and in the process he developed an iconographic style that blended traditional ideas with his personal visionary experiences. These sources are eclectically combined with Western European painting conventions and with pan-Native American Indian symbolism. He worked predominantly in acrylic paint on paper or canvas. Following his first Toronto exhibition in 1962 (which inaugurated the so-called Woodland School), Morrisseau introduced new aesthetic dimensions into Ojibwe artistic traditions: psychological studies, syncretic Native American Indian–Christian iconography, politico-historical revision, and ecological and pan-Native American Indian themes. Morrisseau's symbolic palate draws from, and often blends, Roman Catholic and Ojibwe traditions and

Eckankar concepts (a syncretic cult focusing on soul travel). His work deals largely with invoking such shamanic experiences as soul travel, depicting multiple levels of reality and visions of self-transformation. Characterized by its spiritual concern, Morrisseau's painting often symbolizes mankind's link with the supernatural. His distinctive style and rich imagistic tradition have fostered a new tradition of Woodland painting in the second half of the 20th century and inaugurated a renaissance of other native Canadian Woodland arts.

See also NATIVE NORTH AMERICAN ART, §IV, 2.

BIBLIOGRAPHY
L. Sinclair and J. Pollack: *The Art of Norval Morrisseau* (Toronto, 1979)
E. McLuhan and T. Hill: *Norval Morrisseau and the Emergence of the Image Makers* (Toronto, 1984)
R. Phillips: 'From Midé Scroll to Easel Painting: Norval Morrisseau's Early Phase' [Unpublished paper, Native Art Studies Association, Denver, 1987]
M. L. V. Vogel: *Spirits Speaking Through: Frames of Reference in the Ethnohistory and Interpretation of Native American Traditions and Arts* (Stockholm, 1994)

VANESSA VOGEL

Morse, Edward Sylvester (*b* Portland, MA, 18 June 1838; *d* Salem, MA, 20 Dec 1925). American zoologist, archaeologist and museum director. From his youth he was an avid collector and student of mollusc shells, but after being expelled from every school he attended, he became an apprentice draughtsman. His sincere interest in biology and his artistic abilities won him an assistantship with Louis Agassiz (1807–73) at Harvard University in 1859. He left Harvard in 1867 without a degree to accept a post at the new Peabody Museum at Salem, MA. In 1875 Morse began research on Pacific brachiopods, which led him to Japan in 1877. To support his work Morse gave public lectures, which he illustrated with free-hand chalk drawings. These lectures were so successful in Japan that he was offered a two-year post to establish a zoology programme at the then new Tokyo Imperial University. Shortly after arriving in Japan Morse noticed a concentration of seashells near Ōmori along the railway tracks between Yokohama and Tokyo (*see* ŌMORI SHELL-MOUND). He recognized this as a prehistoric shell midden (*kaizuka*), and with his students' help he excavated the site between September 1877 and March 1878. His well-illustrated description of this work, *Shell Mounds of Ōmori*, was issued shortly before he returned to America in 1879. The Ōmori report established archaeology as a scientific discipline in Japan and introduced the idea of a 'prehistoric' past to the Japanese (*see* JAPAN, §XX). Morse's work also led to the establishment of an archaeology programme and eventually a museum of natural history at Tokyo University. After leaving Japan, he returned to the Peabody Museum, where he became Director and remained until his retirement in 1914. He travelled to Japan in 1882 but did no more archaeological work there. Morse began to assemble a personal collection of ancient to contemporary Japanese ceramics in 1877. He became an expert on this subject, published several catalogues, and sold his collection to the Boston Museum of Fine Arts in 1890. In 1898 he was awarded the Order of the Rising Sun and, in 1922, the Order of the Sacred Treasure.

For a portrait *see* JAPAN, fig. 251.

WRITINGS

Shell Mounds of Ōmori, I/i of *Memoirs of the Science Department, University of Tokyo* (Tokyo, 1879)

Japanese Homes and their Surroundings (London, 1885)

Japan Day by Day: 1877, 1878–79, 1882–83, 2 vols (Boston, MA, 1917)

BIBLIOGRAPHY

D. G. Wayman: *Edward Sylvester Morse: A Biography* (Cambridge, MA, 1942)

Japan Day by Day: An Exhibition in Honor of E. S. Morse (exh. cat. by M. Hickman and P. Fetchko, Salem, MA, Peabody Essex Mus., 1977)

T. Moriya: *Kyōdō kenkyū Morsu to Nihon* [Collaborative partnership: Morse and Japan] (Tokyo, 1988)

PETER BLEED

Morse, Samuel F(inley) B(reese) (*b* Charlestown, MA, 27 April 1791; *d* New York, 2 April 1872). American painter and inventor. The son of a Calvinist minister, he began amateur sketching while a student at Yale College, New Haven, CT. After graduating in 1810 he returned to Charlestown, MA, to paint family portraits. In Boston in the same year he met Washington Allston, recently returned from Italy, under whose tutelage he executed his first history painting, the *Landing of the Pilgrims at Plymouth* (*c.* 1810–11; Boston, MA, Pub. Lib.). He joined Allston on his trip to London in 1811, enrolled in the Royal Academy Schools and also studied privately with Allston and Benjamin West. Morse's *Dying Hercules* (1812–13; New Haven, CT, Yale U. A.G.), based on the pose and musculature of the *Laokoon* (Rome, Vatican, Mus. Pio-Clementino) and the theory evident in Allston's *Dead Man Restored to Life by Touching the Bones of the Prophet Elisha* (1811–14; Philadelphia, PA Acad. F.A.), was critically

acclaimed when exhibited at the Royal Academy and is indicative of Morse's academic interests. After two trips in 1813 and 1814 to Bristol, where he painted a number of portraits and small subject pieces, Morse ended his period in England with another mythological history painting, the *Judgement of Jupiter* (1814–15; New Haven, CT, Yale U. A.G.).

Morse received critical praise but little financial reward from the exhibition of his London pictures on his return to Boston in 1815, and as a result he turned to portraiture to earn a living. After two difficult years travelling through New England, he made the first of four annual trips early in 1818 to Charleston, SC, where he painted dozens of portraits. That of his wife, *Lucretia Pickering Walker Morse* (*c.* 1818–19; Amherst Coll., MA, Mead A. Mus.), shows the influence of Gilbert Stuart in its painterly technique and bold colour. Morse's later portraits in Charleston are closer in style to the fluid elegance of Thomas Sully.

Having profited both artistically and financially from his time in Charleston, Morse painted his first mature American history picture, the *House of Representatives* (2.20×3.33 m, 1822–3; Washington, DC, Corcoran Gal. A.). His largest work, it depicts Benjamin Henry Latrobe's newly renovated Hall of Congress and over eighty portraits of congressmen, Supreme Court justices, journalists, a Pawnee Indian and the artist's father. Morse hoped to demonstrate to a mass audience the rationality, morality and gentility of the American system of government; but because of its emblematic nature and the narrative expectations of the viewing public, the exhibition of the *House*

Samuel Morse: *Gallery of the Louvre*, oil on canvas, 1.87×2.74 m, 1832–3 (Chicago, IL, Terra Museum of American Art)

in New Haven, Boston and New York was a popular and financial disaster, forcing Morse to return to portraiture.

In New Haven during the early 1820s Morse painted figures in and around the Yale University community, such as *Eli Whitney, Benjamin Silliman* (both New Haven, CT, Yale U. A.G.) and *Noah Webster* (Amherst Coll., MA, Mead A. Mus.). Moving late in 1824 to New York, which became his permanent home, Morse reached the apex of his career. He painted many of the city's literary and political leaders, including romantic portraits of *William Cullen Bryant* (c. 1826; New York, N. Acad. Des.) and *DeWitt Clinton* (1826; New York, Met.). His most important portrait commission of this period, for the City of New York, was of the *Marquis de Lafayette* (1825–6; New York, City Hall), who was on a triumphant tour of the USA on the occasion of the semi-centennial of the American Revolution. Full-length and life-size, the portrait represents a departure in the grand-style American portrait. Unlike the static classical pose that had dominated American portraiture (e.g. Gilbert Stuart's *'Lansdowne' Washington*, 1796; Philadelphia, PA Acad. F.A.), Morse's *Lafayette* shows the figure in action, a style influenced by the portraits of Sir Thomas Lawrence. During this period Morse also worked for literary publications, painted a few landscapes and founded the National Academy of Design, New York, of which he was the first president.

Morse travelled to Europe in 1829, spending a year in Italy, where he studied thousands of Old Master pictures, astutely copied some, including Tintoretto's *Miracle of the Slave* (1548; Venice, Accad.; copy, 1831; Boston, MA, Mus. F.A.), and sketched and painted landscapes such as his beautiful *Chapel of the Virgin at Subiaco* (1831; Worcester, MA, A. Mus.). In mid-1831 he was in Paris, where he began the *Gallery of the Louvre* (1832–3; Chicago, IL, Terra Mus. Amer. A.; see fig.). A pantheon of the Louvre's masterpieces assembled in Morse's imagination in the Salon Carré, the work, exemplifying his artistic skill, is Morse's attempt to provide Americans with an awareness of their artistic patrimony. However, like the *House of Representatives* before it, the *Louvre* was not a popular success when exhibited in New York in 1833.

The failure of the *Louvre*, coupled with the decision of the US Congress not to commission Morse to paint a mural in the Capitol Rotunda, signalled the waning of his artistic career. He continued as President of the National Academy until 1845, was appointed Professor of the Literature of the Arts of Design at New York University in 1834 and painted a few spectacular pictures in the 1830s, such as the chromatically brilliant portrait of his daughter Susan, *The Muse* (1836–7; New York, Met.). Morse's time was increasingly absorbed by politics, science and technology. In 1839, after meeting Daguerre in Paris, Morse publicized the daguerreotype process in the USA and became one of its earliest practitioners, opening a portrait studio with John William Draper (1811–82) in New York in 1840. In the late 1830s he developed the first practical electromagnetic telegraph and signalling code. After successfully demonstrating the revolutionary instrument before Congress in 1844 and building a telegraphic empire, Morse became the most honoured inventor in 19th-century America.

WRITINGS

E. L. Morse, ed.: *Samuel F. B. Morse: His Letters and Journals*, 2 vols (Boston, 1914)
N. Cikoksky jr, ed.: *Lectures on the Affinity of Painting with the Other Fine Arts, by Samuel F. B. Morse* (Columbia, MO, 1983)

BIBLIOGRAPHY

Samuel F. B. Morse: American Painter (exh. cat. by H. B. Wehle, New York, Met., 1932)
C. Mabee: *The American Leonardo: A Life of Samuel F. B. Morse* (New York, 1943)
O. Larkin: *Samuel F. B. Morse and American Democratic Art* (Boston, 1954)
P. J. Staiti: 'Samuel F. B. Morse's Search for a Personal Style', *Winterthur Port..*, xvi (1981), pp. 253–81
Samuel F. B. Morse (exh. cat. by P. J. Staiti, New York U., Grey A.G., 1982)
Samuel F. B. Morse: Educator and Champion of the Arts in America (exh. cat. by N. Cikovsky jr and P. J. Staiti, New York, N. Acad. Des., 1982)
P. J. Staiti: *Samuel F. B. Morse* (Cambridge, MA, 1989)

PAUL J. STAITI

Mortensen, Richard (*b* Copenhagen, 23 Oct 1910; *d* Copenhagen, 12 Jan 1993). Danish painter and stage designer. He studied at the art academy in Copenhagen from 1931 to 1932. In 1932 he visited Berlin with the painter Ejler Bille and saw paintings by Vasily Kandinsky, after which he began to make abstract pictures with pure, geometrical forms. He was also attracted by Surrealism and in his paintings of 1933–4 sometimes incorporated fragments of reality, such as an eye and a pair of lips, in otherwise abstract compositions, which gave them a fantastic and erotic character. In 1934 he made some paintings that were purely Surrealist (influenced by Salvador Dalí and Yves Tanguy) as well as drawings of an automatist nature; his works were already exceptionally striking in colour.

From January 1934 Mortensen was associated with the magazine *Linien*, edited by Vilhelm Bjerke-Petersen, and from September 1934 he became its co-editor with Bille. By 1935 he had turned against the more naturalistic kinds of Surrealism; he was inspired by two summers spent on the island of Bornholm to paint a series of pictures based on fantastic impressions of botanical forms, with vigorous interwoven patterns and rich colours. In 1937 he visited Paris, where he met André Breton, Max Ernst, Alberto Giacometti and Yves Tanguy, and in the same year he became joint organizer of an exhibition in Copenhagen that introduced contemporary European painting to Denmark, including works by Kandinsky, Joan Miró, Hans Arp, Ernst, Piet Mondrian and Paul Klee.

The deepening international tensions from 1938 were reflected in the increasing expressionism and violence of Mortensen's work. Following the German invasion of Denmark in 1940 he was one of the small circle of Danish artists including Bille, Asger Jorn and Egill Jacobsen who developed a proto-Cobra style based on the subconscious and automatism, with a seething chaos of colour and brushstrokes, in which recognizable imagery evoked a world of fantasy and nightmare, seen, for example, in *Sacrifice, Night* (1945; Copenhagen, Stat. Mus. Kst; see fig.). From 1942 to 1946 he was also active as a stage designer, his bold, highly patterned and colourful designs including sets and costumes for Stravinsky's *The Nightingale* and *The Soldier's Tale*.

After the war Mortensen changed his style to express the new more optimistic and constructive mood. In 1947

Richard Mortensen: *Sacrifice, Night*, oil on canvas, 1105×1505 mm, 1945 (Copenhagen, Statens Museum for Kunst)

he moved to Paris, where he soon joined the group of abstract artists centred round the Galerie Denise René, including Arp, Auguste Herbin, Alberto Magnelli, Serge Poliakoff and Victor Vasarely, and he began again to make totally abstract pictures with sharp-edged but sometimes fragmented forms. His works tended at first to be crowded and complex in composition, but by 1950–51 they contained large, clearly delineated areas of uniform pure colour, though often with perspectival ambiguities of overlapping and receding planes, for example *Terrorized Complementary Spaces* (1950; Humlebæk, Louisiana Mus.). Their linear structure was sometimes composed of straight lines and sometimes mainly of curves, while the colours were notable for their calm radiance and saturation. In 1950 he organized a large Kandinsky exhibition that toured Scandinavia. After 17 years in France, including periods in Normandy and the south, and at Ajaccio in Corsica, he returned in 1964 to Denmark and divided his time between Copenhagen and Ejby. His later works tend to be more curvilinear and irregular in their shapes and include a large mural for the University at Århus (1964).

BIBLIOGRAPHY
E. Johansson: *Richard Mortensen* (Copenhagen, 1962)
Richard Mortensen (exh. cat., Kolding, Kstmus. Trapholt, 1985)

RONALD ALLEY

Mortimer, John Hamilton (*b* Eastbourne, 17 Sept 1740; *d* London, 4 Feb 1779). English painter, draughtsman and etcher. He was closely involved with the Society of Artists of Great Britain, becoming its president in 1774, and his flamboyant personality, radical politics and romantic penchant for depictions of picturesque *banditti* led contemporaries to perceive him as a latter-day Salvator Rosa. Mortimer's works include portraiture, decorative interiors and book illustration, but he was first and foremost a history painter. Unlike most fellow artists in this genre, however, he derived much of his subject-matter from Anglo-Saxon history rather than from antiquity.

1. LIFE AND WORK.

(i) Early career and history paintings. Mortimer was the son of an excise officer, while his uncle, Roger Mortimer (1700–69), was a painter of portraits and altarpieces (e.g. *Moses and Aaron*, 1721; St Clement's, Hastings, E. Sussex); it may have been this example that first drew his nephew to the visual arts. By 1757 Mortimer was in London, working in Thomas Hudson's studio; his fellow pupils included Joseph Wright (i), who became a lifelong friend. Mortimer, characteristically, moved on before the end of his three-year term with Hudson—in 1759 he was studying with Robert Edge Pine. That year he won the earliest of his many awards: one for a life drawing at the St Martin's Lane Academy, another for a drawing after the Antique made in the sculpture gallery in Whitehall, London, established by Charles Lennox, 3rd Duke of Richmond. In 1760–62 he continued to carry off prizes at the St

Martin's Lane Academy. He also studied at William Shipley's Academy in the Strand, where he became friends with Thomas Jones. In 1763 he won second prize at the Society of Arts competition for a painting from English history, with *Edward the Confessor Stripping his Mother of her Effects* (San Marino, CA, Huntington A.G.); the following year he won first prize in the same competition for *St Paul Preaching to the Ancient Britons* (High Wycombe, Guildhall), an accomplished painting in the somewhat Italianate grand manner then in vogue. With this success he was marked out as one of the rising stars of English painting.

In 1765 Mortimer was elected a Fellow of the Society of Artists of Great Britain, to whose annual exhibitions he was a regular contributor; he became its vice-president in 1770 and president in 1774. He was thus very much a part of the art establishment of his day and supported the prevailing academic doctrine, one that acknowledged history to be the most prestigious of genres of painting. For most of his contemporaries this meant antiquity above all, and for that reason most artists thought it necessary to study in Rome. Mortimer stood almost entirely apart from this bias towards Neo-classicism: he never went to Italy, and only rarely did he depict scenes from Classical history or mythology, preferring instead to draw upon the Anglo-Saxon past. His *Edward the Confessor* and *St Paul* admittedly were painted for an annual competition specifically limited to events taken from British history; but even when not bound by such restrictions he continued to specialize in like subjects. The *Discovery of Prince Arthur's Tomb by the Inscription on the Leaden Cross* (1760s;

John Hamilton Mortimer: *Discovery of Prince Arthur's Tomb by the Inscription on the Leaden Cross*, pen and ink, 390×312 mm, 1760s (London, Victoria and Albert Museum)

untraced; sketch, Edinburgh, N.G.; finished drawing, London, V&A; see fig.), *King John Delivering the Magna Charta to the Barons* (1766; version, Belvoir Castle, Leics) and *Vortigern and Rowena* (exh. RA 1779; untraced; see Sunderland, 1988, fig. 202) are typical of his output in this vein, scenes that demonstrate the cupidity, folly or loss of power of earlier rulers. Mortimer's depictions of national history, undertaken at a time when Britain and its American colonies were drifting towards civil war, certainly implied anti-monarchist sentiments. When on occasion Mortimer did turn to Classical history for subject-matter, it was not in search of the 'noble simplicity and calm grandeur' that Johann Joachim Winckelmann identified as the *locus* of antique greatness. Instead Mortimer dwelt on defeat and spoliation, as in his *Belisarius* (exh. Soc. Artists 1772) and *Caius Marius on the Ruins of Carthage* (exh. Soc. Artists 1774), commissioned by Edward Sacheverell Pole to hang in his Saloon at Radburne Hall, Derbys (*in situ*; see Sunderland, 1988, figs 101, 103), or as in his *Sextus, the Son of Pompey, Applying to Erictho to Know the Fate of the Battle of Pharsalia* (exh. Soc. Artists 1771; untraced), a painting showing the horrific extremes of necrophiliac sorcery, of which a mezzotint was made in 1776 by Robert Dunkarton (1744–1811).

(ii) Banditti subjects and portraits. For Mortimer's contemporaries and, according to anecdote, for the artist also, his life and art were foreshadowed by the picaresque career of the 17th-century Italian painter Salvator Rosa, best known for his paintings and etchings of *banditti* and pirates. Some early commentators supposed this link between the two artists predestined, since Mortimer's own boyhood was spent on the Sussex coast, then a haven for smugglers and the setting for numerous encounters with the excise officers sent against them. The legends surrounding Rosa's life, and his depictions of raffish soldiers and wild gypsies on the Neapolitan shore, provided Mortimer with his model, and during the 1770s he fashioned a new genre of '*banditti*' subjects. A large number of such works survive, some in oils (e.g. *Bandit Taking up his Post*, c. 1775–8; Detroit, MI, Inst. A.), but many more are pen-and-ink drawings and include the large group collected by the connoisseur Richard Payne Knight (e.g. *Banditti Going Out*, *Banditti Returning* and *Soldier's Family*, all 1775; London, BM). Typically, these depict heavily muscled men, often bearded, garbed in bits of armour and carrying assorted weaponry, with a few loosely dressed women and children included for picturesque contrast. The settings are rocky landscapes, occasionally with a part-ruinous Classical building, wreathed in vegetation, in the background.

Mortimer also produced portraits, evidently with no great enthusiasm. Group portraits, such as his *Rev. Charles Everard and Two Others Playing Billiards* (c. 1769; Upton House, Warwicks, NT), are conventional adaptations of Johan Zoffany's conversation pieces; in his self-portraits, however, Mortimer found a more congenial vehicle for his talents. The pen-and-ink drawing, *Self-portrait in Character* (c. 1775–8; London, V&A; version in oils, Eastbourne, Towner A.G. & Local Hist. Mus.), shows him loosely dressed in Shakespearean garb, with dishevelled locks clustered around his face; the expression is animated, part quizzical, part challenging. During the 1770s Mortimer was also involved in several collaborative ventures, while his other works included scenes and characters inspired by Shakespeare, book illustration, 'progress' paintings in a vein of sentimental moral realism, and etchings. He collaborated with Thomas Jones, for example on the *Death of Orpheus* (exh. Soc. Artists 1770; version, New Haven, CT, Yale Cent. Brit. A.), and supplied figures for sets of marine pictures by Richard Paton (1717–91), including *Five Views of the Royal Dockyards* (*c.* 1770–75; London, Buckingham Pal., Royal Col.) and *Four Views of the Victory of the Russian Fleet over the Turks at Chesème Bay* (*c.* 1771; St Petersburg, Peter's Pal.). About 1771–3 Mortimer, James Durno (*c.* 1745–95), Jones and Francis Wheatley decorated the Saloon ceiling at Brocket Hall, Herts (recently rebuilt by James Paine), for Peniston Lamb, 1st Viscount Melbourne (1748–1819), with Rococo-style panels of arabesques and personifications influenced by the contemporary work of Robert Adam (i) and Giovanni Battista Cipriani. As for Mortimer's interest in Shakespeare, this had begun early—for example a *Scene in 'King John'* (exh. Soc. Artists 1768; London, Garrick Club)—and in 1775 he etched and published 12 heads of characters from Shakespeare's plays, including *Lear*, *Ophelia* and *Caliban*, made after his own drawings (London, V&A, and elsewhere). The heads are fantastic, almost to the point of caricature—a mode in which Mortimer also practised from time to time, for example in his Hogarth-like pen-and-ink *Choir and Orchestra* (Windsor Castle, Royal Lib.). He also worked in book illustration, designing 41 of the frontispieces for John Bell's extensive series, the *Poets of Great Britain* (1777–82); engravers on this project included Charles Grignion.

2. CHARACTER, REPUTATION AND INFLUENCE. Mortimer led a giddy, even dangerous life: ship wrecks narrowly avoided, a tussle in which a swordstroke nearly cost him a hand, and various feats of strenuous athleticism interspersed with equally strenuous bouts of drunkenness. His marriage in 1775 is believed to have tempered these excesses, though there are some signs of change in his art before this date. In 1774 he exhibited at the Society of Artists four pictures under the heading *The Progress of Vice* (two untraced; two in priv. col.; see Sunderland, 1986, figs 138, 142). The following year he exhibited a matched quartet, *The Progress of Virtue* (London, Tate). The latter group in particular is cast in a form of sentimental realism that suggests the influence of Jean-Baptiste Greuze and is quite different from Mortimer's previous work. Three years later he defected to the Royal Academy, celebrating his election as ARA by publishing a series of 15 etchings dedicated to the Academy's president, Joshua Reynolds; eight works by Mortimer were shown there posthumously in the exhibition of 1779.

Mortimer's style, both in his oil paintings and in his drawings, is fairly restrained: surprisingly so, given the often unconventional, even radical nature of his subject-matter. His portraits, as one might expect, are the least original in composition; for his *banditti* and other exotic subjects Mortimer's compositions are more dynamic. But his paint surfaces remained elegantly calm, the colours low in key and close in value. More than one critic has likened

Mortimer's paint to clay. According to contemporary anecdote, his drawings were dashed off with breathtaking facility and speed. But they are not the bold washes of such an artist as George Romney nor the cursory notations of a Johann Heinrich Füseli, both contemporaries of his. Instead, Mortimer's drawings are tightly finished, and an elaborate system of crosshatching is used to capture and fix the forms. Romantic, idiosyncratic, even demoniac subjects are depicted in both paintings and drawings in a style that is rational and refined. Tension between subject-matter and style is one of the more powerful qualities of Mortimer's art. He had no pupils and no close followers. His impact on English art was restricted, although it affected his close friend Joseph Wright (i), and was mainly exerted by way of encouraging other artists to explore exotic and emotionally charged subject-matter. Even the archetype of the Romantic artist, which Mortimer had helped to create, was one that found its subsequent expression in Britain more among poets than among painters.

BIBLIOGRAPHY
A. Cunningham: *The Lives of the Most Eminent British Painters, Sculptors, and Architects* (London, 1832), v, pp. 186–203
G. Grigson: 'Painters of the Abyss', *Archit. Rev.*, cvii (1950), pp. 215–20
John Hamilton Mortimer, ARA: 1740–1779 (exh. cat., ed. B. Nicolson; Eastbourne, Towner A.G. & Local Hist. Mus.; London, Kenwood House; 1968)
J. Sunderland: 'John Hamilton Mortimer and Salvator Rosa', *Burl. Mag.*, cxii (1970), pp. 520–31
——: 'Mortimer, Pine and Some Political Aspects of English Painting', *Burl. Mag.*, cxvi (1974), pp. 317–26
——: 'John Hamilton Mortimer's "Progress of Vice"', *Burl. Mag.*, cxviii (1976), pp. 768–71
——: 'John Hamilton Mortimer: His Life and Works', *Walpole Soc.*, lii (1986) [whole issue]
PETER WALCH

Mortimer & Hunt. *See under* STORR, PAUL.

Mortlake Tapestry Factory. English tapestry factory on the River Thames at Mortlake (nr London) in Surrey. It was established in 1619 by Sir Francis Crane (*c.* 1579–1636), on the instigation of James I and his son Charles, Prince of Wales (later Charles I), and inspired by the workshops set up by Henry IV in Paris. The workshop initially wove copies of old cartoons and was run by Flemish workers including Philip de Maecht (*d* 1655), who was appointed master weaver. Charles took great interest in the factory and organized the purchase of the *Acts of the Apostles* cartoons (London, V&A) by Raphael, from which several sets were woven (*see* ENGLAND, fig. 90). FRANCIS CLEYN was employed at the factory to create new tapestry designs and in 1626 was appointed chief designer. Despite the patronage of the Crown and such eminent patrons as George Villiers, Marquis of Buckingham (later 1st Duke of Buckingham), the factory had financial difficulties. With the accession of Charles I (1625) the situation improved slightly, although when Crane's younger brother, Captain Richard Crane (*d* 1645), took over the works in 1636 the factory sank further into debt, and in 1638 it was purchased by the Crown and styled the King's Works. The factory suffered very badly during the Civil War (1642–6) when it lost the royal patronage and the workers sought work elsewhere. Although the Council of State under Oliver Cromwell ordered such tapestry series as the *Story of Abraham* (London, V&A), production was on a much reduced scale. Things did not improve with the Restoration (1660): Charles II took little interest in the factory despite the efforts of Ralph Montagu (later 1st Duke of Montagu) to attract the King's patronage, and the competition from such foreign factories as the Gobelins of France and the new independent factories set up in London by such ex-Mortlake workers as William Benood (*fl* 1645–75) proved to be too much for the concern, which finally closed in 1703. (For further discussion *see* ENGLAND, §XI, 1.)

BIBLIOGRAPHY

J. E. Anderson: *A Short Account of the Tapestry Works at Mortlake* (London, 1894)

A. F. Kendrick: 'An English Tapestry', *Burl. Mag.*, xxxiii (1918), pp. 158–63

W. G. Thomson: *A History of Tapestry* (London, 1930)

M. E. Jones: *British and American Tapestries* (Hadleigh, 1952)

A. Haynes: 'The Mortlake Tapestry Factory', *Hist. Today*, xxiv (1974), pp. 32–40

DIANA FOWLE

Morto da Feltre. *See under* LUZZO, LORENZO.

Morton, Ree (*b* Ossining, NY, 3 Aug 1936; *d* Chicago, 30 April 1977). American conceptual artist, draughtwoman and sculptor. She trained but never practised as a nurse. In 1960 she took her first art classes at the Jacksonville Museum, Jacksonville, FL. Morton then attended the University of Rhode Island, Kingston (1965–8), where she received her BFA, and the Tyler School of Art, Temple University, Philadelphia (MFA, 1970). Having first exhibited at the McLennon Community College, Waco, TX, in 1969, in 1970 she showed work in the Contemporary American Sculpture Annual at the Whitney Museum of American Art in New York. In 1972 Morton moved to New York. In her work she explored an inter-disciplinary approach in installations. She acknowledged the influences of Robert Morris (ii), Bruce Nauman, Eva Hesse, Louise Bourgeois, Claes Oldenberg and Richard Artschwager. Her formal concerns centred on spaces, enclosures and boundaries and included pictures, found objects, sculptures and her signature trait—delineations of spaces with dotted lines, usually tape, on gallery walls and floors in loosely ordered arrangements. In many of her installations there are strong mythological and metaphorical suggestions, evocative of Native American ceremonies, mysterious rituals and Japanese gardens. Her installation *Sister Perpetua's Lie* (first exh. 1973, Philadelphia, U. PA, ICA) was inspired by Raymond Roussel's *Impressions of Africa* (1910), a complex and descriptive account of African peoples' ceremonies and ritual, and in particular by its narrative style and weaving together of bizarre events. Having rejected a conventional life for an intense involvement in art, Morton, a mother of three children, was a role-model for many American women artists. Tragically she died prematurely in a car accident.

BIBLIOGRAPHY

Ree Morton: Retrospective, 1971–77 (exh. cat., New York, New Mus. Contemp. A.; Boulder, U. CO, Mus.; Buffalo, NY, Albright–Knox A.G.; 1980) [incl. critical overview by A. Schwartzman and K. Thomas and friends' reminiscences]

Ree Morton: A New Acquisition: 'Signs of Love' (exh. cat., New York, Whitney, 1990)

Moryn Claessone. *See under* REYMERSWAELE, MARINUS VAN.

Mosaic. Closely spaced polychrome or monochrome particles (tesserae) of near uniform size embedded in a binder, such as mortar or cement. Mosaic has been used as a decorative medium on walls, floors and columns for over 5000 years. A wide range of natural and artificial materials may be used for the tesserae: pebbles, hardstone, shells, vitreous paste, terracotta, mother-of-pearl, enamels and turquoise. The shapes are usually fairly regular: rectangles, squares, triangles or trapezoids. They normally vary in size from a few millimetres to more than 1 cm sq. The terms 'tile mosaic' and 'mosaic faience' are applied to a technique used in the decoration of Islamic buildings from the 11th century onwards, in which tiles of different colours were cut to form a design (*see* ISLAMIC ART, §II, 9(iv)). For the inlay technique of *opus sectile*, where stone pieces were cut into pattern shapes, *see* ROME, ANCIENT, §VI, 1. For Florentine mosaic, *see* FLORENCE, §IV, 1(ii)(b).

For colour plates for this article *see* vol. 21.

I. Materials and techniques. II. Historical survey. III. Conservation.

I. Materials and techniques.

1. Western world. 2. Pre-Columbian Americas.

1. WESTERN WORLD.

(i) Classical. (ii) Post-Antique and medieval. (iii) The Renaissance to the 20th century.

(i) Classical. The term 'mosaic' is taken from the Greek: mosaic pieces were called *abakiskoi* by the Greeks and *abaculi*, *tesserae* or *tessellae* by the Romans. The list of artisans in Diocletian's *Edict on Prices* (AD 301) distinguishes between the *tessellarii*, who laid mosaic pavements, and the *museiarii*, the makers of wall and vault mosaics. The latter term was universally adopted to include both types of artisans in the post-Antique period.

An understanding of how mosaics were produced in antiquity is based almost entirely on the surviving physical evidence (apart from the *Edict on Prices* and some passages in Vitruvius' *On Architecture*) and on the epigraphic evidence from various mosaic projects. It is generally believed that the ancient floor mosaics were produced *in situ*, as suggested, for example, by the archaeological evidence from the 4th-century AD nymphaeum at Neapolis (now Nabeul, Tunisia), where chippings and strips of the polychrome marble used in the pavement were discovered on site. A further proof of this direct method of production is found in the Late Antique relief from Ostia, which may illustrate the *in situ* production of a floor mosaic: it shows the master mosaicist directing two porters who carry sacks of mosaic material, and two mosaicists who cut tesserae on the ground. In fact, it has been suggested that corporations of mosaicists were responsible for the pavements in private buildings, as indicated by inscriptions that include such terms as *ex officina* followed by the name of the artisan (see Balmelle and Damon).

As stone dominated the early history of mosaic production, it is not surprising that its natural colours provided the basic range of hues for the artist. The practice of using stone or marble for certain parts of a mosaic—faces, hands

1. Mosaic emblemata depicting doves drinking, 1st century BC (Rome, Museo Capitolino)

and feet—continued into the Middle Ages in both the East (i.e. Byzantium) and the West.

For the pebble mosaics at Olynthos (*c.* 5th century BC), fairly uniform stones were selected with diameters from 10 to 20 mm (*see* OLYNTHOS, §2). The pebble mosaics from Pella (4th century BC) are made of natural pebbles (*see* PELLA (ii), §2), but in places the mosaicists found it necessary to use strips of lead to outline some of the inner markings and contours. Shaped tesserae from the 3rd century BC are found in the House of Ganymede at Morgantina, Italy, and tessellated mosaic pavements had gradually superseded pebble floors by the end of that century.

While the majority of mosaic pavements in antiquity were laid directly on site, a number of floors display emblemata, which are inset panels of images or ornamental motifs made of fine, precisely set tesserae that could be produced in another location. Emblemata were normally preset on trays of stone or terracotta, which were then embedded in the setting-bed. They are usually of very high quality, as may be seen in the 1st-century BC copy of the mosaic by Sosos of doves drinking (Rome, Mus. Capitolino; see fig. 1).

The technique known as *opus vermiculatum* is so-called from the wormlike look of the close-set rows of undulating tesserae; it first appears in Alexandrian floor mosaics of the late 3rd–early 2nd century BC (*see* ALEXANDRIA, fig. 2). The most famous example of this type of work is the late 2nd-century BC *Alexander* mosaic depicting the battle of Alexander and Darius at Issus found in the House of the Faun at Pompeii (*see* POMPEII, §V and fig. 7). Mosaics of this sort were undoubtedly luxury items.

Glass tesserae first appeared on floor and wall mosaics between the 3rd and 1st centuries BC. They brought unlimited colour possibilities to this art form, but their brittleness made them unsuitable for floor mosaics.

(ii) Post-Antique and medieval. The character of mosaic was altered irrevocably by the widespread use of gold and silver tesserae, and with these craftsmen developed considerable practical experience in how mosaics could serve the laws of optics. Glass for this kind of tesserae had a piece of metal foil applied on to or, better, embedded in it. Pieces of gold leaf were used, or, in the case of silver tesserae, pieces of silver or tin. Both types of tesserae impart a luminous, reflective quality of high intensity; they

were usually used to suggest the idea of light emanating from God (see ICON, colour pl. II, fig. 3). Gold was first used in floor and vault decoration in late antiquity; one of the earliest instances of the use of gold to depict the light of God is found in the representation of Christ as Helios in a 3rd-century mausoleum under St Peter's.

Coloured glass tesserae were prepared by glassmakers, who employed a mixture of sand, soda or potash, and lime, with varying amounts of metallic oxides to obtain the different hues of glass. A number of ancient and medieval treatises have survived that discuss how to colour and manufacture glass tesserae. The 12th-century monk Theophilus, for example, described this process in his treatise *De diversis artibus*. He stated that sheets of glass were prepared using the 'muff' technique of glassmaking, and that these were later cut into the appropriate shapes and sizes. The documents for the 14th-century mosaics on the façade of Orvieto Cathedral corroborate his assertion that some medieval glassmakers used the 'muff' technique rather than casting to make sheets of glass. However, two 12th-century *linguae* or tongues of cast glass, intended for the mosaics at S Marco, Venice, have survived to this day, so production methods obviously varied from site to site.

The provision of the other tesserae also varied. The mosaic decoration of AD 965 in the mosque at Córdoba, for example, was probably executed by Greek mosaicists, and the emperor Nikephoros II Phokas (*reg* 963–9) sent a substantial quantity of tesserae with the workers. After the conquest of Constantinople (now Istanbul) in 1204 the Venetians sent tesserae and other pieces of stone and marble back to Venice, presumably for use at S Marco. That mosaic tesserae were in short supply at certain periods, even in Constantinople, may be deduced from sources that inform us that, for the decoration of the Nea Ekklesia (destr.) within the Great Palace there, Basil I (867–86) had mosaic tesserae and marble slabs removed from Justinian's mausoleum at the church of the Holy Apostles (destr.). On other occasions, various ad hoc solutions were found. For instance, some of the materials for the 11th-century mosaics in the cathedral of St Sophia in Kiev (*see* KIEV, fig. 3), such as coloured glass tesserae, may have been produced locally in a workshop that included a glass furnace. However, the gold tesserae at Kiev are cut with such precision that it has been suggested that they were produced elsewhere, perhaps in Constantinople, where the manufacture of such tesserae was a long and established practice (see LAZAREV). But tesserae may also have been cut, if not produced, *in situ* for a number of medieval mosaic schemes; new evidence shows that this was the case at Monreale during the late 12th century (see ANDALORO).

The evidence from Orvieto indicates that glass tesserae were produced and cut on site there. In fact, between 1321 and 1390, cathedral officials at Orvieto paid for the construction and maintenance of at least one furnace, which was near the bishop's palace across from the cathedral. The officials also sent to Venice for supplies of coloured glass; in addition, tesserae were produced at a small forest glassworks at Monteleone, near Orvieto. By contrast, in Pisa during the early 14th century itinerant merchants supplied cathedral officials with glass and stone for the apse mosaic.

There has been much debate as to how mosaics were produced during the Middle Ages. Until the late 1950s it was thought by some scholars that they were created by the indirect method, in which the tesserae were attached to a cartoon in the studio and then transferred to the wall. While this method was often used for post-medieval mosaics (particularly in the 19th century), a survey carried out in 1957–9 of the unfinished mosaics of the church of the Pammakaristos (now the Fethiye mosque; *see* ISTAN-BUL, fig. 12) led Byzantine scholars to revise their opinions in favour of the direct method, in which artists did preliminary drawings on the wall and then set the tesserae directly on to this surface. It is now generally agreed that both Byzantine and Western mosaics were produced in this manner.

A reasonable amount of information about underdrawings and the composition of mosaic setting-beds is provided by analyses of various mosaic projects. The setting-beds were usually built up of two or three layers of mortar, and in the case of walls and vaults the supporting surfaces were reinforced with iron nails. The documentation for the mosaics on the façade of Orvieto Cathedral makes frequent reference to the purchase of materials for the mortar, as well as to reinforcing nails and clamps for the tops of the gabled surfaces. Nails and clamps have been found at the tops of walls and vaults in a number of medieval mosaic projects in both East and West.

To guide the mosaicists in the setting of the tesserae it was a common practice to paint detailed preparatory drawings directly on to the setting-bed. There is, however, extant physical evidence to suggest that sometimes both Byzantine and Western mosaicists executed a preliminary compositional sketch either on the masonry itself or on one of the preliminary coats of plaster (*see* SINOPIA). The Orvietan evidence reveals an interesting and somewhat different approach to this phase of the work, one that may reflect a moment of transition in mosaic production that would lead ultimately to its transformation during the Renaissance. The documents suggest that a CARTOON or auxiliary drawing was used in conjunction with the *sinopia* to establish the main elements of the composition. Regrettably neither the auxiliary drawings nor a preparatory sketch have been preserved at Orvieto. Iconographic guides and motif books were also used in the early planning stages, as evidenced by the use of a manuscript of the Cotton Genesis type to complete some of the atrium mosaics at S Marco in Venice during the early 13th century.

It seems that the development of wall and vault mosaics in antiquity led to experimentation with the spacing and angling of tesserae (see NORDHAGEN, 1976). Floor mosaics required a close, solid setting, but this was not such a key factor for wall and vault mosaics so the artisans could adopt a much looser approach to the setting. Between the 5th century AD and the 8th, tesserae were placed quite far apart and set at irregular angles to one another, so that the overall effect is one of diverse facets and angles. This may be seen, for example, in the mosaics of the 7th-century chapel of S Venanzio in the Lateran Baptistery, Rome.

2. Deësis mosaic (detail), south gallery, Hagia Sophia, Istanbul, c. 1260–1300

The mosaics produced in the Byzantine empire during the Palaiologan period, such as the Deësis mosaic (c. 1260–1300; see fig. 2 and colour pl. III, fig. 2) at Hagia Sophia, Constantinople, illustrate the care and precision used to set the tiny particles of stone and marble for the faces and hands. In general, Palaiologan mosaicists used small tesserae in their work, and they abandoned hard contours and outlines to achieve effects of soft modelling and subtle transitions of colour. They would also touch up the finished result with paint, if they felt it was needed. In the Renaissance, in accordance with Giorgio Vasari's idea that mosaic was painting for eternity, the tesserae were set as closely as possible, to minimize the abrupt transitions in colour and form that had been so highly prized by earlier mosaicists.

Another matter for debate is how mosaic workshops were organized in the Middle Ages. Deichmann has suggested that Diocletian's *Edict on Prices* cannot be used as a guide, and indeed one medieval reference, a Carolingian manuscript in Leiden, describes a different system of production. It distinguishes between the *pictor*, who supervised the laying of the mortar and possibly the initial drawings on the wall, and the *artifex*, who did the laying-out and setting of the tesserae on the plaster bed.

The evidence from 14th-century work at Orvieto confirms Kitzinger's hypothesis (1960) of a hierarchical division of labour, with the master mosaicists and their assistants working together with a team of glasscutters, as well as collaborating with master glaziers employed by the Orvietan officials. Each gable of mosaic was carried out by one or two highly skilled artisans, who were assisted by several individuals on the more routine tasks, such as the setting of backgrounds, other uniform surfaces, landscape details or ornament. Another group of craftsmen was engaged in the preparation of the setting-bed and in the preparation and cutting of the tesserae. These individuals were paid either a daily or a piece-work rate, and they had little financial security should construction work be discontinued at any time. A third team took charge of the manufacture of the glass tesserae, maintaining the furnaces and ensuring that the master mosaicists were supplied with sufficient material. These master glassmakers produced the glass tesserae at their own expense, although they were also granted certain fringe benefits, such as a house, some bedding and the use of a furnace. At the top of this hierarchy were the master mosaicists, who enjoyed the highest wages and the best conditions of employment, including the luxury of a negotiated contract and a *lodo*, or independent assessment by committee, to determine the final price of their work.

However, the 12th-century inscription on the mosaics in the church of the Nativity in Bethlehem names as executant one Ephraim, painter and mosaicist, thus implying that in some decorative schemes an artist might carry out most of the tasks himself, from the drawing of the images to the setting of the tesserae.

Useful information on the relative costs of producing a mosaic as against those involved in fresco production is provided by the Orvietan evidence. Between 1359 and 1364 comparative costs of production suggest that the mosaics were approximately four times as expensive to manufacture, so that a decision to use mosaic rather than fresco would have had important cost implications for prospective patrons.

(iii) The Renaissance to the 20th century. Mosaic lost its popularity in Italy at the beginning of the Renaissance. Essentially, it became an imitation of painting, and the unique optical possibilities of the medium were not used to best advantage, particularly since the artists, striving for pictorial realism, rebelled against the use of gold. In addition, the distinction between the artist responsible for the project and the setters of the tesserae became more pronounced, and the preparatory work became divorced from the execution. The artist submitted his cartoon and left its transposition to artisans, as occurred in Venice during the 15th and 16th centuries. On-the-spot decisions about setting angles and distances between tesserae were no longer the concern of a master mosaicist.

3. Mosaic designed by Raphael, dome (1516) of the Chigi Chapel, S Maria del Popolo, Rome

Many of the great painters of the Renaissance made designs for mosaics—Raphael, for instance, designed decorations representing God the Father, angels and the seven planets (executed in 1516 by the Venetian Luigi di Pace) for the dome of the Chigi Chapel in S Maria del Popolo

4. Mosaic by Antoni Gaudí made up of fragments of glass and ceramics, from Park Güell, Barcelona, 1900–14

in Rome (see fig. 3). During the late 16th century the dome of St Peter's in Rome was lined with mosaic. This location gradually became an important centre for the manufacture of mosaics, and it remained so in the late 20th century, together with the mosaic studios at Spilimbergo, Ravenna and Venice.

During the 19th century a renewed sense of historicism and an interest in craft techniques led to a demand for mosaic. Tesserae were mass-produced in workshops such as those of Antonio Salviati in Venice or August Wagner in Germany: both used the indirect system of setting tesserae on a prepared base, so that an entire mosaic could be produced in the workshop and then shipped to its final destination. In the 20th century surface texture and mixed materials returned to favour. Antoni Gaudí at the Park Güell (1900–14), Barcelona, for example, arranged pieces of broken glazed tiles with fragments of glass bottles and china plates as a decorative coating over walls and other structures (see fig. 4 and colour pl. IV, fig. 2). Mexican artists, particularly Juan O'Gorman and Diego Rivera, used extensive areas of mosaic, made largely of stone, to cover large, unbroken architectural surfaces. Later in the century, mosaic workshops in Rome and Ravenna promoted the use of mosaic as independent 'panels' or on walls and vaults. The mosaics produced for the 1988 exhibition in the Castello Estense at Mésola were manufactured by artists using the direct method: cubes of glass and stone, shells and pieces of mirrors were combined to exploit the aesthetic possibilities of different materials, shapes, sizes, setting angles and distances.

See also §II, 5 below.

2. PRE-COLUMBIAN AMERICAS. The workers who produced Pre-Columbian mosaics used obsidian, garnet, quartz, beryl, malachite, jadeite, marcasite, gold, mother-of-pearl and shell for their work, but turquoise was preferred above all as a material that conferred prestige and status on the wearer. These various materials were laid on objects made of wood, stone, gold, shell, pottery and leather and were held in place by a vegetal pitch or some kind of cement. In the turquoise-covered mask of Quetzalcóatl (14th–15th centuries; London, Mus. Mankind; see colour pl. IV, fig. 1) tiny pieces of the precious stone have been encrusted all over the surface, cabochon turquoises have been laid on the nose and in lines around the eyes and mouth, and shell inlay represents the eyes and teeth (see also MESOAMERICA, PRE-COLUMBIAN, fig. 41). Mosaic was also used for exterior wall-cladding. At MITLA in Oaxaca, for example, striking geometrical and animal patterns were produced on the 14th-century palaces by fitting together small stones of different shapes and sizes: each stone was cut for the spot it occupies, and some are more deeply embedded than others so that the designs stand out in sharp relief.

See also §II, 6 below.

II. Historical survey.

Mosaic was used to decorate architectural surfaces c. 3500 BC. The walls of the Sumerian sanctuary of Eanna at URUK, Iraq, were decorated in a mosaic-like technique with terracotta cones pressed into surfaces of mud brick until only their bases showed. The cones helped to consolidate and strengthen the wall by providing protection from the elements, and they also had a decorative function in that they were arranged in geometric patterns of triangles, lozenges and zigzags resembling woven textiles.

Actual tesserae (small squares cut from flat plates of stone and shell) were combined with inlay work in the decoration of the Temple of Ninkhursag at Tel Al'Abeid in Sumeria during the same period (3000 BC). The wooden columns and some of the walls of the temple were coated with bitumen: small pieces of stone and shell, which had copper loops attached to their backs, were then pressed into the adhesive. Other walls in the temple were decorated with a frieze of birds and animals cut from shell and limestone, set against an overall background of mosaic. A combination of stone and tile inlays with tesserae was also used in Egypt around 2000 BC, but the technique seems to have had little influence on later developments in mosaic.

The use of coloured stones to decorate a floor first occurred in Greece and Asia Minor. In the town of GORDION, near Ankara, houses from the 8th century BC have been excavated that have pebble floors set in mortar. The motifs used include swastikas, lozenges, interlocking triangles and the key pattern, all of which were to become standard elements in the mosaicist's repertory throughout antiquity. Here, however, they are combined in a random fashion: the concept of the floor mosaic as a unified, centralized composition apparently did not emerge until the 5th century BC.

1. Western world. 2. Pre-Columbian Americas.

1. WESTERN WORLD.

(i) Ancient Greece. (ii) Ancient Rome. (iii) Early Christian and Byzantine. (iv) Medieval. (v) The Renaissance to the 20th century.

(i) Ancient Greece. The first major stage in the development of mosaic art in antiquity occurred in Greece, where the pebble mosaic (*see* §I, 1 above) emerged as an important art form. Pebble mosaics are preserved in large numbers at two sites in particular, Olynthos and Pella in northern Greece. Those at Olynthos, datable to the 5th century BC, feature rectangular or circular compositions, with simple borders and figured friezes arranged around a central element or figural panel illustrating subjects from Classical mythology (*see* OLYNTHOS, §2). The use of light and dark pebbles in this location is quite sophisticated. The forms are created with white or slightly tinted stones against a dark ground of black or blue–black; smaller black pebbles serve as outlines. The pebbles are uniform in size and not shaped in any way. A number of the compositions feature an arrangement of figures that interlock and overlap, with some emphasis on detail.

The pebble mosaics at Pella are considerably later than those at Olynthos, since they are datable to the 4th century BC (*see* PELLA (ii), §2). A distinct difference in the approach to floor mosaics has taken place here: the mosaic is conceived as a picture placed on the floor rather than

5. Mosaic *trompe l'oeil* pavement of an unswept floor (detail), in the style of Sosos, from the Aventine Hill, 2nd century AD (Rome, Vatican)

remaining a flat ornamental or figured design on the surface. These works reveal a more plastic sense of form, as evidenced in the wider range of colour and the use of shading to suggest modelling on the bodies and drapery. A technical development in the treatment of the pebbles aided these efforts at greater naturalism: some of the stones were painted in desired tones—in this instance, green and red—and they have a depression sunk in the middle to protect the layer of paint. In one example the mosaicist sought to give greater definition to the forms by using strips of terracotta or lead wire for some of the contours and inner details, and in another, curls of terracotta were formed for hair.

The introduction of shaped tesserae was gradual. The floor in the Temple of Zeus at Olympia, for example, is composed largely of pebbles, although cut stones are used in those parts of the figures where greater definition was needed. Since this floor has been variously dated from the 4th century BC to the 2nd, it is difficult to know if this is the first instance of the use of shaped tesserae. In other locations, pebbles were chipped into tiny pieces for areas where greater detail was needed, thereby permitting a much closer fit of the individual units. An example of this is found in the 3rd-century BC mosaics of the House of Ganymede at Morgantina, Italy. Tesserae of different materials—stone, baked clay and glass—also provided a new range of colours for mosaic workshops.

By the beginning of the 3rd century BC the transition to tessellated floors had taken place independently in several centres. A high level of technical proficiency was soon reached, as shown by the mosaic (Alexandria, Gr.-Rom. Mus.) signed by the artist SOPHILOS and depicting a woman in military dress (see ALEXANDRIA, §2(iii) and fig. 2). It is the earliest known example of an emblema in the technique of *opus vermiculatum* (see §I, 1 above).

A century later the art of mosaic had spread to the main Hellenistic commercial centres. The literary evidence indicates that Pergamon was particularly famous for its mosaics, and according to Pliny the younger, SOSOS, one of the most proficient mosaicists of antiquity, worked in this city. None of his mosaics survives, although numerous replicas provide some sense of his achievements. Pliny recounted the artist's superior ability to create *trompe l'oeil* effects, in particular in his representations of the unswept floor (*asarotos oikos*) of a banquet hall and of doves drinking. These were widely imitated and adapted throughout Italy and elsewhere (see fig. 5; see also fig. 1 above).

On the island of Delos the houses of wealthy merchants were richly decorated with elaborately worked polychrome motifs set as emblemata (see §I, 1 above) against a background of coarser tesserae. Two of these 2nd-century mosaics depict Dionysiac figures riding on a tiger and a panther, their forms set off against a dark background (see DELOS, §3). Made of stone and glass tesserae, these emblemata usually resemble the illusionistic effects of painting; indeed, many of them are direct imitations of actual paintings. The mosaicist used very small tesserae and paid great attention to fine detail, supplementing the colours of the stone with bits of glass. Emblemata such as these were much sought after, as evidenced by the many adaptations and copies of work by Sosos.

(ii) Ancient Rome. The earliest mosaics of Italy continue in the Hellenistic tradition. One of the most famous is the *Alexander Mosaic*, depicting the battle of Alexander and Darius at Issus datable to the late 2nd century BC (see POMPEII, §V). This is the largest of all known works, measuring about 3.13×5.82 m, and occupying the whole floor of a room specially designed to fit it. The representation of masses of figures engaged in battle, shown in violent movement through the use of dramatic foreshortening, and the concern with complex spatial recession reveal a sophisticated use of *opus vermiculatum*. The mosaicist has sought to imitate the illusionism of contemporary painting, and the work was clearly meant to be looked at as a picture, for it can be appreciated from one angle alone. In fact, it may even be a copy of a painting of *c.* 300 BC, perhaps the famous picture by Philoxenos of Eretria. It seems likely that it was carried out by Greek artists and either imported to Pompeii from one of the great Hellenistic centres or, as its large size suggests, made locally. Works such as this are further evidence that fine mosaics were highly prized, and their placement was designed to show them off to best advantage. A mosaic of this size and quality was undoubtedly a luxury item because of the skill, time and resources required to produce it. This is certainly evident in the mosaic depicting the Nile from the period of Sulla (82–79 BC; see PRAENESTE, fig. 2): the vast panoramic landscape is filled with human figures, architecture and the animals of Egypt.

The practice of mosaic became much more widespread under the Romans, extending throughout the Empire to Spain, France, Britain, Germany (see colour pl. III, fig. 1), North Africa and Syria. As Dunbabin has suggested, the subsequent history of mosaics in the Roman period can be seen as a series of attempts to break away from the limitations inherent in the traditional ways of making them. Different methods of designing a floor were devised that were simpler and more practical. Precious emblemata were not meant to be subjected to hard wear, and although in Italy they were used occasionally as luxury items for some time (e.g. the polychrome emblemata of the 2nd century AD used to great effect at Hadrian's Villa; see TIVOLI, §2(iii)), floors of purely ornamental designs were far more common. These were made by local schools of craftsmen who specialized in such work; other artists produced emblemata for export (as, for example, the imported Italian emblemata in the 2nd-century AD pavement at Brive-la-Gaillarde, France). Ornamental patterns, usually in black and white and not polychrome, were adopted as substitutes for emblemata. Houses of every sort displayed these designs, until eventually artists began to cover the entire surface of the floor with patterns. In time, the tesserae became coarser and increasingly limited in colour to black and white, probably out of consideration of the cost in laying the floor. Some of the best examples of this style datable from the 2nd century AD are preserved at Ostia, which was once the port city of Rome (see OSTIA, §2 and fig. 4, and ROME, ANCIENT, fig. 93). Masterpieces were still produced on occasion in Late Antiquity, as in the mosaics (early 4th century AD) of the Villa Imperiale at Casale near Piazza Armerina in Sicily (see PIAZZA ARMERINA, §2).

Mosaic was also used for surfaces other than floors in the Hellenistic period. In particular, it was employed to striking effect on garden architecture, such as walls and vaults of fountains, niches and grottoes. Examples of this work may be seen in the mansions at Herculaneum and Pompeii, datable to the 1st century AD (*see* HERCULANEUM, §V, and POMPEII, §V). The archaeological evidence indicates that mosaic was gradually introduced into large architectural spaces as well, such as in the vaults of bathhouses.

(iii) Early Christian and Byzantine. The practice of using mosaic for religious subjects appeared in the 3rd century AD: the Temple of Mithras at Ostia has a niche mosaic, and the mausoleum under St Peter's, Rome, has a representation of Christ as Helios. It has been suggested that the cultic mosaic took over the function of the Roman cult statue during this period, perhaps because mosaic seemed better suited to express the new religious ideals (see Nordhagen, 1976).

Among the earliest Christian wall mosaics in Rome are those in the mausoleum of Constantina (now the church of S Costanza; *see* ROME, §V, 18(i)) built *c.* 320–30; only those on the fascia round the vault of the ambulatory survive. A 17th-century drawing by Giovanni Ciampini records that Old and New Testament scenes were portrayed around the dome, but the surviving panels feature pastoral or Dionysiac motifs and other pagan subjects. Obviously a specifically Christian pictorial programme for buildings of this size and complexity had not yet been devised; in lieu of that, a Dionysiac programme was chosen because the allusion to the symbolism of wine could be interpreted in the light of Christian doctrine.

The earliest known apse mosaic dates to the early 5th century and is found at S Pudenziana. Owing to extensive restoration over the years, it is difficult to assess the style of the whole. The iconographic programme features a symbolic representation of Jerusalem, with Christ flanked by the apostles, and two female figures that denote the Church (*ecclesia ex gentibus*) and Synagogue (*ecclesia ex circumsione*). This composition marks a transitional stage in the development of Christian iconographic programmes, and the subject did not become part of the usual repertory of images.

Extant mosaic programmes in locations such as Rome, Ravenna, Naples and Milan indicate the presence of workshops with high artistic standards. Gradually, a systematic approach was taken to the programme of Christian structures. In cupolas, the centre was reserved for depictions of Christ on the cross. In apses, the dominant trend was to show standing figures of Christ, the apostles and venerated saints. The triumphal arch leading to the apse of the church was also an important location for apocalyptic scenes. Scenes from the Old and New Testaments were used on nave walls, as in the decoration of S Maria Maggiore, Rome (432–40), and the church of S Apollinare Nuovo, Ravenna (*c.* 520–50). At times, church exteriors were covered with mosaic, either directly above the entrance, in the narthex or vestibule, or else on the upper part of the façade, as in the case of the now lost 5th-century mosaics of the *Twenty-four Elders of the Apocalypse* at Old Saint Peter's and S Paolo fuori le Mura, Rome, or

6. Mosaic of *Emperor Justinian and his Retinue*, from the apse of S Vitale, Ravenna, *c.* AD 546–7

the badly damaged 6th-century mosaic of the Transfiguration on the exterior of the cathedral at Parenzo (Poreč). Even the floors of churches were decorated with mosaic, as in the cases of Aquileia and Grado (1st half of the 4th century), where scenes of the *Good Shepherd* and *Jonah and the Whale* are shown in combination with other Christian symbols. These pictorial compositions were gradually abandoned, however, in favour of much simpler motifs, for example the crosses used on church floors in Palestine from the late 6th century and early 7th.

Ravenna became the foremost centre of mosaic production during the 5th century, under the patronage of the Ostrogoth king Theodoric (493–526). He was responsible for the decoration of the Arian Baptistery and the church of S Apollinare Nuovo (*see* RAVENNA, §2(i) and (vi)). An important development took place in these commissions: both works feature gold backgrounds, and this became a standard feature of most medieval mosaics. The complete integration of architecture and mosaic may best be seen in the choir of S Vitale (*see* RAVENNA, §2(vii)). Representations of Emperor Justinian and his wife Theodora (*c.* 546–7; see fig. 6 and EARLY CHRISTIAN AND BYZANTINE ART, fig. 39) are placed in the sanctuary area, where they seem to participate in the sacred mysteries for eternity.

In the East little remains of the 6th-century decoration of Hagia Sophia, Constantinople (now Istanbul): only a few crosses on a gold background survive in the narthex and aisles. Literary evidence indicates that these mosaics were regarded as representations of the heavenly vision, with the materials exerting an anagogical function of raising the mind to higher matters. The Great Palace of the emperors in Constantinople (*see* ISTANBUL, §III, 12)

7. Mosaic of *Christ Pantokrator*, from the dome of the Katholikon, Dafni, 11th century

testifies to the persistence of the Classical tradition in the city: the mosaic pavement (Istanbul, Mosaic Mus.), which probably dates from the 6th century, features hunting and pastoral scenes combined with figures from mythology.

Other provincial centres of importance for the early history of Christian mosaic are Thessaloniki and Mount Sinai. In the former, two 6th-century churches, Hagios Georgios and Hagios Demetrios (*see* THESSALONIKI, §III, 2(ii) and 3(ii)), feature extensive programmes relating to the veneration of Christ and the saints; the basilica of Hagios Demetrios once had mosaic decoration on its exterior. Under the patronage of Emperor Justinian, the 6th-century apse mosaic (destr.) at St Catherine's Monastery on Mount Sinai featured the *Transfiguration of Christ*, a composition that achieves new dramatic power and majesty in the use of its wide expanse of gold background.

The further decoration of Hagia Sophia in Constantinople (*see* ISTANBUL, §III, 1(ii)(b)) was undertaken by the Byzantine emperors, who embellished the interior space after the Iconoclastic Controversy of 725–842. In the 9th-century *Virgin and Child* the figures are placed in a vast field of gold tesserae in the apse. The idea of using icon-like compositions became a leading principle in church decoration after the 9th century. By the 10th century a canon of mosaic decoration for the centrally planned church had been developed and was repeated with some variation all over the Byzantine empire. In Middle Byzantine iconographic programmes each figure or scene in the hierarchy of images occupies a specific place in the architecture. The 11th-century Katholikon at Dafni, Greece, provides an example of this programme of imagery. The celestial sphere of the architecture is indicated in the dome by the bust of *Christ Pantokrator* (see fig. 7) and in the apse by a representation of the *Virgin and Child*. Scenes from the *Life of Christ* and the *Life of the Virgin* are depicted in the squinches below the great dome and the walls of the naos display further episodes from the *Life of the Virgin*. Various bishops, priests and deacons, important representatives of Christ's message on earth, are depicted in the subsidiary chapels flanking the apse.

The narthex has another cycle of events from the *Passion* and the *Life of the Virgin*, but only six scenes survive. This idea was less rigidly followed in the West, but the Byzantines considered the use of images to be intimately linked with the symbolism of the building, particularly in the distinction between the heavenly and earthly spheres—the dome and apse, for instance, represented the celestial sphere, with Christ Pantokrator placed in the highest level. Each representation was bound up with fundamental assumptions about its rank and function in this scheme. There are a number of variations on this scheme throughout the Byzantine empire, as in the 11th-century churches of Hosios Loukas in Phocis, Nea Moni in Chios or the cathedral of St Sophia, Kiev.

(iv) Medieval. During the Iconoclastic Controversy in the East a number of mosaic programmes were undertaken in the West, particularly in Rome. The mosaics commissioned by Pope John VII for a chapel in St Peter's (705–7) are in a fragmentary condition, but their style suggests that Byzantine artists were brought over to work on the scheme (*see* ROME, §V, 14(i)(b)). The influence of Byzantium was felt as far afield as France, possibly evidenced by the apse mosaic at Germigny-des-Prés of between 799 and 818 (*see* GERMIGNY-DES-PRÉS, §3). Byzantine mosaicists were reportedly summoned to decorate Islamic buildings such as the Dome of the Rock in Jerusalem (692), the Great Mosque of Damascus (707) and the Great Mosque of Córdoba (extended 965), and wall mosaics occurred sporadically in Islamic buildings until the 13th century. The Classical tradition of floor mosaics also continued in Islamic Syria and Palestine and produced such masterpieces as the scene of lions hunting gazelles under a tree in the bath at Khirbat al-Mafjar (second quarter of the 8th century). This scene is part of the largest single floor mosaic to have survived from the ancient world; it is exceptional in portraying animals, for the Islamic mosaic tradition was predominantly non-figural (*see also* ISLAMIC ART, §II, 9(iv)).

During the 11th century Abbot Desiderius of Montecassino imported Greek mosaicists, who were responsible for decorating the apse, triumphal arch and vestibule of the monastery in imitation of Early Christian programmes of decoration; they were also required to train local craftsmen who by then had lost the art of mosaic.

Another important centre of mosaic production in the West was Sicily, where the Norman rulers sought to compete with the splendours of the Byzantine capital. They imported Greek mosaicists to work at Cefalú (*c.* 1148) (*see* CEFALÚ, §2(ii)), Monreale (*c.* 1180–90) and Palermo (in the Cappella Palatina and the Martorana, both *c.* 1143). The example of Monreale indicates how the canon of decoration could be adapted to fit a basilican plan (*see* MONREALE CATHEDRAL, §3): Christ Pantokrator fills the conch of the apse and scenes from the lives of the Apostles are displayed on the nave walls. Every surface has been covered with mosaic. Similarly ambitious schemes dating from the 11th and 12th centuries and based loosely on the Middle Byzantine programme of decoration are found in Venice at S Marco (*see* VENICE, §IV, 1(iii)).

The many different mosaic schemes executed in Rome during the 12th to 14th centuries indicate the strength of the revival of interest in this medium, with local craftsmen executing important decorative cycles such as those at S Clemente, S Maria Trastevere (1130–41; also Pietro Cavallini's additions of c. 1291) and Old St Peter's (apse, 1198–1216; façade, 1227–41; see ROME, §V, 14(i)(b)).

Byzantine influence played a key role in the revival of wall and vault mosaics in Sicily, Venice and Montecassino, and it may also have been partly responsible for the renewed interest in elaborate mosaic pavements in the West. The most important Romanesque pavements are found in northern and southern Italy, France and the Rhineland. The range of subjects depicted in some churches is enormous, as in the 12th-century mosaics at Otranto, Italy, which illustrate scenes from the Bible, ancient mythology and the labours of the months, but the churches of Rome were normally paved with geometric mosaics produced by the workshops of the Cosmati and made of natural stone and marble (see ROME, fig. 42 and STONE, colour pl. XII). A particularly fine example of a Byzantine-inspired floor mosaic (11th century to early 12th) is found at St Marco (see VENICE, §IV, 1(iii)). During the 12th century Abbot Suger of Saint-Denis had his abbey church decorated with a lunette mosaic above the left-hand entrance and a mosaic pavement in the ambulatory.

The interest in mosaic persisted in both the East and the West into the 14th century, after which this art form was largely superseded by the much quicker, less expensive technique of wall painting. In Istanbul, the Deësis mosaic in the south gallery of Hagia Sophia (c. 1260–1300) is a masterpiece of fine mosaic: minute tesserae were used, and the mosaicist attempted to model the forms as softly and convincingly as possible (see ISTANBUL, §III, 1(ii)(b)). Another commission of great importance in Istanbul was the decoration of the church of Christ the Saviour in Chora (now the Kariye Museum; see ISTANBUL, §III, 3(ii)), paid for by the powerful patron Theodore Metochites in the early 14th century. No mosaic in the Palaiologan style has survived outside Byzantium, but a number of portable mosaics composed of extremely fine tesserae were produced in Byzantium during this period (e.g. the two 14th-century panels depicting the main feasts of the liturgical year; Florence, Mus. Opera Duomo).

In Italy, Giotto completed the decoration of St Peter's, Rome, in the early 14th century with his composition on the retrofaçade of the gate-house of the navicella (or St Peter Walking on the Water)—a theme with important symbolism for the troubled state of the church at this time. Various towns in central Italy had their cathedral façades covered with representational mosaics, as at Siena (early 14th century), Pisa (c. 1301) and Orvieto (c. 1320–90). An ambitious scheme, illustrating scenes from the Old and New Testament and the Life of John the Baptist, was undertaken for the Baptistery in Florence between the 13th century and the early 14th (see FLORENCE, §IV, 1(ii)(b)). The Venetians continued to embellish S Marco during the 13th and 14th centuries with mosaics in the Baptistery and chapel of S Isidore (see VENICE, §IV, 1(iii)). Venetian craftsmen worked on the cathedral of St Vitus in Prague during the 14th century.

(v) The Renaissance to the 20th century. A change in production methods in Europe during the Renaissance reduced mosaic to a less successful art form, which sought to imitate painting (see §I, 3 above). The practice of designing the mosaic became an increasingly separate activity, with artists providing cartoons for the work and other craftsmen setting the tesserae. This is demonstrated in the decoration of 1430 in the Mascoli Chapel in the north transept of S Marco (see VENICE, §IV, 1(iii)). There the mosaic of the Death of the Virgin was designed by the Florentine artist Andrea del Castagno, and the tesserae were set by the Venetian mosaicist Michele Giambono. The deep space of the composition seems totally unrelated to the shape of the vault and shows how mosaic came to rely increasingly on the artistic conventions established by Renaissance painters. A century later, masters such as Titian and Tintoretto designed cartoons for other sections of S Marco, often destroying the medieval mosaics. According to tradition, the idea of replacing these mosaics with work in the new, Renaissance style was suggested by Titian. Another Renaissance master, Raphael, provided cartoons for Luigi di Pace's mosaics in the Cappella Chigi of S Maria del Popolo, Rome (1516).

During the 19th century three centres of importance for mosaic emerged in Europe. The first of these was Paris, where a mosaic workshop was established under the direction of an Italian master to decorate the Melpomene Room in the Palais du Louvre (1810). E. Gerspach, the author of a book on mosaics (1881), helped to set up the Ecole Nationale de la Mosaïque in 1876. Venetian mosaicists were responsible for decorating the Paris Opéra between 1861 and 1874.

In Venice a workshop was founded around 1860 by Antonio Salviati. This put the creation of mosaics on an industrial and commercial basis since the indirect method, which he was the first to use, allowed for the pre-assembly of the mosaic before shipping it to its final destination. The firm of Salviati was responsible for the mosaics of the Albert Memorial and St Paul's Cathedral in London; among the mosaics in St Paul's are those designed by G. F. Watts and Alfred Stevens in 1864.

In Germany, August Warner founded a mosaic company in 1889 that operated until 1969. The firm produced tesserae in 15,000 shades, and the mosaics, also produced by the indirect method, were shipped all over the world. A fine example of their work was the decoration of the Kaiser-Wilhelm-Gedächtniskirche (destr. 1945) in Berlin. A number of 19th-century artists and architects recognized the potential of mosaic. In Gustav Klimt's mural of 1911 for the Palais Stoclet in Brussels smalti or glass-paste tesserae were combined with painted sections and large tiles (see KLIMT, GUSTAV, fig. 2). Antoni Gaudí also used a mixed technique of mosaic smalti, fragments of glass and china plates, as on the pinnacles of the towers of the Templo Expiatorio de la Sagrada Familia, Barcelona (1925; see fig. 8). Other 20th-century artists have explored the different approaches required in mosaic for the handling of colour, pattern, texture and two-dimensionality. This is noticeable in the efforts of Georges Braque, Henri Matisse, Marc Chagall and Fernand Léger.

The greatest use of mosaic as mural decoration is in Mexico, where in the 1930s and 1940s the government

8. Mosaic *smalti* technique used by Antoni Gaudí on the exterior of the Templo Expiatorio de la Sagrada Familia, Barcelona, 1925

supported the use of mosaic for historical and political themes to decorate public buildings. In the 1950s mosaics were increasingly designed by mural painters, such as Diego Rivera, who in 1953 was responsible for the mosaic *A Popular History of Mexico* on the façade of the Teatro de los Insurgentes in Mexico City. The schools of medicine and dentistry were decorated in 1957 with historical mosaics by Francisco Eppens. Juan O'Gorman was a prolific mosaicist who did many works for Mexico City, using mosaic like coloured wrapping paper to cover the architectural structure completely (for illustration *see* O'GORMAN, JUAN). The concern for themes of social realism and the durability of this medium are used to their full potential in this location.

By the late 20th century mosaic was in a stage of transition. Artists were returning to traditional methods of production, such as the use of the direct method. The exhibition in 1988 at the Castello Estense at Mésola, for instance, revealed an awareness of the importance of materials chosen for the tesserae: cubes of stone, glass, shell and other substances were fitted together, sometimes with wide gaps, over panels or walls.

2. PRE-COLUMBIAN AMERICAS. In Mesoamerica mosaic was used during the Pre-Columbian era in architectural

decoration and as a covering for a wide assortment of ceremonial objects. Dating from the time of the Aztec Empire (*c.* 1376–1519), these objects include masks, shields, helmets, knife-handles, other objects of personal ornament and even cult statues. Precious materials, such as obsidian, garnet, mother-of-pearl and turquoise, were glued to a support of wood, stone or pottery. One of the finest examples of this use of turquoise mosaic is the 14th/15th–century mask of Quetzalcóatl (see colour pl. IV, fig. 1). Buildings were also covered with mosaic, as at the site of Mitla in Oaxaca. Here bands of ornament were composed using small stones of different shapes and sizes. Other elaborate Maya façades, as at Uxmal and Chichén Itzá in Yucatán, demonstrate the use of geometric and animal motifs on the exteriors of the buildings.

See also ANCIENT NEAR EAST, §II, 9; EARLY CHRISTIAN AND BYZ-ANTINE ART, §III; GREECE, ANCIENT, §VII; MESOAMERICA, PRE-COLUMBIAN, §X, 5; ROMANESQUE §V; ROME, ANCIENT, §VI. For further illustration *see* AFRICA, fig. 115; ANCIENT AND NEAR EAST, fig. 24; CYPRUS, fig. 22; ISLAMIC ART, fig. 82; TORRITI, JACOPO.

BIBLIOGRAPHY

GENERAL

G. B. De Rossi: *Musaici cristiani e saggi dei pavimenti delle chiese di Roma anteriori al secolo XV*, 27 parts (Rome, 1872–99)

E. Gerspach: *La Mosaïque* (Paris, 1881)

M. van Berchem and E. Clouzot: *Mosaïques chrétiennes du IV au X siècle* (Geneva, 1924)

E. Diez and O. Demus: *Byzantine Mosaics in Greece: Hosios Lucas and Daphni* (Cambridge, MA, 1931)

E. W. Anthony: *A History of Mosaics* (Boston, 1935)

C. R. Morey: *The Mosaics of Antioch* (London and New York, 1938)

J. W. Crowfoot: *Early Churches in Palestine* (London, 1941)

D. Levi: *Antioch Mosaic Pavements*, 2 vols (Princeton, 1947)

O. Demus: *The Mosaics of Norman Sicily* (London, 1950)

H. Frankworth: *The Art and Architecture of the Ancient Orient* (Harmondsworth, 1954)

O. Demus: *Byzantine Mosaic Decoration* (Boston, 1955)

B. R. Brown: *Ptolemaic Paintings and Mosaics and the Alexandrian Style* (Cambridge, MA, 1957)

H. Stern: *Gallia, Sup. X*, i of *Recueil général des mosaïques de la Gaule* (Paris, 1957)

F. Deichmann: *Ravenna: Hauptstadt des spätantiken Abendlandes*, 4 vols (Wiesbaden, 1958–76)

Theophilus, also called Rugerus: *De diversis artibus*; ed. and trans. by C. R. Dodwell as *On Divers Arts* (London, 1961)

Colloque international pour l'étude de la mosaïque antique. La mosaïque greco-romaine: Paris, 1963

J. M. C. Toynbee: *Art in Britain under the Romans* (Oxford, 1964)

V. Lazarev: *Old Russian Murals and Mosaics* (London, 1966)

H. P. L'Orange and P. J. Nordhagen: *Mosaic* (London, 1966)

G. Matthiae: *Mosaici medioevali delle chiese di Roma* (Rome, 1967)

A. Balil: *Mosaicos romanos de Hispania citerior* (Santiago de Compostela, 1971)

2e Colloque international pour l'étude de la mosaïque antique. La mosaïque greco-romaine: Paris, 1975

P. J. Nordhagen: 'Mosaic', *New Encyclopedia Britannica*, xii (Chicago, rev. 15/1976), pp. 462–74

J. Wilpert: *Die römischen Mosaiken der kirchlichen Bauten von IV–XIII Jahrhundert*; rev. ed. W. Schumacher (Vienna, 1976)

K. Dunbabin: *The Mosaics of Roman North Africa* (Oxford, 1978)

J. R. Clarke: *Roman Black and White Figural Mosaics* (New York, 1979)

I. Furlan: *Le icone bizantine a mosaico* (Milan, 1979)

E. Alfoldi-Rosenblum: *Justinian Mosaic Pavements in Cyrenaican Churches* (Rome, 1980)

A. Ovadiah: *Geometric and Floral Patterns in Ancient Mosaics* (Rome, 1980)

D. S. Neal: *Roman Mosaics in Britain* (Sutton, 1981)

D. Salzmann: *Untersuchungen zu den antiken Kieselmosaiken* (Berlin, 1982)

D. von Boeselager: *Antike Mosaiken in Sizilien* (Rome, 1983)

Mosaïque: Recueil d'hommages à Henri Stern (Paris, 1983)

D. Parrish: *Seasons Mosaics of Roman North Africa* (Rome, 1984)

I. Kriseleit: *Antike Mosaiken* (Berlin, 1985)

M. Alfieri and others: *Mosaici minuti romani del '700 e dell'800* (Vatican City, 1986)

P. C. Claussen: *Magistri doctissimi Romani* (Stuttgart, 1987)

MATERIALS AND TECHNIQUES

G. Milanesi: *Dell'arte del vetro per musaico* (Bologna, 1864)

H. Hedfors, ed.: *Compositiones ad tingenda musiva* (Uppsala, 1932)

F. Forlati: 'La tecnica dei primi mosaici marciani', *A. Ven.*, iii (1949), pp. 85–7

A. Diem: 'Techniken des Mittelalters zur Herstellung von Glas und Mosaik', *Artigianato e tecnica nella società dell'alto medioevo occidentale. Settimane di studio del Centro italiano di studi sull'alto medioevo: Spoleto, 1970*, pp. 609–32

I. Roncuzzi Fiorentini: *Arte e tecnologia* (Ravenna, 1971)

E. Kitzinger: 'Mosaic Technique', *Encyclopedia of World Art*, x (New York, Toronto, London, 1972), cols 325–7

J. Mellentin-Haswell: *Van Nostrand Reinhold Manual of Mosaic* (London, 1973)

C. Balmelle and J. P. Damon: 'L'Artisan-mosaïste dans l'Antiquité Tardive', *Artistes, artisans et production artistique au moyen âge*, ed. X. Barral I Altet, 2 vols (Paris, 1986)

C. Harding: 'The Production of Medieval Mosaics', *Dumbarton Oaks Pap.* (1989)

SPECIALIST STUDIES

G. Trenta: *I musaici del duomo di Pisa e i loro autori* (Florence, 1896)

H. Saville: *Turquoise Mosaic Art in Ancient Mexico* (New York, 1922)

M. van Berchem: 'The Mosaics of the Dome of the Rock at Jerusalem and of the Great Mosque at Damascus', *Early Muslim Architecture*, ed. K. A. C. Creswell, i (London, 1932), pp. 149–252

T. Whittemore: *The Mosaics of St Sophia at Istanbul*, 4 vols (Oxford, 1933–52)

G. Brett: 'The Mosaic', *The Great Palace of the Byzantine Emperors. First Report*, ed. D. Talbot Rice (Oxford, 1947), pp. 64–97

O. Grabar: 'The Umayyad Dome of the Rock in Jerusalem', *A. Orient.*, iii (1959), pp. 33–62

E. Kitzinger: *The Mosaics of Monreale* (Palermo, 1960)

M. Muraro: 'The Statutes of the Venetian *Arti* and the Mosaics of the Mascoli Chapel', *A. Bull.*, xliii (1961), pp. 263–74

C. Mango: *The Mosaics of St Sophia at Istanbul* (Washington, 1962)

P. J. Nordhagen: 'The Mosaics of John VII (705–707 A.D.)', *Acta ad archeologiam et Artium Historiam Pertinentia*, ii (1965), pp. 121–66

P. Underwood: *The Kariye Djami*, 4 vols (New York, 1966–75)

F. Difederico: *The Mosaics of St Peter's* (London, 1983)

R. J. A. Wilson: *Piazza Armerina* (London, 1983)

O. Demus: *The Mosaics of San Marco in Venice*, 4 vols (Chicago, 1984)

D. Mouriki: *The Mosaics of Nea Moni on Chios* (Athens, 1985)

M. Andaloro: 'I mosaici di Monreale, restauri e scoperte (1965–1982)', *XIII catalogo di opere d'arte restaurate, Bollettino Beni Culturali Ambientali (Sicilia)*, iv (1986)

C. Harding: 'Economic Dimensions in Art: Mosaic versus Wall Painting in Trecento Orvieto', *Florence and Italy: Renaissance Studies in Honour of Nicolai Rubenstein*, ed. P. Denley and C. Elam (London, 1988), pp. 503–14

III. Conservation.

A summary of the restoration procedures adopted in antiquity and the Middle Ages reveals that whenever earlier mosaics were restored or altered mosaicists usually did not try to disguise the resultant differences in style and technique, although certain signs of restoration, for example the joints in the setting-bed, were concealed if possible. Also, written sources indicate that on occasion mosaics were lifted and transported far afield, as when Charlemagne removed mosaics from Ravenna to decorate the Palatine Chapel (now the cathedral) at Aachen during the late 8th century. There are a number of instances before the Renaissance when early mosaics were destroyed and the tesserae reused in other locations, particularly in the Byzantine empire.

The normal course of restoration for wall and vault mosaics, until even relatively recently, is exemplified in the practices of Alesso Baldovinetti, who repaired the mosaics of the Baptistery in Florence during the mid-15th century by gouging out decayed mortar, consolidating the setting-bed with iron clamps and nails, and patching the originals; he did not attempt to make his restorations resemble the late medieval originals. At times, however, restorers would try to reproduce the style of the originals as closely as possible, as occurred during the early 16th century in Venice, when certain sections of the S Marco mosaics had to be remade after a fire. The mosaicist, known only as Petrus, sought to reproduce the style of the 12th-century originals. Attitudes there to restoration changed drastically during the course of the century. Instead of restoring the mosaics, workshops began to replace damaged work with compositions that were designed by contemporary artists but followed the iconographic scheme of the originals. The Venetian authorities decided to stop this practice in 1610. Attitudes such as these persisted until relatively recently, however, as in the case of the 13th-century mosaics at S Miniato, Florence, where in the 19th century restorers replaced the originals with faithful copies.

Modern conservators try, wherever possible, to respect the original in its setting, whatever its date, and to provide only a minimal amount of intervention when restoration is required. The conservation of mosaics is always closely related to the supporting architectural framework or foundation. Roofs, walls and vaults must be sound and must not permit water to enter the supporting layers of mortar. If the mortar is badly decayed it may be injected with a consolidating substance, such as a mixture of lime, crushed marble and brick mixed with a little acrylic resin, to fill the gaps between the tesserae and the support plaster and to bind the mortar to the masonry or floor. Clamps and nails are used only rarely to hold in the setting-bed.

The *stacco* technique of detachment, in which whole sections of mosaic are removed and reset, is now used only rarely because of the potential disturbance to the surface texture of the work. If the mosaics have to be detached, impressions are taken beforehand and often painted to obtain faithful copies. The *stacco* method is recommended only when the slight pressure used in the injection of the wall or floor causes extensive areas of tesserae to break away.

Apart from the treatment of the different layers of mortar, the conservation process also includes the cleaning of tesserae and their interstices and the reinsertion of any individual tesserae that have fallen out. Patching may be carried out with reused tesserae or closely matched modern tesserae. New tesserae must be clearly recognizable and not made to look old. If the restorer leaves a gap in the tesserae, this is filled with plaster and the missing portions indicated in paint.

Exterior mosaics pose special conservation problems. Floor mosaics, for example, must be kept free and clean from algae and mosses, especially in northern Europe, where conservators cannot seal the surface of the floor because of continual rising moisture from the subsoil. Restorers must also prevent dramatic changes in temperature and ensure the circulation of air to maintain a constant level of humidity.

BIBLIOGRAPHY

I. Andreescu: 'La Mosaïque murale: Histoire des restaurations, évolutions de ses techniques', and L. Majewski: 'Nettoyage, consolidation et traitement des mosaïques murales', *Mosaïque: Détérioration et conservation* (Rome, 1977), pp. 19–33, 50–56

I. Roncuzzi Fiorentini: *Il mosaico: Materiali e tecniche dalle origini a oggi* (Ravenna, 1984)

G. Fumo: 'The Mosaics in the Basilica of Santa Maria Assunta on Torcello', *Twenty Years of Restoration in Venice* (Venice, 1987)

CATHERINE HARDING

Mosca. Italian family of artists. The earliest known family members, both masons, were Francesco di Simone Mosca, also known as Francesco delle Pecore (*b* nr Settignano, early 1470s; last documented 1504), and his brother Jacopo di Simone delle Pecore, who is documented as having matriculated in October 1506. They and three subsequent generations of the family were active in central Italy. Francesco's son, (1) Simone Mosca, also known as 'il Moschini', was a sculptor, as was his son (2) Francesco Mosca, also known as 'il Moschino'. It was the latter's son (3) Simone Mosca Moschino, however, that had the strongest artistic personality.

(1) Simone Mosca [il Moschini] (*b* Settignano, 1492; *d* Orvieto, April 1553). Sculptor. He went to Rome with Antonio da Sangallo (ii) and participated in the building and decoration of S Giovanni dei Fiorentini and the Cesia Chapel in S Maria della Pace. He was also associated with the workshop of Andrea Sansovino and assisted in the decoration of the Santa Casa of Loreto. Around 1525 he travelled to Bologna with Niccolò Tribolo and assisted with reliefs for churches there. Simone's free use of garlands, richly carved cornices and friezes and other classicizing motifs was highly praised by contemporaries. During the late 1520s and early 1530s he assisted Michelangelo on the decoration of the Medici Chapel, Florence. Some time after 1533 Vasari unsuccessfully attempted to obtain for him the commission for the *Del Monte* monument for S Pietro in Montorio, Rome. In collaboration with Benedetto da Rovezzano, Simone carved the base for Baccio Bandinelli's statue of *Orpheus* (Florence, Pal. Medici-Riccardi, main courtyard). His last years were spent mainly in Orvieto, where he executed altars and decorative carvings for the cathedral.

(2) Francesco Mosca [il Moschino] (*b* ?1546; *d* Pisa, 28 Sept 1578). Sculptor, son of (1) Simone Mosca. He also worked in Orvieto, and he may have completed his father's unfinished commissions. For the cathedral there he executed a nude statue of *St Sebastian* and figures of *St Peter* and *St Paul*. He also executed statues for Pisa Cathedral (a *Virgin and Child* and *Angel* in the chapel of the Annunciation) and in 1577 travelled to Parma, where he was employed briefly by the Farnese as court sculptor. A marble relief of *Diane and Acteon* (Florence, Bargello) and a free-standing group of *Atalanta and Meleager* (Kansas City, MO, Nelson–Atkins Mus. A.) reflect Francesco's indebtedness to mid-16th-century Mannerism.

BIBLIOGRAPHY

G. Vasari: *Vite* (1550, rev. 2/1568); ed. G. Milanesi (1878–85)

J. Burckhardt: *Il Cicerone* (Basle, 1855)

K. Weil-Garris: *The Santa Casa di Loreto: Problems in Cinquecento Sculpture* (New York, 1977)

M. Butzek: *Die kommunalen Repräsentationsstatuen der Päpste des 16. Jahrhunderts in Bologna, Perugia und Rom* (Bad Honnef, 1978)

G. Magnani: *Abbazia benedettina di S Giovanni Evangelista a Parma*, ed. B. Adorni (Milan, 1979)

STEVEN BULE

(3) Simone Mosca Moschino (*bapt* Orvieto, 12 Nov 1553; *d* Parma, 20 June 1610). Sculptor and architect, son of (2) Francesco Mosca. He gained experience at an early age, working for Pier Francesco ('Vicino') Orsini (*d* 1585) as a sculptor at Bomarzo (*see* BOMARZO, SACRO BOSCO). In 1578 he was recommended by Orsini to Ottavio Farnese, 2nd Duke of Parma, who appointed him to succeed his father as court sculptor. While he was employed at Bomarzo and during his visits to Rome in 1594, 1597 and 1599–1600, Moschino had the opportunity to become acquainted at first hand with the works of Michelangelo, and this had a personal if superficial impact on his sculpture. Together with his experience at Bomarzo and his youthful contact, through his family, with Florentine Mannerism, and in particular with Bartolomeo Ammanati and Bernardo Buontalenti, this new influence contributed to the evolution of his style towards a determined anti-classicism, which disconcerted his contemporaries (and later also Burckhardt).

Under Ottavio Farnese, Moschino was responsible in particular for the sculptural decoration of Giovanni Boscoli's great fountain, which backs on to the Palazzo del Giardino, Parma. His activity broadened at the end of the century under Ranuccio I, 4th Duke of Parma, who appointed him general superintendent of art and architecture. For Ranuccio he enlarged the Palazzo del Giardino built by Jacopo Vignola, and he probably (under the Duke's precise instructions) also designed the Pilotta next to the ducal palace. This immense construction was a service building housing stables, the wardrobe, armoury and several courtyards for playing pelota and *archetto*. Moschino was responsible for the entrance stairway (1604) to the armoury; the armoury itself was later converted into the Teatro Farnese (1618–19) by Giovanni Battista Aleotti. This grand and complex staircase has a large, domed octagonal space on the main landing, which once possessed a lantern, almost as if it were a large, centralized chapel. Other works by Moschino include the funerary monument of *Margaret of Parma* (*d* 1586) in S Sisto, Piacenza; the enlargement of the Benedictine convent of S Alessandro (1593; destr.) at Parma; a statue of *Duke Alessandro Farnese* (1594; Caserta, Pal. Reale); and a great marble door (from 1596) for the citadel of Parma. From 1604 to 1607 he built the façade of the church of S Giovanni Evangelista, Parma, begun in 1490; here the rigid skeleton of superimposed orders is contrasted with an assortment of niches with statues, small pediments, frames and various motifs taken from Michelangelo; a lively exterior profile supports a medallion with the eagle of St John the Evangelist. Also attributable to Moschino is the bell-tower (1616) of S Sepolcro, Parma, where his anti-classical and anti-architectonic style assumed a particularly violent character.

UNPUBLISHED SOURCES

Munich, Staatl. Graph. Samml. [drawings by Moschino]

BIBLIOGRAPHY

J. Burckhardt: *Il Cicerone* (Basle, 1855)

A. Ronchini: 'Francesco e Simone Moschini', *Atti & Mem. RR. Deput. Stor. Patria Prov. Moden. & Parmen.*, viii (1876), pp. 97–111

A. Sorrentino: 'L'autore del gruppo marmoreo "Alessandro Farnese incoronato dalla vittoria"', *Aurea Parma*, xxiii (1939), pp. 20–25

B. Adorni: *L'architettura farnesiana a Parma, 1545–1630* (Parma, 1974), pp. 45–7, 55–62, 167–83

——: *L'architettura farnesiana a Piacenza, 1545–1600* (Parma, 1982), pp. 409–12

H. Bredekamp: *Vicino Orsini e il sacro bosco di Bomarzo* (Rome, 1989), pp. 66, 69, 71, 76, 120, 123, 128, 131, 143, 152–3, 155, 179, 256, 274, 302, 340–1

B. Adorni: 'I giardini farnesiani a Parma e a Piacenza', *Gli arti farnesiani sul Palatino* (Rome, 1990), pp. 516–17

BRUNO ADORNI

Mosca Padovano, Giovanni Maria [Gianmaria] [Padoan, Zuan Maria; Padovano, Jan Maria] (*b* Padua, *c.* 1493/5; *d* Kraków, after 31 March 1574). Italian sculptor, medallist and architect, active in Poland. He is first documented in 1507, when he was apprenticed for six years to the Paduan sculptor Giovanni d'Antonio Minello de' Bardi. Released early from this contract, he also trained with the sculptor Bartolomeo Mantello (*fl* early 16th century). His first documented work is a bronze relief of the *Beheading of St John the Baptist* (1516; Padua Cathedral). In Padua he also executed a marble relief of the *Judgement of Solomon* (Paris, Louvre) for Giambattista Leon. However, a commission dated 28 April 1520 for a marble relief of the *Miracle of the Unbroken Goblet* (Padua, Santo, Chapel of St Anthony) describes him as a resident of Venice, working on the high altar of S Rocco in that city. Mosca's work on the relief proceeded from 1523 to 1529, when the almost completed relief was finished by Paolo Stella after Mosca's final departure. In S Rocco, the lower register of the high altar contains two small marble works by Mosca, *St John the Baptist* (often identified as *St Pantaleon*) and *St Sebastian*. The powerfully contorted and pathetic *St Sebastian* is his first mature statement departing from the calm, static manner of earlier reliefs by Minello and the influential Tullio Lombardo. Mosca is documented in Venice in 1522, when he received payments for a *Virgin* (untraced) on the house of Paolo de Monte. Other works of this period include several marble reliefs, such as *Venus Anadyomene* (London, V&A), *Portia* (Venice, Ca' d'Oro) and *Mucius Scaevola* (Florence, Bargello).

In 1529 Mosca left Venice, possibly because of ill-will between himself and Jacopo Sansovino. He was given patronage by Sigismund I (*reg* 1506–48), King of Poland, and his Italian wife Bona Sforza, and he set up a workshop in Kraków. His earliest works there were reliefs of *David* and *Solomon* (begun 1529), after a design by Bartolomeo Berrecci, and an effigy intended for the tomb of *Sigismund I* (1529–31), now in the Sigismund Chapel in Wawel Cathedral, Kraków. He also executed portrait medals depicting *Sigismund I*, *Bona Sforza* and their children (1532; Modena, Gal. & Mus. Estense).

Mosca worked principally on funerary sculpture. The hauntingly beautiful tomb of *Barbara Tarnowska* (*c.* 1536; Tarnów Cathedral) is one of his finest works. In 1538 he executed the monument of *Andrzej Krzycki*, the Primate of Poland, in Gniezno Cathedral, of which there remain only the effigy of the deceased and a relief of the *Virgin and Child*; and the funerary monument (1540; destr.) of *Bishop Stanisław Oleśnicki* in Poznań Cathedral. His tombs of bishops in Wawel Cathedral, Kraków, include that of

Piotr Tomicki (1533–5); of *Piotr Gamrat* (1545–7) commissioned by Queen Bona; and of *Samuel Maciejowski* (1552). In 1546 the Crown Prince, later Sigismund II Augustus, asked Mosca to execute a monument (destr.) to his first wife, *Elizabeth of Habsburg* (*d* 1545), and in 1553 commissioned, as king, a monument (1562; destr.) in the castle church of SS Anne and Barbara in Vilnius to his second wife, *Barbara Radziwiłł*. The two large tabernacles that Mosca produced in 1533–6 for Wawel Cathedral have been destroyed.

In 1558–60 Mosca executed the signed monument of *Jan Kamieniecki* (Krosno, Franciscan church), and in 1561–70 he sculpted the finest Polish tomb of the 16th century, that of *Jan Tarnowski*, Great Hetman of the Crown, and of his son, *Jan Krzysztof Tarnowski* (Tarnów Cathedral; see fig.); the two tombs are superimposed on one another,

Giovanni Maria Mosca Padovano: tombs of *Jan Tarnowski* and *Jan Krzysztof Tarnowski*, 1561–70 (Tarnów Cathedral)

creating a two-tiered effect. His last sepulchral work was probably the model for the tomb of *Sigismund II Augustus* (1571); the actual tomb in the Sigismund Chapel of Wawel Cathedral was executed by Santi Gucci and placed above Mosca's monument of *Sigismund I*, to form a double tomb. Mosca also executed an architectural model for Bishop Samuel Maciejowski's villa (1551), built at Prądnik, near Kraków, and a design for the exterior staircase and loggia of the Cloth Hall on the Grand Square in Kraków.

Mosca introduced the influence of the classicizing art of Tullio Lombardo to Poland. His funerary monuments, based on the rectangular aedicule, are without ornaments. The artist modelled his saints and allegorical figures *all'antica*, while portraying the deceased more naturalistically, reclining as if asleep, after the type popularized by Jacopo Sansovino, which Mosca himself also brought to Poland. Mosca also popularized the use of the Classical orders in Poland. Though safeguarded by royal privilege, he also belonged to a guild in Kraków; numerous Poles, including the talented Jan Michałowicz z Urzędowa, trained in his workshop.

BIBLIOGRAPHY

PSB; Thieme–Becker [with bibliog. to date]

A. Venturi: *Storia* (1901–40)

E. Rigoni: 'Notizie riguardanti Bartolomeo Bellano e altri scultori padovani', *Atti & Mem. Reale Accad., Sci., Lett. & A. Padova*, n. s., xlix (1932–3); also in *L'arte rinascimentale in Padova: Studi e documenti, Medioevo e umanesimo*, ix (Padua, 1970), pp. 127–8, 138–9

F. Kopera: 'Jan Maria Padovano', *Prac. Kom. Hist. Sztuki*, vii (1937), pp. 219–61

J. Zarnecki: 'Renaissance Sculpture in Poland: Padovano and Michałowicz', *Burl. Mag.*, lxxxvi (1945), pp. 10–16

H. Kozakiewicz: 'Jan Maria Padovano: Życie i działalność we Włoszech' [Life and activity in Italy], *Biul. Hist. Sztuki*, xxiv (1964), pp. 153–68 [with It. summary]

G. Fiocco: 'Il Mosca a Padova', *Venezia e la Polonia nei secoli dal XVII al XIX*, xix (Venice and Rome, 1968), pp. 43–52

J. Białostocki: *The Art of the Renaissance in Eastern Europe* (Oxford, 1976)

M. Rożek: 'Jan Maria Padovano: Twórca Nagrobka Prymasa Andrzeja Krzyckiego w Gnieźnie [Author of the tomb of Archbishop Andrzej Krycki], *Biul. Hist. Sztuki*, xlv (1983), pp. 49–54 [Fr. summary]

S. Wilk: 'La decorazione cinquecentesca della Cappella dell'Arca di S Antonio', *Le sculture del Santo di Padova*, ed. G. Lorenzoni (Padua, 1984), pp. 134–6

A. M. Schulz: 'Paolo Stella Milanese', *Mitt. Ksthist. Inst. Florenz*, xxix (1985), pp. 79–110

JERZY KOWALCZYK, THOMAS MARTIN

Moscoso y Guzmán. *See under* ALTAMIRA, Condes de.

Moscovitz, Shalom. *See* SAFED, SHALOM VON.

Moscow [Rus. Moskva]. Capital of Russia and former capital of the USSR (1918–91). The largest industrial, scientific and cultural centre in Russia, it covers 875 sq. km and has a population of over 8 million (1988). Situated on the Moskva River, it is built on a radial-concentric pattern with the main thoroughfares radiating outwards from the Kremlin. Western European styles were introduced on a wide scale after *c.* 1700, following the reforms of Peter I, while another major turning-point was brought about by the Revolution of 1917. Many churches, monasteries and secular buildings have survived in the historical heart of Moscow, within the Garden Ring.

I. History and urban development. II. Art life and organization. III. Centre of production. IV. Buildings.

I. History and urban development.

1. Before *c.* 1700. 2. *c.* 1700–1917. 3. After 1917.

1. BEFORE *c.* 1700. According to archaeological evidence, primitive settlements on the site of Moscow date to the 4th and 3rd millennia BC. Fortified settlements with ramparts and ditches belong to the D'yakovo culture (5th century BC to 7th century AD), which takes its name from excavations in the village of D'yakovo (now inside the boundaries of Moscow); traces of this culture have been found on the site of the Kremlin. Slavonic colonization along the rivers Moskva and Oka from the 10th century led to the building of the 11th-century fortified settlement on Borovitsky Hill, a high promontory at the confluence of the rivers Neglinnaya and Moskva. In the 12th century this territory came under the rule of the principality of Vladimir–Suzdal', and in 1147 the border town of 'Moskov' is mentioned in the chronicles for the first time. In 1156 Prince Andrey Bogolyubsky (*reg* 1157–75) built the earliest-known wooden walls of the growing town with its ramparts and ditches, parts of which have been excavated. In 1237 Moscow and its adjacent monasteries and villages were burnt down by Batu Khan (*reg* 1227–55), marking the beginning of Tatar-Mongol suzerainty (*see* RUSSIA, §III, 1).

In the mid-13th century, after the collapse of the principality of Vladimir, Moscow became the capital of one of the independent principalities under Prince Mikhail Khorobrit. Under his grandson, Prince Ivan Kalita (*reg* 1328–41), Moscow became the centre of a bigger and stronger principality, leader of associated Russian territories and the residence of the head of the Russian Church. A new Kremlin was built, covering a larger area and encircled by oak walls, while a suburb to the north-east covered part of the present Kitay-gorod. The first stone buildings in the Kremlin were erected, the cathedrals of the Dormition (Uspensky) and of the Archangel Michael (*see* §IV, 1(ii) and (iii) below), as was the bell-tower church of Ioann Lestvichnik (1329; destr.). Stone monastic churches were also constructed, such as that of the Saviour (Spas na Boru; 1333; destr.) in the Kremlin. In the second half of the 14th century and early 15th, the city expanded and acquired, under Dmitry Donskoy (*reg* 1359–89), its first stone walls, close in configuration and location to the present walls. The settlement to the north-east of the Kremlin, called Veliky (the Great), then covered the entire area of Kitay-gorod, and in 1394 it was enclosed by a rampart, ditch and stockade; a part of it, Zarech'ye ('Across the river'), spread across the River Moskva and another, Zaneglimen'ye, beyond the Neglinnaya. New stone churches were built in the Kremlin (the cathedral of the Annunciation [Blagoveshchensky]; *see* §IV, 1(iv) below; and the church of the Birth of the Virgin [Bogoroditsa]; destr.) as well as in the newly founded monasteries of the Ascension (Vozneseniye; 1393; destr.) and of the Miracles (1358; destr.). The city was surrounded by many villages and settlements as well as by monasteries that served as outposts, such as the Danilov, Andronikov and Simonov monasteries, several of which had stone churches. A particular style of architecture evolved during the second half of the 14th century and early 15th that is usually known as early Muscovite.

Further development took place from the mid-15th century to the early 16th, when Moscow finally freed itself from the Tatar-Mongol yoke (1480) and united under its leadership all the Russian territories, becoming capital of a powerful Russian state. There was an upsurge of building in stone in Moscow, while brick also began to be used. Several stone buildings were erected in the Kremlin in the mid-15th century, including, besides churches, the first stone ceremonial palaces and residences for the ruling princes, the metropolitan, boyars and merchants. Construction began to be more varied, as shown by the decoration of the main gate-tower of the Kremlin, the Frolov Gate (replaced by the Saviour Gate), with its stone equestrian sculptures of SS George and Dmitry.

IVAN III (*reg* 1462–1505) carried out a radical rebuilding programme in the capital, attracting architects and master builders from all over Russia, as well as from Italy, ensuring that Moscow was now in the forefront of Russian architecture. The Kremlin acquired massive brick walls and towers in 1485–99. Built by Italian masters on the basis of the principle of regularity and the latest advances in fortification, the walls embraced a large territory in the form of an unequal triangle, giving the Kremlin the appearance it largely retains. At the same time, larger and grander structures replaced the earlier cathedrals in the Kremlin: the cathedrals of the Dormition (Uspensky; 1475–9; by ARISTOTELE FIORAVANTI), the Annunciation (1484–9; by masons from Pskov), the Archangel Michael (1505–8; Aleviz [Alevisio] Novy) and the bell-tower of Ivan the Great (1505–8; see fig. 1) by Bon Friazin (who is by some identified as Marco Bono). Alongside were built ceremonial court buildings, including the Faceted Palace (Granovitaya Palata; 1487–91; by Marco Ruffo and Pietro Antonio Solari). New stone monastic and court churches were built on the main streets of the Kremlin, as were palaces and other buildings of the aristocracy.

The second most important area of the capital was the suburb Veliky; its main streets, Nikol'skaya, Il'inka and Varvarka, were laid out in the early 16th century, and they ran from the gate-towers of the Kremlin. A large market was located against the east wall of the Kremlin, but it was not rebuilt after the fire of 1453. The streets were lined by the houses of boyars and rich merchants, gradually forcing out the artisans who had previously been the main inhabitants. Stone monastic and parish churches (11 of them by Aleviz Novy) rose above the wooden houses. Other distinctive suburban areas were Zaneglimen'ye, with its Sretenskaya Street, Cannon House (Pushechny Dvor) and Pushkarskaya settlement, and Zarech'ye, with its Pyatnitskaya Street. The Yauza district included the settlement of Goncharnaya and the church of St Nikita the Martyr. To the east of Veliky lay the monarch's gardens and palace (destr.); close by stands the church of St Vladimir (1510; by Aleviz Novy) and the Ivanovsky Convent (16th century; rebuilt 1861–78).

Rapid growth in Moscow in the 16th century led to the erection of fortifications that enclosed parts of the city, thus transforming it into an architectural whole. In 1535–8 massive stone walls were built by the architect Petrok

1. Moscow, Kremlin, bell-tower of Ivan the Great, 1505–8

Maly around Veliky, now renamed Kitay-gorod ('Chinatown'). Magnificent churches were built on the royal estates on the River Moskva: the votive hipped-roof church of the Ascension (1530–32; for illustration *see* KOLOMENSKOYE) and St John the Baptist in D'yakovo (1547) with its half columns and chapels. Close to the main gates of the Kremlin the votive church of the Protective Veil (Pokrov; 1551–61; attributed to Barma and Postnik) was erected to commemorate victory over the khanate of Kazan'. It is now known as St Basil's Cathedral (*see* §IV, 2 below).

Several large public buildings were erected in Kitay-gorod, such as the covered market (Gostiny Dvor; destr.) between Il'inka and Varvarka streets, the English Merchants' House (Angliysky Kupechesky Dvor) on Varvarka Street and the Printing Office (Pechatny Dvor) on Nikol'skaya Street. The entire western side of Zaneglimen'ye was settled by followers of Ivan IV (*reg* 1533–84), who built the Oprichny Palace there. The court's bakers, picklers and grooms settled further to the north; their names were later to be given to many streets and alleys.

Under Fyodor I (*reg* 1584–98) and Boris Godunov (*reg* 1598–1605) major building work was carried out in Moscow: a stone wall (1586–93; destr. late 18th century by Fyodor Kon') was built around the White Town (Bely

Gorod), the district adjacent to the Kremlin and Kitay-gorod, and a wooden wall on an earth rampart, the Skorodom, ringed the settlement around the city. This territory, newly attached to Moscow and still little populated, was criss-crossed by streets that ran through the gate-towers to the central nucleus of the Kremlin and Kitay-gorod. Thus, a radial-concentric street pattern was formed. This can be seen clearly in the first plans of Moscow at the turn of the 16th and 17th centuries, the Petrov and Godunov drawings.

The Stonework Department (Kamenny Prikaz), founded in 1584, controlled building works, builders and building materials, as well as establishing standards. The width of streets and alleys was also regulated. Among major buildings of this time were the new palace for Boris Godunov in the Kremlin and the superstructure (1600) of the bell-tower of Ivan the Great, which was then the dominant vertical feature of the town. Settlements grew up beyond the Skorodom ring: Dorogomilovskaya, Tverskaya and Rogozhskaya. The Time of Troubles (1605–13) brought fire and other destruction to Moscow, but the city was relatively quickly restored, and building work restarted in the 1620s. The city's growth was mainly in the suburbs and as a result of absorbing outlying villages and settlements. Court and military settlements developed in Zemlyanoy Gorod; beyond it lay the foreigners' settlement: the German (Nemetskaya) beyond the Yauza and, following the war with Poland, settlements of Belarusian emigrants, Panskaya and Meshchanskaya. Streets were built to a regular plan, and a series of edicts in the 1680s in respect of Kitay-gorod and the White Town prescribed that for aesthetic reasons, and as a protection against fire, residences on the main streets should be of stone.

The appearance of old districts in the city changed as large public and commercial buildings were erected, for example the Mint (Monetny Dvor; 1697) in Kitay-gorod. On Red Square (Krasnaya Ploshchad'), which was gradually becoming the city's main square, a covered market (Gostiny Dvor) was built, as were the Kazan' Cathedral (1635–6; destr.) and the nearby Gates of the Resurrection. The Kremlin towers were given elegant hipped roofs, while, within the Kremlin itself, the Terem (or Belvedere) Palace (1635–6), the government offices (Prikazy; destr.) and the Patriarch's Palace (1645–55) greatly enriched the ensemble. The Stone (Kamenny) Bridge was built near by, the first fixed structure of its type in Moscow.

The Terem Palace inspired the widespread building of stone houses in Moscow. Mansions were built by the boyar Miloslavsky in the Kremlin, by the Golitsyns and Troyekurovs in Hunters' Row (Okhotny Ryad), by Metropolitan Jonah in Krutitskoye podvor'ye and by the deacon Averky Kirillov and the Ukrainian landowner Sverchkov on Pokrovka Street. Stone parish churches were built in many parts of the town by the aristocracy and priesthood, by landowners and rich merchants, and often formed striking ensembles together with their patrons' palaces. The architecture of these churches, with their tall bell-towers, loggias and galleries, usually oriented towards the street, became important elements in the overall townscape; examples are the church of the Trinity in Nikitniki (1635–53; rest. 1968) and St Gregory of Neocaesarea (1667–9) on Bol'shaya Polyanka Street.

In the development of monasteries emphasis was placed on the creation of picturesque ensembles, as in the Simonov, Vysoko-Petrovsky and Don monasteries and the Novospassky (New Monastery of the Saviour) and Novodevichy (New Convent of the Virgin; founded 1524; see fig. 2) complexes. Sited in the White Town and Zemlyanoy Gorod, as well as in the suburbs, they formed a virtual ring around parts of Moscow. The out-of-town estates of the Tsar and his retinue were particularly luxurious and decorative, with their complex clusters of buildings, churches, palaces, mansions, walls and gates, flower gardens and kitchen gardens, in Kolomenskoye, Pokrovskoye, Izmaylovo, Alekseyevskoye. The large wooden palace (1667–8; destr.) built for Tsar Aleksey Mikhaylovich (*reg* 1645–76) in Kolomenskoye by Russian carpenters was considered by contemporaries the eighth wonder of the world (*see* RUSSIA, fig. 9).

At the turn of the 17th and 18th centuries a new style of architecture developed on the estates belonging to the Tsar's relatives, the Naryshkins (e.g. at Fili and Petrovskoye-Razumovskoye). Muscovite or Naryshkin Baroque is distinguished by its elegance and inventiveness of form, and by the delicacy of its decoration. This transitional style, linking Old Russian architecture with contemporary innovations, brought about an upsurge of building in stone, which within 30 years spread to every type of building and created a number of original forms such as tiered churches of the type known as eight-on-four (an octagon above a cube), centrally planned and quatrefoil, with vast, pillarless refectories. Notable examples of this architecture were the Sukharev Tower (1692–5; destr.);

2. Moscow, Novodevichy Convent (New Convent of the Virgin), cathedral of the Virgin of Smolensk, 1524–5, with 17th-century domes

the churches of the Dormition (Uspenskaya; 1696–9; destr.) on Pokrovka Street, St Nicholas (Nikola Bol'shoy Krest; 1680–89) on Il'inka Street, of the Protective Veil (Pokrov; *c.* 1693) in Fili and of the Trinity (1698–1704) at Troitsko-Lykov; the cathedral (1684–93) of the Don Monastery; the refectory (completed 1680s) of the Simonov Monastery and that attached to the church of the Dormition (1685–7) at the Novodevichy Convent; the Troyekurov House; and the Lefort Palace (1697–8; rebuilt 1707–10).

2. *c.* 1700–1917. The reforms of Peter I (*reg* 1682–1725) in the early 18th century, when the capital was transferred to the newly built St Petersburg, inevitably affected Moscow. The scale and pace of building in the city decreased sharply, new types of buildings predominated, mainly for public or commercial use, methods of construction changed and architecture turned towards western European styles, above all to the Baroque. Numerous building edicts affected urban development in Moscow. Stone paving replaced the wooden surfaces of the main streets, and houses were either of stone or had façades of stucco imitating stone. The St Petersburg practice of unbroken street façades was not followed in Moscow where houses retained their surrounding gardens, and standard building designs were less frequently used.

In the first third of the 18th century the Kremlin fell into dilapidation. Only the Arsenal (1702–36; rebuilt 1830s), the biggest construction of the new type of geometrically accurate design, exemplified the new ideals of urban planning. The focus of life in the city moved to the north-eastern outskirts, to the villages favoured by Peter, Preobrazhenskoye, Semyonovskoye and Lefortovo, as well as the German settlement. Colonies of soldiers were established in the villages, and the Tsar's entourage and rich merchants had their residences within the German settlement, as well as on Maroseyka Street and Pokrovka Street that ran into it. The secular and ecclesiastical buildings they erected were in the new Baroque style, the magnificence of which gradually increased towards the mid-18th century. The imposing Apraksin House (1768) at the Pokrovsky Gates demonstrates the considerable changes in artistic taste at that time.

Among the most interesting churches of the Petrine period are that of the Archangel Gabriel, known as the Menshikov Tower (1704–7; by IVAN ZARUDNY), and SS Peter and Paul on Novaya Basmannaya Street (1707–17); both were surmounted by spires, and the former was the tallest building in Moscow (*see* RUSSIA, fig. 10). These two churches stand in contrast to later churches decorated in mature Baroque style, such as St Nikita the Martyr (from 1750) on Staraya Basmannaya Street and St Clement (1754–74) on Pyatnitskaya Street. Tall bell-towers alongside churches such as that of the Trinity (1781; by Karl Blank) in Serebryaniki and St Nicholas in Zvonari (1762–81; by Blank) dominated the skyline. Celebrations to mark military victories, coronations and other events were an important feature of the life of the city in the first half of the 18th century, for which special wooden triumphal arches were built. Some of these were later rebuilt in stone, such as the Red (or Beautiful) Gates (Krasnyye Vorota;

1753–7; destr.; by DMITRY UKHTOMSKY), thus adorning the city and helping to disseminate Baroque architecture.

The city's development was considerably affected by the first geodesic plan (1731–9) by I. A. Mordvinov and Ivan Michurin. In 1742 a new city boundary was established along the Kamer-Kollezhsky Rampart, encompassing a wide territory beyond Zemlyanoy Gorod, with customs posts on the main roads for the collection of duties. All construction in Moscow was put under strict control, and supervision of the regulations was carried out by an 'architectural team' under the police department.

A new stage in the development of Moscow began in the 1760s under the influence of Neo-classicism. The Commission for Masonry Construction in St Petersburg and Moscow produced a fixed plan for the city (the Gorikhvostov Plan; 1767) and then a plan (1775) for a system of formal squares and streets around the Kremlin to be executed by a specially created organization, the new Kamenny Prikaz (Department of Stonework). In 1768–75 VASILY BAZHENOV prepared a grandiose scheme (unrealized) to rebuild the Kremlin, with a large palace surrounded by an oval plaza and avenues.

In the second half of the 18th century and early 19th, large public buildings, strictly designed on Neo-classical models, led to changes in the planned nodal points of the city. These buildings included the Senate in the Kremlin (1776–87; by MATVEY KAZAKOV) and Moscow University on Mokhovaya Street (1782–93; also by Kazakov), the Nobles' Club on Hunters' Row (1780s; by Kazakov), the Foundling Home (Vospitatel'ny Dom; 1764–70; by Karl Blank) on the River Moskva and the Almshouse beyond Zemlyanoy Gorod (1794–1807; by Ye. S. Nazarov and Giacomo Quarenghi). Several large hospital complexes were built on the periphery of the city: the Military Hospital in Lefortovo (1798–1802; by IVAN YEGOTOV) and the Golitsyn (1794–1801; for illustration *see* KAZAKOV, MATVEY) and Pavlovsky (1802–7) hospitals, both by Kazakov, within the Kamer-Kollezhsky Rampart. The Peter (Petrovsky) Palace (1775–82; by Kazakov; see fig. 3) was built on the road from St Petersburg in a mixture of Gothic Revival and Old Russian styles. Kazakov played a major part in shaping the appearance of Moscow in the period 1780–1812. In the village of Tsaritsyno, then outside Moscow, Bazhenov built an imperial palace (unfinished) in similar style, surrounded by many pavilions set in parkland.

The rapid development of country estates (the best examples are at KUSKOVO and OSTANKINO, then lying outside the city boundaries) influenced all aspects of architecture in Moscow, including residential buildings. The appearance of main streets such as the Tverskaya or Vozdvizhenka streets owed much to the large mansions of the Golitsyns, Demidovs, Sheremet'yevs and others. These houses, whether standing directly on the street or behind impressive courtyards, expressed the prestige of their owners. A variety of Neo-classical forms was blended with great freedom, while various kinds of portico, colonnade and cupola articulated the architecture as a whole. Among the most impressive of these buildings are the Pashkov House on Mokhovaya Street (1784–6; by Bazhenov; for illustration *see* BAZHENOV, VASILY), the Gubin House on Petrovka Street and the Demidov House on

3. Peter (Petrovsky) Palace, near Moscow, by Matvey Kazakov, 1775–82

Gorokhovsky Lane, both built in the 1780s–90s by Kazakov. Merchants' houses with built-in shops were also constructed at this time, as were blocks of flats. Standard architectural designs were widely used in the building of ordinary houses, many of them of wood.

The fire of 1812 destroyed much of the city, and a basic plan for reconstruction was prepared by the Commission for Construction in Moscow under OSIP BOVE in 1817. Bove created an ensemble of squares and public buildings in a semicircle around the Kremlin and Red Square: Teatral'naya (Theatre) Square with the Bol'shoy Theatre (1818–24) connected with Manezhnaya (Manège) Square and the Manezh building (1825), and the restored university (1817–24) led to the Aleksandrovsky Gardens. Red Square was transformed into a spacious and impressive area: the shops along the Kremlin walls were removed, the trading rows (or covered market) were rebuilt and a bronze monument to *Minin and Pozharsky* (1804–18; by Ivan Martos) was erected facing the Senate Tower.

The Council of Guardians (Opekunsky Soviet) building was erected on Solyanka Street in 1821–6 by Domenico Gillardi as part of the Foundling Home ensemble. A triumphal arch (1827–34; by Bove) was placed at the entrance to Moscow from St Petersburg in commemoration of the victory over Napoleon (later rebuilt in Victory Square; for illustration *see* BOVE, OSIP). When the walls of the White Town were taken down in the late 18th century, the ring of boulevards became a favourite place for public promenades. The Zemlyanoy Rampart had been destroyed earlier; the ditch was filled in and a second ring road around Moscow was created, with squares at the intersections of radial streets and with fenced gardens around the houses, hence the name Garden Ring (Sadovoye Kol'tso).

Residential building regulations became stricter. The city was divided into zones in which the economic status of owners determined the number of storeys that could be built and the materials to be used. A new standard type of small detached house for merchants and the middle classes was introduced. Along with standard designs there was also the widespread use of a range of basic decorative elements, which gave some individuality to otherwise identical buildings. The increase in building directly on to streets, the style of façades, the simplification of forms, together with standardization of decoration, demonstrate a clear trend in urban planning, consolidated as the Muscovite Empire style. Major examples of this style are the Gagarin House on Novinsky Boulevard (1817; destr. 1941; by Bove), the Lunin House on Nikitsky (later Suvorovsky) Boulevard (1818–23; by Domenico Gillardi) and the Khrushchov House on Prechistenka (later Kropotkin) Street (1815–17; now the Pushkin Museum) by AFANASY GRIGOR'YEV. Less common were large estates such as the Usachev-Naydyonov House and estate on the River Yauza (1829–31; by Domenico Gillardi). Among commercial buildings, the most striking was the complex of Provisions Warehouses (1832–5; by Vasily Stasov and F. M. Shestakov) on the Garden Ring.

In the mid-19th century a new period of construction accompanied the growth of trade and industry. Rapid expansion took place, and a range of buildings was erected, with differing functions and styles. Strict state controls and earlier concern for the unity of ensembles gave way to private construction in a variety of styles from earlier periods. The high cost of land led to taller buildings and a greater density of streets, often of unbroken façades, all of which greatly altered the scale and proportions of the townscape. The central districts of Moscow now contained multistorey offices and banks, shops and commercial buildings. The business centre of Moscow was Kitay-gorod, while large hotels and theatres, apartment buildings and luxurious town houses were built along the streets of the White Town and Zemlyanoy gorod. On the outskirts, and also on land close to the Kamer-Kollezhsky Rampart, factories and workshops were built; the largest complexes of this kind were in the Kozhevniki and Presnya districts. In suburbs such as Perovo, Kuntsevo and Tsaritsyno, settlements of dachas, a new type of out-of-town development for the better-off, sprang up.

At the very centre of Moscow numerous large new buildings greatly altered the city's appearance. The Great (Bol'shoy) Kremlin Palace (1838–49) and, near by on the banks of the River Moskva, the huge cathedral of Christ the Redeemer (1832–80; destr. 1934; rebuilt from 1994) were both built by KONSTANTIN TON in the official Russo-Byzantine style. On Red Square were erected trading rows (1889–93; later GUM; by ALEKSANDR POMERANTSEV and ROMAN KLEIN), the Historical Museum (1875–81; by Vladimir Shervud; see fig. 4) and opposite this the City Hall (1836–94; by Dmitry Chichagov; later the Central Lenin Museum). The Polytechnical Museum (1875–7; by Ippolit Monigetti and N. A. Shokhin) was built on New Square (Novaya Ploshchad') facing Kitay-gorod. All these buildings were in Russian Revival style, which in the second half of the 19th century was the most popular. Merchants' houses, villas and wooden buildings were also built in this style, 'Ropetism' (*ropetovshchina*), after the architect IVAN ROPET. At the end of the 19th century the

Gothic Revival style became popular, notably in the work of FYODOR SHEKHTEL' and A. E. Erikhson, graphically illustrated in the houses of the aristocracy and merchants in the areas between the Bol'shaya Nikitskaya (later Herzen) and Povarskaya (later Vorovsky) streets and Bol'shaya Polyanka Street and also in specific commercial buildings such as the Muir & Mirrielees department store (1906–8; later TsUM; by Roman Klein).

At the turn of the 20th century numerous buildings were constructed in Art Nouveau style (Rus. *Stil' modern*), including the Metropole Hotel by William Walcot (V. F. Val'kot), the Ryabushinsky House (1900–02; for illustration *see* SHEKHTEL', FYODOR) and the Derozhinsky House (1902; by Shekhtel'). At the same time the Russian Revival style was becoming widespread, as in the Kazan' Station (1912–26; by ALEKSEY SHCHUSEV), the Yaroslavl' Station (1902; by Shekhtel'), and the Pertsev apartment house (1905–7; by Sergey Malyutin). The colourful and imaginative quality of these buildings, especially of churches such as that of the Martha and Mary Mission Convent (1908–12; by Shchusev) and the Old Believers' churches by IL'YA BONDARENKO, wonderfully matched the traditions of early Muscovite architecture.

Examples of Modernist architecture, moving away from the decorative towards a greater simplicity, concision and clarity, were above all to be found among office and commercial buildings such as the Northern Insurance Company's building on Il'inka Street (1910–11; by Ivan Rerberg, Mar'yan Peretyatkovich and Vyacheslav Oltarzhevsky), the *Utro Rossii* printing house (1907; *see* RUSSIA, fig. 13) and the Moscow Trading Company building (1909; both by Shekhtel'), as well as the Business House (Delovoy Dvor'; 1912–13; by I. S. Kuznetsov). During the same period a return to classicizing forms was also apparent in a number of buildings, such as the Shanyavsky People's University (1910–13; by ILLARION IVANOV-SHITS), on Myusskaya Square, often mixed with the methods and style of Art Nouveau, as in the Merchants' Club (1905–9; by Ivanov Shits) on Malaya Dmitrovka Street.

3. AFTER 1917. The Revolution of 1917 set architecture a series of new tasks. In the years immediately following the Revolution a general plan for the reconstruction of the city was drawn up, the 'New Moscow' plan by Ivan Zholtovsky and Aleksey Shchusev, as well as a development plan, 'Greater Moscow', by S. Shestakov. In the difficult conditions of the time, however, the implementation of the general plan amounted only to the removal of several slums, the restoration of the Kremlin, which had been damaged by shelling, and the transformation of Soviet Square (Sovetskaya Ploshchad') with the raising of a monument to *Freedom* (1919; removed 1930s; by N. A. Andreyev). The All-Russian Agricultural and Industrial Exhibition was organized in 1923; among its mostly traditional or stylized buildings the wooden Makhorka pavilion by the Constructivist KONSTANTIN MEL'NIKOV stood out for its original and dynamic forms. On Shabolovka Street stands the striking 160-m steel radio tower by V. G. Shukhov (1923), constituting a distinctive parallel to Vladimir Tatlin's model for a *Monument to the Third International* (1919–20; *see* TATLIN, VLADIMIR, fig. 2). The Lenin Mausoleum on Red Square (timber,

4. Moscow, Red Square, Historical Museum, by Vladimir Shervud, 1875–81

1924; rebuilt in stone, 1929–30, by Shchusev; *see* MAU-SOLEUM, fig. 6) became a special tribune for various celebrations.

Vast residential estates, at first of individual cottages (the village of Sokol) and then of large prefabricated blocks of flats (Usachovka, Shchabolovka, Dubrovka), were built on the outskirts of the capital in the mid-1920s. The main trends of the period were embodied in, for example, the communal housing designed by the Con-structivists, who combined residential units with commu-nal facilities, as on Novinsky and Gogolevsky boulevards and in the student hostel on Donskaya Street. It was only at the beginning of the 1930s and in certain buildings, such as the residential complex on the Bersenev Embank-ment (1928–30; by BORIS IOFAN), that a more realistic approach emerged to deal with the problems of collectiv-ization in daily life.

The most notable architectural achievement of these years were the six workers' clubs, the Rusakov, Frunze and Kauchuk (1927), Svoboda and Pravda (1928) and Burevestnik (1929), all by Konstantin Mel'nikov; the Zuyev Club (for illustration *see* GOLOSOV, (2)) and the Palace of Culture (1931–7; by the VESNIN brothers) for the Proletarsky region. Among other civic buildings, the most interesting are the Gostorg (Ministry of Trade) building (1927; by B. Velikovsky; see fig. 5) on Myasnit-skaya Street, the Planetarium (1928; by Mikhail Barshch

5. Moscow, Myasnitskaya Street, Gostorg (Ministry of Trade) build-ing, by B. Velikovsky, 1927

and M. I. Sinyavsky), the Pravda building (Pantaleymon Golosov), the Izvestiya building (G. Barchin), the Dinamo Stadium (A. Langman and L. Cherikover), the Mossoviet building (for illustration *see* FOMIN, (1)) and the Dinamo Sports Club (both 1928; by Ivan Fomin), in all of which Constructivist motifs predominate. This development was frequently accompanied by the destruction of many fine monuments of the past, including Kazan' Cathedral and the church of the Dormition na Pokrovke (1696–9).

In 1934–41 Moscow grew rapidly as a result of the increasing pressure for urban development and the trend towards large-scale designs. The general plan for the reconstruction of Moscow (1931; ratified 1935; by Vla-dimir Semyonov and Sergey Chernyshov) called for the territorial expansion of the city, its division into zones, the systematization of its streets and squares, and their recon-struction. Simultaneously the style of Soviet architecture changed, with emphasis laid on the picturesque and the traditional, which often resulted in ostentation. The main arteries of Moscow (Gor'ky [now Tverskaya] Street, Lenin Prospect [now Bol'shaya Kaluzhskaya Street], Prospect Mira [now 1-ya Meshchanskaya], the Garden Ring, the Leningrad and Mozhaysky highroads) were lined with multistorey buildings. The centre of the town was re-planned to create large squares and massive public build-ings such as the Council of People's Commissars and the Hotel Moskva on Hunters' Row. New bridges were built across the River Moskva, including the Crimean (Krym-sky) Bridge (1936–8; by Aleksandr Vlasov), and a remod-elling of the river banks led to the creation of several major parks, including Gor'ky Park. The capital became a port for five seas with the building of the Moskva–Volga canal and the River Terminal (1937) at Khimki. The metropolitan underground railway system was built, with stations of grand architectural design. Among the largest public buildings of this period were the Frunze Military Academy (1932–7; by LEV RUDNEV and Viktor O. Munts), the State Lenin (now Russian State) Library (1928–37; by VLADIMIR SHCHUKO and VLADIMIR GEL'FREYKH) and the Red Army Theatre (1934–40; by Karo Alabyan and VASILY SIMBIRTSEV). Of particular interest was the project for a grandiose Palace of the Soviets (h. over 400 m) with a gigantic 500-m statue of Lenin at its apex, which epitomized the excessive triumphalism of Soviet architec-ture of that time. The palace was to be built on the site of the demolished Cathedral of Christ the Redeemer; the foundations, however, proved unable to support such a structure.

After World War II construction in Moscow followed the same lines of development, with special emphasis on new housing, while the seven 'High Buildings' of Moscow State University gave a new skyline to the city (see fig. 6). A new ten-year plan was prepared in 1949–51 by DMITRY CHECHULIN, but it was radically revised in 1972 by MIKHAIL POSOKHIN and others. The boundaries of Mos-cow were extended to the ring motorway, beyond which lay a belt of woods and parks. The entire territory was divided into zones, each with its own specific plan and infrastructure. The move to mass-produced buildings meant a gradual rejection of grand façades and decoration and the use of functional designs. Several new districts were created, including Khimki-Khovrino, Tyoply Stan,

6. Moscow State University, Lenin (now Vorobyov) Hills, by Lev Rudnev and others, 1949–53

Novyye Cheryomushki and Khoroshovo-Mnevniki. Komsomol'sky Prospect was built in a south-westerly direction towards the new sports complex at Luzhniki. In the centre Kalinin Prospect (now New Arbat Street) was created with its tall residential and administrative buildings, and the former Comecon headquarters on the embankment. In the Kremlin itself the Palace of Congresses (Dvorets S'yezdov; 1959–61; by Posokhin and Ashot Mndoyants) was built, and the Hotel Rossiya (1958–65; by Chechulin) in the Zarad'ye district, east of the Kremlin. The Ostankino Tower, the All-Union Radio-Television Centre (completed 1967), and the Palace of Pioneers on the Lenin Hills were built in 1958–62.

In the 1970s and 1980s much attention was given to the problems of blending function and artistic design in large building projects. The architecture of new residential districts became more expressive, as, for example, at Yasenevo, Chertanovo-Severnoye, Veshnyaki-Vladykino, Strogino, Troparevo and Bibirevo-Lyanozovo. Public buildings showed more originality of form; examples include theatres (Moscow Arts Theatre, Taganka Theatre, Children's Music Theatre, Central Puppet Theatre); sports complexes (cycle track at Krylatskoye and Olimpysky Sports' Complex); hotels (Kosmos Hotel and the hotel complex at Izmaylovo); the Tass and Novosty buildings and the department store Moskovsky. The Arbat was turned into a pedestrian zone and its historic appearance restored. In addition, many architectural monuments were restored and fully integrated into the structure of the contemporary city.

For further illustrations *see* SHCHUSEV, ALEKSEY, and RUSSIA, fig. 15.

BIBLIOGRAPHY

GENERAL

I. Mashkov, ed.: *Putevoditel' po Moskve* [A guide to Moscow] (Moscow, 1913)

N. A. Skvortsov: *Arkheologiya i topografiya Moskvy* ([The archaeology and topography of Moscow] (Moscow, 1913)

M. I. Aleksandrovsky: *Ukazatel' moskovskikh tserkvey* [An index of Moscow's churches] (Moscow, 1925)

V. V. Zgura: *Monumental'nyye pamyatniki Moskvy* [The monuments of Moscow] (Moscow, 1926)

V. L. Snegiryov: *Moskovskoye zodchestvo: Ocherki po istorii russkogo zodchestva XIV–XIX v.* [The architecture of Moscow: studies in the history of Russian architecture of the 14th to 19th centuries] (Moscow, 1948)

N. I. Fal'kovsky: *Moskva v istorii tekhniki* [Moscow, a technical history] (Moscow, 1950)

P. V. Sytin: *Istoriya planirovki i zastroyki Moskvy* [A history of the planning and building of Moscow], 3 vols (Moscow, 1950–72)

Moskva: Arkhitekturnyy putevoditel' [Moscow: an architectural guide] (Moscow, 1960)

N. Voronin: *Palaces and Churches of the Kremlin* (London, 1965)

S. Fauchereau, ed.: *Moscow: 1909–1930* (Leningrad, [1980s])

Moskva: Entsiklopediya [Moscow: an encyclopedia] (Moscow, 1980)

I. S. Iaralov and S. M. Zemtsov, eds.: *Zodchiye Moskvy* [Architects of Moscow], 2 vols (Moscow, 1981–8)

A. I. Komech: *Pamyatniki arkhitektury Moskvy: Kreml', Kitay-gorod, tsentral'nyye ploshchadi* [Architectural monuments of Moscow: the Kremlin, Kitay-gorod, the central squares] (Moscow, 1982, 2/1983)

Ye. I. Kirichenko: *Naryad moskovskikh fasadov* [The decoration of Moscow façades] (Moscow, 1987)

A. J. Schmidt: *The Architecture and Planning of Classical Moscow: A Cultural History* (Philadelphia, PA, 1989)

P. Berton: *Moscow: An Architectural History* (Leningrad, 1990)

A. Latour: *Mosca: Guida dell'architettura moderna* (Bologna, 1992)

M. P. Kudryatsev: *Moskva: Tretiy Rim, istoriko-gradostroitel'noye issledovaniye* [Moscow: the third Rome, research into the history of its construction] (Moscow, 1994)

BEFORE *c.* 1700

I. I. Gol'denberg: *Staraya Moskva* [Old Moscow] (Moscow, 1947)

M. N. Tikhomirov: *Drevnyaya Moskva* [Early Moscow] (Moscow, 1947)

S. A. Toropov and N. Brynov: *Arkhitekturnyye pamyatniki Moskvy XV–XVII v.* [Architectural monuments of Moscow from the 15th to 17th centuries] (Moscow, 1948)

M. N. Tikhomirov: *Srednevekovaya Moskva v XIV–XV vekakh* [Medieval Moscow in the 14th and 15th centuries] (Moscow, 1957)

M. G. Rabinovich: *O drevney Moskve* [On early Moscow] (Moscow, 1964)

M. A. Il'in: *Moskva: Pamyatniki arkhitektury XIV–XVII v.* [Moscow: monuments of architecture of the 14th to 17th centuries] (Moscow, 1973)

A. V. Ikonnikov: *Kamennaya letopis' Moskvy* [The chronicle of Moscow in stone] (Moscow, 1978)

V. P. Vygolov: *Arkhitektura moskovskoy Rusi serediny XV veka* [The architecture of Muscovite Rus' in the mid-15th century] (Moscow, 1988)

c. 1700–1917

I. Fomin: 'Moskovskiy klassitsizm' [Moscow classicism], *Mir Isk.* (1904), no. 7, pp. 149–98

M. Ye. Bondarenko: *Arkhitekturnyye pamyatniki Moskvy* [Architectural monuments of Moscow], 3 vols (Moscow, 1904–5)

Moskva na rubezhe dvukh vekov (XIX–XX) [Moscow at the turn of two centuries (19th–20th)] (Moscow, 1910)

P. Gol'denberg and B. Gol'denberg: *Planirovka zhilogo kvartala Moskvy XVII–XIX vv.* [The planning of a residential district of Moscow from the 17th to 19th centuries] (Moscow, 1935)

L. I. Rempel' and T. V. Vyaznikovtseva: *Epokha moderna v Moskve* [The era of Art Nouveau in Moscow], *Arkhit. SSSR* (1935), nos 10–11, pp. 90–93

M. Budylina: *Planirovka i zastroyka Moskvy posle pozhara 1812 goda* [The planning and building of Moscow after the fire of 1812], *Arkhit. Nasledstvo* (1951), no. 1, pp. 135–74

A. A. Fyodorov-Davydov: *Arkhitektura Moskvy posle Otechestvennoy voyny 1812 g.* [The architecture of Moscow after the war of 1812] (Moscow, 1953)

M. A. Il'in: *Arkhitektura Moskvy XVIII veka* [The architecture of 18th-century Moscow] (Moscow, 1953)

——: *Moskva: Pamyatniki arkhitektury XVIII–pervoy treti XIX veka* [Moscow: architectural monuments from the 18th century to the first third of the 19th] (Moscow, 1975)

Ye. V. Nikolayev: *Klassicheskaya Moskva* [Classical Moscow] (Moscow, 1975)

K. Berton: *Moscow: An Architectural History* (London, 1977)

Ye. I. Kirichenko: *Moskva na rubezhe stoletiya* [Moscow at the turn of the century] (Moscow, 1977)

——: *Moskva: Pamyatniki arkhitektury 1830–1910 godov* [Moscow: architectural monuments of the years 1830–1910] (Moscow, 1977)

AFTER 1917

V. Semyonov: 'Arkhitekturnaya rekonstruktsiya Moskvy' [The architectural rebuilding of Moscow], *Voprosy arkhitektury* [Architectural questions] (Moscow, 1935), pp. 119–58

A. M. Zhuravlyov, A. V. Ikonnikov and A. G. Pochegov: *Arkhitektura sovetskoy Rossii* [The architecture of Soviet Russia] (Moscow, 1987)

A. V. Ikonnikov: *Russian Architecture of the Soviet Period* (Moscow, 1988)

II. Art life and organization.

1. Before *c.* 1700. 2. *c.* 1700–1917. 3. After 1917.

1. BEFORE *c.* 1700. Surviving examples of manuscript illumination and icon painting dating to the first half of the 14th century, as well as references in the chronicles to wall painting in the earliest cathedrals in the Moscow Kremlin, are evidence that both Russian and Greek artists were at work there at the time. A local school of painting developed in Moscow in the second half of the 14th century and early 15th and became one of the high points of Old Russian art. ANDREY RUBLYOV, Prokhor from Gorodets, Daniil Chorny and Theophanes the Greek were representatives of the school, which produced major works of wall and panel painting as well as excelling in the art of book production.

Internecine wars in the second quarter of the 15th century brought about a decline in the artistic life of Moscow that was reversed in the second half of the 15th century, leading to great activity in the early 16th. With the establishment of Moscow as capital of the Russian state there was an upsurge in icon painting and wall decoration in line with an increase in building. Artists from Moscow, led by DIONISY, also worked in a number of regional towns and influenced local schools. In the 16th century Moscow became the artistic centre of Russia, with the most important artists working in the palaces of the tsar and the metropolitan. A major fire in the Kremlin in 1547 encouraged such concentration as the work of restoration drew in artists from all over the country.

Two trends stand out in the art of this period: first, an increase in realism and, second, the growing dominance of the church, embodied in the instructions deriving from the Council of the Hundred Chapters (Stoglavy Sobor) of 1551, which led to a richer iconography, more complex compositions and the use of allegorical subjects interpreted in symbolic and theological terms. Along with the development of book illumination, which included hagiographical and historical subjects, as in the chronicles, woodcuts began to appear in books and acted as a channel for Western influence. At the turn of the 16th and 17th centuries, monumental painting was revived by the so-called Godunov school (*see* RUSSIA, §IV, 1), while detailed small-scale painting flourished in the work of the STROGANOV SCHOOL (see fig. 7).

The transitional character of Russian 17th-century art, with its growing links with western Europe, was most clearly manifested in Moscow. The Time of Troubles (1605–13) interrupted artistic development in the capital,

7. Stroganov school: *SS Boris and Gleb*, panel, 17th century (Moscow, Tret'yakov Gallery)

but it was resumed in the second quarter of the 17th century. The main centre of art was the Kremlin Armoury (Oruzheynaya Palata), which housed the first government workshops for icon painting from the mid-1640s. Various works of art were produced there, mainly for the tsar's court, by artists not only from Moscow but also from other Russian towns, as well as from Holland, Poland, Germany and elsewhere. The Armoury also trained artists and was thus the first state school of art in Russia. In 1654–80 it was headed by the boyar B. M. Khitrovo.

The main artistic undertaking of the period was the decoration of the Kremlin cathedrals and numerous estate and monastery churches with wall paintings and icons. Among the artists involved were SIMON USHAKOV, Iosif Vladimirov, Tikhon Filat'yev, Kirill Ulanov (*d* 1751) and Fyodor Zubov. Their work reveals a keen interest in the surrounding world and in communicating spatial forms, realistic tendencies that are most clearly evident in the new, secular genre of portraiture. The spread of printed books resulted in a sharp reduction in the number of illuminated manuscripts produced, which were mainly luxurious folios for the higher nobility and modest manuscripts for the merchant class. The new realism is most notable in prints linked with the work of the Printing Office (Pechatny Dvor), where copper plate engraving was developing. Imported LUBOK prints circulated in Moscow and were frequently used to decorate the rooms of the nobility. The art world of 17th-century Moscow was strongly influenced by immigrants from Ukraine and Belorussia (now Belarus'), whose work introduced new forms of Western art.

2. *c.* 1700–1917. With the transfer of the capital to St Petersburg by Peter I and the removal there of the artists of the Kremlin Armoury, Moscow lost its leading position in the arts, a change confirmed by the establishment of the Academy of Arts in St Petersburg in 1757. The new secular art found fertile soil in Moscow as well as St Petersburg, although in the former it was more influenced by earlier traditions and was closer to popular culture. Portraiture predominated in painting, while icon painting began to incorporate some of the characteristics of western European art, in particular in the use of perspective and chiaroscuro, and the depiction of landscape. Wall paintings, panels, sculptures and reliefs in Baroque and, later, Neo-classical style decorated the nobility's palaces and houses in Moscow as well as their country mansions. The work was carried out by well-known artists and sculptors, principally from St Petersburg. The most important local artists were serfs of noble families, above all of the Sheremet'yevs, working mainly on their estates of KUS KOVO and OSTANKINO.

8. Vasily Perov: *Easter Procession*, oil on canvas, 1861 (Moscow, Tret'yakov Gallery)

By the turn of the 18th and 19th centuries Moscow was on an equal footing with the capital as a centre of artistic life and showed itself to be independent of St Petersburg in the freedom of its artistic tastes. This position was strengthened by the independent system of art education that existed in Moscow. The S. G. Stroganov School of Art was founded in 1825 (from 1860 the Stroganov School of Applied Art); in 1833 the art class at the Moscow Arts Society was established, and in 1866 it was transformed into the Moscow School of Painting, Sculpture and Architecture. These schools were notable for their democratic spirit, even accepting serfs as pupils, and for their special interest in Realism. The founder of the Moscow school of painting was VASILY TROPININ, whose portraits reflect a gentle and lyrical view of everyday life. The Muscovite Vasily Perov was one of the founders of the WANDERERS group, which employed travelling exhibitions and emphasized the portrayal of everyday scenes (see fig. 8). A leading role in the Wanderers art movement was played by other Moscow artists, such as Nikolay Nevryov, Illarion Pryanishnikov, L. L. Kamenev and Aleksey Savrasov, as well as by the collector PAVEL TRET'YAKOV who began his collection of Russian realistic art in 1856. From the 1870s to 1890s Moscow's artistic life was influenced by a circle of artists around the industrialist and art patron SAVVA MAMONTOV; his estate of ABRAMTSEVO was the working location of such artists as Il'ya Repin, Viktor Vasnetsov, Mikhail Vrubel' and Konstantin Korovin. Major historical works were produced in Moscow by Vasily Surikov (*see* RUSSIA, fig. 24), while the work of Vasily Polenov, Isaak Levitan and Mikhail Nesterov was entirely associated with Moscow.

An important event in the artistic life of Moscow was the ceremonial unveiling of the monument to *Aleksandr Pushkin* (1880; by Aleksandr Opekushin) in Tverskoy Boulevard (now in Pushkin Square). In 1892 Tret'yakov made a gift of his collection of paintings to the city, a gesture that led to the convening of the first congress of Russian artists, thus marking the significance of Moscow in the development of national art. In 1905 the collector Ivan Shchukin (1869–1908), brother of Sergey Shchukin (*see* SHCHUKIN, (1)), presented his collection to the Historical Museum. In 1912 the Alexander III Museum of Fine Arts (now Pushkin Museum of Fine Arts) was opened; a year later, the art collections of M. Ye. Tsvetkov, IL'YA OSTROUKHOV and the Botkin family were opened.

In 1903 members of the Muscovite Wanderers combined with those of the St Petersburg World of Art group to create the UNION OF RUSSIAN ARTISTS, including Abram Arkhipov, Korovin, Sergey Ivanov, Valentin Serov and Konstantin Yuon. The Revolution of 1905 provoked a vigorous response from artists in Moscow, expressed in the work of many painters and sculptors, but above all graphic artists. In the ensuing years a series of avant-garde groups were formed: in 1907 BLUE ROSE, with Pavel Kuznetsov, Nikolay Sapunov and Nikolay Krymov, among others; in 1910 JACK OF DIAMONDS, with Pyotr Konchalovsky, Aleksandr Kuprin, Aristarkh Lentulov and Robert Fal'k, out of which emerged in 1912 the Futurist group DONKEY'S TAIL, with Natal'ya Goncharova and Mikhail Larionov among others. The first abstract works

appeared in the 1910s by artists such as Vasily Kandinsky, Kazimir Malevich and Ivan Klyun.

3. AFTER 1917. Moscow became the capital of the new Soviet state in 1918, and artistic life in the city developed vigorously. In 1918 the national studios for free art (Svomas) were established, based in the Stroganov School of Applied Art and the Moscow School of Painting, Sculpture and Architecture; in 1920 they merged to form Vkhutemas (Higher State Art and Technical Workshops). Lenin's Plan of Monumental Propaganda of 1918 led to the razing of monuments on many streets and squares. There was much use of AGITPROP art, principally in preparing the capital for revolutionary festivals, which attracted the city's most accomplished artists. From the Civil War onwards poster art flourished (*see* POSTER), and the All-Russian Agricultural and Industrial Exhibition of 1923 had a stimulating effect on monumental and decorative arts.

In the 1920s artists formed themselves into numerous groups that occasionally fought bitterly over new trends in art and frequently dissolved: the ASSOCIATION OF ARTISTS OF REVOLUTIONARY RUSSIA (AKhRR; 1922–32); the SOCIETY OF EASEL PAINTERS (OST; 1925–32); the Society of Young Artists (Obmokhu; from 1919); Being (Bytiyo; 1921–30); Heat-Colour (Zhar-tsvet; 1923–9); MAKOVETS (1921–6); the Moscow Painters (1925–8); the New Society of Painters (NOKh; 1921–4); the Society of Moscow Artists (OMKh; 1921–32); the Society of Russian Sculptors (ORS; 1926–32); the Association of Realist Artists (OKhR; 1927–32); the Painters' Atelier (1926–30); the FOUR ARTS SOCIETY OF ARTISTS (1924–31). The contradictions among these groups were further emphasized by the establishment of PROLETKUL'T and of the group Left Front of the Arts (LeF; 1922–9), with its idea of Production art or Productivism (*see* CONSTRUCTIVISM, §2). By the mid-1920s the architectural groups that were to determine the course of Soviet architecture had formed: the ASNOVA group (1923–32) was headed by Nikolay Ladovsky, and it described itself as rationalist; in 1925 OSA was founded, headed by Moisey Ginzburg and the Vesnin brothers, and in opposition to the 'left-wing' views of these two groups, the Moscow Society of Architects (MAO) united the traditionalists.

In 1932 the decree 'On the Restructuring of Literary and Artistic Organizations' did away with these multifarious trends in art in Moscow. Later a simple Union of Artists (Soyuz Khudozhnikov) was founded, which advocated Socialist Realism. This change greatly impoverished the artistic life of the capital and encouraged pomposity, especially in large thematic paintings and in formal portraits shown at major exhibitions in the 1930s, such as *Fifteen Years of RKKA* (Workers' and Peasants' Red Army; 1933), *Twenty Years of RKKA and the Navy* (1938) and *Industry and Socialism* (1939). In this context the portraits by Nesterov and Pavel Korin and the landscapes of Igor' Grabar', Kuprin and Yuon are notable for their greater depth. Book illustration was a successful genre, as in the work of Vladimir Favorsky. Monumental art developed considerably as Moscow was rebuilt and expanded, as in the work of Lev Bruni, Aleksandr Deyneka, Yevgeny Lansere and Vera Mukhina (*see* RUSSIA, fig. 27).

After World War II artistic life quickly revived. The Academy of Arts of the USSR was founded in Moscow in 1947. From the second half of the 1950s the number of exhibitions centred on the Central Exhibition Hall in the Manezh building increased. Numerous and varied exhibitions were put on by the Tret'yakov Gallery, the Pushkin Museum of Fine Arts and the Museum of Oriental Art. Several new museums were opened, including the Andrey Rublyov Museum of Ancient Russian Art (1960), the Museum of the Moscow Kremlin (1961) and the A. V. Shchusev State Research and Scientific Museum of Russian Architecture (1964).

Various younger artists, including the avant-garde, worked successfully alongside the older generation and

9. Moscow, Prospect Mira, *Space Obelisk* by A. Faydysh-Krandiyevsky, titanium, h. 100 m, 1964

frequently organized their own exhibitions: at the end of the 1970s and beginning of the 1980s the most important were the *Exhibition of the 23* and the *Seventeen Youth Exhibition*. Monumental artists embellished streets and squares with numerous monuments and decorative sculptures, while paintings and reliefs appeared on the façades, and especially in the interiors, of many large new buildings. Moscow became the centre of a great development that took place in design from the 1960s (see fig. 9).

BIBLIOGRAPHY

N. Geynike and others, eds: *Po Moskve: Progulka po Moskve i yeyo khudozhestvennym i prosvetitel'nym uchrezhdeniyam* [Around Moscow: a walk around Moscow and its artistic and educational institutions] (Moscow, 1917)

V. A. Nikol'sky: *Staraya Moskva: Istoriko-kul'turnyy putevoditel'* [Old Moscow: a historical and cultural guide] (Leningrad, 1924)

Muzei i dostoprimechatel'nosti Moskvy: Putevoditel' [Museums and sights of Moscow: a guidebook] (Moscow, 1926)

A. I. Nekrasov: *Khudozhestvennyye pamyatniki Moskvy i gorodov moskovskoy gubernii* [Artistic monuments of Moscow and the towns of Moscow province] (Moscow, 1928)

——: *Vozniknoveniye moskovskogo iskusstva* [The rise of Muscovite art], i (Moscow, 1929)

Istoriya Moskvy [A history of Moscow], 6 vols (Moscow, 1952–9)

A. S. Loginova: *Khudozhestvennyye sokrovishcha muzeyev Moskvy* [Art treasures of Moscow museums] (Moscow, 1981)

B. Brodsky: *Sokrovishcha Moskvy* [The treasures of Moscow] (Moscow, 1985)

Drugoye iskusstvo: Moskva, 1956–76. K kronike khudozhestvennoy zhizni [A different art: Moscow, 1956–76. Towards a chronicle of artistic life], 2 vols (Moscow, 1991)

VSEVOLOD VYGOLOV

III. Centre of production.

1. GOLD AND SILVER. Moscow's political prominence in the later 15th century and the 16th brought with it a ceremonial splendour that also influenced the art of the goldsmith. Workshops grew around the tsar's court in the Kremlin, which attracted goldsmiths from all parts of Russia. They were accommodated in some of the Kremlin palaces, where they worked both for the tsar and for the court of the patriarch. Production was distinguished by outstanding enamelwork (*see* RUSSIA, §X, 1) and niello, used on both silver and gold objects. Ornament was dominated by stylized floral motifs. Moscow's central position also attracted goldsmiths from Western Europe and the Middle East who introduced new types of ornament; from the West, for example, printed graphics provided patterns for engraving and niello; from Turkey and Persia came decorative motifs derived from brocade fabrics.

During the Time of Troubles (1598–1613) the goldsmithing trade was partly disrupted, but from 1612 the workshops of the Kremlin were re-established and techniques were further perfected on such typically Russian vessels as the *kovsh* (a boat-shaped drinking vessel) or the *bratina* (a rounded drinking bowl). The first Russian hallmarks were used in Moscow c. 1651. The hallmark of work from the tsar's workshop first showed the double-headed eagle, the mark of the patriarch was of a blessing hand. From 1741 the hallmark was of the city's coat of arms of St George.

Towards the end of the 17th century the influence of Western art increased due to the enthusiasm of Peter I for Western culture; new forms of goblets and tankards and bowls were introduced, some showing embossed scenes (e.g. embossed dish, Moscow, Kremlin, Armoury,

MR 156; see 1989 exh. cat., no. 66). After the transfer of the capital to St Petersburg in 1712 the workshops of gold and silversmiths in the Kremlin were closed and the importance of Moscow as a centre of metalwork production declined. Nevertheless, the city remained important for the national market in southern Russia and for exports to the Middle East. It was more closely linked to native traditions. This is seen, for example, in the niello technique, which became popular again from the beginning of the 19th century (e.g. cup and saucer, Moscow, Kremlin, Armoury, 49331, 49332; see 1989 exh. cat., no. 22). With the revival of historical styles from c. 1850 Moscow again became an important centre of enamel production, specializing in cloisonné or filigree enamel work. The leading firms at this time were Ovchinnikov, Khlebnikov and Sazikov, who produced large silver items as well as enamelwork (see RUSSIA, fig. 47). The All Russian Exhibition of Art and Industry in Moscow of 1882 was of far-reaching importance for the establishment of Russian historicism.

About 1900 Art Nouveau was particularly cultivated by goldsmiths in Moscow. Traditional Russian forms and techniques were combined with Art Nouveau motifs. Typical examples of such work are found in the enamel-work of Fyodor Rückert I (fl 1890–1917), who succeeded in detaching this traditional technique from pure historicism to develop a new style.

BIBLIOGRAPHY
T. D. Filimonov: *Opis' moskovskoy Oruzheynoy Palaty* [Inventory of the Armoury in Moscow] (Moscow, 1884)
V. K. Troytsky: *Slovar' moskovskikh masterov zolotogo, serebryanogo i almaznogo dela XVII v.* [Dictionary of Moscow gold, silver and diamond masters of the 17th century] (Moscow, 1930)
T. V. Nikolayeva: *Prikladnoye iskusstvo moskovskoy Rusi* [Applied art of Muscovite Rus'] (Moscow, 1976)
A. von Solodkoff: *Russian Gold and Silver* (Fribourg and London, 1981)
S. Ya. Kovarskaya, I. D. Kostina and Ye. V. Shakurova: *Russkoye zoloto XIV–nachala XXV v.* [Russian gold of the 14th century to the early 15th] (Moscow, 1987)
Tradizioni nella gioielleria russa (exh. cat., Alessandria, 1988)
G. Hill, G. G. Smorodinova and B. L. Ulyanova: *Fabergé and the Russian Master Goldsmiths* (New York, 1989)
Dar Gold aus dem Kreml (exh. cat., Bremen, Übersee-Mus., 1989)

ALEXANDER VON SOLODKOFF

2. CERAMICS. Simple earthenwares and tiles were produced in Moscow from medieval times. Large-scale production began in the 18th century. In 1766 Francis Gardner (fl 1746–86) was granted an imperial privilege to make porcelain, and he established a factory in Verbilki, near Moscow. Under the patronage of Catherine II (reg 1762–96) its success was ensured, and it became the main competitor of St Petersburg Imperial Porcelain Factory, producing table-services and figures. Many factories were established during the 19th century, including those of Prince NIKOLAY YUSUPOV on his estate of Arkhangel'skoye, where blanks from St Petersburg were decorated with flowers, portraits and simple patterns; the Novy Factory in Kuzyayevo, where both faience and porcelain were made until c. 1850; and the Popov Porcelain Factory (est. 1806), which was bought by Aleksandr Popov (fl 1811–c. 1850) in 1811, and which manufactured both faience and porcelain. In 1818 N. S. Kudinov (fl 1818–25) established a porcelain factory at Lystsovo, which produced wares similar to those of the Gardner factory. In the late 19th century most of the factories were merged with the consortium of factories established in 1889 by Mikhail Kuznetsov (fl 1864–89). (For further discussion see RUSSIA, §VII.)

BIBLIOGRAPHY
M. C. Ross: *Russian Porcelains* (Boston, MA, 1968)
L. Nikiforova: *Russian Porcelain in the Hermitage Collection* (Leningrad, 1973)
V. A. Popov: *Russkiy farfor* [Russian porcelain] (Moscow, 1980)

3. GLASS. In 1632 the Swedish gunmaker Paul Kunckel established a glass factory in Dukhanino near Moscow for the production of pharmaceutical and crown glass. The Izmaylovsky Glassworks (est. 1668) outside Moscow were more successful and produced luxury tablewares for the Russian Imperial family until they closed c. 1725. During the early 18th century many new glass factories were established in and around Moscow, but they were forced to close down after the decree of 1747 prohibiting the manufacture of glass in the vicinity of Moscow in order to protect the rapidly decreasing forests.

BIBLIOGRAPHY
Russian Glass of the 17th–20th Century (exh. cat., Corning, NY, Mus. Glass, 1990)

BRUCE TATTERSALL

IV. Buildings.

1. The Kremlin. 2. St Basil's Cathedral.

1. THE KREMLIN.

(i) Introduction. (ii) Cathedral of the Dormition. (iii) Cathedral of the Archangel Michael. (iv) Cathedral of the Annunciation.

(i) Introduction. The earliest development of the Moscow Kremlin by the Slavs, from the 10th century to the 13th, is known only from archaeological excavations and from the chronicles (see §I, 1 above). The rise of Moscow in the 14th century and early 15th, and its transformation into one of the strongest principalities of Rus', was accompanied by the development of stone buildings: white-stone cathedrals were erected in the 1320s–30s, followed by walls and towers (late 1360s), churches and various secular buildings. With the formation of a powerful Russian state centred on Moscow in the second half of the 15th century and early 16th, extensive building took place in the Kremlin, and the asymmetrical triangle of high walls and towers with the Cathedral Square (for illustration see ALEKSEYEV, FYODOR) at the centre and four roads running to the main gates was constructed. The fine cathedrals in the main square, those of the Dormition, the Archangel Michael and the Annunciation (see §(ii)-(iv) below), harmonized well with the bell-tower of Ivan the Great (1505–8) and the Faceted Palace (Granovitaya Palata; 1487–91), as well as with monasteries such as those of the Ascension, Miracles, and Epiphany, which have not survived. The key position of the Kremlin in the growth of Moscow was further emphasized in the 17th century by the superstructure (c. 1600) of the Ivan the Great bell-tower and by the hipped roofs that were added to the gate-towers. Numerous court buildings (the Teremnoy, Poteshny and Patriarch's palaces), administrative buildings such as the Armoury (Oruzheynaya Palata) and churches with Muscovite decorative carving were also built in the 17th century.

10. Moscow Kremlin with the Great Kremlin Palace (1838–49) by Konstantin Ton in the centre; view from the River Moskva

The Arsenal (1702–36; rebuilt 1830s), with its regularity of design, introduced new lines into the ensemble. The transfer of the capital to St Petersburg in the early 18th century, however, saved the Kremlin from major reconstruction. Later, the Neo-classical style was introduced into the Kremlin by Matvey Kazakov's Moscow Senate building (1776–87). During the occupation of Moscow by the French in 1812 the Kremlin suffered considerable damage, and, as the French withdrew, several buildings and walls were destroyed. The restoration of these was carried out by the Commission for Construction in Moscow, headed by Osip Bove. The largest new building was the Great Kremlin Palace (1838–49; by Konstantin Ton) in Russo-Byzantine style, which dominates the view of the Kremlin from the River Moskva (see fig. 10). During its construction several court buildings were demolished; those remaining are inside the new palace. A new Armoury (1844–51) was erected to a plan by Konstantin Ton.

In March 1918 the Kremlin became the residence of the Soviet government, which was transferred to Moscow. Buildings damaged by artillery shelling were restored, while in the late 1920s and 1930s several monasteries, churches and secular buildings were pulled down and replaced by the Military School of the Central Executive Committee. Several areas were laid out with plants in the ensuing years. The Palace of Congresses (1959–61; by a group of architects headed by Mikhail Posokhin) replaced several demolished buildings near the Trinity Tower, seriously distorting the appearance of the Kremlin. Research, restoration and archaeological work began in 1918, however, and returned many buildings to their original appearance.

BIBLIOGRAPHY

A. Vel'tman: *Dostopamyatnosti moskovskogo Kremlya* [Memorabilia of the Moscow Kremlin] (Moscow, 1843)
M. Fabritsius: *Kreml' v Moskve: Ocherki i kartiny proshlogo i nastoyashchego* [The Kremlin in Moscow: studies and pictures of the past and present] (Moscow, 1883)
S. P. Bartenev: *Moskovskiy Kreml' v starinu i teper'* [The Moscow Kremlin in olden times and now], 2 vols (Moscow, 1913–16)
——: *Bol'shoy kremlyovskiy dvorets, dvortsovyye tserkvi i pridvornyye sobory* [The Great Kremlin Palace, court churches and cathedrals] (Moscow, 1916)
N. I. Brunov: *Moskovskiy Kreml'* [The Moscow Kremlin] (Moscow, 1948)
L. Birzite: *Razvitiye natsional'nykh form v arkhitekture moskovskogo Kremlya* [The development of national forms in the architecture of the Moscow Kremlin] (Riga, 1954)
A. Voyce: *The Moscow Kremlin: Its History, Architecture and Art Treasures* (Los Angeles, 1954)
D. S. Likhachev: *Khudozhestvennyye pamyatniki moskovskogo Kremlya* [Artistic monuments of the Moscow Kremlin] (Moscow, 1956)
V. Snegirer, N. Mnera and S. Borovkora: *Kreml' Moskvy* [The Moscow Kremlin] (Moscow, 1957)
N. Ya. Tikhomirov and V. N. Ivanov: *Moskovskiy Kreml': Istoriya arkhitektury* [The Moscow Kremlin: the history of its architecture] (Moscow, 1967)
V. N. Ivanov: *Moskovskiy Kreml'* [The Moscow Kremlin] (Moscow, 1971)
V. P. Vygolov: *Arkhitektura moskovskoy Rusi serediny XV veka* [The architecture of Muscovite Rus' in the mid-15th century] (Moscow, 1988)

(ii) Cathedral of the Dormition. The principal cathedral of Moscow and of the Russian state from the 14th century to the 17th, it was used for the most important religious and state ceremonies. The first stone cathedral of the Dormition (Uspensky sobor) in the Kremlin was built in 1326–7 on the order of Metropolitan Peter and Prince Ivan Kalita (*reg* 1328–40), and it was one of the earliest stone buildings in Moscow. Archaeological excavations show that it was a small single-domed, four-pier church with three apses, three porches and a chapel on the north-eastern side, and was close in style to the cathedral of St George in Yur'yev-Pol'sky (1230–34). By the mid-15th century it had fallen into dilapidation, and in 1472–4 it was replaced by a large new building by the Muscovite architects I. Krivtsov and Myshkin, under the patronage of Metropolitan Feognost, and modelled on the cathedral of the Dormition in Vladimir. The newly built structure collapsed in a minor earthquake in 1474.

On the invitation of Ivan III (*reg* 1462–1505), the Italian engineer and architect ARISTOTELE FIORAVANTI rebuilt the cathedral in 1475–9 using the same model. The foundations were laid at considerable depth (over 4 m) and strengthened with oak beams. The walls were of large white-stone blocks with a rubble fill; the piers, vaults and drums of the domes were of specially durable brick, made to the architect's specifications. The walls were additionally strengthened by iron tie-rods. Techniques and tools new to Russia, such as ruler and compasses, were also used. In 1481 a team of artists headed by DIONISY painted a *Deësis* (destr.) for the iconostasis and decorated two chapels with wall paintings (*see* POST-BYZANTINE ART, fig. 7); the decoration of the interior was completed by 1513–15.

During the 16th and 17th centuries the cathedral underwent several alterations: after the fire of 1547 during repairs to the roof, the domes received their onion shapes and gilt-copper covering; in 1624–6 groin vaults were added, with iron tie-rods, and the capitals of the piers were chiselled smooth; in 1642–3 new wall paintings replaced most of the original decoration; in the 1670s–80s the window surrounds were planed smooth and the south-eastern area of the altar was rebuilt. Restoration and renovation in the 18th and 19th centuries introduced several further significant changes in the architecture of the cathedral. Moreover, it was repeatedly restored in the late 19th century and early 20th, as well as during the Soviet period.

The cathedral is a large, three-aisled building with five low apses and five massive domes to the east. This type of church, clearly based on a 12th-century model, was innovative for its time. Its interpretation of its model is also original and differs from the domed-cross type of church. The six piers (four of them round) divide the interior into 12 equal square bays roofed with groin vaults new to Russia, or with domes. The traditional internal galleries have been omitted in order to achieve unprecedented spaciousness that is evenly and well lit by the windows in the walls and in the drums (for illustration *see* FIORAVANTI, ARISTOTELE).

The exterior is more traditional, and it is divided into equal sections by pilasters ending in *zakomary*. There are two tiers of slit windows and a belt of blind arcading midway up the walls. The arcading is clearly based on that of the model, as are the recessed portals, yet the clarity, precision and regular proportions of the whole design demonstrate the architect's Italian training. Renaissance features are evident in the design of the elegant porch with its double suspended arches at the west entrance. Fioravanti's brilliance can also be seen in the integration of the five apses into the three-aisled plan. The cathedral had a great influence on later Russian churches such as the cathedral of the Virgin of Smolensk in the Novodevichy Convent (see fig. 2 above).

BIBLIOGRAPHY

I. M. Snegiryov: *Uspensky sobor v Moskve* [The cathedral of the Dormition in Moscow] (Moscow, 1856)

A. G. Levshin: *Istoricheskoye opisaniye pervoprestol'nogo v Rossii khrama moskovskogo bol'shogo Uspenskogo sobora* [A historical description of the principal court church in Russia, the great cathedral of the Dormition in Moscow] (Moscow, 1873)

V. Uspensky and S. Pisarev: *Osnovaniye moskovskogo Uspenskogo sobora i predstavleniye Petra mitropolita* [The founding of the cathedral of the Dormition in Moscow and the presentation of Metropolitan Peter] (St Petersburg, 1908)

N. Brunoff: 'Due cattedrali del Cremlino costruite da italiani', *Archit. & A. Dec.*, vi/3 (1926), pp. 97–100

V. L. Snegiryov: *Aristotel' Fioravanti i perestroyka moskovskogo Kremlya* [Aristotel' Fioravanti and the rebuilding of the Moscow Kremlin] (Moscow, 1935)

M. A. Iljin: 'La cattedrale dell'Assunzione di Mosca: Precedenti culturali', *A. Lombarda*, xliv–xlv (1976), pp. 185–7

T. V. Tolstaya: *Uspensky sobor moskovskogo Kremlya* [The Uspensky cathedral of the Dormition in the Moscow Kremlin] (Moscow, 1979)

Unikal'nomu pamyatniku russkoy kul'tury Uspenskomu soboru moskovskogo Kremlya 500 let. Tozisy nauchnoy konferentsii: Moskva, 1979 [The 500th anniversary of the cathedral of the Dormition, a unique monument of Russian culture. Papers of a scientific conference: Moscow, 1979]

Uspensky sobor moskovskogo Kremlya: Materialy i issledovaniya [The Uspensky cathedral of the Dormition in the Moscow Kremlin: materials and research], ed. Ye. S. Smirkova (Moscow, 1985)

V. I. Fyodorov: 'K rekonstruktsii planov glavnogo sobora moskovskogo Kremlya' [Towards the reconstruction of the plans of the main cathedral of the Moscow Kremlin], *Pamyatniki kul'tury: Novyye otkrytiya/ Monuments of Culture: New Discoveries*, ed. T. B. Kiyazevskaya (Leningrad, 1987), pp. 459–71

V. P. Vygolov: *Arkhitektura moskovskoy Rusi serediny XV veka* [The architecture of Muscovite Rus' in the mid-15th century] (Moscow, 1988)

(iii) Cathedral of the Archangel Michael. Its basic plan is traditional, but the exterior is conceived in the spirit of the Italian Renaissance, and it was the first church in Russia to make broad use of the decorative orders. After the cathedral of the Dormition (*see* §(ii) above), it is the second most important building in the Cathedral Square, and it is the burial place of the grand-princes, later the tsars.

The first stone cathedral on the site was built in 1333 by Prince Ivan Kalita (*reg* 1328–40) and was decorated with wall paintings in 1344–6. In 1505–8 the Venetian architect Aleviz Novy (possibly Alevisio Lamberti da Montagnano) built a new cathedral to replace the dilapidated one; the interior was decorated in 1564–5. In the 16th century chapels were added to the side apses. In 1652–66 new wall paintings replaced the earlier decoration.

11. Moscow, Kremlin, cathedral of the Archangel Michael by Aleviz Novy, north and west façades, 1505–8

After the Kremlin fire of 1737, the galleries to the north and west of the cathedral were removed, and in 1773 buttresses were built against the south wall. In the 18th century the goblet-shaped pinnacles (*fialy*) over the *zakomary* were removed, and the main dome was given its onion shape. Partial restoration of the cathedral took place in the Soviet period.

The cathedral is a domed cross in plan, with six rectangular piers, three aisles and five domes. The nave is wider than the aisles, and little natural light enters through the narrow windows. The domes are displaced towards the east; the central dome is the largest, while the west pair of domes are larger than the east pair. A unique feature of the cathedral is its three-tiered narthex at the west end. The lower tier opens on to the façade in an arched porch; the second tier includes small chapels and an annexe (added in 1826) with windows on to both the interior and exterior; the third tier is in the form of a narrow gallery lit by circular windows.

The two-tiered façade is divided vertically by pilasters with Corinthian capitals decorated with volutes and surmounted by *zakomary* in the form of Venetian-style scallop shells. The façade is divided horizontally by two elaborate cornices: the lower tier is decorated with arches, the upper with recessed panels (see fig. 11). The fine carving of the portals and capitals is in white stone, which was all the more distinctive against the original red-brick walls (now plastered). The interior of the cathedral is less affected by the decorative use of orders; the piers were given massive pedestals and cornices, as were the corresponding pilasters in the aisles.

The cathedral's architectural decoration was highly influential in the development of early Russian architecture and in many ways directly affected the style of the Godunov period at the turn of the 16th and 17th centuries.

BIBLIOGRAPHY

I. M. Snegiryov: *Arkhangel'sky sobor v moskovskom Kremle* [The cathedral of the Archangel Michael in the Moscow Kremlin] (Moscow, 1865)

A. Lebedev: *Moskovskiy kafedral'nyy Arkhangel'sky sobor* [The Moscow cathedral of the Archangel Michael] (Moscow, 1880)

N. D. Izvekov: *Moskovskiy pridvornyy Arkhangel'sky sobor* [The Moscow court cathedral of the Archangel Michael] (Sergiyev Posad, 1916)

A. I. Vlasyuk: 'O rabote zodchego Aleviza Novogo v Bakhchisaraye i v moskovskom Kremle' [On the work of the architect Aleviz Novy in Bakhchisaray and in the Moscow Kremlin], *Arkhit. Nasledstvo*, x (1958), pp. 101–10

Ye. S. Sizov: 'Novyye materialy po Arkhangel'skomu soboru: Kogda byl postroyen Arkhangel'sky sobor?' [New materials on the cathedral of the Archangel Michael: when was the cathedral of the Archangel Michael built?], *Arkhit. Nasledstvo*, xv (1963), pp. 176–7

A. V. Vorob'yov and V. A. Smyslova: 'O galereye Arkhangel'skogo sobora' [On the gallery of the cathedral of the Archangel Michael], *Arkhit. Nasledstvo*, xv (1963), pp. 178–81

G. V. Popov, ed.: *Drevnerusskoye iskusstvo: Zarubezhnyye svyazi* [Old Russian art: foreign connections] (Moscow, 1975), pp. 252–81

I. S. Nenarokamova, ed.: *Gosudarstvennyye muzei moskovskogo Kremlya: Materialy i issledovaniya* [The State museums of the Moscow Kremlin: materials and research], iii (Moscow, 1980), pp. 76–105

(iv) Cathedral of the Annunciation. One of the major buildings in the Cathedral Square, it served as the household church of the grand-princes, later the tsars, and it is connected by passages to the palace apartments. The first stone cathedral of the Annunciation (Blagoveshchensky) was built on this site in the late 14th century and is mentioned in the chronicles in the early 15th. It was a small, white-stone church, with a single dome, corner buttresses and single apse above a crypt. In 1405 it was decorated by Theophanes the Greek, Prokhor from Gorodets and Andrey Rublyov. In 1416 it was entirely rebuilt, the walls of the crypt were faced, and the enlarged church included four piers and three apses. In 1482–3 it was pulled down to the level of the crypt, and in 1484–9 masons from Pskov built the present cathedral on the existing foundations.

The cathedral is a typical example of Muscovite architecture of the time: a brick domed-cross church with four piers and three apses and with façades divided into three sections surmounted by *zakomary*. Its special features include the three original domes, evidently derived from the architecture of Vladimir–Suzdal', the octagonal base under the central drum, borrowed from Pskov but reworked in Muscovite style with ogee-shaped *kokoshniki*, and the vaulted promenade-gallery on three sides. The decorative blend of various forms is also notable. Blind arcading on the apses is clearly derived from the cathedral of the Dormition. Typically Muscovite is the ornamental frieze above the arcading (see fig. 12); it was originally ceramic but was replaced in white stone by F. F. Richter in the 19th century. The south portal with its carved columns and capitals is also Muscovite in style, while Pskov influence is evident in the decorative friezes around the drums. The later north and west portals (1564), with their splendid Renaissance carving, are similar to those of the cathedral of the Archangel Michael and are clearly of Italian workmanship. The interior of the building is small and cramped by the low vaults over the side aisles and the gallery for the grand-prince's family at the west end.

12. Moscow, Kremlin, cathedral of the Annunciation, east façade, 1484–9

In 1562–4 the chapel in the south gallery was renovated, its entrance was closed in and four single-domed chapels were built over the corners of the gallery. The chapels' panelled two-tiered façades were modelled on those of the cathedral of the Archangel Michael. At the same time a further two domes were added to the west part of the roof. In 1572 the chapel in the south gallery became the private prayer-chapel of Ivan IV (*reg* 1533–84), and it was sumptuously decorated. The jasper floor of the cathedral came from the church of Rostov the Great (Rostov Veliky) in the mid-16th century.

The cathedral was decorated in 1508 by a team of painters from the Iosifo-Volokolamsky Monastery led by Feodosy, son of Dionisy. The wall paintings were restored after the Kremlin fire of 1547 by artists from Pskov, and again in 1648 by a team of icon painters led by T. Filat'yev. Wall paintings in oil dating to 1771 were uncovered during restoration in the 1980s. Restoration of the building was carried out under F. F. Richter in 1863–7, and again in the Soviet period.

BIBLIOGRAPHY

I. M. Snegiryov: *Blagoveshchensky sobor v Moskve* [The cathedral of the Annunciation in Moscow] (Moscow, 1854)

N. D. Izvekov: *Moskovskiy pridvornyy Blagoveshchensky sobor* [The Moscow court cathedral of the Annunciation] (Moscow, 1911)

N. N. Voronin: *Zodchestvo severo-vostochnoy Rusi XII–XV vv* [The architecture of north-eastern Russia from the 12th century to the 15th], ii (Moscow, 1962), pp. 245–52

V. N. Lazarev and others, ed.: *Drevnerusskoye iskusstvo: Khudozhestvennaya kul'tura Pskova* [Old Russian art: the artistic culture of Pskov] (Moscow, 1968), pp. 174–96

V. I. Fyodorov and N. S. Shelyapina: 'Drevneyshaya istoriya Blagoveshchenskogo sobora moskovskogo Kremlya' [The earliest history of the cathedral of the Annunciation in the Moscow Kremlin], *Sov. Arkheol.* (1972), no. 4, pp. 223–35

M. Kh. Aleshkovsky and B. L. Al'tshuller: 'Blagoveshchensky sobor, a ne pridel Vasiliya Kesariyskogo' [The cathedral of the Annunciation and

13. Moscow, St Basil's Cathedral, attributed to Barma and Postnik, 1555–61, with later additions

not the chapel of Vasily Kesariysky], *Sov. Arkheol.* (1973), no. 2, pp. 88–99

I. S. Nenarokamova, ed.: *Gosudarstvennyye muzei moskovskogo Kremlya: Materialy i issledovaniya* [The State museums of the Moscow Kremlin: materials and research], i (Moscow, 1973), pp. 73–85

V. I. Fyodorov: 'Blagoveshchensky sobor moskovskogo Kremlya v svete issledovaniy 1960–1972 gg' [The cathedral of the Annunciation of the Moscow Kremlin in the light of research of 1960–72], *Sov. Arkheol.* (1974), no. 4, pp. 112–31

2. ST BASIL'S CATHEDRAL. In 1553–4, at the command of Ivan IV (*reg* 1533–84), the stone church of the Trinity on the Fosse (Troitsa na Rvu) was built in Red Square to commemorate the capture of Kazan'. It had seven wooden chapels. In 1555–61, however, the new brick cathedral of the Protective Veil on the Fosse (Pokrov na Rvu), attributed to the architects Barma and Postnik, was built with eight stone chapels symmetrically arranged on a common foundation around this central part. Another chapel was built in the north-east corner over the grave of the 'holy fool' of Moscow, Basil the Blessed (Vasily Blazhenny), in 1588, since when the cathedral has been popularly known by his name. At this time the free-standing bell-tower at the south-east corner of the building was erected. The ornamented domes over the chapels were added in 1593. In 1672 a chapel was built in the south-east corner over the grave of another 'holy fool', John the Blessed (Ioann Blazhenny). In the 1680s a covered gallery with columns and four vestibules was added. The bell-tower was entirely rebuilt. The outside walls of the gallery and the window casings were ornamentally painted, and a polychrome carved frieze with inscriptions was placed below the cornice. In the 18th century the ceramic inscriptions were removed during repairs, as well as the small domes at the base of the central hipped roof. Restoration work, begun in the 1890s, continued in the Soviet period.

The church's astonishing appearance symbolized a heavenly Jerusalem embodying in its forms the idea of the church-city, and to a large extent governed the original conception of the church as a multi-chapel creation. The eight chapels are arranged on a high base symmetrically around the central tower-church, an eight-on-four construction (octagon on a square or cube) with a stellar upper section surmounted by a slender hipped roof and dome. Four octagonal tiered chapels with large domes are placed on the main axes with, between them, smaller chapels surmounted by domes with circular drums above three rows of *kokoshniki* (see fig. 13). The result is a dynamic structure designed to be viewed from every angle. The rich and colourful decoration of the façades is unique, and the cathedral combines the panelled treatment of the chapel walls with rows of *kokoshniki*, varied cornices side by side with pointed gables, columns, window frames decorated with circlets and beads, and polychrome insets.

The interior of the cathedral is also unusual, consisting of separate small churches without piers, connected by covered passages. Such cramped premises, originally embellished not with thematic wall paintings but with rather inadequate non-figurative decoration, were not appropriate for church ceremonies, hence the emphasis on the exterior of the building with its impact on the ensemble of Red Square and on the panorama of the capital.

BIBLIOGRAPHY

A. Ye. Belyankin: *Istoricheskiye zapiski i svedeniya o Pokrovskom i svyatom Vasiliya Blazhennogo sobore v stolichnom grade Moskve, osnovannyye na vernykh faktakh i pocherpnutyye iz dostoverneyshikh istochnikov* [Historical notes and information about the cathedral of the Protective Veil and of St Basil in the capital city Moscow, based on true facts and drawn from reliable sources] (Moscow, 1847, 2/1867)

I. Kuznetsov: *Moskovskiy Pokrovsky i svyatogo Blazhennogo Vasiliya, chto na Rvu, sobor* [The Moscow cathedral of the Protective Veil and of St Basil on the Fosse] (Moscow, 1895)

V. V. Suslov: *Khram Vasiliya Blazhennogo v Moskve (Pokrovsky sobor)* [St Basil's Cathedral in Moscow (the cathedral of the Protective Veil)] (St Petersburg, 1901)

N. H. Sobolev, ed.: *Pamyatniki russkoy arkhitektury: Vasily Blazhenny* [Monuments of Russian architecture: St Basil] (Moscow, 1942)

N. N. Sobolev: *Vasily Blazhenny (Pokrovsky sobor)* [St Basil's (the cathedral of the Protective Veil)] (Moscow, 1949)

V. L. Snegiryov: *Pamyatnik arkhitektury khram Vasiliya Blazhennogo* [The architectural monument, St Basil's Cathedral] (Moscow, 1953)

N. I. Brunov: *Khram Vasiliya Blazhennogo, Pokrovsky sobor* [St Basil's Cathedral, the cathedral of the Protective Veil] (Moscow, 1988)

VSEVOLOD VYGOLOV

Moser (i). English family of artists of Swiss origin.

(1) George Michael Moser (*b* Schaffhausen, 1706; *d* London, 1783). Engraver, chaser, designer, teacher and Swiss medallist. He trained in Geneva as a coppersmith and later as a chaser and engraver. He is thought to have arrived in London in 1726 but is not recorded until his marriage to Mary Guynier in 1729/30. He is best known for the elaborately chased and enamelled gold boxes and watch-cases that he produced in London; some extant examples (Gilbert Col., on loan to Los Angeles, CA, Co. Mus. A.) are signed. Some of his designs for watch-cases also survive (London, V&A). His work, carried out in the continental manner, is often highly sculptural, and he is said to have been influential in spreading the Rococo style in England. Four unmarked caryatid silver candlesticks (1740–45; *see* ENGLAND, fig. 78) on the theme of Apollo's pursuit of Daphne are based on a drawing signed by Moser (all London, V&A) and are rare examples of the execution of a fully Rococo English silver design. Moser was one of the founder-members of the Royal Academy, London, and became its first Keeper in 1768. He is also known to have taught, alongside the French engraver Gravelot, at the St Martin's Lane Academy, London (of which he was manager and treasurer), and acted as drawing master to the British royal family. He influenced a number of his contemporaries, for example Augustin Heckel (*c.* 1690–1770), George Daniel Gaab (*fl* 1744–84) and Peter Glazier (*fl* 1748–52). At his funeral he was described by Sir Joshua Reynolds as the 'Father of the present race of Artists'.

BIBLIOGRAPHY

C. Blair, ed.: *The History of Silver* (London, 1987)

P. Glanville: *Silver in England* (London, 1987)

A. K. Snowman: *Eighteenth-century Gold Boxes of Europe* (Woodbridge, 1990)

C. Truman: *The Gilbert Collection of Gold Boxes*, Los Angeles, CA, Co. Mus. A. cat. (Los Angeles, 1991)

EMMA PACKER

(2) Mary Moser [Lloyd, Mrs Hugh] (*b* London, 27 Oct 1744; *d* London, 2 May 1819). Painter, daughter of (1) George Michael Moser. She painted in oil and water-colour and was one of the founder-members of the British Royal Academy. She probably received her early training from her father. In 1758 and 1759 one of her drawings won an award from the Society of Arts, and from 1760 to 1768 she exhibited at the Society of Artists. She exhibited at the Royal Academy in most years from 1769 to 1802. As a woman, she was not expected to take part in the running of the Academy but took an active role in its proceedings, attending the General Assemblies and voting in elections.

Although Moser was very short-sighted her work was technically meticulous, as can be seen in her floral still-lifes (two examples of *c.* 1769; London, RA), which are in the tradition of Jean-Baptiste Monnoyer and Rachel Ruysch. In the late 1770s her subject-matter appears to have taken a more noble turn, and she exhibited almost exclusively history paintings, showing only an occasional flower picture or portrait. However, her only surviving works are of flowers, the most important being the complete decoration of a room at Frogmore House, Berks, for her friend Queen Charlotte (oil on canvas and paper; *c.* 1795).

In the early years of the Royal Academy her affection for Henry Fuseli was common knowledge. In 1793 she married Captain Hugh Lloyd and exhibited as Mrs Hugh Lloyd from 1797. Moser suffered a stroke that paralysed her right side in 1810 but was working again, albeit with difficulty, by 1814.

BIBLIOGRAPHY

Waterhouse: *18th C.*

J. Farington: *Diaries* (1793–1821); ed. K. Garlick and A. Macintyre (i–vi) and K. Cave (vii–xvi) as *The Diaries of Joseph Farington*, 16 vols (New Haven and London, 1978–84)

J. T. Smith: *Nollekens and his Times* (London, 1828/*R* 1986)

M. Zweig: 'Mary Moser', *Connoisseur Yb.* (1956), pp. 104–10

P. Mitchell: *European Flower Painters* (London, 1973), pp. 182–3, pl. 257

JOHN WILSON

Moser (ii). Swiss family of architects. Johann Moser (1798–1855) was a master builder active in Baden, Aargau, whose son (1) Robert Moser became an architect. (2) Karl Moser, the son of Robert, was one of the most influential architects in Switzerland after 1900 and was known as the father of Swiss Modernism, which he actively supported in his later work and in his teaching. (3) Werner Moser, Karl's son, who was also an influential teacher, introduced the architecture of the USA, and of Frank Lloyd Wright in particular, to Switzerland, and his buildings reflected the development of a regional approach in Swiss Modernism. Werner's son Lorenz Moser continued the family tradition. Their work was concentrated mostly in the German-speaking part of Switzerland, and church building was a particular interest of the family.

(1) Robert Moser (*b* Baden, Aargau, Sept 1833; *d* Zurich, 5 Dec 1901). He studied architecture at the Bauschule, Karlsruhe, where his teachers included Friedrich Eisenlohr and Heinrich Lang (1824–93). His earliest building, a school (1856–7) in Baden, was designed in a neo-classical style echoing Lang's work. Moser then made study trips to Paris, Belgium and Italy. His most important architectural works are public buildings; his prisons at Lenzburg and Basle, for example, were the first in the region to use a centralized, panoptical layout and were regarded as fundamental to future developments in this field. The Kursaal (1871–5), Baden, is a prominent example of Swiss Renaissance Revival architecture in the canton of Aargau. In 1894, under the guidance of Rudolf Rahn (1841–1912), one of the founders of Swiss art history, Moser restored the Klosterkirche in Königsfelden Abbey, Brugg, an outstanding example of the medieval architecture of the mendicant orders in Switzerland.

SKL

BIBLIOGRAPHY

G. Gull: 'Nekrolog', *Schweiz. Bauztg*, xxxviii/25 (1901), pp. 275–6
U. Münzel: 'Robert Moser', *Biographisches Lexikon des Kantons Aargau, 1803–1957* (Aarau, 1958)

(2) Karl Moser (*b* Baden, 10 Aug 1860; *d* Zurich, 28 Feb 1936). Son of (1) Robert Moser. He studied architecture (1878–82) at the Polytechnische Schule, Zurich, under Alfred Bluntschli, a pupil of Gottfried Semper. Moser spent a short period at the Ecole des Beaux-Arts, Paris, and worked in the studio of Jean-Louis Pascal. He then opened a practice in Wiesbaden, where he met his future partner Robert Curjel (1856–1925). In 1887 he travelled in Italy, studying architecture and sculpture and producing watercolours, with the painter Albert Anker among others. His talent as a watercolourist was encouraged by Adolf Rudolf Holzhalb (1835–88) and Julius Jakob Stadler (1828–1904) at the Zurich Bauschule, leading to several exhibitions in Zurich, Karlsruhe and Baden. His watercolours document his development towards an abstract conception of space and form.

In 1888 Karl Moser and Curjel formed an architectural partnership Curjel & Moser, in Karlsruhe, which lasted until 1915. Their buildings, mainly in south-west Germany and German-speaking Switzerland, show stylistic features typical of the period, for example Gothic Revival, Romanesque Revival, nationalist, neo-Baroque, *Jugendstil* and even neo-classical. Curjel's contribution lay in the development of urban residential and commercial buildings, including the Bank Homburger (1898–1901), Karlsruhe, and the Ersparniskasse, Aarau. Moser's main interest was in church design, using the 'Wiesbaden Programme'—named from the Ringkirche (1892–4), Wiesbaden, by JOHANNES OTZEN—for guidance in his Protestant churches. Examples include the Christuskirche (1896–1904) and Lukaskirche (1906), both in Karlsruhe, the Pauluskirche (1898–1901), Basle, and churches at Zug, St Gall and Flawil. Among the firm's many villas and public buildings, Moser was responsible for the Kunsthaus (1909–10; remodelled 1923) and the Universität (1911–14), both in Zurich.

Karl Moser's appointment as professor (1915–28) at the Eidgenössische Technische Hochschule (ETH), Zurich, ended the partnership. He was a gifted teacher but did not follow any obvious doctrine, teaching initially from a historical viewpoint and focusing on architectural theories, from the Renaissance to contemporary historicism. He continued to work as an architect and became interested in residential estates and blocks of flats, designing the complex of Protestant church and residential buildings (1925–6) at Fluntern, Zurich. Moser also experimented with new materials and techniques, and he designed the innovative Antoniuskirche (1924–31), Basle, the first Swiss church to use exposed concrete, although the interior follows traditional models (see fig.). This design, influenced by contemporary French and Dutch architecture,

Karl Moser: interior of the Antoniuskirche, Basle, 1924–31

particularly by Auguste Perret and W. M. Dudok, reflected a new understanding of the relationship of building to urban context. Moser's later buildings show the influence of the young Le Corbusier, and his radical design (1933) for the redevelopment of the Niederdorf, Zurich, makes reference to Le Corbusier's *ville radieuse*. In his role at the ETH he reorganized the training of architects in Switzerland, making possible the breakthrough of modern attitudes, and the most important protagonists of Swiss Modernism were among his pupils. He was a member of the international judging panel in the competition for the Palace of the League of Nations, Geneva, in 1927, supporting the project by Le Corbusier and Pierre Jeanneret, and he was the first president of CIAM (1928–30).

WRITINGS

'Neue holländische Architektur, Bauten von W. M. Dudok, Hilversum', *Werk*, 11 (1922), pp. 205–14

BIBLIOGRAPHY

S. Giedion: 'Nekrolog', *Neue Zürch. Ztg*, 396 (1936)
L. Birchler: 'Karl Moser und der moderne katholische Kirchenbau', *Schweiz. Rundschau* (1936–7), pp. 633–9
Universität Zürich (Kunstführer) (Basle, 1980)
S. von Moos: 'Karl Moser and the Swiss Architectural Avant-garde', *RIBA Trans.*, iii/2 (1984), pp. 74–81
E. Strebel: 'Karl Mosers neuklassizistische Architektur', *Fünf Punkte in der Architekturgeschichte* (Basle, 1985), pp. 230–47

(3) Werner (Max) Moser (*b* Karlsruhe, 16 July 1896; *d* Zurich, 24 Aug 1970). Son of (2) Karl Moser. He studied architecture (1915–19) with his father in Zurich and with Paul Bonatz in Stuttgart, then worked with Marinus Jan Granpré Molière in Holland and finally spent three years

(1923–6) in the USA, at least two of them with Frank Lloyd Wright. He then returned to Zurich. His first buildings were single-family houses, often built on a slope. Their clear, simple overall shapes contrast with delicate details such as banisters, partitions and furniture, and with the surrounding environment. Werner Moser was a founder-member of CIAM (*see* CIAM, fig. 1), and after the late 1920s he worked with other Modernist architects such as Emil Roth (1929) and Mart Stam (1930). He was involved in the Neubühl housing project (1930–32), Zurich, the first Modernist estate in Switzerland, together with Paul Artaria, Hans Schmidt and Max Haefeli and Rudolf Steiger. Moser also made outstanding contributions to church and school building, and in *Das Kind und sein Schulhaus* (1933) he emphasized the importance of school architecture in modern education. His design for the Protestant church (1938–41), Altstätten, Zurich, an extension of the original 18th-century building, reflects his appreciation of regional factors. His use of modern constructional techniques and forms, together with local materials and a sensitivity to the environment, and the creative tension achieved by his asymmetrical spatial arrangements, pointed the way to a new approach to building in Switzerland.

In 1937 Moser formed a partnership with MAX HAEFELI and RUDOLF STEIGER to design the Kongresshaus (1937–9), Zurich, commissioned in connection with the *Landesausstellung* of 1939. Other important buildings resulted from the partnership (HMS), for example the Kantonsspital (1942–51), Zurich, and it became known for introducing elements that were identified as distinctively Swiss (e.g. decorative features or materials) to their fundamentally Modernist buildings. Their 'Zur Palme' commercial building (1960–64), Zurich, reflects some important ideas on urban building from the 1950s and Moser's enduring interest in Wright: it is an open composition with a variety of building volumes, including a striking high-rise section, on a windmill-shaped ground-plan. Like his father, Werner Moser was an influential teacher. After working as a visiting professor (1955) at Harvard University, Cambridge, MA, he was appointed Professor of Architecture at the Eidgenössische Technische Hochschule in Zurich in 1958. His reorganization of architectural education led to the introduction of a foundation course under B. Hoesli (1923–84) and a chair of planning studies.

WRITINGS

with W. Gonzenbach: *Das Kind und sein Schulhaus* (Zurich, 1933)
Frank Lloyd Wright: Sechzig Jahre lebendige Architektur (Winterthur, 1952)

BIBLIOGRAPHY

H. Curjel: 'Nekrolog', *Werk*, 10 (1970), p. 639
'Werner M. Moser, 1896–1970', *Schweiz. Bauztg*, 33 (1972), pp. 793–7; 35 (1972), pp. 831–40
'Haefeli, Moser, Steiger', *Archithese*, 2 (1980) [whole issue]

ERNST STREBEL

Moser, Kolo(man) (*b* Vienna, 30 March 1868; *d* Vienna, 18 Oct 1918). Austrian decorative artist and painter. He first studied commerce at the Gewerbeschule at Wieden following his parents' wishes, but from 1885 he attended the Akademie der Bildenden Künste, after passing the entrance examination. In March of that year he joined the painting course run by Professor Franz Rumpler (1848–1922). From 1888 Moser worked in his own studio on the Rennweg, producing fashion drawings and illustrations for *Wiener Mode* and *Meggendorfers Humoristische Blätter*. In 1892 he transferred to the Kunstgewerbeschule of the Museum für Kunst und Industrie, Vienna (now the Hochschule für Angewandte Kunst). A post as drawing teacher at Schloss Wartholz, where he taught the children of Archduke Karl Ludwig, allowed him to continue his studies. In 1894 he joined the future members of the Vienna Secession to form a loose discussion group called the SIEBENERKLUB at the Café Sperl.

On the invitation of the publisher Martin Gerlach in 1895 he produced 11 plates on various themes for the collection *Allegorien, Neue Folge* (Vienna, 1896), for example plate 15, *Summer* (Vienna, Hist. Mus.). After a brief period in Munich, he returned to Vienna in 1895, working mainly in the field of book illustration. In 1897 he was one of the founder-members of the Wiener Secession-Vereinigung Bildender Künstler Österreichs (*see* SECESSION, §3), and he was put in charge of the design of *Ver Sacrum* (see Fenz, p. 8), the group's information sheet. With Joseph Maria Olbrich he was involved in the design of the Secession building on the Gefreidemarkt in 1898, being responsible for the glass windows, friezes and ornamentation. In the same year he made his first contact with the Josef Böck porcelain factory, supplying numerous designs for services in collaboration with his pupils. In 1899 he took up a teaching post at the Kunstgewerbeschule in Vienna. At the same time he worked on interior design and decoration, both with his pupils and in collaboration with textile, glass and furniture factories, taking pains to maintain a high standard of finish. In 1900 he showed a glass tableware set at the Exposition Universelle in Paris, for which he received a prize. In the same year he designed a tubular cotton fabric, *Flower Awakening* (Vienna, Mus. Angewandte Kst), which was manufactured by Johann Backhausen & Söhne (*see* AUSTRIA, fig. 42).

With Josef Hoffmann and the industrialist Fritz Wärndorfer Moser founded the WIENER WERKSTÄTTE cooperative in Vienna (1903). In the same year, with Hoffmann, Alfred Roller, Otto Wagner and Hermann Bahr, he worked on designs for a Festspielhaus in Salzburg, where he wished to be responsible for the stage sets. Moser designed the interior of the Purkersdorf sanatorium (1903–5) built by Josef Hoffmann. He was also commissioned to produce the windows and altar of a church at Steinhof begun by Otto Wagner in 1904. Work on the designs dragged on for several years as the client was dissatisfied with the execution, although the main reason for the client's boycott was Moser's change of religious affiliation on his marriage to Editha Mautner-Markhof in summer 1905. At this time he was also designing objects for the Wiener Werkstätte, for example a brass vase (1903–4; Vienna, Mus. Angewandte Kst; for illustration *see* WIENER WERKSTÄTTE). In 1906 he produced various paintings on glass for Hoffmann's buildings. A year later, however, he withdrew from the Wiener Werkstätte because of financial difficulties, although he continued to supply designs.

In 1907 Moser's unexecuted design for the Heiliger-Geist-Kirche in Düsseldorf was awarded a prize (see Fenz, pp. 206–7). In the following years he was involved in theatre design, including the costumes for the Fledermaus cabaret in Vienna (1908) and sets for plays at the Vienna Hofoper in 1910–11. At the same time he drew and painted, for example *The Wanderer* (oil on canvas, 1916; Vienna, Hist. Mus.). During World War I his main output was the design of postage stamps.

BIBLIOGRAPHY

Koloman Moser, 1868–1918 (exh. cat., Vienna, Hochsch. Angewandte Kst, 1979)

W. Fenz: *Koloman Moser: Graphik—Kunstgewerbe—Malerei* (Vienna, 1984)

For further bibliography *see* WIENER WERKSTÄTTE.

GABRIELE RAMSAUER

Moser, Lukas [Lucas] (*fl c.* 1430). German painter. His name is known only through an inscription on the frame of the altarpiece above the altar of St Mary Magdalene in the parish church at Tiefenbronn, near Pforzheim. This altarpiece is as important to the art of German-speaking lands as van Eyck's Ghent Altarpiece is to that of the Netherlands. Both were completed in 1432.

The Tiefenbronn Altarpiece was produced at a time when standard forms of Late Gothic retable were beginning to emerge. Unique in form and unconventional in construction, it is a winged altarpiece (*Wandelaltar*) with a shrine for carved figures, a set of hinged wings and a plinth-like predella. It is in its original position, and its distinctive overall shape, a wide, pointed arch, follows the dimensions and outline of the earlier fresco (*c.* 1400) above the altar, remnants of which it conceals.

Lukas Moser: Tiefenbronn Altarpiece: (top) *Supper at Bethany*; (left) *Sea Voyage of the Bethanian Saints*, (centre, closed) *Arrival of the Saints in Marseille*; (right) *Bishop Maximinus Giving the Last Communion to Mary Magdalene in Aix Cathedral*; (below) *Christ and the Wise and Foolish Virgins*, tempera and oil on parchment and panel with gold and silver, 2.96×2.37 m, 1432 (Tiefenbronn, St Maria Magdalena)

When the altarpiece is closed, five picture fields are visible (see fig.). Almost all are surrounded by the original wide framework. The predella shows *Christ and the Wise and Foolish Virgins*, while the four remaining scenes are taken from the legend of Mary Magdalene in Jacopo da Voragine's *Golden Legend*: the lunette contains the *Supper at Bethany*, and beneath this, from left to right in front of a continuous landscape, are the *Sea Voyage of the Bethanian Saints*, the *Arrival of the Saints in Marseille* (on the outer sides of the movable wings) and *Bishop Maximinus Giving the Last Communion to Mary Magdalene in Aix Cathedral*. When the wings are open, the lunette and the predella are still visible, while the insides of the wings show a bishop saint on the right and a female saint on the left. The inscriptions on their haloes, identifying them as Lazarus and Martha, are not original. The central carved group, showing the penitent Mary Magdalene raised in the air by angels, dates from the first third of the 16th century, when the casing of the shrine and the wings were enlarged.

Technical investigations have proved the work to be well preserved, though limited modifications to the construction of the retable and a few instances of overpaint have affected the inscriptions on the horizontal moulding of the frame, the haloes and the hems of the garments. Epigraphic and philological research has confirmed that the much-discussed vertical inscriptions on the frame are genuine. One of these, *lucas moser maler von wil maister dez werx bit got vir in* ('Lukas Moser painter from Weil, master of the work, pray God for him'), confirms that his workshop was in Weil der Stadt, near Tiefenbronn. The significance of the inscription *schri kunst schri und klag dich ser din begert iecz niemen mer so o we 1432* ('cry out, art, cry out and lament greatly, for no one wants you any longer, alas! 1432') is still disputed; the added date of 1432, correctly deciphered by Piccard, refers to the date of completion. The coats of arms on the predella probably belong to the donors of the altarpiece. These were possibly Bernhard von Stein von Steinegg and his wife Engelin or Agnes Maiser von Berg, members of the nobility who owned land around Tiefenbronn.

Moser used the best materials in an almost extravagant way, for example gold and silver grounds. His unusual painting support of parchment glued to the oak panels has led to the conclusion that he also worked as an illuminator. His style shows direct connections with Franco-Flemish book illumination (e.g. Jacquemart de Hesdin, the Boucicaut Master and the de Limbourg brothers). On the other hand Moser's studious dependence on the style of the Master of Flémalle is evident, for example in the realistic organization of the legend scenes through precise representation of setting and in the careful construction of the picture space. The foregrounds are filled with large figures, while the seascapes stretch into the distance and the complicated architecture climbs steeply to the high horizon. Figures are shown as solid forms modelled by light, and the physical quality of all the objects and components of the scenes, whether textiles, water, masonry or wood, is carefully depicted. Furthermore, Moser's familiarity with architectural symbolism and the 'disguised symbolism' of early Netherlandish painting is shown in the portal sculptures and the construction of Aix Cathedral in the scene of the *Last Communion*.

Along with his contemporaries Konrad Witz and Hans Multscher, both active in south-west Germany, Moser was a leading representative of a stylistically progressive group of painters, exponents of the realism that had been developing since the beginning of the 15th century. These artists were receptive to the influence of Franco-Flemish painting, which they had probably seen during their *Wanderjahre*. Their intention to represent contemporary reality in paintings on Christian themes was achieved in an original, expressive and varied way.

BIBLIOGRAPHY

LK; Thieme–Becker

H. Rott: *Quellen und Forschungen zur südwestdeutschen und schweizerischen Kunstgeschichte im 15. und 16. Jarhundert*, ii: *Alt-Schwaben und die Reichsstätte* (Stuttgart, 1934), pp. viii–xi, li–lii, 6–8, 45, 71, 231

J. von Waldburg-Wolfegg: *Lucas Moser* (Berlin, 1939)

J. Sauer: 'Die Instandsetzung des Magdalenenaltars von Lukas Moser in Tiefenbronn', *Dt. Kst & Dkmlpf.* (1939–40), pp. 174–84

K. Bauch: *Der Tiefenbronner Altar des Lucas Moser* (Bremen, 1940)

W. Boeck: *Der Tiefenbronner Altar von Lucas Moser* (Munich, 1951)

A. Stange: *Deutsche Malerei der Gotik*, iv: *Südwestdeutschland in der Zeit der Gotik von 1400 bis 1450* (Berlin, 1951), pp. 91–101

——: 'Lucas Moser', *Kindlers Malerei Lexikon*, iv (Zurich, 1966), pp. 508–10

G. Piccard: *Der Magdalenenaltar des 'Lukas Moser' in Tiefenbronn* (Wiesbaden, 1969)

R. E. Straub: 'Einige technologische Untersuchungen am Tiefenbronner Magdalenenaltar des Lukas Moser', *Jb. Staatl. Kstsamml. Baden-Württemberg*, vii (1970), pp. 31–56

R. Hausherr: 'Der Magdalenenaltar in Tiefenbronn', *Kunstchronik*, xxiv (1971), pp. 177–212

E.-L. Richter: 'Zur Rekonstruktion des Tiefenbronner Magdalenenaltars', *Pantheon*, xxx/1 (1972), pp. 33–8

C. Sterling: 'Observations on Moser's Tiefenbronn Altarpiece', *Pantheon*, xxx/1 (1972), pp. 19–32

DIETMAR LÜDKE

Moses, Grandma [née Robertson, Anna Mary] (*b* Greenwich, NY, 7 Sept 1860; *d* Hoosick Falls, NY, 13 Dec 1961). American painter. The third of ten children, she was encouraged as a child by her father to paint and draw. She worked on a neighbouring farm from the age of 12 until her marriage to Thomas Salmon Moses in 1887. The couple became farmers in Virginia and in 1905 purchased a farm in Eagle Bridge, NY. She decorated certain objects in her home with painted scenes, but it was only in her 70s, with no previous training, that she began to make pictures with embroidered yarn; finding that stiffness in her hands made it difficult to hold a needle, she soon started painting in oils.

In 1938 some pictures by Moses were seen at the Woman's Exchange of a drugstore at Hoosick Falls, NY, by the collector Louis J. Caldor (1900–73), who brought them to the attention of Sidney Janis and Otto Kallir (1894–1978). Janis included three of her paintings in the exhibition *Contemporary Unknown American Painters* held in 1939 in the Members' Rooms of MOMA, NY, and devoted a chapter to her in his study of American primitive painters published three years later; Kallir presented her first one-woman exhibition, *What a Farm Wife Painted*, at Galerie St Etienne in New York in 1940. It was in a review of the latter exhibition in the *New York Herald Tribune* that she was first referred to in print as Grandma Moses. Soon afterwards she enjoyed great public success with an exhibition at Gimbel's, a New York department store, and became a celebrity in the USA.

Moses's pictures, painted in oil on board and widely distributed as reproductions on greeting cards, fabrics, tiles and wallpapers, generally treated rural scenes drawn from her own experience or painted in response to the words of old songs. In her lyrical landscapes, usually inspired by her farm and its view of the Green Mountains in neighbouring Vermont, she concentrated her attention on conveying atmosphere and seasonal changes but also used dabs of paint to depict figures in a variety of activities; a typical example is *Wash Day* (1945; Providence, RI, Sch. Des., Mus. A.), in which women and children are shown washing and folding sheets and clothing in front of farm buildings, with a wealth of incidental detail.

In many cases Moses copied details from lithographs published by Currier & Ives, from newspapers and magazine illustrations and from other forms of popular illustration as elements in her original compositions. The contrast between the rather primitive treatment of figures and buildings and the relative naturalism of the landscape elements, which may be regarded as typical of much NAIVE ART, can be ascribed to the fact that she was self-taught. Her works often suggest a bygone era, especially as they often depict horse-drawn vehicles and women in long dresses. She repeated themes on request but changed each version, for example by varying the season. In winter scenes such as *Hoosick Falls, NY in Winter* (1944; Washington, DC, Phillips Col.) she used pale greys for the winter skies and flaked mica to depict the glitter of the snow. She also produced pictures on historical themes, landscapes inspired by memories of Virginia and a few indoor scenes.

BIBLIOGRAPHY

S. Janis: *They Taught themselves: American Primitive Painters of the 20th Century* (New York, 1942)

O. Kallir, ed.: *Grandma Moses, American Primitive* (New York, 1946) [incl. autobiography of artist]

O. Kallir: *Grandma Moses* (New York, 1973)

J. Kallir: *Grandma Moses: The Artist behind the Myth* (New York, 1982)

RUTH BASS

Moses, (James) Kivetoruk [*Kivetoruk*: 'Bark Dye'] (*b* nr Cape Espenberger, AK, 10 Feb 1903; *d* Nome, AK, 1982). Native American Inupiat painter and carver. His father, Kivoluk, a well-known hunter and trapper, established a string of whaling stations along the Arctic coast, but both of Moses's parents died when he was young. He was brought up by an uncle, who taught him hunting and trapping. He attended elementary school at Shishmaref, AK, the famous carving centre. Although his sketches of Eskimo life became highly popular, he felt he could do better financially as a trapper and hunter, and abandoned art. He married Bessie Ahgupuk, of the celebrated Aghupuk family of sculptors and painters, in 1932; they had two sons, Charles and James. He took up sketching again in 1953 while recuperating from a plane crash. At first his work was primarily pen and ink on sealskin, but he branched out over the years, and in time became the best-known artist in Nome, AK. He turned to full-time art production in 1954 to support his family. His work in pen and ink, watercolour and lithographic pencil are prized examples of Native American genre art. Much of his subject-matter was drawn from Inupiat folklore and shamanistic accounts, especially a well-known series based on the mythical *Sedna* theme, a traditional Eskimo legend recounting the origin of the goddess of the sea creatures. As his physical condition deteriorated (a pacemaker was installed in 1975), he was unable to paint after 1978.

For general discussion of Native American painting in the 20th century *see* NATIVE NORTH AMERICAN ART, §IV, 2.

BIBLIOGRAPHY
J. Yorba: *James Kivetoruk Moses* (San Francisco, 1990)

FREDERICK J. DOCKSTADER

Mosko, Sokrat (Llaqi) (*b* Fier, 10 Oct 1931). Albanian architect and writer. After finishing his secondary education in Tiranë (1952), he continued his studies at the Moscow Institute of Architecture, where he graduated in 1958. Returning to Albania he became a representative of the second generation of post-war Albanian architects who carried on the large-scale government modernization programme and played a decisive role in shaping late 20th-century Albanian architecture. The Modernist character of Mosko's work was established with the design of the 'functional–aesthetic' interior of the Great Palace of Culture (1965), Tiranë. The cinema and theatre hall (1971), Fier, and the Art Gallery in Tiranë (1975; with E. Faja) are notable for their rational functionalism and an exterior surface that is characterized by the emphasized volume of the façade, geometrical decorations and chiaroscuro effects. He continued in this direction with the National Historical Museum (1981), Tiranë, where he led the group of designers. He also published many articles on Albanian contemporary architecture.

UNPUBLISHED SOURCES
Tiranë, U., Archv Chair Archit., MS. (*Historia e Arkitektures Shqiptare* [History of Albanian architecture])

WRITINGS
'Për një nivel më të lartë në krijimtarinë tonë urbanistike dhe arkitektonike' [On a higher level of our urban planning and architecture], *Nëntori*, 6 (1971), pp. 5–29

GJERGJ FRASHËRI

Mosman, William (*fl* 1727; *d* nr Aberdeen, 26 Nov 1771). Scottish painter. In 1727 he studied briefly in London with William Aikman. From *c.* 1732 to 1738 he was in Rome, where he studied under Francesco Imperiali, acquiring a fashionable manner similar to Allan Ramsay's, but somewhat awkwardly handled. He is said to have worked for a time in Edinburgh. From *c.* 1740 his principal clients were from north-eastern Scotland; among the pictures painted for these was a pair of portraits, one of *William Duff, 1st Earl of Fife* and the other of his wife and their children (1741; Kinnaird Castle, Tayside). The full-length of *Sir Thomas Kennedy of Culzean, 9th Earl of Cassillis* (1746; Culzean Castle, Strathclyde, NT Scotland) is more confidently handled. A fine example of Mosman's later style is *John Campbell 'of the Bank'* (1749; Edinburgh, Royal Bank of Scotland). By the early 1750s he had settled in Aberdeen, where he ran a drawing school in the 1760s; few portraits from this period survived. The Art Gallery in Aberdeen has some landscapes by him.

BIBLIOGRAPHY
Waterhouse: *18th C.*
D. Irwin and F. Irwin: *Scottish Painters at Home and Abroad, 1700–1900* (London, 1975)

J. Halsby and P. Harris: *The Dictionary of Scottish Painters, 1600–1960* (Edinburgh and Oxford, 1990)
A Patron of Art: Paintings and Prints from the Collection of the Royal Bank of Scotland (Edinburgh, 1990)

ELIZABETH ALLEN

Mosnier [Monier]. French family of artists. (1) Jean Mosnier and his son (2) Pierre Mosnier were decorative and history painters. Another of Jean's sons, Jacques Mosnier (1643–before 1700), was also a painter, specializing in flowers and animals; a third son, Michel Mosnier (*d* 1686), was a sculptor.

(1) Jean Mosnier (*b* Blois, *bapt* 11 March 1600; *d* Blois, 1656). Painter. He came from a family of stained-glass painters and received his early training from his father, also named Jean. In 1617 Marie de' Medici, the Queen Mother, who was in exile in Blois, commissioned Mosnier to paint a copy (Blois, Mus. B.-A.) of Andrea Solario's *Virgin with the Green Cushion* (*c.* 1505; Paris, Louvre). Pleased with the result, she paid for Mosnier to go to Italy. From 1618 to 1622 he was in Florence where, according to Félibien, he studied with Cristofano Allori, Lodovico Cigoli and Domenico Passignano; from 1623 to 1625, in Rome, he discovered Raphael and the painters of the Romano-Bolognese school. After his return he worked for Marie de' Medici in the Palais du Luxembourg in Paris, probably painting the ceiling that now hangs over the Salle du Livre d'Or. This shows not only Florentine influence but also that of Rubens's recently completed decorative cycle for the palace (Paris, Louvre). Mosnier was also active as a copyist (e.g. *Diana the Huntress*, after Orazio Gentileschi; New York, priv. col.). In 1628 he was calling himself 'Peintre de la Reine Mère'.

In 1630, however, Mosnier returned to settle in Blois; subsequently, as the region's principal painter, he worked also in Tours, Chinon and Chartres. He executed paintings for the clergy, including an *Adoration of the Magi* (Blois, St Nicolas) and a *Holy Family* (Chartres, St Brice); for the aldermen of Blois, such as the *Ex-voto for the Plague of 1631* (1634; Blois, St Saturnin); and also for the local nobility, for whom he carried out decorative schemes such as that for the château of Cheverny (*in situ*), Loir-et-Cher, and the château of Fenailles (Toledo, OH, Mus. A.).

BIBLIOGRAPHY
A. Félibien: *Entretiens sur les vies et les ouvrages des plus excellents peintres anciens et modernes* (Paris, 1685–8, rev. 1725/*R* London, 1967), iv, p. 104
M.-P. Durand: *Recherches sur Jean III Mosnier, peintre blésois (1600–1656)* (MA thesis, U. Paris IV, 1980)
Marie de Médicis et le Palais du Luxembourg (exh. cat. by M.-N. Baudouin-Matuszek, Paris, Mus. Luxembourg, 1991–2), pp. 202, 216

(2) Pierre Mosnier (*b* Blois, *bapt* 2 March 1641; *d* Paris, 29 Dec 1703). Painter, son of (1) Jean Mosnier. He first trained with his father in Blois and then (probably after 1654) entered Sébastien Bourdon's studio in Paris. He probably contributed to the decoration (1657–63) of the gallery in the Hôtel de Bretonvilliers. His *Jason Capturing the Golden Fleece* (Paris, Ecole N. Sup. B.-A.) enabled him to become one of the first students of the Académie de France in Rome (opened in 1666). There he studied the Antique, also admiring the work of Raphael (whom he copied), and that of the Carracci; all of these would become part of the traditional curriculum for the Académie de France. Returning to Paris, Mosnier was accepted (*reçu*) by the Académie in 1674 with *Hercules Presenting Arms to Four Gods* (Paris, Ecole N. Sup. B.-A.). In 1678 he was appointed assistant professor, and professor in 1686, giving numerous lectures on antique art. In 1679 he executed a *Homage to Louis XIV* (Paris, Mus. Assist. Pub.) commissioned for the hospital of La Salpétrière. In 1680 he took part in the fresco decoration of the façade of the château of Marly with François Bonnemer (1638–89) and Jean Nocret; then he collaborated (1684–6) on tapestries of the *Loves of Psyche*, woven at the Gobelins after Giulio Romano's cartoons: *Dance* (Arras, Mus. B.-A.) and *Music* (Grenoble, Mus. Grenoble; preparatory drawing Angers, Mus. Turpin de Crissé). In 1697 Mosnier executed for Notre-Dame de Paris a votive painting which depicted a session of Parlement assembled to try a case, with St Yves in glory interceding on behalf of the Lord (untraced; preparatory drawing Moscow, Pushkin Mus. F.A.). It is impossible to date the *Virgin being Adored by the Angels* (untraced) for St Sulpice, Paris; the *Adoration of the Magi* (untraced) for the convent of the Ste Perrine de Chaillot; and the *Martyrdom of St Ursula* (Troyes, St Pantaléon).

In 1698 Mosnier published his collected lectures as *Histoire des arts qui ont rapport au dessin*: this title shows which side Mosnier took in the contemporary academic debate about the relative values of colour and drawing. A second volume, which was to have been a study of art since 1600, was never published. Mosnier took part in the 1699 Salon with two versions (untraced) of *Christ Summoning the Little Children*. His son Nicolas Mosnier was a pupil of Nicolas de Largillierre.

WRITINGS
Histoire des arts qui ont rapport au dessin (Paris, 1698)

BIBLIOGRAPHY
P. de Chennevières-Pointel: *Recherches sur la vie et les ouvrages de quelques peintres provinciaux de l'ancienne France*, ii (Paris, 1850), pp. 190–97
B. Lépicié and H. Hulst: *Mémoires inédits sur la vie et les ouvrages des membres de l'Académie royale de peinture et de sculpture*, i (Paris, 1854), pp. 8–10
B. Teyssèdre: *Roger de Piles et les débats sur le coloris au siècle de Louis XIV* (Paris, 1957), pp. 604–5 [list of Mosnier's lectures]
P. Rosenberg: 'A Drawing by Pierre Mosnier', *Burl. Mag.* (1985), pp. 786–9

THIERRY BAJOU

Mosnier, Jean-Laurent (*b* Paris, 1743 or 1744; *d* St Petersburg, 10 April 1808). French painter. He was a student at the Académie de St Luc, Paris, where he trained as a miniature painter. In 1776 he was appointed Peintre de la Reine to Marie-Antoinette. He was approved (*agréé*) by the Académie Royale in 1786 and received (*reçu*) as a full member in 1788, presenting two portraits of Academicians, the sculptor *Charles-Antoine Bridan* (Paris, Ecole N. Sup. B.-A.; version, Chartres, Mus. B.-A.) and the painter *Louis Lagrenée I* (Versailles, Château). He exhibited a *Self-portrait* (St Petersburg, Hermitage) at the Salon of 1786, showing himself relaxed and confident at the centre of his studio, flanked by two canvases, which are being admired by his two daughters. After the outbreak of the French Revolution, Mosnier fled to London in 1790 and exhibited at the Royal Academy from 1791 to 1796. His English portraits make some concession to current English taste: *George, 7th Marquess of Tweedale* (priv. col., see Waterhouse, p. 250), for example, is shown full-length in

an outdoor setting; Edwards, however, considered these pictures laboured, 'too mechanical in their execution, to stand in competition with the portraits of the English artists'. From London Mosnier went to Hamburg, where he stayed four years, and then, in 1801, to St Petersburg, a favourite destination for French émigré artists. A potential rival, Elisabeth Vigée-Lebrun, left the city later that year, and Mosnier assumed an influential position. In 1802 he was accepted into the St Petersburg Academy, and he was made a professor there in 1806. His portrait sitters included the imperial family (e.g. *The Empress Elizabeth, Wife of Alexander I, as a Girl*; ex-Cathcart Coll.). This charming and delicate three-quarter-length portrait has the Empress wearing a white Empire dress, with her profile seen in a mirror on the left. Mosnier was a versatile and prolific portrait painter, capable of modifying his style in accordance with changed geographical circumstances, and using his skill as a trained miniaturist to good effect in his highly polished and detailed full-size portraits.

BIBLIOGRAPHY
Waterhouse: *18th C.*
E. Edwards: *Anecdotes of Painters who Have Resided or Been Born in England* (London, 1808), p. 255
D. Roche: 'Jean-Laurent Mosnier et ses portraits à l'huile', *Ren. A. Fr. & Ind. Luxe* (1921), pp. 169–76
G. Marlier: 'Les Séjours à Londres et à Hambourg de Jean-Laurent Mosnier', *Actes du XIXe Congrès international d'histoire de l'art: Paris, 1958*, pp. 405–11

SIMON LEE

Mosque [Arab. *masjid*]. Muslim house of prayer. Islam requires no physical structure for valid prayer, which may be performed anywhere, and a minimal *masjid* ('place of prostration') may consist only of lines marked on the ground, but a building constructed especially for the purpose is preferred, in particular for congregational prayer at Friday noon, the principal weekly service. Such a building may be called a *masjid* or a *jāmi* (Turk. *cami*), from *masjid al-jāmi'* (Pers. *masjid-i jāmi'*; Urdu *jāmi' masjid*), meaning 'congregational mosque'. This term is often rendered in English as 'great mosque', or 'Friday mosque', a translation of *masjid-i juma'*, a Persian variant. The word *masjid* may also be applied to any place where prayer is appropriate, for example the Masjid al-Haram, the enclosed area around the Ka'ba in Mecca. Large buildings constructed for other religious purposes, such as madrasas and *khānaqāh*s, usually contain prayer-halls arranged like free-standing mosques. In cities throughout the Islamic world, the daily needs of the residents of particular quarters have been served by small mosques; they are often reduced versions of the major types of mosque that were most popular locally at the time of their construction. This article is concerned primarily with major structures built specifically for congregational prayer. For further bibliography and information on mosques in other types of buildings, *see* KHĀNAQĀH, KÜLLIYE, MADRASA and MUSALLA; on the historical development of mosques, *see* ISLAMIC ART, §II; on component parts of mosques, *see* MAQSŪRA, MIHRAB, MINARET and MINBAR; on particular buildings, *see* individual site-entries.

1. Introduction. 2. Typology.

1. INTRODUCTION. There is no prescribed form for a mosque, but mosques are adapted to the needs of Islamic prayer. Worshippers must wash before prayer, so water and a place for these ablutions (Arab. *mīḍa'*) are usually provided. During a prayer service, worshippers line up in rows facing the direction of Mecca (Arab. *qibla*) and, following a prayer leader, repeat a series of prayers and perform a set of prostrations. Thus a mosque is normally a rectangular, covered and paved space with one side oriented to Mecca. The qibla wall almost always has one or more mihrabs, the principal one in the centre. The mihrab is usually a concave niche, but in historic mosques in Spain and western North Africa the mihrab is often a small room. In those mosques in which Friday-noon prayer is performed, a minbar, or pulpit for the prayer leader, stands usually to the right of the mihrab, and from it a sermon is read. As the times of the five daily prayers are fixed in relation to the rising and setting of the sun and thus vary from one day to the next, mosques are usually equipped with devices to tell time: sundials or clepsydrae in the pre-modern period, wall or grandfather clocks in the present.

In many mosques the side of the prayer-hall opposite the qibla wall opens on to a courtyard, which is arcaded on the remaining three sides and has a fountain in the centre, although facilities for ablution may be located elsewhere. There are also usually one or more minarets, or towers, from which an official of the mosque, the muezzin, calls the congregation to prayer before each service. The call to prayer may be performed from other locations, such as the roof of the mosque, and at present the minaret is usually equipped with loudspeakers, the muezzin remaining below or being replaced by a recording.

Aside from these elements, mosques take many forms and have been built in all the various historical and regional styles of Islamic architecture. The most elaborately decorated elements are normally the portals, the mihrab, the minbar and the minaret. No form of Islamic art, however, is specific only to mosques and other religious structures, and virtually all media of Islamic art apart from book illustration are represented in mosques, for Islam forbids representations of animate beings (i.e. humans and animals) in contexts where such representations might be mistaken for objects of devotion. Artistically significant elements in the prayer-hall of a mosque may include carved and painted inscriptions, calligraphed and embellished manuscripts of the Koran, boxes or cabinets in which manuscripts are kept, a raised platform (Arab. *dikka*) of wood or stone from which the Koran or responses to the prayer leader are recited, suspended lamps of glass, metal or ceramic, rugs on the floor, gigantic candlesticks and candles kept burning throughout Ramadan, the month of fasting, screens (Arab. *maqṣūra*, 'separated [area]') surrounding several bays near the mihrab and windows of coloured glass. A very few prayer-halls have funerary shrines: Muhammad's tomb has been incorporated in the prayer-hall of the mosque of the Prophet in Medina, and a shrine to the head of John the Baptist stands in the prayer-hall of the Great Mosque of Damascus. In some Cairene mosques built by members of the Mamluk dynasty

(*reg* 1250–1517), the founder's tomb directly adjoins the prayer-hall.

2. TYPOLOGY. The first mosque, a building that Muhammad erected at MEDINA in 622, is usually described as the Prophet's house but was probably intended from the outset as a community centre as well. Initially, it was a rectangular enclosure of unbaked brick, a little over 50 m square, but a portico of palm trunks supporting a roof of palm-frond thatch was quickly erected on the north side of the court, facing Jerusalem, the first qibla, or direction in which Muslims sent their prayers (*see* ISLAMIC ART, fig. 16). When in 624 the qibla was changed to Mecca, another such arcade was built on the south side, facing that city. Muhammad and his family lived in rooms built on to one side of the enclosure, and Muhammad was buried in one of these rooms in 632. During the 7th and early 8th centuries, Muhammad's mosque was repeatedly enlarged and rebuilt, becoming a flat-roofed hypostyle structure with a central court and a prayer-hall deeper than the three other porticos. The first concave mihrab was built in the qibla wall of the Medina mosque in 707; the bay in front of it was covered with a dome. The qibla wall and the aisle leading to the mihrab, which was wider than the other aisles, were highly decorated. Muhammad's minbar was enlarged, and the mosque was given four slender minarets. The Medina mosque was destroyed almost completely by fire in 1256 and again in 1481.

The form of the mosque of the Prophet was closely imitated in the early congregational mosques built in the Iraqi cities of Wasit, Kufa and Basra, and in the mosque built at Daybul in Sind (now Banbhore, Pakistan). In some cities, particularly in Syria, mosques were initially established for the Muslim community in converted churches (e.g. Hama) or parts of churches (e.g. Damascus), or in other significant buildings, such as the *apadana*, or hypostyle hall, at Persepolis in Iran. Other early mosques were built in the ethnically and tribally segregated quarters of the new cities founded by the Arabs, or as special constructions for particular religious groups and their leaders; but in each city the official and public mosque was the one known as the *masjid al-jāmi'*, in which all males of an age to do so joined in prayer at midday on Friday. In time, as the populations of Muslim cities grew, it became impossible to assemble everyone in a single mosque, and multiple congregational mosques came to be built in large urban agglomerations. Some theologians, particularly of the Shafi'ite school, condemned this practice, but many others allowed it. For example, a 15th-century source lists nearly 90 congregational mosques in Cairo, one of the largest cities in the medieval world.

(i) Hypostyle mosques. (ii) Four-iwan mosques. (iii) Domed mosques.

(i) Hypostyle mosques. The wide distribution of the hypostyle mosque throughout the lands of the Middle East and North Africa where Arabic is spoken has led some to call them 'Arab-type' mosques, although they are also known in Iran and Anatolia where other distinctive mosque plans evolved. The mosque of the Prophet in Medina was only one of several prototypes for hypostyle mosques; other prototypes include the Great Mosque of Damascus, the Aqsa Mosque in Jerusalem and the Great Mosques of

1. Aqsa Mosque, Jerusalem, view from the north-west

Samarra'. The Great Mosque of Damascus (see DAMASCUS, §3) was constructed by the Umayyad caliph al-Walid (reg 705–15) within the peribolus of the ancient Temple of Jupiter, which had already been replaced by the Byzantine church of St John the Baptist. A large oblong courtyard is surrounded on the north, east and west by arcades. Facing the courtyard, on the south, is the arcuated façade of the prayer-hall, with a higher central nave (see ISLAMIC ART, fig. 18). The prayer-hall consists of three wide, gabled aisles parallel to the qibla wall, borne on a double arcade and cut transversely by the nave leading to the mihrab. The central bay of this nave is domed; the corresponding dome of the original structure may have been over the bay in front of the mihrab. The qibla wall was originally revetted in quartered marble and glass mosaic, as were the vestibules, the interiors of the arcades and all façades of the courtyard. The fragmentary remains show an experimental phase in the decoration of mosques: they depict landscapes filled with trees and buildings. The meaning of these mosaics is uncertain, although they are best interpreted as representing paradise. This mosque, which combines Byzantine architectural forms and decorative media in a new way, was imitated in many Syrian and Anatolian mosques into the 14th century, most notably the Isa Bey Mosque at Selçuk, near Ephesos (1374; see ISLAMIC ART, fig. 54).

The Aqsa Mosque, at the southern end of the Haram al-Sharif (Temple Mount) in Jerusalem (see JERUSALEM, §II, 1(iv)), was built on the site identified by Muslims of the 7th century with the site of the unnamed 'furthest mosque' (Arab. masjid al-aqsā'), Muhammad's miraculous journey to which is recounted in Koran xvii.1. By 670 a makeshift mosque had been constructed in the ruins of the Herodian stoa on this side of the Haram, and this version of the mosque was replaced in the early 8th century. Much modified by later rebuilding, the Aqsa Mosque (see fig. 1) develops the form of the mosque of the Prophet in Medina, although it is unusual because it has no integral court, undoubtedly due to the peculiarities of its situation. The essential form of the building, a gable-roofed hypostyle mosque on arcades supported by marble columns, with a wider axial nave and a dome before the mihrab, was repeated far afield in the congregational mosques of Fustat (Old Cairo) in Egypt, KAIROUAN in Tunisia (see ISLAMIC ART, fig. 25) and Córdoba in Spain, although these later buildings all feature integral courts.

The Great Mosque of Córdoba (see CÓRDOBA (i), §3(i)(a), and ISLAMIC ART, fig. 26) was founded in 785 by 'Abd al-Rahman I, the Umayyad ruler of Spain, and repeatedly extended by his successors. The most notable among them was al-Hakam II (reg 961–76), who was responsible for the present mihrab area and its magnificent mosaic decoration, undoubtedly ordered in imitation of Umayyad precedents in Syria, although the Cordoban geometric and vegetal ornament shares little with the naturalism of the prototypes. The mosque is unique in its system of supports, with double arcades of alternating brick and stone voussoirs, and its intersecting lobed arches that screen off the bays in front and on either side of the mihrab (see ISLAMIC ART, fig. 45). The arrangement of the mihrab as a small room behind an open arch, however, and the scheme of the decoration around that arch set a model for later mosques in the western Islamic world, such as the Great Mosque of TLEMCEN (rebuilt 1136) in

2. Friday Mosque, Varamin, 1322–6

Algeria. The Great Mosque of Tlemcen is representative of many North African congregational mosques of the 12th to 14th centuries, which comprise a distinctive subtype. They have a mihrab formed as a room, a recess for the minbar when not in use, rectangular brick piers supporting simple and complex arcades of varying profiles, a central aisle hardly wider than the other bays, an elaborate dome over the bay in front of the mihrab, a gabled tile roof and little emphasis on the portals or exterior façades. The minarets of these mosques are square towers, often placed, as at Kairouan, in the centre of the arcade opposite the qibla wall.

The mosques of Damascus and Jerusalem also served as models for Cairene mosques of the 11th to the 15th centuries, although many variations were introduced. Such examples as the mosques of al-Hakim (989/90–1013; see CAIRO, §III, 4, and ISLAMIC ART, fig. 36) and of al-Mu'ayyad Shaykh (1415–20) retain the wider central aisle and hypostyle plans but show increased height, elaborately decorated portals and multiple minarets. Egyptian mosques are generally flat-roofed, as the dry climate does not demand vaulting or gabled roofing.

A fourth prototype for hypostyle mosques is represented by the two congregational mosques at Samarra', the 9th-century capital built by the Abbasid caliphs on the Tigris north of Baghdad. The one called the mosque of Abu Dulaf was of yet another type, longer than it was wide and covered with a flat roof borne on rectangular brick piers. This form, including its separate, helicoidal minaret, was the model for the mosque of Ibn Tulun in Cairo (879; see CAIRO, §III, 2) and, with the exception of the minaret, for many early congregational mosques in Iran and Central Asia, such as the Tarik-Khana at DAMGHAN (9th century; see ISLAMIC ART, fig. 23) and the 9th-century mosque at Isfahan (see ISFAHAN, §3(i)).

(ii) *Four-iwan mosques.* A second major type of congregational mosque, particularly favoured in Iran and western Central Asia, developed out of the hypostyle mosque. Beginning in the 11th century, some major hypostyle mosques were substantially remodelled. This process can be seen most clearly at the Friday Mosque at Isfahan (see ISLAMIC ART, fig. 29), but it can be documented elsewhere, as at the congregational mosque in HERAT, Afghanistan. In the late 11th century, after the Saljuqs (reg 1038–1194) had made Isfahan their capital, a large dome was constructed over many of the bays in front and on either side of the mihrab, probably as a *maqsūra* for the sultan. Some years later, probably after a fire in the early 12th century, the original hypostyle plan was further modified by the introduction of iwans, or open vaulted halls (see IWAN), in the middle of each side of the court's four sides. Many later additions to the Isfahan mosque extended its boundaries and resulted in an irregularly shaped mass closely integrated with the surrounding urban fabric, but the arrangement of a central court with iwans on each of the four sides, the one on the qibla side leading to a dome chamber, became the standard plan for Iranian mosques. It was adopted almost immediately for mosques in the Isfahan region, such as those at Zavara (1135–6) and ARDISTAN (1158–60). This type was further developed with the addition of grand portals corresponding in volume to the iwans (see PĪSHTĀQ), as at the congregational mosque at YAZD (14th century). Slender towers and supplementary dome chambers are added in later Persian and Central Asian examples, such as the congregational mosque at VARAMIN (1322–6; see fig. 2 and ISLAMIC ART, §II, 6(ii)(a)), the mosque of Bibi Khanum at Samarkand (1399–1405; see SAMARKAND, §3(ii)), Gawharshad's mosque for the shrine of Imam Riza at MASHHAD (1418–19; see SHRINE, colour pl. IV, fig. 1) and the Shah Mosque at Isfahan (begun 1611; see ISFAHAN, §3(iii)).

Although the Iranian type of four-iwan and qibla-dome mosque is found on the Indian subcontinent (e.g. Thatta, Friday Mosque, 1644), its essential features were more often adapted to create a distinctive regional type more suited to the Indian climate, such as the Atala Mosque (1377–1404), JAUNPUR, or the Badshahi Mosque, LAHORE (1673), said to be the largest on the subcontinent. This type of courtyard mosque is normally raised on a high plinth and comprises a vast walled court with minarets set at the corners. Portal blocks on the main and lateral axes are approached by flights of steps and are topped with small minaret-like towers and open pavilions (*chatri*). Within the court, which is often devoid of any surrounding arcade, the covered prayer-hall projects from the qibla wall, often occupying most but not all of its width. It is usually fairly shallow and comprises a central iwan-like portal in front of a dome chamber for the mihrab. This principal element is usually flanked by smaller versions of it, other domed bays and towers linked together behind a screenlike façade.

(iii) Domed mosques. A distinctive type of mosque, in which the major element is a large domed space, developed in Anatolia and Thrace under the patronage of the Ottoman dynasty (*reg* 1281–1924). Mosques erected in Anatolia after the Turkish invasion in the 11th century had been built to a variety of plans, ranging from simple, single-domed units with porticos (e.g. Iznik, mosque of Hacı Özbek, 1333; *see* IZNIK, §2) to hypostyle plans with many bays built largely in stone (e.g. KONYA, mosque of Alaeddin, 1156–1220) or in wood (e.g. Beyşehir, Eşrefoğlu Mosque, 1297; *see* ISLAMIC ART, §II, 6(ii)(a)). A more complex organization of parts may be seen in the Bursa-type or *zāwiya* (Turk. *zaviyeli*) mosque, a distinctive Anatolian type usually associated with a dervish cloister (Arab. *zāwiya*). Exemplified by the Yeşil Cami ('Green Mosque'; 1419–24) at BURSA, this type replaces the open court of the hypostyle or four-iwan type with a domed central space complete with a fountain, and the prayer-hall extends from it like an iwan, with corresponding iwan-like spaces to the left and right that could be used for teaching etc. Other chambers in the corners, often furnished with fireplaces, were used as lodgings for itinerant dervishes. This completely covered mosque type was well suited to the rigorous Anatolian climate.

In the 15th and 16th centuries the sultans of the Ottoman dynasty sponsored a series of immense domed congregational mosques, in which the motifs of completely covered space (as at Bursa), the large dome before the mihrab (most apparent in Persian and Central Asian mosques) and the open arcaded forecourt are combined in buildings that were the centrepieces of large religious and charitable foundations. The earliest examples (e.g. the Üç Şerefeli Mosque in EDIRNE, 1437–47, see fig. 3 and ISLAMIC ART, §II, 6(iii)(b)) are essentially vast domes with low subsidiary spaces, but the best-known examples are creative responses to Byzantine architecture, above all the great church of Hagia Sophia in Istanbul, founded by Constantine and rebuilt in the 6th century by the emperor

3. Üç Şerefeli Mosque, Edirne, 1437–47

Justinian (*see* ISTANBUL, §III, 1). Immediately after the conquest of Constantinople in 1453 by the Ottoman emperor Mehmed II, it was converted into the city's first congregational mosque by the addition of a mihrab, minbar and minarets. The Süleymaniye Mosque in Istanbul (1550–57; *see* ISTANBUL, §III, 10 and ISLAMIC ART, fig. 63), a masterpiece of Ottoman architecture by the great architect Sinan, for example, employs an immense central dome buttressed by semi-domes and opened up by many windows to create a strongly centralized space, in contrast to the strongly directional one of the prototype. On the exterior the mosque appears as a cascade of domes and buttresses punctuated by slender minarets and enveloped in the domes of the adjacent religious and charitable foundations, which include the tomb of the founder. Similar though simpler mosques (and complexes) were built in the capital cities of the Ottoman empire, sometimes incorporating local architectural motifs, such as the striped masonry used in Ottoman constructions in Damascus. This Ottoman mosque type has been adapted throughout the Islamic world in the 19th and 20th centuries and is the most popular basis for the design of new mosques.

In other regions with large Muslim communities, such as East Africa, West Africa, Indonesia, South-east Asia and China, mosques generally follow indigenous architectural styles, with suitable modifications for the requirements of Islamic prayer. For example, Indonesian mosques are usually wooden structures with tiered roofs and no minarets, while some Chinese mosques outwardly resemble Chinese temples. No single style characterizes modern mosque architecture in Europe and America.

BIBLIOGRAPHY

Enc. Islam/2: 'Masdjid'
J. Sauvaget: *La Mosquée omeyyade de Médine* (Paris, 1947)
E. Herzfeld: 'Damascus: Studies in Architecture-IV', *A. Islam.*, xiii–xiv (1948), pp. 118–38
E. Kühnel: *Die Moschee, Bedeutung, Einrichtung und kunsthistorische Entwicklung der islamischen Kultstätte* (Berlin, 1949)
O. Grabar: 'The Architecture of the Middle Eastern City from Past to Present: The Case of the Mosque', *Middle Eastern Cities*, ed. I. M. Lapidus (Berkeley and Los Angeles, 1969), pp. 26–46
B. Finster: 'Die Mosaiken der Umayyadenmoschee', *Kst Orients*, vii (1970), pp. 83–141
E. Galdieri: *Isfahān: Masǧid-i Ǧum'a*, 2 vols (Rome, 1972–3)
D. Kuban: *Muslim Religious Architecture*, 2 vols (Leiden, 1974–85)
U. Vogt Göknil: *Die Moschee. Grundformen sakraler Baukunst* (Zurich, 1978)
R. Hillenbrand: 'The Mosque in Medieval Islamic Architecture', *Architecture in Continuity: Building in the Islamic World Today*, ed. Sherban Cantacuzino (New York, 1985), pp. 33–50
M. Frishman and H.-U. Khan: *The Mosque: History, Architectural Development and Regional Diversity* (London, 1994)
R. Hillenbrand: *Islamic Architecture: Form, Function and Meaning* (Edinburgh, 1994), pp. 31–128

□

Mossi. Voltaic-speaking, agricultural people, numbering about 2.3 million, living in central Burkina Faso, West Africa. Art-historically best known for their wooden dolls, they also produce masks and crests, wooden and brass figures and a variety of other arts. Examples of Mossi art are held in numerous public collections (e.g., especially for Mossi dolls, Detroit, MI, Inst. A.; Paris, Mus. de l'Homme).

1. Introduction. 2. Masks and masquerades. 3. Figure sculpture. 4. Dolls. 5. Other arts.

1. INTRODUCTION. The diversity of Mossi art styles reflects the diverse origins of the Mossi people. Rather than creating art forms in one major ethnic style, which can be illustrated as 'archetypal' or 'textbook', the Mossi have created three major styles and several substyles, whose geographical distribution mirrors that of the several groups of farmers who were conquered by invaders in about 1500 and amalgamated into a new group called Mossi.

Mossiland is flat and dry, with clay soils and just enough rainfall in the months from May to September to grow millet, sorghum, maize and groundnuts. Traditionally, the Mossi were organized into exogamous, polygynous, patrilocal clans and were politically centralized, with a number of small kingdoms and a system of chiefs owing allegiance to the Mossi emperor in Ouagadougou, the capital of Burkina Faso. Each chief controlled a pyramidal, official bureaucracy responsible for the various districts, the military and the royal tombs.

The Mossi kingdoms were founded at the end of the 15th century when several small bands of mounted warriors, perhaps the younger sons of rulers from northern Ghana, rode north into the upper basin of the Volta rivers seeking new lands to occupy and peoples to subjugate. These horsemen, called *nakomse*, encountered four major groups of farmers: in the south-west they fought and gradually conquered peoples they called 'Gurunsi', including the Nuna, Winiama and Lela. In the north, they conquered and either assimilated or drove off the Dogon and the Kurumba. In the east, they conquered large numbers of Gurmantche.

In each area the invaders imposed their language on the defeated groups, but left most of the existing social structure intact. Where there was any pre-existing political authority, the local leader was incorporated in the new Mossi society as the 'earth priest', a ritual specialist who, by right of first occupation of the land, held the right to distribute farming land to local families. The original inhabitants retained the power to manipulate the forces of nature, especially lightning and tornadoes, so as to strike their enemies; the descendants of the invaders still fear the magical powers of their subjects. Among the most important social institutions the invaders found in place was the use of masks to represent spirits. The descendants of the conquered peoples, who are now called *nyonyose*, or 'the ancient ones', continue to carve masks that are stylistic survivals of the masks carved before the conquest in 1500.

2. MASKS AND MASQUERADES. The best known Mossi mask style is found in the north-western Mossi kingdom called Yatenga, an area once occupied by the Dogon. Here, the *nyonyose* who remained behind when the majority of Dogon fled to the Bandiagara cliffs were amalgamated into Mossi society. Their descendants carve masks that are vertically orientated, with a tall, slender plank that rises above the face of the mask and is decorated with red, white and black geometric patterns (see fig. 1). The face of the Mossi mask is a concave oval, bisected vertically with a dentate ridge, the face painted white. Dogon masks are concave and rectangular, with a similar vertical ridge.

1. Mossi mask of northern style at a funeral, Burkina Faso; from a photograph by Christopher D. Roy, 1977

Certain Dogon masks are surmounted by a vertical plank that is similar to the plank on Mossi masks from Yatenga. In addition, there are types, such as the mask surmounted by a female figure, that occur among both groups and are stylistically related.

In other northern areas to the east of Yatenga, groups of Kurumba were conquered and assimilated into Mossi society. The masks of their *nyonyose* descendants include the same oval, convex face and complex plank that appear on southern Kurumba masks. Geometric patterns are painted roughly, just as they are among the Kurumba who live to the north.

In the south-western Mossi area, in the kingdom of Ouagadougou, ruled by the Mossi emperor from the capital city, the *nyonyose* are descended from ancient Nuna, Winiama and Lela farmers. These Mossi carve red, white and black animal masks that lack the thin, vertical plank of the northern Mossi styles. These masks appear to represent such animals as the antelope, bush-pig, hawk, hornbill, crocodile and hyena, as well as human characters such as the Fulani woman or albino, or spirits that take no recognizable animal or human forms but which combine the features of many creatures. These masks are related stylistically to the animal and human masks of the contemporary Nuna and Lela who now live to the east of the Mossi. There are certain style traits that serve to distinguish the masks of the south-western Mossi from those of their

neighbours. The Nuna and Winiama use patterns of concentric red, white and black circles that do not appear on Mossi masks.

Finally, in the far eastern Mossi area of the kingdom of Boulsa, the Mossi carve masks that consist of a half-cylinder of wood worn vertically, with a thick costume of red or black fibre. These are exceptions to the rule that Mossi masks are survivals of the carving styles of the ancient inhabitants, for in this area the ancient inhabitants never used masks, and the style has entered Mossi country from the south.

The Mossi use masks at burials, funerals and initiations, and at annual year-end ancestral sacrifices. They represent spirits from the wild bush areas surrounding the village, which may appear to humans as animals. Men and women encounter these spirits while hunting or gathering firewood, and spirits that play an important role in the history of the lineage or clan are honoured by being represented by masks. Clan members will not kill or eat the flesh of the animal spirit, for when such an animal dies, a member of the clan will also die.

When masks are not being worn in performances they are placed on ancestral shrines in the *kimse roogo*, or ancestral spirit house of the family that owns them. Sacrifices may be made on the mask to obtain the blessings of the spirit that the mask represents. Men and women, adults and children alike have access to the masks for sacrifice, although all sacrifices are administered by a man. The spirits protect the family from disease, accident and natural disaster, its crops from insects and drought, its women from infertility, and generally ensure success in life.

Mossi masks appear most frequently at funerals, when masks that belong to the clan of the deceased appear to honour the dead and to participate in the blood sacrifices that free the spirit of the dead to leave the world of the living and travel to the world of the ancestral spirits.

3. FIGURE SCULPTURE. The Mossi both carve figures in wood and cast them in brass. Such figures are political art, used as symbols of their royal ancestors by the descendants of the invading horsemen in displays that reaffirm the allegiance to the chief of all members of the community. Some figures are carved as finials to the posts that are set into the ground at each side of the door to the chief's home, as jamb figures supporting the straw mat that serves to close the entrance at night. These posts appear as male and female pairs, with the female distinguished by a tall ridge from the front to the back of the head, representing the women's hairstyle. Both male and female figures bear traditional Mossi scars on face and body.

At the royal tombs of the Mossi emperors, north-west of Ouagadougou, cast-brass equestrian portraits of the Mossi emperors, perhaps dating as far back as the emperor Oubri in the early 16th century, are displayed once a year to provide the blessings of the royal ancestors for all the Mossi people. These figures are cast by the *nyogsan*, the brass-casters of Mande origin who have lived in a neighbourhood on the north side of Ouagadougou for centuries (for illustration *see* BURKINA FASO).

While Mossi masks can be attributed to a geographic origin on stylistic grounds, figures do not conform to geographic style areas, for they are used by a group that has spread over the entire Mossi plateau. While masks are public projects, and are seen by many artists who are influenced by the various styles, figures are more private and conform to the particular demands of the patron. Mossi figures are therefore stylistically more idiosyncratic than are Mossi masks.

4. DOLLS. The most famous Mossi art objects are the small, stylized figures that little girls play with as dolls. These are carved in a variety of styles, but all consist of a cylinder of wood with a semicircular head and pendulous breasts; legs and arms are almost never included. Virtually all the figures are female. They are made to be used as playthings by Mossi girls, who call them *biiga* ('child') and treat them as they will their own children when they become women. The doll is washed, fed, dressed, put to bed at night, and even given the enema that is a common feature of Mossi infant care. The dolls are cared for only as long as the little girl maintains her interest; when she is distracted the toy may be abandoned in a corner of the family courtyard. Little or no importance is attached to the way a child treats her doll and they become dusty, abraded and worn. Such figures represent the largest proportion of the dolls in museum collections outside Burkina Faso.

There are also, however, other small dolls that are used by young women with problems of fertility. A woman who has just married but is having trouble conceiving her first child may carry a doll, like those used by little girls, tucked in the cloth wrapper at her back. She may carry the figure for days or weeks, and when she finally bears a child, the doll is placed on her sleeping-mat next to her, before being replaced by the newborn infant. Dolls that have been used for fertility purposes are carefully cared for and passed on from generation to generation, acquiring a dark, glossy patina that is quite different from the dusty grey surface of girls' playthings.

Like Mossi masks, dolls can be assigned to geographic style areas. Such attributions are difficult, however, because dolls are carried by their owners when they marry, sometimes many miles from the village where they were carved. It is possible to purchase dolls directly from the artists who make them—blacksmiths who, as elsewhere in Africa, specialize in carving wood as well as forging iron. Smiths travel from market to market selling their work, but it is possible to question them about their personal styles, and to assign styles to the artists' villages of origin.

The best known Mossi doll style is produced near the town of Kaya, in the north-east. The curve of the *geyonfo* hairstyle extends from the front of the head down the back in an unbroken curve and is balanced by the opposing curve of the pendulous breasts. Elsewhere, large numbers of dolls are carved in Ziniare, on the road between Ouagadougou and Kaya. Dolls from Ziniare have a semicircular head with smaller semicircles on each side, forming large masses of hair over the ears (see fig. 2). Finally, in the Boulsa area, dolls have a flat, disc-shaped head with a shallow segment carved away to form the

2. Mossi doll, wood, h. 255 mm, from Ziniare, Burkina Faso, mid-20th century (Iowa City, IA, University of Iowa Museum of Art)

face. The shoulders are very square, and the breasts seem to hang from the shoulders.

5. OTHER ARTS. The Mossi seem to have acquired a further sculptural tradition from their Bamana neighbours to the north-west. In the area of the villages of Kongoussi and Kwaltangen, young men join voluntary associations whose purpose is to aid members of the community in time of need and to provide social cohesion for men of a particular age. These young men wear carved wooden crests in the form of small antelope, with other smaller animal heads facing the rear of the crests. These *zazaido* (sing. *zazaigo*) crests are similar to the *chi wara kun* worn by Bamana men's societies, and seem to have similar purposes.

Although most rural Mossi homes contain few material possessions of great beauty, the Mossi continue to produce pottery, baskets, weaving, cast-brass bracelets and horse-trappings, leatherwork and carved wooden furniture that show great care and skill in manufacture. Weaving is dominated by a segment of Mossi society descended from immigrant Mande weavers from the north-west. The Yarse weave cotton blankets on horizontal, narrow-warp men's looms of the common West African type. Patterns conform to the ubiquitous warp stripes and large black and white chequerwork patterns produced by Mande weavers in the valley of the Niger River. Pottery is made by both men and women, depending on geographical area, using both moulding and modelling techniques.

BIBLIOGRAPHY

L. Marc: *Le Pays Mossi* (Paris, 1909)
L. Tauxier: *Le Noir du Yatenga: Mossis, Nioniossés, Samos, Yarsés, Silmi-Mossis, Peuls*, Etudes Soudanaises (Paris, 1917)
A. A. Dim Delobsom: 'Le Mogho Naba et sa cour', *Bull. Com. Etud. Hist. & Sci. A. O. F.*, xi/3 (1928), pp. 386–421
——: 'Les "Nioniossé" de Goupana (Canton de Sao, Subdivision Ouaga-dougou): 1er article', *Outre-mer*, i/4 (1929), pp. 419–46
——: 'Les Danses mossies et leur signification', *Rev. Anthropol.*, xlii (1932), pp. 169–93
——: *L'Empire du Mogho-Naba: Coutumes des Mossi de la Haute-Volta*, Etudes de Sociologie et d'Ethnologie Juridiques, xi (Paris, 1933)
——: *Les Secrets des sorciers noirs*, Collection Science et Magique, 5 (Paris, 1934)
R. Pageard: 'Recherches sur les Nioniossé', *Etud. Volta.*, n. s., iv (1963), pp. 5–71
J. D. Fage: 'Reflections on the Early History of the Mossi-Dagomba Group of States', *The Historian in Tropical Africa*, eds J. Vansina, R. Mauny and L. V. Thomas (London, 1964), pp. 177–92
E. P. Skinner: *The Mossi of the Upper Volta: The Political Development of a Sudanese People* (Stanford, 1964)
P. B. Hammond: *Yatenga: Technology in the Culture of a West African Kingdom* (New York, 1966)
M. Izard: *Introduction à l'histoire des royaumes mossi*, 2 vols, Recherches Voltaïques, 12 and 13 (Paris and Ouagadougou, 1970)
S. Lallemand: 'Symbolisme des poupées et acceptation de la maternité chez les Mossi', *Obj. & Mondes*, xiii/4 (1973), pp. 235–46
C. D. Roy: *Mossi Masks and Crests* (diss., Bloomington, IN U., 1979)
G. Pallier: *Géographie générale de la Haute-Volta* (Limoges, 1981)
C. D. Roy: 'Mossi Dolls', *Afr. A.*, xiv/4 (1981), pp. 47–51, 88
——: 'Mossi Mask Styles', *IA Stud. Afr. A.*, v/1 (1984)
M. Izard: *Gens du pouvoir, gens de la terre: Les Institutions politiques de l'ancien royaume du Yatenga (Bassin de la Volta Blanche)* (Paris and Cambridge, 1985)
——: *Le Yatenga précolonial: Un Ancien Royaume du Burkina* (Paris, 1985)
C. D. Roy: *Art of the Upper Volta Rivers* (Meudon, 1987)

CHRISTOPHER D. ROY

Mossop. Irish family of medallists. William Mossop (*b* Dublin, 1751; *d* Dublin, 28 Jan 1805) trained as a die-sinker in Dublin and made button and seal dies for the Dublin Linen Board before turning his attention to medals. His first medal, portraying the actor *Thomas Ryder* (silver, bronze and gilt bronze, 1782; see Brown, no. 242), is an accomplished piece, especially given Mossop's lack of training in this field. In the 1790s he worked for the Dublin firm of Camac, Kyan & Camac, cutting dies for its copper halfpenny. He also produced dies for seals and worked in ivory and precious stones. Some of his medal designs are borrowed, but many are original works. His Cunningham medal (gold, silver and bronze, 1776; see Brown, no. 267), an award given by the Royal Irish Academy and portraying its founder *James Caulfeild, 1st Earl of Charlemont*, is one of the finest of Irish medals. His son William Stephen Mossop (*b* Dublin, *bapt* 22 May 1788; *d* Dublin, 11 Aug 1827) trained under the teacher

Samuel Whyte (1733–1811) and later at the art school of the Royal Dublin Society and under Francis West (?1749–1809). His first medal die, for the Incorporated Society for Charter Schools in Ireland, was engraved under the direction of his father. His medals include commissions from societies, military medals and a number of political medals, including one of *Daniel O'Connell* (silver, bronze and white metal, 1816; see Brown, no. 914), and a projected series of distinguished Irishmen. Of the series, only five medals, including those of *Jonathan Swift* (silver, bronze and white metal, 1820; see Brown, nos 1049–50) and *Richard Brinsley Sheridan* (bronze and white metal, 1820; see Brown, no. 1048) were completed, but they show Mossop's mastery of the Neo-classical style.

BIBLIOGRAPHY

DNB; Strickland
H. R. Dawson: 'A Memoir of the Medals and Medallists Connected with Ireland', *Trans. Royal Irish Acad.*, xix (1839), pp. 13–19
W. Frazer: 'The Medallists of Ireland and their Work', *J. Royal Hist. & Archaeol. Assoc. Ireland*, xvii (1886), pp. 443–66
L. Forrer: *Biographical Dictionary of Medallists* (London, 1902–30), iv, pp. 164–72; viii, pp. 80–83
A. E. Went: *Irish Coins and Medals* (Dublin, 1978)
L. Brown: *British Historical Medals*, i (London, 1980)

PHILIP ATTWOOD

Mostaert. North Netherlandish family of painters. (1) Jan Mostaert was closely linked with the early Haarlem school of painting and the tradition of Geertgen tot Sint Jans. According to van Mander, one of Jan's descendants was a painter and the father of the twin painters (2) Gillis Mostaert and Frans Mostaert (*c.* 1528/9–1560). Although born in Hulst, in the northern Netherlands, van Mander claimed that both Gillis and Frans trained in Antwerp, Gillis with Jan Mandijn, Frans with Herri met de Bles. This would explain both Gillis's attachment to the tradition of Hieronymus Bosch and Frans's specialization in landscape painting.

BIBLIOGRAPHY

S. Pierron: *Les Mostaert* (Brussels, 1912)

CARL VAN DE VELDE

(1) Jan (Jansz.) Mostaert (*fl c.* 1475–1555/6). According to van Mander, Mostaert came from a famous noble family in Haarlem and learnt his craft from Jacob van Haarlem, a painter who may be identical with the anonymous MASTER OF THE BRUNSWICK DIPTYCH (*see* MASTERS, ANONYMOUS, AND MONOGRAMMISTS, §I). In 1500 Mostaert was commissioned to paint the shutters (destr.) of a reliquary housing the relics of St Bavo in the Groote Kerck, Haarlem. From this date his name appears frequently in the records of the painters' guild. In 1507 he was named deacon, a position he held again in 1543 and 1544.

The earliest paintings attributed to Mostaert clearly display the influence of the earlier Haarlem painter Geertgen tot Sint Jans and his immediate followers. The colourful *Tree of Jesse* (Amsterdam, Rijksmus.) is considered by some to mark the start of Mostaert's activity, but there are good reasons for attributing it to Geertgen since it is more characteristic of Geertgen's refined technique and innovative compositions than of the clumsy figures with stunted proportions that appear in Mostaert's earliest paintings of *c.* 1500–10. Works by Mostaert of this period include two wings of a triptych with *St Peter* and *St Paul and Donors* (Amsterdam, Rijksmus., on dep. Haarlem, Frans Halsmus.), two panels with the prophets *Isaiah* and *Jeremiah* (Rotterdam, Boymans–van Beuningen) and two portraits, *(?) Jacob Jansz. van der Meer* and *Jacqueline of Bavaria* (both Copenhagen, Stat. Mus. Kst).

Between *c.* 1510 and 1516 Mostaert developed a delicate style with minuscule brushstrokes describing elegantly dressed doll-like figures in landscape settings under scalloped clouds against a bright blue sky. The *Adoration of the Magi* (Amsterdam, Rijksmus.) presents three-quarter-length figures including a bland Virgin in the style of Geertgen seated before a curious antique arch decorated with Old Testament stories from the *Speculum humanae salvationis* ('Mirror of human salvation'), alluding to the Epiphany. Mostaert's portraits of this period include *Abel van de Coulster* (Brussels, Mus. A. Anc.), in which the elegant, thin-faced nobleman stands before an equally elegant palace. In the adjacent courtyard is a subsidiary scene of the vision of Augustus. Mostaert's most ambitious work of this period is the triptych of Aelbrecht Adriaensz. van Adrichem (Brussels, Mus. A. Anc.) showing the *Descent from the Cross* with the *Mocking of Christ* and the *Ecce homo* and, when closed, *Christ Carrying the Cross.* The central *Descent from the Cross* is a weak derivation from the famous *Descent from the Cross* by Rogier van der Weyden (Madrid, Prado; *see* WEYDEN, VAN DER, (1), fig. 2). The painting is overcrowded with decorative details,

and the sluggish figures are packed into a shallow foreground, detracting from any sense of monumentality. More compatible with Mostaert's refined style is the *Last Judgement* triptych (Bonn, Rhein. Landesmus.) painted for Anna van Noordwijk, *c.* 1514, for the family chapel in the Dominican church in Haarlem. Here the meticulously rendered portraits of the donor and her family fill the foreground of the three panels, which are dominated by a broad landscape where the Last Judgement takes place. Mostaert also painted a number of small panels of Christ as the *Man of Sorrows* (e.g. London, N.G.) and a curious *Head of St John the Baptist* (London, N.G.).

According to van Mander, Mostaert served for 18 years as a portrait painter at the court of Margaret of Austria, Governor of the Netherlands. This is an exaggeration: his name is missing in the Haarlem archives between 1516 and 1526, and only two documents, dated 1519 and 1521, record his activity at her court during that period. For Margaret, Mostaert executed a number of copies after original court portraits, including those of her third husband *Philibert II of Savoy* (*d* 1504; Madrid, Prado, on dep. Toledo, Mus. Santa Cruz), the young *Charles V* (Madrid, Prado) and *Philip the Fair* (known only in prints). He also painted a small diptych for Margaret; its unusual iconography may be based in part on the mystic literature of the Spanish court (e.g. Sor Isabel de Villena: *Vita Christi, c.* 1490) with which Margaret had close connections. In the left panel Christ takes leave of his mother in

Jan Mostaert: diptych with portraits of *Hendrik van Merode* and his wife *Franziska van Brederode*, oil on panel, each 686×432 mm, *c.* 1525 (Geel, St Dimpnakerk)

the company of angels (Enschede, Rijksmus. Twenthe); in the right panel a court lady, perhaps Mary of Burgundy, is shown at a prie-dieu with the redeemed souls of the Old Testament (Madrid, Col. Thyssen-Bornemisza).

Mostaert's name is mentioned several times in the Haarlem archives between 1527 and 1554. As a renowned court portrait painter, he enjoyed a steady patronage, and he is probably best known for his bust portraits with the sitter in three-quarter pose, resting his or her hands on a cushion before a low parapet against a sweeping landscape background. These include a number of elegant marriage portraits in diptych form, such as *Hendrik van Merode* and his wife *Franziska van Brederode* (Geel, St Dimpnakerk; see fig.).

During the 1520s Mostaert emulated the large panoramic landscapes of Antwerp Mannerist painters such as Joachim Patinir, to whom Mostaert's *St Christopher* (Antwerp, Mus. Mayer van den Bergh), with its broad river valley receding into a mountainous distance, was formerly attributed. The *Expulsion of Hagar and Ishmael* (Madrid, Col. Thyssen-Bornemisza), originally signed and dated I.M. *1525* (or 1527), combines a large-scale figure group in the left foreground with a distant landscape of lakes and mountains. Mostaert's most ambitious landscape is the '*West Indies Landscape*' (Haarlem, Frans Halsmus.), described by van Mander. Variously identified as the landing of Columbus on the island of Goanin in 1493, the exploits of Cortez in central Mexico and the invasion of Brazil by the Portuguese, the subject-matter is actually the expedition of Coronado in Arizona and New Mexico in 1540–42 and was based on literary accounts of the unsuccessful quest for the seven cities of gold of Cibola and not on drawings of the site brought back to Europe, as some scholars have suggested. As a composition it belongs to the tradition of the Mannerist landscapes of Joachim Patinir and Herri met de Bles. The last documented reference to Mostaert is in 1549, when he petitioned the Haarlem town council for permission to take up residence in Hoorn to complete work on an altarpiece there.

BIBLIOGRAPHY

K. van Mander: *Schilder-boeck* ([1603]–04), fol. 229r–229v

G. J. Hoogewerff: *De Noord-Nederlandsche schilderkunst*, ii (The Hague, 1937), pp. 434–503

A. van Schendel: 'De *Boom van Jesse* en het probleem van Geertgen tot Sint Jans', *Oud-Holland*, v (1957), pp. 75–83

Middeleeuwse kunst der noordelijke Nederlanden (exh. cat., ed. R. Luttervelt; Amsterdam, Rijksmus., 1958), pp. 84–9

F. Winkler: 'Zur Kenntnis und Würdigung des Jan Mostaerts', *Z. Kstwiss.*, xiii (1959), pp. 177–214

M. Thierry de Bye Dólleman: 'Jan Jansz. Mostaert, schilder, een beroemd Haarlemmer', *Jb. Cent. Bureau Geneal.*, xvii (1963), pp. 123–36

K. G. Boon: 'Geertgen tot Sint Jans of Mostaert', *Oud-Holland*, lxxxi (1966), pp. 61–72

M. J. Friedländer: *Early Netherlandish* (1967–76), x, pp. 11–20

J. Duverger: 'Jan Mostaert, ereschilder van Margareta van Oostenrijk', *Aachen. Kstbl.*, xli (1971), pp. 113–17

J. Snyder: 'The Early Haarlem School of Painting, III: The Problem of Geertgen tot Sint Jans and Jan Mostaert', *A. Bull.*, liii (1971), pp. 44–58

——: 'Jan Mostaert's *West Indies Landscape*', *First Images of America: The Impact of the New World on the Old*, i (Berkeley, 1976), pp. 495–502

JAMES SNYDER

(2) Gillis Mostaert (*b* Hulst, *c.* 1528–9; *d* Antwerp, 28 Dec 1598). Descendant of (1) Jan Mostaert. He was enlisted as a master in the Antwerp Guild of St Luke in

1554–5. On 28 October 1563 he married Margareta Baes in St Walburgakerk, and between 1564 and 1572 six children were christened in the same church. From 1575 onwards, and until 1588 (the registers are missing between 1579 and 1584), several more were christened in the St Joriskerk. A tax list of 1584 indicates that the painter was then living in a rented house near that church. No named pupils of Mostaert are recorded in the guild lists, but in 1572 Hendrik Pieters, a young artist who intended to travel to Italy, admitted that he had studied with Mostaert in the latter's house for more than a year. Several other artists can also be associated with Mostaert: Cornelis van Dalem, to whom he introduced Bartholomäus Spranger as a pupil and into whose landscapes he occasionally painted the staffage figures; Peeter Baltens and Crispin van den Broeck, who were godfathers to children of Mostaert in 1571 and 1588.

Gillis Mostaert is a more prolific and versatile artist than has usually been assumed. Apart from landscapes and villages, close to Pieter Bruegel I's example, he also painted Hell and fire scenes, biblical subjects, saints and mythological themes. His role as an imitator of Bosch has become more clearly defined. For instance he painted several versions of the *Haywain* (e.g. Madrid, Prado), using as a model one of the five tapestries after Bosch that were woven for Cardinal Granvelle in 1566 in Brussels (Madrid, Escorial), after older designs inspired by Bosch that existed already before 1542. Mostaert was probably also the inventor, at least the only known exponent, of pictures with flat, *trompe l'oeil* wooden frames on which figures and scenes are depicted surrounding the central theme of the painting. Mostaert made such composite paintings from the 1570s onwards. Many are described in 17th-century inventories in Antwerp. Such paintings were formerly often ascribed incorrectly to Frans Francken the younger.

According to van Mander, Mostaert signed his will on 28 December 1598, and on 15 January 1599 his widow admitted before the city magistrates of Antwerp that she had recklessly accepted his inheritance, not knowing it was burdened by heavy debts. This might explain why in 1614 Philip van Valckenisse, possibly one of the main creditors of Mostaert at his death, possessed *c.* 120 of his paintings, both originals and copies, probably almost the complete remains of his studio.

BIBLIOGRAPHY

Thieme–Becker

G. T. Faggin: 'Gillis Mostaert als landschapschilder', *Jb.: Kon. Mus. S. Kst.* (1964), pp. 89–106

F. Baudouin: 'Een Michelangelo-motief bij Gillis Mostaert', *Miscellanea I. Q. van Regteren Altena* (Amsterdam, 1969), pp. 67–9, 284–5

A. Monballieu: 'De *Kermis van Hoboken* bij P. Bruegel, J. Grimmer en G. Mostaert', *Jb.: Kon. Mus. S. Kst.* (1974), pp. 139–69

C. Van de Velde: 'Taferelen met grisaillelijsten van Gillis Mostaert [Panel paintings with grisaille frames by Gillis Mostaert]', *Essays in Northern European Art Presented to Egbert Haverkamp-Begemann* (Doornspijk, 1983), pp. 276–82

E. Mai: 'Neuzugänge am Wallraf-Richartz-Museum: Dauerleihgaben aus Privatbesitz', *Mus. Stadt Köln*, vi (1984), pp. 77–81

C. Van de Velde: '*Et mundus eum cognovit*: De monogrammist TG', *Liber amicorum Leon Voet* (Antwerp, 1985), pp. 595–612

A. Zwollo: 'Enkele nieuwe tekeningen van Gillis Mostaert', *Rubens and his World* (Antwerp, 1985), pp. 61–9

CARL VAN DE VELDE

Mosui. *See* KARAKHOTO.

Mosul [Mawṣil]. City in northern Iraq. Located on the west bank of the Tigris River, opposite the ancient city of Nineveh, Mosul is surrounded by fertile plains. It replaced Nineveh under Byzantine rule and was conquered in AD 637 by Muslim Arabs, who used it as a base from which to conquer Azerbaijan and Armenia and as an important entrepôt for overland trade between Iran and Syria. It served as the capital of the Hamdanid (*reg* 905–91) and 'Uqaylid (*reg* 992–1096) dynasties, and, after a brief interregnum, became the capital of the Zangids (*reg* 1127–1222). 'Imad al-Din Zangi (*reg* 1127–46) restored the fortifications and expanded the city. Under Nur al-Din Zangi (*reg* 1146–74) several important buildings were erected (*see* ISLAMIC ART, §II, 5(ii)(e)), but most have been extensively rebuilt. The most important was the congregational mosque (1170–72), of which the only medieval parts to remain are the brick minaret, some columns and the mihrab (1148), which came from another mosque. The Mujahidi (Khidr Ilyas) Mosque preserves a fine mihrab (1180). Power passed to the atabeg Badr al-Din Lu'lu' (*reg* 1222–59), whose palace had three iwans overlooking the Tigris. Several shrines to minor Shi'ite saints, such as those of Imam Yahya ibn al-Qasim (1239) and Imam 'Awn al-Din (1248), are square buildings containing tiled mihrabs and covered with *muqarnas* vaults under pyramidal roofs. The typical building material in the medieval period was rubble masonry revetted with stone and vaulted with brick. Zangid buildings were often decorated with a wide inscription band made of deep-blue marble inlaid with white alabaster. Following the Mongol attack in 1262 the city declined in importance. After a period of Mongol rule, the city passed to the Aqqoyunlu Turkomans in the 15th century, the Safavids of Iran in 1508 and the Ottomans in 1535. The opening of the Suez Canal in 1869 destroyed its trade position, but the discovery of oil in the region has made it the third-largest city in Iraq.

Mosul was known in medieval sources for fine textiles called *mawṣilīn*, from which the word muslin is derived, although these luxury fabrics with gold and silver threads were quite different from the cottons and silks usually associated with this term. Under the patronage of the Zangids and of Badr al-Din Lu'lu', fine illustrated manuscripts were produced at Mosul (*see* ISLAMIC ART, §III, 4(iv)(c)). They continue the Classical tradition of technical and naturalistic illustration and often have frontispieces depicting the enthroned sovereign. A school of metalwork also flourished there in the 12th and 13th centuries (*see* ISLAMIC ART, §IV, 3(ii)), and the epithet *al-Mawṣilī* came to be associated with the finest practitioners of the craft. Inlaid with gold and silver, vessels of copper alloy were decorated with scenes of the hunt, pleasures of the court and signs of the zodiac. The city was also known for its fine woodwork, such as a pair of wooden doors from the mosque of Nabi Jirjis and a minbar (1153) from the 'Amadiyya Mosque (both Baghdad, Iraq Mus.; *see* ISLAMIC ART, §VII, 1(i)(b)).

BIBLIOGRAPHY

Enc. Islam/2: 'Mawṣil'

F. Sarre and E. Herzfeld: *Archäologische Reise im Euphrat- und Tigris-Gebiet*, 4 vols (Berlin, 1911–20), ii, pp. 203–305

S. al-Daywahji [Dewachi]: 'Jāmi' al-nabī Jurjīs fī'l-Mawṣil' [The mosque of Nabi Jurjis in Mosul], *Sumer*, xvii (1960), pp. 100–12

——: 'Mashhad al-imām Yaḥyā b. al-Qāsīm' [The shrine of the Imam Yahya ibn al-Qasim], *Sumer*, xxiv (1968), pp. 171–81

N. Y. al-Tutunji: 'Jāmi' al-mujāhidi fī'l-Mawṣil' [The Mujahidi mosque in Mosul], *Sumer*, xxviii (1972), pp. 193–200

SAEED AL-DEWACHI

Moszyński, August Fryderyk (*b* Dresden, 25 Jan 1731; *d* Padua, June–July 1786). Polish architect, artistic administrator and writer. The son of Frederica Alexandra, natural daughter of King Frederick-Augustus I of Saxony and Poland, he was educated at military school in Dresden and trained in architecture by Gaetano Chiaveri. In 1747 he travelled to France, England and Italy (where he took part in excavations at Naples and Herculaneum). Moszyński's first designs were for Dominican churches in Ternopol, Ukraine (1755–70), and Mikulintsy, Ukraine (1761–79). From 1764 he administered the collections of King Stanislav II Poniatowski, and in 1765–72 he was director of the Polish Royal Buildings. His many unrealized plans include designs for a public theatre in Warsaw (*c.* 1772) and for the reconstruction of the collegiate church of St John, Warsaw (*c.* 1770–80; both U. Warsaw, Lib.), also plans for an attempt to found a royal academy of fine art in the 1780s. Moszyński's 'Essai sur le jardinage angloise' (1774), dedicated to the Polish King, was modelled on Thomas Whatley's *Observations on Modern Gardening* (London, 1770). Aside from his interests in architecture and collecting, Moszyński also busied himself with the sciences and, among other things, organized the royal physics and astronomy collection as well as the chemical laboratory. An active freemason, he was elected Grand Master of the Great Warsaw Lodge in 1769. In March 1785 he left for Italy. His travel diaries contain interesting reflections on the fine arts.

WRITINGS

M. Zboińska-Daszyńska, ed.: *Dzienniki podróży do Francji i Włoch* [Diaries of travels to France and Italy] (Kraków, 1970)

A. Morawińska, ed.: *Rozprawa o ogrodnictwie angielskim* [Treatise on English gardening] (Wrocław, 1977) [incl. Pol. and Fr. versions]

PSB

BIBLIOGRAPHY

T. Mańkowski: 'August Moszyński: Architekt polski XVIII stulecia', *Prace Kom. Hist. Sztuki*, iv (1928), no. 2, pp. 169–230

ANDRZEJ ROTTERMUND

Mota, António Augusto da. *See* COSTA MOTA, ANTÓNIO AUGUSTO DA.

Motesiczky, Marie-Louise (von) (*b* Vienna, 24 Oct 1906). Austrian painter, active in Germany and England. She was born into a prosperous Viennese family. Motesiczky's friendship with Max Beckmann provided the impetus for her to begin painting seriously. She had studied art in The Hague and Vienna until 1922 and spent the years between 1924 and 1926 in Paris, before joining Beckmann's master class in Frankfurt am Main in 1927. He provided a model for an approach based on the humanity of figurative painting. Her work reflects her association with him and their common interests. She was interested in the narrative, symbolic and psychological content of her subjects rather than their formal qualities. She often painted portraits (e.g. *Elias Canetti*, oil on canvas, 490×390 mm, 1960; Vienna, Hist. Mus.; *At the Dressmaker's*, 1930; Cambridge, Fitzwilliam; *Self-portrait* *with Pears*, oil on canvas, 610×460 mm, 1965; Linz, Neue Gal.) or mythological subject-matter. Her work is characterized by a sculptural awareness of light and shade. Forced to leave Vienna by the Nazi threat, she moved to England in 1939 and continued to paint with great sensitivity and humanity. Her first solo show was held at Beaux Arts Gallery, London, in 1960, but she remained relatively unknown, despite a large output of paintings, until a retrospective in 1985 (London, Goethe Inst.).

BIBLIOGRAPHY
Marie-Louise von Motesiczky: Paintings Vienna 1925–London 1985 (exh. cat., intro. R. Calvocoressi; London, Goethe Inst., 1985) [incl. texts by E. H. Gombrich, G. Büsch and Motesiczky]

Mother-of-pearl. Type of iridescent substance lining the shell of some molluscs and other marine invertebrates.

1. Material, sources and techniques. 2. Uses.

1. MATERIAL, SOURCES AND TECHNIQUES. Mother-of-pearl is composed of thin, flat calcium-carbonate plates secreted by certain bivalve molluscs (as well as cuttlefish and snails) and arranged in layers around the inside of the shell. The outside of the shell is composed of a brown, horny substance, known as conchiolin. The iridescence of mother-of-pearl is a result of the refraction of light through the many layers. The waters in which the shell is fished determine the colour of mother-of-pearl: in warmer seas near the Equator colours range from pink through amber to black, although white mother-of-pearl has always been the most prized. Pigments that create various markings on the shell are also secreted by the mollusc. The established source of mother-of-pearl, as well as pearls, is the large saltwater pearl oyster (*Aricula margaritifera* or *Meleagrina margaritifera*), found mainly in the Red Sea, Persian Gulf, the Indian Ocean, South China Sea, Celebes Sea and North Pacific Ocean at a depth of between 10 and 70 m. The freshwater pearl oyster (*Unio margaritifera*) is found in rivers and lakes throughout Europe, Asia and North America. Other sources of mother-of-pearl are the shells of the cuttlefish (*Nautilus pompilus*), found in tropical waters, and the red abalone (*Haliotis iris*), found in the Pacific. The shells of turbinate snails also produce mother-of-pearl: these were traditionally fished by divers until the Japanese developed commercial oyster farming in the 1920s. The hard outer layer of conchiolin must be removed before the mother-of-pearl can be worked. This can be achieved either by the use of acid or by grinding with a stone in a water-filled trough. As a soft material, mother-of-pearl can be carved by hand or dissolved in acid, those areas to remain in relief being protected by wax. The mother-of-pearl can then be polished with abrasives or acid to regain its lustre. Carving and engraving can be carried out with goldsmiths' tools. Mother-of-pearl will lose its iridescence on exposure to sunlight and will effervesce in acid; the outer layers can be damaged by prolonged exposure to heat (over 100°C), humidity and dryness.

For pearls *see under* GEM-ENGRAVING.

2. USES.

(i) *Europe*. One of the oldest items of secular jewellery to be found in Europe, thought to be palaeolithic, is made of mussel shells and pearls, with remaining traces of etching. The use of mother-of-pearl as a material for mosaic work may have originated in the East but was employed in the Roman Empire (e.g. mother-of-pearl mosaics, 6th century AD; Ravenna, S Apollinare). There is insufficient evidence to allow attribution of Late Gothic works in mother-of-pearl to a particular artist or workshop, but goldsmiths or gem-cutters may have carved mother-of-pearl, as they would have had the necessary tools and techniques. Most surviving examples of carved mother-of-pearl lamellae are relief carvings; only a few objects carved in the round are known, of which the oldest extant work (1406) is a silver reliquary inset with mother-of-pearl figures carved in the round (Prague, former Benedictine monastery of St Margaret). Mother-of-pearl carving increased after the mid-15th century, and the work is mostly circular or polygonal in form, occasionally pierced or in the *plique à jour* style. Mother-of-pearl, usually set in silver or brass, was used in plaques, reliquaries or family altars, or in rosaries, medallions and secular jewellery; it was not usually painted, but a few examples survive that show traces of paint or gilding (e.g. *Reading Saint*; Graz, Joanneum). The thinness of the material usually only allowed carving on one side, but there are examples of lamellae with carving on both sides in the Österreichisches Museum für Angewandte Kunst, Vienna. Pieces carved on one side are frequently found in settings that are enclosed at the back and engraved (e.g. *Lamentation*, Basle, Hist. Mus.; *Death of the Virgin*, Prague Cathedral, St Vitus's Treasury). The subject-matter of mother-of-pearl carving is usually ecclesiastical, and of the approximately 400 lamellae known by the late 20th century, scenes of the *Annunciation*, *Birth of Christ*, *Crucifixion* and *St George* were well represented in the major collections in London (V&A), Berlin (Skulpgal.), Munich (Bayer. Nmus.), Cologne (Schnütgen-Mus.) and Nuremberg (Ger. Nmus.). The E. Kofler-Truniger Collection in Lucerne has a few important examples.

During the 15th century centres specializing in goldsmiths' work also produced mother-of-pearl carving. Israhel van Meckenem the younger (*see* MECKENHEM, (2)), probably active in Cleve in 1465, is thought to be responsible for a number of mother-of-pearl carvings, among which are a silver-gilt pax with a mother-of-pearl relief of the *Adoration of the Magi* (Cleve, Städt. Mus. Haus Koekkoek) and the *Birth of Christ* (Munich, Bayer. Nmus.). Mother-of-pearl reliefs carved in Basle (*see* SWITZERLAND, §X) are similar in style to silver medallions produced in the Upper Rhine area, for example the *Annunciation* (London, V&A), *Birth of Christ* (Brussels, Musées Royaux A. & Hist.) and a reliquary with a mother-of-pearl relief depicting the *Man of Sorrows* (Basle, Hist. Mus.). The Bistritz pax with a mother-of-pearl relief of *St George* (Budapest, N. Mus.) may have been produced in Nuremberg, and a reliquary (1486; Innsbruck, Premonstratensian Abbey) with a pierced mother-of-pearl relief of the *Crucifixion* is also linked with this city. The Augsburg tax records mention a Claus 'Berlachmuterschneider' in

1484, who may possibly have been responsible for the *Death of the Virgin* on the Rechberg Pax (Augsburg, Maximilianmus.), although the exact source of this work remains unclear. Salzburg was another centre of production. Part of the private altar with mother-of-pearl reliefs (1494; New York, Met.) has been attributed to the goldsmith Bertold Schauer (*d* 1496), while other pieces attributed to Salzburg workshops are the *St Erintrudis* and the *Man of Sorrows* (Vienna, Österreich. Mus. Angewandte Kst.). Although gem-cutters and seal-makers were active in Cologne in the 15th century, it remains unclear whether mother-of-pearl carving was also produced in the area.

Some mother-of-pearl carving is based on 15th-century engravings by Master E. S. or Martin Schongauer, although the engraving and carving may not have been produced in the same place; for example the engraving by Schongauer (Lehrs, no. 363) and the carving of *Death of the Virgin* (Innsbruck, Tirol. Landesmus.). Other carved lamellae are more loosely based on engravings by Schongauer, for example *Christ Carrying the Cross* and *Christ before St Anne*, which decorate the silver tabernacle triptych made for the monastery of St Peter, Salzburg (see fig.). There may be a connection between the mother-of-pearl reliefs on an altar and the work of Master E. S. (Berliner, no. 13, pl. 10), as a surviving fragment depicting *St George* (Baltimore, MD, Walters A.G.) can be connected to an extant drawing (Berliner, no. 52, pl. 25c). In the wake of humanist thought, ecclesiastical subject-matter gave way to secular themes, the portrait being especially popular. Many more named artists were known. The carving of shell-cameos also became widespread during this period and, as with the shell-cameo, there was an interest in creating a multi-coloured surface. Consequently, the dark, outer layer of the shell was occasionally used (e.g. half-length portraits of *Philip II* and *Charles V*, 1556; Hamburg, Mus. Kst & Gew.), although the white, iridescent surface soon regained its popularity (e.g. portrait of *Emperor Matthias of Hungary* by Dionysio Miseroni, 1613, Vienna, Ksthist. Mus.; portrait of *Henry III*, Berlin, Skulpgal.).

During the late Renaissance and Baroque periods, nautilus shells (*see* NAUTILUS CUP), turbo shells and trochus shells were frequently mounted in goldsmiths' work; examples include a nautilus cup in the form of a snail (*c.* 1630; Hartford, CT, Wadsworth Atheneum), by Jeremias Ritter of Nuremberg, and a turbo shell with silver-gilt mounts (late 16th century; Madrid, Mus. Thyssen-Bornemisza), possibly by Claus Harders of Lüneburg. The Jamnitzer workshop in Nuremberg was a specialist centre for curiosities of this type (e.g. trochus shell in silver-gilt mounts, *c.* 1570; Munich, Residenz; *see* SHELL, colour pl. I, fig. 1; *see also* JAMNITZER, (1)). The towns of Nuremberg and Augsburg were the main centres of production for mounted shells during the 16th and 17th centuries, but Antwerp (e.g. nautilus shell, 1555–6; London, BM), London (e.g. salt, *c.* 1750; London, V&A) and Paris (*see* FRANCE, fig. 74) also produced pieces of comparable workmanship and complexity of design. The shell could be polished flat, etched with acid to leave patterns in relief, or engraved, with a pigment comprising coal dust, oil or wax creating additional definition (examples in Vienna, Ksthist. Mus.; Munich, Residenz). Mother-of-pearl relief carvings with additional black line-engravings

Mother-of-pearl lamellae (detail) on a tabernacle triptych, silver, parcel gilt and enamel, h. 692 mm, from the Benedictine monastery of St Peter, Salzburg (New York, Metropolitan Museum of Art)

of mythological or genre scenes were produced in the Belkein family workshop in Amsterdam (e.g. shell depicting *Perseus and Andromeda*; Stuttgart, Württemberg. Landesmus.). Another method of working was to use the prismatic layers of the mother-of-pearl as a contrast to the flat relief.

From the 17th century onwards mother-of-pearl was frequently used in Europe as a material for inlay or marquetry. Known craftsmen included Bernhard Strauss (*fl* 1662–81) in Augsburg and Dirk van Ryswyck (1596–1679), a leading craftsman in Amsterdam working in mother-of-pearl marquetry, signed examples of whose work can be seen in the Grünes Gewölbe, Dresden. Van Ryswyck had immediate access to the material through the Dutch East India Co. trade. Musical instruments, mirror frames and weapons were also inlaid with mother-of-pearl, often in conjunction with such other materials as brass, tortoiseshell and pewter (e.g. wheel lock and stock, early 17th century; Stuttgart, Württemberg. Landesmus.).

Vessels embellished with mother-of-pearl originated in Paris but were produced throughout Europe. The lamellae could be attached with studs or with more complex metal ornament (e.g. vessel in the form of a partridge; Copenhagen, Nmus.). In 18th-century Paris mother-of-pearl was an extremely fashionable material for snuff boxes, étuis and gold-mounted boxes of all types (examples in Madrid, Mus. Thyssen-Bornemisza; Paris, Mus. A. Déc.; Waddesdon Manor, Bucks, NT; *see also* FRANCE, §X, 2 and SHELL, colour pl. I, fig. 2). In the 19th century mother-of-pearl was used extensively as decoration to simulate inlay in a wide variety of papier-mâché work, ranging from furniture (e.g. papier-mâché settee with mother-of-pearl decoration; London, V&A) to boxes and trays (*see* PAPIER-MÂCHÉ, §§1 and 2 and fig.). Mother-of-pearl was also frequently used as inlay in wood furniture from the late 19th century until the 1930s (*see* MARQUETRY, §§1 and 2). A mother-of-pearl industry had been established in Austria in the 18th century, two notable craftsmen being Veit Pnotsch and Leopold Rauch (both active in 1768). Wood-turned objects, for example buttons and other fashion accessories, were produced, and by the end of the 19th century such items as pipe-bowls and walking-stick handles were popular. The use of the colourful haliotis shell in the 19th century led to new techniques in which the material, in the form of thin lamellae, was placed between layers of white mother-of-pearl (e.g. visiting-card holder; Stuttgart, Württemberg. Landesmus.). Mother-of-pearl inlay was also used in such religious souvenirs as Jerusalem crosses (e.g. Freiburg im Breisgau, Augustinmus.) or models of the Church of the Holy Sepulchre, Jerusalem (examples in London, BM; Munich, Bayer. Nmus.). In the Art Nouveau period mother-of-pearl was used extensively by such craftsmen and designers as Koloman Moser (e.g. mother-of-pearl letter rack and inkwell, *c*. 1900; Klein and Bishop, fig. 5) and C. R. Ashbee, and the nautilus shell continued to be mounted in novel settings (e.g. silvered pewter and nautilus shell desk lamp, 1904; Klein and Bishop, fig. 3).

(ii) America, Asia and Islamic lands. In Pre-Columbian Mesoamerica and in Native American art mother-of-pearl was used, among other shells, to make beads for necklaces and other body ornaments (*see* NATIVE NORTH AMERICAN

ART, §IX, 4 and 5). It was also used as inlay in masks and stone sculptures and included in élite tomb offerings. One of the most famous examples is a large pair of artificial pearls from the Temple of Inscriptions at Maya Palenque, each made from two hollow mother-of-pearl pieces, filled and glued with a limestone paste (Mexico City, Mus. N. Antropol.; *see also* MESOAMERICA, PRE-COLUMBIAN, §IX, 4 and 6). In South-east Asia mother-of-pearl inlay is widely used to decorate jewellery, boxes, utensils, weapons, furniture, screens, doors and window shutters. The art of mother-of-pearl inlay has reached a particularly high level of refinement and technical skill in Thailand (*see* THAILAND, §X, 10 and fig. 32). In the Philippines mother-of-pearl inlay and other nacreous shells are also used to decorate such diverse objects as boats, weapons, guitars and other musical instruments. In East Asia mother-of-pearl was used in conjunction with lacquer (*see* CHINA, §IX, 3 and 5 and JAPAN, §X and figs 177 and 180), while in the Ottoman court it was used as an inlay on wooden furniture (*see* ISLAMIC ART, §VII, 2(iv)).

BIBLIOGRAPHY

H. Grunn: *Perlmutterkunst in alter und neuer Zeit. 73. Sonderausstellung des Niederösterreichischen Landesmuseums* (Vienna, n.d.)
M. Lehrs: *Geschichte und kritischer Katalog des deutschen, niederländischen und französischen Kupferstichs im XV. Jahrhundert*, v (Vienna, 1925)
P. H. Halm and R. Berliner: *Das Hallesche Heiltum* (Berlin, 1931)
G. E. Pazaurek: *Perlmutter* (Berlin, 1937)
A. Stifft-Gottlieb: 'Linearkeramische Gräber mit Spondylusschmuck aus Eggenburg, Nierdonau', *Mitt. Antropol. Ges. Wien*, lxix (1939), p. 149f
M. C. Ross: 'A Late XVth-century Mother-of-pearl Carving', *J. Walters A.G.*, vii–viii (1944–5), pp. 125–6
L. Ehret: *Seeschwäbische Goldschmiedekunst im 15. und 16. Jahrhundert* (Freiburg im Breisgau, 1954)
H. Muller: 'Augsburger Goldschmiedekunst der Zeit Hans Holbein d. Ä.', *Hans I Iolbein der Ältere und die Kunst der Spätgotik* (exh. cat., Augsburg, Rathaus, 1965), pp. 194–5
H. Kohlsausen: *Nürnberger Goldschmiedekunst des Mittelalters und der Dürerzeit: 1240–1540* (Berlin, 1968)
G. Smith: 'Reflections of a Pattern Print by Master E. S.: Passion Cycles in Mother-of-pearl', *Pantheon* (Jan–Feb 1968), pp. 430–39
C. I. A. Ritchie: *Carving Shells and Cameos* (London, 1970)
——: *Shell Carving: History and Techniques* (London, 1974)
F. Wagner: 'Goldschmiedekunst: Spätgotik in Salzburg: Skulptur und Kunstgewerbe', *Jschr. Salzburg. Mus. Carolino Augusteum*, xxi (1975), pp. 75–92
J. F. Hayward: *Virtuoso Goldsmiths and the Triumph of Mannerism: 1540–1620* (London, 1976)
J. Rasmussen: 'Untersuchungen zum Halleschen Heiltum des Kardinal Albrecht von Brandenburg', *Münchn. Jb. Bild. Kst*, xvii (1976), pp. 59–118; xviii (1977), pp. 91–132
A. Limpinsky: 'Exotische Meeresschnecken in der europäischen Goldschmiedekunst des 16. und 17. Jahrhunderts', *Alte & Mod. Kst*, xxii (1977), p. 151
J. Schlosser: *Kunst- und Wunderkammern*, 2 vols (Brunswick, 1978)
E. Scheicher: *Die Kunst- und Wunderkammern der Habsburger* (Zurich, 1979)
Die Muschel in der Kunst (exh. cat., Zurich, Mus. Bellerive, 1985)
D. Klein and M. Bishop: *Decorative Art: 1880–1980* (Oxford, 1986)

MICHAELA SLATNER-PRÜCKL

Motherwell, Robert (*b* Aberdeen, WA, 24 Jan 1915; *d* Princetown, MA, 16 July 1991). American painter, printmaker and editor. A major figure of the Abstract Expressionist generation (*see* ABSTRACT EXPRESSIONISM), in his mature work he encompassed both the expressive brushwork of action painting and the breadth of scale and saturated hues of colour field painting, often with a marked emphasis on European traditions of decorative abstraction.

Robert Motherwell: *Reconciliation Elegy*, acrylic on canvas, 3.05×9.27 m, 1978 (Washington, DC, National Gallery of Art)

Motherwell was sent to school in the dry climate of central California to combat severe asthmatic attacks and developed a love for the broad spaces and bright colours that later emerged as essential characteristics of his abstract paintings. His later concern with themes of mortality can likewise be traced to his frail health as a child. From 1932 he studied literature, psychology and philosophy at Stanford University, CA, and encountered in the poetry of the French Symbolists an expression of moods that dispensed with traditional narrative. He paid tribute to these writers in later paintings such as *Mallarmé's Swan* (1944; Cleveland, OH, Mus. A.) and *The Voyage* (1949; New York, MOMA), named after Baudelaire's poem. As a postgraduate student of philosophy at Harvard University, Cambridge, MA, in 1937–8, he found further justification for abstraction in writings by John Dewey, Alfred North Whitehead and David Prall, later relating their views on the expression of individual identity through immediate experiences to his own urge to reveal his personality through the gestures of his brushwork (*see* ACTION PAINTING).

Motherwell decided to become an artist after seeing modern French painting during a trip to Paris in 1938–9, but in order to satisfy his father's demands for a secure career he first studied art history from 1940 to 1941 under Meyer Schapiro at Columbia University, NY. Through Schapiro he met Roberto Matta and other exiled European artists associated with Surrealism; their use of automatism as a means of registering subconscious impulses was to have a lasting effect on Motherwell and on other American painters such as Jackson Pollock, Lee Krasner and William Baziotes, whom he befriended in New York after a trip to Mexico in 1941 with Matta.

While in Mexico, Motherwell executed his first known works, the *Mexican Sketchbook* of 11 pen-and-ink drawings in black and white (artist's col.; for first page, see Arnason, 1982, p. 29). These were influenced by Matta but were more abstract and spontaneous in appearance. The appeal of automatist spontaneity, however, was complemented for him by the clear structure, simple shapes and broad areas of flat colour in paintings by Piet Mondrian, Picasso and Matisse.

The interaction of emotionally charged brushwork with severity of structure began to emerge in paintings such as the *Little Spanish Prison* (1941–4; New York, MOMA), a deceptively simple composition of slightly undulating vertical stripes in yellow and white interrupted by a single horizontal bar.

In 1943 Motherwell produced a series of dark, menacing works of torn and paint-stained paper in response to the wartime atmosphere. *Surprise and Inspiration* (Venice, Guggenheim), originally called *Wounded Personage*, equated the act of tearing with killing and the paint-soaked paper with bandages. These collages, which heralded his lifelong commitment to the medium, were presented as the focal point of his first one-man exhibition held in 1944 at Peggy Guggenheim's Art of This Century Gallery, New York.

During the 1940s, like many of his colleagues in the New York School, Motherwell remained devoted to recognizable imagery, to the expressive potential of calligraphic marks and to subject-matter of a literary and of a political nature, as in *Pancho Villa, Dead and Alive* (gouache and oil with collage on cardboard, 1943; New York, MOMA). The abstract paintings for which he is best known, such as *Elegy to the Spanish Republic XXXIV* (1953–4; Buffalo, NY, Albright–Knox A.G.), one of a series of more than 140 large canvases initiated in 1949, expressed a nostalgia that he shared with many of his generation for the lost cause of the Spanish Civil War. The works in this series typically consist of black, organic ovals squeezed by stiff, vertical bars against a white ground, retaining the unpremeditated quality of an ink sketch even when enlarged to enormous dimensions, as in the much later *Reconciliation Elegy* (see fig.). He conceived of the shapes as elements within an almost musical rhythm, rich in associations with archetypal imagery of figures or body parts but sufficiently generalized to convey a mood rather than a specific representation.

During the late 1940s and 1950s Motherwell spent much of his time lecturing and teaching; he taught at BLACK MOUNTAIN COLLEGE, NC, in 1950, and from 1951 to 1959 at Hunter College, New York. He also worked on three influential editorial projects: the Documents of Modern Art series, which he initiated in 1944 and which included his most important literary contribution to the history of modern art, *The Dada Painters and Poets: An Anthology* (New York, 1951); *Possibilities* magazine, from

1947; and *Modern Artists in America* (New York, 1951), which he co-authored with Ad Reinhardt.

By the time that he returned fully to his art in the late 1950s, Motherwell had developed various different series. The *Elegies*, severe in their concentration on black and white and in their ever-growing scale, were the vehicle of his most profound emotions, while the small oil paintings occasioned by the decay of his second marriage, the *Je t'aime* series of 1954–8 (e.g. *Je t'aime IIA*, 1955; New York, Grossman priv. col., see Sandler, 1970, p. 246), expressed more intimate and private feelings. His collages, which he began to reproduce also by lithographic means in the 1960s, began to incorporate material from his studio life, such as cigarette packets and labels from artists' supplies, so as to become records of his daily experiences (e.g. *Summer Lights Series* published by Gemini GEL in 1973; see Arnason, 1982, pp. 203–6). The coastline near the artists' colony of Provincetown, MA, where Motherwell began to spend his summers in 1962, inspired works such as *Beside the Sea No. 5* (1962; artist's col., see Sandler, 1970, p. 209), a series of 64 pictures in which he splashed oil paint against rag paper with the full force of his arm as a physical equivalent for the action of sea spray on the bulkhead in front of his studio.

From 1968 to 1972 Motherwell worked on a series of paintings with the generic title *Open* as a personal response to the colour field painting made by younger abstract painters in the 1960s. Typical of this more contemplative strain of his art is *Open No. 17: In Ultramarine with Charcoal Line* (polymer paint and charcoal on canvas, 1968; artist's col., see H. Geldzahler: *New York Painting and Sculpture: 1940–1970*, New York, 1969, p. 236), which consists of a surface of a single colour on to which he has drawn three sides of a rectangle in charcoal lines: an abstract equivalent to the views through open windows favoured by European painters such as Matisse as metaphors for the relationship between the interior world of the emotions and the external world of the senses.

Motherwell's first important print, the lithograph *Poet I* (London, Tate), was published by Tatyana Grossman's Universal Art Editions in 1961. He subsequently produced an important body of printed work, notably *A la pintura* (1972; London, BM), a limited edition book of 24 unbound pages printed in letterpress, etching and colour aquatint, in which he exploited the medium's capacity for combinations of rich colour and exacting line to approximate the sensuous effects of his paintings. One of Motherwell's most significant, late series of paintings and drawings was the *Hollow Men*. While the title of these works is taken from T. S. Eliot's poem of despair for Cassius in Shakespeare's *Julius Caesar*, Motherwell's paintings evoke a different spirit: the artist's desire to slice through superficiality and reveal the essence of his art. As such, the *Hollow Men* incorporates both the style of the *Elegies* and that of the *Opens*. The organic forms of the *Elegies* are now translucent rather than solid, and consequently more exposed; they are set against a threatening black ground. In these shapes, Motherwell has also revealed more of his automatic drawing, which he believed was the essence of his artistic personality, than in any large-scale works since the 1950s. The *Hollow Men* stands

as one of Motherwell's final attempts to assert the authenticity of his Abstract Expressionist art.

BIBLIOGRAPHY
I. Sandler: *Abstract Expressionism* (London, 1970)
Robert Motherwell (exh. cat. by R. C. Hobbs, Düsseldorf, Städt. Ksthalle, 1976)
H. H. Arnason: *Robert Motherwell* (New York, 1977, rev. 2/1982)
J. Fineberg: 'Death and Maternal Love: Psychological Speculations on Robert Motherwell's art', *Artforum*, xvii (1978), pp. 52–7
E. A. Carmean jr, ed.: *Robert Motherwell: The Reconciliation Energy* (New York, 1980)
R. S. Mattison: 'The Emperor of China: Symbols of Power and Vulnerability in the Art of Robert Motherwell during the 1940s', *A. Int.*, xxv (1982), pp. 8–14
Robert Motherwell (exh. cat., ed. R. T. Buck; Buffalo, Albright–Knox A.G., 1983)
S. Terenzio and D. C. Belknap: *The Prints of Robert Motherwell: A Catalogue Raisonné, 1943–1984* (New York, 1984)
R. S. Mattison: 'A Voyage: Robert Motherwell's Earliest Works', *A. Mag.*, lix (1985), pp. 90–93
For further bibliography *see* ABSTRACT EXPRESSIONISM, ACTION PAINTING and COLOUR FIELD PAINTING.
ROBERT SALTONSTALL MATTISON

Motonobu. *See* KANŌ, (2).

Motsurin. *See* SHŌTŌ BOKUSAI.

Motta, Fabrizio Carini. *See* CARINI MOTTA, FABRIZIO.

Motta, Raffaello. *See* REGGIO, RAFFAELLINO DA.

Mottez, Victor(-Louis) (*b* Lille, 13 Feb 1809; *d* Bièvres, near Paris, 7 June 1897). French painter. In Lille he studied with his father Louis Mottez and with Edouard Liénard (1779–1840), the director of the art school and a former student of Jacques-Louis David. Mottez went to Paris at the end of 1828, when, according to Giard, he met the future king Louis-Philippe, then Duc d'Orléans and a student at the Collège Henri IV; their friendship is one reason for the many decorative commissions that Mottez received during the July Monarchy. In March 1829 Mottez entered the Ecole des Beaux-Arts, where he studied with Jean-Auguste-Dominique Ingres and François-Edouard Picot. He exhibited at the Paris Salon from 1833, gaining a first-class medal for history painting in 1838 and a second-class medal in 1845. He was awarded the Légion d'honneur in 1846.

Mottez travelled widely and frequently in order to educate himself in the techniques of fresco and mural painting. In Florence in 1833 he came to appreciate the work of Giotto and the Italian primitives. In 1858 he published a translation of Cennini's *Il libro dell'arte*. He also studied northern European decorative painting, travelling to Belgium in 1833 and to Germany in 1842. It is possible that he met Peter Joseph Cornelius at this time. During the Second Republic, between 1848 and 1852, Mottez lived in England, where he was exposed to Pre-Raphaelite painting.

Mottez's early works are small-scale, literary genre subjects in the Romantic style. He exhibited a scene from Walter Scott's *A Legend of Montrose* and the *Quarrel between Gurth and Cedric* from Scott's *Ivanhoe* at Douai in 1829 (both untraced). His mature style is heavily indebted to Ingres in the strong contours, the distilled essence of physiognomy and idealized approach to form, the media of fresco and mural decoration, and the selection of subjects from Classical history or mythology or from religion. Between 1839 and 1846 Mottez frescoed the porch (destr.) of St Germain-l'Auxerrois and, near the ambulatory, painted *St Martin Dividing his Cloak* (*in situ*). He also decorated the chapels of St François de Sales and the Immaculate Conception in St-Séverin, Paris (commission given 1852), the chapel of St Martin in St-Sulpice (1859–63; *in situ*) and, for Ste Catherine in Lille, the *Four Evangelists*, the *Denial of St Peter* and the *Agony in the Garden* (untraced). The majority of his surviving decorative paintings are in a bad state of preservation; however, photographs of 1854 (see Foucart, 1969) of *Dance* and *Music*, a pair of frescoes painted in 1846–7 for the apartment of Armand Bertin (destr. 1854), reveal Mottez's iconography (the Bertin family and their friends in the arts, including both Ingres and Victor Hugo as Olympian gods) and style (similar to Ingres's *Apotheosis of Homer*, Paris, Louvre, and *Golden Age*, Dampierre, Château).

Among Mottez's mature easel paintings are: the *Martyrdom of St Stephen* (exh. Salon 1838; untraced), *Ulysses and the Sirens* (1848; Nantes, Mus. B.-A.), *Melitus Accusing Socrates* (exh. Salon 1857; Lille, Mus. B.-A.), *Zeuxis Taking the Most Beautiful Maidens of Agrigento for his Models* (exh. Salon 1859; Lyon, Mus. B.-A.) and *Phryne Before the Judges of the Areopagus* (exh. Salon 1859; Dijon, Mus. B.-A.). The Musée Wicar, Lille, has a collection of his sketchbooks.

WRITINGS

trans.: *Le Livre de l'art ou traité de peinture* (Paris, 1858) [trans. of C. Cennini: *Il libro dell'arte* (*c.* 1390)]

BIBLIOGRAPHY

R. Giard: *Le Peintre Victor Mottez d'après sa correspondance (1809–1897)* (Lille, 1934)
B. Foucart: 'Victor Mottez et les fresques du salon Bertin', *Bull. Soc. Hist. A. Fr.* (1969), pp. 153–73
J. Lacambre: 'Les Elèves d'Ingres et la critique du temps', *Actes du colloque Ingres: Montauban, 1969*, pp. 104, 109
B. Foucart: *Le Renouveau de la peinture religieuse en France (1800–60)* (Paris, 1987)
A. Haudiquet and others: 'Répertoire des artistes', *Les Salons retrouvés: Eclat de la vie artistique dans la France du Nord, 1815–1848*, ii (1993), p. 130

BETH S. WRIGHT

Mottram, Charles (*b* 1807; *d* London, 30 Aug 1876). English engraver. Examples of his line-engravings include his reduced-size plate (Thomas Landseer had already produced a larger version) after Edwin Landseer's *The Challenge* (Alnwick Castle, Northumb.) and his large plate after Rosa Bonheur's *Breton Oxen* (untraced), both declared for publication by Henry Graves & Co. in 1862. He reproduced in mezzotint Thomas Jones Barker's *Morning before the Battle* and *Evening after the Battle* (both untraced; declared for publication by Graves in, respectively, 1865 and 1866). His most celebrated works, however, are the three mixed mezzotint plates reproducing John Martin's *Last Judgement* (1853), *Plains of Heaven* (1851–3) and *Great Day of His Wrath* (1851–3; all London, Tate). The three subjects were published in 1225 sets by Thomas McLean in 1854, and their popularity endured well into the 20th century. Mottram was an expert in the application to steel plates of 'sky tints' with the use of a ruling machine.

DNB
Victorian Engravings (exh. cat. by H. Beck, London, V&A, 1973), p. 55

ANTHONY DYSON

Moucheron, de. Dutch family of artists of French descent. Both (1) Frederik de Moucheron and his son (2) Isaac de Moucheron specialized in Italianate landscape views with park-like settings. These were particularly used to decorate the walls in houses of the well-to-do in Amsterdam.

(1) Frederik de Moucheron (*b* Emden, Germany, 1633; *bur* Amsterdam, 5 Jan 1686). Painter. After training with Jan Asselijn in Amsterdam, he settled and worked in France for several years, where in 1656 he was recorded as staying in Paris and Lyon. He returned to Amsterdam after a brief period in Antwerp. In 1659 he married Marieke de Jouderville, daughter of the painter Isaac de Jouderville; they had 12 children. Frederik was strongly influenced by the work of the second generation of DUTCH ITALIANATES, particularly Asselijn and Jan Both. His landscapes also show similarities with the late work of Adam Pynacker. Dirck Helmbreker, Johannes Lingelbach, Adriaen van de Velde and Nicolaes Berchem all provided staffage for his paintings.

De Moucheron's work is appreciated primarily for its picturesque, decorative qualities, his paintings often rendered attractively atmospheric by use of silvery touches (e.g. *Italianate Landscape*, 1670s; Hannover, Niedersächs. Landesmus.). Towards the end of his life he painted landscapes for three *saletkamer* walls in a doll's house, which was made and furnished in Amsterdam for Adam Oortmans and Petronella de la Court between *c.* 1674 and 1690 (Utrecht, Cent. Mus.). These show how such landscape wall panels would have looked *in situ*, although to find an actual room so decorated as early as this would have been rare. In 1678 and 1679 he completed, with Berchem, several works by Willem Schellinks, who had died in 1678.

BIBLIOGRAPHY

Thieme-Becker; Wurzbach
I. H. van Eeghen: 'Het poppenhuis van Petronella de la Court, huisvrouw van Adam Oortmans', *Jb. Amstelodamum*, xlvii (1960), pp. 159–67
Nederlandse 17e-eeuwse Italianiserende landschapschilders (exh. cat., ed. A. Blankert; Utrecht, Cent. Mus., 1965); rev. and trans. as *Dutch 17th-century Italianate Landscape Painters* (Soest, 1978)
L. Salerno: *Pittori di paesaggio del seicento a Roma*, 3 vols (Rome, 1977–80), ii, pp. 760–67; iii, p. 1060
Die Niederländer in Italien: Italienisante Niederländer des 17. Jahrhunderts aus Österreichischem Besitz (exh. cat. by R. Trnek, Salzburg, Residenzgal.; Vienna, Gemäldegal. Akad. Bild. Kst.; 1986), pp. 144–50
Masters of 17th-century Dutch Landscape Painting (exh. cat. by P. C. Sutton and others, Amsterdam, Rijksmus.; Boston, MA, Mus. F.A.; Philadelphia, PA, Mus. A.; 1987–8), pp. 378–80, pl. 121

TRUDY VAN ZADELHOFF

(2) Isaac de Moucheron (*bapt* Amsterdam, 23 Nov 1667; *d* Amsterdam, 1744). Painter, draughtsman, etcher and architect. Son of (1) Frederik de Moucheron. He was apprenticed to his father, before going to Italy, where he arrived *c.* 1695 and stayed for at least two years. He worked mainly in Rome in company with other northern artists, who gave him the Bent-name 'Ordonantie' (*see* SCHILDERSBENT). He specialized in vedute, such as *View of the River Tiber* (*c.* 1696; Warsaw, N. Mus.), which shows an

Isaac de Moucheron: *Statues and Buildings on the Water in a Park*, oil on canvas, 1.3×1.6 m (Amsterdam, Rijksmuseum: on deposit at Amsterdam, Museum Willet-Holthuysen)

atmospheric view of Rome from the south. In making Roman townscapes the main subject of his paintings he followed the singular example of Gaspar van Wittel. Isaac also copied paintings by Nicolas Poussin and, on his return to Amsterdam in 1697, made a series of etchings after Gaspard Dughet. His interest in these classicist French masters had a clearly recognizable effect on his own work.

In the Netherlands Isaac became known, as had his father, primarily for the painted wall decorations he made for wealthy patricians' houses. However, through his pictures he introduced a new theme to landscape painting, in which parks containing prominent architectural features are the main subject. His *Statues and Buildings on the Water in a Park* (Amsterdam, Rijksmus., on dep. Mus. Willet-Holthuysen; see fig.), with its geometrically designed garden, its lake and architectural elements, made for the Hortus Botanicus in Amsterdam, is a typical example of the new theme.

Over the years many of Isaac's wall decorations have been lost, but those done for two houses in Amsterdam are still *in situ*: at Herengracht 168 (now Ned. Theat. Inst.) and 475. Those at 168, five paintings of the *Story of Jephthah*, were installed *c.* 1730 and include figures painted

by Jacob de Wit. The harmonious colours show that the artists took into consideration how individual rooms were lit, and the scenes create the illusion that the walls have been broken through to reveal open space beyond. The strong classical French influence is also apparent in such works as *Southern Landscape* (1698; Montpellier, Mus. Fabre), painted in Dughet's style, with a timeless, arcadian character.

Isaac was also an important draughtsman. Besides preparatory studies, a number of his finished drawings are known, most in pen and ink with watercolour, such as *Italian Villa with Park* (Hamburg, Ksthalle), in which he achieved beautiful results. Among his etchings is one made after his own wall decoration: *Park with Fountains*. As an architect he made several designs for the Logement van Amsterdam in The Hague (1737 and 1741), and he may also have produced garden designs.

BIBLIOGRAPHY

Hollstein: *Dut. & Flem.*
A. Staring: 'Isaac de Moucheron als ontwerper van gevels en tuinen' [Isaac de Moucheron as designer of façades and gardens], *Oud-Holland*, lxv (1950), pp. 85–104
Nederlandse 17e-eeuwse Italianiserende landschapschilders (exh. cat., ed. A. Blankert; Utrecht, Cent. Mus., 1965); rev. and trans. as *Dutch 17th-century Italianate Landscape Painters* (Soest, 1978)

A. Zwollo: *Hollandse en Vlaamse veduteschilders te Rome* (Assen, 1973), pp. 39–56

D. Freedberg: *Dutch Landscape Prints of the Seventeenth Century* (London, 1980), p. 67, pls 143–4

LUUK BOS

Mouchette. Curved, daggerlike motif in Gothic TRACERY.

☐

Mouchy, Louis-Philippe (*b* Paris, 31 March 1734; *d* Paris, 10 Dec 1801). French sculptor. He owed his very successful official career to the protection of his teacher, Jean-Baptiste Pigalle, whose niece he married in 1764, after he returned from a stay in Italy. Accepted (*agréé*) by the Académie Royale in 1766, he was received (*reçu*) as a full member in 1768 on presentation of the statuette *Shepherd at Rest* (marble, exh. Salon 1769; Paris, Louvre), the physiological realism of which, inspired by Pigalle, was far removed from the classical canon to which Mouchy was indebted in later such works as the bland *Harpocrates, God of Silence* (marble, 1789; Paris, Pal. Luxembourg).

Mouchy was associated with Pigalle on a number of projects: working on the pedimental sculpture of the Hôtel des Fermes in the Place Royale, Reims (*c.* 1756); modelling reductions of several of Pigalle's works to be reproduced in biscuit porcelain, including the bronze monument to *Louis XV* (1765) in the Place Royale, Reims; and carving the minor figures and the *Glory* surrounding Pigalle's statue of the *Virgin and Child* (marble, 1774; Paris, St Sulpice). His busts of *Voltaire* and of the *Maréchal de Saxe* (both 1778–9) (marble, Versailles, Château) were heavily influenced by Pigalle's realistic portrait style, and were once attributed to him. Mouchy was also responsible for carving a copy of Edme Bouchardon's *Cupid Carving his Bow from the Club of Hercules* for the gardens of the Petit Trianon, Versailles (marble, 1778; *in situ*). In 1787 he collaborated with Louis-Simon Boizot on a number of works for St Sulpice in Paris, chief among them being four plaster female statues personifying *Faith, Hope, Resignation* and *Humility* and the relief of the *Death of St Joseph* (*in situ*).

Among Mouchy's best-known independent works are the three life-size historical portrait statues commissioned by the Comte d'Angiviller, director of the Bâtiments du Roi, for the series of 'Illustrious Frenchmen'. The standing *Maximilien de Béthune, Duc de Sully* (marble, exh. Salon 1777; Paris, Inst. France) is perhaps the best of these. It is a sober work, stripped of the historical accessories that encumber the seated *Charles, Duc de Montausier* (marble, exh. Salon 1789; Paris, Louvre), and free of the theatrical heroics of the standing *Maréchal François-Henri de Montmorency-Bouteville, Duc de Luxembourg* (marble, exh. Salon 1791; Versailles, Château). Mouchy was also responsible for a statue of *Apollo* (marble, 1779; Paris, Louvre), commissioned in 1774 by the Abbé Terray together with a pendant statue of *Mercury* by Pigalle (Paris, Louvre), the two works symbolizing Terray's dual function as director of the Bâtiments du Roi and Minister of Finance.

During the French Revolution, Mouchy was an active member of the Commission des Monuments. His last work was a bust of the *Duc de Sully* (marble, exh. Salon 1801; Versailles, Château) executed for the Galerie des Consuls in the Tuileries Palace, Paris. He was a competent and successful artist, but his work, oscillating between the naturalistic and Neo-classical trends of French sculpture in the later 18th century, is without real individuality.

BIBLIOGRAPHY

Lami

M.-F. Raynaud, ed.: 'Inventaire des sculptures exécutées au XVIIIe siècle pour la direction des Bâtiments du Roi', *Archv A. Fr.*, xiv (Paris, 1927), pp. 220–34

J. Thirion: 'L'Apollon de Mouchy', *Rev. Louvre*, i (1976), pp. 35–40

Diderot et l'art de Boucher à David (exh. cat., Paris, Hôtel de la Monnaie, 1984), pp. 467–9 [entry by J.-R. Gaborit]

GUILHEM SCHERF

Moudarres, Fateh [Mudarris, Fātiḥ] (*b* Aleppo, 1922). Syrian painter and sculptor. Initially a self-taught painter working in a realistic style, he was inspired by Surrealism in the 1940s and 1950s, and he explained his work in verse and prose to the public. After studying at the Accademia di Belle Arti, Rome (1954–60), he returned to Syria and developed a highly personal style that he described as 'surrealistic and figurative with a strong element of abstraction' (see Ali, 1989, p. 131). Moudarres's work was influenced by the icons of the Eastern Orthodox Church and Syrian Classical art, which he studied in the National Museum of Damascus. His work became increasingly abstract in the 1960s, although after 1967 he expressed political themes. From 1969 to 1972 he studied at the Ecole des Beaux-Arts in Paris. His paintings have an accomplished sense of composition and balance of colour. As one of the leaders of the modern art movement in Syria, Moudarres trained several generations of artists in his classes at the College of Fine Arts at the University of Damascus.

BIBLIOGRAPHY

W. Ali: 'Contemporary Art from the Islamic World', *Scorpion* (London, 1989)

——: *A Survey of Modern Painting in the Islamic World and the Development of the Contemporary Calligraphic School* (diss., U. London, SOAS, 1993)

W. ALI

Mouka. See MUTISO, DAVID.

Moukhtar, Mahmoud. See MUKHTAR, MAHMUD.

Mould, Jacob Wrey (*b* Chislehurst, Kent, 1825; *d* New York, 14 June 1886). English architect and designer, active in the USA. He claimed to have been an assistant to Owen Jones in London. In 1852 he emigrated to New York where he designed All Souls' Unitarian Church (1853–5; destr.). The banded red brick and white sandstone of the Italian Romanesque design introduced polychromy to American architecture. In subsequent years Mould designed less flamboyant churches, notably West Presbyterian Church (1863; destr.) in New York and First Presbyterian Church (1874) in Bath, NY. His talent as a designer led him to work in the decorative arts. He made designs for stained glass, book bindings, banknotes, textiles and other items. His taste for non-Western design motifs anticipated the American Aesthetic Movement. Unfortunately little remains as evidence of Mould's inventive manipulation of colour and ornament. His most enduring works as a decorator are the carvings he designed for the Terrace (1858–70) in Central Park, New York, a structure designed by Calvert Vaux. Mould also collaborated with Vaux on the design of the Metropolitan Museum of Art (begun 1874) and the American Museum of Natural History (begun 1874), both in New York. For a brief period in the early 1870s, he served as architect-in-chief of Central Park. In 1874–9 he lived in Lima, Peru, where he planned the municipal park system and designed a polychromatic brick and stone house (c. 1879). Mould enjoyed the reputation of a genius among his liberal-minded colleagues. His unconventional way of life, however—he lived openly with a woman who was not his wife—put off many influential clients. Among his more important extant works are Trinity Church Parish School (1860; now the Serbian Eastern Orthodox Cathedral of St Sava), New York; the Sheepfold (1870; now the Tavern-on-the-Green restaurant) in Central Park; and St Mary's Church (1874), Luzerne, NY.

MEA

BIBLIOGRAPHY

H.-R. Hitchcock: 'Ruskin and American Architecture, or Regeneration Long Delayed', *Concerning Architecture: Essays on Architectural Writers and Writing Presented to Nikolaus Pevsner*, ed. J. Summerson (London, 1968)

D. Van Zanten: 'Jacob Wrey Mould: Echoes of Owen Jones and the High Victorian Styles in New York, 1853–1865', *J. Soc. Archit. Hist.*, xxviii (1969), pp. 41–57

FRANCIS R. KOWSKY

Moulding. Abstract ornament of continuous section used both monumentally and decoratively to enrich a surface or disguise a join. Mouldings can be applied to flat or curved surfaces, and they are integral to many architectural features including arches, piers and bases. They appear in all developed forms of architecture, in some periods following strict rules of application. As an ornamental device to decorate walls, ceilings, wood-, metal- and plasterwork, they were particularly varied in the 18th and 19th centuries, when techniques of casting and wood-turning became more sophisticated.

In ancient Greek and Roman architecture and again in the Renaissance and early 18th century, mouldings were attributes of the Classical orders and were restricted largely to entablatures and bases. In the Middle Ages, however, the variety of types and applications increased remarkably, encouraged by the invention of new architectural features such as vault ribs and window mullions. They enlivened surfaces and reduced the mass through subtle modulations of light and shade. Mouldings are therefore studied as an important stylistic indicator in Romanesque and Gothic architecture from the 11th century to the early 16th in northern Europe, especially in England.

This article discusses architectural mouldings of the medieval period; for information on Classical mouldings *see* GREECE, ANCIENT, §II, 1(iii)(b).

See also ORDERS, ARCHITECTURAL, especially §I, 1.

I. Introduction. II. Types. III. History and development.

I. Introduction.

A profile is a section drawing of a moulding. Most published profiles have been derived from examples in stone and from churches following the ecclesiological bias of the GOTHIC REVIVAL. Nonetheless mouldings exist in other materials (e.g. wood and brick) and in secular buildings, especially in the later Middle Ages. In some areas of Europe, such as northern Germany and Poland,

brick mouldings were already quite sophisticated by the late 13th century. Profiles from secular buildings may be simple, such as chamfer-moulded ribs in vaulted undercrofts (Morris, 1986), and some moulding types are perhaps more characteristic of secular architecture (e.g. quadrant mouldings in England). Other mouldings encountered in a secular context are up to date with ecclesiastical examples, if they do not actually set the trend themselves, such as the use from 1283 of wave and sunk chamfer mouldings in the Welsh castles of Edward I (Morris, 1978; *see* CAERNARFON CASTLE and JAMES OF ST GEORGE).

The study of medieval mouldings has centred on those countries in which Gothic architecture flourished: France, Germany and England, but most notably the latter, where the Gothic Revival had its roots and encouraged antiquarian studies of the subject. As early as 1480 William Worcestre, the English antiquary, described the mouldings of two contemporary doorways of Bristol churches. In the later 18th century there was a revival of interest in recording the details of medieval buildings, and the drawings of profiles by the antiquarian draughtsman John Carter set a high standard for accuracy. It was not until the mid-19th century, however, that medieval mouldings were afforded detailed archaeological study and classification. In England, Robert Willis analysed their nomenclature in 1844; F. A. Paley (1815–88) compiled a manual that is still a standard work; and Edmund Sharpe (1809–77) published surveys of full-size profiles of an unsurpassed quality. Many splendid profile drawings are also to be found in various 19th-century 'sketchbook' publications, such as the *Architectural Association Sketchbook* (London, 1867–1906; see *Topographical Index to Measured Drawings* …). At this time an accurate knowledge of Gothic mouldings was essential for a British architect (e.g. Bond). Meanwhile, various studies appeared in Europe, especially France, containing useful information about continental mouldings (e.g. Viollet-le-Duc; Dehio and von Bezold; Enlart); but no extensive national surveys were published equivalent to Paley's for England.

Mouldings were usually carved with a chisel, although for brick the shape was generally created by impressing in a mould. The mason was guided by a template (Med. 'molde') designed as a full-size profile and cut from a thin material such as wooden board in the Middle Ages and zinc in modern times (e.g. the collection of post-medieval templates in the masons' tracing shop at York Minster; see Shelby). Medieval templates are shown in contemporary illustrations such as those in Villard de Honnecourt's portfolio (1220–35; Paris, Bib. N., MS. Fr. 19093). Late medieval drawings of profiles exist, especially in Germany and Austria (see Bucher), and bequests of templates are recorded in craftsmen's wills. The practice of the master mason designing templates goes back at least to the 12th century, when William of Sens delivered moulds (Lat. 'formas') for shaping the stones to 'sculptors' for rebuilding Canterbury Cathedral choir in 1175 (Willis). It is generally presumed that this remained standard practice during the Middle Ages (Salzman), but some delegation of the design of mouldings is also probable (Morris, 1990).

Several methods have been used since the 19th century to obtain accurate full-size profiles of mouldings *in situ* in historic buildings (Paley). Professional architects have generally advocated measured drawings (Roberts), but accurate copies are obtained more quickly by the use of a 'template former' ('mouldings comb'), a device pushed against the moulded surface to produce an exact impression (see *Recording Worked Stones*). Lead wire is less practicable if many mouldings are to be drawn. A recent development is the production of profile drawings by photogrammetric survey (Crosby).

In the 19th century medieval mouldings were studied primarily to supply exemplars for Gothic Revival architects. In modern times their value lies mainly in assisting art historians and archaeologists in matters of dating and provenance, especially where other forms of evidence are lacking. No scientific method exists for dating stone, unlike wood, whereas in favourable circumstances a typological study of profiles can provide a date within 20 or 30 years (Morris, 1990) and evidence for a sequence of building phases (Rigold). Mouldings may reveal the hand of the architect as brushwork does that of the painter (Harvey, 1961), so that often a group of profiles can be attributed to a particular workshop (Morris, 1978, 1979), although less frequently to a specific master craftsman (Roberts; Morris, 1990).

BIBLIOGRAPHY

Papworth: 'Mould', 'Moulding'
W. Worcestre: *Itineraries* [*c*. 1480]; ed. J. H. Harvey (Oxford, 1969), pp. 314–17
R. Willis: *Architectural Nomenclature of the Middle Ages* (Cambridge, 1844)
F. A. Paley: *Manual of Gothic Mouldings* (London, 1847, rev. 3/1865)
E. Sharpe: *Supplement to Architectural Parallels in the 12th and 13th Centuries* (London, 1848)
E.-E. Viollet-le-Duc: *Dictionnaire raisonné de l'architecture française du XIe au XVIe siècle*, 10 vols (Paris, 1867–70) [esp. 'profil'; further inf. in entries throughout vols i–ix, e.g. 'arc', 'base', 'chapiteau']
E. Sharpe: *The Mouldings of the Six Periods of British Architecture from the Conquest to the Reformation*, 3 vols (London, 1871–4) [incomplete]
G. Dehio and G. von Bezold: *Die kirchliche Baukunst des Abendlandes*, 5 vols (Stuttgart, 1887–1901) [plates]
F. Bond: *Gothic Architecture in England* (London, 1906), pp. 658–707 [excellent collection of profiles]
Topographical Index to Measured Drawings of Architecture in Principal British Architectural Publications, London, V&A (London, 1908)
C. Enlart: *Architecture religieuse*, 3 vols (1924–7), i of *Manuel d'archéologie française depuis les temps mérovingiens jusqu'à la Renaissance*, 4 vols (Paris, 1902–27)
H. R. Hahnloser, ed.: *Villard de Honnecourt: Kritische Gesamtausgabe des Bauhüttenbuches MS. Fr. 19093 der Pariser Nationalbibliothek* (Vienna, 1935, Graz, 2/1972)
L. F. Salzman: *Building in England down to 1540: A Documentary History* (Oxford, 1952, rev. 2/1967), pp. 20–22
J. H. Harvey: 'Origins of the Perpendicular Style', *Studies in Building History: Essays in Recognition of the Work of B. H. St J. O'Neil*, ed. E. M. Jope (London, 1961), pp. 134–65 [early Perpendicular mouldings]
F. Bucher: 'Design in Gothic Architecture: A Preliminary Assessment', *J. Soc. Archit. Historians*, xxvii/1 (1968), pp. 49–71 [medieval drawings of profiles]
L. Shelby: 'Medieval masons' templates', *J. Soc. Archit. Historians*, xxx/2 (1971), pp. 140–54
S. E. Rigold: 'Romanesque Bases in and South-east of the Limestone Belt', *Ancient Monuments and their Interpretation: Essays Presented to A. J. Taylor* (London, 1977), pp. 99–137
E. Roberts: 'Moulding Analysis and Architectural Research: The Late Middle Ages', *Archit. Hist.*, xx (1977), pp. 1–13
R. K. Morris: 'The Development of Later Gothic Mouldings in England, *c*. 1250–1400', *Archit. Hist.*, xxi (1978), pp. 18–57; xxii (1979), pp. 1–48
S. McK. Crosby: 'Some Uses of Photogrammetry by the Historian of Art', *Etudes d'art médiéval offertes à Louis Grodecki*, ed. S. McK. Crosby and others (Paris, 1981), pp. 119–28
R. K. Morris: 'The Architecture of the Earls of Warwick', *England in the 14th Century*, ed. W. M. Ormrod (Woodbridge, 1986), pp. 161–74
Recording Worked Stones, Council for British Archaeology (London, 1987), pp. 23–39
R. K. Morris: 'Mouldings and the Analysis of Medieval Style', *Medieval Architecture and its Intellectual Context: Studies in Honour of Peter Kidson*, ed. E. Fernie and P. Crossley (London, 1990), pp. 239–47
——:'An English Glossary of Medieval Mouldings, with an Introduction to Mouldings *c*. 1040–1240', *Archit. Hist.*, xxxv (1992), pp. 1–17

1. Arch mouldings: (a) crossing, St Etienne, Caen, France (schematic); (b) choir arcade, Durham Cathedral, England (after Bilson); (c) chancel, All Saints, Wittering, Cambridgeshire, England (after Taylor); (d) north transept, Furness Abbey, Lancashire, England (after Bilson); (e) keep, Castle Hedingham, Essex, England (after Bond); (f) arcade, east end, Malines Cathedral, Belgium; (g) main arcade, St Hugh's choir, Lincoln Cathedral, England; (h) choir arcade, Bristol Cathedral, England; (i) dado, east end, St Urbain, Troyes, France; (j) main arcade, Reims Cathedral, France (after Dehio); (k) main arcade (inner order), east end, Salisbury Cathedral, England

II. Types.

A combination of two or more mouldings is described as a 'group' (Paley) or 'moulding formation' (Morris, 1978). A group frequently coincides with an architectural component, such as a rib or the order of an arch (see figs 1i and 2g). A typical group consists of a centrally placed moulding and one projecting on either side (2g). Willis called the centrally placed moulding 'on the keel' and the one projecting on either side 'on the wing'.

Various terms are used to locate a moulding on an arch or related architectural feature. 'Soffit', 'face' and 'angle' are more usually applied in Romanesque and Early and High Gothic (see fig. 2f). The soffit of an arch may coincide with the axial moulding. An angle moulding, such as an angle roll, occurs where the arch profile is essentially rectangular in section. In later Gothic the block is characteristically chamfered, and the angle is replaced by mouldings worked on the chamfer plane (1j).

Angle-fillet (Bilson). A wedge-shaped moulding (see fig. 3xxiv), typically a subsidiary component in a Romanesque or Early Gothic moulding group (1e). In later Gothic it is usually undercut on one or both sides by hollow mouldings (3xxx), and it is mainly a continental form. It is rare after the 13th century in England, except for capitals ('chisel-nosed'; Morris, 1979). See also *chamfered mitre, spiked hollow.*

Angle roll [edge roll (Paley); quirked roll (Bilson)]. A roll moulding on the corner of a profile, usually of an arch (2f), used in Romanesque and Early and High Gothic architecture.

Bead [little bowtell (Willis)]. A small roll moulding of continuous section (3xxix), typically less than 25 mm in diameter.

Beak [hook (Stalley); horn (Wilson, 1986); peaked (Paley)]. A delicate moulding resembling a bird's beak (3xx), found especially as the lateral moulding of ribs in the 12th and 13th centuries. The term 'beaked half-roll' has been applied especially to larger examples (see also *beaked roll*). Small examples (e.g. for abaci; see fig. 2m) have been described as forming a 'convex lip' (Bilson) or 'tongue-shaped member' (Paley).

Beaked half-roll. See *beak.*

Beaked roll. A roll moulding typically undercut on both sides (3xiii), used in Early English architecture, mainly on arches and ribs. The term could also be applied to other roll-type mouldings, such as the beaked ogee keel (3xiv) and the beaked roll-and-fillet (3xv).

Bowtell. See *bead, roll.*

Casement. A late medieval term for a hollow moulding (Willis), it is now applied specifically to a large hollow of compound curve, often flanked by fillets (3xxviii) and mainly used in Late Gothic architecture. See also *wave.*

Cavetto. See *hollow mouldings.*

Chamfer [plain chamfer (Paley)]. A moulding produced by cutting the right angle of the block of stone on a diagonal plane (3xxxiii), used early in abaci and sub-bases. From the 13th century it was regularly used for arches, ribs and mullions. The angle of the chamfer-type mouldings generally became narrower from the 14th century (3xxxii). See also *chamfered mitre, hollow chamfer, sunk chamfer.*

Chamfered mitre (Jansen, 1984; Ger. 'dreikanter', 'Kletzl') [polygonal termination (Morris, 1979)]. An angle-fillet with a flat termination and undercut by hollows (3xxxi). It was commonly used as the axial moulding of ribs and

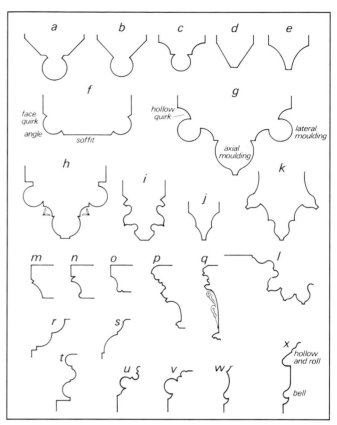

2. Architectural moulding applications: Mullions: (a-b) roll and chamfer mullion; (c) roll and hollow-chamfer mullion; (d) chamfer mullion; (e) hollow-chamfer mullion. Ribs and arches: (f) arch with angle rolls; (g) transverse arch, nave vault, Amiens Cathedral, France (after Durand); (h) diagonal rib, main vault, east arm, Canterbury Cathedral, England; (i) tierceron rib, nave aisle, Lincoln Cathedral, England; (j) rib, Tachov, Bohemia (after Mend); (k) arch, east chapels, Notre-Dame, Caudebec-en-Caux, France; (l) respond, St Catherine's Chapel, Strasbourg Cathedral, France (after Recht). Abaci: (m) quirk and hollow-chamfer abacus, crypt, Bayeux Cathedral, France (after Ruprich-Robert); (n) hollow and bead abacus, north transept, Furness Abbey, England (after Bilson); (o) cyma recta abacus, nave, Holme Cultram Abbey, Cumbria, England (after Wilson). Capitals: (p) capital, main arcade, east end, Exeter Cathedral, England; (q) capital, east chapels, St Urbain, Troyes, France. Bases: (r) double-hollow base, Westminster Abbey, England (after R.C.H.M.); (s) modified Attic base, nave, Gloucester Cathedral, England (after Rigold); (t) Attic base, St Remi, Reims, France (after Viollet-le-Duc); (u) water-holding base, nave, Glastonbury Abbey, England; (v) triple-roll base, east end, Salisbury Cathedral, England; (w) bell base, nave, St Maclou, Rouen, France; (x) hollow and roll base with bell sub-base, apsidal chapels, Notre-Dame, Paris, France (after Viollet-le-Duc)

mullions in later Gothic, especially in continental Europe (1f).

Channelled roll. See *grooved roll.*

Chisel-nosed. See *angle-fillet.*

Convex lip. See *beak.*

Concave mouldings. See *hollow mouldings.*

Cyma recta. See *ogee.*

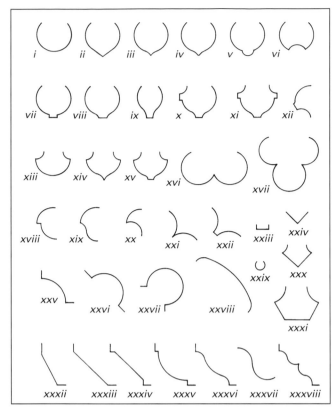

3. Moulding types: (i) roll; (ii) keel; (iii) ogee keel; (iv–v) rounded ogee keel; (vi) grooved roll; (vii–ix) roll-and-fillet; (x) roll with two fillets; (xi) roll with three fillets; (xii) demi-roll-and-fillet; (xiii) beaked roll; (xiv) beaked ogee keel; (xv) beaked roll-and-fillet; (xvi) double roll; (xvii) triple roll; (xviii–xix) scroll; (xx) beak; (xxi) spiked hollow; (xxii) free-standing fillet; (xxiii) fillet; (xxiv) angle-fillet; (xxv) hollow chamfer; (xxvi) semicircular hollow; (xxvii) three-quarter hollow; (xxviii) casement; (xxix) bead; (xxx) undercut angle-fillet; (xxxi) chamfered mitre; (xxxii–xxxiii) chamfer; (xxxiv) sunk chamfer; (xxxv) quadrant; (xxxvi) wave; (xxxvii) ogee; (xxxviii) double ogee

Double ogee. Two ogee mouldings brought together to form a 'cupid's bow' profile (3xxxviii), used in Late Gothic architecture, especially in England. See also *ogee*.

Edge roll. See *angle roll*.

Face roll. A half-roll on the face of an arch (1a), used in early Romanesque architecture, especially in England and Normandy.

Fillet. A projecting flat strip of continuous section (3xxiii). It is typically less than 40 mm wide (e.g. roll-and-fillet; see fig. 3vii), but it can be broader, especially in the Early and High Gothic periods (1j). See also *angle-fillet*. The term 'fillet base' is used for a base with a prominent fillet in plan, mainly found in continental Late Gothic (Neagley).

Fillet moulding. See *roll-and-fillet*.

Filleted roll. See *roll-and-fillet*.

Free-standing fillet. A fillet standing alone, typically between two hollow mouldings (3xxii), found in the later Gothic period.

Grooved roll (Morris, 1978) [channelled roll (Wilson, 1986)]. A roll moulding with a continuous curved recess (3vi). It is a rare form, distinctive to Early Gothic, and usually deployed for arches and ribs.

Half roll-and-fillet. See *quadrant*.

Hollow [concave] *mouldings.* See also *casement, spiked hollow.*

Hollow chamfer (Paley) [It. cavetto]. A hollow carved on the chamfer plane, typically of a quarter circle (3xxv), used commonly in Gothic architecture.

Hollow roll (Fernie). A term used for some hollow mouldings (except the hollow chamfer) in Romanesque architecture that are generally carved on the face. It was used especially in England and Normandy.

Semicircular hollow [sunken semi-circle (Paley)]. A hollow moulding flanked by fillets or flat surfaces (3xxvi), used mainly from the 12th to the 14th centuries for arches, ribs, piers etc.

Three-quarter hollow. A hollow of more than a semicircle (characteristically about three-quarters of a circle). It is primarily an English form, used in the 13th and 14th centuries, and typically flanked by fillets after *c.* 1250 (3xxvii).

Hollow quirk. See *quirk.*

Hook. See *beak.*

Horn. See *beak.*

Keel [keeled]. A roll moulding with an arris resembling the keeled hull of a ship in section. The term has been applied to two different profiles, causing frequent confusion in the literature, especially as applied to Cistercian and related architecture in the British Isles.

Keel [keeled roll (Wilson, 1986); pointed bowtell (Paley); pointed or keel-shaped (Bilson)]. In this form the surfaces flanking the arris are flattish (3ii). It is mainly characteristic of Early Gothic architecture.

Ogee keel [nib, nibbed, nibbing (Wilson, 1986); ogee keeling (Wilson, 1978)]. In this usage the surfaces flanking the arris are concave (3iii). Paley called it a 'keel' but clearly differentiated it from keel. Bilson described it as a 'sharp fillet' or 'sharp arris formed by a sharp reverse curve'. The ogee keel was popular in Early English architecture but did not occur on the Continent until the later Gothic period. See also *beaked roll, pear.*

Keeled roll. See *keel.*

Nib. See *keel.*

Ogee [Class. cyma recta; cyma reversa]. An S-curve profile (3xxxvii), found mainly in Late Gothic architecture (*see* OGEE). See also *double ogee, wave.*

Ogee casement. See *wave.*

Ogee keel. See *keel.*

Ovolo. See *quadrant.*

Peaked. See *beak.*

Pear (Ger.: 'birnstab'). A general term to describe a moulding incorporating two opposed ogee ('half pear') curves, such as an elongated roll-and-fillet (3ix) or an ogee keel. It was used especially in continental Late Gothic architecture for shafts, arches and ribs. The term is also used to refer to the pear-shaped profile (3iv) of an ogee keel with a slightly rounded tip, here termed a 'rounded ogee keel'; Paley called it 'a coarse keel mould'. An Early Gothic form, it is often hard to distinguish from an ogee keel. A version with a more rounded tip (3v) occurs occasionally in later Gothic.

Polygonal termination. See *chamfered mitre*.

Pointed bowtell. See *keel*.

Pointed or keel-shaped. See *keel*.

Quadrant [half roll-and-fillet (Paley); Class. ovolo; quarter-round moulding]. A convex moulding of quarter-circle profile, usually terminated by fillets (3xxxv), occurring mainly in the later 12th century and the 13th.

Quarter-round moulding. See *quadrant*.

Quirk. An angular incision (2f), found mainly in Romanesque and Early Gothic architecture. 'Hollow quirk' (Bilson) is used for larger, concave-sided examples (2g). See also *angle roll*.

Quirked roll. See *angle roll*.

Roll. A large convex moulding, usually semicircular or three-quarters of a circle in section (3i). Willis used the late medieval terms 'bowtell' and 'great bowtell' (now archaic) to describe the latter form. The roll is one of the commonest moulding types, from which many other roll-type mouldings derive: see *angle roll, head, beaked roll, face roll, grooved roll, keel, pear, roll-and-fillet, scroll, soffit roll*. Composite roll mouldings are termed 'double' (3xvi) or 'triple' (3xvii) if the rolls are contiguous, or 'paired' if they are separated by another feature (1e).

Roll-and-fillet [filleted roll]. A roll moulding with a single axial fillet (Paley). It was prevalent from the 13th century, especially in arches and ribs. In earlier examples the junction between the fillet and roll is often angular (3vii); in later Gothic it may be curved and closer to the profile of an ogee (3viii). It frequently assumes an elongated 'almond' shape in Late Gothic, and French examples have been termed 'fillet mouldings' (Murray, Neagley; see fig. 3ix); see also *pear*. Composite forms found in England are the roll with two fillets (termed 'side-filleted' by Paley; fig. 3x), the roll with three fillets (termed 'roll-and-triple-fillet' by Paley; fig. 3xi), the demi-roll-and-fillet (3xii) and the beaked roll-and-fillet (3xv). See also *quadrant*.

Scroll. A moulding resembling in section the end of a rolled scroll; the overlapping edge may be either angular or curved (3xviii–xix). It is perhaps derived from the keel moulding and is distinctively English, being used in Decorated buildings between 1250 and 1350, especially for capitals, string courses and some arches.

Semicircular hollow. See *hollow mouldings*.

Sharp fillet. See *keel*.

Side-filleted. See *roll-and-fillet*.

Soffit roll. A roll moulding, usually semicircular, used on the soffit of an arch in Romanesque architecture (1a).

Spiked hollow (Morris, 1978). An arris ('spike') flanked by hollows (3xxi). It is related to the use of fluting for shafts and bases, and appears especially in Late Gothic architecture, such as French Flamboyant.

Sunk chamfer. A chamfer moulding with a shallow, flat recess and raised edges (3xxxiv), used in English architecture between 1280 and 1350.

Sunken semi-circle. See *hollow mouldings*.

Three-quarter hollow. See *hollow mouldings*.

Tongue-shaped member. See *beak*.

Wave [ogee casement (Roberts)]. An undulating moulding, consisting of shallow concave/convex/concave curves (3xxxvi), used in later Gothic architecture, predominantly in England between 1280 and 1380. See also *casement*.

III. History and development.

1. Romanesque. 2. Early and High Gothic. 3. Later Gothic.

1. ROMANESQUE. A significant development in Romanesque architecture (11th and 12th centuries) was the rediscovery of the roll moulding and its application to arches. It may be inferred from its appearance on arches in early Islamic buildings that this usage was known in Roman architecture, although the most common use of the roll in Classical antiquity is the torus moulding in bases. The origin of Romanesque experimentation was probably the application of the Roman half column to wall surfaces, which led to the early medieval compound pier, consisting of a square or cruciform core with a half column attached to each face. This design, which had appeared in eastern France as early as the 11th century, was to be the basis for the articulation of mature Romanesque church interiors, but usually the arches above the half columns had flat soffits, for example in the nave of Jumièges Abbey (1050–65; *see* JUMIÈGES ABBEY, fig. 1). At an early stage in northeast France, the half-column profile was extended to the arch as the soffit roll (e.g. Auxerre Cathedral, crypt; *c.* 1030). This fundamental development eventually led to the most typical form of Gothic arch profile, centred on an axial roll moulding (see fig. 1j above). More immediately, it prefigured the application of roll mouldings to other parts of the arch, such as the angle roll, which assumed a smaller diameter more comparable to the Classical torus. Its use suggests a desire to imbue arches with the same quality as the increasingly complex compound piers that supported them.

St Etienne (*c.* 1070), Caen, in Normandy is regarded as an important building in this development, although the full potential of the roll moulding was realized in England only after the late 11th century. The soffit roll had been introduced into Normandy by *c.* 1040 (e.g. Bernay Abbey). At St Etienne the angle roll occurs apparently for the first time, separated from the wall face by a quirk (fig. 2f), for example in the nave arcades (*see* CAEN, fig. 1); this combination became the hallmark of the 'Caennais school'.

The possibility of Anglo-Saxon influence in these developments cannot be excluded (Fernie). The crossing-arch profile at St Etienne is more remarkable, in that it combines a soffit roll with face rolls and two orders of angle rolls (fig. 1a). As the arch was recut in the 12th century, its 11th-century authenticity is questionable, and certainly such a complex profile is rare in continental Europe before the Early Gothic period. During the 12th century, various forms of heavy angle rolls became common for the exterior frames of windows and portals, but arcade arches generally remained rectangular in section, following the square shape of the abacus. This is the probable reason why the soffit roll had no further important influence on the Continent in the 11th century.

By contrast, the soffit roll flourished in England as a consequence of the decorative environment of late Anglo-Saxon architecture. In the second half of the 11th century the soffit roll, probably derived from Normandy, was combined with the face roll and the hollow chamfer to create elaborate arch profiles, such as in the chancel arch of All Saints, Wittering, Cambs (1060–80; fig. 1c). In the great churches built immediately after the Norman Conquest of 1066, however, arcades remained unadorned in typical continental fashion, and it was not until 1090–1140 that roll mouldings, including angle rolls, reappeared in what has been viewed as an 'Anglo-Saxon revival' (Bony; e.g. Durham Cathedral; from 1093; fig. 1b; see also DUR-HAM, fig. 2). Variations on the soffit roll were a particular feature of this period: used with hollow chamfers, especially in the Durham group, and employed also for ribs; paired as double soffit rolls in the more sculptural decorative style of south and west England (e.g. Christchurch Priory, Hants; c. 1120); and double rolls separated by an angle-fillet, especially popular in early ribs, as at Gloucester Cathedral (1120–30; see also fig. 1e above). From c. 1120 the soffit roll was taken up again in Normandy under English influence, for example at Evreux Cathedral (after 1119); outliers of this development occur at St Vincent (c. 1100), Soignies, Belgium, and in Norman Sicily in the cloister (1180s) at Monreale Cathedral. In the second quarter of the 12th century it became a significant element in Early Gothic buildings in the Paris basin (e.g. Paris, St Martin-des-Champs; Saint-Denis Abbey), and after c. 1150 bold roll mouldings spread to Cistercian architecture in Burgundy and elsewhere, such as the chapter house at Fontenay Abbey.

The mouldings of capitals and bases were mainly, if loosely, derived from antique and Early Christian models. The Attic form of base predominates (fig. 2t), but numerous meaningful variations of it exist, such as the 'modified Attic' (fig. 2s; Rigold, see §I above). Entirely different designs such as the 'double hollow base' (fig. 2r) are also significant, especially in Normandy (Deshoulières, Rigold). Carved spurs on sub-bases, a motif occasionally found in antiquity, were revived in the 11th century (e.g. Hildesheim, St Michael; 1001–33) and became prevalent in the 12th century in Romanesque and Gothic in many parts of Europe, although rare in England. Fine examples occur particularly in the Ile de France and the Rhineland in the 12th century (e.g. Etampes, Notre-Dame; Strasbourg Cathedral). The abaci of capitals were typically square in plan and generally prominent in size, or they have impost blocks (of Byzantine derivation) above, the latter occurring mainly in Italy and southern and central France. Abaci and imposts provide the only mouldings associated with capitals: the bottom edge is commonly chamfered and from c. 1050 the quirk and hollow chamfer were introduced, as in Normandy and post-Conquest England (e.g. Bayeux Cathedral, crypt; fig. 2m). Capitals were commonly carved with foliage, but the undecorated cubic capital ('cushion' capital in England) is distinctive in northern Europe and Lombardy (see CAPITAL, fig. 1).

BIBLIOGRAPHY

V. Ruprich-Robert: *L'Architecture normande aux XIe et XIIe siècles*, 2 vols (Paris, 1884–9)
F. Deshoulières: 'Essai sur les bases romanes', *Bull. Mnmtl*, lxxv (1911), pp. 77–101
A. Clapham: *English Romanesque Architecture: After the Conquest* (Oxford, 1934), pp. 113–24
H. M. Taylor and J. Taylor: *Anglo-Saxon Architecture*, 3 vols (Cambridge, 1965–78)
J. Bony: 'Durham et la tradition saxonne', *Etudes d'art médiéval offertes à Louis Grodecki*, ed. S. McK. Crosby and others (Paris, 1981), pp. 79–85 [incl. material from Bony's important unpubd paper 'The Soffit-roll in Saxon and Norman Architecture']
E. Fernie: *Architecture of the Anglo-Saxons* (London, 1983), pp. 81–9, 124–73

2. EARLY AND HIGH GOTHIC.

(i) Development of types. (ii) Vault ribs. (iii) Capitals and bases.

(i) Development of types. During the 12th and 13th centuries a series of new mouldings based on the roll moulding was invented and developed. None has any real precedent in antiquity, and they are the essential vocabulary of a distinctively northern Gothic architecture. The examples derive predominantly from northern France, the pioneering area (1140–75), and England; Cistercian architecture in Burgundy also assumed a significant role in the 12th century. The acceptance of the style of Chartres Cathedral, with its simple mouldings, as the model for High Gothic churches tended to stultify further development in northern France in the early 13th century, but invention continued unabated in England and influenced Normandy.

(a) Keel. The keel is distinctive to the first century of Gothic and may have been the earliest new moulding to appear. It occurs in the piers of St Etienne, Beauvais (1130–40; Enlart), where it may have originated. It spread rapidly in northern French Gothic, employed mainly as the axial moulding for vault ribs (e.g. Saint-Denis Abbey, western block; 1137–40), and in this usage was common in many regions of France and elsewhere, including Burgundy and the Rhineland, until supplanted by ogee-keel or roll-and-fillet mouldings in the later 13th century. It often assumed an almond shape, in contrast to the blunter form usually found in Early Gothic in England. Probably under Burgundian Cistercian influence, the keel spread to Spain (e.g. Cuenca Cathedral; from c. 1200) and later to Bohemia, where it occurs in conjunction with other mouldings (beak) of similar derivation (e.g. Mnichovo Hradiště Abbey, cloister; 1250–60; Mencl, 1952). However it was taken up pre-eminently in the Cistercian environment of northern England from the 1160s, brought there by masons with northern French experience (e.g. Roche Abbey, S. Yorks; Ripon Minster, N. Yorks; Wilson, 1986). From there it was introduced to Scotland (e.g. St

Andrews Cathedral; from 1162) and to Norway (Trondheim Cathedral; 1170–80). In northern England it was incorporated into more elaborate arch profiles than in France (e.g. Byland Abbey, N. Yorks, nave; 1180s), and a particular feature of the region was its use in clustered piers well into the 13th century (e.g. Whitby Abbey, N. Yorks; c. 1220). It is less frequent elsewhere in England: roll mouldings and detached shafts were preferred in the south and ogee-keel mouldings in the west.

(b) Grooved roll and beak. The grooved roll and beak mouldings were invented in northern France almost simultaneously with the keel, and they often appear together in Early Gothic buildings (e.g. Saint Leu-d'Esserent priory church, Ile de France, narthex; c. 1140). From the 1150s they spread to England (York Minster, choir; c. 1160), and thence to Ireland (e.g. Mellifont Abbey, Co. Louth; c. 1200) and Norway. The grooved roll is regarded (Lasteyrie; Wilson, 1986) as an indication of Early Gothic influence from the Ile de France, Picardy and the Soissonnais (e.g. at Cologne, St Gereon), and is seldom encountered after 1200 except in Bohemia (Mencl, 1952). The beak moulding, however, continued in use in the 13th century, especially as a lateral moulding in ribs in some French regional workshops (e.g. Burgundy) and in Bohemia, Austria and the Rhineland (e.g. Maulbronn Abbey; see Dehio and Bezold), but most notably in England. The beaked roll appears to have been invented there (e.g. Furness Abbey, Lancs, transept; c. 1180; fig. 1d above), for it is virtually unknown on the Continent, and with the beak moulding it became a hallmark of Gothic in south and west England between 1200 and 1250 (e.g. Salisbury Cathedral, from 1220; Jansen, 1984).

(c) Ogee keel and roll-and-fillet. The appearance of the ogee-keel and roll-and fillet mouldings was more significant ultimately for the development of the Gothic style, and for Paley the roll-and-fillet symbolized the 'revolution' leading to the complex moulding profiles of later Gothic. Some early but isolated examples are recorded for ribs in northern France (e.g. Saint-Denis Abbey, narthex, c. 1140, filleted roll; Chartres Cathedral, south-west tower, c. 1150, ogee keel); but their main development occurred in England from the 1160s, with the ogee keel generally preceding the roll-and-fillet. The first English usage of the former was in northern England for shafts (e.g. Ripon Minster; 1160s), followed in the same area by roll-and-fillet mouldings for ribs in the late 12th century (e.g. Byland Abbey), leading to combinations of keeled and filleted shafts for piers characteristic of the north in the 13th century, for example at Whitby Abbey (from c. 1220). In south-west England the ogee keel occurs from c. 1175 in piers and arch profiles, as in the west bays of Worcester Cathedral, and multiple groups of ogee-keeled shafts are a feature of the 12th-century 'west country school', for example the choir (c. 1185) of Glastonbury Abbey. Meanwhile the roll-and-fillet appeared in ribs and arches in the south-east, for example at Canterbury Cathedral in the work of William the Englishman in 1179–84, and it occurred more widely after c. 1200. In particular, filleted multiple shafts replaced ogee-keeled ones in the 'west country school' (e.g. Shrewsbury, St Mary, c. 1200; Dublin,

Christ Church Cathedral, c. 1216–34). In the 13th century, the ogee keel (1200–1250) and the roll-and-fillet (from 1220) typified Early English arches and ribs, and further embellishments, such as the roll with multiple fillets (see fig. 3xi) and the beaked ogee keel (fig. 3xiv), are entirely distinctive to England.

In French Gothic, ogee-keeled and filleted shafts are unknown until the later 13th century, and the inclusion of the ogee keel in arches and ribs is rare before the advent of Rayonnant architecture (an early example is Troyes Cathedral, 1210–28; Bongartz). Nonetheless, in northern France a significant step was taken with the introduction of a prominent roll-and-fillet as the axial moulding of the main arcade arch profile at Reims Cathedral (from 1211; fig. 1j above; *see also* REIMS, fig. 3). Occasional earlier instances are known, for example in the east transept (c. 1180) at Canterbury Cathedral and the south transept (c. 1176–90) of Soissons Cathedral, which has a combination of roll-and-fillet and grooved roll, but they were not employed in the main arcade. Villard de Honnecourt recorded the Reims profile (Hahnloser, *see* §I above), and it spread during the 13th century to become the basis of 14th-century arcade arches. At the same time in northern France there was renewed interest in applying the roll-and-fillet to vaults (e.g. Amiens Cathedral, 1220–36; fig. 2g).

(d) Angle roll. Nonetheless, between 1140 and 1240 the most common moulding for all types of arch was the angle roll. The robust angle roll of Anglo-Norman Romanesque was refined in such innovative designs of French Gothic as the work of the second master (1140–44) at Saint-Denis Abbey (Gardner). Typically it relieved the angles of arcade-arch profiles, which retained an overall rectangular shape in section throughout this period. The classic High Gothic arcade arch consists of two orders with angle rolls and a flat soffit, popularized at Chartres Cathedral (from 1194; see fig. 2f). It was remarkably persistent in 13th-century France and French-influenced architecture (e.g. Spain, León Cathedral, c. 1255), despite the appearance of the axial roll-and-fillet design at Reims. Occasional variations exist in 12th-century France, such as the use of a semicircular hollow for the soffit at St Remi, Reims (1162–80; Lasteyrie), but the main area for experiment was England. There the soffit roll flanked by angle rolls (fig. 1d) formed the basis for more elaborate designs from c. 1160 in the Cistercian-related churches of the north, such as Ripon Minster (Bilson; Wilson, 1986). Before 1200 remarkable arcade-arch profiles had been produced in two key centres in the west and north of England, respectively at Wells Cathedral (c. 1175) and in St Hugh's choir at Lincoln Cathedral (from 1192; fig. 1g). These anticipate later Gothic in the way that multiple rolls and hollow mouldings are deployed to disguise the rectangular shape of the orders, and they prefigure the undulating profiles with deep hollows that characterize 13th-century English Gothic, for example at Salisbury Cathedral (1220–66). A reflection of these ideas is also found in north-west France and Normandy (e.g. Le Mans Cathedral; 1217–54); Lasteyrie termed such profiles 'irrational'. Nonetheless, the basic premise of French High Gothic arch profiles, namely some form of paired rolls for the soffit, predominated in

Early English arches into the 13th century (fig. 1k). It was not until the 1230s that a prominent axial moulding (the descendant of the soffit roll) became the focal point of arcade-arch design (e.g. London, Temple Church, choir), and in this respect English Gothic is not in advance of developments in northern France.

(ii) Vault ribs. Vault ribs were the main new architectural components to be established in this period. Their designs generally relate to arcade arches, although in some instances designs were first applied to ribs: for example, the roll-and-fillet was employed as the axial moulding in diagonal rib profiles, such as in the east arm of Canterbury Cathedral (1175–84; see fig. 2h above), well before its acceptance in arcade arches. Two main types of rib profile are encountered: rectangular in section with paired angle rolls separated by an angle-fillet (fig. 2f; e.g. Sens Cathedral, ambulatory; *c.* 1150), by a large fillet or by a hollow (e.g. Chartres Cathedral, high vaults; 1194–1235, both patterns); and triangular in section, with a single axial roll moulding, frequently flanked by a pair of lateral mouldings in a stepped formation (fig. 2g). A characteristic form of the latter in 12th-century Romanesque and in Early Gothic in northern France and England is the triple-roll rib (e.g. Paris, St Martin-des-Champs; 1130–40; Bilson). By the early 13th century the form common in later Gothic, with hollow mouldings separating the rolls, was evolving, especially in England (e.g. Winchester Cathedral, retrochoir; 1200–20) and then in France (e.g. Amiens Cathedral, nave; 1220–36; fig. 2g).

The deployment of the two types of profile is significant. In early rib vaults, such as in the aisles of Durham Cathedral (1093–6) and at St Etienne, Beauvais (1125–30), it was common to combine the angle-roll type for transverse arches with the axial-roll type for diagonal ribs; this remained popular in the aisles of High Gothic cathedrals (e.g. Chartres) and in English high vaults to *c.* 1250 (e.g. Lincoln Cathedral, nave). In French Gothic, however, the angle-roll type was employed in the high vault for all ribs (e.g. Sens and Chartres cathedrals), although still differentiating in detail between transverse and diagonal. This formula is found less frequently in England (e.g. Wells Cathedral). In the early 13th century the axial type was adopted occasionally for all the ribs of high vaults (e.g. Bourges Cathedral), anticipating the sharper profiles of later Gothic, and it appeared in English high vaults slightly later (e.g. London, Temple Church; *c.* 1230). In French High Gothic examples, the transverse arch generally remained larger than the diagonal rib in this period, but uniform profiles, consisting of a single axial roll, occurred early in the more decorative Angevin rib vaults of western France, for example at St Serge, Angers (1210–20; Mussat).

(iii) Capitals and bases. A greater variety of mouldings appeared in the abaci of capitals, and the same designs were also applied to string courses and hood mouldings. The 'hollow and bead' abacus (see fig. 2n above; Bilson) is typical in northern France and England from the mid-12th century, and the 'cyma recta' abacus (fig. 2o; Wilson, 1986) appeared in Burgundy *c.* 1150 and in northern England from the 1160s. The lip extended into a beak moulding was characteristic of abaci 1160–1200 (e.g. Paris, Notre-Dame; Wells Cathedral). By *c.* 1200, the lip usually

consisted of a roll moulding, often a keel or ogee keel in England, with the roll-and-fillet soon becoming popular there in the 13th century; the plain roll remained usual in France until *c.* 1240. For bases, the Attic design remained dominant. The main development was the revival of a more correct classical design ('Neo-Attic') in northern France by *c.* 1150 (e.g. Sens Cathedral) and this was brought to England by William of Sens at Canterbury Cathedral in 1175. It became the basis of the characteristic Early English 'water-holding' base (fig. 2u) and was also adapted for the mouldings of stone shaft-rings, which came into fashion from *c.* 1160 with the advent of detached shafts. The mouldings of sub-bases often received additional roll mouldings from the later 12th century, as in the east transept (from 1192) of Lincoln Cathedral and at Reims Cathedral (from 1211).

Important developments occurred in the plan shape of capitals and bases. Although square abaci and sub-bases remained standard for main arcades in many parts of Europe, including the Ile de France, circular and octagonal plans emerged in areas that experimented with less orthodox pier and arch forms (e.g. Picardy, Burgundy, Normandy, England). The use of columnar and clustered piers was influential, and also arch profiles that emphasized the diagonal plane (as in fig. 1g above). Circular sub-bases appeared in Picardy *c.* 1140 and circular abaci shortly after, particularly in Cistercian contexts, for example in England in the dormitory of Kirkstall Abbey, W. Yorks (from 1152) and in Spain at Moreruela Abbey, Zamora (from 1158; Wilson, 1986). By *c.* 1180 circular abaci and sub-bases were in use in southern England (e.g. Canterbury Cathedral, east transept; 1179–84), and in the 13th century both were distinctive components of Early English Gothic, especially in the south and usually with undecorated moulded capitals (e.g. Salisbury Cathedral, 1220–66; Jansen, 1984). The 13th-century occurrence of circular moulded capitals in Brittany and Normandy, for example at Coutances Cathedral (*c.* 1220–33), is related to English usage.

In the mid-12th century the Cistercians also experimented with octagonal abaci and sub-bases (e.g. Fontenay Abbey, chapter house), and early examples occur in northern France and northern England, as in the nave abaci at Fountains Abbey (from 1150; Wilson, 1986). Between 1180 and 1220 part-octagonal abaci and sub-bases became features of the English west country school, related to the clustered shafts of the piers (e.g. Wells Cathedral, 1175–1220), and a strikingly similar usage occurs in Normandy and Maine after 1200 (e.g. Le Mans Cathedral, 1217–54). Elsewhere in France, octagonal forms often appear in conjunction with columnar piers from the end of the 12th century (e.g. Braine, St Yved, *c.* 1190). An exceptional instance of part-octagonal abaci on *piliers cantonnés* occurs at Reims Cathedral (from 1211), presumably connected with the adoption of a single axial moulding for the arch soffit. Part-octagonal abaci were generally shunned in the main elevations of High Gothic churches well into the 13th century, but sub-bases of part-octagonal plan were adopted for the shafts of *piliers cantonnés* from the 1220s (e.g. Amiens Cathedral, nave), and this change, together with the developments in

England, was an indication of the growing interest in diagonal planes typical of later Gothic.

BIBLIOGRAPHY

G. Durand: *Monographie de l'église Notre-Dame cathédrale d'Amiens*, 2 vols (Amiens, 1901–3)

J. Bilson: 'The Architecture of the Cistercians with Special Reference to Some of their Earlier Churches in England', *Archaeol. J.*, lxvi (1909), pp. 185–280

R. de Lasteyrie: *L'Architecture religieuse en France à l'époque gothique*, 2 vols (Paris, 1926–7)

J. Brakspear: 'A West Country School of Masons', *Archaeologia*, lxxxi (1931), pp. 1–18

V. Mencl: 'Tvary klenebních žeber v české gotické architectuře' [Proportions of rib vaults in Bohemian Gothic architecture], *Zprávy Památkové Péče*, xi (1952), pp. 268–81

R. Branner: *Burgundian Gothic Architecture* (London, 1960)

V. Mencl: 'Vývoj středověkého portálu v českých zemích' [Development of medieval portals in Bohemia], *Zprávy Památkové Péče*, xx (1960), pp. 8–26, 112–53

A. Mussat: *Le Style gothique de l'ouest de la France: XIIe–XIIIe siècles* (Paris, 1963)

G. Fischer: *Domkirken i Trondheim*, 2 vols (Oslo, 1965)

C. Wilson: 'Sources for the Late 12th-century Work at Worcester Cathedral', *British Archaeological Association Conference Transactions: Medieval Art and Architecture at Worcester Cathedral: Worcester, 1975*, pp. 80–90 (83)

N. Bongartz: *Die frühen Bauteile der Kathedral in Troyes* (Stuttgart, 1979)

S. Gardner: 'Two Campaigns in Suger's Western Block at St Denis', *A. Bull.*, lxvi/4 (1984), pp. 574–87

V. Jansen: 'Architectural Remains of King John's Abbey, Beaulieu (Hampshire)', *Studies in Cistercian Art and Architecture*, ed. M. P. Lillich (Kalamazoo, 1984), i, pp. 76–114

C. Wilson: 'The Cistercians as "Missionaries of Gothic" in Northern England', *Cistercian Art and Architecture in Britain*, ed. E. C. Norton and D. Park (Cambridge, 1986), pp. 86–116

R. Stalley: *The Cistercian Monasteries of Ireland* (London, 1987), pp. 252–9 [profile drgs]

3. Later Gothic.

(i) Development of types. (ii) Capitals and bases.

(i) Development of types. Later Gothic mouldings from the 13th century to the early 16th display more variety and elaboration than in any previous period. They are characterized by combinations of concave and convex shapes, creating both angular profiles and soft undulating curves. Prototypes for such mouldings appeared during the 13th century and justify treating this period as a whole. Another unifying feature from the mid-13th century is the universal acceptance of bar tracery, which introduced the mullion as an essential architectural component for the application of mouldings.

From *c.* 1240 the Rayonnant style in France established new standards of refinement in the detail of mouldings, particularly at the Sainte-Chapelle (1241–8), Paris. These qualities are also manifest in various regional schools in France during the 13th century, notably Picardy and Burgundy, but the emaciated, linear style of mouldings that typifies French Flamboyant architecture developed only in the late 14th century. The development of Late Gothic mouldings advanced more rapidly in the Rhineland (including the Netherlands), central Europe and England. In particular, the variety and bold design of mouldings in Bohemian churches deserve to be better known (see Mencl, 1960, §2 above) in relation to comparable developments in England. During the 14th century, in the hands of the Parler family, these ideas mixed with more conventional French Rayonnant mouldings, which had been assimilated in Rhineland lodges such as those of the

cathedrals of Cologne and Strasbourg, to establish the vocabulary of German Late Gothic (Crossley; Recht). Moreover, German masons exported features of this style to Spain and northern Italy in the 15th century. In many respects, however, England was the real pioneer of Late Gothic mouldings. Already in the Early to High Gothic period, innovations such as piers with filleted and keeled mouldings were consistently employed, and in the Decorated period more new mouldings were created in England than anywhere else in Europe, some of which continued into the Perpendicular style (e.g. the double ogee; Morris, 1978, 1979; *see* §I above). English moulding types did, however, generally remain insular, so that those of the Perpendicular style seldom emulated the sharp, angular profiles characteristic of French Flamboyant and German *Sondergotik*.

(a) Ogee keel and roll-and-fillet. On the Continent the route to Late Gothic was pioneered initially through a wider application of ogee-keel and roll-and-fillet mouldings. In French Rayonnant the ogee keel became more common in rib and arch profiles as the 13th century progressed, with important early examples in the Sainte-Chapelle, Paris (rib, dado arches; 1241–8), and related churches in the Paris area (e.g. St Sulpice-de-Favières; *c.* 1245). From 1270 to 1350 this usage was extended to some shafts of responds and piers, especially in eastern France (e.g. Auxerre, St Germain; from 1277). The roll-and-fillet moulding followed a similar pattern of development, with its inclusion in arcade arches and ribs (e.g. fig. 1j above) preceding its appearance in responds and piers. Early instances of the latter usage occur at Narbonne Cathedral (from 1272) and St Germain, Auxerre, and during the 14th century it became common in France. It can be found slightly earlier for the jambs of more ornamental features such as portals and dados (e.g. Troyes, St Urbain; 1262–6; see fig. 1i). Central Europe also provides important early examples. Mencl (1960) illustrates roll-and-fillet mouldings in portal jambs in Bohemia from *c.* 1270, and filleted shafts are a feature of the choir piers of Heiligenkreuz Abbey, Austria (consecrated 1295). Ogee-keel mouldings were used too in this period in the German lands, but during the 14th century they were generally replaced by roll-and-fillet mouldings, following the European trend. Occasionally later ogee-keel mouldings in various parts of Europe have a rounded profile to the tip (fig. 3v); examples are found in the crypt of St Stephen's Chapel (from 1292; rest.) in the Palace of Westminster, London, and in the nave (from 1302) of Bayonne Cathedral. With the wide acceptance of the roll-and-fillet during the 14th century, it was characteristic on the Continent to accentuate its sinuous shape by projecting it forwards from deep hollow mouldings, such as in the Dominican church at Strasbourg (from 1307; Recht). This treatment became typical of Late Gothic in central Europe, for example in the Wenceslas Chapel (1356–67) designed by Peter Parler at Prague Cathedral, and in France, for example at Notre-Dame, Caudebec-en-Caux (from 1426; fig. 2k).

(b) Curvilinear mouldings. The increasing emphasis on undulating shapes is part of a general Late Gothic preference for curvilinear profiles, epitomized by the OGEE moulding. The earliest significant examples appear to be in England, in the main arcades of Winchester Cathedral presbytery and Bristol Cathedral choir (both *c.* 1315; see fig. 1h). The double-ogee moulding was pioneered in England during the same period, for example on the Eleanor cross (1290s) at Geddington, Northants, and through its use by royal masons such as William Ramsey it was established as a feature of the Perpendicular style, as in the nave (1379–1405) of Canterbury Cathedral. The double ogee is virtually unknown on the Continent, a rare instance in Kraków Cathedral, Poland (choir piers, from 1320), apparently arising from the interest found in central Europe for combinations of roll-and-fillet and hollow mouldings. Monumental single-ogee mouldings like those at Bristol Cathedral are also unusual, although examples occur in French Flamboyant (e.g. Cléry, Notre-Dame; *c.* 1450). More characteristic of continental Late Gothic is the ogee as a demi-roll-and-fillet moulding deployed to terminate a respond at the junction with a wall surface, especially in Germany and the Netherlands (e.g. Soest, St Maria zur Wiese; from 1331; see also fig. 2l), and in French Flamboyant (e.g. Alençon, Notre-Dame; from 1477).

Various other curvilinear profiles were invented during the period. A prototype for the ogee was a delicate S-curve moulding that appeared in Paris during the 1240s, for example in the north transept of Notre-Dame, and became a regular feature of Rayonnant architecture in France and elsewhere by 1300, as at St Urbain, Troyes (1262–6; fig. 1i), Westminster Abbey (1245–72) and the nave of Strasbourg Cathedral (1240–75). During the 14th century its hollow moulding was enlarged disproportionately, for example on the south-west tower pier (*c.* 1320) of Cologne Cathedral and in Belgium at Notre-Dame, Hal (1341–1409); this form of ogee remained popular in Late Gothic, particularly in Germany and the Netherlands (fig. 1f). The wave moulding had been developed in England at the same time, being employed especially for arches (e.g. Caernarfon Castle; 1238–92). This was the most typical moulding of the later Decorated style between 1310 and 1360 (Morris, 1978). It demonstrates how English masons anticipated the vocabulary of Late Gothic without directly influencing it, for the wave moulding is unknown on the Continent in this period. The only comparison is with a large, undulating profile (concave/convex/concave) found occasionally in 14th-century France incorporated in piers and arches, for example at Auxerre in both the Cathedral and St Germain (after 1313; Morris, 1978). This is a likely source of inspiration for the monumental, undulating pier profiles that are more common in later Flamboyant, as in the work of Martin Chambiges (e.g. Beauvais Cathedral; from *c.* 1500; Murray).

(c) Angular mouldings. Late Gothic architecture is very diversified in detail, and curvilinear mouldings represent only one trend. Angularity is as dominant a principle of design and manifests itself in the variations on two mouldings that gained greatly in popularity in this period: the chamfer and the hollow chamfer. Isolated and less conspicuous examples of their use exist in the earlier periods: hollow chamfers had appeared at Durham Cathedral (1093–1133; see fig. 1b), and small chamfers were standard in Romanesque abaci. Both mouldings, however, became more common from the 13th century, especially in window tracery. The earliest mullion profiles are typically of the roll and chamfer variety (figs 2a and 2b), starting at Reims Cathedral (from 1211) and regularly used in 13th-century French Rayonnant. It was supplanted in the 14th century by the roll and hollow chamfer (fig. 2c), which first appeared *c.* 1240, for example in the blind tracery of the east end of Amiens Cathedral. Later Gothic mullions in England and in certain parts of Europe (e.g. the Netherlands) were based on this design, frequently with a filleted roll, which appeared first in England *c.* 1260. A more radical departure from tradition was to omit the roll moulding and employ only plain or hollow chamfers separated by a narrow fillet (figs 2d and 2e): various combinations of chamfer are encountered (Morris, 1979). This idea was developed in the first half of the 14th century, particularly in England and Germany (e.g. Soest, St Maria zur Wiese; from 1331), and was commonplace in Europe by the 15th century. These trends may also be observed in rib profiles, but the mullion was the most important component for the development of Late Gothic mouldings. Mullions consistently used the chamfer plane and the single axial roll when most High Gothic ribs still kept to paired rolls (*see* §2(ii) above); ultimately the abandonment of the axial roll established the linear aesthetic of Late Gothic.

The employment of chamfer mouldings on main arcade arches appeared in England during the 12th century and was fairly common there from 1200 to 1250 (e.g. Romsey Abbey, Hants; *c.* 1230), also spreading to Normandy and the Netherlands (e.g. Hambye Abbey; *c.* 1240). Conceptually this represents a significant move towards Late Gothic arch design, but in practice arches made up entirely of chamfer mouldings tend to be restricted to provincial or more austere churches, such as those of the Cistercian Order. For more sophisticated arch profiles, the most distinctive form of chamfer moulding in Late Gothic is the chamfered mitre, which was pioneered in Early English Gothic at the same time as the undercut angle-fillet. The latter appears occasionally in southern England before *c.* 1250, for example in the refectory (*c.* 1225) of Beaulieu Abbey, Hants, but the chamfered mitre was more prevalent. Lincoln Cathedral is an important early centre, where it occurs inconspicuously between paired mouldings in the arcade arches of St Hugh's choir (*c.* 1200; fig. 1g) and more overtly as the axial moulding in some of the nave aisle ribs (*c.* 1230; fig. 2i). This probably connects with its appearance as the axial moulding for mullions in Picardy from the mid-13th century (Morris, 1979). It is also recorded for ribs in Bohemia (Mencl, 1952) and from *c.* 1300 for ribs and the soffit of arcade arches in eastern France, Germany and the Netherlands, such as in the choir (from 1351) at the Cathedral of the Holy Cross, Schwäbisch Gmünd, and at Antwerp Cathedral (from 1352; Recht, Crossley). The undercut angle-fillet also found favour in 14th-century German architecture (e.g. Soest, St Pauli; *c.* 1350). A natural development was to apply the chamfered mitre to piers, especially in the

Netherlands and in German Late Gothic (e.g. Soest, St Maria zur Wiese; from 1331). Its stylish simplicity appealed to the mendicant orders, for example in the nave of the second Dominican church at Strasbourg (from 1307), and the popularity of octagonal piers in Late Gothic may be seen as part of this move to prismatic shapes (e.g. Florence, Santa Croce; from 1294). In the English Perpendicular style the chamfered mitre is rare for arcades but common in mullions and window frames (e.g. Winchester Cathedral, nave; from 1350), a usage also common in the Netherlands and Germany in the same period (Morris, 1979).

(d) Hollow mouldings. In the Late Gothic period designers increasingly emphasized hollow mouldings, the antithesis of the solid, rounded forms inherited from Classical antiquity. The three-quarter hollow moulding, noted as a feature of the Early English and Decorated styles (Morris, 1978), apparently existed on the Continent in the 13th century only in Bohemia from *c.* 1270. The latter examples influenced the deep hollow mouldings found in the Rhineland and in the work of Peter Parler in the 14th century (Crossley). Meanwhile Rayonnant architecture spread the popularity of the semicircular hollow after *c.* 1250, often combined with a bead to create an ogee moulding (e.g. fig. 1i above). From the later 14th century the casement hollow was preferred in English Perpendicular, originating in the 1320s, and this tendency towards wider, shallower hollow mouldings is general in European Late Gothic.

Another trend was to juxtapose concave mouldings to create sharp edges, expressing line rather than mass. The increasing use of the hollow chamfer is an aspect of this development, such as at Chester Cathedral (*c.* 1280; Jansen, 1982), but it is best represented by the spiked hollow moulding. This is found from *c.* 1260 in eastern France (e.g. Saint-Thibault-en-Auxois, side chapel), and from the 1290s in eastern England (e.g. Lincoln Cathedral, cloister), Normandy, the Netherlands and Germany (e.g. Schwäbisch Gmünd, Cathedral of the Holy Cross; from 1320; Morris, 1978).

In several areas to which it spread, the taste for linear profiles was already observable in their use of the freestanding fillet. The latter may have originated in England *c.* 1200 (e.g. Lincoln Cathedral, St Hugh's choir; see fig. 1g) and it continued in north-east England into the 14th century. Its main area, however, was in Germany, the Netherlands and Bohemia from *c.* 1250, for example at Tournai Cathedral (1243–55) and in the Franciscan church (*c.* 1260) at Cologne. In the 14th century it became common throughout this area, but it was supplanted by the spiked hollow during the 15th century. The design favoured in German Late Gothic was a pair of opposed spiked hollows separated by a fillet, used typically for rib profiles (fig. 2j). Bohemian examples range from the 14th century to the early 16th, including the work of Benedikt Ried (*c.* 1500), and examples in vault ribs are frequent elsewhere, such as the St Laurent chapel (1515) at Strasbourg Cathedral. In France this design was also adopted for ribs, mullions and responds from the later 14th century (e.g. Riom, Sainte Chapelle; *c.* 1380). The version most characteristic of Flamboyant is an almond-shaped roll-and-fillet moulding flanked by spiked hollows, for example

at Notre-Dame, Caudebec-en-Caux (from 1426; fig. 2k): a perfect combination of the two main traits of Late Gothic, undulation and delineation. Despite the pioneering role of England in both these fields, the Perpendicular style made hardly any use of the spiked hollow.

(ii) Capitals and bases. Major changes took place in the design of later Gothic bases. The derivatives of the Attic base were gradually abandoned in 13th-century France in favour of a softer profile, here termed the 'hollow and roll' base (see fig. 2x). It originated in northern French Rayonnant, as in the Sainte Chapelle (1241–8), Paris, and rapidly spread to other regions of France and elsewhere (e.g. Strasbourg Cathedral, 1240–75). In England it was the most typical base of the Decorated style (e.g. York Minster, from 1291), but it was preceded between 1250 and 1290 by the 'triple roll' base, which also moved away from the Attic profile by replacing the centre hollow (scotia) with a roll (fig. 2v). This base seems unknown in France, although examples occur later in Germany, such as at the Katharinenkirche, Oppenheim (from 1317). Two features consistently found with the hollow and roll base in France are sub-bases of polygonal plan and bell-shaped sub-bases. The most common plan is octagonal (*see* §2(iii) above), which became standard in Europe in the 14th century, but the hexagon also appeared after *c.* 1250, probably originating in Paris, for example in the aisle chapels at Notre-Dame. Late Gothic architects appreciated the angular effects afforded by its shape, seen in Martin Chambiges's design of the transept piers in Beauvais Cathedral (*c.* 1510; Murray). The bell-shaped sub-base, originating in France about 1240 (e.g. Paris, Sainte Chapelle, lower chapel), was the dominant form there by *c.* 1300 (fig. 2x). During the early 14th century in England and Germany, bell shapes were applied to the main base as well (e.g. Ely Cathedral, choir; from 1322), which became standard in Late Gothic usage. A characteristic 15th-century profile has a small hollow at the neck of the bell, for example in the nave piers at St Maclou, Rouen (from 1432; fig. 2w), in tune with the concave surfaces and sharp edges of Late Gothic. These qualities are also manifest in the 'fillet base' typical of the Flamboyant architecture of France and the Netherlands and in the fluted plinths used in the bases particularly of German and Bohemian Late Gothic (e.g. Schwäbisch Gmünd, Cathedral of the Holy Cross, choir; from 1351).

During the 15th century, bases became both higher and more complex in design, standing up to 2 m above floor level and with a variety of sizes and levels for the component parts. This trait was not confined to the traditional Gothic areas but may also be found in Italy (Bologna, S Petronio; from 1390) and Spain (Salamanca, New Cathedral; from 1513). Conversely, a functionalist approach was adopted, whereby traditional base profiles were completely omitted and the vertical mouldings of the pier or jamb were allowed to die into a plain socle. This idea had been applied to door- and window-frames during the 13th century, especially in England and in conjunction with the increasing use of chamfer mouldings; but the piers of great churches were not treated in this fashion until the 14th century, for example at Bristol Cathedral (1310–20) and in St Maria zur Wiese, Soest (from 1331).

The angle-fillet was the most significant new profile in capitals, popularized by Parisian Rayonnant of the mid-13th century (e.g. Paris, Sainte Chapelle). Two slightly different versions exist in 13th-century France, one used invariably in the necking, the other used in the bell or abacus (fig. 2q). Their sharp edges reduced the bulk of the capital, and during the 13th and 14th centuries the number of capitals was also reduced in those areas influenced by French Rayonnant, except for England, where prominent moulded capitals, often with a large mid-roll, remained popular. Their characteristic moulding up to c. 1350 was the scroll, developed in north-east England apparently as a variant of the ogee keel and used initially in arches (e.g. Lincoln Cathedral, St Hugh's choir; c. 1200), before becoming more usual in capitals and string courses from c. 1250 (e.g. Exeter Cathedral; c. 1280; fig. 2p). The scroll moulding is unique to English Gothic, and moulded capitals without foliage carving are also rare in Late Gothic on the Continent (e.g. Narbonne Cathedral; from 1272). The use of octagonal abaci for capitals was not generally accepted in France or elsewhere on the Continent until the later 13th century. Meanwhile the hexagonal abacus with a prominent salient angle (Fr. à bec) had been invented in northern France, for instance in the nave triforium (1220–36) at Amiens Cathedral. It suited the angular aesthetic of Late Gothic and was accepted throughout France during the 13th century and elsewhere in Europe in the 14th (e.g. Prague Cathedral, choir clerestory; c. 1380).

The ultimate, if negative, development concerning capitals was their omission, which removed the last point of reference to Classical architecture and produced a purely Gothic style. The west of England experimented with this at an early date, with main arcades partly or completely devoid of capitals c. 1200 (e.g. Llanthony Priory, Gwent; c. 1210). The continuous orders thus created consist mainly of chamfer mouldings, emphasizing the crucial link between the development of Late Gothic and the wider acceptance of mouldings set on the chamfer plane. Early English prototypes, however, probably had little direct influence on the appearance of the continuous order in continental Late Gothic, where the key experiments took place in eastern France, Germany and central Europe c. 1300. Several buildings with a fully developed continuous order were built in eastern France during the late 13th century (e.g. Auxerre, St Germain; from 1277); and by the early 14th century in the Rhineland around Strasbourg (see Recht) and in southern Germany. This sudden interest in the idea may derive from central Europe, where by c. 1270 portals in Bohemian churches had continuous orders reminiscent of the earlier examples in western England and created particularly under Cistercian patronage (Mencl, 1960). In the same period the mendicant orders in Germany and France adopted a functionalist approach by allowing arcade arch mouldings to die into simple columnar piers without intermediary capitals (e.g. Freiburg im Breisgau, Franciscan church; c. 1300). 'Dying mouldings' became one of the fundamental characteristics of Late Gothic, and experiments with this idea, while retaining the capitals, can be traced back to c. 1220, especially in England (e.g. Salisbury Cathedral; Jansen, 1982). Nonetheless, with rare exceptions (e.g. Bristol

Cathedral, 1310–20), dying mouldings and continuous orders were never accepted in English Late Gothic. In the Perpendicular style capitals were retained for the shafts of main arcades, and English masons showed more interest in a rich variety of mouldings than in the gaunt minimalism characteristic of parts of the Continent. From c. 1350 continuous mouldings were widely accepted in such influential centres as Prague (e.g. Prague Cathedral, sacristy; 1355–60) and the court of Jean, Duc de Berry (e.g. Riom, Sainte Chapelle; c. 1380). By the early 15th century the total omission of capitals was standard in central Europe, Germany, the Netherlands and northern France. The capital only re-emerged as a regular feature in these areas with the arrival of Renaissance influences, but then it was part of a style that encouraged a formalist rather than creative approach to mouldings.

BIBLIOGRAPHY
O. Kletzl: *Planfragmente aus der deutschen Dombauhütte von Prag in Stuttgart und Ulm* (Stuttgart, 1939)
R. Recht: *L'Alsace gothique de 1300 à 1365* (Colmar, 1974)
P. Crossley: 'Wells, the West Country, and Central European Late Gothic', *British Archaeological Association Conference Transactions: Medieval Art and Architecture at Wells and Glastonbury: Wells, 1978*, pp. 81–109 (87–8)
J. H. Harvey: *The Perpendicular Style, 1330–1485* (London, 1978), pp. 246–65 [profiles of major Perpendicular churches]
V. Jansen: 'Dying Mouldings, Unarticulated Springer Blocks, and Hollow Chamfers in 13th-century Architecture', *J. Brit. Archaeol. Assoc.*, cxxxv (1982), pp. 35–54
S. Murray: *Building Troyes Cathedral: The Late Gothic Campaigns* (Bloomington, IN, 1987)
L. E. Neagley: 'The Flamboyant Architecture of St Maclou, Rouen, and the Development of a Style', *J. Soc. Archit. Historians*, xlvii/4 (1988), pp. 374–96
R. K. MORRIS

Moulthrop, Reuben (*b* East Haven, CT, 1763; *d* East Haven, 1814). American painter. As proprietor of a waxworks museum and travelling waxworks exhibition he was interested in modelling in wax in his early years. While moving around his native state he was exposed to several artistic influences, beginning with Winthrop Chandler. His earliest portraits seem to date from about 1788, when he completed *Mr and Mrs Samuel Hathaway* (1788; New Haven, CT, Colony Hist. Soc. Mus.). Its dark, heavy outlines, its flatness and almost geometric forms derive from Chandler. The quality of Moulthrop's paintings was extremely uneven; many of the best of the surviving body of about 50 works date from around 1800. *The Rev. Thomas Robbins* (1801; Hartford, CT Hist. Soc. Mus.), which depicts the sitter's direct gaze and contains more detail than the earlier portraits, shows the artist at his most accomplished. In the last years of his brief career he appears to have been influenced by William Jennys and John Durand, but he remained wedded to the flat conservative style seemingly favoured by his subjects.

BIBLIOGRAPHY
S. Sawitzky: 'New Light on the Early Work of Reuben Moulthrop', *A. America*, xliv (1956), pp. 9–11, 55
R. W. Thomas: 'Reuben Moulthrop, 1763–1814', *CT Hist. Soc. Bull.*, xxi (1956), pp. 97–111
DAVID M. SOKOL

Mount, William Sidney (*b* Setauket, NY, 26 Nov 1807; *d* Setauket, 18 Nov 1868). American painter. America's first major genre painter and one of the most accomplished

William Sidney Mount: *Bargaining for a Horse*, oil on canvas, 609×762 mm, 1835 (New York, New-York Historical Society)

of his era (rivalled only by George Caleb Bingham), he spent most of his life on rural Long Island. He was apprenticed as a sign painter in 1825 to his brother, Henry Mount (1802–41) in New York. In 1826, frustrated by the limitations of sign painting, he enrolled for drawing classes at the newly established National Academy of Design, where he aspired to be a painter of historical subjects. His first efforts in painting were portraits; the historical scenes that followed, such as *Saul and the Witch of Endor* (1828; Washington, DC, N. Mus. Amer. A.), were similarly linear, flat and brightly coloured. In 1827 he returned to live on Long Island, and from then onwards he alternated between the city and the country. He began to make the yeomen of Long Island his subject-matter, perhaps inspired by the popularity of engravings after David Wilkie and 17th-century genre painters.

Mount's first attempt at a genre painting, *Rustic Dance after a Sleigh Ride* (1830; Boston, MA, Mus. F.A.), which he exhibited at the National Academy in New York that year, was a great success. It depicts a farm parlour full of dancing male and female 'rustics', lightly caricatured in their dress and expressions. Amusing as his New York audience found country manners, however, he soon realized that he could probe a deeper vein in this agrarian ideal. On the one hand, Americans considered the landowning and hardworking farmer to be the ideal American;

on the other, because political, social and economic decision-makers (and patrons of the arts) tended to be city people, they saw the rural citizen as a shrewd bumpkin. This characterization could also be referred back to the city dwellers. Mount's first painting highlighting this comic discrepancy was so well received that it set the pattern for the rest of his career. His *Bargaining for a Horse* (1835; New York, NY Hist. Soc.; see fig.) shows two farmers in a barnyard whittling to disguise their strategy in working out a deal. The negotiation is overtly for the horse near by, but in the new era of political bargaining and economic speculation that America had entered in the early 1830s, the painting also encouraged the viewer to laugh at many kinds of 'horsetrading' in which American citizens were involved.

Mount followed this huge success—the painting was engraved twice, once for the American Art Union—with a succession of paintings that were rooted in national self-criticism and popular expression. *Farmers Nooning* (1836; Stony Brook, NY, Mus.) embodied the apprehensions that were held about slavery and emancipation and highlighted the self-indulgent black worker as a major American labour problem. *Cider Making* (1841; New York, Met.) showed farmers directing all the phases of cider-making, a clever allegory for the party machinery of the Whigs, who had used cider (the drink of the 'common man') as one of their major symbols in the 1840 election campaign. *Herald in the Country* (or *The Politics of 1852: Who Let down the Bars?*, 1853; Stony Brook, NY, Mus.) shows a country man and a city man on opposite sides of a partially dismantled rail fence; the city man is reading a newspaper, *The Herald*, a clue that, alongside Mount's alternative title, suggests the painting laughs at the Democratic election victory over the Whigs in 1852, a victory made possible by the huge influx of immigrants who voted Democrat. Although he himself was a Democrat, Mount's paintings usually rose above party issues to laugh at the political process in general.

In many of his paintings, Mount turned to other themes of rural life. He created several works that celebrated rural music-making. One of his favourite formats was fiddle-playing (Mount was himself a violinist) or the fiddle-accompanied dance inside the country barn, visible from the outside of the barn through a large rectangular open door. In one of his best-known paintings in this format, *The Power of Music* (1847; Cleveland, OH, Mus. A.), a black person leans against the outside wall of the barn, absorbed in the attraction of the music. Mount was unusual in depicting the listener without caricature. Recognizing the attractiveness of this point of view, in the 1850s the art dealer William Schaus commissioned from Mount a number of images of black musicians for distribution in Europe as lithographs.

Mount received commissions from the most influential patrons in New York City, including Luman Reed and Jonathan Sturges (who took *Farmers Nooning*), and many of his works were engraved. He was a favourite of the newspaper and journal critics, who held him up as a model. The wit with which he carried out national self-criticism was unique among American artists; imitators such as Francis Edmonds and James Clonney failed to capture the spirit of his paintings. His clear draughtsmanship, small, precise brushstrokes, abstemious application of paint and choice of bright colours all contributed greatly to his success. Extraordinarily self-conscious about painting methods, he kept journals in which he recorded experiments with pigments and brushes. He sketched extensively in notebooks and painted *plein-air* oil sketches for several works, devising a studio-wagon in which he travelled over Long Island. In his journals and extensive correspondence he considered a number of ideas for subjects. Although he made a large number of sketches of city characters, he only ever painted rural scenes, as these were what his audience wanted.

Mount never married. Throughout his life he continued to paint portraits; so many of them were posthumous that he once commented that his best patron was death. Although his genre paintings were very much in demand, he went for long stretches without painting—particularly after the Civil War—possibly because of the limited number of popular puns and concerns that he could exploit pictorially.

UNPUBLISHED SOURCES

Stony Brook, NY, Mus. [ntbks, journals, corr.]

BIBLIOGRAPHY

K. Adams: 'The Black Image in the Paintings of William Sidney Mount', *Amer. A. J.*, vii/2 (1975), pp. 42–59

A. Frankenstein: *William Sidney Mount* (New York, 1975)

J. Hudson jr: 'Banks, Politics, Hard Cider and Paint: The Political Origins of William Sidney Mount's *Cider Making*', *Met. Mus. J.*, x (1975), pp. 107–18

D. Cassedy and G. Schrott: *William Sidney Mount: Annotated Bibliography and Listings of Archival Holdings of the Museums at Stony Brook* (Stony Brook, NY, 1983)

——: *William Sidney Mount: Works in the Collection of the Museums at Stony Brook* (Stony Brook, NY, 1983)

J. Armstrong, ed.: *Catching the Tune: Music and William Sidney Mount* (Stony Brook, NY, 1984)

E. Johns: *American Genre Painting: The Politics of Everyday Life* (New Haven, CT, and London, 1991)

ELIZABETH JOHNS

Mt Abu [Ābu; anc. Arbuda; Arbudagiri]. Rocky plateau with lakes, an ancient fort and temples in Sirohi District, Rajasthan, India, which flourished from *c*. the 8th century.

1. HISTORY. Folklore recounts that the clan of Rajputs known as Agni-Kula (fire-pit) originated from the flames of a sacred fire on Mt Abu. The earliest evidence suggests the mountain and the sacred lake of Nakhi Talav were a stronghold of Shaivism. This is attested by the *Arbuda Mahātmya* of the *Skanda Purāṇa*, and epigraphs beginning in the 8th century AD. The continuous history of Abu begins only in the second half of the 10th century when the mountain was annexed by the PARAMARA king Vakpati II Munja (*reg c*. AD 973–94). He put his son Aranyaraja on the throne of Chandravati, the capital of the area. The Paramaras built the fort of Achalgarh, about 10 km north-east of Nakhi Talav. Inside are two heavily renovated Jaina temples. At the base of the fort is the tank called Mandakini Kunda and Achaleshvara temple, mostly a modern structure, surrounded by a host of minor shrines. A brass Nandi in front of the temple is dated 1408. The Paramara kings were defeated *c*. 1022 by the SOLANKI monarch Bhimadeva (*reg c*. 1022–64). He appointed Vimala of the Pragata family as his minister (Skt *daṇḍanāyaka*). Through Vimala's intercession, Abu was restored to the Paramara ruler Dhanduka. Vimala founded a Jaina temple at Dilwara (*see* §2 below), and in later centuries Abu became an important centre of Jainism. In 1197 King Dharavarsha suffered defeat near the foot of the mountain at the hands of Khusrau, the general of Qutb al-Din Aybak. Abu passed into the hands of Chahamana (Chauhan) Lutiga of south Marwar sometime before 1320. Rana Kumbha occupied Abu in the 15th century, enlarging the fort at Achalgarh and adding two equestrian statues beside the tank. Abu came under Mughal rule and was later used as the summer headquarters of the British Agent-General for Rajputana. Numerous palatial residences were built here by the British and the leading Rajput princes in colonial times.

2. TEMPLES AT DILWARA. Four main temples were constructed at Dilwara, *c*. 3 km north-east of Nakhi Talav. The earliest, known as the Vimala Vasahi, was begun in 1032 by Vimala, the minister of the Solanki monarch Bhimadeva. Much of the present structure was probably executed *c*. 12th century. One of the finest Jaina temples in western India, it is set in a quadrangular cloister lined with image niches. The temple building consists of a black stone sanctum containing a large metal image of Adinatha (installed during the restoration of 1322), preceded by a closed hall (Skt *gūḍha-maṇḍapa*) and two open pillared halls. The open halls, built of translucent white marble,

have richly carved pillars and intricate ornamental arches (*vandana-mālikā*). The main domical ceiling (diam. 7 m) is trabeate and consists of concentric rings carved with a spellbinding variety of figures, floral devices, pendants and architectural motifs. Large struts are carved as standing female figures, and the apex of the dome carries a spectacular stamen-like drop-finial (*padma-śilā*). The ceiling panels in the side aisles also carry a lively array of figures and floral patterns. An octagonal domed porch was added in the 13th century. It contains ten portrait images of Vimala and members of his family seated on elephants.

A second temple was begun at Dilwara in 1230 by the wealthy banker Tejapala, brother of Vastupala, a minister of the Vaghelas of Gujarat. Dedicated to Neminatha, the temple is known also as the Luna Vasahi. It follows the pattern of the Vimala Vasahi but is distinguished by an increased variety and density in the sculptural ornament. The stone screens in the cloister walk and the main dome in the hall are particularly fine (for illustration of the latter, *see* INDIAN SUBCONTINENT, fig. 71). The Adinatha temple, placed adjacent to the Luna Vashai, was built in the 14th century. Like its neighbour, it follows the Vimala Vasahi in its essential features. Carving is found only on the doors and pillars, for the temple was left unfinished. The shrine contains a massive metal Jaina image. The last temple at Dilwara dates to 1459 and is dedicated to Parshvanatha. Unlike the earlier temples, it follows a *caturmukha* ('four-mouthed') plan, with an opening and porch on each of its four sides. The superstructure is dilapidated. The building is surrounded by cruciform halls with ornate ceilings. The enclosing cloister wall characteristic of the Vimala and Luna Vasahi is absent.

See also INDIAN SUBCONTINENT, §§III, 6(i)(b) and IV, 7(iii)(a).

BIBLIOGRAPHY
A. V. Pandya: *Abu in Bombay State* (Bombay, n.d.)
F. Kielhorn: 'Mount Abu Vimala Temple Inscription of (Vikrama) Samvat 1378', *Epig. Ind.*, ix (1907–8), p. 149
H. Cousens: *Architectural Antiquities of Western India* (London, 1926)
P. Brown: *Indian Architecture, Buddhist and Hindu Periods* (?Bombay [1941], rev. Bombay 1956)
Muni Shri Jayantavijayi: *Tīrtharāja Abu*; Eng. trans. by U. P. Shah as *Holy Abu: A Tourist's Guide to Mount Abu and its Jaina Shrines* (Bhavnagar, 1954)
U. P. Shah: *Studies in Jaina Art* (Varanasi, 1955)
M. A. Dhaky: 'The Ceilings in the Temples of Gujarat', *Bull. Baroda Mus. & Pict. Gall.*, xvi–xvii (1963) [entire volume a monograph by Dhaky]
U. P. Shah: 'Some Mediaeval Sculptures from Gujarat and Rajasthan', *J. Ind. Soc. Orient. A.* (1965–6), pp. 52–87 [special issue, *Western Indian Art*]
D. Sharma, ed.: *Rajasthan through the Ages*, i (Bikaner, 1966)
A. Volwahsen: *Living Architecture: India* (New York, 1969)
M. A. Dhaky: 'Vimalavasahīnī Ketalīka Samasyāo', *Svādhyāya*, ix (1972), pp. 349–68; Eng. trans. by M. Desai and M. Desai as *Complexities Surrounding the Vimalavasahī Temple at Mt Abu*, Occas. Pap. Ser., Dept South Asia Reg. Stud., U. Pennsylvania (Philadelphia, 1980)
K. C. Jain: *Ancient Cities and Towns of Rajasthan* (Delhi, 1972)
A. Ghosh, ed.: *Jaina Art and Architecture*, 3 vols (Delhi, 1974)
S. Huntington and J. Huntington: *The Art of Ancient India* (New York, 1985), pp. 490–97
G. Michell and P. Davies: *The Penguin Guide to the Monuments of India*, 2 vols (London, 1989)

ASOK KUMAR DAS

Mt Athos [anc. Akte]. The easternmost of the three southern promontories of Chalkidiki in northern Greece, inhabited since the 7th century AD by Eastern Orthodox monks. According to legend the name is derived from the rebellious giant Athos, who dared to challenge Poseidon and was then buried under the rock hurled against him by the furious god. At its north-west end the peninsula (w. 5–10 km; l. *c.* 47.5 km) is joined to the mainland by a low and narrow isthmus (w. 2.5 km), through which King Xerxes of Persia (*reg* 486–465 BC) cut a canal before 480 BC, distinct traces of which still exist. From this point a hilly and then mountainous ridge stretches south-east, dividing the peninsula into two main slopes—the northeast and south-west, on which lie all the monastic communities—and terminating in Mt Athos (h. 2033 m). According to Herodotos (*Histories*, vii, 22) the Pelasgians from the island of Lemnos founded five cities on the peninsula. Colonies were also established by the inhabitants of Eretria. Of the towns known to have stood on the isthmus, only the remains of Akanthos are known. The beginning of monastic life on Athos is lost in a confusion of legend, the monks by tradition attributing the first religious institutions to the reign of Constantine the Great (*reg* 306–37). By at least the 7th century AD the inaccessible and inhospitable nature of the peninsula had begun to attract Christian contemplatives wishing to practise the rigours of the ascetic life. The earliest documented reference to it as a monastic centre is in the acts of the Council of 843 convened by Empress THEODORA at Constantinople (now Istanbul) to discuss the restoration of the icons; by the mid-11th century the whole peninsula was known as the Holy Mountain (Agion Oros). Today it remains an area dedicated to the monastic life, and, apart from a few State officials and lay workers, all its permanent inhabitants are monks; only male visitors are allowed entry. Athos preserves a wealth and variety of Byzantine architecture, painting, manuscripts and sculpture amassed in the centuries before and after the fall of Constantinople to the Turks in 1453.

1. History and organization. 2. Architecture. 3. Monumental painting and mosaic. 4. Icons. 5. Illuminated manuscripts. 6. Sculpture.

1. HISTORY AND ORGANIZATION. The earliest religious inhabitants of Athos lived as hermits. The present-day monasterial organization was established on Athos with the foundation in 962 by St Athanasios the Athonite (*c.* 915–1002) of the Great Lavra, which remains the chief monastery of the peninsula. St Athanasios introduced the cenobitic system, in contrast to the life lived by the solitaries, who were alone or in a lavra (a group of huts), and imposed a strict constitutional charter (*typikon*), granted by the monastery's benefactor Emperor Nikephoras II Phokas (*reg* 963–9) and similar to that of the monastery of St John Stoudios in Constantinople. The zenith of Athonite prosperity was reached in the 10th to the 12th centuries; as many as 180 monasteries were founded, and the community, taking the shape of a monastic confederation, acquired a pan-Orthodox character from the numerous Georgian, south Italian, Russian, Serbian and Bulgarian monks who either joined existing monasteries or founded national houses. All settlements could be grouped hierarchically: the ruling monasteries of the cenobitic or idiorhythmic rule; the *sketae*, subordinate to a ruling monastery, with the layout of a village or the shape of a monastery; the *kellia*, *kalyves* and *kathismata*, in the form of a cottage; and the *hesichasteria* or *asketeria*, small huts or caves housing one monk and situated in the most inaccessible spots.

Monastic life carried on in such a harsh environment as Athos and with organizational strictness that nevertheless demanded splendid surroundings required continuous patronage. Thus the monasteries were supported legally by *chrysobulls*, or imperial documents, and economically by continuous grants, and the Great Lavra received an annual income by imperial decree. Individual works of art were also supported, for example the 16th-century mural decoration for the catholikon of the Great Lavra was made possible thanks to a grant by a bishop; his name is mentioned in the dedicatory inscription, together with those of the then patriarch of Constantinople, of the abbot of the monastery and of the painter.

As a result of Frankish raids during the Latin occupation of the empire (1204–61), the efforts of Emperor Michael VIII Palaiologos (*reg* 1259–82) to force the monks into union with the Western Church and the plundering of Athos by Catalan mercenaries in 1307–9, the number of monasteries was reduced to 25. The Ottoman occupiers (1430–1912) allowed the monks to retain privileges, which, taken together with the strict yoke imposed outside Athos, explains why the mountain developed into a national centre of the Orthodox world. The monastic tradition on Athos has been maintained up to the late 20th century, and the peninsula is a self-governing community under the protection of Greece.

2. ARCHITECTURE. From afar, most Athonite monasteries, with their defensive towers, look like medieval fortresses. They follow the typical plan of a Byzantine monastery, which was itself based on such earlier models as the monastery of St Catherine on Mt Sinai (*see* SINAI, §2(i)); a primary purpose was to protect the monks from enemy attack. The layout of an Athonite monastery comprises a circuit of buildings and defensive walling that forms a rectangular or polygonal enclosure (see fig. 1). The outer walls are blank, massively built and fortresslike, and furnished with small turrets, embrasures and machicolations; a footway on top of walls behind battlements and machicolations can still be seen at the Great Lavra, Chilandar and Xenophontos. There is usually a substantial tower on one wall of the enclosure, often protecting the main entrance, which gives access to the central courtyard and in modern times usually houses the library. In the centre of the courtyard stands the monastery's principal church, the katholikon. Most katholika are free-standing and built in the so-called 'Athonite style', which is based on the four-columned cross-in-square type common in Constantinople but with three additional features: the central space has side apses to accommodate the singers; there are one or two narthexes, or one wide narthex (*lite*); and there are one or two annexed side chapels. The earliest example of this style is the katholikon (963) of the Great Lavra where recent excavations have shown that the side apses were added in 1002, apparently merely for reasons of function, and were therefore not part of the original

1. Mt Athos, Monastery of Dionysiou, 1370–74; aerial view

2. Mt Athos, Monastery of Vatopedi, 972–85; interior of refectory

structure (Mylonas, 1976). Another adaptation, again for reasons of function, can be seen at the church of the Protaton (principal church) at Karyes. Here a simple 9th-century three-aisled basilica under a wooden roof was transformed (?965) into a domeless roofed cross-in-square in plan alone by taking away the two middle pillars, thus instituting a transept, the cross arms of which could be used as choirs. There are also still on Athos 10th- and 11th-century churches (e.g. Stavronikita, St Vasileios) without side apses, further proof that the 'Athonite style' is an adaptation of the Constantinopolitan cross-in-square and that this evolution occurred on Athos alone, between the 11th and 14th centuries. This new type then spread to Macedonia, mainland Greece and Serbia, and from Serbia influenced 15th- and 16th-century churches in the regions around the Danube. These latter types in turn influenced Athos churches of the 16th century. Some katholika have rendered exterior walls that are painted a deep red to symbolize the Blood of Christ; some are built in the cloisonné technique (*see* BRICK, §II, 2). Many of the façades are decorated with ceramic inserts (17th–18th century) inlaid with rosettes, circles or spiral patterns, low reliefs and painted scenes.

The next most important building after the katholikon is the refectory where the monks eat their communal meals (see fig. 2). It is usually sited close to the church. The refectories vary in plan; some are rectangular, others are built in the shape of a cross or are T-shaped. Many terminate in an apse, in which is placed the table for the abbot and his senior monks. Close to the refectory are the

kitchen, bakery, and liquid and cereal stores. Sometimes between the katholikon and refectory, but always near the former, is the *phiale*, a holy well or fountain set in an open arcade. The cells for the monks are usually laid out in the multistorey buildings that run along the outside wall. When the wall served a real defensive purpose, it was not pierced by windows, but in recent centuries windows and strutted balconies have been built through the outer walls.

3. MONUMENTAL PAINTING AND MOSAIC. The 11th-century mosaics of the *Annunciation* and *Deësis* in the katholikon of Vatopedi are probably the only examples of monumental art on Athos pre-dating the 12th century. Another *Annunciation* mosaic in the church dates to the 14th century. Of greater significance than these mosaics are the wall paintings of the 12th to 20th centuries that decorate the interior walls of many katholika, small chapels, refectories and libraries. These wall paintings reflect the various artistic movements of successive ages, of which the Macedonian and Cretan schools are particularly well represented: most paintings have, however, been re-touched many times since they were originally executed. The themes depicted are the traditional iconographical cycles illustrating Orthodox church doctrine, their content and arrangement in successive horizontal tiers following the prescriptions laid down by DIONYSIOS OF FURNA. Even so, cycles were altered to fit the characteristics of a building: at the katholikon of the Great Lavra (a low building) there are four tiers of paintings, whereas the tall

buildings of Dionysiou and Stavronikita accommodate six tiers.

The earliest fragments of wall paintings are in the library at Vatopedi and depict the heads of SS Peter and Paul (12th century). Later in date (?1220) are the full-length portraits of the same two saints at Ravdouchos near Karyes. Examples of the art from the school of Thessaloniki, to which most Macedonian works of the period owe their origin, are to be found in the katholika of Vatopedi (1312) and Chilandar (1319; attributed to Georgios Kallergis) and the Protaton at Karyes (late 13th century or early 14th; *see* EARLY CHRISTIAN AND BYZANTINE ART, fig. 46). The paintings in the Protaton at Karyes have been attributed to Manuel Panselinos and are considered to be the finest on Athos. The principal characteristics of these wall paintings are their naturalism, mobility of facial expression and the use of bright colours.

Athonite wall painting reached its acme between the 16th century and the 18th when the Cretan school held sway (*see* POST-BYZANTINE, §II). In contrast to the Macedonian school, the gestures and movements of the Cretan figures are more restrained, and the palette of colours is subtler. The most renowned representative of the Cretan school was THEOPHANES THE CRETAN whose frescoes decorate the refectories and katholika of the Great Lavra (*c*. 1535–40 and ?1530–35 respectively; *see* POST-BYZANTINE, fig. 4) and Stavronikita (1546). Other Cretan painters were Tzortzis, who decorated the katholikon of Dionysiou (1547), and an unknown painter, who decorated the katholikon of Docheiariou (1568); Antonios, who decorated the katholikon of Xenophontos (1544) and the chapel of St George at St Paul's (1552) but in a divergent style stemming from mainland Greece; and Frangos Katellanos, who decorated the chapel of St Nicholas at the Lavra (1560). Katellanos' style of painting is less classicizing than that of the others and is closer to the expressionistic style of Georgie Mitrofanović's work in the chapel of St Tryphon (1621) and the refectory (1662) at Chilandar.

In the early 18th century Dionysios of Furna encouraged a return to the techniques of Panselinos, thus instigating a final renaissance of Byzantine fresco painting. After this period, however, both architecture and painting were increasingly influenced by Western Baroque and Rococo mannerisms, which in some cases were combined with Byzantine traditions to produce a charmingly naive kind of painting, as in the chapel of Hagia Zoni at Vatopedi (1794).

4. ICONS. There are about 20,000 icons of various sizes, styles and artistic value ranging from the 12th century to the 20th. Some hang in the katholika and small chapels; others are stored in the monasteries' treasuries. Of the few mosaic icons, two of *St George* and *St Demetrios* (late 11th century) in the inner narthex of the katholikon at Xenophontos were originally part of the wall decoration. Among other mosaic icons are a *Virgin Hodegetria* (12th–13th century) at Chilandar, *St John the Theologian* (14th century) at the Great Lavra and *St Nicholas Stridas* (14th century) at Stavronikita.

The remaining icons are painted on wooden panels, many of which are displayed on stands in the katholika or

in chapels named after them. Numerous tales are told about the arrival and miracle-working qualities of such icons as the *Virgin Tricherousa* (Of the Three Hands) at Chilandar, which is even said to be the work of St Luke the Evangelist. Icons predating the Ottoman conquest also survive in the collections at Chilandar, Vatopedi, Iviron and the Great Lavra (e.g. a 13th-century icon of *St Panteleimon*). They reflect the styles and techniques associated with Constantinople and Thessaloniki.

As in Athonite wall painting, some of the most impressive icons are by artists of the Cretan school. They include among others the *Great Deësis* (1542) at Dionysiou, consisting of five icons by the painter Euphrosynos; at least one (1542) on the iconostasis in the Protaton; and two cycles of the *Twelve Feasts* at the Great Lavra (?1535) and Stavronikita (?1546), both of which are attributed to Theophanes the Cretan.

5. ILLUMINATED MANUSCRIPTS. Of the 12,000 manuscripts kept in the monasteries' libraries and treasuries 800 are illuminated. Most of these contain religious and ecclesiastical subject-matter; a few monasteries also possess illuminated liturgical scrolls written on parchment, such as Cod. 2 at the Great Lavra and Cod. 101 and 105 at Dionysiou. They date mainly from the 9th to the 11th century and consist of headpieces at the beginning of the text, narrative scenes relating to the text, author portraits and initial letters. The decoration of the headpieces and initial letters is particularly rich, with multicoloured vegetal and geometric designs. Scenes from daily life and groups of animals, birds and fish are also common. Some of the finest illuminated manuscripts belong to the Great Lavra (e.g. 11th-century lectionary, the so-called 'Gospel of Nikephoros Phokas'), Vatopedi (e.g. Cod. 602, 655 and 1199), Iviron (e.g. cod. 1, 55 and 874), Dionysiou (e.g. 11th-century Gospel book), Esphigmenou (e.g. 11th-century Menologion with 80 miniatures) and St Panteleimon (e.g. Cod. 6, the *Homilies of St Gregory the Theologian*), Iviron (e.g. Cod. 463, 12th-century narrative of *Barlaam and Joasaph* with 80 miniatures) and Vatopedi (e.g. 13th-century Octateuch).

For illustration *see* EARLY CHRISTIAN AND BYZANTINE ART, fig. 60.

6. SCULPTURE. The use of architectural sculpture on Athos is limited to a few columns, capitals, parapet slabs and relief plaques. Some of these pieces, such as the double-zoned capitals with animal *protomes* (6th century; *see* EARLY CHRISTIAN AND BYZANTINE ART, §IV, 2) in the katholikon at Iviron, have been reused. Most parapet slabs enclose the basin of a *phiale* like the one at the Great Lavra, which bears relief decoration of vegetal and geometric patterns, crosses and groups of birds. Marble or stone plaques with relief figures or decorative patterns are frequently found in the façades and walls of churches. One of the finest examples is a middle Byzantine marble relief showing a full-length portrait of *St Demetrios* in the west wall of the katholikon at Xeropotamou. It seems likely that this plaque and most of the other sculptural pieces were imported into Athos.

The treasuries also preserve many small carvings in stone, wood and ivory, as well as works in bronze, gold and silver. Among the most renowned examples is a steatite paten (diam. 150 mm) supposedly presented by Empress Pulcheria (*reg* 399–453) to the monastery of Xeropotamou and depicting the *Divine Liturgy*. Other objects include a 10th-century ivory carving of the *Crucifixion* and a 13th-century wood-carved cover of a Psalter (Cod. 31), both at Dionysiou; two sets of bronze-relief doors in the katholika of the Great Lavra and Vatopedi; and numerous gold and silver caskets containing fragments of the True Cross or relics of saints, such as the many-domed church reliquary said to be the gift of Nikephoros II Phokas to the Great Lavra.

BIBLIOGRAPHY

GENERAL

V. G. Barskij: *Stranstvovanija svjatym městam vestoka s 1723 po 1747* [Wanderings around the Holy Places of the East from 1723 to 1747], 2 vols (St Petersburg, 1778); ed. N. Barsukov, 4 vols (St Petersburg, 1885–7) [vols 1 and 3 contain the accounts of visits to Athos, with many important architectural illustrations]

H. Brockhaus: *Die Kunst in der Athosklöstern* (Leipzig, 1891, 2/1924)

P. Meyer: *Die Haupturkunden für die Geschichte der Athosklöster* (Amsterdam, 1894, 2/1965)

G. Millet, J. Pargoire and L. Petit: *Recueil des inscriptions chrétiennes de l'Athos* (Paris, 1904)

F. W. Hasluck: *Athos and its Monasteries* (London, 1924)

F. Dölger and others: *Mönchsland Athos* (Munich, 1943)

Le Millénaire du Mont Athos, 963–1963: Etudes et mélanges, i–ii (Chevetogne, 1963–4)

Chilandar. Zborn., i– (1966–)

P. Huber: *Athos: Leben, Glaube, Kunst* (Zurich, 1969)

ARCHITECTURE

G. Millet: 'Recherches au Mont Athos', *Bull. Corr. Hell.*, xxix (1905), pp. 55–141

P. M. Mylonas: *L'Architecture du Mont Athos* (Venice, 1963)

——: 'Research on Athos: Memorandum of Works Accomplished and Projected', *Praktika tou IE' diethnous synedriou byzantinon spoudon* [Proceedings of the 15th International Congress of Byzantine Studies], *Athens 1976*, ii, pp. 529–44

——: 'Two Middle-Byzantine Churches on Athos', ibid., ii, pp. 545–74

——: 'Les Etapes successives de construction du Protaton au Mont Athos', *Cah. Archéol.*, xxviii (1979), pp. 143–60

——: 'Notice sur le catholicon d'Iviron', *Actes d'Iviron*, i (Paris, 1985), xiv of *Archives de l'Athos*, ed. P. Lemerle (1970–)

——: 'Remarques architecturales sur le catholicon de Chilandar', *Chilandar. Zborn.*, vi (1986), pp. 8–38

——: 'Le Trapéza de la Gr. Lavra, au Mont Athos', *Cah. Archéol.*, xxxv (1987), pp. 143–57

PAINTING

G. Millet: *Les Peintures*, i of *Monuments de l'Athos* (Paris, 1927)

J. Renaud: *Le Cycle de l'apocalypse de Dionysiou* (Paris, 1943)

V. Djuric: 'Fresques médiévales à Chilandar', *Actes du XII congrès international d'études byzantines, Ochrid 1961*, iii, pp. 59–98

A. Xyngopoulos: 'La Peinture monumentale au Mont-Athos', *Corsi Cult. A. Ravenn. & Biz.*, xi (1964), pp. 491–30

A. Deroko and S. Nenadović: 'Konaci manastira Hilandara' [The dormitory buildings of Chilandar monastery], Srpska akademi ja nauka, *Spomenik*, cxx (Belgrade, 1971), pp. 19–37

S. Nenadović: 'Arhitektura Hilandara: Crkve i paraklisi' [The architecture of Chilandar: the churches and the chapels], *Hilandarski zbornik*, iii (1974), pp. 85–196

C. G. Patrinelis, A. Karakatsani and M. Theochari: *Mone Stauroniketa: Istoria, eikones, chrysokentemata* [Monastery of Stavronikita: history, icons, gold objects] (Athens, 1974)

ILLUMINATED MANUSCRIPTS

K. Weitzmann: *Aus den Bibliotheken des Athos* (Hamburg, 1963)

P. Huber: *Bild und Botschaft: Altes und Neues Testament* (Zurich, 1973)

S. M. Pelekanides and others: *Oi thesauroi tou Agiou Orous: Eikonografemena* [The treasures of Mount Athos: illuminated manuscripts], i–ii (Athens, 1973; Eng. trans., Athens, 1974), iii (Athens, 1979)

Mt Athos Painters' Guide. *See under* DIONYSIOS OF FURNA.

Mt Cameron West. Complex of Aboriginal sites on the north-west coast of Tasmania, Australia. It has the best-known and largest collection of Aboriginal petroglyphs in Tasmania, with six individual sites where engravings (as they are also known) have been carved on rocky outcrops at, or just above, the high-water level and close to a freshwater creek. Since the petroglyphs are exposed to windblown beach sands, salt spray and the surf of very high tides and are associated with shell-midden deposits characteristic of the more recent prehistory of Tasmania (i.e. not earlier than *c.* 1000 BC), they are probably of relatively recent origin. Shifting beach and dune sands partially bury the rocks, and their exposure and visibility can vary significantly. The Mt Cameron West engravings were almost certainly entirely covered in the early 19th century when George Augustus travelled in the region. In the early 1930s they were partially exposed and the Tasmanian antiquarian A. L. Meston first recognized their significance as Aboriginal carvings. Since the soft rock of Mt Cameron West is very friable and decays rapidly when exposed, a number of blocks were removed from the site in the 1930s and stored in the Tasmanian Museum and Art Gallery, Hobart, and the Queen Victoria Museum and Art Gallery, Launceston. Excavations undertaken in 1969 in an attempt to date the petroglyphs yielded no reliable dating evidence, but a large section of the panels was exposed, revealing the complexity of the motif arrangements. However, owing to their fragility and the exposed location, the petroglyphs were reburied under dune sand, which has been carefully planted with vegetation to ensure its stability. Few petroglyphs are now visible at the site.

Unlike other known petroglyph sites, the rock at Mt Cameron West is a poorly indurated sandstone and the motifs are thus deeply gouged out. The range of motifs, consisting almost exclusively of circles, pits, arcs and amorphous patches of pounded rock, corresponds to that of other sites (*see* ABORIGINAL AUSTRALIA, §II, 2). Yet these basic design elements are elaborated at Mt Cameron West with the addition of dividing lines within circles, radiating lines, circular enclosures and a large outline containing a number of merging circular patterns. No other Tasmanian rock art site has yielded similar elaboration, which may have been facilitated here by the nature of the rock. Some stones also contain long, linear patterns that end in three prongs and resemble a simple bird-track schema. There are, however, no unambiguous track patterns of birds, animals or humans. There is no indigenous information on the sites' original significance.

BIBLIOGRAPHY

A. L. Meston: 'Aboriginal Rock Carvings in Tasmania', *Pap. & Proc. Royal Soc. Tasmania* (1932), pp. 1–6

ANDRÉE ROSENFELD

Mountford, E(dward) W(illiam) (*b* Shipston-on-Stour, Warwicks, 22 Sept 1855; *d* London, 7 Feb 1908). English architect. Mountford was a conventionally successful architect; he served on the council of the RIBA, was elected president of the Architectural Association (1893–5) and won a silver medal at the Paris Exposition Universelle of 1900. Most of his work was for municipal and other public buildings where his talent for providing commonsense answers to complex planning problems was revealed. In his designs he preferred to combine elements of the Renaissance and Classical revivals; and until about 1900 he avoided the more dramatic effects of the Baroque in favour of restrained and finely modelled work. He was also, justly, praised for his sensitivity in using sculpture and painting to decorate buildings, working for preference with the sculptor F. W. Pomeroy.

He began his career in 1872 in the office of Habershon & Pite, setting up on his own in 1881. He first achieved national recognition with his winning design for Sheffield Town Hall in 1890. Of his early works only a few offered much scope for his talents (e.g. a hospital at Stratford-on-Avon, 1883; clubhouse at Shipston-on-Stour, 1888; St Andrew, Wandsworth, 1888). His style is seen at its best in Sheffield Town Hall (1890–99), Battersea Town Hall (1892), St Olave's School, Southwark (1893), City Polytechnic, Clerkenwell (1893), Central Criminal Court, Old Bailey, London (1902), and in unbuilt designs for the New States House, Guernsey (1899), and County Hall, London (c. 1906). His last major work, the new town hall at Lancaster (1906), was his most nearly Baroque design, completed after his death by his assistant F. Dare Clapham (1875–1914).

BIBLIOGRAPHY
Obituary, *Builder* (15 Feb 1908), p. 190

COLIN CUNNINGHAM

Mountfort, Benjamin Woolfield (*b* Wolverhampton, 13 March 1825; *d* Christchurch, 15 March 1898). New Zealand architect of English birth. The pre-eminent Gothic Revival architect of 19th-century New Zealand, he was articled to R. C. Carpenter in 1844. From Carpenter he gained a sound knowledge of Gothic design and an understanding of ecclesiological principles, to which he adhered throughout his career. By 1848 he was practising in London. A devout Anglo-Catholic, Mountfort emigrated in 1850 to Canterbury, South Island, New Zealand, a colony promoted by the Church of England. He practised in Christchurch for the rest of his career. Mountfort's first major commission, Holy Trinity (1852; destr. 1857), Lyttelton, was an over-ambitious, timber-framed church, which quickly deteriorated through the shrinkage of unseasoned timber. Despite this setback, he continued to design churches for the predominantly Anglican colonists, including St Bartholomew's (1855), Kaiapoi, and St Mary's (1863), Halswell. St Mary's, a small, ecclesiologically correct parish church, Early English in style, picturesque in composition, with a timber frame and vertical board-and-batten sidings, became the model for Mountfort's subsequent wooden churches. Although derived from Carpenter's design for a timber church in the Ecclesiological Society's *Instrumenta Ecclesiastica* (2nd ser., 1856), Mountfort's churches, erected throughout the Christchurch Diocese and further afield, are distinctive in character and diverse in form. They are among his major achievements and are a significant contribution to the Gothic Revival. In 1857 Mountfort became architect to the Province of Canterbury and designed the Canterbury Provincial Government Buildings (1858–65), Christchurch. Built in three stages, first in timber and later in stone, the complex reflects the rapid architectural development of the colony in its formative years. The stone Council Chamber (1865),

the outstanding achievement of Mountfort's career, is the earliest and finest example of High Victorian Gothic in New Zealand. The exterior, vigorously modelled with dramatic changes in scale, contrasts with the lofty, richly polychromed interior.

Always an inventive designer, Mountfort, in his works for Canterbury College, Christchurch (now a centre for the arts), including the Entrance Block (1877) and Great Hall (1882), abandoned Gothic precedent for free design based on the segmental arch. His Canterbury Museum (1870–82), Christchurch, combines influences from G. E. Street's Howsham Church (1859), N. Yorks, and Deane & Woodward's Oxford Museum (1855–61; now University Museum). These public buildings helped define the character of Victorian Christchurch and created a precinct of Gothic Revival buildings unequalled in New Zealand. During the latter stages of his career Mountfort was recognized as the leading designer of Anglican churches in New Zealand and was increasingly able to build in brick and stone. Three churches in Christchurch—Trinity Congregational (1874), an aggressively muscular stone church in the Early French style; Holy Trinity (1876), Avonside, with its richly embellished chancel; and the church of the Good Shepherd (1884), Phillipstown, built in finely detailed brick—reveal the range and variety of his later churches. As supervising architect for Christchurch Cathedral from 1873 Mountfort enlivened Sir George Gilbert I Scott (ii)'s design of 1863, notably by adding balconies to the tower and pinnacles to the spire. St John's Cathedral (1886; destr. 1931), Napier, an austere brick design with massive internal buttresses, inspired by Albi Cathedral, France, bears comparison with St Bartholomew's (1874), Brighton, by Edmund Scott (*d* 1895). The largest and most impressive of Mountfort's timber churches, St Mary's Pro-Cathedral (1887–98), Auckland, fittingly culminated his career. In 1872 he became the founding president of the Canterbury Association of Architects, the earliest professional body of architects in New Zealand. Mountfort's professionalism, his commitment to principles of design, and the high quality of his buildings have been an example to subsequent generations of New Zealand architects, including Samuel Hurst Seager and Peter Beaven.

BIBLIOGRAPHY
I. J. Lochhead: *The Early Works of Benjamin Woolfield Mountfort, 1850–65* (diss., U. Auckland, 1975)
——: 'Gilbert Scott, Benjamin Mountfort and the Building of Christchurch Cathedral', *Bull. NZ A. Hist.*, iv (1976), pp. 2–15
W. J. A. Brittenden: 'Canterbury Provincial Government Buildings', *Historic Buildings of New Zealand: South Island*, ed. F. Porter (Auckland, 1983), pp. 94–9
J. Mané: 'Pilgrim Churches', *Historic Buildings of New Zealand: South Island*, ed. F. Porter (Auckland, 1983), pp. 68–81
I. J. Lochhead: *Antipodean Gothic: The Architecture of Benjamin Woolfield Mountfort* (in preparation)

IAN J. LOCHHEAD

Mt Fuji [Fujisan]. Japan's highest mountain (elevation of 3776 m), on the border between Shizuoka and Yamanashi prefectures. It is a semi-dormant volcano that last erupted in 1707. The graceful, nearly symmetrical cone of Mt Fuji, with its usually snow-capped peak, dominates the surrounding landscape and has for centuries captured the Japanese imagination. Mt Fuji has inspired art, poetry,

Thunderstorm beneath the Summit by Katsushika Hokusai, from his *Fugaku sanjurokkei* ('Thirty-six views of Mt Fuji'), polychrome woodblock print, 250×380 mm, early 1830s (London, Victoria and Albert Museum)

religious veneration, popular affection and national pride for so long that it is for many a symbol of Japan itself.

Mt Fuji has been sacred to Japan's indigenous religion, SHINTO, for over 1000 years. Shrines to its spirit, which was regarded as the principal mountain deity (*kami*) of Japan, were established at its peak and later at its base. One such is the Sengen Shrine in Fujinomiya, Shizuoka Prefecture. The ascent of the mountain became an important pilgrimage, especially among adherents of the syncretistic Shinto–Buddhist sect Shugendō (*see* JAPAN, §II, 7), which maintained that climbing sacred mountains was a means of religious purification and a necessary goal during one's lifetime. The practice began as early as the Heian period (AD 794–1185) and was widespread during the Edo period (1600–1868). Ascents of Mt Fuji were depicted in such paintings as the *Fuji Pilgrimage Maṇḍala* (16th century; Sengen Shrine, Shizuoka).

Mt Fuji is mentioned in early poetry anthologies, beginning with the *Man'yōshū* (*c.* 759), as well as in such narratives as the 10th-century *Tales of Ise*. Although it was a *meisho* (famous place celebrated in poetry), its distance from traditional centres of culture meant that it was rarely depicted in painting until the Edo period. Its earliest surviving representations are in the *Shōtoku taishi eden* ('Illustrated biography of Prince Shōtoku'; 1069; Tokyo, N. Mus.) and the *Ippen shōnin eden* ('Illustrated biography of the monk Ippen'; 1299; Kyoto, Kangikōji). Paintings proliferated after the establishment of Edo as the headquarters of the Tokugawa shogunate in 1603. Some, such as those by artists of the Rinpa school, showed the

mountain in a stylized manner reflecting the *meisho* tradition of landscape painting, while others, such as the work of the literati painter Ike Taiga, were based on first-hand observation. The artist KATSUSHIKA HOKUSAI produced the woodblock-printed series *Fugaku sanjūrokkei* ('Thirty-six views of Mt Fuji'), which contains by far the most familiar images of Mt Fuji known in the West (see fig.). Published in 1830–32 and eventually comprising 46 scenes, the series presents the celebrated mountain in different aspects: on clear days and stormy days; on land and over water; in monumental solitude or as a backdrop for travellers, townspeople, artisans or oarsmen facing the force of a great, overarching wave. A notable ceramic representation of the mountain is the *Fujisan* teabowl (*c.* 1615; Tokyo, Sakai priv. col.) by another Rinpa artist, Hon'ami Kōetsu (*see* HON'AMI, (1)). Mt Fuji was also mentioned in early poetry anthologies, such as the *Man'yōshū* (the earliest anthology of Japanese poetry, completed AD 759), and was the subject of many poems written in the Kamakura period (1185–1333).

BIBLIOGRAPHY
Fuji no e [Paintings of Mt Fuji] (exh. cat., Nara, Yamato Bunkakan, 1980)
S. E. Lee: 'Early Sites and Views: Landscape as Subject', *Reflections of Reality in Japanese Art* (exh. cat. by S. E. Lee, M. R. Cunningham and J. T. Ulak, Cleveland, OH, Mus. A., 1983), pp. 143–52
Katsushika Hokusai: One Hundred Views of Mount Fuji, intro. by H. Smith (New York, 1988)

JOAN H. O'MARA

Mt Grenfell. Site of Aboriginal activity, *c.* 50 km northwest of Cobar, western New South Wales, south-east

Australia. The Cobar Plain is a broad, semi-arid plain south of the Darling River. Intermittent rains have eroded the sandstone to produce short, narrow valleys with low cliffs and rock shelters. Permanent water-holes in the vicinity were important centres for Aboriginal activity with concentrations of campsites and painted rock shelters. Eight of the shelters clustered around Mt Grenfell have paintings; two of the largest also have evidence of habitation.

Most of the figures, painted in red, yellow or white, are fairly small (h. 100–300 mm). The paint was not always evenly ground and was generally applied thickly either with a finger or with a blunt object such as a frayed stick brush, but some paintings in red have much finer lines, possibly requiring the use of a hair brush. Human figures predominate, but a range of animal motifs also occurs, mainly macropods and emu, with dingo, fish and others more difficult to identify. The images are in plain silhouette with little detail, and they appear to have been sketched in rapidly. Most of the human figures are shown frontally, often in rows or groups with bent legs and arms, as if jumping or dancing. The latter interpretation is strengthened by the occasional addition of seated figures with arms raised in front as if clapping or holding clapsticks. Despite the high degree of schematization, varying limb positions and body angles suggest an extensive range of postures, with the occasional use of profiles to provide a greater variety. The paintings are lively and dynamic, although few activities can be identified precisely. Apart from a probable predominance of dance, some associated human and animal figures suggest hunting scenes, but animals, both isolated and in groups, are not often clearly related to the humans. A pair of red macropods (one in a very upright position), facing each other and holding clapsticks, clearly indicates that not all the animal images are to be read literally as potential prey. There are also sequences of tracks, complex designs resembling mazes that have no obvious iconic origin, hand stencils and some object stencils.

Excavations at one of the shelters yielded a range of stone artefacts of the recent past, axe-grinding grooves and small, round, mortar stones, but it is not clear whether these were for grinding seeds or pigments. The few bones recovered indicate that a wide range of small animals was hunted, with a clear preference for possum. The entire assemblage and the often fresh appearance of the pigments suggest that the activities of the site have taken place within the last four hundred years, a view strengthened by the results of radiocarbon dating.

See also ABORIGINAL AUSTRALIA, §II, 2(ii)(b).

BIBLIOGRAPHY
F. D. McCarthy: *Rock Art of the Cobar Pediplain* (Canberra, 1976)
ANDRÉE ROSENFELD

Mounting. Attachment of a work of art to a support or setting, or the application of accessories or decoration as embellishment. In many types of mount, these two distinct concepts may be combined, and the mount serves both a functional and decorative purpose.

1. Introduction. 2. East Asia. 3. Islamic lands and India. 4. Western world.

1. INTRODUCTION. Although the term 'mounting' may apply to the support or fixing of three-dimensional art, this article is concerned with the description and history of the mounting of two-dimensional or flat format pictorial and other graphic material. In East and Eastern Central Asia this includes paintings and calligraphy in scroll, screen, fan, album and banner formats, as well as prints of various sorts; in India and the Islamic world, calligraphy, painted decoration, miniatures and various kinds of banner painting; in the West, mainly prints, drawings and watercolours. The chief substances used in the fabrication of these works of art are such materials as paper and woven silk. These form the original, or primary, support for the pigment with which the pictorial image or script is created. The pigment, usually mixed with a binding medium, may be applied directly to the surface of the support, as in an East Asian scroll painting or European engraved print, or the support may first be coated with a preparation or ground as in a Renaissance metalpoint drawing, an Indian or Islamic miniature painting or a Tibetan tangka. In their unmounted state, all these works of art are fragile and vulnerable to damage from handling and other environmental effects of unprotected storage or display, and adequate physical support in the form of a mount became necessary once people sought to preserve them. In some civilizations mounting evolved with the art form itself, as in the case of East Asian scrolls; elsewhere methods evolved from the need to organize and display collections, initially in the form of albums and later by fixing into a cut-out cardboard surround or 'window' mount (USA: mat). In the West this practice developed when collections of drawings and prints began to be assembled from the 15th century onwards. Since then, the 'window' mount style of mounting has evolved in conjunction with the increasing practice of framing and displaying graphic art.

The underlying reason, therefore, for mounting works of art is that of conservation, but this may be overshadowed where cultural tradition dictates the format for the presentation of works of art. Additional reasons arise from more abstract, aesthetic considerations. In many forms of mounting, the mount comprises or includes a border area surrounding the art work itself. Like the picture frame, this serves the dual purpose of defining or emphasizing the physical boundary of the image and isolating it from its immediate surroundings, thus allowing the viewer to focus on the work with minimal distraction or confusion from background detail. Equally, a lavishly decorated mount or one made of rare or expensive materials may serve to indicate the high regard of the owner for the piece as a work of art, or its status as an object of veneration.

The forms and methods of construction of mounts are related to the type of object and its use or function in the culture in which it originated. Although a few East Asian hanging scrolls or hand scrolls were displayed in imperial, domestic or religious interiors, most were normally stored rolled and brought out only on special occasions, such as for private viewing or literary gatherings. The same is true of Tibetan tangkas, which have a religious function as a focus for Buddhist worship and meditation; even when exhibited, the image is usually concealed with a cover, which is attached to and forms part of the silk mount. The shape, size and materials of painting and mount, together with accessories such as rods and hanging cord, are fixed by traditional rules and religious custom. In Japan a major consideration in the design of fine art forms was that of portability, owing to the conventions of use and to the high risk of earthquake and fire in dwelling houses. Hence a type of painting made of lightweight materials that could be rolled up in a compact, easily transportable form was an obvious advantage when the work needed to be either changed, as scrolls often were according to season or special occasion, or saved in the event of sudden evacuation.

The choice of materials for mounting is also influenced by availability, cost, physical compatibility and aesthetics. For example, luxurious materials such as patterned silk are used to form the 'frame' around East Asian scroll paintings and for the two strips that hang from the top of the scroll (*see* SCROLL, §1 and 2). This is a product of the same civilization as the painting and is readily available, if costly. Not only does it enhance and embellish the painting by providing a harmonious setting, but it also has an essential structural role because it behaves physically in the same way as the support of the painting, whether paper-backed woven silk or paper. This together with appropriate paper backings and adhesive allow the scroll to be rolled, unrolled and hung without causing distortion. In contrast, card board made from mechanical woodpulp has been used in the West for mounting prints and drawings since the mid-19th century. As a material, it has low chemical stability, but its cheapness and ready availability recommend it to commercial mounters. In recent decades, with a growing concern for factors affecting the long-term preservation of works of art, the need for high chemical stability and purity in mounting material has assumed a greater priority.

In the West from the late 18th century onwards works of art from all over the world were amassed in private and public collections. Partly from the requirement for display in Western-style picture frames and partly though a tendency in museums and art galleries to impose uniformity of storage format, this has led to the Western-style cardboard mount becoming adopted worldwide as the preferred storage and display format for many types of graphic and pictorial art.

ALAN DONNITHORNE

2. EAST ASIA. The tradition of mounting works of art in East Asia began *c.* the 1st–2nd century AD in China with the construction of book rolls, comprising a series of images joined to form a long roll; these were intended to simplify storage. For the next five centuries the sole purpose of mounting was to strengthen paintings or texts.

(i) China. The Chinese hanging scroll is a remarkably complex object. Structurally it is three-dimensional when rolled and two-dimensional when unrolled. Mechanically, it must perform two distinct functions: it must be easily rolled and stored for extended periods without damage, and it must remain straight when hung for viewing. A scroll must also enhance the painting it supports: taste and style in scroll mountings changed as different influences were absorbed by artists and scroll mounters.

Chinese hanging scroll mountings are much thinner than those of Japan. Since the Cultural Revolution (1966–76) the range of silks available has been much reduced, and Chinese silks are generally thinner than those used in Japan, with plain-coloured silks or subtly patterned shadow silks (*ling zhi*) most extensively used. Rarely are more than two types of silk combined in a mounting, although

1. Japanese scroll painting of a Buddhist deity of music, watercolour on silk, 2.05×0.74 m, 15th century (London, British Museum)

occasionally a fine band of rich brocade is used to highlight the sides of the painting. The paper that supports the silk is also very thin. Usually sandalwood (*tan*) is used to produce a thin, smooth, short-fibred paper; it has little strength when wet and consequently is generally applied dry to a pasted painting (*see also* CHINA, §XIII, 18). Thin Chinese paper and silks are also ideally suited to the handscroll format (for both hanging scrolls and handscrolls *see* SCROLL, §1 and 2(i)).

Albums, in accordion or butterfly format, were used in China by the late 10th century for remounting calligraphy and painting. Later, artists painted directly on to them (*see* ALBUM, §1). Two types of fan, the rigid flat fan and the folding fan, were also used for mounting paintings (*see* FAN, §II).

(ii) Japan and Korea. Techniques for scroll mounting were first introduced into Japan from China in the 6th century AD, beginning with Buddhist texts mounted as handscrolls. Thereafter scroll mounting was influenced variously by architectural developments, Zen Buddhism and the Japanese tea ceremony (*see* JAPAN, §XIV). Different styles of mounting were devised according to the degree of formality of the painting subject: the most formal and complicated mounts, often featuring gold brocade and gilt fittings, were for Buddhist subjects (see fig. 1); the simplest, including those made entirely from paper, were for secular themes. Japanese scroll mounts use a much wider range of silks, brocades and damasks than Chinese; three distinct types of silk are often used together for hanging scrolls, with different weaves, colours, thicknesses and decorative motifs. Usually paper made from mulberry is used, which is long fibred and thin but very strong (*see* JAPAN, §XVI, 18). Adhesive is generally a gluten-free wheat-starch paste, but for the final layers of backing a dilute form of a ten-year aged starch paste is used. Papers are pounded together with a heavy brush to form a strong but flexible support. Japanese scrolls are usually given two or more lining layers. The proportions of Japanese mountings tend to be smaller than Chinese ones, as the absence of chairs in Japanese houses and the low ceilings tended to reduce the dimensions of the silk mount surrounding the painting (religious paintings hung in temples were longer). Nevertheless, the ratio between 'heaven' and 'earth' (*see* SCROLL, §1) remained constant: the upper band ('heaven') is always almost twice as wide as the lower band ('earth'). The same proportions occur in handscrolls, which in Japan rarely exceed 8 m in length.

Another pictorial format developed by the Japanese is that of the folding screen, commonly with two or eight folds. These, like Japanese sliding doors, are constructed using a cedar lattice covered in many layers of strong paper. They are never displayed flat, but opened out in a zigzag fashion; they need careful handling, as the hinges are constructed entirely from paper (*see* SCREEN (ii), §1).

The mounting tradition in Korea has suffered many interruptions, and there is no longer a particular style identifiable as Korean. The many Korean paintings in Japan generally have Japanese-style mountings, whereas those remaining in Korea seem to favour a thinner Chinese style of mount (*see also* KOREA, §IV, 1).

2. Tibetan *tangka* painting of a *maṇḍala* (circular ritual diagram), gouache on gesso cotton, mounted using Chinese brocades, 1.32×0.80 m, 19th century (London, British Museum); the protective veils are in a raised position at the top of the painting

(iii) Tibet. The Tibetan *tangka* (*see* TIBET, §IV) is a scroll painting in so far as it is rolled for storage and hung for display, but it lacks the structural sophistication of the Chinese or Japanese scroll. The image is invariably Tibetan Buddhist in theme and is painted on a gesso cotton in a type of gouache. It is set in a border of Chinese silk brocade, generally sewn into place rather than adhered; crude rollers often have brass terminals. In correspondence to the sanctity of the image, up to seven silk veils may be sewn to hang in front of it, serving to protect it from both dirt and profane eyes (see fig. 2).

BIBLIOGRAPHY

H. P. Bowie: *Japanese Painting* (New York, 1952)
N. J. Irons: *Fans of Imperial China* (Hong Kong, 1982)
Emaki Narrative Scrolls from Japan (exh. cat. by M. Murase, New York, Asia Soc. Gals, 1984)
P. Pal: *Tibetan Paintings* (London, 1984)
Treasures from Korea (exh. cat., ed. R. Whitfield, intro. R. Goepper; London, BM, 1984)
R. H. van Gulik: *Chinese Pictorial Art* (New York, 1989)

ANDREW THOMPSON

3. ISLAMIC LANDS AND INDIA. In the early Islamic era the texts of manuscripts and their borders were one continuous sheet, but by the 11th century rulings often separated the text block from the margin in manuscripts of the Koran and other books (*see* ISLAMIC ART, §III, 3). Perhaps as a result of the corrosive pigments (e.g. verdigris) used for marginal rulings, the paper often split, separating the text block from the borders. The necessity of repairing such damage seems to have led to the practice of setting the text, and later the illustrations, into new borders, thus providing mounts for manuscript pages. Separate margins are found in bound manuscripts and albums (Arab. *muraqqa'*; *see* ALBUM, §§2 and 3).

Carefully made mounts consist of two single sheets of paper with identical windows slightly smaller than the text or illustration that was affixed between them. On hastily crafted margins, four overlapping strips of paper surround the text or illustration on the *recto* of a folio, glued to four equivalent strips on the *verso*. The most celebrated Islamic and Indian mounts are borders from albums. The format of the standard album, established by the 15th century, consists of facing pages of calligraphy alternating with paintings or drawings mounted in borders with the same decorative patterns, even if the colour of the paper varies.

A typical mounting for an Islamic or Indian album page comprises three zones. In the centre is the text or picture. This then is surrounded by one or more narrow transitional borders, either plain or decorated with arabesques or cartouches of calligraphy: first comes a narrow border in strips pasted over the edges of the central zone, followed by two narrow coloured borders; the inner one, overlapped by the first border, likewise overlaps the outer. The wide outer borders, the third stage, are made from a thick sheet of laminated paper with a window cut in the centre or nearer the spine, overlapped on its inner edges by the outer transitional border. A folio-sized sheet would then be glued to the back, and the completed page would be joined to its *recto* or *verso*. Many albums, bound either in codex or concertina form, were intended to be expandable, and only the most expensive albums appear to have been planned as an entity.

Many album borders are made of coloured paper sprinkled with gold and are separated from the paintings by narrow bands of arabesque. Elaborate examples of border decoration produced in the royal studio under the SAFAVID dynasty of Iran include a copy of Sa'di's *Gulistān* ('Rose-garden'; *c.* 1525–30; dispersed) with fine border paintings of wild and mythical animals in a landscape painted in two shades of gold and silver on coloured paper. Such borders apparently inspired a whole class of marginal decoration in Safavid Iran as well as the courts of their contemporaries to the west and east, the Ottoman and Mughal dynasties. Similarly, borders with geometric and floral arabesques, the most common of Iranian decorative mounts, found favour under the Ottomans and Mughals in the 16th century and were adapted to fit local styles.

In an album produced for the Ottoman sultan Murad III (*reg* 1574–95; see fig. 3), the opulent variety of the floral arabesque and geometric borders rivals that of the finest Ottoman textiles and ceramics (*see* ISLAMIC ART, fig. 192). These borders are painted in gold and polychrome on coloured or plain paper. Two other forms of mounting used under the Ottomans are marbled borders and those with cut-out decoration. Marbled borders, which also figure in 17th-century Mughal albums, appear in many Ottoman books (*see* ISLAMIC ART, fig. 134), while cut-out decoration is found in the borders of the album compiled for the Englishman Peter Mundy (1618; London, BM, 1974 6–17 013).

Mughal artists adopted and maintained the various Persian styles of border decoration during most of the 16th century, but by 1599 leading artists under Prince Salim (later the emperor Jahangir, *reg* 1605–27) revolutionized the art of album mounts by creating border scenes ranging from European-inspired figures in landscapes to craftsmen producing a manuscript (*see* INDIAN SUBCONTINENT, fig. 265). Another distinctive feature associated with this workshop was the depiction of birds or flowers in polychrome on borders otherwise painted only in gold. These borders are found in the Gulshan Album (Tehran, Gulistan Pal. Lib.), the Berlin Album (Berlin, Staatsbib.) and a third album (Tehran, priv. col.). Under Jahangir's successor, Shah Jahan (*reg* 1628–58), a new style of border decoration developed. Consisting of polychrome flowering plants with gold outlines and recalling the pietra dura

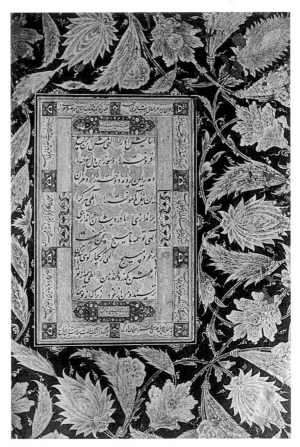

3. Islamic mounted page of calligraphy from an album assembled for the Ottoman sultan Murad III (*reg* 1574–95), gold on coloured paper, 334×222 mm, late 16th century (Vienna, Österreichische National-bibliothek, Codex Mixtus 313, fol. 17*v*)

inlay of contemporary buildings such as the Taj Mahal (*see* AGRA, §II, 1), these borders can be found in the Kevorkian Album (Washington, DC, Freer, and New York, Met.), the Wantage Album (London, V&A) and the Minto Album (London, V&A, and Dublin, Chester Beatty Lib.). The decoration of Islamic Indian album mounts from the late 17th century onwards was rarely innovative and derived mostly from earlier geometric and floral arabesque patterns.

BIBLIOGRAPHY

Enc. Islam/2: 'Murakka" [Album]
Wonders of the Age (exh. cat. by S. C. Welch, Cambridge, MA, Fogg, 1979–80)
M. C. Beach: *The Imperial Image: Paintings for the Mughal Court* (Washington, DC, 1981)
Y. Petsopoulos, ed.: *Tulips, Arabesques and Turbans: Decorative Arts from the Ottoman Empire* (London, 1982)
M. S. Simpson: 'The Production and Patronage of the *Haft Aurang* by Jami in the Freer Gallery of Art', *A. Orient.*, xiii (1982), pp. 93–119
S. C. Welch and others: *The Emperors' Album* (New York, 1987)
M. S. Simpson: 'Codicology in the Service of Chronology: The Case of Some Safavid Manuscripts', *Les Manuscrits du Moyen-Orient: Essais de codicologie et de paléographie*, ed. F. Déroche (Istanbul, 1989), pp. 133–7

SHEILA R. CANBY

4. WESTERN WORLD.

(i) Historical origins. In the West the mounting of graphic works of art began towards the end of the 15th century, when drawings and prints began to be collected in appreciable quantity. At first, drawings were no doubt kept loose or in portfolios in the artist's workshop. In this state many drawings would have become damaged as a result of excessive handling and may have been pasted to another sheet of paper as a means of preservation. As paper became cheaper, this method of mounting became more common, allowing works of differing sizes to be organized into one or more standard mount sizes. Later, as collections grew too large to handle in the form of loose sheets, they were frequently pasted into albums.

The most famous early collector and mounter of drawings was Giorgio Vasari (*see* VASARI, (1)), whose *Libro de' disegni* is referred to in *Le vite de' più eccelenti pittori, scultori ed architettori* (Florence, 1550). Although the five volumes of the *Libro* were subsequently broken up and the individual drawings dispersed, some 560 can be identified in present-day collections (see Kurz; Ragghianti Collobi). This task was much helped by Vasari's characteristic mounting style: a unique elaborate ornamental frame drawn in pen and wash round the margins of the drawing with an inscription giving the attribution and sometimes a pasted-in woodcut portrait of the artist (see fig. 4).

Vasari's example was followed by many later collectors, although few took the trouble to produce unique designs for each drawing. Some of the mounts of Padre SEBASTIANO RESTA have a pseudo-architectural border, but his mounts are also recognizable by a wash-line border, a style imitated by the artist and collector Jonathan Richardson the elder. These mounts, and those of his son Jonathan Richardson the younger (1694–1771), are characterized by a painted gold band abutting the edges of the drawing, surrounded by a series of ruled ink lines and a wide band of watercolour wash, in a colour chosen to complement

the general tone of the drawing. Similar styles were adopted by other English collectors.

A most distinctive mounting style was that of the French collector Pierre-Jean Mariette (*see* MARIETTE, (4)). The drawing was pasted to a thin, three-ply card with the space between the drawing and the edges of the mount filled with wide strips of blue paper. The design was completed with a band of gold leaf and ruled lines in black ink, the name of the artist being enclosed in an ornamental cartouche.

Other collectors who used characteristic styles of mount include EVERARD JABACH, Filippo Baldinucci, Pierre Crozat, John Talman (*see* TALMAN, (2)), Anton Maria Zanetti (i), Joshua Reynolds, Thomas Lawrence and William Young Ottley. Examples of their mounts are found in most public and private collections (see James and others). Many artists of the late 18th century and the early 19th also mounted their drawings and watercolours in a similar manner (see Nicholson).

(ii) Techniques. Even at an early date some drawings and prints were pasted to wooden, paperboard or textile supports and framed. Canvas linings were useful for displaying outsize works such as cartoons, and laying down on to calico was a cheaper and simpler means of mounting prints—by stretching them over a wooden strainer—until ready-made mounting board became commonly available in the second quarter of the 19th century. Exhibition watercolours were often mounted on stretched canvas and framed 'close' in an attempt to emulate the appearance of oil paintings (see Bayard). Later, it became common to show watercolours with a gilt 'slip' or 'flat' around the edge, inside the frame. Originally made of wood, these later came to be made of cardboard, the most commonly used type consisting of a core of inferior pulp covered on both sides with thin, good-quality paper.

Cardboard mounts usually consist of two parts: a backing sheet to which the print or drawing is attached and a cover sheet—often referred to as a 'mat'—in which an aperture or 'window' is cut to expose the work. The aperture, usually cut with a bevelled edge, is generally placed so that its geometric centre is higher than the centre of the sheet. Originally, hand-held knives were used, but by the mid-20th century various mount-cutting devices were available. These consist of a straight-edge with a sliding jig that holds the blade, together with some means of clamping the board. Modifications include wall-mounted units and devices for cutting circular and oval apertures. Some mounters also use metal templates for set sizes; these are particularly appropriate for photographs, for which many standard formats exist.

Once mounted, the work is usually fixed in a glazed frame. The mount therefore has two main functions: to provide a 'neutral' gap between the pictorial composition and its display surroundings, and to keep the surface of the work from touching the glass (most important in the case of 'soft' drawing media such as charcoal, pastel and chalks). This method of mounting was endorsed by John Ruskin in a letter to *The Times* of 28 October 1856, by which time artists' suppliers and stationers were already advertising various grades of 'mounting board'. Towards the end of the 19th century the fashion for gilt mounts

4. Page from Vasari's *Libro de' disegni*, with an *Allegorical Scene* (pen and grey-brown ink, 198×187 mm), formerly attributed to Vittore Carpaccio, mounted below a woodcut portrait of the artist; the mount itself is drawn in pen and brown ink and brown wash, over black chalk, and is inscribed *Anno 1495*, 571×442 mm, assembled after 1568 (London, British Museum)

gave way to plain cream or white (see Hardie), and in the 20th century there was a revival of wash-line decoration, applied to the surface of the mat itself. There has also been a proliferation in the variety of colours and surface textures of mounting board, including textile coverings. Unfortunately, the commercialization of mounting has had an adverse effect on the quality of the product. Early mounting boards, such as 'Bristol' board (see Krill), were made from good-quality fibre such as rags, but from 1850, following the introduction of mechanically processed woodpulp (an acidic material), the quality rapidly declined. It tended to be only in museums and galleries that finer, acid-free quality boards continued to be used to any great extent.

A slightly different style of cardboard mount is sometimes used in large public collections where the main method of storage of prints and drawings is by boxing rather than framing. This type of mount, called a 'raised', 'sunk' or 'solid' mount, was developed in the 1850s at the British Museum, London (see Willshire). The drawing or print is pasted around its edges to a backboard and the bevelled mat pasted solidly around the edges of the backboard, forming a kind of thin, wide tray with the art work 'sunk' into its centre. This type of mount affords adequate protection from the hazards of handling and protects the surface of the work from abrasion when several mounts are stacked together in their solander boxes.

A variety of methods and materials has been used to attach graphic works of art to their mounts. The traditional adhesive was flour paste, although animal glue and even sealing wax have been used. Some mounters used spots of paste at the corners, with extra spots along the edges for larger works. More careful mounters first adhered small rectangles of paper to the back of a drawing before attaching it to the mount, as is characteristic of Bouverie mounts (see 1991 exh. cat.). A later development was the continuous hinge or 'guard' of thin paper fixed around all four edges (see Plenderleith 1937 and 1952). An alternative method of attachment is by means of a false margin or 'inlay': the drawing is pasted around the edges to a sheet of paper with an aperture slightly smaller than the drawing, thus exposing the *verso* of the work (see Harding). Alternatively, the aperture in the margin may be cut just larger than the drawing and the latter attached to the inlay using narrow strips of thin paper, such as Japanese *kōzo* (mulberry) paper. In the case of double-sided drawings, a window may be cut in the back of the mount, incorporating a sheet of transparent acrylic plastic as glazing (earlier examples made use of hardened gelatin or cellulose acetate).

However, the most commonly recommended method of attachment is by means of paper hinges, Japanese papers being favoured because they are thin, strong and flexible. Hinges (see fig. 5) are either folded (like a stamp-hinge) or pendant (flat). In the latter case, the part of the hinge attached to the mount is visible, the print appearing to hang from it. Sometimes it is advisable to place another strip of Japanese paper at right angles over the pendant hinge, making a T-hinge. Pure starch paste is a recommended adhesive, although several cellulose ether gels, for

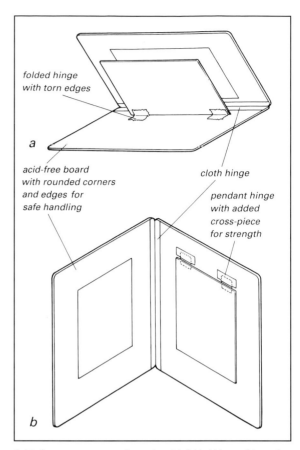

5. Modern museum mounting styles: (a) folded hinge; (b) pendant hinge

example methylcellulose, are also archivally durable. Animal glue, rubber and pressure-sensitive tapes should be avoided as these deteriorate, causing eventual staining of the art work. With hinged as well as inlaid material, it is customary to attach the mat to the backboard with a cloth hinge.

BIBLIOGRAPHY

G. Vasari: *Vite* (1550, rev. 2/1568); ed. G. Milanesi (1878–85)
F. Nicholson: *The Practice of Drawing and Painting Landscape from Nature in Watercolours* (London, 1820, 2/1823), pp. 96–105 [discussion of the mounting and varnishing of watercolours]
[J. Maberly]: *The Print Collector* (London, 1845, rev. 2/New York, 1880), chap. vi
W. H. Willshire: *An Introduction to the Study and Collection of Ancient Prints* (London, 1874)
J. Meder: *Die Handzeichnung: Ihre Technik und Entwicklung* (Vienna, 1919/R 1923); Eng. trans., rev. and ed. by W. Ames as *The Mastery of Drawing* (New York, 1978) [chap. 17 gives an account of the history of drawing collectors and collections]
F. Lugt: *Marques* (1921)
A. E. Popham: 'Sebastiano Resta and his Collections', *Old Master Drgs*, xli (1936), pp. 1–19 [18 pls]
O. Kurz: 'Giorgio Vasari's *Libro de' disegni*', *Old Master Drgs*, xlv (1937), pp. 1–15 [16 pls]; xlvii (1937), pp. 32–44 [16 pls]
H. J. Plenderleith: *The Conservation of Prints, Drawings and Manuscripts* (London, 1937), pp. 13–27
——: *The Conservation of Antiquities and Works of Art* (Oxford, 1952); rev. with A. E. A. Werner (Oxford, 1972)
M. Hardie: *Watercolour Painting in Britain*, 2 vols (London, 1956–67), ii, pp. 40–43
F. Lugt: *Marques*, suppl. (1956)

The figure labels read: folded hinge with torn edges; acid-free board with rounded corners and edges for safe handling; cloth hinge; pendant hinge with added cross-piece for strength; a; b.

C. Zigrosser and C. Gaehde: *A Guide to the Collecting and Care of Original Prints* (New York, 1965), pp. 99–109

E. G. Harding: *The Mounting of Prints and Drawings*, Museums Association Information Sheet, xii (London, 1972, rev. 2/1980)

A. F. Clapp: *The Curatorial Care of Works of Art on Paper* (Oberlin, 1973, rev. 2/1974, rev. 3/1978, rev.4/New York, 1987)

L. Ragghianti Collobi: *Il Libro de' disegni del Vasari* (Florence, 1974)

J. Bayard: *Works of Splendour and Imagination: The Exhibition Watercolour, 1770–1870* (New Haven, 1981)

A. Petrioli Tofani: 'I montaggi', *Restauro e conservazione delle opere d'arte su carta* (Florence, 1981), pp. 161–80 [eight illus. of various historical mounting styles]

M. A. Smith: *Matting and Hinging Works of Art on Paper* (Washington, DC, 1981)

L. Keefe and D. Inch: *The Life of a Photograph* (London and New York, 1984/R 1990) [incl. long section on techniques of mount-cutting]

D. Le Marois: 'Les Montages de dessins au XVIIIe siècle: L'Exemple de Mariette', *Bull. Soc. Hist. A. Fr.* (1984), pp. 87–96

M. H. Ellis: *The Care of Prints and Drawings* (Nashville, 1987), pp. 13–50

J. Krill: *English Artists' Paper* (London, 1987), pp. 139–41

C. Monbeig Goguel: 'Le Dessin encadré', *Rev. A.* [Paris], lxxvi (1987), pp. 25–31

C. James and others: *Manuale per la conservazione e il restauro di disegni e stampe antichi* (Florence, 1991) [chap. 1 gives well-illustrated descriptions of a great many mounting styles]

Drawings by Guercino from British Collections (exh. cat. by N. Turner and C. Plazzotta, London, BM, 1991), pp. 25ff [history of Bouverie collection mounts, formerly called 'Casa Gennari' mounts]

ALAN DONNITHORNE

Mt Izla. *See* Tur 'Abdin.

Mt Mai-chi. *See* Mt Maiji.

Mt Maiji [Mt Mai-chi; Maiji shan; Mai-chi shan]. Site of 194 Chinese Buddhist cave-temples, carved into the south cliff of Mt Maiji in Gansu Province. The area is prone to seismic activity, and the collapse of the central portion of the cliff during an earthquake in AD 734 divided the site into east and west sections. Access to the caves is by means of scaffold-like timber walkways. The cave temples house the second largest collection of Chinese clay statuary, after Dunhuang. While the figures follow the style of mainstream Chinese sculpture found at the central Chinese sites of Gong xian, Longmen and Yungang, the artists at Mt Maiji exercised more freedom and imagination in the modelling of the Buddhas and their groupings. The figures and walls were once painted, and about 900 sq. m of wall paintings survive, though in very poor condition.

The Buddhist activities at the site lasted from the 5th century AD to the Song period (960–1279). During later periods the main focus was on restoration, which continued until the Qing period (1644–1911). Of the 194 cave-temples, 89 were carved during the Northern Wei period (AD 386–534), and 42 during the Northern Zhou period (AD 557–81). The few remaining early 5th-century caves are on the west side and have conical ceilings. The figures in these caves have round faces and broad features. The Buddhas sit erect with shoulders square and legs crossed, their clothing consisting of a thick robe with rhythmic lines draped over an undergarment. Their *uṣṇīṣa*s (Buddha's cranial bump) and heads are shaved. The *bodhisattva*s stand erect with broad shoulders and narrow hips. They each wear a tall crown, neckwear, a scarf draped over the left shoulder and a *dhoti*-like garment marked by rhythmic lines over the lower body.

The caves built in the first quarter of the 6th century AD are mainly square but include a few rectangular caves

laid out in the same manner. In several caves the Buddhas are placed in deep niches carved into the walls. They are usually accompanied by monks or *bodhisattva*s, and all wear Chinese clothing. In some caves a stele bearing a Buddha carved in high relief is placed against a wall without a niche. An unusual feature of these caves is that the main image is accompanied by one monk or one *bodhisattva*, a break with traditional Buddhist iconography, in which the Buddha is accompanied by two *bodhisattva*s or two monks, or two *bodhisattva*s and two monks. In a few caves, images of Vajrāpaṇi (Buddha's protector in Ghandaran sculpture) accompany the Buddha. The walls outside the niches are often decorated with paintings or combinations of paintings and relief carvings. Stelae and clay figures were occasionally added in later periods. The clay figures from the late Northern Wei period project an intimacy that is unique to Mt Maiji: their faces are softly moulded, usually with the hint of a smile, and thick garments flow easily over their bodies, just as they do over the small figures of worshippers.

The second phase of activity at the site, during the Northern Zhou period, resulted in large, rectangular caves. The façades are elaborately carved in forms from Chinese architecture, sometimes decorated with larger-than-life figures of Vajrapani. Inside, deep niches are carved on the back walls. The expressions of the figures show restraint, and the intimacy of the Northern Wei figures is absent. The eyes are narrow slits that look downwards, and even the fierce expressions of the Vajrapani figures do not look outwards.

See also China, §III, 1(ii)(b) and Temple, §IV, 1(i).

BIBLIOGRAPHY

Y. Natori: *Bakusekisan sekkutsu* [Cave temples at Mt Maiji] (Tokyo, 1957)

M. Sullivan: *The Cave Temples of Maichishan* (Stanford, 1969)

The Cave Temples at Maichishan, Five Thousand Years of Chinese Art (Taipei, 1983)

Yan Wenru, ed.: *Maiji shan shiku* [Cave temples at Mt Maiji] (1984)

Chūgoku sekkustu: Bakusekisan sekkutsu [Chinese cave temples: cave temples at Mt Maiji], Tianshui Maiji shan Shiku Yishu Yanjiusuo (Tokyo, 1987)

MOLLY SIUPING HO

Mt Masius. *See* Tur 'Abdin.

Mt Song. *See under* Dengfeng.

Mt Tianlong [Mt T'ien-lung; Tianlong shan; T'ien-lung shan]. Cave temple site about 25 km south of Taiyuan in Shanxi Province, China. This complex of relatively small caves is carved in a fairly homogeneous style displaying Indian influences. It was discovered by the Japanese scholar Tadashi Sekino (1868–1935) in 1918 and subsequently studied and photographed extensively. Thereafter, most of the sculptures were stolen piecemeal and acquired for various collections throughout the world, notably the Fogg Art Museum, Cambridge, MA; the Museum of Fine Arts, Boston, MA; the Van der Heidt collection, Museum Rietberg, Zurich; the Nelson-Atkins Museum of Art, Kansas City, MO; the M. H. de Young Memorial Museum, San Francisco, CA; and the National Museum, Tokyo.

Most of the caves are dated stylistically to a span of approximately 300 years: Caves 1, 2, 3, 10 and 16 date to the Northern Qi period (AD 550–77), Cave 4 to the Sui period (581–618), and others to the Tang period (618–907). The Tang caves are further identified as comprising two groups chronologically 20 years apart. Osvald Sirén dated them to the early 7th century AD, but the Japanese placed them a century later. Only Cave 9 is much later, dating to the Liao (907–1125) or Song (960–1279) period.

The sculptures were carved in fine white sandstone in high or low relief. For the most part, they consisted of groups of three, five or seven images arranged symmetrically along three of the four walls of each cave. Additional monks and *lokapāla*s (guardian generals) were depicted in the later caves. General consistency in style suggests rapid execution of the figures according to an overall plan for each cave. In the Northern Qi caves *apsarasas* (celestial nymphs) and monks were carved in lower relief than the major deities. In general, faces are rounder and bodies plumper than contemporary examples at LONGMEN. Columnar figures, e.g. those from Cave 2, stand rigidly with their weight evenly distributed. Their frontality contrasts with the transitional triple bend posture of a *bodhisattva* from the west wall of Cave 3. The seated Buddha from the north wall of Cave 2 offers a prototype for the Japanese Tori Busshi-style sculpture of the HORYUJI temple and is also similar to that of Longmen.

Gupta influence (*see* INDIAN SUBCONTINENT, §V, 6) is especially strong in the Tang sculptures, carved either by Indian or Indian-trained artisans. For the first time the Indian aesthetic, which imparts a feeling of swelling life into sculpture, achieves a compromise with the Chinese sense of linear rhythm. Stone is treated almost like clay. Figures stand in relaxed *tribhanga* (contrapposto) or sit in versions of *lalitāsana* (posture of royal ease). The plasticity of Indian-style voluptuousness synthesizes with the plump Tang ideal beauty, as in the figures originally in Cave 14. Earlier linear tensions disappear, and there is a new regard for anatomy: although figures are still not anatomically correct, there is a sense of form and potential movement. For the first time, deities are depicted semi-nude, with transparent *dhoti*s (Indian garments) defining the body in clinging rhythmic patterns. Ornamental scarves and jewellery are directly related to Indian prototypes. The refinement of this earlier group of Tang sculptures in Cave 14 contrasts with the heaviness and clumsiness of the later group, illustrated by the figures of Cave 21.

BIBLIOGRAPHY

T. Sekino: 'Tenryuzan sekkutsu' [The grottoes at Mt Tianlong], *Kokka*, 375 (1921)

S. Tanka: *Tenryuzan sekkutsu* [The grottoes at Mt Tianlong] (1922)

O. Sirén: *Chinese Sculpture from the Fifth to the Fourteenth Century*, 4 vols (London, 1925/R New York, 1970), pls 206–29, 293–9, 485–504

D. Tokiwa and T. Sekino: *Shina bukkyō shiseki* [Buddhist monuments in China], iii (Tokyo, 1926), pp. 17–35

Sadajirō Yamanaka: *Tenryuzan sekibutsu* [Stone Buddhas at Mt Tianlong] (Osaka, 1928)

H. Vanderstappen and M. Rhie: 'The Sculpture of Tien Lung Shan: Reconstruction and Dating', *Artibus Asiae*, xxvii/3 (1964–5), pp. 189–220

MARY S. LAWTON

Mt T'ien-lung. *See* MT TIANLONG.

Mt Washington Glass Works. American glass factory founded in 1837 by Deming Jarves (1790–1869), who was also instrumental in establishing the New England Glass Co. and the Boston & Sandwich Glass Co. Located in South Boston, the Mt Washington Glass Works was operated by Luther Russell until his death. Jarves's son, George D. Jarves, was a partner in the firm with others from 1846 until it was sold in 1861 to William L. Libbey (1827–83) and Timothy Howe (*d* 1866). In 1866 Libbey became sole proprietor, and in 1870 he moved the works to a modern factory in New Bedford, MA. Although the early products were apparently mundane, including lamps, tubes for table lamps, shades and table glass, the art wares produced after 1880 established the firm's reputation. Beginning in 1878 the company patented several types of opal and shaded effects including 'Lava', 'Burmese', 'Peachblow', 'Albertine', 'Royal Flemish' and 'Crown Milano'. Often these wares were fitted with silver-plated covers or holders. In the 1880s the company agent Frederick Stacey Shirley promoted the firm's place as a leading manufacturer of art glass.

In 1894 the firm was purchased by the Pairpoint Manufacturing Co. Established in 1880, Pairpoint had been using Mt Washington glass as inserts and shades for its silver-plated products. This association continued until 1938, when a former glassworker, Robert M. Gundersen, purchased the glassworks from a salvage company that had obtained it from Pairpoint. Under Gundersen the glassworks flourished until his death in 1952. Glassmaking ceased when the property was condemned in 1957.

BIBLIOGRAPHY

K. M. Wilson: *New England Glass and Glassmaking* (New York, 1972)

ELLEN PAUL DENKER

Mt Wenshu [Wen-shu]. *See under* JIUQUAN.

Mt Wutai [Mt Wu-t'ai; Wutai shan; Wu-t'ai shan]. Monastic site in Wutai County in the north-east of Shanxi Province, China, approximately 150 km north-east of the provincial capital, Taiyuan. It is one of the four Buddhist holy mountains and centres of Buddhist pilgrimage of China (the others are Mt Emei, Sichuan Province; Mt Putuo, Zhejiang Province; and Mt Jiuhua, Anhui Province). Manjushri (Wenshu), *bodhisattva* of wisdom, is said to have appeared on Mt Wutai, whose major temples are therefore devoted to the deity. As Manjushri is a favoured deity of Lamaist Buddhism, Mt Wutai was also a major place of pilgrimage for Lamaist Mongols from Inner Mongolia, which borders Shanxi Province to the north.

Five major peaks (about 3000 m above sea-level) surround a depression in which stands Taihuai zhen, now the centre of a much diminished Buddhist community. During the Tang Period (AD 618–907), when Buddhism was at the height of its power in China, and Japanese and Korean monks came on pilgrimages, over 200 temples were set in an area of some 250 sq. km; by the late 20th century only 47 were reasonably well preserved. The persecution of Buddhism in AD 845 badly affected Mt Wutai, and in subsequent periods—notably the Ming (1368–1644) and Qing (1644–1911)—imperial patronage was restricted to the temples around Taihuai zhen. Some more distant temples survived, however, and lack of imperial patronage meant that they were preserved without extensive rebuilding.

The two earliest surviving timber halls in China are the main hall of the Nanchan Temple (Nanchan si) in Lijia zhuang, built in AD 782, and the main hall of the Foguang Temple (Foguang si; *see* CHINA, §II, 2(iv) and fig. 20) near Doucun xiang, built in AD 857; both dates are inscribed on roof beams in the halls.

The main hall of the Nanchan Temple is a small three-bay (*jian*) building standing on a high brick platform. It is roughly square in plan, 11.6×9.9 m, with a gabled half-hipped roof, the main and subsidiary ridges built up with flat grey tiles and an incurling owl's tail (*chiwei*) at each end of the main ridge. Unusually, the central bay is considerably wider than the side bays, a feature rarely seen in later Chinese building but which adds grandeur to the small hall. The façade of the central bay and its door are timber, the side bays have brick apron walls surmounted by lattice windows with a simple row of vertical timbers. It is probable that the façade is a modern reconstruction in the style of the Tang Period (probably based on wall paintings at the Buddhist cave-temple at Dunhuang, Gansu Province), since photographs in the first site report (*Wenwu cankao ziliao*, 11, 1954, pp. 38–43) show a brick façade with arched windows. The projecting eaves are supported on bracket sets (*dougong*) on top of the columns, with no intercolumnar bracketing. There are no interior columns, and there is no ceiling, so the roof construction is visible. It reveals the inverted V-post positioned on top of the highest cross beam (replaced in later periods by the king post), a feature of Tang Period building. The stucco figures in the hall, a Buddha flanked by Manjushri, Samantabhadra (the *bodhisattva* of universal benevolence) and attendant *bodhisattva*s and guardians, also date to the Tang Period.

The main hall of the Foguang Temple is a far grander building, seven bays wide (all the bays of equal span) and four bays deep, with interior columns and a remarkable eaves projection (about 7 m beyond the columns of the façade), necessitating bracket sets with cantilevers (*ang*) and bracket sets between the columns. Inside the hall are frescoes and stucco figures, also said to date from the Tang Period. The adjoining Manjushri (Wenshu) Hall, dedicated to Manjushri, is of the Jin Period (1115–1234).

Other important buildings in the Mt Wutai area are mostly found in Taihuai zhen. The Tayuan Temple, which has a pagoda in the courtyard, is dominated by a massive 50 m-high white dagoba in the courtyard of which the original date of construction is unknown but which was rebuilt in the Wanli reign (1573–1619) of the Ming Dynasty. A smaller dagoba is said to contain the hair of Manjushri, and the two-storey library building houses a wooden revolving *sūtra* bookcase of 33 'storeys'. The nearby Xiantong Temple includes a two-storey brick-vaulted hall of the Ming Period, unusual in that Chinese architecture was dominated by timber construction: other examples include the Beamless Hall (Wuliang dian) in Nanjing (Jiangsu Province) and side halls at the Shuangta Temple, Taiyuan. On one of the upper terraces of the same temple is a miniature hall (1573–1620; just over 5 m high) constructed entirely from cast bronze in imitation of timber. The interior is covered with tiny Buddhas: externally, the window lattices, door panels with carved bird-and-flower designs and details of architectural construction are rendered both accurately and elegantly. The bronze hall is flanked by two Ming Period bronze pagodas (of the dagoba type).

BIBLIOGRAPHY
Liang Sicheng: 'Ji Wutai shan Foguang si jianzhu' [On the four buildings of the Foguang Temple at Mt Wutai], *Bull. Soc. Res. Chin. Archit.*, vii (1945), nos 1 and 2
Qi Yingtao: 'Liang nian lai Shanxi sheng xin faxian de gu jianzhu' [An ancient building discovered within the last two years in Shanxi province], *Wenwu cankao ziliao* (1954), no. 11, pp. 38–43
M. Rhie: *The Fo-kuang ssu: Literary Evidences and Buddhist Images* (London and New York, 1977)
Wutai shan (Beijing, 1984)

FRANCES WOOD

Mounychia. *See under* PEIRAEUS.

Moura y Corte Real, Manuel de, 2nd Marqués de Castel Rodrigo. *See* CASTEL RODRIGO.

Moure, Francisco de (*b* Santiago de Compostela, *c.* 1576; *d* Monforte de Lemos, 1636). Spanish sculptor. He spent his life in Galicia, remaining based in Orense after moving there as a child. In Orense he trained under Alonso Martinez de Montanchez (*fl* 1594–before 1615), but as early as 1598 he was already accepting commissions, including the *St Roque* in Orense Cathedral. Moure visited Castile, where he was deeply influenced by the work of Juan de Juni, and this is apparent in the retable with the figure of *St Esteban* (1603) for the church in Villar de Sandias. Moure's work slowly developed towards an expressive and detailed realism, which led him to depict hair and wrinkles, veins and tendons as well as blood and tears in an almost exaggerated manner; this is seen in *St Bartolomé* of 1608 in S Maria de Beade, Rivadavia, and later in the *St Mary of Egypt* (1621–5) in the choir-stalls of Lugo Cathedral. In 1615 he carved five retables, including the high altar, in the monastery of Samos, Lugo, of which two have survived, those dedicated to the *Immaculate Conception* and *St Benito*, with the figures of *St John the Baptist* and *St Catherine*. In 1621 he received his most important commission, the choir-stalls of Lugo Cathedral; the reliefs carved in walnut include a fine *Coronation of the Virgin*, a *Virgin Appearing to St Bernardo* and panels of the *Apostles*; all are remarkable for their vivid realism and expressive qualities. In 1625 Moure carved the principal retable for the Jesuit Colegio del Cardenal in Monforte de Lemos. This work was completed by his son, also named Francisco, after Moure's death in 1636.

BIBLIOGRAPHY
C. Cid: 'El escultor Francisco de Moure', *Bol. Com. Prov. Mnmts Orense*, vii (1923–5), pp. 273–300
P. Pérez Constanti: *Diccionario de artistas que florecieron en Galicia durante los siglos XVI y XVII* (Santiago de Compostela, 1930), p. 398
Francisco de Moure (exh. cat. by F. Fariña Busto and M. D. Vila Jato, Orense, Mus. Arqueol. Prov., 1977)

G. RAMALLO ASENSIO

Mourner. *See* WEEPER.

Mouron, Adolphe Jean-Marie. *See* CASSANDRE.

Mousa. Fortified stone tower (broch) of the 1st century BC–2nd century AD on the small island of Mousa off the east coast of mainland Shetland, Scotland. The isolated location has contributed to the outstanding state of preservation of this broch, which was built on a rocky promontory with its entrance facing the sea; another broch stood on the opposite coast across the sound. Mousa is virtually intact and demonstrates the height that could be achieved by the unique drystone building method used for brochs, in which an inner and an outer skin of walling were bonded together by horizontal lintels. It was cleared of debris in 1861, but few artefacts were found and no precise dating evidence was obtained.

The tower is 15.0 m in external diameter and it rises to a height of 13.3 m; its original height was probably *c.* 15 m. An entrance at the base is the only opening into this formidable building. The wall is 4.5 m thick at the base and narrows as it rises, creating a smoothly tapering profile. At floor-level, the interior of the tower is 6.1 m in diameter, and there are doorways into three oval cells within the thickness of the wall. Two ledges run round the internal wall-face and these are thought to have supported a timber gallery. There is no evidence as to whether the tower was roofed. The wall is solidly built to a height of 3.7 m, thereafter rising as a double wall with a hollow core, the two faces bonded at intervals of *c.* 2 m by stone lintels. These form a series of galleries, through which a stair leads upwards to the top of the tower. Mousa was later modified internally before being abandoned at some time before the mid-1st millennium AD. Icelandic sagas relate that it was used as a defensive refuge by Norsemen on two occasions in the 10th and 11th centuries AD.

BIBLIOGRAPHY

Inventory of Shetland, Royal Commission on the Ancient Monuments of Scotland (Edinburgh, 1946), pp. 48–55

ANNA RITCHIE

Moustiers. French centre of faience production. The commercial success of the potteries in Moustiers, Provence, was ensured by an abundance of local clay, ample wood for kilns and a nearby market at Beaucaire. Earthenware was manufactured by the mid-17th century, and tin-glazing was probably introduced by Italian maiolica potters. Pierre Clérissy (1651–1728) first produced faience *c.* 1679, and the factory was managed by four succeeding generations. At least 12 other potteries operated in Moustiers, many founded by workers trained at the Clèrissy factory. The ceramic body is finer than that of the rival potteries in Rouen, and the glaze is bright white. During the early period blue-and-white wares decorated with armorial or historical scenes, based on engravings by the Italian printmaker Antonio Tempesta, were produced; from *c.* 1710 wares decorated with strapwork and lambrequin borders in the style of Jean Bérain I were predominant (e.g. faience dish, *c.* 1710; London, BM). In 1738 another factory was founded by Joseph Olerys (1697–1749), formerly director of the factory in Alcora, Spain, who introduced the fashion for high-fired polychrome decoration in the Spanish tradition; the wares have a distinctive palette of yellow, green and purple (e.g. faience dish, *c.* 1750–60; Paris, Louvre). Two potters from the Olerys factory, Joseph Fouque (*b* 1720) and Jean-François Pelloquin (1715–75), founded their own factory in 1749. The soft palette of high-fired colours, however, had fallen from fashion by the 1780s. The factory of the Ferrat brothers (est. 1718) popularized chinoiserie motifs in the last quarter of the century and imitated the bright palette of faience

and porcelain from Strasbourg. Only the factory of Gaspard Férand (est. 1779) produced wares in the Neoclassical style. The industry had dwindled by the 19th century, but from *c.* 1970 the production of tin-glaze was revived.

BIBLIOGRAPHY

J. Mompeut: *Les Faïences de Moustiers du XVIIe siècle à nos jours* (Aix-en-Provence, 1980)

ELLENOR ALCORN

Movimento arte concreta [MAC]. Italian art movement founded in Milan in December 1948 by the critic (and at that time painter) Gillo Dorfles (*b* 1910), the artist and architect Gianni Monnet (1912–58; the originator and leader of the group), Bruno Munari and Atanasio Soldati (1896–1953), a painter who had been working in an abstract idiom during the 1930s. They were inspired by the growth of CONCRETE ART in Switzerland and immediately attracted a large following with other Italian artists, among them Galliano Mazzon (*b* 1896), Luigi Veronesi, Mario Nigro (*b* 1917), Mauro Reggiani (*b* 1897), Ettore Sottsass and Amalia Garau. In Turin, Naples and Florence, other groups of Concrete artists formed that had links with the Milan group, which disbanded after Monnet's death in 1958. MAC had no rigid programme or manifesto: despite its name, its adherents did not discriminate rigorously between what they termed 'Concrete art' and more generic abstract or geometric art, which did not flourish in Italy. In Milan the group brought together those few artists who had rejected the tradition of Novecento Italiano and who did not accept the artistic and ideological attitudes of social realism. Similarly, some years after its foundation, when non-representational art became prominent, MAC defended the positions of rationalism and perceptive rigour and was in fact responsible for the diffusion in Italy of the theories of Gestalt psychology and rejected automatism, irrationalism and profusion of sentiment in nonfigurative works. MAC's theoretical antagonism towards non-representational art was not, however, borne out coherently in the works produced by its members, which, particularly after 1954, reflected the influence of action painting. The most interesting of MAC's activities was the publication of their monthly and, from 1954, annual bulletins, the graphics, typography and layout of which were truly innovative: they included such features as a square format, transparent paper and pages cut into shapes or sewn together (for which Munari was mainly responsible), and they contained articles on design, on visual perception, on the synthesis of the arts and on the reproducibility of art work.

WRITINGS

Arte concreta (1948–53)
Documenti d'arte oggi (1954–8)
G. Monnet: *L'arte moderna dall'A alla Z* (Milan, 1955)

BIBLIOGRAPHY

P. Fossati: *Il movimento arte concreta* (Turin, 1980)
M. Meneguzzo: *Il MAC, 1948/1958: Direzioni, contraddizioni e linee di sviluppo di una poetica aperta* (Ascoli Piceno, 1981)
L. Caramel: *MAC* (Milan, 1984)

MARCO MENEGUZZO

Movimento Italiano per l'Architettura Razionale. *See* MIAR.

Movimento nucleare. *See* ARTE NUCLEARE.

Moya, Hidalgo. *See under* POWELL AND MOYA.

Moyne de Morgues, Jacques Le. *See* LE MOYNE DE MORGUES, JACQUES.

Moynihan, Rodrigo (*b* Tenerife, Canary Islands, 17 Oct 1910; *d* 6 Nov 1990). English painter. He lived in the USA and Rome before studying at the Slade School of Fine Art, London (1928–31). Early acclaim in the 1930s resulted from his part in the formation of the OBJECTIVE ABSTRACTION group. With the development of Social Realism in the late 1930s, Moynihan abandoned abstraction as increasingly isolating and from 1937 became closely associated with the Euston Road School.

As Official War Artist (1943), ARA (1944) and Professor of Painting at the Royal College of Art, London (1948–57), Moynihan received important portrait commissions, but his large group portrait, *The Teaching Staff of the Painting School at the Royal College of Art, 1949–50* (2.13×3.35 m; London, Tate), is particularly remarkable for its centralized composition and treatment of the figures, who each assume an individual pose; in the far left in the background is a self-portrait. In the mid-1950s Moynihan again painted abstract pictures such as *Red Painting, February 1959* (priv. col., see 1978 exh. cat., p. 42). After working in a richly impastoed style with a lighter palette, *c.* 1961 he adopted smoother surfaces with broad areas of saturated colour punctuated by personal symbols or motifs. From 1964 to 1968 he was an editor for the journal *Art and Literature*.

In the early 1970s Moynihan returned to figuration, taking as his preferred subject his unordered studio shelves in works such as *Oval Still-life: Roll of Paper and Paintbox* (1974–5; priv. col., see 1978 exh. cat., p. 52). His tools and materials are precisely depicted in austere and sombre tones, viewed obliquely throwing the horizontal plane into deep perspective. He also turned again to portraits of friends, to self-portraits, and to commissioned portraits such as that of *Margaret Thatcher* (1983; London, N.P.G.). From 1957 Moynihan lived and worked in France, Spain, the USA and Britain.

WRITINGS

'Abstract Background—A Self Interview', *ARTnews Annu.*, 65 (1966), pp. 41, 65–6

BIBLIOGRAPHY

Rodrigo Moynihan: Still-life Paintings (exh. cat., intro. R. Rosenblum; London, Fischer F.A., 1973)
Rodrigo Moynihan: A Retrospective Exhibition (exh. cat., essay L. Gowing, interview D. Sylvester; London, RA, 1978) [excellent pls]
Rodrigo Moynihan: Recent Paintings (exh. cat.; London, Fischer F.A., 1982)

INGRID SWENSON

Moyon (*fl* Paris, 1825–38). French dealer and print-publisher. From 1825 to 1838 he conducted business at his premises at 5, Rue de l'Université, Paris. The first artist with whom he was particularly associated was Jean-Augustin Franquelin (1798–1839), who was also admired by the art historian and collector Alexandre du Sommerard. In 1827 Moyon sent two genre subjects by Franquelin to the Salon and in 1831 he sent four, one of which (untraced) was a scene from Pierre-Augustin de Beaumarchais's play *Le Mariage de Figaro* depicting Comtesse Almaviva drying Chérubin's tears. Such other dealers as François-Simon-Alphonse Giroux, Amédée Susse, Jean Marie Fortuné Durand-Ruel, Louis-Auguste Asse and P. Souty followed suit in buying these pleasant and undemanding works and in the 1830s regularly submitted Franquelin's paintings to the Salons. Moyon, however, continued to send the largest number of Franquelin's works, some of which reappeared in his closing sale; this suggests, in view of their evident popularity, that he had not intended them for sale but rather for hire, probably for the purposes of copying. Several landscapes, which were also a specialization of his gallery, were certainly intended for this purpose. He owned almost the entire oeuvre of Jules Coignet (1798–1860), which consisted primarily of studies and paintings of trees, rocks, plants and architectural fragments, and he also issued a collection of lithographs of landscape studies, some of which were after Coignet. His gallery was particularly associated with studies of this kind, which were made available for the use of artists. He also kept a stock of works popular at the time, such as paintings of Gothic interiors by Charles Arrowsmith (*b* 1798) and Charles Renoux (1795–1846) and literary subjects by Alexander Colin and Camille Roqueplan. Moyon's business expanded in the early years of the July Monarchy (1830–48); by 1832 it was advertised as being under the patronage of one of the royal princesses, and by 1835 he was listing the opening hours of his gallery, a new practice. However, his business may have started to lose money, as on 12–14 December 1837 and 16–18 January 1838 he wound up his affairs with a sale of his entire stock.

LINDA WHITELEY

Moysis, Costanzo de. *See* COSTANZO DA FERRARA.

Mozambique, People's Republic of [República de Moçambique]. Country in south-eastern Africa bordered by Tanzania to the north, Malawi, Zambia and Zimbabwe to the west and South Africa and Swaziland to the west and south. Its eastern border comprises a 2000 km Indian Ocean shoreline. The capital is Maputo (formerly Lourenço Marques), founded in 1545. The country gained independence from Portuguese colonization in 1975.

1. Geography and cultural history. 2. Sculpture. 3. Painting. 4. Architecture. 5. Art institutions.

1. GEOGRAPHY AND CULTURAL HISTORY. Mozambique's total area of 784,961 sq. km includes a 300 km-wide coastal strip, temperate uplands and the Zambezi Valley and Basin, which has some swampy, malarial areas. The country has high temperatures and a monsoon climate. Of the 15,200,000 inhabitants (est. 1989), 85% live in rural areas. The main ethnic groups are Makua-Lomwe (40%) and Tsonga (24%). Traditional African religions are followed by 60% of Mozambicans; 20% are Christian and 15% Muslim. The official language is Portuguese.

Although abundant stone and rock paintings bear witness to earlier, nomadic societies, the present population mainly descends from Bantu agriculturalist immigrants, who settled in the first centuries AD. From AD 900 Arab, Persian and Swahili gold and ivory traders established settlements along the coast and the rivers. In 1498

Vasco da Gama initiated 450 years of Portuguese colonial rule, slave trading and conscript labour. Upon independence the multiracial Frente de Libertação de Moçambique (FRELIMO) government was established. In the early 1990s Mozambique turned into a multi-party state with a market economy policy.

Traditional Mozambican art was intimately related to self-supporting farming societies, where craftsmen made wooden domestic utensils and decorated them with geometric motifs and inlays. Such traditional ritual objects as wooden masks, beadwork worn by women during ceremonies and calabashes covered with beadwork, which were used as medicine containers, were also developed and continued to be made into the 1990s. Others are no longer made, for example the woven and dyed textile art, with its expressive geometrical and figurative design, which was once produced in Zambezia Province.

This entry covers the art produced in the area since colonial times. For art of the region in earlier periods *see* AFRICA, §VII, 8. *See also* MAKONDE.

2. SCULPTURE. While only the work of modern Makonde sculptors has become widely known, Mozambican sculpture has a longer and richer history. In early colonial times authentic carvings were sought after as souvenirs by foreign missionaries and administrators. They were also shown at colonial exhibitions in Europe. This market was at first supplied with sculpture and furniture made from valuable wood, often with talent and skill, especially in northern Mozambique. A mass immigration of Portuguese settlers in the 1940s contributed to an expansion in this activity. Unfortunately, increasing demand has, largely, reduced the quality of the sculptures and confined production to decorative objects, stereotyped Christian saints, busts of colonialists and figures from African nature or village life. Around the capital, however, one type of carving for ritual and domestic use (the *Psikelekhedana*), which developed in the early 20th century and is now produced as a souvenir, has retained a certain vitality. Popular motifs include animals, warriors and masks carved from whitewood and then burnt or painted black and red.

Late 20th-century Mozambican sculpture is rooted in rural and historical beliefs. Local carvings and traditional Makonde art inspired artists and encouraged them in their use of wood, while the struggle against colonialism provided such new subjects as the disasters of war and poverty. An appreciation of the qualities inherent in the wood is a feature of both traditional and later carvings. This awareness is seen in the work of such artists as Chissano (*b* 1936), who began his career in 1965. His groups of figures appear to be extracted from, rather than imposed on, the grain of the wood. The sculptures of Naftal Langa (*b* 1933) tell stories of love and family life, his figures softly, even tenderly linked in contrast with the aggressive, straggling works of Gowane (*b* 1954). Sansão Makamo (*b* 1957) dramatically reduces human figures to a few gestures of hands and faces, while the ceramic work of Reinata Chadimba (*b* 1945) is based on tradition and integrates geometric design with human and animal forms. The 'surreal' cement sculptures of Massinguitana (*b* 1926) have also attracted international attention.

3. PAINTING. At the end of World War II the colonial intelligentsia launched cultural action against the 'back to the origin' movement. A painting movement appeared, which emanated from the Maputo artists' association Núcleo de Arte and can be seen as the rise of modern Mozambican painting. Bertina Lopes (*b* 1927), a black drawing teacher, was the first Mozambican painter to offer local socio-political appeal. After two appearances in collective exhibitions, the first black painter of repute, Malangatana Valente Ngwenya (*b* 1936), who was to be influential in later years, appeared in his own exhibition in 1960. The outbreak of guerrilla war in northern Mozambique in the mid-1960s, resulting in the colonial regime's brutal repression, paradoxically fostered the emergence of Mozambican art. Artists working in this oppressive regime produced representations of their fears and anxieties using distorted bodies in crowded compositions that resembled the swarming figures in Makonde sculptures, for example Malangatana's *Requiem for Flower-growers on Bomb-torn Lands* (see fig.), dedicated to Picasso on the centenary of his birth. During the independence struggles Mankeu Mahumana (*b* 1934) painted naturalistic records of the hardship caused by starvation and mutilation. After the

Malangatana Valente Ngwenya: *Requiem for Flower-growers on Bomb-torn Lands*, oil on canvas, 1.00×0.58 m, 1981 (Maputo, Museu de Arte)

liberation he used more varied colours and rounded forms to portray such themes as the role of women in preparing for a new society. Other artists who portrayed a heroic, suffering people include Abdias Muchanga (*b* 1942), Shikhani (*b* 1934) and Sansão Cossa (*b* 1946). The latter's scenes from traditional life are related to Mankeu's early work in their use of earth colours.

The generation of artists that emerged in Mozambique after independence was conscious of both its heritage and recent political events. The realistic paintings of Neto (né Ernesto Tembe; *b* 1960) show his anthropological awareness as well as his technical skill. One of the spokesmen for the colonized, Idasse (*b* 1955), created drawings and paintings imbued with ritual and tradition, while Nurdino Ubisse (*b* 1957), after studies at the Universidad Complutense, Madrid (1986–7), used a Cubist-inspired pictorial language to portray his victorious, though suffering, compatriots. The paintings and batiks of Fernando Rosa (*b* 1957) convey a similar sensitivity to recent events in their portrayal of the impact of social change on traditional rural life. Delicate depictions of daily life in colonial Lourenço Marques by Isabel Martins (*b* 1950) contrast with her sad pictures of a terrorist-haunted Maputo.

A strong interest in social and physical human relations is apparent in the work of Samate (*b* 1939), whose paintings convey a sense of space that is echoed in his metal sculptures, and in that of the painter Robert Chichorro (*b* 1941), in his scenes of a coarse but cheerful suburban life. Naguib (*b* 1953) depicted mainly sensuous women in warm colours, while the work of Victor Sousa (*b* 1952) includes ceramics and paintings of different colours and moods in which music and, later, sensual presentations of the figure play an important part. The naive painter Estevão Mucavele (*b* 1941) re-created memories of South Africa, using a palette knife to apply thick layers of paint.

Graphic artists Gilberto Cossa (*b* 1961) and Francisco Conde (*b* 1957) are also known as painters. In recent years artists have turned to abstraction as a means of expression, a style that was earlier followed only by Eugénio Lemos (*b* 1930) and Fátima Fernandes (*b* 1955). A wide range of posters, comic strips and murals (the most impressive example, 6×95 m, is situated near Maputo airport) take inspiration from the liberation struggle and the consolidation of independence. Art of this type is vital for information and education in a still largely illiterate society; much of it is of a high artistic quality.

4. ARCHITECTURE. Traditional architectural forms include round or square straw-covered huts and the Arab-influenced, rectangular, flat-roofed house. Portuguese rule brought European and Indian construction and decorative elements to upper-class housing, trading houses and institutions. In Nampula Province the world heritage monument Ilha de Moçambique is a fairly well-preserved, 400-year-old town, with traditional palm-thatched houses and brick buildings in Euro-Indian inspired styles. In Maputo colonial buildings include such landmarks as Mercado Municipal (1903; by architects David & Carvalho), Casa de Ferro (an early 20th-century iron house imported from Belgium), the railway station (1916; by M. Weiga, A. A. Lisboa de Lima and J. C. Ferreira da

Costa) and Hotel Clube (1898; by Eduardo de Almeida Saldanha), as well as Functionalist enclaves from the 1950s and high-rise blocks from the 1960s. In the late 1950s Amancio Guedes added Macua, Tsonga and Maconde patterns to his buildings. José Forjas adapted a country club into the Presidential Palace. In 1991 the first architects, including Miguel Cesar, Maria do Rosario, João Tique and Victor Tomaz, graduated from Maputo School of Architecture (founded 1986).

5. ART INSTITUTIONS. In Maputo the Museu de História Natural (founded 1911), part of the university, has an ethnographic collection, and the Museu de Arte (founded 1976, opened 1985), houses *c.* 1000 works, including colonial period pieces, paintings, sculptures and drawings. Other important art centres are the Museu de Nampula (founded 1956), the Museu Municipal (in Beira; founded 1960s), the Palácio de São Paolo (founded 1971) and the Museu de Arte Sacra (founded 1969), Ilha de Moçambique. Collections of contemporary art are owned by such bodies as Telecomunicações de Moçambique, Linhas Aéreas de Moçambique and Banco de Moçambique. In addition, the studios of Malangatana (Bairro do Aeroporto, Rua Luís de Camões) and Chissano (Bairro Sial, Rua Tórres Valles) can also be regarded as museums, housing a variety of contemporary Mozambican art.

In the early 1990s exhibitions, workshops and other art programmes were arranged by the Museu de Arte and the artists' association Núcleu de Arte, as well as Casa Velha, Centro de Estudos Brasileiros and such galleries as Afritique, Circulo and Associação Moçambicana de Fotografia (all Maputo).

In the late 1970s the school of general cultural education, Centro de Estudos Culturais, Maputo, opened a graphic design department, and from 1983 a three-year art course in textile, ceramic and graphic arts was offered at the Escola de Artes Visuais. In the 1990s students relied on scholarships for studies abroad for advanced art education. The university in Maputo offers a three-year course for drawing teachers entering the general school system.

BIBLIOGRAPHY

B. Schneider: 'Massinguitana of Mozambique', *Afr. A.*, x/1 (1976), pp. 24–9

Ilha de Moçambique Report: 1982-5 [pubd by Secretaria de Estado da Cultura, Mozambique, and School of Architecture, Århus, Denmark; Port. and Eng. text]

A. Sachs: *Images of a Revolution* (Harare, 1983)

A. *Ilha de Moçambique em perigo de desaparecimento* (exh. cat., Lisbon, Fund. Gulbenkian, 1983)

Semana de Moçambique no Estoril (exh. cat., Estoril, Casino, 1983)

Moçambique: Arte di un popolo (exh. cat., ed. E. Corsa; Rome, Pal. Venezia, 1986)

E. A. Alpers: 'Representation and Historical Consciousness in the Art of Modern Mozambique', *Can. J. Afr. Stud.*, xxii/1 (1988), pp. 73–94

Mozambique! (exh. cat., ed. K. Danielsson; Stockholm, Kulthuset, 1988)

Art/Images in Southern Africa (exh. cat., ed. K. Danielsson; Stockholm, Kulthuset, 1989)

B. Sahlström: *Political Posters in Ethiopia and Mozambique: Visual Imagery in a Revolutionary Context*, Acta Universitas Upsaliensis, n. s. 24 (Stockholm, 1990)

Art from the Frontline: Contemporary Art from Southern Africa (exh. cat., Glasgow, A.G. & Mus.; Salford, Mus. & A.G.; Dublin, City Cent.; London, Commonwealth Inst.; 1990)

FILMS
R. Goncalves, director: *Pintores moçambicanos* (Maputo, 1986)
X. Lara, director: *Salão dos escultores* (Maputo, 1986)

KERSTIN DANIELSSON

Mozarabic [Sp. *mozárabe*]. Term traditionally used to describe the art of Christians living in the areas of the Iberian peninsula ruled by Muslims in the 10th and 11th centuries. The Castilian word derives from the Arabic *musta'rib* ('Arabized') and is to be contrasted with MU-DÉJAR, the term used to describe the art of Islamic inspiration produced for non-Muslim patrons in the areas of the Iberian peninsula reconquered by Christians between 1085 and the 16th century. Very few surviving works of art fit this strict definition of Mozarabic art, and it is difficult to characterize them. The only substantial building is the ruined three-aisled basilica at Mesas de Villaverde (Málaga; often identified as 'Bobastro'), which preserves its rock-cut foundations and walls (*see* SPAIN, §II, 2). The two illuminated manuscripts surviving from this period are quite different in style. The Biblia Hispalense (Madrid, Bib. N., Cod. Vit. 13–1), copied *c.* 900 at or near Seville by or for Bishop Servandus and completed in 988 when figures of three prophets were added, shows some naturalism in the presentation of the symbols of the Evangelists. Ildefonsus's *Treatise on the Virginity of Mary* (Florence, Bib. Medicea-Laurenziana, MS. Ashb. 17), copied in Toledo by the archpriest Salomon in 1067, has distinctly Islamic-style foliage although the iconography is Hispanic.

The term Mozarabic has also been applied more generally to the art and culture of Christians who had emigrated in the 10th century from Muslim areas to resettle areas of northern Spain that had recently been reconquered. Because of this historical background, the term 'resettlement' (Sp. *reboplación*) is more appropriate, although others have preferred *condal, fronterizo* or simply '10th-century'. This art made use of the glorious monuments of old Visigothic towns and buildings and represents a reassertion of traditional Visigothic culture (*see* VISIGOTHIC ART), primarily in architecture. The revival of forms was partly due to the desire by the Asturian kings (*reg* 718–1037) to see themselves as heirs to the ancient Visigothic kingdom destroyed by the Muslim conquest in the 8th century. The religious communities of the repopulated areas sought out buildings founded by the fathers of the Hispanic Church and settled there, venerating the sanctuaries and their ruins. This period, which began in the late 9th century, was prolonged variously in different Christian states of the peninsula: until *c.* 1000 in the Catalan counties and some parts of Aragon, and until the last third of the 11th century in the rest of Iberia. The distinctly Hispanic Mozarabic tradition was eventually integrated into the international Romanesque style (*see* ROMANESQUE, §II, 4).

1. ARCHITECTURE. When the Asturian kings established their court at Oviedo in 794, they chose the old Roman praetorium of the city. They restored defensive walls, churches and dwellings and used spolia for new construction. In the process the builders became familiar with old forms and techniques, contributing to the continuity of traditional building formulae. The survival of building traditions was assured in the east, where depopulation was less of a problem. Churches conform to the classical type for the Visigothic liturgy, which continued to be used until the adoption of the Roman rite and the introduction of the Romanesque style. The nave was divided by an iconostasis, a furnishing or fabric screen that separated the choir or presbytery near the altar from the area intended for the congregation. The only surviving example is at the monastery of SAN MIGUEL DE ESCALADA (913; near León), where the triple arch would have been hung with curtains. Adjoining the presbytery were small sacristies or possibly penitential areas. Some churches may have had another apse on the west, a feature that had been introduced from North Africa in the 6th century. Its funerary significance can be seen in such churches as that of Santiago de Peñalba (León).

The forms used were already known in the Visigothic period: cubic projections enclosing rectangular, semicircular or horseshoe apses; and a single nave or a nave flanked by aisles, generally with an area meant as a kind of transept and marked not by projections on the exterior but by a wider span on the main axis. The availability of materials and local building practices determined regional variants. Common features include the use of spolia columns, horseshoe arches, domes, barrel vaults with a horseshoe profile, and projecting cornices with brackets decorated with rosettes and trilobes. The inspiration of contemporary Islamic architecture in southern Spain (*see* ISLAMIC ART, §II, 5(iv)(a)) is evident in the use of rectangular frames around arches (Sp. *alfiz*) and intersecting ribbed vaults. This type of vault, first used in the extension (961–6) of the mosque of Córdoba by al-Hakam II (*reg* 961–76), was repeated at the end of the 10th century and in the 11th at such buildings as the church at San Millán de la Cogolla (Rioja) and the church of S Baudelio, near Berlanga de Duero (Soria).

Buildings were painted on both the interior and exterior. Bright colours accented the architectural lines and details, such as arches, mouldings, capitals and reliefs. At the church of S María de Bamba (Valladolid), an attempt was made to reproduce the pattern of an Islamic textile: a lozenge border frames a criss-cross pattern of roundels containing geometric and animal motifs. Geometric decoration survives at Santiago de Peñalba (see fig.) and S Cebrián de Mazote (Valladolid), where there is also a small relief that gives some idea of monumental sculpture, although its iconography is unclear (*see* SPAIN, §IV, 2). Another example of pre-Romanesque monumental sculpture is a crude, chip-carved relief in Luesia (Saragossa) showing a king carrying a cross; the iconography is similar to that found in contemporary book illustration.

The architecture of León and Castile changed radically when the Asturian court moved to the city of León in the early 10th century. The Leonese (later Leonese–Castilian) court erected large buildings, chiefly in the Duero Valley. Documentary evidence and some archaeological remains indicate that palatine types, such as the royal pantheon of Oviedo, continued to be used, but most surviving architecture from the period is related to the activity of the monks of the resettlement, who erected buildings on old

Mozarabic decoration around a horseshoe arch, Santiago de Peñalba, near Ponferrada, León, Spain, 10th century

foundations and repeatedly enlarged them. The largest examples are such basilicas as S Miguel de Escalada, S Cebrián de Mazote, S María de Bamba and, in Cantabria, S María de Lebeña. In the mid-11th century the abbot of S Domingo at Silos enlarged his monastic church from one to three aisles, following traditional models. The existence of ancient and venerated rock hermitages led to the construction of new sanctuaries built around chambers cut out of the rock. This resulted in such curious solutions as the twin-naved church at San Millán de Cogolla, although its plan has also been explained as a provision for male and female monastic communities. Many small churches had a single nave and horseshoe-shaped apse within an orthogonal projection. The most important for their complex vaulting and religious and political significance are S Miguel de Celanova (Orense), built by St Rudesind, founder of Galician monasticism, and Santiago de Peñalba, built by St Gennadius, restorer of Visigothic monastic rule and creator of the 'Leonese Thebaid'. The church of S Baudelio, near Berlanga (second half of the 11th century), represents an unusual type with a square plan and an enormous central column supporting ribbed vaults and surmounted by a small vaulted aedicule. A tribune with a small altar-sanctuary occupies nearly half the interior. The original form of other buildings, such as S María de Peñalba, indicates that this unusual type was

more common than had previously been thought. S Baudelio was probably built for a small religious community, although some scholars, relying on its extensive cycle of Romanesque murals, think it may have had some royal function.

All of the churches in Navarre and Aragon have been remodelled except for a group in Galicia. The pre-Romanesque church of the monastery of Leyre must have been remodelled like the one at Silos. The small church of S Juan de la Peña, with two naves and partly cut into the cliff-side, is reminiscent of that at San Millán de la Cogolla. The churches in the Gállego Valley are later in date. Built in a popular and archaizing style, they use traditional Visigothic forms but also show early Romanesque features.

Most surviving buildings in the Catalan counties (including some in modern France) are simple structures based on pre-Islamic building practices. In the mid-10th century a modest type of church with a single nave and a rectangular apse, often with irregular sides, became popular throughout the region (e.g. S Juan de Boada). S Quirce de Pedret and S María de Marquet have more complex plans. The former Benedictine abbey church of SAINT-MICHEL-DE-CUXA in Roussillon, France (ded. 974; subsequently enlarged), has five apses along a large transept. Although the technique of construction is local and Mozarabic motifs such as the horseshoe arch are in evidence, the building was modelled on the chevet of the second monastic church ('Cluny II') of the Benedictine abbey at Cluny in France, for Cuxa pioneered the introduction of the Cluniac rite into Spain.

2. DECORATIVE ARTS. Book illustrations produced in the Christian kingdoms are distinct from those attributed to Mozarabic artists, for the iconography seems to rely on Visigothic prototypes, although these are poorly known (*see* SPAIN, §III, 2). The principal products were copies of the Bible and of the *Commentary on the Apocalypse* (8th century) by the monk Beatus of Liébana (now Lebeña). These manuscripts provide abundant information about scribes and artists, places of production and scriptoria. A fragment of a *Beatus* manuscript (Silos, Monastery of S Domingo) is considered one of the earliest examples (late 9th century), but its venerable appearance may be due to the crude and clumsy workmanship rather than to its age. The early style is typified by a Bible of 920 (León Cathedral, MS. 6), supervised by the monk Vimara and executed by the scribe and painter Ioannes. Characteristic are the flat metallic figures executed with brilliant and intense colours without shading and backgrounds of bands of plain colours.

The apogee of the style was reached in such manuscripts as the Morgan *Beatus* (mid-10th century; New York, Pierpont Morgan Lib., MS. M. 644), copied and illustrated by the monk Magius. The scribe Florentius, who transcribed and illustrated a copy of Pope Gregory I's commentary on the Book of Job, *Moralia in Job* (945; Madrid, Bib. N., Cod. 80) in the monastery of Valeránica, started a process of minimal naturalism, and some influence of Carolingian illumination can be seen. In the Girona *Beatus* (975; Girona Cathedral, MS. 7), there are Carolingian influences not only in the decorative details but also in the large illustrations of *Christ in Majesty* (fol. 2*r*) and the *Crucifixion* (fol. 16*v*). During the 11th century scriptoria continued to produce works of marked transitional character, but Romanesque formulae were gradually adopted. A magnificent *Beatus* (London, BL, Add. MS. 11695) with beautiful coloured line-drawing was produced at a monastery in Silos between 1091 and 1109, but there is disagreement as to whether it is traditional or Romanesque.

Other decorative arts include a few ivories produced at the monastery of San Millán de la Cogolla: a portable altar (Madrid, Mus. Arqueol. N.) and the arms of a cross (Paris, Louvre; Madrid, Mus. Arqueol. N.) are decorated with animal and floral motifs reminiscent of contemporary European ivories (*see* ROMANESQUE, §VIII) and Islamic ones (*see* ISLAMIC ART, §VIII, 7). Metal wares include a brass cross offered by Ramiro II (*reg* 931–51) to Santiago de Peñalba (León, Mus. Arqueol. Prov.), which continues the flat form of Asturian examples. A portable silver altar (Girona, Mus. Dioc.), probably originally commissioned for the abbey of S Pere de Rodes and given by Josué and Elimburga to Girona Cathedral at the end of the 10th century, is decorated with crudely worked figures of Christ and angels. The great chalice of S Domingo de Silos (late 11th century; Silos Abbey, Treasury) is of the conventional type with two semi-ovoids joined by a shaft with a central knop; it is entirely decorated with silver filigree forming little horseshoe arches. (*See also* ROMANESQUE, §VI, 7.)

BIBLIOGRAPHY

M. Gómez-Moreno: *Iglesias mozárabes* (Madrid, 1919)
——: *El arte árabe español hasta los almohades, arte mozárabe*, A. Hisp., iii (Madrid, 1951)
G. Menéndez Pidal: 'Mozárabes y asturianos', *Bol. Real Acad. Hist.* (1954), pp. 137–291
J. Camón Aznar: 'Arquitectura española del siglo X: Mozárabe y de la repoblación', *Goya*, 52 (1963), pp. 206–19
E. Junyent: *L'arquitectura religiosa en la Catalunya carolingia* (Barcelona, 1963)
J. Camón Aznar: 'El arte de la miniatura española en el siglo X', *Goya*, 64–5 (1964), pp. 266–87
J. E. Uranga and F. Iñiguez Almech: *Arte medieval navarro* (Pamplona, 1971)
J. Fernández Arenas: *Arquitectura mozárabe* (Barcelona, 1972)
A. Durán Gudiol: *Arte altoaragonés de los siglos X–XI* (Sabiñánigo, 1973)
I. G. Bango Torviso: 'Arquitectura de la décima centuria: ¿Repoblación o mozárabe?', *Goya*, 122 (1974), pp. 68–75
J. Ainaud de Lasarte: *Los templos visigótico-románicos de Tarrasa* (Madrid, 1976)
M. Mentré: *Contribución al estudio de la miniatura en León Castilla en la alta edad media* (León, 1976)
J. Fontaine: *L'art mozarabe* (Yonne, 1977)
J. Williams: *Early Spanish Manuscript Illumination* (New York, 1977)
Actas del simposio para el estudio de los Códices del 'Comentario al Apocalipsis' de Beato de Liébana, 2 vols (Madrid, 1978)
I. G. Bango Torviso: 'El neovisigotismo artístico de los siglos IX–X: La restauración de ciudades y templos', *Rev. Ideas Estét.*, xxxvii (1979), pp. 319–38
J. Yarza: *Arte y arquitectura en España, 500/1250* (Madrid, 1979)
X. Barral y Altet: *L'art prerromanic a Catalunya (segles IX–X)* (Barcelona, 1981)
S. Silva y Verástegui: *Iconografía del siglo X en el reino de Pamplona–Nájera* (Pamplona, 1984)
J. Yarza-Luaces: *Arte asturiano, arte mozárabe* (Extremadura, 1985)
B. Cabañero and F. Galtier Marti: '"Tuis exercitibus crux Christi semper adsistat": El relieve real prerrománico de Luesia', *Artigrama*, lxxxix (1986), pp. 11–28
S. Noack: 'En torno al arte "mozárabe"', *Actas del II congreso de arqueología medieval española: Madrid, 1987*, iii, pp. 581–8
R. Puertas Tricas: 'Iglesias represtres de Málaga', *Actas del II congreso de arqueología medieval española: Madrid, 1987*, i, pp. 99–152
I. G. Bango Torviso: 'La part oriental dels temples de l'abat-bisbe Oliba', *Quad. Estud. Med.*, iv (1988), pp. 51–66
——: *Alta edad media: De la tradición hispanogoda al románico* (Madrid, 1989)
J. A. Gutiérrez González: 'Sistemas defensivos y de repoblación en el reino de León', *Actas del III congreso de arqueología medieval española: Oviedo, 1989*
M. Nuñez Rodriguez: *San Miguel de Celanova* (Santiago de Compostela, 1989)
F. Olaguer-Feliú: *El arte medieval hasta el año mil* (Madrid, 1989)
J. D. Dodds: *Architecture and Ideology in Early Medieval Spain* (University Park, PA, and London, 1990)

I. G. BANGO TORVISO

Mozart, Anton (*b* ?Augsburg, 1573; *d* Augsburg, 13 May 1625). German painter and draughtsman. The son and pupil of Christoph Mozart II (*d c.* 1590), a craftsman painter, he may have visited Venice and Treviso in the 1590s. The stylistic proximity to the Frankenthal school or Frederik van Valckenborch (*c.* 1570–1623) of his earliest landscape, the *Sermon of John the Baptist* (1602; Augsburg, Schaezlerpal.), is due more to common period factors than to any direct influence. In 1598 Mozart became a master in Augsburg, where he remained except for short journeys. He painted small-format cabinet pictures and repository pieces, mostly on copper or wood, occasionally on alabaster or lapis lazuli. His verified works comprise only about 25 paintings and miniatures, a similar number of drawings and a few pages for dynastic albums, often with the distinctive monogram A under M, and the date.

Mozart's diverse output as a painter includes *Head-landscape* (1590s), a picture puzzle in the style of Giuseppe Arcimboldo, of which there are many versions, mostly from the later engraving (Hollstein, no. 405) by Matthäus Merian I. While the earliest dated picture, *Christ before Pilate* (1600; ex-art market, Vienna, 1986), is set in a complicated Late Gothic interior, the aforementioned *Sermon* includes a wide landscape and a self-portrait on the lower edge. Mozart's unusually dense, heavily populated *Adoration of the Magi* (1608; Salzburg, Residenzgal.) has a wealth of technical ornamentation on the lower edge, probably by Augsburg artists. Eight pictures remain of Mozart's contribution to the *Pomeranian Cabinet* (1617; Berlin, Kstgewmus.; other parts destr. 1945; *see* WAL-BAUM, MATTHIAS and AUGSBURG, fig. 3); of these, the main picture, a depiction of the handing-over of the cabinet to Duke Philipp I von Pomern-Stettin, can claim independent artistic standing, through its 41 portraits of those who collaborated to produce the piece. The other pictures form such an uneven group that the use of external models is suspected, especially as the depiction of *Air*, from the series of the *Four Elements*, is copied, directly or indirectly, from a painting by Jan Breughel I. It is unlikely that Mozart, as has been claimed, collaborated on other pieces from the Walbaum workshop. The painting of the *Feeding of the Five Thousand* (1620s; Augsburg, Schaezlerpal.; see fig.), preceded by a preparatory drawing (Coburg, Veste Coburg), serves to illustrate the economical nature of Mozart's work procedures: a probably earlier miniature on parchment presents an almost identical scene. Similarly a *Tower of Babel* exists in three versions: as a painting (Zurich, Gal. Koller, 1979), as a miniature (Berlin) and as a drawing (Karlsruhe, Staatl. Ksthalle; Brentel album, inv. no. 1965–10).

Mozart's drawings (several monogrammed, permitting positive attribution of others on stylistic grounds) show the same pattern of development. The tall figures with expressive gestures and faces of the first decade of the 17th century (influenced by Josef Heintz I) can also be seen in the above paintings and in a small domestic altar (*c.* 1610; Munich, Bayer. Nmus.). The drawings after 1610 are freer in style, their shorthand reminiscent of Hans Rottenhammer I, and present densely peopled scenes in landscapes and interiors. Through a preparatory drawing, *Wide Seascape with Harbour* (Schloss Wolfegg, Furstl. Kstsamml.), Mozart's small oeuvre has been extended (see exh. cat.) to include a particularly impressive picture, *View of a Sea-Port* (Paris, Louvre). Close to this scene in stylistic terms is an alabaster tablet (Innsbruck, Schloss Ambras) painted on both sides, incorporating the grain of the stone, depicting the *Gathering of Manna* and the *Crossing of the Red Sea*. It conforms to the evaluation of the Augsburg art dealer Philipp Hainhofer, who in his correspondence frequently recommended Mozart as a miniaturist, heraldic painter and illustrator of albums (e.g. Augsburg, Staats. & Stadtbib., Matthäus Müller album).

BIBLIOGRAPHY
Hollstein: *Ger.*
L. Wegele: *Der Augsburger Maler Anton Mozart* (Augsburg, 1969)
E. von Knorre: 'Zwei unbekannte Gemälde von Anton Mozart', *Acta Mozartiana*, xviii (1971), pp. 37–40

Anton Mozart: *Feeding of the Five Thousand*, tempera on paper, 155×190 mm, 1620s (Munich, Bayerische Staatsgemäldesammlungen: on deposit at Augsburg, Schaezlerpalais)

Zeichnung in Deutschland: Deutsche Zeichner, 1540–1640 (exh. cat. by H. Geissler, Stuttgart, Staatsgal., 1979–80), no. F 20

GODE KRÄMER

Mozetto, Girolamo. *See* MOCETTO, GIROLAMO

Mozuna, Kikō [Monta] (*b* Kushiro, Hokkaido, 14 Nov 1941). Japanese architect and teacher. He studied architecture with Masaya Mukai at Kobe University, graduating in 1965; he then taught at the university from 1965 to 1976. He set up his own practice, Monta Mozuna Mobile Molgue, in Kobe in 1969, opening the Monta Mozuna (later Kikō Mozuna) Atelier in Tokyo in 1977. His first work, his own Anti-dwelling Box House (1972), Kushiro, established him as one of Japan's leading Post-modernists. His other notable buildings include the Yin-yang House (1983), Kushiro, the Akan Wagoto Museum (1983), Teshikago, the Kushiro Marshland Observatory (1984), the Kushiro City Museum (1984), Kushiro Fisherman's Wharf (1987) and the Kushiro Higashi Middle School (1989). Mozuna often interpreted his work in terms of Esoteric Buddhist philosophy or natural symbolism. He compared the form of the Kushiro City Museum, for example, to that of a bird with its wings wrapped around its eggs and described its three display levels as representing earth, man and the heavens and its double-spiral staircases as referring to the double helix of DNA.

BIBLIOGRAPHY
P. Portoghesi: *Post Modern* (New York, 1983)
H. Suzuki, R. Banham and K. Kobayashi: *Contemporary Architecture of Japan, 1958–1984* (New York, 1985)
H. Watanabe: *Amazing Architecture from Japan* (New York, 1991)

KEN BROWN

Mozzetta. *See under* VESTMENTS, ECCLESIASTICAL, §1(iii).

Mrauk U. *See under* ARAKAN.

Mrkusich, Milan (*b* Dargaville, 5 April 1925). New Zealand painter. He was self-taught as a painter but had training in commercial art in Auckland. He began painting in the 1940s and was able to do so full-time from 1958. He painted in a consistently non-figurative abstract style but he vacillated between such gestural, expressive imagery as can be seen in his paintings of 1961 and the *Emblem* series (1962–4; e.g. *Golden Centre: Earth Emblem*, oil on canvas, 1962–3; Auckland, C.A.G.), and the geometric abstraction of his *Elements* series (1965–6; e.g. *Four Elements Above (Crimson)*, oil on canvas, 1965; Auckland, C.A.G.). His painting, meditative in mood, is distinguished by an intense feeling for colour, especially deep resonant greens and crimsons.

In his *Corner* paintings, begun in 1968, Mrkusich eliminated drawing and composition by the use of a given format, usually a square canvas with coloured, triangular elements in the corners. In these works he stained the central field with layerings of colour, sometimes atmospheric, sometimes opaque and two-dimensional in effect, as in *Painting Ochre* (1974; U. Auckland). Among his later series are the *Journey* paintings, begun in 1986, an example of which is *Journey No. 1* (Hamilton, NZ, Chartwell Trust Col.). These introduce an asymmetrical, less formal presentation to his art.

BIBLIOGRAPHY
Milan Mrkusich: Paintings, 1946–1972 (exh. cat. by M. Dunn and P. Vuletic, Auckland, C.A.G., 1972)
Milan Mrkusich: A Decade Further on (exh. cat. by R. T. L. Wilson and P. Leech, Auckland, C.A.G., 1985)

MICHAEL DUNN

Mrohaung. *See under* ARAKAN.

Mshatta [Mshattā; Mushatta; Qaṣr al-Mshattā]. Unfinished Islamic palace 25 km south of Amman, Jordan. The outer enclosure is a square (147 m externally) of fine ashlar masonry with regularly spaced half-round buttresses and, on the south, a gate flanked by two semi-octagonal towers. The interior is divided into three tracts, of which only the central one was laid out, again in three parts. The gate-block appears to have consisted of an enclosed hall, a small court and a mosque, but only the base courses were laid out. The second part comprised a large open court. The third block had a triple-arched façade in front of an audience hall containing two rows of grey–green marble columns terminating in a triconch. The hall, of which the plan derives from a late Roman type, was flanked by four suites (Arab. *bayt*) of four vaulted rooms around a court. The walls, which rested on three courses of limestone masonry, were built of fired brick and supported slightly pointed pitched-brick vaults of Mesopotamian style.

The most notable feature is the richly carved south façade (*see* ISLAMIC ART, fig. 252) presented by the Ottoman sultan 'Abd al-Hamid II (*reg* 1876–1909) to Emperor William II; at J. Strzygowski's urging, W. von Bode accepted it for Berlin (Pergamonmus.). The façade is divided by a zigzag moulding into 40 triangles 2.95 m high, in various stages of completion. Each triangle has a central rosette in high relief, and the remainder of the field is sculpted in low relief with chalices, vines, lions, birds and griffons. Rediscovered by Europeans several times in the 19th century, the building was variously attributed to the Ghassanid and the Lakhmid dynasties in the 6th century AD or to the Sasanian occupation of Syria in the early 7th.

An attribution to Islamic times, however, is certain because of the integral presence of the mosque and is supported by the find of two bricks fired with Arabic graffiti and one with an Arabic stamp impression. Mshatta may have been built by the caliph al-Walid II (*reg* 743–4) to welcome pilgrims returning from Mecca.

BIBLIOGRAPHY
K. A. C. Cresswell: *Early Muslim Architecture*, i (Oxford, 1932/*R* and enlarged 1969), pp. 578–606, 614–41
G. Bishei: 'Qaṣr al-Mshatta in the Light of a Recently Found Inscription', *Studies in the Archaeology and History of Jordan*, iii, ed. A. Hadidi (Amman, 1986), pp. 193–7

ALASTAIR NORTHEDGE

mtho gling. *See* THOLING.

Mtskheta. Town in Georgia near the confluence of the rivers Kura and Aragvi, 21 km north of Tbilisi. Mtskheta and the surrounding district, known as Great Mtskheta, contain some of the earliest settlements in Georgia dating to the Early Bronze Age (3rd millennium BC). The town developed into an economic and cultural centre and served as the capital of the kingdom of Kartli (Iberia) from the 4th century BC to the 5th century AD. With the adoption of Christianity as the official religion of the kingdom in the 330s, Mtskheta also became its religious centre and the residence of the head of the Georgian Church, the Katholikos-patriarch. Although Great Mtskheta attracted the interest of archaeologists in the 1870s, a systematic programme of excavation was not undertaken until 1937. Among the excavated architectural remains are the fortifications of the acropolis, which covers 30 ha on Bagineti Hill on the right bank of the River Kura, and where the kings resided, several richly decorated tombs, a bathhouse (2nd–3rd centuries AD) and a small stone mausoleum of the late 1st century–early 2nd century AD. This has a barrel vault of dressed stone blocks and a gabled roof of large tiles reinforced with mortar. Inside were found the bones of a woman and child accompanied by grave goods, including a gold buckle with inset stones, pendants, buttons and a hoard of silver and gold coins. Most of the finds are in the State Museum of the History of Georgia in Tbilisi.

The earliest church in Mtskheta was built of wood in the 330s, but it was replaced by a larger, three-aisled basilica of stone in the 5th century. Another monument of the 4th century was the large wooden cross erected at the top of the hill on the left bank of the River Aragvi. A chapel built next to the cross by King Guaram I (*reg* 588–90) was replaced under his son Stephan I (*reg* 590–627) by the present-day Jvari (Cross) church (586–605; see fig.); the cross was housed at its centre, although only the base survives. The church is a tetraconch set in a square and surmounted by an octagonal dome (diam. 9 m) resting on a system of squinches. The walls, which are built of level rows of carefully cut stone blocks, are plain inside, although the east conch of the altar may originally have borne mosaics or wall paintings. The external form of the building reflects its internal arrangement with apses projecting from the façades. Three reliefs depicting the donors and one of the *Ascension of the Cross with Angels* lie above the three windows of the eastern apse and in the tympanum over the south entrance respectively. In its simple grandeur this church represents the earliest attempt by Georgian architects to reconcile the functional aspects of the building's interior with an aesthetically pleasing exterior. Its form was copied and developed in numerous churches, including those of ATENI, Dzveli Shuamta in Kakheti and Martvili in western Georgia. The closest parallels to this architectural type are at Avan, Aramus, Sisian and the St Hrip'sime church at EDJMIADZIN in Armenia. The cathedral served as the burial place of the Georgian kings.

Between 1010 and 1029 the present cathedral of the Life-creating Pillar (Svetitskhoveli) was built, replacing the 5th-century three-aisled basilica. Inscriptions and surviving documents indicate that the church's donor was the Katholikos-patriarch Melchisedek and that the architect was Arsukisdze. In the 13th century the cathedral was damaged by an earthquake and looted in the late 14th century by the forces of Tamerlane (*reg* 1336–1405); it was partly rebuilt under Alexander I (*reg* 1408–42). It is the largest church in Georgia (25×51 m; external h. *c.* 50 m) and a typical example of medieval Georgian architecture. Its rectangular plan is crowned by a single dome on a tall drum and supported by four piers. The deep altar apse is contained within the church's walls and preserves the only surviving frescoes (16th–17th centuries); choirs occupy the west end. The walls are built of hewn blocks of sandy-coloured stone interspersed with bright red blocks. The exterior decoration comprises a system of arches and windows framed by richly carved surrounds; the five-arched 'formula' on the east façade includes two deep niches, a typical feature of Georgian architecture.

Near by is the smaller Samtavro church (first half of the 11th century). It is also rectangular in plan with two columns and two buttresses on the corners of the altar apse supporting the dome. The carved window surrounds of the north and south façades are particularly well executed.

BIBLIOGRAPHY

G. N. Chubinashvili: *Pamyatniki tipa Dzhvari* [Monuments of the Jvari type] (Tbilisi, 1948)

A. M. Apakidze and others: *Arkheologicheskiye pamyatniki Armaziskhevi po raskopkam 1937–1946* [Archaeological monuments of Armaziskhevi from the excavations of 1937–46] (1958), i of *Mtskheta: Itogi arkheologicheskikh issledovaniy* [Mtskheta: results of the archaeological investigations] (Tbilisi, 1958–)

G. N. Chubinashvili: 'Gruzinskaya srednevekovaya arkhitektura i tri yeyo velichayshikh kafedrala' [Medieval Georgian architecture and three of its greatest cathedrals], *Voprosy Istor. Isk.*, i (1970), pp. 262–78

V. Béridzé: 'Une Fois encore au sujet de l'église de Djavari', *Bedi Kartlisa*, xxviii (1971), pp. 122–32

V. BERIDZE

Mualla, Fikret (*b* Istanbul, 1903; *d* Nice, 20 July 1967). Turkish painter. After attending high school in Istanbul, he continued his education in Germany, where he became increasingly interested in painting, and in Paris, where he studied under André Lhote. On returning to Turkey, he designed costumes for operettas and worked on illustrations for books and magazines. His life, however, was severely affected by a childhood accident, and later by alcoholism; his health deteriorated in the mid-1930s, and he was committed to a mental hospital near Istanbul. During this period, however, his work began to be recognized in Turkey, and he painted up to 30 pictures of Istanbul for the Turkish Pavilion at the international

Mtskheta, Jvari church, view from the south-east, 586–605

exhibition in New York in 1939. From 1940 onwards he lived in Paris. The first exhibition there of his paintings was held at the Galerie Dina Vierny in 1954, after which his reputation as an artist increased. His subjects included Parisian cafés and bars, street scenes, places of entertainment, landscapes and a few portraits. He worked quickly in an Expressionist manner, using bright colours in gouache, usually on small sheets of paper. His oil paintings were fewer in number; they included *The Musicians* (*c.* 1940; Istanbul, Mimar Sinan U., Mus. Ptg & Sculp.).

BIBLIOGRAPHY

A. Dino and A. Güler: *Fikret Mualla* (Istanbul, 1980) [Turk. text]

G. Renda and others: *A History of Turkish Painting* (Geneva, Seattle and London, 1988), pp. 223–7

□

Muang Thai. *See* THAILAND.

Muan Xingtao. *See* MOKUAN SHŌTŌ.

Mucha, Alphonse [Alfons] (*b* Ivančice, Moravia, 24 July 1860; *d* Prague, 14 July 1939). Czech graphic artist and painter, active in France. In 1877 he attempted unsuccessfully to enter the Academy of Fine Arts, Prague, and afterwards set about travelling and working. He went first to Vienna, where he worked for a company that produced stage sets, and where he discovered the work of Hans Makart. After being made redundant he left in 1882 for Mikulov, where he earned a living painting portraits of important local figures. He met Count Khuen-Belassi, who invited him to paint murals at his home (1882–4; some panels in Brno, Mus. City), later sending him to the Akademie der Bildenden Künste in Munich (1885–7) and to Paris in autumn 1888. Mucha enrolled at the Académie Julian and worked in the studios of Jules Lefebvre and Jean-Paul Laurens. When his grant was cut off at the end of 1889, he stayed in Paris and briefly attended the Académie Colarossi; to finance himself he produced a variety of illustrations, collaborating on *La Vie populaire* and the children's review *Le Petit Français illustré.*

Mucha exhibited at the Salon des Artistes Français in 1894 and won a medal of honour. In the same year he began teaching at the Académie Colarossi, and he designed the poster *Gismonda* (colour lithograph 2.13×.75 m, 1894; see Bridges, pl. A1) for a production at the Théâtre de la Renaissance, Paris. He had already designed three posters, for soap, toothpaste and stationery; but the *Gismonda* poster, intended for Sarah Bernhardt who was playing the title role and was also theatre manager, ratified him, taking him out of the more anonymous world of illustrators and into that of the great poster designers. His desire to create a life-size image of the actress led him to choose a large, elongated format; he took his inspiration from Byzantine mosaics to make Bernhardt into a magnificent, proud figure, which aroused surprise when it appeared on the walls of Paris in January 1895. This poster contrasted radically with the work of Jules Chéret or Théophile-Alexandre Steinlen. Seduced by this new image of herself, Bernhardt signed a six-year contract with Mucha; he made six other large theatre posters for her (e.g. *Amants*, 1895; see fig.), as well as undertaking designs for sets, costumes and jewellery. Having established himself, he received many commissions. While working for Bernhardt, he made posters for commercial firms including those for *Job* (1898; see Bridges, pl. A36) and *Moët et Chandon* (1899; see Bridges, pl. A39); he also designed a large number of stamps, vignettes, calendars, illustrations and 'decorative panels', a lithographic type developed for Mucha (e.g. *Morning Awakening*, colour lithograph, 1899; see Bridges, p. 28). Mucha shared with his peers the desire to make art popular and acceptable. In this spirit he co-founded, with Eugènc-Samucl Grassct, René Lalique, Gallé and Horta, the Société Internationale de l'Art Populaire, and with James McNeill Whistler he founded the Académie Carmen in 1898 (closed 1901).

The influence of Hans Makart, Eugène-Samuel Grasset and the Pre-Raphaelites contributed to Mucha's style, which was characterized by a sense of ornamentation, a balancing of realist and stylized elements and a certain *horror vacui*. His taste for Byzantine art can be seen in the mosaic backgrounds and in the portrayal of gorgeous garments laden with gold and precious gems. All these elements, used to enhance a femininity that was more mystical than avant-garde, created a style that was perceived as typically Art Nouveau, despite Mucha's assertion that 'art is eternal, it cannot be new', and his rejection of any direct links with the movement. Fifty-eight posters by

Alphonse Mucha: *Amants*, lithograph, 1895 (London, Victoria and Albert Museum)

Mucha were printed in Paris, usually by the firm Champenois. In all his commissions he gave free rein to his taste for female figures in theatrical poses, flamboyant curving lines, floral motifs and delicate interwoven designs. He had two exhibitions in 1897, including *Alphonse Mucha et son oeuvre* (Paris, Salon des Cent), organized by *La Plume*.

The period 1895 to 1900 was Mucha's most prolific. His posters were of primary importance, but he continued to illustrate numerous books and published several series of decorative panels. In addition, he made designs for wallpaper and furniture. He was actively involved with the Exposition Universelle in 1900; he designed jewellery and a shop (1900–01; destr.) for Georges Fouquet (1862–1957) and undertook the decoration of the pavilion for Bosnia and Herzegovina, a task that aroused his patriotic spirit. In 1910 he returned to Bohemia. He started working on the *Slav Epic* (1913; Moravský Krumlov Castle), a series of 20 paintings, which he gave to the town of Prague in 1928. He saw himself as inheriting the decorative traditions of his native country, and he was convinced of the need to use his art to express his devoted attachment to ideals and traditions. He continued painting until his death.

BIBLIOGRAPHY

J. Mucha: *Alphonse Mucha: The Master of Art Nouveau* (Prague, 1966)
J. Mucha, M. Henderson and A. Scharf: *Alphonse Mucha* (London and New York, 1974)
J. Mucha: *Mucha* (Paris, 1977)
A. Bridges, ed.: *Alphonse Mucha: The Complete Graphic Works* (London and New York, 1980)
Mucha, 1860–1939: Peintures, illustrations, affiches, arts décoratifs (exh. cat. by J. Kotalík and J. Brabcová, Paris, Grand Pal.; Darmstadt, Ausstellhallen Matildenhöhe; Prague, Jízdárna Pražského Hradu; 1980)
J. Rennert and A. Weill: *Alphonse Mucha: The Complete Posters and Panels* (Boston and Paris, 1984)

MICHÈLE LAVALLÉE

Muche, Georg (*b* Querfurt, 8 May 1895; *d* 1987). German painter and teacher. His father was an amateur painter and art collector who became known as the naive painter Felix Ramholz. In 1913 Muche began studying painting at the Azbe-Kunstschule in Munich. His work was entirely conventional until 1914, when he moved to Berlin and became Herwarth Walden's exhibitions assistant at the Sturm-Galerie. After his introduction to Expressionist circles, he began to paint intensively, plunging into a heady abstraction that combined a Cubist approach to form with the rich saturated colours of the work of Der Blaue Reiter and Marc Chagall.

By 1915–16 Muche had developed his own abstract style using smudgy, blurred patches of colour in conjunction with hard outlines. This lends his compositions a highly atmospheric and primeval quality that was not lost on his contemporaries. Herwarth Walden dubbed one of his most dramatic compositions '*And God Divided Light from Dark*' (1916; destr.; see 1980 exh. cat., p. 25, no. M28).

He exhibited at the Sturm-Galerie alongside figures such as Max Ernst, Paul Klee and Alexander Archipenko. Although he was referred to by his contemporaries as an Expressionist, at this time it was a broad term denoting modern art that was thought to centre on the vision of the inner eye. Muche chose to use the elements of art themselves and, in particular, colour to express this inner revelation. His compositions became increasingly complex and frequently included a chequer-board or grid motif, as in *Surface Spaces: Composition* (1916; Duisburg, Lehmbruck-Mus.).

From 1917, Muche served in the Infantry and in 1919 he suffered a nervous collapse. After recovering he returned to Berlin, where he renewed contact with the Sturm circle and met members of the Novembergruppe and Dadaists. He resumed his abstract painting and further enriched his compositions. Having considered entering a monastery, in April 1920 he joined the staff of the Bauhaus at Weimar, where he developed a close friendship with Johannes Itten and assisted him in teaching the preliminary course.

In their own work both Muche and Itten returned to figuration, fearing that abstraction could mean an end to the tradition of European painting. They decided that the challenge was to depict the visible world without trespassing on the territory of photography. This return to figuration was part of the general tendency of Neue Sachlichkeit. Muche experimented with photography, photograms and mirrors in order to pinpoint the differences between photography and painting, and he decided that painting concerned the world of experience, ordered by memory and then re-created in a picture. A strong classicism runs through his figurative work, along with Surrealist elements and spatial ambiguities. *Breakfast Outdoors* (1926; destr.; see 1980 exh. cat., no. M74) sums up a number of his favourite themes and motifs: people, nature, still-life, classical profiles and amphorae. It is a contemplative kind of figuration, in which the physical is frequently a vessel for the metaphysical.

Although he had no architectural training, Muche designed the Haus am Horn, an experimental house for the Bauhaus exhibition of 1923; it is a symmetrical villa designed for servantless family life, with small rooms grouped around a larger central room, which is lit by clerestory windows. At Dessau in 1926 he collaborated with Richard Paulick to build a house from prefabricated steel components. Muche disagreed with some aspects of Bauhaus ideology, and his leadership of the weaving workshop was unsuccessful, largely because he disdained craft work. In 1927 he began teaching at the Ittenschule in Berlin and in 1931 he was appointed Professor at the Staatliche Akademie für Kunst und Kunstgewerbe in Breslau. After his dismissal in 1933 he taught at Hugo Häring's Kunst und Werkschule in Berlin and became increasingly interested in fresco painting, which he researched in some detail in Italy.

During the Nazi regime Muche's work became increasingly despairing, dwelling on the theme of catastrophe and conflict. He embarked on a series of monochrome works called *Panels of Guilt*, which he gave to the Nationalgalerie in East Berlin in 1973. His frescoes (a number of which perished during World War II) were a serene antidote to this treatment of suffering and disaster. He hoped his work would reach ordinary people and yet was painfully aware of the limitations of the influence of art. From 1933 until 1959 he gave a masterclass at the Krefeld Textile Engineering School. In 1943 he worked at the Institut für Malstoffkunde in Wuppertal, along with Oscar Schlemmer and Willi Baumeister. In his later years he became increasingly interested in art theory and in particular in the relationship between art and technology. He produced many drawings, for example the series, *NEMI SEE–Eye of Diana, Variation F* (1964; see 1977 exh. cat., p. 27), which in 1965 he transformed into mysterious abstract engravings as part of his experiments in Variographie, an electrotype process.

WRITINGS
Buonfresco: Briefe aus Italien über Handwerk und Stil der echten Frescomalerei (Berlin, 1938)
Blickpunkt Sturm Dada Bauhaus Gegenwart (Tübingen, 1965)

BIBLIOGRAPHY
Georg Muche: Der Zeichner (exh. cat. by G. Thiem, Stuttgart, Staatsgal., 1977)
Georg Muche: Das künstlerische Werk, 1912–1927 (exh. cat. by M. Droste, W. Berlin, Bauhaus-Archv, 1980) [extensive bibliog.]
Georg Muche: Das malerische Werk, 1928–1982 (exh. cat., foreword H. Wingler; W. Berlin, Bauhaus-Archv, 1983)

ANNA ROWLAND

Mu-ch'i. *See* MUQI.

Mudarris, Fātiḥ. *See* MOUDARRES, FATEH.

Mudéjar. Spanish term used to describe the architecture and art of Islamic inspiration produced in the areas of the Iberian peninsula reconquered by Christians between 1085, when Alfonso VI of Castile-León (*reg* 1072–1109) seized Toledo from the Muslims, and the 16th century. The Castilian word derives from the Arabic *mudajjan* ('permitted to remain'), and it was initially thought that *Mudéjar* art was produced only by Muslims for Christian masters, but the term has come to be applied to a broader range of works produced by Muslims, Christians and Jews for Christian and Jewish patrons. *Mudéjar* may be contrasted to MOZARABIC, which, in its strictest sense, refers to the art of Christians living under Muslim rule in the peninsula in the 10th and 11th centuries. The distinctive and eclectic style of *Mudéjar* brick, stucco and timber architecture developed in many regions of Spain throughout the long Spanish Middle Ages (*see* SPAIN, §II, 1). *Mudéjar* buildings are related to contemporary Islamic buildings in appearance and techniques of construction and decoration, but their structure is closer to Romanesque and Gothic architecture. The many long periods of peaceful co-existence during the lengthy wars of the Reconquest are attested not only in architectural borrowing but also in the paintings to the *Cantigas de Santa María* (Madrid, Escorial, Bib. Monasterio S Lorenzo, MS. J.b.2), a collection of lyrics compiled for Alfonso X (*reg* 1252–84).

Mudéjar art lasted for so many centuries because the Islamic art from which it drew its inspiration was itself deeply rooted in the Iberian peninsula (*see* ISLAMIC ART, §II, 4(iv) and 5(iv)). The Christian monarchs, the Church and the populace admired mosques, palaces and mansions in the reconquered cities: mosques were consecrated and adapted to Christian worship without major architectural change, while palaces became the residences of kings and aristocrats. New buildings, including churches, archiepiscopal palaces and even synagogues, were decorated in stucco carved with arabesques and geometric patterns and inscribed with Latin or Hebrew phrases juxtaposed to such Arabic ones as 'happiness and prosperity' or the name Muhammad. Palaces were adorned with horseshoe arches, trefoil arches of exquisite design, gardens with two water channels crossing at the centre, wide porticoed patios with a large central cistern, comfortable baths and central throne-rooms. This nucleus was decorated with fine ribbed cupolas, multicoloured carved stucco, niches or cupboards for glazed ceramic jars, and with MUQARNAS and arabesques. Gradually this Islamic style of decoration gave way to a more naturalistic style inspired by Gothic art of the 13th and 14th centuries. Multicoloured glazed tiles, which were already used on the exterior of the brick towers of Toledo and Aragon, adorned the floors and walls of many palaces and private houses. In this respect *Mudéjar* art went beyond the Islamic tradition, and the demand for glazed tiles became so great that manufacturing centres were established in Valencia, Málaga, the Triana district of Seville, Toledo and El Puente del Arzobispo (Toledo), Teruel and Muel.

Mudéjar religious architecture developed in TOLEDO after the conquest of the city in 1085, when it became the residence of the kings of Castile and the ecclesiastical centre of Spain. Brick and stone masonry between brick courses became popular, along with horseshoe and trefoil arches and façades similar to those found on mosques. The small mosque of Bab al-Mardum (999–1000) was transformed into the church of Cristo de la Luz in *c.* 1187 by the addition of a voluminous apse to its east side. Like the mosque, the apse was constructed of brick and articulated on the exterior with two storeys of blind arcades, the upper one cusped. It differed from the mosque, however, in the extensive mural decoration on the interior. The church of S Román, rebuilt in 1221 for Archbishop Jiménez de Rada in the same brickwork technique, had horseshoe arches with voussoirs alternately painted in red and white and extensive figural paintings surrounded by Arabic and Latin inscriptions. At the church of Santiago del Arrabal (before 1256), horseshoe arches were replaced by pointed ones, while a *Mudéjar* belfry was added to the tower, which had served as a minaret, as at S Bartolomé (rest. early 14th century). These adapted minarets gave way to newly built monumental bell-towers decorated with friezes of arches, as at S Román (late 13th century or early 14th) and S Tomé (early 14th century).

The Jewish communities in Toledo and such other cities as Segovia, Córdoba, Seville and Granada erected synagogues in the *Mudéjar* style, although only a few have survived (*see* JEWISH ART, §II, 1(iii)(a)). The Ibn Shoshan synagogue of Toledo (13th century), later transformed into the church of S María la Blanca, is a trapezoidal hypostyle brick building. Twenty-four octagonal brick piers support four arcades of horseshoe arches; the capitals, spandrels and upper walls are richly decorated with carved stucco. A similar and probably contemporary synagogue in Segovia was transformed into the church of Corpus Christi (destr. 1899). The small (6.95×6.37 m) synagogue of Córdoba (early 14th century; *see* CÓRDOBA (i), §3(ii)) has a patio and an entrance hall; the interior walls are decorated with carved Hebrew inscriptions and stucco panels surrounding cusped and lambrequin arches. A second Toledan synagogue (1366) built by Samuel Leví, finance minister to Peter the Cruel, and later consecrated as the church of Nuestra Señora del Tránsito, has a spacious hall (23×12 m) with magnificent carved plasterwork on the walls and a fine wooden roof. Hebrew and Arabic inscriptions are integrated into the extraordinarily complex ornament, which includes the arms of Castile among the *muqarnas*, arabesque and geometric patterns.

In Old Castile and León, *Mudéjar* architecture appeared during the reign of Alfonso VIII (*reg* 1158–1214), who won the battle of Navas de Tolosa (1212), effectively ending Almohad rule in Spain. In 1187 he had founded the monastery of Las Huelgas (*see* BURGOS, §2(ii)) and an adjoining palace; these were decorated in the purest Almohad style by master builders from Toledo and Seville. The Capilla de la Asunción, for example, has rich stucco of lambrequin arches supporting ribbed and *muqarnas* domes; the stucco-covered pointed barrel vaults over the cloister of S Fernando (13th century) were decorated with a textile-like pattern of roundels enclosing birds and other animals. *Mudéjar* masters also built brick churches on Romanesque lines, such as those of S Tirso (12th century) and S Lorenzo (*c.* 1200), both at Sahagún. They have three semicylindrical apses and square towers above the transept and are decorated on the exterior with recessed arched panels in the Toledan style.

After the conquest of Córdoba in 1236, the famed vaults with interlaced ribs at the Great Mosque (*see* CÓRDOBA (i), §3(i)(a)) provided inspiration for vaults in churches in Toledo, Soria, Navarra and Saragossa, as well as at the hospital of San Blas, near Oloron, and Havarrens in southern France. With the conquest of Seville by Fernando III (*reg* 1217–52) in 1248, Christians had access to the great monuments of Almohad Andalucía, and *Mudéjar* architecture in this region retained a greater Islamic element, especially in Seville where an old Almohad minaret, the Giralda (*see* BRICK, fig. 13), provided a model for *Mudéjar* towers, as at the churches of Omnium Sanctorum and S Marcos. In such profoundly Arabized areas as the Aljarafe of Seville, Islamic-style domes were erected in many chapels and more complex churches, such as the chapel of the Magdalena, the Piedad de S Marina and the narrow Quinta of S Pablo. Alfonso XI (*reg* 1312–50), who defeated the Marinids at the Battle of Salado (1340), together with his son Peter the Cruel (*reg* 1350–69), had workers from Toledo, Seville and Granada build several lavish palaces in Tordesillas, Astudillo (Palencia), Córdoba and Seville. Façades exuberantly decorated in stone or stucco surrounded patios and gardens with crossed water channels, an arrangement undoubtedly inspired by the Patio de los Leones in the Alhambra (*see* GRANADA, fig. 4). The Alhambra, the greatest monument of the Nasrids (*reg* 1230–1492), was an inexhaustible source of exotic artistry that *Mudéjar* master builders adapted for new construction in Toledo and Aragon. Following the example of his friend and ally the Nasrid sultan Muhammad V (*reg* 1354–91 with interruption), Peter the Cruel had magnificent throne-rooms built in the midst of his gardens. The finest of his palaces was the Alcázar of Seville (*see* SEVILLE, §IV, 2); its splendid Salón de Embajadores (see fig.) is one of the finest examples of the *Mudéjar* style. The Alhambra and the Alcázar of Seville were the inspiration for 14th-century renovations to the palaces of Toledo, where many large and lavish reception

Mudéjar architecture of the Salón de Embajadores, the Alcázar, Seville, Spain, mid-14th century

halls (Sp. *tarbea*) were built, such as the Taller del Moro, the Casa de Mesa and the hall of the Corral de Don Diego. All of these show the new, naturalistic decoration, with silhouettes of animals and animated scenes, first seen in the Leví synagogue in Toledo and the palace of Tordesillas.

In the province of Huelva such churches as Villalba del Alcor and S Clara de Moguer were built resembling the fortress–monasteries (Arab. *ribāt*) of the Arabs. Their robust appearance contrasted with their fragile interior patios, designed in the style of mosque courtyards. The cloister of the monastery of La Rábida at Huelva is a particularly attractive example. The Hieronymite monastery at GUADALUPE (14–15th century) was built by emigrés from Seville and master builders from Toledo; its outstanding two-storey cloister (1402–12) has arcades of horseshoe arches and a *Mudéjar* pavilion (1405) in its centre, surmounted by a spire in three stages built of brick, stucco and glazed tiles.

In Aragon during the 13th and 14th centuries, *Mudéjar* churches were built in brick with variegated exterior decoration, revealing that medieval Aragonese builders owed much to Andalusian models, such as the Giralda at Seville. The more archaic churches of S Domingo and Santiago de Daroca (12th–13th century) and the bell-towers of Belmonte and S María de Ateca gave way to the richly decorated churches of the Magdalena at Saragossa, S Pedro and S Salvador in Teruel. The style came to an end with the majestic towers of S María at Calatayud (15th century) and the Torre Nueva at Saragossa (16th century; destr. 1892), a 55.6 m clock-tower built by Christian master builders together with one Jewish and two Muslim master builders.

At the beginning of the 15th century *Mudéjar* architecture began to blend first into Late Gothic and then into the first manifestations of Renaissance or PLATERESQUE styles associated with Queen Isabella I of Castile and León and Cardinal FRANCISCO JIMÉNEZ DE CISNEROS (*see also* HISPANO-FLEMISH STYLE). Among the finest examples are the palace of Peñaranda de Duero (Burgos), the chapel of S Ildefonso (1510) and the Paraninfo (Great Hall; 1518–19) at the university in ALCALÁ DE HENARES, the palace of Cárdenas de Ocaña (Toledo) and the Casa de Pilatos (*see* SEVILLE, §IV, 3). In Andalucía the houses of the Moors who were baptized and remained in Granada after 1492 remained true to Islamic styles, with patios with two porticos and decoration resembling that of the Alhambra (e.g. Casa de Chapiz and the houses of Horno de Oro Street).

In addition to architectural decoration in carved, joined and painted wood (*see* ARTESONADO) and in brick, glazed ceramic tiles, plaster and paint, *Mudéjar* artists produced textiles, carpets, crockery, furniture, metal wares and arms and armour. *Mudéjar* textiles are closely related to those produced for Islamic patrons (*see* ISLAMIC ART, §VI, 2(ii)(a)). Carpets were knotted for Christian and Jewish patrons, and many of the designs are Spanish versions of Turkish rugs (*see* SPAIN, §XI, 1, and CARPET, §II, 2(i) and (ii)). In addition to tiles, *Mudéjar* potters produced earthenwares overglaze-painted in lustre. After production ceased at Málaga, the major centre under Muslim control, some time before the mid-15th century, the production of lustrewares continued elsewhere under Christian patronage, especially in Valencia (*see* SPAIN, §VII, 1).

BIBLIOGRAPHY

D. Angulo Iñiguez: *Arquitectura mudéjar sevillana de los siglos XII, XIII, XIV y XV* (Seville, 1932)

L. Torres Balbas: *Arte almohade, arte nazarí, arte mudéjar*, A. Hisp., iv (Madrid, 1949)

F. Chueca Goitia: *Historia de la arquitectura española: Edad antigua y edad media* (Madrid, 1965)

B. Pavón Maldonado: *Arte toledano: Islámico y mudéjar* (Madrid, 1973, rev. 2/1988)

——: *Arte mudéjar en Castilla la vieja y León* (Madrid, 1975)

M. Fraga: *Arquitectura mudéjar en la baja Andalucía* (Santa Cruz de Tenerife, 1977)

G. M. Borrás Gualis: *Arte mudéjar aragonés*, 3 vols (Saragossa, 1978, rev. 1985)

M. Aguilar: *Málaga mudéjar: Arquitectura religiosa y civil* (Málaga, 1979)

B. Martínez Caviro: *Mudéjar toledano: Palacios y conventos* (Madrid, 1980)

M. Valdés Fernández: *Arquitectura mudéjar en León y Castilla* (León, 1981, rev. 2/1984)

Actas I–II y III de simposio internacional de mudéjarismo (Teruel, 1981–4)

P. Mogollón: *El mudéjar en Extremadura* (Extremadura, 1987)

J. Dodds: 'The Mudejar Tradition in Architecture', *The Legacy of Muslim Spain*, ed. S. K. Jayyusi (Leiden, 1992), pp. 592–7

V. B. Mann, T. F. Glick and J. D. Dodds, eds: *Convivencia: Jews, Muslims, and Christians in Medieval Spain* (New York, 1992)

BASILIO PAVÓN MALDONADO

Mudéjar revival. Term used to describe a style of architecture and the decorative arts employed by some artists in Spain and its colonies in the 19th century. It was based on the medieval work of Spanish *mudajjan*, an Arabic word denoting Muslims living under Christian rule (*see also* MUDÉJAR), and was particularly prevalent in such centres as Burgos, Seville and Toledo (e.g. Toledo Railway Station), which were rich in important examples of Islamic architecture. Nationalism during this period, however, led to the style being used in other cities throughout the Iberian peninsula and in the Spanish colonies (e.g. masonic temple, San Pedro Sula, Honduras). In other parts of Europe and the Western world a similar revival is usually called MOORISH STYLE.

□

Mudo, el. *See* NAVARRETE, JUAN FERNÁNDEZ DE.

Muehl [Mühl], Otto (*b* Grodnau, Burgenland, 16 June 1925). Austrian performance artist, painter, writer and film maker. He served with the German Army between 1943 and 1945, during which time he reached the rank of Lieutenant and was awarded both the Infantry Storm decoration and the Iron Cross; this period fuelled the subsequent direction of his work in many ways. He attended the University of Vienna (1947–52) and the Akademie der Bildenden Künste in Vienna (1952–7). After beginning to work as a drawing therapist and mathematics tutor at the University of Vienna, where he remained until 1968, he soon became dissatisfied with painting, which for him had always involved violent and energetic activity and unorthodox techniques, and after experimenting with Junk sculpture he began creating performances or *Aktionen*. These involved an expressive use of the male and female body, both of which he subjected to a variety of forms of ritualistic physical abuse. By 1964 the body had become more objectified as part of a still-life in a series of performances intended for photographic documentation, such as *Material Action No. 10: Still-life with a Woman's Head and a Pig's Head*, and it was at this time that he helped found the AKTIONISMUS group with Hermann Nitsch, Günter Brus and Rudolf Schwarzkogler. In 1964 Muehl also met the film maker Kurt Kren (*b* 1920), who subsequently filmed a number of his and Brus's *Aktionen*, but, because Kren transformed the meaning of their performances, Muehl and Brus both broke off their collaborations. In 1965 Muehl employed Ernst Schmidt (*b* 1938) to film his *Aktionen* strictly under his own direction.

By this time Muehl had moved towards a more direct confrontation with the social taboos surrounding sexuality in such performances as *Material Action No. 13: Leda and the Swan* and *Material Action No. 15: Cosine Alpha*. These revealed how far he was moving from the concerns of Nitsch and some of the other members of Aktionismus, grounding his work within a framework of behavioural analysis that blurred the relationship between art and life. After 1966 he moved even further in this direction and was a founder-member of the Institut für Direkte Kunst. Many of his actions became so extreme that they could not be performed and were realized almost exclusively on film: one of his few *Aktionen* performed for an audience, *Art and Revolution* (performed at the University of Vienna in July 1968), led to arrests.

By the late 1960s the stress of Muehl's largely spontaneous performances moved from the *Aktion* itself to the analysis of action as the motivating force behind an alternative society. Believing that most artists attempt in their work to come to terms with a troubled past, he stated that 'It is the assignment of the artist to destroy art and come closer to reality. The artist has the responsibility to change himself and society as well.' In this he was reiterating one of the central tenets of Aktionismus, that art should have a cathartic, curative function within society. His aim in such works as *SS and Jewish Star Aktion* (1971) was a form of social therapy through an act of self-abasement for the Nazi period, a liberating reinterpretation of the self and society. In the 1970s Muehl withdrew from the art world and formed the Aktions Analytischen Kommune at Friedrichshof in Burgenland, which proposed a utopian, collective community in which a unity of art and life could be achieved.

WRITINGS
Omen Super: Materialaktion, Totalaktion, Superaktion (Vienna, 1967)
Zock: Aspekte einer Totalrevolution (Vienna, 1968)
Mama & Papa: Materialaktion, 63–69 (Frankfurt am Main, 1969)
Zock: Aspekte einer Totalrevolution, 66/71 (Munich, 1971)
Das AA-Modell (Neusiedl am See, 1976)
Weg aus dem Sumpf (Nuremberg, 1977)

BIBLIOGRAPHY
H. Klocker: *Otto Muehl: Ausgewahlte Arbeiten, 1963–1986* (Zurndorf, rev. 2/1987)

For further bibliography *see* AKTIONISMUS.

ANDREW WILSON

Muelenbroec, Willem. *See* MASTERS, ANONYMOUS, AND MONOGRAMMISTS, §I: MASTER OF THE MANSI MAGDALENE.

Muelich, Hans. *See* MIELICH, HANS.

Mueller [Müller], **Otto** (*b* Licbau, Silesia [now Libawka, Poland], 16 Oct 1874; *d* Breslau [now Wrocław, Poland], 24 Sept 1930). German painter and printmaker. His mother was said to have been a gypsy, although this was never proved. He began his artistic training with an apprenticeship as a lithographer from 1890 until 1894 in Görlitz, Silesia. From 1894 to 1896 he studied at the Kunstakademie in Dresden. He returned to Silesia, however, travelling occasionally, for example to Switzerland, Italy and Munich. Towards the end of 1908 he moved to Berlin, where he joined the Neue Sezession, an exhibiting group formed in 1910 in protest at the rejection of younger artists' work by the Berliner Sezession (*see* SECESSION, §2), which had a conservative tendency. In this circle he met some of the painters of DIE BRÜCKE and he became a member of the group in 1910.

As each artist moved from Dresden to Berlin, Mueller's contact with Die Brücke intensified. In 1911 he worked in Berlin with Ernst Ludwig Kirchner and Max Pechstein. He travelled to Bohemia with Kirchner and spent the summer with Kirchner and Erich Heckel on the Baltic island of Fehmarn. After the early influences of Symbolism and Post-Impressionism, and in particular the art of Arnold Böcklin and Ludwig von Hofmann (1861–1945), from 1910 he found his characteristic painting and drawing styles and his personal subject-matter through Die Brücke. His most common theme was models painted in nature, one that other group members had painted at the Moritzburg lakes near Dresden and on the beaches of the Baltic Sea: naked women and men, painted in couples or groups,

resting in the reeds or under the trees, or swimming in the water, as in *Bathers* (1912; Essen, Mus. Flkwang).

Mueller removed all realistic description from his portrayals of these scenes, instead taking the theme to an arcadian sphere so that it represented a yearning for the innocent union of humanity and nature. While the theme had been a representation of spontaneous life for many of the artists of Die Brücke and, in the case of Kirchner and Heckel, radical provocations of bourgeois life, Mueller depicted the subject in terms of peaceful idylls. His style was, however, Expressionist in being very two-dimensional and graphic with a marked tendency to formal stylization. This is illustrated particularly well in his prints, for example *Three Girls Seated* (woodcut, 1912; see Buchheim, p. 63). As with many members of Die Brücke, his bright palette changed to gentler colouring around 1911, losing its provocative harshness, for example in *Nude Standing under Trees* (1915; Düsseldorf, Kstsamml. Nordrhein-Westfalen).

An innovation with which Mueller influenced the other artists of Die Brücke was his use of distemper, a glue-based paint, instead of traditional oil paint. Distemper proved more fluid and flexible, and better suited to Mueller's fast and graphic style of painting. It also enabled

Otto Mueller: *Two Girls*, distemper on burlap, 1.75×1.11 m, *c.* 1925–8 (Berlin, Neue Nationalgalerie)

him to achieve a matt surface, an effect that the other painters of Die Brücke also found suitable for their work.

In 1919 after his military service (1916–18), Mueller became a professor at the Kunstakademie of Breslau. His subject-matter and style changed little, and he continued to paint the female nude in a landscape, for example *Two Girls* (*c.* 1925–8; Berlin, Neue N.G.; see fig.). Because he seldom dated his works, it is difficult to arrange them chronologically. In the 1920s he travelled to Romania, Bulgaria and Hungary, spending some time living among gypsies. He produced numerous paintings of gypsy life, which seemed a logical progression from the theme of naked figures moving about freely in the open. His choice of this subject-matter has led to further speculation about his mother's identity. As well as paintings, such as *Gypsy Woman with Sunflower* (Saarbrücken, Saarland-Mus.), he produced many lithographs, including the *Zigeunermappe* portfolio of 1927 (see Buchheim, nos 160–68) of nine colour lithographs.

In Nazi Germany, Mueller's work was designated as 'degenerate art' (*see* ENTARTETE KUNST). Many of his works were removed from museums. After World War II, however, his stylized painting and drawing style became very popular in Germany and in the 1950s influenced many illustrators and fashion designers.

BIBLIOGRAPHY

W. Scheidig: *Otto Mueller: Zigeunermappe* (Dresden, 1958)
L.-G. Buchheim: *Otto Mueller: Leben und Werk* (Feldafing, 1963) [incl. cat. of graphic work]
F. Karsch: *Otto Mueller: Das graphische Gesamtwerk* (Berlin, 1974)
H. Jähner: *Künstlergruppe Brücke: Geschichte einer Gemeinschaft und das Lebenswerk ihrer Repräsentanten* (Berlin, 1984), pp. 218–49, 445

LUCIUS GRISEBACH

Mug, Mount. *See under* KALA-I MUG.

Muggeridge, Edward James. *See* MUYBRIDGE, EADWEARD.

Mughal [Moghul; Mogul]. Dynasty of Central Asian origin that ruled portions of the Indian subcontinent from 1526 to 1857. The patronage of the Mughal emperors had a significant impact on the development of architecture, painting and a variety of other arts (*see* INDIAN SUBCONTINENT, §§III, 7(i); V, 4(i); and VII, 1(ii), 3, 6(iii), 9–12, 15 and 17).

The Mughal dynasty was founded by Babur (*reg* 1526–30), a prince descended from Timur and Chingiz Khan. Having lost his Central Asian kingdom of FERGHANA, Babur conquered KABUL and then in 1526 Delhi (*see* DELHI, §I). He was a collector of books and his interests in art are apparent in his memoirs, the *Bāburnāma*, written in Chagatay Turkish. Babur built palace pavilions and laid out gardens. The latter, divided into four parts by water courses (Ind.-Pers. *chār-bāgh*, a four-plot garden), became a model for subsequent Mughal gardens.

Babur was succeeded by Humayun (*reg* 1530–40, 1555–6), who initiated a number of building projects, most notably the Purana Qila' in Delhi. Sher Shah usurped the throne and drove Humayun into exile in 1540. During the SUR (ii) interregnum, Humayun travelled to Iran where he was able to attract a number of Safavid court artists to his service. In 1545 he re-established Mughal power in the subcontinent with the capture of Kabul, which was the centre of Humayun's court until he took Delhi in 1555. Little is known of the Kabul period, but painters from Iran arrived there, and apparently some manuscripts were produced. Humayun died in 1556, shortly after his return to Delhi.

Akbar (*reg* 1556–1605) inherited a small and precarious kingdom, but by the time of his death in 1605 it had been transformed into a vast empire stretching from Kabul to the Deccan. A ruler of genius, Akbar established political, administrative and cultural institutions that endured until the 19th century. The history of his reign and the details of its institutions were recorded by his courtier Abu'l al-Fazl in the *Akbarnāma* and *Āyīn-i Akbarī*. Akbar introduced active state patronage of craft manufacture and textile production. His interest in the imperial painting workshops apparently encouraged the development of a new composite style (*see* 'ABD AL-SAMAD and fig.). Numerous manuscripts were created for the imperial court, and their style was imitated in works produced for the nobility. Akbar's contribution to architecture included an impressive series of forts and palaces exhibiting a fascinating blend of Persian and Indian styles, the most important built at AGRA, LAHORE and FATEHPUR SIKRI. He was also interested in music and attracted outstanding musicians to his court, including the famous Tansen of Gwalior.

Jahangir (*reg* 1605–27) continued the policies set in place by his father and, for the most part, did not interfere with the institutions of state. As a patron, he had an active interest in painting, architecture and gardens, as indicated by surviving pictures and monuments and his memoirs, the *Tūzuk-i Jahāngīrī*. Like earlier emperors, he was an acute observer of the everyday world and took a special delight in curiosities from distant lands that were arriving in India. His connoisseur's eye for painting is revealed by the attributions, written in his own hand, that are found on many pictures. Splendid pieces of carved jade and other precious objects made for Jahangir attest an impressive level of craftsmanship and the opulence of the emperor's material surroundings.

The dynasty's greatest patron of architecture, Shah Jahan (*reg* 1628–58), established an entirely new city at Delhi and undertook the wholesale reconstruction of the palaces at Agra and Lahore. His most famous project was the Taj Mahal at Agra (*see* AGRA, §II, 1), a stunning mausoleum of white marble built for his wife. All these buildings exhibit a careful synthesis of diverse Indian and Persian elements. The formality of Shah Jahan's architecture was paralleled in painting and the decorative arts. Miniatures of the court exhibit a cool grandeur, as do the paintings in the *Shāh Jahānnāma* (Windsor Castle, Royal Lib.), an illustrated history of the reign. Of the many precious objects made for the court, perhaps the most impressive is the Emperor's white jade wine cup (London, V&A).

Aurangzeb (*reg* 1658–1707) ascended the throne after imprisoning his father and eliminating his brothers and nephews. In the early part of his reign, patronage continued as before, with portraits of the Emperor following the conventions established in the time of Shah Jahan. Aurangzeb's rule, however, was marked by a gradual increase in Islamic orthodoxy. Painting and music were discouraged at court; artists began to rely on the nobility for patronage, some migrating to regional centres. Aurangzeb added little to the imperial palaces built by his forebears but commissioned the construction of a number of mosques. The best-known example is the Badshahi Mosque at Lahore, a building of extraordinary scale. Wars in the Deccan against Bijapur and Golconda occupied much of Aurangzeb's rule, and portions of the empire in the north-west began to slip from Mughal hands.

The rule of the later Mughals (1707–1857) was marked by political disintegration. The Marathas gained control of Maharashtra and central India, the British slowly expanded their holdings in Bengal and the Sikhs emerged as a militant force in Punjab. The Nizam of Hyderabad broke away in 1724, and Sind was ruled by its own emirs. The Nawabs of Murshidabad and Lucknow, while ostensibly vassals, were independent for all practical purposes. A devastating blow came in 1739 during the reign of Muhammad Shah (1719–48) when Nadir Shah of Iran sacked the Mughal capital. With relatively little territory or revenue, the Mughal court ceased to set the standard in the arts.

BIBLIOGRAPHY

EARLY SOURCES

Zahir al-Din Muhammad Babur: *Bāburnāma* (*c.* 1530) Eng. trans. and ed. by A. S. Beveridge, 2 vols (London, 1922/*R* New Delhi, 1970)
Abu'l al-Fazl: *Āyīn-i Akbarī* [Annals of Akbar] (*c.* 1596–1602); Eng. trans. in 3 vols: vol. i, trans. H. Blochmann, ed. S. L. Gloomer ([Calcutta], 1871/*R* Delhi, 1965); vols ii–iii, trans. H. S. Jarrett, ed. J. Sarkar (1948–9/*R* New Delhi, 1972–3)
——: *Akbarnāma* (*c.* 1596–1602); Eng. trans. H. Beveridge, 3 vols (Calcutta, 1907–39/*R* New Delhi, 1972–3)
Nur al Din Muhammad Jahangir: *Tūzuk-i Jahāngīrī* [Memoirs of Jahangir] (*c.* 1624); Eng. trans. A. Rogers, ed. H. Beveridge (London, 1904–14/*R* Delhi, 1968)
'Abd al-Hamid Lahauri: *Pādshāhnāma* [Emperor's book] (*c.* 1654–5); ed. K. Ahmad and A. Rahim, 2 vols (Calcutta, 1865–8)

GENERAL

B. Prasad: *History of Jahangir* (London and Madras, 1922, rev. Allahabad, 5/1962)
J. Sarkar: *History of Aurangzeb*, 5 vols (Calcutta, 1925–34)
——: *Fall of the Mughal Empire*, 3 vols (Calcutta, 1932–50)
I. Habib: *The Agrarian System of Mughal India* (Bombay, 1963)
M. Athar Ali: *The Mughal Nobility under Aurangzeb* (Bombay, 1968)
S. A. A. Rizvi: *The Religious and Intellectual History of the Muslims in Akbar's Reign* (Delhi, 1975)
A. R. Khan: *The Chieftains in the Mughal Empire during the Reign of Akbar* (Simla, 1977)
A. J. Qaisar: *The Indian Response to European Technology and Culture, 1498–1707* (Delhi, 1982)
T. Raychaudhari and I. Habib, eds: *The Cambridge Economic History of India*, i (Cambridge, 1982)
M. Hasan: *Babur, the Founder of the Mughal Empire in India* (Delhi, 1986)
D. Streusand: *The Formation of the Mughal Empire* (Oxford, 1989)
W. E. Begley, ed.: *Shah Jahan Nama of Inayat Khan: An Abridged History of the Mughal Emperor Shah Jahan* (New Delhi, 1990)
J. Richards: *The Mughal Empire* (Cambridge, 1993)

R. NATH

Mug Tepe. *See under* URA TYUBE.

Muhammad 'Ali (i) [Muḥammad 'Alī Muzahhib] (*fl c.* 1600–10). Persian painter, active in India. He has been identified from three inscribed works bearing his name: a *Seated Poet* (Boston, MA, Mus. F.A.), a *Seated Youth* (Washington, DC, Freer) and the drawing of *A Girl* in the Binney Collection (San Diego, CA, Mus. A.). The latter, signed Muhammad 'Ali Jahangir Shahi with the

presumed regnal date 5 (AD 1610–11), shows that he worked for the Mughal emperor Jahangir (*reg* 1605–27) early in his reign. The painting of a *Young Prince Riding* (Geneva, Prince Sadruddin Aga Khan priv. col.) has also been attributed to him. This is close in style to the painting in the Freer Gallery of Art, and the two share a competent but bland indebtedness to the work of FARRUKH BEG. The equestrian portrait of *Ibrahim 'Adil Shah II*, attributed to Muhammad 'Ali by S. C. Welch, is now known to be a signed work of Farrukh Beg. Muhammad 'Ali's small oeuvre, technical skill and dependence on another's artistic personality suggest that he was primarily an illuminator, namely the Muhammad 'Ali Muzahhib of Shiraz whose portrait was drawn by Reza 'Abbasi in AH 1020 (AD 1611–12) following his return from India.

BIBLIOGRAPHY

Indian Miniature Painting from the Collection of Edwin Binney, 3rd: The Mughal and Deccani Schools with Some Related Sultanate Material (exh. cat. by E. Binney, Portland, OR, A. Mus., 1973), no. 123
B. W. Robinson, ed.: *The Keir Collection: Islamic Painting and the Arts of the Book* (London, 1976), pt III, no. 351
The Grand Mogul: Imperial Painting in India, 1600–1660 (exh. cat. by M. C. Beach, Williamstown, MA, Clark A. Inst.; Baltimore, MD, Walters A.G.; Boston, MA, Mus. F.A.; New York, Asia Soc. Gals; 1978–9)
S. C. Welch: 'Reflections on Muhammad 'Ali', *Gott ist schön und er liebt die Schönheit: Festschrift für Annemarie Schimmel*, ed. A. Giese and C. Bürgel (Berne, 1994), pp. 407–20

ROBERT SKELTON

Muhammad 'Ali (ii) [Muḥammad 'Alī al-Mashhadī ibn Malik Ḥusayn al-Iṣfahānī] (*fl* Isfahan, 1645–60). Persian illustrator. The son of a painter, Muhammad 'Ali became one of the most popular and prolific painters at the court of the Safavid monarch 'Abbas II (*reg* 1642–66). Muhammad 'Ali was a skilled and competent artist who preferred rounded contours and simple forms. Although he was not as innovative in form and style as his contemporary MU'IN, Muhammad 'Ali's figures convey tremendous charm, animation and vitality. Eight of his paintings illustrate his own copy (Baltimore, MD, Walters A.G., MS 649) of Muhammad Riza Naw'i's *Sūz u gudāz* ('Burning and consuming'). The largest number of the artist's ink drawings highlighted with colour washes and gold illustrate a copy (Istanbul, Topkapı Pal. Lib., H. 1010) of Hafiz's *Dīvān* (collected poetry). His album pages include standard figures of youths, elderly men and lovers as well as more unusual group scenes, such as one of bears imitating a court.

BIBLIOGRAPHY

T. Falk, ed.: *Treasures of Islam* (Geneva, 1985), no. 93
M. Farhad: *Safavid Single Page Painting, 1628–1666* (diss., Cambridge, MA, Harvard U., 1987), pp. 102–19 and cat. nos 12–27

Muhammad 'Ali (ibn Muhammad Zaman) (iii). *See under* MUHAMMAD ZAMAN.

Muhammad Baqir (i). *See* BAQIR.

Muhammad Baqir (ii) [Muḥammad Bāqir] (*fl* 1750s–1760s). Persian painter. He is known for decorations in the margins of manuscripts, copies of European prints and 17th-century paintings, and wash drawings. His subjects range from floral sprays to nudes, such as the watercolour of a sleeping nymph (1765; Dublin, Chester Beatty Lib., cat. no. 282.VI). He contributed paintings and marginal decorations to a sumptuous album (1758–9; St Petersburg, Hermitage), probably compiled for the Afsharid court historian Mirza Mahdi Khan Astarabadi. Muhammad Baqir's punning signature there suggests that he was a pupil of 'ALI ASHRAF. Muhammad Baqir signed one of the finest marginal paintings in a smaller but similar album (1764; dispersed; sold Hôtel Drouot, Paris, 23 June 1982) and may have been responsible for all of them, which include rose sprays and copies of *Susannah and the Elders*. Muhammad Baqir is sometimes said to have continued to work under the Qajar ruler Fath 'Ali Shah (*reg* 1797–1834), for the impressive varnished covers that the ruler ordered to replace the original binding on the famous copy (London, BL, Or. MS. 2265) of Nizami's *Khamsa* ('Five poems') made for the Safavid shah Tahmasp I in 1539–43 are signed by Muhammad Baqir and SAYYID MIRZA. As the date of the binding (the late 1820s) would extend Muhammad Baqir's career beyond reasonable limits, it is more likely that the painter of the varnished covers should be identified with the enameller BAQIR.

BIBLIOGRAPHY

B. W. Robinson: 'Persian Painting in the Qajar Period', *Highlights of Persian Art*, ed. R. Ettinghausen and E. Yarshater (Boulder, CO, 1979), pp. 331–62

M. A. Karīmzāda Tabrīzī: *Aḥvāl u āthār-i naqqāshān-i qadīm-i īrān* [The lives and art of old painters of Iran] (London, 1985), no. 943

L. S. Diba: 'Lacquerwork', *The Arts of Persia*, ed. R. W. Ferrier (New Haven and London, 1989), pp. 243–54

——: 'Persian Painting in the Eighteenth Century: Tradition and Transmission', *Muqarnas*, vi (1989), pp. 147–60

B. W. Robinson: 'Persian Painting under the Zand and Qājār Dynasties', *From Nadir Shah to the Islamic Republic* (1991), vii of *The Cambridge History of Iran* (Cambridge, 1968–91), pp. 870–90

Muhammad Ghaffari. *See* GHAFFARI, (3).

Muhammad Hasan Afshar [Muḥammad Ḥasan Khān Afshār] (*fl c.* 1835–*c.* 1865). Persian painter. A noted court painter and portraitist under the Qajar rulers Muhammad Shah (*reg* 1834–48) and Nasir al-Din (*reg* 1848–96), Muhammad Hasan Afshar was awarded the title Painter Laureate (Pers. *naqqāsh bāshī*). A portrait dated 1847 in the Churchill Album (London, BL, Or. MS. 4938) depicts Muhammad Shah seated in a red tunic with blue sash and flashing diamonds. The artist's most remarkable works are three life-size oil portraits of Nasir al-Din (Tehran, Gulistan Pal.; Tehran, Moghaddam priv. col. (see Robinson, 1991, fig. 30a); and Isfahan, Chihil Sutun Palace, dated 1860). The artist also painted small varnished objects, such as a penbox dated 1846 (priv. col., see Robinson, 1989, fig. 16a), which has a scene of the Last Judgement on the top and a Napoleonic battle scene on one side. The penbox was only finished in 1861 by ISMA'IL JALAYIR, who added a scene of the Qajar monarch Muhammad Shah in battle on the other side and a design and inscription on the base. Other members of the Afshar family also painted similar objects, such as another penbox with a scene of the Last Judgement (Los Angeles, CA, Co. Mus. A., 73.5.159).

BIBLIOGRAPHY

B. W. Robinson: *Persian Miniature Painting from Collections in the British Isles* (London, 1967)

M. A. Karīmzāda Tabrīzī: *Aḥvāl u āthār-i naqqāshān-i qadīm-i īrān* [The lives and art of old painters of Iran] (London, 1985), no. 988

B. W. Robinson: 'Qajar Lacquer', *Muqarnas*, vi (1989), pp. 131–46

——: 'Persian Painting under the Zand and Qājār Dynasties', *From Nadir Shah to the Islamic Republic* (1991), vii of *The Cambridge History of Iran* (Cambridge, 1968–91), pp. 870–90

Muhammad Hasan Khan [Muḥammad Ḥasan Khān] (*fl c.* 1800–40). Persian painter. He signed a number of large oil paintings (Tehran, Nigaristan Mus.; ex-Amery priv. col.), including two life-size portraits of princes and a painting of *Shaykh San'an and the Christian Maiden*. Other paintings that can be attributed to the artist on stylistic grounds include a third portrait of a prince in the same collection and two paintings of women (Tbilisi, Mus. A. Georg.). His style is characterized by a soft rendering of features, fondness for reddish brown and a hallmark vase of flowers. He also produced miniature paintings in the form of monochrome portraits. European travellers in Tehran in the 19th century erroneously attributed to him the large mural in the Nigaristan Palace depicting the court of the Qajar monarch Fath 'Ali Shah (*reg* 1797–1834), but this painting is now considered the work of 'ABDALLAH KHAN.

BIBLIOGRAPHY

S. Y. Amiranashvili: *Iranskaya stankovaya zhivopis'* [Iranian wall painting] (Tbilisi, 1940)

B. W. Robinson: 'The Court Painters of Fatḥ 'Alī Shāh', *Eretz-Israel*, vii (1964), pp. 94–105

S. J. Falk: *Qajar Paintings: Persian Oil Paintings of the 18th and 19th Centuries* (London, 1972)

B. W. Robinson: 'Persian Painting in the Qajar Period', *Highlights of Persian Art*, ed. R. Ettinghausen and E. Yarshater (Boulder, CO, 1979), pp. 331–62

M. A. Karīmzāda Tabrīzī: *Aḥvāl u āthār-i naqqāshān-i qadīm-i īrān* [The lives and art of old painters of Iran] (London, 1985), no. 987

B. W. Robinson: 'Persian Painting under the Zand and Qājār Dynasties', *From Nadir Shah to the Islamic Republic* (1991), vii of *The Cambridge History of Iran* (Cambridge, 1968–91), pp. 870–90

S. J. VERNOIT

Muhammadi [Muḥammadī Haravī] (*fl* Qazvin, *c.* 1570–78; Herat, *c.* 1578–87). Persian draughtsman and illustrator. Although the Ottoman historian Mustafa 'Ali identified Muhammadi as a son of SULTAN-MUHAMMAD (quoted in Armenag Bey Sakisian: *La Miniature Persane* (Paris and Brussels, 1929), p. 123), such a kinship is unlikely in light of Muhammadi's epithet *Haravī* (from Herat) used in an inscription on a painting after Muhammadi (Istanbul, Topkapı Pal. Lib., H. 2140, fol. 5*r*) of a seated youth with a falcon. As A. Welch has reconstructed Muhammadi's life, he worked at the studio of the Safavid ruler Isma'il II (*reg* 1576–8) at Qazvin but after the accession of Muhammad Khudabanda (*reg* 1578–88) left for Khurasan. Muhammadi's subsequent itinerary is suggested by his portrait (Istanbul, Topkapı Pal. Lib., H. 2155, fol. 20*v*) of 'Aliquli Khan dated 1584, while he was governor of HERAT (1581–7). B. W. Robinson places his *floruit* entirely in Herat from *c.* 1560 to *c.* 1590. Although Muhammadi worked on at least one manuscript, a copy (Istanbul, Topkapı Pal. Lib., H. 777) of Nizami's *Khamsa* ('Five poems'), he is best known for his portraits (e.g. London, BL, Orient. & India Office Lib., 28–14) and bucolic scenes (e.g. Paris, Mus. Guimet, no. 7111). His figural style conforms to that associated with Qazvin *c.* 1575, in which long-necked, round-cheeked youths and girls sway to music or towards one another. Often his figures appear off-balance, as if rocking on their heels. Although his hunting or encampment scenes are composed as a series of vignettes rather than as a unified whole, they and his slightly awkward portraits exerted a strong influence on the artists at the court of Shah 'Abbas I (*see* ISLAMIC ART, §III, 4(vi)(a)).

BIBLIOGRAPHY
A. Welch: 'Painting and Patronage under Shah 'Abbas I', *Iran. Stud.*, vii (1974), pp. 466–70
B. W. Robinson: 'Muhammadī and the Khurāsān Style', *Iran*, xxx (1992), pp. 17–30

SHEILA R. CANBY

Muhammad ibn al-Zayn [Muh'ammad ibn al-Zayn; Ibn al-Zayn] (*fl* early 14th century). Arab metalworker. He is known from signatures on two undated inlaid wares, the Baptistère de St Louis (Paris, Louvre, LP 16; *see* ISLAMIC ART, fig. 153, signed in six places) and the Vasselot Bowl (Paris, Louvre, MAO 331, signed once). His style is characterized by bold compositions of large figures encrusted with silver plaques on which details are elaborately chased. His repertory develops themes characteristic of later 13th-century metalwork from Mosul (*see* ISLAMIC ART, §IV, 3(ii) and (iii))—mounted or enthroned rulers, bands of running or prowling animals, an elaborate Nilotic composition, courtiers bearing insignia of office, and battle scenes on scroll grounds with strikingly naturalistic fauna. His work is marked by a realism of facial expression, in which Turco-Mongolian physiognomy, dress, headgear and even coiffure are prominent, and a vigour of movement, gesture or stance that enlivens and transforms even the running animals and rows of standing courtiers, some in Frankish costume. The technique and style of these pieces allow their attribution to the Bahri Mamluk period in Egypt and Syria (*c.* 1250–*c.* 1350), but the absence of owners' inscriptions suggests that they were not made for a Mamluk sultan. The exceptional naturalism has encouraged scholars to date the Baptistère by identifying the figures depicted. Rice, for example, suggested that the basin was made for the amir Salar (*d* 1310) on the basis of the emblems worn by one figure, but other scholars have suggested dates ranging from the mid-13th century to the mid-14th. Other works in the same distinctive style have been attributed to his workshop, such as a basin (Jerusalem, Mayer Mem. Inst. Islam. A.), a steel mirror inlaid with gold and silver and decorated with inscriptions and signs of the zodiac (Istanbul, Topkapı Pal. Mus.; *see* MIRROR, fig. 6) and an incense burner found at Qus (Cairo, Mus. Islam. A.). A forged iron screen in the Is'ardiyya Madrasa (before 1345) in Jerusalem is inscribed with the name of Muhammad ibn al-Zayn, but the date of the screen and its relationship to the inlaid wares are uncertain.

BIBLIOGRAPHY
D. S. Rice: 'The Blazons of the "Baptistère de Saint Louis"', *Bull. SOAS*, xiii (1950), pp. 367–80
——: *Le Baptistère de Saint Louis* (Paris, 1951)
Renaissance of Islam: Art of the Mamluks (exh. cat. by E. Atıl, Washington, DC, N. Mus. Nat. Hist.; Minneapolis, MN, Inst. A.; New York, Met. and elsewhere; 1981), nos 20, 21
J. M. Bloom: 'A Mamluk Basin in the L. A. Mayer Memorial Institute', *Islam. A.*, ii (1987), pp. 19–26
D. Behrens-Abouseif: 'The Baptistère de Saint Louis: A Reinterpretation', *Islam. A.*, iii (1988–9), pp. 3–9

J. M. ROGERS

Muhammad Ibrahim (ibn Hajji Yusuf). *See under* MUHAMMAD ZAMAN.

Muhammad Isma'il. *See* ISFAHANI, (2).

Muhammad Ja'far [Muhammad Ja'far] (*fl c.* 1800–30). Persian painter. He was the most prolific painter in enamels at the court of the Qajar monarch Fath 'Ali Shah (*reg* 1797–1834), but unlike his contemporaries BAQIR and 'ALI, Muhammad Ja'far did not attach a title to his name when he signed his work. One of his earliest works is an inkpot for a penbox (1805; sold Paris, Hôtel Drouot, 25 May 1964, lot 2) decorated with busts of a young man and a girl. His most impressive pieces are large objects made for official presentation to foreign dignitaries. He enamelled several large gold dishes that are decorated with a lion and sun in the centre panel surrounded by alternating birds and floral swags. One (1813; ex-Kazrouni priv. col.; sold London, Sotheby's, March 1954, lot 867) was presented to Sir Gore Ouseley, the British ambassador to Iran, and another made of solid gold and weighing more than six pounds (1817–18; London, V&A, I.S.09406) was presented to the Court of Directors of the British East India Company on 18 June 1819. Muhammad Ja'far also painted a number of smaller objects such as the bowl and base of a waterpipe or hooka (Pers. *qaliyān*) and a jewelled snuffbox made in 1814 for the Crown Prince 'Abbas Mirza (all sold Paris, Hôtel Drouot, 25 May 1964, lots 29, 54 and 17 respectively). Muhammad Ja'far's painting is very fine, although his drawing is occasionally stiff and his shading harsh.

BIBLIOGRAPHY
B. W. Robinson: 'The Royal Gifts of Fath 'Alī Shāh', *Apollo*, lii (1950), pp. 66–8
V. B. Meen and A. D. Tushingham: *The Crown Jewels of Iran* (Toronto, 1968)
B. W. Robinson: 'Qājār Painted Enamels', *Paintings from Islamic Lands*, ed. R. Pinder-Wilson (Oxford, 1969), pp. 187–204

S. J. VERNOIT

Muhammad Qasim [Muhammad Qāsim Tabrīzī] (*b* ?Tabriz; *d* 1659). Persian illustrator, painter and poet. He was the most important painter in mid-17th-century Isfahan after MU'IN. Muhammad Qasim contributed illustrations to several manuscripts, including many tinted drawings for two copies (1640; Istanbul, Topkapı Pal. Lib., H. 1010; and *c.* 1650; Dublin, Chester Beatty Lib., MS. 299) of Hafiz's *Dīvān* (collected poetry) and 42 paintings to a copy (1648; Windsor Castle, Royal Lib., MS. A/6, Holmes 151) of the *Shāhnāma* ('Book of kings'). The artist also painted several murals of single figures and groups of picnickers in the side room (P4) adjoining the reception hall of the Chihil Sutun Palace (1647; *see* ISFAHAN, §3(vii)). He is best known for his album paintings of single figures or small groups; they often include short poems or letters that reflect his reputation as a celebrated poet. He was an accomplished draughtsman and sensitive colourist who repeated a few carefully controlled hues to create overall balance and harmony, but his elegant figures are somewhat stiff and his landscapes mere backdrops.

BIBLIOGRAPHY

I. Stchoukine: *Les Peintures des manuscrits de Shah 'Abbas 1er à la fin des Safavis* (Paris, 1964)
T. Falk, ed.: *Treasures of Islam* (Geneva, 1985), no. 89
B. Gray: 'The Arts in the Safavid Period', *The Timurid and Safavid Periods*, ed. P. Jackson (1986), vi of *The Cambridge History of Iran* (Cambridge, 1968–91), pp. 903–4
M. Farhad: *Safavid Single Page Painting, 1628–1666* (diss., Cambridge, MA, Harvard U., 1987), pp. 120–49 and cat. nos 28–40

Muhammad Sadiq [Muḥammad Ṣādiq; Mulla Sadiq; Sadiq] (*fl c.* 1750–1800). Persian painter. The foremost painter at the court of Karim Khan (*reg* 1750–79), the Zand ruler in Shiraz, he worked in a variety of media, from large oil paintings to miniatures, and painted and varnished ('lacquered') objects (*see* ISLAMIC ART, fig. 242). His name has become synonymous with the Zand style. His reputation was so great that many works by different hands have been attributed to him. Works signed with his name range in date from the 1730s to the 1790s, an improbably long time, and it is likely that some are by other artists. Muhammad Sadiq was apparently a pupil of 'ALI ASHRAF, for one of his earliest works, a circular box depicting a young woman in early 18th-century dress on the interior (Tehran, Nigaristan Mus.), is painted on the exterior with birds and flowers in the style of his master and has a punning signature that invokes his master's name. Other early work includes several of the splendid marginal designs in a sumptuous album (1758–9; St Petersburg, Hermitage). Muhammad Sadiq produced several oil paintings, including two signed works (ex-Amery priv. col.; Tehran, Nigaristan Mus.) depicting lovers drinking at a window and a prince on horseback attacked by a dragon. Several of the murals from Karim Khan's mausoleum (Shiraz, Pars Mus.) are signed by him. He also worked in miniature, for a mirror-case (1775–6; London, V&A, 763–1888) has a punning signature that invokes his namesake Ja'far al-Sadiq (*d* 765), the sixth Shi'ite imam. The front covers are decorated with a hunting scene, and the inside and back covers show amorous couples on a terrace.

After Karim Khan's death, Muhammad Sadiq continued to work for the Qajar monarch Agha Muhammad (*reg* 1779–97), and, on the Shah's orders, Muhammad Sadiq repaired the mural in the Chihil Sutun Palace in Isfahan that depicts Nadir Shah's defeat of the Mughal armies at the Battle of Karnal in 1738. Several of the artist's painted objects, such as an octagonal mirror-case (1792–3; Tehran, Nigaristan Mus., 75.5.32), show that the Zand style continued into the early Qajar period. A signed mirror-case (1795–6; Berne, Hist. Mus., 72/13) has Christian scenes of the *Annunciation*, the *Presentation in the Temple* and the *Adoration of the Magi*, but another signed mirror-case dated the following year (Berne, Hist. Mus., 641) may be the work of his pupil. Figures play a predominant role in Muhammad Sadiq's style, which is notable for its fine detail, intimate atmosphere and poetic qualities. European features, such as shading, modelling, drapery and atmospheric perspective, remain superficial. His meticulous figural style made a great impression on his contemporaries, and his name was renowned many years after his death. His style was refined and developed

by the miniature painter Najaf 'Ali Isfahani (*see* ISFAHANI, (1)).

BIBLIOGRAPHY

B. W. Robinson: 'Persian Lacquer in the Bern Historical Museum', *Iran*, viii (1970), pp. 47–50
S. J. Falk: *Qajar Paintings: Persian Oil Paintings of the 18th and 19th Centuries* (London, 1972)
L. S. Diba: 'Lacquerwork', *The Arts of Persia*, ed. R. W. Ferrier (New Haven and London, 1989), pp. 243–54
——: 'Persian Painting in the Eighteenth Century: Tradition and Transmission', *Muqarnas*, vi (1989), pp. 147–60
B. W. Robinson: 'Painting in the Post-Safavid Period', *The Arts of Persia*, ed. R. W. Ferrier (New Haven and London, 1989), pp. 225–31
——: 'Persian Painting under the Zand and Qājār Dynasties', *From Nadir Shah to the Islamic Republic* (1991), vii of *The Cambridge History of Iran* (Cambridge, 1968–91), pp. 870–90

Muhammad Shafi' [Muḥammad Shafī' 'Abbāsī; Shafī' 'Abbāsī] (*fl* Isfahan, 1628–*c.* 1674). Persian painter. The son of RIZA, Muhammad Shafi' developed and popularized bird-and-flower painting, a genre his father had introduced to the Isfahan school. *Youth Painting a Flower* (*c.* 1635; Washington, DC, Freer, 53.17) is probably a self-portrait; mounted beside a sketch of an elderly bespectacled man identified as Riza, it corroborates the claim of Muhammad Shafi''s kinship to Riza, also established by an inscribed drawing in Los Angeles (Co. Mus. A.). Muhammad Shafi' also completed at least one of his father's late drawings, *The Poet, the Robber and the Dogs* (Ham, Surrey, Keir priv. col., III.387). The quality of line in Muhammad Shafi''s drawings is somewhat dry, but paintings such as *Bird, Butterflies and Blossom* (1651–2; Cleveland, OH, Mus. A.) exhibit a sensitive palette and subtly modelled forms, which were derived from European sources, including English engravings. The botanical studies of Muhammad Shafi' are exemplified by a group of flower drawings, many signed and dated between 1640 and 1671, included in an album (London, BM, 1988, 4-23 01-056); they are the forerunners of a versatile new decorative genre which was continued by such late 17th-century painters as MUHAMMAD ZAMAN and 'ALIQULI JABBADAR and translated into intricate textile patterns. A velvet panel of pairs of standing females in a landscape of flowering plants (New York, Sotheby's, 11 Dec 1994, lot 87) bears Shafi' 'Abbasi's signature, confirming his role as a textile designer.

BIBLIOGRAPHY

B. Gray: 'An Album of Designs for Persian Textiles', *Aus der Welt der islamischen Kunst, Festschrift Ernst Kühnel* (Berlin, 1959), pp. 219–25
B. W. Robinson, ed.: *Islamic Painting and the Arts of the Book* (London, 1976), pp. 208–10 [Keir col.]
E. Atıl: *The Brush of the Masters: Drawings from Iran and India* (Washington, DC, 1978), p. 83
Islamic Art and Design, 1500–1700 (exh. cat. by J. M. Rogers, London, BM, 1983), no. 58
M. Farhad: *Safavid Single Page Painting, 1629–1666* (diss., Cambridge, MA, Harvard U., 1987), pp. 187–205 and cat. nos 64–77

SHEILA R. CANBY

Muḥammad Shafīq. See MEHMED ṢEFIK.

Muhammad Sharif (*fl c.* 1580–1625). Indian miniature painter, son of 'ABD AL-SAMAD. Of noble descent and an accomplished courtier, he is not on the list of 17 highly prized artists compiled by Abu'l Fazl, the biographer of the Mughal emperor Akbar (*reg* 1556–1605), in the *Āyīn-i*

Akbarī, a contemporary account of court matters. The earliest manuscript with inscriptions naming Muhammad Sharif as a painter is the *Khamsa* ('Five poems') of Nizami (*c.* 1585; Pontresina, Keir priv. col.). The style of miniatures assigned to him (fols 73b, 157) suggests a painter at the beginning of his career. The work is mostly carefully contained within the margin, with rather primitive stylized animals, but where it breaks the margin more freedom of movement and greater realism appears. Muhammad Sharif acted as the designer/outliner in three miniatures in the *Razmnāma* ('Book of wars'; *c.* 1582–6; Jaipur, Maharaja Sawai Man Singh II Mus., MS. AG. 1683–1850): he collaborated with Bhanwari (fol. 122), Kesu Khurd (fol. 118) and Munir (fol. 68). Few other examples can be firmly assigned to him.

For illustration of work *see* ISLAMIC ART, fig. 131.

BIBLIOGRAPHY

The Grand Mogul: Imperial Painting in India 1600–1660 (exh. cat. by M. C. Beach, Williamstown, MA, Clark A. Inst.; Baltimore, MD, Walters A.G.; Boston, MA, Mus. F.A.; New York, Asia Soc. Gals; 1978–9)
The Imperial Image: Paintings for the Mughal Court (exh. cat. by M. C. Beach, Washington, DC, Freer, 1981)

HEATHER ELGOOD

Muḥammad Shawqī. *See* MEHMED ŞEVKI.

Muhammad Shirin [Muḥammad, the 'Shirin' Painter] (*fl c.* 1825–50). Persian painter. He painted in a distinctive, bold style and is known for his depiction of plump moon-faced women. He has been assigned the name Muhammad on the basis of the punning signature, *yā muḥammad* ('O Muhammad') on a painting of a reclining woman (1842; Foroughi priv. col.). The artist is also known as the 'Shirin' Painter, a name derived from a painting of a woman (Tehran, Nigaristan Mus., ex-Amery priv. col.) inscribed with the name Shirin. Several other paintings (Tehran, Nigaristan Mus.; Tbilisi, Mus. A. Georg.; London, V&A) can be assigned to him on stylistic grounds, and his output seems to have quite large. He excelled in the depiction of women (e.g. a dancing woman with castanets; Tehran, Nigaristan Mus., ex-Amery priv. col.); his male figures are less successful.

BIBLIOGRAPHY

S. Y. Amiranashvili: *Iranskaya stankovaya zhivopis'* [Iranian wall painting] (Tbilisi, 1940)
B. W. Robinson: 'The Court Painters of Fatḥ 'Alī Shāh', *Eretz-Israel*, vii (1964), pp. 94–105
S. J. Falk: *Qajar Paintings: Persian Oil Paintings of the 18th and 19th Centuries* (London, 1972)
B. W. Robinson: 'Persian Painting in the Qajar Period', *Highlights of Persian Art*, ed. R. Ettinghausen and E. Yarshater (Boulder, CO, 1979), pp. 331–62
M. A. Karīmzāda Tabrīzī: *Aḥvāl u āthār-i naqqāshān-i qadīm-i īrān* [The lives and art of old painters of Iran] (London, 1985), no. 880
Treasures of Islam (exh. cat., ed. T. Falk; Geneva, Mus. A. & Hist., 1985), nos 185–6
B. W. Robinson: 'Painting in the Post-Safavid Period', *The Arts of Persia*, ed. R. W. Ferrier (New Haven and London, 1989), pp. 225–31
——: 'Persian Painting under the Zand and Qājār Dynasties', *From Nadir Shah to the Islamic Republic* (1991), vii of *The Cambridge History of Iran* (Cambridge, 1968–91), pp. 879–80 and fig. 21a

Muhammad Taqi. *See under* SHAYKH 'ABBASI.

Muhammad Yusuf [Mir Muḥammad Yūsuf al-Ḥusaynī Muṣavvir] (*fl* Isfahan, 1636–66). Persian painter. A prolific artist during the reigns of the Safavid shahs Safi (*reg* 1629–42) and 'Abbas II (*reg* 1642–66), Muhammad Yusuf worked in a variety of styles. His earliest works, including the eight illustrations in a copy (1636; London, BL, Add. MS. 7922) of Baqi's *Dīvān* (collected poetry) and single-page drawings and paintings (e.g. *Youth Holding a Cane*; Boston, MA, Mus. F.A., 14.637), exhibit fine draughtsmanship and a bright palette. In the 1640s he adopted a bolder calligraphic style for tinted drawings, such as the ones illustrating a copy of Hafiz's *Dīvān* (1640; Istanbul, Topkapı Pal. Lib., H. 1010) and several single-page compositions (e.g. Paris, Bib. N., MS. arabe 6074, fols 3*r*, 4*v* and 5*r*). This change from the artistic ideals of the early 17th century to a new linear style may have resulted from exposure to the work of his contemporary MUHAMMAD QASIM, with whom he collaborated on several manuscripts, including the *Dīvān* of Hafiz in Istanbul.

BIBLIOGRAPHY

I. Stchoukine: *Les Peintures des manuscrits de Shah 'Abbas 1er à la fin des Safavis* (Paris, 1964)
B. Gray: 'The Arts in the Safavid Period', *The Timurid and Safavid Periods*, ed. P. Jackson (1986), vi of *The Cambridge History of Iran* (Cambridge, 1968–91), p. 904 and pl. 65b
M. Farhad: *Safavid Single Page Painting, 1628–1666* (diss., Cambridge, MA, Harvard U., 1987), pp. 150–69 and cat. nos 41–52

Muhammad Zaman [Muḥammad Zamān ibn Ḥājjī Yūsuf Qumī] (*fl* 1649–1704; *d* before 1720–21/AH 1133). Persian painter. He was the foremost practitioner of stylistic eclecticism in 17th-century Safavid painting (*see* ISLAMIC ART, §III, 4(vi)(a)). In 20th-century writing on Persian painting he was confused with a Persian Christian called Muhammad-Paolo Zaman, who is mentioned in the *Storia do Mogor*, a history of Mughal India by the Venetian adventurer Niccolas Manucci (?1639–after 1712). According to Martin, for instance, Muhammad Zaman was sent by Shah 'Abbas II to study painting in Rome in the 1640s; he returned a convert to Christianity and had to take refuge at the court of the Mughal emperor, Shah Jahan, who gave him an official post in Kashmir. This theory would account for the distinctive features in his painting, such as figures in European dress, an interest in atmosphere, night scenes and cast shadows, and an elusive but pervasive flavour of Mughal India. In 1962, however, this account was discredited by the publication of the Leningrad (now St Petersburg) Album (St Petersburg, Hermitage, E-14), and Muhammad Zaman's paintings remain the only source of information on his career.

Muhammad Zaman's spidery, black signature, usually referring to himself in one of the standard Persian formulae of self-deprecation, occurs on no fewer than 40 works. The most important include a *Night Scene* mounted in the Davis Album (New York, Met., 30.95.174.1), a series of penboxes and other papier-mâché objects dated between 1659 and 1674 (Tehran, priv. cols, see Zukā', figs 2–7 and 50–57) and six fine miniatures added to two unfinished royal manuscripts of the 16th century, five of which are dated AH 1086 (1675–6). Four of these were inserted in a copy of the *Khamsa* ('Five poems') of Nizami made for Shah Tahmasp between 1539 and 1543 (three in London, BL, Or. MS. 2265; the fourth, Soudavar priv. col.); the other two are in a fragmentary copy of the *Shāhnāma*

('Book of kings') of Firdawsi associated with Shah 'Abbas I and datable to *c.* 1587 (Dublin, Chester Beatty Lib., Pers. MS. 277). Despite their traditional subject-matter, the use of perspective, modelling with colours, landscape elements and other conventions drawn from Western painting in these miniatures creates an unsettling contrast with the original 16th-century illustrations.

Other outstanding examples of Muhammad Zaman's work are the 16 miniatures of 1675–8 that he painted for an undedicated copy of Nizami's *Khamsa* (15 in New York, Pierpont Morgan Lib., MS. M. 469; one in a priv. col.) and six extraordinary and highly eclectic paintings based on Flemish and Italian prints, five of which bear dates between 1682 and 1689 (three mounted in the St Petersburg Album, fols 86, 89 and 94; one in Cambridge, MA, Fogg, inv. no. 1966.6; one Switzerland, priv. col.; the last untraced). All these are in a remarkably homogeneous, highly polished and finished style that does not need to be explained by a sojourn in Rome. Rather the artist's consistent mannerisms suggest that the European elements in his art were learnt in Iran from European prints, whose compositions were either selectively mined for details or copied in their entirety. Prints by Egbert van Panderen, Lucas Vorsterman I (reproducing a painting by Rubens), Raphael Sadeler I and others based on paintings by Italian masters, including one by Guido Reni, have been identified as the sources for some of Muhammad Zaman's paintings. The same Europeanizing style appears on papier-mâché objects painted by Muhammad Zaman and his brother Muhammad Ibrahim (ibn Hajji Yusuf) (*see* ISLAMIC ART, §VIII, 10). A son, Muhammad 'Ali (ibn Muhammad Zaman), also painted in his father's manner, as in a painting depicting the *New Year Audience of Shah Sultan Husayn* (1772; London, BM).

Mühlhausen, St Maria, south transept façade, *Elizabeth of Pomerania*

BIBLIOGRAPHY

N. Manucci: *Storia do Mogor* (MS.; 1699–1709); Eng. trans. by W. Irvine as *Storia do Mogor, or Mogul India*, ii (London, 1907/R New Delhi, 1981), pp. 17–18
F. R. Martin: *The Miniature Painting and Painters of Persia, India and Turkey from the 8th to the 18th Century*, 2 vols (London, 1912), i, p. 76; ii, pl. 173
A. A. Ivanov: 'Persidskiye miniatyury' [The Persian miniatures], *Al'bom indiyskikh i persidskikh miniatyur XVI–XVIII vv.* [An album of Indian and Persian miniatures of the 16th–18th centuries], ed. L. T. Guzal'yan (Moscow, 1962), pp. 44–55, pls 83–90
Y. Zukā': 'Muḥammad Zaman, nakhustīn nigārgar-i īrānī ki ba Urūpā firistāda shud' [Muhammad Zaman, the first Iranian artist to be sent to Europe], *Nigāh ba nigārgarī-i Īrān dar sadahā-yi davāzdahum va sizdahum* [A look at painting in Iran in the 12th and 13th centuries AH] (Tehran, Iran. Solar 1353/1975), pp. 37–79
E. G. Sims: 'Five Seventeenth-century Persian Oil Paintings', *Persian and Mughal Art*, ed. M. Goedhuis (London, 1976), pp. 228–30
——: 'Late Safavid Painting: The Chetel Sutun, the Armenian Houses, the Oil Paintings', *Akten des VII. internationalen Kongresses für iranische Kunst und Archäologie: München, 1976*, pp. 408–18
A. A. Ivanov: 'The Life of Muhammad Zaman: A Reconsideration', *Iran*, xvii (1979), pp. 65–70
E. G. Sims: 'The European Print Sources of Paintings by the Seventeenth-century Persian Painter, Muhammad Zaman ibn Haji Yusuf of Qum', *Le stampe e la diffusione delle immagini e degli stili*, ed. H. Zerner (Bologna, 1983), pp. 73–83, pls 76–83
Treasures of Islam/Trésors d'Islam (exh. cat., ed. T. Falk; Geneva, 1985), p. 129, no. 102 [ptg related to the works in the St Petersburg Album]
A. Soudavar: *Art of the Persian Courts* (New York, 1992), pp. 374–5, fig. 151
O. Akimuškin and others: *Il Murakka' di San Pietroburgo: Album di miniature indiane e persiane del XVI–XVIII secolo* (St Petersburg, Lugano and Milan, 1994) pp. 20, 69, 71, 73, 78, 83, 84, 109–114

ELEANOR SIMS

Mühl, Otto. *See* MUEHL, OTTO.

Mühlhausen. German town in Thuringia. It was first documented in 775 as a village under the protection of a Frankish castle. In 1180 it became a free imperial city and was a member of the Hanseatic League from 1418. The town was the centre of the Peasants' War (1524–5) under the leadership of Thomas Müntzer (*c.* 1489–1525). Much of the medieval town wall survives.

1. ST MARIA. The main parish church of the Neustadt district, St Maria, dating from the 12th century, was transferred in 1243 to the Teutonic Order, which also took over the Blasiuskirche in the Altstadt district in 1246. The 12th-century church was a cruciform basilica with nave and aisles, and with transeptal apses; only the north tower (*c.* 1190–1200) and the lowest floor of the south tower have survived. In the second quarter of the 13th century masons from the Maulbronn lodge worked on the church, their influence being especially noticeable in details and a heraldic console with affronted half-moons on the south tower.

The present church was built after the town was seriously damaged in 1315; a letter of indulgence of 1317 may mark the beginning of the work. It is a five-aisled, rib-vaulted hall church of five bays, with a transept, elongated hall chancel and two side chapels, with three west towers, the third added in the early 16th century. On stylistic evidence the chancel was probably built before the middle of the 14th century. The delicate tracery in the gables between the pier buttresses of the chancel is noteworthy, and the influence of the Cologne building lodge is discernible. Building continued after the mid-century, and two outer aisles were added to the plan of the old structure, which is marked by the line of the inner piers. The richly articulated piers and the fully moulded profiles are, like some of the exterior forms, influenced by the Parler workshop in Prague. The rich traceried gables of the chancel exterior were replaced in the later work by plain stepped gables, which continue the motif of the south transept gable (see below) and recall secular buildings.

The real show façade is that of the south transept, which is of very idiosyncratic design. It is framed by two massive pier buttresses, with a recessed portal. The jamb figures, the *Virgin and Child* in the trumeau and the *Crucifixion* group in the tympanum, are late 19th-century restorations, replacing those destroyed during the Peasants' War. The layer of blind arcading above the portal supports an inaccessible gallery with traceried balustrade, over which lean sculptured figures of the Emperor Charles IV and Empress (see fig.), attended by a lord- and lady-in-waiting. Although the original polychromy has disappeared, all the figures give a strong impression of actuality in their fashionable contemporary dress. Between the three windows above, figures of the *Adoration of the Magi* are set on corbels and under canopies. In the stepped gable is a small balcony, above which appears *Christ* in the mandorla, with a sword and a lily issuing from his mouth and two damned souls cowering at his feet. Intercessory figures of the *Virgin* and *St John the Baptist* flank the base of the mandorla with two angels blowing trumpets above them. The programme was intended to demonstrate the city's loyalty to the Emperor, symbolizing him receiving the annual homage of the town council. It was probably influenced by the Frauenkirche (1355–8), Nuremberg, founded by Charles IV, and the town side of the Old Town bridge tower (begun 1373) in Prague. The sculpture (1370–80) is stylistically related to that of the Parlers, the workshop of the Severikirche, Erfurt, and to sculptures in the cathedrals of Magdeburg and Halberstadt.

BIBLIOGRAPHY

K. Sellmann: 'Beiträge zur Baugeschichte der Marienkirche in Mühlhausen in Thüringen', *Mühlhäuser Geschbl.*, v (1904–5) [whole issue]

E. Badstübner: *Die Marienkirche zu Mühlhausen* (Berlin, 1971)

BETTINA GEORGI, ERNST ULLMANN

Muiden Castle. Moated castle situated on the River Vecht in the central Netherlands, built *c.* 1280. It acted as a defence post for the county of Holland, halting the territorial encroachments of the bishops of Utrecht. Its quadrangular plan, with four corner towers and a fortified entrance (see fig.), is related to such castles as Harlech, built by Edward I of England (*see* JAMES OF ST GEORGE), and to the bastions built in France during the reign of Philipp II Augustus (*reg* 1180–1223). Like the older type with a donjon, this variety did not appear in the Netherlands until after 1250. Floris V, Count of Holland (*reg* 1256–96), the patron of the castle, was influenced by the ideas of Edward I, with whom he was intimately associated, but Muiden also shows significant French influence.

The brick-built castle measures 32×35 m. Of the four corner towers (diam. *c.* 8.5 m) the western tower, the

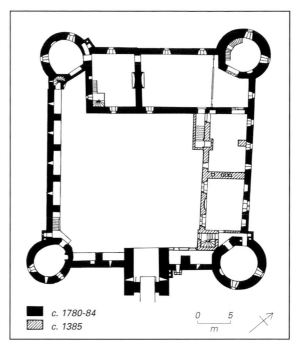

Muiden Castle, ground-plan, begun *c.* 1280

highest, is the least effective defensively as it is the least projecting. The south tower, the watch-tower, is oval in shape and therefore the strongest. The tower walls are up to 1.5 m thick. The gateway in the middle of the east wall has machicolation with three murder holes, and the walls on the landward side have wall-walks and crenellations. The west wall-walk was restored in the 19th century. The domestic quarters, a large hall and three smaller rooms, are located on the protected river side to the north-west and north-east.

The castle underwent long periods of neglect, and its building history is uncertain. It was probably begun between 1280 and 1284, but it may well have been razed by the Bishop of Utrecht in or shortly after 1296, when Count Floris V was murdered. Excavation has shown that the foundations date from the late 13th century but that the walls date from after 1350; this tallies with its disappearance from written sources from 1296 until after 1364. Builders' accounts from 1373 show that rebuilding was going on at this time. The reconstruction took place in stages. The walls, corner towers, the gate-tower and the large hall were built first; the rooms on the east side were added *c.* 1385; the fortifications at the entrance in 1476. The castle was also used as a state prison, but this did not prevent the States-General from neglecting it, so that the caretakers were regularly obliged to beg for money to maintain the fabric.

In the early 19th century the castle ceased to have an official function, but although it became extremely dilapidated the state did not grant any money for restoration until 1863. The first restoration period (1895–1909) was originally supervised by P. J. H. Cuypers and later by J. W. H. Berden. The latter, in particular, believed that the building must conform to the idealized image of a medieval castle, so that many post-1500 features were destroyed, including the entrance portal giving on to the courtyard, which had been built between 1609 and 1647, when the castle caretaker was P. C. Hooft, the poet and historian. The portal was, however, restored during the second period (1956–72), when many architectural details from both before and after 1500 were returned as close as possible to their original state, in an attempt to do justice to all the castle's architectural phases. Muiden Castle is now a museum.

BIBLIOGRAPHY

J. G. N. Renaud: 'De bouwgeschiedenis van het Muiderslot', *Bull. & Nieuws-bull. Kon. Ned. Oudhdknd. Bond*, 6th ser., 7 (1954), pp. 193–213
——: 'Graf Floris V als burchtenbouwer', *Ber. Rijksdienst Oudhdknd. Bodemonderzoek* (1957–8), pp. 159–72
T. Koot: *Het Muiderslot* (The Hague, 1977)
——: *Het Mysterie van Muiden* (The Hague, 1977)
P. van Mensch and H. Nieuwenhuis: *Muiderslot*, Nederlandse Kastelen, xlii (1980)

J. M. M. KLYSTRA-WIELINGA

Mu'in [Mu'īn Muṣavvir] (*b c.* 1617; *fl* Isfahan, 1635–97). Persian illustrator and painter. Numerous works clearly signed in black ink *mu'īn muṣavvir* ('Mu'in the painter') establish the dates of this artist's activity. He codified the style developed by his teacher RIZA and remained impervious to the eclecticism of late 17th-century art (*see* ISLAMIC ART, §III, 4(vi)(a)). Mu'in often drew in magenta; his art had a firm ground in calligraphy and an equally firm colourism, but his palette is less intense than Riza's and less deep in tonality; his figures are also less mannered in form and less extravagant in line than Riza's and the males often sport the broad moustaches made fashionable by 'Abbas I (*reg* 1588–1629). Signed works include copiously illustrated manuscripts, nearly 60 single-figure paintings and ink drawings, and painted and varnished bookbindings (*see* ISLAMIC ART, §VIII, 10). Many of the manuscripts (e.g. Dublin, Chester Beatty Lib., P. 270, dated 1656) are copies of Firdawsi's *Shāhnāma* ('Book of kings'). Such drawings as *A Lion Attacking a Youth* (1672; Boston, MA, Mus. F.A.) and *Portrait of Riza* (1635–73; Princeton U., NJ, Lib.), both of which have long, informative and highly personal inscriptions, convey the essence of the man. Mu'in's style is also evident in contemporary mural paintings, especially those in the Chihil Sutun pavilion (*see* ISFAHAN, §3(vii)). A prolific artist with many followers, he would have finished, and signed, many pictures alone, while assistants such as Fazl'ali, whose signature appears together with Mu'in's on some illustrations in the Cochran *Shāhnāma* (New York, Met.), and others still anonymous, would have finished other pictures that bear Mu'in's signature or are in his distinctive style.

BIBLIOGRAPHY

E. Kühnel: 'Der Maler Mu'in', *Pantheon*, xxix (1942), pp. 108–14
I. Stchoukine: *Les Peintures des manuscrits de Shāh 'Abbās Ier à la fin des Safavis* (Paris, 1964), pp. 62–71 and *passim*
B. W. Robinson: 'The Shāhnāmeh Manuscript Cochran 4 in the Metropolitan Museum of Art', *Islamic Art in the Metropolitan Museum of Art*, ed. R. Ettinghausen (New York, 1972), pp. 73–86
E. J. Grube and E. G. Sims: 'Wall Paintings in the Seventeenth-century Monuments of Isfahan', *Iran. Stud.*, vii (1974), pp. 511–42, figs 1–5
M. Farhad: 'The Art of Mu'in Musavvir: A Mirror of his Time', *Persian Masters: Five Centuries of Painting*, ed. S. R. Canby (Bombay, 1990), pp. 113–28
——: 'An Artist's Impression: Mu'in Musavvir's *Tiger Attacking a Youth*', *Muqarnas*, ix (1992), pp. 116–23

ELEANOR SIMS

Muisca [Chibcha]. Pre-Columbian people of the high plateaux of the Eastern Cordillera of Colombia, around Bogotá and Tunja. They flourished from *c.* AD 800 to the 16th century, when the Spaniards found a dense aboriginal population that, in terms of social, religious and political complexity, had evolved beyond the level of neighbouring groups. Historical documents describe palisaded towns whose rulers and temple priests were rich in gold items and emeralds, many of which they deposited in shrines, caches or sacred lagoons. Lake Guatavita was a place of supreme power. On taking office, each new chief was consecrated there in a splendid ceremony: coated with resin and covered with gold dust, he was rowed out into the lagoon on a raft laden with offerings; there the gifts were thrown into the water and the new ruler submerged to wash off his gilded body. This ceremony probably lies behind the many legends of 'El Dorado' ('The gilded man'), and votive offerings have been recovered during various attempts to drain Lake Guatavita. Muisca archaeology is unspectacular, for the wooden buildings and most artefacts of organic origin have disappeared. Beside pottery and stone tools, finds include a few crude stone statues, human mummies, textiles and wooden idols from burials in dry caves, and many little votive figurines (*tunjos*) of cast gold, copper or their alloys. There was no attempt at modelling in the round; the figures consist of flat plaques with wirelike details applied to the front. There are also miniature artefacts and, occasionally, scenes. One *tunjo*, the centrepiece of the Museo del Oro in Bogotá, depicts figures on a raft, one of which may represent the Gilded Man himself (*see* SOUTH AMERICA, PRE-COLUMBIAN, fig. 56). As offerings, *tunjos* were not intended for human sight and therefore appear crude and unfinished by comparison with Muisca jewellery. However, they provide valuable information about costume, tools, weapons and everyday life.

For discussion of Pre-Columbian Colombia *see also* PRE-COLUMBIAN SOUTH AMERICA, §II.

BIBLIOGRAPHY

A. L. Kroeber: 'The Chibcha', *Hb. S. Amer. Ind.*, ii, Bureau Amer. Ethnol. Bull., cxliii (1946), pp. 887–909
J. Pérez de Barradas: *Los Muiscas antes de la conquista*, 2 vols (Madrid, 1950–51)
——: *Orfebrería prehispánica de Colombia: Estilos Tolima y Muisca*, 2 vols (Madrid, 1958)
G. Reichel-Dolmatoff: *Colombia* (London, 1965), pp. 158–68
The Gold of El Dorado (exh. cat. by W. Bray, London, RA, 1978)

WARWICK BRAY

Mu'izzi Mamluks of Delhi. *See* MAMLUK, §I.

Mukachevo. *See* MUNKÁCS.

Mukhalingam [anc. Kaliṅganagara]. Temple site of the 8th–12th century AD in north-eastern Andhra Pradesh, India. It was the capital of the Eastern Ganga dynasty until the first quarter of the 12th century, and numerous inscriptions on the Madhukeshvara Temple (see below) show that it housed the dynastic deity, Madhikeshvara.

Although the town's religious importance probably declined when King Anantavarman Chodaganga (*reg* 1078–1150) transferred his capital to central Orissa *c.* 1120, inscriptions on the Madhukeshvara recording donations as late as 1434 indicate its continued importance as a pilgrimage site.

The three Mukhalingam temples are of importance as probable examples of the Kalinga 'order', described in ancient architectural texts. They are typified by curvilinear spires (Skt *śikharas*) divided into registers of horizontal bands. The largest temple, the Madhukeshvara complex (*c.* 700–850; *see* INDIAN SUBCONTINENT, §III, 5(i)(e)), is housed within a walled enclosure. Two free-standing shrines (*vimānas*) stand on either side of the main temple's east-facing entrance, with two further shrines attached to the north-western and south-western corners of the enclosure; rectangular shrines are built into its northern, southern and western walls. An eastern gateway leads into a forecourt with a second gateway beyond. The superstructures of the four corner shrines resemble contemporary Orissan architecture, most notably that of the mid-10th-century Parashurameshvara Temple at Bhubaneshwar (*see* BHUBANESHWAR, §2(i)), but are less elaborately sculpted. The main temple comprises a portico (*maṇḍapa*) with six interior columns and a sanctum with plain exterior walls articulated by three broad vertical divisions. The superstructure is characterized by the distinctive Kalinga horizontal mouldings. Throughout the complex, exuberant reliefs of religious and secular subjects are carved on doorframes and gateways and in the large 'window' medallions (*candraśālās*) found on the superstructures of the buildings. These figures are distinguished by boldly conceived angular forms expressing a high sense of movement and expression (*see* INDIAN SUBCONTINENT, fig. 227). The late 9th-century Someshvara Temple is a free-standing *vimāna* shrine. The lower walls feature large central niches flanked by smaller ones. These niches, which contain Shaiva images, are framed by wide bands and supported by base mouldings resembling those on the mid-10th-century Mukteshvara Temple at Bhubaneshwar. The unfinished superstructure is a squarish, less sculptural variant of the contemporary Orissan type. The Bhimeshvara Temple, architecturally the most severe of the Mukhalingam monuments, comprises a shrine preceded by a portico. The similarity of its shrine to that of the Madhukeshvara Temple suggests a date of *c.* 700, although the portico and the central niches are probably later additions of the 11th century.

See also INDIAN SUBCONTINENT, §IV, 7(vi)(d).

BIBLIOGRAPHY
D. Barrett: *Mukhalingam Temples* (Bombay, 1960)
H. Kulke: 'Royal Temple Policy and the Structure of Medieval Hindu Kingdoms', *The Cult of Jagannath and the Regional Traditions of Orissa* (New Delhi, 1978), pp. 199–208
B. Masthanaiah: *The Temples of Mukhalingam* (Delhi, 1978)
T. E. Donaldson: *Hindu Temple Art of Orissa*, i (Leiden, 1985)
M. F. Linda: 'The Kaliṅga Temple Form', *A. Orient.*, xx (1990), pp. 87–112)

WALTER SMITH

Mukherjee, Benode Behari (*b* Behala, nr Calcutta, 7 Feb 1904; *d* Delhi, 19 Nov 1980). Indian painter and writer. Disregarding his weak eyesight he studied (1919–24) under NANDALAL BOSE at Shantiniketan, Bengal, and later became his colleague. His early work, landscapes and figure paintings, were influenced by Expressionism (e.g. *The Bridge*, tempera on cloth, 1932; New Dehli, N.G. Mod. A.) and shared among other things the graphic quality of the German expressionists, especially of the Die Brücke group. In 1936–7 he visited Japan and was greatly impressed by the paintings of Toba Sojo (1053–1140), Toyo Sesshu and Tawaraya Sotatsu. Following this his style became more relaxed and calligraphic. His painted ceiling (1940) at the Kala Bhavan hostel, Shantiniketan, depicting the rural Bengal landscape in a personalized calligraphic idiom is the first work of his maturity. He continued painting murals, experimenting with techniques, themes and structures. His major work is the monumental 1947 mural at the Hindi Bhavan, Shantiniketan, based on the lives of medieval Indian saints and painted without cartoons. With its conceptual breadth and synthesis of elements from Giotto and Tawaraya Sotatsu, as well as from the art of such ancient Indian sites as AJANTA and MAMALLAPURAM, it is among the greatest achievements in contemporary Indian painting.

During the 1950s Mukherjee explored the fusion of art with craft. This interest is reflected in his subsequent works, including the mural at Vanastali Vidyapith (1950), Rajasthan, and the programme he drew up for his short-lived Training Centre of Art and Craft, Mussoorie. He lost his eyesight in 1957 but continued to draw and to make wax sculptures, papercuts and even a mural in ceramic tiles (1972) at Kala Bhavan, Shantiniketan. In addition to his art and teaching he wrote perceptive art criticism, a history of modern art education in India and a highly acclaimed fictionalized autobiography in Bengali. In 1972 the Calcutta film maker Satyajit Ray produced a documentary film about Mukherjee entitled *Inner Eye*.

WRITINGS
Adunik Silpa Siksha [Modern Indian art education] (Calcutta, 1972)
'My Experiments with Murals', *Lalit Kala Contemp.*, xii (1972), pp. 3–8
Chitrakar [The picture maker] (Calcutta, 1979)
Chitrakatha [About art] (Calcutta, 1984) [collection of essays]

BIBLIOGRAPHY
Benode Behari Mukherjee (exh. cat., Calcutta, Santiniketan Ashramik Sangha, 1959)
P. Neogy: *Benode Behari Mukherjee* (New Delhi, 1965)
Benode Behari Mukherjee (exh. cat., New Delhi, India Int. Cent., 1969)
G. M. Sheikh: 'Viewer's View: Looking at Pictures', *J. A. & Ideas*, iii (1983), pp. 5–20 [Hindi Bhavan mural reproduced in full]

R. SIVA KUMAR

Mukherjee, Meera (*b* Calcutta, 12 May 1923). Indian sculptor. After studying at the Government School of Art in Calcutta and the Delhi Polytechnic, Delhi, she received in 1953 a scholarship to study at the Bayerische Akademie der Schönen Künste in Munich, where she worked under Toni Stadler and Heinrich Kirchner. On returning to India she began to work from 1957 with the tribal artisans of Bastar and to learn techniques from bell metal craftsmen in Bihar and Madhya Pradesh. By the 1960s she had achieved recognition for her work and in 1968 was awarded the President's Award of Master Craftsman in metalwork. From 1969 she funded her own tours in Madhya Pradesh but later received a two-year stipend from the Anthropological Survey of India to assist her research. She documented ritual vessels and items in bell metal and surveyed the work of indigenous metal craftsmen in India and Nepal. Like the metalworkers she studied, she employed the lost-wax process for her metal sculptures and worked seasonally, taking a year on each image and casting no more than six or seven in a year. She worked on large- and small-scale works, and her sculpted figures often have a quiet poise (e.g. standing figure of a woman; bronze, h. *c* 1.35 m; New Delhi, N.G. Mod. A.). Her style is influenced by the folk art she encountered, and her repertory includes such archetypal figures as the archer, bowman and boatswain, as well as figures from daily life. Based in Calcutta, she exhibited her work in solo and group exhibitions throughout the world (e.g. New Delhi, N.G. Mod. A.; Frankfurt am Main, Hermann Abs Mus.). She also received an Emeritus Fellowship from the Indian government. Her works are in a number of private and public collections in India and abroad.

BIBLIOGRAPHY
G. Sen: 'Bronzes by Meera Mukherjee: The Relation of Tradition to Contemporary Sculpture', *Lalit Kala Contemp.*, xxvii (1979), pp. 5–7
Meera and the Indian Tradition: Meera Mukherjee—A Retrospective, 1963–83 (exh. cat., intro. J. Appasamy; Bombay, Jehangir A.G., 1983)
The Sculpted Image: A Panorama of Contemporary Indian Sculpture (exh. cat. by N. Malani and R. Shahani, Bombay, Nehru Cent., 1987)
Artists Alert (exh. cat. by G. Kapur, New Delhi, 1989)

ANIS FAROOQI

Mukhina, Vera (Ignat'yevna) (*b* Riga, 19 June 1889; *d* Moscow, 6 Oct 1953). Russian sculptor and decorative artist of Latvian birth. From the mid-1900s until 1912 she attended various private art schools in Moscow, including that of Il'ya Mashkov, but her real training as a sculptor began in 1912, when she travelled to Paris. Until 1914 she took an active part in the artistic life of Paris, attending the Académie de la Grande Chaumière, taking lessons from Emile-Antoine Bourdelle, and making many acquaintances, among them Ossip Zadkine, Jacques Lipchitz, and also Lyubov' Popova, with whom she travelled to Italy in 1914. After returning to Moscow following the outbreak of World War I, Mukhina worked for a time as scenographic assistant to Alexandra Exter in the Kamerny Theatre of Aleksandr Tairov (1885–1950) and also designed costumes independently for a number of plays, none of which was produced. Mukhina again joined forces with Exter in 1923, when both women worked on fabric and dress designs for the newly opened Atel'ye Mody (Atelier of Fashion) in Moscow; she also helped Exter with the costumes for the film *Aelita* (1924).

Mukhina realized her true vocation as a monumental sculptor in the 1920s, thanks in part to her involvement in the Monumental Propaganda Plan, in which her project for a monument to Yakov Sverdlov, *Flame of Revolution* (1922; Moscow, Cent. Mus. Revolution), can be included. Although she was well aware of the achievements of the Cubists and of Constantin Brancusi, and demonstrated a strong interest in Cubism and Futurism in her stage designs of 1915–16, Mukhina was slow to accept avant-garde experiments and remained devoted to a more conventional figuration. Consequently, shortly after the Revolution, she responded easily to the call for Realist sculpture, and in

the 1920s to 1940s produced many busts and full-length statues with both a documentary value (e.g. the architect *Sergey Zamkov*, 1934, and the surgeon *Nikolay Burdenko*, 1943; both Moscow, Tret'yakov Gal.) and allegorical value (e.g. *Wind*, 1926; Moscow, Tret'yakov Gal.; and the sculptural ensemble *Bread* for the new Moscow River Bridge, Moskovoretsky Most, 1939).

Mukhina's reputation as the Soviet Union's foremost Socialist Realist sculptor was established with the enormous *Worker and Collective Farm Woman* (h. *c*. 24 m), erected on top of the Soviet pavilion at the Exposition Universelle, Paris, in 1937 (now in Moscow at the main entrance to the former Exhibition of Economic Achievements; *see* RUSSIA, fig. 27). Aesthetically connected to Stalin's passion of the 1930s for the monumental, this stainless steel colossus expressed Mukhina's love of the dynamic and the histrionic. Although she continued to produce important monuments until her death (e.g. *Tchaikovsky*, 1945–53; in front of the Great Hall of the Tchaikovsky Conservatory, Moscow), she never again produced such a single impressive work. During the 1940s Mukhina also designed glass figurines and vases, some of which were mass-produced.

WRITINGS
R. Klimov, ed.: *Khudozhestvennoye i literaturno-kriticheskoye naslediye* [Artistic and literary-critical heritage], 3 vols (Moscow, 1959–60)
A Sculptor's Thoughts (Moscow, n.d.) [in Eng.]

BIBLIOGRAPHY
N. I. Vorkunova: *Simvol novogo mira: Skul'ptura 'Rabochiy i Kolkhoznitsa' V. I. Mukhinoy* [Symbol of a new world: V. I. Mukhina's sculpture *Worker and Collective Farm Woman*] (Moscow, 1965)
O. Voronova: *V. I. Mukhina* (Moscow, 1976)
P. Suzdalev: *Vera Ignat'yevna Mukhina* (Moscow, 1981)
N. V. Voronov: *Vera Mukhina* (Moscow, 1989)

JOHN E. BOWLT

Mukhtar, Mahmud [Mukhtār, Maḥmūd; Moukhtar, Mahmoud] (*b* Tanyra, 10 May 1891; *d* Cairo, 27 March 1934). Egyptian sculptor. He studied at the School of Fine Arts, Cairo, and after graduating was sent in 1911 by the founder of the School, Prince Yusuf Kamal, to study sculpture at the Ecole des Beaux-Arts, Paris. Although Mukhtar was at ease in France, and regularly exhibited at the Salon des Artistes Français, his aim increasingly was to search for an Egyptian identity in art. In order to re-establish an Egyptian style in monumental sculpture he developed a 'neo-pharaonic' style, and became the first Egyptian artist to use granite since Ancient Egyptian times. His massive pink granite statue *Egyptian Awakening* (1919–28; *see* EGYPT, fig. 2), the most official of his works, was placed at the gateway to Cairo University. It shows a sphinx about to rise, and a woman unveiling.

During the 1920s Mukhtar became an influential figure in modern Egyptian art, and prominent in the group La Chimère, founded in 1927, which included the painters Raghib Ayyad (1892–1982), Muhammad Naghi and Mahmud Said. In addition to his 'neo-pharaonic' sculptures, he also produced works in other styles; for example *The Nile Bride* (Paris, Mus. Grévin), a marble figure of the late 1920s, was inspired by the Greco-Roman tradition. He also executed caricature sculptures and a series of cartoon drawings which appeared in the satirical paper *al-Kashkul*. He carved two statues of the nationalist leader Sa'd Zaghlul

(1857–1927), one in Cairo and the other in Alexandria. In Cairo the Mukhtar Museum (opened 1964), in a building designed by the Egyptian architect Ramses Wissa Wassef (1911–74), contains a range of his sculptures, including *Khamsin Winds* (limestone, late 1920s), *The Blind* (bronze, 1929), *Fellaha Lifting Jug* (limestone, 1929) and *Siesta* (red porphyry, early 1930s).

BIBLIOGRAPHY

Badr El-Dine Abou Ghazi and G. Boctor: *Moukhtar, ou le réveil de l'Egypte* (Cairo, 1949)

M. S. al-Jabakhanji: *Tārīkh al-ḥaraka al-fanniyya fī miṣr ilā 'aynām 1945* [A history of the artistic movement in Egypt to 1945] (Cairo, 1986)

L. Karnouk: *Modern Egyptian Art: The Emergence of a National Style* (Cairo, 1988)

S. J. VERNOIT

Mukund [Mukunda] (*fl c.* 1570–1600). Indian miniature painter. All known works by Mukund were painted under the patronage of the Mughal emperor Akbar (*reg* 1556–1605). He must have joined the court atelier before the time of the *Razmnāma* ('Book of wars'; 1582–6; Jaipur, Maharaja Sawai Singh II Mus., MS. AG. 1683–1850), for the earliest works ascribed to him record the rare assignment of both the design and execution of six illustrations in that manuscript and another five in the *Khamsa* ('Five poems') of Nizami of *c.* 1585 (London, priv. col.). His prominence in the atelier is affirmed by ascriptions in all major manuscripts of the 1580s and 1590s and his inclusion among the 17 painters named in the *Āyīn-i Akbarī*, a contemporary account of Akbar's administration.

Like most Mughal painters, Mukund was capable of working in a variety of styles, from the relatively open composition, stocky figures, and *nīm qalam* (uncoloured) style of the *Akbarnāma* ('History of Akbar'; 1596–7; Dublin, Chester Beatty Lib., MS. 3, fol. 202b; alternatively dated *c.* 1604) to the deep landscapes and nervous forms of the *Khamsa* of Nizami of 1595 (London, BL, Or. MS. 12208, fol. 19r). Nevertheless, his architectural settings and townscapes are consistently a flattened jumble of pastel walls and skewed pavilions. His figures often display a similar awkwardness, especially when incited to action or dramatic gestures. For example, Mukund's design for two paintings in an *Akbarnāma* (*c.* 1590; London, V&A, IS. 2-1986, 70, 71/117) links a row of onlookers by means of interlocked arms, a formulaic solution whose tediousness is relieved in the latter work only by superior painting by Manohar. Mukund retained the facial conventions of the 1580s until the end of his career *c.* 1600, making his lightly modelled figures in three-quarter profile somewhat less expressive than those of his contemporaries.

BIBLIOGRAPHY

The Imperial Image: Paintings for the Mughal Court (exh. cat. by M. C. Beach, Washington, DC, Freer, 1981)

D. Walker and E. Smart: *Pride of the Princes: Indian Art of the Mughal Era in the Cincinnati Art Museum* (Cincinnati, OH, 1985)

M. C. Beach: *Early Mughal Painting* (Cambridge, MA, 1987)

JOHN SEYLLER

Mulas, Ugo (*b* Pozzolengo, Brescia, 28 Aug 1928; *d* Milan, 2 March 1973). Italian photographer. He studied drawing at the Accademia di Brera in Milan (1951–2), at the same time frequenting the Bar Giamaica, a meeting place for avant-garde artists and intellectuals. He was a self-taught photographer but became a professional in 1954, when he was commissioned to make a photographic documentary of the Venice Biennale. From this date he photographed mostly architecture, and fashion and theatre designs, also working as a photojournalist. The lives and works of artists were, however, his main interests; he continued to document their activities, sometimes abroad.

In the USA Mulas was particularly influenced by the work of Lee Friedlander and Robert Frank. In New York between 1964 and 1967 he took a series of photographs of Pop artists and their world, from which he produced a book entitled *New York, arte e persone* (Milan, 1967) that established him internationally. In New York he met, among others, Marcel Duchamp, whose work greatly influenced him, and whose intellectual and artistic bearing inspired him to review the relationship between image and meaning in his own art. Unlike other photographers in Italy in the post-war years, who were concerned with the debate between formalism and neo-realism, Mulas concentrated on the language of photography, which became his main area of study and which he examined systematically through a series of *Verifiche* photographs that he worked on between 1970 and 1972, for example *Verifiche 1: Homage to Niépce* (1970; see 1983 exh. cat., p. 350).

PHOTOGRAPHIC PUBLICATIONS

Invito a Venezia (Milan, 1960)

with H. H. Arnason: *Calder* (New York, 1971)

BIBLIOGRAPHY

P. Fossati: *Ugo Mulas: La fotografia* (Turin, 1973)

Ugo Mulas: Immagini e testi (exh. cat. by A. C. Quintavalle, U. Parma, 1973)

Kunst mit Photographie (exh. cat. by R. H. Krauss, M. Schmalriede and M. Schwarz, W. Berlin, N.G.; Cologne, Kstver.; Munich, Stadtmus.; Kiel, Christian Albrechts-U., Ksthalle; 1983), pp. 72–3, 350

Ugo Mulas: Fotografo, 1928–1973 (exh. cat. by H. Teicher, Geneva, Mus. Rath; Zurich, Ksthaus; 1984)

ITALO ZANNIER

Muldenfaltenstil [Ger.: 'troughfold style']. Term used to describe a convention of drapery representation in the figurative arts in north-western Europe between *c.* 1180 and *c.* 1240. It was typical of metalwork, sculpture and painting executed in the region between the River Meuse and the Ile-de-France and is one of the most distinctive features of art of the so-called Transitional period between Romanesque and Gothic (*see* TRANSITIONAL STYLE). In this style cloth hangs around figures in deep looped troughs, clinging to limbs but also partially concealing them. The emergence of the style coincided with a renewed interest in antique forms, displacing the more abstract linear conventions of the Byzantine 'dampfold' styles of the mid-12th century (*see* ROMANESQUE, §IV, 2). Although this new tendency towards rounder, more sculptural forms was widespread in north-western Europe around 1200, the occurrence of true *Muldenfaltenstil* work was geographically more restricted. It appears not to have occurred in England, for example.

The first mature work in this idiom was the enamelled pulpit made in 1181 by the Mosan goldsmith NICHOLAS OF VERDUN for the Austrian abbey of Klosterneuburg. Nicholas's champlevé enamels are marked by an antique gravity and show how this style was intimately linked to the broad, muscular anatomies and humanistic head types of Roman art. Roman antecedents for the style may be found in sculpture of the 1st century AD, such as the Ara Pacis in Rome. The *Muldenfaltenstil* remained in vogue in metalwork of the late 12th and early 13th centuries, notably the shrine of the Three Kings at Cologne Cathedral and the shrines of the Virgin Mary in the cathedral treasuries at Tournai and Aachen (*see* SHRINE, colour pl. IV, fig. 2).

The iconographic programmes of Mosan metalwork found favour with late 12th-century French sculptors, and as a result of this liaison the *Muldenfaltenstil* passed into French monumental sculpture, being found on the south transept portal of Strasbourg Cathedral (*c.* 1230), and in its purest form on the north transept *Judgement* and *Calixtus* portals (1220s) and the *Visitation* group on the west front of Reims Cathedral, *c.* 1230. From Reims the style spread to Germany (Bamberg Cathedral, figures of the *Virgin* and *St Elizabeth*). Works such as the Reims *Visitation* group, with its *contrapposto* stances, imply familiarity with antique sarcophagi or other remnants of Roman art in France; but the interpretation given is fundamentally in keeping with Gothic sentiment.

The *Muldenfaltenstil* became common in painting after 1200. It is found in French wall painting (Chamalières-sur-Loire, Haute Loire) and stained glass (the *Seven Sleepers of Ephesus* window at Rouen Cathedral), and in some work in the Ingeborg Psalter of *c.* 1200 (Chantilly, Mus. Condé, MS. 9/1695). It occurs in the extensive Parisian programmes of interpretative Bible illustration in the *Bibles moralisées* (*see* BIBLE, §I, 3(i)) of the 1220s and 1230s. The last celebrated examples are the drawings in the Portfolio of Villard de Honnecourt. In the 1240s the style was displaced in monumental sculpture produced in Paris and Champagne by the 'broadfold' idiom, which simplified carved surfaces and contributed to the crisper silhouettes and sharper delineation of mature Gothic sculpture and painting.

BIBLIOGRAPHY
H. R. Hahnloser: *Villard de Honnecourt: Kritische Gesamtausgabe des Bauhüttenbuches MS. Fr. 19093 der Pariser Nationalbibliothek* (Vienna, 1935, rev. Graz, 1972)
F. Deuchler: *Der Ingeborgpsalter* (Berlin, 1967)
W. Sauerländer: *Gotische Skulptur in Frankreich, 1140–1270* (Munich, 1970; Eng. trans., London, 1972)
The Year 1200 (exh. cat. by K. Hoffmann and F. Deuchler, New York, Met., 1970)
The Year 1200: A Symposium. New York, 1970 (New York, 1975)
R. Branner: *Manuscript Painting in Paris during the Reign of Saint Louis* (Berkeley, CA, 1977)
H. Buschhausen: *Der Verduner Altar: Das Emailwerk des Nikolaus von Verdun im Stift Klosterneuburg* (Vienna, 1980)

PAUL BINSKI

Mulla Sadiq. *See* MUHAMMAD SADIQ.

Muller. Stone or glass implement with a flat base, used to grind paints by hand on a hard flat surface or slab. Mullers and slabs of hard stone are first recorded in ancient Egypt. Large glass mullers were used for the commercial preparation of paints until the 19th century. Pigments could be ground on their own for use in fresco or aqueous media or ground in oil for later use.

RUPERT FEATHERSTONE

Muller, Emile (*b* Altkirch, Alsace, 21 Sept 1823; *d* Nice, 11 Nov 1889). French architect, ceramics manufacturer and writer. He trained at the Ecole Centrale des Arts et Manufactures, Paris, and became a civil engineer, his first project being the building of 300 dwellings (1852–97) for the Jean Dollfuss workers' housing estate in Mulhouse. In 1853 he proposed model workers' housing estates called 'cités circulaires', composed of prefabricated timber houses, but none was ever built. After these early experiments in social housing Muller became one of the undisputed specialists in the field, publishing his ideas in 1855 and 1879.

It was in the industrialized production of ceramic products, however, that Muller played his most significant role. In 1854 he founded his own tile factory, La Grande Tuilerie d'Ivry, producing the first industrial tiles, which were exhibited at the Exposition Universelle, Paris, in 1855. He produced industrial tiles in different colours, ridge-tiles and made-to-measure roofing for the Menier factory (1871–2) in Noisiel, Seine-et-Marne. Designed by the architect Jules Saulnier and admired by Viollet-le-Duc, this was one of the first buildings constructed with an exposed metal framework. Muller's business eventually comprised seven factories, which mass-produced tiles, piping, cast components, heat-resistant products and numerous architectural ornaments. He also set up a small research workshop in which he developed a highly durable glazed ceramic body, which it was possible to fire in large sections. Thereafter he sought to produce whole architectural components that could be incorporated structurally into buildings and he rejected the use of such cladding materials as small tiles, the joints of which he considered to be unsightly. Matt or glossy, his ceramic components shimmered with intense polychromatic effects. He even suggested to his clients that they themselves should design the article to be produced and afterwards destroy the mould, for Muller rejected the 'vulgarity of repeated models'. Thus, a semi-industrial artefact, which logically belonged to the realm of mass production, was promoted to the rank of a work of art. The first attempt to use monumental polychrome ceramic was carried out by the architect C. Jacotin on the Ramleh-Casino in Alexandria. Muller's works came to public attention at the Exposition Universelle, Paris, in 1889, at which they won a major prize. People were particularly appreciative of the beauty of multi-coloured materials used in the Palais des Beaux-Arts et des Arts Libéraux. Muller cast ornamental finials, ridge-tiles, balustrades and cartouches for the greatest architects of his time, including Henri Labrouste, Eugène-Emmanuel Viollet-le-Duc and Théodore Ballu. Some of these afterwards agreed to market their designs. Thus, the balustrades designed by Labrouste for the Bibliothèque Nationale were sold at 40 francs per metre, at a weight of 110 kg. Muller launched himself simultaneously into the production of unique items of art and into mass production. He began by copying works by Old Masters, and at the World's Columbian Exhibition, Chicago, of 1893, he launched in polychrome stoneware works derived from such Renaissance artists as Donatello and Verrochio, as well as sphinxes and seats in an antique style. In 1894 he added to his output reproductions of works by such contemporary artists as Eugène-Samuel Grasset, ALEXANDRE CHARPENTIER, Hector Guimard and Henri de Toulouse-Lautrec.

In addition to his work as an architect and manufacturer, Muller taught civil construction at the Ecole Centrale, where he founded the civil engineering department. He also co-founded the Ecole Spéciale d'Architecture (1863) and the Institut des Sciences Politiques, both in Paris. His son Louis Muller succeeded him in the business and produced the frieze entitled *Labour* for the monumental gateway designed by René Binet (1866–1911) as the entrance to the Exposition Universelle of 1900, after designs by the sculptor Anatole Guillot (1865–1911).

WRITINGS

Habitations ouvrières (Paris, 1855)
with E. Cacheux: *Les Habitations ouvrières en tous pays* (Paris, 1879, rev. 1889)
Produits céramiques pour constructions et industries (Paris, 1895)

BIBLIOGRAPHY

H. de Chennevières: 'Exposition Universelle de 1889. La Céramique monumentale: M. Emile Muller', *Rev. A. Déc.*, iv (1888–9), pp. 129–36
'Emile Muller et Cie', *Arts Décoratifs Modernes* (exh. cat., Paris, Gal. Petit, 1894)
R. Borrmann: *Moderne Keramik* (Leipzig, *c.* 1902)
Grande Tuilerie d'Ivry (Ivry, 1904)

HÉLÈNE GUÉNÉ-LOYER

Müller, (Johann) Friedrich [Maler Müller] (*b* Kreuznach, 13 Jan 1749; *d* Rome, 23 April 1825). German painter, engraver, draughtsman, poet and playwright. From about 1765 he was taught by Daniel Hien (1724–73), court painter to Christian IV, Duke of Zweibrücken, with 17th-century Dutch painting as his model. Müller showed a talent for realistic depiction of animals, especially horses, and landscape, including farm scenes. The Duke gave him an allowance so that, from 1769, he was able to attend the Mannheim Akademie. Müller's friendship there with Ferdinand Kobell and Franz Kobell (1749–1822) led to a considerable mutual influence in the work of all three. Müller also established himself as a poet at this time, becoming one of the representatives of the late 18th-century German literary movement known as Sturm und Drang. In the course of the 1770s Müller wrote a celebrated series of idylls, the lyric drama *Niobe* and the first parts of his *Fausts Leben dramatisiert*, all issued in editions with his own engraved illustrations. Life drawings and etchings from this period are in Mannheim (Städt. Reiss-Mus.), Frankfurt am Main (Goethemus.) and Monaco-Ville (Archvs Pal. Princier). At this time, however, Müller's work as a poet and dramatist was more widely known and admired than his work as an artist. His study of the famous collection of casts of antique sculptures in the Antikensaal at Mannheim, and of paintings in the picture gallery belonging to the Elector Charles Theodore, directed Müller's interest, however, towards antique art and the Italian painting of the Renaissance and Mannerist periods, and induced a longing to visit Rome. After he had been appointed Kabinettsmaler to the Elector in 1777, Müller was awarded a grant for travel to Italy. In August 1778 he travelled to Rome, where he was based for the rest of his life.

In Rome, Müller set to work with a zeal that seriously endangered his health. In 1779 he painted the *Birth of Flora* and the *Triumph of Flora* (both untraced). Other early Roman paintings were on the subject of the life of Moses; all are now untraced, except for a watercolour of *Moses Drawing Water from the Rock* (Weimar, Schlossmus.). Financial hardship stemming from the transfer of the Elector's court from Mannheim to Munich, and later from the general political situation, kept Müller in Rome; soon he had to earn his living by acting as a guide for foreign visitors and from writing on art. Meanwhile, his own painting output steadily declined. Of his work of the 1780s almost all is untraced, although contemporary Roman reviews and Müller's own descriptions record paintings of the *Rape of the Daughters of Leucippus* (1783/4), *Alexander the Great and his Physician Philip* (1784/5), *Hercules and Omphale* (1786) and *Jason* (1787). Of these mythological subjects only the painting *Hymen* (1799; Munich, Neue Pin.; see fig.), which had *Amor* as its counterpart, has survived. Both paintings had been bought by Lord Bristol, and, when his estate was auctioned in Rome in 1804, Müller bought them back and reworked them over a period of several years. His last great painting, *Ulysses in the Underworld* (1805–19), is also untraced. He also painted portraits. In Rome Müller embraced the classical ideals of Anton Raphael Mengs and Johann Joachim Winckelmann. Like his friends Joseph Anton Koch and Johann Christian Reinhart, Müller rejected the religious-cum-patriotic art of the Lukasbrüder, although he did discuss their ideas in some of his unpublished writings (Frankfurt am Main, Goethemus.). Both during and after his lifetime the drawings, etchings and paintings from Müller's first, German period had been admired, while his work in Rome received only partial praise from

Friedrich Muller: *Hymen*, oil on canvas, 1.37×1.00, 1799 (Munich, Neue Pinakothek)

his contemporaries and was soon forgotten after his death. Between 1805 and 1810 Müller worked as an agent for the future King Ludwig I of Bavaria, arranging the first purchase of antique Roman sculptures for the Glyptothek in Munich.

WRITINGS
F. Batt, J. P. Le Pique and L. Tieck, eds: *Schriften*, 3 vols (1811–25)
H. Hettner, ed.: *Dichtungen*, 2 vols (1868/R 1968)

BIBLIOGRAPHY
F. Denk: *Friedrich Müller: Der Malerdichter und Dichtermaler* (Speyer, 1930)
K. Unverricht: *Die Radierungen des Maler Müller* (1931)
F. Gross: 'Zwischen niederem Stil und klassischem Ausdruck: Die Revolte des Malers Müller', *Idea: Jb. Hamburg. Ksthalle*, iv (1985), pp. 83–106
I. Sattel Bernardini and W. Schlegel: *Friedrich Müller, 1749–1825: Der Maler* (Landau, 1986)
G. Sauder, R. Paulus and C. Weiss, eds: *Maler Müller in neuer Sicht* (St Ingbert, 1990)
I. Sattel Bernardini: 'Friedrich Müller, detto Maler Müller, e il commercio romano d'antichità all'inizio dell'ottocento', *Boll. Mnmt. Mus. & Gal. Pont.*, xiii (1993), pp. 127–57

INGRID SATTEL BERNARDINI

Müller, Hélène. *See* KRÖLLER-MÜLLER, HÉLÈNE.

Muller, Jan (Harmensz.) (*b* Amsterdam, 1 July 1571; *d* Amsterdam, 18 April 1628). Dutch engraver, draughtsman and painter. He was the eldest son of Harmen Jansz. Muller (1540–1617), the Amsterdam book printer, engraver and publisher. The family business, called De Vergulde Passer ('The gilded compasses'), was situated in Warmoesstraat, and Jan Muller worked there for many years. He may have been apprenticed to Hendrik Goltzius in Haarlem. Between 1594 and 1602 he is thought to have gone to Italy, where he stayed in Rome and Naples. He was related by marriage to the Dutch sculptor Adriaen de Vries, who was a pupil of Giambologna. He also maintained contacts with Bartholomeus Spranger and other artists in Prague, which under the rule of Emperor Rudolf II had become a flourishing centre of the arts. In 1602 he made an unsuccessful attempt to mediate on behalf of Rudolf II, who wanted to buy Lucas van Leyden's *Last Judgement* (Leiden, Stedel. Mus. Lakenhal). When Harmen Jansz. Muller died, he left the entire stock of his shop, including a number of copperplates, to his bachelor son Jan.

One hundred engravings by Muller are catalogued in Hollstein. Relatively few of the prints are based on the artist's own designs: the majority seem to have been after works by Haarlem Mannerists such as Goltzius and Cornelis van Haarlem, by Lucas van Leyden and Abraham Bloemaert, and by Rudolfine artists such as Adriaen de Vries, Spranger and Hans von Aachen. After *c.* 1590 Muller mastered and applied with great virtuosity Goltzius's volumetric engraving technique based on swelling and diminishing lines. This technique can be seen, for example, in a number of engravings after the early sculptural figure groups made by Adriaen de Vries in Prague (see fig.). Muller's finest engraving is possibly *Belshazzar's Feast* (Hollstein, no. 11), a night scene with beautiful light inspired by Tintoretto's *Last Supper* (Venice, S Giorgio Maggiore). Muller made the design (Amsterdam, Rijksmus.) for this print himself. Later he also made engravings after younger artists such as Michiel van Mierevelt, Thomas de Keyser and Peter Paul Rubens. In these he shows

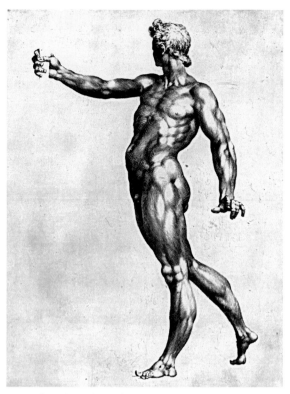

Jan Muller (after Adriaen de Vries): *Apollo*, engraving, 1st state, 410×302 mm (Amsterdam, Rijksmuseum)

himself adept at reproductive techniques. The largest collection of engravings by Muller, including a number of early states and prints not yet described, is in the Albertina, Vienna.

There are 60 known drawings by the artist. Muller used a variety of drawing media, often in combination: pen and ink, wash and chalk. Apart from the series of four allegorical drawings he made as a youth in the manner of Maarten van Heemskerck (London, BM), his early development as a draughtsman was influenced by his contact with Goltzius and his knowledge of compositions by Spranger. Lagging behind the general trend away from Mannerism, he drew in an exaggerated style similar to that of Spranger and the young Cornelis van Haarlem. During his stay in Italy his style changed; after *c.* 1600 he moved away from the extreme, unnatural stylization and developed a kind of pseudo-realism. Around this time he achieved some remarkable results using chalk. Among his drawings there is a series of outstanding *vanitas* portraits in the manner of Goltzius's *Federkunststücke*, pen-and-ink drawings imitating the technique of engraving (e.g. Haarlem, Teylers Mus.). The artist's last drawings in pen and ink, for instance the *Magdalene* (Gorssel, J. U. de Kempenaar family priv. col., see Reznicek, 1956, fig. 26), are strongly influenced by Lucas van Leyden. There are also a number of studies and designs for engravings.

It is clear from the artist's will and various inventories of the period that Muller was also active as a painter. According to the inventory of his household effects in

1624, four years before his death, he left two large paintings from his Italian period to his sister. The first painting to be firmly attributed to him is the *Joseph and his Family before Pharaoh* (Dunkirk, Mus. B.-A.), which before 1975 was thought to be by Karel van Mander.

BIBLIOGRAPHY

ENGRAVINGS

Hollstein: *Dut. & Flem.*

Zwischen Renaissance und Barock (exh. cat., ed. K. Oberhuber; Vienna, Albertina, 1976), pp. 227–31

W. L. Strauss: *Netherlandish Artists*, 4 [III/ii] of *The Illustrated Bartsch*, ed. W. L. Strauss (New York, 1980)

DRAWINGS

E. K. J. Reznicek: 'Jan Harmensz. Muller als tekenaar', *Ned. Ksthist. Jb.*, vii (1956), pp. 65–110

——: 'Jan Harmensz. Muller as Draughtsman: Addenda', *Master Drgs*, xviii/2 (1980), pp. 115–33; xix/4 (1981), pp. 460–61

E. K. J. REZNICEK

Müller, Johann Georg (Wilhelm) (*b* Mosnang, nr St Gall, 15 Sept 1822; *d* Vienna, 2 May 1849). Swiss architect and writer. He trained under F. W. Kubly in St Gall (1837) and Georg Friedrich Ziebland in Munich (1838–41). In 1842–3 he travelled to Italy, staying mainly in Florence. In 1844–5 he opposed the rebuilding of the Laurenzenkirche at St Gall, which was instead restored (1849–55), basically in accordance with his ideas. Before going to Vienna in 1847, he designed several private houses and some railway stations (including those at Zurich and Winterthur). An article he wrote in 1847 attracted attention to his views on the reconstruction of the façade of the cathedral in Florence, based on the marble facings of Giotto's campanile. It was translated into Italian after his death, and its proposals seem to have been seriously considered though never realized. In 1847 Müller was elected to the Akademie der Bildende Künste, Vienna, and two years later he became a professor at the Ingenieurs-Akademie, due in part to a controversial pamphlet concerning the rebuilding of the new parish church at Altlerchenfeld, Vienna (*Zu den sieben Zufluchten*), published in 1848 by the newly founded Wiener Architektenverein: in it, Müller criticized the work already begun by Paul Eduard Sprenger for the inappropriateness of its style, advocating the Middle Ages rather than pagan antiquity or the Renaissance as an appropriate source for contemporary sacred architecture. Although the work at Altlerchenfeld had already reached the foundation level, Sprenger's opponents were successful, and the work continued (1850–60) to Müller's designs. Against the background of revolution in 1848 the church at Altlerchenfeld is to be seen as a Romantic *Gesamtkunstwerk*: externally a partly plastered, brick building of basilica type with Renaissance forms at the foundation level (by Sprenger), but with Romanesque features in the upper parts, including the two-tower façade and the octagonal crossing tower. The interior, which bears a resemblance to Friedrich Gärtner's Ludwigskirche (1829–40) in Munich, was embellished with elaborate frescoes (1853–61) designed by Joseph von Führich. After Müller's death, his plans were continued by Franz Sitte (1818–79).

WRITINGS

'Über die einstige Vollendung des Florentiner Domes', *Allg. Bauztg Abbild.*, xi (1847), pp. 179–213

Der deutsche Kirchenbau und die neu zu erbauenden Renaissance-Kirche in Altlerchenfeld (Vienna, 1848)

'Über die italienisch-mittelalterlichen Grabdenkmäler', *Allg. Bauztg Abbild.*, xii (1848), pp. 153–62

BIBLIOGRAPHY

E. Förster: *J. G. Müller: Ein Dichter- und Künstlerleben* (St Gall, 1851)

M. Ziegler: *Aus dem künstlerischen Nachlasse von J. G. Müller* (Winterthur, 1860)

C. Sitte: 'Die neuere kirchliche Architektur in Österreich und Ungarn', *Österreich.-Ung. Rev.*, iii (1887), pp. 65–87

F. Rieger: *Die Altlerchenfelder Kirche* (Vienna, 1911)

U. Hilber: *Aus den Briefen J. G. Müllers* (St Gall, 1922)

E. Poeschel: *Die Stadt St Gallen* (1957), iii of *Die Kunstdenkmäler des Kantons St Gallen*, 4 vols (Basle, 1951–66), pp. 102–4 [Laurenzenkirche]

A. Reine: 'J. G. Müller: Ein Schweizer Neugotiker', *Das Werk*, iv (1962), pp. 146–8

G. R. Crasemann Collins and C. Crasemann Collins: *Camillo Sitte and the Birth of Modern City Planning* (London, 1965), pp. 6ff

A. Meyer: *Neugotik und Neuromanik in der schweizer Architektur des 19. Jahrhunderts* (Zurich, 1973), pp. 49ff

B. Richarz: *Die Altlerchenfelder Kirche in Wien* (Karlsruhe, 1981)

U. Klären: *Der schweizer Architekt J. G. Müller (1822–49)* (in preparation)

MICHAEL BOLLÉ

Müller, Johann Gotthard von (*b* Bernhausen, nr Stuttgart, 4 May 1747; *d* Stuttgart, 14 March 1830). German draughtsman and engraver. He studied painting from 1764 to 1770 under Nicolas Guibal with the encouragement of Charles Eugene, Duke of Württemberg, at the latter's academy of arts in Ludwigsburg, and engraving from 1770 to 1776 under Jean Georges Wille in Paris. In 1776 he became a member of the Académie Royale de Peinture et de Sculpture in Paris and returned to Stuttgart, where he became Director of the engraving class at the 'Hohe Carlsschule', the academy of arts founded by the Duke in Stuttgart in 1761. After its closure in 1798, Müller continued to run the engraving school and printing press as an independent venture. Müller, with Wille and Georg Friedrich Schmidt among the outstanding engravers of the period, was recognized in his own day and awarded numerous distinctions. The portrait of *King Louis XVI of France* after Jean-Claude Duplessis (1790) and the *Battle of Bunker Hill near Boston, 17 June 1775* (London, 1798) are regarded as his masterpieces. His son Johann Friedrich Wilhelm Müller (1782–1816) was also an engraver.

BIBLIOGRAPHY

E. Petermann: 'Johann Gotthard Müller und die Kupferstichschule der Hohe Carlsschule', *Die Hohe Carlsschule* (exh. cat., Stuttgart, Württemberg. Landesmuseums, 1959), pp. 71–81

EBBA KRULL

Müller, Otto. *See* MUELLER, OTTO.

Muller, Peter (Neil) (*b* Adelaide, 3 July 1927). Australian architect. After training at the universities of Adelaide and Pennsylvania, he practised in Sydney, building houses sympathetically related to their sites and exhibiting his understanding of the spatial compositions of the work of Frank Lloyd Wright. Of these, Audette House (1952), Castlecrag, Sydney, the Richardson house (1956), Palm Beach, Sydney, and his own house at Whale Beach (1954), Sydney, were the most accomplished. In this, his most significant period, he helped lay the foundations for an organic approach to design sympathetic to the Australian environment. Although his buildings exhibit a love of natural materials, he was content to use less expensive substitutes to further sound design in low cost dwellings. Muller visited Japan in 1961 and 1963, where he studied

Buddhist philosophy. This reinforced his prior interest in Japanese culture and design. His own office (1961), Paddington, Sydney, most clearly testifies to this influence, which later led to projects in Asia, the Middle East and the South Pacific. The Kayu Aya Hotel (1973), Bali, demonstrates his continuing love for fine craftsmanship and concern for the natural beauty of sites.

Between 1964 and 1968 Muller was involved in commercial architecture, especially theatres, and buildings such as Hoyts Cinema Centre (1967), Melbourne, which shows the continuance of the early influences in his work. In 1975–7 he was Director of the National Planning Development Commission, Canberra, where he acted as an advocate in support of Walter Burley Griffin's proposals for the city.

BIBLIOGRAPHY

Contemp. Architects
Archit. & A. (1955) [supernumerary issue]
J. C. Urford: *Peter Muller: Domestic Architecture to 1964* (diss., U. Sydney, 1984)
J. Taylor: *An Australian Identity: Houses for Sydney, 1953–63* (Sydney, 1972, rev. 1985)

JENNIFER TAYLOR

Müller, Philipp Heinrich (*b* Augsburg, 2 Oct 1654; *d* Augsburg, 17 Jan 1719). German medallist and diecutter. He learnt the craft of silversmith in Augsburg but soon turned his attention to cutting dies for medals. His earliest signed medal for the *Betrothal of the Holy Roman Emperor Leopold I* dates from 1677. Some ten years later Müller joined the medal workshop of Caspar Gottlieb Lauffer (*fl c.* 1700) in Nuremberg, where the majority of his works were produced. Lauffer's insistence that the medallists who worked for him should adhere to the style of the workshop left little room for individual artistic development. In his catalogue von Forster lists about 400 medals by Müller: besides medals portraying clerical and secular rulers, there were numerous medals commemorating the Turkish Wars and the battles of the War of the Spanish Succession. From the latter set of dies were produced series of wooden game pieces. Müller cut the dies for 102 medals in Lauffer's series of 250 papal portraits. He also produced dies for the coins of 25 states, mostly in South Germany, but his medals are the artistic high point of his work.

BIBLIOGRAPHY

Forrer; Thieme–Becker
A. von Forster: *Die Erzeugnisse der Stempelschneidekunst in Augsburg und Ph. H. Müllers* (Leipzig, 1910), pp. 85–142
Eugenius in Nummis: Kriegs- und Friedenstaten des Prinzen Eugen in der Medaille (exh. cat. by L. Popelka, Vienna, Heeresgesch. Mus., 1986)

HERMANN MAUÉ

Müller, Robert (*b* Zurich, 17 June 1920). Swiss sculptor, draughtsman and engraver. He entered the studio of Germaine Richier and Otto Bänninger (1897–1973) in Zurich in 1939 and was interested in the work of Marino Marini. Müller lived in Genoa (1947–8) before settling in Paris (1949), where Richier invited him to become her assistant. He executed his first works in repoussé iron in 1951, and in 1952 he underwent an apprenticeship as a smith in order to explore the expressive qualities of iron. His first works, abstract but clearly influenced by Richier's fantastic imagination, earned him official selection for the

Venice Biennale of 1956. After his award at the São Paulo Biennale in 1957 he was considered the leading light of the first Swiss 'iron generation'. However, he gradually gave up forging to concentrate on the welding and riveting of heterogeneous pieces. His object sculptures (from 1957) polarized two opposed three-dimensional impulses: the force of expansion expressed by a core appearing to push out and dilate, and the force of contraction expressed by an outer shell appearing to squeeze and enclose the core. This metaphor of Gros brought to Müller a new notoriety, confirmed by invitations to take part in such international exhibitions as *European Art Today* in the United States, the *Documenta* in Kassel, the Surrealist exhibition *Eros* in Paris, and *Bewogen* (1961) at the Stedelijk Museum in Amsterdam, where his erotic *Cyclist's Widow* (1957; priv. col.) caused a scandal and had to be withdrawn. His assemblages of the 1960s and 1970s were often on a monumental scale and sometimes involved materials such as concrete, as in *Fanfare* (1968–70; Zurich, in front of the Kunsthaus). After 1975 Müller placed more emphasis on drawing and engraving, the possibilities of which he has been exploring since 1958.

BIBLIOGRAPHY

P. Descargues: *Robert Müller: Catalogue des sculptures établi par Myriam Prévot* (Brussels, 1971)
Robert Müller: 'L'Oeuvre gravé du début à 1981 (exh. cat. by R. M. Mason, Geneva, Cab. Est. Mus. A. & Hist., 1982)
P.-A. Jaccard, ed.: 'La Génération du fer', *La Sculpture*, vii of *Ars Helvetica. Arts et culture visuels en Suisse*, ed. F. Deuchler (Distentis, 1987–92), pp. 270–73
Robert Müller: Kreta, Zeichnungen, 1978–1987 (exh. cat., Solothurn, Kstmus., 1990)   □

Müller, William James (*b* Bristol, 28 June 1812; *d* Bristol, 8 Sept 1845). English painter and draughtsman of Prussian descent. He was the son of a Prussian émigré and his Bristol-born wife. He began drawing at an early age and in 1827 was apprenticed to James Baker Pyne, a follower of Turner. By the early 1830s Müller had acquired a reputation for the rapidity and proficiency of his sketching. His first subjects were predominantly the picturesque back streets of Bristol and the woods and lanes of the surrounding countryside. While influenced by the landscapes of older Bristol colleagues such as Samuel Jackson (1794–1869), Müller also adopted stylistic elements from other artists, including Samuel Prout and John Sell Cotman. This eclecticism was to continue throughout Müller's career and was both a strength and a weakness in his art.

From 1834 to 1835 Müller and a fellow artist, George Fripp (1813–96), travelled through the Low Countries, down the Rhine and across the Alps to Italy, where Venice and Tivoli most inspired Müller. The high quality of draughtsmanship in his pencil drawings from this trip was not generally matched by the oil paintings produced after his return to England, although these did have some success among local patrons. So far, Müller's excursions had fallen within a well-established tradition among British artists, but in 1838 he determined to explore a subject that was less familiar but that held great romantic appeal: the Near East. That autumn and winter he visited Greece and then Egypt, becoming one of the first British artists to set out to depict realistically the rich and varied world of the Orient. Like other travellers, Müller was impressed by the colourful bazaars and ancient ruins of Egypt, but he responded with greater sensitivity to the Nile and desert landscapes (e.g. London, BM).

Soon after his return to England in 1839, Müller moved to London and exhibited Egyptian subjects at the Royal Academy and British Institution. Again, many of these display his awkward handling of oil paint, although a few, for example *Carpet Bazaar, Cairo* (1843; Bristol, Mus. & A.G.), are notable for their rendering of light and colour. Such pictures found favour with individual critics and patrons but were not well received at the Academy. Müller, meanwhile, had turned to new subjects: in 1840 he and a friend and pupil, W. E. Dighton (1822–53), visited northern France to gather material for a series of lithographs published the following year as the *Age of Francis I*, an example of the contemporary taste for historical genre. Also in the early 1840s he made a number of sketching trips along the Thames and to Somerset and Wales.

Müller's last and most interesting expedition combined the two most potent sources of inspiration of his art: the Orient and wild, untamed nature. In 1843, on the invitation of the archaeologist Charles Fellows, Müller travelled to Lycia, a remote corner of south-west Anatolia. Müller's watercolours vividly evoked the spirit of the place, portraying the shifting nuances of light and colour in weather conditions varying between torrential rain and bright sunshine, the rugged, mountainous landscape, the ancient rock-cut tombs and the exotic costumes and possessions of the nomadic people (e.g. London, Tate and BM). Like the watercolours made in France and Wales, these show Müller at his best, exhibiting the fluency and vigour of brushwork for which he was renowned. Müller's studio sale took place at Christie's, 1–3 April 1846.

WRITINGS
'An Artist's Tour in Egypt', *Art-Union*, i (1839), pp. 131–2
'Letter from Xanthus', *Art-Union*, vi (1844), pp. 41–2
'The Artist in Xanthus: Days and Nights in Tloss', *Art-Union*, vi (1844), pp. 209–11
'Letters from Xanthus', *Art-Union*, vi (1844), pp. 356–8

BIBLIOGRAPHY
N. Neal Solly: *Memoir of the Life of William James Müller* (London, 1875)
William James Müller (exh. cat., Birmingham, Mus. & A.G., 1896)
William James Müller, 1812–1845 (exh. cat., Bristol, Mus. & A.G., 1962)
D. G. Wilson: *Drawings and Watercolors of William James Müller in the Henry E. Huntington Collection* (MA thesis, Los Angeles, UCLA, 1974)
B. Llewellyn: *William James Müller and the Middle East* (MA thesis, U. London, Courtauld Inst., 1981)
William Müller, 1812–1845 (exh. cat. by B. Llewellyn, London, Tate, 1985)
W. J. Müller, 1812–1845 (exh. cat. by F. Greenacre and S. Stoddard, Bristol, Mus. & A.G., 1991)

BRIONY LLEWELLYN

Mullett, Alfred B(ult) (*b* Taunton, Somerset, 8 April 1834; *d* Washington, DC, 20 Oct 1890). American architect of English birth. He emigrated to the USA with his family in 1844 and settled in Glendale, OH, located just to the north of Cincinnati. He received training in technical drawing and mathematics from Farmers' College, Hamilton Co., OH, and in 1856 began his architectural career in the office of Isaiah Rogers in Cincinnati. After four years with the firm, Mullett left for a grand tour of Europe. In June 1861, soon after the outbreak of the Civil War, he was hired as a clerk by the US Treasury Department. Two years later he was transferred to the Office of the Supervising Architect, then part of the Treasury Department, which was headed by Rogers. Mullett succeeded Rogers as Supervising Architect in 1866. During the eight years that Mullett served in that position, he was in charge of the design and construction of important federal government buildings, including custom houses, court-houses, post offices, branch mints and assay offices, located throughout the country. Several of his earliest federal government buildings were designed in classical styles, such as the Greek Revival San Francisco Mint (1869–74) and the Court House and Post Office in Portland, ME (1869–73; destr. 1965).

Mullett is best remembered for his massive Second Empire style buildings constructed in several of the USA's larger cities. Outstanding examples include the Post Office and Custom House (1872–84) in St Louis, MO, the Post Office and Court House (1869–75; destr. 1939) in New York and the State, War and Navy Building (1871–86) on the block immediately to the west of the President's House (now the White House) in Washington, DC. Mullett oversaw the design of 40 new federal government buildings. He resigned from his position in 1874, after a change in the administration of the Treasury Department and in the midst of severe criticism voiced by private architects about his authority over federal government buildings. During the remainder of his life, Mullett designed many private buildings in Washington, DC, and elsewhere. Among his most significant private commissions in the capital are the Sun Building (1885–6) and the Central National Bank Building (1887–8; now the Apex Building), both in the Romanesque Revival style.

BIBLIOGRAPHY
D. J. Lehman: *Executive Office Building*, General Services Administration Historical Study, 3 (Washington, DC, 1970)
L. Wodehouse: 'Alfred B. Mullett and his French Style Government Buildings', *J. Soc. Archit. Hist.*, xxxi (1972), pp. 22–37

ANTOINETTE J. LEE

Mullgardt, Louis C(hristian) (*b* Washington, MO, 1866; *d* Stockton, CA, 1942). American architect. His career began at the age of 15 when he became an apprentice with the architectural firm of Wilhelmi & Janssen, followed by work in the office of James Stewart & Co., both offices in St Louis, MO. In 1887 he moved to Brookline, MA, to work for the firm of Shepley, Rutan & Coolidge, successors to the practice of H. H. Richardson. His work in that office included designs for the Stanford University campus, which brought his attention to the idea of developing a uniquely Californian style. In 1889 he entered Harvard College, Cambridge, MA, but left before graduation due to illness.

In 1891 Mullgardt joined the Chicago office of Henry Ives Cobb where he designed buildings in many styles, including the Newberry Library (1892), Chicago, in the Romanesque style and the Athletic Club (1892), Chicago, in Venetian style. He also worked on buildings in Gothic style for the University of Chicago (1891–3) and was responsible for the decorative detail of Cobb's Fisheries building (1893) for the World's Columbia Exposition, Chicago. From 1892 to 1894 he was a partner in the firm of Stewart, McClure & Mullgardt in St Louis, designing the American Colonial style Arlington Hotel (1892–4; destr.) of Hot Springs, AR.

After travelling in Europe in 1894 and 1895, Mullgardt returned to a practice in St Louis. From 1903 to 1904 he was in England serving as a consultant on architectural structural design. In 1905 he returned to the USA and opened an office in San Francisco in 1906 where he carried out some of his most influential work. The small Ernest A. Evans house (1907) in Mill Valley, CA, and the vast mansion (1908–10; destr. 1935; see *Macmillan Enc. Architects*, p. 253) for Henry W. Taylor in Berkeley are examples of Mullgardt's efforts to achieve a California style through the amalgamation of such diverse influences as English Arts and Crafts work, the white walls and tile roofs of the Spanish California missions and the developing bungalow style that became typical of much work in the San Francisco Bay Area.

In 1912 Mullgardt became a member of the group planning the Panama–Pacific Exposition of 1915. He was responsible for the design of the grouping known as the Court of the Ages, a garden courtyard surrounded by arcades with a giant central tower richly decorated with ornament inspired by natural forms, loosely based on Spanish Renaissance and Moorish precedents. This was a temporary building that seems to have set Mullgardt's thinking towards the ornate plaster detailing that characterized much of his subsequent work, such as the President's house (1915–18) for Stanford University and the M. H. de Young Memorial Museum (1916–21) in the Golden Gate Park, San Francisco. The rich decorative detail of the latter building soon fell into disrepair and was largely removed in the 1940s.

In 1917 Mullgardt became involved in the planning and design of a business centre for Honolulu. He proposed the invention of a mid-Pacific Hawaiian Renaissance style, in which colourful, decorative terracotta in green and yellow would form the surface of Italian Renaissance palace-like structures built in reinforced concrete. Of the seven planned buildings, he executed only one, the Theodore H. Davies building (1917–21), a large four-storey wholesale warehouse covering an entire city block. After travelling around the world in 1922–3, Mullgardt returned to San Francisco to resume practice. In 1924 he developed a proposal for a bay bridge whose piers would incorporate skyscraper towers to serve as hotels, office buildings and factories. After the rejection of this scheme his practice was limited to a few minor works as tastes turned away from the ornate and eccentric historicism that was his forte in later years, in favour of the Functionalism of the Modern Movement of the late 1920s and 1930s.

BIBLIOGRAPHY

Macmillan Enc. Architects

R. J. Clark: 'Louis Christian Mullgardt and the Court of the Ages', *J. Soc. Archit. Historians*, xxi/4 (1962), pp. 171–8

——: *Louis Christian Mullgardt: 1866–1942* (Santa Barbara, 1966)

JOHN F. PILE

Mulready. British family of artists. (1) William Mulready was, with James Barry and Francis Danby, among the most talented and distinguished of the numerous Irish artists who moved to London in the late 18th century and the 19th century. In 1802 he married the painter Elizabeth

VARLEY. Of their four sons, the eldest, Paul Augustus (1805–64), was the father of (2) A. E. Mulready, while William (1805–78) and Michael (1807–89) also became professional artists.

(1) William Mulready (*b* Ennis, Co. Clare, 1 April 1786; *d* London, 7 July 1863). Irish painter and draughtsman, active in England.

1. LIFE AND WORK. He was the son of an Irish leather breeches maker who settled in the Bayswater area of London *c*. 1792. From 1799 to *c*. 1804 he worked on Robert Ker Porter's panoramas; his precocious talent and the assistance of the sculptor Charles Bell earned him a place at the Royal Academy Schools in 1800. In 1804 he first exhibited at the Royal Academy; while he appears to have attempted history painting, only preparatory drawings in this genre survive (e.g. the *Disobedient Prophet*, 1804; London, V&A), and his energies were devoted to still-lifes (untraced) and cottage subjects.

It was in this last category that Mulready began to make a reputation. In the company of his close friend David Wilkie, he visited private collections and copied works by Adriaen van Ostade and Pieter de Hooch. His earliest known dated painting, *The Rattle* (1808; London, Tate), reveals a pronounced debt to both artists, while also demonstrating both his impressive technical skill and the direction his art would take. His earliest cottage subjects (e.g. *Cottage in St Albans*, 1805–6; London, V&A) explore the varied textures and uneven surfaces of dilapidated houses in London and its environs (he drew in the company of John Linnell, William Henry Hunt and the Varley brothers at Hampstead Heath, Millbank and St

1. William Mulready: *The Wolf and the Lamb*, 1820 (London, Buckingham Palace, Royal Collection)

2. William Mulready: *The Last in*, oil on panel, 612×750 mm, 1835 (London, Tate Gallery)

Albans), representing the vernacular in a carefully orchestrated essay in the picturesque. Afterwards he turned to the interior of the cottage and to the lives of its inhabitants for his subject-matter. Between 1805 and 1812 he supported himself by illustrating children's books for William Godwin's Juvenile Library; *Lamb's Tales from Shakespeare* (1822), for example, contains engravings by William Blake made from Mulready's designs.

Despite winning a silver medal at the Royal Academy as a student (1806), Mulready experienced difficulty in gaining official recognition: he failed to win the coveted British Institution premium in 1808 with *The Rattle* and in 1809 with the *Carpenter's Shop* (untraced; see 1986 exh. cat., p. 107); *The Mall* (1811) and *Near the Mall* (1812; both London, V&A), both Dutch-inspired views of his home territory of Kensington Gravel Pits (i.e. Notting Hill Gate), were rejected by the patron who had commissioned them; and he failed in his bid for election as ARA in 1813. Mulready attributed some of his professional difficulties to public knowledge about the irregularities of his private life. At 17 he had married Elizabeth Varley (whose brother John Varley was Mulready's first teacher and remained a lifelong friend); with the collapse of their marriage in 1810, the couple quarrelled violently over the

custody of the children. The four sons were brought up by Mulready in a substantial house in London, which he rented from 1828 until his death.

By 1814 Mulready had gained a degree of professional security; that year he met Sir John Swinburne (*d* 1860) and his family, who, with John Sheepshanks, became his most liberal patrons. In 1815 he was elected ARA with *Idle Boys* (untraced; see Heleniak, p. 199), a schoolroom scene, and in 1816 he became an RA with *Village Buffoon* (London, RA), a depiction of an eccentric old man courting a young cottage girl, set against the encircling walls of Kensington Gardens.

During the 1820s Mulready had outstanding successes and significant failures. Viewers often complained of the obscurity and of the risqué quality of some of his paintings. Ruskin remarked that Mulready painted subjects 'unfit for pictorial representation'. *The Wolf and the Lamb* (1820; Brit. Royal Col.; see fig. 1), a drama of a bully and his victim, was purchased from the Royal Academy by George IV in 1820. However, *The Widow* (1823; Sir Richard Proby priv. col.) remained unsold after its exhibition at the Royal Academy, condemned by an anonymous reviewer: 'We cannot admit that the extreme cleverness displayed in this picture throughout atones for the scarcely covert grossness of it.'

The subject-matter of many of Mulready's mature works concerns childhood and education. As Mulready was for most of his life a single parent, biography and iconography are inextricably linked in his art. A work such as *The Last In* (1835; London, Tate; see fig. 2) reveals the qualities that made Mulready a model for the later generation of the Pre-Raphaelite Brotherhood. The low-life narrative and composition of this work also has much in common with works by David Wilkie, such as *Blind Man's Buff* (1811–13; Brit. Royal Col.). The tense drama of Mulready's picture is emphasized by the large central window, focusing the viewer's attention on the moral dilemma between the relative educational values of the village classroom and Nature outside.

Mulready was highly regarded as a draughtsman and was frequently called upon in this capacity. In the early 1830s he was working for the publisher Robert Cadell on a series of illustrations for the first complete illustrated edition of Sir Walter Scott's novels. His most successful exercise in this genre was his set of illustrations for John van Voorst's edition of Oliver Goldsmith's *The Vicar of Wakefield* (1843). Three paintings followed the engravings: *The Whistonian Controversy* (1843; Lord Northbrook priv. col.); *Choosing the Wedding Gown* (1845; London, V&A); and *Haymaking* (1846–7; Lord Northbrook priv. col.). These were very popular and were frequently reproduced; for example, the last mentioned was used to decorate a milk jug in 1842 by Henry Cole's Art Manufactures.

Mulready's least successful venture was the Mulready postal envelope, designed in December 1839 for a commission from Henry Cole. The envelope shows Britannia sending angelic messengers to the furthest corners of the Empire. After its issue in early May 1840, dozens of caricatures were produced, many of them explicitly anti-Irish and some of them satirizing the conventions of high art that Mulready had employed; Cole later admitted that the design was not suitable for its purpose.

In 1848 Mulready was honoured by a retrospective exhibition at the Society of Arts. Subsequently he painted few new subject pictures. *The Butt* (exh. RA 1848) and *A Mother Teaching her Son* (exh. RA 1858; both London, V&A) are exceptions. Mulready worked mostly in the life class at the Royal Academy; he was devoted to the Academy and performed his duties as Visitor with a conscientiousness rarely seen at the time. *The Bathers* (1848–9; Dublin, Hugh Lane Mun. Gal.) and *Bathers Surprised* (1852–3; Dublin, N.G.) as well as a very large drawing on several pieces of paper stuck together (Edinburgh, N.G.) testify to Mulready's preoccupation with depicting the female nude on a grand scale. An exhibition of his drawings at Gore House, London, in 1853 attracted much attention and royal patronage for his life studies. Exhibits at the Academy were, however, often either replicas or re-workings.

Mulready died shortly after giving evidence, in support of the life class as central to academic education, before the Royal Commission Enquiry into the Royal Academy.

2. WORKING METHODS AND TECHNIQUE. Preparation for a composition often involved written notations of a theme (many examples in U. Manchester, Whitworth A.G.). At the same time Mulready would make annotated drawings of a strictly empirical kind; these studies of, for example, clothing, uniforms, footwear and working equipment were the basis from which a concentrated pictorial narrative would be constructed. A series of small pen-and-ink sketches outlining the composition and working-out details of figures and groups was the next stage. The composition might then be given a working title, which, differing from the exhibition title, reveals the thematic core of the work. One of the sketches for *The Last In*, for example, is inscribed 'Master Jack Lag, y/ Innocent Master Jack', indicating that irony, epitomized by the schoolmaster's bowing to the late entrant, was central from the work's inception. The more rhetorical title was introduced, along with an intensified lyricism and grandeur in the treatment of the figures, only in the final stages. A highly finished chalk drawing seems to have served as a cartoon. He used a very small oil sketch (often no more than 82×70 mm, as with *Interior of an English Cottage*, 1828; London, Tate) to block in the areas of light and shade and establish the tonal relations of the finished painting.

Mulready's early work is sombre in colour range and varies from the extraordinarily freely handled studies of Hampstead Heath on millboard (1806; London, V&A) to the flat application of a mosaic of pigment carefully controlled and safely varnished as with *The Rattle*. In the 1830s Mulready began painting on a white ground with transparent glazes, his palette rich in reds and browns, creating sensuous effects by scumbling. Working in oil, often on panel rather than canvas, he lavished great attention on the surface of his works, and most of them are stable and, when cleaned, brilliant in colour.

The contents of Mulready's studio were auctioned at Christie's, London, on 28 April 1864. The Victoria and Albert Museum, London, has the largest collection of his work, as well as his account book (1805–c. 1861), correspondence and personal papers.

UNPUBLISHED SOURCES
London, V&A [account bk, corr. & personal pap.]

BIBLIOGRAPHY
T. Marcliffe [W. Godwin]: *The Looking Glass: The True History of an Artist* (London, 1805) [based on conversations between Mulready and Godwin]
F. G. Stephens: *Masterpieces of Mulready: Memorials of W. Mulready* (London, 1867, rev. 3/1890)
J. Dafforne: *Pictures by William Mulready RA* (London, 1872)
Drawings by William Mulready (exh. cat. by A. Rorimer, London, V&A, 1972)
K. M. Heleniak: *William Mulready* (New Haven, 1980) [with cat. rais.]
Mulready (exh. cat. by M. Pointon, London, V&A, 1986)

MARCIA POINTON

(2) A(ugustus) E(dwin) Mulready (*b* 23 Feb 1844; *d* after 1903). English painter, grandson of (1) William Mulready. He studied at the South Kensington Schools and entered the Royal Academy Schools, London, in December 1861 on the recommendation of J. C. Horsley. In 1863 he won the silver medal for drawing from the Antique. Horsley was prominent in the artists' colony at Cranbrook in Kent (*see* CRANBROOK COLONY), where

Mulready was recorded in 1870 and 1872 although no rural scenes by him are known. He exhibited at the Royal Academy between 1863 and 1880, and he was still active in November 1903.

Mulready's first Royal Academy entries were portraits, but he is best known for his sentimental London street scenes. His favourite subjects were children, particularly crossing-sweepers and flower-sellers, always rosy-cheeked and healthy, their rags clean (e.g. *A London Crossing-sweeper and a Flower-girl*, 1884; London, Mus. London). The paintings often contain unsubtle rich–poor contrasts, as in *Our Good-natured Cousins* (n.d.; priv. col., see Casteras, fig. 22), in which an upper-class trio walks past a flower-girl, ostentatiously ignoring her. Across the street an undertaker's shop advertises cheap rates for children, hinting at the girl's fate. A frequent, lightly ironical device is the contrasting of figures with theatrical posters: in *A Sunny Day* (1874; priv. col., see Reynolds, pl. 34), the relationship of the two women to their male escort is made explicit by the sandwich-board advertising Sheridan's *The Rivals*. Mulready resumed portraiture late in his career when his sentimental street scenes became less fashionable.

BIBLIOGRAPHY

'Augustus Edwin Mulready', *Biog. & Rev.*, 1 (Jan 1879), pp. 51–5
G. Reynolds: *Victorian Painting* (London, 1966, rev. 2/1987)
The Cranbrook Colony (exh. cat. by A. Greg, Wolverhampton, A.G., 1977)
S. P. Casteras: *Images of Victorian Womanhood in English Art* (London, 1987)

PHILIP MCEVANSONEYA

Multan. Town in Pakistan. It was an ancient stronghold of the GANDHARA kingdom that was annexed to the Achaemenid empire by Darius (*reg* 522–486 BC) and, after Alexander the Great (*reg* 336–323 BC), was controlled successively by Bactrian, Indo-Parthian and Kushana dynasties. Traces of these cultures are buried beneath the core of the old citadel. The Buddhist remains in the region include the ruins of the town of Tulamba and a monastery and tower at the site of Sui Vihara. Ancient Multan probably had a concentric plan, with the citadel containing a stupa or temple in the centre, similar in layout to Tulamba. With a revival of Hinduism in the 6th century AD, Multan fell under the sway of that faith, notably the worship of the sun god; in 641 the Chinese Buddhist pilgrim Xuanzang recorded that the worship of Buddha had almost disappeared. In the Arab invasion of Sind in 711 Multan was taken by Muhammad ibn Qasim, but in the 10th century the geographer al-Istakhri described the town as still predominantly Hindu, with the great temple known as Bayt al-dhahab (House of Gold) in the centre of the town, while the Arab ruler lived 3 km away. Multan, however, was reconstructed and its plan adapted to that of an Islamic town, with the site of the old citadel incorporated in the ramparts of the Islamic fort at one side of the town. Together with Sind, Multan became a stronghold of the Shi'ites, who were later suppressed under the Ghaznavids (*reg* 977–1186). Subsequently the town was under the Khalji sultans of Delhi (*reg* 1290–1320) and the Mughals (*reg* 1526–1857). After the annexation of the Punjab by the British in 1849, an obelisk and other memorials were erected, but the fort was demolished. The high mound of the citadel still dominates the city,

however, and preserves within its core the original street layout.

Multan has a tradition of brick architecture with characteristic battered walls and corner towers, a style associated with Khurasan rather than India. The earliest Muslim building is the 12th-century mosque of Khalid Walid, a plain, ruinous building with an exceptionally fine mihrab of cut and moulded brick decorated with Kufic inscriptions. Other pre-Mughal buildings are the shrine of Shah Yusuf Gardizi, which was built in 1152 and then restored and covered with tiles in 1548, and the tombs of Shaikh Baha al-Haqq Zakariya (*d* 1262), Shadna Shahid (*d* 1270) and Shams al-din Tabrizi (*d* 1276). These tombs, in the form of square, domed chambers, greatly influenced the later tomb architecture of India. The most celebrated tomb of Multan is that of Rukn-i 'Alam (1320–24; *see* INDIAN SUBCONTINENT, fig. 86). It consists of an octagonal tomb chamber with a hemispherical dome and tapering towers at each corner. Its finely carved wooden mihrab is unparalleled in Islamic India. The Mughal tombs of Multan are strongly influenced by earlier forms, particularly that of the tomb of Rukn-i 'Alam. Examples are the tombs of Sultan 'Ali Akbar, Sa'id Khan Quraishi and Ma'i Mihraban. The Sawi Mosque and the 'Idgah combine the Mughal style with the local architectural tradition of brick and ceramic tiles.

See also INDIAN SUBCONTINENT, §III, 6(ii)(a).

BIBLIOGRAPHY

A. Cunningham: *The Ancient Geography of India* (London, 1871), pp. 230–41
——: *Archaeol. Surv. India Rep.*, v (1875), pp. 114–36
J. Marshall: 'The Monuments of Muslim India', *The Cambridge History of India*, iii (Cambridge, 1928), pp. 597–9
V. V. Mirashi: 'Three Ancient and Famous Temples of the Sun', *Purāṇa*, viii (1966), pp. 38–51
A. Nabi Khan: *Multan: History and Architecture* (Islamabad, 1983)

NATALIE H. SHOKOOHY

Multimedia. Term used in an art-historical context to describe art forms that include a variety of media, often unconventional. It is used mainly where a complete description of media would be too lengthy. Multimedia may also comprise live or PERFORMANCE ART, Happenings, ENVIRONMENTAL ART, VIDEO ART and INSTALLATION. The origins of multimedia may be traced to DADA, especially the activity in 1916 in Zurich of the Cabaret Voltaire. The concept was developed further by artists associated with SURREALISM, for example at the Exposition Internationale du Surréalisme (1938) at the Galerie des Beaux-Arts, Paris: works were exhibited in a series of 'environments', such as the display of Salvador Dalí's *Rainy Taxi*, which was positioned under a localized rainstorm and contained a female dummy and live, crawling snails; in another room Marcel Duchamp hung 1200 coal-sacks from the ceiling, covered the floor with dead leaves and moss and installed a lily pond surrounded by firs and reeds. Duchamp in particular opened the way for artists to explore new art forms and combinations of multimedia. In the second half of the 20th century groups or movements that advanced the concept of multimedia included the Situationists (*see* SITUATION), FLUXUS, the INDEPENDENT GROUP, POP ART, NOUVEAU RÉALISME and AKTIONISMUS.

BIBLIOGRAPHY

Dada, Surrealism and their Heritage (exh. cat. by W. S. Rubin, New York, MOMA, 1968)

L. Lippard: ed.: *Six Years: The Dematerialization of the Art Object from 1966 to 1972* (London, 1973)

A. Henri: *Environments and Happenings* (London, 1974)

Dada and Surrealism Reviewed (exh. cat., London, Hayward Gal., 1978)

S. C. Foster, ed.: *'Event' Arts and Art Events* (Ann Arbor and London, 1988)

Multiple. *See* LIMITED EDITION, §2.

Multscher, Hans (*b* Reichenhofen, Bavaria, *c.* 1400; *d* Ulm, before 13 March 1467). German sculptor.

1. Life. 2. Work. 3. Influence.

1. LIFE. Multscher mentions his birthplace on the inscribed band, originally a predella, of the Karg altarpiece in Ulm Cathedral (1433) and on two wings of the so-called 'Wurzach Altar' (1437) at Reichenhofen in the Allgäu. The town archives of Leutkirch, written between 1405 and 1437, record that Multscher belonged to the 'Freien Leute auf Leutkircher Heide', a commune of free peasants who had been able to preserve their independence because they were the direct descendants of *Königsfreie*, who had always been free. Under a charter of Emperor Ludwig in 1337, these men were direct subjects of the Empire and had the right of free movement 'to Imperial cities or other towns'.

This inherited liberty was very important to Multscher, since it enabled him eventually to go to Ulm as a man free and equal from birth. This status, rare in the Middle Ages, may explain the pride with which he mentions his home; and it probably also partly explains why he was admitted as a freeman of Ulm in 1427 without paying any dues. He also fulfilled the legal requirements for citizenship in Ulm: he had an excellent training as a craftsman and artist, married in 1427 Adelheid Kitzin, a member of a family of sculptors known in Ulm from 1370, and at his marriage he already owned a house on a prime corner site near the cathedral square. A letter of 1468 (Ulm, Stadtarchv) 'concerning the redemption of the one and a half gulden' reveals that he additionally possessed 'land and goods' to the value of 37 gulden, 2 ort in Ulm currency, and these possessions, together with his free imperial status and his artistic qualifications, were to prove very important with regard to his position in Ulm.

Multscher had a large workshop that produced altarpieces. A letter of recommendation from the City Council to the Council of Nördlingen dated 25 April 1430 mentions a brother, Heinrich, who was also a sculptor and employed in Hans's workshop. Although Multscher is described as a sculptor and carver, the *bozzetto* for the tomb of *Duke Ludwig the Bearded* (*c.* 1430; Munich, Bayer. Nmus.) and some bronze figures show that he was also a modeller. It is not certain if he was a painter. A lost Ulm document of 1431 described him as a 'Bildmacher und geschworener Werkhmann' ('maker of images and a sworn artisan'), but in Middle High German 'Bild' means a three-dimensional figure. As to the 'geschworener Werkhmann', Multscher was a Free Master, his workshop including craftsmen in all the trades necessary for the production of altarpieces without the compulsory membership of a guild. The 'sworn artisan', an honorary office, was an officially sworn assessor for the trades of sculptor and carver for the Ulm City Council. Multscher's hereditary authority as a Royal Freeman, together with his other qualifications, must have predestined him for this office, and he evidently possessed the necessary incorruptibility and disinterest to carry it out.

Multscher is next documented in the memorial book of the Charterhouse of Güterstein near Urach, where a perpetual memorial day (the anniversary of 14 Aug 1449) is entered for him and his wife. The sisters recorded that Multscher gave them a reduction of 8 gulden on the price of an altar he produced for them in return. On 9 February 1456 Multscher met at Innsbruck Thomas Luenczner, the representative of the parish of Sterzing (now Vipiteno) in the Brenner Pass, to discuss the commission for the planned high altar, for which Multscher received a down payment of 5 Berne marks. From July 1458 to 7 or 9 January 1459 Multscher was in Sterzing with several journeymen to erect the high altar (Vipiteno, Unserer Lieben Frau im Moos), which had been made in sections in Ulm. On 8 January 1459 the accounts were worked out according to ancient German custom 'at the table' with food and drink, and Multscher was given a further payment. The rest of the money was sent to him in several

1. Hans Multscher: *Holy Trinity*, alabaster relief with oil and tempera, 285×163×102 mm, *c.* 1427–30 (Frankfurt am Main, Liebieghaus)

instalments via Ulm merchants, and the dates of payment are the only documentary evidence for the last eight years of his life. Two Ulm documents of 1467 and 1468 establish the approximate date of his death.

2. WORK. At the height of Multscher's workshop activity up to 16 collaborators can be traced, and the number of surviving school works and others in his style is correspondingly large (for illustration *see* PALMESEL). They are important reference points in the attempt to follow the formation of his style. None of Multscher's own works has survived from the so-called 'dark decade' after 1437, during which he apparently moved away from the Soft style to develop a 'new Realism'.

From his early works it appears that, after a possible apprenticeship in the Allgäu, Multscher travelled extensively in the main artistic centres of the day, northern France, Burgundy and the Low Countries, returning to the Allgäu before settling in Ulm. The influence of these regions is clear in the stylistic details of his early works, which are outstanding in contemporary Swabian art. Three works have been identified: an angel on a console in Aachen Cathedral (before 1420), a *Virgin and Child* (1420–25; Aachen, Suermondt-Ludwig-Mus.) and an enthroned *Virgin and Child* from a Middle Rhenish church (*c.* 1420; Riggisberg, Switzerland, Abegg-Stift.) that is similar to the wooden *Miraculous Elevation of St Mary Magdalene* (1420–25; ex-Bodemus., Berlin), especially in the facial structure. The last is one of a series of wood-carvings produced in the Allgäu after Multscher's return from his travels. These include: a standing *Virgin and Child* from Kempten (1420–25; Stuttgart, Württemberg. Landesmus.), a standing *Virgin and Child* (1425–7; Reichenhofen im Allgäu, parish church) and a standing bishop/saint (*c.* 1425–30; Rohrdorf im Allgäu, parish church).

Statuary attributable to the period after Multscher became a citizen of Ulm includes: the group on the east side of the Ulm Rathaus, of Charlemagne accompanied by two squires and the Kings of Hungary and Bohemia (*c.* 1427–30), the *Holy Trinity* relief in alabaster from Sandizell (*c.* 1427–30; Frankfurt am Main, Liebieghaus; see fig. 1), the *Man of Sorrows* beside the west doorway of Ulm Cathedral (1429; *see* GOTHIC, fig. 37, and ULM, fig. 3), the bronze statuette of a standing *Virgin and Child* (*c.* 1430; Munich, Bayer. Nmus.), the Karg Retable (1433; Ulm Cathedral) and a Crucifix (*c.* 1435; ex-Bodemus., Berlin).

Multscher's early period ended with the Landsberg *Virgin and Child* (1437; Landsberg am Lech, St Maria Himmelfahrt; see fig. 2). It was originally the main figure in the central panel of the so-called 'Wurzach Altar', once the high altar retable in Landsberg church. A female saint, formerly standing, which exists as a three-quarter figure (Augsburg, Maximilianmus.), also seems to have been part of the Landsberg altar group, as it is very close to the Landsberg *Virgin and Child* not only in style and quality but also in its technical execution.

It is at the stylistic level of the Landsberg *Virgin and Child* and the Augsburg female saint that the decisive phase in Multscher's attempt completely to overcome the influence of the Soft style and his clear adoption of the 'new Realism' can be seen to begin. It culminates in the

2. Hans Multscher: *Virgin and Child*, limewood, 1437 (Landsberg am Lech, St Maria Himmelfahrt)

two female saints of *c.* 1450 from Heiligkreuztal Abbey near Riedlingen (Rottweil, Dominikanermus.). As well as being of high quality, they are of great importance for the development of Multscher's style, showing that he had finally freed himself from the last traces of the Soft style and achieved the breakthrough to the naturalistic attention to realistic detail that characterizes his late period. They adumbrate the style of the Sterzing altar figures. The stone *Virgin* from Ummendorf near Biberach and the funerary figure of the *Countess Mechthild* in the Stiftskirche in Tübingen have survived from 1450–55, the period of Multscher's mature stylistic development. The Sterzing altar (1456–8/9) marks the beginning of the transition to the work he produced in old age. Although it was thought that the remains of the Sterzing altar represented the last surviving works of Multscher and his collaborators, a bronze reliquary bust (New York, Frick) may be by Multscher's own hand, produced about 1460. At about this time Multscher appears also to have executed the model for a small beaten plaque, which survives in two slightly differing examples. The standing *Virgin* from Bihlafingen (Ulm, Ulm. Mus.) must also on stylistic evidence have been produced shortly after the Sterzing altar figures. The female saint (possibly Mary Magdalene) in the Liebieghaus in Frankfurt, stylistically very different from the Sterzing figures, was probably, like two more female saints (Mülheim an der Ruhr, Härle priv. col.), executed during the first half of the 1460s.

3. INFLUENCE. Multscher was an innovator, producing works of an individual character. During his 40 years in Ulm his statuary and, above all, his carved altarpieces introduced into southern Germany the traditions of the artistic centres of western Europe, which had led the way since 1400. Through his inspired combination of south German and Western stylistic elements he made Ulm the leading artistic centre in the whole country. At the same time he developed new methods of producing altarpieces, and he also trained his fellow craftsmen to lead work teams that could cope with the future requirements of increased demand for works with multiple figures of individual character and above average quality. It was owing to Multscher's keen foresight that the increased production of south German carved altars in the Late Gothic style in the last third of the 15th century did not degenerate into mass-production, as was the case with the altars exported from the Netherlands.

BIBLIOGRAPHY
K. Gerstenberg: *Hans Multscher* (Leipzig, 1928)
A. Schädler: 'Die Frühwerke Hans Multschers', *Z. Württemberg. Landesgesch.*, xiv (1955), pp. 385–444
M. Schröder: *Das plastische Werk Multschers in seiner chronologischen Entwicklung* (Tübingen, 1955)
W. Paatz: *Süddeutsche Schnitzaltäre der Spätgotik* (Heidelberg, 1963)
A. Schädler: 'Beiträge zum Werk Hans Multschers', *Anz. Ger. Nmus.* (1969), pp. 40–62
M. Tripps: *Hans Multscher: Seine Ulmer Schaffenszeit, 1427–1467* (Weissenhorn, 1969)
——: 'Das dunkle Jahrzehnt in der Stilbildung Multschers', *Z. Württemberg. Landesgesch.*, xxix (1970), pp. 1–14
——: 'Unbekannte Mitarbeiter der Ulmer Multscherwerkstatt und die von ihnen erzeugten Schulströmungen', *Ruperto–Carola*, xxii/46 (1970), pp. 43–54
A. Schädler: 'Bronzebildwerke von Hans Multscher', *Intuition und Kunstwissenschaft: Festschrift für Hanns Swarzenski* (Berlin, 1973), pp. 391–408
M. Tripps: 'Eine Reihe thronender Gottesmütter und deren Verbindung zum frühen Schaffen Multschers', *Schwäb. Heimat*, xxv/1 (1974), pp. 17–36
H. Schindler: *Der Schnitzaltar: Meisterwerke und Meister in Süddeutschland, Österreich und Südtirol* (Regensburg, 1978)
M. Tripps: 'Die thronende Muttergottes mit Kind in der Abegg-Stiftung Bern in Riggisberg: Ein Frühwerk von Hans Multscher?', *Z. Württemberg. Landesgesch.*, xlviii (1988), pp. 113–26
H. Beck and M. Buckling: *Hans Multschers Frankfurter Trinitätsrelief: Ein Zeugnis spekulativer Künstlerindividualität* (Frankfurt am Main, 1988)
Hans Multscher, Meister der Spätgotik: Sein Werk, seine Schule, seine Zeit (exh. cat. by M. Tripps, Leutkirch im Allgäu, 1993)

MANFRED TRIPPS

Mulvany, John Skipton (*b* Dublin, *c*. 1813; *d* Dublin, 1870). Irish architect. He completed his articles to the architect William Deane Butler (*d* 1859) in 1833 and by 1836 was working for the Dublin and Kingstown Railway Company. In 1842 he designed the classical pavilion that was the Kingstown terminus of the line. The Royal Irish Yacht Club, another classical ornament to Kingstown (Dún Laoghaire) harbour, was completed in 1850. In 1845 he was appointed architect to the Midland Great Western Railway Company with an annual salary of £250. Some of his finest work was done for the company, in particular the Greco–Egyptian terminus at Broadstone, Dublin, which Craig called 'the last building in Dublin to partake of the sublime'. Mulvany also designed stations along the line, the most important being at Athlone (1851), and the terminus and grand Railway Hotel at Galway (1850–52). He had a considerable practice designing grand Italianate villas for wealthy industrialists, including several for the Malcomson family in Co. Waterford in the 1860s.

Mulvany was a great admirer of James Gandon and handled the classical vocabulary with assurance. He was at his best when designing in the most severe Neo-classical style. His only major departure was for the lunatic asylum at Mullingar (1850–55), which is in a rather dessicated Gothic style, as the Board of Works had recommended Gothic rather than classical. Towards the end of his life Mulvany did less architectural work, devoting himself more to business, and to being a railway arbitrator and valuer.

BIBLIOGRAPHY
Obituary, *Irish Builder*, xii (1870), p. 115
M. Craig: *Dublin, 1660–1860* (London, 1952), p. 300
J. Sheehy: 'Railway Architecture', *J. Irish Rlwy Rec. Soc.*, xii/68 (1975), pp. 125–38
F. O'Dwyer: 'John Skipton Mulvany, Architect, 1813–70', *Martello* (Summer, 1988)

JEANNE SHEEHY

Mumbai. *See* BOMBAY.

Mumford, Lewis (*b* Flushing, NY, 19 Oct 1895; *d* Amenia, NY, 26 Jan 1990). American critic and theorist. Following the turn-of-the-century trends of romantic radicalism and progressivism, which inspired William Morris, Ebenezer Howard and Patrick Geddes among others, he advocated an architecture that would integrate work and play, art and labour, rural and urban life in a new culture fostering a democratic community. Like John Dewey he tried to translate the Transcendentalists' interest in a democratic art into an aesthetic of democratic 'experience' appropriate to the modern age. Although he helped to organize the exhibition *International Style* at MOMA, New York (1932), which introduced many Americans to Modernism, by the 1940s he had emerged as a vocal critic of the International Style, particularly of the wing of the movement inspired by Le Corbusier's vision of the 'Cité

Radieuse'. Beginning with *Sticks and Stones* (1922), one of the first published histories of American architecture, he repeatedly called for an indigenous American architectural style. While embracing functionalism as an antidote to the florid ornamentation of Beaux-Arts style, he grew increasingly critical of the minimalist tendencies in European Modernism. His arguments for a type of functionalism that would draw on local techniques and materials to unite function and expression owe much to the aesthetics of Louis Sullivan and Frank Lloyd Wright, despite his criticism of specific elements of their work.

Mumford also championed an updated version of Howard's garden-city ideal, arguing in favour of decentralized regional planning and of smaller settlements combining the best features of rural and urban culture. As the dominant intellectual figure within the Regional Planning Association of America (RPAA; 1923–33), he formulated the ideas that Clarence Stein (1883–1977), Henry Wright (1878–1936) and other RPAA members sought to realize. *The Culture of Cities* (1938) immediately became a key text for advocates of green-belt cities within the New Deal and also influenced the work of Frederic J. Osborn (1885–1978) with the Garden Cities and Town Planning Association in Great Britain in the post-war New Towns movement. In the 1950s and 1960s Mumford emerged as one of the most outspoken critics of 'bigness' in urban planning, and he used his 'Sky Line' column in the *New Yorker* to attack the devastation of the traditional city centre and surrounding areas by the skyscraper, major roads and dormitory suburbs. *The City in History* (1961) drew together the various themes in his life's work in a critical chronicle of the undermining of Western urban culture by the technological culture of industrialization. The industrial megalopolis, in his view, was both disintegrative and homogenizing; it gutted the public space of the agora and the medieval town, while forsaking the diversity of urban culture for the uniformity of dispersed suburbs. His influence as a critic is difficult to ascertain. His work provides little comfort for either conventional Modernists or advocates of a playful Post-modernism. Neither group committed itself to the communitarian principles underlying Mumford's urbanism, nor to the search for a democratic form that plays such a central role in his aesthetic theory.

WRITINGS

Sticks and Stones: A Study of American Architecture and Civilization (New York, 1922)
The Culture of Cities (New York, 1938)
The City in History: Its Origins, its Transformations, and its Prospects (London and New York, 1961/ *R* London, 1984)
Technics and Human Development, i of *The Myth of the Machine* (New York, 1967)
The Pentagon of Power, ii of *The Myth of the Machine* (New York, 1970)

BIBLIOGRAPHY

E. S. Newman: *Lewis Mumford: A Bibliography, 1914–1970* (New York, 1971)
C. Sussman, ed.: *Planning the Fourth Migration: The Neglected Vision of the Regional Planning Association of America* (Cambridge, MA, 1976)
D. L. Miller, ed.: *The Lewis Mumford Reader* (New York, 1986)
D. L. Miller: *Lewis Mumford: A Life* (New York, 1989)
C. N. Blake: *Beloved Community: The Cultural Criticism of Randolph Bourne, Van Wyck Brooks, Waldo Frank and Lewis Mumford* (Chapel Hill, NC, 1990)

CASEY BLAKE

Mummy, Egyptian. Artificially preserved human and animal remains. Mummification was practised in Egypt from the Early Dynastic period (*c.* 2925–*c.* 2575 BC). It is believed that the development of mummification was stimulated by observation of the natural desiccation that occurred in bodies buried in shallow pits in the hot sand of the desert. Over time, the preservation of the body came to be regarded as a prerequisite for survival in the afterlife, and artificial methods of conservation evolved. These were applied both to humans and to animals, especially those interred in mass burials as part of certain religious cults. The practice of mummification continued into the Greco-Roman period (332 BC–AD 395) but was gradually abandoned with the advent of Christianity. (*See also* EGYPT, ANCIENT, §XIII.)

1. HUMAN. In humans, the fully developed mummification technique involved the removal of the brain and viscera, the latter being preserved separately in vessels known as canopic jars (*see* EGYPT, ANCIENT, §XII, 2(vi)). The body was then dried with natron, after which treatment oils were rubbed into the skin to restore suppleness. Sometimes such devices as the addition of padding or artificial eyes were employed to re-create a lifelike appearance. The corpse was next wrapped in linen bandages;

1. Mummy of Irtyertia from Panopolis, Ptolemaic period, 304–30 BC (New York, Metropolitan Museum of Art)

various amulets were incorporated into the linen wrappings to provide it with magical protection. Finally, a modelled funerary headpiece was added to give protection to the head and neck. Although this basic process altered little over time, substantial changes took place in the wrapping and presentation of the mummy.

The earliest known example of artificial mummification comes from a tomb at Saqqara of the 2nd Dynasty (*c.* 2775–*c.* 2650 BC), but the amorphous mass of corroded linen wrappings prevents accurate description of the configuration of the bandaging. However, a female mummy (Boston, MA, Mus. F.A.) of the Old Kingdom (*c.* 2575–*c.* 2150 BC) found in Mastaba G 2220 at Giza is better preserved. The arms and the head (on which the nose and lips had first been fleshed out with linen) were individually

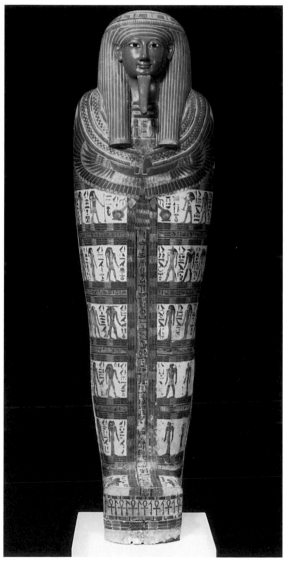

2. Mummy of Nespanetjerenpere, painted cartonnage (linen or papyrus mixed with plaster), with eyes and eyebrows inlaid with glass and lapis lazuli, l. 1.77 m, Third Intermediate Period, 22nd Dynasty, *c.* 950–*c.* 730 BC (New York, Brooklyn Museum)

wrapped as the upper chest, thorax, lower abdomen and legs were successively bandaged. A thin dress was then placed over the body and the whole covered with a shroud. Some Old Kingdom mummies had facial features painted on to the wrappings of the head, while in other cases the features were modelled in plaster on to the bandages and then painted.

The quantity of linen employed in the wrapping of the mummy of Wah (New York, Met., 20.3.203), an official at Thebes during the Middle Kingdom (*c.* 2008–*c.* 1630 BC), amounted to 375 sq. m. After the head, torso and limbs had been wrapped separately and covered with resins, a broad collar of blue-green beads and matching bracelets and anklets were added: this choice of colour was symbolic, suggesting the regenerative powers of the plant world. As the bandaging continued, five additional necklaces of silver, gold, faience and hardstones were laid about the neck. In the final stages of wrapping a large silver scarab inscribed with Wah's name and titles was placed on his head. Over this was eventually positioned a gilded headpiece made of cartonnage, moulded linen and plaster (*see* EGYPT, ANCIENT, §XII, 2(iii)). Royal tombs of the 12th Dynasty (*c.* 1938–*c.* 1756 BC), such as that of the Princess Sithathoriunet at Dahshur, have yielded examples of funerary jewellery of unparalleled quality (*see* EGYPT, ANCIENT, §XIV, 3), some of which would have been placed on the mummies.

The best-preserved royal mummy of the Egyptian New Kingdom (*c.* 1540–*c.* 1075 BC) belonged to Tutankhamun (*reg c.* 1332–*c.* 1323 BC). Although the wrappings were too damaged to present a clear picture of their configuration, they yielded a rich array of jewellery and amulets (*see* EGYPT, ANCIENT, §XIV, 4), including a beaded skullcap adorned with two cobras. On the King's forearms were 13 bracelets, several of which were decorated either with the *wadjet* (symbolizing the concept of well-being) or with the scarab (a solar symbol of rebirth). This solar symbolism is also reflected in the extensive use of gold in the funerary equipment, especially in the famous funerary mask. Around the waist of the King were placed a series of girdles, or belts, made of chased bands of gold; around his head was a fillet and on his fingers an assortment of 15 rings. Two daggers, several gold collars and necklaces and various amulets were also placed on the body. The principal decorative motifs were the vulture and the cobra, the symbols of Upper and Lower Egypt, and all the pieces were encrusted with inlays in a variety of materials (all Cairo, Egyp. Mus.).

During the Third Intermediate Period (*c.* 1075–*c.* 750 BC), when the embalmer's craft reached its apogee, the outer wrappings of mummies generally comprised large sheets wound around the corpse and held in place by a series of horizontal linen straps linked by a single vertical band.

The necropolis at Tanis contained several unplundered royal burials, the mummies of which were equipped with an extraordinary array of jewellery (*see* EGYPT, ANCIENT, §XIV, 5). That of Psusennes I (*reg c.* 1040–*c.* 997 BC) contained, in addition to a gold head covering with inlaid eyes, gold 'fingerstalls', a bead necklace of gold and lapis lazuli, gold bracelets and pectorals, an inlaid ring and several amulets in the shape of miniature collars. Small golden images of deities, among them Bastet and Isis, were also found on mummies at Tanis (all Cairo, Egyp. Mus.). A falcon pectoral (Cairo, Egyp. Mus., JE 86036) found on the mummy of Amenemope (*reg c.* 993–*c.* 989 BC), also at Tanis, is an extraordinary orchestration of coloured inlays.

In the 26th Dynasty (664–525 BC) 'heart scarabs' (*see* EGYPT, ANCIENT, §XII, 3(vi)) inscribed with texts intended to assist the deceased in the afterlife became more common (e.g. Boston, MA, Mus. F.A., 1974.566). Also during this period the bandages began to be wrapped decoratively around the mummy in interesting diamond-shaped patterns that ultimately evolved into the intricate lozenge designs found on some mummies of Roman Egypt (e.g. London, BM, 13595; *see* EGYPT, ANCIENT, §XII, 2(v)). Amulets of faience, hardstones or gold (many in London, U. Coll., Petrie Mus.) were often placed within the bandages of Late Period mummies in a more or less established pattern. At the same time, beadwork covers of blue or green faience in the form of reticulated nets bearing the motif of a winged scarab and/or images of the protector deities known as the Four Sons of Horus (e.g. Boston, MA, Mus. F.A., 95.1407a, 72.3019 and 94.255–58) were frequently placed over the mummy.

In the Late Ptolemaic period, the use of cartonnage ensembles that enveloped the entire mummy was adopted (*see* EGYPT, ANCIENT, §XII, 2(iv)). Some of these covers, from both the 1st and the 2nd century AD (e.g. Boston, MA, Mus. F.A., 03.1859 and 1977.175), have gilded faces, but the majority rely on paint to articulate facial details (e.g. Boston, MA, Mus. F.A., 54.638). Although at first glance the faces appear to be individualized, when regarded as a series each belongs to a recognizable group conforming to contemporary tastes in coiffures and jewellery; they are not, therefore, portraits. The covers were also made as separate pieces for the chest, abdomen, legs and feet (see fig. 1); the last sometimes take the form of sandals (e.g. Boston, MA, Mus. F.A., 59.1071). Scenes representing the trampling of enemies, symbolic of the triumph of the deceased in the afterlife, are also common on foot-cases (e.g. Boston, MA, Mus. F.A., 1971.217). On occasion, the entire mummy might be enveloped in a single piece of cartonnage, a practice known from the Third Intermediate Period (e.g. New York, Brooklyn Mus., 36.1265; see fig. 2) but more common in the Roman period (e.g. London, BM, 29584–5).

Related to these cartonnage masks are the 'Faiyum portraits': funerary masks rendered in the encaustic technique, in which pigments suspended in melted wax are applied to thin, flat wooden panels (*see* TEMPERA, colour pl. V, fig. 1). These, too, conform to established typologies, despite their lifelike appearance. They were often added to the mummy with bandages (e.g. London, BM, 13595) or incorporated into a cartonnage 'envelope' (e.g. London, BM, 21810).

2. ANIMAL. Copious evidence of animal mummification has been recovered from the numerous sacred animal cemeteries scattered throughout Egypt (*see* EGYPT, ANCIENT, §VIII, 2(iii)). Although animal cults—in which either individual creatures or all the members of a species were regarded as divine incarnations—existed from the

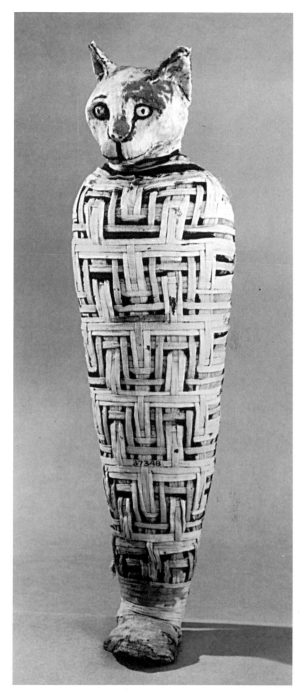

3. Mummified cat, wrapped in linen, h. 460 mm, from Abydos, Roman period, 30 BC–AD 395 (London, British Museum)

Early Dynastic period (*c.* 2925–*c.* 2575 BC), the earliest surviving animal mummies date from the New Kingdom (*c.* 1540–*c.* 1075 BC). The vast majority of specimens, however, belong to the Late and Greco-Roman periods (*c.* 750 BC–AD 395), when animal cults gained enormous popularity.

The species found vary according to locality, reflecting the birds and animals associated with particular deities.

Thus, the ibises and baboons associated with Thoth occur in number at his cult centre of Hermopolis Magna, while cats, sacred to the feline goddess Bastet, predominate at her city of Bubastis. However, a single cemetery may contain many species: the important animal necropolis at Saqqara, for example, has so far yielded the mummified remains of more than four million ibises, along with baboons, cows, cats, dogs and falcons, among others.

The most celebrated animal cult at Saqqara belonged to the Apis bulls buried in the Serapeum. No Apis mummies survive, but finds of gold jewellery and amulets in some of their coffins confirm that they were equipped in a similar fashion to those of humans. The remains of a 26th Dynasty Apis embalming house at Memphis include the huge alabaster tables—sloped to allow drainage—that were used during mummification, and a demotic papyrus now in Vienna describes the care lavished on their preservation. The process employed was similar to that used for humans, except that the bodies of the bulls were arranged in a kneeling position on wooden boards, to which they were attached by means of bronze or iron clamps, before bandaging. Although some of the early Apis burials were provided with canopic vessels, there is no evidence that evisceration actually took place.

The presentation of some animal mummies was extremely elaborate. The plastered and gilded heads of the Buchis bulls of Armant, dating from the Late and Greco-Roman periods, had artificial eyes of glass or stone set in bronze; a gilded wooden crown was placed between each animal's horns. Similarly, some of the falcon mummies from Saqqara had painted plaster headpieces over the facial area. Animal mummies of Roman date sometimes display the intricate geometrical bandaging common in contemporary human mummies, as in the case of a fine cat mummy from Abydos in the British Museum (see fig. 3). Others, however, were more crudely treated: in the Faiyum, the bodies of crocodiles sacred to the god Sebek were preserved by a simple coating of black pitch.

BIBLIOGRAPHY

G. E. Smith: *Catalogue général des antiquités égyptiennes du Musée du Caire nos 61051–61100: The Royal Mummies* (Cairo, 1912)
H. Carter: *The Tomb of Tutankhamun*, ii (London, 1927)
S. Smith: *A Handbook to the Egyptian Mummies and Coffins Exhibited in the British Museum* (London, 1938)
W. C. Hayes: *The Scepter of Egypt*, i (New York, 1953)
A. F. Shore: *Portrait Paintings from Roman Egypt* (London, 1972)
H. E. Winlock: 'The Mummy of Wah Unwrapped', *Bull. Met.*, lxxiv (1975), pp. 72–6
R. S. Bianchi: 'Egyptian Mummies: Myth and Reality', *Archaeology*, xxxv (1982), pp. 18–25
Mummies and Magic: The Funerary Arts of Ancient Egypt (exh. cat. by S. D'Auria, P. Lacovara and C. H. Roehrig, Boston, MA, Mus. F.A., 1988)

ROBERT S. BIANCHI

Mumuye. Cluster of peoples numbering *c.* 100,000, speaking related languages of the Adamawa branch of the Adamawa–Ubangi family. They occupy the hilly area between the towns of Jalingo and Mayo Belwa, south of the Benue River in Gongola State, north-eastern Nigeria. Art-historically, the Mumuye are known for their masks and figure carvings. Published information on Mumuye art is limited (see bibliography).

1. GEOGRAPHY AND CULTURAL HISTORY. Mumuye groups have had important religious and political links with the Jukun of Kona, their neighbours to the west. Bounding the Mumuye to the north are the related Yendang and, across the Benue River, the Jen and the disparate populations grouped together as Wurkun. Their neighbours to the east are the Verre and, to the south, various sub-groups of the Chamba. Sizeable concentrations of settled Fulani live interspersed among the Mumuye, while pastoral Fulani groups move their herds through the area in search of seasonal pasturage.

Although traditional ways of life changed drastically during the colonial period and even more so after Nigerian independence in 1960, most Mumuye were still sedentary agriculturalists in the late 1980s. Formerly, the Mumuye lived in dispersed hamlets located, for defensive purposes, in difficult, rocky terrain. Compounds, housing extended families, consisted of clusters of circular houses and granaries made of mud, surrounded with woven grass-mat fences. The conical roofs of the houses were thatched with grass. These traditional patterns have increasingly given way to those typical of northern Nigeria. Compact settlements have grown up on the plains, usually near main roads, with rectangular houses made of mud bricks plastered with cement and roofed with corrugated metal.

Traditional political organization was essentially non-centralized, with authority based on religious sanctions and primarily vested in the rainmaker–priest. The institution of secular chiefship, introduced during the colonial period, has gradually increased in importance. In addition to language ties and structural affinities in the realm of political and social organization, most Mumuye groups shared such cultural practices as the use of bovine masks in connection with the initiation of male age-sets and the production of carved images in human form. On a local and sub-group level, however, a considerable diversity of beliefs and practices is evident. Moreover, as the Mumuye have come to participate more in the cosmopolitan world of modern Nigeria, individualism and stratification have progressively compromised the formerly egalitarian structure of their society. Artistically, these tendencies have been reflected in the appearance of such prestige wood-carvings, incorporating human figures, as pipe-stems and stools.

2. MASK AND MASQUERADE. Traditionally among the Mumuye, subsistence activities, self-defence and rites of passage were organized by age-sets composed of males who had gone through septennial initiations together. Each new age-set would commission a carved wooden bovine mask, regarded as male and usually called Va or Vabo (see fig.). These horizontally aligned helmet masks have horns projecting to the rear and mouth planes that curve around the longitudinal axis, with a vision-port between them. The masks are coloured with various combinations of red and white and are worn with a thick, hibiscus-fibre mantle. They are danced by members of the age-set at subsequent initiations and at such events as memorial rites and harvest festivals. Each masker is given an individual name, usually referring to strength, aggression or determination. He may be accompanied by a 'wife', also wearing a horizontally positioned mask, but one based

Mumuye ceremonial procession with two Vabo maskers, musicians and an attendant carrying a *vatopo* memorial ceramic vessel, Sawa, Gongola State, Nigeria; from a photograph by Arnold Rubin, 1970

on a simian or avian motif. Other 'female' masks were carved in the form of 'yokes': small heads, with prominent representations of distended pierced earlobes, on long necks rising from U-shaped structures with a vision-port in the front panel. Around the town of Zing such masks are given the name Sukuru. Women and uninitiated boys were allowed to observe certain performances of the female maskers, which were mostly for entertainment, but in most groups they were forbidden to see the male versions.

Although styles vary, the bovine masks of the Mumuye form part of a continuous distribution of similar masks among peoples living along the western flank of the mountains on the border between Nigeria and Cameroon. The traditions involved include those of the Chamba, Mambila and several Jukunoid populations living around the town of Takum. Although documentation is scanty, yoke-shaped masks similar to those of the Mumuye appear to have been concentrated north of the Benue, among the Jukun (*see* JUKUN, §3), Jen and Wurkun. Their attribution to the Waja is erroneous.

3. FIGURE SCULPTURE. Carved wooden figures are used by rainmakers, heads of families or divine healers as prestige objects or visual foci of their status or vocation. Such images, characterized by angular legs and a complex

spatial relationship between arms and torso, exhibit a vast range of sculptural variation. The heads often exhibit the prominent distended pierced earlobes that both men and women formerly had. Such figures were originally attributed to the Chamba (*see* CHAMBA (ii)), neighbours of the Mumuye. Many examples appeared on the art markets of Europe and the USA during and after the Biafran War (1967–70), following the breakdown of administrative controls on the export of antiquities. Their main stylistic affinities are with the carved ancestor representations venerated by the JUKUN of the Upper Benue River and with some figurative sculptures of the Mambila.

4. CERAMICS. Around the town of Sawa ceramic vessels surmounted by finials in the shape of Vabo masks are used to mourn important male elders. Such vessels (*vatopo*) are made or purchased by each of the deceased's sisters for use in two successive ceremonies held annually at the end of the dry season. For a few days before the actual ceremony, the vessels are displayed at a shrine or altar in the centre of the deceased's compound, along with his heritable goods. On the appointed day, a procession of male relatives of the deceased, accompanied by Vabo maskers and musicians playing gourd trumpets, convey the vessels to a site outside the town, where they are ceremonially smashed (see fig.). After these procedures have been carried out twice, the estate of the deceased is divided among his heirs, and his widows are permitted to remarry. Similarly decorated ceramic vessels are found among many of the peoples of the Upper Benue and Gongola river basins.

BIBLIOGRAPHY
C. K. Meek: 'The Mumuye and Neighbouring Tribes', *Tribal Studies in Northern Nigeria*, i (London, 1931), pp. 446–73
P. Fry: 'Essai sur la statuaire mumuye', *Obj. & Mondes*, x (1970), pp. 3–28

ARNOLD RUBIN

Munakata, Shikō (*b* Aomori, 5 Sept 1903; *d* Kamakura, Kanagawa Prefect., 13 Sept 1975). Japanese printmaker. Inspired by the works of Vincent van Gogh, he went to Tokyo in 1924 with the hopes of becoming a Western-style painter. In 1926 he saw and was impressed by a book of woodblock-printed poems and pictures by the artist Sumio Kawakami (1895–1972) and in 1928 he visited the printmaker Un'ichi Hiratsuka (*b* 1895) and received instruction in the woodblock printing technique. In the same year he was selected for the first time to submit an oil painting to the 9th Teiten (Imperial Art Exhibition). In 1936 Muneyoshi Yanagi, a theologian and philosopher who founded the Mingei (folk arts) movement, and the ceramicists Shōji Hamada and Kanjirō Kawai acknowledged his prints and from that time they encouraged him. In turn he was spiritually and ideologically influenced by the spokesman of Japanese Romanticism, Yojūrō Yasuda (1910–81), who praised Japanese art and aesthetics rather than the contemporary Western mentality that was popular at the time. At this time, he also seriously considered the importance of traditional folk customs.

The subjects of Munakata's works were drawn from Japanese mythology, folk tales and Buddhist scripture, for example the well-known series *Ten Great Disciples of Buddha* (1939). These works were, before World War II, also influenced by the thinking of his close literary friends. However, Munakata was perhaps unique in his energy, which was marked by an exuberance of life and provincial sentiment. The self-absorbed, expressionistic manner in which he worked disregarded any attempts at a calculated design; however, his excess artistic energy was often restrained by the medium of the woodblock. His characteristic expression of human sentiment, which has been acknowledged as generally divorced from Japanese regionalism, was quickly reappraised on an international scale after World War II.

In 1938 Munakata received his first special selection in the 2nd Shin Bunten (New Ministry of Education Exhibition). In 1955 he was awarded a prize at the São Paulo Biennale and in 1956 he received the grand prize in the print section of the Venice Biennale. In 1959 he was invited to go to the USA for the first time where he had one-man shows in New York and Boston. In 1960 he also held solo exhibitions at such institutions as the Cleveland Museum of Fine Arts and, subsequently, he frequently displayed his works in Europe and the USA. In 1970 he was awarded the Bunka kunshō, the country's highest honour in the arts. In 1985 a large-scale exhibition, which toured Tokyo, Nagoya and Nishinomiya, was organized by the Tokyo Museum of Modern Art.

WRITINGS
Hangokudō (Tokyo, 1964)

BIBLIOGRAPHY
Munakata Shikō zenshū [Complete works of Shikō Munakata], 11 vols (Tokyo, 1972–9)
Munakata Shikō ten [Shikō Munakata exhibition] (exh. cat., Tokyo, N. Mus. Mod. A., 1985)

ATSUSHI TANAKA

Munari, Bruno (*b* Milan, 24 Oct 1907). Italian sculptor, painter, film maker and designer. His artistic ambition was influenced by Filippo Tommaso Marinetti whom he met in Milan in the mid-1920s. Munari formally allied himself with the second generation of Futurists in 1927 and continued to exhibit with them into the 1930s (*see* FUTURISM, §1 and AEROPITTURA). Few works of Munari's remain from this period, as most were made from transient materials. One extant work in tempera from 1932 (see Tanchis, p. 13) suggests that Munari had fully adopted Futurist aesthetics. Several other examples from the 1930s, however, show a clear debt to Surrealism.

In his sculpture from 1930 Munari adopted a different attitude. *Aerial Machine* (1930; see Tanchis, p. 21), for example, indicates a move towards a Constructivist aesthetic. This elegant object is a precursor of his *Useless Machines*, the first of which was executed in 1933. Constructed of painted cardboard and other lightweight materials, they served to liberate abstract forms in three dimensions. Moreover, they were meant to integrate with the surrounding environment through their kinetic action.

After World War II Munari concentrated on industrial design. An early example is *X Hour* (1945; see Tanchis, pp. 72–3), an alarm clock with rotating half-discs in lieu of hands. In 1963, as part of an effort to bring the best in design to the Italian public, *X Hour* was produced as a multiple. Other objects by Munari that were not strictly utilitarian were also mass-produced, such as the *Flexy* (1968; see 1986 exh. cat., pp. 82–3), a flexible metal wire

structure that could be set in any number of positions. After 1949 Munari began to investigate *Gestalt* theory through a series of experimental works entitled *Negative Positive*, in which he attempted to achieve absolute parity between figure and ground. In *Negative Positive* (1950; see Tanchis, p. 55), for example, the areas of dark and light are equal.

As early as the 1930s, Munari had been trying out radical innovations in graphics and typography, but it was not until after World War II that he began to design and produce book-objects. His children's books were simple, provocative learning tools. His books for adults, on the other hand, were useless objects, *Unreadable Books*, which were meant to challenge the very concept of a book. In 1950 Munari began to experiment with light projection through coloured plastic to create coloured-light compositions. The use of polarized light, special lenses and motorization enabled him to achieve more complex and variable results and led to the production of his first coloured-light film, *I colori della luce* (1963) with electronic music.

The principle of public access to the means of visual communication was very important to Munari, who believed anyone could produce objects of aesthetic value, given the proper technological advantages. Following this principle, in 1964 Munari began to install photocopiers at exhibition sites, including the Central Pavilion of the 35th Venice Biennale in 1970.

WRITINGS
Discovery of the Circle (New York, 1965)
Discovery of the Square (New York, 1965)

BIBLIOGRAPHY
C. Tisdall: 'Statements by Munari', *Studio Int.*, clxxx (Oct 1970), pp. 135–9
Bruno Munari: Ricerche visive/Design/Visuelle Formfindung (exh. cat., ed. W. Skreiner; Graz, Neue Gal., 1970)
Bruno Munari: Opere, 1930–1986 (exh. cat., ed. M. Meneguzzo and T. Quirico; Milan, Pal. Reale, 1986)
A. Tanchis: *Bruno Munari: Design as Art* (Cambridge, MA, 1987)

LAURAL WEINTRAUB

Munari, Cristoforo [Monari, Monarico; Cristofano] (*b* Reggio Emilia, *bapt* 21 July 1667; *d* Pisa, 3 June 1720). Italian painter. A specialist in still-life painting, until 1703 he apparently worked in his native city, a protégé of Rinaldo I d'Este, Duke of Modena (*reg* 1694–1737). In 1703 he went to Rome, 'where he took a wife and where he served the Very Eminent Cardinal Imperiali and other princes and lords' (F. M. N. Gaburri: *Vite de' pittori*, Florence, Bib. N. Cent., MS. Palat. E.B.9.5; ii, p. 618). He remained there until at least June 1706. He then moved to Florence, where for about a decade he was attached to the court of Ferdinand de' Medici. There is a *Self-portrait* (1710; Florence, Depositi Gal.) from this period, during which he also worked for Cosimo III and Cardinal Francesco Maria de' Medici (1667–1710), for whom he painted, among many other similar works, the *Still-life with Musical Instruments* (1709; Florence, Uffizi). Munari's style is characterized by a realistic treatment of detail and a subtle play of reflections and transparencies, suggestive of the manner of such Dutch artists as Jan de Heem. Typical of Munari is the pair of paintings (Florence, Mus. Bardini, inv. nos 1149–1150) in which Chinese porcelains, silver and cut-glass objects are juxtaposed with richly coloured fruits. In 1715 he moved to Pisa, where he worked not only as a painter but also as a restorer of paintings in the cathedral. At his death he was buried in the Camposanto, Pisa.

BIBLIOGRAPHY

G. de Logu: 'Cristofano Monari o Monarico? Monari o Munari?', *Emporium*, cxxi (1955), pp. 249–58

Cristoforo Munari e la natura morta emiliana (exh. cat. by A. Ghidiglia Quintavalle, Parma, 1964)

L. Salerno: *La natura morta italiana* (Rome, 1984), pp. 336–40

D. Biagi Maino: 'Cristoforo Munari', *La natura morta in Italia*, ed. F. Zeri, i (Milan, 1989), pp. 412–20

FRANCO MORO

Munch, Edvard (*b* Løten, Hedmark, 12 Dec 1863; *d* Oslo, 23 Jan 1944). Norwegian painter, printmaker and draughtsman. Especially concerned with the expressive representation of emotions and personal relationships, he was associated with the international development of Symbolism during the 1890s and recognized as a precursor of Expressionism, particularly in his paintings and woodcuts.

1. Childhood and early work, to 1884. 2. The Kristiania Bohème and the first one-man exhibition, 1884–9. 3. Paris, 1889–92. 4. Berlin and the major cycles, 1892–1907. 5. 1908–44.

1. CHILDHOOD AND EARLY WORK, TO 1884. Edvard Munch was born the second of five children to Laura Cathrine Bjølstad and Dr Christian Munch, a military doctor. Living in tenement houses in the workers' suburbs of Christiania (which became Kristiania in 1877 and Oslo in 1925), the family, descended from Norway's cultural aristocracy but economically impoverished, was doubly alienated. Unable to move freely among the educated and social élite, they experienced at the same time the illnesses impacted most severely on the Scandinavian urban working class: tuberculosis and bronchitis. Weakened after the birth of her fifth child, Edvard Munch's mother succumbed to tuberculosis in 1868, as did her oldest child, Sophie, in 1877. After the deaths of his wife and daughter, Dr Munch suffered periodic fits of deep depression and violent temper, accompanied by fanatical visions of his own and his surviving children's eternal damnation in hell. An extreme Christian fundamentalist, Dr Munch saw the bouts of severe, life-threatening bronchitis and tuberculosis suffered by Edvard and the other children as God's 'punishing illnesses' to which the sole response could be penitential prayer and remorseful submission. The constant experience of illness, hallucination, death and rejection, but also of determined and desperate resistance, provided the fundamental shape of Edvard Munch's character: 'I was born dying', he recalled shortly after his 70th birthday, 'Sickness, insanity and death were the dark angels standing guard at my cradle and they have followed me throughout my life.' This dramatic self-representation also gives retrospective shape to his art and grants it an overarching unity fusing and denying the disparity of efforts marking his long career as an artist.

After briefly studying engineering in accordance with his father's wishes, Munch entered the Tegneskole in Kristiania in 1881, studying sculpture under Julius Middelthun. In 1882 he rented a studio with six other artists,

supervised by the painter Christian Krohg, and in autumn 1883 he attended Frits Thaulow's Friluftsakademi at Modum. Munch soon added to his academic training experiments in a semi-Impressionist Naturalism, as advocated by Krohg and Thaulow in their efforts to create a national landscape style based on *plein-air* painting and influenced by the contemporary art of Paris. As practised by them, and by Munch in his paintings *Young Servant Girl Kindling a Stove* (1883; Oslo, priv. col., see Eggum, 1983, p. 33) and *Morning* (1884; Bergen, Meyers Saml.), this new style also underlined the process of Norwegian independence from Sweden, linked with parliamentary liberalism and ideas of radical social reform. In 1882 Munch took part in the organization of the first Høstutstilling, free of the Norwegian Kunstforening's sponsorship and censorship; as subject-matter the artists exhibiting selected the life of the urban poor in addition to Norwegian landscapes.

2. THE KRISTIANIA BOHÈME AND THE FIRST ONE-MAN EXHIBITION, 1884–9. Artists, writers and students who opposed bourgeois society and morality formed a loose association referred to as the Kristiania Bohème. The spokesman for the group was Hans Jaeger, an anarchist writer who advocated an anti-bourgeois life style of emancipation and freedom focused on sexual liberation, social equality and the rejection of Christianity. Demoralized, however, by government repression and deprived of a political base, the artists turned away from socially engaged art to a fundamentally subjective and introspective art. Munch spent much of 1885–6, the most active and public years of the Kristiania Bohème, working on a single painting, *The Sick Child* (Oslo, N.G.; see fig. 1). It depicts a teenaged girl propped up against a pillow in a large armchair, next to an older woman who bows her head in despair and grief. Grounded in Munch's recollections of his sister's death *c.* ten years earlier, in accordance with Jaeger's dictum of the primacy of personal experience, and possibly influenced by the contemporary success of thematically similar paintings in Scandinavia and Central Europe, *The Sick Child* was conceived in a variation of Impressionist technique, but in the course of a year-long alteration Munch built up thick coagulations of paint into which the final remaining image was more scratched than painted, and over which a veil of thin rivulets of paint was placed (to be removed during a partial repainting *c.* 1893). In his experimentation Munch created effects similar to those achieved in the late 1880s by James Ensor and Vincent van Gogh in works today recognized as precursors of 20th-century Expressionism. In Norway in 1886, however, there was no measure by which *The Sick Child* could be judged. Exhibited at the 1886 Høstutstilling in Kristiania as *A Study*, the painting was vehemently attacked by critics and fellow artists alike, so that only Hans Jaeger in the newspaper *Dagen* dared to defend it, describing it as an intuitive work of genius.

Other works by Munch of the period of the Kristiania Bohème focus on his experience of sexual relationships, in particular his jealousy-ridden affair with Emily 'Milly' Ihlen, the wife of his cousin Captain Carl Thaulow and identified as 'Mrs Heiberg' after 1890 in fragmentary,

1. Edvard Munch: *The Sick Child*, oil on canvas, 1.20×1.18 m, 1885–6 (Oslo, Nasjonalgalleri)

diary-like, semi-fictional notes modelled on Jaeger's no-vellas. In the paintings *Hulda* (1886; destr.) and *The Day After* (1886; destr.; 1894–5 version, Oslo, N.G.) he posed women aggressively proffering their naked bodies or in abandoned sleep on rumpled beds next to nightstands filled with empty liquor bottles. Private icons of the Kristiania Bohème's faith in free love, such images hung in Munch's studio as objects of personal devotion and melancholy recollections of failed romance, unable to find public audiences while government efforts at censorship were renewed.

Devastated and disappointed by the reception and rejection of *The Sick Child*, his erotic motifs repressed, Munch reverted to a more common Naturalist style after 1886 in renditions of subjectively evocative landscapes and in portraits that more readily found a market than did his experimental bohemian works. In a daringly provoca-tive, speculative gesture he collected his works into a large one-man exhibition at the Studentersamfund, Kristiania, in April and May 1889, an event unprecedented in Norway except in the contemporary celebration of the renowned, elderly academic landscape painter Hans Fredrik Gude. The works Munch exhibited demonstrated his move from Impressionist experiment with form dissolved in the summer sun towards a more firmly modelled Naturalism in which effects of light were manipulated for emotive value. In place of the failed *Sick Child* he substituted a massive new painting on the same theme, *Spring* (1.69×2.64 m, 1889; Oslo, N.G.), in which Munch con-centrated on effects of sunlight pouring in through a brightly illuminated window, an emblem of hope set in contrast to the desperation of the convalescent girl and her concerned companion. With this remarkable demonstration of painterly bravura and a monumental portrait of *Hans Jaeger* after his release from prison (1.10×0.84 m, 1889; Oslo, N.G.) as its centrepieces, the exhibition succeeded in obtaining for Munch a state grant to study drawing with Léon Bonnat in Paris. In 1889 Munch spent his first summer at Åsgårdstrand on Kristianiafjord (now Oslofjord), a retreat to which he consistently returned and that for 20 years provided the setting for innumerable paintings.

3. PARIS, 1889–92. Although Munch had briefly visited exhibitions in Antwerp and Paris in 1885, the Exposition Universelle of 1889 and associated art exhibitions provided extensive experience of contemporary painting for him on his arrival in Paris. Almost immediately, however, he entered a period of debilitating depression and grief after being informed that his father had died suddenly. He was unable to paint and isolated himself in a room in Saint-Cloud, where he jotted down recollections of his father and of his affair with 'Mrs Heiberg' and engaged in ruminations on art, love, death and immortality with the equally disillusioned Danish poet Emanuel Goldstein. The combination of his grieving process and Goldstein's discovery of French Decadent and Symbolist poetry caused Munch to reform his own views on art, so that he rejected the Naturalism of the Kristiania Bohème for a more subjective form of Symbolism conjoined with his monist views of a pantheistic life-force inherent in all matter, forbidding death in a process of material transformation. The transmission of life in sexual intercourse was a primary principle in Munch's new-found pseudo-scientific faith, and in projects for its depiction he formulated the transformed purpose of his art (Munch, 1929, p. 17):

A strong naked arm—a tanned powerful neck—a young woman rests her head on the arching chest. . . . These two in that moment when they are not themselves, but only one of thousands of sexual links tying one generation to another generation. People should understand the sanctity, the grandeur of it, and would take off their hats as if in a church. I would make a number of such paintings. No longer would interiors, people who read and women who knit, be painted.

The conversion of emotions into works of art culminated during the spring of 1890 in two paintings, *Night* (Oslo, N.G.) and *Spring Day on Karl Johan Street* (Bergen, Billedgal.), both adapting principles of Neo-Impressionism to subjective images representing, respectively, death and grief on the one hand and life and joy on the other: the one as a scene tinged in blue, depicting a lone figure seated in a dark interior while a window permits a view on to a nocturnal winter cityscape, the other a springtime view of Kristiania's main thoroughfare with groups of people promenading in bright sunshine. In 1891 he used similar variations on Neo-Impressionist technique, depicting scenes of city life, as in *Rue Lafayette* (Oslo, N.G.), in order to project his emotional response to contemporary urban existence. Late in the year, however, he began to assimilate aspects of SYNTHETISM, largely based on his

experience of works by the Scandinavian followers of Paul Gauguin, such as Jens F. Willumsen and Ivan Aguéli, into his artistic vocabulary, most notably in his drawings of 1891–2 for a collection of Goldstein's poetry, *Alruner* ('Mandrake'), and in the mixed-media painting *Melancholy* (Oslo, Munch-Mus.), which is derived from the drawings. In these works, as well as in the drawings intended for publication along with (but not directly illustrating) the poems of the Norwegian poets Sigbjørn Obstfelder and Vilhelm Krag, and in his initial paintings of a *Kiss* (1892; Oslo, N.G.) and *Despair* (1892; Stockholm, Thielska Gal.), Munch outlined a range of emotional subject-matter that he was to work on again and again and that here formed the foundation of a series of paintings he grouped together under the title *Love*.

4. BERLIN AND THE MAJOR CYCLES, 1892–1907. Munch arrived in Berlin in autumn 1892, after he was invited to exhibit by the Verein Berliner Künstler. His exhibition there was dominated by paintings emulating various French Impressionist and Post-Impressionist tendencies, but a majority of the members of the Verein voted to close it after one week, mainly in response to the uncompromising personal subject-matter. The 'Munch Affair' aggravated already existing splits within Berlin's art community and led to the establishment, under the leadership of the engraver Karl Koepping, of the Freie Vereinigung Berliner Künstler in protest. The 'Affair' also provided Munch with unprecedented publicity, which appeared to promise a significant German market for his art. He was invited to exhibit elsewhere in Germany, finally exhibiting in Berlin at the Equitable Palast in December of the same year.

Apart from the summers painting in Norway, Munch spent the next three years in Germany in extensive, almost frenetic, exhibition activity, through which he gained a small but influential clientele of patrons, such as Eberhard von Bodenhausen, Walther Rathenau (ii) and Harry Count Kessler (1868–1937), and critics associated with the innovative literary and artistic periodical *Pan*. He also befriended *Pan*'s editor, Julius Meier-Graefe, August Strindberg and the Polish writer Stanisław Przybyszewski, who were resident in Berlin at that time. Together with the German poet Richard Dehmel, they formed the core—augmented by Przybyszewski's future wife, Dagny Juell, and periodically by other Scandinavian, French, Polish and German critics, poets and artists—of a bohemian group meeting at a bierkeller called Zum schwarzen Ferkel. It was from within this fermenting artistic milieu, with shared obsessions in monism and the psychology of sexuality, that Munch formed the beginnings of his cycle of paintings initially entitled *Love*, which was extended and exhibited at the Berlin Secession in 1902 as a frieze of 22 paintings on motifs of love and death unified by their Åsgårdstrand setting and later identified as *The Frieze of Life*. This visualized philosophy of sexuality, the psychology of love, the generation of life and the effects of death influenced most of Munch's major paintings of the 1890s, including *The Voice* (1893; Boston, MA, Mus. F.A.), *The Vampire* (1893; Göteborg, Kstmus.), *Ashes* (1894; Oslo, N.G.; see fig. 2), *Madonna* (1894–5; Oslo, N.G.), *The Scream* (1893; Oslo, N.G.), *Three Stages of Woman (Sphinx)* (1893–5;

2. Edvard Munch: *Ashes*, oil and tempera on canvas, 1.21×1.41 m, 1894 (Oslo, Nasjonalgalleri)

Bergen, Meyers Saml.) and *Death Enters the Sickroom* (1893–4; Oslo, N.G.). The cycle demonstrates above all how Munch extended the obsessive personal nature of his subjects into universal symbols of emotional states.

The same motifs provided the material for Munch's initial attempts at printmaking. Munch had learnt to make drypoints in 1894 for financial reasons, and he printed his first colour lithographs and woodcuts in 1896. As an artist he had a rare ability to master various printmaking techniques at the same time. An initial portfolio of eight drypoints was published in 1895 by Meier-Graefe and Bodenhausen, but a more ambitious project for a portfolio of 20 lithographs and woodcuts to be entitled *Speilet* ('the mirror'), although announced for publication in 1897, was never completed (examples in Oslo, Munch-Mus.). In 1909 he published the series of lithographs illustrating his own story of the life and death of a couple, the first and last human inhabitants of an island, *Alpha og Omega*. Prints of various types became important foundations for Munch's investigation of the same motifs throughout his life. Through the prints, and especially through his woodcuts (e.g. *Workers in the Snow*, 1911; Oslo, Munch-Mus.;

see fig. 3), he was able to exploit various effects he also used in his paintings, for example stylization and chiaroscuro, which were allied to a great expressiveness of line. His use of woodcut was innovative, in that he began to exploit the structure of the wood itself, thus emphasizing the expressiveness of the material. Munch's woodcuts had a marked influence on later artists, especially the German Expressionists, and they did much to foster a revival of the technique. From the time he made his first prints, the prints and the paintings largely fed off one another.

Munch had also become interested in photography after his meeting with Strindberg in 1892. He used photographs for documenting his work and his surroundings but also as the basis for portraits and other compositions. Although he never regarded his photography as the equal of his prints and paintings, he considered it, following Strindberg, as particularly revealing of character, and he made extensive use of self-portraits (especially in the period 1902–8) after he bought a small camera in Berlin in 1902. His photographs, for example *Self-portrait, Åsgårdstrand* (1904; Oslo, Munch-Mus.; see fig. 4), are often more experimental than his other works, especially in their treatment of light, and he made particular use of blur and double exposure.

Constant travel in France and Germany after 1895 and a dramatic romantic involvement with a Norwegian woman, Tulla Larsen, beginning in 1898 caused Munch to seek to restore his nervous and physical strength in the sanatorium of Kornhaug in Gudbrandsdalen in 1899–1900. He continued to work on *Frieze of Life* motifs and their variations but also began to receive an increasing number of portrait commissions from Germany and to gain significant patronage as well as critical recognition there. Despite the traumatic end of his relationship with Tulla Larsen in 1902, which resulted in his being shot in the hand and which inaugurated a period of intense psychological turmoil for him, Munch fulfilled his varied commissions. These included a frieze of 12 tempera paintings for the Kammerspielhaus of Max Reinhardt (1873–1943), for whom he also executed stage designs, in Berlin (1907; now Berlin, Neue N.G.). Another frieze intended for the room of the children of the German collector Max Linde (1862–1940) (now Oslo, Munch-Mus.) was completed in 1904, although Munch's use of the same subject-matter meant that Linde (who wanted landscapes) did not accept it. At this time Munch also painted a new cycle on love relationships, entitled *The Green Room*, for example *Consolation (The Green Room)* (1907; Oslo, Munch-Mus.). Manifesting varied stylistic approaches, the painting cycles continued to explore the motifs of *The Frieze of Life*, but with shifting emphases that began to accentuate group dynamics rather than individual relationships. The same is true of the monumental triptych *Bathing Men (The Ages of Life)* (1907–8), in which the paintings *Youth* (Bergen, Meyers Saml.),

3. Edvard Munch: *Workers in the Snow*, woodcut, *c.* 600×495 mm, 1911 (Oslo, Munch-Museum)

4. Edvard Munch: *Self-portrait, Åsgårdstrand*, gelatin-silver print, 88×94 mm, 1904 (Oslo, Munch-Museum)

Maturity (Bathing Men) (Helsinki, Athenaeum A. Mus.) and *Old Age* (Oslo, Munch-Mus.) are a celebration of masculinity and virility manifested in fraternal association, naked in intense sunlight.

5. 1908–44. Munch's fragile psychological and physical health broke down under the aggravation of excessive alcohol consumption and nicotine poisoning in 1908, and he entered the sanatorium of Dr Daniel Jacobsen in Copenhagen to effect a cure of what Munch himself identified as his 'nerve crisis'. The enforced rest and recuperation were used by him to continue a series of full-length portraits, to arrange major sales of works to Norwegian collectors and to prepare an extensive retrospective exhibition in Kristiania. Once released from the clinic, Munch moved in 1909 to an isolated estate in Kragerø on the southern Norwegian coast, and he entered the competition for the wall paintings in the newly constructed University Aula in Kristiania. After lengthy public debate, and after he was invited by the Sonderbund of Düsseldorf to exhibit in an exhibition in 1912 in Cologne intended to present a survey of Expressionism, of which he was proclaimed a precursor, with 32 paintings on show, Munch received the commission. The paintings, the most important of which were *History*, *Alma Mater* and *The Sun*, were finally installed in 1916. The imagery is centred in the painting *The Sun*, derived from landscape studies and paintings of the massive boulders on the seashore of Kragerø, and presents original allegories of the faculties of history and science as rooted in the folk wisdom of the Norwegian people. They demonstrate another facet of Munch's adaptability of style to setting; the broadly painted, highly simplified form of the Aula paintings, intended to be seen at a distance, contrasts with the exploration of spatial disjuncture and heavily massed forms in other works of the time. Here style, as a relative

entity, was manipulated and altered from image to image, and Munch frequently cited practices from his earlier works as if he were making memory visible.

Isolated from his German patrons during World War I, Munch found a Norwegian audience to be his most attentive for the first time since the 1880s. Portraits of such industrialists and ship-owners as *Rolf Stenersen* (1922) and *Heinrich Hudt-Wackler* (1919) and their families, who found new wealth during Norway's wartime neutrality, became his major means of support as new commissions of the stature of the Aula murals, such as wall paintings for a planned city hall in Oslo, failed to materialize. During the 1920s Munch overcame his isolation in a series of extensive exhibitions in Switzerland and Germany, where he was now accepted as a member of the Kunstakademien of Prussia and Bavaria. Established as a precursor of modern art, Munch also sought to orchestrate the myth being formed around him. In 1915 he collected together poeticized autobiographical and philosophical and artistic thoughts, which he later augmented with drawings and prints in a massive bound portfolio he called *The Tree of the Knowledge of Good and Evil* (Oslo, Kommunes Kstsaml., MS. T 2547). He also pulled new impressions of earlier prints, reworked or repainted paintings and motifs of the 1890s and early 1900s, although continuing to experiment, and formulated the contents of retrospective exhibitions such as that of 1927 in Berlin (Tiergarten, N.G.) and, enlarged, in Oslo (N.G.).

Munch's 70th birthday in 1933 received official recognition internationally and was the occasion of the publication of two monographs on his work. The years following, however, as Nazism triumphed in Germany and political turmoil marked Norwegian life as well, proved less productive or profitable for Munch. He had recurring problems with cysts in his eyes, causing temporary partial blindness; his art was removed from German museums and classified as 'degenerate' (*see* ENTARTETE KUNST); the opportunities for exhibition, whether in Norway or elsewhere, decreased dramatically, although auctions of his works from German collections demonstrated continued demand for his art. By the time Germany invaded and occupied Norway in 1940 Munch had withdrawn into an isolated existence that focussed on his increasingly self-referential art and on growing crops at his estates in Ekely, at Skøyen on the outskirts of Oslo, and Hvitsten on Oslofjord. Norwegian museums also removed his paintings and prints from view, although regular attempts were made by some in the German and Norwegian press sympathetic to Nazism to rehabilitate his work and his life as exemplary of Nordic traits. Munch, however, refused to participate in these or other efforts to recruit him in the cause of the Third Reich and its allies. He became fatally ill after an explosion at the munitions depot at Filipstad near Ekely broke the windows in his house. In his will he bequeathed most of his work—over 1000 paintings, some 15,400 prints and a large number of their plates, 5000 watercolours and drawings, and 6 sculptures—to the Municipality of Oslo. The collection became available to the public after the opening of the Munch-Museet in Oslo in 1963.

UNPUBLISHED SOURCES
Oslo, Munch-Mus. [var. manuscript mat.]

WRITINGS
Livs-frisen [The Frieze of Life] (Kristiania, [1918])
Livs-frisens tilblivelse [The genesis of *The Frieze of Life*] (Oslo, 1929)
I. Munch, ed.: *Edvard Munchs brev: Familien* [The letters of Edvard Munch: the family], Munch-Museet Skrifter, 1 (Oslo, 1949)
G. Lindtke, ed.: *Edvard Munch—Dr Max Linde: Briefwechsel, 1902–1928* (Lübeck, [1974])
A. Eggum, ed.: *Munch, Edvard/Schiefler, Gustav: Briefwechsel, 1902–14* (Hamburg, 1987)

BIBLIOGRAPHY
MONOGRAPHS
S. Przybyszewski and others: *Edvard Munch: Vier Beiträge* (Berlin, 1894)
H. Dedekam: *Edvard Munch* (Kristiania, 1909)
P. Gauguin: *Edvard Munch* (Oslo, 1933, rev. 1946)
J. Thiis: *Edvard Munch og hans samtid: Slekten, livet og kunsten* [Edvard Munch and his contemporaries: origins, life and art] (Oslo, 1933)
C. Dahl and others: *Edvard Munch: Mennesket og kunstneren* [Edvard Munch: the man and the artist] (Oslo, 1946)
Edvard Munch som vi kjente ham: Vennene forteller [Edvard Munch as we knew him: reminiscences by his friends] (Oslo, 1946)
R. E. Stenersen: *Edvard Munch: Naerbilde av et geni* [Edvard Munch: close-up of a genius] (Oslo, 1946, 2/1964; Eng. trans., Oslo, 1969)
J. P. Hodin: *Edvard Munch: Der Genius des Nordens* (Stockholm, 1948, 2/Berlin and Mainz, 1963)
H. E. Gerlach: *Edvard Munch: Sein Leben und sein Werk* (Hamburg, 1955)
A. Moen: *Edvard Munch*, 3 vols (Oslo, 1956–8)
O. Benesch: *Edvard Munch* (Cologne and London, 1960)
J. B. Smith: *Edvard Munch, 1863–1944* (Berlin, 1962)
'Edvard Munch: 100 år', *Oslo Kommunes Kstsaml. Årbok* (1963) [whole issue]
G. Svenaeus: *Edvard Munch: Das Universum des Melancholie* (Lund, 1967)
R. A. Boe: *Edvard Munch, his Life and Work from 1880 to 1920* (diss., New York U., 1970)
N. Stang: *Edvard Munch* (Oslo, 1971–2)
J. P. Hodin: *Edvard Munch* (London and New York, 1972)
H. Bock and G. Busch, eds: *Edvard Munch: Probleme—Forschungen—Thesen* (Munich, 1973)
G. Svennaeus: *Edvard Munch: Im männlichen Gehirn*, 2 vols (Lund, 1973)
J. Selz: *Edvard Munch* (Paris, 1974)
J. B. Smith: *Munch* (Oxford and New York, 1977)
R. T. Stang: *Edvard Munch: Mennesket og kunstneren* [Edvard Munch: the man and the artist] (Oslo, 1977; Eng. trans., New York, 1979)
A. Eggum: *Edvard Munch: Malerier—skisser og studier* [Edvard Munch: paintings—sketches and studies] (Oslo, 1983; Eng. trans., New York, 1984)
A. Carlsson: *Edvard Munch: Leben und Werk* (Stuttgart and Zurich, 1984)
R. Heller: *Munch: His Life and Work* (Chicago and London, 1984)
B. Torjusen: *Edvard Munch: Words and Images* (Chelsea, VT, 1986)

SPECIALIST STUDIES
G. Schiefler: *Verzeichnis des graphischen Werks Edvard Munchs, bis 1906* (Berlin, 1907/R Oslo, 1974)
——: *Edvard Munch: Das graphische Werk, 1906–1926* (Berlin, 1928/R Oslo, 1974)
P. Gauguin: *Grafikeren Edvard Munch* [Edvard Munch the printmaker] (Trondheim, 1946)
J. H. Langaard and R. Vaering: *Edvard Munchs selvportretter* (Oslo, 1947)
O. Sarvig: *Edvard Munchs grafik* (Copenhagen, 1948, 3/1980)
S. Willoch: *Edvard Munchs raderinger* [Edvard Munch's etchings], Munch-Museet Skrifter, 2 (Oslo, 1950)
O. Kokoschka: 'Edvard Munchs ekspresjonisme', *Kst & Kult.* [Oslo] (1952), pp. 129–50; Eng. trans., *Coll. A. J.*, xii/4 (sum. 1953), pp. 312–20; xiii/7 (aut. 1953), pp. 15–18
W. Hofmann: 'Zu einem Bildmittel Edvard Munchs', *Alte & Neue Kst*, iii/1 (1954), pp. 20–40; also in W. Hofmann: *Bruchlinien: Aufsätze zur Kunst des 19. Jahrhunderts* (Munich, 1979)
G. W. Digby: *Meaning and Symbol in Three Modern Artists: Edvard Munch, Henry Moore, Paul Nash* (London, 1955)
E. Goepel: *Edvard Munch: Selbstbildnisse und Dokumente* (Munich, 1955)
J. H. Langaard and R. Revold: *Edvard Munch som tegner* [Edvard Munch as a draughtsman] (Oslo, 1958)
——: *Edvard Munch fra år til år: En håndbok* [Edvard Munch from year to year: a handbook] (Oslo, 1961)
E. Greve: *Edvard Munch: Liv og verk i lys av tresnittene* [Edvard Munch: life and work in the light of the woodcuts] (Oslo, 1963)

J. H. Langaard and R. Revold: *Mesterverker i Munch-museet* [Masterworks in the Munch-Museum] (Oslo, 1963; Eng. trans., New York, 1964)

H. Burckhardt: 'Angst und Eros bei Edvard Munch', *Dt. Ärztebl.:Ärztl. Mitt.*, lxii/39 (25 Sept 1965), pp. 1098–2101

E. Hoffmann: 'Some Sources for Munch's Symbolism', *Apollo*, 81 (1965), pp. 87–93

J. Askeland: 'Angstmotivet i Edvard Munchs kunst' [The fear motif in Edvard Munch's art], *Kst Idag*, xx/4 (1966), pp. 4–57 [with Eng. summary]

R. Heller: *Edvard Munch's 'Frieze of Life': Its Beginnings and Origins* (diss., Bloomington, IN U., 1968)

T. Nergaard: *Refleksjon og vision: Naturalismens dilemma i Edvard Munchs kunst, 1889–1894* [Reflection and vision: the dilemma of Naturalism in the art of Edvard Munch, 1889–1894] (diss., U. Oslo, 1968)

W. Timm: *Edvard Munch: Graphik* (Berlin, 1969); Eng. trans. as *The Graphic Art of Edvard Munch* (Greenwich, CT, 1969)

I. A. Gloersen: *Lykkehuset: Edvard Munch og Åsgårdstrand* [The house of fortune: Edvard Munch and Åsgårdstrand] (Oslo, 1970)

J. A. Schmoll gen. Eisenwerth: *Malerei nach Fotografie* (Munich, 1970), pp. 125–31

R. Heller: *Munch: The Scream* (London, 1973)

P. Hougen: *Edvard Munch: Handzeichnungen* (Hamburg and New York, 1976)

R. Heller: 'Edvard Munch's *Night*, the Aesthetics of Decadence and the Content of Biography', *A. Mag.*, liii/2 (Oct 1978), pp. 80–105

A. Eggum: 'Munch and Photography', *The Frozen Image: Scandinavian Photography* (exh. cat., intro. M. Friedman; Minneapolis, Walker A. Cent.; Rochester, NY, Int. Mus. Phot.; Los Angeles, UCLA, Wight A.G.; Portland, A. Mus.; 1982–3), pp. 108–14

E. Prelinger: *Edvard Munch, Master Printmaker* (New York, London, Toronto, 1983)

A. Eggum: *Munch og fotografi* [Munch and photography] (Oslo, 1987; Eng. trans., New Haven, CT, and London, 1989)

EXHIBITION CATALOGUES

Edvard Munch (exh. cat., Oslo, Blomqvist Ksthandel, 1929) [contains Munch's *Livs-frisens tilblivelse* and extracts from diaries]

Edvard Munch (exh. cat., essay F. B. Deknatel, intro. J. H. Langaard, New York, MOMA; Boston, MA, ICA; 1950)

Edvard Munch (exh. cat., texts S. Willoch, J. H. Langaard, L. A. Svendsen; New York, Guggenheim, 1965–6)

Edvard Munch: Lithographs, Etchings, Woodcuts (exh. cat., intro. W. S. Liebermann, notes E. Feinblatt; Los Angeles, Co. Mus. A., 1969)

Edvard Munch: Das zeichnerische Werk (exh. cat. by P. Hougen, Bremen, Ksthalle, 1970)

Edvard Munch: Tegninger, skisser og studier [Edvard Munch: drawings, sketches and studies] (exh. cat. by P. Hougen, Oslo, Munch-Mus., 1973)

Edvard Munch: The Major Graphics (exh. cat., essays A. Eggum, G. Woll; Washington, DC, Smithsonian Inst., Traveling Exh. Serv., 1976–8)

Edvard Munch (exh. cat., essays A. Eggum, G. Woll; Stockholm, Liljevalchs Ksthall; Stockholm, Kulthuset; 1977)

Die Brücke—Edvard Munch (exh. cat., essays A. Eggum, G. Woll; Oslo, Munch-Mus., 1978)

Edvards Munchs Arbeiterbilder, 1910–1930 (exh. cat., essay U. Schneede; Hamburg, Kstver., 1978)

Edvard Munch: Symbols and Images (exh. cat., essays A. Eggum and others; Washington, DC, N.G.A., 1978–9)

Edvard Munch and his Literary Associates (exh. cat. by C. Lathe, Norwich, U. E. Anglia, Sainsbury Cent., 1979)

Edvard Munch: Tegninger og akvareller (exh. cat., essays A. Eggum, G. Woll; Copenhagen, Kstforen., 1979)

Edvard Munch: Liebe, Angst, Tod (exh. cat., essays A. Eggum and others; Bielefeld, Städt. Ksthalle, 1980)

Munch Exhibition (exh. cat., essays A. Eggum and G. Woll; Tokyo, N. Mus. Mod. A., 1981)

Munch (exh. cat.; Milan, Pal. Reale; Milan, Fond. Bagatti Valsecchi, 1985–6)

Munch, 1863–1944 (exh. cat., Barcelona, Cent. Cult. Caixa Pensions, 1987)

Edvard Munch (exh. cat., Essen, Mus. Flkwang; Zurich, Ksthaus; 1987–8)

Edvard Munch og hans modeller, 1912–1943 (exh. cat., Oslo, Munch-Mus., 1988–9)

Munch and Photography (exh. cat. by A. Eggum, U. Newcastle upon Tyne, Hatton Gal. and Newcastle upon Tyne, Poly. Gal.; Edinburgh, City A. Cent.; Manchester, C.A.G.; Oxford, MOMA; 1989–90)

Edvard Munch: Master Prints from the Epstein Family Collection (exh. cat., Washington, DC, N.G.A., 1990–91)

Edvard Munch: The Frieze of Life (exh. cat., ed. M.-H. Wood, essays A. Eggum and others; London, N. G., 1992–3)

For further bibliography see *Oslo Komm. Kstsaml. Ab.* (1946–60, 1963) and A. Eggum: 'Litteraturen om Edvard Munch gjennom nitti år' [The literature on Edvard Munch over 90 years], *Kst & Kult.* [Oslo] (1982), pp. 270–79

REINHOLD HELLER

Munchak Tepe. *See under* KURKAT.

Munch'ung. *See* NAM KU-MAN.

Mun-ch'ŏng. *See* BUNSEI.

Munck, Jan de (*b* Hulst, 12 Sept 1687; *d* Middelburg, 24 Feb 1768). Dutch architect. He probably trained as a carpenter. In 1715 he settled in Middelburg, where he was appointed dean of the carpenters' guild in 1723. Five years later he was made controller of surveyors to the province of Zeeland, and in 1730 he was appointed municipal architect of Middelburg. In this capacity he designed, among other works, the Office of Weights and Measures (1739; destr.), the Lutherse Kerk (1742) with adjoining houses, as well as a new town crane (1746). De Munck designed façades for distinguished private houses in a simple, provincial, late Louis XIV style. A typical example of this is his own house (1736) in Middelburg. The wide façade, with rusticated angle pilasters and topped with a straight cornice, was in keeping with the prevailing style of the time in this town. Façades of this type were more popular in Middelburg than, for example, in Amsterdam, probably as a result of municipal building regulations. Next door to his own house he built an observatory (1736; destr. 1775). De Munck was an amateur astronomer of some note, and in 1747 was appointed 'astronomicus and observer of celestial motions and astronomy' to William IV, Stadholder of the Netherlands.

BIBLIOGRAPHY

BWN

W. S. Unger: 'Aantekeningen betreffende enkele oud-Nederlandse bouwmeesters' [Notes about some old Dutch architects], *Oud-Holland*, xl (1922), pp. 161–7

PAUL H. REM

Munday, Richard (*b* ?Newport, RI, *c*. 1685 ; *d* Newport, 1739). American architect. Records show that he was married in Newport in 1713. In 1719 he was listed as an innkeeper and in 1721 as a house carpenter, becoming a freeman in 1722. In the early 1730s he lived at Bristol, RI, but he had returned to Newport by 1738. Munday's high reputation among the craftsmen–architects of New England rests mainly on two buildings in Newport: Trinity Church (1725–6) and the Colony House (1739–41). Trinity Church is a timber structure, resembling Christopher Wren's St James, Piccadilly, London, which was also the model for the Old North Church, Boston, begun in 1723. Old North Church, rather than St James, Piccadilly, was clearly Munday's source. The spire, designed in 1726 but not built until 1741, has much in common with the spire of Old North, which is itself a taller version of the spire of Wren's St Lawrence Jewry, London. A contemporary document shows that Munday was to be paid £25 for 'draughting a plan' for the Colony House. The style and scale of this brick and stone civic building are predominantly domestic, with motifs associated with local domestic architecture. In Godfrey Malbone's house (1727; destr.) in Newport Munday had employed a broad gambrel roof and a cupola, and the Thomas Hancock House (Joshua Blanchard, builder; 1737–40; destr. 1863), Boston, had a façade with a balcony at first-floor level. To the Colony House, Munday again gave a cupola and front balcony. The civil courtroom occupied the ground floor; on the first floor, the middle room, behind the balcony, was flanked by the Deputies' Room to the west and the Council Room to the east.

BIBLIOGRAPHY

Macmillan Enc. Architects
H. R. Hitchcock: *Rhode Island Architecture* (Providence, 1939/R New York, 1968)
A. F. Downing and V. J. Scully jr: *The Architectural Heritage of Newport, Rhode Island, 1640–1915* (Cambridge, MA, 1952, rev. New York, 1967)

MARCUS WHIFFEN

Mündler, Otto (*b* Kempten, 3 Feb 1811; *d* Paris, 14 April 1870). German art historian and dealer. The son of a school-teacher, he studied theology and languages at the universities of Munich and Erlangen from 1828 to 1833. By 1835 he had moved to Paris where he abandoned theology to pursue his art-historical studies as a dealer. In the 1840s he became friendly with Giovanni Morelli, Ralph Wornum (1812–77; then in Paris to write the first scholarly catalogue of the National Gallery, London) and Emmanuel Sano (*d* 1878), a Belgian marine artist with whom he formed a business association. Mündler acquired a considerable knowledge of Old Master paintings that he demonstrated in his first publication, a lengthy essay (1850) on the Italian collection in the Louvre, Paris. This established him as one of the leading critics of museum policies, for he showed that the Louvre had been indifferently administered, its conservation neglected and the recently published catalogue (1849) by the Director, Frédéric Villot, contained numerous errors of dating and absurd attributions. Mündler had an excellent eye for stylistic differences and an impressive knowledge of documentary sources, and his theological background informed his writing on religious imagery. The most important criterion of his method of connoisseurship was the analysis of the morphology of artists' signatures; he collected material for a dictionary of painters' monograms and signatures, which was never published.

On 2 July 1855, partly as a result of the success of his Louvre volume, Mündler was appointed travelling agent for the National Gallery, London, by Charles Lock Eastlake, its first Director, to obtain the earliest possible information about works of art when they were offered for sale on the Continent. He was required to keep a travel diary for the Trustees concerning possible acquisitions; this has become an important source of information about contemporary collectors, dealers, restorers and museum directors, as well as about Renaissance paintings and their provenances. In terms of acquisitions (which included such masterpieces as Veronese's the *Family of Darius before Alexander*; London, N.G.) the new office was a success, but there was unjustified criticism of Mündler in the press, and his post was abolished by the House of Commons in 1858. He continued to work on an occasional

basis for Eastlake and his successor, William Boxall, reporting on collections in Germany and France in 1864. When Eastlake died, Mündler wrote a generous and perceptive tribute to him (1869).

After his dismissal Mündler returned to Paris, where he acted as a dealer for German museums, especially those in Berlin, where he hoped to succeed his mentor Gustav F. Waagen as Director of the Gemäldegalerie. In 1861 he completed a catalogue of the Galleria Sabauda in Turin for Morelli and Giuseppe Molteni, the conservator at the Brera, Milan. In his last years he met Théophile Thoré, whom he admired, and influenced the early work of Wilhelm Lübke and Alfred Woltmann. Mündler's volume on the Louvre, as well as his later articles, the critical study of Rudolf Marggraff's catalogue of the Alte Pinakothek, Munich (1865), and his lengthy revision of the attributions in Jacob Burckhardt's *Cicerone* (1869), made a considerable impact on the development of art history. They were the stimulus for a series of critical editions of Burckhardt's guidebook and were the models for Morelli's *Kunstkritische Studien* (1890–93).

UNPUBLISHED SOURCES

London, N.G. [MS., *Report of a Tour through Parts of Germany and France in Autumn 1864*]

WRITINGS

Essai d'une analyse critique de la notice des tableaux italiens du Musée national du Louvre accompagné d'observations et de documents relatifs à ces mêmes tableaux (Paris, 1850)
'Die Apokryphen der Münchener Pinakothek und der neue Katalog', *Recens. & Mitt. Bild. Kst*, xlv (1865), pp. 353–7; xlvii (1867), pp. 369–74
'Beiträge zu Burckhardts *Cicerone*', *Jb. Kstwiss.*, ii (1869), pp. 259–324
'Charles Lock Eastlake', *Z. Bild. Kst*, iv (1869), pp. 93–101
C. Tognieri Dowd, ed.: 'The Travel Diaries of Otto Mündler, 1855–1858', intro. J. Anderson, *Walpole Soc.*, li (1985) [whole issue; incl. bibliog. of Mündler's pubns]

BIBLIOGRAPHY

C. von Lützow: 'Otto Mündler', *Z. Bild. Kst*, v (1870), pp. 113–15 [insert]
A. Woltmann: 'Otto Mündler', *Berlin. N.-Ztg* (8 May 1870), pp. 1–2
T. Borenius: 'Eastlake's Travelling Agent for the National Gallery', *Burl. Mag.*, lxxxiii (1943), pp. 211–16
D. Robertson: *Sir Charles Eastlake and the Victorian Art World* (Princeton, 1978)
R. Kultzen: 'Otto Mündler als Briefpartner Wilhelm Von Bodes', *Martin Gosebruch zu Ehren*, ed. F. Neidhart (Munich, 1984), pp. 184–91
——: 'Giovanni Morelli als Briefpartner von Otto Mündler', *Z. Kstgesch.*, lii (1989), pp. 373–400
——: 'Einiges über die kunsthistorischen Leitbilder Otto Mündlers', *Hülle und Fülle: Festschrift für Tilmann Buddensieg*, ed. A. Beyer, V. M. Lampugnani and G. Schweikhart (1993), pp. 323–35

JAYNIE ANDERSON

Munehiro. *See* KŌRA MUNEHIRO BUNGO.

Munggenast, Joseph (*b* Schnann, Tyrol, 5 March 1680; *d* St Pölten, Lower Austria, 3 May 1741). Austrian architect. He settled in St Pölten and was granted citizenship and his master's certificate in 1717. He worked for Jakob Prandtauer, at first acting as his clerk of works on such projects as the pilgrimage church at Sonntagberg; he was subsequently entrusted with the execution of commissions for Prandtauer on a basis that allowed considerably more artistic freedom (e.g. Dürnstein Abbey Church), and he gradually achieved the status of an independent architect. On Prandtauer's death in 1726, Munggenast was responsible for completing most of his unfinished schemes, including the monastery buildings at Melk Abbey, Herzogenburg and St Pölten. He was thus brought into contact with those commissioning building work in the monasteries and monastic foundations of Lower and Upper Austria, and from about 1730 he became one of the leading architects in Lower Austria, outside Vienna.

The new monastic buildings at Seitenstetten, begun by Munggenast in 1718, were an independent achievement based on Prandtauer's design ideas. At the abbeys of Dürnstein (begun 1718) and Zwettl (begun 1722), however, Munggenast's work shows the influence of Matthias Steinl, his collaborator on these projects, who used sculptural devices borrowed from the Roman High Baroque. At Dürnstein, in addition to his executive role and his detailed plans and revisions to Steinl's project for the tower, Munggenast may also have designed the choir, which features gallery arches that bow outwards, with pierced vaults behind. At Zwettl Abbey Church he carried out Baroque alterations to the nave and produced projects for the façade of the tower and for the high altar. Munggenast also produced several unexecuted schemes for the remodelling of existing monastery buildings and abbey churches, and these typically show a centralized three-bay layout with a central dome. A number of variations were proposed for the monastery church at Herzogenburg (from 1727); for Wilhering Abbey Church (from 1733); and for the Klosterkirche at Maria Langegg (*c.* 1733).

Munggenast's most important work was carried out in the church and library at Altenburg Abbey, which he redeveloped in the Baroque style from 1730 and where he succeeded in combining simple architectural forms with three-dimensional animation through the use of rich decoration. The nave of the church is a central longitudinal oval articulated by pilasters; these continue as a minor order above the entablature to give the effect of a drum, which the dome in fact lacks, and the frescoes by Paul Troger on the soffit of the dome thereby exert greater impact below. This elaboration of a simple basic shape occurs again in the library, where an elongated rectangle has diagonally placed columns along the walls, their entablatures surmounted by rearing horses and other figures; three domes separated by barrel vaults roof the space. Other late works by Munggenast include the extension of buildings at Geras Abbey (1736–40); plans to rebuild the abbey and church at Mondsee (1736–8); a prelate's building and bishop's gate (1739) at St Pölten Abbey; and a project (1740) for a new building at Siebenlinden Parish Church. The incorporation of nature into the building, characteristic of Munggenast's late work, can be seen most clearly in the courtyard of Melk Abbey Church, with the opening in the great loggia. In his interiors, as at Altenburg and Melk, he used sculptural decoration and painting to achieve his intended effects, with colour making a considerable contribution; they are among the major achievements of the Austrian Baroque in its final phase.

Other members of Munggenast's family were also active as architects and builders: his brother Sigismund Munggenast (1694–1770) worked in Luxemburg, and his sons Franz Munggenast (1724–48) and Matthias Munggenast (1729–98) worked in Lower Austria.

BIBLIOGRAPHY

Thieme–Becker

G. Wagner: *Joseph Munggenast, 1680–1741* (diss., U. Vienna, 1940)

R. Feuchtmüller: 'Joseph Munggenast: Das barocke Gesamtkunstwerk zur Zeit Paul Trogers', *Paul Troger und die österreichische Barockkunst* (exh. cat., Altenburg, Benedictine Abbey, 1963), pp. 13–26

E. Munggenast: *Joseph Munggenast: Der Stiftsbaumeister* (Vienna, 1963)

B. Grimschitz: 'Joseph und Franz Munggenasts Pläne zur Stiftskirche in Herzogenburg', *Alte & Mod. Kst*, lxxv (1964), pp. 20–23

L. Pühringer-Zwanowetz: *Matthias Steinl* (Vienna and Munich, 1966)

——: 'Die Baugeschichte des Augustiner-Chorherrenstiftes Dürnstein und das "neue Kloster" des Propstes Hieronymus Übelbacher', *Wien. Jb. Kstgesch.*, xxvi (1973), pp. 96–198

W. G. Rizzi: 'Zur Sakralarchitektur Johann Michael Prunners', *Wien. Jb. Kstgesch.*, xxxii (1979), pp. 99–133

L. Pühringer-Zwanowetz: 'Zur Baugeschichte des Augustiner-Chorherrenstiftes Herzogenburg', *Stift Herzogenburg und seine Kunstschätze* (St Pölten, 1982)

W. GEORG RIZZI

Mung Thai. *See* THAILAND.

Munich [Ger. München]. Capital city of Bavaria, Germany. It is also the administrative district of Upper Bavaria and is situated on the River Isar near the foothills of the Alps. With a population of *c.* 1,350,000 it is an important university city and one of the largest industrial cities in Germany.

I. History and urban development. II. Art life and organization. III. Centre of production. IV. Buildings.

I. History and urban development.

1. Before *c.* 1505. 2. *c.* 1505–*c.* 1799. 3. *c.* 1799 and after.

1. BEFORE *c.* 1505. Munich was founded in 1158 by Henry the Lion, who destroyed the bridge over the Isar at Oberföhring and established a new bridge, a salt market and a mint on the site of a small monastic settlement known as *ad munichen* or *ze de Munichen*. Few traces remain of the settlement near the Peterskirche dating from before the foundation of the city. The present street pattern established under Henry the Lion follows the near-oval ring of the first fortifications of *c.* 1170, enclosing 17 ha, which had five gates (destr. 1691–1944; Unteres Tor reconstructed 1972). The town was planned with individual plots of land, as at Lübeck, with two intersecting main streets: the economically important Salzstrasse running from east to west (from Salzburg to Augsburg) and the Schwabinger Landstrasse running from north to south (from Nuremberg to Italy). At their intersection was a market-place (originally the Schrannenplatz, from 1854 the Marienplatz).

Bavaria was seized in 1180 by the house of WITTELSBACH, whose artistic and cultural policies decisively influenced the town's appearance. Dominant features were the Petersbergl, the ducal residence later known as the Alter Hof at the north-east corner, and the Frauenplatz. A devastating fire in 1221 was followed by an economic and building boom. After *c.* 1230 the Marienkapelle on the Frauenplatz was replaced by a Romanesque basilica, which, owing to the increased population, became a second parish church (*see* §IV, 1 below) in 1271. The establishment (1255) of the Wittelsbach court in Munich as seat of the part-duchy of Bavaria–Munich (Upper Bavaria) was of great importance to the development of the town. The Alter Hof became the official residence of Duke Ludwig

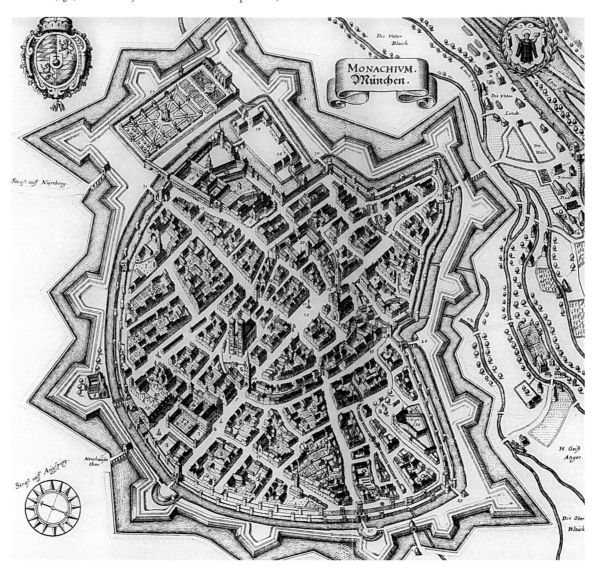

1. Munich, plan engraved by Matthäus Merian (i), 1640 (Munich, Bayerische Staatsbibliothek)

II ('the Severe'; *reg* 1253–94), who also extended the old central road grid, creating an outer town with a second fortification wall. Church leaders were also prominent building patrons in the second half of the 13th century: a Franciscan monastery (originally on the site of the present Nationaltheater; relocated outside the old north wall 1284; destr. 1327; new building dedicated 1375; destr. 1803); the Augustinian church (begun 1291; now the Deutsches Jagd- und Fischerei-Museum); the Heiliggeistspital (begun 1208; enlarged from 1250); and St Jakob am Anger (*c.* 1250; destr. 1944; rebuilt 1955–6). Under Ludwig IV ('the Bavarian'; *reg* 1294–1347) Munich became an imperial residence and an important spiritual and economic centre. Ludwig extended the residence at the Alter Hof, building the Lorenzkapelle, and completed the new fortifications in 1337. There were four gates: the Isartor (east, rest. 1972), the Schwabinger Tor (west, now the Karlstor), the Neuhauser Tor (north, destr.) and the Sendlinger Tor

(south-west). The city was now six times as large as in the 1170s, and Ludwig's decree in 1315 that the Marienplatz must be left free of buildings in perpetuity was crucial to its future development. An imperial 'golden bull' of 1332 granted Munich a salt monopoly, and in 1340 it was granted the 'Great Charter'.

Much of the eastern part of the inner city was rebuilt (after a fire in 1327), mostly in the second half of the 14th century: the Peterskirche (dedicated 1368), the Heilig-geistkirche (completed by Gabriel Ridler in 1392, rebuilt 1723–30) and the Altes Rathaus (enlarged 1392–4; destr. 1944–5; rebuilt). As a result of the city's expansion the Alter Hof was no longer at the edge of the city, and with increasing civic disturbances at the end of the 14th century, notably the burghers' uprising of 1385, the Wittelsbachs established the Neuveste (new fortress) at the new north-east boundary. This square, moated castle, progressively enlarged in the following centuries and demolished only in the 19th, forms the basis of the complex development of the Residenz (*see* §IV, 2 below). At the end of the 14th century the town had four distinct economic sectors, the Kreuzviertel in the north-west (church affairs), the Garggenauerviertel in the north-east (the nobility), the Hackenviertel in the south-east and the Angerviertel in the south-west (tradesmen and merchants). Prominent merchants were now rivalling the court as patrons. They commissioned from the town architect JÖRG VON HALSBACH the most important building of this period and still the city's symbol: the brick Frauenkirche (*see* §IV, 1 below). Another sign of their prosperity is the Altes Rathaus (rest. 19th century) on the site of the Unteres Tor within Henry the Lion's city walls. This was built by von Halsbach in the 1470s to replace an earlier building and contained a dance hall. From the late 15th century, however, enthusiasm for building gradually waned. The building materials for the medieval city came from the immediate vicinity: limestone for more sophisticated buildings and wood for ordinary houses. In contrast to Landshut and the towns along the River Inn, the eaves generally faced the street.

VERENA BEAUCAMP

2. *c.* 1505–*c.* 1799. In 1505 the part-duchies of Upper and Lower Bavaria were reunited with Munich as the capital. From the end of the Late Gothic period to *c.* 1570 there were few changes in the general appearance of Munich as recorded in the model of the city (1570; Munich, Bayer. Nmus.) by Jakob Sandtner (*fl c.* 1561–74). One development, however, was a new style of burgher house with a roof recessed behind crenellations. Larger residences often had arcaded courtyards. Surviving houses include the Stadtschreiberei (now the Weinstadl), enlarged 1550–52 by Hans Aernhofer the elder with a façade painting designed by Hans Müelich; and the Eilles Hof, built in 1560–70. The broadly conceived 'Landschaftshaus' (destr.) on the market-place (on the site of the Neues Rathaus) consisted until 1568 of two burgher houses with arcades on the ground floor and façade painting. The Marstall was built in 1563–7 by WILHELM EGCKL in Italian Renaissance style, as a link between the Neuveste and the Alter Hof. It housed the art collections and library of Duke Albert V (*see* WITTELSBACH, §I(3)) and later served as a mint. Of this once extensive complex, which included the ducal stables, only the arcaded courtyard survives. Alterations to the Neuveste resulted in space restrictions that led Albert V in 1569 to have the Antiquarium built outside the fortress. This was the first stage of the Residenz (*see* §IV, 2 below).

Munich developed into a centre of the Counter-Reformation after the mid-16th century. Under Duke William V, during several periods of building from 1583 or 1585, the Jesuit Michaelskirche and college were constructed (*see* WITTELSBACH, §I(4)). In the last years of his reign the Wilhelminische Veste (1593–6; later the Herzog-Max-Burg) was built on the north-west edge of the town. On outer walls were areas of coloured stucco (largely destr. 1944) in the Florentine manner. An outstanding landmark of the city is the long west façade of the Residenz, built 1611–19 under Maximilian I, Elector of Bavaria. Until the 19th century it was the building's only decorative

front. In 1618–19, in anticipation of war, new town fortifications were built under the direction of HEINRICH SCHÖN; they determined the appearance of the town (see fig. 1) until *c.* 1800. Schön also designed the Hofgarten (1613–17). Munich was the electors' official residence from 1623. In 1632 it was occupied by the Swedes, but they had been ousted by 1637–9, and Maximilian had the *Column of Mary* erected in the Marienplatz as a token of thanksgiving.

In the period after the Thirty Years War (1618–48) the Carmelite monastery (*c.* 1657–60) was built by Marx Schinnagel (1612–81) to designs by Hans Conrad Asper (*b* 1588). With its strict, sober style the monastery church is Munich's first Baroque church. Schinnagel also built the Turnierhaus (tournament building; 1660–61) on the west side of the Hofgarten. The Opernhaus was built to designs by Asper under Schinnagel's direction from 1651. The interior decoration was by the Venetian painter Francesco Santurini (1627–82).

Under Elector Ferdinand, Agostino Barelli was commissioned in 1662 to build the Theatine church of St Kajetan (1662–8; completed by Enrico Zuccalli; façade added 1765–7 by François de Cuvilliés I; *see* WITTELSBACH, §I(6); for further discussion and illustration *see* BARELLI, AGOSTINO). Meanwhile, from 1664, Schloss Nymphenburg (*see* §IV, 3 below) was being built to plans by Barelli. The reign of Elector Maximilian II Emanuel led to a boom in private secular building (*see* WITTELSBACH, §I(7)). In the exterior decoration a clear, sculptural architectural style replaced the earlier façade painting; after relatively small-scale beginnings, this culminated in the 1690s in the development of Italianate palaces around the Residenz. The most important architect of this period was ENRICO ZUCCALLI, who designed the Palais Portia (1693–4).

West of the Jesuit college, the Bürgersaalkirche was built in 1709–10 by Johann Georg Ettenhofer to plans by GIOVANNI ANTONIO VISCARDI, who also supplied plans for the Dreifaltigkeitskirche (1711–14). The strongly projecting sculptural façade of the latter lends a Roman accent to the town. The palaces built for the nobility in following years were, however, influenced by French architecture. The Palais Preysing, the first Rococo palace in Munich, was built 1723–9 to plans by Josef Effner (*see also* ZIMMERMANN, JOHANN BAPTIST). Its exterior façade was decorated with rich stucco, as were the interior walls. Among the most important surviving palaces by FRANÇOIS DE CUVILLIÉS I is the Palais Holnstein (1733–7; now the archbishop's palace) with its harmonious arrangement of rooms and façade structure.

Artists' houses form a separate group. The house (*c.* 1730) of Johann Baptist Gunetzrhainer (1692–1763) on the Promenadenplatz has a Rococo façade articulated by plasterwork, with delicate Régence-style stucco ornament. The façade (*c.* 1735) of the Asam-Haus in the Sendlinger Strasse is liberally decorated with allegorical stuccowork.

After 1725 there was a resurgence of church architecture. Munich's first Rococo church, the Hieronymite monastery church of St Anna, was built 1727–33 in the eastern suburb of Lehel. The architect, JOHANN MICHAEL FISCHER, developed a style independent of Italian practice.

Equally original, though more dependent upon Italian architecture, is the Damenstiftkirche of St Anna (1732–5) by Gunetzrhainer. The church of St Johann Nepomuk was begun by the Asam brothers (*see* ASAM, §I) in 1729 (completed 1746) as a private church for burgher artists. The slightly concave façade, with its sculpturally accentuated centre and lively curved pediment, fits between the neighbouring houses without disrupting the profile of the Sendlinger Strasse.

In his Rococo Residenztheater (Cuvilliés-Theater; 1750–53; destr. World War II; rebuilt on a different site), inspired by the opera house (1745–8) by Joseph de Saint-Pierre in Bayreuth and the theatre project (after 1748) by Anges-Jacques Gabriel for Versailles, de Cuvilliés produced a building of genius, developing the Baroque idiom into a flowing style of surface ornament. Of the palaces built for the nobility from the mid-18th century, the only surviving example is the Palais Gise (*c.* 1765) by Karl Albert von Lespilliez (1723–96), which shows the influence of de Cuvilliés. In the second half of the 18th century building activity virtually ceased. In 1789 Friedrich Ludwig von Sckell began laying out the Englischer Garten: the Chinesischer Turm (1789–90) is one of its outstanding features. In 1791, in response to increasing population, Elector Charles Theodore decided to demolish the ramparts, thus allowing the town to spread.

JOSEF STRASSER

3. *c.* 1799 AND AFTER. When Elector Charles Theodore died in 1799, he was succeeded by Maximilian IV Joseph (*reg* 1799–1825, later Maximilian I Joseph, King of Bavaria), and with him came the Frenchman Freiherr von Montgelas (1759–1838), from 1799 to 1817 the Elector's ruling minister of state, who was to lead Bavaria into a century of enlightenment. The secularization of church property in 1803 released monastic lands for redevelopment. Bavaria broke off its alliance with Napoleon in 1806 and became a kingdom. Munich, as its capital and royal residence, expanded rapidly. In 1821 the seat of the bishop was transferred from Freising to Munich.

King Ludwig I (*see* WITTELSBACH, §III(3)) had ambitions to turn Munich into a capital of the arts, akin to Paris. During his rule the city was given a classicist appearance by such architects as KARL VON FISCHER, LEO VON KLENZE and Friedrich von Gärtner (*see* GÄRTNER, (2)). Grand squares (Karolinenplatz, 1810–33; Königsplatz, begun 1812) and districts on a gridplan were linked by magnificent streets. The last included the 1-km Ludwigstrasse (1816–52; *see* RUNDBOGENSTIL; for illustration *see* GÄRTNER, (2)) between the Feldherrnhalle (1840) and the Siegestor (1843–52), leading north towards Schwabing; and the Brienner Strasse (begun under Maximilian IV Joseph after 1808 as Königstrasse; Brienner Strasse from 1828), leading to Schloss Nymphenburg (*see* §IV, 3 below), which lay on the outskirts of the city. The Königsplatz was also located well outside the city centre and, over a period of almost 50 years, was enclosed with Greek Revival buildings such as the Glyptothek (1816–30; rest. 1972; *see* KLENZE, LEO VON, fig. 1), the Staatliche Antikensammlungen (1838–45) and the Propyläen (1854–62). Not far away was built the Alte Pinakothek (1825–36; *see* MUSEUM, fig. 5), housing one of the finest collections of paintings in the world. Ludwig I also extended the Residenz (1826–35; *see* §IV, 2 below); commissioned the Ruhmeshalle (1843–53) above the Theresienwiese, outside which is the monumental figure of *Bavaria* (1844–50) designed by Ludwig von Schwanthaler (*see* SCHWANTHALER, (4)); and founded the Neue Pinakothek (1846–53; *see* §II, 2 below).

Ludwig's elaborate projects, financed by taxes levied from an essentially agricultural country, were a heavy burden on the citizens. Twelve factories, of which the NYMPHENBURG PORCELAIN FACTORY is best known, brought revenue to the state but at the same time inhibited industrial initiatives by the townspeople. Financial services were centred on the city, however, and, because of its position at the intersection of the routes linking Paris with Vienna and Berlin with Rome, Munich became the south German centre for trade in cereals, livestock and fruit.

Ludwig's successor, Maximilian II (*reg* 1848–64), began to expand the areas to the east and south of Munich. Between 1852 and 1875 the neo-Gothic Maximilianstrasse was developed as a third axis by FRIEDRICH BÜRKLEIN, who had also designed the Hauptbahnhof (1847–9; destr. 1945); the street ended at the Maximilianeum (1856–74). With a façade by Gottfried Semper, this building stands high above the banks of the Isar and is now the Bavarian parliament building (see fig. 2). The new street improved trade with the villages east of the river, bringing them increased prosperity.

Munich had been linked by rail to Augsburg since 1839. By 1873 seven other lines had been built. The western Hauptbahnhof was connected with the Ostbahnhof by a circle line, providing railway links for incipient industrialization and predetermining future commercial and industrial zones. With the growth of capitalism and the influence of the expanding middle classes came the demand for

2. Munich, Maximilianeum (1856–74), façade by Gottfried Semper; now the Bavarian parliament building

buildings subdivided into small units that could be let as housing or for commercial enterprises. The 1863 Munich building regulations, however, forbade the construction of tenement housing of the type found in Berlin and Vienna. From 1860 came the development of the Gärtnerplatzviertel, centred on a new 'people's' theatre named the Gärtnerplatztheater, the Ostbahnhof district; and the Wiesenviertel on the Theresienwiese, famous for the October Festival.

Under Prince Luitpold of Bavaria (Prince Regent, 1886–1912), Prinzregentenstrasse was begun in 1890. Parallel to, but 600 m north of Maximilianstrasse, it was the last of the grand avenues, culminating in a victory column surmounted by the *Angel of Peace* (1899) by Heinrich Düll (*b* 1867). A number of important public buildings were constructed in the late 19th century. The new Rathaus was built in a Gothic Revival style by GEORGE JOSEPH VON HAUBERISSER after he had won the competition in 1866. Extensions were added to it in 1888–93 and 1899–1908, and it was the first major Gothic Revival public building in Munich. In the same style he also designed the Stadtpfarrkirche St Paul (1892–1906). In 1887 FRIEDRICH VON THIERSCH was commissioned by Luitpold to build the Justizpalast (1887–97), executed in the Baroque Revival style. Other historicist works by him include the new Stock Exchange (1898–1901) and the new Justizgebäude (1902–5). Slightly later are the works of MAX LITTMANN, who built the Schauspielhaus (1900–01), one of the outstanding examples of *Jugendstil* architecture, and also the severe Bau der Anatomie (1905–8), one of the first buildings to use exposed reinforced concrete.

Between the accession of Ludwig II (1864) and *c.* 1900 the population of Munich rose from *c.* 150,000 to almost half a million, and outlying parishes were incorporated into the city. The graded building regulation of 1904, permitting four enclosed and four open styles of building and no more than five storeys, resulted in residential areas with wide, closely built streets, radiating out from squares, where there was commercial provision for local needs. Green areas were kept free of development and remain so today. Industrialization continued on a relatively modest scale until World War I, and Munich remained a lower-middle-class city. Revolution (1918) put an end to the rule and artistic policies of the Wittelsbachs. The only products of Hitler's 12 years in power from 1933 and his massive plan to expand Munich as his party headquarters were the two 'Führer' buildings (now the Hochschule für Musik in München and the Staatliche Graphische Sammlung) in German Renaissance Revival style on the Königsplatz and the Haus der Kunst (1933–7) in the Prinzregentenstrasse (*see* §II, 2 below). World War II reduced much of the old city to rubble.

After the war Munich became the capital of the Free State of Bavaria under a new constitution. A period of industrial growth followed. The next turning point for urban development, however, was not until the 1972 Olympic Games, which prompted the construction not only of an Olympic park, which carries conviction both functionally and architecturally, but also of a transport infrastructure of trains, underground, trams and buses. Underground railway tunnels enabled the creation of one of the largest pedestrian areas in Europe, which includes the open-air market.

Further industrialization in the late 20th century had led to the sprawl of commuter suburbs into the surrounding area. The modern city is divided: in the south an affluent population lives in garden cities, well provided with cultural facilities; in the less attractive north are concentrated service and other industries, motorway intersections and a large new airport. This dichotomy has not, however, affected the high-profile image of modern Munich. Now that Berlin has again become the capital of Germany, Munich may have lost its role as the 'secret capital'. It should, however, retain its role as a metropolis of European culture.

ROBERT GEIPEL

BIBLIOGRAPHY

L. von Westenrieder: *Beschreibung der Haupt- und Residenzstadt München* (Munich, 1783)

T. Dombart: *Das Werden und Wachsen des Stadtbildes* (Munich, 1931)

P. Dirr: *Grundlagen der Münchner Stadtgeschichte* (Munich, 1937)

D. Österreicher: *Die Entstehung und Entwicklung des Stadtgrundrisses von München* (diss., Munich, Tech. Hochsch., 1949)

M. Megele: *Baugeschichtlicher Atlas der Landeshauptstadt München* (Munich, 1951)

Der Mönch im Wappen: Aus Geschichte und Gegenwart des katholischen München (Munich, 1960)

K. Bösl: *München: Bürgerstadt, Residenz, heimliche Hauptstadt Deutschlands* (Stuttgart, 1971)

G. Ruhl: *Das Image von München als Faktor für den Zuzug* (Kallmünz, 1971)

N. Lieb and H.-J. Sauermost: *Münchens Kirchen* (Munich, 1973)

G. Muske: *Motive für die Wahl des Studienortes München* (Kallmünz, 1975)

M. Schattenhofer: 'Die Anfänge Münchens', *Abensberger Vorträge, 1977* (Munich, 1978)

K. Gallas: *München* (Cologne, 1979)

Wittelsbach und Bayern, 6 vols (exh. cat., ed. H. Glaser; Munich, Residenz, 1980)

H.-P. Rasp: *Eine Stadt für 1000 Jahre* (Munich, 1981)

J. Dramm: *München: Mit Schloss und Park Schleissheim* (Zurich and Munich, 1983)

J. Pohl and R. Geipel: *Umweltqualität im Münchner Norden* (Kallmünz, 1983)

H. Habel, H. Himen and H. W. Lübbeke: *Landeshauptstadt München* (1985), i/1 of *Denkmäler in Bayern*, ed. M. Petzet, 7 vols (Munich, 1985–6)

R. Geipel and G. Heinritz: *München: Ein sozialgeographischer Exkursionsführer* (Kallmünz, 1987)

N. Huse: *Kleine Kunstgeschichte Münchens* (Munich, 1990, rev. 2/1992)

R. Bauer, ed.: *Geschichte der Stadt München* (Munich, 1992)

R. Geipel, I. Helbrecht and J. Pohl: *Die Münchner Olympischen Spiele von 1972 als Instrument der Stadtentwicklungspolitik* (Opladen, 1993)

VERENA BEAUCAMP, JOSEF STRASSER

II. Art life and organization.

1. Before *c.* 1799. 2. *c.* 1799 and after.

1. BEFORE *c.* 1799. Art life in Munich began to flourish only in the 16th century. In the period from 1496 to 1532 the outstanding glass-painter was Jakob Kistenfeger, examples of whose work can be found in the Salvatorkirche and the Frauenkirche. In the early 16th century Erasmus Grasser and his workshop continued to dominate sculpture in the city, although the Master of the Blutenburg Apostles (*fl c.* 1483–*c.* 1505) was also important. The gradual transition from the Late Gothic to Renaissance is seen in the sculpture of the Master of Rabenden (*fl c.* 1500–30). The death of Jan Polack in 1519 concluded the first high period of the city's painting; subsequently Munich was long overshadowed by the great artistic centres of

Nuremberg and Augsburg. Polack's followers Jakob Heitzinger (*fl c*. 1500–10) and Niklas Schlesitzer are documented as having been in Munich in the early 16th century. The Court Painter Hans Ostendorfer the elder (*d* 1524), who had been in the city from as early as 1503, introduced a new impetus and assimilated the formal vocabulary of the Renaissance.

The important impulses came from outside Munich, however. Albrecht Altdorfer, Hans Wertinger and Wolfgang Huber all produced influential work in the town. Barthel Beham (*see* BEHAM, (2)), who was granted citizenship in 1528 and became court painter soon afterwards, was active there slightly later, as was LUDWIG REFINGER. The monumental history cycle (after 1528) commissioned by Duke William IV (*see* WITTELSBACH, §I(2)) was decisive in the gradual development of a court art. Its execution was shared by Beham, Refinger, Jörg Breu (*see* BREU, (1)), MELCHIOR FESELEN, Hans Burgkmair I and others. The outstanding work in the series is the *Battle of Alexander* (1529; Munich, Alte Pin.) by Albrecht Altdorfer. The first important 16th-century artist native to Munich was HANS MIELICH, who combined the traditions of Munich and Nuremberg with Italian influences to produce an idiom of his own.

In the era of Duke Albert V (*see* WITTELSBACH, §I(3)), such German artists as Hans Aesslinger (Court Sculptor 1550–52), Hans Wiesreither, Caspar Weinhart (*fl* after *c*. 1556; *d c*. 1597), Hans Wörner and Hans Aernhofer the elder were active. When Duke William V (*see* WITTELSBACH, §I(4)) took over the regency in 1579, however, they received increasing competition from itinerant artists from Italy and the Netherlands, and the city became a centre for Mannerism. A number of works were produced under the direction of Friedrich Sustris (*see* SUSTRIS, (2)) when he became court painter to William V. Second to Sustris was the German painter CHRISTOPH SCHWARZ, while the outstanding sculptor of the period was the Netherlandish HUBERT GERHARD. His most important works in Munich include the Perseus Fountain (*c*. 1585) of the Grottenhof at the Residenz, *St Michael and Lucifer* (1588; *see* GERHARD, HUBERT, fig. 1) on the façade of the Michaelskirche, *Bavaria* (1594), also at the Grottenhof, and the *Virgin* (1595) on the *Column of Mary* in the Marienplatz. The tomb of *William V* (begun 1592) has a crucifix by Giambologna, a *Mary Magdalene* (1595) by Hans Reichle (*see* REICHLE, HANS, §2) and an *Angel Bearing the Holy Water Stoup* (1593–6) and several reliefs and figures by Gerhard. Outstanding among the goldsmiths' work of this period is the mounted statuette of *St George* (Munich, Residenz) by Hans Schleich (*fl* after *c*. 1582; *d* 1616). The painter PIETER CANDID, summoned to Munich in 1586, distanced himself from Mannerism, his personal style combining elements of Netherlandish realism and Italian idealism. He also produced designs for the carpet factory (founded 1604).

Unlike his father, Elector Maximilian I favoured local Munich artists, including the painter HANS WERL, appointed court artist in 1594, and Johann Ulrich Loth. Well-known artists from outside Munich, however, such as Joachim von Sandrart and Johann Heinrich Schönfeld, also received commissions from the court and the clergy. In sculpture the monumental work of HANS KRUMPER

was in contrast to the small-scale carvings of Christoph Angermair (court sculptor 1623; *see* ANGERMAIR, CHRISTOPH, fig. 2). In 1656 Michael Gumpp (1636–79) arrived from Innsbruck, and in 1661 he became court painter. From Nuremberg came the engravers Michael Wening (1645–1718) and Carl Gustav Amling.

Under Elector Ferdinand (*see* WITTELSBACH, §I(6)) a succession of Italian artists arrived, among them the painter Antonio Domenico Triva (1626–99), who worked in Schloss Lustheim near Munich (*see* SCHLEISSHEIM, SCHLOSS). They were soon followed by such French artists as the architect and painter Jean Delamonce (1635–1708) and the painter Paul Mignard (1639–91). From 1675 the painter Johann Anton Gumpp (*see* GUMPP, (3)) was active in Munich; the painters Johann Kaspar Sing (1651–1729) and Hans Georg Asam arrived in 1679–80. Bavarian sculptors, especially wood-carvers, also came into favour under Elector Ferdinand, among them Tobias Pader (*fl* 1651; *d* ?1690); Balthasar Ableithner (1613–75), who produced sculptures (1670–72) in the Theatinerkirche; and Andreas Faistenberger II (1647–1736), examples of whose work survive in the Theatinerkirche and the Institut der Englischen Fräulein in Berg am Laim. Johann Andreas Wolff became court painter to Maximilian II Emanuel in 1680. His successor was the Frenchman Joseph Vivien. The Weilheim ivory carvers Dominikus Stainhart and Matthias Loth (1675–1738) were active from 1690 and 1705 respectively.

After the return from exile (1715) of Elector Maximilian II Emanuel, court painting was given a new impetus by Franz Joachim Beich, Jacopo Amigoni, Heinrich von Waterschoot (*d* 1748) and Peter Jacob Horemans (appointed court painter, 1727), and Munich became a centre for French artists. Numerous foreign sculptors came to the town, including Giuseppe Volpini (*d* 1729); CHARLES-CLAUDE DUBUT; GUILLIELMUS DE GROF, who became Court Sculptor; Egid Verhelst I; and Jakob Gerstens (*fl c*. 1730). Towards the end of Maximilian's reign, such German artists as NIKOLAUS GOTTFRIED STUBER, his cousin Cosmas Damian Asam and Balthasar Augustin Albrecht rose in importance; they enjoyed still greater favour under his successor Elector Charles (*reg* 1726–45). At this time the stuccoist and painter Johann Baptist Zimmermann (*see* ZIMMERMANN, (1)) was active in the city.

German sculptors significant in the transition from Baroque to Rococo and active in Munich include Johann Georg Greif (*c*. 1693–1753), Gabriel Luidl (*fl* 1720; *d* 1741) and, above all, Egid Quirin Asam, while the Rococo painter Georges Desmarées was appointed court painter in 1730. Important works by Asam in Munich are the high altar (1732–4) of the Peterskirche and the confessional group and *Seat of Mercy* (1733–46) in the church of St Johann Neopomuk (also known as the Asamkirche). With the appointment of Johann Baptist Straub as Court Sculptor in 1737, the Rococo reached an apogee (see fig. 3; *see also* STRAUB, (1)). Straub's pupil IGNAZ GÜNTHER was one of the most gifted masters of Bavarian Rococo. After Günther's death, ROMAN ANTON BOOS was the leading sculptor in Munich. (*See also* NYMPHENBURG PORCELAIN FACTORY and BUSTELLI, FRANZ ANTON.)

3. Johann Baptist Straub: *Minerva*, wood, h. *c.* 2.6 m, 1772 (Munich, Hauptpost)

Christian Thomas Wink (1738–97), court painter from 1769, also supplied designs (1767–80; Munich, Residenz) for tapestries (Munich, Residenz; Munich, Bayer. Mus.) produced by the reorganized Gobelin factory (*see* §IV, 2 below). The landscape and genre painter JOHANN JAKOB DORNER I, a native of Breisgau, became official Inspector of Galleries in 1770 and later (1788) organized the first public art exhibition in the town. The portraits of Josef Georg von Edlinger (1741–1819), who arrived in 1770–71, are influenced by the Enlightenment.

The artists who came to Munich after the accession (in 1777) of Elector Charles Theodore included the

QUAGLIO family. The transition from Rococo to Neo-classicism is seen after 1785 in the work of Franz Jakob Schwanthaler, who had worked in the studio of Boos. The work of the Upper-Bavarian landscape painters JOHANN GEORG VON DILLIS and Max Joseph Wagenbauer (1774–1829) led Munich into the 19th century.

BIBLIOGRAPHY

N. Lieb: *München: Lebensbild einer Stadtkultur* (Munich, 1952/*R* 1972)
——: *München: Die Geschichte seiner Kunst* (Munich, 1971, rev. 4/1988)
J. H. Biller and H.-P. Rasp: *München: Kunst und Kultur-Lexikon* (Munich, 1972, rev. 2/1985)
W. Braunfels: *Die weltlichen Fürstentümer* (1979), i of *Die Kunst im Heiligen Römischen Reich Deutscher Nation* (Munich, 1979–89), pp. 161–208

JOSEF STRASSER

2. *c.* 1799 AND AFTER. Munich's artistic importance increased greatly when Bavaria became (1806) a kingdom with large new territories, and the arts flourished under the first Wittelsbach kings Maximilian I Joseph and Ludwig I. Ludwig, an active patron until his death in 1868, enlisted many artists to decorate his new monumental streets and buildings, among them the painters PETER CORNELIUS, CARL ROTTMANN and Julius Schnorr von Carolsfeld and the sculptor Ludwig von Schwanthaler (*see* SCHWAN-THALER, (4)).

The Akademie der Bildenden Künste was refounded in 1808 and by the mid-19th century had become central Europe's premier training institution under the leadership (1849–74) of Wilhelm Kaulbach (*see* KAULBACH, (1)) and especially (1874–86) Karl Theodor von Piloty, attracting students from all over Germany, eastern and northern Europe, Russia and the USA.

Ludwig I founded the Alte Pinakothek (1825–36; by Klenze; *see* MUSEUM, §II and fig. 5), which came to house the finest works from the huge Wittelsbach collection of Old Masters, swelled by the contents of the former Düsseldorf gallery (which Ludwig acquired through inheritance in 1788), the secularization of church property and Ludwig's purchases, particularly the BOISSERÉE collection (purchased in 1827). Ludwig I also founded the Neue Pinakothek (1846–53; destr. World War II; rebuilt 1975–81), built by AUGUST VON VOIT and containing contemporary paintings; and the Glyptothek (1816–30; rest. 1972; *see* KLENZE, LEO VON, fig. 1), the museum of Classical sculpture. The Bayerisches Nationalmuseum was founded in 1853 by Maximilian II, and the private collection of 19th-century painting assembled by ADOLF FRIEDRICH VON SCHACK was later opened to the public.

The Kunstverein founded in 1824 became an important centre for genre and landscape painting. The city's first academic salon had been held in 1788 (*see* §II, 1 above), and the Akademie mounted fairly regular exhibitions in the first half of the 19th century. By the 1850s, however, Munich's numerous and self-confident independent artists were gaining greater influence, and in 1858 they joined with the Akademie and the Kunstverein in organizing Germany's important first national art exhibition. The responsibility for salons was later transferred from the Akademie to the Künstlergenossenschaft, the main artists' society, which organized an international show in 1863. Particularly important for Munich's reputation was the second international salon held in 1869, which included work by the Barbizon school, Courbet and Manet. The 1860s, 1870s and 1880s were the heyday of the Munich school. Artistic activity benefited from the strength of the local economy, and from the 1860s dealers (Ackermann, Fleischmann, Heinemann and others) became increasingly active alongside the Kunstverein and the salons in the Munich Glaspalast (1853–4; by Voit; destr. 1931). WIL-HELM LEIBL, FRANZ DUVENECK and other important Realists were active during the 1870s. By the death of Ludwig II (1886) there were almost a thousand painters and sculptors resident in the city, headed by the genre specialists FRANZ VON DEFREGGER (see fig. 4), Wilhelm von Diez (1839–1907) and Eduard Grützner (*b* 1846), and the portraitists FRANZ VON LENBACH and Friedrich August von Kaulbach (1850–1920).

During the regency (1886–1912) of Prince Luitpold that followed the death of Ludwig II, Munich faced both competition from Berlin and other centres and uncertainties about the international market. These concerns, combined with tensions within the Künstlergenossenschaft, led to the formation in April 1892 of Germany's first Secession (*see* SECESSION, §1), the Verein Bildender Künstler Münchens. From 1893 it held one or more exhibitions a year, independently of the Glaspalast salons. Although the Secession became increasingly conservative, its foundation began a process of fragmentation within the art community that continued until World War I. Other groups included the Freie Vereinigung (1904), Neu-Dachau (1897), PHALANX (1901), the Juryfreien (1907), the NEUE KÜNSTLERVEREINIGUNG MÜNCHEN (1909), the BLAUE REITER (1911–14) and the New Secession

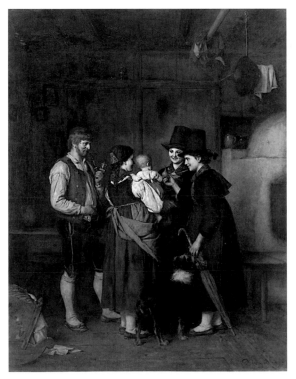

4. Franz von Defregger: *The Visit*, oil on canvas, 930×720 mm, 1875 (Munich, Neue Pinakothek)

(1913). (*See also* STEFFAN, JOHANN GOTTFRIED, and, SCHOLLE, DIE.) Both the Secession and later also the avant-garde groups around FRANZ MARC and Vasily Kandinsky (*see* KANDINSKY, VASILY) were linked with the modern graphic and applied arts movement that began in the mid-1890s and was associated with such illustrated papers as *Jugend*, founded in 1895 by GEORG HIRTH, and Albert Langen's *Simplicissimus* (1896); such organizations as the Vereinigte Werkstätte (1897–8); and such private schools as that started by HERMANN OBRIST and WILHELM VON DEBSCHITZ in 1901–2. The DEUTSCHER WERKBUND was founded in Munich in 1907. Nevertheless, painting continued to dominate the scene, although Germany's most important sculptor, Adolf von Hildebrand, lived in Munich between 1891 and 1921 (*see also* HAHN, HERMANN). By 1914 the city was Germany's largest centre for the export of pictures and part of an increasingly integrated national and international market, hence the ability of Kandinsky and his friends to work in Bavaria, while from 1912 showing and selling their pictures mainly through their Berlin dealer Herwarth Walden.

Ludwig II's lack of interest in the royal collections and his heavy expenditure on buildings had necessitated increasing state financial support of museums during the 1880s. Yet rising art prices (partly caused by vigorous buying by museums all over Germany), shortage of space, difficulties with Parliament and the insistence of local artists that state funds be spent mainly on their work hindered the development of a consistent purchasing policy. Nevertheless, HUGO VON TSCHUDI during his brief (1909–11) and controversial period as director of the Bayerische Staatsgemäldesammlungen thoroughly reorganized the collections and, with the help of private donors, acquired major Realist and Impressionist works that consolidated the international reputation of the Neue Pinakothek.

After World War I Munich lost its cosmopolitan atmosphere, and, with exports and tourism greatly reduced, plans for new galleries and exhibition facilities were shelved. The 1920s were overshadowed by post-war political and economic upheavals, the market was sluggish and the art community divided. Many artists left Munich for Berlin, where the dominant mode was less conservative, although in Munich representatives of NEUE SACH-LICHKEIT such as Alexander Kanoldt (1881–1939), Georg Schrimpf, Christian Schad and Wilhelm Heise (1892–1965) were associated with such groups as the Juryfreien (1928) and the New Secession. In 1929 a municipal gallery, the Lenbachhaus, opened in Lenbach's former villa (completed 1891); in 1931 the Glaspalast was destroyed by fire. During the Nazi period Hitler, who liked conventional Munich art, such as that of Eduard Grützner (*b* 1846) and CARL SPITZWEG, made the city Germany's artistic capital. Its status was symbolized by the new Haus der Kunst (1933–7) by Paul Ludwig Troost, opened with elaborate pageantry on 18 July 1937. State patronage and a reviving private art market brought prosperity to officially approved artists, but radical tendencies were banned, and all pre-Nazi artists' organizations were eventually disbanded. One positive achievement was the establishment in 1938 of the Dörner Institut for research into painting materials and techniques.

After 1945 many old organizations reappeared, and new ones (the Neue Gruppe, the Neue Künstlergenossenschaft) were founded. Links with the USA were created by exhibitions in the Haus der Kunst (where Munich's main annual salons were later also held) and in the Amerikahaus; such circles as ZEN 49 (established 1949) became points of contact with abstract movements in Europe and the USA. Since the 1950s Munich has become a city of international importance as a centre of the art market. Museum collections broken up by the Nazis have been reconstituted and expanded using public, private and commercial funds, and wartime destruction has been gradually made good. The restored Alte Pinakothek reopened in 1957, and a new gallery by Alexander von Branca, completed in 1981, replaced the completely destroyed Neue Pinakothek; in the 1990s the Moderne Staatsgalerie of 20th-century art still remained temporarily housed in a wing of Troost's Haus der Kunst. The municipal gallery in the Lenbachhaus, greatly enriched by large donations of works by Kandinsky, Marc, GABRIELE MÜNTER and their friends, regularly hosts major exhibitions of 19th-century, 20th-century and contemporary art.

BIBLIOGRAPHY

H. Ludwig: *Münchener Malerei im 19. Jahrhundert* (Munich, 1978)
P. Weiss: *Kandinsky in Munich: The Formative Jugendstil Years* (Princeton, NJ, 1979)
Die Münchener Schule, 1850–1914 (exh. cat., Munich, Haus Kst, 1979)
Die zwanziger Jahre in München (exh. cat., ed. C. Stolz; Munich, Stadtmus., 1979)
R. Lenman: 'A Community in Transition: Painters in Munich, 1886–1914', *Cent. Eur. Hist.*, xv (1982), pp. 3–33
M. Makela: *The Munich Secession: Art and Artists in Turn of the Century Munich* (Princeton, NJ, 1990)
R. Lenman: *Die Kunst, die Macht und das Geld* (Frankfurt am Main, 1994)

ROBIN LENMAN

III. Centre of production.

1. GOLD AND SILVER. The rapid expansion of the city after its foundation in 1158 and the patronage of the ruling house of Wittelsbach encouraged goldsmiths to move to Munich in the Middle Ages. Regulations concerning goldsmiths dating from 1365 are related to those governing Viennese goldsmiths, and there were also links between craftsmen in Munich and those in the nearby towns of Augsburg, Nuremberg, Ulm, Regensburg, Salzburg and Bozen (now Bolzano). Among the earliest surviving goldsmiths' works made in Munich are a reliquary monstrance and a reliquary in the form of a cross that were donations from Duke John II of Bavaria (*reg* 1375–97) to the Benedictine abbey at Andechs (*in situ*). Among the medieval silver belonging to the city council are two goblets (Munich, Stadtmus.) with the coat of arms of the city of Munich in enamel by Gabriel Graispach (*d* 1472). Two ornaments (Munich, Stadtmus.) from a marksman's chain with Bavarian coats of arms in enamel are dated 1463 and 1473.

Albert V, Duke of Bavaria (*see* WITTELSBACH, §I(3)), fond of splendour, a collector and patron who had a particular interest in goldsmithing, founded the Bavarian Schatzkammer in Munich. Outstanding immigrant artists, from north Germany in particular, including Jörg Stain from Königsberg (now Kaliningrad), Albrect Krauss from

Prussia, Hans Reimer from Schwerin, Hans Schwechenmacher from Hamburg, Eckhart Vollmann from Lüneburg and Isaak Melper, who was apprenticed in Berlin, as well as the artistic influence of the court painter Hans Mielich, developed Munich as an important centre of goldsmithing. One important piece from this period is a magnificent standing-cup by Hans Reimer (*fl* 1555; *d* 1604) made of gold and enamel and set with gemstones (Munich, Residenz). This tradition of magnificence was continued by the succeeding dukes. One of the finest examples of goldsmithing of this period is the reliquary (Munich, Residenz) created for Albert's successor, William V, Duke of Bavaria, a statuette of *St George* made of gold, enamel and gemstones. It may have been designed by Friedrich Sustris; like Pieter Candid, he was inspired by the Italian and Flemish Renaissance styles and was a pre-eminent artist at the court of William V. Hans von Schwanenburg (*d* 1597), a Dutchman, is recorded as Court Goldsmith in 1591, and his compatriot Paulus van Vianen was made a member of the guild of goldsmiths despite the opposition of native masters.

The Reiche Kapelle erected by Maximilian I, Elector of Bavaria, in 1607 was largely furnished and equipped with plate (*in situ*) by goldsmiths in Munich. Italian grotesque ornament is combined with such indigenous elements as scrolling in high relief. After the Thirty Years War (1618–48), the court, which was under Italian influence, commissioned mainly table silver to replace destroyed pieces and jewellery. In the reign of Maximilian II Emanuel, Elector of Bavaria, the court was modelled on that of Louis XIV; there was continued prosperity, but for the first time most commissions were given to goldsmiths in Augsburg. The Court Jeweller, Johann Strobel (*fl* 1666–1703), however, had large orders for *Gnadenpfennige* ('grace' pennies, decorated coins, usually of gold, awarded as a decoration, especially in the 17th century), portrait snuff-boxes and jewellery. The activities of the guild of goldsmiths in Munich were revived by the arrival of several goldsmiths from Bregenz, for example Franz Kessler, who was active in Munich between 1664 and 1717; the change of style in the Baroque period is reflected in his work, for example his bust of *St Korbinian* (1685; Freising, SS Maria and Korbinian), of which mostly ecclesiastical silver has been preserved.

Hard-pressed by competition from court artists and imported goods, the guild of goldsmiths tried to gain a monopoly of the craft in Munich in the 18th century, and a distinction was made between the operations of goldsmiths and silversmiths for the first time in 1738. The south German Rococo was the predominant style, for example in the four busts of saints by Joseph Friedrich Canzler (*fl* 1743–56), based on models by Ignaz Günther, in silver rocaille frames (Munich, Bürgersaal). At the end of the 18th century the Empire style emanating from France became popular in Munich. The Napoleonic Wars, however, resulted in a decline in the use of luxury wares. Gold- and silverwork produced in the Biedermeier and Historismus periods in the early and mid-19th century was of local importance only. In the 20th century Franz Richert (*b* 1904) and his student Hermann Jünger (*b* 1928) were notable in the development of goldsmithing as a subject of study in art schools.

BIBLIOGRAPHY

M. Frankenburger: *Die Alt-Münchner Goldschmiede und ihre Kunst* (Munich, 1912)

U. Krempel: 'Augsburger und Münchner Emailarbeiten des Manierismus: Aus dem Besitz der Bayerischen Herzöge Albrecht V, Wilhelm V und Maximilian I', *Münch. Jb. Bild. Kst*, n. s. 2, xviii (1967), pp. 111–86

FABIAN STEIN

2. TAPESTRY. Tapestries were made in Munich between 1604 and 1615 and from 1718 to 1818 (*see* GERMANY, §XI, 3(iii) and (iv)).

☐

3. OBJECTS OF VERTU. For centuries members of the ruling house of Wittelsbach (*see* WITTELSBACH, §I) were active as patrons and collectors of precious gems and other objects of vertu, which have been preserved mainly in the Schatzkammer of the Residenz in Munich. The Wittelsbach collections served 19th-century jewellers as models. Decorative art in Munich flourished particularly during the reign of King Ludwig II of Bavaria (*reg* 1864–86), who ordered a large amount of jewellery, orders, watches, Easter eggs and similar objects of vertu, magnificently decorated with gemstones and enamel. Like the goldsmiths favoured by the royal court—Gottfried Merk (1817–90), Adam Hausinger (1820–1908) and Julius Elchinger (1842–92)—most jewellers in Munich made individual pieces by hand that differed markedly from the industrial mass production of other German towns, such as Pforzheim, Hanau and Schwäbisch Gmünd. As well as the French-influenced neo-Baroque style (e.g. Karl Blum: pendant, 1882; Pforzheim, Schmuckmus.) that Ludwig II preferred, the neo-Renaissance style, with its characteristic *plique à jour* ornament and use of coloured gemstones and pearls, predominated in late 19th-century ornament in Munich.

The influence of reform movements such as the Arts and Crafts movements in England, France and Belgium in particular led to a fundamental change of style shortly before the end of the century. Historicism was replaced by a fanciful, decorative naturalism, drawing a wealth of motifs from indigenous flora and fauna. The jeweller Karl Rothmüller (1860–1930) especially achieved an international reputation with pendants, brooches (1905; Pforzheim, Schmuckmus.) and rings; as small-scale, sculptural compositions of great artistic merit notable for their sophisticated touches of colour, his work was compared at the time with the creations of René Lalique. Besides Rothmüller, Nikolaus Thallmayr (1875–1925) was also prominent at important international exhibitions of the time, where his belt buckles and hatpins in plant forms, often made from gilt silver (vermeil) in yellow and green shades, attracted the admiration of his contemporaries. Objects made by such designers as Friedrich Adler (1878–(?)1942), Gertraud von Schnellenbühel (1878–1959) and Fritz Schmoll von Eisenwerth (1883–1963), who emerged from the Lehr- und Versuchs-Ateliers für Angewandte und Freie Kunst of what was known as the Debschitz school, occupy an important place in *Jugendstil* decorative art both in and beyond Munich. Their brilliantly abstract necklaces, pendants and brooches give vivid expression to the decorative charm of the forms and forces of nature.

BIBLIOGRAPHY

Katalog 125 Jahre bayerischer Kunstgewerbeverein (exh. cat., Munich, Stadtmus., 1976)

H. Eisenwerth [Schmoll]: 'Die Münchener Debschitz-Schule', *Kunstschulreform, 1900–1933*, ed. H. M. Wingler (Berlin, 1977), pp. 68–92

U. von Hase: *Schmuck in Deutschland und Österreich, 1895–1914: Symbolismus, Jugendstil, Neohistorismus* (Munich, 1977/*R* 1985)

L. Seelig: 'Gold und Silber, Bronze und Zink: Zur Metallkunst unter König Ludwig II', *Katalog König Ludwig II: Museum Herrenchiemsee*, ed. G. Hojer (Munich, 1986), pp. 95–125

K. B. Hiesinger, ed.: *Katalog der Meister des Münchner Jugendstils* (Munich, 1988)

G. Dry: *Katalog Münchner Schmuck, 1900–1940* (Munich, 1990)

MICHAEL KOCH

IV. Buildings.

1. Frauenkirche. 2. Residenz. 3. Schloss Nymphenburg.

1. FRAUENKIRCHE. In the first half of the 13th century the Marienkapelle was replaced by a second parish church, the Marienkirche, which was an aisled basilica with two west towers and no transept. In the first quarter of the 14th century the sanctuary was converted into a long chancel. In 1468, however, the city council decided to replace the church. JÖRG VON HALSBACH was appointed municipal architect charged with the construction of the new Frauenkirche, a brick building 109 m long. The walls and piers were built by 1473, and Mathes Roriczer was consulted over the construction of the vault, as were, in 1474, Moritz Ensinger, Conrad Roriczer, Friedrich Sphys of Ingolstadt and Michael Sallinger of Eggenfelden. The roof was erected 1477–8 by Heinrich von Straubing. The towers were complete by Jörg's death (1488), and the church was consecrated in 1494. The bulbous cupolas were added in 1524–5. When the see of Freising was transferred to Munich (1821) the Frauenkirche became a cathedral. Serious war damage (1943–5) necessitated restoration (1947–57), involving a new vault and the reconstruction in reinforced concrete of the bulbous cupolas.

The cathedral is a long, aisled hall church with ten nave bays and an ambulatory, with high side chapels. The apse has a 5/10 formation, and the unified exterior has shallow pilasters. The powerful octagonal piers support a star vault in the nave. Of the few remaining Gothic fittings, the most important is the stained glass, much of which came from the old church, as did some of the carvings (*see also* GRASSER, ERASMUS). On the west wall is the grave slab of the architect.

See also KRUMPPER, HANS; SCHÖN, HEINRICH; and ROTTENHAMMER, HANS, I, §2.

BIBLIOGRAPHY

K. Abenthum: *Der Münchner Liebfrauendom nach seiner Wiederherstellung* (Munich, 1966)

E. von Witzleben: *Die Frauenkirche in München: Glasmalereien einer bedeutenden Kirche* (Augsburg, 1969)

N. Knopp: *Die Frauenkirche zu München und St Peter* (Stuttgart, 1970)

N. Lieb and H.-J. Sauermost: *Münchens Kirchen* (Munich, 1973), pp. 53–68

FRIEDRICH KOBLER

2. RESIDENZ. This complex, built between the 16th century and the 19th, exemplifies every architectural style from the late Renaissance to Neo-classicism and is one of the outstanding examples of court culture in Europe. In the design of the 16th-century building the Wittelsbachs were the first German princes to give display precedence

over defence, making the transition from the fortified medieval castle to the modern residential palace. Until 1918 the Residenz was the seat of the Wittelsbach dukes, electors and kings.

The Neuveste (*see* §I, 1 above), built after the burghers' uprising of 1385, formed the basis of the complex development of the Residenz. In 1559–60 Duke Albert V (*see* WITTELSBACH, §I(3)) had a ballroom (destr.) built at the south-east corner of the Neuveste. Of much greater importance, however, was the building from 1569 of the Antiquarium (see fig. 5). The Augsburg architects Bernhard and Simon ZWITZEL, assisted by the ducal architect WILHELM EGCKL, used designs by Jacopo Strada in this 69 m barrel-vaulted chamber, the largest and most important secular structure of the German Renaissance. It housed the ducal library in the upper rooms and ancient sculptures on the ground floor.

In 1580–81 Duke William V had a two-storey building erected on the Schwabinger Gasse as a residence for the widowed Duchess Anna. Residential rooms replaced the library on the upper storey of the Antiquarium, the floor of which was lowered by Friedrich Sustris (*see* SUSTRIS, (2)) in 1586. These rooms were linked *c.* 1590 to the Schwarzer Saal, and *c.* 1600 the Schwarzer Saal staircase, one of the earliest examples north of the Alps of an Italian staircase with opposed flights, was constructed. William's most important contribution, however, was the Grottenhof building built by Sustris in 1581–6 around a quadrangle, south-west of the Antiquarium. Of the two arcaded halls, only the eastern one (with Mannerist grotesque ornamentation, mosaic and shell facing and wall painting) survived the alterations (*c.* 1730) by François de Cuvilliés I. The Gartensaal (*c.* 1581) by Sustris was replaced in 1726–31 by the Ahnengalerie. The Grottenhof wing was enhanced by artistically designed gardens ornamented with bronzes. In subsequent years the Grottenhof building was extended towards the Schwabinger Gasse, for example by the Erbprinz buildings (*c.* 1590).

With Elector Maximilian I one of the most important periods in the construction of the Residenz began. First the new Hofkapelle (1601–3) and the lavishly decorated Reiche Kapelle (consecrated 1607; probably extended after 1609 by Hans Krumpper) were built. Then the Elector had the separate buildings linked by various wings to form the inner courtyards characteristic of the whole complex. The linking of the Antiquarium with the southern parts of the Neuveste resulted in the octagonal Brunnenhof with the clock-tower (1612–15) to the north-west, while the construction of the Breite Treppe, the Alter Herkulessaal and the Hofdamenstock created the former 'Jägergassl' bordering the Kapellenhof. North of this was built Maximilian's next and most important contribution: the Kaiserhof. On the upper floors of the west and east wings were the main living quarters: the Steinzimmer (west wing) and the Trierzimmer (east wing). On the north side was an imperial wing containing the ceremonial Kaisersaal, Vierschimmelsaal, named after a ceiling painting (destr.) of *Apollo in his Chariot Drawn by Four White Horses*, and Kaisertreppe (1616), one of the first monumental staircases outside Italy. The Apothekenhof was surrounded by the Grosser Hirschgang (1614; the corridor

5. Munich, Residenz, the Antiquarium by Wilhelm Egckl, after 1569

linking the imperial wing with the Neuveste) and the Charlottengang (1612).

The buildings of the imperial wing provided the basis for a unified west façade (1611–19). Until the 19th century this was the only ornamental façade of the structure, consisting of two main floors with rectangular and round windows providing lighting from above, a mezzanine and an immense saddle roof. The 33-bay façade is divided by the niche containing Hans Krumpper's *Patrona Boiariae* (1616) and two bronze figures above the monumental portals. The whole exterior of the Residenz was executed in brick, enhanced with contrasting plasterwork, painting and ashlar. To the north a new Hofgarten was laid out in 1613–17, to plans by HEINRICH SCHÖN.

Maximilian I's successors made only slight changes, mainly concerning the interior. Maximilian II Emanuel commissioned changes from 1725, the Grottenhof being remodelled by de Cuvilliés in 1730–31; Charles refurbished the rooms damaged in the fire of 1729, the Reiche Zimmer and the Ahnengalerie (1730–37). The Grüne Galerie to the east of the present Königsbauhof was built in 1733–7. Its two-storey façade with round-arched windows is regarded as one of de Cuvilliés's most important works.

Under Elector Maximilian III Joseph the Kurfürstenzimmer (elector's rooms) above the Antiquarium were altered (1746–8) by Johann Baptist Gunetzrhainer (1692–1763) and again (1760–63) by de Cuvilliés. To replace the Georgssaal, destroyed by the Neuveste fire of 1750, the Elector had the Residenztheater (1750–53; now Cuvilliés-Theater; rebuilt 1957–8 in the Apothekentrakt), one of the finest Rococo theatre buildings, built to plans by de Cuvilliés (*see* WITTELSBACH, §I(10) and §I, 2 above).

During the reign of Maximilian IV Joseph the Hofgarten rooms (destr.) were incorporated into the imperial wing in 1799, the architect being Charles Pierre Puille (1731–1805). This involved eliminating the Kaisersaal and the Vierschimmelsaal (now reconstructed). The Alter Herkulessaal (now the Max-Joseph-Saal) was rebuilt by Andreas Gärtner in 1803. Probably between 1803 and 1809 the west part of the north front of the Residenz was given a façade of restrained simplicity. South of the Cuvilliés-Theater, outside the Residenz complex itself, the royal Hof- und Nationaltheater was erected by Karl von Fischer (1811–18; destr. 1823; rebuilt by Leo von Klenze from 1823 to 1825).

The Residenz acquired its definitive form under Ludwig I. Between 1826 and 1835 LEO VON KLENZE created the classicist Königsbau on the model of Florentine Renaissance palaces; this was the residence of the king, which closed the south side of the complex facing the Max-Joseph-Platz. The monumental two- and three-storey façade with rustication and round-arched windows is articulated on the upper floors by Ionic and Corinthian pilasters. On the ground floor are the Nibelung rooms decorated with monumental paintings of the *Nibelungenlied* (1827–34, 1843–67) by Julius Schnorr von Carolsfeld with Friedrich von Olivier and Wilhelm Hauschild. Between 1826 and 1837 the Allerheiligen-Hofkirche was built to plans by Klenze on the south side of the Residenz.

The Grosser Hirschgang had to be demolished when Klenze extended (1832–42) the north side with the Festsaal wing. Its 252 m façade is articulated by two corner pavilions and a central block with projecting portico, adorned with statues by Ludwig von Schwanthaler. The Schlachtensaal, the ballroom and the Schönheitengalerie Ludwig I (from which paintings, by Joseph Karl Stieler, are now in Schloss Nymphenburg) had been added to the east wing before its destruction in 1944; the central building contained the throne room, on the site of which the modern Neuer Herkulessaal was built between 1952 and 1958. From 1837 to 1842 the façade system was continued along the east side of the Apothekenhof, where the Cuvilliés-Theater is now situated. Under Ludwig II a winter garden was erected (1866–8) on the roof of the Residenz by August von Voit, and this became world famous, although it was removed in 1897. The Residenz, heavily damaged in World War II, had been rebuilt by 1985.

For discussion of interior design and decoration *see* BARELLI, AGOSTINO; CUVILLIÉS, FRANÇOIS DE, I; EFFNER, JOSEF; FOLTZ, PHILIPP VON.

BIBLIOGRAPHY

R. Pallavicino: *I trionfi dell' architettura nella sontuosa residenza di Monaco descritti e rappresentati all' Altezza Seren. di Ferdinando Maria Duca dell' una e altra Baviera, Conte Palatino del Reno, Elettore del S.R.I. & C.* (Munich, 1667)

J. Schmidt: *Triumphierendes Wunder-Gebaew der Chur-Fuerstlichen Residenz zu München* (Munich, 1685)

C. Haeutle: *Geschichte der Residenz in München von ihren frühesten Zeiten bis herab zum Jahre 1777* (Leipzig, 1883)

Festschrift zur Eröffnung des Fest- und Konzertsaales in der Münchener Residenz am 3. März 1953 (Munich, 1953)

Vierte Festschrift zum Wiederaufbau der Residenz München (Munich, 1959)

H. Brunner, G. Hojer and L. Seelig: *Residenz München* (Munich, 1986) [official guide]

G. Hojer and L. Seelig: *Die Appartements Ludwigs I im Königsbau der Münchener Residenz* (Munich, 1986)

T. Walz, O. Meitinger and T. Beil: *Die Residenz zu München: Entstehung, Zerstörung, Wiederaufbau* (Munich, 1987)

3. SCHLOSS NYMPHENBURG. The extensive summer residence of the Bavarian electors and kings is one of the most individualistic but significant palaces in Europe, and its excellent decoration has remained almost intact. (*See also* NYMPHENBURG PORCELAIN FACTORY.)

On the birth in 1662 of his heir Maximilian Emanuel, Elector Ferdinand gave his wife, Henrietta Adelaide of Savoy (1636–76), some land for a palace west of Munich. In 1664 the foundation stone was laid for a villa suburbana in the Italian style, the 'Borgo delle Ninfe'. Under the direction of Agostino Barelli and from 1673 of Enrico Zuccalli, the central cubic block was erected, with domed pavilions linked to it by galleries. Its five storeys were separated by string courses; and for a short time it had a roof with dormers (removed 1678). A symmetrical external staircase with twin flights led to the central portal. An Italian garden lay to the east.

The internal arrangement has changed little. At the centre was the Steinerner Saal, adjoined by the electoral suites. Antonio Triva (1626–99), Joseph Werner II, Antonio Zanchi, Stefano Catani (*fl* 1669 and later) and others collaborated in the decorative paintings (destr.). Building work slackened on the electress's death and ceased in 1680, to be resumed only in 1701 when Maximilian II Emanuel returned from the Netherlands and commissioned Enrico Zuccalli to plan the next stage, directed from 1702 by Giovanni Antonio Viscardi. To the existing main building the Elector added two slightly projecting cubic side pavilions, probably on the foundations of the earlier ones, connected to the central pavilion by arcaded galleries. The loose linking of the buildings and the view of the park from the arcades and the passage through the socle storey of the middle building distinguish the Nymphenburg, as a garden-palace, from such closed structures as Versailles. Its models were not French, however, but Netherlandish, Maximilian II Emanuel's ideas having been influenced, in particular, by HET LOO (1685–92) at Apeldorn.

During the same period the middle pavilion was altered on both the town and the park side, the five middle bays being reduced to three and large, round arched windows added on the first and second floors (see fig. 6). Inside, arcades opened from the two rooms one above the other on the garden side, into the Steinerner Saal, which thus received more light. Articulated with colossal pilasters, the Steinerner Saal had a decorative scheme by Johann Anton Gumpp (1701–3; apparently replaced 1726 by paintings on leather [destr.] by Domenico Valeriani: *d* before 1771; and Giuseppe Valeriani: *d* 1761), similar to that in Schloss Lustheim (*see* SCHLEISSHEIM, SCHLOSS), showing scenes from the myth of Diana.

Further enlargement was delayed by the outbreak of the War of the Spanish Succession (1704) and fully resumed only in 1715, under Josef Effner. He converted the lesenes of the main pavilion into pilasters and on the garden side extended them to the cornice. The four bays

6. Schloss Nymphenburg, near Munich, view from the east

on either side of the central section were reduced to three, and large triangular pediments (removed 1826) were added above the three central bays. In 1715 16 Effner elaborated the interior and produced plans (unexecuted) for subsidiary buildings on each side. One of the first rooms to receive Régence panelling, by Johann Adam Pichler (*fl c.* 1716–61), was the north antcroom, from *c.* 1716. The Marstall (now Marstallmuseum) with courtiers' accommodation was built to the south (1716–19), the orangerie (1723–4) with other buildings to the north, while the galleries over the canals, which linked the whole complex together, were not constructed until 1739 and 1747. The gardens underwent modifications in 1701–4 by Charles Carbonet (*fl* 1700–15) and by DOMINIQUE GIRARD in 1715. Three pavilions (the Pagodenburg, the Badenburg and the Magdalenenklause) were designed by JOSEPH EFFNER, and the fourth and most important, the Amalienburg, by François de Cuvilliés I (for discussion and illustration *see* CUVILLIÉS, FRANÇOIS DE, I). Artists involved in the decoration of the pavilions included CHARLES-CLAUDE DUBUT, GUILLIELMUS DE GROF, Peter Jacob Horemans (*see* HOREMANS, (2)) and Johann Baptist Zimmermann (*see* ZIMMERMANN, (1)).

The long façades with middle and corner pavilions, the blind arcades and the segmental arched windows clearly show the influence of such French architects as Robert de Cotte and, especially, Germain Boffrand. A plan (after 1728) of 'Carlstadt', centred on the palace (*see* EFFNER, JOSEF), was produced under Elector Charles and realized only in the ten central pavilions, one of which accommodated the porcelain factory after 1761.

Under Elector Maximilian III Joseph, some rooms were altered and redecorated. The most important work of this phase is the decoration (1755–7) of the Steinerner Saal by Zimmermann and de Cuvilliés, focusing on Zimmerman's fresco *Nymphs Paying Homage to the Goddess Flora* (1755–7; *in situ*). The decoration of the Gartensaal and the Emporensaal was designed by de Cuvilliés.

From 1804 to 1823 the Baroque garden, made up of symmetrical groups of shrubbery, was extensively modified by FRIEDRICH LUDWIG VON SCKELL in the style of an English landscape garden. The last phase of alterations to the palace took place under Maximilian IV Joseph, who chose it as his favourite residence after he became king (1806). Karl Ludwig Puille (*d* 1858) began remodelling the rooms of the first pavilions to the north and south from 1806. In 1826 Klenze adapted the central building to the Neo-classical style.

BIBLIOGRAPHY
L. Hager: *Nymphenburg: Schloss, Park und Burgen* (Munich, 1955)
G. Hojer: 'Die Baugeschichte des Schlosses Nymphenburg' *Schloss Nymphenburg*, ed. F. Schlapper and others (Munich, 1972), pp. 108–16
M. Petzet: 'Entwürfe für Nymphenburg', *Zwischen Donau und Alpen: Festschrift für Norbert Lieb* (Munich, 1972), pp. 202–12
P. Vierl: 'Neue Erkenntnisse zur Baugeschichte des Schlosses Nymphenburg', *Jb. Bayer. Dkmlpf.*, xxix (1972–4), pp. 97–115
G. Hojer and E. D. Schmid: *Nymphenburg: Schloss, Park und Burgen* (Munich, 1975; rev. 16/1985) [official guide]
E. D. Schmid: *Nymphenburg: Schloss und Garten, Pagodenburg, Badenburg, Magdalenenklause, Amalienburg* (Munich, 1981)
D. von Frank: *Effners Pagodenburg* (Munich, 1985)
A. Bauer-Wild: *Die erste Bau- und Ausstattungsphase des Schlosses Nymphenburg, 1663–1680* (Munich, 1986)
G. von Deessen: *Die Badenburg im Park von Nymphenburg* (Munich, 1986)

JOSEF STRASSER

Munich Secession. *See* SECESSION, §1.

Munjang. *See* SŎNG SE-CH'ANG.

Munjong [Yi Ku; *cha* Huiji] (*b* 1414; *reg* 1450–52; *d* 1452). Korean king and calligrapher. The son of SEJONG, he was the fifth king of the Chosŏn dynasty (1392–1910). He was known for his learning and respect for scholarship; his interests ranged from Neo-Confucian philosophy to astronomy and mathematics. Munjong was famous for his calligraphy in the regular, clerical and grass scripts in the style of Zhao Mengfu (*see* ZHAO, (1)),the Chinese statesman, painter and calligrapher of the Yuan period (1279–1368). *Songsŏl-ch'e*, named after Zhao's sobriquet, was the most influential style of calligraphy in Korea for centuries. Occasionally Munjong also tried ink paintings. Although none of his works survive, it is recorded that he gave a painting of plum blossoms in snow to his brother, Prince Anp'yŏng (*see* YI YŎNG), the most talented of Sejong's sons.

BIBLIOGRAPHY
Kim Yong-yun: *Hanguk sŏhwa inmyŏng sasŏ* [Biographical dictionary of Korean painters and calligraphers] (Seoul, 1959), p. 66
Kim Ki-sŭng: *Hanguk sŏyesa* [History of Korean calligraphy] (Seoul, 1975), pp. 387–8

YI SŎNG-MI

Munkács [Munkats]. Name applied to a type of cast-iron ware produced until the end of the 19th century at Munkács (Munkats), Hungary (now Mukachevo, Ukraine). The first foundry was established around 1670, but the peak period of production was at the beginning of the 19th century. Before the employment (*c.* 1848) of the Hungarian sculptor András Schlossel (*d* 1874), the types of product made were influenced by the styles and forms used by ironworkers in Berlin, Gleiwitz and Mariazell. The foundry produced a wide variety of small ornaments and articles for everyday use, including vases, dishes, candlesticks and animal and human figures in the Neo-classical and Gothic Revival styles, for example a bust of *Lajos Kossuth, Governor of Hungary* (1848; Budapest, Mus. Applied A.). The work produced there is marked with the name MUNKÁTS, later MUNKÁCS. Cast-iron goods were also made in the surrounding towns of Munkács-Szelesztó and Munkács-Frigyesfalva (both now part of Mukachevo).

BIBLIOGRAPHY
L. Pusztai: *Magyar öntöttvasművesség* [Hungarian cast iron] (Budapest, 1978)

FERENC BATÁRI

Munkacsi, Martin [Marmorstein, Martin] (*b* Kolozsvar, Munkacsi, Hungary [now Cluj-Napoca, Romania], 18 May 1896; *d* New York, 14 July 1963). American photographer. From 1911 to 1913 he worked as an apprentice house painter before moving to Budapest in 1913. From 1914 to 1921 he was a reporter for *Az Est*, *Pesti Napló* and *Szinházi Elet*. A self-taught photographer, in 1921 he began to contribute photographs, as well as reports, on sport to *Az Est* and also photographs to the weekly review *Theatre Life*. In 1923 he was awarded a three-year contract with Ullstein Verlag in Berlin, during which time he contributed to *Berliner Illustrierte Zeitung*, *Die Dame*, *Koralle*, *Uhu* and other Ullstein publications, travelling widely abroad. From 1930 to 1933 he worked as a freelance photographer, contributing to *The Studio*, *Harper's Bazaar*, *Deutsche Lichtbild*, *Photographie* and others, producing such striking images as *Mid-Morning Coffee Break* (1933; see White and Esten, p. 17) for the *Deutsche Lichtbild*.

In 1934, with Nazism on the rise, Munkacsi emigrated to America, where he worked as a fashion photographer for *Harper's Bazaar*, *Town and Country*, *Pictorial Review*

and *Life Magazine* until 1940. He had first visited the USA in 1933 on a contract for the *Berliner Illustrierte Zeitung* and had been offered a fashion assignment by Carmel Snow, editor of *Harper's Bazaar*. This resulted in the photograph of *Lucille Brokaw* (1933; New York, Liza Cowan and Sharon Mumby priv. col., see White and Esten, p. 25). Taken outdoors with the model running, this was a revolutionary departure from the static studio images of traditional fashion photography, and showed how effectively the action technique he had used for sports could be applied to other subjects. From 1940 to 1946 he worked for *Ladies Home Journal* and thereafter as a freelance photographer, though a heart attack in 1943 severely restricted his activities. In this latter period he published several books, including the autobiography *Fool's Apprentice* (1945) and *Munkacsi: Nudes* (1951).

WRITINGS
Fool's Apprentice (New York, 1945)

PHOTOGRAPHS
Munkacsi: Nudes (New York, 1951)

BIBLIOGRAPHY
N. White and J. Esten: *Style in Motion: Munkacsi Photographs of the '20s, '30s and '40s* (New York, 1979)

□

Munkácsy [Lieb], **Mihály** [Michael] **(von)** (*b* Munkács [now Mukachevo, Ukraine], 20 Feb 1844; *d* Endenich, nr Bonn, 1 May 1900). Hungarian painter. Orphaned at an early age, he learnt carpentry but, even as an apprentice, was a keen draughtsman. He took regular lessons in Gyula from an itinerant painter, Elek Szamossy (1826–88). After going to Pest in 1863 he spent half a year at the Akademie der Bildenden Künste in Vienna in 1864, where he befriended László Paál and János Jankó (1833–96), whose drawings later inspired several of his genre paintings. His Biedermeier-style *Outlaw in Sorrow* (Debrecen, Déri Mus.) dates from 1865. From 1866 he spent two years in Munich, first attending classes by Sándor Wagner (1838–1919) at the Akademie, then at Adam Eugen's private school for painting battle-scenes. Wilhelm Leibl's influence dates from about this time. Munkácsy changed his name from Lieb in 1868, after which he spent three years in Düsseldorf in the circle of Ludwig Knaus. There he became accustomed to using a bitumenized base, which still undermines the state of many of his pictures.

In the large-scale study (Budapest, N.G.) for *Yawning Apprentice* (1868–9; untraced) Munkácsy had already abandoned the Romanticism that characterizes his early work. His later figure-studies are also large, but the scale is always appropriate. In 1870 he won a gold medal at the Paris Salon for *Death Row* (Budapest, N.G.), which made him famous almost overnight. He prepared several portrait-like sketches for this picture, as well as studies suggesting different compositional solutions. This painting displays for the first time his outstanding ability to produce dramatic tension through the skilful juxtaposition of dark and light colours. His depiction of character is equally strong and is full of psychological tension. His most significant picture with several figures is *Lint Makers* (1872; Budapest, N.G.), a nostalgic evocation of the fight against the Habsburgs in 1848, where women sitting at a long table make lint while listening to the stories of a wounded soldier. Apart from using the 'romantic outlaw' type popular in contemporary literature, Munkácsy also drew inspiration from his own youth and childhood experiences. The critical tone of his figure studies became sharpest in two-figure compositions such as *Woman Churning* and *Parting* (both 1872–3; Budapest, N.G.).

From 1871 Munkácsy lived in Paris, and after his marriage to the widow of Baron De Marches his life took a different turn. The only urban painting with a critical tone in this period is his *Pawn Shop* (1874; ex-Met, New York; figure study in Budapest, N.G., see fig.). He painted several portraits and at least 50 drawing-room interiors, or perhaps more, for by this time he sold his pictures almost as soon as they were finished. He had now developed a virtuoso technique, and he still painted excellent flower still-lifes as preparatory sketches, though his character portrayal became lacklustre. In 1878 he signed a ten-year contract with the art dealer Charles Sedelmeyer, to whom he committed all his paintings and whom he even agreed to consult about the choice of themes. The head studies (Budapest, N.G.) for his *Milton* (1878; New York, Pub. Lib.) are successful portraits, while the final large composition, where the blind poet is dictating to his daughter, has the air of theatricality recommended by Sedelmeyer. It was also on Sedelmeyer's initiative that Munkácsy painted *Christ Before Pilate* (1881) and *Golgotha* (1884; both Budapest, N.G.). After consulting Ary Renan for his interpretation of the figure of Christ, he decided to treat the theme as an everyday situation. The considerably less

successful *Ecce homo* (1896; Debrecen, Déri Mus.) completed this trilogy of paintings on the life of Christ.

Following the death of Hans Makart, Munkácsy was commissioned to paint the 100 sq. m stairwell ceiling of the Kunsthistorisches Museum in Vienna, which he finished in 1890. In many aspects this work is unresolved, partly due to his lack of experience in such tasks and partly to the anachronistic nature of the subject, the *Victory of Light over Darkness*. Munkácsy was also commissioned at this time to paint a picture for one of the rooms in the new Parliament building in Budapest. This painting, *Taking the Land*, which refers to the conquest of the Carpathian Basin by Magyar tribes in the 9th century, was finished in 1893 and subsequently exhibited in Paris and Budapest. The picture was severely criticized, not for its lack of quality, but for its particular historical perspective, which ignored the national tensions of Central Europe.

Only a small fraction of Munkácsy's portrait work is known, though a small study of the painter *László Paál* (1877; Budapest, N.G.), one of his masterpieces, suggests new sensibilities in Munkácsy's realism. It is equally difficult to comprehend why Munkácsy rejected landscape painting, for among his very few landscapes are several masterpieces, such as *Dusty Road* (Budapest, N.G.), which displays a Turner-like sensitivity. Munkácsy's paintings of forest edges and tree-lined alleys are close to the later mature style of the Barbizon school and Courbet, as in *Alley* and *Park in Colpach* (both 1886; Budapest, N.G.). One of his last works was a painting of the novel theme of an illuminated landscape: *Parc Monceau at Night* (1895; Budapest, N.G.).

In his lifetime Munkácsy enjoyed great international popularity, partly due to his personal accomplishments and partly due to the promotions of his dealer. He never took pupils and he had no followers. Though he was sometimes hailed as the greatest painter of his age, his work is sometimes regarded as merely a belated condensation of Academicism.

Mihály Munkácsy: figure study for *Pawn Shop*, oil on canvas, 920×723 mm, 1874 (Budapest, Hungarian National Gallery)

WRITINGS

Souvenirs: L'Enfance, foreword B. d'Argent (Paris, 1897)
Emlékezéseim [My recollections] (Budapest, 1950)
Z. Farkas, ed.: *Munkácsy M. válogatott levelei* [Selected letters of M. Munkácsy] (Budapest, 1952)

BIBLIOGRAPHY

D. Malonyay: *Munkácsy Mihály élete és munkái* [The life and works of Mihály Munkácsy] (Budapest, 1898)
C. Sedelmeyer: *Michael von Munkácsy* (Paris, 1914)
Munkácsy Mihály emlékkiállítás [Mihály Munkácsy: commemorative exhibition] (exh. cat. cd. I. Oltványi; Budapest, A. Hall, 1952)
L. Végvári: *Munkácsy Mihály élete és művei* [The life and works of Mihály Munkácsy] (Budapest, 1958) [comprehensive monograph with complete list of works]
L. S. Alyoshina: *Mihály Munkácsy* (Moscow, 1960)
G. Perneczky: *Munkácsy Mihály* (Budapest, 1970)
S. Kürti Katalin: *Munkácsy Mihály Krisztus-trilógiája* [Mihály Munkácsy's Christ trilogy] (Budapest, 1989)

NÓRA ARADI

Munnichhoeven [Monnickes; Münichhoven; Munnichofen; Munnichhoven; Munnekus; Munniks], **Hendrik** [Hendrick] (*fl* Utrecht, 1622; *d* Stockholm, Aug 1664). Dutch painter. In 1622 he was living in Utrecht, where he became dean of the painters' guild in 1643; none of his works of this period is known. In November 1648 he was in Prague, in the service of Count Magnus Gabriel De la

Gardie, and in 1650 he arrived in Stockholm and entered the service of Queen Christina. An inventory of that year records mythological works, depicting *Hercules*, *Venus and Cupid* and *Mars*, reflecting the Italian influence of his artistic environment in Utrecht. He did not sign his paintings, and his known oeuvre has been compiled through archival evidence and stylistic comparison, comprising exclusively the portraits he executed for the Swedish court and aristocracy. His most important achievement was the double full-length portrait of *Magnus Gabriel De la Gardie and his Wife, Countess Palatine Maria Euphrosyne* (1652; Stockholm, Nmus.; exh. Mariefred, Gripsholm Slott) showing the couple on a terrace; stylistically the portrait has a realistic character when compared with the Baroque tendencies inspired by Anthony van Dyck that were just being introduced in Sweden. But Munnichhoeven tried to keep up with the new trends, as can be seen from his portrait of *Beata Elisabeth von Königsmarck* (1654; Bålsta, Skoklosters Slott), in which floral symbolism contributes to the impression of sweet melancholy.

BIBLIOGRAPHY

A. Bredius: *Künstler-Inventare: II*, Quellenstudien zur holländischen Kunstgeschichte, vi (The Hague, 1916)

K. E. Steneberg: *Kristinatidens måleri* [Painters of the time of Christina] (Malmö, 1955)

ALLAN ELLENIUS

Munnings, Sir **Alfred (James)** (*b* Mendham, Suffolk, 8 Oct 1878; *d* Dedham, Essex, 17 July 1959). English painter. He grew up in the countryside of the Waveney Valley and left school at the age of 14 for a six-year apprenticeship with a firm of lithographers in Norwich, where he came to excel as a lithographic draughtsman while also studying painting in evening classes. He left the printing business after his apprenticeship, supporting himself through freelance poster work and occasional sales of paintings. The loss of sight in his right eye in an accident in 1898 did not deflect his determination to paint, and in 1899 two of his pictures were shown at the Royal Academy Summer Exhibition.

A visit to the Lavenham Horse Fair sparked off Munnings's lifelong fascination with painting horses and stimulated his first major composition, *A Suffolk Horse Fair* (1901; Dedham, Essex, Munnings A. Mus.). Country fairs became a frequent subject, and *A Gala Day* (1902; Preston, Harris Mus. & A.G.) shows a bright palette, suggestive brushwork and an acute eye for the characterization of the figures. For short periods in 1902 and 1903 Munnings studied at the Académie Julian in Paris, where he received little tuition but drew inspiration from the paintings he saw there. Still based in the Suffolk countryside he continued to paint landscapes and scenes from local life, occasionally in watercolour but mainly in oils. *The Path to the Orchard* (1908; Dedham, Essex, Munnings A. Mus.) reveals the fluid use of paint that became characteristic of his mature style. In 1909 Munnings visited Munich, where he was struck by the broad brushwork and sense of movement in a painting by the German painter Henrich von Zügel (1850–1941); he endeavoured to achieve similar effects in works such as *The Ford* (1910; Dedham, Essex, Munnings A. Mus.). In 1911 he joined the artists' colony at Newlyn, Cornwall, where he shared the common enthusiasm for painting directly from nature.

His subject-matter there continued to centre on horses and also on gypsy life, as in *The Departure of the Hoppickers* (1913; Melbourne, N.G. Victoria).

Munnings was turned down for active service in World War I but was sent to France in 1918 to record the actions of the Canadian Cavalry Brigade. *General Seeley on Horseback* (1918; Ottawa, Can. War Mus.), exhibited after the war, created a demand for his equestrian portraits. In 1920 he painted the Belvoir Hunt, notably in his *Belvoir Point-to-point Meeting on Borrowby Hill* (1920; Paul Mellon priv. col., see Booth, p. 31), which shows an unerring sensitivity to light and landscape and a mastery of suggested movement. This painting and other similar subjects formed a successful exhibition at the Alpine Club in London in 1921. On visiting the USA for six months in 1924 he was besieged with society commissions, and in 1925 he was invited by Queen Mary to paint *The Ascot Procession Crossing Windsor Park* (1925; Brit. Royal Col.). In 1926 he was elected RA.

Many of Munnings's commissioned works lack the vitality of subjects of his own choosing, although the challenge of painting horses was a constant motivation. *Son-in-law* (1927; Cape Town, N.G.) is a fine example of his horse portraiture as a study of both light and equine temperament. He was elected President of the Royal Academy in 1944, using the office as a platform for his reactionary views concerning modern art, which caused embarrassment and controversy in a speech broadcast in 1949, in which he attacked Picasso. In his old age he continued to record the tension and excitement of racing in pictures such as *Under Starter's Orders* (1957; Dedham, Essex, Munnings A. Mus.). After his death his wife turned their home in Dedham into a museum of his work.

WRITINGS

An Artist's Life (London, 1950)
The Second Burst (London, 1951)
The Finish (London, 1952)

BIBLIOGRAPHY

S. Booth: *Sir Alfred Munnings, 1878–1959: An Appreciation of the Artist* (London, 1986)

J. Goodman: *What A Go!* (London, 1988)

RICHARD F. NEWBURY

Muñoz, Fernão [Fernando] (*b* Tuy, Galicia, *c*. 1480; *d* ?Lisbon, *c*. 1550). Spanish sculptor and wood-carver, active in Portugal. In 1508 he worked in collaboration with the Flemish sculptor Olivier of Ghent on the choir-stalls at the church of the Military Order of Christ, Tomar (fragments *in situ*). In 1512, on the death of Olivier, Muñoz completed the stalls and the statues begun by the former in the Templars' Rotunda at Tomar. Muñoz can also be linked to the sculptures depicting the Prophets and to the elegant polychromed wooden angel bearing a shield, all situated between the large painted panels on the exterior wall of the passage surrounding the octagonal Church of the Templars, now the apse, Tomar. Here he kept close to the art of the Netherlandish sculptors who, in the early 16th century, were an important influence on the art of the western regions of the Iberian Peninsula. Muñoz is known to have lived in Lisbon in 1545, at which time he was denounced by the Inquisition.

BIBLIOGRAPHY
V. Correia: 'A escultura em Portugal no primeiro terço do século XVI', *A. & Arqueol.*, 1 (1930), pp. 29–48
R. dos Santos: *A escultura em Portugal* (Lisbon, 1950–51)
P. Dias: *O manuelino*, v of *História da arte em Portugal* (Lisbon, 1986), pp. 93–115

PEDRO DIAS

Muñoz, Gerónimo Fures y. *See* FURES Y MUÑOZ, GERÓNIMO.

Muñoz, Lucio (*b* Madrid, 27 Dec 1929). Spanish painter and printmaker. He studied drawing at the Academia de Bellas Artes de San Fernando in Madrid from 1949 to 1954. Freeing himself gradually from academic discipline, he became acquainted with Cubism, Expressionism, abstract art and other modernist tendencies and also experimented with collage. After taking part in a group show in Madrid in 1955 he spent a year in Paris (1955–6), where he became involved with *Art informel* and matter painting, taking a particular interest in the textures of his materials. He was particularly innovative in his prints and in works on wood rather than in oil paintings. Far from assigning a merely supportive role to wood, he incorporated it fully into the overall concept of works such as *Panel 21* (1959; London, Tate), sometimes scorching it, scratching deep cuts into it or covering it with a thick layer of oil paint into which he mixed marble dust, sawdust and pulverized minerals. He referred to these works by the ironic term *Pseudo-paintings*.

BIBLIOGRAPHY
G. Ureña: *Las vanguardias artísticas en la postguerra española, 1940–1959* (Madrid, 1982)

MARÍA TERESA DABRIO GONZALEZ

Muñoz, Sebastián (*b* Navalcarnero, Segovia, *c.* 1654; *d* Madrid, 1690). Spanish painter. He trained first in Madrid as a pupil of Claudio Coello and then in Rome, where he spent four years in the studio of Carlo Maratti. He returned to Spain in 1684 and associated with Coello again, collaborating with him on the frescoes in the Manteria church in Saragossa (*in situ*). His fame rapidly spread in Madrid, and he was summoned by Charles II to work in the Palacio Real. There, in different rooms, he executed paintings based on the stories of Angelica and Medoro and of Cupid and Psyche, which were destroyed in the fire at the old Alcázar in 1734. Muñoz also painted skilful portraits of Charles II, Queen María Luisa and many members of the court, as a result of which the King appointed him Pintor de Cámara in 1688. The eight scenes of the *Life of St Eligius*, which he painted in the church of S Salvador in Madrid, have not survived. The *Martyrdom of St Sebastian* that he painted in 1687 for the convent of the Calced Carmelites in Madrid may be the same as a *St Sebastian* in a private collection in Bordeaux. The only other surviving work by Muñoz is the excellent *Funeral of Queen María Luisa* (1689; New York, Hisp. Soc. America). Muñoz died at the age of 36 when he fell from the scaffolding while retouching frescoes (destr.) by Francisco de Herrera (ii) in the dome of the chapel of Nuestra Señora de Atocha in Madrid.

BIBLIOGRAPHY
Ceán Bermúdez
D. Angulo Iñiguez: *Pintura del siglo XVII*, A. Hisp. (Madrid, 1971), pp. 318–19
A. E. Pérez Sánchez: *Pintura barroca española* (Madrid, 1992), p. 328

ENRIQUE VALDIVIESO

Muñoz, Fray Vicente (*b* Seville, 1699; *d* ? Buenos Aires, 1784). Spanish architect, active in Argentina. In 1741 he joined the Franciscan Order in Buenos Aires. When he took his vows it was noted that he was a 'mason–architect', and he worked in this capacity in Buenos Aires, Córdoba and Salta. From 1730 he designed the vaulting for S Francisco, Buenos Aires, following the plans of the original architect Andrea Bianchi, who had begun it *c.* 1724. The dome (1752) of Córdoba Cathedral is attributed to Muñoz. As has been noted, it is a majestic cupola reminiscent of those of Toro Cathedral in Spain or the Old Cathedral in Salamanca (Spain). Its corner turrets are designed in the Romanesque style, although its skilful interplay of curves and counter-curves, onion-shaped crown and base strengthened by a balustered ring are derived from Piedmontese Baroque (Gallardo). In 1754 Muñoz was involved in the construction of S Roque Chapel, Buenos Aires, designed by Antonio Massella, and in 1758 he drew up the design for, and was the builder of, S Francisco (destr.), Salta, a forerunner of the present cathedral (1858–82) by Giovanni Soldati. S Francisco had a dome similar to that of Córdoba Cathedral.

BIBLIOGRAPHY
G. Furlong: *Arquitectos argentinos durante la dominación hispánica* (1946)
R. Gallardo: *Las iglesias antiguas de Córdoba* (1990)

JOSÉ MARÍA PEÑA

Muñoz Degrain, Antonio (*b* Valencia, 18 Nov 1840; *d* Málaga, 12 Oct 1924). Spanish painter. He trained at the Academia in Valencia and later at the Accademia di San Luca in Rome. Between 1862 and 1915 he regularly participated in both national and international exhibitions and was an admired teacher in Málaga and Madrid. From 1879 he taught landscape painting at the Escuela de Bellas Artes de San Fernando in Madrid, in 1901 becoming Director. He received most official recognition for his history paintings (e.g. *Othello and Desdemona*, 1881). Subsequently, however, he was more highly regarded for his landscapes, which owe a great deal to the Realist works of Carlos de Haes but also extend beyond Realism, approaching Symbolism in their heightened atmosphere. *Squall in Granada* (1881; Granada, Mus. A. Mod.) uses pink, violet and grey tones (criticized by contemporaries as excessively bright) to evoke the mysterious and alien character of natural forces. Muñoz Degrain's landscapes encompass a range of moods: lyrical, as in *Rio Piedra*, dramatic, as in *Roncesvalles*, or dream-like, as in *The Sultana's Bridge* (1914; Málaga, Mus. Prov. B.A.). A scene from the Middle East, *The Jordan*, recalls the Orientalist works of William Holman Hunt, while *The Valkyries* (1915; Valencia, Mus. B.A.) is a fantasy based on Richard Wagner's music from the *Ring* cycle. While successful during his lifetime, Muñoz Degrain was soon forgotten after his death and came to be negatively regarded as a representative of 19th-century academicism, notably by Surrealist artists such as Salvador Dalí.

See also under PINTURA DE LA LUZ.

BIBLIOGRAPHY
J. de Siles: 'Muñoz Degrain y Martínez Cubells', *Bellas A.*, iv (1887)
Sala Muñoz Degrain, Málaga, Mus. Prov. B.A. cat. (Málaga, 1916)
S. Rodríguez Garcia: *Antonio Muñoz Degrain: Pintor valenciano* (Valencia, 1966)
                                        JESÚS GUTIÉRREZ BURÓN

Muñoz Suárez, David (*b* San Miguel de Allende, Guanajuato, 28 Dec 1924). Mexican architect, urban planner and teacher. At first he worked, like his father, as a mason, before studying architecture (1946–8) at the Universidad Nacional Autónoma de México, Mexico City, where he later taught (1955–80). He planned the Ciudad Sahagún industrial and housing complex (1961) in the state of Hidalgo, based on the urban planning ideas of Carlos Lazo, who was influenced by Ludwig Hilbersheimer. He also designed the new headquarters of the Lotería Nacional (1970; with R. Torres and S. Santacruz), Mexico City, a high triangular prism of steel and glass quite different from his other work. Between 1976 and 1981 he planned the interdisciplinary unit of the Instituto Politécnico Nacional, Iztacalco, Mexico City, and two schools, each for *c*. 18,000 students, at the Universidad Autónoma Metropolitana, Mexico City, on the Azcapotzalco and Xochimilco campuses. He also designed the Palacio de Gobierno (1979) in Tuxtla Gutiérrez. Evident in these is his preference for horizontal masses and the placing of passageways around interior courtyards. Muñoz Suárez also worked with Pedro Ramírez Vázquez and Jorge Campuzano on the new Palacio Legislativo (1982), Mexico City, and on five missionary buildings (1985) in Dodoma, Tanzania. The Seguros Azteca Building (1987), Xochimilco, Mexico City, has a façade formed of a remarkable articulation of expanses of blank concrete.

WRITINGS
'Otras búsquedas contemporáneas', *Cuad. Arquit. Mesoamer.*, ix (1987), p. 92
                                        ALBERTO GONZÁLEZ POZO

Munro, Alexander (*b* Inverness, Scotland, 26 Oct 1825; *d* Cannes, 1 Jan 1871). Scottish sculptor, active in England. With the help of Harriet Egerton, Duchess of Sutherland, he obtained work in London, where in 1844 he assisted with carving in the Houses of Parliament, then being rebuilt following destruction by fire. After working under Edward Hodges Baily, he enrolled in 1847 at the Royal Academy Schools, where he met members of the Pre-Raphaelite circle; he befriended Dante Gabriel Rossetti and shared his studio with Arthur Hughes. Munro's most obviously Pre-Raphaelite work is *Paolo and Francesca* (marble, 1851–2; Birmingham, Mus. & A.G.). Although it is traditionally seen as following Rossetti, it preceded the latter's *Paolo and Francesca da Rimini* (1855; London, Tate) and reflected Munro's admiration of John Flaxman. Pre-Raphaelitism is evident in Paolo's gauche pose and the work's emotional intensity; the unrealistically smooth modelling emphasizes its visionary and poetic qualities. Munro's stone tympanum relief *King Arthur and the Knights of the Round Table* (1857–8; Oxford, Un. Soc.) was executed from Rossetti's design. Its primitive stiffness

and its theme make it a major example of Gothic Revival sculpture. It was intended to fuse stylistically with the architecture of the Oxford Union building, the work of Thomas Deane and Benjamin Woodward. Similar qualities are found in Munro's six marble statues of scientists (1863) in the same architects' University Museum, Oxford, although these figures make a greater compromise with realism. Munro's marble portrait medallions, such as *Pauline, Lady Trevelyan* (1857; Wallington House, Northumb., NT) and *Benjamin Woodward* (*c.* 1861; Oxford, U. Mus.), were admired by John Ruskin; they combine verisimilitude with idealization and retain the intensity of *Paolo and Francesca*.

BIBLIOGRAPHY
J. A. Gere: 'Alexander Munro's "Paolo and Francesca"', *Burl. Mag.*, cv (1963), pp. 509–10
H. B. Simon: 'A Millais Portrait Relief by Alexander Munro at the Ashmolean Museum, Oxford', *Apollo*, cxiii (1981), p. 115
B. Read: *Victorian Sculpture* (New Haven and London, 1982)
——: 'Was there Pre-Raphaelite Sculpture?', *Pre-Raphaelite Papers*, ed. L. Parris (London, 1984), pp. 97–110
The Pre-Raphaelites (exh. cat., London, Tate, 1984)
B. Read and J. Barnes, eds: *Pre-Raphaelite Sculpture: Nature and Imagination in British Sculpture, 1848–1914* (London, 1991), pp. 46–8, 57–65, 111–30
                                        MARK STOCKER

Munro [Munro of Novar]**, H(ugh) A(ndrew) J(ohnstone)** (*b* London, 13 Feb 1797; *d* Novar, Scotland, 22 Nov 1864). Scottish collector and painter. He inherited a painting by Murillo as well as the family estates at Novar, Scotland, from his father in 1810. By 1826 he was a friend of J. M. W. Turner and he also invited artists to Novar: Turner (1831), Edwin Henry Landseer, Théodore Gudin and Károly Brocky (whom he brought over from Paris to London in 1838). He went sketching with Turner in Italy in 1836 and painted alongside other artists in his studio in London. He was well regarded as a painter; Gustav Friedrich Waagen said that he painted in the style of Jean-Baptiste Greuze. In the 1850s he exhibited his works in the Amateur Artists shows held at 121 Pall Mall, London, though no surviving works by him have been traced. By 1830 Munro was collecting works by Turner, building up a major collection of his paintings (e.g. *Juliet and her Nurse*, 1835; Argentina, Fortabat priv. col.) and watercolours (notably Swiss scenes from the 1840s). He also bought prints from John Constable's *English Scenery* in 1832 and was a keen collector of the works of Thomas Stothard, Richard Parkes Bonington (e.g. *Grand Canal, Venice*, priv. col.) and William Etty (e.g. *Aurora and Zephyr*, 1845; Port Sunlight, Lady Lever A.G.). He was an equally avid collector of Old Master works. The most famous of these, though not so highly regarded in the late 20th century, were two paintings attributed to Raphael: a version of the *Madonna dei Candelabri* (Baltimore, MD, Walters A.G.) and the *Novar Virgin* or *Virgin of the Legend*. The collection embraced the Venetian, Bolognese, Roman, Dutch, Flemish, French and Spanish schools, including authentic works by Claude, Titian, Rembrandt and Rubens. Most interesting was his taste for such artists as Giambattista Tiepolo (the *Martyrdom of St Agatha*, Berlin, Gemäldegal.) and Watteau (*Spring*, destr.). On his death his collection was inherited by his sister, Mrs Butler Johnstone, and her husband, and was sold at Christie's in the 1860s and 1870s. The repute of the collection was diminished when it was sold by the number of works of dubious attribution.

BIBLIOGRAPHY
DNB
G. F. Waagen: *Treasures in Great Britain*, ii (London, 1854), pp. 131–42
W. E. Frost and H. Reeve: *A Complete Catalogue of the Paintings, Watercolour Drawings, Drawings, and Prints, in the Collection of the Late Hugh Andrew Johnstone Munro, Esq., of Novar, at the Time of his Death Deposited in his House, No. 6, Hamilton Place, London; with Some Additional Paintings at Novar* (London, 1865)
S. Whittingham: 'Munro of Novar: Man, Artist and Collector', *J. M. W. Turner, R.A.* (in preparation)

SELBY WHITTINGHAM

Munsŏng. *See* YI (i), (2).

Münster. German university town on the River Aa in Westphalia with a population of *c.* 280,000. The settlement of Mimigernaford, originally founded on the site by Saxons in the 7th century AD, first achieved importance in the Saxon Wars of Charlemagne in 772–804. St Ludger, sent to Westphalia as a missionary by Charlemagne *c.* 792–3, founded a religious house, or *monasterium* (Lat.: 'monastery'), from which the city's name is derived, and he was ordained as Münster's first bishop in 805. Because of its advantageous location at the intersection of two major trade routes, as a member of the Hanseatic League Münster flourished in the Middle Ages until the 15th century. During this period the present Late Romanesque cathedral of St Paulus (*c.* 1225–64) was built (*see* §1(i) below). The impressive Prinzipalmarkt, with its gabled stone houses, was at the heart of the medieval city. The Rathaus is part of this complex and has a splendid, stepped gable façade (14th century). Additionally, such collegiate and parish churches as the Überwasserkirche (*see* §1(ii) below) were built, and important panel paintings and sculptures were produced. During the Reformation Anabaptists controlled the city (1534–5), and damaged churches and works of art in iconoclastic riots before their defeat by the Prince–bishop. Among the important artists of the town in the 16th century were the tom Ring family of painters, the sculptors Johann and Franz Brabender and the engraver Heinrich Aldegrever. The Peace of Westphalia treaty (1648) was signed in the Rathaus, bringing the Thirty Years War to an end. The PICTORIUS family of architects was active from the mid-17th century to the 18th; at the same time the Gröninger family of sculptors participated in artistic life. In the 18th century numerous Baroque buildings were constructed, among them the church of St Clemens (1745–53; destr.; rebuilt 1956), the Erbdrostenhof (1749–57; rest.; *see* SCHLAUN, JOHANN CONRAD and fig.) and the Residenzschloss of the Prince–bishops (from 1767; destr. 1945; rest.; now part of the university), all by Johann Conrad Schlaun. The university was founded in 1771. In the 19th century the city was controlled by the French and then the Prussians. 90% of the old city was destroyed during World War II, but it has been rebuilt to reproduce its former structure and appearance. HARALD DEILMANN was part of the team that designed the Stadttheater (1954–6). Late 20th-century architecture is represented by the new Stadtbibliothek (1993), designed by Bolles-Wilson & Partner, and the townscape is shaped by numerous sculptures created by such contemporary artists as Chillida, Oldenburg and Judd.

BIBLIOGRAPHY
M. Geisberg: *Die Stadt Münster*, Bau- und Kunstdenkmäler in Westfalen, 6 vols (Münster, 1932–41)
G. Dehio: *Handbuch der deutschen Kunstdenkmäler: Westfalen*, ed. D. Kluge and W. Hansmann (Munich and Berlin, 1966/*R* 1986)
F.-J. Jakoby, ed.: *Geschichte der Stadt Münster*, 3 vols (Münster, 1993)
J. Poeschke, C. Syndikus and T. Weigel: *Mittelalterliche Kirchen in Münster* (Munich, 1993)

GUIDO MARKUS KOHLENBACH

1. CATHEDRAL. The foundation stone of the present building, which is the third on the site, was laid in 1225, and the cathedral was consecrated in 1265. The cathedral sculptures, dating from the 1230s to the 16th century, give an overview of Westphalian Gothic sculpture. In the paradise, or narthex (1230–50), which is situated to the south of the west transept, is a double portal with *Christ the Judge* depicted on the tympanum and *St Paul* on the trumeau (with an addition of 1536 in the original style); there are five *Apostle* figures (h. 2.25 m; see fig.) against the wall on either side of the doorway. The ensemble is

Münster Cathedral, *Apostle* figures in the narthex, h. 2.25 m, 1230–50

one of the richest portal figure cycles of 13th-century Germany. The figures, heavy and with some lingering Romanesque stylistic features, are nevertheless clearly derived from early 13th-century French cathedral sculpture (e.g. Chartres and Laon cathedrals). In niches near the entrance area figures associated with the diocese are depicted in a later style: *St Mary Magdalene* and a *Knight* on the west wall and *Bishop Dietrich of Isenberg* and *St Lawrence* on the east wall. It is uncertain whether this was the original location of these works. Other surviving 13th-century sculpture includes a head of *St Paul* and a *Lion and Lamb* from the southern exterior of the west transept (now Münster, Westfäl. Landesmus.); the *Head of St John the Baptist on a Platter* (southern tower chapel); a *Wolf and Crane* (Münster, Domschatz); the *Evangelists* on the four crossing piers; and reliefs and portal sculpture in the cloister. Heinrich Brabender produced a monumental figure group depicting the *Entry into Jerusalem* (*c.* 1516; now Münster, Westfäl. Landesmus.). After the Anabaptist iconoclasm, Johann Brabender made many single figures, the nine angels (*c.* 1554) on the chandelier in the chancel ambulatory and the sculptures for the choir-screen (*c.* 1545; dismantled 1870; damaged World War II; now Münster, Westfäl. Landesmus.). Other 16th-century works include the memorial plaques to *Albert Reining* (*fl* 1540–*c.* 1583/4), *Hans Lacke* (*fl* 1569–1618) and *Bernt Katmann* (*fl* 1598–1609), and the monumental figure cycle of the *Virgin* (1592) produced for the former west portal (now south-west crossing pier), which originally incorporated the *Wise and Foolish Virgins* (now cloister). The memorial plaque to *Otto von Dorgelo* (*d* 1625; h. *c.* 7.5 m; south-eastern pier of west transept) by Melchior Kribbe (*d* 1635) has reliefs with scenes from the *Passion* and the *Life of St Paul*. It is a typical Renaissance memorial plaque, with a two-storey architectonic structure. Much notable 17th- and early 18th-century sculpture in the cathedral was executed by members of the Gröninger family (*see* GRÖNINGER).

BIBLIOGRAPHY
A. Schroer, ed.: *Monasterium: Festschrift zum siebenhundertjährigen Weihegedächtnis des Paulus-Domes zu Münster* (Münster, 1966)
R. Budde: *Der Skulpturenschmuck des 13. Jahrhunderts im Dom zu Münster; Ein Beitrag zur Plastik in Westfalen* (Cologne, 1969)
——: 'Die Statuen der Evangelisten Markus und Lukas in der Vierung des Domes zu Münster und ihre stilistische Nachfolge', *Wallraf-Richartz-Jb.*, xxxii (1970), pp. 67–98
W. Sauerländer: 'Die kunstgeschichtliche Stellung der Figurenportale des 13. Jahrhunderts in Westfalen', *Westfalen: Hft. Gesch., Kst & Vlksknd.*, il (1971), pp. 1–76
P. Pieper: *Heinrich Brabender: Ein Bildhauer der Spätgotik in Münster* (Münster, 1984)
U. Grote: *Johann Mauritz Gröninger: Ein Beitrag zur Plastik des Hochbarock in Westfalen* (diss., U. Münster, 1987)

2. ÜBERWASSERKIRCHE. Dedicated to St Mary, this is a three-aisled hall church, built 1340–46, with figured vault bosses depicting heads in foliage, *Christ*, the *Trinity* and the *Lamb of God*. The remains of an *Apostle* cycle from the portal of the west tower (now Münster, Westfäl. Landesmus.) are among the most outstanding sculptures of the region. Carved of Baumberg sandstone, they were made from 1364 and probably put in place in 1374. They were damaged in the Anabaptist destructions of the 1530s and were discovered in 1898 during excavations based on information given in chronicles of the Anabaptist period.

The sculptures consist of the *Virgin and Child* from the trumeau, seven *Apostle* figures and two torsos. The cycle was disposed over the door jambs and the two buttresses flanking the portal. The ensemble is firmly dated by inscriptions on the lintel and on the reliquary held by the Virgin. The workshop was influenced by sculpture in France, the Upper Rhine and Cologne Cathedral, in particular the St Peter Portal of this last (*see* COLOGNE, §IV, 1(ii)). Until 1878 a series of 15th- and 16th-century sculptures adorned each of the four main storeys of the west tower, but these were replaced during Hilger Hertel's restorations (from 1878), mostly with sculptures of similar subjects (the *Good Shepherd*, *Crucifixion*, *Resurrection* and figures of saints). The tomb sculpture consists of a worn slab, produced in the 1180s and probably from the tomb of *Bishop Hermann I* (*reg* 1032–46), set into the westernmost buttress on the south side of the church; and several 17th-century memorial plaques, in particular those of the *Kerkering Brothers* (*d* 1600) and *Bernhard Hansmann* (*d* 1626), both from the circle of Gerhard Gröninger's workshop.

BIBLIOGRAPHY
H. Apfelstaedt: 'Die Skulpturen der Überwasserkirche zu Münster in Westfalen', *Marburger Jb. Kstwiss.*, viii–ix (1936), pp. 391–470
K. Noehles: 'Die angebliche Grabplatte Bischof Hermanns I. an der Überwasserkirche zu Münster', *Westfalen: Hft. Gesch., Kst & Vlksknd.*, xxxii (1954), pp. 184–8
Die Parler und der Schöne Stil, 1350–1400: Europäische Kunst unter den Luxemburgern, i (exh. cat., ed. A. Legner; Cologne, Schnütgen-Mus., 1978)

F. NIEHOFF

Munsterhjelm, (Magnus) Hjalmar (*b* Tuulos, 19 Oct 1840; *d* Helsinki, 2 April 1905). Finnish painter. His father owned an estate in central Finland, the area that was to inspire most of his landscapes. He admired the work of Werner Holmberg, which prompted him to study at the Kunstakademie in Düsseldorf. He attended the Akademie between 1860 and 1865, first as a pupil of Hans Fredrik Gude and then under Oswald Achenbach. From 1865 to 1870 he worked under Gude in Karlsruhe, producing such works as *Road in Finland* (1865; Helsinki, Athenaeum A. Mus.). During this period he was influenced by Gude's Realism as well as by the Nordic Romanticism of the older generation of artists in Düsseldorf.

On his return to Finland Munsterhjelm's large, atmospheric paintings of Finnish subjects, such as *Landscape with Rye Stooks* (1877) and *Landscape in Tuulos* (1877; both Helsinki, Athenaeum A. Mus.), earned him a reputation as one of the most popular landscape artists of the day. In the 1870s he continued to paint Finnish themes in Munich. During this period he also won fame in Europe and sold several of his large canvases. He spent some time in Paris in 1881–2, but he found the city disagreeable and decided to maintain the German idiom in his art by persevering with studio painting. Towards the turn of the century his colours gradually grew brighter, and the creation of light became more central to his work.

Munsterhjelm was an extremely productive landscape painter who strove to satisfy the desires of his public. He was technically very accomplished but did not always have the patience to be thorough in his work; his output is therefore uneven and at times shows the strain of commercial considerations. The beloved idyll of Finnish lakeside scenery is characteristic of his landscapes. His work is at its most romantic in moonlit scenes (e.g. *Forest Pond by Moonlight*, 1888; Turku, A. Mus.) and autumnal moods, while his seascapes display the more Realist influence of Gude. He produced over 1400 works, most of which are in private collections. From the 1880s Munsterhjelm was severely criticized by the younger generation, but he retained his popularity with the public to the very last.

BIBLIOGRAPHY
Hjalmar Munsterhjelm (exh. cat., essay A. Reitala; Hämeenlinna, A. Mus., 1983)

AIMO REITALA

Münsterman [Münstermann], **Ludwig** (*b* ?Bremen, ?*c.* 1575; *d* Hamburg, *c.* 1637). German sculptor. He was the most original sculptor active in northern Germany during the early 17th century. Fliedner (1956) suggested that he descended from Bremen wood-carvers and carpenters and that he was born in the early 1560s; however, the first definite record of the artist is of 1599, when he joined the wood-turners (*Drechsleramt*) in Hamburg. Münsterman lived in Hamburg until his death, though most of his sculptures are for churches and palaces in the nearby county of Oldenburg.

Münsterman worked primarily in wood or stone, but a few miniature carvings in ivory from 1600–10 (Oldenburg, Landesmus.) and an amber *Apostle* (sold London, Sotheby's, 7 April 1977) are attributed to him. He enjoyed noble patronage throughout his career, producing his earliest dated work, the elaborately figured organ frame (1608; now Bremen, Focke-Mus.) for the palace chapel in Rotenburg of Philipp Sigismund, Bishop of Verden and Osnabrück. Between 1607 and 1612 he carved architectural sculpture for the Schloss Oldenburg of Anton Günther, Graf von Oldenburg und Delmenhorst, who in 1612 also ordered a stone and wood pulpit for S Ulrichskirche, Rastede. In 1613–18 Münsterman created his finest ensemble, still largely intact, for the palace church in Varel. His other works here include the stone and wood pulpit, signed and dated 161(?3), the high altar (1614; stone and wood), the organ case (1615), the wooden prayer benches of Graf Anton II von Delmenhorst, the baptismal font (1618; stone and alabaster) and the lectern (wood). Only fragments of the organ case survive; these include figures of trumpeting angels and a winged woman holding a church (Varel) and *Apollo* (Berlin, Skulpgal.). Münsterman carved similar decorations in the Protestant churches of Hohenkirchen (altar, 1620; and pulpit, 1628), Rodenkirchen (altar, 1629; and pulpit, 1631) and Holle (baptismal font and cover, *c.* 1623–4; and pulpit, 1637), among others.

Münsterman's inventive style is based on an eclectic combination of Mannerist architectural and ornamental patterns with a highly personal vision. In early works, such as the Rotenburg organ case, the grotesques and strapwork forms derive from prints by Cornelis Floris and Wendel Dietterlin; however, their application to an organ and their association with the angel-headed volutes and the fully rounded figures of King David and Apollo are peculiar to Münsterman. His figures became increasingly elongated and more expressive as his style developed: the seated Apollo of the Rotenburg organ is calm in comparison with the standing Apollo of the Varel organ, made about seven years later, which is attenuated, demonstrating Münsterman's deviation from more natural human proportions and expressions. As in many of his figures, such as the Lindenwood *Adam and Eve* from the Holle font cover (*c.* 1623–4; Oldenburg, Landesmus.), a deliberately crude manner of carving and unfinished appearance intensify the expressive effect: the roughly formed figures are scarcely more advanced than the crude Tree of Life behind them.

The origins of Münsterman's style are difficult to determine. The elongated figures and dramatic gestures of the work of the Bremen stone-sculptor Hans Winter (*fl* 1560–*c.* 1595) may have influenced him; however, the uncertainty about Münsterman's birthdate and the chronology of Winter's works of the 1580s and early 1590s makes it difficult to ascertain their relationship, if any. Münsterman's heavy architectural framework, niche statues and vertically stacked reliefs in the Varel altar are reminiscent of the work of Christopher Dehne in Magdeburg and the epitaphs and pulpits by Jürgen Röttger (*c.* 1550–1623) in Braunschweig (Martinikirche, Brüdernkirche, Katharinenkirche), which were influential on north German sculpture of the late 16th century.

Münsterman's sons Johan (*b* Hamburg, *c.* 1600) and Claus (*b* 1601 or 1602) helped to carve the wooden Rodenkirchen pulpit of 1631 and perpetuated their father's style in their own works. His assistant, Onnen Dirksen (*fl* 1631–40), also became an independent master after Münsterman's death.

BIBLIOGRAPHY
M. Riesebieter: *Ludwig Münsterman: Ein Beitrag zur Geschichte der frühen niederdeutschen Barockplastik* (Berlin, [1930])
S. Fliedner: 'Ludwig Münsterman', *Z. Kstgesch.*, xix (1956), pp. 35–47
U. Kultermann: 'Der Vareler Altar von Ludwig Münsterman', *Z. Kstgesch.*, xix (1956), pp. 201–5
S. Fliedner: *Welt im Zwielicht: Das Werk des Bildhauers Ludwig Münstermann* (Oldenburg, 1962)
Barockplastik in Norddeutschland (exh. cat. by J. Rasmussen, Hamburg, Ksthalle, 1977), pp. 252–61
H.-R. Aukschun: *Die Schlosskirche in Varel und ihre Münsterman-Werke* (Varel, 1983)
H. Reimers: *Ludwig Münstermann* (Marburg, 1993)

JEFFREY CHIPPS SMITH

Muntaner. Spanish family of artists. Juan Montaner (*d* Rome, 1730) was a Mallorcan painter who settled in Rome. His son Lorenzo Muntaner Yupe (*b* Rome; *d* Palma de Mallorca, 1768), an engraver of devotional pictures, was the father of three engravers, all born in Palma de Mallorca. The oldest, Francesco Muntaner Moner (*b* 1743; *d* Madrid, 1805), studied in Madrid in 1767 under Juan Bernabé Palomino, and he was made an associate member of the Real Academia de S Fernando the same year, becoming a full member in 1771. He helped illustrate editions of Sallust (Madrid, 1772) and *Don Quixote* (Madrid, 1780), and he also produced devotional pictures and engraved the plates for the *Diseños de la Catedral de Malaga* (Madrid, 1785). Francesco's brother José Muntaner Moner (*b* 1745; *d* Madrid, 1788) worked both in Palma de Mallorca, where he was Director of the Escuela de Disegno, and in Madrid, and he was an associate member of the Real Academia de S Fernando. In 1785 he was commissioned by Cardinal

Despuig to make a detailed map of Mallorca. Juan Muntaner Moner (*b* 1750; *d* Palma de Mallorca, 1795), the youngest brother, was an engraver, painter and priest. José Muntaner's son Lorenzo María Muntaner y Diez de Armendariz (*b* Palma de Mallorca, 1782; *d* Palma de Mallorca, 1848) was a canon of Palma de Mallorca Cathedral and engraved maps and plans of Mallorca.

BIBLIOGRAPHY

M. Osorio y Bernard: *Galería biográfica de artistas españoles del siglo XIX* (Madrid, 1868)
J. J. Tous: *Grabadores mallorquines* (Palma de Mallorca, 1977)
A. Gallego: *Historia del grabado en España* (Madrid, 1979), pp. 311–12
E. Páez Ríos: *Repertorio* (1981–3)
A. Tomás and M. S. Silvestre: *Estampas y planchas de la Real Academia en el Museo de Bellas Artes de Valencia* (Valencia, 1982)
J. Carrete, F. Checa and V. Bozal: *El grabado en España: Siglos XV al XVIII*, Summa A., xxxi (1987)

BLANCA GARCÍA VEGA

Münter, Gabriele (*b* Berlin, 19 Feb 1877; *d* Murnau, Bavaria, 19 May 1962). German painter. Her formal art education began in Düsseldorf in 1897 at the Malschule für Damen. While in the USA (1898–1900), Münter developed a proficiency in sketching casual poses with an economic use of line, for example *Aunt Lou in Plainview* (1899; Munich, Lenbachhaus). On returning to Germany she enrolled in 1901 at the Künstlerinnen-Verein in Munich. In 1902 she entered the recently established Phalanxschule, which closely followed the arts and crafts tradition of *Jugendstil*. Münter first encountered still-life painting in evening classes taught by the Director of the school, Vasily Kandinsky, and during the summers of 1902 and 1903 she attended courses in landscape painting under his guidance. During this period they became engaged, but they never married. From 1904 to 1908 they travelled extensively outside Germany, visiting Sèvres in 1906–7. Münter attempted larger landscape paintings that acquired greater atmospheric qualities as a result of her contact with French Impressionist painting. She also experimented with colour linocuts, and a group of portraits in this medium were exhibited at the Salon d'Automne in 1907, including a portrait of *Kandinsky* (1906; New York, Leonard Hutton Gals).

In 1908 Münter and Kandinsky returned to Berlin and subsequently settled in Munich. The house that Münter acquired in the Bavarian village of Murnau in 1909 became a popular venue for meetings with the Russian artists Alexei Jawlenski and Marianne Werefkin. Münter's contribution to the Neue Künstlervereinigung (NKV) exhibitions of 1909 and 1910 in Munich included oil paintings and prints of landscape, still-life and portraiture. Traditional Bavarian *Hinterglasbilder* (Ger.: 'paintings behind glass') influenced the tendency towards simplification of line, the use of heightened colour effects and the rejection of Impressionist values, which characterized her production at this time. The naive imagery of the *Hinterglasbilder* also provided the subject-matter for still-life arrangements, such as *Still-life with St George* (1911; Munich, Lenbachhaus). Unlike Kandinsky, Münter saw the need for only a limited degree of abstraction. Dissension within the NKV in late 1911 caused Franz Marc, Münter and Kandinsky to withdraw and to arrange the Blaue Reiter group exhibitions. In 1913 Münter held solo exhibitions in Munich, Dresden, Frankfurt am Main and Stuttgart. In general, newspaper reviews were negative, linking her work with Expressionist trends in German art.

At the outbreak of World War I Münter and Kandinsky moved to Switzerland. He subsequently returned to Russia, while she settled in Stockholm. After a brief reunion in 1916, they separated permanently. During this difficult transitional period Münter created a group of paintings of women in interiors, for example *Reflecting* (1917; Munich, Lenbachhaus). Between 1917 and 1920, while living in Copenhagen, she achieved recognition as a major contributor to the Blaue Reiter group. Münter produced very little work during the 1920s, but her ensuing friendship with the art historian Johannes Eichner was a catalyst in making her resume her career with more vigour. An exhibition of her work at the Münchner Kunstverein was closed by the Nazi district leader in 1937. The post-war period was marked by increasing recognition of her work and she received several honours. In Münter's later work, executed in comparative seclusion at Murnau, contemporary trends were largely ignored in favour of a continued concern with traditional subjects: landscape and still-life, for example *Flowers on a Black Ground* (*c.* 1950; Munich, Lenbachhaus).

BIBLIOGRAPHY

Thieme–Becker; Vollmer
J. Eichner: *Kandinsky und Gabriele Münter: Von Ursprüngen moderner Kunst* (Munich, 1957)
E. Roditi: *Dialogues on Art* (London, 1960)
R. Gollek: *Der Blaue Reiter im Lenbachhaus München* (Munich, 1974)
E. Pfeiffer-Belliand and S. Helms: *Gabriele Münter: Zeichnungen und Aquarelle* (Berlin, 1979)
A. Comini: 'State of the Field: The Woman Artists of German Expressionism', *A. Mag.*, lv/3 (1980), pp. 147–53
R. Gollek: *Gabriele Münter, 1877–1962: Gemälde, Zeichnungen, Hinterglasbilder und Volkskunst aus ihrem Besitz* (Munich, 1980)
A. Mochon: *Gabriele Münter: Between Munich and Murnau* (Harvard, 1980)
U. Evers: *Deutsche Künstlerinnen des 20. Jahrhunderts* (Hamburg, 1983)
S. Behr: *Women Expressionists* (Oxford, 1988)
G. Kleine: *Gabriele Münter und Wassily Kandinsky* (Frankfurt am Main, 1990)
A. Hoberg and H. Friedel, eds: *Gabriele Münter, 1877–1962: Retrospektive* (Munich, 1992)

SHULAMITH BEHR

Munthe, Gerhard (Peter Frantz Wilhelm) (*b* Skanshagen at Elverum, 19 July 1849; *d* Baerum, 15 Jan 1929). Norwegian painter and designer. He trained as a landscape painter at the art school in Christiania (after 1877 Kristiania, now Oslo) run by J. F. Eckersberg and his followers from 1870 to 1874. He travelled widely throughout his career but was most attracted to eastern Norway, where he had been born. His first ambition was to paint in a realistic style that would also accommodate impulses from fantasy and literature. During the winters of 1874–5 and 1875–6 he visited his relative the painter Ludvig Munthe at Düsseldorf and was impressed by his work. An *Autumn Landscape* (1876; Bergen, Meyers Saml.) was Gerhard Munthe's first major painting. During a long stay at Munich (1877–82) he studied the Old Masters as well as contemporary art. He painted about 70 oils, mainly dark in tone but quite varied in content. They are largely based on impressions of the coastal towns or interior of Norway rather than being inspired by German motifs. *Suburb* (1879; Oslo, N.G.) and *Nevlunghavn* (1881; Bergen,

Meyers Saml.) are good examples of Munthe's work of this time. With such paintings he emerged as one of Norway's leading artists. Returning to Kristiania in 1882, he started to use lighter colours and adopted a more realistic style. He was introduced to French Realism by his Norwegian friend the painter Erik Theodor Werenskiold and others. Such pictures by Munthe as *Summer Day* (1884) and *Garden of the Farm* (1889; both Oslo, N.G.) appealed to the patriotic sentiments of Norwegians.

After 1890 Munthe's landscapes reflected the contemporary trend towards simplification of form and the use of expressive colours. His brushwork was generally energetic, but he also achieved subtle effects in watercolour. After 1892 he produced some decorative watercolours in the tradition of European Art Nouveau, a series of 'fairy-tale moods' intended to appeal to the viewer's subconscious and depict subjects that could not be expressed through a naturalistic approach. The style was to some extent based on old Norwegian art, mainly peasant rugs from the 18th century, but Munthe was also influenced by the work of modern French painters such as Pierre Puvis de Chavannes and Paul Gauguin. There are literary allusions to medieval Norwegian folk poetry as well as the work of the Belgian Symbolist poet and dramatist Maurice Maeterlinck. Perspective is discarded and firm, curved outlines surround areas of strong and unmixed colours. The colours are used to evoke particular moods and were also chosen as seeming typically Norwegian. His first series of watercolours, exhibited in 1893, included the *Horse of Death*, *Afraid of the Dark* and the *Daughters of the Northern Lights and their Suitors* (all Oslo, N.G.). Some of these compositions were subsequently made into designs for tapestry, and Munthe also made designs for other kinds of applied art, especially books (e.g. illustrations for Snorri Sturluson's *Sagas of the Norse Kings*, 1896–9) and the decoration of such interiors as the Fairy-tale Room in the hotel at Holmenkollen (1896; destr. 1914, see Bakken, 1946, p. 227) and the King Haakon's Hall in Bergen (1910–15; destr. 1944, see Bakken, 1946, pp. 287, 297 and 299). Because of his interest in the decorative arts and the influence he had at the turn of the century, Munthe has been called the 'William Morris of Norway'. He also resembled Morris in being active in various artistic organizations and writing on art and design.

See also NORWAY, §§V and VI. For portrait see KROHG, (1).

WRITINGS
Minder og meninger [Memories and opinions] (Oslo, 1919)

BIBLIOGRAPHY
NKL
J. Thiis: *Gerhard Munthe* (Trondheim, 1904)
E. Lexow: *Haakonshallen* (Bergen, 1929)
H. Bakken: *Gerhard Munthes dekorative kunst* (Oslo, 1946)
——: *Gerhard Munthe* (Oslo, 1952)

VIDAR POULSSON

Munthe, Holm (Hansen) (*b* Stange, 1 Jan 1848; *d* Christiania [now Oslo], 23 May 1898). Norwegian architect. He trained first at Wilhelm von Hanno's School of Design in Christiania and later as an architect in Hannover, Germany, from 1872 to 1877. He started his own practice in Christiania in 1878 and became a teacher at the Royal School of Design in 1885. From 1897 to his death he served as city architect for Christiania. With Henrik Nissen the elder (1845–1915), Munthe designed a number of important Renaissance Revival buildings in Oslo, such as the former Commercial High School, which has a red brick façade with granite and plaster details. He is best known, however, as the creator of the 'Dragon style', a fusion of the Chalet style (known in Norway as the 'Swiss style') and traditional Norwegian timber architectural forms, such as the characteristic two-storey front of the rural *loft* (Norw.: 'store-house'). The name of the style is derived from the use of dragon heads (a motif taken from medieval stave churches) to crown the gables. Munthe's bathing house (1880) at Larvik, his first work in this style, was immediately recognized as a significant contribution to the development of a Norwegian national identity in the arts. Munthe continued to develop what was then called the 'national wood' or 'stabbur' (Norw.: 'store-house on pillars') style, which culminated in the group of buildings he designed around 1890 for the heights of Holmenkollen and Frognerseteren, overlooking Oslo. Among these were the restaurant (1891) at Frognerseteren and the Holmenkollen Tourist Hotel (1889–90; destr.). With overhanging upper storeys, and made from notched, dark-stained logs, these buildings aroused great admiration among foreign visitors to these exclusive resort areas. Emperor William II subsequently commissioned a hunting-lodge and a stave church (both 1891) at Rominten, East Prussia, among other buildings, from Munthe. The Dragon style was employed for about a decade after Munthe's death, notably by his former assistants Ole Sverre (1865–1952) and Holger Sinding-Larsen (1869–1938).

NKL
BIBLIOGRAPHY
L. Dietrichson and H. Munthe: *Die Holzbaukunst Norwegens in Vergangenheit und Gegenwart* (Berlin, 1893)
S. Tschudi-Madsen: 'Veien hjem: Norsk arkitektur, 1870–1914' [The way home: Norwegian architecture, 1870–1914], Norges Kunsthistorie, v (Oslo, 1981)

CHRISTIAN NORBERG-SCHULZ

Munthe, General J(ohan) W(ilhelm) N(ormann) (*b* Bergen, 27 July 1864; *d* Beijing, 13 May 1935). Norwegian officer and collector. After training at the cavalry's non-commissioned officers' school in Kristiania (now Oslo) from 1884 to 1886, he travelled to China in 1886 and was appointed to the Chinese customs and excise service in 1887. Munthe remained in China and took part in various military actions. He was also adjutant to Yuan Shikai, then viceroy of Zhili, Hebei Province (1900–08), and then customs director in Tianjin (1909–11). After the Revolution (1911), Munthe was again adjutant and adviser to Yuan Shikai, first President of the Republic of China (1912–16). Munthe was the head of the protective guard of the legation district in Beijing, adviser to the Ministry of War and a Chinese lieutenant general. During the 1920s he was director of the Sino-Scandinavian Bank. The honours he received included the Russian St George's Cross, the British China Expedition Medal and the Norwegian Cross of the Commander of the Norwegian Order of St Olav. From 1907 to 1935 Munthe sent Chinese art to the Vestlandske Kunstindustrimuseum, Bergen, where his collection is housed. It comprises *c.* 2500 objects from all periods of Chinese art, the emphasis being on the last thousand years. It includes some 300 bronzes, 400 jades, 900 ceramic or porcelain pieces, around 750 paintings, 50 textile works and 20 carved marble plinths from the Yuanming Yuan summer palace, Beijing. Most notable are some 80 Buddhist sculptures, of which around 20 are of monumental works in white marble (provenance unknown but probably Hebei Province, Liao-Jin dynasties, 11–12th century). In 1994 the collection was newly arranged in the Vestlandske Kunstindustrimuseum.

UNPUBLISHED SOURCES
Bergen, Vestlandske Kstindustmus. Archv [corr. between Gen. Munthe and museum's directors, 1907–16 and 1930–35]

NBL   BIBLIOGRAPHY
R. Kloster: 'General J. W. N. Munthes etterlatte samlinger i USA' [General J. W. N. Munthe's posthumous collections in the USA], *Vestlandske kunstindustrimuseum 100 år* (Bergen, 1987)

MONIKA P. THOWSEN

Munthe, Ludvig (*b* Aaroey in Sogndal, 11 March 1841; *d* Düsseldorf, 30 March 1896). Norwegian painter. He trained under Franz Wilhelm Schiertz (1813–87) in Bergen from 1859 to 1860 and then went to Düsseldorf in 1861, studying there for a short time with local painters and then settling permanently. He also travelled in the Netherlands, attracted by the landscape and impressed by earlier Dutch art in the galleries. After 1870 he developed a style of his own, a form of Realism similar in some respects to that of Charles-François Daubigny or the Hungarians Michael Munkacsy (1844–1909) and Laszlo Paal. Munthe rejected complicated structures and bright colours, favouring grey and ochre pigments. His effects were based on a careful choice of colour harmonies and not on a scale of brightness and shadow. He preferred to paint winter landscapes in the afternoon or evening with the sky as the major focus for the colour scheme. He also favoured autumn landscapes showing people engaged in their daily tasks, for example *Potato Gatherers* (1873) and *Autumn in the Forest* (1882; both Oslo, N.G.). Munthe's work became popular with art critics and collectors all over Europe and during his last years it tended to be repetitive. At their best, however, his paintings testify to the enduring style of the mid-19th-century Düsseldorf school.

NKL   BIBLIOGRAPHY
M. Malmanger: *Norsk malerkunst fra klassisisme til tidlig realisme* [Norwegian painting from classicism to early realism] (Oslo, 1981), pp. 204–6

VIDAR POULSSON

Munthe-Kaas, Herman. *See under* BLAKSTAD & MUNTHE-KAAS.

Müntz, Eugène (*b* Soultz-sous-Forêts, 11 June 1845; *d* Paris, 30 October 1902). French art historian. He was one of the most prolific of 19th-century French art historians. In 1857 he went to study law in Paris, where he also worked as a notary. Although he completed his legal studies, Müntz became increasingly interested in art, and by 1867 he had devoted himself exclusively to this discipline. After initial studies in Athens, Müntz enrolled in 1875 at the Ecole Française in Rome. He returned to Paris in 1876 as the assistant librarian at the Ecole des Beaux-Arts; two years later, he became principal librarian as well as keeper of the archives and collections. From 1885 to 1892, he held a professorship in aesthetics and the history of art at the Ecole des Beaux-Arts, and in 1893 he entered the French Institute. Beginning in 1869 and extending to 1902, Müntz's art-historical bibliography numbered over 200 items. His scholarly interests were chronologically and geographically diverse, ranging from Roman and Early Christian art and architecture to contemporary art movements in France and Great Britain. The majority of Müntz's publications concern the Italian Renaissance, and even within this speciality, his interests were broad. Müntz published on Italian artists of the 14th, 15th and 16th centuries with a particular emphasis on the Florentine school and the art of Leonardo and Raphael. Müntz also published extensively on art at the papal court in Avignon and on the history of tapestry in Flanders, France and Italy. Another of Müntz's principal interests was the history of collecting, particularly of the popes and the Medici family. In these researches, but not exclusive to them, he made pioneering use of archival documents. Besides archives, which he praised as the 'sanctuaries of the science', his researches benefited from an immense personal library and a substantial photograph collection.

BIBLIOGRAPHY
Bibliothek Eugen Muentz hervorragende Sammlung von Werken zur Geschichte und Theorie der Kunst (Frankfurt am Main, 1903–5)
E. Josi: 'Eugène Müntz', *Enc. Catt.*, viii (Florence, 1952), cols 1519–22

ROGER J. CRUM

Müntz, Johann Heinrich (*b* Mulhouse, 28 Sept 1727; *d* Kassel, *bur* May 1798). Swiss architect, painter, draughtsman and writer. He served as an engineer in the French army (1748–54) and drew Gothic monuments in Spain (1748) and copied ancient vases and painted idyllic landscapes in Rome (1749–54). He then stayed from 1755 to 1759 with Horace Walpole at Strawberry Hill, where he worked as a topographical artist, portrait painter and architectural draughtsman. Having left Walpole after a domestic dispute, Müntz attempted to support himself through commissions, producing drawings of a Gothic cathedral and possibly the Alhambra for Kew Gardens, a dining room and cloister (New Haven, CT, Yale U., Lewis Walpole Lib.) for Richard Bateman, and an oval room for Lord Charlemont, to complement his vase collection. All were in the Gothic style, as were a number of architectural drawings later used in a guide by Robert Manwaring (1760). Müntz left England in 1762 and spent a year recording monuments in Greece and Jerusalem before settling in Holland, where he worked until 1778 as a metallurgist while continuing to paint imaginary scenes. Following a period of patronage by Polish royalty (1778–85), for whom he acted as a topographical artist, architect and adviser, in 1786 Müntz went to Wilhelmshöhe, where he spent the remainder of his life recording the gardens and surrounding landscape. He wrote three complete treatises and two treatise proposals, and he contributed illustrations to a treatise on engraving by Johann Heinrich Tischbein II (1742–1808). Other subjects included ancient vases and the oval, encaustic painting, smelting, Gothic architecture and practical painting. Müntz's works display three common characteristics: a technical approach to art, a knowledge of antiquity and a sense of what interested his contemporaries.

UNPUBLISHED SOURCES

London, BL, Add. MS. 6771, fols 215–16 [*Proposals for Publishing by Subscription a Course of Gothic Architecture*, 1760; printed copy]

London, V&A , MS., inv. no. [26.6] 1868. Ref. no. 86 FF56 [*Voorstellung van een assortiment van de allerfraysten aloudsten en zeldsamstern Egyptisen, Hetrurisen, Grieksen en Romeinsen vasen en urnen*, 1772]

U. Warsaw, Lib. [*Voyages pittoresques de la Pologne*, 1781/3]

WRITINGS

Encaustic, or Count Caylus' Method of Painting in the Manner of the Ancients (London, 1760)

PRINTS

R. Manwaring: *Carpenters Compleat Guide to the Whole System of Gothic Railing* (London, 1760)

J. H. Tischbein: *Kurzgefasste Abhandlung über die Ätz-Kunst und die geätzten 84 Blätter welche durch Johann Heinrich Tischbein . . . herausgeben sind* (Kassel, 1790)

BIBLIOGRAPHY

Thieme–Becker

E. Budzinksa: *Jana Henryka Müntza podróże malownicze po Polsce i Ukrainie, 1781–3* [Johann Heinrich Müntz's painterly travels through Poland and the Ukraine, 1781–3] (Warsaw, 1982)

T. Watts: *The Life and Work of Johann Heinrich Müntz, 1727–98* (diss., U. Toronto, 1986)

M. McCarthy: *The Origins of the Gothic Revival* (New Haven, 1987)

TERESA S. WATTS

Muqarnas [Arab. *muqarnas*; *muqarnaṣ*; *muqarbaṣ*; Sp. *mocarabes*]. Three-dimensional decorative device used widely in Islamic architecture, in which tiers of individual elements, including niche-like cells, brackets and pendants, are projected over those below. *Muqarnas* decoration, executed in stucco, brick, wood and stone, was consistently applied to cornices, squinches, pendentives, the inner surfaces of vaults and other parts of buildings throughout the Islamic world from the 12th century. Seen from below, the *muqarnas* presents a stunning visual effect as light plays over the deeply sculpted but regularly composed surface; this explains the comparison of *muqarnas* in European languages with 'stalactite vaulting' (Ger. *Stalak-titentengewölbe*) or 'honeycombs' (Fr. *alvéoles*). The Arabic term *muqarnas* first appears in the 12th century, but a related verb had been used a century earlier to describe deeply carved and moulded stucco ornament on Islamic architecture. It has been suggested and widely accepted that the word derives from the Greek *koronis* ('cornice'), although this derivation is not confirmed in any Arabic or Persian source. The Arabic lexicographer Firuzabadi (*d* 1415) defined *muqarnas* as a form with stepped or serrated edges and the related word *qirnās* as a projecting rock on a mountain. These two definitions encompass the most salient features of all *muqarnas* decoration, namely fragmentation and seemingly unsupported projection. Scholars have focused their attention on the history and development of this most characteristic feature of Islamic architecture, and some have seen *muqarnas* as a manifestation of basic principles in the formation of an Islamic aesthetic.

1. Before *c.* 1100. 2. After *c.* 1100.

1. BEFORE *c.* 1100. The earliest ensembles of *muqarnas* decoration survive on 11th-century buildings in Iran and western Central Asia, North Africa, Upper Egypt and Iraq, but the broad geographical distribution of these examples and their technical sophistication suggest that the form had evolved in one of these regions at least a century earlier and was then diffused to other Islamic lands. Such

early scholars as Rosintal, Creswell and Marçais, however, interpreted the data as evidence of spontaneous and parallel developments in Iran, Egypt and North Africa.

The earliest known evidence for *muqarnas*-like decoration consists of concave triangular pieces of stucco excavated at Nishapur in north-east Iran, datable to the 9th or 10th century, and tentatively reassembled by the excavators to form a tripartite squinch. This reconstruction remains conjectural, and the earliest tripartite squinch *in situ* is found at the Arab-Ata Mausoleum at Tim (977–8) in the Zarafshan Valley of Uzbekistan, where niche-like elements, built of brick but similar in form to those found at Nishapur, have been combined within a trefoil arch. This type of tripartite squinch was successfully utilized in several 11th-century Iranian buildings, such as the GUNBAD-I QABUS (1006–7), where it appears over the portal, and the dome chamber of the Duvazdah Imam Mausoleum in Yazd (1037–8). The tripartite squinch was fully exploited in the two dome chambers added in the late 11th century to the Friday Mosque at Isfahan (*see* ISLAMIC ART, fig. 31). At the Friday Mosque (1105–18) at Golpayegan, the squinches in the dome chamber enclose heptafoil arches formed by four tiers of projecting elements, and five tiers, for example, are used over the portal to the Ghaffariyya tomb tower (14th century) at Maragha.

Niche-like elements were also combined in Iranian architecture to form cornices separating the roof from the shaft of a tomb tower and the storeys of a minaret. At the Gunbad-i 'Ali (1056) in Abarquh, for example, three tiers of niche-like elements project above the inscription band to form a highly sculpted cornice, which contrasts sharply with the smooth surfaces of the octagonal shaft and hemispheric dome. The cornice at Abarquh is constructed of mortared rubble, but most Iranian examples, such as the tomb tower at Risgit (*c.* 1100), are built of brick, as are the deeply sculpted cornices on Iranian minarets, although that of the Muhammad Mosque (1081–2) at Baku in Azerbaijan is made of stone. The use of deeply sculpted cornices of niche-like elements to separate the parts of buildings may have developed from the local building tradition in which courses of shaped and angled bricks were corbelled to differentiate parts of buildings (e.g. Damghan, Pir-i 'Alamdar tomb tower, 1026–7).

Excavations at the 11th-century site of QAL'AT BANI HAMMAD in Algeria yielded several, small, baked ceramic parallelepipeds (47×47×160 mm), fluted on three or four sides. Marçais reconstructed them in pendant clusters that would have hung from the juncture of a flat ceiling and a wall, but this reconstruction remains conjectural, and these elements stand outside the main development of *muqarnas*. Concave stucco cells grouped with brackets were also found at the site and dated to the mid-11th century. Golvin reconstructed them in corbelled tiers to show similarities to later *muqarnas* vaults in Iraq, North Africa and Sicily. It is quite unlikely, however, that such an important form originated in this remote North African site, and the technical sophistication of these fragmentary remains suggests that the form had an earlier history.

The earliest *muqarnas* cornice to survive in Egypt is found on the minaret of the Mashhad al-Juyushi (1085) in Cairo, where two (or perhaps three) tiers of niche-like elements separate the storeys of the shaft. Painted plaster *muqarnas* elements were found in the ruins of the bath of Abu'l-Su'ud in Fustat (Old Cairo) and have been dated to the late 11th century. In several mausolea at Aswan in Upper Egypt and in Cairo, some of which date from the late 11th century, the zones of transition are variously elaborated, sometimes even approximating the appearance of *muqarnas*. They seem to reflect the now-lost architecture of the Hijaz, to which Upper Egypt was connected by the pilgrimage route across the Red Sea. The Hijaz, again, is an unlikely source for the origin of the form, and it was probably imported there as it was to central North Africa.

The earliest extant dome constructed entirely of *muqarnas* elements is the shrine of Imam Dur (1085–90), built by the 'Uqaylid prince Muslim ibn Quraysh in the tiny village of Dur, some 20 km north of Samarra' in Iraq. An elongated square (h. 12 m) topped by a vault of almost equal height, the chamber is transformed into an octagon by four squinches and four arches. The upper vault is composed of four eight-celled tiers of diminishing size, each rotated 45 degrees. The internal organization is reflected on the exterior by the tiered pyramid of alternating rounded and angular projections. The layering of increasingly small cells with multiple profiles makes the interior of the vault appear insubstantial, as the play of light on its intricate surfaces dissolves the mass. Such visual display is one of the novel characteristics of the *muqarnas* dome and distinguishes it from 11th-century Iranian domes, in which the use of *muqarnas* elements is restricted to the zone of transition. The sophisticated application of *muqarnas* in this small village shrine argues for the existence of earlier models elsewhere. The most likely place is the nearby capital of Baghdad, which underwent a cultural and political revival in the early 11th century under the stridently Sunni leadership of the Abbasid caliph al-Qadir (*reg* 991–1031), although none of its monuments from this period has survived. Tabbaa has suggested that during al-Qadir's reign *muqarnas* elements were first combined to form a dome, a fragmented and ephemeral structure that was a suitable metaphor for the atomistic theology propagated by the caliph's chief apologist, al-Baqillani. The relationship of the *muqarnas* dome to earlier elements, such as the tripartite squinch, the *muqarnas* cornice and the scattered fragments, is still unclear, but by the 12th century *muqarnas* had become a ubiquitous decorative device in Islamic architecture, used for a variety of purposes.

2. AFTER *c.* 1100. The popularity of *muqarnas* from the 12th century on allows several distinct regional types to be delineated. The type used in southern Iraq follows the example of the shrine of Imam Dur and has tall conical brick vaults in which the inner articulation is reflected on the exterior, creating a pine-cone appearance. In the shrine of Zumurrud Khatun at Baghdad, built by the Abbasid caliph al-Nasir (*reg* 1180–1225), the vault springs from an octagonal base. The type used in northern Iraq and northeast Syria consists of a brick or stucco *muqarnas* vault covered by a pyramidal brick roof, which is sometimes glazed. The finest example in Mosul is the shrine of Imam 'Awn al-Din (1245), in which the central vault rests on four little *murqarnas* vaults at the corners. The individual cells of the central vault are made of small rectangular

strips of glazed brick, a colouristic effect that enhances the sumptuousness of the interior. This vault, or one like it, may have provided the model for a technically related *muqarnas* vault over the tomb of Shaykh 'Abd al-Samad at Natanz (1307) in central Iran (*see* ISLAMIC ART, fig. 49). The stucco vault at Natanz epitomizes the variety and complexity of form and richness of decoration of such structures erected in Iran under the Ilkhanid dynasty (*reg* 1256–1353). The earliest *muqarnas* portal vaults to survive in Iran date from the same time, and their high degree of development presupposes the existence of earlier examples. An incised plaster plan for a *muqarnas* vault and stucco fragments were excavated from the ruins of the Ilkhanid palace (*c.* 1275) at Takht-i Sulayman in northwest Iran; they indicate that the precision and complexity of these vaults were achieved by sketching out the plan beforehand in order to facilitate construction. The popularity of the form in Iran is attested by the lyric poet Hafiz (*d* 1389), who often used the expression *falak-i muqarnas* to refer to the dome of heaven.

Some spectacular *muqarnas* vaults were erected in the eastern Islamic world under the Timurid dynasty (*reg* 1370–1506). At the shrine of Ahmad Yasavi at TURKESTAN, for example, the large central room, the mosque and the tomb have *muqarnas* vaults, but the radial organization and emphasis on the ribbed crown differentiate them from earlier examples. Tiers of *muqarnas* cells were also used on exteriors to make the transition between the tall cylindrical drum and the base of the ribbed dome, creating the characteristic swelling profile of Timurid buildings. Tiers of cells continued to be used to separate the stages of minarets. Under the Timurids a new type of ribbed vault was developed, in which *muqarnas* cells were sometimes used to fill the interstitial surfaces. Although *muqarnas* vaulting seems to have lost some of its appeal in this period, the earliest treatise on the *muqarnas* vault to survive, the *Miftāh al-hisāb* ('Key to arithmetic'), was written by the Timurid mathematician Ghiyath al-Din al-Kashi in 1427. One chapter of his work presents a typology of *muqarnas* vaults known in his time and analyses them in terms of their individual elements and overall design.

Under the Safavid dynasty (*reg* 1501–1732) in Iran, *muqarnas* continued to be used for the vaults of large iwans, and the cells are often covered with tile mosaic, creating an unparalleled shimmering effect (e.g. Isfahan, Friday Mosque; for illustration *see* IWAN). *Muqarnas* vaults were, however, often eliminated from the interiors of religious buildings in favour of flat surfaces covered with brilliantly coloured tile mosaic, as in the mosque of Shaykh Lutfallah (1603–19), Isfahan. In the 18th century another stage in the evolution of *muqarnas* decoration in Iran began as the individual cells were covered with mirror glass (Pers. *ā'ina-kārī*). One of the earliest examples is the portal to the Chihil Sutun Palace (rest. 1706–7; *see* ISFAHAN, §3, (vii)). Mirror-work *muqarnas* was often used for portals and vaults at the shrines of important Shi'ite martyrs, such as that for al-Husayn in Karbala' in southern Iraq, where they create an oppressive, hypnotic effect.

In Syria the pine-cone type of *muqarnas* vault used in Iraq was initially favoured in such buildings as the hospital at Damascus built by the Zangid ruler Nur al-Din (1154). The vestibule is covered by a *muqarnas* dome clearly modelled on Iraqi prototypes and is flanked by two niches covered with *muqarnas* vaults. Made of stucco and suspended from the load-bearing roof by a wooden framework, the vaults contain pendants and terminate in eight-pointed stars. *Muqarnas* is also used to decorate the shallow hood of the portal, the earliest extant example of a feature that became extremely popular in later times. The translation of the brick and stucco *muqarnas* tradition into stone was concomitant with the development of the vigorous stereotomic tradition in Aleppo that began in the last quarter of the 12th century, and stone *muqarnas* became one of the hallmarks of architecture in Syria and Egypt under the Ayyubid (*reg* 1169–1260) and Mamluk (*reg* 1250–1517) dynasties. Herzfeld differentiated *muqarnas* domes of the Ayyubid period into Western and Iranian types, depending on the support system used. The vault of the Western type rises from *muqarnas* pendentives, whereas the vault of the Iranian type rests on squinches themselves made of *muqarnas* cells; both end with a scalloped semi-dome. Visually, the Western type presents a smooth transition from pendentive to staggered rows of cells and brackets to the little dome; the Iranian type, with a more abrupt beginning, looks more like a suspended vault. The Western type seems to be the earlier of the two—the first example being the portal vault of the Shadbakhtiyya Madrasa (1193) in Aleppo—but both types were used simultaneously in Damascus and Aleppo from the beginning of the 13th century. All of the fully developed examples in the 13th century, such as the Firdaws Madrasa (1235) in Aleppo and the Zahiriyya Madrasa in Damascus (1274), are of the Iranian type. *Muqarnas* was also applied to capitals of columns; some of the earliest are the enormous stone capitals (late 12th century) from the Great Mosque of Harran, now in south-east Turkey. The earliest evolved *muqarnas* capitals known adorn the Firdaws Madrasa in Aleppo (1235–7; *see* ISLAMIC ART, fig. 41), whence the innovation may have spread north to Anatolia.

Muqarnas decoration was introduced to Anatolia following its conquest in the late 11th century, and examples were executed in wood, stucco and stone following precedents from neighbouring Iran and Syria. The hoods of mihrabs were decorated with *muqarnas* in glazed tile (e.g. Konya, Sahib Ata Mosque, 1258); portals had *muqarnas* hoods sculpted in stone (e.g. Sivas, Çifte Minareli Madrasa, 1271; *see* fig. 1); several tiers of *muqarnas* were used to mark the transition between shaft and roof on tomb towers (e.g. Kayseri, Döner Künbed, *c.* 1275); the capitals of columns were decorated with *muqarnas* (e.g. Afyon, Ulu Cami, 1273); and *muqarnas* supported the balconies of minarets (e.g. Konya, Ince Minareli Madrasa, 1260–65). It was not normally used for pendentives or squinches, as the transition from base to dome was typically effected with a belt of prismatic consoles (*see* ISLAMIC ART, §II, 6(ii)). *Muqarnas* continued to be used in buildings erected under the Ottoman dynasty (*reg* 1281–1924), but it was only one of many decorative devices used in classical Ottoman architecture of the 16th century (e.g. Istanbul, Süleymaniye Mosque, 1550–57). The use of *muqarnas* was gradually abandoned in the 18th century in favour of Europeanizing ornament.

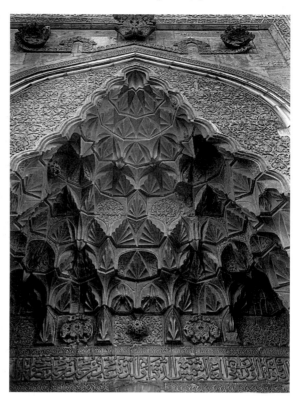

1. *Muqarnas* hood, portal of the Çifte Minareli Madrasa, Sivas, Turkey, 1271

In Egypt the first complete and sophisticated example of *muqarnas* is found on the Aqmar Mosque (1125) in Cairo, erected under the patronage of the Fatimid dynasty (*reg* 969–1171). A rectangular panel on the façade is carved with four tiers of *muqarnas*, and the chamfered corner of the building terminates in a hood with two tiers of inscribed *muqarnas*. This building was, however, exceptional, for *muqarnas* decoration became popular only in the mid-13th century. *Muqarnas* squinches in wood may have been used as early as 1211 for the original dome (rest.) over the tomb of Imam al-Shafi'i in Cairo; they were indisputably used there for the dome over the tomb of the Ayyubid sultan al-Salih Najm al-Din Ayyub (*reg* 1240–49). Stone domes carried on pendentives decorated with *muqarnas* were typical of funerary architecture of the Mamluks, as in the mausoleum of Sultan Qa'itbay (1472–4; *see* fig. 2 and CAIRO, §III, 10). The Mamluk sultan Baybars I (*reg* 1260–77) is credited with introducing the fashion for a stone portal with a *muqarnas* hood from Syria into Egypt, where it quickly became a major feature of architectural decoration. Stunning *muqarnas* hoods and vaults carved in stone were used to embellish the portals of religious buildings (e.g. complex of Sultan Hasan, 1356–62; *see* CAIRO, §III, 9) and palaces (e.g. palace of Yashbak, 1337).

By the mid-12th century complete *muqarnas* domes and vaults were used in North Africa and Sicily. The lobed dome of the Barudiyyin cupola (1107–43) in Marrakesh, Morocco, rests on an octagon created by the intersecting ribs of two rotated squares. Little spaces in the corners are

2. *Muqarnas* on the dome of the mausoleum of Sultan Qa'itbay, Cairo, 1472–4

covered by *muqarnas* cupolas, and the transition to the central dome is so highly elaborated with lobed arches and vegetal ornament that the whole produces the insubstantial effect of a *muqarnas* dome. Although not a true *muqarnas* dome, it could not have been constructed without some knowledge of the type of *muqarnas* domes used in Iraq, such as that of Imam Dur. The filigree-stucco dome over the bay in front of the mihrab at the Great Mosque (1136) at Tlemcen, Algeria, rests on *muqarnas* squinches and is capped by a *muqarnas* cupola. A series of superbly crafted and varied *muqarnas* vaults, all made of carved stucco, was added to the axial nave of the Qarawiyyin Mosque at Fez, Morocco, when it was rebuilt in 1134–43. *Muqarnas* vaults are also found in 12th-century buildings erected under Norman patronage in Sicily, one of the few instances where *muqarnas* decoration was used in structures commissioned by non-Muslim patrons. Its use there confirms the continuing importance of North African models in Sicilian architecture of the period. The vault covering the nave of the Palatine Chapel (1131–53; *see* PALERMO, §II, 2(ii) and ISLAMIC ART, fig. 35) is the largest and most famous example. Made of wood and worked on seven levels, the scheme comprises three rows of eleven cupolas separated by two rows of ten stellate octagons. The individual elements are superbly painted with figural,

vegetal and epigraphic motifs. Other examples of *muqarnas* vaults at the Ziza Palace (*c.* 1165–7) in Palermo are executed in stucco or stone. The stone vault over the fountain there resembles a *muqarnas* vault of stucco, as it was not assembled from individually carved stone blocks but was carved after construction.

The tradition of *muqarnas* vaulting in the Muslim West attained its greatest sophistication in the vaults and domes of the Alhambra (*see* GRANADA, §III, 1). The *muqarnas* domes in the Sala de los Abencerrajes and the Sala de Dos Hermanas (1354–9) expand the concepts of fragmentation and ephemerality, already evident in the earliest *muqarnas* dome, beyond the limits of logic. A great number of tiny cells in a variety of shapes, including a high proportion of pendants, and brightly coloured in blue, ochre and gold, have been joined in intricate compositions. Carefully illuminated by modulated sources of lighting, these ever-changing domes appear to defy gravity, leading such scholars as Grabar to consider them architectural representations of the dome of heaven. The ubiquitous *muqarnas* passed into the architecture of Christian Spain (*see* MUDÉJAR), where it was used in such buildings as the Alcázar of Seville (1364–6), and it was occasionally imitated in European and North American Orientalist architecture (e.g. Columbus, OH, Ohio Theater, 1928). Modern architects in the Islamic world, such as Halim Abdelhalim, have experimented with new forms of the *muqarnas* (e.g. his 1981 entry for the Osman ibn Affan Mosque competition in Doha, Qatar; *see* ISLAMIC ART, fig. 76).

BIBLIOGRAPHY

Enc. Islam/2: 'Muḳarbaṣ', 'Muḳarnas'
Ghiyāth al-Dīn Jamshīd al-Kāshī (*d* 1429): *Miftāḥ al-ḥisāb* ['Key to arithmetic'], ed. with Rus. trans. by B. A. Rosenfeld, V. S. Segal and A. P. Yushkevich (Moscow, 1951)
F. Sarre and E. Herzfeld: *Archäologische Reise im Euphrat- und Tigris-Gebiet*, ii (Berlin, 1920)
J. Rosintal: *Pendentifs, trompes et stalactites dans l'architecture orientale* (Paris, 1928)
E. Herzfeld: 'Damascus: Studies in Architecture, I', *A. Islam.*, ix (1942), pp. 10–40
K. A. C. Creswell: *The Muslim Architecture of Egypt*, 2 vols (Oxford, 1952–9)
G. Marçais: *L'Architecture musulmane d'Occident* (Paris, 1954)
L. Golvin: *Recherches archéologiques à la Qal'a des Banu Hammād* (Paris, 1965)
D. Jones: 'The Cappella Palatina in Palermo: Problems of Attribution', *A. & Archaeol. Res. Pap.*, ii (1972), pp. 41–57
O. Grabar: *The Alhambra* (Cambridge, MA, 1978)
U. Harb: *Ilkhanidische Stalaktitengewölbe: Beiträge zu Entwurf und Bautechnik* (Berlin, 1978)
A. Paccard: *Le Maroc et l'artisanat traditionnel islamique dans l'architecture*, 2 vols (St-Jorioz, 1979)
Y. Tabbaa: 'The Muqarnas Dome: Its Origin and Meaning', *Muqarnas*, iii (1985), pp. 61–74
C. K. Wilkinson: *Nishapur: Some Early Islamic Buildings and their Decoration* (New York, 1986)
J. M. Bloom: 'The Introduction of the Muqarnas into Egypt', *Muqarnas*, v (1988), pp. 21–8
L. Golombek and D. Wilber: *The Timurid Architecture of Iran and Turan* (Princeton, 1988)

YASSER TABBAA

Muqi [Mu-ch'i; Fachang] (*b c.* 1210; *d* after 1269). Chinese painter and Chan (Jap. Zen) Buddhist monk. Muqi's family name (*xing*) is not known; his monastic name was Fachang; the name Muqi was a sobriquet (*hao*).

Muqi originated from Sichuan Province; it is assumed that he was born there. His most famous surviving painting, *White-robed Guanyin*, part of a triptych (see fig.), is signed the 'monk from Shu [Sichuan]'. The first textual affirmation of Muqi's connection with Sichuan occurs in Wu Taisu's *Songzhai meipu* (Songzhai's plum manual; 1351), preserved in Japan. The connection is further confirmed by hints in surviving poetry. It is thought that as a young man, possibly in the 1230s, when Mongol invasions threatened Sichuan, Muqi travelled down the Yangzi River to Hangzhou in Zhejiang Province. Poetry commenting on his painting indicates that it evoked feelings both of the Yangzi gorges and the broad reaches of the Xiao and Xiang rivers: Liu Ji (1311–75) remarked, 'in it are a thousand *li* of Xiao and Xiang autumn'. Later, in Japan, much of Muqi's fame was to rest on the assertion that he painted this scenery. Four superb paintings surviving from an original handscroll, *Eight Views of Xiao and Xiang*, are attributed to him: *Returning Sails off a Distant Coast* (Hinohara Col.); *Sunset over a Fishing Village* (Tokyo, Nezu A. Mus.); *Wild Geese Alighting* (Tokyo, Idemitsu Mus. A.); and *Evening Bell from a Distant Temple* (Tokyo, Hatakeyama Col.).

Chan genealogies claim that in Hangzhou Muqi was a disciple of the great Chan master Wujun Shifan (*c.* 1178–1249), the abbot of Jingshan si, and then became abbot himself at Liutong si in the wooded area south of West Lake, where he was responsible for its restoration. Muqi's monastic position must have carried some weight, for Wu Taisu in the *Songzhai meipu* notes that he was accused of slandering the Prime Minister, Jia Sidao (1213–75), and was forced to go into hiding in the home of a Zhejiang

Muqi: *Crane and Bamboo*, *White-robed Guanyin*, *Gibbon and Child*, triptych composed of three hanging scrolls, ink on silk, each scroll 1.75×0.99 m, 13th century (Kyoto, Daitokuji)

family named Qiu. This probably took place in Jia's first years of office (1260–62). Wu also states that Muqi died in the Zhiyuan era (1264–94). A dated inscription on Muqi's diptych *Dragon and Tiger* (Kyoto, Daitokuji), if reliable, indicates that he lived at least until 1269. However, there is no evidence of his painting in the Yuan period (1279–1368), and the early Yuan Daoist recluse Ma Zhen (*b* 1254) wrote that in his youth he had seen Muqi's 'hand painting' but that the artist had 'long' been dead.

In general, Muqi's paintings have been little acclaimed in China, and no certain examples survive there. Initially, however, they were admired, as reflected in poems by not only near contemporaries such as the Chan monk Wuwen Daocan (*d* 1271) and the Daoist Ma Zhen but prominent mid-14th century figures such as Zhang Yu (1289–1371), Song Lian (1310–81) and Liu Ji. Wu Taisu remarked that 'scholar-officials from Jiangnan [south of the Yangzi] still today preserve his paintings, although his bamboo is rare and of his reeds and geese many are forgeries'. The Japanese ink-painter Mokuan Reien, who was in China from 1326 or 1328, was praised as a reborn Muqi and given the latter's seals. Whether there was a 'school' of followers is not certain, although the fine hanging scroll, *Rooster and Bamboo* (Tokyo, N. Mus.), signed by the monk Luochuang from Muqi's monastery, suggests there may have been from as early as the later part of the Song period (960–1279). Even in Ming-period (1368–1643) China, Muqi's contribution was not entirely forgotten. Two handscrolls, generally considered copies, illustrate the continuation of his ideals into the 15th and 16th centuries: *Fruit, Birds and Fish* (Beijing, Pal. Mus.) and *Sketches from Life* (Taipei, N. Pal. Mus.). The former has a colophon by Shen Zhou and the latter has approving encomiums by the famous collector Xiang Yuanbian and the 17th-century painter Zha Shibiao, who praised the painting as ink-play (*moxi*) and suggested Muqi's influence on Suzhou painters of such subjects.

Muqi's increasing obscurity in China can be accounted for by the fact that his painting never truly met the literati ideals that came to dominate art in post-Song China. Even early on, some critics rejected him: Zhuang Su (1298) considered that he lacked refinement and was suitable only for a secluded temple atmosphere; Tang Hou (1330) wrote that his bamboo displayed 'a crudeness beyond compare'; and Xia Wenyan (1365) condemned him for coarseness, a lack of elegance and deficiency in the techniques of the old masters. Such criticism may reflect aspects of Muqi's style as indicated by Wu Taisu. The artist sometimes used 'sugar-cane fibres' to apply ink; in general he strove for simplicity, was careless of physical likeness and displayed an easy brush and dotting of ink. Such methods had aroused both admiration and condemnation in China as early as the Tang dynasty (AD 618–907) in Zhang Yanyuan's *Lidai minghua ji* ('Record of famous painters of all periods'; preface dated AD 847). For some, the absence of the structure of clearly traceable brushwork removed such art from the category of painting altogether. Muqi's unorthodox methods are typified in *Sunset over a Fishing Village*; in *White-robed Guanyin* his use of the brush is more careful and controlled.

In Japan taste was not in the same way governed by literati ideals, and in the atmosphere of enthusiasm for Chan Buddhism, Muqi paintings were prized. In 1365 the temple inventory *Butsunichi an kubutsu mokuroku* cited some Muqi paintings; a century later the curator's manual and catalogue of the shōgun collection, Shinnō Nōami's *Gyomotsu on'e mokuroku*, cited 103 works. Many were imitations, some close, some distant, as is the case regarding Muqi attributions both in Japan and elsewhere in modern times. Important paintings by or attributed to Muqi other than those mentioned above include: *Luohan in Meditation*, with a Muqi seal (Tokyo, Seikadō Bunko); *Chestnuts* (Kyoto, Ryūkō-in); *Six Persimmons* (Kyoto, Ryūkō-in; *see* CHINA, fig. 112); *Hibiscus in Rain* (Kyoto, Daitokuji); *Qianzi with a Shrimp*, with a Muqi seal, though doubted (Baron Masuda priv. col.); *Mynah on a Pine-trunk*, with a Muqi seal (Tokyo, Setsu Gatodo priv. col.); and *Sparrows and Bamboo* (Tokyo, Nezu A. Mus.).

EWA: 'Mu-ch'i'

BIBLIOGRAPHY

Zhuang Su: *Hua ji buyi* [Painting continued: a supplement] (1298); *Hua ji, Hua ji buyi*, ed. Deng Chun and Zhuang Su (Beijing, 1963), pp. 6–7
Tang Hou: *Huajian* [Mirror of painting] (*c.* 1330/R Beijing, 1959), p. 54
Xia Wenyan: *Tuhui baojian* [Precious mirror for examining painting] (1365/R Shanghai, 1963), p. 74
O. Sirén: *Chinese Painting: Leading Masters and Principles* (London and New York, 1956–8), ii, pp. 59, 138–42; iii, pls 336–9
Sōgen no kaiga [Paintings of Song and Yuan] (Tokyo, 1962), pls 22–5, 69–75
Gugong shuhua lu [Record of calligraphy and painting in the Palace Museum], 4 vols (Taipei, 1965), ii, pp. 38–9
J. Fontein and M. Hickman: *Zen Painting and Calligraphy* (Boston, 1970), pp. 28–34
T. Toda: *Mokkei, Gyokan* [Muqi and Yujian], iii of *Suiboku bijutsu taikei* [Compendium of the art of ink painting] (Tokyo, 1973)
N. Wei, *Mu-ch'i and Zen painting* (PhD diss., U. Chicago, 1974)
K. Suzuki: *Chūgoku kaiga shi* [History of Chinese painting], ii (Tokyo, 1985), pp. 208–18; pls 160–71

RICHARD EDWARDS

Mur, Ramon de. *See* RAMON DE MUR.

Mura, Francesco de (*b* Naples, 1696; *d* Naples, 1782). Italian painter. He was educated initially in the workshop of Domenico Viola at Naples, but in 1708 he entered the school of Francesco Solimena, whose favourite pupil and most trusted collaborator he became. At first he followed closely Solimena's monumental Baroque manner, as in the frescoes (1715) in S Nicola alla Carità in Naples, but later developed a more controlled and refined style of rhythmical lines, light and airy colours and delicate psychological overtones. He employed this new style in his ten canvases of the *Virtues* and his vast *Adoration of the Magi* (all 1728; Naples, S Maria Donnaromita) and, above all, in his frescoes of the *Adoration of the Magi* in the apsidal dome of the church of the Nunziatella, Naples (1732; *in situ*). De Mura was also active as a portrait painter; his *Portrait of the Artist's Wife* (*c.* 1730; Naples, Pio Monte della Misericordia) and *Self-portrait* (*c.* 1730; Florence, Uffizi) are both very much in Solimena's manner.

In 1737–8 de Mura executed two allegorical ceiling paintings in the Palazzo Reale, Naples, where the vast *Allegory of the Monarchy* remains, and in 1738 he began the fresco decoration of the church of SS Severino e Sossio, Naples, with scenes from the *Life of St Benedict*. From 1741 to 1743 he worked in Turin, where he decorated a series of rooms at the Palazzo Reale with scenes from Greek history and mythology; among the most beautiful, and in the finest state of preservation, is the decoration of the Sala delle Macchine with *Stories of Theseus*. On his return to Naples, he completed the vast decorative scheme of SS Severino e Sossio with a series of canvases. All this vast quantity of work shows his constant preference for a subtle and intimate manner, both worldly and elegant, which eschews heroics and subtly conveys the most delicate emotion. However, his work in Turin, with its pale, radiant colours and arcadian landscapes, also marked a clear moderation of the late Baroque classicism of Solimena towards the most recent European Rococo, similar to that in the contemporary work of Corrado Giaquinto.

In 1751 de Mura resumed work on the church of the Nunziatella, frescoing the ceiling with a grandiose *Assumption of the Virgin* (see fig.). He continued to paint portraits, and his depiction of *Cardinal Antonio Sersale* (1756; USA, priv. col., see 1979–80 exh. cat., p. 194) and the *Blessed Francesco de Gerolamo* (1758; Naples, Pio Monte della Misericordia) are mature examples of intense psychological interpretation, made vivid by delicate chromatic harmonies. In other surviving works of this period, such as the *bozzetti* for the destroyed frescoes in the Sedile di Porto, the overdoor paintings of *Allegories of the Virtues* for the Palazzo Reale, Turin (*in situ*), which were sent from Naples in 1758, and the designs for tapestries manufactured in both Naples and Turin, for example the *Allegory of Modesty* (1764; Caserta, Pal. Reale), a notably academic approach is evident, which some critics have seen as a progressive decline in ideas. In fact de Mura demonstrated, through this more systematic classicism, his adherence to the enlightened rationalism prevalent in later 18th-century European culture; indeed, sometimes he even anticipated aspects of Neo-classicism. This is especially evident in mythological and allegorical paintings, such as the *Bacchus and Ceres* (early 1760s; U. Notre Dame, IN, Snite Mus. A.) and the *Princes Ascending to the Temple of Immortality*, painted in 1767–8 (Naples, Pio Monte della Misericordia).

Towards the end of his long and prestigious career, de Mura's expressive and formal standards declined irreversibly, and he produced weak and frigidly academic works. As the head of a large workshop, he influenced a number of the Neapolitan artists active in the second half of the 18th century, among them Pietro Bardellino, Fedele Fischetti and Giacinto Diana.

BIBLIOGRAPHY
Bolaffi; Thieme–Becker
B. de Dominici: *Vite* (Naples, 1742–5)
F. Bologna: *Francesco Solimena* (Naples, 1958), pp. 149–50
A. Griseri: 'Francesco de Mura fra le corti di Napoli, Madrid e Torino', *Paragone*, xiii/155 (1962), pp. 22–43
R. Engass: 'Francesco de Mura alla Nunziatella', *Boll. A.*, xlix (1964), pp. 133–48
R. Causa: *Opere d'arte nel Pio Monte della Misericordia* (Cava dei Tirreni, 1970), pp. 63–84, 107–17 [with bibliog.]
N. Spinosa: 'A propos d'un tableau de Francesco de Mura au Louvre', *Rev. Louvre*, xxv (1975), pp. 368–76
V. Rizzo: 'L'opera giovanile di Francesco de Mura', *Napoli Nob.*, xvii–xviii (1978), pp. 93–113
Civiltà del settecento a Napoli, 1734–1799 (exh. cat., Naples, Capodimonte and Pal. Reale, 1979–80), i, pp. 192–205, 384–5; ii, pp. 432–3
V. Rizzo: 'La maturità di Francesco de Mura', *Napoli Nob.*, xix–xx (1980), pp. 29–47

ROBERTO MIDDIONE

Francesco de Mura: *Assumption of the Virgin* (1751), ceiling fresco, church of the Nunziatella, Naples

Murabitun, al-. *See* ALMORAVID.

Murad III. *See* OTTOMAN, §II(4).

Murak, Teresa (*b* Kielczewice, nr Lublin, 5 July 1949). Polish sculptor and conceptual artist. She studied at the Academy of Fine Arts, Warsaw, from 1971 to 1976. Her works *Procession* (1974), featuring sowings of motherwort on a suit of clothes, *Cradle* (1975), on the flat of the hand, and on a 70 m Easter tapestry or carpet for the church in her native Kielczewice (1974), are meditative in character and draw on the fundamental laws of nature and the elements, the life-giving qualities of water and the transformational power of the sun's light. *Sculpture for the Earth* (1974; Ubbenboga, Sweden) contains a hemisphere hollowed out in the earth, juxtaposed with a hemispherical mound. Negative and positive are reiterated in cross-section by graphic Yin and Yang symbols. In the next *Sculpture for the Earth* (begun 1976) a simple geometric quadrilateral encloses the source of a river; two of its sides pass into the side of a mountain, while the other two form a clay wall. The essence of *Intermediate Space* (1986) is the muddiness of the form-creating material (water and earth), the movements of the palm of the hand above it, the action of the light that dries and crystallizes the form while drawing it from the darkness and making it visible. After 1986 Murak worked with bread leavens mixed with earth (e.g. *Longing, Doing, Vigilance*), compositions that illustrate the relationship between grain, earth and water. The process of natural growth and ripening is connected with the full range of human activity towards nature and the shaped form, as is shown in *Crater* (1987; Lillehammer, Bys Malerisaml.).

BIBLIOGRAPHY
J. Brach-Czajna: *Etos nowej sztuki* [Ethos of new art] (Warsaw, 1984), pp. 201–2
Teresa Murak: Rysunki 'Dla ziemii' [Teresa Murak: *For the Earth* drawings] (exh. cat., ed. W. Wierzchowska and M. Selmowicz; Warsaw, Pokaz Gal., 1987) [interview with the artist]

EWA MIKINA

Murakami, Kagaku (*b* Osaka, 3 July 1888; *d* Kobe, 11 Nov 1939). Japanese painter. In 1907 he graduated from the Kyoto Municipal Painting School. After learning the realistic painting techniques of the Maruyama–Shijō school, he studied such traditional Japanese schools of painting as Yamatoe, Rinpa and Ukiyoe as well as classical Indian and Chinese painting, incorporating elements of all these traditions in his work to create an individual style. In 1918 he became a member of the National Creative Painting Society (Kokuga sōsaku kyōkai), a group formed in Kyoto that aimed at the creation of a new Japanese painting style (*Nihonga*) (*see* JAPAN, §VI, 5(iii)). He became afflicted with chronic asthma, and in 1927 he moved to Kobe and severed his ties with artistic circles, exhibiting rarely after this time. Murakami's subject-matter included the mountains of Kobe, Buddhist images and flowers such as peonies and camellias. His remaining works, such as *Portrait of the Hidakagawa Princess* (1919; Tokyo, N. Mus. Mod. A.), are introspective and spiritual.

WRITINGS
Garon [Discussions on painting] (Tokyo, 1968)

BIBLIOGRAPHY
M. Kawakita: *Murakami Kagaku* (Tokyo, 1969)
Murakami Kagaku (exh. cat., foreword K. Adachi and K. Morita; Tokyo, N. Mus. Mod. A., 1984)

YOSHIKAZU IWASAKI

Mural. Painting applied to an exterior or interior wall surface, especially in a public building or space. During the 19th century a growing sense of national identity in many countries, especially in Europe, and the emergence of new patrons, both private and public, stimulated a revival in didactic and historical mural painting that was closely linked with revivalist movements in architecture. The mural subsequently became a significant art form throughout the modern Western world, where its potential accessibility for a large viewing public and, in some cases, its ability to stimulate public response led to its use in the promotion of a variety of social and political causes. This article discusses the history of this modern development. For discussion of the techniques used in mural painting, and of their development from antiquity to modern times, *see* WALL PAINTING and FRESCO. For discussion of the important role of mural painting in a number of cultures outside the Western world *see under* the survey article on the appropriate country or civilization.

1. Europe. 2. Latin America. 3. North America.

1. EUROPE.

(i) *c.* 1810–*c.* 1930. (ii) After *c.* 1930.

(i) c. 1810–c. 1930. The modern revival of mural painting in Europe was led by the NAZARENES in Rome and Munich, using true fresco according to Italian Renaissance techniques (*see* FRESCO). Renouncing Rococo and Neoclassical ideals for a naive style based on medieval and early Renaissance sources, Friedrich Overbeck, Peter Cornelius, Wilhelm Schadow and Philipp Veit illustrated the *Story of Joseph* (1816–18) at the Casa Bartholdy in Rome, and Julius Schnorr von Carolsfeld painted scenes from Ariosto's *Orlando furioso* in 1817 (for illustration *see* SCHNORR VON CAROLSFELD, (2)) at the Villa Massimo. Their style was adopted by King Ludwig I of Bavaria as a symbol of German identity in such commissions as Cornelius's *Prometheus* and *Trojan War* murals (1820–30; *see* CORNELIUS, PETER, fig. 2) for the Glyptothek, Munich, and Schnorr von Carolsfeld's scenes based on the Nibelung legend in the Königsbau in the Residenz in Munich (from 1827; see fig. 1). Cornelius also advised on the murals of British history and legend promoted by Prince Albert at the new Palace of Westminster, London, from 1845, where they were intended to complement Charles Barry's and A. W. N. Pugin's Gothic Revival architecture. The chief artists were William Dyce and Daniel Maclise. The Nazarenes' example was also followed by Melchior Paul von Deschwanden in Switzerland and by Moritz von Schwind at the Staatsoper, Vienna (1863–7). Historical subjects were also adopted in Spain (e.g. by Vicente López

1. Murals illustrating the Nibelung legend (1845) by Julius Schnorr von Carolsfeld: the *Room of Betrayal* and *Siegfried's Death*, fresco, 4.75×5.29 m, Residenz, Munich

y Portaña at the Palacio Real, Madrid, 1825–8) and in Sweden (e.g. by Johann Gustav Sandberg (1782–1854) at Uppsala Cathedral, 1831–8), although Baroque styles persisted in Bohemia (e.g in Josef Matěj Navrátil's work of the 1830s to 1850s).

In France, meanwhile, Delacroix and Ingres developed a strong national tradition of mural painting that dated back to Eustache Le Sueur and Charles Le Brun (1619–90). In Paris, Delacroix gave a Romantic interpretation to classical iconography in his commissions at the Palais-Bourbon (from 1833), the Palais du Luxembourg (from 1840) and the Louvre (1849–61), and his colour experiments at St Sulpice (1850–61) were later influential for the Impressionists and Post-Impressionists. He also contributed, with Ingres, to the decoration (1849–53; destr. 1871) of the Hôtel de Ville, Paris. Ingres's pupils developed a number of influential mural styles, as in Hippolyte Flandrin's simplified, monumental figures, often in frieze format, for Viollet-le-Duc's church restorations (e.g. St Vincent-de-Paul, Paris, 1849–53), which can be seen as the direct precedent for the work of Pierre Puvis de Chavannes (e.g. the Musée Napoléon (now Musée de Picardie), Amiens, 1861–4 and 1880–82). Paul Delaroche introduced a new element of realism in his *Hemicycle* (from 1837) at the Ecole des Beaux-Arts, Paris, and Théodore Chassériau combined aspects of Ingres with Delacroix's sense of colour in such works as the panels (1844–8; destr. 1871; fragments in Paris, Louvre) for the staircase of the Cour des Comptes, Palais d'Orsay.

The majority of these French works were executed in oil on canvas, attached to the wall by the process of marouflage (*see* WALL PAINTING, §I, 4(iv)), and as Paris emerged during the mid-19th century as the European centre for art training, this mural technique gained widespread currency. Mural painting became closely associated with easel styles, and the trend to realism in Delaroche's *Hemicycle* was emulated in such works as the *Artists of Antwerp* mural (1862–72) by Nicaise De Keyser in the Koninklijk Museum voor Schone Kunsten, Antwerp. Under Gustaf Wappers, Director of the Antwerp Academie from 1840 to 1855, a revival of a colouristic style derived from Rubens and the Flemish Baroque was fused with historical and psychological realism in the oil murals of such artists as Henri Leys, Jan Swerts (1820–79) and Gottfried Egide Guffens (1823–1901). Another of Wappers's pupils, Ernst Stückelberg, later developed a highly dramatic realism in his illustrations (completed 1883) of Schiller's *William Tell* for the Tellskapelle on Lake Urner in Switzerland. Wappers also taught Anselm Feuerbach, who as Director of the Akademie der Bildenden Künste, Vienna, evolved a somewhat insipid neo-Baroque in his *Fall of the Titans* ceiling (1874–80) for the academy's Great Hall.

In Germany, reaction to the Nazarenes' primitivism was expressed in a shift of focus from Munich to Düsseldorf, which became, with Antwerp, the chief centre outside Paris for training in mural painting. In Düsseldorf Delaroche's realism was highly influential, for example in the work of Carl Friedrich Lessing, Heinrich Karl Anton Mücke (1806–91) and Hermann Freihold Plüddemann (1809–68) at Heltorf Castle (1829–30). The murals painted by ALFRED RETHEL in 1847–9 for the Rathaus, Aachen,

continued the use of fresco, but Rethel's fusion of religious sentiment, national identity and contemporary political reference was new and was also imbued with a sense of the elemental and the mystical, expressed in an angular stylism derived from early German woodcuts. Another Düsseldorf artist, Eduard Bendemann, developed more classical tendencies in his murals (1855) for the Königsschloss, Dresden, and the discoveries at Herculaneum and Pompeii inspired the academic Neo-classicism of Wilhelm von Kaulbach's frescoes (1847–63) in the Neues Museum, Berlin. By the 1880s the work of Peter Janssen, who became Director of the Düsseldorf Academy in 1895, can be seen as part of a widespread historical mural style, shared by Karl Theodor von Piloty and in France by Jean-Joseph Weerts (1847–1927), Francis Tattegrain (1852–1912), Theóbald Chartran (1849–1907) and others, some of whom had studied in Düsseldorf as well as in Paris. Janssen's major work was at the town halls of Krefeld (1869–73) and Erfurt (1878–81), and at the university in Marburg (1887–92).

It was in fresco that the mystical aspects of Rethel's work were developed, principally in relation to the stricter revivalist styles that were developed from around the mid-19th century and encouraged by the translation of Renaissance treatises by such artists as VICTOR MOTTEZ in France and Mary Philadelphia Merrifield in Britain. Arnold Böcklin's study of antique work, for example, resulted in a highly personal use of fresco to achieve direct and spiritual 'communion' between the painter and his themes. Böcklin's allegories of the *Fruitfulness of Mother Earth* in the Museum für Natur- und Völkerkunde, Basle, which were commissioned by the art historian Jacob Burckhardt in 1868, were also a deliberate attempt to harmonize with the Renaissance Revival architecture of the new building. The concern with the integration of architecture and decoration was given added impetus by Hegel's theories of architecture as the 'mother art', which inspired such artists as Charles Blanc in France, by the revival of craftsmanship by William Morris and his followers in their experiments with fresco at the Oxford Union in 1857, by the 'National Theatre generation' in Prague (which included František Ženíšek), and by the development of the idea of the GESAMTKUNSTWERK by Richard Wagner and others. This last development joined with the example of Böcklin to form a key ingredient in the evolution of Symbolism. Perhaps the most significant revivals of fresco, however, were at the Beuron Cloister in Switzerland and in other works in Prague, Montecassino, Stuttgart and Teplice in Bohemia by Peter Lenz (1832–1928), Jacob Wüger (1829–92) and Fridolin Steiner (1849–1906). These artists drew inspiration from Byzantine and Early Christian art and later influenced the Nabis and the Ateliers d'Art Sacré of MAURICE DENIS in the 20th century. The Scandinavian fresco revival includes the Stockholm National Museum murals by Carl Larsson and others and culminates in the work (1920–23) of the Fresco Brothers in the Bergen Exchange in Norway.

Aspects of Böcklin's idealism were developed in Hans Reinhard von Marées's frescoes (1873; with Adolf von Hildebrand) in the library of the Zoological Institute in Naples, which were sponsored by Konrad Fiedler. These landscape idylls, intended to recreate the spirit of a lost golden age, led to Marées's late experiments with the fusion of wall and easel painting through the concept of the triptych. Other Symbolists such as Giovanni Segantini, Ferdinand Hodler and Cuno Amiet also developed what might be termed 'murals without walls' in response to the preference of Joséphin Peladan's Salon de la Rose + Croix for 'work that has a mural-like character'. Max Klinger, Franz von Stuck and other members of the Berlin and Munich Secessions developed this form of art, and Edvard Munch's *Frieze of Life* cycle (1893–1902; Oslo, Nasjonalgalleriet) formed the basis of his murals in Oslo University Festival Hall (1911–16).

During the late 19th century, France assumed a leading role in the use of oil-based murals. Following the Weltausstellung of 1873 in Vienna, at which German and Austrian murals had been shown prior to installation, mural painting was promoted by CHARLES-PHILIPPE DE CHENNEVIÈRES, as a means to regenerate French art. His scheme of 'religio-historico' murals, commissioned from 1874 to decorate the Panthéon in Paris, was executed by artists from the Ecole des Beaux-Arts and by others felt to represent modern academic French achievement. Among the panels, not completed until 1901, those on the subject of St Genevieve (1874–8 and 1893–8) by PIERRE PUVIS DE CHAVANNES were of international influence, with their attempt to emulate in oil the light tonalities and simplified figure style of early Italian frescoes (see fig. 2). Puvis emerged as the principal French mural painter of the period and is perhaps best known for his *Sacred Wood* (1887), an allegory of the arts and sciences in the Sorbonne, Paris. The eclectic revivalism used by Charles Garnier in his design for the new Opéra in Paris was paralleled by the Mannerist and Michelangelesque Opéra murals (1866–74) by Paul Baudry and others, which formed part of a highly integrated symbolic scheme of architecture and decoration. This eclecticism reached its climax in the civic project at the Hôtel de Ville, Paris, where from 1887 to 1902 more than 50 artists were involved, ranging from Puvis to the historical realists such as Tattegrain, the social realist Léon Lhermitte and the proto-Divisionist work of Henri Martin, though Manet's offer of murals on themes from Zola, made prior to the scheme in 1879, was not taken up. This was probably the most ambitious town hall decoration in Europe and marked a distinctive French trend towards contemporary iconography that was echoed by ALBERT BESNARD's work (1884–7) at the Ecole de Pharmacie and culminated in the neo-Impressionist murals painted by HENRI MARTIN in the early 20th century in the Palais Royal, Paris.

Although modern iconography was incorporated in some German civic schemes as an expression of national unity, the majority of such projects retained the Düsseldorf school style of historical realism. In Vienna and Britain too, contemporary subjects were slow to be accepted. During the 1890s GUSTAV KLIMT, in partnership with Ernst Klimt (1864–92) and Franz Matsch (1861–1942), illustrated historical and Classical material in the Burgtheater and the Kunsthistorisches Museum, Vienna, where new sources of inspiration from Byzantine and early German art were grafted on to the colourism of Hans Makart, with whom the partnership had trained. These

2. Mural by Pierre Puvis de Chavannes: *St Genevieve Keeping Watch over the Sleeping Paris* (1898), marouflaged canvas, 4.62×2.26 m, Panthéon, Paris

reached full development in Gustav Klimt's radical *Beethoven Frieze* for the Vienna Sezession Building in 1902. Klimt was also commissioned to decorate the Universität, Vienna, in a move to identify the new political regime with progressive art, but his uncompromising exposure of contemporary mores caused an outcry. The Neo-classical work executed by Alois Hans Schram (1864–1919) at the Parlament (1909–11) and the symbolic personifications eventually painted by Matsch for the Universität (1905–7) represented the official preference.

Following the experiment with fresco at the Palace of Westminster, there was a revival of British mural painting in the 19th century, including much church decoration, G. F. Watts's *Lawgivers* fresco (1853–9) at Lincoln's Inn, London, work in many public buildings, and such private schemes as Whistler's *Harmony in Blue and Gold: The Peacock Room* (1876–7; Washington, DC, Freer) and that by John Duncan (1866–1945) and others for Sir Patrick Geddes at Ramsay Garden, Edinburgh. Ford Madox Brown's historical scheme (1878–93) at Manchester Town Hall (*see* BROWN, FORD MADOX) was a late survival of Nazarene principles but used the 'spirit fresco' medium developed by THOMAS GAMBIER-PARRY. This was popularized as a more durable alternative to true fresco in the allegorical lunettes (1878–83) for the South Kensington Museum (now Victoria and Albert Museum), London, by Frederic Leighton, whose emulation of French precedents in the collaborative historical scheme at the Royal Exchange (1892–1927), London, marked a new trend in the mural revival in Britain. This directly inspired the principal public work of the period, a series of schemes at the Palace of Westminster from 1906 to 1927, but it also influenced the iconography of Frank Brangwyn's first major commission at Skinners' Hall in London (1901–9). Brangwyn's colouristic synthesis of Baroque, Realist and Symbolist elements remained closer to continental than British traditions (*see* BRANGWYN, FRANK), and much of his work was for American patrons and foreign exhibitions. His style contrasted strongly with the Pre-Raphaelite and neo-classical tendencies given preference at Westminster, but it had a number of emulators, including Gerald Edward Moira (1867–1959).

The European revival of mural painting reached its peak in the years 1890–1914, when the integration of art and architecture characteristic of the Arts and Crafts Movement, Art Nouveau and *Jugendstil* coincided with economic prosperity and the strengthening of the nationalist and political independence movements. These aspects found focus in the Exposition Universelle of 1900 in Paris, where the Finnish pavilion was decorated with Akseli Gallen-Kallela's *Kalevala* legend frescoes (destr.; sketches in Helsinki, Athenaeum A. Mus.; larger versions (1928) in Helsinki, N. Mus.). Later nationalist mural schemes included the Czech Alphonse Mucha's *Slav Epic* panels (1913; Prague, Moravský Krumlov Castle).

A number of schemes commenced before and just after World War I reflected stylistic developments in European painting. These included Angelo Jank's murals at the Reichstag in Munich and the Cubist and Fauvist designs proposed for the Stockholm Law Courts in 1912–13 by Georg Pauli (1855–1935) and others, which were rejected in favour of more traditional styles by Filip Mansson (1864–1933). Henri Matisse completed Fauvist panels for Sergei Shchukin in Moscow in 1908–11 on the themes of *Dance* and *Music* (both St Petersburg, Hermitage), and Ivan Morozov and Savva Mamontov commissioned Russian avant-garde artists such as Mikhail Vrubel'. Cubism and Vorticism found mural exponents in Emile-Antoine Bourdelle (e.g. the Théâtre des Champs Elysées, Paris, 1912; for illustration *see* BOURDELLE, EMILE-ANTOINE) and Wyndham Lewis and in the Omega Workshops artists working for private patrons in Britain. Amédée Ozenfant collaborated with Le Corbusier on a number of schemes in France, and elements of Neue Sachlichkeit are present in Hilding Linnqvist's murals (1928) at the Stadsbibliothek in Stockholm. There was little Expressionist mural work, however, apart from that by Munch, the Kamerny State

Jewish Theatre murals (1920–21) in Moscow by Marc Chagall and a few private commissions executed by Ernst Ludwig Kirchner and Max Pechstein.

In the 1920s the didactic and propagandist role formerly played by much public mural painting passed increasingly to posters and films, and mural painting began to serve a more purely decorative function. At the Exposition Internationale des Arts Décoratifs et Industriels Modernes of 1925 in Paris, the future of mural art was seen as being in cheaper modern media using non-representational styles. With the rise of Functionalism in architecture, the role of mural painting was seriously challenged and further developments depended heavily on architectural initiative. Examples include Piet Mondrian's and El Lissitzky's attempts to unify architecture and painting in their abstract rooms, Willi Baumeister's *Wall Pictures* (1920–23) and Oskar Schlemmer's work for the Bauhaus at Weimar.

BIBLIOGRAPHY

A. Champeaux: *Histoire de la peinture décorative* (Paris, 1890)
G. Pauli: *Monumentalmåleriets utveckling i Sverige från 1800: talets senare del* (Stockholm, 1933)
M. Pfister-Burkhalter: *Arnold Böcklin: Die Basler Museumsfresken* (Basle, 1951)
T. S. R. Boase: 'The Decoration of the New Palace of Westminster, 1841–63', *J. Warb. & Court. Inst.*, xvii (1954), pp. 319–58
B. Degenhart: *Hans von Marées: Die Fresken in Neapel* (Munich, 1959)
R. Josephson: *Bilden på muren* (Stockholm, 1965)
H. von Einem: 'Die Tragödie der Karlsfresken Alfred Rethels', *Karl der Grosse*, iv (1967), pp. 306–25
P. Werner: *Pompeii und die Wanddekorationen der Goethezeit* (Munich, 1970)
F. Zelger: *Die Fresken Ernst Stückelbergs in der Tellskapelle am Vierwaldstättersee* (Berne, 1972)
M. Bisanz Prakken: *Gustav Klimt: Der Beethovenfries: Geschichte, Funktion und Bedeutung* (Salzburg, 1977)
R. Gordon and C. F. Stuckey: 'Blossoms and Blunders: Monet and the State', pt 1, *A. America* (Jan–Feb 1979); pt. 2, *A. America* (Sept 1979)
Die Düsseldorfer Malerschule (exh. cat., ed. R. Andrée and others; Düsseldorf, Kstmus., 1979)
P. Vaisse: *La Troisième République et les peintres* (diss., Paris IV, 1979)
J. Foucart: *Les Peintures de l'Opéra de Paris de Baudry à Chagall* (Paris, 1980)
Le Moyen-Age et les peintres français de la fin du XIXe siècle (exh. cat., ed. G. Lacambre and others; Cagnes-sur-Mer, Château-Mus., 1980)
W. Kitlitshka: *Die Malerei der Wiener Ringstrasse* (Wiesbaden, 1981)
H. T. Wappenschmidt: *Studien zur Ausstattung des deutschen Rathaussaales in der 2. Hälfte des 19. Jahrhunderts bis 1918* (Bonn, 1981)
C. A. P. Willsdon: 'Scotland's Mural Renascence', *Scot. Rev.*, xxix (1983), pp. 15–22
H. Smith: *Decorative Painting in the Domestic Interior in England and Wales, c. 1850–1890* (New York and London, 1984)
Hippolyte, Auguste et Paul Flandrin: Une Fraternité picturale au XIXe siècle (exh. cat., ed. J. Foucart; Paris, Mus. Luxembourg, 1984)
Le Triomphe des mairies (exh. cat., ed. T. Burollet, D. Imbert and F. Folliot; Paris, Petit Pal., 1986–7)
C. A. P. Willsdon: *Aspects of Mural Painting in London, 1890–1930* (diss., U. Cambridge, 1988)
M. C. Chaudonneret: 'Historicism and Heritage in the Louvre: From the Musée Charles X to the Galerie d'Apollon', *A. Hist.*, xiv/4 (1991), pp. 488–520
W. H. Robinson: 'Puvis de Chavannes' Summer and the Symbolist Avant-garde', *Bull. Cleveland Mus. A.*, lxxviii (1991), pp. 2–27
C. A. P. Willsdon: 'Klimt's Beethoven Frieze: Goethe, "Tempelkunst" and the Fulfilment of Wishes', *A. Hist.*, xix/1 (March 1996)
——: 'The Mural Paintings of the Royal Exchange, London', *The Royal Exchange, London*, ed. A. Saunders, London Topographical Society monograph (London, 1997)
——: *Mural Painting in Britain 1840–1940* (Oxford, in preparation)
CLARE A. P. WILLSDON

(ii) After c. 1930. During the 1930s there was a worldwide trend towards making art public and accessible as a reaction

against what was perceived as the hermetic and introspective development of modern art. This trend was particularly pronounced in Mexico and the USA, where it was supported through government sponsorship, but it was also evident in Britain, France and Portugal. In Italy a desire on the part of some artists to return to Classical and Renaissance sources was supported by Mussolini, who harnessed it to his propagandist political purposes (*see* FASCISM, §2). Mario Sironi was a leading figure in the didactic muralism that ensued, publishing his *Manifesto of Mural Painting* in 1933. He also commissioned murals in a variety of styles by such artists as De Chirico and Carrà, including non-propagandist works such as Carrà's *Universal Justice* of 1938 in the Palazzo di Giustizia, Milan. In Germany and the USSR public art also largely reflected the totalitarian propaganda of the State, for example in the titles of such works as Rudolf Hengstenberg's *Comradeship* of 1937 and the collaborative *Comrade Stalin together with the Leading Workers of the Party and the Government Inspect the Work of a Soviet Tractor of a New Type* of 1939. Elsewhere in Europe there was a parallel rise of artists and groups supporting Socialist causes. In Spain, for example, José María Sert (1874–1945) used the dramatic manner of Goya and Tiepolo in his anti-Fascist murals (e.g. *Elegies to the Basque People*, 1929–34; San Sebastián, Mus. Mun. S Telmo). In 1933 Artists International (later the ARTISTS INTERNATIONAL ASSOCIATION [AIA]) was established in Britain with the aim of achieving 'the unity of artists against Fascism and war and the suppression of culture'. The organization's membership embraced all stylistic tendencies and various political attitudes; the dominant style, though, was social realism, incorporating influences from Mexico and the USA through Diego Rivera's apprentices Jack Hastings and Clifford Wight. Cliff Rowe (*b* 1904) and other members of the Communist Party adhered to influences from Moscow. Among the notable exhibitions organized by the AIA was *Art for the People*, held at the Whitechapel Art Gallery, London, in 1939. Not all murals produced during this period were politically motivated, however. There were also many private commissions for purely decorative work for stately homes, educational institutions and places of entertainment, often in the classical and rococo styles made fashionable by such artists as Duncan Grant, Vanessa Bell and Rex Whistler. A notable stylistic exception was Stanley Spencer, who expressed wartime themes in his murals (1927–32) for the Sandham Memorial Chapel in Burghclere, Hants. Perhaps the most significant European event of the 1930s for mural painting, however, was the Exposition Universelle in Paris in 1937, for which many leading painters were commissioned to execute murals: Fernand Léger, for example, was commissioned to produce two works, including one for the pavilion of the Union des Artistes Modernes. Among the more avant-garde contributions was Picasso's *Guernica*, exhibited in the Spanish pavilion. In Britain the degree to which mural painting had become an accepted art form was demonstrated by the photographic exhibition *Mural Painting in Great Britain, 1919–39*, held at the Tate Gallery, London, in 1939.

During World War II many commissions were revoked in Britain, although many artists continued to work either as war artists or independently. The AIA established a policy aimed at providing financial aid to artists and at broadening the accessibility of art, introducing programmes of mural decoration for temporary or converted buildings used for wartime administration, such as workers' hostels, barracks, NAAFI canteens and government-subsidized restaurants (e.g. Kenneth Rowntree: untitled mural (*c.* 1943) for British Restaurant, Acton, London; see Feibusch, pl. xlix). The projects involved collective design and execution, and the subjects depicted were derived from the location and use of the buildings. In the case of hostels funding came from residents, but other projects were instigated by the Council for the Encouragement of Music and the Arts (CEMA), in an attempt to establish a policy of government sponsorship for public art works. An important figure in Portugal in the 1940s was Almada Negreiros, who produced frescoes for the Gare Marítima de Alcântara (1943–5) and the Gare Marítima da Rocha (1946–8) in the port of Lisbon; he used various modernist styles to depict port life and to treat the subject of emigration.

Despite the provision of instruction in numerous art schools, mural painting declined in the post-war years. Murals painted for the Festival of Britain (1951) were in a decorative style, and most were either private or civic commissions. A discretionary levy on the cost of new civic buildings financed many art projects, notably the murals painted in schools for Hertfordshire County Council by Fred Millett and Ceri Richards. In the Netherlands, the Rotterdamse Kunststichting commissioned such works as Karel Appel's *Wall of Energy* (1955) as part of a programme of post-war reconstruction. A more general re-emergence of mural painting in the 1960s and 1970s, however, echoed many of the attitudes of the 1930s. Artists, architects and planners sought to anchor themselves more firmly within the fabric of society and to join workers, tenants and students in an attempt to reverse the isolating hold of professionalism and to establish self-determination and control. The trend was visible throughout Europe, and while initially it developed spontaneously in separate countries, artists gradually made definite links between countries, creating a spirit of mutual interest and support. Major influences during this period were the Mexican mural painters Diego Rivera, David Alfaro Siqueiros and José Clemente Orozco (*see* §2 below), as well as African-American and Latin American artists based in the USA. The principal features of the movement were that the murals were predominantly painted on the flank walls of local buildings; the subject-matter was governed by the interests of the working classes, with murals deliberately located in working-class areas; and the movement promoted collaborative work between artists and non-artists in an effort to diminish the élitist status of art and to establish artistic training outside formal educational institutions. A notable government-led scheme of this period was the Statens Kunstfond, set up in Denmark in 1964 to provide funding for public decoration schemes.

By 1974 various mural workshops had been established throughout Europe, based either on collective or cooperative management, and many more independent artists worked to commission from neighbourhood or community groups and art organizations. In Britain political and social issues, community action, racial and cultural pride and harmony, pacifism and ecological concerns dominated the subject-matter of murals, for example the Greenwich Mural Workshop's depiction of the struggle against Fascism, the *Battle of Cable Street* (1978–83; London, Tower Hamlets, St George's Town Hall; see fig. 3). The Rotterdamse Kunstichting, the Senate of Bremen and the Arts Council of Great Britain, together with the Regional Arts Board, all supported programmes including the funding of murals, aimed at the social and artistic involvement of people within their own communities. The cities of Stockholm, Newcastle and London commissioned extensive programmes to decorate their metro systems, involving both community artists and professionals (e.g. Siri Derkert's untitled work of 1961 at Östermalmstorg Station, Stockholm). In Amsterdam the Artists' Union organized the creation of a series of murals protesting against a planned metro system that was to entail the demolition of residential areas. School and hospital mural projects were established in many countries, involving residencies for artists, while in France the mass use of screenprinted posters during the uprisings of May 1968 developed into 'wall newspapers' produced by Atelier Populaire. Murals in France and the Netherlands were distinguished by their partial use of a wall, whereas in England and Germany all of the flank wall was used to maximize the effect on the street environment. Social realism was again the predominant style, although *trompe l'oeil* techniques were sometimes used. In the subterranean entertainment and shopping complex developed at Les Halles, Paris, in 1979, murals were in a Pop art style. Also during the 1970s murals were used by exiled Chilean artists in Europe to protest against military interventionism in their country. The revolution in Portugal in 1974 likewise produced a mass of spontaneous protest murals.

Despite the waning in the 1980s of the earlier fervour, interest in mural painting continued. The Public Art Development Trust was set up in Britain in 1983 to promote public art. Additional funding through programmes aimed at creating youth employment boosted the numbers of artists and non-artists producing murals, and local government encouraged the decoration of unattractive areas as a cheap means of environmental improvement. Artists became more aware of potential areas of employment in non-traditional art forms, and this broadening of interests led to a dilution of social activism in mural painting and an increase in the variety of media used, including fresco, terracotta, enamels and mosaics (e.g. Eduardo Paolozzi's work at Tottenham Court Road Station, London, 1980–88). Active state patronage of public art schemes continued during this period in various European countries, including France, where the state would allocate 1% of the construction cost of new public buildings towards their artistic decoration. In spite of reductions in state subsidy in the late 1980s and increased government pressure to use industrial and commercial sponsorship to fund the arts, particularly in Britain, there

3. Mural by the Greenwich Mural Workshop: *Battle of Cable Street* (1978–83), St George's Town Hall, Cable St, Tower Hamlets, London

was a revival in interest in public art; the Art for Architecture scheme, established in the 1990s, was a joint initiative between the Royal Society of Arts and the Department of the Environment to make financial awards to architects and developers, enabling them to commission works of art for integration into new buildings.

BIBLIOGRAPHY

Mural Painting in Great Britain, 1919–1939: An Exhibition of Photographs (exh. cat., London, Tate, 1939)
H. Feibusch: *Mural Painting* (London, 1946)
M. Regouin and M. Roelofs: *Couleur locale: Stadsschilderingen in Rotterdam* (Rotterdam, 1978)
G. Cooper and D. Sargent: *Painting the Town* (Oxford, 1979)
V. Barthelmeh: *Kunst an der Wand: Wandmalerei in der Bundesrepublik Deutschland* (Frankfurt, 1980)
M. Benn, L. Benn and A. Lindberg: *Konstnären mittibland oss* [The artist among us] (Stockholm, 1981)
F. Chatel and others: *L'Art public: Peintures murales contemporaines, peintures populaires traditionnelles* (Paris, 1981)
The Story of the Artists International Association, 1933–1953 (exh. cat. by L. Morris and R. Radford, Oxford, MOMA, 1983)
C. Kenna: *Murals in London* (London, 1985)
C. Kenna and S. Lobb: *Mural Manual* (London, 1985)
E. Lucie-Smith: *Art of the 1930s* (London, 1985)
R. Radford: *Art for a Purpose: The Artists International Association, 1933–1953* (Winchester, 1987)

CAROL KENNA

2. LATIN AMERICA. During the late 19th century mural painting in Mexico spread from its colonial role in church decoration and began to be used for secular decorations endorsing the positivist ideology that dominated education and political thought. Such murals as Juan Cordero's *Triumph of Science and Labour over Envy and Ignorance* (1874; Mexico City, Escuela N. Prep.; destr.) were painted in educational institutions and state buildings. After the Mexican Revolution (1910–20), the Secretary of State for Education (1921–4), José Vasconcelos (1882–1959), allocated a substantial budget for the decoration of public buildings with murals, demonstrating his belief in

4. Mural by Roberto Montenegro: *Tree of Life* (1922), tempera, former church of SS Pedro y Pablo, Mexico City

the edifying function of art. ROBERTO MONTENEGRO, DIEGO RIVERA and DAVID ALFARO SIQUEIROS were among those who received the first major mural commissions; they had spent time in Spain during the early 1900s and were familiar with *modernista* mural decorations in Barcelona. The influence of these is evident in the first large-scale mural commission, in which Montenegro, Adolfo Best Maugard and the Guatemalan Carlos Mérida decorated (1921–2) the former church of SS Pedro y Pablo in Mexico City. The artists depicted motifs drawn from regional craftworks, and Montenegro painted *Tree of Life* in tempera on the main wall, using Symbolist imagery heavily influenced by *Modernista* paintings (see fig. 4). Similar influences are evident in Diego Rivera's *Creation* (encaustic and gold leaf, 1922–3; Mexico City, Anfiteatro Bolívar, Escuela N. Prep.), while a series of frescoes by JOSÉ CLEMENTE OROZCO were expressionistic in style and treated esoteric themes (e.g. *Struggle of Man against Nature*, 1923; Mexico City, Escuela N. Prep.; destr.).

The influence of *modernismo* declined as nationalist themes became prominent; several mural artists sought to develop nationalist styles based on images and forms from Pre-Columbian and indigenous popular art, as in JEAN CHARLOT's *Conquest of Tenochtitlán* (fresco, 1922–3; Mexico City, Escuela N. Prep., stairway) and FERNANDO LEAL's *Festival at Chalma* (fresco, 1922–3; Mexico City, Escuela N. Prep., stairway). At the same time a more militant tendency was also discernible: many leading mural artists, notably Rivera and Siqueiros, had joined the Mexican Communist Party and in 1922 had helped form the Sindicato de Obreros Técnicos, Pintores y Escultores. The Sindicato issued a manifesto in its periodical, *El Machete*, stating that mural painting should be Socialist in orientation, both in terms of imagery and in methods of execution. Rivera's murals in the Ministry of Education building, Mexico City, started in 1923 on three storeys of the two main courtyards, initially depicted peasant life but gradually became more militant, showing images of work and of the Revolution. Orozco also painted images of the Revolution at the Escuela Nacional Preparatoria; his first version of the *Revolutionary Trinity* (1923–4) was destroyed by hostile students, but he replaced it in 1926–7. Orozco became increasingly overt in his criticism of the exploitation of the working classes, and the left-wing orientation of the muralists' work led to hostility from the government between 1925 and 1933. Consequently, activity in this area was greatly reduced.

A revival in commissions for murals in schools, union buildings and open public areas in the mid-1930s was the result of a united response of the government and artists to the rise of Fascism in Europe. The political emphasis of the murals from this period lessened, however, in the late 1940s, when commissions came from many private institutions as well as for government buildings (for illustration *see* OROZCO, JOSÉ CLEMENTE). Such artists as Rufino Tamayo and JUAN O'GORMAN were less overtly political than Orozco, Rivera or Siqueiros had been, and their murals often reflected a more decorative, folkloric approach. Particularly striking is O'Gorman's mosaic decoration *Historical Representation of Culture* (1948–50), created around the exterior walls of the central library at the Ciudad Universitaria, Mexico City. O'Gorman's use of mosaic was typical of a move towards using different materials and a more technical approach. Siqueiros had encouraged experimentation in the USA in the early 1930s with such approaches and techniques as the use of nitro-cellulose pyroxaline paint, photographic projection, air-brushes, curvilinear perspective and collective work. His innovations were demonstrated in *For a Complete Social Security for all Mexicans* (1954; Mexico City, Hospital de la Raza).

The impact of Mexican muralism was felt throughout Latin America in the post-war period. In Argentina, since 1971, more than 400 murals have been painted in schools, regional museums and union buildings by such groups as La Pena in Mar del Plata and Greda in Buenos Aires. A significant example is the mural by Rodolfo Campondon-ica (*b* 1938) on the history of Argentina, the *Path of Humanity* (1973–80), at the municipal palace at Trenque Lauquen. Against the backdrop of radical political events, many mural artists in Latin America also took to painting on walls in the streets. This occurred in Chile during the government of President Allende (1970–73), when mural artists formed themselves into brigades to protest at military interventionism. Also in the 1970s the Colectivo Acciones de Arte (CADA) was set up in Chile with the aim of producing art collectively in public spaces. In Nicaragua, where the influence of Mexican mural painting was felt most strongly following the Sandinista revolution (1979), such mural painters as Alejandro Canales turned to political and revolutionary themes, as in his vast mural *Communication Past and Present* (30×14 m) on the Telcor Building, Managua. The example of Mexico also inspired the Anteo group in Bolivia to create murals on public, university and school buildings, which took a Marxist stance and idealized Pre-Columbian Bolivia. The group's members included Gil Imaná, Solón Romero (*b* 1925) and Lorgio Vaca (*b* 1930).

See also MEXICO, §IV, 2(iv)(a).

BIBLIOGRAPHY

A. Brenner: *Idols behind Altars* (Boston, 1929, rev. 1970)
B. Myers: *Mexican Painting in our Time* (New York, 1956)
J. Charlot: *The Mexican Mural Renaissance, 1920–1925* (New Haven, 1963)
L. Cardoza y Aragón: *México: Pintura de hoy* (Mexico City, 1966)
E. Edwards: *Painted Walls of Mexico from Pre-Historic Times until Today* (Austin, TX, and London, 1966), pp. 166–276
A. Rodríguez: *A History of Mexican Mural Painting* (New York and London, 1969)
J. Franco: *The Modern Culture of Latin America* (London, 1970)
O. Suárez: *Inventario del muralismo mexicano* (Mexico City, 1972)
F. Chatel and others: *L'Art public: Peintures murales contemporaines, peintures populaires traditionnelles* (Paris, 1981)
Comm. Murals Mag. (1981–7)
J. Fernández: *El arte del siglo XIX en México* (Mexico City, 1983)
N. Coleby: 'La construcción de una estética: El Ateneo de la Juventud, Vasconcelos y la primera etapa de la pintura mural postrevolucionaria, 1921–24' (MA thesis, Mexico City, U. N. Autónoma, 1986)
Art in Latin America: The Modern Era, 1820–1980 (exh. cat. by D. Ades and others, London, Hayward Gal., 1989), pp. 151–79, 323–4
D. Rochfort: *Mexican Muralists: Orozco, Rivera, Siqueiros* (London, 1993)

NICOLA COLEBY, DESMOND ROCHFORT

3. NORTH AMERICA. Although murals had been painted in the USA from colonial times, it was in the 19th century that significant public murals were commissioned from such artists as Edward Austin Abbey and Constantino Brumidi, who in 1878 began painting the rotunda frieze of the Capitol, Washington, DC, depicting American history (completed 1953; *see* WASHINGTON, DC, fig. 5). In the early 20th century George A. Reid produced murals in Canada, such as the Parliament Buildings in Ottawa (1905). Between 1934 and 1943 federal programmes supporting unemployed artists were established in the USA. They were unprecedented in scope. Such programmes as the FAP (Federal Art Program) of the WPA (Works Progress Administration) and the PWAP (Public Works of Art Project) sponsored thousands of murals in local government buildings and such public locations as post offices, court-houses, schools, libraries, railway stations and prisons (*see* UNITED STATES OF AMERICA, §III, 3). Artists' salaries were paid federally, and within government guidelines themes and designs were developed with local officials or groups. The subject-matter was diverse but often included local historical events, attractions, pastimes and industries (e.g. Thomas Hart Benton's *Politics and Agriculture*, 1936; Jefferson City, Missouri State Capitol). Specifically African American themes were also represented (*see* AFRICAN AMERICAN ART, §2) by such artists as Hale Woodruff (1900–80) and Charles Alston (1907–78). The programmes were discontinued during World War II. Although in Canada there was no equivalent of the New Deal murals, notable individual commissions there included *Endocrinology* (1940) by Marian Scott (*b* 1906) for the McGill University medical building in Montreal. Alfred Pellan painted his first mural in 1957 for the City Centre Building, also in Montreal.

Many of the murals of this period were representational and narrative, in keeping with the current popularity of realism. However, the stylistic range was great, including several abstract designs, notably those by Willem De Kooning and Stuart Davis (e.g. untitled mural, 1939; New York, Met.; for illustration *see* DAVIS, STUART). In the USA the influence of the New Deal murals and the ubiquitous wall paintings in restaurants, meat markets, theatres and other privately owned public spaces established a presence for public images that, along with the work of the Mexican muralists (*see* §2 above), led to a flowering of community-based murals in the late 1960s and early 1970s. At the time residents of poor neighbourhoods, people of colour, women, members of trade unions, schools, clubs and churches and political activists painted on community walls without government control to express their sense of pride and concern for neglected social and cultural issues. Mass political activism relating to the Vietnam War, civil rights, women's liberation, ethnic pride and working-class rights provided a supportive social atmosphere. The result was a broadening of the term 'mural' to include any individually or collectively produced community-interactive art project. The earliest community murals were painted in Denver, CO, and in California (*see* fig. 5). These projects set the pattern for community murals of individual trained artists or a group of artists working alone or with local people to develop themes, select images, finalize designs and execute them in a collaborative interaction, with the artist working as guide and organizer. Subsequently, 'walls of respect' were painted by people of Latin American origin, in particular Chicanos (*see* LATIN AMERICAN ARTISTS OF THE USA, §2), and by Asians, native American Indians, African Americans,

5. Mural by Commonarts (Osha Neumann, O'Brian Thiele, Ray Patlan, Anna de Leon): *Song of Unity* (1978; restored and slightly revised 1989), Berkeley, CA

women and other activist artists. These murals typically connected repressed images of traditional cultures with the daily lives of local people. Other popular themes were criticisms of racism, sexism and economic exploitation, and the celebration of multi-racial and multi-ethnic communities. Sometimes groups of artists painted clusters of a dozen or more murals about a unified theme at a single site (e.g. Clarion Alley, San Francisco).

Funding was always sparse for such projects, which initially depended on local donations of materials and cash. From the mid-1970s, however, government agencies, responding to political pressures, offered support (perceived by many as a strategy to reduce the images' political impact), and money from foundations became available in the 1980s. The artists involved utilized whatever materials were available, although in the 1970s special mural acrylics became popular. In the 1980s muralists also turned to other media and techniques, including mosaic, fresco, cast concrete and even fabricated steel and polyurethane epoxy paints. By this time the social circumstances that had produced a national protest art had subsided, and many muralists had turned to other forms of protest expression. While community-based murals were still painted, they stressed celebration of traditional cultures rather than the sharp political criticism of earlier periods. The popularity of community-based murals encouraged the painting of murals with other orientations, such as commercial, decorative, *trompe l'oeil* and private works. Public walls also provided a suitable location for GRAFFITI ART, which attracted attention as a form of expression in its own right.

BIBLIOGRAPHY

M. Rogovin, M. Burton and H. Highfill: *Mural Manual: How to Paint Murals for the Classroom, Community Center, and Street Corner* (Boston, 1973)

F. V. O'Connor, ed.: *Art for the Millions: Essays from the 1930s by Artists and Administrators of the WPA Federal Arts Project* (Boston, 1975)

E. Cockcroft, J. Weber and J. Cockcroft: *Towards a People's Art: The Contemporary Mural Movement* (New York, 1977)

Comm. Murals Mag. (San Francisco and Berkeley, CA, 1981–7)

V. Barthelmeh: *Street Murals* (New York, 1982)

K. A. Marling: *Wall-to-wall America: A Cultural History of Post Office Murals in the Great Depression* (Minneapolis, 1982)

A. W. Barnett: *Community Murals: The People's Art* (Philadelphia, New York and London, 1984)

M. Park and G. E. Markowitz: *Democratic Vistas: Post Offices and Public Art in the New Deal* (Philadelphia, 1984)

S. M. Goldman and T. Ybarra-Frausto: *Arte Chicano: A Comprehensive Annotated Bibliography of Chicano Art, 1965–1981* (Berkeley, CA, 1985)

TIMOTHY W. DRESCHER

Murano. *See* VENICE, §III, 3.

Murano, Tōgo (*b* Karatsu, Saga Prefect., 15 May 1891; *d* Ashiya, Osaka, 26 Nov 1984). Japanese architect. After graduating from Waseda University, Tokyo, he worked in the office of the architect Setsu Watanabe in Osaka (1918–29) and then established his own office in Osaka. During this time he spent periods of study in the USA and Europe. An early example of his work is the Sogō department store (1936) in Osaka, the first modern building of its kind in the city. Its façade of slender vertical louvres and mosaic revealed his particular interest in the quality of surface textures. Murano, whose practice became Murano & Mori in 1949, was a Modernist who was distinguished by his commitment to a humanistic architecture, creating spaces that were practical yet richly expressive; he aimed to provide a bridge between the expectations of his clients and those of the public who used his buildings. As well as several department stores in Osaka, Kobe, Nagoya and Tokyo, he also built hotels, theatres, office buildings and the World Peace Memorial Cathedral (1953) in Hiroshima; this is an austerely simple building with an exposed frame of concrete columns and beams with infill walls of grey cement bricks made with ash from the atomic bomb explosion. Other major works include the Miyako Hotel (1934 and 1960), Kyoto; the New Kabuki Theatre (1958), Osaka, with traditional Japanese roof forms; and the Nippon Life Insurance Co. offices (1963), Tokyo, a granite-faced block with ornate window openings containing the Gaudíesque Nissei Theatre, with free-form walls and fantastic Art Nouveau decoration of seashells and glass mosaic. He also designed head offices for the Chiyoda Life Insurance Co. (1966) and Nihon Kangyo Bank (1974), both in Tokyo. Murano was a master of the *sukiya* (tea house) style (*see* JAPAN, §XIV, 2), a reinterpretation of traditional Japanese residential architecture; examples of this work include the Kasuien Annexe (1959) of the Miyako Hotel, Kyoto, and the Nadaman Tea House (1977) in the gardens of the New Otani Hotel, Tokyo.

WRITINGS
Murano Tōgo: Wafū kenchikushu [Tōgo Murano: collected works of traditional architecture] (Tokyo, 1978)

BIBLIOGRAPHY
Murano Tōgo, Gendai Nihon kenchikuka zenshū [Complete collection of modern Japanese architects], 2 (Tokyo, 1971)
T. Muramatsu: 'A Dialogue with Tōgo Murano', *Japan Architect*, 207 (1974), pp. 89–96
Murano Tōgo, 2 vols (Tokyo, 1983–4)

KATSUYOSHI ARAI

Muraro, Michelangelo (*b* Sossano Veneto, nr Vicenza, 8 Aug 1913; *d* Venice, 15 May 1991). Italian art historian. He studied under Giuseppe Fiocco at the University of Padua (thesis 1937), from 1939 at the Scuola Archeologica Italiana, Athens, and from 1941 at the Scuola Storica e Filologica delle Venezie. His academic subjects included Venetian architecture in the eastern Mediterranean and the work of Giulio Carpioni and Pietro Selvatico. After World War II Muraro began his career at the Soprintendenza ai Monumenti di Venezia, where he assumed responsibility for the preservation of the artistic and architectural heritage of Venice. To raise awareness of the importance of this preservation he organized various exhibitions (e.g. *Pitture murali nel Veneto e tecnica dell'affresco*, Venice, Fond. Cini, 1960), some of which were based on the results of his initiative to restore a number of fresco cycles in Venice and the Veneto. He also organized the first exhibition (Treviso, 1952) devoted to Renaissance villas in the Veneto, with the aim of publicizing their state of neglect. At the instigation of Erwin Panofsky, he spent 1956–7 at Princeton in the USA, where he was able to disseminate his ideas to a wider audience. From 1963, as Director of the Galleria Giorgio Franchetti, Venice, he was instrumental in successfully converting the celebrated Ca' d'Oro into a museum without disturbing its architectural integrity. Muraro's complete list of publications, given in his *Festschrift* (1984), attests to his breadth of scholarship. He brought his profound insight

to such diverse topics as the art of Squarcione, Carpaccio, Titian, Giorgione and Pordenone, the buildings of S Marco and S Maria della Salute, medieval Venetian sculpture and particularly Venetian drawings of the 17th and 18th centuries.

WRITINGS
'Il Pilastro del miracolo e il secondo programma dei mosaici marcioni', *A. Ven.*, xxix (1975), pp. 60–65
'Giorgione e la civiltà delle ville venete', *Giorgione: Atti del convegno internazionale di studio per il 50 centenario della nascita: 29–31 maggio, 1978*

BIBLIOGRAPHY
D. Rosand, ed.: *Interpretazioni veneziane: Studi di storia dell'arte in onore di Michelangelo Muraro* (Venice, 1984) [esp. D. Puppulin: 'Bibliografia degli scritti di Michelangelo Muraro', p. 173]
D. Rosand: 'Michelangelo Muraro, 1913–1991', *Burl. Mag.*, cxxxiii (1991), pp. 517–18

Murase Taiitsu [Murase Taiichi] (*b* Kōzuchi [now Mino City], nr Nagoya, 1803; *d* Inuyama, nr Nagoya, 1881). Japanese painter, poet and calligrapher. He became one of the most notable and eccentric exponents of literati painting (*Bunjinga* or *Nanga*, see JAPAN, §VI, 4(vi)(d)) of the early Meiji period (1868–1912). He was educated in Confucianism and Buddhism from the monk Kaigen at the temple of Zen'oji. He was also influenced by his uncles Murase Tōjō (1791–1853), Murase Ryūsai (1792/4–1876) and Murase Shunsui (1795–1876). Through Tōjō's introduction, Taiitsu studied under the poet, calligrapher and historian Rai San'yō from 1829 until San'yō's death in 1832. Taiitsu then returned to his native village, but in 1837 he moved to Nagoya to open his own Confucian academy. In 1844 Taiitsu became the teacher at the Naruse clan school in Nagoya, remaining there until feudal schools were abolished at the beginning of the Meiji period.

From 1879 until his death Taiitsu lived in Inuyama near Nagoya. Most of his paintings and calligraphy date from his years there, where he fashioned a reputation as a scholarly eccentric who delighted in brushwork. Taiitsu painted as the spirit moved him: apparently on a paper lantern on a street corner, on a *tansu* (wooden chest) prepared for his daughter's wedding and on toilet paper in a bathroom during a banquet. Although he occasionally painted literati subjects such as bamboo and orchids, his work consists mainly of landscapes in the literati style and figure paintings. While most Japanese literati artists either avoided figure paintings or restricted their portrayal to Chinese sages and poets, Taiitsu enjoyed depicting Japanese historical and literary figures and subjects. These works, such as the hanging scrolls *The Six Oppositions* (1871; New Orleans, LA, Mus. A.) and *Saigyō and the Silver Cat* (New Orleans, LA, priv. col.; see JAPAN, fig. 99), are tinged with wit and humour. In the landscapes Taiitsu followed past literati models, although his own brushwork was more spontaneous, free-flowing and generally rapid. Colophons on several of his paintings, such as the undated hanging scroll *My Natural Place* (Virginia, Shōka priv. col.), help to explain his attitude towards art, expressed in his statement: 'All methods that restrict men do not apply to me.' His style was extremely calligraphic, with a predominant use of line and only occasional addition of wash. He almost always used varied ink tones without colour.

Despite the poverty of his final years, when he eked out a marginal living giving private lessons in the Confucian classics and poetry, Taiitsu seems to have maintained his equilibrium. His paintings enjoyed a period of popularity in Inuyama and Nagoya in the decades following his death, after which time they fell from favour. In the later 20th century more attention was focused on Taiitsu, whose bold and spontaneous style is considered exemplary of one trend of Meiji period literati painting.

BIBLIOGRAPHY

G. Yoshida: *Murase Taiitsu no shōgai* [The life of Murase Taiitsu] (Inuyama, 1964)

A Japanese Eccentric: The Three Arts of Murase Taiitsu (exh. cat. by S. Addiss, New Orleans, LA, Mus. A., 1979)

S. Makai: *Murase Taiitsu* (Nagoya, 1981)

STEPHEN ADDISS

Murashko, Oleksandr [Aleksandr] (*b* Kiev, 1875; *d* Kiev, 14th June 1919). Ukrainian painter. He trained at the icon workshop in Kiev and helped decorate the cathedral of St Volodymyr under Viktor Vasnetsov and Adrian Prakhov (1846–1916). Murashko's transition from icon painting to secular easel art occurred in 1894, when he enrolled in the Academy of Arts in St Petersburg. After graduating from the Academy, he entered the workshop of Il'ya Repin, whose influence can be seen in Murashko's portraiture and in his award-winning painting, *Funeral of the Cossack Kosh Otaman* (1900; Kiev, Mus. Ukrain. A.), which won him a travel grant to work in A. Ažbe's studio in Munich (1901) and then in Paris (1902–4). Returning to St Petersburg, Murashko joined the New Association of Artists and took part in their annual exhibitions. Two more trips abroad were funded by the Academy before he returned to Kiev in 1907. He received a gold medal for his painting *Carousel* at the Munich Glaspalast in 1909; and in 1910 and 1911 he had one-man exhibitions in Berlin, Cologne and Düsseldorf; from 1911 he became a regular contributor to the Munich Secession. After 1910 he participated in the exhibitions of the Association of Russian Artists, and in Kiev he became a teacher at the drawing school of Mykola Murashko, his adoptive uncle. In 1913, to counter the influence of the Wanderers (Peredvizhniki), together with Anna Krüger-Prakhova (1876–1962) and others, he founded his own studio and infused a Western European and modernist character into Ukrainian painting. In 1916 he founded the Association of Kiev Artists, an organization that served a younger generation of painters before the establishment in 1918 of the Ukrainian Academy of Arts, where he taught.

BIBLIOGRAPHY

L. Chlenova: *Oleksandr Murashko* (Kiev, 1980)

MYROSLAVA M. MUDRAK

Murat, Joachim, King of Naples (*b* Labastide-Fortunière (now Labastide-Murat), Lot, 25 March 1767; *d* Pizzo, Calabria, 13 Oct 1815). French soldier and ruler and patron in Italy. Having been a soldier of the French Revolution, he became one of Napoleon's most devoted followers. On 20 January 1800 he married Caroline Bonaparte (*b* Ajaccio, 25 March 1782; *d* Florence, 19 May 1839), Napoleon's third sister, and this marriage opened to him an outstanding career. He served with distinction as one of Napoleon's commanders during the Italian campaign; while in Florence in 1801 he assembled a collection of Italian Old Master paintings that included a painting by Raphael from the Vatican collections, a gift from Pius VII. Murat also sought out sculptures by Canova, acquiring *Cupid Awakening Psyche* (*see* CANOVA, ANTONIO, fig. 1) and *Cupid and Psyche Standing* (both Paris, Louvre). In 1806 Murat became Grand Duc de Berg; in February 1808 Napoleon sent him to carry out the French occupation of Spain. In a vain attempt to secure Murat's favour, Manuel Godoy, Chief Minister of the Spanish Crown, gave him several of his finest paintings, including Correggio's *Mercury Instructing Cupid before Venus* (London, N.G.). Having secured the Spanish throne for Joseph Bonaparte, his brother-in-law, Murat took his place as King of Naples. Napoleon then obliged him to give up his estates in France. A part of his collection—e.g. the *Rape of Europa* after Francesco Albani (Paris, Louvre) and the *Holy Family*, attributed to Raphael (St Petersburg, Hermitage)—went to augment Empress Josephine's collection; other works—e.g. Correggio's *Girl Bathing* and the *Confinement and Death of Rachel* after Francesco Furini (Paris, Louvre)—were given to national collections.

Caroline Murat built up a new collection in Naples in which the Italian masters mingled with works by contemporary artists under her patronage, some of them Frenchmen at the Académie de France in Rome; one such was Ingres, who painted the *Betrothal of Raphael* (Baltimore, MD, Walters A.G.) and the *Grande Odalisque* (Paris, Louvre) for the Murat collection. In 1815, following the defeat of Napoleon, Murat was overthrown by Ferdinand I (1751–1825) and fled; subsequently, attempting to regain his throne, he was captured and executed. His widow succeeded in carrying away some of their paintings, while Ferdinand seized the remainder. Some works that were subsequently sold to Henri d'Orléans, Duc d'Aumale, are now in the Musée Condé, Château de Chantilly; they include Ingres's *Paolo and Francesca* and the *Three Ages* by François Gérard. Caroline Murat, in exile in Austria, lived by selling her pictures. In 1822 she sold Correggio's *Ecce homo* (London, N.G.), together with some paintings by Guido Reni, Annibale Carracci and Domenichino, to Robert Stewart, 2nd Marquess of Londonderry (1769–1822).

UNPUBLISHED SOURCES

Paris, Bib. Thiers, fond. Masson, MS. Carton 58

BIBLIOGRAPHY

P. Le Brethon, ed.: *Lettres et documents pour servir à l'histoire de Joachim Murat, publiés par S.A. le prince Murat*, 8 vols (Paris, 1908–14)

P. Marmottan: *Murat à l'Elysée* (Paris, 1919)

GUY COUPET

Murata Shukō [Jukō] (*b* Nara, *c.* 1422; *d* Kyoto, 1502). Japanese tea master. He is credited with establishing the *wabicha* tea-ceremony style, based on the concept of *wabi* ('simple', 'lonely') taste, which was taken up by TAKENO JŌŌ and culminated in the tea practices of SEN NO RIKYŪ (*see* JAPAN, §XIV, 1). According to the *Yamanoue Sōjiki*, a diary by Yamanoue Sōji (1544–90), Shukō was the son of a Buddhist priest and entered the Pure Land Buddhist monastery of Shomyōji (nr Nara) at an early age. He was later adopted by a merchant family named Murata. He is said to have met the painter and connoisseur Nōami (*see*

AMI, (1)), who fled from Kyoto to Nara during the Ōnin Wars (1467–77) and who instructed him in the tea-ceremony practices of the *dōbōshū* ('comrades'; unofficial artistic advisers) of the retired shogun Ashikaga Yoshimasa (1436–90). Shukō then studied under the Zen master IKKYŪ SŌJUN of Daitokuji in Kyoto. Shukō may have become a *dōbōshū* to Yoshimasa and served him tea in the Dōjinsai room of the Tōgūdō pavilion of Ginkakuji (*see* KYOTO, §IV, 8), which is usually cited as the model for all standard four-and-a-half-mat (9 sq. m) tea-rooms. Shukō's use of Yoshimasa's collection of Chinese and Japanese tea utensils established the conventions for later tea ceremonies.

In around 1488 Shukō described some of his ideas concerning the tea ceremony in *Kokoro no fumi* ('Letter of the heart-mind'; ex-Hirase priv. col., 1908), a letter to the priest Furuichi Harima (1452–1508). He used words such as *hie* ('cool'), *kare* ('withered') and *yase* ('lean') to describe the qualities of inner beauty of tea utensils and felt that no distinction should be made between utensils imported from China and objects made in Japan, as long as they all reflect a proper spirit and aesthetic taste. To appreciate the understated aspects of things, Shukō wrote, was to master one's heart and mind, and he warned against self-satisfaction. Although Shukō did not use the term *wabi*, his ideas appear consistent with this important aesthetic concept, which was developed further by his followers in tea, Takeno Jōō and Jōō's student Sen no Rikyū. Shukō was seen by later generations of tea masters as the man who shifted the focus of the tea ceremony away from the connoisseurship of expensive utensils to a heightened awareness of the inner beauty of objects and to the spiritual communion engendered among the participants.

BIBLIOGRAPHY
S. Tanaka: *The Tea Ceremony* (Tokyo and New York, 1973)
D. Hirota: 'Heart's Mastery: Kokoro no Fumi', *Chanoyu Q.*, 22 (1979), pp. 7–24
BRUCE A. COATS

Muratov, Pavel (Pavlovich) (*b* March 1881; *d* Oct 1950). Russian historian and critic. In 1906 he left Russia for Paris, having become interested in modern art, and his art criticism was published in *Zolotoye runo*, *Apollon*, *Vesy* and *Staryye gody*. In 1908–11 he lived in Italy, where he began work on his most important book, *Obrazy Italii* ('Images of Italy'), which included an analysis of outstanding medieval and Renaissance monuments. In 1917–22, after war service, he worked in museum administration for the State Commission for the Preservation of Monuments, and for the Institute of Archaeology and Art affiliated to Moscow University; he was also head of the Institute of Italian Culture. In the early 1920s he published monographs on the artists Pyotr Konchalovsky and Nikolay Ul'yanov, a novel, short stories and a play, while his articles 'Kinematograf' and 'Anti-iskusstvo' ('Against art'), published in *Sovremennyye zapiski*, dealt with questions of modern culture. In 1922 he left for Berlin where he collaborated with other Russian emigré writers. He also wrote essays and memoirs and gave lectures on Russian art in Oxford and Cambridge. During World War II he was a war correspondent in England. After the war, he

moved to Ireland where he studied the relations between England and Russia in the 16th century.

WRITINGS
Obrazy Italii [Images of Italy], 3 vols (Vols 1 & 2 Moscow, 1912; vol. 3 Leipzig, 1924)
Ikonopis' pri pervom tsare iz doma Romanovykh [Icon painting under the first tsar of the house of the Romanovs] (Moscow, 1913)
Drevnerusskaya ikonopis' [Old Russian icon painting] (Moscow, 1914)
Zhivopis' Konchalovskogo [The paintings of Konchalovsky] (Moscow, 1923)
N. Ul'yanov (Moscow, 1923)

BIBLIOGRAPHY
A. Vetlugin: *Novaya russkaya kniga* [The new Russian book], iv (Berlin, 1922)
B. Zaytsev: 'P. Muratov: *Obrazy Italii*', *Sovremennyye zapiski*, xxii (1924)
V. S. TURCHIN

Murayama, Tomoyoshi (*b* Tokyo, 18 Jan 1901; *d* Tokyo, 22 March 1977). Japanese writer, director and painter. Although he entered Tokyo Imperial University in 1921 with the intention of studying philosophy, he soon left to study in Berlin, where he became absorbed in painting and drama. Initially fascinated by the work of Vasily Kandinsky and by Constructivism, he later became dissatisfied with the detachment of Constructivist works from the concrete properties of objects; he decided it was possible to provoke concrete associations, and to obtain a variety of sensory effects using real or 'ready-made' objects. He named this method (a kind of collage or assemblage) 'conscious constructivism'. An example of this is *Construction* (1925; Tokyo, N. Mus. Mod. A.).

On returning to Japan in 1923, he formed the small avant-garde group Mavo. He continued to exhibit works while publishing provocative criticism in art magazines and the *Mavo* magazine (founded in 1924). He immediately became a central figure in the avant-garde art movement of the Taisho period (1912–26) and participated in the formation of the Sanka group. In 1924 he designed a Constructivist set for a production of Georg Kaiser's *Von Morgen bis Mitternachts* at the Tsukiji Little Theatre. At the second Sanka exhibition he and other members of the MAVO group showed Dadaist works; their radical tendencies were, however, one reason for the group's dissolution, after which Murayama turned his attention to drama, based on Marxist ideas of art.

BIBLIOGRAPHY
T. Asano: *Zen'ei kaiga* [Avant-garde painting] (1978), viii of *Genshoku gendai Nihon no bijutsu* [Modern Japanese art in colour] (Tokyo, 1978–80)
Murayama Tomoyoshi no bijutsu no shigoto [The artistic works of Tomoyoshi Murayama, ed.], Murayama Tomoyoshi no bijutsu no shigoto kankōiinkai [Committee for the publication of the artistic works of Tomoyoshi Murayama] (Tokyo, 1985)
TORU ASANO

Murcutt, Glenn (Marcus) (*b* London, 25 July 1936). Australian architect. He spent his childhood on the Upper Watut in the Morobe district of New Guinea and this experience shaped not only his life but to a marked degree his architecture. He studied architecture at the University of New South Wales, Sydney (1956–61); after spending two years in Europe (1962–4) he was apprenticed to various offices in the Sydney area, including Ancher, Mortlock, Murray & Woolley. Early in his life, his thought and outlook were also influenced by his father who

Müridoğlu, Zühtü (*b* Istanbul, 29 Jan 1906; *d* 1992). Turkish sculptor. He studied at the Fine Arts Academy, Istanbul, under the sculptor Ihsan Özsoy (1867–1944). From 1928 to 1932 he continued his studies in Paris, working in the studio of the sculptor Marcel Gimond (*b* 1894) and at the Académie Colarossi. He also attended courses in aesthetics at the Sorbonne and art history at the Ecole du Louvre, and he exhibited work at the Salon d'Automne (1931 and 1932). On returning to Turkey he taught painting at the Samsun High School (1932) and in 1933 was a founder-member of the D Group in Istanbul. In 1936 Müridoğlu worked at the Arkeoloji Müzesi in Istanbul and in 1939 went to teach at the Gazi Teachers' College in Ankara. From 1940 he taught at the Fine Arts Academy in Istanbul. From 1947 to 1949 he stayed in Paris where he participated in the Salon des Indépendants in 1949 and 1950. After returning to Istanbul he taught sculpture at the Fine Arts Academy with Ali Hadi Bara and in 1952 exhibited his work at the Maya Gallery. His early sculptures were influenced by the work of Gimond and Charles Despiau, but he later developed his style in both statues and abstract works. With Bara he worked on the statue of the 16th-century Ottoman admiral *Barbarossa* in Beşiktaş, Istanbul, erected in 1946 on the 400th anniversary of Barbarossa's death, and on the monument to *Atatürk and Ismet Inönü on Horseback* in Zonguldak. He also worked on the reliefs on the steps of the Atatürk Mausoleum (1953), and on the monuments to *Atatürk* at Büyükada, Istanbul, in Muş (1965), and in Eyüp (1966). Müridoğlu continued to exhibit sculpture in Europe, at such exhibitions as the Venice Biennale (1956) and the second Exposition Internationale de Sculpture Contemporaine at the Musée Rodin, Paris (1961).

BIBLIOGRAPHY

2e Exposition internationale de sculpture contemporaine (exh. cat., Paris, Mus. Rodin, 1961)

S. Tansuğ: *Çağdaş Türk sanatı* [Contemporary Turkish art] (Istanbul, 1986)

K. Giray: 'Heykel Sanatımızın Müridi: Zühtü Müritoğlu', *Kült. Ve Sanat*, 17 (March 1993), pp. 32–5

S. J. VERNOIT

Murillo, Bartolomé Esteban (*b* Seville, *bapt* 1 Jan 1618; *d* Seville, 28 March 1682). Spanish painter and draughtsman. He combined 17th-century realism with a taste for serene, sweet and sentimental beauty. His large output of religious works included numerous treatments of the Immaculate Conception, and he was also one of the greatest portrait painters of his time. However, his fame abroad was established most especially by his genre pictures of children. His works were highly prized by collectors, particularly in the 18th century, and his painting, which was well known in other European countries, particularly England and France, served as an example to such artists as Gainsborough, Reynolds and Greuze.

1. Life and work. 2. Working methods and technique.

1. LIFE AND WORK.

(i) Before 1645. (ii) 1645–57. (iii) 1658–*c*. 1665. (iv) *c*. 1665–1682.

(i) Before 1645. Born in the last days of 1617, he was the youngest child of Gaspar Esteban of Seville, a barber-surgeon, and María Pérez, but adopted the surname of his maternal grandmother, Elvira Murillo, and rarely signed or used that of his father. The family enjoyed a degree of social status and wealth and in 1607 Gaspar was described as a 'rich and thrifty man'. One of Murillo's uncles, Antonio Pérez, was a painter and was married to the daughter of Vasco de Pereira, a Sevillian artist, and their daughters likewise married painters. Murillo's parents died within a few months of each other in 1627 and 1628, and he became the ward of his brother-in-law Juan Agustín Lagares. In early 1633 Murillo drew up his will in preparation for a journey to America, where some of his family had already emigrated, but there is no documentary evidence that he undertook the voyage.

It is said by Palomino that Murillo trained in the Seville studio of Juan del Castillo (who was related to him on his mother's side), but no apprenticeship contract has survived. The general practice in Spain was for apprentices to enter a studio at the age of 12 or 13, so it is likely that Murillo would have joined Castillo *c*. 1630. Certainly, the style of his first documented works (e.g. the *Vision of Friar Lauterio*, *c*. 1638, Cambridge, Fitzwilliam; the *Virgin Presenting the Rosary to St Dominic*, *c*. 1638, Seville, Pal. Arzobisp.) directly emulates the manner of Castillo. Castillo's links with the Sevillian artistic community (he worked in Seville until 1638) were extensive and, according to Palomino, he had long been a close friend of Alonso Cano. This network could have facilitated Murillo's first independent commissions, while the strong personality of Cano must have been attractive, as was his painting. Though different from Murillo's, certain aspects of Cano's painting can be related to those of the younger artist.

Palomino wrote that Murillo first worked as a 'festival painter', producing ephemeral decorations and works for festivities, that he executed a 'consignment of paintings to be transported to the Indies', and that he visited Madrid (this last claim was taken up and elaborated by Ceán Bermúdez). However, the visit cannot be confirmed. It is difficult to accept the idea that Murillo could have spent much time in Madrid, as contemporary documents specifically state that he had 'all his life been a parishioner of la Magdalena [in Seville] without any notable absence'. Furthermore, his early work shows no knowledge of the work of Rubens, Velázquez or the Venetian artists, that he would surely have seen on any visit to Madrid.

(ii) 1645–57. In 1645 Murillo married Beatriz Cabrera y Villalobos. The couple were married for 20 years and had 11 children. Also in 1645 Murillo received his first important commission, for the series of 11 canvases for the small cloister of the convent of S Francisco, Seville, and he took on an apprentice to help him. In these works, which narrate miracles of Franciscan saints, Murillo blended the influences of the painting of Francisco de Herrera the elder and, above all, the naturalism and powerful tenebrism of Zurbarán's work. In the two large-scale canvases, the *Levitation of St Giles* (usually known as the 'Angel's Kitchen', Paris, Louvre) and the *Death of St Clare* (Dresden, Gemäldegal. Alte Meister), the characteristic elements of Murillo's work are already evident: the elegance and beauty of the female figures and the angels, the realism of the still-life details and the fusion of reality with the spiritual world, which is extraordinarily well

developed in some of the compositions. Some canvases echo Zurbarán, for example the *Ecstasy of St Francis* (Madrid, Real Acad. S Fernando, Mus.) or *St Junípero and the Beggar* (Paris, Louvre), but others, such as the *Death of St Clare*, display a light and luminous technique, full of soft shades of colour, already revealing the change towards Murillo's characteristic treatment. Also from this period is the *Boy Delousing himself* (Paris, Louvre; see fig. 1), in which there are echoes of the Sevillian work of Velázquez, rather than that of Zurbarán. This is the first of Murillo's numerous canvases depicting children.

In 1648 Murillo moved to the parish of S Isidoro, the church of which contained Juan de Roelas's great canvas of the *Death of St Isidore* (1613; *in situ*). This, which takes the form of a Gloria, is one of the most spectacular works in 17th-century Sevillian painting and must subsequently have exercised a decisive influence on the young Murillo. He began to develop his contacts with Seville's intellectual circles: Don Miguel de Mañara Vicentelo de Leca, who was responsible for the revival of the Hospital de la Caridád, became (1650) the godfather to one of his sons. However, from the spring of 1649 until 1650 Seville suffered a devastating plague epidemic, which seriously affected artistic and cultural life. Despite this, Murillo produced a number of works, including the early *Self-portrait* (1649; USA, priv. col., see Angulo Iñiguez, 1981, no. 413) and the portrait of *Juan de Saavedra* (1649; Córdoba, Marqués de Viana priv. col., see Angulo Iñiguez, 1981, no. 454). Both of these paintings are derived from Flemish and Dutch prints, in which the face or bust of the sitter is set in an oval 'frame' inscribed with the subject's name. Of about the same date is the *Holy Family with a Little Bird* (Madrid, Prado), a work that marks the artist's

1. Bartolomé Esteban Murillo: *Boy Delousing himself*, oil on canvas, 1.37×1.15 m, *c.* 1645 (Paris, Musée du Louvre)

move towards a greater naturalism. It is possible that he used the Barocci *Virgin and Child with St Joseph and the Infant Baptist* (the '*Madonna del Gatto*', London, N.G.) as a model; this was known through an engraving (1577) by Cornelis Cort. However, Murillo produced an entirely personal example of the representation of a religious subject through an everyday domestic scene, and for the first time there appear certain elements with a delicate gracefulness, tenderness and reality, tempered with senti-mentality—all to become the most characteristic aspects of his mature work. Murillo, in his depiction of paternal love, may have followed the text of the Carmelite Graciano de la Madre de Dios's book on St Joseph (1597), which describes the devoted familial intimacy found in Murillo's painting and claims that the saint never returned to his house without a present for the Child, such as a bird or apples. Very similar in style are the *Flight into Egypt* (Detroit, MI, Inst. A.) and the *Virgin of the Rosary* (*c.* 1649–50; Castres, Mus. Goya), perhaps the earliest of the three compositions of the same theme (others Madrid, Prado; Florence, Pitti) which may be linked to Murillo's association from 1644 with the Confraternity of the Virgin of the Rosary. The *Last Supper* (*c.* 1650; Seville, S María la Blanca) clearly displays the influence of northern artists, principally Dutch (e.g. Gerrit van Honthorst and Hendrick ter Brugghen), whose work he may have seen in Seville.

In these years around 1650 Murillo painted various pictures that contain what were to become his most popular subjects, for example the *Two Boys Eating Fruit* (Munich, Alte Pin.), the *Immaculate Conception* (the '*Large Conception*' painted for the church of the convent of S Francisco, Seville, Mus. B.A.) and the *Immaculate Conception with Friar Juan de Quirós* (*c.* 1652; Seville, Pal. Arzobisp.). The '*Large Conception*' may have been influenced by engravings of Ribera's *Immaculate Conception* (1635) in the Augustinian Convent, Salamanca. In both of these Immaculate Conceptions, the Virgin is a young girl of exquisite beauty, dressed in white and blue, with her cape blowing in the wind, flying above the clouds and surrounded by putti. In its expression this work would become the model for a subject favoured by both Spanish art and religion. The *Immaculate Conception with Friar Juan de Quirós*, painted for the convent of S Francisco, shows the renowned Franciscan monk and defender of the doctrine of the Immaculate Conception in the act of writing his *Glorias de María*. In this unusual type of portrait both reality and spirituality are fused with the artist's characteristic facility.

During the 1650s Murillo frequently moved house, possibly to accommodate the births (and deaths) of his many children. In 1652, during the aftermath of the plague, there was an uprising among the textile workers of the city, which was suppressed by the Marqués de Villaman-rique (one of Murillo's patrons). Despite all these distur-bances, Murillo was at the height of his success in Seville and received a stream of major commissions. In 1655 the archdeacon of the cathedral, Don Juan Federigui, paid for the paintings of *St Isidore* and *St Leander* for the church's sacristy (*in situ*) and stated that they would be 'by the hand of the best painter in Seville' (in spite of the fact that Zurbarán was still in the city). Ceán Bermúdez referred to Antonio de la Cuesta's book in manuscript form, *Tesoro de la catedral de Sevilla*, in which he says that the face of *St Isidore* is in fact a portrait of the ecclesiastic Francisco López Talabán, who died in the year that the work was executed; *St Leander*, according to tradition, is a portrait of Alonso de Herrera, registrar of the cathedral choir.

Two vast altarpieces, the *Virgin with St Bernard* and *St Ildefonsus Receiving the Chasuble* (both Madrid, Prado; see fig. 2), must also date from these years, and were possibly painted for the Cistercian convent of S Clemente in Seville. The interpretation of light and use of chiaroscuro and the models used for these works link them to others of the period. In the *St Bernard* there is a broad and luminous fissure of 'glory'; the *St Ildefonsus* figures, which are strongly realistic, are very like those in the *Adoration of the Shepherds* (Madrid, Prado), in which there is still a predominance of strong luminous contrasts and great realism in the representation of the figures and the still-life elements. In both the *Adoration* and the *Resurrection* (Madrid, Real Acad. S Fernando) of the same period Murillo employs the Caravaggesque device of giving the shepherds and soldiers dirty feet, which suggests that he had some knowledge of Caravaggio's work, perhaps through the many contemporary copies then in the city.

In 1656, following the success of the *St Leander* and *St Isidore*, Murillo received another commission for the cathedral: an altarpiece for the baptismal chapel dedicated to St Anthony of Padua (*in situ*; see fig. 3). In this, the largest canvas that had ever been seen in Seville, Murillo created a composition in which the impressive glory, with the Christ child appearing before the saint surrounded by a multitude of angels, occupies more than half the upper

3. Bartolomé Esteban Murillo: *Vision of St Anthony of Padua*, oil on canvas, 5.60×3.69 m, 1656 (Seville Cathedral)

2. Bartolomé Esteban Murillo: *St Ildefonsus Receiving the Chasuble*, oil on canvas, 3.0×2.5 m, *c.* 1655 (Madrid, Museo del Prado)

part of the canvas; the strong chiaroscuro has gone and he employed a more even lighting and a new technique, shedding his earlier dryness, that is indebted to the influence of new trends from Italy introduced by Francisco de Herrera the younger (*see* HERRERA, (2)).

(iii) 1658–c. 1665. Murillo is documented as being in Madrid in April 1658, but by the beginning of December he was back in Seville. The reason for the visit is unrecorded, but it was perhaps to establish himself at court and make contact with the other Sevillian artists there—Zurbarán, Alonso Cano and Diego Velázquez. What is more certain is that Murillo, probably through the influence of Velázquez, was able to study the royal and aristocratic collections, which were to have an undoubtable influence in transforming his art. In the years following the *Vision of St Anthony of Padua* he attained public recognition for his art and a comfortable financial position, as well as executing some of his most beautiful compositions. The *Virgin and Child in the Clouds* (*c.* 1658; Amsterdam, Rijksmus.) marks an appreciable change from his previous representations of this subject. The figures are positioned against a reddish, luminous sky containing vaporous clouds, producing a sensation of unreal incandescence and contrasting with the serene beauty of the mother holding the Infant in her lap. The remote calm of the two figures, less tender and sentimental than in earlier representations of the theme, reflects the religious ideal of divine contemplation.

In January 1660 the Real Academia de Belles Artes de S Isabel de Hungría opened in Seville. Murillo had long worked for the establishment of an academy of art, and Seville achieved the distinction of the first official organization in Spain, modelled on those of Italy. The principal function of the academy was to teach drawing and to encourage its students to copy and study models from the life. On its opening the academy had teachers of painting, sculpture and gilding, and at first it had two presidents, Murillo and Francisco Herrera the younger. Its patron, initially the Conde de Arenales, was from 1673 the Marqués de Villamanrique. By November 1660 Herrera had gone to Madrid, and in 1663 Valdés Leal was appointed President. From then on Murillo seems to have distanced himself from the academy, and according to Palomino, 'he held it in his house, so as not to have to have dealings with the arrogant character [of Valdés Leal]'. It may be that Murillo was simply too busy to be closely involved.

Possibly from 1660 is one of Murillo's most emblematic works. In the painting of *St John the Baptist, the Good Shepherd* (Madrid, Prado), he takes one of his genre-like, street scene representations of a child and unites this with a religious image. Though the work belongs within the realm of a simple and popular faith, it retains its value as a devotional image through the way the artist endows the beautiful child with a mysterious and intimate enchantment, thus elevating him above the reality of the shepherd's life. This way of expressing a religious subject through one that is profane is apparent in *St Justa* and *St Rufina* (both Dallas, TX, S. Methodist U., Meadows Mus. & Gal.), small works of private devotion that represent the patron saints of Seville in the manner of portraits of beautiful young women of the period. The large (1.79×3.49 m) canvas of the *Birth of the Virgin* (1660; Paris, Louvre) was painted for the Capilla de la Concepción in the cathedral. This great Baroque painting, filled with figures, would seem to reflect Murillo's earlier visit to the court of Madrid, and combined here for the first time are the compositional grandeur of Venetian painting and the rich colouring and technique of Rubens that he would have seen there.

In 1662 Murillo became a lay member of the Venerable Orden Tercera de S Francisco, and in the registration document was described as a 'famous painter who is the admiration of Europe, only in Spain, his land, is he unknown and less esteemed'. The major commission to Murillo in 1662 for a series of paintings for the church of S María la Blanca is connected to the renovation of the church begun in the same year. The difficult and awkward canvases for S María la Blanca must have taken up a great deal of his time during the next three years. The large lunettes narrating the foundation of the Roman basilica of S María Maggiore (the *Dream of the Patrician* and *Patrician John and his Wife before Pope Liberius*, both Madrid, Prado) and two smaller ones of the *Immaculate Conception* (Paris, Louvre) and the *Triumph of the Eucharist* (Buscot Park, Oxon, NT) encapsulate the central stylistic, narrative and thematic preoccupations of Murillo's entire life. Chiaroscuro is used with masterly ease in the *Dream of the Patrician*, in which the naturalism of the domestic interior and the extraordinary composition of the sleeping patrician

and his wife are balanced against the celestial vision of the Virgin and Child. Once again the sacred and the profane are combined seamlessly in a world that Murillo appears to imagine with great ease. In *Patrician John and his Wife before Pope Liberius* the artist represents the grandeur of the head of the Church and the humble simplicity of the pious, who are confident in the faith and goodness of the Pope. For the same church he executed an *Infant St John* (possibly the one now in London, N.G.) and its pendant, the *Good Shepherd* (Peterborough, Lane priv. col.), commissioned for a temporary altar dedicated to the Virgin. Both are superb examples of child-like grace, anticipating 18th-century sensibility.

During this same period Murillo produced works of a more intimate character, on a smaller scale and with gentle themes. Among these are the *Mystic Marriage of St Catherine* (Lisbon, Mus. N. A. Ant.), two versions of the *Annunciation* (Madrid, Prado; St Petersburg, Hermitage) and three versions of the *Holy Family* (Budapest, Mus. F.A.; Chatsworth, Derbys; Munich, priv. col.). These are works of refined naturalism and silent, serene meditation on family life and work. The *Virgin and Child* ('*Virgin of the Cloth*'; Seville, Mus. B.A.) is a masterly example of simplicity, grace and naturalism in which the vivaciousness of the child is outstanding.

The *Immaculate Conception of the Escorial* (c. 1660–65; Madrid, Prado) is an outstanding version in the series of Immaculate Conceptions painted by Murillo throughout his career. The dogma of the Virgin's immaculate conception, though staunchly defended by the Franciscan Order, was a subject of considerable discussion in early 17th-century Spain, and in 1661, largely as a result of Spanish pressure, a papal bull was issued clarifying this (the dogma was not confirmed until 1854). Murillo, who was closely involved with the Franciscans and became a lay member of the Venerable Orden Tercera de S Francisco in 1662, always represented the Immaculate Conception according to the vision of Beatriz de Silva, to whom the Virgin appeared dressed in white, with a blue cloak (the form also recommended by Pacheco). Nevertheless, his compositions varied throughout his career; the Escorial *Immaculate Conception* breaks with the rigid pedestal-like designs of earlier artists, and the angels supporting the clouds in the lower half of the picture are presented in an open and dynamic composition as if playing among them. A number of other paintings of the same subject executed during the 1660s and 1670s exist, including those at Kansas City, MO (Nelson–Atkins Mus. A.), St Petersburg (Hermitage), Detroit, MI (Inst. A.) and Ponce (Mus. A.). Of the two in Seville, that in the Museo des Bellas Artes (1668) is a more complex version of the youthful image in Paris (1665; Louvre); the other shows the Virgin with black hair and a modest expression and was painted (c. 1667–8) for the cathedral (*in situ*).

In 1663 Murillo moved to the parish of S Bartolomé, near the church of S María la Blanca; his wife died in December of the same year. The artist had some company during the years that followed the death of his wife: Don Miguel de Mañara lived in the same parish, as did the Marqués de Villamanrique. There was also Don Antonio Hurtado de Salcedo, the Marqués de Legarda, of whom the painter executed the portrait in huntsman's dress (*c.* 1664; Vitoria, priv. col.; see Angulo Iñiguez, 1981, no. 410). This is one of Murillo's most unusual portraits, in which, next to the hunting marqués, he introduced the figure of his servant leading the dogs; the severe and imposing figure of the nobleman contrasts with that of the boy, executed in a profoundly naturalistic manner. In the central years of his life, Murillo's activity as a portraitist achieved its most personal and characteristic expression. His portraits can be divided into various types, and there exists in them a clear evolution from early naturalist tenebrism to the late tonal and luminous elegance. A work exceptional for its intensity is the portrait of *Don Justino de Neve* (1665; London, N.G.), whose sitter had commissioned Murillo for the works in S María la Blanca. De Neve is shown seated at his desk, on which a clock is ostentatiously placed. A dog at his feet raises its head towards its master, and in the background the architecture and landscape lend monumentality and grandeur to the composition. The light falling on the head and hands of the figure reveals the solidity and serenity of his character, attributes that were recognized by his contemporaries, and the accuracy with which the sitter's psychology is captured places Murillo among the great portrait painters of his time.

(iv) c. 1665–1682. The decade after finishing the works for S María la Blanca was Murillo's period of greatest activity. About 1665 he painted a series of four large canvases on the subject of the *Story of Jacob* (dispersed; three of the canvases: Dallas, TX, Mus. F.A.; Cleveland, OH, Mus. A.; St Petersburg, Hermitage), for the Marqués de Villamanrique. These works display his mastery of large-scale composition and his abilities as a landscape artist: the small figures and landscapes indicate a knowledge of Flemish landscape painting, with its great variety and naturalism, rather than the ideal classical landscape in the Italian manner. Also in 1665 Murillo received the commission to paint a cycle of works for the convent of the Capuchinos, Seville (finished 1666), with its exquisite canvases dedicated to the Sevillian saints *SS Justa and Rufina* and *SS Leander and Bonaventure* (both Seville, Mus. B.A.) and others. The works executed for the church of S Agustín must be dated between 1666 and 1670; they are now dispersed but include *St Thomas of Villanueva as a Child, Dividing his Clothes among Beggar Boys* (Cincinnati, OH, A. Mus.) and *St Thomas of Villanueva Giving Alms* (Los Angeles, CA, Norton Simon Found.). After 1668 Murillo executed the magnificent canvases for the second cycle commissioned by the Convent of the Capuchinos for its church. Of the nine large-scale canvases that remain (eight in Seville, Mus. B.A.) those that are distinguished by their beauty and by the singularity of their compositions are the *Adoration of the Shepherds*, the *Vision of St Francis at the Portiuncula* (Cologne, Wallraf-Richertz-Mus.) and the *St Thomas of Villanueva Giving Alms*. These are mature works, whose gravity and mysticism are expressed through a profound naturalism in a way that is unique to Murillo, as is seen in the detail of the mother with her child and the beggars in the *St Thomas*.

Finally, the most important series that Murillo undertook for Seville was the series of 11 canvases for the interior of the church of the Hospital de la Caridád, funded by Don Miguel de Mañara (*see* SEVILLE, §IV, 4). The decorations were commissioned principally from Murillo, who executed compositions from the Old and New Testaments. However, two works by Valdés Leal were also commissioned: *In Ictu oculi* (*see* VALDES LÉAL, (1), fig. 2) and *Finis gloria mundi*, which in their cruel and merciless depiction of death contrast vividly with the beautiful and serene canvases of Murillo, which depict acts of mercy and charity. The largest canvases, almost 6 m long, are *Moses Drawing Water from the Rock* and the *Miracle of the Loaves and the Fishes*. Other works of lesser dimensions for the altars are the *Return of the Prodigal Son* (Washington, DC, N.G.A.), *Christ Healing the Paralytic at the Pool of Bethesda* (London, N.G.), the *Liberation of St Peter* (St Petersburg, Hermitage), *Abraham and the Three Angels* (Ottawa, N.G.), *St John of God Assisting the Sick Man* and *St Elizabeth of Hungary Healing the Sick* (both *in situ*). In these works Murillo moved towards the perfect realization of an aerial perspective, as achieved by Velázquez shortly before in *Las Meninas* (*see* VELÁZQUEZ, DIEGO, fig. 10). All the scenes chosen by the artist allowed him to depict the types of figure in which he excelled: poor people, beggars and charitable saints.

Between 1665 and 1675 Murillo executed most of his depictions of children (the earlier *Boy Delousing Himself* is an exception). They range from scruffy street urchins, such as *Children Eating Melon and Grapes* and *Children Playing at Dice* (both Munich, Alte Pin.), to young girls selling fruit and flowers, for example the *Young Fruitseller* (St Petersburg, Hermitage) and the *Girl with Fruit* (London, Dulwich Pict. Gal.). One of the most masterly works in the genre is the *Boy with a Dog* (*c.* 1660; St Petersburg, Hermitage). There appears to be no social message in these compositions, merely the artist's interest in depicting the vitality and beauty of children. It is difficult to define the border between the sacred and profane in some of the works of this kind, especially in the representations of the Good Shepherd and St John as a boy as well as the *St Thomas de Villanueva as a Boy*. Such pictures as the *Family Group* (Fort Worth, TX, Kimbell A. Mus.) and the *Two Girls at a Window* (Washington, DC, N.G.A.; see fig. 4) fall midway between genre and portraiture. The former shows a woman delousing a child seated in her lap while a young woman and a man look at the viewer, the woman winking in a gesture of complicity. The *Family Group* cannot be considered a portrait, but its content may have some significance that is now unknown. The figures, however, with their spontaneous vivaciousness, naturalness and intimacy, seem simply to represent a family from the artist's environment.

Murillo's late *Self-portrait* (1670–75; London, N.G.) and the portrait of *Nicolás de Omazur* (1672; Madrid, Prado) are further examples of the artist's interest in the Flemish-style oval portrait; Omazur, a Fleming living in Seville, is depicted holding a skull, a *vanitas* symbol particularly popular in northern European portraiture. An echo of van Dyck's work may be seen in some of the portraits where the subject is presented full-length in an architectural setting with swags of drapery (e.g. *Josua van Belle*, 1670; Dublin, N.G.). In other portraits of knights and gentlemen, however, Murillo follows the very austere Spanish tradition, in which the sitter is presented in an indeterminate

4. Bartolomé Esteban Murillo: *Two Girls at a Window*, oil on canvas, 1.25×1.04 m, 1665–75 (Washington, DC, National Gallery of Art)

space leaning on a desk or table, accentuated by extremes of light and shade (e.g. *Don Diego F. de Esquivel*, Denver, CO, A. Mus.; *Knight of the Order of Alcántara*, New York, Met.; and *Portrait of a Knight*, Madrid, Prado).

From 1670 until his death Murillo painted some of his most intimate works. The compositions contain fewer figures in very ample spaces, creating a sense of tranquillity and contemplation far removed from the colouristic and lively animation of earlier years. From this period is the *Infant Christ Asleep on the Cross* (Sheffield, Mappin A.G.), a common iconographic theme of the 17th century, which Murillo interprets with his usual sensitivity towards childhood; also from these years is *St Rosa of Lima with the Infant Christ* (*c.* 1670; Madrid, Mus. Lázaro Galdiano), in which he may have been portraying his daughter Francisca, who became a nun in 1671. During this period Murillo also executed the large altarpiece of the *Two Trinities* (London, N.G.), in which he depicts God the Father surrounded by angels, with the Holy Spirit in the upper part and the Holy Family in the lower part; this displays once again Murillo's compositional ability in large-scale works. In 1678 Murillo executed for the Hospital de los Venerables, Seville, the *Immaculate Conception* (Madrid, Prado), also known as the '*Soult Immaculate Conception*' after it was taken to France by Marshal Soult during the Napoleonic invasion. Also for the Venerables he painted the *Virgin and Child Distributing Bread to a Priest* (Budapest, Mus. F.A.) for the hospital refectory. The extraordinary portrait of *Don Juan Antonio de Miranda y Ramírez de Vergara* (Madrid, Col. Duque de Alba), grave and austere, dates from 1680. In the following year Murillo received the commission for the main altar of the church of the Capuchines in Cádiz, but he fell from the scaffolding

while still painting the great central canvas of the *Mystic Marriage of St Catherine* (Cádiz, Mus. B.A.), and died a few months later while making his will. 'I saw that he was dying', said the scribe, 'when I asked him at the given moment whether or not he had made any other will, and he did not answer me, and expired a short while afterwards.'

2. WORKING METHODS AND TECHNIQUE. Murillo's earliest works are painted in a manner derived from his teacher Castillo and such established artists as Zurbarán and Cano. However, in works such as the *Death of St Clare* of *c.* 1645 he was already using the soft shades of colour that were to become his hallmark. It was not until the mid-1650s that he abandoned the tenebrism of his early years, and thereafter his scenes are bathed in a luminous light that defines the composition's depth, as in the landscape backgrounds of the three remaining canvases of the four scenes from the *Life of St John the Baptist* (1655; Cambridge, Fitzwilliam; Berlin, Gemäldegal.; Chicago, IL, A. Inst.). After his visit to Madrid, Murillo began to adopt the richer colouring and brilliant technique of Rubens and this was augmented by his study of the works of Genoese artists (numerous in Sevillian collections and churches) with their use of warm tones, thick brushstrokes and dazzling white highlights. During the last decade of his career Murillo refined and purified his style: the range of tones was reduced and he used fewer colours, with carmine, mauve, and grey and brown shades predominating. His brushwork became much looser and at times gives the canvases an unfinished appearance. The most impressive examples of the loose technique of his final years are the pair of a *Child Laughing* (London, N.G.) and the *Girl Lifting her Bonnet* (London, Carras priv. col., see Angulo Iñiguez, 1981, no. 396), as well as the *Martyrdom of St Andrew* (*c.* 1680; Madrid, Prado), which in its delicate colouring and light and vaporous brushwork recalls the work of Rubens.

Unusually for a Spanish artist, a considerable number (*c.* 100) of drawings by Murillo still exist. His working methods followed the practice of the time: he made quick notes of his ideas in black chalk or pen, while for the more finished compositions with studies of light and shade he employed pen with wash or red and black chalk. An exceptionally highly finished work such as the *Mystic Marriage of St Catherine* (*c.* 1655; Hamburg, Ksthalle) is in black and red chalk. He produced a number of detailed figure studies for his works, some of which are of great beauty and have an energetic strength of execution, for example the pen sketch of *St Isidore* (Paris, Louvre), the *Archangel Michael* (London, BM) and the *Virgin and Child* (Cleveland, OH, Mus. A.), which is a preparatory sketch for the painting (New York, Met.). The series of *Angels with Symbols of the Passion* (Paris, Louvre; Bayonne, Mus. Bonnat) are fine examples of the use of pen and watercolour. However, the *Crucifixion* (London, Sir Brinsley Ford priv. col., see 1982–3 exh. cat., no. D13) is undoubtedly the most impressive of Murillo's drawings, both for its size and for the beauty of its technique (a mixture of red and black chalk). Apart from making preparatory drawings, Murillo also produced oil sketches in a refined technique with vaporous brushstrokes and soft colouring that anticipate 18th-century works (e.g. the *Virgin and Child in Glory with Saints*, London, Wallace Col.).

BIBLIOGRAPHY

EARLY SOURCES

Ceán Bermúdez
D. Ortiz de Zuñiga: *Anales eclesiásticos y seculares de las más noble y muy leal ciudad de Sevilla . . . desde el ano de 1246 hasta el de 1671* (Seville, 1677)
A. A. Palomino de Castro y Velasco: *Museo pictórico* (1715–24)
A. Ponz: *Viaje* (1772–94); ed. C. M. de Rivero (1947)
J. A. Ceán Bermúdez: *Carta de D. Agustín Ceán Bermúdez a un amigo suyo sobre el estilo y gusto en la pintura de la escuela sevillana y sobre el grado de perfección a que se elevó Bartolomé Esteban Murillo cuya vida se inserta, y se describen sus obras en Sevilla* (Cádiz, 1806/R Seville, 1968)
E. Davies: *The Life of B. Esteban Murillo: Compiled from the Writings of Various Authors* (London, 1819)
D. Angulo Iñiguez: 'Bartolomé Murillo: Inventario de sus bienes', *Bol. Acad. N. Hist.* (1966), pp. 147ff

GENERAL

Gestoso y Perez
F. Quilliet: *Dictionnaire des peintres espagnols* (Paris, 1816), pp. 96–103
W. Buchanan: *Memoirs of Painting with Chronological History of the Importation of Pictures by the Great Masters into England since the French Revolution*, ii (London, 1824), pp. 281–3
C. B. Curtis: *Velázquez and Murillo: A Description and Historical Catalogue of the Works* (London and New York, 1883)
M. Gomez Imaz: *Inventario de los cuadros sustraídos por el Gobierno intruso en Sevilla el ano 1810* (Seville, 1896, rev. 1916/R 1972), pp. 1–49
El Greco to Goya. The Taste for Spanish Paintings in Britain and Ireland (exh. cat. by A. Braham, London, N.G., 1981)
La época de Murillo: Antecedentes y consecuentes de su pintura (exh. cat. by E. Valdivieso and J. M. Serrera, Seville, Pal. Arzobisp., 1982)

MONOGRAPHS

T. Gautier: *Esteban Bartolomé Murillo: Les Dieux et les demi-dieux de la peinture* (Paris, 1864)
F. M. Tubino: *Murillo: Su epoca, su vida, sus cuadros* (Seville, 1864)
W. Bell Scott: *Murillo and the Spanish School of Painting* (1873)
W. Stirling-Maxwell: *Murillo* (London, 1873)
L. Alfonso: *Murillo: El hombre, el artista, las obras* (Barcelona, 1883)
C. Justi: *Murillo* (Bonn, 1892, rev. Leipzig, 1904)
P. Lefort: *Murillo et ses élèves* (Paris, 1892)
A. F. Calvert: *Murillo: A Biography and Appreciation* (London and New York, 1907)
P. Lafond: *Murillo* (Paris, 1907)
A. L. Mayer: *Murillo* (Berlin, 1923)
S. Montoto: *Murillo* (Seville, 1923)
B. De Pantorba: *Murillo* (Madrid, 1947)
A. Dotor: *Murillo* (Madrid, 1964)
D. Angulo Iñiguez: *Murillo y su escuela* (Seville, 1975)
E. Young: *Die grossen Meister der Malerei: Bartolomé Murillo* (Berlin, 1980)
D. Angulo Iñiguez: *Murillo: Su vida, su arte, su obra*, 3 vols (Madrid, 1981)
——: *Murillo*, A. Hisp. (Seville, 1982)
Murillo (1617–1682) (exh. cat. by D. Angulo Iñiguez and others, Madrid, Prado; London, RA; 1982–3)
N. Ayala Mallory: *Bartolomé Esteban Murillo* (Madrid, 1983)

SPECIALIST STUDIES

J. Burckhardt: 'Über Murillo', *Atlantis*, ix (1837), p. 482
J. M. Alvarez: 'Noticias biográficas de Murillo', *Sevilla Mariana*, ii (1882), pp. 384, 421
P. Madrazo: 'Murillo y Rafael: Discurso en la velada con que se conmemoró en Madrid el segundo centenario del eminente pintor sevillano', *Bol. Acad. B. A.* (1882), p. 12
S. Montoto: 'La biblioteca de Murillo', *Bibliog. Hisp.* (July 1946), pp. 465ff
F. Abbad: *Las Inmaculadas de Murillo* (Barcelona, 1948)
J. Guerrero: 'Murillo y Assereto', *Archv. Esp. A.*, xxiii (1950), p. 133
J. Elizalde: *Las Inmaculadas de Murillo* (Madrid, 1955)
D. Angulo Iñiguez: 'La piedad de Murillo: El viaje del pintor a Madrid', *Archv. Esp. A.*, xxxii (1961), pp. 146–9
A. de la Banda: 'Los estatutos de la academia de Murillo', *Ana. U. Hispal.* (1961), pp. 107–20
D. Angulo Iñiguez: 'Towards a Revaluation of Murillo', *Apollo*, xxix (1964), pp. 27–30
A. Braham: 'The Early Style of Murillo', *Burl. Mag.*, cvii (1965), pp. 445–51

D. Angulo Iñiguez: 'El viaje de Murillo a Tierra Firme en 1633', *Archv. Esp. A.*, xlvi (1973), pp. 354–8
——: 'Alguno dibujos de Murillo', *Archv. Esp. A.*, xlvii (1974), pp. 97–108
Murillo and his Drawings (exh. cat. by J. Brown, Princeton U., NJ, A. Mus., 1976)
Murillo dans les musées français (exh. cat. by C. Resort, Paris, Louvre, 1983)

MANUELA MENA

Murillo, Gerardo. *See* ATL, DR.

Murlo. *See* POGGIO CIVITATE.

Muro, José Antonio Fernández. *See* FERNÁNDEZ MURO, JOSÉ ANTONIO.

Murōji [Nyon'in Kōya: 'Women's Mt Kōya']. Japanese temple in Uda County, Nara Prefecture, *c.* 25 km southeast of Nara. It serves the Buzan branch of the Shingon sect of Esoteric Buddhism (*see* BUDDHISM, §III, 10). Before recorded history, the site was believed to have been sacred to a local water-dragon deity, to which the nearby shrine Ryūketsu Jinja is dedicated. A temple may have been founded at the site in the late 7th century AD by the wandering monk En no Gyōja (*b* 634); another traditional account claims that Murōji itself was established during the 8th century by a priest from Kōfukuji, the tutelary temple of the powerful Fujiwara family in Nara (*see* NARA, §III, 7). It did, in fact, enjoy a close affiliation with Kōfukuji. Murōji's remote setting on a mountain slope made it an important centre of Esoteric Buddhist teaching and practice, although it did not formally become a Shingon temple until 1694. Unlike Kōyasan (Mt Kōya), principal monastic complex of the Shingon sect, Murōji permitted women to enter and worship within its grounds, a custom that earned it its popular name.

The precinct of Murōji contains superb examples of early Heian period (794–1185) architecture and sculpture. Unlike those of other temples of Nara, the buildings do not follow a symmetrical ground-plan, but they are arranged according to the topography of the mountainside, with steep flights of stone steps leading from one to another. Murōji's oldest extant structure is the five-storey pagoda, which dates from the late 8th century to the early 9th and, at 16.2 m high, is the smallest temple pagoda in Japan. Each of its roofs is smaller than the one below. The *kondō* ('golden hall'), which dates from the 9th century, is also small; later Edo period (1600–1868) additions to its façade and verandah include an extra bay, constructed in 1672 to serve as a *raidō* ('worship hall') and supported by wooden pillars set on a stone terrace. Both the *kondō* and the pagoda are roofed with cedar rather than with ceramic tiles. Additional buildings include the Mirokudō (Hall of Miroku [Skt Maitreya] Buddha) and Mieidō (Founder's Hall), both of the Kamakura period (1185–1333).

Among the sculptures at Murōji are such masterpieces as the temple's central image, a 9th-century standing *Shaka Buddha* (Skt Shakyamuni), carved from a solid block of wood. The Mirokudō houses a 9th-century seated *Shaka*, sculpted in cedar in the same single-block fashion, the draperies of which exemplify the *Honpa* ('Rolling-wave') style of carving (*see* JAPAN, §V, 3(iii)), with rounded folds separated by sharp ridges. Other works of sculpture include a *Jūichimen Kannon* (Eleven-headed Kannon; Skt

Ekadashamukha Avalokiteshvara), a *Yakushi Buddha* (Skt Bhaishajyaguru) and a *Jizō Bodhisattva* (Skt Kshitigarbha), all dating from the Heian period. Smaller images of the *Jūnishinsho* (Twelve Divine Generals), housed in the *kondō*, date from the Kamakura period.

BIBLIOGRAPHY

T. Domon and M. Katagawa: *Murōji* (Tokyo, 1954); Eng. trans. by R. A. Miller as *Murōji: An Eighth Century Japanese Temple: Its Art and History* (Tokyo, 1954)

M. Ooka: *Nara no tera*, Nihon no bijutsu [Arts of Japan], vii (Tokyo, 1965); Eng. trans. by D. Lishka as *Temples of Nara and their Art*, Heibonsha Surv. Jap. A., vii (New York and Tokyo, 1973)

B. Kurata: *Mikkyō jiin to Jōgan chōkoku* [The sculpture of Esoteric Buddhism], Genshoku Nihon no bijutsu [Arts of Japan, illustrated], v (Tokyo, 1967)

STEPHANIE S. WADA

Murom. Russian town 300 km east of Moscow on the left bank of the River Oka first mentioned in AD 862. It was already a sizeable settlement at the beginning of the 11th century when Yaroslav I (*reg* 1019–54) gave it to his son Gleb. Murom became a religious centre after the murder and subsequent canonization of Gleb, and numerous churches were built, although the surviving buildings date from the 16th and 17th centuries. These churches were built close to the steep riverbank, forming the impressive river frontage of the town. The austere five-domed cathedral of the Transfiguration of the Saviour (Spaso-Preobrazhensky) and the tower church of SS Cosmas and Damian, a small cuboid building surmounted by a stone hipped roof, both date from the second half of the 16th century. The most important buildings of the 17th century are the monasteries of the Trinity (Troitsky) and the Annunciation (Blagoveshchensky). Both feature monumental walls and towers and central five-domed cathedrals: the cathedral of the Trinity (1642–3) and that of the Annunciation (1664), single-domed churches built over the gateways and belfries with hipped roofs. They are lavishly decorated in brick and stone as well as polychrome tiles. Parish churches were also rich in ornament, for example the churches of the Resurrection (Voskresenskaya; 1658) and of the Presentation (Vvedenskaya; 1659). Old Russian traditions together with Baroque features predominated in Murom throughout the 18th-century architecture. Buildings in Neo-classical style date from the early 19th century; examples are the new church of SS Cosmas and Damian (1804–38), the Zvorykin House (1830s) and the Karatygin House (1840s). In 1912 Aleksey Shchusev built the railway station in the style of an Old Russian fortress. Traditional Russian architecture was popular in Murom at the turn of the 20th century, and many timber houses combine historical elements with modern features.

BIBLIOGRAPHY

N. Bespalov: *Murom* (Yaroslavl', 1971)

S. Maslenitsyn: *Murom* (Moscow, 1971)

G. Vagner: *Po Oke ot Kolomny do Muroma* [Along the Oka from Kolomna to Murom] (Moscow, 1980)

N. Bespalov: *Murom: Pamyatniki arkhitektury i iskusstva* [Murom: architectural and artistic monuments] (Moscow, 1990)

D. O. SHVIDKOVSKY

Muromachi period. Period in Japanese history, 1333–1568 (*see also* JAPAN, §I, 2). It was ushered in by Ashikaga Takauji (1305–58), leader of an important military family near Kamakura, and the ambitious young Emperor GoDaigo (*reg* 1318–39). For centuries the office of emperor had been dominated by aristocratic regents or military rulers. GoDaigo, determined to challenge the Hōjō regents in Kamakura, requested the aid of the ASHIKAGA family. Victory came through this alliance, and GoDaigo reigned briefly as master of his own court. However, in 1335 Takauji exiled GoDaigo and placed his own candidate on the throne. The period from 1336 to 1392, when two legitimate lines claimed their equal right to the throne, is termed the Nanbokuchō ('period of the north–south dynasties'). It represents the only split in the Japanese imperial line in nearly two millennia, making it the longest surviving such line in the world.

Takauji made two decisions that affected the aesthetic taste and artistic styles of Muromachi arts and left a permanent mark on Japanese cultural history. First, he transferred his military headquarters back to the imperial capital of Kyoto, to the Muromachi section (from which the period takes its name). Second, in 1342, Takauji reopened formal relations with China, which had been greatly diminished since Kublai Khan, leader of the Yuan dynasty, twice threatened to invade Japan in 1274 and 1281. From the first decision blossomed an extraordinary synthesis of military and aristocratic values in the arts. This was begun during the reign of the third shogun, Ashikaga Yoshimitsu (1358–1408), who led the Ashikaga government to the peak of its power. In 1395 he retired to the Kitayama suburb (northern hills) of Kyoto, where he brought together many artists, craftsmen and performers. The *nō* theatre, an early form of the tea ceremony, garden design and the structure of the Kinkakuji (Golden Pavilion) are among the accomplishments of the Kitayama *bunka* (culture), which grew out of Yoshimitsu's generous patronage of the arts.

From the trade with China there developed guilds (*za*) to handle the flow of imported and exported goods. Certain warehouse owners specializing in the handling and evaluating of imported Chinese wares became acknowledged connoisseurs of Chinese paintings, porcelains and other *objets d'art*. By the time of the eighth shogun, Ashikaga Yoshimasa (1436–90), these specialists (*dōbōshū*) formed the intimate circle of the shogunal court. Yoshimasa aspired to emulate the political accomplishments of his grandfather Yoshimitsu, but presided over such setbacks as the burning of Kyoto during the Ōnin War (1467–77). Where Yoshimasa failed in politics, however, he achieved brilliantly as a patron of the arts. His retirement villa, the Ginkakuji (Silver Pavilion), which still stands in the eastern hills of Kyoto, was the centre of his Higashiyama *bunka* ('culture of the eastern hills'). Under his patronage, such activities as garden design, *nō* acting, the tea ceremony and connoisseurship were elevated to the level of fine arts, establishing traditions of styles and lineages of masters that would continue through the centuries (*see also* JAPAN, §§XIII and XIV).

Buddhism continued to exert an important influence on Japanese culture. Of particular significance during this period was the growth and spread of Zen Buddhism (*see* BUDDHISM, §III, 10(iv)), particularly among the military class. Zen temples in Kyoto were centres of Chinese culture, where Chinese poetry, history, Confucian doctrine and a tradition of *suibokuga* (brush and ink painting; *see* JAPAN, §VI, 4(iii)) were actively practised.

BIBLIOGRAPHY
T. Matsushita: *Ink Painting* (Tokyo, 1974)
Japanese Ink Painting (exh. cat., ed. Y. Shimizu; Princeton U., NJ, A. Mus., 1976)
J. Hall, ed.: *Japan in the Muromachi Age* (Berkeley, CA, 1977)
M. Collcutt: *Five Mountains: The Rinzai Zen Monastic Institution in Medieval Japan* (Cambridge, MA, 1981)
H. Varley: *Japanese Culture* (Honolulu, 1984)

BONNIE ABIKO

Murphy, Anna. *See* JAMESON, ANNA BROWNELL.

Murphy, Gerald (*b* Boston, MA, 26 March 1888; *d* East Hampton, Long Island, NY, 17 Oct 1964). American painter. He graduated from Yale University, New Haven, CT, in 1912 and from 1919 to 1921 attended a course in landscape design at Harvard Graduate School, Cambridge, MA. In September 1921 he arrived in Paris with his family and soon afterwards saw an exhibition at the Galerie Paul Rosenberg of works by Picasso, Braque, Matisse and Gris, which inspired him to become a painter. Having no prior training, he took lessons with Natalia Goncharova until spring 1922. He soon became involved in the flamboyant lifestyle of Paris in the 1920s and his friends included Picasso, Léger and Igor Stravinsky. By 1924 he was based at the Villa America in Antibes, and from 1923 to 1926 he exhibited annually at the Salon des Indépendants. Murphy's output was very small and averaged only about two paintings a year during his short painting life from 1922 to 1929, some of which are lost. One of his most impressive early works is the large-scale *Boatdeck* (5.4×3.6 m, 1923; untraced; see 1974 exh. cat., p. 23). It depicts the funnels and other vents of an ocean liner in Murphy's characteristic precise, graphic and impersonal style. Like many of his works it has a general affinity with the paintings of the American Precisionists. In 1923 Murphy was asked by Rolf de Maré to produce an 'American Ballet' for the Ballets Suédois. The result was *Within the Quota*, with music by Cole Porter and costumes and scenery by Murphy. It received its first performance at the Théâtre des Champs Elysées in Paris the same year. The painting *Razor* (1924; Dallas, TX, Mus. F.A.) shows the influence of Cubism through its flattened, abstracted forms, and it has a poster-like quality in its graphic depiction of manufactured objects. Murphy's last-known work is *Wasp and Pear* (1929; New York, MOMA), which includes a close-up of a wasp's foot, reflecting his interest in natural forms. Murphy gave up painting in 1929 as a result of family and business problems and returned to New York in the Depression in order to save the family firm Mark Cross and Co. His total output, possibly as few as 14 works, which were largely neglected until the end of his life, shows an original assimilation and development of Cubism and Purism; in their cool depiction of largely prosaic objects they presage elements of Pop art.

BIBLIOGRAPHY
C. Tomkins: *Living Well is the Best Revenge: Two Americans in Paris, 1921–1933* (New York, 1971) [biog.]
The Paintings of Gerald Murphy (exh. cat. by W. Rubin, New York, MOMA, 1974)

Murphy, J(ohn) Francis (*b* Oswego, NY, 11 Dec 1853; *d* New York, 10 June 1921). American painter. A self-taught artist, he depicted the coastal flatlands of New York and New Jersey and similar countryside in New England. His early work until *c.* 1885 was based on direct observation of nature and was often small-scale, for example *Summer Afternoon* (1875; Salt Lake City, U. UT, Mus. F.A.). In middle-period works such as *New England Landscapes* (n.d.; Springville, UT, Mus. A.) Murphy was influenced by A. H. Wyant, George Inness, Homer Dodge Martin and the Barbizon school painters Corot, Rousseau and Daubigny. He spent summers at Arkville in the Catskill mountains from 1887, and Wyant's presence there between 1889 and 1892 had a pronounced influence on Murphy's developing Tonalist style. His work of this time consists of spare expressions of barren wind-blown land painted with a limited palette. Murphy typically prepared his canvases early to give time for the underpaint to dry and then applied brown and gold, which he flattened with a palette-knife as a basis for later stages of rubbing (with pumice), lacquering and glazing. After 1900 Murphy painted some of his finest oils, including *Sprout Lake* (1915; Washington, DC, N. Mus. Amer. A.), in which he achieved an almost pure tonal unity.

BIBLIOGRAPHY
E. Clark: *J. Francis Murphy* (New York, 1926)
American Art in the Barbizon Mood (exh. cat. by P. Bermingham, Washington, DC, Smithsonian Inst., 1975)
M. Muir: *Tonal Painting, Tonalism and Tonal Impressionism* (MA thesis, U. Utah, 1978)
Tonalism: An American Experience (exh. cat., ed. J. Davern; New York, Grand Cent. A. Gals, 1982)

ROBERT S. OLPIN

Murphy/Jahn. *See* JAHN, HELMUT.

Murr, Christoph Gottlieb von (*b* Nuremberg, 6 Aug 1733; *d* Nuremberg, 8 April 1811). German publisher, writer and art historian. After obtaining a doctorate in law from the University of Altdorf, he travelled (1756–7) to Strasbourg, the Netherlands and England, where he met well-known figures in science, art and politics. In 1758 he set off again from Nuremberg to Vienna and northern Italy. Besides his employment as a Nuremberg weighmaster and customs official from 1760, Murr wrote about German art history and culture. He also published various magazines such as the weekly *Der Zufriedene* (Nuremberg, 1763–4), the *Journal zur Kunstgeschichte und zur allgemeine Litteratur* (Nuremberg, 1775–89) and the *Neues Journal zur Literatur und Kunstgeschichte* (Nuremberg, 1798–9). Stimulated by his wide-ranging correspondence with leading figures within and outside Europe, these contained many articles on the art history and culture of other countries. His work also encompassed linguistic surveys, political and historical subjects and writings about the Jesuit order. He was the author of 82 titles, though his own literary experiments remained insignificant. Murr became a member of the Königliches Historisches Institut, Göttingen, in 1765, and later of other learned societies in Berlin, Strasbourg and Munich.

WRITINGS
Bibliothèque de peinture, de sculpture et de gravure (Frankfurt am Main and Leipzig, 1770)

Beschreibung der vornehmsten Merkwürdigkeiten in der . . . Stadt Nürnberg und auf der hohen Schule zu Altdorf, i (Nuremberg, 1778), ii (1802)
Beschreibung der sämtlichen Reichskleinodien und Heligthümer, welche in . . . Nürnberg aufbewahret werden (Nuremberg, 1790)
Merkwürdigkeiten der fürstbischöflichen Residenzstadt Bamberg (Nuremberg, 1799)

BIBLIOGRAPHY
ADB
H. W. Rotermund: *Fortsetzung und Ergänzungen zu Christian Gottlieb Jöchers allgemeinen Gelehrten-Lexicon,* v (Bremen, 1816)
C. von Imhoff: *Berühmte Nürnberger aus neun Jahrhunderten* (Nuremberg, 1984)

ANGELA LOHREY

Murray, Charles (Oliver) (*b* Denholm, Borders, 1842; *d* Croydon, 11 Dec 1924). British illustrator and etcher. He was a prolific and successful etcher both in working after other painters and as an original artist. He studied at the Edinburgh School of Design and the Royal Scottish Academy Schools, winning the Keith prize and medals for anatomical studies and drawing from the Antique. He was soon in demand as an illustrator and in 1881 was a founder-member of the Royal Society of Painter-Etchers. From 1872 to 1924 he was a frequent exhibitor at the Royal Academy, London, showing original works and etchings after popular contemporary artists. He worked in landscape and genre but excelled as an interpreter of architecture (e.g. *St Mark's, Venice,* 1892; *Canterbury Cathedral,* 1887; *Burgos Cathedral,* 1910; all London, V&A). His work was included regularly in the specialized graphic periodicals, *The Etcher, The Portfolio* and *English Etchings.*

BIBLIOGRAPHY
H. Beck: *Victorian Engravings* (London, 1973)
R. K. Engen: *Dictionary of Victorian Engravers, Print Publishers and their Works* (Cambridge and Teaneck, NJ, 1979)

Murray, Charles Fairfax (*b* 30 Sept 1849; *d* London, 25 Jan 1919). English painter, draughtsman and collector. He came from a poor family and worked for most of his youth in an engineer's office in London. When he was in his teens he attracted the attention of Dante Gabriel Rossetti, Philip Webb and William Morris and became an assistant in the studios of Rossetti, Edward Burne-Jones and G. F. Watts. He transferred Burne-Jones's cartoons on to glass for Morris, Marshall, Faulkner & Co. (from 1875 Morris & Co.) and executed designs for Christina Rossetti's *Goblin Market and Other Poems* (1862) and Morris's *The Earthly Paradise* (1868–70). He went to Italy to copy Old Master paintings for Ruskin, who described him as 'a heaven-born copyist' (examples, after Carpaccio and Botticelli, Sheffield, Ruskin Gal. Col. Guild of St George). In 1867 he began exhibiting at the Royal Academy, London, and after 1877 at the Grosvenor Gallery, London. His paintings (e.g. *St George and the Dragon;* Birmingham, Mus. & A.G.) were strongly influenced by the Pre-Raphaelites. Murray had homes in London and Paris and spent much of his life in Italy, where he developed a reputation as an art expert and connoisseur. He advised dealers and various collectors, among them Ruskin, and was a consultant to Thos Agnew & Sons, London, for whom he bought a *Pietà* (1490; Washington, DC, N.G.A.) by Fra Filippo Lippi. He had a long association with the American cotton manufacturer Samuel Bancroft jr (1840–1915), assisting him in the formation of

his collection of Pre-Raphaelite art (now Wilmington, DE, A. Mus.). In 1894 he published a catalogue of the collection of William John Cavendish-Bentinck, 5th Duke of Portland. In addition to paintings, Murray collected rare books and Old Master drawings, on which he privately published catalogues. His collection of books, which included early French, German, Dutch, Flemish, Swiss and Austro-Hungarian printed books, effectively traced the progress of woodcut illustration in Europe from the 15th to the 17th century. He was a generous man and made significant gifts to public collections, for example Titian's *Tarquin and Lucretia* (*c.* 1570) to the Fitzwilliam Museum, Cambridge, and several pictures by such English portrait painters as Gerard Soest and John Riley to the Dulwich Picture Gallery, London. When the City of Birmingham Art Gallery purchased part of his collection of works by Rossetti and Burne-Jones, he donated an equal amount. In 1910 his collection of Old Master drawings, books and correspondence was sold to J. Pierpont Morgan and later became part of the Pierpont Morgan Library in New York. His collection of paintings was partly dispersed at auction in 1914 (Paris, Gal. Georges Petit, 15 June). Among those sold were Reynolds's study for the *Death of Dido* (exh. RA 1781; British Royal Col.), van Dyck's portrait of *Lucas Vorsterman the Elder* (*c.* 1626–32; Lisbon, Mus. N.A. Ant.), Dürer's *Salvator mundi* (*c.* 1503; New York, Met.) and Boucher's *Young Woman Lying on a Sofa* (1751; Cologne, Wallraf-Richartz-Mus.). Further parts of the collection were sold at Christie's, London (17–19 Dec 1917, 28–29 Jan and 2 Feb 1920).

UNPUBLISHED SOURCES
Austin, U. TX [MSS notebooks]
WRITINGS
J. Pierpont Morgan Collection of Drawings by the Old Masters, Formed by C. Fairfax Murray, 4 vols (London, 1905–12)
BIBLIOGRAPHY
Obituary, *The Times* (28 Jan 1919), p. 11
D. Robinson: 'Burne-Jones, Fairfax Murray and Siena', *Apollo,* cii (1975), pp. 348–51
R. Elzea, ed.: *The Correspondence between Samuel Bancroft, jr. and Charles Fairfax Murray, 1892–1916,* Delaware Art Museum Occasional Paper, 2 ([Wilmington, DE], 1980)
D. Sutton: 'From Ottley to Eastlake', *Apollo,* cxxii (1985), pp. 122–3
The Last Romantics: The Romantic Tradition in British Art (exh. cat., ed. J. Christian; London, Barbican A.G., 1989)

Murray, Elizabeth (*b* Chicago, IL, 6 Sept 1940). American painter, printmaker and draughtsman. She studied at the Art Institute of Chicago (1958–62) and at Mills College, Oakland, CA (1962–4). As a student she was influenced by many painters, ranging from Cézanne to Robert Rauschenberg and Jasper Johns. In 1967 Murray moved to New York and first exhibited in 1971 in the Whitney Museum of American Art Annual Exhibition. Her first mature works included *Children Meeting* (oil on canvas, 2.56×3.22 m, 1978; New York, Whitney), and they evoke human characteristics, personalities or pure feeling through an interaction of non-figurative shapes, colour and lines. Murray is particularly well known for her shaped canvases, which date from 1976, on to which are painted both figurative and non-figurative elements: *Sail Baby* (1983; Minneapolis, MN, Walker A. Cent.) is effectively a collage of the image of a brightly painted yellow cup together with three biomorphic, interlocking canvases.

The perceptual play of image and constructed object/ground is characteristic of Murray's highly inventive and personal visual language.

BIBLIOGRAPHY

Elizabeth Murray: Drawings, 1980–1986 (exh. cat., Pittsburgh, PA, Carnegie–Mellon U.A.G., 1986)
Elizabeth Murray: Paintings and Drawings (exh. cat., Dallas, TX, Mus. A., and elsewhere, 1987)

Murray, John (*b* London, 16 April 1808; *d* London, 2 April 1892). English publisher and writer. He was the son of the publisher John Murray II (1778–1843) and was educated at Charterhouse School, London, and, for one year (1827), at Edinburgh University. In 1829 he made the first of many trips to the Continent, visiting Holland, Belgium and northern Germany, during which he became aware of the need for a guide book to aid English tourists. He set about gathering relevant information: in 1830 he visited northern and central France, in 1831 Milan, Venice, Salzburg, Munich and elsewhere, and in 1836 he travelled down the Danube to the borders of Turkey and Wallachia. The result of his travels was the famous series of Murray handbooks, in their distinctive red covers. The first title was *A Handbook for Travellers on the Continent: Being a Guide through Holland, Belgium, Prussia and Northern Germany, and along the Rhine, from Holland to Switzerland* (1836). Like the subsequent titles, it contained a mixture of practical and cultural information, arranged according to a number of suggested routes. He followed it with guides to southern Germany (1837), Switzerland and the Alps (1838) and France (1843). He commissioned other writers for further handbooks, including Francis Palgrave for northern Italy, RICHARD FORD for Spain, and the explorer and Egyptologist John Gardner Wilkinson (1787–1875) for Egypt. The Murray series inspired the Baedeker travel books, the first of which appeared in 1839, early issues of Baedeker being virtually translations of the equivalent Murray handbooks. On the death of his father in 1843, John Murray III succeeded to the family business and under his management the company published such notable works as Charles Darwin's *Origin of Species* (London, 1859), the *Handbooks of the History of Painting* series, based on Franz Kugler's *Handbuch der Kunstgeschichte* (Stuttgart, 1842), and translations of Heinrich Schliemann's books on his excavations at Troy, Tiryns and elsewhere.

See also GUIDEBOOK.

WRITINGS

A Handbook for Travellers on the Continent: Being a Guide through Holland, Belgium, Prussia and Northern Germany, and along the Rhine from Holland to Switzerland (London, 1836)
A Handbook for Travellers in Southern Germany (London, 1837)
A Handbook for Travellers in Switzerland and the Alps of Savoy and Piedmont, including the Protestant Valleys of Waldenses (London, 1838)
A Handbook for Travellers in France (London, 1843)

BIBLIOGRAPHY
DNB
J. Murray IV: *John Murray III, 1808–1892; A Brief Memoir* (London, 1919)
G. Paston [Miss E. M. Symonds]: *At John Murray's: Records of a Literary Circle, 1843–1892* (London, 1932)

Murray [Murrey], Thomas (*b* ?Scotland, 1663; *d* London, 1 June 1735). ?Scottish painter. He was active in London, where he studied with a member of the de Critz family before becoming a pupil of John Riley, much of whose style he assimilated. His more satisfactory portraits date from the 1690s and include *William Dampier* (*c*. 1697–8; London, NPG) and *Edmund Halley* (*c*. 1695; London, Royal Soc.) as well as the full-length portrait of *Thomas Doggett* (*c*. 1692; Sherbourne Castle, Dorset, Col. Simon Wingfield Digby). The portrait of Doggett, sharply observed in the manner of Riley, shows him in the role of Nincompoop in D'Urfey's *Love for Money*, the earliest known English portrait of an actor in character before a scenic backdrop. Murray's portraits of women were far less successful. Towards 1700 he attempted a more elegant if somewhat flaccid style, as in *Richard Waller* (*c*. 1700–11; London, Royal Soc.). His increasing dependence on studio assistance led to a serious loss in individuality, particularly in the mass production of ceremonial full-length portraits.

An astute businessman, who increased his profits by shrewd speculation, Murray was not above accepting hack commissions such as the provision of benefactors' portraits for Oxford colleges, and his studio produced royal portraits after Kneller: examples are *William III* (1725; London, Middle Temple) and *Queen Anne* (1703; London, Middle Temple; variant at Royal Hosp.). A number of his portraits were engraved, and he maintained his popularity in academic circles, resulting in dull portraits of *Halley* again (*c*. 1713; Oxford, Bodleian Lib.), *Sir Isaac Newton* (1718; Cambridge, Trinity Coll.) and *Sir Hans Sloane* (*c*. 1725–8; London, Royal Coll. of Physicians).

In 1726, when he was a childless widower, Murray owned a town house in Holborn, London, as well as his studio in the Piazza, Covent Garden. He provided George Vertue with information about earlier painters, but the younger man was more impressed by his parsimony, which yielded the painter a fortune, estimated at more than £40,000 at his death.

BIBLIOGRAPHY

DNB; Waterhouse: *18thC*
G. Vertue: 'The Note Books of George Vertue', *Walp. Soc.*, xviii (1929–30) [autobiog.], xx (1931–2), xxii (1933–4) and xxiv (1935–6)
E. K. Waterhouse: *Painting in Britain, 1530 to 1790* (Harmondsworth, 1953, 4/1978), p. 149

RICHARD JEFFREE

Murray, William Staite (*b* London, 9 Sept 1881; *d* Umtali, South Rhodesia [now Zimbabwe], 20 Feb 1962). English potter. He attended evening classes in pottery at the Camberwell School of Art, London (*c*. 1909–12). About 1915–16 he joined Cuthbert Hamilton at the Yeoman Pottery in Kensington, London (closed 1920). After World War I he set up his own pottery at the family engineering firm in Rotherhithe in 1919, moving in 1924 to a new workshop in south-east London where he developed a high-firing, oil-burning kiln, which he patented in 1926. He made large, often wide-shouldered earthenware and stoneware pots and vases, freely painted with abstract designs ('Wheel of Life', 1937–9; London, V&A), which he regarded as art forms rather than functional pots. In the 1920s and 1930s he showed his highly priced pots in fine-art galleries with such painters as Ben and Winifred Nicholson and Christopher Wood. From 1926 he was

Head of the pottery department at the Royal College of Art, where he was an inspiring if eccentric teacher. In 1939 he settled at Odzi, in South Rhodesia (now Zimbabwe), where he embraced Buddhism and never potted again. He returned to England briefly in 1957 to prepare an exhibition of the last of his pre-war work at the Leicester Galleries, London (1958).

BIBLIOGRAPHY
E. Cooper: *A History of World Pottery* (London, 1972, rev. 3/1988)
William Staite Murray (exh. cat. by M. Haslam, London, Crafts Council Gal., 1984)
R. Hyne: 'William Staite Murray: Potter and Artist', *Cer. Rev.*, 92 (1985), pp. 10–15

Murtić, Edo (*b* Velika Pisanica, nr Bjelovar, 4 May 1921). Croatian painter, printmaker, stage designer, graphic designer and illustrator. Before World War II he studied at the Zagreb Academy. In 1943 he joined the partisan forces where he founded, together with another painter Zlatko Prica (*b* 1916), an engraver's printshop and edited a portfolio of prints in illustration of the epic poem *Pit* by I. G. Kovačić. In 1951 he abandoned his Post-Impressionist style of painting Adriatic landscapes after a stay in the USA and Canada. In 1953 he exhibited in Belgrade and Zagreb the cycle *Experience of America* (1950–51), which contained about 30 paintings and was greatly criticized. These pictures (now Zagreb, Gal. Mod. A. and Mun. A. G.; Belgrade, Min. Foreign Affairs; priv. cols) conveyed impressions of American megalopoles such as Pittsburgh and New York in the manner of American Abstract Expressionism. Mimetic elements began to disappear from his work, and by the late 1950s Murtić developed his own dramatic brushwork. Around 1960 he approached *Art informel* with his predominantly earth tones and wilfully plain handling.

In the 1960s Murtić painted mostly abstract pictures, in which the physical gesture was turning into the artist's characteristic sign. The dramatic effect was heightened by sweeps of black colour, rhythmically and harmoniously applied to the picture surface. Clear touches of bright colour in a great variety of contrasting tones remained characteristic throughout this period. In the late 1970s his abstract forms represented Mediterranean landscape again.

BIBLIOGRAPHY
B. Bek: *Edo Murtić* (Zagreb, 1958)
V. Maleković: *Murtić* (Pordenone, 1978)
M. Gibson: *Edo Murtić* (Zagreb, 1989)
JURE MIKUŽ

Muru, Selwyn (*b* Te Hapua, N. Auckland, NZ, 1939). Maori painter, sculptor, writer and film maker. His tribal affiliation is Ngati Kuri, Te Aupouri, Te Paatu, Ngati Rehia, Murikahara, Te Whakatohea. He studied at Ardmore and Dunedin Teachers' College, but he left teaching in 1962 to concentrate on his art, holding his first one-man show at the Ikon Gallery in Auckland in the same year. He was largely self-taught as a painter and sculptor, believing 'all creative artists are self-taught'. His philosophy of art closely followed the view of Picasso, whom he much admired, that artists should be honest to their own personal experiences and strengths. Muru's paintings have often been characterized by their narrative political content,

from the series telling the story of Parihaka (1972) to the 14 panels of *Whakapapa*, painted for the *Kohia ko taikaka anake* exhibition at the National Art Gallery in Wellington, NZ, in 1990. In later years he increasingly combined his skills as an orator and a painter, making extensive use of language in his works to address issues concerning the status of the *tangata whenua* (first people) within New Zealand. As a sculptor he is well known for *Waharoa*, a large gateway outside the Aotea Centre in the central Civic Square in Auckland.

BIBLIOGRAPHY
E. Bett: *New Zealand Art, A Modern Perspective* (Auckland, 1986), p. 172
K. Mataira: *Seven Maori Artists* (Wellington, 1986), p. 66
Maori Art Today (exh. cat., Auckland, Inst. & Mus., 1987)
Kohia ko taikaka anake: Artists Construct New Directions. New Zealand's Largest Exhibition of Contemporary Maori Art (exh. cat., Wellington, NZ, N.A.G., 1990–91)
MEGAN TAMATI-QUENNELL

Mus, Paul (*b* 1902; *d* Murs, Provence, 9 Aug 1969). French art historian and teacher. Born into a family of teachers, he first went to Indo-China as a child. In 1927 he became a member of the Ecole Française d'Extrême-Orient, and in 1933 he completed his doctoral thesis on the archaeology and architectural iconography of the Buddhist stupa in Borobudur. In 1937 he became Director of Studies at the Ecole Pratique des Hautes Etudes in Paris. His career was interrupted by employment with the Services Spéciaux in Hanoi during World War II, but it resumed when he became Director of the Ecole Nationale de la France d'Outre-Mer. In 1946 he was appointed to the chair of Far Eastern civilizations at the Collège de France; he also taught at the University of Yale. His linguistic studies of Sanskrit, Tibetan, Chinese, Siamese and Vietnamese were combined with studies in the comparative religion, history of religion, archaeology, ethnography and iconography of Hinduism and Buddhism in India and South-east Asia. As an art historian he concentrated on the religious significance of architectural monuments in Buddhist ritual, their cosmic symbolism and their mystic aspects. He also took a sociological and political interest in the analysis of Indo-China, especially the problems relating to decolonization and the war in Vietnam.

WRITINGS
Barabudur: Esquisse d'une histoire du bouddhisme fondée sur la critique archéologique des textes, 2 vols (Hanoi, 1935)
BIBLIOGRAPHY
G. Moréchand: Obituary, *Bull. Ecole Fr. Extrême-Orient*, lvii (1970), pp. 25–42 [with bibliography]
S. J. VERNOIT

Musa-i Logar. *See* GULDARA.

Musalla [Arab. *muṣallā*; Pers. *ʿīdgāh*]. Large open-air space where prayers are held on the occasion of the two major religious festivals in Islam, ʿId al-Fitr and ʿId al-Adha. In eastern Islamic lands, including Iran and the Indian subcontinent, the Arabic term *muṣallā* ('place of prayer') is often replaced by the Persian *ʿīdgāh* ('place of the festival'). A *muṣallā* must be large enough to contain all the males of a city who are old enough to engage in prayer; it may be walled and equipped with a free-standing mihrab and minbar constructed of durable materials, but it need have no other significant architectural form. Not every Islamic city has an architecturally formalized *muṣallā*. Normally located outside a city or town, a *muṣallā* may occasionally be found within the walls of a city; in any event, the site of a city's *muṣallā* generally reflected changes in urban development. *Muṣallā*s are often placed next to cemeteries (which are usually outside the walls, too); for this reason, or because prayers for the dead were performed at the *muṣallā* in Medina in Muhammad's day, funerary mosques are sometimes found at these sites. In some cities an open *muṣallā* was replaced with a mosque on the same site.

*Muṣallā*s are seldom accorded prominence in urban topographies, but many historical examples are known. Muhammad prayed at a *muṣallā* in Mecca and established another at Medina, outside the city wall to the south-west. Under the early Abbasid caliphs, Baghdad had a *muṣallā* outside the wall on the east side of the city, adjacent to the Malikiya cemetery. An *'īdgāh* was established at Delhi after its conquest by Muslims in the late 12th century. In the 12th century Damascus had a *muṣallā* outside the walls to the south; Aleppo also had an extramural example. In the 15th century Cairo, then one of the largest Islamic cities, had no fewer than eight places of prayer called *muṣallā*s.

The case of HERAT in Afghanistan shows how the function of the *muṣallā* can be fulfilled in different ways at various times. An *'īdgāh* existed there in the 13th century, just north of the city walls. An iwan was constructed at the *'īdgāh* in the mid-15th century, when it is known to have been in a district of tombs and cemeteries, well to the north-west of the city. At this time it was also called a *muṣallā* and a *namāzgāh* (Pers.: 'place of prayer'). In the 19th century the 'Id prayers were held at the ruins of the great Timurid religious monuments north of the city, and this area was then called the *muṣallā*, although it was without any architectural embellishment suited to the purpose. Finally, after the Great Mosque was renovated in the 1940s and the adjoining city wall was sliced through to create a large park, this new location proved large enough to accommodate the male population, and so the 'Id prayer services came to be held there.

Other *muṣallā*s with some substantial architectural features exist, or are known to have existed, at Bukhara, Isfahan, Mashhad, Shiraz, Samarkand and many other smaller towns in Iran and Central Asia. Free-standing iwans housing the mihrab, sometimes with open, flanking chambers, are common at these sites, but the minbar stands outside the structure.

BIBLIOGRAPHY

Enc. Islam/2: 'Muṣallā'
E. Galdieri: 'A Hitherto Unreported Architectural Complex at Iṣfahān: The So-called "Lesān al-'arz" Preliminary Report', *E. & W.*, n. s., xxiii (1973), pp. 249–64   ☐

Musashi. *See* MIYAMOTO MUSASHI NITEN.

Muscat and Oman. *See* OMAN.

Museifneh. *See under* ESKI MOSUL REGION.

Museum. Institution primarily for the preservation, display and study of works of cultural interest, but increasingly characterized by a broader range of social functions. The origins of the modern museum can be traced to Classical times. It was only after the Renaissance, however, that it came to be regarded as a vital public institution. Although museum history has traditionally been surveyed in the context of the history of COLLECTING and of the temporary EXHIBITION, the substantial growth in knowledge of each topic warrants their separate treatment. Architecturally, this institutional history has been accompanied by the development of an important building type. More detailed studies of major individual museums may be found under the headings for the cities in which they are located, while national historical overviews are contained within country and regional survey articles.

I. History. II. Architecture.

I. *History.*

1. Classical origins. 2. Renaissance microcosms of the world. 3. Egalitarianism and instruction. 4. Cultural monuments: the creation of the Musée du Louvre and repercussions in Europe. 5. Linear display versus period room. 6. The rise of the American museum. 7. Modern reassessments of function.

1. CLASSICAL ORIGINS. *Mouseion* (Gr.), the etymological root of 'museum', was the term for ancient Greek temples dedicated to the muses of the arts and sciences, which by *c.* 500–450 BC were usually sites for funerary cult ceremonies as well as competitions among members of literary societies. Literary activities associated with the *mouseion* may have contributed to a broadening of its meaning to encompass other non-religious functions, particularly in the context of Hellenistic academies *c.* 400–300 BC. During this time Aristotle began his pioneering biological studies, which included the collection and taxonomy of specimens. His method of inquiry, grounded in observation and the promulgation of theories based exclusively on material evidence, marked a sharp departure from Plato's procedure of investigation through dialogue and induction. Aristotle's technique figured prominently in his lyceum, and it was advanced after his death by his student Theophrastus (*c.* 371–287 BC). A *mouseion* is documented as part of the lyceum's study and teaching facilities in Theophrastus' will (Diogenes Laertius: *Lives*, v. 51–7).

Knowledge of the lyceum and its *mouseion* reached Ptolemy I Soter (*c.* 367–283 BC), who incorporated and vastly enlarged the innovations in his plans for the new city of Alexandria. Primary functions of Ptolemy's *mouseion* (*c.* 290–48 BC) included the recovery and preservation of texts and objects endangered by 4th-century BC political turmoil, the collection of biological samples and the production of new knowledge through organized study. The scope of the institution's collecting was nearly universal, and classification of holdings was a major preoccupation. The place of honour accorded the *mouseion* of Alexandria in the corpus of Classical learning ensured that the meaning of 'museum' would thereafter include these activities.

2. RENAISSANCE MICROCOSMS OF THE WORLD. Despite evidence of the widespread adoption of the Alexandrian model for museum-like institutions during the Ptolemaic period and the Roman Empire, by the 14th

1. *Musei Wormiani Historia*, frontispiece, engraving, 275×356 mm (London, British Library); from *Lugduni Batavorum* (Leiden, 1655)

century AD only a historical knowledge of them remained. Although the Renaissance retrieval of Classical learning secured a lasting familiarity with the Alexandrian museum among educated persons from that time to the beginning of the 20th century, 'museum' was recoined during the Renaissance as a learned shorthand for both a variety of rooms containing objects, and books filled with descriptions of objects. Renaissance museums, whether edifices or texts, comprised a scholarly response to the appearance of unfamiliar objects in the urban centres of Europe. Natural specimens and human artefacts, yielded by voyages of discovery abroad and explorations closer to home, were gathered into collections often called *Wunderkammern*, *cabinets de curiosité* or 'cabinets of curiosity'. In this context 'museum' was an empirical frame that served scholars' efforts to crowd together, sort and regard bewildering arrays of objects that otherwise defied ready comprehension. Renaissance museums were often understood by their creators to be microcosms of an expanding world of distant lands and remote pasts. By labelling their collections 'museums', organizers drew on the authority and prestige of Classical antiquity's greatest institution to set a learned context for their superficially confusing aggregations. The museum of the Danish physician Olaf Worm (1588–1654) was typical of the period's collections in its emphasis on what would later be called natural history,

depicted in the frontispiece to the museum's inventory (see fig. 1).

During the 16th, 17th and 18th centuries paintings and statuary were collected and displayed as decorative, albeit precious, furnishings. Collections were usually formed by royalty, landed aristocracy and the Church. *Kunstkammern* and galleries appeared with growing frequency in this period (*see* KUNSTKAMMER), and records detailing their contents reveal important information about the history of taste (e.g. the addition, censuring, removal and reinstallation of statuary) in the Cortile del Belvedere (subsequently the Museo Pio-Clementino, Rome, *c.* 1500–1790), the use of art to communicate social prestige and political power (e.g. the *Kunstkammer* of the Holy Roman Emperor Rudolf II) and the study of history through the lives of important figures (e.g. the collection of portraits and portrait copies that the Italian cleric and humanist Paolo Giovio arranged and labelled to valorize sovereigns, church fathers, warriors, scholars and others). The Medici family collection, one of the few Renaissance collections to survive intact to modern times in its original quarters, was installed during the 1570s in the Galleria degli Uffizi, a series of ducal offices designed some years earlier by Giorgio Vasari the elder for Cosimo I de' Medici, Grand Duke of Tuscany (*see* FLORENCE, §IV, 10). A subsequent alteration to the Uffizi's loggia, the addition of the Tribuna and the commissioning of specialized interior fittings to receive the vast Medici collections set influential standards for purpose-built displays of paintings and statuary. Although Vasari, Giovio's protégé, did not live to help arrange the works in the Uffizi, his narration of the rise and development of Renaissance art, *Le vite de' più eccelenti pittori scultori ed architettori* . . . (Florence, 1550), may have guided the selection and display of works there.

3. EGALITARIANISM AND INSTRUCTION. The opening of many royal, aristocratic and church collections to 'public' access, which began in the 17th century, and contemporary gifts of collections to art academies, associations, universities and government bodies were often motivated by the same egalitarian beliefs that fuelled the English Revolution and later the French Revolution (1789–95). However, 'public' during the period usually meant restricted to the privileged classes, artists, connoisseurs and students. One of the first private collections permanently made public in the spirit of human equality was that with which the Ashmolean Museum in Oxford was founded in 1683 (*see* ASHMOLE, ELIAS). Its primary constituency, however, remained Oxford University's faculty and students, whom the museum served as a type of laboratory. At first the Ashmolean resembled a 16th-century cabinet of curiosity writ large, and although

precious things were among its earliest holdings, works of art *per se* were not a collecting priority.

The British Museum, London, began its existence in 1753, also as a public collection. It was established with a gift to the British people, which stipulated that Parliament's acceptance should include the foundation of a public museum. Travellers' accounts and museum policy statements reveal, however, that access was usually limited to scholars, artists and the privileged well into the 19th century. The British Museum began with a considerable variety of collecting interests, which came to include antiquities, portraits and ethnographic artefacts, and it has always functioned, like its Alexandrian predecessor, as a research facility, including a library collection. During the 18th century numerous other collections were opened to outsiders, including that of the Medici in the Uffizi (1743), the Vatican's in the Capitoline Museum (1734) and Museo Pio-Clementino (1772–3), and the Habsburgs' in Schloss Belvedere, Vienna (*c.* 1781). Of equal importance to the democratization of access was an accompanying Enlightenment emphasis on educational utility, which found expression in the arrangement and labelling of displays and the separation of paintings, sculptures and *objets de luxe* from other types of objects.

The opening of the Medici collections was followed in the late 1760s by the order of the then Grand Duke of Tuscany, the future Holy Roman Emperor Leopold II, to

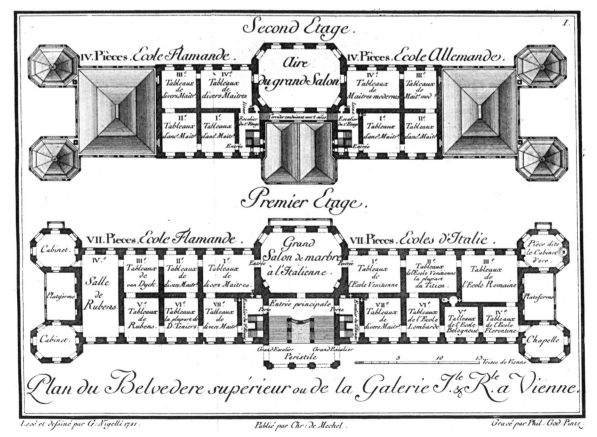

2. Christian von Mechel: *The Imperial Gallery . . . Vienna*, engraving, 179×245 mm (London, British Library); published Basle, 1784

cull them for works of art to be shown exclusively in the Uffizi. Armour, scientific instruments, natural history specimens and curios were removed from the Uffizi to make way for paintings brought from the Palazzo Pitti, the Guardaroba and the Villa Poggio Imperiale. Supervised by two guardians appointed in 1775, the accumulation of works of art in the Uffizi was gradually reorganized in accordance with pedagogical and historical principles subsequently articulated by the deputy guardian, Luigi Lanzi, in his *Storia pittorica della Italia inferiore* (Florence, 1792). He argued that works of art must be displayed 'systematically' to facilitate students' appreciation of their stylistic as well as historical relations. However, the Grand Duke of Tuscany may also have suggested installation designs after viewing the enterprising display of the Habsburg collections in Schloss Belvedere, Vienna.

To create the Schloss Belvedere gallery (forerunner to the Kunsthistorisches Museum), the Holy Roman Emperor Joseph II (1741–90) authorized the gathering together of the most significant and desirable works of art from Habsburg holdings then located in castles throughout the family empire (*see* VIENNA, §V, 6). The chronological breadth, national diversity and stylistic variety of the resulting collection enabled the Emperor's adviser, Christian von Mechel, a Swiss engraver and print publisher, to devise in his plan of the layout of the Belvedere a 'visible history of art' composed of chronological narratives of artistic development within separate national schools (see fig. 2). His historical arrangement of the collection, informed by a similar rehanging of the Düsseldorf gallery in 1755 and the innovative scholarship of his friend the German art historian Johann Joachim Winckelmann, was designed to embody, and thereby provide instruction in, art history. Although von Mechel's 'systematic' approach was consistent with the 18th century's predisposition to ordering knowledge, evidenced in such texts as the *Encyclopédie* (Paris, 1751–65) of Denis Diderot and Jean Le Rond d'Alembert (1717–83), it was attacked by connoisseurs who favoured a method that accentuated aesthetic relationships, determined by comparisons of paintings based on composition, design, colour and subject. The latter type of arrangement appears quite disorderly in surviving depictions, but mid-18th-century guides to domestic furnishing reveal a set of subtle standards that were shaped by such theories as Roger de Piles' taxonomy of the elements of great art, as presented in his *Cours de peinture par principes* (Paris, 1708). These 'eclectic' standards were based on formal, thematic and scale relationships designed both to cultivate refined aesthetic sensibility and to result in balanced, often symmetrical arrangements. The debate continued in France following the formation of the Musée du Louvre in the second half of the 18th century.

4. CULTURAL MONUMENTS: THE CREATION OF THE MUSÉE DU LOUVRE AND REPERCUSSIONS IN EUROPE. The establishment of the Musée du Louvre resulted from nearly 50 years of efforts to increase public access to royal art collections in Paris. The process began in 1750 in the Palais du Luxembourg, where an eclectic display was opened to the public for two days a week until 1779. That year the palace was reclaimed for private use by the royal family, and plans for a more ambitious display in the

Grande Galerie of the Palais du Louvre were begun. A new installation, possibly inspired by the Schloss Belvedere gallery, was mapped to survey art history as represented in three schools of painting: Italian, French and northern European. Work was delayed by the beginning of the French Revolution in 1789, and with the fall of the monarchy in 1792 the Louvre and its contents were declared national property. The Assemblée Nationale soon authorized the establishment of a public art museum in the Louvre. The successful opening of the museum in 1793 was calculated to signal to domestic critics and foreign observers the Revolutionary government's stability, power and efficient guardianship of the national patrimony. Internal debate erupted, however, over the extent to which the museum was truly accessible, with regard not to entry days and hours but rather to the pedagogical utility of its installations. The new display, which celebrated the sumptuousness and extent of the nation's artistic wealth, was 'eclectic'. Those favouring a more 'systematic' approach argued that the nation's collections would not be fully accessible if the average citizen could not comprehend the display. They also politicized the conflict by identifying their position with the Revolutionary principle of public participation in all aspects of national life, while characterizing defenders of the eclectic scheme as élitists. These arguments proved successful, and the collections were culled, apparently reinstalled by school and stylistic development, and they reopened in 1801. However, the new installation offended more ardent Revolutionaries, because it included numerous religious images and royal portraits. Those charged with rehanging the collections countered that the 'systematic' arrangement neutralized the iconographic potency of the offending works by removing them from their original settings and exploiting them as stylistic and historical examples. More than any other event, the use of the Louvre as a sign of egalitarian purpose and civic constancy fixed in the modern mind the notion of the 'museum' as inherently public, religiously and politically 'neutral' and symbolic of social and cultural durability.

In 1801 fifteen other museums were established among French départements by government decree to receive from the Louvre surplus works crowded out by Revolutionary confiscations from private and church collections in France and expropriations from lands conquered by Napoleon. They included the museums of Bordeaux and Marseille (1804), Lyon (1806) and Rouen and Caen (1809). Often set up adjacent to local art schools, the museums were intended to project on a modest scale the type of historical and stylistic breadth possessed by the Louvre and for the same egalitarian and pedagogical reasons. Moreover, Napoleon's military campaigns and subsequent pillaging of collections throughout Europe contributed to the chronological breadth and artistic diversity of the displays of the Louvre and its satellite museums. The French authorities' centralized administration, nationalization of church and royal property and confiscation of nobles' wealth also led to the establishment of museums in cities occupied by Napoleon: the Galleria dell' Accademia (1807), Venice; the Pinacoteca di Brera (1809), Milan; the predecessor of the Rijksmuseum (1808), Amsterdam; and the Museo del Prado (1809), Madrid. Several other early 19th-century museums resulted from France's seizure and subsequent return of art, including the Altes Museum in Berlin.

Despite the opening by Frederick William II, King of Prussia, of royal Prussian collections to artists and pupils of the Berlin Akademie der Künste in 1790, there were calls here too for a more public museum. The archaeologist Aloys Hirt, who taught at the Berlin academy, presented a museum plan to display a comprehensive art survey in a 'systematic classification' as a 'school for the cultivation of taste' in artists and patrons alike, for the advancement of Prussian fine and manufacturing arts. The plan was abandoned when Napoleon seized royal collections for the Louvre. After Napoleon's defeat in 1815, the return of these works was celebrated in a popular public exhibition at the academy. Frederick William III, King of Prussia, perhaps inspired by his visit to the Louvre during peace negotiations, called for an expansion of the academy building in Berlin to create a national Prussian museum, the Altes Museum. The plan was replaced by a design for an entirely new building proposed by Karl Friedrich Schinkel, professor of architecture and the Berlin city planner (see §II, 1 below), but the project was soon clouded in debate over the objects to be included in the museum and the organization of its displays. While Hirt's ambitions for universality would have been achieved through the use of casts and copies as well as original works by both greater and lesser masters, Schinkel and one of the earliest trained art historians, Gustav Friedrich Waagen, argued

for the display of only original works of art and only then of universally appreciable 'masterpieces'. Further, Schinkel and Waagen presented their museum plan as a tool for promoting social unity in the wake of failed Prussian political reforms between 1815 and 1819. Their views prevailed, and by 1830 the selection and installation of works were completed for the museum opening. In suggesting that the government-sponsored museum could unify the public by orienting citizens to a shared experience of aesthetic reverence, Schinkel and Waagen brought the museum into line with the political objective of averting anti-government dissent. The Altes Museum thus obtained official sanction by identifying an almost religious veneration of artistic masterpieces with government patronage.

The large, public, comprehensive and pedagogically oriented museum was a direct result of French political and administrative reforms. It was also one of the few institutions to survive Napoleon's retreat from the nations he had conquered. Most subsequent art museums throughout the world have been guided by this formulation of civic, cultural and administrative values. Examples of national collections embodying these concerns that appeared during the 19th century include the National Gallery, London (1824), the National Gallery of Victoria, Melbourne (1856), the National Museum, Tokyo (1872), and the National Gallery of Canada, Ottawa (1880).

5. LINEAR DISPLAY VERSUS PERIOD ROOM. Although most 18th- and 19th-century museums appeared to the untrained eye as haphazard arrangements of art (see fig. 3), one system of display or another was often at work.

3. Giuseppe Castiglione: *Salon Carré, the Louvre*, oil on canvas, 0.69×1.03 m, 1865 (Paris, Musée du Louvre)

However, whether 'eclectic' (e.g. based on thematic or formal relationships or canvas size) or 'systematic' (e.g. based on national schools, master–student relationships and chronological development), the arrangements usually employed individual works to represent an artist's career or an entire genre. Thus a portrait by Rembrandt would be used to evoke the artist's total output in a room of Dutch art by several masters or 17th-century Dutch painting in a room of northern European art.

Early in the 19th century the French official and collector Alexandre Du Sommerard began acquiring, among other works, medieval *objets d'art*, which he arranged for public view in 1832 in the Hôtel de Cluny, Paris. Rather than attempt an art-historical narrative of the Middle Ages, he arranged his collection to envelop the visitor in an experience of a moment in medieval culture. Thus religious images and ceremonial objects were shown together in the former chapel of the Gothic structure, eating utensils, faience and pottery in the former dining-room and so on. Although certainly romanticized, Du Sommerard's creation (received by the French government as the Musée de Cluny in 1843) enabled visitors to pass through his medieval environment as a lived experience as opposed to passing by objects arranged in a sequential distillation of medieval art history. His approach persisted in the form of 'period rooms' in modern European and American museums, often interspersed among more typical displays of art history as a continuous narrative of artistic development and the transmission of influences within and across schools, nations and centuries.

6. THE RISE OF THE AMERICAN MUSEUM. During the late 19th century and early 20th, history's largest transfer of cultural wealth from one hemisphere to another took place. In the USA in the final decades of the 19th century, the convergence of industry and people in such urban centres as New York, Boston, Philadelphia, Detroit and Chicago concentrated great wealth among a handful of mercantilists, industrialists and financiers, who began collecting European art at an unparalleled pace. Within a generation they had amassed many of the nation's, and the world's, greatest private collections and the material resources for numerous subsequent public collections. The businessmen or their wives who possessed the wealth to buy European art also possessed the civic influence to found cultural institutions modelled on those of Europe, including museums. A disproportionate emphasis on creating art museums as opposed to other types has been attributed to cultural leaders' concern about the inferiority of the USA's cultural attainments. This explanation may also account for the preference of early collectors for works by European Old Masters rather than creations by contemporary American and European artists.

Although some museums were established during the first half of the 19th century, including the Brooklyn Museum, New York (1823), and the Wadsworth Atheneum, Hartford, CT (1842), many of the nation's major museums were created during a torrent of institutional foundings that began in the 1870s: the Museum of Fine Arts, Boston (1870), the Metropolitan Museum of Art, New York (1870), the Philadelphia Museum of Art (1876) and the Art Institute of Chicago (1879). Museums founded

in the late 19th century often shared several traits: the provision of public instruction in the arts for a variety of purposes, including the training of artists and improvement of manufacturing design, the orientation of recent immigrant populations to a unifying culture, and the elevation of manners and morals; they were created as non-governmental, non-profit-making institutions overseen by self-perpetuating boards of trustees composed of business, civic, educational and cultural leaders; their collections included reproductions and casts alongside a limited number of authentic objects. The dominant concern was the fortification of the spiritual life of ordinary citizens, and museums were envisaged as potential surrogate religious institutions, calculated to help preserve family and social values. This conviction held that human improvement could be obtained through knowledge of the past and eternal, especially religious, verities exemplified in great paintings and sculptures. Further economic growth enabled a large number of museum foundings after 1900, including the Los Angeles County Museum of Art (1910), the Cleveland Museum of Art (1916) and the National Gallery of Art, Washington, DC (1937). In each instance founders' statements identified the museum and its patrons, private and public, with civic virtues of public service, cultural attainment and social stability.

Between the World Wars American museums gradually disposed of copies in favour of original works, as gifts of patrons' collections and cash endowments grew to help museums fill gaps in their representations of artistic traditions. Collections were cultivated to provide comprehensive historical and geographic overviews of Western European art and, in many institutions, East, South Asian and Middle Eastern art. The ambitions of most American museums of the period, no matter how small, to create 'universal surveys' of art history, no matter how abridged, distinguish them as a group from European institutions.

7. MODERN REASSESSMENTS OF FUNCTION. Consistent with the increasing specialization of academic disciplines in the late 19th century, new museums in Europe and the USA focused on discrete areas of the 'human sciences' such as natural history, technology and industry, national or regional history, as well as art. Definitions of 'art' to determine what might be included in an art museum varied, but they were generally limited to European painting, sculpture and *objets de luxe*. However, the compelling visual attraction of the material culture of tribal societies for artists and others in Paris from *c.* 1904–5 began a process that unsettled the collecting and display functions of Western museums in the 20th century. As European artists' appropriation of East Asian, especially Japanese, art in the late 19th century popularized those forms, early 20th-century artists' adoption of the visual power of tribal sculptures enlarged audiences for 'primitive' art. A dramatic expansion of museum collecting interests resulted. Although the material productions of tribal peoples ranging from Africa to the Americas and the painting and statuary of South and East Asian cultures were assiduously collected and displayed in natural history museums from the mid-19th century, such objects did not fall within the self-defined purviews of art museums until later. By 1919, however, African and Oceanic works were

presented as art for collectors in Paris, and by the early 1920s museums in Europe and the USA began exhibiting African sculpture as art. In the intervening years many European and American art museums also began exhibiting Native American art.

The display of tribal art objects within art museums posed numerous problems, most of them due to profound conflicts between Western empirical practices, including museum display conventions and native traditions that prohibit showing sacred objects to others. After World War II the reassertion of sovereign rights by native peoples in the Americas and Australia was accompanied by efforts to reclaim objects housed in museum collections. Beginning in the 1970s, the native American Zuni tribe legally removed altar god figures from numerous North American and European museums to return the carvings to Zuni shrines, which, according to tribal beliefs, are open to the sky so that the figures may be consumed by the forces of nature. The Zuni reclamations contradicted centuries of Western empirical principles integral to the museum concept: collecting for the purposes of scholarly investigation and public education, display of authentic objects and permanent preservation of objects for future generations.

Faltering acceptance of avant-garde art by museum curators and patrons motivated artists and collectors of modern Western art to advocate new museums devoted exclusively to such works: the Museum of Modern Art, New York (1929), the Musée National d'Art Moderne, Paris (1936), and more recently the Los Angeles Museum of Contemporary Art (1979) and the Museum Ludwig, Cologne (1986). Unlike the many institutions exhibiting only work by previously recognized and well-established masters, contemporary art museums in particular became aggressive participants in the discovery, patronage and interpretation of new talent. New art museums of all kinds were established at an extraordinary rate throughout the world after World War II, accompanied by an almost exponential growth in museum collections, interpretative programmes and museum audiences in each subsequent decade. Museums became major sponsors of art scholarship in the form of journals, collection and special exhibition catalogues and conferences (see also ART HISTORY, §I). Nonetheless, like their 19th-century predecessors, museums in the 20th century continued to be sites of controversy. From the 1970s in particular, when scholars began questioning the methodological assumptions of historical research and writing in many disciplines, the role of museums in embodying disputable models of art history became the subject of especially intense scrutiny and debate. Scholars examining the historiography of art questioned such topics as the role of museum-based connoisseurship in separating objects from their historical and social contexts or museums' narrative summaries of art history that set works of art in quasi-biological cycles of stylistic development characterized by decline and renewal. Sociologists also questioned the extent to which museum programmes successfully reach the disadvantaged and minorities within modern society. As the principal location for preserving, displaying and interpreting art, the museum increasingly became the subject of critical inquiries into the nature of art as a separate academic subject or isolated cultural phenomenon.

See also DISPLAY OF ART.

BIBLIOGRAPHY

R. Goldwater: *Primitivism in Modern Art* (New York, 1938, rev. Cambridge, MA, 1986)
A. Wittlin: *The Museum: Its History and its Tasks in Education* (London, 1949, rev. Cambridge, MA, 1970)
D. Fox: *Engines of Culture: Philanthropy and Art Museums* (Madison, WI, 1963)
G. Bazin: *Le Temps des musées* (Brussels, 1967; Eng. trans., Brussels, 1967)
N. von Holst: *Creators, Collectors and Connoisseurs* (New York, 1967)
P. Bourdieu and others: *L'Amour de l'art: Les Musées d'art européens et leur public* (Paris, 1969; Eng. trans., Cambridge, 1990)
P. Fraser: *Ptolemaic Alexandria*, 2 vols (Oxford, 1972), pp. 305–35
N. Burt: *Palaces for the People: A Social History of the American Art Museum* (Boston, 1977)
B. Denecke and R. Kahsnitz, eds: *Das kunst- und kulturgeschichtliche Museum im 19. Jahrhundert* (Munich, 1977)
T. Kaufman: 'Remarks on the Collections of Rudolf II: The *Kunstkammer* as a Form of *representatio*', *A. J.* [New York], xxxviii (1978), pp. 22–8
C. Duncan and A. Wallach: 'The Universal Survey Museum', *A. Hist.*, iii (1980), pp. 448–69
F. Haskell, ed.: *Saloni, gallerie, musei e loro influenza sullo sviluppo dell'arte dei secoli XIX e XX. Atti del XXIV congresso C.I.H.A.: Bologna, 1979*
F. Haskell and N. Penny: *Taste and the Antique: The Lure of Classical Sculpture, 1500-1900* (New Haven, 1981)
S. Bann: *The Clothing of Clio: A Study of the Representation of History in Nineteenth-century Britain and France* (Cambridge, 1984), pp. 77–92
O. Impey and A. MacGregor, eds: *The Origins of Museums: The Cabinet of Curiosities in Sixteenth- and Seventeenth-century Europe* (Oxford, 1985)
B. O'Doherty: *Inside the White Cube: The Ideology of the Gallery Space* (San Francisco, 1986)
K. Pomian: *Collectionneurs, amateurs et curieux* (Paris, 1986; Eng. trans., Cambridge, 1990)
C. Bailey: 'Conventions of the Eighteenth-century *cabinet de tableaux*: Blondel d'Azincourt's *La Première idée de la curiosité*, *A. Bull.*, lxix (1987), pp. 431–47
V. Jackson, ed.: *Art Museums of the World*, 2 vols (Westport, 1987)
J. Clifford: *The Predicament of Culture: Twentieth-century Ethnography, Literature and Art* (Cambridge, MA, 1988), pp. 189–251
A. McClellan: 'The Musée du Louvre as Revolutionary Metaphor during the Terror', *A. Bull.*, lxx (1988), pp. 300–13
P. Findlen: 'The Museum: Its Classical Etymology and Renaissance Genealogy', *J. Hist. Col.*, i (1989), pp. 59–78
S. Price: *Primitive Art in Civilized Places* (Chicago, 1989)
D. Sherman: *Worthy Monuments: Art Museums and the Politics of Culture in Nineteenth-century France* (Cambridge, MA, 1989)
P. Woodhead and G. Stansfield: *Keyguide to Information Sources in Museum Studies* (London, 1989)
S. Moyano: 'Quality vs. History: Schinkel's Altes Museum and Prussian Arts Policy', *A. Bull.*, lxxii (1990), pp. 585–608
L. S. Klinger: *The Portrait Collection of Paolo Giovio* (diss., Princeton U., 1991)
K. D. McCarthy: *Women's Culture: American Philanthropy and Art, 1830-1930* (Chicago, 1991)
E. Hooper-Greenhill: *Museums and the Shaping of Knowledge* (London, 1992)
A. McClellan: *Inventing the Louvre: Art, Politics, and the Origins of the Modern Museum in Eighteenth-century Paris* (Cambridge, 1994)
T. Bennett: *The Birth of the Museum: History, Theory, Politics* (London, 1995)
C. Duncan: *Civilizing Rituals: Inside Public Art Museums* (London, 1995)
JEFFREY ABT

II. Architecture.

The museum emerged as a distinct building type in Europe in the second half of the 18th century, and by the mid-19th century it had become an indispensable component of the modern city. Initially, museum architecture was typologically consistent and functionally pure. Imposing and lofty edifices were built to exhibit objects in strictly controlled settings. Changing historical and epistemological conditions, however, gradually deformed the orthodox museum structure. As institutions became more democratic in their audience and more diverse in their activities, assuming more active roles as purveyors of education and entertainment, architectural compositions altered. Sustained disagreement about the best methods of circulation, illumination and display insured further heterogeneity in museum design. The most important issue of all has not, however, been resolved: should the museum building be a monument, a work of art in its own right that celebrates the elevated nature of the institution and its collections and reflects the cherished values of a given epoch? Or should it be a neutral container, a warehouse that neither comments on nor competes with its contents? Each of these extremes, and the gamut between, has been represented in museum architecture.

1. Before 1850. 2. 1850–1940. 3. After 1940.

1. BEFORE 1850. The architectural origins of the museum are hybrid. The first museums were housed in existing buildings, frequently palatial in scale and function, that contained the long, narrow 'galleries' and small 'cabinets of curiosity' that for centuries had been used in Europe to display private collections of art objects and scientific specimens (*see* KUNSTKAMMER). The two most important forerunners of the modern museum building were the Villa Albani by Carlo Marchionni for Cardinal Alessandro Albani (completed *c.* 1762; for illustration *see* MARCHIONNI, CARLO; *see also* ROME, §V, 27) and the Museum Fridericianum (1769–79) in Kassel, designed by Simon Louis Du Ry for Frederick II, Landgrave of Hesse-Kassel (for illustration *see* DU RY, SIMON LOUIS). Although they were both built in Late Baroque style, they differed in conception. The Villa Albani was reserved for the display of antiquities (thus anticipating the specialized art museum), while the Fridericianum, with its library and mixed collections of scholarly curiosities and works of art, was an encyclopedic museum.

Construction of the first public museums took place in the age of NEO-CLASSICISM, and since collections of these institutions emphasized antiquity and the Renaissance, the buildings and their contents were perfectly matched. Architects combined the formal vocabulary and structural systems of Greek and Roman architecture—colonnades, vaults and domes—with Renaissance spatial types—cabinets, galleries and courtyards—to produce the plan and

4. Museo Pio-Clementino, Vatican, Rome, by Alessandro Dori, Michelangelo Simonetti and Giuseppe Camporese, begun 1770

formal image required by the programme of the public museum. The first purpose-built art museum was probably the Museo Pio-Clementino, Rome, constructed in stages from 1770 under the pontificates of Clement XIV and Pius VI to successive designs by Alessandro Dori (d 1771), Michelangelo Simonetti and Giuseppe Camporese. In the process basic formats were established that would be used for generations. An appendage to the Vatican Palace in Rome, the Pio-Clementino incorporated in remarkably pure form features that would be incessantly repeated in free-standing museums: a grand staircase, a domed, Pantheon-like rotunda (see fig. 4), an open courtyard (in the case of the Pio-Clementino, created from the pre-existing Cortile del Belvedere by Bramante) and long rooms, based on the palatial gallery but made more monumental by majestic vaults and sumptuous materials. The embryonic formats to be found in the Pio-Clementino were made systematic and given monumental expression in France. In 1802–5 Jean-Nicolas-Louis Durand published the ultimate codification in his *Précis des leçons*. Durand's design for a 'museum', with a central rotunda and vaulted galleries symmetrically arranged around four courtyards, was to have international influence.

These ideal museum schemes were first realized in actual buildings by ambitious rulers in the German-speaking territories. New art museums in Munich (e.g. the Glyptothek, 1816–30, by LEO VON KLENZE) and Berlin

5. Alte Pinakothek, Munich, by Leo von Klenze, 1825–36; interior view showing the Rubens Gallery

(e.g. the Altes Museum, 1823–30, by KARL FRIEDRICH SCHINKEL; or the Neues Museum, 1843–50, by FRIEDRICH AUGUST STÜLER) played an integral role in the urban layout of their respective cities. German architects acquired such expertise in museum design that they were in demand elsewhere: Klenze designed a vast new wing for the Hermitage (1839–51) in St Petersburg and Stüler the Nationalmuseum (1850–66) in Stockholm. The Glyptothek in Munich was built to display sculpture; its founder, Ludwig I, King of Bavaria, chose the building scheme, a miniaturization of Durand's grand prototype, submitted by Klenze in a competition of 1814–15. Schinkel's Altes Museum in Berlin offered a more original interpretation of Durand. The prismatic volume of its exterior concealed two light courts placed to either side of a rotunda in which sculpture was exhibited. On the first floor, colonnaded halls surrounding the courts housed statues, gems and coins; paintings were placed in side-lit rooms on the second level, where space for displays was augmented by an ingenious system of panels set perpendicular to the outer walls. Schinkel blended classical motifs into a new synthesis: the main façade, its Ionic order transposed from the Erechtheion in Athens, was based on Greek stoa, while the rotunda has a soaring dome with an oculus inspired by the Pantheon in Rome. The monumental flight of stairs leading up to the entrance was copied in museum architecture for more than a century.

In England museums built in the second and third decades of the 19th century represented a more archaeological phase of Neo-classicism. Examples of this include the British Museum (1823–48) by Robert Smirke (ii) (*see* SMIRKE, (2)) and William Wilkins's National Gallery (1832–8), both in London. The universities of Cambridge and Oxford both held competitions for museum buildings, and the winning entries interpreted antique architecture in a more vigorous, eclectic manner. GEORGE BASEVI won the commission (1834) for the Fitzwilliam Museum, Cambridge, and in 1840 C. R. Cockerell won the contest underwritten by Oxford University for the Ashmolean Museum and Taylorian Institute (*see* COCKERELL, (2), fig. 2). Instructions to the entrants of the Oxford competition specified that the design be 'of Grecian character', and Cockerell's first-hand acquaintance with Hellenic ruins gave him a manifest advantage. The first public gallery of pictures, the Dulwich Picture Gallery (1811–14) in south London, by Sir JOHN SOANE, presented a more personal and idiosyncratic classicism than the museums previously cited. Its interior arrangement became very influential, and the galleries, arranged in enfilade in an alternating sequence of square and rectangular rooms, were top-lit by a novel system of clerestory monitors. Although experts disagreed over the best methods of illumination, by the end of the 18th century many preferred zenithal to raked light. (Proposals to transform the Palais du Louvre in Paris into a public art museum were to reflect this preference; *see* §I, 4 above.)

The Dulwich Picture Gallery includes a mausoleum, intended for the remains of its benefactors. This identification of the museum with the mausoleum is not unique: one of the most magnificent of these musea–mausolea is Thorvaldsens Museum (1839–47), Copenhagen, by Gottlieb Bindesbøll. This museum, influenced by Schinkel's

Altes Museum, is more welcoming and less hieratic than most, because its entrance is at street level and not screened by a colonnade (for illustration *see* BINDESBØLL, (1)); one enters directly through splayed portals that have their origins in the Egyptian pylon and the Greek temple doorway. Unlike previous museums, the walls of Thorvaldsens Museum were painted in contrasting hues; this followed on from the rediscovery of the use of polychromy in the Classical period. Completed shortly after the death of Bertel Thorvaldsen, the museum was intended to be this sculptor's memorial. His tomb is in the courtyard, the walls of which are frescoed with arboreal and floral images symbolizing transcendence over death.

Such an evocative decorative programme was typical of 19th-century practice, in which museum decoration frequently celebrated the achievement of those artists whose work was displayed within or, in the case of science museums, displayed two- and three-dimensional specimens. An early, complete example of the former is provided by the Alte Pinakothek, Munich (see fig. 5; *see also* LEO VON KLENZE, fig. 2), the second museum that Leo von Klenze built (1825–36) for Ludwig I. No less exemplary than its decorative consistency is the Pinakothek's organization. A sequence of large galleries is arranged along a central spine, framed on the north by a series of cabinet-sized rooms for small objects and on the south by a corridor, or loggia, that allowed random access to the central galleries, which could also be traversed enfilade. These were top-lit, those to either side taking advantage of the raking light admitted by the generous windows; works of art were arranged in chronological order and by national school. Constructed of brick with terracotta trim, the Renaissance Revival style Pinakothek influenced a number of subsequent museums, among them the Staatliche Kunsthalle (1837–46), Karlsruhe, by HEINRICH HÜBSCH; the Neue Pinakothek (1846–54; destr.), Munich, designed for Ludwig I by August von Voit; and the Gemäldegalerie Alte Meister (1847–55), Dresden, by GOTTFRIED SEMPER.

2. 1850–1940. By the mid-19th century the classical vocabulary no longer reigned supreme in museum architecture. The winning design by DEANE & WOODWARD, submitted to the competition (1854) for the University Museum (built 1855–61), Oxford, introduced the Venetian Gothic style promoted by John Ruskin. Its expensive ornamentation was also inspired by Ruskin's theories, for the representations in stone and wrought iron of flora and fauna offered vivid visual lessons on the natural world. The Natural History Museum (1872), London, by ALFRED WATERHOUSE, similarly reflected Ruskin's belief that decoration should be at once copious and didactic. Here, however, the historical vocabulary is Romanesque, and, instead of using hand-carved stone, the building is faced entirely in cream and blue–grey terracotta. Cast into this material is a delightful menagerie of extant and extinct animals. The use in both these museums of ferro-vitreous construction was no doubt inspired by the vast buildings erected for the international exhibitions that were held with increasing frequency from the mid-century onwards. A revised planning paradigm was developed; behind the

masonry shells that continued to protect museums, elongated courts covered over by iron-and-glass roofs were set. This provided well-lit weatherproof spaces for display, whether of art objects, historical documents, scientific instruments or natural history specimens. The hitherto compact volume of the museum was stretched laterally to accommodate such courts, generally placed to either side of a monumental staircase.

In some cases buildings erected for specific exhibitions were retained and used as museums. Philadelphia's Memorial Hall by Henry J. Swartzmann, built in 1876 for the city's Centennial International Exhibition, became an exhibition gallery, as did the Petit Palais, Paris, built by CHARLES-LOUIS GIRAULT for the Exposition Universelle of 1900. The St Louis Art Museum was installed in a building designed by Cass Gilbert for the Louisiana Purchase International Exposition of 1904, and the Austrian Pavilion, designed by KARL SCHWANZER for the Exposition Universelle et Internationale of 1958, was afterwards dismantled and re-erected in Vienna in 1964 as the Museum des 20. Jahrhunderts.

It was not only the architecture of the international exhibitions that was influential for museums but also the very nature of their displays, in which the distinction between art, technology and manufactures was blurred (*see* INTERNATIONAL EXHIBITION). Paintings, sculptures, machines and commercial products were often displayed in close proximity in large iron-framed glass sheds, as at the South Kensington Museum, London, originally housed in a temporary structure—the 'Brompton Boilers' of 1856—that mimicked other exhibition buildings. A similar mixture of contents prevailed in the museums of cultural or national history. The Bayerisches Nationalmuseum (1897–9) in Munich, the subject of a competition of 1893 won by Gabriel von Seidl, exhibits together objects of various kinds and widely differing monetary values, just as the building itself incorporates stylistic elements from various periods of German architecture. The Bayerisches Nationalmuseum was also one of the first to create period rooms, in which works of fine art were installed along with crafts products and useful objects from the same era to offer the visitor a sense of historical context.

In addition to this response to the impact made by the architecture of the international exhibitions, purpose-built museums were transformed stylistically to accommodate the extravagant eclecticism that characterized the second half of the 19th century. The introduction of museums of arts and crafts, or applied and industrial arts, whose contents were drawn from many different periods, further undermined the hegemony of classicism. These buildings served as demonstrations as well as repositories of the decorative arts. The first permanent structure for the South Kensington Museum (later the Victoria & Albert Museum), London (*see* ENGLAND, §XIV), designed from 1860 by Captain FRANCIS FOWKE and completed in 1869 by General H. Y. D. Scott (1822–83), had lavish ornament designed by students at the South Kensington art schools. Other applied arts museums followed this example, using exposed brick with terracotta trim; they include the Kunstgewerbemuseum (1866–71), Vienna, by HEINRICH VON FERSTEL, and the Kunstgewerbemuseum (1877–81), Berlin, by Martin Gropius.

6. Prince of Wales Museum of Western India, Bombay, by George Wittet, 1905–14 (extended 1937); interior

These eclectic manifestations, found among every type of museum, often carried nationalistic overtones. In the two museums built in Vienna during the reign of Emperor Francis-Joseph—the Kunsthistorisches Museum (1871–82) and the Naturhistorisches Museum (1872–89)—Semper and KARL HASENAUER provided a rich blend of Mannerist and Baroque elements appropriate for Austro-Hungarian imperial grandeur. Their designs, almost identical except for the representational ornament, had been submitted to a closed competition, as had that of the Rijksmuseum, Amsterdam. The entrants for the Rijksmuseum competition were charged with developing a national Dutch style, and for this purpose the winner, P. J. H. Cuypers (see CUYPERS, (1)), combined Late Gothic ribbed vaults with Northern Renaissance features (1876–85). Cuypers also used ferro-vitreous construction for the Rijksmuseum's two large courtyards and established two schools on-site for training craftsmen to design and execute an exhaustive decorative programme illustrating the history of Dutch art and culture.

The export of the quintessentially Western museum idea to European colonies in another hemisphere added some interesting variants to the canon. The British in India sought a style with an indigenous flavour. The Lahore Museum (1890–94), by Sardar Bhai Ram Singh and John Lockwood Kipling (1837–1911), was designed in the mixed Anglo-Indian style. Its symmetrical plan and massing, with framing pavilions and a dome, resembles that of contemporary European museums, such as the two in Vienna, but the shape of the domes, the filigree carving on the white stone gate fronting the brick walls and the detailing of the arches are Mughal in style. In the Prince of Wales Museum of Western India, Bombay, begun in 1905, GEORGE WITTET, consultant architect to the Government of Bombay, offered a more scholarly interpretation of local traditions based on Indian architecture of the 15th, 16th and 17th centuries (see fig. 6). The vast complex is dominated by a monumental dome, appropriately based on the mausoleum known as Gol Gumbaz (1656) at Bijapur, and regional blue and yellow basalt was used for the walls.

Indian rulers also appreciated the cultural opportunities offered by a museum. The Maharaja Sayaji Rao III Gaikwar founded the Baroda Museum (now the Museum and Picture Gallery, Vadodara) in 1894. The design is hybrid: in silhouette and materials (a timber frame filled in with brick) it reflects local traditions, but the ground floor was given a cornice embellished with a cast of the Parthenon frieze. A far 'purer' example of the adaptation of local materials and structure to a new programme is the National

Museum of Phnom Penh. Constructed in 1917 in the Cambodian vernacular style, it thus offered a sympathetic setting for its splendid art collections drawn mainly from the 5th to the 13th centuries, the period of classic Khmer production.

In the late 19th century and early 20th, when the search for a fresh alternative to the historicism that had dominated 19th-century design manifested itself in a number of Art Nouveau designs, a few galleries were constructed that challenged the conventional image of museum architecture. In London CHARLES HARRISON TOWNSEND introduced a new decorative vocabulary based directly on natural forms in his design for the Whitechapel Art Gallery (1895–1901), while also maintaining the monumentality associated with institutional architecture through a few Romanesque Revival details. Fittingly, in the exhibition building created for the Vienna Secession, on which the motto 'To each Time its Art, to Art its Freedom' was inscribed over its entrance, Joseph Maria Olbrich made a novel interpretation of the Temple of the Muses (see AUSTRIA, fig. 9). He gave his symmetrical Secession gallery (1897–8) an imposing crowning centrepiece, an open-work sphere of gilded-metal laurel leaves, rather than the type of masonry dome usually designed for museums. The interior organization is equally innovative: both top- and sidelighting are available, and movable non-load-bearing walls permit complete flexibility with regard to the size and illumination of galleries.

This interval of originality was short-lived, however, and there was soon a return to the classical tradition of museum design, especially in the USA and Australia. Most American museums built between 1893 and the 1930s were indebted to Beaux-Arts principles of organization, and rarely did architects deviate from the established format of twin courts or naves surrounded by a single or double row of galleries. Examples include the Museum of Fine Arts (1907–1915), Boston, by Guy Lowell, and the Cleveland Museum of Art (1916), OH, by Benjamin S. Hubbell (1867–1953) and W. Dominick Benes (1857–c. 1935) (for illustration see CLEVELAND). Although the outside façades and inner public spaces of these buildings followed classical prototypes, the increasingly popular period rooms installed within them provided stylistic variety. This paradigm prevailed until around 1940, for example in the National Gallery of Art, Washington, DC, completed in 1943 to John Russell Pope's designs (see fig. 7). After this date, the classical verities on which the museum had so frequently been based were challenged by representatives of the Modern Movement in architecture.

In 1929 Le Corbusier had proposed a radical design to display the interrelationship between scientific objects, historical documents and works of art. This, his Musée Mondial project (part of a Mundaneum or world cultural centre conceived for Geneva), was in the form of a ziggurat, the summit of which visitors first reached by an elevator. From there, a series of three-aisled, right-angled ramps led them through an encyclopedic survey of the human race and its environment from earliest times through to the present. Although this ambitious project was not executed, Le Corbusier subsequently built three museums outside Europe that reflected aspects of his Musée Mondial design: a museum in Ahmadabad (1951–

7. National Gallery of Art, Washington, DC, aerial view showing West Wing (1941–3; centre) by John Russell Pope, and East Wing (1967–78; top) by I. M. Pei

8), India; the National Museum of Western Art (1956–9), Tokyo; and the Government Museum and Art Gallery, Chandigarh (1964–8), India.

Le Corbusier's museums, however inventive, retained the sense of monumentality traditionally associated with museums. In the USA George Howe and William Edmond Lescaze made six projects for the Museum of Modern Art (MOMA) in New York. These broke with the previous typology completely in their resemblance to office or apartment buildings in an existing streetscape. Other unexecuted museum projects of the period (all competition designs), although modernist in vocabulary, were less bold in conception, in that their designers continued with free-standing, horizontal compositions. These unexecuted designs included the Imperial Museum (1931), Tokyo, by Kunio Maekawa (built 1937 by Hitoshi Watanabe as the main part of the National Museum); the Museo de Arte Moderno (1934), Madrid, by members of Gatepac; the Tallinn City Museum (1937), Tallinn, Estonia, by Alvar Aalto; and the Smithsonian Art Gallery (1939), Washington, DC (1939), by Eliel Saarinen and Eero Saarinen. Although the MOMA building, as realized in 1939 to the designs of Philip L. Goodwin (1885–1958) and EDWARD DURELL STONE, was less iconoclastic than originally projected, it nevertheless represented a break with traditional museum architecture. After 1950, when a (still unabated) global explosion of museum construction commenced, the pioneering example of MOMA had a lasting impact.

3. AFTER 1940. During the period that followed the end of World War II, the most powerful concept governing museum architecture was the glazed universal space, derived from the 19th-century exhibition building. Since such a construction could be subdivided to fit changing spatial requirements, it offered a flexibility deemed advantageous in an era when the temporary exhibition, often a major international artistic event, was an important attraction. Notable examples are the additions made since 1967

8. Exterior of the north wing, Louisiana Museum, Humlebæk, near Copenhagen, by Bo & Wohlert, 1958–82

to the Metropolitan Museum of Art, New York, by Kevin Roche and John Dinkeloo (1918–81; for illustration *see* ROCHE, KEVIN); the Centre National d'Art et de Culture Georges Pompidou (completed 1977; *see* PARIS, fig. 14), by RICHARD ROGERS and Renzo Piano; and the Sainsbury Centre for Visual Arts (1977) at the University of East Anglia, Norwich, England, by NORMAN FOSTER. The purest example constructed along these lines is, however, the Nationalgalerie (1965–8) in Berlin by Ludwig Mies van der Rohe. Eight columns support a steel roof-truss, allowing for a completely open hall, measuring 2500 sq. m. Since the walls are made entirely of glass, paintings are hung from the ceiling or fixed to free-standing panels. Buried under the podium of this steel-framed 'temple' is an area housing the permanent collection. The ideal of the universal space also governs the Museu de Arte de São Paulo Assis Chateaubriand in Brazil (1968; for illustration *see* SÃO PAULO) by Lina Bardi, where a two-storey exhibition hall is raised high above the ground to create a covered plaza for outdoor displays. Both Mies van der Rohe and Bardi exploited the latest materials and technology for their wide-span structures, so as to generate a dramatic, modern image for museums.

These popular loft-spaces were contained within opaque as well as within transparent enclosures, as at the Whitney Museum of American Art (1963–6), New York, by MARCEL BREUER and Hamilton Smith (*b* 1925). Most of the

illumination in such buildings, which resemble strongboxes, is necessarily artificial. A variant was provided for the National Air and Space Museum (1971–5), Washington, DC, by George F. Hellmuth (*b* 1907), Gyo Obata (*b* 1923) and George E. Kassabaum (HOK); this museum consists of a row of four huge, opaque boxes connected by three intervening transparent volumes. The enormous spaces thus created allowed the museum to set up spectacular permanent displays of air- and spacecraft, some of which are suspended by steel cabling.

Post-war design has been influenced by museums built in countries not constrained by the architectural traditions of Europe and North America. Working with limited budgets, on projects where the presentation of collections as precious objects was rarely a consideration, designers were free to jettison conventional wisdom and start afresh. One solution, frequently applied, was the provision of a loosely grouped aggregate of buildings or pavilions, rather than a single, symmetrically planned monument. The enclosed type of museum courtyard that had prevailed for two centuries was replaced by an open patio. This new arrangement governed the planning of the Israel Museum (1959–65), Jerusalem, by AL MANSFELD and Dora Gad; the Museo Nacional de Antropología (1964), Mexico City, by Pedro Ramírez Vásquez with Jorge Campuzano and Rafael Mijares (*see* MEXICO CITY, fig. 6); and the National Museum (1977), Kuwait City, designed by Michel Ecochard (*b* 1905). A similar organizational concept can be found in the proposed National Museum of Ghana for Accra, designed by Franco Minissi in 1963.

Since the 1950s some museums have been built outside towns or cities, in more pastoral settings. The Louisiana Museum, Humlebæk, near Copenhagen, by BO & WOHLERT, is intimately related to its natural surroundings (see fig. 8). Built in five campaigns between 1958 and 1982—a factor that contributed to the relaxed character of the plan—the glass walls of the pavilions permit constant views of the surrounding landscape. The Louisiana Museum was also one of the first for which rustic materials sympathetic to its sylvan site were extensively used in construction. Other institutions that have made a natural setting into an integral part of the visitor's itinerary include the Museum of Anthropology (1971–6), University of British Columbia, Vancouver, by ARTHUR ERICKSON, and the Burrell Collection museum in Glasgow (see SCOTLAND, fig. 7), based on a competition design of 1972 by Barry Gasson (b 1936) and completed in 1983. For the Museum of Anthropology, Erickson used resolutely contemporary materials—precast concrete posts and precast, post-tensioned beams—sensitively fitted together to recall the simple frames of the Kwakiutl longhouses that the museum shelters. For the Burrell Collection, Gasson mixed glass and stainless steel with materials that have more traditional associations, such as stone and wood.

The opposite approach governs such inwardly focused buildings as the Solomon R. Guggenheim Museum (1943–60), New York, by Frank Lloyd Wright. While its soaring, luminous central space looks back to the rotundas of the first art museums, circulation in this museum, managed by means of ramps (adumbrated in Le Corbusier's project of 1929 for the Musée Mondiale), was novel. Although its slanting walls and ramps were severely criticized on functional grounds, Wright's system of movement does alleviate congestion, and it also allows works to be seen from across the rotunda as well as in close proximity. Architects who admired the Guggenheim emulated its virtues elsewhere and 'corrected' its shortcomings. In the University Art Museum of the University of California at Berkeley (1962–70) by Mario Ciampi (b 1907), ramps are angular rather than curvilinear, whereas in the High Museum of Art (1980–84), Atlanta, RICHARD MEIER placed the curving ramps in a quadrant (for illustration see ATLANTA). In both cases, ramps are used exclusively for circulation rather than for viewing works of art. The rough, grey concrete of Ciampi's museum reflected the Brutalist style current in the 1960s and 1970s, exemplified by the museums executed after World War II by Le Corbusier, while Meier's radiantly white forms, clad in the porcelain-enamelled steel panels that he also used for the Museum für Kunsthandwerk (1979–85), Frankfurt am Main, and for additions to the Art Center (1984), Des Moines, IA, look back to the 1920s and the heroic period of Modernism.

The East Wing (1967–78) of the National Gallery of Art, Washington, DC, by I. M. PEI, was also composed around a skylit central space. Although its concrete frame is clad in the same Tennessee marble as Pope's original building (now called the West Wing), Pei's East Wing offers a striking contrast. Because of the site, the ground-plan is composed of triangles, which enforces a more

dynamic image than the serene rectangularity of the West Wing (see fig. 7 above). The irregular shapes of the temporary galleries provide large open spaces, although this requires a mini-museum to be constructed within the East Wing for each temporary exhibition. Pei's East Wing has been compared with designs for airports and shopping malls, and indeed its escalators, bridges and atrium full of bustle imply that a museum should not be a sacred precinct set apart from daily life, but a place intimately involved with modern consumer culture.

A contrasting but equally pervasive trend in museum design from the 1960s on was the return to historical models, led by Philip Johnson and Louis I. Kahn. Johnson was one of the first to resurrect the classical language and symmetrical planning of the first museums, as in his Sheldon Memorial Art Gallery (1963), in the University of Nebraska, Lincoln, NE. Kahn maintained a more Modernist vocabulary, but he reintroduced structural and spatial typologies taken from the traditional museum, and he subtly blended artificial and natural light. In the Kimbell Art Museum (1966–72), Fort Worth, TX (for illustration see KAHN, LOUIS I.), he reintroduced the top-lit, barrel-vaulted galleries that had found favour in such classical museums as the Glyptothek in Munich, but Kahn endowed these galleries with a new flexibility by supporting them on widely spaced columns. Since then the vault has reappeared, singly or in multiples, in a host of museums, among them the Kunstmuseum (1976–81), Holstebro, Denmark, by Hanne Kjaerholm, and the Museum of Fine Arts (1977–83), Dallas, TX, by Edward Larrabee Barnes, as well as the Okanoyama Graphic Art Museum (1982–4), Nishiwaki, Japan, and the Museum of Contemporary Art (1982–7), Los Angeles, both by Arata Isozaki.

In the Yale Center for British Art (1969–77), New Haven, CT, on the other hand, one of the first museums to incorporate commercial rental space, Kahn revised for a late 20th-century audience the ideal of the two-court plan that had reigned from Schinkel's Altes Museum to Pope's National Gallery of Art. Again Kahn used a reinforced-concrete frame to achieve flexibility, in this case creating a series of square bays that could be organized according to need into cabinet-sized rooms or into larger galleries. Kahn was particularly sensitive to the importance of natural light, and he worked with lighting engineers to evolve materials and devices to tame its potentially destructive force. Henry N. Cobb (b 1926), of I. M. Pei and Partners, also studied the problem; the system of monitor lighting that he devised for the new wing of the Museum of Art (1978–82), Portland, ME, drew inspiration from Soane's Dulwich Picture Gallery, while for the plan he combined aspects of Kahn's Kimbell and Yale museums.

Another architect preoccupied with bringing natural illumination safely into the museum setting was James Stirling, who with his partner Michael Wilford designed three major additions: the Staatsgalerie (1977–82), Stuttgart, which includes provision for a theatre, music school, auditorium, restaurant and administration area; the Arthur M. Sackler Museum (1979–84), Harvard University, Cambridge, MA (for illustration see STIRLING, JAMES); and the Clore Wing (1980–85) of the Tate Gallery, London. All

9. Städtisches Museum Abteiberg, Mönchengladbach, Germany, by Hans Hollein, 1972–82

three invoke the magisterial exemplars of the past while exploiting the technical resources available in the present. The plan of the Staatsgalerie directly invoked that of the Altes Museum, thus emphasizing the historical and institutional continuity of the museum as a building type. At the same time, the transformations Stirling wrought in his versions of the modern museum are acknowledgement of modern ambivalence concerning cultural heritage.

A late 20th century phenomenon was the provision of additional exhibition space wholly or partially underground, in order to leave undisturbed an existing site above ground. This is demonstrated in museums that otherwise have little in common: the DeWitt Wallace Decorative Arts Gallery (1982–6), Williamsburg, VA, by Kevin Roche; extensions (1980–87) to the Smithsonian Institution, Washington, DC (1980–87), by Jean-Paul Carlhian (*b* 1919); and extensions (1983–9) for the Louvre, Paris, by I. M. Pei. Another museum that is partially underground, though for a different reason (to incorporate into the building fabric the remains of Roman villas on the site), is the Museo Nacional de Arte Romano (1980–85), Mérida, Spain, by RAFAEL MONEO, where the space is structured by semi-circular and segmental brick arches that recall the architecture of ancient Rome.

The divergent trends visible in modern museum architecture are perhaps most tellingly summarized in the Städtisches Museum Abteiberg (1972–82), Mönchengladbach (see fig. 9), by Hans Hollein, where conventional verities are combined with brilliantly inventive strokes. For a collection that focuses on contemporary art, Hollein produced a unique structure that addresses itself to the town on one side and the abbey gardens on the other. He achieved flexibility not exclusively through open loft spaces, although these exist, but also by providing a variety of room shapes and sizes: square galleries lined up at the

corner angles, curvilinear rooms, double and single height spaces and underground cabinets. Natural light, from above and the side, co-exists with incandescent and fluorescent lighting. Wholly sympathetic to its contents, Hollein's museum proclaims itself a playful monument, at once avant-garde and traditional, an excellent model for a building type that preserves the old while encouraging the production of the new in an age when the museum has become the intellectual and spiritual centre of the community.

BIBLIOGRAPHY

GENERAL

B. I. Gilman: *Museum Ideals of Purpose and Method* (Cambridge, MA, 1923)

H.-R. Hitchcock: *Early Museum Architecture* (Hartford, 1934) [mus. pamphlet]

Muséographie: Architecture et aménagement des musées d'art. Conférence internationale d'études: Madrid, 1934

A. S. Wittlin: *The Museum: Its History and its Tasks in Education* (London, 1949, rev. 3/1974)

H. Seling: *Die Entstehung des Kunstmuseums* (Freiburg, 1953)

R. Aloi: *Musei: Architettura, tecnica* (Milan, 1962) [well illustrated text in It. and Eng.]

M. Brawne: *The New Museum: Architecture and Display* (New York, 1965)

N. von Holst: *Creators, Collectors and Connoisseurs* (London, 1967)

L. Glaeser: *Architecture of Museums* (New York, 1968)

N. Pevsner: *A History of Building Types* (London, 1976), pp. 111–38

B. Deneke and R. Kahsnitz, eds: *Das kunst- und kulturgeschichtliche Museum im 19. Jahrhundert* (Munich, 1977)

P. Hetherington: 'Pantheons in the *Mouseion*: An Aspect of the History of Taste', *A. Hist.*, i (1978), pp. 214–28

J. Robinson and M. Filler, eds: *Buildings for the Arts* (New York, 1978)

F. Haskell, ed.: *Saloni, gallerie, musei e loro influenza sullo sviluppo dell'arte dei secoli XIX e XX. Atti del XXIV congreso C. I. H. A.: Bologna, 1979*

J. M. Daven, ed.: *Architecture, 1970–1980: A Decade of Change* (New York, 1980)

M. Brawne: *The Museum Interior* (New York, 1982)

A. Piva: *La costruzione del museo contemporaneo* (Milan, 1982)

E. P. Alexander: *Museum Masters: Their Museums and their Influence* (Nashville, 1983)

M. D. Levin: *The Modern Museum: Temple or Showroom* (Tel Aviv, 1983)

F. Minissi: *Il museo negli anni '80* (Rome, 1983)

B. O'Doherty: *Inside the White Cube: The Ideology of the Gallery Space* (San Francisco, CA, 1986)

J. M. Montaner and J. Oliveras: *The Museums of the Last Generation* (Stuttgart, 1986)

S. Stephens, ed.: *Building the New Museum* (New York, 1986)

K. Hudson: *Museums of Influence* (Cambridge, 1987)

V. Jackson, ed.: *Art Museums of the World*, 2 vols (New York, 1987)

D. Davis: *The Museum Transformed: Design and Culture in the Post-Pompidou Age* (New York, 1991)

J. M. Montaner: *New Museums* (New York, 1991)

SPECIALIST STUDIES

England

J. Jones: 'Museum and Art Gallery Buildings in England, 1845–1914', *Mus. J.*, lxv (1965), pp. 230–38; (1966), pp. 271–80

France

J. L. Connelly: 'The Grand Gallery of the Louvre and the Museum Project: Architectural Problems', *J. Soc. Archit. Hist.*, xxxi (1972), pp. 120–32

C. Duncan and A. Wallach: 'The Universal Survey Museum', *A. Hist.*, iii (1980), pp. 448–69

A. L. McClellan: 'The Politics and Aesthetics of Display: Museums in Paris 1750–1800', *A. Hist.*, vii (1984), pp. 438–63

D. J. Sherman: 'The Bourgeoisie, Cultural Appropriation, and the Art Museum in Nineteenth-century France', *Radical Hist.*, xxxviii (1987), pp. 38–58

Germany

V. Plagemann: *Das deutsche Kunstmuseum, 1790–1870: Lage, Baukörper, Raumorganisation, Bildprogramm*, iii of *Studien zur Kunst des 19. Jahrhunderts* (Munich, 1967)

P. Böttger: *Die Alte Pinakothek in München* (Munich, 1972)

B. Mundt: *Die deutschen Kunstgewerbemuseum im 19. Jahrhundert* (Munich, 1974)

H. Klotz and W. Krase: *New Museum Buildings in the Federal Republic of Germany* (Stuttgart, 1985)

V. M. Lampugnani, ed.: *Museum Architecture in Frankfurt, 1980–1990* (Munich, 1991)

Italy

C. Pietrangeli: *I musei vaticani: Cinque secoli di storia* (Rome, 1985)

Netherlands

R. van Lutterwelt: *The Rijksmuseum and other Dutch Museums* (London, 1967)

Spain

'Concurso para un museo de arte moderno', *Doc. Actividad Contemp.*, xiii (1934), pp. 32–41

Switzerland

U. Jehle-Schulte Strathaus: *Das Zürcher Kunsthaus: Ein Museumsbau von Karl Moser* (Basle, 1983)

USA

C. Brewer: 'American Museum Buildings', *J. RIBA*, n.s. 3 (1913), pp. 365–403

L. V. Coleman: *Museum Buildings* (Washington, DC, 1950)

J. Cantor: 'Temples of the Arts: Museum Architecture in Nineteenth-century America', *MOMA Bull.*, xxviii (1970), pp. 331–54

H. M. Stewart, ed.: *American Architecture for the Arts* (Dallas, 1978)

H. Searing: *New American Art Museums* (Berkeley, 1982)

E. R. Gaddis, ed.: *Avery Memorial Wadsworth Atheneum: The First Modern Museum* (Hartford, 1984)

D. Ricciotti: 'The 1939 Building of the Museum of Modern Art: The Goodwin-Stone Collaboration', *Amer. A. J.*, xvii (1985), pp. 51–76

HELEN SEARING

Mushatta. *See* MSHATTA.

Musi, Agostino dei [Agostino Veneziano] (*b* Venice, *c*. 1490; *d* ?Rome, after 1536). Italian engraver and draughtsman. His monogram ('A.V.') and in five instances his full name appear on 141 prints. Of these 85 are dated from 1514 to 1536. He began his career in Venice. His earliest dated prints (1514) are copies after Giulio Campagnola (*The Astrologer*; B. 411) and Dürer (*Last Supper*; B. 25). A print dated 1515 after Baccio Bandinelli (*Cleopatra*; B. 193) and another dated 1516 after Andrea del Sarto (the *Dead Christ Supported by Three Angels*; B. 40) indicate his presence in Florence in these years.

In 1516 Agostino went to Rome, where over the next ten years he produced numerous prints after Raphael (e.g. *Blinding of Elymas*, 1516; B. 43), Michelangelo, Giulio Romano and Rosso Fiorentino. He left Rome at the time of the Sack in 1527 and went to Venice, where he worked on illustrations (later rejected; B. 525–33) for a book on architecture by Sebastiano Serlio (unpublished); he also visited Mantua, where he engraved prints after Giulio Romano (e.g. *Hercules and the Nemean Lion*, 1528; B. 287), and Florence. Between 1531 and 1536 he worked in Rome, where he produced numerous prints, including a set of 12 *Antique Vases* (1531; B. 541–52) and several contemporary portraits (e.g. *Francis I, King of France*, 1536; B. 519).

BIBLIOGRAPHY

DBI: 'De' Musi, Agostini'

B. Hedergott: 'Eine Braunschweiger Zeichnung von Agostino Veneziano: Gedanken zur Physiognomik der Groteske', *Beitr. Kstgesch.* (1960), pp. 126–54

K. Oberhuber: *Graphische Sammlung Albertina: Die Kunst der Graphik III: Renaissance in Italien 16. Jahrhundert* (Vienna, 1966)

——: *Marcantonio Raimondi*, 2 vols (New York, 1978), 26 [14–1] and 27 [14–2] of *The Illustrated Bartsch*, ed. W. Strauss (New York, 1978–) [B.]

D. Minonzio: 'Novità e apporti per Agostino Veneziano', *Rass. Stud. & Not.*, viii (1980), pp. 273–320

S. Massari: *Tra mito e allegoria* (Rome, 1989)

CHRISTOPHER L. C. E. WITCOMBE

Music, printed. Reproduced musical notation. Musical notation may be seen in printed books as early as the Psalter (Mainz, 1457) of Johannes Fust (*fl* 1457–66) and Peter Schoeffer (*c*. 1425–1502), although in this work the music was intended to be added in manuscript. Early printers devised various solutions to the complex layout problems of signs on the staff lines. Woodcuts were occasionally seen, as in the *Musices opusculum* (Bologna, 1487) of Nicolaus Burtius (*c*. 1436–1528). Occasionally either the lines or notes alone were printed, the other intended to be added by hand, as in the *Grammatica brevis* (Venice, 1480) of Franciscus Niger (*fl* 1480; *d* 1513). Multiple impressions for lines, notes and often text as well are first seen in a south German Gradual (*c*. 1472) and in a Missal (Rome, 1476) printed by Ulrich Han (*fl* 1438; *d c*. 1478). Multiple-impression printing reached a high point in the superb editions (Venice and Fossombrone, 1501–20; see fig.) of Ottaviano dei Petrucci (1466–1539), in which the Renaissance masterworks of Josquin Desprez (*c*. 1440–1521) and his contemporaries are presented.

Simpler single-impression printing for music, probably introduced just before 1520 by John Rastell (1475–1536) in London, was used extensively from 1526, at first particularly by Pierre Attaingnant (*c*. 1484–1551/2) in Paris. This process was adopted in the 1530s and 1540s in Nuremberg, Venice and Antwerp and in dozens of other cities in the 17th and 18th centuries. Movable type remained fundamentally awkward for music printing, and by the time Johann Sebastian Bach (1685–1750) came to prominence, even the works of major composers were seldom printed but circulated and preserved in manuscript.

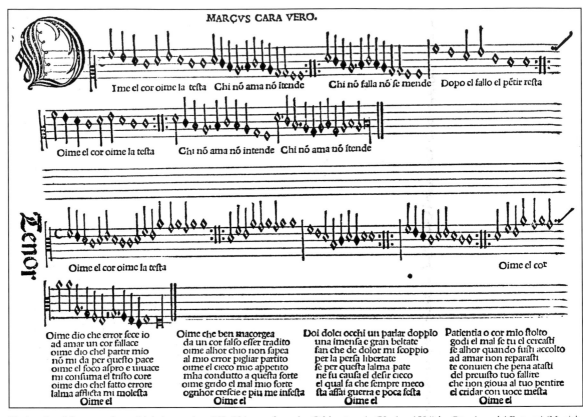

Music printed from type by multiple impression, 165×234 mm; from the *Odehecaton*, xiv (Venice, 1504) by Ottaviano dei Petrucci (Munich, Bayerische Staatsbibliothek); cantus and tenor parts of *Oimè el cor oimè la testa* by Marchetto Cara

Such other innovations as the complicated conceptions involving type arranged as a mosaic rather than in a linear sequence, introduced *c*. 1750 by Johan Gottlob Immanuel Breitkopf (1719–94), Pierre-Simon Fournier (1712–68), Johannes Enschedé (1708–80) and others, proved less than adequate for the increasing complications of musical notation.

The engraving process has proved far better suited than movable type for displaying musical notation. The earliest-known engraving of music is a book of *Intavolatura da leuto* (Venice, ?1530s) compiled by Francesco Canova da Milano (1497–1543). Later experiments include superb decorative pictorial plates by Jan Sadeler (i) in Antwerp in the late 1580s, entire music books engraved by Simone Verovio (*fl*1575–1608) in Rome from the 1580s and several dozen other splendid books produced over the next century that are mostly anthologies of instrumental music, including the celebrated *Parthenia* (London, *c*. 1612). Before 1700 engraving of music was usually sumptuous, with finely drawn signs cut by hand in hard copper, in contrast to the popular engraved song sheets with signs from specially cut punches impressed into soft pewter, introduced by John Walsh (*c*. 1665/6–1736) in London in the late 17th century.

The music-publishing industry slowly spread across Europe, beginning in London in the time of George Frideric Handel (1685–1759) and extending by the mid-18th century to Paris and later to Vienna and other German centres in the period of Franz Joseph Haydn (1732–1809), Wolfgang Amadeus Mozart (1756–91) and Ludwig van Beethoven (1770–1827), about the same time to the USA and several decades later to Italy. During the 19th century the output proliferated and expanded to accommodate the many repertories of music. A brief fascination with lithography *c*. 1800, stimulated by Alois Senefelder's ambitious hopes for the widespread application of his invention, soon receded, due mostly to the technical skills of music engravers, who continued to engrave plates that were then transferred, in the interests of mass production, to faster presses. The annual output of printed music, which in the late 19th century came close to surpassing that of printed books, has slowly declined in the late 20th century, due mostly to the rise of sound recording.

The visual aspects of printed music have rarely been more than routinely functional. The few graphic conceptions that have aspired to artistic distinction have rarely been imitated, and no outstanding artist has been involved in music printing. Music title-pages and covers have a more notable history, both for their beauty and as records of cultural history. Major artists numbered among the producers of woodcut and copperplate illustrations for early music books, mostly in dedicatory images. In the 18th century George Bickham's *Musical Entertainer* (London, 1737–9) showed his craft at its best. In the 19th century music covers, by then intended mostly to attract customers, also featured noteworthy lithographs by Tony

Johannot (1803–82), Henri de Toulouse-Lautrec and Gustave Doré in Paris, Alfred Concanen (1835–86) and John Brandard (1872–63) in London and Winslow Homer and Currier & Ives in the USA. The work of Max Klinger in late editions of the works of Johannes Brahms (1833–97) and of Pablo Picasso for Igor Fedorovich Stravinsky (1882–1971) has also been celebrated.

BIBLIOGRAPHY
A. B. Barksdale: *The Printed Note: 500 Years of Music Printing and Engraving* (Toledo, OH, 1957/*R* New York, 1981)
A. H. King: *Four Hundred Years of Music Printing* (London, 1964)
G. Fraenkel: *Decorative Music Title Pages: 201 Examples from 1500 to 1800* (New York, 1969)
D. W. Krummel and S. Sadie: *The New Grove Handbooks in Music: Music Printing and Publishing* (London, 1990)

D. W. KRUMMEL

Musić, Zoran Anton [Antonio] (*b* Görz, Carniola [now Gorizia, Italy], 12 Feb 1909). Italian painter, draughtsman and printmaker of Carniolan origin. As a child he experienced the confluence of Slavic, Germanic and Italian culture, but as an artist he later drew from French influences. His first encounters with art were in the 1920s, in Vienna with the style of the Secession, and in Prague with Impressionism. From 1930 to 1935 he studied at the School of Fine Arts in Zagreb under Ljubo Babic (1890–1974), a pupil of Franz von Stuck. In 1935 he travelled to Spain, where he was profoundly impressed by the works of El Greco and Goya. At the outbreak of the Civil War he returned to the barren countryside of Dalmatia, which became a major and continuing source of inspiration. It was the experience of World War II, however, which marked his life: he was arrested by the Gestapo and interned at Dachau from 1944 to 1945. There he made a series of drawings, *Dachau* (artist's col., see 1977 exh. cat., pp. 1–12), an extraordinary document of concentration-camp life. His first works after his release were watercolours and gouaches of Venice and paintings of the Sienese countryside. In such paintings as *Dalmatian Motif* (1950; Venice, Ca' Pesaro) the influence of the landscape emerged more clearly in gentle hills, painted in delicate colours. Musić borrowed elements from Byzantine art (for example at Ravenna) and the earth colours and dry handling of fresco painting, a technique that he improved in working with the Venetian painter Guido Cadorin (1892–1976), whose assistant he became in 1946, and whose daughter, the painter Ida Barbarigo (*b* 1923), he was to marry in 1949. Musić's first major exhibitions were the Venice Biennale of 1948, and in Paris at the Galerie de France in 1952. In the mid-1950s and the 1960s he underwent a period of crisis because of the pressures placed on his natural inclination towards representation by the dominance of the abstraction of the Ecole de Paris. In his prints of this period he returned to the themes of the 1940s. In the series of paintings, prints and drawings *We Are Not the Last* (1970–76; examples, Paris, Pompidou, and Munich, Neue Pin.), he returned decisively to his origins as a figurative artist in a painful meditation on the terror of Dachau. It was followed by such series as *Rocky Landscapes* (from 1976), views of Venice (the Giudecca and the Dogana) in 1981, and *Church Interiors* in 1984. After 1985 he worked intensely on self-portraits and double portraits of himself and his wife.

BIBLIOGRAPHY
J. Grenier: *Musić* (Paris, 1970)
Musić: Malerei—Zeichnung—Graphik (exh. cat. by E. Steingräber and B. Krimmel, Darmstadt, Ausstellhallen Mathildenhöhe, 1977)
G. Mazzariol: *Musić* (Milan, 1980)
Musić: Opere, 1946–1982 (exh. cat. by G. Mazzariol and J. Leymarie, Venice, Correr, 1985)

JEAN CLAIR

Musical instruments. Although created primarily for the production of sound, many musical instruments are equally valued for their visual appeal. Considered from a musicological point of view, the study of instruments is usually based on categorization by structure and/or method of sound production. This article, however, is mainly concerned with the visual aspects of musical instruments and the inherent implications for those who design or decorate

1. Carnyxes, detail from a Celtic silver cauldron found at Gundestrup, Jutland, Denmark, 1st or 2nd century BC (Copenhagen, Nationalmuseum)

them. Instruments are, of course, usually conceived as functional objects: they are made to be played. Their design must satisfy demands external to visual considerations, which may both significantly restrict and create opportunities for the designer. Undecorated instruments may have an undeniable beauty derived from their materials and acoustically determined shapes, but these are beyond the scope of this article, as are ornamental non-functional instruments, such as a violin made of Delft faience (?17th century; Amsterdam, Rijksmus.).

1. Western. 2. Other civilizations. 3. Restoration and collections.

1. WESTERN.

(i) Pre-16th century. (ii) 16th century to mid-20th. (iii) Late 20th century.

(i) Pre-16th century. While relatively few Western instruments survive from any period before the Renaissance, those that do, as well as descriptions and representations, provide ample evidence that the decorative aspect could be significant. Even crude prehistoric clay rattles were sometimes painted or sculpted as figurines. The instruments of ancient Mesopotamia could be considerably more sophisticated; harps and lyres devoted to ceremonial use in Sumeria employed gold and lapis lazuli and were fitted with a distinctive bull's head and figurative inlaid plaques (*see* ANCIENT NEAR EAST, §II, 11). Many Egyptian musical instruments survived as funerary equipment. The treasures of Tutankhamun include two precious-metal trumpets ornamented with geometric patterns and hieroglyphics (Cairo, Egyp. Mus.). There are also examples of sistra (ceremonial cymbal-rattles) that bear the likeness of the goddess Hathor and have yokes richly engraved with figurative motifs and inscriptions inlaid with gold (Paris, Louvre; Boston, MA, Mus. F.A.). Texts describe harps boasting ebony, gold, silver and precious stones. Anthropomorphic Egyptian instruments include paired wood and ivory clappers in the form of arms and hands (*see* EGYPT, ANCIENT, §XVI, 12). Only fragmentary evidence survives from instruments of ancient Greco-Roman times; certain amphorae, for instance, show representations of the kithara (a wooden string instrument akin to the lyre; *see also* GREECE, ANCIENT, fig. 166a and b) with sculptural ornamentation (e.g. 5th-century red-figure vase; Oxford, Ashmolean). Most ancient cultures produced small metal bells, sometimes of precious metals, decorated with relief inscriptions or figures, or made in a descriptive form such as the phallus or lotus.

Among early European wind instruments were the late Nordic Bronze Age lurs, great twisted metal horns in mirror-image pairs, and the ancient Celtic carnyx (see fig. 1), characterized by a curved speaking-end that often represented an animal's head. This high level of metalwork was revealed also by the 5th-century short gold horns found in Denmark. Gilt-bronze was the material of decorative animal-style bosses discovered as part of the remains of a wooden lyre (London, BM) in the 7th-century SUTTON HOO royal ship burial.

The nature of medieval instruments is known chiefly from iconographic sources (see Praetorius and Mersenne), which suggest that they were generally plain, at least until the Late Gothic. At that time such architectural ornament as rosettes and tracery was applied to some instruments

(e.g. portative organs) and a wealth of capricious carving to others (e.g. gittern; London, BM; *see* WOOD, colour pl. I, fig. 2). Medieval and ceremonial carved ivory horns, called oliphants (*see* OLIPHANT), survive in several public collections; these were often used as reliquaries rather than as instruments.

(ii) 16th century to mid-20th.

(a) Keyboard instruments. (b) Stringed instruments. (c) Woodwind and brass instruments. (d) Percussion and mechanical instruments.

(a) Keyboard instruments. Because almost all keyboard instruments are enclosed in some manner of large cabinet or permanent case, they are susceptible as a group to similar kinds of decorative treatment. Of all Western instruments, they are most responsive to changing concepts in furniture, interior design and architecture. The earliest surviving stringed keyboard instruments are Italian harpsichords and spinets of the 16th century; the 'arpicembalo che fà il piano e il forte' (i.e. the first documented reference to the piano, 1698) was invented in Florence by Bartolomeo Cristofori (1655–1731). During the 17th and 18th centuries important centres of keyboard manufacture were also established in northern Europe. Be it Renaissance strapwork or Rococo chinoiseries, the decoration varied greatly according to fashion. An old instrument might be redecorated one or more times, so dating an instrument solely by artistic style is inadvisable.

Craft techniques applied to keyboard instruments are almost limitless and include (besides fine joinery) carving,

2. Harpsichord, by Hans Ruckers the younger of Antwerp, with paintings on wooden lid by Jan Breughel I, Hendrick van Balen and Paul Bril and on soundboard by Frans Francken II, 1612, with 18th-century stand (Paris, Musée Instrumental du Conservatoire National Supérieur de Musique)

casting, inlay, marquetry, matched veneer, gilding, japanning, tooled leatherwork and the application of fabrics or printed papers. Painting on keyboard instruments is more common than on any other type of musical instrument, mostly because of the possibilities inherent in the range and extent of flat surfaces. Particularly favoured are lid interiors, keyboard well panels and soundboards. A plain exterior may belie a rich interior, but any flat surface, inside or outside, can be painted. This painting could take the form of marbling, false tortoiseshell, arabesques, grotesques, scattered chinoiserie motifs, fruit and flowers and mottoes. Often the painting is pictorial; indeed, some such works have outlived their instruments as gallery pictures. While lid panels are often rectangular, those that are triangular pose a compositional challenge. Subjects, often music-related, may include Apollo with the muses or contesting Pan, Orpheus, Arion, Amphion, Venus the Mother of Harmony, allegories of the arts or the senses, aristocratic or rustic musicians in formal gardens or pastoral settings respectively and King David and famous musicians. Non-musical iconography includes landscapes, maritime, urban or hunting scenes, allegories of the seasons and images of illustrious persons in history or government. Some well-known names are associated with harpsichord painting: Agnolo Bronzino, Peter Paul Rubens, Antoine Watteau and Roger Fry (c.g. 1917–18; U. London, Courtauld Inst. Gals) are among them. One harpsichord (1612; Paris, Mus. Instr. Conserv. N. Sup. Musique; see fig. 2), made by Hans Ruckers the younger (1578–1643), features paintings by Jan Breughel I, Hendrick van Balen, Paul Bril and Frans Francken II. If a painter of even modest repute could not be afforded, pictorial engravings glued to the lid interior might provide an alternative.

Some decorative procedures are unique to keyboard instruments: in Italy, the key ends were often ornamentally arcaded, while in northern Europe cast metal roses (impractical for lutes) were set into harpsichord soundboards. A few instruments went far beyond mere decoration; a spinetta of 1577 (London, V&A) by Annibale Rossi (*fl c.* 1550–80) is set with nearly 2000 gemstones, while the exuberant *Macchina di Polifemo e Galatea* (1676; New York, Met.) by Michele Todini (*c.* 1625–*c.* 1689) was conceived as a full-scale, gilded sculptural group in three parts into which a harpsichord has been introduced. At the opposite extreme from such conspicuous wealth are those modest keyboard instruments concealed in or disguised as a table, sewing-box, chest of drawers or some other item of everyday furniture. Miniature pianos could be similarly masked.

As the pianoforte inherited the harpsichord's musical and social stature, it too became subject to visual elaboration. The relative reticence of 18th-century Neo-classicism, in which an Angelica Kauffman painting or some Wedgwood plaques might represent the extreme in ornament, was quickly overtaken by Romantic extravagance. Nineteenth-century pianos could display Egyptian sphinxes, Roman columns, Gothic tracery or Renaissance strapwork with equal liberty. From this period of glorious excess comes the neo-Baroque satinwood piano (*c.* 1840; New York, Met.) with marquetry and sculptural embellishments by the Erard firm and the 'Byzantine' grand piano

3. Organ with sculpture and shutter paintings attributed to Philipp Tidemann, 1692 (Middelburg, Nieuwe Kerk)

(1878; destr. World War II) built by the Broadwood Co. for, and partially decorated by, Lawrence Alma-Tadema.

An alternative to this profusion of decorative styles and to the increasingly bland industrial piano was offered by the Arts and Crafts Movement. The Broadwood 'Manxman' upright model, by M. H. Baillie Scott, was a study in creative cabinetry; Broadwood also offered its 'Orpheus' model grand with a crisp, architectural case designed in part by Edward Burne-Jones. The prototype, built in 1879–80 for William Graham, features paintings by Burne-Jones of the legend of Orpheus and Eurydice in roundels on the side and *Terra omniparens* on the lid (priv. col., for illustration see *Burne-Jones*, exh. cat., ACEng, 1975–6, fig. 208). Equally distinctive is an Art Nouveau grand piano made by Alexandre Charpentier in 1902 (Nice, Mus. B.-A.). While the 20th-century piano has on occasion either reverted to 19th-century revivalist splendour or received the attention of such modern artists as Marc Chagall, the impersonal, decoratively restrained, ebonized grand piano is the norm in the concert hall.

The long and involved history of the organ (strictly speaking a wind instrument) has embraced more vicissitudes of taste than virtually any other instrument. Its structural complexity has yielded opportunities for designers to express each of the major arts on a grand scale:

architecture, as seen in columns, entablatures, turrets etc; painting, most likely on shutters hinged to open like those of a triptych (*see* ORGAN SHUTTERS); and sculpture, in the form of musical angels, putti and biblical or allegorical figures (see fig. 3). The organ case developed from the rectangular box at the dawn of the Renaissance to elaborate formal conceptions in the late Baroque. One strikingly unarchitectonic design is the organ by Gianlorenzo Bernini in S Maria del Popolo, Rome, in the form of a leafy oak tree. Painters who have turned their attention to organs include Veronese (1558–60; Venice, S Sebastiano), Tintoretto (1551–4; Venice, Madonna del Orto) and Hans Holbein (ii). The *sine qua non* of organ design is the judicious arrangement of visible pipework, often in multiple fields on several levels. Façade pipes, usually functional, may be polished, painted, gilded or embossed, and their proportions may be altered for visual effect. Early treatises that discuss organ design or decoration include Giovanni Paolo Lomazzo's *Trattato dell'arte de la pittura* (Milan, 1584) and Jakob Adlung's *Musica mechanica organeodi* (Berlin, 1768). Thomas Chippendale (i) included six chamber-organ designs in *The Gentleman's and Cabinet Maker's Director* (London, 1754). Early 20th-century organs were often relegated to invisibility in chambers, but later in the century there was a revival of artistic case design. Some small continuo organs, designed for table-top use, display the intricate or subtle ornament of the harpsichord.

(b) Stringed instruments. Among string instruments with fingered necks (e.g. the lute, guitar, viol and violin families) the peg-box was most prone to elaboration, often carved as a human figure or head, more rarely as an animal. The reinforcing block at the base of the neck might also be carved. A carved belly or back, however, as seen on the celebrated violin (1687) and cello (1691; both Modena, Gal. & Mus. Estense) by Domenico Galli, is very rare because the acoustical function of the thin-shelled resonator is impaired. The body was more likely ornamented with geometric or pictorial inlay using ivory, mother-of-pearl, tortoiseshell, soft metals and exotic woods (especially ebony). Bold striped patterns are the most common. The viol (Brussels, Mus. Instr. Conserv. Royale; see fig. 4), formerly attributed to Gaspar Tieffenbrücker the elder (1514–71) and thought to have belonged to Francis I on the basis of a 19th-century inscription, is nevertheless interesting for its marquetry flowers, birds and insects on the belly and an aerial view of 16th-century Paris on the back. Joachim Tielke (1641–1719) of Hamburg is considered to be the greatest master of intarsia decoration on stringed instruments (examples in London, V&A).

For plucked instruments (lutes, guitars, citterns etc) an intricate rose is usually centred in the belly. The instrument's visual focus, this rose may be cut directly from the soundboard or inset, flat or sunken, and formed as Gothic tracery or as a geometric interlace pattern betraying the Arabic origins of the lute. The familiar silhouettes of string instruments have been modified and elaborated for visual effect; particularly notable are the convoluted outlines of some German viols. Decorated mute, bow, case or other original accessories are rare, although the porcelain case of the flute made for Frederick II, King of Prussia, by

4. 'Viol of Francis I', wood with marquetry, l. 1.25 m; 19th-century reconstruction (Brussels, Musée Instrumental du Conservatoire Royale)

Johann Joachim Quantz (1697–1773) survives (Washington, DC, Lib. Congr.).

The structure of the harp offers sculptural or even architectural possibilities for the design of the frame. As an 18th- or 19th-century salon instrument, the harp strongly reflected taste in high society. The broad, painted soundboard might bear Rococo musical trophies or chinoiseries, the pillar a Classical order or a Gothic pavilion; the pillar of the Barberini harp (c.1625; Rome, Pal. Barberini), for example, consists of superimposed caryatid groups sculpted in the round.

(c) Woodwind and brass instruments. Whether they are made of wood, ivory, porcelain, metal or some other material, instruments of the woodwind family (recorders, flutes, oboes, bassoons etc) are almost never painted because the surfaces are small and constant handling would efface the work. Occasionally the body of a woodwind instrument derives its visual appeal from elaborate turning or the presence of rings in a contrasting material. While three-dimensional carving is rare, a recorder beak may be carved to suggest a fish mouth, and reliefs may be found on an oboe bell. Figurative or abstract motifs may be engraved on the body or displayed on metal (perhaps silver) keywork. Among wind instruments found in zoomorphic form are the musette, a small bagpipe often featuring at the top of the chanter pipe a carved goat-head attached to a shaggy animal-hide bag; the only known set

of *Tartölten* (16th century; Vienna, Ksthist. Mus.), in which the instruments are constructed and painted to resemble dragons whose bodies conceal the instruments' coils; and the common ceramic whistle-flute, usually in bird form.

Largely because of their military and aristocratic associations, brass instruments (usually of brass but sometimes silver or other metal) are often richly ornamented with relief and engraving concentrated on bell, ferrules and sleeves; in general the ornament is more boldly three-dimensional in Renaissance examples than in later ones. Surviving instruments show a wide variety of decorative motifs, often heraldic, occasionally with the engraved date and maker's name. A trumpet could even be set with gems or glass 'stones', for example the trumpet in F by Michael Hainleinn (1697; Berlin, Staatl. Inst. Musikforsch. Preuss. Kultbes., cat. no. 4497), while a hefty, distinctive knob, or boss, would often be placed at the instrument's centre of gravity. Trumpet tubing would be wrapped with a brightly coloured cord terminating in dangling tassels; a pennant or banner might also be suspended from a ceremonial trumpet. The instruments of Renaissance Nuremberg are considered the finest pre-industrial brasses. Bells of some 19th-century parade instruments, especially serpents (bass-keyed bugles), are shaped as dragon heads with gaping mouths; this idea could be extended as a pattern of scales cut into the entire body of the instrument. The interior of the widely flared orchestral horn bell could display coloured lacquer or enamel ornament.

(d) Percussion and mechanical instruments. Military drums, since they are generally subjected to rough use, are usually plain but could display appropriate painted (or stencilled) coats of arms, regimental emblems, flags and mottoes. The metal shells of timpani might boast engraved images or inscriptions as well as exuberantly shaped flanged lugs.

Encased musical automata also lend themselves well to painted or sculpted ornament, ranging from musical clocks (*see* CLOCKS AND WATCHES and fig. 8) to musical boxes (*see* AUTOMATA) and various other types of mechanical instrument. These had their heyday in the 18th century and may be regarded as precursors of the 20th-century jukebox (which is no less a visual expression of its time).

(iii) Late 20th century. In the 20th century the decline of artistic invention in musical instruments may be attributed in part to mass production, to larger concert halls, which distance audience and instruments, and to the unornamented machine aesthetic. Musical objects and the visual arts have not, however, completely parted company. Some makers of traditional instruments are aware that there is a place for individual visual statement in their craft. Frequently made to commission and generally not in collections, one area of ornamentation that seems rather lively is specially crafted guitars, for use by rock'n'roll and country-and-western musicians (e.g. William 'grit' Laskin's pictorial mother-of-pearl and shell inlays). Equally, church organs never completely succumbed to the sameness of mass production and offer many examples of visually distinctive work (e.g. the Fritts-Richard instrument, 1987; St Alphonsus, Seattle, WA).

Some avant-garde artists and musicians have pursued independently the creation of 'sound sculptures': objects may be activated by wind, water or some external element or mechanically manipulated to produce various types of sound. Some are dependent on sophisticated technology, while others have a simplicity inspired by the instruments of early civilizations. Some classics in this area include the untitled 'structures sonores' by the Baschet brothers in France during the 1950s and later several works by Jean Tinguely, including *Metaharmonie II* (1979; Basle, Ksthalle). Other interesting examples are a four-acre sound–sculpture garden at Lake Placid, NY, installed by Bill and Mary Buchen, and a 'Wave Organ' installed by Peter Richards in the surf at San Francisco, CA.

2. OTHER CIVILIZATIONS. Many ancient civilizations and non-Western cultures created and continue to create musical instruments of considerable visual interest. Some of the materials used are unexpected: feathers, beads, leaves, snakeskins and animal or human skulls; in post-contact times such artefacts as roofing metal or oil-drums have served as instruments in themselves. Wood, bone or horn and ceramics, however, are the most prevalent materials. Surface ornament includes beadwork, painting and cut or burnt engraving; the design repertory stretches from abstract to realistic. Surfaces may also be polished or scorched overall. Relief carving is common, and figurative sculpture in the round may either be appended to an instrument (such as African drum stands representing lions, elephants and humans) or form the instrument body itself. Examples of sculptural instrument types include the African slit-drum in animal form (see fig. 5) and the ceramic Maya flute in human/deity form (*see* MESO-AMERICA, PRE-COLUMBIAN, §IX, 7). The human figure may also form the resonator for various harps, drums and lamellaphones. There are some objects, such as the *mumbira* of the Central African Nyanga people (*see* AFRICA, §VI, 8), that are essentially ritual sculpture to which a secondary musical function has been appended.

As in other forms of ethnographic art, the design of musical instruments usually expresses a ceremonial or folklore tradition, which gives the object much of its societal value. Some instruments are used only in secret societies; both their sound and appearance are known

5. Arambo slit-drum, from Zaïre (New York, American Museum of Natural History)

only to initiates. Other instruments are intended for public display. Both music and visual images are frequently thought to contain potent magic in the right contexts, and the combination of the two would be deemed particularly powerful; some instruments are considered sacred objects in their own right. The sound and appearance of an instrument may proclaim the high status of a leader.

The wind and percussion instruments of South Asian civilizations may bear colourful painted or dyed fibre bands around their cylindrical forms. A bright fabric jacket may be provided for some Indian drums and for the Javanese lute (*rebab*). The Javanese gamelan expresses its courtly status partially through the florid wood-carving of the instruments' supporting stands. Cast-bronze prayer bells from Java may be richly adorned; in some cases a plain bulbous bell-cup is surmounted by an ornamental ringed stem, suggesting the ritual architecture of a stupa. Cast bronze is also used by the Karen peoples of Laos, Burma (*see* BURMA, §IX, 1, 9 and 12) and Thailand in their distinctive and highly prized frog drums, which present a rich repertory of incised and relief animal motifs. In India the most elaborately decorated instruments are those belonging to the vina family, which embraces chordophones as diverse as harps, lutes, zithers and bowed string instruments. Varying greatly according to type and regional tradition, their ornament may include painting or gilding, peg-boxes featuring animal heads relating to Hindu mythology, ivory inlay and relief carving. Structural details are seldom standardized, but examples of the bowed sarangi are known in which the bridge is carved in the form of an elephant. Similarly seven-pointed leaves carved in relief may spread over the gourd resonators of the sitar and related instruments. Other zoomorphic instruments include the *dilrubā*, a fretted fiddle (New York, Met.); some 19th-century examples used at court have resonators shaped and painted as a peacock, to which genuine peacock tail-feathers that spread behind the fingerboard are appended.

In China the impulse towards rich ornament and material can be found throughout the highly developed family of idiophones (bells and gongs; *see* BELL, §1), favoured in ritual for their evocation of elemental natural forces (*see* CHINA, §VI, 1 and 3(iii)). Archaeologically recovered cast bronze bells of the Zhou period (*c.* 1050–256 BC) display high relief. Sets of musical bars made of jade were particularly treasured. By custom, such instruments are supported by elaborate cast bronze or wooden stands. In China and Korea, such carved and painted stands could feature the sun or moon, dragons, tigers, cranes, pavilion or gateway forms and tassels. Music is closely connected in the Chinese oral tradition with the dragon and phoenix; these creatures thus figure prominently in the decoration of Chinese ceremonial orchestral instruments. The oldest extant string instrument with this kind of ornamentation is a lute (*qin*), which may date from the 5th century AD and which entered the Japanese treasury at the Shōsōin, Nara, in AD 817 (*see* CHINA, fig. 245). It features intricate inlaid pictorial designs in lacquer and silver and gold paint, representing a Buddhist enlightenment or paradise scene.

A prized element in the home of the contemplative Confucian scholar would be a seemingly simple *qin*, chosen by the owner–connoisseur for its pleasing shape, varnish crackle patterns, polish, colour (usually of lacquer) and its single overtly decorative feature, calligraphy. Every important *qin* featured an inscription, cut into the bottom board and highlighted with paint. A *qin* that displayed inscriptions or gold-lacquer characters on the top board would be considered excessively ostentatious by the discriminating literatus. The *qin* was treasured primarily as a subtle *objet d'art*, evocative of the learning of the ancients and of intimate, poetic reverie. The scholar might also collect rubbings of inscriptions found on the backs of instruments owned by others.

For further illustrations *see* ASANTE AND RELATED PEOPLES, fig. 6 and MESOAMERICA, PRE-COLUMBIAN, fig. 42. *See also* JAPAN, §XVI, 16; MONGOLIA, §IV, 8; SOUTH AMERICA, PRE-COLUMBIAN, §VIII, 6; and TIBET, §V, 7.

3. RESTORATION AND COLLECTIONS. Materials used in constructing and decorating musical instruments include wood, leather, parchment, hairs and bristles, gut, quills, bone and ivory, shell, textiles, base and precious metals, ceramics, glass and even stone and gems. The problems of conservation and restoration are thus particularly complex. Instruments must be protected from the adverse effects of light, extreme temperature and humidity, air pollution, parasites and particularly dust. Mechanical damage from use, past or present, is also a concern. While preparation for mute display is certainly demanding, restoration to performance condition should be entrusted only to the most experienced, specialized restorers and is less important than preserving the original fabric. Hard decisions may be faced if the replacement of original parts is desirable for mechanical or acoustical reasons, and removed parts must be kept as a record.

Instrument collections have been formed to satisfy the performance needs of such institutions as church or court. In Europe, collecting instruments as *objets d'art* or as curiosities dates from the Renaissance, when instruments might be featured in a *Wunderkammer* or *studio di musica*. Inventory descriptions suggest a fascination with costly materials and extravagant skill. At that time the principal collections included those of Isabella d'Este in Mantua and the Fugger family of merchants and bankers at Augsburg. Some major collections, among them that of the Kunsthistorisches Museum, Vienna, owe the core of their holdings to such princely collections. Other collections were donated to museums by wealthy amateurs (Crosby Brown Collection, New York, Met.), professional musicians or scholars (Curt Sachs Collection, Berlin Musikinstr.-Mus., Staatl. Inst. Musikforsch. Preuss. Kultbes.). The field work of archaeologists and anthropologists accounts for the largest tabulated instrument collections in the world, seen at the Koninklijk Museum voor Midden-Afrika, Tervuren (*c.* 10,000 items), the British Museum, London (*c.* 7800 items), and the Musée de l'Homme, Paris (*c.* 7000 items). Other respected musical-instrument collections include those at the Musée Instrumental du Conservatoire Royale, Brussels; the Musée Instrumental du Conservatoire National Supérieur de Musique, Paris; the Germanisches Nationalmuseum, Nuremberg; the Musikmuseet, Stockholm; the Horniman Museum, Victoria and Albert Museum and the Royal

College of Music, all in London; the National Museum of American History, Smithsonian Institution, Washington, DC; the Stearns Collection of Musical Instruments, University of Michigan, Ann Arbor; and the Shrine to Music Museum, Vermillion, SD.

See also MUSIC AND ART.

BIBLIOGRAPHY

Grove Instr.

M. Praetorius: *Syntagma musicum*, ii (Wolfenbüttel, 1618, 2/1619/*R* 1980)

M. Mersenne: *Harmonie universelle*, 2 vols (Paris, 1636–7/*R* 1963)

R. H. van Gulik: *The Lore of the Chinese Lute: An Essay in the Ideology of the Ch'in* (Tokyo, 1940, rev. 1969)

J. E. Blanton: *The Revival of the Organ Case* (Albany, TX, 1965)

B. W. Dietz and M. B. Olatunji: *Musical Instruments of Africa: Their Nature, Use and Place in the Life of a Deeply Musical People* (New York, 1965)

A. Berner and others: *Preservation and Restoration of Musical Instruments: Provisional Recommendations* (London, 1967)

E. Winternitz: *Musical Instruments of the Western World* (New York, 1967)

R. Clemencic: *Old Musical Instruments* (London, 1968)

P. Thornton: *Musical Instruments as Works of Art* (London, 1968, rev. 1982)

J. Rimmer: *Ancient Musical Instruments of Western Asia in the Department of Western Asiatic Antiquities, British Museum* (London, 1969)

W. Lichtenwanger, ed.: *A Survey of Musical Instrument Collections in the United States and Canada* (Ann Arbor, 1974)

J. Jenkins, ed.: *International Directory of Musical Instrument Collections* (Buren, 1977) [does not incl. USA or Canada]

M. I. Wilson: *Organ Cases of Western Europe* (London, 1979)

G. Bauer and L. Bauer: 'Bernini's Organ-case for S Maria del Popolo', *A. Bull.*, lxii (1980), pp. 115–23

P. T. Young: *The Look of Music: Rare Musical Instruments, 1500–1900* (Seattle, 1980)

J. Coover: *Musical Instruments Collections: Catalogs and Cognate Literature* (Detroit, 1981)

Lee Hye-gu, ed.: *Korean Musical Instruments* (Seoul, 1982)

C. Reuger: *Musikinstrument und Dekor: Kostbarkeiten europäischer Kulturgeschichte* (Gütersloh, 1982; Eng. trans., Cincinnati, 1986)

B. Sonnaillon: *L'Orgue, instrument et musiciens* (Fribourg, 1984); Eng. trans. as *King of Instruments: A History of the Organ* (New York, 1985)

Experimental Musical Instruments: Newsletter for the Design, Construction, & Enjoyment of New Sound Sources (Nicasio, CA, 1985–)

J. Yorke: *Keyboard Instruments at the Victoria and Albert Museum* (London, 1986)

M.-T. Brincard and others, eds: *Sounding Forms: African Musical Instruments* (New York, 1989)

RONALD D. RARICK

Music and art. Within the European tradition, philosophers and critics, artists and musicians have at different times envisaged a profound relationship between music and other art forms. For many centuries, however, from ancient Greece until the High Renaissance, music was more closely allied with what were termed the 'liberal' arts—arithmetic, geometry and astronomy—than with painting or sculpture, which were regarded as merely 'mechanical' and therefore inferior occupations. The exalted status music enjoyed was due largely to its seemingly inherent logical or mathematical character. Particularly significant was the discovery, often associated with Pythagoras, that the primary consonances—the octave, the fifth, the fourth—may be expressed by the ratios of the smallest whole numbers: 1:2, 2:3, 3:4. In the *Timaeus*, Plato devoted some space to a discussion of this phenomenon and its implications. Subsequent philosophers, including the Italian Neo-Platonists of the 16th century, constructed elaborate (and often improbable) cosmologies upon this simple fact of acoustics. The 'hidden order' of music seemed to them proof of divine intervention both

in the creation of mankind and in the ordering of the universe—although to what extent often-repeated images like that of the 'harmony' between microcosm and macrocosm, or the 'music of the spheres', were meant to be understood literally rather than metaphorically remains a matter for debate.

See also SOUND AND ART.

1. 15th and 16th centuries. 2. 17th and 18th centuries. 3. 19th century. 4. 20th century.

1. 15TH AND 16TH CENTURIES. Renaissance artists were intrigued by the fact that the same set of numerical relationships could be translated into a proportional system that, it was thought, might confer on the visual arts—and especially architecture (*see* ARCHITECTURAL PROPORTION, §II)—a similarly elevated character (see fig. 1). Such ideas were widespread from *c*. 1490 in the writings of such theorists as Pomponius Gauricus and Francesco Lancilotti, and especially in the *Hypnerotomachia Poliphili* (Venice, 1499), thought to be by Francesco Colonna, which exerted a considerable influence in the early 16th century. The book draws a specific parallel between the architectural orders and the musical 'modes' of antiquity, comparing the activity of the composer with that of the architect—not as builder (again, a merely manual occupation) but as

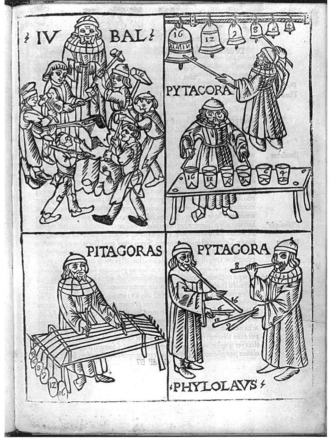

1. *Tubalcain, Pythagoras, Philolaos*; from Franchino Gaffurio: *Theorica musice* (1492)

designer. However, many such assertions and analogies did not overstep the realms of theory; only in the work of Alberti had similar notions been translated into reality. In writing about his design for the façade of S Francesco in Rimini (*c.* 1453), Alberti employed a specifically musical metaphor, observing that nothing should be altered, in particular the proportions of the pilasters, lest in so doing 'all this music' be destroyed (*see* RIMINI, §1(i) and figs 1 and 2). Furthermore, in the plan for the nave of S Andrea in Mantua, he employed a numerical system governing the depth and width of the bays, as well as the height of the arches, likewise based on those 'divine' ratios that produce the primary musical consonances (*see* ALBERTI, LEON BATTISTA, fig. 6).

Alberti's plan for S Andrea may be compared with perhaps the most famous example of 'musical architecture', Jacopo Sansovino's design (1534) for S Francesco della Vigna, Venice. Sansovino adhered closely to a proposal by the Neo-Platonist Francesco Giorgi, friar of the Franciscan Observant order (see Wittkower). This envisaged a system of proportional relationships between the principal parts of the church—between the length of the nave and its width, the width of the nave and the width of the side chapels—which Giorgi expressed in terms of musical consonances: 'diapason' and 'diapente', octave and fifth. There is no doubt that these relationships or ratios were meant to be perceptible to the eye: Giorgi insisted: 'All the measurements of the plan should be in perfect consonance. They will necessarily delight all those who observe them, unless their sight be dense and disproportionate.' That the same carefully calculated ratios were intended to govern every aspect of the building may be judged from the fact that when, in 1562, Andrea Palladio added the façade of the church, he too observed Giorgi's system of 'harmonic' proportions.

Such ideas could also be applied, albeit in a more limited way, to painting. With the advent of perspective, and the desire to show the 'determined relationship' between bodies in space, a complex set of mathematical rules was needed in order that, as Alberti wrote, 'objects in a painting should appear like real objects'. Another Renaissance theorist, Luca Pacioli, drew an explicit parallel between music and perspective, observing that 'if the one art exploits harmonic proportions, the other exploits arithmetical and geometrical ones'. Leonardo, who was closely associated with Pacioli, likewise demanded that if music were to be placed among the liberal arts, then so too must painting. A complex proportional schema based on musical ratios is thought to underlie the fresco of the *Last Supper* (*c.* 1495–7; Milan, S Maria delle Grazie).

2. 17TH AND 18TH CENTURIES. Until the end of the 16th century, parallels between music and visual art continued to be drawn by such architects as Jacopo Vignola and theorists like Giovanni Paolo Lomazzo (who attributed the mastery of proportion displayed by both Leonardo and Michelangelo to their knowledge of music). In the 17th century elements of Lomazzo's theory were further adapted to the French context by writers, including Charles Le Brun and André Félibien. The latter was also responsible for publicizing and commenting on Nicolas Poussin's theories concerning the 'harmony' of painting— although by this time terms such as 'harmony' and 'proportion' seem to have lost any relation to older ideas of cosmic harmonies. Instead, Poussin drew specifically on a more recent source, Gioseffo Zarlino's *Le istituzioni harmoniche* (Venice, 1558), for his discussion of the relationship between painting and the antique 'modes' (Dorian, Lydian etc). In a letter of 1647 to his patron Paul Fréart de Chantelou, he wrote: 'I hope by the end of the year to have painted a subject in the Phrygian mode, that is to say a mode which is violent and furious, very severe and calculated to produce amazement.' In the same letter, he also discusses the character of the Lydian, Hypolydian, Dorian and Ionian modes.

Ironically, little was known at this time about the music of the ancients, which research has concluded bore little resemblance to the modes employed in medieval church music, despite the survival of the antique nomenclature. Rather than any very exact musical analogy, Poussin probably had in mind the unity and decorum of pictorial composition, the 'modes' being associated with those moods appropriate to the subject-matter, as if a picture could be 'tuned' to the right emotional key by means of the unity of action, gesture and expression. Later writers, however, interpreted Poussin's observations in a more 'modern' fashion, equating the 'modes' with the 'abstract' elements of painting, notably colour, composition and proportion, seeing the effect of a picture as depending as much on an appeal to the senses as to the mind. Antoine Coypel, in what is probably the best-known 18th-century definition of the modes in painting, wrote: 'What musicians call *modes* or *dessins* are graceful, strong or terrible. The same applies to pictures. What should move the heart by passing through the ears should also move it by passing through the eyes. The first impression of a picture must determine its character.'

3. 19TH CENTURY. From the 18th century onwards new musical forms, notably the sonata, the symphony and the fugue, led artists to seek their pictorial equivalents in the invention of new structures for painting, employing such devices as the repetition or imitation of forms upon which, for example, the fugue depends. The German Romantic painter Philipp Otto Runge believed that the principles of fugal composition could be applied to painting, as in the *Nightingale's Music Lesson* (1804–5; Hamburg, Ksthalle; see fig. 2) where, in his own words, he allowed the underlying 'musical idea' to appear in 'different variations' throughout the composition. He also envisaged a synthesis of the arts, as exemplified by his project for a cycle of paintings, the *Four Times of Day*, which he dreamt of installing in a specially designed building in which accompanying music was to be performed. This project, never carried to completion, marks the beginning of a long tradition, lasting until well into the 20th century, of 'cyclical' works inspired by music, among them Max Klinger's graphic cycle *Brahms-Fantasie* (1894; Hamburg, Staats- & Ubib.) and Gustav Klimt's *Beethoven Frieze* (1902; Vienna, Belvedere).

To some extent, Runge's ideas foreshadow those of Richard Wagner, who aimed to re-unite the different arts, long separated from one another, in the service of a new art form that he called 'music drama'. Wagner's ideas and

2. Philipp Otto Runge: *Nightingale's Music Lesson*, oil on canvas, 1047×855 mm, 1804–5 (Hamburg, Hamburger Kunsthalle)

his music profoundly influenced later 19th-century artists, both in the representation of Wagnerian subjects (Fantin-Latour, Renoir, Cézanne), and in the widespread ambition to create a new form of synthetic art or 'total work of art' (*see* GESAMTKUNSTWERK). Such aims were reinforced by the characteristically *fin-de-siècle* preoccupation with synaesthesia or *audition colorée*: 'hearing' colours, 'seeing' notes, etc—a preoccupation prefigured by a number of 19th-century writers. The German novelist Ernst Theodor Amadeus Hoffmann (1776–1822) described a dreamlike state in which 'colours, sounds and perfumes coalesce', a notion also given poetic expression by Baudelaire who, in an article of 1861 on Wagner, wrote: 'It would be amazing if sound could not suggest colour, or colours could not give the idea of melody . . . such things have always been expressed by reciprocal analogy.'

At the same time, music was increasingly seen to possess, by its very nature, advantages that the painter might envy—especially its non-material aspect. Goethe, for example, extolled music because it had, in his words, 'no material which need be discounted'. By 'material' (Ger. *Stoff*) he meant on the one hand substance, the fact that music is not 'weighed down' by any material embodiment, unlike architecture or sculpture, which were increasingly seen as inferior forms of art. But *Stoff* also means subject-matter; and with the rise of movements such as Realism, Impressionism and Post-Impressionism and the corresponding decline in the importance of narrative, painting might be thought to be able to survive by offering, as the English critic Philip Gilbert Hamerton put it, 'nothing but its own merchandize'. 'The vision of the world', wrote Hamerton, 'becomes. . .what Wordsworth aptly termed

'eye music''. . .painting is then no longer a study of tangible things at all, but a dream, like the dreams of a musician.'

4. 20TH CENTURY. Comparisons between music and art were to dominate discussions about art well into the 20th century. Critics from Ruskin via Maurice Denis to Hermann Bahr and Roger Fry, artists from Delacroix to Gauguin and van Gogh, Kandinsky and František Kupka all wrote about the 'musicality' of painting, by which they meant principally its colouristic and compositional, as opposed to its narrative aspect. Whistler declared his 'whole aim' in painting to be 'to bring about a certain harmony of colour'; he also gave musical titles to his paintings, calling his picture the *White Girl*, for example, *Symphony in White No. 1* (1861; Washington, DC, NGA). Kandinsky wrote about how easily representational aims could be dispensed with in music that, echoing Goethe, he called 'the least material of the arts today'. In a letter to the composer Arnold Schoenberg (who was also an amateur painter), he wrote: 'How fortunate are musicians in their art. . .how lucky in being able to renounce entirely purely practical aims. How long will it take painting to accomplish the same?' If music, so the argument went, could succeed in communicating with the listener without recourse to stories or allegories or subject-matter of any kind, why should painting not do likewise? Why should there not exist in painting also the possibility of an expressive art based on nothing other than colours and forms—what Fry called 'pure visual music'?

Even painters not wedded to abstraction sought to link their art in one way or another with music. The Expressionist August Macke wrote of the 'undreamed-of power

3. August Macke: *Coloured Composition I (Homage to J. S. Bach)*, oil on canvas, 1.01×0.82 mm, 1912 (Ludwigshafen, Wilhelm Hack-Museum und Städtische Kunstsammlungen)

one would possess if one could organize colours into a system, like notes'. He also painted an abstract colour composition subtitled *Homage to J. S. Bach* (1912; Ludwigshafen, Hack-Mus. & Städt. Kstsamml.; see fig. 3). A number of artists experimented with both painting and musical composition, for example the painter-composer Mikhail Matiushin and Mikalojus Čiurlionis who, between 1907 and 1908, worked on a series of seven cycles of pictures that he called 'Sonatas'. Others announced their ambition to incorporate specifically musical attributes such as 'rhythm' and 'tempo' into works of visual art. The painter Léopold Survage wrote: 'I will animate my painting, I will give it movement, I will introduce rhythm into the concrete action of my abstract painting...I will execute the "scores" of my visions, corresponding to my state of mind.' He also undertook a succession of studies to which he gave the title *Coloured Rhythm* (e.g. the ink wash drawing, 1913; Paris, Pompidou).

At times, such experiments seem to cross the boundaries between visual art and performance, as in the case of Duncan Grant's *Abstract Kinetic Collage Painting with Sound* (1914; London, Tate), a long scroll-like work intended to be slowly unrolled by mechanical means to the accompaniment of music. Other artists too, among them Viking Eggeling and Hans Richter, made abstract scroll paintings (e.g. Eggeling's *Horizontal-Vertical Orchestra I*, 1919–21; lost, copy in Basle, Kstmus.), leading to the first experiments in the field of abstract animated film. Abstract colour and shape also sometimes featured as an integral part of musical performances. The composer Aleksandr Skryabin (1892–1915) believed that the 'cosmic effect' of his compositions would be enhanced by the addition of colours, to which he attributed mystical associations. His *Prometheus: The Poem of Fire* (first perf. Moscow, 1911) included a part for 'colour organ', an instrument that produced no sound, but which was linked to a system for projecting coloured lights, individual colours 'corresponding' to particular notes on the keyboard; while Skryabin's compatriot Vladimir Baranoff-Rossiné invented an 'optophonic piano' (Paris, Pompidou), which, likewise activated by a conventional keyboard, projected light through rotating, hand-painted glass discs. This received its première at a 'colour–sound' concert at the Meierkhold Theatre in Moscow in 1923.

The colour organ demanded by Skryabin was, however, no new-fangled contraption: attempts to create an apparatus that might demonstrate the supposed physical analogy between colour wavelengths and the vibrations that determine the pitch of musical tones go back at least as far as the 17th century. In 1734 a Jesuit priest, Father Bertrand Castel, apparently exhibited a model for a 'colour keyboard' or *clavecin oculaire*, an instrument described by the composer Georg Philipp Telemann (1681–1767). For a long time, such devices remained reliant on relatively feeble light sources, and little further progress was made until the advent of electricity. Thereafter, inventors like Alexander Wallace Rimington, Thomas Wilfred and others produced a bewildering variety of instruments dependent on the principle of projecting coloured light by means of powerful lenses and even more powerful lamps (see fig. 4). 'Colour–light performances' enjoyed an extraordinary vogue during the 1890s and early 1900s, competing in

4. Alexander Wallace Rimington and his colour organ; photograph from A. B. Klein: *Colour Music: The Art of Light* (London, 1926)

popularity with the early cinema, with whose evolution they were in many respects closely linked. They were also taken very seriously by writers on art; one of the most influential surveys of avant-garde painting, Arthur Eddy's *Cubists and Post-Impressionism* (Chicago, 1914), devoted a whole chapter to the art of 'colour music'. During the years immediately after the Great War, artists including Alexander László (*b* 1895) and Ludwig Hirschfeld-Mack continued to experiment both with new kinds of apparatus and with the creation of colour–light compositions, now regarded as an autonomous art form in their own right.

As the 20th century progressed, artists' interest in music to some extent polarized. Some painters returned to an analogy with music because of its mathematical basis. (Johannes Itten, for example, wrote on one of his 'musical' drawings: 'Proportion is the level on which music and painting meet'.) Others sought (as in the early Romantic period) a visual equivalent for its purely formal structures. It has been suggested that few, if any, of the Cubist painters had any detailed understanding of music; yet virtually all of them paid tribute to Bach, whose music enjoyed a widespread revival during the first decades of the 20th century. Many artists produced 'fugue' paintings: not only the Cubists, but also Kupka (*Amorpha: Fugue in Two Colours*, 1912; Prague, N. Tech. Mus.; for illustration *see* ORPHISM), Kandinsky (*Fugue*, 1914; New York, Guggenheim) and Klee. But it was Klee who produced perhaps the most complex and sophisticated 'translations' of musical forms into their graphic equivalent, not only in paintings such as *Fugue in Red* (1921; Berne, F. Klee priv. col., see 1985 exh. cat., no. 14), but also in drawings inspired by musical subjects such as the 'two-part' *Once Emerged from the Grey of Night* (Berne, Kstmus.), which mimics the arrangement of notes on the musical stave. Other artists like Marsden Hartley created even more specific imitations of particular works of music, as in his *Musical Theme No. 2: Bach, Preludes and Fugues* (1912; Madrid, Mus. Thyssen-Bornemisza), being outdone in literalness only by the monumental sculpture (model, 1928) by Heinrich Neugeboren (1901–59) entitled *Plastic Representation of Bars 52–55 of the Fugue in E-flat by J. S. Bach*. During the post-war period other artists including Luigi Veronesi, Günther Uecker and Karl Duschek (*b* 1947) again turned to specific works of Bach for inspiration.

From *c.* 1950 several new tendencies can be detected, particularly among artists of the New Realism and Fluxus movements, several of whom were also musicians. Just as composers such as John Cage and Karlheinz Stockhausen (*b* 1928) wrote for 'prepared' instruments whose sound character was deliberately changed or distorted, artists too began to 'prepare' musical instruments, for example by wrapping them (Joseph Beuys, *Homogeneous Infiltration for 'Cello*, 1967; Remscheid, W. Feelisch priv. col., see 1985 exh. cat., no. 457), or sometimes effectively destroying them, as in the case of Arman's *Spanish Capriccio* (1962; Cologne, Gal. Reckeman), a guitar sawn into pieces and mounted on board, or *Burnt Violin* (1967; Darmstadt, Hess. Landesmus.). Others, including Cage himself, exploited the graphic aspect of music by turning notes and staves into visual representations in their own right, bearing little if any relation to actual performance (e.g. Sigmar Polke, *The Fifties*, 1969; Darmstadt, Hess. Landesmus., and Jiří Kolář, *Partitur H3361*, 1961; Nuremberg, Gal. Johanna Ricard). Yet others, conversely, created sculptures or constructions specifically intended for 'performance' by creating sounds or noises of various kinds (Jean Tinguely, *My Stars: Concert for Seven Paintings*, 1958; artist's estate), recalling the *bruitiste* 'concerts' of Italian Futurists, and the bizarre instruments—*ululatori, crepitatori* etc—devised by Luigi Russolo and his companions. From the 1960s a significant number of artists occupied themselves with the performance aspect of music, and with staged 'events' of a kind that united various types of aesthetic (or anti-aesthetic) experience. Of these, the most notable manifestations were the celebrated Fluxus concerts and Happenings of the mid-1960s, which lead to the multiplicity of contradictory conventions and anti-conventions of performance and video art (*see* PERFORMANCE ART).

BIBLIOGRAPHY

Grove 6: 'Colour and Music'

G. P. Telemann: *Beschreibung der Augen-Orgel oder des Augen-Clavicimbels* (Hamburg, 1739; repr. in L. Mizler: *Musikalische Bibliothek*, ii/2 (1742/R), pp. 269–74

A. Wallace Rimington: *Colour Music: The Art of Mobile Colour* (London, 1911)

A. B. Klein: *Colour Music: The Art of Light* (London, 1926, 2/1930)

A. Alfassa: 'L'Origine de la lettre de Poussin sur les modes d'après un travail récent', *Bull. Soc. Hist. A. Fr.* (1933), pp. 125–43

R. Wittkower: *Architectural Principles in the Age of Humanism* (London, 1949, rev. 3/1962)

J. M. Stein: *Richard Wagner and the Synthesis of the Arts* (Detroit, 1960/R Westport, 1973)

J. Białostocki: 'Das Modusproblem in den bildenden Künsten', *Z. Kstgesch.*, xxiv (1961), pp. 128–41

R. Lee: *Ut pictura poesis: The Humanistic Theory of Painting* (New York, 1967)

J. Kissane: 'Art Historians and Art Critics—IX: P. G. Hamerton, Victorian Art Critic', *Burl. Mag.*, cxiv (1972), pp. 22–8

E. Lockspeiser: *Music and Painting: A Study in Comparative Ideas from Turner to Schoenberg* (London, 1973)

E. Winternitz: 'Leonardo and Music', *The Unknown Leonardo*, ed. L. Reti (New York, 1974)

F. Würtenberger: *Musik und Malerei: Die Geschichte des Verhaltens zweier Künste zueinander* (Frankfurt, 1979)

S. Selwood: *The Development from Abstract Art to Abstract Animated Film* (diss., Colchester, U. Essex, 1981)

A. Kagan: *Paul Klee: Art and Music* (Ithaca, NY, 1983)

Der Hang zum Gesamtkunstwerk (exh. cat., ed. H. Szeemann; Zurich, Ksthaus, 1983)

J. Hahl-Koch, ed.: *Arnold Schoenberg—Wassily Kandinsky: Letters, Pictures and Documents* (London, 1984)

J. Onians: 'On How to Listen to High Renaissance Art', *A. Hist.*, vii (1984), pp. 410–37

T. Puttfarken: *Roger de Piles' Theory of Art* (New Haven and London, 1985)

Vom Klang der Bilder: Die Musik in der Kunst des 20. Jahrhunderts (exh. cat., ed. K. von Maur; Stuttgart, Staatsgal., 1985)

K. von Maur: 'Music and Theatre in the Work of Juan Gris', *Juan Gris* (exh. cat., ed. C. Green; London, Whitechapel A.G., 1992), pp. 268–82

PETER VERGO

Muskau. Landscape garden set out between 1815 and 1845 by HERMANN VON PÜCKLER-MUSKAU on his estate at Muskau, near Cottbus. The River Neisse, which runs through the park, became part of the German–Polish border in 1945; about two-thirds of its total area (545 ha) lies in Poland and a third in Germany. One of the last great creations of the mature style of German landscape gardening, it surrounds the town of Muskau and its Schloss, rising to a moderate height on both sides of the Neisse Valley, in varied scenery with mixed gradients. At the centre, in an oval area between a bend of the river and the town, lies the Schlosspark, which is continued in the Bergpark, beyond the town to the west. The larger part of the park, including the Oberpark, a broad strip along the river, and the Arboretum, further off on high ground, lies to the east, on the Polish side of the Neisse. Pückler's basic notion for the park was to restore a Utopian ideal: he wanted to display the life of his family (i.e. of the aristocracy) in a romanticized and aesthetically idealized setting, at a time when the middle classes were gaining increasing power. The park should therefore be seen to represent a microcosm of a hierarchical, patriarchal society: a sham castle (unexecuted) on the eastern hills was intended to be the spatial and historical opposite of the industrial landscape incorporating an alum mine in the western Bergpark. Immediately surrounding the palace are pleasure gardens, which include flower gardens, a winter garden, greenhouses and vegetable gardens. Pückler's treatment of the park boundary is conservative: it is designed not to open the gardens to their surroundings but to isolate the ideal society within from the outside world. The boundary was, in the main, marked by an impenetrable wall of densely planted bushes and trees. However, in 1845 Pückler-Muskau suffered financial ruin and was obliged to sell Muskau, leaving his overall plan uncompleted. Between 1852 and 1881 the landscaped area was extended by Eduard Petzold (1815–91). After 1945 only the German side of the park was kept up.

BIBLIOGRAPHY
H. von Pückler-Muskau: *Andeutungen über Landschaftsgärtnerei* (Stuttgart, 1834/*R* Berlin, 1984)
J. Fait and D. Karg, eds: *Hermann Ludwig Heinrich, Fürst von Pückler-Muskau: Gartenkunst und Denkmalpflege* (Weimar, 1989)

REINHARD ZIMMERMANN

Muslim [Muslim ibn al-Dahhān] (*fl* Cairo, *c*. 1000). Arab potter. Twenty complete or fragmentary lustreware vessels signed by Muslim are known. A fragmentary plate with birds in a floral scroll (Athens, Benaki Mus., 11122) is inscribed on the rim '[the work of] Muslim ibn al-Dahhan to please . . . Hassan Iqbal al-Hakimi'. Although the patron has not been identified, his epithet al-Hakimi suggests that he was a courtier of the Fatimid caliph al-Hakim (*reg* 996–1021). The other pieces, bowls or bases from them, are decorated with animals, birds, interlaced bands, inscriptions and floral motifs. One complete bowl (New York, Met., 63.178.1) shows a heraldic eagle, a second (Cairo, Mus. Islam. A., 14930) has a central griffin surrounded by palmettes, and a third (Cairo, Mus. Islam. A., 15958) has a design of four white leaves surrounded by an inscription in kufic offering good wishes. Muslim also countersigned objects made by other potters and may have been the master of an important workshop. His work represents the zenith in the animal, floral and abstract decoration of Egyptian lustrewares of the Fatimid period (969–1171), for after him Fatimid potters increasingly depicted figural subjects (*see* ISLAMIC ART, §V, 3(i)).

BIBLIOGRAPHY
A. A. Yusuf: 'Khazzāfūn min al-'aṣr al-fāṭimī wa asālībuhum al-fannīya' [Ceramicists of the Fatimid period and their artistic styles], *Bull. Fac. A., Cairo U.*, xx (1958), pp. 173–279
M. Jenkins: 'Muslim: An Early Fatimid Ceramicist', *Bull. Met.*, xxvi (1968), pp. 359–69

Musō Sōseki (*b* Ise Prov. [now in Mie Prefect.], 1275; *d* Kyoto, 1351). Japanese Zen master, poet, scholar and garden designer. As spiritual adviser to both Emperor GoDaigo (*reg* 1318–39) and the military leaders who overthrew him, Musō was politically influential and acted as mediator during the civil wars of the 1330s. At various times in his life Musō served as abbot of Nanzenji, one of the various Gozan (Five Mountains) Zen monasteries including Nanzenji in Kyoto (*see* KYOTO, §IV, 4). The support of both imperial and shogunal courts enabled him to found many new Rinzai Zen temples. He was instrumental in popularizing Zen teachings, though also criticized for the secularization of some Zen institutions. Three times during his life and four times posthumously he was given the honorific title *kokushi* (National Master).

Musō began Buddhist studies at the age of three. Although his early training was in the Esoteric Tendai and Shingon doctrines, attraction to Zen brought him to Kamakura, where he received instruction from the Japanese disciples of distinguished Chinese Chan (Jap. Zen) monks, including Kōhō Kennichi (1316–41), imperial prince–abbot of Engakuji. Musō's most illustrious teacher, however, was the Chinese monk Yishan Yining [Issan Ichinei] (1247–1317), who was deeply versed in the philosophy and literature of Song period (AD 960–1279)

China. Musō thus became, in part thanks to Yishan's tutelage, perhaps the first Japanese master to assimilate the Neo-Confucian philosophy and aesthetic canons and poetic styles of Song-period literature without studying in China.

He also ranks as one of Japan's great innovators in garden design (*see* GARDEN, §VI, 3). His great love of nature is evident in his poems about the scenery and gardens surrounding temples. In designing Rinzai Zen temples and their gardens, Musō chose sites and placed structures so as to achieve a harmonious relationship among the various halls and their settings. He selected materials for the gardens that were consonant with the natural landscape. He also sought to re-create, in his gardens, places described in Buddhist *sutra*s, and he named garden features and pavilions after sites mentioned in Zen texts. His garden designs reflect his belief that the natural environment encouraged the self-discipline and introspection necessary for attaining enlightenment. The best-preserved example of his gardens is at Eihōji, outside Nagoya. In 1314, a year after the temple's foundation, he erected the Kannonkaku, a small chapel dedicated to the *bodhisattva* Kannon (Skt Avalokiteshvara), who is sometimes pictured sitting at the base of a waterfall meditating on the reflection of the moon in the water. By placing the chapel against a sheer cliff, diverting water to create a waterfall and making a large pond garden in front of the hall, Musō literally re-created an appropriate setting for the sacred image, an environment symbolic of spiritual enlightenment. At Zuisenji, near Kamakura, he hollowed out a cave where he could sit in meditation, emulating the Zen patriarch Bodhidharma (Jap. Daruma). Musō's most famous gardens belong to Tenryūji and Saihōji (*see* KYOTO, §IV, 2), both Rinzai Zen temples in Kyoto established in 1339. These gardens have been heavily restored over the centuries, but their original forms reflected his fascination with China and inspired the designs of dry-landscape gardens found in many later Zen temples. Tenryūji, of which Musō was founding abbot, was dedicated to the spiritual well-being of the deposed emperor GoDaigo. It was constructed between 1340 and 1344 on the site of a suburban estate that the emperor had owned. Musō incorporated an existing pond garden into the layout, adding some clusters of rocks to its western shore, where he set enormous boulders into an artificial hill and positioned their craggy edges to suggest a mountain ravine. The rockwork was designed to be seen as a dry landscape, but there was also a conduit to bring water for the falls. In front of the cascade Musō clustered stones into dramatic island formations; their towering peaks seemed to re-create the landscape of China as he had seen it rendered in the Chinese ink paintings then being imported into Japan. At Saihōji, located near Tenryūji, Musō built pavilions around a pond garden and designed rock arrangements on the hillside, where he could meditate.

Musō was also renowned as an author of Zen treatises and as a poet in Chinese and Japanese. His poems are included in many surviving collections, including imperially commissioned anthologies. Strength of character, intellectual brilliance, a considerable gift for diplomacy and doubtless a certain ambition ensured not only Musō's prominence in his day but also the lasting continuation of his lineage. Many of his disciples were themselves men of profound achievement and great fame. The tradition of landscape design that he established—emphasizing gardens as environments conducive to Zen practice and the harmonious integration of buildings with their settings—was part of his legacy.

BIBLIOGRAPHY

T. Tamamura: *Musō Sōseki* (Kyoto, 1958)
K. Kawase: *Musō Kokushi, Zen to teien* [National Teacher Musō, Zen and gardens] (Tokyo, 1968)

BRUCE A. COATS

Musscher, Michiel van (*b* Rotterdam, 27 Jan 1645; *d* Amsterdam, 20 June 1705). Dutch painter and printmaker. According to Houbraken, van Musscher received his eclectic artistic training in Amsterdam, studying first with the history painter Martinus Zaagmolen (*c.* 1620–69) in 1660, then with Abraham van den Tempel in 1661, followed by lessons with Gabriel Metsu in 1665. He completed his studies in 1667 in the studio of Adriaen van Ostade. The following year van Musscher returned briefly to Rotterdam before settling permanently in Amsterdam.

Van Musscher's earliest dated painting, *Adriaen Corver and Rijckje Theulingh* (1666; Warsaw, N. Mus.), is a simple and sensitive double portrait reminiscent of works by Gerard ter Borch (ii). During the 1660s he produced both portraits and genre paintings; notable among the latter are representations of ladies with their maids and scholars in their studies, variously showing the influences of Metsu, van Ostade, Nicolaes Maes, Frans van Mieris (i) and Johannes Vermeer. By the 1670s van Musscher was painting almost exclusively portraits. The most striking of these, such as the portrait of *Thomas Hees* (1687; Amsterdam, Rijksmus.), retain an aspect of genre painting by depicting the sitter in his own environment, surrounded by everyday attributes that visually amplify his identity. Among these are several portraits of artists in their studios, including *Willem van de Velde the Younger in his Studio* (*c.* 1665–7; England, Lord Northbrook priv. col., see *Treasure Houses of Britain*, exh. cat., ed. G. Jackson-Stops; Washington, DC, N.G.A., 1985, no. 305), and a series of self-portraits dating from 1669 (Moscow, Pushkin Mus. F.A.) to 1692 (Florence, Uffizi) and possibly later. In style, technique and composition these self-portraits trace van Musscher's development from a simple craftsman to an elegant and sophisticated artist. Many of his late works are characterized by a cool, hard, almost metallic tone.

Eight prints by van Musscher are known, all of them portraits: five mezzotints (e.g. *Self-portrait in a Frame with Allegories*, 1685), two engravings (e.g. *Joost van den Vondel*) and an etching (*Johan Maurits, Count of Nassau-Siegen*, 1673). Among his pupils were Ottmar Elliger II and Dirck van Valkenburg (1675–1721). The contents of van Musscher's studio were auctioned a year after his death on 12 April 1706.

BIBLIOGRAPHY

A. Houbraken: *De groote schouburgh*, iii (1721), pp. 210–12
A. Bredius: 'Inventare von Michiel van Musscher', *Künstler-Inventare: Urkunden zur Geschichte der holländischen Kunst des XVIten, XVIIten und XVIIIten Jahrhunderts* (The Hague, 1915–21), iii, pp. 987–90; vii, pp. 165–6
P. J. J. van Thiel: 'Michiel van Musscher's vroegste werk naar aanleiding van zijn portret van het echtpaar Comans' [Michiel van Musscher's earliest work with reference to his portrait of the Comans family], *Bull. Rijksmus.*, xvii (1969), pp. 3–35
——: 'Andermaal Michiel van Musscher: Zijn zelfportretten' [Michiel van Musscher again: his self-portraits], *Bull. Rijksmus.*, xxii (1974), pp. 131–49
Masters of Seventeenth-century Dutch Genre Painting (exh. cat., ed. P. C. Sutton; Philadelphia, Mus. A.; W. Berlin, Gemäldegal.; London, RA; 1984), pp. 266–7

MARJORIE E. WIESEMAN

Mussini, Luigi (*b* Berlin, 19 Dec 1813; *d* Siena, 18 June 1888). Italian painter and administrator. The son of Natale Mussini, chapel-master at the Prussian court in Berlin, he was sent to Florence, where he was educated in art, music and literature. He first studied art under his older brother Cesare Mussini (1804–79) and later, at the Accademia delle Belle Arti in Florence, he attended courses given by Pietro Benvenuti and Giuseppe Bezzuoli. He was more attracted by a direct study of the great Tuscan masters of the 14th and 15th centuries, whose works he admired for their purity and expressive dignity, than by the practice of copying from classical casts according to Neo-classical teaching. In *Saul Anointed by Samuel* (1835–6), Mussini already displayed a sensitivity towards the theories of *Purismo* through his commitment to studying from nature and ignoring the practice of copying. In 1840 he won a scholarship to Rome, where he was introduced to Ingres and painted his first serious work, *Holy Music* (1842; Florence, Pitti), clearly inspired by Raphael. He returned to Florence in 1844 and, with his friend Franz Adolph von Stürler (1802–81), opened a small art school based on the workshops of the early Renaissance, where they practised a form of 'free teaching' in opposition to the strict rules of the academies. He fought in the Revolutions of 1848 and the following year decided to leave for Paris, where he became close friends with Ingres and those of his school, including Hippolyte Flandrin, Jean-Léon Gérôme, Auguste Gendron and the engraver William Haussoullier (*c.* 1818–1891). His paintings *Holy Music* and the *Triumph of Truth* (1848; Milan, Brera) were exhibited at the Salon of 1849 and were so successful that he was commissioned by the Ministry of Fine Arts to make copies of them (e.g. *Holy Music*, *c.* 1873–5, priv. col.) as well as to do another painting on a subject of his choice. For this he chose a theme particularly dear to the artists of the *Purismo* movement: the *Commemorative Celebration of the Birth of Plato Held at Lorenzo the Magnificent's Villa di Careggi* (1851; Bourg-en-Bresse, Mus. Ain). In this work he decided to emphasize the importance of the ideals of Neo-Platonism and of Florentine humanism and to render the painting in an austere manner of drawing derived from Ingres. At the same time he employed a rich and luxurious colour inspired by the masters of the 16th century, quite unlike the dry quality in Nazarene painting. In 1851 he became Director of the Istituto d'Arte in Siena. While there he painted modern interpretations of *Purismo*, responding to the theories of Ingres and to a new faith in the absolute value of form, as in the difficult *Eudoro and Cimodoce* (Florence, Pitti), inspired by Chateaubriand's prose epic *Les Martyrs* (Paris, 1809). It was exhibited at the Salon of 1857 in Paris and later in Florence in 1861 and was admired by critics for its emotional content, formal qualities and deep velvety tones. During the 1860s he executed the *Mater dolorosa* (1856; Siena, Pal. Pub.), a work painted on panel against a gold background, and produced various copies of the *Commemorative Celebration of the Birth of Plato* (e.g. 1862; Turin, Gal. Civ. A. Mod.). Other paintings done during these years in Siena include *Spartan Education* (1869; Montauban, Mus. Ingres), exhibited at the Ecole des Beaux-Arts in Paris and later bought by the French government for the Musée du Luxembourg, and the characteristic *St Crescentio* (1867), an altarpiece for Siena Cathedral. He also took part in the artistic and cultural life of Siena, in particular helping to restore the ancient monuments of the city, and he set up a school of *Purismo*, whose best representatives were Alessandro Franchi, Angelo Visconti (1829–61) and Amos Cassioli (1832–91). His wife Luigia Mussini-Piaggio (1830–65) and daughter Luisa Mussini-Franchi (*b* 1864 or 1865) were also painters.

WRITINGS
'Cenni autobiografici', *In memoria di Luigi Mussini pittore* (Siena, 1888), pp. 1–8
Epistolario artistico di Luigi Mussini colla vita di lui scritta da Luisa Anzoletti (Siena, 1893)

BIBLIOGRAPHY
N. Mengozzi: *Lettere intime di artisti senesi* (Siena, 1908)
Disegni italiani del XIX secolo (exh. cat. by C. Del Bravo, Florence, Uffizi, 1971), pp. 92–3
Cultura neoclassica e romantica nella Toscana granducale (exh. cat. by S. Pinto, Florence, Cent. Di, 1972), pp. 80–83
E. Spalletti: *Gli anni del Caffè Michelangelo* (Rome, 1985)
G. Uzzani: 'Luigi Mussini: Formazione purista ed esiti senesi', *Siena tra Purismo e Liberty* (exh. cat., ed. M. Batazzi; Siena, Pal. Pub., 1988), pp. 81–6
E. Spalletti: 'La pittura dell'ottocento in Toscana', *La pittura in Italia: L'ottocento*, i (Milan, 1991), pp. 288–366 [biog. in vol. ii, pp. 935–6]

GIOVANNA UZZANI

Musso, Niccolò [Nicolò] (*b* ?Casale Monferrato, *c.* 1595; *d* after 1622). Italian painter. Early sources suggest, and this is confirmed by his works, that he was trained in Caravaggesque circles in Rome in the early 1600s. There he was probably also in contact with the Piedmontese Giovanni Antonio Molineri (1577–1645), active in Rome in 1615. A *Veronica* (Bassano Romano, Pal. Odescalchi) seems to be an early Roman work by Musso, and he can probably be identified with an otherwise unknown Francesco Casale mentioned in the inventories of the collection of the Marchese Vincenzo Giustiniani.

By 1618 Musso had already returned to Casale, where he painted a *Virgin of the Rosary* for S Domenico, which reveals the influence of both Orazio Gentileschi and Carlo Saraceni, with echoes of Orazio Borgianni. He also executed a series of robustly painted works such as the *Virgin and Child* (ex-priv. col., USA), which is clearly influenced by Gentileschi. Another important religious work is the *St Francis at the Foot of the Cross* in S Ilario, Casale, in which the composition, spaciously arranged against the sky, appears innovative by comparison with more traditional contemporary Piedmontese art, partly due to the inspiration of the Caraveggesque art of Molineri.

Musso's later works are less distinguished, partly because of the provincial climate in which he was now working, which was dominated by the archaizing Counter-Reformation art of Moncalvo. Thus the *Virgin of the Carmine* in S Ilario blends Caravaggesque elements, partly mediated by Antonio d'Enrico Tanzio da Varallo, with borrowings from Moncalvo, as does the *Annunciation*

(1622; Ticineto, Assunta). Both Moncalvo and his pupil Giorgio Alberini (*b* 1606), however, also responded to Musso's art, and he, perhaps, did not work in complete isolation.

BIBLIOGRAPHY
P. D'Ancona: 'Un ignoto discepolo di Michelangelo da Caravaggio (Niccolò Musso da Casalmonferrato)', *L'Arte*, xix (1916), pp. 175–8
L. Salerno: 'The Picture Gallery of Vincenzo Giustiniani, II: The Inventory, Part I', *Burl. Mag.*, cii (1960), pp. 21, 93–104, 135–48
G. Romano: 'Niccolò Musso a Roma e a Casale', *Paragone*, xxii/255 (1971), pp. 44–60
——: 'Orientamenti della pittura casalese da G. M. Spanzotti alla fine del cinquecento', *Quarto congresso di antichità e d'arte: Casale Monferrato, 1974*

UGO RUGGERI

Mustafa Ağa [Meremetçi: 'the Mender'] (*d* Istanbul, *c.* 1665). Ottoman architect. Known as the 'Mender', owing to his early career as a repairer and restorer, he was appointed chief imperial architect on the removal of Kasım Ağa in 1644, although he reportedly spent so much on building stables at Üsküdar for Ibrahim (*reg* 1640–48) that he was dismissed the following year. Reappointed in 1651, he was charged with the rebuilding of the Dardanelles fortresses at Çanakkale (1659–61). His major commission, executed between 1660 and 1663, was to complete the Yeni Valide Mosque at Eminönü in Istanbul, begun by Davud Ağa in 1594. Mustafa Ağa added its associated pavilion, public fountains, primary school, Koran school, the tomb of its founder and nearby Mısır Çarşı (Egyptian Bazaar). He supervised construction of the pavilion (Turk. *kasr*) of Davud Pasha (1665) and was responsible for the construction of the fountain (Turk. *sebil*) of Mustafa Ağa (1664; destr.) in the courtyard of the mosque of Mahmud Pasha, and the Çamlıca Kiosk (1665; destr.). The single monument inscribed with the name of Mustafa Ağa is the Mustafa Ağa Çeşmesi (1660), a fountain in the Cibali district of Istanbul. The traveller Evliya Çelebi (1611–84) records the existence of a waterside residence (Turk. *yalı*) belonging to Mustafa Ağa on the Bosphorus at Ortaköy.

BIBLIOGRAPHY
Evliya Çelebi: *Seyāhatnāme* [Book of travels] (MS. *c.* 1684; Istanbul, 1928), i, p. 451; v, p. 17
İ. Kumbaracılar: *İstanbul Sebilleri* [Fountains of Istanbul] (Istanbul, 1936), p. 27
A. Refik: *Türk Mimarları* [Turkish architects] (Istanbul, 1936), pp. 49–56
İ. H. Tanışık: *İstanbul Çeşmeleri* [Fountains of Istanbul], i (Istanbul, 1943), p. 80
L. A. Mayer: *Islamic Architects and their Works* (Geneva, 1956), p. 111
G. Goodwin: *A History of Ottoman Architecture* (Baltimore and London, 1971), pp. 356–60
Z. Nayır: *Osmanlı Mimarlığında Sultan Ahmed Külliyesi ve sonrası, 1609–1690* [The Sultan Ahmed Complex and its successors in Ottoman architecture, 1609–1690] (Istanbul, 1975), pp. 140–41

HOWARD CRANE

Mustafa İzzet [İzzet Efendi; Kadıasker Mustafa İzzet; Muṣṭafā 'Izzat] (*b* Tosya, 1801; *d* Istanbul, 1876). Ottoman calligrapher. He went to Istanbul at a young age and caught the attention of the Ottoman sultan Mahmud II (*reg* 1808–39), who, on hearing the youth's fine voice, took him into the Topkapı Palace to be trained and educated. He learnt *thuluth* and *naskh* scripts from the calligrapher Mustafa Vasif (*d* 1852), from whom he received a diploma (Turk. *icazet*). Mustafa İzzet, who was a distinguished musician and became military judge (*kadıasker*) of Anatolia, tutored Sultan Abdülmecid (*reg* 1839–61) and granted him an *icazet* in *thuluth*. Mustafa İzzet produced 11 copies of the Koran, several books of Koranic quotations and prayers, some 200 calligraphic compositions describing the features and qualities of the Prophet Muhammad (*hilye*), and panels in a fine *naskh* in the style of HAFIZ OSMAN. He was also responsible for the large calligraphic roundels that adorn Hagia Sophia and he restored the inscription on the dome (*see* ISTANBUL, §III, 1(iii)). Among his many pupils were MEHMED ŞEFIK, Muhsinzade Abdullah (1832–99), Abdullah Zühdü (*d* 1879), Kayışzade Osman, Arif of Çarşamba (*d* 1892) and Mehmed Hilmi. A follower of the Nakshbandi order of dervishes, Mustafa İzzet was buried in the graveyard of the Kadiri dervish convent in Tophane, Istanbul.

BIBLIOGRAPHY
A. S. Ünver: *Hattat Kazasker Mustafa İzzet: Hayatı ve eserleri* [The calligrapher Kazasker Mustafa İzzet: his life and works] (Istanbul, 1953)
Ş. Rado: *Türk hattatları* [Turkish calligraphers] (Istanbul, n.d.), pp. 216–17

Mustafa Raqim [Muṣṭafā Rāqim; Mustafa Rakım] (*b* Ünye, 1757; *d* Istanbul, 1826). Ottoman calligrapher. Together with his elder brother, the calligrapher Isma'il Zühdü Efendi (*d* 1806), he went to Istanbul, where he studied with several masters and obtained his diploma at the age of 12. He rose through the Ottoman civil service and eventually held a number of high government offices. He and his brother are generally recognized as freeing Islamic calligraphy from the style canonized by HAFIZ OSMAN (*see* ISLAMIC ART, §III, 2(iv)(a) and (v)). His calligraphic works include a well-known picture of the invocation of the name of God (Arab. *basmala*; Turk. *besmele*) in the form of a crane and TUGHRAs for the sultans Mustafa IV (*reg* 1807–8) and Mahmud II (*reg* 1808–39). He also crafted the inscriptions on the tomb complex of Mahmud's mother, Nakşidil Sultan, in Istanbul.

BIBLIOGRAPHY
Ş. Rado: *Türk hattatları* [Turkish calligraphers] (Istanbul, n.d.), pp. 196–9
A. Schimmel: *Calligraphy and Islamic Culture* (New York, 1984)
WALTER B. DENNY

Müstair [Münster], **St Johann.** Monastery church in the Swiss canton of Graubünden. The church, remarkable for its fresco decoration, was built *c.* AD 800 as a simple, rectangular nave, *c.* 20 m long, with three tall eastern apses; two rows of columns introduced in the 15th century divided it into nave and aisles, and groin vaults replaced the timber ceiling. Probably in the second quarter of the 9th century the church was frescoed throughout. Much of this work is preserved, although awkwardly restored, on the north, south and west walls. While of mediocre quality, these frescoes are the most extensive group of Carolingian wall paintings to survive (*see* CAROLINGIAN ART, §IV, 1). The *Last Judgement* on the west wall is the oldest example of the subject in this position. The narrative scenes on the side walls are arranged in five registers. These originally included scenes from the *Life of David* (Zürich, Schweizer. Landesmus.). The other registers, now partly indecipherable, had 50 or 60 episodes from the *Life of Christ*, one of the largest extant Christological cycles in medieval wall painting. The apses were repainted, probably between 1165 and 1180; the upper parts of this Romanesque work

have broken away, revealing the original Carolingian images in those areas; in the semi-dome of the central apse is *Christ in Majesty* with the story of *John the Baptist* below; in the semi-dome of the left apse is the *Traditio Legis* with scenes from the apostles' lives below; and in the semi-dome of the right apse the *Cross* is represented with the story of *St Stephen* below. In the cloister of the church are very poorly preserved fragments of murals depicting the *Crucifixion* and *Descent from the Cross*; these have been dated to the late 11th century.

BIBLIOGRAPHY
E. Poeschel: *Die Kunstdenkmäler der Schweiz: Die Kunstdenkmäler des Kantons Graubünden* (Basle, 1937–48), v, pp. 292–370; vii, pp. 453–6
L. Birchler: 'Zur karolingischen Architektur und Malerei in Münster-Müstair', *Frühmittelalterliche Kunst in den Alpenländern: Akten zum III. internationalen Kongress für Frühmittelalterforschung: Lausanne, 1954*, pp. 167–252
B. Brenk: *Die romanische Wandmalerei in der Schweiz* (Berne, 1963), pp. 16–20, 28–61
O. Demus: *Romanesque Mural Painting* (London, 1970), pp. 308–10, pls. 83–4, fig. 11
DON DENNY

Mutesellim, Tell el-. *See* MEGIDDO.

Muther, Richard (*b* Ohrdruf, Saxe-Coburg, 20/25 Feb 1860; *d* Wölfesgrund, Silesia [now in Poland], 28 June 1909). German art historian. He studied philology, history and art history at the universities of Berlin and Leipzig and was a friend of Rainer Rilke. He became the curator of the Print Room at the Alte Pinakothek in Munich in 1885 and ten years later was appointed to the chair of art history at the university of Breslau (now Wrocław, Poland). He was a prolific writer and dealt with all areas of art. His approach to art history was distinguished by the attention that he paid to historical context and by his ability to relate artistic style to a wider cultural environment. In the preface to *Geschichte der Malerei* (1900–02) he described his aim as 'to explain from the psychology (so to speak) of each period its dominant style and to interpret the works of art as "human documents"'. He argued, for example, that the religious painting of Velázquez and Zurbarán reflected the two dominant tendencies of the Spanish monarchy, Catholicism and absolutism.

Geschichte der Malerei im XIX Jahrhundert (1893–4) became a standard work on 19th-century art. In this book Muther surveyed the whole century, which he believed to mark 'a new section of universal history'. The prevalent opinion that it had no distinctive style but was a diverse mixture of old and new was, he claimed, an error that resulted from a failure to distinguish between 'the eclectic and personal, the derived and the independent'. His study therefore attempted to make clear 'the logic and sequence of its evolution'. He also wrote many monographs, including works on Leonardo and Rembrandt.

WRITINGS
Geschichte der Malerei im XIX. Jahrhundert, 3 vols (Munich, 1893–4); Eng. trans. as *The History of Modern Painting*, 3 vols, London, 1895–6)
Geschichte der Malerei, 5 vols (Leipzig, 1900–02; Eng. trans., 2 vols, London and New York, 1907)
Geschichte der englischen Malerei (Berlin, 1903)
Leonardo da Vinci (Berlin, 1903; Eng. trans., London, 1907)
Die belgische Malerei im neunzehnten Jahrhundert (Berlin, 1904)
Rembrandt (Berlin, 1904)

BIBLIOGRAPHY
J. Mack: *Wie Muther Kunstkritiker wurde: Ein Beitrag zur Psychologie des Grössenwahns* (Leipzig, 1896)
P. Augé, ed.: *Larousse du XXe siècle*, iv (Paris, 1931), p. 1055
H. Rupp and C. L. Lang, eds.: *Deutsches Literatur-Lexikon*, x (Berne, 1986)

Muthesius, Hermann (*b* Grossneuhaus, 20 April 1861; *d* Berlin, 26 Oct 1927). German architect, architectural historian, theorist and critic. He worked with Ende & Böckmann, one of the leading architectural firms in Berlin, who employed him in Tokyo (1887–91), where he designed a Gothic Revival German church. On his return to Germany he joined the Ministry of Public Works and was appointed technical attaché (1896–1903) to the German Embassy in London. In England he studied the work of the English country-house architects from about 1870: the earlier figures, Philip Webb and R. Norman Shaw, and his own contemporaries C. F. A. Voysey, Edwin Lutyens and W. R. Lethaby. He published several accounts of his investigations of English architectural culture, most notably the three-volume *Das englische Haus* (Berlin, 1904–05). This detailed study, which considers the house, and architecture in general, as an expression of the society of which it is a part, expressed Muthesius's enthusiasm for England and his belief that the immediate future belonged to this style of building. It was much admired in England, but its effect in Germany was to provoke controversy; even in the 1920s a copy was still kept locked away from students of the Technische Hochschule, Berlin. Although keen to promote an awareness of the functional and practical in architecture, Muthesius did not go so far as to see the form of a house as merely the result of fulfilling functional needs. He never denied that the architect was an artist, motivated by the desire to give a convincing visual expression. Indeed his admiration went to artistically minded architects, such as Lutyens and Charles Rennie Mackintosh, who became a close friend, rather than to the more severely rational, such as Voysey.

Muthesius's own architectural career continued after his return to Germany in 1903 and strongly reflected his experiences in England. His first commission, the Seefeld House (1904), Berlin, was dubbed by some 'the house in the English country-house style'. It was followed by the Schuckmann and Velsen houses in the suburbs of Berlin, and by his own house and the neighbouring Freudenberg on the Rehwiese, Nikolassee, Berlin. These differed from their English prototypes in that they were situated in the suburbs rather than the country and were built for city workers. Muthesius was consequently more concerned than his English colleagues to provide a certain amount of prestige. This entailed some adherence to conventional forms; in the Freudenberg House, for example, rooms of irregular shape are forced within a symmetrical outline. More successful are the smaller houses, in which each room stands alone, while the whole building nevertheless gives an impression of unity, as in the De Burlet House (1911) in Schlachtensee (Berlin). Continually inquiring into new possibilities, in 1912 Muthesius began to experiment with neo-Baroque houses, as in the neighbouring Mohrbutter House, Schlactensee. In some ways Muthesius's houses do not match his own advanced theories, however, particularly his proposal that they should conform to standard types. They were nevertheless among the finest examples of 20th-century German architecture in terms of relation to the landscape, accessibility and practicality, and they established his reputation among the educated middle classes.

Parallel to his work as an architect, Muthesius devoted much attention to the problem of maintaining standards of craftsmanship in an industrial age. His treatise *Stilarchitektur und Baukunst* (Mühlheim-Ruhr, 1902), a tract written against all artistic styles, was particularly critical of the newly fashionable *Jugendstil*. Against this, he extolled William Morris's idea of honest craftsmanship and extended it by not excluding the machine and its products as Morris had done, and by anticipating the concept of industrial design. Muthesius had a similarly positive attitude towards new construction methods and materials, such as steel and reinforced concrete. He continued to promote these ideas in his capacity as an official of the Prussian Ministry of Trade, to which he had been appointed on his return to Germany, and his lecture in 1907, given at the Handelshochschule, Berlin, criticizing the state of the German craft industries led to the formation of the DEUTSCHER WERKBUND. This nationalist association comprised not only architects but also artists, craftsmen, teachers, economists, businesses and politicians; it was opposed, however, by some who disagreed with its doctrine of modest ornamentation. The Werkbund also wanted to subject German citizens to a thoroughgoing aesthetic re-education, in a contemporary phrase, 'from the sofa cushion to the city', in which functionality was paramount. In the Werkbund annuals, which came out from 1912, such diverse subjects as shop-windows, the shape of silos and the design of vehicles, including aeroplanes, were discussed. There were disagreements between members of the group, however: at the Werkbund Conference at Cologne in 1914 Muthesius's proposal that the group should concern itself with mass-production and industrial design was rejected by members, such as Henry Van de Velde, who believed in maintaining a certain exclusivity. By the end of World War I much of the Werkbund's work seemed obsolete, however, as did Muthesius's opulent country-house architecture. He continued to work and write, however, until his death in a road accident.

WRITINGS
'Deutsche evangelische Kirche in Tokyo', *Zentralbl. Bauverwalt.*, xi (1891), pp. 337–9

BIBLIOGRAPHY
R. Breuer: 'Einige Häuser von Hermann Muthesius', *Berlin. Architwelt*, xiii/6 (1911), pp. 211–20
H. Busch: 'Hermann Muthesius', *Die Dt. Berufs- & Fachsch.*, xlvi/11 (1950), pp. 827–30
J. Posener: 'Hermann Muthesius', *Architect's Y-b.*, x (1961), pp. 45–51
M. Kubiszky: 'Das Formproblem in der Theorie von Hermann Muthesius', *Baum + Wohnen*, ix (1968), pp. 1–4

JULIUS POSENER

Mutiso, David [Mouka] (*b* Machakos, nr Nairobi, 17 Sept 1932). Kenyan architect and town planner. He was educated at the University of Sheffield's School of Architecture from 1954 to 1959. After graduation, he served apprenticeships with J. Womersley, City Architect of the Sheffield Corporation (1959–60), Professor Quaroni in

Italy and Richard Hughes in Kenya (1961–2). Between 1964 and 1974 he was the Chief Architect of the Kenya Ministry of Works, and he was responsible for a number of public projects, of which the Kenyatta Conference Centre (1974) remains the major architectural landmark. A member of the RIBA and, from 1956 to 1970, of the National Housing Corporation, Mutiso was also a founder-member of the Architectural Association of Kenya in 1967. Between 1965 and 1974 he was Chairman of the Kenya Board of Registration of Architects and Quantity Surveyors, as well as being an external examiner for the Department of Architecture at the University of Nairobi. In 1967 he was registered to practise architecture in Kenya. Mutiso opened his own practice in 1974 and created a portfolio of projects impressive for its range and diversity as well as for the exceptional quality of his buildings and the sensitivity of the siting and landscaping. The United Nations accommodation of 1975, comprising the head-quarters of the UN Centre for Human Settlements as well as the regional offices of UNESCO and UNICEF, sited on 40 ha of undulating landscape at Gigiri, is remarkable for its interplay of structure and non-structural enclosure planes. With the Kenya Technical Teachers College (1978), also in Gigiri, he achieved another level of clarity with contrasting planes of colour: vertical white walls for accent, delineating volumes, and horizontal planes of monopitch, dark red concrete roof tiles, defining various levels of spatial volumes that peak into a flat-topped pyramid over the amphitheatre. The horizontal linear shadow of the roof over the fenestration provides a subdued effect accentuated by the vertical window mullions.

For general discussion of modern Kenyan architecture *see* KENYA, §2.

BIBLIOGRAPHY

U. Kultermann: *New Directions in African Architecture* (New York, 1969)

DAVID ARADEON

Mutters, H(ermanus) P(ieter) (*b* The Hague, 20 Nov 1829; *d* The Hague, 16 Jan 1913). Dutch furniture manufacturer. He founded the well-known Koninklijke Nederlandsche Meubelenfabriek in 1867 in The Hague, which produced furniture largely for private customers. The company was particularly renowned for richly ornamented furnishings, many designed in imitation of French examples by successive generations of the Mutters family. The factory supplied both woodwork and upholstery and received large commissions, including those from the royal family for exhibition pavilions. Until the 1920s the factory also provided interior fittings for ocean liners. The factory's immense popularity at the end of the 19th century was superseded several decades later by the firm of H. PANDER & Zonen.

BIBLIOGRAPHY

J. Gram: *'s Gravenhage in onze tijd* [The Hague in our times] (The Hague, 1893), pp. 84–90

J. M. W. van Voorst tot Voorst: 'Haagse meubelmakers en negentiende-eeuwse meubelstijlen' [Furniture-makers in The Hague and 19th-century furniture styles], *Antiek*, iii (1974), pp. 237–62

——: 'Twee Haagse meubelfabrieken' [Two furniture factories in The Hague], *Antiek*, iv (1974), pp. 357–75

MONIQUE D. J. M. TEUNISSEN

Muttoni, Francesco (*b* Lacima [now Cima], Lake Lugano, 22 Jan 1669; *d* Vicenza, 21 Feb 1747). Italian architect, architectural editor and expositor, landscape designer, draughtsman and cartographer. His work represents the transition from late Venetian Baroque to Neo-classicism, which his studies of Palladio did much to promote in its early stages. His style, however, was never entirely free of the Baroque elements acquired during his formative years.

Muttoni was the son of a builder, and in 1696 he went to work in Vicenza, as members of his family had done since the 16th century, enrolling that year in the stonemasons' guild. From the beginning of the 18th century he was active as an expert consultant ('*perito*') and cartographer, as is exemplified by the plan of the fortifications of Vicenza that he drew in 1701 for the Venetian government (Vicenza, Archv Stor. Mun.). Throughout his life he continued to undertake various small professional commissions for surveys and on-site studies. His first major commission, however, was the majestic Palazzo Repeta (1701–12; now the Bank of Italy) in Piazza S Lorenzo, Vicenza, for Scipione Repeta. Its imposing façade has echoes of Michele Sanmicheli and Andrea Palladio. The rusticated ground floor characterizes many of Muttoni's subsequent works, while the windows of the *piano nobile* are embellished by Baroque details at their heads. Inside is a grand staircase decorated with frescoes by Louis Dorigny and a sculptural group by Orazio Marinali.

Around the same time Muttoni began a project (1702–27) for Benedetto Valmarana to rebuild the vast complex of the Villa Valmarana Morosini (known as La Morosina), at Altavilla, Vicentina. Detailed autograph drawings of the handsome stables there are preserved at Chatsworth, Derbys, England. The Palazzo Angarano alle Fontanelle, Vicenza, also dates from the beginning of the century (*c.* 1701–31; destr.), and in 1703 Muttoni designed the Biblioteca Bertoliana, Vicenza, which was built under his supervision between 1704 and 1706. The small adjacent church of S Vincenzo was also enlarged, under his guidance, with the chapel of the high altar (1704–8). In 1706 construction began on the Palazzo Velo Vettore, Vicenza (see fig.), commissioned by Giacomo Velo, but work was interrupted probably by Velo's death in 1708, and only the part between Contrà Lodi and Contrà Contorana was executed. The building was intended to be an exuberant variation of Palladio's Palazzo Chiericati in Vicenza, 'corrected' by the use of an architrave in the portico and by filling in the upper loggias. The use of Baroque elements is characteristically limited to the decoration of the windows.

Around 1708 Thomas Twisden, an English amateur architect, commissioned from Muttoni a series of drawings of ancient monuments in Rome and Palladian buildings. In 1708 Muttoni excavated at the Colosseum and around the Arch of Constantine in Rome and surveyed a number of ancient buildings. This gave him the opportunity to verify some unpublished original drawings by Palladio of the antiquities of Rome, which he had acquired at the beginning of the century. This was the beginning of his great task in editing Palladio's theoretical and architectural works, which were published anonymously in eight volumes by the Venetian publisher Angelo Pasinelli in the

Francesco Muttoni: Palazzo Velo Vettore, Vicenza, begun 1706

1740s, with fine plates engraved by the architect Giorgio Fossati (1706–78), the engraver Francesco Zucchi and others. The edition included a reprint of Palladio's *Quattro libri* (Venice, 1570) and Muttoni's comments, in which he stresses the differences between the actual buildings and the corresponding drawings in Palladio's treatise, with accurate drawings of his own that provide valuable information on the state of Palladio's buildings at the beginning of the 18th century. Also included were the 'unpublished buildings' executed by Palladio in Venice and a treatise on the five orders of architecture as exemplified by ancient and modern authorities. The ninth volume, devoted to the many other 'unpublished buildings' attributed to Palladio and edited by Giorgio Fossati, was not published until 1760. The preparatory drawings for the tenth volume, which was never printed, include works by architects following Palladio and plans by Muttoni himself. Muttoni also published in 1741 a smaller version of the volume on the five orders of architecture, which was a more convenient manual for professionals.

On returning from Rome, Muttoni resumed his architectural work. He planned a grandiose royal palace with a square floor plan surrounding a circular court surmounted by a dome for Frederick IV of Denmark, who was in Vicenza at the end of 1708. Between 1708 and 1710 he laid out with great sensitivity the vast complex of buildings and gardens of Villa Fracanzan at Orgiano, Vicenza, for Giovanni Battista Fracanzan, and around this time he was also working on the magnificent stables of the Villa Porto Colleoni at Thiene, Vicenza, both of which projects included statues by Orazio Marinali. In 1709 he was appointed 'Architect and Public Surveyor' of Vicenza, and he proceeded to draw up a plan (1713; unexecuted, Bib. Civ. Bertoliana) for the redevelopment of the Campo Marzo area of the city to accommodate a new site for the annual fair. In 1712, for Ottavio and Giuseppe Trento, Muttoni produced the first drawings for the Palazzo Trento Valmarana, Vicenza, which was built under his continuous supervision (1713–17; interior destr. 1945). This palazzo, which is considered his masterpiece, reveals Muttoni's ability to experiment, notably in the façade overlooking the garden, where Baroque detailing is again used at the windows. He is also credited with a design of a radically different style for the simple and harmonious Villa Da Porto (1714–15), known as La Favorita, in Monticello di Fara, Vicenza, which is designed on Palladian lines, with a slightly projecting porch and paired Ionic columns, and he worked in 1717–18 on the country estates of the Trento family at Costozza di Longare, Vicenza. His subsequent skilful planning (1718–46) of the avenues, courts, belvederes, ponds, parterres and gates in the two Trissino villas, Vicenza, constitutes one of the most important landscaping projects in the Veneto and further confirmed his reputation as a landscape designer. Muttoni also worked on a number of Palladio's villas: at the Villa Rotonda, Vicenza, between 1725 and 1740, he transformed the third floor into small rooms suitable for living space (*see also* VICENZA, §2); early in the 18th century he extended the Villa Thiene Valmarana at Quinto Vicentino, of which he possessed Palladio's original drawing; and in the Villa Pojana at Pojana Maggiore, Vicenza, he created a new wing of the building with a corner turret for the stairs (before 1740).

Muttoni also carried out numerous minor projects in churches and convents in Vicenza and the surrounding area, and he executed the parish churches of Rossano Veneto (1746; façade altered), Vicenza, and of Leffe (1767; refaced 1834) in Val Seriana, Bergamo. Another important, and controversial, late work was the Portici di Monte Berico (1746–c. 1778) in Vicenza, a long passage covered by simple, severe arches, running uphill from the city to the sanctuary of the Madonna. Muttoni published an essay on the subject in 1741, but in 1746, as construction work was beginning, the project was opposed by the Vicenza academic and architect Enea Arnaldi (1716–94). Appeal was made to the judgement of the Paduan scientist Giovanni Poleni, who ruled in favour of Muttoni's plan. Many other buildings in and around Vicenza are referred or provisionally attributed to Muttoni, who at his death left his books, manuscripts, prints, drawings and drawing instruments (all now in Porlezza, Archv Com.) to his native town for the use of architectural students.

UNPUBLISHED SOURCES

Vicenza, Cent. Int. Stud. Archit. Palladio [*Disegni et annotationi fatte di commissione del Sig.r K. re Tomaso Tuixden inglese*]

Washington, DC, Lib. Congr. [*Disegni originali dell'edizione di Palladio . . . che dovevano formare il X libro non uscito*]

WRITINGS

Architettura di Andrea Palladio Vicentino di nuovo ristampata, e di figure in rame diligentemente intagliate arrichita, corretta e accresciuta di moltissime fabbriche inedite: Con le osservazioni dell'architetto N. N. e con la traduzione francese, 8 vols (Venice, 1740–48)

Osservazioni intorno alle fabbriche fatte o da eseguirsi in onore della Beata Vergine Maria di Monte Berico a Vicenza (Vicenza, 1741)

BIBLIOGRAPHY

F. Barbieri: 'Per il regesto di Francesco Muttoni: Il distrutto palazzo Angaran alle Fontanelle', *Vita Vicentina*, ix (1954), pp. 287–92

F. Franco: 'Francesco Muttoni: L'architetto di Vicenza N. N.', *Boll. Cent. Int. Stud. Archit. Andrea Palladio*, iv (1962), pp. 147–55

M. Tafuri: 'Il parco della villa Trissino a Trissino e l'opera di Francesco Muttoni', *Archit.: Chron. & Stor.*, cxic (1965), pp. 832–41

R. Cevese: *Ville della provincia di Vicenza*, 2 vols (Milan, 1971)

F. Barbieri: *Illuministi e neoclassici a Vicenza* (Vicenza, 1972), pp. 3–23

L. Puppi: 'La "Morosina" d'Altavilla', *Riv. Ist. N. Archeol. & Stor. A.*, xix–xx (1972–3), pp. 219–319

G. Mantese: 'L'architetto Francesco Muttoni fu difendente', *Memorie storiche della chiesa vicentina*, iv (Vicenza, 1974), pp. 1371–87

L. Puppi: 'La prima redazione della mappa del Chiampo di Francesco Muttoni', *Valle del Chiampo: Antologia* (1974), pp. 187–204

D. Lewis: 'A New Book of Drawings by Francesco Muttoni', *A. Ven.*, xxx (1976), pp. 132–46

L. Olivato: 'Francesco Muttoni, Ottavio Bertotti Scamozzi', *Vicenza illustrata*, ed. N. Pozza (Vicenza, 1976), pp. 351–62

U. Soragni: 'La fiera "incompiuta" del Campo Marzo', *Vicenza*, v (1976), p. 19

——: 'Una pianta di Vicenza del 1701 di Francesco Muttoni', *Storia della città*, v (1977), pp. 54–62

F. Barbieri: 'I disegni di Francesco Muttoni a Chatsworth: Qualche appunto sui disegni muttoniani di Washington: Un possibile aggancio per una ipotesi palladiana?', *A. Lombarda*, lv–lvii (1980), pp. 219–35

L. Puppi: 'Alle origini del Neopalladianesimo: Il contributo comasco di Francesco Muttoni', *A. Lombarda*, lv–lvii (1980), pp. 336–42

M. Azzi Visentini, ed.: *Il giardino veneto* (Milano, 1988), pp. 145–48, 294, 301

C. M. Sicca: 'A Lost Drawing by Francesco Muttoni for the Staircase and Garden at the Castello di Trissino', *An. Archit. Cent. Int. Stud. Archit. Andrea Palladio*, i (1989), pp. 122–25

F. Barbieri, N. Grilli: 'Francesco Muttoni: 289 disegni inediti dell'archivio di Porlezza', *Il disegno di architettura*, ii (1990), pp. 8–12

I Tiepolo e il settecento vicentino (exh. cat., ed. Electa, Vicenza, 1990), pp. 194, 204–5, 207

N. Grilli: *Un archivio inedito dell'architetto Francesco Muttoni a Porlezza* (Florence, 1991)

L. Puppi: 'Francesco Muttoni scenografo nel Teatro olimpico e nel giardino Valmarana a Vicenza', *Venezia Arti*, vi (1992), pp. 45–52

M. Azzi Visentini: 'Francesco Muttoni architetto di giardini: Villa Trissino-Marzotto a Trissino', *A. Ven.*, xliv (1993), pp. 34–47

VALERIA FARINATI

Muttoni, Pietro. *See under* VECCHIA, PIETRO DELLA.

Mutule. Projecting block on the underside of a Doric cornice (*see* GREECE, ANCIENT, fig. 9j and ORDERS, ARCHITECTURAL, fig. 1xvii), often decorated with rows of guttae (*see* Gutta; *see also* POLYCHROMY, colour pl. I, fig. 1). ☐

Muwahhidun, al-. *See* ALMOHAD.

Muybridge, Eadweard [Muggeridge, Edward James] (*b* Kingston-on-Thames, 9 April 1830; *d* Kingston-on-Thames, 8 May 1904). English photographer, active in the USA. He was the first to analyse motion successfully by using a sequence of photographs and resynthesizing them to produce moving pictures on a screen. His work has been described as the inspiration behind the invention of the motion picture. Born Edward James Muggeridge, he emigrated around 1852 to the USA, where he first worked for a firm of publishers and later became a book dealer. After a stagecoach accident in Texas in 1860, he returned to England, where he took up photography. By 1867 he was back in California, describing himself as 'Eadweard Muybridge, artist–photographer'. During the next five years he took over 2000 photographs, selling many of them under the pseudonym Helios. Muybridge made his

Eadweard Muybridge: photograph of a horse ('Occident') trotting, 1877 (London, Science Museum)

name as a photographer with a successful series of views, *Scenery of the Yosemite Valley*, published in 1868. In 1872 he was commissioned by a former governor of California, Leland Stanford, to photograph his horse, Occident, trotting at speed. The aim was to test Stanford's theory that at some stage in its trot the horse would have all four feet off the ground. Muybridge's first photographs were inconclusive but further attempts in 1873 appeared to prove the point, at least to Stanford's satisfaction. Work was interrupted by a dramatic crisis when Muybridge, tried for killing his wife's lover and acquitted, found it prudent to make a photographic expedition to Central America.

In 1877 Muybridge returned to the problem of the trotting horse and began the work which was to make him famous. He designed an improved shutter to work at the astonishing speed of one-thousandth of a second and used all his experience to sensitize his plates for the shortest possible exposure. When the resulting retouched picture of Occident in arrested motion was published in July 1877, it was so different from the traditional artist's impression that it created a minor sensation (see fig.). The next year Muybridge embarked on an even more ambitious series of experiments. In order to secure a sequence of photographs of horses in various stages of trotting, he set up a battery of 12 cameras fitted with electromagnetic shutters. These were activated by strings stretched across the track. Muybridge later repeated his experiments using 24 cameras. The subsequent photographs were widely reproduced in publications throughout America and Europe. The publicity led Muybridge to design a projecting device based on an optical toy by which drawings derived from his photographs could be projected on to a screen as moving pictures. During the early 1880s he toured Europe with this instrument, termed the zoopraxiscope, and a large collection of lantern slides. With the latter he was able to demonstrate that artists throughout the ages had depicted the horse in attitudes which were completely false. On his return to America Muybridge quarrelled with Stanford, but in 1884 he was able to begin work at the University of Pennsylvania using elaborate banks of cameras to analyse animal and human motion by means of photographs. He took over 100,000 photographs, 20,000 of which were reproduced in his major publication, *Animal Locomotion* (London, 1887; for example *see* PHOTOGRAPHY, fig. 17). This 11-volume work had a tremendous impact, not least on artists, who were forced to reassess completely the manner in which they depicted animal movement.

Muybridge finally returned to England in 1900. He bequeathed numerous relics of his work to Kingston-on-Thames Public Library, a great proportion of which is on loan to the Science Museum, London. Other major repositories of Muybridge's work include the Bancroft Library at the University of California, Berkeley, the Stanford University Library and the Stanford University Art Gallery and Museum.

BIBLIOGRAPHY
J. M. Eder: *Geschichte der Photographie* (Vienna, 1905, rev. Halle 4/1932; Eng. trans., 1945/R 1972)
G. Hendricks: *The Edison Motion Picture Myth* (Berkeley, 1961)
The Painter and the Photograph (exh. cat., ed. Van Deren Coke; Albuquerque, U. NM, A. Mus., 1964)
A. Scharf: *Art and Photography* (London, 1968)
Eadweard Muybridge: The Stanford Years, 1872–1882 (exh. cat., ed. A. V. Mozley, R. B. Haas and F. Forster-Hahn; Stanford U., A.G. & Mus., 1972, rev. 1973)
R. B. Haas: *Muybridge, Man in Motion* (Berkeley, 1975)
G. Hendricks: *Eadweard Muybridge, the Father of the Motion Picture* (London, 1975)
Muybridge's Complete Human and Animal Locomotion, 3 vols (New York, 1979) [reprint of *Animal Locomotion* and *Prospectus and Catalogue of Plates* (London, 1887), with intro. by A. V. Mozley]
B. Coe: *The History of Movie Photography* (London, 1981)

J. P. WARD

Muyden, Evert (Louis) van (*b* Albano, Laziale, nr Rome, 18 July 1853; *d* Orsay, nr Paris, 27 Feb 1922). Swiss engraver, illustrator and painter. He began his studies with his father, the painter Alfred van Muyden (1818–98), and then studied in Geneva, Berlin and Paris. From 1879 to 1884 he worked in Rome, where he painted mainly landscapes, typical of which is *View of the Piazza del Olmo at Tivoli* (*c*. 1880; Basle, Kstmus.), which shows the influence of Corot. From 1885 he lived in Paris and painted animals in the manner of Antoine-Louis Barye. He made hundreds of drawings and engravings of plants and animals from the Muséum National d'Histoire Naturelle in Paris and the Zoologischer Garten in Basle. The double portrait of his dog *Sultan* (1889; Basle, Kstmus.) demonstrates his fluid style rooted in naturalism based on direct observation. He illustrated many books, including Champfleury's *Contes choisis* (Paris, 1899) and Emil Frey's *Die Kriegstaten der Schweiz* (Neuchâtel, 1905). Although he produced isolated portraits and various sculptures, only his engravings and book illustrations are well known.

BIBLIOGRAPHY
H. v. M. [Henri van Muyden]: 'Evert van Muyden: Artiste animalier, 1853–1922', *Page A.*, ix (1923), pp. 243–62

WILLIAM HAUPTMAN

Muzaffar 'Ali [Muzaffar 'Alī ibn Haydar 'Alī al-Tabrīzī] (*fl* late 1520s–70s; *d* Qazvin, *c*. 1576). Persian calligrapher, illustrator, painter and poet. He was a versatile artist who belonged to the second generation working for Tahmasp I (*reg* 1524–76) at the Safavid court in north-west Iran (*see* ISLAMIC ART, §III, 4(vi)(a)). His career has been reconstructed by Dickson and Welch on the basis of brief notices by Safavid artists and historians, signed calligraphies and ascribed paintings. He studied calligraphy with the master Rustam 'Ali, and several folios in the album compiled for Bahram Mirza in 1544–5 (Istanbul, Topkapı Pal. Lib., H. 2154) are signed jointly by Rustam 'Ali for the writing and Muzaffar 'Ali for the *découpage* (Arab. *qat'*). He was a master of *nasta'līq* script, and two examples in the album prepared for Amir Ghayb Beg in 1564–5 (Istanbul, Topkapı Pal. Lib., H. 2161) are signed by him. In the introduction to this album, Malik Daylami wrote of his skill in calligraphic decoration and gold illumination, and the chronicler Qazi Ahmad reported that he also excelled in gold-flecking, gilding and varnished painting. Muzaffar 'Ali reportedly studied painting with the renowned master BIHZAD, who was his great-uncle. Two paintings in London, one in a copy (BL, Or. MS. 2265, fol. 211*r*) of Nizami's *Khamsa* ('Five poems') dated 1539–43 and one in a copy (BL, Or. MS. 12985, fol. 5*r*) of Asadi's *Garshāspnāma* ('Book of Garshasp') of 1573–4, are ascribed to him. Welch attributed to him nine paintings (fols 294*r*, 385*v*, 538*r*, 553*r*, 602*v*, 622*r*, 629*r*, 654*r*, 708*v*) from the monumental *Shāhnāma* ('Book of kings') made for Tahmasp (ex-Houghton priv. col., dispersed) and four (fols 30*r*, 105*r*, 110*v*, 231*r*) in the splendid copy (Washington, DC, Freer, 46.12) of Jami's *Haft awrang* ('Seven thrones') of 1556–65. Welch identified the artist's work as lyrical and smooth, with loose compositions and thinly applied pigments. According to the historian Iskandar Munshi, the artist also designed the paintings for the Safavid royal palace in QAZVIN and the wall paintings for the Chihil Sutun Pavilion (both destr.), and personally executed much of the brushwork. He was the teacher of SADIQI and SIYAVUSH.

BIBLIOGRAPHY

Malik Daylami: Preface to the Amir Husayn Beg Album (1560–61; Istanbul, Topkapı Pal. Lib., H. 2151), partial Eng. trans. by W. M. Thackston in *A Century of Princes: Sources on Timurid History and Art* (Cambridge, MA, 1989), pp. 351–2

Qazi Ahmad ibn Mir Munshi: *Gulistān-i hunar* [Garden of the arts] (*c.* 1606), ed. A. Suhayli (Tehran, Iran. Solar 1352/1974), p. 137; Eng. trans. by V. Minorsky as *Calligraphers and Painters* (Washington, DC, 1959), pp. 186, 191

Iskandar Munshi: *Tārīkh-i 'ālamārā-yi 'abbāsī* [History of the world-conquering 'Abbas] (1629); Eng. trans. by R. Savory as *History of Shah 'Abbas the Great* (Boulder, 1978), p. 271

M. B. Dickson and S. C. Welch: *The Houghton Shahnameh* (Cambridge, MA, 1981), pp. 154–64, pls 168, 190, 221, 226, 237, 240, 241, 247, 255

M. Bayani: *Ahvāl va āthār-i khushnivīsān* [Biographies and examples of calligraphers] (Tehran, Iran. Solar 1363/1985), pp. 209, 912

SHEILA S. BLAIR

Muzaffarid. Islamic dynasty that ruled in southern Iran and Kurdistan from 1314 to 1393. The founder, Sharaf al-Din Muzaffar, was a native of Khurasan and after holding several posts at the Ilkhanid court was appointed governor of Maybud near Isfahan. In 1314 his son Mubariz al-Din Muhammad (*reg* 1314–58; *d* 1364) succeeded him in this post, and in turn added Yazd (1319), Kirman (1340), Shiraz (1354) and finally Isfahan (1356) to his domains, wresting much of southern Iran from the control of the Inju governors and even briefly holding Tabriz. He was thus the major political figure in central and southern Iran until deposed and blinded by his son Shah Shuja' (*reg* 1364–84), whose reign was dominated by conflicts with his own brother (the governor of Isfahan) and the JALAYIRID rulers of western Iran. Shah Shuja' divided his territories between his son 'Ali (*reg* 1384–7) and his brother Ahmad (*reg* 1384–93 in Kirman), but other members of the family, Yahya (*reg* 1387–93 in Yazd) and Mansur (*reg* 1387–93 in Isfahan, Fars and Iraq), pressed their claims by force and thus weakened Muzaffarid power. Meanwhile, to the north, the TIMURID menace was growing, and although both 'Ali and Ahmad submitted to Timur, a local rebellion in Isfahan against Timur's tax collectors provoked an appalling massacre in which reputedly 200,000 people perished. Mansur fell in battle against Timur, who promptly executed the remaining 70 members of the royal house.

In the cultural sphere, the Muzaffarid rulers were notable patrons of architecture, and dozens of their buildings—including mud-brick tombs with fresco ornament, congregational mosques and madrasas—survive, especially in the areas of Isfahan (*see* ISFAHAN, §3(i)), YAZD and ABARQUH (*see* ISLAMIC ART, §II, 6(i)(a)). The great poet Hafiz (1325–90) lived at the court of Shah

Shuja', and in this period Ilkhanid modes of book painting gave way to those associated with the Timurids (*see* ISLAMIC ART, §III, 4(v)(c)). Metalwork under the Muzaffarids continued the tradition established under the Injus, featuring figural themes borrowed from book painting and etiolated inscriptions derived from Mamluk models.

BIBLIOGRAPHY

Enc. Islam/2

S. Album: 'Power and Legitimacy: The Coinage of the Mubāriz al-Dīn Muḥammad ibn al-Muzaffar at Yazd and Kirman', *Monde Iran. & Islam*, ii (1974), pp. 157–71

S. S. Blair: 'Artists and Patronage in Late Fourteenth-century Iran in the Light of Two Catalogues of Islamic Metalwork', *Bull. SOAS*, xlviii (1985), pp. 53–9

ROBERT HILLENBRAND

Muziano, Girolamo (*b* Brescia, 1532; *d* Rome, 27 April 1592). Italian painter and draughtsman. He trained as a landscape painter in Padua and Venice, but from 1549 he worked in Rome. In 1550–51 he skilfully completed the background of Battista Franco's altarpiece of the *Resurrection* in the Gabrielli Chapel, S Maria sopra Minerva, Rome, with a rustic scene of woods, mill and stream in the style of Titian and of Domenico Campagnola, rendered in rhythmic, luminous strokes reminiscent of Tintoretto and Andrea Schiavone; on the entrance pilasters he executed the rather laboured frescoes of *Prophets* and *Seers*, derived from Michelangelo. Around 1554–5 he frescoed the *Prophets* and *Dream of Joseph* (Rome, S Caterina della Rota). The angel in the latter is related to elaborate Mannerist figures by Taddeo Zuccaro and Pellegrino Tibaldi, but Muziano's clear illustration of the subject and careful characterization of the protagonists reflect the sombre classicizing style of Girolamo Siciolante da Sermoneta and the artistic tenets of the Counter-Reformation. The monumental forest setting and dramatic lighting, reminiscent of Titian, do not seem to have been appreciated in Rome; for a few years Muziano worked only outside the city, and subsequently he reduced the role of landscape in his religious paintings.

In Subiaco, Muziano painted a *Raising of Lazarus* (Rome, Pin. Vaticana; see fig.), which was exhibited in Rome in 1555. Its large dimensions, dramatic light effects and varied textures still show Venetian influence, but he used an eloquent background of Classical ruins and wove sufficient variety and complexity into his design and use of colour to please the sophisticated Mannerist taste of his Roman audience without compromising the solemnity of the subject. The picture earned him Michelangelo's praise (Turner, p. 131) and brought him other major commissions. Between 1555 and 1558 for Orvieto Cathedral Muziano painted two large altarpieces, another *Raising of Lazarus* and a *Road to Calvary* (*in situ*), and chapel decorations (destr.). An altarpiece (untraced) for Foligno Cathedral also dates from this period. He declined to collaborate with Zuccaro and others on the decoration of Villa Farnese at Caprarola, and after refusing further commissions in Orvieto he returned to Rome.

Between 1560 and 1566 Muziano painted original and highly influential landscape frescoes in Cardinal Ippolito II d'Este's villas in Rome and Tivoli. None survives, but drawings, such as one in the Uffizi, Florence (512), suggest that in these landscapes he initiated the revival of the Classical genre of the idealized landscape, adapting it to

Girolamo Muziano: *Raising of Lazarus*, oil on canvas, 2.95×4.40 m, exh. 1555 (Rome, Pinacoteca Vaticana)

contemporary Roman taste with a picturesque blend of natural forms and evocative antique ruins in scenes derived from the local countryside and accented with Venetian contrasts of scale.

Subsequently Muziano concentrated on religious subjects, further developing his interpretation of the spiritual values of the Counter-Reformation. Responding to the growing market for popular devotional images, he designed many engravings, notably nine scenes from the *Life of Christ* and two versions of the *Stigmatization of St Francis*, all issued by Cornelis Cort in 1567–8, and seven plates of *Penitent Saints* in large landscapes, issued by Cort in 1573–5 (London, BM; Hollstein, nos 77, 80–81, 83, 86–7, 128–9, 135). All in vertical format, the *Penitent Saints* are tightly organized on the surface and in depth, using both aerial perspective and a series of overlapping planes; framing and accentuating the tiny figures are richly varied landscape forms, some boldly exaggerated but naturalistically described, which create dramatic contrasts and a moody play of light and shade and which evoke the awesome aspects of the wilderness.

In his many small devotional paintings (for which he received high prices) Muziano relied on vibrant atmospheric effects rather than detailed descriptions of figures or background to communicate mood. Even in large paintings, such as *St Francis* (Rome, S Maria della Concezione) and *St Jerome* (Bologna, Pin. N.), where the figures dominate the landscape, shifting coloured lights and shadow convey a sense of brooding and expectation. For narrative subjects in the early 1560s, such as *Christ Raising*

the Daughter of Jairus (Madrid, Escorial), painted for Philip II of Spain, Muziano had developed a style of classically balanced composition and naturalistic representation of action similar to that of Zuccaro, but he later turned towards a more poetic form of communication. Beginning with his paintings (*c.* 1569) in the Ruiz Chapel, S Caterina dei Funari, Rome, he limited action to a few grave gestures and arranged his figures in simple planar designs of graceful geometric shapes connected in gentle rhythms. Later treatments of narrative subjects, for example *Christ Receiving Envoys from John the Baptist* (*c.* 1570–75; Loreto, S Casa), are enlivened with soft colours and textures and flickering rose and gold light.

In the late 1570s and the 1580s the patronage of Gregory XIII ensured that Muziano was the foremost religious artist in Rome, and in 1577 he persuaded the Pope to establish the Accademia di S Luca. From 1576 Muziano painted numerous canvases for the papal court and supervised the making of mosaics from his own designs in the Cappella Gregoriana, the first chapel completed in the new St Peter's. He did not participate in the decoration of the Galleria Geografica in the Vatican, another of the collaborative projects he disliked. His altarpieces were in great demand, especially among Roman families ordered by the Pope to improve their chapels: the *Ascension* (1580–81; Rome, S Maria in Vallicella); the *Donation of the Keys to St Peter* (*c.* 1584; Rome, S Maria degli Angeli); the *Ascension*, *St Paul* and the *Immaculate Conception* (*c.* 1581–4; all now Rome, Carmelite Coll.); and in the Mattei Chapel (*c.* 1582–9; Rome, S Maria d'Aracoeli).

The only commission Muziano received after Gregory XIII's death (1585) was the *Circumcision* for the high altar of Il Gesù (1587–9; Rome, Pal. Gesù). He died after a long illness, leaving many paintings unfinished. His altarpieces for St Peter's were completed by artists he had inspired, the *Mass of St Gregory* (untraced) by his former pupil Cesare Nebbia and the *Six Hermit Saints* (Rome, S Maria degli Angeli) by Paul Bril.

BIBLIOGRAPHY

Hollstein: *Dut. & Flem.*; Thieme–Becker

G. Vasari: *Vite* (1550, rev. 2/1568); ed. G. Milanesi (1878–85), v, p. 432; vi, p. 508; vii, p. 87

R. Borghini: *Il riposo*, iii (Florence, 1584/*R* 1807), pp. 145–9; 2nd edn A. M. Biscioni and G. G. Bottari (Florence, 1730), pp. 469–72

G. Baglione: *Vite* (1642); ed. V. Mariani (1935), pp. 49–52

U. da Como: *Girolamo Muziano, 1528–1592: Note e documenti* (Bergamo, 1930)

U. Procacci: 'Una *Vita* inedita del Muziano', *A. Ven.*, viii (1954), pp. 242–64

F. da Morrovalle: 'Girolamo Muziano a Loreto', *A. Ant. & Mod.*, viii (1965), pp. 385f

A. R. Turner: *The Vision of Landscape in Renaissance Italy* (Princeton, 1966), pp. 116–18, 131–2, 175–8

R. E. Mack: 'Girolamo Muziano and Cesare Nebbia at Orvieto', *A. Bull.*, lvi (1974), pp. 410–13

G. L. Masetti Zannini: *Pittori della seconda metà del cinquecento* (Rome, 1974), pp. 61–9

J. Heideman: 'Observations on Girolamo Muziano's Decoration of the Mattei Chapel in S Maria in Aracoeli', *Burl. Mag.*, cxix (1977), pp. 686–94

G. Fusconi and S. Prosperi Valenti Rodinò: 'Note in margine ad una schedatura: I disegni del Fondo Corsini nel Gabinetto Nazionale delle Stampe', *Boll. A.*, xvi (1982), pp. 81–118

J. A. Gere and P. M. R. Pouncey: *Italian Drawings in the Department of Prints and Drawings in the British Museum*, i (London, 1983), pp. 129–31

ROSAMOND E. MACK

Muzika, František (*b* Prague, 26 June 1900; *d* Prague, 1 Nov 1974). Czech painter, draughtsman, typographer, stage designer, writer and teacher. He studied at the Academy of Fine Arts in Prague from 1919 to 1924, under Jakub Obrovský (1882–1949), Karel Krattner (1862–1926) and, later on, Jan Štursa. In 1921 he became a member of the important group of avant-garde artists Devětsil, and in 1922 he participated in their Spring exhibition with a group of 12 paintings. In 1923 he also joined the Mánes Union of Artists. After graduating from the Academy he spent a year at the Académie des Beaux-Arts in Paris. He attended lectures by František Kupka and was in contact with Josef Šíma and Jan Zrzavý. In 1927 he started working with the Prague publishing house Aventinum as a book designer, typographer, caricaturist and art critic. At the same time he began to work for the theatre, and from 1927 to 1947 he created 107 stage designs. He took part in the international Surrealist exhibition *Poesie 1932* in Prague. From 1945 to 1970 he taught at the Academy of Applied Arts in Prague, where he was the head of the School of Book Design, Poster Art and Calligraphy. His long interest in calligraphy and typography resulted in *Krásné písmo ve vývoji latinky* (1958).

Muzika's work is rooted in the avant-garde tradition between the Wars; it evolved, however, into an individual style of poetic or lyrical Surrealism. After the poetic, naive and later neo-classical style of his early Devětsil years, Muzika went through a period of lyrical Cubism influenced by Picasso in the late 1920s, and in the 1930s approached Surrealism and imaginative painting. During World War II he painted a number of imaginary landscapes, with torsos or fragments of human bodies surrounded by, or growing out of, rocks and stones. After the War his paintings drew their inspiration from elementary microbiological forms; later, in the 1960s, he created several series of *Tumuli*, *Totems*, *Citadels*, *Elsinores* and other evocations of the cult monuments of ancient civilizations. In the late 1960s he added series of *Windstorms*, *Larvae*, *Jellyfish* and *Staircases*. He exhibited widely from the mid-1960s on.

WRITINGS

Krásné písmo ve vývoji latinky [Fine calligraphy in the development of the Roman script], 2 vols (Prague, 1958; Ger. trans., 1965)

BIBLIOGRAPHY

J. Pečírka: *František Muzika* (Prague, 1947)

F. Šmejkal: *František Muzika* (Prague, 1966)

František Muzika (exh. cat., intro. F. Šmejkal; Cologne, Baukst-Gal., 1972)

František Muzika: Kresby [František Muzika: drawings] (exh. cat., intro. F. Šmejkal; Brno, House A., 1978)

František Muzika: Obrazy, kresby, scénické návrhy, knižní grafika [František Muzika: paintings, drawings, stage and book designs] (exh. cat., intro. F. Šmejkal; Prague, N.G., 1981)

F. Šmejkal: *František Muzika: Kresby, scénická a knižní tvorba* [František Muzika: drawings, stage and book designs] (Prague, 1984)

JIŘÍ BUREŠ

Muzio, Giovanni (*b* Milan, 12 Feb 1893; *d* Milan, 21 May 1982). Italian architect. He was the son of the architect Virginio Muzio (*d* 1904), and, after graduating from the Politecnico di Milano (1915), he served during World War I, returning in 1919. He set up practice in Milan in 1920. He was the most influential member of the group of Italian architects associated with the NOVECENTO ITALIANO, both through his numerous buildings and through his writing, although it was not until 1931 (in an article in *Dedalo*) that he expressed the movement's architectural aims. Muzio was invited to design a vast residential building in the Quartiere Moscova in Milan, perhaps the best-known example of Novecento architecture, the Ca' Brutta (completed 1922). Its unflattering name arose from the eccentric display of mannerist intricacy using diverse classical elements across the surfaces of five-storey façades: arches (real and applied), shallow niches, brackets, mock balconies, deep and shallow window recesses, decoratively framed and pedimented or with emblazoned heads, all set out in bands of stucco in restrained colours above a travertine ground floor. The vast site was divided into unequal parts by a new road, which Muzio bridged with a simplified Palladian archway leading into the inner courtyard. A series of buildings in the same vein followed: the Milan Tennis Club (1923–9), the headquarters of the Banca Bergamasca (1924–7; for illustration *see* FASCISM), Bergamo, and a beautifully proportioned house on Via Giuriati (1930), Milan. Also in this early period Muzio was successful in urban development competitions (Milan, 1926, second premium, and Bolzano, 1930, first prize). He was also responsible for exhibition buildings (with Gio Ponti and Mario Sironi) for the Triennale of 1930.

By the 1930s the multiplicity of classical motifs was being abandoned in favour of lightly modelled panels made up of stylized classical features such as shallow pilasters, friezes and mouldings, precisely worked in the characteristic clinker bricks of the region. The most important building of this period on which Muzio worked for 15 years (from 1928) was the Università Cattolica del Sacro Cuore in Milan. It is a model for the efficient planning of complex combinations of spaces and incorporates the Renaissance cloisters of S Ambrogio into a classroom block. The Cinquecento entrance to the university (designed 1929) contrasts markedly with the severe and regular brick façade, at one end of which it is set: it is a pale coloured granite clock and bell tower, set almost flush into the four-storey building. Paired two-storey Tuscan columns flank the entrance archway and are surmounted by a niche and segmental arch to cornice level. An inscribed granite attic panel carries the brick clock-storey and a complete distyle aedile housing the bell. It is an early example of Muzio complementing the modern with the traditional in the same composition. In later blocks, such as the dormitories (1934), he developed the idea further: a square grid is drawn upon the main (stucco) surfaces, which are reminiscent of contemporary *razionalismo* and began to qualify for the name 'geometric Novecento'. It is largely for buildings like these that Muzio is known and many official Fascist buildings in Milan follow this pattern, including the Palazzo dell'Arte (1932–3), Parco Sempione, Milan, and the Palazzo del Popolo d'Italia (1938), Milan. Nevertheless Muzio did occasionally quote literally from the Rationalist vocabulary by using cantilevered roofs and large areas of glazing, especially in utilitarian buildings such as the Barnabone Garage (1934), Lodi, and in some parts of the Palazzo dell'Arte. After World War II, he continued to work until 1979, disdaining obvious modernity, building mainly for the Church: shrines, convents and chapels. From the 1970s his work, with that of others of the Novecento movement, was reassessed, and was viewed by some as precursors of Postmodernism.

WRITINGS

'Alcuni architetti d'oggi in Lombardia', *Dedalo*, xi (1931), pp. 1082–1119; repr. in *Architettura in Italia, 1919–1943: Le polemiche*, ed. L. Patetta (Milan, 1972), pp. 78–86

BIBLIOGRAPHY

G. Mezzanotte: *Giovanni Muzio: Architettura francescana* (Milan, 1974)
G. Contessi: 'Giovanni Muzio: Architetture civili, 1921–1940', *Quad. Archit. & Des.*, 2 (Dec 1979)
R. Airoldi: 'L'idea di architettura nelle opere di Giovanni Muzio (1922–1940)', *Casabella*, 454 (Jan 1980), pp. 56–60
G. Gambirasio and B. Minardi, eds: *Giovanni Muzio, opere e scritti* (Milan, 1982)
G. Muratore, ed.: *Giovanni Muzio, tre case a Milano* (Rome, 1987)

GUIDO ZUCCONI

Myan ma [Myanmar]. *See* BURMA.

Myasoyedov, Grigory (Grigor'yevich) (*b* Pan'kovo, Tula province [now in Orlov region], 19 April 1834; *d* Poltava, Ukraine, 31 Dec 1911). Russian painter. The son of a small village landowner, he studied from 1853 to 1862 at the St Petersburg Academy of Art under Timofey Andreyevich Neff (1805–76) and Aleksey Tarasovich Markov (1802–78). At the end of the 1850s he became friendly with Ivan Kramskoy and his circle of progressive students. Myasoyedov had his first significant success with the painting *Congratulating the Young People in the Landowner's House* (1861; St Petersburg, Rus. Mus.), which is

executed within the traditions of idyllic genre painting of the 1850s. In the competition for the Grand Gold Medal in 1862 Myasoyedov submitted the historical work depicting the *Flight of Grigory Otrep'yev from the Tavern on the Lithuanian Border* (St Petersburg, A. S. Pushkin Apartment Mus.), inspired by a scene in Pushkin's drama *Boris Godunov*. The picture, an attempt at social and historical authenticity, won the artist a six-year scholarship to France, Germany and Italy. In Florence in 1867 Myasoyedov became acquainted with the artist Nicolay Ge and his circle of liberal Russian intellectuals, students and admirers of the writings of Alexander Hertzen and Mikhail Bakunin. In 1869 Myasoyedov and Ge, among others, put forward the idea of forming the WANDERERS (actually founded 1870), with support from Moscow and St Petersburg realist artists. From this time Myasoyedov was intimately involved with the affairs of the Wanderers, and he remained an active member and exhibitor to the end of his life. Myasoyedov became an Academician in 1870, and the decade 1870–80 was a time of great public acclaim for him. With Konstantin Savitsky, Vasily Maksimov and Il'ya Repin, he formed the main principles of Wanderers realism in genre painting: an obligatory socio-analytical approach to the subject, with clearly expressed sympathy towards the peasantry. In the painting of the *Zemstvo at Dinner* (1872; Moscow, Tret'yakov Gal.), his most significant work, he laid bare the roots of social inequality in pre-reform Russia. In numerous works he created a broad gallery of impressive and dignified peasant characters; the beauty and grandeur of peasant labour in *The Scythers* (1887; St Petersburg, Rus. Mus.), for example, transforms them and humanizes nature. The style of Myasoyedov's genre paintings is distinguished by its emotional restraint and severity, and by the accentuated ordinariness of his serious, down-to-earth narrative. He constantly adopted historical subject-matter, as in *The Self-immolators* (1884; Moscow, Tret'yakov Gal.), and he painted portraits and landscapes. During the 1890s Myasoyedov, who had proved unable to adopt the new ideals of the young factions of the Wanderers, occupied an inflexible conservative position in the association, for which he was criticized.

WRITINGS

L. I. Iovleva, ed.: *Grigory Grigor'yevich Myasoyedov: Pis'ma, dokumenty vospominaniya* [Grigory Grigor'yevich Myasoyedov: letters, documents, reminiscences] (Leningrad, 1972)

BIBLIOGRAPHY

I. N. Shuvlova: *Myasoyedov* (Leningrad, 1971)

L. I. IOVLEVA

Myauk U. *See under* ARAKAN.

Mycenae. Site in the north-eastern Peloponnese in southern Greece, 30 km south-west of Corinth. It is renowned for its Late Bronze Age (LBA) palace, tombs and fortifications. In Homeric epic it was the capital city of Agamemnon, leader of the Greek forces at Troy, and it now gives its name to the Mycenaean civilization (*see* HELLADIC, §I, 4(iii)(b)).

In this article relative dates for the Bronze Age are used; for discussion of chronology *see* HELLADIC, §I, 4.

1. INTRODUCTION. Mycenae stands on an isolated hill separated by two ravines from Mt Zara and Mt Ayios Ilias and forms a natural strongpoint controlling the route from the Peloponnese to central Greece. Combined with its proximity to the sea, this made Mycenae the key point on the trade routes between the Aegean and the eastern Mediterranean on one side and Greece and central Europe on the other. Originally occupied in the Neolithic period, the area was thickly settled after Early Helladic (EH) III, and the hill became the seat of increasingly powerful rulers. The first fortification wall was built in Late Helladic (LH) IIIA, turning the rock into a citadel (see fig. 1), and a network of roads was established, leading inland and to the ports. Mycenae soon became a powerful state and the cultural centre of LBA Greece, subordinating many mainland strongholds and Aegean islands, including the Cyclades and Crete (see HELLADIC, §I, 4(iii)(b), CYCLADIC, §I, 4(iii) and MINOAN, §I, 4(iii)). In LH IIIB, at the height of its prosperity, the city was devastated by an earthquake, though most buildings were reconstructed and more were added. A succession of later fires, however, destroyed various structures, which could not be repaired owing to the decline of Mycenaean palace civilization. The site was gradually abandoned in LH IIIC, and Mycenae later re-emerged as a mere village. A few Geometric (c. 900–

c. 700 BC) huts were set up over the ruined palace, followed by an Archaic temple (6th century BC). Small Mycenaean contingents fought at Thermopylai (480 BC) and Plataia (479 BC), but in 468 BC the village was destroyed by the Argives. It was resettled in the 3rd century BC by farmers, who reconstructed the temple and built a theatre and fountain house outside the walls; it was finally deserted after the 2nd century AD. The site was rediscovered in the 18th century, and in 1841 the Archaeological Society at Athens cleared the Lion Gate (figs 1b and 2). Systematic excavations (1874, 1876) were initiated by HEINRICH SCHLIEMANN and have been continued by the Greek Archaeological Society and the British School at Athens.

2. THE SITE OUTSIDE THE CITADEL. On the southern approach is a truncated sub-Mycenaean viaduct across the Chavos ravine, built of flat blocks in almost level courses. The remains of an earlier Cyclopean bridge lie further north. Beyond the ravine, the Panayia ridge and the ground to its west and north are honeycombed with chamber tombs of the LH IIA–LH IIIC periods. There are nine tholos tombs LH I–IIIB. Six, on both sides of the ridge, are named after their architectural forms, location or alleged occupants: the Treasury of Atreus (for illustration see HELLADIC, fig. 5, and THOLOS TOMB), the Tomb of the Genii, the Epano Phournos and Kato Phournos, the Cyclopean Tomb and the Panayia Tomb. Three further tholoi (the

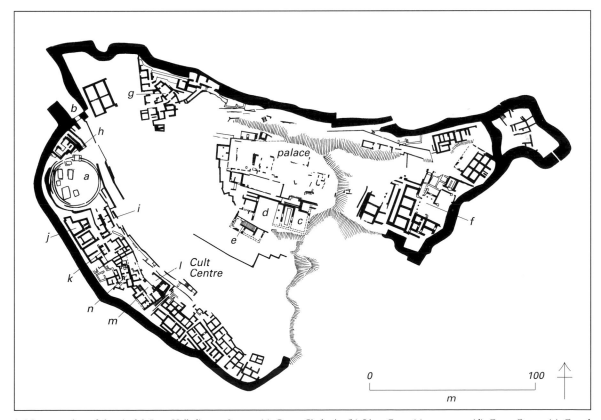

0   100
m

1. Mycenae, plan of the citadel, Late Helladic IIIA:2–IIIC: (a) Grave Circle A; (b) Lion Gate; (c) megaron; (d) Great Court; (e) Grand Staircase; (f) House of Columns; (g) House M; (h) granary; (i) Ramp House; (j) House of the Warrior Vase; (k) South House; (l) temple; (m) Tsountas's House; (n) sanctuaries

2. Mycenae, Lion Gate, LH IIIB

B listing quantities of oil and herbs were found near by (all artefacts now in Athens, N. Archaeol. Mus., unless stated otherwise). Of the other three houses only the basements survive. The House of Sphinxes contained stone vases, ivory inlays and further tablets mentioning spices; the House of the Oil Merchant, where the fire had been fed by the oil stored in jars in the basement, contained 38 inscribed tablets relating to oil, wool, spices and a list of bakers, all fallen from the living-quarters above; and from the House of Shields, built on a massive terrace, came 24 stone vases, cracked and discoloured by the fire. The house at Plakes consisted of a row of four rooms behind a court, with three basement rooms below them. The earthquake precipitated part of it downhill, and its basement rooms were filled with falling debris, which crushed beneath it three adults and a child.

A short distance past the Oil Merchant's quarter the road to the citadel formed a loop around Grave Circle B, which was surrounded by a strong circular wall and contained 14 richly furnished shaft graves, marked with funerary stelai. Between the shafts were 12 individual burials in shallow cists. The enclosure clearly formed part of an MH cemetery that extended eastwards to the foot of the citadel hill. There lay the other royal burial enclosure, Grave Circle A (see fig. 1a) containing six shaft graves and mistakenly identified by Schliemann as belonging to Agamemnon and his entourage. Grave Circle B predates it by a generation or two, but they were used concurrently during the LH I period, when the Tomb of Aigisthos was also built near by. In LH IIA Shaft Grave Rho in Grave Circle B was dug up and extended to accommodate a built tomb of a type otherwise known only from Cyprus and Ugarit. Then when the Tomb of Klytemnestra was built (LH IIIB), its dome demolished part of the enclosure of the no longer visible Grave Circle B. The last three tholos tombs (i.e. the Treasury of Atreus, the Tomb of the Genii and the Tomb of Klytemnestra), built in the same style as the citadel's Lion Gate (see fig. 2), have walls of square-cut blocks lining their entrance passages, ashlar façades with sculptural decoration and vaults of polished conglomerate ashlars laid in regular horizontal courses. The use of sawn blocks of locally quarried conglomerate is a feature unique to Mycenaean architecture when compared with that of other Helladic sites.

Tomb of Aigisthos, the Tomb of Klytemnestra and the Lion Tomb) are situated on the west slope of the citadel hill. Near by are the House of Lead, Lisa's House and the Panayia houses. Further north lies the Oil Merchant's quarter, and some distance north-west of the citadel were Petsas' House (probably a potter's workshop) and the House of the Wine Merchant. One more house was excavated at Plakes, on the west slope of Mt Ayios Ilias. Only the Panayia houses, the Oil Merchant's quarter and the Plakes house have been thoroughly investigated. The first two groups were built along the ancient road to the citadel, in an area already settled in Middle Helladic (MH) times and reoccupied in LH IIB–IIIB. The Panayia group consists of three houses (LH IIIB) built close together. Of these, House I is a megaron-type building (see MEGARON) fronted by a small court. In LH IIIB it was destroyed by the earthquake, as were House II and House III, which have less clear and more cramped plans. Both the latter were repaired, but House II was burnt down shortly afterwards. House III survived in use for some time.

The Oil Merchant's quarter (LH IIIB) was a complex comprising four buildings, all eventually destroyed by fire: the House of the Oil Merchant, the House of Sphinxes and the House of Shields were built in a row and are named after some oil jars, some ivory plaques representing sphinxes and some others representing shields found in their ruins. Behind them and higher up the slope is the West House, the earliest of the group. Built partly on top of an MH structure, it had a paved court in front of a megaron, which was separated by a corridor from a row of five rooms along its west side. Behind its rear wall there was a large double fireplace, which clearly formed part of a perfume workshop, since clay tablets inscribed in Linear

3. THE CITADEL. MH graves and remains of buildings on the west, north and north-east slopes of the citadel hill show that at the time of the grave circles it was already inhabited, and some rock cuttings on the summit suggest that there may have been a palace there. The hill, however, was not fortified until LH IIIA, when the first Cyclopean circuit wall was built along the brow of the rock. The main gate seems to have been above Grave Circle A, with another entrance at the north-east corner. About this time the peak was surrounded with terraces built to support a new palace, approached by a stairway on the north side. The south-west fortification wall was dismantled in LH IIIB, and a new entrance, the Lion Gate (see figs 1b and 2 above), was erected, protected by an outwork on the right. The regular courses of rectangular stone blocks around the Lion Gate and the North Gate contrast strikingly with the rough Cyclopean masonry of the earlier fortification

wall. From the outwork a new wall was built around the foot of the hill, taking in the west slope and Grave Circle A, which was filled in to the level of the new entrance and embellished with a parapet of stone slabs. Inside the gate, a steep ramp rising southwards replaced the old approach to the palace, while another gate, also flanked by an outwork, was built in the north wall. In LH IIIB the fortifications were extended to the north-east, mainly to protect the underground fountain that provided the citadel with a constant supply of water. Meanwhile, the palace, which had been damaged by fire, was repaired and extended by the addition of a megaron (1c; for illustration of plan *see* MEGARON) and the Great Court (1d) on the south side, accessible through a new approach, the Grand Staircase (1e). It expanded also to the east as far as the circuit wall. In its final form, it comprised four wings, separated by corridors and open spaces. The north wing, of which practically nothing survives, apparently housed the royal quarters, while the middle area formed a terrace in front of them and the south wing contained the state apartments. Workshops, store-rooms, the House of Columns (1f) and two other structures were located in the east wing. All were destroyed by fire in LH IIIB but were immediately repaired and reoccupied. House M (1g), built on the north slope after the reconstruction of the palace and used until its final abandonment, seems to have been another palace dependency. Three further houses within the circuit wall above the Lion Gate were damaged by the great earthquake and are preserved only to basement level.

Buildings on the west slope include the granary (1h), the Ramp House (1i), the House of the Warrior Vase (1j) and the South House (1k). All date from LH IIIB, were built around Grave Circle A (1a) and continued in use until LH IIIC, after being damaged and rebuilt. The block of buildings next to the South House constituted the cult centre of the citadel, accessible by a processional road leading to a square temple (1l), which had an altar and a flat stone in front of it. At a later date the walls of the temple had to be reinforced from inside, while the altar area was filled in, and a new altar was erected near the precinct's entrance. From the temple, a few steps led down to Tsountas's House (1m; named after its excavator), which was probably occupied by a religious official. Lower still were LH IIIB sanctuaries (1n) containing idols (Navplion, Archaeol. Mus.) and religious frescoes, organized around a small court with a circular altar in the middle. Soon after the sanctuaries' construction, the altar was buried under an accumulation of debris and plastered over with white clay, while the doors to the court were blocked. Some walls, however, were shored up, and new floors were laid, and the shrines continued in use until they were burnt in LH IIIB:2, together with Tsountas's House and part of an adjacent building to the south. The area was then reoccupied until the citadel was finally abandoned. Further south the slope was covered with houses, built in LH IIIB and arranged in superimposed levels. No traces of burning are apparent, and the houses were finally deserted without having been destroyed.

For further discussion of Mycenaean architecture *see* HELLADIC, §II.

4. ARTEFACTS. The best works of Late Helladic (LH) art were found at Mycenae. They come from three main find groups, which succeed and complement each other: the royal shaft graves (LH I); the chamber tombs of the civilian population (LH I–IIIC); and the non-funerary buildings (LH IIIB–IIIC). The first group reflects the impact of Minoan and Cycladic artistic styles on the plain MH local styles at a stage when the copying of Cretan prototypes had given way to the attempt to master foreign techniques and to amalgamate the Minoan elegance of style with Helladic subject-matter, full of action and movement.

By LH II, however, Mycenaean artists had developed their own artistic tradition, distinguished by the tectonic arrangement of shapes and by frugal ornament, evolving from realism to formal stylization. The magnificent hammered, inlaid and cloisonné gold and silver artefacts from the shaft graves (see fig. 3) are followed by the silver cup inlaid with bulls' heads in gold and niello (probably LH IIIB) and by the repoussé, granulated and enamelled jewellery from the chamber tombs. The masterpieces of ivory-carving, such as the tusk engraved with a man and a tree flanked by ibexes (probably LH IIIA–B), also found in the chamber tombs, were paralleled by artefacts from the houses and palace, including a group of two women (apparently goddesses) and a child (LH II or IIIA; *see* HELLADIC, fig. 16). The only surviving larger-scale sculptures, however, are the primitive stelai, carved in low relief, from the grave circles, the fragmentary decoration from

3. Mycenae, 'Lion Hunt' dagger, bronze with inlaid decoration of gold, niello and silver, l. 240 mm, from Grave Circle A, LH I (Athens, National Archaeological Museum)

the façade of the Treasury of Atreus (London, BM), the Lion Relief, and the plaster head from the cult area (LH IIIB; *see* HELLADIC, fig. 14).

The buildings were decorated with frescoes representing scenes of battle, hunting or ritual processions, of which the fragment known as the '*Mykenaia*' (LH IIIB; *see* HELLADIC, fig. 1) is justly famous for the elegance of its pose and its fine workmanship. Nothing of quality seems to have been created after LH IIIB.

BIBLIOGRAPHY

H. Schliemann: *Mykenae* (Leipzig, 1878/*R* Darmstadt, 1966)
A. J. B. Wace and others: 'Excavations at Mycenae', *Annu. Brit. Sch. Athens*, xxv (1921–3) [whole vol.]
G. Karo: *Die Schachtgräber von Mykenai* (Munich, 1930–33)
A. J. B. Wace: *Chamber Tombs at Mycenae* (Oxford, 1932)
——: *Mycenae: An Archaeological History and Guide* (Princeton, 1949)
G. E. Mylonas: *Ancient Mycenae: The Capital City of Agamemnon* (Princeton, 1957)
——: *Mycenae and the Mycenaean Age* (Princeton, 1966)
——: *O Taphikos Kyklos B ton Mykenon* [Grave Circle B at Mycenae] (Athens, 1973) [Eng. summary]
W. D. Taylour: *The Excavations* (1981), i of *Well-built Mycenae* (Warminster, 1981–)
S. E. Iakovidis: *Late Helladic Citadels on Mainland Greece* (Leiden, 1983), pp. 23–72
G. E. Mylonas: *Mycenae Rich in Gold* (Athens, 1983)
A. Xenaki-Sakellariou: *Oi thalamokoi taphoi ton Mykenon: Anaskaphes Chr. Tsountas, 1887–1898* [The chamber tombs of Mycenae: excavations of C. Tsountas, 1887–1898] (Paris, 1985) [Fr. summary]
I. Mylonas-Shear: *The Panagia Houses at Mycenae* (Philadelphia, 1987)

Mycenaean [Achaean]. Civilization that flourished in the Late Bronze Age (*c.* 1600–*c.* 1100 BC) on the Greek mainland. *See* HELLADIC, esp. §I, 4(iii).

☐

Mycerinus (*reg c.* 2490–*c.* 2472 BC). Egyptian king of the 4th Dynasty (*c* 2475–*c.* 2465 BC), whose pyramid was the third and smallest of the group at Giza (*see* GIZA, §1). The tomb of Mycerinus may have actually been more extravagant than those of his predecessors, since he seems to have intended to case it entirely in red granite. However, he died before the pyramid could be completed, and its upper courses were cased in limestone, while the attached temple complex was finished in mud brick by his successor, Shepseskaf (*reg c.* 2472–*c.* 2465 BC).

Mycerinus' complex, as was typical for the period, consisted of a mortuary temple at the base of the pyramid's eastern face, a valley temple at the western edge of the cultivated fields and a causeway connecting the two (for a plan of the temple *see* EGYPT, ANCIENT, fig. 37). Here the cult of the dead king was enacted throughout the Old Kingdom, despite the encroachment of the houses of his funerary priests into most of the available space in the valley temple. When the site was excavated by George Reisner, between 1906 and 1909, a stele of King Pepy II (*reg c.* 2246–*c.* 2150 BC) of the 6th Dynasty was found at the entrance to the complex. The inscription on the stele exempted the inhabitants from taxes and forced labour.

The major finds of the excavation, however, were the fine statue groups that originally decorated the valley temple and are now divided between the Egyptian Museum, Cairo, and the Museum of Fine Arts, Boston. The most interesting of these are six triads (two fragmentary) of greywacke, each depicting the king with a figure representing one of the provinces and the goddess Hathor, who was worshipped as Mistress of the Sycamore near by. These triads were probably part of a larger series demonstrating the king's dominion over all parts of Egypt. The presence of Hathor may be related to the growth of the sun cult, in which she played an important role in the 5th Dynasty (*c.* 2465–*c.* 2325 BC). A dyad in the same stone represents Mycerinus with his queen; this is one of the greatest masterpieces of Egyptian sculpture, despite its unfinished condition (Boston, MA, Mus. F.A.; see fig.).

There were also several statues of the king carved in white alabaster, from both the valley temple and the mortuary temple, including an oddly proportioned colossal seated figure that was presumably the main cult statue of the mortuary temple. Traces of paint on all of these sculptures suggest that the dramatic contrast between the colour of their materials was less obvious in antiquity.

According to some accounts, a small statue of Mycerinus (Cairo, Egyp. Mus.) was taken from the Ptah Temple at the capital city of Memphis. This king may therefore also have contributed to the buildings there.

BIBLIOGRAPHY

L. Borchardt: *Statuen und Statuetten von Königen und Privatleuten im Museum von Kairo*, i (Berlin, 1911), p. 39, pl. 11
G. A. Reisner: *Mycerinus: The Temples of the Third Pyramid at Giza* (Cambridge, 1931), pp. 49–54
W. Wood: 'A Reconstruction of the Triads of Mycerinus', *J. Egyp. Archaeol.*, lx (1974), pp. 82–93
P. Lacovara and C. N. Reeves: 'The Colossal Statue of Mycerinus Reconsidered', *Rev. Egyp.*, xxxviii (1987), pp. 111–15

ANN MACY ROTH

Myers, Elijah E. (*b* Philadelphia, 22 Dec 1832; *d* Detroit, 5 March 1909). American architect. Having worked as a carpenter in Philadelphia, he studied architecture in the office of Samuel Sloan and at the Franklin Institute, Philadelphia. His career as an architect began after the Civil War, during which he served as an engineer in the Union Army. He designed a number of churches, hospitals, city halls, court-houses and, most notably, several state capitols. For a short time he had an office in Springfield, IL, where he won the competition for the design of the Michigan State Capitol (1873–9), Lansing; he moved to Detroit to supervise construction of this building, which is in the Renaissance Revival style on a cruciform plan. He went on to win competitions for the Idaho Territorial Capitol (1885), Boise, and the Colorado State Capitol (1890–96), Denver, also to Renaissance Revival designs. His most important work is the Texas Capitol (1882–8), Austin, similarly inspired by the US Capitol (1792–1830, 1855–65), Washington, DC. Built with walls faced on the exterior with pink granite, the Texas Capitol is a monumental work on a cruciform plan, 171 m long and 87 m wide. It is crowned with a colonnaded drum and a hemispherical dome terminated with a lantern. Myers's career was shadowed by accusations of malpractice, but his Renaissance Revival public buildings rank high among 19th-century civic architecture in America.

BIBLIOGRAPHY

The Michigan State Capitol, Michigan Historical Commission (Lansing, 1969)
M. A. K. Koellner: *Elijah E. Myers (1832–1909): Architect* (MA thesis, Macomb, W. IL U., 1972)

King Mycerinus and Queen Khamerernebt, greywacke with traces of paint, h. 1.42 m, *c.* 2480 BC (Boston, MA, Museum of Fine Arts)

W. B. Robinson: *Texas Public Buildings of the Nineteenth Century* (Austin, 1974)
P. Goeldner: 'The Designing Architect: Elijah E. Myers', *SW Hist. Q.*, xcii (1988), pp. 271–87

WILLARD B. ROBINSON

Myers, George Hewitt (*b* Cleveland, OH, 10 Sept 1875; *d* Washington, DC, 23 Dec 1957). American collector. An heir to the Bristol–Myers pharmaceutical fortune, Myers began collecting Oriental carpets while an undergraduate at Yale University, New Haven, CT. He began to collect seriously from 1909, and in 1925 he founded The Textile Museum, housed in the residence that JOHN RUSSELL POPE had designed for him in Washington, DC, and the adjacent structure. His collection then comprised 275 carpets, and he continued to enrich the museum until his death, when it included some five hundred carpets and thousands of textiles. Avoiding in large part the acquisition of then fashionable and costly showpieces, Myers built a collection of historical and traditional textiles from Asia and Central and South America that is virtually without parallel in its richness and quality.

BIBLIOGRAPHY
S. P. Collins: 'George Hewitt Myers, 1875–1957', *Hali*, xxvii (1985), pp. 6–7
M. McWilliam: 'One Man's Romance with Fiber Created the Textile Museum', *Smithsonian*, xvii/12 (March 1987), pp. 109–17

WALTER B. DENNY

Mylne. Scottish family of masons and architects. Their involvement in construction stretched over ten generations and 300 years, from its obscure beginnings in the 15th century to the 18th, the most notable member being (1) Robert Mylne the younger. John Mylne I (*d* 1621), son of Thomas Mylne, Master Mason of Dundee, was a Burgess of Dundee, Freeman of Perth, Master of the mason's lodge at Scone and, like his father, Master Mason to the king of Scotland. His known works include the elegant, polygonal Dundee Mercat Cross (1586) and the Tay Bridge (1604; destr. 1621) at Perth. His son John Mylne II (*d* 1657), Master of the Scone Lodge and Burgess of both Dundee and Edinburgh, was involved in church and fortification repair. Although his known works include the re-erection of the Mercat Cross (1617), Edinburgh, and two elaborate sundials in the Scots necromantic tradition—Drummond Castle (1630) and Holyrood (1633)—his main significance lies in his involvement in the family's sizeable firm of masons, which worked on crown contracts throughout Scotland for most of the 17th century. John Mylne III (1611–67) succeeded his father, John Mylne II, as Master Mason to the King in 1636 and rose to prominence as a member of the Scottish Parliament and as a Commissioner to negotiate a treaty of union with England. His notable legacy includes a new openwork spire or crown (1648) for St Giles' Cathedral, Edinburgh; the great Cromwellian citadel of Leith (1649–50; a gate survives); works at Heriot's Hospital and at Holyrood House in Edinburgh; the delightful Cowane's Hospital (1637), Stirling; the strikingly Netherlandish Tron Church (1637–47; altered 1728 and 1824)—a T-plan building with inventive Late Gothic tracery, classical pilasters and doorway, and splendid roof; Fort Charlotte (1665), Lerwick—an advanced pentagonal design; and Panmure House

(from 1666; destr. 1960), Angus, the drawings for which reveal a modern plan beneath Scottish trappings, the first of a group of late 17th-century houses characterized by a front of twin gables tied together by a balustraded, flat-roofed centre.

Robert Mylne I (1633–1710) succeeded his uncle John Mylne III as Master Mason to the King in 1668. His field of activity was similar to that of his predecessors, except for his excursion into speculation in desirable high-density courtyard developments, for example at Mylne's Court (1690), Lawnmarket, and Milne's Square, High Street, Edinburgh, and his work (from 1671) on the new palace of Holyrood House from 1671, nominally as Master Mason under William Bruce (although Mylne not only drew but also signed the plans). He also worked with Bruce for the Duke of Lauderdale at Thirlestane (*c.* 1670–80), Lauder, and Ham House (*c.* 1682), Surrey. He repaired Edinburgh Castle (1662–85), worked with his uncle on the great Leslie Palace (*c.* 1667–8), Fife, provided a new Mercat Cross in Perth (1688), extended Wemyss Castle (1669–72), Fife, and designed the Trotter tombstone (1709) in Greyfriars' churchyard, Edinburgh. In 1679 his daughter Janet Mylne, 'a good drawer and very clever', married the rising architect James Smith, and Robert may have withdrawn to allow his son-in-law to prosper. Robert's son William Mylne I (1662–1728) and grandson Thomas Mylne (*d* 1763) were both masons, but his great-grandsons Robert Mylne the younger and William Mylne II (1734–90) rose further, with William designing the bridge (1759) at Fernilee, Selkirk, and assisting with Jamaica Bridge (1768), Glasgow, before emigrating to the USA. He returned to become engineer to Dublin Water Works.

(1) Robert Mylne the younger (*b* Edinburgh, 4 Jan 1733; *d* London, 5 May 1811). He travelled with his brother William Mylne I to Rome in 1754, hoping to become an architect. In 1758 he won the Silver Medal for architecture at the Accademia di S Luca, and he became a member of the academies of Rome, Florence and Bologna before returning to London in 1759. He won the competition of 1760 for Blackfriars Bridge, London, with a design spanning the Thames in nine arches, the piers being decorated with Ionic columns. He was also involved with the Gloucester and Berkeley Ship Canal and the Worcester Canal (1790), and he designed twelve other bridges, including Jamaica Bridge (1768–72), Glasgow, two bridges at Inveraray, Strathclyde, and major ones in Hexham (1785–93), Northumb., and Newcastle upon Tyne (1774–81). In 1767 he became Surveyor to the New River Company, and later to St Paul's Cathedral and the Stationers' Company (both in London), and to Canterbury Cathedral. Elected FRS in 1767, he became a prominent member of the Society of Civil Engineers.

Mylne's public buildings include St Cecilia's Hall (1761), Cowgate, Edinburgh, the City of London Hospital (1770) and Stationers Hall (1800), London. The simple temple-like church of 1795 at Inveraray is notable for containing two separate churches: one Scottish and one Gaelic, entered from either end. Other work at Inveraray included the gorgeous redecoration (from 1782) of the castle's principal reception rooms, the semi-circular Maam Steading of farm buildings (1787), some tenements within the town and the great screen wall (1787) facing Loch Fyne. He was also a fashionable country house architect, although only nine of his forty-eight such commissions were in Scotland. He provided probably no more than a sketch for the flamboyantly castellated Blaise Castle (1766), near Bristol, and preferred a spare elegance that looked forward to later Neo-classicism: the grandeur of the hall (1763) at Cally, Dumfriesshire, was one example of this approach, which was developed more fully at the tall, austere Tusmore Park (1760; destr. 1960), Oxon. His grandest town house was at 1 Stratton Street (1763; destr. 1925), Westminster, London. He was also commissioned for significant alterations to 15 buildings, notably Wormleybury (1767), Herts; Addington (1773), Surrey; and Bickley Place (1780), Kent. His son William Mylne III (1781–1863) succeeded him as Surveyor to the Stationers Hall and the New River Company; for the latter William developed Myddleton Square, Inglebert Street and River Street, Amwell, with St Mark's Church (1826) and the Charity School. He was also responsible for Harpole Rectory (1816) and Flint House (1842), Amwell, and he was elected an FRS in 1826. His own son William Mylne IV (1817–90) was also an architect and engineer.

BIBLIOGRAPHY

Colvin
R. S. Mylne: *The Master Masons to the Crown of Scotland* (Edinburgh, 1893)
W. G. Blaikie Murdoch: 'A Scottish Architect of the Caroline Period: John Mylne, 1611–1667', *Royal Incorp. Architects Scotland, Q*, xliv (1933), pp. 5–10
C. McKean and D. Walker: *Dundee: An Illustrated Architectural Guide* (Edinburgh, 1984)

CHARLES MCKEAN

Myn, van der. *See* MIJN, VAN DER.

Myohaung. *See under* ARAKAN.

Myōman Mokujiki [Mokujiki Gogyō; Mokujiki Gyōdō; Mokujiki Meiman] (*b* Marubatake, Kai Province [now Yamashi Prefecture], 1718; *d* 1810). Japanese sculptor and Buddhist monk. He was an ascetic priest of the Shingon sect (*see* BUDDHISM, §III, 10) during the Edo period (1600–1868) and apparently functioned as an itinerant monk (*hijiri*) in early adulthood. At the age of 45 he took vows as a 'wood-eater' (*mokujiki*), one who abstained not only from meat, fish and fowl but also from grains, eating only nuts, roots and berries. In 1773, after taking an additional vow to travel throughout Japan, he embarked on a programme of missionary activity that took him from Hokkaido in the north to Kyushu in the south. Mokujiki was already in his early 60s when he began sculpting devotional images for the communities he visited, apparently following the example of his predecessor ENKŪ. Interestingly, he avoided localities where Enkū had made images. Mokujiki enjoyed excellent health and continued to produce sculptures until he was over 90 years old.

The sculpture of Mokujiki was rediscovered during the Taishō period (1912–26) by MUNEYOSHI YANAGI, the founder of the MINGEI (folk art) movement (*see also* JAPAN, §XV, 1). By this chance association, Mokujiki's work was placed within the folk tradition, which was not strictly its source. Mokujiki's earliest carving was somewhat awkward, but he rapidly developed a studied and polished style characterized by a fluid, curvilinear treatment of the surfaces, and to this style he clung, with little variation, for some 30 years. Notable examples of his work are the *Fudō* (Skt Acala; Tokyo, Flk Crafts Mus.) and the *Sixteen Rakan* (Skt *arhat*; enlightened persons; Kyoto, Yagi, Seigenji). The extensive documentation available for Mokujiki, including detailed diaries of his travels, makes his career invaluable for the study of Buddhism in the Edo period.

BIBLIOGRAPHY

M. Yanagi: *Mokujiki Gogyō shōnin ryakuden* [A short biography of the priest Mokujiki] (Tokyo, 1925)
S. Gorai: *Bishō butsu: Mokujiki no shōgai* [The smiling Buddha: the life of Mokujiki] (Kyoto, 1966)
M. Honma: *Enkū to Mokujiki* [Enkū and Mokujiki], Nihon no bijutsu: Butsukusu obu butsukusu [Book of books], xxxv (Tokyo, 1974)
T. Kuno: *Sekibutsu* [Buddhist stone sculpture], Nihon no bijutsu: Butsukusu obu butsukusu [Book of books], xxxvi (Tokyo, 1975)

DONALD F. MCCALLUM

Myōjō. *See* FUJIWARA (ii), (7).

Myra. Site in LYCIA, Turkey, 1.5 km north of Demre. The inscriptions and rock-cut tombs indicate that it was an important settlement at least as early as the 5th century BC. In the 2nd century BC it became a member of the Lycian League and continued to flourish under Roman rule (1st century BC–3rd century AD). The miracles performed by its bishop, St Nicholas (*b c.* 300), brought Myra widespread fame, and under Theodosios II (*reg* 408–50) it became the provincial capital of Lycia. The rock-cut tombs include a wide variety of types that imitate local wooden and masonry techniques.

Among the more elaborate examples are seven tombs decorated with external reliefs that reflect the process of Hellenization in the 4th century BC. Contrary to earlier scholarly opinion, the façades of these tombs are not based on Lycian houses or Greek temples, but on the banqueting halls within Lycian dwellings. The reliefs frequently contain lifesize figures in a mixed setting such as that of a battle scene combined with a funeral repast.

The town's prosperity under the Romans is demonstrated by the marble sarcophagi imported from Athens and Pamphylia (south-west Turkey) and by the theatre (diam. 120 m), much of which is well preserved, including the stage building with its frieze of theatrical masks. Myra's importance in the administration of imperial grain is reflected by Hadrian's granary (60×30 m) in the harbour of Andriake, 2.5 km to the south-west.

At the western edge of Demre is the church of Hagios Nikolaos (?8th century) with a crypt that may date to the time of the bishop. The present building has undergone many alterations and repairs; it contains a late example of a synthronon and is decorated with mosaics and wall paintings of church councils, Apostles, a warrior saint, a *Harrowing of Hell* and a *Dormition*, as well as rich architectural ornament of various dates within the Byzantine period.

BIBLIOGRAPHY

E. Petersen and F. von Luschan: *Reisen im südwestlichen Kleinasien*, ii (1889), pp. 28ff
G. Anrich: *Hagios Nikolaos: Der heilige Nikolaos in der griechischen Kirche*, 2 vols (Leipzig, 1913–17)
U. Peschlow: 'Die Kirche des hl. Nikolaos in Myra', *Ant. Welt*, v (1974), pp. 15–25

J. Borchhardt: *Myra. Eine lykische Metropole in antiker und byzantinischer Zeit* (Berlin, 1975)
C. Bruns-Özgan: *Lykische Grabreliefs des 5. und 4. Jahrhunderts v. Chr.* (Tübingen, 1987)

JURGEN BORCHHARDT

Myricenis [Myricinus, Myriginus], **Petrus.** *See* HEYDEN, PIETER VAN DER.

Myron of Eleutherai (*fl c.* 470–*c.* 440 BC). Greek sculptor. He was a leading Early Classical bronze sculptor of the Attic school (*see also* GREECE, ANCIENT, §III, 2(iii)(a)). Pliny (*Natural History* XXIV.xix.49) dated his floruit to 420–417 BC, but this is probably inaccurate. The only firm dates for his career are statues of Olympic victors in 456 BC, 448 BC and perhaps 444 BC. Epigraphic evidence suggests that his son Lykios was active in the 440s and 430s BC. These dates suggest that Myron began his career around 470 BC at the latest, and there is no evidence that he worked after *c.* 440 BC.

Later writers counted Myron among the most distinguished Greek sculptors, listing him, together with Pheidias and Polykleitos, as a pupil of Agelades of Argos and comparing him to Pythagoras of Rhegion, perhaps a slightly older contemporary, as a rival (Pliny: *Natural History* XXXIV.xix.57–9). In their analyses of the development of sculptural forms, Cicero (*Brutus* xviii.70) and Quintilian (*Principles of Oratory* XII.x.7) placed him after Kalamis but before Polykleitos. An obscure passage in Pliny's *Natural History* (XXXIV.xix.58) indicates that the sculptor considerably expanded the compositional repertory and that, in the number of his formal schemes and possibly also in the methods used to determine their proportions, he contrasted with Polykleitos. Indeed, the subject-matter of the works attributed to him suggests a range and versatility unequalled among Early Classical sculptors.

Myron's statues of athletes were greatly admired, especially that of the runner *Ladas* (untraced). Its daring pose and sense of physical exertion were celebrated in epigrams (*Greek Anthology: Planudean Appendix* IV.54; Catullus, *Poems* lviiib.3), suggesting similarities with his *Diskobolos* (Discus-thrower). The latter was described in detail by Lucian (*Philopseudeis* xviii) and has been securely identified in Roman copies (e.g. Rome, Mus. N. Romano; *see* GREECE, ANCIENT, fig. 38). The most famous example of Myron's ability to imbue sculpture with an almost deceptive naturalism was his *Heifer* on the Athenian Acropolis. His statues of divinities, however, were criticized for a lack of spiritual depth. His colossal *Apollo* at Ephesos (untraced) and the mid-5th century BC group of the *Introduction of Herakles to Olympos* at Samos, the base of which still survives, indicate his willingness to experiment in scale as well as in pose. Another *Apollo* was a prized possession of the people of Akragas. A group of *Athena and Marsyas* attributed by Pliny to Myron (*Natural History* XXXIV.xix.57) was probably the one seen by Pausanias (*Guide to Greece* I.xxiv.1) on the Athenian Acropolis. The modern restoration of the group from Roman copies of individual figures (*Athena*, Frankfurt am Main, Liebieghaus; *Marsyas*, Rome, Vatican, Mus. Gregoriano Profano) is usually accepted as correct, though doubts still remain (see Carpenter). Surviving marble heads (London,

BM; Rome, Mus. Conserv.) may be copies of his famous *Perseus after the Killing of Medusa*, which stood on the Athenian Acropolis (Pausanias: *Guide to Greece* I.xxiii.8). The Riccardi *Hero* (Rome, Villa Borghese) may also be based on his work, since it is similar to the head of the *Diskobolos*. Attempts to identify copies of figures from the Samian group, however, have proved unconvincing. It is plausible that Myron's skills were needed for architectural sculptures during the mid-5th-century BC Periclean building programme at Athens; the metopes of the Hephaisteion and the south metopes of the Parthenon have subjects in which his talent for momentary poses and for animal sculpture would have been put to good use.

BIBLIOGRAPHY
Enc. A. Ant.; Pauly–Wissowa; Thieme–Becker
R. Carpenter: 'Observations on Familiar Statuary in Rome', *Mem. Amer. Acad. Rome*, xviii (1941), pp. 3–25
B. S. Ridgway: *The Severe Style in Greek Sculpture* (Princeton, NJ, 1970), pp. 84–6
M. Robertson: *A History of Greek Art* (Cambridge, 1975), pp. 339–44

CHARLES M. EDWARDS

Myrtos. Village on the river of the same name on the south coast of Crete, 17 km from Ierapetra. It has two important Minoan settlements (Pyrgos and Phournou Koriphi), as well as a large Roman baths (2nd century AD) and residential area, both with mosaic pavements. Pyrgos, half a kilometre east of the modern village, on a prominent hill above the mouth of the river, was a long-lived (Early Minoan [EM] II to Late Minoan [LM] I, *c.* 2900/2600–*c.* 1425 BC) and prosperous settlement measuring at least 95×70 m. Excavated by G. Cadogan, largely between 1970 and 1973, the settlement has four principal Minoan phases, of which three (Pyrgos I: EM II, *c.* 2900/2600–*c.* 2200 BC; Pyrgos III: Middle Minoan [MM] II–III, *c.* 1800–*c.* 1600 BC; Pyrgos IV: LM I, *c.* 1600–*c.* 1425 BC) ended in the site's destruction by fire.

The earliest architectural remains are of Pyrgos II (EM III–MM I, *c.* 2200–*c.* 1800 BC), when a house-like communal tomb, similar to those at GOURNIA and MOCHLOS, was built at the south-west corner of the settlement, with a paved yard approached by a stairway and road from the top of the hill. A clay dove rhyton (Knossos, Stratig. Mus.) was part of a probable foundation deposit for this tomb, which continued in use intermittently throughout the Minoan occupation of the settlement. Pyrgos III shared a pottery style, and probably a regional culture, with Mallia, Gournia and other sites in and around the Lasithi Mountains. Finds included a remarkable lobed kantharos (Herakleion, Archaeol. Mus.) containing miniature versions of the same shape. The principal extant monuments of Pyrgos III are two cisterns and a square tower.

In Pyrgos IV a grand country house (which may have had a predecessor in Pyrgos III) built in ashlar masonry was terraced into the hilltop above the settlement, facing south across a courtyard towards the Libyan Sea, its position comparable to that of the contemporary 'palace' at Gournia. Its architecture displays interesting polychrome effects. At the heart of the building is a light well bordered by a gypsum staircase with a stepped parapet, as in the palace at Knossos. A gypsum bench faces the light well. A room on an upper floor probably served as a shrine; its contents included a Linear A tablet (Ayios

Nikolaos, Archaeol. Mus.), a red-glazed faience triton shell (Herakleion, Archaeol. Mus.) comparable to one from Grave Circle A at Mycenae (Athens, N. Archaeol. Mus.), two clay sealings (Herakleion, Archaeol. Mus.), a Marine style jug (LM IB, c. 1480–c. 1425 BC) and four clay tubular stands, with fixed or movable bowls for offerings (Herakleion, Archaeol. Mus.). However, no cult image was found. Another upstairs room, above the house's storerooms, contained stone vases, a pair of elaborate clay amphorae with decoration copying similar vases in marble and three Cycladic jugs, probably imported from Thera (all in Knossos, Stratig. Mus.). The Pyrgos IV settlement was built with streets following the contours of the hill and with a block system comparable to that at Gournia. Objects discovered there include a Cycladic Black-and-Red bird jug and a large globular alabastron with conglomerate decoration (LM IB; Knossos, Stratig. Mus.). A Hellenistic shrine (from Pyrgos V) of Hermes and Aphrodite was built over the ruins of the country house. On top of that stood Pyrgos VI, the Venetian and Turkish watchtower (Gr. *pyrgos*) that gives the site its name.

Phournou Koriphi is about 2 km east of Pyrgos. Uncovered by P. Warren in 1967–8, it is the only completely excavated EM II settlement. Some 90 rooms and associated spaces have been preserved in an area of about 55×35 m, representing two EM II phases of occupation. As at Pyrgos, the second phase ended in destruction by fire, but, unlike Pyrgos, Phournou Koriphi was not reoccupied except by a solitary circular building on the top of the hill (date and function uncertain). Finds from Phournou Koriphi provide important evidence for dating the earliest Minoan stone vases and seals. A vase in the shape of a goddess (Ayios Nikolaos, Archaeol. Mus.) from the settlement's shrine holds a miniature jug of the Myrtos ware type used during EM II at both the Myrtos settlements.

BIBLIOGRAPHY

G. Cadogan: 'Clay Tubes in Minoan Religion', *Praktika tou tritou diethnous Kritologikou synedriou· Rethymnon, 1971* [Proceedings of the third international Cretan congress: Rethymnon, 1971], i, pp. 34–8

P. Warren: *Myrtos: An Early Bronze Age Settlement in Crete*, British School at Athens Suppl. Paper, vii (London, 1972)

V. Hankey: 'Stone Vessels at Myrtos Pyrgos', *Praktika tou tetartou diethnous Kritologikou synedriou: Heraklio, 1976* [Proceedings of the fourth international Cretan congress: Herakleion, 1976], i, pp. 210–15

G. Cadogan: 'Pyrgos, Crete, 1970–77', *J. Archaeol. Rep.*, xxiv (1977–8), pp. 70–84

T. M. Whitelaw: *Community Structure and Social Organization at Fournou Korifi, Myrtos* (MA thesis, U. Southampton, 1979)

G. Cadogan: 'A Probable Shrine in the Country House at Pyrgos', *Sanctuaries and Cults in the Aegean Bronze Age: Proceedings of the First International Symposium at the Swedish Institute: Athens, 1980*, pp. 169–71

T. M. Whitelaw: 'The Settlement at Fournou Korifi, Myrtos and Aspects of Early Minoan Social Organization', *Minoan Society: Proceedings of the Cambridge Colloquium: Cambridge, 1981*, pp. 323–45

I. F. Sanders: *Roman Crete* (Warminster, 1982), pp. 18, 138

V. Hankey: 'Pyrgos: The Communal Tomb in Pyrgos IV (Late Minoan I)', *Bull. Inst. Class. Stud. U. London*, xxxiii (1986), pp. 135–7

G. Cadogan: 'Myrtos-Pyrgos', *The Aerial Atlas of Ancient Crete*, ed. J. W. Myers, E. E. Myers and G. Cadogan (Berkeley, 1992), pp. 200–09

P. Warren: 'Myrtos-Phournou Koryphi', *The Aerial Atlas of Ancient Crete*, ed. J. W. Myers, E. E. Myers and G. Cadogan (Berkeley, 1992), pp. 196–9

GERALD CADOGAN

Myslbek, Josef Václav (*b* Prague, 20 June 1848; *d* Prague, 2 June 1922). Bohemian sculptor. He was the founder of modern Bohemian sculpture, and his work is mainly housed in Zbraslav Castle, Prague. He began his career as an assistant in the Prague sculpture workshops of Tomáš Seidan (1830–90) and of the more remarkable Václav Levý (1820–70). In 1868 he entered the Prague Academy of Fine Arts, which at the time did not have a department of sculpture, and in 1869 he designed his first monument, an *Allegory of Health* for Gräfenberg (now Jeseník), in Neoclassical style. In the early 1870s he began showing sketches on themes from Bohemian folklore at Prague exhibitions, thus associating himself with the legacy of Josef Mánes. He thereby declared his adherence to the political and cultural programme of the Bohemian national revival, which brought him both respect and commissions. His reclining figures of *Drama* and *Opera* (1871–4) in the National Theatre in Prague indicate that his bent was not so much for decorative as for monumental sculpture. In his first monument to a national hero, the leader of the Hussites, *Jan Žižka of Trocnov* (1874–7), for the town of Tábor, Myslbek produced a new type of heroic figure in the spirit of historical realism. His second memorial to *Jan Žižka*, for the town of Čáslav, further intensified the monumentality of his approach. In 1878 he visited Paris for the Exposition Universelle and became acquainted with the work of new wave of French monumental sculptors, notably Emmanuel Frémiet and Paul Dubois (i), which profoundly influenced his later work, although he also drew substantially on the Bohemian Baroque tradition.

By the 1880s Myslbek was beginning to be recognized internationally. In 1884 he exhibited the sculpture *Devotion* (Prague, N.G., Zbraslav Castle) at the Künstlerhaus, Vienna; it had originally been commissioned as decoration for the Viennese Parliament, and later, when worked in marble, it won the prestigious Reichl Prize (1886). In 1887 his *Christ with St Joseph* (Prague, N.G., Zbraslav Castle) won a *mention honorable* at the Paris salon, and in 1888 it won the gold medal at Munich. His greatest success came with his *Crucifixion* (Prague, N.G., Zbraslav Castle), which won awards at Vienna, Berlin, Paris and Chicago in 1890–93. In 1885 Myslbek was appointed professor of sculpture at the Prague School of Applied Arts and in 1896 professor of sculpture at the Prague Academy of Fine Arts. His mature work was infused with national feeling. He sculpted grandiose heroic figures from Bohemian history for the Palacký Bridge in Prague (competition models: 1881; realization: 1887–97; now Prague, Vyšehrad Park). His allegorical statue of *Music* (Prague, N. Theat.; see fig.), which he first designed in 1892–4 in a style approaching French Symbolism, was reworked by him in 1907–12 in a style reminiscent of that of Josef Mánes. His attachment to the monumental, however, is at its most intense in his equestrian statue of the founder of the state of Bohemia, *St Wenceslas*, a commission that he won in close competition (1894) with Bohuslav Schnirch. He began work on the statue in 1900–04 and it was unveiled, unfinished, on Wenceslas Square, Prague, in 1913. He continued working on the statue until his death. It has since become the most significant of Czech monuments, for both political and artistic reasons (*see* PRAGUE, fig. 10).

Myslbek was also a distinguished portraitist. In addition to medallions and busts (e.g. *Self-portrait*, 1902–3; Prague,

Josef Václav Myslbek: *Music*, bronze, h. 2.25 m, 1907–12 (Prague, National Theatre)

N.G., Zbraslav Castle), his output includes full-length portraits (e.g. the kneeling figure of *Cardinal Bedřich, Prince Schwarzenberg*, 1892–5; Prague, N.G., Zbraslav Castle) and portraits of statesmen (e.g. *František Rieger*, 1913–14; Prague, Vinohrady, Riegrovy Sady).

BIBLIOGRAPHY
V. Volavka: *Josef Václav Myslbek* (Prague, 1942)
A. Lodr, ed.: *J. V. Myslbek: Korespondence* (Prague, 1960)

PETR WITTLICH

Myson Painter. *See* Vase painters, §II.

Mysore [Maisūr; Mahiṣūrul]. City and temple site in Karnataka, India. It rose to prominence under the Wodeyar princes, who ruled locally from the 15th century and regionally off and on from the fall of the Vijayanagara empire in the late 16th century until the establishment of the Republic of India. Its name is derived from *Mahiṣūru*, meaning the 'place [Kannada *ūru*] of the Buffalo demon Mahisha', and its oldest temple, located on a hill outside the city, is dedicated to the goddess Chamundi, the slayer of the demon Mahisha. The temple, built in a southern (Skt *drāviḍa*) style, was supposed locally to have been founded in the 12th century. The current gateway was finished in 1827. Near the top of the hill is a colossal sculpture of the bull Nandi (h. 5 m, the largest of its type in India), cut from a single boulder on the order of Dodda Devaraja Wodeyar (*reg* 1659–72). Its symbolic purpose is to serve as a vehicle for Shiva, consort of the goddess in the temple.

The major monument within the city is the Ambavilas Palace. Inscriptions suggest that the temple of Lakshmiramana, built in a southern style and standing within the palace grounds, was already in existence by 1499. All temples in the palace are built of granite with brick superstructures displaying local variations of the southern style. The goddess shrine at the Varahasvami temple is notable as an archaizing version of the style developed under the Hoysala rulers. The latest structure is a triple-shrined temple (1953) dedicated to Savitri, Gayatri and Lakshmi (*see* Indian subcontinent, §III, 8(ii)).

The original fortifications of the palace were built in the 16th century, but most of these structures were replaced between 1897 and 1912. The new palace, designed by the British architect Henry Irwin (1841–1922), is a marvellous Beaux-Arts fantasy in the 'Indo-Saracenic' manner. The audience hall, facing east, is tall enough to admit the elephants used in traditional state processions. Onion domes and arched balconies recall Islamic art, while the central tower and double corner bastions give hints of late Renaissance Europe. This benign eclecticism is completed by imported Art Nouveau stained glass, cast-iron pillars from Glasgow, and local stone- and wood-carving in the time-honoured manner. Of particular note are paintings and sculptures by V. Venkatapa, Silpi Siddalingasvami, Y. Subramanya Raju and Ravi Varma.

The city's other monuments include Government House (1805), built by the British, an important early example of Palladian architecture in India. As in most colonial centres, there are picturesque bungalows dating to the late 19th century. The Roman Catholic cathedral of St Philomina (1931) is a Gothic Revival building. E. W. Fritchly's palace, the Lalitamahal (1930), has been described as 'American Renaissance'. Later buildings are in an international modern style. The city has a handicraft industry, specializing in weaving and sandalwood-carving, a legacy of Wodeyar patronage.

BIBLIOGRAPHY
B. L. Rice, ed.: 'Mysore and Coorg', *Imperial Gazetteer of India* (Calcutta, 1908)

Ann. Rep. Mysore Archaeol. Dept (1912), pp. 37–9; (1916), pp. 27–8; (1918), p. 29, pls viii and ix; (1919), pp. 17–18; (1920), pp. 2–3 [authoritative source on temples]

H. Rao: *Mysore Gazetteer*, ii (Mysore, 1927–30) [authoritative study of history and inscriptions]

C. E. Parsons: *Mysore City* (London, 1930)

P. B. Desai, ed.: *A History of Karnataka* (Dharwar, 1970)

F. Gaekwad and V. Fass: *The Palaces of India* (New York, 1980), pp. 140–47

M. S. Nagraja Rao: 'The Mysore Palace: Its History and Architecture', *Dasarah Cultural Festivities, 1980 Souvenir* (Mysore, 1980), pp. 23–34

P. Davies: *Splendours of the Raj: British Architecture in India, 1660–1947* (London, 1985)

M. S. Nagaraja Rao: *The Mysore Palace: A Visitor's Guide* (Mysore, 1989)

GARY MICHAEL TARTAKOV

Mystras [Mistra; Mistras; Myzithras]. Site of the Byzantine capital of the Morea (Peloponnese, Greece), on a foothill of the Taygetos range, *c.* 5 km south-west of Sparta. It was originally called Myzithras, but this name was later corrupted to Mystras ('mistress').

1. History and urban development. 2. Buildings.

1. HISTORY AND URBAN DEVELOPMENT. The castle of Mystras was founded in 1249 by William II of Villehardouin (*reg* 1246–78), prince of the Frankish principality of Achaea. In 1259 he was defeated and captured by Michael II, Despot of Epiros (*reg* 1236–71), at the Battle of Pelagonia in northern Greece; in 1262, in order to pay his own ransom, William was forced to concede the castle of Mystras to the Byzantine emperor Michael VIII Palaiologos (*reg* 1261–82). Soon afterwards Mystras became the capital of the growing Greek province of the Morea and expanded to accommodate the inhabitants of the vale of Sparta, who moved there for greater protection during the continual warfare between the Franks and Greeks. At first it was governed by a resident Byzantine general. In 1348, however, Emperor John VI Kantakouzenos (*reg* 1347–54) appointed his son Manuel (*reg* 1348–80) as governor of the Morea, giving him the title of despot. The despotate of the Kantakouzenoi (1348–84) was followed by that of the Palaiologoi (1384–1460). In its heyday between the late 13th century and the mid-15th, Mystras was an important centre of learning and the arts, as well as a focal point in the cultural development of Europe: it was frequently visited by outstanding political and ecclesiastical figures from Constantinople and was home to numerous artists, scribes and copyists, connoisseurs and intellectuals. A prominent figure after *c.* 1407 was the philosopher Georgios Gemistos Plethon (*c.* 1360–1452), who held a high position in government.

In 1460, seven years after the fall of Constantinople to the Ottoman Turks, the last Palaiologoi of Mystras were forced to cede the city to Muhammad II (*reg* 1451–81). It remained under Turkish control until 1687, when it fell to the Venetians, only to be recaptured by the Turks in 1714. In the Russo-Turkish War (1768–74), Mystras was briefly occupied by the Russians (1770) before being burnt by Albanian troops in the same year. It was finally destroyed in 1825 by Ibrahim Pasha during the war of independence. The site was largely abandoned except for the southernmost part of the outer city, which is occupied by the present small town of Mystras.

The castle of Villehardouin was built on the summit of the hill. Few elements from the original building survive, since works done by the Byzantines and the Turks have changed its form almost entirely. The first settlement, later known as the Town or Upper Town, was built on the steep slopes outside the castle wall, probably in the second half of the 13th century. It was surrounded by a high wall with two entrances, the Monemvasia Gate to the east and the Nauplia Gate to the west, which were connected by a central street 3 m wide. As the city developed outside the wall a second fortification was built to protect the new settlement, the Middle or Lower Town. A third settlement, the Outer Town, established beyond the second wall, was inhabited until *c.* 1830.

In the square at the northern end of the Upper Town stands the Palace of the Despots (13th–15th centuries), a large complex of buildings with two wings joined almost at a right angle. The north wing dates to the second half of the 14th century and served as the apartments of the despot and his family. The west wing was probably added in the 15th century and contains the ruins of the Great Hall (39×12 m). Originally, on the building's south façade there was a two-storey gallery with a balcony on top. The palace is similar to official Byzantine buildings of the 13th and 14th centuries, such as the late 13th-century Tekfur Saray in Constantinople, but its circular and ogee headed windows are reminiscent of styles in Venice. The houses in the Lower Town are two-storey, long and rectangular and originally had gabled roofs. Some have a verandah on the façade overlooking the valley; others are the mansions of noblemen with strong protective towers; a third group has neither verandah nor tower. The domestic quarters were on the first floor, with the ground-floor used as a store room or stable.

2. BUILDINGS. The city's most important monuments are its churches of the 13th to 15th centuries.

(i) Hagios Demetrios. (ii) The monastery of the Brontochion. (iii) Hagia Sophia. (iv) The Peribleptos. (v) The Evangelistria. (vi) The Pantanassa.

(i) Hagios Demetrios. The church (also known as the Metropolis) stands at the north-eastern edge of the Lower Town and was originally built as a basilica with three aisles by Metropolitan Eugenios (1263–72), who is probably portrayed in the apse. Metropolitan Nikephoros Moschopoulos (1286–1315) added the narthex, and during the 15th century another Metropolitan, Matthew, tried to adapt the basilica to the plan of the churches of the Hodegetria (or Aphentiko) and the Pantanassa (see §§(ii) and (vi) below) by adding an upper storey in the shape of a cross-in-square church with five domes. A dedicatory inscription referring to the second phase of the building, and containing the date 1291–2, is preserved in the church.

The painted decoration of the church was completed in two consecutive phases. Phase A (1272–88) includes the wall paintings of the *Virgin and Child* in the apse; scenes from the *Life of St Demetrios* (see fig. 1), the *Miracles of Christ* and various bishops and saints in the prothesis and north aisle; a *Christ in Majesty*, the *Hetoimasia* with angels in adoration, the *Miracles of SS Cosmas and Damian* in the diakonikon; and scenes from the *Life of the Virgin*, *Christ among the Doctors*, the *Marriage at Cana* and saints in the south aisle. These paintings are distinguished by the

1. Mystras, Hagios Demetrios (founded 1263–72), wall painting showing scenes from the *Life of St Demetrios*, 1272–88

presence of different stylistic trends, some of which are classicizing, while in the more important scenes a cuboid conception of form dominates. The architectural background in some scenes reflects the influence of Western art, for example the *Miracles of St Demetrios* in the north nave in which the buildings are like tall, narrow, densely grouped towers with many small, narrow windows and with a recession reminiscent of representations in Gothic art.

Phase B (1291/2–1315) includes scenes from the *Life of Christ* in the central aisle, which were partly destroyed by the addition of the upper storey; the *Miracles of Christ* in Galilee and the apostles in the south aisle; and a *Last Judgement* in the narthex. The figures have refined expressions and elegant poses, and some of them are characterized by animated movements. The buildings in the scenes are unrealistically depicted and are linked together by a red curtain. Daring contrasts of colour are another feature of these paintings. The charm and spaciousness of the representations recall in some cases the 'aristocratic' wall painting and mosaic (*c.* 1316–21) of the katholikon of the monastery of Chora in Constantinople (*see* ISTANBUL, §III, 3).

(ii) The monastery of the Brontochion. This large complex occupies the northernmost corner of the Lower Town and served as a cultural centre and burial place of the despots. It has two churches, Hagioi Theodoroi and the

Hodegetria, also known as Aphentiko. Hagioi Theodoroi combines a cruciform plan with a domed octagon. According to an inscription, it was built *c.* 1290–95. Only poorly preserved fragments of the original wall paintings have survived. They reveal four zones of painting: the topmost zone depicts scenes from the *Passion* and the *Resurrection*; the zone below showed another group of scenes, of which only the archangel of the *Annunciation* and fragments from the *Life of the Virgin* are preserved; the third zone has a procession of full-length, larger than life-size military saints; and the lowest zone (h. *c.* 1 m from floor level) is painted with imitation marble veneer. These wall paintings are reminiscent of those in the north aisle of Hagios Demetrios (*see* §(i) above), and are executed in a free manner with warm colours; the shading of the faces is green, and the figures, especially those of the military saints, are strong and full of vitality. The church has four funerary chapels; the north-east chapel contains representations of an emperor, probably Manuel II Palaiologos (*reg* 1391–1425), while the south-east chapel has portraits of two noblemen wearing conical hats that are among the most interesting paintings in Mystras.

The second Brontochion church is that of the Hodegetria or Aphentiko (1310–22; *see* EARLY CHRISTIAN AND BYZANTINE ART, fig. 28). This ambitious building was the model of what has been called the 'Mystras type' of church: the ground-plan is that of a three-aisled basilica with a narthex, while the upper storey is in the form of a cross-in-square church with five domes. The wall paintings of the Hodegetria are among the most pretentious of the early 14th century in Mystras and bear the closest resemblance to the art of Constantinople, as represented by the mosaics and wall paintings of the monastery of Chora. On the basis of documentary evidence the decoration of the Hodegetria can be assigned to between 1311–12 and 1322. The donor was Pachomios, the enterprising abbot (c. 1310–22) of the Brontochion Monastery, who obtained important privileges from the Byzantine emperors Andronikos II (reg 1282–1328) and Michael IX (reg 1295–1320).

The iconographic programme of the sanctuary contains such traditional subjects as the *Virgin Enthroned with Two Archangels*, the *Communion of the Apostles*, bishops and episodes connected with the *Resurrection*. In the upper storey the *Gospel* cycle unfolds on the barrel vaults; 70 apostles, patriarchs and prophets (scc fig. 2) are depicted in the galleries, while the bust of the *Virgin* surrounded by prophets and seraphim appears in the dome of the west gallery; saints, martyrs and prophets are portrayed in the two lateral aisles. On the ground floor the walls were originally covered with polychrome marble decoration supplemented by wall paintings with standing prelates and saints. Scenes from the *Life of Christ*, with special emphasis on the miracles, are painted on the walls and in the vaults

of the narthex. The style of the paintings reveals the work of several artists. The multi-figured compositions are full of movement and colour contrasts, which create a dramatic atmosphere. Of special interest is the iconography of the *Baptism*, with its personifications of the River Jordan and of the sea, and an unusual fishing scene. These details are based on classical Nilotic scenes, but they also reveal a close observation of nature. The figures are elegant and imitate Classical models. The principal colours are applied in a free manner in broad brushstrokes, and their complementary tones are combined in an almost impressionistic way.

The funerary chapel in the north-west corner contains the tombs of the abbot Pachomios and of Despot Theodoros I Palaiologos (reg 1407–43). The wall paintings show a procession of martyrs, prophets, patriarchs, apostles and saints who, together with the *Virgin* and *St John the Baptist* in the south tympanum, address a prayer to *Christ the Judge* in the eastern conch; a *Pantokrator* occupies the dome. The paintings have been dated on grounds of style to c. 1320. Some of the figures (e.g. the martyrs on the west wall of the chapel) are particularly elegant and bear a close resemblance to the mosaics in the narthex of the katholikon of the Chora Monastery. The colours are gradated in many soft hues, giving the appearance of velvet. The wall paintings in the south-east chapcl include the *Virgin and Child*, the *Last Supper* and the *Vision of*

2. Mystras, church of the Hodegetria (1310–22), wall painting of the prophet *Zachariah*, 1311/12–22

John of Euchaita together with the 4th-century bishops Basil the Great, Gregory of Nazianzos and John Chrysostomos. On the basis of the monogram of the abbot Kyprianos, they are dated to 1366. The domical vault of the south-west chapel is painted with four angels, who originally held a circular mandorla of Christ (destr.). Copies of four chrysobulls granted by the Byzantine emperors between 1312–13 and 1322 and detailing the foundation, properties and privileges of the monastery have been painted on the walls.

The south gallery, which also became a funerary chapel, is decorated with portraits of noblemen, scenes from the *Life of Christ* and the *Dormition of the Virgin* (second half of the 14th century).

(iii) Hagia Sophia. This simple two-column cross-in-square church (1350–65) has a two-storey narthex and lies to the west of the palace. It served as both the palace chapel and the katholikon of a small monastery associated with the first despot, Manuel Kantakouzenos. From the few remaining fragments of wall painting it is possible to reconstruct an iconographic programme comparable to that of the Peribleptos (*see* §(iv) below). A *Christ Enthroned*, eucharistic scenes, the *Ascension* and bishops are depicted in the sanctuary. A zone (h. 1.5 m) of painted decoration imitating marble revetment covers the lower part of the walls. In the nave, scenes of the *Dodekaeorton* and the *Passion* are preserved. Stylistically, the paintings are similar to those in the Peribleptos, both decorations belonging to the third quarter of the 14th century.

(iv) The Peribleptos. This domed cross-in-square church (second half of the 14th century) lies at the south end of the Lower Town with a view eastwards. Its construction is distinctive as it is partly built into the rock. The main entrance lies beside the northernmost of the three pentagonal apses and leads through a low, narrow corridor into the church, beneath the north arm of the cross. The wall paintings are usually dated to the reign of Manuel Kantakouzenos, and their close stylistic affinity with the illustrations in a copy of the theological works of John VI Kantakouzenos (1370–75; Paris, Bib. N., gr. 1242) may indicate a more precise date in the 1370s. Above the sanctuary is the *Ascension*; the central apse has a *Virgin and Child* with liturgical scenes and figures of bishops and saints on the adjacent walls. The central dome shows the *Pantokrator*, who is surrounded by prophets, the *Hetoimasia*, the *Virgin* and angels. Scenes from the *Dodekaeorton*, the *Passion* and the *Life of the Virgin* occupy the upper zones of the nave. The zone below has full-length saints, while on the west wall is the founding couple offering a model of the church to the Virgin. The lowest part of the walls is decorated with a painted dado imitating marble revetment.

The iconography of the wall paintings emphasizes the liturgy and the *Life of the Virgin*, which is represented in 25 scenes, making it one of the richest of its kind in monumental painting. The role of the Virgin in the incarnation is also given prominence in the paintings in the dome and through the texts on scrolls and the symbolical objects held by the prophets. The aristocratic figures have slightly wistful expressions, while the subtle gradations in colour of the faces, the graceful movements

of the bodies and the symmetry in the compositions indicate a deliberate return by an accomplished workshop to the classicizing tendency of the Palaiologan painting of the first quarter of the 14th century.

(v) The Evangelistria. It is of the cross-in-square type and lies to the north of the Metropolitan church in the Lower Town. Its poorly preserved wall paintings probably date to the early 15th century and depict a programme that differs little from those in Hagia Sophia and the Peribleptos, but it lacks their beauty.

(vi) The Pantanassa. It is situated on a terrace immediately below the Upper Town, has a superb view to the east and is the best-preserved and most picturesque of all the churches at Mystras. It was built and decorated *c.* 1430 by Ioannis Frangopoulos, who held an office equivalent to that of prime minister in the despotate. His identity is revealed in the form of six painted monograms on the west façade of the church. The building imitates the design of the Hodegetria (*see* §(ii) above), comprising a three-aisled basilica on the ground floor surmounted by a cross-in-square church with five domes. Its exterior is decorated with small columns, Gothic arches, garlands and *rinceau* ornament. The wall paintings preserved in the gallery illustrate several trends and can be attributed to more than one artist. The original decoration of the ground floor was never completed, and the existing wall paintings date to the 17th and 18th centuries.

The painted decoration of *c.* 1430 is modelled on that in the Hodegetria and the Peribleptos (*see* §§(ii) and (iv) above). As in the Hodegetria, the main apse is decorated with the *Virgin Enthroned with Two Archangels*. The pendentives show the Evangelists, while prophets, patriarchs and cherubim occupy the domical vaults of the galleries. The Church Feasts are depicted in the barrel vaults of the arms of the cross, while the *Ascension* and the *Pentecost* decorate the sanctuary. In the galleries 70 apostles, prophets and saints are depicted, and in the dome of the west gallery is a bust of the *Virgin* surrounded by seraphim, with prophets around the drum and with apostles in medallions on the pendentives (see fig. 3). Although scenes in the Pantanassa include compositional devices and iconographic features similar to those found in corresponding scenes in the Peribleptos, the wall paintings of the Pantanassa incorporate more anecdotal images, which distract the viewer from the principal theme of the compositions. The use of grisaille, the depiction of elements from everyday life and antiquarian masks and motifs are all characteristics of the Pantanassa paintings.

The classicizing and subdued expression of the figures reflects a return to the early 14th-century style of painting represented by the mosaics and wall paintings in the katholikon of the Chora Monastery. Many other stylistic features, however, are borrowed from the decoration of the Hodegetria. The faces in the Pantanassa are fleshy and earth-bound, and the treatment of colour and light enhances the volume and the dynamic and decorative aspect of the paintings. Sienese influence is evident in some aspects of the composition and in the use of colour. The Panatassa wall paintings are the most important survivals from the last phase of Byzantine paintings. The atmosphere of a dream world created through the use of colour

3. Mystras, church of the Pantanassa, medallion wall painting of an apostle, *c.* 1430

and the numerous anecdotal details owe much to the philosophy of Georgios Gemistos Plethon, which encouraged a return to the Classical past.

BIBLIOGRAPHY

G. Millet: 'Inscriptions byzantines de Mistra', *Bull. Corr. Hell.*, xxiii (1899), pp. 97–156

——: 'Inscriptions inédites de Mistra', *Bull. Corr. Hell.*, xxx (1906), pp. 453–66

——: *Monuments byzantins de Mistra* (Paris, 1910)

——: *Recherches sur l'iconographie de l'Evangile aux XIVe, XVe et XVIe siècles* (Paris, 1916)

D. Zakythinos: *Le Despotat grec de Morée*, i (Paris, 1932), ii (Athens, 1953, rev. London, 1975)

A. Orlandos: 'Daniel, o protos ktitor ton Agion Theodoron tou Mystra' [Daniel, the first founder of Hagioi Theodoroi at Mystras], *Epeteris Etaireias Byz. Spoudon*, xii (1936), pp. 443–8

——: 'Ta palatia kai ta spitia tou Mystra' [The palaces and the houses in Mystras], *Archeion Byz. Mnimeion Ellados*, iii (1937), pp. 3–114

M. Chatzidakis: *Mystras: Istoria, mnimeia, techni* [Mystras: history, monuments, painting] (Athens, 1948); Eng. trans. as *Mystras: The Medieval City and the Castle: A Complete Guide to the Churches, Palaces and the Castle* (Athens, 1981)

M. I. Manousakas: 'I chronologia tis ktirorikis epigrafis tou Agiou Dimitriou tou Mystra' [The date of the foundation inscription in Hagios Demetrios at Mystras], *Deltion Christ. Archaiol. Etaireias* (1959), pp. 72–80

C. Delvoye: 'Mistra', *Corsi di cultura sull'arte ravennate e bizantina* (Ravenna, 1964), pp. 126–38

D. Mouriki: 'Tessares mi meletitheisai skinai tou viou tis Panagias eis tin Periblepton tou Mystra' [Four unpublished scenes from the Life of the Virgin in the Peribleptos at Mystras], *Archaiol. Ephimeris* (1968), *Archaiol. Chron.*, suppl., pp. 1–6

S. Dufrenne: *Les Programmes iconographiques des églises byzantines de Mistra* (Paris, 1970)

D. Mouriki: 'Ai biblikai proikoniseis tis Panagias eis ton troullon tis Peribleptou tou Mystra' [The biblical representation of the Virgin in the dome of the Peribleptos at Mystras], *Archaiol. Deltion*, xxv (1970), pp. 217–51

M. Chatzidakis: 'Classicisme et tendances populaires au XIVe siècle: Les Recherches sur l'évolution du style', *Actes du XIVe Congrès international des études byzantines: Bucarest, 1974*, i, pp. 153–88

——: 'Neotera apo ti Mitropoli tou Mystra' [New finds from the Metropolis at Mystras], *Deltion Christ. Archaiol. Etaireias*, ix (1977–9), pp. 143–79

S. Runciman: *Mistra: Byzantine Capital of the Peloponnese* (London, 1980)

D. Mouriki: 'The Mask Motif in the Wall Paintings of Mistra', *Deltion Christ. Archaiol. Etaireias*, x (1980–81), pp. 307–38

R. Etzeoglou: 'Quelques Remarques sur les portraits figurés dans les églises de Mistra', *XVI. Internationaler Byzantinistenkongress, Wien: 1981*, ii/5, pp. 513–21

D. Mouriki: 'Revival Themes with Elements of Daily Life in Two Palaeologan Frescoes Depicting the Baptism', *Okeanos: Essays Presented to Ihor Ševčenko* (Cambridge, MA, 1983), pp. 458–88

A. Kalligas and H. Kalligas: 'To spiti tou Laskari sto Mystra' [The house of Laskaris at Mystras], *Deltion Christ. Archaiol. Etaireias*, xiii (1985–6), pp. 261–78

D. Mouriki: 'Palaeologan Mistra and the West', *Byzantium and Europe: First International Byzantine Conference: Delphi, 1985* (Athens, 1987), pp. 209–46

S. Sinos: 'Organisation und Form des Palastes von Mystras', *Archit.: Z. Gesch. Archit.*, xvii (1987), pp. 105–28

——: 'Gotische Fensterformen in der Architektur der byzantinischen Stadt von Mystras', *Istanbul. Mitt.*, xxxix (1989), pp. 523–34

D. Mouriki: 'The Wall Paintings of the Pantanassa at Mistra: Models of a Painters' Workshop in the Fifteenth Century', *The Twilight of Byzantium: Aspects of Cultural and Religious History in the Late Byzantine Empire*, ed. S. Ćurčić and D. Mouriki (Princeton, 1991), pp. 217–50

MELITA EMMANUEL

Mytens. *See* MIJTENS.

Mythological painting and sculpture. Term used to describe art forms that draw on myth for their subject-matter. The term 'myth' refers to a story that attempts in more or less symbolic form to explain the mystery of the origins of the cosmos, the earth and humanity, the issue of life and death, and the causes and meanings of natural phenomena, all of which have bewildered humanity since ancient times. Humankind uses myth as an attempt to express its relation to nature. Closely related to myth is the saga or legend, which is based on historical events and which is by definition associated with a place and time, so lacking the universality of the myth. A legend or saga can, however, accumulate so much mythical material that the divide becomes blurred. This article concentrates on Greco-Roman mythology and its particular significance for contemporary and for later Western art and culture. There was a fundamental difference in attitude to mythology during these two periods: whereas in antiquity mythology was inextricably linked with religion, in post-antiquity it became primarily a source of inspiration for a variety of themes in art and literature. The diversity and universality of these themes, combined with the inexhaustible, metaphorical possibilities of the ancient myths, ensure the survival of mythology in Western art up to the present day. For a discussion of mythology and its relationship with religions and beliefs in other civilizations and cultures, *see* articles within the appropriate survey, especially the subsections on iconography and subject-matter.

1. Classical antiquity, before *c.* AD 300. 2. The medieval period, *c.* AD 300–*c.* 1400. 3. The Renaissance, *c.* 1400–*c.* 1595. 4. The Baroque period, *c.* 1595–*c.* 1700. 5. Late Baroque and Neo-classicism, *c.* 1700–*c.* 1800. 6. Romanticism, Symbolism and modern art, *c.* 1800 and after.

1. CLASSICAL ANTIQUITY, BEFORE *c.* AD 300. Greek mythology is distinguished by its rational nature and anthropomorphism. Human form is attributed to both gods and heroes; the gods became more human and humanity more divine. The first literary expressions of mythology, the Homeric epics, the *Iliad* and the *Odyssey*, and Hesiod's *Theogony*, were probably formulated in the 8th century BC, and the earliest visual representation of mythical scenes occurs on pottery of the Geometric period (*c.* 900–*c.* 700 BC). In this early period there was no question of an iconographic tradition, which came into being only in the Archaic period, 600 BC. The figures on vases were identified by their context and by written inscriptions. In the 6th century BC the use of fixed attributes and postures became widespread. Not until the Classical period (5th century BC) was harmony established between attribute and context.

Greek vase painters were inspired by stories from Homeric epic, a popular literary source, as in the krater by Aristonothos showing *Odysseus and his Friends Blinding the Cyclops* (mid-7th century BC; Rome, Mus. Conserv.). The narrative structure of Archaic vase painting was confined to the illustration of climactic moments: the beginning and end, the cause and effect of a story. These moments, summarized in a single picture, sometimes led to an elision of differences in space and time, as in the kylix by the Boston Polyphemos Painter showing the story of *Odysseus and Circe* (*c.* 550 BC; Boston, MA, Mus. F.A.; see fig. 1). Exekias (*c.* 540 BC), by concentrating on the moment immediately preceding the climax of the story, created a new emphasis on psychological insight, as in the amphorae showing the *Suicide of Ajax* (Boulogne, Mus. Mun., 558) and *Ajax and Achilles Playing a Board-game* (Rome, Vatican, Mus. Gregoriana Etrus., 344; for illustration *see* VASE PAINTERS, §II: EXEKIAS).

Around 500 BC the Greek concept of divinity changed fundamentally (Schefold with Jung, 1981). The static world picture, which conveyed faith in the divine order of the universe, was replaced by the dynamic world picture of tragedy and satire, in which history (both human and divine) developed in accordance with Fate. Painters and

1. *Odysseus and Circe*, from the kylix by the Boston Polyphemos Painter, h. 132 mm, diam. 217 mm, *c.* 550 BC (Boston, MA, Museum of Fine Arts)

2. *Alcestis*, from the sarcophagus of C. Junius Euhodus and Metilia Acte, 2.1×0.8×0.9 m, AD 160–70 (Rome, Vatican, Museo Chiaramonti)

sculptors attempted to convey the spiritual meaning of the events they depicted and to explore the relationship between visible and invisible and between humanity and an ideal image and ideal truth. These philosophical themes inspired the sculptors of the east pediment of the Temple of Zeus at Olympia (*c.* 470–457 BC; Olympia, Archaeol. Mus.; *see* GREECE, ANCIENT, fig. 45) and of the pediment and frieze of the Parthenon, Athens (447–432 BC; London, BM; *see* FRIEZE, fig. 1). In the same period satyric drama, which burlesqued the loves of the gods, is reflected in vase painting, as in the lewdly revelling satyrs on a wine-cooler signed Douris (490–480 BC; now London, BM). In the Late Classical period scenes of Dionysiac ecstasy, and of the power of Eros, emphasize how those forces that determine the behaviour of the gods also affect the activities of humanity.

During the Hellenistic period (late 4th century to 1st century BC), the possibility of interpreting myth as political allegory was enlarged by the theories of Euhemeros and his students. They believed that myths recorded historical facts. Political interpretation of myth inspired, for example, the frieze representing a *Gigantomachy* on the 'Great Altar' at Pergamon (*c.* 180 BC; Berlin, Pergamonmus.; *see* PER-GAMON, fig. 5).

The Romans studied Late Classical mythographers; they admired Greek art and owned copies of Classical and Hellenistic paintings and sculptures, from which were made example-books of Hellenistic models and positive plaster casts to work from. Their art was deeply indebted to that of the Greeks (*see* ROME, ANCIENT, §V, 2), but it also exhibited obvious differences. Mythology lost its narrative power and formed part of moral allegories; the artists who decorated the walls and gardens of the villas at Pompeii emphasized decorative beauty and expressive power rather than mythological content.

The decoration of sarcophagi in the 2nd century AD (see fig. 2) offered opportunities for a new use of myth, to glorify the dead and to suggest the promise of immortality. Such sculptures may include demons, allegorical personifications and a mythological portrait of the deceased; the mythological figures may function as moral exemplars, for example Hercules symbolizing triumph over death (*see* SARCOPHAGUS, fig. 2). From the end of

the 2nd century motifs became more decorative, and scenes of the apotheosis yielded to more picturesque themes, such as the Seasons. After Christianity became the official religion of the Empire (AD 312–13), artists of the Early Christian period attempted to unite Classical themes and forms with the demands of a new religious art. Certain Fathers of the Church, including Tertullian (*c.* 160–*c.* 230), Eusebius (4th century) and St Augustine (354–430), fulminated against both literal and allegorical interpretations of mythology. Nevertheless, some mythological figures and themes continued to play a limited role in Early Christian mosaics, wall painting and metalwork; for example, Orpheus was used as a symbol of the triumph of good over evil, and as a type of Christ, as in the Catacomb of Priscilla in Rome. From the 4th century the use of pagan gods in Christian art became increasingly taboo (*see* CHRISTIANITY, §III, 1), though there are exceptions (*see* EARLY CHRISTIAN AND BYZANTINE ART, figs 8–9).

2. THE MEDIEVAL PERIOD, *c.* AD 300–*c.* 1400. During the Middle Ages the Classical gods did not disappear from human consciousness. A knowledge of Classical literature persisted, for the discipline of grammar included a reading of Latin texts and their associated commentaries. Three influential interpretations of mythology, themselves derived from Late Antiquity, also ensured the survival of Classical mythology (Seznec, 1940). The euhemeristic interpretation, first used by the Fathers of the Church as a weapon against paganism, was elaborated in the encyclopedic *Etymologiae* by Isidore of Seville (*c.* 560–636; ed. W. M. Lindsay, 1911), who placed the gods in historical time. His doctrine encouraged many nations and families to seek their ancestry in the demigods and heroes of a fabulous past. A second tradition identified the gods with the planets, as the Greeks and Romans had done. A structure developed of moral and intellectual thought, in which the planets and signs of the zodiac controlled all knowledge; they were related to the seasons, humours and temperaments, and were associated with the Virtues and the liberal arts. In the sculptures that decorate the Campanile of Florence Cathedral the planetary gods, medieval in appearance, appear among repre-

sentations of the Virtues and Sciences. From the 14th century astrological cycles, in which enthroned stellar gods are accompanied by the 'children of the planet', reflect these relationships, and such themes remained popular until the end of the 16th century (e.g. Francesco del Cossa's allegorical frescoes of *Aries, Taurus* and *Gemini*, before 1470; Ferrara, Pal. Schifanoia, Salone dei Mesi; *see* FERRARA, fig. 3). Finally, the Neo-Platonists interpreted mythology allegorically, often seeking hidden Christian truths in the adventures of the gods. This approach above all others became fundamental to the mythography of the Middle Ages, as demonstrated in the Latin grammarian Servius' lengthy allegorical commentary on the *Aeneid* of Virgil; Macrobius' *Saturnalia* and *Commentarii in somnium Scipionis*, Martianus Capella's *De nuptuis Mercurii et Philologiae* and Fulgentius' *Mythologiae*.

The figures of the gods themselves were kept alive in the visual arts, especially in manuscript illumination, and the representation of mythological figures based on antique models survived in various ways, particularly in the Carolingian period. First there were the personifications that appeared in Christian art: Sol, Luna, Tellus and Oceanus, as well as angels, which derive from Classical Victories.

Second, pagan idols, distinguished by their nudity and by their standing on pedestals, gesturing, were represented in such Christian themes as the *Flight into Egypt*. Third, the gods feature in illustrations to astrological manuscripts, such as the *Calendar of 354* (destr.; known from copies, e.g. 15th century, Vienna, Staatsbib. 3416), and to the various *Aratea* manuscripts (e.g. 9th century, Leiden, U. Lib., MS. Voss. Kat. Q. 79) that comprise the Latin translation of the *Phaenomena* by Aratus of Soli (*fl c.* 310–*c.* 240 BC), describing the myths of the stars. In the 12th and 13th centuries the orientalizing illustrations of Arabian manuscripts added new images, and such scholars as Michael Scotus (*c.* 1175–1234), astrologer at the court of Frederick II, were no longer aware of the Classical forms. A 14th-century copy of his popular treatise *Liber introductorius* (Munich, Bayer. Staatsbib., MS. 10268) is illustrated by misunderstood figures, such as Mercury portrayed as a bishop. (*See also* ASTROLOGICAL AND ASTRONOMICAL MANUSCRIPTS.)

Another pictorial tradition, independent of Classical models and inspired instead by literary descriptions, developed from the 11th century. Remigius of Auxerre's commentary (*c.* 1100) on Martianus Capella is illustrated by images of the gods in medieval dress, with attributes (sometimes incorrectly interpreted) derived from the text. This type of illustration, where Classical form and Classical subject are separated, persisted into the later Middle Ages. A sense of continuity between the Classical past and Christian present prevented archaeologically correct rendering of Classical subjects. Pagan gods, to whom Christian meanings had been attributed, were now portrayed as the knights and damsels of medieval chivalry. Benoît de Sainte-Maure's *Roman de Troie*, an epic and popular poem of *c.* 1160, exists in illustrated copies (e.g. early 14th century; Paris, Bib. N., MS. fr. 782) that depict the legendary history of the Trojan War in a context that is often recognizable as 12th-century feudal society.

In the 14th century the search for hidden Christian truths flourished. John Ridewall in *Fulgentius metaforalis* (*c.* 1330) explicitly identified the gods with Christian Virtues and Vices. A Christian interpretation of OVID was first applied in the anonymous French poem *Ovide moralisé* (*c.* 1316–28), which suggested that Ovidian stories could be read as prefigurations of the events of the New Testament. This approach was taken further by Petrus Berchorius in the Latin prose *Ovidius moralizatus* (*c.* 1340), on which was based the *Libellus de imaginibus deorum* (*c.* 1400), a widely influential handbook of the gods. The illustrations to this initiated a lively pictorial tradition that found expression in such 15th-century works as the *Tarocchi* (*c.* 1465) and Francesco del Cossa's decorations (before 1470) of the Palazzo Schianoia in Ferrara. The *De genealogia deorum gentilium* (1350–75) of GIOVANNI BOCCACCIO inherited this tradition and became the most influential mythographical handbook until the mid-16th century. Boccaccio retained the Christian allegorical exegesis of the medieval period yet cast a more critical eye on his sources than his predecessors.

3. THE RENAISSANCE, *c.* 1400–*c.* 1595. Renaissance humanists, in emulation of Boccaccio, made use of Late Antique rather than Greek authors; as a result medieval interpretations of mythology outlined above were largely retained. Euhemerism remained a living tradition in numerous princely genealogies, some of which, such as the *Florentine Picture Chronicle* (*c.* 1460; London, BM), were accompanied by drawings of mythological figures (formerly attrib. Maso Finiguerra). Astrology became more important: Baldassare Peruzzi's ceiling decoration of the Loggia di Galatea in the Villa Farnesina, Rome, uses mythological figures (e.g. *Perseus Slaying Medusa*, 1510–11) to represent the constellations showing the aspect of the sky on the patron's date of birth (1 Dec 1466), hence illustrating Agostino Chigi (i)'s horoscope. Myths continued to convey moral allegories, as in Andrea Mantegna's *Pallas Expelling the Vices from the Garden of Virtue* (*c.* 1499–1502; Paris, Louvre), the subject of his decoration of the *studiolo* of Isabella d'Este. Hercules was particularly popular. The legend of Hercules at the crossroads made it possible for Hercules to personify Virtue, and this provided an opportunity for political allegories in which he represents the ideal ruler. The search for concealed wisdom in myth retained its fascination, and the Florentine Neo-Platonists, most significantly MARSILIO FICINO, ANGELO POLIZIANO and Giovanni Pico della Mirandola (1463–94), sought to reveal, through a complex symbolic language, a fundamental affinity between pagan mythology and Christian theology. The key term in Ficino's philosophy is love: originating in God, it is the power that holds together body and soul. Love can be manifest as spiritual or sensual, as exemplified in the concept of the two Venuses, the heavenly and the earthly. Neo-Platonism found its mirror in the work of painters, including Sandro Botticelli's *Primavera* (*see* BOTTICELLI, SANDRO, fig. 2), *Birth of Venus* (*see* BOTTICELLI, SANDRO, fig. 3), *Pallas and the Centaur* (all Florence, Uffizi) and *Mars and Venus* (London, N.G.; *see* BOTTICELLI, SANDRO, fig. 6). Cristoforo Landino's allegorical exegesis of Virgil's *Aeneid*, the Neo-Platonist *Disputationes Camaldulensis* (Florence,

3. *Wedding of Cupid and Psyche* (1517–18) by Raphael, ceiling fresco, Villa Farnesina, Rome

c. 1474), interprets the legend as the ascent of the soul from the *vita activa* to the *vita contemplativa* and remained influential into the 17th century. Through a long process, begun above all by Francesco Petrarch, there emerged a growing realization of the historical distance of the present from antiquity. This led to an idealization of the ancient world, which came to be seen as a harmonious, longed-for universe, separate from reality. It is the depiction of this unattainable harmony that separates Raphael's *Parnassus* (Rome, Vatican, Stanza della Segnatura) from the medieval works that precede it, although the allegorical programme of the Stanza della Segnatura is the culmination of a medieval encyclopedic tradition.

Although *cassoni* (bridal chests) and *deschi da parto* continued to be painted or carved with scenes from Greek and Roman myth and history, in which the figures are shown wearing fashionable contemporary dress (*see* CASSONE), the archaeological rediscovery of the ancient world, which gradually increased in the early 15th-century, encouraged a reintegration of Classical form and subject. Classical motifs were included incidentally by such artists as Gentile da Fabriano, and in the art of Michelangelo there is complete harmony between form and subject. Albrecht Dürer was among the northern European artists to convey both the spirit and form of antiquity, in such drawings as the *Death of Orpheus* (1494; Hamburg, Ksthalle). Yet despite the revival of antique forms, changes in meaning originating in the Middle Ages could still persist, as for example in Saturn's transformation into Father Time. At the same time a conception *all'antica* could be quasi-Classical, because it actually originated in medieval iconography: thus the nakedness of many Renaissance goddesses would have been impossible in antiquity and derived partly from medieval iconographical concepts of idols, partly from medieval allegorical personifications (Himmelmann, 1986).

The union of Classical form and Classical subject also reflected a growing interest in the physical characteristics of humankind. This itself reflected a new Renaissance sense of the power of the individual, and such legends as

Hercules at the crossroads were now used to illustrate the possibility of a choice between good and evil, a concept that earlier would have been inconceivable.

According to Leon Battista Alberti (1452) in his *De re aedificatoria* (*c.* 1450), the decoration of palaces and villas should reflect the status of the patron, the function of the building and the function of the rooms within the building. The choice of mythological subjects also followed this rule, as restated in Giovanni Paolo Lomazzo's *Trattato dell'arte della pittura* (1584; *see* LOMAZZO, GIOVANNI PAOLO, §2); this was largely adhered to in practice (de Jong, 1987). It was recommended that palace rooms with an official function should be decorated with scenes representing Virtue, heroic ancestry or acts of outstanding statesmanship. The legend of Aeneas, whom Boccaccio described not only as the founder of Rome but also as an exemplar of resolution in opposition to passionate feeling, could be brilliantly adapted to such themes, as in Nicolò dell'Abate's cycle of *Scenes from the Aeneid* (Modena, Gal. & Mus. Estense).

Lighter, amusing subjects, such as love scenes and metamorphoses, inspired by Ovid or by Apuleius' story of Cupid and Psyche, were recommended for the decoration of country villas, and for the private rooms in both villas and palaces. Outstanding among such decorations are Correggio's *Loves of Jupiter*, commissioned by Federico Gonzaga II, which includes *Ganymede* and *Io* (both *c.* 1532; Vienna, Ksthist. Mus.; *see* CORREGGIO, fig. 6); Giulio Romano's decoration of the Palazzo del Te at Mantua (*see* GIULIO ROMANO, figs 4–5); and Raphael's decoration of the Villa Farnesina, Rome, whose theme of 'Amor vincit omnia' encompassed such ceiling frescoes as the *Wedding of Cupid and Psyche* (see fig. 3).

Depiction of straightforward eroticism without any deeper implications was a distinctively Venetian tradition. Titian's paintings, most importantly the cycle (1519–25; London, N.G.; Madrid, Prado; *see* TITIAN, figs 3–5) for the *camerino* of Alfonso I d'Este and the *Poesie* (1550–62; Madrid, Prado) for Philip II, are an incomparably sensual illustration of all-conquering love. In his correspondence with Philip II, Titian described his mythological paintings as *poesie, nude* and *paesi*; this was a new concept, one that he, together with Giorgione, initiated and one that would be popular in the 17th century: the mythological pastoral. The tendency towards undisguisedly erotic depictions of mythological scenes also persisted in the art of Fontainebleau and Prague, and in Lucas Cranach I's paintings for the court at Wittenberg (*see* CRANACH, (1), fig. 4).

The mythographical works of Lilio Gregorio Giraldi (1548), Natale Conti (1551) and VINCENZO CARTARI (1556, 2/1571) took over the role first played by Boccaccio's *Genealogia* as handbooks of mythography. In addition, they followed the earlier work's style of explaining mythology as an assemblage of truths and ancient wisdom veiled in fable. The contributions of studies of the hieroglyphs engraved on obelisks, such as the Egyptian priest Horapollo Niliacus' *Hieroglyphica* (*c.* 2nd-4th century AD; discovered in 1419 and published in Venice, 1505), eventually led to a strong emphasis on oriental divinities. The engravings in Cartari's *Imagini* (2/1571) were particularly influential (e.g. in their effect on mythological costume designs for ceremonial processions). Writers, including Lomazzo, considered a knowledge of mythology as a necessity for artists; such knowledge was also promoted by numerous illustrated translations of Ovid, among them an important edition published in Lyon (1557) with woodcuts by Bernard Salomon. Reworkings and allegorical exegeses of Classical authors also became an important source of emblematic material.

At the same time a reaction against mythology was encouraged by the Counter-Reformation. Yet the attitudes of the high officials of the Church were ambivalent; mythology continued to provide material for the decoration of their palaces. The Church could not stem the rising tide of mythological content in the arts; the moralized Ovid (but not the original) was placed on the *Index librorum prohibitorum*, but nonetheless, allegorical explanation remained the supreme justification for mythological scenes. The Jesuits, in particular, were aware of the allegorical possibilities offered by mythology and exploited them for the greater glory of God. The pagan gods were taken from their context and used as symbols of concepts or philosophical truths. The elaborate symbolic language of such images, developed by Cartari, was extended in the *Iconologia* (1593, 2/1603) of CESARE RIPA, thus ensuring the gods' survival in the art of the future.

4. THE BAROQUE PERIOD, *c.* 1595–*c.* 1700. Annibale Carracci's radiant and sensual mythological frescoed decoration (1597–1600) of the loves of the gods in the Galleria Farnese in Rome (*see* CARRACI, (3), fig. 5 and ITALY, fig. 36) continues the theme of 'Amor vincit omnia' that had inspired Raphael's decoration of the Villa Farnesina. The scenes could be interpreted neo-platonically, and in the 17th century the Renaissance desire to justify sensual mythological scenes allegorically and to stress the importance of decorum in choosing decorative schemes for the palaces of high churchmen, secular rulers and noble patrons persisted. Carracci's revival of both antique spirit and Classical forms deeply influenced Gianlorenzo Bernini, whose marble groups of *Aeneas, Anchises and Ascanius Leaving Troy* (1618–19), *Pluto and Proserpina* (1621–2)

and *Apollo and Daphne* (1622–4; all Rome, Gal. Borghese; *see* BERNINI, (2), fig. 1) are immediate and dramatic illustrations of Classical myths, inspired by his intense response to the realism of Hellenistic sculpture. Mythology was also used to glorify the patron and his or her family. Carracci's *Hercules at the Crossroads* (Naples, Capodimonte), for example, does this indirectly, while portraits of monarchs in the guise of mythological figures could accomplish it more obviously. Henry IV of France was frequently represented as Hercules, especially on medals (see Vivanti, 1967). Following these examples Pietro da Cortona glorified the Medici family in his series of rooms dedicated to the planetary deities in the Palazzo Pitti, Florence (1641–7; *in situ*; *see* CORTONA, PIETRO DA, fig. 2) and in the Galleria Doria-Pamphili, Rome (1651–4), as did Luca Giordano at the Galleria Riccardiana (1682–5; Florence, Pal. Medici–Riccardi).

In the work of Peter Paul Rubens, mythology achieved simultaneously its most spontaneous and most triumphant expression (*see* RUBENS, PETER PAUL, fig. 5). Rubens's Baroque style became the touchstone of mythological painting for later generations. As vision becomes reality in his religious works, reality and the supernatural are brought into perfect harmony in mythological paintings. Rubens achieved this by means of compositional devices, strengthened by his vivid, human rendering of mythological characters, which strikes the viewer even when the gods are personifications of abstract concepts, as in the *Allegory of War and Peace* (1629–30; London, N.G.; *see* ALLEGORY, fig. 7). In Rubens's most extensive mythological cycle, the Ovid series (1636–7) for the Torre de la Parada, Philip IV of Spain's hunting-lodge, the gods behave like human beings and convey a wide range of emotion. In this work Rubens achieved that which Classical art theory considered art's highest goal: to illustrate emotions by means of the actions and expressions of the figures. This achievement is even more remarkable in the preparatory oil sketches he made for the series, for example the scene showing the *Rape of Proserpina* (see fig. 4), in which the girl's fear is vividly conveyed.

In contrast to Rubens's dramatic art, the mythological scenes of Nicolas Poussin are tightly controlled within a poetic, elegiac atmosphere. Poussin interpreted myth both poetically and philosophically, inspired by such Classical poets as Ovid and Lucretius, and by his contemporary Giambattista Marino, as in the *Kingdom of Flora* (1630–31; Dresden, Gemäldegal. Alte Meister), the *Triumph of Neptune* (1635–6; Philadelphia, PA, Mus. A.) and the *Triumph of Pan* (1636; London, N.G.; *see* POUSSIN, NICOLAS, fig. 2). His later 'mythological' landscapes (Blunt, 1967) reflect a Stoic attitude towards nature, and mythical figures symbolize the forces of nature, as in the *Birth of Bacchus* (1657; Cambridge, MA, Fogg) and *Apollo and Daphne* (*c.* 1664; Paris, Louvre). In his early pastoral scenes Claude Lorrain, like many 17th-century landscape painters, envisaged the Ovidian landscape as a carefree woodland scene where nymphs and shepherds play; his later romantic mythologies, such as the *Enchanted Castle* (1664; London, N.G.), are more poignant and elegiac, and his late pictures, many inspired by Virgil's *Aeneid*, suggest both the beauty of the Roman Campagna and its rich mythological associations.

4. *Rape of Proserpina* by Peter Paul Rubens, sketch for the Torre de la Parada cycle, oil on panel, 260×370 mm, 1636–7 (Bayonne, Musée Bonnat)

5. LATE BAROQUE AND NEO-CLASSICISM, *c.* 1700–*c.* 1800. During the 18th century the division between two steadily emergent interpretations of mythology became much wider: on the one hand a scientific approach, as represented in Gerard Vossius's *De theologia gentili et physiologia christiana* (1641), developed into comparative mythology and theology; and on the other an increasing emphasis on the decorative aspects of mythological painting led to the mythologies of Giambattista Tiepolo (*see* TIEPOLO, (1), fig. 3) and the sensuous nymphs and goddesses of François Boucher (*see* BOUCHER, FRANÇOIS, figs 3–4) and Jean-Honoré Fragonard. The Enlightenment, however, brought about a significant change in the way mythology was valued. Antoine Banier's *La Mythologie et les fables expliquées par l'histoire* (1738–40), a collection of non-allegorical fables, constituted a breakthrough for rationalism in the field of mythological investigation. As archaeology developed, works that illustrated mythology from archaeological sources, such as Bernard de Montfaucon's *L'Antiquité expliquée et représentée en figures* (10 vols, 1719) and Johann Joachim Winckelmann's *Monumenti antichi inediti* (1767) and *Versuch einer Allegorie, besonders für die Kunst* (1766), rendered traditional mythological iconography increasingly old-fashioned. Around the mid-18th century artists began to seek inspiration in the Homeric epics rather than in Ovid, a shift of preference reflected in Charles Rollin's *De la Manière d'enseigner et d'étudier les belles-lettres* (1726–8); Rollin valued in Homer

precisely those elements that originally had led to the poet's rejection in favour of Ovid: the naturalism and human qualities of the characters. The Comte de Caylus's *Tableaux tirés de l'Iliade, de l'Odyssée d'Homère* (1757) inspired many renderings of Homeric scenes. Gavin Hamilton painted such themes (for illustration *see* HAMILTON, GAVIN), and he and Caylus, both of whom admired the austere art of Poussin, embodied a critical attack on the decorative art of the Rococo.

Towards the end of the 18th century these developments led to the creation of Neo-classicism, a style characterized by a closer adherence to Classical art, by concentration on the essential elements of a narrative and by simplicity of composition and form. This simplicity is epitomized by John Flaxman's illustrations to the *Iliad* (1793) and *Odyssey* (1795), which are pure outline drawings in the manner of the illustrations in archaeological publications. Antonio Canova similarly attempted to emulate the simplicity of Greek sculpture (e.g. *Theseus and the Minotaur*, 1781–3; London, V&A), and his *Cupid Awakening Psyche* (1783–93; *see* CANOVA, ANTONIO, fig. 1) and *Cupid and Psyche Standing* (1796–1800; both Paris, Louvre) suggest the soul's search for divine love. Bertel Thorvaldsen, who followed Canova as one of the foremost Neo-classical sculptors, continued to explore these themes well into the 19th century (e.g. *Three Graces with Cupid*, 1817–19; and *Jason with the Golden Fleece*, 1803–28; both Copenhagen, Thorvaldsen Mus.; for the latter *see* THORVALDSEN, BERTEL, fig. 1). For other artists mythological subjects came to be seen as frivolous and immoral, and such painters as Jacques-Louis David began to focus on the heroic actions of men rather than the loves of the gods; they moved from light-hearted subjects and chose elevated themes of a predominantly tragic character.

6. ROMANTICISM, SYMBOLISM AND MODERN ART, *c.* 1800 AND AFTER. In the 19th century mythological themes acquired an unmistakably Romantic tone, with an appeal to the emotions as a primary characteristic: Eugène Delacroix was among the artists to treat the tragic fate of humanity, lamentation of the dead and heroic or tragic female figures (e.g. *Medea*, 1838; Lille, Mus. B.-A.; *see* DELACROIX, EUGÈNE, fig. 4). The heroism that dominated mythological scenes was parodied by such artists as Honoré Daumier (e.g. the *Drunkenness of Silenus*, 1863; Calais, Mus. B.-A.). In the second half of the 19th century in England such Aesthetic Movement painters as Frederic Leighton, Lawrence Alma-Tadema and Albert Joseph Moore stressed that formal organization of a picture was more important than its subject; they nevertheless chose mythological scenes to convey their artistic ideals (e.g. Leighton's *Garden of the Hesperides*, *c.* 1892; Port Sunlight, Lady Lever A.G.). Symbolist artists, in a reaction against Realism in art and the empirical in science, sought to depict the spiritual through mythological subjects (*see* SYMBOLISM). The melancholy art of Edward Burne-Jones and of the French Symbolists, notably Odilon Redon and Gustave Moreau, poignantly conveys a sense of the end of a tradition. Moreau's mythological works, for example *Oedipus and the Sphinx* (*c.* 1864; New York, Met.) and *Hercules and the Hydra of Lerna* (1876; Chicago, IL, A. Inst.), symbolize such universal themes as life versus death, male versus female and the conflict between good and evil. His many paintings of Orpheus explore the theme of artistic creation and of the poet's role in a hostile society. Redon used mythical allusions to convey a sense of the origin of things: the sirens, centaurs and bound Pegasus of his volume of lithographs *Origins* (1883) suggest the mystery of creation; his fantastic and monstrous images are indebted to the art of Goya. In Arnold Böcklin's landscapes mythological figures and sea creatures embody the vitality of nature (e.g. *Pan in the Reeds*, 1856–8; Munich, Neue Pin.; *see* BÖCKLIN, ARNOLD, fig. 1).

In 20th-century art there was less emphasis on narrative mythological scenes. Artists used mythological subjects to symbolize universal themes, such as life versus death, and Orphic and Bacchic subjects recurred. The relationship between myth and dream as explored by Sigmund Freud and Carl Gustav Jung also had a significant effect on 20th-century artists; the Surrealists, indebted to Freud, illustrated such myths as Narcissus and Echo, Oedipus and Theseus and the Minotaur. André Masson produced numerous paintings and drawings of the myth of Theseus and the Minotaur, and the Cretan labyrinth became a symbol of the unconscious. The subject also attracted Picasso, who produced besides drawings (*see* DRAWING, colour pl. II, fig. 1) a series of etchings of *Metamorphoses of Ovid* (1933), the *Tauromachia* (1934) and the *Minotauromachia* (1935). From the 1930s Max Beckmann treated mythological subjects in a number of his paintings (e.g.

Odysseus and Calypso, 1943; Hamburg, Ksthalle); like many of his works, these have an expressive realism yet can be interpreted allegorically. The use of myth to express and validate a personal psychology continued to interest some succeeding 20th-century artists.

BIBLIOGRAPHY

SOURCES

[Servius]: *Servii grammatici qui feruntur in Vergilii Carmina commentarii* (4th–5th centuries AD); ed. G. Thilo and H. Hagen (Leipzig, 1881/*R* Hildesheim, 1961)

Macrobius: *Commentarii in somnium Scipionis* (5th century AD); ed. J. Willis, 2 vols (Leipzig, 1963, 2/1970) [incl. *Saturnalia*]

Martianus Capella: *De nuptiis Mercurii et Philologiae* (5th century AD); ed. A. Dick (Leipzig, 1925, 2/1969)

Fulgentius: *Mythologiae* (late 5th century AD–early 6th); ed. R. Helm (Leipzig, 1898)

[Remigius of Auxerre]: *Remigii Autissiodorensis commentum in Martianum Capellam* (*c.* late 9th–early 10th century; MS. *c.* 1100; Munich, Bayer. Staatsbib., clm 14271); ed. C. E. Lutz, 2 vols (Leiden, 1962–5)

Ovide moralisé (*c.* 1316–28); ed. C. de Boer in *Verhand. Kon. Acad. Wet. Afd. Lettknd.*, n. s., xv (1915); xxi (1920); xxx (1931); xxxvi–xxxvii (1936); xliii (1938); prose version, ed. C. de Boer, ibid., lxi (1954)

J. Ridewall: *Fulgentius metaforalis* (*c.* 1330); see also H. Liebeschütz (1926)

P. Berchorius: *Ovidius moralizatus* (*c.* 1340); ed. J. Engels, Werkmateriaal, 1–3 (Utrecht, 1960–66)

G. Boccaccio: *De genealogia deorum gentilium libri* (Venice, 1372), ed. V. Romano, 2 vols (Bari, 1951)

Libellus de imaginibus deorum (*c.* 1400); see also H. Liebeschütz (1926) [incl. texts of *Libellus* and John Ridewall's *Fulgentius metaforalis* with comment.]

L. G. Giraldi: *De deis gentium varia et multiplex historia in qua simul de eorum imaginibus et cognominibus agitur* (Basle, 1548/*R* New York, 1976)

N. Conti: *Mythologiae, sive explicationis fabularum libri decem* (Venice, 1551, 1567/*R* New York, 1976)

V. Cartari: *Le imagini, con la spositione de i dei de gli antichi* (Venice, 1556, 2/1571/*R* New York, 1976); facs. ed. M. Bussagli (Genoa, 1987)

C. Ripa: *Iconologia* (Rome, 1593, 2/1603/*R* New York, 1976)

B. de Montfaucon: *L'Antiquité expliquée et représentée en figures*, 10 vols (Paris, 1719, 2/1722–4; Eng. trans., London, 1721–5/*R* New York, 1976)

C. Rollin: *De la Manière d'enseigner et d'étudier les belles-lettres*, 4 vols (Paris, 1726–8; Eng. trans., London, 1734)

A. Banier: *La Mythologie et les fables expliquées par l'histoire*, 4 vols (Paris, 1738–40; Eng. trans., London, 1739–40/*R* New York, 1976)

J. J. Winckelmann: *Versuch einer Allegorie, besonders für die Kunst* (Dresden, 1766/*R* 1964)

Comte de Caylus: *Tableaux tirés de l'Iliade de l'Odyssée d'Homère et de l'Enéide de Virgile: Avec des observations générales sur le costume* (Paris, 1757)

J. J. Winckelmann: *Monumenti antichi inediti*, 2 vols (Rome, 1767/*R* 1967)

S. Orgel, ed.: *The Renaissance and the Gods: A Comprehensive Collection of Renaissance Mythographies, Iconologies and Iconographies, with a Selection of Works from the Enlightenment*, 55 vols (New York, 1976) [reprints of treatises from the late 15th century to the 18th]

GENERAL

EWA: 'Myth and Fable' [with extensive bibliography]

A. Pigler: *Barockthemen: Eine Auswahl von Verzeichnissen zur Ikonographie des 17. und 18. Jahrhunderts*, 2 vols (Budapest, 1956, rev. and enlarged in 3 vols, 2/1974)

A. Henkel and A. Schöne, eds: *Emblemata: Handbuch zur Sinnbildkunst des XVI. und XVII. Jahrhunderts* (Stuttgart, 1967, rev. 2/1976/*R* 1978)

J. de Bie, ed.: *Griekse mythologie en Europese cultuur*, Lustrumuitgave Nederlands Klassiek Verbond 1938–1978 (Antwerp, 1979)

K. Hübner: *Die Wahrheit als Mythos* (Munich, 1985)

J. D. Reid: *The Oxford Guide to Classical Mythology in the Arts, 1300–1990s*, 2 vols (New York and Oxford, 1993)

SPECIALIST STUDIES
Bibliography

M. Lurker: *Bibliographie zur Symbolik, Ikonographie und Mythologie: Internationales Referateorgan* (Baden-Baden, 1968–)

H. van de Waal: *Iconclass: An Iconographic Classification System*, 17 vols (Amsterdam, 1973–85)

Classical Antiquity and Etruscan

R. Hinks: *Myth and Allegory in Ancient Art*, Stud. Warb. Inst., vi (London, 1939)

C. M. Dawson: *Romano-Campanian Mythological Landscape Painting*, Yale Class. Stud., ix (New Haven, 1944/R Rome, 1965)

F. Brommer: *Vasenlisten zur griechischen Heldensage* (Marburg, 1956, rev. 3/1973)

K. Schefold: *Frühgriechische Sagenbilder* (Munich, 1964; Eng. trans., London, 1966)

F. Brommer: *Denkmälerlisten zur griechischen Heldensage*, 3 vols (Marburg, 1971–6)

H. Sichtermann and G. Koch: *Griechische Mythen auf römischen Sarkophagen*, 5–6, Bilderheft des Dt. Archäol. Inst., Rom (Tübingen, 1975)

K. Schefold and L. Giuliani: *Götter- und Heldensagen der Griechen in der spätarchaischen Kunst* (Munich, 1978)

K. Schefold and F. Jung: *Die Göttersage in der klassischen und hellenistischen Kunst* (Munich, 1981)

LIMC: *Lexicon iconographicum mythologiae classicae* (Zurich and Munich, 1981–)

W. G. Moon, ed.: *Ancient Greek Art and Iconography* (Madison, 1983)

K. Schefold and F. Jung: *Die Urkönige, Perseus, Bellerophon, Herakles und Theseus in der klassischen und hellenistischen Kunst* (Munich, 1988)

——: *Die Sagen von den Argonauten, von Theben und Troia in der klassischen und hellenistischen Kunst* (Munich, 1989)

Late Antique, Early Christian, Byzantine

K. Weitzmann: *Greek Mythology in Byzantine Art*, Stud. MS. Illum., iv (Princeton, 1951/R 1984)

——: 'The Survival of Mythological Representations in Early Christian and Byzantine Art and their Impact on Christian Iconography', *Dumbarton Oaks Pap.*, xiv (1960), pp. 43–68

Survival of the Classical Tradition

F. Saxl: 'Rinascimento di antiquità: Studien zu den Arbeiten A. Warburgs', *Repert. Kstwiss.*, xliii (1922), pp. 220–72

M. D. Henkel: 'Illustrierte Ausgaben von Ovids Metamorphosen im XV., XVI. und XVII. Jahrhundert', *Vorträge Bib. Warburg*, vi (1926–7), pp. 58–144

E. Panofsky: *Hercules am Scheidewege und andere antike Bildstoffe in der neueren Kunst*, Stud. Bib. Warburg, xviii (Leipzig, 1930)

A. M. Warburg: *Gesammelte Schriften: Die Erneuerung der heidnischen Antike*, 2 vols (Berlin and Leipzig, 1932/R Nendeln, 1969)

E. Panofsky: *Studies in Iconology: Humanistic Themes in the Art of the Renaissance* (New York, 1939/R 1962)

J. Seznec: *La Survivance des dieux antiques: Essai sur le rôle de la tradition mythologique dans l'humanisme et dans l'art de la Renaissance*, Stud. Warburg Inst., xi (London, 1940; Eng. trans., New York, 1953/R Princeton, 1972)

F. Saxl: *Lectures*, 2 vols (London, 1957)

E. Panofsky: *Renaissance and Renascences in Western Art* (Stockholm, 1960/R New York, 1972)

G. K. Galinsky: *The Hercules Theme* (Oxford, 1972)

Medieval

F. Saxl: *Verzeichnis astrologischer und mythologischer illustrierter Handschriften des lateinischen Mittelalters*, i: *Römischen Bibliotheken* (Heidelberg, 1915); ii: *Die Handschriften der National-Bibliothek in Wien* (Heidelberg, 1927); iii, with H. Meier, ed. H. Bober: *Handschriften in englischen Bibliotheken* (London, 1953/R 1978); iv, by P. McGurk: *Astrological Manuscripts in Italian Libraries (other than Rome)* (London, 1966)

F. von Bezold: *Das Fortleben der antiken Götter im mittelalterlichen Humanismus* (Bonn, 1922/R Aalen, 1962)

H. Liebeschütz: *Fulgentius Metaforalis: Ein Beitrag zur Geschichte der antiken Mythologie im Mittelalter*, Stud. Bib. Warb., iv (Leipzig and Berlin, 1926)

E. Panofsky and F. Saxl: 'Classical Mythology in Mediaeval Art', *Met. Mus. Stud.*, iv (1932–3), pp. 228–80

K. Heitmann: 'Typen der Deformierung antiker Mythen im Mittelalter: Am Beispiel der Orpheussage', *Romanist. Jb.*, xiv (1963), pp. 45–77

H. Buchthal: *Historia Troiana: Studies in the History of Mediaeval Secular Illustration*, Stud. Warb. Inst., xxxii (London, 1971/R Nendeln, 1978)

N. Himmelmann: *Antike Götter im Mittelalter* (Mainz, 1986)

Renaissance

P. Schubring: *Cassoni: Truhen und Truhenbilder in der italienischen Frührenaissance: Ein Beitrag zur Profanmalerei im Quattrocento*, 2 vols (Leipzig, 1915) [suppl. 1923]

C. Vivanti: 'Henry IV, the Gallic Hercules', *J. Warb. & Court. Inst.*, xxx (1967), pp. 176–97, figs 18b, g and h

D. C. Allen: *Mysteriously Meant: The Rediscovery of Pagan Symbolism and Allegorical Interpretation in the Renaissance* (Baltimore and London, 1970)

L. D. Ettlinger: 'Hercules Florentinus', *Mitt. Ksthist. Inst. Florenz*, xvi (1972), pp. 119–42

E. H. Gombrich: *Symbolic Images: Studies in the Art of the Renaissance* (London, 1972)

B. Guthmüller: 'Picta poesis Ovidiana', *Renatae litterae: Studien zum Nachleben der Antike und zur europäischen Renaissance: [Festschrift] August Buck* (Frankfurt, 1973), pp. 171–92

L. Cheney: *Quattrocento Neo-Platonism and Medici Humanism in Botticelli's Mythological Paintings* (New York and London, 1985)

P. P. Bober and R. Rubinstein: *Renaissance Artists and Antique Sculpture: A Handbook of Sources* (London, 1986, 2/1987)

J. L. de Jong: *De oudheid in fresco: De interpretatie van klassieke onderwerpen in de Italiaanse wandschilderkunst, inzonderheid te Rome, circa 1370–1555* (diss., U. Leiden, 1987)

17th and 18th centuries

H. Bardon: 'Les Peintures à sujets antiques au XVIIIe siècle d'après les livrets de Salons', *Gaz. B.-A.*, n. s. 5 (1963), pp. 217–50

J. R. Martin: *The Farnese Gallery*, Princeton Monographs A. Archaeol., 36 (Princeton, 1965)

S. Alpers: 'Manner and Meaning in Some Rubens Mythologies', *J. Warb. & Court. Inst.*, xxx (1967), pp. 272–95

A. Blunt: *Nicolas Poussin* (London and New York, 1967)

C. Dempsey: '"Et nos cedamus amori": Observations on the Farnese Gallery', *A. Bull.*, 1 (1968), pp. 363–74

S. Alpers: *The Decoration of the Torre de la Parada*, Corpus Rubenianum Ludwig Burchard, ix (London and New York, 1971)

F. Bardon: *Le Portrait mythologique à la cour de France sous Henri IV et Louis XIII: Mythologie et politique* (Paris, 1974)

Gods, Saints and Heroes: Dutch Painting in the Age of Rembrandt (exh. cat., ed. A. Blankert; Washington, DC, N.G.A.; Detroit, MI, Inst. A.; Amsterdam, Rijksmus.; 1980–81)

R. López Torrijos: *La mitología en la pintura española del siglo de oro* (Madrid, 1985)

F. J. Sluijter: *De 'heydensche fabulen' in de Noordnederlandse schilderkunst circa 1590–1670: Een proeve van beschrijving en interpretatie van schilderijen met verhalende onderwerpen uit de klassieke mythologie* (diss., U. Leiden, 1986)

Les Amours des dieux: La Peinture mythologique de Watteau à David (exh. cat., ed. C. B. Bailey; Paris, Grand Pal.; Philadelphia, PA, Mus. A.; Fort Worth, TX, Kimbell A. Mus.; 1991–2)

19th–20th centuries

H. Falkner von Sonnenburg: *Die antike Mythologie in der Malerei des 19. Jahrhunderts* (diss., U. Munich, 1952)

D. Wiebenson: 'Subjects from Homer's Iliad in Neo-classical Art', *A. Bull.*, xlvi (1964), pp. 23–37

John Flaxman: Mythologie und Industrie (exh. cat., ed. W. Hofmann; Hamburg, Ksthalle, 1979)

W. Chadwick: *Myth in Surrealist Painting, 1929–1939* (Ann Arbor, 1980)

WILLEM F. LASH

Mytilene. *See under* LESBOS.

Myzithras. *See* MYSTRAS.

N

Naarden. Dutch town, 20 km east of Amsterdam. It is one of the best-preserved fortified towns in Europe, presenting an almost regular form of large bastions. Viewed from the air, it is revealed as an extended, slightly irregular hexagon, protected by ravelins and a broad, double, wet ditch with two stretches of water separated by a wide *fausse-braye* (lower protective wall). The town dates back to the mid-14th century, and it was fortified during the late 16th century and the early 17th as a result of the War of Independence (1568–1648) against Spain. Its defences were completely rebuilt after 1676, and four of its six bastions with their intervening curtains were remodelled on the French style, with orillons, high and low flanks and with revetted scarp walls. The work was probably done by Paul Storff, a German engineer who also worked in England and Ireland, but it was completed in 1685 by the two Dutch engineers Adriaen Dortsman and Willem Paen. Some of the flanking gun positions are gracefully curved in the manner advocated by Menno van Coehoorn, but it is unlikely that he was actively involved in the project. After the Napoleonic Wars, in the 19th century Naarden became the northern pivot of the New Dutch Waterline, the main line of defence for the Netherlands, a great water barrier linked to the lower Rhine. Part of the fortress was modernized in the 1870s, when bomb-proof barracks and mortar casemates were built. The sole remaining gate is the powerful stone Utrecht Gate, built in 1877, its entrance passage defended by numerous musketry loopholes and with a splendid Gothic façade towards the town. Naarden is also noted for its Grote Kerk (1380–1440, rebuilt 1479), which has fine vault paintings from the early 16th century and a wooden choir-screen (1513), and the Stadhuis (1601), which has two stepped gables and fine interior decoration.

BIBLIOGRAPHY

A. C. J. de Vrankrijker: *De historie van de vesting Naarden* (Bussum, 1965)

QUENTIN HUGHES

Nabarrayal, Lofty (*b* W. Arnhem Land, N. Territory, 1926). Australian Aboriginal painter. His father painted on rock surfaces in the region of the upper reaches of the Liverpool River, and as a youth Nabarrayal was trained to paint at a number of caves in this area. His bark paintings, like those of Dick Ngulayngulay, have strong affinities to the rock art of Western Arnhem Land. For many years researchers had visited Oenpelli, one of the two major towns in the region, to collect art, and the production of art and craft had become a major community occupation during the 1960s. It was then that Nabarrayal began painting works for sale while he was living at the Oenpelli Mission, using as his materials natural ochres on sheets of the bark of the Eucalyptus tetradonta tree. Such works as *Animals Feeding* (*c.* 1975; Canberra, N. Mus.) are characterized by the exquisite detail given to features of his animal figures. Animals and mimi spirits are common subjects, but Nabarrayal became well known for painting images of Ngalyod or Yingarna, the original creator being of Western Arnhem Land's religion. In a work such as *Ngalyod the Rainbow Serpent* (Darwin, N. Territ. Mus. A. & Sci.) he painted a fantastic body form that includes the features of many species, expressing the way this being is conceived as a 'mother' of all species and of humans. Sections of the figure are infilled with parallel-line hatching, invariably in red ochre.

BIBLIOGRAPHY

R. Edwards, ed.: *Oenpelli Bark Paintings* (Sydney, 1979), p. 49

LUKE TAYLOR

Nabataea. Kingdom in north-west Arabia (now Jordan and north-west Saudi Arabia) that flourished from the 4th century BC to the 4th century AD and became one of the greatest trading kingdoms of the Ancient Near East. By the late 4th century BC a group of pastoral nomads had settled in the region in the ancient Edomite stronghold of PETRA, and they were known as the Nabatu or Nabataeans. As nomads, the Nabataeans had gained wide experience of the Arabian caravan routes; they monopolized the lucrative frankincense and myrrh trade from the south and then expanded it to include other luxury items prized by the hellenized West. A royal line developed in the 2nd century BC, and Petra became the capital city of the kingdom, which remained virtually autonomous until Roman annexation by the emperor Trajan (*reg* AD 98–117) in AD 106. Even then Nabataean culture survived at Petra, until the city was destroyed by an earthquake in AD 363. Due perhaps to the previously nomadic lives of the people, as well as to their unusual talent, Nabataean culture developed an eclectic character, most obvious in art and architecture. Public and private monumental architecture abounded, the former including theatres, temples, roads and hydraulic systems, the latter including the tomb façades that have become the Nabataeans' most famous architectural relics.

1. ARCHITECTURE. Earlier studies of Nabataean architecture concentrated mainly on the rock-cut funerary

monuments at Petra and MADA' IN SALIH. With the excavation of temples and other public buildings at Petra and elsewhere, however, knowledge of Nabataean building methods, decoration, models and influences has increased. The initial work on the numerous tomb façades, by Rudolph E. Brünnow, Alfred von Domaszewski and others, produced only broad typologies, which were neither firm chronologies nor true pictures of actual architectural development. They did recognize, however, that the Nabataeans adapted elements from Mesopotamia, Egypt and the hellenized West and incorporated them into their own structures; examples of this are the crow-step, the Egyptian cavetto, the Corinthian column and, finally, Roman orders, modified to suit Nabataean taste. The Nabataean capital, for example, is distinctive, composed of projecting 'horns' instead of the volutes of the Corinthian order. Less obvious modifications are reductions in standard heights and in module sizes, and the lack of columnar entasis, apparent only after careful analysis. By contrast, the lavish use of floral decoration, often with applied elements, the typical diagonal dressing of interior walls and the sheer size of the façades and tomb chambers are typically Nabataean contributions.

Nabataean buildings were more varied in their construction techniques and quality than the superbly carved rock tombs. Heavy plastering often covered rather poorly fitted blocks or took the place of elements that might be expected to have been stone-carved, for example in the interior of the Temple of Allat (the Temple of the Winged Lions) at Petra. At the same time innovative approaches to construction can be seen in the use of numbers and letters of the alphabet to designate the location for ashlars and column drums, in the use of ring-bases for columns, in the keying nails and tacks used in plastering walls and in the devices used for affixing *crustae* (plaster wall attachments).

Certain features in Nabataean architecture, at least in the reign of Aretas IV (9 BC–AD 40), were probably based on examples in Vitruvius' *On Architecture*, either directly or indirectly via artisans trained in Rome. Hence the plans of such buildings as theatres and temples tend to conform to those commonly found throughout the hellenized Roman Empire. The impressive architectural contributions made by Aretas IV were perhaps the result of rivalry with the equally impressive record of HEROD THE GREAT (*reg* 37–4 BC), himself part Nabataean, in the nearby kingdom of Judaea.

Architectural decoration was similarly eclectic. Scattered fragments of reliefs, often copies of Hellenistic works showing Greek deities, sculpture in the round, patterned mosaic floors, mystery-cult fresco panels, scrolls depicting faces and animals, naturalistic or highly conventionalized cult images, vine-covered column drums and other examples intermingle throughout Nabataean territory. Oriental elements are apparent in the pouting lips and protruding eyes of faces and in the use of attributes to symbolize deities. Purely Nabataean are the eye-idols (stylized faces with prominent eyes) and the Dushara blocks (rectangular blocks of rock in niches symbolizing the chief male deity) still *in situ* in Petra.

In hydraulic engineering the Nabataeans surpassed most other cultures in the neighbouring regions, especially in their incorporation of natural features into water-supply systems. Innumerable dams, cisterns and other devices for storing water have been found throughout Nabataea. These are most remarkable at Petra. In drier regions circles of stone may have been an architectural feature designed to curtail run-off and permit the arid soil to soak up the maximum amount of rainfall.

2. SCULPTURE, CERAMICS AND OTHER ARTS. Although the names of sometimes successive generations of tomb-façade artisans are known (e.g. at Mada' in Salih), the authorship of the innumerable examples of other types of sculpture found in the region is not. It is difficult, therefore, to determine whether any given sculpture is the work of a local artist or that of an itinerant one. If the work is of local stone, the place of execution is obvious, but the origin of the artist is not. Classical motifs, such as deities, or symmetrical arrangement could have been executed by either local or visiting artists, as could local motifs. The Nabataeans were skilled in many other crafts, suggesting they also possessed technological and artistic ability in the realm of sculpture, but it is not possible to be certain of this. Examples of sculpture found in the region can be seen on Nabataean sites, in the Petra Museum and in the Jordan Archaeological Museum, Amman (*see* PETRA, fig. 1). The basalt head in the Louvre

1. Nabataean sculpture of a male head, basalt, h. 200 mm, from Seia, 33/32–2/1 BC (Paris, Musée du Louvre)

(see fig. 1) shows the typical almond-shaped eyes and Nabataean hairstyle but lacks the characteristic 'pouting' lips that are often found.

Nabataean ceramics are distinctive. The fine, thin, red-painted wares were first identified with the culture by Horsfield and Horsfield, who looked to Persia for their origin, although their affinity in form with the West Slope ware of the Athenian Agora (*see* GREECE, ANCIENT, §V, 9) suggests a Western source. They display a remarkably high level of expertise in clay preparation, throwing, standardization of size and shape, wall thinness, slip-paint decoration and firing. Decorated plates are common, but a wide variety of small cups, jugs and bowls also occur (see fig. 2). Decoration includes floral, linear and occasional zoomorphic motifs. In the early examples (1st century BC–1st century AD), which represent the highest technological level achieved, the decoration appears in red tones. Later, the decoration on generally less well-executed specimens (late 4th century AD) is done in black, although this may simply represent poor firing. The fine ware class appeared suddenly, probably in the last quarter of the 1st century BC, and represented an advanced stage of ceramic production. The transition to the black decorated class occurred probably around the last quarter of the 1st century AD.

The common wares found on Nabataean sites sometimes followed the forms of the fine ware class (especially the small plates), but proliferated according to the demands of domestic need. Thus cooking pots, strainer jugs, jars, storage jars, 'pilgrim flasks', bowls and other everyday vessels are found. In general, these conform to similar assemblages found throughout the Middle East, as well as in the West, during the Roman period and later. Decoration includes coloured slips, combing and ribbing, along with occasional examples of 'drip' painting on exteriors. Especially notable in the common ware class are the containers thought to be for ointments and known as *unguentaria*.

Early examples at Petra (probably 4th century BC) were in the typical Hellenistic form of the spindle bottle, but these were later completely replaced by a series of high-necked types with round to ovoid bodies of varying and apparently standardized forms (1st century BC onwards). The quantity present at Petra in particular suggests local manufacture, linked to the local production of myrrh and other unguents that the Nabataeans traded. The appearance of the same forms in Western sites also suggests that the Nabataeans may have traded in finished products, as well as in raw materials. Some examples of local duplication of imported items have also been found, for example varieties of *terra sigillata* and Roman red wares, indicating that the local potters were aware of techniques not generally used in their own productions.

Allied to the production of household ceramics was the production in large quantities of figurines and lamps. These were commonly made in two moulds and joined before firing. The figurines include naturalistic examples of animals (particularly the horse and camel—the animals of desert caravan transport—but also monkey and ibex), deities, warriors and other motifs. The lamps, typically with slash-and-rosette or similar decoraton, had short nozzles decorated with volutes, round bodies and wide filling holes. They are based on types prevalent during the Roman period (*see* ROME, ANCIENT, §X, 6).

Nabataean coins are also derivative (examples in London, BM, and Petra Mus.). The earliest coins—those of Harithath II (*reg* 110–95 BC) until Maliku II (*reg c.* 50–28 BC)—portray the head of the king on the obverse but with reverse types borrowed from types issued by their Seleucid neighbours. Later, from the reign of Obidath III (28–9 BC) onwards, the reverses began to show individuality, and they were inscribed with the name of the monarch and, eventually, with that of his queen. The quality of the obverse designs tends to be rather primitive, although successive issues show some variation in features.

2. Nabataean ceramic bowl, diam. 170 mm, from Petra, 1st century AD (Munich, Prähistorische Staatssammlung)

Metalwork items, both commonplace and artistic, have been recovered from Nabataean sites. The range includes architectural fixtures for *crustae*, nails for plastering, door keys, chains, diminutive bells and household vessels, as well as cast busts of deities and mythological creatures. The degree of refinement of the metals (especially copper) found in these artefacts is astonishing. It is highly probable that some objects were of local manufacture, but the origin of certain well-made pieces of jewellery and of the finely cast bronze busts is uncertain. None of the art works displays unique stylistic or obviously developmental features; the motifs vary in style from Hellenistic to oriental.

BIBLIOGRAPHY

R. E. Brünnow and A. von Domaszewski: *Die Provincia Arabia*, 3 vols (Strasbourg, 1901–9)

J. Cantineau: *Le Nabatéen* (Paris, 1930)

G. Horsfield and A. Horsfield: *Q. Dept. Art. Palestine*, ix (1941), pp. 105–218 ['Sela-Petra, the Rock of Edom and Nabatene, IV: The Finds'; 'Excavations in Palestine and Trans-Jordan, 1938–9'; 'Bibliography of Excavations in Palestine and Trans-Jordan, 1938–9']

N. Glueck: *Deities and Dolphins: The Story of the Nabataeans* (London, 1966) [good pls]

P. C. Hammond: *The Nabataeans: Their History, Culture and Archaeology* (Göteborg, 1973)

A. Negev: *The Nabataean Potters' Workshop at Oboda* (Bonn, 1974)

G. Bowersock: *Roman Arabia* (Cambridge, MA, 1983)

PHILIP C. HAMMOND

Nabeshima. Type of Japanese porcelain. It was produced at the Nabeshima clan's kiln at Ōkawauchiyama (Hizen Prov., now Saga Prefect.) from *c.* 1677 to 1871. Production consisted of *sometsuke* (underglaze cobalt blue, blue-and-white), *aoki* (celadon) and *iroe* (polychrome overglaze enamel) wares, of which the most representative polychrome pieces are *iro Nabeshima* ('coloured Nabeshima') wares (see JAPAN, §VIII, 3(iii)). In addition to developing original decorative processes, the kiln succeeded in copying Chinese *doucai* techniques (see CHINA, §VII, 3(vi)), in which designs were outlined in underglaze blue. Early Nabeshima designs were often taken from textiles, but these were superseded by bird-and-flower, landscape and geometrical motifs. The principal Nabeshima ware types were plates in several standard sizes and small bowls; a limited quantity of vases and tea kettles were also made. The kiln lost clan patronage after the abolition of the feudal domains in 1871, but in the 1990s the ware was still being made by the 13th-generation head of the Imaizumi family, Imaizumi Imaemon (*b* 1926).

BIBLIOGRAPHY

Two Hundred Years of Japanese Porcelain (exh. cat. by R. Cleveland, St Louis, MO, A. Mus.; Kansas City, MO, Nelson–Atkins Mus. A.; 1970)

HIROKO NISHIDA

Nabis [Heb.: 'prophets']. Group of artists, predominantly French, active *c.* 1888–1900. Dedicated to pursuing the Synthetist example of Gauguin, the Nabis were a disaffected group of art students at the Académie Julian in Paris who formed themselves into a secret brotherhood in 1888–9. The movement's first adherents were PAUL SÉRUSIER, the group's founder, Maurice Denis, Pierre Bonnard, PAUL RANSON and Henri-Gabriel Ibels. Returning to Paris from Pont-Aven in the autumn term of 1888, Sérusier revealed to his friends a new Synthetist use of

colour and design exemplified in the *Bois d'Amour at Pont-Aven* (Paris, Mus. d'Orsay; for illustration *see* SÉRUSIER, PAUL), a boldly simplified landscape painted on a cigar-box lid under Gauguin's directions that later became known as *The Talisman*. Already drawn together by their common interest in idealist philosophy and in recent Symbolist developments in literature, they adopted their esoteric name from the Hebrew word for prophets—a private designation rather than a public label—at the suggestion of Henri Cazalis, a Hebrew scholar. The name aptly described the enthusiastic zeal with which they greeted and then disseminated the revolutionary teachings of Gauguin. Their youthful desire to shake off the taint of academicism—in their case the quasi-photographic naturalism taught by their masters William-Adolphe Bouguereau and Jules Lefebvre—and revert to the pure decorative roots of art had loose, though possibly conscious, parallels with earlier artistic brotherhoods, notably the German Nazarenes and the English Pre-Raphaelites.

The original group was soon augmented by new recruits, Ker-Xavier Roussel and Edouard Vuillard, friends from the Ecole des Beaux-Arts, Paris, and in 1891–2 a number of foreign artists, including the Dutch Jan Verkade, Danish Mogens Ballin, Swiss Félix Vallotton and Hungarian József Rippl-Rónai. These in their turn introduced the sculptor Georges Lacombe and Aristide Maillol, whose Nabi experiments in a variety of media preceded his career as a sculptor. A few writers and musicians such as Charles Morice (1861–1919) and Pierre Hermant were affiliated to the Nabi group, and Gauguin, then in Tahiti, was made an honorary member. Although he never took any active part in Nabi activities, he gave them his encouragement and appreciated their moral support.

Early meetings were held at a bistro, the L'Os à Moelle near the Académie Julian, and after 1890 monthly reunions took place in Ranson's studio at 25 Boulevard du Montparnasse, jokingly referred to as 'Le Temple'. Nicknames were adopted, and certain esoteric words were used, mainly by the more committed members of the group, Ranson, Sérusier and Verkade, as a means of setting themselves and their 'icônes' (pictures) apart from the uncomprehending 'pelichtim' (bourgeoisie).

Although at no stage can one identify a true group style, between 1890 and 1892, when Sérusier, Bonnard, Vuillard and Denis shared the use of a small studio in the Rue Pigalle, there was a common exploration of certain decorative stylistic features: simplified drawing, flat patches of colour and bold contours inspired by the work of Gauguin and Emile Bernard, as well as arabesques and other patterning devices inspired by Japanese prints. One finds such stylistic features combined in Denis's *Mme Ranson with a Cat* (1892; Saint-Germain-en-Laye, Mus. Dépt. Prieuré), which was painted on to a vertical panel suitable for a folding screen rather than on to a regular size of canvas. They frequently painted on unconventional supports, cardboard or even velvet and explored a wide spectrum of decorative work, ranging from posters, screens, wallpaper and lampshades to scenery painting or costume design for the Symbolist theatre. The Symbolist poet and dramatist Paul Fort (1872–1960) made use of their talents from 1891 to 1893 at his Théâtre d'Art, and from 1893 they were closely involved with the Théâtre de l'Oeuvre, managed by Denis's former school-friend the actor Aurélien Lugné-Poe. The *Revue blanche*, an anarchic and eclectic journal founded in 1891 by the brothers Thadée and Alexandre Natanson (*see* NATANSON, THADEÉ), did much to promote the Nabis: as well as sponsoring group printmaking ventures, the Natansons were responsible for offering Vuillard some of his earliest major decorative commissions. In 1895 Siegfried Bing commissioned stained-glass designs from Sérusier, Denis, Vuillard, Bonnard, Ibels, Roussel and Vallotton, which were made up in Tiffany glass and exhibited at his Salon de l'Art Nouveau, while the art dealer Ambroise Vollard encouraged Denis, Bonnard, Vuillard and Roussel to experiment in the novel medium of colour lithography.

The first group exhibition, arranged by Denis, was held at the château of Saint-Germain-en-Laye in 1891; thereafter until 1896 group shows were held regularly in the gallery of the dealer Louis Le Barc de Boutteville, where the Nabis, identified as Symbolists, hung work alongside the Neo-Impressionists and independent figures such as Toulouse-Lautrec. During the 1890s the Nabis also exhibited, either together or separately, in Toulouse, Antwerp and Brussels. Denis's *Définition du Néo-traditionnisme* (*A. & Crit.*, May 1890), published as a defence of Gauguin and asserting the right of the painter to deform and simplify nature in the pursuit of decorative beauty, served as a loose stylistic credo; and in 1892 an important article by the critic Georges-Albert Aurier hailed the Nabis as inheritors of Gauguin's teaching and creators of a truly Symbolist art.

The lack of a clear programme or unified aesthetic aim left the way open for individual members to pursue their own independent paths, though the exact date at which the group disintegrated is unclear. Whereas Sérusier, who was essentially responsible for the group's existence, felt his initial vision of a unified brotherhood had been disappointed as early as 1892, and Nabi meetings after that date occurred less frequently, close collaboration over exhibitions and other projects continued until 1900; shows such as the Durand-Ruel group show of March 1899, which marked a decade of group activity, had a cohesive effect.

There were two main artistic divisions within the group: artists such as Sérusier, Denis and Ranson saw an essential connection between their Nabi ideas and their religious or theosophical beliefs and tended to draw their subjects from myth, religion or tradition; on the other hand, artists such as Vallotton, Vuillard and Bonnard, whose commitment to the esoteric, symbolist side of the Nabi aesthetic was weaker, drew their art more directly from nature and the modern world. Whereas the former maintained their roles into the 20th century as disseminators of the Nabi aesthetic through teaching and religious painting, the two most successful members of the group, Bonnard and Vuillard, departed radically from their periods of Nabi experimentation and developed luminous and subjective styles that built on the Impressionists' use of colour (*see* INTIMISME). Yet even in their 20th-century portraits and fashionable paintings of and for bourgeois interiors, both artists retained something of the original emphasis on the flat, decorative purpose of painting that was the legacy of their Nabi beginnings.

BIBLIOGRAPHY

G.-A. Aurier: 'Les Symbolistes', *Rev. Enc.*, xxxii (1892), pp. 474–86; also in *Oeuvres posthumes*, ed. R. de Gowmont (Paris, 1893)

A. Humbert: *Les Nabis et leur époque* (Geneva, 1954)

Bonnard, Vuillard et les Nabis (exh. cat., Paris, Mus. N. A. Mod., 1955)

C. Chassé: *Les Nabis et leur époque* (Paris, 1960; Eng. trans., London, 1969)

The Nabis and their Circle (exh. cat., Minneapolis, MN, Inst. A., 1962)

Die Nabis und ihre Freunde (exh. cat., Mannheim, Städt. Ksthalle, 1963–4)

Neo-Impressionists and Nabis in the Collection of Arthur G. Altschul (exh. cat., New Haven, CT, Yale U. A.G., 1965)

U. Perucchi-Petri: *Die Nabis und Japan: Das Frühwerk von Bonnard, Vuillard und Denis* (Munich, 1976)

G. Mauner: *The Nabis: Their History and their Art, 1888–1896* (New York, 1978)

Nabi Prints (exh. cat., New Brunswick, NJ, Rutgers U., Zimmerli A. Mus., 1988–9; Amsterdam, Rijksmus. van Gogh; 1989)

Les Nabis (exh. cat., Paris, Mus. d'Orsay; Zurich, Ksthaus; 1993)

BELINDA THOMSON

Naccherino [Nacherino], **Michelangelo** (*b* Florence, 6 March 1550; *d* Naples, ?Feb 1622). Italian sculptor. He was a pupil of Giambologna in Florence, as he stated in a testimony in which he accused his master of impiety. He settled in Naples in 1573 and for half a century was the city's leading sculptor. In 1575–7 he worked on the statue of the *River Papyrus*, a *Nereid* and other minor elements for the fountain in the Piazza Pretoria in Palermo. This fountain was executed in the 1550s by the Florentine sculptor Francesco Camilliani (*d* 1586) and was moved in 1574 from Florence to Palermo, where it was enlarged under the direction of Francesco's son CAMILLO CAMILLIANI. Naccherino soon introduced into his work expressive features more suitable to the spiritual climate of Naples, which was deeply influenced by the Counter-Reformation (Wittkower). In the funerary monument to *Alfonso Sánchez* (1588–9; Naples, SS Annunziata) and the *Immaculate Virgin* (1594; Cava dei Tirreni, Salerno, S Francesco da Paola), formal Mannerist elegance and pious sentiment are combined. His major work during this period is a marble *Crucifix* (1599) for the church of the Spirito Santo (Naples, S Carlo all'Arena). A wooden version (1601) is in the church of S Maria Incoronata, Naples.

In 1600–01 Naccherino collaborated with Pietro Bernini on the execution of the Medina Fountain, Naples, and the decoration of the façade of the Monte di Pietà chapel in Naples, for which he sculpted the group of the *Pietà*. A spirit of rivalry developed between the two Florentine sculptors, which prompted Naccherino to develop a more monumental style, resulting in the grandiose pomp of the bronze statues of *St Andrew* (1602–4; Amalfi Cathedral) and *St Matthew* (1606; Salerno Cathedral).

The funerary monument to *Fabrizio Pignatelli* (1596–1607; Naples, S Maria Mater Domini) created a new prototype that was adopted in Naples in the 17th century, in particular the concept of the bronze statue of the deceased kneeling in an attitude of devout resignation. Numerous commissions in Naples, both religious and secular, such as the S Lucia Fountain (1606–9), consolidated Naccherino's reputation, and in 1614 he executed, in collaboration with Tommaso Montani (*fl* 1599–1645), the statues of *Christ at the Column* (Madrid, Mus. Galdiano) and the *Virgin and Child* (El Pito, Cudillero, Asturias, nr the church of Gesù Nazareno) for Philip III of Spain. These were sent to Madrid in 1616 and were originally placed in the convent of the Trinity. Naccherino made other versions of those two statues in 1616 for the Grand Duke Cosimo II de' Medici: only a *Christ at the Column* (which the sculptor may have personally carried to Florence in 1617) survives (Montelupo Fiorentino, SS Quirico e Lucia). Also for Cosimo de' Medici, he sculpted a marble group of *Adam and Eve Tempted by the Serpent* in 1616, which was placed in the Boboli Gardens in Florence. These last works show a return by Naccherino to the 'mannerist classicism' (Wittkower) of his early Tuscan training, with an anachronistic elegance also found in the gigantic *Risen Christ* (1617; Naples, cloister of the Certosa di S Martino).

Naccherino fell ill in 1617, while working on two small statues of the *Christ Child* (untraced), commissioned by Andrea Cioli, secretary of Cosimo de' Medici, and by Cosimo del Sera, an agent of the Grand Duke in Naples. The works were completed by Tommaso Montani, and their identification with two signed statuettes of the *Christ Child* (Burgos, Mus. Arqueol. Prov.; Sotilla de la Ribera, parish church) is a mere hypothesis. No other works by Naccherino can be dated after 1618.

BIBLIOGRAPHY
B. de Dominici: *Vite* (1742–5/*R* Bologna, 1979), ii, p. 142
A. Venturi: *Storia* (1901–40/*R* 1967), x/2, pp. 583–609
A. Maresca di Serracapriola: *M. Naccherino, scultore fiorentino allievo di Giambologna* (Naples, 1924)
R. Wittkower: *Art and Architecture in Italy, 1600–1750*, Pelican Hist. A. (Harmondsworth, 1958), pp. 87–8
E. Santiago Paez: 'Algunas esculturas napolitanas del siglo XVII en España', *Archv Esp. A.*, xi (1967), pp. 115–32
A. Parronchi: 'Sculture e progetti di Michelangelo Naccherino', *Prospettiva* [Florence], xx (1980), pp. 34–46
M. I. Catalano: 'Michelangelo Naccherino', *Civiltà del seicento a Napoli* (exh. cat., Naples, Capodimonte and Villa Pignatelli, 1984–5), ii, pp. 219–23
——: 'Scultori toscani a Napoli alle fine del cinquecento: Considerazioni e problemi', *Stor. A.*, liv (1985), pp. 123–32

ORESTE FERRARI

Nachna [Nāchnā; Nāchnā-Kuṭharā]. Temple site in Panna District, Madhya Pradesh, India, that flourished during the 5th century. The site is best known for its Parvati Temple (second half of the 5th century). Though ruined and subject to misguided renovation, the original features of the building can be determined. The square cella, now empty, once carried an upper chamber and superstructure. The cella was surrounded by a space for circumambulation, enclosed by walls and lit by small window openings. This is the earliest known instance of a temple type, common in the medieval period, known as *Sāndhāra* (Skt: 'bright ambulatory'). The temple stands on a high moulded platform. The stone blocks of the platform are sculpted in an unusual rusticated fashion to suggest the irregular surface of a mountain. This ornamentation, suggesting the mythical mountain where the gods reside, was originally continued into the ambulatory walls. The sculpture of the elaborate doorway, on the west side, exemplifies the finest Gupta-period work. In the centre of the lintel are small seated images of Shiva and Parvati. The river goddesses are seen at the base of the jambs (*see* INDIAN SUBCONTINENT, fig. 28).

In the Mahadeva Temple (9th century) the elevation follows the usual northern pattern for the period, but two large window panels of the 5th century were incorporated into the north and south walls. The forehall of the Mahadeva Temple belongs to the 20th century. Earlier work is also incorporated in the modern Kumramath Temple near by.

Some sculpture and architectural fragments are housed in the site museum, and other pieces have been removed to the National Museum, New Delhi, and the Tulasi Museum, Ramvan. The most important include panels bearing scenes from the *Rāmāyaṇa*, a four-faced linga, Jaina figures (indicating this faith was also represented at the site) and doorjambs and a lintel that may have belonged to a temple of Surya-Narayana.

See also INDIAN SUBCONTINENT, §IV, 6(iv)(b) and for further illustration INDIAN SUBCONTINENT, fig. 134.

BIBLIOGRAPHY
A. Cunningham: *Archaeol. Surv. India Rep.*, xxi (1883–5), pp. 95–9
K. Deva: 'Chaturmukha Mahādeva Temple at Nachna Kuthara', *J. Madhya Pradesh Itihasa Parishad*, i (1959), pp. 69–73
K. D. Bajpai: 'Some Interesting Gaṇa Figures from Panna', *Lalit Kala*, x (1961), pp. 21–4
W. Spink: 'A Temple with Four Uchchakalpa (?) Doorways at Nāchnā Kuṭharā', *Chhavi, Golden Jubilee Volume, Bharat Kala Bhavan, 1920–1970*, ed. A. Krishna (Varanasi, 1971), pp. 161–72
J. Williams: 'Two New Gupta Jina Images', *Orient. A.*, xviii/4 (1972), pp. 378–80
J. Harle: *Gupta Sculpture* (Oxford, 1973)
J. Williams: *The Art of Gupta India: Empire and Province* (Princeton, 1982)

DONALD M. STADTNER

Nacht-Samborski, (Stefan) Artur (*b* Kraków, 26 May 1898; *d* Warsaw, 9 Oct 1974). Polish painter. He trained at the Kraków Academy of Fine Arts (1917–19) under Wojciech Weiss and Józef Mehoffer, then went to Berlin (1920–23) and on his return to Kraków continued his studies (1923–4) under Felicjan Kowarski and Józef Pankiewicz. The *Portrait of a Woman in a Green Dress* (1924; Warsaw, N. Mus.), one of his first paintings, is not so much a portrait—the sitter does not show her face—as a pretext for applying colour. He remained primarily concerned with colour, understood in Post-Impressionist terms. Between 1924 and 1939 he was associated with the KAPISTS in Paris and thereafter adhered to their characteristic technique and subject-matter. During World War II, hiding in Lwów (now L'viv) and Warsaw, he painted joyful portraits of girls and young women with flowers. After the war he was appointed professor at the Sopot Higher School of Art and the Warsaw Academy of Fine Arts. He was a prolific artist. In his still-lifes he favoured painting flowers and leaves (e.g. *Still-life with a White Jug*, 1962; Łódź, Mus. A.). Some of his paintings (e.g. *White Portrait*, 1962; Kraków, N. Mus.) and drawings (e.g. *Nika Bloc Avamo*, sketchbook, 1960s; Łódź, Mus. A.) belong to the world of fantasy inhabited by strange, masked creatures, phantoms and puppets.

BIBLIOGRAPHY
Artur Nacht-Samborski, 1898–1974 (exh. cat., ed. M. Kaczanowska, H. Piprek and B. Szajna-Sierosławska; Warsaw, N. Mus., 1977)
Artur Nacht-Samborski (exh. cat., ed. J. Ładnowska; Łódź, Mus. A., 1989)

ANNA BENTKOWSKA

Nadar [Tournachon, (Gaspard) Félix] (*b* Paris, 8 April 1820; *d* Paris, 21 March 1910). French photographer, printmaker, draughtsman, writer and balloonist. He was born into a family of printers and became familiar with the world of letters very early in life. He abandoned his study of medicine for journalism, working first in Lyon and then in Paris. In the 1840s Nadar moved in socialist, bohemian circles and developed strong republican convictions. Around this time he adopted the pseudonym Nadar (from 'Tourne à dard', a nickname he gained because of his talent for caricature). For his friend Charles Baudelaire, Nadar personified 'the most astonishing expression of vitality'. In 1845 he published his first novel, *La Robe de Déjanira*, and the following year he embarked on his career as a caricaturist, working for *La Silhouette* and *Le Charivari* and subsequently for the *Revue comique* (1848) and Charles Philipon's *Journal pour rire* (1849), which later became the *Journal amusant* (1856). In London in 1863 Nadar discovered the drawings in *Punch* and met the illustrators Paul Gavarni and Constantin Guys, who became a friend. Nadar ended his career as a caricaturist in 1865, by which time he had become famous as a photographer.

Nadar became well known for his *Panthéon Nadar*, a lithographic panorama of contemporary French cultural celebrities, published on two occasions, once in the *Lanterne magique* (1854) and once in *Le Figaro* (1858), but unfinished. For some of the *c.* 300 figures (Honoré de Balzac and Victor Hugo, for example) Nadar had recourse to already existing portrait photographs. Following this use of photography, Nadar decided to establish himself as a photographer, initially with his brother Adrien Tournachon (1825–1903), whom he apprenticed to the photographer Gustave Le Gray in 1853, before himself training with Camille d'Arnaud and Auguste Bertsch (*d* 1871). In 1854–5 the two brothers produced a series of portraits of the mime artist Charles Deburau, illustrating various expressions, for example *Surprise* and *Terror*. In translating the emotions, according to the studies of the neurologist Guillaume Benjamin Duchenne de Boulogne, Adrien, with his interest in theatre, played an important role in this partnership. A number of his own portraits, for example that of the critic *Jules Husson Champfleury*, and his self-portraits have nothing to fear from comparison with those by Félix. Subsequently, relations between the two brothers deteriorated and led to two lawsuits in 1856–7, during the course of which Félix claimed exclusive right to the pseudonym Nadar. This affair showed a lack of solidarity between them from which the weaker Adrien never recovered.

Nadar's first photographs were portraits of friends made in 1854–5: of the writers *Alfred de Vigny, Théophile Gautier, Gérard de Nerval* (the only known photograph of him) and *Charles Baudelaire*, for example. He rapidly became known as the portrait photographer who took as his subjects the most interesting personalities of his day. *Gustave Doré* (1855 and 1859), *Honoré Daumier* (1856), *Sarah Bernhardt* (*c.* 1860), *Edouard Manet, Gustave Courbet* and many others were taken by him. He also produced some remarkable images of his family, for example of his wife *Ernestine*, his son *Paul*, his servants and numerous self-portraits. Nadar and his brother were the first French photographers to create a purely photographic aesthetic for their portraits. It is in total contrast to the rigid and conventional style that had made the fortune of numerous other practitioners. Nadar's portraiture is characterized by the rejection of any artifice such as the use of accessories, painted backdrops or retouching (e.g. his simple portrait of a *Young West Indian Woman*, 1855, Paris, Mus. d'Orsay; see fig.). His direct approach to his sitters shows his concern to grasp their inner life. The most successful and often most beautiful images are those that reveal an intimacy between photographer and model. This is the case in all his early work, where he made particular use of side lighting and where the light and shade alone create an almost romantic atmosphere around the figure. Influenced by his early contacts with Deburau and Duchenne de Boulogne and by his experience as a caricaturist, he focused above all on the faces, and the gaze of the sitter sometimes assumes a disturbing intensity, as in, for example, the portraits of *Gérard de Nerval, Charles Baudelaire* and *Ernestine*. Nadar used the wet collodion glass negative process (and from 1861 dry collodion), which at that time had supplanted the daguerreotype as the most appropriate for portraiture.

In order to cater for an increasing clientele, Nadar was forced to change his premises. His first studio was at 113 rue St Lazare, but the best known was that at 25 boulevard des Capucines, where he moved in 1860. These premises

Nadar: *Young West Indian Woman*, salt paper print, 250×190 mm, 1855 (Paris, Musée d'Orsay)

became a meeting-place for artists and intellectuals opposed to the imperial regime, and Nadar also rented the studio out for exhibitions, notably the first public showing of the group who were later to be christened Impressionists (April–May 1874). In the 1860s Nadar was so much in demand as a portrait photographer that he had to employ assistants. He then took a less active part in the production of his portraits. He also had to resort to the commercial formula of making *cartes de visite*, abandoning his larger format of 180×240 mm. Financially ruined by the War of 1870, the Paris Commune (for which he provided a balloon postal and observation service at his own expense) and his attempts at ballooning, Nadar took on a more broadly based clientele made up of the bourgeoisie and people who were not acquaintances. This had an effect on his output: his portraits, made more rapidly, became less sensitive. Towards 1885, he had more or less regained his former wealth, and from 1887 his son Paul Nadar (1856–1939) began to relieve him in the studio, carrying on his father's activity in a very different spirit, gravitating towards more glamorous and artificial portrayals, as in his portrait of *Lillie Langtry* (Paris, Bib. N.).

Nadar was a pioneer in other photographic fields besides portraiture, in particular aerial photography, which he practised from his various balloons (e.g. *Avenue de l'Impératrice*). He also attempted underground photography in artificial light (electric arc lamps and bunsen batteries), producing *c.* 100 pictures of the catacombs and sewers of Paris (1861–2; Paris, Bib. N.). These experiments were accompanied by other technical researches: microphotography, snaps in artificial light using magnesium and aerial navigation. Nadar was one of the first to conceive of the 'photographic interview': the series of eight photographs (taken on roll film by his son Paul) of his conversation with the chemist and colour theorist *Michel-Eugène Chevreul* on the eve of his 100th birthday appeared in the *Journal illustré* in September 1886 (original 27 images in Paris, Bib. N.).

After staying in Marseille from 1895 to 1904, where he opened a studio, Nadar returned to the region of Paris. He remained interested in what was happening in France in the field of photography and founded the journal *Paris photographe*, edited by Paul, in 1891. In 1899 he published his memoirs *Quand j'étais photographe*. He remains a crucial figure in the history of photography for having created a type of modern portrait based on the direct psychological approach to his subject and for his pioneering technical feats and championing of the medium. With few exceptions, Nadar's negatives are held in the Caisse Nationale des Monuments Historiques et des Sites (head office, Hôtel de Sully, Paris); studio prints are held in the Bibliothèque Nationale, Paris.

For further illustration *see* MERV, fig. 2.

WRITINGS
Quand j'étais photographe (Paris, 1899)

PHOTOGRAPHIC PUBLICATIONS
J. Illus. (Sept 1886), p. 137 [photographic interview of Michel-Eugène Chevreul]

BIBLIOGRAPHY
J. Prinet and A. Dilasser: *Nadar* (Paris, 1966)
N. Gosling: *Nadar* (London, 1976)
A. Jammes: 'Duchenne de Boulogne, la grimace provoquée et Nadar', *Gaz. B.-A.*, n. s. 6, xcii (1978), pp. 215–20
P. Néagu and J. J. Poulet-Allamagny: *Nadar*, 2 vols (Paris, 1979)
R. Greaves: *Nadar ou le paradoxe vital* (Paris, 1980)
Le Paris souterrain de Félix Nadar (exh. cat., text P. Néagu and J. J. Poulet-Allamagny; Paris, Caisse N. Mnmts Hist. & Sites, 1982)
A. Jammes: *Nadar* (Paris, 1983)
U. Keller: 'Nadar as Portraitist', *Gaz. B.-A.*, n. s. 6, cvii (1986), pp. 133–56
Nadar (exh. cat. by M. M. Hambourg, F. Heilbrun and P. Néagu, Paris, Mus. d'Orsay; New York, Met., 1994)

HÉLÈNE BOCARD

Nadelman, Elie (*b* Warsaw, 20 Feb 1882; *d* Riverdale, NY, 28 Dec 1946). American sculptor, draughtsman and collector of Polish birth. After studying briefly in Warsaw he visited Munich in 1902, where he became interested in the Classical antiquities at the Glyptothek. He lived in Paris from 1904 to 1914 and was closely involved there with the avant-garde, exhibiting at the Salon des Indépendants and at the Salon d'Automne from 1905 to 1908. At his first one-man exhibition at the Galerie Druet, Paris, in 1909 he exhibited a large series of plaster and bronze classical female heads and full-length standing nudes, as well as somewhat mannered Cubist drawings; a number of the latter were purchased by Leo Stein, who had brought Picasso to Nadelman's studio in 1908. During this period Nadelman also benefited from the patronage of the Natanson brothers. By the time he left Paris for New York at the outbreak of World War I, Nadelman had already produced groups of works in a variety of styles, including generalizations from the Antique, tubular nudes and primitive animals, inspired by a visit to the cave paintings in Dordogne in 1911. For Nadelman, formal considerations took precedence over materials and methods; as he explained in a statement published in 1910: 'I employ no other line than the curve, which possesses freshness and force. I compose the curves so as to bring them in accord in opposition to each other.'

One of Nadelman's sculptures and twelve of his drawings were selected by Arthur B. Davies for inclusion in the Armory Show, the first large-scale show of European art that started in New York in 1913. Supported by Helena Rubinstein, who in 1911 had purchased the complete contents of his exhibition at the Patterson Gallery in London, Nadelman moved to New York in 1914. He was immediately drawn to the city's popular culture, to its theatre, jazz, dancers, circus performers and society types, as a source of subject-matter. His most important early work, *Man in the Open Air* (1914–15; New York, MOMA; see fig.), combines an elegant figure style indebted to the work of Georges Seurat with an American naivety and humour; dressed only in a bowler hat and a curly bow-tie, the man is supported by a tree trunk whose branch appears to grow through his arm. This witty rendition of *Apollo Sauroktonos* by Praxiteles, which was first exhibited in December 1915 at Alfred Stieglitz's Gallery 291, combines a genius for gesture with an aristocratic simplification of form. Nadelman's growing interest in American folk art, combined with his daily observations of society types, resulted in an important series of figures carved from wood and then stained and painted; among the most popular are *Woman at the Piano* (*c.* 1917; New York, MOMA) and *Orchestra Conductor* (*c.* 1919; Washington,

Elie Nadelman: *Man in the Open Air*, bronze, h. 1.38 m, 1914–15 (New York, Museum of Modern Art)

DC, Hirshhorn). These figures represented Nadelman's halcyon years, in which he was widely exhibited and financially secure.

After marriage in 1919 to Viola M. Spiess (1878–1962), formerly Mrs Joseph Flannery, a wealthy widow, Nadelman purchased Alderbrook, an estate at Riverdale, NY, and a town house on 93rd Street in New York, where he set up a studio with three assistants to do much of his preliminary carving. He and his wife spent over £500,000 on American folk art between 1921 and 1924 and built a museum for the collection on their estate in 1924. Nadelman became an American citizen in 1927 and retired to Riverdale in 1929. During the remainder of his life he became increasingly reclusive and removed from the art world; he held his last one-man exhibition in 1930 (Paris, Bernheim-Jeune) and after two architectural commissions in 1935 worked only on small ceramics and clay figures. The stock market collapse forced him to sell his home in Manhattan and his folk art collection, and in 1935 many of his plaster figures and wood-carvings were destroyed by workmen sent to remodel his studio. Nadelman packed away all his pre-1935 work in the attic and cellar of his home in Riverdale and left it there to disintegrate, but this sculpture was restored after his death under the supervision of Lincoln Kirstein and reintroduced to a wide American public in 1948 in a retrospective at MOMA, New York.

WRITINGS
'Statement on Drawings', *Cam. Work*, 32 (1910), p. 41
'Statement for Exhibition at Photo-Secession', *Cam. Work*, 48 (1916), p. 10

BIBLIOGRAPHY
G. Apollinaire: *Anecdotiques* (Paris, 1926), p. 10
A. Gide: *The Journals of André Gide* (New York, 1947), pp. 234–7
The Sculpture of Elie Nadelman (exh. cat. by L. Kirstein, New York, MOMA, 1948)
L. Kirstein: *Elie Nadelman: Drawings* (New York, 1949)
——: *Elie Nadelman* (New York, 1973)
The Sculpture and Drawings of Elie Nadelman (exh. cat. by J.I.H. Baur, New York, Whitney, 1975)

FRANCINE KOSLOW MILLER

Nadorp, Franz (Johann Heinrich) (*b* Anholt, Westphalia, 23 June 1794; *d* Rome, 13 Sept 1876). German painter and sculptor. He studied at the Academy of Visual Arts in Prague (1814–27) under Josef Bergler, where in 1819 he met Joseph von Führich. In 1822 he was awarded the Academy's gold medal; he aspired to become a history painter, but his figure compositions were mostly weak and theatrical, and his real talent was for portrait painting, for example *Josef Bergler* (Prague, N. Mus.). In 1827 he accompanied Prince Franz zu Salm-Salm, whose father, Prince Konstantin zu Salm-Salm, had supported him in Prague, on a journey to Italy. He arrived in Rome in 1828, where he remained for the rest of his life, leaving only to make excursions in Umbria, Tuscany, Naples and Pompeii, and to visit Germany in 1862. The death of his patron shortly after his arrival in Rome left Nadorp in precarious financial circumstances, exacerbated by the fact that as a subject of the prince of Salm-Salm he received no state commissions from either Austria or Prussia. In 1859 Frederick William IV, King of Prussia, became a patron. Although his paintings were often highly praised, for example *Raphael's Villa at Rome* (1850; Munich, Neue Pin.), sales were rare. He also produced some sculpture, for example a design for a *Pietà* (Anholt, Fürst Salm-Salm, Mus. Wasserburg-Anholt).

As commissions for portraits dwindled, Nadorp was obliged to earn his living as a drawing tutor until shortly before his death, when he was granted a modest state pension. He played an active role in the social and professional life of the German artists' colony in Rome, and he was a leading member of several artists' societies. He and Führich were closely associated with the Lukasbrüder (Nazarenes), especially Friedrich Overbeck and Peter Cornelius, and he was also a friend of Bertel Thorvaldsen.

BIBLIOGRAPHY
Thieme–Becker
H. van Os, ed.: *Der Zeichner Franz Nadorp, 1794–1876: Ein romantischer Künstler aus Anholt* (Amsterdam, 1976)
U. Eichler: 'Raffaels Villa bei Rom: Gedanken zu einem Gemälde von Franz Nadorp', *Die Weltkunst*, xlix (1979), pp. 1566–7

COLIN J. BAILEY

Nagadipa. *See* JAFFNA.

Nagaoka [Nagaokakyō; Nagaoka no miya]. Site in Japan of an 8th-century AD capital city. It is now within the city of Nagaokakyō, Otokuni District, Kyoto Prefecture, near the confluence of the Katsura, Uji and Kizu rivers, which merge into the Yodo River. This region was originally the western central part of ancient Yamashiro Province. The *Nihon no shoki* ('Chronicle of Japan'; AD 720) and other sources record that Nagaoka was the seat of the ancient Japanese monarchy and central government from 784 to

794, during the reign of Emperor Kanmu (*reg* 781–806). Kanmu's accession to the throne in 781 was followed by an era of factional strife and court scandal, much abetted by competing Buddhist prelates at Tōdaiji (*see* NARA, §III, 4) and other powerful Nara-based temple–shrine complexes. It also marked the downfall of the royal lineage of Tenmu (*reg* 672–86) and the rise of Kanmu's own, deriving from the monarch Tenji (*reg* 668–71).

Kanmu, apparently unhappy with the Heijōkyō (now Nara; *see* NARA, §I) environment, where he had hitherto been based, and desirous of a royal city for his own lineage, ordered the construction of a new capital and palace in Nagaoka in 784. Responsibility for the project was assigned to Fujiwara no Tanetsugu (737–85), an ally and close friend. The choice of Nagaoka was judged appropriate for two reasons: its location granted access via the Yodo River to Osaka Bay and thus to the Inland Sea, an important route for continental trade; and the region was inhabited by a large number of *kikajin* ('naturalized subjects') from China and Korea, a point emphasized by some scholars because the mothers of both Kanmu and Tanetsugu came from powerful 'naturalized' lineages. The history of the capital was beset by tragedy, however. In 785 Tanetsugu was assassinated by rivals at court, and, although Kanmu ordered Saeki no Emishi (719–90) and others to complete the project, little progress seems to have been made. Soon it was rumoured that Nagaoka was under the curse of the deceased Prince Sawara (*d* 785), who had starved himself to death in protest when Kanmu, certain that Sawara was responsible for Tanetsugu's death, had removed him as crown prince. Next Kanmu's mother and then his consorts died. Finally, in 792, Nagaoka was inundated when the Yodo River burst its banks. In 793 Kanmu jettisoned further plans for Nagaoka and turned his attention to the construction of another capital, Heian (now Kyoto; *see* KYOTO, §I), not far to the north.

The Nagaoka site has been minimally excavated, and therefore little is known in detail about its appearance. It was rapidly built from timbers and other materials from the old palace at Naniwa (*see* OSAKA, §I, 2), and scholars conjecture that it was laid out in a grid pattern, with the Daidairi (Palace Compound) located in the northern central sector of the city. Unlike the palace compounds at Fujiwara (*see* FUJIWARA (i)) and other ancient capitals, the Daidairi at Nagaoka had two completely separate sectors: the Chōdōin (Ministries Compound) and Daigokuden (Great Audience Hall) in one precinct to the west; and the Dairi (Inner Palace), where the sovereign and his family lived, in an independent precinct that bordered the Daigokuden on the east. It is believed that Nagaoka resembled early Heian in layout and in size, measuring *c.* 4.5 km east–west×5.2 km north–south (*see* JAPAN, fig. 43e).

BIBLIOGRAPHY

Y. Kudō: *Fujiwara no miya* (Tokyo, 1967)

M. Ueda: 'Miyako no shutsugen to chiiki no bunka' [Regional culture and the emergence of capital palace cities], *Asuka, Hakuhō, zusetsu Nihon bunka no rekishi* [An illustrated history of Japanese culture], ed. M. Ueda and others, ii (Tokyo, 1979), pp. 45–64

K. Tsuboi: *Kinki-hen* [The home provinces] (1985), iv of *Zusetsu hakkutsu ga kataru Nihonshi* [An illustrated history of Japan as revealed through excavations] (Tokyo, 1985–7)

MIMI HALL YIENGPRUKSAWAN

Nagappattinam [Nāgapaṭṭinam; Nāgapaṭṭaṇam; Nāgipaṭṭaṇam]. Seaport and centre of Buddhism in Thanjavur District, Tamil Nadu, India. Nagappattinam had significant connections with China, with Sri Lanka and with the kingdom of Srivijaya in Sumatra from the 7th century AD to the 15th. The earliest reference dates to the time of the Pallava king Narasimhavarman II Rajasimha (*reg* 690–728), during whose rule a temple was built for Chinese Buddhists who had come to India for trading purposes. Mahayana Buddhism was also encouraged by members of the Javanese Shailendra dynasty, who in the mid-9th century extended their rule into Sumatra (Suvarnadvipa). In the 11th century they provided grants for the construction of shrines (Skt *caitya*s). These were built under the patronage of the contemporary kings of the Chola dynasty and named Rajaraja-perum-palli and Rajendra-Chola-perum-palli after Rajaraja I (*reg c.* 985–1014) and Rajendra I (*reg* 1012–44) respectively. None of these monuments survives. The last remarkable Buddhist temple, a brick-built tower-like structure, perhaps dating to Pallava times, was pulled down in the mid-19th century, but its appearance is preserved in a sketch of 1846. The Kayarohana and Tyagaraja temples, both of the 11th century, are typical Chola-period buildings. In the 13th century Marco Polo referred to Nagappattinam as Pa-tan and described a stupa at the site. A noteworthy find at Nagappattinam was a cache of about 350 metal images (*see* Ramachandran). These were found at the site of a monastery built by Shri Maravijayottungavarman on the orders of his father, the Shailendra ruler Chudamanivarman. The objects include miniature votive stupas and a wide assortment of Buddhist divinities exhibiting a range of styles and influences; they are in various collections (particularly Madras, Govt Mus. & N.A.G.).

BIBLIOGRAPHY

T. N. Ramachandran: *The Nāgapaṭṭinam and Other Buddhist Bronzes in the Madras Museum*, Bull. Madras Govt Mus., n. s., general section 7, no. 1 (Madras, 1965)

D. Mitra: *Buddhist Monuments* (Delhi, 1970)

J. Guy: *The Lost Temples of Nagapattinam and Quanzhou: A Study in Sino-Indian Relations*, Silk Road Art and Archaeology, iii (Kamakura, 1993–4), pp. 291–310

Nagarjunakonda [Nāgārjunakoṇḍa; Nagarjunikonda]. Buddhist centre and capital of the Ikshvaku dynasty in Guntur District, Andhra Pradesh, India. It flourished in the 3rd–4th century AD. Nagarjunakonda was one of several Buddhist settlements (another being AMARAVATI) that developed along the Krishna River between the 2nd century BC and the 3rd century AD. The hills—offshoots of the Nallamala range of the Eastern Ghats—flanking the valley of Nagarjunakonda provided formidable natural fortifications, and in the 3rd century AD Vijayapuri ('city of victory') was established as the capital of the Ikshvaku kings, successors to the SATAVAHANA dynasty. The city lay west of a hill known as Shriparvata. According to Tibetan tradition, it was in a monastery on Shriparvata that Nagarjuna, the great Buddhist philosopher of the 2nd century AD, lived towards the end of his life. The Ikshvaku kings patronized Brahmanical rites, but their queens, daughters and relatives were adherents of Buddhism. The valley was filled with Buddhist edifices as a result of their benefactions.

Nagarjunakonda was discovered in 1926, by which time it was in ruins. A series of excavations, of which that by A. H. Longhurst was the most noteworthy, culminated in a seven-year campaign begun in 1954 by the Archaeological Survey of India. The purpose of this campaign was to gather information and salvage artefacts prior to the inundation of the valley as part of the project to build the Nagarjunasagar Dam. The most important structure, the main stupa (Pkt *mahācetiya*; diam. *c.* 27.5 m), was built of large bricks (*c.* 510×255×80 mm). The dome was covered in carved plaster. A platform at the four cardinal points projected outwards and supported five pillars (*ayaka-khambha*s), some with inscriptions of the Ikshvakus. Stone low-reliefs depicting Buddhist subjects were applied to the lower portions of the exterior. Other buildings included monasteries, shrines and stupas, often arranged as units. Some stupas were decorated with a mixture of stone-carving and stuccowork (*see* STUCCO AND PLASTERWORK, §III, 6). Bone relics were found in a number of stupas at Nagarjunakonda in either a gold reliquary or a silver casket, along with other precious offerings. Before the flooding of the valley some important monuments were reconstructed with ancient material on Nagarjunakonda Hill (now an island) and on the eastern bank of the reservoir. Small-scale replicas of several monuments were also erected, and the Archaeological Museum was built to house the excavated finds.

See also INDIAN SUBCONTINENT, §§III, 3(ii)(a) and IV, 5(vi); and STUPA, §1.

BIBLIOGRAPHY
A. H. Longhurst: *The Buddhist Antiquities of Nāgārjunakoṇḍa, Madras Presidency*, Mem. Archaeol. Surv. India, liv (Delhi, 1938)
T. N. Ramachandran: *Nāgārjunakoṇḍa*, Mem. Archaeol. Surv. India, lxxi (Calcutta, 1953)
D. Mitra: *Buddhist Monuments* (Calcutta, 1971)
G. Schopen: 'On the Buddha and his Bones: The Conception of the Relic in the Inscriptions of Nāgārjunakoṇḍa', *J. Amer. Orient. Soc.*, 108 (1988), pp. 527–37

G. BHATTACHARYA

Nagarjuni. *See under* BARABAR AND NAGARJUNI.

Nagasaki. Japanese city on the hilly Nagasaki Peninsula in north-western Kyushu; it is the capital of Nagasaki Prefecture. Between 1641 and 1869 it was the only Japanese port open to foreign trade and residence. Its role as a port declined rapidly after the Meiji Restoration of 1868. By the 20th century it had become a major shipbuilding centre, making it a target for nuclear attack in 1945 during World War II.

At the end of the 12th century the site on the sheltered inlet was occupied by a small fishing village, variously known as Tamanotsu, Fukaestu and Fukutominotsu, with an excellent natural harbour. The name Nagasaki appears to date from the Kamakura period (1185–1333) when the samurai clan of Nagasaki settled in the area. From the 16th century onwards wealth from major gold and silver mines in various parts of the country supported a lucrative trade, via Nagasaki, in Chinese silk thread exchanged for Japanese silver. This trade was dominated by Chinese and Japanese carriers until the second half of the 16th century, when the Portuguese and, later, the Spanish, Dutch and English began to compete for a share as middlemen. Along with the European traders, Christian missionaries also entered the country. A number of daimyo converted to Catholicism, some because it opened up trade possibilities, others out of a genuine interest in the religion. One of those baptized was Ōmura Sumitada (1533–87), who in 1571 established a town in Nagasaki for the Portuguese. In 1580 he donated the town and environs to the Society of Jesus (the Jesuits) in the hope of securing access to the wealth and military technology guaranteed by trade. In 1587 TOYOTOMI HIDEYOSHI confiscated the settlement and instituted the first ban on Catholicism. In 1597 a group of 26 martyrs were killed on Nishisaka Hill. A century after their canonization a memorial hall was erected to them on the spot in 1962.

The systematic suppression of Christianity began in 1614, by which time the Tokugawa shogunate (Edo period; 1600–1868) had assumed control of Nagasaki. Until 1614 Nagasaki had 11 churches, a seminary, a printing press that produced books in Latin, Portuguese and Japanese, and at one stage a Jesuit university. Much European art, music, science and technology imported into Japan appeared first in Nagasaki. Artistic production by Japanese and foreigners included devotional objects (e.g. an engraving of the *Virgin and Child* (1597) in the collection of Ōura Tenshudō (a 19th-century church)) and secular pieces such as *Nanban byōbu* ('southern barbarian screens'), which illustrated the activities of Portuguese traders and missionaries (*see* JAPAN, §VI, 4(vi)(a)).

After 1614 the shogunate banned the activities of Western missionaries. In 1622 the public execution of 51 Christians in the city and in 1637–8 the massacre of the Shimabara uprising in Shimabaro Domain (now Nagasaki Prefecture) effectively extinguished Catholicism and the influence of Portuguese culture in Nagasaki. In 1639 the shogunate banned trade with the Portuguese and implemented their closed-door policy (*sakoku*; 'secluded country'), which forbade Japanese to travel abroad and restricted entry of foreign vessels, except into Nagasaki. The Dutch were the only Europeans permitted to remain in Japan and they were restricted to Dejima (or Deshima; see fig.), an artificial island built in Nagasaki Harbour between 1634 and 1636. Chinese traders lived freely in the city until 1689, when they were restricted to a special compound. By the late 17th century Japanese mines were becoming exhausted, and the wealth of the country was further depleted by the unabated outflow of bullion through foreign trade. The shogunate therefore sought to limit the volume of trade. The population of Nagasaki reflected this change, decreasing from 64,523 in 1696 to 27,343 in 1853. Conversely, the city's cultural activities increased in importance. The influx of Chinese traders resulted in the introduction of Chinese cuisine, dragon dances and dragon-boat festivals. The Chinese crafts of tortoiseshell-carving, mother-of-pearl inlay and glass-blowing became Nagasaki specialities.

During this period the city was also home to a significant number of artists working in a diversity of styles: their works are loosely referred to as the Nagasaki school (*see* JAPAN, §VI, 4(vi)(c)). The Appraisal Bureau of Foreign Paintings was established in 1697 to appraise all imported paintings, and the painters employed there (*karae mekiki*) produced works illustrating foreign objects and scenes in

Nagasaki, *Bird's-eye View of Dejima* by Kawahara Keiga, first half of the 19th century (Leiden, Rijksmuseum voor Volkenkunde)

and around Nagasaki. The Chinese monks of the Huangbo (Ōbaku) sect of Chan (Jap. Zen) Buddhism who settled in Nagasaki (*see also* MANPUKUJI) were instrumental in disseminating Ming-period (1368–1644) culture, arts and architecture. The most noteworthy of the three Nagasaki Ōbaku temples, Sōfukuji (1629), preserves examples of Ming-period architecture. The bird-and-flower paintings of the Qing-period (1644–1911) artist SHEN NANPIN, who visited Nagasaki in 1731–3, were faithful copies from nature. His work and that of his student Kumashiro Yūhi (1713–72) had a major impact on Japanese approaches to realism and the use of colour. Nagasaki prints (*Nagasaki miyage*; 'souvenirs') illustrated the activities of the city's foreigners and were generally designed by anonymous artists and published by established publishers such as Hariya or Toshiyama (*see* JAPAN, §IX, 2). Kawahara Keiga (1786–*c*. 1860s) was one of the individualists whose artistic services were offered to the Dutch residents on Dejima and who were commissioned by foreigners such as Dr PHILIPP FRANZ VON SIEBOLD of the Dutch East India Company. Keiga's realistic paintings, for example the watercolour *Nagasaki Mask Dancers* (Leiden, Rijksmus. Vlkenknd.), are invaluable contemporary records of everyday life among both the Japanese and foreign inhabitants.

The East India Company served not only as a window on the West for Japan but also as a vehicle for the export to the West of Japanese art, especially lacquerware and porcelain from ARITA. Arita ware later influenced several European kilns, notably those in Delft (*see* DELFT, §3) and London (*see* CHELSEA PORCELAIN FACTORY).

The breakdown of Tokugawa restrictions on foreign relations in 1859 signalled the end of Nagasaki's importance as an international port. Although the dockyard established in 1860 by the shogunate was the largest in

eastern Asia, by 1914 Nagasaki accounted for only 1% of the country's foreign trade. Nonetheless, a large foreign community developed in the Ōura district, sections of which survive, such as the Glover Mansion (1863), the residence of the British merchant Thomas Glover (1838–1911). On 9 August 1945 an atom bomb was dropped by Allied forces on the city, killing over 70,000 people; the city's hilly terrain, however, limited damage to 36% of the urban area. After 1945 the Mitsubishi shipyards led a revival of the city's economy, and in 1949 Nagasaki was designated a city of international culture. Since 1974, however, a general depression in the shipbuilding industry has caused the city to stagnate.

BIBLIOGRAPHY
M. Hosono: *Yōfūhanga* [Western-style prints], Nihon no bijutsu [Arts of Japan], xxxvi (Tokyo, 1969); Eng. trans. by L. R. Craighill as *Nagasaki Prints and Early Copperplates*, Japanese Arts Library, vi, ed. J. Rosenfield (Tokyo, New York and San Francisco, 1978)
T. Nagami: *Nagasaki no bijutsushi* [The history of Nagasaki art] (Kyoto, 1974)
T. Etchū and Y. Ōto: *Nagasaki, Yokohama* (1976), *Edo jidai zushi* [A pictorial history of the Edo period] (Tokyo)
C. French: *Through Closed Doors: Western Influence on Japanese Art, 1639–1853* (New York, 1977)

J. F. MORRIS

Nagasawa. *See* HAKUIN EKAKU.

Nagasawa Rosetsu [Gyosha; Inkyo; Kanshū; Rosetsu] (*b* Yamashiro, 1754; *d* Osaka, 1799). Japanese painter. He was born into a low-ranking samurai family of the Yodo clan. When he was about 25, he began to study painting under the founder of the Maruyama school, MARUYAMA ŌKYO, becoming one of Ōkyo's 'Ten Great Disciples', but he had achieved independent status by the age of 29. His early works closely resemble those of Ōkyo, being tight, meticulous representations of birds and flowers, figures and animals, although stylistic differences were already visible. His treatment of the human figure was less idealized and more orthodox than his teacher's.

Rosetsu was a lay practitioner of Zen. In 1786 and 1787 Ōkyo sent him to the southern Kii peninsula (now Wakayama Prefect.), where he painted about 180 wall paintings (*shōhekiga*) for Zen temples, including his famous *Dragon and Tiger* and *Chinese Children Imitating the Four Scholarly Pastimes* (Kishimoto, Muryōji). Rosetsu's painting style at this time diverged from Ōkyo's more controlled manner, becoming freer and more creative. He used Ōkyo's innovative brush techniques for shading forms in the *mokkotsu* ('boneless') manner, not, as Ōkyo did, for three-dimensional effect but for their expressive possibilities.

Rosetsu's late works were marked by even greater eccentricity. The brushwork is soft and fluid, and the compositions are bold, loosely constructed and spontaneous, playfully combining elements of realism and abstraction. Characteristic of these works is his album of *Eight Famous Views of Miyajima, Hiroshima* (1794; Hiroshima, C. Yasuda priv. col.; see 1980 exh. cat., pls 42a–e). Rosetsu died at the age of 45, reputedly poisoned by a rival. He is not known to have had any followers.

See also JAPAN, §VI, 4(viii).

BIBLIOGRAPHY
T. Kobayashi and others, eds: *Jakuchū, Shohaku, Rosetsu* (1973), vi of *Suiboku bijutsu taikei* [Compendium of the art of ink painting], ed. I. Tanaka and others (Tokyo, 1973–7)
Rosetsu (exh. cat. by R. Moes, Denver, CO, A. Mus., 1973)
J. Hillier: *The Uninhibited Brush: Japanese Art in the Shijō Style* (London, 1974)
Ōkyo and the Maruyama–Shijō School of Japanese Painting (exh. cat. by J. Sasaki, St Louis, MO, A. Mus., 1980)

PATRICIA J. GRAHAM

Nagda. *See under* EKLINGJI AND NAGDA.

Nagel, Otto (*b* Berlin, 27 Sept 1894; *d* Berlin, 12 July 1967). German painter, printmaker and writer. He showed talent as a draughtsman at an early age. After showing Bruno Paul some drawings in 1908, he was promised a free place in the education department of the Kunstgewerbemuseum, Berlin, following his training as a craftsman. He studied briefly in a stained-glass workshop (1908–10) but abandoned this to work as a studio assistant (1910–21). From 1913 to 1914 he also attended evening classes in drawing. As a pacifist he refused military service and was temporarily imprisoned. In 1919 his application to the Hochschule für Bildende Künste in Charlottenburg, Berlin, was rejected.

At the home of the architect and art critic Adolf Behne (1855–1948) Nagel saw for the first time paintings by August Macke, whose bold use of colour made a lasting impression on his work, for example *Self-portrait with Hat* (oil on cardboard, 1920; Berlin, priv. col., see 1984 exh. cat., p. 53). However, in his socio-critical works of this time he strove for a more sombre appearance. In the early 1920s he became an independent artist and participated in numerous exhibitions, meeting Käthe Kollwitz, Heinrich Zille, El Lissitzky and others. He was strongly committed to the Communist Party and became secretary of the

Internationale Arbeiterhilfe (IAH). In 1925, commissioned by the IAH's Künstlerhilfe, he accompanied the first German art exhibition to the USSR.

In his prints and his paintings Nagel took themes from the life of the common man: *Employment Agency* (oil on canvas, 1925; lost; see exh. cat., pl. 8), *End of the Working Day* (oil on canvas, 1928; untraced, see 1984 exh. cat., p. 18) and *Early Shift* (oil on canvas, *c.* 1929; Dresden, Gemäldegal. Neue Meister) are frank depictions of despair and the joyless existence of the factory worker. His major works include *Wedding Family* (oil on canvas, polyptych, 1930–31: *The Worker-Athlete*, Berlin, Akad. Kst. DDR, on loan to Frankfurt an der Oder, Gal. Junge Kst.; *The Grandfather*, Berlin, Mus. Dt. Gesch.; *The Young Communist*, Berlin, S. Schallenberg-Nagel priv. col.), which shows three generations of proletarian families, and *The 70th Birthday of the Forestry Worker Scharf* (oil on canvas, 1934; Berlin, Staatl. Museen, N.G.). Nagel taught at the Marxist Arbeiterschule and helped to found the Rotenkabaretts and, with Zille, the satirical magazine *Eulenspiegel*. In 1929 he finished the outline for the film *Mutter Krausens Fahrt ins Glück*, and in 1931 and 1932 he organized exhibitions of the work of Kollwitz in Berlin, Moscow and Leningrad (now St Petersburg). In 1933 he was chairperson of the Reichsverband Bildender Künstler Deutschlands for only 12 hours since his election was declared invalid by the Nazis. Because he was forbidden to paint in his studio, he had to turn to architectural motifs and landscapes, painting *en plein air*, working in oil and in pastel. In 1937 he was sent temporarily to the Sachsenhausen concentration camp. The 'degenerate' art policy of the Nazis (*see* ENTARTETE KUNST) destroyed 27 of his works.

After the fall of the Third Reich, Nagel devoted himself with great energy to cultural and political reconstruction in Germany. The small number of paintings that he produced included a series of portraits, which lack the expressiveness of his pre-war work. He became a professor and President of the Akademie der Künste, Berlin, and a member of parliament in the Volkskammer. He also made a living editing books on Kollwitz and Zille. From 1973 his artistic estate was housed in the Otto-Nagel-Haus.

WRITINGS
Leben und Werk (Berlin, 1952)

BIBLIOGRAPHY
E. Frommhold: *Otto Nagel: Zeit—Leben—Werk* (Berlin, 1974)
S. Schallenberg-Nagel and G. Schallenberg: *Otto Nagel: Gemälde und Pastelle* (Berlin, 1974)
W. Nagel: *Das darfst du nicht! Erinnerungen* (Halle and Leipzig, 1983) [Mem. by Nagel's wife]
Otto Nagel: Gemälde, Pastelle, Zeichnungen (exh. cat. by C. Hoffmeister, Berlin, Staatl Museen, N.G., 1984)

SEPP KERN

Nagel, Peter. *See under* ZEBRA.

Nag el-Deir [Naga-ed-Der; Arab. Nag' al-Dayr]. Site of an ancient necropolis on the east bank of the Nile in Upper Egypt, opposite the modern town of Girgā. The tombs range in date from the Predynastic period (late 4th millennium BC) to the Middle Kingdom (*c.* 2008–*c.* 1630 BC). Nag el-Deir, excavated by George Reisner (1901–2), was one of the major cemeteries of the 8th nome. People of many different social levels were buried there.

A large amount of very fine jewellery of the Early Dynastic period (*c*. 2925–*c*. 2575 BC) was found, including gold amulets and necklaces (Cairo, Egyp. Mus.) from a 1st-dynasty tomb. The four rolls of the Reisner Papyri, from a Middle Kingdom tomb (N 408), shed light on the accounting and administrative processes of that time. The late Old Kingdom and First Intermediate Period (*c*. 2300–*c*. 2008 BC) tombs contained stone stelae, including one decorated in painted sunk relief (Philadelphia, U. PA, Mus.). These stelae are important as sources for the development of provincial art styles at that time. The tomb of the nomarch Tjamerery, dated to the very late Old Kingdom (*c*. 2150 BC), is decorated with reliefs in the elegant and harmonious Memphite style, but with signs of the deteriorating skill of provincial artists. Prominent features of the local style are the depiction of long and thin figures with very large eyes and the carving of many hieroglyphs in a very exaggerated fashion.

BIBLIOGRAPHY

LÄ: 'Naga (Nag')-ed-Der'

D. Dunham: *Naga-ed-Der Stelae of the First Intermediate Period* (Oxford, 1937)

C. N. Peck: *Some Decorated Tombs of the First Intermediate Period at Naga ed-Dêr* (Ann Arbor, 1970)

NIGEL STRUDWICK

Naghi [Nagui; Nagy; Nājī], **Mohammed** [Muḥammad] (*b* Alexandria, 1888; *d* Cairo, 1956). Egyptian painter. He was educated at the Université de Lyon in France, where he studied law, and also at the School of Fine Arts, Cairo, and at Giverny under Monet. During the 1920s he worked for the Egyptian diplomatic service at embassies abroad, but increasingly devoted himself to painting, developing an Impressionist style and in 1927 becoming a member of a group of artists in Cairo called La Chimère, which included the sculptor Mahmud Mukhtar, and the painters Mahmud Said and Raghib Ayyad (1892–1982). Among his paintings of this period was the canvas mural *The Village* (1928; Alexandria, Mus. F.A. & Cult. Cent.). In 1930, not long after a diplomatic mission in Brazil, he left for Abyssinia [now Ethiopia], where he spent a year at the embassy in Addis Ababa. He studied the landscape of the country and painted portraits of Emperor Haile Selassie I and other notable figures. Around this time also he studied indigenous Egyptian art. These and other influences led to works such as the *Bread Bakers* (1934; Alexandria, Mus. F.A.). After his Abyssinian expedition he became increasingly involved in painting murals for a number of public buildings, notably the *Renaissance of Egypt* (1935; Cairo, Senate), which depicts a slow colourful procession. In the early 1950s he formed the Atelier Group, which had branches in Cairo and Alexandria. He spent much of his life travelling and painting abroad, and in Egypt set up studios in Alexandria, Luxor, Memphis and in Cairo, where his old studio has become the Mohammed Naghi Museum.

BIBLIOGRAPHY

E. J. Finbert: 'Mohammed Naghi', *A. Vivant* (Jan 1924)

Mohammed Naghi Retrospective Exhibition Catalogue (exh. cat., Prague, Higher Council F.A., 1958)

S. J. VERNOIT

Nagler, G(ustav) K(aspar) (*b* Oberfiesbach, Oberbayern, 6 Jan 1801; *d* Munich, 20 Jan 1866). German art historian and bookseller. Through his marriage to Johanna Ehrenreich, a widow from Munich, he became a dealer in secondhand books and joint owner of her business. In 1829 he graduated as a doctor of philosophy from the Universität Erlangen. He began to write regular articles on art for the *Bayerische Nationalzeitung*. The material he collected while researching in the Bayerische Staatsbibliothek in Munich and which he obtained from the books in his shop formed the basis of his *Neues allgemeines Künstler-Lexikon* (1835–52). From 1857 to 1878 he published the five-volume *Die Monogrammisten und diejenigen bekannten und unbekannten Künstler aller Schulen . . .*, which he envisaged as a supplement to his dictionary of artists. By modern standards *Die Monogrammisten* appears to be partly speculative, especially in the way in which the monograms are deciphered. However, it represents an initial attempt to approach art in a modern systematic way. It was prompted by the recent opening of collections to the public and the growing interest in art history in the academic world. Alongside his work on the dictionary and his business as a bookseller, Nagler lectured twice a week from 1836 at the Königliche Baugewerbschule in Munich on the history of architecture. His lectures dealt mostly with buildings in Munich.

WRITINGS

Neues allgemeines Künstler-Lexikon oder Nachrichten von dem Leben und den Werken der Maler, Bildhauer, Baumeister, Kupferstecher, Formschneider, Lithographen, Zeichner, Medailleure, Elfenbeinarbeiter, etc., 22 vols (Munich, 1835–52, repr. Leipzig and Vienna, 1924)

Michel-Angelo Buonarroti als Künstler (Munich, 1836)

Rafael als Mensch und Künstler (Munich, 1836)

Die Monogrammisten und diejenigen bekannten und unbekannten Künstler aller Schulen, welchen sich zur Bezeichnung ihrer Werke eines figürlichen Zeichens, der Initiale des Namens, der Abbreviatur desselben, etc., 5 vols (vols 1–4, Munich, 1857–76, vol. 5, Leipzig, 1878; rev. Munich, 2/1860–79/R 1966)

Regular contributions to *Bayer. Nztg*

BIBLIOGRAPHY

ADB

R. Marggraff: Obituary, *Jber. Hist. Ver. Oberbayern*, xxix (1866), pp. 118ff

BARBARA LANGE

Nagoya. City in Japan, between Osaka and Tokyo, situated on the Nōbi Plain and the Ise Bay, and at the centre of the Chūkyō Industrial Zone. It is the capital of Aichi Prefecture and the third largest Japanese city. Nagoya has a rich cultural heritage, and it possessed the sole surviving example of a 17th-century main castle enceinte until 1945, when it was destroyed by bombing, along with many other art treasures.

1. BEFORE 1610. During the Kofun period (*c*. AD 300–710) a number of tomb mounds were constructed on the site now occupied by the city, including the Shiratori ryō (or Shiratori no Misasagi), the supposed tomb of the legendary Prince Yamatotakeru. From early in the region's history, the hills to the east of the city produced high-quality clay and abundant timber to support a flourishing pottery industry, which has continued into modern times. The fertile region of Nagoya contains a number of Shinto shrines, including the important Atsuta Shrine (5th or 6th century AD), which purportedly houses one of the three imperial insignia, the *kusanagi no tsurugi* ('grass-cutting sword'). The first written record of the name Nagoya dates from the late 12th century. Buddhist temples such as

Shōtokuji, Enpukuji, Honnōji and Chōboji date from the Muromachi period (1333–1568). In 1521 the daimyo Imagawa Ujichika (1473–1526) began to build a castle in the city; the site was later taken over by the military leader Nobuhide Nobunaga (1510–41), father of ODA NOBUNAGA.

2. 1610–1871. The modern city of Nagoya dates from 1610, when the first Tokugawa shogun, Ieyasu (1542–1616), ordered a new castle and castle town (see JAPAN, §IV, 3) to be built for his ninth son Yoshinao (1600–50) to replace the stronghold of Kiyosu, some 8 km to the west, and to be a bastion against the rival Toyotomi family at Osaka Castle (see OSAKA, §I, 3). Twenty daimyo were ordered to participate in the construction of the castle's earth- and stoneworks, as was the famous tea master and director of Tokugawa buildings, KOBORI ENSHŪ. The basic parts of the castle and town were completed in 1612 (see fig.). Nagoya remained the capital of the Owari branch of the Tokugawa family, the largest of Tokugawa branches, until the abolition of domains in 1871. It was the fourth largest domain in the Edo period (1600–1868).

Nagoya Castle (also called Kinkōjō and Hosajō) was one of the largest and most elaborate in Japan (see JAPAN, §III, 4(ii)(c)). It was a *hirajiro* ('castle on a plain') type and comprised five enceintes covering an area of some 35 ha. The two donjons in the Main Enceinte (Honmaru) are connected by a fortified corridor, and the main donjon (*tenshukaku*) was five storeys (48.5 m) high. The roof tiles of the main donjon were faced with copper on two storeys, and their decorative gables and the top of the building were surmounted by two gilded, dolphin-like creatures (*shachi*). The residential palace buildings of the Main

Nagoya Castle, original palace and donjon buildings, early 17th century (destr. World War II)

Enceinte were constructed in the *shoin zukuri* ('book hall or study construction') and lavishly decorated with paintings in gold leaf and colour and in monochrome ink on thick paper sliding panels (*fusuma*) and wooden sliding doors. These were done principally by the members of the KANŌ SCHOOL and were representative of Momoyama period (1568–1600) and Edo period (1600–1868) styles. Many of these works survived the 1945 bombing, and they are now housed in the reconstructed concrete main donjon (1959). The northern part of the garden in the Second Enceinte (Ninomaru), which is attributed to Kobori Enshū, has been largely restored. It covers 5900 sq m and is an important surviving example of a daimyo castle garden.

Unlike many castle towns, Nagoya was laid out systematically. The main commercial district to the south of the castle was laid out on a grid plan resembling that of Kyoto, with the principal thoroughfare (w. 27 m) leading from the castle and bisecting the city. Since its width made it hard to restrict movement at night, as was common in other castle towns, the southern end of the main street was lined with street stalls and vendors. The population is estimated to have been *c.* 100,000 by the early 18th century.

Tokugawa Yoshinao was a highly cultivated man, instrumental in establishing a rich tradition of patronage and scholarship in Nagoya. Under Tokugawa and merchant patronage, Nagoya became a centre for émigré scholars and artists who had fled China at the end of the Ming period (1368–1644). This cosmopolitan environment was further fostered by its location along the Tōkaidō road. In 1783 the city became the site of a domain academy of Confucian studies, a private medical school and a school of Dutch studies. In the early 19th century Nagoya also became an important centre of literati painting; its chief exponents were Nakabayashi Chikutō (1776–1853) and Yamamoto Baiitsu.

Several important academic publishers, such as Fugetsu Magosuke and Eirakuya Tōshirō, were based in Nagoya, which became one of Japan's largest publishing centres outside of Edo; and the Taisō in Nagoya was reputedly the largest commercial book-lending shop in the country. Several important secular and religious collections of books still exist, the largest being the Hōsa Library, begun by Tokugawa Ieyasu and developed by Yoshinao when he inherited the collection. It contains over 80,000 volumes, including books from the Kamakura (1185–1333) to Meiji (1868–1912) periods in Japan and from China of the Song (AD 960–1279) and Qing (1644–1911) periods, books of Dutch studies, ancient documents, a number of Korean *katsujibon* (books printed using movable type; see JAPAN, §IX, 2) and books of the *gozan* ('five mountains'; the highest-ranking temple–monasteries). Also notable is the Ōsu Library of the temple Hōshōin, which includes among its important treasures a complete set of *sūtras* from the Buddhist temple Nanatsudera (Chōfukuji), which was founded in the 8th century AD and moved to Nagoya in the early 17th century.

The Owari Tokugawa were important patrons of the arts. The heads of the Takayasu school of *nō* drama, the Nishikawara school of dance and the Matsu school of *chanoyu* (tea ceremony) were based in Nagoya. The family also amassed a large art collection of over 10,000 items, which was donated to the city in 1935 and is housed in the Tokugawa Art Museum (*see* JAPAN, §XXI, 2). Two of its important works are the 43 segments of the Heian period (AD 794–1185) illustrated *Tale of Genji Scroll* (*Genji monogatari emaki*) and the Kamakura period illustrated *Tales of Saigyō Scroll* (*Saigyō monogatari emaki*). The museum also houses the world's finest collection of Japanese swords.

3. AFTER 1871. After Tokugawa rule in Nagoya was abolished in 1871, the castle passed under the control of the army, and the residences and gardens outside the Main Enceinte were demolished. The city itself changed comparatively little until World War II, when some 70% of it was destroyed by bombing. Nagoya's original systematic layout, unlike that of most former castle towns, enabled redevelopment to take place on the old city plan. Only after 1945 was there any major development beyond the original city limits. Upgrading of Nagoya's port stimulated the growth of chemical and heavy industries, and since the 1960s Nagoya has formed its own independent industrial belt, incorporating neighbouring cities such as Toyota.

BIBLIOGRAPHY

Kenzōbutsu hen [Architecture] and *Bijutsu kōgei hen* [Arts and crafts], *Sensai tō ni yoru shōshitsu bunkazai* [Cultural properties lost through war and other disasters], 2 vols, Agency of Cultural Affairs (Kyoto, 1983)

P. Graham: 'Nanga Painters of Nagoya', *Orientations* (Oct 1984), pp. 34–48

A. Naitō, ed.: *Nagoya* (Tokyo, 1985), iii of *Nihon meijō shusei* [Famous castles of Japan] (Tokyo, 1984–6)

J. F. MORRIS

Nagy, István (*b* Csikmindszent, 28 March 1873; *d* Baja, 13 Feb 1937). Hungarian painter and draughtsman. He studied in Kolozsvár (now Cluj-Napoca, Romania) and then at the Budapest School of Design (1895–8) under Bertalan Székely; he continued his studies at the Akademie der Bildenden Künste in Munich under Franz von Lenbach and L. Herrterich. After briefly attending the Académie Julian in Paris, he went on a study trip to Italy. He worked in Transylvania (1903–20), painting local landscape and people in muted colours, ignoring current artistic trends. From 1905 his work became more dramatic, and he tended to use pastels and charcoal rather than oils, as in *Fiume Landscape* (1911; Budapest, priv. col.). During World War I he worked as a war artist on the Galician and Italian fronts, depicting the human aspects of the conflict. His portraits, especially drawings of his mother (1918; Budapest, priv. col.), evoke profound love. In 1920 he began to paint the villages and pastoral life of the Hungarian plains. He worked at first with József Koszta in Szentes, but although both artists are associated with the genre of GREAT PLAINS PAINTING, they remained isolated figures. In 1923 a one-man show of his work from this period was held at the National Salon in Budapest. In 1924 he painted beside Lake Balaton and met József Egry. His representations made monumental events of the everyday, revealing his self-discipline, expressive spirituality and sensitivity to the countryside. He was interested in the structure of painting, and his organization of space and perspective was influenced by Hungarian folk art. Apart from still-lifes and portraits he depicted mainly mountainous landscapes, sometimes including animals. His most successful works were done in blue and yellow pastels (e.g. *Landscape in Winter*, 1927; Budapest, N.G.). In the late 1920s he painted in Yugoslavia and finally settled in Baja. His figures became increasingly abstract with time; he returned to portraiture in his later years to support himself.

BIBLIOGRAPHY

G. Pap: *Nagy István* (Budapest, 1965)

Nagy István emlékkiállítás [István Nagy retrospective show] (exh. cat., intro. I. Solymár; Budapest, N.G., 1967)

I. Solymár: *Nagy István* (Budapest, 1977)

ÉVA BAJKAY

Nagy, Sándor (*b* Németbánya, 18 May 1869; *d* Gödöllő, 14 March 1950). Hungarian painter, draughtsman, designer and illustrator. He studied at the school of design drawing, Mintarajziskola, Budapest, under Bertalan Székely. In 1890 he travelled to Rome on a two-year scholarship, where he met the Hungarian painters Ferenc Szoldatics and Aladár Körösfői-Kriesch. From 1892 he attended the Académie Julian in Paris and in 1900 returned to Hungary, settling in Veszprém. From 1907 he worked at the GÖDÖLLŐ COLONY with his wife, the artist Laura Kriesch, the sister of Körösfői-Kriesch. Nagy's works are characterized by a zeal for experimentation, particularly with materials and techniques. He was especially concerned with the edifying role of art for the individual and society. He was influenced by Ruskin and Tolstoy and also by anarchism. His works of art incorporate a mystical symbolism, while some designs use a Secessionist style incorporating elements of Hungarian folklore.

In his early drawings and paintings Nagy sought to represent the road to moral and spiritual purification (e.g. *On and on . . .*, 1902, and *Ave Myriam*, 1904; both Budapest, N.G.). He continued the Hungarian romantic, historical tradition by drawing on Hungarian mythology for his subject-matter, as in the sgraffito *Hunor and Magor* (1909; Veszprém, Petőfi Theatre). He continued the same trend in his tapestries (e.g. *Toldi*, after 1915; Budapest, Mus. Applied A.). He also designed successful works in leather, executed by Léo Belmonte. He did illustrations in collaboration with Körösfői-Kriesch, and with his wife he followed English examples in creating an individual style in the illustration of children's books (e.g. *Móka bácsi meséi* ('Tales of Uncle Wisecrack'), Budapest, 1903). Nagy designed interiors in collaboration with Körösfői-Kriesch in the 1910s. One of his major works is the set of stained-glass windows he designed in 1913 for the Culture Palace in Marosvásárhely (now Tîrgu Mureş, Romania), representing Székely folk ballads.

Nagy and his wife took over the textile workshop at Gödöllő after the death of Körösfői-Kriesch in 1920. From 1938 to 1941 Nagy executed frescoes that retain the earlier Secessionist Symbolist style. His drawings, however, range from this style to Surrealism. His pastel and watercolour landscapes from the 1920s and 1930s display a mystical atmosphere and a fresh experience of nature unlike the decorative pastels of his early period. From 1943 he taught fresco painting, tapestry and mosaic design at the Academy of Fine Arts, Budapest. He also wrote articles dealing with folklore and art education.

WRITINGS
Az élet művészetéről [The art of life] (Budapest, 1911)

BIBLIOGRAPHY
G. Ruzsa: 'Adalékok Nagy Sándor festő és iparművész életéhez' [Contributions to the life of the painter and designer Sándor Nagy], *Művészettörténeti Értesítő* (1974), pp. 152–5
K. Gellér: *Nagy Sándor* (Budapest, 1978)
Nagy Sándor (1869–1950) (exh. cat., Veszprém, Bakonyi Mus., 1980)
'Hungarian Stained Glass of the Early 20th Century', *J. Stained Glass*, xviii/2 (1986–7), pp. 201–14

KATALIN GELLÉR

Nagybánya colony. Hungarian painters' colony, founded in 1896 in north-eastern Hungary. The idea of the colony was conceived in Simon Hollósy's painting academy in Munich, when János Thorma (1870–1937) and István Réti persuaded Hollósy to choose the small mining town of Nagybánya (now Baia Mare, Romania) for his private summer school. Béla Iványi Grünwald and Károly Ferenczy also helped to found the colony. For Hollósy and his associates the small town soon became more than a convenient location for their summer workshop, and they eventually settled there. In the next six years Hollósy continued to attract Hungarian and foreign pupils from Munich to Nagybánya every summer. After his departure in 1902 the colony abolished tuition fees and continued to attract 50 to 70 students per year.

The Nagybánya colony was of great importance for the development of Hungarian art, and its establishment signalled the beginning of a new era. The colony had excellent teachers practising free-school methods and a surrounding landscape rich in motifs and colours similar to those found in Provence, France—a combination that greatly enhanced the artistic impact of Nagybánya. Critics referred to Nagybánya as the 'Hungarian Barbizon', although its members could have been influenced by French painting only indirectly via Munich. *Plein-air* painting may provide a link, but in Hungary the exodus also came from the desire of some painters to avoid the official celebrations in Budapest in 1896 of the 1000th anniversary of the taking of the land by Magyar tribes.

The colony's first exhibition was held in 1897. On display were paintings and illustrations to poems by József Kiss. Although initially greeted with ridicule by the critics, the Nagybánya representation of nature—so different from academic or salon painting—had within a few years influenced a significant number of Hungarian painters. The founder-members possessed different styles and thematic interests, although while working in Munich they were equally attracted to the refined naturalism of Jules Bastien-Lepage. Undoubtedly the strongest personality of the colony was Károly Ferenczy (*see* FERENCZY, (1)), whose particular method of achieving a unity of emotion and atmosphere between man and landscape became the artistic standard of the Nagybánya school.

The high ethical and qualitative standards of the founders ensured a great esteem for the colony in its own time and a long-lasting impact. Réti, the self-appointed chronicler of the colony, distinguished three generations among its artists. The first comprised the founders and the artists who joined them, for example István Csók and Oszkár Glatz (1872–1958); the second included all the painter-pupils from 1902; and the third consisted of artists who arrived at the end of the 1910s. Of the second generation, Jenő Maticska (1885–1906), a talented painter who died young, showed the greatest promise. Réti applied the term 'loyal Nagybánya artist' to those second-generation painters who decided to settle in Nagybánya and who were prepared to uphold for a lifetime the ideals of style and landscape developed by Ferenczy. By around 1905, however, this ideal had changed into a rigid type of conservatism, peculiar to the Nagybánya colony, and the most accomplished painters of the second generation, in particular the 'neos' Béla Czóbel, Vilmos Perlrott Csaba and Sándor Ziffer (1880–1962) among others, turned against this ossified tradition. The works they exhibited in 1906 marked a new period in the history of Hungarian painting. They drew on German art, in particular on Expressionism, but they were most attracted to Parisian painters, such as Cézanne and Matisse. From 1907 even first-generation painters underwent a change in style, although they all showed some interest in Secessionist forms. Around 1910 Iványi Grünwald managed to attract some of the artists who left Nagybánya to his newly formed KECSKEMÉT COLONY.

From this period the remaining three founders, Ferenczy, Réti and Thorma, continued correcting students' work in the art school. It was mostly Thorma who fulfilled this role, however, as first Ferenczy, then Réti started teaching at the Academy of Fine Arts in Budapest. In the decade after 1910 the art school received increasingly younger painters, probably because of travelling difficulties brought about by World War I. After the Treaty of Versailles Nagybánya became part of Romania, and the school took both Hungarian and Romanian pupils, in some years up to 150. In 1927 the school was re-established under second-generation members as the School of Fine Arts (Szépművészeti Iskola). Although the colony's achievements in painting had been surpassed by the time of the jubilee exhibition (1912), its ethical stance, based on the particular relationship between man and the landscape, continued in the work of the 'post-Nagybánya' school (*see* GRESHAM GROUP) and the Szinyei Merse Society. Although the colony ceased to exist as such in the 1930s, its ideals persisted in art-school teaching methods in Hungary in the 1940s and 1950s.

BIBLIOGRAPHY
Nagybányai jubiláris képkiállítás [Jubilee picture exhibition of the Nagybánya colony] (exh. cat., foreword I. Réti; Nagybánya, 1912) [first summary of the colony's history]
B. Szokolay: *A nagybányai művésztelep* [The Nagybánya artists' colony] (Cluj, 1926)
I. Genthon: 'A nagybányai iskola' [The Nagybánya school], *Szépművészet* (1944), pp. 1–8
N. Aradi: 'Nagybánya értékeléséhez' [Towards an assessment of the Nagybánya school], *Művészettörténeti Tanulmányok* (1954), pp. 423–34
I. Réti: *A nagybányai művésztelep* [The Nagybánya artists' colony] (Budapest, 1954) [incl. detailed inf. on the everyday life of the colony and list of pupils, 1896–1933]

NÓRA ARADI

Nagyszeben. *See* SIBIU.

Nagyszentmiklós Treasure. Hoard of gold (Vienna, Ksthist. Mus.), discovered in 1799 in a swamp region near Nagyszentmiklós (now Sînnicolau Mare, Romania) and the largest known gold hoard from the early Middle Ages. In the same year it went to Vienna, where it became part of the Imperial collection. The hoard comprises 23 gold vessels (see fig.) with an average standard of 20–22 carats and a total weight of almost 10 kg. There are ten different types of vessel: seven pitchers (nos 1–7 in Hampel and later publications; not the museum inventory nos), four bowls with clasps (nos 9, 10, 20, 21), two bowls with handles (nos 15, 16), an oval bowl (no. 8), a small bellied bowl (no. 19), two bull's head bowls (nos 13, 14), a footless bull's head bowl (no. 18), two goblets (nos 22, 23), two truncated-cone shaped cups (nos 11, 12) and a drinking horn (no. 17).

The vessels are richly decorated. All are embossed, and all except nos 11, 12, 17, 22 and 23 are partly chased; some have figurative designs. The most interesting examples, in the four medallions on one of the pitchers (no. 2), include an armoured nomad rider holding a lance and seizing a captive by the top of his head, with another severed head at his saddle; an eagle carrying off a woman holding a flower in her hand; a rider on a fantastic winged creature shooting a panther with a bow; and a griffin bringing down a doe. The medallions on the flat pitcher (no. 7) show Ganymede being carried off by the eagle, while on the narrow sides centaurs are shown fighting and waterfowl are depicted on the neck. The medallions on the bowls with handles (nos 15 and 16) and the bowl with clasps (no. 20), as well as the body of the small bellied bowl (no. 19) and the handle of the oval bowl (no. 8), are decorated with such mythical and fantastic creatures as griffins and fish-tailed lions. Fighting animals (e.g. a winged lion bringing down a stag) appear on the medallion of the bowl with clasps (no. 21), which also has a Greek cross surrounded by an inscription in Greek letters on the inside. Several vessels bear Greek, Turkish and rune-like carved inscriptions that had not yet been interpreted by the late 1990s; neither the Greek inscriptions on two bowls (nos 9 and 10) of a liturgical character (indicated by the cross) nor the Turkish or perhaps Old Bulgarian inscription in Greek letters on another bowl (no. 21) have been satisfactorily translated. Notched inscriptions on 13 of the vessels—probably in a Turkish script related to late Avar and Hungarian—were engraved or incised later (except on the oval bowl); they probably specify the name (or perhaps rank) of the owner or donor.

The vessels were made over an extended period in at least four different workshops that may have been late Sasanian or Bactrian, or influenced by these. The extraordinary quality of most of the vessels reveals a superb mastery of goldsmithswork that was based on a long tradition and that reflects the diversity of cultural connections in the Balkans in the 7th to 9th centuries. The hoard comprises works displaying the most diverse cultural, stylistic and religious influences: Avar, Sasanian, mid-Asian and Islamic elements beside Greco-Roman and Byzantine ones; pagan features appear beside Christian ones. The large pitchers have forms based on Sasanian prototypes, and they are decorated with a complicated mixture of late Sasanian and mid-Asian motifs from the 7th to 8th centuries, as well as Islamic ones from the 9th century. The representation of animals and mythical beasts is uncommon in Middle Eastern art but characteristic of the art of the nomads of the steppes (e.g. in late Avar

Nagyszentmiklós Treasure (selection of vessels), gold, ?late 8th century (Vienna, Kunsthistorisches Museum)

work), and demonstrates the close contact of these cultures, as does the representation of Asian mythological scenes. The forms of the drinking horn, bowls and cup recall the nomad, chiefly Avar tradition of the 7th century, while Byzantine elements are also apparent in the representations of the cross, the Greek inscriptions and the use of Greek characters in the Turkish inscriptions.

Owing to the differences between the individual pieces and the lack of strictly comparable works, the ethnic and art-historical context of the treasure is still uncertain, despite the numerous studies that have been written on the subject. In the 19th century the hoard was known as 'the treasure of Attila', but in the 20th century it was ascribed to 7th-century Kuvratbulgars, 7th- or 8th century late Avars, 9th-century Balkanbulgars and 10th- to 11th-century Hungarians (Pechenegs). On the basis of all the evidence, especially the animal and human representations and the floral motifs, the hoard should probably be dated to the late 8th century and the 9th, and linked with the late Avar-Hungarian-Bulgar cultural circle; the conversion of the Bulgars to Christianity in 864 could explain the co-existence of Christian and pagan motifs. The treasure, which is thought originally to have been expensive tableware and later used for liturgical purposes, was no doubt buried during the Hungarian attack of 896. The attempts of Hungarian researchers to associate the vessels with Hungarian royal goldsmith workshops are not convincing.

BIBLIOGRAPHY

J. Hampel: *A nagyszentmiklósi kincs* [The Nagyszentmiklós Treasure] (Budapest, 1884)

J. Németh: *Die Inschriften des Schatzes von Nagy-Szent-Miklós* (Budapest, 1932)

N. Mavrodinov: *Le Trésor protobulgare de Nagyszentmiklós* (Budapest, 1943)

G. László and I. Rácz: *A nagyszentmiklósi kincs* [The Nagyszentmiklós Treasure] (Budapest, 1977; Eng. trans., Budapest, 1984)

K. Horedt: 'Zur Zeitstellung des Schatzfundes von Sinnicolau Mare (Nagyszentmiklós)', *Archäol. Korrbl.*, xiii (1983), pp. 503–5

H.-W. Haussig: 'Die Runen des Schatzes von Nagy-Szent Miklós in ihrer Bedeutung für die Runenschrift Osteuropas', *Runen, Tamgas und Graffiti aus Asien und Osteuropa*, ed. K. Röhrbohn and W. Veenker (Wiesbaden, 1985), pp. 17–52

B. Marschak: *Silberschätze des Orients: Metallkunst des 3.–13. Jahrhunderts und ihre Kontinuität* (Leipzig, 1986)

ALFRED BERNHARD-WALCHER

Nagyszombat. *See* TRNAVA.

Nahl, Johann August, *der Ältere* (*b* Berlin, 22 Aug 1710; *d* Kassel, 22 Oct 1781). German sculptor and stuccoist. He was first trained by his father, the sculptor Johann Samuel Nahl (1664–1727), who since 1704 had been court sculptor to Frederick I in Berlin. At the age of 18 Nahl set out as a journeyman, travelling via Sigmaringen and Berne to Strasbourg, where from 1728 he worked as an assistant to Robert Le Lorrain. In 1731 he went to Paris, where he spent two years studying ornament. In 1734 he spent a year in Rome, then travelled in Italy. In 1735 he moved to Schaffhausen, where he executed various stuccowork projects that cannot now be identified; he then returned to Strasbourg, where he set up as an independent sculptor and decorator. He worked first for the royal praetor Klinglin, and subsequently for Cardinal Armand-Gaston de Rohan-Soubise on the episcopal palace, now known as the Palais Rohan, which had been started in 1731. In 1736 Nahl was granted citizenship of Strasbourg and was married; one of his sons, Samuel Nahl (1748–1813), likewise became a sculptor, and another, Johann August Nahl *der Jüngere*, became a painter.

In response to a summons from Frederick II (*see* GERMANY, §V, 3) Nahl moved in 1741 to Berlin, where he collaborated on the interior decoration of the New Wing at Schloss Charlottenburg. He took part in the decoration of the King's First Apartment: the Silver Anteroom, library and study. At first he carried out other decorators' designs but subsequently was able to implement his own ideas, as in the ceiling decoration of the main staircase of the New Wing. His contribution to the Golden Gallery (completed in 1746, reconstructed after war damage) was chiefly confined, however, to execution and detailing, the design of that superb banqueting room being the work of Georg Wenceslaus von Knobelsdorff. The four rooms comprising what was known as Frederick II's Second Apartment were based on Nahl's designs, executed after his departure by the Hoppenhaupt brothers.

Nahl worked more or less independently in the renovation of the royal apartments in the west and east wings of the Stadtschloss at Potsdam. The first project was the decoration of the western apartment, intended as a guest suite, on the first floor of the palace; he provided designs for all seven rooms. Only the ceiling decoration of what was known as the Bronzesaal was extant at the time of the building's destruction in World War II; it displayed an elegant fluency reminiscent of Nahl's work at Charlottenburg. Some of his most beautiful decorative work in Potsdam was to be found in the exquisitely executed decorations of the six rooms (destr.) of the Winter Apartments, for example the decorative schemes of the concert room and the bedroom. In the same period Nahl, who had been promoted to 'Directeur des ornements', carried out the decorative work in the apartment of Sophie

Dorothea, Frederick the Great's mother, on the third floor of the Berliner Schloss (destr.). Nahl's final project in Prussia was the rich decoration of the concert room at Schloss Sanssouci, but his designs were carried out by Johann Michael Hoppenhaupt II, as in 1746 Nahl more or less fled from Prussia to Strasbourg, because of the burden of the working conditions imposed on him by Frederick II.

In the autumn of 1746 Nahl moved to Berne. In the creative period that followed, sculptural work tended to predominate. His first commission was the epitaph for *Mayor Beat Ludwig May* (1747) in the town church of Thun. Two years later he received his first public commission, to build the new organ screen and overhaul the organ case in Berne Cathedral. However, the massive ornamentation does not much resemble Nahl's decorative work in Prussia, suggesting that his emigration had brought about some artistic decline. Between 1749 and 1752 he worked mainly for Albert Friedrich von Erlach, carrying out the stuccowork in the banqueting room of the Erlach house in Berne and designing several wrought-iron items, including the splendid balcony railing on the south front of the courtyard side of the building. For the same patron Nahl created lions and sphinxes (1748–52) for the park of Schloss Hindelbank. The tomb of *Hieronymus von Erlach* in the church at Hindelbank (1750–51) dates from about the same period. Nahl's most important work in Switzerland was the tomb of *Maria Magdalena Langhans* (1751–2) in the same church, depicting the resurrection of Maria Magdalena and her child. It was much celebrated: its rather sentimental style made it especially appealing to contemporary taste. Nahl's other works around that time included models for ornamental gun decorations (1750), various examples of stuccowork in the houses of patrician families (1752–4), a model for a seal for the canton of Berne (1754) and the design and model for the ceremonial goblet of the guild of carpenters (1752), one of the most beautiful pieces of decorative art from that period. Nahl also worked as an architect, as shown by some design sketches for the two garden pavilions (1756) at the Frischingshaus in the Junkergasse, Berne.

In 1755 Nahl moved to Kassel, entering the service of Landgrave William VIII (*reg* 1751–60), on whose behalf he travelled in 1756 to Switzerland and, via Lausanne and Genoa, to Carrara. Nahl's most important work in Kassel was the design of the rich interior decoration of Schloss Wilhelmsthal (1755–61); in its elegance it reflected his earlier achievements in Prussia. The decoration of the breakfast room in the hotel 'Zum Schwan' in Karlshafen (completed 1765), which is ascribed to him, is simpler in effect. In addition, Nahl produced a series of sculptures, including two colossal groups with sea monsters for the grotto in front of Wilhelmsthal, transferred in 1795 to the *Pluto* grotto in the park at Wilhelmshöhe. He also worked on a vase (1757; not completed) in the park of Wilhelmsthal and executed two statues of a *Lion-tamer* (*c.* 1767) in the Wilhelmsaue at Kassel. His last large work, which was actually completed by his son Samuel Nahl, was the statue of *Landgrave Frederick II*, erected in 1783 on the Friedrichsplatz in Kassel.

During his years in Kassel, Nahl carried out numerous commissions outside the town. As early as 1756 he

Johann August Nahl: façade of the artist's house at 41 Königsstrasse (Friedrichsplatz), Kassel, 1771 (destr. after 1950)

provided the wax models for the decoration of the principal façade of the town church at Yverdon, Switzerland. From 1760 he apparently worked for some time for Schloss Seehof near Bamberg. He was probably also involved in the interior furnishing of Schlösschen Frankenstein (1761–3, destr. 1867) in the grounds of Seehof; from this only a superb stove (New York, Met.) has been preserved. By 1771 Nahl was rich enough to build himself an imposing residence at 41 Königsstrasse, Kassel (destr. after 1950; see fig.), with a richly decorated façade designed by himself. Another façade that he created for the Königsplatz house of the stuccoist Johann Michael Brühl was destroyed in World War II. In addition to being appointed court sculptor, Nahl became in 1777 director of the Kassel academy of art, and also a councillor.

Both as a sculptor of figures and a decorative sculptor, Nahl was one of the most important artistic personalities of the 18th century in Germany; as a decorator in particular he was a stylistic pioneer. Together with Knobelsdorff, he created the interior decoration and furnishing of the Frederican era, which occupies a special position within European Rococo.

BIBLIOGRAPHY

Thieme–Becker
Hartwig and Sprengel: *Sprengels Handwerk und Künste in Tabellen*, 9 vols (Berlin, 1772), p. 211
H. Manger: *Baugeschichte von Potsdam* (Berlin, 1789), pp. 44, 53, 62
F. Nicolai: *Nachrichten von Baumeistern, Bildhauern, Kupferstechern, Malern, Stukkateuren und anderen Künstlern* (Berlin and Stettin, 1789), p. 151
P. Seidel: 'Johann August Nahl', *Centbl. Bauverwalt.*, xiii (1893), pp. 494–6
A. Worringer: 'Das Standbild des Landgrafen Friedrich II auf dem Friedrichsplatz zu Kassel', *Hessenland*, xxxviii (1919)
H. Kania: 'Ein Meister des deutschen Rokoko: Johann August Nahl', *Potsdam. Tagztg*, 2 (1921)
F. Bleibaum: 'Schloss Wilhelmsthal', *Die Bau- und Kunstdenkmäler im Regierungsbezirk Cassel*, vii (Kassel, 1926)
——: *Johann August Nahl: Der Künstler Friedrichs des Grossen und der Landgrafen von Hessen-Kassel* (Baden and Berlin, 1933)
P. Hofer and L. Mojon: *Die Kunstdenkmale des Kantons Bern: Die Stadt Bern*, i–v (Basle, 1947–69)
C. R. Dautermann: 'The Frankenstein Dragon Stove', *Bull. Met.* (1960), pp. 168–70
M. Grandjean: 'Les Deux Projets de décoration du tympan d'Yverdon et l'iconographie protestante', *Unsere Kstdkml.*, xiv (1963), pp. 58ff
E. Goens: 'Die Gartenskulpturen von Schloss Hindelbank', *Marburg. Jb. Kstwiss.*, xviii (1969), pp. 153–60
E. M. Fallet: *Der Bildhauer Johann August Nahl der Ältere: Seine Berner Jahre von 1746–1755* (Berne, 1970)
J.-D. Ludmann: 'Le Décor intérieur du palais Rohan de Strasbourg', *Inf. Hist. A.*, iii (1972), pp. 119–38

T. EGGELING

Na'in [Nā'īn; Nayin]. Town in central Iran. Na'in lies on the edge of the central desert to the east of Isfahan on the route from Qum to Yazd. The town has two buildings of architectural importance: the congregational mosque and a ruined palace. The mosque has been much rebuilt, but the original foundation can be dated *c.* AD 960 on the basis of its hypostyle plan and stucco decoration; it is one of the earliest congregational mosques to survive in Iran (*see*

ISLAMIC ART, §II, 5(i)(a)). It has a small court surrounded by arcades and a roof supported by barrel vaults that are pointed with a noticeable stilt. A minaret with a square base and a tapering octagonal shaft is set in the south-east corner. The mihrab and the six bays around it are richly revetted with carved stucco. Motifs include vine scrolls, rosettes and acanthus typical of the style of carving associated with the Abbasid capital at Samarra' and inscriptions in foliated kufic script framing the arches and bays. The piers on the qibla side of the court are decorated with small bricks laid in relief in diamond, zigzag and other geometric patterns. This style of brickwork is also found in the restorations to the congregational mosque at Isfahan done under the Buyids (reg 932–1062), and this suggests that, as at Isfahan, the court façade of the mosque at Na'in was redone soon after its construction. The three bays in front of the mihrab are covered by domical vaults, which may have been rebuilt later, perhaps at the same time that the fine wooden minbar was donated by a local merchant in 1311.

The two-storey palace in Na'in has been dated c. 1560 on the style of the painted decoration, and it is one of the earliest examples of secular architecture built by the Safavids (reg 1501–1732) to survive (see ISLAMIC ART, §II, 7(ii)(a)). It has a sunken courtyard with two iwans on each of the longer façades. The largest iwan has intricate squinch-net vaulting rising from blind niches; both the stellate vaults and the niches are covered with figural designs of white stucco cut away to reveal a dark ground. The traces of colour that survive may be later. The scenes depicted, such as events from Persian poetry, enthroned royal couples, polo matches, banquets and the hunt, are typical of Safavid book painting (see ISLAMIC ART, §III, 4(vi)(a)), while the vaults are decorated with chinoiserie themes of dragons, phoenixes and flying ducks.

BIBLIOGRAPHY
H. Viollet and S. Flury: 'Un Monument des premiers siècles de l'hégire en Perse', *Syria*, ii (1921), pp. 226–34, 305–16
S. Flury: 'La Mosquée de Nāyin', *Syria*, xi (1930), pp. 43–58
M. B. Smith: 'The Wood Mimbar in the Masdjid-i Djami', Nāīn', *A. Islam.*, v (1938), pp. 21–35
A. U. Pope and P. Ackerman, eds: *Survey of Persian Art* (Oxford, 1938–9, rev. Shiraz, 2/1964–7), pp. 934–9
I. Luschey-Schmeisser: 'Der Wand- und Deckenschmuck eines safavidischen Palastes in Nayin', *Archäol. Mitt. Iran*, n. s., ii (1969), pp. 183–92
——: 'Ein neuer Raum in Nayin', *Archäol. Mitt. Iran*, v (1972), pp. 309–14

Nain, Le. *See* LE NAIN.

Nainsukh (*b* Guler, *c.* 1710; *d* Basohli, 1778). Indian painter. He was the younger son of PANDIT SEU. He remains, justly perhaps, the Pahari painter about whom most is known. Growing up in an atmosphere of experimentation and change, Nainsukh seems to have matured early and taken enthusiastically to the fluent naturalism of Mughal painting that came to the hill region at this time. Moving much further in this direction than did his father or elder brother, MANAKU, he brought the family painting

Nainsukh: *Nainsukh Standing Respectfully behind his Patron, Raja Balwant Singh of Jasrota, while He Examines a Painting*, gouache on paper, 210×300 mm, *c.* 1748 (Zurich, Museum Rietberg Zürich)

style to a point where it established norms, affecting painting throughout the hills. Leaving his home in Guler *c.* 1740, Nainsukh entered the service of Prince Balwant Singh of Jasrota, a discriminating patron whom he served until his death in 1763. In 1763 Nainsukh went on a pilgrimage to Hardwar, where Balwant Singh's ashes were taken for immersion, and made an uncommonly long and informative entry in the priest's register, adding a tiny but brilliant impromptu drawing on the same page. Around 1765 he moved to Basohli, where he seems to have remained until his own death. A *Self-portrait*, done before he was 20 years old, has survived, as have portraits of his father and his elder brother. Several works inscribed in Nainsukh's hand and some bearing his name have survived. He had four sons—Kama, Gandhu, Nikka and Ranjha—who, together with Fattu and Khushala, Manaku's sons, continued to work in the family style that had been established *c.* 1760.

Nainsukh is known chiefly for the evocative and singularly sensitive studies through which he captured the atmosphere of a small princely court and rendered politically the routine, rather unspectacular life of his patron, Balwant Singh (see fig.; *see also* INDIAN SUBCONTINENT, fig. 299). This large group of paintings and drawings is not only marked by extraordinary powers of observation and wit, but also by the deep humanity that informed Nainsukh's work throughout his life. His eye seems to have been uncommonly sharp in picking up details; this gift he uses when he renders sensitive, individual faces and captures the movements, gestures and personal foibles that impart such warmth to his work. Using supple line to great effect, he was able to make the most complex of compositions appear as if they were the easiest things to do. In his outdoor studies, there is a feeling of openness, of airy expanse, that lifts the viewer's spirits. Devices and mannerisms associated with Nainsukh include: a preference for uncoloured grounds; shading through a light wash that imparts volume and weight to figures and groups; a fine horizontal line that separates ground from background; a rich green in which his landscapes are usually bathed; a bush with flat circular leaves that he often introduces; a peculiar loop of the long stem of a *hooka*; and a minor figure often introduced in a two-thirds profile. To Nainsukh can also be attributed the invention of an idealized female type, the face rendered with porcelain delicacy, the body youthful and singularly well-proportioned, creating a general aspect of soft, melting grace. This female type was to be used with great effect by members of his family in the following two generations.

See also INDIAN SUBCONTINENT, §V, 4(iv).

BIBLIOGRAPHY
B. N. Goswamy: 'The Problem of the Artist Nainsukh of Jasrota', *Asiae Artibus*, xxviii (1966), pp. 205–10
W. G. Archer: *Indian Paintings from the Punjab Hills*, i (London, 1973)
R. W. Skelton: *The Indian Heritage: Court Life and Arts under Mughal Rule* (exh. cat., London, V&A, 1982)
Pahari-Meister (exh. cat. by B. N. Goswamy and E. Fischer, Zurich, Mus. Rietberg, 1990)

B. N. GOSWAMY

Nairn, James M(cLachlan) (*b* Aberfoyle, nr Glasgow, 18 Nov 1859; *d* Wellington, 22 Feb 1904). Scottish painter, active in New Zealand. Having trained at the Glasgow School of Art, he worked with the Glasgow Boys. He also studied at the Académie Julian in Paris during the 1880s. Both the style and the imagery of his work indicate a knowledge of Impressionist painting, particularly Monet and Camille Pissarro, as well as the work of Millet, Courbet and Bastien-Lepage. By the time he arrived in New Zealand in 1890, Nairn had developed a subdued type of *plein-air* realism that was concerned with light and atmosphere but not the dissolution of form under the effects of light that was the essence of Impressionism. *Hutt River* (1892; Wellington, Mus. NZ, Te Papa Tongarewa) is typical of his brand of Scottish Impressionism. New Zealand artists were stimulated by the first-hand contact Nairn provided with innovative European styles. He was among the first artists in New Zealand who lived solely from the sale of their art. His flair, independence and professionalism encouraged a considerable following in Wellington, where he lived for the remainder of his short life. Nairn was prominent in art circles, teaching at the local art school, exhibiting his work regularly and forming an art group that favoured freedom of expression.

Despite his early death, Nairn was an important catalyst for the early 20th-century direction and development of New Zealand art. The National Art Gallery in Wellington holds a large collection of his works, two of the most outstanding examples being *Winter Morning*, *Wellington Harbour* (*c.* 1900) and a *Summer Idyll* (1903).

BIBLIOGRAPHY
S. H. Edwards and J. Magurk: 'James Nairn: Artist', *A. NZ*, xii (1940), pp. 220–25
G. Docking: *Two Hundred Years of New Zealand Painting* (Wellington, 1971), pp. 76–80
F. Pound: *Frames on the Land* (Auckland, 1983), pp. 84–90

TONY MACKLE

Nairne, George Colvill. *See under* McCARTER NAIRNE.

Naive art. Term applied to the work of non-professional, self-taught artists who, while lacking orthodox skills, apply themselves to their art in a resolute and independent spirit.

1. Introduction. 2. Characteristics and examples. 3. Distribution and impact.

1. INTRODUCTION. The history of naive art is both the history of the complex evolution of the many art forms lying outside the fine arts tradition and of the critical attempts to disentangle a distinct strand from this broader fabric. In the course of the 19th century in Europe, the arts and crafts of rural peoples (normally termed FOLK ART, or sometimes 'peasant art') and the urban traditions of semi-skilled craftsmen gradually faltered in the face of growing industrialization. Factory products enfeebled the individual impulse to fashion handmade artefacts; itinerant portrait painters ('limners') found their trade dwindling after the advent of photography; and in general the rise of an industry-based economy and the growth of cities sapped the vitality of vernacular and communally recognized artwork such as embroidery, toymaking, the carving of ships' figureheads, painted targets and so forth. Similar developments took place in North America, though at a slower pace, partly determined by a wilful defence of inherited models on the part of culture-conscious immigrants.

A precise line of demarcation between folk and naive art has yet to be universally ratified. It is above all notable that in North America the term 'folk art' continues to be applied, quite indiscriminately, to work of both the 19th and 20th centuries ranging from early anonymous quilts and painted decoy ducks of folk inspiration through naive paintings proper and on to extravagant psychotic drawings more usefully classifiable as ART BRUT. Nonetheless, there seems to be a fairly clear correlation in both North America and Europe between the erosion of communal folk traditions in the last decades of the 19th century and the incidence of unschooled artists whose works begin to shed their kinship with comforting stereotypes and to reveal a bolder, more individual aesthetic investment, in short, a personal touch.

If naive artists first emerged in the late 19th century, a framework for their appreciation had in a sense long been established by virtue of concepts and values dating back as far as Jean-Jacques Rousseau's eulogies of the 'noble savage' and the unschooled peasant, men uncorrupted by urban civilization. The equation of the naive with the innocent and the authentic may similarly be traced to the debates of Schiller and Goethe on the benefits of instinct and spontaneity; their ideas flowed into the wider stream of a German Romantic revaluation of folklore and popular creativity. Yet it turned out to be in France that naive art was first decisively recognized, with the emergence of an outstanding and irreducibly authentic naive artist, Henri Rousseau ('Le Douanier'). At first patronized, in ways that ironically admitted his talent while mocking his amateurishness, Rousseau took himself extremely seriously and worked hard to produce canvases that in due time won the admiration and support of the modernist avant-garde (Guillaume Apollinaire, Picasso, Robert Delaunay; for illustration see ROUSSEAU, HENRI). Rousseau was subsequently taken up by the critic and collector Wilhelm Uhde, who was fortunate (and discriminating) enough to discover the work of four other major French naive painters of the time—Louis Vivin, André Bauchant, Camille Bombois and Séraphine. Uhde's enthusiastic sponsorship of these artists was a major step towards the public acceptance of naive art as a distinct category.

Although Uhde later admitted the shortcomings of his own terminology, the first major exhibition of these five artists' work took place at the Galerie des Quatre Chemins in Paris in 1928 under the heading *Les Peintres du coeur sacré*, a sentimental allusion to innocence and a religiosity not in fact appropriate to all five. For several decades, the search for a clearcut label marked each new exhibition or book title. The Paris exhibition of 1937 at the Salle Royale was launched with the title *Les Maîtres populaires de la réalité*, implying that these were artists of the people who treated their subjects in a realist style. The expression 'Sunday painter' had some currency until it was pointed out that naive artists are often unemployed and do not see their art as a mere hobby. The term *Laienmaler* ('lay painter') had some resonance in German-speaking countries. 'Primitive' has been widely used as a synonym of 'naive', although the obvious dangers of confusion with early Italian painting (e.g. Cimabue) or again with non-Western art (e.g. Polynesian ritual carvings) has prompted the more cautious variants 'neo-primitive' or 'modern

primitive' (*see* PRIMITIVISM, §2). The organizers of the Bratislava Triennale for naive art sponsored the neologism *insitné umenie*, from the Latin *insitus*, meaning 'innate', 'unschooled', or 'undiluted' art. One of the most impressive theorists, Vladimir Maleković, spoke of 'primal art', a creativity springing from the innermost resources of the individual. However, since at least the late 1950s (with the large international exhibition *La Peinture naïve* at Knokke-Het Zoute in 1958 and Oto Bihalji-Merin's influential book *Das naive Bild der Welt*, 1959), the term 'naive art' may be said to have established itself as the most widely accepted term, being by now stripped of any pejorative connotations of ineptness or stupidity and functioning in a strictly classificatory sense.

2. CHARACTERISTICS AND EXAMPLES. The ramifications of this terminological survey reflect something of the inherent paradox of the phenomenon. One might suppose a naive artist to be unsophisticated by definition, yet arguably he or she frequently develops modes of operating that are highly sophisticated; the work might seem awkward or clumsy by academic standards, yet, through what Rosenberg called the 'skilled use of unskill' (see 1974 exh. cat., review), the artist can achieve exceptional results. Essentially, the virtue of naive art rests in the fact that deficiencies, such as a poor grasp of anatomy or conventional perspective, are turned to aesthetic account; Jean Lipman suggested that technical inabilities can lead to a compensatory emphasis on pure design.

What does seem paramount in the best naive work is the commingling of the intuitive and the intellectual, the spontaneous and the disciplined. As Maleković pointed out in his discussion of Rousseau, there is a clear basis of intuition in the conception of the image and yet a formidable deliberateness about its execution. It is a keynote of naive painting that it should appear complete in every part, with an even accentuation of each last detail; it is often this studied concern for minutiae at the expense of overall balance, combined with deviations from the naturalistic norm—awkward contours, incorrect colouring—that creates its characteristic aesthetic impact. Several commentators speak of naive artists as operating in regard to a mental idea of their subject rather than a visual impression, rather like children. Thus the artists transliterate what they know or feel rather than what they see; they often consider their work to be realistic, where others notice only its deviance from actuality. Many critics from Uhde onwards have referred to some form of ecstatic experience that precedes, or is encoded within, the painting: a high proportion of naive works present sharply outlined yet somehow insubstantial objects that float in an ambience of luminosity, offering the viewer a preternaturally enhanced version of a scene that nonetheless remains identifiably derived from ordinary experience.

A few examples of naive work may clarify these generalizations. The paintings of the Croatian Emerik Feješ (1904–69) were copied from postcard views of foreign cities he had never seen. His piece-by-piece reconstruction of the architecture of *Milan Cathedral* (1966; Zagreb, Gal. Primitive A.; see fig.) leads to an ungainly overall shape; and the colouring-in of each tiny zone within the ensemble disregards plausibility, to produce a kaleidoscopic array of conflicting hues at once unsettling and strangely appealing. There are many instances of naive artists who work from a ready-made image. Ernst Damitz (1805–83) produced magical versions of landscapes taken from engravings, and Josef Wittlich (*b* 1903) transcribed images from popular magazines to garish yet grandiose effect. Other artists work from memory to produce documentary or narrative work recording the detail of acquaintances or seasonal events, usually within a small-town setting. Grandma Moses, Orneore Metelli (1872–1939) and Germain Tessier (1895–1981) painted homespun scenes typical of their respective environments, while the paintings of Horace Pippin (1888–1946) offer intense insight into the public and private experience of the African American, for example *John Brown Going to his Hanging* (1942; Philadelphia, PA Acad. F.A.).

Although it is tempting to divide naive painters into two broad types, realists and fantasists, the division cannot be absolute. Whereas some gravitate towards a clarity of finish that denotes a concern for scrupulous accuracy, and others are drawn to expressions of almost irresponsible eccentricity, the hallmark of the naive lies in the co-existence of extremes within the same work. Thus, where the high gloss renderings of wild-life of Adolf Dietrich (1877–1957) move towards naturalism, the very sharpness of his finish has a certain uncanny quality; and when Matija Skurjeni (*b* 1898) presents an exotic dream of a journey to Paris, there remains a certain amount of legible reference (the Eiffel Tower) to give credence to the fantasy. Some naive art has been called visionary, such as the hypnotic flower paintings of Séraphine, for example the *Tree of Paradise* (1929; Paris, Mus. A. Mod. Ville Paris), or the rapturous floating landscapes of Ivan Rabuzin (*b* 1921), as in *On the Hills, Virgin Wood* (1960; Zagreb, Gal. Primitive A.). Their example prompts the thought that naive artists may be concerned not with making images that are intensely real, or conversely intensely unreal, but with producing mythic transpositions of the world, invocations of the 'superreal', an idealized, timeless and yet still accessible reality. Elemental or essential qualities blend in a vision of utopian harmony; and if there are sometimes aggressive or disruptive images (for instance, the bristling 'devil houses' drawn by the convict Frank Jones (1901–69)), there is also almost always both a superficial charm that flatters the casual gaze and a cool, distinctive luminosity, an aura or 'poetic halo', in Maleković's phrase, of genuine aesthetic value.

Works of art in media other than paint, most commonly wood or stone, may equally qualify as naive art. These include the multi-figured logs shaped by Bogosav Živković (*b* 1920), the *Adam and Eve* cycle carved by Edgar Tolson (*b* 1904) and the voodoo-inspired cult figures cut by Louco (Boaventura da Silva Filho) (*b* 1932). The lesser-known field of environmental work created in naive or *Art brut* styles has yet to be properly classified, though the ambitious *Garden of Eden* constructed by Samuel Perry Dinsmoor (1843–1932) and the pebblework village assembled by Marcel Landreau (*b* 1922) are valid contributions to naive art.

Naive art by Emerik Feješ: *Milan Cathedral*, tempera on canvas, 455×625 mm, 1966 (Zagreb, Gallery of Primitive Art)

3. DISTRIBUTION AND IMPACT. Critical awareness of naive art has increased to a point where it has become necessary to envisage it as a worldwide phenomenon. The *World Encyclopedia of Naive Art* (1984) lists hundreds of artists from dozens of countries, from Canada to Poland, from Brazil to China. It has been possible to identify clusters of naive painters working in such places as Haiti, the Italian village of Luzzara (nr Mantua) and the village of Hlebine in Croatia; those working in the last-named have been dubbed the HLEBINE SCHOOL, and a definite local style can be discerned. Nonetheless, a more typical quality of naive art is its singularity, the fact that most of its exponents work in relative isolation, albeit—and this is crucial in differentiating them from exponents of *Art brut*—without veering towards a pitch of self-indulgence such as entirely to lose track of a potential audience. In the main, naive artists are keen to be recognized and exhibited and, in certain cases, as with Rousseau, will blithely assume a position on a par with established artists.

Professionals have frequently shown a direct interest in naive art and have sometimes drawn creatively on its example. The work of such painters as Marc Chagall or L. S. Lowry is partly dependent on naive or folk models. Pioneers of Modernism, including Kandinsky, Malevich, Klee and Léger, have explicitly or implicitly aligned their creative endeavours with qualities they associated with the naive idiom. The mature inventions of Rousseau have been seen as significant predecessors of the Surrealists, of whom Giorgio de Chirico and Victor Brauner, for example, exploited, doubtless in a more knowing than innocent manner, certain naive features. The crudely executed marine paintings of Alfred Wallis were highly prized by Christopher Wood and Ben Nicholson. The peasant artists of Hlebine, including their leader, Ivan Generalić, came to prominence largely thanks to Krsto Hegedušić, who first invited them to participate in shows alongside members of his own LAND GROUP. Later, the Chicago Imagist group was to show a lively interest in the productions of untutored artists such as Henry Darger (1892–1973).

Each time the naive artist experiences public attention, his or her spontaneous naivety is at once placed at risk. It is arguable that sympathetic concern for an artist's singular effort may be every bit as intrusive as its cynical exploitation. Some naive artists adjust smoothly to the marketplace and make a satisfactory transition into professionalism, often thereby renouncing their naive qualities. Others respond to the commercial lure by selling replicas of their best pictures, repeating them until all trace of spontaneity is lost. The selling power of naive art has influenced both tourism and the expanding gallery trade in kitsch: a veritable industry of pseudo-naive work has evolved, of minimal artistic value. Partisans of authenticity would wish to protest at such exploitation and to impute negative value to any work made by rote. Nevertheless, the most stimulating and consistent works are those made by individuals who abide by their original vision. The best naive art demonstrates that timelessness and discipline are not easily faked.

See also CSONTVÁRY, TIVADAR; HIRSHFIELD, MORRIS; KANE, JOHN; PICKETT, JOSEPH; SAFED, SHALOM VON; TYTGAT, EDGARD.

BIBLIOGRAPHY

Les Peintres du coeur sacré (exh. cat., ed. W. Uhde; Paris, Gal. Quatre Chemins, 1928)
S. Janis: *They Taught themselves: American Primitive Painters of the Twentieth Century* (New York, 1942)
J. Lipman: *American Primitive Painting* (New York, 1942)
W. Uhde: *Fünf primitive Meister* (Zurich, 1947; Eng. trans., New York, 1949)
A. Jakovsky: *Les Peintres naïfs* (Paris, 1956)
O. Bihalji-Merin: *Das naive Bild der Welt* (Cologne, 1959); Eng. trans. as *Modern Primitives: Masters of Naive Painting* (New York, 1959)
A. Jakovsky: *Peintres naïfs: Lexique des peintres naïfs du monde entier* (Basle, 1967)
A. Phribný and S. Tkáč: *Naive Painters of Czechoslovakia* (Prague, 1967)
B. Kelemen: *Yugoslav Naive Painting* (Zagreb, 1969)
S. Tkáč: *Svetové insitné umenie* [World insitné art] (Bratislava, 1969)
S. Williams: *Voodoo and the Art of Haiti* (London, 1969)
A. Dasnoy: *Exégèse de la peinture naïve* (Brussels, 1970)
O. Bihalji-Merin: *Modern Primitives: Naive Painting from the Late Seventeenth Century to the Present Day* (London, 1971)
H. W. Hemphill jr and J. Weissman: *Twentieth-century American Folk Art and Artists* (New York, 1974)
V. Maleković: *Croatian Naive Art* (Zagreb, 1974)
The Flowering of American Folk Art, 1776–1876 (exh. cat. by J. Lipman and A. Winchester, New York, Whitney, 1974); review by H. Rosenberg in *New Yorker* (25 March 1974), pp. 128–32
J. Kind: 'The Naive Imagination', *Naive Art in Illinois, 1830–1976* (exh. cat., Chicago, IL A. Council, 1976)
B. Lassus: *Jardins imaginaires* (Paris, 1977)
E. Lister and S. Williams: *Twentieth-century British Naive and Primitive Artists* (London, 1977)
S. Rodman: *Genius in the Backlands: Popular Artists of Brazil* (Old Greenwich, 1977)
S. Rosen: *In Celebration of ourselves* (San Francisco, 1979)
J. Ayres: *English Naive Painting, 1750–1900* (London, 1980)
D. Zdunić, ed.: *Primitive Painting: An Anthology of the World's Naive Painters* (New York, 1980)
J. Pierre: *Les Peintres naïfs* (Paris, 1983)
O. Bihalji-Merin and N.-B. Tomašević, eds: *World Encyclopedia of Naive Art: A Hundred Years of Naive Art* (London, 1984)

ROGER CARDINAL

Naiveu [Neveu], **Matthijs** (*b* Leiden, *bapt* 16 April 1647; *d* Amsterdam, 4 June 1726). Dutch painter. He was the son of a wine merchant from Rotterdam and began his training with Abraham Toorenvliet (*c.* 1620–92), a glass painter and drawing master in Leiden. From 1667 to 1669 Naiveu was apprenticed to the Leiden 'Fine' painter Gerrit Dou, who received 100 guilders a year (an exceptionally high sum) for instructing Naiveu. In 1671 Naiveu entered the Leiden Guild of St Luke, of which he became the head in 1677 and again in 1678, the year in which he moved to Amsterdam, where he was later appointed hop inspector. This work did not prevent him producing a considerable number of paintings; the earliest known work by Naiveu is dated 1668, the latest 1721. There are dated paintings for almost every year in between; his most productive periods were 1675–9 and 1705–12.

Naiveu's subject-matter and the fine and detailed manner of painting in his early work reveal the influence of Dou and, to a lesser degree, that of Dou's older pupils Frans van Mieris (i) and Pieter van Slingeland. Typical early subjects include a girl spinning, market vendors and women customers, children blowing bubbles and groups of elegant people in luxurious interiors (none of which is in public collections). In the 1670s, however, Naiveu—unlike most of Dou's other pupils—began to distance himself increasingly from the example of his master. He continued to work in a fairly detailed manner, but his technique became noticeably less refined and polished, while his palette became brighter. Later on he occasionally returned to themes that were typical of Leiden 'Fine' painters: scenes of children, women or couples standing at a window (e.g. *Children Blowing Bubbles at a Window*, Boston, MA, Mus. F.A.). However, his windows were heavily decorated with pilasters, consoles, festoons and other carved work, giving these scenes an extravagance that is altogether uncharacteristic of the simple arched niches of Dou's pictures.

From the end of the 1670s Naiveu began to depict scenes rare in Dutch painting at the time, such as delivery rooms (e.g. *Visitors after the Birth*, 1675; New York, Met.), street parties with adults and children (e.g. *Street Festivities* and the *Morning after the Party*, both 1710; priv. col., see 1988 exh. cat., nos 60–61) and, above all, outdoor scenes of theatrical performances with harlequins and other comic figures from the *commedia dell'arte*, as in *Theatrical Performance outside the Town* (Amsterdam, Rijksmus., on loan to Amsterdam, Toneel Mus.) and *Theatrical Performance in a Dutch Town* (Geneva, Mus. A. & Hist.). Most of these theatrical scenes are set on an outdoor stage in a Dutch town or village; occasionally, however, the background is Italian—whether Naiveu actually visited Italy is unknown. These later paintings are strikingly original. From time to time there is a similarity to the work of Jan Steen; possibly Naiveu was also influenced by the *bamboccianti*, but it is very difficult to name any specific source of inspiration. Naiveu had no pupils of importance, but his street scenes and scenes with figures from the *commedia dell'arte* had a marked influence on Cornelis Troost. Naiveu's work also includes the occasional biblical, mythological and allegorical scene, a number of portraits and a few still-lifes; there are no known drawings by him.

BIBLIOGRAPHY

A. Houbraken: *De groote schouburgh*, iii (Amsterdam, 1721), pp. 228–9
Leidse fijnschilders: Van Gerrit Dou tot Frans van Mieris de Jonge, 1630–1760 (exh. cat. by E. J. Sluijter, M. Enklaar and P. Nieuwenhuizen, Leiden, Stedel. Mus. Lakenhal, 1988), pp. 12–13, 42, 72–3, 186–95

ERIC J. SLUIJTER

Naiwincx [Naiwinx; Nauwjncx; Naywinck; Nouwjnx], **Herman** [Harman] (*b* Schoonhoven, 27 Oct 1623; *d* ?Hamburg, after 1651). Dutch draughtsman, etcher, painter and carpet dealer of Flemish origin. His success as an etcher is based on two series of landscape prints after his own designs, which were published in Amsterdam (Hollstein, nos 1–16), and on two other etchings (Hollstein, nos 17 and 18). These all represent hilly wooded landscapes, some with a panoramic viewpoint, and show the artist's familiarity with both the Italianate tradition of landscape painting, practised by such artists as Jan Asselijn and Adam Pynacker, and the more Dutch works of Jacob van Ruisdael and Jacob Salomonsz. van Ruysdael (*c.* 1630–81). Of the 16 landscape drawings now attributed to Naiwincx, most are executed in chalk and wash (e.g. *River Landscape*, Paris, Fond. Custodia, Inst. Néer.); two are in pen and ink. Apart from a few drawings that evidently served as studies for etchings or paintings by the artist, his highly finished drawings must have been intended as works of art in their own right. His earliest work is thought to be a group of Dutch landscape scenes with farmhouses. Naiwincx's paintings clearly demonstrate his eclecticism; he made ingenious use of motifs borrowed from other artists and variations on them. The clumsiness of his figures is usually not noticed because they are so tiny, except when he tried to enlarge them, as in his *Baptism of the Eunuch* (Paris, Louvre), where the figure group is borrowed from Rembrandt's etching of the same subject (Hollstein, no. 98). In other paintings by Naiwincx, the figures were added by Willem Schellinks or Gerbrand van den Eeckhout. After 1651 there is no trace of Naiwincx, and his supposed residency in Hamburg could well be based on his business trips there as a merchant.

BIBLIOGRAPHY
Hollstein: *Dut. & Flem.*; Thieme–Becker
A. Blankert and A. Nystad: 'Herman Nauwincx als schilder en tekenaar', *Tableau*, i/5 (1979), pp. 48–58 [with cat. of ptgs & drgs]
A. Kuyper: 'Twee tekeningen door Herman Nauwincx', *Leids Ksthist. Jb.* (1984), pp. 237–42
                                         CHRISTIAAN SCHUCKMAN

Najaf ʿAli. *See* ISFAHANI, (1).

Nájera, Duquesa de. *See under* SANTAMARCA.

Nájera, Andrés de. *See* ANDRÉS DE NÁJERA.

Nājī, Muḥammad. *See* NAGHI, MOHAMMED.

Naj Tunich. Pre-Columbian MAYA cave shrine in the Lowland Maya area, *c.* 30 km east of Poptún in Petén, Guatemala. Naj Tunich (Maya: 'stone house') lies at an elevation of 650 m along part of a spectacular upland karst zone (limestone terrain characterized by water-formed caverns) containing some of the longest caves in Central America. It was rediscovered in 1980, and archaeological work began in 1981. The 3 km of broad passages yielded a wealth of ancient remains including rock-cut architecture and artefacts of pottery, jade, shell, obsidian and other materials. The major find, however, was a remarkable collection of Late Classic period (*c.* AD 600–*c.* 900) cave paintings, which distinguished Naj Tunich as one of the most important cave-painting sites of the New World. Unfortunately, many of these have since been damaged or erased by vandals. The ritual use of Naj Tunich was greatest between *c.* 50 BC and *c.* AD 250, at the end of the Late Pre-Classic period (sometimes called the Proto-Classic). It centred around two locations: a spring deep within the cave and an elevated terrace overlooking the entrance hall. The terrace supported six manmade structures, three of which were built of limestone slabs and may have functioned as tombs. The concentration of such structures, including retaining walls, is among the highest found at any Maya cave site.

It was during a brief florescence in the Late Classic period that the body of paintings and petroglyphs, totalling 90–100, was made. The images are located deep within the tunnel system, where, paradoxically, Late Classic period artefacts are scarce and seldom occur in association with the paintings. The paintings vary greatly in complexity and size, the largest measuring over 1 m in height and the smallest a mere 40 mm. Leaving aside such variants, the consistent style of the paintings indicates that they belong to a single epoch, a conclusion supported by hieroglyphic dates corresponding to the period AD 692–771. This stylistic consistency extends to the use of an organic black pigment to define images crisply against the cream-coloured limestone wall, in a monochrome, linear style reminiscent of Maya vase painting, which suggests that the artists may have been painters of ceramics.

The paintings of Naj Tunich fall into two major categories: hieroglyphic texts and human images. The 47 texts, containing *c.* 450 hieroglyphs, are exceptional as a body of sacred writings appearing within a cave. The significance of the context is underlined by the importance of caves in the Maya world view. The texts contain 21

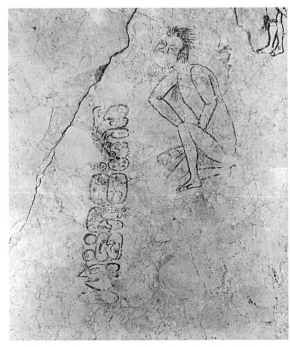

Naj Tunich, Maya cave painting depicting ithyphallic figure, 300×180 mm, *c.* AD 750; the three-quarter profile shown is rare in Maya art

hieroglyphic dates of the type known as a Calendar Round. These cyclical dates can be anchored to two Maya Long Count period-endings corresponding to AD 692 and 741 (*see* MESOAMERICA, PRE-COLUMBIAN, §II). The pictorial images show 44 simply clad human figures, who may well be participants in ritual. Compared with the baroque complexity of Classic Maya art, the Naj Tunich scenes are dramatic in their simplicity. Their blunt naturalism is illustrated in several paintings that show nude or semi-nude figures engaged in acts of sexual stimulation or genital mutilation, probably for ritual bloodletting purposes (see fig.). These images, exceptional for their graphic anatomical depictions, provide further evidence that the cave was acknowledged as a private, supernatural sanctuary. A remote labyrinthine passage revealed a painted hieroglyphic inscription above a stone altar, testifying to the ritual function of the paintings.

Several paintings with clear iconographic contexts correspond closely to Maya cave lore. For example, four ballplayer scenes appear at Naj Tunich, and it is well known that ballcourts were identified with the underworld and caves. Two dwarfs are also portrayed at the site: in Maya thought the dwarf was often believed to inhabit caves. The paintings of Naj Tunich therefore provide a unique window into ancient Maya ritual life, in which caves played an extremely important role.

BIBLIOGRAPHY
G. Stuart: 'Maya Art Treasures Discovered in Cave', *N. Geog.*, clx/4 (1981), pp. 220–35
A. Stone: 'Recent Discoveries from Naj Tunich', *Mexicon*, iv/5–6 (1982), pp. 93–9
——: 'Epigraphic Patterns in the Inscriptions of Naj Tunich', *Recent Contributions to Maya Hieroglyphic Decipherment*, ed. S. Houston (New Haven, 1983), pp. 83–103
——: 'The Moon Goddess at Naj Tunich', *Mexicon*, vii/2 (1985), pp. 23–9
J. Brady and A. Stone: 'Naj Tunich: Entrance to the Maya Underworld', *Archaeology*, xxix/6 (1986), pp. 18–25
J. Brady: *An Investigation of Maya Ritual Cave Use with Special Reference to Naj Tunich, Petén, Guatemala* (diss., UCLA, 1989)
ANDREA STONE

Nakahara, Teijirō (*b* Hokkaido, 4 Oct 1888; *d* Tokyo, 28 March 1921). Japanese sculptor. His early years were spent in Asahikawa, Hokkaido. In 1905 he left school in Sapporo and went to Tokyo intending to become a painter. In 1906 he joined the Hakubakai (White Horse Society), where he made friends with Tsune Nakamura. In 1907 he moved to the Pacific Academy of Western Art. The following year he met Morie Ogiwara who had returned to Japan after studying under Rodin in France. With Nakamura he frequently visited Ogiwara's studio, and he was greatly influenced by him. After Ogiwara's death, in 1910 he moved from painting to sculpture, receiving instruction from Taketarō Shinkai (1868–1927) at the sculpture and carving department of the Pacific Academy of Western Art. In the same year his sculpture *Head of an Old Man* (bronze, h. 570 mm, 1910; Asahikawa, Educ. Cttee) was accepted for the fourth Bunten (Ministry of Education Art exhibition). In 1912 he saw three sculptures by Rodin at the *Shirakaba* (White Birch) art exhibition, which made a lasting impression on him. In 1916 he entered the sculpture department of the Japan Art Institute. In the same year he exhibited a statue of *Ishii Tsuruzō*

(bronze, h. 395 mm, 1916; Asahikawa, Educ. Cttee) at the third In-ten (exhibition of the Japan Art Institute), receiving the *Chōgyū* prize. In 1918 he became a member of the Japan Art Institute. In 1919 he produced one of his most important works, *Youth from the Kavkaz* (bronze, h. 425 mm, 1919; Tokyo, N. Mus. Mod. A.), using a Russian model called Ninska, who was living in exile in Japan.

WRITINGS
Chōkoku no seimei [Living sculpture] (Tokyo, 1969)

BIBLIOGRAPHY
Seitan hyakunen kinen: Nakahara Teijirō to sono yūjintachi [100th birthday memorial exhibition: Teijirō Nakahara and his friends] (exh. cat., essays by H. Takumi and Y. Asakawa; Asahikawa, Hokkaido Mus. A., 1988)
YASUYOSHI SAITO

Nakamura, Tsune (*b* Mito, 3 July 1887; *d* Tokyo, 24 Dec 1924). Japanese painter. He abandoned his plan to be a professional soldier after contracting pulmonary tuberculosis at the age of 17 and instead studied oil painting and drawing at the Western painting study centres of the Hakubakai (White Horse Society) and the Taiheiyō Gakai (Pacific Painting Society) groups in Tokyo. In 1908 he met the sculptor Morie Ogiwara, who had been impressed by the sculpture of Auguste Rodin during his stay in Paris. Ogiwara greatly influenced Nakamura by his assertion of art as an expression of inner life. He also came to admire Rembrandt and the work of Renoir and the Impressionists, which he knew through reproductions. Nakamura's career was brief but eclectic, progressing from early self-portaits in the manner of Rembrandt, such as *Self-portrait Wearing Hat* (1909; Tokyo, Bridgestone A. Mus.), to paintings influenced by Renoir and Vincent van Gogh, and also Paul Cézanne, whose style is reflected in the brushwork of *Ōshima Landscape* (1914–15; Tokyo, priv. col., see Asano and others, pl. 12). In spite of these many sources and his progressive illness, Nakamura's work retained a distinctive clarity, individuality of vision and sense of well-being. He produced landscapes and still-lifes, but his finest works were portraits such as *Girl* (1914; Tokyo, priv. col.), for which his girlfriend served as a model, and those of the elderly physicist *Dr Tanakadate* (1916; Tokyo, N. Mus. Mod. A.) and the blind Russian poet *Vasily Yaroshenko* (1920; Tokyo, N. Mus. Mod. A.). Both of these show an awareness of the work of Renoir and reveal his profound compassion for humanity.

WRITINGS
Geijutsu no mugenkan [The infinite feeling of art] (Tokyo, 1926, rev. 1977)

BIBLIOGRAPHY
H. Suzuki: *Nakamura Tsune* (Tokyo, 1967)
T. Asano and others: *Nakamura Tsune gashū* [Collected paintings of Tsune Nakamura] (Tokyo, 1984)
TORU ASANO

Nakanishi, Natsuyuki. *See under* HI-RED CENTER.

Nakayama, Iwata (*b* Yanagawa, 3 Aug 1895; *d* Ashiya, 20 Jan 1949). Japanese photographer. He was the first student to graduate from the photography course of the Tokyo School of Fine Art (now Tokyo University of Fine Arts and Music), after which he was sent by the Ministry of Agriculture and Trade to train in the USA. In 1921 he opened the Laquan Studio on Fifth Avenue, New York, and was active as a portrait photographer, taking such pictures as *Dancer, New York* (1922; see 1979 exh. cat., no. 46). In 1926, at the suggestion of Nyota Inyoka, a dancer he had known in New York, he went to Paris and took fashion and theatre photographs for the magazine *Femina*. At that time he photographed the stage sets and costumes of Enrico Prampolini. While in New York and Paris, Nakayama absorbed much from contemporary avant-garde art and went on to establish his own style.

In 1927 Nakayama returned to Japan and established a studio in Ashiya, Hyōgo prefecture, in 1929. He entered the work *Fukusuke Tabi Socks* (see *A Century of Japanese Photography*, p. 312) in the First International Advertising Photography Exhibition (1930) sponsored by the Asahi Newspaper Company and received first prize. This geometrical pattern, formed from the outlines of *tabi* socks and emphasizing the feeling of modern design, had a profound impact on contemporary photographers. In the same year he formed the Ashiya Camera Club with Kanbei Hanaya, Kichinosuke Benitani, Jūzō Matsubara and others, and they began to hold yearly photographic exhibitions. In 1932, with Yasuzō Nojima and Ihei Kimura, he founded the photographic magazine *Kōga*, in which he published a number of photomontages. During this period, he also produced some masterpieces of portrait photography, such as *Woman from Shanghai* (1936; see fig.).

In 1940 Nakayama became a member of the photography division of the National Painting Association and showed his work mainly at their exhibitions. From this time his works developed a spiritual element, with shapes such as eggs or spheres, flowers such as mimosa and roses and symbolic objects such as shells, butterflies and seahorses freely arranged on the picture area (for example *Butterflies*, 1941; see 1979 exh. cat., no. 60). One of his greatest works, *Festival of the Demons* (1948; see 1979 exh. cat., p. 72), is a combination of shells and nudes with a hint of eroticism.

Nakayama's distinctive career as a photographer was an accumulation of attempts to transmit to Japan the modernist sensibility that he had absorbed in Europe and the USA. In the troubled years leading up to World War II it was no doubt difficult to make a true assessment of his work. His distinctive photomontages, were, however reevaluated in the 1980s.

PHOTOGRAPHIC PUBLICATIONS

Nakayama Iwata shashinshū: Hikari no dandizumu [Collected photographs of Iwata Nakayama: the dandyism of light] (Tokyo, 1987)

BIBLIOGRAPHY

Nihon Shashin Shi, 1840–1945 (Tokyo, 1971; Eng. trans. as *A Century of Japanese Photography*, intro. J. W. Dower, London, 1981)

Japanese Photography Today and its Origin (exh. cat. by A. Colombo and I. Donisello; Bologna, Gal. A. Mod.; Milan, ex-Pal. Reale; Brussels, Pal. B.-A.; London, ICA; 1979)

K. Kuwubara, ed.: *The Complete History of Japanese Photography*, iii: *The Modern Photography Movement in Japan* (Tokyo, 1986)

Iwata Nakayama (exh. cat., Hyōgo, Prefect. MOMA, 1987)

KOHTARO IIZAWA

Nakhchyvan [Nakhchivan; Nakhčiwān; Nakhichevan]. Town and region in Azerbaijan. Set in a mountainous area known for good hunting and natural beauty, it is located in Transcaucasia north-west of the great southern bend of the Araxes River, which has formed the border with Iran since 1834. Archaeological excavations reveal that the town was founded in the 6th century BC. It reached its apogee in the 12th century AD, when it became an important political and trading centre between Transcaucasia, Iran and Anatolia and the capital of the Eldigüzid (Ildegizid) rulers of Azerbaijan (*reg* 1137–1225).

The medieval town developed within fortified walls (10th–14th century). The anonymous 13th-century author of *Ajā'ib al-dunyā* ('Wonders of the world') mentioned the construction near the town of a stone fortress with a madrasa and mosque and a source of water. In the town itself were the palace and government building. A local school of architecture, characterized by the use of engaged columns and glazed brick, developed for commemorative and religious buildings in the 12th century under 'Ajami ibn Abu Bakr, who designed the octagonal mausoleum of Yusuf ibn Kusayr (1162–3). The sides have reveals elaborately decorated with strapwork, and a frieze with a kufic inscription below the pyramidal roof and the three-line inscription over the door are done in terracotta. 'Ajami ibn Abu Bakr also designed the mausoleum (1186) for Mu'mina Khatun, wife of one of the Eldigüzids. The architect gave the decagonal tower (h. 25 m) monumental form by setting it on a socle faced with red diorite. He also used more elaborate decoration: the sides have pointed reveals with *muqarnas* hoods and several types of geometric patterns; the wide frieze below the *muqarnas* cornice is decorated with a kufic inscription composed of

Iwata Nakayama: *Woman from Shanghai*, gelatin silver print, 1936

turquoise-glazed tiles. On the interior, a cylindrical chamber surmounts the crypt covered by a system of pointed arches. As part of the mausoleum for Mu'mina Khatun, 'Ajami ibn Abu Bakr also designed a mosque, now in ruins, which had a tall portal with a pointed arch flanked by tapering minarets.

Nakhchyvan was devastated by the Mongols in the 13th century. According to the 17th-century traveller Evliya Čelebi, it had 10,200 houses, 40 mosques, 20 caravanserais, 7 baths, some 1000 shops and 33 minarets, but the town plan (1827) drawn up by Russian military engineers shows only the remains of these buildings in the centre of town, where there was a square with the mausoleum of Mu'mina Khatun, a palace and commercial structures (destr.). The Imamzada complex with three mausolea was begun in the 18th century. The first mausoleum comprises a cubic socle, an octagon shaft, a round drum and a helmet-shaped cupola. The drum is decorated with dark violet glazed brick in *bannā'ī* technique. Two more mausolea were added in the 19th century. One, built of brick, is square with a cylindrical vault. The other, built of brick and stone, is a domed octagon with pointed reveals on the interior. A 19th-century mosque, now ruined, had a complex plan and façades articulated with pointed niches. The typical house in Nakhchyvan was a two-storey square with passages leading from a central vestibule to corner rooms. The staircase leading to the first floor opened into a broad hall covered with a flat roof. The houses were set in courtyards, with the main façade looking on to the garden and an iwan-type gateway. In 1968 the architects U. Ibrahimov and N. Mamedbeyli drew up a town plan that determined all subsequent construction. The Musical Dramatic Theatre, designed (1964) by I. Ismailov and G. Medjidov, has a portico with four paired columns topped with *muqarnas* capitals.

BIBLIOGRAPHY

Enc. Islam/2: 'Naḵḥčiwān'

V. M. Sysoyev: *Nakhchyvan' na Arakse i drevnosti Nakhchyvanskoy avtonomnoy sotsialisticheskoy respubliki* [Nakhchyvan on the Araxes and the antiquities of the Nakhchyvan' autonomous socialist republic] (Baku, 1928)

A. V. Salamzade: *Adzhemi syn Abubekra Nakhchyvani* ['Ajami son of Abu Bakr Nakhchyvani] (Baku, 1976)

A. V. Salamzade and K. M. Mamedzade: *Pamyatniki nakhchyvanskoy shkoly azerbaydzhanskogo zodchestva* [Monuments of the Nakhchyvan school of Azerbaijani architecture] (Baku, 1985)

E. R. SALMANOV

Nakht, tomb of. Painted ancient Egyptian tomb chapel (TT 52) in the Theban necropolis (now Luxor). The walls of the rock-cut chapel of the scribe Nakht (*fl c.* 1400 BC) are decorated with wall paintings on mud plaster. The scenes in the transverse hall, though unfinished, are particularly fine, with lively depictions of daily life and well-preserved colouring. On the left-hand wall Nakht superintends agricultural operations; the grain is shown being measured and winnowed, and the corn reaped and pressed into large panniers. Of particular interest is the figure of a man shown leaping into the air to force the corn tightly into the basket. In the scene below men are shown clearing trees, breaking up the earth and ploughing with teams of oxen before sowing the seed. On the facing wall are the remains of a banqueting scene, including a blind harper and a well-balanced group of three female musicians; in defiance of convention the painter has represented the torso of the central girl partly in frontal view. Another attractive detail is the depiction of a pet cat eating a fish beneath its mistress's chair. On the rear right-hand wall is a fine scene of Nakht and his family fishing and fowling in the papyrus marshes, while below are represented the trapping, plucking and cleaning of birds and the gathering and treading of grapes to make wine. Further scenes of offerings being presented to Nakht and his wife complete the decoration. The unpainted inner room gave access to the subterranean burial chamber, from which a few fragments of the original funerary equipment were recovered.

BIBLIOGRAPHY

N. de G. Davies: *The Tomb of Nakht at Thebes* (New York, 1917)

J. H. TAYLOR

Nakian, Reuben (*b* College Point, NY, 10 Aug 1897; *d* Stamford, CT, 4 Dec 1986). American sculptor. He was the son of Armenian parents who emigrated to the USA from Turkey. In 1916 he was accepted as an apprentice in the studio of Paul Manship in New York. There he worked with Manship's assistant, Gaston Lachaise, with whom he later shared a studio. The subjects of his early work were free-flowing, stylized animals, for example *Seal* (1930; New York, Whitney). In the 1930s he produced a series of life-size portrait busts of artists, collectors and members of President Roosevelt's first cabinet. In 1934 he exhibited a plaster sculpture, 2.44 m high, of the baseball hero *Babe Ruth*. The piece was greeted by much fanfare but never cast in bronze and was subsequently destroyed. Long unrecognized and on the brink of poverty, he nonetheless gradually developed a unique style under the influence of his friends Gorky and Stuart Davis. His most significant work was done after 1945. Using methods which combined 'Renaissance studio practice and the immediacy of Oriental calligraphers', he created 'a land of his own', said the poet-critic Frank O'Hara (*Nakian*, 1966). Drawing was always central to Nakian's production. Inspired by ancient Mediterranean art, he preferred to execute his imagery rapidly in the wet media of plaster and clay. Beginning in the late 1940s, he articulated his surfaces with action and gesture, linking his work with de Kooning and Abstract Expressionism. He worked spontaneously and considered each piece complete at the moment of inspiration. He was his own harshest critic and destroyed much of his work. In most of the surviving drawings and sculptures, uninhibited, voluptuous women and animals cohabit in an atmosphere of lyric sensuality; Leda and the Swan (e.g. *Leda and the Swan*, h. 318 mm, 1963; New York, Egan Gal.), nymph and satyr, Europa and the Bull are repeated mythical themes. There are an outgoing eroticism and at times a pastoral innocence or comic abandon in the brush drawing or freely cut ceramic line.

BIBLIOGRAPHY

T. B. Hess: 'November Contrasts: Reuben Nakian', *ARTnews*, lxiii/7 (Nov 1964), pp. 30, 65

Nakian (exh. cat., intro. F. O'Hara; New York, MOMA, 1966)

G. Glueck: 'Art People: Reuben Nakian', *NY Times* (11 Nov 1977)

BURT CHERNOW

Nakkaş Hasan. *See* HASAN PASHA, NAKKAŞ.

Nakkaş Osman. *See* OSMAN.

Nakp'a. *See* YI (ii), (1).

Nakşi, Ahmed. *See* AHMED NAKŞİ.

Naksŏ. *See* YUN, (2).

Nalanda [Nālandā]. Buddhist monastery in Bihar, India. Literary accounts trace the history of Nalanda back to the time of the Buddha, but no remains have been found predating the Gupta period (*c.* 5th century AD). By that time Nalanda had become the most important Buddhist monastery in Asia, attracting pilgrims from as far as China and Java. Nalanda continued in active use until the end of the 12th century, when it was sacked by Bhaktiyar Khalji. Although this event is regarded as ending Nalanda's history, the monastery was not altogether abandoned.

The monastery, constructed throughout of brick, has an essentially rectangular layout set on a north–south axis. Along the western side are the structures used for worship, consisting of the great stupa at the north end and three large temples located further south. Two monastic structures, probably the original ones on the site, are on the perimeter of the northern side; eight more monasteries are arranged along the eastern side to face the temples. The monastic structures have the usual plan, with small cells for monks arrayed around a courtyard for communal activities. Among the ritual structures, the great stupa was the most important and still dominates the site today. Probably begun when Nalanda was first established, the stupa was modified six times subsequently. In its fifth modification (*c.* early 7th century), it was enlarged substantially, and towers were added at its four corners. Stucco images were placed on the walls and would have been passed by devotees as they circumambulated the stupa prior to ascending the stairs to a shrine on the summit. Each of the three temples to the south of the great stupa enshrined enormous clay images (several times life-size), but only the lowest portions remain. Two other temples are located to the east, outside the main rectangle of the monastery. One, the temple of Site 2, dates to the 7th century and is best known for its stone plinth adorned with more than 200 reliefs. The other, datable to about the same time and known as the temple of the Serai mound, has paintings on the huge pedestal of the damaged clay image. These are the only surviving murals in eastern India. A number of illustrated manuscripts produced at Nalanda also survive, probably only a fraction of those originally created. Examples with colophons indicating that they were copied and illuminated at Nalanda include two 12th-century manuscripts of the *Aṣṭasāhasrikā Prajñāpāramitā* (London, V&A and Royal Asiat. Soc.).

More than 100 bronzes (Nalanda, Archaeol. Mus., and Patna Mus.), mostly datable to the 8th and 9th centuries, were found within the cells of the monasteries. Many are Buddha images, but *bodhisattvas* and other deities of the Buddhist pantheon are also represented. Stone sculptures, some life-size, were found mainly in the vicinity of the temples, often in small shrines. These include a tall Lokanatha and a superb Avalokiteshvara (both Nalanda, Archaeol. Mus.). Many Hindu images are enshrined in the Surya temple of Bargaon village, adjacent to the site. Other sculptures (both Buddhist and Hindu) are found in nearby villages and may have been brought from Nalanda. Among these is a life-size seated Buddha at Jagdishpur; its backslab is decorated with reliefs depicting the Buddha's life.

See also INDIAN SUBCONTINENT, §IV, 7(v).

BIBLIOGRAPHY
A. M. Broadley: *Ruins of the Nālandā Monasteries at Burgaon, Sub-division Bihar, Zillah Patna* (Calcutta, 1872)
A. Ghosh: *A Guide to Nālandā* (Delhi, 1929/*R* 1971)
A. J. Bernet-Kempers: *The Bronzes at Nālandā and Hindu-Javanese Art* (Leiden, 1933)
H. D. Sankalia: *The Nālandā University* (Madras, 1934, rev. Delhi, 1972)
H. Sastri: *Nālandā and its Epigraphic Material*, Mem. Archaeol. Surv. India, lxvi (Delhi, 1942/*R* 1986)
R. K. Mookerji: 'The University of Nālandā', *J. Bihar & Orissa Res. Soc.*, xxx (1944), pp. 126–59
D. Mitra: *Buddhist Monuments* (Calcutta, 1971)
F. M. Asher: *The Art of Eastern India, 300–800* (Minneapolis, 1980)
Buddhism: Art and Faith (exh. cat., ed. W. Zwalf; London, BM, 1985)
M. Stewart: *Nālandā Muhāvihāra: A Study of an Indian Pāla Period Buddhist Site and British Historical Archaeology* (Oxford, 1989)

FREDERICK M. ASHER

Naldini, Giovan Battista [Giovanbattista] (*b* Fiesole, *c.* 1537; *d* Florence, 18 Feb 1591). Italian painter and draughtsman. He was the artistic heir of Jacopo Pontormo, with whom he trained from 1549 to 1556. While maintaining an allegiance to the ideals of Andrea del Sarto and Pontormo, he also worked in the vocabularies of Bronzino and Vasari. From these sources he forged an individual style of drawing indebted to del Sarto in its loose handling of chalk and reminiscent of Pontormo in its schematic figures defined by firm contours and modelled with loose hatching or spots of wash. There are an analogous stylization and an expressive freedom in his treatment of serpentine figures, which are sculptural in form but painterly in detail, arranged in compact compositions with concentrated lights revealing passages of warm yellows, reds and greens. Particularly characteristic is the *Christ Carrying the Cross* (1566; Florence, S Maria Assunta), which is distinguished in its colouring and expressive figures from the chill linearity and metallic forms of Bronzino, Vasari and Alessandro Allori.

Naldini had numerous patrons in Florence and elsewhere in Tuscany, but he worked largely for the Medici as one of the artists under Vasari's supervision. He was in Rome after Pontormo's death in 1557 but returned to Florence *c.* 1562 to assist Vasari in the decorations for the Palazzo Vecchio, working in the *studiolo* (e.g. *Allegory of Dreams* and *Gathering Ambergris*, both 1570–71; see fig.) and in the Sala del Cinquecento. His work with Vasari included decorations for the obsequies of Michelangelo in 1564 and for the marriage of Francesco I de' Medici, Grand Duke of Tuscany, in 1565, as well as participation in the renovations of Santa Croce (*Pietà*, tomb of Michelangelo) and of S Maria Novella (*Pietà*, 1572; *Nativity*, 1573; *Presentation in the Temple*, 1577). He was in Rome again in the late 1570s, painting frescoes with Giovanni Balducci of scenes from the *Life of St John the Baptist* (1577–80) in the Altoviti Chapel, Santa Trinità dei Monti. Contemporary and later examples of his painting, reflecting the influence of the Council of Trent, are the *Pietà* (*c.* 1577; Bologna, Col. Molinari Pradelli, see 1980 exh.

Giovan Battista Naldini: *Gathering Ambergris*, oil on slate, 1270×890 mm, 1570–71 (Florence, Palazzo Vecchio, *studiolo*)

cat., ed. L. Berti, p. 150), the *Virgin and Child with Saints* (1580s; Granaiolo, nr Castelfiorentino, S Matteo) and the *Calling of St Matthew* (1588; Florence, S Marco, Cappella Salviati). In 1590, again with Balducci, he worked on the *Presentation of the Virgin* in Volterra Cathedral (*in situ*). Although responsive to late Mannerism and to the reforms of the Council of Trent, Naldini remained an anomaly, a highly individual Mannerist. He was a founder-member in 1563 of the Accademia del Disegno, in which he was active throughout his career, and he had pupils who influenced 17th-century Florentine art: Giovanni Balducci, Valerio Marucelli (1563–1620), Cosimo Gamberucci (*d* 1620), Francesco Curradi and Domenico Passignano.

BIBLIOGRAPHY

Colnaghi; Thieme–Becker

G. Vasari: *Vite* (1550, rev. 2/1568); ed. G. Milanesi (1878–85), vi, p. 288; vii, pp. 99, 308, 610; viii, pp. 619–20

R. Borghini: *Il riposo* (Florence, 1584); ed. M. Rosci (Milan, 1968), esp. pp. 613–19

F. Baldinucci: *Notizie* (1681–1728); ed. F. Ranalli (1845–7); rev. P. Barocchi (1974), esp. iii, pp. 511–19

P. Barocchi: 'Itinerario di Giovan Battista Naldini', *A. Ant. & Mod.*, 31–2 (1965), pp. 244–88

A. Forlani Tempesti: 'Alcuni disegni di Giovanbattista Naldini', *Festschrift Ulrich Middeldorf* (Berlin, 1968), pp. 294–300

G. Thiem: 'Neuentdeckte Zeichnungen Vasaris und Naldinis für die Sala Grande des Palazzo Vecchio in Florenz', *Z. Kstgesch.*, xxxi (1968), pp. 143–50

E. Pillsbury: 'The Sala Grande Drawings by Vasari and his Workshop: Some Documents and New Attributions', *Master Drgs*, xiv (1976), pp. 127–46

Palazzo Vecchio: Committenza e collezionismo medicei (exh. cat., ed. P. Barocchi; Florence, Pal. Vecchio, 1980), pp. 280–81 [entries by M. Collareta]

Il primato del disegno (exh. cat., ed. L. Berti; Florence, Pal. Strozzi, 1980), pp. 148–52 [entries by A. Petrioli Tofani]

Florentine Drawings of the Sixteenth Century (exh. cat. by N. Turner, London, BM, 1986), pp. 210–14

Sixteenth-century Tuscan Drawings from the Uffizi (exh. cat. by A. Petrioli Tofani and G. Smith, Detroit, MI, Inst. A., 1988–9), pp. 128–35

From Studio to Studiolo: Florentine Draftsmanship under the First Medici Grand Dukes (exh. cat. by L. J. Feinberg and K.-E. Barrman, Oberlin Coll., OH, Allen Mem. A. Mus., 1991), pp. 129–39

MILES L. CHAPPELL

Naldini, Lorenzo [Regnauldin, Laurent] (*fl* 1534; *d* between 7 Feb and 28 June 1567). Italian sculptor, stuccoist and painter, active in France. He was a pupil of Giovanni Francesco Rustici, whom he accompanied to France, and he is usually identified as the 'Laurent Regnauldin' recorded from 1534 as a Florentine painter at the château of Fontainebleau. His actual role seems to have been that of a sculptor and stucco modeller in the team of artists directed by Francesco Primaticcio that was responsible for the decoration of the Chambre du Roi (1535; destr.), the Chambre de la Reine (1535–6; destr. except for the chimney-piece) and the room above the Porte Dorée (destr.).

According to Vasari, Naldini was in Florence in 1540. Between 1540 and 1550 he was employed regularly by the French Crown as a restorer of antique sculpture and of the coral carvings in the Cabinet du Roi. From 1542 he collaborated with Simon Le Roy (*fl* from 1534) on carved decoration for the rood screen (destr. 1745) at St Germain-l'Auxerrois, Paris, for which Jean Goujon provided the principal sculptures. From 1564 to 1566 Naldini was part of the team working under Goujon on the tomb of *Henry II* in the Abbey Church of St Denis (marble and bronze; *in situ*; see SAINT-DENIS ABBEY, §II, 2(ii)). Shortly before his death he received a commission for a monument to *Charles de Bourbon, Prince of La Roche-sur-Yonne, and his Family* (marble; destr.) for Belle-Fontaine Abbey, near Angers. Beaulieu suggested that the four marble low reliefs of the *Evangelists* (after 1547) in the chapel of the château of Ecouen, Val-d'Oise, variations on those by Goujon for the rood screen at St Germain-l'Auxerrois (Paris, Louvre), should be attributed to Naldini and Le Roy.

BIBLIOGRAPHY

Lami

G. Vasari: *Vite* (1550, rev. 2/1568); ed. G. Milanesi (1878–85), v, p. 170; vi, pp. 609, 619, 621

L. Dimier: *Le Primatice: Peintre, sculpteur et architecte des rois de France* (Paris, 1900)

Le Roi, la sculpture et la mort: Gisants et tombeaux de la basilique de Saint-Denis (exh. cat by A. Erlande-Brandenburg and others, Saint-Denis, Maison Cult., 1976)

M. Beaulieu: *La Renaissance française*, Description raisonnée des sculptures du Musée du Louvre (Paris, 1978)

C. Grodecki: *Documents du Minutier central des notaires de Paris: Histoire de l'art au XVIe siècle, 1540–1600*, ii (Paris, 1986)

PHILIPPE ROUILLARD

Naldini, Paolo. *See* BALDINI, PIETRO PAOLO.

Naldo, Niccolò di. *See* NICCOLÒ DI NALDO.

Naliboki [Radziwiłł] **Glassworks.** Glassworks situated in Naliboki, Poland (now Belarus'). Established by Princess Anna Radziwiłł (1676–1746), it was in production from 1722 to 1862. The Naliboki Glassworks, managed by Constantin François Fremel (*c.* 1670–1750), produced ruby glass and high-quality crystal glass that had a tendency to crizzling and specialized in vessels and candlesticks. It practised relief engraving, and surviving documents record that it also produced wares decorated with applied relief ornament of pressed glass. The goblets were, to a certain degree, modelled on glass produced in Dresden and Berlin. Engraved ornament features figural scenes (examples in Tarnów, Dist. Mus.), portraits and coats of arms, usually of the Radziwiłł family and Augustus III (examples in Corning, NY, Mus. Glass; Växjö, Smålands Mus.; *see* POLAND, fig. 20). The Naliboki Glassworks occasionally used the services of Dresden engravers: Johann Heinrich Heintze (*fl c.* 1715–48) between 1725 and 1727; Johann Christof Dreher from 1728 to 1732; and Andreas Heinrich Heintze from 1743 to 1744. They trained local masters, including Mikołaj Dubicki (*fl c.* 1739–94) and Jan Dubicki (*fl c.* 1735–84), Mikołaj Stasiewicz (*fl c.* 1732–43) and Jan Tarnapowicz (*fl c.* 1728–78).

About 1740 the Naliboki Glassworks began production in association with the URZECZE GLASSWORKS, and in the mid-18th century emerged an original local, late Baroque style, known as the Urzecze-Naliboki style. Goblets produced in this style (1750–70) are characterized by bold shapes with undulating lines and decoration comprising coats of arms and military motifs (examples in Kraków, N. Mus.; Warsaw, N. Mus.).

BIBLIOGRAPHY

B. Smoleńska: 'Materiały do dziejów huty szklanej w Nalibokach z XVIII wieku' [Materials on the history of the glassworks at Naliboki in the 18th century], *Teki archiwalne*, i (1953), pp. 79–147

K. Buczkowski: *Dawne szkła artystyczne w Polsce* [Old artistic glass in Poland] (Kraków, 1958)

H. Chojnacka and P. Chrzanowska: 'La Verrerie polonaise baroque et ses contacts avec l'Europe centrale', *Annales du 5e congrès de l'Association internationale pour l'histoire du verre: Prague, 1970*, pp. 187–96

—: 'Nalibockie szkła wypukło szlifowane' [Relief engraved glass from Naliboki], *O rzemiośle artystycznym w Polsce* [Artistic craft in Poland] (Warsaw, 1976), pp. 185–208

M. M. Janickaja: *Belaruskae mastackae šklo (XVI–XVIII stst.)* [Belarussian artistic glass (XVI–XVIII cent.)] (Mińsk, 1977)

A. Kasprzak: 'Produkcja szkieł rubinowych w Nalibokach w I poł. XVIII w.' [Production of ruby glass in Naliboki in the first half of the 18th century], *Roc. Muz. N. Warszaw./Annu. Mus. N. Varsovie*, xxxviii (1995)

HALINA CHOJNACKA

Namakkal. Fortified mountain, site of two 8th-century AD cave temples, 50 km south of Salem in Tamil Nadu, south India. Commissioned by a feudatory of the PALLAVA dynasty, both cave temples are stylistically akin to the 7th-century monuments at MAMALLAPURAM. Their iconographic schemes, however, are reminiscent of Karnataka traditions (*see* INDIAN SUBCONTINENT, §V, 7(vi)(c)), in keeping with the site's intermediate location between the two regions. In particular, the west-facing cave (8×8 m), dedicated to Vishnu's man–lion incarnation Narasimha, recalls the late 6th-century Vaishnava cave temples at BADAMI in its configuration of narrative tableaux. These include depictions of Vishnu seated on the serpent Ananta Varaha (Vishnu's boar incarnation) rescuing the earth goddess and of Vamana, the dwarf, taking possession of the cosmos in three strides. The east-facing cave is oblong, rather than square, in plan in order to accommodate in its sanctum a colossal image of Narayana Vishnu sleeping on the serpent Ananta prior to the act of creation. The inclusion of many witnessing gods and sages (named in inscriptions) is consistent with other depictions of this type in Tamil Nadu, including those found in the roughly contemporary cave temples at Singavaram, Malaiyatippatti and Tirumayam.

BIBLIOGRAPHY

P. R. Srinivasan: 'Sculptures in the Two Rock-cut Vaisnava Cave Temples of Namakkal', *Artibus Asiae*, xxiv (1961), pp. 107–16

V. Dehejia: *Namakkal Caves* (Madras, 1977)

MICHAEL D. RABE

Namatjira, Albert (*b* nr Hermannsburg Mission Station [then South Australia; from 1911 in the Northern Territory], 28 July 1902; *d* Alice Springs, 8 Aug 1959). Aboriginal draughtsman and watercolourist. He was of the Aranda (Arunta) people. He was educated by Lutheran missionaries and worked as a camel driver and stockman in central Australia. Already a practised draughtsman, he began painting in 1934 when Lutheran Pastor Albrecht gave him watercolours, following a visit to the region by Rex Battarbee (1893–1973) and John Gardner (1906–87), painters from Victoria. Battarbee returned in 1936, employed Namatjira as guide for a painting expedition and taught him watercolour techniques. At a Lutheran conference in South Australia the following year Pastor Albrecht sold works by Namatjira, and Battarbee included others in his exhibition in Adelaide. Namatjira had his first solo exhibitions in Melbourne in 1938 and Adelaide in 1939.

Despite artistic success, Namatjira was not able to handle his own affairs until granted citizenship in 1957, because Aborigines were not, in general, legal citizens until 1967, only wards of state. In 1958 he was convicted of illegally supplying alcoholic drink to Aborigines—an outcome of fulfilling tribal obligations to share material resources with his ethnic group. Resulting psychological stress probably contributed to his death in 1959. He was the first Aboriginal artist to gain personal renown in the white community.

Because of superficial formal resemblance of Namatjira's watercolours to those of Battarbee, his work was formerly widely considered as completely derivative from Western art but is now commonly recognized to embody authentic elements of traditional Aboriginal culture (Sutton). Namatjira's example inspired a distinct Aranda school of painting, including members of his immediate family; his five sons and one son-in-law, eight grandchildren and other descendants also became artists.

BIBLIOGRAPHY

C. Mountford: *The Art of Albert Namatjira* (Melbourne, 1944)

R. Battarbee: *Modern Australian Aboriginal Art* (Sydney, 1951)

N. Amadio, ed.: *Albert Namatjira: The Life and Work of an Australian Painter* (Melbourne, 1986)

P. Sutton, ed.: *Dreamings: The Art of Aboriginal Australia* (Melbourne, 1988)

Aratjara: The Art of the First Australians (exh. cat., ed. B. Luthi; Düsseldorf, Kstsamml. Nordrhein–Westfalen; London, Hayward Gal.; Humlebaek, Louisiana Mus.; Melbourne, N.G. Victoria; 1993–4)

ROBERT SMITH

Namch'ang. *See* KIM HYŎN-SŎNG.

Namibia, Republic of [formerly South West Africa]. Country in south-west Africa bordered by Angola and Zambia to the north, Botswana to the east and South Africa to the south. Namibia also has a long Atlantic Ocean coastline. Namibia became independent from South Africa in 1990. Although rich in minerals, it is a vast and arid land (of *c.* 824,292 sq. km) with the inhospitable Namib Desert on the west and the Kalahari Desert to the east. The capital is Windhoek and the population is *c.* 1,500,000 (estimate, 1990). Namibia was a German protectorate from 1880 to 1915 and subsequently was placed under South African mandate during World War I. Its status was then disputed until it achieved independence. This entry covers the art produced in the country since colonial times. For art of the area in earlier periods *see* AFRICA, §VII, 8.

Although the colonizers introduced new expressive forms and artistic styles, lack of an understanding of African aesthetics and a misguided belief in the superiority of their own art led to the negation of indigenous traditional art forms and the alienation of the people from their aesthetic heritage. There were a number of artists among the colonial settlers, primarily from Germany and later from South Africa. The country's landscape and wildlife inspired an expressive tradition that continued in the late 20th century. Of the initial group, Adolph Jentsch (1880–1977) and Fritz Krampe (1913–66), painting landscapes and wildlife respectively, were the most acclaimed.

The Germans also introduced a turn-of-the-century European architectural style, a few well-preserved examples of which have survived, such as the Gathemann Building (1913), Windhoek, by Willy Sander and the Woermann House (1900–05), Swakopmund, by Hermann Muthesius. Moreover, aspects of this style feature prominently in some recent Post-modernist buildings in the capital, including Mutual Platz (1991), designed by Stauch and Partners. Of more recent artists, John Muafangejo (1943–87) was the most successful in breaking away from the landscape/wildlife tradition, offering a very personalized view of Namibian life in his internationally acclaimed linocuts, though some of these also treated traditional subjects (see fig.).

By the late 20th century it was still too early to evaluate the impact of independence on the art of Namibia, although a much-needed revival was anticipated, aided by the falling away of cultural boycotts, a new national awareness and the introduction of art and cultural programmes to schools. In the early 1990s financial support from government, donor agencies and private individuals ensured the reintroduction of traditional art and the establishment of new crafts as expressive art forms in their own right. The full effects of this activity should be the introduction of a new approach to Namibian aesthetics and the decentralization of art production. In addition to the Staatsmuseum and Arts Association Gallery in Windhoek, there is a smaller museum and the Swakopmund Arts Association in Swakopmund.

BIBLIOGRAPHY
O. Levinson: *Adolph Jentsch* (Cape Town, 1973)
N. Roos: *Art in South West Africa* (Pretoria, 1978)

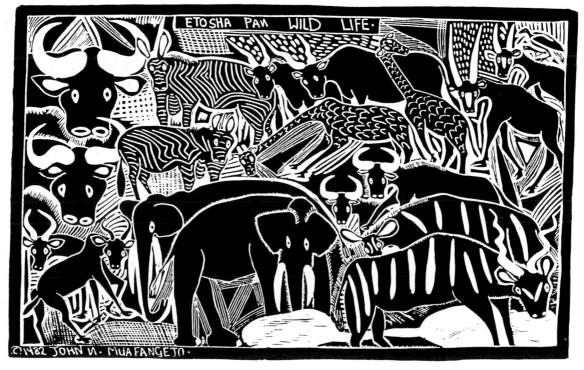

John Muafangejo: *Etosha Pan Wildlife*, linocut, 440×696 mm, 1982

Namibian Arts and Crafts Symposium (Windhoek, 1980)
L. Heinze and U. Oldorf: *Painters SWA/Namibia* (Roodepoort, 1983)
Culture in Namibia, an Overview (Windhoek, 1991)
O. Levinson: *I Was Lonelyness: The Complete Graphic Works of John Muafangejo* (Cape Town, 1992) [cat. rais.]
——: *The African Dream: Visions of Love and Sorrow: The Art of John Muafangejo* (London, 1992)

FRANÇOIS DE NECKER

Nam Ku-man [*cha* Unro; *ho* Yakchŏn, Mijae; posthumous title Munch'ung] (*b* Uinyŏng, South Kyŏngsang Province, 1629; *d* 1711). Korean calligrapher, literati painter and scholar–official. Active during the Chosŏn period (1392–1910), he passed the civil service examination in 1656 and served in many important posts, such as governor of Hamgyŏng Province, before becoming chief minister. In calligraphy he followed the famous mid-17th-century Korean calligrapher, Song Chun-gil (1606–71). In the 17th century Korean calligraphers developed styles independent of Chinese influence as a result of the Manchu invasion of Korea in 1636 and the ensuing struggle for independence by the Koreans. The *Ssangsu-jong Kijok-pi* (1708), a stele erected to commemorate the pacification of Yi Kwal's uprising (1624) in Kongju, South Ch'ungch'ŏng Province, shows Nam Ku-man's unique style of character composition: each character conveys a great sense of movement even though it is in regular script, which is usually regarded as stable. Each stroke has greater modulation and curve than are usual in regular script, especially in strokes that curve to the right. Nam's other calligraphic works include the *Chwasang Nam Chi* stele and the signboards for the Kaesim Temple, Yanghwa Pavilion and Yongsong Pavilion. He also left an eight-fold screen of landscape paintings.

BIBLIOGRAPHY
O Se-ch'ang, ed.: *Kŭnyŏk sŏhwa ching* [Dictionary of Korean painters and calligraphers] (Taegu, 1928/*R* Seoul, 1975), p. 149
Kim Ki-sŭng: *Han'guk sŏyesa* [History of Korean calligraphy] (Seoul, 1975), p. 640

YI SŎNG-MI

Nam Kye-u [*ho* Ilho] (*b* 1811; *d* 1888). Korean painter. He was a member of the aristocracy with official rank at court during the late Chosŏn period (1392–1910). His butterfly paintings were outstanding in literati painting for their incredible accuracy and detail and for the realism and correct habitat of the flowers and rocks painted in the background. Since he also enjoyed writing about these insects, he earned the nickname 'Butterfly Nam'. He painted most of his compositions on long, narrow, vertical screens. Examples of his work are the four panels comprising *Butterflies* (each 1279×288 mm, colour on paper; Seoul, N. Mus.; see Hwi-joon Ahn, p. 146).

BIBLIOGRAPHY
Ahn Hwi-joon [An Hwi-jun]: 'Traditional Korean Painting/Hanguk chŏnt'ong hoehwa-ŭi byŏnch'ŏn', *Korean Art Tradition/Hanguk-ŭi yesul chŏnt'ong*, ed. Young Ick Lew [Ryu Yŏng-ik] (Seoul, 1993), pp. 139–40, 146 [bilingual text]

HONG SŎN-P'YO

Nampeyo: group of vessels and pots (clockwise from left): pottery bowl, black and light brown design, diam. 237 mm; canteen-shaped pot, black and brown design, h. 190 mm; small bowl, black design, hole diam. 43 mm; pottery bowl, diam. 240 mm; small olla, black and light brown design, hole diam. 420 mm (Milwaukee, WI, Public Museum)

Nampeyo (*b* Tewa Village, First Mesa, Hopi Reservation, AZ, *c.* 1860; *d* Polacca, Hopi Reservation, 20 July 1942). Native American Hopi–Tewa potter. In the 1890s she began to incorporate forms and motifs adapted from Sikyatki, Awatovi and other prehistoric Southwest pottery traditions (*see* NATIVE NORTH AMERICAN ART, §V, 1(i)) in her work. By *c.* 1900 Nampeyo had elevated the new revival style to an independent art form, later designated Hano Polychrome. She worked in the traditional coil-and-scrape method with local clay. She formed vessels ranging from small seed jars and bowls to low-shouldered jars as large as 500 mm in diameter and ollas (large-mouthed water or grain jars) up to 460 mm high. On the surfaces she painted designs of stylized birds, feathers and graceful curvilinear motifs, inspired by ancient pottery, in finely ground mineral pigments and boiled vegetal matter, using a fibrous yucca-leaf, chewed at the end to form a brush (e.g. Samuel Barrett collection, Milwaukee, WI, Pub. Mus.; see fig.). She fired the vessels outdoors with dried sheep dung or, less frequently, with coal; they turned a warm honey colour with red and black designs, occasionally with white accents. Nampeyo also made a smaller number of vessels with clay that fired red and during her early years sometimes laid a white slip on the surface before painting the design. She did not sign her work. In 1905 and 1907 the Fred Harvey Company, hotel and dining-room managers for the Santa Fe Railroad, took Nampeyo to demonstrate pottery-making at the Grand Canyon Hopi House, which had a salesroom and exhibition and demonstration space for Indian arts and crafts; and in 1910 to Chicago as part of the Santa Fe Railroad exhibit of the United States Land and Irrigation Exhibition. Nampeyo and her Hopi husband Lesso (*b c.* 1862; *d* 1930) had three daughters, who became potters in their mother's tradition: Annie Healing (*c.* 1884–*c.* 1968); Nellie Douma (*c.* 1894–1979); and Fannie Polacca (*c.* 1902–87). After Nampeyo lost her sight in the 1920s, other members of her family painted her vessels, and generations of Nampeyo's descendants have continued her pottery style.

BIBLIOGRAPHY

B. Kramer: 'Nampeyo, Hopi House and the Chicago Land Show', *Amer. Ind. A.*, xiv/1 (1988), pp. 46–53

——: *She Left No Words: Nampeyo and her Pottery* (Albuquerque, 1995)

BARBARA KRAMER

Namri. *See* KIM TU-RYANG.

Namur [Flem. Namen]. Belgian city and capital of the province of the same name. It is situated at the confluence of the Meuse and Sombre rivers. Namur was important from Roman times, and it was recorded in the 7th century as a Merovingian fortress. From 908 until 1420 it was the seat of the counts of Namur, before passing to Burgundy. The city became part of independent Belgium in 1830. Namur is notable for its production of furniture, gold and silver.

1. FURNITURE. Medieval and 16th- and 17th-century furniture from Namur is very scarce. Production expanded under the influence of the Louis XIV style until *c.* 1780. There were few master furniture-makers, and the work was done by draughtsmen, architects and sculptors. Because masons and furniture-makers used the same patterns, there are parallels between carvings in stone and on furniture. Unlike in Liège and its surroundings, the decorative ornament of furniture made in Namur was exceptional or absent and was not carved through the full thickness of the wood. Specific Namur pieces can be distinguished by their elaborately worked wide copings and profile frames above and below.

See also BELGIUM, §VI.

BIBLIOGRAPHY

E. Nemery: *Le Meuble namurois au XIIe siècle* (Gembloux, 1970)

STÉPHANE VANDENBERGHE

2. GOLD AND SILVER. Philip the Good, Duke of Burgundy, in his capacity as Count of Namur, awarded the gold- and silversmiths of Namur their own charter in 1440, although the trade was already well established. In addition the city received a special hallmark, consisting of a lion rampant, crowned with the Burgundian thunderbolt (*Vuurslag*). The peak period of production was the 17th and 18th centuries; Namur silverwork from this period is exceptional not so much for its innovative qualities as for the assimilation, in constant response to prevailing trends, of the various stylistic influences. Silversmiths in Namur, however, could not compete with those in Liège and nearby German cities, where alloys of a lower silver content were permitted. Among the most important 17th- and 18th-century gold- and silversmiths working in Namur were Nicolas-François Rosart (*fl* 1683–?1724) and the families of Ancheval, Bachuys, Bodart, Bodson, Cloes and Wodon. The plate engraved with masters' names and marks was lost during World War I, which created difficulties in the identification of the various silversmiths, although a later detailed study of the archives greatly alleviated this problem.

BIBLIOGRAPHY

G. Poskin and P. Stokart: *Orfèvres namurois* (Namur, 1982)

Orfèvreries namuroises, 1500–1800 (exh. cat. by P. Stokart, Namur, 1994)

LEO DE REN

Namuth, Hans (*b* Essen, 17 March 1915; *d* East Hampton, NY, 13 Oct 1990). American photographer and film maker. He worked in France and Spain as a freelance photographer for *Life*, *Vu* and other magazines from 1935 to 1938, during which time he photographed the Spanish Civil War (1936–9). He settled in the USA in 1951 and studied under Alexey Brodovitch (1898–1971) at the New School for Social Research, New York. In the late 1940s he worked in Guatemala, where he later returned repeatedly, taking portraits of the inhabitants of the village of Todos Santos. In the 1950s he began taking photographic portraits of prominent American painters and sculptors. Much of Namuth's career focused on recording the working techniques of the Abstract Expressionist painters, particularly Jackson Pollock, who was the subject of his first film in 1951. His own work was characterized by its calm intimacy, reflecting the influence of August Sander.

PHOTOGRAPHIC PUBLICATIONS

Pollock Painting (New York, 1980)

Artists, 1950–81: A Personal View (New York, 1981)

BIBLIOGRAPHY
Contemp. Phots
V. Williams: Obituary, *The Independent* (29 Oct 1990), p. 20

ELIZABETH MITCHELL WALTER

Nan-ching. *See* NANJING.

Nancy. City in north-east France, capital of the Meurthe-et-Moselle *département* and former capital of the Duchy of Lorraine (12th century to 1766). It is situated in the valley of the Meurthe River, not far from its confluence with the Moselle, and is dominated to the west by the densely wooded hills of the Forest of Haye.

1. History and urban development. 2. Art life and organization. 3. Centre of tapestry production.

1. HISTORY AND URBAN DEVELOPMENT. The derivation of its name was deduced from the discovery of three Merovingian coins bearing the inscription NANCIACO. In 1895 several Alemannic graves from the end of the 6th century or the beginning of the 7th were discovered on the site of the 'Vieil-Aître' (built before 1158), which was a property of the Knights Hospitaller. However, it was not possible positively to identify these graves with the origins of the future town, of which the earliest record dates from 1061. Another document, dated 1073, refers to 'the exercise from Nancy of a role of command' and is the first indirect evidence of the presence there of a ducal power. This would confirm the tradition that Gerard of Alsace (*reg* 1048–70) was the founder of the ducal palace of Nancy. The palace formed the south-west corner of the developing town and was sited some 20 m above the flood-level of the Meurthe, separated from the river by a mere quarter of a league of marshland. The founding of the priory of Notre-Dame *c.* 1090 and the building of the church of St Evre before 1145 provide evidence of the growth of the community, which was seized and burnt in 1218 by the Holy Roman Emperor Frederick II as part of his struggle against Theobald I (*reg* 1213–20). In 1298 the original palace was abandoned and became a Dominican monastery. A new ducal residence was built on the same site as the present Palais Ducal (now the Musée Historique Lorrain; from 1501; rest. early 19th century).

In the 14th century the ramparts completely enclosed what would become the Old Town. The reigns of Raoul (*reg* 1329–46) and Charles II (*reg* 1390–1431) were particularly prosperous periods: in 1339 the collegiate church of St Georges was built adjoining the palace (it later became the burial place of the dukes of Lorraine); urban planning was undertaken; a new hospital was constructed to supplement the 12th-century Maison-Dieu and the hospital of St Julien (1336); and the marshland on the banks of the Meurthe was drained. At the time of Charles II's death, Nancy had 1200 inhabitants and covered an area of 16 ha within its walls. For over a century it had functioned as the capital of the Duchy of Lorraine. In 1477 Charles the Bold, 4th Duke of Burgundy, besieged Nancy, but his troops were defeated by those of René II (*reg* 1473–1508). A period of expansion followed: in 1485 a large church was built for the convent of the Cordeliers (Franciscans), and from 1501 the dilapidated Palais Ducal was rebuilt to a square plan that gave the Grande-Rue part of its present appearance.

In 1522 the Carrière (Race-course) was created on a large open space to the south of the palace. Buildings with identical façades were erected surrounding the area, which provided an ideal venue for cavalcades and tournaments. This urban project was linked to the partial rebuilding of the fortifications—made necessary by the improvements in artillery—that was being carried out by Italian engineers. From 1549 to 1567 new defences continued to evolve, the only remaining trace of which is the Vaudémont bastion that protected the south-east of the town. The bastion des Dames appears in an etching (1625) by Jacques Callot showing the *parterre à l'italienne*, which it contained to the rear of the palace. The area inside the city walls remained practically unchanged, with the suburbs absorbing the increase in population. As the suburbs could have proved a danger to Nancy in wartime, Charles III (*reg* 1545–1608) enlarged the town, encircling it with impressive fortifications incorporating the southern suburbs and transferring into the town the inhabitants of the village of Saint-Dizier to the north, which was then to be demolished. In about 1588 the engineer Jeronimo Citoni (*fl c.* 1580s) drew up plans for the New Town, which was arranged on a north–south axis that led towards the adjoining Old Town. With the exception of the main thoroughfare of the suburb of Saint-Nicholas, the streets follow a grid running between predominantly rectangular blocks of buildings. A formidable ring of moats and bastions built by the Italian Giovanni Battista Stabili (*d* 1611) provided a link to the Old Town, which retained its defences with the addition of a citadel to the north. This vast urban plan was completed in 1620. All the gates survive except one, and the 15th-century Porte de la Craffe, which was newly reinforced, remains as part of the new ramparts. As population growth was slow, Charles III brought in religious orders to inhabit the New Town; 16 monasteries were established between 1590 and 1634.

During the reign of Charles IV (*reg* 1625–75), plague, war and occupation by French troops impeded the development of Nancy. The ramparts were dismantled by order of Louis XIV and then rebuilt by Sébastian Leprestre de Vauban, and those of the New Town were demolished and replaced by a simple boundary wall. From the late 18th century the ramparts of the Old Town gradually disappeared.

The arrival of Duke Leopold (*reg* 1697–1729) in the territories that had entered his possession under the Treaty of Rijswijk (1697) resulted in a remarkable period of building: the alignment and height of buildings became subject to regulations, and many fine *hôtels* were constructed. A project by Jules Hardouin Mansart, followed by a more ambitious one by Germain Boffrand (both unrealized), was to have replaced the partly demolished Palais Ducal with a larger palace for Leopold modelled on the Palais du Louvre in Paris. The long façade was to have extended along the Carrière, where the Hôtel de Craon (1714) by Boffrand occupied the eastern side. The Primatiale (now the cathedral) was modified by Hardouin Mansart in 1706 and completed by Boffrand in 1742, and the church of St Sébastien was rebuilt from 1720 to 1731. The Esplanade, a tree-lined area between the two parts of the town, allowed for construction of two new roads. The suburbs spread to the south as far as Notre-Dame de

1. Nancy, aerial view from the west, showing the Place du Gouvernement (the Hémicycle; *c.* 1750–57) by Emmanuel Héré with the Palais du Gouvernement (Palais d'Intendance; 1751–3) by Richard Mique on the left; part of the Palais Ducal (now Musée Historique Lorrain; from 1501, restored early 19th century) in the left foreground; and the public garden, La Pépinière (1765), in the distance

Bonsecours (built by EMMANUEL HÉRÉ in 1738–41) and north towards Metz. In 1739 the church of the Premonstratensians was built, with a façade inspired by Il Gesù in Rome.

Between 1751 and 1755 Nancy's most successful piece of urban planning was realized: the skilful linking together of existing architectural elements to form a monumental group of three squares—the Place Royale, the Place de la Carrière and the Place du Gouvernement. This project was begun by STANISLAV I LESZCZYŃSKI, former king of Poland and titular Grand Duke of Lorraine (*reg* 1736–66), who succeeded to the latter title following the renunciation by Francis III (*reg* 1729–36) of his hereditary territories. Grand Duke Stanislas (as Stanislav became known) helped to establish Nancy's reputation as a centre of culture. A magnificent new quarter facing the Old Town was also developed to the north-east of the New Town. The Place Royale (now Place Stanislas) was dedicated to Louis XV of France, the effective ruler of Nancy, and a bronze statue of him (1755; destr. 1792) by Barthélemy Guibal was erected in the centre. Emmanuel Héré's Hôtel de Ville (1752–6) occupies the entire south-east side of the square (for illustration *see* HÉRÉ, EMMANUEL). Through an Arc de Triomphe set into the reduced ramparts the Place Stanislas leads to the Place de la Carrière, the buildings of which have completely renovated façades. The central strip was converted into an enclosed garden. The north

end of the Place de la Carrière opens on to the Place du Gouvernement (the Hémicycle) by Héré, with the semicircular colonnades of the Palais du Gouvernement (Palais d'Intendance; 1751–3) creating an elliptical space (see fig. 1). To the east of the complex, the Place d'Alliance (1753), also by Héré and with a Baroque-inspired fountain by Guibal, commemorates the reconciliation of the two houses of France and Austria, which had been rivals for so long. La Pépinière, a large public garden adjoining the Place du Gouvernement, was created in 1765 from a former tree-nursery and was completed in 1772 (see fig. 1). In the 1780s the enthusiasm for urban planning continued in the western part of Nancy with the creation of the Cours Léopold, an immense open space with tree-lined avenues opening out in the direction of Metz through the Porte Saint-Louis (1784; now Porte Desilles). In 1783 the Neo-classical chapel of the Visitation was built to designs by the Parisian architect Jacques-Denis Antoine.

During the 19th century the Paris–Strasbourg railway line was constructed further to the west, and in 1852 the railway station was opened. At the same time, the canal connecting the Marne with the Rhine was being excavated to the east. The annexation of Alsace–Lorraine to Germany in 1871 increased the population of the town, which in 1881 was 70,000. For more than 40 years Nancy continued to develop in an uncontrolled way before urban-planning regulations were brought into force. After World War II construction did not begin again until 1957, when a group of long blocks on the elevated site of the Haut-de-Lièvre were built. The south-west part of the New Town, totally rebuilt between 1964 and 1976, bristled with high-rise blocks and was also the site of a new shopping centre. The area around the railway station escaped radical development, and the Tour Frantel (the only modern building to be constructed there) did not meet with public approval. In the late 20th century the dilapidated buildings of the Old Town underwent cleaning and restoration, and the area around the canal was improved.

2. ART LIFE AND ORGANIZATION. The principal surviving example of art from the Romanesque period is the portal of the former church of the priory of Notre-Dame. The interior of the late medieval church of the Cordeliers has Gothic vaults combined with Renaissance pilasters. The interior of the church also contains the tomb of *René II* (artist unknown, 1512; *in situ*), an example of Renaissance influence on Gothic sculpture. The gate-lodge of the Palais Ducal and the gallery on to the garden (both *c*. 1512) also combine aspects of the Gothic and Renaissance styles. Important sculptors of the early 16th century include Mansuy Gauvain (*fl* 1506–43), who executed a *Madonna of Mercy* (1506; Notre-Dame de Bonse-cours), and Jan Crocq (*fl* 1486–1511), a sculptor of Flemish origin (various sculptures, Nancy, Mus. Hist. Lorrain). The most important late Renaissance sculptor is Florent Drouin (*c*. 1540–1612), among whose works are the statues (after 1587) for the tomb of *Cardinal de*

Vaudémont in the church of the Cordeliers. In the 16th century the painter and printmaker Gabriel Salmon (*fl* 1504–42) worked in Nancy, while 200 painters are documented as working in Nancy between 1590 and 1660, among them Jacques Bellange, Jean Leclerc and Claude Deruet, who were also printmakers. The painter Charles Mellin was apprenticed in Nancy, and Claude Lorrain stayed briefly in the city (1625–6), employed by Deruet to paint illusionistic architectural frames on the ceiling of the Carmelite church (destr. during French Revolution). The painter and printmaker Georges Lallemant worked in Nancy before his move to Paris in 1601, while the etcher Jacques Callot, a native of the city, also worked there.

During the early 17th century the octagonal sepulchral chapel of the dukes of Lorraine (1607) adjoining the church of the Cordeliers was constructed, as was the Hôtel de Lillebonne. The brothers David de Chaligny (*d* 1631) and Antoine de Chaligny (*d* 1651) designed the equestrian statue (begun 1621) of *Duke Charles III* (Nancy, Mus. Hist. Lorrain). In 1698 a tapestry factory was set up, the majority of its production going to Vienna (*see* §3 below). In the 18th century the early classical Primatiale (now the cathedral) was built by Hardouin Mansart and Boffrand (*see* §1 above). Baroque-influenced towers were completed for the façades of St Sébastien by Jean-Nicolas Jennesson (1686–1755) and Notre-Dame de Bonsecours by Héré. The latter church contains the tombs of *Stanislav I Leszczyński* (begun 1768) by Louis-Claude Vassé, and his wife *Catherina Opalinska* (1749) by Nicolas-Sébastien Adam (ii). Among important 18th-century painters and

2. Nancy, Place Stanislas, wrought-iron grilles (*c*. 1755) by Jean Lamour

engravers are Claude Jacquart (1686–1736), who frescoed the dome of the cathedral, Claude Charles (1661–1747), who executed paintings for the apse, and Jean-Charles François. In the Place Stanislas, Barthélemy Guibal and Paul-Louis Cyfflé (1724–1806) designed the gilt lead fountains of *Neptune* and *Amphitrite* (both *c.* 1750–55) in two of the corners, and Jean Lamour (1698–1771) created the wrought-iron grilles at the corners of the square (see fig. 2). In other parts of the town there are numerous statues and reliefs by Adrien Lépy, Barthélemy Mesny (*c.* 1650–1724) and Johann Joseph Söntgen (*d* 1788).

The best-known sculptor from Nancy was Clodion, who was born there in 1738 and lived there in 1793–8. Important painters of the later 18th century and the 19th and 20th centuries include Jean-Baptiste Isabey (whose career was formed mostly in Paris), the Impressionist Charles de Meixmoron (1839–1912), Emile Friant (1863–1932), Victor Guillaume (1880–1924) and Etienne Cornault (1891–1948).

Nancy, however, was most closely associated with the rebirth of the decorative arts in France at the end of the 19th century. Members of the Alliance Provinciale des Industries d'Art (later called the Ecole de Nancy) included the glassmaker Emile Gallé, the group's founder in 1901; Auguste Daum, also a glassmaker; the cabinetmakers Louis Majorelle and Eugène Vallin; Victor Prouvé, who produced decorative work and designs for bookbindings; the stained-glassmaker Jacques Gruber (1870–1936); and the architects Emile André, Désiré Bourgon (1855–1915) and Lucien Weissenburger (1860–1929).

BIBLIOGRAPHY

E. Nicolas: 'L'Architecture et le mobilier architectural modernes à Nancy', *Lorraine Artiste* (1–15 June 1902), pp. 163–70, 177–81
C. Pfister: *Histoire de Nancy*, 3 vols (Nancy, 1902–8)
E. Nicolas: 'L'Ecole de Nancy', *Rev. Lorraine Ill.*, 9 (1908), pp. 1–48
C. Schmid: *Nouvelles Constructions de Nancy: Recueil de façades de style moderne édifiées à Nancy* (Paris, 1908)
P. Marot: *La Genèse de la Place Royale de Nancy* (Nancy, 1954)
——: *Le Vieux Nancy* (Nancy, 1970)
R. Taveneaux, ed.: *Histoire de Nancy* (Toulouse, 1978)
F.-T. Charpentier: *Musée de l'Ecole de Nancy* (Nancy, 1983)
P. Simonin and R. Clément: *L'Ensemble architectural de Stanislas* (Nancy, 1985)
J.-L. Fray: *Nancy-le-Duc: Essor d'une résidence princière dans les dernières années du moyen âge* (Nancy, 1986)
F.-T. Charpentier: *Art nouveau: L'Ecole de Nancy* (Nancy, 1987)
J.-L. Fray: 'Nancy du XIe au début du XVe siècle: Naissance et évolution de la ville médiévale', *Le Pays lorrain*, iii (1987), pp. 117–30
'La Vie artistique', *Encyclopédie illustrée de la Lorraine*, ed. H. Collin (Nancy, 1987)

For further bibliography see HÉRÉ, EMMANUEL.

PIERRE SIMONIN

3. CENTRE OF TAPESTRY PRODUCTION. In 1604 and 1613 tapestry-weavers from Brussels were called to Nancy by Leopold, Duke of Lorraine. Of the works executed in the court workshop at this time, the only ones to survive are four of the *Story of St Paul*. It is very likely that the turmoil caused by the Thirty Years War (1618–48) brought about the dispersion of this establishment, and it was only after the restoration of Duke Leopold (*reg* 1698–1729) that there were favourable economic conditions for the flowering of such an expensive industry as tapestry-weaving.

The standard of tapestries at this time was set by the great hangings designed by Charles Le Brun at the Gobelins in Paris. Inspired by the tapestries of the *Conquests of Louis XIV* (*c.* 1690) made by the factory of Beauvais in France, Leopold decided to commission a set of tapestries illustrating the military successes of his father, Charles V, nominal Duke of Lorraine, against the Turks. Five paintings by Charles Herbel (*c.* 1650–1702) were delivered by 1701. In August 1698 Leopold had appointed Charles Mité (*d* 1736), an inhabitant of Nancy, as 'tapissier de son hôtel'. The first task of the new workshop was the restoration of the ducal tapestries, and it was not until 1703 that work began on the 'small hanging' series of the *Victories of Charles V* (1703–10; Vienna, Ksthist. Mus.; *see* FRANCE, fig. 93). Relatively modest in size, and somewhat clumsily woven, these compositions, although realistic, lacked the monumentality sought by Leopold. The hanging was not delivered until 1710, but from 1707 the French painter Jean-Baptiste Durup (*c.* 1672–1709) had been commissioned to produce new models. After his death in December 1709, when he had only completed a single painting, Durup was immediately succeeded by Jean-Baptiste Martin I, who, with Jean-Louis Guyon (*c.* 1672–1736), produced eighteen cartoons in seven years. These were in a more monumental style suitable for the subject and had much more ambitious compositions, in which great artistry was allied with a notable attention to detail and historical accuracy. In 1711, in order to produce a weaving worthy of these new cartoons, 12 workers from the Gobelins were enlisted specifically to the project. After the tapestry, the 'large hanging' series of the *Victories of Charles V* (1711–18; Vienna, Ksthist. Mus.), was finished in 1718, dissension broke out. Under the leadership of Sigisbert Mengin (*fl* 1712–25) and a Frenchman, Josse Bacor (*fl* 1681–1737), a new workshop was set up in the neighbouring town of Lunéville. In 1718 work began on the *Portières aux trophées turcs* (Vienna, Ksthist. Mus.): on a red and yellow background, the valances, colonettes and arabesques to some extent recall the gracious compositions made by Claude Audran III for the Gobelins, and the high standard of weaving rivals its best productions.

In 1723 Bacor left Lunéville and was taken on in the workshop established in the old ducal château of La Malgrange, on the outskirts of Nancy. The first task of this relatively modest workshop was to re-weave two tapestries of the *Victories of Charles V*, which had been burnt in a fire of 1719. It was then decided to produce a new version of the famous Brussels tapestry series the *Grotesque Months* after Giulio Romano. Mité's workshop had already produced a somewhat curious adaptation of these hangings, in which the figures of the gods had been replaced by imaginary architecture, based on designs by Francesco Bibiena (1659–1739). In the new cartoons (Vienna, Ksthist. Mus., and Prague, Hradčany Castle) they were replaced by landscapes painted by Dieudonné Coquelet (1677–1743). In 1737 François III abandoned his Duchy of Lorraine for Tuscany, and the three weavers who were still working at La Malgrange probably went to work for him in Florence. The Nancy factory was primarily attached to the ducal court: altogether some 70 pieces can be attributed to it, most of which are in the Kunsthistorisches Museum, Vienna.

BIBLIOGRAPHY
L. Baldass: *Die Wiener Gobelinssammlung* (Vienna, 1920)
M. Antoine: *Les Manufactures de tapisseries des ducs de Lorraine au XVIIIe siècle* (Nancy, 1965)
E. Mahl: 'Die Mosesfolge der Tapisseriensammlung des Kunsthistorischen Museums in Wien', *Jb. Ksthist. Samml. Wien*, lxiii (1967), pp. 7–38
Historische Schlachten (exh. cat., Vienna, Schloss Halbturn, 1976)

ISABELLE DENIS

Nandangarh. *See* LAURIYA NANDANGARH.

Nanggan-kŏsa. *See* YI YŎNG.

Nanggok. *See* KIM (iv), (2).

Nangulay, Dick. *See* NGULAYNGULAY, DICK.

Nanha [Nānhā] (*fl c.* 1582–1635). Indian miniature painter. His works epitomize the stylistic and typological changes that occurred in Mughal painting during the reigns of the three emperors who were his patrons: Akbar (*reg* 1556–1605), Jahangir (*reg* 1605–27) and Shah Jahan (*reg* 1628–57). His earliest known works appear in the *Dārābnāma* ('History of Darab'; *c.* 1580; London, BL, Or. Ms. 4615); the *Razmnāma* ('Book of war'; 1582–6; Jaipur, Maharaja Sawai Man Singh II Mus., MS. AG. 1683–1850), a translation of the Hindu epic the *Mahābhārata* commissioned by Akbar; and the *Tārīkh-i Khāndān-i Tīmūriyya* ('History of the house of Timur'; *c.* 1584; Bankipur, Patna, Khuda Bakhsh Lib.). Nanha is not among the 17 artists singled out for praise in the *Āyīn-i Akbarī*, a contemporary account of Akbar's reign, but his multiple roles as designer, painter and portraitist in the *Akbarnāma* of *c.* 1590 ('History of Akbar'; London, V&A, MS. IS. 2-1896) suggest that he ranked high in the atelier's second tier of artists. He contributed more often to profusely illustrated manuscripts than to de luxe projects; however, one painting in Akbar's fine, small *Dīvān* (collected poems) of Anvari (1588; Cambridge, MA, Sackler Mus., MS. 1960.117.15) has been attributed to him and four paintings in the *Khamsa* ('Five poems') of Nizami (1595; London, BL, Or. MS. 12208, fols 63*v*, 159*r*, and 305*v* (signed on a scroll held by a seated figure in yellow); and Baltimore, MD, Walters A.G., MS. W.613, fol. 16*v*) bear inscriptions naming him as the artist. Nanha's work displays two distinctive figure types: one whose thickset neck and shoulders impart a notable stockiness and another whose slender physique is accentuated by strong contours and a small but heavily modelled face.

Nanha is known particularly for his portraiture, which was well-suited to the taste of Jahangir. It has been suggested that he left the imperial workshop to join Jahangir when as a rebelling prince he established a separate court at Allahabad. This theory is based on the paucity of works in imperial projects about 1600; an illustration in the *Dīvān* of Amir Hasan Dihlavi (1602; Baltimore, MD, Walters A.G., MS. W.650); and a single illustration (fol. 280*v*) late in the manuscript of the *Anvar-i Suhaylī* ('Lights of Canopus'; 1604–10/11, London, BL, Add. MS. 18579).

Unlike his more famous nephew, BISHAN DAS, also known for his portraiture, Nanha produced relatively few paintings for Jahangir and Shah Jahan. His self-portrait is included in an illustration for the *Jahāngīrnāma* ('History of Jahangir'; London, V&A, IS. 185-1984), which shows him as a middle-aged, dark-complexioned attendant kneeling among the figures surrounding Prince Khurram (the future Shah Jahan). A later work shows Shah Jahan with Prince Dara Shikoh (New York, Met., 55.121.10.36*v*). Portraits of nobles with inscriptions naming Nanha as the artist include those of *Zulfiqar Khan* from the Minto Album (*c.* 1635; London, V&A) and *Sayf Khan Barha* (New York, Met., 55.121.10.4*v*). Nanha also developed a minor speciality of scenes of lion attacks, one of his finest being *Perils of the Hunt* (Philadelphia, PA, Free Lib., M.36), painted uncharacteristically on silk.

Nanha's artistic identity has been somewhat obscured by his erroneous association with other artists with similar names. These include a lesser Akbar-period painter known from inscriptions as Nama or Naman. It has also been proposed (Losty, 1982) that Nanha is synonymous with the artist Kanha, explaining the orthographic difference as a variant Persian transliteration of regional pronunciations of the proper Hindu name Jnana. Although this view can be supported somewhat on stylistic grounds, its plausibility is undermined by the inscription on one painting (57/117) of the *Akbarnāma* of *c.* 1586–7 (or *c.* 1590) which lists Kanha and Nanha as the respective designer and painter, a formula never used when a single artist served both roles.

See also INDIAN SUBCONTINENT, §V, 4(i)(c).

BIBLIOGRAPHY
The Grand Mogul: Imperial Painting in India, 1600–1660 (exh. cat. by M. C. Beach, Williamstown, MA, Clark A. Inst.; Baltimore, MD, Walters A.G.; Boston, MA, Mus. F.A.; New York, Asia House Gals; 1978–9)
The Imperial Image: Paintings for the Mughal Court (exh. cat. by M. C. Beach, Washington, DC, Freer, 1981)
The Art of the Book in India (exh. cat. by J. Losty, London, BL, 1982)
A. Schimmel and S. C. Welch: *Anvari's Divan: A Pocket Book for Akbar* (New York, 1983)
V&A Mus. Album, Occasional paper, 4 (1985), p. 16
S. C. Welch and others: *The Emperors' Album* (New York, 1987)

JOHN SEYLLER

Naniwa [Naniwakyō]. *See* OSAKA, §I, 2.

Nanjing [Nanking; Nan-ching]. Modern capital of Jiangsu Province, China, and capital of China at various times between AD 222 and 1949. It is situated on the southern bank of the Yangzi River, with the smaller Qinhuai River to the west and south. Several nearby lakes include Lake Mochou to the west and Lake Xuanwu just north of the old city walls.

The history of Nanjing goes back to the Eastern Zhou period (771–256 BC), when it was under the control successively of the states of Wu, Yue and Chu. When China was unified under the Qin (221–206 BC) it was known as Jinling, a name the conquerors changed to Moling. Under the Han dynasty (206 BC–AD 220) the name was changed to Danyang. During the Three Kingdoms period (AD 220–80) Nanjing gradually became the most important centre of culture in southern China, and in AD 229 it was made the capital of the kingdom of Wu (AD 222–80). In AD 317 the state of Eastern Jin established itself in south China with Nanjing as its capital under the name Jiankang. Traditional Chinese culture flourished, and in the distinctive southern intellectual climate Buddho–Daoist groups such as Xuanxue (Obscure Learning), Mingjiao (Teaching of Names) and Qingtan (Pure Conversation) evolved. Numerous scholars lived in Nanjing, including the celebrated calligrapher Wang Xizhi and the painter Gu Kaizhi.

In AD 420 the Eastern Jin dynasty fell to the Liu Song (AD 420–79), which continued the cultural development begun by the Jin. With the establishment of the Liang dynasty (AD 502–57), the city came under strong Buddhist influence. Emperor Wudi (*reg* AD 502–49) was a devout Buddhist under whose patronage numerous new temples and monasteries were built. He is known to have copied Buddhist scriptures in his own hand and to have been ceremoniously ordained on several occasions.

With the establishment of the Sui dynasty (AD 581–618) Nanjing lost its position as capital city and became instead a prefectural capital. Under the Tang dynasty (AD 618–907) the city was relatively unimportant, although Buddhism flourished in the area. When the state of Southern Tang (AD 937–75) was established, Nanjing enjoyed again for a short time the status of capital and underwent renewed construction and development of the local waterways. During the Southern Song period (1127–1279) the city regained some of its political and strategic importance: it was used by the Song as a military base from which to attack the territory held by the Jin north of the Yangzi River.

Nanjing became the capital of China with the founding of the Ming dynasty (1368–1644). Immediately upon his ascension to the throne the Hongwu emperor (*reg* 1368–98) decided to expand and strengthen the city, and to this end he ordered the construction of a city wall. This wall, measuring 33.4 km in circumference, the longest such city wall in the world, was to a large extent built upon the remains of earlier walls; it had 13 gates, encompassing an area totalling more than 42 sq. km. The project took more than 20 years to complete, and as much as two thirds of the wall still stands. In contrast to the usual square or rectangular layouts of Chinese cities, the city wall of Nanjing is somewhat irregular, encompassing such topographical and strategic features in the landscape as hills and streams. Among the important features of the city wall are the Heping Gate in the north and the Zhonghua Gate in the south, a near impregnable two-storey building with entry through three succeeding vaulted gates, each with its own courtyard.

When the Hongwu emperor established himself in Nanjing, he had built for himself a magnificent palace that supposedly outshone all previous imperial palaces. Although very little remains of this once imposing complex of great halls, galleries and gates, it is thought that it could easily have compared with the later imperial palace begun during the reign of the Yongle emperor (*reg* 1403–24) in Beijing (*see* CHINA, fig. 79). Nanjing ('Southern Capital') was given its present name in 1421, when the Yongle emperor moved the capital to Beijing. As the secondary capital of the Ming dynasty, Nanjing became one of the most important cultural, artistic and intellectual centres of the empire. Gong Xian, for example, who was one of the most important painters of the 17th century, was a Nanjing artist.

With the establishment of the Qing dynasty (1644–1911) Nanjing became the provincial capital of the Jiangnan area, which covered the modern provinces of Jiangsu, Jiangxi and Anhui. The peace declaration ending the First Opium War was signed in the city in 1842. In 1852 it was occupied by the Taiping army and became the capital of their Empire of Heavenly Peace. Under the rule of the Taipings much of Nanjing was destroyed or plundered, and the retaking of the city by a combined imperial army and a foreign expedition corps in 1864 only caused further damage. In 1911 the city was made the capital of the Republic of China (1911–49).

Among the oldest historical sites in Nanjing is the burial site of Bian Kun (AD 280–327), a loyal hero of the Eastern Jin dynasty. Memorial halls for him were built as late as the Song (960–1279) and Ming periods, though nothing remains beyond two stelae from the Northern Song period (960–1127) and the late Qing. There are several Buddhist temples near the city, some of which date to the Liang dynasty. The most famous of these is the Qixia Temple on Mt She, 20 km to the east of Nanjing; the caves around it house Buddhist sculptures from the Southern Qi (AD 479–502) to Ming periods. There are altogether some 294 caves and niches with a total of 515 images, ranging in size from the colossal images in the Sansheng Cave (h. *c.* 13 m) to relatively insignificant sculptures less than a metre high. In the course of time the statues have been badly damaged, and poorly executed repairs from the Republican period have disfigured many of them considerably. The carvings, however, are very important, as they are virtually the only old Buddhist stone sculptures in southern China. Another important monument in the Qixia Temple itself is the Sheli ta, an octagonal, five-storey stone stupa (h. 15 m), said to date from AD 601 but restored during the Southern Tang dynasty (see fig.). Reliefs of guardian spirits are carved on four of its sides, in addition to the scenes of the eight major events in the life of Shakyamuni Buddha.

Among the non-Buddhist relics from the Liang period (AD 502–557) is the imperial burial ground located to the north-east of Nanjing. Divided into two main sections, it contains the tombs of Liang Wudi (AD 502–49), his father and son (in Danyang) and those of his cousin and younger brothers (in Shiyuecun, Ganjiaxing). Although many of these tombs are no longer preserved in their original shape, each of them originally featured a spirit road with beasts, mythical animals and stelae carved in stone flanking the passage to the tomb. The most prominent beast among the tomb guardians from the Liu Song and Liang dynasties is the chimera, the stylized winged lion that originally came from Persia.

Mt Niushou (Niutou), located 12 km south of the city, was an important centre for Chan Buddhism during the early Tang period; the pagoda of the Hongjue Temple (Hongjue si; AD 774) can still be seen on the southern slopes of the mountain. There are several Chan Buddhist sites on the mountain itself, including meditation caves and inscriptions.

The tombs of two of the kings of the Southern Tang dynasty—Li Bian (*reg* AD 937–43) and Li Jing (*reg* AD 943–61)—can be found 15 km south of Nanjing, at the foot of Mt Zutang. Each tomb consists of a sloping entry ramp up to the tomb, with stone sculptures of animals, mythic beasts, martial figures and dignitaries facing each other only 3 m apart. The compound surrounding the tomb is enclosed by a high wall with a large gate, which opens out to a courtyard where there once stood a huge memorial hall; now only the stone platform remains. From the first courtyard one enters the inner compound, with an arched marble bridge and a monumental tower-like brick building. At the end of a rectangular enclosure lies the huge tumulus surrounded by a stone wall enclosing an area 350 m in diameter. The tomb itself has not been excavated, but it is thought to resemble that of the Wanli emperor (*reg* 1573–1620) outside Beijing. There are also several tombs of important dignitaries, officials and military figures in the hills surrounding the city.

The Baoensi (Debt of Gratitude Temple) in Nanjing once housed the famous Porcelain Pagoda, built with white-glazed bricks by the Yongle emperor (*reg* 1403–24) in memory of his mother; it was destroyed during the Taiping Rebellion. Other Ming buildings of importance in the city include the drum tower and the examination hall. There are only a few notable Qing-period remains, mostly buildings and murals from the Taiping Kingdom.

See also NANJING SCHOOL.

BIBLIOGRAPHY
P. M. Tchang: *Tombeau des Liang* (Shanghai, 1912)
K. W. Kwok: *The Splendours of Historic Nanking* (Shanghai, 1933)
J. Prip-Møller: 'The Hall of Lin Ku Ssu, Nanking', *Artes*, iii (1934) [whole issue]
——: *Chinese Buddhist Monasteries* (Copenhagen, 1937)
D. Tokiwa and T. Sekino: *Shina Bukkyō Shiseki* [Buddhist monuments in China], iv (Tokyo, 1937), pp. 1–24
Zhu Jiexian, ed.: *Qixia si zhi* [Record of Qixia Temple] (Hong Kong, 1962)
Jiangsu sheng chutu wenwu xuanji [Selection of material on archaeological finds in Jiangsu Province], Nanjing, Jiangsu Prov. Mus. (Beijing, 1963)
F. W. Mote: 'The Transformation of Nanking, 1350–1400', *The City in Late Imperial China*, ed. G. W. Skinner (Stanford, CA, 1977)
Chūgoku bukkyō no ryo [A Journey of Chinese Buddhism], ii (Kyoto, 1980), pp. 67–76
Jiang Zanchu: *Nanjing shihua* [A History of Nanjing] (Nanjing, 1980)
B. Till: *In Search of Old Nanking* (Hong Kong, 1982)
A. Paludan: *The Chinese Spirit Road: The Classical Tradition of Stone Tomb Statuary* (New Haven and London, 1991)

HENRIK H. SØRENSEN

Nanjing, Qixia Temple, Sheli ta stone stupa, h. 15 m, possibly AD 601, restored during the Southern Tang period (AD 937–75)

and three vaulted chambers, with several small side chambers for grave goods. The tombs are roughly similar in layout and construction and are modelled on the standard Tang tombs, although on a much smaller and less sophisticated scale.

On Mt Zijin, 5–6 km east of Nanjing, lies the Lingguku si (Wondrous Bones Temple), originally founded in 1384 by the Ming Hongwu emperor (*reg* 1368–98). Its name refers to the enshrined relics of the great pilgrim–monk Xuanzang (AD 600–64). By the late Qing period the temple had been abandoned and was more or less in ruins; most of the existing structures date from the 20th century. All that remains of the original Ming structure is the massive main hall made of bricks (l. 46 m), the Wuliang dian (Beamless Hall), which takes its name from the unusual fact that it has no supporting wooden beams.

The tomb of the first Ming emperor is also located on the slopes of Mt Zijin (*see also* MING DYNASTY). In 1381 the Hongwu emperor began the construction of his own tomb, and it was finished *c.* 1415, together with its memorial temple. There is a long, winding spirit road leading

Nanjing school. Term used to refer to a group of Chinese painters active in Nanjing chiefly in the second half of the 17th century, at the start of the Qing period (1644–1912). The Nanjing school was roughly contemporaneous with the ANHUI SCHOOL, which was active in the adjacent Anhui Province. By the late 17th century the leading painters of the school were already identified as the Eight Masters of Jinling [Nanjing] (*Jinling bajia*). The earliest extant listing of the eight is by Zhang Geng (1685–1760) in his 1739 *Guochao hua zheng lu* ('Catalogue of painting in our dynasty'); most were born elsewhere, but all were active in Nanjing as professional artists. Later lists vary, but the painters most often included are GONG XIAN, the leader of the school; Fan Qih (1615/16–*c.* 1694) from Nanjing; Gao Cen (*fl* 1670s; *d* 1689) from Hangzhou in Zhejiang Province; Zou Zhe (*fl c.* 1641–84) from Suzhou, Jiangsu Province; Ye Xin (*fl* 1650s–70s) from Huating, modern Songjiang; Wu Hong (*fl* 1670s–1680s) from Junqi,

Jiangsu Province; Xie Sun (*fl* 1679) from Jiangning, Guangxi Province; and Hu Cao (*fl* 1681) from Jiangning. Others sometimes associated with the school include Lu Qian (*fl* 1660s–80s) from Suiming, Sichuan Province; Wu Dan and Liu Yu (both *fl* 1670s–80s), Nanjing natives; and Gong Xian's pupil Wang Gai (*fl* 1670s–90s) from Xiushui, Zhejiang Province.

1. SUBJECT-MATTER AND STYLE. Nanjing masters produced mostly landscapes, although some of them painted flowers and occasionally figures. Like the masters of the Anhui school, they often depicted the local scenery: densely wooded hills, the banks of the Yangzi River, temples and shrines, and the Qin Huai pleasure district of Nanjing. In addition to the local tradition, two outside currents deeply influenced their styles. One was the landscape tradition of the Northern Song period (AD 960–1127), with its imposing compositions made up of richly textured earth masses and its emphasis on fine technique (*see also* CHINA, §V, 3(iv)(a)). The other was the European pictorial tradition, known to Chinese artists of the time, especially in the Nanjing region, chiefly through engravings in books brought by Jesuit missionaries from the late Ming period (1368–1644) onwards. The latter influence can be seen in many features typical of Nanjing school painting: strong effects of light and shadow; non-traditional ways of depicting spatial recessions; river scenes with clearly drawn horizon lines over which ships are sometimes shown disappearing; foreshortened and three-dimensional drawing of boats and bridges; and representations of houses in which the interior spaces can be discerned. These features, together with the use of heavy dotting (often more like Western stippling than Chinese texture strokes; *see* STIPPLE (i), §1) and certain compositional devices—the use of trees, mountainsides etc—to divide the picture space with strong diagonals into triangular, rhomboid and other geometric shapes, make works of the Nanjing school immediately recognizable.

2. HISTORICAL DEVELOPMENT. Located on the east bank of the Yangzi River in western Jiangsu Province, Nanjing was an important centre of painting in the Ming period. It was the second, southern capital of the Ming (the primary, northern capital was Beijing), and the city's rich patronage and cultural life attracted professional artists. Also of note were the amateur painters among the scholar-officials attached to the shadow court at Nanjing (*see also* CHINA, §V, 4(ii)). Some Ming painters who held positions in the imperial court academy in Beijing, such as Wu Wei and Wu Bin, seem to have chosen to spend more time in Nanjing than in Beijing. Wu Bin and several other late Ming masters were responsible for reviving the monumental landscape style of the Northern Song period, a revival made possible by the presence in the city of major collections of early paintings.

Nanjing escaped the destruction and massacre suffered by other southern cities during the Ming–Qing transition, and by the early 1660s the city was once more a gathering-place for scholars and officials both in and out of office, as well as writers and artists. The great patron of painters Zhou Lianggong spent much of his time there from 1661, attracting to his circle such notable artists as Hu Yukun, who lived for years as Zhou's house guest, and the Orthodox school master Wang Hui, who enjoyed Zhou's patronage from around 1667. Other painters not usually numbered among masters of the Nanjing school were active there at this time, including Zhang Feng, Cheng Zhengkui and the Buddhist monk-artists Kuncan and Daoji. By 1669 Gong Xian, the leading master of the school, could write that Nanjing 'has several tens of eminent painters, but if we count all those who can paint, the number exceeds one thousand'.

After Gong Xian, the most distinguished and interesting of the Nanjing masters is Fan Qih, who once received scant recognition by Chinese writers but who, as more of his works became known, emerged as one of the neglected, versatile professional masters whose reputations suffered because of the bias of Chinese critics in favour of amateur

Nanjing school painting by Fan Qih: untitled handscroll (detail), ink on silk, 345×1625 mm (Berlin, Museum für Ostasiatische Kunst)

scholar-painters. A handscroll by him (1546; San Francisco, CA, Asian A. Mus.) begins and ends with passages of fantastic landscape in the style created by Wu Bin, and an undated album of landscapes (New York, Met.) shows him at his most refined. Another undated handscroll (Berlin, Mus. Ostasiat. Kst; see fig.) represents his somewhat Westernized, illusionist manner. The sense of mass and tactile surface imparted to the heavily eroded earth banks depends partly on texture strokes and volumetric drawing in the Song manner and partly on European-style shading.

Nanjing was a centre of pictorial printing in this period. The first part of the *Mustard Seed Garden Manual of Painting* (*Jieziyuan huazhuan*; published 1679 and 1701) was compiled there by Wang Gai, following the example of his teacher Gong Xian, who had produced a number of hand-painted teaching manuals. In addition to providing models for painting rocks and trees in the styles of old masters, it codified the style of the Nanjing school into learnable type-forms and brought about the wide propagation of that style by making it accessible to innumerable artists of later times, including the Nanga masters of Edo-period Japan (*see* JAPAN, §VI, 4(vi)(d)).

BIBLIOGRAPHY

Hongnam Kim: *Chou Liang-kung and his* Tu-hualu *(Lives of Painters): Patron-critic and Painters in Seventeenth Century China* (diss., New Haven, CT, Yale U., 1955)

A. Lippe: 'Kung Hsien and the Nanking School', *Orient. A.*, n. s., ii (1956), pp. 21–9; iv (1958), pp. 159–70

O. Sirén: *Chinese Painting: Leading Masters and Principles* (London and New York, 1956–8), v, pp. 128–37

JAMES CAHILL

Nankai. *See* GION NANKAI.

Nanking. *See* NANJING.

Nankok. *See* CHŎNG SŎN.

Nanni, Giovanni. *See* UDINE, GIOVANNI DA.

Nanni, Ser Ricciardo di. *See* RICCIARDO DI NANNI, SER.

Nanni di Baccio Bigio. *See* BIGIO, NANNI DI BACCIO.

Nanni di Banco (*b* Florence, *c.* 1380–85; *d* Florence, 1421). Italian sculptor. His father, Antonio di Banco (*d* 1415), a stone-carver at Florence Cathedral with whom he trained, was married in 1368, which provides a *terminus post quem* for Nanni's birth. On 2 February 1405 Nanni matriculated in the Arte di Pietra e Legname, the masons' guild, presumably to allow him into the cathedral workshops. He is first documented there on 31 December 1407, working with his father on the archivolt sculpture of the Porta della Mandorla.

On 24 January 1408 Nanni and his father were both commissioned to carve a figure of *Isaiah* for the exterior of the north tribune of the cathedral (now inside). Despite both names on the document, it is likely that the statue was intended to be by Nanni alone, since his father seems to have been a *lastraiuolo* (stone-carver), not a figural sculptor. Nanni and his father probably operated a joint workshop. Nanni is first referred to by the title *magister* in a document of February 1408, in which Donatello was

Nanni di Banco: *Four Crowned Saints*, marble, Orsanmichele, Florence, *c.* 1416

commissioned to carve a marble *David* (Florence, Bargello) as a companion figure to the *Isaiah*, which itself was completed by 15 December 1408, when Nanni's father received payment for his son. Despite the long, curving lines of the Late Gothic style, there is a hint in the *Isaiah*, as in Donatello's *David*, of an active contrapposto pose derived from antique sculpture.

On 19 December 1408 Nanni was commissioned to carve a seated marble *St Luke* for one of the niches flanking the main doors of the cathedral, while Donatello was assigned a companion figure of *St John the Evangelist* and Niccolò di Piero Lamberti a figure of *St Mark* (all Florence, Mus. Opera Duomo). Work on these statues progressed fitfully, and the *St Luke* was not completed and paid for until 16 February 1413. It also owes much to Nanni's study of Classical prototypes and, with Donatello's *St John*, marks a turning-point towards the early Renaissance style. Nanni's only other known documented figural work is the high relief of the *Assumption of the Virgin* for the tympanum of the Porta della Mandorla, a work that is full of robust movement and was much admired by Vasari. Begun in 1414, the relief was substantially complete by the sculptor's death in 1421. Taking into account the intervention of pupils (among whom may have been Luca della Robbia) in the carving, the relief features gothicizing drapery patterns that may reflect Nanni's response to the style of the portal into which it was to be inserted, rather than any significant shift in his late style.

Three other figures in marble are universally accepted as Nanni's work, though their dating and ordering are controversial: the *St Philip*, the *Four Crowned Saints* (see fig.) and the *St Eligius*, all for the trade guild niches on the exterior of Orsanmichele, Florence (*in situ*). Given the delays in the carving of the *St Luke*, it is possible that Nanni's work at Orsanmichele was competing for his attention. The *St Philip* (*c.* 1412–15) for the Arte dei Calzolai is comparable in pose to Donatello's nearby *St Mark* (1411), just as the two artists' *Isaiah* and *David* for the tribune are essentially mirror images. Since they worked closely together in the cathedral workshops, they undoubtedly also shared ideas for their sculpture at Orsanmichele. Their sculpture seems to have developed along parallel lines, even though Nanni may have been older and may well have initiated the stylistic changes normally ascribed to Donatello's fertile imagination. Nanni's *Four Crowned Saints*, with its overtly classicizing forms, is important as the first sculptural group in Renaissance Florence. The relief beneath the group showing stone-carvers at work is instructive for collaborative workshop practices during the early 15th century.

From May to August 1414 Nanni served as consul for the guild of the Maestri di Pietra e Legname, the guild that commissioned the *Four Crowned Saints*. He also held the civic office of podestà of Montagna for six months from 22 August 1414 and of Castelfranco di Sopra from 9 July 1416. He was proposed for the same office for Tizzana (1414) and Buggiano (1415) but was not elected.

Nanni's shop must have been active, although records remain only for six carved coats of arms of the wool guild in 1419: two for S Maria Novella and four for their guildhall. The same year, with Donatello and Brunelleschi, Nanni provided a model for the new dome of Florence Cathedral, a fact that further testifies to the active collaboration between the leading sculptural workshops of the city.

BIBLIOGRAPHY

G. Vasari: *Vite* (1550, rev. 2/1568); ed. G. Milanesi (1878–85), ii, pp. 161–5, 344, 351

H. Semper: *Donatello, seine Zeit und Schule*, Quellenschr. Kstgesch. & Ksttech., ix (Vienna, 1875)

G. Poggi: *Il Duomo di Firenze*, It. Forsch. Kstgesch., ii (Berlin, 1909/*R* Florence, 1988)

O. Wulff: 'Nanni d'Antonio di Banco und sein Verhältnis zu Donatello', *Kstgesch. Ges.*, v (1909), pp. 27–9

——: 'Giovanni d'Antonio di Banco und die Anfänge der Renaissance-plastik in Florenz', *Jb. Kön.-Preuss. Kstsamml.*, xxxiii (1913), pp. 99–164

G. Brunetti: 'Un'opera sconosciuta di Nanni di Banco e nuovi documenti relativi all'artista', *Riv. A.*, xii (1930), pp. 229–37

J. Lanyi: 'Il Profeta Isaia di Nanni di Banco', *Riv. A.*, xviii (1936), pp. 137–78

——: 'Zur Pragmatik der Florentiner Quattrocentoplastik', *Krit. Ber.*, vi (1937), p. 128

W. R. Valentiner: 'Donatello and Ghiberti', *A. Q.* [Detroit], iii (1940), pp. 182–215

L. Planiscig: 'I profeti sulla Porta della Mandorla del Duomo fiorentino', *Riv. A.*, xxiv (1942), pp. 125–42

——: *Nanni di Banco* (Florence, 1946)

W. R. Valentiner: 'Donatello or Nanni di Banco', *Crit. A.*, xxvii (1949), pp. 25–31

P. Vaccarino: *Nanni* (Florence, 1950)

W. R. Valentiner: 'Notes on the Early Works of Donatello', *A. Q.* [Detroit], xiv (1951), pp. 307–25

M. Wundram: 'Antonio di Banco', *Mitt. Ksthist. Inst. Florenz*, x (1961), pp. 23–32

H. von Einem: 'Bemerkungen zur Bildhauerdarstellung des Nanni di Banco', *Festschrift für Hans Sedlmayr* (Munich, 1962), pp. 68–79

M. Phillips: 'A New Interpretation of the Early Style of Nanni di Banco', *Marsyas*, xi (1962–4), pp. 63–6

H. W. Janson: 'Nanni di Banco's *Assumption of the Virgin* on the Porta della Mandorla', *Studies in Western Art: Acts of the Twentieth Congress of the History of Art: Princeton, 1963*, ii, pp. 98–107; also in H. W. Janson: *Sixteen Studies* (New York, 1973), pp. 91–7

M. Wundram: *Donatello und Nanni di Banco* (Berlin, 1969)

V. Herzner: 'Donatello und Nanni di Banco', *Mitt. Ksthist. Inst. Florenz*, xvii (1973), pp. 1–28

M. Lisner: 'Josua und David—Nannis und Donatellos Statuen für den Tribuna-Zyklus des Florentiner Doms', *Pantheon*, xxxii (1974), pp. 232–43

A. Parronchi: 'L'autore del Crocifisso di Santa Croce: Nanni di Banco', *Prospettiva*, vi (1976), pp. 50–55

J. T. Paoletti: '"Nella mia giovanile età mi partì . . . da Firenze"', *Lorenzo Ghiberti nel suo tempo: Atti del convegno internazionale di studi, Firenze, 1978*, i, pp. 99–110

R. Munman: 'The Evangelists from the Cathedral of Florence: A Renaissance Arrangement Recovered', *A. Bull.*, lxii (1980), pp. 207–17

M. L. Dunkelman: 'Nanni di Banco', *Italian Renaissance Sculpture in the Time of Donatello* (exh. cat., ed. A. Darr and G. Bonsanti; Detroit, MI, Inst. A.; Fort Worth, TX, Kimball A. Mus.; Florence, Forte Belvedere; 1985–6), pp. 83–5 (103–4, It. ed.)

M Bergstein: 'La vita civica di Nanni di Banco', *Riv. A.*, xxxix (1987), pp. 55–82

——: 'The Date of Nanni di Banco's "Quattro santi coronati"', *Burl. Mag.*, cxxx (1988), pp. 910–13

C. King: 'Narrative in the Representation of the Four Crowned Martyrs: Or San Michele and the Doge's Palace', *A. Crist.*, dccxliii (1991), pp. 81–9

JOHN T. PAOLETTI

Nanni [Giovanni] **di Bartolo** [il Rosso] (*fl* 1419–35). Italian sculptor. He was the son of a Fra Bartolo. From 1419 to 1424 he worked on various figures for the façade and campanile of Florence Cathedral. In July 1419, with Pietro Uberti Baldassarre degli Albizzi as his guarantor, he was commissioned to sculpt a figure for the cathedral façade, which was completed in March 1420. Its subject is not stated, but it may perhaps be identified as the *St John the Baptist* (Florence, Mus. Opera Duomo). On 30 April 1420 Nanni was asked to complete a statue of Joshua begun by Bernardo Ciuffagni in 1415 for the east side of the campanile. The identity of this figure is uncertain.

It has been suggested that Nanni was trained in the workshop of Niccolò di Pietro Lamberti, who, with Antonio di Banco and his son Nanni, completed the Porta della Mandorla on the north side of Florence Cathedral (1406–9). Brunetti (1934–5) attributed some of the reliefs in the frieze to the left of the door to Nanni, but they have also been attributed to Nanni di Banco or Jacopo della Quercia. The attribution (Brunetti, 1934–5) to Nanni of two small prophets (Florence, Mus. Opera Duomo), originally on pinnacles flanking the door of the campanile, has also been questioned. These figures, with their thickly curled hair and beards, undulating borders to their cloaks, hooked folds in their robes and exaggerated curvature of their posture, resemble the figure style of Ghiberti's contemporary relief panels on the north door of the Baptistery. A group of terracotta sculptures, stylistically dependent on Ghiberti, has also been attributed to Nanni. It includes a standing *Virgin and Child* (destr.; ex-Kaiser-Friedrich Mus., Berlin) and a half-length *Virgin and Child* (Berlin, Skulpgal.) and can probably be dated between 1415 and 1420.

In 1421–2 Nanni collaborated with Donatello on the group of *Abraham and Isaac* (Florence, Mus. Opera Duomo) for the east side of the campanile. Donatello's strong artistic personality inspired a change in Nanni's style, which is visible in his only signed Florentine work, the *Obadiah* (Florence, Mus. Opera Duomo, see fig.),

Nanni di Bartolo: *Obadiah* (Florence, Museo Opera Duomo)

Another group of terracotta and stucco figures attributed to Nanni combines features taken from Ghiberti with the rhythmic quality of Donatello's early works. This includes the *Virgin and Child* (Florence, Mus. Ognissanti), originally in S Miniato, Florence, the beautiful *Virgin and Child Enthroned* (Krefeld, Kaiser Wilhelm Mus.) and five stucco versions of the *Virgin and Child* (e.g. Florence, Mus. Stibbert), presumably made from the same prototype (see Bellini and Schlegel).

Nanni di Bartolo had left Florence before 11 February 1424 leaving unpaid debts behind him and, according to a document of that date, was engaged on a project in Venice that would take a long time to complete. This project has not been identified, but he may have worked on three gargoyles on the north face of S Marco. The document also says that he was resident in Volterra, but this was probably a mistake on the part of the scribe, for on 14 May 1424 Nanni was present when the Venetian Doge received Rinaldo degli Albizzi, the Florentine ambassador in Venice (Gilbert).

Nanni's only certain work in north Italy is the signed Brenzoni monument (*c.* 1426) in S Fermo, Verona. The harmonious relationship between Nanni's sculpted scene of the *Resurrection of Christ* and Pisanello's fresco of the *Annunciation* above it gives the impression that the two artists formed a well-integrated team (Longhi and Del Bravo). It seems probable that Nanni designed the highly pictorial scene, based on Ghiberti's relief of the same subject on the north doors of the Florentine Baptistery, but left part of the execution to an assistant. Several works in Venice are attributed to Nanni; among the most probable attributions are the four statues on the left of the façade of S Maria dell'Orto and the large group depicting the *Judgement of Solomon* above the capital of Justice on the exterior of the Doge's Palace.

Nanni di Bartolo was in the Veneto again in 1435, as is shown by the inscription over the portal of S Niccolò at Tolentino, in the Marches, erected by him. It seems, however, that his role there was limited to assembling various pieces of statuary, which had been carved by other artists in the Veneto and brought to Tolentino by the brother of the condottiere Niccolò da Tolentino after the latter's death in 1435. The *Virgin and Child* and the two saints in the lunette show the influence of Jacopo della Quercia and have been attributed to Nanni, but they bear no stylistic relationship to his certain works. The relief of the *Baptism* in the lunette above the tomb of the Blessed Pacifico (1437; S Maria dei Frari) has also been attributed to him (see Wolters).

Nanni's date of death is uncertain. A document of 1451 has been used to prove that he was active in Carrara at that date, but Gilbert believed that it provides no evidence to suggest that he was still alive.

BIBLIOGRAPHY

Thieme–Becker

R. Longhi: 'Recensione: Lettera pittorica a Giuseppe Fiocco', *Vita Artistica*, i (1926), pp. 127–39

F. Schottmüller: 'Nanni di Bartolo, il Rosso', *Miscellanea di storia dell'arte in onore di Igino Benvenuto Supino* (Florence, 1933), pp. 295–304

G. Brunetti: 'Ricerche su Nanni di Bartolo "il Rosso"', *Boll. A.*, xxviii (1934–5), pp. 258–72

J. Lányi: 'Le statue quattrocentesche dei profeti nel campanile e nell'antica facciata di Santa Maria del Fiore', *Riv. A.*, xvii (1935), pp. 120–59, 245–80

originally on the west side of the campanile. The youthful prophet is well characterized, and his movement graceful and balanced, but the figure lacks Donatello's dramatic power.

M. Wundram: 'Donatello und Ciuffagni', *Z. Kstgesch.*, xxii (1959), pp. 85–101

C. Del Bravo: 'Proposte e appunti per Nanni di Bartolo', *Paragone*, xii/137 (1961), pp. 26–32

R. Stang and N. Stang: 'Donatello il Giosuè', *Acta Archaeol. & A. Hist. Pertinentia*, i (1962), pp. 113–30

L. Becherucci and G. Brunetti: *Il Museo dell'Opera del Duomo a Firenze*, i (Milan, 1970), pp. 258–60, 264–7

R. Chiarelli: 'Note pisanelliane', *Ant. Viva*, ii (1972), pp. 3–25

C. Gilbert: 'La presenza a Venezia di Nanni di Bartolo il Rosso', *Studi di storia dell'arte in onore di Antonio Morassi* (Venice, 1972), pp. 35–9

F. Bellini: 'Da Federighi a Nanni di Bartolo? Riesame di un gruppo di terracotte fiorentine', *Jacopo della Quercia fra gotico e rinascimento. Atti del convegno di studi: Siena, 1975*, pp. 180–88

G. Brunetti: 'Sull'attività di Nanni di Bartolo nell'Italia settentrionale', *Jacopo della Quercia fra gotico e rinascimento. Atti del convegno di studi: Siena, 1975*, pp. 189–200

W. Wolters: *La scultura veneziana gotica, 1300–1460* (Venice, 1976), pp. 90–93, 267–71

U. Schlegel: 'Dalla cerchia del Ghiberti: Rappresentazione della Madonna di Nanni di Bartolo', *Ant. Viva*, xviii/1 (1979), pp. 21–6

G. C. Gentilini: 'Nella rinascita delle antichità', *La civiltà del cotto* (exh. cat., Impruneta, 1980), pp. 93–4

E. Neri Lusanna and L. Faedo: *Il Museo Bardini a Firenze: Le sculture* (Milan, 1986), pp. 247–8

L. Bellosi: 'Da una costola di Donatello: Nanni di Bartolo', *Prospettiva* [Florence], 53–6 (1988–9), pp. 22–13

F. Landi: 'Per Nanni di Bartolo, il Rosso', *Ant. Viva*, xxxi/2 (1992), pp. 27–31

FRANCESCA PETRUCCI

Nanni di Pietro. *See* GIOVANNI DI PIETRO (ii).

Nanninga, Jaap [Jacob] (*b* Winschoten, 19 Nov 1904; *d* The Hague, 6 Jan 1962). Dutch painter. He studied at the Vrije Academie in Groningen (1929), where he had contact with members of De Ploeg (The Plough). He made a living as a painter–decorator, window-dresser and cartoonist. After travelling in Germany and Poland (1937–8), he moved to The Hague (1938), where he trained at the Academie voor Beeldende Kunsten (1939–44). His first exhibition took place in a private gallery, Les Beaux-Arts, The Hague, in March 1946. At that time his work comprised picturesque scenes in soft colours. He travelled to Paris and the south of France, where he began to appreciate the work of Georges Braque, Marc Chagall, Georges Rouault and Vincent van Gogh. He produced his first abstract canvases from 1948. Initially he painted triangles and circles, but later, influenced by primitive and non-Western art, totems and signs. From 1950 he made spontaneous drawings, in which the influence of Corneille and Karel Appel is evident. He also designed tapestries and stained-glass windows. A retrospective of his work was held at the Gemeentemuseum, The Hague, in 1987.

BIBLIOGRAPHY

E. Slagter: *Jaap Nanninga* (Amsterdam, 1987) [incl. Eng. summary]

JOHN STEEN

Nanpin Shen. *See* SHEN NANPIN.

Nantes. French city at the confluence of the rivers Erdre and Loire, préfecture of Loire–Atlantique, with a population of *c.* 250,000. The capital of the Namnetes was succeeded by Roman Portus Namnetum, where Christianity arrived in the 3rd century AD. Alan II, Count of Brittany (*reg* 937–52), decisively ended Norman attempts to control the city. The first Duke of Brittany, Peter I of Dreux (*reg* 1213–37), pragmatically chose Nantes as his capital, since it was already wealthy from Atlantic trade. The Montfort dukes used art for political as well as cultural ends. The Nantais bourgeoisie, more receptive than Breton aristocrats to the influences of the French and English courts, patronized the arts in order to affirm their status.

The new cathedral of St Pierre and Château des Ducs de Bretagne contributed to the city's 15th-century apotheosis. In 1434 John V (*reg* 1399–1442) laid the first stone of the cathedral. Guillaume de Dammartin's use of the Flamboyant style represents a radical departure from traditional Breton style. The nave was given the illusion of height by the small triforium, the columns rising uninterrupted to the vaults, and the use of white Loire limestone. The façade, with its two towers and three portals, is reminiscent of the English Perpendicular style in its simplicity of line. The 13th-century château was rebuilt from 1466; a formidable defensive work, it was furnished sumptuously in imitation of aristocratic building on both sides of the Channel. The Tour de la Couronne d'Or, with its Italianate loggias, was the work of the cathedral architect Mathelin Rodier (*d* before 1483). Anne of Brittany (*d* 1514), Queen of France, added the Flamboyant Grand-Logis, decorated with granite fleurs-de-lis (symbolizing her marriage to Louis XII), and five ornate dormer windows.

Artists and craftsmen found patronage in Nantes: a school of illuminators is thought to have emigrated there from Paris; English sculptors created the tomb of *John IV of Montfort* (1408), whose effigy resembles that of *Edward the Black Prince* (*d* 1376; Canterbury Cathedral); and more than 15 master goldsmiths were active. Sculpture is represented by the fine funerary monument to *Francis II, 10th Duke of Brittany, and Marguerite of Foix* (marble, 1497–1507; Nantes Cathedral) by Michel Colombe (for illustration *see* COLOMBE, (1)). In 1598 Henry IV (*reg* 1589–1610) signed the Edict of Nantes (revoked 1685) in the city, ending the Wars of Religion and giving Protestants certain rights.

The urban aristocracy supported a wealth of ecclesiastical building: the 15th-century Dominican chapel and convent, the charterhouse (all destr.) and the Baroque Oratorian Chapel (*c.* 1639; now archives). Civil architecture benefited, too, with the first system of grand boulevards, half-timbered houses decorated with carved corner posts and such elaborately decorated hôtels as the Hôtel Aignan (1500) and the Hôtel de Rosmadec (1653; now part of the town hall), which has a massive internal staircase turning around a central space.

Ambitious plans in 1720 translated the city's wealth (based on the slave trade) into Baroque architectural masterpieces. Ornate wrought-iron balconies created an impression of depth on the tall buildings that lined the waterfront and narrow streets. A second campaign—both more grandiose and more austere, inspired by Jean-Louis Graslin (1728–90)—focused on the Neo-classical Grand Théâtre (1788; rest. 1811) and the Palais de la Bourse (1792–1810; partly rebuilt) by MATHURIN CRUCY.

The Gothic Revival influenced the church of St Nicolas (1844–54) by Jean-Baptiste-Antoine Lassus and the completion of the cathedral (1893), even while much of the medieval city was being demolished in the wake of industrial development.

BIBLIOGRAPHY
G. Durville: *Etudes sur vieux Nantes*, 2 vols (Vannes, 1900)
P. Lelièvre: *Nantes au XVIIIe siècle: Urbanisme et architecture* (Nantes, 1942)
M. Le Marié: 'La Construction à Nantes au XVe siècle', *An. Bretagne*, lxviii (1961), pp. 361–402
P. Musset: *Arts et cultures de Bretagne: Un Millénaire* (Paris, 1979)

Nanteuil [Leboeuf], Charles-François (*b* Paris, 9 Aug 1792; *d* Paris, 1 Nov 1865). French sculptor. He studied with Pierre Cartellier at the Ecole des Beaux-Arts, assimilating a classicizing notion of 'ideal beauty' that lasted throughout his career. He won the Prix de Rome in 1817 and in Rome in 1822 carved the marble *Dying Eurydice* (Paris, Louvre), which made a notable début at the Salon of 1824 and later inspired Auguste Clésinger's erotic marble *Woman Bitten by a Snake* (1847; Paris, Mus. d'Orsay). Nanteuil was an accomplished portrait sculptor, producing many busts, including those of the painter *Prud'hon* (marble, 1828; Paris, Louvre) and of his fellow-fighter against Romanticism, the Neo-classical art critic *Quatremère de Quincy* (marble, Salon of 1850; Paris, Inst. France).

Nanteuil regularly received commissions for large-scale sculpture from the State, such as the group *Commerce and Industry* for the Senate in Paris—inspired by the antique sculpture *Castor and Pollux*—or statues for the historical museum of Louis-Philippe at Versailles, such as the seated *Montesquieu* (marble, 1840; Paris, Pal. Luxembourg; plaster, Versailles, Château). Among his commemorative monuments is an impressive statue of *General Desaix* (bronze, 1844; Clermont-Ferrand, Place de Jaude). Under the Second Empirc (1851–70) his increasingly rigorous sculpture helped embellish the Gare du Nord, the Paris Opéra and the rebuilt Louvre.

Nanteuil's most important ecclesiastical commissions were for the pedimental sculpture of Notre-Dame-de-Lorette, Paris (*Homage to the Virgin*, stone, commissioned 1830), and for St Vincent de Paul (*Glorification of St Vincent de Paul*, stone, commissioned 1846). These pediments, decorated with free-standing statues and groups carved from single blocks of stone in the studio, show the influence both of early Renaissance Italian sculpture and of sculptures from Aegina and the Parthenon. Nanteuil was also involved, during the 1840s, in the decoration of the chapel at Dreux built to commemorate Ferdinand-Philippe, Duc d'Orléans, and he carved colossal stone statues of *St Louis* (1843) and *St Philip* (1844) for the principal entrance of the church of the Madeleine, Paris.

BIBLIOGRAPHY
Lami

ISABELLE LEMAISTRE

Nanteuil, Robert (*b* Reims, 1623; *d* Paris, 9 Dec 1678). French engraver, draughtsman and pastellist. He was the son of Lancelot Nanteuil, a wool merchant, and submitted his thesis in philosophy, for which he engraved the headpiece, at the Jesuit College of Reims, in 1645. He went on to work in the studio of Nicolas Regnesson, whose sister he married in 1646, before moving to Paris in 1647. His early work mainly consisted of portrait drawings in black lead on parchment (e.g. Paris, Louvre), and he continued to draw throughout his career. He took

155 of his 221 portraits directly from life. His drawing style was influenced by Philippe de Champaigne, and he based his engraving technique on the work of Claude Mellan and Jean Morin. By 1652 he had developed his own technique (*see* ENGRAVING, §II, 4), and his engraving of *Cardinal Mazarin* of that year gained him official recognition (for illustration *see* MAZARIN, (1)). The size of his engravings increased, and after 1664 he produced mainly life-size heads. In 1658 he was appointed Dessinateur et Graveur Ordinaire du Roi.

Nanteuil's best work dates from the years immediately after 1657, when his subjects included royalty as well as high-ranking members of society. He engraved 11 portraits of *Louis XIV* and many plates of *Mazarin, Michel le Tellier* and *Jean-Baptiste Colbert*. Through his campaigning engravers received in 1660 the Edict of St Jean-de-Luz, which raised engraving to the status of a liberal art in France. His philosophical education is apparent in the *Maximes et réflexions* preserved by his only pupil Domenico Tempesti: 'time and trouble do not make fine works of art so much as a good disposition and intelligence' is typical. It was always his aim to capture the character of his subject; one of his most searching engraved portraits is of *Simon Arnauld, Marquis de Pomponne* (see fig.). Nanteuil's style dominated French portrait engraving until the end of the 18th century. Most of his portraits are set in a simple oval resting on an architectural plinth. Accessories are almost eliminated and costume invariably simple, so that nothing can distract from the facial character. Nanteuil's complete mastery of the burin led him away from extravagant effects, and he tried to make his subjects appear tranquil and highminded; he liked to talk to them amusingly in his studio. His finest works include his

Robert Nanteuil: *Simon Arnauld, Marquis de Pomponne*, engraving, 510×429 mm, 1675 (Paris, Bibliothèque Nationale)

portraits of *François Lotin, Seigneur de Charny* (1657; after Florent Le Comte), *Jean Loret* and *Claude Regnauldin, Seigneur de Béru* (both 1658) and *François de la Mothe le Vayer* (1661). In addition to his skills as a portrait engraver, he was the most accomplished pastellist of the 18th century in France, bringing the art to a high degree of refinement in such portraits as those of *Jean Dorieu* (1660) and *Dominique de Ligny* (both Paris, Louvre).

BIBLIOGRAPHY
C. Petitjean and C. Wickert: *Catalogue de l'oeuvre gravé de Robert Nanteuil* (Paris, 1925)
Y. Fromrich: 'Robert Nanteuil, dessinateur', *Gaz. B.-A.*, n.s. 4, xlix (1957), p. 209
J. M. PINKERTON

Nanto. *See* NARA.

Nanto, Francesco de [da] (*fl c.* 1520–32). Italian woodcutter. He was active in the Venice area, but his origins in the Savoy are indicated by the signature FRANCISCVS/DE NANTO/DE SABAVDIA on the print of the *Healing of the Gouty Man* (London, BM). Stylistic comparisons suggest a date between 1520 and 1525 for a series of 13 woodcuts of scenes from the *Life of Christ* (London, BM), taken from designs by Girolamo da Treviso the younger. A few other prints by him are known, after works by Amico Aspertini and Francesco Francia. The frame decorated with grotesques and allegorical motifs, signed DE NANTO, in the edition of Ludovico Ariosto's *Orlando furioso* published in Ferrara in 1532 by Francesco Rosso da Valenza indicates his activity in book production. This frame is used for the title-page and again for the portrait of *Ariosto*, reputedly based on a design by Titian. The portrait itself was once considered to be the work of de Nanto, but it does not show the traces of wormholes that are apparent in the frame, which has led to the suggestion (see exh. cat.) that it may have been cut after the frame. The elegant and refined technique of the portrait also contrasts strongly with de Nanto's sometimes harsh and irregular manner.

BIBLIOGRAPHY
F. Zava Boccazzi: 'Tracce per Girolamo da Treviso il Giovane in alcune xilografie di Francesco de Nanto', *A. Ven.*, xii (1958), pp. 70–78
N. Nanni: 'Uno xilografo italiano del cinquecento: Francesco da Nanto', *Rass. Graf.*, 118 (1963), pp. 24ff
Tiziano e la silografia veneziana del cinquecento (exh. cat. by M. Muraro and D. Rosand, Venice, Fond. Cini; Washington, DC, N.G.A.; 1976–7), pp. 84, 109, 117
FELICIANO BENVENUTI

Nanyue [Nan-yüeh]. Independent Chinese state established in modern Guangdong Province at the end of the Qin period (221–206 BC). It was absorbed into the Han empire (206 BC–AD 220) in 111 BC. The tomb of King Zhao Mo (*d c.* 122 BC) was discovered in Guangzhou (Canton) in 1983. It comprises seven chambers cut into a natural hill and lined with stone slabs on which traces of murals survive. The undisturbed tomb was richly furnished with jades, bronzes, ceramics and iron objects; traces of lacquerwares and textiles were also found. Most of the pieces were imported from metropolitan centres of northern China or fashioned in imitation of imported models, reflecting Zhao Mo's cultural and political aspirations and providing evidence of the flourishing trade in luxury items between northern and southern China. The most remarkable finds are the jades, including the first example of a complete jade 'suit', in which Zhao Mo's body was encased (for illustration of another Han-period jade burial suit *see* MANCHENG), as well as plaques, pendants, sword fittings and a number of rare vessels, in all comprising the most important group of Han jades known. The suit is made of small pieces of nephrite backed with hemp cloth and sewn together with silk thread. The presence of many jade *bi* (perforated discs), including one inset into the suit, attests to their importance in funerary rituals. The most spectacular of the jade plaques is a *tao tie* monster mask with a ring handle and a reticulated asymmetrical pendant incorporating a phoenix standing on a *bi*. The position of many of the pendants shows that they were originally strung together to form elaborate pectorals, often incorporating a variety of forms and materials: openwork *bi* with dragons and phoenixes, *huang* arcs, small gold figurines and beads, jade, black amber and glass. The jade vessels include an unprecedented rhyton with relief and intaglio decoration, a box and cover, and a tall beaker set into a bronze basin with gold and silver mounts. While the majority of the jades are probably imports, the jade suit may have been made locally (*see* CHINA, §VIII, 1). The large number of sword fittings, some of which are mounted on to iron swords placed in Zhao Mo's coffin, include some executed in high relief with sinuous, convoluted dragons reminiscent of Chu wood-carving (*see* CHINA, §XIII, 26). This mastery of three-dimensional representation indicates an advance on the two-dimensional work of the preceding Shang and Zhou periods.

The bronze, gold and silver objects can be divided into imported and local types. A gilt bronze *hu* and two *fang* (a square version of the *hu*) are vessel types known from the Chu tradition, while gold, silver and turquoise-inlaid weapons and belthooks also follow closely styles current in the traditional centres. Chimes of shanked bells (*yong zhong*) and bells with a central loop (*niu zhong*; *see* CHINA, §VI, 1(ii)) attest to the Nanyue's retention of Eastern Zhou (771–256 BC) musical and ritual objects after their demise further north. On the other hand, a number of gold and jade seals, one inscribed with Zhao Mo's self-proclaimed imperial title, show that this new symbol of political authority had been adopted in Nanyue. Other exotic objects include a set of leaf-shaped gold plaques decorated in steppe style and a silver-gilt repoussé box and cover of Iranian manufacture. An impressive chime of bells with upward-facing mouths known as *gou diao*, on the other hand, are characteristic Yue products, as are large, slim-legged *ding* tripods with dished mouth-rims, and straight-sided wine buckets. The ceramics, mainly unglazed and decorated with incised, impressed or rouletted patterns, are clearly also of local manufacture.

BIBLIOGRAPHY
'Xi Han Nanyue wang mu fajue chubu baogao' [Preliminary report on the excavation of a royal tomb of the Nanyue kingdom of the Western Han dynasty at Guangzhou], *Kaogu* (1984), no. 3, pp. 222–30, pls 1–4
P. Swart: 'The Tomb of the King of Nan Yue', *Orientations*, xxi/6 (1990), pp. 56–66
Xi Han Nanyue wang mu [Nanyue king's tomb of the Western Han], 2 vols (Beijing, 1991)

Jades from the Tomb of the King of Nanyue/Nanyue wang mu yuqi (exh. cat., Hong Kong, Chin. U., A.G., 1991)

COLIN MACKENZIE

Nan-yüeh. *See* NANYUE.

Naogram. *See* RANIGAT.

Naong. *See* YI CHŎNG (ii).

Naonobu. *See* KANŌ, (12).

Naophorous statue. *See* EGYPT, ANCIENT, §IX, 2(i)(h).

Naos. Term for the architectural core or sanctuary of a building. In ancient Greek architecture it refers to the cella or main sanctuary of a temple, while in Byzantine architecture it is used for that area of a centrally planned church that is reserved for the performance of the liturgy.

Naotake Odano. *See* ODANO NAOTAKE.

Năpăruş, Georgeta (*b* Comarnic, 23 Oct 1930). Romanian painter. She studied painting at the Institute of Fine Arts 'Nicolae Grigorescu' in Bucharest (1951–7) and subsequently took part in many exhibitions in Romania and abroad. Her formative years coincided with the freeing of Romanian painting from the restrictions of Socialist Realism and a corresponding absorption of trends in European art that had been ignored since World War II. In 1964–6 Năpăruş became familiar with the work of Picasso, Klee and the Surrealists, as reflected in her modifications of the figure in such works as *Women in Comarnic* (1967; Bucharest, Mus. A.). While she continued to work with the figure, the hieratic poses and rich patterns of folk art and Arabic arts influenced her painting after 1970 (e.g. *Textile Workers*, 1979; Ploieşti, Mus. A.). Unlike other artists of her generation she did not disdain everyday reality in her work but subjected it to metamorphoses and transformations, sometimes with simulated and colourful naivety but in a process always controlled by a sophisticated intelligence and humour.

BIBLIOGRAPHY

I. Frunzetti: 'Georgeta Năpăruş: Logica legendei şi basmului' [Georgeta Năpăruş: the logic of legend and fairy tale], *Romania Lit.* (14 Oct 1971)

Georgeta Năpăruş (exh. cat. by N. Cassian, Oradea, Crişana Mus., 1976)

R. Bogdan: *Georgeta Năpăruş* (Bucharest, 1983)

IOANA VLASIU

Napata. Site in Dongola Province, Sudan, that was an early capital and religious centre of Kush *c.* 1440 BC–*c.* AD 300 (*see* NUBIA, §IV, 1–3). Napata was established in the mid-15th century BC as the southernmost limit of Egyptian imperial rule. The site consists of the town of Napata itself and a nearby mountain, now called Gebel Barkal, where temples of the Theban god Amun were built. By the 8th century BC Napata had become the capital of an independent Kushite kingdom and the seat of a local monarchy (modelled on that in Egypt), which conquered Egypt *c.* 715 BC and established itself as Egypt's 25th Dynasty (*c.* 750–*c.* 656 BC). Expelled from Egypt by Assyria in 664 BC, the Kushites retreated to Napata and there maintained an Egyptian court in exile until 591 BC, when an Egyptian army of the 26th Dynasty King, Psammetichus II (*reg* 595–589 BC), invaded Kush and ravaged the city. Henceforth the political axis of Kush moved southwards to MEROE, but Napata remained the site of the royal coronations and burials until the early 3rd century BC. In the 1st century BC Napata again became a royal residence, only to be destroyed in 23 BC by a Roman army. Two or three decades later it was restored by the Meroitic King Natakamani, and it seems to have flourished until the end of the Meroitic kingdom in the 4th century AD.

The main settlement of Napata, still unexcavated, probably sprawled along the bank of the Nile immediately to the south of Gebel Barkal. Excavations at the edge of the cultivation, by F. Donadoni of the University of Rome (1972–7), revealed an area of private houses as well as two temples of the Meroitic period (*c.* 300 BC–*c.* AD 360). Other sites associated with the city extend 15 km upstream and downstream on both banks. One important settlement, with a cemetery, a Temple of Amon-Re and a royal treasury, was excavated by F. Griffith (1912–13) at Sanam. The finds (including sculpture, metal and faience objects and jewellery), primarily dating to the 25th Dynasty and Napatan period, are in the Ashmolean Museum, Oxford, and the National Museum, Khartoum.

From 1916 to 1920 G. Reisner cleared the Gebel Barkal temples and recovered many sculptures and inscribed monuments dating from the New Kingdom to the late Meroitic period, including ten large Kushite royal statues (Khartoum, N. Mus.; Boston, MA, Mus. F.A.; Richmond, VA Mus. F.A.; Toledo, OH, Mus. A.). Other important stelae and statues found at Gebel Barkal in the 19th century are at the Egyptian Museum, Cairo, the Louvre, Paris, the British Museum, London, and the Bodemuseum, Berlin. The three royal cemeteries of Napata (el-Kurru, Nuri and Gebel Barkal), also cleared by the Reisner expedition, contained an unbroken line of Kushite royal burials from the 9th to the 3rd century BC, with some at Gebel Barkal dating to the 2nd and 1st centuries BC. These pyramid tombs contained a great diversity of funerary material, including gold foil and coloured stone inlays from decayed wooden coffins, two large granite sarcophagi, thousands of carved *shabti* figures, stone and metal vessels, gold, silver and faience jewellery and amulets (Khartoum, N. Mus.; Boston, MA, Mus. F.A.). In 1978 the Donadoni expedition began work near the Gebel Barkal temples, clearing a Meroitic palace, dating to the late 1st century AD. In 1986 this team was joined by an expedition led by Timothy Kendall from the Museum of Fine Arts, Boston, recording all the preserved reliefs in the Gebel Barkal temples.

BIBLIOGRAPHY

LÄ: 'Gebel Barkal', 'Napata'

D. Dunham: *The Royal Cemeteries of Kush*, 4 vols (Boston, 1950–57)

——: *The Barkal Temples* (Boston, 1970)

Orientalia, xliii– (1974–) [preliminary excavation report from Gebel Barkal by J. Leclant]

N. Geog., clxxviii (Nov 1990), pp. 90–125

For further bibliography *see* NUBIA, §§I and IV, 1–3.

TIMOTHY KENDALL

Napier. New Zealand city on the east coast of North Island, famous for its Art Deco architecture. Napier was established in the 1840s with the arrival of missionary and trading settlers, and by the 1920s, with a population of 16,000, it was the main administrative centre and port of Hawke's Bay province, with a reputation as a resort due to its attractive seaside location, spectacular hilltop residential areas and Mediterranean climate. On 3 February 1931 a violent earthquake measuring 7.9 on the Richter scale convulsed the region, destroying all but recently built reinforced concrete buildings in the city centre. Fires broke out and completed the devastation.

The city was rebuilt in 1932–3, following a building moratorium while plans for the new Napier were considered. All services were placed underground, street corners splayed and standard verandah heights set for commercial buildings. The restriction on building heights to two storeys and the use of reinforced concrete for safety reasons resulted in a townscape remarkably cohesive in scale and materials. Because the collapse of ornate embellishments on Victorian and Edwardian buildings had caused many of the 162 deaths and countless injuries in the city, the new buildings were designed in simple but, for a small isolated city, radically modern styles (see fig.). The four local architectural practices formed a loose association to share resources and bring a unity of purpose to the task of rebuilding, although each firm tended to prefer a particular style. Finch & Westerholm preferred the Spanish Mission Revival, Natusch & Sons designed

the simplest buildings, E. A. Williams created the best of the Art Deco designs, and the work of Louis Hay (1881–1948) was inspired by that of Frank Lloyd Wright illustrated in the Wasmuth Folio (Berlin, 1910). Later, borough architect J. T. Watson (1882–1960) designed in the Art Deco and stripped classical styles. The offices of national companies were usually designed by architects from Wellington.

The architecture of Napier is enhanced by the city's beautiful setting, its straightforward topography and an unusually favourable relationship with the sea. The foreshore was landscaped in fine 1930s style over earthquake rubble, and once the rebuilding of the commercial area had been completed in 1934, architectural features were added to the seafront, creating a promenade for which Napier had become renowned by the end of the decade. Few buildings were demolished or substantially altered before 1980, but a nationwide building boom in the early 1980s resulted in some losses. This eventually spurred a small group of citizens, who later established the Art Deco Trust, to begin in 1985 to publicize the aesthetic and historical importance of the city, as well as its potential for tourism. With the support of the Hawke's Bay Museum, the regional museum of art and history, the Art Deco Trust inspired a revival of civic pride in Napier's architecture, encouraged by increasing tourist and media interest.

Napier, Dalton Street, showing (from left to right) Kidson's Building (1933), Dalton Chambers (1933), Hotel Central (1932), Napier Building (1932) and Public Trust Office (1922); from a photograph of 1933 (Napier, Hawke's Bay Museum)

The city in turn introduced planning ordinances that encourage preservation and refurbishment.

BIBLIOGRAPHY
Napier: The City Beautiful (Napier, 1933)
G. Conly: *The Shock of '31* (Auckland, 1980)
H. Ives: *The Art Deco Architecture of Napier* (Wellington, 1982)
P. Shaw and P. Hallett: *Art Deco Napier: Styles of the Thirties* (Auckland, 1987)
R. McGregor: *The Great Quake* (Napier, 1989)

ROBERT MCGREGOR

Naples [Napoli]. Italian city. The largest and most important city in South Italy, Naples is situated on the Bay of Naples, overlooking the Tyrrhenian Sea, to the west of Mt Vesuvius. It has had a varied and lively history, starting as a Greek colony and being ruled by the Romans, the Norman kings of Sicily, the Ghibelline house of Hohenstaufen, the Angevins, the house of Aragon, the French, the Spaniards and the Bourbons, until becoming part of united Italy in 1860. In art Naples is most famous for its exuberant Baroque paintings, sculpture and buildings of the 17th–18th centuries. Despite rapid industrialization after World War II, the city is still relatively poor, hugely overcrowded and the victim of social and environmental problems.

I. History and urban development. II. Art life and organization. III. Centre of production. IV. Buildings.

I. History and urban development.

1. Before AD 552. 2. AD 552–1442. 3. 1443–*c.* 1600. 4. *c.* 1600–*c.* 1880. 5. *c.* 1880 and after.

1. BEFORE AD 552. Naples began as a Greek settlement. When the Greek colony of Cumae reached its optimum size in the mid-6th century BC the residents established a new settlement to the south. Known either as Parthenope in honour of the siren or as Palaiopolis (Gr.: 'the old city'), this settlement on the Bay of Naples was encompassed by a protective tufa wall. When more immigrants arrived in the mid-5th century BC they established Neapolis ('the new city') to the north-east; Palaiopolis became a mere suburb. The new city had a Hippodamean grid (*see* HIPPODAMOS) with narrow rectangular blocks within an irregularly shaped city wall. Three broad streets (*decumani*) ran east–west, crossed by *c.* 20 narrower north–south streets. With an excellent harbour Neapolis assumed a leading role among the colonies of South Italy. The Greek town covered approximately 60 ha and had a population of *c.* 30,000. Only a few traces of Greek houses, temples and burials have been discovered under the modern city. In 326 BC the Romans occupied Palaiopolis; Neapolis surrendered without resistance and became a favoured ally of Rome. Hellenic influence remained strong: Greek was commonly spoken, and the city boasted a Greek-style gymnasium erected in the Augustan age (27 BC–AD 14). Most notable of the few Roman urban buildings visible today is the Temple to the Dioscuri, erected under Tiberius (*reg* AD 14–37) and clearly evident within the later church of S Paolo Maggiore. Wealthy citizens from Rome spent winters in the pleasant environment of Naples. The surrounding areas boasts hundreds of villas, including that of L. Licinius Lucullus with its famous fishponds in the area of Palaiopolis. In

AD 79 the eruption of Vesuvius damaged the town. Soon after, Rome settled a contingent of veterans on the site and awarded Neapolis the title and benefits of a Roman colony. The Imperial city spread over 100 ha with a population of *c.* 35,000. During the late Empire repeated barbarian onslaughts compelled the residents to strengthen the city walls. In AD 552 Neapolis came under Byzantine suzerainty. Ancient art and archaeological material from the area are on display in the grand Museo Archeologico Nazionale.

BIBLIOGRAPHY
M. Napoli: *Napoli greco-romana* (Naples, 1959)
A. G. McKay: *Naples and Campania* (Exeter, NH, 1962)
J. D'Arms: *Romans on the Bay of Naples* (Cambridge, MA, 1970)
C. De Seta: *Storia della città di Napoli* (Rome and Bari, 1973)
S. De Caro and A. Greco: *Campania*, Guide archeologiche Laterza (Bari, 1981)

DIANE FAVRO

2. AD 552–1442. Naples was the seat of a Byzantine duchy from 554 to 1139. The urban centres were the fortified ducal palace and the bishop's residence, which was established in Early Christian times around an arcaded courtyard, on to which looked the 4th-century basilica of S Restituta (now part of the cathedral), with the baptistery of S Giovanni attached, and the basilica of La Stefania (destr.). The main nucleus of the Byzantine community was concentrated in the upper region in the north-east, while the town's expansion continued within the city walls, which had been restored (440) under Valentinianus III. There is evidence of the walls being lengthened and restored, but the total extent of this work is uncertain. During the 10th century sizeable population growth, arising from peace with the Lombards and the Arabs, led to a revival of trade and manufacturing. This resulted in the construction of appropriate new defence structures, the modernization of port facilities and the emergence of small, built-up urban nuclei. From the 10th to the 12th century the ducal city had a high concentration of urban churches (e.g. S Aspreno, with its marble iconostasis) and monasteries, which regulated the activity of farmers in the surrounding countryside. The principal churches outside the town included SS Severino e Sossio, founded by Bishop Calvo of Naples between 748 and 761 (enlarged 1494–1561), and the Early Christian basilica of S Gennaro, where a Benedictine monastery was founded in the mid-9th century. The proto-Romanesque bell-tower of the 5th-century church of S Maria Maggiore (rebuilt 17th century) is the only surviving example of Neapolitan architecture from the 6th to the 12th centuries.

The extraordinary development of Naples in the Angevin period (1266–1442) continued some of the initiatives made by the Norman Hauteville dynasty and the Swabian kings (1139–94 and 1194–1266 respectively), which were dictated by strategic necessities, but which nevertheless opened the city to its hinterland and created a new upsurge of building development out towards the plain. After the conquest of the Duchy of Naples by King Roger II of Sicily in 1139, one of the first Norman works undertaken was the Castel Capuano (*c.* 1165), built by William I (*reg* 1154–66) to replace a Byzantine fort on the edge of the plain to the west of the city. It was completed by Emperor Frederick II (*reg* 1194–1250), and since 1540 it has been the Court of Justice. The other was the occupation of the islet of Salvatore, previously inhabited by a monastic community, which was transferred to Naples to allow the construction of Castel dell'Ovo, a fortified stronghold built on the foundations of the Roman villa of L. Licinius Lucullus, where the court was installed before it moved to the royal residence of Castel Capuano. With these fortresses the Normans established two points of surveillance, one facing the hinterland and the other looking out to sea, working together in a defensive system based on strongpoints around the city at Pozzuoli, Aversa, Acerra and Afragola. Due to tensions between Norman and Swabian dynasties and the papacy, little religious architecture was built in Naples in the 12th and 13th centuries. However, the rebuilt church of S Giovanni a Mare, and the hospital of the Knights of St John of Jerusalem beside it, were both constructed during the Norman period. Under Emperor Frederick II, Naples regained its position as a major city (*see* HOHENSTAUFEN, (2)). He founded the University of Naples in 1224, which helped to reconfirm the city's cultural status.

With the succession of the Angevins in 1266, Naples was the capital of a great kingdom, and there are records of a further increase in the population: in 1278 there were nearly 30,000 inhabitants. Under Charles I (*reg* 1266–85) Castel Capuano was restored, and the southern stretch of city walls was enlarged, while Castel dell'Ovo was transformed into a public building and became the seat of the Treasury. Between 1279 and 1283 construction work began on a new royal palace: Castelnuovo (see fig. 1 and §IV, 4 below). The strong tie between the Angevins and the papacy paved the way for a religious revival. S Lorenzo Maggiore (*see* §IV, 2 below) was built during the reign of Charles I, and incorporated the Early Christian church erected on the Roman basilica. The complete reconstruction of the cathedral, which continued for many years, was initiated in 1294 on the site of La Stefania. The old city centre increasingly assumed the character of a religious, conventual area, while the commercial and governmental district moved to the surroundings of Castelnuovo. Under kings Charles II and Robert (*see* ANJOU §I(1) and (2)) the enlargement of the western walls continued, as did a vast programme of public works: streets, manufacturing businesses, harbour works (from 1302), a market-place and exchanges. During the 14th century a number of important

Gothic churches were started, including S Maria Donna Regina (1307–20), S Eligio Maggiore, S Chiara (1313–40; built at the wish of Queen Sancha), S Domenico Maggiore (1289–1324) and S Pietro a Maiella. The Certosa di S Martino (*see* §IV, 3 below) was founded in 1325. A seaquake in 1343 did not damage the city, but it necessitated repairs to the harbour structures, which were carried out in 1347. Between 1348 and 1411 repeated plague epidemics led to a decline in public investment in urban planning and development. Furthermore, Naples and its strongholds suffered immense damage in the course of dynastic struggles between the Angevins and Aragonese, resulting in a lengthy siege that ended in 1442 with the city's capitulation to Alfonso I (*see* ARAGON, (2)).

BIBLIOGRAPHY

G. M. Fusco: *Riflessioni sulla topografia della città di Napoli nel medio evo* (Naples, 1865)
B. Capasso: *Topografia della città di Napoli nell'XI secolo* (Naples, 1895)
M. Schipa: *Storia del ducato napolitano* (Naples, 1895)
G. Russo: *Napoli come città* (Naples, 1966)
L. Santoro: *Le mura di Napoli* (Rome, 1984)

ROBERTO CORONEO

3. 1443–*c.* 1600. Naples recovered quickly from the siege of 1442 to become the principal Aragonese military and commercial power in the Mediterranean. Between 1443 and 1458 Alfonso I rebuilt Castelnuovo to repair damage and to meet new military requirements, thus creating the actual and symbolic highpoint of Renaissance Naples. An earthquake in 1450 devastated the old centre of the city, but the reconstruction of the harbour areas and the restoration of the Castel dell'Ovo were complete by the time of Alfonso's death in 1458. Naples was already substantially the city that in 1464 was to be depicted in the Tavola Strozzi (see fig. 1).

Alfonso's successor King Ferdinand I and his son Alfonso, Duke of Calabria (later King Alfonso II), further strengthened the city's defences with a modern system of wall construction. Under Alfonso's supervision, two major extensions were effected. In the first (1484) the whole eastern range was moved forwards from the Castello del Carmine (formerly Forte dello Sperona) to Porta S Gennaro, involving the construction of 22 round towers. Alfonso also commissioned the court architect, Giuliano da Maiano, to construct a large triumphal arch (1484; see

1. Naples, the Tavola Strozzi, showing the Old City and Castelnuovo, panel, 1464 (Naples, Museo e Gallerie Nazionali di Capodimonte)

2. Naples, Porta Capuana, by Giuliano da Maiano, 1484; from a 19th-century photograph

fig. 2) for the Porta Capuana. The second extension (1499–1501) ran from the Porta Reale (now Piazza del Gesù) part of the way down the present Via Toledo and ended at Castelnuovo. Areas of the Greco-Roman city were also redeveloped, and restorations were made to the fabric of the city that had been damaged during the Angevin–Durazzo wars, filling the old centre with magnificent residences in a Catalan Durazzo-Renaissance style (e.g. Palazzo Carafa Santangelo, 1466; the portal of Palazzo Bonifacio at Porta Nuova, early 15th century; rusticated façade of Palazzo Sanseverino, begun 1470, remodelled 1584–1601, now the Gesù Nuovo).

Many Neapolitan buildings from the late 15th century demonstrate an influx of Tuscan influences, due mainly to the intensification of political and cultural ties between the Kingdom of Naples and Florence. Tuscan styles later permeated the city's whole artistic output of the early 16th century, even after the Kingdom of Naples passed under Spanish imperial dominion (1504). This can be seen in the Palazzo Cuomo (begun 1466), designed probably by Giuliano da Maiano on Florentine lines; again at Palazzo Orsini di Gravina (begun 1513) by Neapolitan craftsmen; and even at the Pontano chapel (1492), or the cathedral crypt (1497–1506) by Tommaso Malvito. Alfonso built a number of royal villas on the outskirts of Naples, including one at Poggio Reale (from 1487; destr. late 18th century) to designs by Giuliano da Maiano, and La Duchesca (destr. ?16th century), which was a casino built in the gardens of the Castel Capuano.

The arrival of the Spaniards in Naples brought the greatest expansion of the urban fabric before the 19th century. They governed under a system of viceroys. The Viceroy Don Pedro Alvarez de Toledo, Marqués de Villafranca (reg 1532–53), created a new road, the Via Toledo, which connected the area of Porta Reale (now Piazza Dante) and the open space around Castelnuovo. He also planned the layout of the Spanish Quarter, where troops and administrative personnel were accommodated. Thus the directional centre of the city was created, between the Collina di Pizzofalcone, the later Palazzo Reale, Castelnuovo and the Aragonese port, all of which were defended by the new star-shaped ramparts of the fortress of Sant'Elmo (1537–46). Under Don Pedro Naples became the western fulcrum of the Mediterranean military politics of imperial Spain, and it was transformed into a great administrative capital, characterized by high urban density due to the influx of immigrants from the provinces.

The ever increasing presence of the religious orders in the social life of the metropolis led to the expansion or foundation of dozens of monastic complexes, mostly situated near the Greco-Roman *polis*, a trend that continued throughout the 17th century (*see* §4 below). It was during this time that such complexes as S Gregorio Armeno, S Maria di Montevergine, S Caterina at Formiello and many others were enlarged, and they continued to be extended until the early 18th century. At the same time the Neapolitan aristocracy were producing buildings that were manifestly influenced by Tuscan styles (e.g. Palazzo Marigliano, *c.* 1512; Palazzo del Panormita, late 16th century). Neapolitan Baroque, however, characterized the reconstructions of such palaces as the Carafa di Maddaloni in Via Toledo, Palazzo del Pio Monte della Misericordia and many other noble residences in the old city centre.

BIBLIOGRAPHY

N. Cortese: *Cultura e politica a Napoli dal cinquecento al settecento* (Naples, 1965)

G. L. Hersey: *Alfonso II and the Artistic Renewal of Naples, 1485–95* (New Haven and London, 1969)

A. Ryder: *The Kingdom of Naples under Alfonso the Magnificent* (Oxford, 1976)

4. *c.* 1600–*c.* 1880. Naples was, in this period, one of the capitals of modern Europe, initially the principal city of the most important satellite kingdom of the Spanish crown (1504–1707), then of the Habsburg Empire (1707–34), next an independent kingdom under the Bourbon dynasty (1734–99), then the Bonaparte family, until the Unification of Italy in 1860 removed its independence.

Naples continued to be governed under a system of viceroys in the 17th century, and in their dual capacity of principal public patrons and private collectors these viceroys contributed in varying degrees to the urban and cultural significance of the city. Their role was at times of fundamental importance; significant viceroys included Manuel de Acevedo y Zúñiga, 6th Conde de MONTERREY (*reg* 1631–7), and the Duque de Medina da las Torres (*reg* 1637–44), who exported large numbers of Neapolitan paintings to the palace of El Buen Retiro, near Madrid. A later viceroy, the 7th Marqués del Carpio (*reg* 1682–7), was also an influential collector and patron, and he too shipped many works back to Spain. The Austrian viceroys who succeeded these men continued their system of patronage and development. As public patrons, the viceroys employed a number of court engineers and architects. The most important royal building scheme of the early 17th century was the completion of the Palazzo Reale (1600–02) by Domenico Fontana and his son Giulio Cesare Fontana (*fl* 1593–1627) at the centre of the city.

No further extensions to the city walls were undertaken, but new suburbs continued to spread beyond the city gates throughout the 17th and 18th centuries. It is generally impossible, however, to link the progress of the great artistic commissions, the construction of the great religious establishments and even the building projects of the nobility and royalty in Naples to the general economic situation, which fluctuated constantly at this time. The realization of Neapolitan Baroque works of art benefited from time to time from funds received through the devotion of the public, from generous legacies or through revenues from heavy taxation. One building programme that can, however, be directly related to the rise in economic fortunes eventually found its expression in the grand projects instigated by Charles III (*reg* 1734–59),

subsequently pursued, albeit with ever decreasing vigour, by his son Ferdinand I (*reg* 1759–1825).

There was, however, a significant link between the major building and planning developments and earthquakes. There was invariably a flurry of building activity in the wake of frequent earthquakes in Naples, which also affected other centres in the region. The majority of the works carried out consisted of rebuilding schemes, which demonstrated an awareness of the historic significance of those buildings that were restored rather than pulled down. Under such circumstances Baroque architects, decorators and painters had to tackle the problem of restoring architecture in the 'old-fashioned manner', using stucco decoration, which maintained the general characteristics of buildings while still conforming to the dictates of contemporary fashion.

Naples had a tight network of religious communities within the city centre, and many of these groups were important patrons. The available census material records 92 convents in Naples in 1585, with over 3700 residents. After the plague of 1656 there were 304 churches, 33 convent schools and 11 hospitals with *c.* 4600 members of various orders. By the end of the 17th century there were 104 monasteries and 40 convents. Between parish churches, confraternities, monasteries, charitable institutions and hospitals, according to contemporary guidebooks, the number of churches had risen to 504, while in 1742 the population of religious personnel in Naples totalled almost 15,000. It was during this phase that intellectuals referred to Naples as a 'New Oxyrhynchus', after the ancient Egyptian city populated by 20,000 monks and 20,000 nuns. This massive religious presence had a formative effect on the social, political and cultural aspects of Neapolitan life as well as on its customs during the 17th and 18th centuries. The most important religious building scheme was the continuation and completion of the Certosa di S Martino, which provided commissions for artists from all over Italy as well as local Neapolitans. Other notable churches included two by GIOVANNI GIACOMO DI CONFORTO, S Teresa degli Studi (1603–12) and S Agostino degli Scalzi (1612–30); and S Giorgio dei Genovesi (completed 1620) by Bartolomeo Picchiati.

In the 17th and 18th centuries there was an increasing migration of the nobility towards Naples because of the patronage awarded by the court. A so-called 'City of Barons' was created, its 16th-century residences in a state of continual change, often bought and sold by nobles old and new. Even if it never reached the pervasiveness and extent of its religious counterpart, secular architecture was nevertheless the other major factor in Neapolitan urban development. The influx of nobles transformed the city, which experienced a proliferation of craft activities related to the luxurious embellishment of the noble palaces. Despite this, examples of newly built 17th- and 18th-century palaces are relatively few: it was common practice to refurbish earlier buildings, usually slowly and often without preserving the integrity of formal expression. Furthermore, building activities tended to be heavily concentrated in certain quarters of the city, moving outwards from the old centre towards Via Toledo and the Collina di Pizzofalcone and finally, during the 18th century, towards the Chiaia Quarter. This process did not favour

Como. The chapel, its attendant sculpture and its wall decoration mark a highpoint of Renaissance style in Naples. In painting the city also saw a shift from the Late Gothic and Flemish work of the Neapolitan Niccolò Colantonio to that of Antonio Solario and his student Andrea da Salerno (*c.* 1490–1530) in the Venetian style, seen in such works as Solario's cycle of 20 scenes from the *Life of St Benedict* (*c.* 1515; now in Naples, Archv Stato) in the cloister of SS Severino e Sosio.

After the Spanish conquest in 1506, the city's ports, walls and infrastructure were greatly expanded and modernized to fit its new status as a southern capital of the Habsburg empire. Throughout the 16th century one development that went hand-in-hand with new imperial patronage and the Late Renaissance style was the emergence of southern Italian and native Neapolitan artists who worked for both foreign masters and the native nobility. This coincided with the patronage of such new and reformed religious orders as the Theatines, Oratorian Fathers and Jesuits, as the Counter-Reformation sought to match the austerity of Protestant reform with a new sensuality of colour, material and form that well fitted the sensibilities of the south. Examples of the collaboration between northerners and regional artists include Malvito's designs and Giovanni Marigliano's sculpture (1517) in the Caracciolo Chapel (S Giovanni a Carbonara). The sculpture of such Spanish artists as Bartolomé Ordoñez, who carved the marble altarpiece in the Caracciolo Chapel, helped to create a Neapolitan art that mirrored the cosmopolitan nature of its political rule and patronage. Yet this very hybridization of artistic currents led to something of a decline in Neapolitan arts at the end of the 16th century as reform turned into the formulae of Mannerism and orthodoxy into a reliance upon often archaizing trends. The arrival in Naples of the sculptor Pietro Bernini (*c.* 1584), the painter Caravaggio (1606) and the architect COSIMO FANZAGO (1608) coincided with Domenico Fontana's completion of the massive Palazzo Reale in 1602. These all served to consolidate the end of the Renaissance impulse and to give fresh impetus to the Baroque.

BIBLIOGRAPHY

R. Pane: *Architettura dell'età barocca in Napoli* (Naples, 1939)
P. Causa: *Pittura napoletana dal XV al XIX secolo* (Bergamo, 1957)
N. Cortese: *Cultura e politica a Napoli dal cinque al settecento* (Naples, 1965)
G. L. H. Hersey: *Renewal of Naples, 1485–1495* (New Haven and London, 1969)
A. Blunt: *Neapolitan and Baroque Architecture* (London, 1975)
G. d'Agostino: *La capitale ambigua: Napoli dal 1458 al 1580* (Naples, 1979)
J. H. Bentley: *Politics and Culture in Renaissance Naples* (Princeton, NJ, 1987)
A. Ryder: *Alfonso the Magnanimous, King of Aragon, Naples and Sicily, 1396–1458* (Oxford and New York, 1990)

RONALD G. MUSTO

3. *c.* 1600–*c.* 1700. Although Neapolitan art in this period was heavily influenced by Spanish forms imported by the Spanish rulers, it also absorbed a wide variety of styles and ideas, managing to express an individual style of its own. The artistic movements of the Counter-Reformation are best represented in Naples by two Florentines active in the city from the late 16th century: Pietro Bernini and Michelangelo Naccherino. They were

6. Naples, church of Monteoliveto, Piccolomini Chapel, carved altarpiece of the *Nativity* (1475), by Antonio Rossellino

active principally in the field of portraiture and monumental sculpture, producing a synthesis between the style of the last works of Michelangelo, aspects of southern Italian 15th-century sculpture and of Spanish devotional sculpture from the same period. Although they formed close links with Roman art, particularly in the field of portraiture, Naccherino and Bernini gave a wholly Neapolitan flavour to the sculpture of southern Italy.

The decorative settings prepared by the marble workers who collaborated with these two sculptors still reflected, however, the Florentine cultural background of their creators. Naccherino and Bernini also influenced greatly two naturalized foreigners who were champions of two different schools of expression and who together determined the character of the local environment: COSIMO FANZAGO and Giuliano Finelli. Fanzago created the spandrels over the doors depicting *Holy Bishops and Carthusians* (1623–31 and 1631–56) in S Martino. His innovations would have influenced such decorators as Jacopo Lazzari and Dionisio Lazzari, who maintained close links with their Tuscan roots. Artists who had trained outside Naples often brought influential new styles to the city, and they were frequently commissioned to execute important works in Naples, for instance Andrea Bolgi carved the four portrait busts of the *Founders of the de Caro-Cace Family* (1653) in the family chapel in S Lorenzo Maggiore. After the plague of 1656, a group of native Neapolitan sculptors became established, including Gian Domenico Vinaccia, who learnt from Fanzago the art of working in a variety of media. His altarpiece of the *Translation of the Relics of St Gennaro* (1692–5; see fig. 7) in the cathedral was one of the fundamental texts for the

7. Naples Cathedral, chapel of St Gennaro, altarpiece of the *Translation of the Relics of St Gennaro* (1692–5), by Gian Domenico Vinaccia

interpretation of late Neapolitan Baroque sculpture. Another important local artist was Lorenzo Vaccaro (*see* VACCARO, (1)), who demonstrated his accomplishment and modernity in the large statues he carved for S Martino (*see* §IV, 3 below).

The turning-point of 17th-century Neapolitan painting hinges on two visits made by Caravaggio to the city, in 1606–7 and 1609–10. His innovations were absorbed much more quickly by Neapolitan painters than by those in other Italian artistic centres, even though the late Mannerist style prevailed in the works of such painters as Fabrizio Santafede, Giovanni Bernardino Azzolino and above all Belisario Corenzio. One important young artist who took up Caravaggio's style was GIOVANNI BATTISTA CARAC-CIOLO, who worked in Caravaggio's workshop in Naples in 1610 and managed to capture the most profound aspects of Caravaggio's style. Carlo Sellitto was closely related in style to Caracciolo, and he was in full possession of the Caravaggian cultural legacy. Another highly influential painter of the early 17th century in Naples was the Spaniard Jusepe de Ribera, who moved to Naples *c.* 1615, and his works were consistently of the highest standard.

The emergent Baroque style was introduced to Naples by Guido Reni, and Bolognese classicism became known due to the presence (1630–41) of Domenichino, as well as through a massive importation of works of art for sale. These works included examples by Nicolas Poussin, known in Naples through the Filomarino collection and for the *Adoration of the Golden Calf* (destr. 1647). In the field of decorative wall painting the Baroque movement was most influential for such Neapolitan painters as MASSIMO STANZIONE. The most dedicated exponent of the early Baroque in Rome, Giovanni Lanfranco, was active in Naples from 1634 to 1646 at S Martino, the Gesù Nuovo, the Cappella del Tesoro in S Gennaro and at SS Apostoli.

There were a number of important collectors in Naples at this time. The merchant GASPAR ROOMER owned a variety of important works by such artists as van Dyck and Rubens, and these helped to disseminate northern European and Italian styles to artists working in Naples. Another important collector was Bartolomeo PICCHIATI, who owned the most famous Neapolitan *Wunderkammer* and who also collected architectural drawings. Roomer's collection influenced Aniello Falcone, who was outstanding for the authoritativeness and quality of his research, as well as for the variety of the disciplines within which he operated. He was inspired by the Bamboccianti painters and in turn greatly influenced his pupil Salvator Rosa.

Neapolitan artists who specialized in smaller-scale painting included Scipione Compagni, Filippo Napoletano and, above all, Micco Spadaro, who was also influenced by the neo-Mannerist figures of Johann Heinrich Schoenfeldt (1609–83), active in Naples from 1638 to *c.* 1648. Numerous artists began to specialize in still-lifes, including Luca Forte, Paolo Porpora and Giacomo Recco and Giovan Battista Recco. It was, however, Ribera who provided the most authoritative reference point for the revival of Venetian forms in Naples: while Velázquez was in Italy in 1630 he worked in Ribera's studio, where the cultural exchanges between the two artists were intense and far-reaching for the Neapolitan art world: the artists most affected by this encounter were Falcone and Francesco Guarino.

Towards the middle of the 17th century there emerged in Naples one of the most important painters of the time: BERNARDO CAVALLINO, who produced principally small works depicting scenes from the Old Testament, or half-figures of saints in the style of Simon Vouet and Stanzione. This production stands out for its poetic gentleness, for the profundity of its psychological perceptiveness in the subjects portrayed and for its exquisite pictorial quality, which embodies all the Neapolitan tendencies of the period. From *c.* 1645 until the plague of 1665 Neapolitan painting in all its forms enjoyed a period of ever increasing quality and variety, to the point of acquiring the authoritativeness of one of the major areas of Italian and European figurative expression. Stanzione in particular demonstrated himself to be the most accomplished of the Neapolitan decorators and fresco artists, working in many Neapolitan churches within the context of a synthesis of Roman and Bolognese influences.

The combination of realism and colour first demonstrated by Ribera became the hallmark of one of the most noted painters of the Italian Late Baroque: LUCA GIORDANO. He served his apprenticeship under Ribera and then travelled to all the major centres in the Italian peninsula to broaden his experience. He also brought Spanish styles back to Naples, having served as court painter to Charles II, King of Spain. Mattia Preti was another influential painter in mid-17th century Naples. Together with Giordano he introduced Neapolitan art to the styles of such north Italian painters as Pietro da Cortona and Paolo Veronese. Several local artists followed the styles of Preti and Giordano, including Francesco di Maria, Giacomo Farelli, Giovan Battista Beinaschi and Nicola Vaccaro (1637–1717). In still-life painting Giuseppe Recco, Giovanni Battista Ruoppolo and Andrea Belvedere upheld the traditions created by their predecessors at the beginning of the century. These artists constituted in many ways only the soil from which sprang the most international figure in Neapolitan painting of the 17th and 18th centuries: Francesco Solimena (*see* SOLIMENA, (2)). He produced paintings of great distinction in Naples, and he was responsible for one of the highpoints in Neapolitan painting of the period, the fresco of the *Banishment of Heliodorus from the Temple* (1725), in the Gesù Nuovo.

BIBLIOGRAPHY

Painting in Naples, 1606–1705: From Caravaggio to Giordano (exh. cat., ed. C. Whitfield and J. Martineau; London, RA; Washington, DC, N.G.A; Paris, Grand Pal.; Turin, Fond. Agnelli; 1982–4)

D. Pasculli Ferrara: *Arte napoletana in Puglia dal XVI and XVIII secolo* (Fasano, 1983)

For further bibliography *see* §4 below.

4. *c.* 1700–*c.* 1860. Neapolitan sculpture in the 18th century was linked to the great architectural commissions (e.g. S Martino, the Concezione at Montcalvario). Domenico Antonio Vaccaro cultivated an impressive team of sculptors and marble workers, including Matteo Bottiglieri (1684–1756) and Francesco Pagano (*d* 1764), who were capable of developing their own forms of expression, even in the field of portraiture. These artists were important for the high level of their professionalism, and they form a link between the two Vaccaros and the other great 18th-century Neapolitan sculptor, GIUSEPPE SANMARTINO, who was awarded the most prestigious private commissions available in Naples. Paolo de Matteis, Domenico Antonio Vaccaro and Giacomo del Po all contributed in their various ways towards freeing Neapolitan painting from its late Baroque mood and allowing it to develop a new, more typically 18th-century dimension. Although Charles VII, King of Naples (later Charles III, King of Spain), had excluded from his patronage those architects who had links with the previous political regime, he did make good use of the Neapolitan painters who had acquired an international reputation. Thus he engaged Solimena, Francesco de Mura, Nicola Maria Rossi and Domenico Antonio Vaccaro to fresco the reception rooms of the Palazzo Reale in Naples for his wedding to Maria Amalia of Saxony.

De Mura was an apprentice of Solimena, and he became the most important Neapolitan painter of the mid-18th century. He went to Turin (1741–3), and on his return to Naples he continued to subject his painting to a greater degree of classicism, which, towards the end of his career, drew him closer to the academic tendencies of the pre-Neo-classical period. Other painters made significant contributions in this period. GIUSEPPE BONITO, after an apprenticeship under Solimena, managed to obtain major commissions from the court and in 1755 became the principal of the Accademia del Disegno founded shortly before by Charles VII. He was an accomplished painter in every discipline. His scenes from modern life, although they lack the critical tensions typical of Gaspare Traversi, constitute a perceptive documentation of 18th-century Neapolitan life outside high-ranking aristocratic circles. Equally clear and socially provocative was Traversi's study of the under-privileged and the habits and rituals of the bourgeoisie.

Solimena's numerous pupils did not lack patronage throughout the late 18th century, particularly from the religious orders. The dominant stylistic tendency was one of combining the compositional structures of Solimena with the pleasant arcadianism of de Mura. Such a course was followed by Leonardo Olivieri (1689–*c.* 1750), Lorenzo de Caro, Jacopo Cestaro (1718–78), Domenico Mondo, Pietro Bardellino, Filippo Falciatore (*fl* 1728–68) and, above all, Giacinto Diana. It was, however, the powerful influence of Luigi Vanvitelli, the 'director' of royal artistic tastes in Naples, as well as the greater degree of authority assumed first by Maria Amalia and subsequently by Maria Carolina in matters of royal patronage, that resulted in a weakening of the resistance of Neapolitan art to the ever increasing onslaught of academic classicism and the advent of Neo-classicism. During the first phase of this change the part played by Sebastiano Conca was of considerable importance; following his apprenticeship with Solimena, he returned to Naples *c.* 1753 and was active in the Bourbon court until his death. Equally important was the later career of CORRADO GIAQUINTO, who also worked for the court. These two painters were exponents of the Rococo, a movement that had begun in Rome with Pompeo Batoni, who in 1763 sent works to the Palazzo Reale in Caserta and was well known in Naples also through the derivations of Anton Raphael Mengs, himself invited to Naples by the Royal Court in 1759. Other influential painters active in Naples included Francesco Liani, Angelica Kauffman, Heinrich Friedrich Füger, Elisabeth-Louise Vigée Le Brun and the British painters Joshua Reynolds and Gavin Hamilton.

The key exponent of Neo-classicism as the state art was Wilhelm Tischbein, who accompanied Goethe in the southern stages of his Italian tour. Tischbein was appointed Director of the Accademia di Belle Arti in 1789 and imposed on that institution a Neo-classical direction, signalling a final break with the Neapolitan late Baroque and Rococo schools. In the early 19th century Sanmartino's pupils pressed forwards with high-quality creations that concluded with great dignity the history of Neapolitan Baroque sculpture. New movements in sculpture were popularized by Filippo Tagliolini (*fl* 1781–1812), who, although he never worked on any monumental sculptures, designed a number of important works in biscuit for the royal porcelain factories (*see* §III, 3 below). The sculptors in the mainstream of international classicism included Antonio Cali (1788–1866; e.g. bronze bust of *Charles III*; Naples, Capodimonte), Gennaro Cali (1799–1877) and Tito Angelini (*b* 1806).

A clear break was made away from academicism by ACHILLE D'ORSI, who leant towards social realism in such works as *Proximus tuus* (bronze plaster cast; Rome, G.N.A. Mod.). All of these competent professional figures were, however, eclipsed by VINCENZO GEMITO, who was in contact with such artists as Mariano Fortuny and with the landscape artists of the Scuola di Resina. He produced sculptures of an intimate style (e.g. *Little Fisherman*, bronze; Naples, Gal. Accad. B.A.), but he also worked in the graphic arts. From the end of the 18th century to the early 19th Naples became the primary focus for landscape artists drawn there by the fame of the Classical sites of Herculaneum and Pompeii and the better-known quarters of the capital and its suburbs. Most of these artists enjoyed no real relationship with the local artistic community and moved on to the more picturesque locations in Campania, where they produced works of varying stylistic and cultural quality, while sharing the common aim of faithfully representing the picturesque and landscape qualities of some of the most loved scenery in Europe. Local production of varying degrees of popularity in watercolour and gouache by such artists as Gabriele Ricciardelli, Ruiz, Saverio della Gatta and Titta Lusieri prepared the cultural terrain of the late 18th century into which the SCUOLA DI POSILLIPO was to be born.

From its inception the Scuola di Posillipo found a place in the local economy selling landscapes to tourists; it rejected great historical compositions and large format painting in favour of small pictures on board or on paper glued to wood, but nevertheless retaining a higher level of pictorial quality compared with the gouache paintings. The first exponent of the Scuola was Anton Sminck Pitloo, who moved to Naples from Paris in 1816. Pitloo's teaching at the Accademia di Belle Arti was formative in the experience of the most accomplished of the local exponents, particularly GIACINTO GIGANTE, who was active as a landscape painter, producing luminous watercolour views of the most picturesque corners of Naples. Gigante's collaborators included such artists as Achille Vianelli,

Consalvo Carelli (1818–1900) and Giuseppe Carelli (1859–1921), Vincenzo Franceschini (*fl* 1812), Teodoro Duclere (1816–69) and Gabriele Smargiassi (1798–1882). Their works were characterized by the same tendency towards a gradual disintegration of the concrete forms of pictorial contours in favour of a technique of 'dots' (*di macchia*), achieved using a series of rapid brushstrokes.

Towards the mid-19th century the SCUOLA DI RESINA began to flourish. This movement took its name from a small village near Portici, which was the home of Consalvo Carelli. Painters trained under the school included Marco De Gregorio (1829–75), Federico Rossano (1835–1912) and Giuseppe De Nittis. Their common aim was the promotion primarily of the *Macchiaioli* painter Adriano Cecioni, who linked this group to contemporary experiences in Tuscany. The tendencies of the Resina group were also a reaction against academicism, particularly the organizational power of DOMENICO MORELLI, whose romantic realism embodied in historical scenes represented, together with the work of Filippo Palizzi (*see* PALIZZI, (2)), the apotheosis of Neapolitan academic painting, linked with the Barbizon school and capable of holding its own alongside the best of European artistic expression. Other Resina artists who followed Palizzi and Morelli, adding their own individual emphases, included Giuseppe Mancinelli (1813–75), Giuseppe De Nigris (1832–1903) and, above all, Francesco Saverio Altamura (1822–97).

BIBLIOGRAPHY
C. De Seta: *Arti e civiltà del settecento a Napoli* (Rome, 1982)
Gouaches napoletane del settecento e dell'ottocento (exh. cat., Naples, Villa Pignatelli, 1985)
A Taste for Angels: Neapolitan Painting in North America, 1650–1750 (exh. cat., New Haven, CT, Yale U. A.G.; Sarasota, FL, Ringling Mus. A.; Kansas City, MO, Nelson–Atkins Mus. A.; 1987)

RICCARDO LATTUARDA

5. *c.* 1860 AND AFTER. The political upheavals following the Unification of Italy (1860) contributed to a vibrant, if somewhat confused, cultural identity in Naples. However, several artistic periodicals were founded, including *Società di storia patria* (1875) and *Napoli nobilissima* (1892–1906/1920–22). Neapolitan art demonstrated a strong antipathy towards academic painting (which had been latent since the early 19th century with the Scuola di Posillipo) and an affinity towards French Realism, notably Gustave Courbet and the work of the *Macchiaioli* group in Tuscany. The younger generation of painters tried to emulate such artists as Domenico Morelli, and a new interest in depicting contemporary subjects emerged, for example the Risorgimento battle scenes by MICHELE CAMMARANO and the scenes of everyday life by Eduardo Dalbono. Other influential painters included Gioacchino Toma and Antonio Mancini. Sculpture was dominated by Vincenzo Gemito, whose naturalistic depictions marked a total break with academically refined work. A number of artists left Naples to work abroad, notably Giuseppe De Nittis who settled in Paris and combined Neapolitan audacity with French elegance. No particular school of painting emerged, due largely to the artistic dominance of Paris throughout the 19th century. The most outstanding artistic traits in Naples were the move towards Naturalism, known as *Verismo*, combined with a strong sense of the

decorative (the influence of Mariano Fortuny) and expressive qualities of colour. Such innovative 20th-century movements as Futurism no longer needed a local base from which to progress, and, although Neapolitan artists always participated in later developments, central and particularly northern Italy (Milan and Turin) increasingly dominated the artistic scene as the century progressed.

BIBLIOGRAPHY

A. Venturi: *Storia* (1901–40)

A. Schettini: *La pittura napoletana dell'ottocento* (Rome, 1967)

III. Centre of production.

1. TAPESTRY. During the rule of Frederick IV of Naples (*reg* 1496–1501) there was apparently a royal tapestry workshop in the Castelnuovo (documented 1498), but by the late 1990s nothing was known of its works. Among the ambitious artistic projects of Charles VII, King of Naples (later Charles III, King of Spain), was the foundation of a royal Neapolitan tapestry workshop. In 1737, after the initial closing of the Arazzeria Medicea in Florence, Charles invited Domenico del Rosso (*fl* 1736–68) and Giovanni Francesco Pieri (*fl* 1732–8), two of the master weavers, to Naples, and they called a number of Florentine workers to help them. At first the production was limited to the same tapestry types produced during the final years in Florence: allegories of *The Elements* (1739–63; Naples, Pal. Reale); portraits, notably *Charles of Bourbon* (1739–41; Naples, Capodimonte), woven by Giuseppe de Filippis (*fl* 1739–41) and Rosso; and copies of such paintings from the important Farnese collection as the *Virgin Adoring the Christ Child* (1742; Naples, Capodimonte) after Guido Reni and woven by Carlo Mugnai. In 1753–4 the Milanese weaver Michelangelo Cavanna (*fl* 1753; *d* 1772), who specialized in virtuoso reproductions of paintings, joined the factory and produced such tapestries as *St Jerome* (1758–9; Naples, Capodimonte) after Guercino.

For the Palazzo Reale at Caserta, near Naples, begun in 1751, Charles and his architect, Luigi Vanvitelli, planned extensive tapestry decorations; in 1757 Pietro Duranti (*d* 1799) was brought from Rome to direct a new workshop of weavers from Rome and Turin. Duranti was also charged with reorganizing the entire factory. It was decided to enlarge Charles's set of 12 Gobelins tapestries depicting the *Story of Don Quixote* (1730–33; Naples, Capodimonte and Pal. Reale, and Rome, Pal. Quirinale) based on cartoons by Charles-Antoine Coypel: new designs for the centre vignettes were added after designs by the court painter Giuseppe Bonito and such other painters as Antonio Dominici (*b c.* 1730; *d* before 1800) and Giovan Battista Rossi (*fl* 1758–77). Duranti's workshop wove at least 41 large tapestries and numerous smaller overdoors and other assorted companion pieces between 1758 and 1779 (31 tapestries; Naples, Capodimonte). At this time Duranti's workshop produced some of the most successful Neapolitan tapestries, including the *Allegories of the Virtues* (1762–6; examples in Naples, Capodimonte) from cartoons by Francesco de Mura, Pietro Bardellino and Bonito and later the *Story of Cupid and Psyche* (1783–*c.* 1786; Naples, Pal. Reale) and the *Life of Henry IV of Bourbon*

(*c.* 1791; Naples, Capodimonte) from cartoons by Fedele Fischetti. The final, large set produced by the factory was the *Royal Apotheosis* (1794–8; Naples, Capodimonte and Pal. Reale), for which Desiderio de Angelis (*fl* 1784–1808) made the cartoons. Duranti's son, Giovanni Duranti (*fl c.* 1799), inherited his father's position in 1799, but little more weaving was done because Ferdinand IV, King of Naples (*reg* 1759–1806), fled to Sicily in fear of a French invasion. The factory was finally closed in 1806.

BIBLIOGRAPHY

R. Filangieri: *Rassegna delle fonti per Castelnuovo* (Naples, 1939), p. 65

O. Ferrari: *Arazzi italiani del seicento e settecento* (Milan, 1968), pp. 39–44, 98–114

N. Spinosa: *L'Arazzeria napoletana* (Naples, 1971)

——: 'Gli arazzi del Belvedere a Palazzo Reale', *Antol. B.A.*, ii/5 (1978), pp. 96–106

M. Siniscalco Spinosa: 'Arazzi', *Civiltà del '700 a Napoli, 1734–1799* (exh. cat., Naples, Capodimonte, 1979–80), pp. 96–106

——: 'Italia', *Gli arazzi*, ed. A. González-Palacios (Milan, 1981), pp. 23, 25–7

CANDACE J. ADELSON

2. HARDSTONES. The Real Laboratorio delle Pietre Dure was established in 1738 by Charles VII, King of Naples (later Charles III of Spain). He brought to Naples ten Florentine craftsmen who were experts in carving and working hardstones into mosaics. Francesco Ghinghi headed the Neapolitan Laboratorio from its foundation until his death in 1762. The other craftsmen who came with him were Giovanni Battista Zucconi (*d* 1743), Giuseppe Carli, Francesco Bichi (*d* 1769), Zanobio Ciani, Giuseppe Minchioni (*d* 1755), Francesco Campi (*d* 1761), Raffaele Muffati, Giovanni Scarpettini (*d* 1756) and Gaspare Donnini (*d* 1780). The last mentioned, a specialist in cabinet work, succeeded Ghinghi as head of the Laboratorio from 1762 to 1780. It was later run by Giovanni Mugnai (1780–1805), Antonio Lombardo (1806), Filippo Rega, Orazio Angelini (1833–49), Pietro Valente and Luigi Arnaud (1859–61).

Assisted by a small crew of apprentices, the Florentine craftsmen worked on intaglio and mosaic productions following the style that prevailed in Florence. Documentary sources, including a letter from Ghinghi that includes autobiographical information (González-Palacios, *Antol. B.A.*, 1977), record that among the earliest works (all untraced) produced by the Neapolitan workshop were: a chalcedony intaglio carved by Ghinghi with the insignia of Charles and Maria Amalia of Saxony, whom he married in 1738; an octagonal plaque with flower, bird and fruit motifs on a black background; an intaglio with the arms of the sovereign and a large cameo with his portrait; a pair of small tables; and a holy-water basin designed by the Florentine Giovanni Antonio Noferi. Works that have been traced include a plaque with the Annunciation, crowned by an exuberantly decorated bronze pinnacle (Madrid, Pal. Real), and two black marble tables (Madrid, Prado) with bases of ebony and bronze, ornamented with lively floral rocaille decorations and a necklace of pearls at the centre. These were inspired by a table (Florence, Pitti) produced in Florence in 1716. Similar motifs of flowers and birds recur in another pair of Neapolitan tables with legs in the shape of goat's feet (Madrid, Prado), finished under Donnini's direction. A pair of table-tops with central designs of fruit (Palermo, Pal. Cinese) was also made in the 1760s; another table (Caserta, Pal. Reale), based on a design by the painter Gennaro Cappella using the already antiquated motifs of flowers and pearls on a black background, dates from between 1773 and 1787.

A new orientation can be seen in the works of the late 18th century, when Neo-classical taste favoured table-tops displaying a fascinating variety of hardstones rather than a virtuoso display of figurative mosaic work. This can be seen in two Sicilian tables inlaid with varieties of jasper (Caserta, Pal. Reale) and in an oval table (Palermo, Pal. Normanni) with a wood top inlaid with petrified wood, a material that also appears in a table-top with a chessboard (Naples, Capodimonte), made in 1811 and mounted in 1834–5 on marble supports recovered from ancient Roman ruins. With the Restoration the activity of the workshop, which had never been very regular, was further diminished. Its last project was the monumental tabernacle for the Palatine Chapel at the Palazzo Reale at Caserta, which was begun in 1753 but never finished. In 1861, following the end of the Kingdom of the Two Sicilies, the workshop was closed, and its stocks of precious materials were turned over to the Opificio delle Pietre Dure in Florence.

BIBLIOGRAPHY

A. González-Palacios: 'Un'autobiografia del Ghinghi', *Antol. B.A.*, iii (1977), pp. 271–81
——: 'The Laboratorio delle Pietre Dure in Naples, 1738–1805', *Connoisseur*, cxcvi (1977), pp. 119–29
——: *Le arti figurative a Napoli nel settecento* (Naples, 1979), pp. 71–151
F. Strazzullo: *Le manifatture d'arte di Carlo di Borbone* (Naples, 1979), pp. 93–143
Civiltà del '700 a Napoli, 1734–1799, ii (exh. cat., Naples, Capodimonte, 1979–80), pp. 178–86
A. González-Palacios: *Mosaici e pietre dure*, ii (Milan, 1981), pp. 51–75
R. Valeriani: 'Il Real Laboratorio delle Pietre Dure a Napoli', *Splendori di pietre dure: L'arte di corte nella Firenze dei granduchi* (exh. cat., ed. A. M. Giusti; Florence, Pitti, 1988–9), pp. 250–53

ANNAMARIA GIUSTI

3. PORCELAIN. After the CAPODIMONTE PORCELAIN FACTORY closed in 1759, the Real Fabbrica della Porcellana was founded in 1771 in Pórtici by Ferdinand I, King of Naples and the Two Sicilies (Ferdinand IV of Naples); it was moved to Naples in 1772. Between 1772 and 1779 the director was Tommaso Perez (*d* 1779), and the principal modeller and painter was Francesco Celebrano (*fl* 1772–90). The factory employed workmen from Capodimonte, and early production continued in the Rococo style used there. The Neo-classical style was introduced after the appointment of Domenico Venuti (1745–1817) as director (1779) and Filippo Tagliolini (1745–1808) as chief modeller (1781). The forms and decoration of the tableware and biscuit figures were based on Classical models, especially those excavated at Herculaneum. Such table-services as the 'Herculaneum' service (1781; untraced) for Charles III, King of Spain, and the 'Etruscan' service (1785–7; Windsor Castle, Berks, Royal Col.) for George III, King of England, were important commissions. Commercial production included tea services painted with views, figures in contemporary costume, polychrome figures and groups and satirical biscuit figures. The factory experimented with several soft-paste formulae, and between 1784 and *c.* 1790 a tin-glazed body of the type made at Doccia was produced. Between 1771 and *c.* 1790 wares were marked RF or FRF, usually with a crown,

the entire mark then being either incised or in underglaze blue, and thereafter a crowned N in underglaze blue. The factory ceased production in 1806, and the following year it was sold to Giovanni Poulard Prad, who produced tablewares in the French style until 1821.

BIBLIOGRAPHY

A. Caròla-Perrotti: *La porcellana della real fabbrica ferdinandea* (Dimauro, 1978)
A. Gonzáles-Palacios: 'La real fabbrica della porcellana di Napoli', *Civiltà del '700 a Napoli, 1734–1799* (exh. cat., Naples, Capodimonte, 1979–80), pp. 126–60
A. Caròla-Perrotti: *Le porcellane dei Borbone di Napoli* (Naples, 1986)
——: *Le porcellane napoletane dell'ottocento, 1801–1860* (Naples, 1990)
Porcellane di Capodimonte: La real fabbrica di Carlo di Borbone, 1743–1759 (exh. cat., ed. L. Ambrosio; Naples, Mus. N. Cer., 1993)

CLARE LE CORBEILLER

IV. Buildings.

1. Catacombs. 2. S Lorenzo Maggiore. 3. Certosa di S Martino. 4. Castelnuovo.

1. CATACOMBS. Naples contains some of the few catacombs in Italy outside Rome. The four surviving catacombs are all located in the Capodimonte area: S Gennaro (St Januarius; 2nd century AD); S Gaudioso (5th century), which is beneath the church of S Maria della Sanità (1602–13); S Efebo (S Eufemio), near the church of S Efamo Vecchio; and S Severo alla Sanità. The Neapolitan catacombs have wider, more open spaces than the numerous long, narrow galleries of the Roman examples. Those in Naples also have certain examples of the baldacchino type of construction, which was more widespread in the catacombs in Malta and Sicily but almost non-existent in Rome. The Neapolitan catacombs also remained in use longer than those in Rome. From the 5th century AD they demonstrate less and less affinity with Roman catacomb paintings, and, unusually for catacomb images, the Neapolitan cubicula are sometimes embellished with mosaic. Also dating from this period are images of the individuals in the tombs, or of saints, which look more like icons than the sign-pictures, or picture-writing, that are more typical of Roman and earlier Neapolitan images.

By far the largest and best preserved of the Neapolitan catacombs is that of S Gennaro or St Januarius, patron saint of Naples. It was originally the tomb of a private family, expanding to accommodate a larger community in later years. The remains of the saint were brought to Naples by Bishop Giovanni I (*reg* 413–32), and for *c.* 400 years the catacomb was the centre of the cult of S Gennaro. In 831, however, the relics were removed to Benevento, and the catacomb declined in use until it was abandoned in the 13th century. It is constructed on two levels, the passages lined with the usual arcosolia and *loculi* (shelf-like burial spaces). Important features include the 'small basilica' of S Agrippino and the so-called 'Bishop's crypt', which contains images, in mosaic and in paint, of early Neapolitan bishops. Painted images survive throughout the catacomb, some having been restored in the 20th century (for illustration *see* CATACOMB).

The catacomb of S Gaudioso contains the most extensive remains. It is named after Septimus Caelius Gaudiosus, an African bishop exiled by Genseric in AD 439, whose mortal remains were buried here. It is difficult to determine the original ground-plan of the catacomb, for it underwent several modifications under the direction of Dominican monks from the early 17th century. A few frescoes and mosaics survive, however, including mosaic portrait busts, similar to some in S Gennaro, and symbolic compositions with vines, crosses, lambs, peacocks and, possibly, eagles. The plans of the catacombs of S Severo and S Efebo are even more obscure than that of S Gaudioso, and S Efebo contains just two surviving frescoes. At S Severo there are a few more remains, but so damaged as to be difficult to decipher. As with Roman examples, scholars have not agreed as to how much can be deduced from the Neapolitan catacombs about the number of Christians in the area at the time. It is questionable whether there were enough Christians to carry out all the construction and embellishment work, especially during the earlier centuries. Pagans and Christians may have been buried together.

BIBLIOGRAPHY

A. Bellucci: 'Ritrovamenti archeologici nelle catacombe di San Gaudioso e di Sant'Eufebio a Napoli', *Riv. Archaeol. Crist.*, xi (1934), pp. 74–118
——: 'Ritrovamento della catacomba di San Eufebio e di nuova zone nella catacomba di San Gaudioso a Napoli', *Atti del III congreso internazionale di archeologia cristiana: Roma, 1934*, pp. 327–70
H. Achelis: *Die Katakomben von Neapel* (Leipzig, 1935–6)
R. Calvino: *La catacomba di S Gennaro in Napoli* (Naples, 1970)
U. M. Fasola: *Le catacombe de S Gennaro a Capodimonte* (Rome, 1975) [good photographs and useful bibliog.]
R. Calvino: 'Peintures et mosaïques des catacombes napolitaines', *Doss. Archéol.*, 19 (Nov–Dec 1976), pp. 22–33
P. N. Ciavolino: 'Dans le Sol de Naples, des galeries monumentales', *Doss. Archéol.*, 19 (Nov–Dec 1976), pp. 8–21

2. S LORENZO MAGGIORE. A Franciscan church (see fig. 8), the finest extant Gothic monument in Naples, it was probably begun *c*. 1275–80 and is often associated with King Charles I of Anjou (*reg* 1266–85) and his court, although there is no documentary evidence for royal patronage before 1284. Members of the family were buried there up to 1323. The church was heavily damaged in successive earthquakes, especially those of 1349 and 1456, and it has been restored several times. From 1639 the nave and transept received a complete Baroque decoration (the chevet at that point was closed off and abandoned); but more recent restorations have returned the church to its medieval appearance.

The original church was founded in the old Roman forum between *c*. 534 and 554 by Bishop John of Naples. The nave (*c*. 10×24 m) was flanked on either side by aisles 4 m wide. The large apse, about 9 m wide at the junction with the transept, was flanked on the left by a prothesis (5×5.3 m) and on the right by a diakonikon (8×4.5 m), both decorated by a lavish mosaic pavement. The nave arcade was supported by columns and capitals reused from Roman monuments, presumably spolia from the forum itself, and these materials were used once again in the nave of the Gothic building. By the mid-11th century the church of S Lorenzo belonged to the chapter of Aversa, but in November 1234 it was given to the Franciscan Order. The reconstruction of the church was begun about 40 years later. The earliest references to the reconstruction appear in the donations of Charles, Prince of Salerno (the future Charles II of Anjou), in 1284 for its completion and repair. He made another donation in 1300

8. Naples, S Lorenzo Maggiore, interior view looking east, begun *c*. 1275–80

for the completion of the building, which suggests that work advanced slowly; the façade was erected only in 1324.

S Lorenzo Maggiore is built of local yellow tufa and grey lava (*piperno*). The total external length of the church is *c*. 80 m. It is a rare example in Italy of a church with an ambulatory and seven radiating chapels. The inspiration for the plan of the chevet derives directly from models in France, comparing most closely with that of the Cistercian church of Valmagne (Hérault), built in the third quarter of the 13th century. The two-storey elevation of the chevet, with flat panels of wall between the arcade and clerestory windows, also recalls the elevation of the chevet of the Cistercian church at Ourscamp (Oise) of the 1230s. The rib vaulting of the apse, ambulatory and radiating chapels, the carving of the capitals, bases and plinths, and the bar tracery of the chevet windows reveal French workmanship in the design and much of the execution of the earliest parts of the monument. The westernmost bay of the chevet was modified during construction to create a higher vault, which permitted the insertion of an oculus in the flat span of wall before the hemicycle vaults, a counterpart to the oculi in the east wall of the transept. This work is probably contemporary with the building of the transept, which was itself modified a number of times during construction. The effect of the lighting at the east end of the church provided by these windows is very similar to that often found in Cistercian monuments, for example Fontenay in Burgundy.

The later nave of S Lorenzo Maggiore (c. 1295–1300) differs sharply from the chevet. Consisting of one wide unvaulted volume flanked by chapels, it has often been attributed to an Italian architect. The different conception of space, the absence of vaults over the main volume and the reuse of spolia from the older church all suggest an Italian master. The consistency in handling the plinths and capitals in the side chapels, however, indicates that many of the workmen may have remained the same. Any interruption between the building of the chevet and the nave was therefore not prolonged. The nave design is similar to that of the Franciscan church at Messina, begun in the mid-13th century, and it was frequently repeated in other mendicant churches in Naples, for example the nave of S Chiara.

BIBLIOGRAPHY

L. de la Ville sur-Yllon: 'L'abside della chiesa si S Lorenzo Maggiore', *Napoli Nob.*, iv (1895), pp. 37–41

E. Bertaux: 'Les Artistes français au service des rois angevins de Naples', *Gaz. B.-A.*, xxxiv (1905), pp. 313–25

R. Wagner-Rieger: 'Der Chor von S Lorenzo Maggiore in Neapel', *Actes du XIXe congrès international d'histoire de l'art: Paris, 1958*, pp. 139–44

——: 'S Lorenzo Maggiore in Neapel und die suditalienische Architektur unter den ersten Königen aus dem Hause Anjou', *Misc. Bib. Hertz.* (1961), pp. 131–43

——: 'S Lorenzo Maggiore: Il coro', *Napoli Nob.*, 3rd ser., i (1961–2), pp. 1–7

W. Johannowsky: 'Recente scoperte archeologiche in San Lorenzo Maggiore in Napoli', *Napoli Nob.*, 3rd ser., i (1961–2), pp. 8–12

G. Recupido [Hirpinus]: 'S Lorenzo Maggiore a Napoli: Ritrovamenti paleocristiani e altomedioevali', *Napoli Nob.*, 3rd ser., i (1961–2), pp. 13–21

A. Venditti: *Urbanistica e architettura angioina*, Storia di Napoli, iii (Naples, 1969), pp. 665–888

J. Kruger: *S Lorenzo Maggiore in Neapel: Eine Franziskanerkirche zwischen Ordensideal und Herrschaftsarchitektur* (Werl, 1985)

C. BRUZELIUS

3. CERTOSA DI S MARTINO. The Carthusian certosa (charterhouse) on the Vómero Hill, site of the Museo di S Martino, was founded in 1325. It was built in close relation to the surrounding landscape, with magnificent gardens (rest. after World War II) overlooking the city. From the late 16th century to the late 18th the certosa underwent transformations that almost obliterated its medieval form and made it one of the most remarkable European Baroque monuments. The 14th-century structure of the certosa is attributed to Tino di Camaino and Francesco di Vito (or di Vico) for the period 1325–37, and to Atanasio Primario and Balduccio de Bacza for the period 1336–46. The only 14th-century remains are the powerful substructures of the present great cloister and the wings of the buildings around it. Giovanni Giacomo di Conforto and Giovanni Antonio Dosio restructured the certosa in the late 16th century. Dosio designed the great arched and columned Chiostro Grande (1591–1609; see fig. 9), on which Cosimo Fanzago, who directed the works 1631–56, placed the fluted panels over the columns, the statues on the portico and the corner doors inside the ambulatory, articulated in a system of mouldings and fantastic plant and animal motifs including the small marble tongues used as keystones to the arches. These elements, part architectural and part decorative, serve to frame the series of busts of Carthusian saints over the doors. Five of these busts, carved by Fanzago, are works of major importance for early 17th-century Neapolitan sculpture, especially the marble *Blessed Nicola Albergati* (1623–43; *see* FANZAGO, COSIMO, fig. 1). Fanzago also created the balustrade of the monks' cemetery, in which the ephemerality of earthly life is emphasized by laurel-wreathed skulls on the top.

The church of the certosa, with its treasury, sacristy and chapter house, is a key example of the main trends in 17th- and 18th-century Neapolitan art. The reconstructions that began in the late 16th century are attributed to Dosio. The monks' choir behind the main altar was doubled in size by reducing the area of the great cloister. The nave of the 14th-century church was retained, while in the aisles six chapels were built with round arches on pillars, following an old Tuscan style that was also used in many Neapolitan structures from the Counter-Reformation period. The first late 16th-century elements of the system, Pietro Bernini's *Active Life* (1596–8) and *Purity* (*Contemplative Life*) attributed to Giovanni Battista Caccini on the end wall of the monks' choir, illustrate allegories of labour and meditation, essential elements of the Carthusian life. The programme started by Dosio is continued in the decoration of all the chapels, with pairs of virtues or *concetti* (literary themes) linked with the hagiography of the saint for whom the chapel was named. The inlaid wooden wardrobes in the sacristy, which were built in 1587–1600 by a Flemish and Neapolitan consortium, are untypical of the late 16th century. The inlaid doors, with images of fantastic architecture in the lower panels and scenes from the Apocalypse and the scriptures in the upper ones, are a fine example of 'international' Mannerism. In the late 16th century Cavaliere d'Arpino and Bernardino Cesari (1571–1622) frescoed the ceiling of the monks' choir and the small vault of the passage between the parlatory and chapter house. In this phase the Carthusians chose such artists active in Rome or Genoa as Luca Cambiaso and his pupil Lazzaro Tavarone, who painted much of the decoration of the sacristy. Parts of the church were frescoed by Belisario Corenzio, who decorated the chapel of S Nicola (1632).

A large number of important painters worked at the certosa, including Giovanni Battista Caracciolo (*Christ Washing the Feet of the Disciples*, completed 1622, in the choir) and Paolo Domenico Finoglia, who painted ten lunettes with *Founders of Religious Orders* (1620–c. 1626) and the brilliantly coloured, late-Mannerist frescoes (c. 1632) in the chapel of St Martin. Massimo Stanzione painted the *Adoration of the Shepherds* (1630s) in the chapter house, the frescoes and canvases (c. 1630–37) in the chapel of St Bruno, the lunettes and fresco (1642–4) of the chapel of St John the Baptist and the *Virgin with SS Hugo and Anthelmus* (1644; *in situ*) in the chapel of the Rosary (1644). Jusepe de Ribera and Andrea Vaccaro also worked here. Ribera painted the *Pietà* (1637) in the treasury, *Prophets* (1638–43) on the arcades leading to the chapels and the solidly monumental *Moses and Elijah* (1638) on the interior façade. Vaccaro painted the *Penitent Magdalen* (1636; *in situ*) and two canvases of *Stories of St Hugh* (1652) in the chapel of the Magdalen (*in situ*).

As patrons, the Carthusians also took an interest in the best art being produced outside Naples. Many foreign

9. Naples, Certosa di S Martino, Chiostro Grande, designed by Giovanni Antonio Dosio, 1591–1609, with further decoration by Cosimo Fanzago, 1631–56

artists were engaged, including Simon Vouet, who painted the *Virgin Appearing to St Bruno* (1626) in the monks' chapter house (*in situ*). Guido Reni painted the *Adoration of the Shepherds* (1642; unfinished) on the wall of the tribune (*in situ*). GIOVANNI LANFRANCO was commissioned in 1637 to fresco the nave of the church and the interior façade of the choir. He transformed the structural constraint imposed by the groined vaults of the original church into an architectural framework, in which he 'opened' enormous circular windows revealing an infinite space filled with a celestial jubilation inspired by Correggio. On the interior façade of the choir he painted a dramatic *Crucifixion*. The church interior is almost entirely decorated with polychrome marblework by Fanzago. He was succeeded in 1656 by Bonaventura Presti (*d* 1685), who finished the inlaid polychrome marble pavement and the top of the late 16th-century lectern in the choir.

The church is characterized mainly by great sculpture from the late 17th century and early 18th. Lorenzo and Domenico Antonio Vaccaro decorated the chapels of the Baptist, St Bruno, S Gennaro, St Joseph and the Rosary. The chapel of S Gennaro contains a superb marble ensemble (1709–*c*. 1719) by Domenico Antonio Vaccaro, which is a work of key importance for Neapolitan art. It is almost contemporary with the other two chapels that he created—those of St Joseph and the Rosary. The former

resembles a late-Baroque central European interior, and the chapel of the Rosary is illuminated by the use of white and light-green plaster to unify the sculptural and decorative elements (columns and life-size angels holding garlands) with canvases also by Vaccaro. Other 18th-century sculptures include the four busts of Carthusian saints (1720–25) by Matteo Bottiglieri (*fl* 1720–54) in the chapel of St Hugo (*in situ*), the marble *Charity* and *Fortitude* (1757) by Giuseppe Sanmartino in the chapel of S Martino and his *Virginity and Reward* (1757) in the chapel of the Assumption (*in situ*). In the ceiling of the chapel of the treasury is the cycle of scenes from the *Life of Judith* (1704), one of the last works of Luca Giordano.

The Prior governed the religious, administrative and ceremonial life of the monastery from the so-called 'Quarto' (apartment) of the Priors, and he was the only one allowed to communicate with the outside world. In the 18th century the Quarto reached such a degree of splendour in its furnishings and painted decorations that it was often compared by visitors to a prince's apartment. It contained a gallery, bedrooms for illustrious guests, a loggia, the oratory, the library and a hanging garden. It now houses the Museo Nazionale di San Martino. That the Carthusians constantly kept up to date in commissioning works of art is evident in the former library, where the ceiling fresco of an allegory of the *Triumph of the Catholic Faith over Heresy* is attributed to Crescenzo la Gamba or Leonardo Olivieri (1692–1745), and other decorations, attributed to Gaetano Magri, are in the chinoiserie style of the mid-18th century. The maiolica pavement (1741) with the monogram of the Carthusian Order, in perfect harmony with the rest of the room, was made by the workshop of Giuseppe Massa (*d* 1738). The pavement of the Hall of the Meridiana (1771) displays the signs of the zodiac and is attributed to Leonardo Chiaiese. The present arrangement of the Quarto includes works from the Prior's picture gallery, which 18th-century travellers considered one of the richest in Naples. The collection was dispersed among public bodies and museums after 1806, and only in the 20th century did scholars begin to identify the paintings and objects that belonged to it. Artists represented in the collection include Giovanni Battista Caracciolo, Massimo Stanzione, Jusepe de Ribera, Francesco Guarino, Andrea Vaccaro and Micco Spadaro. The collection also included late works by Pietro Bernini.

BIBLIOGRAPHY

R. Causa: *L'arte della certosa di San Martino a Napoli* (Cava dei Tireni, 1973)
Civiltà del settecento a Napoli, 1734–1799, 2 vols (Florence, 1978–9)
G. Cantone: *Napoli barocca e Cosimo Fanzago* (Naples, 1984), pp. 53–101
T. Fittipaldi: 'Il Quarto del Priore e le sezioni storico-artistiche nella certosa di San Martino a Napoli', *A. Crist.*, xxii (1984), pp. 267–335
R. Lattuada: 'La certosa', *Napoli: Una storia per immagini* (Naples, 1985), pp. 273–95
L. Arbace, F. Capobianco and R. Pastorelli: *La certosa di San Martino: Il seicento* (Naples, 1986)
——: *Museo della certosa di San Martino: Il Quarto del Priore* (Naples, 1986)

RICCARDO LATTUADA

4. CASTELNUOVO. The fortified residence was built in 1281 by the architects Pierre de Chaule and Pierre d'Agincourt for Charles I of Anjou (*reg* 1266–85), who elevated Naples to the status of capital of the Kingdom of Sicily and Naples. The site combined proximity to the city with direct access to the sea. The original structure must have resembled contemporary French castles in Provence, which were characterized by extremely high towers and walls crowned with crenellations, embrasures, a moat and all the other defensive devices of the period. Total remodelling during the 15th century retained only the basic square plan around a large central courtyard; the chapel of St Barbara, or Palatine Chapel, is the only surviving part of the original castle. Constructed in the Gothic style under the supervision of Giovanni Caracciolo and Gualtiero Seripando, it was decorated throughout with frescoes by Giotto and Maso di Banco, but this work had already been destroyed by the mid-15th century. Only the medallions of *Angels* and *Saints* remain in the splayed jambs of the high, single-light windows.

Castelnuovo was inhabited by the Angevins until 1382, when Charles III di Durazzo took it as Pretender to the succession of Joanna. Two low-arched gateways constructed in peperino stone remain from the Durazzo era. The castle was the stage for various dynastic struggles that endured until 1442, when Alfonso V of Aragon (later Alfonso I, King of Naples and Sicily) conquered Naples. From 1443 he began the demolition of a large part of Castelnuovo (already seriously damaged during the hostilities) in order to rebuild it on a trapezoidal plan within the same area encircled by the moats. Another motive for the reconstruction was the evolution of warfare: the use of bombards and subsequently of gunpowder necessitated low and bulky towers able to resist the grazing fire of the cannonballs. At first the work did not follow a unified plan, and it was only with the arrival of Guillem Sagrera in 1447 and his introduction of military engineering technology based on the practice of Catalan fortification specialists in Mallorca (derived ultimately from Burgundy) that a radical transformation of the castle was carried out to a predetermined plan. Sagrera devised the system of five massive round towers, their bases decorated with scale-like tiles and concave spiral grooves, to prevent scaling-ladders from being placed against the walls and to present a fearsome appearance (*see* MILITARY ARCHITECTURE AND FORTIFICATION, fig. 11). His finest achievement at Castelnuovo is the Great Hall, or Barons' Hall, a superb room on a square plan, covered by an octagonal stellar vault with ribbing that dies into the wall without the intervention of corbels. In the place of a keystone, an oculus admits the light in an analogy of the domes of the Roman baths at Baia and Tripergola in the nearby Phlegrean Fields.

The triumphal arch (*c.* 1452–71; see fig. 10), built in marble to celebrate and immortalize Alfonso's triumphal entry into Naples (26 Feb 1443), is both the frontispiece and the entrance to the castle. Squeezed in between the two towers faced in peperino on the western wall looking towards Naples, the monument comprises four superimposed zones, including two distinct arches, which belong to separate periods. The first zone consists of a triumphal arch resting on paired Corinthian columns and decorated in the pendentives by two rampant griffins bearing the Aragon royal coat of arms over the centre of the arch. In the second zone a frieze in high relief depicts the *Triumph*

10. Naples, Castelnuovo, triumphal arch of Alfonso I, *c.* 1452–71

of King Alfonso. The third zone is composed of another open arch flanked by paired columns with Winged Victories in the pendentives. Four shell niches, separated by plaster strips and containing statues of the Cardinal Virtues, make up the fourth zone. The arch culminates in a curved pediment with two allegorical figures of Rivers and, at the very top, a statue of St Michael. From the vestibule, the entrance arch opens into the castle, and above this is a high relief of the Coronation of Ferrante. The sculpture of the triumphal arch was executed by at least nine different artists, including Domenico Gagini, Isaia da Pisa and Paolo Romano, and their numerous assistants. The design of the arch itself has been attributed to Pietro di Martino da Milano, who was also responsible for several of the reliefs. Inspired by Classical models such as the Arch of Trajan at Benevento and the Arch of the Sergi at Pola, and by medieval examples such as the Gate of Frederick II at Capua, the arch at Castelnuovo is a complex work of architecture and sculpture that represents an extremely rich interweaving of Late Gothic and humanistic cultures.

From 1453 Castelnuovo was protected by a low solid barbican, an enclosure of crenellated walls with towers, but in 1494 Francesco di Giorgio Martini, and subsequently his pupil Antonio Marchesi da Settignano (1451–1522), redesigned the outer defences of the castle by constructing a proper fortified enclosure, which was to render the castle impregnable (destr.). After the Kingdom of Naples became a province of the Spanish empire in 1503, Castelnuovo served as the temporary seat of the viceroys, who continued work on the fortifications until 1537. From the late 16th century it was used as a military store and as a barracks. In successive centuries further work was carried out to rebuild and repair the defensive walls and the castle itself, and many new buildings were also added, including an arsenal, a foundry and an armoury. At the behest of the Bourbon Ferdinand I, King of the Two Sicilies (Ferdinand IV, King of Naples, reg 1759–1806) a major restoration programme was executed between 1767 and 1774, and again in 1823. In 1870, after the Unification of Italy, Castelnuovo was granted to the city of Naples, and work began on the demolition of the outworks and the subsequent restoration of the Palazzo Reale. This work continued intermittently until c. 1950 and was aimed at restoring the building to its original Aragonese state. Work on Alfonso's arch was completed in 1988.

BIBLIOGRAPHY

G. Ceci: Bibliografia per la storia delle arti figurative nell'Italia meridionale (Bari, 1911, 2/1937) [with complete bibliog. to date]

R. Filangieri: 'La città della aragonese e il recinto bastionato di Castelnuovo', Atti Accad. Pontaniana, n. s. 1, xxxiv (1929), pp. 49–73

——: Castelnuovo: Reggia angioina ed aragonese di Napoli (Naples, 1934)

——: 'Rassegna critica delle fonti per la storia di Castelnuovo', Archv Stor. Prov. Napolet., lxi (1936), pp. 251–3; lxii (1937), pp. 267–333; lxiii (1938), pp. 258–342

G. Rosi: 'Il restauro del Castelnuovo a Napoli', Arti: Rass. Bimest. A. Ant. & Mod., iv (1942), pp. 284–7

F. Bologna: I pittori alla corte angioina di Napoli (Rome, 1969)

G. Alomar: Guillem Sagrera y la arquitectura gotica de siglo XV (Barcelona, 1970)

R. Causa: 'Sagrera, Fouquet, Laurana e l'arco di Castelnuovo', Atti del IX congresso di storia della corona d'Aragona: Napoli, 1973

G. L. Hersey: The Aragonese Arch at Naples, 1443–1475 (New Haven, 1973) [with comprehensive bibliog. and doc.]

H. W. Kruft and M. Malmanger: Der Triumphbogen Alfonsos in Neapel, Acta Archaeol. & A. Hist. Pertinentia, vi (Rome, 1976), pp. 213–88

F. Bologna: Napoli e le Rotte Mediterranee della pittura da Alfonso il Magnanimo a Ferdinando il Cattolico (Naples, 1977)

L. Santoro: Castelli angioini e aragonesi (Milan, 1982)

G. Cassese: 'Il dibattito storico-critico sull'arco di Alfonso d'Aragona: Problemi generali e questioni di metodo', Quad. Ist. N. Stud. Rinascimento Merid., ii (1985), pp. 7–44

A. Alabiso and others: L'arco di trionfo di Alfonso d'Aragona e il suo restauro (Rome, 1987)

GIOVANNA CASSESE

Napoca. See CLUJ-NAPOCA.

Napoleon I, Emperor of the French. See BONAPARTE, (1).

Napoleon III, Emperor of the French. See BONAPARTE, (8).

Napoletano, Filippo [d'Angeli, d'Angelo, de Liagno, de Llano; Teodor] (b Naples or Rome, c. 1587; d Rome, 1629). Italian painter and engraver. From 1600 until at least 1613 he was in Naples, where the naturalism of landscape painters from northern Europe, particularly Paul Bril, Goffredo Wals (fl 1615–31) and Adam Elsheimer, influenced his early development. After 1614 he was in Rome and became acquainted with the landscapes and seascapes of Agostino Tassi. In 1617 Cosimo II de' Medici summoned him to Florence, where he worked closely with Jacques Callot. Filippo sketched in the Tuscan countryside, and pen-and-wash drawings such as the Landscape with a Rustic House (Florence, Uffizi) capture effects of bright sunlight. He developed a new kind of realistic landscape, showing small scenes that suggest the charm of country life; examples are the Country Dance (1618; Florence, Uffizi), the Mill (Florence, Pitti) and the Fair at Impruneta (Florence, Pitti). In 1620–21 he produced a series of etchings of Skeletons of Animals, dedicated to the scientist Johann Faber, and in 1622 twelve etchings of Caprices and Military Uniforms (signed Teodor Filippo de Liagno). He was interested in macabre subjects (Mancini) and had a small Wunderkammer, or museum of curiosities.

By 1622 Filippo was back in Rome, where he executed landscape frescoes (1622–3; in situ) in the palace of Cardinal Guido Bentivoglio (now the Palazzo Rospigliosi-Pallavacini; see Salerno, 1970, figs 22–5) and was patronized by the Barberini. He probably made a second visit to Naples (Baglione) between 1624 and 1625, and there his fresh vision influenced Micco Spadaro and Salvator Rosa. He was the first Italian painter to paint from nature at Tivoli (Baglione), and his naturalism was important for later Dutch Italianate painters and for Claude Lorrain.

BIBLIOGRAPHY

G. Mancini: Considerazioni sulla pittura (Rome, 1616–24); ed. A. Marucchi and L. Salerno (Rome, 1956–7), i, pp. 97, 255; iii, pp. 47, 156

G. Baglione: Vite (1642); ed. V. Mariani (1935), p. 335

R. Longhi: 'Una traccia per Filippo Napoletano', Paragone, ix/95 (1957), pp. 32–62

L. Salerno: 'Il vero Filippo Napoletano e il vero Tassi', Stor. A., vi (1970), pp. 139–50

——: Pittori di paesaggio del seicento a Roma, i (Rome, 1977), pp. 132–5 [with pls and good bibliog.]

M. R. Nappi: 'Note sull'attività giovanile de Filippo Napoletano', Prospettiva, xxxvii (1984), pp. 33–43

Il seicento fiorentino: Arte a Firenze da Ferdinando I a Cosimo II (exh. cat., Florence, Pal. Strozzi, 1986–7), pp. 27–9, 193–9 [with bibliog.]

GIOVANNA CASSESE

Napoli, Giovanni da. *See* MARIGLIANO, GIOVANNI.

Nappel'baum, Moisey (Solomonovich) (*b* Minsk, 26 Dec 1869; *d* Moscow, 13 June 1958). Russian photographer of Belorussian birth. He learnt portrait photography in the studio of the Italian firm Boretti in Minsk, afterwards working in Smolensk, Moscow, Odessa, Warsaw and Vilnius before leaving for the USA to further his experience. After working in New York, Philadelphia and Pittsburgh, he returned to Minsk in 1895 and opened his own portrait studio. In 1910 his work was used by the press, and his portraits of prominent personalities in politics, science and the arts were published in *Solntse Rossii*, one of the most prestigious magazines of the period. Unlike many of his profession he did not flee from Russia after the Revolution in 1917 but offered his services to the Soviet government. He made his portrait *V. I. Lenin, Petrograd, 31 January 1918* (see 1982 exh. cat., p. 40) in order to familiarize the public with the leader's face. In the fashion of the time the final print showed only the oval of the face with the bust sketched in. In spring 1918 a big exhibition of his portraits was held in Petrograd (now St Petersburg). It included images not only of revolutionary leaders but also of poets, writers, dramatists, painters and film makers.

When the Soviet seat of government moved to Moscow in 1919, Nappel'baum also went there and set up the first state photographic studio. In the following years he built up his own portrait gallery, which in its range and importance had no parallel in Russian photography. Nappel'baum largely followed the classical Russian tradition of studio portraiture, but his portraits testify to his ability to capture the essence of strong human personalities. His use of a single light source, which often illuminated only the face, impressed his photographs with an enigmatic quality and a singular depth of feeling, as in his portrait of the producer *Vsevolod Meyerhold* (1920s; see Morozov and Lloyd, p. 139). Although under Stalin portraiture fell into disfavour as a 'bourgeois relic', Nappel'baum remained faithful to the genre and assisted in its later revival. His book *Ot remesla k iskusstvu* ('From craft to art') was published in Moscow in the year of his death. In it he related his life story along with comments on portraiture and the transformation of Russian society.

BIBLIOGRAPHY
Early Soviet Photographers (exh. cat. by D. Mrázková and V. Remeš, Oxford, MOMA, 1982)
S. Morozov and V. Lloyd, eds: *Soviet Photography, 1917–1940: The New Photojournalism* (London, 1984)

DANIELA MRÁZKOVÁ

Naqada [anc. Egyp. Nubt; Gr. Ombos]. Site of an Egyptian cemetery and settlement, on the west bank of the Nile 33 km north of Luxor. Predynastic Naqada was the type site for the two Naqada phases (*c.* 4000–2925 BC). FLINDERS PETRIE conducted the first excavations at the site in 1894–5, systematically recording 2200 graves, which he identified as the necropolis of a 'New Race' who, he believed, invaded Egypt during the First Intermediate Period (*c.* 2150–*c.* 2008 BC). In 1896, however, Jacques de Morgan identified similar graves at Abydos as Predynastic, and Petrie eventually became convinced of the correctness of this view.

The Predynastic graves at Naqada belong to two periods, Naqada I (or Amratian; *c.* 4000–*c.* 3500 BC) and Naqada II (or Gerzean; *c.* 3500–2925 BC). The deceased were buried in shallow rectangular pits, roofed with branches and then covered with sand. The bodies, preserved by the desiccating effect of the sand, were usually placed in a foetal position, with the head at the south end of the tomb and the face towards the west. The most common grave good was pottery, which, in the Naqada I phase, was 'Red Polished' (often with a black top). Sometimes the vessels were decorated with white cross-lined geometric patterns (*see* EGYPT, ANCIENT, fig. 88). The funerary equipment also included finely carved ivory combs and pressure-flaked flint blades of exceptional quality, the best examples of which were almost transparent.

In the Naqada II period there is evidence of stronger links with Syria–Palestine and Mesopotamia. Graves became more elaborate, some incorporating wooden planking into the structure. The pottery began to include buff-coloured wares with reddish-brown painted decoration depicting stylized humans, animals and boats. Ceramic human figurines were also produced. Slate palettes, formerly lozenge-shaped, were fashioned in animal shapes, while mace heads, formerly discoid, became pear-shaped. Flint working continued to be of a high quality, but copper artefacts were increasingly common.

In 'Cemetery T' at Naqada there were a few brick-lined burials, which were forerunners of the Early Dynastic (*c.* 2925–*c.* 2575 BC) tombs at Abydos and Saqqara. In 1896 de Morgan discovered the culmination of this sequence in the form of the tomb of the 1st Dynasty Queen Neithhotep (*fl c.* 2920 BC), with its accompanying

Naqada, ivory plaque from the tomb of Queen Neithhotep recording events in the reign of King Aha, 48×56 mm, Early Dynastic period, *c.* 2920 BC (Cairo, Egyptian Museum, CG 14142)

sacrificial burials. Among the objects from this tomb was an ivory plaque commemorating the Unification of Upper and Lower Egypt (see fig.). The southern part of the site ('South Town') also preserves evidence of a Naqada II settlement. Central Naqada eventually developed into the Old Kingdom (*c.* 2575–*c.* 2150 BC) town of Nubt, a centre for the gold trade.

BIBLIOGRAPHY

W. M. F. Petrie and J. E. Quibell: *Naqada and Ballas, 1895* (London, 1896)

J. De Morgan: *Ethnographie préhistorique et tombeau royal de Négadah* (Paris, 1897)

E. Baumgartel: *Petrie's Naqada Excavation: A Supplement* (London, 1970)

M. Hoffman: *Egypt before the Pharaohs* (London, 1980)

B. Adams: *Predynastic Egypt* (Aylesbury, 1988)

PAUL T. NICHOLSON

Naqsh, Jamil (*b* Kairana, India, 1937). Pakistani painter. His father, the painter Abdul Basit, introduced him to miniature painting. He devoted much of his two years at the National College of Arts, Lahore, to an internship with Mohammad Haji Sharif (1889–1978), the last of the old-guard miniature painters in Pakistan. Naqsh's first major exhibition was held in Lahore (1962); he then moved to Karachi.

Naqsh is among the most accomplished draughtsmen in Pakistan, equally skilled in pencil, pen and ink, water-colour, oil and mixed media. His early figurative work is slightly abstract, reflecting the influence of another mentor, Shakir 'Ali. Colour schemes are often monochromatic or bichromatic in brilliant blues and reds. Other paintings in lighter, more neutral tones suggest the influence of Karachi painter 'Ali Imam (*b* 1924).

Naqsh claims no symbolism for his ubiquitous rendering of women and pigeons (usually in combination), depicted realistically as well as abstractly. In *Woman and Pigeon* (colour on paper, 0.78×0.63 m, 1980s; Minoo Marker priv. col.), a stoic model with a pigeon on her knee reveals Jamil's consummate draughtsmanship in a simplified tonal composition. While most painters returned to figurative art and realism in the late 1980s, Jamil embarked upon a colourful, lyrical series of non-objective paintings.

See also PAKISTAN, §III.

BIBLIOGRAPHY

B. Ashraf: 'An Introduction to Jamil Naqsh', *The Sun* (2 May 1971), pp. 1–5

Nina: 'Jamil Naqsh—Our Most Complete Artist', *Focus Pakistan*, iii/3 (1976), pp. 23–8

S. Ashraf: 'Naqsh: Seeking Perfection', *The Herald* (Nov 1979), pp. 34–6

Paintings from Pakistan (Islamabad, 1982)

M. Nesom-Sirhandi: *Contemporary Painting in Pakistan* (Lahore, 1992)

MARCELLA NESOM-SIRHANDI

Nara [Heijō; Heijōkyō; Nanto; Naramachi]. City in Japan, in the Kinki region, in northern Nara Prefecture, on flat land at the end of the Nara (Yamato) Basin. This area once comprised the ancient province of Yamato, the centre of several ancient and early Japanese states, and is thus often called the 'cradle of Japanese civilization'. Like Heian (now KYOTO) and KAMAKURA, Nara gives its name to a period in Japanese history (the NARA PERIOD, AD 710–94), during which it was the national capital, and it ranks with these cities in its historical importance as a political, commercial and cultural centre. The modern city of Nara

corresponds to the outlying eastern sector of the 8th-century capital, Heijō (see §I below).

I. History and urban development. II. Art life and organization. III. Buildings.

I. History and urban development.

1. BEFORE AD 708. Archaeological records indicate that Nara was settled as early as the Jōmon period (*c.* 10,000–*c.* 300 BC). A large number of finds from the Kofun period (*c.* AD 300–710)—namely, the groups of tumuli at Mimoroyama (now Sakurai), Katsuragi (now Gose) and especially Saki no Tatanami (in Nara proper)— suggest that the Nara Plain was a base for several regimes and master lineages of the early Yamato rulers. There are seven royal tombs, all of the keyhole-shaped construction (*zenpōkōenfun*, 'squared front, rounded back'; *see* JAPAN, §III, 2(ii) and fig. 13), at Saki no Tatanami alone. However, the Nara Plain was not developed into a palace city and capital proper until relatively late in its history as a political and economic centre.

On the basis of an important citation in the *Nihon shoki* ('Chronicle of Japan'; AD 720) and other early references, it appears that the name Nara (which occurs in at least ten different ideographic forms in classical texts) is derived from the verb *narashi/narasu* ('to flatten'; *Nihon shoki*, Sujin 10.9.27), presumably because of its flat-land site. Some scholars, however, believe that it derives from the Old Korean word *nara* ('capital' or 'country'). This raises one of the major problems in early Japanese history, namely, the role of Korean lineages in the formation of the Yamato state. During the period when Nara was the national capital, it was known as Heijō or Heijōkyō, once the name of the capital in the Chinese Northern Wei period (AD 386–535), Pingcheng (now Datong, northern Shanxi Prov.). Heijō also means 'flat-land fortification' and, in the Japanese native (*kun*) phonetic system, the first ideograph of the word, *hei*, is read as *nara*.

2. AD 708–94.

(*i*) *Planning and construction.* The compilers of the *Shoku Nihongi* ('Chronicle of Japan, continued'; AD 797) attribute to Empress Genmei (*reg* 707–15) the decision in 708 to move the royal court and government to Heijō from FUJIWARA 20 km to the south. However, she was almost certainly guided by the wishes of her recently deceased son Monmu (*reg* 697–707); by concern over the future of Monmu's son Obito (the future Emperor SHŌMU); and by the lobbying of an influential ally, Obito's maternal grandfather, Fujiwara no Fuhito (659–720), whose increasingly powerful family had built up a regional alliance and headquarters at Heijō. Other considerations may have included: the overpopulation of Fujiwarakyō; a prolonged outbreak there of the pestilence that had taken Monmu's life; the need for more space for new office buildings to house the expanded government bureaucracy that had emerged with the promulgation in 701 and 702 of legal codes based on those of Tang-period (618–907) China; the Heijō region's optimal riverine and overland communications and superior strategic position; and, finally, the desire to construct a grand city that would rival the legendary Chinese Tang capital at Chang'an (now XI'AN), described by diplomats returning to court in 701, and mark the dawn of a new age.

Scholars agree that Chang'an was the principal model for Heijō, although numerous features derived from Fujiwara. The project began with the institution in 708 of two administrative offices to oversee the building: the Office of Heijō Construction (Zō Heijōkyō Shi) and the Bureau of Palace Construction (Zōgūshō). The city was laid out in a rectangular format that measured approximately 4.8 km north–south and 4.3 km east–west, about twice the size of Fujiwara but only about a third that of Chang'an (see JAPAN, §IV, 2(ii) and fig. 44). Like Fujiwara, it was situated along the two principal regional highways, the Nakatsumichi and Shimotsumichi, which ran from north to south through the Yamato Basin (see JAPAN, fig. 43). Heijō's northern border was defined by the Saki no Tatanami tomb group and the Nara hills; to its east stood two important mountains, Kasuga and Wakakusa; to its west was Mt Ikoma; and to the south it opened on the Nara Basin. Two rivers, the Saho and the Akishino, traversed the Heijō site, their courses having been altered to flow southwards through the city.

Again like Fujiwara, Heijō consisted of two zones: the Daidairi (palace compound; see §III, 1, below) in the north of the city and, to the sides and south of this precinct, the city proper, laid out in a regular grid pattern of boulevards and avenues. Heijō was traversed by eight boulevards (ōji) on a north–south axis and 12 avenues (jō) on an east–west axis; sectors formed by the intersection of boulevards and avenues were called bō (blocks). The main north–south thoroughfare was Suzaku Ōji, which was c. 72 m wide and ran north for some 3.8 km from the city's immense southernmost gate, Rajōmon (plan c. 38×20 m), to Suzakumon, the main gate of the Daidairi. Suzaku Ōji divided the city into two sectors: Ukyō ('right' or 'west capital') and Sakyō ('left' or 'east capital'). Each sector measured nine blocks north–south by four blocks east–west.

(ii) The new capital. Formal occupation of Heijō took place in 710, with the arrival of Genmei and her entourage, but construction of palace and government structures continued throughout the 740s. Once the court was firmly established at Heijō, the principal state and private Buddhist temples of the Asuka (see ASUKA-HAKUHŌ PERIOD) and Fujiwara capitals were transferred there. Apparently to accommodate some of these establishments, an Outer Capital (Gekyō or Gaikyō) had been laid out to the east of the Sakyō. This sector measured 2.2 km north–south by 1.6 km east–west.

In 710 Fujiwara no Fuhito relocated his clan temple, Yamashinadera or Umayasakadera, into the Outer Capital as Kōfukuji (see fig. 1; see also §III, 7, below). In 716 Daikan Daiji was moved from Takaichi in Asuka, rebuilt in the Sakyō and renamed Daianji (see §III, 6, below). In 718 Yakushiji (see §III, 5, below) was moved from Fujiwara and rebuilt in the Ukyō at a site opposite Daianji and four blocks away. In the same year Asukadera (Hōkōji) was brought from Asuka to the Outer Capital and rebuilt, as Gangōji, to the south of Kōfukuji. Collectively these were called the Four Great Temples (Shi Daiji) of Heijō, and

1. Nara, Kōfukuji, view across Sarusawanoike Pond

work continued on all of them, as on palace and government structures, throughout the reigns of Genshō (reg 715–24) and Shōmu (reg 724–49).

In 741 the devout Shōmu, in association with Empress KŌMYŌ and their confidants Fujiwara no Nakamaro (706–64) and the monks Genbō (d 746) and Rōben (689–773), instituted the system of provincial state monasteries (kokubunji) and convents (kokubun niji). This was modelled on a similar system in Tang-period China and expressed an ideology ascribing a religious mandate to the Nara imperium. For Shōmu and his associates, the principal scriptural foundations in this endeavour were the Konkōmyō saishōōkyō sūtra (Skt Suvarṇa prabhāsottama sūtrendra rāja sūtra) and the Hokkekyō or Myōhō renge kyō (Skt Saddharmapuṇḍarīka sūtra; Lotus Sutra), two sūtras revered for their supposed powers of national protection; and the Kegongyō (Skt Avataṃsaka sūtra), which sets forth the practices of a bodhisattva and teaches that all beings possess the 'Buddha nature'. The prime temples of Shōmu's kokubunji provincial network were built at Heijō: the monastery Tōdaiji (full title Konkōmyō Shi Tennō Gogoku no Tera, 'Temple for the Protection of the Nation by the Four Guardian Kings of the Konkōmyō saishōōkyō'; see §III, 4, below), which was under construction from 745 onwards on the eastern perimeter of the Outer Capital; and the convent Hokkeji (full title Hokke Metsuzai no Tera, 'Temple for the Eradication of Sin through the Hokkekyō'), built in 745 just east of the Daidairi. Other prominent Heijō temples constructed during the regimes of Shōmu and his equally devout daughter Shōtoku (reg

749–58 (as Kōken), 764–70 (as Shōtoku) were Shinyakushi-ji (*see* §III, 8 below), built in 747 by Kōmyō on the eastern perimeter of the Outer Capital; Tōshōdaiji (*see* §III, 9, below), built in 759 in the Sakyō just north of Yakushiji; and Saidaiji, built in 764 by Shōtoku on the site of her villa in the Sakyō, two blocks west of the Daidairi.

Two major Shinto centres were also constructed during this period, in affiliation with monastic complexes. In 749 the deity Usa Hachiman was made tutelary god of the Tōdaiji complex and the occupant of the temple's new Hachiman shrine (which survived into modern times as Tamukeyama Shrine). In 768 the Fujiwara house arranged the consecration of Kasuga (see fig. 2; *see also* §III, 2, below), the tutelary shrine of both their clan, and the Kōfukuji complex, in the hills to the east of the Outer Capital.

Like Fujiwara and the earlier palace–city capitals, and despite its comparatively enormous scale and structural complexity, Heijō was the national seat of the monarchy for less than a century. Nonetheless, during the city's prime, in the 740s and 750s, its population numbered around 200,000, making it probably one of the largest cities in the world at that time. Unlike the earlier palace–city capitals, however, Heijō remained culturally and—because of the militancy of the Buddhist clergy at Tōdaiji and Kōfukuji—politically viable long after the removal of the capital to NAGAOKA in 784 and Kyoto in 794.

3. AFTER AD 794. When Emperor Kanmu (*reg* 781–806) moved the capital to Kyoto, the great temples and their clergy, once the seat of state Buddhism, were left behind in Nara, thus diminishing their dominance at court. In time their presence in Nara vouchsafed the very existence of the city, which became known as Nanto or Nankyō (Southern Capital) and nicknamed *shaji no miyako* ('a capital of temples and shrines'). By the 12th century the Nanto Shichidaiji (Seven Great Temples of the Southern Capital)—Tōdaiji, Kōfukuji, Gangōji, Daianji, Saidaiji, Yakushiji and Hōryūji—as well as the Kasuga Shrine complex, were the sites of both pilgrimage and public ritual for the inhabitants of Nara and Kyoto alike. By the 9th century Tōdaiji and the Kōfukuji–Kasuga complex, affiliated to the Fujiwara house and its allies, had emerged as political forces in their own right, powerful opponents of the militant ENRYAKUJI complex on Mt Hiei.

In 1180, at the height of the Genpei or Taira–Minamoto War (1180–85), the warrior Taira no Shigehira (1156–85) and his soldiers put Tōdaiji and Kōfukuji to the torch. Most of the city was destroyed in the conflagration that followed. Under the Minamoto and their retainers, Tōdaiji and Kōfukuji were rebuilt, including the urban enclaves (*monzenmachi*: 'villages before the gates' or 'temple towns') that had grown up around them. These enclaves flourished and, dominated by Tōdaiji and the Kōfukuji–Kasuga complex, became a new city, Naramachi, on the site of what was once the Outer Capital.

By the 14th century Naramachi, structured around a system of guilds (*za*) affiliated to the temples, had emerged as a commercial and industrial centre. Until the arrival of ODA NOBUNAGA, who in 1559 broke Kōfukuji's admin-istrative hold on the city, the temple ruled Naramachi and

2. Nara, *nanmon* ('southern gate') of the Kasuga Grand Shrine

the province of Yamato without contest. It had become far more powerful than Tōdaiji and was supported by a force of 60,000 young monks, in effect its metropolitan police. Modern Nara, still very much the *shaji no miyako*, has developed from feudal Naramachi but retains, in its temples and their museum collections as well as its place-names, much of the classical tenor of old Heijō.

II. Art life and organization.

There is much evidence that, of Japan's capitals before 1600, Heijō was the most cosmopolitan: its rulers were profoundly influenced by continental culture and politics, and its residents were familiar with the numerous Korean, Chinese, Central Asian, Indian and other foreign monks and emissaries visiting the city. In 724, in an effort to make Heijō better resemble the splendid Chinese capitals at Chang'an and LUOYANG, Shōmu ordered that the tile roofs of the city's buildings be painted vermilion. It was during this time, specifically during the Tenpyō era (729–48), that a flowering of the arts occurred that was to exert a sustained influence on Japanese culture for more than a millennium.

As at Luoyang and Chang'an, the key factors in the planning of Heijō were its secular and ecclesiastical seats: the Daidairi (palace compound; *see* §III, 1, below) and the primary state shrine–temple complexes (*see* §III, 2–9, below). It was at these sites that artistic and cultural activities were centred and that the standards of classical Japanese culture were gradually developed.

While the Daidairi was the seat of the Nara monarchy, the principal Heijō temples were the locus of its religious mandate, where a highly articulated ecclesiastical hierarchy attended to the various Buddhist and Shinto deities, whose presence protected state and family. Like the great temples of Luoyang and Chang'an, the shrine–temple complexes of Heijō were laid out in a grand flat-land format that typically involved one or more pagodas (*tō*); a main hall called the *kondō* ('golden hall'); a lecture hall (*kōdō*); a *sūtra* repository (*kyōzō*); a belfry (*shurō*); a refectory

3. Nara, Shōsōin

In the centre of the corridor on the south side of the precinct is a two-storey *nanmon* ('southern gate'), which serves as the front entrance. There are three gates along the western corridor, all one-storey and identical in size. Only the southernmost gate—the *keigamon*—has a ceiling. The *kairō* and the gates, which are painted vermilion, were rebuilt in 1382–5. The eastern corridor collapsed later and was re-erected *c*. 1613. In ancient times, the *orō* and *kairō* were enclosed by a *mizugaki* ('sacred fence'). The middle gate and the *nanmon* were originally plain *torii* (post-and-lintel gates); however, styles gradually changed, and they assumed their present-day form when they were rebuilt in 1179.

An entrance path to the shrine (*sandō*) approaches from the west before turning north to the *nanmon*. Along this path, to the south-west of the shrine, are two similar, plain, unpainted buildings, the *chakutōden* and the *kurumaya*, which were used during pilgrimages to the shrine by the aristocracy. They were reconstructed in 1413 and 1632 respectively. An enormous wooden *torii*, painted vermilion, stands 1200 m west of the *nanmon*, indicating the entrance to the shrine compound. The Wakamiya Shrine is 150 m to the south of the *nanmon*. It is part of the Kasuga Shrine and is dedicated to the worship of the son of Amenokoyane no mikoto, one of the Kasuga Shrine *kami*. It was first erected in 1135 and has a main sanctuary identical to the Kasuga Shrine. Like the Kasuga Shrine, it was reconstructed in 1863. During ancient times there were two five-storey pagodas in the shrine compound; neither exists today.

BIBLIOGRAPHY

T. Fukuyama: *Nihon kenchikushi no kenkyū* [Research on the history of Japanese architecture] (Kyoto, 1943)
E. Inagaki: *Jinja to reibyō* [Shinto shrines and mausolea], Genshoku Nihon no bijutsu [Arts of Japan, illustrated], xvi (Tokyo, 1968)
N. Kuroda: *Kasuga taisha kenchiku shiron* [Monograph on the architectural history of Kasuga Shrine] (Kyoto, 1978)
S. C. Tyler: *The Cult of Kasuga Seen through its Art* (Ann Arbor, 1992)

MASAYUKI MIURA

3. SHŌSŌIN. The Shōsōin (see fig. 3) is both an architectural monument and the site of a collection of 8th-century Japanese art works and artefacts. It stands on the north-western perimeter of Tōdaiji (*see* §4 below). The Shōsōin is a key monument of Buddhist architecture of the Nara period (710–94), and its rich collection once belonged to Emperor SHŌMU, to his associates and to his temple, Tōdaiji. It was constructed as one of several storehouses on the precincts of Tōdaiji, and both the building and its holdings constitute exceptionally fine examples of the cosmopolitan Buddhist culture of the Nara period. Since 1875 it has been under the jurisdiction of the Kunaichō (Imperial Household Agency), which periodically sponsors exhibitions of its treasures.

The Shōsōin itself was originally Tōdaiji's *shōsō* (principal storehouse), one of several structures in a precinct (*in*) located north-west of the Daibutsuden (hall of the *Daibutsu*). By the end of the Heian period (794–1185) the *shōsō*, having survived all the other buildings in its precinct, came to be called Shōsōin. The present Shōsōin was extensively restored in 1913 and is one of very few structures to survive of the original Tōdaiji complex. It has occupied its present site for at least 1200 years.

It has 9×3 bays and measures 33.1 m wide, 9.3 m deep and is 13.9 m high. It is built in the hipped-gable roof construction style (*yosemune zukuri*), with a raised floor (2.7 m) and tile roofing. The building is of the log storehouse construction (*azekura zukuri*), which is common for storehouses. Its logs (*azeki*) of Japanese cypress are triangular in cross-section, with the flat back facing inwards. Divided into three units, each measuring 3×3 bays, the Shōsōin conforms to the 'long double-chamber' storehouse arrangement (*narabi kura*), in which a central open space separates two enclosed storage areas. However, it is also called a 'triple-chamber' storehouse (*mitsugura*), because in this case the central space has been enclosed. It is believed that the Shōsōin was originally constructed as a two-chamber storehouse: its two outer chambers are in the *azekura zukuri* format, whereas the walls of the central chamber have been rendered simply with wooden planks (*itakura*).

The collection housed in the Shōsōin began with a set of treasures donated by the widowed Empress KŌMYŌ in 756, during the rituals to mark the end of the 49 days of mourning after her husband Shōmu's death. These treasures had been collected by Shōmu and were donated to the colossal gilt-bronze statue of the *Great Buddha* (*Daibutsu* or *Birushana*; Skt *Vairocana*) that he had commissioned (consecrated 752). The collection was placed in Tōdaiji's *shōsō* (see above), and over the next two years Kōmyō presented more objects.

The present-day Shōsōin collection numbers almost 9000 items, which are divided into four groups according to their source: the original set of treasures presented in 756–8 by Kōmyō; a collection transferred in 950 from the storehouse of the Tōdaiji subtemple, Kenzakuin; items belonging to the administrative division of Tōdaiji; and documents, maps and various other materials belonging to the Tōdaiji archives. Shōmu's collection comprised some 700 items, ranging from implements for Buddhist ritual to musical instruments and chess sets, and was placed in the Shōsōin's northern chamber. Only 100 or so of these treasures and some medicine bundles survive; and these, with items from the other groups in the Shōsōin collection, are now housed in a separate facility for better conservation. The collection from Kenzakuin includes implements, furnishings, musical instruments, masks and costumes that were used in the consecration ceremony for the *Daibutsu* in 752, as well as items presented by Kōmyō and by her daughter Shōtoku (*reg* 749–58 (as Kōken), 764–70 (as Shōtoku)) to Tōdaiji, either in memory of Shōmu or to mark their own pilgrimages there. The Kenzakuin collection was originally housed in the southern chamber.

Most of the surviving Shōsōin treasures have been maintained in a state close to their original condition, because the collection was sealed by imperial decree (i.e. admission was only by imperial authorization). They have been classified into 12 groups by H. Doi (1968) and others: documents; stationery; musical instruments; Buddhist implements and items of monastic usage, such as robes and rosaries; items used in the annual celebrations called *nenchū gyōji*; chess sets and other objects for amusement; armour and weaponry; clothing and accessories; furnishings; utensils for food and drink (*see* JAPAN, fig. 141); medicines; and tools used by artisans. The Shōsōin collection is noted for several features invaluable to scholars: many of the objects have a clear provenance and are well documented; most are of an extremely high technical quality; many of the materials used in their construction—sandalwood, tortoise-shell, mother-of-pearl—are precious; the collection is vast; and, perhaps most interesting, a significant number of the Shōsōin treasures are continental in provenance, their origins ranging from China and Korea to kingdoms along the Silk Route and even Sasanian Persia.

BIBLIOGRAPHY

Shōsōin no shoseki [Calligraphy in the Shōsōin], Shōsōin Office (Nara, 1964)

Shōsōin no garasu [Glass in the Shōsōin], Shōsōin Office (Nara, 1965)

R. Hayashi: *Shiruku rōdo Shōsōin* [The Silk Road and the Shōsōin], Nihon no bijutsu [Arts of Japan], vi (Tokyo, 1966); Eng. trans. by R. Ricketts as *The Silk Road and the Shōsōin*, Heibonsha Surv. Jap. A., vi (New York and Tokyo, 1975)

Shōsōin no gakki [Musical instruments in the Shōsōin], Shōsōin Office (Nara, 1967)

H. Doi: *Shōsōin*, Genshoku Nihon no bijutsu [Japanese arts, illustrated], iv (Tokyo, 1968)

Shōsōin no kaiga [Paintings in the Shōsōin], Shōsōin Office (Nara, 1968)

Shōsōin no toki [Ceramics in the Shōsōin], Shōsōin Office (Nara, 1971)

Shōsōin no tōken [Sword blades in the Shōsōin], Shōsōin Office (Nara, 1974)

Shōsōin no kinkō [Metalwork in the Shōsōin], Shōsōin Office (Nara, 1976)

Shōsōin no mokkō [Woodwork objects in the Shōsōin], Shōsōin Office (Nara, 1978)

4. TŌDAIJI. A Buddhist temple at the foot of Mt Mikasa (see fig. 4), it is one of the Seven Great Temples of Nara (Nanto Shichidaiji). Tōdaiji (Daikegonji; Konkōmyō Shi Tennō Gokoku no Tera; Sōkokubunji) is the head temple (*honzan*) of the Kegon sect, of which it has been a seat since its consecration in the 8th century AD. The name Tōdaiji (or 'Higashi no Ōtera' in the *kun* phonetics; 'East Great Temple') refers to the temple's location on the eastern edge of Nara. It has occupied the same site for some 1200 years, during which time it has been one of the pre-eminent institutions of Japanese Buddhism. The modern temple is noted for its *Daibutsu*

4. Nara, Tōdaiji, restoration model

(*Great Buddha*; see fig. 5 below), a colossal bronze sculpture (h. 14.9 m) of the seated Buddha Rushana (Skt Vairocana), housed in the Daibutsuden (Great Buddha Hall; 57×47×52 m). The original *Daibutsu* was 16 m high, but was burnt and recast twice. The fact that Tōdaiji has been reconstructed several times with state sanction, as well as razed to the ground several times at the hands of sundry military powers, bespeaks the temple's profound association with both the good of the nation and its political realities.

(i) History and development. (ii) Principal buildings and monuments.

(i) History and development.

(a) To AD *756.* Sources such as *Shoku Nihongi* ('Chronicle of Japan, continued'; AD 797), the set of Nara-period documents called *Shōsōin monjo* ('The Shōsōin texts'; 8th century) and the compendium of Nara- and Heian- (794–1185) period documents called *Tōdaiji yōroku* ('Tōdaiji compendium'; 1106) record the early history of the temple. It was largely dictated by the *Daibutsu*, for the great state temple that came to be called Tōdaiji was originally conceived as part of a project to build and consecrate a colossal gilt-bronze sculpture of Rushana in the Nara region. The conceptual framework for this project lay in the *Kegongyō* (Skt *Avataṃsakasūtra*), with its celebration of the Cosmic Buddha Rushana as the organizing principle of the universe. The *Daibutsu* at Tōdaiji would come to symbolize the concern of Emperor Shōmu to establish a righteous Buddhist state under his rule and, no doubt, to provide his regime with an abiding religious mandate.

In 740 Shōmu visited the temple Chishikiji in Kawachi Province (now in Osaka Prefect.), where he saw the temple's monumental sculpture of *Rushana* and pledged himself to build a Daibutsu. A year later, in association with his wife Kōmyō, the Buddhist monks Genbō (*d* 746) and Rōben (689–773) and a coterie of confidants from the high-ranking FUJIWARA family, Shōmu instituted the *kokubunji* system of provincial state monasteries (*kokubunji*) and convents (*kokubun niji*). At the centre of this construct was the *Daibutsu*, which, like the *kokubunji* system itself, had received an impetus from China, where monumental sculptures had been commissioned by the state at sites such as the temple Fengxiansi at LONGMEN (now in Henan Prov.).

Work on the *Daibutsu* began in 743 at Kōgadera, a temple near Shōmu's detached palace complex at Shigaraki in Ōmi Province (now Shiga Prefect.), which the sovereign, driven out of Heijō (now Nara) by state and personal difficulties, was then promoting as the new national capital. In 745 Shōmu returned to Heijō, to which was brought the *Daibutsu* in its first stage of construction. The new site chosen for the sculpture was Rōben's temple Konshōji (or Konshuji) on the slopes of Mt Mikasa, whose principal patron was Kōmyō. By 747, as the work went forward, Konshōji had been renamed Konkōmyō Shi Tennō Gogoku no Tera (Temple for the Protection of the Nation by the Four Guardian Kings of the *Konkōmyō saishōōkyō*), and the Daibutsuden, which was to be the temple's *kondō* ('golden hall'), was in the early stages of construction. Most scholars agree that the shorter name 'Tōdaiji' came into use at about this time. In 748 the government's Zō

Tōdaiji-shi (Office of Tōdaiji Construction) was established. The area allotted to the temple was about 100 ha, equivalent to that of Shōmu's palace complex at Heijō, the Daidairi (*see* §1 above), and twice as big as Kōfukuji and Yakushiji (*see* §§7 and 5 below).

By 750 the *Daibutsu* had been cast and stood some 11 m high. Construction of the Daibutsuden was completed a year later. Gilding of the *Daibutsu* began early in 752, not to be finished until 757, although consecration of the sculpture and of Tōdaiji took place in 752. The rites held at the Daibutsuden, as recorded in *Shoku Nihongi*, were a reflection of the cosmopolitan flavour of the age: the principal ceremony attended by Shōmu and his entourage was officiated by Bodhisena, an Indian monk, along with Korean and Chinese monks of high standing.

(b) After AD *756.* Tōdaiji continued to evolve well beyond Shōmu's death in 756, flourishing as a seat of Kegon, Sanron, Jōjitsu, Kusha, Ritsu and other schools of Buddhism. By the late 760s the core complex had been built at the north-eastern edge of Nara's Outer Capital (Gekyō or Gaikyō) in the eastern sector of the city. Its outer perimeter was defined by a roofed earthen wall (*tsuiji*). Apart from the Daibutsuden, the principal structures were two seven-storey pagodas (*tō*), each some 100 m high; a *kōdō* ('lecture hall'); a *kaidan'in* ('ordination hall'); a *hokkedō* (*hokke-zanmai-dō*; 'hall for meditations on the *Hokkekyō*' (Lotus Sutra; Skt *Saddharmapuṇḍarīka sūtra*), which was the main hall of a precinct called Kenjakuin that had been established on the old site of Konshōji; the royal depository called Shōsōin (*see* §3 above), in which was housed Shōmu's collection of personal treasures, offered in devotion to the Great Buddha by Kōmyō on her husband's death; a *shurō* (belfry); a *kyōzō* ('*sūtra* repository'); monks' quarters; a *jikidō* (refectory); and, on a hillside just south-east of the *hokkedō*, the Tamukeyama Shrine dedicated to the temple's tutelary deity, Hachiman.

Although Tōdaiji continued to grow during the Heian period, most government sponsorship had been withdrawn by the 790s, in keeping with the policies of the new regime that had moved the national capital from Nara to Nagaoka and then to Kyoto. The Tōdaiji workshop was closed in 789. Nonetheless, Tōdaiji remained a great power, with large landholdings in some 23 provinces, as well as an influential clergy, whose leaders continued to figure in court politics and ritual and whose growing army of riotous mercenary soldier–monks (*sōhei*) threatened not only their rival monasteries—principally ENRYAKUJI, ONJŌJI and Kōfukuji, themselves possessed of considerable armies—and the common good but also Tōdaiji itself. It is for these reasons that very little of the original Tōdaiji complex remains.

In 1180, in the course of the Genpei or Taira–Minamoto War, Tōdaiji was set on fire by Taira forces. Most of the temple was lost, including the Daibutsuden; the head of the *Daibutsu* fell to the ground. In 1181 restorations were ordered by the retired emperor GoShirakawa (*reg* 1155–8) and financed by the newly emergent military leader Minamoto no Yoritomo (1147–99), his retainers and Kyoto patricians such as Kujō Kanezane (1149–1207). The project was supervised by the monk Chōgen [Shunjōbō

Chōgen] (1121–1206), recently returned from a trip to China.

The Tōdaiji restoration marked a watershed in the history of Buddhist art and architecture. Already the tastes and sensibilities that were to develop more fully in the 13th century were in evidence. Most of the sculpture restoration was in the hands of KŌKEI, UNKEI and KAIKEI, of the prime lineage of the KEI school; beside them worked artists from China; and, no doubt with the encouragement of Chōgen, Chinese Song-period (960–1279) formal elements were incorporated both in sculpture (for example in the Guardian figures by Unkei and Kaikei in the *nandaimon* or 'southern main gate', dating from 1196–1202) and in the stark 'Indianizing style' (*Tenjikuyō*) of architecture. In 1195 the new Daibutsuden was consecrated; by 1203 the restoration project was complete.

Tōdaiji was burnt down again in 1567 by Matsunaga Hisahide (1510–77) in his war with the successors of Miyoshi Nagayoshi (1523–64). Yamada Dōan (*d* 1573), another warlord, financed partial restorations from 1568 to 1570, including repairs to the cracked and damaged *Daibutsu*, which had again lost its head. A century later the temple remained in a state of disrepair. In 1684 the Tōdaiji monk Kōkei (1648–1705), granted permission to collect donations, began restorations in earnest. Donations had earlier been sought for the construction and restoration of Tōdaiji by Gyōgi and Chōgen. In 1692 a new *Daibutsu* was completed; in 1709 its new Daibutsuden was consecrated. The extant *Daibutsu* and Daibutsuden at Tōdaiji are these Edo-period (1600–1868) works.

(ii) Principal buildings and monuments.

(a) Layout. Recent excavations and research, as well as citations and diagrams in *Shōsōin monjo*, *Tōdaiji yōroku* and Ōe no Chikamichi's (*d* 1151) *Shichidaiji nikki* ('Diary of a visit to the Seven Great Temples'; 1106) and *Shichidaiji junrei shiki* ('Diary of my pilgrimage to the Seven Great Temples'; 1140) provide a good idea of what the temple looked like in the Nara and Heian periods. Its nuclear buildings were arranged in what is called the Tōdaiji-style temple plan (see fig. 4). This was a variant of the plan at Kōfukuji and at Daianji (*see* §§6 and 7 below). The principal structures were arranged along a north–south axis bounded, on the south, by the two main gates of southern access—the *nandaimon* and the *nanchūmon* ('southern middle gate')—and, on the north, by the *hokuchūmon* ('northern middle gate') opening on the *kōdō*. At the centre of the complex stood the *kondō*, the Daibutsuden, within its own rectangular compound defined by a *kairō* (roofed corridor). On the approach to the Daibutsuden between the *nandaimon* and *nanchūmon* were the temple's twin pagodas, one to the east, one to the west, within their own compounds. North of the Daibutsuden compound was that of the *kōdō*, formed on the south by the northern span of the Daibutsuden *kairō* and, to the east, west and north, by the buildings of the monks' quarters. Within this compound, to the east and west, respectively, of the *kōdō* stood the *kyōzō* and the belfry. To the east of the core complex, on the hilly slope of Mt Mikasa, stood the *hokkedō*, where it remains. To the west of the Daibutsuden,

in its own precinct, was the *kaidan'in*. The Shōsōin occupies its original site to the north-east of the *kōdō*.

(b) Construction of the 'Daibutsu' and Daibutsuden. There is little question that the construction of the *Daibutsu* (see fig. 5) was a technological feat worthy of the dreams of its patron (*see also* JAPAN, §V, 3(ii)(b)). Its preparation, which took 11 years, involved four stages and was supervised by a team of artists, most notably the sculptors KUNINAKA NO MURAJI KIMIMARO and Sueda no Jimaro and the bronzesmiths Takechi no Ōkuni and Kakimoto no Otana. The project also involved the erection, in 745, of a clay-and-sand (*hanchiku*) podium capable of supporting a sculpture that would weigh close to 250 tonnes.

The first stage in the *Daibutsu* project was construction of a wooden 'skeleton' (*taikotsu zukuri*), over which layers of bamboo matting were affixed. In 745 this wooden frame was brought from Kōgadera to its new site at Konshōji. Next, a clay core (*nakago*) was formed over the wooden frame (*sozō zukuri*, 'clay construction'). The clay, mixed with straw, was built up to a thickness of 200 to 300 mm and then painted with a paste of ash, clay and starch (*shikkui*), which gave a protective, lacquer-like coating. The clay core, itself a huge sculpture, seems to have been complete by 746.

Next came the double process of preparing the clay outer mould (*sotogata zukuri*), followed by casting (*chūzō*). This was done in eight stages and took three years, from 747 to 749. Beginning in sections at the bottom of the now hardened clay core, a part of the surface of the core was coated with a paste of mica or talc; over this, a layer of fine clay was applied; next came a layer of coarser clay mixed with straw, wood or metal shavings applied to a thickness of some 300 mm; then the section was allowed

5. Nara, Tōdaiji, gilt-bronze statue of *Daibutsu* (*Great Buddha*), h. 14.9 m, consecrated *c.* 752

to dry. Once dry, the section was removed, and about 60 mm were shaved from its inner surface to form a matrix (*nakago zukuri*) for the molten metal. Numerous such sections, each measuring perhaps 1800×300× 900 mm, were taken in a band around the clay *Daibutsu*. They were then returned to their original positions along the clay core; earth was packed around them to hold them in place; and the molten metal, arriving via flues from furnaces operated near by, was poured into the 60-mm matrix (*igata*).

This double process was repeated eight times. When bronze casting was finished in 749, the *Daibutsu* stood covered by a 16-m mound of earth. (The sculpture's hands were cast separately in four stages.) Once the earth had been removed, the surface of the sculpture was polished as the Daibutsuden was being constructed over the huge icon. In 752 the gilding process (*tokin*) began: sections of the bronze surface were washed with plum vinegar and then painted with an amalgam of gold and mercury (in a ratio of *c.* 1:5). Heating evaporated the mercury, and the remaining gold surface was then polished.

The structure erected to house the resulting gilt-bronze *Daibutsu* was appropriately monumental. It had 11×7 bays and measured at least 87×47×52 m. The present Daibutsuden, consecrated in 1709, is considerably smaller (7×7 bays) and, with features such as its ornamental 'Chinese' gable (*karahafu*) with bronze roofing, preserves little of the ambience of its Nara-period prototype. The building is a one-storey structure built in the hipped-gable roof construction format (*yosemune zukuri*) with tile roofing (*hongawarabuki*) and a *mokoshi* (walled outer corridor equipped with a small subsidiary roof construction) along its ground-floor. Its corbelled bracketing, in the starkly tiered *Tenjikuyō* style, places the structure outside the Nara architectural tradition.

(c) Other structures. There are several buildings at modern Tōdaiji that have survived in their 8th-century form: the Tegaimon; the Honbō *sūtra* repository (*kyōzō*); and the *hokkedō*.

Tegaimon. This building, used primarily by monks, was the northernmost gate into the Tōdaiji complex from the west. It is a three-bay, 'eight-legged' gate (*hakkyakumon*; a gate with eight posts) with one door and a tiled roof in the gabled-roof construction format (*kirizuma zukuri*; 16.7×10.6×8.3 m). Typical Nara-period features are seen in the gate's roof-support system, which involves double rainbow beams (*nijū-kōryō*) with frog-leg struts (*kaerumata*). The ceilingless interior of each bay reveals the reverse of a 'hidden cosmetic roof' (*keshōyane*). In the 1190s, in the course of the Tōdaiji restoration project, the Tegaimon underwent repairs, at which time its bracket complexes were altered from three-on-one (*mitsudogumi*, or *mitsudo-tokyō*) to one-stepped (*degumi*) (*see* BRACKET SYSTEM, §3).

Honbō sūtra repository. This building, just south of the *hokkedō*, is a 3×2-bay storehouse (8.9×10.3×5.9 m) in the *yosemune zukuri*, with a raised floor (*takayuka*) and tile roofing. The building is of log storehouse construction (*azekura zukuri*); its logs (*azeki*) are triangular in cross-section, with the base of the triangle facing the storehouse

interior, and are stacked in the interlocking 'well-crib' format (*seirōgata*), in which log ends overlap. It is considered to be a representative example of a Nara-period storehouse.

Hokkedō. According to *Tōdaiji yōroku* and other sources, the *hokkedō* was the main hall at Rōben's temple Konshōji. It was the site of annual rites celebrating the *Hokkekyō*; it was also called the Sangatsudō (Third-month Hall) because these rites were held in the third month of the lunar year. The current structure is believed to have been built between 746 and 748. Its *honzon* (principal object of worship) is a 3.62 m high sculpture in the lacquer technique called *dakkatsu kanshitsu* ('removed-core [dry] lacquer', in which layers of lacquer-soaked hemp cloth are applied over a clay core, which is later removed) of the bodhisattva *Fukūkenjaku Kannon* (Skt Amoghapasha Avalokiteshvara). This icon, one of an important group of 8th-century lacquer sculptures now housed in the building, is believed to have been produced at the Tōdaiji workshop of Kuninaka no Muraji Kimimaro, which was also responsible for the *Daibutsu*. Most scholars agree that the *Fukūkenjaku* sculpture was ready by the time of the first *Hokkekyō* rite at the *hokkedō* in 748.

The *hokkedō* consists of two units, the original 8th-century *seidō* ('main hall') and, in front of it, the *raidō* ('worship chapel'), a structure added during the restorations of the late 12th century. The *seidō*, in the *yosemune zukuri* with tile roofing, measures 5×8 bays; the *raidō*, which measures 5×2 bays, is built in the hip-and-gable roof construction format (*irimoya zukuri*), also with tile roofing (full size 18.4×25.2 m). Originally the *seidō* and the *raidō* were separate structures, but they were connected as 'twin halls' (*narabidono*) in the 1190s. The *seidō*, completed *c.* 746, is noted for its simplicity and clarity of execution, features that are emblematic of the architecture of the classical era known as Tenpyō (AD 729–49). This is especially evident in the one-stepped bracket complexes and in the squared rendering of rafters.

Belfry, kaisandō and nandaimon. A number of buildings at Tōdaiji are important monuments of Kamakura-period (1185–1333) architecture, including the belfry, the *kaisandō* ('founder's hall') and the *nandaimon*. The belfry was constructed between 1207 and 1210, in the *irimoya zukuri* with tile roofing. It measures one bay square (7.6×7.6 m), stands on a stone podium of the *danjōzumi* type, in which stones are cut square and arranged in a stepped, rectangular format, and is open on all four sides (*shimen fukihanachi*). Structural reinforcements—to support the huge bronze bell (h. 3.86 m, diam. 2.76 m; cast in 750)—include supplementary pillars (*mabashira*) and tie-beams (*nuki*) as well as immense frog-leg struts. Elements of the *Tenjikuyō* style are seen in the downward slant (*kurigata*) of the tie-beam ends and in the circular rendering of the frog-leg struts in cross-section.

The *kaisandō* is a one-storey, 3-bay-square structure in the pyramidal-roof construction format (*hōgyō zukuri*) with tile roofing. It enshrines a noted wooden sculpture of Rōben, believed to have been completed *c.* 1019, when Tōdaiji officials staged the first temple memorial in honour of the prelate. The *kaisandō* may have been built in the 1190s, during Chōgen's tenure at Tōdaiji. It was originally a much smaller chapel, measuring only one bay square; it was enlarged to its present size in 1250 with the addition of the *gejin* (outer sanctuary) (full size 7.2×7.2 m). The building is a fine example of the simple *Tenjikuyō* style: the bracketing is restrained, but the overall ambience—with the pillars rising abruptly to the roof—is one of boldness and stark clarity.

The *nandaimon* is one of Tōdaiji's more celebrated buildings. Like the *kaisandō*, it is regarded as a key example of Chōgen's influence and taste as manifested during the Tōdaiji restoration project of 1181–1203. The *nandaimon* is a colossal structure, standing some 25 m high and measuring five bays (28.8 m) wide and two bays (10.8 m) deep. It consists of two storeys of equal size, an unusual design (the upper storey was traditionally smaller) but with suitably monumental effect, and is constructed in the *irimoya zukuri* with tile roofing. Temple records indicate that work on the *nandaimon* began in 1196; it was completed around 1199 and consecrated in 1203. The building's three centre bays serve as the gate proper; the outer bays are enclosed. In each outer bay is one of a pair of wooden *Kongō rikishi* (guardians called 'adamantine strengths'; Skt Vajradhara), measuring 8.36 and 8.42 m, sculpted in 1203 by the Kei-school masters Unkei and Kaikei and their apprentices.

The *nandaimon* is outstanding as an example of the fully developed *Tenjikuyō* style. The roof rests on stout, towering pillars; its deep eaves are supported by six-stepped bracket complexes (*mutesaki*), which rise in tiers and without bracket arms, the lateral bracing being accomplished through penetrating tie-beams. As in the belfry, the tie-beam ends (*kibana*) are cut in a downward slant. Tail rafters (*odaruki*), which bear the weight of the eaves, are seen only at the corners of the building. The roof has been rendered without the usual framework of hidden rafters (*noyane*), leaving the roof exposed (*keshōyane*) and without a ceiling, a feature considered revolutionary in view of earlier architectural custom. The overall effect is one of enormous proportion and grandeur.

BIBLIOGRAPHY

Tōdaiji, ix–xi of *Nara rokudaiji taikan* [General survey of the six great Buddhist temples of Nara] (Tokyo, 1970–72/*R* 1979–80)
I. Ishino: '*Daibutsu konryū*' [Construction of the *Daibutsu*], *Nihon bunka no rekishi, 3: Nara*, ed. M. Mayuzumi (Tokyo, 1979), pp. 106–8
'*Daibutsu konryū to Tenpyō no seiki*' [The construction of the *Daibutsu* and the age of Tenpyō], *Rekishi Tokuhon*, xxv/14 (1980)
K. Suzuki: *Early Buddhist Architecture in Japan* (New York, 1980)
M. Mushakōji: *Tenpyō geijutsu no kōbō* [Art studios in the Tenpyō era] (Tokyo, 1981)
H. Ota, ed.: *Tōdaiji Shin Yakushiji* (1984), xi of *Zenshū Nihon no koji* [Collection of ancient temples of Japan] (Tokyo)
The Great Eastern Temple: Treasures of Japanese Buddhist Art from Tōdaiji (exh. cat. by Y. Mino, with contributions by J. M. Rosenfield, W. H. Coaldrake, S. C. Morse and C. M. E. Guth; Chicago, IL, A. Inst., 1986)

MIMI HALL YIENGPRUKSAWAN

5. YAKUSHIJI. This temple, ranking with Kōfukuji (*see* §7 below), is one of the two head temples (*honzan*) of the Hossō sect of Buddhism. It is dedicated to Yakushi (Skt Bhaishajyaguru), the Buddha of healing. Located in Nishinokyō, just west of Nara city, the compound was originally constructed as a temple–monastery in the Asuka region, when Emperor Tenmu (*reg* AD 672–86) commissioned an image of Yakushi in the hope of curing the illness of his consort, the future Empress Jitō (*reg* 690–97). Construction of Yakushiji, the temple intended to house the image, was begun about 687, and in 697 the installation ceremony was held for the precinct's principal sculptural icon. The temple was essentially complete by 698, but some 12 years later the capital was moved to Nara (initially known as Heijōkyō, 'Heijō capital'), and it was decided to move three of the so-called Four Great Temples of the Asuka area—Daianji (*see* §6 below), Gangōji and Yakushiji—to the new city. This relocation was initiated about 718; the Yakushiji compound was rebuilt on its present site, mostly in the 720s. The first Yakushiji complex, which became known as Moto-Yakushiji, endured until the middle of the Heian period (794–1185); only traces of its foundation remain.

The plan of the 8th-century temple closely matches that of the Moto-Yakushiji in Asuka. The south-facing *kondō* ('golden hall') is prominently placed in the centre of the main courtyard with a pagoda on either side. The two pagodas, one to the east (see fig. 6), one to the west, are set somewhat in front of the *kondō*, close to the corners of the courtyard; this type of layout was evidently derived from that found in Korean temples of the Unified Silla dynasty (668–935). In this respect, Yakushiji differed from earlier, Asuka-period (552–710) temples such as HŌRYŪJI, in which pagoda and *kondō* share a central location in the

6. Nara, Yakushiji, East Pagoda, 8th century AD

courtyard, or Shitennōji, where the pagoda is directly in front of the *kondō*. The Yakushiji precinct also contained a *nandaimon* ('southern main gate'), a *chūmon* ('middle gate'), a lecture hall, refectory, *sūtra* repository, belfry and living-quarters for monks.

Of Yakushiji's Nara-period (710–94) buildings, only the east pagoda is extant. The west pagoda was demolished in the civil wars of the early 16th century; the other 8th-century structures were destroyed by fires and natural disasters and rebuilt during later periods in different styles. The east pagoda, constructed in 730, is a three-storey structure, 34.14 m high. Each storey features a walled outer corridor (*mokoshi*) equipped with a small subsidiary roof. These three small sub-roofs, constructed beneath each of the three main roofs, provide a sense of height and lightness. Above the nine rings of the pagoda's mast stands an unusual gilt-bronze finial (*sōrin*), decorated with a water-flame design and *apsara*s (celestial beings playing musical instruments), which also dates from about 730. The interior of the building was decorated with painted motifs typical of the Nara period, such as the *hosoge* (imaginary floral pattern).

Of the 8th-century *kondō* only foundation stones remain. These suggest that the building measured seven bays wide by four bays deep. According to an account by Ōe no Chikamichi (*d* 1151) in his *Shichidaiji junrei shiki* ('Diary of my pilgrimage to the Seven Great Temples'; 1140), this *kondō* was a two-storey building, which, like the pagoda, featured secondary roof eaves beneath the primary roofs to give the impression of a four-storey structure. The original lecture hall was single-storey but also had a secondary roof.

Other structures in the Yakushiji compound include a *tōindō* ('eastern precinct hall') dating from 1285, a treasury and a *bussokudō* ('hall of the Buddha's footprint'). The latter houses a stone monument, erected in 752 and carved with footprints of Shaka (Skt Shakyamuni) Buddha. The present-day *kondō* and west pagoda were constructed in the 20th century. A Shinto shrine dedicated to the deity Hachiman also stands within the precincts of the temple. It was first built during the 9th century by the monk Eishō, but the present structure dates from the Edo period (1600–1868).

Yakushiji contains masterpieces of Hakuhō (645–710) and Nara-period sculpture, among them an imposing, larger-than-life-size *Yakushi Triad* in cast bronze, originally gilded (late 7th century–early 8th), which is the main icon of the *kondō*. In this work, the seated deity is flanked by two standing *bodhisattva*s, Nikkō (Skt Suryaprabha) and Gakkō (Skt Chandraprabha), whose bodies sway in a graceful contrapposto stance. The rectangular dais beneath the Yakushi is ornamented with motifs of scrolling grapevines; grotesque, semi-nude, demonic (or barbarian) figures; and the Chinese symbols of the four cardinal directions—the dragon (east), tiger (west), phoenix (south) and entwined serpent and tortoise (north). The *tōindō* contains a graceful standing bronze *Shō Kannon* (Skt Arya Avalokiteshvara), which may have been cast slightly earlier than the triad. Both works exhibit the influence of China's sensuous, full-bodied, Tang-period (618–907) sculptural style.

The treasury houses a number of important works of Buddhist and Shinto art. Among them is a famous 8th-century painting on hemp cloth, depicting Kichijōten (Skt Sri Lakshmi), the goddess of fecundity, beauty and wealth. Executed in a style inspired by Chinese Tang-period figure painting, with brilliant colours highlighted with gold leaf, it depicts the goddess as a lady in fashionable Chinese court dress and an elaborate crown of floral ornaments. The Hachiman shrine contains a *Triad* of wooden figures dating from the late 9th century, which are among the earliest extant works of Shinto sculpture. These polychromed images, each carved from a single block of wood, represent Hachiman, the goddess Nakatsuhime and the legendary Empress Jingū. Hachiman is depicted in the guise of a Buddhist monk (Sōgyō Hachiman); the female deities are clad in elegant, courtly garments.

A number of important Buddhist rituals and ceremonies are still conducted in the Yakushiji precinct. Particularly notable are the Saishōe, a three-day annual event focusing on the *Konkōmyō saishōōkyō sūtra* (Skt *Suvarṇa prabhāsottama sūtrendra rāja sūtra*; 'Sūtra of the sovereign kings of the golden light ray'), the Kichijō-kekae, held in honour of Kichijōten, and the Jion'e, a memorial to Jion Daishi (Chin. Faxiang, *fl* 7th–8th century), first patriarch of the Hossō sect.

BIBLIOGRAPHY

K. Machida: *Yakushiji* (Tokyo, 1960)
M. Ooka: *Nara no tera*, Nihon no bijutsu [Arts of Japan], vii (Tokyo, 1964); Eng. trans. by D. Lishka as *Temples of Nara and their Art*, Heibonsha Surv. Jap. A., vii (New York and Tokyo, 1973)
——: *Nanto Shichidaiji no kenkyū* [A study of the Seven Great Temples of Nara] (Tokyo, 1966)
M. Inoue: *Nihon Kenchiku no Kukan* [Space in Japanese Architecture]; Eng. trans. by H. Watanabe (New York and Tokyo, 1985)

STEPHANIE S. WADA

6. DAIANJI. It is one of the oldest temples in Japan, said to have been founded in AD 617, at Kumagori, by PRINCE SHŌTOKU as a centre for the Sanron school of Buddhism introduced from Korea. Moved to the banks of the River Kudara, Daianji (Kudaradaiji; Takechidaiji; Daikandaiji) was rebuilt in an expanded version in 639. Among the buildings of the new temple was a large nine-storey pagoda, possibly in Korean style, thought to have been the first of its kind in Yamato (the early nation state of Japan). The temple was an imperial cloister, until a fire razed it during the reign of Empress Kōgyoku (*reg* 642–5). Rebuilt again, it was moved in 673 to Takaichi. With the formal occupation of Nara (Heijō) in 710, the temple was relocated once more, and it reverted to its old status as an imperial cloister. New buildings were added *c.* 718, when the monk Dōji (*d* 744) was installed as its abbot. At that time Daianji received its present name and became one of the seven major Buddhist institutions in the capital.

After a period of prosperity and expansion the temple began to decline when Heian (now Kyoto) was established. In the early 11th century Daianji was partly destroyed by a great fire, and during the ensuing centuries it fell gradually in ruins. By the 18th century only a small hermitage remained on the site. Excavations during the 1950s and 1960s showed that the temple's plan closely resembled that of the other major Nara temples including Tōdaiji and Shinyakushiji (*see* §4 above and §8 below). A large southern gate gave access through the outer wall to the temple area, which was divided into several lesser enclosures. In the largest of these, the first court, was a pair of seven-storey pagodas. To the north on the same axis was the main temple compound with a *kōdō* ('lecture hall'), a two-storey *kondō* ('golden hall') and a double pair of monks' quarters, comprising six individual buildings at the back and on the sides. A refectory and other minor buildings completed this gigantic complex. The temple had several gates on the northern, eastern and western sides. This layout seems to have been based on a Chinese Tang-period (618–907) model, probably introduced by Dōji, who was acquainted with the Chinese capital. Nothing remains of the temple, on the site of which stands a modern building housing an important group of 8th-century statues.

BIBLIOGRAPHY

A. C. Soper: *The Evolution of Buddhist Architecture in Japan* (Princeton and London, 1942), pp. 43, 53–4, 65

M. Ooka: *Nara no tera*, Nihon no bijutsu [Arts of Japan], vii (Tokyo, 1964); Eng. trans. by D. Lishka as *Temples of Nara and their Art*, Heibonsha Surv. Jap. A., vii (New York and Tokyo, 1973)

K. Suzuki: *Jōdai no jiin kenchiku* [Early Buddhist architecture], Nihon no bijutsu [Arts of Japan], lxvi (Tokyo, 1971); Eng. trans. by M. N. Parent and N. S. Steinhardt as *Early Buddhist Architecture*, Jap. A. Lib., ix (New York and Tokyo, 1980), pp. 84–5, 88, 194, 196, 200–01

J. E. Kidder jr: *Early Buddhist Japan* (London, 1972), pp. 38, 45, 67, 86, 106–7, 110, 112–15, 120, 158

——: *The Making of the Past: Ancient Japan* (Oxford, 1977), pp. 82, 100, 102, 126

H. Ota and others: *Yamato koji taikan* [A general view of the ancient temples of Yamato], iii (Tokyo, 1977)

HENRIK H. SØRENSEN

7. KŌFUKUJI. This temple ranks with Yakushiji (*see* §5 above) as one of two headquarters (*honzan*) for the Hossō sect of Buddhism. Kōfukuji (Yamashinadera; Umayasakadera) is in the north-eastern section of Nara. Its origin dates from AD 669, when Kagami no Ōkimi (*d* 683), the consort of Fujiwara no Kamatari (614–69), a celebrated statesman and founder of the aristocratic and influential FUJIWARA family, established a temple known as Yamashinadera in what is now Kyoto Prefecture. The temple was later moved to the Asuka region south of Nara and named Umayasakadera. After the capital was moved to Nara in 710, the temple was moved to its present site, probably during the Reikō (715–17) or Yōro (717–24) eras, and named Kōfukuji. Kōfukuji prospered as an *ujidera* ('clan temple') of the Fujiwara family.

The buildings of the temple–monastery were arranged in a layout characteristic of Nara-period (710–94) design: the principal structures of the complex were a *chūkondō* ('centre main hall'), a *kōdō* ('lecture hall') and monks' quarters situated on a north–south axis behind an inner gate and the *nandaimon* ('southern main gate'). A *jikidō* (refectory), a *nanendō* ('southern round hall') and a west main hall were built on either side of the central complex. In 721 the construction of a *hokuendō* ('northern round hall') was ordered by Empress Genshō (*reg* 715–24) and dedicated to the Buddha Miroku (Skt Maitreya). The *tōkondō* ('eastern main hall') was established in 726 by Emperor Shōmu; he had an image of *Yakushi* (Skt Bhaishajyaguru), the Buddha of healing, enshrined there as a pious act intended for the recovery of the ailing Empress Genshō. In 730 a five-storey pagoda was constructed in the south-eastern corner of the compound.

The doctrines of the Hossō sect, based on the Indian Buddhist school Vijnanavada ('Consciousness doctrine'; Jap. Yuishikishū), were introduced at Kōfukuji by Genbō (*d* 746), a monk who had studied Buddhism in China. Apart from Kōfukuji and Yakushiji, the other major tutelary sanctuary of the Fujiwara family was the Kasuga Grand Shrine (*see* §2 above), founded in the 8th century. Since Kasuga Shrine and Kōfukuji were supported by the Fujiwara nobility, from the late Heian period (794–1185) onwards the *kami* (deities) of Kasuga became associated with the tutelary Buddhist deities of Kōfukuji in keeping with a religious belief known as *honji suijaku* ('true form provisional manifestation').

As the power of the Fujiwara family strengthened during the Heian period, Kōfukuji became the most influential of the Nara temples. At the height of its prosperity there were as many as 175 buildings within its precincts. Although various fires destroyed temple buildings in the 11th century, they were soon rebuilt. During the conflicts that arose between the Taira (Heike) and Minamoto (Genji) clans (the Genpei or Taira–Minamoto War (1180–85)), the Kōfukuji complex was burnt to the ground by Taira forces in 1180. Afterwards, three phases of reconstruction ensued. The second programme of rebuilding was initiated by Kujō Kanezane [Fujiwara Kanezane] (1148–1207), who eventually won support for the project from the new military ruler Minamoto no Yoritomo (1147–99). The only buildings that survive from this general period of reconstruction are the *hokuendō* (1210) and the three-storey pagoda (first half of the 13th century); these structures are designated National Treasures. During the latter part of the Kamakura period (1185–1333) and the Nanbokuchō period (1336–92), Kōfukuji was repeatedly devastated by fires, and, although buildings were reconstructed, the temple's power gradually declined. The *tōkondō*, rebuilt in 1415, and the five-storey pagoda, rebuilt at about the same time, are the only extant structures from the Muromachi period (1333–1568); these are also National Treasures. During the Edo period (1600–1868), Kōfukuji's estate decreased, and in 1717 a major fire destroyed much of the compound.

Kōfukuji possesses an outstanding collection of Buddhist sculptures, some of which are displayed in the Kokuhōkan (National Treasure Hall); many are National Treasures. The earliest sculpture is a bronze head of *Yakushi* dated 685. Other major masterpieces of the collection include rare examples of Nara-period dry-lacquer statues and sculptures by members of the *Nara busshi* (Buddhist master sculptors), a professional guild of sculptors represented by the KEI school whose activities were centred at Kōfukuji and nearby Tōdaiji (*see* §4 above and JAPAN, §V, 3(iii)). The dry-lacquer sculptures, the finest extant examples in Japan, include two groups: the *Hachibushū* (Skt Dharmapala; 'Eight heavenly beings') and the *Ten Great Disciples of Shaka Buddha* (Skt Shakyamuni; 734). A famous example from the latter group is a figure of *Asura* (Skt Ashura), which has multiple faces and arms. Kamakura period sculptures are represented by the works of Kei-school artists, whose expressive style was inspired by Nara-period naturalism, and who competed with *Kyōto busshi* for commissions to replace statues at Kōfukuji that were lost in the devastation of 1180.

KŌKEI, head of the Kei school at that time, was asked to produce sculptures for the *nanendō*. These works include a *Fukūkenjaku Kannon* (Skt Amoghapasha Avalokiteshvara) and the *Hossō rokuso* ('Six patriarchs of the Hossō sect'), which are dated 1189. He also produced a group of *Shitennō* (Skt Caturmahārājika; Four Guardian Kings) for the *chūkondō*. Kōkei's son UNKEI was later commissioned to execute sculptures for the *hokuendō* and by 1212 had completed images of *Miroku* and of the Indian theologians *Muchaku* (Skt Asanga) and *Seshin* (Skt Vasubandhu). Associated with Unkei's third son Kōben (*fl* early 13th century) are a pair of demon sculptures known as *Ryūtōki* ('Demon carrying a lantern on his head') and *Tentōki* ('Demon shouldering a lantern'). A sculpture of *Yuima* (Skt Vimalakirti) by Unkei's pupil Jōkei (*fl* 1224–56) is also in the temple's collection.

BIBLIOGRAPHY
H. Mori: *Unkei to Kamakura chōkoku*, Nihon no bijutsu [Arts of Japan], xi (Tokyo, 1964); Eng. trans. by K. Eickmann as *Sculpture of the Kamakura Period*, Heibonsha Surv. Jap. A., xi (New York and Tokyo, 1974)
M. Ooka: *Nara no tera*, Nihon no bijutsu [Arts of Japan], vii (Tokyo, 1964); Eng. trans. by D. Lishka as *Temples of Nara and their Art*, Heibonsha Surv. Jap. A., vii (New York and Tokyo, 1973)
Kōfukuji, Nara Rokudaiji Taikan Kankō-kai (1969–70), vii–viii of *Nara rokudaiji taikan* [General survey of the six great Buddhist temples of Nara] (Tokyo, 1969–73)
K. Mizuno and others, eds: *Unkei to Kaikei* [Unkei and Kaikei], x of *Nihon bijutsu zenshu* [Complete collection of Japanese art] (Tokyo, 1991)

GRATIA WILLIAMS NAKAHASHI

8. SHINYAKUSHIJI. The temple of Shinyakushiji ('new Yakushiji') was founded *c.* AD 747 by Empress KŌMYŌ in order to petition for the recovery of her husband, Emperor SHŌMU, who was supposedly suffering from a disease in one eye. It was dedicated to Bhaishajyaguru (Jap. Yakushi or Yakushi Nyorai), the Buddha of healing. Shinyakushiji belongs to the Kegon sect of Buddhism, which was the most prominent of the Buddhist denominations in Nara during the Tenpyō era (729–49).

The only extant original building is the *hondō* ('main hall'), which is a low, unadorned hall, probably built at the very end of the Nara period (710–94). It measures 7×3 bays, with the three central bays constituting the entrance. It employs a basic bracket system (*daito-hijiki*) (*see* BRACKET SYSTEM, §3), consisting of a bearing block on which rests a large, boat-shaped bracket arm. The inner construction consists of a simple strut with diagonal bracing. The floor is made of tiles in accordance with the old Korean and Chinese models known elsewhere in the Nara temples. The hall appears to retain most of its original features, including the low inclining roof. The *hondō* houses a 2 m high gilt-wood statue of Yakushi Nyorai seated on a circular altar originally made of clay (later cement) and surrounded by lesser images of the Twelve Divine Generals of the zodiac. These statues date from the Heian period (794–1185) and may have been made at the time the hall was built.

Other buildings in the temple include the two-storey belfry (*shurō*) dating from the Kamakura period (1185–1333) (with later modifications), which features an exposed ridge with hidden, flying rafters, a two-legged east gate with a gable roof and no bracket system, the Jizōdō (hall for the worship of the *bodhisattva* Jizō) from 1266

with a hip-and-gable roof, and a four-legged south gate featuring a gable roof. All the buildings underwent major repairs in the course of the 20th century.

BIBLIOGRAPHY
A. C. Soper: *The Evolution of Buddhist Architecture in Japan* (Princeton and London, 1942)
M. Ooka: *Nara no tera*, Nihon no bijutsu [Arts of Japan], vii (Tokyo, 1964); Eng. trans. by D. Lishka as *Temples of Nara and their Art*, Heibonsha Surv. Jap. A., vii (New York and Tokyo, 1973)
K. Suzuki: *Jōdai no jiin kenchiku* [Early Buddhist architecture], Nihon no bijutsu [Arts of Japan], lxvi (Tokyo, 1971); Eng. trans. by M. N. Parent and N. S. Steinhardt as *Early Buddhist Architecture*, Jap. A. Lib., ix (New York and Tokyo, 1980), pp. 125–6, 183, 205
M. N. Parent: *The Roof in Japanese Buddhist Architecture* (New York and Tokyo, 1983), pp. 32, 34, 53–5, 64, 78, 121–3, 142, 145

9. TŌSHŌDAIJI. Tōshōdaiji ('temple for lodging monks from Tang'), in the western area of Nara, was established in AD 759 by the Chinese monk Jianzhen (688–763) on land donated by the imperial family. Jianzhen, who had arrived in Japan three years before and was the *de facto* founder of the Japanese Ritsu sect of Buddhism, presided in his temple at one of the greatest ordination ceremonies held in Nara and had a new platform built for the occasion. Empress Kōken (718–70) and several government officials received the *bodhisattva* precepts at Tōshōdaiji. After Jianzhen's death the temple continued to prosper, and it was one of the most prominent temples in Japan at the beginning of the Heian period (AD 794–1185). Its halls contain important Buddhist sculptures in wood. With the rise of the Tendai and Shingon sects during the 9th century, both the Ritsu school and Tōshōdaiji entered a period of decline that lasted well into the 12th century. During this interval many of the buildings in the temple fell into decay and disrepair because of neglect.

With the general renaissance of the Nara schools of Buddhism during the late Heian and early Kamakura (1185–1333) periods, Tōshōdaiji was restored to some of its former glory. Under the eminent monks Gedatsu (1155–1213) and Kakujō (1194–1249), the temple was repaired, and several buildings were rebuilt or reconstructed with the help of the Kamakura shogunate. During the Edo period (1600–1868) the old roof of the *kondō* ('golden hall') was dismantled and replaced by a new roof with a steeper incline. The raising of the ridge by 2.5 m gave the roof a rather 'heavy' look. The original upturned 'fishes'-tail' ridge ends (*shibi*) were preserved.

The *kondō* of Tōshōdaiji is the only surviving building from the Tenpyō period (729–49) in Japan. It measures 7×4 bays (28.0×14.6 m). Since the temple was originally small, the *kondō* has only a single storey, unlike most main halls of the period, which had two. As such, the *kondō* represents a new type of Buddhist hall, displaying the beginnings of a distinct native style (*Wayō*). It has an open porch, one bay deep, across the front, which allows the worshippers to get near the images inside without actually entering the hall. The front entrance is in the centre of the building, with the gaps between wooden pillars gradually narrowing to both sides. This uneven spacing conveys a sense of stability and weight. Originally the *kondō* had a pair of large doors, but these have long since been removed. The perfection and balance of late-Tenpyō architecture are further seen in the arrangement of the eaves and brackets as well as in the sturdy frame of the building. The *kondō* has a slightly reduced but compact three-bracket system and features double eaves consisting of rounded base rafters and square flying rafters. Each of the bracket arms sit on one bearing block (*masuto*) with the strut support (*shiringeta*) sitting on the second outer level in the bracket structure. This creates an orderly supporting system running the length of the hall.

Other buildings include the *kōdō* ('lecture hall'; see fig. 7), which was originally an assembly hall (*chōshūden*) in the imperial palace. It was rebuilt in Tōshōdaiji in 760. The present building dates from the 13th century and only partly reflects Tenpyō-period secular architecture, most notably in the double rainbow beams inside the hall. This building houses some of the most important Buddhist sculptures from the late Nara period. The parallel treasure building (*hōzō*) and the *sūtra* repository (*kyōzō*) are small, square log buildings raised on stilts. Both are said to date from the 8th century. The temple has also a founder's hall (*mieidō*), which features a dry-lacquer image of Jianzhen seated in meditation. The building itself dates from the Kamakura period. Also noteworthy is the two-storey drum tower originally raised in 1240.

7. Nara, Tōshōdaiji, *kōdō* ('lecture hall')

BIBLIOGRAPHY

A. C. Soper: *The Evolution of Buddhist Architecture in Japan* (Princeton and London, 1942), pp. 72–4, 77–8, 88–9, 105–8, 117–21, 123–4
R. T. Paine and A. Soper: *The Art and Architecture of Japan*, Pelican Hist. A. (Harmondsworth and New York, 1955, rev. 1981), pp. 309–10, 319–22, 361–2, 444–5
J. E. Kidder jr: *Japanese Temples: Sculpture, Paintings, Gardens and Architecture* (London, 1964), pp. 25–36, 149–84
Ars Buddhica, lxiv (1967) [whole issue]
T. Kobayashi: 'Tōshōdai-ji no Kamakura fukkō' [The restoration of the Tōshōdaiji during the Kamakura period], *Ars Buddhica*, lxix (1968), pp. 38–55
K. Suzuki: *Jōdai no jiin kenchiku* [Early Buddhist architecture], Nihon no bijutsu [Arts of Japan], lxvi (Tokyo, 1971); Eng. trans. by M. N. Parent and N. S. Steinhardt as *Early Buddhist Architecture*, Jap. A. Lib., ix (New York and Tokyo, 1980), pp. 110–32
Wu Wen, ed.: *Jianzhen* [Ganjin] (Beijing, 1980)
M. N. Parent: *The Roof in Japanese Buddhist Architecture* (New York and Tokyo, 1983), pp. 17–18, 36–9, 50–52, 64, 123–4, 142–8

HENRIK H. SØRENSEN

Narahara, Ikko (*b* Omuta, 3 Nov 1931). Japanese photographer. He studied art history at Waseda University, Tokyo (1954–9), and a one-man exhibition of his work was held at the Matsushima Gallery in 1956. His theme of man and the land gained him attention as a rising photographer. It was an intensely personal record of the life of the people of Hashima (popularly known as 'Warship Island'), an island in Nagasaki Prefecture created artificially for coal mining, and of the people of the village of Kurokami, Kagoshima Prefecture, suffering the fall-out of volcanic ash from Sakurajima. The works were later published as *Ningen no tochi* ('Man and his land'). From 1959 to 1962 he was one of the members of the Vivo group, which included EIKOH HOSOE and Shomei Tomatsu. He signed his prints 'Ikko'.

Ikko lived in Europe between 1962 and 1965, and from 1970 to 1974 in the USA, earning international recognition. In 1969 he photographed the Zen temple Sojiji, at Tsurumi, with a new awareness of his Japanese identity. His photographic publications demonstrated a balance between intellect and emotion. In *Yoroppa, seishi shita jikan* ('Europe, where time has stopped') he recorded the continent through its historic perspective, which unlike devastated Japan had retained some of its landmarks after World War II. One of his most famous photographs, of two metal dustbins being blown down a street in a ghost town in New Mexico, was published in the series *Shōmetsu shita jikan* ('Where time has vanished'); the collection has a surrealist tone, and Ikko focuses on space and time as much as the subject. His other collections include *España gran tarde*, *Japanesuku* ('Japanesque'), *Ōkoku* ('Domains'), *Venetsuia no yoru* ('Venice night scenes') and *Kū* ('Emptiness').

PRINTS

Yoroppa, seishi shita jikan [Europe, where time has stopped] (Tokyo, 1967)
España gran tarde (Tokyo, 1969)
Japanesuku [Japanesque] (Tokyo, 1970)
Ningen no tochi [Man and his land] (Tokyo, 1971)
Shōmetsu shita jikan [Where time has vanished] (Tokyo, 1975)
Ōkoku [Domains] (Tokyo, 1978)
Venetsuia no yoru [Venice night scenes] (Tokyo, 1985)
Kū [Emptiness] (Tokyo, 1994)

BIBLIOGRAPHY

New Japanese Photography (exh. cat. by S. Yamagishi, New York, MOMA, 1973), pp. 74–9
Japan: A Self-portrait (exh. cat. by C. Capa, T. Tamioka and S. Yamagishi, New York, Int. Cent. Phot., 1979), pp. 19–27

KOHTARO IIZAWA

Nara period. Period in Japanese history, AD 710–94, named after the city that in 710 became the first permanent capital in Japan (*see* JAPAN, §I, 2). Before this, a new capital had been built for the enthronement of each emperor (*see* JAPAN, §IV, 1). The history of the 8th century is spiced with stories of the courage and energy of the travellers sent on Japanese government missions to China—students, Buddhist clerics, scholars, craftsmen—to study, absorb and return home with a knowledge of the great Tang civilization (618–907). The SILK ROUTE linked China with Central Asia, India, Persia and the Arab civilizations as far west as the Mediterranean coast and brought a flow of people, ideas and exotic goods into Xi'an, capital of Tang-period China and the most cosmopolitan city of its day. Through the travellers to China thousands of items found their way to Japan, where they exerted a decisive influence on the development of Nara-period arts. Some 9000 objects from this period, many originating from markets along these great caravan routes, are preserved in the Shōsōin in Nara (*see* NARA, §III, 3).

The original Shōsōin storehouse was erected on the grounds of the Tōdaiji (*see* NARA, §III, 4), a structure of impressive scale. Buddhism, which had been officially received into Japan in the mid-6th century (*see* ASUKA-HAKUHŌ PERIOD), was in the 8th century nearly embraced as a state religion. These two monuments reflect the desire of Emperor SHŌMU, a dedicated Buddhist and beneficent patron of Tōdaiji, to bring Yamato, the early Japanese state, into the larger Asian sphere. The Tōdaiji was erected to house a colossal (h. 14.9 m) seated bronze image of the *Great Buddha* (Daibutsu; Skt Vairocama), the cosmic creator and central Buddha of the Kegon sect (*see* JAPAN, §V, 3(ii) and NARA, fig. 5). Colossal Buddha figures had long since been carved out of stone in the Chinese cave temples. Buddhist images made of clay and dry lacquer, of which there are a number surrounding the Vairocana and in other Nara temples, are evidence of a widened pantheon of divinities and a variety of sculptural materials brought from China.

In 753 the Chinese monk Jianzhen (689–765) arrived in Japan at Shōmu's invitation after no fewer than five attempts, aborted for reasons including shipwreck and piracy. After fulfilling Shōmu's desire that an Ordination Hall (Kaidan'in) be constructed for the proper induction of Buddhist clergy, Jianzhen lived out his years at the Tōshōdaiji, a small, exquisite temple complex (*see* NARA, §III, 9). A dry-lacquer figure, rendered with extraordinary realism and reverence, of the old and blind Jianzhen, seated in meditation, seems to embody the spirit of the period and the courage and stamina required by its people.

BIBLIOGRAPHY

M. Ooka: *Nara no tera*, Nihon no bijutsu [Arts of Japan], vii (Tokyo, 1964); Eng. trans. by D. Lishka as *Temples of Nara and their Art*, Heibonsha Surv. Jap. A., vii (New York and Tokyo, 1973)
J. Sugiyama: *Tempyō chōkoku*, Nihon no bijutsu [Arts of Japan], xv (Tokyo, 1967); Eng. trans. by S. C. Morse as *Classic Buddhist Sculpture: The Tempyō Period* (New York, 1982)
R. Hayashi: *The Silk Road and the Shōsōin* (Tokyo, 1975)
The Great Eastern Temple: Treasures of Japanese Buddhist Art from Tōdai-ji (exh. cat. by M. Yutaka; Eng. trans. by C. J. Bogel and others; Chicago, IL, A. Inst., 1986)

BONNIE ABIKO

Narashige Koide. *See* KOIDE, NARASHIGE.

Narbonne [anc. Narbo Martius]. French city in Aude, situated in the south-east, 13 km from the Mediterranean Sea. It was the first Roman colony in Gaul (118 BC) and became capital of the province of southern Gaul, Gallia Narbonensis, and an important port. There was a further influx of Roman settlers in 46 BC; the city flourished under the Empire, and it became renowned for its beauty. Traces of the once famous Capitol and an early amphitheatre have been uncovered. Christianity may have been introduced to Narbonne as early as the 1st century AD, and a bishopric (dissolved 1790) was established there by the 4th century; remains of an Early Christian necropolis with numerous marble sarcophagi and carvings survive. From 413 to the late 7th century the city was under Visigothic rule; traces of their fortifications and of a 5th-century cathedral have been excavated. Narbonne was subsequently occupied by the Saracens and then by the Franks, becoming the capital of the duchy of Gothia or Septimania in the 9th century. During the Middle Ages, government of the city was divided between the counts of Toulouse and the archbishops, and there was an important Jewish community (expelled 1306). Surviving monuments from the 12th century to the 14th include the fortified Palais des Archevêques, the Early Gothic church of St Paul-Serge and the cathedral (*see* §1 below).

Narbonne remained an important port throughout the Middle Ages, but in 1320 the area was flooded by the River Aude; disease and epidemics spread as a result, the harbour silted up and the city gradually declined. It was incorporated into the kingdom of France in 1509. In the mid-19th century the city walls were demolished, and boulevards were laid out, but the inner network of medieval streets has been preserved. Narbonne is now a trading centre for the surrounding wine-growing districts.

☐

1. CATHEDRAL.

(i) Architecture. The first stone of the cathedral of SS Just and Pasteur, sent from Rome by Pope Clement IV, was laid on 13 April 1272 by Maurin, Clement's successor as Archbishop of Narbonne. The new building was intended to replace the Carolingian cathedral built in 890 by Archbishop Théodard (*reg* 885–93) and finally razed in 1354. Construction was slow and was never finished,

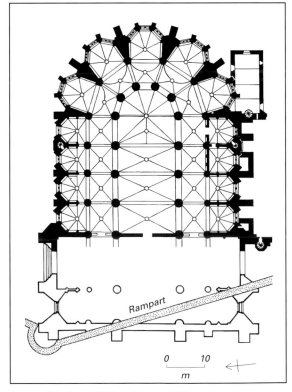

1. Plan of Narbonne Cathedral, begun 1272

2. Narbonne Cathedral (begun 1272), choir looking east

because the city consuls refused to pull down part of the town rampart to make way for the nave. Situated near the former bed of the River Aude in the part of the Cité that was a dependency of the archbishopric, the cathedral is bounded to the south and east by the archbishop's palace (11th–14th century) and the cloister (14th–15th century). The town rampart that checked its construction in 1349 lay to the west.

In 1286 Jean Deschamps, who was also the architect of the cathedral of Clermont Ferrand (see DESCHAMPS), arrived on the site. He was succeeded by Dominique de Faveran (1295–1309), Jacques de Faveran (1309–36) and Raymond Aicard (1336–49), but it is difficult to determine the role of each in the stages of construction.

The present building comprises the choir and the beginning of the transept. The four straight bays of the choir have aisles flanked by chapels on the north and south; those on the north are linked by a passage. The apse has an ambulatory and five radiating chapels (see fig. 1). Although the layout of Narbonne imitates the great cathedral choirs of northern France, the building is particularly interesting for its elevation: the arcades occupy half the total height; there is a blind triforium (at a time when glazed triforia were widespread); and each clerestory window is flanked by expanses of wall (see fig. 2). The treatment of the arcades was also new: the strict relationship between the mouldings of ribs, arcades and piers was abandoned in favour of arcade mouldings that die into a

circular pier, which has only a few slender shafts attached to it (this design was incised into the floor of the axial chapel; for illustration see TRACING FLOOR, TRACING HOUSE). The tension created by clusters of colonnettes continuing through to the vault disappeared and was replaced by a more relaxed system that anticipated the developments of Late Gothic. On the exterior, the traditional pyramidal arrangement of side chapels, aisles and central vessel was supplanted by a section on two levels, in which the central vessel rises above side chapels, aisles and ambulatory of equal height. The effect of two massive, juxtaposed volumes is heightened by the terraces over the chapels, ambulatory and aisles, which break the vertical emphasis.

In addition to these preoccupations, which are characteristic of early 14th-century Gothic, the builders integrated local traditions. Southern Gothic tends to reject light and stresses the squat, almost defensive aspect of buildings. At Narbonne, the rejection of light is expressed by the use of smallish windows and a blind triforium; the defensive character is perceptible in the lower parts of the buttresses, which contain guard-rooms provided with arrow loops, while the upper parts of the buttresses are connected to one another by a crenellated parapet walk.

(ii) Stained glass. The oldest glass, in the central window of the chapel of St Pierre, was reused from the previous building. Dating from the 1260s, it represents the *Life of St Peter* and includes standing figures of the cathedral's patron saints. The stained-glass windows of the radiating chapels and the hemicycle constitute, with those of St Nazaire, Carcassonne, the largest surviving collection in Languedoc. They are divided stylistically and chronologically into two main groups: one from 1295 to 1310, and the other, influenced by Norman models, from 1320 to 1335. Glass from the first group decorates the chapel of St Michel (*c.* 1300), representing, in an iconography rare in 14th-century stained glass, the *Legend of the Archangel*; it is also to be found in the axial chapel of Notre-Dame-de-Bethléem, which has cycles of the *Nativity*, *Epiphany* and the *Massacre of the Innocents*, with SS Pasteur and Just, each flanked by two angels on a grisaille ground in the side windows; and also in the central window of the adjoining Trinity Chapel (*c.* 1310), depicting in three lancet windows the Father, the Son and the Holy Ghost, with grisaille windows to the right and to the left.

Glass from the second group is found in the chapel of St Pierre (SS Peter and Paul, each flanked by two apostles) and the hemicycle clerestory, where saints stand against a grisaille ground. In the course of the 14th century medallions increasingly gave way to grisaille and large standing figures, and the architectural decoration and canopies represented in the glass imitated contemporary architectural forms used in the construction of the cathedral.

(iii) Furnishings and treasury. The architectural sculpture of Narbonne Cathedral is of fairly poor quality, except for the boss of the hemicycle vault, which represents Christ showing his wounds (1340). There is also a series of tombs, of which the most important is that of *King Philip III* (d 1285), installed in 1344 in the central vessel. One weeper and the canopy over the head of the King (cathedral treasury) survived the Revolution (1789–95).

The work is attributable to the Master of Rieux, sculptor of the apostles from the chapel of Jean Tissandier in the Franciscan convent in Toulouse. The tombs of the archbishops form a screen round the choir hemicycle. The best preserved is that of *Cardinal Pierre de la Jugie*, executed between 1347 and 1375, during his lifetime. Inspired by work at Avignon, the baldacchino, set between two hemicycle piers, the canopy and the low reliefs on the tomb chest representing a funeral procession of bishops and canons all survive. The forms, already High Gothic, are precocious, but they also show the enduring influence of the Master of Rieux.

In 1981 a sculptured and painted décor, which had been allowed to decay during the 18th century, was discovered in the chapel of Notre-Dame-de-Bethléem. A cycle of paintings depicting the *Childhood of Christ*, along with an exceptionally fine series of scenes of Hell and Purgatory with angels and apostles interspersed, can be seen under the Late Gothic arcades. Certain sculptural and iconographic details date these paintings to the mid-14th century. Later a statue of a standing *Virgin and Child*, typical of workshops connected with the Master of Rieux, was placed in the centre of this décor. This sculptural decoration is completed by contemporary paintings executed in an Italianate style, stylistically related to the paintings from the tomb of *Bernard de Fargues* and those representing the Church Fathers giving the Rule to a monk and a canon, on the west face of the first two hemicycle piers. They are illustrative of the importance of the Italianate style in the Languedoc part of Midi in the 14th century.

The cloister to the south of the cathedral was planned in 1349 but was still underway in 1417. Its four walks, surmounted by terraces, are rib-vaulted and have buttresses topped with High Gothic pinnacles. To the east is the former chapter house, now the chapel of the Annonciade, the nine bays of which are also rib-vaulted. The cathedral treasury contains tapestries (the *Trinity*, the *Seven Days of Creation*), a 10th-century Arab casket from Cuenca (Spain), 11th-century ivory binding boards representing *Christ on the Cross* surrounded by scenes of the *Passion*, and the Pontifical of Pierre de La Jugie, illuminated in 1351 by four different painters, one of whom came from Catalonia.

BIBLIOGRAPHY

V. Mortet: 'Notes historiques et archéologiques sur la cathédrale, le cloître et le palais archiépiscopal de Narbonne', *An. Midi* (1899), pp. 252–302
L. Narbonne: *La Cathédrale Saint-Just de Narbonne* (Narbonne, 1901)
L. Sigal: 'Contribution à l'histoire de la cathédrale Saint-Just de Narbonne', *Bull. Comm. Archéol. Narbonne*, xv (1921–3), pp. 11–153
R. Rey: 'La Cathédrale de Narbonne', *Congr. Archéol. France*, cxii (1954), pp. 446–75
P. Pradel: 'Un Relief provenant du tombeau des "chairs" du roi Philippe III au musée de Narbonne', *Rev. Archéol.*, i (1964), pp. 33–46
M. Schlumberger: 'Le Tombeau des "chairs" du roi Philippe III le Hardi à la cathédrale de Narbonne', *Actes du 96ème congrès national des sociétés savantes: Toulouse, 1971*
Narbonne au moyen-âge. XLVème Congrès de la fédération historique du Languedoc méditerranéen et du Roussillon: Montpellier, 1973 [vol. ii incl. M. Durliat: 'La Signification de la cathédrale de Narbonne et sa place dans l'architecture gothique', pp. 209–16; M. Pradalier-Schlumberger: 'Le Tombeau du cardinal Pierre de la Jugie à Narbonne', pp. 271–88; M.-C. Gept: 'La Mise au tombeau de la cathédrale Saint-Just de Narbonne', pp. 289–96; J.-P. Suau: 'Les Vitraux du XIVème siècle de la cathèdrale de Narbonne', pp. 237–69]

Y. Carbonell-Lamothe: 'Architecture languedocienne et majorquine au début du XIVème siècle', *LIIIème Congrès de la fédération historique du Languedoc méditerranéen et du Roussillon: Montpellier, 1982*, pp. 61–76
J. Pauc: 'Le Décor de la chapelle Nôtre-Dame-de-Bethléem à Saint-Just de Narbonne', *Mnmt Hist. France*, cxxvii (1983), pp. 28–34
Les Bâtisseurs des cathédrales gothiques (exh. cat., ed. R. Recht; Strasbourg, Mus. A. Mod., 1989) [incl. C. Freigang: 'Le Chantier de Narbonne', pp. 127–32]
Le Grand Retable de Narbonne (Narbonne, 1990), pp. 27–44, 57–76
C. Freigang: 'Jean Deschamps et le Midi', *Bull. Mnmtl*, 149 (1991), pp. 265–98
——: *Imitare ecclesias nobiles: Die Kathedralen von Narbonne, Toulouse und Rodez und die nordfranzösische Rayonnantgotik in Languedoc* (Worms, 1992)
Les Vitraux de Narbonne (Narbonne, 1992)

HENRI PRADALIER

Narbut, Georgy (Ivanovych) [Yegor Ivanovich] (*b* Narbutovka [now in Sumy region, Ukraine], 26 Feb 1886; *d* Kiev, 23 May 1920). Ukrainian graphic designer and book designer. He received no special artistic training, but his tastes and later his style were formed under the influence of artists from the World of Art (Mir Iskusstva) group, particularly Ivan Bilibin. The influence of Bilibin's style is apparent in Narbut's illustrations to the tale about *Yegor Khorobr* (1904) and to Aleksandr Pushkin's poem *Ruslan and Ludmila* (1905; both Kiev, Mus. Ukrain. A.). In 1910, having travelled abroad, Narbut spent some time in the studio of Simon Hollósy in Munich. On his return to St Petersburg, where he was based from 1906 to 1917, he created several fantastic compositions that incorporated architectural motifs and were imbued with a sense of disquiet, such as *Landscape with a Comet* (watercolour, 1910; St Petersburg, Rus. Mus.). In his later years Georgy Narbut illustrated and designed books of Ivan Krylov's fables (Moscow, 1912) and Hans Christian Andersen's fairy tales (Moscow, 1912–13). In his illustrations to the book *The Year 1812 in Krylov's Fables* (Moscow, 1912) he perfected the technique of representing images as silhouettes against a contrasting background, which he also used in a number of portraits and compositions from the years 1913 to 1918.

Narbut had a deep interest in the past of his homeland and soon became an expert in this field. This interest is clear in the design of the books *Gerby getmanov Malorosii* ('Coats of arms of the hetmen of Little Russia'; Petrograd, 1915) and *Starinnyye usad'by Khar'kovskogo gubernii* ('Old estates of the Khar'kov province'; Petrograd, 1917) by G. Lukomsky among others. In the cycle *Ukrainskaya azbuka* ('The Ukrainian alphabet', India ink, 1917; Kharkiv, Mus. F.A.) Narbut expertly combined motifs from folk art with real and fantastic elements of architecture and landscape. From 1917, when he moved back to Ukraine, he took an active part in Ukrainian artistic life and educational work. In his drawings in India ink for the covers of the magazine *Nashe mynule* (1918) and *Solntse truda* (1919; both Kiev, Mus. Ukrain. A.) and the frontispiece of the magazine *Mystetstvo* (1919; Kharkiv, Mus. F.A.) he reworked motifs from Ukrainian baroque art and made a great contribution to the style of contemporary Ukrainian art.

BIBLIOGRAPHY

E. Gollerbach: *Siluety G. I. Narbuta* [Silhouettes by G. I. Narbut] (Leningrad, 1926)

A. A. Sidorov: 'G. I. Narbut', *Mastera sovremennoy gravyury i grafiki* [Masters of contemporary engraving and graphic art], ed. V. Polonsky (Moscow, 1928)

A. Efros: 'Narbut', *Profili* [Profiles] (Moscow, 1930), pp. 237–44

P. Beletsky: *G. I. Narbut* (Leningrad, 1985)

V. P. TSEL'TNER

Nardi, Angelo (*b* Razzo, Vaglia di Mugello, Tuscany, 1584; *d* Madrid, between March 1663 and July 1665). Italian painter, active in Spain. Born into a noble Florentine family, he was probably trained in the Florentine circle of painters that included Lodovico Cigoli, Domenico Passignano and Gregorio Pagani, and from 1600 he spent several years in Venice. By 1607 Nardi was in Madrid, and in 1615 he was commissioned to paint the *Reception of the Princesses of France and Spain at Irun* (untraced), a descriptive painting of a historical subject for the Spanish court. Between 1619 and 1620 he worked on an important series of paintings for the convent of Las Bernardas in Alcalá de Henares, founded by the powerful Cardinal Bernardo de Sandoval y Rojas, Archbishop of Toledo. In these his art is already mature. The monumental nudes in the *Stoning of St Stephen* and the solemn, balanced compositions of the *Betrothal of the Virgin*, *Ascension* and *Immaculate Conception* show Tuscan elements, while Venetian influences, particularly of the Bassano family, are evident in the *Adoration of the Shepherds* and the *Martyrdom of St Lawrence* (all *in situ*). There is also an intense naturalism in the depiction of some of the faces, and an interest in the use of light, probably due to a knowledge of the work of Michelangelo Caravaggio and his followers.

In 1623 Nardi married a daughter of Marcos de Aguilera, in whose studio he had been working, but in October 1625 he obtained an annulment. The volume of his work for the court increased during the 1620s, and on 4 July 1625 he was appointed Pintor del Rey without salary. In 1627 he took part in a competition for the painting of an *Expulsion of the Moriscos* (untraced), which was won by Diego Velázquez, and in the same year he applied for the court post left vacant by the death of Bartolomé González. Vicente Carducho, Eugenio Cajés and Velázquez voted initially for Antonio Lanchares, but it was probably through the influence of Velázquez that, when Lanchares died in 1630, Nardi obtained the appointment in the following year. Velázquez remained a close friend, as is revealed in an informative document of 1658, when Nardi supported the award to Velázquez of the Order of Santiago.

Among the fresco decorations Nardi executed in 1632 in the chapel of the Conception in the church of La Guardia, Toledo, are the *Fathers of the Church*, *Justice* and *Charity*; his works on canvas for the same chapel include the *Annunciation*, the *Assumption of the Virgin*, *St Sebastian* and *St Ildefonso* (all *in situ*). In 1634 he painted the lateral altarpieces (including an *Assumption of the Virgin* and an *Annunciation*) in the convent of Las Bernardas in Jaén, a foundation, like that of La Guardia, that was connected with Cardinal Sandoval. The works at Jaén are Tuscan in manner, similar to those he had painted in Alcalá; the frescoes here show a mastery of the technique, although they are dated stylistically, resembling the earlier Mannerist work of Giuseppe Cesari, Cavaliere d'Arpino, in Rome. In the Jaén *Assumption of the Virgin* and in the *Assumption*

of *St Mary Magdalene* (1639) of the retable in the Magdalena Church at Getafe, Madrid, there is a perceptible enrichment of his style. The symmetrical arrangement of the earlier Alcalá paintings is abandoned in favour of a more oblique composition, and the greater dynamism and depth are more in keeping with the general development of contemporary painting in Madrid.

In 1640 Nardi painted the large canvas of *St Diego of Alcalá Served by Angels* for the collegiate church of Sta María de Jesús in Alcalá de Henares (destr. 1941); this was his finest work, an admirably balanced composition with excellent passages of naturalism apparent in the faces and in the still-lifes. His later paintings, such as the altarpiece with *St Clare Defending the Convent from an Attack by the Moors*, an *Adoration of the Shepherds* and the *Adoration of the Magi* (all 1647; destr. 1936; see Angulo Iñiguez and Pérez Sánchez, pls 230–31) in the convent of Las Claras, Alcalá de Henares, and the *Adoration of the Shepherds* (1650; Madrid, priv. col., see Pérez Sánchez, pl. 30), indicate his inability to develop; the rather dull compositions are in the manner of the Bassano family and show a certain hardness and sterility.

Nardi remained faithful to Tuscan and Venetian traditions, not developing beyond the stylistic phase represented by Pedro Orrente or Carducho, whom he outlived by 20 and 30 years respectively. He was highly esteemed for his perceptive and accurate knowledge of Italian painting and was frequently asked to make attributions of works coming from Italy. He was regarded as a man of good character and was much in demand as an assessor of painting, sometimes being chosen by both sides in litigation or in valuations for contracted work. In 1638 Nardi and Carducho were involved in a defence of artists against their liability to pay taxes because they produced saleable goods; they succeeded on the grounds that painting is a liberal art.

BIBLIOGRAPHY

A. E. Pérez Sánchez: *Borgianni, Cavarozzi y Nardi en España* (Madrid, 1964), pp. 25–39, nos 24–48

D. Angulo Iñiguez and A. E. Pérez Sánchez: *Historia della pintura española: Escuela madrileña del primo tercio del siglo XVII* (Madrid, 1969), pp. 271–98

ALFONSO E. PÉREZ SÁNCHEZ

Nardo, Mariotto di. *See* MARIOTTO DI NARDO.

Nardo di Cione. *See* CIONE, (2).

Narice [Narici], **Francesco** (*b* Genoa, *c.* 1719; *d* Genoa, 1785). Italian painter. He was educated in Naples. Alizeri described him as a pupil of Solimena, but it has also been suggested that he knew Francesco de Mura and especially Jacopo Cestaro (1718–78) and Domenico Mondo. The artist's activity in Campania has been traced through several works dated between 1751 and 1779 (see Spinosa, 1973).

The two portraits of members of the Monticelli family, the *Gentleman* and *Gentlewoman* (before 1751; Genoa, Mus. Accad. Ligustica B.A.), show a stylistic derivation from the late 17th-century French mode of portraiture, with traces of Piedmontese Rococo (Sborgi, 1974), and the formal elegance of de Mura's portraits produced after his visit to Turin (Spinosa, 1979–80). The influence of the

Neapolitan school is revealed in the chiaroscuro contrasts, in the compositions with raking light and in the tendency towards pastel colouring, all of which characterize Narice's paintings for Genoese churches. These include *St John of Sanfacondo Saving a Child* (S Maria della Consolazione) and the *Ecstasy of the Blessed Marinonio* (S Giorgio), both datable around 1760; *St Jerome Emiliani in Glory*, probably painted in 1767 (ex-Santo Spirito, Genoa; Genoa, Villa Imp. Terralba); six paintings with scenes from the *Life of St Zita* (1777; S Zita) and two canvases of *St John of God* (ex-S Carlo, Genoa; Genoa, S Stefano, Sopr. Beni A. & Stor. Liguria, Depositi). Preparatory drawings and *bozzetti*, some related to the paintings mentioned and others to pictures now dispersed, are considered an important part of Narice's work.

BIBLIOGRAPHY
F. Alizeri: *Notizie dei professori del disegno in Liguria dalla fondazione dell'Accademia* (Genoa, 1864–6), i, pp. 165–7
A. M. Stoppiglia: *Memorie della soppressa chiesa di S Spirito in Genova* (Genoa, 1933), pp. 18–21
K. Andrews: *Catalogue of Italian Drawings*, Edinburgh, N.G. (Cambridge, 1968), i, p. 79; ii, p. 99
F. R. Pesenti: 'L'illuminismo e l'età neoclassica', *La pittura a Genova e in Liguria*, ed. C. Bozzo Dufour and others (Genoa, 1970, rev. 2/1987), ii, pp. 350, 373
M. Newcome: *Genoese Baroque Drawings* (Binghamton, 1972), p. 55, nn. 148, 148a
G. Godi: *Dipinti e disegni genovesi dal '500 al '700* (Parma, 1973), pp. 128–31, nn. 31, 31a; 132–3, n. 32
N. Spinosa: 'Un pittore genovese nella Napoli del secondo settecento: Francesco Narici', *Napoli Nob.*, v (1973), pp. 165–76
F. Sborgi: 'Pittura e cultura artistica nell'Accademia Ligustica a Genova, 1751/1920', *Quad. Ist. Stor. A. U. Genova*, 7 (1974), p. 20
N. Spinosa: 'Francesco Narici', *Civiltà del settecento a Napoli, 1734–1799* (Naples, 1979–80), i, p. 304; ii, p. 441
M. Newcome: 'Genoese Neapolitan Connections in the Settecento: Palmieri, Campora and Narice', *Ant. Viva*, xx/1 (1981), pp. 19–22
E. Baccheschi: *Il Museo dell'Accademia Ligustica di Belle Arti: La Pinacoteca* (Genoa, 1983), p. 57, figs 146–7
J. Garms and S. Prosperi Valenti Rodinò: *Due raccolte di disegni di recente acquisizione* (Rome, 1985), pp. 51–2

RITA DUGONI

Narjoux, Félix (*b* Chalons-sur-Saône, 19 Dec 1832; *d* Sèvres, 14 Aug 1891). French architect and writer. In 1857 he was put in charge of the restoration of Limoges Cathedral and two years later became inspector of diocesan buildings. In 1860 he settled in Nice as civic architect, where he completed the slaughterhouse, among other projects, before moving to Paris in 1864 to join the municipal administration. From 1870 until his death he was responsible for highway maintenance but did not belong to the official group of Paris architects. Nevertheless, after he was awarded a prize in the *Encyclopédie d'architecture* competition for his essay 'La Construction et l'installation des écoles primaires' (1872; pubd 1873), he was entrusted with the building of primary schools. He built one (1875) on the Rue Curial (now 41, Rue de Tanger) and another (1880) at 12–16, Rue Titon. He was deeply influenced by the lessons of Viollet-le-Duc; there are no flourishes in his style, where decoration issues from the rational use of materials: stone for the load-bearing parts of the structure and coloured brick as infill, with a few Gothic details, as in his own house (1889) at 3, Rue Littré. Narjoux became more famous from his writings than from his municipal work. He published several books on school architecture and was the author of a series of volumes entitled *Paris: Monuments élevés par la Ville entre 1850 et 1880*, in which his Rue Curial school appears, as well as other structures intended for children. These books were created very much in the image of those published by Viollet-le-Duc. Narjoux's son André (1867–1934) was also an architect and collaborated with Victor Laloux on the Crédit Lyonnais building, Rue Quatre Septembre, Paris.

WRITINGS
Construction et installation des écoles primaires (Paris, 1873)
Les Ecoles publiques: Construction et installation en France et en Angleterre (Paris, 1877)
Histoire d'une ferme (Paris, 1882)
Paris: Monuments élevés par la Ville entre 1850 et 1880, 4 vols (Paris, 1883)

BIBLIOGRAPHY
Obituary, *La Construction moderne* (12 Sept 1891), p. 588
A. M. Châtelet: 'Trois biographies exemplaires', *L'Ecole primaire à Paris, 1970–1914* (exh. cat., Paris, Mus. A. Mod. Ville Paris, 1985)

A. M. CHÂTELET

Narkompros [Narodnyy Komissariat Prosveshcheniya; Rus.: People's Commissariat for Enlightenment]. Soviet government agency established in Russia in 1917. When the Bolshevik Party took power following the Revolution of October 1917, it inaugurated a new set of administrative bodies or People's Commissariats. Narkompros was set up under Anatoly Lunacharsky on 26 October 1917 to take responsibility for the administration of education and the arts, including the maintenance of museums and ancient monuments. It was divided into various departments: Music (MUZO), Photography and Film (FOTO-KINO), Literature (LITO), Theatre (TEO) and Fine Arts (IZO), which was set up in Petrograd (now St Petersburg) in early 1918.

IZO was run by an Arts Board or Collegium, which consisted of David Shterenberg (President), Natan Al't-man, Nikolay Punin, Sergey Chekhonin, Aleksandr Matveyev, Aleksey Karev and Grigory Yatmanov. Later members included Vladimir Baranoff-Rossiné, Iosif Shkol'nik (1883–1926), Vladimir Mayakovsky and Osip Brik, and five architects including Vladimir Shchuko. Another Arts Board was organized in Moscow, headed by Vladimir Tatlin, who acted as Shterenberg's assistant. The Moscow Board included such artists as Kazimir Malevich, Robert Fal'k, Il'ya Mashkov, Ol'ga Rozanova, Aleksandr Rodchenko and Vasily Kandinsky. In both cities the Collegium organized various subsections to administer different aspects of artistic life, including the teaching of art in schools, the publication of art books and journals such as the Petrograd IZO's journal *Iskusstvo kommuny* ('Art of the commune'), which ran from 1918 to 1919, the revitalization of architecture and the promotion of art in industrial production, craft and design.

In 1918–21, during the years of the Civil War, the All-Russian Central Exhibitions Bureau of Narkompros managed to arrange 28 jury-free exhibitions. The first of these, which opened in April 1919 in Petrograd, included almost 300 artists of all tendencies and a total of 1826 works. The Museums Bureau, set up in Moscow in early 1918 and run by Rodchenko with the assistance of Varvara Stepanova, bought 1926 works from 415 artists and organized 30 provincial museums, to which it sent 1211 works. The

Subsection for Artistic Work registered artistic organizations that would undertake government propaganda projects. It organized competitions for various agitational projects including news kiosks and monuments to important political figures to be erected in all the major cities as part of Lenin's Plan for Monumental Propaganda inaugurated in April 1918 (*see* AGITPROP). It also commissioned stencil posters for different propaganda campaigns, including almost 2000 for the Abolition of Illiteracy Campaign, and it collaborated with the city soviets on arranging street decorations for the Revolutionary festivals of May Day and the anniversary of the Revolution. The Art and Production Subsection was directed by Rozanova, who, with Rodchenko, visited craft studios in and around Moscow and raised money to revitalize them.

IZO was also responsible for formulating a cultural policy for the new Socialist society. In 1919 it published a general statement of its aesthetic position and considered the nature and types of artistic forums that should be established. Among other proposals it suggested the setting up of a Scientific and Theoretical Department in the Central Section of the Academy of Fine Arts (AKIZO) in order to maintain contact with the latest technological and scientific ideas, while acknowledging that INKHUK, the Institute of Artistic Culture, was to be responsible for 'questions relating to the science of art'. Although avant-garde artists provided the majority of workers in IZO between 1918 and 1921, their aesthetic values were not accepted by the Party, and criticisms of Futurism, along with warnings about its adoption as the official aesthetic doctrine, were printed in *Pravda*, the Party newspaper, as early as November 1918. Lenin was particularly opposed to avant-garde ideas, and in 1921, having won the Civil War, the Party was free to reorganize and to purge IZO of avant-garde elements. From then on, the control of the arts by Narkompros became less innovative and more bureaucratic. Lunacharsky left in 1929.

BIBLIOGRAPHY
S. Fitzpatrick: *The Commissariat of Enlightenment: Soviet Organization of Education and the Arts under Lunacharsky, October 1917–1921* (Cambridge, 1970)
C. Lodder: *Russian Constructivism* (New Haven, 1983)

CHRISTINA LODDER

Narmer (*reg c.* 3000 BC). Ancient Egyptian ruler. A series of small sculptures bear the name of Narmer, who was the last predynastic king of Egypt and who is identified by some with the traditional first pharaoh, Menes. Objects bearing Narmer's name were found at Abydos in and near Tomb B10, generally thought to have been his burial-place, but also in Queen Neithhotpe's tomb at Naqada. The most important monuments of his reign come from Hierakonpolis (Egyp. Nekhen), the ancient Upper Egyptian capital.

'Narmer Palette', schist, h. 635 mm, from Hierakonpolis, *c.* 3000 BC (Cairo, Egyptian Museum)

A large macehead (Oxford, Ashmolean), bearing relief decoration, shows Narmer in his jubilee cloak and the red crown of Lower Egypt; dignitaries stand behind his throne and standard-bearers approach him; large numbers of men, oxen and goats are enumerated, and there are other hieroglyphic signs. Another mace head from Hierakonpolis also bears Narmer's name, while a third shows a dyke being cut by a king labelled 'Scorpion', perhaps another name for Narmer. By far the most impressive of the relics from Hierakonpolis is the great votive 'Narmer Palette' carved in schist (Cairo, Egyp. Mus.; see fig.). It celebrates the triumph of the King over his enemies. Wearing the white crown he strides forward in a heroic pose, which was to become a stereotype in Egyptian sculpture. His right hand grasps a mace, his left holds a prisoner by the hair, and above, in the guise of a hawk, he dominates 6000 fallen foes. At the top of the palette his name is flanked by horned heads, perhaps symbols of the goddess Hathor. On the other side, the circular depression for grinding eye-paint is flanked by captive monsters; the King, this time in the red crown, witnesses the march of standard-bearers towards a row of decapitated prisoners; below, as a bull, he breaks down the wall of a fort. It is not known what historical event the palette is commemorating, but its importance lies in the fact that it is Egypt's first great work of art. Already the artist has evolved the classic Egyptian formula for rendering the human figure in relief: head, hips and legs in profile and shoulders square to the front. Here also is the canon of proportion that was to be observed in Egypt for centuries to come (see EGYPT, ANCIENT, §IV, 3).

BIBLIOGRAPHY

J. E. Quibell: *Hierakonpolis* (London, 1900–02), i, pl. 26, 29; ii, pp. 41–3

W. B. Emery: *Archaic Egypt* (Harmondsworth, 1961), pp. 32–7, 42–7

W. Kaiser: 'Einige Bemerkungen zur ägyptischen Frühzeit III', *Z. Ägyp. Sprache & Altertknd.*, xci (1964), pp. 86–125

I. E. S. Edwards: 'The Early Monarchy and the Unification of Egypt', *Early History of the Middle East*, Cambridge Anc. Hist., i/2 (Cambridge, 3/1971)

B. J. Kemp: *Ancient Egypt: Anatomy of a Civilization* (London and New York, 1989), pp. 42ff

M. S. DROWER

Narrative art. Term used to describe art that provides a visual representation of some kind of story, sometimes based on literary work. It is found throughout the world, and it appears not only as an art form in its own right in both two and three dimensions but also as decoration on a variety of objects. Narration, the relating of an event as it unfolds over time, is in principle a difficult task for the visual arts, since a work of art usually lacks an obvious beginning, middle and end, essential features of any story. Nevertheless, since ancient times many works of art have had as their subjects figures or tales from mythology, legend or history. The artists overcame the inherent limitations of visual narrative by representing stories that the viewer might be expected to know and would therefore retell in his or her mind while taking in the representation.

BIBLIOGRAPHY

A. Thomas: *The Illustrated Dictionary of Narrative Painting* (London, 1994) [based on the col. of the N.G., London]

I. Ancient world. II. Islamic lands. III. Indian subcontinent. IV. Pre-Columbian Americas. V. Western world.

I. Ancient world.

1. Near East. 2. Egypt. 3. Greece and Rome.

1. NEAR EAST. In the Ancient Near East narrative art illustrated three main themes: royal hunts, banquets and war. The scenes were depicted in bands and registers that generally read from bottom to top and from left to right, although in some cases the direction varies from register to register to create the impression of a winding procession or succession of events. Often, however, consecutive events are shown taking place simultaneously. The reliefs of the Assyrian kings at Nimrud, Khorsabad and Nineveh (9th to 7th century BC), often accompanied by explanatory captions in the cuneiform script, were the vehicles for extremely sophisticated narrative art, fully integrated in the architecture. Probably the earliest example of narrative art in the Ancient Near East is a painted scene on the interior of a bowl (Baghdad, Iraq Mus.) of the Halaf period (*c.* 5000 BC), excavated at Tell Arpachiyah in northern Iraq. As the bowl is turned the scene unwinds of two alluring, naked women, who stand on either side of a fenced enclosure, towards which a bull is approaching; beyond, an archer is shooting an arrow at an attacking lion or leopard. The protection of livestock from predators was probably the prerogative of the leader of the community, and the theme reappears on a stone stele from Uruk in southern Iraq (*c.* 3100 BC; Baghdad, Iraq Mus.), where the priest-king is shown shooting an arrow at one lion and spearing another. Millennia later the Assyrian king Assurbanipal (*reg* 668–627 BC) is depicted on the famous lion-hunt reliefs from Nineveh (London, BM) killing lions from a chariot, using a bow, sword and spear. The chariot is shown several times, first travelling in one direction, then in another, to convey the feeling of action and speed; on one occasion a lion grasping a wheel of the chariot in its jaws and paws is lifted off the ground as the chariot advances. The preparations leading up to the hunt are depicted in detail (selection of arrows, stringing of bows, harnessing of horses, arrival of the onlookers with their picnics); its religious aftermath, accompanied by a framed explanatory caption in the cuneiform script, is also depicted on another set of reliefs, where the king is shown pouring libations over the dead lions while priests play harps. On cylinder seals of all periods, but particularly in the 3rd millennium BC, heroes are depicted protecting animals from attack by lions and leopards (*see* ANCIENT NEAR EAST, §II, 1(ii)).

Religious banquets connected with agrarian festivals are depicted in abbreviated form from *c.* 3100 BC on a cylinder seal from Chogha Mami and on the bands of relief decoration on a stone vessel known as the Warka Vase (Baghdad, Iraq Mus.). The latter show water, plants and ears of wheat on the fourth and lowest register; sheep moving to the right on the third; nude priests moving to the left, bearing vessels full of offerings, on the second; and, on the uppermost register, a nude priest with offerings, the 'priest-king' and an attendant, all moving towards the right, approaching the goddess Inanna, who stands before the reed bundles identifying her temple, in which stand her ritual vessels and altars. The motif of a procession, culminating in a banquet accompanied by musicians,

1. Ancient Near Eastern narrative scene depicting the flight of Teumman and his son after the Battle of the River Ulai, detail of an Assyrian limestone relief from Nineveh, h. 1.80 m, 7th century BC (London, British Museum)

and often including a ship or chariot, is found on votive plaques between *c.* 2800 and *c.* 2500 BC (e.g. Baghdad, Iraq Mus.). Two cult vessels from Bitik and Inandık in central Anatolia (*c.* 1600 BC; Ankara, Mus. Anatol. Civiliz.) show similar religious processions in several registers, but the ceremonies are connected with marriage or ritual sex. Around 1000 BC the funerary meal entered the iconography of the Near East, probably from Egypt, sometimes, as on the Ahiram sarcophagus (Beirut, Mus. N.), as the focus of a funerary procession.

Battles were also generally accompanied by victory banquets. Although often condensed into one scene, as on an ivory box from Megiddo in Israel (12th century BC; Jerusalem, Rockefeller Mus.), the expanded version provides ample scope for the development of narrative. The 'Royal Standard of Ur' (*c.* 2600 BC; London, BM; *see* UR, fig. 2) consists of two rectangular panels back-to-back, divided into three registers, made up of red (limestone), white (shell) and blue (lapis lazuli) inlays set in bitumen. On the 'war' side four chariots drive towards the right over the fallen enemy (bottom), and infantry escort prisoners towards the right (middle); on the top register the prisoners are led from the right towards the victorious ruler, who has alighted from his chariot. On the 'peace' side figures with booty and food for the banquet are approaching from the left on the two lower registers; on the top register musicians play, and high officials raise

cups towards the ruler who sits facing right. On both sides the ruler is shown larger than his entourage, and he even overlaps the frame in the 'war' frieze.

Again, it is in the reliefs of King Assurbanipal that this type of narrative finds its fullest expression. The sequence depicting the Battle of the River Ulai (London, BM) is accompanied by captions like a strip-cartoon: it shows the capture of Til Tuba by the Assyrians, leading to their victory over the Elamites. The wounded Elamite king, Teumman, flees with his son; their chariot overturns in a forest (see fig. 1), the son is clubbed to death; Teumman is beheaded, the head is identified, carried in a chariot to Assurbanipal and hung round the neck of a captive. Meanwhile the River Ulai is clogged with the bodies of the dead, the city of Madaktu surrenders, a pro-Assyrian governor is installed, the Elamites' allies are tortured and killed, and—the whole aim of these reliefs—the cautionary message is passed on to ambassadors from Urartu. The final scene, known as the 'Garden Party' relief, shows Assurbanipal reclining at a feast (the earliest depiction of the reclining banquet), while his wife sits beside him, musicians play, birds and crickets sing in the trees—and in one of the trees hangs the head of Teumman.

BIBLIOGRAPHY
I. J. Winter: 'Royal Rhetoric and the Development of Historical Narrative in Neo-Assyrian Reliefs', *Stud. Visual Communic.*, vii/2 (1981), pp. 2–38

——: 'After the Battle is Over: The *Stele of the Vultures* and the Beginning of Historical Narrative in the Art of the Ancient Near East', *Pictorial Narrative in Antiquity and the Middle Ages*, ed. H. L. Kessler and M. S. Simpson, Stud. Hist. A., xvi (Washington, DC, 1985), pp. 11–32

M. I. Marcus: 'Geography as an Organizing Principle in the Imperial Art of Shalmaneser III', *Iraq*, xlix (1988), pp. 77–90

C. Breniquet: 'A propos du vase halafien de la Tombe G2 de Tell Arpachiyah', *Iraq*, liv (1992), pp. 69–78

D. Collon: 'Banquets in the Art of the Ancient Near East', *Banquets d'Orient*, ed. R. Gyselen, Res Orientales, iv (Leuven, 1992), pp. 23–30

DOMINIQUE COLLON

2. EGYPT. The Egyptians' conception of pictorial art was closely linked with their understanding of the world in general, which, in turn, was conditioned by historical, social and psychological factors. The Egyptians regarded the universe as a static entity in which current events were mere repetitions of things that had happened in the 'First Time' (the moment of the world's creation). Life was therefore considered to be permanent and unchangeable rather than transitory. The Egyptian artist created scenes that were usually typical illustrations of archetypal actions rather than being strictly narrative.

The reliefs on the walls of Egyptian temples are mostly depictions of characteristic rituals performed daily or annually by gods or kings. In private tombs most of the subjects are concerned with aspects of daily life, such as agriculture, craftsmanship, fowling, fishing, offerings and banquets (although there was usually an underlying religious significance). These funerary scenes form an elaborate sequence of pictures usually expressing matter-of-fact statements rather than specific events. Even scenes that recall particular events, such as the death of the tomb owner, became standardized and repetitive, so that they lost the specific qualities of narrative.

However, the extensive repertory of Egyptian art included other subject-matter beyond the depiction of religious ritual and daily life. In the Predynastic period (*c.* 6000–*c.* 2925 BC), for instance, Egyptian artists carved scenes with narrative content on such small monuments as slate palettes, knife handles and mace heads (*see* EGYPT, ANCIENT, §IX, 3(i); *see also* NARMER). The establishment of divine kingship at the beginning of the Dynastic period (*c.* 2925 BC), with its emphasis on the non-ephemeral nature of the king, led to the introduction of rigid pictorial conventions (*see* EGYPT, ANCIENT, §IV, 2). Scenes that were intended to record definite historical events, such as the first unification of Egypt, were rendered without indications of time or place.

With the king's assumption of absolute power in the Old Kingdom (*c.* 2575–*c.* 2150 BC), the grip of the artistic conventions grew stronger, and narrative scenes became extremely rare. Even scenes referring to specific events, such as mining or quarrying expeditions, foreign trade missions and military campaigns, were made to fit into the general scheme of typical decorations. Towards the end of the Old Kingdom, scenes including elements of narrative began to reappear, perhaps coinciding with the gradual rise in the importance of the individual, and the attitude to narrative remained substantially the same during the Middle Kingdom (*c.* 2008–*c.* 1630 BC).

The pharaohs of the New Kingdom (*c.* 1540–*c.* 1075 BC) pursued an expansionist policy, and, with Egypt's transformation into a world power, fresh ideas began to enrich and stimulate Egyptian culture. Narrative scenes, though not abundant, gradually increased on both royal and private monuments. In the Amarna period (*c.* 1353–*c.* 1332 BC) there was an almost complete break with the traditional conventions, in the search for 'truth' (Egyp. *maat*) in both

2. Ancient Egyptian narrative scene depicting Ramesses II at the Battle of Qadesh, sandstone relief in the Great Temple at Abu Simbel, *c.* 1260 BC

religion and art. For King Akhenaten (*reg c.* 1353–*c.* 1332 BC), the propagator of the new doctrines, 'truth' in art meant the visual rather than conceptual rendition of nature. Although this attitude might seem to have been a potentially fruitful source of narrative art, the alternative repertory of Amarna art was so limited that narrative scenes tended to assume a repetitive character.

The Ramesside era (*c.* 1292–*c.* 1075 BC) was in many ways the golden age of Egyptian narrative art, since the 19th and 20th Dynasty pharaohs devoted whole walls of temples to scenes of warfare intended to emphasize their military prowess as champions of Egypt. The traditional scene of the king crushing his enemies with one blow was effectively expanded to show him charging in his chariot, capturing foreign forts and returning home triumphantly to offer prisoners and spoils of war to the principal deities of Egypt (*see* ABU SIMBEL; ABYDOS; and THEBES (i), §§VI and VII). Most Egyptian narrative scenes depict 'multiple scenes' of events as they unfolded. Others, however, portray the 'culminating scene' (i.e. the results of an action), particularly when it is not intended to depict the protagonists directly involved. Whenever space permitted, the artists preferred 'multiple scenes', consisting of a number of episodes of a given event, depicted in a comprehensive and sequential manner on the walls of a temple or tomb. The treatment of the scenes was always simple and straightforward, with summary treatment of both the setting (*see* EGYPT, ANCIENT, §VI, 17) and the participants. In war scenes, for instance, only the pharaoh was shown engaged in battle (see fig. 2), although later in the Ramesside period the royal children were also shown in action.

Hieroglyphic inscriptions played an important role in Egyptian narrative art by explaining certain events and specifying particular persons, places and dates, but in many cases the various episodes were clear enough so that their meaning could be easily comprehended.

BIBLIOGRAPHY

H. A. Groenewegen-Frankfort: *Arrest and Movement: An Essay on Space and Time in the Representational Art of the Ancient Near East* (London, 1951/*R* New York, 1972); review by J. Baines in *J. Egyp. Archaeol.*, lx (1971), pp. 272–6

H. Kantor: 'Narration in Egyptian Art', *Amer. J. Archaeol.*, lxi (1957), pp. 44–54

G. A. Gaballa: *Narrative in Egyptian Art* (Mainz, 1976)

G. A. GABALLA

3. GREECE AND ROME. Much of the scholarship on narration in ancient Greek and Roman art consists of attempts to classify the various techniques employed by artists to convey stories visually. The multiplicity and complexity of these techniques is due mainly to two factors: the changing means by which stories were transmitted in antiquity; and the great variety of media and formats in which ancient art occurs. Concurrent with the development of narrative art, Greek culture gradually transformed itself from a culture reliant upon an oral tradition into a literate society; public performance of poetry and song gave way to erudition and to private enjoyment of literature in books (although this was restricted to a small literate minority). These profound changes in the ways that myths and stories were experienced inevitably led to changes in the techniques of visual

narration. As for the diversity of media and of forms, narrative art was represented in sculptural friezes, metopes and pediments, for example the *Gigantomachy* from the north frieze of the Siphnian Treasury at Delphi (*see* GREECE, ANCIENT, fig. 83); and on sarcophagi and funerary urns; some narrative statuary groups also exist. Narrative scenes were represented in monumental wall paintings (untraced) for public buildings and in wall paintings and mosaics for private houses, for example the pebble mosaic from Olynthos depicting *Thetis Bringing Armour to Achilles* (*see* GREECE, ANCIENT, fig. 140). The largest number of representations of narrative art from Ancient Greece consist of the decorative schemes on thousands of painted vases from Athens and South Italy, such as that of *Ajax and Achilles Playing a Board Game* by Exekias on an amphora (Rome, Vatican, Mus. Gregoriano Etrus.; for illustration *see* VASE PAINTERS, §II: EXEKIAS). (For further discussion *see* GREECE, ANCIENT, esp. §V, 5 and 6.) Different formats encouraged the use of different narrative techniques: tondi and statuary groups permitted the representation of only a few figures and a single episode in a story, whereas sculptural friezes and wall paintings almost required the proliferation of figures and scenes.

The earliest figural scenes in Greek art are those on Geometric pottery of the 8th century BC (*see* GREECE, ANCIENT, figs 85–87), but they are problematic with respect to narrative. They may be purely descriptive scenes of everyday life, rather than representations of specific narratives. If they are narrative scenes, it is difficult to determine whether the events depicted are contemporary or legendary because of the lack of individualization of the figures and actions. The contemporary viewer would have had information external to the images themselves, such as the specific contexts in which they were viewed, to indicate whether they were narrative scenes.

By contrast, in the Archaic period (*c.* 700–480 BC) the narrative content of many works of painting and sculpture manifests itself through the use of attributes and inscriptions to identify specific figures, usually gods or heroes, and through the depiction of actions and situations unique to specific stories. A characteristic feature is the depiction of objects, events or figures from several different moments in the tale, rather than the representation of a single moment in a story. This is often described as the simultaneous, or synoptic, method, and its aim was to render a narrative scene more immediately or more fully intelligible through the inclusion of as much detail as possible from a story. This method has been compared to epic poetry, which is similarly characterized by a great interest in detail.

During the Classical period (*c.* 480–323 BC) the content or action of a narrative scene was often expressed through subtle details of appearance and gesture; the climactic moment in the story was often passed over in favour of a quiet moment before or after the main action, as in the metope scene from the Temple of Zeus at Olympia showing *Atlas Presenting Herakles with the Apples of the Hesperides* (*c.* 470–457 BC; Olympia, Archaeol. Mus.; *see* OLYMPIA, fig. 4). This approach is sometimes called narration by allusion, and its purpose is to draw attention to the nature or state of mind of the characters in a story and thereby not only to relate what happened but also to indicate why it happened. Narrative art of this period also

3. Hellenistic narrative scene depicting the *Building of the Boat for Auge* (detail), marble, from the Telephos frieze of the Great Altar, Pergamon, *c.* 180–*c.* 160 BC (Berlin, Pergamonmuseum, Ostasiatische Sammlung)

tended to represent one moment in a story, rather than several, and to include in a scene only those figures and objects relevant to that one moment; this method of visual narration, often called the monoscenic method, is closer to written narrative than the simultaneous method is, in so far as it visually maintains the temporal distinctions between successive events in a narrative text. This development, as well as the interest in character and internal states of mind, has been thought to be related to the rise of Athenian drama in the 5th century BC. As means of representing stories, drama and art are similar in that both rely on visual spectacle. Drama, however, also relies for its full effect on the orderly unfolding of events over time (including, for example, dramatic peripeteia or reversal of fortune), and this heightened concern for the temporal aspect of the narrative may have influenced Classical artists. The staging, choreography and costumes of Athenian drama were only occasionally represented in art, but the many reworkings of traditional stories by Athenian dramatic poets served as the point of departure for much narrative art from the 4th century BC on.

Two further developments in narrative art during the Classical period should be noted. First, narrative scenes in painting began to include not only figures but also simple indications of setting, such as landscape and architectural features; in a few instances they seem to have conveyed not merely the location of the action but also a sense of the space in which it occurred. Most examples of these are lost, but references to them exist in literary sources. Second, in addition to representations from legend and mythology, there were representations of actual historical events, the mid-5th-century BC painting (untraced) of the

Battle of Marathon by PANAINOS, originally in the Painted Stoa (Stoa Poikile) at Athens, being perhaps the earliest known example. This new type of subject-matter remained exceptional until the second half of the 4th century BC, when it seems to have greatly increased in importance due to Macedonian patronage, as, for example, in the *Alexander Mosaic* (*c.* 100 BC; Naples, Mus. Archeol. N.; *see* POMPEII, fig. 7) from the House of the Faun at Pompeii, which probably represents the Battle of Issus between Alexander the Great and Darius III and was copied from an earlier painting of the ?4th/3rd century BC.

In the Hellenistic period (323–7 BC) a far-reaching development in narrative art was the practice of illuminating texts. Illuminated texts appear to have served as sources for many works of narrative art in this and in the Roman period, and to have increased the number of situations in Greek myth and legend that were given visual form. This type of visual narrative, sometimes called the cyclic method, presumes that the viewer has a detailed knowledge of the specific textual source of a narrative scene, since the representation was originally embedded in the text itself. As a result, works of art based on these manuscript illuminations are very often obscure, learned in character and less immediately comprehensible than earlier works of narrative art.

The technique of continuous narrative, in which a figure appears more than once in the same setting, was also developed during the Hellenistic period. It can be seen in the Telephos frieze showing the *Building of the Boat for Auge* (*c.* 180–*c.* 160 BC; Berlin, Pergamonmus.; *see* fig. 3) from the Great Altar at Pergamon. Use of continuous narrative was, however, a characteristic feature of Roman art, and it has been the subject of frequent debate since Franz Wickhoff (1895) advanced the argument that it was a uniquely Roman, rather than Greek, development. Studies in the 20th century by Kurt Weitzmann (1947) and Peter Heinrich von Blanckenhagen (1957) have shown that continuous narrative was a Hellenistic, not Roman, innovation. The principal development of narrative in the Roman period is that of the relation of figure to background. Many Roman paintings of the 1st century BC and the 1st century AD are characterized by expansive landscapes peopled with diminutive figures from Greek mythology, whose actions are subordinate to the setting and the general ambience; the best-known example is the painting showing scenes from the *Odyssey* (*c.* 40–*c.* 20 BC; Rome, Vatican, Sala della Nozze Aldobrandine; *see* LANDSCAPE PAINTING, fig. 1; *see also* ROME, ANCIENT, §V, 1(i)). While the concern for setting and mood is not completely unattested in Greek art, it was of great interest and importance to Roman patrons. The representation of historical events became the most important function of public narrative art in the Roman Imperial period, the scenes on Trajan's Column (AD 112–13) being well-known examples (*see* ROME, ANCIENT, §IV, 2(v); *see also* ROME, §V, 7 and fig. 25).

BIBLIOGRAPHY
C. Robert: *Bild und Lied: Archäologische Beiträge zur Geschichte der griechischen Heldensage*, Philologische Untersuchungen, v (Berlin, 1881/*R* New York, 1975)
F. Wickhoff: *Die Wiener Genesis* (Vienna, 1895); Eng. trans. by E. Strong as *Roman Art: Some of its Principles and their Application to Early Christian Painting* (London, 1900)

K. Weitzmann: *Illustrations in Roll and Codex: A Study of the Origin and Method of Text Illustration*, Stud. MS. Illum., ii (Princeton, 1947, rev. 1970)

P. H. von Blanckenhagen: 'Narration in Hellenistic and Roman Art', *Amer. J. Archaeol.*, lxi (1957), pp. 78–83

G. M. A. Hanfmann: 'Narration in Greek Art', *Amer. J. Archaeol.*, lxi (1957), pp. 71–8

N. Himmelmann-Wildschütz: 'Erzählung und Figur in der archäischen Kunst', *Abh. Geistes- & Sozwiss. Kl.* (1967), pp. 73–100

A. M. Snodgrass: *Narration and Allusion in Archaic Greek Art* (London, 1982)

R. Brilliant: *Visual Narratives: Storytelling in Etruscan and Roman Art* (Ithaca, NY, and London, 1984)

GUY HEDREEN

II. Islamic lands.

Narrative imagery in Islamic lands continued an artistic tradition of the pictorialization of stories and historical events that had long prevailed throughout western Asia and the Mediterranean region. The earliest examples of recognizable narrative may be found among the frescoes in the bath complex at QUSAYR 'AMRA, an 8th-century site in the Jordanian desert. The diverse programme of monumental decoration includes three hunting scenes, the first depicting a Bedouin round-up of onagers, and the other two depicting the killing (or perhaps branding) and butchering of the captured animals. Although the wall paintings are on different walls, they seem to represent a sequence or progression of related events that may well have taken place in the vicinity of the estate.

Virtually no examples of buildings decorated with narrative scenes survive from later periods, although some fragmentary remains and literary descriptions, such as those in the *Shāhnāma* ('Book of kings') compiled by the poet Firdawsi between *c.* 980 and *c.* 994 and revised *c.* 1010, may attest to the continuation of this imagery. In order to trace the history of narrative images through the medieval and later Islamic periods, it is necessary to turn to three-dimensional objects, particularly ceramics, metalwork and illustrated manuscripts. The vast corpus of Islamic objects includes various pieces decorated with identifiable narrative scenes, or at least with images that may be presumed to refer to some kind of story or actual event. A number of pieces of lustreware made in Egypt in the 11th and 12th centuries, for example, are said to represent genre scenes (*see* ISLAMIC ART, §V, 3(i)), including cock fights and men wrestling, but these might just as easily represent fables or local legends. Scenes from the *Life of Christ* appear on a group of inlaid brasses from 13th-century Syria and Egypt, while the exploits of specific heroes figure on Iranian metalwork and enamelled and lustre-painted ceramics dating from the 12th century until the 14th (*see* ISLAMIC ART, §V, 4(i)(a)). In these works the decoration comprises extracted, and occasionally conflated or epitomized, narratives rendered as discrete images. The emphasis on the single narrative moment, as opposed to serial narration, suggests that the iconography was sufficiently familiar, so that anyone looking at such works would be able to identify the complete narrative. The representation of a solitary figure riding a humped, horned cow, for instance, on the interior of a lustre-painted bowl (e.g. bowl from Iran, 12th–13th century; Leipzig, Kstgewmus.) would have been enough to conjure up the entire story of how the legendary Iranian hero Faridun captured

the evil usurper Zahhak with the help of the blacksmith Kawa. The depiction of narrative sequence sometimes occurs, as in the famous enamelled beaker from Iran (early 13th century; h. 120 mm, diam. 112 mm; Washington, DC, Freer) decorated with the tale of Bizhan and Manizha 'told' in comic-strip style of three superimposed registers with small linked panels. Even here, however, only a few, select moments in the story, known from the *Shāhnāma*, are represented, and it is left to the viewer to fill in the narrative lacunae and reconstruct the entire heroic tale.

Pictorial narrative in Islamic illustrated manuscripts was also based on selection and extraction. Although Arab codices of the 13th century, such as a copy (Paris, Bib. N., MS. arabe 5847) of al-Hariri's *Maqāmāt* ('Seances'), contain narrative scenes, these generally were not required by the text and seem to derive from an interest in recording aspects of everyday life. Narrative painting as an artistic genre within the Islamic art of the book really developed and flourished in volumes of Persian and Turkish literature, including histories, epics, romances and mystical allegories, written in both prose and poetry. Illustrations in such texts not only depict the action of a story but also invoke mood, express emotion and interpret abstract themes.

The earliest known manuscript with narrative paintings is the well-known copy (Istanbul, Topkapı Pal. Lib., H841; *see* ISLAMIC ART, fig. 125) of *Varga and Gulshah*, datable

4. Islamic narrative scene depicting *Khosrow Seeing Shirin Bathing*; illustration from Nizami: *Khamsa* ('Five poems'), from Iran, early 15th century (Washington, DC, Freer Gallery of Art)

to the early 13th century. The Persian story of two star-crossed lovers contains 72 narrow illustrations set between lines of text. The majority of these compositions are in close proximity to the verses they illustrate and follow the content and sequence of the text—a principle that obtained throughout the history of the pictorial narrative in Iran and neighbouring regions. Another noteworthy feature of this manuscript is its high rate of illustration, with narrative scenes coming in rapid succession. This approach towards narrative illustration prevailed until the middle of the 14th century. Thereafter, illustrated manuscripts tended to have a much smaller selection of scenes, with greater emphasis placed on the landscape setting and other features of individual narrative compositions.

Manuscript painters evidently had considerable freedom in the choice of narrative episodes to be illustrated, and virtually no two volumes of the same text, be it the epic *Shāhnāma* by Firdawsi, Nizami's romances collected in the *Khamsa* ('Five poems'; see fig. 4) or Jami's mystical *Haft awrang* ('Seven thrones'), have the same set of illustrations. Invariably, certain favourite stories were illustrated again and again, leading to the formulation of standardized, and instantly recognizable, images. Such narrative topoi, however repetitive or iconographically formulaic, could evoke the entire progression of a story, including the overall plot, dramatic action and cast of characters. Narrative imagery in Islamic manuscripts goes beyond 'mere' illustration. It also involves the use of visual metaphors, intended to enhance complex literary themes and mystical ideas. This is, perhaps, the most distinctive feature of Islamic narrative painting, through which it can rightly be acclaimed as one of the most imaginative narrative traditions in the history of art.

BIBLIOGRAPHY

A. S. Melikian-Chirvani: 'Le Roman de Varqe et Golsah', *A. Asiatiques*, xxii (1970), pp. 1–262
——: 'Conceptual Art in Iranian Painting and Metalwork', *Akten des VII internationalen Kongresses für iranische Kunst und Archäologie: Berlin, 1979*, pp. 392–400
M. S. Simpson: 'The Narrative Structure of a Medieval Iranian Beaker', *A. Orient.*, xii (1981), pp. 15–24
——: 'Narrative Allusion and Metaphor in the Decoration of Medieval Islamic Objects', *Pictorial Narrative in Antiquity and the Middle Ages*, ed. H. L. Kessler and M. S. Simpson, Stud. Hist. A., xvi (Washington, DC, 1985), pp. 131–49
A. S. Melikian-Chirvani: 'Khwaje Mirak Naqqash', *J. Asiat.*, cclxxvi (1988), pp. 97–146
E. Baer: *Ayyubid Metalwork with Christian Images* (Leiden, 1989)

MARIANNA S. SIMPSON

III. Indian subcontinent.

Although India has a strong story-telling tradition, religious subjects (stories of deities and accounts of miracles, saints, holy men or devotees) have predominated in narrative art. Chronological accounts of events in secular time had little importance at moments of political flux, and the Hindu, Buddhist and Jaina religions ascribe no ultimate value to life in the world. In local and regional folk traditions, however, the histories of heroes, kings and communities flourished, and secular histories emerged as important subjects for depiction under the influence of West and Central Asian and European traditions. The belief in recurring cycles of time, common to Hinduism, Jainism and Buddhism, also influenced modes of narrative expression.

The sacrificial religion described in the Vedas, India's earliest literature, depended initially on oral transmission and did not develop a narrative art (*see* INDIAN SUBCONTINENT, §I, 2(i)). Jainism and Buddhism, both of which emerged in the 6th century BC, introduced life stories of personages whose teachings were central to their philosophies. Sculptural representations of incidents in the Buddha's life—his birth, departure from the palace, first sermon, miracles and death—preceded the appearance of the Buddha image itself. These and *jātaka* scenes (stories of the Buddha's previous births) appear, for example, on the railings and great *torana*s (Skt: gateways) of the stupas at BHARHUT in north-central India (*c.* 2nd century BC), at SANCHI in central India (2nd century BC–1st century AD; *see* INDIAN SUBCONTINENT, figs 17 and 23) and at AMARAVATI in the Deccan (3rd century BC–4th century AD). In each instance a number of successive episodes are shown within the confines of a single panel or in panels one above the other, but rarely in chronological order. By contrast, Buddhist narrative art of the 1st–4th centuries AD in Gandhara (present-day north-west India, Pakistan and Afghanistan) is linear, a sequence of arrested moments, separated by such artistic devices as Corinthian pilasters, thus reflecting Hellenistic influence from Bactria and Parthia and contact with Rome. The most famous examples of Buddhist narrative painting are in the cave complex at Ajanta in the western Deccan. The earliest *jātaka* scenes there date to the 2nd century BC, but most of the paintings are late 5th century AD (*see* AJANTA, §2(i)). Buddhist narrative paintings at BAGH in Malwa date from between the 6th century AD and the first half of the 7th.

By this period the important texts of popular Hinduism, the *Rāmāyaṇa* (the story of Rama, one of the incarnations of the Hindu god Vishnu), the historical narrative known as *Mahābhārata* (with its appendix, the *Harivaṃśa*), the *Bhāgavata purāṇa* and other key Puranas (mythological and legendary histories), had been composed, bringing together a wide range of legends and religious teachings. A temple culture and a complex sacred iconography had been established. Many gods were depicted in scenes from myths and legends: deities in terrifying postures slaying their enemies (e.g. the goddess Durga killing the buffalo-demon Mahishasura); the moment of rescue or miraculous manifestation (e.g. the god Shiva emerging from the fiery *linga*, his phallic emblem); stories of creation, usually associated with the god Vishnu; forest and battle scenes and legends of the deity Krishna (*see* INDIAN SUBCONTINENT, figs 256 and 292), especially episodes from his childhood and youthful dalliance with the cow-herd Radha. Hindu narrative sculpture, not normally worshipped, was confined to horizontal friezes on beams, the bases of walls and the gateways of temples. Superb 15th-century examples can be seen at the Ramachandra Temple at Vijayanagara in the Deccan (*see* HAMPI). Sculpted wall panels illustrating the *Rāmāyaṇa* run around the *maṇḍapa* (pillared porch) and antechamber in three tiers. Mythological scenes also appear in painted form on south Indian temple walls from the medieval period to the present, and on painted, printed and dyed cloths used in ritual performances, which sometimes combine narrative depictions with iconic representations of deities. Episodes are rarely arranged in a simple linear sequence (*see* INDIAN SUBCONTINENT, §VII, 3).

Narrative depiction in the form of book illustration appears in both courtly and religious contexts. The earliest surviving illustrated palm-leaf manuscripts and book covers date from the 11th century. They consist of eastern Indian Vajrayana Buddhist texts of the Pala period (*see* PALA AND SENA); the wooden covers occasionally depict a *jātaka* story (*see* INDIAN SUBCONTINENT, §VI, 3(ii)(c)). Western Indian Jaina paintings from the late 14th century—the earliest narrative illustrations on paper—depict the life of the *tīrthaṅkara* (divine master) Mahavira and other *jina*s (liberated souls who had conquered vice) and accounts of monks such as Kalaka. The earliest extant illustrated Hindu texts date to the 15th century. The latter two traditions continued under mercantile and court patronage, respectively, until the 19th century.

Muslim rulers of West and Central Asian origin introduced a secular and nationalist narrative tradition into India (*see* INDIAN SUBCONTINENT, §VI, 3(ii)(d)). The Sultanate rulers (13th–16th century) of north India commissioned illustrations of the Persian 'national epic', Firdawsi's *Shāhnāma* ('Book of kings'), and books of fables and stories. The Mughal ruler Akbar (*reg* 1556–1605), once his Indian empire had been secured, commissioned illustrations to his grandfather Babur's biography (see fig. 5), to the *Ḥamzanāma* (a Persian romance) and to the account of his own rule, the *Akbarnāma*, as well as to Hindu epics and other texts. Subsequent Mughal emperors and provincial Muslim rulers continued the practice of illustrating events in their reigns. Examples include the *Tūzuk-i Jahāngīrī* (*c.* 1620), the memoirs of Jahangir (*reg* 1605–27) and the *Pādshāhnāma* (*c.* 1646/50), an account of the reign (1628–58) of Shah Jahan (*see* INDIAN SUBCONTINENT, figs 259, 262–3 and 268).

As the European trading powers fought for control of India in the 18th century, European artists working at the courts of local rulers strengthened interest in the depiction of particular events. Haydar 'Ali, the Sultan of Mysore (*reg* ?1761–82), and Tipu Sultan (*reg* 1782–99) commissioned wall paintings to celebrate their defeat of the British at Polillur in 1780. As real power diminished, Hindu rulers of the north-west commissioned paintings of ceremonies and festivals, subject-matter that was taken over by photographers in the second half of the 19th century.

At the local level in modern India, women depict mythological scenes on house walls at festive times. Travelling picture-showmen in many parts of India (Gujarat, Rajasthan, Bengal, Orissa, Maharashtra, Andhra Pradesh) still narrate local and community histories and Puranic legends illustrated by paintings, in sequences of single episodes on paper scrolls or single sheets, or in multiple-scene compositions on cloth; in the 1990s the film and television industries threatened their demise. Artists of the 19th century and early 20th at pilgrimage centres, such as Kalighat in Calcutta, produced satirical images of topical events and mythological scenes in watercolour and block-print (*see* CALCUTTA, §3). In the late 20th century mythological scenes were printed in the form of calendars for the popular market.

The genre of narrative painting in the Western sense did not exist in India, although *Rāgamāla* ('Garland of

5. Indian narrative scene depicting a *Royal Entertainment with Wrestling and Animal Contests*; illustration from a manuscript copy of the *Baburnāma* ('Memoirs of Babur'), Akbar period, *c.* 1590 (London, Victoria and Albert Museum)

melodies'; personifications of musical modes) and related religious paintings did utilize techniques for the depiction of emotion (*see* INDIAN SUBCONTINENT, fig. 278). Upper- and middle-class art-school-trained artists drawing on both European and Indian traditions since the late 19th century have at times used this narrative mode, and historical narratives in various media celebrate nationalist themes.

See also BUDDHISM, §III, 1; HINDUISM, §1; JAINISM; and INDIAN SUBCONTINENT, §§II and V, 1.

BIBLIOGRAPHY
H. C. Ackermann: *Narrative Reliefs from Gandhara in the Victoria and Albert Museum London* (Rome, 1975)
J. P. Losty: *The Art of the Book in India* (London, 1982)
L. Nehru: *Origins of the Gandharan Style* (Delhi, 1989)
V. Dehejia: 'Narrative Modes in Ajanta Cave 17: A Preliminary Study', *S. Asian Stud.*, vii (1991), pp. 45–57
A. L. Dallapiccola and others: *The Ramachandra Temple of Vijayanagar* (Delhi, 1992)

D. A. SWALLOW

IV. Pre-Columbian Americas.

Narration permeates many aspects of Pre-Columbian art, but in some cultures the vast majority of art appears to be

6. Pre-Columbian American narrative scene depicting the *Migration of the Mexica: Island Homeland of the Mexica (Aztlán)*; reconstructed detail from the Codex Boturini, roll manuscript, 198×5490 mm (Mexico City, Museo Nacional de Antropología)

not so much concerned with telling a story as with representing symbol and meaning in a cosmic sense. Nevertheless, narrative scenes, both religious and secular, are presented on wall paintings in palaces, residences, tombs and, in a few cases, on cave walls; in carved stone, plaster and mud-plaster on monumental walls, on stelae and on benches within rooms; and in ceramics, and sometimes in metals, either as painted scenes on vessels or as groups of figures.

Narration was presented in a variety of compositional formats. It could be shown as a single moment in time, but, characteristically, as part of an entire sequence of actions (e.g. the installation of the king depicted on the Leiden Plaque from Palenque (Leiden, Rijksmus. Vlkenknd.), or the capture of a city shown on many Mesoamerican stelae); as a continuous sequence of moments that move from one scene to another (e.g. the battle, ritual and celebratory scenes at Maya BONAMPAK, or the series of six carved panels along the sides of the principal ballcourt at TAJÍN, showing sacrifice); as contrasting episodes from different parts of a sequence of actions; or as what might be called simultaneous narration. In the last type, a single scene is shown, but the elements in it are a composite of several different stages of a

sequence. For example, in Mesoamerican art a war captive, shown at the time of capture with his captor dominating the scene over him, is often depicted in the state of a captive ready for sacrifice, although his state of dress and other regalia would not, of course, be so until some time after his capture, when sacrificial rituals were begun.

In continuous sequences of narrative art, attention is sometimes focused on three points in time: an inceptive moment just before or as the sequence of the ritual, mythological or historical action begins, a progressive moment or moments in which part of an ongoing action is shown, and perhaps a completive moment when the ritual or event is done. In other cases the 'sequence' is implied by a continuous stream, as in scenes of running humans and animals, pumas attacking, boats, and birds in flight in Mochica paintings of northern Peru.

The narration in most Mesoamerican art is, at least on one level, an obvious depiction of a story, be it 'actual' or mythological/legendary (e.g the investiture of a ruler, the Maya myth of the hero twins, the capture of a city, a battle, or a sacrifice or other ritual). In contrast, the art of TEOTIHUACÁN appears not so much to tell a story as to depict ideals. It assumed a local audience already familiar with the symbols shown. It did not suggest dramatic or explanatory strategies for a wider audience. For example, one of the most common themes in Teotihuacán art is the human heart, shown on a sacrificial knife, in front of the jaws of an animal or simply on its own. Whereas other Mesoamerican cultures depicted war captives with their captors, at Teotihuacán it is the concept of capture and sacrifice that is primary. Conquest and sacrifice were central to the well-being of the state, but they are removed from historical representation and shown in their cosmological interpretation. In the same way, most of Teotihuacán's art emphasizes in symbol the themes of natural bounty, social order and harmony. Narration in Aztec art is found mainly in the codices. In these, historical and ritual sequences are depicted linearly on the sheets and from one sheet to another. Movement and the progression of events are shown through such symbols as lines of footprints to indicate movements and journeys, lines of dates and speech scrolls, and through the repetition of figures in successive scenes (see fig. 6).

Narration, at least as interpreted by archaeologists, can also often be said to be implied in a single piece or group of pieces. For example, the unique set of sixteen stone figures with a backdrop of six jade celts found in an offering at the Olmec site of LA VENTA (Mexico City, Mus. N. Antropol.)has been interpreted as showing a ritual scene with a principal figure, possibly regarded in a hostile way by a file of participants, and a jostle of onlookers. The Chibcha (Colombia) cast-gold raft holding a dignitary and his officials (Bogotá, Mus. Oro) can be interpreted as representative of the entire ritual of rulership investiture and gold offerings known to have been performed in Lake Guatavita. The many groups of pottery figures in the western cultures of Mesoamerica also depict scenes of ritual and daily activities (e.g. an entire Mesoamerican ballgame, itself a ritual, from Nayarit; New Haven, CT, Yale U. A.G.).

BIBLIOGRAPHY

G. Kubler: *The Art and Architecture of Ancient America*, Pelican Hist. A. (Harmondsworth, 1962, rev. 3/1984)

M. P. Weaver: *The Aztecs, Maya and their Predecessors: Archaeology of Mesoamerica* (New York, 1972, rev. 3/1993)

D. Bonavia: *Ricchata quellccani: Pinturas murales prehispánicas* (Lima, 1974); Eng. trans. by P. J. Lyon as *Mural Painting in Ancient Peru* (Bloomington, IN, 1985)

W. Bray: *The Gold of El Dorado* (London, 1978)

E. Pasztory: *Aztec Art* (New York, 1983)

L. Schele and M. E. Miller: *The Blood of Kings: Dynasty and Ritual in Maya Art* (Fort Worth, 1986, rev. London, 1992)

M. E. Moseley: *The Incas and their Ancestors: The Archaeology of Peru* (London, 1992)

E. Pasztory: 'Teotihuacán Unmasked: A View through Art', *Teotihuacán: Art from the City of the Gods*, ed. K. Berrin and E. Pasztory (London, 1993), pp. 45–63

DAVID M. JONES

V. Western world.

1. Early Christian and Byzantine, *c.* AD 250–1453. 2. Medieval Europe, *c.* AD 700–*c.* 1300. 3. Late medieval and later, *c.* 1300 and after.

1. EARLY CHRISTIAN AND BYZANTINE, *c.* AD 250–1453. Most of the art that has survived from the Early Christian and Byzantine period is religious. Artists drew primarily from the Bible or from popular religious texts for their subject-matter. The juxtaposition of Old and New Testament episodes, simple, two-figure compositions and multiple layers of meaning were threads that ran throughout the narrative art of the Early Christian period. One of the earliest surviving examples comes from a mid-3rd-century Christian meeting house (*domus ecclesia*), from Dura Europos, Syria (restored at New Haven, CT, Yale U. A.G.; *see* DURA EUROPOS, §4). Only fragments of Old and New Testament scenes survive on the walls of a room that served as a baptistery, and the overriding theme was one of Christian salvation. Often narrative and non-narrative images appeared together, as in the painted ceiling of the catacomb of SS Pietro and Marcellino in Rome (4th century), where four episodes from the story of Jonah formed part of a composition that also contained orant figures and an allegorical image of Christ as the Good Shepherd (*see also* ROME, §V, 13).

Richly illustrated manuscripts of individual biblical books, such as the COTTON GENESIS (5th/6th century; London, BL, Cotton MS. Oth. B. VI), now fragmentary, were filled with animated scenes. Either separate pictures framed by plain borders were set within the text columns, beneath the text, or several scenes were joined to fill a single page, as in a fragmentary manuscript of the Book of Kings, the so-called Quedlinburg Itala (early 5th century; Berlin, Staatsbib., MS. theol. lat. fol. 485; *see* EARLY CHRISTIAN AND BYZANTINE ART, §V, 1). The walls of Early Christian churches were decorated with lavish biblical narrative illustrations, perhaps derived from manuscripts. In S Maria Maggiore in Rome, as in other Roman churches, Old Testament cycles in mosaic lined the two walls of the nave and culminated in a cycle on the triumphal-arch wall devoted to the *Infancy of Christ*, a popular narrative subject. Passion and Miracle cycles also frequently adorned sarcophagi (*see* SARCOPHAGUS, §III, 1), churches and small ivory plaques.

In the 6th century a more hieratic and ceremonial approach to narrative art prevailed, as on the lead oil flask (ampulla) from Palestine (6th century), now in the Cathedral Treasury in Monza, where the *Adoration of the Magi* and the *Annunciation to the Shepherds* were composed as a single, centralized image.

Narrative episodes were often chosen for their liturgical value. In the presbytery mosaics in S Vitale (*c.* 547) in Ravenna, Italy, the *Sacrifice of Melchizedek*, the *Sacrifice of Isaac* and the *Hospitality of Abraham* prefigured the Eucharist. Later in Byzantine art, entire feast cycles were developed, based on the church calendar and drawn from historical cycles, with scenes such as the *Annunciation*, *Baptism* and *Ascension*, as in the katholikon or main monastery church (*c.* 1000) of HOSIOS LOUKAS, near Delphi, Greece. Narrative episodes were also used for political purposes. Eight silver plates discovered in Cyprus (now New York, Met.) embossed with scenes from the *Life of David* were produced in Constantinople (now Istanbul) under Heraklios, the Byzantine emperor, between 613 and 629/30, as an ensemble to glorify the kingly, and therefore imperial, triumphs. The line between religious and secular art in this case (as in others) was vague.

In manuscripts of this period there was a progressive separation of text and illustration. Half-page or full-page miniatures illustrated Old Testament or Gospel texts. Among the most beautiful of the early manuscripts are the VIENNA GENESIS (Vienna, Österreich. Nbib., Cod. theol. gr. 31), the ROSSANO GOSPELS (Rossano, Mus. Dioc.) and the RABBULA GOSPELS (Florence, Bib. Medicea-Laurenziana, MS. Plut. 1, 56), all from the 6th century. In manuscripts of later date, such as the Homilies of St Gregory Nazianzus (880–86; Paris, Bib. N., MS. gr. 510; see PARIS GREGORY), the Psalter of Basil II (c. 1017; Venice, Bib. N. Marciana, MS. gr. 17), and the PARIS PSALTER (mid-10th century; Paris, Bib. N., MS. gr. 139), full-page narrative illustrations are found, sometimes imitating monumental art, together with scenes distributed over several registers, in imitation of Early Christian models.

Undoubtedly the most elaborate Byzantine narrative art dates from the 9th century, after the iconoclastic controversy (see ICONOCLASM). The vaults and walls of 9th- and 10th-century rock-cut chapels in Cappadocia, in modern-day Turkey, were painted with complex series of scenes arranged side by side, and sometimes in rows, drawing on Early Christian models (see CAPPADOCIA, §2(ii)). Slightly later, in the Komnenian period (1057–1185), church walls were covered with Old and New Testament cycles at St Sophia, OHRID, in the churches of ST GEORGE, KURBINOVO, ST PANTELEIMON, NEREZI, and S Marco, Venice, and, in Sicily, in the Cappella Palatina at Palermo and the cathedral of Monreale. During the Palaiologan period (1259–1453) the church of Christ the Saviour in Chora, Constantinople (see ISTANBUL, §III, 3(ii) and WALL PAINTING, colour pl. II, fig. 1), and churches in Mistra, Greece, were adorned with mosaics and frescoes illustrating magnificent and elaborate cycles of the lives of Christ and the Virgin, two of the most important narrative themes in Byzantine art. Although few secular works survive from the Byzantine period, those that do continue the Roman tradition of illustrating contemporary themes: marriage ceremonies, circus and hunt scenes, and Classical literary themes.

2. MEDIEVAL EUROPE, c. AD 700–c. 1300. Medieval art of the West perpetuated Early Christian and Byzantine iconographic traditions, but to the narrative repertory were added cycles of the lives and martyrdom of saints. These began to appear as early as the 8th and 9th centuries in Rome in, for example, the churches of S Prassede and the chapel of S Maria Antiqua, the latter a Greek monastery where Greek and Latin artists worked side by side (see ROME, §V, 19). Lives of saints and stories of martyrdom appeared frequently in later medieval churches in Italy, for example in S Vincenzo (c. 1007), Galliano, and in northern Europe, as in the PRIORY CHAPEL, BERZÉ-LA-VILLE (early 12th century), in France. They were also illustrated in manuscripts (see SAINTS' LIVES). Besides flanking naves, in the Romanesque period Old Testament cycles began also to cover nave vaults in correspondence with architectural developments in vaulted ceilings, as in SAINT-SAVIN-SUR-GARTEMPE (c. 1100). Narrative art was found also in apses and narthexes.

In manuscripts, full-page illustrations with several rows of scenes to be read from left to right and from top to bottom, like a text, were one of the formats used for narrative illustration in this period, with examples ranging

from the late 6th-century St Augustine Gospels (Cambridge, Corpus Christi Coll., MS. 286; see EARLY CHRISTIAN AND BYZANTINE ART, fig. 57) to the 9th-century Tours Bibles, in which scene after scene appeared against a unified and continuous background in a sequence typical of cyclical and historical depictions. In some cases single episodes occupied entire pages, such as the *Annunciation to the Shepherds* in the Ottonian Pericopes of Henry II (1002–14; Munich, Bayer. Staatsbib., Clm. 4452, fol. 8v).

Narrative biblical cycles decorated the 9th-century 'Golden Altar' of S Ambrogio, Milan (see CAROLINGIAN ART, fig. 11), numerous Carolingian ivories (see fig. 7; see also CAROLINGIAN ART, figs 13 and 15) and the bronze doors of the Ottonian church of St Michael at Hildesheim (c. 1001–31; see DOOR, fig. 3). Biblical stories and stories about the lives of religious personages and heroes appeared on all types of objects from crystals to glass and from jewels to gravestones.

In Romanesque sculpture New Testament scenes were depicted around sculpted capitals in naves and cloisters (see ROMANESQUE, §III). These novel designs illustrated whole cycles with scenes running in succession down the nave, where smooth wall surfaces had been replaced by articulated or skeletal structures. Portal sculpture also provided a suitable medium for narrative images that ran across lintels or were enlarged as scenes (e.g. the Last Judgement) spanning the semicircular spaces of tympana.

The few secular narratives that are known include the 69 m long BAYEUX TAPESTRY on which the Norman Conquest of 1066 was woven in precise detail. Battle scenes had long been favourite subjects for secular narratives.

7. Carolingian narrative scenes of the *Passion*, ivory book cover from Metz, 244×171 mm, mid-9th century (Paris, Bibliothèque Nationale)

BIBLIOGRAPHY

A. Grabar: *Christian Iconography: A Study of its Origins*, The A. W. Mellon Lectures in the Fine Arts, 1961, Bollingen Series, xxxv/10 (Princeton, 1968) [good overview]

K. Weitzmann, W. Loerke, E. Kitzinger and H. Buchthal: *The Place of Book Illumination in Byzantine Art* (Princeton, 1975)

Age of Spirituality: Late Antique and Early Christian Art, Third to Seventh Century (exh. cat., ed. K. Weitzmann; New York, Met., 1979) [excellent pls]

F. Andersen and others, eds: *Medieval Iconography and Narrative: A Symposium* (Odense, 1980)

H. L. Kessler and M. S. Simpson, eds: *Pictorial Narrative in Antiquity and the Middle Ages*, Stud. Hist. A., xvi (Washington, DC, 1985)

H. Kessler: 'On the State of Medieval Art', *A. Bull.*, lxx (1988), pp. 166–87 [recent bibliog.]

M. Lavin: *The Place of Narrative: Mural Decoration in Italian Churches, 431–1600* (Chicago and London, 1990)

PAULA D. LEVETO

3. LATE MEDIEVAL AND LATER, *c.* 1300 AND AFTER. In the period before 1500, narrative art was characterized by complex forms of relating historical events. Influenced by the medieval visual tradition, Renaissance narrative art developed a very sophisticated iconographic vocabulary based on biblical stories. Even illiterate Christians understood the stories the artists' visual symbols represented. Giotto in his fresco of the *Raising of Lazarus* (*c.* 1305) in the Arena Chapel in Padua (*see* PADUA, §4(ii)) depicted the culmination of the miracle, when Lazarus emerged from the tomb, as described in the Gospel of St John, 11 (*see* GIOTTO, §I, 3(i)), and this treatment of the narrative can be described as the culmination method, since it shows the end or resolution of an event that happened at one time and in one place. An episodic method of narrative depicts several scenes from the same event separated much like a comic-strip. By reading the series of episodes, this method suggests time passing. For instance, the *St Francis* cycle of frescoes (*c.* 1320) by an anonymous master in S Francesco, Assisi, shows the chronology of events from the madman's recognition of St Francis's sanctity to the latter's death (*see* ASSISI, §II, 2).

In the continuous form of narrative, events are depicted as separated by time but involving the same character within the same visual setting. Each new event is identified by the visual repetition of this character: for example, in the *Tribute Money* (*c.* 1425–7; *see* MASACCIO, fig. 6) in the Brancacci Chapel in S Maria del Carmine, Florence, Masaccio depicted events from Matthew 27: 24–7, in which Christ instructs St Peter to find tax money in a fish's mouth; Peter, identified by his tightly curled white hair and beard, orange robe and green undergarment, appears in the centre of the composition receiving his instructions. On the left, on the same ground plane and apparently at the same time, St Peter reappears, taking the money from the fish's mouth; on the right he appears again, giving it to the Roman tax collector.

The simultaneous narrative is characterized by depicting in the same work two or more distinct events known to have taken place at different times and/or places. However, it uses events involving different people, avoiding the use of repeated figures. The *Annunciation* (see fig. 8) by Fra Angelico for S Domenico in Cortona narrates Luke 1:35, in which the Angel Gabriel tells the Virgin that she will be the mother of Christ. In this painting the New Testament theme of the Annunciation dominates the composition's foreground, while in the distance (the upper left corner) is depicted the Expulsion from the Garden of Eden, an Old Testament subject. In symbolic narrative, the second major category of narrative art during the Renaissance, specific contemporary events are depicted. There are several examples of this form in the Renaissance, notably Uccello's three panels on the subject of the *Rout* (or *Battle*) *of San Romano* (*c.* mid-1430s; London, N.G.; Florence, Uffizi; Paris, Louvre; *see* UCCELLO, PAOLO, fig. 3), illustrating the events of 1432. The landscape in the background is recognizable as the Arno Valley near San Romano, and the man on horseback in the centre of the version in the National Gallery in London is clearly a portrait of Niccolò da Tolentino, commander of the Florentine forces. In a type of 'pseudo-narrative' form of art, there are two types: allegorical and genre. The allegorical form, in which abstract themes or concepts (e.g. virtues and vices) are symbolically represented, is illustrated by the *Birth of Venus* (*c.* 1484; Florence, Uffizi) by Botticelli, in which Beauty is personified by Venus on a cockleshell, and the wind is personified as a floating human figure issuing a puff of breath from his cheeks (*see* BOTTICELLI, SANDRO, fig. 3). The genre form represents common yet significant events, such as hunting, dancing and feasting.

In his famous frescoes on the Sistine Chapel ceiling (1508–12; Rome, Vatican), Michelangelo used the episodic form of narrative in his overall plan of the ceiling, depicting the nine stories from Genesis. He used the culmination form in many of the separate scenes; for example, the *Creation of Adam* and the *Creation of the Sun and Moon* (*see* MICHELANGELO, fig. 7) show the end of the respective stories. Michelangelo also used the simultaneous narrative form in the *Fall and Expulsion*, in which he depicted the Serpent tempting Adam and Eve on one side of the Tree, while on the other side, within the same landscape, the angel expels them from the Garden of Eden. After *c.* 1520 and the period of the High Renaissance, painters ceased to use the simultaneous form, but they continued to use the episodic form in ceiling paintings. Use of the culmination form persisted, however. It maintained its popularity in the narrative art of the Baroque period, particularly in its religious paintings. Notable examples include the *Conversion of St Paul* (1601) painted by Caravaggio for the chapel of Pope Clement VIII's General Treasurer, Monsignor Tiberio Cerasi, in the Augustinian church of S Maria del Popolo, Rome, in which Saul is shown being knocked off his horse by a blinding, divine light at the moment of his conversion to Christianity (*see* CARAVAGGIO, MICHELANGELO MERISI DA, fig. 6). Rubens's the *Rape of the Daughters of Leucippus* (*c.* 1617; Munich, Alte Pin.) illustrates the violent act of the women being abducted by the Roman soldiers (*see* RUBENS, PETER PAUL, fig. 5). Rembrandt's the *Blinding of Samson* (1636; Frankfurt am Main, Städel. Kstinst. & Städt. Gal.) shows the moment of peak action in the story when Samson's eyes are gouged out.

In northern Europe in the 16th and 17th centuries, narrative art flourished in the work of several artists in particular. The period was dominated by Albrecht Dürer and Pieter Bruegel I, whose narrative works are categorized as iconographic and genre, respectively. Dürer's iconographic narrative relied on a language of symbols and the audience's knowledge and understanding of those symbols. His work therefore inevitably appealed to a limited audience. In the engraving of the *Fall of Man* (1504; for illustration *see* STATES) he illustrated the Temptation. As well as the usual characters and motifs of Adam, Eve, the Serpent, the Apple and the Tree, animals not usually associated with the story from Genesis are present: a cat, a mouse, an elk, a parrot, an ox and, perched on a pinnacle in the distance, a mountain goat. While a commoner would recognize the story, he probably would not understand the significance of these seemingly extraneous characters; a wealthier, educated person would recognize the animals as associated with the four temperaments, the sins and the diseases associated with them, or metaphorical references from the Bible (Cuttler, p. 340). In the 17th century Bruegel's genre narrative form, using commonplace events for subject-matter, gained considerable popularity. Scenes from the everyday life of common people—hunting scenes, weddings, harvests—are typical subjects of Bruegel's paintings (*see* BRUEGEL, (1), fig. 7). Unlike Dürer's work, Bruegel's paintings appealed to a wide audience, whose experiences were similar to those shown. *Hunters in the Snow* (1565; Vienna, Ksthist. Mus.) is Bruegel's genre form at its best: hunters trudge through the snow followed by their dogs, tails tucked between their legs, while peasant women tend the cooking fire. In the distant valley below, skaters may be seen on an icy lake. Not only does Bruegel show a typical day in the lives of these people but he also evokes the feeling of a cold, sunless winter day (Cuttler, p. 480).

Historical narrative paintings became very popular from *c.* 1775 in the Neo-classical period. This narrative form illustrates a factual event. One of the earliest examples is Jacques-Louis David's *Oath of the Horatii* (1784–5; Paris, Louvre), in which he depicted the three brothers receiving the oath and their swords from their father (*see* DAVID, JACQUES-LOUIS, fig. 1), an event documented by Roman historians (Hartt, p. 789). Many of David's paintings are historical in nature: the *Death of Marat* (1793; Brussels, Mus. A. Anc.; *see* FRANCE, fig. 25) and the *Coronation of Napoleon in Notre Dame* (1805–7; Paris, Louvre; *see* DAVID, JACQUES-LOUIS, fig. 4) are also very good examples of this form. A particularly expressive example of historical narrative is Francisco de Goya's *Third of May*,

8. Narrative scene by Fra Angelico: *Annunciation*, tempera on panel, *c.* 1432 (Cortona, Museo Diocesano)

1808 (1814; Madrid, Prado), representing the execution by Napoleon's soldiers of Madrid rebels on Principe Pio Mountain (*see* GOYA, FRANCISCO DE, fig. 4). A single lantern illuminates a grisly scene of a man about to be executed, standing amid the bodies of those shot before him by a faceless firing squad. Others hide their faces from the terror. Although Goya took liberties for effective, expressive purposes, the gruesome details are based on his own observations, thus adding credence to the narrative.

By the late 19th century artists focused less on the narrative and more on expression of either emotion or of colour and light captured in paint. The traditional narrative forms of the Renaissance were transformed into a form emphasizing mood and expression. The primary purpose of modern narrative art became the expression of an artist's feelings towards an event, often using a personal iconography that omitted certain signs connecting the elements of the narrative and encouraging the viewer to construct his own narrative by relating the images to his own experience. In *Guernica* (1937; Madrid, Prado) Picasso painted his response to the Nazi bombing in April 1937 of an innocent Spanish village. While the title of *Guernica* enhanced the semi-abstract narrative content of the painting, in some works text also becomes part of the image, as in the *Pencil Story* (1972–3; New York, Bulgari priv. col.), in which John Baldessari elevated the mundane act of sharpening a pencil by including a written narrative underneath two photographs of the same pencil; on the left it is dull, on the right it has been sharpened. The text describes the action between the two points in time represented by each image. Personal narratives were depicted by Paula Rego in such works as *Snare* (1987; see fig. 9), in which she drew on childhood memories of scenes that are often imbued with a sense of the macabre. Other artists, such as Öyvind Fahlström and Jess (*b* 1923), took up traditional but modern means of depicting narrative by using the form of COMIC-STRIP ART, yet simultaneously altering or recycling the episodes the strips illustrated. Comini identified two literary devices that modern narrative artists borrowed: metonymy and synecdoche. With metonymy, an image represents a concept, much as a metaphor does in language. For example, in *Old House Lane=9* (1986; New York, Paula Cooper Gal.) Jennifer Bartlett realistically portrays three views of the same picket fence and behind it a quaint, white house. Depending upon the viewer's past experience, the sun-dappled, white picket fence could represent tranquillity, security or safety for whomever is in the house; another interpretation might see the fence as an aggressive barrier to whomever is standing outside. In synecdoche a part is used to represent the whole. For instance, a crown represents the king. In *The Accident* (1957; New York, Joseph E. Seagram and Sons, Inc., priv. col.) by Larry Rivers, the viewer may construct a narrative disaster from its disjointed images, each of which represents the whole concept of 'accident'.

BIBLIOGRAPHY
C. D. Cuttler: *Northern Painting* (New York, 1968)
F. Hartt: *History of Italian Renaissance Art* (New York, 1969, rev. Englewood Cliffs, NJ, 3/1987)
E. Panofsky: *Early Netherlandish Painting* (New York, 1971)
A. Comini: 'From Apparatus to Apparition in 19th and 20th Century Art', *Arts* [New York], liv (1980), pp. 145–51

9. Narrative painting by Paula Rego: *Snare*, acrylic on canvas, 1.5×1.5 m, 1987 (London, British Council)

C. Owens: 'Telling Stories: A Recent Collocation of John Baldessari's Narrative Art', *A. America*, lxix (1981), pp. 129–35
J. Marter: 'Narrative Painting, Language, and Ora Lerman's Trilogies', *Arts* [New York], lvi (1982), pp. 90–94
K. Linker: 'Eric Fischl—Involuted Narratives', *Flash A.*, cxv (1984), pp. 56–8
A. Cook: *Changing the Signs: The Fifteenth Century Breakthrough* (Lincoln, NE, 1985)
A. C. Danto: 'Giotto and the Stench of Lazarus', *Antæus*, liv (1985), pp. 7–20
M. Kozloff: 'Through the Narrative Portal', *Artforum*, xxiv (1986), pp. 86–97
P. Fortini Brown: *Venetian Narrative in the Age of Carpaccio* (New Haven, CT, 1988)

RANDY R. BECKER

Narthex. Single-storey porch or vestibule at the western end of a church, usually spanning its entire width, either inside the main structure or abutted to the façade.

□

Narváez, Francisco (*b* Porlamar, 4 Oct 1905; *d* Caracas, 7 July 1982). Venezuelan sculptor, painter and teacher. He studied at the Academia de Bellas Artes, Caracas, from 1922 to 1927. In 1928 he had his first one-man show in the Club Venezuela, Caracas, after which he went to Paris, where he studied at the Académie Julian and in the studio of the French sculptor Paul Landowski (1875–1961). He also met François Pompon and studied the work of Rodin, Aristide Maillol, Emile-Antoine Bourdelle, Mateo Hernández, Charles Despiau and Pablo Gargallo. On his return to Caracas in 1931, Narváez set up a workshop, which was active until 1943. Between 1936 and 1956 he taught at the Escuela de Artes Plásticas y Aplicadas in Caracas, for the last three years as its director. From 1938 he produced decorative work for various architectural projects in Caracas under the direction of Carlos Raúl Villanueva, notably on the reliefs for the façades of the Museo de Ciencias Naturales (*Man* and *Woman*) and the Galería de Arte Nacional, the Toninas Fountain (mythological figures; artificial stone) and on murals (*in situ*, except for n. 42 (destr.)) at the Ciudad Universitaria. He was awarded the Official Prize for Sculpture in 1940 for *Decorative Figure* (mahogany, 790×300×300 mm; Caracas, Gal. A. N.), a work that shows his progression from the stylization of Art Deco to a Creole-inspired phase. In 1948 he won the National Prize for Painting. In his later work he abandoned figuration for an interest in abstraction based on textured volumes (e.g. *3 Volumes*, bronze, 1.36×0.82×0.73 m, 1981; Caracas, Mus. A. Contemp.).

BIBLIOGRAPHY

F. Paz Castillo and R. Rojas Guardia, eds: *Diccionario de las artes visuales en Venezuela*, i (Caracas, 1973), pp. 171–3

R. Pineda: *Francisco Narváez: El maestrazo* (Caracas, 1976)

ANA TAPIAS

Nasca. *See* NAZCA.

Nash. English family of artists.

(1) Paul Nash (*b* London, 11 May 1889; *d* Boscombe, Hants, 11 July 1946). Painter, printmaker, designer, writer and photographer. Although he briefly attended the Slade School, London, in 1910, he was essentially self-taught. His first one-man show was held in 1912 at the Carfax Gallery, London, where he showed a set of shadowy landscapes and imaginative drawings that look back to the Pre-Raphaelites and late 19th-century illustration. Between 1910 and 1914 he paid little attention to Post-Impressionism and the modern movements in London.

During World War I he served as an officer on the Western Front and as an Official War Artist in 1917–18. His artistic reputation was confirmed by his exhibition 'Void of War' at the Leicester Galleries, London, in 1918. His pastel drawings of the Passchendaele battlefields were bitter reflections on the carnage of war, graphically communicated through the obliteration of natural features and their replacement by swamps of mud and water-filled shell holes. He received commissions for large canvases from the British and Canadian War Records, notably *The Menin Road* (1918–19; London, Imperial War Mus.) and *A Night Bombardment* (1919–20; Ottawa, N.G.). Though inexperienced in oil painting, he rapidly taught himself to design with clarity on a large scale without losing the passion and drama of the first experience.

After the war, when living at Dymchurch, Kent, next to the sea-wall that protected Romney Marsh, Nash found a new landscape that could be interpreted on canvas as a metaphor for emotions. But generally his landscapes of the 1920s were less imbued with personal feeling than earlier ones and, in line with the current taste for classicism, were more objective and ordered. Influenced by, though not affiliated to, the Bloomsbury group, he concentrated on formal problems. Paul Cézanne was also a major influence, especially on his watercolours.

In the late 1920s the ending of a conservative phase in post-war taste made more radical innovation possible, and Nash, with several well-received exhibitions behind him, was ready to take the lead in forging new links between English artists and European avant-garde movements. He was greatly stimulated by the Pittura Metafisica of Giorgio

de Chirico and the latter's sense of drama and presentiment. In such pictures as *Landscape at Iden* (1929; London, Tate) he began to isolate particular objects from their contexts and focus on them, giving them special status and hinting at hidden meaning behind external experience. These objects, which sometimes have human or animal overtones, mark the beginnings of his Surrealism and his concept of what he later called the 'object personage'.

Encouraged by further successes, he went beyond landscape painting, temporarily extending his interest in mystery and ambiguity into the urban scene in such pictures as *Harbour and Room* (1932–6; London, Tate; see fig.), where ideas about mirrors and reflections are considered in relation to the world of dream. He also explored Cubism more fully, pushing it to the borders of abstraction in *Kinetic Feature* (1931; London, Tate). He soon came to realize, however, that his literary, poetic mind made him unsuited to non-figurative art, and this line was not pursued.

Nash was the main force behind the formation in 1933 of UNIT ONE, which brought together the abstract and Surrealist tendencies in British art. When Unit One split up after a single exhibition, he moved further towards Surrealism, becoming a member of the committee of the International Surrealist Exhibition in London in 1936 and developing his interest in 'found objects' such as flints, bones, driftwood and jetsam. He felt that these objects possessed their own animation, hinting at bird or animal forms or exhibiting vitality in some other way, and he used them to imply that the landscape was not just a scene or view but a living force with hidden energy that could be

Paul Nash: *Harbour and Room*, 914×711 mm, 1932–6 (London, Tate Gallery)

brought to the surface by means of these metaphors for natural power.

During World War II Nash was again an Official War Artist, working mainly for the Air Ministry. Surrealism survives in *Totes Meer* (1940–1; London, Tate), which shows a dump of wrecked German aircraft metamorphosed into a dark and threatening sea. Nash's last paintings develop earlier interests in seasonal cycles, the ebb and flow of tides and the rising and setting of sun and moon. The symbolism and mythological references in these last pictures are complex, but the canvases speak strongly for themselves and can be enjoyed without a complete understanding of their hidden meaning.

Nash's projection of personal feelings on to nature and interpretations of landscape mood relate to traditions of poetry as well as painting, while his identification with the spirit of individual places has affinities with earlier English landscape painters such as Samuel Palmer. Nevertheless, he was avowedly a modernist. He was a critic and essayist on art, a wood-engraver and designer of textiles and posters. He was interested in photography both as an art form in itself and as a way of recording ideas for pictures.

WRITINGS
Outline: An Autobiography and Other Writings (London, 1949)

BIBLIOGRAPHY
M. Eates, ed.: *Paul Nash: Paintings, Drawings and Illustrations* (London, 1948)
A. Bertram: *Paul Nash: The Portrait of an Artist* (London, 1955)
M. Eates: *Paul Nash: Master of the Image* (London, 1973)
A. Postan: *The Complete Graphic Work of Paul Nash* (London, 1973)
Paul Nash (exh. cat., London, Tate, 1975)
A. Causey: *Paul Nash* (Oxford, 1980)
Paul Nash Book Designs (exh. cat., ed. C. Colvin; Colchester, Minories, 1982)
A Bitter Truth: Avant-garde Art and the Great War (exh. cat. by R. Cork, Berlin, Altes Mus.; London, Barbican A.G.; 1994)

(2) John Nash (*b* London, 11 April 1893; *d* Colchester, 23 Sept 1977). Painter, wood-engraver and illustrator, brother of (1) Paul Nash. He had no formal art training but was urged by his brother to develop his natural talent as a draughtsman. His early work was in watercolour and included biblical scenes, comic drawings and landscapes. A joint exhibition with Paul at the Dorien Leigh Gallery, London, in 1913 was successful, and John was invited to become a founder-member of the LONDON GROUP in 1914 and to join the CUMBERLAND MARKET GROUP in 1915. He began painting in oils with the encouragement of Harold Gilman, whose meticulous craftsmanship influenced his finest landscapes such as *The Cornfield* (1918; London, Tate).

After service in the trenches during World War I, John was appointed Official War Artist in 1918. His two major commissions, *Over the Top: 1st Artists Rifles at Marcoing* (1918–19) and the larger *Oppy Wood 1917: Evening* (1918; both London, Imp. War Mus.), exemplify the primitivizing tendency in his early works, with their firm drawing, sharp colouring and self-contained forms.

John Nash was perhaps most successful in the 1920s. As an oil painter he drew ideas from French landscape painters such as Jean Marchand who were being promoted by Roger Fry and the Bloomsbury group, developing a landscape style that was evocative and atmospheric yet tightly constructed. He was prominent in the post-war

revival of wood-engraving, and his major sets of prints, notably the outstanding *Poisonous Plants* (1927), are confidently executed with clean, elegant lines. His close-up images of flowers have a rich, silky quality that is both sensuous and, sometimes, sinister. His painting style changed little after 1930, though his botanical drawings in pencil with watercolour are distinguished. He was elected ARA in 1940, RA in 1951 and, in 1967, was given a major retrospective exhibition at the Royal Academy, London.

BIBLIOGRAPHY
Exhibition of Paintings and Drawings by John Nash CBE, RA (exh. cat., preface W. T. Monnington; intro. F. Gore; London, RA, 1967)
J. Lewis: *John Nash: The Painter as Illustrator* (London, 1978)
John Nash (exh. cat., ed. C. Colvin; Colchester, Minories, 1983)
J. Rothenstein: *John Nash* (London, 1983)

ANDREW CAUSEY

Nash, David (*b* Esher, Surrey, 14 Nov 1945). English sculptor, land artist and draughtsman. He studied at Kingston College of Art (1963), Brighton College (BA, 1964–7) and Chelsea School of Art (MFA, 1969–70). In 1967 he moved to Blaenau Ffestiniog, Gwynned, a slate-quarrying village, motivated by a desire to escape the 'unnecessarily competitive' metropolitan art world. As a student Nash became interested in the art and writing of China, particularly the text of the Dao de Jing by Laozi (*see* CHINA, §I, 5); other interests include the painting of Abstract Expressionist Arshile Gorky, as well as the theoretical implications of Minimalism, although he found much Minimalist work 'completely devoid of the human spirit'. Nash's early works were in part a response to both Minimalism and the sculpture in the *New Generation 65* exhibition (1965; London, Whitechapel A.G.), which included work by Philip King and William Tucker. From the late 1960s he developed his holistic approach to art; his first exhibition *Briefly Cooked Apples* (1973; York Festival) revealed his belief that his activity was a collaboration with nature. The free-standing sculptures were accompanied by a leaflet reproducing his sketches, including some of ways of ordering wood in bundles, stacks or rows. Wood became Nash's primary material, being used in both temporary and permanent land-based works (*see* LAND ART); for *Black Dome* (1986) 900 lengths of charred larch formed a low dome (*c.* 7 m diameter) that would eventually be reabsorbed into the soil in the Forest of Dean, England. Nash also had numerous artist residencies in sculpture parks in England.

BIBLIOGRAPHY
Sixty Seasons (exh. cat., ed. M. Tooby and C. Carell; Glasgow, Third Eye Cent.; Edinburgh, Fruitmarket Gal.; Llandudno, Mostyn A.G.; Swansea, Vivian A.G. & Mus.; Stoke-on-Trent, City Mus. & A.G.; 1983)
David Nash: Sculpture, 1971–90 (exh. cat., essay by N. Lynton, London, Serpentine Gal.; Cardiff, N. Mus.; Edinburgh, N.G. Mod. A.; 1990)
David Nash: Voyages and Vessels (exh. cat. by G. W. J. Beal, essay by Marina Warner, Omaha, NE, Joslyn A. Mus.; San Diego, CA, Mus. Contemp. A.; Honolulu, HI, Contemp. Mus.; 1994)

□

Nash, John (*b* London, 1752; *d* E. Cowes, Isle of Wight, 13 May 1835). English architect and urban planner. Immensely prolific, he enjoyed the patronage of George IV, and the architecture of the Regency period is particularly associated with his work. He followed the ideas of the PICTURESQUE movement and produced some of its best-known and most influential architectural effects at Blaise Hamlet, near Bristol, the Royal Pavilion, Brighton, and Regents Park and Regent Street, London.

1. Life and work. 2. Critical reception and posthumous reputation.

1. LIFE AND WORK.

(i) Early career and country-house practice, to c. 1810. (ii) Work for the Crown, c. 1810 and after.

(i) Early career and country-house practice, to c. *1810.* Nash was the son of a Lambeth millwright and came from a family of Welsh origins. He spent about seven years in the office of Robert Taylor in London before setting up practice as a speculative builder and architect in 1777. In 1777–8 he designed and built a row of houses in Great Russell Street, London, followed c. 1782 by the remodelling of 17 Bloomsbury Square. These houses were notable for their precocious use of stucco, but the speculation failed, and, following the collapse of a disastrous first marriage, Nash went bankrupt in 1783 and moved to Carmarthenshire. In the eight years from c. 1787 to 1796 he built up a modestly successful practice in south-west Wales, made up of public buildings (e.g. Carmarthen gaol, 1789–92; destr.) and country villas of classical appearance for the local squires. After about 1793, Nash's architecture began to be influenced by the Picturesque doctrines of Richard Payne Knight and Sir Uvedale Price, the second of whom he met through working at Thomas Johnes's Gothic villa at Hafod, Dyfed, where he designed the octagonal library (destr.); in about 1795 he designed a castellated triangular villa, the Castle House (destr. 1958), for Price on the seafront at Aberystwyth. He moved to London in 1795 and established a partnership with the landscape designer HUMPHRY REPTON, taking two of Repton's sons, John Adey Repton (1775–1860) and George Stanley Repton (1786–1858), into his office as assistants. A series of important country-house commissions followed, through which he was soon established as one of the most successful domestic architects in the

country. The partnership broke up in 1800 amid recriminations, but Nash continued to attract commissions on his own and built up a large practice that extended over much of England, Wales and Ireland.

As an architect of country houses, Nash responded to a growing taste for comfortable residences whose external appearance would complement the picturesque landscapes in which they were set, and whose layout would enable the owner to enjoy the views. His houses were designed to be enjoyed, and visual effect was paramount. In a few of his houses, such as Southgate Grove (1797–8), Southgate, north London, he used the Classical orders to good effect, and he was capable of designing noble and sumptuous classical interiors such as those at Caledon (1808–10), Co. Tyrone. But more often he broke free of classical restraint, abandoning symmetry and achieving an effect of contrived informality through the artful grouping of differently shaped blocks, often punctuated by carefully placed (though functionally useless) towers. Favourite features were the bay window, the conservatory and the long, ground-floor gallery; all three appeared in his own castellated villa (begun 1798; destr. 1950) at East Cowes in the Isle of Wight. He was adventurous in his choice of materials, employing stucco or rough blocks of stone as the occasion demanded and making considerable use of cast iron for staircases, even, in the picture gallery at Attingham Park (1807–10), Salop, in conjunction with glass roofs.

To achieve the desired effect, Nash made use of several different styles. In an age when universally accepted standards of architectural taste were collapsing, he offered and gave each consumer what he wanted. In a small group of irregular Italianate villas, such as Cronkhill (c. 1802; see fig. 1), Salop, and Sandridge Park (c. 1805), Devon, he successfully realized the arcadian 'Claudian' ideal later publicized by Payne Knight in his *Analytical Inquiry into the Principles of Taste* (London, 1805); these relatively modest houses anticipate much Victorian and even later domestic architecture. He also employed the already popular idioms of medieval revivalism, either Tudor Gothic as at Longner Hall (c. 1805), Salop, rich in bargeboards and plaster fan vaults, or, more commonly, the castellated style pioneered by Payne Knight at Downton Castle (1772–8), Hereford & Worcs. The best of Nash's 'castles', such as Luscombe (1800–04), Devon, Caerhayes (c. 1808), Cornwall, and Lough Cutra (1811; altered), Co. Galway, are among the most engaging examples of this often ponderous genre. He was also one of the first architects to restore a Tudor character to houses altered in the 18th century, as at Helmingham Hall (1800), Suffolk, and Parnham (1807–11), Dorset; here, as in most of his Gothic Revival works, he left much of the detailing to his assistants.

In many of his smaller houses, Nash took up the idiom of the picturesque rustic cottage (*see* COTTAGE ORNÉ), showing great sensitivity to texture and outline and anticipating by more than half a century the architects of the late Victorian domestic revival. He took particular care over the design of lodges and estate buildings, and at Blaise Hamlet (1810–11), Henbury, Bristol, he designed an exquisite village of thatched stone cottages for the retired pensioners of the Quaker banker John Scandrett

1. John Nash: Cronkhill, near Cross Houses, Shrewsbury, Salop, from the north east, c. 1802

Harford; in its artfully arranged informality and exploitation of vernacular idiom, this can be seen as a paradigm for many 19th-century estate villages and, more distantly, for the publicly financed housing estates of the 20th century. Here, as in certain other respects, Nash was a harbinger of later developments in the provision of domestic architecture for a mass society.

(ii) Work for the Crown, c. 1810 and after.

(a) Buildings for royalty. Even if he had designed nothing after 1810 (when he was 58 years old), Nash would still be remembered as an innovative and inventive domestic architect. But in his sixties his career began to take a new direction. In 1806, while his domestic practice was in full spate, he acquired a minor salaried post as architect in the Office of Woods and Forests, probably through the patronage of Lord Robert Spencer, Surveyor of Woods and Forests in the 'Ministry of all the talents'. In this capacity he made plans in 1811 for the long-anticipated development of the Crown's estate in Marylebone Park (Regents Park), London. They were implemented, and for the rest of his working life he was intimately associated with plans to develop and reshape the West End of London.

Nash had meanwhile attracted the attention of the Prince Regent (later George IV; *see* HANOVER, (4)), who embarked on a series of large-scale building schemes after becoming *de facto* head of state in 1811. In 1813 Nash received his first direct royal commission, for a *cottage orné* in Windsor Great Park, Berks; this became the nucleus of the Royal Lodge (largely remodelled 1830). He was then commissioned to extend two buildings by Henry Holland, also for the Prince Regent: Carlton House, London (1814, destr.; 1827–8), and the Royal Pavilion (1815–22) at Brighton. In 1815 he was also made one of the three 'Attached Architects' in the Office of Works, along with John Soane and Robert Smirke, after which time he virtually stopped taking private commissions.

Nash's witty, insouciant and reckless temperament found a counterpart in that of the Prince Regent. His alterations to the Royal Pavilion transformed the exterior of Holland's restrained seaside villa into a riotous, Mughal-inspired extravaganza dominated by a row of bizarre onion domes, imaginative enough to transmit the heady spirit of Regency Brighton to posterity, yet masking a cast-iron constructional system of considerable ingenuity. For the interiors of the Pavilion he provided an appropriately lavish architectural framework for the bewilderingly rich Chinese-inspired decoration carried out by Frederick Crace (1779–1859), then in charge of his family's firm of decorators in London (for illustrations *see* BRIGHTON and OVERDOOR).

An almost equally ornate effect was achieved in Nash's additions to Carlton House, but the work here was very short-lived, and in 1825 George IV decided to abandon the house. Its demolition was followed by the redevelopment of the site for housing by the Commissioners of Woods and Forests, and the conversion of the largely 18th-century Buckingham House into the main royal residence in London. These commissions were entrusted to Nash, and over the next five years he turned Buckingham House into a palace, adding a set of rooms of Baroque magnificence to the garden front and creating an entrance courtyard facing The Mall, flanked by projecting wings and entered through a triumphal arch of Roman derivation (the Marble Arch (*see* TRIUMPHAL ARCH, fig. 2), moved to Cumberland Gate, Hyde Park, in 1851). The interiors of Buckingham Palace were more successful than the exterior, which attracted widespread criticism. The rebuilding was planned and executed with an impetuous haste, and Nash, the master of scenic effects and picturesque grouping, failed to impart enough monumental gravity to the façades.

With the evaporation of the confidence that followed the end of the Napoleonic Wars, fears of excessive public spending led to a parliamentary inquiry (1828) into Nash's building activities. When George IV died (1830), and the Whigs came to power, Nash was exposed to a series of attacks that stripped him of his position in the Office of Works and, in 1831, deprived him of the Buckingham Palace commission. Though vindicated in his handling of structural iron in the palace, he was condemned by a Select Committee for 'inexcusable irregularity and great negligence' in the framing of building contracts (in the 2nd Report of the Select Committee on Windsor Castle and Buckingham Palace, *British Parliamentary Papers*, iv (1831) [329]). The garden front was completed by Edward Blore to a slightly altered design in 1832–7, and the main façade to the Mall, hidden from view by Blore's east range (1847–50), itself remodelled by Aston Webb in 1912–13.

(b) Metropolitan improvements. The greatest achievements of Nash's later years lay in the sphere of urban planning. Blaise Hamlet showed his mastery of picturesque grouping. Regents Park gave him an opportunity to bring Repton's aristocratic landscape-garden ideas to the town. The effect was one of contrived informality made up of a lake, winding paths and clumps of trees interspersed with buildings, and it became a model for countless public parks in England and elsewhere. His plans for the park were approved in 1812 and, with the credit boom following the end of the Napoleonic Wars, he was able to develop the Crown land surrounding the park with profitable housing for the rich. Here, overlooking the park, he produced a series of highly inventive variations on the theme of the Georgian terrace. Park Crescent (1812), Sussex Place (1822), Chester Terrace (1825) and Cumberland Terrace (1825; see fig. 2) are palatial-looking structures that conceal commonplace construction and planning behind a display of Roman-inspired architecture in stucco. However, as urban scenery they are second to none in London. In 1826 Nash designed the equally impressive Carlton House Terrace overlooking St James's Park, which he then proceeded to remodel after the fashion of Regents Park as a suitable foreground to Buckingham Palace.

Spectacular though these developments were, the Park Village, built after 1825 on a site at the north-western corner of Regents Park, was even more influential. In this urbanized derivative of Blaise Hamlet, stuccoed villas in a variety of Gothic and Italianate styles (many of them built

2. John Nash: Cumberland Terrace, Regents Park, London, 1825; engraving by James Tingle after drawing by Thomas H. Shepherd from T. H. Shepherd and J. Elmes: *Metropolitan Improvements, or London in the 19th Century* (London, 1827)

in the 1830s under the supervision of JAMES PENNE-THORNE, who took over Nash's practice) were grouped irregularly on either side of the Regent's Canal. In its completed form the 'village' can be seen as a prototype for the Victorian middle-class suburb.

Nash's talents as a planner were displayed to the greatest effect in Regent Street. His first scheme for a new street linking Regents Park with Carlton House and the West End was made in 1812. The street was built under the supervision of the Commissioners of Woods and Forests, using government revenue and loans, and, as their surveyor, Nash was made responsible for purchasing property, making bargains with builders and supervising—and, in many cases, designing—the architectural elevations. The layout and architecture display many of the felicities of the picturesque approach to design: variety, surprise, changes of texture and style and the artful management of vistas. The street transformed the face of the West End, demarcating fashionable Mayfair from the shabbier districts to the east, providing sites for shops and creating some of the focal points of modern London: Oxford Circus, Piccadilly Circus and Waterloo Place. In order to ensure its rapid completion Nash acted both as designer and as speculative developer for some of the crucial sites, notably the colonnaded Quadrant (1818–20; destr. 1848 and 1906; *see* LONDON, fig. 7) that carried the street north-west from Piccadilly towards Regents Park. Elsewhere he relied greatly on the assistance of the builder James Burton (1761–1837). All the original blocks flanking the street have been replaced, most of them when the Crown leases fell in after World War I. Only some of the public buildings remain, including Nash's church, All Souls (1822), Langham Place, whose curved peristyle and pointed steeple still

close the northern vista from Oxford Circus, and his astylar United Services Club (1826–8; now the Institute of Directors), facing Decimus Burton's Athenaeum Club across Waterloo Place at the southern end.

With Regent Street largely completed, Nash prepared designs in 1826 for a new phase of metropolitan improvements. They included the formation of a new square (Trafalgar Square) on the site of the Royal Mews at the northern end of Whitehall and the remodelling of the western end of the Strand. The blocks of houses and shops in this part of the Strand, including the block (later altered) opposite Charing Cross Station occupied by Coutts Bank, were built by William Herbert (*c.* 1792–1863) to Nash's designs and completed in 1831; they represent the best surviving examples of Nash's street architecture. The architectural development of Trafalgar Square owed nothing to Nash, and the rest of his street improvement plans fell victim to economies enforced by the governments of the 1830s. Nash retired to the Isle of Wight in 1830, leaving his office in the hands of James Pennethorne, and in 1834 he formally made over what remained of his practice to the younger man.

2. CRITICAL RECEPTION AND POSTHUMOUS REPUTATION. It is not difficult to account for Nash's success as an architect. Humphry Repton said that he had 'powers of fascination beyond anyone I had ever met with'. He was ambitious, adept at pleasing patrons, good at understanding the social functions of buildings from palaces down to cottages, financially astute, especially in the management of urban building operations, and far-sighted in the organization of his architectural practice, which he ran like a design team. Much of his skill as an architect lay

in his mastery of planning, grouping, outline and the relationship of buildings to their context: skills more usually associated with the painter and designer than with the architect. His approach to design was essentially experimental, and he was more alive than most of his contemporaries to the potential of new materials, especially stucco and iron. However, he was careless in the handling of detail, much of which he left to his office staff or contracted out to others, occasionally slipshod in his methods and apt to cut corners in the management of building contracts. His career fell foul of a growing wish to separate architectural design from speculative building, a division that was unknown in the 18th century when he grew up. Nash's architecture is of a piece with his character and epitomizes the glamour of the Regency era, for which reason it fell into disfavour for most of the rest of the 19th century. Yet, for all his shortcomings, Nash played a major part in the evolution of domestic design in England and did more than any architect since Wren to improve the face of London. With the growing understanding in the 20th century of the need to link architecture to its wider environment, appreciation of his achievement has steadily increased.

BIBLIOGRAPHY

T. H. Shepherd and J. Elmes: *Metropolitan Improvements, or London in the 19th Century* (London, 1827/*R* New York, 1978) [partial repr. as *Shepherd's London*, ed. J. F. C. Phillips]
H. Clifford Smith: *Buckingham Palace* (London, 1931)
J. Summerson: *Georgian London* (London, 1945, rev. 1970)
T. Davis: *The Architecture of John Nash* (London, 1960)
——: *John Nash: The Prince Regent's Architect* (London, 1966, 2/1973), [contains excellent photographs]
A. Saunders: *Regents Park* (London, 1969)
J. M. Crook and M. H. Port: *The History of the King's Works*, vi (London, 1973), pp. 261–99 [Buckingham Palace], 307–22 [Carlton House]
G. Tyack: 'John Nash and the Park Village', *Georgian Group Journal* (1973), pp. 68–73
H. Hobhouse: *The History of Regent Street* (London, 1975)
J. Dinkel: *The Royal Pavilion, Brighton* (Brighton, 1979, 2/1983)
N. Temple: *John Nash and the Village Picturesque* (Gloucester, 1979)
J. Summerson: *The Life and Work of John Nash, Architect* (London, 1980) [the definitive study]
M. Mansbridge: *John Nash: A Complete Catalogue* (London, 1991)

GEOFFREY C. TYACK

Nasik [Nāsika; Nāsikka; Gulshanābād]. Pilgrimage centre and cave-temple site in Maharashtra, India. It was inhabited since Chalcolithic times (*c*. 1500 BC). The earliest monumental remains at Nasik are a series of rock-cut monasteries (Skt *vihāra*) and a prayer-hall (*caitya gṛha*) clustered on a hill. The prayer-hall (1st century BC) is a modest apsidal excavation enshrining a stupa. The octagonal pillars of the hall (some bearing inscriptions) rise out of pots on stepped bases. The roof is undecorated, but mortices suggest that wooden ribs were originally installed there. The façade has a large arched window and a richly carved entrance door flanked by single standing figures (*see* INDIAN SUBCONTINENT, §V, 4(iii)). Cave 19, a small monastery with six cells, has an inscription of the SATAVAHANA king Kanha (*reg c*. 1st century BC). Two larger monasteries (nos 3 and 10) belong to the 1st century AD. Both have pillared verandahs fronting on a series of monks' cells arrayed around a court. Cave 10, which has inscriptions of the Kshaharata king Nahapana (*reg c*. first quarter of the 2nd century AD), has a stone railing across the verandah and a gate-like door flanked by guardian figures. Subsequent additions to many caves document the appearance of Mahayana doctrine.

During the rule of the Yadava dynasty, at the end of the 12th century, Jainism flourished at Nasik. The places known as Anjaneri and Chamar-lena were developed, the former containing a sizeable number of structural temples. Chamar-lena has numerous Jaina caves and sculptures of the 12th–13th centuries. During this period the Buddhist caves were appropriated and additions made. Cave 11, for example, has a figure of a Tirthamkara (Jaina teacher) of the 12th century. In the 18th century, under the Marathas, Nasik became an important place of pilgrimage due to its identification with the place known as Janasthana in the *Rāmāyaṇa*. The site was studded with temples, bathing ghats and pools. A number of mansions were also built, notably the Sarkarwada associated with the Peshwas, hereditary ministers and *de facto* kings of the Marathas.

See also INDIAN SUBCONTINENT, §IV, 4(iii) and 5(iii)(b).

BIBLIOGRAPHY

J. Fergusson and J. Burgess: *The Cave Temples of India* (London, 1880), pp. 263–79
M. S. Mate: *Maratha Architecture (1650 AD–1850 AD)* (Pune, 1959), pp. 89–94
V. Dehejia: *Early Buddhist Rock Temples: A Chronology* (London, 1972), pp. 159–60
R. Salomon: 'The Kṣatrapas and Mahākṣatrapas of India', *Wien. Z. Knd. Südasiens & Archv Ind. Philos.*, xvii (1973), pp. 5–25
S. Nagaraju: *Buddhist Architecture of Western India (c. 250 BC–AD 300)* (New Delhi, 1981), pp. 258–81, 306–7, 343–5

A. P. JAMKHEDKAR

Nasimovich, Nikolay (Fyodorovich). *See* CHUZHAK, NIKOLAY.

Nasini, Giuseppe Nicola (*b* Castel del Piano, 1657; *d* Siena, 1736). Italian painter and draughtsman. He was the son of the artist Francesco Nasini (1621–95) and was responsible for the revival of Baroque painting in Siena at the end of the 17th century. Between 1681 and 1688 he attended the Accademia Fiorentina, Rome, sponsored by that institution's founder, Cosimo III de' Medici, who commissioned from him the *Death of St Peter of Alcántara* (1682; Montelupo Fiorentino, convent of the Ambrogiana), a work clearly influenced by Ciro Ferri, director of the Accademia and Nasini's teacher. In 1685–6 Nasini was in Siena and painted, assisted by his brother Antonio Nasini (1643–1715), the fresco on the Antiporta di Camollia, which he subsequently restored (1699; destr. 1944). A *bozzetto* survives by Antonio Nasini (Siena, Col. Chigi-Saracini); there is also a drawing (Paris, Louvre) by Giuseppe Nicola Nasini that is probably connected with the work's restoration. In the autumn of 1686, after a brief stay in Bologna, Nasini went to Venice, where he remained until 1688. He drew inspiration from Venetian 16th-century painting and frescoed a chapel in the church of the Umiltà and a lunette depicting *St Peter in Prison* in the convent of S Giorgio (both destr.).

After a series of visits to towns in the Po Valley, Nasini began to work for the Medici court in Florence. He painted highly praised canvases for the Palazzo Pitti depicting the

Giuseppe Nicola Nasini: *Apotheosis of St Catherine* (1701; detail), fresco, oratory of the Crocifisso, sanctuary of S Caterina, Siena

Day of Judgement (1690–94; untraced) and *St John Chrysostom* (1691; Florence, S Spirito), and he painted illusionistic frescoes, inspired by Veronese and Tintoretto, of *Jupiter Launching Thunderbolts against the Giants* and *Hercules at the Crossroads* (both 1691; Florence, Pal. Medici–Riccardi). In the Palazzo Medici–Riccardi he studied the works of Luca Giordano, whose influence can be seen in Nasini's fine frescoes painted in the late 1690s, after his return to Siena, in the oratory of SS Trinità, Siena. In these years Nasini became the foremost painter in Siena and one who inspired many young Sienese artists: he painted frescoes in the oratory of the Crocifisso of the sanctuary of S Catherina, including the *Apotheosis of St Catherine* (1701; see fig.); also in the apse of Santo Spirito (1704; *in situ*), in the church of the Visitazione (1704–5; *in situ*) and in the Venturini Chapel in the church of S Domenico (1705; destr.); these works were all highly acclaimed (della Valle). In 1707 he executed a *Virgin Enthroned between SS Charles and Philip* for the Collegio Romano di Propaganda Fide in Siena, and in 1712 he painted the *Stations of the Cross* in a series of frescoes along the road leading from the centre of Perugia to the monastery of Monte Morcino (*in situ*).

Around 1715 Nasini moved to Rome, where in 1716 he painted a canvas of the *Baptism* (Rome; S Lorenzo in Lucina, baptistery). In 1718 he painted the frescoes in the Gran Sala of the Cancelleria Apostolica in the Vatican (*in situ*), celebrating Pope Clement's role as a patron of

architecture, and also a canvas of the *Prophet Amos* (Rome; S Giovanni in Laterano), part of a decorative cycle on which the greatest painters in Rome at the time also worked. Nasini was commissioned in 1719 to make a mosaic version of Domenico Passignano's *Crucifixion* in St Peter's (*in situ*). During this time he also studied the new painting techniques of Sebastiano Conca, Giovanni Odazzi and, most notably, Benedetto Luti. His good fortune in Rome did not last for long, however. The mediocrity of his frescoes in the Odescalchi Chapel (1721–2; Rome, SS Apostoli) so dented his reputation that he was obliged to return to Siena in 1723. Here he created frescoes for the collegiate church at Provenzano (*in situ*), for the church of S Mustiola and the convent of Santo Spirito. In 1726 he painted a fresco of the *Virgin* in the church of the Incoronata, Arcidosso, and, in 1728, a *Pietà* in the local Capuchin convent. After 1729 Nasini painted the frescoes for the Malati Chapel in the Spedale di S Maria della Scala, Siena (*in situ*); for the same church he presented (1730) a preparatory sketch of a fresco for the tribune, but the commission had already been given to Conca. During the 1730s Nasini, by now approaching 80, worked in Siena, first in S Gaetano Thiene and later in the Carthusian monastery at Maggiano, assisted by his son Apollonio Nasini.

BIBLIOGRAPHY

G. della Valle: *Lettere senesi*, iii (Rome, 1786), pp. 51–5

E. Romagnoli: *Biografia cronologica de' bellartisti senesi dal secolo XII a tutto il XVIII* (before 1835/*R* Florence, 1976)

S. Rudolph: 'The Gran Sala in the Cancellaria Apostolica: A Homage to the Artistic Patronage of Clement XI', *Burl. Mag.*, cxx (1978), pp. 593–60

G. Casale: 'Giuseppe Nicola Nasini pittore senese: Opere conservate a Roma', *Annu. Ist. Stor. A.* (1981–2), pp. 43–52

Bernardino Mei e la pittura barocca a Siena (exh. cat., ed. F. Bisogni and M. Ciampolini; Siena, Pal. Chigi-Saraceni, 1987), pp. 221–36 [with bibliog. to 1987]

M. Gregori and E. Schleier, eds: *La pittura in Italia: Il seicento*, 2 vols (Milan, 1989), p. 826 [with bibliog.]

MARCO CIAMPOLINI

Nasir al-Din. *See* QAJAR, (2).

Nāṣir al-Dīn Hasan. *See* MAMLUK, §II, 2(5).

Nasir Muhammad, al-. *See* MAMLUK, §II, 2(3).

Nasmyth. Scottish family of artists. Michael Naesmyth was the head of a family firm of architect–builders. With his father he built many Edinburgh houses, notably in St Andrew Square and George Square. (1) Alexander Nasmyth was his second son and the most notable artist of the family. He was the father of 11 children, among whom (2) Patrick Nasmyth was the best-known painter. The others were Jane (1788–1867), Barbara (1790–1870), Margaret (1791–1869), Elizabeth (1793–1862), Anne (1798–1874), Charlotte (1804–84), Alexander (1805–*c*. 1816), George (1807–*c*. 1860), James (1808–90) and Mary (1810–11). Jane, Barbara, Margaret and Charlotte assisted their father in running the art classes at 47 York Place; like their sisters Anne and Elizabeth, they all painted. Alexander's fourth son, James, painted but was best known for his invention of the steam hammer. His works include a portrait of his father (Aberdeen, A.G.), painted in 1884 from a sketch by William Nicholson (1784–1844).

(1) Alexander Nasmyth (*b* Edinburgh, 9 Sept 1758; *d* Edinburgh, 10 April 1840). Painter, illustrator, landscape gardener and engineer. He was educated for a career in architecture, but at an early age he showed artistic talent, and in 1773 he was apprenticed to James Cummyng (*c.* 1730–92), a house decorator and antiquarian. Nasmyth painted panels for carriages at Alexander Crichton's coach-works and attended evening classes at the Trustees' Academy. When Allan Ramsay visited Crichton in 1774, he was impressed with Nasmyth's ability. Nasmyth subsequently accompanied Ramsay to his London studio where he continued his apprenticeship for four years.

Nasmyth returned to Edinburgh at the end of 1778 and soon obtained ample employment as a portrait painter. His earliest works, for example *John Scott of Malleny* (1781; Malleny House, Lothian, NT Scotland), followed Ramsay's practice of showing the head and shoulders of the sitter against a plain background, but Nasmyth gradually liberated himself from the conventions of his master, and within a few years he was placing his figures within landscape settings, lavishing as much care on the landscape details as on the sitters. He painted *Patrick Miller and his Children* (1782; Dalswinton, Dumfries & Galloway, priv. col.) around the theme of a shooting-party, with the family set in their own parkland. Miller, a retired banker, discovered Nasmyth's scientific capabilities and loaned him £500 with which to broaden his artistic education on the Continent.

Nasmyth arrived in Rome in April 1783. Views painted by him in later life from sketches made on the Continent suggest that he also visited the Bay of Naples, Bolsena, Ancona and Tivoli. His homeward route may be traced through pictures of *Lake Lausanne, Lake Lucerne, Lake Geneva from the Jura Mountains* and *Haarlem*. His sketches were the basis of many paintings by his children. He returned to Edinburgh at the end of 1784 and resumed painting portraits, the best known being of his close friend *Robert Burns* (1787; Edinburgh, N.G.). *The Gordon Family at Braid* (*c.* 1790; Cluny Castle, Grampian) represents the high point of Nasmyth's portraiture. The handling of the dresses and attention to the details of the house in its landscape setting are particularly fine.

Nasmyth's liberal politics and outspokenness on the glaring abuses of the government embarrassed his aristocratic patrons. Despite warnings that commissions would cease, he persisted in expressing his beliefs, even 'refusing to paint their…faces, preferring instead the beautiful face of nature'. His portrait of *Thomas, 7th Earl of Haddington and his Brothers* (*c.* 1792; Mellerstain, Borders) remained half complete in Nasmyth's studio at his death. Henry Raeburn's dominance of portrait painting in Edinburgh during this period further encouraged Nasmyth to turn to landscape painting.

As early as 1788 Nasmyth described himself in the Edinburgh directories as 'portrait and landscape painter'. His predominant theme was the Scottish landscape, usually containing an architectural feature often seen across water, the distance bathed in mist, for example *Lugar Water* (Aberdeen, A.G.) and *Loch Tay with Kenmore Bridge* (1810; Tayside, priv. col.). A fine foreign view is the *Ponte Molle on the Sylvan Side of Rome* (1810; Manchester, C.A.G.). In the 1820s he turned his attention to Edinburgh street scenes, recording fashions, daily activity and architecture, such as *Princes Street, with the Royal Institution Building under Construction* (1825; Edinburgh, N.G.; *see* EDINBURGH, fig. 4). *Edinburgh with the High Street and Lawnmarket* (exh. RA 1824; Balmoral, Grampian, Royal Col.) and its companion *Shipping at Leith* (exh. RA 1824; Edinburgh, City Chambers) were probably painted to mark the visit of George IV to Edinburgh in 1822.

Nasmyth's style appears to have been moulded principally on that of Claude Lorrain in arrangement, colour and mood, and on Jacob van Ruysdael in the handling of water, trees and foreground details. Rather than paint directly what he saw, Nasmyth would generally follow prevalent Picturesque theories as propounded by William Gilpin, first searching out the finest view and then editing or improving it to achieve a harmonious balance. He painted his pictures in the studio, working from small pencil sketches often made many years earlier. The paintings were then worked up from several layers of pigment and glazing to achieve a feeling of layered depth, the top leaves painted in minute and regular clusters of three or four. Throughout his life he used greens, browns and russet for the trees and foreground; pinks and browns for the paths and buildings; blue, grey–white, pinks and oranges for the skies, which were often the most colourful part of the composition. Nasmyth's style, once formulated, displayed a remarkable consistency in both vision and technique throughout his career. From 1832 he suffered from gout and rheumatism, and the effects of old age rendered his later works less precise.

Admired during his lifetime as 'the father of landscape painting in Scotland', Nasmyth was later accused of repetitiveness. He frequently painted the same view several times, only varying the positions of the figures. Few of his works are signed, and because many 'Nasmyths' contain the hand of one or more of his talented children, care must be exercised in attributing lesser works to him, particularly as they vary considerably in quality. His best works, however, are distinguished by a rare interpretation of local weather conditions, which gives them an indefinable aura of romance, poetry and tranquillity. He sent his most ambitious pictures to London and also exhibited in Edinburgh, Manchester, Carlisle and Liverpool.

Nasmyth owned the upper floors of 47 York Place, which included a large studio, from 1799. As the Napoleonic Wars rendered the Continent unsafe for travel, Edinburgh assumed greater importance as a cultural centre, and Nasmyth responded to an increased demand for art classes. Among his pupils were David Wilkie, David Roberts, Clarkson Stanfield, William Allan, Andrew Robertson, Andrew Geddes, Hugh William Williams and John Thomson (i). Nasmyth's teaching methods involved short instructive talks at the easel combined with copying objects, sometimes using the camera obscura. He did not take on apprentices in the conventional sense, and his relationships with pupils were informal.

Nasmyth was often called on to paint a large house or castle in its landscape: for example *Castle Huntly* (Dundee, McManus Gals). At times he was employed to help his clients improve the landscape appearance of their estates by making the garden or park resemble his pictures of them. He made sketches and models to demonstrate how vistas might be opened up by judicious pruning, emphasizing the importance of preserving mature trees. He was often asked to select a suitable site for a new house, looking through the eyes of what Sir Uvedale Price termed the 'architetto-pittore', or to modernize an old castle. Between 1800 and 1810 he provided designs for follies, bridges, stable complexes and grand mansions, the latter including Taymouth Castle (Tayside), Dunglass House (Lothian), Loudoun Castle (Strathclyde), Dreghorn Castle (Lothian) and Rosneath (Dumbartonshire).

Nasmyth also produced the stock scenery for the principal Scottish theatres and those in Drury Lane in London. His scenery for Glasgow, which consisted of streets, houses, cottages, palaces, interiors and landscapes, 'excited universal admiration', according to David Roberts. Possibly as a result of the success in 1818 of the scenery for *The Heart of Midlothian* (sketches in Edinburgh, N.G.), Nasmyth was commissioned by Walter Scott through his publisher Archibald Constable to provide vignette engravings for the 1821 edition of the *Waverley* novels. In all Nasmyth contributed over 60 illustrations to Scott's works.

Nasmyth had considerable talents as an engineer. He designed a tunnel under the Forth (*Scots Mag.*, 1807, pp. 189, 243) and made designs for bridges and bridge-building (Edinburgh, N.G.). The bow-and-string bridge and arch, used commonly for spanning rivers or the roofs of factories and railway stations, was his invention (1794), as was compression riveting (1816). He appears in John Graham Gilbert's *The Distinguished Men of Science of Great Britain Living in 1807/8* (London, N.P.G.) beside Sir William Herschel, John Dalton, Isambard Kingdom Brunel, James Watt and Thomas Telford.

Nasmyth continued the family tradition of beautifying his native city. He designed St Bernard's Well, the small temple over the Waters of Leith, and provided the original design for the Dean Bridge. He was keenly interested in the progress of the New Town, frequently making suggestions and models and discussing his ideas with the architects and builders. *Princes Street from Hanover Street with the Foundation of the Royal Institution* (exh. RA 1826; Edinburgh, priv. col.) and *Edinburgh from the Calton Hill* (exh. RA 1826; Glasgow, Clydesdale Bank) show the progress of the New Town. *Edinburgh from St Anthony's Chapel* (1832; Dalmeny House, Lothian) depicts in great detail the Old and completed New Towns side by side.

(2) Patrick [Peter] **Nasmyth** (*b* Edinburgh, 1787; *d* London, 1831). Painter, son of (1) Alexander Nasmyth. He was trained by his father and settled in London in 1810. He lost the use of his right hand as a result of an accident on a sketching trip, changed to painting with his left hand with no great difficulty and overcame youthful deafness. He lived the rather erratic life of a bachelor artist, mixing chiefly with other Scottish artists including David Roberts, Clarkson Stanfield and David Wilkie. Extracts of his conversations with other artists in John Burnet's *Progress of a Painter* (1854) give considerable insight into his artistic attitudes. He was always careless in financial dealings and never profited by his art. He generally painted small domestic scenes in a style comparable with that of his father, although his brushstrokes were more minute, and he used more oil on his brush. He paid great attention to details of brickwork and foreground plants. His paintings, of which *Heathland near Godstone* (F. J. Nettleford priv. col.) is a fine example, are mostly in private collections. The Tate Gallery, London, has a number of small-scale works by Patrick, including the *New Forest* (1815).

WRITINGS
S. Smiles, ed.: *James Nasmyth, Engineer: An Autobiography* (London, 1883)

BIBLIOGRAPHY
J. L. Caw: 'Alexander Nasmyth, 1758–1840', *Scots Mag.*, n. s., xxxii (1940), pp. 325–35
The Works of the Nasmyth Family, (1719–1890) (exh. cat., Edinburgh, Saltire Soc., 1948)
B. Skinner: 'Nasmyth Revalued', *Scot. A. Rev.*, x/3 (1966), pp. 10–13
M. Kemp: 'Alexander Nasmyth and the Style of Graphic Eloquence', *Connoisseur*, clxxiii (1970), pp. 93–100
Alexander Nasmyth and his Family (exh. cat. by M. Patry, Eccles, Monks Hall Mus., 1973)
F. Irwin: 'Lady Amateurs and their Masters in Scott's Edinburgh', *Connoisseur*, clxxxvii (1974), pp. 229–37
The Nasmyth Family of Painters (exh. cat., London, Oscar & Peter Johnson, 1974)
D. Irwin and F. Irwin: *Scottish Painters at Home and Abroad, 1700–1900* (London, 1975), pp. 138–45, 238–40
P. Johnson and E. Money: *The Nasmyth Family of Painters* (Leigh-on-Sea, 1977)
The Discovery of Scotland (exh. cat. by L. Errington and J. Holloway, Edinburgh, N.G., 1978), pp. 27, 54–5, 73–9
Alexander Nasmyth, 1758–1840 (exh. cat. by J. C. B. Cooksey, U. St Andrews, Crawford Cent. A., 1979)
Painting in Scotland: The Golden Age (exh. cat. by D. Macmillan, U. Edinburgh, Talbot Rice Gal.; London, Tate; 1986), pp. 140–51; cat. nos 134–45
J. C. B. Cooksey: *Alexander Nasmyth H.R.S.A., 1758–1840: A Man of the Scottish Renaissance* (Haddington, 1991)

JANET COOKSEY

Nasoni, Nicolau [Nasoni, Niccolò; Nazzoni, Niccolò] (*b* San Giovanni, Valderno di Sopra, Tuscany, 1691; *d* (?Oporto), 1773). Italian architect, painter and designer, active in Portugal. He was one of the most influential figures of the Portuguese Baroque. Immensely productive and imaginative, he was essentially a decorator who revealed in his buildings the decorative vocabulary of Tuscan Baroque. He was called 'Dom Nicolau' by the people of Oporto as a tribute to his inventiveness and originality and to his transformation of Oporto, which he found a medieval town and converted into one of the most Baroque of Portuguese cities. He endowed it with churches and houses based on the formula of a literal translation into granite of the complex ornament in his painting. Nasoni was theatrical in his designs for staircases and portals as well as in the realism of his decorative motifs, and he established in Oporto architecture and wood-carving a tradition of extremely dramatic effects combined with the richest ornamentation seen in Portugal since the Manueline style.

1. EARLY TRAINING AND PAINTING. Between 1713 and 1720 Nasoni lived in Siena, where he distinguished himself in the construction of catafalques and triumphal arches in which the sense of theatre that was to characterize his later work was already evident. At the same time he was studying architecture and painting with Giuseppe Nicola Nasini, and it was as a painter that he travelled first to Rome and then to Malta. There, from 1722 to 1725, he worked for the Portuguese nobleman Dom Antonio

Manuel de Vilhena, Grand Master of the Order of Malta (appointed Master 1722, *d* 1736), painting ceilings in the Palace of the Order of Malta, Valletta, with decorative *quadratura* painting of Tuscan origin. While in Malta he met the brother of the Dean of the diocese of Oporto, Dom Jerónimo de Távora e Noronha Leme Cernache (1690–1754), and it was through the invitation of the Dean that he went, about 1725, to Oporto to direct the redecoration and modernization of the Romanesque cathedral.

Nasoni's first paintings in fresco were for the walls of the chancel of Oporto Cathedral (*in situ*, damaged) in which he created illusionist perspectives intended to enlarge its medieval spaces. The painted decorations of the chancel arch are composed of asymmetrical volutes and acanthus foliage. Nasoni was later to translate into stone these heavy yet lively ornamental motifs. His frescoes on the vaults of the nave (destr.) probably inspired the false cupolas of those of Lamego Cathedral (1738–43; *in situ*), the nave of which he painted during the years that he was responsible for rebuilding the interior of the cathedral. These Old Testament Scenes are depicted with a variety and richness of decoration, a sense of depth and a predilection for asymmetry, and they are important for introducing Italian illusionistic ceiling painting to northern Portugal. Other commissions from clerical circles included the frescoes with scenes from the *Apocalypse* (1739; destr.) on the ceiling of the nave in the church of Sta Eulália, Cumeeira, Trás-os-Montes.

2. ARCHITECTURE. For two doorcases in the apse of Oporto Cathedral, Nasoni used reversed pediments with either rigid or slightly curved profiles, reminiscent of wings, and these designs go back to the work of the Florentine Bernardo Buontalenti, from whom Nasoni drew numerous elements of dramatic fantasy. The handsome doorcases in the cloister (1733–6) show Nasoni's theatrical use of ornamental vases and naturalistic sculptured cloths and tassels that recall the designs of Jean Bérain I. The frames of these doors also brought to Oporto the taste for fantastic shapes and profiles that had been created by Francesco Borromini. Above the granite porch (1736) in the form of a Palladian arcade, which he added to the north side of Oporto Cathedral, Nasoni introduced a dramatic design of volutes and obelisks. He also designed the grand, double divided staircase (1733–6) that connects the cathedral cloisters with the chapter house. Here, on a severe granite frame with Doric frieze and a solid parapet, he used a rich variety of ornament that also derived from Buontalenti. The renovation of the cathedral precinct was completed by the building of the vast Bishop's Palace, begun in 1741 to Nasoni's designs of 1734, though only part of the façade was completed in the architect's lifetime. The palace of S João Novo, Oporto, attributed on stylistic grounds to Nasoni, was erected *c.* 1727–33 for the magistrate Pedro da Costa Lima, whose son Miguel was treasurer of Oporto Cathedral. The granite façade presents a contrast between the simple Doric framework and the rich ornament used.

In 1731 Nasoni was commissioned by the brotherhood of the clergy of Oporto, the Clérigos, led by Jerónimo de Távora e Noronha, to design their first church and the seat of the Order. Its construction was the most important

Nicolau Nasoni: façade of S Pedro dos Clérigos, Oporto, completed *c.* 1750

architectural event in Oporto during a period of urban expansion and renovation in the first half of the 18th century. Many aspects of the church, completed *c.* 1750, were innovative. The ground-plan is in the form of an oval, a space rare in Portugal and not repeated by Nasoni. The exterior divided staircase leads to the principal entrance at the side of the building. The façade is based on a Roman scheme of the early 17th century with an indented broken pediment and is decorated with heavy garlands and shells, including a rich profusion of sculptured ornament (see fig.). The central frieze displays the symbols of worship, and these, like the incense boat, were modelled on Baroque silver vessels. The House of the Clergy, begun in 1754, links the apse of the church with the bell-tower. The tower, 75.6 m high, was built between 1757 and 1763 in six sections. It was inspired by Nasoni's native Tuscan campanile, and it both dominates the city and is its symbol. As in much of Nasoni's late work, the ornament has become simpler, and everything is subordinated to the strong lines and volume of the great structure.

In 1743 Nasoni designed the new façade of Bom Jesus, Matosinhos, to which he added a new element of horizontality, rarely found in Portuguese architecture, and a rhythmic design of broad Ionic capitals that frame the doorways and carved niches. Three years later, in 1746, he was working on the designs for the church of the orphanage of Nossa Senhora da Esperança. The simple lines of the façade are enriched with sculptured forms that abound in plasticity and in places suggest the designs of contemporary furniture and silver, as for instance in the windows that recall the frames of looking-glasses. In 1749 Nasoni prepared the first plan for rebuilding the church of Santa Casa de Misericórdia, Oporto. The existing preparatory drawings (Archv. of the Brotherhood) show that the building as it stands represents a compromise between the wishes of artist and client. As planned, there is a concentration of ornament on the façade, which is carved in deep relief with shells and cartouches surmounted by the royal coat of arms. But the unrealized design for the upper section, rejected for reasons of economy, was more elaborate, with the figures of Hope and Charity seated on reversed pediments.

Nasoni's reputation as an architect of churches and palaces led to further commissions for country residences near Oporto from the same circle of clerics and their relatives, some of whom belonged to the boards of brotherhoods who had previously commissioned work from the architect. In these, Nasoni recreated the spirit of the Italian villa, designing houses that were in harmony with, and linked by exterior staircases to, their surroundings. He planned their gardens and filled them with fountains and statues from his own designs. At the Quinta do Chantre, to the west of Oporto, built c. 1743 for the cleric Fernando Barbara de Albuquerque, the garden walls and fountains line a central axis leading to the house. Nasoni combined these innovations with Portuguese elements: the house is a large rectangular block with the traditional central tower. The design of the Quinta de Ramalde, near Oporto, built c. 1746 for Florência Leite Pereiro de Melo (who inherited the property in 1745 and died in 1777), is another conservative plan to which Nasoni introduced imaginative neo-Gothic elements such as the medieval battlements on the central tower. The Quinta da Prelada, near Oporto, built before 1758 for Dom Antonio de Mesquita de Melo (not completed), is one of Nasoni's most theatrical schemes. Here he demonstrated the ideals of Italian and French estate planning, seen in the way the residence is set in the middle of a great central axis that dominates the garden and its cascades, obelisks, pyramids, maze and large lake. Nasoni is attributed on stylistic grounds with the Palace of Mateus, near Vila Real, Trás-os-Montes, probably built 1739–43 for Antonio José Botelho Mourão (1688–1746), where the carved granite ornament on the main façade gives an air of festive decoration to the building.

Nasoni's most important and refined secular work of c. 1749–54 is the Palacio do Freixo, Campanhã, built for his principal patron, Dom Jerónimo de Távora e Noronha, and formally set in grounds that descended in a series of terraces to the River Douro. Nasoni planned an oblique spatial procession from the gateway of the park to the house, treating the landscape as a theatrical stage. For the house, Nasoni used a ground-plan that he first employed at Mateus with a vaulted central ground-level passage bisecting the building. Each of the four façades has a different design, the most dramatic being the east front, where the central section has a wide exterior stairway leading to monumental doors.

3. SCULPTURE AND WOOD-CARVING. Nasoni was active as a designer of sculpture and wood-carving. The designs were to be executed in the local dark, hard granite and have simplified, stylized forms. They form an integral part of Nasoni's concept for the design of country houses and, like the fountain of the Tortoise, Quinta da Prelada, near Oporto, c. 1758, are full of fantasy and invention. His fountains designed to be placed against a wall include that (c. 1738) for Nossa Senhora dos Remedios, Lamego, which takes the form of a fantastic broken pediment decorated with garlands. Another fine example is the Chimera Fountain (c. 1746–58) in the garden of Quinta do Viso,

Matosinhos, with four elegant granite statues representing the *Seasons*.

In the design of gilded wood-carving Nasoni found an ideal vehicle to express his decorative ideas and for the diffusion of a wealth of ornament. He probably exercised more influence in this field than in any other. In his design for retables he introduced the concave plan as well as the undulant profile of the arch at the top; both forms derive from Andrea Pozzo and were widely imitated in northern Portugal. These elements are seen in the retable that he designed in 1745 for the high altar of S Ildefonso, Oporto, where he used the same decorative vocabulary that he had used in his architecture, including asymmetrical shells, volutes, husks and leaves, to which he added new motifs such as angels in flight. His style of wood-sculpture had a marked influence on contemporary Oporto silver. Nasoni's own designs for ecclesiastical silver include the drawings of c. 1739–42 and c. 1751 (untraced) for completing the silver altarpiece in Oporto Cathedral in which he used the same flying angels, garlands and acanthus foliage that appear in his stone- and wood- carving. These motifs are repeated in the beautiful iron railings and gates he designed in 1754 for the chancel arch in the cathedral.

Nasoni did not found a school in Oporto, nor did he train pupils, but in his double role as architect and painter he had enormous influence in northern Portugal. His successors gained from his work, in particular José de Figueiredo Seixas, who worked under his direction and who also began his career as a painter.

BIBLIOGRAPHY

G. Bazin: 'Réflexions sur l'origine et l'évolution du Baroque dans le nord du Portugal', *Belas A.*, ii (1950), pp. 5–8
J. Bury: 'Late Baroque and Rococo in North Portugal', *J. Soc. Archit. Hist.*, xv (1956)
J. M. Pereira de Oliveira: 'Nasoni e a igreja da Misericórdia', *St. Gen.*, viii/2 (1961), pp. 57–67
B. Xavier Continho: 'A igreja e a Irmandade dos Clérigos', *Doc. & Mem. Hist. Porto*, xxxvi (1965), p. 97
R. Smith: *Nicolau Nasoni, arquitecto do Porto* (Lisbon, 1966)
——: 'Nicolau Nasoni, 1691–1773', *Bracara Augusta*, lxiv (1973)
M. T. Mandroux França: 'Quatre Phases de l'urbanisation du Porto', *Bol. Cult. Câmara Mun. Porto*, 2nd ser., ii (1984)
J. Fernandes Pereira: *Arquitectura barroca em Portugal* (Lisbon, 1986)
Niccolò Nasoni: Un artista italiano a Oporto, III centenario della nascita (exh. cat. by S. Andreine, S. Casciu and G. Piras, Arezzo, Com. S Giovanne Valdarno; Oporto, Cam. Mun.; 1991)

JOSÉ FERNANDES PEREIRA

Nasrid [Banū Naṣr; Banū'l-Aḥmar]. Islamic dynasty that ruled in southern Spain from 1230 to 1492. The Nasrids rose to power after the defeat of the Almohads (*reg* 1130–1269) at the battle of Las Navas de Tolosa (1212) and ruled over a kingdom that extended from the Straits of Gibraltar and Almería in the south to the mountains of the Serrania de Ronda and the Sierra d'Elvira in the north. In 1238 Granada (*see* GRANADA, §I, 1) was captured and adopted as capital by the Nasrid ruler Muhammad I (*reg* 1232–72). As vassal to the Christian king Ferdinand III of Castile and León (*reg* 1217–52) and later to Alfonso X (*reg* 1252–84), Muhammad I witnessed their victories in Southern Spain, while many Spanish Muslim refugees were attracted to his kingdom. After the reign of Muhammad I the Nasrids alternated between submission to Castile and alliance with the Muslim MARINID dynasty of Fez, which resulted in four Marinid expeditions to the Iberian peninsula. The Nasrids became weakened by factional strife, and when Christian Spain was united by the marriage of Ferdinand II of Aragon to Isabella I of Castile in 1469, the Nasrid position grew precarious. After a series of defeats, the Nasrid kingdom dwindled, and under Abu'l-Hasan 'Ali (*reg* 1464–85 with interruption) there was a succession struggle. Nearly eight centuries of Muslim rule in Spain came to an end with the Christian conquest of Granada in 1492, and the last Nasrid ruler, Muhammad XI (*reg* 1482–92 with interruption), known to the West as Boabdil, became an exile in Morocco.

Architecture flourished under Nasrid rule, especially in Granada in the 14th century. The Nasrids are principally remembered for the construction of the citadel known as the Alhambra (*see* GRANADA, §III, 1(i)), which comprised a palace–city; but there are remains of several other Nasrid buildings in Granada and elsewhere in the kingdom (*see* ISLAMIC ART, §II, 6(iv)(a)). Under Muhammad II (*reg* 1272–1302) the garden palace known as the Generalife was added and the palace known as the Dar al-Manjara al-Kubra (now the Cuarto Real de S Domingo) built in the city. Muhammad III (*reg* 1302–8) built the Great Mosque (destr.) in Granada as well as the Partal Palace and the Torre de las Damas at the Alhambra, and Isma'il I (*reg* 1313–25) rebuilt the Generalife and began work on the Mexuar. It was, however, during the reigns of Yusuf I (*reg* 1333–54) and Muhammad V (*reg* 1354–91 with interruption) that the most spectacular additions were made at the Alhambra, including the Comares and Lion palaces. Yusuf also built a madrasa (rest.) in Granada.

Patronage of the decorative arts was equally important under the Nasrids, and splendid examples of ceramics, textiles, metalwork and jewellery survive, many inscribed with the Nasrid motto (*lā ghālib ilā'llah*: 'There is no victor save God'). The Nasrids commissioned immense lustre-painted objects, including earthenware jars known as Alhambra vases, and tile panels such as the Fortuny Tablet (1.08×0.63 m; Madrid, Inst. Valencia Don Juan), which bears an inscription dating it to the reign of Yusuf III (*reg* 1407–17; *see* ISLAMIC ART, §V, 4(iv)). Nasrid silk textiles were among the finest produced and were prized by Muslims and Christians alike (*see* ISLAMIC ART, §VI, 2(ii)(a) and TEXTILE, colour pl. VII, fig. 1), as were large knotted woollen carpets (*see* CARPET, §II, 2(i)). Splendid swords, daggers, knives and shields richly decorated with cloisonné enamels exemplify the quality of Nasrid metalwork (*see* ISLAMIC ART, §§IV, 3(iv) and IX). Few manuscripts survived the Christian reconquest, but rare copies of the Koran (e.g. 1304; Paris, Bib. N., MS. arab. 385) give some idea of the richness of Nasrid decoration and the distinctive style of calligraphy.

See also MARQUETRY, colour pl. VIII, fig. 3.

Enc. Islam/2
BIBLIOGRAPHY
L. Torres Balbás: *Arte almohade: Arte nazarí: Arte mudéjar*, A. Hisp., iv (Madrid, 1949)
——: *La Alhambra y el Generalife* (Madrid, 1950)
R. Arié: *L'Espagne musulmane au temps des Nasrides, 1232–1492* (Paris, 1973, 2/1990)
O. Grabar: *The Alhambra* (Cambridge, MA, and London, 1978)
S. S. Kenesson: 'Nasrid Luster Pottery: The Alhambra Vases', *Muqarnas*, ix (1992), pp. 93–115

Al-Andalus: The Art of Islamic Spain (exh. cat., ed. J. D. Dodds; Granada, Alhambra; New York, Met.; 1992)

S. J. VERNOIT

Nassau, House of. Netherlandish family of patrons of German origin. The Counts of Nassau came from an area of Germany between the rivers Rhine and Main but by prudent marriages acquired extensive properties in the Netherlands, centred on Breda. Engelbrecht II, Count of Nassau (1451–1504), owned several Books of Hours, which were illustrated by the most prominent illuminators of the period, including the Master of Mary of Burgundy, and his portrait (1487; Amsterdam, Rijksmus.) was painted by the Master of the Portraits of Princes. Hendrik III, Count of Nassau (1483–1538), who succeeded his uncle, Engelbrecht II, was a friend of Emperor Charles V and a member of the Order of the Golden Fleece. In 1515 he was created Stadholder of Holland, Zeeland and Franche Comté. He owned paintings by such artists as Jan Gossart and Jan van Scorel and is believed to have commissioned Hieronymus Bosch's *Garden of Earthly Delights* (*c.* 1504; Madrid, Prado; *see* BOSCH, HIERONYMUS, fig. 3). His most important commission was the series of tapestries, known as the *Nassau Genealogy*, designed for him by Bernard van Orley and depicting members of the House of Nassau on horseback. These tapestries, which symbolized the power and status of the family, are lost, but drawings by van Orley survive, for instance in the Staatliche Graphische Sammlung, Munich, and the Musée des Beaux-Arts, Rennes. Hendrik also undertook the modernization of BREDA CASTLE *c.* 1515–21, the first known example of Renaissance architecture in the northern Netherlands. From 1536, however, Hendrik began to replace the old castle with a completely new Renaissance palace, for which his architect was possibly the painter Tommaso di Andrea Vincidor. By Hendrik's marriage to Claudia of Chalon, Princess of Orange (1498–1521), the principality of Orange passed to the Nassau family. Their son, René of Chalon, Prince of Orange (1519–44), died childless and the principality transferred to the German branch of the family, members of which became rulers of the Netherlands (*see* ORANGE NASSAU).

BIBLIOGRAPHY
J. Rosenberg, S. Slive and E. H. ter Kuile: *Dutch Art and Architecture, 1600–1800*, Pelican Hist. A. (Harmondsworth, 1966, rev. 3/1977), pp. 372–6
J. K. Steppe: 'Jheronimus Bosch: Bijdrage tot de historische ikonografische stidie van zijn werk' [Hieronymus Bosch: a contribution to the historical and iconographic study of his work], *Bijdragen bij gelegenheid van de herdenkingstentoonstelling te 's-Hertogenbosch* [Collected essays for the occasion of the memorial exhibition in 's-Hertogenbosch] ('s Hertogenbosch, 1967), pp. 5–41
C. W. Fock: 'Nieuws over de tapijten, bekend als de Nassause Genealogie' [New information about the tapestries known as the Nassau Genealogy], *Oud-Holland*, lxxxiv (1969), pp. 1–28
S. W. A. Drossaers and T. H. Lunsingh Scheurleer: *Inventarissen van de inboedels in de verblijven van de Oranjes* [Inventories of the contents of the residences of the Oranges], 3 vols (The Hague, 1974–6)

(1) Johan Maurits, Count of Nassau-Siegen (*b* Dillenburg, 1604; *d* 1679). He was the youngest son of an impoverished branch of the Nassau family. In 1620 he joined the Dutch army led by his cousin, Prince Maurice of Orange (*see* ORANGE NASSAU, (2)). Johan Maurits's career progressed rapidly, and in 1636 he became Governor of the Dutch colony in north-east Brazil. He remained a skilful soldier all his life and as late as 1672 served as field-marshal in the army of the Stadholder William III of Orange.

In 1633 Johan Maurits purchased a much sought-after piece of land in The Hague between the Binnenhof and the Stadholder's gardens. A few years later Constantijn Huygens the elder, secretary to Stadholder Frederick Henry, acquired the adjoining piece of land. Jacob van Campen advised Huygens on the building of his house, Hofwijck, and also designed that of Johan Maurits. The plans for the Mauritshuis (for illustration *see* CAMPEN, JACOB VAN), as it is known, were based on Italian classical treatises of the 16th century, especially those of Scamozzi. Construction was supervised by Pieter Post. The building is of brick, a typically Dutch feature, while its classical elements, for example the pilasters and tympana, are of stone. When Johan Maurits went to Brazil in 1636, the house was unfinished, and it was completed and decorated under Huygens's supervision. Portraits dominated the decoration of the interior: kings, members of the House of Nassau and contemporary and historical figures. In addition there were many battle scenes, often hung below the portraits. The staircase was decorated with topographical wall paintings depicting views of exotic countries and people. These paintings and murals would have formed a reflection of the perceived world order. Johan Maurits lived in this residence in The Hague with periodic breaks. After his death, the house was rented by the States General of the United Provinces, who used it to accommodate state guests. During a visit by the English ambassador in 1704, the building caught fire, and the interior, including all the decorations, was destroyed. The present interior of the building (now the city's gallery of Old Master paintings), in particular the Great Hall, was redecorated in an austere Louis XIV style between 1704 and 1718.

Johan Maurits governed Dutch Brazil for seven years as an enlightened monarch (*see* BRAZIL, §§I and IV, 1(i)). He devoted himself with much enthusiasm to the building of towns and fortifications. As Governor he built himself a palace, as well as a country house, surrounded by extensive gardens. The most important aspect, however, of his Brazilian period was the scientific work by people he had invited at his own expense, among them Georg Marggraf, a natural scientist and cartographer, Willem Piso, a doctor, and the artists Frans Post (*see* POST, (2)) and ALBERT ECKHOUT, who, with almost naive precision, carefully recorded the landscape, the native population and the country's flora and fauna in hundreds of drawings, gouaches and paintings: the *Theatrum rerum naturalium Brasíliae* (Kraków, Jagiellonian U. Lib.) consists of nearly 1500 oil sketches by Post and Eckhout. The result of their efforts was the monumental *Historia naturalis Brasíliae* (1648), a pioneering publication due to the systematic approach underlying the research, which was to remain the standard work on Brazilian natural history until the 19th century.

Johan Maurits's Brazilian adventure was not long-lived: his employers, the West India Company, regarded him as too independent and not sufficiently interested in making profits. In 1643 he resigned as Governor and returned to the Netherlands, taking with him an extensive collection from which he later made important donations to Elector Frederick William of Brandenburg (1652; a donation that was, in fact, more like a sale), to Frederick III, King of Denmark (1654), and to Louis XIV, King of France (1679). This explains the presence of a series of portraits of Brazilians (e.g. *Negro Woman and Child*, 1641; Copenhagen, Stat. Mus. Kst) and a few still-lifes by Albert Eckhout in Copenhagen. Another series of paintings by Eckhout, given to Louis XIV, became the model on which two of the most popular sets of Gobelins tapestries, *Les Anciennes Indes* and *Les Nouvelles Indes*, were based.

In 1647 the Elector of Brandenburg appointed Johan Maurits as Stadholder of Cleve. He employed architects to build houses in the city and to lay out gardens (*see* CLEVE), including a zoo with a classical semicircular gallery, later known as the 'Amphitheatre'. He also rebuilt the castle and, in those areas of the city that had been damaged most severely during the Thirty Years War (1618–48), laid out avenues similar to those in The Hague. In 1652 Johan Maurits became Grand Master of the Order of St John, a function he retained until his death. Between 1661 and 1668 he was responsible for the complete rebuilding of the castle of the Order in Sonnenburg according to a design by Maurits Post; Johan Maurits also built a hospital and renovated houses and churches in Sonnenburg. He was portrayed by such leading portrait painters in The Hague as Pieter Nason (1612–88/91) and Jan de Baen (Brussels, Mus. A. Anc.; The Hague, Mauritshuis).

BIBLIOGRAPHY

T. Thomsen: *Albert Eckhout: Ein niederländischer Maler und sein Gönner Moritz der Brasíliner* (Copenhagen, 1938)
E. van den Boogaart, ed.: *Johan Maurits van Nassau-Siegen, 1604–1679: A Humanist Prince in Europe and Brazil* (The Hague, 1979)
Johan Maurits van Nassau-Siegen, 1604–1679 (exh. cat., The Hague, Mauritshuis, 1979)
Soweit der Erdkreis reicht: Johann Moritz von Nassau-Siegen, 1604–1679 (exh. cat., Cleve, Stadt. Mus. Haus Koekkoek, 1979)

B. BRENNINKMEYER-DE ROOIJ

Nast, Thomas (*b* Landau, Bavaria, 27 Sept 1840; *d* Guayaquil, Ecuador, 7 Dec 1902). American illustrator of German birth. His family emigrated to the USA and settled in New York when he was six. Precocious at drawing, Nast was taught by the German-born history painter Theodore Kaufmann (*b* 1814) and later studied briefly at the National Academy of Design. In 1855, aged 15, he began to work for *Leslie's Illustrated Weekly Magazine*, which continued to publish his political cartoons until 1858.

In 1860 Nast reported the Heenan–Sayers prize-fight in England for the *New York Illustrated News* and spent four months covering Garibaldi's campaign in Sicily and southern Italy for the *News* and the *Illustrated London News*. In 1862 Nast joined the staff of *Harper's Weekly*, where he worked until 1886. During that time he established the power of the American political cartoon. His Civil War drawings for *Harper's* were primarily trenchant propaganda against the South. Abraham Lincoln called Nast 'the Union's best recruiting sergeant'. His drawings mixed patriotism and sentiment, although a few achieved a broader humanistic statement about war.

Nast's style was fully developed by 1870. His drawings concentrated on a single strong image, in contrast to his earlier work, which attempted to combine several incidents. The directness of his mature style may be due to his increased interest in painting and book illustration. Incisive lines reinforced the pointed wit of his subject-matter, and bold images translated more effectively into wood-engraving. After 1865 he based his portrait caricatures on photographs, as other British and American cartoonists had done. Nast subtly insinuated character traits and personal weaknesses into the expressions of the well-known public figures that were his subject-matter. This combination of truth and exaggeration made provocative concrete imagery out of abstract ideas. The point was reinforced by short satirical captions. The enormous public response to his work gave Nast greater influence than any other cartoonist.

Beginning with Lincoln in 1861, each of the six presidential candidates backed by Nast and *Harper's* was elected, earning Nast the name of 'president maker'. He also originated the Democratic donkey and the Republican elephant as party symbols and helped to shape popular American images of Santa Claus, Uncle Sam and Columbia. While Nast's political cartoons relate to earlier American ephemera, his more direct stylistic influence was the British illustrated press. The caricatures in *Punch* and the line drawings of John Tenniel were of particular importance to his mature style.

Nast is most famous for his relentless battle from 1869 to 1871 against the 'Tweed Ring', a gang of corrupt politicians who controlled the government of New York. Headed by 'Boss' William Marcy Tweed, the Ring defrauded the city of some £200 million. It was broken as the result of the overwhelming public campaign aroused by Nast's devastating cartoons. 'Boss' Tweed was sentenced to prison but escaped to Spain, where, ironically, he was arrested after being identified from one of Nast's cartoons.

By the mid-1880s interest in Nast's style had declined as popular attention was drawn to the cartoons in Joseph Keppler's *Puck*, a comic weekly illustrated with colour lithographs. In 1886 Nast left *Harper's*; resuming his interest in illustration and painting, he published a book, *Thomas Nast's Christmas Drawings for the Human Race* (New York, 1890, rev. 1978). In 1902 President Theodore Roosevelt, an admirer, appointed Nast American Consul to Guayaquil, Ecuador, where six months later he died of yellow fever.

BIBLIOGRAPHY
A. B. Paine: *Thomas Nast: His Period and Pictures* (New York, 1904/R 1974)
F. Weitenkampf: 'Thomas Nast, Artist in Caricature', *Bull. NY Pub. Lib.*, xxxvii (1933), pp. 770–74
J. C. Vinson: *Thomas Nast: Political Cartoonist* (Athens, GA, 1967)
M. Keller: *The Art and Politics of Thomas Nast* (New York, 1968)
A. Boime: 'Thomas Nast and French Art', *Amer. A.J.*, iv (1972), pp. 43–65

EDWARD BRYANT

Nasuh Matrakçı [Naṣūḥ al-Silāḥī al-Matrāqī; Naṣūḥ ibn Qaragöz ibn 'Abdallāh al-Būsnawī] (*b* Visoko, Bosnia; *fl* 1517; *d* 28 April 1564). Ottoman soldier, writer, copyist and illustrator. He initiated the topographical style of painting that became characteristic of the illustrated histories produced at the Ottoman court in the 1550s (*see* ISLAMIC ART, §III, 4(vi)(e)). As a youth he was recruited into the imperial service in a forced levy (*devşirme*) and was trained as a page in the household of Sultan Bayazid II (*reg* 1481–1512). He later served as an officer in the Ottoman army, where he was noted as a swordsman. He was also celebrated as the inventor of new forms of the game of *matrak*, played by throwing sticks or weapons as a form of military training.

Nasuh was a prolific writer on mathematics, swordsmanship and history. In 1520 he began the translation from Arabic into Turkish of al-Tabari's *Majura' al-tawārīkh* ('Compendium of histories'), to which he added a section covering the history of the Ottomans to 1551. He transcribed and illustrated at least three volumes of this section on the Ottomans. Only one, an account of the campaigns of 1534–6 in Iraq and Iran with 128 illustrations, is signed, but a history of Sultan Bayazid II with 10 scenes and an account of the Hungarian campaign of 1543 and of operations by the Ottoman navy in the Mediterranean are identical in style. The latter has 32 illustrations. His paintings show views of cities devoid of figures, but with detailed, if schematic, representations of their major monuments and the surrounding countryside. They reflect influences of European maps but record Nasuh's own impressions of the sites.

UNPUBLISHED SOURCES
Istanbul, Topkapı Pal. Lib. [*Tarih-i Sultan Bayezid* ('History of Sultan Bayazid'); *c.* 1540; MS. R. 1272]

WRITINGS
Beyân-i menâzil-i sefer-i Irâkeyn-i Sultan Süleyman Han [Description of the stages on the campaign of Sultan Süleyman Khan in the two Iraqs] (1537; Istanbul, U. Lib., T. 5964); facs. edn H. G. Yurdaydın (Ankara, 1976)
Tarih-i Feth-i Şikloş, Estergon ve İstol(n)i Belgrad or *Süleyman-name* [History of the conquest of Siklos, Esztergom and Székesfehérvár or Book of Süleyman] (*c.* 1545; Istanbul, Topkapı Pal. Lib., H.1608); facs. edn (Ankara, 1987) [pubd as work of Sinan Çavuş]

BIBLIOGRAPHY
*Enc. Islam/*2
H. G. Yurdaydın: *Matrakçı Nasuh* (Ankara, 1963)
Z. Akalay: 'Tarihi konularda ilk Osmanlı minyatürleri' [The first Ottoman miniatures on historical subjects], *Sanat Tarihi Yıllığı*, ii (1966–8), pp. 102–15
E. Atıl: *The Age of Sultan Süleyman the Magnificent* (Washington and New York, 1987), pp. 82–6

ESIN ATIL

Natalini, Adolfo. *See under* SUPERSTUDIO.

Natanson, Thadée (*b* Warsaw, 28 March 1868; *d* Paris, 1951). French critic and collector. The second son of a wealthy Polish Jewish banking family (his father emigrated to Paris in the early 1870s), he was educated and spent most of his life in France. With his brothers Alexandre and Alfred he ran the *Revue blanche* (1891–1903), the most wide-ranging and intellectually adventurous journal of its day. Natanson was largely responsible for the art reviews and for the *Revue blanche*'s active and lively support of such artists as the Nabis and Toulouse-Lautrec.

The *Revue blanche* began as a school magazine, the brainchild of a group of pupils at the Lycée Condorcet in Paris, and its first issues were published in Liège in 1889–90. In 1891 the journal moved to Paris, where its financial management was taken over by the Natanson brothers, and Thadée became editor-in-chief. Although his early ambitions were literary (extracts from his novel *Pour l'ombre* appeared in the first Paris editions), Natanson was the journal's regular art correspondent between 1893 and 1900, a role he seems to have taken on by default, having sought unsuccessfully to interest Maurice Denis in the job. As Félix Fénéon noted in 1923, Natanson defended 'Neo-Impressionism, Post-Impressionism and Impressionism (it was still necessary to do so)'. More particularly he is remembered for his intelligent and passionate support for the Nabi group, several of whose members became close friends, notably Vuillard, Bonnard and Vallotton. His close involvement with these artists intensified following his marriage, in 1893, to Misia Godebska, a young Polish pianist whom he had known since childhood. Misia's charm and musical talent attracted these artists who regarded her as their Muse, her kittenish profile appearing in many of their paintings in the mid-1890s. On Natanson's initiative his artist friends were commissioned to produce individual prints as frontispieces for the *Revue blanche*, which were offered to subscribers monthly during 1893–4. The series was published as a portfolio, *L'Album de la Revue blanche*, which quickly became a collectors' item. Natanson also commissioned highly successful colour lithograph posters for the journal from Bonnard and Toulouse-Lautrec, and ran an occasional satirical appendix 'Nib', to which Lautrec, Bonnard and Vallotton contributed sketches.

In 1895 Natanson commissioned Vuillard to produce a series of small decorative paintings on the theme *Women and Flowers* and over the years acquired a considerable collection of small-scale easel paintings and portraits by his Nabi friends. His own portrait was painted on several occasions, notably by Vallotton in 1897 (Geneva, Petit Pal.), in an austere style reminiscent of Holbein, and by Bonnard the same year (Paris, priv. col.). Many of Vuillard's interiors of the mid-1890s depict Thadée and Misia Natanson's Paris apartment in the Rue St Florentin, or their two country homes, first at Valvins (where Stéphane Mallarmé was a close neighbour and friend), and subsequently at Le Relais, Villeneuve-sur-Yonne, the setting for the two major decorative panels Vuillard painted for Jean Schopfer in 1898, *Figures in the Garden* (priv. col.).

In the later 1890s Natanson was increasingly drawn to politics, helping to ensure the *Revue blanche*'s adherence to an anarchistic and staunchly Dreyfusard line. After 1900 he abandoned journalism, handing over the editorship of the *Revue blanche* to Fénéon and the art criticism to Charles Saunier and Félicien Fagus; the journal ceased publication in 1903. Subsequently, he ran a coal mine in Hungary, a somewhat utopian project for which he seems to have had little aptitude and which was a financial failure. His financial backer was the millionaire Alfred Edwards, whose assiduous courtship of Misia eventually led to the break-up of the Natanson marriage in 1904. Ensuing financial difficulties forced Thadée Natanson to sell off his collection of paintings in 1908. He was more successful as director of the Lazare-Levy munitions factory in Lyon during World War I. Natanson continued to publish occasional literary portraits of the artists with whom he had been acquainted. These were collected and published in 1948 as *Peints à leur tour*, a valuable source of first-hand information about *fin-de-siècle* French artists.

WRITINGS
Peints à leur tour (Paris, 1948)
Un Henri de Toulouse-Lautrec (Geneva, 1951)
Regular contributions to *Rev. Blanche* (1891–1902)

BIBLIOGRAPHY
A. B. Jackson: 'Thadée Natanson, critique d'art, et les peintres de *La Revue Blanche*', *Rev. Lett. Mod.*, iv/25–6 (1957), pp. 17–27
E. Nattier Natanson: *Les Amitiés de la Revue blanche et quelques autres* (Vincennes, 1959)
R. Fizdale and A. Gold: *Misia* (London, 1980)

BELINDA THOMSON

Natanz [Naṭanz]. Town in central Iran, 130 km north of Isfahan. The antiquity of the town, situated on the eastern slopes of the Karkaz Mountains, is attested by the ruins of a fire-temple of the Sasanian period (AD 224–632). A dependency of Isfahan in the Islamic period, the town preserves the oldest dated dome (999) in central Iran, probably built as an octagonal tomb for a local saint and later incorporated into the Friday mosque as the sanctuary dome. 'Abd al-Samad (*d* ?1299), a mystic of the Suhrawardi order, lived near the mosque, and after his death, an Ilkhanid vizier enlarged it (1304–9) and constructed the adjacent shrine complex, comprising the mystic's tomb, with a superb *muqarnas* vault (1307–8), and a *khānaqāh* with a splendid tile mosaic façade (1307–8; *see* ISLAMIC ART, §II, 6(i)(a) and fig. 49). A minaret was added in 1324–5. The complex was decorated with stucco inscriptions designed by the renowned calligrapher HAYDAR and lustre tiles, including a mihrab hood (London, V&A, 71-1885), a cenotaph cover (New York, Met., 09.87) and a frieze (dispersed), identifiable by its headless birds, defaced by a later iconoclast.

BIBLIOGRAPHY
Enc. Islam/2
A. Godard: 'Naṭanz', *Āthār-ē-Īrān*, i (1936), pp. 75–106
H. Naraqi: *Āthār-i ta'rīkhī-yi shahristānhā-yi Kāshān u Naṭanz* [Historical monuments of Kashan and Natanz] (Tehran, Iran. Solar 1348/1970)
S. S. Blair: 'The Octagonal Pavilion at Natanz', *Muqarnas*, i (1983), pp. 69–94
——: 'A Medieval Persian Builder', *J. Soc. Archit. Historians*, xlv (1986), pp. 389–95
——: *The Ilkhanid Shrine Complex at Natanz, Iran* (Cambridge, MA, 1986)
——: 'Sufi Saints and Shrine Architecture in the Early Fourteenth Century', *Muqarnas*, vii (1990), pp. 35–49
——: *The Monumental Inscriptions of Early Islamic Iran and Transoxiana* (Leiden, 1992), no. 58

SHEILA S. BLAIR

Natchez. North American city in Mississippi, USA, built on a 70 m bluff on the east bank of the Mississippi River. Its associated port is the semi-independent village of Natchez-under-the-Hill. It was a centre of late Mississippian culture and of the complex chiefdom of the Natchez Indians, whose Emerald Mound, near Natchez, is the second largest, late prehistoric earthwork in North America (*see* NATIVE NORTH AMERICAN ART). It was then successively a French fort (1716–29), British settlement (1763–79), under Spanish occupation, and then the extreme south-eastern outpost of the USA and capital (1789–1802) of the Mississippi Territory. After 1800 it became the principal centre of American cotton production and an important river port, enjoying an extraordinary prosperity resulting from the fertility of the land and the successive introductions of the cotton gin (1798), West Indian cotton, and especially steamboat transportation (1811).

At Natchez, uniquely in the South before the Civil War (1861–5), although the cotton plantations were continuously expanded towards the interior, the planters concentrated their residences in this political, commercial and cultural metropolis. The city therefore possesses, disposed on a grid-plan originally laid out (1787–91) by the Spanish, the American South's finest collection of grandiose private buildings erected before the War. The FEDERAL STYLE dominated the city until the early 1830s. Natchez pioneered the architectural image of the 'Cotton Kingdom' with the brick-built mansion Texada (1790s), which introduced to the southern states the delicate refinements of Federal style detailing; while Gloucester (1803) by John Scott, with façade (1808) by Levi Weeks, epitomizes the style; Auburn (1812) by Weeks, first adumbrated a free-standing double-galleried portico with a colossal columnar order; and Rosalie (1820–23; see fig.) by James S. Griffin and named after the French fort on the site of which it stands, established the classic form of a tall cubic block with colonnaded galleries front and back. Among the most interesting refinements of these basic forms were matched dependencies arranged symmetrically around a rear courtyard, creating domestic ensembles of unusual extensiveness, complexity and sophistication. A contrasting style was provided by the Greek Revival, which dates from the Agricultural Bank (1833) and is particularly accomplished in the mansions D'Evereux (1840) and Melrose (1845), the latter being the nucleus of the Natchez National Historical Park established 1990. The Greek Revival reached its highpoint with Stanton Hall (1851–7), attributed to Thomas Rose, the largest and most lavishly decorated of the mansions in Natchez, of which the grillwork and fluted columns of the portico are particularly notable. Longwood (1860–62) by Samuel Sloan is exceptional, being of octagonal plan with an onion-shaped dome and combining a fully developed Italianate villa idiom, which was current from c. 1855, with elements of Oriental exoticism. The outbreak of the Civil War, which led to Longwood's abandonment when nearly complete, also marked the end of the prosperity of the Natchez cotton planters and their architectural achievements. In the poverty following the War even the houses' interiors could not be modernized, so that they continue to display an essentially unrestored domestic architectural and decorative heritage that is unmatched in the USA.

BIBLIOGRAPHY

Mississippi: The WPA Guide to the Magnolia State, Federal Writers Project (New York, 1938/*R* Jackson, MS, and London, 1988)

J. W. Gandy and T. H. Gandy: *Norman's Natchez: An Early Photographer and his Town* (Jackson, MS, 1978) [photography of Henry C. Norman (1850–1913)]

M. W. Miller and R. W. Miller: *The Great Houses of Natchez* (Jackson, MS, and London, 1986)

N. Polk, ed.: *Natchez before 1830* (Jackson, MS, and London, 1989)

DOUGLAS LEWIS

National Art Society of Bulgaria [Rodno Izkustwo; Society of Artists of Bulgaria]. Bulgarian group of artists

Natchez, MS, Rosalie (1820–23), by James S. Griffin

active from 1893. Founded on 24 June 1893 as the Society of Artists of Bulgaria, it was the first arts society to be established in Bulgaria. Having in its ranks the best-known intellectuals and artists of the time, its aim was to organize and develop the nation's artistic life. One of its principal goals was to expand the artistic outlook and develop the aesthetic sense of Bulgarian artists and the public by making them aware of the works of western European Old Masters. It initiated group exhibitions in 1894, 1897, 1898 and 1900, and in 1895 founded *Izkustwo*, the first magazine in Bulgaria to devote itself to art criticism. In 1895 the Society prepared a draft bill dealing with the establishment of an academy of the arts in Sofia; this led to the formation of the National Academy of Arts (Nationalna Hudozhestvena Academia). After other artists' organizations were founded in the first three decades of the 20th century—among them Contemporary Art (1904), the Society of Artists of Southern Bulgaria (1912), the Society of Independent Artists (1919), National Art (1919), the Society of Artists of Northern Bulgaria (1921) and the NEW ARTISTS' SOCIETY (1931)—the National Art Society of Bulgaria continued its existence within the framework of the Union of the Societies of Artists of Bulgaria (founded in 1932), which in 1959 was renamed the Union of Bulgarian Artists. Until 1990 the Union of Bulgarian Artists was a very centralized arts organization, controlled by an executive council and its congress, and its members could only be professionally recognized artists who held a degree or had a specialized education in the arts and who actively participated in exhibitions. The Union was the sole sponsor of the arts and maintained complete control over all aspects of Bulgaria's art life, imposing its artistic criteria on what type of art was to be exhibited both in Bulgaria and abroad. It provided the funds for purchases of art by Bulgarian art galleries and also ensured the professional status of artists. The Union's function changed after 1990, when Bulgaria embraced democratic reforms: its structure became decentralized, and the conditions for its membership became more democratic. At the same time, however, it lost control over financial matters and sponsorship of artists and arts events.

BIBLIOGRAPHY

Catalogue of Joint Exhibitions (exh. cat., Sofia, Society of Artists of Bulgaria, 1922)

Proceedings of the Congresses of the Union of Bulgarian Artists: Sofia, 1970, 1973, 1976, 1979, 1982, 1985 and 1988

JULIANA NEDEVA-WEGENER

National Romanticism. Term that suggests the merging of national boundaries and the indigenous 'ethnic essence' of a nation rather than a particular school or style. National Romanticism was a mid- and late 19th-century coalescence of two potent ideologies and was linked to the struggle for political legitimacy for a circumscribed geographic region. Its tenet was that the indigenous arts, history, music and folk traditions of a nation contributed to the spiritual and political survival of its people. It was manifest in the arts of those countries or regions of northern and central Europe, such as Scandinavia and Germany, that were once subject to foreign domination or had experienced recent unification. Thus, National Romanticism arose in response to a sense of intrusive internationalism that was perceived to weaken a sense of unity within a single geographic group. With its sources in German Romantic philosophy, this theoretical movement was introduced in the mid-19th century to Denmark through the writings of Adam Oehlensläger (1779–1850), to Norway by Henrik Wergeland (1808–45), to Sweden by the German poet and philosopher Friedrich Leopold von Hardenberg (1772–1801) under his pseudonym Novalis and, somewhat later, to Iceland by Sigurður Guðmundsson (1833–74). The notions of *Volksgeist* propelling a nation's culture expounded by JOHANN GOTTFRIED HERDER and Johann Gottfried Fichte (1762–1814), and the theories of HIPPOLYTE TAINE linking race and milieu, were important underpinnings for the affirmation of National Romanticism: a nation's faith in a unified culture and in the uniqueness of its people.

The term 'National Romanticism' was later used in the 1880s and 1890s in Norway, Sweden and Finland to define the artistic and literary vanguard. In Sweden, the term *Nyromantik* (Neo-Romanticism), associated with a 'Swedish Renaissance', defined an anti-naturalist movement in the arts. The validity of national or regional legitimacy was asserted by identifying and exploiting subjects, materials and media that were perceived as unique to a nation. In the pictorial arts two basic strategies can be traced: the representation of landscape as a signifier of national essence and the 'high art' revival of native folk art. In landscape painting, the idea of an unspoilt wilderness served as a corrective to the ills of urbanization through its evocation of an eternal national spirit. The landscape paintings of the Swedish artists KARL NORDSTRÖM, Richard Bergh, (*see* BERGH, (2)) NILS KREUGER and Gustaf Fjaestad, the Norwegian Harald Oskar Sohlberg and the Finn PEKKA HALONEN (e.g. *Wilderness, Karelian Landscape*, 1899; Turku A. Mus.; *see* FINLAND, fig. 6) suggested such mystical and redemptive readings. Artists represented nature as the source of collective identity by painting works with motifs chosen for their monumentality and topographic uniqueness, as in Sohlberg's *Winter Night in*

Rondane (1914; Oslo, N.G.); for their political and historical resonance, as in Nordström's *Varberg Fort* (1893; Stockholm, Prins Eugens Waldemarsudde); or for their evocation of mysticism through localized meteorological or light effects, as in Fjaestad's *Snow* (1900; Göteborg, Kstmus.; see fig.). The scholarly rediscovery of the works of the Norwegian artist J. C. Dahl and the Germans Caspar David Friedrich and Philipp Otto Runge by the Norwegian art historian Andreas Aubert (1851–1913) supported this interpretation of landscape as primordial national soul.

Folk art was a crucial element in the definition of National Romantic movements throughout Europe and was perceived as an unbroken link with a pure native past. Decorative and utilitarian objects were collected from rural regions and used to inspire modern investigation. Those who produced these works were understood by urban intellectuals to be living legacies of a mythic past and the conservators of indigenous traditions. This veneration for folk culture led to the founding of such open-air architectural museums in northern Europe as the extensive Skansen complex (1891) in Stockholm. In Norway, the paintings of Erik Werenskiold (e.g. *Girls of Telemark*, 1883; Oslo, N.G.; for illustration *see* WERENSKIOLD, ERIK) and GERHARD MUNTHE (e.g. the *Horse of Death*, 1893; Oslo, N.G.) adapted medieval folk motifs, colour structures and rhythmical patterning, as did the tapestries of Munthe and Frida Hansen (1855–1935) (e.g. *Blue in White*, 1899; Oslo, Kstindustmus.), those of Fjaestad in Sweden (e.g. *Running Water*, 1906; Göteborg, Kstmus.) and the Friends of Finnish Handicrafts, founded in 1879 (e.g. Sigrid Wickström's embroidered sledge-cover, 1912; Helsinki, Mus. Applied A.) (*see* FINLAND, §XI). National Romantic scholarship, in the work of the Norwegian historian Peter Andreas Munch (1810–63), created a shift away from the historical study of aristocracy towards the consideration of daily life and the extraction of national characteristics among individual groups. An increased interest in national history, folk literature and folk language in mid-19th-century scholarship also introduced National Romanticism as a re-examination of native orthographies. The impulse to collect folk legends and incorporate their motifs into art came initially from such folklorists as the brothers Jakob Grimm (1785–1863) and Wilhelm Grimm (1786–1859) in Germany, Elias Lönnrot (1802–84) in Finland and Peter C. Asbjørnson (1812–85) and Jörgen Moe (1813–82) in Norway. In Finland AKSELI GALLEN-KALLELA and the sculptor Alpo Sailo (1877–1955) took the legends and ballads of the *Kalevala* as sources for much of their work, in keeping with National Romantic impulses (e.g. Gallen-Kallela's *Aino*, 1891; Helsinki, Athenaeum A. Mus.). Munthe, Werenskiold and Halfdan Egedius used *Snorre Sturlasons Kongesagaer* [Snorri Sturlason's sagas of the Norse kings] (Kristiania [now Oslo], 1896–9) as the basis for some of their illustrated work. Such musicians as Edvard Grieg (1843–1907) and Jean Sibelius (1865–1957) also incorporated folk melodies and rhythms into their compositions to communicate a sense of continuity with native traditions.

National Romantic architecture embodied a retrospective view of indigenous building forms. It was identified with folk forms and with wooden architecture rather than with such institutionalized or official architectural revivals

Gustaf Fjaestad: *Snow*, oil on canvas, 0.99×1.41 m, 1900 (Göteborg, Göteborgs Konstmuseum)

as seen in the buildings of the *Dragestil* [Dragon-style] in Norway (*c.* 1840–1900), the artists' colony in Darmstadt (1899–1903) and Ragnar Östberg's City Hall (1913) in Stockholm. In Finland, National Romanticism described the national manifestation of *Jugendstil* and incorporated indigenous decorative motifs and wood construction. Gallen-Kallela's design for his studio, *Kalela*, in Ruovesi (1895), the Finnish Pavilion at the Exposition Universelle in Paris (1900) by GESELLIUS, LINDGREN, SAARINEN and the church of St John (1902–7; now Tampere Cathedral) in Tampere by Lars Sonck are examples.

BIBLIOGRAPHY

A. Bramsen: 'Rasen, Kulturen och Konsten', *Ord & Bild*, x (1901), pp. 354–73
C. Hayes: *Essays on Nationalism* (New York, 1926)
O. Falnes: *National Romanticism in Norway* (New York, 1933)
L. Ostby: *Frå naturalisme til nyromantik: En studie i norsk malerkunst i tiden ca. 1885–1895* [From nationalism to neo-romanticism: a study in Norwegian painting from *c.* 1885–95] (Oslo, 1934)
E. M. Earle, ed.: *Nationalism and Internationalism: Essays Inscribed to Carleton Hayes* (New York, 1950)
C. Hayes: *Nationalism: A Religion* (New York, 1960)
S. Strömbom: *National-romantik och radikalism: Konstnärforbundets historia, 1891–1920* [National Romanticism and radicalism: the history of the Artists' League, 1891–1920] (Udevalla, 1965)
J. I. Kolehmainen: *Epic of the North: The Story of Finland's National Epic* (New York, 1973)
E. Gellner: *Nations and Nationalism* (Ithaca, NY, 1983)
F. Scott: *Sweden, The Nation's History* (Dexter, MI, 1983)
A. Ellenius: 'Aspekter på bildkonsten och den nationela romantiken vid sekelskiftet' [Aspects of painting and National Romanticism at the turn of the century], *Att vara svensk* [To be Swedish], Kungliga Vitterhets Historie och Antikvitets Akademien (Stockholm, 1984), pp. 65–72
The Mystic North: Symbolist Landscape Painting in Northern Europe and North America, 1890–1940 (exh. cat. by R. Nasgaard, Toronto, A.G. Ont.; Cincinnati, OH, A. Mus.; 1984)

PATRICIA G. BERMAN

National Socialism. *See* NAZISM.

Native North American art. Term used for the indigenous artistic traditions of North America, both before and after European contact. The area covered in this survey includes present-day Canada, the United States and, at some periods, northern Mexico. The art of the Pre-Columbian Americas from Mexico southwards is discussed elsewhere in this dictionary (*see* MESOAMERICA, PRE-COLUMBIAN, and SOUTH AMERICA, PRE-COLUMBIAN).

I. Introduction. II. Dwellings and other structures. III. Carving and sculpture. IV. Painting. V. Pottery. VI. Metalwork. VII. Textiles. VIII. Dress and personal adornment. IX. Beadwork and shellwork. X. Embroidery. XI. Quillwork. XII. Featherwork. XIII. Hide. XIV. Basketwork. XV. Other late 20th-century developments. XVI. Archaeology. XVII. Historiography. XVIII. Museums, collections and patronage. XIX. Exhibitions.

I. Introduction.

1. Geography and peoples. 2. History. 3. Religion. 4. Iconography. 5. Concept of art. 6. Status of art and role of the artist.

1. GEOGRAPHY AND PEOPLES. The study of Native American peoples and their art can be divided according to a combination of traditional areas of cultural and economic coherence, linguistic groupings and natural

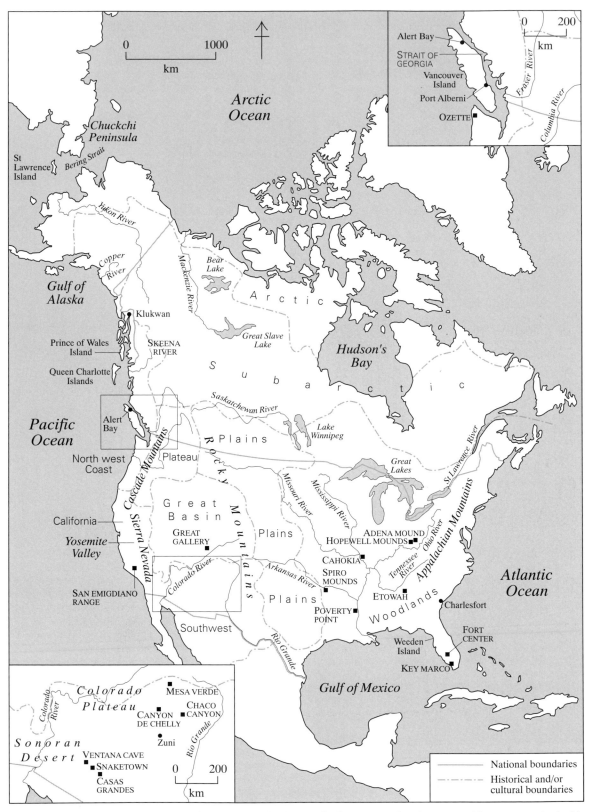

1. Map of North America, showing main culture-areas and distribution of indigenous peoples; those areas with separate entries in this dictionary are distinguished by CROSS-REFERENCE TYPE

geographic boundaries (see fig. 1). The boundaries, however, are not rigidly fixed, and there is considerable overlap among the various regions.

(i) Arctic. (ii) Subarctic. (iii) Northwest Coast. (iv) Plateau. (v) Great Basin. (vi) California. (vii) Southwest. (viii) Plains. (ix) Woodlands.

(i) Arctic. This region comprises the Arctic coasts of Alaska and Canada (see fig. 1) and is part of a wider culture-area that also includes the Arctic coasts of Siberia and Greenland. It has been inhabited for over four thousand years by Eskimo and Aleut peoples, who have adjusted to the severe climatic conditions of the far north. These peoples have been biologically classified as Arctic Mongoloids. Although they have long been called Eskimos by explorers and historians, they prefer their own nomenclature: those living along the eastern shores of the Chuckchi Peninsula of Siberia, the western shores of Alaska and on the islands in between call themselves Yuit (or Yupik); inhabitants of northern Alaska are Inupiat (or Inupiak); and Canadian and Greenlandic populations are Inuit. As a result of intermarriage with other ethnic groups, most are now of mixed descent. A high degree of uniformity in their culture is the result of migrations from Alaska to Greenland *c.* 2000 BC and *c.* AD 900 and counter-migration back to Alaska *c.* AD 1300. A single language with regional dialects is spoken from northern Alaska to Greenland; only the Yuit language is distinct. Linguists believe that the mother-tongue, which has been named Eskaleutian, underwent a split *c.* 4000 BC, perhaps around the time of the separation of Aleuts (in the Aleutian Islands and extreme south-west of Alaska) and Eskimos. A second split first millennium AD resulted in the two Eskimo languages.

Authorities differ on how and when these peoples reached North America. Genetic studies of dental traits and blood types suggest two or three waves of immigrants who originated in an area encompassing the Amur River Valley in Manchuria, North China, Mongolia and eastern Siberia. Archaeologists theorize that immigration waves occurred as early as *c.* 12,000–*c.* 8000 BC. Since the Bering Land Bridge was submerged by this time, crossings must have been over frozen sea ice in winter or in boats in the summer. It appears that the Northwest Coast and Athapaskan Native Americans arrived earlier than the ancestral Eskimo–Aleuts during these waves of infiltration. Comparison reveals striking similarities between Northwest Coast and Eskimo art and the art styles of both the Late Palaeolithic and Mesolithic periods in Siberia (9000–3000 BC) and the Neolithic period of northern China (from *c.* 5000 BC).

Eskimo art was first defined by the tastes of the early 18th-century and 19th-century explorers, although most of what they were allowed to see and purchase comprised articles newly made for trade. Information on more authentic art styles resulted from finds of prehistoric artefacts in 20th-century excavations. Eskimo art performed a magico-religious function, for example providing protection from evil spirits and promoting success in the hunt; elaborately decorated hunting tools were considered necessary to attract animals who would then allow themselves to be taken for food. A strong belief in sympathetic magic is evident in such practices as the elaborate Bear Cult ceremonies in Canada, in which an eviscerated bear was hung in the home, decorated with beads and fed choice morsels of food, so that its reincarnated spirit would again allow itself to be killed for food. Festivals and religious ceremonies were also an integral part of Eskimo life. In Alaska, particularly along the Bering Sea, dancers wore complicated, highly symbolic masks, which aimed at making the unreal world visible. One such mask (see fig. 2) depicts a grotesque human face, surmounted by a seal's face; above this is the simplified seal's body, with remnants of a rib cage and, at the very top, a small human face, perhaps the *inua* (soul) of the seal.

Although archaeologists have identified Eskimo cultures as early as *c.* 4000 BC, the most significant prehistoric

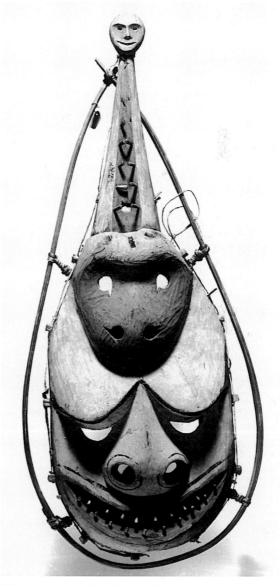

2. Eskimo mask, wood and leather with red, green, black and ochre pigments, h. 775 mm, collected south of Lower Yukon River, Alaska, 1877 (Washington, DC, Smithsonian Institution)

art from the region is found in the Okvik and Old Bering Sea cultures of Bering Strait and St Lawrence Island in Alaska (*c.* 500 BC–*c.* AD 500), the Ipiutak culture of North Alaska of approximately the same period and the Dorset culture of Canada (*c.* 800 BC–*c.* AD 1400). The Thule culture of both Alaska and Canada began *c.* 800 BC and lasted until *c.* AD 1700. The deeply rooted traditions of Thule culture gave way in the 19th century to the massive influences of Western civilization. New tools, materials and opportunities for trade created a 'mini-renaissance' of mask-making, ivory-carving and engraving, all produced with an economic incentive. While a few Eskimos, with limited education and travel, still produce objects in the style of their ancestors, many of the well-educated acculturated Eskimos are producing fine art, which is a blend of 20th-century styles and techniques overlaid with the subject-matter and myths of their forefathers.

BIBLIOGRAPHY

E. W. Nelson: 'The Eskimo about Bering Strait', *Annu. Rep. Bureau Amer. Ethnol. Secretary Smithsonian Inst.*, xviii (1899/R 1983)
H. B. Collins: 'Eskimo Cultures', *EWA*, v (1962), pp. 1–28
H. G. Bandi: *Eskimo Prehistory* (Stuttgart, 1964; Eng. trans., Fairbanks, 1969)
H. Larson: 'Some Examples of Bear Cult among the Eskimo and Other Northern Peoples', *Folk*, xi–xii (1969–70), pp. 27–42
H. B. Collins and others: 'Eskimo Art', *The Far North: 2000 Years of American Eskimo and Indian Art* (exh. cat., Washington, DC, N.G.A., 1973), pp. 1–129
A. Okladnikov: *Art of the Amur* (New York and Leningrad, 1981)
W. W. Fitzhugh and S. A. Kaplan: *Inua: Spirit World of the Bering Sea Eskimo* (exh. cat., Washington, DC, N. Mus. Nat. Hist., 1982)
W. W. Fitzhugh and A. Crowell: *Crossroads of Continents* (exh. cat., Washington, DC, N. Mus. Nat. Hist., 1988)

SARADELL ARD

(ii) Subarctic. This region stretches across North America from the Labrador and Newfoundland coasts to the Bering Sea (see fig. 1 above). It comprises tundra–woodland and boreal forest, mountain ranges and the Hudson's Bay, and has long severe winters and short warm summers. Human habitation dates to at least *c.* 7000 BC and may be much earlier in the west. The Canadian Shield and associated Hudson Bay Lowlands and Mackenzie Borderlands, making up three-quarters of the Subarctic landmass, have been the homeland of the Algonquian-speaking Naskapi, Montagnais, Cree, Northern Ojibwa and Saulteaux peoples, and, west of Hudson's Bay, of the Athapaskan-speaking Chipewyan, Slavey, Beaver, Dogrib, Yellowknife, Hare (including Bear Lake) and Mountain peoples. The people of the Cordillera, the mountainous area between the Mackenzie Lowlands and Yukon River plateau, are the Athapaskan-speaking Chilcotin, Carrier, Sekani, Kaska, Tahltan, Inland Tlingit, Tagish, Tutchone, Han and Kutchin. The Athapaskans of the Alaska Plateau are the Tanana, Upper Tanana, Koyukon, Ingalik and Kolchan, and, south of the Alaska Range, the Tanaina and Ahtna.

Climatic uniformity has dictated similar adaptation for both Athapaskans and Algonquians. Traditionally, they were frequently on the move and subsisted primarily on moose, caribou, hare and fish. They lived in easily erected, transportable shelters, which were usually conical and covered with skins, bark or brush. Women made skin clothing, tailored to protect against the climate, and the painted or porcupine-quill ornamentation of clothing were highly developed arts. Minimally ornamented bone and antler tools were made, and birch-bark containers and, in some areas, coiled spruce-root baskets were used for collecting and cooking. Traditional Subarctic cultural traits included a high value placed on adaptiveness and personal autonomy, a religion based on animism, shamanism, female puberty rites, and burial with new clothes and whatever the soul might need in the afterlife.

The first European contacts date to the early 16th century along the Gulf of St Lawrence, 1670 in the western Shield region and the early 18th century in what soon became Russian America (later Alaska). European goods and diseases preceded the actual Europeans, whose numbers slowly increased as traders pushed further into the Subarctic interior seeking new sources for furs. Furs were traded for Western technology, especially guns, knives, kettles, fabrics and beads. In 1821 the Hudson's Bay Company secured a trade monopoly.

Many families eventually chose to forgo nomadic life, and different groups became associated with particular trading-posts. During the 19th century Anglican and Oblate Catholic missionaries established churches and schools across the Subarctic in fur trading-posts, encouraging European ways of living. European–Native intermarriage was common, and mixed-blood families often served as brokers between cultures. Although mixed heritage has become prevalent across the Subarctic, it is primarily those of the Lake Winnipeg and Great Slave Lake who call themselves Metis ('mixed-bloods'). Metis around Lake Winnipeg tried unsuccessfully to organize politically late in the 19th century.

The 'modern era' began about 1945 with a continued decline in the fur trade and the Canadian government's assumption from the Church of responsibility for Native American health, education and welfare needs in Canada. In Alaska the government has been responsible for Native American education since about 1900. The need to interact within Euro-American governmental and economic institutions has fundamentally altered social roles, and specialized jobs carried out in a non-kin social setting have replaced traditional economic interdependence within the family. Increased pressures towards urban-living styles and standards have dramatically altered the traditional outlook. Since the 1960s Subarctic Native Americans have been increasingly involved in political activism, litigation over land claims and acquisition of the economic and political power to control the valuable hydro and mineral resources of their regions.

BIBLIOGRAPHY

J. Helm and N. Laurie: 'The Hunting Tribes of Subarctic Canada', *North American Indians in Historical Perspective*, ed. E. Leacock and N. Laurie (New York, 1971), pp. 343–74
J. Van Stone: *Athapaskan Adaptations* (Chicago, 1974)
J. Helm and others: 'The Contact History of the Subarctic Athapaskans: An Overview', *Proceedings: Northern Athapaskan Conference*, Canadian Ethnology Service Paper xxvii (1975), pp. 302–49
J. Helm, ed.: 'Subarctic', *Hb. N. Amer. Ind.*, vi (1981) [whole issue]

KATE C. DUNCAN

(iii) Northwest Coast. The Northwest Coast culture area comprises the offshore islands and the thin strip of land between the Pacific Ocean and the coastal mountain range from the Copper River on the Gulf of Alaska to the Chetco River on the southern Oregon coast (see fig. 1 above). Despite the effects of acculturation, much that

was traditional has remained on the Northwest Coast, including clan affiliation, ranking and, in some areas, artistic production. Scholars divide Northwest Coast peoples and art into three provinces: northern, central and southern.

The three groups of the northern province share a matrilineal organization, in which exogamous social units define themselves with images of and myths about crest animals. The display of these crests (see fig. 3) constitutes one of the two principal motivations for creating art. The other purpose for art in this area is for use by shamans during their magical rituals.

The Tlingit are the northernmost people. They are divided into two moieties, the Ravens and the Wolves, each subdivided into a number of clans with distinctive crests. High-ranking families lived in communal houses of up to 50 residents. In most Tlingit villages there was a shaman, usually male, whose responsibility it was to cure the sick, control the weather, guarantee success in warfare and ensure adequate fish runs. During his ceremonies the shaman manipulated an array of art objects that had profound supernatural power, as the spirits depicted on them were felt to be present at seances.

The Haida live on the Queen Charlotte Islands and the southern part of Prince of Wales Island in Alaska. They are divided into two matrilineal moieties, the Eagles and the Ravens, each composed of a number of localized lineages. They were renowned for their skill in carving totem poles and making ocean-going canoes: 19th-century photographs show large Haida villages with forests of totem poles and rows of canoes lining the shore. The Haida are also noted for carvings, made for trade with Euro-Americans, of a black fine-textured shale called argillite.

The third northern group, the Tsimshian, are divided into the Tsimshian proper, who live on the coast of northern British Columbia, the Nishga of the Nass River and the Gitksan of the Skeena. The Tsimshian and Nishga are divided into four phratries—the Eagle, Raven, Wolf and Blackfish—while the Gitksan are divided into three clans—the Frog-Raven, Wolf and Fireweed. They too made totem poles, elaborate architectural paintings, and sculptures and clan crests. Tsimshian sculptors were known especially for the fineness of their headdress frontlets, as well as their raven rattles. They also made masks representing hereditary spirits called Naxnox.

Between the northern and central provinces are some transitional groups that display characteristics of both areas. The Haisla and Haihais who live around Douglas and Gardner canals, directly south of the Tsimshian, have a matrilineal social organization and produced art in a classic northern style.

The central province is characterized socially by a bilateral lineage system. The Bella Bella or Heiltsuk, who

3. Northwest Coast, Chilkat blanket, made by Tlingit people from cedar bark and mountain-goat wool, black, yellow and blue-green dyes, l. 1.17 m, from Alaska, c. 1890–c. 1910 (Washington, DC, National Museum of Natural History)

live between the Haisla and Kwakiutl in central British Columbia, share some of the characteristics of the central province but produced art closer to that of their northern neighbours. The Bella Coola, who are Salish-speakers, live inland in the Bella Coola River region and made art to depict their elaborate mythology. The Kwakiutl are distributed from the northern end of Vancouver Island to Campell River and the mainland opposite. They claim descent from both parents, often inheriting social rank from the father and ceremonial privileges from the mother. Totem poles, painted house façades, freestanding figural sculptures and costumes are all used to display status. Some masks illustrate family legends; an intense interest in cuisine at ceremonials led to the creation of large carved food bowls. Kwakiutl of high status inherit the right to be initiated into dancing societies, which have associated costumes, masks and stage props. The initiate is said to have been kidnapped by a spirit, who infuses him or her with inhuman drives. The initiate returns to the village in a frenzied state and must be tamed and reintegrated back into society during an elaborate ceremonial, which involves sleight-of-hand tricks, ventriloquism, puppetry and the display of numerous masks.

The Nuu-chah-nuulth or Nootkan people live from the Brooks Peninsula on the south-west coast of western Vancouver Island. Like the Kwakiutl, they dramatize inherited privileges in masquerades. The best known of these is the wolf ceremony, in which masked dancers representing supernatural wolves take into the woods an initiate, who must then be returned to the village.

The southern province is inhabited by the Coast Salish and Chinookans. There are three sub-areas: Georgia Strait, Puget Sound and Southwest Washington–Lower Columbia. The Georgia Strait Salish made rattles and masks for cleansing rituals officiated by priests. Carvings associated with architecture as well as grave monuments depicted visions or ancestors. The Puget Sound Salish made art for the spirit canoe ceremony, including painted boards and power figures representing the supernaturals who assisted shamans in their curing rituals.

BIBLIOGRAPHY

F. Boas: 'The Social Organization and Secret Societies of the Kwakiutl Indians', *Report of the United States National Museum, 1895* (Washington, DC, 1897)
B. Holm: *Northwest Coast Indian Art: An Analysis of Form* (Seattle, 1965)
E. Gunther: *Art in the Life of the Northwest Coast Indians* (Portland, 1966)
P. Macnair, A. Hoover and K. Neary: *The Legacy* (Victoria, BC, 1980)
R. Carlson, ed.: *Indian Art Traditions of the Northwest Coast* (Burnaby, BC, 1983)
B. Holm: *Spirit and Ancestor: A Century of Northwest Coast Indian Art at the Burke Museum* (Seattle, 1987)
A. Jonaitis: *From the Land of the Totem Poles: The Northwest Coast Indian Art Collection at the American Museum of Natural History* (Seattle, 1988)

ALDONA JONAITIS

(iv) Plateau. The Plateau region of the north-western USA and south-western Canada encompasses the land drained by the Columbia River and its tributaries in the states of British Columbia, Oregon, Washington, Idaho and Montana, as well as the Thompson and Fraser river drainages in British Columbia (see fig. 1 above). With rainfall cut off by the Cascade Mountains on the west, much of the region

is dry. The open lowlands were covered with sagebrush and grass at the time of contact with the first non-Native Americans. Timbered highlands and mountains surround the central plains.

The languages spoken on the Plateau were from four linguistic groupings: dialects of the Salish language family in the northern region, Sahaptian and Waiilatpuan in the south and a small number of Upper Chinookan speakers along the Columbia River on the west. In spite of the language differences, the shared climate and close social relations of the people produced a distinct culture marked by equality within groups and peaceful contact with others.

Traditionally, the peoples of the Plateau moved within their territory in a regular seasonal round. In the winter, families lived in small autonomous settlements in sheltered locations near rivers and streams, where they made or repaired baskets, clothing, nets and tools, told the winter stories and joined neighbouring families for religious ceremonies. In the spring, they gathered at traditional fishing places, usually where there was a waterfall or cascade to impede the upriver migration of the salmon and steelhead. The women dug food roots on the hills and dried roots and fish for trade or for winter use. In summer and autumn, large groups moved to the mountains to hunt and to pick and dry huckleberries and other fruits. There they visited, traded and participated in races and other games.

Before the horse was introduced in the early 18th century, these inter-group gatherings were largely limited to those living along the same rivers and streams. The Upper Chinookan-speaking Wasco and Wishxam shared the Plateau way of life, but their culture also reflected frequent contact with Northwest Coast groups (*see* §(iii) above) at the mouth of the Columbia River to the west. With the new mobility that horses allowed, the Salish and Sahaptian people began to travel greater distances for trading and socializing. Hunting parties travelled as far as the Plains for buffalo, resulting in access to other cultural influences from the east, including influences brought to the Plateau by European settlers in the mid-1800s. However, many aspects of traditional culture have been sustained by periodic celebrations, in which style of dress, fine beadwork and basketry and other objects of material culture provide a link with the past.

BIBLIOGRAPHY

V. F. Ray: *Cultural Relations in the Plateau of North America* (Los Angeles, 1939)
A. Anastasio: *The Southern Plateau: An Ecological Analysis of Intergroup Relations* (Moscow, ID, 1975)

MARY D. SCHLICK

(v) Great Basin. The vast semi-arid desert steppe of the Great Basin (see fig. 1 above) lies east of the Sierra Nevada and Cascade mountain ranges and west of the Rocky Mountains. Its northern boundary is the uplift of the Columbia Plateau in central Idaho and Oregon, and its southern boundary lies roughly along the Colorado River in Utah and Arizona. From *c.* 10,000 BC the Great Basin was occupied by peoples of unknown language affiliation, who were principally hunters, gatherers and fishermen. A few peoples, ultimately affiliated with those of the Southwest region, also farmed parts of the eastern and southern Great Basin *c.* AD 500–1200.

At an unknown time the development of these peoples and/or the arrival of new peoples resulted in the tribal and linguistic groups recorded at the time of disruption of the Native American way of life by Euro-American expansion and settlement *c.* 1830–60. Various groups made their living by hunting, by gathering vegetable foods and by fishing where possible. The groups included the Washoe, centred around Lake Tahoe in the central Sierra Nevada; the Northern Paiute and Owens Valley Paiute of western Nevada, southern Oregon and southern California; the Northern and Western Shoshone of southern Idaho, central Nevada and southern California; the Southern Paiute (including the Chemehuevi) of southern California, southern Utah and northern Arizona; and the Ute of western and eastern Utah and adjacent western Colorado. All of these groups, except the Washoe, speak related languages, ultimately affiliated with the widespread Uto-Aztecan family of languages. The Washoe speak a Hokan language related to others in California and elsewhere.

Although at various times and places some Great Basin groups enjoyed more favourable subsistence, most were required to move at least seasonally in search of foods. Movement affected material culture, limiting its variety and making portability a prime factor. Camps of five to ten families were typical in most seasons, although winter might bring more to favoured locations for fuel, food and water. Housing was more permanent in winter, usually consisting of domed or conical dwellings of brush, grass or bark. Only in good years, and at times of communal game drives, major fish runs or piñon-nut harvests, did people come together in numbers of 100 or more. At those times, and with a reserve of food, they gathered to feast, offer thanksgiving prayers, dance, play games and socialize generally.

Particularly prominent among Great Basin arts at the time of Euro-American contact were non-material forms, such as story-telling and singing. The material arts were nonetheless important, including basketry, carving and sculpture, and, in western areas, featherwork. Non-portable art was confined principally to rock art, of which both painted (pictographs) and incised or pecked (petroglyphs) varieties occurred. Rock art, however, appears to have been more characteristic of peoples earlier than the historic tribes. In the post-contact period work in glass beads became prominent.

BIBLIOGRAPHY
J. Jennings: *Prehistory of Utah and the Eastern Great Basin* (Salt Lake City, 1978)
W. d'Azevedo: 'Introduction', *Hb. N. Amer. Ind.*, xi (1986), pp. 1–14

CATHERINE S. FOWLER

(vi) California. This culture area (see fig. 1 above) is roughly equivalent to the modern state of California. It was home to more than 60 main groups, each of which comprised numerous smaller autonomous ones, speaking different dialects or, in some cases, different languages. The peoples can be grouped into several different cultural areas.

North-western California included the Karok, Yurok, Hupa, Wiyot and Tolowa, and was culturally an extension of the North-west Coast area (*see* §(iii) above). Extensive woodworking industries developed in this region, and other characteristic features include the production of twined basketry, stone-handled adzes, elkhorn wedges, woven rod armour and dentalium shell currency, as well as salmon fishing with nets, traps, weirs and harpoons. There was a focus on the acquisition of wealth as a means of attaining power and status, and affluence in the form of rare albino deerskins, large bi-pointed obsidian blades and regalia made of scarlet woodpecker scalps and shells would have been displayed in World Renewal rites, such as the White Deerskin Dance.

North-eastern California was the area of the Achomawi and Atsugewi. It was characterized by a hunter–gatherer culture with affiliations mainly to the north, with the Klamath Lake people. Extensive use was made of desert, swamp and wetland ecosystems. Characteristic products were twined basketry, in a variety of forms, simple wooden dugout canoes and fine bows.

In central California, the Pomo, Miwok, Maidu, Nisenan, Patwin, Yokuts and Costanoan maintained a rich hunter–gatherer culture. These people made extensive use of both twined and coiled baskets. Their houses were thatched with brush or grass, or were earth-covered and semi-subterranean or constructed of conifer-bark slabs. World Renewal rites were held at prescribed times of the year, and ceremonial regalia included a broad array of featherwork items (see fig. 4). Objects exchanged in a vast

4. California, featherwork, shell and glass-bead regalia worn by Chief Lemee (Chris Brown) of the Southern Miwok, Yosemite Valley, *c.* 1930

intertribal trade network included finely made coiled baskets, belts woven of cordage and incorporating shell beads, tiny red and green bird feathers and a variety of shell beads and ornaments.

East of the Sierra Nevada Mountains, the high desert was inhabited by a variety of Paiute peoples and was an extension of the Great Basin culture area (*see* §(v) above). Southern California peoples include the Luiseno, Cahuilla, Tipai, Ipai and others. They lived in brush or grass thatched houses, placed an emphasis on coiled basketry and made some pottery and some featherwork ceremonial regalia. The Chumash of the Santa Barbara area, and to a lesser extent the neighbouring Gabrielino, exploited ocean resources, making canoes of split wooden planks, sewn together and caulked with pitch and asphaltum. They also made twined and coiled baskets, shell beads and ornaments, and highly polished and often inlaid wood-burl bowls. They produced an astounding variety of polychrome rock art, primarily in caves and sheltered outcrops, and developed refined stoneworking arts, primarily using steatite. Along the Colorado River, peoples such as the Quechan were in contact with Southwest groups and, like these, practised agriculture and made pottery.

BIBLIOGRAPHY
R. F. Heizer, ed.: 'California', *Hb. N. Amer. Ind.*, viii (1978) [whole issue]

CRAIG D. BATES

(vii) Southwest. This area comprises 777,200 sq. km, including New Mexico, Arizona, southern Colorado and Utah, west Texas and eastern Nevada, forming the geographic north-western frontier of Mexico (see fig. 1 above). It is an arid land drained by the Rio Grande and Colorado rivers. Major geographical features include the Sonoran Desert, 900 m to 1200 m above sea-level, and the Colorado Plateau, 1675 m to 2130 m high. Mesas (table-shaped hills), deep canyons, volcanic formations and mountain ranges that rise above 4000 m create an ecological mosaic of great variety. From *c.* 10,000 BC the area has been settled by many different peoples, each isolated somewhat from all others, but until the 20th century the population probably never exceeded 200,000. There were no written languages until after the 16th-century Spanish invasions, and all peoples made art that was applied to useful objects, had social and ritual functions, and served as visual metaphors of a shared world view. Information on this area before the European arrival is based entirely on excavated objects interpreted by archaeology, ethnology and the traditions of several dozen intact indigenous groups that still live in their ancient homeland.

Soon after *c.* 6000 BC modern warm, dry climatic conditions took hold, ushering in the Desert-culture era. Desert-culture art was of two sorts: highly structured, geometrical designs on textiles, basketry and other domestic objects, and ritual art that was often casually composed, representational and ephemeral. It included feathered sticks, wooden animal figurines, enormous paintings of spectral figures in caves and rock shelters, and similar engravings at open-air sites.

By *c.* 1000 BC some Desert-culture hunter–gatherers acquired maize from Mesoamerican cultures to the south and began the transition to an agricultural, sedentary way of life. Many different farming cultures thrived in oasis-like enclaves from *c.* AD 200 to the late 16th century, each with its own artistic traditions and history. The Colorado Plateau and central and southern Arizona and New Mexico were population centres of, among others, Anasazi, Mogollon and Hohokam people until *c.* 1300. The Hohokam then withdrew to southern Arizona, and Anasazi and Mogollon people resettled along the upper Rio Grande Valley and the southern margin of the Colorado Plateau. Domestic art forms in all areas included painted pottery, basketry and weaving. Architecture became important, especially on the Colorado Plateau after *c.* 950 (*see* §II below). Ritual art became especially elaborate after *c.* 1300. Rock art is ubiquitous in all areas.

In the 16th century the Spaniards called the Anasazi farmers living in about a hundred towns of the Rio Grande Valley and southern Colorado Plateau 'Pueblo people'. They admired their architecture, painted pottery and textiles, but were disturbed by their ritual paintings, masked *kachina* (essences or spirits of different elements in the Pueblo world) dances and other ceremonial arts. About 20 Pueblo groups that survive in New Mexico and Arizona still maintain their traditional way of life and many traditional arts. They spoke nine or ten distinctly different languages at the time of contact with Europeans, of which six (Hopi, Zuni, Keresan, Tiwa, Towa and Tewa) are still spoken. While Pueblo people and groups such as the Piman-speaking Pima and Tohono O'Odham of southern Arizona have been in the Southwest for a very long time, other groups, such as the Athapaskan-speaking Navajo and Apache, arrived more recently. The art forms for which they are now famous, for example Apache basketwork and Navajo sand painting, weaving and silverwork, derive from the Southwest. In each case the art tradition was transformed and then integrated into the life of a people new to the region, and this ability to transform novel modes and integrate them with indigenous social patterns characterizes all Southwestern Native American art.

BIBLIOGRAPHY
C. L. Tanner: *Prehistoric Southwestern Craft Arts* (Tucson, 1976)
A. Ortiz, ed.: 'Southwest', *Hb. N. Amer. Ind.*, ix (1979) [whole issue]
L. S. Cordell: *Prehistory of the Southwest* (Orlando, 1984)
W. M. Ferguson and A. H. Rohn: *Anasazi Ruins of the Southwest in Color* (Albuquerque, 1986)
J. J. Brody: *Anasazi and Pueblo Painting* (Albuquerque, 1991)

J. J. BRODY

(viii) Plains. The North American Plains cover *c.* 2,600,000 sq. km, extending from the Rocky Mountains eastward to the Mississippi Valley and from the Saskatchewan River south into Texas (see fig. 1 above). Within this region the western High Plains are arid, with trees growing mainly in the valleys of the few meandering rivers. Surrounding the High Plains are other sub-regions: the forested foothills of the Rocky Mountains, the parklands to the north, the lush prairies east of the Missouri River and the near desert to the south. These sub-regions are gradual transition zones between the heartland of the Plains and the surrounding areas.

The vast Plains region, predominantly grassland, was inhabited by immense herds of bison, antelopes and various types of deer. Attracted by these natural resources small bands of nomadic hunters have roamed the Plains for thousands of years. After *c.* AD 200 these people developed a distinct style of pottery, derived from eastern Woodland prototypes. Ceramics and other archaeological evidence indicate cultural relationships with regions beyond the Plains. Drives and other communal hunting techniques were employed in the exploitation of the bison herds. Such activities required cooperation among the widely dispersed bands, stimulating the formation of tribal societies.

Originating from the lower Mississippi Valley, agriculture spread along the Missouri River and its main tributaries by AD 900. Some farmers were migrants from the south-east, introducing a Mississippian culture pattern that was adopted to some extent by the local population. The farmers established semi-permanent villages of earth-covered lodges, often surrounded by palisades. Although much of their food came from the gardens in the valleys, hunting remained a necessity. They made basketry and pottery, and their small stone sculpture related to cosmological concepts of south-eastern origin. The influence of these Mississippian cultures were felt as far away as the northern Plains, as indicated by artefacts found in Manitoba burial mounds. The riverine villages became centres in an extensive trade network and functioned in the dissemination of a complex ritualism among the Plains nomadic hunters, who frequented these market-places and maintained a symbiotic relationship with the agrarian village communities along the Missouri River.

The first European influences reached the Plains through the Native American trade network in the 17th century. From the Spanish colonies in the south horses spread slowly northward. In the 1730s they reached the villages along the middle Missouri, where they were exchanged against the first European trade goods that arrived from French and British establishments in the north-eastern parts of the continent. For more than a century the fur trade was the sole medium of contact between the expanding Euro-American society and the Plains Native Americans.

In the 18th century horses, the fur trade and indirect Euro-American colonial pressure caused Native American groups from surrounding regions to make their home on the Plains. The diverse origins of these populations is reflected in their different languages. Algonquian languages originating from the north-eastern Woodlands are spoken by the Blackfoot, Plains Cree, Plains Ojibwa, Cheyenne, Arapaho and Gros Ventres; Siouan languages originating from the upper Mississippi region are represented by the Mandan, Hidatsa, Crow, Assiniboin, Yankton, Yanktonai, Teton, Iowa, Oto, Missouri, Omaha, Ponca, Kansa, Osage and Quapaw; from the far north came the Sarsi, Kiowa–Apache and Lipan Apache, who spoke Athapaskan languages; Caddoan languages from the south-east were spoken by the Wichita, Pawnee and Arikara; from west of the Rocky Mountains came the Ute, Shoshoni and Comanche, who spoke Uto-Aztecan languages; the Kiowa spoke a language that was distantly related to Tanoan in New Mexico, and the Tonkawa in Texas may have spoken a Coahuiltecan language of northern Mexico. In view of these many different languages and the prevailing nomadic lifestyle, a well-developed hand-sign language served as a lingua franca.

Horses, fire-arms, an increasing range of European imports and the exposure to European fashions, behaviour and ideas created a new way of life for Plains peoples, which was dependent on the buffalo herds as much as on European trade, yet distinctly Native American in character. The cultural focus shifted from the riverine farmers to the nomadic hunters. It is this historical phenomenon that is commonly referred to as Plains Native American culture. Horses and fire-arms made life easier for the hunters; beads, cloth and other imports stimulated artistic production, and much time was spent in ceremonial activities. Historic Plains Native American culture was increasingly motivated by the achieving of honour in intertribal warfare and the acquisition of material wealth, to be ostentatiously displayed in tribal ceremonialism.

When buffalo hides became a major export product the fate of the herds was sealed; between 1830 and 1870 the buffalo dwindled from an estimated thirty million to a few thousand. While the traders pulled out, American settlement gathered momentum after the Civil War (1861–5) and the extension of railroad tracks. Following a desperate resistance, the Native American people were forced to sign treaties and settle on reservations. Half a century followed in which a paternalistic government endeavoured to suppress all expressions of Native American culture. From over 100,000 in the early 19th century, the Native American population decreased to *c.* 54,000 in 1900. Only since World War II have living conditions improved for the rapidly increasing Native American population (*c.* 164,300 in 1970), and Native American culture has shown a surprising vitality.

BIBLIOGRAPHY
H. Hartmann: *Die Plains- und Prärieindianer Nordamerikas* (Berlin, 1973)
N. Bancroft-Hunter and W. Forman: *The Indians of the Great Plains* (London, 1982)
J. C. Ewers: *Plains Indian Sculpture* (Washington, DC, 1986)
E. M. Maurer, ed.: *Visions of the People: A Pictorial History of Plains Indian Life* (Minneapolis, MN, 1992)

T. J. BRASSER

(ix) *Woodlands.* South of the coniferous forests of the Subarctic region and east of the grasslands of the Plains region there extends an area of temperate deciduous forests, usually referred to as the Woodlands region (see fig. 1 above). It stretches from the St Lawrence River and the Great Lakes to the Gulf of Mexico, and from the Atlantic Ocean to the Mississippi River. The Appalachian Mountains, which form the watershed between the Atlantic and the Mississippi, rise to *c.* 1800 m in the south and to *c.* 600 m in the north. Along their eastern flank, the foothills rise above the tidewater area of the coastal plain. In the west, the Appalachian Plateau borders on the interior plains of the Ohio Valley and the Great Lakes. With annual rainfall ranging from *c.* 720 mm in the north to *c.* 1540 mm in the south, climates vary from humid continental to humid subtropical. Parts of southern Florida extend into the tropical region. The northern boundary of the Woodlands region coincides with the limit of native horticulture.

The earliest human inhabitants of the Woodlands were Palaeo-Native American big-game hunters, who entered the area before 10,000 BC. Adaptation to changing environmental conditions led to a variety of hunting and gathering traditions and, from the 3rd millennium BC in restricted areas, to sedentary lifestyles with horticulture and pottery. European contact on the Atlantic Coast began during the 16th century and had reached the western Great Lakes by the early 17th century.

Among the tribes of the Woodlands, two major language groups are represented: Macro-Algonquian includes the Algonquian language family of the north-east (with relatives in the Subarctic and Plains regions) and the Gulf-Muskogean language stock of the south-east. The Algonquians, whose origin c. 1000 BC has been traced to an area north of the Great Lakes, include the Eastern Algonquians on the Atlantic Coast (e.g. the Abnaki, New England

Algonquians, Delaware, Virginia and North Carolina Algonquians) and the Central Algonquians around and south of the western Great Lakes (e.g. Ottawa, Ojibwa, Menominee, Sauk, Fox, Potawatomi, Miami, Illinois and Shawnee). The Muskogeans (Creek, Choctaw and Chickasaw) were more distantly related to the Gulf languages of the south-east (Natchez, Tunica, Chitimacha and Atakapa). The Iroquois–Caddo–Sioux group has members of all three composite language families in the Woodlands. It includes such northern groups as the Erie, Neutral, Huron and the five nations of the late prehistoric–early historic period League of the Iroquois (Mohawk, Oneida, Onondaga, Cayuga and Seneca); their close relatives the Tuscarora, in North Carolina, who later joined the League; and the southern Cherokee in the Appalachian region of the south-east. Relatively small groups of Siouans lived scattered throughout the region from the Winnebago in the western Great Lakes area, to the Catawba of the Carolinas and the Biloxi of the lower Mississippi Valley. Like the Siouans, the Caddo of western Louisiana and Arkansas had more numerous relatives living in the Plains region. Apart from members of the two major language groups, there were speakers of isolated languages, such as the Timucua of Florida and the Yuchi (whose connection may be with Siouan), and peoples whose linguistic affiliation will remain unknown because their speech was extinguished before adequate records had been made. Nothing is known about the peoples of the Ohio Valley, whose villages were deserted, probably following epidemic diseases spreading in front of the advancing Europeans.

Substantial cultural variation existed within the Woodlands region. Cultivation of corn, beans, squash and other plants on burnt-over clearings was almost universally the basis for a sedentary life, but varied greatly in relative importance. Without animal husbandry, meat had to be supplied by hunting, which was done by the men. Men also dominated in fishing, which was of first importance along the Atlantic and Gulf coasts and in the Great Lakes. Throughout the Woodlands, nuts, roots and the seeds of grasses were gathered by the women, helping to stabilize the food economy. Of special importance was the gathering of wild rice (*Zizania aquatica*) in the western Great Lakes region, where it was a staple food. Women usually also planted the fields, except for the public 'town fields' in the south-east, which were worked by both sexes. Agriculture may have supplied up to half the food in the south-east but was of marginal importance in the western Great Lakes area.

The dominance of the women in subsistence activities over much of the Woodlands region is only partly reflected in social organization. Matrilineal descent is found among the Iroquois and their immediate neighbours and generally in the south-east; patrilineality is typical for the western Great Lakes; while bilateral reckoning of descent occurred among the northern coastal Algonquians. Leadership positions were commonly inherited, although a person's status could often be improved through economic or military achievements. Social composition ranged from near equality to strictly defined social classes, with craft specialization showing a similar and related variation.

Shared features in the material cultures of the Woodlands were the presence of pottery and the predominance

5. Woodlands region, village of Secoton, showing houses, fields of maize at three different stages of growth, inhabitants dancing around a circle of posts with carved faces and (bottom left) a mortuary temple; detail from a watercolour by John White, 324×199 mm, 1585 (London, British Museum)

of the use of skin for clothing, which only in the south and east was supplemented by vegetal fibres. Wood-carving was significantly more important than work in stone, and, in the absence of weaving, basketry played a major role. Multi-family houses were the rule throughout the region, but forms and construction materials varied widely, reflecting both the intensity of sedentism and the adaptation to the habitat (see fig. 5). Transportation was mostly over waterways; wooden dugout canoes predominated, except for the northern part of the area where light bark boats prevailed.

Introduced diseases dramatically affected tribal populations. Fire-arms changed the military balance of power, and European trade redirected traditional economic strategies. European colonial settlement caused major redistributions of population. While some tribes disappeared, new groups (such as the Seminole of Florida) were formed. During the first half of the 19th century, but especially after the Indian Removal Act of 1830, many of the surviving indigenous populations (especially of the southeast) were relocated to lands west of the Mississippi River (mostly in Kansas and Oklahoma). Due to these changes, and to the early destruction of whole populations, the arts of the Woodlands remain imperfectly known, although some of the earliest documented collections of Native American objects were made in this region.

BIBLIOGRAPHY

C. Hudson: *The Southeastern Indians* (Knoxville, 1976)

B. G. Trigger, ed.: 'Northeast', *Hb. N. Amer. Ind.*, xv (1978) [whole issue]

CHRISTIAN F. FEEST

2. HISTORY. The first written reports of the indigenous cultures of North America were compiled by Europeans from the 16th through to the end of the 18th century. Strictly speaking, it is with those records that historical documentation across the region began at very different times. Earlier evidence, provided by archaeological or art-historical inference, while extensive, remains relatively incomplete. Unlike the urban civilizations of PRE-COLUMBIAN MESOAMERICA and PRE-COLUMBIAN SOUTH AMERICA, most non-ceramic North American artefacts, now considered art objects, were made of perishable materials. Further, with the exception of the Southwest region (*see* §(i) below), stone architecture was not used, even in the largest of North America's prehistoric urban settlements or ceremonial sites.

(i) Before European contact. (ii) After European contact.

(i) Before European contact. The final glaciation of the Late Pleistocene period (*c.* 80,000–*c.* 10,000 BP) is known in North America as the Wisconsinan. During this time the water held as ice caused sea-levels to fall by at least 85 m, opening up a land bridge, known as Beringia, between Siberia and Alaska. Despite questionable claims for a few earlier sites, the first significant population migration into North America apparently began *c.* 20,000–15,000 BP. Small groups of ancestral Mongolians crossed the 1600 km wide tundra connecting eastern Siberia and western Alaska, now the Bering Strait, and moved south along the Rocky Mountains' east slope. The first Palaeo-Native Americans hunted mammoths, horses, camelids and giant bison at

water-holes across the plains and prairies, using spear-shafts tipped with fluted flint points and stone, bone or antler tools similar to those used in the Eurasian Upper Palaeolithic period (*c.* 40,000–*c.* 10,000 BP). A few mountain sites include ochre-covered burials or cremations with large, fine points. While bone remains or tools are rare and burials unknown, the distributions of tools and structural elements at numerous sites in the eastern Woodlands suggest repeated short occupations by small, mobile groups as long ago as *c.* 12,000 BP. Early hunters and gatherers followed caribou herds along the retreating glaciers of the Great Lakes–St Lawrence River drainage. By *c.* 10,500 BP other Palaeo-Native Americans had reached Tierra del Fuego.

About 9500 BP modern flora and fauna had developed across North America. On plains and prairies as far east as the Great Lakes, hundreds of bison were hunted by being driven over cliffs and riverbanks or into canyons. In the western mountains and throughout the Great Basin small bands met on the shores of vast lakes to hunt and fish, then moved seasonally to rock shelters at higher elevations to collect piñon nuts. Along the major rivers of the Pacific north-west, spawning salmon and a variety of indigenous plants with starchy roots and bulbs supported larger and larger seasonal groups. Throughout California localized populations exploited acorns and deer, and in the south-western deserts and mountains small groups moved seasonally from valley to upland to hunt and collect seeds. In the eastern Woodlands larger and denser populations collected nuts and hunted in limited territories, returning seasonally to sites near mussel beds in the major rivers or gathering at the rivermouths and bays of oceans and lakes to net or spear spawning fish. Such regional economic specialization, much of which remained relatively unchanged for millennia, was aided by new ground stone adzes, grooved axes, mortars and grinding stones, and notched or barbed stone points and knives showing only slight differences across large areas. Around 6000 BP the spear-thrower came into use, and a variety of bone and antler hooks and stylized stone handles and weights were developed to improve its performance.

Although the western lakes disappeared and grasslands replaced many earlier forests during a warm, dry climatic episode that began *c.* 5000 BP (*c.* 3000 BC), only in the Great Basin were populations reduced to a fixed economy. Along the islands and estuaries of the Pacific coasts, marine mammals and spawning fish, along with roots or acorns, supported rather sedentary groups, who traded their abundant foodstuffs for stone and animal products with groups from the drier and higher interior. By *c.* 1000 BC the people of the Windmiller culture in California's Central Valley, peoples of the Straits of Georgia tradition along the Northwest Coast, and even some cultural groups in the northern plateau, were living in permanent villages, from which richly diverse natural environments were exploited and trade with other groups was controlled. The bison hunters on the plains spent more of their year at streams in the eastern Rocky Mountains or along east-flowing rivers in the prairies. These regional patterns persisted up to European contact.

After *c.* 3000 BC, across most of the Southwest, isolated bands of small game hunters and seed gatherers moved seasonally from stream bottom camps to small villages in the mountains or on plateau rims, and by *c.* 2000 BC contact with developing civilizations of PRE-COLUMBIAN MESOAMERICA introduced the cultivation of maize, beans and squash, and then pottery, to similar groups in the southern deserts and mountains. By *c.* 1500 BC eastern Woodlands hunter–gatherers were also cultivating squash and gourds, and harvesting native seed plants and nuts. Permanent settlements began along rich southern rivers, where some burials contained exotic stone artefacts. Between *c.* 1500 and *c.* 200 BC, as pottery appeared in the Southeast, growing populations began inter-group exchange to maintain access to territorially restricted resources. Some individuals received mound burial or were buried with increasing quantities of exotic materials (or both), which, by *c.* 1000 BC, included tools cold-hammered from Great Lakes copper and marine shell ornaments.

Between *c.* 200 BC and *c.* AD 500, groups of such newly agricultural peoples established permanent pit-house villages along the major rivers of the south-western deserts and in the south-western mountains. By *c.* AD 700, probably owing to Mesoamerican influences, large irrigation systems and ceremonial public architecture were constructed; these are associated with the sophisticated regional stoneworking and pottery of the Hohokam and Mogollon traditions. Trade to the south and west provided exotic material for ornaments, and trade to the north initiated the agricultural and architectural changes from Basketmaker to Early Pueblo culture that characterized the Anasazi tradition of the Colorado Plateau (*see* §1, 1(vii) above).

While hunting and fishing dominated aboriginal life along the northern lakes and oceans, from *c.* 200 BC to *c.* AD 500 minimally horticultural societies in the more temperate eastern Woodlands region increasingly integrated an elaborate exchange of ritual objects into élite mortuary ceremonies and public constructions, many of which display seasonal celestial significance. Differing networks and levels of exchange for an extraordinary assemblage of iconographic artefacts reached an apogee in Ohio Hopewellian ritual sites, which existed more for exchange than for subsistence (*see* HOPEWELL MOUNDS). Hopewellian traits were widely incorporated into cultures with local social and economic patterns. After *c.* AD 500, however, bow hunting and self-sufficient maize agriculture developed and spread, and population density grew throughout the eastern Woodlands. Small agricultural villages spread west along major rivers far into the Plains region. There were increasingly distinct regional cultural economies and styles, and except for related societies along the Gulf Coast and lower Mississippi Valley nearly all exchange of exotic material or mortuary ceremony ended.

From *c.* AD 1000 to *c.* 1400 new cultures developed. In the deserts of the Southwest, extensive systems of irrigation agriculture supported large Hohokam towns, with pyramidal mounds and ballcourts. These centres participated in an exchange system reaching south to Aztec Tenochtitlán (*see* MEXICO CITY, §1). More sedentary pit-house and stone-built agricultural villages were established in stylistically distinct regional Pueblo traditions on the Colorado Plateau (*see also* §II, 2, below). In the CHACO CANYON region, well-maintained roadways linked a hierarchical system of small villages and complex, multi-storey architectural habitation and ritual centres into a system of local and distant trade for exotic products, foodstuffs and minerals.

In the Mississippi River Valley, after *c.* AD 1000, societies with some unknown degree of indirect Mesoamerican influence built large towns surrounding sets of multi-stage, flat-topped and ramped mounds, upon which temples or civic buildings stood. These Mississippian cultures became increasingly urbanized, socially hierarchical societies with intensive multi-cropping of maize, beans and squash. Dense populations lived in planned communities with sophisticated and increasingly specialized ceramic and lithic technology, and a quasi-theocratic social organization. After *c.* AD 1350, however, in both the Southwest and in the eastern Woodlands, climatic disturbances produced significant cultural repercussions.

In the Southwest, years of intermittent drought were accompanied by the appearance of Navajo and Apache, the southernmost penetration of a second influx of Asiatic hunting and gathering peoples. By *c.* 1400 expansion on to the northern plateau and into the southern mountains, the construction of public architecture other than defensive fortification and trade in exotic luxury objects had ended. Warfare brought the abandonment of nearly all intervening territory; populations concentrated into a few isolated mesa-top sites along the Pecos, Rio Grande and Little Colorado rivers, where they were found by 16th-century Spanish explorers.

Mississippian earthwork construction and status-differentiation also ended by *c.* 1350. An élite ceremonial cult to maintain relationships among economically stressed societies appeared and spread across the Southeast. Within most political territories there was a widespread shift to fortified sites in central, defensive locations, including some of the northern groups, who never practised the intensive agriculture or the rigid socio-ceremonial patterns of Mississippian culture. Yet, many tribes of the upper Mississippi or of the South Atlantic coast, and nearly all south-eastern tribes, retained a diffuse Mississippian culture when they were encountered by Spanish conquistadors in the 16th century. Mississippian-influenced cultures also developed and coalesced in the mid-Ohio and Missouri river valleys, the Appalachian highlands and the Middle Atlantic states; but apart from a few stylistic influences, Mississippian culture did not spread into the Great Lakes or New England areas, where hunting–fishing–horticultural groups diversified into the various tribes met in the 17th century by English and French explorers.

BIBLIOGRAPHY

J. D. Jennings, ed.: *Ancient North Americans* (New York, 1983, rev. 1990)
M. Coe, D. Snow and E. Benson: *Atlas of Ancient America* (Oxford, 1986)

DAVID S. BROSE

(ii) After European contact.

(a) Introduction. Sustained encounter between the native peoples of North America and Euro-Americans began at different times, ranging from the late 15th century on the northern Atlantic coast to the late 19th century in the

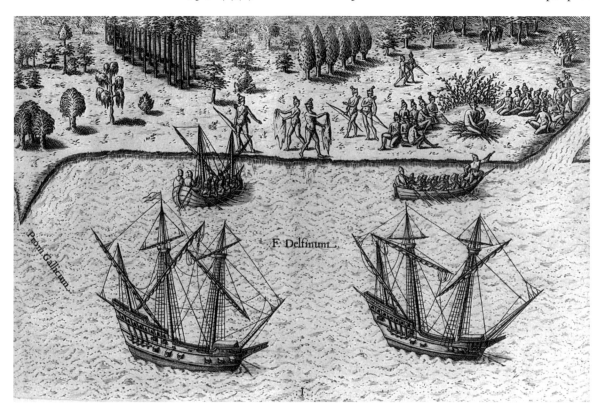

6. First French landing in Florida, 1562, when the short-lived settlement of Charlesfort (near Beaufort, South Carolina) was established by Jean Ribaut; engraving by Theodor de Bry, from *Bevis narratioeorum quae in Florida America Provicia Gallis acciderunt, secunda in illam nauigatione anno MDLXIII quae es secunda pars America* (Frankfurt am Main, 1591), pl. 1 (London, British Museum)

central Arctic. Although the results of such contacts were broadly similar, cultural differences on the part of the indigenous peoples and the divergent strategic goals of colonization are responsible for substantial regional variation. Before the establishment of permanent European colonies in North America, most contacts along the east coast of the continent were with fishermen, explorers and slave raiders of various western European nations. Early in the 16th century Spain established its first colony in Florida and undertook several exploratory expeditions into the interior Southeast as well as to the Southwest, where the colony of New Mexico was established in 1598. French and English attempts to gain a permanent foothold in North America failed during the 16th century (see fig. 6) but succeeded with the establishment of Virginia in 1607 (followed by others from the New England colonies in the north to Georgia in the south) and of New France in 1609, later followed by Louisiana. Short-lived colonial attempts in eastern North America included the 17th-century colonies of the New Netherlands and New Sweden. During the 1720s Denmark began to colonize Greenland; beginning with the 1740s Russia extended its Siberian empire to include Alaska; and Spain stepped up its military and missionary activities from north-western Mexico to California during the last quarter of the 18th century.

In 1763 Canada fell to Great Britain (which was to lose its other North American colonies to the newly established United States in 1783), while Spain gained temporary control over Louisiana (including much of the trans-Mississippi West), which in 1803 was purchased by the United States from Napoleon. The United States also obtained Florida in 1818, annexed Texas in 1845, gained the remaining Hispanic portions of North America from Mexico in 1849 and purchased Alaska from Russia in 1867. In the same year the confederation of the British colonies in Canada (including Quebec) and the establishment of a second nation state ended the period of colonial empires in North America, but not of internal colonization of the indigenous peoples.

(b) Effects of contact on Native American peoples. One of the first results of the colonial encounter was the introduction of new epidemic diseases, to which significant portions of Native American populations fell victim, sometimes even before direct contact with Europeans. As a consequence of depopulation rates of up to and sometimes above 90%, some Native peoples were completely wiped out, while others realigned themselves through alliances, fusion and other ethnogenetic processes. New peoples also emerged from widespread intermarriages between natives and newcomers: some of the largest indigenous groups of the late 20th century (such as the Métis of Manitoba or the Lumbee of North Carolina) are of post-contact origin.

The ethnographic map of North America was further changed by the military and economic conquest brought about by colonialism. The rapid expansion of English settlements led to the establishment of the reservation system in the 17th century, which, mostly on the basis of treaties, secured especially protected tracts of land for the remaining Native populations. The treaty system was later adopted by the USA (which abandoned it in 1871, but continued to create reservations by executive order) and by Canada (which entered into a series of numbered treaties with Native peoples, mostly between 1871 and 1877). In the USA Native land loss was compounded by systematic attempts to remove tribes from lands east of the Mississippi River (especially in conjunction with the Indian Removal Act of 1830) and by the General Allotment Act of 1887, which enforced individual against communal Native land ownership. By the end of the 20th century less than 2% of land in the USA was still owned by Native American peoples. Of *c.* 300 reservations in the USA, the Navajo Reservation is larger than Switzerland, while the Golden Hill Reservation in Connecticut measures just a quarter of an acre. In Canada most of the more than 2000 reservations are small, but Native lands in British Columbia and most of the north remain unceded; the Nunavut Agreement of 1993 provided for the creation in 1999 of the new Territory of Nunavut, in which the Inuit would have *de facto* self-government. Greenland with its dominant Inuit population gained home rule from Denmark in 1979 and subsequently left the European Community in order to protect its fishing rights.

Since the 17th century many Native peoples of the North American Woodlands, Subarctic, and later also the Northwest Coast, were drawn into the European fur trade, dominated by such commercial monopolies as the Hudson Bay Company. The fur trade provided access to European commodities highly valued by Native peoples, such as iron tools, firearms, glass beads, cloth or alcohol, and generally helped to intensify traditional forms of cultural expression. In the long run, however, the fur trade also created economic dependencies, especially whenever subsistence hunting was given up in order to increase the harvest of furs. On the Plains the introduction of the horse from Spanish sources likewise led to a period of cultural and economic prosperity based on a nomadic and hunting way of life, which ended in poverty and deprivation when the immense bison herds were virtually exterminated within a few decades in the late 19th century.

While economic prosperity tended to strengthen cultural diversity and differences with Euro-American lifestyles, both Christian missionaries and government officials generally saw themselves as agents of Western 'civilization' and sought to transform Native societies in order to assimilate them to their own image. There was a wide spectrum of Native reactions, from selective acceptance of Euro-American cultural influences to resistance to them. Whereas for some groups, for example the Micmac of Nova Scotia, Roman Catholicism became the exclusive substitute for their tribal religion, the enforced conversion of the Pueblo Indians of the Southwest had led to a compartmentalized coexistence between Christianity and traditional beliefs and practices. In addition there were syncretistic movements (such as the pan-Indian Peyote religion), which organically combined features of both the old and the new.

In the second half of the 20th century there was a dramatic resurgence of pride on the part of Native peoples in their traditional heritage and in their identity as generalized 'Indians' or as members of specific groups. It was partly based on a reversal of demographic trends, but had also contributed to them. In 1990 there were three million Native people north of the Rio Grande, compared to less than a million in 1900. Less than half of these, however, lived on reservations or spoke an indigenous language. Cultural and social diversity, often based on different premises than that encountered 500 years ago, remained a major characteristic of Native North American peoples.

BIBLIOGRAPHY

W. E. Washburn, ed.: 'History of Indian–White Relations', *Hb. N. Amer. Ind.*, iv (1988) [whole vol.]

CHRISTIAN F. FEEST

3. RELIGION. The indigenous religions of North America comprise a variety of individual, tribal and regional patterns of belief and expression. At the time of European contact, there was general belief in the pervasive existence of invisible forces, persons and realms. Spiritual entities revealed themselves through such natural phenomena as stones, rapids, animals, trees, winds and the sun, as well as through human beings. Indeed, these spirits were embedded so thoroughly in the material world that they cannot be described entirely as 'supernaturals'. Such entities as the Navajo 'holy persons', the Ojibwa *manitos*, the Lakota *wakan tanka* and the Iroquois *orenda* constituted the ultimate sources of existence. Without these entities, life was felt to be impossible; hence, Native Americans sought to understand them, and to enter relations with them that would benefit not only individuals and communities but also the larger community of life. At the same time, the existence of spiritual entities was posited within each living creature, and there was the same compulsion to know and maintain harmony with these animating, consciousness-enhancing souls, in order to live healthy and long lives. Grounded in these beliefs, Native American religion, at least ideally, centred on life-promoting relations with the ultimate sources of existence.

(i) Cosmology. (ii) Ritual. (iii) Development after European contact.

(i) Cosmology. Ideas about the structure of the cosmos were expressed most prominently through the medium of oral mythological narratives but also through art, architecture, ritual and social institutions. Indigenous cosmologies stated that matter was the primal substance of the universe; that primordial beings fashioned matter into the forms that presently exist; that the visible earth is but one of several layers of existence (others being both above and below it); that human life came into this world from other layers (e.g. falling from the sky world or emerging from underground); that the world is replete with animate beings who can aid or hinder humans; and that there are means by which humans can please, placate or coerce these beings to foster life. These means traditionally constitute a large part of the religious life of the community, and cosmological ideas were expressed in terms of local environments. For example, the Inuit of the Arctic region told of Sedna, the woman who dwells unhappily beneath the icy water (having been mutilated and left for dead by her father), whose finger-joints are seals, walruses

and whales, and who releases or withholds them from hunters, depending upon the moral and ritual propriety of the local community. The Iroquoian cosmogony of the north-east forest held that a pregnant woman fell from the sky, was cushioned by waterfowl and landed upon a great turtle's back. Diving animals brought mud from the depths and created the world, where the woman's grandsons—the Good Mind and Evil Mind—worked their wills into the shapes of present reality, such as forests, hills, streams, rocks, deer, snakes and herbs. From their dead mother's body grew corn, beans, squash and other crops. The Pueblo farmers of the Southwestern desert (e.g. the Hopis) spoke of their ancestral history in worlds beneath this one. Emerging upwards into this world, they formed clans and searched for their destined homeland, learning along the way the rituals necessary to bring fertilizing rain. The first death in this world made it possible for ancestors to become the spirits of rainclouds, who in turn could cause life-sustaining crops to grow.

Like the Arctic hunters, the horticulturalist–hunter–gatherers of the Northeast and the farmers of the Southwest, diverse Native American peoples possessed world views that portrayed their local ecosystems and provided knowledge perceived as essential for their lives. Native American myth-tellers narrated the vivid details of these cosmologies: girls marry stars; bears adopt boys; warrior twins defeat monsters; culture heroes provide their tribes with fire or medicines; tricksters derive creativity from their sanguinary breaking of taboos; husbands are unable to revive their spouses from the land of the dead. There were stories of the cyclical struggles between summer and winter; of the quarrels between women and men; of the interplay between hunters and their prey, or between diseases and their cures; of the origins of such rituals as smoking the pipe and purifying oneself in the sweat lodge. Elders and officials in each community passed down religious knowledge concerning the spiritual masters and mistresses of fish and animals, herbs and cultivated foods; concerning thunderers and underwater serpents; or about spider grandmothers and cannibal ogres. They laid out their villages to coordinate with constellations; they kept track of the solstices, equinoxes and moons; and they informed each generation regarding the proper ways to approach the spirits and cherish values in accord with cosmic patterns and principles.

(ii) Ritual. Native Americans brought to their religious life a range of attitudes, from the entreaties of pitiful dependence uttered by Lakota vision questers, to the assertive confidence of Navajo singers, who trusted in the compulsive efficacy of their ritual acts. Ideally, however, their religious practices were supposed to convey an affirmation of the cosmos and the spiritual entities inhabiting it. Particularly in the gathering and hunting cultures of the north, Native Americans trained themselves and their children to make face-to-face contact with the spirits through visions. At puberty, or repeatedly through life, they fasted, removed themselves to isolated, wild and dangerous locales, perhaps engaged in self-mutilation or self-torture and thereby invited the spirits to appear, offering protection and powers. These guardian spirits provided the visionary with guidance and foresight, health

7. Medicine pouch, hide, feathers, beads and weasel skins, from the weasel chapter of the Crow Tobacco Society, Plains Indian (Cody, WY, Buffalo Bill Historical Center)

and old age; a relationship between guardian and visionary might last a lifetime. The visionary displayed the identity of the guardian on shields, pennants and other regalia, through songs, titles and dance behaviour, in the contents of personal medicine pouches (see fig. 7) and in demonstrations of prowess. In some cultures (e.g. in the Plains region) visions were sought not only in private but also in such public ceremonials as the Sundance. In other cultures (e.g. in the Northwest Coast region), individuals inherited their guardians from their lineages, rather than attaining them through vision quests. Even in cultures without dominant vision-questing complexes (e.g. the Iroquois of the north-east Woodlands region) individuals paid close attention to the content of their dreams, regarding them as communication from the spiritual entities—deities or souls—who constituted their sources of existence.

The emphasis in Native American religions upon dreams and visions culminated in SHAMANISM (see fig. 8). In many communities, certain individuals possessed the ability to attain ecstatic trances, during which time they believed their souls capable of travelling to distant locations throughout the cosmos—even to the afterworld—in order to aid their tribesmen. They found lost objects of importance; they located scarce game during starving time; they tracked down enemies; they recovered souls that had wandered away, or that had been stolen by sorcerers; and they practised healing. Arctic Inuit shamans were renowned for their ability to send their soul to Sedna's quarters beneath the sea (while their body lay comatose above ground) in order to persuade her to release sea mammals to be hunted. Shamans acted as mediators between the underwater goddess and the community, eliciting confessions from their fellows whose

8. Northwest Coast shaman wearing a Tsimshian mask (Hull, Qué., Canadian Museum of Civilization)

misdeeds had angered Sedna into withholding the sea beasts. Subarctic Ojibwa shamans employed the technique of the 'shaking tent' to conjure the spirits so that they might speak with humankind. The shaman sat entranced in a conical tent, while drumming and chanting for the spirits to come. As the spirits entered the tent, it shook vigorously, and they made their voices heard among the people sitting outside. Then the community questioned the deities, with the shaman serving as mediating ventriloquist. Whether shamans engaged in soul flight or conjuring, their contribution to the tribe was their acute knowledge of the cosmos and its spiritual inhabitants.

Shamanic rituals were only the most dramatic forms of ceremonial expression among the northern hunters and gatherers. Rituals marked the passages along the road of individual lives, from naming ceremonies for infants, through first menstruation seclusion and celebration, and feasts for the first kill of young hunters, to mourning and burial rites. Ceremonies also accompanied seasonal subsistence activities: hunters not only divined the whereabouts of game animals and purified themselves for the chase, but they also apologized to the slain prey (and their spirit masters) and gave them tobacco and burnt offerings. Fishermen of the Northwest Coast region engaged in elaborate ceremonialism to honour the salmon; Plains Native Americans masqueraded as bison in order to display their admiration; bear ceremonials throughout North America demonstrated the reverence for these animals; and Native American doctors were sure to show their respect for herbs by leaving gifts whenever they gathered their medicines. In these ways Native Americans suffused their life-activities with religiousness.

Seasonal ceremonialism was further elaborated among the farming peoples of the south. The Creeks of the Southeast performed an annual midsummer new year's fast and feast at the ripening of their corn crop. As the new year approached, they cleaned out their houses and village squares, put out their fires and emptied their bellies by fasting and vomiting. Then when the new corn was green, they exulted in the temporal re-creation of the cosmos by feasting and dancing. Further north, the horticultural Iroquois thanked the wild maples for their sap and the wild strawberries for their fruits, as well as the domesticated corn for its grain. In the Southwest the Pueblo people periodically invited deer and buffalo spirits into their villages; however, the dominant concern of Pueblo ritual life was for agricultural bounty. The liturgical year contained numerous masquerades, through which Pueblo dancers in their plazas and *kiva*s (semi-subterranean circular ritual rooms; *see* §II, 2 below) embodied the fertilizing spirits so the crops would grow and community life might persist. Pueblo priests kept track of calendars and watched over the ritual propriety of the life-promoting activities, encouraging their congregations to be of good will during the performances.

Despite attempts through life-cycle and seasonal-cycle rituals to maintain good relations with the spirits, crises arose that compelled individuals and communities to turn to yet another set of ceremonial forms. Rites of crisis included divination, through scapulimancy, scrying, stargazing, hand-trembling and other practices to determine the causes of the disequilibrium; shamanistic conjuring to assess the disposition of the spirits; offerings and sacrifices to propitiate offended deities; and exorcisms to drive away evils. The most prominent rites of crisis, however, focused upon the curing of diseases. The Navajos of the Southwest region relied upon a system of healing ceremonials, all of which were said to owe their origin to the mythic exploits of heroes who received their powers from the spirits. Conducted by trained singers and their helpers, and lasting from one to nine nights, these rituals attempted to identify the patient with the mythic hero, and hence with the spiritual powers that cause and cure illness. The climax of many Navajo 'sings' was the creation of sand paintings depicting the cosmic forces at the heart of disease and health. The singer made the patient sit on the designs, which were then transferred to the patient's body, thereby effecting a cure according to the compelling power of ritual symbolism.

Underlying most Native American ceremonials were two widespread ritual items: the pipe and the sweat lodge. Pipes filled with tobacco and other substances were smoked as a means of communicating with the spiritual realms. It was believed that the spirits enjoyed the smoke, which served as a partially visible, partially invisible prayer; offering smoke was a means of maintaining relations with the cosmic forces. Inside sweat lodges Native Americans sought to purify themselves of their ills and misdeeds, and to enter communion with their deities (*see also* §II, 3 below). Both pipe and sweat lodge—like other kinds of ceremonialism—also had the function of binding religious congregants together in shared acts of piety.

(iii) Development after European contact. Native American religious phenomena were never static; nevertheless, the European invasion of America brought about wide-ranging and long-lasting changes in Native American religious life. The introduction of such animals as the horse and the influx of trade goods altered the environmental relations, economic life and social structure of many Native groups. Without the horse, the Sundance would not have flourished as the ceremonial centrepiece of Plains culture. Without trade, wealth in the Northwest Coast, the extravagant giveaways of the potlatch (gift-giving, perhaps with deliberate destruction of hoarded surpluses for status validation) during the winter ceremonial season would not have developed in their most competitive forms. Various prophetic movements spread across tribal lines, as Native Americans looked eagerly toward gaining the mysterious and fabled products of the West in order to promote local life.

Christian missionary activity, alongside European diseases, ecological devastation, demographic displacement and political domination, undermined native religious complexes in a series of cultural crises. Healers were unable to treat the new epidemics, and the consequence was a crisis of faith in ritual medicine and in the very existence of the aboriginal spirits (ironically, at times when Native American health was at its worst). The annihilation of such traditional food sources as the bison led to starvation and despair, and no religious activities could bring them back. As the Euro-Americans removed Native Americans from their lands, many tribes lost the intimate contact they had had with their ancient sources of existence and suffered from spiritual anomie in strange locales. As US and Canadian authorities gained control, they prevented the free exercise of Native American religions. Sundances, potlatches and other ritual forms were outlawed and practitioners prosecuted. Throughout these crises, Christian missionaries exhorted Native American groups to obliterate their aboriginal beliefs and practices and adopt Christian worship. By criticizing traditional forms of faith, the missionaries weakened the old complexes. By offering a convincing and powerful alternative to the old forms, they persuaded many Native Americans to reorient themselves to Christian cosmology and ritual. Some Native American Christians combined Native and Christian modes; others kept their Native American and Christian lives separate, at least in practice if not in concept. Still other Christian Native Americans over the generations erased most or all aspects of traditional spirituality so that Christianity became for them the traditional religion.

At the same time Christian motifs were used in creating new religious movements. Some of these were virulently anti-Christian in their ideology, for example Pope's Pueblo nativism of 1680, the Delaware Prophet's revival of the 1760s, Tenskwatawa's pan-Native American insurgency of the early 19th century and Smohalla's reactionary movement in the 1870s. Others, like Handsome Lake's Longhouse religion among the Iroquois (begun with his ecstatic vision of 1799) or John and Mary Slocum's Native American Shaker religion (begun among the Coast Salish of the North-west Coast region in 1882), made liberal use of Christianity to adapt Native American groups peacefully to their altered conditions. Some new religions (e.g. the

Paiute Wovoka's Ghost Dance of the 1890s) promised millennial return to the ways of the past. Others, such as the peyote religion that has flourished for well over a century in the USA and Canada, encouraged Native Americans to seek moral transformation and personal redemption through visionary introspection. Despite the continued spread of Christianity and of new movements, aboriginal Native American spirituality still has vitality in many Native American communities.

BIBLIOGRAPHY
P. Beck and A. Walters: *The Sacred* (Tsaile, AZ, 1977)
Å. Hultkrantz: *Belief and Worship in Native North America* (Syracuse, NY, 1981)
——: *The Study of American Indian Religions* (New York, 1983)
C. Vecsey: *Imagine ourselves Richly: Mythic Narratives of North American Indians* (New York, 1988)

CHRISTOPHER VECSEY

4. ICONOGRAPHY. The first efforts to interpret the iconography of Native American art were made by FRANZ BOAS and his students in the late 19th century and early 20th. Since their studies, however, no comprehensive view has been offered. The several reasons for this are the great number of independent ethnic groups, cultures and religious ideologies; the diversity of materials and techniques; and differentiation in male–female specialization, which determined the object to be decorated and the style used. Explicit meaning makes sense only when dealing with the works of a specific tribe; and understanding can only be achieved through detailed analysis of the ethnography.

(i) Early rock art. The earliest widespread art form of imagery was rock art. The oldest styles from *c.* 8000 BC were probably simple circular grooves and small pits or holes. Curvilinear abstract styles developed later. In the Woodland region few early petroglyphs include human figures, but in the eastern Subarctic rock paintings in red and petroglyphs include abstract and representational designs in equal numbers. Many of those found on lake shores were obviously made by early Algonquians, whose historic descendants continued to use the same imagery on other media.

Polychrome rock painting, developed alongside simpler variants, was exclusive to the Southwest and California (*see also* §IV, 1(iii) below). The earliest example is the Pecos River style of southern Texas (before *c.* AD 600), with its monumental anthropomorphic figures carrying spear-throwers. The closest iconographic similarities are found more than 1000 km away and several hundred years later in the Barrier Canyon style associated with the Fremont culture of Utah (*see* GREAT GALLERY, BARRIER CANYON). In the Southwest, the Jornada style (*c.* AD 1000) of the Mogollon culture (*c.* AD 200–*c.* 1350) included a repertory of horned masks, rectilinear human figures and 'kachina blankets' in a non-representational style similar to that used on Mimbres pottery (*see* §V, 1(i) below). After *c.* 1300 the rock art of the Rio Grande Pueblo area was influenced by the Jornada style but shows more rounded forms, and some masks are identifiable with those of historic *kachinas* (masked beings who bring rain and protection; *see also* §III, 4 below). The polychrome rock paintings of the Santa Barbara style of (18th and 19th centuries) of the California Chumash includes elaborate curvilinear and angular elements in abstract or highly conventionalized anthropomorphic and zoomorphic designs. Recent archaeoastronomical studies have postulated solar and other astronomical significance for some of the designs. Similarly, human and animal imagery, in red or black paint or incised, on rock faces in the Great Plains shows a close relationship with later 19th-century Plains pictographic art on leather, canvas and paper (see §IV, 1(iv) and 2 below).

(ii) Northwest Coast. The iconography of this region forms a distinct tradition. One motif is known as 'split representation', in which a face is formed by two confronting beings in profile. Another image results from the atomizing or dismembering of several figurative elements, or 'rearrangement of anatomical parts'. A third motif, the 'X-ray image', portrays the essential but unseen internal structure of an animal or being. All of these motifs may represent manifestations of a shamanic world view. They appear equally in sacred and secular art and have a metaphoric quality that alludes to the ritual process of exchange in both sacred and secular spheres.

(iii) Southwest. In this region it is the prehistoric Mimbres painting tradition (*c.* AD 1000–*c.* 1200) that has most influenced later Pueblo art. During its development the Mimbres style, a branch of the greater Mogollon cultural tradition of southern New Mexico and north-west Mexico, borrowed heavily from contemporary neighbouring cultures, including Hohokam in eastern Arizona and Anasazi in northern Arizona–New Mexico and southern Utah–Colorado. The Classic Mimbres style on pottery comprised two distinct but interrelated types of subject-matter: sophisticated, technically exacting geometric forms; and naive but realistic representations of people, mammals, birds, reptiles, amphibians, fishes, insects and other invertebrates, various composite beings and, more rarely, plants and artefacts. Most unidentifiable animal subjects have features of two or more species, suggesting that the paintings were deliberately unnatural. While some scholars attribute Mimbres figurative painting to Mesoamerican influence (especially to Aztec and Maya religious beliefs; *see* MESOAMERICA, PRE-COLUMBIAN, §I, 4(i)), others insist that the meanings of the representations are directly related to indigenous Pueblo Zuni myths, suggesting continuity between archaeological past and ethnographic present. In the late 14th century Pueblo pottery decoration gradually changed to a flamboyant polychrome style, but still often included birds, animals and people. Many of the figures resemble *kachinas*. During the 17th century European and Mexican shapes and designs were incorporated into Pueblo pottery, and in the 1880s and 1890s new and old shapes and designs were combined to create what may be termed a tourist or commercial style.

Navajo dry-painting or 'sandpainting' (with various ground minerals) represents a second Southwest iconographic tradition (*see also* §IV, 1(iii) below). The Navajo were relative late-comers to the region (from *c.* 1500 or perhaps a century earlier) and supposedly adopted the practice from the Pueblo peoples. Nevertheless, they elaborated it into a flamboyant style and continue to use it, accompanied by recitations and songs, as a central part of their curing ceremonies. The composition of dry-paintings is normally centrifugal and radial, intended to

create and maintain harmony with the cosmos. The painting is usually enclosed in a frame, with carefully controlled lines isolating the colour fields. Subject-matter is highly stylized and may include plants, animals, astral bodies and supernatural beings.

(iv) Plains. The earliest imagery came from rock art (*see* §(i) above). Human and animal figures were of central importance. Vision-inspired figurative painting is one of the oldest Plains art forms. Painted tepees were reported by Spanish explorers in the mid-16th century, and the tepee-painting tradition lasted until the second half of the 19th century among the Kiowa, Cheyenne and Lakota; and the Blackfeet continue to use painted tepees on ceremonial occasions. Usually, the central section of the tepee was decorated with the visionary scenes (figures of animals and/or spiritual beings), while paintings on the top and bottom referred to the Upperworld and the Lowerworld. Abstract forms (circles, crescents, Maltese crosses) were also used with symbolic meanings, mainly to represent astronomical entities.

Painted designs on rawhide shields were also dictated by individual visions and have specific characteristics that can be deciphered in terms of tribal cosmologies. For example, the horned beings (black and red) on a Cheyenne shield (Indianapolis, IN, Eiteljorg Mus. Amer. Ind. & W. A.; *see* §XIII and fig. 64 below) are certainly personifications of Thunder and Hail, respectively, while the four lizards represent the cardinal directions. Pale-green horned and winged forms on another shield depict green darner dragonflies (*c.* 1870; Prague, Náprstek Mus. Asian, Afr. & Amer. Cult., 44.603).

Geometric motifs were prominent in quill- and bead-embroidery, including stepped triangles, crosses, hourglass motifs, parallel lines and circles. On bison robes and on garments associated with war deeds or social status such designs could have highly symbolic meanings. The polychrome painting tradition of geometric motifs (rectangles, triangles, circles and dots) and of floral designs is known as a female style, and it seems to indicate tribal and band affiliation. The male style is pictographic: the Lakota and Kiowa Native Americans had a tradition of calendric painting or 'winter counts', in which each year was designated with an important event and was executed in a highly stylized manner; and the warriors of most Plains groups depicted war honours on the outsides of leather and canvas tepees, on interior dew cloths (leather or canvas lining inside a lodge to block draughts and dew) and on leather robes. These traditions were transferred to other media introduced by Euro-Americans during the second half of the 19th century (*see* §IV, 2 below). During the 1880s and 1890s the Peyote cult introduced new iconographic elements, including the water turkey, scissor-tailed flycatcher, macaw and some Christian motifs. The Ghost Dance movement of the same time period revitalized former symbols and designs, combining them in new iconographic contexts.

(v) Woodlands. The prehistoric Southern Cult, from *c.* AD 1000 to *c.* 1700, was focused on the three principal centres of SPIRO MOUNDS, Moundville and ETOWAH and their subsidiary sites. A visual unity in their art suggests a shared iconography among the divergent regional styles.

The earlier Adena–Hopewell cultural complex (*c.* 500 BC–*c.* AD 700) may have provided the gestation of the cult in several, generalized common images (birds, snakes and felines and composite forms of these; and human–animal relationships, reflecting such shamanistic phenomena as transformation and personification), which seem to have been crucial in shell-engraving. Projecting backwards from historical ethnographic examples, some of the most frequent figures of Southern Cult shellwork, such as the Birdman, or mythic feline, may be early examples of the Thunderbird, or Underwater Panther, suggesting mythic continuity between the archaeological past and the ethnographic present. Both beings were represented as anthropomorphic forms that stress animal attributes and as humans dressed in costumes to represent a thunderbird or panther.

To the north, in Great Lakes Native American cosmology, the Thunderbird and Underwater Panther represent the dominant spirits of the Upperworld and the Lowerworld respectively. Their images were used to decorate the two sides of twined bags to establish symbolic identity with the two worlds. Between the surfaces power objects or medicines were believed to affect the earth itself. In contrast to the uninterrupted connection of Southeast imagery, however, after contact with Europeans in the 17th century, continuity was broken by the introduction of such new materials as painted cotton thread and glass beads, which began to be used to decorate bags with geometric motifs (*see also* §IX, 7 below): hour-glass forms were used beside Thunderbirds and zigzag, or castellated lines beside Underwater Panthers. In the 19th century geometric, non-representational forms gradually replaced the Thunderbird and Underwater Panther images altogether.

BIBLIOGRAPHY

J. M. Vastokas and R. K. Vastokas: *Sacred Art of the Algonkians* (Peterborough, 1973)
J. Goldman: *Mouth of Heaven: An Introduction to Kwakiutl Religious Thought* (New York, 1975)
I Wear the Morning Star: An Exhibition of American Indian Ghost Dance Objects (exh. cat., Minneapolis, MN, Inst. A., 1976)
J. J. Brody: *Mimbres Painted Pottery* (Santa Fe, 1977)
E. M. Maurer: *The Native American Heritage: A Survey of North American Indian Art* (Chicago, 1977)
Sacred Circles: Two Thousand Years of North American Indian Art (exh. cat. by R. T. Coe, London, Hayward Gal.; Kansas City, MO, W. Rockhill Nelson Gal.; 1977)
P. Phillips and J. A. Brown: *Pre-Columbian Shell Engravings from the Craig Mound at Spiro, Oklahoma* (Cambridge, MA, 1978, 2/1984)
T. J. Brasser: 'The Pedigree of the Hugging Bear Tipi in the Blackfoot Camp', *Amer. Ind. A.*, v/1 (1979), pp. 32–9
Z. P. Matthews and A. Jonaitis, eds: *Native North American Art History* (Palo Alto, 1982)
R. A. Williamson: *Living the Sky: The Cosmos of the American Indian* (Norman, 1984)
L. A. Wilson: 'Southern Cult Images of Composite Human and Animal Figures', *Amer. Ind. A.*, xi/1 (1985), pp. 46–57
R. B. Phillips: 'Dreams and Designs: Iconographic Problems in Great Lakes Twined Bags', *Bull. Detroit Inst. A.*, lxii/1 (1986), pp. 27–37
E. L. Wade, ed.: *The Arts of the North American Indian: Native Traditions in Evolution* (New York, 1986)
A. Jonaitis: *Art of the Northern Tlingit* (Seattle and London, 1986)
J. M. Vastokas: 'Native Art as Art History: Meaning and Time from Unwritten Sources', *J. Can. Stud.*, xxi/4 (1987), pp. 7–36
N. L. Fagin: 'The James Mooney Collection of Cheyenne Tipi Models at Field Museum of Natural History', *Plains Anthropologist*, xxxiii/120 (1988), pp. 261–78

IMRE NAGY

5. CONCEPT OF ART. In Native American cultures the visual arts were essential expressions of social and sacred systems, and concepts of beauty were an important and integral element of people's lives. Given this importance and the need for accurate communication, people developed commonly held ideals concerning the standards of beauty they valued in works of art. These standards determined regional and tribal styles of clothing, ceramics, sculpture, painting and all other utilitarian and specialized modes of decoration and visual representation. Since there were no schools or academies of art, technical expertise and aesthetic values were passed down from one generation to another. The aesthetics of Native American societies were determined by the physical characteristics of a work of art as well as by its meaning and the manner in which it was created. Native Americans were sensitive to such factors as colour, shape, proportion, symmetry, construction and finish as basic aesthetic elements that constituted the beauty of a work of art. Recognizable styles of art developed, based on commonly held conventions or rules about the use of colour, form and balance; all artists in a given group had to use a common group of visual elements in their work. In this type of system success depends on an individual's ability to create inventive solutions to the problems of integrating a two-dimensional design system to three-dimensional forms. In their study of Northwest Coast carving, Holm and Reid (1976) demonstrated how the success of an individual work of art closely depends on the artist's ability to manipulate the guiding aesthetic conventions while also expressing the beauty of their spiritual associations.

Native American artists throughout North America used colour to create visual effects and as a powerful reference to the vital natural forces that provided the basic structure of their lives. Among the Plains groups, for example, colours had some generally held references, such as yellow for the sun, blue for sky or water and red for the earth. As these essential elements of nature were imbued with great spiritual power, their associated colours also carried a high charge of religious importance that became part of their overall aesthetic effect. Through the prehistoric and early historic periods the sources of colour were natural pigments made from clays, crushed minerals and a great variety of plants. The Plains groups applied them to finely finished hide garments, creating fields of rich, soft colour; the pleasing visual effect this produced implied by extension a meaningful reference to powerful sacred forces. Tones of rich terracotta red were also used throughout North America for the decoration of objects and adornment of the body, both for aesthetic and for sacred reasons. With the introduction of industrially produced pigments and materials from Europe, the soft natural colours were gradually superseded by brighter colours available from the traders. However, tribal stylistic preferences and natural associative symbolism remained important factors in indigenous art. Colour was also used by Plains groups as a visual reference for the cardinal directions, which were considered potent sacred forces. Unlike the references to the sun or the earth, colour associations with directions often varied from tribe to tribe.

The proportions, balance and symmetry of designs also had many variations in different parts of the continent.

The vital energy expressed by powerful asymmetrical designs and arrangements of colour were favoured as a positive aesthetic in the beadwork of the Delaware in the eastern Woodlands region and of the Kiowa in the southern Plains region. Asymmetry still characterizes the designs of the Hopi potters of Arizona, who have used it since at least the Sikyatki style of the 17th century (see §V below). Other peoples, such as the Menominee of the Great Lakes region or the Lakota of the Plains region, favoured symmetrical elements that give a sense of solid balance to their designs in quills, beads, weaving and painting.

The construction and finish of a work of art were also integral elements of its aesthetic success. All Native American peoples valued fine workmanship, as reflected in the equivalent terms for artist in their various languages, which generally mean one who has skill, talent and understanding in work (see §6 below). Ruth Bunzel reported that among Hopi potters, for example, concerns for the technical skill in creating an object ranked even higher in their evaluation of a work of art than the aesthetics of its decoration. For the Hopi, the ceramic's visual attraction was negated if it were made by a poor technique.

6. STATUS OF ART AND ROLE OF THE ARTIST. In Native American cultures of all periods the creative arts were an integral and admired part of life because they were associated with primary social and sacred systems (see §5 above). Works of art, however, were not separated from their basic cultural functions or considered as statements of individual self-expression. The arts were a basic form of social communication, used to indicate status or rank, membership in group associations and personal achievements. In the south-east Woodlands during the Mississippian period (c. AD 700–c. 1700; see §2(i) above) individuals of high status associated with large communities were identified by special clothing and ornaments and by the high-quality ceramics, sculptures, elaborately engraved shells and embossed copper objects placed in their burials (see TOMB, §VI, 1). In the fertile regions of the Northwest Coast the highly stratified social structure was symbolically expressed by a large and diverse range of artistic creations. These included carved, painted and woven representations of heraldic animals associated with clans and families, as well as richly adorned objects that conveyed the rank and position of the bearer. Among the tribal groups of the Plains region, association with important male warrior societies was indicated by the structure and ornamentation of special garments and objects used by members. These same individuals expressed their personal achievements as courageous warriors with beautifully drawn representations of their acts of bravery and daring applied to such articles of clothing as robes or shirts as well as to tepee covers and liners.

Works of art were sometimes accumulated and distributed as status objects integral to the bonding of social groups. The most extreme example of this tradition was the potlatch gift exchange of the Northwest Coast, in which great quantities of works of art, other valuable objects and food were given away, or sometimes deliberately destroyed, as part of an intricate system of social support and interrelationship. The tradition of exchanging works of art as gifts is still an important element of Native American life, and at times of communal interaction the display of fine objects and clothing remains a valued way for both men and women to demonstrate their skills and achievements. This characteristic was noted by 18th- and 19th-century European observers of the peoples of the Woodlands and Plains regions and was developed into a major element of cultural identity during the reservation period, a tradition that continues to the present day. In an allied sense, art objects in Native American society have also been valued and venerated for their age and the collective force of ancestral traditions that are associated with them. For example, Pueblo peoples in the Southwest show deep respect towards older ceramics and other objects used in ritual ceremonies.

Works of art were also highly valued in the extensive system of intertribal and inter-regional trade that existed from ancient times. Archaeological evidence in the Southwest indicates that fine ceramics were an important part of a trade system extending south into Mexico and west to the California coast (see §V, 1(i) below). Fine-quality ceramics and woven textiles are still one of the mainstays of the Pueblo commercial system, whose market since the late 19th century has been mainly established in the non-Native American world (see §XV below). This commercial development of works of art for the non-Native American market has been common to many tribal peoples living in all areas of the USA.

In traditional Native American cultures every aspect of the peoples' lives was animated by spiritual power. Human activity was also deemed important to the natural order, and proper social and ritual behaviour was necessary to maintain the course and harmony of the world (see §3

9. Shield, painted rawhide, diam. 533 mm, made by Crow artist Humped Wolf, 19th century (Minneapolis, MN, Minneapolis Institute of Arts)

above). Works of art were important carriers of spiritual power, prime examples being masks, notably the masks created for rituals of healing and myth of the False Face Medicine societies found among the Iroquois nations of the north-east Woodlands or those of the *kachina* dancers of the Hopi in the Southwest, whose elaborate yearly performances mark the cycle of nature (*see also* §III, 4 and 6 below). Forces of spiritual power in all indigenous North American cultures have also been represented by sculpture, painting, engraved petroglyphs and other media.

In the Great Lakes the Midewiwin Grand Medicine Society utilized a variety of works of art as elements of their ritual ceremonies. Spiritual forces called *manitos* were represented by animals and anthropomorphic figures made in a variety of media by male and female artists. Art as an expression of sacred power was also a vital element of Plains life. The great communal ceremonies of natural renewal called the Sundance used effigies and symbolically decorated objects to mark the essential elements of the ritual. This tradition is also found in the paraphernalia of the Crow Tobacco Society and in the elaborately painted clothing of the Ghost Dance societies. The Plains warrior also used art to represent the sacred powers that he hoped to attract in personal spirit quests (*see also* §I, 3 above). Revealed in dreams and visions, these images were painted on leather shields (see fig. 9), which were carried into battle more as elements of magical than physical protection.

Most members of traditional Native American societies were able to produce the essential goods and materials of everyday life; art was based on these utilitarian models but distinguished from them by quality and symbolic decoration. People with special skills at making things were admired for their creative talent, often being asked to produce objects for ritual and sacred purposes. On the Plains, women who combined great skill in quill and bead decoration with exemplary personal conduct were asked to join a special group, whose honour it was to produce decorated clothing and containers for priests and ritual objects.

Some Native American groups developed a class of professional artists whose special talents and skills were necessary to fulfil commercial demands as well as the needs of elaborate social and religious rituals. In the Southwest Pueblos, professionally produced ceramics have been traded since *c.* AD 1000 (*see* §V, 1(i) below). Perhaps the outstanding example of the professional artist was found among North-west Coast peoples, whose elaborate social and ritual lives depended on the visual arts.

Another important role of the artist in Native American cultures was established by their association with shamanic healing ceremonies (*see* §3(ii) above). Shamans from the cultures of the Great Lakes to the Northwest Coast regions and from the Arctic Eskimo culture created powerful works of art depicting their spirit allies. By objectifying the supernatural, these healer–artists made a great variety of masks, sculptures and paintings that still have the power to move the beholder both aesthetically and emotionally. Another extraordinary example of the artistic genius of the healer–artist can still be found in traditional Navajo culture, where the sacred singers who lead the curing ceremonies create sand paintings of great beauty and complexity that bring people back into natural harmony with themselves and the world.

BIBLIOGRAPHY

R. L. Bunzel: *The Pueblo Potter: A Study of the Creative Imagination in Primitive Art*, Columbia University Contributions to Anthropology, viii (New York, 1929)

B. Holm and B. Reid: *Indian Art of the Northwest Coast: A Dialogue on Craftsmanship and Aesthetics* (Houston, 1976)

E. M. Maurer: 'Determining Quality in Native American Art', *The Arts of the North American Indian*, ed. E. L. Wade (New York, 1986)

E. L. Wade, ed.: *The Arts of the North American Indian* (New York, 1986)

EVAN M. MAURER

II. Dwellings and other structures.

North American dwellings took numerous forms, depending on environmental, social and other factors. They range from permanent buildings made of stone and adobe to temporary or portable structures, such as the tepee. This article also discusses the use of such buildings and other structures for ceremonial, funerary, storage and other purposes.

1. Northwest Coast. 2. Southwest. 3. Plains. 4. Woodlands.

1. NORTHWEST COAST.

(i) Introduction. (ii) House types.

(i) Introduction. In a region characterized by temperate maritime climate, rich marine resources and dense rain-forests, Northwest Coast peoples developed a highly skilled woodworking technology, capable of producing seagoing dugout canoes and great plank houses. The construction of their dwellings was influenced by their cultural emphasis on the acquisition and display of wealth; their division of society into nobles, commoners and slaves; and their spectacular ceremonies and highly developed art. The plank house was the most distinctive feature of Northwest Coast material culture and a prerequisite to several other basic features—economic, social and aesthetic. It was not only a dwelling—its form and functions relating to the social group that occupied it—but also, in a wet climate, a food-processing and storage plant. Further, the house served as a stage for public ceremonies and as a medium for the display of symbols of privilege and power. The plank house and its complement the canoe, required by the yearly round of movements to and from fishing, hunting and gathering sites, were both important integral elements of Northwest Coast culture.

Throughout most of the area the material commonly used was western red cedar (*Thuja plicata*). This tree grows to great size, and its wood is easily split, light and durable. Beyond the range of red cedar to the north, spruce and hemlock were used, and to the south redwood. When Europeans first arrived in the late 18th century, Northwest Coast peoples already had some iron, but most of their woodworking tools were of stone, bone, antler and shell. With these they produced the huge planks that determined the rectangular shape of the house. The Northwest Coast house consisted of a framework of posts and beams, a roof and walls of planks, and, inside, a bed platform extending around the walls, with food-drying racks suspended from the beams. It was usually occupied by several families, each with its own space.

(ii) House types. Houses were built in several regional types, varying in the form of the roof, attachment of wall planks, excavation of the floor, number of hearths and other features. In the early 19th century gable (two-pitched) roofs were usual everywhere along the coast except for a region of shed (single-pitched) roofs in southern British Columbia and northern Washington state. In the north, wall planks were fitted into an outer frame. In a central region, including the southern part of the northern gable-roof region and shed-roof region, wall planks were slung horizontally, separate from the frame holding the roof, and easily removed. And in the southern region of gable-roof houses, wall planks were set vertically into the ground and helped to support the roof. Removing planks from the winter house for use at summer sites was practised widely but most easily done in the central region. Roof form and wall attachment thus define four major house types: a northern gable-roof house with fitted wall planks; a central gable-roof house with loose wall planks; a shed-roof with loose wall planks; and a southern gable-roof house with sunken wall planks. Each type coincides with a different form of social organization and cultural practices.

Other house types of restricted distribution include the Bella Coola house with a huge false front, the Puget Sound gambrel- (or mansard-) roof house with a nearly flat central roof and four steeper slopes extending away from it and the north-western California rich man's house with a three-pitch roof—a gable roof with the peak truncated at an angle. By the late 19th century the traditional hand-hewn planks and cedar-withe ropes were replaced nearly everywhere by milled boards and nails. For a time, the internal plan remained the same, but in a few decades the old-style houses were abandoned for single-family frame houses.

(a) Northern gable-roof. Used by the Tlingit, Haida, Tsimshian, Haisla and Heiltsuk, this type was nearly square in plan, 10–18 m on each side. A gable end faced the shore, with the entrance in the centre. The interior of a chief's house was often excavated, with two or more levels of planked floors. There was a single central hearth on the lowest level and a single permanent smoke-hole in the peak of the roof above it. Strips of bark weighted by stones often substituted for roof planks. At some sites, as along rivers with steep banks and seasonal flooding, houses were built with their rear ends set into the hillside and their fronts supported by pilings or cribworks of logs.

The most common subtype, the two-beam version, had a central framework of four posts and two long beams to support crossbeams and a single or double ridge-pole; and an outer framework of four corner posts, often with posts at the centre of each side as well, all connected by plates and sills. The wall planks were fitted either horizontally or vertically into slots in the outer frame. The front and rear gable plates or bargeboards rose to the peak of the roof. The roof was supported at the peak by the central frame and bargeboards, and at the eaves by the corner posts and side plates. In Tlingit and Tsimshian houses the rear of the house, opposite the door, was often screened off as the living compartment of the house chief, and sometimes his younger brothers had screened rooms at the sides.

A late Southern Haida subtype, the six-beam version (see fig. 10), had no central frame. Posts at the four corners, a pair at the centre of the front and another pair at the centre of the rear were connected by plates and sills. The gable plates supported six long beams, which supported the roof and projected beyond the roof at the front and rear. The plates and sills were carefully mortised into the posts, and the wall planks were fitted vertically into slots in the plates and sills, the whole forming a strong yet open structure. Usually a tall carved pole with a circular entrance stood in the centre of the front, flanked by the posts holding the plates, and a carved post was installed inside between the pair of posts at the centre of the rear wall.

The northern household might consist of the house head, his younger brothers, his sisters' grown sons, the wives and minor children of these men and his slaves. The head's family occupied the upper level at the rear, his brothers the sides and lower-ranking persons the lower level by the fire. This household, with its hierarchical structure and single hearth, was a close-knit social group, its adult free males being members of the same matrilineal line. For ceremonial events, the excavated house of a chief served as an amphitheatre, with guests and hosts seated according to lineage membership and rank.

The house was decorated with the crests of the lineage—paintings and carvings representing animals or other beings encountered by ancestors (see §§III, 2 and IV, 1(i) below). The front of a Tlingit or Tsimshian house was often painted, and the interior posts were carved. If a wooden screen separated the chief's compartment, it was painted

10. Northwest Coast, Haida six-beam house (Western-style doorway added), 'house where people always want to go', Haina village, Queen Charlotte Islands; photograph by R. Maynard, 1888 (Victoria, BC, Provincial Museum)

or carved. Haida house fronts were less often painted, a frontal pole serving to display the crests instead. In the six-beam house, carving was generally confined to the frontal pole and rear post. Separate mortuary poles and memorial poles ('totem poles') might be erected in front of the house.

(b) Central gable-roof. This type was used by the Kwakiutl, Northern and Central Nootkans and some Northern Coast Salish. Its central framework consisted either of four posts supporting two long beams that served as a double ridge-pole, or of three posts—two at the front topped with a lintel and one at the rear—supporting a single ridge-pole. A set of smaller posts on each side supported smaller beams holding the eaves. The walls consisted of planks tied horizontally, overlapping, between pairs of vertical poles; they were quite separate from the frame, which served only to support the roof. The floor was usually not excavated. There were usually several hearths with smoke-holes made by shifting the roof planks above them.

In the late 18th century houses of this type were often much longer than wide, stood parallel to the shore and had nearly flat roofs. By the late 19th century, Kwakiutl houses were built more like Northern houses—nearly square, with the gable end facing the shore, a steeper roof, the walls more solidly attached and a projecting deck.

The household consisted of permanent members—the families of the house head, his brothers and others holding positions in his cognatic kin group, and temporary members, such as the families of relatives without positions, who might move on if the fortunes of the house declined. In the Nootkan house the permanent families lived in the corners, which were ranked in value, while the temporary residents occupied spaces between. House posts were decorated with carvings and façades with paintings representing animals or other beings standing in a special relationship to the kin group, as ancestors or their non-human protectors. By the mid-19th century the Kwakiutl were also erecting separate memorial poles.

(c) Shed-roof. This type was used by most of the Coast Salish of the Strait of Georgia–Puget Sound region and by the Nitinaht, Makah and Quileute on the outer coast. It was generally oblong and built parallel to the shore. Pairs of posts were set in the ground in two rows of unequal height. Usually each pair of posts held a crossbeam, and these supported stringers, which supported the roof planks, laid on parallel to the crossbeams and often interlocking like tiles. The walls, floor and hearths were as in the central gable-roof house. Gaps in the wall planks served as doors where needed. Family sections were separated by waist-high plank partitions. In winter the walls were lined with mats and family sections wholly enclosed with mats. Some Coast Salish shed-roof houses were up to 20 m wide and 200 m long. These longer structures were divided by plank partitions into segments and might be better identified as rows of houses sharing common walls.

The Coast Salish household consisted of families related through either males or females. Status differences among them were reflected only in the larger section needed by a wealthy man for his several wives and slaves. The families cooperated in social and ceremonial activities, but each family had its own stores and hearth and might separate seasonally from the others, taking its own planks from the house frame, laying them across a pair of canoes to raft its equipment to a summer camp and cover another house frame there. A family might also leave permanently, taking its planks to another house in another village. The shed-roof house could be adapted to such shifts by shortening or lengthening it through the subtraction or addition of pairs of posts and beams. For a summer potlatch (the display of inherited privileges and the payment of witnesses who serve to validate the status and ownership of the hosts, later, by the end of the 19th century, perhaps with deliberate destruction of hoarded surpluses for status validation), the nearly flat roof served as a stage, from which the hosts distributed wealth. For a winter spirit dance, the fires of the individual families were consolidated as a central fire under a new smoke-hole. Wealthy men had their house posts carved or painted to show ancestors grasping ritual possessions (especially in the Georgia Strait region) or to symbolize their guardian spirits (especially in the Puget Sound region), and a few had carved entrance posts and painted walls.

(d) Southern gable-roof. Used by the Quinault and other Coast Salish of south-western Washington, by the Chinookan tribes of the lower Columbia River and by the tribes of the Oregon Coast and of north-western California, this type commonly had a floor excavated to a depth approaching the height of the walls. The wall planks were set vertically into the ground, the ridge-pole was supported by central posts, and the roof planks were laid parallel to the ridge-pole and held in place by poles running from ridge-pole to eaves. Some houses built by the Chinookans were over 100 m long, but most southern houses were relatively small. The longer houses were built parallel to the shore and had multiple hearths. The household was composed of the families of men related through the male line, led by a wealthy headman. In the Lower Columbia River region, carvings representing guardian spirits (two surviving examples in New York, Amer. Mus. Nat. Hist.) were executed on house posts and on boards set up before the beds of shamans. A late 18th-century explorer reported doorways made to represent huge mouths. Decorated houses are not reported far south of the Columbia River.

BIBLIOGRAPHY

F. Boas: 'The Houses of the Kwakiutl Indians, British Columbia', *Proceedings of the United States National Museum for 1888* (Washington, DC, 1888), pp. 187–213

L. Shotridge and F. Shotridge: 'Chilkat Houses: House Posts and Screens and their Heraldry', *Mus. J.*, v (1913), pp. 81–99

T. T. Waterman and R. Greiner: *Indian Houses of Puget Sound*, Indian Notes and Monographs, Museum of the American Indian (New York, 1921)

P. Drucker: 'The Northern and Central Nootkan Tribes', *Bureau Amer. Ethnol. Bull.*, cxliv (1951) [whole issue]

——: *Indians of the North-west Coast* (New York, 1955)

J. M. Vastokas: *Architecture of the North-west Coast Indians of America* (diss., New York, Columbia U., 1966)

M. B. Blackman: *'Nei:wins*, the "Monster" House of Chief *Wi:ha*: An Exercise in Ethnohistorical, Archaeological and Ethnological Reasoning', *Syesis*, v (1972), pp. 211–25

J. Smyly and C. Smyly: *Those Born at Koona: The Totem Poles of the Haida Village Skedans, Queen Charlotte Islands* (Saanichton, BC, 1973/*R* as *The Totem Poles of Skedans*, Seattle, 1974)

J. E. Mauger: *Shed Roof Houses at the Ozette Archaeological Site: A Protohistoric Architectural System* (diss., Washington State U., 1978)

G. F. MacDonald: *Haida Monumental Art: Villages of the Queen Charlotte Islands* (Vancouver, 1983)

——: *Ninstints: Haida World Heritage Site*, U. BC Museum of Anthropology Museum Note, xii (Vancouver, 1983)

H. Stewart: *Cedar: Tree of Life to the Northwest Coast Indians* (Vancouver, 1984)

W. Suttles, ed.: 'North-west Coast', *Hb. N. Amer. Ind.*, vii (1990)

W. Suttles: 'The Shed-roof House', *A Time of Gathering: Native Heritage of Washington State*, ed. R. Wright (Seattle, 1993) pp. 32–45

WAYNE SUTTLES

2. SOUTHWEST. Indigenous architecture appeared early in the Southwest culture area. While the region has topographical variety, it is marked by an overall climatic aridity. When the indigenous peoples became sedentary agriculturalists (*see* §I, 2(i) above), they built permanent houses for residential purposes. These massed, communal buildings were later termed 'Pueblos' ('towns') by the first Spanish explorers. The principles by which they were constructed, including their environmentally suitable relationship to the landscape and passive solar heating properties, are an enduring architectural legacy.

(i) Before European contact. (ii) European influence and traditional forms up to World War II. (iii) Post-war developments.

(i) Before European contact. The prehistoric Southwest was home to three dominant cultural groups: the Mogollon of south-western New Mexico and central Arizona, the Hohokam of central Arizona and the Anasazi of the Colorado Plateau and along the Rio Grande and its tributaries. The first form of residential structure, the pithouse, was common to the Mogollon and Anasazi cultures. The earliest pithouses were Mogollon and date before *c.* AD 100. Pithouses were excavated into the ground, from 0.60 to 1.8 m in depth, with a circular, rectangular or ovoid floor-plan. Walls were made with a framework of brush and twigs and covered with mud. Most pithouses had one or more centre posts to support the roof, and beams were laid over the posts to carry the earth-covered roof elements. The interior was a single room with a fire pit, deflector slabs and, particularly in Anasazi construction, a *sipapu*, a small ceremonial hole that represented the passageway from the underworld. Entry to the dwelling was by the smoke-hole, although some pithouses were built with an enclosed vestibule or passageway, a device that was later modified into a ventilator shaft *c.* AD 450. Interior earthen walls were lined with upright stone slabs or had cribbed-log braces. The pithouse form contained useful thermal properties and gradually became standardized in most areas. By *c.* AD 700–*c.* 850, however, building emphasis had shifted to above-ground, contiguously walled, free-standing communal dwelling units, sited in the open or against cliff walls.

Mogollon mountain and plateau settlements contained from five to fifty semi-subterranean structures and used masonry walls for fortification. As these villages grew, they were apparently influenced by Anasazi and Mesoamerican building practices: by *c.* AD 1000 rooms were joined, and walls employed cobbles in mud mortar and became multi-storey. Architectural developments from the south may have been brought to the Mogollon through their active commercial trade ties with Pacquimé, on the Casas Grandes site near Chihuahua, Mexico, where a sophisticated trading city flourished from *c.* AD 1060–*c.* 1340. Mogollon society declined and eventually disappeared by *c.* AD 1450.

The Hohokam of the desert valleys of central Arizona employed extensive canal irrigation and interacted with neighbouring Sinagua, Salado and Anasazi groups. Sonoran influence can be seen in Arizona in the settlement patterns and construction of Casa Grande (*c.* AD 1350–*c.* 1450) and SNAKETOWN, the latter site occupied continuously for nearly 700 years (*c.* AD 300–*c.* 1000). Hohokam houses were not pithouses but had excavated floors with wattle-and-daub on framework walls. As Hohokam settlements grew, they acquired several features that point to Mesoamerican origins: enclosed compounds, platform mounds and ritual ballcourts.

However, it was the Anasazi who produced the most elaborate and enduring native architecture of the region. Their settlements were permanent unit pueblos comprising surface-built rooms made of stone and adobe, forming adjoining cubicles with shared walls. The masonry surface rooms had a minimal number of windows or doors and were usually arranged around an irregular plaza area, with a ceremonial chamber known as a KIVA and a rubbish mound. Such pueblos rose from one to four storeys in height, were often terraced with setbacks (recessed chambers or rooms) and varied in size. Entrance into individual dwellings was by ladder, and the sturdily built roofs served as a main living area.

From *c.* AD 1100 to *c.* 1300 the Anasazi created monumental house-blocks and used the vestigial pithouse form for their *kiva*s. The most notable remnants of this development are the cliff dwellings of MESA VERDE and the 12 'Great House' communities at CHACO CANYON. The pueblos at Chaco Canyon show varying forms of finely fitted masonry technique in evolution. Core masonry techniques, using rubble hearting with a veneer of dressed stones to provide smooth facing, can be seen in the Great Houses and Great *Kiva*s. One of the Great Houses, Pueblo Bonito, had a D-shaped plan and was constructed using cored, veneered masonry with interlocking stone. The walls were raised to four storeys at the rear. Occupying two acres by *c.* AD 1070, Pueblo Bonito contained 800 rooms, 37 *kiva*s and a plaza area with two Great *Kiva*s. Refined stone masonry was also employed at such large fortified sites as Mesa Verde, Aztec Pueblo and Betatakin. Circular and square masonry towers, such as those at Hovenweep National Monument, may have been constructed for the same defensive or ritual purposes that moved the Anasazi to site their buildings on cliff ledges.

One of the most important Anasazi contributions to indigenous architecture was the transformation of the pithouse form into the *kiva* chamber. This semi-subterranean room has survived into modern times and is used for sacred or social purposes by the Pueblo Native Americans. Interiors were lined with adobe benches and sometimes had wall paintings. Elements from the *kiva*'s early origins retain symbolic functions, as in the use of the fire pit and *sipapu*.

Anasazi Great Houses and large population sites were abandoned by the late 13th century, and its peoples, who may be the ancestors of the various Pueblo groups, began a period of eastward migration to the area of the present-day pueblos. Residential mobility is evident through all phases of Anasazi culture, but the reasons for this final abandonment are not fully known. This period has been called a 'regressive' phase, largely because of the retreat from building on a large scale. The new communities reflect a transitional approach to pueblo construction; buildings were single-storey or irregularly shaped house-blocks, partly enclosing a courtyard or plaza and opening to the south. Each community usually had at least one *kiva*; a rectangular shape was employed in the western pueblos, while the eastern settlements used circular *kivas*.

(ii) European influence and traditional forms up to World War II. The pueblos encountered by Spanish conquistadors upon their arrival in the Southwest in the mid-16th century were the result of the transitional 'regressive' phase. The newcomers found small communal adobe and sandstone towns, built in clusters with connecting rooftop and interior passageways. The Pueblo Native American groups used their living spaces efficiently, utilizing areas for water and grain storage, and other areas for work, social and ceremonial activities. Acoma and Old Oraibi Pueblos vie for the title of 'oldest continually occupied town' in the USA.

For about the next 140 years, Pueblo Native American architecture was influenced by the Spanish conquerors, and this was still true in the 1880s, when ethnographic records of building styles began (see fig. 11). The Spaniards taught the Pueblos how to manufacture adobe bricks of mud with a straw binder, moulded into forms. In the eastern pueblos moulded adobe bricks were used in masonry style, while in the western pueblos wet adobe was preferred, being used as mortar and plaster. Franciscan missionaries used Pueblo Native American labour to construct the first churches in the region, but did not attempt to teach European methods of stone construction.

The Pueblo Native Americans incorporated new European architectural ideas without abandoning their traditional construction or spatial practices. Much indigenous architecture was preserved by the Spanish colonists' refusal to live among the natives: many traditional methods continued to be used into the 19th and 20th centuries and can be seen in the new Hopi towns of Hotevilla, Bacavi and Moenkopi in Arizona. Nevertheless, with the end of the need for defensive positioning, pueblos acquired more windows and doors, using such imported building materials as milled lumber, and more free-standing individual houses were built. In New Mexico, Taos Pueblo's two house-blocks most closely resemble building before the Spanish Conquest, but the modern pueblos are an amalgam of traditional and acculturated forms.

The indigenous building practices of the other tribes of the Southwest reveal different traditions. The Pima and Papago of southern Arizona, possible descendants of the Hohokam, made partly excavated, brush-covered 'ki' dwellings up to 3 m in diameter. In summer, both groups used arbors, or ramadas, for outdoor living. By the reservation period, the Pima and Papago were encouraged to utilize a form of acculturated 'sandwich house', made from lathe-and-mud and adobe wadded between one-by-four timbers. Mud-walling techniques using ocotillo stalks or willow thatch and were applied to create rectangular houses, and plaster filling was used for finishing. The ki house type did not die out completely but became the sacred *vahki* (rain-house) used for ceremonial gatherings.

The nomadic Western Apache groups and the Navajo constructed less permanent dwellings. The Apache made wikiups, grass and brush shelters lashed together by frame poles or crossbeams. Such structures were portable, until larger, more permanent examples were made when the Apache were settled on to reservations. The Navajo were relative newcomers to the region, migrating from the

11. Southwest region, Zuni Pueblo, Block I; photograph by A. C. Vroman, 1899 (Washington, DC, National Museum of American History)

north-west and arriving only shortly before the Spaniards. They brought with them the domed dwelling known as the 'hogan', which they believed had its origins in religious instruction, but which did not really evolve into its unique shape until the Navajo settled in the Southwest. Unlike the Pueblo Native Americans, the Navajo traditionally lived in dispersed seasonal camps or homesteads and did not begin to live in fixed communities on reservations until the early 20th century. The oldest form is the 'male' hogan, a conical forked-pole shape with four posts positioned at the cardinal directions. Another variation is a hogan of leaning logs, derived from a ceremonial structure and in use by the 1870s. The 'female' hogan was the most common form after the 1880s and is still in use; it is six-sided and has a corbelled log roof. Every hogan type shares common interior features that were determined by tradition: a single room heated by a central floor fireplace or stove, a smoke-hole and the door facing the east. The plank hogan is the most recent evolution of the form, strongly influenced by the Euro-American frame house, and took root on the reservations by the mid-1930s.

(iii) Post-war developments. The tenor of post-war life has accelerated changes in Southwest Native American housing, and indigenous structural integrity has often been compromised. While adobe walls and exposed timber roofs were a constant construction feature of most Pueblo architecture from prehistoric times, after World War II these features were frequently abandoned for newer and more durable materials. Cement blocks, wooden frames and aluminium have replaced stone and adobe, and the house-block form has been altered by fenestration and modular planning, as, for example, at Zuni, Acoma and Isleta Pueblos in New Mexico. A successful example of modern construction is the Hopi Cultural Center on the Second Mesa, Arizona, built in 1970–71 by Gonzales Associates. While the Pueblo groups continue to build on traditional sites, reusing existing structures, their use of Federal Government housing programmes and Anglo-American carpentry techniques has changed the look of their communities.

The hogan has remained the core of Navajo housing, but post-war building practices reflect increased acculturation. Traditional structures such as cribbed-log storage huts, corrals and sweat baths are made much as they have been for centuries. Polygonal hogans were increasingly preferred to the conical type after 1946, and by the 1950s modern hogans had tar paper and plank roofs, and chimneys replaced smoke-holes. By then, the Navajo used sawed lumber, and the tribal council permitted an approved form of trailer (caravan) home. Government-subsidized housing was brought to the reservation, with concrete blocks as a basic building element. While Navajo architecture of the late 20th century demonstrates active cultural fusion, builders may still observe traditional taboos during construction. At Navajo Community College, Tsaile, Arizona, both the campus-plan and the Ned Hatathli Center (built by Chambers, Campbell, Isaacson and Chaplin in 1972) are based on the hogan shape.

The enduring beauty and practicality of indigenous architectural practices had a powerful effect on non-Native American architects. Regional architecture in the Southwest borrowed many elements from traditional Pueblo construction. A number of architects, from Mary Colter of the Fred Harvey Company to John Gaw Meem and Isaac Hamilton Rapp, combined Pueblo construction techniques with modern decorative features to create a 'Pueblo Style'. FRANK LLOYD WRIGHT incorporated the stepped pyramid form into his architectural vocabulary. The most elaborate tribute to indigenous building was the 'Pueblo Deco' movement of the 20th century.

BIBLIOGRAPHY

V. Mindeleff: 'A Study of Pueblo Architecture: Tusayan and Cibola', *Bureau of Ethnology, Annual Report*, viii (Washington, DC, 1891), pp. 3–228
G. Kubler: *The Religious Architecture of New Mexico in the Colonial Period and since the American Occupation* (Albuquerque, 1940)
T. E. Sanford: *The Architecture of the Southwest: Indian, Spanish, American* (New York, 1950)
M. A. Tremblay: 'Navaho Housing in Transition', *América Indíg.*, xiv (1954), pp. 182–219
C. Kluckhohn with W. W. Hill and L. W. Kluckhohn: 'House Types', *Navaho Material Culture* (Cambridge, MA, 1971), pp. 143–57
V. Scully: *Pueblo, Mountain, Village, Dance* (New York, 1975)
B. Bunting: *Early Architecture in New Mexico* (Albuquerque, 1976)
S. Jett and V. Spencer: *Navajo Architecture: Forms, History, Distributions* (Tucson, 1981)
L. S. Cordell: *Prehistory of the Southwest* (New York, 1984)
S. Lekson: *Great Pueblo Architecture of Chaco Canyon, New Mexico* (Albuquerque, 1984)
P. Nabokov: *Americas Indigena* (New York, 1989)
N. C. Markovich, ed.: *Pueblo Style and Regional Architecture* (New York, 1990)

PAULA A. BAXTER

3. PLAINS. Dwellings and ceremonial structures among the Native Americas Plains groups usually had a round or oval ground-plan. The construction of dwellings reflected the two basic culture patterns of the region: nomadic hunters camped in transportable tents, called tepees, while permanent lodges were used by riverine farmers in the eastern Plains. After the tribes settled on reservations their traditional dwelling types slowly disappeared as people moved into log cabins and houses of a Euro-American type. Only the tepee has survived, though its use is restricted to festivities in the summer.

(i) Tepees and earth lodges. The tepee is a modified version of the bark-covered wigwam used in circumpolar regions (see fig. 12). It consists of a conical frame of straight poles covered by a semicircular tarpaulin of buffalo skins sewn together. The close-fitting cover is pulled around the frame as a mantle, the straight edges meeting in front, where they are held together by wooden pins. The most distinctive feature of the tepee are the two wings or ears around the smoke-hole at the top; by moving the two poles that hold them, the draught from the central fireplace can be regulated or the vent closed up in bad weather. The tepee was pitched with the front poles set at a slope, while the back poles were set more vertically, against the prevailing westerly wind. This resulted in a tilted cone shape and provided stability against the strong winds on the high Plains. For the same reason the poles were set up in a definite order so that they would lock one another in place.

A skin lining was erected inside the tepee cover, reaching from the ground to *c.* 2 m high, and served to keep out the draught; a layer of grass between lining and tepee cover provided extra insulation in winter. A flange along

12. Plains region, Shoshoni camp tepees; from a photograph by W. H. Jackson, 1870 (Washington, DC, Smithsonian Institution)

the lower rim of the skin cover was held down by a ring of stones, betraying the residence of people long after they had moved away. Thousands of such tepee rings have been found on the western high Plains. Both the outside of the tepee cover and the inner lining could be decorated by paintings, referring either to spiritual visions or to the war records of the male resident and his friends (*see* §IV, 1(iv) below).

Before European contact, tepees were small, the weight of poles and tent cover being restricted by the strength of the pack-dogs used in transport. Most common was a tepee with a ground diameter of *c*. 3 m. In the 18th century the acquisition of horses enabled Native American Plains groups to increase the size and comfort of their tepees with a floor-plan of *c*. 4.5 m in diameter. The extermination of the buffalo herds forced the Native American Plains groups to adopt canvas tepee covers, as early as 1850 on the southern and central Plains and some 30 years later in more northern areas. In the sewing of the canvas cover the old pattern was maintained. At the same time, the use of stones to hold down the flange was replaced by the use of wooden pegs. Modern means of transport allow the use of tepees with a ground diameter of *c*. 6 m and an impressive crown of long poles. Tepee use today is restricted to the tradition-orientated minority in each Native American group when attending the summer ceremonials.

Owing to wear from transport and constant use, neither the poles nor the cover of the tepee lasted much longer than a year, and their replacement was a regular enterprise in spring. Making, erecting and transporting the tepee was strictly the work of the woman, and the tepee was considered her property. The seats and sleeping places of household members and visitors were assigned according to strict rules of etiquette, the men to the north and the women to the south of the eastward-facing entrance. Opposite the entrance was the place of honour, reserved for the host and his medicine bundles.

For much of the year the nomadic hunters moved around in small bands, their tepees pitched close together for protection against the elements and enemies. Once a year, however, the bands of each group assembled their tepees in one large circular camp to celebrate the Sundance and associated ceremonies (*see* §I, 3 above). Shelter for a large public meeting or ceremonial was created by combining two tepees to create a large lodge. For the annual Sundance several groups constructed a special temple consisting of a tall pole in the centre of a circular wall of green brush. Connecting the temple and the lodge were long rafters, decorated with individual ex-votos of brightly coloured cloth and feather ornaments. In the early 1900s large circular wooden dance halls were constructed by some groups in North Dakota and Oklahoma.

Several groups along the Missouri River lived in earth-covered lodges during the farming season. The earth lodge was a circular, dome-shaped structure averaging *c*. 12 m in diameter, with an earth floor at least 0.6 m below ground-level and entered by a tunnel-like passage. Four to eight posts of from 3 to 4.5 m high surrounded the central parlour, also used as the cooking place. A smoke-hole was left in the roof above the central fireplace. Long rafters connected this area to a surrounding wall of shorter posts, and the entire wooden structure was covered with a heavy layer of earth on top of a matting of willow boughs and grass. A shrine and bed benches were situated opposite the entrance, along the outer wall of the peripheral space, which also contained storages for food, firewood, garden tools and a small horse corral. Most of the winter supply of food was stored in pits lined with split logs and grass, dug in the ground outside the lodge. Several related nuclear families inhabited a single such dwelling, which had a lifespan from ten to twenty years. Villages of 30 to 200 earth lodges were usually sited on high promontories and were fortified by trenches and stockades. In the centre of each village was an earth lodge twice as large as a normal dwelling, used for public meetings and ceremonies. The villages were abandoned during the autumn, when the people left on hunting expeditions and lived in tepees.

The parts of the earth lodge and of the tepee were related to cosmic symbolism. The conical or dome-shaped wall of the earth lodge represented the sky, which was believed to rest as a dome upon the earth, symbolized by the floor of the lodge. Tepee poles and rafters linked earth and sky, and they symbolized the trails along which the prayers of the people reached the spirits. Entrances faced east, towards the sunrise, heralding the day and new life. Widespread in North America, this symbolism of the lodge as a microcosm played a role in the rituals performed within them.

(ii) Other structures. Round grass houses were used on the south-eastern Plains. Their 'gothic' dome shapes, about 4.5 m high, were formed by a bent frame of long flexible poles tied together at the top. Four of the poles were somewhat longer than the others, their top sections extending towards the four cardinal directions, symbolizing the gods of the four world quarters. Horizontal rods encircled the frame at intervals, and the whole was carefully covered with grass thatch. Sleeping platforms were constructed around the inside of the wall. Grass houses were from 4.5 to 9 m in diameter and were occupied by a number of related families. Several groups in the eastern Prairies lived in mat- or bark-covered dome-shaped lodges as used in the adjoining Woodlands region (*see* §4 below). Such lodges were *c.* 3 m high, up to 30 m long and *c.* 5.5 m wide.

Other structures erected by Native American Plains groups included small bark- or brush-covered conical shelters made by war parties at secluded locations in enemy territory. These were large enough to accommodate ten to twelve warriors and sufficiently strong to provide protection in case of an attack. They served as a supply base in preparation for surprise raids on enemy camps. Sweat lodges were made for taking steam-baths, frequently with ritual overtones. Such a lodge consisted of a dome-shaped frame of branches, *c.* 1.4 m high, covered with buffalo skins or blankets. The floor was covered with sage grass, except for a hole in the centre, in which hot stones were placed. The bather(s) crouched inside and sprinkled water on the stones to create steam in the airtight hut.

In late prehistoric times (i.e. just before European contact) the use of burial mounds spread from the south-east Woodlands region northward as far as Manitoba. The use of small versions survived up to early historic times among the agricultural communities in the lower Missouri region. Prevailing throughout the Plains, however, was the use of scaffolds and trees for burial practices; and among the nomadic hunters the tepee served as a burial lodge for important individuals.

BIBLIOGRAPHY
R. H. Lowie: *Indians of the Plains* (New York, 1954)
K. Laubin and G. Laubin: *The Indian Tepee* (Norman, 1957)

T. J. BRASSER

4. WOODLANDS. Hundreds of Native American groups lived in the vast Woodlands region (*see* §I, 1(ix) above). Differences in climate and environment, and changes in society, economy and ideology, were reflected by differences in the forms and functions of domestic and ritual structures, spaces and locations.

(i) Archaic. (ii) Adena–Hopewell. (iii) Mississippi–Late Woodland.

(i) Archaic. Little is known concerning even domestic structures at any archaeological site before *c.* 4500 BC. Only the scattered remains in rock shelters and traces of hunting sites and quarries survive from apparently mobile peoples who followed retreating glaciers into the Woodlands region, though they unquestionably had weatherproof shelters of some kind. No Palaeo-Native American site with evidence for public or ceremonial architecture or space is known in the Woodlands. Distribution of tools and chipping debris suggests that most domestic sites were diffuse occupations by three to five nuclear families, each using a living area *c.* 20 m in diameter, each such area being about 20 m from the next. The few early sites to yield architectural evidence contain only mundane structures. In the 3rd and 2nd millennia BC at the Wapanuckett No. 6 site in Massachusetts and the Koster Farm site in the lower Illinois Valley, two to six small domestic structures were occupied for much of each year by a single extended family of localized hunter–gatherers. At both sites oval houses, *c.* 4×5 m with central open hearths, were built of single-set wooden posts, probably tied together at their tops. At other, coeval sites throughout the region, fragmentary remains suggest that this was the common plan.

Most ritual or civic use of space during the 1st millennium BC was apparently unplanned. Fishing and gathering peoples on many of the South Atlantic coastal islands lived on uniformly sized and shaped annular and penannular shell middens, 20–30 m in diameter, with what are taken to be deliberately cleaned central plazas. While a few post-hole remains have been identified, the size and shape of the houses is unknown. By *c.* 500 BC, on several island sites off the Georgia coast, repetitive interments in restricted areas led to the creation of low sand and shell mounds over multi-family burials of the Deptford culture. In much the same way, in the Midwest and Great Lakes region between *c.* 1200 and *c.* 400 BC, the ritual burial of generations of presumptive lineage leaders in particular gravel knolls and glacial kames (conical hills of glacial deposits formed at the edge of the ice sheet) resulted in the creation of less than impressive artificial burial mounds.

The earliest and one of the most imposing planned ceremonial sites in the eastern Woodlands is the POVERTY POINT site in north-eastern Louisiana. There, along Bayou Maçon, a huge series of earthworks covers nearly 20 ha with five-eighths of an octagon composed of from four to six discontinuous concentric ridges over 3 m high (the rest may have eroded away). Most of the dates from this site suggest that the earthworks were built over several generations between *c.* 1100 and *c.* 800 BC, although at least one of the adjoining mounds is probably more recent. Few post-holes or hearths have been found on these imposing walls, and the secular architecture of the occupants of the site is entirely unknown.

(ii) Adena–Hopewell. While a few houses and simple mounds of earth over burials are known from the 3rd and 2nd millennia BC, domestic and sacred architectural structures and spaces became common during the succeeding Woodland periods. In the Ohio and Tennessee river valleys conical burial mounds, such as Grave Creek, West Virginia, or the ADENA MOUND in Ohio, were up to 22 m high, in an annular or penannular ditch and embankment 50 m or more across. Below such characteristic Early Woodland (*c.* 1000–*c.* 100 BC) mounds, tombs had been placed within circular paired sets of out-slanted wooden posts, but whether the structures represented were roofed or not,

and whether they reflect domestic as well as mortuary architecture, is unclear. In Kentucky an intermittent ditch and over 12,000 posts enclosed the free-form Peter Site, where ritually important minerals were mined.

Vast free-form ditches and stone-revetted embankments also enclosed Hopewell sites on plateaux and hilltops in southern Ohio (*c.* 100 BC–*c.* AD 500). But far more impressive were the vast, regular geometric enclosures forming connected and isolated squares and octagons with small conical mounds at breaks in the walls. There were open and closed circles and ellipses, and additional sets of parallel earthen walls having open or closed ends of various shapes, many with celestially significant orientations. Within these enclosures many Hopewell mounds in Ohio and many related Middle Woodland (*c.* 100 BC–*c.* AD 500) mounds in the Southeast were built over series of complex ritual spaces and wooden post structures, often reflecting the earthwork motifs. Further, within many of the conical burial mounds of the Middle Woodland period, structures had stood and rituals were performed on flat earthen platforms. Some of these were later incorporated into other such platforms, and

13. Woodlands region, aerial view of Great Serpent Mound, southern Ohio

most finally incorporated into a conical or loaf-shaped mound.

In southern Ohio and in Tennessee, Alabama, Georgia and in north-western Florida sites that participated in the exchange of Hopewell ritual iconography and objects, there were rectangular flat-topped mounds within discontinuous square enclosures, some with ramped graded ways from the enclosure to the river edge. In the lower Mississippi Valley, multi-staged Hopewellian mounds stood within large semicircular earthen embankments abutting the river, while in the Florida Everglades, sites with complex circular and radial ditches and embankments enclosed ceremonial centres, often containing low, flat-topped mounds built over community charnel houses. At the same time, along the islands off the south Florida Gulf Coast, dense populations were beginning to live in such communities as KEY MARCO, where conch and whelk shell middens were combined into house platforms and built into dikes, canals and boat slips.

The construction of Adena or Hopewellian mounds and related ritual spaces and buildings, and the acquisition, distribution and disposal of material and artefacts, represented competitive personal achievement by the leaders of socially equivalent family groups. The acquisition of many exotic materials and artefacts, and perhaps awareness of their complex iconographic significance, were probably restricted to those particular participants.

This sacred or civic architecture and sense of space is quite different from that seen at the few excavated non-ceremonial Hopewell sites, where a few randomly placed secular houses show a simple rectangular or square plan (sides 4–6 m), each with one or two hearths for a single nuclear or extended family. Built of closely placed, single-set wooden posts, with several larger internal support posts, they probably had some form of gabled roof. At Hopewellian-related sites in the mid-south, similar square houses and clay-plastered circular houses of equal area appear to represent both summer and winter use of the sites.

While few burial mounds in the northern Woodlands postdate the Middle Woodland period, along the upper Mississippi River there are fields of from five to fifty low mounds, 10–20 m long, in the form of birds, mammals and reptiles, usually with a single burial at the head or heart. There are no materials of secure archaeological provenance from the base of the 100-m long coiled Great Serpent Mound on a high ridge in southern Ohio (see fig. 13), but fragments of domestic ceramics (Columbus, OH, Hist. Soc.) in its upper layers suggest that it too was constructed in the cultural hiatus between the Hopewellian and Mississippian florescences.

(iii) Mississippi–Late Woodland. After AD 1200, at numerous sites on the fertile river bottom terraces throughout the south-east Woodlands and along the lower Ohio and Missouri river valleys, Mississippian societies built large towns surrounding sets of normally square or rectangular, flat-topped (and often steeply ramped) mounds, on which stood temples or civic buildings, oriented to the cardinal directions. At a few large Mississippian sites, such as CAHOKIA across from St Louis, there were numerous plazas formed by pyramidal temple mounds along with conical mounds and long, ridged mounds containing élite burials. There were also circles more than 100 m across, composed of large wooden posts, the largest of which cast shadows demarcating summer or winter solstice sunrise along the faces or edges of particular mounds. Many such isolated wooden posts were also set as gnomons in or adjacent to the large cleared plazas about which most Mississippian towns were planned or grew. While a few large and unusual ramped helical mounds supporting temples or charnel houses appear to have been conceived and constructed as a single project, most mounds were built and rebuilt, layer upon layer, over a complex series of public ritual spaces and/or structures. In the southern Appalachians, Mississippian temples and council houses were often rebuilt into towering mounds over partially subterranean structures.

Unlike earlier sacred religious buildings, all such Mississippian mound and temple structures were built by organized group effort. Although the use and display of their sacred and civic contents may have been restricted to particular individuals, these mounds represent fully corporate icons. Within every Mississippian polity, ritual and exchange, as well as some level of economic and political control, were held by the élite members of one or a few lineages; together, mound, structure, space and artefact functioned as hierarchical symbols reflecting the socially unifying role of ritual.

Although the spatial arrangement of houses within towns and villages and the layout of settlements changed in response to economic and ceremonial demands, from c. AD 1200, virtually all the regional varieties of domestic architecture that persisted in the eastern Woodlands until European contact had been developed. Villages of huge, randomly placed multi-family earth lodges were built by Missouri River Valley farmers (see §3 above). Square semi-subterranean single-family wall-trench buildings plastered with clay characterized all Mississippian settlements, from the dense, planned many-templed towns, to the small single-mound regional centres, to the family farmsteads along the Mississippi, lower Ohio, Tennessee and Alabama river valleys. Open-sided, palmetto-thatched rectangular houses on stilts served small families of ancient Native Americans in the deep south, while along the lower Great Lakes and St Lawrence River generations of matrilocal families lived down the partitioned centres of nearly airtight, bark-covered arched-roof houses as much as 8 m high and 35 m long. Throughout the eastern Woodlands skin, bark and reed mats covered small, temporary or special-purpose structures of vaguely circular plan and domed elevation.

Equally widespread were the changes in location and defensive posture of sites in response to the climatic, economic and, eventually, military pressures that began in the 15th century (see MILITARY ARCHITECTURE AND FORTIFICATION, §X). Within the more densely settled southern riverine area, while individual farmsteads persisted, most outlying political centres were abandoned, and central towns were enclosed in multiple lines of wooden palisades, complete with closely set, square projecting bastions. Across most of the mid-continent, in the

Appalachian valleys and in the mid-Atlantic region, open farming villages were realigned within circular stockades as concentric rings of houses, activity areas and burials about a central plaza. Open agricultural villages in the upper Ohio and Mississippi valleys and across southern portions of the Great Lakes were relocated away from the major river valleys on to high promontories isolated by defensive ditches and embankments. Even temporary seasonal camps in this region appear to have been protected by the end of the 16th century.

BIBLIOGRAPHY

B. Fagan: *In the Beginning: An Introduction to Archaeology* (Boston, 1972); rev. as *Introduction to American Archaeology* (San Francisco, 1992)

W. N. Morgan: *Prehistoric Architecture of the Eastern United States* (Cambridge, MA, 1980)

D. S. Brose, J. A. Brown and D. W. Penney: *Ancient Art of the American Woodland Indians* (New York, 1985)

J. D. Jennings: *Ancient North Americans* (New York, 1990)

B. D. Smith: *Rivers of Change* (Washington, DC, 1992)

DAVID S. BROSE

III. Carving and sculpture.

Native American sculpture of monumental proportions is rare in North America. Apart from the carving of totem poles and plank walls among Northwest Coast peoples, most other carving and sculpture was done on small, portable objects. Until the advent of carving for the tourist trade, almost all carving was in some way connected to a ritual or magico-religious function. In some regions, such as California and the Far West, carving played virtually no role.

1. Arctic. 2. Northwest Coast. 3. Great Basin. 4. Southwest. 5. Plains. 6. Woodlands.

1. ARCTIC. Eskimo sculpture has been evolving constantly over three millennia, changing in response to local cultural influences and to contacts with Siberian travellers. Prehistoric trade routes for the exchange of goods with other Arctic tribes existed from Siberia through Alaska into Canada, and new ideas moved with the prehistoric migrations of Eskimos from Alaska to Greenland and with counter-migrations from Greenland to Alaska. Thus, there is both continuity and diversity, including regional art forms developed by isolated groups. Perhaps because of the abundance of sea mammals and land animals, the fullest development of the Eskimo culture took place in Alaska, around the shores of the Bering Sea. Leisure time allowed for the development of art and ceremony. In Canada, where living conditions were less favourable, more time was devoted to survival and less to the decoration of implements or the fabrication of elaborate masks.

(i) Before European contact. (ii) After European contact.

(i) Before European contact. Before the arrival of white explorers, there was a close integration of art with everyday life and belief. Carvings in stone, bone, ivory and, occasionally, wood were created for magico-religious use and can be divided into three groups. The first group comprises: miniature female figurines used as fertility charms; small replicas of cooking pots, carved and stored carefully to insure against breakage of full-sized pots; and amulets to serve as personal good-luck charms. It is possible that

14. Arctic carved mask, wood with painted decoration, h. 320 mm, Pastolik (South Alaskan Eskimo), late 19th century (Washington, DC, Smithsonian Institution)

some of these miniatures served as sympathetic magic. For example, human figures and animals have been found with a sliver inserted to indicate a spear. Canadian Inuit Eskimos produced small animals and amulets in abundance, and at least some of these had a magico-religious function. The second group comprises carvings on hunting and fishing implements. Intricate surface designs were carved on these, as it was believed that animals preferred to be killed by a beautiful weapon. In many cases, the entire or partial image of a creature whose attributes were useful to the hunter was added; for example, the sharp eyes of a bird or the strength of a bear. The third group is composed of ceremonial masks and shamanistic paraphernalia, used in dances and in seasonal festivals, and designed to please the animals killed and to ensure their continued regeneration. The shaman, who possessed an intimate knowledge of the supernatural, designed most of the masks, which were usually carved from driftwood, frequently with feathers or other appendages (see fig. 14). It was believed that animals were originally able to transform themselves into humans or to pull back their outer skins to reveal a small human face (*inua*). For this reason, many masks, in addition to the larger main image of a bird or animal, have a small human face inserted to indicate the *inua*.

(a) Alaska. Prehistoric Eskimo carving in Alaska can be divided into distinct stylistic periods. Little artistic evidence remains from the Arctic Small Tool tradition (2500–1000 BC), the first identifiable Eskimo culture. It spread from Alaska—perhaps from an origin in Siberia— all the way to Greenland by *c.* 2000 BC, but archaeologists believe some sort of art style existed. Art objects dated *c.* 500 BC–*c.* AD 500 have been found along the Gulf of Alaska, but most have been unearthed further north, near

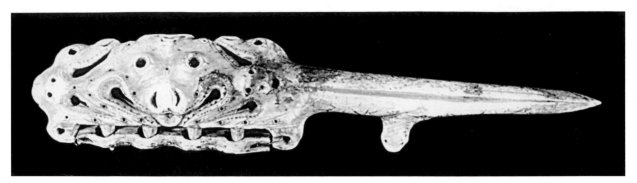

15. Arctic carved ceremonial comb, ivory, 55×260 mm, Ipiutak, from Point Spencer, Seward Peninsula, Alaska, *c.* AD 350–*c.* 400 (Fairbanks, Alaska, University of Alaska Museum)

the coast of the Bering Sea, the Chukchi Sea and the Arctic Ocean. Distinct periods have been identified: Choris (*c.* 1400–600 BC), Norton (*c.* 600–100 BC), Okvik (*c.* 500 BC–AD 500), Old Bering Sea (*c.* 500 BC–AD 500), Ipiutak (*c.* AD 1–500), Punuk (*c.* AD 600–1500), Birnirk (*c.* AD 600–1000) and Thule (*c.* AD 700–1700), ranging from *c.* 1400 BC to *c.* AD 1700. Of these, the greatest abundance of highly artistic carvings come from the Okvik, Old Bering Sea and Ipiutak periods, and most have been unearthed since the 1920s.

Since only a fraction of the land has been excavated, it can be assumed that vast treasures remain to be discovered. Certainly, the most dramatic find was the Ipiutak prehistoric village near Point Hope, Alaska, where about 600 houses and over 100 graves provided over 10,000 artefacts. The ornate carvings from this site suggest links to the prehistoric art of northern China. The Ipiutak ceremonial comb (see fig. 15) has been dated at *c.* AD 350–*c.* 400. When it is compared with the *taotie* masks found on Shang dynasty ritual vessels (*c.* 1600–*c.* 1050 BC), definite influence is apparent (*see* CHINA, §VI, 3(ii)(a)). The bear's head is intact, and the split body extends on each side with clearly delineated front paws and hind legs in the same composition as the *taotie* mask. However, the Eskimo artist omitted the elaborate quilled tail of the dragon, substituting fanciful animal heads above and inserting small faces at either end. Several such combs were excavated. The carving style, embellished with incised border designs, is typically Ipiutak. Drilled holes were originally inset with jet or baleen. When viewed upside down, a second animal face utilizing the bear's eyes but with separate nostrils and mouth can be seen; this is typical of the visual punning enjoyed by Eskimos. Helge Larsen hypothesized that these combs were used to comb and clean the fur of a bear in the ceremonies of the Bear Cult in a monograph on the Bear Cult in 1969.

Okvik and Old Bering Sea artefacts also have Siberian similarities, for example, a series of Okvik dolls, some representing pregnant women. One, originally holding either an infant child or a bear cub, has been variously named the 'Okvik Madonna' or the 'Bear Mother' (Fairbanks, U. AK Mus.), after a widespread myth of a woman who married a bear and bore a vicious bear cub. Numerous other less elaborate female figures, of ivory or wood, have also been found; these were reportedly carried in fishing boats and fed appeasing morsels of food to ensure success in the expedition. Small dolls were also carved by shamans and given to childless women to induce pregnancy. It seems likely that all these small dolls were descendants of Siberian Neolithic female figures, assumed to have been fertility figures.

In the Old Bering Sea period the ornate 'winged' objects, which served as counterweights on harpoon shafts, have curvilinear designs engraved on the carved surfaces, the emphasis being on flowing lines and symmetry. Concentric circles and ellipses abound, and the centres are usually elevated and have drilled holes with insets to suggest eyes in much the same fashion as Chinese Shang and Zhou bronzes. There are no two identical winged objects, but all have a well-planned three-part division. The evolution of these counterweights can be traced from the Okvik period, in which the 'wings' first appeared, through the prolific Old Bering Sea period and into the Punuk period, in which the wings disappear, leaving only the central portion in a bottle-like shape. Such changes in shape and weight suggest functional adaptations.

Shamanistic paraphernalia have been found in Old Bering Sea and Ipiutak graves. Of particular interest are a masklike set of ivory carvings (New York, Amer. Mus. Nat. Hist.) found in an Ipiutak grave, ivory mouth covers, nose plugs and artificial eyes inset with jade; these suggest a belief that the spirit must be contained in the corpse. Equally puzzling were a number of finger-sized human heads and skulls (Copenhagen, Nmus.). Small naturalistic carvings of polar bears and seals were also found (New York, Amer. Mus. Nat. Hist.). One carving of a baby walrus is decorated with a surface design indicating the skeleton and oval bosses indicating joints. In addition, dozens of 'pretzel-like' ivory carvings were found, and chains and swivels carved of ivory appear to be derived from metal models, which were often attached to the clothing of Siberian shamans. Following these peak periods of design, in the Punuk, Birnirk and Thule periods the carving of functional objects persisted, but decoration became more sparse and geometric. At one Punuk site, in addition to occasional naturalistic whale and seal figures, the torso of a pregnant woman was found, which is reminiscent of Upper Palaeolithic sculptures from Siberia.

(b) Canada. The sequence of prehistoric art production in Canada is somewhat simpler. A few carvings from the

Arctic Small Tool tradition (c. 2200–1400 BC) and the Pre-Dorset culture (c. 1450–800 BC) have been unearthed, but the preponderance of artefacts come from the Dorset culture (c. 800 BC–c. AD 1300), which displays considerable artistic achievement. Most sculptures, though small, are carved in a vigorous style ranging from naturalistic to grotesque. Bone, ivory and wood were used to carve both human and animal figures, many of which displayed the skeletal view and joint marks. However, in Canada joint marks were indicated by an 'X' rather than by an oval boss. The carvings can be divided into two categories: ritual or ceremonial objects produced by or for the shaman and miniature models or toys. The shaman's paraphernalia ranged from carvings of his 'helping spirits' (bears, birds and sea mammals) to sucking tubes ('soul catchers') of bone and ivory, carved with surface decorations of human and animal faces. Other shaman's devices, employed during a trance, included false teeth with protruding walrus tusks, to indicate that he was under the spell of the walrus spirit; masks, carved by the shaman and worn as a disguise; and belts with attached carved images of spirit helpers. Numerous small sculptures of birds, animals, fish and humans may have been carved as toys for children, as amulets to ensure personal safety or as figures for use in 'sympathetic magic'. Some human figures have slots in the throat or chest into which spear-like slivers have been inserted, and several have red ochre stains to symbolize blood. Further remarkable discoveries, clearly Dorset, are c. 95 carved petroglyphs of human faces, cut into an outcrop of soapstone near Wakeham Bay to the south of Hudson Bay. Two other similar sites are known, all with petroglyphs representing human or animal faces and masks.

A migration by the Thule people from Alaska to Canada began c. AD 900. As the end product of several peak cultural periods in Alaska, one would expect the Thule culture (AD 900–1400) to produce a more distinguished art style rather than the gradual transition to a simpler, more geometric style that ensued. In Canada, Thule art replaced and absorbed the Dorset culture over a wide area, but there are few artefacts that can be classified as art: only dolls and dozens of tiny, flat-bottomed birds. Utilitarian objects, such as combs, were occasionally decorated with carved, simplified figures.

(ii) After European contact. The first written accounts of Canadian Eskimos are Norse records of c. AD 1000. English explorers in the later 16th century mention small carvings in wood of humans, kayaks and animals. In Alaska, recorded history begins with early Russian discoveries from 1711 to 1741, the date of Vitus Bering's 'official discovery'. In the following century, explorers, traders and missionaries collected thousands of Eskimo objects, now housed in Russian, European and North American museums. Before outside contact, carvings were based on culturally shared meaning, usually spiritual. Opportunities for trade provided a new impetus and resulted in increased production. Prehistoric carvings were small (50 mm to 70 mm high) owing to the limitations in size of ivory and to a semi-nomadic existence. But with the new incentives for trade, Eskimos in Alaska and Canada began to carve tiny replicas of humans, animals and kayaks, and even

guns and teapots. Others carved miniature scenes of hunter and hunted, of snow houses and of village life. Alaskan Eskimos, more exposed to the foreigners, began to adjust the subject-matter to the tastes of the buyers, creating a stereotyped version of Eskimo life that still exists today as 'tourist art'. At the same time, formerly functional items, such as drill bows and pipes, became decorative rather than functional and were produced in quantity for commercial sale. The situation for masks was somewhat different. Originally, these were burnt after use in ceremony or dance, and at first Alaskan Eskimos refused requests for purchase. Later, however, using ingenious reasoning, they sold the masks and burnt an equivalent amount of wood.

The most prominent and prolific period for Alaskan Eskimo art was the 19th century. A renaissance in sculpture in Canada occurred in the 1950s. The catalyst for this resurgence was James Houston (b 1921), who first collected small carvings in the Hudson Bay area in 1948. He was so impressed by the tiny sculptures that he persuaded the Canadian Handicrafts Guild to underwrite a return trip to collect items for sale, thus providing income for impoverished Eskimos. His collection of 1000 carvings sold out in three days, and thereafter the Canadian government began to underwrite an aggressive programme to encourage carving and provide for sales to a world market. White artists were hired as instructors, and cooperatives were formed throughout the Canadian Arctic.

Houston noted considerable skill but a lack of invention. He encouraged bold designs and lively subject-matter, and style changed from the somewhat crude style of the 1950s to more sophisticated, highly polished productions in the 1970s. Sculptures of stone became larger, some measuring up to 400 or 500 mm. In the 1980s, twisting movement reminiscent of European Baroque art appeared, and traces of Mannerism were noted as artists became more proficient. The success of this venture has been well publicized; the best sculptures have been collected in museums around the world, and individual artists have been recognized.

The situation is somewhat different in Alaska. Unlike certain isolated and uneducated Canadian Eskimos, nearly all Alaskan Eskimos have been exposed to outside, Western, influences since the mid-19th century, and most have attended school with English-speaking teachers. Although many still carve repetitious bears, birds and hunters for the souvenir market, a few well-trained artists also produce exceptional, highly creative sculpture. Their work is also collected by museums and exhibited around the world. In comparison with the millions of dollars spent by the Canadian government to promote Eskimo sculpture, only a fraction of that amount has been devoted to specialized training for Alaskans. Workshops and extension programmes have been poorly funded. In the case of Alaskan artists it was George Fedoroff (b 1906), former Alaskan representative of the Indian Arts and Crafts Board, Department of the Interior, who influenced their lives, encouraged them, enlarged their vision and made arrangements for advanced training.

Much of the work produced by modern Alaskan carvers contains a deliberate inclusion of prehistoric devices, such as the skeletal view and the life line. Nevertheless, the style is comparable to that of international sculptors, and as such, it is sometimes not immediately recognized as Eskimo art. These artists are the product of many influences: the deeply rooted traditions of their culture, the new techniques and aesthetic standards of Western civilization and the pressures of the 20th century to depart from tradition and develop highly personal forms of expression.

BIBLIOGRAPHY

EWA: 'Eskimo Cultures'

W. H. Dall: 'On Masks, Labrets and Certain Aboriginal Customs', *Bureau Amer. Ethnol. An. Rep.*, iii (Washington, DC, 1882)

E. W. Nelson: 'The Eskimo about Bering Strait', *Bureau Amer. Ethnol. An. Rep.*, xviii (Washington, DC, 1899/R 1983)

H. E. Larsen and F. G. Rainey: 'Ipiutak and the Arctic Whale Hunting Culture', *Anthropol. Pap. Amer. Mus. Nat. Hist.*, xlii (1948) [whole vol.]

H. G. Bandi: *Eskimo Prehistory* (Stuttgart, 1964; Eng. trans. Juneau, 1969)

D. J. Ray and A. A. Blaker: *Eskimo Masks: Art and Ceremony* (Seattle, 1967)

H. E. Larsen: 'Some Examples of Bear Cult among the Eskimo and Other Northern Peoples', *Folk*, xi–xii (1969–70), pp. 27–42

S. Ard Frederick: 'Alaskan Eskimo Art Today', *Alaska J.*, ii/4 (1972), pp. 30–41

The Far North: 2000 Years of American Eskimo and Indian Art (exh. cat. by H. B. Collins and others, Washington, DC, N.G.A., 1973)

S. Ard Frederick: 'Inuit Sculpture', *Alaska J.*, x/3 (1980), pp. 28–31

Inua: Spirit World of the Bering Sea Eskimo (exh. cat. by W. W. Fitzhugh and S. A. Kaplan, Washington, DC, N. Mus. Nat. Hist., 1982)

Crossroads of Continents (exh. cat. by W. W. Fitzhugh and A. Crowell, Washington, DC, N. Mus. Nat. Hist., 1988)

G. Swinton: *Sculpture of the Inuit* (Toronto, 1992)

S. Ard: *Eskimo Art around the Arctic Circle* [in preparation]

SARADELL ARD

2. NORTHWEST COAST.

(i) Introduction. (ii) Southern. (iii) Central. (iv) Northern. (v) Contemporary developments.

(i) Introduction. The sculptural arts of the indigenous peoples of the Northwest Coast range from monumental totem poles to mechanical transformation masks to delicate amulets. At the time of the arrival of Europeans in the late 18th century, carvers throughout the Northwest Coast excelled at the manipulation of wood, horn and bone. Many different types of wooden canoes, bentwood boxes, chests and bowls, and horn spoons, ladles and bowls were produced using steaming and bending techniques unique to this area. The northern and central groups carved monumental poles and house posts and a variety of ceremonial, shamans' and warriors' equipment that displayed inherited crests and spiritual helpers. In the south, monumental sculpture was used primarily to represent personal supernatural spirit helpers in the form of carved house posts, staffs and figures.

The first human occupants of the region, *c.* 10,000–*c.* 2500 BC, made chipped and ground stone tools with little or no embellishment. The earliest archaeological evidence for the production of art comprises anthropomorphic and zoomorphic bone, horn and stone carvings dated *c.* 2500–2000 BC (for illustration see Carlson, p. 24, fig. 1.5). The appearance of art on the Northwest Coast is associated with dramatic changes in the environment, including the stabilization of sea-levels, the development of stable riverine and near-shore ecosystems, including salmon, eulachon and shellfish, and the first appearance of western red-cedar forests. Woodworking and carving tools, such as ground stone adze blades, antler wedges and

chisels, and beaver tooth knives, also appear for the first time in the later part of this period.

Between *c.* 1500 BC and *c.* AD 500 Northwest Coast culture began to exhibit most of the features that have since distinguished it: plank house architecture (*see* §II, 1 above), social stratification based on the accumulation of wealth and the prolific decoration of tools and utensils with crest figures, symbols of social status and/or spiritual power. During this period a distinctive style of carving developed, based on the representation of animal or human forms in a flat, low-relief style. Negative areas were cut away to delineate broad, flat positive lines that outline the body parts. Heads are often exaggerated in size, limbs are frequently shown in a flexed or crouching position, and there is an emphasis on the facial features (Fladmark, pls 22 and 23). Pointed eyelid lines and an X-ray view of skeletal structure also distinguish the style. The style seems to have existed in widely dispersed areas of the coast, from the north near Prince Rupert in northern British Columbia as far south as the Columbia River. From the prehistoric style, well established by *c.* AD 500, several regionally distinctive styles had developed by the time of European contact.

(ii) Southern. The southern Northwest Coast region extended from the Chinookan-speaking peoples of the lower Columbia River in the south to Coast Salish-speaking peoples in southern British Columbia in the north. With the exception of weaving and basketwork (*see* §§VII, 1 and XIV, 3 below) fewer art objects were produced in this area, and its sculpture is less common in museum collections than that from the central and northern Northwest Coast (*see* §§(iii) and (iv) below). With a social structure less rigid than those in central and northern Northwest Coast areas, status and the display of crests and inherited privileges were less important. Large-scale sculpture in the south was produced primarily to display personal spirit power and as such was private. Rather than being displayed publicly or passed down as heirlooms, as crest objects were in the north, carvings were kept hidden when not in use and were often left in the forest to disintegrate or placed with the grave at the death of the owner. In addition, the people on the southern Northwest Coast were affected earlier and more severely by diseases and by Euro-American colonization. Their populations had been severely reduced, and some traditional southern Northwest Coast sculptural forms had ceased to be made well before the late 19th-century period of intensive collecting by the world's ethnological museums.

The sculpture of the southern region is most closely linked to prehistoric styles. The human body is carved in a flat, frontal manner, and the human face is usually represented with a flat-oval principal form, the facial features defined with two or three stepped planes. With the two-step structure, the forehead is on one plane, then steps back at the brow line to the cheek and chin plane. The three-step structure has an additional step below the cheeks, with the chin and mouth recessed further. The nose is generally handled as a thin ridge extending from the forehead plane. The eyes are small and round, set close to the nose under the brow ridge. The mouth is usually a thin slit with no lip projections. Limbs are handled in minimal fashion, and there are often V-shaped ribs indicated on the chest.

Within the southern Northwest Coast region, several styles existed. The Chinookan-speaking peoples of the Columbia River shared a common sculptural style with the Coast Salish of the Pacific Coast and Puget Sound areas of Washington state. In these areas, carved or painted geometric surface decoration is typical. Concentric circles, chevrons and zigzag lines created by carving negative interlocking triangles were frequently used on bowls, spoons and figures. Columbia River human figures carved in bone, horn and wood (for illustration see Wright, ed., 1991, pls 49–51, 55–7, 59, 64, 73–4 and 77) are often associated with cremation or burial sites. Their form is consistent: the heads have a flat-oval or circular principal form with two- or three-step facial structure; the bodies are skeletal, often with collar-bone and ribs clearly indicated. The skeletal form of these figures, as well as their association with burials, suggests a religious function, although such an interpretation can only be conjectural. Before about the mid-19th century on the lower Columbia River, bowls and spoons or ladles made from wood and from steamed and spread mountain sheep horn were frequently decorated with skeletal human or animal figures combined with geometric zigzags, chevrons and circles similar to prehistoric examples. The style is also closely related to historical basketwork styles from this area (see §XIV, 3 below), which incorporate skeletal human figures and geometric animals on their twined surfaces.

Further north, Quinault shamans on the Pacific Coast of Washington state carved human figures representing their personal spirit helpers on staffs or wands. These are similar in style to Columbia River sculpture, though less skeletal in form. They also resemble the Coast Salish Spirit Canoe figures made by shamans in the central Puget Sound area. These figures were owned by individual shamans, who worked in a group to journey to the land of the dead in order to recover the souls of sick people. House posts from this region are rare, but interior house posts occasionally displayed a human spirit helper or an abstract design relating to spirit power (for illustration see Suttles, 1991, figs 4 and 6; Suttles, 1983, figs 4.7–4.12).

In the central Coast Salish areas of the Strait of Juan de Fuca and the Georgia Straits, the Halkomelem-speaking people had a more curvilinear carving style. Human figures were handled frontally but are generally naturalistic in proportion, with fully fleshed bodies. Human faces have a flat-oval principal form but are generally more rounded and filled out than those of their southern neighbours. Nevertheless, they do have two- or three-step facial structures, with the eye on the cheek plane and minimal mouth projections. House posts displaying supernatural spirit helpers and grave-guardian figures are more common from this area, and monumental sculpture generally increases in frequency as one moves north along the coast.

The central Coast Salish area is distinguished by the only indigenous Coast Salish masking tradition, still active today. Skhwaikhwey masks are used in purification rituals. The right to perform the masked dance is an inherited privilege, but anyone can hire the dancers to perform at such events as marriage, memorial or naming ceremonies. The carved wooden masks display a consistent style, with

16. Northwest Coast spindle-whorl, wood, Coast Salish, 19th century (New York, DeMenil private collection)

projecting cylindrical peglike eyes, two bird or animal heads extending above the masklike ears and a broad, flat projection—like an abstract extended tongue—at the bottom. Noses are frequently developed into a secondary figure, such as a bird or fisher. A feathered ruff and projecting horns around the mask, a completely feathered body costume with birdskin leggings, deer-hoof leg rattles and a scallop shell rattle held in the hand complete the costume.

The surface of Skhwaikhwey masks is often decorated with low-relief carving in the 'Salish formline' style. This two-dimensional design system is remarkably similar to prehistoric carving styles found throughout the coast. In historic times it is associated specifically with the Halkomelem-speaking Salish. It was used primarily on ceremonial mountain sheep horn rattles, wooden combs, clubs, spindle-whorls (see fig. 16) and other tools and is characterized by flat, low-relief carving, defining human, bird and animal forms with negative crescent and T- or wedge-shapes. Pointed eyelid lines and the use of circles or ovals for eyes and joints link this style with the northern Northwest Coast formline style (see §(iv) below) and suggest that they had common antecedents.

(iii) Central. The central Northwest Coast includes the Wakashan-speaking Makah in Washington state and the Nootka of western Vancouver Island, the Kwakiutl of northern Vancouver Island and the adjacent mainland of British Columbia, and the Salish-speaking Bella Coola in central British Columbia. In some ways the Makah and Nootka might equally be included in the southern Northwest Coast region: they are close neighbours of the Coast Salish, and their prehistoric art is remarkably similar to historic Halkomelem art. However, their linguistic and cultural similarities with the Wakashan-speaking Kwakiutl place them culturally in the central area.

17. Northwest Coast wolf mask, wood with cedar-bark and painted cloth attachments, l. 1.17 m, Makah (New York, National Museum of the American Indian)

Excavations that have been dated to *c.* AD 1500 at the wet site of OZETTE on the north-west tip of Washington state have unearthed the largest collection of prehistoric wood sculpture from the Northwest Coast (Neah Bay, WA, Makah Cult. & Res. Cent.). Flat, low-relief carvings on chests, combs, retaining planks, clubs, spindle whorls and other tools reveal the use of negative crescents and of T- and wedge-shapes to define the positive outlines of animal and human forms. Whalebone war-clubs from the site are identical in style to clubs collected by the earliest European explorers on the coast at Nootka Sound on Vancouver Island. Hooked-beak thunderbirds with pointed eyelid lines decorate the pommels, and the blades frequently display negative triangular and crescent shapes that define jointlike circular forms or zigzag lines.

The treatment of the human figure on the central Northwest Coast is more three-dimensional than in southern Coast Salish or Chinookan art (*see* §(ii) above). Makah and Nootka human figures in house posts and freestanding figures are naturalistic, rounded and frontally oriented, similar to those of the central and northern Coast Salish. However, the structure of the face, rather than being flat as in Salish sculpture, is based on a prismatic principal form. The sides of the face slant back from the central ridge of the nose, forehead and chin. Lips are drawn back along the planes of the face. The underbrow plane is long and slanted, rather than being sharply stepped-back as in Salish sculpture. The eyes are large with pointed eyelid lines (often slanting up at the front and down at the back of the eye) and are placed flat on the cheek plane with no projecting eyeball. The planes of the face are smooth and minimally carved, and the surface is frequently decorated with painted sweeping geometric patterns. The earliest Nootkan masks (London, BM) collected in the late 18th century have less deeply carved faces than late 19th-century masks, but their long, slanting underbrow and back-swept cheeks prefigure the deep prismatic masks of the late 19th century.

The Nootka and Makah also carved masks or headdresses for use during their major winter ceremonial, the Wolf Dance, called Klookwalli (Makah) or Tlookwana (Nootka). The principal masks are wolf headdresses, carved from a solid block of wood, with long snouts, narrow lips, many teeth and large eyes with pointed eyelid lines. Lightning serpent, thunderbird and a variety of humanoid masks representing inherited privileges were also used during the wolf dances. From the late 19th century onwards, wolf, lightning serpent and thunderbird masks have sometimes been made of flat boards, later plywood, joined together at the nose. Facial details are painted on the surface, and piercing in the mouth, teeth and along the forehead crest adds to the elegance of the masks (see fig. 17). Globular rattles representing grouse and other birds are also made by Makah and Nootka artists.

Late 19th-century Kwakiutl sculpture is dramatically different from the more southern styles. While Nootka and Coast Salish sculpture is characterized by smooth, nearly flat planes, late 19th-century Kwakiutl sculpture has rounded and deeply carved surfaces. The typical facial form is half-cylindrical with the forehead rounded back above the brow. The eyeball is pronounced and bulging, and the planes of the eye-socket and mouth are sharply defined; nostrils and lips are sharply defined, the mouth projection intersects with the forecheek plane in a sharp cheek line, and the sides of the eye-socket are sharply cut. Painting generally follows the carved lines of the face.

Kwakiutl sculpture includes interior house posts, memorial poles and standing human figures representing crests or ancestors. These monumental sculptures are fully three-dimensional. Human figures are generally naturalistic in proportion, except for their enlarged heads. The arms, wings, fins and beaks of figures were often carved from separate pieces of wood and attached as extensions to the central pole, adding a dynamic aspect (see fig. 18). Most

18. Northwest Coast memorial pole (1931), red cedar wood, by the Kwakiutl artist Willie Seaweed, Alert Bay cemetery, British Columbia

spectacular are the masks made for the ceremonial dance complexes known as the Tseyka (Red Cedar Bark dances) and Tlasula (Feather dances). These are highly dramatic and theatrical performances that display the inherited privileges of the host family. Huge human-eating bird masks appear during the Hamatsa dances, the most important dances of the Tseyka. The Tlasula involves the use of dancing headdresses with long ermine skin trailers. These headdresses, which have carved masklike frontlets, representing the dancer's crests, attached above the forehead, are made by all groups from the Kwakiutl north to the Tlingit and are generally used in a peace or welcoming dance. When used in the Tlasula, their appearance is followed by the arrival of a masked dancer representing a supernatural being.

The Bella Coola people are Salish speakers, and their complex cosmology includes a vast range of mythical beings. While this mythology differs somewhat from that of their neighbours, their art styles reflect their close association with the neighbouring Kwakwala-speaking and Northern Wakashan-speaking peoples. The Bella Coola have two ceremonial complexes that are roughly equivalent to the Kwakiutl Tseyka (Kusioot) and Tlasula (Sisaok) and provide occasions for the display of inherited privileges. Bella Coola sculpture, like that of their neighbours, includes house posts and house frontal poles (although apparently no fully sculpted poles), headdress frontlets and a wide variety of masks. Humanoid masks are generally naturalistic but distinctive in style. The forehead and chin both slope backwards from the prominent nose, giving masks a hemispherical principal form. The pronounced eyeballs resemble truncated cones. The underbrow plane slopes down on the outer side of the eye, intersecting with the upper cheek plane in a sharply carved line. The cheek below this intersection bulges at the point where the cheek-bone would be in natural anatomy. Holm (1983) described this feature as the 'Bella Coola bulge'. Lips have a conical outward projection and are frequently open with a diamond-like appearance. Eyebrows are generally heavy and slant downwards on the temple. The painting on Bella Coola masks differs significantly from that of Kwakiutl masks in that it extends in broad U-form lobes across the carved surfaces of the face (see §IV, 1(i) below).

(iv) Northern. The northern Northwest Coast region includes the Northern Wakashan-speaking peoples (linguistically related to the Kwakiutl and to the Nootka), the Tsimshian of northern British Columbia, the Haida of the Queen Charlotte Islands and the Tlingit of south-east Alaska. The art of this area is unified by its close adherence to the two-dimensional system known as 'northern formline design' (*see* §IV, 1(i) below). House posts, house frontal poles, memorial poles, masks, frontlets, rattles, staffs, boxes, chests, bowls and spoons were all carved. Humanoid masks have a half-cylindrical principal form and are frequently naturalistic, even portrait-like.

The Northern Wakashan linguistic area includes the Haisla, Haihais and Heiltsuk groups. Haisla and Haihais sculpture is similar to Tsimshian and Haida art, while Heiltsuk sculpture more closely resembles the Heiltsuk art to the south. Consequently, no unified sculptural system can be assigned to this area. Most distinctive are the humanoid masks made by the artists from the village of Bella Bella. While similar to Nuxalk masks, the eyeballs are larger and more flattened, with narrow and sharply carved surrounding upper cheek and underbrow planes. Additionally, Heiltsuk masks lack the 'Nuxalk bulge' (*see* §(iii) above).

Tsimshian masks and frontlets (and those made by their Haisla and Haihais neighbours) have large rounded eyeballs, with eyelids defined by a single-edged incision, rather than the wide, painted eyelid line used elsewhere on the northern coast. The cheek area has a pyramidal form, in which the side, upper and forecheek merge. Masks were produced in a wide range of humanoid forms and used to dramatize the appearance of spirits in a display of power called Nakhnokh. Figures on Tsimshian totem poles tend to be more naturalistic than Haida or Tlingit sculpture. The limbs are rounded, and the figures stand in a more upright position, rather than crouching with knees drawn up, and are separated, rather than interlocked as on Haida poles. Tsimshian artists also specialized in producing raven rattles. Used throughout the northern Northwest Coast and as far south as Vancouver Island, these elaborate chief's rattles take the form of a raven with a human figure reclining on the back. Shaman's equipment produced by Tsimshian artists includes tubular bone soulcatchers, also carved in low-relief formline design.

Haida sculpture ranges from highly stylized to fully naturalistic. While Haida artists were perhaps the most skilled portraitists on the Northwest Coast, they were also capable of adhering strictly to the rules of the formline system of design (*see* §IV, 1(i) below). Famous for their 'forests' of monumental totem poles, Haida artists were equally skilled at small-scale sculpture on mountain goat horn spoon handles. Totem poles were treated in a flat, two-dimensional way, as if a flat formline design were wrapped around the cylindrical pole, with negative areas between the formlines carved away. Figures crouch in compact stances with knees drawn up, often touching elbows. Figures on poles, spoon handles and other forms are frequently interlocked, grasping each other with beak, mouth or claws, and with the hands and feet of one figure extending through the ears and mouths of its neighbours.

During the 19th century Haida artists began to carve argillite, a soft black stone, in the form of tobacco pipes, which were sold to visiting Euro-American fur traders. Soon they were producing elaborate non-functional pipes, platters and figural sculpture, including images of ships and Euro-Americans; these objects became the first specifically 'tourist' art of the Northwest Coast. During the late 19th century, when full-sized totem poles had ceased to be made, small model totem poles, model houses and

19. Northwest Coast, carved interior of Whale House, Klukwan, Alaska, by the Tlingit wood-carver Cádjisdu'axtc, early 19th century; photograph by Lloyd L. Winter and Edwin P. Pond, 1895

figures representing Haida chiefs and shamans were produced in both wood and argillite for sale to outsiders. Argillite carving has remained an active art form for Haida artists throughout the 20th century (*see* §(v) below).

As with other northern groups, Tlingit sculpture could be naturalistic and portrait-like, yet human facial features in Tlingit masks can be distinguished from those of their neighbours. The features are rounded; large eyes with rounded orbs frequently have unconstricted or open eyelid lines. Lips are wide and form a continuous band, often raised at the corners of the mouth. The upper cheek plane frequently slopes in an uninterrupted line from the eye to the raised lip-band. Masks were made both for the display of inherited crests and as shaman's equipment. Masklike faces representing frightening creatures or imposing humans were also carved on warriors' helmets. Other warriors' equipment, such as dagger handles, and shamans' paraphernalia in the form of amulets and rattles were elaborately sculpted with supernatural spirit helpers that could be interpreted only by the owners. Inherited crest art also included headdresses and crest hats, bowls, spoons, pipes, staffs and house posts. Few exterior totem poles were carved in the more northern Tlingit areas, but interior house posts and screens were elaborate representations of inherited crests. Some, such as the interior posts and screen of the Klukwan Whale House (see fig. 19) and the house posts from Chief Shakes's house in Wrangell, are exceptionally fine. Like the Haida, Tlingit carvers exploited the developing tourist trade in the late 19th century and the 20th, carving models of poles, shaman figures and silver jewellery.

(v) Contemporary developments. During the 20th century sculpture on the Northwest Coast has continued to be produced, with Native American artists creating spectacular works that range from monumental to delicate, and from traditional to innovative. Carving and sculpture remain vital elements of the cultural heritage of the peoples of the Northwest Coast. After the devastating smallpox epidemics of the 1860s, missionary activity that discouraged such traditional social and religious practices as the potlatch and shamanism, and the banning of the potlatch by both the US and Canadian governments in the 1880s, many tribes experienced a decline in their traditional arts, continuing only those arts that produced objects for sale to outsiders: basketwork, silverwork, argillite carving and model-making. Remarkably, however, several groups succeeded in preserving their ceremonial arts. Most successfully, the Kwakiutl continued their potlatching traditions, even though they had to be practised in secret until the 1950s, when the anti-potlatch law was reversed. During the early 20th century such master artists as CHARLIE JAMES, WILLIE SEAWEED, MUNGO MARTIN and others produced traditional masks for ceremonial use as well as memorial poles and model poles made for sale (see fig. 18 above).

Groups that had experienced a decline in the traditional arts—the Haida, Tlingit, Tsimshian, Nootka and Coast Salish—have experienced strong revivals of their arts since the 1960s. BILL REID, ROBERT DAVIDSON, Nathan Jackson (*b* 1941), Norman Tait (*b* 1941), JOE DAVID and Art Thompson (*b* 1948) are at the forefront of this revival.

BIBLIOGRAPHY

B. Holm: *Northwest Coast Indian Art: An Analysis of Form* (Seattle, 1965)
Boxes and Bowls: Decorated Containers by Nineteenth-century Haida, Tlingit, Bella Bella and Tsimshian Indian Artists (exh. cat. by W. C. Sturtevant, Washington, DC, Renwick Gal., 1974)
The Legacy: Continuing Traditions of Canadian North-west Coast Indian Art (exh. cat. by P. Macnair, A. Hoover and K. Neary, Victoria, BC, Prov. Mus., 1980); rev. as *The Legacy: Tradition and Innovation in North-west Coast Indian Art* (Seattle, 1984)
P. Nuytten: *The Totem Carvers: Charlie James, Ellen Neel and Mungo Martin* (Vancouver, 1982)
R. K. Wright: 'Haida Argillite Carved for Sale', *Amer. Ind. A.*, viii/1 (1982), pp. 48–55
R. Carlson, ed.: *Indian Art Traditions of the North-west Coast* (Burnaby, BC, 1983)
B. Holm: 'Form in North-west Coast Indian Art', *Indian Art Traditions of the North-west Coast*, ed. R. Carlson (Burnaby, BC, 1983), pp. 33–46
——: *Smoky-Top: The Art and Times of Willie Seaweed* (Seattle, 1983)
W. Suttles: 'Productivity and its Constraints: A Coast Salish Case', *Indian Art Traditions of the North-west Coast*, ed. R. Carlson (Burnaby, BC, 1983), pp. 67–88
D. Cole: *Captured Heritage: The Scramble for North-west Coast Artifacts* (Vancouver, 1985)
K. R. Fladmark: *British Columbian Prehistory* (Ottawa, 1986)
S. Brown: 'From Taquan to Klukwan: Tracing the Work of an Early Tlingit Master Artist', *Faces, Voices and Dreams: A Celebration of the Centennial of the Sheldon Jackson Museum*, ed. P. Corey (Juneau, 1987), pp. 157–76
B. Holm: 'The Head Canoe', *Faces, Voices and Dreams: A Celebration of the Centennial of the Sheldon Jackson Museum*, ed. P. Corey (Juneau, 1987), pp. 143–56
J. Miller: *Shamanic Odyssey: The Lushootseed Salish Journey to the Land of the Dead* (Menlo Park, 1988)
D. Cole and I. Chaikin: *An Iron Hand upon the People: The Law against the Potlatch on the North-west Coast* (Vancouver and Seattle, 1990)
B. Holm: 'Art', *Hb. N. Amer. Ind.*, vii (1990), pp. 602–32
——: 'Kwakiutl: Winter Ceremonies', *Hb. N. Amer. Ind.*, vii (1990), pp. 378–86
——: 'Historical, Salish Canoes', *A Time of Gathering: Native Heritage in Washington State*, ed. R. K. Wright (Seattle, 1991)
A. Jonaitis: *Chiefly Feasts* (Seattle, 1991), pp. 238–47
W. Suttles: 'The Shed-Roof House', *A Time of Gathering: Native Heritage in Washington State*, ed. R. K. Wright (Seattle, 1991), pp. 212–22

ROBIN K. WRIGHT

3. GREAT BASIN. The carving and sculpture of the Great Basin comprises large-scale petroglyphic rock art and small, portable objects in stone, bone, wood, clay, feathers and plant parts. Because works range in age from *c.* 6000 BC to the 19th century and represent a diversity of forms and images, their cultural affiliations and exact functions are not always known. Some portable items include possible pendants, which may have been purely decorative; others, which appear to echo themes in rock art or are found cached in seemingly unusual locations, may reflect religious practices.

Petroglyphic rock art, although not strictly carving or sculpture, is related by technique of manufacture and sometimes imagery. Although flat rather than volumetric, it sometimes takes advantage of natural rock contours or has places within the image that might be enhanced with some extra work. Petroglyphs were made by pecking with a stone tool the outline of an image and sometimes the full surface of the image on a highly patinated stone surface. In the Great Basin at least two styles of such work have been identified along with several minor or regional variants. These are a curvilinear style, with motifs including concentric circles, sun discs, meanders, snakes etc, and a rectilinear style, typified by rectangular grids, dots, rakes, crosshatches etc (Heizer and Baumhoff). Both of these feature abstract images, although what is called the representational style is sometimes found in association with them. This style has identifiable birds, big-horn sheep, anthropomorphs, mammals etc. A scratched style, featuring images made with a sharp implement, is sometimes seen in the same locations. Very limited chronological control suggests curvilinear motifs may be earlier than rectilinear, and that scratched may be the latest. Specific representational styles appear to be correlated with Fremont and Anasazi occupations of the region (AD 500–1200), but others are undoubtedly older (Schaafsma). As with Great Basin pictographic art, there is a tendency for images to be clustered in certain locations, only in part controlled by suitable base materials. Relationships to hunting sites and game trails have been noted, but there are undoubtedly other functions as well. Small, portable stone slabs, sometimes with similar pecked and scratched motifs and sometimes not, also occur over much of the area around springs and in the fill of archaeological sites. Their purpose is unknown.

Among the small, free-standing carvings and sculptures are several from archaeological sites throughout the region, in particular from western Nevada. These include what appear to be fish, horned lizards, grasshoppers or locusts, snakes, birds, rabbits and big-horn sheep, as well as more abstract forms (Carson City, NV, Mus.). Most are in stone—carefully pecked and incised—or in bone (bird, big-horn sheep) that has been cut to shape and incised with lines, dots and other forms. A few show evidence of pigment in depressions, as if they were once painted. Important areas of provenance include the Humboldt, Carson and Pyramid Lake basins in western Nevada, known to have been focal points for the Lovelock culture, dated *c.* 1000 BC to *c.* AD 1000. Although some of these items are surface finds and thus not datable, a few come from Lovelock culture contexts in caves and rock shelters. Some have possible associations with shamanism.

Equally conjectural is the function of the split-twig figurines of the eastern and southern Great Basin, which have particular charm. Caches of these figures, made by ingeniously splitting and wrapping single, or occasionally multiple, stems of willow or lemonade berry (*Rhus trilobata*) into zoomorphic forms, were first discovered in caves in the Grand Canyon in northern Arizona in the 1930s (Grand N. Park, AZ). Since then they have been found singly or in groups in about 15 archaeological localities in southern California, southern Nevada, northern Arizona and eastern Utah, mostly in contexts dated *c.* 2000–*c.* 1100 BC. The animals represented are difficult to identify, although some with horns may be deer or big-horn sheep. Some Grand Canyon specimens contain within the wrapped body cavities faecal pellets of deer, big-horn sheep or mountain goats. One from Newberry Cave in southern California (San Bernardino, CA, Co. Mus.) contains a worked stone flake. At least one figurine (Grand N. Park, AZ) from the Grand Canyon has what appears to be a spear thrust into it (Schroedl, 1977). Grand Canyon specimens are often found grouped in caves that lack other evidence of human occupation; some are contained in rock cairns that also suggest religious functions. Finds outside of this region may be associated with other types of living debris and thus suggest more secular

uses. All known sites date from *c.* 9500 BC–*c.* AD 500) but cannot be given a more precise cultural affiliation.

Although also of unknown function, two sculptural forms from the eastern Great Basin can be assigned to the Fremont culture. This was partly agricultural, partly sedentary (occupying multi-roomed adobe and stone structures) and loosely affiliated with the cultures of the Southwest (*see* §§I, 1(v) and (vii), and 2(i) above). It flourished over much of Utah and parts of adjacent Colorado from *c.* AD 500 to *c.* 1200. The sculptural forms produced by Fremont peoples include baked and unbaked clay figurines with elaborate decoration, and small soft-fibre pieces, consisting of plant materials wrapped around a central core and displaying horns and feathers. Both these forms, but especially the clay figurines, resemble decorated and/or horned anthropomorphic figures in Fremont painted rock art (*see* §IV, 1(ii) below). The clay figurines are occasionally found cached in groups at Fremont sites.

The peoples occupying the Great Basin at the time of Euro-American contact in the late 18th–early 19th century apparently produced little carving and sculpture. The Northern and Southern Paiute made small unbaked clay figurines and clay utensils as children's toys, and bone carvings and shellwork pendants and earrings are also known from all groups, as are stone and clay pipes.

BIBLIOGRAPHY

S. Wheeler: 'Prehistoric Miniatures', *The Masterkey*, xi (1937), p. 181
R. F. Heizer and M. A. Baumhoff: *Prehistoric Rock Art of Nevada and Eastern California* (Berkeley, 1962)
A. Schroedl: 'The Grand Canyon Figurine Complex', *Amer. Ant.*, xlii (1977), pp. 254–65
D. Tuohy: 'Portable Art Objects', *Hb. N. Amer. Ind.*, xi (1986), pp. 227–37
P. Schaafsma: 'Rock Art', *Hb. N. Amer. Ind.*, xi (1986), pp. 215–26

CATHERINE S. FOWLER

4. SOUTHWEST.

(i) Introduction. The principal type of Southwest sculpture is the wooden *kachina* doll or *tihu*. Such dolls have been of interest to Euro-Americans since the Spanish attempted to eradicate them as heathen idols in the late 16th century. By the mid-19th century attitudes had changed, and the first doll was collected by Dr Edward Palmer of the US Army and subsequently presented to the National Museum of American Art, Washington, DC. Rooted in the Pueblo culture of northern New Mexico and Arizona, the beginnings of the *kachina* cult remain unknown, although archaeologists perceive similarities to artefacts of the 10th and 11th centuries AD; it is only from the 1850s onwards that this evolving art form can be studied in detail.

Kachinas themselves are not gods but the essences or spirits of different elements in the Pueblo world. Neither good nor evil in themselves, they are intercessors between men and deities. In addition to their special natures, *kachinas* may cause or cure various diseases or promote increase, but they are always rain-bringers, fulfilling the most imperative need of farmers in an arid land. They take three forms: an invisible spirit, a masked male dancer and a wooden doll or *tihu* (see fig. 20). When Pueblo men don mask and costume to become one with the spirit they portray, they give visual form to the *kachina* (see fig. 21). The small carved wooden *tihu* is a replica of the dancer's

this evolution of use, changes in carving tools, paints and supplementary materials have occurred; but more importantly there has been a shift in what the dolls represent. They no longer represent just the symbolic characteristics of *kachina* spirits but have become instead artistic renditions more freely inspired by *kachina*s. Within a century *kachina* dolls have evolved from strictly religious artefacts to a diverse art form that ranges from the true *tihu* to triumphs of expressive wood-carving, even including political satires.

(ii) Chronological development. The sequence of *kachina* dolls can be divided into six main periods. While Spanish records after 1630 document fully carved dolls, no such early examples survive. Rare examples of flat dolls exist, as do ceramic representations of *kachina*s. The earliest extant *tihu*s are from the Early Classic period (1850–85). These are roughly carved, with emphasis on an over-large head, and are often nude, with the genitalia indicated. The arms and hands are rudimentary; legs may be shaped, but feet are not. These dolls are painted entirely with native pigments.

By the Late Classic period (1885–1910), 'Victorian' morality had apparently eradicated the nude figure. New materials were being introduced, such as poster paint and dyed feathers, and some dolls were dressed in miniature clothing. The legs, arms and feet were often carved

20. Southwest region doll representing a *kachina* spirit (*tihu*), painted wood and feathers, h. 382 mm, Hopi, collected before 1894 (Copenhagen, Nationalmuseum)

appearance. This doll is given to infants of both sexes while they are still babes in arms, but thereafter only to girls. The first dolls given to infants are flat tablets, sometimes with faces carved in low relief at one end and with painted indications of hands and arms but no feet or legs. As the girls grow older they receive fully carved dolls. The doll is not, as sometimes stated, a device to teach the females about *kachina*s but a token of bonding between mortal and supernatural.

Hopi *tihu*s are carved of cottonwood, a tree whose roots reach deep in search of water. The wood of the root is light, easily carved, difficult to split and, above all, psychologically satisfying, since it seeks water just as the Hopi farmer does. The ritual carving of *tihu*s continues as an integral part of Hopi Native American religion, but in the 1890s some sale of dolls began, despite tribal disapproval, and this practice has steadily increased. Collected first as objects of anthropological interest, then as tourist curios, they have also become examples of fine art. During

21. Southwest region, Hopi *kachina* dancers of the Powamu or bean-planting ceremony; from a photograph of 1893 (Washington, DC, Smithsonian Institution)

separately and then glued, nailed or pegged on as though wood were in short supply.

From the Early Traditional period (1910–45) onwards dolls were bought as curios. Although only a few were made for the tourist trade, many *tihu*s were purchased after their ritual presentation to girls. The Great Depression of the 1930s brought this trade almost to an end, but the ritual use of *tihu*s continued unabated. Dolls of this period are more standardized in appearance than earlier dolls and are often carved in one piece, with the exception of the arms. Proportions are better, and hands, feet and limbs are more naturalistic. Tempera replaced all native pigments.

In the Late Traditional period (1945–60) Hopi veterans of World War II brought home new ideas. One of their first efforts was to make a doll that would stand alone rather than hang from a wall, suspended by a string around its neck. Because the feet could not make dolls stable enough to stand, bases were developed, opening the way for further significant changes in style. Although the figures stood flat-footed, knees were often bent or arms carved in an outstretched position; and objects were more often carved or placed in the doll's hands. Casein was tried as a new paint, but tempera remained the most frequent choice. A few unpainted carvings were also done, and in a radical new departure some Hopi began to sign their works. Children were supposed to believe that *tihu*s came from the *kachina*s.

The Early Florescent period (1960–75) was a time of great experimentation, expanding concepts and a rekindled public interest in purchasing the dolls. The 'Action' doll, portraying the dancers' movements in increasingly naturalistic poses, was introduced, and new materials were used to enhance the lifelike quality. Imported shells began to be used, as did felts and plastics, beads and bells, and exotic furs and leathers. The *kachina* doll's neck ruff is characteristic of the Hopi carvers' experimentation. From the usual evergreen foliage, which dried and fell off, they changed to plastic imitations, then to English seaweed, then to green yarn and finally to carved wood. Ethnically correct feathers, the use of which was discouraged by the Endangered Species Act of 1974, had to be abandoned and chicken, pheasant and other domestic bird feathers substituted. Carvings from single pieces of wood began, acrylic paints replaced tempera, and fixatives were used to hold or brighten the colours. The increased demands of non-Hopi people produced many eccentric carvings of erotic dolls, jumping toys, Disney creations, elements of folk-tales and other untraditional ideas. For several years dolls increased steadily in both size and price, but when this market declined, large-scale *kachina*s were quickly replaced with miniature carvings. A few dolls of this period were cast in bronze. However, despite the experiments and changing fashions the dolls retained their essential identity and continued to grow in popularity.

The Late Florescent period (1975–) began with more sophisticated experimentation, involving not only paint but also form and concept, and it included the final change from *tihu* to art object. Carvings cut from a single piece of wood were continued, with increasing complexity, often embodying two or more *kachina*s from a single ceremony. Wood stains and artists' dyes were tried by various artists for different effects. Some pieces were even left completely unpainted to show the wood. Such muted dolls were an instant commercial success and almost immediately replaced those painted with acrylics; they were avidly sought by art galleries. During this interval Dremel cutting tools and the burning iron were introduced, speeding up and enhancing the artists' work. However, the ritually given *tihu* remained a simpler carving, usually painted with acrylics.

Wider exposure to the art world brought several developments. Experimentation with form resulted in attenuated figures, whose bodies were enormously lengthened, and the delineation of hands, arms or feet was deleted. The bodies were left as long clean lines of wood, or small pueblo scenes or other devices were carved in low relief in the blank expanses of the bodies. First made as single figures, they were soon grouped in multiples of similar figures. In another experimental form the *kachina* body disappeared completely. Traditional symbols or implied associations with other objects were incorporated in a single carving. The result is not a *kachina* doll but a piece of expressionistic sculpture. The carving of clowns has resulted in a distinctive satirical form, in which political issues are 'dramatized', usually by figurines of clowns.

Although fashions have changed, and new forms have been established, dolls that resemble the earliest *tihu*s are still made, and most *tihu*s are still carved by the men of the villages to be ritually presented to the girls.

BIBLIOGRAPHY
A. Ortiz, ed.: 'Southwest', *Hb. N. Amer. Ind.*, ix (1979) [whole vol.]
——: 'Southwest', *Hb. N. Amer. Ind.*, x (1983) [whole vol.]

B. WRIGHT

5. PLAINS. Most Plains Native American sculpture was in miniature. While the nomadism of the most typical Plains tribes, such as the Sioux, Blackfeet and Crow, was probably a significant factor in explaining the desire for portable three-dimensional artwork, even among the more sedentary tribes, such as the Mandan, Arikara and Hidatsa of the Missouri River region, no large carved sculpture has been found. One notable exception to this custom was the Plains Cree and Ojibwa use of human effigy spirit posts, which were observed as early as 1700 in the vicinity of the Beaver River in eastern Alberta, by the fur-trader Peter Fidler (MacGregor, p. 115). Such posts, which were generally life-size, had crudely carved heads and were referred to as 'Mantokan', from the Algonquian *maniot*, a term for the mysterious life powers of the universe. Fidler reported that the Native Americans erected them in the hope that 'the great Menneto will grant them and their families health while they remain in these parts'. Before the arrival of Europeans, the carving of objects in the round was done with stone implements; however, bone and possibly pieces of copper obtained in trade may also have been employed. While appearing primitive, such tools were considerably more efficient in the hands of a skilled craftsman than might be imagined.

Some of the finest Plains Native American carvings, in the form of pipe-bowls, are of catlinite (see fig. 22). The artist and explorer GEORGE CATLIN (after whom the stone was named) expressed the opinion in 1832 that the Pawnee were probably the 'most ingenious' of all the Plains peoples

22. Plains region pipe-bowl, carved catlinite, 85×187 mm, Ojibwa, c. 1830 (Rome, Museo Nazionale Preistorico ed Etnografico Luigi Pigorini)

in the production of such articles. More recently, however, several examples have been located that suggest that some members of the Eastern Sioux tribes—possibly Santee—were also adept carvers of effigy pipes (Ewers, 1981). In 1841 Catlin described how the Plains groups, whom he had observed in the early 1830s, drilled their pipe-bowls: 'the Indian makes a hole in the bowl of the pipe, by drilling into it a hard stick, shaped to the desired size, with a quantity of sharp sand and water kept constantly in the hole' (Catlin, i, p. 234). Experiments show that such work was very time consuming. For example, a cone-shaped hole some 25 mm in depth, drilled into catlinite employing this method, took one hour (West, 1934, pp. 341-2).

Studies of Plains Native American horse effigies show that horses were often depicted on mirrors and pipes and that carved replicas of weapons were also popular, such as wooden models of guns or lances and clubs (West, 1978 and 1979). In his studies West identified the carver of several horse effigy sticks, which were coloured with various clays and juices from fruits, as a Hunkpapa Sioux called No Two Horns, who was renowned as a wood-carver. No Two Horns was also remembered for the dolls and miniature weapons he carved for his grandchildren.

A survey of Woodland sculpture (Ritzenthaler) has revealed that carved objects from that region were rarely more than 300 mm long and that woodworking was carried out by men. After the arrival of Europeans, the chipped-stone tool kits anciently used by these people were quickly replaced with their steel and iron counterparts. The bowls, ladles, fish lures (carved and painted wooden figures simulating frogs or minnows), pipe-stems, flutes and clubs produced were frequently embellished with a single carved effigy. Magico-religious carvings were also produced for use by shamans. Comparison of such work with Plains sculpture has led to the conclusion that numerous characteristics were shared by Plains Native American sculpture (Ewers, 1986, p. 11), although Plains Native American

sculpture was not necessarily simply a westward extension of that of the Woodlands region (see §6 below).

It is not known how much wooden sculpture the early Plains people produced; the general rapid deterioration of wood in the ground would explain the absence of effigy carvings in archaeological sites on the Great Plains. On the other hand, effigy carvings made of catlinite (a soft red stone quarried in Minnesota) have been found in Plains archaeological sites dated earlier than the late 15th century (Ewers, 1986, pp. 12, 15).

BIBLIOGRAPHY
G. Catlin: Letters and Notes on the Manners, Customs and Condition of the North American Indian, 2 vols (London, 1841)
G. West: 'Tobacco Pipes and Smoking Customs of the American Indians', Bull. Pub. Mus. City Milwaukee, xvii (1934) [whole issue]
J. G. MacGregor: Peter Fidler: Canada's Forgotten Surveyor, 1769–1822 (Toronto, 1966)
R. Ritzenthaler: 'Woodland Sculpture', Amer. Ind. A., iv (1976), pp. 34–41
I. West: 'Plains Indian Horse Sticks', Amer. Ind. A., iii (1978), pp. 58–67
——: 'Tributes to a Horse Nation: Plains Indian Horse Effigies', SD Hist., ix/4 (1979) [whole issue]
J. C. Ewers: 'Pipes for the Presidents', Amer. Ind. A., vi/3 (1981), pp. 66–70
——: Plains Indian Sculpture (Washington, DC, 1986)

COLIN TAYLOR

6. WOODLANDS. The Woodland Native Americans have had a rich artistic tradition of sculpture from at least the Late Archaic period (c. 4000–c. 1000 BC). The archaeological record includes sculpture in stone, wood, bone and shell. Sculpturally embellished artefacts were used for both ritual and utilitarian purposes. Many items are sophisticated works of art, for example the highly stylized birdstones of the Late Archaic and Early Woodland periods (c. 4000–c. 100 BC), often characterized by elongated beaks, fan tails or 'popeyes'; or the platform pipes of the Middle Woodland period (c. 100 BC–c. AD 500) with

their realistic bird and animal images. The tradition continued to grow and evolve during the historic period, after
c. 1600.

At the time of their first contact with Europeans,
Woodland Native Americans led a semi-nomadic life, with
hunting and fishing grounds spread over a wide territory
and an intimate knowledge of the natural environment
that resulted in their highly successful adaptation to the
land. A nomadic lifestyle dictated that possessions be
limited to the necessities of life and be easily transportable.
Both utilitarian and ritual objects were decorated. While
women made and decorated clothing (*see* §VIII below),
men concentrated on the manufacture of ritual and
utilitarian items. The creative ability and personal choice
of the individual artist determined decorative ideas but
were tempered by the dictates of cultural tradition and
confined within the broad limits of tribal preference. The
introduction of metal tools by Europeans (knives, saws,
files etc) opened technical possibilities for more complex
designs and stimulated an increase in artistic production.

Wooden bowls, spoons and ladles were among the
items chosen for sculptural treatment. The preferred
materials were ash and maple burl, because the close-knit
burl grain was a strong and durable product, and the grain
pattern also added to the aesthetic appeal of the finished
piece. Sculptural representations of birds, animals or
mythical beings were usually placed above the rims of
bowls. Occasionally the entire bowl was carved to suggest
an animal lying on its back with its head, tail and feet
extending above the rim. In other examples the animal's
legs were carved in low relief along the sides, with its head
and tail protruding from opposite ends. Spoons, ladles
and stirring sticks were carved in a similar style with bird,
animal or human figures decorating the handle.

Wooden war-clubs were also sculpted: the two most
popular styles were the ball-head club and the gunstock
club. Ball-head clubs were carved from young trees
growing on steep hillsides or along riverbanks. If the wood
had been carefully selected, the grain pattern followed the
curve of the club, and a strong weapon was produced by
shaping the ball from the root and the handle from the
trunk. The club was often carved to represent an animal
holding the ball in its jaws. The handles were sometimes
decorated with an animal form in relief next to the ball.
The gunstock club was named from its musket-shaped
profile. It was made from a flat piece of wood and often
decorated with incised carving, including birds, animals,
the heavenly bodies and geometric designs. Occasionally
the decoration was pictorial, representing the life experiences of the owner.

Pipe-bowls were another favourite item for carved
decoration. The preferred material was soft sedimentary
stone (red, grey or black in colour) that could be easily
worked (e.g. catlinite). The sculptural forms of pipe-bowls
range from elegant versions of the basic form (a funnel-
shaped bowl, a short tapering prow and a shank, which
might have a raised fin) to both realistic and stylized
images of humans and animals. The pipe-bowl was often
carved in the shape of a human head usually facing the
smoker (see fig. 23). Artists also produced realistic zoomorphic forms on pipes, making identification of the
particular animal possible. Pipe-stems were usually made

23. Woodlands region pipe-bowl, carved catlinite, 79×66 mm, Miami,
c. 1750–1800 (Detroit, MI, Detroit Institute of Arts)

from an ashwood sapling. One popular idea was to carve
the stem to suggest that the wood had been twisted in a
corkscrew fashion. Other examples depict animals in low
relief along the length of the stem.

The curved shape of the crooked knife handle also
suggested a variety of carved motifs to Woodland artists.
Human and animal bodies lent themselves to the flowing
form of the handle and were used with remarkable effects.
Heddles and awls were other tools given similar treatment.

Religious and ritual items, also produced exclusively by
men, comprise another important part of the sculptural
tradition. Perhaps the best-known examples are the
wooden masks of the Iroquois False Face Society, in which
human and animal faces were depicted in a contorted,
occasionally grotesque, manner. Native Americans from
the western Great Lakes produced carved human figures
associated with the Midewiwin Society (the Grand Medicine Lodge). Miniature carved wooden items, such as war-
clubs, bows and arrows, were placed in sacred bundles
referred to as 'man's business' and probably served as
sympathetic magic to ensure the success of a hunt or war
party. Under the influence of Christianity and pressures
from the encroaching Euro-American society, traditional
Woodland cultures changed, and by the early years of the
20th century many traditional forms and techniques had
disappeared.

BIBLIOGRAPHY

R. E. Ritzenthaler and P. Ritzenthaler: *The Woodland Indians of the Western
    Great Lakes* (New York, 1970)
Art of the Great Lakes Indians, Flint Institute of Arts (Flint, MI, 1973)
D. S. Brose, J. A. Brown and D. W. Penney: *Ancient Art of the American
    Woodland Indians* (New York, 1985)
W. N. Fenton: *The False Faces of the Iroquois* (Norman, 1987)
D. W. Penney, ed.: *Great Lakes Indian Art* (Detroit, 1989)

RICHARD A. POHRT

IV. Painting.

Before European contact, Native American painting was endowed with a variety of ritual and social purposes by diverse cultural groups throughout the continent. Despite the ravages brought by Euro-American invaders and settlers, many Native American painting traditions survived and evolved into new art forms. Painting traditions continued in the Southwest, on the Plains and the North-west Coast, often retaining their ritual function, while new styles influenced by Euro-American painting traditions, new materials and new audiences catered to the new market, while providing a means of perserving cultural identities (*see* §2 below).

1. Before European contact. 2. After European contact.

1. BEFORE EUROPEAN CONTACT. Painting as 'fine art' was not a distinct category of Native American art before European contact. There were no such terms as 'decorative art', 'fine art', 'folk art' or 'primitive art'; nor did Native American languages have specific terms for 'artist' or 'painter' (*see also* §I, 5 and 6 above). A Native American artist was simply a person who worked for the general well-being of the community, attempting to harmonize the temporal and spiritual worlds through the creation of beautiful objects.

(i) Northwest Coast. (ii) Great Basin. (iii) Southwest. (iv) Plains.

(i) Northwest Coast.

(a) Materials and techniques. (b) Origins. (c) Regional survey. (d) Contemporary developments.

(a) Materials and techniques. Native American paints were made from naturally occurring mineral pigments, primarily black, obtained from lignite, graphite and charcoal, red from ochres and haematite, and blue or blue-green from copper minerals or soladinite, a blue-green iron-based mineral. The binder used was primarily fish-egg tempera, obtained by chewing salmon eggs wrapped in cedar bark and spitting the saliva and egg juices into the paint dish. After trade materials became available in the late 18th century, imported pigments were rapidly adopted, especially Chinese vermilion, Prussian blue, ultramarine and Reckitts commercial laundry blueing. White and yellow were rarely used on the northern Northwest Coast but became popular further south, especially in Kwakiutl art during the late 19th century. Shiny enamel paints became popular in the early 20th century, and by the end of the century artists worked in a variety of media, including acrylics. Brushes were traditionally made of animal hair (often porcupine hairs) bound on wooden handles with split spruce or cedar roots.

(b) Origins. The two-dimensional design used in North-west Coast sculpture (*see* §III, 2 above) may have had its origins in painting on hide, bark and wood, but little of this material survives, and when it does, little or no paint remains. Perhaps shallow incised designs were first scratched on the surfaces of bone, wood and horn, and later filled in with pigments to emphasize their forms. However, historical evidence from the northern Northwest Coast suggests that by the 19th century painted designs were generally applied to the surface first, to define designs that were only later carved in order to emphasize the edges of the painted design. New techniques developed to excavate wet sites, where organic materials are preserved, may reveal more about the origins of Northwest Coast painting. The Hoko River site, Washington, has produced a carved wooden tool handle, dated before 500 BC, that has low-relief carving and retains traces of paint (Holm, 1990, p. 611; Carlson, fig. 11.9). Stone bowls of the type used in historical times for grinding pigments also occur, suggesting that painting developed concurrently with carving styles between *c.* 1500 BC and *c.* AD 500 (Fladmark, pp. 66–85). Totem poles, house fronts, boxes, oil bowls and chests made and collected during the late 18th century and the early 19th often show traces of paint, but the effects of handling, oil saturation, weathering and wear quickly remove the original paint. While prehistoric styles throughout the Northwest Coast show strong similarities in basic design elements, by the late 18th century distinctive regional painting styles were fully developed. These can be divided into three regional styles, within which both tribal and individual artists' styles are discernible.

(c) Regional survey.

Northern. This region includes the Haida, Tlingit, Tsimshian and Northern Wakashan-speaking peoples. The strict adherence to a set of two-dimensional design rules unifies the painting in this area, and differences in tribal art styles are discernible primarily in three-dimensional sculptural forms (*see* §III, 2 above). Painting on flat surfaces includes painted interior house screens and planks, bentwood chests and boxes, tanned moose- or caribou-hide robes, tunics, dance aprons and armour. These painted 'formline' designs almost always represent animal or human forms. Two-dimensional painted designs are frequently combined with low-relief carving. Three-dimensional sculptural forms, such as totem poles, house posts, masks, headdresses, rattles and bowls, are almost always painted. The figures represent supernatural, mythical or ancestral beings associated with either family history or shamanic practice. The display of inherited crest figures on poles, house posts, screens, masks or feast dishes established the social status of the family and was the primary motivation for the production of art on the northern and central Northwest Coast (*see also* §I, 5 and 6 above).

A 'formline' is a flat, semi-angular, bandlike element that tapers and swells in a continuous curvilinear gridlike design representing abstract animal or human figures (Holm, 1965). The two basic formline shapes are ovoids (oval forms that are convex at the top, flat or slightly concave at the bottom and symmetrical from side to side) and U-forms. When combined with straight lines, S- and L-shapes, these two forms provide the basic components of the design system. Ovoids are used for both eyes and joint areas. Formline ovoids contain inner ovoids that float non-concentrically above the centre. The primary formline design is generally painted black. Within the areas gridded by the primary formlines, secondary formline designs, generally painted red, join the primary formlines at their corners to make a continuous pattern. Thin black tertiary lines are used for eyelid lines, to outline the floating inner ovoids, or for bordering or splitting U- or S-shapes. The background area or tertiary space is either left in the ground colour or painted blue or blue-green. If the object is carved, the blue tertiary area is generally cut back or hollowed before it is painted. The primary and secondary formlines are generally on the plane surface, and only the tertiary and ground spaces are cut away. In order to avoid heaviness in the design, formlines either taper and bend or swell in junctures, with swelling junctures relieved with negative crescent, T- or circular shapes.

Within this system designs range from naturalistic profiles (configurative designs) to expansive designs, where a profile remains but the body parts are out of proportion and exaggerated to fill the space, to distributive designs that fill an entire surface space and distort the body parts to near abstraction. Differences in the thickness and proportions of formlines, the handling of tertiary spaces and variations on the basic formline rules make it possible to distinguish not only subtle differences in tribal styles but also changes in styles through time and the styles of individual artists.

Central. This area includes the Coast Salish-speaking Bella Coola and the Wakashan-speaking Kwakiutl, Makah and Nootka peoples, each of whom developed distinctive painting styles. Bella Coola painting adheres fairly closely to the northern formline style of art but has more freedom. House fronts were painted in the formline style, and masks were decorated with broad lobes of ultramarine blue paint in U-form and split-U designs that extend across their carved surfaces. The influence of the northern formline painting style is thought to have spread south to the

Kwakiutl and Nootka during the mid-19th century, perhaps through the intermediaries of the Northern Wakashan and Bella Coola artists. By the late 19th century painted house fronts, boxes, chests, canoes, paddles and screens clearly show northern-style ovoids and U-forms, but the formline system as practised in the north was adapted to a more flamboyant and free-flowing style by Kwakiutl artists. Formlines were frequently unconnected and non-continuous; tertiary lines were eliminated, and a broader palette of colours was adopted. By the late 19th century white was frequently used as a background, yellow for beaks, feet and bodies, and green became favoured for eye sockets. In the early 20th century some Kwakiutl artists, such as WILLIE SEAWEED, began to use commercial oil enamel paints with a glossy finish (Holm, 1983).

Because early collections of Kwakiutl art are rare (fur traders rarely travelled to the interior of Vancouver Island, limiting their trade to the more accessible west coast), only early Nootka painting provides a clue to the nature of earlier styles. The painting of screens, originally made of cedar planks and later of canvas, was a highly developed art form among the Nootka during the 19th century (see fig. 24). Nootka painting includes naturalistic, representational depictions of mythical creatures, particularly of the whale, thunderbird, lightning serpent and wolf. These creatures were depicted on family screens to display inherited privileges or family histories during potlatches (the display of inherited privileges and the payment of witnesses who serve to validate the ownership and status of the hosts, later, by the end of the 19th century, perhaps involving the deliberate destruction of wealth) and other ceremonial occasions. Abstract, perhaps non-representational, angular designs, including blocks, crosses, spirals,

24. Northwest Coast painted cedar-plank screen with traditional designs, depicting the wolf, thunderbird, whale and lightning serpent, 1.73m×2.99m, Nootka, collected at Port Alberni, mid-19th century (New York, American Museum of Natural History)

circles and dots, were used as borders or fillers. The animal forms are often handled in an X-ray manner, allowing the viewer to see through the skin to the internal organs and skeleton of the creature. U-form feathers, oval eyes, crescent and T-reliefs, pointed eyelid lines and thin black outlines used to delineate the profiles of creatures resemble more closely the prehistoric low-relief carving local to the area than the northern formline system introduced later in the 19th century. In the late 19th century Nootka artists, particularly one Chulatus, created designs more directly influenced by the northern styles. These more structured compositions are less naturalistic than earlier styles, but they retain a freedom drawn from earlier traditions.

Southern. Painting was less important among the Coast Salish and Chinookan-speaking peoples of southern British Columbia and Washington than it was further north. While the Halkomelem artists had a distinctive two-dimensional design system, it is represented primarily in unpainted low-relief carving, such as spindle whorls, mountain sheep horn rattles, combs and other objects. There is evidence that on certain ritual occasions mountain sheep horn rattles were used as stamps, dipped in pigment and pressed on the body of a person to leave the image of the carved low relief design on their skin (Suttles, p. 73).

Further south, among the southern Coast Salish, paintings were done on wood, primarily for religious purposes. The most elaborate paintings from the Puget Sound area are painted boards used in the Spirit Canoe Ceremony (*see* §III, 2 above). Performed by a group of shamans working together, this ceremony involved a journey to the land of the dead to recover lost souls. Carved human figures representing spirit helpers were used in association with flat painted boards that had the silhouette of a creature with a projecting snout. Both the figures and boards were painted with images of birds, animals, anthropomorphic beings and symbols of spiritual power. The paintings were generally red and black, sometimes blue, on a white background. Only the shaman owner of the board and figure could interpret them, although some symbols seem to have had standard meanings, such as rows of dots coming from the mouth used to represent songs. Sometimes spoons, canoe paddles, boxes and gambling equipment were painted as well, generally in a geometric decorative manner. There is little evidence of painting from the lower Columbia River area, although, as with the Halkomelem, the two-dimensional design system in this area was highly developed.

(d) Contemporary developments. In the early 20th century the impact of diseases, missionary activity, colonization and the banning of traditional cultural and religious practices by governmental agencies caused the decline of traditional painting in most areas of the Northwest Coast. Remarkable exceptions to this include the Kwakiutl artists who continued their arts and traditions throughout the early 20th century. Some of their most innovative artists, such as Willie Seaweed and MUNGO MARTIN, produced art both for sale and for ceremonial use during this period, despite the banning of the potlatch. Paintings and drawings of crest figures were made by Kwakiutl artists during the first half of the 20th century, and artists such as Henry

Speck (1908–71) experimented with the use of traditional Kwakiutl motifs, such as button blankets and cedar-bark head and neck-rings, in Christian scenes such as the Nativity and the Crucifixion. In the 1960s there was a revival in traditional art styles among many Northwest Coast tribes. In part this can be traced to the publication of Bill Holm's *Northwest Coast Indian Art: An Analysis of Style* (1965), the first formal analysis of the complex northern formline system. Also during this period, in part related to the civil-rights movements elsewhere in North America, Native American people re-established a pride in their culture that had been suppressed during the early 20th-century period of forced boarding-school attendance and assimilation policies. This pride motivated a generation of artists to investigate their traditional art styles and to produce art that both drew on these traditions and carried them to new innovative levels. During the 1970s and 1980s the primary new medium used by Northwest Coast artists was the screenprint, which is ideally suited to the traditional two-dimensional design systems with sharply demarcated colours. Haida artists BILL REID and ROBERT DAVIDSON and Kwakiutl artist Tony Hunt (*b* 1942) pioneered this medium. JOE DAVID, Art Thompson (*b* 1948) and Tim Paul (*b* 1950) have based their work on the early naturalistic and geometric styles of Nootka art, and the late 19th-century formline-influenced styles of Chulatus, but they have gone on to innovate in painting as well as carving and printmaking. During the 1980s Coast Salish artists Susan Point (*b* 1952), Rod Modeste (*b* 1946), Stan Greene (*b* 1953) and others joined the growing number of Native American artists producing innovative paintings and screenprints.

BIBLIOGRAPHY
B. Holm: *Northwest Coast Indian Art: An Analysis of Form* (Seattle, 1965)
The Legacy: Continuing Traditions of Canadian North-west Coast Indian Art (exh. cat. by P. Macnair, A. Hoover and K. Neary, Victoria, BC, Prov. Mus., 1980); rev. as *The Legacy: Tradition and Innovation in Northwest Coast Indian Art* (Seattle, 1984)
M. Blackman, E. S. Hall and V. Rickard: *North-west Coast Indian Graphics: An Introduction to Silk Screen Painting* (Seattle, 1981)
R. Carlson: *Indian Art Traditions of the North-west Coast* (Burnaby, BC, 1983)
B. Holm: *Smoky-Top: The Art and Times of Willie Seaweed* (Seattle, 1983)
W. Suttles: 'Productivity and its Constraints: A Coast Salish Case', *Indian Art Traditions of the North-west Coast*, ed. R. Carlson (Burnaby, BC, 1983), pp. 67–88
K. R. Fladmark: *British Columbian Prehistory* (Ottawa, 1986)
B. Holm: 'Art', *Hb. N. Amer. Ind.*, vii (1990), pp. 602–32
ROBIN K. WRIGHT

(ii) Great Basin. With the exception of works by contemporary Native American artists, Great Basin painting is largely confined to the rock art of its prehistoric cultures. This has a long and complex history in the region, closely related to that of the region's petroglyphic rock art (*see* §III, 3 above). On the whole, rock painting is less common than petroglyphic work; although it is suggested that the latter, being more resistant to weathering, persists longer, perhaps creating a false impression as to relative age.

Great Basin rock art in general appears to be of considerable antiquity, although as with rock art elsewhere, precise dating is often impossible. The region has been occupied by hunters and gatherers since at least *c.* 9000 BC, and some rock art may be that early (Schaafsma, p. 218).

However, the first painted images appear to belong to what has been termed the Great Basin Abstract style (Curvilinear and Rectangular sub-styles), which dates to perhaps *c.* 2500 BC and later (Heizer and Baumhoff). Common curvilinear motifs are circles (whole and part), sun-discs, curvilinear meanders, wavy lines or snakes and star figures. Rectilinear motifs include dots, rectangular grids, bird tracks, rakes and crosshatching. Most common in painting are circles and parallel lines, arguably elements from both. Identified pigments are haematite (red), goethite (yellow), charcoal (black) and gypsum (white) (McKee and Thomas). The Great Basin Abstract style (including painted versions) occurs over much of the region, at least as far east as the Wasatch Range in Utah. It also seems to be represented on pebbles and small stone slabs found in archaeological sites (Tuohy).

Rock paintings of a better defined style occur in the eastern Great Basin and are seemingly later. These consist of representational figures, possibly associated with the horticulturally based Fremont culture, dated *c.* AD 500– *c.* 1200. The commonest motifs are anthropomorphic figures with triangular or trapezoidal bodies. They appear to wear headdresses with paired horns and carry shields, plants or other objects. They occur singly or in multiples, often dominating the paintings or occurring without other motifs. They are known from sites in extreme western and southern Nevada and much of Utah, coinciding with the distribution of the Fremont culture. Haematite is one pigment used in these images, but they also commonly occur in pecked and incised versions. The Barrier Canyon painted anthropomorphs of eastern Utah show similarities but are more circumscribed in distribution and possibly older.

Native American peoples present in the Great Basin at the time of Euro-American contact usually deny authorship or specific knowledge of the rock art. Most attribute the work to peoples who came before them, or to mythical figures such as Coyote or Water Babies. Nevertheless, a few sites with motifs clearly of post-contact date, such as horses, suggest involvement by ancestors of present-day tribal members. There is also some evidence that the rock art was the work of specialists, such as shamans and curers or leaders of hunts for big game (big-horn sheep, deer, antelope). The association of Great Basin rock art, including abstract paintings, with game trails has long been recognized, and the hypothesis that it was associated with hunting has been well developed (Heizer and Baumhoff, p. 219). Rock-art sites are considered by Great Basin Native Americans to be important cultural resources.

BIBLIOGRAPHY

R. Heizer and M. Baumhoff: *Prehistoric Rock Art of Nevada and Eastern California* (Berkeley, 1962)
D. Thomas and T. Thomas: 'New Data on Rock Art Chronology in the Central Great Basin', *Tebiwa*, xv (1972), pp. 64–71
E. McKee and D. Thomas: 'X-ray Diffraction Analysis of Pictograph Pigments from Toquima Cave', *Amer. Ant.*, xxxviii (1973), pp. 112–13
P. Schaafsma: 'Rock Art', *Hb. N. Amer. Ind.*, xi (1986), pp. 215–26
D. Tuohy: 'Portable Rock Art', *Hb. N. Amer. Ind.*, xi (1986), pp. 227–37

CATHERINE S. FOWLER

(iii) Southwest.

(a) Introduction. Southwest Native American painting covers a great variety of forms, techniques and media that are not easily classifiable. While all forms must be understood within the context of specific local cultural and temporal traditions, there are common features throughout the Southwest. All painting from the region can be viewed as a form of visual prayer, whose specific meaning is closely tied to tradition. Paintings are produced to serve social purposes, from honouring a deity to signifying group solidarity. Because of this, painting from the Southwest has often been mistakenly dismissed as merely utilitarian and decorative.

Southwest Native American painting existed for centuries before European contact. The earliest works are huge paintings of figures in caves and rock shelters dating to *c.* 4000 BC. Rock art has continued to the present day as a record of historical journeys and events, clan and kinship designations, mnemonic devices, astronomical symbols and images of both supernatural and natural phenomena.

All prehistoric and historic groups have left an extensive record of rock paintings and engravings that can be found at numerous locations throughout the Southwest. Painting still continues in traditional form as a vivid means of expression (*see also* §2 below). Many objects and surfaces are painted: ceramic vessels and figurines, masks, sculpture and carvings (such as *kachina* dolls; *see* §III, 4 above), shields, ritual equipment, musical instruments, hide and woven clothing, the human body, sacred chambers, and cliffs and rocks. All of these are decorated with vegetable and mineral pigments in representational and abstract forms that show a clear and highly developed understanding of composition as it relates to multi-dimensional surfaces. Painters adapt their compositions to the natural outlines of the materials, incorporating the form with precise drawings.

In general, Southwest painting is dominated by abstract geometric designs or highly conventionalized treatments of natural phenomena, although it is always the essence, rather than the physical characteristics, that is portrayed. The most naturalistic expression appears on objects used in daily life or in non-ritual situations, such as pottery, followed by ceremonial costumes and masks depicting spirits, and wall paintings inside Pueblo religious structures, called *kivas* (*see* KIVA). On the latter, brilliant pigments are applied with a fibre brush to wood, clay or white plastered walls in a dry-fresco technique. Painted *kivas* occur from *c.* 1350 onwards, and the most famous are at AWATOVI and Kuauá, where deities and religious symbols are painted in a flat style in outline areas without shading or modelling.

Religious objects are always symbolic, using abstract geometrics as signs. Most esoteric are *pahos*, altars, tablitas, large cloth screens and fetishes. Equally linear or radial in composition, Southwestern religious art is strongly conventionalized, for as it represents gifts of the Holy People, there must be little artistic experimentation. The symbols are often depicted repetitively, a device that produces rhythm, symmetry and balance, while the use of colour produces contrast.

(b) Dry-painting. A remarkable Southwest painting tradition is dry-painting. While made by most Puebloan, Piman, Cahitan and Athapaskan peoples, dry-paintings are

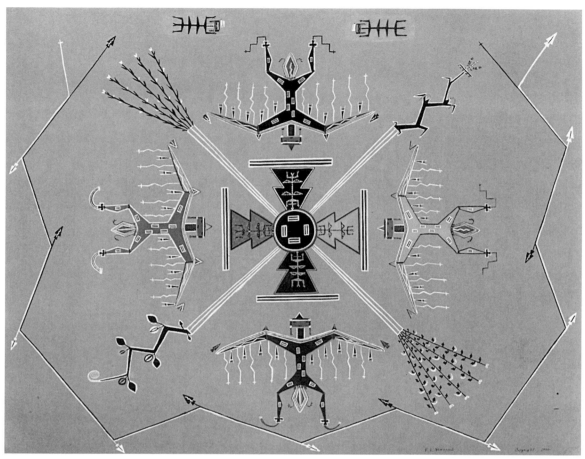

25. Traditional Southwest region dry-painting (sand-painting) design, representing Four Thunders and Four Sacred Plants (1932); used in the Male Shootingway ceremonial (Santa Fe, NM, Wheelwright Museum of the American Indian)

most diverse, complex and prominent among the Navajo, who since their arrival in the Southwest in the 16th century have created a repertory of over 1200 distinct paintings. Dry-paintings are holy, representing deities within symbolic and mythological landscapes. They are used only during curing ceremonies in order to restore harmony and balance. Dry-paintings are ephemeral and are executed only under the direction of a religious specialist with colourful powdered minerals and vegetal pigments, including pollen and pulverized flower blossoms. A small amount of colour is strewn between the index finger and the thumb in a controlled trickle. Lines and outlined colour areas are laid out in circular, centred or rectangular compositions on a prepared layer of neutral river-bed sand, or sometimes on a buckskin spread on the floor of ceremonial areas. Sizes range from 1 to 2 m and occasionally to 6.5 m.

On completion, the singer consecrates the design, which becomes holy or, in Navajo terms, 'the place where the gods come and go', and is capable of curing and restoring harmony. Mnemonic in nature, showing mythological events, dry-painting designs portray the Holy People—a class of legendary beings who taught the Navajo to live in balance with the world. In addition to the Holy People,

who are depicted as anthropomorphic beings stylized to curved or angular geometric shapes, other symbolic motifs include comparatively naturalistic images of animals and plants, zigzag lightning, crosses, swastikas, stars and circular solar symbols within a frame always open to the east. Designs are formal, geometric and abstract, and their symbolism inherent in placement of figures, composition and colour, being associated with the cardinal directions, seasonality, gender and other important concepts (see fig. 25). These designs, characterized by order and clarity, rhythmic repetition and balanced asymmetry, are standardized with little room for variation: they have to be exact in order to become efficacious, and no significant style changes have been noted since they were first recorded in the mid-1880s.

(c) Contemporary developments. During the second half of the 19th century, Euro-Americans had introduced new media and concepts into Southwest Native American art (see §2 below). In 1932 Dorothy Dunn founded The Studio at the Santa Fe Indian School to encourage artistic development and pride in native heritage. Students were taught to paint the stylized, two-dimensional compositions that have come to be regarded as 'traditional' Native

American painting. Subject-matter was culture specific but always focused on ceremonial and daily life, the environment and symbolic representations from dry-paintings and rock art; Dunn believed that some forms, especially animals, plants and anthropomorphic beings, were prototypically 'Native American' and should be the basic stylistic components. In the 1950s the Institute of American Indian Arts in Santa Fe assumed the lead in educational training in the arts, and by the 1960s painters were questioning the value of strict adherence to established conventions of Native American painting that were often reinforced by Euro-American controlled markets and juried shows. By the late 20th century the main problem facing all Southwest Native American painters was misplaced purism. While traditionalists often suspect innovative painters of abandoning their traditions, purism is centred in the art market where patrons, museums and galleries have tried to persuade Native American artists to conform to ethnically identifiable subjects and styles, thereby reinforcing the 1930s Studio tradition. 'Traditional' art produced in this context is in danger of simply conforming to types that consumers see as 'Native American'. Nevertheless, Native American artists continue to produce paintings as murals, on pottery, and as dry-painting and rock art. The reasons for continuing past techniques are still present, as are the opportunities for new forms to convey new messages.

BIBLIOGRAPHY

D. Dunn: *American Indian Painting of the Southwest and Plains Areas* (Albuquerque, 1968)
J. Brody: *Indian Painters and White Patrons* (Albuquerque, 1971)
C. L. Tanner: *Southwest Indian Painting: A Changing Art* (Tucson, 1973)
J. Highwater: *Songs of the Earth: American Indian Painting* (Boston, 1976)
P. Schaafsma: *Indian Rock Art of the Southwest* (Albuquerque, 1980)
N. J. Parezo: *Navajo Sandpaintings: From Religious Act to Commercial Art* (Tucson, 1983)
L. C. Wyman: *Southwest Indian Drypainting* (Albuquerque, 1983)

NANCY J. PAREZO

(iv) Plains.

(a) Early development. The origins of Plains Native American painting are to be found in the images on boulders, cliff faces and rock shelters scattered from Alberta, Canada, to Texas. Although the Plains artistic tradition is probably of greater antiquity, the earliest work in such sites as the Pictographic Cave and Castle Butte, Montana, and Writing-on-Stone, Alberta, Canada, dates from *c.* AD 500–*c.* 1800. Pre-European contact subject-matter, dating from before the acquisition of horses, includes men bearing decorated shields covering the entire body. The shield designs often depict humans, animals and geometric patterns. Later rock art includes scenes of mounted combat, with warriors armed with both lances and flintlock guns. The images were painted in a non-realistic pictographic style: sticklike riders with knobby, featureless heads were shown either legless or with both legs on the near side of the horse. There was no attempt to describe clothing or horse trappings.

Surviving early Plains hide paintings are in the rock art pictographic tradition. There are 16th-century Spanish references to painted hides, but none survives. The earliest extant hide paintings, which date from the 18th century, are in the Musée de l'Homme, Paris. The oldest documented hide painting in the United States is the Mandan

26. Traditional Plains region painting, the Mandan Robe (detail showing a battle of 1797), pigment on native-tanned buffalo hide, 2.59×2.39 m, *c.* 1805 (Cambridge, MA, Harvard University, Peabody Museum of Archaeology and Ethnology)

Robe, collected from the Mandan by the explorers Lewis and Clark in 1805, in the Peabody Museum of Archaeology and Ethnology, Harvard University, Cambridge, MA (see fig. 26). It portrays a battle in 1797 and is an example of traditional Plains Native American painting untouched by non-Native American stylistic influences (Ewers).

Figural hide paintings were executed by men and were mainly concerned with the recording of individual and tribal military accomplishments. Abstract geometric compositions were painted by women on hide robes and utilitarian items such as parfleches (folded rectangular rawhide containers used to store dried meat and household items). Men sometimes sought mystical assurances of protection and success by painting shields and tepees with designs obtained in dreams and visions. Among the Sioux and Kiowa, chronicles were kept in pictographic winter counts or calendar counts that recorded significant events. Occasionally, pictorial messages were left to inform following members of hunting and war parties.

(b) After c. 1800. In the first decades of the 19th century, delegations of Native Americans were exposed to non-Native American art during visits to Washington, DC, and other cities. On the Plains, with increased opportunities to study examples of non-Native American art during encounters with traders and explorers, some Native American artists began to paint and draw in a manner influenced by new models. The best-documented examples of early Euro-American influence on Plains Native American painting concern the artists GEORGE CATLIN and KARL BODMER. Four Bears (Matatope) was the chief and artist befriended by them both, some of whose works on paper are in the Joslyn Art Museum, Omaha (*see* §IV, 2 below). During most of the 19th

century, however, Plains Native American art, while tending to become more naturalistic, remained essentially conservative in form and function. Likenesses were not valued. Colours, sparingly used, were applied evenly without modelling or shading. Pictorial conventions were commonly used to indicate direction, numbers, intentions, proper names, tribal affiliation and other features. The style remained a narrative one, well suited to conveying specific information.

Towards the end of the 19th century, a flowering of Plains Native American art occurred with the advent of Plains ledger drawing, so-called because many of the drawings were executed in ruled ledger-books. During a period of almost constant warfare, when camps were being sacked and burnt by the US Army and the only possessions that could be saved were those that could be carried on one's person, ledger-books were particularly convenient for preserving records of warfare. Books, pencils, inks and paints were secured by trade and, at times, as spoils of war. War was the prevalent subject, although, fuelled by nostalgia for the more tranquil past, new subject-matter was introduced: reminiscences of childhood, youthful escapades, courting scenes and ceremonials. Such books, recording the lives and martial accomplishments of the artists and their friends, who often contributed drawings, were created for a Native American audience. Notable examples of early ledger art, such as the Dog Soldier or Summit Springs ledger-book (1869; Denver, CO Hist. Soc.) or the Little Fingernail ledger-book (1879; New York, Amer. Mus. Nat. Hist.), passed to non-Native American hands only as spoils of war. Later, ledger drawings conforming to early prototypes were, at times, made specifically for sale to outsiders.

Of all the ledger drawings, perhaps the most significant, because of their impact on the later development of Plains paintings, were those made from 1875 to 1878 by a group of Southern Plains Native Americans imprisoned after the Red River War (1874–5) in the military prison at Fort Marion, Florida. Encouraged by the officer in charge, Captain Richard Henry Pratt, who provided art supplies, many prisoners drew and painted in sketchbooks, which were sold to visitors. Pratt also provided teachers who taught the prisoners English. Fort Marion art is relatively free of the Plains preoccupation with warfare, demonstrating new wide-ranging subject-matter and new styles. In addition to the nostalgic recalling of hunts, ceremonials and courting scenes, there were scenes of encounters with Euro-American civilization, such as the journey from Oklahoma to prison and activities at Fort Marion, including its classrooms, chapel, beaches, sailing boats and the prisoners in army uniforms as members of the 'Indian Company'. Although there was no art instruction at Fort Marion, art was readily accessible in newspapers, magazines, photographs, religious pictures and other educational material ordered by Pratt for the classrooms. Most Fort Marion work does not reveal a concern with narrative and the conveying of specific information. The evocation of mood and the painting of beautiful compositions became major concerns. Balance and symmetry are evident in many carefully planned works. Colour was used profusely. A number of works depicting ceremonial occasions weave patterns of shapes and colours into decorative

compositions. Although most pictorial conventions were abandoned, some traditional devices were still used occasionally, such as foot and animal tracks and indications of speech and animal sounds.

The gentle Fort Marion style did not survive the Fort Marion experience. Afterwards, owing to the disillusioning conditions on the reservations, Native American art acquired its compensatory mechanism—extolling and idealizing the past while blotting out the generally unsatisfactory present. On the Plains, artists kept to more conservative styles, with painterly or aesthetic considerations being less important than subject-matter. Warfare maintained some of its prominence as old warriors, especially those active in resisting Euro-American encroachment, sought to validate their claims to leadership by recounting their former accomplishments. The collectors, mostly army officers and travellers looking for souvenirs of Native American warfare, valued Plains Native American art for its documentary content.

BIBLIOGRAPHY
A Chronicle of the Kiowa Indians (1832–1882) (Berkeley, n.d.)
R. H. Pratt: Battlefield and Classroom: Four Decades with the American Indian, 1867–1904, ed. R. M. Utley (New Haven, 1964)
H. H. Blish: A Pictographic History of the Oglala Sioux (Lincoln, NE, 1967)
C. Grant: Rock Art of the American Indian (New York, 1967)
D. Dunn: American Indian Painting of the Southwest and Plains Areas (Albuquerque, 1968)
J. C. Ewers: 'Plains Indian Painting: The History and Development of an American Art Form', Howling Wolf: A Cheyenne Warrior's Graphic Interpretation of his People, ed. D. Dunn (Palo Alto, 1968), pp. 5–19
K. D. Petersen: Plains Indian Art from Fort Marion (Norman, 1971)
P. J. Powell: They Drew from Power: An Introduction to Northern Cheyenne Ledger Book Art (Los Angeles, 1976)
One Hundred Years of Native American Painting (exh. cat. by A. Silberman, Oklahoma City, OK Mus. A., 1978)
A. Silberman: 'The Art of Fort Marion', Native Peoples (Summer 1993), pp. 32–9
ARTHUR SILBERMAN

2. AFTER EUROPEAN CONTACT. The adoption of easel painting by indigenous artists was an inevitable post-contact development. As Native Americans were instructed in this new form of expression, they also absorbed related Euro-American artistic values. One of the most prominent of these concepts was the idea of the artist as a named individual, whose unique vision created a special place for him or her in society. Modern Native American fine-art painting is the result of various cultural, educational, economic, political and religious influences.

(i) Euro-American influence, c. 1870–1900. (ii) Early narrative genre painting, c. 1900–30. (iii) Institutionalized art instruction, c. 1930–45. (iv) Post-war developments and pan-Native American activism, 1945–70. (v) After 1970.

(i) Euro-American influence, c. 1870–1900. Early easel painting was the product of Native American–White relationships. The first painters were self-taught and usually engaged in tentative attempts to record historical events. The clash between Native Americans and their conquerors was frequently depicted. Painting on hides by Plains Native Americans were usually picture-writing genre narratives of ceremonials, battles and winter counts (see §1(iv) above). Walks-in-the-Light (Sioux) produced early work on hide and cloth (1870s; e.g. Washington, DC, Smithsonian Inst., Archvs Amer. A.; New York, Mus. Amer. Ind.). In the 1870s Plains warriors imprisoned at

Fort Marion, Florida, made ledger-book drawings with materials supplied by their captors (*see* §1(iv) above). Captain Richard Pratt, supervisor of the Fort Marion prisoners, encouraged their artistic efforts, and his experiences induced him to open the Carlisle Indian School in Pennsylvania. This action inaugurated the Native American boarding-school system, where many young Native Americans were introduced to Euro-American painting methods. Other artists experimented wih coloured pencils and paper: Carl Sweezy (Arapaho; 1881–1953) made naive-style drawings based on works by the Fort Marion painters; and one youth, Choh (Navajo; *fl* 1880s), was reportedly drawing imaginary scenes at a New Mexico trading post *c.* 1885 (Dunn, p. 189).

A number of Native Americans began painting without formal art training. Sweezy's contributions were an important link in the development of Native American professional artists. He used a narrative genre style to illuminate personal and group experiences, as in his *Peyote Road Man* (*c.* 1927; see fig. 27). Another self-taught painter, Ernest

27. Carl Sweezy: *Peyote Road Man*, house paint and pencil on board, 696×394 mm, *c.* 1927 (Phoenix, AZ, Heard Museum)

Spybuck (Shawnee; 1883–1949), produced richly detailed genre scenes. Works from this early phase of Native American painting show attempts to portray what was personally important.

Euro-American patronage assisted these endeavours. A formal art education programme for Native Americans was started in 1892, at St Patrick's Mission School in Anadarko, OK, where students could study drawing and painting techniques. The US government evolved a number of Native American educational policies through its Bureau of Indian Affairs in the late 19th century. Art was taught intermittently in Native American boarding schools and was later introduced into day schools on a more regular basis.

(ii) Early narrative genre painting, c. 1900–30. New Mexico contained a large indigenous population in interactive proximity with Euro-American residents, school teachers and visiting anthropologists. A wave of newcomers started active art colonies in Taos and Santa Fe. Euro-American patronage also helped to create the San Ildefonso Watercolor Movement (1900–10) in northern New Mexico, which began after educator Elizabeth Richard established an art programme at the San Ildefonso Pueblo's Day School. San Ildefonso artists such as Cresencio Martinez (*d* 1918), Alfonso Roybal/Awa Tsireh (1898–1955), and TONITA PEÑA/Quah Ah created a style that can be considered 'traditional'. Their works were stylized and conventionalized, usually omitting background and foreground. This treatment was adopted by other Pueblo artists and patronized by various Euro-American supporters. Alfredo Montoya (San Ildefonso; *d* 1931) was commissioned to make a series of drawings of native dances for the School of American Research in Santa Fe.

In 1902 anthropologist Jesse Walter Fewkes commissioned four Hopi artists to paint over 200 representations of *kachina* dolls for an ethnological report, and Dr Kenneth Chapman hired Apie Begay (Navajo) to make drawings from sand paintings. Initially, there was some religious resistance to the adoption of this new secular painting, most notably in the case of VELINO HERRERA. The occasional recovery of ancient *kiva* wall-painting fragments (as at the Frijoles Canyon ruins, excavated from 1901–14; Los Alamos Co., NM, Bandelier N. Mnmt) provided additional sources of inspiration to Native American artists (*see* §1(iii) above). Self-taught Pueblo artists, active from 1910 to 1930, produced a standard style of easel painting that was popular with Euro-American buyers.

Painting activity expanded throughout the Southwest and was vigorous from 1920 to 1962. It is often termed 'The Southwest Movement'. Elizabeth DeHuff's art programme at the Santa Fe Indian Day School, started in 1917, became a seminal event. Also in 1917, Dr Edgar Hewett commissioned from Cresencio Martinez a series of paintings of Pueblo ceremonies, exhibited at the Museum of New Mexico, Santa Fe, NM, and at the American Museum of Natural History in New York City. After Martinez's death in 1918, Alfonso Roybal continued the commission. Many distinctly individual artists emerged from this period of artistic development. Their styles were mostly subordinated to a growing orthodoxy of institutionalized art instruction, supported by the US government and avid Euro-American collectors. The so-called 'traditional' style usually employed flat, two-dimensional scenes, idealized subject-matter and the use of solid colour and strong outlines. DeHuff student FRED KABOTIE (Hopi; 1900–86) painted scenes within established standards for traditional painting, and, along with Otis Polelonema (Hopi; 1902–81), was an inspiration to young Hopi painters. Marina Lujan/Pop Chalee (Taos; b 1908) created a widely imitated—and later ridiculed—'Bambi' style of decorative painting. Her use of animal imagery became an enduring theme. At the same time, such works as Waldo Mootzka's (Hopi; 1903–38) *Pollination of the Corn* (1938; Tulsa, OK, Gilcrease Inst. Amer. Hist. & A.) were influenced by the contemporary Art Deco style and show a rising triumph of originality over otherwise formulaic subject-matter.

Related events were occurring in Oklahoma, which possessed a large and diverse Native American population. During the 1920s Susie Peters, field matron at St Michael's Mission School at Anadarko, encouraged five Kiowa youths to enrol in a special art programme at the University of Oklahoma. The five students, Spencer Asah (1905–54), James Auchiah (1906–75), Jack Hokeah (1902–73), STEPHEN MOPOPE and Monroe Tsatoke (1904–81), received advanced painting training from Edith Mahier and Oscar B. Jacobson. A sixth student, Lois Smoky (1907–81), joined the group later and had a brief, active career as an artist. Their work typified an 'Oklahoma' style of Native American painting, flat and decorative in nature, with flowing and illustrative use of lines and forms, depicting nostalgic subject-matter. Many paintings romanticized 19th-century Plains Native American life. The Kiowas, whose influence on Oklahoma-area Native American painters was strong up to the 1940s, were celebrated at home and abroad. Their works were exhibited at a 1928 international art show in Prague, and Jacobson extended their fame with *Kiowa Indian Art* (1929).

Non-Native American patrons were eager to support and promulgate the emerging traditional style of Native American easel painting, as evidenced by exhibitions in the 1920s of Native American art in the Annual Exhibition of the Society of Independent Artists, and the American Museum of Natural History, both in New York, the Arts Club of Chicago and Washington, DC (*see also* §XIX, 4 below). Simultaneously, promotion of Native American commercial arts helped to 'freeze' preconceptions of what Native American fine-art painting should look like. The sentimental nature of early 20th-century Native American paintings said as much about Euro-American patrons' expectations as those of the artists: works were expected to depict tribal culture, often integrating traditional religious and decorative symbolism, but were primarily addressed to a non-Native American audience. Early White teachers encouraged their Native American students to use conventionalized techniques, which were adopted by later artists. However, the growth of commercial success for both the Oklahoma and Southwest Native American painting styles led to an eventual decline in quality, and works were reduced to formulaic tenets.

(iii) Institutionalized art instruction, c. *1930–45.* In the 1930s the institutionalization of Native American painting instruction was firmly established. The US government's Miriam Report (1928) had urged federal encouragement of Native American arts, particularly a 'crafts revival'. The Indian Reorganization Act (1934) officially sanctioned art teaching in government Native American schools. The Indian Arts and Crafts Board was formed in 1935. A dedicated White teacher, Dorothy Dunn, founded The Studio at the Santa Fe Indian School in 1932 and remained its director until 1937. Under her tuition, many notable students were exposed to the mechanics of what Dunn felt was Native American painting, particularly her belief in fundamental Native American design prototypes. She influenced her students to adopt a flat, two-dimensional style and use blocks of pastel colour; their efforts became a pervasive aesthetic widely perceived as 'true' Native American painting. Dunn's teaching techniques were followed by many instructors in US Native American schools.

Many prominent artists emerged from training at The Studio: Oqwa Pi, PABLITA VELARDE, Andy Tsihnahjinnie (b 1918), Sybil Yazzie, ALLAN HOUSER, Ben Quintana (1923–44), Geronima Cruz Montoya (b 1915), Eva Mirabel (1920–67), HARRISON BEGAY, Pop Chalee (b 1908), Popovi Da (c. 1920–71), Beatin Yazz (b 1928), Gerald Nailor (1917–52) and QUINCY TAHOMA. Two painters, Joe Herrera (Cochiti; b 1923) and OSCAR HOWE, were among the first to absorb the traditional style and later to break with its conventions. Herrera, the son of Tonita Pena, imbued his early works with the mannerisms of the Southwest style of painting. He went on to study with non-Native American artist Raymond Jonson, and was influenced by European modernism. Howe was one of the first Native American individualists in his approach to painting. Studio-educated Quincy Tahoma also brought his personal vision to his subject-matter.

Another important centre for art education was established in 1935 at the Bacone Junior College Art Department in Muskogee, OK. This small, sectarian school institutionalized the study of Native American painting in the region. Acee Blue Eagle (Creek/Pawnee; 1907–59), a student of Oscar B. Jacobson, founded and chaired the Art Department from 1935 to 1938. Blue Eagle and his successors, Woody Crumbo (Potawatomi; b 1912) and RICHARD WEST (Cheyenne; b 1912), trained many promising Native American artists in a regional Oklahoma version of traditional painting. This form of painting was generally static and decorative in technique. Some notable students from Bacone include Blackbear Bosin (Kiowa/Comanche; 1921–80), Cecil Dick (Cherokee; b 1915), Fred Beaver (Creek; 1911–80) and JOAN HILL, whose *Creek White Feather Dance* is representative of the style (see fig. 28). There were strong stylistic and aesthetic ties between the work of these Bacone-trained Oklahoma painters and the Southwest artists. The works of Dick and Beaver, in particular, incorporate events from the history of the Five Civilized Tribes, depicted somewhat less romantically than art from the early Oklahoma artists period.

The establishment of two major, interactive regional centres for art instruction helped to define, and even

28. Joan Hill: *Creek White Feather Dance*, watercolour on paper, 1962 (Phoenix, AZ, Heard Museum)

institutionalize, 'traditional' painting. Pictures usually portrayed an idealized version of bygone Indian life. Most paintings were stylized in their use of form, colour and outline. Contemporary traditional painters still attempt to provide accuracy in historical detail, but they have eliminated decorative compositional elements in favour of background and perspective. Non-Native Americans viewed such 'traditional' painting as a specific style; one measure of its acceptance was the exhibition *Indian Art of the United States* (1941) at the Museum of Modern Art, New York.

During the 1930s a separate Alaskan Movement also developed. Artists chose to work in naive or genre modes similar to other early 20th-century Native American painting. The Alaskan Movement's practitioners produced humorous, everyday-life narrative scenes. Self-taught painters Florence Nupok Chauncey/Malewotkuk (Eskimo; 1906–71) and George Ahgupuk (Eskimo; *b* 1911) were influential in the creation of native Alaskan painting. Ahgupuk associated with illustrator ROCKWELL KENT and with Kent's assistance became a member of the American Artist Group. Inuit, or Eskimo, art has been greatly commercialized since the 1950s, and this has overshadowed public understanding of the nature of the Alaskan Movement.

(iv) Post-war developments and pan-Native American activism, 1945–70. With World War II came dramatic changes for Native American artists and their societies. Many painters entered the services; some died, and some that returned did not pursue their art. A realistic portrait of this cultural upheaval can be seen in Quincy Tahoma's *First Furlough* (1943; Washington, DC, N. Mus. Amer. Indian, Smithsonian Inst.). By 1944 many Native Americans had migrated to urban centres to do war-related work. A number of Native American artists later used the 1945 GI Bill to attend school. Also of significance was the Philbrook Art Center's (Tulsa, OK) adoption in 1946 of an annual competition for Native American artists. Many Bacone-trained painters participated in this activity. The National Exhibition of American Indian Painting continued (with slight changes of name) until 1980.

While Native American painting in the early 1950s was characterized by its representational, stylized content, there was also the beginning of a reaction by painters. Increasingly exposed to other contemporary art trends, many Native American painters chose to create alternative, individualistic visions. While some adhered to traditionalism, others began to explore mainstream techniques, using modernist styles and enlarging their range of subject-matter. Inevitably, clashes occurred. Oscar Howe sent a work incorporating abstraction to the 1958 Philbrook annual, only to have it rejected because it was in 'a non-traditional Indian style'. Howe protested, as did other painters in similar situations. They were opposed by a non-Native American-dominated world of curators, collectors and other patrons who wished to see Native American painting as a prescribed, ethnic style. Many Native American painters began to espouse individualism as a right of artistic freedom. Joe Herrera's explorations of non-objective, or even abstract, forms were taken up by others. Patrick DesJarlait's (Chippewa; 1921–73) work reflected the influence of Cubism and the Mexican muralists. During this time, George Morrison (Ojibway; *b* 1919) experimented with modern abstract techniques. Morrison was prominent in the mainstream New York art scene and became an influential educator. Southwestern artist Patrick Swazo Hinds (Tesuque; 1924–74) was another early defector from traditional style.

The transformation of Native American attitudes towards their art brought concern about the future. In 1959 the Rockefeller Foundation funded the conference *Directions in Indian Art* at the University of Arizona. Its organizers were seeking ways to expand the ethnic art market; among the topics discussed was the changing stylistic direction of younger Native American artists. A result of the conference was the Southwest Indian Art Project, composed of programmes held in the summers of 1961–2. Young artists received special art instruction that included traditional Native American and mainstream art forms. The Project also led to the establishment of the Institute of American Indian Art (IAIA) in Santa Fe in 1962. Other developments included the founding of the Scottsdale National Indian Arts Exhibitions (1961–72) and the addition of a non-traditional painting category to the Philbrook Annual Exhibition. Important alumni of the Southwest Indian Art Project were HELEN HARDIN

(Santa Clara), Mary Morez (Navajo; *b* 1938) and Michael Kabotie (Hopi; *b* 1942).

The creation of the Institute of American Indian Art had major repercussions for contemporary Native American painting. Its first director, Lloyd Kiva New, developed a programme of formal art education incorporating learning from tribal heritage and mainstream modern movements. Students could pursue avant-garde interests and work on the integration of their uniquely Native American vision within contemporary aesthetic technique. Innovation was valued, while respect for traditional modes was encouraged. New's tenure (1962–7) offered a training ground for an important generation of artists. Young artists at the IAIA pursued easel painting as a valid part of changing Native American culture. Among the new breed of idiosyncratic painters, at home with mainstream art world styles and philosophies, were T. C. Cannon (Caddo/Kiowa; 1946–78), Jerome Tiger (Creek/Seminole; 1946–67) and Valjean Hessing (Choctaw; *b* 1934), whose *Choctaw Removal* (1966; Tulsa, OK, Philbrook A. Cent.) combines traditional and modernist effects.

Native American activism and pan-Native American identity grew in the 1960s. In the wake of the Civil Rights Movement, some Native Americans formed groups to address their concerns, for example the National Indian Youth Council and the militant American Indian Movement (AIM). As Native Americans met socially at pow-wows and other events, many were encouraged to adopt a pan-Native American stance, in which being a Native American took social and cultural precedence over tribal identification. These attitudes influenced contemporary Native American painters: young artists produced works that reflected political anger, irony and concern about the treatment of Native American peoples.

In contrast to the USA, Canadian Native American fine-art painting has had a long struggle to be recognized. While there are a few reported cases of 19th-century painting in the European mode—such as the works Zacharie Vincent (Huron) made after he observed artist ANTOINE PLAMONDON—most Canadian Native Americans were too engaged in the struggle for survival to pursue painterly skills. Canada's various termination and assimilation policies made governmental encouragement of First Nations arts difficult. Native Americans were forced to adapt their artistic production to suit White buyers' demands.

The Canadian government employed a number of tactics in promoting Native American arts; Native American crafts, especially Inuit art, received the most attention and were marketed vigorously. The Massey Commission (1949) was an early statement of national cultural policy. Its efforts were followed by the commissioning of a *Report on Contemporary Art of the Canadian Indian* in 1950. These studies established the groundwork for a governmental sanction of indigenous arts. The Department of Indian Affairs created a Cultural Affairs Division in 1964 to promote artistic efforts, organize Native American art exhibitions and arrange scholarships. The Division's mandate accelerated after Native American communities rejected the proposed termination policies of the government's 1969 White Paper.

True patronage for modern Canadian Native American painting began in the 1960s. Ontario, the Plains provinces and the Northwest Coast were the main artistic centres of activity. North-western Ontario was the originating point for the Image Makers school of painting. The rise of pictorial thematic painting took place on the prairies, including Alberta, Saskatchewan and western Manitoba, while Northwest Coast art centred on collective visions inspired by traditional sculpture and graphics. Works produced before the 1960s were usually valued by non-Native American consumers for their anthropological veracity, and Native American artists did not make explicit political or social commentary. The prosperous era of the 1960s made 'ethnicity' a revalidated expression of nationalism—indigenous arts could be seen as truly Canadian. Arts in this era were highly individualistic but retained an identifiable Native American content. While Native American communities accepted art as an expression of their identity, non-Native Americans continued to be the major economic force behind the collection of this art.

One individual, NORVAL MORRISSEAU, greatly stimulated interest in Canadian Native American painting when his one-man show at the Pollock Gallery (Toronto) sold out in 1962. Morrisseau was an innovator, and his art was inspired by a combination of Ojibwa oral tradition, aboriginal rock art and Midewin scroll pictographs. He founded the school of Algonquin Legend Painters; his personal vision, which broke tribal taboos against non-Native Americans viewing pictorial depiction of legends, influenced many Ojibwa, Odawa and Cree painters. The 'Morrisseau School' was established by the late 1960s and represented a powerful public view of Native American nationalism. Legend painting, while reviving traditional art forms, also allowed its practitioners to work on a new means of expressing 'Native Americanness'. The international public was given an opportunity to see this new style of imagery when Morrisseau and follower Carl Ray (Cree; 1943–79) painted a large mural for the Indian Pavilion at Expo 67 in Montreal. The Pavilion, a controversial project encouraged by Native American administrators for the Cultural Affairs Division, introduced Canadians to the visual themes of the contemporary Native American artist. The work of Variationist painters, pioneered by Daphne Odjig (Odawa; *b* 1925), came into being in a geographically peripheral area, north-western Ontario and Manitoulin Island. Influential artists inspired by Morrisseau included Odjig, Goyce Kakegamic (Cree; *b* 1948) and Jackson Beardy (Ojibway; *b* 1944).

Another tradition of painting in the central Canadian provinces was animated by the region's large Cree population. Cree artists produced representational pictures of reservation life as experienced by tribal elders. Paintings from the 1960s depicted realistic and anecdotal scenes of everyday life in earlier decades. Genre painter Allen Sapp (Cree; *b* 1929) was a major figure; his work won him election to membership in the Royal Canadian Academy of Arts (RCAA) in 1975. Gerald Tailfeathers (Blood; 1925–74) gained recognition in the 1950s for his nostalgic scenes of late 19th-century tribal activities. Young art school-educated Native American artists were quick to adopt modernist painting styles. Alex Janvier (Chippewa; *b* 1935), working in Alberta, was influential for his activities in art and education. Janvier's non-objective image painting emphasized colour and movement. He worked for a time in the Department of Indian Affairs and was a champion of Native American artists' work on the Expo 67 Indian Pavilion. Janvier, Morrisseau and other artists were interested in seeing Native American painting become part of the Canadian artistic mainstream.

(v) After 1970. The Canadian government enacted multiculturalism as a federal policy in October 1971. While Native American fine artists struggled to place their works in mainstream cultural institutions, several art exhibitions and cultural education centres were created to promote Native American art. Exhibitions that emphasized aesthetics over anthropological viewpoints began to be mounted, as in *Canadian Indian Art '74* (Toronto, Royal Ont. Mus.). An Indian Art Centre was created within the Department of Indian Affairs to collect resources and documentation. In the 1970s there was also a more complete shift from tribal expression to individualistic and politically motivated painting. Art from Native American communities combined various interests, schools of thought and expressive modes. As in the USA, Native American painters had become more sophisticated, were more often trained in art schools and were more aware of cultural issues within and outside their reserve community. Ties were established between developing Canadian Native American art colleges and the IAIA in Santa Fe. Artist–educators, such as Alez Janvier (Cree/Ojibway; *b* 1948), represented a new breed of ideologically aware Native American painters. Modernist principles were taught in such schools as Manitou College in Quebec and Saskatchewan Cultural College in Saskatoon, now at the University of Saskatchewan in Regina.

Native American art activism continued in the 1970s and 1980s. In 1975 the McMichael Canadian Collection at Kleinburg opened the first permanent exhibition gallery devoted to contemporary Native American painting. The first Native Artist Conference was held on Manitoulin Island, where there is a large Native American artists colony, in October 1978. Controversial subjects were still being discussed at the 1983 Third Native Artist Conference in Hazleton, BC. Native American fine artists often felt opposed by the government's emphasis on marketing craft works. In Winnipeg, a 'Group of Seven' painters banded together in the mid-1970s as a reaction to governmental programmes and the predominance of the Ottawa–Toronto art scene. The Society for Canadian Artists of Native Ancestry (SCANA) became an official national organization in 1985. Indian Cultural Educational Centres, developed in various geographical locations contiguous to Native American populations, brought increased opportunities for art study and exhibitions.

By the 1980s Canadian Native American painting reflected a number of styles, from traditionally rendered legend painting, based on the recollection of tribal elders, to the kind of politically charged expressionism shown in Bob Boyer's (Metis; *b* 1948) *A Minor Sport in Canada* (1985; Ottawa, N.G.). Painters of the 1980s and 1990s worked with a selective and personal incorporation of Native American vision and international modernist art styles. While most Native American painters strove to be part of the mainstream Canadian art world, they were also engaged in evoking an aesthetic ideology that included their Native American consciousness. This diversity of form and imagery can be seen in the works of many contemporary painters: Carl Beam (Ojibway; *b* 1943), Robert Houle (Saulteaux/Ojibway; *b* 1947), Jane Ash Poitras (Chippewa; *b* 1951), Samuel Ash (Ojibway; *b* 1951), Gerald McMaster (Cree; *b* 1953), Luke Simon (Micmac; *b* 1953), Blake Debassige (Ojibway; *b* 1956), Maxine Noel/Ioyan Mani (Sioux; *b* 1946), Cyril Assiniboine (Saulteaux) and Lawrence Paul (Salish/Okanaga; *b* 1957).

In general, Native American painting in the USA and Canada became more diverse and independent in the 1970s. A greater number of Native American painters were professionally trained; and they were well grounded in technical and art- historical modes. As a result, postwar generation Native American artists grew tired of being asked to display their Native Americanness. While many continued to be interested in capturing the dual cultural identity of contemporary Native American life, painters could choose between new forms of expression in the traditional style, or use modernist, and often abstract, techniques. Traditional design motifs were often used; social commentary on modern Native American life appeared more frequently, and preconceived views of Native American painting were challenged afresh by a new generation of artists.

During the 1970s RUDOLPH CARL GORMAN and FRITZ SCHOLDER (Luiseno Mission) became so influential that many viewers felt their work to be representative of Native American painting as a whole. Gorman's elegant, linear portraits of Navajo women and tribal objects are so distinctive that his style has been greatly imitated (see fig. 29). While essentially a fine artist, Gorman successfully commercialized his work, thereby giving it a wider audience. This brought criticism from the fine-art community, but his technical ability has inspired many young Native American artists. Scholder, first a student and then an instructor in the Southwest Indian Art Project, painted bold, colourful canvases with powerful imagery. His works show the influence of Oscar Howe, Francis Bacon and Wayne Thiebaud. Scholder turned to Native American subject-matter around 1964, when he became an instructor at the IAIA. His paintings are ironic, and somewhat militantly iconic, portrayals of Native Americans. Scholder's images mock Native American stereotypes and have aroused controversy; like Gorman's, his evocative style inspires general interest in the new look of Native American painting.

Native American artists have engaged in various collaborative ventures since the 1970s. One of the most notable cooperative groups, the Artists Hopid, was organized by Michael Kabotie, Terrance Talaswaima (Hopi; *b* 1939) and Neil David sr (Hopi; *b* 1944); they joined together in 1973 and exhibited regularly thereafter, adding other artists in time. About 1977 the Grey Canyon Collective emerged in Albuquerque, NM. Institutionally unaffiliated groups of Native American artists began collaborating in the 1970s. A California-based network of non-Southwestern artists began in 1974. In addition, Native American artists

29. Rudolph Carl Gorman: *Navajo Woman*, watercolour on paper, 1.02×0.86 m (including frame), 1973 (Phoenix, AZ, Heard Museum)

received increased exhibition opportunities, although Native American fine-art exhibitions have often been shunted to anthropologically oriented museums and galleries. The Scottsdale National Indian Arts Council reinitiated its National Indian Arts Exhibition in 1974. The Commission of Indian Affairs authorized a two-year AA degree for the IAIA in 1975. A San Francisco commercial gallery, American Indian Contemporary Art, began in the 1980s to boost the profile of Native American arts. An important venue, the Native American Fine Arts Invitational Biennial, was established in 1983 at the Heard Museum in Phoenix, AZ.

However, Native American fine-art painters have faced continuing obstacles to their general success: the powerful ethnic art market, and lack of public education combined with tourist demand, have hampered contemporary Native American artists' battles against outdated stereotypes. Native American painters working in avant-garde modes have suffered from misperceptions about how their work should be seen; the viewing public has been baffled by Native Americans working in abstract and non-objective styles, and Native American artists' style has been confused with iconography. One of the most controversial developments in the Native American art world was the adoption in 1990 of the Indian Arts and Crafts Act (US Public Law 101–644), federal legislation created to ensure that Native American art is made by 'authentic' Native Americans, as a means of stemming the persistent problem of fakes. In order to qualify, Native American artists must be enrolled and certified by their groups. However, this registration bars artists without group documentation or

those in groups not officially recognized by the government, and many Native American artists have condemned the Act as divisive.

Despite the problems inherent in Native American fine-art painting's growth and dissemination, there exists a vigorous group of practitioners. These diverse painters aim for an idiom of timelessness that incorporates traditional and modern consciousness. Contemporary works of the 1980s and 1990s eschew the idea of a unified Native American painting style. Several women became inspirational leaders in fine-art painting: Kay WalkingStick (Cherokee; *b* 1935), JAUNE QUICK-TO-SEE SMITH (Cree/Flathead/Shoshone), Linda Lomaheftewa (Hopi; *b* 1940), Phyllis Fife (Creek; *b* 1948) and Emmi Whitehorse (Navajo; *b* 1957). Others broke new ground in their chosen medium. James Havard (Choctaw/Chippewa; *b* 1937) forged a successful career as an abstract illusionist painter without reference to his Native American heritage. George Morrison worked in the abstract expressionist style, and George Longfish (Seneca/Tuscarora; *b* 1942) and Dan Namingha (Hopi; *b* 1950) were leading exponents of individualistically styled painting imbued with Native American aesthetics.

Native American fine-art painters gained ground in the last decades of the 20th century. Awareness of contemporary Native American arts grew, fuelled in part by the vigorous crafts industry and increasing American acceptance of multiculturalism. Exhibitions of Native American painting at Canadian institutions, such as the Art Gallery of Ontario, Toronto, and the Canadian Museum of Civilization, Ottawa, increased steadily. A National Museum of the Native North American is due to open in Washington, DC, by 1999.

BIBLIOGRAPHY

GENERAL
O. B. Jacobson: *American Indian Painters* (Nice, 1950)
N. Feder: *North American Indian Painting* (New York, 1967)
D. Dowdy: *Annotated Bibliography of American Indian Painting* (New York, 1968)
Native American Arts, United States Department of the Interior (Washington, DC, 1968)
J. Snodgrass: *American Indian Painters: A Biographical Directory* (New York, 1968)
J. Highwater: *Song from the Earth: American Indian Painting* (Boston, 1976)
A. Silberman: *100 Years of Native American Painting* (Oklahoma City, 1978)
P. Broder: *American Indian Painting and Sculpture* (New York, 1981)
E. Wade, ed.: *The Arts of the North American Indian: Native Traditions in Evolution* (Tulsa, 1986)
E. Wade: 'What Is Native American Art?' *SWA.*, xvi (October 1986), pp. 108–17

SPECIALIZED STUDIES
K. Chapman: *Pueblo Indian Painters* (Nice, 1936)
F. Dockstader, ed.: *Directions in Indian Art* (Tucson, 1959)
D. Dunn: *American Indian Painting of the Southwest and the Plains Areas* (Albuquerque, 1968)
J. J. Brody: *Indian Painters and White Patrons* (Albuquerque, 1971)
M. Nelson: *Future Directions in Native American Art* (Santa Fe, 1972)
C. L. Tanner: *Southwest Indian Painting: A Changing Art* (Tucson, 1973)
G. Monthan and D. Monthan: *Art and Indian Individualists* (Flagstaff, 1975)
P. Broder: *Hopi Painting: The World of the Hopis* (New York, 1978)
E. Wade and R. Strickland: *Magic Images: Contemporary Native American Art* (Norman, 1981)
R. Schrader: *The Indian Arts and Crafts Board* (Albuquerque, 1983)
M. E. Southcott: *The Sound of the Drum: The Sacred Art of the Anishnabec* (Erin, Ontario, 1984)

R. Strickland: 'Where Have All the Blue Deer Gone? Depth and Diversity in Postwar Indian Painting', *Amer. Ind. A.*, x (1985), pp. 36–45
L. Jacka and J. Jacka: *Beyond Tradition: Contemporary Indian Art and its Evolution* (Flagstaff, 1988)
J. Berlo, ed.: *The Early Years of Native American Art History: The Politics of Scholarship and Collecting* (Seattle, 1992)

EXHIBITION CATALOGUES
Contemporary American Indian Painting (exh. cat., Washington, DC, N.G.A., 1953)
Native American Painting: Selections from the Museum of the American Indian (exh. cat. by D. Fawcett and L. Callander, New York, Mus. Amer. Ind., 1982)
Norval Morrisseau and the Emergence of the Image Makers (exh. cat. by E. McLuhan and T. Hill, Toronto, A.G. Ont., 1984)
Women of Sweetgrass, Cedar and Sage: Contemporary Art by Native American Women (exh. cat., New York, Gal. Amer. Ind. Comm. House, 1985)
Portfolio: Eleven American Indian Artists (exh. cat., San Francisco, CA, Amer. Ind. Contemp. A., 1986)
A Celebration of Contemporary Canadian Native Art (exh. cat. by T. Hill, Brantford, Ont., Woodlands Ind. Cult. Educ. Cent., 1987)
Beyond History (exh. cat. by K. Duffeck, Vancouver, A.G., 1989)
Our Land/Ourselves (exh. cat., Albany, SUNY, U. A.G., 1990)
5th Biennial Native American Fine Arts Invitational (exh. cat. by M. Archuleta, Phoenix, AZ, Heard Mus., 1991)
Shared Visions: Native American Painters and Sculptures in the Twentieth Century (exh. cat. by M. Archuleta and R. Strickland, Phoenix, AZ, Heard Mus., 1991)
E. Wade: 'Native American Paintings and Sculpture', *The Philbrook Museum of Art Handbook of the Collections* (Tulsa, 1991), pp. 195–221
Creativity is our Tradition: Three Decades of Contemporary Indian Art at the Institute of American Indian Arts (exh. cat. by R. Hill, Santa Fe, NM, Inst. Amer. Ind. A., 1992)
MARGARET ARCHULETA, PAULA A. BAXTER

V. Pottery.

Ceramics played a prominent part in many but not all Native American cultures. In those areas where pottery was not used, or used almost incidentally for utilitarian purposes only, other materials, such as stone, gourds, wood, horn, skins and baskets, were employed as vessels and containers. In the Southwest cultures and in the complex array of cultures in the eastern half of the USA, however, ceramics played an important role in utilitarian material culture and in trade, ceremony and art.

1. Southwest. 2. Woodlands.

1. SOUTHWEST.

(i) Before European contact. (ii) After European contact.

(i) Before European contact. Pottery is the most common form of material culture recovered from late prehistoric settlements in the North American Southwest. It has therefore been studied extensively by generations of archaeologists, and its complex classification of forms has become the backbone of most cultural historical reconstructions for the region. Southwestern specialists on prehistoric ceramics recognize well over 1500 distinct pottery types, and pottery classification has been used to distinguish areas of apparent cultural uniformity and ethnic–linguistic identity. Although the simple equation of ceramic style with ethnicity can be challenged on both empirical as well as theoretical grounds, it remains implicit in most discussions of prehistoric Southwestern pottery. Three major and several minor prehistoric pottery traditions have been recognized within the region. The three major traditions include the Hohokam of southern Arizona and northern Sonora; the Mogollon of south-east Arizona, southern New Mexico and northern Chihuahua;

and the Anasazi of the northern Southwest, including northern New Mexico and the 'Four Corners' area, where Utah, Colorado, Arizona and New Mexico meet. The minor traditions are less widely recognized, but designations such as Hakataya, Patayan, Salado, Sinagua and Jornado Mogollon have variously been proposed and described. Although each of these archaeologically defined 'cultures' is presumed to reflect a unique ethnic and historical trajectory within the region, in reality there appears to have been much temporal and spatial blurring of identity between these material traditions. This blurring is especially apparent towards the end of the pre-contact sequence.

(a) Early Village period (*c.* AD 200–*c.* 900). (b) Regional Integration period (*c.* AD 900–*c.* 1300). (c) Aggregated Town period (*c.* 1300–*c.* 1600).

*(a) Early Village period (*c.* 200–c. 900).* The earliest currently accepted dates associated with pottery in the North American Southwest cluster around AD 200. The start of ceramic production seems to be closely linked to the spread of maize agriculture into the region, and, as with domesticated maize, its origins can probably be traced to early highland farming villages in Mesoamerica (*see* MESOAMERICA, PRE-COLUMBIAN, §II, 2(i)). Throughout the Southwest pottery was produced almost exclusively within domestic contexts and primarily for household use. Two general functional categories are recognized: utility ware vessels, generally in the form of wide-mouthed jars, had either rough or intentionally textured surfaces, coarsely textured pastes and were used primarily for cooking and storage; service wares, on the other hand, were more durable and usually in the form of bowls or, less frequently, jars, with fine-textured pastes and well-finished surfaces that were usually slipped and painted. Painted pottery appears to have been used primarily for preparing and serving food, carrying and storing water, and for specialized functions, such as religious rituals.

Despite archaeological problems that cloud interpretations of its earliest occurrences, pottery-making appears to have been widespread throughout the Southwest by *c.* AD 500, by which time the Hohokam, Mogollon and Anasazi traditions were each well established. The first ceramics were predominantly simple, undecorated bowls, ollas (globular water-jars with flaring necks), seed-jars and ladles that mimicked contemporary gourd and basketwork containers. As the traditions matured, adding a slip or painted decoration to one or more surface became common, and distinctions between decorated service wares and undecorated utility wares became apparent.

Mogollon. From its earliest occurrences Mogollon pottery was made from local, fine-textured, residual clays that fired brown in an oxidizing atmosphere. After *c.* AD 550, a slipped and polished redware was added to the repertory, and before the 10th century such red-slipped vessels, often with smudged and polished black interiors, were the most common service ware throughout much of the Mogollon region. In contrast, Mogollon painted pottery was relatively rare. About AD 700 potters in the Mimbres area began to paint simple red designs on polished brown backgrounds. Shortly thereafter, probably as a result of influence from the Anasazi, white slips were added as a background to the painted surfaces of vessels and within another generation or so black paint replaced red. This black-on-white style remained relatively constant for the next 350 years, although changes occurred in the composition and quality of painted designs. Early examples of the style are characterized by bold, heavy motifs of broad, barbed, straight or wavy lines, forming interlocking scrolls, spirals and concentric circles. Design layouts generally comprise a single field or quartered layout covering the entire interior surface of bowls and are strongly reminiscent of early Hohokam designs.

Brown utility pottery continued to be produced throughout the Mogollon area after the introduction of slipped and painted wares. Increasingly, however, potters began to experiment with ways to manipulate the exterior surface of these simple vessels. At first, decoration was limited to a few incised lines or rows of punching or scoring around the necks of jars. Later, these were replaced by a few broad rows of unfinished neck-coils. Such early jars are generally small and often have braided or strap handles. Over time, neck-bands became increasingly narrow and covered more of the surface of the pot; and by the 10th century corrugations covered the entire top-half of jars, and vessel sizes were considerably larger.

Anasazi. Anasazi wares followed a contemporary and parallel development. The earliest pottery on Anasazi sites was Mogollon brownware. Anasazi potters, however, rapidly began to experiment with local materials. North of the Mogollon rim the most common clays are sedimentary in origin and generally fire light to dark grey in colour. Unlike the fine-textured residual clays to the south, these sedimentary clays required the addition of crushed rock or sand to make them workable. As a result, exterior surfaces on Anasazi pots tended to be coarser and more difficult to polish. This physical limitation may have led Anasazi potters to begin adding a fine white or, much more rarely, red slip to their service vessels to create a smooth surface for the application of black painted designs.

Two variations of the Anasazi black-on-white tradition developed quite early, defined primarily on the basis of the pigment used. Although there are many exceptions and much overlap, in general, northern and western Anasazi pots are characterized by the use of vegetal-based pigments that fired with a soft, translucent, grey-to-black tone, while to the south and east, a denser, iron-based mineral paint was preferred, which allowed for better control and finer linework. The earliest Anasazi designs are characteristic of those woven into basketwork, featuring free-form, isolated figures and graceful, often asymmetrical, curving elements. Within a few generations, however, the Anasazi had developed a much more precise and controlled style. Painting on pottery was generally non-figurative, incorporating a limited number of geometric motifs within carefully defined and framed zones. The zones are usually laid out with an arithmetic symmetry that tends to reinforce the form of the vessel. The overall effect is 'stately, rhythmically predictable, and emotionally under control' (Brody, 1991, p. 33). In those rare cases where human, animal or other life forms are incorporated within the design, they are usually rendered with more expressive freedom than their geometric counterparts. These representational images resemble contemporary rock art designs in both style and subject-matter.

Early Anasazi utility ware consists primarily of small, grey jars and jugs, with or without handles. Over time, the coils or corrugations around the necks and upper shoulders of pots were accentuated intentionally, following the similar trend in Mogollon brownware, but with some regional variation. The exterior surfaces of Anasazi utility jars are often sooted black from use over cooking fires.

Hohokam. While Anasazi and Mogollon potters formed their pots by building up successive coils of clay, which were thinned by drawing and scraping with a special tool, such as a gourd rind, Hohokam potters thinned their coil-built pots by the 'paddle-and-anvil' technique. This distinction is generally interpreted as indicative of a separate origin for the Hohokam tradition. The earliest Hohokam ceramics consist of simple, plain brown or buff vessels, occasionally covered by a polished red slip. Painting began by reducing the red slip to a series of broad parallel bands or chevrons. Early linework was predominantly rectilinear but became progressively narrower and more closely spaced over time. Much of the charm and vitality of Hohokam pottery can be attributed to its simple but dynamic portrayal of life forms, including birds, reptiles, mammals and human figures. Hohokam potters also developed a stunning array of small geometric motifs that were repeated to create eye-dazzling overall designs (see fig. 30).

Motifs tended to be distributed evenly over painted surfaces, so that there was little sense of a single dominant image or bounded space. Interior spaces or zones for decoration were divided into four or more segments that radiated out from the centre to the rim. Exterior surfaces were organized into diagonally repeating patterns or into a series of concentric rings. This preference for overall patterning and for the use of expanding designs, as opposed to zonal subdivisions and restricted pictorial

30. Santa Cruz red-on-buff jar, diam. 126 mm, from Snaketown, Arizona, Hohokam tradition, *c.* AD 700–*c.* 900 (Tucson, AZ, Arizona State Museum)

fields, distinguishes the Hohokam tradition. The Hohokam potter was 'master of the extemporaneous stroke, using her brush in truly creative delineation, whereas the Pueblo [Anasazi] decorator used hers as a methodical generator of prim lines in formal geometric figures. The latter is a well-schooled draughtsman, the former an unschooled artist' (Amsden, p. 44).

Standard Hohokam utility ware, known as Gila Plain, comprised simple, undecorated brown to grey vessels that appear to have undergone negligible stylistic change during the millennium or more of their production. At SNAKETOWN, Haury (1976) noted a slight tendency for vessel walls to become thicker through time. This trend may be related to an increase in the average size of storage vessels, particularly during the 10th and 11th centuries as the size of permanent agricultural villages grew.

(b) Regional Integration period (c. AD 900–c. 1300). During the second half of the 11th century a large part of the northern Southwest came under the domination of a complex system of political and economic interaction centred at CHACO CANYON in north-eastern New Mexico. Other regional systems developed in the vicinity of CASAS GRANDES in northern Chihuahua and among the Hohokam of the Gila and Salt Basins in southern Arizona. But despite such political systems and their widespread influences, most continued to live in more simply organized communities, such as the Classic Mimbres settlements of south-western New Mexico.

During this period pottery styles throughout the Southwest were characterized by an elaboration and refinement of earlier trends and increasing regional variation. In particular, distinctions between the two major variants of the Anasazi black-on-white tradition intensified. The mineral-painted pottery that dominated the Cibola–Chaco area stressed the use of fine lines on a surface that was usually chalky white, while the vegetal-painted variants of the MESA VERDE and Kayenta areas emphasized heavy black solid elements on a surface that was usually highly polished. While both variants shared fundamental motifs and the same basic linear, rhythmic and symmetrical design structure, the fine-line designs tended to be lighter in tone and tenser in character (see fig. 31) than the heavier and strongly negative designs on vegetal-painted vessels.

The fine-line 'Chaco' style dominated painted pottery on sites within a 100 km radius of Chaco Canyon from the end of the 8th century to the mid-12th. Local copies of this style were produced throughout north-eastern and north-central New Mexico and adjacent parts of Colorado, Utah and Arizona. What the widespread distribution of this style meant in social and economic terms remains an object of much speculation. About AD 1130, the Chaco political sphere appears to have collapsed, and with it the mineral-paint tradition of the central Anasazi area came to an abrupt end, although related pottery continued to be produced to the south and west in the Cibola and Acoma provinces. In parts of the Anasazi area, red or orange slips were used, occasionally with black paint. Designs generally paralleled the local black-on-white tradition. Such wares appear to have been extremely popular as gift or trade items and often reached settlements far from their point of manufacture. Whether they held some special significance or served some purpose outside the standard domestic context remains unknown. Also during this period, surface texturing on the standard Anasazi grey utility pottery underwent a transition from simple neckbanding to increasingly complex variants of all-over indented corrugation.

During the 11th and 12th centuries Mimbres potters in south-western New Mexico developed a highly refined style of black-on-white painted pottery, known as 'Classic Mimbres'. Its geometric variant shows strong influence from the Anasazi tradition, with the incorporation of framing lines and clearly bounded linear design panels. Designs are characterized by a dynamic tension achieved by the careful balancing and symmetrical opposition of solid black and finely hatched elements; after *c.* AD 1000 figurative motifs became increasingly common. In some cases animals, birds, fish, insects and human forms were incorporated as elements within otherwise geometric design panels. More often, single or multiple figures were drawn in the centre of the open field on the bottom of a bowl, the geometric band acting as an elaborate frame. The most unique examples of Classic Mimbres painting, however, use this open field as a picture space for complex, dynamic, narrative scenes (see fig. 32), apparently a mix of scenes from daily life and episodes from mythic narratives or ritual performances. Images that blur the distinction between natural and supernatural, human and animal are common. LeBlanc (1983, pp. 119–20) argues convincingly that these scenes must be viewed without standard reference to Western canons of representational art: for example, Hopi informants consistently saw these

31. Chaco black-on-white pitcher, h. 172 mm, max. diam. 148 mm, Anasazi Mineral Paint tradition, *c.* AD 1075–*c.* 1130 (Santa Fe, NM, Museum of New Mexico)

scenes as metaphors for the relationship between human groups in society and between man and nature, showing how the lives of humans and animals are symbiotically intertwined.

Alongside the Classic Mimbres style, Mogollon potters, both within and beyond the Mimbres Valley, experimented with a variety of exterior surface treatments on their utility brownware. Most vessels were corrugated over their entire surface, but some potters alternated rows of plain and indented corrugated coils or selectively indented parts of each coil to create rectilinear scrolls and lozenge-shaped figures. During the 13th century some potters in east-central Arizona even added a thick white slip to accentuate certain aspects of the indented patterns. Towards the end of the 12th century sites began to be abandoned throughout the Mogollon area, and the Mogollon pottery tradition declined, although elements of it continued to influence Southwest pottery well into post-contact times (see §V, 1(ii) below).

In the 12th and 13th centuries Casas Grandes also became the centre of a large regional system, whose influence extended at least as far north as south-western New Mexico. Casas Grandes painted pottery (see fig. 33) came to be characterized by highly polished polychrome vessels decorated with stylized macaw heads, snakes, feathered serpents and a variety of feather and corn motifs. Animal and human effigy vessels were also common. The Casas Grandes regional system appears to have collapsed by the mid-14th century, but polychrome pottery strongly influenced by the Casas Grandes style continued to be produced in northern Chihuahua and adjacent areas of south-western New Mexico and southern Arizona well into the 16th century.

The peak of excellence in the Hohokam red-on-buff tradition came with the production of Santa Cruz Red-on-buff in the 9th century. Succeeding types show a trend towards larger vessels, and coarse linework and layout that appears to be correlated with an increasingly high level of production. During the 10th to 12th centuries design panels were often set at right angles to each other in apparently overlapping, expanding and dynamic patterns that resemble twillweave basketwork, but there is little in the way of new or innovative motifs. By the end of the 14th century Hohokam potters were producing only a small fraction of the painted pottery made previously, and this lacked the flamboyant spontaneity of earlier types. Forms were limited and patterns stiffly rectilinear in a tightly controlled style reminiscent of the Anasazi tradition.

(c) Aggregated Town period (c. 1300–c. 1600). At the end of the 13th century there was a massive redistribution of population throughout the Southwest. Former centres of regional systems were abandoned, and large aggregated communities were established in areas that had previously been only sparsely populated. Because people of diverse origins came together to form new communities, the cultural designations used to identify the ceramic traditions of earlier periods no longer apply. Instead, Southwest pottery during this period was characterized by the development of a few innovative and closely related decorative styles that were produced, copied and traded over enormous distances. These ceramics are marked by a dramatic

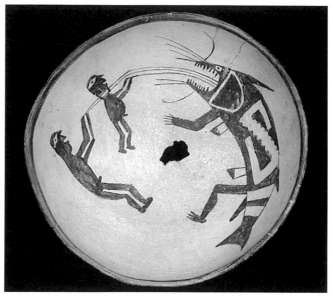

32. Classic Mimbres black-on-white figural bowl, diam. 200 mm, Mogollon tradition, *c.* AD 1000–*c.* 1150 (Boulder, CO, University of Colorado)

33. Jar, h. 220 mm, from Casas Grandes, Chihuahua, Mexico, ?*c.* AD 1300 (Prague, Náprstek Museum of Asian, African and American Culture)

use of colour and the incorporation of more obviously iconographic and symbolic elements within decorative motifs. The distribution of each new polychrome type may reflect the emergence of increasingly complex regional systems of socio-political and economic integration that cut across traditional cultural and ethnic boundaries.

Pottery styles that developed between *c.* 1300 and *c.* 1600 formed the basis for most of the historic ceramic traditions in the Southwest. Many of the technological and stylistic innovations in ceramic production that characterize this period can be traced to the Cibola region of

34. Sikyatki Polychrome bowl, diam. 263 mm, from Kawaika-a, Arizona, Hopi Province, *c.* AD 1400–*c.* 1700 (Philadelphia, PA, University of Pennsylvania, University Museum)

western New Mexico and east-central Arizona, along the former border between the Anasazi and Mogollon traditions. Popular and widely traded red-slipped variants of local black-on-white types had been produced in this area since the beginning of the 11th century. By the 13th century white paint was occasionally added to bowl exteriors to create polychrome designs. Among these White Mountain Redwares six partially overlapping temporal styles have been defined (Carlson). The latest style, Fourmile, reflects a radical departure from all earlier Southwest styles: on bowls, the focus of decoration was shifted from the walls to the centre, and single dominant motifs became more common; many designs lack the overall symmetry of earlier styles. In addition, the line between abstraction and representation is often blurred, with traditional geometric motifs, such as stepped figures or interlocking spirals, recombined to become feathers, birds, sun symbols, horned serpents or other elements of Pueblo sacred iconography. The Fourmile style originated in the Cibola area during the 14th century but appears to have spread rapidly, influencing other contemporaneous polychrome traditions throughout the Southwest.

This influence is most strongly seen in Sikyatki Polychrome (see fig. 34), produced on the Hopi mesas of north-eastern Arizona between the 15th century and the 17th. The distinctive hard, buff-to-yellow pastes that characterize Sikyatki and other Hopi painted pottery are produced by firing the pots in an oxidizing atmosphere, using coal instead of wood as fuel. Designs can be extraordinarily complex and dynamic, and the combinations of colours and application techniques used give them a sense of texture and depth that is unique among Southwest painted pottery. Production appears to have

been limited to the Hopi mesas, but Sikyatki Polychrome and related Hopi yellow-ware pottery were widely traded throughout the Southwest during the 14th to 16th centuries.

Some iconographic aspects of the Fourmile–Sikyatki style, along with its use of colour contrast, are reminiscent of Casas Grandes polychromes, but most specialists believe the two styles developed independently from a common Southwest base. Either or both styles may have influenced the production and design of Gila Polychrome (*c.* 1300–1600), the most important and widely distributed of the 'Salado Polychromes'. Gila Polychrome bowls have orange-slipped, unpainted exteriors and white-slipped interiors with black-painted designs. Design layouts generally cover the entire interior, and geometric elements often represent abstract birds, serpents, masks or other symbolic motifs. Gila Polychrome is found over an enormous area from Casas Grandes to north of Phoenix, Arizona, and from the Gila–Salt Basin in Arizona to the Mimbres Valley in New Mexico. In some areas these vessels appear to have been produced locally, alongside other decorated ceramic types, while in other areas they appear to have been imported. The production and distribution of Salado Polychromes has been interpreted as a marker of participation in a broad interaction sphere, the context and function of which remains uncertain.

Another important technological innovation that occurred in the Cibola–Zuni area during the late 13th century was the development of glaze-painted pottery. The black mineral paint used in this area contained impurities that occasionally caused it to fuse when fired. Potters learnt to control the fusing, so that a true glaze was consistently formed. By the beginning of the 14th century glaze-paint technology had spread from the Zuni area eastward to Acoma and the middle Rio Grande. The related bichrome and polychrome types produced in these areas between the 14th century and the 17th were characterized, initially, by dark red and orange slips, and, later, by light pink, yellow and white slips, to which were added a variety of coloured matte and translucent glaze paints. The luminous quality of the vitrified paints added texture to the painted surfaces of pots. Over time, the glazes became increasingly runny, flowing over and interfering with the linear designs that still dominated Pueblo painted pottery. Like other late polychrome styles, glaze-painted pottery was widely traded. Mineralogical studies in the middle and northern Rio Grande suggest that a few provinces controlled its production and distribution throughout the region.

North of the Santa Fe River in the northern Rio Grande Valley, vegetal-based matte-painted pottery continued to be made through the 17th century, but these late black-on-white types are less appealing aesthetically. Vessel walls are generally thick, and slips, when present, vary from a streaky, dirty white to a thick, crackled, creamy yellow. Designs are still confined to linear bands, but lines are wider and less angularly precise and the draughtsmanship more casual and, at times, quite sloppy. During the late 17th century and the early 18th the black-on-white tradition of the north merged with the glaze polychrome tradition of the south and west, resulting in the development of the matte-painted polychromes that came to dominate the historic pottery traditions of Acoma, Zuni and the Eastern Pueblos. The production of unpainted polished red and black wares became increasingly common in the northern Rio Grande area during this period as well.

Late pre-contact utility ware in both the Eastern and Western Pueblo areas was characterized by a tendency to smear over or obliterate the carefully indented corrugations on vessel exteriors. By the 16th century this trend resulted in a return to the production of utility pottery with generally smooth, untextured surfaces. In the northern Rio Grande area, utility pottery made with residual clays from the foothills of the Sangre de Cristo Mountains became increasingly popular from the beginning of the 14th century. These highly micaceous clays gave vessels an appealing and distinctive lustrous quality. By the 17th century recent migrant Apache groups were producing similar micaceous utility pottery in the foothills and plains adjacent to the Eastern Pueblo settlements of New Mexico.

BIBLIOGRAPHY

A. V. Kidder and C. A. Amsden: *The Pottery of Pecos*, i (New Haven, 1931)
C. A. Amsden: *An Analysis of Hohokam Pottery Design* (Globe, 1936)
A. V. Kidder and A. O. Shepard: *The Pottery of Pecos*, ii (New Haven, 1936)
A. O. Shepard: *Rio Grande Glaze Paint Ware* (Washington, DC, 1942)
W. Smith, R. B. Woodbury and N. F. S. Woodbury: *The Excavation of Hawikuh by Frederick Webb Hodge* (New York, 1966)
R. L. Carlson: *White Mountain Redware: A Pottery Tradition of East-Central Arizona and Western New Mexico* (Tucson, 1970)
W. Smith: *Painted Ceramics of the Western Mound at Awatovi* (Cambridge, 1971)
E. W. Haury: *The Hohokam: Desert Farmers and Craftsmen: Excavations at Snaketown, 1964–1965* (Tucson, 1976/R 1978)
J. J. Brody: *Mimbres Painted Pottery* (Albuquerque, 1977)
A. H. Schroeder, ed.: *Southwestern Ceramics: A Comparative Review* (Phoenix, 1982)
S. A. LeBlanc: *The Mimbres People: Ancient Pueblo Painters of the American Southwest* (London, 1983)
L. S. Cordell: *Prehistory of the Southwest* (New York, 1984)
S. Peckham: *From this Earth: The Ancient Art of Pueblo Pottery* (Santa Fe, 1990)
E. C. Adams: *The Origin and Development of the Pueblo Katsina Cult* (Tucson, 1991)
J. J. Brody: *Anasazi and Pueblo Painting* (Albuquerque, 1991)
J. A. Habicht-Mauche: *The Pottery from Arroyo Hondo Pueblo: Tribalization and Trade in the Northern Rio Grande* (Santa Fe, 1993)

JUDITH A. HABICHT-MAUCHE

(ii) After European contact. Pottery-making, universal in the historic Southwest, has been a continuous tradition since European contact. Information on it is limited, however, due to the semi-sedentary lifestyle of some peoples, the late date at which collecting began in the region and the lack of interest in certain undecorated wares.

(a) Pima, Yuma, Navajo and Apache. (b) Pueblo.

(a) Pima, Yuma, Navajo and Apache. Piman and Yuman peoples of Arizona and south-eastern California have long made simply decorated pottery. Prehistoric antecedents are seldom apparent, but they do exist; for example, Piman designs are derived from those of the prehistoric Hohokam, who occupied the same region (*see* §(i) above and I, 2(i)). The pottery of some of these peoples has been called mediocre or unimaginative, but the Mohaves and Quechans made charming ceramic dolls now treasured by collectors. All of the Athapaskan-speaking Navajos and Apaches made pottery, but some, for example the Western Apaches and Mescalero Apaches, made so little that only

a few examples exist. The Jicarilla Apaches of northern New Mexico made unpainted culinary ware, which they traded to Pueblo Native Americans of the northern Rio Grande Valley. The Navajos still make unpainted culinary ware, often waterproofed with pine resin. The unpainted pottery of the Navajos and Apaches was often decorated with filleted rims and with appliqué strands or roundels of clay impressed with designs. The Navajos also made painted pottery, but taboos governing it were so numerous that it approached extinction in the early 20th century. The currently thriving market for Native American arts has revived Navajo pottery. Appliqué horned toads and corralled cows are among the fanciful interpretations of the tradition by Betty Manygoats, Silas Claw and others, while superbly crafted, sensuous shapes typify the work of Christine McHorse.

(b) Pueblo.

Introduction. The sedentary Pueblo Native Americans of more than 30 distinct communities of New Mexico and Arizona, descendants of the Anasazi (*see* §I, 2(i) above), have been the region's most prolific potters. Pottery has probably been made to some extent in almost every pueblo, but potters in only about half of them excel at the craft today. Although knowledge of Pueblo pottery is greater than that of other Southwest peoples, it is nonetheless limited, especially for the period 1500 to 1700, due to the rarity of whole vessels and the paucity of reliable archaeological data. The Spanish Conquest and raids by nomadic peoples led to abandonment of many pueblos in the 17th century, and increasing pressures precipitated the Pueblo Revolt in 1680, in which the Pueblos drove the Spanish from the region. Spanish Reconquest in the 1690s never enforced the control that obtained before the Revolt. Almost all the pueblos occupied in 1700 remain so, and excavations in them have been limited. Consequently most surviving historic pots made before 1870, when museums began to collect, were preserved as heirlooms. Few sites provide dates to establish a chronology of historic pottery.

Since the Spanish Conquest, the broad regional styles of prehistoric times have yielded to localized styles found in clusters of villages sharing a common language. In the 20th century Euro-American preoccupation with individualism, named artists and signed works of art brought innovations to pottery and fame to potters; even so, the traditional conformity that appears to have been foremost in the prehistoric potter's mind has not been abandoned by even the most innovative potters. Although other crafts declined under Spanish rule, the difficulty of transporting pottery from Mexico caused Spanish settlers to use pottery made by Pueblo women. Pueblo pottery remained unchanged from pre-contact styles until the late 17th century, although new shapes were introduced, including ecclesiastical vessels, such as chalices and candlesticks, and incense boats, censers and spoons.

Economic adjustments led to other changes. With Reconquest, the Spanish seized control of mineral resources, and the Pueblo glaze-paint tradition came to a halt. In the 18th century adoption of European traditions added more new vessel forms, in particular the dough bowl and the storage jar. The appearance of the dough bowl in the late 18th century or early 19th marks the adoption of wheat and leavened bread from the Spaniards. The storage jar came into use about the same time, and, although it has generally been used for storage, it may originally have had other purposes. Several early, excavated storage jars were recovered not from sites where they were made but in areas to which they were traded, suggesting that they were used to transport grain or other trade goods from pueblo to pueblo. Completion of the transcontinental railroad to New Mexico in 1880 brought metalware and other goods that supplanted pottery in Pueblo homes. Pottery-making declined quickly. Potters began making such tourist objects as ceramic ashtrays and moccasins, but by 1900 few potters were active. Interaction between them and concerned outsiders led to a number of revivals that have kept the craft viable. Some pueblos have become noted for their pottery and were the homes of notable individual potters.

Tiwa. Tiwa-speaking potters of Taos and Picuris, the northernmost pueblos, and of Sandía and Isleta, near Albuquerque, have traditionally made undecorated pottery. Taos and Picuris potters made a culinary ware similar to that of the Jicarilla Apaches. In the 20th century most pottery at Taos has been acquired through trade, while at Picuris pottery-making has remained a more lively tradition. Potters at Sandía made a coarse culinary ware but have long been inactive. At Isleta potters made wares resembling Tewa types (see below), either partially red-slipped or deliberately smudged, until about 1950. Isleta is better known for polychrome pottery, which was introduced from Laguna Pueblo about 1880, when a faction left Laguna and established a village on Isleta land. Typical pots by Lagunas and their Isleta students are small vessels or figurines for the tourist trade, sold for many years by their makers at Albuquerque railroad station. In the 1970s and 1980s Isleta became known for pottery in non-traditional pastel colours.

Tewa. Pottery made by Tewa-speaking potters of San Juan, Santa Clara, San Ildefonso, Nambe, Pojoaque and Tesuque pueblos north-west of Santa Fe represents a tradition uninterrupted since ancient times. White-slipped vessels with designs in black and varying amounts of red can be traced back for centuries and were made until the 1980s. Black paint was derived from sugar-rich plants, such as Rocky Mountain bee plant and tansy mustard. Red, used since the Tewas moved in the 16th century from their ancestral homelands on the Pajarito Plateau to their current villages on the Rio Grande, was made from red clay obtained in trade from Keresans further south on the Rio Grande. In the 17th century Tewa potters added red to white-slipped vessels and invented two new types: a red-slipped ware fired in an oxidizing atmosphere, and a red-slipped ware deliberately smudged. The decorative zones implied by the contours of jars, bowls, plates and other shapes, together with the use of white, red and black, allowed Tewa potters to make a variety of types. Every type was probably originally made in all Tewa pueblos, but by the late 19th century each village specialized in one or a few. Polished red and polished black were preferred at San Juan and Santa Clara, while at Tesuque the predominant type was white-slipped polychrome. The greatest

variety was made at San Ildefonso: polychrome, polished red and polished black. Pottery at Nambe and Pojoaque became nearly extinct.

Some of the most famous Pueblo potters have been Tewa, not because they are more gifted but because they were accessible to traders and museum personnel of Santa Fe earlier than potters of other pueblos. As early as the 1870s traders in Santa Fe specialized in pottery as a commodity for tourists. Potters of Tesuque and San Juan provided much of this pottery and made non-traditional vessels to satisfy the new consumers, for example flower-pots with drainage holes and ceramic figures called 'rain gods'. The typical rain god is a seated figure with its legs together and extended. Its eyes are usually depicted as though it is squinting, and its mouth is open as if speaking or singing. Rain gods often have objects on their laps, most commonly pots. They were made profusely in the late 19th century and early 20th and are thus common in museum collections (e.g. Colorado Springs, CO, Taylor Mus.). Nevertheless, by the early 20th century, few skilled Tewa potters were active, few young people were learning, and traders, archaeologists and others became alarmed at the speed of the craft's decline. Some intervened by encouraging potters to study old pottery and by paying more than asking prices for potters' best work. The best-known Tewa potters are Maria Martinez and Julian Martinez (*see* MARTINEZ) of San Ildefonso. However, Maria Martinez considered her predecessors Martina Montoya and Florentino Montoya (1858–1917) to have been the greatest, and she and Julian were closely rivalled by Tonita Roybal (1892–1945) and Juan Cruz Roybal (1896–1990). Other well-known Tewa potters are Margaret Tafoya (*b* 1904) of Santa Clara and ROSE GONZALES of San Ildefonso. Lonnie Vigil of Nambe and Tina Garcia-Trujillo of Santa Clara are among the few Tewa potters who made traditional vessels in the 20th century that can withstand use. In order to preserve the high polish preferred by collectors, polished black and red pots are fired at low temperatures and are no longer waterproof. Santa Clara is the source of most polished black and red vessels, and some families there have produced generations of masters. Among young descendants of Margaret Tafoya are Nathan Youngblood and his sister Nancy Youngblood Cutler. Their pottery is untraditional in archaeological terms, but it can be traced through four generations and from their perspective is well established. Few Pueblo potters have pushed the bounds of tradition further than Jody Folwell and her sister Nora Naranjo-Morse of Santa Clara; these two are foremost among potters who are immersed in tradition, but who incorporate into their work reflections upon their experiences in urban society.

Keres. Keres pueblos fall into three ceramic provinces: the north-east Keres pueblos of San Felipe, Cóchiti and Santo Domingo; the Puname pueblos of Zia and Santa Ana; and the western Keres pueblos of Acoma and Laguna. In early historic times, the north-east Keres pueblos produced glaze-painted pottery, made only for local use, and of which the few known examples (e.g. Santa Fe, NM, SW Cult. Resources Cent., Lab. Anthropol., cat. no. 8551/11) are from sites occupied *c.* 1680–94 (for illustration of a site near San Felipe, see *Pottery...*, Batkin,

1987). From at least 1700 until *c.* 1825 pottery of north-east Keres resembled that of the Tewa pueblos in clay, slip, paint and designs but was not traded. Only fragments are known, and they can often be distinguished from Tewa examples only through analysis of materials. Since the mid-19th century the north-east Keres and Tewa traditions have diverged.

For more than a century Cóchiti potters have made secular vessels painted with such ceremonial symbols as clouds and rainfall, a practice not considered appropriate in other Rio Grande pueblos. Since the 1870s, Cóchiti potters have made ceramic figures and effigy vessels sold in great quantity by Santa Fe traders. Figurines are still made, but their popularity had diminished until the 1980s. The tradition received a boost through Helen Cordero, who invented the 'story-teller', a figure of an adult with children on its lap, legs, arms and shoulders. Story-tellers are now made at several pueblos, but those made by Helen Cordero are the most highly sought-after. Santo Domingo is a conservative pueblo, and in contrast to nearby Cóchiti its pottery has been decorated without reference to ceremonialism. A limited range of geometric, floral and bird designs have been used since the late 19th century, and because the designs are repetitious, few potters stand out as innovators. Among the most notable are Felipita Aguilar García, her sister Asuncion Aguilar Cate and their sister-in-law Mrs Ramos Aguilar, who invented a new style, now termed Aguilar, in the early 20th century. Monica Silva, a member of the Tafoya family of Santa Clara, moved to Santo Domingo before 1920 and continued to make pottery in Tewa styles. These have enjoyed limited popularity among other potters since the late 1920s. In the 1980s the leading potter was Robert Tenorio, whose style favours that invented by the Aguilars.

Potters in Zia and Santa Ana, originally near one another, made glaze-painted ware in the late 16th century and the 17th. Santa Ana was destroyed in 1687, reoccupied after the reconquest and then moved to a new site on the Rio Grande with the old site preserved for ceremonial use. Zia and Santa Ana potters have used a dense red clay since late prehistoric times, but, after moving, Santa Ana potters began using sand temper instead of the crushed basalt of the Puname province. The dark-brown pigment used since the Spanish Reconquest is haematite mixed with black carbon paint; it has also been used at Acoma, Laguna, Jémez, Zuni and the Hopi villages. It is prepared by placing a few drops of the vegetal solution on a stone palette and grinding a small lump of haematite on the surface until an adequate amount has become mixed.

Shapes and designs changed dramatically between late prehistoric times and 1700. The round-bottomed, short-necked water jar of the 15th century yielded to a tall-necked variety with indented base and low-placed bulge, clearly influenced by jars of the Tewas. The movement of Pueblo peoples during the Revolt and Reconquest increased contact between Keresans and the Zunis and Hopis to the west, and led to Puname adoption of stylized feather motifs. Styles from the western pueblos continued at Zia during the 18th century, but the situation at Santa Ana is almost unknown because only a half dozen 18th-century pots from Santa Ana exist (Santa Fe, NM, Sch. Amer. Res., 2773; and (fragments) Albuquerque, U. NM,

A. Mus.), and they feature an unusually simple, blocky design system that remains in use. After 1800 birds and floral designs derived from European folk arts became increasingly popular at Zia and by 1900 were standard. The precise origins of these have not been determined: although logical sources were Spanish–Mexican, they may also have been Germanic, because nearly 400 German Jews established trading-posts and other enterprises in New Mexico in the 19th century, and several worked directly with the Pueblo Native Americans.

Few potters have been active at Santa Ana since 1900, and Eudora Montoya single-handedly maintained the tradition for decades. Pottery also declined at Zia after 1900, although a few families kept the art alive. Potters of the Medina family, for example, can be traced more than a hundred years, and of these Trinidad Medina was one of the great masters of the 20th century. Her most active descendants are Elizabeth Medina, who makes and paints beautiful traditional jars, and her husband Marcellus, who paints some of her vessels with acrylics after firing.

Acoma and Laguna potters have made almost indistinguishable vessels since *c.* 1700. Fine white clay and crushed pot-sherd temper produce light, thin-walled vessels, for which they are famed. Some potters at Laguna used crushed rock for temper, and some potters of both villages used sand, the variety of tempers being attributable to the movement of people during the Revolt and Reconquest. Laguna was founded by people of several pueblos in the late 1690s. Acoma's ceramic tradition was allied with Zuni's until the Revolt; during the 18th century it shared traits with Zuni, Laguna and Zia traditions, and since 1800 it has remained similar to Laguna and Zia, while Zuni

35. Southwest region pottery, polychrome water-jar, from Acoma, *c.* 1890 (Los Angeles, CA, Southwest Museum)

pottery has become distinct. Such convergence and divergence of trends in historic times is linked to political alliances and other causes.

As at Zia, Acoma potters have since the late 19th century decorated water-jars with floral designs and birds derived from European folk arts. Their beautifully crafted water-jars were favoured as trade items well into the 20th century and are still sought as collectors' items (see fig. 35). One of the best-known Acoma potters for more than 50 years of the 20th century was Mary Histia (1881–1973). As her production declined, her fame became overshadowed by LUCY LEWIS. Descendants of these and other masters were still active at the end of the 20th century. Barbara and Joe Cerno make exceptional water-jars and storage jars in the style of the 19th century, while other potters have adopted new designs influenced by prehistoric pottery of the Mimbres culture or the fine-line designs invented by Lucy Lewis and her contemporaries. The most famous Laguna potter of the 1980s is Gladys Paquin, who has studied old pots in Santa Fe's museums for inspiration. Half Zuni, born at Laguna, Paquin was raised at Santa Ana; her pots, painted in Laguna styles, are made using Santa Ana techniques. The best Laguna potter of the 19th century was a male transvestite whose pots mimic Zuni style. At least 12 examples of his work are known, of which the most important is a large storage jar in the collection of the School of American Research, Santa Fe, NM. Transvestites, known as 'men–women' in the pueblos, were among the best potters at several villages for two centuries and presumably longer. Unlike other men, who help gather materials and paint the pots of their wives and other female relatives, men–women participated at every level of the process.

Towa. Jemez is the last occupied Towa pueblo. Of several destroyed by the Spanish or abandoned since colonization, three have provided information on early historic Towa pottery: Giusewa and Astialakwa, both near Jemez, and Pecos, south-east of Santa Fe, whose last

surviving residents moved to Jemez in 1838. Jemez potters made a simple type, Jemez black-on-white, for at least 300 years until the late 17th century or early 18th. From then on, pottery was imported, principally from Zia. Only about a dozen 19th-century Jemez pots exist (Washington, DC, N. Mus. Nat. Hist. cat. nos 47192, 47196, 47199, 47207 and 47208); these were made with materials similar to those at Zia, but they are crude. Jemez pottery was first revived in 1924, and the tradition has faltered and been revived several times since. Among the gifted potters active in the late 20th century were Marie Romero, who adopted the story-teller tradition in the 1960s, and her daughters Maxine Toya and Laura Gachupin, who work together on figurative pieces. Evelyn Vigil has revived the ancient glaze-painted pottery of Pecos.

Zuni. Zuni pottery is legendary for its beauty and variety of designs, which have been copied by potters of other pueblos for generations. The ceramic sequence at Zuni is better known than at any other pueblo. Hawikuh, one of six Zuni cities abandoned at the time of the Revolt, was excavated between 1917 and 1923, and vessels (New York, Mus. Amer. Ind.) from it provide a complete picture of ceramic development from prehistoric times to 1680. Ethnologists from the Smithsonian Institution, Washington, DC, collected more than 5000 vessels at Zuni between 1879 and 1904, of which dozens were heirlooms dating as early as the Revolt. Zunis influenced the potters of a vast region and were inspired by distant traditions. From 1475 to the late 1600s Zunis abandoned glaze paints and made a type called Matsaki Polychrome. Matsaki Polychrome, though peculiar to Zuni, is similar to ancient Hopi pottery types. In the late 1600s Zunis revived glaze paint and made a type called Hawikuh Glaze Polychrome, practically identical to a contemporaneous type at Acoma. In the 18th century Zunis made a bewildering variety of types resembling those of Hopi, Acoma and other regions, including the Tewa pueblos.

A unique Zuni style began to emerge by the early 19th century (see fig. 36). Typical water-jars are decorated with only a few repetitive designs, including a rosette derived from Spanish New Mexican furniture or architectural elements and a deer or antelope painted with a 'heartline', an arrow-shaped device extending from the chest cavity to the mouth and signifying the life-force. Pottery is still made in this style. However, in the late 1800s, when metalware and other goods began to supplant pottery, the tradition declined nearly to extinction.

Because Zuni was remote, there was little outside support to preserve the tradition, and one trader, C. G. Wallace, who began working there in 1918 deliberately discouraged the making of pottery in order to promote new crafts, which he introduced. The talents of the remaining few potters, however, did not escape his attention, and he commissioned them to make 'museum pieces'. The most notable was Tsayutitsa, who made several large, beautiful pots. Others preserved pottery by teaching either informally at home or in Zuni schools. Among these have been Catalina Zunie; Daisy Hooee, a Hopi–Tewa married to a Zuni; and Jenny Laate, an Acoma also married into Zuni. Among leading potters are Josephine Nahohai, her sons Milford and Randy, and Randy's

36. Southwest region pottery, polychrome water-jar, diam. 300 mm, from Zuni, *c.* 1825–40 (Colorado Springs, CO, Fine Arts Center)

wife Rowena; Randy Nahohai is particularly creative and has experimented extensively with materials and an electric kiln. Modern forms are also made: meat platters, gravy boats and other accessories from Creative Arts of Zuni, whose young Zuni craftspeople decorate commercial slip-cast ware with Zuni designs before glazing and firing.

Hopi. At the time of the Spanish Conquest, potters of the Hopi villages of Arizona made polychrome pottery, known from excavations of the ancient sites of Sikyatki and AWATOVI. Sikyatki Polychrome jars (Washington, DC, N. Mus. Nat. Hist.) are delicately shaped with round bases, flat upper surfaces and short vertical necks. These and accompanying bowls, canteens and other vessels are elaborately decorated with stylized birds and other creatures, and with symbolic references to *kachinas*, the spiritual messengers between men and gods (*see also* §III, 4, above). Traditional Pueblo brushes (leaves or 'spears' of the yucca plant, chewed to remove the fleshy matter between fibres and trimmed to required width) were used to draw and stipple; paint was sprayed from the mouth; and other details were achieved by *sgraffito.*

Hopi pottery shows some Spanish influences, but Spanish presence was never strong in this remote region. Hopi pottery from *c.* 1680 to 1800 shows numerous traits shared with pottery of Zuni, Acoma, Laguna and Zia. During this period, Hopi design characteristics reached the Rio Grande pueblos, while Tewa shapes, translated by various groups, became present in the Hopi region. The sharing of painted motifs was so extensive at this time that identifying the source for any is difficult. Most 19th-century Hopi pottery bears strong resemblances to Zuni pottery. This is due to one or more temporary migrations by Hopis to Zuni to escape smallpox epidemics between 1775 and 1854. Despite the practice of referring to 19th-century pottery as Hopi, only a few Hopi villages have produced more than a nominal amount. The most productive potters are not Hopi by ancestry, but Tewa. These are descendants of Tewas from the Rio Grande who migrated to Hopi in the 17th century.

The most famous potter of Hano, a Tewa village at First Mesa, was NAMPEYO. Details about her life are obscure. She was making pottery by the early 1890s, apparently seeking inspiration from fragments of vessels at Sikyatki, and before long she had revived the tradition of the ancient Hopis, not only painting designs derived from Sikyatki Polychrome but also making vessels of clay from the finest old sources—clay that required neither temper nor slip. She was eventually assisted to varying degrees by daughters Annie, Fannie and Nellie, and by her husband Lesou, and it is consequently difficult to determine exactly who made or painted what after 1900. Nevertheless, she was undoubtedly responsible for the Hopi pottery revival. One of the greatest potters among Nampeyo's descendants is her great-granddaughter Dextra Quotskuyva, whose exceptional pots are rarely exhibited because they are invariably sold before they are finished. Mark Tahbo, great-grandson of Nampeyo's neighbour Grace Chapella, makes beautiful water-jars; other potters make only a few shapes. Joy Navasie (Frog Woman) and her sister-in-law Helen Naha (Feather Woman) have

specialized in making the difficult 'wedding jar', a double-spouted vessel with tall necks and with a stirrup handle that connects the spouts, which probably originated at Santa Clara Pueblo in the 1880s or 1890s. Polingaysi Qoyawayma (Elizabeth White) invented a beautiful style of vessel with sculpted corn cobs on the surface, a shape continued by her nephew, Al Qoyawayma, who has expanded the range to include large jars in Sikyatki Polychrome shapes.

BIBLIOGRAPHY

C. E. Guthe: *Pueblo Pottery-making: A Study at the Village of San Ildefonso* (New Haven, 1925)

O. Halseth: 'The Revival of Pueblo Pottery Making', *El Palacio*, xxi (1926), pp. 135–54

R. Bunzel: *The Pueblo Potter: A Study of Creative Imagination in Primitive Art* (New York, 1929)

A. V. Kidder: *The Pottery of Pecos*, i (New Haven, 1931)

A. V. Kidder and A. O. Shepard: *The Pottery of Pecos*, ii (New Haven, 1936)

K. Chapman: *The Pottery of Santo Domingo Pueblo: A Detailed Study of its Decoration* (Santa Fe, 1938, 2/1953/*R* 1977)

H. P. Mera: *Style Trends of Pueblo Pottery in the Rio Grande and Little Colorado Cultural Areas from the Sixteenth to the Nineteenth Century* (Santa Fe, 1939)

W. Smith, R. B. Woodbury and N. F. S. Woodbury: *The Excavation of Hawikuh by Frederick Webb Hodge: Report of the Hendricks–Hodge Expedition, 1917–1923* (New York, 1966)

K. Chapman: *The Pottery of San Ildefonso Pueblo* (Albuquerque, 1970/*R* 1977)

F. H. Harlow: *Matte-paint Pottery of the Tewa, Keres and Zuni Pueblos* (Santa Fe, 1973)

B. LeFree: *Santa Clara Pottery Today* (Albuquerque, 1975/*R* 1990)

K. Gratz: 'Origins of the Tesuque Rain God', *El Palacio*, lxxxii/3 (1976), pp. 3–8

N. Fox: 'Rose Gonzales', *Amer. Ind. A.*, ii/4 (1977), pp. 52–7

F. H. Harlow: *Modern Pueblo Pottery, 1880–1960* (Flagstaff, 1977)

S. Peterson: *The Living Tradition of Maria Martinez* (Tokyo, 1977)

R. Spivey: *Maria* (Flagstaff, 1979, rev. 2/[1989])

E. L. Wade and L. S. McChesney: *Historic Hopi Ceramics: The Thomas V. Keam Collection of the Peabody Museum of Archaeology and Ethnology* (Cambridge, MA, 1981)

M. A. Hardin: *Gifts of Mother Earth: Ceramics in the Zuni Tradition* (Phoenix, 1983)

L. G. Allen: *Contemporary Hopi Pottery* (Flagstaff, 1984)

S. Peterson: *Lucy M. Lewis, American Indian Potter* (Tokyo, 1984)

B. Babcock, G. Monthan and D. Monthan: *The Pueblo Storyteller. Development of a Figurative Ceramic Tradition* (Tucson, 1986)

M. E. Blair and L. Blair: *Margaret Tafoya: A Tewa Potter's Heritage and Legacy* (West Chester, 1986)

M. Rodee and J. Ostler: *Zuni Pottery* (West Chester, 1986)

R. P. Hartman and J. Musial: *Navajo Pottery: Traditions and Innovations* (Flagstaff, 1987)

S. Trimble: *Talking with the Clay: The Art of Pueblo Pottery* (Santa Fe, 1987)

J. Batkin: 'Martina Vigil and Florentino Montoya: Master Potters of San Ildefonso and Cochiti Pueblos', *Amer. Ind. A.*, xii/4 (1987), pp. 28–37

——: *Pottery of the Pueblos of New Mexico, 1700–1940* (Colorado Springs, 1987)

S. Peckham: *From this Earth: The Ancient Art of Pueblo Pottery* (Santa Fe, 1990)

J. Batkin: 'Three Great Potters of San Ildefonso and their Legacy: Tonita Peña, Marianita Roybal and Dominguita Pino', *Amer. Ind. A.*, xvi/4 (1991), pp. 56–69, 85

R. Dillingham: *Acoma and Laguna Pottery* (Santa Fe, 1992)

JONATHAN BATKIN

2. WOODLANDS. The earliest pottery in the Woodlands region appeared towards the end of the Archaic period, *c.* 1500 BC in the south-east. Peoples in the north-east began making pottery a little later, at the beginning of the Woodland period (*c.* 1000 BC–*c.* AD 1000). Early ceramics were handmade by coiling and comprised mainly flat-bottomed, flaring-sided dishes, often with lug handles. Deeper bowls and jars soon followed, and early decoration included cord-marking and net-impression. Vessels were pit-fired (placed in an open fire and covered with hot coals), a method that produced vessels strong enough for cooking, holding liquids, storing food and other uses.

(i) Woodland period (*c.* 1000 BC–*c.* AD 1000). (ii) Mississippian or Late period (*c.* AD 1000–1600).

(i) Woodland period (c. *1000* BC–c. AD *1000*).

(a) Introduction. Ceramic production during the Woodland period was characterized by distinct regional variations and an elaboration of technique and decoration. Pottery continued to be handmade by the coiling and pit-fired methods. Tempering agents included sand, grit, quartz, fibre and pulverized fired clay or stone, added to the clay paste for strength. Sizes ranged from small vessels only a few centimetres high to large bowls and effigy figures measuring over 300 mm high. Shapes included bowls, jars, cups and specialized ceramic pieces, such as effigy figures and statuettes. Rim treatments also varied considerably: rims might be thickened, flared, flattened, pinched or decorated with animal or human effigies. Surface decoration included incising or punctating with a sharp instrument to create lines, checks, crosshatching or dots; fingernail, comb or reed impressions; and designs made by pressing cord or fabric-wrapped paddles or carved wooden paddles against the still damp clay. Carved paddles made stamped designs referred to as dentate, crenulate, roulette, rocker, checker, parallel and complicated. In addition, some vessels were painted or slipped with black, white or red designs.

Woodland period ceramics can be divided into two categories—secular and sacred. Secular wares were utilitarian, usually either undecorated or with simple patterns, and are found in village sites or middens. Sacred ceramics are often elaborate, extensively decorated, frequently non-utilitarian and are associated with ceremonial or burial sites. Animal and human effigies and ceremonial pipes fall into the second category. The spread of ceramic styles and techniques and the development of regional variations in design are two of the cultural characteristics used to define the Early, Middle and Late Woodland periods. There were, however, few abrupt changes in ceramic technology. Rather, a continuous development over time led to the emergence of new artefact styles and innovations in materials that coalesced into regionally differing cultural complexes.

(b) Early (c. 1000–c. 100 BC). During this period four cultural patterns emerged, based on ceramic styles and ceremonial traditions: Alexander, in the middle Tennessee River Valley; Tchefuncte, in the lower Mississippi River Valley; Morton, in the central and lower Illinois River Valley; and Adena, in the middle and upper Ohio River Valley (*see* ADENA MOUND). Alexander pottery often took the form of thin, well-fired globular jars with flared rims decorated with dentate rocker stamping or punctated designs. There was a preference for separating the base, body and rim of the vessel into different decorative zones. Tchefuncte ceramics may have been influenced by the development of Alexander pottery, for there is a noted continuity of style between the two regions. However, Tchefuncte potters experimented with a variety of shapes and designs, including incising, punctating, pinching and stamping, and painting with red slip. Morton ceramics also exhibit connections with the lower Mississippi River Valley, blending northern materials and techniques with zoned decorations characteristic of the Delta region and the Gulf Coast. The Adena complex was produced by the most elaborate of the Early Woodland period societies. Adena ceramics, however, are generally plain with little decoration beyond cord-marking, diagonal incised lines or check stamping. Pottery was not included in Adena graves, although it was apparently used in graveside rituals.

(c) Middle (c. 100 BC–c. AD *500).* During this period ceramic techniques and decorative motifs appeared in the south-east Woodlands and the Midwest. New designs were characterized by zones of stamped or punctated decoration separated from plain areas by broad curvilinear lines. This approach divided the surface into positive and negative areas, creating a figure–background relationship between the outlined areas and the decorative 'filler'. Frequently, the incised designs take the form of birds or serpents, although swastikas, hearts, ovals and abstracted zoomorphic forms also appeared. After *c.* 100 BC these new designs are called Marksville in the lower Mississippi Valley, Porter in the Mobile Bay area and Havana in central Illinois. These and other cultures of the period are often grouped together with the Ohio Hopewell tradition, which was centred in the Chillicothe area of southern Ohio (*see* HOPEWELL MOUNDS).

The Ohio Hopewell earthworks sites and ceremonial complexes in the Scioto River Valley date from as early as *c.* 100 BC to as late as *c.* 600 AD and were part of a widespread trade network in the eastern half of the USA, known as the Hopewell Interaction Sphere, for such rare or exotic items as mica, obsidian and other non-local stone, copper and marine shells. A number of the designs on Hopewell pottery from Ohio, Illinois and the Gulf Coast use a bird image, frequently executed in a complex, zoned style. According to Penney (1985), two kinds of bird image appeared during the Middle Woodland period—a raptorial bird with a curving beak and a broad-billed duck. All three Hopewell pottery traditions—Havana, Marksville and Ohio Hopewell—include pots with both of these designs. Penney pointed out that these designs complement each other—the raptor associated with the sky, the duck with the watery underworld. Ducks and raptorial birds comprise the only representational imagery on Hopewell pottery. Besides vessels, other ceramic forms appeared during this period, including ceramic pipes and small human figurines representing both male and female figures in seated or kneeling positions. The function of these figurines is unknown, but they are usually associated with burial sites.

Between the 1st and 6th centuries AD large Middle Woodland populations lived in villages scattered along the entire Gulf Coast. These people produced a rich assortment of pottery, some modelled with naturalistic bird and animal forms. Ceramic beakers, bowls and jars were buried intact or deliberately 'killed' by breaking prior to interment.

A few ceramic types, such as bird and human effigies, were apparently used only as grave goods, since they have no apparent utilitarian function. Although the Gulf Coast sites in Alabama and Florida are known by a variety of names such as Santa Rosa–Swift Creek, Porter, Yent and Green Point, Brose (1985) has suggested that the entire complex might be better termed the Crystal River–Kolomoki complex, after the larger sites in north Florida and south-west Georgia.

(d) Late (c. 500–c. 1000). During this period there seem to have been rather abrupt changes in the ceramics produced at the Ohio Hopewell centres. Elaborate vessel shapes and special ceremonial wares were discontinued after *c.* AD 600, and only the non-mortuary plain or cord-marked vessels were still manufactured. The same phenomena existed in the Illinois ceramics of the Havana tradition. In addition, the far-flung trade network that had characterized the Early and Middle Woodland periods appears to have withered, and Late Woodland societies yield little evidence of exchange of raw materials, finished artefacts or specialized designs. While these trends have been cited as evidence that the Late Woodland period was one of cultural decline, there are many exceptions. In several areas, especially along the Gulf Coast, in the lower Mississippi Valley and in the Florida–Georgia region, there was a growth and elaboration of ceremonial activity and the development of new technical and stylistic trends in ceramics. The Late Woodland period was, then, one of transition marked by growing regional variation and autonomy, rather than one of decline.

In particular, the Weeden Island culture of the south Georgia–north Florida region emerged as stylistically and technically innovative. This culture flourished from *c.* AD 300 to *c.* 1000 and occupied a large area from Tampa Bay westward along the Gulf Coast to the Alabama border and inland to southern Georgia. Within this region numerous sites have been found, ranging from small villages to large ceremonial complexes. One of the most impressive of the large complexes is the Kolomoki site in south-western Georgia. Kolomoki represented an extensive multi-mound and village complex and includes several burial mounds that contained examples of ceremonial ceramics (*in situ*; Gainesville, U. FL, Mus. Nat. Hist.; Tallahassee, Mus. FL Hist.).

The Weeden Island culture was preceded in the area by the Santa Rosa–Swift Creek culture, which, along with other regional variations such as Porter, Yent and Green Point, was part of the Hopewellian sphere of influence. Ceramic decoration in the region made use of hand, eye, swastika and shell motifs, which, along with the use of negative painting, resemble decorative devices associated with Hopewellian artefacts from elsewhere in the eastern USA. However, in the Weeden Island culture these traits were largely absent, and there is a marked increase in the use of local materials and designs. Weeden Island culture continued to exhibit the secular–sacred dichotomy in ceramic production. Ceremonial vessels differ in quality, form and decoration from the simple utilitarian wares and are associated almost entirely with ceremonial and burial sites as opposed to village areas. Sacred ceramics were also apparently associated with certain lineages or families and

37. Woodlands region pottery, human effigy urn, h. *c.* 360 mm, from Buck Mounds, Okaloosa County, Florida, Weeden Island period, *c.* AD 300–*c.* 800 (Fort Walton Beach, FL, Temple Mound Museum)

may have been treated as family heirlooms or status symbols. Placed in high-status tombs, these exotic vessels, along with other sumptuous artefacts, were periodically removed from circulation within society.

Effigy vessels provide the most elaborate examples of the ceramic tradition associated with Weeden Island, and probably the most spectacular is an unusual human effigy vessel (Fort Walton Beach, FL, Temple Mound Mus.; see fig. 37) recovered from the Buck Mounds, a Weeden Island site near Fort Walton Beach, Florida. The vessel is over 360 mm high, covered with red paste and zone-painted in white and black. Two methods were employed in its construction—the legs are slab built and hollow, while the body is coil constructed. This unusual polychrome piece resembles vessels of Mesoamerican manufacture, while its masklike face and feathered 'cape' seem to presage the elaborate 'falcon impersonator' artefacts of the Mississippian period.

Weeden Island potters also produced a series of zoomorphic ceramic figures, with birds as the predominant subject (see fig. 38). An openwork vessel with two birds' heads on the rim (*c.* AD 200–750; New York, N. Mus.

38. Woodlands region pottery, bird effigy bowl, from Buck Mounds, Okaloosa County, Florida, Weeden Island period, c. AD 300–c. 800 (Fort Walton Beach, FL, Temple Mound Museum)

Amer. Ind.) is an excellent example. Owls were a favourite group, but turkeys, woodpeckers, doves, waterfowl, quails and buzzards were also represented. Animal subjects included panther, opossum and bobcat. The serpent was also depicted on Weeden Island ceramics, generally highly conventionalized into a series of sinuous, serpentine patterns incised on the body of the vessel. Decorative techniques combine modelling, incised lines, perforations, punctations and filler motifs, and the use of paint to accentuate figure–background relationships. Some vessels have cut-out areas in the body of the pot and may have functioned as lanterns or as incense burners. Many vessels probably also served as cult objects or as guardian figures within the context of the group's ceremonial life.

*(ii) Mississippian or Late period (*c. AD *1000–1600).* In the south-east Woodlands, painted pottery first appeared towards the end of the Late Woodland and beginning of the Mississippian period (*c.* AD 1000–1600). Some scholars argue that the techniques necessary came directly from Mesoamerica, perhaps with indirect influence from the Southwest (*see* §1(i) above and MESOAMERICA, PRE-COLUMBIAN, §VII, 1). Most of the designs were used on vessels of Mesoamerican-type forms, including narrow-necked jars or vases, short straight-necked jars, annular-based vases, tripartite globular-footed vases and various effigy vessels. Many are bichrome, using the negative painting technique of applying a primary colour, then a design in wax before dipping the vessel in a second colour that only adheres where the wax has not been applied.

From *c.* AD 700 to *c.* 1000, in the middle Mississippi Valley, the Fort Ancient complex had produced a variety of shell-tempered jars, bowls, pans and occasionally plates. In the early Mississippian period of the upper Mississippi Valley, cord-impressed decorations on the rims of vessels began to be used on the collars of jars. A variety of such cord-impressed patterns and notched rims were used by cultures in Wisconsin, Illinois and adjacent regions. In the Oneota complex (*c.* AD 1000–*c.* 1200) of the Wisconsin–Iowa area pottery was mainly shell-tempered, with plain surfaces. Burial vessels included small, loop handles and

notched rim decoration. Further east, in Ohio–Pennsylvania–West Virginia the wide-mouth jar was the dominant form, to which a variety of rim shapes and impressed decorations were applied.

In the north-east Woodlands from *c.* AD 1000 to *c.* 1600 Iroquoian ceramics were dominated by collared globular jar shapes, varying from rounded bases to slightly pointed bases. Decoration was primarily restricted to collars and rims and included a wide variety of cord-marking, punched and incised patterns. Rims were either plain or formed into castellated or scalloped shapes. Various decorative patterns are identified with different tribes or nations, such as the St Lawrence Iroquois, Mohawk, Oneida, Onondaga, Cayuga, Seneca, Susquehannock, Wenro, Erie, Neutral, Petun and Huron, that existed by the time of European contacts.

BIBLIOGRAPHY
W. Sears: 'The Sacred and the Secular in Prehistoric Ceramics', *Illinois Archaeological Survey*, ed. D. Lathrop and J. Douglas (Springfield, IL, 1973), pp. 31–42
D. Snow: *The Archaeology of North America: American Indians and their Origins* (London and New York, 1976, rev./1980)
J. B. Griffin: 'The Midlands and Northeastern United States', *Ancient Native Americans*, ed. J. D. Jennings (San Francisco, 1978), pp. 221–79
J. D. Muller: 'The Southeast', *Ancient Native Americans*, ed. J. D. Jennings (San Francisco, 1978), pp. 280–325
B. G. Trigger, ed.: 'Northeast', *Hb. N. Amer. Ind.*, xv (1978) [whole issue]
Y. Lazarus: *The Buck Burial Mound: A Mound of the Weeden Island Culture* (Fort Walton Beach, FL, 1979)
J. Milanich and C. Fairbanks: *Florida Archaeology* (New York, 1980)
D. Brose, J. Brown and D. Penny: *Ancient Art of the American Woodland Indians* (New York, 1985)
MALLORY MCCANE-O'CONNOR

VI. Metalwork.

Metal-smelting technology was generally unknown to Native American peoples before European contact. The exception was the Southwest region, where small moulded copper bells and a few other copper objects were imported from Mesoamerica (*see* MESOAMERICA, PRE-COLUMBIAN, §IX, 5); eventually these were manufactured locally (*see* §2 below).

1. Northwest Coast. 2. Southwest. 3. Plains. 4. Woodlands.

1. NORTHWEST COAST.

(i) Before European contact. Evidence for the use of metals on the Northwest Coast in the pre-contact period is found in the archaeological record. Excavations from the Broadwalk site, Prince Rupert Harbour, in the Tsimshian area, have yielded copper artefacts dating from at least 500 BC. These include bracelets, pendants, earrings and small pieces of beaten copper wrapped around a wooden core. Evidence also exists for pre-contact use of iron, although this post-dates the use of copper.

In the pre-contact period metal was available from various sources. Rich deposits of 'native' copper (copper existing in the environment in its metallic state) occur in the region, particularly around the upper reaches of the White and Copper rivers of Alaska, north of the Tlingit area. The Chilkat Tlingit obtained native copper through trade with their Atna and Eyak neighbours. The copper was then traded to other Northwest Coast groups living south of the Tlingit. Non-native metals were also available, through well-established intertribal trade networks. Russian metals and Siberian iron may have been obtained from northern trading partners, while Spanish metal may have reached the Northwest Coast through trade to the south. The oral traditions of coastal populations record that the sea also provided Northwest Coast peoples with metal: Pacific currents washed shipwreck debris from Japanese waters to the Northwest Coast, and coastal peoples searched for metal among debris washed up on the shore.

(ii) After European contact. European explorers first contacted Northwest Coast peoples in 1774, and early accounts of the area frequently mention metal items in the possession of indigenous people. Observations from the early contact period indicate that metal was used primarily for weapons, tools and personal ornaments. Artefacts collected in this period corroborate such observations. In addition metal was occasionally used to decorate masks and frontlets. A Tlingit wooden frontlet collected in 1791 is decorated with elaborately engraved copper plaques (Madrid, Mus. América; see also Gunther).

The artefactual record from the early contact period is meagre but suggests that metal objects were relatively plain in style. Iron and copper necklaces and bracelets consisted of heavy single pieces of metal or metal bands twisted together. Daggers, worn around the necks of Tlingit men as a status symbol, consisted of a one-piece metal blade, hilt and pommel, and, while early examples have little decoration, their carefully crafted blades exhibit outstanding workmanship. Among the earliest known is a dagger (1596) in the collection of the Museo de América, Madrid, thought to have been collected between 1776 and 1792. Its pommel is decorated with a simple face with a mouth of inlaid copper.

The first expeditions to the Northwest Coast stimulated European economic interest in the area, leading firstly to seasonal fur trading and eventually to permanent European settlement. In the initial years of the fur trade, metal items were almost the only articles of trade accepted by the indigenous population in return for sea-otter furs. The desire for metal cannot be seen simply in terms of demand for a functionally useful, but previously scarce, commodity. Both intertribal trading networks and trading links with Europeans were controlled by those in positions of political authority, and therefore ownership of items only available through trade was associated with prestige and power. The ways in which metal was used in the post-contact period indicate that, before European contact, metal was already regarded as a prestige item with established socio-political connotations.

In the 19th century the increased availability of metal enabled it to be used more frequently to make objects associated with high status, such as masks, frontlets, rattles and hats. The eyebrows, mouths and other features of totemic animals depicted in such objects were often fashioned from metal strips. The introduction of new European types and forms of metal also led to innovation and change in Northwest Coast metalwork. Large quantities of European sheet metal, particularly copper, were obtained through trade, enabling indigenous metalsmiths to make much larger metal objects than had previously been possible. Especially in the second half of the 19th century, masks, rattles and even hats were sometimes made entirely from sheet metal, which was used in the place of such traditional materials as wood, horn and woven spruce roots.

European sheet copper was also used in the manufacture of 'coppers', one of the most distinctive metal objects of the Northwest Coast (see fig. 39). The earliest-known record of coppers dates from 1804, so it is unclear whether they existed before European contact. The copper illustrated shows a highly characteristic shape and the typical way in which the upper and lower portions are divided by the top of a protruding T-shaped ridge of metal; the reason for this shape is not known. The upper portions of coppers are often painted or incised with totemic emblems. Coppers were used as items of exchange by all Northwest Coast groups except the Nootka and Salish. The role and symbolism of coppers varied from group to group, although generally they were associated with great wealth and prestige. In the post-contact period metal items were also made from European trade goods, which were modified and crafted by Native American metalsmiths

39. Northwest Coast 'copper', worked sheet-copper, h. 800 mm, 19th century (London, British Museum)

into indigenous forms. For example, European knives were used to make Tlingit-style daggers. In the 19th century the pommels of these daggers were often elaborately worked to represent totemic animals, and the blades were elaborately fluted.

Silver was introduced in the post-contact period in the form of coinage, but silver items of Native American manufacture did not become common until the mid-19th century, when permanent trading-posts were established, and money became a more common trade item. Coins were melted down, and the silver obtained was used particularly to make jewellery. Bracelets, pendants and earrings were popular with both the indigenous population and European settlers. The designs used in their decoration reflected this dual market, being either traditional northern formline designs (see §III, 2 above) or Euro-American designs, such as floral patterns. The Haida, in particular, produced especially fine silverwork. In the 20th century, metalwork, like all artistic production on the North-west Coast, suffered through several factors, including serious depletion of the population by disease and the suppression of Native American traditions by the Canadian government. However, from the 1950s there was a resurgence in metalwork, particularly in gold- and silversmithing.

BIBLIOGRAPHY

T. A. Rickard: 'The Use of Iron and Copper by the Indians of British Columbia', *BC Hist Q.*, iii (1939)

E. Gunther: *Indian Life on the Northwest Coast of North America, as Seen by the Early Explorers and Fur Traders During the Last Decades of the Eighteenth Century* (Chicago and London, 1972)

G. Macdonald: 'Prehistoric Art of the Northern North-west Coast', *Indian Art Traditions of the North-west Coast*, ed. R. Carlson (Burnaby, BC, 1976)

N. Harris: 'Reflections on North-west Coast Silver', *The Legacy: Continuing Traditions of Canadian North-west Coast Indian Art*, ed. P. L. Macnair (Victoria, BC, 1980)

C. J. Jopling: 'The Coppers of the North-west Coast Indians: Their Origin, Development and Possible Antecedents', *Trans. Amer. Philos. Soc.*, n. s., lxxix (1989)

M. L. Wayman, J. G. H. King and P. T. Craddock: *Aspects of Early North American Metallurgy*, British Museum Occasional Paper, lxxix (London, 1992)

KATE JAEGER

2. SOUTHWEST. Metalwork from the Southwest mainly comprises jewellery, which combines old traditions of personal adornment in shell, hardstones and other lapidary materials with European introduced techniques of silversmithing. In the Pre-Columbian period metalworking was characteristic of Mesoamerica rather than of the Southwest, although Mesoamerican copper bells were imported by the Hohokam culture from c. AD 900, and there is evidence that nugget copper was used by them to produce their own bells by cold hammering (see MESOAMERICA, PRE-COLUMBIAN, §IX, 5). The first use of iron to make tools and ornaments came via trade with European settlers. Native American groups borrowed forms, materials and techniques and gave them new vitality. By the end of the 20th century the best-known silversmiths were Navajo, Zuni and Hopi. Other groups, such as the Santo Domingo, continued to concentrate on their lapidary traditions.

(i) c. 1800–c. 1890. Metalworking was introduced into the Southwest through blacksmithing. By working the forges for Mexican smiths, through formal apprenticeships and by observation of itinerant smiths, Native American boys became wheelwrights and smiths themselves. Zuni Pueblo had a shop run by a Mexican in the 1830s. It was not uncommon for blacksmiths to produce basic household utensils, axes and hoes, and simple ornaments. The Navajos became interested in metal jewellery through trade with Plains groups (see §3 below), as well as with the Spaniards and Mexicans. By 1855 all Navajos were wearing leather belts with metal discs, and several Navajo smiths had begun to practise independently in the 1850s–60s. The first was Atsidi Sani (d 1918), who became a blacksmith and jeweller c. 1853. Most Navajo smiths first worked in copper and brass, and later switched to silver, which they considered a more beautiful metal. Navajo smiths were influenced by the designs they saw in Mexican work, such as 'squash blossom beads' (pomegranate flower shapes), conchas, bridle ornaments, *najas* (crescent-shaped pendants), crosses, buttons and tobacco canteens. Their tools were few and rudimentary, and this limited design techniques to incising, scratching and filing. By the 1880s smiths acquired the skills of annealing, hammering and soldering, and began to produce the hollow beads for which they are justly famous and had developed distinctive styles. By 1893 they were setting turquoise and crafting a large variety of objects.

Even though by the end of the 20th century many artists worked in gold, silver was always the metal of choice for Southwestern jewellers. In the 1880s Navajo smiths obtained silver from coins, which they melted down or cold hammered into buttons. When the defacing of coins was outlawed, slug and sheet silver was obtained from traders. Cast and wrought jewellery became more elaborate as tools improved and jewellers grew more skilful. Smiths began making stamps to impress designs into the metal. Turquoise, garnet, jet and malachite were set in silver mountings, reflecting a Navajo love of colour, also evident in their rug weaving (see §VII, 2, below).

The Zuni learnt silversmithing from the Navajos in the 1870s and 1880s. It is generally accepted that the Navajo smith credited with producing the first silver belt and mounted bridle, Atsidi Chon, taught the Zuni smith, Lanyade, in 1872. Zunis made Navajo-style jewellery at first, but they went on to develop their own cultural styles and designs by the beginning of the 20th century. The Hopi soon learnt from the Zuni—the Zuni smith Laniyati taught the Hopi Sikyatala in the 1890s—and followed the same developmental pattern. Several other Pueblo groups also developed metalworking traditions from these groups, or from working with Mexican or Euro-American smiths.

A special category of jewellery, known as pawn, was developed in the late 19th century. Navajo income was seasonal, coming mainly from temporary wage work or the sale of lambs and shorn wool. Smiths used the income to purchase silver and pay off debts from the purchase of manufactured goods and food incurred during the rest of the year. Jewellery was pawned as collateral during the months when credit was extended; when income increased, pawn items were redeemed or new jewellery purchased. Thus 'pawn' does not designate a particular style of jewellery, but rather a piece that was not redeemed by a Navajo smith or his family. 'Dead pawn' was jewellery not redeemed in a specified period of time; it could therefore be sold to outsiders. Many collectors valued pawn because of its previous use.

(ii) After c. *1890.* Before the 1890s jewellery was made for internal use and for trade with other tribes. The commercialization of Native American silver began in the 1890s, when the Fred Harvey Company began commissioning light, small pieces and esoteric forms for the growing tourist trade. The growth of this market played a key role in the florescence of Southwestern metalwork. Subsequently, manufacture for Euro-American and European markets dominated Southwest metalwork. Part of the commercial modification was the increasing use of turquoise and the adoption of designs, such as swastikas and arrows, that consumers and traders considered 'Indian'. Such designs reflected the preconceptions of Euro-Americans rather than Navajo or Zuni artists. With the introduction of more sophisticated tools and greater supplies of silver and stones, styles developed rapidly and became extremely sophisticated. From the 1920s Navajo and Zuni smiths revived forms and diversified their work. Some smiths continued to produce for the tourist market, others for the fine-art and connoisseur market, which developed in the second half of the 20th century. Some artists developed what are known as 'revival period' styles: pieces than can be distinguished by an adherence to the simplicity and beauty of the earliest designs.

Navajos use wrought metal, filing, casting, stamping, cold-chiselling, soldering, hammering and repoussé; wirework is still done, especially for bracelets (see fig. 40). Designs and styles fluctuated with alternating periods of simplicity and almost 'baroque' ornateness. In general, designs are not symbolic or representational but rather abstract and formal. Jewellery is sculptural and hierarchical, with a clear central motif and different scales of stones. Emphasis is placed on the form; dynamic alternations of mass and space predominate, with a strong sense of proportion, order, balance and strength. Massiveness, which emphasizes the soft glow of the polished silver, is highly prized, as are the graceful rhythms of curvilinear and geometric forms. Bold decorative designs emphasize bilateral symmetry in highly polished or textural designs.

Navajo jewellery is characterized by silver embellished by stones, while Zuni smiths emphasize stones in minimized settings. Clusters of turquoise are set in the silver using mounting techniques perfected in the 1920s for metalwork, but which had been used in Pre-Columbian times in other media. Turquoise—regarded as a symbol of beauty and harmony for all Southwestern groups—is highly prized, and the Zuni value the strong colour contrasts it makes with silver. Delicate channel work, *petit point*, cluster, needlepoint and mosaic are the hallmarks of Zuni Pueblo's cultural style. Zuni smiths rarely stamp or extensively file silver. Navajos are more likely to use larger pieces or nuggets of turquoise that are not so highly formed and allow more of the silver to carry the design. Sometimes Navajo and Zuni smiths collaborate on a piece: the Zuni artist carves the stone and places it in the silver setting produced by the Navajo artist.

Hopi smiths did not develop a distinctive style until Hopi and Euro-American museum curators and artists introduced overlay after World War II, considering it well suited to Hopi jewellery. In overlay, two pieces of silver are soldered together, and a design is cut out of the top layer. The bottom is blackened through oxidation and burnished. Hopi designs may be representational, symbolic or abstract; many stem from their pottery, basketry, pictographic, religious and weaving traditions, and represent a greater diversity of motif than found in Zuni or Navajo pieces. As with the Navajo, the emphasis is on the metal and its textural qualities. Hopi silver is characterized by movement and grace seen in fluid curving lines, frets and spirals. Many shapes are irregular, so that the works alternate between the symmetrical and the asymmetrical.

Several talented and famous jewellers were at work by the second half of the 20th century; all developed highly distinctive individual styles. Some were traditionalists,

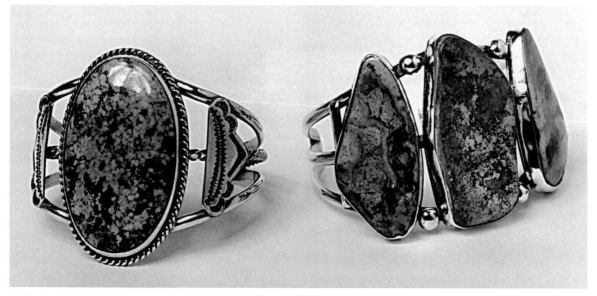

40. Southwest region bracelets, turquoise and silver, Navajo (London, British Museum)

while others were distinctly pan-Native American and even international in taste. Yet all were situated in cultural concepts of beauty and their feeling for metal and stone: Charles Loloma (*b* 1921), Gail Bird, Yazzie Johnson, Kenneth Begay, Lawrence Saufkie and Gracilda Saufkie, Preston Monongye, to name but a few, developed what has been called 'The New Indian' style. This emphasizes experimentation in design, materials and technique. In a single piece can be seen bold clean styles, stressing the beauty of textures, and combinations of stones and techniques. Motifs are abstract, symbolic and representational, and technical perfection is a salient aesthetic feature. These innovative styles transcend the confines of tradition, for by the 20th century cross-cultural interaction brought about an unparalleled florescence of metalwork in the Southwest.

BIBLIOGRAPHY
J. Adair: *The Navajo and Pueblo Silversmiths* (Norman, 1944, 2/1973)
A. Woodward: *Navajo Silver: Brief History of Navajo Silversmithing* (Flagstaff, 1971)
M. Wright: *Hopi Silver: The History and Hallmarks of Hopi Silversmithing* (Flagstaff, 1972)
M. Bedinger: *Indian Silver: Navajo and Pueblo Jewelers* (Albuquerque, 1973)
J. W. Jernigan: *White Metal Universe: Navajo Silver from the Fred Harvey Collection*, Phoenix, AZ, Heard Mus. cat. (Phoenix, 1981)

NANCY J. PAREZO

3. PLAINS. The Plains Native Americans never learnt to melt metals in order to mould them. In Pre-Columbian times, embossed and engraved copper cut-outs had reached the Plains region from the south-east Woodlands, but characteristic Plains metalwork developed only after the introduction of European trade goods in the early 18th century. Through a well-established intertribal trade network, metalworkers received files, brass wires, coins and pieces of various metals. Their major techniques involved pounding, cutting and filing, which were developed from *c.* 1700, with early Euro-American contact. An early British

account (*c.* 1795) relates that certain Prairie tribes, such as the Iowa, Kansas and Osage, visited Fort Michilimaquinac on the Great Lakes to receive gifts in silverware from the English, but such silver trade items were never prized for their pawn value on the Great Plains. However, before 1850, when metal of any sort was scarce, silver, brass, copper or iron were valued for prestige and later strictly for their decorative qualities.

The first reference to Plains Native Americans working metal into tools or ornaments was made by François-Antoine Larocque, a French-Canadian trader, in his *Yellowstone Journal* (1805). He referred to the Crow Native Americans making knives out of a broken piece of iron and then to a more westerly group, the Flatheads, who cut up brass kettles into small pieces, which they used to decorate their garments and hair. The flow of trade metal pieces was continuous up to the last decades of the 19th century, while Plains metalwork became widespread only after 1865. About this time, instead of silverware, German silver, a non-ferrous alloy of copper, nickel and zinc, was introduced to the Plains in sheet form. In the following years a highly productive metalwork output began, documented in photographs of the period. German silver pieces were used as personal decoration by both men and women. Hair plates—discs attached, decreasing in size, to a strip of leather—were worn by men on the scalp lock at the back of the head. About 1870 similar sets were worn by women as belts, and circular conchas of equal size were attached to the front of the boot-moccasins of Arapaho, Cheyenne and Comanche women.

Cloud-shaped pectorals (see fig. 41) were worn by men, either attached to their bone breast plates or used as kerchief ties. These items were often decorated with engraved designs, as in the illustrated piece, which, although attributed to the Kiowa, bears on the back an engraving that depicts the typical visionary experience of a member of the Elk Dreamers' Cult of the Lakota Sioux. Both single- and double-barred crosses were worn by Plains Native American men, in the same way as pectorals. These were often decorated with crescent-shaped ornaments at the lower edge of the bars and at the bottom. Silver-mounted headstalls were combined from several pieces of German silver ornaments, which could be used at one time or another, for various purposes. Many other smaller ornaments were also produced by Plains metalworkers, such as finger rings, bracelets, arm-bands, earrings, tweezers for pulling whiskers and women's awl cases.

From about 1880 there was a gradual decline in the production of Plains metalwork, as metal ornaments were no longer difficult to obtain and therefore lost their prestige value. About 1900 a new impetus came from the Peyote religious movement, and new types of metal ornaments became widespread in the Plains region: Peyote tie slides, Peyote earrings and women's combs. The iconography of such Peyote jewellery was influenced by the doctrines of the Native American Church. The most talented and innovative Plains metalsmith of the later 20th century was the Pawnee, Julius Caesar (*b* 1910), who worked in German silver.

41. Plains region cloud-shaped silver pectoral, 131×142 mm, attributed to Kiowa, probably Lakota Sioux, *c.* 1870 (New York, Museum of the American Indian)

BIBLIOGRAPHY
F. H. Douglas and A. Marriott: 'Metal Jewelry of the Peyote Cult', *Material Culture Notes*, ed. F. H. Douglas (Denver, 1942, rev. 1969)
A. P. Nasatir: *Before Lewis and Clark: Documents Illustrating the History of the Missouri, 1784–1804*, 2 vols (St Louis, 1952)
N. Feder: 'Plains Indian Metalworking', *Amer. Ind. Trad.*, viii (1962), pp. 55–76, 93–108
J. A. Hanson: *Metal Weapons: Tools and Ornaments of the Teton Dakota Indians* (Lincoln, 1975)
R. Ellison: 'The Artistry and Genius of Julius Caesar', *Amer. Ind. A.*, iii/4 (1978), pp. 56–61, 75
C. F. Feest: *Native Arts of North America* (New York, 1980)
R. W. Wood and T. D. Thiessen, eds: *Early Fur Trade on the Northern Plains: Canadian Traders among the Mandan and Hidatsa Indians, 1738–1818* (Norman, 1985)

IMRE NAGY

4. WOODLANDS. Throughout Pre-Columbian times, copper was used almost exclusively in connection with ritual. It also played an important role in the formation of religio-political alliances. The archaeological record and early historic documents suggest that the special status of copper was derived from its colour and metallic properties, as well as from the contexts in which it was found and from the techniques used to work it.

The earliest evidence of metallurgy in the eastern Woodlands occurs in the Lake Superior area *c.* 3000 BC. The metal extracted from mines there was almost pure native copper. Mines were of two types: deep pits excavated through a rocky matrix and long trenches dug into less resistant matrices. Cold hammering, forging and annealing techniques were used, but there is no convincing evidence of smelting.

The first Native American groups to utilize copper are referred to as the Old Copper culture, based in the mining region. Various forms were produced, *c.* 20,000 examples of which have been discovered. Most common are large spear-points, varying in design from simple blades to heavy socketed points of triangular section. Other forms include rings, bracelets and headdresses, as well as woodworking tools. Implement forms often replicate items made from more mundane materials. Evidence from burials, often in natural knolls and kames, indicates that only a minority of the population owned and used metal objects, despite their numbers and utilitarian appearance.

About 1500 BC the metallurgy of the Old Copper culture groups reached its most complex level, after which the use of metals waned. At the same time, the ritual manifestation known as Adena began to develop further south (*see also* ADENA MOUND). Members of what was probably a religious élite began to be buried in specially constructed earth mounds, accompanied by copper rings and bracelets, small rectangular and crescent-shaped gorgets, headdresses, ceremonial weaponry and other metal objects. The use of copper was limited exclusively to this ritual context.

By *c.* 300 BC Adena patterns began to wane, replaced by the even more elaborate rituals of Hopewell and related cultures (*see also* HOPEWELL MOUNDS), scattered through the river valleys of Ohio and Illinois. Once again, the most prominent feature of the culture was its elaborate burial tradition. Metalwork from Hopewell-related burial mounds (Columbus, OH State U.; Chicago, IL, Field Mus.

42. Woodlands region openwork copper disc, diam. 200 mm, Hopewell culture, from Hopewell Mound group, Ross County, Ohio, *c.* 200 BC–*c.* AD 400 (Chicago, IL, Field Museum of Natural History)

Nat. Hist.) includes cymbal-shaped ear ornaments, trapezoidal breastplates, bracelets, headdresses, rings, copper-clad panpipes and a few copper birds and human appendages. There are also hundreds of copper tinkling cones, buttons, bear teeth, antlers and complex geometric designs (see fig. 42). Refined copper celts and adzes have also been found, although none shows much evidence of use. Stone pipes were also decorated with inlays and bands of copper. Related groups throughout much of the southeast Woodlands produced similar metalwork and also placed it in burial mounds. Hopewellian influence extended as far north as Wisconsin and Michigan and west into Iowa and Missouri. Its pervasive nature suggests that there may have been political implications in the adoption of the rituals associated with copper.

Virtually all the copper used during these early periods came from the Lake Superior region. By *c.* AD 600 the rituals associated with Hopewell and its sophisticated metalwork had almost disappeared. Nevertheless, knowledge of both the technology and the source of the raw material was not completely lost, and when the Southern Ceremonial Complex developed in the south-east Woodlands *c.* AD 900, complex ritual metallurgy again became important. The technology involved was from the outset so sophisticated as to suggest that it was passed across the centuries by a handful of religious specialists and reintroduced on a large scale when circumstances demanded. At first copper was imported from the area around Lake Superior, but local sources later became increasingly important. Most Southern Ceremonial Complex metalwork (Cartersville, GA, Etowah Mounds Archaeol. Area; Norman, OK, U. OK Mus.; Moundville, AL, Delf Norona Mus. & Cult. Cent.; New York, N. Mus. Amer. Ind.; Washington, DC, N. Mus. Amer. Hist.) is thinner and more fragile than earlier examples, reflecting the limited size of copper nuggets available from south-east Woodlands sources.

The objects made were similar to Hopewell types and were also exclusively for ritual use. Copper breastplates are circular instead of trapezoidal and usually include cruciform designs. Ear ornaments are larger, carved from wood or stone, and the use of copper on them is limited to a thin sheet covering the surface. Motifs are mostly in repoussé instead of the openwork more characteristic of Hopewellian design. Human imagery, rare in Hopewellian metalwork, is common and usually combined with references to the peregrine falcon. Deer and bear imagery is scarce, a shift that may reflect the change from Hopewellian hunting-and-gathering subsistence patterns to the intensive agriculture practised in the south-east Woodlands. Copper tools and weapons are emphatically ceremonial, either miniaturized or highly attenuated.

When Europeans arrived, Native Americans along the eastern seaboard, as well as many interior groups, still made and used objects hammered from native copper. Early documents indicate that the ritual significance of the metal and its use was similar to prehistoric tradition, although the elaborate mound complexes were no longer occupied. Ceremonial copper weaponry was stored in ritual centres, along with sacred images hung with copper ornaments. Copper also continued to be important in the forging of military and political alliances. At first the Native Americans used European metals in essentially the same way they used those obtained locally. The Native American preference for brass and copper in trade is testimony to the relationship between early trade interests and the ancient tradition.

In the mid-18th century, rather suddenly, silver and silver-coloured metals replaced copper. Silver was worked in much the same way and into forms clearly related to pre-contact metallurgy—circular and crescent-shaped gorgets, ear ornaments, bracelets and headbands, often with openwork and engraved decoration. Silver-coloured metal was also used for tinkling cones and inlays on carved stone pipe-bowls. Sacred images, such as the Delaware 'Naneetis, Guardian of Health' (New York, N. Mus. Amer. Ind.), were hung with dozens of silver ornaments. There is even evidence of a continuing association between metal and political relationships. The metaphor of the silver 'Covenant Chain', a series of alliances between the Iroquois and the British, probably derived from these traditions. By the end of the 20th century metalwork was still produced by a few Native American artisans in the eastern Woodlands, and silver ornaments were used as costume elements, although silver's role in ritual was negligible.

BIBLIOGRAPHY
W. Strachey: *The Historie of Travaile into Virginia Britannia* (London, 1849)
J. R. Swanton: 'Aboriginal Culture of the Southeast', *42nd Annual Report of the Smithsonian Institution Bureau of American Ethnology* (Washington, DC, 1928), pp. 490–91, 507–10, *passim*
A. J. Waring and P. Holder: 'A Prehistoric Ceremonial Complex in the Southeastern United States', *Amer. Anthropologist*, xlvii (1945), pp. 1–34
W. L. Wittry and R. E. Ritzenthaler: 'The Old Copper Complex: An Archaic Manifestation in Wisconsin', *WI Archaeologist*, xxxviii/4 (1957), pp. 311–29
R. W. Drier and O. J. duTemple: *Prehistoric Copper Mining in the Lake Superior Region: A Collection of Reference Articles* (1961)
G. I. Quimby: *Indian Culture and European Trade Goods* (Madison, 1966)
J. H. Howard: 'The Southeastern Ceremonial Complex and its Interpretation', *MO Archaeol. Soc. Mem.*, vi (1968)
H. W. Hamilton, J. T. Hamilton and E. F. Chapman: 'Spiro Mound Copper', *MO Archaeol. Soc. Mem.*, xi (1974)
S. Goad: *Exchange Networks in the Prehistoric Eastern United States* (diss., U. Georgia, 1978)
M. F. Seaman: *The Hopewell Interaction Sphere: The Evidence for Interregional Trade and Structural Complexity*, Indiana Historical Society Prehistoric Research Series, v/2 (Indianapolis, IN, 1979)
J. Walthall: *Prehistoric Indians of the Southeast: The Archaeology of Alabama and the Middle South* (Tuscaloosa, AL, 1980)
D. T. Price and J. A. Brown, eds: *Prehistoric Hunter–Gatherers: The Emergence of Cultural Complexity* (New York, 1985)
A. Trevelyan: *Prehistoric Native American Copperwork from the Eastern United States* (diss., Los Angeles, UCLA, 1987)
AMELIA M. TREVELYAN

VII. Textiles.

Native American textiles are soft, two-dimensional fabrics, woven either by hand or with specialized equipment. Both before and after European contact twining was the most common technique of fabrication. Braiding or finger-weaving a single set of elements was the second most common technique. Twining declined or disappeared in some areas when weaving on a true loom was introduced.

1. Northwest Coast. 2. Southwest. 3. Woodlands.

1. NORTHWEST COAST. The earliest 'textiles' of the Northwest Coast cultures comprised the weaving of baskets (*see* §XIV, 3 below). Techniques included single-, double- and triple-twined wefts. Everyday clothing was made of leather or twined cedar bark. Robes, skirts and rain capes were twined from the inner bark of the yellow cedar tree. The bark was shredded and twisted together to form the warp yarns; the weft yarns were thigh-spun from bark, which had been boiled to remove the pitch and then split into thin strips. On special robes, mountain-goat wool was added to the wefts, which were dyed black and yellow; geometric patterns were twined into the borders and heraldic designs painted on the surface.

(i) Ravenstail robes. (ii) Chilkat dancing robes. (iii) Development after European contact.

(i) Ravenstail robes. Through the 18th century woollen weaving was a direct reflection of the basketmaker's art. Ceremonial robes, made from the downy underwool and fleece of the mountain goat (*Oreamnos americanus*), were twined and decorated in techniques directly borrowed from basketry. Known as 'Ravenstail' robes, these were the garments of the élite, worn on special occasions with great display and dignity.

The making of Ravenstail robes was the art of the women. Like baskets, robes were adorned with designs that reflected the natural world, interpreted in geometric patterns. Traditionally, Northwest Coast people believed that a spirit dwelt in every object and action, and the names of their designs were based on the world they lived in: the 'track' of the woodworm, the 'wings' of the butterfly or the 'backbone' of the halibut. The name Ravenstail, which now designates a whole style of weaving, comes from a translation of the Tlingit word for the robes, *yeil koowu*. Ravenstail robes were the main products of the Northwest Coast women's looms before and during the years of initial European contact. When their production started is impossible to determine from the historic record; descriptions in the journals of explorers and drawings by the artists employed to record their travels describe production at the time of contact. One such artist, the Russian Mikhail Tikhanov, drew the Tlingit warrior chief Katlian and another chief, Aichunk, during the voyage of the Russian sloop *Kamchatka* in 1816 (see Shur and Pierce). From such records it is known that the robes were being worn, and probably still being made, in the early 19th century. Only 15 records of actual Ravenstail robes exist. They are distributed around the world in the homelands of the explorers and traders who collected them in the late 18th century and early 19th. Three are drawings, and one is a photograph, leaving only eleven examples of the actual cloth. Six of the eleven are complete robes; the other five are only fragments.

Ravenstail robes are rectangular, with fringes on the sides and bottom and a sea-otter fur wrapping along the top edge (see fig. 43). They are marked by strong linear black-and-white patterns and have thick, long tassels, which hang pendant-like from figures in the central design field. The wool was separated from the long guard hairs and made into roving (slightly twisted slivers of wool) before being spun. The warp yarns are two-ply, Z-twist strands, handspun on the thigh without a spindle. Two-plys were spun from metre-long pieces of roving; they were rolled parallel and simultaneously down the thigh, and then plied with an upward motion on the spinner's leg. New pieces of mountain-goat wool were added about every metre. Very fine, two-ply weft yarns were spun on a small shin-spindle, which was rolled on the spinner's shin with her right hand, the left hand guiding the spinning of the wool. It would take a spinner from six months to a year to prepare all of the yarns for the weaving of a robe.

The outer border of a Ravenstail robe is white, the undyed colour of mountain-goat wool; the design elements are woven in black, white and yellow. Black dye was probably obtained from an initial dyebath of freshly stripped hemlock bark, simmered in water that contained a considerable amount of the mineral iron. The white wool was dyed first in this bath and then overdyed in a bath in which copper had been oxidized in old urine. The yellow colour was obtained from a lichen, *Evernia vulpina*, commonly called 'wolf moss', which grows on the boughs of the coniferous pine. These trees do not grow in the wet rain-forests of the coast but rather on the drier mountains of the interior, and therefore the moss had to be obtained in trade from the people who dwelt near the pine forests.

43. Northwest Coast, Ravenstail robe, known as the Swift Robe, mountain-goat wool with sea-otter fur wrapping at the top edge (Cambridge, MA, Harvard University, Peabody Museum)

The dyestuff was boiled in fresh urine and strained; then the wool was placed in the liquor for ten minutes to obtain the desired colour. Wolf moss yellow is very fugitive in light, and therefore in most of the surviving robes it is considerably faded.

Two-strand and three-strand twining form the basis of the weaving technique, with as many as nine variations, which gave the weaver a tremendous flexibility in design. Unlike basket-weaving, where the weaver can hold her work in her lap, the warp yarns need to be hung from a board the width of the weaving. This was done by using a single bar loom (a horizontal beam held by two upright posts). Groups of warp yarns were hung from the beam and bundled into bags at the bottom of the weaving to keep them clean and orderly. On the Northwest Coast the warp yarns were not weighted, as the technique requires no vertical tension other than that provided by the weaver's hands. The production of a Ravenstail robe was extremely clean. Twining was started at the top edge of the robe and worked in individual rows from left to right. At the end of each row a knot was tied in the wefts, the remaining length becoming side fringe. Additional short fringes were added between the rows on the left. Each horizontal row built, geometrically, the pattern established in the designer's mind. Each row was complete; there were no ends to work in when the twining was finished, since the total length of every strand of yarn was utilized in the design. Ravenstail robes demanded a row-by-row solution to their development; there was a close marriage between design and technique. It took a weaver from four months to a year to complete a robe, depending on the complexity of the design. Two of the surviving robes differ from the others in that they are completely covered on one side in sea-otter fur. This was accomplished by cutting sea-otter pelts in long, thin strips and hanging them on the loom alongside the woollen warp yarns. Due to the nature of sea-otter fur and the thickness of the hide, the weavers were able to twine a pattern on one side of the robe while confining the fur entirely to the other side.

Great value was placed on the work of the weavers and on the special use of mountain-goat wool. As weaving was slow, Ravenstail robes were relatively scarce, and it took considerable wealth to commission a robe. The possession and display of one was a sign of distinction. Surrounded as they were by a prolific totemic art form (see §III, 2 above), weavers felt challenged to develop a technique that would allow them to weave similar curvilinear designs. The strength, beauty and power of Ravenstail robes was ultimately eclipsed by the display of status in crest designs. These were carved or painted by men and might adorn practically every object of daily or ceremonial use, including cedar-bark and leather garments.

(ii) *Chilkat dancing robes.* Chilkat robes succeeded Ravenstail robes. The Tsimshian women were reputedly the first to succeed in twining ceremonial garments with crest designs. The Tsimshian term *gus-halai't* for such weaving is translated as 'dancing blanket'. Later, knowledge of this type of weaving travelled through intermarriage to Tlingit families, who know them as *nakheen* ('fringe about the body'), obviously referring to the long warp fringe, which sways about the body of the dancer when the robe is worn in ceremony. In the late 19th century European and American traders called the garments 'Chilkat blankets' due to the fact the most prolific weavers at that time came from the villages of the Chilkat Tlingit. By the mid-20th century the production of Chilkat blankets had almost stopped.

A Chilkat blanket, or dancing robe, is rectangular at the top and sides, with the bottom edge shaped in a shallow V (see fig. 44). Across the top it is bordered with a wrapping of sea-otter fur; plaits with attached fringes frame each side, and a long warp fringe extends from the lower V. Black and yellow borders surround a central design field, in which a crest animal is depicted. Some of the designs are easily recognized, but most are stylized in such a way as to make them difficult to interpret. Crests were owned by families and clans; individuals could only display designs that they owned. Such crest animals as raven, eagle, whale, frog or beaver were first designed and then woven on commission for a specific individual. Eventually, however, patterns were reused; for example, individuals of the killer-whale clan could commission a robe from a weaver known to own a pattern of that design.

Male artists painted the patterns, which the weavers copied directly. These pattern boards, drawn to scale, depicted just over one-half of the figure shown in the central design field, as one side of the design mirrors the other. The pattern board was painted only in black; the weaver, understanding the design conventions, filled in the appropriate colours.

The earliest 'dancing blankets' were black, yellow, white and a soft yellow-green. The yellow and black were dyed with the same recipes used in the Ravenstail robes. The yellow-green was obtained by first dyeing the wool in the copper and urine bath, and then overdyeing it quickly in the wolf moss dye. When commercially woven blue trade cloth became available, yellow-green was replaced by a blue-green obtained from extracting dye from the trade cloth, dyeing the wool initially in this bath and then overdyeing it with wolf moss yellow. Occasionally Chilkat robes have red in them, but this is rare and is done with commercially spun and dyed yarn. Other commercial dyes were also experimented with, but the colours they produced tended to be garish, and they did not completely replace the use of native dyes.

The oldest Chilkat robes are twined entirely from weft yarns made from the downy undercoat of the mountain goat. The weft yarns, spun on a shin-spindle, were a very fine two-ply Z-twist yarn. In the finest blankets their count might be as many as 20 rows per centimetre. When they became available, commercially spun four-ply S-twist weft yarns, made from sheep's wool, were often used. The Tlingit name *nakheen* emphasizes the important role played by the fringe when the blanket is used in dance. The warp fringe was long, sometimes as long as one-quarter the length of the robe. When danced in it came to life, swaying magnificently around the body of the dancer. The warp yarns themselves are dense and strong, owing to the inclusion of a core of yellow cedar bark with the mountain-goat wool, and the success of their movement in the dance is due in part to their weight. Compared to the weft yarns, the warp yarns are large. They are thigh-spun, using the same technique as for Ravenstail warp yarn, except for the

44. Northwest Coast Chilkat blanket, known as the Skatins Robe, mountain-goat wool (Toronto, Royal Ontario Museum)

addition of yellow cedar bark. The bark is boiled, stripped and spun down the leg when wet; it is then left to dry before being laid inside each roving of mountain-goat wool as the warp is made. The spinning of both warp and weft yarns for a dancing blanket could take six months to a year to complete; over a year would be spent on the actual weaving.

Compared to the designs painted on bark and leather garments, there is an extraordinary richness in woven garments; the weight, drape and magnificence of the material can only be discerned when it is seen next to its painted counterpart. Another characteristic of woven designs that cannot be duplicated in leather and paint is that the weaving creates an effect of low relief, and in this aspect it echoes the carved and painted wooden panels made by Woodlands men. In both robes and panels, rich curvilinear patterns are enhanced and given shape by subtle changes in surface depth, giving both a special distinction.

Holm (1965) described Northwest Coast design and the artistic conventions that form the basis for individual expression. He called the main element of the design the 'primary formline', a gracefully swelling and curving line that defines the major figures. Within the primary formline, inner shapes follow the stylistic principles governing the formline and are used to colour, fill and balance the design. In most painted designs the primary formline is black. The

inner shapes, composed of secondary and tertiary lines, are usually red and blue when painted and yellow and blue when woven.

The master weavers of the Chilkat tradition developed a weave structure that coped magnificently with the curvilinear design forms of Northwest Coast art. With the use of small outline braids that travelled at any angle over the surface of the twined fabric, they could overcome the problem of creating a circle on a graph. Such a circle is, in fact, a composite of an upper crescent, a central rectangle and a lower crescent. The outline braids create a perfect circle by travelling in the warp around the upper crescent, moving to the front of the web and travelling through the weft at the sides of the circle, then moving back into the warp to finish the curve around the lower crescent. On the sides of the circle, the outline braids do not appear on the back of the fabric. The fact that they ride on the front of the web on top of the ground wefts also gives life to the low-relief feature of the weaving. They actually form corded ridges, raised 1–2 mm above the main surface of the weave. An extension of this concept to all curved lines created the design freedom the Chilkat women weavers needed to copy the curvilinear forms of the men's art.

Owing to the outline braids, the number of weft strands in each horizontal row made weaving impossible. To weave a shape beautifully, the weaver needed the freedom to concentrate on that shape alone, and therefore another technique was developed. Small threads, called draw-strings, were introduced in a special manner along any vertical line in the pattern. When these threads (originally made of sinew and later of seine twine) were inserted, the weaver did not have to weave the adjoining segment of the design. She could concentrate on the forms found between two drawstrings and then, when she went to weave the adjacent forms, draw out a loop in the draw-string, insert the weft in it and pull the loop tight. This woven join, often mistaken as sewing, allowed the weaver to work in separate sections, then weave the sections together as the weaving progressed. Thus, in Chilkat weaving, no row between the heading and footing is continuous border to border. Because of the low relief achieved with the braid technique, there are innumerable ends to be worked in as each section is completed.

(iii) Development after European contact. Chilkat robes and Ravenstail robes were the glory of the Native American women's woven art. Magnificent in design, spectacular in performance, they gave pride and esteem both to the people who wore them and to the women who wove them. After contact with Euro-American cultures the lives of the people of the coast changed rapidly. An initial result of exchange between Northwest Coast peoples and ex-plorers and traders was a vastly increased production of Native American art. Men and women artists realized that, with steel knives, axe blades and ready-spun wool, the time their work took was greatly reduced. Traders and collectors wanted works of art, and a new market was opened. Native American artists were willing to experi-ment, and, because of their intellectual curiosity and open-mindedness, their art flourished.

Changes in lifestyle and values were too often forced on Native Americans by over-zealous missionaries or government officials who sought to destroy Native Amer-ican traditions. Their language was forbidden, their cere-monies outlawed, their art confiscated, and disease and alcohol took a heavy toll. For a time Northwest Coast traditions became dormant; but their strength, power and vitality have been given new life. By the mid-20th century only a handful of women knew the secrets of Chilkat blanket twining. From the 1960s, however, a revival in the traditional art forms swept the Northwest Coast. With the inquisitive minds of creative perfectionists, the artists retained or discard new ideas while honouring traditional conventions of the art. In the 1980s a tremendous revival took place. Ravenstail robes, long unknown even among the Native Americans, were again woven and danced in. Weavers living in the communities that originally devel-oped the designs and techniques are mastering the tech-nology and the concepts of an art form that allow them to weave today's song.

BIBLIOGRAPHY

G. T. Emmons: 'The Basketry of the Tlingit', *Mem. Amer. Mus. Nat. Hist.*, iii/2 (1903) [whole issue]
——: 'The Chilkat Blanket', *Mem. Amer. Mus. Nat. Hist.*, iii/4 (1907) [whole issue]
C. C. Willoughby: 'A New Type of Ceremonial Blanket from the North-west Coast', *Amer. Anthropologist*, xii (1910), pp. 1–10
M. L. Kissel: 'The Early Geometric Patterned Chilkat', *Amer. Anthropol-ogist*, xxx (1928), pp. 116–20
F. Paul: *Spruce Root Basketry of the Alaska Tlingit* (Washington, DC, 1944)
F. De Laguna and others: 'Archaeology of the Yakutat Bay Area, Alaska', *Bureau Amer. Ethnol. Bull.*, cxcii (1964) [whole issue]
B. Holm: *Northwest Coast Indian Art: An Analysis of Form* (Seattle, 1965)
E. Gunther: *Indian Life on the Northwest Coast of America, as Seen by the Early Explorers and Fur Traders during the Last Decades of the Eighteenth Century* (Chicago, 1972)
L. A. Shur and R. A. Pierce: 'Artists in Russian America: Mikhail Tikhanov (1818)', *Alaska J.* (1976)
B. Holm: 'A Woolen Mantle Neatly Wrought: The Early Historic Record of Northwest Coast Pattern-twined Textiles, 1774–1850', *Amer. Ind. A.* (1982)
C. Samuel: *The Chilkat Dancing Blanket* (Seattle, 1982, Norman, 2/1990)
——: 'From Baskets to Blankets: Old Style Ceremonial Weaving from the Northwest Coast', *Threads Mag.*, v (1986)
——: 'The Knight Island Robe', *The Raven's Journey*, ed. S. Kaplan and K. Barsness (Philadelphia, 1986)
——: *The Raven's Tail* (Vancouver, 1987)

CHERYL SAMUEL

2. SOUTHWEST. The US Southwest was in many respects a continuation of the high-culture area of PRE-COLUMBIAN MESOAMERICA. Like Mesoamerica, its peo-ples depended on agriculture for their main subsistence and practised the arts of basketry, pottery and weaving.

(i) Before European contact. (ii) After European contact.

(i) Before European contact. As elsewhere in North America, the first 'textiles' in the Southwest were plaited and twined fibres for baskets, ropes and sashes. A number of fabrics were also produced by finger-weaving techniques. The Anasazi and the Mogollon made robes large enough to wrap around the body from fibre cords wrapped with narrow strips of fur, usually of rabbit, while the Hohokam made short fur robes. Later, robes were made from cordage, incorporating feathers. Several kinds of fringed aprons were made for women by the Anasazi, the Sinagua and Salado. Some consisted merely of shredded juniper bark hung over waist cords of braided human hair, but others had panels of finger-woven tapestry in geometric patterns. Braided sashes of dog and rabbit hair were used as belts. Sandals of complex weaves were made with geometric woven patterns on the upper surface and patterns of knots on the soles, the designs and shapes of which changed through time. Large, egg-shaped bags were made by weft twining, adding warps to increase the diameter of the bag and deleting them to narrow the bags at the mouth. Decoration usually consisted of weft stripes in red and black on the tan background of yucca and *apocynum* fibre, but they were sometimes painted. Small cloth blankets in plain weave were sometimes made of yucca and *apocynum* fibre as well.

By *c.* AD 1 looms for weaving narrow widths of cloth were introduced into the southern part of the Southwest from Mesoamerica, along with the cultivation of cotton, which replaced the use of fibre from yuccas and other undomesticated plants. Both loom and cotton had reached the Anasazi by *c.* AD 600, and by 1100 a wide loom had been developed. A variety of textiles were woven on both the wide and narrow looms. All Southwest peoples wove cotton blankets to be worn as cloaks or dresses: Anasazi, Sinagua and Salado blankets were nearly square, while those of the Hohokam were long rectangles, sometimes of two pieces sewn together. Selvage cords were woven in along the edges to strengthen them. Some Anasazi blankets were woven in twill weave, with stripe decoration, but others were in plain weave decorated by painting, embroidery or tie-dyeing, or as woven plaidlike patterns and solid colours. Miniature cotton blankets were woven by the Hohokam, who used them to wrap around cane cigarettes (sections of cane filled with tobacco). Most of the southern peoples depended on varied and complex weaves, such as gauze and weft-wrap openwork, for decoration. The Anasazi, however, depended more on painting; the painted designs on their shirts and blankets were sometimes laid out in offset quartered patterns, much like the designs of their contemporary ceramics. Shirts were usually made of two pieces sewn together with flaplike sleeves. Ponchos were made in a single piece with a neck hole woven or cut in the centre.

Breech cloths of several kinds were woven: some were short with fringes, but others were long and narrow, and a few had tapered ends. They were held in place by belts or sashes, either decorated with designs in warp-float technique or some in the sprang technique. Smaller, tapelike fabrics served as garters and hair-ties. As garters they secured socks made from human hair by simple looping, or leggings made with a single continuous element by knitting or crocheting. Rectangular fabrics were woven as kiltlike garments, earlier in the south but also by the Anasazi by the 1300s, and were depicted commonly in the *kiva* wall paintings of the period (*see* §IV, 1(iii) above).

(ii) After European contact.

(a) Early Pueblo weaving. (b) Early Navajo weaving. (c) Late 18th-century and early 19th-century designs. (d) Navajo rugs. (e) Spanish and Pueblo weaving, 19th–20th centuries.

(a) Early Pueblo weaving. When Spanish explorers under Coronado entered the Southwest in 1540, the village-dwelling Native Americans they termed Pueblos were well dressed in clothing of cotton and other fibres. These were generally the same sorts of garments worn by the Anasazi and other earlier Southwest peoples. Men wore shirts, kiltlike skirts and breech cloths; women wore cotton blankets, or mantas, over one shoulder and under the opposite arm, clasped by a warp-faced belt around the waist. Cotton belts braided in the sprang technique were still made. Both sexes wore mantas as cloaks in cold weather and leather moccasins or woven sandals. As in earlier times the mantas were decorated by coloured stripes, by painted designs or by embroidery. Tie-dyed patterns seem to have ceased, as had many of the more complex weaves. To the south, the Native Americans who lived along the Gila River and its tributaries still wove large white cotton blankets on a loom built horizontally just above the ground.

In 1598 Spanish settlers along the Rio Grande brought sheep and goats into the Southwest for both meat and wool. They also introduced the European treadle loom for their own weaving, making it from local materials. Although the spinning-wheel was used in Spain and Mexico, the Spanish settlers adopted the use of Pueblo hand spindles. The treadle loom was well adapted to the weaving of long lengths of coarse cloth called *jerga* or serge. Plaidlike and chequered patterns were woven in both plain and twill weaves. Because the Spanish looms

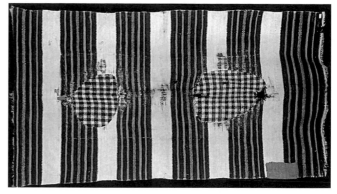

45. Southwest region wool blanket, patched with wool *jerga*, 1.08×2.10 m, Spanish colonial, from Rio Grande Valley, *c.* 1860 (Boulder, CO, University of Colorado Museum)

were narrow, blankets were usually woven in plain weft-faced weave in two halves and sewn together. Although single-ply warps were normally used for cloth, blankets had two-ply warps and single-ply wefts. Decoration frequently consisted of panels of alternating brown and indigo blue stripes separated by zones of white (see fig. 45).

With the assignment of Spanish priests to the Pueblo villages in the 1620s, sheep were allotted to the Pueblos, and by 1625 the Pueblo Native Americans were weaving in wool as well as cotton. Wool became the preferred material for everyday garments and for some decorative embroidered mantas (see fig. 46), while cotton was eventually used almost exclusively for ceremonial garments. The Pueblos continued to use their traditional spindle for spinning and vertical loom for weaving. Nevertheless, they began to weave wool blankets that were longer than they were wide, like those of the Spaniards, and often decorated them with alternating brown and blue stripes. This pattern came to be called Moki, after the Spanish name for the

46. Southwest region wool manta, embroidered with lac-dyed ravelled *bayeta*, 1.08×1.55 m, from Acoma Pueblo, *c.* 1850 (Boulder, CO, University of Colorado Museum)

Hopi Native Americans of Arizona. Both warp and weft of these blankets were single-ply.

(b) Early Navajo weaving. Around and between the settled Pueblo villages were a number of semi-nomadic, rather warlike tribes who depended on hunting and gathering for their subsistence. Most of these were Apache, part of the Athapaskan stock that had arrived in the Southwest a little before the Spaniards. One tribe inhabiting the mountainous region west and north of Santa Fe had taken over agriculture from the Pueblos and was known as Apaches de Navaju (Apaches of the big fields), eventually shortened to Navajo. When the Navajo entered the historical record in 1626 they were not known as weavers, although they may have been weaving baskets. From about 1640 they began to acquire sheep in raids on Spanish settlements in retaliation for Spanish slaving raids. During the same period many Pueblo Native Americans fled the Rio Grande villages and took refuge with the Navajo, and it was probably from these refugees that the Navajo learnt to weave in the second half of the 17th century. The Navajo adopted the Pueblo vertical loom with its heddle controls, the spindle, and both wool and cotton. They also adopted Pueblo dress, including wool mantas, shirts and belts.

During much of the 17th century the Pueblos traded with Plains Native Americans in textiles and other goods. Under considerable Spanish pressure—including attempts by Catholic priests to abolish Pueblo religion, an annual tax of one cotton manta per family and being forced to knit great quantities of cotton and woollen hose for the Spaniards—the Pueblos and Navajos rebelled in 1680. By 1696 the Spaniards had quelled the revolt, but many things had changed. Pueblo weaving became largely a matter of supplying only their own needs plus blankets and mantas for trade to other Native Americans. By the early 18th century the Navajo had established weaving as a cottage industry and were trading surplus cloth and blankets to both Pueblos and Spanish, as well as weaving cotton and wool mantas, shirts and belts of the types produced by the Pueblos.

They continued to use the vertical loom but began to make changes in technique. Where the Pueblos had woven a selvage of three two-ply cords, the Navajo began using two three-ply selvage cords. Instead of weaving each weft pick continuously from side to side, the Navajo began to weave the fabric in sections leaving a diagonal 'lazy-line' between each segment. Most Pueblo and early Navajo fabrics were woven in balanced plain- or twill-weave, in which both warp and weft were equally visible. During the 18th century the Navajo began to weave both their plain and twill cloth in weft-face or tapestry technique, in which the larger, softer wefts concealed smaller warps. This emphasis on weft-faced weaves may have come from the Spaniards, along with longer-than-wide blankets. Other changes occurred as two-piece dresses, with identical front and rear small blankets, began to replace the one-piece manta as a dress. The manta, however, continued to be made and used as a shawl or shoulder blanket. Early woollen mantas had black centres of diagonal twill and end panels of diamond twill, dyed dark blue with indigo traded from the Spaniards. While the Pueblos continued

this fashion, the Navajo began to weave decorative panels using a red background rather than blue. As there was no source of red dye in the Southwest, the Navajo began to unravel a solid red commercial cloth known as *bayeta* (baize) in order to obtain crimson red threads to use as wefts in their own fabrics. *Bayeta* was a loosely woven variety of flannel and was produced in several colours in various countries, including England, France, Spain, Turkey, Mexico and even New Mexico.

(c) Late 18th-century and early 19th-century designs. The decoration of most early weaving in the Southwest, whether Pueblo, Spanish or Navajo, consisted of weft-stripes that could be made simply by changing the colour of the weft. Such stripes were usually white, dark brown or black, with intermediate shades produced by carding light and dark wools together to make grey or tan. Indigo was frequently the only dyed colour, but occasionally locally procured vegetal dyes were used to provide yellows and greens; and imported brazil wood and, rarely, cochineal were used for reds by the Spaniards and possibly by the Pueblos. Stripe patterns varied from simple alternations, such as the brown and blue of the Moki pattern, to fairly complex stripe sequences, utilizing several colours in various rhythms.

Weft-stripes could be used in both plain and weft-face weaves, but the development of tapestry weave (see below), in which the design was produced by using discontinuous wefts, introducing a new colour at each place a design change was desired, made it possible to weave very complex figures. By the late 18th century the Navajo had begun to use tapestry technique to create designs based on terraced-edged figures, such as solid and hollow diamonds and triangles, which they had previously used on their basketry. When triangles were opposed apex to apex, diamond spaces were created; while offset opposed triangles created zigzag figures. Positive and negative designs were created by the alternation of colours. The layout of such figures normally ran from edge to edge of the textile with no border. In one-piece shawls, often woven in weft-faced twill, and two-piece dresses, usually of plain weft-faced tapestry, decoration in blue or blue-on-red was normally confined to panels or ends, with the central part woven in dark brown-black or, occasionally, white.

Chief blankets. During the 19th century the Navajo continued to weave shoulder blankets in wider-than-long proportions. In addition to manta shawls they wove larger blankets, the so-called 'Chief blankets', made for men. The earliest of these were decorated only with alternating stripes of black and white, but by 1800 the end and central stripes were made wider, with paired narrow blue stripes at the ends and two pairs across the wider central band. This simple, elegant 'first phase' Chief blanket became a favourite item of trade to the Plains Native Americans and to the Great Basin Utes, and it is often termed the 'Ute blanket'. Sometimes the blue stripes were edged by a few weft picks of ravelled crimson *bayeta*.

About the mid-19th century another design change occurred, in which small rectangles or concentric rectangles of red were inserted at the ends and centres of each of the blue stripes to make a 'second phase' Chief blanket. By 1860 these end and centre motifs were being made larger, so that they encroached on the field of broad black-and-white stripes. At this point the Navajo began to introduce the large terraced diamonds, previously used in sarapes, into the Chief blanket; a full diamond at the centre, quarter-diamonds at each corner and half-diamonds in between produced a 'third phase' Chief blanket. The Navajo also wove variations of these classic patterns. A smaller version of the Chief blanket was woven for women and followed the same developmental stages. Although the same layout and design elements were used, the background stripes on the women's blankets were narrower and in black and grey.

Navajo tapestry-woven blankets, c. 1800–63. Although the Navajo produced many textiles in the wider-than-long proportions, their finest achievements in weaving were the longer-than-wide, tapestry-woven blankets adapted from the Spanish serape. There were two sorts of serape: the common utility type, called *diyugi* ('soft fluffy blanket') by the Navajo, and a finer type. The *diyugi* was woven for heavy use, as it served as a bed blanket at night, as a wearing blanket by day, or as a carrying bag for firewood, clipped wool or babies. For every fine serape there were dozens of *diyugis* woven, used, worn out and discarded. Most of these blankets, like the utility blankets of the Spaniards and Pueblos, were decorated with weft-stripes in simple rhythms and colour schemes composed of white, black and indigo, with yellow and perhaps a few other native vegetal dye colours. When aniline dyes came into the Southwest in the early 1860s, the colour palette increased dramatically, and more complex zones of stripes were woven. Sometimes stripes were embellished with geometric figures.

Textiles of the period *c.* 1800–63 is known as the Classic period, and Navajo serapes woven during this time have never been equalled in the Southwest. Some of these were ponchos, woven with a slit in the centre for the wearer's head. Most Classic period serapes had a crimson background, unravelled from a fine-threaded worsted *bayeta* known as 100-thread *bayeta*, of unknown origin, dyed with the South-east Asian insect dye, lac, or with a combination of lac and cochineal. Designs were worked in indigo and white, and much more rarely in other colours. Designs included stripes, stepped or terraced triangles, hollow or solid terraced diamonds or zigzags arranged in rows or zones to compose an overall pattern. The field was frequently divided into three or five zones, but the patterns of one zone often merged with or reflected that of the next. The end zones often had quarter-diamonds at the corners and one or more half-diamonds in between. The layout of the centre usually consisted of terraced-edged diamonds with half-diamonds at the sides (see fig. 47). Occasionally, a network of large hollow diamonds covered the entire centre of the serape and might have smaller figures nested within the diamonds across the centre. Negative figures were often made by the placement of the terraced figures and the contrast of the blue and white colours.

Navajo weaving, 1863–8. The Classic period ended in 1863 with Navajo internment at Fort Sumner, or Bosque Redondo, in eastern New Mexico, in retaliation for raids on the Pueblos and on Spanish settlements along the Rio Grande to steal horses and sheep, or to take slaves. Most of the Navajo's sheep had been destroyed in the campaign against them, and there was insufficient wool for weaving. The annuity system, which had been established some years before the internment, became the chief source of materials for weaving and comprised soft, thick woollen *bayeta* woven in England and the north-eastern USA, flannel from Mexico and three-ply, later four-ply, commercial yarn named after Germantown, Pennsylvania, where some of it was spun.

Many design changes were introduced into Navajo weaving during their five years of internment. Most of the terraced design elements of the Classic period continued in use, but they tended to be smaller and arranged in tightly controlled bands divided by narrow stripes. Many figures became very elaborate. Elements once composed of solid colour lines were broken into chequer-board figures or were made up of short units of alternating colours. More and more colours, mostly derived from commercial plied yarns, were incorporated into the designs. Several new design motifs were also introduced, some of which also appeared on baskets: meanders, simple and elaborate crosses, chevrons and short, vertical zigzags arranged in horizontal stripes. The thicker, woollen yarns and the larger plied yarns being used made for thicker, coarser blankets. A trend towards smaller blankets also began at this time.

About 1868 a new design system was introduced, picked up from earlier Spanish colonial coarse woven copies of elaborate sarapes made in the Saltillo region of northern Mexico. These had a large, centre-dominant motif, usually of concentric diamonds with serrated edges, on a background of vertically oriented zigzag stripes, 'butterfly' figures or a grid of spaced dots, all surrounded by a figured border. Navajo designs had always gone from edge to edge and consisted of elements arrayed in horizontal zones, stripes, zigzags and terraced figures. Borders were rarely used. But the new style with all its serrations was not adopted completely. Rather, terraced-edged triangles

47. Southwest region serape, lac-dyed ravelled *bayeta*, white and indigo dyed handspun wool yarns, 1.27×1.93 m, Navajo Classic period, *c.* 1840 (Boulder, CO, University of Colorado Museum)

and zigzags were replaced by identical figures with serrated edges. Rows of vertical zigzags were truncated and made into horizontal stripes; or occasionally the vertical zigzags were made into the total design of the blanket. Thus, even though some terraced-edged figures continued to be woven, by 1885 serrated blankets with a border dominated Navajo weaving. Brightly coloured Germantown four-ply yarns were used in profusion, often to outline each of the motifs in a different colour. Handspun yarns still predominated but were brightly coloured with the recently introduced synthetic dyes. Such textiles, transitional between late Classic blankets and rugs, appropriately came to be called 'eye dazzlers' (*see* TEXTILE, colour pl. VIII, fig. 2).

Other new kinds of textiles were also woven. Two-faced blankets, with a different design on each face were developed, and various eccentric-weaves, in which stripes were woven diagonally to the warp, became known as wedge-weave. Tufts of wool or angora hair were inserted along the weft to make a long pile to produce a kind of imitation sheepskin. Pictorial elements had occasionally been inserted into blankets that otherwise had a regular layout, but pictorial blankets now became a popular genre in their own right. Twill-weaves, which had been mainly used for saddle blankets, served for rugs; and small, fancy saddle throws were also developed.

(d) Navajo rugs. By the time the Navajo returned to their own country in 1868, they had become accustomed to wearing clothing of commercial cotton cloth, velveteen or lightweight wool. Pendleton or other commercial shawls began to replace blankets of Navajo manufacture. Rather than see weaving die out, traders began to encourage the Navajo to weave heavier fabrics for use as rugs. From *c.* 1900 oriental carpets were in great demand, and some traders, notably John Bradford Moore at Crystal, New Mexico, and J. Lorenzo Hubbell at Ganado, Arizona, developed rugs in simplified oriental patterns that could be ordered in any size and colour scheme desired. From the early 20th century several regional Navajo rug styles developed. Around the trading-posts at Ganado, Teecnos-pos and Kayenta (Arizona) and Two Grey Hills and Crystal (New Mexico) distinctive rugs were made, with designs based largely on oriental carpet patterns. From *c.* 1920, starting at Chinle, Arizona, rugs featuring the use of vegetal dyes and borderless layout were developed. By the end of the 20th century many professional Navajo weavers specialized in fine tapestries.

(e) Spanish and Pueblo weaving, 19th–20th centuries. During the 19th century the Rio Grande Spanish settlers maintained a lively commerce in cloth and blankets. Thousands of simply decorated common blankets and fine blankets with designs copied from Saltillo and Navajo sarapes were woven. Most were sold in the mining districts of northern Mexico, in California and, after 1846, to the US Indian Service for distribution to the Apaches and Utes. After 1900 the Rio Grande weavers developed a curio trade around the village of Chimayo in northern New Mexico. Native American and Spanish designs were combined, and commercial yarns were used. The Pueblo Native Americans almost ceased to weave during the late 19th century. Only the Hopi continued to weave traditional

garments, especially for ceremonial use, and to trade them to other Pueblos. Instead, fine blankets were obtained from the Navajo.

BIBLIOGRAPHY
G. S. Maxwell: *Navajo Rugs: Past, Present and Future* (Palm Desert, 1963)
A. Berlant and M. H. Kahlenberg: *Walk in Beauty: The Navajo and their Blanket* (Boston, 1977)
H. P. Mera and J. B. Wheat: *The Alfred I. Barton Collection of Southwestern Textiles* (Miami, 1978)
K. P. Kent: *Prehistoric Textiles of the Southwest* (Santa Fe, 1983)
——: *Pueblo Indian Textiles: A Living Tradition* (Santa Fe, 1983)
J. B. Wheat: *The Gift of Spiderwoman: Southwestern Textiles, the Navajo Tradition* (Philadelphia, 1984)
K. P. Kent: *Navajo Weaving: Three Centuries of Change* (Santa Fe, 1985)
M. Rodee: *Weaving of the Southwest* (Westchester, 1987)
N. J. Blomberg: *Navajo Textiles: The William Randolph Hearst Collection* (Tucson, 1988)

JOE BEN WHEAT

3. WOODLANDS.

(i) Materials and techniques. (ii) Regional survey.

(i) Materials and techniques. Twining and braiding were the preferred techniques of the Woodlands Indians and are still practised. Twining is hand-weaving, in which a weft, or filling material, is twisted (or twined) over the warp, or foundation strands. Many variations and derivatives of this technique are found in Woodlands textile production. Spaced-weft twining, for example, uses warps of basswood or other bark fibre, which are secured by twisting two spaced wefts of nettle, milkweed, hemp or cotton thread around them. The design can be varied by alternating the colour of the bark warp. Spaced alternate pair weft twining (or alternate-pair twining) involves double or paired warps of different colours that switch position to create contrasts of dark and light in the pattern. The resulting designs vary from simple vertical stripes to more complex geometrical patterning. Traditionally, twined textiles were created by hanging the warps over a horizontal stick or cord (the so-called suspension loom) and then twining the warps together in a gradual downward spiral. When the twining was completed, the stick was removed.

Plaiting was used for warp-faced mats, in which only the warp is visible. These were made by using reeds or cat-tail warps and thin bast fibre wefts. Simple chequered weave mats were also produced, often of bark strips, and the suspension loom was often used to aid their production. Finger-weaving was the most frequent form of plaiting, in which the active warp was braided to make fabrics. Belts, sashes, garters and bags were made in this way, originally of native fibres such as buffalo wool and later of commercial yarn. Mats were also occasionally finger-woven.

The hole and slot heddle was introduced by Europeans to the Woodland Native Americans shortly after contact. The heddle separated fixed warps so that a perpendicular weft could be inserted. It was most often used to create woven beadwork (*see* §IX, 7 below). The introduction of the loom, in combination with the availability of European trade cloth and blankets, led to the decline of Woodlands textile manufacture. Important collections of Woodlands textiles are held in: New York (Mus. Amer. Ind.), Washington, DC, (Smithsonian Inst.), Ottawa (Can. Mus. Civiliz.), Cambridge, MA, Harvard U. (Peabody Mus.), Milwaukee, WI (Pub. Mus.), Vienna (Mus. Vlkerknd.), Montreal, McGill U. (McCord Mus.), Oxford U. (Pitt

Rivers Mus.) and St Petersburg (Peter the Great Mus. Anthropol. & Ethnog.).

(ii) Regional survey.

(a) Central. In Ohio and Illinois, complex weaves using hemp, cat-tail and rush existed as early as 250 BC. Twining was ubiquitous before European contact. Fibres were spun in an 'S' twist, combined in pairs and reversed in a 'Z' twist to create weft cordage. A great variety of weaves existed, and many disparate fibres—including human hair, bison hair, nettle, cedar, elm and basswood bark—were used in combination. The suspension loom was used, but no heddles have been excavated at pre-contact sites. Accounts by early explorers record large quantities of Native American cloth in the 16th and 17th centuries. Woven and twined mats, bags, burden straps and sashes were made of materials such as bullrushes, basswood and other bark fibres, Indian hemp, nettle, buffalo and animal hair. The introduction of European textiles and designs caused central Woodlands peoples to abandon their own fabrics and clothing styles almost overnight. Little traditional weaving was practised by the beginning of the 18th century, and wool and linen were used instead of indigenous materials. Nevertheless, articles such as arm-bands, sashes, belts and garters continued to incorporate traditional designs.

Rush matting and coverings made on a suspension loom were produced throughout the central Woodlands, especially among the Ottawa, Mississauga, Chippewa, Menomini, Sauk, Fox and Potawatomi peoples. Plaited reed mats were produced by the Ottawa, with designs resembling those created by alternate-pair twining. Simple chequered-weave plaited bags and mats were also produced by the Ottawa using strips of cedar bark. Geometric or naturalistic designs in soft vegetable colours were often woven into the plaited mats. The introduction of aniline dyes made possible stronger coloration, and today rush mats have designs in bright blue, green, purple and maroon. Coarser mats were used as a covering for dome-shaped dwellings, bed and floor coverings and interior house linings. Finely woven mats were displayed as decorative hangings and used as wrappings and for giving-away ceremonies.

Fibre bags were made in endless variety. Bast fibre, made from the beaten inner bark of the basswood, cedar or slippery elm, was boiled in a solution of lye, which separated the fibres. These were then dried and twisted or spun into cordage for weaving. Such bags were of loose weave, had a coarse appearance and were often left unpatterned. They were used to store food and personal possessions.

Softer, more finely woven bags were made from nettle, bison hair, Indian hemp or, after European contact, commercial cotton twine. Vegetal dyes coloured some bags, while commercial dyes created strong colour contrast in others. Such closely woven bags, created by alternate-pair twining, were more carefully finished than the coarser bags. Those that were not of a utilitarian nature were embellished with woven geometric designs of animals, birds and occasionally humans. Mythical beings, such as the Thunderbird or the Great Underwater Panther, were frequently depicted. Different designs were used for either side of the bag; as a rule a zoomorphic or mythical design is interwoven on one side and a geometric or linear pattern on the other. If both sides of the bag are decorated with geometric designs, each is different. The designs are usually woven on a square central panel in brown on a buff background, with multicoloured lines flanking the central panel to form the borders.

Such twined bags were common throughout the central Woodlands and especially among the central tribes, the Ojibwa (especially of the Southern and Mississuaga bands), the Delaware, the New York Coastal Algonquin and the Iroquois. The greatest variety in technique and design of soft twined bags was found among the Algonquin tribes of the western Great Lakes and some of the Dakota, while the most sophisticated mastery of twining occurred in the south-western Great Lakes region. The people of this region were noted for a method of twining in which discontinuous wool wefts were used to make tapestry twined bags. Their use of diamonds and serrated lines resembled the geometric motifs created in silk and ribbon appliqué work. Medicine pouches were made in the same way as bags and were decorated with thunderbirds, underwater panthers, horned serpents, suns, turtles, fish, beavers, zigzags and wavy lines. Many of the patterns were borrowed from the vocabulary of body tattooing, which had all but died out by the 18th century.

The form of bags and pouches was altered significantly with the use of European wool and commercial cording. As early as the 18th century woollen trade blankets were unravelled by the Great Lakes tribes to produce yarn, which was then used for both warp and weft. The old fibre bags and pouches woven on suspension looms were, in effect, seamless pockets; the loose ends were braided together to form the rim of the bag or pouch. The new wool bags were created by hanging the warp threads over a cord stretched between two vertical poles, producing a flat cylinder as the wefts were twined around the warp threads; the bottom was sewn shut to form the pouch. Bags made in this way were simply decorated in horizontal bands of coloured cording of changing widths. New techniques were also possible using the new materials: for example, weft threads could be given a full twist between each warp strand, showing only the short vertical twists and making the horizontal wefts invisible. Geometric designs increased with the use of commercial yarn, while representational motifs decreased. Nevertheless, each side of such bags still displayed a different pattern.

Finger-woven sashes, belts and garters, made of bast and wool and decorated with geometric patterns, were also made in the central Woodlands. Many beaded sashes and belts were made by interweaving trade beads into the textile, but others were made on a bead loom. Finger-woven sashes were still made at the end of the 20th century by the Native Americans of Wisconsin and Oklahoma, and the craft has also been revived by French Canadians, who adopted the technique from the Native Americans in the mid-18th century. Traditional textile arts were being enthusiastically revived in the later 20th century by Native American communities across the central Woodlands.

the *qulittaq* (outer layer), made with the fur facing outward. Each part of the ensemble fitted together in order to eliminate cold draughts. Garments were designed to trap warm air and funnel the air up towards the hood opening where it escapes. The details of length, hood and tailoring changed from region to region.

Parkas for men and women differed. The design of the man's parka symbolized the relationship between man and animal in a hunting culture; the woman's parka symbolized the woman as mother. Children's parkas echoed the parka design of the appropriate sex. The skin of caribou, seal and small mammals, such as the ground squirrel or muskrat, were used to make the man's hooded and evenly hemmed parka, with the highly prized fur of the wolverine used for trimming in some areas of the Arctic. Trousers of matching fur and boots with soles of sealskin or skins of other animals and fur or skin uppers completed the hunter's costume. Similarly the triangular tusklike gussets at the front may symbolize the strength of the walrus, the hunter's most formidable prey.

The woman's parka was made of the same skins, and in some regions they featured long, scalloped panels that formed the front apron and back tail. The *amaut* (pouch) was incorporated into the back of parkas from some regions, forming a symbolic second womb in which to carry an infant. Trousers and boots completed the woman's outfit.

Waterproof garments of sea-mammal gut were also made, as well as parkas and hats made from the skins of birds, fish, seals and sea otters. Personal ornamentation included belts of feather quills, crab shells, wolverine toes, ptarmigan feet and caribou incisor teeth strung or sewn together. Ornaments and facial jewellery of beads and shells, and ivory jewellery were worn mostly by women, while body painting was a tradition among men. For example, in Alaska Yuit and Inupiat decorated their faces with tattoos and ivory or bone labrets (worn by men and a few women), inserted through the skin near the lips. A few tattooed elders were still alive in the 1980s, but this tradition has been discontinued since the early part of the 20th century. By the late 20th century women used mass-produced commercial jewellery and make-up.

(ii) Contemporary variations. By the late 20th century traditional Arctic clothing designs remained an integral part of daily life in the north. In addition, clothing served as a medium to record history through design features and through the symbolic meaning attached to decorative details. In Canada, Inuit and Inuvialuit seamstresses created works of art in the form of clothing. Some seamstresses continued to produce clothing from skins, including seal, caribou, squirrel, bird, wolf, wolverine and eider duck. Skins were dried and scraped, and some were chewed until pliable. In the western region ochre, fabric dye and wet crêpe paper were a few items used to stain skins before using them to decorate garments. The availability of natural resources, cultural traditions and the end use of the garment influenced the type of skins used. For example, seal and walrus intestines were traditionally used to produce waterproof clothing for summer use. By the late 20th century many women used fabric to produce clothing worn within the community. Skin clothing was

still extremely important for people travelling in cold weather conditions.

Temporal, regional and gender variations result in clothing styles that reveal cultural identity. In the late 20th century parkas with tails were used by some women in the central and eastern Canadian Arctic. MacKenzie Delta Inuvialuit and Copper Inuit women in the western Canadian Arctic used parkas with broad parka ruffs made by piecing together tiny pieces of wolfskin. This band is finished with a broad strip of wolverine-skin, producing a 'sunburst ruff' (see fig. 48). In the central and eastern Canadian Arctic women's parkas were made with a pouch sewn into the back panel, where young children were carried. Such parkas were also used occasionally by men when babysitting young children.

Along the Arctic coastline of Alaska, Yuit and Inupiat seamstresses used a combination of sea and land animals in their clothing. Moose, fish, wolf, mountain goat, polar bear, seal and black bear were some of the skins used for

48. Arctic woman wearing a caribou-skin parka with tassels and hemline in wolverine-skin and a 'sunburst ruff' of wolverine skins on the wolfskin hood, made by June Klengenberg, Coppermine, Northwest Territories, 1987

skin boots. Extensive intersettlement trade between inland, island and coastal Yuit and Inupiat communities enabled seamstresses to obtain a wide variety of materials.

As in Canada, Alaskan seamstresses use clothing and personal adornment as one medium to express creatively their group identity, age, gender, marital status and other aspects of life. Seasonal variations, end usage of garments, historical factors and available resources influence the type of materials and clothing styles produced. For example, in the past, the Bering Sea Inupiat removed the fat from puffin-skins by soaking them in urine. Skins were then rubbed with fish roe and natural dyes to improve the water-repellent qualities. Birdskin clothing is rarely used today, but in the past it was used primarily by groups who had little access to caribou- or reindeer-skins. In contrast, Kobuk River Valley Inupiat rubbed their caribou leg skin boots with fat and stained the skin with alder bark to improve the water-repellent qualities of their footwear when sealskins were unavailable through intersettlement trade.

By the late 20th century Yuit and Inupiat rarely used birdskin parkas. Instead, they created spectacular parkas from muskrat, reindeer, commercial calf, ground squirrel and other skins. Decoration is provided by tassels cut from wolverine-skins, stained, as in western Canada, with ochre, wet crêpe paper or alder bark. Traditionally, the tassels represented friendship and the number of children or grandchildren in the wearer's family. The hemline, hood, back and sleeves are decorated with geometric pieces of light- and dark-haired skins, sewn together into intricate patterns, which vary regionally and demonstrate group affiliation. Small clusters of beads strung on to a skin or piece of red yarn are also used as decoration; similar skin and beaded tassels are attached to skin boots, especially those used for special occasions.

Important collections of Arctic clothing are held in Seattle (WA State Mus.), Oxford U. (Pitt Rivers Mus.), London (BM), Helsinki (N. Mus.), Anchorage, AL (Hist. & F.A. Mus.), New York (Amer. Mus. Nat. Hist.), Ottawa (Can. Mus. Civiliz.), Glasgow (A.G. & Mus.), Copenhagen (Nmus.), Toronto (Bata Shoe Mus.) and Washington, DC (N. Mus. Nat. Hist.).

BIBLIOGRAPHY

T. Manning and E. Manning: 'The Preparation of Skins and Clothing in the Eastern Canadian Arctic', *Polar Rec.*, iv/28 (1944), pp. 156–69
G. Hatt: 'Arctic Skin Clothing in Eurasia and America: An Ethnographic Study', *Arctic Anthropol.*, v/2 (1969), pp. 3–132
M. Angugatiaq: 'Caribou Garments', *Inummarit*, ii/1 (1973), p. 6
The Far North: 2000 Years of American and Indian Art (exh. cat. by H. Collins and others, Washington, DC, N.G.A., 1973)
D. J. Ray: *Aleut and Eskimo Art: Tradition and Innovation in South Alaska* (Seattle, 1977/R Seattle and London, 1981)
B. Driscoll and G. Swinton: *The Inuit Amautik: I Like my Hood to Be Full* (Winnipeg, 1980)
D. J. Ray: *Eskimo Art: Tradition and Innovation in North Alaska* (Seattle, 1980)
L. Black: *Aleut Art* (Anchorage, 1982)
D. Damas, ed.: 'Arctic', *Hb. N. Amer. Ind.*, v (1985) [whole issue]
B. Driscoll: 'Pretending to Be Caribou: The Inuit Parka as an Artistic Tradition', *The Spirit Sings: Artistic Traditions of Canada's First Peoples* (Toronto, 1987), pp. 83–102
J. Oakes: *Factors Influencing Skin Boot Production in Arctic Bay, N. W. T.*, Can. Ethnol. Serv. Pap., cvii (1987), pp. 1–54
——: *Copper and Caribou Inuit Skin Clothing Production* (diss., U. Manitoba, 1988)
——: 'Regional Variations in Bird Skin Preparation Techniques and Parka Design', *Home Econ. Res. J.*, xx/2 (1991), pp. 119–32
——: 'Eider Skin Garments Used by Ungava Inuit from the Belcher Islands, Northwest Territories', *Cloth. & Textiles Res. J.*, x/2 (1992), pp. 1–10

JOANNE DANFORD-CORDINGLEY, JILL OAKES

3. SUBARCTIC. For the semi-nomadic hunting peoples of the Subarctic regions, clothing was not only essential for survival in a harsh northern environment but also provided the principal means of artistic expression. Traditionally, garments were made from the tanned skins of large land mammals, mainly moose and caribou. Styles varied according to region and season, but the upper garment was usually a long-sleeved, pullover tunic, worn with leggings or trousers (see fig. 49). Moccasins were either separate, or sewn as one with the legging. Other costume elements included hoods, mittens, bags and knife sheaths.

In the making and decoration of such garments seamstresses displayed great technical skill and highly developed aesthetic sensibilities. Hides were made supple and soft through a laborious process of scraping, soaking, stretching and rubbing with a caribou-brain tanning mixture. For winter clothing the fur was retained; for summer wear hides were dehaired and either frost-dried, which produced a white hide, or smoke-tanned to a golden brown. Garments were decorated by painting with pigments derived from earth ochres and plant and berry juices, by the attachment of bands of sewn or woven porcupine quills dyed red, green, brown and purple, and by the incorporation of fringes embellished with porcupine quills, seed beads, animal hoofs and claws, and feathers (*see also*, §XI, 2 below).

Garment decoration varied according to region and purpose. To propitiate and honour the spirit of the caribou, Naskapi hunters of the eastern Subarctic wore coats of white caribou-skin elaborately painted with symbolic curvilinear and parallel line motifs in red, green and yellow paint. Far to the west, well-to-do Kutchin wore tunics of white caribou-hide decorated with curving yokes of appliqué porcupine quills and long fringes wrapped with porcupine quills and strung with small seed beads (see fig. 49). Garment seams and opening edges were outlined with red ochre, highly valued for its decorative qualities and spiritual power.

Face painting and tattooing were significant ritual and aesthetic expressions, constituting another method of proclaiming social identity and honouring the spirit inhabitants of an animistic universe. Tattooing was accomplished by piercing the skin with a porcupine quill or fine sharp bone, then slowly drawing a length of animal sinew coated with charcoal under the surface. Face painting was an even more common method of self-adornment. The main colours were red and black, generally derived from ochre and charcoal. The raw material was reduced to a fine powder, then usually mixed with water and applied with a finger to the face.

Hairdressing was also important: well-cared-for, carefully arranged and decorated hair conveyed distinction and status. The men of some western Subarctic groups wore their hair long, bound at the nape of the neck with a band of dentalium shells. The hair was greased and sprinkled

49. Subarctic man's summer outfit of tunic, moccasin trousers, mittens and knife-sheath, made of caribou-hide with glass trade beads, dentalium shell and red ochre, and sewn with sinew, h. 1.2 m, Kutchin, collected 1862 (Hull, Québec, Canadian Museum of Civilization)

with fine bird down, the parting marked with red ochre. Nose ornaments, earrings, necklaces, hair ties and pendants were worn by men and women. These were often made of precious materials, such as imported shells, silver, copper and glass beads.

With increased contact between Subarctic peoples and Euro-American traders, explorers and missionaries in the 18th and 19th centuries, Native American self-adornment and clothing changed dramatically. Facial painting, tattooing and elaborate hairdressing were discouraged by traders and missionaries and often given up soon after contact. Native American fashions reflected the increased availability of such European trade goods as woven cloth, glass

beads, ribbons, steel needles and scissors, as well as the exposure of Native American seamstresses to embroidery skills, decorative motifs and clothing fashions of European origin. Brightly coloured floral patterns in glass beads or embroidery floss replaced geometric-patterned porcupine quillwork as the dominant decorative art. As with earlier work, Subarctic decorative art of the fur-trade era exhibits great technical skill and aesthetically pleasing combinations of colours and materials. Traditional skin clothing was, for the most part, eventually relinquished in favour of cloth garments, although some indigenous forms survived in modified versions. For example, jackets, moccasins and mittens of heavily smoked hide decorated with floral beadwork were popular throughout the fur-trade era and continue to be made.

BIBLIOGRAPHY
T. Brasser: 'Bo'jou Neejee!': Profiles of Canadian Indian Art (Ottawa, 1976)
R. Phillips: '"Like a Star I Shine": Northern Woodlands Artistic Traditions', The Spirit Sings: Artistic Traditions of Canada's First Peoples (Toronto, 1987), pp. 51–92
J. Thompson: '"No Little Variety of Ornament": Northern Athapaskan Artistic Traditions', The Spirit Sings: Artistic Traditions of Canada's First Peoples (Toronto, 1987), pp. 133–68
K. Duncan: Northern Athapaskan Art: A Beadwork Tradition (Seattle and London, 1989)

JUDY THOMPSON

4. NORTHWEST COAST. There are shared characteristics in dress and adornment among the various Northwest Coast groups. Typical to all these groups is the use of cedar-bark fibres and mountain-goat wool to weave robes and blankets (see §VII, 1 above). Dress consists primarily of the robe or blanket fixed about the shoulders; leggings, aprons, hats, capes and skirts are also worn. Ornamentation is made from various objects such as shell, bones, bird beaks and copper. Northwest Coast peoples all celebrate the potlatch, have a stratified society and use crests and totemic images to represent their clan or extended family. Differences among Northwest Coast groups can be seen in their use of clan symbols and totems and their weaving style.

Northern groups (Tlingit, Tsimshian, Haida, Kwakiutl (now known as Kwakwaka'wakw) and Bella Coola (now Known as Nuxalk)) use clan symbols to decorate almost all personal and communal objects. Each part of their dress may include representations of their clan animal or personal totem. The resulting motifs are individual, despite rigid canons of design; these are abstract in design but always include a definite figure.

Southern groups (Nootka (now known as Nuu-chah-nulth), Coast Salish) depict clan symbols on personal items such as jewellery and weaving whorls, but their blankets remain plain. Elaboration is done with weaving techniques (i.e. herringbone or twill-weave) rather than with the inclusion of designs. With the introduction of coloured yarns to the Coast Salish, abstract multicoloured blankets were created. Coast Salish were unique in their use of dog hair in weaving their blankets; these dogs were specifically raised for their hair, and their ownership was limited to nobility.

For bibliography see §VII, 1 above.

NICHOLETTE PRINCE

5. PLATEAU. Although people have lived in the Plateau for several millennia, little is known about their ancient dress. According to Native American tradition, clothing such as fringed skirts was first made of vegetable fibres, but archaeologists have found remains only of fibre sandals and leather moccasins cut in various patterns. Women probably made brimless twined basketry caps.

Between c. 1650 and 1800 basic Plateau clothing forms developed. Both sexes wore moccasins made with sole and upper in one folded piece, sewn along the outside from toe to heel. Women wore long dresses made of two large animal skins, one for front and one for back, covering them almost to the ankles, and tubular leather leggings from the ankles to up over the calves. Men wore longer leggings rising to their hips. Men also wore breech cloths—long leather strips passing between the legs, under a belt front and back, and with covering ends like aprons—and simple leather shirts with identical fronts and backs falling to mid-thigh, with sleeves to the wrist. As horses were introduced into the Plateau at this time, women's longer, fuller dresses may have facilitated riding astride. Both sexes used leather and fur blankets for outer coverings, and women regularly wore their fez-shaped basketry caps.

The introduction of horses also brought Plateau people into contact with the Plains tribes from c. 1800. It has been suggested that Plateau culture was modified by this contact, but Plains influences were actually superficial. The basic design of garments changed little, but new items, such as feather headdresses, were introduced (see also §XII, 2 below).

There is little evidence for decoration of clothing among Plateau peoples until after c. 1800. Porcupine-quill embroidery was limited and applied mostly to smaller garments, such as moccasins, while others were painted with earth pigments (see §XI, 3 below). One garment form peculiar to the Plateau is the perforated leather shirt: parallel vertical rows of round or diamond-shaped holes about 10 mm long were cut into the leather. The reason for this is unknown. Another unique Plateau ornament is the bride's headdress of dentalium shells, worn by the Chinookan and Sahaptian-speaking groups. Necklaces of flat shell discs about 15 mm in diameter were also common. Plateau decorative practices flourished when the European traders arrived early in the 19th century with glass beads, cloth, ribbons and other such items. By the 1880s women were adding heavy decorations of beads to leather and trade cloth garments (see also §IX, 6, below). By the 1990s Plateau women still produced many decorated garments and horse trappings for use by themselves and family members.

BIBLIOGRAPHY
V. F. Ray: *The Sanpoil and Nespelem: Salishan Peoples of Northeastern Washington*, University of Washington Publications in Anthropology, v (Seattle, 1932)
R. G. Conn: *A Persistent Vision: Art of the Reservation Days* (Denver, 1986)

RICHARD G. CONN

6. GREAT BASIN. As elsewhere, clothing and personal adornment varied in the Great Basin, depending on availability of materials, season of the year, and the sex and age of the wearer. Geographic or regional styles were common and cut across tribal lines. Except in the north and east, where contact with Plains groups led to the adoption of Plains styles, there was little differentiation of wealth, rank or status expressed in Great Basin clothing.

Clothing of plant fibres was common to several Great Basin peoples. The Northern Paiute of western Nevada made shirts, aprons and leg wrappings for men, and front and back aprons for women, of twined sagebrush bark or tules. Southern Paiute groups in southern Utah and northern Arizona made similar garments of cliffrose bark, including a two-piece dress with shoulder straps for women and a sleeveless shirt and breech cloth for men. In areas where deer or antelope were more readily available, such as parts of Western Shoshone country in central Nevada and the mountain areas of the Washoe, Northern Paiute and Southern Paiute, the man's plant-fibre shirt was replaced by one made of one large or two small skins, worn poncho-style with a belt at the waist. Such shirts had short sleeves in the western Great Basin and longer ones in the east and south. Women's aprons in these areas were made of a single skin, sometimes tanned with the hair left on. Some women had longer dresses made of two skins. In all areas, men and women wore capes or robes of twined rabbit-skins in winter. People in mountain areas had capes of tanned bobcat- or bear-hide. In marshy zones, capes of twined or tanned duckskin or gooseskin were alternatives. Footwear included sandals of tules, sagebrush or yucca (depending on the area), or moccasins of deer, antelope or bighorn sheep hide. Men's moccasins were ankle high; those of women came to mid-calf. They, like the skin clothing, were plain in pre-European contact times but decorated with geometric and floral patterns in glass beads after that time.

Children's clothing mirrored that of adults, although children commonly wore little clothing before puberty, except in winter. Rabbit-skin capes were made in children's sizes, and they, like adults, used them as blankets at night. Headbands of buckskin and necklaces and earrings of shells were commonly worn by children and adults. Headbands had painted geometric designs or feather mosaic patterns. Men often wore skin caps and women basketry caps.

The hair of both sexes was combed loose; men occasionally braided their hair. Fur or buckskin wraps or shell disks were used to cover and tie the braids. Facial tattooing was not uncommon and usually consisted of a few lines from the mouth or eyes. Facial painting for ceremonial occasions was much more elaborate and was influenced among the Ute and Shoshone groups by contact with Plains tribes.

Plains-style buckskin beaded and quilled shirts and dresses were common among the Ute, and Northern Shoshone and Wind River Shoshone. Shoshone beadwork on these garments was similar to Crow styles with the late (1890s) overlay of northern floral patterns. Ute work was closer to that of the southern and central Plains and primarily geometric.

See also §§VIII, 9, IX, 6 and XI, 3 below.

BIBLIOGRAPHY
A. M. Smith: *Ethnography of the Northern Utes*, Papers in Anthropology, xvii (Santa Fe, 1974)
W. L. d'Azevedo, ed.: 'Great Basin', *Hb. N. Amer. Ind.*, xi (1986) [whole vol.]

C. S. Fowler, ed.: *Willard Z. Park's Ethnographic Notes on the Northern Paiute of Western Nevada, 1933–1940*, Anthropological Papers of the University of Utah, cxiv (Salt Lake City, 1989)

CATHERINE S. FOWLER

7. CALIFORNIA. Daily dress was minimal throughout the California area. Men wore breech cloths of tanned hide, if anything, while women wore skirts or two-piece aprons of diverse materials, including fringed deerskin, shredded tree bark or tule. Ceremonial regalia differed between regions. In southern California a netted skirt, fringed with eagle or condor feathers, was an important part of the dance regalia for men in the whirling dance of the Cahuilla and their neighbours. In central California, headbands of the stripped, salmon-orange quills of the flicker were worn in conjunction with an array of head plumes, feather topknots and shell-bead necklaces in World Renewal ceremonies. In north-west California, World Renewal ceremonies provided an occasion to show off accumulated wealth in the form of ceremonial finery: women wore finely woven basketry caps, fringed deerskin skirts laden with shell, bead and woven grass decoration, and multitudes of shell bead necklaces; men wore a variety of headdresses, including one with projecting sea-lion teeth, a headband of painted leather fringed with wolf fur and a wide headband decorated with scarlet woodpecker scalps, along with many dentalium shell necklaces. Dance regalia among the groups in north-east California and in the high desert east of the Sierra Nevada mountain range was extremely limited before 1900; by the 1990s many of those groups had adopted pan-Native American style clothing for Native American gatherings.

BIBLIOGRAPHY

R. F. Heizer, ed.: 'California', *Hb. N. Amer. Ind.*, viii (1978) [whole vol.]
C. D. Bates: 'Dressing the Part: A Brief Look at the Development of Stereotypical Indian Clothing among Native Peoples in the Far West', *J. California & Gt Basin Anthropol.*, iv/1 (1982), pp. 55–6
——: *Feathered Regalia of Central California: Wealth and Power*, Occasional Papers of the Redding Museum, ii (Redding, CA, 1982)
C. D. Bates and B. Bibby: 'Beauty and Omnipotence: Traditional Dance Regalia of Northern California', *The Extension of Tradition: Contemporary Northern California Native American Art in Cultural Perspective* (exh. cat., ed. F. R. La Peña and J. T. Driesbach; Sacramento, CA, Crocker A. Mus.), pp. 28–37

CRAIG D. BATES

8. SOUTHWEST. Clothing in the Southwest has, from pre-European contact times, been geographically differentiated and culturally specific. Each of the Greater Southwest's 44 cultures had styles that marked an individual as a member of a group, distinctive from all others. Similarly, each society had elaborate costumes for special occasions and rituals. Clothing as protection from the elements was also influenced by climate, available technology and raw materials. The earliest clothing was of animal skins and gathered plant materials. Weaving techniques were developed after the introduction of domesticated cotton from Mesoamerica *c.* AD 1000 and applied to wool after the introduction of sheep by the Spaniards in the late 16th century (*see* §VII, 2 above). By the late 20th century commercially manufactured garments were the norm, and costumes in modified traditional designs were used only for ceremonial and special occasions.

People inhabiting the hottest desert areas, such as the Seri and River Yumans, wore little clothing: loincloths, deerskin skirts, woven fibre aprons, twined and coiled basketry hats and sandals. The main form of body decoration was body painting and tattooing, in a wide variety of patterns, supplemented by beads. Non-agricultural groups living in upland and mountainous regions, such as the Walapai and Havasupai, wore skin shirts, breech cloths, leggings and moccasins. Women's dress consisted of a fringed skin reaching from neck to ankles under a short apron, held in place with a Hopi sash. Moccasins were worn and, in inclement weather, rabbit-skin blankets. Hunters and pastoralists, such as the Apacheans, also wore clothing made of fringed and painted skins: shirts and leggings for men; two-piece dresses for women. In warm weather men wore only breech cloths and women a short skirt. The knee-length moccasins were decorated with culturally specific designs. Hair was held in place by a buckskin or cloth band. Men occasionally wore brightly painted buckskin caps. Jewellery was predominantly beads, showing heavy Plains and Pueblo influence.

Navajo clothing has changed considerably through time. Following contact with Pueblo groups, skin clothing was replaced by cotton and then wool garments (see fig. 50). Men wore loose cotton trousers split to the knee, fastened with silver buttons. In the late 19th century solid-coloured velveteen or coloured calico shirts for both sexes, Stetson hats and blue jeans for men, and full long cotton skirts for women became standard and highly distinctive apparel. Ankle-high moccasins, fastened across the instep by a silver button, were worn by both sexes. Hair was long, tied in an hour-glass bun worn low on the neck. Long narrow handwoven belts, garters and hair ties were characteristic as decoration, combined with large quantities of silver, shell and turquoise jewellery. Manufactured blankets and coats replaced the Navajo blanket, which was itself superseded by rugs (*see* §VII, 2 above).

The agricultural Pueblo peoples relied on woven cloth for their clothing. Pueblo men wore loose white cotton trousers, loincloths or kilts—rectangular pieces of cloth wound around the waist. In cool weather a plain or embroidered poncho-style shirt, along with woven robes of rabbitskin, cotton or wool, were added. Robes were especially conspicuous at Taos Pueblo: one moiety (social clan) wore white, the other red. Most Pueblo men cut their hair in bangs (or fringes), knotted back or secured with a strip of cloth. Footless knitted stockings were worn with coloured hide and beaded moccasins. Pueblo women wore handwoven dresses that went under the left arm and fastened above the right shoulder. Called mantas, these dresses were made of black or dark blue wool, decorated along the edge in diamond or diagonal weaves, and secured around the waist by a long, narrow belt. By the 1990s a calico sleeved blouse was worn underneath, and fancy aprons were added for special occasions, while large shawls were draped over the head. Female hairstyles and footwear signify age and social status. Jewellery for both sexes included silver, shell and turquoise necklaces, belts, earrings, rings, bracelets and buttons (*see also* §VI, 2 above). Men generally made and wore more jewellery than women.

50. Navajo dress, late 19th century; the men wear headbands, cotton shirts, cloth trousers, concho belts, necklaces and moccasins; the women wear velveteen blouses, cotton skirts, shawls, woollen belts, concho belts, hair ties, silver buttons and moccasins

BIBLIOGRAPHY
C. Wissler: 'Indian Costumes in the United States: A Guide to the Study of the Collections in the Museum', *Amer. Mus. Nat. Hist. Bull.*, lxiii (1926) [whole issue]
A. Ortiz, ed.: 'Southwest', *Hb. N. Amer. Ind.*, ix (1979) [whole vol.]
——: 'Southwest', *Hb. N. Amer. Ind.*, x (1983) [whole vol.]
K. P. Kent: *Pueblo Indian Textiles: A Living Tradition* (Santa Fe, 1983)
L. S. Cordell: *Prehistory of the Southwest* (New York, 1984)

NANCY J. PAREZO

9. PLAINS. In the mid-19th century the clothing of the Plains Native American was almost exclusively made of soft tanned skins of deer, antelope, elk and buffalo. The smaller, largely untrimmed, hides were used to make shirts, leggings and dresses, which were laced or tied together with thongs or sewn with sinew. Larger hides were tanned virtually entirely and used as robes. Footwear consisted of moccasins, which at this time on both the central and northern Plains were generally made from a single piece of hide having an outer side seam and soft sole.

While there were some variations on these basic styles, ceremonial regalia was generally an elaboration of everyday wear, although the undecorated shirt had only limited distribution. Regional, frequently tribal, styles existed, however, and specialized skills and resources were transmitted through the several complex trade networks across the Plains. Certain modes of dress, ornaments and weapons were not uncommonly used by tribes who did not actually make them. Some particularly innovative centres for elaborate regalia were the Crow villages in the Yellowstone River region.

Grizzly-bear claw necklaces were sometimes worn by distinguished warriors, and both sexes wore ornaments of shells, which were obtained in trade; dentalium and discs of conch were particularly popular. Tattooing was fairly common to both sexes and employed as a sign of rank or status; it tended to be limited to the chest and arms for men and to the face for women. Hairstyles varied considerably: some of the more commonly used styles were roaching, single and double braiding, pompadour and artificial lengthening.

Typical warrior ceremonial regalia consisted of a painted buffalo robe, a quilled shirt, leggings, moccasins, a decorated bag and possibly a headdress, generally embellished with eagle feathers, ermine-skins and sometimes buffalo horns (see fig. 55 below). Additionally, bows and arrows were carried in a combined bowcase and quiver, perhaps made of otter skin and decorated with quills and beads. Robes were often painted with the wearer's exploits and also often displayed a broad band of quillwork separating the upper and lower field (*see* §XI, 3 below); such robes epitomized the fine dress clothing of the Crow. Shirts were made of two complete soft-tanned skins of the deer or bighorn sheep, each being cut into two pieces. The upper third, when folded lengthwise, formed the arms, the lower two-thirds the body; across the shoulders and down the arms were bands of quillwork—later beadwork— to the outer edges of which were attached fringes of buckskin, ermine-skins or hair. Traditionally, all these embellishments were highly symbolic. Crow shirts were often left unpainted; those of the Blackfoot were daubed with red and black earth paint; and the coveted Lakota scalp-shirt was painted blue or green at the top and yellow at the bottom.

Before *c.* 1820 women's dresses were fabricated by simply folding a rectangular-shaped piece of hide and lacing or sewing along the open side; later, this style was replaced by a garment made from two soft-tanned deer-skins with the natural contours retained, the edges were then fringed and elk teeth or beads sewn to the upper part. Children's dress, although more limited in the ceremonial context, was similar to that of their parents, not infrequently reflecting the wealth and prestige of the family.

BIBLIOGRAPHY

C. Wissler: 'Costumes of the Plains Indians', *Anthropol. Pap. Amer. Mus. Nat. Hist.*, xvii/2 (1915), pp. 39–91
R. Lowie: *Indians of the Plains* (New York, 1954)
C. Taylor: 'Analysis and Classification of the Plains Indian Ceremonial Shirt: John C. Ewers' Influence on a Plains Material Culture Project', *Fifth Annual Plains Indian Seminar: Museum of the Plains Indian: Cody, 1981*, pp. 11–40
——: 'Crow Rendezvous', *Crow Indian Art*, ed. R. Lessard and D. Lessard (Mission, SD, 1984), pp. 33–48
——: 'Early Nineteenth-century Crow Warrior Costume', *Jb. Mus. Vlkerknd. Leipzig*, xxxvii (1987), pp. 302–19
W. R. Swagerty: 'Indian Trade in the Trans-Mississippi West to 1870', *Hb. N. Amer. Ind.*, iv (1988), pp. 351–74
C. Taylor: 'Wakanyan: Symbols of Power and Ritual of the Teton Sioux', *Amerind. Cosmol.*, vii/2 (1989), pp. 237–57

COLIN TAYLOR

10. WOODLANDS. Dress and body decoration have been highly important forms of visual aesthetic expression for indigenous Woodlands peoples from pre-European contact times to the present. The dress worn on ceremonial occasions and for dances (such as the modern powwow) is the most elaborate. It consists of finely decorated clothing, jewellery, elaborate coiffures, headdresses, body painting (and, until the mid-18th century, tattooing) and hand-held objects such as decorated pouches, clubs, pipes or shawls.

The sources for the study of dress and personal adornment are highly uneven and diverse. For the pre-European contact period in the south-east Woodlands and Great Lakes evidence is mostly on archaeological materials, such as engraved representations and figural sculptures showing costumed individuals, together with rare surviving textile fragments. For other areas only pottery, shell or stone ornaments are extant. For the early historic period the sources include a small corpus of poorly documented examples of clothing and the highly Europeanized graphic representations and textual descriptions of early travellers (see fig. 51). The establishment of ethnology as a discipline in the 19th century gave rise to a literature recording indigenous material culture—including clothing manufacture—that is informed by the dominant 'vanishing Native American' paradigm of the period. There has as yet been relatively little scholarly attention paid to the continuing evolution of distinctive Native American dress in the 20th century and to the revival of local traditions.

An individual's ceremonial dress is unique and incorporates, now as in the past, tokens or motifs whose specific meanings are private and result from visionary revelations. These elements both symbolize and carry the vitally important powers bestowed by guardian spirits. Speck (1935) found that motifs applied to clothing and utensils by the eastern Cree had the purpose of pleasing the spirits of animals and inducing them to give themselves up to the hunter. Subsequent scholarship has supported his findings and argued that they apply generally to Woodlands clothing and adornment.

Changes in dress publicly signified permanent changes in an individual's status as well as periods of temporary liminality. Following a pattern general in the region people kept their hair ungroomed, wore ragged clothes and blackened their faces during puberty seclusion, on vision quests and during mourning. To marry, to prepare for death and burial or for formal meetings and celebrations an individual wore rich ornaments, fine clothes and red or coloured paints.

Materials and techniques of clothing manufacture varied in different parts of the Woodlands according to the types of animal skins and natural fibres available. In the early European contact period the most important material for clothing was animal skin. Deerskin was widely used, except in northern areas, where moose and caribou were more important. Women were highly skilled in the brain-tanning process and smoked hides to make them water-resistant. The woods used for smoking were chosen to heighten the aesthetic qualities of aroma and colour; regional preferences for shades of brown and black are evident in surviving early examples.

Women cut and sewed hides with sinew to make the basic item of male clothing, the breech cloth, as well as leggings, moccasins and untailored robes or, in the north, tailored coats. For their own use, women made kiltlike wrapped skirts or, in the Great Lakes region, a wrapped, knee-length tunic suspended from shoulder straps and therefore known as a 'strap-dress'. In cold weather they added separate sleeves tied together across chest and back like a bolero jacket.

At the time of European contact women decorated hide clothing with red, black and white mineral paints in striped, geometric or curvilinear patterns; they also ornamented seams and borders with quill embroidery or woven quillwork appliqués (*see* §XI, 4 below). Some south-eastern peoples used cultivated fibres to weave or twine skirts, robes and 'shawls'. They also made elaborate feather cloaks on backings of netted fibre. North-eastern groups twined nettlestalk (Indian hemp) fibre into garters, sashes and pouches, which were often embellished with dyed animal hair, porcupine quills and shell beads.

Contact with Europeans brought about important changes in Woodlands dress. Native American peoples found European manufactures highly attractive, and traders strove to supply trade goods that satisfied their tastes.

51. Woodlands region dress depicted in *A Weroan or Great Lorde of Virginia.III.*, engraving by Theodor de Bry after John White, 149×216 mm (London, British Library); from Thomas Harriot: *A Brief and True Report of the New Found Land of Virginia* (London, 1590)

Early contact-period clothing displays a general preference for red, black and dark-blue wool cloth that conformed to established pre-contact colour usages. People also appreciated the bright, luminous textures and colours of metal ornaments, glass beads and silk ribbon. By the late 18th century these materials had begun to replace hide, porcupine quills and paint in many places. European shirts and coats also became popular additions to dress, although basic garment styles did not change radically until the 19th century.

During the mid-19th century trousers and coats for men and longer skirts and smock dresses for women came to replace earlier garments. A new design vocabulary that innovatively combined Euro-American floral and geometric motifs with indigenous design concepts replaced earlier motifs. During this period, too, policies of directed assimilation actively repressed indigenous religious practices and the ceremonial dress worn by participants.

Native Americans invented new kinds of 'special occasion dress', which, towards the end of the 19th century, increasingly featured pan-Native American elements such as fringing, headbands and feather bonnets derived from stereotypical Plains Native American clothing (*see* §9 above). This dress continued to be worn in pageants and on official occasions into the 1960s. The revitalization of indigenous cultural life after the 1950s brought a renewed interest in local rather than pan-Native American clothing traditions, and a new historicism in clothing was increasingly seen at modern Woodlands powwows and public events.

BIBLIOGRAPHY

F. G. Speck: *Naskapi: The Savage Hunters of the Labrador Peninsula* (1935/R Norman, 1977)

J. R. Swanton: 'The Indians of the South-eastern United States', *Bureau Amer. Ethnol. Bull.*, cxxxvii (1946/R Washington, DC, 1979) [whole issue]

A. Tanner: *Bringing Home Animals: Religious Ideology and Mode of Production of the Mistassini Cree Hunters* (New York, 1979)

T. J. Brasser: 'Pleasing the Spirits: Indian Art around the Great Lakes', *Pleasing the Spirits: A Catalogue of a Collection of American Indian Art*, D. C. Ewing (New York, 1982)

J. C. H. King: *Thunderbird and Lightning: Indian Life in North-eastern North America, 1600–1900* (London, 1982)

R. B. Phillips: ' "Like a Star I Shine": Northern Woodlands Artistic Traditions', *The Spirit Sings: Artistic Traditions of Canada's First Peoples* (Toronto, 1987)

Downs D.: *Art of the Florida Seminole and Miccosukee Indians* (Gainesville, 1995)

RUTH B. PHILLIPS

IX. Beadwork and shellwork.

Beads and pendants were made by virtually all Native American peoples before European contact. A variety of materials was used: stone, bone, teeth, shell and in some areas copper. Wood and other plant materials may also have been used, but they have not survived in the archaeological record. Complex trade networks developed to distribute shells, in particular from the Atlantic or Pacific coast to inland cultures. From the 16th century, after initial contact with European cultures, glass and china trade beads of many colours were distributed rapidly throughout the continent. Opaque china 'pony beads', so called because they arrived on traders' ponies, were *c.* 3.2 mm in diameter, while glass 'seed beads' were even smaller (diam *c.* 1.6 mm). These beads were used widely, replacing traditional materials and influencing the development of Native American designs on everyday and ceremonial garments and accoutrements (*see* BEADWORK, colour pl. I, fig. 1).

1. Arctic. 2. Subarctic. 3. Northwest Coast. 4. California. 5. Southwest. 6. Plains. 7. Woodlands.

1. ARCTIC. Evidence of Arctic shellwork is rare when compared with beadwork. Since the introduction of glass beads from Siberia and Europe, the Inuit have made ingenious use of beads in virtually all their design work. The colourful, linear nature of design in beadwork has also provided inspiration for Inuit graphic art. Traditionally, Pacific Coast abalone shells were traded as far north as Alaska in historic times and were used in personal adornment and in sculpture. Crab shells were also used to make belts in Alaska. Beadwork gained popularity among the Alaskan Inuit with the introduction of trade beads from Siberia. Beads were used to trim almost all Aleut and Inuit products: fur clothing, baskets, hats, headdresses, ivory and wood carvings and sculpture, necklaces, masks and facial jewellery. Items made entirely of beads included ceremonial hats and bands, belts, necklaces and neck- and arm-bands.

In the western Canadian Arctic, blue beads from Siberia were obtained by the Mackenzie-area Inuit from the Alaskan Inuit and were used in hairdressing and in making labrets, earrings, needle cases and men's pipes. Strings of white and blue trade seed beads were used to wrap women's long plaited hair. Dentalium shells from the Pacific were acquired from Athapaskan peoples and were also used in earrings and hairdressing.

In the central Canadian Arctic, during the 19th century, women's plaited hair was wrapped with stroud cloth (European cloth manufactured specifically for Native American trade) adorned with beads obtained through European traders. Elaborate patterns of beadwork were also sewn on to brightly coloured cloth backings, which were then applied to the front panels of the *amautik* or mother's parka (*see* §VIII, 2 above). The inventive and novel beadwork designs of the Inuit seamstress ranged in motif from depictions of tea kettles through high-heeled shoes and ribboned bows to compasses—all icons of the whaling period. Beads were not easily obtainable in the central Arctic until the Hudson Bay outposts began trading them in the 20th century. Beads of violet, green, scarlet, pink, turquoise, lemon, white, black and orange were shipped to the trading-posts in great quantities, and they were used by the Central and Eastern Arctic Inuit in personal adornment and in the decoration of parkas.

In the eastern Canadian Arctic, during the 18th and 19th centuries, the abundance of glass trade beads inspired the creation of elaborate beaded ear ornaments among the Inuit in Labrador. By the mid-19th century beads were a popular trade commodity throughout the eastern Arctic. In the Baffin area beads were strung from shoulder to

shoulder across the front of the *atigi* (inner parka) to form simple patterns of horizontal, coloured bands.

Important collections are held in Seattle, WA (Thomas Burke Mem. WA State Mus.), Juneau, AL (State Mus.), Anchorage, AL (Hist. & F.A. Mus.), Washington, DC (Smithsonian Inst.), New York (Amer. Mus. Nat. Hist.), Toronto (Royal Ont. Mus.), Ottawa (Can. Mus. Civiliz.), Winnipeg (Mannitoba Mus. Man & Nat.), London (BM), Oxford U. (Pitt Rivers Mus.) and Copenhagen (Nmus.).

BIBLIOGRAPHY

D. J. Ray: *Aleut and Eskimo Art: Tradition and Innovation in South Alaska* (Seattle, 1977/*R* Seattle and London, 1981)
R. L. Shalkop: 'Introduction', *Contemporary Native Art of Alaska from the Collection of the Anchorage Historical and Fine Arts Museum* (Anchorage, 1979)
B. Driscoll and G. Swinton: *The Inuit Amautik: I Like my Hood to Be Full* (Winnipeg, 1980)
D. J. Ray: *Eskimo Art: Tradition and Innovation in North Alaska* (Seattle, 1980)
J. Highwater: *Arts of the Indian Americas* (New York, 1983)
B. Driscoll: 'The Inuit Parka', *The Spirit Sings: Artistic Traditions of Canada's First Peoples* (Toronto, 1987)

JOANNE DANFORD-CORDINGLEY

2. SUBARCTIC. Ornamentation of clothing was traditionally the primary art form across the Subarctic, and beads were the most important medium for this in the western and central Subarctic among Algonquian- and Athapaskan-speaking peoples (*see* §§VIII, 3 above and XI, 2 below). The Naskapi of Labrador preferred painting their garments and thus produced only a little beadwork. Shells were rarely used in the Subarctic, except for a short time in the 19th century by western Athapaskans.

(i) Eastern and central. In these regions European-made glass seed beads were introduced early in the 19th century, along with needles, thread and European embroidery traditions, through European trading companies and missionaries. The art of couched floral beadwork quickly spread north and west. As schools were established (beginning in the 1820s in the Cree–Ojibwa Lake Winnipeg area, in the 1860s among the Athapaskans), ministers' wives and nuns taught girls 'fancy work'. Floral beadwork and, in some places, silkwork (*see* §X, 2 below) quickly became important art forms.

Women with closer connection to trading-posts and schools became especially proficient in needlework. In some regions, particularly the Cree–Ojibwa area around Lake Winnipeg, the Metis (of mixed Native American–European descent) became known for their colourfully ornamented clothing and love of floral embroidery. Brasser (1985) called most Subarctic beadwork Metis work; Duncan (1989), citing both Native American and mixed-blood participation in the art and the changing, imprecise use of the term Metis, argued that tribal names (e.g. Cree) must be used in beadwork attribution, with Metis appended (e.g. Cree or Cree-Metis) in areas where mixed-bloods called themselves Metis. In some regions mixed bloods used tribal names rather than the term Metis.

In the central Subarctic, anyone might wear beaded moccasins, but men were the primary users of most beadwork. Women beaded leggings, garters, mittens, gloves, jackets and shot pouches or firebags (for fire-starting implements) for their husbands. In the latter category, the panel bag, a fabric pouch with a woven bead panel below (e.g. Toronto, Royal Ont. Mus., 960.115.2), became established early in the 19th century among Cree and Ojibwa. The 'octopus' bag, a fabric pouch with four sets of free-standing tabs below (e.g. Winnipeg, Manitoba Mus. Man & Nat., H.40.734), was a favourite Cree or Cree-Metis type during the second half of the century.

In the second half of the 19th century in the central Subarctic, silkwork was also important, and bead and floss designs were often closely related. Several recognizable Cree or Cree-Metis floral styles developed. Cree women in the James Bay area wore rectangular fabric hoods beaded with multiple borders of flowered serpentine stems (e.g. Hull, Qué., Can. Mus. Civiliz., II-D-572). Floral sprays characterized by cascading lobes alone or behind petals and leaves appeared on panel bags (e.g. Washington, DC, Mus. Amer. Ind., 17-6924) and other objects c. 1900.

(ii) Western. Large glass beads came to the Alaskan coast through Russian trade late in the 18th century. They soon made their way inland and were welcomed by the Athapaskan inhabitants. In 1847–8 Alexander Murray, who established the Hudson's Bay post at Fort Yukon, sketched and described heavily beaded garments worn by the western Athapaskan who traded there. On slightly later tunics, 'pony' or necklace beads, strung in blocks, were often alternated with blocks of dentalium shells (e.g. Washington, DC, N. Mus. Amer. Hist., 4971). The placement of materials and often the designs reflected long-established pre-contact quillwork traditions (*see* §XI, 2 below). While still rare, beads and dentalia were valuable and for a time functioned as currency; those of stature literally wore their wealth.

In the eastern Athapaskan area white seed beads were first used about the mid-19th century, to edge decorative wool-appliqué borders on hide tunics and bags (e.g. Hull, Qué., Can. Mus. Civiliz. VI-N-3). As the Hudson's Bay Company established a network of posts on Lake Athapaska, Great Slave Lake and down the Mackenzie River, mission schools followed after c. 1850. As in the Cree–Ojibwa area, floral needlework, especially beadwork, was encouraged. By the 1890s women across the entire Athapaskan region were producing beadwork, and distinct regional styles had developed. In the Great Slave Lake–Mackenzie River Region, direct European-based teaching was the strongest, and designs, beaded on black velvet, were closely related to European needlework. Ornate formal bouquets in shaded pastels touched with metal accents ornamented moccasins and mittens, baby moss bags and carrying straps; valances and wall-pockets for household use; and, for men, jackets, hunting bags, tobacco pouches and sets of sled dog blankets displayed on special occasions (see fig. 52).

In Yukon–Tanana Region collections (e.g. Berkeley, U. CA, Hearst Mus. Anthropol., 2-2636), sled bags, gun cases, hunting shirts, jackets and gold pokes (for carrying gold dust) dominate, all beaded rather sparsely with simple, outlined, loosely foliate motifs, united by dominant skeletal stem networks against an open hide or wool background. Colours contrast and often cut across motifs transversely or longitudinally.

Liard–Fraser Region beadwork is typically dense, exuberant and openly experimental in colour use and motif

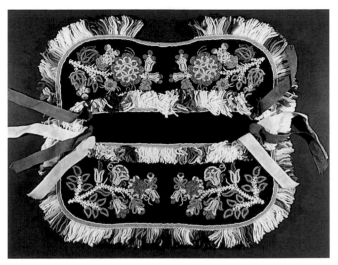

52. Subarctic beadwork on a dog blanket, seed and metal beads couched on to black velvet, with wool-yarn fringes and cotton-canvas backing, 524×508 mm, from the Great Slave Lake–Mackenzie River Athapaskan region, c. 1912 (Montreal, McGill University, McCord Museum)

combination. Designs themselves demonstrate the process of their development, with the contours of established motifs, inspiring new shapes. Sled bags and eared, ruffed firebags (Hull, Qué., Can. Mus. Civiliz., VI-M-2) dominate, and each example is different.

Tahltan beadwork is of two types: a floral style reflects the influence of Cree or Cree-Metis in British Columbia at the end of the 19th century and appears on firebags and knife cases (e.g. Victoria, Royal BC Mus., 14825); and a classic geometric style is based on earlier art forms. Most beadwork is on ceremonial regalia, and the classic style dominates. Panels of angular geometric motifs, which are also found on spruce-root baskets of the neighbouring non-Athapaskan Tlingit tribe, are woven directly on to hide firebags and knife sheaths (e.g. Hull, Qué., Can. Mus. Civiliz., and Victoria, Royal BC Mus.). These same motifs become curvilinear abstract forms when outlined on fabric panels applied to such bags, and to jackets and ceremonial cartridge belts. Classic Tahltan designs often alternate lines of white beads with red, blue or black ones, in an elegant, precisely controlled balance.

Early 20th-century Inland Tlingit bead designs and those of neighbouring Tlingit are hard to distinguish (*see* §3 below). Both outline entire groups of blossoms and cartouche-like leaves in a single band of beads, changing colour with each implied part. Designs on Inland Tlingit octopus bags, moccasins, wall-pockets (e.g. Hull, Qué., Can. Mus. Civiliz., VI-J-5) and shirts are often slightly more angular. Western peripheral Athapaskan groups, such as the Tanana and Ingalik, produced little beadwork.

Beadwork, made both for family and friends, and to sell in craft shops, remains important in the Subarctic. Motifs are usually floral and maintain reference to earlier ones. Among the Cree–Ojibwa, moccasins and pouches dominate. Athapaskans make moccasins, small pouches, barrettes and earrings, all objects that require little or no hard-to-obtain hide. Fort Rae women bead duffle coats.

Baby belts are made at Fort Yukon, and woven-bead ones are made and used at Fort McPherson.

BIBLIOGRAPHY

A. H. Murray: 'Journal of the Yukon, 1847–48', *Pubns Can. Archvs*, iv (1910), pp. 1–125
J. Honigman: 'Expressive Aspects of Subarctic Indian Culture', *Hb. N. Amer. Ind.*, vi (1981), pp. 718–38
J. VanStone: *Athapaskan Clothing and Related Objects in the Collection of the Field Museum of Natural History* (Chicago, 1981)
T. J. Brasser: 'In Search of Metis Art', *The New Peoples: Being and Becoming Metis in North America*, ed. J. Peterson and J. Brown (Winnipeg, 1985), pp. 221–9
W. E. Simeone with J. VanStone: *And He Was Beautiful: Contemporary Athapaskan Material Culture in the Collections of the Field Museum of Natural History* (Chicago, 1986)
The Spirit Sings: Artistic Traditions of Canada's First Peoples (exh. cat., Calgary, Glenbow–Alta. Inst., 1987) [many early examples from Eur. collections]
K. C. Duncan and E. Carney: *A Special Gift: The Kutchin Beadwork Tradition* (Seattle, 1988)
K. C. Duncan: *Northern Athapaskan Art: A Beadwork Tradition* (Seattle and London, 1989)
B. A. Hail and K. C. Duncan: *Out of the North: The Subarctic Collection of the Haffenreffer Museum of Anthropology* (Providence, RI, 1989)

3. NORTHWEST COAST. Shells were important in northern Northwest Coast art from long before European contact. Prehistorically mussel shells were worked to form knives, celts, harpoon and adze blades. Later, Northern and central Northwest Coast people used abalone shells from California on ceremonial clothing, particularly to form the centres of eye ovoids on formline designs painted on hide garments and on appliquéd button blankets. In the 19th century abalone often edged a northern dancing frontlet (e.g. Philadelphia, U. PA, NA 9474) or formed

53. Northwest Coast beaded garments and Chilkat blankets worn by Tlingit hosts and Yakutat guests at the Sitka potlatch, 9 December 1904 (New York, American Museum of Natural History)

the pupils of the eyes on a bowl, mask or headdress frontlet (*see* SHELL, colour pl. II, fig. 1). Locally available red-turban opercula shells were spaced along the upper edges of bent-wood bowls (e.g. St Petersburg, Peter the Great Mus. Anthropol. & Ethnog., 337-28) and on the fronts of chest and box lids. Opercula were also inlaid to form teeth on Tlingit masks. The Tlingit also occasionally sewed folded bands of porcupine quills on to hide tunics and shamans' hats and aprons (*see* §XI, 2 below). Dentalium (*haiqua*) shells, a symbol of wealth, sometimes ornamented button blankets. On the southern coast shells were used less often. The Salish made rattles of scallop shells hung on a ring. By the 19th century Columbia River people were wearing jewellery made from dentalia and beads.

Although glass beads were available to Northwest Coast peoples by the late 18th century, they were rarely used until the later 19th century. About 1880 glass seed beads became important for the ornament of Tlingit dance shirts, bibs and tabbed 'octopus' bags worn on ceremonial occasions (e.g. Washington, DC, N. Mus. Amer. Indian; Sitka, AK, Sheldon Jackson Mus.; Juneau, AK, State Mus.). Cree and Athapaskan influences are evident in the Tlingit beadwork style (*see* §2 above). An open, fluid foliate-scroll style of couched beadwork developed, in which entire foliate-like sprays were outlined in a continuous line of beads, with the colour changing with each implied leaf, blossom or bud. Multicoloured crest figures were also beaded, especially on bibs.

The need for ceremonial clothing by the newly wealthy who lacked inherited regalia of painted skin or Chilkat weaving (*see* §VII, 1 above) may help explain the sudden popularity of beaded items late in the 19th century. Photographs of that time of potlatch ceremonies (extravagant gift-giving occasions for rank validation) picture quantities of beadwork (see fig. 53). At the same time, the popularity of travel up the Inside Passage created a tourist market for mementos, and Tlingit women beaded hundreds of moccasins, wall-pockets and small pouches to sell to visitors (e.g. Washington, DC, N. Mus. Amer. Indian). Beadwork remained an important art form among the Tlingit, especially for ceremonial regalia, and some women have become renowned for their work.

Beadwork was far less prominent among tribes living to the south of the Tlingit. Appliqué forms were sometimes edged with white beads on 19th-century Tsimshian leggings (e.g. Washington, DC, N. Mus. Amer. Indian, 91855); and 20th-century Kwakiutl dance aprons may incorporate beaded foliate forms (e.g. Victoria, Royal BC Mus., 12844). Several elaborately beaded late 19th-century Salish spirit dance garments are also known (e.g. Seattle, WA, Thomas Burke Mem. WA State Mus., BM 1-11479).

BIBLIOGRAPHY

F. deLaguna: *Under Mt St Elias* (Washington, DC, 1972) [Tlingit potlatch photographs]
K. C. Duncan: *Northern Athapaskan Art: A Beadwork Tradition* (Seattle and London, 1989) [Tlingit style]
W. Suttles, ed.: 'Northwest Coast', *Hb. N. Amer. Ind.*, vii (1990) [whole vol.]
J. Thompson: 'Some Curious Dresses of the Natives: A Re-examination of Some Early Garments from the Alaskan Coast', *Amer. Ind. A.*, xvi/3 (1991), pp. 66–76

KATE C. DUNCAN

54. Californian beadwork and shellwork on a Costanoan- (Ohlone-) style basket of sedge-root sewing strands, willow rods and Acorn Woodpecker scalp feathers, decorated with olivella-shell disc beads, h. 64 mm, diam. 241 mm, c. 1800 (London, British Museum)

4. CALIFORNIA. Beadwork and shellwork are popular art forms of Californian Native American peoples. Beads were produced and used as an item of adornment, particularly on baskets (see fig. 54), and exchange for more than 5000 years. Distinctive regional styles developed before European contact, and surviving examples were produced primarily of shell or stone. By the time of intensive contact with Europeans in the 18th century, these styles were centred in three regions. South coast peoples used small discoidal beads made from olivella (*Olivella biplicata*), whole olivella beads, a variety of abalone (*Haliotis*; mother-of-pearl) shell ornaments, and other beads and ornaments of a variety of shells and of steatite. Larger tubes and pendants of steatite were often inlaid with shell beads. Peoples in central California used entire olivella-shell beads and discs, as well as more numerous disc beads made of the Washington clam shell (*Saxidomus nuttailli*) and abalone shell ornaments, while in the southern Sierra Nevada steatite disc beads were made, and in the Clear Lake region of the Coast Range tubes and beads of baked magnesite were produced. In northern California, clam-shell beads were obtained in trade from the south, while dentalium shells (*Dentalium pretiosum*) were obtained in trade from further north. Dentalia were used in conjunction with beads of bull pine (*Pinus sabiniana*) and juniper (*Juniperus occidentalis*) seeds. Nearly all of these bead types in all areas were traded throughout California and beyond.

Glass beads were brought to California early in the 18th century, and by the early 19th century simple necklaces were common. The Pomo and Costanoan were using them to decorate their finest baskets in place of shell beads. By the 1840s Nisenan and Miwok peoples were weaving glass beads into belts and chokers, much as the Pomo had previously used clam-shell disc beads. By the late 1860s woven beadwork, in the form of loom-woven or loose-warp woven bands, was in use in California, made of glass pony beads. As early as 1872 the Mono Lake Paiute were making net beaded collars; and, by 1900, woven bands were being made by a variety of California peoples, particularly those in the north and east.

A northern style of beadwork, using a set of patterns primarily from the eastern USA, was practised by, but not limited to, the Atsugewi, Achomawi, Modoc, Northeastern Maidu and Northern Paiute. Warps and wefts are black or white commercial thread, and the favoured bead colours include black, white and transparent or translucent dark greens, reds and blues. Using the loose-warp technique, purses, baskets and bottles were covered with beadwork. The Mono Lake Paiute, c. 1908, developed a style of netted beadwork to cover baskets; by the 1920s the Washoe, other Paiute and Western Shoshone had also adopted the style.

In the 1960s many of these beadwork styles persisted, although fewer people made shell disc beads. During this time many people relearnt beadwork from Native American art and craft books. Many Yurok, Karok and Hupa people made necklaces of native and glass beads for sale and for their own use. By the 1970s they and others extended beadwork to such things as key-chains, hair barrettes, plastic combs, cigarette cases and caps. In the 1980s the same styles persisted, with some craftsmen creating beadwork based on their own imagination and not on any identifiable tribal style.

BIBLIOGRAPHY
E. Gifford: *California Shell Artifacts*, Anthropological Records, ix/1 (Berkeley, 1947)
C. Bates: 'Beaded Baskets of the Washoe, Paiute and Western Shoshone', *Moccasin Tracks*, v/1 (1978), pp. 4–7
——: 'Beadwork in the Far West: The Continuation of an Eastern Tradition', *Moccasin Tracks*, vi/6 (1979), pp. 4–9, 13
C. D. Bates and M. J. Lee: *Tradition and Innovation: A Basketry History of the Indians of Yosemite-Mono Lake Area* (Yosemite N. Park, CA, 1990)
CRAIG D. BATES

5. SOUTHWEST. During the long pre-agricultural occupation of the Southwest, hunter–gatherers made ornaments of the natural materials they found attractive.

Animal claws and teeth, pieces of bone, stone, wood and horn were drilled and worn as pendants. Sometimes these were ground into simple shapes, such as discs or rectangles, occasionally with engraved geometric patterns. By at least 6000 BC these Desert-culture people were importing shell from the coast of the Gulf of California and from the Pacific coast. Small olivella shells (*Olivella biplicata*) were sometimes strung on knotted cordage and worn as necklaces. Nevertheless, it does not appear that the people of the Desert-culture, who also occupied the Great Basin area, modified and sculpted shell to the extent that their agricultural descendants did.

From *c.* AD 200 the agricultural Hohokam, Mogollon and Anasazi cultures and their neighbours, while sharing with each other much of their basic jewellery repertory, each produced stylistically distinct ornaments as well. Common to the Southwest cultures was the production of round disc beads of shell and claystone, shaped geometric pendants of shell, stone, turquoise and bone—probably worn most commonly as ear pendants—and bracelets and finger-rings of shell, bone and occasionally stone. All of these cultures produced mosaic jewellery by glueing small pieces of turquoise, shell and stone to shell or wood backings; and all used bone hairpins decorated with engraving or turquoise mosaic.

The Hohokam are most notable for their work in shell, and it was they who imported much of the shell traded on to the Mogollon and Anasazi, who lived further from the coast. Using principally a large cockle-like shell, the Hohokam produced many flat pendants filed into disc, rectangle or doughnut shapes. More distinctively, they also produced a menagerie of animal forms. Birds, snakes and lizards are usually rendered as flat silhouettes with minimal detail; but some bird pendants and most quadruped pendants show large, round eyes and engraved lines, indicating feathers, legs or toes. Quadrupeds show lines of drill pits to indicate teeth and an animated, flying-gallop pose. Heavy clamlike shells were pierced to form bracelets and in some cases have raised portions with carved decoration, often taking the form of a frog or a bird, or pair of birds, grasping a rattlesnake in their beaks. During the period *c.* AD 900–*c.* 1150 the Hohokam invented a technique for etching designs on shell, using cactus-fruit acid to etch and tree pitch to resist the acid and form the design.

Mogollon craftsmen seem to have followed Hohokam designs for much of their history. Many shell pieces found in early Mogollon villages may be identified as trade pieces from the Hohokam by the clear and uniform style characteristic of most Hohokam pieces. But, later, Mogollon craftsmen in larger villages in the mountains produced some creditable work of their own in stone and shell. By the period *c.* AD 1150–*c.* 1400 the mountain villagers were producing many small animal pendants, made of various kinds of stone.

After European contact, Southwest Native American jewellery became largely based on silverworking traditions introduced by the Spanish in the late 16th century and the 17th, but turquoise, shell and stone beads and pendants continue to be made and in some cases retain their ceremonial significance (*see* §VI, 2 above).

BIBLIOGRAPHY
E. W. Jernigan: *Jewelry of the Prehistoric Southwest* (Santa Fe, 1978)
                                          E. WESLEY JERNIGAN

6. PLAINS. Before European trade goods reached the Plains, dried berries, shells, claws and animal teeth were made into necklaces and pendants attached to garments. Dentalium shells from the west coast reached the Plains along Native American trade routes. Elk teeth were popular and remained so into the second half of the 20th century. Long tubular bone beads were made by the Sioux, who used them to make breast plates. Glass and porcelain beads from Venice, England and Holland became available to the Great Lakes Native Americans as early as 1600; they reached the north-western Plains in the late 18th century. These early beads were large and thus suitable for necklaces, wristlets and hair ornaments.

About 1800 fur traders introduced opaque china beads of *c.* 3 mm in diameter. They were called 'pony beads' because they arrived in the pony pack trains of the traders. Blue and white beads were most popular, but black and red beads were available as well. Some tribes along the upper Missouri River fashioned beads more to their liking by melting down these pony beads and reshaping them. The size of these beads enabled Native American women to use them in embroidery on garments, but they were neither small enough nor available in sufficiently large numbers to replace the indigenous embroidery using dyed porcupine quills (*see* §XI, 3 below). Pony beads were used to create simple geometric designs; and blue pony beads were used to outline porcupine quillwork.

55. Plains region Blackfoot men from Browning, Montana, showing the use of floral and geometric beadwork designs to decorate clothing as well as other items, such as the tobacco-bag carried by the man in the centre; photograph by De Lancey Gill, 1916 (Washington, DC, Smithsonian Institution)

The introduction of fine steel needles enabled Plains women to use very small glass beads, which became available in a wide range of colours by 1840. These 'seed beads' were about half the size of pony beads, allowing the creation of delicate patterns. As a result the more time-consuming quillwork gradually disappeared. Plains sewing techniques were adapted to the new media, but new techniques were developed as well. In the northern Plains the 'overlay' or 'spot stitch' became most popular, whereas the 'lazy stitch' was typical for the central Plains; the netted 'gourd stitch' was used on the southern Plains and woven beadwork was practised along the eastern margins of the region, primarily by tribes that originated from further east.

After the 1860s beadwork designs became more complex, and both regional styles and tribal peculiarities emerged. Geometric and angular designs remained dominant, but floral patterns of a Great Lakes origin became popular on the northern Plains (see fig. 55) and in the eastern prairie region. Central Plains beadwork of the 1870s may have been influenced by geometric patterns on the oriental rugs used by Euro-American settlers. In the same region a pictorial style emerged in lazy-stitch beadwork, showing realistic representations of humans and animals. Whereas beadwork of the northern and central Plains proliferated to cover garments and horse trappings, beadwork on the southern Plains remained almost restricted to simple geometric designs in narrow bands along the edges of garments. It is mainly on Kiowa cradleboards and the paraphernalia of the Peyote cult that more complex beadwork became noticeable in this sub-region.

By 1900 the great period of beadwork was over, yet in almost every Native American community there are still women who continue to create beadworked costumes for use at powwows and similar festivals.

BIBLIOGRAPHY
B. A. Hail: *Hau, Kola! The Plains Collection of the Haffenreffer Museum of Anthropology* (Brown U., Bristol, RI, 1980)
E. M. Maurer: 'Visions of the People', *A Pictorial History of Plains Indian Life* (exh. cat., ed. E. M. Maurer; Minneapolis, MN, Inst. A.; St Louis, MO, A. Mus.; Omaha, NE, Joslyn A. Mus.; 1992–3), pp. 15–45

T. J. BRASSER

7. WOODLANDS. Woodlands Americans from the Yukon River to the Atlantic coast embellished clothing and other articles with coloured trade beads, dyed porcupine quills and moose and caribou hair. Long before Europeans introduced glass beads, the shiny, hollow quills of the porcupine (*Erethizon dorsatum* in the east and *E. epixanthum* in the west) were dyed with a variety of vegetal materials and worked into designs on skin and birch-bark (*see* §XI, 4 below). A technique unique to the Woodlands was loom weaving, in which flattened quills were worked into a net of cross-woven sinew strung on a bow; when the soft quills are compressed together they look like cylindrical beads.

Glass trade seed beads were sewn throughout the Woodlands area by couching or spot-stitching, at first with sinew and later (*c.* 1650) with commercial thread. Beads were strung on a strand of sinew and arranged to form a design, then stitched in place with a second strand. The technique produces a smooth surface and is very flexible. Common patterns among the eastern tribes include open

56. Woodlands region bandolier bag decorated with trade beads sewn on cloth, 559×406 mm (pouch), made by the Anishinabe tribe, Western Great Lakes, *c.* 1900 (Santa Fe, NM, School of American Research)

foliate patterns and lacy designs with many scrolls. The Iroquois also developed 'embossed' beadwork from about 1860, with raised leaf designs, often padded with paper. The technique was used to decorate caps and pouches, and also on pin-cushions to sell to tourists.

Among the Great Lakes peoples, beads were sewn on pouches, moccasins, leggings, shirts and other clothing. Early patterns were linear and used few beads, but, when beads became more plentiful in the mid-19th century, designs became larger and much more complex. Large designs in many colours represent leaves, flowers and fruits in a semi-realistic style. The most distinctive use of beads in the Great Lakes region was in the large bandolier bags; early examples were woven with geometric designs, but later bags are decorated with dense, elaborate, sewn foliate motifs (see fig. 56). Woven beadwork in a variety of techniques was developed in the Woodlands to produce garters, sashes and arm-bands with complex geometric designs.

Both woven geometric designs and sewn foliate patterns are still produced by Woodlands peoples. The sewn floral patterns were adopted by the western Subarctic peoples and developed into a variety of complex and brilliant styles to decorate their garments of cloth and skin (see §2 above). The floral patterns here tend to be formed with smaller units and more colours than are usually found on the beadwork of the Great Lakes, and they are more often bilaterally symmetrical.

Shells were used from earliest times as scrapers; examples of flat shells carved with effigy faces have been found at archaeological sites (e.g. Potomac Creek, VA); and shells were shaped and drilled into rounded and long and short cylindrical beads. Both animal teeth (e.g. bear, elk) and single large, flat shells were drilled and worn as pendants and gorgets.

Sources for shell included both local coasts and the Atlantic and Great Lakes shores. Atlantic shells were traded inland through a wide-ranging network of middlemen; and shell beads eventually became a medium of exchange, until replaced by wampum from about the 16th century. Wampum beads were strung on hemp between buckskin thongs and arranged into strips or 'belts'. The most commonly used shells for wampum were quahog shells (*Mercenaria mercenaria* for 'black'—actually purple) and whelks (*Busycon carica*, *Busycon canaliculatum* and *Buccinum undatum* for white) from south-eastern Atlantic coasts. The cylindrical shell beads were woven into various geometrical patterns or with repetitive stylized figures and were used as 'currency', as symbolic gifts and as the seal of political alliance in intertribal councils.

BIBLIOGRAPHY

D. Snow: *The Archaeology of North America: American Indians and their Origins* (London and New York, 1976, rev. 1980)
B. G. Trigger, ed.: 'Northeast', *Hb. N. Amer. Ind.*, xv (1978) [whole vol.]

ANDREW HUNTER WHITEFORD

X. Embroidery.

Native Americans used a variety of embroidery materials, both indigenous and introduced, to embellish tanned leather, birch-bark and cloth, to decorate clothing, horse trappings, household objects, tepees and even sacred paraphernalia. Techniques included true sewn embroidery, fringing and false embroidery (external weft wrap).

1. Introduction. 2. Subarctic. 3. Plateau. 4. Woodlands.

1. INTRODUCTION. Before European contact, Native American embroiderers used leather, porcupine and bird quills, feathers, shell and bone, vegetable fibres and animal hair. The use of hair for embroidery by some northeastern Siberian peoples may indicate an ancient Old World connection in the tradition. A widespread form was leather fringe, whether cut directly into the basic object itself or from added pieces. Fringes were often long and very fine, and sometimes each strand was itself embroidered with wrappings of quills, vegetable fibres or other material. In the southern Great Plains two-ply 'twisted fringes', resembling fine cord, were made and attached to clothing, fan handles and other objects. All species of North American native deer have rump patches of hollow white hair that dyes readily and thus was a favourite embroidery medium throughout the northern half of the continent. It was preferred in the north-eastern Woodlands for embroidering black-dyed leather garments. Another widespread material was porcupine quill, also hollow and easily dyed, and applied to many objects in many ways (*see* §XI below). For example, in the Plateau region, bunches of horsehair were wrapped with quills of several colours and placed side by side to decorate panels on men's shirts. Bird quills were used to some extent in the central Plains, generally split lengthwise and trimmed. Small feathers or bits of fluff were often used in conjunction with porcupine quill, especially in the Great Plains. In California, whole Red Woodpecker scalps were massed in decorating ritual headdresses. Vegetable fibres were used for decorating leather clothing in the western USA, especially in California. These included Maidenhair Fern rib, split Beargrass leaves and others. In those regions where indigenous weaving was established, cloth was embroidered with native fibre yarns, feathers and other materials.

After European contact, glass beads were imported in great numbers, and beadwork on clothing and other items is known over most of North America (*see* §IX above). In the Midwest, Native Americans used silk ribbon to create distinctive appliqués by cutting repeated figures from one ribbon and sewing it over another of contrasting colour. Other trade materials, such as metal sequins, brass tacks and buttons, were also widely used for decoration. Along the Northwest Coast, ritual blankets were made by sewing heraldic figures of flannel to woollen blankets and then edging the former with rows of mother-of-pearl buttons. These replaced the iridescent marine shell plaques used earlier.

Over time, there has been a continuous development of embroidery styles, reflecting changes in taste, materials most available and innovations. For example, floral design arose from a mixture of Native American and European ideas in 17th-century eastern Canada and has since established itself over much of the continent. Considerable quantities of Native American embroidery are still produced today.

BIBLIOGRAPHY

W. C. Orchard: *The Technique of Porcupine-quill Decoration among the North American Indians*, Contributions from the Museum of the American Indian, Heye Foundation, iv/1 (New York, 1916/R 1971), pp. 1–53
——: *Beads and Beadwork of the American Indian: A Study Based on Specimens in the Museum of the American Indian, Heye Foundation*, Contributions from the Museum of the American Indian, Heye Foundation, xi (New York, 1929/R 1975)

K. P. Kent: 'The Cultivation and Weaving of Cotton in the Prehistoric Southwestern United States', *Trans. Amer. Philos. Soc.*, n. s., xlvii/3 (1957) [whole issue]
R. G. Conn: *Native American Art in the Denver Museum* (Denver, 1979)
K. C. Duncan: *North Athapaskan Art: A Beadwork Tradition* (Seattle and London, 1989)

RICHARD G. CONN

2. SUBARCTIC. When mission schools were established in the Subarctic in the 19th century, the European art of fancy needlework was taught to Native American and mixed-blood girls (*see* §IX, 2 above). In the central Subarctic, among the Cree and Cree–Metis, silk embroidery became especially popular and continued to be so well into the 20th century. At the end of the 19th century moccasins and slippers, wall-pockets (a hanging pocketed object for holding domestic items, such as letters or combs, in a dwelling with few drawers, which also served as a wall decoration), pouches, picture frames and lamp pads of hide, delicately silk-embroidered, were sold to visitors to the Red River colony at Selkirk and remote locations on Lake Winnipeg accessible only by steamer (examples in Providence, RI, Haffenraffer Mus. Anthropol.).

Two Cree–Cree-Metis styles that were especially prominent are what have been called the 'Lake Winnipeg small flower style' and the 'Norway House style'. The small flower style, found particularly on slippers and small purses, features fluid sprigs of tiny sinuous S-shaped leaves, tendrils and rosettes, alone or partly wrapped with tear-shaped lobes. Reds and greens dominate (e.g. moccasins in Winnipeg, Manitoba Mus. Man & Nat., H.40.791). The related and flamboyant early 20th-century Norway House style (see fig. 57), from the northern Lake Winnipeg Cree–Ojibwa area, was used particularly on moccasins, gloves and jackets. Designs enlarge and emphasize certain motifs of the small flower style; large pink and rose rosettes, composed of concentric layers of petals, and serpentine, broad-veined green leaves partly enclosed in pink scallops dominate. After World War II fine silk floss was rarely available, and beadwork came to dominate in the central Subarctic.

Floss embroidery was a minor and intermittent tradition with Subarctic Athapaskan peoples and was never popular among the Naskapi of Labrador. Athapaskan embroidery was almost exclusively of floral designs, stylistically similar to the beaded designs of the given area. About 1915 Slave Athapaskan women at Hay River embroidered tiny graceful flowers in pastels on to hide wall-pockets and lamp pads (e.g. New York, Amer. Mus. Nat. Hist., 50.1-7726). In the early 20th century some British Columbia Athapaskans, such as the Sekani, embroidered cursory semi-foliate motifs on moccasins and wall-pockets with sewing thread or floss. In the mid-20th century Dogrib women used floss for a time on moccasins and baby belts but then returned to beads.

Early in the 20th century eastern Athapaskan women also embroidered dog blankets with floral designs using wool yarn (e.g. Fort Smith, NWT, N. Hist. Site). By the end of the 20th century some used yarn on *mukluks* and other footwear (Yellowknife, NWT, Prince of Wales N. Her. Cent., 979.63.14). Designs relate to late 19th-century styles but are generally simpler and bolder.

57. Subarctic embroidery on a bibbed jacket, silk floss on tanned hide, made at Berens River Reserve, Manitoba, 1912 (Winnipeg, Manitoba Museum of Man and Nature)

During World War I Slave women began tufting moose hair, imitating European 'punch work'. White moose hairs were dyed, tufted on to hide or velvet and trimmed to form flowers and leaves. Tufting was revived in the 1960s, particularly for frameable pictures, and remained popular into the 1990s and beyond in several Great Slave Lake–Mackenzie River communities (e.g. Colorado Springs, CO, Taylor Mus., 1983.33). At Fort Yukon, AK, women took up the craft in the early 1990s.

BIBLIOGRAPHY
J. Honigman: 'Expressive Aspects of Subarctic Indian Culture', *Hb. N. Amer. Ind.*, vi (1981), pp. 718–38
The Spirit Sings: Artistic Traditions of Canada's First Peoples (exh. cat., Calgary, Glenbow–Alta Inst., 1987) [many early examples from Eur. collections]
K. C. Duncan: *Northern Athapaskan Art: A Beadwork Tradition* (Seattle and London, 1989)
B. A. Hail and K. C. Duncan: *Out of the North: The Subarctic Collection of the Haffenraffer Museum of Anthropology* (Providence, RI, 1989)

KATE C. DUNCAN

3. PLATEAU. From ancient times Plateau weavers used 'false embroidery', or external weft wrap, to create a distinctive textile. The technique, evolved in basketwork, was used primarily to decorate flat, rectangular bags for carrying and storing dried foods and other valuables, vests, arm-bands, belts and other articles of clothing, and horse trappings (see fig. 58). Although some groups in the eastern Woodlands used the technique until the 19th century (*see* §4 below), only peoples of the Sahaptian, Upper Chinook, a few Interior Salish groups on the Plateau and the Tlingit, Tsimshian and Aleut peoples of the North Pacific rim have decorated their baskets in this way in more recent times. False embroidered items, whether

58. Plateau region woman weaving a storage bag using the false embroidery technique, Tygh Valley, Oregon; from a photograph by Fanny van Duyn, *c.* 1907 (Goldendale, WA, Maryhill Museum of Art)

family heirlooms or the product of one of the few artists working in the medium by the end of the 20th century, are carried with great pride at tribal celebrations and ceremonies, and they contribute to the owner's sense of identity and status within the Plateau community.

False embroidery is an elaboration on plain twining. The weaver wraps a decorative third strand around the outside of the twining stitch as the bag is woven, creating a design as the fabric is constructed. Bags for storing clothing were large, some the size of a pillowcase, with smaller bags for dried roots, berries, nuts and other foods. Incorporating the third weaving element into the bag not only allowed the weaver to beautify the utilitarian object but also produced a tight fabric that would resist the sand and dust of the dry Plateau region.

The earliest Plateau bags were twined of kneespun Indian hemp (*Apocynum cannibinum*). Simple geometric designs were applied in false embroidery in the natural colours of native grass. At the beginning of the 19th century explorers and fur traders brought new materials to the people of the Plateau. By the mid-19th century cornhusk had replaced native grasses as a decorative material, and articles woven in this way began to be known as 'cornhusk' work. Cornhusk's ability to accept dyes, as well as the newly acquired ravelled woollens and yarn, allowed the weavers to incorporate colour into the designs. From the mid-19th century the variety of motifs and colours in false embroidery increased, reaching a peak of innovation in the early 20th century. The introduction of canvas, burlap and other carrying and storage bags freed the weavers to apply their skills to making more decorative items, such as women's handbags and the foldover purses worn by both men and women on their belts. A few weavers continued to produce the large storage bags until the 1930s.

Designs in Plateau false embroidery generally fall into five categories: overall repeat motifs; horizontal, vertical or diagonal bands; a unified design that refers to or frames a dominant central motif; a five-part design, usually a large central motif with smaller versions of the motif repeated in each corner; and naturalistic designs. The earliest examples of false embroidered designs are single motifs such as triangles, rhomboids and other simple geometric forms, repeated in columns or bands. On these and later bags, designs are different on each side of the bag.

After European contact, new materials and the opportunity to use a variety of colours allowed weavers to elaborate on basic geometric motifs. Steps were added to triangles, internally and externally; motifs were joined to form complicated designs. Darker colours outlined forms, creating three-dimensional effects. Although the complexity of the designs increased with time, the overall style continued to be formal, marked by symmetry and rhythmic repetition. On many bags the weaver created a complex design on one side and a simple repeat geometric motif on the other. Naturalistic designs were not common until the late 19th century, when they may have been inspired by the surge in floral beadwork on the Plateau (*see* §IX, 3 above). The few Plateau weavers who carry on false embroidery appear to prefer the traditional elaborated geometric motifs for their designs. This continuity of design in Plateau false embroidery may be due to the relative stability of the Plateau lifestyle, where the people have remained on the lands of their ancestors, and the dry climate has helped preserve the weaving and provided many fine examples from earlier generations to serve as inspiration.

BIBLIOGRAPHY
J. M. Gogol: 'Cornhusk Bags and Hats of the Columbia Plateau Indians', *Amer. Ind. Bask.*, i/1 (1979), pp. 4–10
M. D. Schlick: 'Art Treasures of the Columbia Plateau', *Amer. Ind. Bask.*, i/2 (1980), pp. 12–20
G. L. Miller: *Flat Twined Bags of the Plateau* (MA thesis, Seattle, U. WA, 1986)
M. D. Schlick: 'The Flat Twined Bag', *Columbia River Basketry: Gift of the Ancestors, Gift of the Earth*, ed. M. D. Schlick (Seattle, 1994), pp. 133–72
D. Walker, ed.: 'Plateau', *Hb. N. Amer. Ind.*, xii (in preparation)
MARY D. SCHLICK

4. WOODLANDS. Peoples of the Woodlands used embroidery to embellish clothing, everyday utensils and trade wares from before European contact. As women incoporated new trade goods and developed innovative methods and designs under the stimulus of Euro-American and Canadian examples, the techniques and appearance of their embroidery also changed dramatically. Porcupine quills and moose hair were the most widely used materials before European contact (see fig. 69 below). Using both representational and geometric designs, women applied embroidery to the borders and seams of garments, to the vamps and cuffs of moccasins, and to the faces of pouches and other items. They sewed quills to hide by tacking them to the surface with sinew stitches or folded them in complex patterns over double parallel sinew threads, using a bone awl to make holes for the insertion of sinew (*see* §XI, 4 below).

As Turner's careful analysis shows, the use of moose hair for linear embroidery was more limited until the advent of steel trade needles, but Woodlands embroiderers were able to create densely patterned bands of moose-hair ornament with a technique called 'false embroidery', or external weft wrap (*see* §3 above). Hairs dyed in different colours were twisted around the exposed wefts of twined vegetable fibre textiles as the weaving proceeded, producing a tapestry effect that often completely covered the surface. In the 17th and 18th centuries Huron and Iroquois women excelled at this technique, although it may well have been more widespread in the north-east Woodlands. They created intricate geometric patterns with false embroidery on small pouches (see fig. 59), on belts and in the centre sections of burden straps.

Ursuline nuns at Quebec City began to teach embroidery to their Montagnais, Huron and Micmac students in the mid-17th century. The nuns introduced European stitches, floral and figurative motifs, and silk thread into indigenous art. Barbeau argued that the floral motifs that came to dominate indigenous art across the continent during the 19th century had their origin in this convent teaching, a contention that has been much debated among scholars. The nuns were also probably responsible for introducing special types of souvenir artefacts in bark, embroidered in moose hair with pictorial scenes and flowers, which became an exclusively Woodlands Native American production after *c.* 1800. In the central Great Lakes region a parallel production of quill-decorated birch-bark containers—in floral, geometric and representational designs—developed slightly later, beginning *c.* 1820 and still continues (*see* §XI, 4 below).

During the 19th century the availability of steel needles also made it possible for Woodlands Native American women to apply floral embroidery in moose hair, silk and cotton thread to clothing. An even more popular embroidery medium consisted of glass beads laid down in linear patterns, appliquéd to the surface with thread, which could be formed into solid blocks of beadwork by placing successive rows side by side. Regional styles of bead embroidery developed throughout the Woodlands, displaying varying approaches to colour harmony, to the relationship of figure and ground and to the use of specific European stylistic models (*see* §IX, 7 above). The Iroquois, for example, specialized in a style of raised bead embroidery using translucent or iridescent glass beads; this was so heavily influenced by 'Victorian' styles that examples in museum collections have often been mistaken for European work.

Between about 1870 and 1950 missionaries and teachers in Native American schools increased the impact of Euro-American and Canadian styles of embroidery. They held the mastery of embroidery to be an important step in the 'civilizing' of Native American girls, because competence in needlework was so closely linked during this period to the Western ideal of femininity. In embroidery as in other art forms, however, Woodlands artists borrowed Euro-American ideas while continuing to express many indigenous concepts or specific motifs that had once been executed in moose hair or quills.

BIBLIOGRAPHY

W. C. Orchard: *Beads and Beadwork of the American Indians: A Study Based on Specimens in the Museum of the American Indian, Heye Foundation*, Contributions from the Museum of the American Indian, Heye Foundation, xi (New York, 1929/*R* 1975)

M. Barbeau: *Les Brodeuses* (1944), i of *Saintes Artisanes* (Montreal, 1944–6)

G. Turner: *Hair Embroidery in Siberia and North America*, Pitt Rivers Museum Occasional Papers on Technology, vii (Oxford, 1955/*R* 1976)

RUTH B. PHILLIPS

XI. Quillwork.

1. Introduction. 2. Subarctic. 3. Plains. 4. Woodlands.

1. INTRODUCTION. The art of quillwork is distinctively North American. Quills from the porcupine were most often used (*Erethizon dorsatum* in the east and *E. epixanthum* in the west), although bird quills were also worked, and moose hair, coloured grasses and dyed cornhusks were employed in a similar way (*see* §X above). Real quill

59. Woodlands region pouch with strap of Indian hemp, decorated with moose-hair false embroidery in orange, blue, yellow and white and edged with opaque white glass beads, l. 970 mm, Eastern Ojibwa, *c.* 1780; the pouch (220×220 mm) of tanned, black-dyed skin decorated with quillwork, showing three thunderbird motifs (Hull, Qué., Canadian Museum of Civilization)

embroidery was practised throughout most of the habitat of the porcupine, from eastern Alaska across the northern forest to Nova Scotia, and south in the Rocky Mountains, on the Plains and in the Great Lakes region. After European contact, through the second half of the 19th century, imported Venetian trade beads replaced the use of quills in embroidery, but more recently, in the 20th century, Native American cultural pride has brought the return of interest in traditional quillwork techniques.

The quills differed in size, the largest ones coming from the tail of the animal and then decreasing in size across the back to the neck, to slim and delicate quills from the belly. The quills were plucked out of the skin of the animal, and then, after the barb at the tip had been cut off, they were washed and dyed. Dyeing was done simply by boiling the quills and dyeing material together in water until the required colour was obtained. Native materials for dye-making were plentiful and varied from region to region. The inner bark of trees and dried or shredded roots were most often used, frequently mixed with such minerals as black earth, ochre and grindstone dust, all of which contain iron to act as a setting agent (mordant); berries, plants and flowers were also used. Among the Slavey indigo was used for blue, indigo and turmeric for green, turmeric for yellow and cochineal for red. During the second half of the 19th century a wider variety of bright aniline dyes was traded from Europe.

After being washed, dyed and sorted, quills were stored in containers of animal bladder or rawhide. Before the quills were applied to soft tanned leather, they were softened to make them more workable, either in warm water or in the quillworker's mouth. As she needed quills, she drew them out and flattened them between her teeth, with her fingernails or with a bone or wood quill-flattener. The most important techniques for applying the quills to the leather were wrapping, a great variety of sewing, plaiting and, in northern Canada, a type of loom-woven method.

Feder (1987) has shown that the use of bird quills was much more important than Orchard (1916) had originally suggested. Bird quills were often combined with porcupine quills, and on the Plains among the Hidatsa, at least, bird quills were preferred. There were three important centres for bird-quill embroidery: the upper Missouri River area, the upper Mississippi River area and among the Northern Athapaskan, Cree and Eskimo.

Archaeological evidence suggests that porcupine quill-work has long been practised in North America. The earliest and main evidence comes from Nevada and Utah, where specimens preserved in caves suggest the use of quills as a bonding element as early as 530 BC and as decoration on moccasins from the 13th and 14th centuries AD (Loud and Harrington, p. 24; Libby, no. 276; and Martin, Quimby and Collier). Ling Roth has suggested that quillwork possibly had its beginnings in Asia, citing examples of woven mats and baskets from Asia that show the same basic weaving and sewing techniques as employed in quillwork in North America (Roth, pp. 1–4).

Some of the earliest extant examples of quillwork are to be found in European museums, for example: an elaborate quill-embellished shirt, probably from the region just north of Lake Huron and collected prior to 1683

(Oxford, Ashmolean); the Sloane and Christy material in the Museum of Mankind, London (Braunholtz, p. 25 and King, pp. 51, 65); and the collection of early moccasins and headdresses in the Musée de l'Homme, Paris (Fardoulis). Porcupine-quill decorated bags, pouches and robes, dating before 1800 and in the collections of the Museum of the American Indian, Heye Foundation, New York, are described in Orchard (1926, pp. 59–68). While most of these specimens are from a region east of the Great Plains, they exhibit wrapped, woven, and sewn techniques virtually identical to those found on later Plains specimens.

BIBLIOGRAPHY

W. C. Orchard: *The Technique of Porcupine Quill Decoration among the Indians of North America*, Contributions from the Museum of the American Indian, Heye Foundation, iv/1 (New York, 1916/*R* 1971)
H. L. Roth: 'American Quillwork: A Possible Clue to its Origins', *Man* (1923)
W. C. Orchard: *Porcupine-quill Ornamentation*, Indian Notes of the Museum of the American Indian, Heye Foundation, iii/2 (New York, 1926)
L. L. Loud and M. R. Harrington: *Lovelock Cave*, University of California Publications in American Archaeology and Ethnology, xxv/1 (Berkeley, 1929)
C. Lyford: *Quill and Beadwork of the Western Sioux* (Lawrence, 1940)
P. S. Martin, G. I. Quimby and D. Collier: *Indians before Columbus* (Chicago, 1947)
W. F. Libby: 'Radiocarbon Dates, II', *Science*, cxiv (1951), pp. 291–6
G. Turner: *Hair Embroidery in Siberia and North America*, Pitt Rivers Museum Occasional Papers on Technology, vii (Oxford, 1955/*R* 1976)
H. Benndorf and A. Speyer: *Indianer Nordamerikas, 1760–1860* (Offenbach, 1968)
H. J. Braunholtz: *Sir Hans Sloane and Ethnography* (London, 1970)
N. Feder: *American Indian Art* (New York, 1971)
A. Fardoulis: *Le Cabinet du Roi, et les anciens cabinets de curiosités dans les collections du Musée de l'Homme* (Paris, 1979)
J. C. H. King: *Thunderbird and Lightning* (London, 1982)
R. H. Whitehead: *Micmac Quillwork* (Halifax, 1982)
G. Turner: *Tradescant's Rareties* (Oxford, 1983)
N. Feder: 'Bird Quillwork', *Amer. Ind. A.*, xii/3 (1987), pp. 46–57

IMRE NAGY, with COLIN TAYLOR

2. SUBARCTIC. In the Subarctic, quillwork is traditionally a woman's art, produced mainly to decorate garments of tanned skin and articles of adornment. A number of different techniques were used to apply the prepared quills to the object being decorated. The wrapping of garment fringes with quills was practised across the Subarctic region and was probably the principal use of quills among the easternmost Subarctic groups, the Naskapi and Montagnais. Also widespread was the emphasizing of seams and edges by parallel lines of overstitched quills. A more technically demanding technique, that of woven quillwork, was employed extensively by the Cree and Northern Ojibwa of the eastern and central Subarctic, and by many Athapaskan-speaking peoples in the western Subarctic. A frame, formed from a bent stick and strung with a warp of sinew threads, was used for this work, with the completed weaving sewn to a backing of tanned skin. Such bands became belts, headbands, baby-carrying straps and wristlets, or were sewn on garments and pouches (see fig. 60). Another popular technique was appliqué quillwork, which involved stitching flattened and folded quills directly to a garment in parallel rows, using sinew thread.

Traditionally, designs in quillwork were always geometric. Horizontal stripe patterns were worked on fringes, through alteration of contrasting colours. In woven and appliqué quillwork, symmetrical patterns of rectangles, triangles and diamonds were worked in shades of red, blue, green and yellow against a natural white background. The original significance of such motifs is not known, but they may have evolved from stylized representations of animals or other animate or inanimate beings whose assistance was sought by the wearer of the garment.

In the 18th and 19th centuries, with the introduction of European floral patterns and such decorative materials as silk embroidery floss and glass beads, and the adoption by Subarctic peoples of imported clothing, porcupine quill-work was gradually produced less frequently (*see* §§IX, 2 and X, 2 above). It survives mainly in the work of a few Athapaskan women living in the Northwest Territories of Canada. A small amount of loom-woven quillwork is produced, for museum and private collectors, and for a tourist market. Articles of clothing, particularly smoked-hide jackets and footwear, are occasionally decorated with porcupine quillwork in appliqué or oversewn line tech-niques. In these instances, motifs are often floral, imitating those more commonly executed in beadwork.

BIBLIOGRAPHY
W. C. Orchard: *The Technique of Porcupine Quill Decoration among the North American Indians,* Contributions from the Museum of the North American Indian, Heye Foundation, iv/1 (New York, 1916/*R* 1971)
J. Thompson: '"No Little Variety of Ornament": Northern Athapaskan Artistic Traditions', *The Spirit Sings: Artistic Traditions of Canada's First Peoples* (Toronto, 1987), pp. 133–68
K. C. Duncan: *Northern Athapaskan Art: A Beadwork Tradition* (Seattle and London, 1989)
B. Hail and K. C. Duncan: *Out of the North: The Subarctic Collection of the Haffenraffer Museum of Anthropology* (Providence, RI, 1989)

JUDY THOMPSON

3. PLAINS. Large amounts of quillwork were produced in the 19th century by those Plains peoples, such as the Sioux and Cheyenne, who lived in regions where the porcupine was not generally found, the quills being 'a significant trade item' (Best and McClelland, p. 4), al-though more recent zoological scholarship indicates that the porcupine may have been more widely distributed than once thought. In addition to porcupine quills, bird quills were also sometimes used, particularly by groups on the Missouri River, such as the Hidatsa, Mandan and Arikara. Feder has also identified a 'visually distinctive' form of bird quillwork from the region of the Upper Mississippi River, the main producers being the Santee Sioux, although there is some evidence to suggest that the Yankton Sioux, Ojibwa and other tribes in the region also produced such work.

Possibly the earliest account of porcupine quillwork from the Plains region was by Dr Samuel Latham Mitchell, who described in great detail an Assiniboin quilled wapiti skin collected prior to 1817; it exhibits at least three different quill techniques (including wrapping) and both geometrical and animal figures (Fenenga, pp. 19–22 and Orchard, 1926, p. 64).

On the Plains, 16 working techniques were used. As elsewhere, the porcupine quills were softened by moisten-ing, commonly by placing them in the mouth, and were flattened by drawing them between the teeth or fingernails; while some elaborately carved bone or antler flatteners survive (Orchard, 1916, p. 14 and Bebbington, p. 15), most were probably ceremonial in function. The quills were dyed either by boiling them with a suitable vegetal

60. Subarctic sealskin pouch with bands of woven porcupine quillwork and quill-wrapped fringes, h. 240 mm, attributed to Swampy Cree, *c.* 1840 (Hull, Qué., Canadian Museum of Civilization)

or mineral dye or, later, with coloured trade cloth, the colour boiling out of the cloth and penetrating the quills, although this assumption has been disputed by Feder. Aniline dyes were introduced about 1870. Red, yellow and purple were the commonest colours used, these being combined with the natural white and brown-black. Tools were simple; in addition to the possible use of quill flatteners, women quillworkers used bone markers, awls, knives and sinew threads. The marker either simply impressed the surface or was dipped into a coloured fluid and then used as a pen. The sinew thread was used to secure the quills to the hide. Great patience was needed in producing this work, as the quills frequently had to be spliced together.

Eight of the working techniques were very common, although in combination they can frequently be used to determine the tribal origin and date of a particular speci-men (see fig. 61). Wrapping techniques on rawhide strips were common and widely used in the decoration of pipe-bags and hair ornaments, which were particularly favoured by the Sioux (Lyford, p. 43; Best and McClelland, p. 12). More specialized was quill-wrapping on horse hair and the 'plaited technique', both of which were particularly well developed by the Crow for the decoration of shirts, leggings and moccasins but are also found on similar items collected from the Hidatsa, Mandan, Arikara and Nez Perce, who probably acquired most of them in trade from the Crow. Quillwork on bark, common among such

61. Plains region bridle and headstall, with sewn and wrapped porcupine quillwork, northern Plains, *c.*1850 (Copenhagen, Nationalmuseum)

peoples as the Micmac and Ojibwa, was not found on the Plains; however, the use of moose hair, while firmly associated with the Huron and other Woodlands tribes (*see* §4 below), was, on occasions, also made by the Plains Cree (Turner, 1955, pl. vii).

Highly formalized quillworkers' guilds have been identified among such peoples as the Cheyenne and Arapaho (Grinnell, i, p. 163; Kroeber, 1902, 1904, 1907). Within guilds, certain designs were considered sacred and could be produced only by initiated women. Similar customs prevailed among the Blackfeet (Ewers, p. 29), who have traditionally been reported as emphasizing the religious significance of quillwork (Dempsey, p. 52). Quillworkers' guilds appear to have been less formalized among such Sioux tribes as the Lakota, Mandan, Hidatsa and Crow, but several of these tribes, in common with the Plains Algonquians, explain the origin of quillwork in mythological terms (Wissler, p. 92; Simms; Duvall and Wissler, p. 131; and Lyford, p. 55).

With the wholesale introduction of beads to the Plains Native Americans in the mid-19th century, quillwork was progressively displaced as a decorative medium. However, fine traditional costumes decorated with quillwork were still produced in limited amounts as late as the beginning of the 20th century on both the northern and central

Plains. The Hidatsa in particular excelled in its production, and in 1953 J. C. Ewers of the Smithsonian Institution, Washington, DC, found several Gros Ventre and Assiniboin women on the Fort Belknap Reservation, Montana, well informed on the quill techniques of their tribes. In 1974 the Sioux Indian Museum in Rapid City, South Dakota, assembled an exhibition of contemporary Sioux quillwork. Since that time, a number of Sioux quillworkers have found a ready market for their wares.

BIBLIOGRAPHY

A. L. Kroeber: 'The Arapaho', *Bull. Amer. Mus. Nat. Hist.*, xv (1902), pp. 33–5, 64–9
S. C. Simms: *Traditions of the Crows*, Field Museum of Natural History, Chicago, Publication lxxxv (Chicago, 1903)
A. L. Kroeber: 'The Arapaho', *Bull. Amer. Mus. Nat. Hist.*, xvii (1904), pp. 209–10
——: 'The Arapaho', *Bull. Amer. Mus. Nat. Hist.*, xx (1907), pp. 414–18
D. C. Duvall and C. Wissler: *Mythology of the Blackfoot Indians*, i (New York, 1908)
C. Wissler: *Societies and Ceremonial Associations in Oglala Division of the Teton-Dakota*, Anthropol. Pap. Amer. Mus. Nat. Hist., xi (New York, 1912)
W. C. Orchard: *The Technique of Porcupine Quill Decoration among the Indians of North America*, Contributions from the Museum of the American Indian, Heye Foundation, iv/1 (New York, 1916/*R* 1971)
G. B. Grinnell: *The Cheyenne Indians: Their History and Ways of Life*, 2 vols (New Haven, 1923)
H. L. Roth: 'American Quillwork: A Possible Clue to its Origins', *Man*, xxiii/8 (Aug 1923), pp. 113–16
W. C. Orchard: *Porcupine-quill Ornamentation*, Indian Notes of the Museum of the American Indian, Heye Foundation, iii/2 (New York, 1926)
L. L. Loud and M. R. Harrington: *Lovelock Cave*, University of California Publications in American Archaeology and Ethnology, xxv/1 (Berkeley, 1929)
C. A. Lyford: *Quill and Beadwork of the Western Sioux*, US Department of the Interior, Bureau of Indian Affairs, Haskell Institute (Lawrence, 1940)
J. C. Ewers: *Blackfeet Crafts*, US Department of the Interior, Bureau of Indian Affairs, Haskell Institute (Lawrence, 1945)
P. S. Martin, G. I. Quimby and D. Collier: *Indians before Columbus* (Chicago, 1947)
W. F. Libby: 'Radiocarbon Dates, II', *Science*, cxiv (1951), pp. 291–6
G. Turner: *Hair Embroidery in Siberia and North America*, Pitt Rivers Museum Occasional Papers on Technology, vii (Oxford, 1955/*R* 1976)
F. Fenenga: 'An Early Nineteenth-century Account of Assiniboine Quillwork', *Plains Anthropologist*, iv (1959), pp. 19–22
C. Taylor: 'Early Plains Indian Quill Techniques in European Museum Collections', *Plains Anthropologist*, vii (1962), pp. 58–69
H. Dempsey: 'Religious Significance of Blackfoot Quillwork', *Plains Anthropologist*, viii (1963), pp. 52–3
H. J. Braunholtz: *Sir Hans Sloane and Ethnography* (London, 1970)
A. Best and A. McClelland: *Quillwork by Native Peoples in Canada* (Ontario, 1977)
A. Fardoulis: *Le Cabinet du Roi, et les anciens cabinets de curiosités dans les collections du Musée de l'Homme* (Paris, 1979)
C. Taylor: 'Costume with Quill-wrapped Hair: Nez Perce or Crow?', *Amer. Ind. A.*, vi/3 (1981), pp. 42–53
J. N. Bebbington: *Quillwork of the Plains* (Calgary, 1982)
J. C. H. King: *Thunderbird and Lightning* (London, 1982)
R. H. Whitehead: *Micmac Quillwork* (Halifax, 1982)
G. Turner: *Tradescant's Rarities* (Oxford, 1983)
N. Feder: 'Bird Quillwork', *Amer. Ind. A.*, xii/3 (1987), pp. 46–57
C. Taylor: 'Early Nineteenth Century Crow Warrior Costume', *Jb. Mus. Vlkrknde. Leipzig*, xxxvii (1987), pp. 302–19

COLIN TAYLOR

4. WOODLANDS. Porcupine quills were widely available throughout the northern Woodlands as a natural habitat of the porcupine and to other areas through trade. Early European explorers in the North American Woodlands stressed the high value placed on ornaments made of quills (see fig. 62). Lescarbot described the wearing of

quilled necklaces, bracelets, arm-bands and sashes by the Micmac in 1606–7, which were dyed by the women in 'black, white and red colours, as lively as possibly may be'. Other observers describe Micmac people wearing elaborate panels of quillwork *c.* 200 mm square, made with a combination of embroidery, netting and wrapping techniques. Although no examples from the eastern coastal peoples can be identified, similar pieces made by Cree living around Hudson's Bay survive, indicating how widespread this art form was in the northern Woodlands, until it was replaced by beadwork and silk embroidery during the 19th century.

Woodlands women also used porcupine quills to ornament clothing and objects used for sacred and everyday activities. The stitches and techniques used were first described comprehensively by Orchard and have been reanalysed and categorized by Bebbington. The main stitch used for outlining was the simple line, in which a flattened quill was laid in the desired position and then secured to the hide with sinew threads inserted into holes made with a bone awl, using the spot-, back- or loop-stitch. More complex stitches were made by folding flattened quills over and under double lines of sinew threads in different directions. Two of the most common such stitches in Woodlands quillwork were the simple band and the zigzag band stitches. These were used to infill large areas on moccasin vamps and pouch fronts (see fig. 59 above). Patterns of triangles, chevrons and chequer-boards could be produced by combining quills of different colours. Women finished the edges of hide items with borders of one-quill edging or other edging stitches.

Panels of netted quillwork are found on numerous 17th- and 18th-century Woodlands objects: attached to the shoulders of hide coats, made into sashes, and suspended from cradleboard fronts and the bottoms of hide pouches and to basketwork (see fig. 69 below). The netting technique involved slitting a panel of hide into parallel thongs and wrapping them in alternating pairs. Women introduced new colours with great skill so as to create geometric designs and figurative images such as thunderbirds. Quillworkers also wove quills on sinew warps strung on a bow loom. They created intricately patterned bands of geometric motifs, averaging about 80 mm in width, which they sewed to moccasin vamps, knife sheaths, pouch fronts, belts, the shoulders of coats and a wide variety of other items.

Craftswomen used a variety of other techniques to wrap single or doubled thongs and vegetable fibres with quills to make decorative cords, sashes and fringing. Quill-wrapped cords of different colours were also wrapped around pipe-stems and other implements to create striped patterns or more complex motifs. Women also used quills to decorate the spruce-root rims of birch-bark containers. Quills were sometimes interwoven into these wrappings to create decorative chequer-board patterns.

Possibly as early as the late 16th century Micmac women began to adapt ancient techniques for the decorative insertion of quills into bark, to meet the tastes of European travellers and settlers seeking 'Native American curiosities'. They developed a densely patterned, mosaic-like style of quillwork decoration, which entirely covered the lids of bark boxes. The geometric designs were derived from Native American double curve patterns and from European folk-art traditions.

About a century later, when a similar clientele appeared in the central Great Lakes, Ottawa and Ojibwa women developed a parallel but stylistically distinctive tradition of quillwork on bark. During the 19th century they typically ornamented their boxes, wall-pockets and other items with infilled floral designs on a bark ground. Towards the end of the 19th century a fully quilled geometric style exploiting the natural brown and white coloration of undyed quills was introduced, together with an expanding range of representational designs. Although Micmac production ceased early in the 20th century, Ottawa and Ojibwa women from Ontario and Michigan continued to make

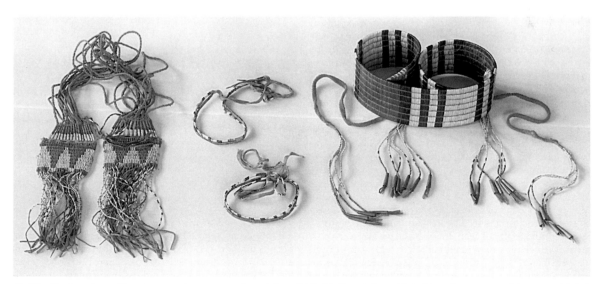

62. Woodlands region quillwork personal ornaments, Central Cree, 1662–76 (from left to right): (a) neck ornament; (b) garters; (c) belt (Canterbury Cathedral)

boxes and other items of birch-bark with a continually evolving repertory of designs.

BIBLIOGRAPHY

W. C. Orchard: *The Technique of Porcupine Quill Decoration among the Indians of North America*, Contributions from the Museum of the American Indian, Heye Foundation, iv/1 (New York, 1916/*R* 1971)
J. M. Bebbington: *Quillwork of the Plains* (Calgary, 1982)
R. H. Whitehead: *Micmac Quillwork* (Halifax, 1982)
Ottawa Quillwork on Birchbark, Harbor Springs Historical Commission (Harbor Springs, MI, 1983)

RUTH B. PHILLIPS

XII. Featherwork.

Most indigenous peoples throughout North America produced FEATHERWORK of some kind; this art, however, was particularly highly developed among the peoples of California and the Plains.

1. CALIFORNIA. Featherwork in diverse styles was produced throughout California. In north-west California, the Yurok and their neighbours made elaborately decorated headbands, ornamented with hundreds of scarlet woodpecker scalps, considered a visible manifestation of wealth. They were used in many ways: to trim women's basketwork, caps and braid ornaments, otter-skin quivers carried in the Brush Dance, white buckskin bandoliers, whole eagle and condor feathers worn at the back of the head by male dancers and the albino deerskins carried in the White Deerskin dance. The scalps were usually trimmed to size, then applied to the object to be decorated, although in some instances—particularly in decorating dentalium shells and in the covering of long, slender antenna-like hairpins called 'rockers'—individual feathers were applied using glue and finely split sinew. The brilliant salmon-orange tail feathers of the flicker were used in fringe-like clusters to decorate foxskin quivers, dance wands and the feet of albino deerskins.

In central California, the Maidu and nearby groups made delicate headbands from hundreds of stripped feather quills of the flicker and capes on a net foundation, decorated with large primary feathers from birds of prey. Elaborate head plumes were decorated with a variety of bird feathers and often hung with small, square mats made of stripped flicker quills. Forehead bands of fur worn by Pomo women were decorated with multiples of these flicker-quill mats. Featherwork skirts, capes, headbands, belts and headdresses were also made by western Great Basin peoples. Topknots, large feather bunches, were worn on top of the head by both men and women, and were made of many types of large bird feathers, including crow, hawk and goose. Elaborate belts, 1.82 m long and 102 mm wide, were woven of native cordage and incorporated tiny scarlet and green bird scalp feathers, along with white shell or, later, glass beads. Some coiled baskets woven by the Pomo, and to a lesser extent by the Maidu, Miwok and Costanoan, were decorated with the inclusion of small bird feathers in their construction. This resulted in the soft covering of feathers over the whole exterior of the basket. The Valley Maidu, Patwin and some Pomo people made large headpieces, often over 1.22 m in diameter, of willow shoots decorated with white waterfowl feathers for use by specific spirit impersonators in the Hesi ceremony, a dance by members of a secret society to give thanks to the spirits and ensure prosperity and health, which is held in the autumn and spring by the Patwin and some of their neighbours. Maidu feather blankets were decorated with striped patterns and were woven of native cordage and waterfowl feathers. Yokut male dancers wore skirts of strings of white down, along with headpieces of iridescent magpie or roadrunner tail feathers, surrounded by stripped black crow feathers.

In southern California featherwork was more limited; ceremonial regalia for men consisted of a network skirt fringed with eagle or condor feathers, and head plumes of great horned owl feathers. The Chumash used regalia like that of the Yokuts and added skirts similar to those used further south. They made feather quill bands used as streamers at ceremonial sites and as bandoliers from flicker, jay, pelican and other bird feathers.

BIBLIOGRAPHY

R. F. Heizer, ed.: *Hb. N. Amer. Ind.*, viii (1978)
C. D. Bates: 'Wealth and Power: Feathered Regalia of Central California', *Pleasing the Spirits: A Catalogue of a Collection of American Indian Art*, ed. D. C. Ewing (New York, 1982), pp. 32–47
C. D. Bates and B. Bibby: 'Beauty and Omnipotence: Traditional Dance Regalia of Northern California', *The Extension of Tradition: Contemporary Northern Californian Native American Art in Cultural Perspective* (exh. cat., ed. F. R. LaPena and J. T. Driesbach; Sacramento, CA, Crocker A. Mus.; Palm Springs, CA, Desert Mus.; 1985–6), pp. 28–37

CRAIG D. BATES

2. PLAINS. It has been suggested that the origin of Plains Native American featherwork was its high degree of development in Pre-Columbian Mesoamerica (*see* MESOAMERICA, PRE-COLUMBIAN, §IX, 3), from which it spread to the Plains. Supporting this hypothesis is the fact that feathers functioned as insignia in a system of war honours both in Aztec Mexico and among the Plains Native Americans.

The behaviour of birds and other animals provided the Plains Native American with a rich source of symbolism, associated with a spiritual intepretation of all natural phenomena. As seasonal migrants most birds were seen as followers of the Thunderbird, who announced his annual return by the first thunder heard in spring. Associated with this warlike spirit, the feathers of these birds served as charms or amulets for warriors. Paramount among these 'war birds' was the eagle, who was the visual representative of the Thunderbird himself. The eagle was admired for its hunting prowess, its solitary dignity and courage. As such the eagle was spoken of as the chief of all raptors and scavenger birds. Among his followers was the owl, admired for its stealthy nocturnal hunting; and the hawk for the speed of its attack. However, the Plains Native American taxonomy of war birds was not limited to birds of prey and scavengers. Flickers owed association with the Thunderbird to their peculiar shrill call when a storm came up; woodpeckers were war birds because of their skill in finding prey, piercing the hard tree as the warrior stabbed an enemy. The qualities of war birds were interpreted as spiritual powers, which could be given to people in their dreams; and the skins and feathers of raptorial birds were kept in 'medicine bundles', to be handled in war rituals. A headdress made of such feathers was believed to protect the warrior against the weapons of his enemies.

Featherwork was done by men, and its products used mainly by men. In gathering the feathers the trapping of eagles was surrounded by ritual, and the danger involved made eagle feathers a highly prized commodity in intertribal trade. They were stored in special rawhide or wooden containers. Feathers were used in the creation of headdresses and also served as meaningful decorations on shields, ceremonial pipe-stems, shirts, leggings, ceremonial regalia and tepee covers. Many of these ornaments were textured collages, in which feathers were combined with fur, hair, bones, quills and other materials, each item having a symbolic function and conveying a particular message.

Plains Native American art in general was created to appear at its best in action, and this holds true in particular for the use of feathers. Feather ornaments were made to be seen in movement, when they acquired an incredible flamboyance. As a fringe along the edges of a shield, eagle feathers were believed to give its owner the swiftness and courage of that bird. While the round shape of the shield symbolized the sun, the eagle feathers around the edge represented the rays of that great patron of warriors.

The shape and materials of a headdress often followed from instructions given by a spirit to the maker in a dream or vision, and as such it had a personal religious significance. Some headdresses consisted of entire birdskins tied to the wearer's hair; other headdresses functioned as distinctive regalia of warrior fraternities or dance clubs, for example, the leader of the Dog Society in the Hidatsa tribe (see fig. 63). Turbans made of the bills and scalps of the ivory-billed woodpecker were popular among tribes on the eastern prairies, while crowns of standing eagle feathers were common on the northern and central Plains. Such 'straight-up' headdresses survived in use among the Blackfeet until recent times (see fig. 55 above), but elsewhere they gave way to a more elegant and prestigious headdress, the 'war bonnet', which indicated the martial prowess of its wearer.

A Native American warrior acquired the right to wear eagle feathers through his performance in battle. The military symbolism of the war bonnet derived from the rating of particular deeds, using a system of trimming, marking and mounting of feathers to indicate specific exploits: an eagle feather worn upright in the hair stood for striking an unwounded enemy, while an eagle feather worn horizontally indicated that a wounded enemy had been hit; a split feather referred to wounds received in battle, while a tuft of hair glued to the tip of the feather indicated the taking of a scalp. The accumulation of many such war honours enabled a man to make himself a war bonnet, though well-known and outstanding war leaders often restricted themselves to a single feather, standing upright at the back of their heads. About 30 eagle tailfeathers were needed to encircle the skullcap of a war bonnet. The feathers were attached to the cap by a string running through the butt ends of the quills, allowing the feathers to flare out and sweep backwards. Such a feather crown symbolized the sun, and its stylized picture was painted on the buffalo robes worn by warriors. Few, if any, men ever acquired enough war honours to wear a war bonnet with a long trail down along the back. In making such a headdress a man invited his comrades to help by

63. Plains region featherwork headdress worn by leader of the Dog Society, Hidatsa, early 19th century, aquatint after a watercolour by Karl Bodmer; from Prince Maximilian of Wied-Neuwied: *Reise in das innere Nord-Amerika in den Jahren 1832 bis 1834*, 2 vols and atlas (Koblenz, 1839–41)

adding feathers of their own. Thus the trailing war bonnet symbolized the combined valour of the wearer and the other members of his warrior fraternity. This style of war bonnet became popular on the central Plains in the early 19th century and was subsequently adopted by all other peoples in the region. As a result of Wild West shows and the film industry it has become the prime iconographic symbol of the Native American.

Among the Omaha and their neighbours the members of certain warrior fraternities wore belts with complex feather ornaments at the back, symbolizing birds who come as scavengers to a battlefield. In the 1880s, after the Native Americans were settled on reservations, this so-called 'Crow Belt' and other ceremonial regalia became part of a costume for the 'Grass Dance' that became popular throughout the central and northern Plains. This was the start of a new era, in which Native Americans from many different tribes met each other at annual dance festivals called 'powwows'. Dances and feather regalia that once were distinctive for one or a few tribes became popular throughout the Plains region, and this blending and borrowing of tribal styles created a pan-Native American culture centred around the intertribal powwow. The featherwork of dance costumes thus lost its old symbolism but became increasingly elaborate. Oklahoma in particular, with its large and heterogeneous Native American population, became a hotbed for the creation of new fashions in dance costumes, which continually changed the pow-wow scene.

From the 1970s, however, there was a noticeable trend among many tribes to revive their own traditional dance regalia, including certain old-fashioned feather ornaments. Most active among the revivalists were younger people who had rediscovered the creations of their ancestors in museum exhibitions. Symbolism has survived mainly in the creation of exquisite feather fans and other regalia used in the Peyote cult, more recently called the Native American Church. The worshippers hold these 'singing fans' and shake them gently as they sing their prayers. The feathers are held in the smoke of incense and then struck on the body in order to transfer spiritual power to the user.

BIBLIOGRAPHY
F. G. Speck: 'Notes on the Functional Basis of Decoration and the Feather Technique of the Oglala Sioux', *Ind. Notes*, v/1 (1928), pp. 1–42

T. J. BRASSER

XIII. Hide.

Animal skins and leathers were used in many types of Native American art productions and were essential materials for diverse utilitarian purposes, including storage utensils, clothing and dwellings (*see also* §§II and VIII above). After removal from the animal, the skin or rawhide was cleansed of muscle and surface fats and left to dry hard. Sometimes the cleaned skin was also cured and stretched, thinned down and manipulated to induce some flexibility in making various items. Native-tanned or semi-tanned leather differs from skin in that it is processed by working oils or vegetable tannins deep into the fibres in order to lubricate and partially stabilize the collagen in the skin. Brain tannage is achieved with brains, or combinations of brains with liver and pancreas. Worked into the skin, these substances produce a napped, suede-like leather, which is much softer than dried skin. Smoking of the skin or leather frequently supplemented native tanning to impart colour, fragrance, additional waterproofing and resistance to insects. For example, the Plateau Native Americans used different smoking processes to induce colouring and could achieve subtle shades of yellow, red or reddish-brown.

In the eastern Woodlands tanned leather was the primary material for both men's and women's clothing, until cloth was introduced by Europeans. Leggings, moccasins and breech-cloths were often decorated with quill-work, later with beads or ribbon appliqué (*see* §§IX, 7; X, 7; and XI, 4 above). The most extensive use of skins and leather was among the Plains peoples. Stiff rawhide containers, usually called *parfleche*, were produced either in cylindrical or envelope forms to store foods, moisture-sensitive resources or clothes. Incised designs were cut into the epidermis on envelope-shaped *parfleches* (e.g. *parfleche*, *c.* 1865; Denver, CO, A. Mus., LCr-l-P) and into the stiff rawhide base of circular shields (e.g. leather shield, *c.* 1820; London, BM, 5202). Later these items were intricately painted with symbolic and/or geometric designs on their outer surface (see fig. 64).

64. Cheyenne shield, buffalo rawhide with deerskin cover, painted with designs in bluish-black, diam. *c.* 450 mm, *c.* 1860 (Rochester, NY, Museum and Science Center)

Full-sized tanned buffalo robes were used by both men and women. Such robes were painted on the flesh side with geometric patterns to indicate the sex, age and social status of the wearer. Men's shirts and leggings were made from the tanned skins of deer and bighorn sheep. These were also decorated with solid painting, quillwork or beadwork and heavy fringe along the seams. Larger, tanned elk hides were used for women's leather dresses, decorated in the characteristic tribal styles (*see* §VIII above). The conical Plains Native American dwelling, the tepee, was also made from several buffalo hides sewn together (*see* §II, 3 above). Among the Northwest Coast group, shamans wore simple hide aprons and shoulder robes. The fringes of the apron were decorated with deer dewclaws and puffin bills. In the Southwest, the Apache used leather extensively, decorating their clothes with pierced patterns, tin cones and intricate paintings. Furs of different animals were used everywhere in North America, and among the Californian Chumash these were an expression of social status. A 20th-century use of hide in Native American art is provided by Arthur Amiotte (*b* 1944), a Sioux artist whose 'banners' are of native tanned leather, combined with cloth, beadwork, silk ribbon and metal pieces.

BIBLIOGRAPHY

B. Loeb: 'Arthur Amiotte's Banners', *Amer. Ind. A.*, x/2 (1985), pp. 54–9

A. Jonaitis: *The Art of the Northern Tlingit* (Seattle, 1986)

A. Howatt-Krahn: 'Skin and Native-tanned Leather', *Amer. Ind. A.*, xii/2 (1987), pp. 44–51

G. Torrence: *The American Indian Parfleche: A Tradition of Abstract Painting* (Seattle, WA, 1994)

IMRE NAGY

XIV. Basketwork.

The Native American peoples have made basketwork since at least *c.* 9000 BC. By *c.* 8000 BC they had invented the three basic basket-making techniques: twining, the oldest, comprises single or double wefts twisted around a group of warps; plaiting is done by weaving splints or stems over and under each other; and coiling is done with bundles of fibres or sticks bent into a spiral, then wrapped and sewn together with finer splints.

1. Arctic. 2. Subarctic. 3. Northwest Coast. 4. California and the Far West. 5. Southwest. 6. Woodlands.

1. ARCTIC. Two basket techniques were used in the Arctic: hand twining and sewn coil. All Aleut basketwork is twined, using the two-strand weave technique, in which a double weft is wound around the warp strands. The baskets are suspended by a string or placed on a stake and worked upside down. The weaver weaves from bottom to top with the fine fringe of the top edge hanging down. Ornamentation is usually sewn on afterwards, using embroidery floss or coloured grasses. Inuit basketry is almost exclusively coiled. Collections of Arctic basketwork are held in Anchorage, AK (Hist. & F.A. Mus.), Vienna (Mus. Vlkerknd), Juneau, AK (State Mus.), Washington, DC (N. Mus. Amer. A.), and New York (Mus. Amer. Ind.).

(i) Aleut. The exact provenance of Aleut baskets is difficult to determine but is judged according to the fineness of the weave, the shape of the basket and the style of the corners and knobs. Aleut women created baskets from wild rye grass, finely split with the fingernail. These were the most delicate baskets made in North America, and their surface texture is often compared to linen; one square inch of the basket fabric could have up to 1300 stitches. Numerous techniques were used to vary the texture of the

weave: plain, open and three-element twining, crossed and divided warps, different coloured weft strands and false embroidery. The Attu women made the finest baskets of all: an example in the Alaska State Museum in Juneau has 1980 meshes to the square inch.

As early as 1805 most Aleut basketwork was created for the souvenir trade and included such basketwork products as mats, miniature baskets, pocket-books, cigar cases and belts. Decoration most often comprised geometric designs, until the 19th century, when floral patterns became popular on items made for the tourist trade. Also in the 19th century imported raffia (fibre made from a type of palm-tree) replaced beach grass as the basic weaving material, and silk replaced reindeer hair as thread. After reaching its peak in the 1880s, Aleut basketwork became more coarse in the 20th century, and only a few skilled weavers remained.

(ii) Inuit.

(a) South Alaskan. Coiled grass basketwork, typically of cylindrical or globular shape, is a traditional Inuit craft. Most of it is made of grass or other materials with contrasting colours woven as part of the weft into the basket itself. Only in the later 20th century were baskets further embellished with imbricated or overlaid decoration in embroidery floss or raffia. Inuit twined and coiled basketry is far coarser than its Aleut counterpart. Yet, as Aleut basketwork declined, South Alaskan Inuit basketwork increased in quantity and improved in quality.

Two Alaskan archaeological sites—Bristol Bay and Cape Denbigh—yielded examples of prehistoric coiled basketwork. After European contact only a few coiled baskets were collected, even though Inuit women made hundreds of them for the souvenir trade, which developed during the gold rush of the Seward Peninsula. Traditional Inuit twined basketwork designs consisted of simple horizontal or vertical patterns, rendered in subtle contrasting colours. Coiled basket designs were also simple originally: tufts of yarn, tiny beads and natural objects, such as bird's feet, were employed in repeat patterns. The type of grass used for the weft was also changed frequently for a mottled effect. In the 1930s basket-making became a chief source of income for South Alaskan Inuit women. Accompanying this expansion was a shift to bolder geometric designs and the use of representational motifs, especially fish, flies, crabs, dogs, birds and sleds.

Coiled basketry among the South Alaskan Inuit reached its height of sophistication during the 1960s and 1970s. Almost any subject-matter was considered suitable: yoyos, dolls, kerosene lamps and dance fans all served as inspiration for basket shapes. Snowmobiles were used as design motifs, and basket lids were made to represent faces. Still more recently, Southwest Native American motifs were incorporated. By the 1980s most Inuit baskets produced for sale were coiled; Mary Black was well known for her grass and sealgut baskets.

(b) North Alaskan. Traditional North Alaskan baskets were made of birch-bark. Their envelope form dates back to *c.* AD 1–500. There is evidence that the western Thule people made twined baskets, but little is known about basketwork in North Alaska after European contact,

except that, at some point before the 19th century, twining was abandoned for coiled basketwork techniques, learnt from the South Alaskans.

Like their South Alaskan counterparts, North Alaskan Inuit women made baskets in response to the demands of the souvenir trade. Decorated with tufts of fur, beads, small ivory carvings and imbrication, their grass coiled baskets were made in miniature and large sizes to the exclusion of any twined basketwork. However, an influenza epidemic in 1918 marked the almost complete abandonment of basketwork by North Alaskan Inuit women and a shift to the sewing of furs.

Baskets of baleen, a flexible, hornlike material found in the mouth of the baleen whale, were made for the tourist trade from 1905. Working baleen baskets takes great strength, and it is therefore men who most often make them. Using a single-rod coiling technique, in which adjacent weft strands alternate over warp strands, a six-inch diameter basket takes approximately fifty hours to finish. Two of the best-known weavers of baleen baskets are Kingoktuk and Marvine Sakvan Peter.

BIBLIOGRAPHY
J. D. Ray: *Eskimo Art: Tradition and Innovation in North Alaska* (Vancouver, 1977)
R. L. Shalkop: 'Introduction', *Contemporary Native Art of Alaska from the Collection of the Anchorage Historical and Fine Arts Museum* (Anchorage, 1979)
C. F. .Feest: *Native Arts of North America* (London, 1980)
J. G. E. Smith: *Arctic Art: Eskimo Ivory* (New York, 1980)
J. D. Ray: *Aleut and Eskimo Art: Tradition and Innovation in South Alaska* (Seattle and London, 1981)
J. Highwater: *Arts of the Indian Americas* (New York, 1983)

JOANNE DANFORD-CORDINGLEY

(c) Labradoran and Québécois. Basketwork of the Inuit in Arctic Canada appears to have been restricted to the sewn-oil technique. At the time of early contact with Europeans, small baskets were used to store women's sewing equipment or tinder for starting fires. In the manufacture of these early baskets a foundation of dried grass, willow twigs or spruce roots was arranged in a spiral and held together by over-and-over sewing with dried grass, spruce root, willow bark or sinew. In the early 19th century Moravian missionaries in Labrador began to encourage the Inuit in their congregations to produce coiled-grass baskets and mats for sale in Europe through the mission trading operation. From that time the development of basketwork as a saleable craft spread throughout northern Labrador and neighbouring Arctic Quebec, where it has since provided a source of cash income to Inuit, mostly women.

The coiled grass plaques and baskets produced for sale display a wide variety of shapes and decorative features. Typical of the Labrador area is the frequent incorporation of zigzag openwork, a form of ornamentation probably introduced from Europe via missionaries or settlers. In Arctic Quebec, basket lids are often provided with handles that have been carved from soapstone, ivory or antler in the shape of birds or animals. Geometric patterns are commonly added to basketwork by using grasses that have natural colour variation, or else have been dyed, and also by incorporating wool, raffia, strips of black sealskin, whale sinew or black vinyl.

BIBLIOGRAPHY
Grass Work of Labrador (exh. cat., ed. E. Goodridge; St John's, Mem. U. Nfld, A.G., 1979)

J. GARTH TAYLOR

2. SUBARCTIC. Basketwork was important in the Subarctic before European contact. Late prehistoric sites have yielded bark basket fragments. Ethnographic evidence reveals that girls perfected basketwork skills during puberty confinement. Throughout the Subarctic, birch-bark was the primary material for containers for berry picking, storage, stone boiling, serving and eating. Bark was cut and folded, usually into rectangular-based, round-rimmed containers. The wrapped spruce-root rim was sometimes coloured in sections. Western Athapaskan bark containers were often ornamented with horizontal bands of lines or triangles scraped away to reveal the lighter inner bark (e.g. Chilcotin containers, New York, Mus. Amer. Ind.). On Algonquian containers foliate and figural motifs were created by scraping away background rather than the motifs themselves. The Naskapi made bark trays. Across the Subarctic basketwork traps were widely used with fish weirs.

Coiled basketwork was more rare. In the mid-19th century some Mackenzie and Cordillera Athapaskans coiled grass baskets (e.g. Slavey baskets, Edinburgh, Royal Scot. Mus.), as occasionally did Southern Shield Algonquians. Chilcotin and Carrier women created coiled imbricated spruce-root baskets similar to those made by the Salish (*see* §3 below).

By the late 20th century, baskets were made primarily for sale. Lower Yukon Athapaskan women coiled willow trays and baskets (e.g. Fairbanks, U. AK Mus.); and Slavey women ornamented large cylindrical birch-bark containers with porcupine quill insertion or incising (e.g. Providence, RI, Haffenraffer Mus. Anthropol.).

BIBLIOGRAPHY
F. G. Speck: *Montagnais Art in Birchbark: A Circumpolar Trait* (New York, 1937)
J. Helm, ed.: 'Subarctic', *Hb. N. Amer. Ind.*, vi (1981) [whole vol.]
J. Steinbright, ed.: *From Skins, Trees, Quills and Beads: The Work of Nine Athapaskans*, Institute of Alaska Native Arts (Fairbanks, 1983)
B. A. Hail and K. C. Duncan: *Out of the North: The Subarctic Collection of the Haffenraffer Museum of Anthropology* (Providence, RI, 1989)

KATE C. DUNCAN

3. NORTHWEST COAST. Native American women of the Northwest Coast developed different approaches to basketwork design within three major traditions: plaited basketry, twined basketry and coiled basketry. The continuity of traditions between 18th-century and 19th-century baskets indicates that basketwork was highly conservative. Nonetheless, the late 19th century and the early 20th century were times of considerable innovation and experimentation with new materials, techniques and forms. In several regions contemporary basket-makers continue to work innovatively in long-established traditions.

Geometric design, executed within an essentially rectangular format, is characteristic of all regions of the coast and developed particularly on plaited bark baskets and mats. The definition of the field ranges from the simple placement of a single motif at the mid-point of a container wall, through stripes executed in a single colour, to a composition in two colours occupying the entire surface of a container or mat. The principal colours are black, appearing alone in contrast to the natural colour of the bark, or black and red in combination. In all regions designs sometimes incorporate optical illusion, achieved through variations in the weave. The basketwork of the Haida and Kwakiutl features design based on optical illusion without added colour, although Haida women also made mats with geometric designs in black and red (see fig. 65). The repertory of geometric motifs is substantial, with some variation from one region to another.

Approaches to design on twined basketwork vary across the region. In the north, Tlingit twined basketwork is distinguished by bands of geometric motifs executed in false embroidery around the walls, the motifs of the upper and lower bands often identical and contrasting with motifs in a central band. Haida basketwork is similar in approach, with the decorative bands composed in solid colours or short vertical or diagonal lines created through the substitution of coloured wefts for plain. The use of false embroidery on Haida basketry is limited and appears to represent innovations by certain basket-makers in the early 20th century. In the late 19th century and early 20th twined basketwork made of cedar bark and decorated in false embroidery was produced in certain Coast Tsimshian communities, particularly Metlakatla, but this had a limited distribution. On these baskets motifs appear individually, rather than in bands. An older tradition of twined spruce-root basketwork was practised among the Gitksan; the few examples that exist show an approach to design different from that of the Tlingit and Haida; geometric motifs are applied with an overlay technique in diagonal bands (Quebec, Mus. Civilis.; Chicago, IL, Field Mus. Nat. Hist.).

The small, wrapped-twine baskets and mats that became common on the west coast of Vancouver Island and the Olympic Peninsula during the 19th century exhibit a distinctive approach to design based on concentric circles (Washington, DC, N. Mus. Nat. Hist.; Chicago, IL, Field Mus. Nat. Hist.; Quebec, Mus. Civilis.; Victoria, Royal BC Mus.). The essential technique is substitution. Motifs in strong colours—green, purple, orange and red—achieved with commerical dyes, are placed against a light background of bleached grass.

Motifs are arranged in bands encircling the basket. Baskets and mats from the early periods often have bands consisting only of coloured lines, with the colours arranged symmetrically within the band. On later baskets geometric or representative motifs appear in bands encircling the basket at the mid-point of the wall, framed above and below with bands of colour. Baskets in this tradition often have lids that are fully incorporated into the composition, with the centre of the lid a focal point of the design. Looking down at a basket, the viewer sees the design in concentric bands with the centre of the lid as the central point. The overall composition of wrapped-twine basketwork design may be derived from the composition of design on the traditional whaler's hat. In the approach to design, particularly of small containers, there are also strong correspondences with Aleut twined grass basketwork of the 19th century (see §1(i) above).

In the later 19th century and early 20th wrapped-twine baskets had bands of colour and geometric motifs. In the

65. Northwest Coast Haida woman weaving a basketwork mat, early 20th century photograph (Chicago, IL, Field Museum of Natural History)

early 20th century the repertory of design expanded to include such representative motifs as ducks and other birds, and whaling scenes reminiscent of those on whalers' hats, and these became prominent. There was also considerable experimentation with stylized representative designs and floral patterns. From the 1890s basket-makers working in this tradition brought an innovative approach to the use of technique and the development of design.

Although there are substantial regional differences between the basketwork from Puget Sound and from the Columbia River area, the twined basketwork of these regions of the southern Northwest Coast is distinguished by an approach to design, in which motifs are arranged in vertical bands beneath a horizontal band following the line of the rim.

Contemporary Coast Salish people recognize the geometric motifs of cedar-root coiled basketwork as part of their heritage. Originally an Interior Salish tradition, coiled baskets have been found in Coast Salish homes for generations. Interior Salish basketwork design is complex, with a large repertory of geometric motifs, the composition of motifs and designs governed by rules concerning the alternation of colour and spacing, and regionally distinct approaches to the definition of the design field. A Coast Salish style, developed in the 19th century, has, as a distinctive decorative feature, representative motifs in black or red, each built from several narrow decorative strips placed against a single coil.

BIBLIOGRAPHY

G. T. Emmons: 'The Basketry of the Tlingit', *Mem. Amer. Mus. Nat. Hist.*, iii (1903), pp. 229–77

F. Boas: 'The Kwakiutl of Vancouver Island', *Mem. Amer. Mus. Nat. Hist.*, v/2 (1909), pp. 389–90

H. K. Haeberlin, J. Teit and H. Roberts: 'Coiled Basketry in British Columbia and Surrounding Regions', *Annu. Rep. Bureau Amer. Ethnol. Secretary Smithsonian Inst.* (Washington, DC, 1928), pp. 119–484

From the Tree Where the Bark Grows: North American Basket Treasures from the Peabody Museum, Harvard University (exh. cat. by J. S. Brandford, Cambridge, MA, Harvard U., Peabody Mus., 1987)

R. L. Hudson: 'Designs in Aleut Basketry', *Faces, Voices and Dreams: A Celebration of the Centennial of the Sheldon Jackson Museum, Sitka Alaska, 1888–1988*, ed. P. L. Corey (Anchorage, 1988), pp. 63–92

F. W. Porter, III, ed.: *The Art of Native American Basketry: A Living Legacy* (New York, 1990)

ANDREA LAFORET

4. CALIFORNIA AND THE FAR WEST.

(i) Introduction. (ii) Regional styles after European contact. (iii) Effects of the curio trade, 19th century and after.

(i) Introduction. Like pottery and other forms of weaving, basketwork in western North America is an art traditionally practised exclusively by women. Two basket-weaving techniques dominate in the Far West: twining, in which the rigid foundation rods radiate from the basket centre like the spokes of a wheel, bound together by two or more flexible wefts passed simultaneously over and under them; and coiling, in which the foundation material spirals outward from the centre like a clockspring, bound together by sewing with a single weft element. In coiling, an awl is used to make the hole through the previous round, through which the flexible material is then passed. In western North America, coiled basketwork predominates in southern California and the Southwestern states, while twining predominates in northern California and the Northwest Coast, with a pocket of coiled basket-weaving in northern Washington and southern British Columbia.

Baskets were created for the care and protection of the family. They are particularly associated with food and may be involved in all stages of procurement, processing, storage, cooking, serving and eating. For example, in California the acorn formed the staple food, and baskets were developed to gather the nut, grind, sift, leach and store the flour, cook it into mush, and serve and eat it. Great Basin peoples relied instead on the piñon nut, which does not require leaching, and developed a similar repertory of food baskets with the addition of trays for parching the nut. The protective and nurturing role of baskets extends to their use as caps and baby carriers.

Designs in California and Far West basketwork are created primarily by variation in colour, using naturally contrasting plant fibres, dyed materials or both. Because the basket is woven in an inexorable spiral from centre to rim, it is not possible to complete a colour area at one time, as in tapestry weaving. The weaver must break off one material and shift to material of contrasting colour according to the dictates of the pattern. The design may be created either by the weft material or by an overlay that is carried simultaneously with it. In coiling, the delineation of design with overlay materials is usually called imbrication and is characteristic of the coiled basket-weaving groups spanning the US–Canadian border. The use of overlay for design in twining, often called false embroidery (*see also* §X, 3 above), is prominent in northern California and the Northwest Coast.

The importance placed on basketwork decoration differs with each group. Where many types of baskets are developed to suit a variety of functions, designs are usually more elaborate on those baskets that receive lighter wear. The most highly ornamented basketwork is that involving social interaction outside the immediate family, such as dress caps, gambling trays and gift or offering baskets. In the latter types, aesthetic appreciation outweighs practical considerations of form or design.

Historically, the most elaborate schemes of ornamentation developed in the valleys and coastal regions of California, where a benificent environment fostered larger and less nomadic populations with more leisure time and opportunity for social interaction. The contrasting simplicity of ornamentation among Great Basin tribes before the development of the curio trade (*see* §(iii) below) correlates with the region's harsher environment, which limited population and required much more mobility in the seasonal round.

Individual elements of design, which were generally named for the sake of verbal communication, are well-recorded in the anthropological literature (e.g. Kroeber). Some enthusiasts ignored the weavers' denial of literal meaning and postulated that the motifs formed the vocabulary of a symbolic system. They assumed that basketwork designs were abstractions of natural forms and thus expressed symbolism in the same way as the representational design of men's ritual arts of North America (James). Other scholars argued that the abstract nature of most women's arts in North America is inherent, the designs being allowed to convey meaning without recourse to overt symbolism. Bright colours and reflective surfaces suggest well-being, while ordered symmetry and the interlocking of light and dark suggest harmony with the structure of the universe. Both elements function on the principle of sympathetic magic to protect and preserve whatever the baskets contain.

(ii) Regional styles after European contact. Basketwork in California and the Far West continued to evolve after European contact. Whereas basketwork containers co-existed with pottery in the Southwest USA and with wood containers along the Northwest Coast, they are the preeminent type of container along the Pacific coast from California to most of Washington state. Rough use and destruction as gifts and funerary offerings has precluded the survival of most pre-European contact and early post-contact examples. Therefore, most baskets in museums and private collections are examples made for the curio trade, which climaxed between *c.* 1885 and *c.* 1925 (*see* §(iii) below). Nevertheless, because the curio trade brought about so many changes in shapes, materials and designs, it is still useful to describe historic or pre-curio styles of basketwork in California and the Far West. Different styles and techniques were developed by the dozens of peoples that occupied the western states. These diverse traditions can be divided into three broad macrostyles and their interfaces, each characterized by a shared preference for certain forms, colours and design arrangements. Significantly, these aesthetic criteria exist independently of the materials selected and at times independently of the weaving technique.

(a) Macrostyles. Mission macrostyle is associated with the mission peoples of southern California. Although the spheroid shape and the preference for black and brown design on light ground is distinctive to the region, the use

of the curved tray and radiating or starlike patterns, which grow naturally from the coiling technique, are shared by the basketwork styles of Arizona (*see* §5 below).

Southern macrostyle is associated with the several Yokut groups, as well as Tubatulabal, Kawaiisu, Koso (Panamint) and Monache (Western Mono). The preferred coiled basket shapes include a flat tray, truncated cooking basket and collared gift basket with distinctive sharp shoulder and short cylindrical neck (see fig. 66d). Designs are usually formed by contrasting stepped rectangles, diamonds or triangles of red and black, or by outlining a red motif with black line. In both cases the black and red are separated by an intervening row of the light ground. These elements are kept small to allow multiple repetitions, arranged in horizontal, diagonal or vertical bands or band segments. Vertical and diagonal bands are often further ornamented by repeating a flaglike motif known as the 'quail plume'. Bands of simple human figures are sometimes ascribed to Euro-American influence. Most baskets combine bands of several different motifs, separated by bands of plain ground, which allows for increase of stitches as the basket expands. Often the scale of the design elements actually decreases as the basket diameter increases. This discontinuity between scale of design and form, like the multiplicity of design elements and the sharply segmented profile of the fanciest gift baskets, arises from a controlling aesthetic of variety and contrast.

Northern macrostyle is associated with groups from San Francisco north to the Canadian border and includes both twined and coiled decorated wares. Best illustrated in the literature are baskets of the Pomo, Maidu and Washoe groups, the lower Klamath River peoples, the Achomawi and Atsugewi, the Modoc of the upper Klamath and Salish imbricated coiled wares of the North-west. Preferred basket shapes include conical gathering or burden baskets, truncated conical cooking vessels and spheroid gift baskets, as well as flat gambling trays, spheroid or conical hats and baby carriers. Designs are usually executed in one dark colour on a light ground—the polychrome style of the Lower Klamath River groups (Hupa, Yurok, Karok etc) representing a spectacular exception (66c). The basic design elements employed are serrated diagonals, variously ornamented and arranged in discontinuous parallel bands or in a continuous zigzag band. Usually a single design element is repeated throughout the basket, with an interlocking and sometimes reciprocal relationship between dark pattern and light ground, and allowed to expand and contract with a basket's diameter. This approach promotes homogeneity and organic unity between shape and design, so that it is not the individual element or band that the eye perceives but the continuous web of pattern.

(b) Interface styles. Some of the most innovative and complicated basketwork traditions developed at the interfaces of the three macrostyles described above. For example, the twined basketwork of the Twana on the west side of Puget Sound and the coiled basketwork of the Klickitat and other groups on the east side combine the serrated diagonal web of the Northern macrostyle with the rectilinear outlines and intricate light–dark contrasts of the Northwest Coast. To the south, Chumash basketwork

66. Californian and Far West regional basketwork (clockwise from top left): (a) Pomoan twined mush bowl, h. 246 mm; (b) Pomoan twined mush bowl, h. 219 mm; (c) Hupa twined woman's work cap, h. 81 mm; (d) Monache coiled bottleneck basket, h. 168 mm (Berkeley, CA, University of California, Phoebe A. Hearst Museum of Anthropology)

combines preferences of the Mission macrostyle, such as the spheroid shape, the brown-black-light colour scheme and complete coverage of the basket with design, with other traits characteristic of the Southern macrostyle, such as the banded, cylindrical-necked gift basket, the flatter tray and the banded arrangements of diverse designs.

Even richer contrasts appear at the interface between the Southern and Northern macrostyles, since many peoples in these regions (Maidu, Washoe, Mono Lake Paiute and the Pomoan groups) make both twined and coiled baskets for different functions. For example, among these groups the conical gathering basket is always twined, while baskets used for cooking acorn mush may be twined or coiled. Among the Washoe and Paiute, Southern banded designs are conventionally applied to twined baskets, while Northern zigzag designs appear in coiling. The greatest diversity appears in basketwork of Pomoan groups, for which three different design schemes have been noted. On twined burden and cooking baskets, the Northern preference for a single dark colour and serrated zigzags is used but arranged according to the Southern scheme in contrasting and separated horizontal bands (66b). Coiled gift baskets are frequently decorated with triangular designs in vertical bands, the overall discontinuity and heterogeneity of which are also characteristic of styles to the south. A third scheme, which appears identically on both twined and coiled Pomoan wares, is the serrated diagonal or zigzag in an expansive, organically unified pattern, with carefully controlled negative spaces that are completely within the aesthetic of the Northern macrostyle (66a).

(iii) Effects of the curio trade, 19th century and after. The consistency of Native American aesthetic preference in basketwork was considerably altered under the impact of the curio trade. The Arts and Crafts Movement, which translated 'Victorian' nostalgia for the noble savage into

visual form, placed a special emphasis on basketwork. As the development of basketwork was known to predate that of pottery, it was considered the oldest human art and thus a window into the purest time in human history. In basketwork, the entire weaving process is visible in the final result, a characteristic that appealed to those interested in manufacture by hand rather than by machinery, and signs of wear or deposition of food particles only added to the charm. Furthermore, as fewer and fewer Native American women learnt the art of basket-weaving to replace those who died, the anticipated demise of basketwork came to symbolize the myth of the vanishing Native American. As collectors scrambled to acquire these supposed remnants of a dying race, the manufacture of basketwork for sale exploded with unprecedented quantity and variety. Metal tools permitted finer stitching, exploited by weavers aiming at a high-class market. Those who publicized basketwork as a dying art obscured this improvement in technique, instead referring to innovators who set higher standards of workmanship as the 'last of the great weavers'. The climax of basketwork in the Far West under the stimulus of the curio trade is largely due to four types of individuals: innovative weavers, traders, publicists and collectors.

(a) Weavers and traders. Weavers of curio baskets were creative in their attempts to appeal to Euro-American tastes. They developed new shapes, especially lidded baskets (see fig. 67d); they tried new sizes, such as miniatures and giant baskets (67a); they developed new weaving techniques, such as gap stitching or covering glass containers with twined basketwork; they employed new decorative materials including dyes, threads and beads

(67b); and they added new designs, especially representational images of birds, flowers and humans (67c). Among some peoples, the Washoe for example, basketwork made for sale constituted a new style, dominated by shapes, materials and designs that were unknown in pre-curio weaving. Cutting across the traditional macrostyle divisions (see §(ii) above), a new representational mode of plant and animal images came to dominate basketwork in regions most visited by tourists, as among the Washoe who sold to tourists at Lake Tahoe, the Mono Lake Paiute who encountered them at Yosemite, the Panamint Shoshone who lived in Death Valley, as well as the peoples of the southern California missions.

Traders provided both the stimulus and the direction of the basketwork craze, gathering thousands of baskets made obsolete by acquisition of metal containers and encouraging continued production for sale. By patronizing gifted weavers and promoting them as individuals, they developed an élite market for baskets as fine art curios. Many dealers carried on their business in the metropolitan centres of the coast, close to their consumers. Grace Nicholson represents the outstanding example, scouring the western states for the finest baskets to sell to her wealthy Pasadena clientele and forming exclusive patronage contracts with the Pomo weavers Mary Benson and William Benson (see BENSON (ii)) and the Karok weavers Louise and ELIZABETH HICKOX. Other traders set up shops at resorts in the harsher mountain regions, where the baskets were made, inviting weavers to form part of the local colour to attract summer tourists. Foremost among these were Amy and Abe Cohn of Carson City. Through their contacts with many Washoe weavers and their patronage of the great innovator DAT SO LA LEE (Louisa Keyser), the Cohns catalyzed the transformation of an impoverished local tradition into one of the most valued curio styles. To make this new style appear authentic, they fabricated a legend around Dat so la lee and developed a symbolic vocabulary of their own to interpret basketwork designs.

(b) Publicists and collectors. The success of dealers and traders in building the curio market is also partially due to the writers who publicized western basketwork in the romantic terms that appealed to 'Victorian' nostalgia. The most influential writer was George Wharton James, who compiled a monumental survey of Native American basketwork, founded a basketwork fraternity—which issued a periodical—promoted the imitation of Native American basketwork by White Americans and expanded the Cohns' symbolic vocabulary into a general theory of basketwork symbolism that he promulgated through public lectures.

Purchasers of curio baskets ranged from travellers collecting an inexpensive souvenir through wealthy, usually eastern North American families furnishing their 'Native American Room', to the basketwork enthusiasts who competed to acquire the most representative collection of western styles. The changing tastes of these consumers affected the evolution of curio weaving. Washburn has shown that curio trade in basketwork progressed through four phases. Although she notes that progress through these phases differed in character and timing for each region, for clarity about a decade or two can be assigned

67. Californian and Far West regional basketwork forms developed for the curio trade (clockwise from top left): (a) oversize basket by Carrie Bethel (Mono Lake Paiute), h. 226 mm, *c.* 1925; (b) beaded bottle by ?Tootsie Dick Sam (Washoe), h. 247 mm, *c.* 1925; (c) bowl with representational design by Maggie Mayo James (Washoe), h. 115 mm, 1920; (d) lidded basket by Elizabeth Hickox (Karok), h. 176 mm, 1913 (California, private collections)

to each phase. The first decade, c. 1885–95, was dominated by the collection of used baskets that weavers no longer needed, since they had acquired metal containers. When the supply of used baskets was exhausted, and baskets began to be made specifically for sale, western basket-weavers attempted to appeal to 'Victorian' decorative tastes. As a result, from 1895 to 1905 many basketwork imitations of Euro-American shapes were produced, such as the goblet or the cup-and-saucer, along with adoption of such western motifs as alphabet letters and flowers. As 'Victorian' taste waned, basketwork enthusiasts came to prefer a more reserved and technically finer approach, which they considered more traditional. Dealers in basketwork and other Native American arts dominated the curio trade in the west, supplying an élite market for expensive fine art curios and inspiring the climax of trade from c. 1905 to c. 1925. Finally, by 1925, a change in attitude engendered by World War I, and the movement to reverse governmental policies of assimilation, led to a decline in the Euro-Americans' nostalgic view of the Native American as a noble savage. In the following decade the élite market declined, and most prominent collectors sold or donated their basketwork to museums. Indeed, most of the older weavers were dead, almost no new weavers emerged, and in each region the repertory of shapes, techniques and designs contracted under the stereotyping influence of the souvenir market.

The number of surviving techniques, as well as surviving weavers, continued to dwindle after 1935. By the 1990s few groups had more than a few basket-weavers. However, Native American interest in preserving basketwork increased steadily. Even among groups that perpetuated styles of weaving developed specifically for the curio trade, basketwork took on profound significance as a symbol of Native American heritage. The origin of this movement in 1960s counter-culture resulted in the association of basketwork and other Native American cultural patterns with shamanism, to the extent that weavers were often regarded as 'medicine women'.

BIBLIOGRAPHY

O. T. Mason: *Aboriginal American Basketry: Studies in a Textile Art without Machinery*, Report of the US National Museum, Smithsonian Institution (Washington, DC, 1904)

A. L. Kroeber: 'Basket Designs of the Indians of Northwestern California', *U. CA Pubns Amer. Archaeol. & Ethnol.*, ii/4 (1905), pp. 105–164

G. W. James: *Indian Basketry, and How to Make Indian and Other Baskets* (New York, 1909/*R* 1972)

D. Washburn: 'Dealers and Collectors of Indian Baskets at the Turn of the Century in California: Their Effect on the Ethnographic Sample', *Emp. Stud. A.*, ii/1 (1984), pp. 51–74

MARVIN COHODAS

5. SOUTHWEST. Peoples of the Palaeo-Indian and Archaic (c. 9000–c. 200 BC) Southwest have made basketwork since c. 9000 BC (Berkeley, U. CA, Hearst Mus. Anthropol.; Salt Lake City, U. UT, Mus. Nat. Hist.; Carson City, NV, State Mus.). By 8000 BC they had invented the various basket-making techniques used in later centuries, including twining and plaiting. These techniques are still used in the Southwest to create many kinds of baskets, using almost every kind of vegetal material: stems, roots, wood, leaves, grass and other materials. Basketmakers had to be knowledgeable botanists to identify and to understand the gathering and preparation of these materials.

The earliest baskets were twined. They were used to gather seeds, nuts and roots, to carry them to camps, to process them by parching and perhaps to cook them with hot stones. Coiled baskets appeared c. 5000 BC and quickly became popular because they were better than twined baskets for parching seeds and nuts.

The ancestors of the Pueblo peoples, the Basketmakers (c. 200 BC–c. AD 700) continued to practise the basket-making traditions of the Archaic period, as did later Pueblo peoples, but the only modern Pueblo people to have preserved the ancient tradition is the Hopi. Most early decoration comprised highly structured geometrical designs. The Hopis make baskets for ceremonial use, to use as gifts among themselves and for sale to collectors and tourists. The villages on Second Mesa produce fine baskets with coils of galleta grass sewn with yucca splints. On Third Mesa brightly coloured wicker baskets are plaited with rabbit-brush wefts over sumac warps. Both kinds of basket are decorated with *kachina* figures, rain symbols and other traditional designs. They also make plaited yucca ring baskets, similar to those made c. AD 1000. In the other Pueblo villages few baskets were still made by the end of the 20th century: yucca ring-baskets and a few coiled baskets at Jemez; openwork plaited wicker bowls at Jemez and several other Rio Grande towns.

The peoples of the circum-Pueblo region also make many kinds of basket. Most of them are coiled on slender sticks or rods—usually three—and sewn with strands of willow or sumac. The Havasupais, Walapais, Yavapais and Chemehuevis decorated their bowls and vase-forms with geometric designs of black 'devil's claws', a technique used also by the Western Apaches. The beautiful baskets the Apaches made until the mid-20th century were covered with geometric patterns and figures of people and animals (see fig. 68). All these people also made twined baskets: squat jars with flat rims by the Walapais; fine conical carriers and water jars by all groups; and bucket-shaped burden baskets by the Apaches. Although coiling almost disappeared among the Apaches, twining survived because the twined burden baskets were used ceremonially. By the 1990s their chief products were conical twined baskets from c. 1 m in height to miniature baskets used on earrings. The Cibecue Apaches in particular still twine water jars and cover them with melted pine gum.

The Eastern Apaches of New Mexico formerly made distinctive baskets. The northern Jicarilla Apaches produce stout baskets coiled with three or five rods and sewn with sumac splints. They are brightly coloured with aniline and vegetal dyes and are important in the economic life of many families. Large shallow bowls are the commonest shapes, and they also make unique water bottles, coated white and sealed only on the inside surface. The Mescalero Apaches of southern New Mexico once made a unique type, coiled with two stacked rods and a bundle of fibre, and sewn with tan yucca splints. Their broad bowls and covered 'boxes' are no longer produced.

The Apaches' linguistic relatives, the Navajos, learnt from the early Pueblo peoples to make baskets with two-rod and bundle coils, but they stopped making them before the start of the 20th century to concentrate on weaving rugs (see §VII, 2 above). Nevertheless, because baskets were important in many Navajo rituals, they turned

68. Southwest region coiled basket of willow and devil's claw, h. 1.22 m, Western Apache, c. 1900 (Cambridge, MA, Harvard University, Peabody Museum of Archaeology and Ethnology)

1970s and 1980s some Papago women produced beautifully made baskets coiled with black and white horsehair and decorated with many tiny figures of snakes and/or people. The Yuman-speaking desert tribes of the lower Rio Grande never made such basketwork, except for fish traps and large coiled granaries. In the rest of the Southwest basket-making continues, and the number of basketmakers may be increasing.

BIBLIOGRAPHY

E. H. Morris and R. F. Burgh: *Anasazi Basketry: Basket Maker II through Pueblo III* (Washington, 1941)
B. Robinson: *The Basket Weavers of Arizona* (Albuquerque, 1954)
J. M. Adavasio: *Basketry Technology: A Guide to Identification and Analysis* (Chicago, 1977)
C. L. Tanner: *Apache Indian Baskets* (Tucson, 1982)
——: *Indian Baskets of the Southwest* (Tucson, 1983)
A. H. Whiteford: *Southwestern Indian Baskets: Their History and their Makers* (Santa Fe, 1988)

ANDREW HUNTER WHITEFORD

6. WOODLANDS. Basketwork is of considerable antiquity in the Woodlands. The earliest evidence for plaiting probably dates to before 8000 BC; coiling (limited to the southern Plains, where it was introduced from the Southwest; *see* §5 above) and twining were practised by the 1st millennium BC at the latest. Plaiting is the most widespread type of basketwork in the Woodlands. In the Southeast, river-cane splints of equal width were generally twilled to produce a wide range of shapes, from shallow winnowing trays to voluminous pack baskets. Besides simple single weaves, there were double-woven baskets consisting of two layers of warps and wefts showing different patterns on the inside and outside. Geometric designs were produced by using black, red (rarely orange and yellow) and natural-coloured splints. While most of these patterns were rectilinear, the complex curvilinear patterns used by the Chitimacha and their neighbours transcended the limitations of the technique.

On technical, stylistic and distributional grounds, a Euro-American origin has been postulated for the woodsplint basketwork of the north-eastern Woodlands. A tradition of plaited bags, mats and perhaps even baskets made of strips of bark before European contact must have favoured the adoption of woodsplint basketwork. However, the manufacture of thin and regular splints of white ash, white oak and other hardwoods was at least greatly simplified by specialized iron implements (splint splitters, gauges and planes). Some constructive features—such as the use of carved wooden handles—and the use of block-stamp decoration also betray European influence. Historically, there is evidence for the presence of Native American woodsplint basketwork in the north-eastern Woodlands since at least the early 18th century, whence the basic technique had spread to the western Great Lakes region by the early 19th century. Among the Cherokee, where it exists side by side with river-cane basketwork, it may have been introduced in the 18th century either from indigenous or European sources.

As in other adopted crafts, there was considerable indigenous innovation, which gave rise to some local peculiarities. Patterns are formed by splints of different width and colour, but since twilling is less common than in cane basketwork, chequerwork and banded designs predominate. Other features that distinguish woodsplint

their basketwork needs over to the Great Basin San Juan Paiutes, who, from that time on, produced most of the famous 'Navajo wedding baskets', the shallow bowls, with encircling red bands with black terraced triangles along each edge, that are used in ceremonies to hold corn meal and/or pollen. In the 1970s these Paiutes and the Navajos produced a notable renaissance of basket-making. Both groups began to produce coiled baskets of varied sizes, decorated with an eclectic assortment of coloured designs: crosses, butterflies, yei figures (the highly stylized human figures representing supernatural spirits that are used in sand paintings) and other attractive patterns that have made their creations an economic success.

A different tradition of coiling is found among the Pimas and Papagos of southern Arizona. In Pima baskets the narrow coils have a foundation of rush fibres, while the Papagos use bear-grass. Both tribes traditionally sewed their baskets with willow splints and used 'devil's claw' for geometric designs. Pima basketwork became almost extinct in the late 20th century, but the Papagos invented a new type of basket with thick coils of Beargrass sewn with splints of yucca leaves. Such baskets could be produced quickly and easily, and sold cheaply. They also created complex new stitches that both enhanced the appearance of the baskets and facilitated their production. In the

basketwork are the use of overlay and false embroidery, hexagonal weaves and the twisting of wefts to produce curls. Painted and stamped decoration—produced by means of potato, cork or wooden stamps—is especially characteristic of New England Algonquian basketwork.

The plaited wickerwork practised by the Cherokee and Virginia Algonquians using honeysuckle or buckbrush vines as wefts over rigid warps is of late 19th-century origin. Although inspired by their Euro-American neighbours, the craft was independently developed by Native American makers, for example in the double-woven root-runner baskets of the Oklahoma Cherokee. Sweetgrass and sweetgrass braids are used with woodsplint warps by the Iroquois and some of their neighbours for plaited wickerwork. Twilled burden baskets of strips of willow and box-elder bark (sometimes also leather) were plaited by the sedentary peoples of the Upper Missouri, exhibiting a limited number of simple geometric, two-colour patterns of diamonds, zigzags and other motifs.

The oldest historically collected baskets (Providence, RI Hist. Soc.; Paris, Mus. Homme; Wörlitz, Schloss) from the north-eastern Woodlands (New England and the Great Lakes), dating from the 17th and 18th centuries, were twined in a variety of techniques, including compact and spaced weft twining (see fig. 69). Designs consisted of horizontal bands of geometric patterns, often in false embroidery with dyed porcupine quills or moose hair as

decorative material. The same techniques and designs were also used in the area for two-dimensional textiles, which survived into the 19th and 20th centuries in the manufacture of soft bags. In three-dimensional basketwork, twining was almost completely replaced by plaited woodsplint basketwork, with the exception of the undecorated, bottle-shaped salt and tobacco containers and some cornhusk masks of the Iroquois, both of which are now more commonly made of sewn coiled husk braids.

Whereas two types of coiled gambling trays were traditionally made on the Plains, coiling seems to be a relatively recent basketwork technique in much of the Woodlands. As products for the tourist trade, coiled sweetgrass baskets appeared in the Great Lakes region in the 19th century and among the Florida Seminole in the 1930s. The latter produced simple designs of parallel rows created by the coloured thread used for stitching to hold the coils; these were modified into stepped geometric patterns by the 1990s. Elsewhere in the south-eastern Woodlands, coiled pine-needle baskets are similarly of 20th-century origin and may have as much Afro-American as Euro-American background. Effigy baskets made in this technique are an even more recent innovation. Yet another post-European contact style in the south-eastern Woodlands is represented by the baskets of braided bands of split palmetto leaves, made by the Houma.

BIBLIOGRAPHY

F. G. Speck: *Decorative Art and Basketry of the Cherokee*, Milwaukee Public Museum Bulletin, ii/2 (Milwaukee, 1920)
M. R. Gilmore: 'Arikara Basketry', *Ind. Notes*, ii (1925), pp. 89–95
F. H. Douglas: 'A Choctaw Pack Basket', *Mat. Cult. Notes*, iv (1937), pp. 15–18
——: 'An Hidatsa Burden Basket', *Mat. Cult. Notes*, xiv (1941), pp. 60–65
——: 'Three Creek Baskets', *Mat. Cult. Notes*, xiv (1941), pp. 66–9
M. Lismer: *Seneca Splint Basketry* (Washington, DC, 1941)
C. Field: *The Art and Romance of Indian Basketry* (Tulsa, 1964)
M. Dean and A. Billiot: 'Palmetto and Spanish Moss Weaving', *Amer. Ind. Crafts & Cult.*, viii/2 (1974), pp. 14–17
T. J. Brasser: *A Basketful of Indian Culture Change*, N. Mus. Man Mercury Series, Canadian Ethnology Service Paper, xxii (Ottawa, 1975)
K. Deagan: 'An Early Seminole Cane Basket', *FL Anthropologist*, xxx/29 (1977), pp. 28–33
C. Medford jr: 'Chitimacha Split Cane Basketry Weaves and Designs', *Amer. Ind. A.*, iii/1 (1977), pp. 56–61, 101
G. Pelletier: *Abenaki Basketry*, Canadian Ethnology Service Paper, National Museum of Man Mercury Series, lxxxv (Ottawa, 1982)
K. Bardwell: 'The Case for an Aboriginal Origin of Northeastern Indian Woodsplint Basketry', *Man NE*, xxxi (1986), pp. 49–67
C. F. Feest: 'Some 18th-century Specimens from Eastern North America in Collections in the German Democratic Republic', *Jb. Mus. Vlkerknd. Leipzig*, xxvii (1987), pp. 281–301
A. McMullen and R. G. Handsman: *A Key into the Language of Woodsplint Baskets* (Washington, CT, 1987)
D. Downs: 'Contemporary Florida Indian Patchwork and Baskets', *Amer. Ind. A.*, xic/4 (1990), pp. 56–63

XV. Other late 20th-century developments.

Many of the factors affecting the development of Native American art in the late 20th century can be traced back to the early stages of European contact, which took place between the 17th century and the 19th, depending on the region. The changes associated with European contact are discussed in terms of particular art forms in the major sections above (*see* esp. §§IV, 2 and V, 1(ii) above), but their general effects are summarized below.

69. Woodlands region twined basket of Indian hemp with false embroidery designs in porcupine quills, h. 220 mm, diam. 165 mm, Great Lakes area, 18th century (Wörlitz, Schloss Wörlitz)

1. INTRODUCTION. Broadly speaking, external influences have affected Native American traditions in four ways: technologically, economically, stylistically and structurally. The creative traditions of Native Americans were in part defined by technical limitations, such as the virtual lack of metal (and, in particular, iron) tools, of the use of true rotary motion and of mechanized means of production. European contact provided access to these and other technologies, as well as to a variety of manufactured goods, such as glass beads (*see* §IX above), various kinds of textiles and commercial dyes (*see* §VII above), thereby offering new choices for the solutions to traditional creative goals. Not all of these new possibilities were equally accepted: for example, whereas iron tools and

70. Northwest Coast Tsimshian portrait mask, carved wood with painted features and chevron and crosshatching designs, h. 220 mm, *c.* 1880–*c.* 1910 (Los Angeles, CA, University of California, Fowler Museum of Cultural History)

implements were almost instantly adopted throughout North America, implements based on rotary motion, such as the potter's wheel or the lathe, were accepted only at a very late date or not at all; glass beads quickly developed into an important medium in the decorative arts east of the Rocky Mountains but remained relatively unimportant elsewhere, particularly in the Pueblo area of the Southwest. The overall effect of most of these innovations was one of instant technical refinement, but some of the initial advantage was lost as the advantages began to be used to increase the quantity, rather than the quality, of the output.

European contact also affected the primarily economic aspects of the arts. Native American societies differed in the principles regulating the division of labour and in the relative importance of markets in the distribution of crafts. In most tribes simple forms of a gender-based division of labour prevailed to the exclusion of full-time crafts specialization (see §I, 5 and 6 above). There was long-distance trade, usually in prestige goods, and local trade, typically in useful products, but works were usually made primarily for personal, domestic or local use. European presence created new outlets for traditional products, such as pottery, which were gradually adapted to non-Native American needs; and the European demand for portable mementos of the New World led to the emergence of works specifically made for this market (see also §3 below). This process happened more quickly in regions with specialized craftspeople, such as on the Northwest Coast. As Native Americans became part of the trade networks of the increasingly dominant Euro-American societies, part- and full-time specialization became more common, and even traditional gender-based rules lost some of their significance. For example, male bead- and quillworkers on the Plains or female carvers on the Northwest Coast, once unheard of, were found by the 1990s.

The exposure to works of a different tradition of visual expression offered Native American artists and artisans new ideas and inspirations. European representational painting, for example, made a lasting impression on many Native Americans (see §IV, 2 above) and was often associated with the idea of supernatural power, or medicine, and thus with prestige. Floral designs, by no means unknown prior to European contact, flourished in new directions after exposure to comparable transatlantic traditions.

In addition to the consequences of technical innovation, for example the rise of polychromy owing to a wider range of available colours, the growing importance of non-Native American markets had implications for stylistic trends. Representational arts were more popular among the new customers and influenced the rise of portrait masks on the Northwest Coast (see fig. 70), of pictorial weaving among the Navajo, of pictographic beadwork on the Plains and of representational basketwork designs in the greater Southwest. Strong stylistic influences were, on the other hand, also transmitted through formal training in schools.

Ultimately, the most profound change affecting Native American traditional arts was the integration of the indigenous societies into the dominant Euro-American society. With it came the acceptance of the idea of 'art' as a separate and separable realm, largely defined by the uniqueness of artistic expression and the creative individuality of the artist, and accompanied by the separation of form from function. During the same general period when Euro-American modern artists 'discovered' what they considered 'primitive art' in an effort to legitimate their deviation from the established canon, some Native Americans discovered 'art' in a Euro-American sense as a new way to express themselves and their identity in a manner meaningful to the larger society.

The result of these developments was generally not the replacement of older traditions by innovations. More typically, various traditions often exist side by side within the same tribal communities. Some works are created primarily for local use, others use new techniques and/or styles to answer the demands of new markets, while in yet other cases the ethnic identity of the artist may be the only 'Native American' element involved in their creation.

BIBLIOGRAPHY

J. C. Ewers: 'Early White Influence upon Plains Indian Painting', *Smithsonian Inst. Misc. Col.*, cxxxiv/7 (1957), pp. 1–11

N. H. H. Graburn, ed.: *Ethnic and Tourist Arts: Cultural Expressions from the Fourth World* (Berkeley and London, 1976)

C. F. Feest: *Native Arts of North America* (London, 1980)

CHRISTIAN F. FEEST

2. RECENT TRENDS AND ATTITUDES.

(i) Introduction. (ii) Principal fields of activity.

(i) Introduction. The definition of contemporary Native American arts has generally been imposed by Euro-American scholars, anthropologists and art-market personnel rather than by Native American artists. There are two major positions: that contemporary Native American arts constitute a logical evolution from traditional arts; or that they are products of an aesthetically vibrant hybrid ethnic art arising from a fusion of Euro-American and Native American aesthetic traditions. Both schools of thought adhere to traditional anthropologically defined culture areas (see §I, 1 above). Despite an increasing awareness that urban Native American and individualistic artistic productions preclude the convenient use of tribal or geographic ascription, most exhibitions and publications still consign objects to such culture areas. Identification by tribal affiliation has imposed restrictive evaluations of what constitutes true Native American art. Innovators such as the sculpture–collage artist Richard Glazer Danay (Mohawk, *b* 1942), sculptor Robert Haozous (Chiricahua Apache/Navajo, *b* 1943) and painter Frank Bigbear jr (Chippewa, *b* 1953) among others have been criticized for pursuing individual aesthetic expression not readily identifiable by cultural ascription.

The concept of 'contemporary' (in the sense of 'new and improved') Native American arts is itself a very late development; until the late 20th century the approach to Native American arts has generally been romantic and subjective, fostered by the perception of Native American art as a 'generic' phenomenon and emphasizing the iconography of ethnicity, especially motifs of now extinct 19th-century Native American cultures and lifestyles. Compounding the issue is the polarization of the Native American arts by the activities of numerous associations, agencies and institutions, each of which claims to be a valid arbiter of the future direction of Native American tradition. Most notable is the increasing politicization of Native American art as national policy through the Institute of American Indian Arts in Santa Fe, New Mexico. The IAIA is an official US government agency directed towards generating new genres of native artistry (*see also* §IV, 2 above); some proponents claim it has had revolutionary impact by encouraging innovation and shattering stereotypes previously associated with Native American arts, while opponents see its role as minor compared with that of the commercial art market.

(ii) Principal fields of activity.

(a) Tribal fine and folk art. Works in this category are perceived as having derived from 19th-century tribal-art traditions. Over 60% of active Native American artists are in this group, which excludes easel painting, graphics and much sculpture. Contemporary Pueblo pottery makers and jewellers are often extremely innovative (*see* §V, 1(ii) above), but they are typically evaluated by the wider public against Native American traditions within their respective communities. The newer works are thus perceived as forms of Native American expression and are often acquired by collectors concerned with ethnographic documentation rather than because they are the work of a unique talent. Within this category a continuum exists

71. Norval Morrisseau: *Virgin Mary with Christ and St John*, acrylic on canvas, 1.02×0.81 m, 1973 (Ottawa, Department of Indian Affairs and Northern Development)

from inexpensive mementos produced by anonymous artisans to the works of artists of acknowledged stature who perpetuate historic tribal fine arts, for example the sculptor and jeweller BILL REID. From the 1920s there was an increasing trend toward folk-art production, especially for Pueblo pottery and Southwest basketwork, in which functional considerations were dismissed, and form, size and surface finish became increasingly standardized. Certain designs and compositions became so closely associated with Pueblo tribes or Navajo guilds that they may become subject to legal copyright restrictions. Object size—especially with pottery, horsehair Pima and Papago basketwork and other products—were intentionally miniaturized, effectively minimizing production time and maximizing profit return.

(b) Sacred objects. These continue to be produced for Native American religions, cults, curing ceremonies and pan-Native American rituals. For example, Pueblo religious practices and the Navajo chantway curing ceremonies involve specific costumes, sacred anthropomorphic and zoomorphic sculptural imagery, wall paintings, masks, sacred vessels and containers, sand paintings and shrine construction. Among the Puget Sound and southern British Columbia Salish, the Smokehouse religion still requires its own complex of spirit-dance costuming, staffs and insignias. For Iroquois and other north-east Woodlands peoples, Longhouse religion continues to support native art production especially that pertaining to False Face curing ceremonies. Few exhibitions or publications have dealt with the contemporary arts made for such continuing traditions; nor is there an accurate survey of the artists responsible for this aesthetic output, who are commonly not artisans involved in the commercial art market.

(c) Decorative commercial fine arts. From the late 1960s there was a pronounced development of professionally trained, commercially orientated, often pan-Native American artists who were attuned stylistically to changing trends within mainstream North American art, architectural interiors and fashionable ethnic interests. They range from curio producers, through such artists as the painter RUDOLPH CARL GORMAN to contemporary movements, such as the Morrisseau (named after founding artist NORVAL MORRISSEAU; see fig. 71) or Legend Painting School. All such artists are distinguished by a pursuit of individualistic imagery, drawn from pan-Native American experiences but marketed through emphasis on the artist's Native American ethnicity. Such ethnographic details as tribally identifiable styles, designs or techniques have been replaced by an emphasis on mainstream art to convey the impressionistic vigour or romanticism of a generalized Native American consciousness. Market centres have increasingly switched from historic and contemporary ethnographic fine arts to these more socially and economically adaptable creations, although artists such as Fritz Scholder (Mission [Luiseno], *b* 1937), whose work dominated this emerging Native American market niche throughout the 1970s, have realized the limitations imposed by this approach and have attempted to divorce ethnicity and its associations from their identity as artists.

During the 1970s and 1980s decorative and commercial fine arts proved to be the most profitable niche. Limited European market centres are clustered throughout Germany and France, with markedly fewer in England, Austria, Spain and Norway. Even though interest in Native American art, both antique and modern, has dramatically increased since the 1960s, as a collecting field it remains highly specialized and, within continental North America, regionalized to urban centres in the West and Midwest.

Since the largest share of profit and career mobility for artists is in the commercial sector, it is logical that this is where the greatest controversies over authenticity of artistic expression and falsified ethnicity occur. In the 1980s there was a rising social awareness of the commercial fabrication of ethnicity as a device to propel particular artists' careers. In 1978 in New Mexico the Indian Arts and Crafts Sales Act was drafted as a protective measure demanding proof of Native American heritage for works labelled 'Native American' but that might actually be mass-produced in Japan and Hong Kong. For Native American artists themselves, verification has become an issue of heated debate; and because of lobbying by Native American political activists, the New Mexico law has been redrafted to prohibit sale of works by individuals claiming to be Native American but with no documentation as to their own heritage.

Two positions have been taken by artists. The Native American Artists Association demands that a Native American artist's heritage be documented through listing on a tribal roll (proof of one-fourth or more Native American ancestry) or recognized by a larger pan-tribal community. The more moderate opposition eschews these restrictions. Artists have been accused of falsifying or exaggerating their native heritage as a career strategy, and the controversy has even extended to include Native American spokesmen, scholars and writers. The central issues, of personal ethnicity, what is or is not legitimate Native American expression, and how one separates a supposed communal tribal aesthetic expression from the personal perceptions and explorations of an individual Native American artist, constitute the fulcrum on which the future of Native American art is balanced. Ultimately, the debate over authentic ethnic expression reveals the artificiality of promoting Native American art on the basis of biology rather than talent.

(d) Individualist. A few Native American artists have pursued their individual visions as artists rather than categorically Native American or ethnic artisans. Their position was summarized by Leon Polk Smith (Chickasaw, *b* 1906): 'I do not make any art but my own art, and I wouldn't want to be lined up with other painters simply on the basis of race any more than I would agree, if I were female, to be exhibited with other female artists' (Highwater, 1978).

Among numerous artists who revel in creating experimental unorthodox compositions, many have had their work excluded from participation in Native American competitions or exhibitions. Many have built on Fritz Scholder's strategy of demanding confrontational debates, introducing radical change within the segregated Native

American market, then launching into the wider international art circle. They demand to be judged on their talent first and their ethnicity second. Increasingly, they are gaining admission to the mainstream North American art world and receiving both economic and critical rewards.

BIBLIOGRAPHY
J. J. Brody: *Indian Painters and their White Patrons* (Albuquerque, 1971)
A. Shulze-Thulin: *Indianische Malerei in Nordamerika 1830–1970* (Stuttgart, 1973)
J. Highwater: *Song from the Earth: American Indian Painting* (Boston, 1975)
G. Monthan and D. Monthan: *Art and Indian Individualists* (Flagstaff, 1975)
Contemporary Native Art of Canada—Manitoulin Island (exh. cat., Toronto, Royal Ont. Mus., 1978)
J. A. Warner: 'Contemporary Algonkian Legend Painting', *Amer. Ind. A.*, iii/3 (1978)
J. Highwater: *The Sweet Grass Lives On: Fifty Contemporary North American Indian Artists* (New York, 1980)
E. L. Wade and R. Strickland: *Magic Images: Contemporary Native American Art* (Norman, 1981)
H. Adams: 'The Golden Indian', *Akwesasne Notes* (July 1984), pp. 10–12
G. Hoffmann, ed.: *Indianische Kunst im 20. Jahrhundert* (Munich, 1985)
E. L. Wade: 'The Ethnic Art Market in the Southwest', *Objects and Others: Essays on Museums and Material Culture*, ed. G. W. Stocking, History of Anthropology, iii (Madison, 1985)
R. T. Coe: *Lost and Found Traditions: Native American Art 1965–1985* (Seattle, 1986)
E. L. Wade, ed.: *The Arts of the North American Indian: Native Traditions in Evolution* (New York, 1986)
C. J. Frisbie: *Navajo Medicine Bundles or Jish: Acquisition, Transmission and Disposition in the Past and Present* (Albuquerque, 1987)
H. Giambruni, ed.: *Craft Int.* (July-Aug-Sept 1987) [whole issue]
S. White, ed.: *New Directions Northwest: Contemporary Native American Art* (Portland, 1987)
R. Hill: *Indian Art Swimming in the Mainstream*, Daybreak (Midwinter, 1988)
J. Jacka and L. Jacka: *Beyond Tradition: Contemporary Indian Art and its Evolution* (Flagstaff, 1988)
L. Weisberg: 'Battleground: Should Indian Artists Have to Prove they're "Genuine"?', *Chicago Tribune* (7 July 1988), sect. 5, pp. 1, 11
J. Arango: 'What's it All About: When Is an Indian not an Indian? Squabbling in Santa Fe', *A. & Ant.*, vi/4 (1989)
L. B. Easton: 'The Only One who Knows: A Separate Vision', *Amer. Ind. A.*, xiv/3 (1989)
H. Pindell: 'Art World Racism: A Documentation', *New A. Examiner*, xvi/7 (1989)
EDWIN L. WADE

3. TOURIST ART.

(i) Introduction. (ii) Regional survey. (iii) Market influences.

(i) Introduction. Native American tourist art can be defined as art made by Native Americans for sale to cultural outsiders; these essentially commercialized works make up a large part of the Native American ethnic art market. From the earliest days of contact, Native American artefacts and art have held great appeal for Europeans and other settlers in North America. Native American communities quickly saw the much needed commercial potential of tourist art, and Euro-American entrepreneurs collaborated with tribal groups to promote art that would be attractive to tourists, with independent Native Americans traders acting as an important catalyst. Tourism is responsible for the revival and enhancement of much traditional Native American artistry that might otherwise have disappeared.

Native American art is extremely diverse, and this is reflected in tourist art, which ranges from handmade goods in traditional or contemporary modes, to manufactured curios and kitsch. Commercialized Native American arts sell primarily as souvenirs, speculative investments or collectible Americana. At the same time, during the 20th century Native American individualist fine artists have emerged and chosen to compete either within or outside this market-place (see §2 above).

Most later 20th-century tourist art, while based on traditional forms, demonstrates the effects of acculturation. Goods originally sold to visitors were utilitarian items made for daily or ceremonial purposes; these items had long been used for trade among tribes. Later, the growing volume of tourist trade led native craftsmen to create works specifically for sale. Native Americans started by creating these souvenirs through traditional means, but they soon saw that they could also sell to tourists various works that carried only the appearance of tradition. Traditional forms were sometimes reworked to accommodate customer convenience and taste, as in the miniaturization of utilitarian and decorative objects. Tourists wanted works that were recognizably 'Native American', portable, decorative or useful and, in many cases, inexpensive. On the positive side, market demand has nurtured indigenous artistic traditions. While some older forms of design and technique have vanished, new expressions have been developed in their place. The purchase of tourist art can encourage a more extensive interest in Native American art.

(ii) Regional survey.

(a) Arctic. Tourist art in the Arctic region is dominated by the Inuit, or Eskimo. The Aleut offered souvenir baskets and miniature kayaks to early tourists, but the Eskimo have been most active in making and adapting art materials and techniques since their initial contact with Europeans and Asians. Eskimo art's humorous and elegant qualities are popular with non-Native Americans. Independent traders, such as the Hudson's Bay Company and the Canadian and US governments, have encouraged Eskimo art production. By the 1940s Eskimo carvings, fur garments and newly introduced prints were being publicized as desirable goods (see §§III, 1 and VIII, 2 above). In the late 20th century, tourism to the Arctic region increased, along with appreciation of local Native American arts. Athapaskan tribes sell these works at shops along the Alaska Highway.

Artefacts from daily life—ulu knives (with curved, broad blades, used by Inuit women for gutting fish and game), beaded clothing, parkas, mukluks (boots made from reindeer-skin or sealskin), dolls, wooden bowls and moose-hair embroidery—are created in regular or miniaturized forms. Eskimo sculpture, carved from walrus ivory, soapstone, wood or bone, is subject to commercialization but sells mainly as a fine art. Overall, Eskimo art has been confusingly marketed, with many cheap and shoddy goods sold to unwary visitors. Some of this has been the result of overproduction, since the income derived from these objects is vital to a people with seasonal and erratic employment.

(b) Northwest Coast. Peoples of this region have revived various arts in recent years. Their works contain rich naturalistic designs and vivid colours. Ceremonial carvings, such as masks and rattles, are considered a fine art in themselves and have been imitated for the tourist trade (see §III, 2 above). The Salish, Nootka and Chinooka have revived some of their older crafts, making masks, figures, boxes and small totems for export. The Kwakiutl and Bella Coola carve bolder, more dramatic sculptures and masks. Reproductions of traditional storage boxes, food bowls and spoons are often the work of the Tlingit and Tsimshian. The Haida are known for their souvenir renderings of argillite pipes and miniaturized totem poles. Tribal handmade craft industries have grown, but so has mass production and fakes, distorting some of the true beauty of Northwest Coast designs through crude execution and overpainting. Totem poles have even been co-opted as souvenirs by other Native American groups.

(c) California. In the West, the Native Americans of California produce and sell tourist items in a market already saturated with the crafts of the south-western tribes. Basketwork is the chief indigenous product of the various California tribes (see §XIV, 4 above). The Pomo are particularly noted for their 'jewel' or 'gift' baskets, which are decorated with shell pendants and feathers. The Yurok, Karok and Mission peoples weave twined baskets with half-twist overlay. Full-twist overlay is employed by the Klamath, Modoc and Maidu. Many younger basket-weavers are carrying on these traditions.

(d) Southwest. Tourist art is a primary industry in the Southwest; the region is the site of an unprecedented collaboration between Native Americans and outsiders that has transformed traditional arts into saleable commodities. Pottery manufacture, jewellery-making, weaving and wood-carving have been deliberately altered as a result of the tourist trade. Through skilful marketing, the reintegrated commercial arts of the Navajo and Pueblo Native Americans of New Mexico and Arizona are recognized internationally. In the late 19th century the Pueblo sold their wares at train stops and on reservations, often as part of the attractions offered by such tour operators as the Fred Harvey Company. Pueblo potters, their craft largely restored by the tourist market, revived older designs and decreased sizes to make their pottery more portable (see §V, 1(ii) above). San Ildefonso Pueblo, NM, was a popular tourist stop, and it became famous for the black-on-black ware of Maria Martinez (see MARTINEZ). Successful tourist pottery from other Pueblos includes Zuni owls, Acoma seed pots and Cochiti 'story-tellers' and other figurines (see fig. 72). The Yuma and Mohave of Arizona make decorated pottery dolls for sale.

Silver-and-turquoise jewellery is one of the most identifiable symbols of Southwest craftsmanship (see §VI, 2 above); and the Navajo dominate the field. After the 1920s tourist demand led to increased use of lightweight silver and alloys, precut turquoise stones and stamp work with 'Native American' symbols. Several Pueblos have also gained distinction for their jewellery-making. The Santo Domingo Pueblo, NM, produces much imitated heishe beads (either machine- or handmade disc-shaped beads, usually of shell, sometimes of semi-precious stone or silver) and 'liquid silver' necklaces (made from thin, tube-shaped silver beads, either machine or hand drawn,

72. Native American tourist art, three figurines of bathers, clay with slip and pigment, h. (left to right) 152 mm, 136 mm, 152 mm, 1984, from Cochiti Pueblo, New Mexico (Santa Fe, NM, Mudd-Carr Gallery)

used in chokers and necklaces). The Zuni are remarkable lapidarists in inlay and channel work. Zuni fetishes—those that are made for sale and that have no religious meaning—have become collectable carvings; strung into popular necklaces, these fetishes also form a popular jewellery style. The Hopi created a distinctive silver overlay jewellery style in the late 1930s.

Traders on and around the Navajo reservation in the 19th century helped develop rug- and blanket-weaving into a lucrative form of tourist art (see §VII, 2 above). Weavers produce specific styles and patterns named for the trading post that actively encouraged rug production. Navajo textiles range from expensive collectors' items to goods available in various sizes and prices at trading posts. While Hopi *kachina* figures (see §III, 4 above) are still made to have religious meaning, in response to buyer preferences these commercial *kachina* dolls, developed to accommodate collectors' tastes, are now carved with fully articulated bodies and finished with bright colours and meticulously detailed features (see §III, 4 above). Basketry also thrives in the works of various tribes. The Hopi are known for their Second Mesa coiled baskets, and Oraibi wicker ware. The Pima, Papago and Havasupai of Arizona are the most well-known basket producers (see XIV, 5 above).

(e) Plains, Great Basin and Plateau. The peoples of these regions have long had tourist appeal. Plains tribes are often considered representative of a typical 'Native American' type, frequently depicted in films, with mythic qualities of nobility, spirituality and ferocity. Art forms from tribes in this region, however, do not have such a homogenous aspect; Plains tribes traded extensively with their neighbours and borrowed pleasing materials and designs at will. For example cultural interaction with the tribes of the Southwest is evident in their tourist metalwork (see §VI, 2 and 3 above). Decorative ceremonial regalia, such as feather headdresses, robes, carved stone pipes and painted shields, excite tourist and collector demand because of their touted spiritual elements (see §§VIII, 9 and XII, 2 above). A popular imitation on the market is the specious 'Native American mandala', based on the Plains tribes' painted-hide vision shields. Tribal co-operatives have been established to meet the demand for authentic Plains art. Beaded garments, moccasins and pouches, incorporating the lazy-stitch sewing technique, whereby beads are strung on and fastened to surface ends, with an arched, angular line effect, are produced for tourist consumption (see §IX, 6 above). The Utes, Jicarilla Apaches and Nez Perce sell fine coiled and twined basketry to visitors. The Sioux, Cheyenne and Arapaho produce distinctive geometric designs on souvenir goods.

(f) Woodlands. On historical artefacts of the Woodlands tribes are based such souvenir kitsch as tomahawks, beadwork resembling wampum strings, and miniature

canoes and wigwams. However, Woodlands fine crafts, including wood-carvings, weaving, decorative beading, leathercraft and basketwork, are also much in demand as tourist goods. Algonquian baskets and featherwork are still made by various tribes. Iroquois crafts, such as cornhusk dolls and German silver jewellery (*see* §VI, 4 above), have been tourist staples since the mid-19th century. The Micmac and Cree of Canada create artful woodcrafts, weaving and screenprints, while the more northern Naskapi are renowned for their beaded garments. The Cherokee and Catawba of North Carolina make and sell pottery in forms that have been influenced by trade with outsiders. The Seminoles' palmetto fibre dolls and colourful patchwork and ribbon appliqué clothing are part of Florida's active tourist trade.

(iii) Market influences. Tourist art is particularly affected by customer preference. This has led to the creation of such new and controversial art forms as portable Navajo sand painting. However, the commercialization of Native American painting, sculpture and graphic art has encouraged a static and limiting approach to subject-matter (*see* §IV, 2 above). Many non-Native American buyers prefer traditional, stereotyped imagery, and paintings and sculpture often perpetuate romanticized and oversimplified views of what 'Native American' art should look like. Depictions of ceremonial rites abound, despite the bitter opposition of conservative Native Americans. However, these commercialized works continue to be sold to enthusiastic and undiscriminating consumers (*see* §2 above).

The governments of Canada and the USA have offered sporadic encouragement to the commercial Native American art market. Nineteenth-century government agents advocated craft production for tribes settling on reservations. In the USA the Indian Arts and Crafts Board was established in 1935 as a governmental means of assistance. The Canadian Indian Affairs Branch has taken a parallel role, with a central purchasing and distribution centre in Ottawa. Native American goods are featured in the exhibitions of Canada's National Gift Show and the Canadian Handicrafts Guild.

Native American tourist art, like all art produced for a market more interested in myth and romance than reality, suffers from exploitation by entrepreneurs. While genuine goods are made for sale and export, many mass-produced and misleadingly labelled objects are churned out by factories in North America, Mexico and Asia. Native American designs and craftsmanship are appropriated freely by non-Native Americans. The Indian Arts and Crafts Association, started in 1974, is a membership organization with a code of ethics for the promotion and sale of authentic work. US government regulations against misrepresentation have been attempted as recently as 1991; however, successful enforcement continues to be problematic (*see* §2 above). One provision of the current law, requiring proof of tribal enrolment, has been criticized by Native Americans and non-Native Americans alike.

BIBLIOGRAPHY
Indian Art of the United States (exh. cat. by F. Douglas and R. d'Harnoncourt, New York, MOMA, 1941)
C. Lyford: *Iroquois Crafts* (Washington, DC, 1945)
The Development of Indian and Eskimo Art and Crafts in the Far North: NOREC Conference: Toronto, 1965
C. Tanner: *Southwest Indian Craft Arts* (Tucson, 1968)
G. Dorfles: *Kitsch: The World of Bad Taste* (New York, 1970)
A. Whiteford: *North American Indian Arts* (New York, 1970)
J. J. Brody: *Indian Painters and White Patrons* (Albuquerque, 1971)
F. Dockstader: *Indian Art in America: The Arts and Crafts of the North American Indian* (New York, 1974)
N. Feder: *American Indian Art* (New York, 1974)
J. Highwater: *Fodor's Indian America* (New York, 1975)
N. Graburn, ed.: *Ethnic and Tourist Arts: Cultural Expressions from the Fourth World* (Berkeley, 1976)
M. Lund: *Indian Jewelry: Fact and Fantasy* (Boulder, 1976)
L. Deitch: 'The Impact of Tourism upon the Arts and Crafts of the Indians of the Southwestern United States', *Hosts and Guests: The Anthropology of Tourism*, ed. V. Smith (Philadelphia, 1977), pp. 173–84
Indian Kitsch: The Use and Misuse of Indian Images (exh. cat. by F. Scholder, Phoenix, AZ, Heard Mus., 1979)
Magic Images: Contemporary Native American Art (exh. cat., ed. E. Wade; Tulsa, OK, Philbrook A. Cent., 1981)
D. J. Ray: *Aleut and Eskimo Art: Tradition and Innovation in South Alaska* (Seattle, 1981)
E. Wade: 'The Ethnic Art Market and the Dilemma of Innovative Indian Artists', *Magic Images: Contemporary Native American Art*, ed. E. Wade (Tulsa, 1981), pp. 9–17
R. Schrader: *The Indian Arts and Crafts Board: An Aspect of New Deal Policy* (Albuquerque, 1983)
R. Coe: *Lost and Found Traditions: Native American Art 1965–1985* (New York, 1986)
E. Wade, ed.: *The Arts of the North American Indian: Native Tradition in Evolution* (New York, 1986)
D. Evans-Pritchard: 'The Portal Case: Authenticity, Tourism, Traditions and the Law', *J. Amer. Flklore*, c (1987), pp. 287–96
J. Jacka: *Beyond Tradition: Contemporary Indian Art and its Evolution* (Flagstaff, 1988)
S. Greer: 'Stereotypes, Native Art and Art', *Artviews*, xiv (March–May 1989), pp. 18–23
R. Phillips: 'Souvenirs from North America: The Miniature as Image of Woodlands Indian Life', *Amer. Ind. A.*, xiv/2 (1989), pp. 52–63, 78–9
Eagle Walking Turtle: *Indian America: A Traveler's Companion* (Santa Fe, NM, 1989, rev. 1991)

PAULA A. BAXTER

4. ARCHITECTURE. From the late 1960s Native Americans commissioned and sometimes designed buildings that acknowledged the architectural heritage of the Native American nations or presented an innovative, self-consciously 'Indian' appearance. The socio-political background to this includes supratribal ('pan-Indian') political activism; an improved legal position; greater numbers of educated Native Americans, including graduates of architecture schools; and Post-modern currents promoting cultural specificity in design. Early examples were the Navajo Community College and the Hopi Cultural Center (*see* §II, 2 above) and the Minneapolis American Indian Center (1975) by the Hodne-Stageberg Partnership. Resurgent interest in Native American language, dance and other aspects of heritage became widespread in the later 20th century and is represented by a wide variety of buildings, especially in the states where Native Americans concentrate: Arizona, New Mexico, California, Washington, Oklahoma, North and South Dakota, Minnesota, Wisconsin and New York. The building types are rarely those used in the past; in some cases, they were unknown before the Indian Reorganization Act of 1934 established forms of Native American government and promoted secular direction of education and health care. The building types include tribal offices; schools; cultural centres and museums; clinics; tribally controlled colleges; libraries; some housing; Native American Churches; bingo halls and casinos ('domestic dependent nations' are not subject to all state-imposed regulations on gambling).

The buildings may be grouped according to the design strategies used to relate Native American tradition or interests to contemporary form. The first group represents the repetition of venerable building types for customary purposes, sometimes using modern materials. (Native Americans have incorporated useful new ideas into their culture without losing their Native identity.) One example is the Pawnee Roundhouse (1971–4) in Pawhuska, Oklahoma, a commodious polygon extended by a vestibule. Inside a shell of wood, its internal steel structure achieves a broad span economically. Hogans (earth-covered log structures) are found in many parts of the Navaho reservation; roundhouses are built in California and other states; groups and individuals erect sweatlodges on many reservations; and longhouses rise in Washington, the large Swinomish example (1990–92) by Cedar Tree Associates being especially beautiful inside.

A second strategy is that of adapting older forms. The Yakima in Washington erected a taller variant of a longhouse; the Swinomish social service building (1970s) is shaped like a longhouse, with a central assembly hall surrounded by banked seats. Don Wedll, an official of the Mille Lacs Band (Ojibwe), designed his home (c. 1980) in Minnesota as a domed wigwam, using modern materials and internal arrangements, with a bedroom balcony above the other rooms. Cuningham, Hamilton, Quiter designed two polygonal wooden ceremonial structures (1992–3) for the Mille Lacs Band, alluding to tradition without imitating it. The Indian Pueblo Cultural Center (1976) in Albuquerque by Hoshour & Pearson has a semicircular plan recalling that of Pueblo Bonito at Chaco Canyon. The San Felipe Pueblo School (c. 1990) by Mimbres Associates is a particularly sensitive version of the indigenous architectural manner, emphasizing juxtaposed geometric forms.

Other buildings employ traditional plans but non-traditional elevations: examples include the Lac du Flambeau Museum (1989), WI, by Fritz Dreger (b 1942), constructed as a centralized roundhouse; or the Lake Mendocino Pomo Visitor Center (1982), CA, by the Promontory Partnership, a handsome round building covered in shingles and embedded in the landscape. Some buildings suggest traditional forms using innovative plans: one example is the Camp Verde Visitor Center (1981), AZ, by Dennis Numkena (b 1941; Hopi), which varies the forms of a loose pueblo grouping and culminates in a tower based upon the ladder of a *kiva*.

Several architects, sometimes at the client's direction, used Native American symbols as the basis of design: among them were Thomas Hodne (b 1927), Dennis Sun Rhodes (b 1947; Arapaho), Richard Thern (b 1930), Denby Deegan (b ?1946; Sioux–Arikara) and David Sloan (b 1949; Navaho). They created the most overtly innovative Native American buildings in the late 20th century. The Native American Cultural Center (1981) in Niagara Falls, NY, by Hodne-Stageberg Partners has the plan of a turtle (a sacred figure for the sponsoring Iroquois) with a geodesic dome as the carapace. Deegan's Four Winds School (1978–83) design at Fort Totten Reservation, ND, is a cylinder quadrisected by corridors, evoking the medicine wheel. In a round Culture Room at the core, a tipi serves as the counselling centre for troubled children.

Other architects emphasized natural materials and harmony with the landscape, as Native American peoples are widely seen as having a special relationship to the earth and cosmos. At Cherokee, NC, Six Associates designed triangular prismatic spaces (1976) recalling the local mountains. The surface is of wood, windows allow broad views, and a rivulet runs along a stone trough on the façade. One Muscogee Creek office building (1980) by Ragsdale, Christenson, Everett, is embedded in a grass-covered mound. The entrance hall of the Warm Springs Museum (1993), OR, by Stastny-Burke emphasizes branching cylindrical, tree-like columns.

Some buildings do not appear specifically Native American but are so regarded because the design and/or building processes were culturally appropriate. Three examples are the wooden Lakota Studies Building (1989) at Oglala Lakota College, SD, by Ron Hernandez (b 1947; Lakota), the Ramah Navajo School, (1975) NM, by Hirshen, Gammill, Trumbo and the Ak-Chin Eco-Museum (1991), AZ, by D. Kristine Woolsey (b1959).

BIBLIOGRAPHY

'Regionalism in the Southwest', *Prog. Archit.*, lv (March, 1974), pp. 70–77 [on Gonzales' Hopi Cultural Center]

E. Gaboury: 'Amerindian Identity: Architects: The Hodne-Stageberg Partners', *Archit. Rev.* [London], cxviii/1002 (1980), pp. 79–86

S. Woodbridge: 'School Designed both with and for a Navajo Community', *J. Amer. Inst. Architects*, lxix/14 (1980), pp. 40–45 [on the Ramah school]

P. West: 'The Miami Indian Tourist Attractions: A History and Analysis of a Transitional Micasuki Seminole Environment', *FL Anthropol.*, 34 (1981), pp. 200–24

J. Stewart: 'Bringing Native Spirit Home', *Archit. MN*, xi/3 (1985), pp. 48–51 [on housing by Hodne and Sun Rhodes]

R. G. Brittain and M. A. Myhrman: 'Toward a Responsive Tohono O'Odham Dwelling', *Arid Lands Newslett.*, 28 (1989), pp. 20–23

J. Amer. Inst. Architects, lxxxii/12 (1993) [esp. pp. 35, 37, 70–71, 93–101]

C. H. Krinsky: *Contemporary Native American Architecture* (New York)

CAROL HERSELLE KRINSKY

XVI. Archaeology.

North American archaeology has always had two objectives. The first was to integrate the linguistic, social and material culture history of Native American groups that were disappearing under the expansion of their recorders' society. The other was to place that cultural history within the contemporary global framework. The initial development of American archaeology, and its dependent relationship to anthropology, can be traced to political history. Questions of origins occupied the first studies of the 16th and 17th centuries; the ecclesiastic decision that Native Americans were equally descended from Adam raised the questions of where they had come from, and when they had arrived in America. Investigations initially began as 'field archaeology' in the two areas of North America in which the most spectacular ancient architectural remains were to be found: the eastern Woodlands and the Southwest.

The first trans-Appalachian explorers were amazed by the ancient earthworks and mounds they encountered (see fig.73). While THOMAS JEFFERSON's mound excavation in 1784 on his Virginia farm left him with the unpopular belief that the mounds' builders were ancestral Native Americans, frontier sentiment, nascent antiquarianism and even federal policy coincided in the conviction that Native

73. John J. Egan : *Dr Dickenson Excavating a Mound*, detail from the panoramic painting *Monumental Grandeur of the Mississippi Valley*, thin flexible paint resembling tempera on muslin sheeting, 2.28×106 m, 1850 (St Louis, MO, Art Museum)

Americans had no legitimate claim to a continent that had once been occupied by a civilized race of 'Moundbuilders', supposed to have come from Ireland, Israel, North Africa or China. In the decades before the American Civil War (1861–5), self-taught archaeologists demonstrated that the mounds and earthworks, and their inclusive artefacts, differed; but varying explanations interpreted every hilltop or closed earthwork as a fort, each geometric mound or ritual object as proof of foreign evangelists and any object from non-local sources as proof of ancient trans-oceanic commercial imperialism.

Between the American Civil War and World War I federal exploration of the West had also revealed the existence of hundreds of masonry ruins in precarious settings. The obvious cultural connections with surviving modern Pueblo groups curtailed any serious belief in a separate race of 'Cliff-Dwellers', and for a generation extensive, if unsystematic, artefact collecting and site recording documented the spatial, stylistic and presumably temporal differences in Southwest prehistory. At the same time, excavations throughout the eastern Woodlands by the Smithsonian Institution and by scholars from Pennsylvania, Mississippi, Wisconsin, Georgia and Massachusetts concluded that the mounds, like the scattered village sites being revealed by agriculture and development, were the works of Native Americans of different times and different cultures.

The issues of relative chronology became an increasing concern in the 20th century. Descriptions of American antiquities concentrated on deriving temporal sequences of mound, cliff dwelling or village by comparing the artefacts they contained. Successive waves of earlier indigenous populations were posited from purported similarities of chosen artefacts; these often found spurious confirmation from physical anthropology. Cruder stone tools from buried river beds or mines had long been compared to materials from European Pleistocene deposits (*c.* 2 million–10,000 BP), but human occupation of the New World was not considered to be of great antiquity. Two issues were crucial: to establish the duration of the American past and to assess the evidence for American artefacts in geological contexts like those in Europe. By the 20th century physical anthropologists had shown that, in many inherited characteristics, Native Americans were most similar to, and were probably descendants of, Mongoloid peoples of north-central Asia. Then, in the 1920s, discovery of artefacts associated with extinct fauna at several western sites demonstrated a respectable antiquity for the occupation of the New World and revealed the material culture of the earliest Native Americans. Still, in the eastern Woodlands, neither fauna nor a layered (stratigraphic) sequence of cultural materials seemed present, limiting temporal interpretation until after World War II.

Between World War I and World War II most American archaeologists followed the broad classificatory approaches of biological and social evolution, using them to recognize and measure social contacts between different prehistoric societies or through time. In the late 1920s the development by A. E. Douglass of a tree-ring chronology gave Southwest archaeology a dating method and an insight into prehistoric social and spatial differences virtually unique in the world. Meanwhile, the detailed archaeological field techniques developed in England were applied to Midwest sites, revealing a new wealth of social and historical data.

During the Great Depression of the 1930s vast Federal Relief Projects used those techniques in the Woodlands, on the Plains and in the Far West and acquired masses of archaeological data. Deep and extensive site exposures and intensive analytical studies became common in American archaeology for the first time. While differing in detail, in both the eastern Woodlands and the Southwest, American archaeologists created complex, Linnean-like, material culture taxonomies, pioneering statistical studies, in which the presence or absence of ritual objects, the similarities of burial details and the minutiae of shared or copied designs on pottery indicated relationships between artefacts, sites and regions. The best interpretations in all areas of the country were structured by attributing the behaviour of historic ethnographic groups to the remains of prehistoric groups, although in most of the eastern Woodlands little direct continuity could be demonstrated.

After World War II, American archaeologists turned to the evaluative criteria based on new techniques for determining the sources, manufacturing methods and functions of archaeological structures and objects. In 1951 W. F. Libby's discovery of the radiocarbon dating method provided the entire continent with the potential, hitherto confined to the Southwest, to determine relative or absolute lapses of time. By the late 1960s new excavation and recovery methods for plant and animal remains from apparently unpromising sites in the Woodlands led to ecological models of cultural change, soon adopted in the western states and then around the world. American archaeology also brought anthropology back into explanation of the past. Interpretation of social roles in prehistoric ritual, exchange structure and social interaction was expressed in terms of what were called the 'law-like generalizations' of sociology, ethnology and cultural geography. By the 1970s this approach incorporated evolutionary operational systems models and concepts advanced as information theory. Such approaches were combined with techniques of remote sensing and computerized geographic displays in predictive models of archaeological site location being demanded by new protective legislation. Most recently, American archaeologists have discarded their brief flirtation with the deconstructive approach, which claimed not only that the meaning of what happened in the past was different for different 'readers' but also that there was no correct way to know what happened in the past at all.

BIBLIOGRAPHY

J. E. Fitting, ed.: *The Development of North American Archaeology* (New York, 1973)

G. R. Willey and J. A. Sabloff: *A History of American Archaeology* (London and San Francisco, 1974; 2/1980)

S. Williams: *Fantastic Archaeology: The Wild Side of North American Prehistory* (Philadelphia, 1991)

DAVID S. BROSE

XVII. Historiography.

The history of the study of Native American art has closely followed the history of anthropological research, principally because most scholars who have studied Native American art have been anthropologists: the first major work on the subject by an art historian was published in 1949 (Wingert). A central concept of early Native American studies was that of the culture area. It was first adopted as a means of organizing artefacts for museum display and was used by Otis Mason, William Henry Holmes and FRANZ BOAS at the Chicago World Columbian Exposition of 1893. The practice soon spread to the National Museum of American Art and the American Museum of Natural

History and became standard for general works on Native American art as well as museum displays.

1. ANTHROPOLOGICAL APPROACHES. Until the 1940s and 1950s American anthropological scholarship tended to be positivist, with little analysis from a theoretical point of view. The Bureau of American Ethnography and the National Museum of American Art in Washington, DC, produced an excellent series of monographs describing the material culture of many Native American peoples. These formed the basis of much of the literature on Native American art during the 20th century. Some, such as Mallery's work on picture writing, Holmes' on Woodland pottery and Mason's on basketwork, were comparative in scope, while others dealt with specific ethnic groups, such as the Apache (Bourke), the Naskapi (Turner), the Eskimo (Nelson, Hoffman), the Cherokee (Mooney), the Zuni (Stevenson), the Hopi (Fewkes) and the Omaha (Fletcher and La Flesche).

Franz Boas was as central to the study of Native American art as he was to American anthropology (Jonaitis, 1994). He began by analyzing the art of the North-west Coast in an attempt to show that the art of this area was the product of complex historical circumstances rather than unilinear degeneration from realism to abstraction favoured by evolutionists. Boas's own work was supplemented by a series of monographs written under his direction for the American Museum of Natural History's Jesup North Pacific Expedition (1897–1902), including Emmons's work on blankets. As Boas's interests expanded, this was reflected in the work of his students. The first generation was mostly engaged with questions of style and symbolism, producing monographs on Arapaho symbols (Kroeber, 1900, 1902), Basketwork designs (Dixon) and the arts of the Crow (Lowie) and the Sioux (Wissler); Kroeber's contribution was particularly important. The second generation was encouraged to study the psychology of the artist and the creative process: Ruth Bunzel's analysis of the Pueblo potter remains a classic and was complemented by other work on individual basketmakers, weavers and potters (O'Neale; Reichard; Marriott).

George Heye, the collector who formed the Museum of the American Indian in New York, was also associated with a group of scholars who studied Native American art from an anthropological perspective. They contributed works to the Museum's publication series, many of which dealt with the peoples of the Great Lakes and eastern North America. These included studies of the double-curve motif (Speck, 1914), quillwork (Orchard, 1916), beadwork (Orchard, 1921), the Menominee (Skinner), the Penobscot (Speck, 1927) and the Naskapi (Speck, 1935). Speck's Naskapi publication was particularly important as an investigation into the relations between cosmology, religion and art. Other noteworthy publications were those on the Eskimo (Ray), the North-west Coast (Gunther) and the Iroquois (Fenton).

During the 1930s new ideas from Europe began to challenge the positivism of American anthropologists. Diffusionism was the first of these theoretical frameworks to gain wide acceptance. Boas had already used the concept of the diffusion of art styles from one group to another within a relatively small geographic area as part of his challenge to evolutionism, but his kind of diffusionism was very different from the more radical form popular from the 1930s to the 1960s. This took the form of a trans-Pacific contact theory, according to which art styles were generated in ancient China and spread throughout the Pacific basin by migration; it was these population movements rather than coincidence that had produced the similarities between the arts of China and those of the New World (Covarrubias, Fraser). Diffusionism was rapidly superseded by the structuralism of Claude Lévi-Strauss (1963, 1982), who held that 'primitive' people were intellectual equals of 'Westerners'. Significant studies of the stone sculpture of British Columbia (Duff), the art of the Navajo (Witherspoon), Eskimo basketwork (Lee) and the art of the Northern Tlingit (Jonaitis, 1986) were written by scholars attempting to discover the underlying structures of Native American art.

2. ART-HISTORICAL APPROACHES. In the 1940s a group of European refugees who belonged to the Surrealist movement opposed the notion of trans-Pacific contact, suggesting that any similarities in style between Chinese art and that of Native Americans were due to similar mythic structures (Paalen). They believed Native American art to be similar in inspiration to their own art, and by making their admiration for this material public they helped to validate it as 'art' (Cowling; Jonaitis, 1981; Maurer, 1984). The Surrealists complemented an American movement aimed at promoting the aesthetic appreciation of Native American art that had been initiated in the 1920s by the artist JOHN SLOAN. In 1931 Sloan and Oliver LaFarge organized the first large-scale exhibition of this material, the *Exposition of Indian Tribal Arts* in New York. This was followed in 1939 by the splendid exhibition of Native American art that Frederic Douglas of the Denver Art Museum and René d'Harnoncourt, general manager of the Indian Arts and Crafts Board, organized for the San Francisco Golden Gate Exposition. Their exhibition at the Museum of Modern Art in New York in 1941, *Indian Art of the United States*, firmly established the artistic nature of this material.

Subsequent surveys of Native American art consisted largely of exhibition catalogues associated with artistically oriented museum displays. Although there have been many exhibitions on single culture areas, particularly those that appeal specially to Western tastes, such as the Northwest Coast (Jonaitis, 1991) and the Inuit, several publications have been produced in association with exhibitions that displayed Native American art in general, including those by Coe (1977), Maurer (1977) and Roosevelt and Smith. *The Spirit Sings* (1987 exh. cat.) was noteworthy as the first major publication devoted to Canadian native art. The growing acceptance of Native American art as 'art' has given rise to monographs that deal with named artists such as the Kwakiutl wood-carver WILLIE SEAWEED (Holm, 1983) and the Haida artists BILL REID (Shadbolt) and ROBERT DAVIDSON (Thom). Recently studies have been made analysing the history of scholarship on Native American art (Berlo, 1992).

3. ANALYSIS OF ACCULTURATION. Boas, like many of his generation, feared the rapid disappearance of Native

American groups and tried to represent them as he supposed they had been in pre-European contact times. Such attempts to describe the art of pristine, unacculturated people led to a bias in favour of 'traditional' art and against any art influenced by Euro-Americans. Since the 1960s a growing body of literature on what is generally termed acculturated art has worked against this bias. In these publications Native American art is seen as a dynamic, changing element of culture that integrates the traditional with the innovative but always remains 'Native American' at its core. The major theoretician on art and acculturation was Nelson Graburn (1976), who proposed several different categories of what he called 'Fourth World' art: traditional art made for the Euro-American market; art that synthesizes Native and non-Native American traditions; and innovative art made for sale. The literature on arts that have been influenced by Euro-American patronage or sales includes works on painting, particularly in the Southwest and the Plains (Tanner; Brody), Inuit carving and printmaking (Swinton; Goetz), Micmac quillwork (Whitehead), Haida argillite carving (Macnair and Hoover), 'tourist art' (Phillips, 1993) and the North-west Coast 'renaissance' (Macnair, Hoover and Neary). Exhibitions of such art have had accompanying catalogues, notably Ralph Coe's *Lost and Found Traditions* and Gerhard Hoffmann's *Indianische Kunst im 20. Jahrhundert*.

BIBLIOGRAPHY

ANTHROPOLOGICAL APPROACHES

J. Bourke: 'Medicine-men of the Apache', *Annu. Rep. Bureau Amer. Ethnol. Secretary Smithsonian Inst.*, ix (1892)

G. Mallery: 'Picture-writing of the American Indians', *Annu. Rep. Bureau Amer. Ethnol. Secretary Smithsonian Inst.*, x (1893)

L. Turner: 'Ethnology of the Ungava District, Hudson Bay Territory', *Annu. Rep. Bureau Amer. Ethnol. Secretary Smithsonian Inst.*, xi (1894)

W. Holmes: 'Aboriginal Pottery of the Eastern United States', *Annu. Rep. Bureau Amer. Ethnol. Secretary Smithsonian Inst.*, xx (1899)

E. W. Nelson: 'The Eskimo Around Bering Strait', *Annu. Rep. Bureau Amer. Ethnol. Secretary Smithsonian Inst.*, xx (1899)

A. B. Kroeber: 'Symbolism of the Arapaho Indians', *Amer. Mus. Nat. Hist. Bull.*, xiii (1900) [whole issue]

J. Mooney: 'Myths of the Cherokee', *Annu. Rep. Bureau Amer. Ethnol. Secretary Smithsonian Inst.*, xix (1900)

W. J. Hoffman: 'The Graphic Art of the Eskimos Based upon the Collections in the National Museum', *Report for 1899: US National Museum* (Washington, DC, 1901)

M. C. Stevenson: 'The Zuni Indians', *Annu. Rep. Bureau Amer. Ethnol. Secretary Smithsonian Inst.*, xxiii (1902)

A. L. Kroeber: 'The Arapaho, ii: Decorative Art and Symbolism', *Amer. Mus. Nat. Hist. Bull.*, xvii (1902) [whole issue]

R. Dixon: 'Basketry Designs of the Indians of Northern California', *Amer. Mus. Nat. Hist. Bull.*, xvii (1902) [whole issue]

W. J. Fewkes: 'Hopi Katcinas, Drawn by Native Artists', *Annu. Rep. Bureau Amer. Ethnol. Secretary Smithsonian Inst.*, xxi (1903)

O. T. Mason: 'Aboriginal American Basketry', *Annual Report for 1902: US National Museum* (Washington, DC, 1904)

C. Wissler: 'Decorative Art of the Sioux Indians'. *Amer. Mus. Nat. Hist. Bull.*, xviii (1904) [whole issue]

A. C. Fletcher and F. La Flesche: 'The Omaha Tribe', *Annu. Rep. Bureau Amer. Ethnol. Secretary Smithsonian Inst.*, xxvii (1906)

G. T. Emmons: *The Chilkat Blanket*, Memoirs of the American Museum of Natural History (New York, 1907)

F. Speck: *The Double-curve Motive in Northeastern Algonkian Art*, Canadian Dept of Mines Geological Survey, Memoir xlii (Ottawa, 1914)

W. C. Orchard: 'The Technique of Porcupine-quill Decoration among the North American Indians', *Contrib. Mus. Amer. Ind., Heye Found.*, iv (1916)

——: 'Beads and Beadwork of the American Indians', *Contrib. Mus. Amer. Ind., Heye Found.*, xi (1921)

A. Skinner: *Material Culture of the Menomini*, Indian Notes and Monographs, misc. ser., xx (1921)

R. Lowie: 'Crow Indian Art', *Amer. Mus. Nat. Hist. Bull.*, xxi (1922)

F. Speck: 'Symbolism in Penobscot Art', *Amer. Mus. Nat. Hist. Bull.*, xxix (1927)

R. Bunzel: *The Pueblo Potter* (New York, 1929)

L. O'Neale: 'Yurok-Karok Basket Weavers', *U. CA Pubns Amer. Archaeol. & Ethnol.*, xxxii (1932) [whole issue]

G. Reichard: *Spider Woman: The Story of Navaho Weavers and Chanters* (New York, 1934)

F. Speck: *Naskapi* (Norman, 1935)

W. Fenton: 'Masked Medicine Societies of the Iroquois', *Annual Report of the Smithsonian Institution for 1940* (Washington, DC, 1940)

A. Marriot: *Maria the Potter of San Ildefonso* (Norman, 1948)

M. Covarrubias: *The Eagle, the Jaguar and the Serpent* (New York, 1954)

C. Lévi-Strauss: *Structural Anthropology* (Garden City, 1963)

E. Gunther: *Art in the Life of the Northwest Coast Indians* (Portland, 1966)

D. J. Ray: *Eskimo Masks* (Seattle, 1967)

D. Fraser: *Early Chinese Art and the Pacific Basin* (New York, 1968)

W. Duff: *Images: Sonte B.C.* (Seattle, 1975)

G. Witherspoon: *Language and Art in the Navaho Universe* (Ann Arbor, 1977)

C. Lévi-Strauss: *The Way of the Masks* (Seattle, 1982)

M. Lee: *Baleen Basketry of the North Alaskan Eskimo* (AK, 1983)

A. Jonaitis: *Art of the Northern Tlingit* (Seattle, 1986)

A. Jonaitis, ed.: *'A Wealth of Thought': Franz Boas on Native American Art History* (Seattle, 1994)

ART-HISTORICAL APPROACHES

J. Sloan and O. LaFarge: *Introduction to American Indian Art* (New York, 1931)

P. Douglas and R. d'Harnoncourt: *Indian Art of the United States* (New York, 1941)

W. Paalen: 'Totem Art', *DYN*, 4–5 (1943), pp. 7–39

P. S. Wingert: *American Indian Sculpture: A Study of the North-west Coast* (New York, 1949)

B. Holm: *Northwest Coast Indian Art: An Analysis of Form* (Seattle, 1965)

Sacred Circles: Two Thousand Years of North American Indian Art (exh. cat. by R. Coe, London, Hayward Gal.; Kansas City, MO, W. Rockhill Nelson Gal.; 1977)

E. Maurer: *The Native American Heritage* (Chicago, 1977)

E. Cowling: 'The Eskimos, the American Indians and the Surrealists', *A. Hist.*, i (1978), pp. 485–99

A. Roosevelt and J. Smith: *The Ancestors: Native Artisans of the Americas* (New York, 1979)

H. Stewart: *Robert Davidson: Haida Printmaker* (Seattle, 1979)

A. Jonaitis: 'Creations of Mystics and Philosophers: The White Man's Perceptions of Northwest Coast Indian Art from the 1930s to the Present', *Amer. Ind. Cult. & Res. J.*, i (1981), pp. 1–48

B. Holm: *Smoky-Top: The Art and Times of Willie Seaweed* (Seattle, 1983)

E. Maurer: 'Dada and Surrealism', *Primitivism in 20th Century Art*, ed. W. Rubin (New York, 1984), pp. 535–95

D. Shadbolt: *Bill Reid* (Seattle, 1986)

The Spirit Sings: Artistic Traditions of Canada's First Peoples (exh. cat., Toronto, Glenbow Mus., 1987)

A. Jonaitis, ed.: *Chiefly Feasts: The Enduring Kwakiutl Potlatch* (Seattle, 1991)

J. Berlo, ed.: *The Early Years of Native American Art History: The Politics of Scholarship and Collecting* (Seattle, 1992)

I. Thom, ed.: *Robert Davidson: Eagle of the Dawn* (Vancouver, 1993)

ANALYSIS OF ACCULTURATION

J. J. Brody: *Indian Painters and White Patrons* (Albuquerque, 1971)

G. Swinton: *Sculpture of the Eskimo* (Toronto, 1972)

C. L. Tanner: *Southwest Indian Painting: A Changing Art* (Tucson, 1973)

N. Graburn: *Ethnic and Tourist Arts* (Berkeley, 1976)

H. Goetz: *The Inuit Print* (Ottawa, 1977)

The Legacy: Continuing Traditions of Canadian Northwest Coast Indian Art (exh. cat. by P. Macnair, A. Hoover and K. Neary, Victoria, BC, Prov. Mus., 1980)

R. Whitehead: *Micmac Quillwork* (Halifax, 1982)

P. Macnair and A. Hoover: *The Magic Leaves: A History of Haida Argillite Carving* (Victoria, BC, 1984)

G. Hoffmann: *Indianische Kunst im 20. Jahrhundert* (Munich, 1985)

R. Coe: *Lost and Found Traditions* (New York, 1986)

R. Phillips: 'Why Not Tourist Art?: Significant Silences in Native American Museum Representation', *After Colonialism: Imperialism and the Colonial Aftermath*, ed. G. Prakash (Princeton, 1993)

ALDONA JONAITIS

XVIII. Museums, collections and patronage.

Before the 19th century, European antiquarians were busy amassing collections of antiquities, exotic and unusual items, many of which became the cores of major European museums. Native American art and material culture items were among those sought. European and British collectors were exposed to these artefacts as the result of the discovery, exploration, trading, missionary and colonizing expeditions to North America being conducted at this time. As Hudson notes, John Tradescant's Closet of Curiosities, also known as Tradescant's Ark, 'reflected the seventeenth-century assumption that everything was potentially interesting and useful' (Hudson, 1987, p. 21). Tradescant's collection, which holds early important material from North America, eventually became the foundation of the Ashmolean Museum, Oxford, which opened its doors in 1683. Some pieces from this collection are also in the Pitt Rivers Museum, Oxford University. Arthur MacGregor discusses a number of significant early collections that included North American material, such as those of Athanasius Kircher (1601–80), a Jesuit priest in Rome; Archduke Ferdinand of Tyrol (1529–95); Father Claude du Molinet at the abbey of St Geneviève in 1692; and John Bargrave (1610–80), a canon of Canterbury Cathedral. An example of an 18th-century museum is the Leverian Museum, London, which grew as a result of material collected by James Cook during his various voyages. The approach was different from the old Cabinet of Curiosities or Wunderkammern-type of display, however. The objects were exhibited as representatives from particular cultures. The collection of the Leverian Museum was auctioned in 1806. The Cook ethnographic artefacts were purchased for the Austrian emperor and formed the basis for the Imperial Natural History Cabinet, Vienna (now in Vienna, Mus. Vlkerknd.). Because it owned the Cook material, the Vienna collection subsequently received two major gifts of similar material, one of Ojibwa culture objects and the other of Eskimo material from Greenland (Feest, 1993, p. 6). The era of intensive organized collecting of Native American art began in the late 19th century and continued into the first decade of the 20th century. Many American museums and research institutions, mostly located in the Midwest and on the east coast, were founded at this time and amassed their archaeological, ethnographic and historic collections through large-scale collecting expeditions. Notable examples include the Smithsonian Institution, Washington, DC (founded 1846), the Peabody Museum at Harvard University, Cambridge, MA (1866), the Field Museum of Natural History, Chicago, IL (1893), the American Museum of Natural History (1869), the Museum of the American Indian, Heye Foundation (1916), and the Brooklyn Museum (1823), all in New York. The first extensive collecting trips to the Pueblos of Arizona and New Mexico by the Bureau of American Ethnology (1879) occurred during this time. European museums continued to purchase North American material and entered into exchanges with the new American museums. Feest noted that it became increasingly difficult for European museums to compete for collections with their younger, American counterparts. The number of major European collecting trips dwindled, with the exceptions of Gustaf Nordenskjöld's expeditions to the Southwest, Adrian Jacobsen's to the Northwest Coast and Léon de Cessac's to California (Feest 1993, pp. 7–8). Besides material culture, research was also conducted on linguistics, social structure, religion and other aspects of Native American life. As Janet Berlo (1992, p. 3) noted in her excellent review of Native American art history, for more than 100 years our ideas of what is Native American art was formed by what these institutions collected.

1. Collection and cultural attitudes, late 19th century–early 20th. 2. Interest in individual artists and contemporary art, 1920–40. 3. Growth of a wider public, 1940–50. 4. Developments after 1950.

1. COLLECTION AND CULTURAL ATTITUDES, LATE 19TH CENTURY–EARLY 20TH. In the late 19th century, anthropologists from the above-mentioned institutions, such as FRANK HAMILTON CUSHING, FRANZ BOAS and Stewart Culin, searched out the 'oldest' and the 'most authentic' Native American objects (Berlo, 1992, p. 3). They believed that Native American cultures were dying out and thus felt an urgency in their collecting. These collectors and the manner in which they collected often influenced, and had serious and complicated consequences for, the groups with which they were involved. Many sought to collect what they conceived were 'traditional' objects, a rather arbitrary definition by anthropologists of objects produced before their arrival in the native community. The Smithsonian Institution, for example, collected 6500 pots between 1880 and 1885 from Acoma and Zuni Pueblos. Such wholesale collecting disrupted pottery-making traditions by removing most pottery design sources from the Pueblos (Batkin, 1987, p. 30). A more positive relationship resulted from Franz Boas's work with Pacific Northwest Coast Native American cultures. Because of Boas's detailed recording of language, myths, ceremonies and art, he left a rich legacy of information that many Northwest Coast Native American peoples use to reinterpret or revive aspects of their culture (Berlo, 1992, p. 3). Similarly, Stewart Culin of the Brooklyn Museum, New York, was so intent in his pursuit of the old and the sacred at Zuni Pueblo that if the real object were not available, he would have replicas made for his collection (Berlo, 1992, p. 4).

On the other hand, contemporary and innovative art being produced at the time of collecting was frequently ignored by these collectors. Furthermore, some ethnographic collections were built of items not actually used by the Native American groups from which they were purchased but were made for trade with other Native Americans or with tourists (see §XV, 3 above). Museums viewed their collections as their property for intellectual and scientific inquiry and as legitimate efforts at preservation. Only from the 1970s has 'repatriation legislation . . . forced museums to recognize this as only one point of view and . . . necessitated new attitudes in museums about their stewardship of the collections in their care' (Welsh, 1992). Nevertheless, from the early 1900s there had been

a growing emphasis on collecting data along with the objects. Research regarding art and its uses within the communities was popular. For example, Matilda Coxe Stephenson (1849–1915) worked at Zuni, Franz Boas with the Kwakiutl and John Swanton (1873–1958) with the Haida. As Berlo (1992, p. 7) notes, a pivotal work in the history of Native American art of the period is the article by Franz Boas, 'The Decorative Art of the Indians of the North Pacific Coast' (1897), in which he discusses meaning, representation, iconography and abstraction in Northwest Coast art.

The study of anthropology and of Native American culture also attracted interested amateurs, who contributed some important early research. George Wharton James (1858–1923), a collector and popular author, wrote *Indian Basketry* in 1901 and *Indian Blankets and their Makers* in 1914. Both books are considered classics and, at the time, contributed to the popularity of collecting. Many collections built by amateurs have ultimately ended up in major museums.

The interest of private collectors and dealers grew up alongside museum collecting and scholarly research. The role of the trader was different, depending on the place and time. Many traders have had great impact on such aspects of Native American art as technique, style, iconography and art production (Berlo, 1992, p. 7). John H. Huckel (1863–1936) joined the Fred Harvey Company in 1898 and soon founded the Indian Department of the Fred Harvey Company, including a company museum and showroom featuring Native American art for sale in Albuquerque, New Mexico. Thomas Keam (1846–1904), a trader in the 1880s and 1890s in Arizona, encouraged Hopi potters to mass-produce their wares for the tourist trade. He was responsible for the introduction of new styles, decoration and the reproduction of prehistoric pottery (Wade and McChesney, 1980, p. 9). As Berlo (1992, p. 8) notes, certain other traders, such as Clinton Neal Cotton (1859–1936), John Bradford Moore (*b* 1855) and Lorenzo Hubbell, are thought to have been directly responsible for changes in Navajo rug weaving as a result of their interest in oriental carpet patterns. These traders regularly influenced weavers in the use of certain yarns and dyes, and provided the weavers with pattern examples to examine.

Traders often benefited from US government-sponsored arts and craft fairs and competitions, and from the great variety of wares from which they could choose for their businesses. The US government and the traders began to set quality standards, and this practice, too, changed native styles and designs. Wade and Strickland note that 'certain traders used this relationship to induce Native American craftsmen to abandon entire art traditions and cheapen and downgrade others' (1981, p. 11). Native American art was big business at the turn of the century.

2. INTEREST IN INDIVIDUAL ARTISTS AND CONTEMPORARY ART, 1920–40. By the 1920s traders and collectors began to appreciate Native American art for more than its utilitarian value. There was also growing interest in individual artists. Ruth Bunzel (1898–1990) was working with Zuni and other Pueblo artists when she wrote *The*

Pueblo Potter (1929), which established the standards for the study of artistry, individuality and ethnoaesthetics in Native American art (Berlo, 1992, p. 10). Working about the same time, Lila O'Neale (1886–1948), studying Yurok–Karok basketwork, is credited with pioneering the practice of researching native aesthetic standards by using art objects or photographs of objects in discussions with Native American artists (Berlo, 1992, p. 11). Another contemporary, Gladys Reichard (1893–1955), explored the role of artists in their traditional cultures, particularly Navajo weavers and sand painters. Her three books on Navajo weaving, written between 1934 and 1939, were geared towards a popular readership.

Artists in the Southwest USA played an important role in the growth of Native American fine art, and many museums in the region were instrumental in promoting native art and artists. In 1919 the Museum of Northern Arizona held its first Native American painting show. The Heard Museum in Phoenix, Arizona, established in 1929, held its first Annual Indian Fair in 1958, its first Indian Art and Craft Show in 1968, and it continues to sponsor major Native American art shows and forums today. The introduction of easel art in 1916 at New Mexico's Santa Fe Indian School was also of long-range impact to Native American art. The school began to offer formal art training in 1932, taught by Dorothy Dunn (1903–92), and established 'The Studio' in 1933 (*see* §IV, 2(iii) above). Having evolved into the Institute of American Indian Arts, it began to sponsor art shows for its students from 1956 to 1965 and continues to do so today. The Inter-tribal Indian Ceremonial was initiated in Gallup, New Mexico, and the first Santa Fe Indian Market was held in 1929. Another major influence in the late 1930s was the establishment of the Indian Arts and Crafts Board in 1935 as part of the Indian Office, under the enthusiastic direction of Commissioner John Collier (1884–1968). The Denver Art Museum, directed by Frederic H. Douglas (1897–1956), established its Indian Art Collection and also began sponsoring local and travelling shows during this period.

In the 1930s and 1940s scholars and the general public showed increased interest in individual artists as well as in Native American art in general. The marketing of Native American art and of individual artists to tourists and collectors was matched by the increasing amount of the art appearing in museums and galleries. Maria Martinez, the great San Ildefonso Pueblo potter, was signing her work as early as the 1920s in response to demands made by the art market. Brody (1971) clearly documents the rise of signed paintings by Pueblo artists and those from Oklahoma at this time.

3. GROWTH OF A WIDER PUBLIC, 1940–50. The Museum of Modern Art in New York held the important exhibition *Indian Art of the US* in 1941. The show was produced by the Indian Arts and Crafts Board under the direction of John Collier's successor, Rene d'Harnoncourt (1901–68). The purpose of the exhibition was to show that Native American art was a living tradition, and work by such innovative artists as FRED KABOTIE and OSCAR HOWE was highlighted. Through the Indian Arts and Crafts Board, d'Harnoncourt worked for more than 20 years at providing a non-native modern context for Native

American art. Such exhibitions captured the interest of non-Native American artists, for many European and American artists were not only aware of Native American art but were also, in fact, collectors themselves. As Berlo (1992, p. 15) notes, Georgia O'Keeffe, for example, had begun to collect Native American art on her trips to New Mexico as early as 1929, and in the 1920s some European Surrealist artists had begun to incorporate Alaskan Eskimo and Northwest Coast mask forms into their paintings.

Interest in, and growing appreciation of, Native American art by scholars, collectors and the general public is also reflected in popular literature, such as the richly illustrated volumes published by the Bureau of American Ethnology that were widely available. *Art and Archaeology*, a popular publication from 1915 to 1934, featured issues in which articles on modern Native American art were found with those written about American archaeological excavations. Art history books began to include sections on Native American art.

4. DEVELOPMENTS AFTER 1950. Although several excellent Native American art shows had been established, J. J. Brody (1971) suggests that the 1950s was a time of discouragement for many curators and collectors. Many collectors felt Native American art as a whole was in decline. In 1959 concern about this situation led to a conference that changed the whole direction of Native American art. *Directions in Indian Art* was held at the University of Arizona in Tucson and was supported by the Rockefeller Foundation. It was attended by Native American craftsmen, artists, traders, educators, administrators and museum and gallery curators. One result was the Southwest Indian Art Project, established at the University of Arizona, which ran from 1960 to 1962, the purpose of which was to explore the future of Native American art.

In contrast to the 1950s, the 1960s and 1970s witnessed a great increase in tourism and concurrently a significant rise in the availability of tourist and ethnic art for sale. Although tourist markets are profitable, some scholars are concerned about the damaging effects long-term participation in these art markets will have on the future of Native American art. Sometimes, however, participation in ethnic art markets can be beneficial. For example, in the mid-1960s William Beaver, a trader and collector, encouraged Navajo potters to produce a variety of vessel forms and to experiment with new decorative motifs. He facilitated a revitalization of Navajo pottery-making, and the market continued to grow with the assistance of interested dealers, collectors and museums. The value of the pottery rose, and by the 1990s it was not uncommon to find examples in art galleries and museums (Musial and Hartman, 1987, p. 2).

By the 1980s many critics and collectors pessimistically predicted the decline and impending death of 'authentic' Native American art. Some scholars, collectors and critics were disturbed by the changing definition of contemporary Native American art. In truth, to quote Rennard Strickland and Edwin Wade, 'Indian art is very much alive. Talent remains; the vision has changed' (1981, p. 5). Through the 1980s and into the 1990s museums, galleries and patrons continued to be important in stimulating further development of Native American art. The Philbrook Art Center had inaugurated an annual competitive nationwide painting exhibition in 1946. Other museums followed, including the Museum of the American Indian, Heye Foundation, New York, the Heard Museum, Phoenix, AZ, and the Sacred Circles gallery in San Francisco. Museums still collect, but their focus and objectives continue to change and be redefined. For example, the Arizona State Museum in Tucson, founded in 1893, collects examples of tourist art and utilitarian objects to document the evolving nature of certain types of Native American art forms. Trading networks in the 1990s included Native American cooperatives and craft guilds, private traders, powwows, Native American markets and dealers. Investment speculation drove Native American art into a multi-million-dollar industry.

Native American art in the 1990s was promoted as both modern and uniquely American. According to Sally Price (1989), the move of Native American art from anthropology and natural history museums to art museums, and the concurrent change from its being viewed strictly in ethnographic terms to its appreciation as art, were clearly associated in the public's mind with its increasing monetary value and with a shift from function to aesthetics as a basis for evaluation (Price, 1989, p. 84). Interest in and concern about 'authenticity' of native-made objects and fine art continue to be important issues: 'The public always has accorded greater value to that which is labelled authentic' (Welsh, 1992, p. 843). The growing popularity of 'heritage' and cultural tourism and the ethnic art market in fact helped promote stereotypes of what is 'traditional' and 'authentic' Native American art. Strickland and Archuleta note that in 1971 J. J. Brody 'identified the colonial nature of a patronage system that narrowly defined and dictated what was "Indian art"', and by the 1990s some collectors began to look to earlier periods for 'real' Native American art (1991, p. 9). However, many Native American artists feel that this externally dictated definition of art must change along with the frequent isolation of Native American art from the wider art community. Native American artists want art historians and critics, not anthropologists, to review their work.

BIBLIOGRAPHY

F. Boas: 'The Decorative Art of the Indians of the North Pacific Coast', *Bull. Amer. Mus. Nat. Hist.*, ix (1897), pp. 123–76
G. W. James: *Indian Basketry* (Pasadena, 1901)
——: *Indian Blankets and their Makers* (Chicago, 1914)
R. L. Bunzel: *The Pueblo Potter: A Study of Creative Imagination in Primitive Art* (New York, 1929)
J. J. Brody: *Indian Painters and White Patrons* (Albuquerque, 1971)
Fred Harvey Fine Arts Collection, Phoenix, AZ, Heard Mus. cat. (Phoenix, 1976)
E. L. Wade and L. S. McChesney: *America's Great Lost Expedition: The Thomas Keam Collection of Hopi Pottery from the Second Hemenway Expedition, 1890–1894* (Phoenix, 1980)
C. M. Hinsley jr: *Savages and Scientists: The Smithsonian Institution and the Development of American Anthropology, 1846–1910* (Washington, DC, 1981)
E. L. Wade and R. Strickland: *Magic Images: Contemporary Native American Art* (Norman, 1981)
A. MacGregor, ed.: *Tradescant's Rarities* (Oxford, 1983)
R. F. Shrader: *The Indian Arts and Crafts Board: An Aspect of the New Deal Indian Policy* (Albuquerque, 1983)
G. Stocking, ed.: *Object and Others: Essays on Museums and Material Culture* (Madison, 1985)
E. L. Wade, ed.: *The Arts of the North American Indian: Native Traditions in Evolution* (New York, 1986)
J. Batkin: *Pottery of the Pueblos of New Mexico, 1700–1940* (Colorado Springs, 1987)
K. Hudson: *Museum of Influence* (Cambridge, 1987)
J. Musial and R. P. Hartman: *Navajo Pottery: Traditions and Innovations* (Flagstaff, 1987)
S. Price: *Primitive Art in Civilized Places* (Chicago, 1989)
M. Archuleta and R. Strickland: *Shared Visions: Native American Painters and Sculptors in the Twentieth Century* (New York, 1991)
N. P. Parezo: *Navajo Sandpainting: From Religious Art to Commercial Art* (Albuquerque, 1991)
J. C. Berlo, ed.: *The Early Years of Native American Art History: The Politics of Scholarship and Collecting* (Seattle, 1992)
P. H. Welsh: 'Repatriation and Cultural Preservation: Potent Objects, Potent Pasts', *U. MI J. Law Reform*, xxv (1992), pp. 837–65
C. F. Feest: 'European Collecting of American Indian Artefacts and Art', *J. Hist. Col.*, v/1 (1993), pp. 1–11

MARY E. GRAHAM

XIX. Exhibitions.

Native American artefacts were collected by Europeans as 'artificial curiosities' from the time of contact, but they were rarely exhibited until the end of the 18th century. Exhibition became common in the 19th century, both as curiosities in anthropological contexts and in theatrical entertainments. Exhibitions of Native American artefacts as art are a 20th-century phenomenon.

Northwest Coast and Alaskan objects collected during Capt. James Cook's third voyage (1776–80) were included in public exhibits of Native American materials held in British private commercial museums, most notably William Bullock's Egyptian Hall (London), early in the 19th century. In the USA, collections of the Lewis and Clark expedition (1804–6) were exhibited in the private commercial museum of the Philadelphia artist and natural philosopher Charles Willson Peale (*see* PEALE, (1)). Peale pioneered the use of museums for popular education, and his may have been the first didactic exhibition of Native American objects.

During the 1830s two important collections were made of Plains Native American materials from the upper Missouri. That of Prince Maximilian of Wied (1833–4; Berlin, Mus. Vlkerknd., and Stuttgart, Linden-Mus.) is the best preserved, although it had virtually no public exposure until after World War II. Of far greater influence was the collection acquired during 1832–3 by the American artist GEORGE CATLIN, which is now largely lost. Catlin intended to document and exhibit what he perceived as 'the last days of a vanishing race', using his paintings to illustrate aboriginal ways of life. He toured his *Indian Gallery* in America in 1838–9, and, when efforts to sell it to the US government failed, he took it to Europe with troupes of Native American performers. He opened in London in 1840 at Bullock's Egyptian Hall and spent the next decade there, in Paris and on tour in Britain. Royal patronage in England and France ensured early popular success, and he later toured Europe and western Asia. Catlin's exhibits, performances and *tableaux vivants* were prototypes for 'Wild West' shows and the colonial villages that featured at World's Fairs later in the 19th century and were influential in dramatizing Plains Native Americans as stereotypical 'noble savages'.

Native American artefacts were included in anthropological exhibits at the natural history museums that proliferated in Europe and America during the second half of the 19th century and early 20th. Two interpretative formats were common. The ahistorical interpretation—exemplified by the Pitt-Rivers Museum, Oxford University—juxtaposes objects of different cultural origins to illustrate a general anthropological theory. A historical interpretation— exemplified by the American Museum of Natural History, New York—selects objects from a single time and place to illustrate the unique qualities of a given society. Far more popular were the Wild West shows that toured Europe and North America following the end of the Plains Wars in 1876. These not only reinforced images of a stereotypical Plains Native American but also creatively influenced Native American powwow art, which played a major role in reintegrating shattered Native American societies. The Plains stereotype was tempered after 1893 by exhibitions of ancient Southwest art at the World's Columbian Exposition in Chicago that year, and craft demonstrations by Southwest Native American artists there and at the World's Fairs in St Louis and in San Diego. Burgeoning interest in Native American craft arts (*see* §XV, 2 and 3 above) helped stimulate modern Native American art traditions.

The acquisition and exhibition of Native American artefacts by art museums lagged behind their interest in exotic objects from Africa and Oceania. Though the ideological transformation of such artefacts into 'art' was made possible by the modernist and arts-and-crafts movements of the late 19th century and early 20th, Native American art had relatively little impact on early modern artists. Only some Surrealists working during the 1930s and 1940s appeared deeply impressed by it, and the redefinition of Native American artefacts as art occurred in the USA largely in response to post-World War I isolationism, regionalism and the desire to create a national artistic identity (*see* §XVII above). The first exhibition of Native American artefacts as art seems to have been of modern Pueblo watercolours in 1920 in New York by the Society of Independent Artists. Other small art exhibitions were held during the 1920s in the USA and Europe, and in 1925 the Denver Art Museum is credited as the first deliberately to collect Native American art.

There were no large Native American art exhibitions until the touring *Exposition of Indian Tribal Arts* (1931–3) was organized by artist JOHN SLOAN, philanthropist Amelia Elizabeth White and novelist Oliver LaFarge. In 1941 the Museum of Modern Art, New York, was the first major art museum to organize a comprehensive exhibition of Native American art, organized by the curators F. H. Douglas of the Denver Art Museum and René d'Harnoncourt of the Museum of Modern Art. Their accompanying catalogue (1941) was the first published overview of Native American art history. The exhibition was as encyclopedic as the Sloan–White–LaFarge *Exposition* and was organized geographically using the historic model of anthropology museums.

Many local exhibitions of Native American art were organized in America and Europe by art and anthropology museums in the three decades following World War II. These increasingly focused on specific artistic traditions in response to greatly refined scholarship and public interest. A new era of interpretative travelling exhibitions, some with international venues, was stimulated by the Bicentennial of American Independence (1976). *Sacred Circles* (1976–7), curated by R. T. Coe of the W. Rockhill Nelson Gallery in Kansas City, MO (now Nelson–Atkins Mus. A.), for the Arts Council of Great Britain, set the tone. Although encyclopedic, it differed from earlier comprehensive exhibitions by emphasizing perceived spiritual expressions in Native American art. That theme subsequently became a major focus of scholarly and popular interpretations.

Even more influential have been the many exhibitions organized since 1977 that have focused on particular, well-defined artistic traditions. Their interpretative emphasis has been on the objective exploration of artistic form, art history and the interactions of history, artistic forms and social content and context. Such exhibitions are typically temporary and accompanied by non-technical, authoritative texts of lasting value. Many travel, and they tend to blur distinctions between the disciplines of art history and anthropology. By emphasizing the extraordinary diversity of Native American art traditions as well as their ordinary social utility, these exhibitions have profoundly altered perceptions of Native American art and life, and at the same time they suggest alternative views concerning the nature of art itself.

BIBLIOGRAPHY

J. Sloan and O. LaFarge: *Introduction to American Art*, 2 vols (New York, 1931)
Indian Art of the United States (exh. cat. by F. H. Douglas and R. d'Harnoncourt, New York, MOMA, 1941)
R. Goldwater: *Primitivism in Modern Art* (New York, 1967)
J. J. Brody: *Indian Painters and White Patrons* (Albuquerque, 1971)
B. Holm and B. Reid: *Form and Freedom* (Houston, 1975)
N. H. H. Graburn: *Ethnic and Tourist Arts: Cultural Expressions from the Fourth World* (Berkeley, 1976)
Sacred Circles: Two Thousand Years of North American Indian Art (exh. cat. by R. T. Coe, London, Hayward Gal.; Kansas City, MO, W. Rockhill Nelson Gal.; 1977)
A. L. Kaeppler: *Artificial Curiosities* (Honolulu, 1978)
E. P. Alexander: *Museums in Motion* (Nashville, 1979)
W. Haberland: *Donnervogel und Raaubwal: Indianische Kunst der nordwestküste Nordamerikas* (Hamburg, 1979)
W. H. Truettner: *The Natural Man Observed: A Study of Catlin's Indian Gallery* (Washington, DC, 1979)
C. F. Feest: *Native Arts of North America* (New York, 1980)
C. Lévi-Strauss: *The Way of the Masks* (Seattle, 1982)
J. J. Brody, C. J. Scott and S. A. LeBlanc: *Mimbres Pottery: Ancient Art of the American Southwest* (New York, 1983)
W. Rubin, ed.: *'Primitivism' in 20th-century Art*, 2 vols (New York, 1984)
D. S. Brose, J. A. Brown and D. W. Penny: *Ancient Art of the American Woodland Indian* (New York, 1985)
J. Maquet: *The Aesthetic Experience* (New Haven, 1986)
A. Wardwell: *Ancient Eskimo Ivories of the Bering Strait* (New York, 1986)
S. Price: *Primitive Art in Civilized Places* (Chicago, 1989)

J. J. BRODY

Nativity group [It. *presepe*; Ger. *Krippe*]. Three-dimensional representation of the events surrounding the birth of Christ. All depictions of the Nativity derive from veneration of the cave in Bethlehem in which Christ was born, and which was visited by pilgrims as early as the 2nd century AD. The first copy in Europe was created in the area of Rome's Liberian basilica (later S Maria Maggiore), which was described in the mid-7th century as 'S Maria ad

Praesepem' (Lat.: manger, crib); fragments of rock from the cave in Bethlehem were venerated there. From the end of the 13th century, Italian records describe fixed, life-size reconstructions of the Nativity in devotional rooms set aside for them. Figures representing the adoration of the Magi were provided for a chapel on the north aisle of S Maria Maggiore in 1291; the church retains most of them, though not *in situ*. A contract of 1384 between Vanni Mainardi from Monterubbiano and Brother Giovanni di Bartolomeo in Fabriano provides the first indication of a criblike scene depicting the night of Christ's birth, alluding to wooden, coloured, roughly half life-size figures representing the Virgin and Child, St Joseph, two angels, a shepherd with his sheep and an ox and donkey. There are fully rounded terracotta figures of the Holy Family and Magi dating from *c.* 1465 in Volterra Cathedral in two niches in front of a background painting by Benozzo Gozzoli. From the 13th century to the 15th there were common factors in Italian representations of the Nativity: into a niche above an altar was inserted a grotto containing marble, wooden or terracotta figures; scenes depicting the annunciation to the shepherds and the journey of the Magi were set on a mountain rising steeply above it, reduced in size at the back in accordance with perspective. Such grottoes often contained fragments of rock from the Bethlehem cave.

St Cajetan of Thiene (1480–1547) built a Nativity scene every year, using individual, freely movable figures. This style of crib, with a number of figures in positions that could be altered, developed in Italy from the mid-16th century and became generally popular in Catholic countries in the course of the 17th century. The figures or groups of figures enacted a scene in an artificially created, illusionistic landscape, generally consisting of a hill with a stable, cave or ruin. Like a stage manager in a theatre, the builder could alter the positions of the figures and the scenes, within set boundaries based on liturgy or custom, to depict the Christmas narrative, from the Annunciation to the massacre of the Innocents, some even adding the wedding at Cana. There were also box cribs, in which miniature figures were arranged by the maker in a fixed position in a wooden box enclosed by glass at the front (e.g. Berchtesgaden, late 18th century; Munich, Bayer. Nmus.). The scenes depicted in these were almost exclusively events central to the Nativity, such as the adoration of the shepherds and Magi.

The building of cribs was first promoted by the Jesuits. In 1560 they set up the first crib in their college at Coimbra in Portugal, and in 1562 there was a crib with clothed figures in the Jesuit church in Prague. By shortly after 1600 the Jesuits had already introduced the crib (and the celebration of Christmas) to Japan, India and China. Philippe de Berlaymont SJ (1576–1637) wrote the first theoretical analysis of the Christmas crib in 1619. Subsequently every predominantly Catholic country developed its own traditions with regard to methods of production and the materials used for the figures. One of the areas in which cribs were earliest documented was Sicily: in Messina in 1609 and Monreale in 1611 the Jesuits constructed a theatre with individual, separate, painted figures, comparable in style to a crib with two-dimensional figures cut out of panels. In 1653 the church of S Domenico at Palermo was the first to have clothed figures. Trapani was by then already a centre for cribs with small figures made of precious materials: ivory, coral, mother-of-pearl. Giovanni Antonio Matera (1653–1718), a celebrated builder of cribs, used lime-wood to create carved, painted figures with clothes glued on to them (e.g. Munich, Bayer. Nmus.).

In the mid-18th century Naples was an important centre for the construction of cribs of high artistic quality. Charles VII, King of Naples (from 1759 Charles III of Spain), personally promoted crib-building by encouraging well-known artists from his porcelain factory at Capodimonte to produce terracotta heads; his own crib was widely copied. The heads of the figures were modelled in terracotta, painted and given inset glass eyes; arms and legs were carved from wood and likewise coloured (examples in Naples, Mus. N. S Martino, and Munich, Bayer. Nmus.; see fig.). Where the figures represent shepherds and the Neapolitan townspeople, they wear clothing that is accurate in detail and made from the original materials; the figures in the suite of the Magi wear oriental robes and real jewellery. Tiny accessories, such as animals, musical instruments and goods for market stalls, were produced by other artists from terracotta, wood, wax and other materials. In Neapolitan cribs the representation of the life of the people is often more dominant than the original religious character.

The plentifulness of wood and the existing carving tradition in the Alps led to a considerable output of carved cribs in southern Germany and Austria (examples in Munich, Bayer. Nmus.; Innsbruck, Tirol. Vlkskstms.; Bressanone, Mus. Dioc.). Two types of figures were found in the 18th and 19th centuries: carved, coloured figures that were generally very small, and articulated wooden dolls up to half life-size, with textile clothing. Until the end of the 18th century, figures intended for cribs wore the clothing of the country in which the crib was made; it was only under the influence of the Nazarene concept of art that the 'Oriental' crib came into being. In the 19th century individual traditions of crib-building evolved all over Europe: *santons* (small clay figures) in Provence, paper figures in Bohemia and Moravia, roughly carved, brightly coloured wooden figures in Poland and ceramic figures in Portugal, Spain and Italy. In the 20th century crib-building extended into Latin America, Africa and Asia, inspired by Catholic missionaries. Indigenous materials such as bamboo, teak, balsawood and shells have been used in these areas, and the Virgin may appear as a Native American, with a dark-skinned baby as Jesus and a tepee in place of the Nativity stable or cave. In the late 20th century colourful cribs with large numbers of figures made of clay were produced in Mexico and Peru and even exported to Europe (e.g. Schleissheim, Altes Schloss). Although 20th-century artists rarely concerned themselves with the theme of the Nativity, Edward Kienholz used *objets trouvés* from a lumber dump for his scenic *Nativity* (1961; artist's priv. col.).

BIBLIOGRAPHY

R. Berliner: *Denkmäler der Krippenkunst* (Augsburg, 1926–30) [issued in 21 pts in port.]

A. Stefanucci: *Storia del presepio* (Rome, 1944)

L. Kretzenbacher: *Weihnachtskrippen in Steiermark*, Veröffentlichungen des Österreichischen Museums für Volkskunde, iii (Vienna, 1953)

R. Berliner: *Die Weihnachtskrippe* (Munich, 1955)

Nativity group by Giuseppe Sanmartino (attrib.), coloured terracotta, h. 290 mm (largest figure), mid-18th century (Munich, Bayerisches Nationalmuseum)

A. Walzer: *Schwäbische Weihnachtskrippen aus der Barockzeit* (Konstanz, 1960)

G. Borelli: *Sanmartino: Scultore per il presepe napoletano* (Naples, 1966)

N. Grass, ed.: *Weihnachtskrippen aus Österreich* (Innsbruck, 1966)

E. Catello: *Francesco Celebrano e l'arte nel presepe napoletano del '700* (Naples, 1969)

G. Borelli: *Il presepe napoletano* (Rome and Naples, 1970)

A. Karasek and J. Lanz: *Krippenkunst in Böhmen und Mähren vom Frühbarock bis zur Gegenwart* (Marburg, 1974)

C. Daxelmüller: *Krippen in Franken* (Würzburg, 1978)

I. Koschier: *Weihnachtskrippen in Kärnten*, Kärntner Museumsschriften (Klagenfurt, 1978)

A. Uccello: *Il presepio popolare in Sicilia* (Palermo, 1979)

G. Gamet: *La Crèche provençale: Le Monde enchanté des santons* (Marseille, 1980)

N. Kuret: *Jaslice na Slovenskem* (Ljubljana, 1981)

E. Egg and H. Menardi: *Das Tiroler Krippenbuch* (Innsbruck and Vienna, 1985)

N. Crockerell: *Krippen im Bayerischen Nationalmuseum* (Munich, 1993, rev. 1994)

NINA GOCKERELL

Natoire, Charles-Joseph (*b* Nimes, 3 March 1700; *d* Castel Gandolfo, 23 or 29 Aug 1777). French painter, draughtsman and teacher, active also in Italy. An exact contemporary of François Boucher, he was a painter of cabinet pictures, decorations and tapestry cartoons and one of the most adept practitioners of Rococo art in 18th-century France. The greater part of his career was spent in Paris, where he received important commissions from Louis XV as well as from private patrons. In 1751 he accepted the post of Director of the Académie de France in Rome. From then on he devoted himself to his teaching duties at the expense of his painting.

1. TRAINING AND EARLY CAREER, TO 1730. After receiving an initial artistic education from his father, the sculptor Florent Natoire (*c.* 1667–1754), Charles-Joseph moved to Paris in 1717 in order to continue his apprenticeship in the studio of Louis Galloche. It was presumably during the period spent with this master that he acquired a pronounced taste for landscape art before moving on to study further under François Lemoyne, a painter whom he admired and who exercised a decisive influence on his career. From Lemoyne, Natoire inherited a sense of composition and a taste for the female nude—a field of endeavour in which Natoire executed figures even more sensual than those depicted by his teacher, as is amply demonstrated by his first known painting, *Manoah Offering a Sacrifice to the Lord* (Paris, Ecole N. Sup. B.-A.). This canvas won him the Prix de Rome of the Académie Royale in 1721. Two years later he arrived at the Académie de France in Rome, where he was soon singled out for his qualities as a draughtsman. In 1725 he was awarded the first prize of the Accademia di S Luca and in 1727 he received a commission from Cardinal Melchior de Polignac for a painting depicting *Christ Driving the Money-changers from the Temple* (Paris, St Médard). Natoire experienced some difficulty in mastering this composition, an ambitious work combining the influence of Lemoyne with that of the great Italian masters, in particular Raphael. At the end of the following year he left Rome for northern Italy and arrived in Paris in 1730.

2. PARIS, 1730–51. On his return to Paris Natoire was approved (*agréé*) by the Académie Royale; he was received (*reçu*) as a full member in 1734, when he submitted the painting *Venus Begging Arms from Vulcan* (Montpellier, Mus. Fabre), which was heavily influenced by Boucher's version of the same subject (Paris, Louvre) painted two years previously. Natoire had already received his first royal commission, an allegory of *Youth and Virtue Presenting France with Two Princesses*, painted for the Chambre de la Reine at the château of Versailles (*in situ*). He executed further works for the royal châteaux of Fontainebleau, Versailles and Marly, and also for the Bibliothèque Royale in Paris. His reputation was, however, established as soon as he returned from Italy by a decorative ensemble that he painted from 1731 to 1740 for Philibert Orry and intended for the Château de La Chapelle-Godefroy (Aube). This consisted of four series of paintings (Moscow, Pushkin Mus. F.A. and Troyes, Mus. B.-A. & Archéol.). Although two of the series, the *History of the Gods* and the *Four Seasons*, are typical of the period in both their subjects and their agreeable style, the second to be executed, the *Story of Clovis*, is more unusual, depicting episodes from national history, a rarity before the 1770s. The fourth series, the *Story of Telemachus*, was inspired by François de La Mothe-Fénelon's novel *Télémaque* (1699). Around 1735 Natoire was asked by the financier Grimod Du Ford to illustrate another novel, Cervantes's *Don Quixote*, by producing cartoons (Compiègne, Château) for Beauvais tapestries (Aix-en-Provence, Mus. Tap.).

From 1737 to 1739, together with Boucher, Carle Vanloo and Pierre-Charles Trémolières, Natoire collaborated with the architect Germain Boffrand on the restoration of the Hôtel de Soubise (now the Archives Nationales) in Paris. He was allocated the decoration of the finest of the rooms, the oval Salon de la Princesse. Here he created eight paintings of the *Story of Psyche* (*in situ*; see fig.) designed to fit into the elaborately shaped spandrels between the arched, mirrored recesses that form the main feature of Boffrand's décor. Natoire's compositions are adapted to the curves of their framing with considerable skill to create a harmonious whole. His talent as a decorative painter was confirmed by his work for Boffrand's chapel of the Hospice des Enfants Trouvés (destr.). This ensemble of architecture and decoration, unique in the Paris of its day, is known through drawings and also through engravings by Etienne Fessard (1714–77). Natoire's contribution, executed between 1741 and 1750, consisted of 14 painted panels, including the *Adoration of the Magi and the Shepherds*, integrated into an elaborate *trompe l'oeil* décor by Gaetano (*d* 1758) and Paolo Antonio Brunetti that included a ruined ceiling whose crumbling and ivy-covered vaults opened on to a cloudy sky.

3. ROME, AFTER 1751. In 1751 Natoire was appointed Director of the Académie de France in Rome, and he spent the rest of his life in Italy. In 1754 he was commissioned to execute the decorations for the ceiling of the church of S Luigi dei Francesi. This was the first time that he had had an opportunity to pit himself against the difficulties of a monumental décor of such size. He turned for inspiration for his fresco of the *Apotheosis of St Louis* to the great Roman late Baroque decorations of his youth; this was at a time when the new Neo-classical style, sharply opposed to the aesthetic that Natoire represented,

Charles-Joseph Natoire: *Psyche Illuminating the Sleeping Figure of Cupid,* oil on canvas, 1738 (Paris, Archives Nationales, formerly the Hôtel de Soubise)

was just making its appearance in Rome. This backward-looking work was Natoire's last great achievement; he made hardly any attempt to modernize his style, which soon passed out of fashion. The series of tapestry cartoons of the *History of Mark Antony,* for example, commissioned for Louis XV in 1740, delivery of which was long delayed, failed to please the new Directeur des Bâtiments du Roi, the Marquis de Marigny, who cancelled the commission. Natoire now began to devote himself increasingly to his role as Director of the Académie. With the aim of encouraging the art of landscape painting, Natoire used to take his pupils to various sites in Rome and to surrounding places such as Frascati and Tivoli so that they could draw from nature. He himself executed a considerable number of fine landscape drawings, tinted with washes and then with watercolour or gouache, which reveal his efforts to achieve picturesque effects (e.g. Paris, Louvre; London, BM; Vienna, Albertina; Berlin, Kstbib. & Mus.). Natoire's *plein-air* classes influenced the development of such young artists as Hubert Robert and Fragonard, both of whom were among his pupils in Rome. He was removed from his post in 1775 and retired to Castel Gandolfo.

See also PARIS, fig. 18.

BIBLIOGRAPHY
F. Boyer: 'Catalogue raisonné de l'oeuvre de Natoire, peintre du roi', *Archvs A. Fr.,* n. s., xxi (1949), pp. 29–106
A.-P. de Mirimonde: 'L'Impromptu du plafond ou *L'Apothéose de Saint-Louis* par Natoire', *Rev. des A.,* viii/6 (1958), pp. 279–84
L. Duclaux: 'La Décoration de la chapelle de l'hospice des Enfants-trouvés à Paris', *Rev. A.* [Paris], 14 (1971), pp. 45–50
Charles-Joseph Natoire (exh. cat., Troyes, Mus. B.-A. & Archéol.; Nîmes, Mus. B.-A.; Rome, Acad. France; 1977)
Don Quichotte vu par un peintre du XVIIIe siècle: Natoire (exh. cat. by O. P. Sebastiani and M.-H. Krotoff, Compiègne, Château; Aix-en-Provence, Mus. Tap.; 1977)

NICOLE PARMENTIER-LALLEMENT

Natsuyuki Nakanishi. *See under* HI-RED CENTER.

Natter, Johann Lorenz (*b* Biberach an der Riss, nr Ulm, 21 March 1705; *d* St Petersburg, 27 Oct 1763). German gem-engraver and medallist. He trained as a goldsmith in Biberach and then learnt seal- and gem-engraving in Berne. In 1730 he travelled to Venice to work as a seal-engraver. In 1732 the antiquary Baron Philipp von Stosch set him to copying ancient carved gems in Florence. To improve his skill, Natter drew after the Antique at the Accademia di San Luca in Rome, developing a style based on Classical models that was to become characteristic of his gem-carving, an example of which is his cornelian bust of *Livia as Ceres* (*c.* 1730; London, V&A). He also became one of the earliest representatives of the Neo-classical medal style. At the end of the 1730s he moved to London, where he produced several noteworthy medals, such as the portrait bust of *Sir Robert Walpole* (silver, copper and lead, 1741; London, BM). In 1743 the Danish Court invited him to Copenhagen, where he carved a number of gems, among which were the portrait busts in chalcedony of *Frederick V of Denmark as Crown Prince* and *Christian VI of Denmark* (both Copenhagen, Rosenborg Pal.). He returned to England in 1744 and by 1745 had visited Stockholm and St Petersburg but received no important commissions. However, he found in William IV of Orange Nassau, Stadholder of the Netherlands, a patron who repeatedly commissioned from him gems and medals. Examples of these are the cornelian portrait busts of *William IV* (1747–51) and *William V as a Child* (1747; both Leiden, Rijksmus. Kon. Penningkab.). In his portrait medals Natter now adopted the Rococo style, which laid great emphasis on the rendering of splendid clothing and elaborate coiffures. After William IV's death in 1751 Natter returned to England. In 1754 his *Traité de la méthode antique de graver en pierres fines* was published in London and brought him the honorary membership of the Society of Antiquaries. In 1756–7 he worked for a while as Chief Engraver at the Mint in Utrecht but then settled in The Hague, where he carved on precious stones the portraits of numerous European princes. He returned briefly to Stockholm in 1757, to work as an art dealer. He died suddenly on a journey to Russia in 1763. The works that can definitely be ascribed to Natter comprise *c.* 145 carved gemstones, many of them signed, and 20 medals.

WRITINGS

Traité de la méthode antique de graver en pierres fines (London, 1754; Eng. trans., London, 1754)

BIBLIOGRAPHY

ADB; Forrer; Thieme–Becker
E. Nau: *Lorenz Natter* (Biberach an der Riss, 1966)

HERMANN MAUÉ

Nattier. French family of painters and draughtsmen. Marc Nattier (*b* 1642; *d* Paris, 24 Oct 1705) was a painter who specialized in portraits and was married to the miniature painter Marie Nattier [née Courtois] (*b c.* 1655; *d* Paris, 13 Oct 1703). He had a royal licence to reproduce Rubens's famous cycle of paintings the *History of Marie de' Medici* (Paris, Louvre), then in the Palais du Luxembourg, Paris. Before he died, Marc made the licence over to his sons, (1) Jean-Baptiste Nattier and (2) Jean-Marc Nattier, who produced a series of drawings after it for some of the foremost engravers of the day, including Gérard Edelinck, Bernard Picart and Gaspard Duchange. The drawings appeared in 1710 under the title *La Galerie du Palais du Luxembourg*. Both painters subsequently worked as history painters, as had been their father's intention, but Jean-Marc is best known for his fashionable portraits.

(1) Jean-Baptiste Nattier (*b* Paris, 27 Sept 1678; *d* Paris, 23 May 1726). He was taught first by his father, then from 1704 to 1709 he was a student at the Académie de France in Rome. In 1712 he became a member of the Académie Royale de Peinture et de Sculpture on presentation of *Joseph and Potiphar's Wife* (St Petersburg, Hermitage). He is principally known for his history paintings, such as *David with the Head of Goliath* (Moscow, Pushkin Mus. F.A.). His career came to an abrupt end when a scandal in his private life resulted in his expulsion from the Académie Royale and his imprisonment in the Bastille, where he took his own life.

(2) Jean-Marc Nattier (*b* Paris, 17 March 1685; *d* Paris, 7 Nov 1766). Brother of (1) Jean-Baptiste Nattier. As well as being taught by his father, he trained with his godfather, Jean Jouvenet, and attended the drawing classes of the Académie Royale, where in 1700 he won the Premier Prix de Dessin. From around 1703 he worked on *La Galerie du Palais du Luxembourg*. The experience of copying the work of Rubens does not, however, seem to have had a liberating effect on his draughtsmanship, which was described by the 18th-century collector Pierre-Jean Mariette as 'cold'. Nattier was commissioned to make further drawings for engravers in the early part of his career, including those after Hyacinthe Rigaud's famous state portrait of *Louis XIV* (1701; Paris, Louvre) in 1710, which indicates that he had established a reputation while he was still quite young. Although he was offered a place at the Académie de France in Rome on the recommendation of Jouvenet, Nattier preferred to remain in Paris and further his career. In 1717 he nevertheless made a trip to Holland, where he painted portraits of *Peter the Great* and the *Empress Catherine* (St Petersburg, Hermitage). The Tsar offered Nattier work at the Russian court, but the artist declined the offer. He remained in Paris for the rest of his life.

Despite the fact that in 1717 he was received (*reçu*) into the Académie Royale as a history painter with *Perseus Petrifying Phineus by Showing him the Head of Medusa* (Tours, Mus. B.-A.), Nattier preferred to build up a practice as a portrait painter. Since portrait painting came relatively low in the academic hierarchy of genres, it is perhaps not surprising that contemporary biographers, such as Nattier's daughter, Mme Tocqué, and the Abbé de Fontenai, felt they had to stress that material necessity made him a portrait painter, although his talents made him worthy of being a history painter. The allegorical or mythologizing portraits by which he is best known combine elements of both genres in a way that caused Mme Tocqué to remark, 'The enlightened public often does not know which to admire more in him, the history painter or the portrait painter.'

In 1724 Nattier married Marie-Madeleine de La Roche, with whom he had four children. His *Family Portrait* (Versailles, Château), started in 1730, shows that by this time he was reasonably well-to-do, but his ultimate success at the French court came to him only gradually. Initially he drew the clientele for his portrait practice from the Paris bourgeoisie, and he completed numerous preparatory drawings for portrait and reproductive engravings. Among these are those after Old-Master paintings in the French royal collection and in the collection of the Regent, Philippe II, Duc d'Orléans, for Pierre Crozat in 1721, and those after Charles Le Brun's decorations in the Galerie des Glaces at the château of Versailles from 1723. He imparted to these works some of his own style, rendering them more agreeable to contemporary taste.

The beginning of Nattier's success as a painter of court society came in 1732, with his mythologizing portrait of *Mlle de Lambesc as Minerva with the Comte de Brionne* (Paris, Louvre). The subject sits in an armchair and holds a helmet, with four attributes of warfare near her; the Comte as a seven-year-old boy stands by her, in armour. With its formal grandeur, the work is firmly within the tradition of the dominant portrait painters of the previous generation, Rigaud and Nicolas de Largillierre, but it is modified by the introduction of mythological attributes and a vaguely classicizing costume, which justified the chic state of undress of the fashionable sitter. The work initiated a whole series of similar portraits, mostly of women, and this flattering and idealizing portrait type remained in vogue for nearly two decades.

From the early 1730s Nattier's large-scale portraits, which he exhibited regularly at the Salons, began to replace the 'portraits d'apparat' that had been popular at Court. In 1735 Jean-Philippe, Chevalier d'Orléans, Grand Prior of the Knights Templar, ordered a series of paintings of the *Muses* (untraced) for his gallery at the Temple, Paris, and at the 1738 Salon Nattier exhibited a full-length portrait of the Chevalier (untraced). In 1740 Nattier's standing at Court was finally confirmed when he painted portraits of the younger sisters of Louis XV's mistress, Louise de Neslé, Comtesse de Mailly: he depicted *Mme de Flavacour as Silence* and *Mme de Chateauroux as Dawn* (both Stockholm, Drottningholms Slott). The costumes of both women and the attributes that indicate their roles underline Nattier's timeless idealization of his sitters.

Nattier went on to paint a number of portraits of the daughters of Louix XV in a similar style: for example *Mme Henriette as Flora* and *Mme Adélaïde as Diana* (1742 and 1745; Versailles, Château). These were intended for the private apartments of their mother, Maria Leczynska, at Versailles. Further commissions from the Court and the royal family followed: in 1744 Nattier painted the large and imposing portrait of the *Duchesse de Chaulnes as Hebe* (Paris, Louvre), which demonstrates well the artist's expressive brushwork and restrained and harmonious colouring, based on opaque local tones, occasionally with lighter accents. The model has a general sense of calm and well-being about her, which is typical of Nattier's sitters.

Somewhat unusual in the context of Nattier's court portraits is his half-length depiction of the Queen, *Maria Leczynska* (1748; Versailles, Château; see fig.), in which she is shown simply dressed, with an open Bible beside her. While the columns and swags of drapery in the background belong to the tradition of the Baroque state portrait, the subject's relaxed, seated pose and natural expression are the first embodiment of a new conception of portraiture that aimed above all at 'naturalness'. The most notable exponent of the style was Maurice-Quentin de La Tour, who was to equal Nattier in fashionable esteem. It is revealing that, whereas in 1748, when Louis XV commissioned a portrait of his mistress, Nattier painted a mythologizing portrait, *Mme de Pompadour as Diana* (Cleveland, OH, Mus. A.), in 1755, when the great patron herself commissioned La Tour to paint her (Paris, Louvre), the younger artist depicted her in a more natural guise as a lover of art and literature.

In 1747 Nattier's daughter had married Louis Tocqué, and the two artists joined forces. However, Tocqué's naturalistic portraits gradually began to receive more favourable attention from the Salon critics than the works of his father-in-law. Although the fashion for the kind of portraits that had made Nattier's fame was dying out, in the 1750s he was nevertheless still receiving royal commissions, and he was still capable of work as impressive

Jean-Marc Nattier: *Maria Leczynska*, oil on canvas, 1.12×1.04 m. 1748 (Versailles, Musée National du Château de Versailles et de Trianon)

as the full-length of *Mme Henriette Playing the Bass Viol* (exh. 1755 Salon; Versailles, Château), which he described as 'one of my best works'. In the last years of his life, however, his fame and success declined, and he died ill and in poverty.

BIBLIOGRAPHY
Bénézit; Mariette; Thieme–Becker
L.-A. de Bonafous, Abbé de Fontenai: *Dictionnaire des artistes*, ii (Paris, 1776), pp. 196ff
L. Dussieux and others, eds: *Mémoires inédites . . . des membres de l'Académie royale* (1854), pp. 348ff
P. de Nolhac: *Jean-Marc Nattier: Peintre de la cour de Louis XV* (Paris, 1925)
G. Huard: 'J.-M. Nattier', *Les Peintres français du XVIIIe siècle*, ed. L. Dimier, ii (Paris, 1930), pp. 93ff

CATHRIN KLINGSÖHR-LE ROY

Naturalism. Term that has been used with many different meanings. It is predominantly applied to painting, and in its broadest sense it describes any art depicting actual, rather than religious and imaginary, subject-matter. It implies a style in which the artist tries to observe and then faithfully record the subject before him without deliberate idealization or stylization. The term has been used more specifically and (sometimes confusingly) in relation to 19th-century art, particularly French art, both as a synonym for REALISM and as a label for certain mutually exclusive subcurrents of it. Nevertheless, a more selfconscious development, Naturalism, can be discerned in the 19th century, which is centred on the ideas of JULES-ANTOINE CASTAGNARY and EMILE ZOLA.

1. GENERAL DEVELOPMENT BEFORE THE 19TH CENTURY. In Classical art the application of the term is complicated by the fact that the religious or mythological overtones of an image cannot always be discounted. Roman art provides the clearest early examples of naturalism, and at Pompeii there are several wall paintings showing everyday scenes, such as that depicting an argument between dice players seated around a table (mid-1st century AD; Pompeii). From the late Republic onwards, a greater naturalism can also be discerned in Roman portraiture, in both painting and sculpture. Naturalist art can be found in the marginalia of late medieval manuscripts. In the Luttrell Psalter (c. 1330–40; London, BL, Add. MS. 42130), for example, although the main images are drawn from traditional Christian iconography, the marginal scenes of peasant life are executed in a contrastingly naturalistic manner. While most Renaissance art depicted idealized Christian (or, increasingly, Classical) subject-matter, its very principles—the systematic, unprejudiced study of the world—brought art down to actuality. Leonardo's studies of nature and anatomy (e.g. *Oak-leaves with Acorns and Dyer's Greenweed*, drawing, c. 1505–8; Windsor Castle, Royal Lib.) reflect this attitude. Renaissance artists frequently subordinated the ostensible subject-matter to the truthful depiction of a scene, creating people who appeared more earthly than divine. This empiricism was particularly popular in northern Europe, as expressed, for example, in the aesthetic of Dürer, who painted extremely detailed studies of animals and plants (e.g. *Large Piece of Turf*, 1503; Vienna, Albertina; *see* DÜRER, (1), fig. 7). The empirical approach also led to the 'disguised symbolism' of some northern European paintings, in which commonplace objects, lovingly reproduced, carried religious meanings to the knowledgeable viewer.

In the 16th century there was a contrary movement in the imaginative transformations of Mannerism, but there was also a steady growth of landscape painting and an increase in illustration, developments often linked to the progress of science and technology. It is, however, in the 17th century that these tendencies reach a climax, and 'naturalism' has often been used to describe aspects of the art of this period. The Dutch townscapes, interiors, still-lifes and landscapes seem taken directly from life, bereft of religious content or ideal beauty. A church interior by Pieter Saenredam (e.g. *Choir of St Bavo's, Haarlem*, 1637; London, N.G.) carries no more significance than a street scene by Jan van der Heyden (e.g. *The Dam, Amsterdam*, c. 1665; Amsterdam, Rijksmus.). Dutch mercantile, bourgeois society has often been seen to prefigure general economic and social developments in the 19th century, and certainly the Realist artists of the latter period studied the earlier Dutch art with enthusiasm. Many such practitioners of the Baroque Grand Manner as Annibale Carracci and Peter Paul Rubens also painted everyday subjects (e.g. Carracci's *Bean Eater*, 1583–4, Rome, Gal. Colonna, *see* CARRACCI, (3), fig. 1; or Rubens's landscapes). Caravaggio created a sensation in Rome with his figures of saints apparently painted after the most ordinary people in the street and his insistence that a good painter knew how 'to imitate natural things well'. He and the art critic Bellori helped launch the concept of naturalism in art, although Bellori's advocation of it was tempered by his reliance on Classical art, and he, in fact, disliked what he thought to be the excessive naturalism of Caravaggio's work. Also, as Walter Friedlaender has pointed out, Caravaggio's melodramatic lighting leads to what can be called 'realistic' or 'naturalistic mysticism'. In 17th-century art generally, naturalism is inextricably bound up with a tendency to use allegory, and therefore the term cannot be applied straightforwardly, although Dutch art may provide exceptions.

The history of modern naturalism begins in the 18th century. The enthusiasm for science and the precipitous decline in religious belief among the educated classes led to a cult of nature, in which it was seen as a source of value in itself and not necessarily as an expression of divine creation. The ferment of analysis and thought led to the creation of modern art history, art criticism and aesthetics. This turmoil inspired Winckelmann and Reynolds to restate the ideal vision of art embodied in the Grand Manner. In Winckelmann's case, however, his theories were based on a belief that the ancient Greeks led lives close to nature, and that the beauty exemplified in Greek art had not been an imaginary ideal but a representation of actual Greek life. Subsequently Winckelmann and Reynolds have become probably the most quoted 18th-century writers on painting and sculpture, but they were fighting a losing battle. Artists became more and more interested in drawing and painting what they saw around them without embellishments, and landscape became the most popular subject in art. For example, certain works by Thomas Jones (e.g. *Wall in Naples*, 1782; priv. col., see Galassi, 1991, p. 33), George Stubbs (e.g. *Newmarket Heath, with a Rubbing-down House*, c. 1765; London, Tate) and Pierre Henri de Valenciennes (e.g. *Rooftop in Sunlight*, 1782–4; Paris, Louvre) lack all grandeur and social commentary and embody exactly the objectivity demanded by such later protagonists of naturalism as Emile Zola. This empirical observation of the world found further advocates at the beginning of the 19th century. William Henry Pyne prefaced *Microcosm* (London, 1806), his collection of etchings of all the labouring occupations of England, with a spirited claim:

> The poet, the painter or the dramatist who makes imaginery nature his model, or any other nature but the nature of common life, if he lives long, will himself live to see his attempts consigned to oblivion. It is strict real nature that has the principle of attraction, and of course, of vitality in it. All the rest is, at best trash, more or less splendid, and sooner or later must die.

There is a characteristic stress on nature and an echo of William Wordsworth's preface to the third edition of *Lyrical Ballads* published in London in 1802. The poet contrasted his own writing with 'the gaudy and inane phraseology of many modern writers' and defined his purpose as being 'to choose incidents and situations from common life, and to relate or describe them throughout, as far as was possible, in a selection of language really used by men' (p. vii). Although naturalism was to reach its climax in France, its beginnings can thus be found in England. In John Constable's writings as well as his paintings, which were to have such an impact in France (e.g. at the Salon of 1824), there is the same concern to depict the ordinary freed from all idealization. He wrote of his desire to develop a 'natural painture', and described his particular subject-matter thus: 'The sound of water escaping from mill-dams etc, willows, old rotten planks, slimy posts and brickwork. I love such things.'

2. DEVELOPMENT IN 19TH-CENTURY FRANCE AND LATER USE OF THE TERM. The words 'nature' and 'natural' were used so broadly in the late 18th century and the early 19th that the word 'realist' seems to have come into favour to provide a more specific term for literature and art drawn from immediate observation and experience. From the 1820s to the 1870s the term 'realism' was in wide use, especially in France. Gustave Courbet, somewhat reluctantly, published a Realist manifesto to accompany his exhibition at the Pavillon du Réalisme in Paris in 1855, and the following year Edmond Duranty launched his magazine *Réalisme*. Edgar Degas, when urging his painter friends to enter works in what came to be called the first Impressionist Exhibition in 1874, referred to it as a 'realist salon'. Realism became the battle cry and identifying slogan for the younger artists and writers who rejected established forms and often also the social system of which they formed a part. At the time of the Revolution of 1848 in particular, to be a Realist meant that one had socialist and democratic leanings and strove to reform society. Thus Realism became a universal term with both an artistic and a social significance. Naturalism consequently returned with a double meaning. It was a useful synonym for Realism (Degas also referred to himself as being part of the 'naturalistic school'), but it was also used for art without a particular political or social significance. In his Salon review of 1863 Jules-Antoine Castagnary chose the term 'naturalist' and wrote (i, pp. 104–5): 'The naturalist school declares that art is the expression of life under all phases and on all levels, and that its sole aim is to reproduce nature by carrying it to its maximum power and intensity: it is truth balanced with science.'

In 1868 Castagnary wrote: 'The word *naturalism*, which I use to define the tendencies of today, is not new in the history of art, and it is one of the reasons that make it preferable to the word *realism*' (i, p. 289). He went on to argue that all the best art had been naturalist, citing Cimabue's use of a living model in the studio, the work of Jan van Eyck and Hubert van Eyck and 17th-century Dutch and Spanish painting. The young Zola followed Castagnary's usage, and in his Salon review of 1868 he had a section headed *The Naturalists*. Zola chose Camille Pissarro to characterize the group, and he wrote a perceptive account of the artist's landscapes, including the claim that 'he is neither poet nor philosopher, but simply a naturalist, a maker of skies and earth.' In this statement by Zola, as in Castagnary's reference to science, is found the concept of objectivity and that of the elimination of any of the political significance that accompanied the Realists of 1848. In 1868 Zola also published the famous preface to the second edition of his novel *Thérèse Raquin*, which had been attacked for immorality. Zola presented himself as a type of scientist, impartially studying society: 'I hope that by now it is becoming clear that my object has been

first and foremost a scientific one' (p. 22). He went on to use such phrases as 'the scientific analysis' and 'the methodical and naturalist critique'. Zola developed his ideas most systematically in his long essay *Le Roman expérimental* (1879). (The title does not translate exactly into English because 'expérimental' means based on experiments in a scientific sense.) He linked his ideas firmly to those found in the French scientist Claude Bernard's *Introduction à l'étude de la médecine expérimentale* (Paris, 1865). Bernard was trying to establish a more scientific form of medicine, and Zola emphasized how innovative this was, as the processes of the human body had previously been thought too complex to be studied by the methods of inorganic chemistry. Zola described the Naturalist novelist as similar to Bernard but investigating the body of society.

Zola separated his method from that of the novelist addressing the reader directly or presenting any kind of moralizing commentary. Thus, in Zola's terms, a novelist like Charles Dickens, who took his materials from an intense observation of the life around him, could be a Realist but not a Naturalist, because of the moralizing presentation of the observations. Zola's theory has several drawbacks. It is, firstly, simplistic, because the novelist does not merely observe events as Zola suggests when he speaks of throwing his characters 'in a violent drama and [noting] down with scrupulous care the sensations and actions of these creatures' and then carrying out 'the analytical method ... that surgeons apply to corpses' (*Thérèse Raquin*, pp. 22–3). Furthermore, in his writings Zola always returned to his belief in the importance of the temperament of the artist, which is scarcely compatible with scientific objectivity. Nevertheless, Zola's vocabulary caught on: the pseudo-scientific arguments appealed because of the contemporary enthusiasm for science. In addition it reflects a plausible distinction between the work of the first generation of Realist artists and that of the Impressionists. Where Courbet and Jean-François Millet obviously composed their subjects, as in, for example, Courbet's *Burial at Ornans* (1849–50; Paris, Mus. d'Orsay; see COURBET, GUSTAVE, fig. 1), the Impressionist glimpse of the riverbank at Argenteuil (e.g. Alfred Sisley's *Bridge at Argenteuil*, 1872; Memphis, TN, Brooks Mus. A.; *see* SISLEY, ALFRED, fig. 1), or the steam and smoke in a railway station (*see* OIL PAINTING, colour pl. IV), does not focus on an event, and the paintings could therefore be described as objective slices of life (although in an unobtrusive way they are, of course, just as composed as the earlier paintings).

An example of an artist from this period who took a sociological approach analogous to Zola's analytical one and who became known as a Naturalist is Jean-François Raffaëlli. A decade younger than such Impressionists as Monet and Renoir, Raffaëlli shared the Naturalist novelists' interest in the outskirts of Paris, where the city was invading the countryside with a dreary mixture of factories and abandoned fields. Here the shacks of the poor and the dispossessed sprang up, and he depicted the workers, the unemployed and the ragpickers without drama or sentimentality, as in *The Ragpicker* (etching, 1911; Columbus, OH, Mus. A.; see fig.). Raffaëlli saw himself as methodically studying these people, and in an essay of

Jean-François Raffaëlli: *The Ragpicker*, etching with watercolour, 222×114 mm, 1911 (Columbus, OH, Museum of Art)

1884 he wrote (Schinman Fields, p. 107): 'The man of our times, the scientific man, tired of the baseless speculations of metaphysicians, wants an analytic examination of nature, of society and of individuals; . . . it is our duty to provide him with the judgments and the insights that we have discovered.' In the mid-1880s came the spectacular rise of Symbolism and Post-Impressionism, and the leading writers and critics rapidly lost interest in the debate over Realism and Naturalism, so that Raffaëlli became a somewhat isolated figure. There was no artistic attempt to develop a systematic study of society, which was taken up instead by sociologists and photographers. The word 'naturalism', having been popularized by Castagnary and Zola, continued to be used indiscriminately for various kinds of realism.

In the 20th century the proceedings of a conference held at Johns Hopkins University in Baltimore, Maryland,

in 1938 was, for example, called *Courbet and the Naturalistic Movement*, using the term for the first generation of Realists. Joseph C. Sloane, acknowledging that Realism and Naturalism had been confusingly interchanged, chose to distinguish Courbet and Millet by calling them 'objective naturalists' in *French Painting between the Past and the Present* (1951). Sloane defined the phrase in his own context and did not claim any absolute justification for his use. Later developments in scholarship have not clarified the vocabulary. For an exhibition in 1980–81 of the whole span of this art from Daumier and Courbet to the end of the 19th century, Gabriel P. Weisberg reasonably chose as title *The Realist Tradition: French Painting and Drawing, 1830–1900*. In the colloquium that accompanied the exhibition, Geneviève Lacambre tried to distinguish the later phase by using Zola's concept of Naturalism but further defining it. She wrote: 'Naturalism was a style that gradually superseded Realism through its advocacy of scientific accuracy, photographic verisimilitude, and largeness of scale. It became the most visible art form by 1880.' Lacambre also included the Impressionists because they abandoned convention to work out of doors in front of the motif: 'The Impressionists can rightfully claim the Naturalist label.' Among the works listed by Lacambre as examples of Naturalism are *La Toussaint* (1888; Nancy, Mus. B.-A.) by Emile Friant (1863–1932), *The Meeting* (1884; Paris, Mus. d'Orsay) by Mariya Konstantinovna Bashkirtseva and *Docks at Cardiff* (1898; Paris, Mus. d'Orsay) by Lionel Walden (1861–1933).

It is difficult to see these painters and the Impressionists as belonging to the same movement, and a further complication was created by the contribution of Kenneth McConkey to the same colloquium. He discussed a type of painting in Britain at the end of the 19th century that he called 'rustic naturalism'. This concentrates on the rural poor and has similarities with the pictures mentioned by Lacambre (e.g. by Jules Bastien-Lepage), but McConkey stressed that these painters aim to move the viewer by the use of pathetic fallacy. He wrote of horses looking at a collapsing ploughman with 'mute sympathy', and of weather and light providing an atmosphere appropriate to the subject. For example, a reviewer in the 1890s found in Henry Herbert La Thangue's *Man with the Scythe* (1896; London, Tate) an 'ingenious combination of symbolic purpose and realistic truth'. This rustic Naturalism seems incompatible with Lacambre's definition, and thus there appears to be no agreement on a common meaning for Naturalism or on its distinction from Realism. The attempt by Castagnary and Zola to give an objective, scientific content to the term did not succeed, partly because they did not discuss the photograph and its relation to the aim of objectivity.

BIBLIOGRAPHY
E. Zola: *Thérèse Raquin* (Paris, 2/1868; Eng. trans., Harmondsworth, 1962) [preface, pp. 21–7]
——: *Le Roman expérimental* (Paris, 1879)
J.-A. Castagnary: *Salons, 1857–1870*, 2 vols (Paris, 1892)
Courbet and the Naturalistic Movement: Baltimore, 1938
J. C. Sloane: *French Painting between the Past and the Present: Artists, Critics and Traditions from 1848 to 1870* (Princeton, 1951)
W. Friedlaender: *Caravaggio Studies* (Princeton, 1955)
A Decade of English Naturalism (exh. cat. by J. Gage, Norwich, Castle Mus., 1969)
J. R. Martin: *Baroque* (London, 1977, 2/1989), pp. 39–72

B. Schinman Fields: *Jean-François Raffaëlli: The Naturalist Artist* (diss., Columbia U., 1979)

Painting from Nature: The Tradition of Open Air Oil Sketching from the 17th to the 19th Centuries (exh. cat. by P. Conisbee, L. Gowing and J. A. Gere, Cambridge, Fitzwilliam; London, RA; 1980–81)

The Realist Tradition: French Painting and Drawing, 1830–1900 (exh. cat. by G. P. Weisberg, Cleveland, OH, Mus. A.; New York, Brooklyn Mus.; St Louis, MO, A. Mus.; Glasgow, A.G. & Mus.; 1980–81)

Before Photography: Painting and the Invention of Naturalism (exh. cat. by P. Galassi, New York, MOMA, 1981)

S. Alpers: *The Art of Describing: Dutch Art in the Seventeenth Century* (Chicago and London, 1983)

P. Galassi: *Corot in Italy: Open Air Painting and the Classical Landscape Tradition* (New Haven and London, 1991), pp. 11–39

G. P. Weisberg: *Beyond Impressionism: The Naturalist Impulse in European Art, 1860–1905* (London, 1992)

R. Thomson: 'Painter and Peasant', *TLS* (2 April 1993), p. 10

GERALD NEEDHAM

Nauen, Heinrich (*b* Krefeld, 1 June 1880; *d* Kalkar, 26 Nov 1940). German painter. He began his artistic training in 1898 at the Kunstakademie in Düsseldorf, attended the private school of Heinrich Knirr (1862–1944) in 1899 and in 1902 completed his studies by attending the class run by Leopold von Kalckreuth at the Königliche Akademie der Bildenden Künste in Stuttgart. From 1902 to 1905 he lived in the Belgian artists' colony of Laethem-Saint-Martin. In works produced at the beginning of the century he concentrated on landscapes and religious subjects. His encounter with Vincent van Gogh's work in 1905 was of decisive importance for the development of his painting. *Self-portrait* (1909; Krefeld, Kaiser Wilhelm Mus.) and *Still-life with Flowers* (1909; Düsseldorf, Kstmus.) both resemble the works van Gogh produced in the south of France. In the years Nauen spent in Berlin (1906–11), where he took part in exhibitions at the Secession and at Paul Cassirer's Kunstsalon, he cultivated contacts with artists such as Max Beckmann, Erich Heckel, Emil Nolde and Karl Schmidt-Rotluff, relieving him from his over-dependence on van Gogh.

From 1911 Nauen lived in the castle of Dillborn, Elmpt, on the Lower Rhine. A visit to Paris and contact with other artists living in the Rhineland stimulated him to develop his art further. In this period from 1912 to 1913, he produced one of his major works, the *Drove Cycle* (Krefeld, Kaiser Wilhelm Mus.), which comprised six tempera paintings and which represented a new concept in mural design. He altered Edwin Suermondt's (1883–1923) original commission—to decorate a room in the wing of the castle of Drove in Düren with a cycle of pictures depicting rural life—by contrasting thematically different works through the main colour underlying each one (e.g. red for an interior, yellow for a picture of a harvest). He combined the impression of colour that these formal contrasts evoked with a spatial structure, neutral oak panelling, a green tiled stove and light coming in through the window to create overall harmony. The works in the *Drove Cycle* revealed an exceptionally lengthened, angular figurative style typical of Nauen. He simplified the forms of the various pictorial objects depicted and brought out their objective qualities through colour contrasts. These stylistic features can also be seen in the portraits that he painted shortly after World War I, which, with still-lifes and landscapes, constitute an important area of subject-matter within his oeuvre. In *The Cellist Polly*

Heckmann (1919; Bonn, Städt. Kstmus.), the exaggeratedly long hands, the expression of concentration on the face and the dominant position of the musical instrument hiding the cellist's body helped to reveal the subject's character.

In 1921 Nauen accepted an appointment at the Kunstakademie in Düsseldorf, where he taught until his retirement in 1937. The works he produced in the 1920s revealed a different attitude to colour. Instead of composing pictorial space through colour contrast, he did so tone by tone through muted colours. From 1925 to 1926 he produced mosaics (destr.) for the exhibition buildings of the Gesolei in Düsseldorf. In 1933 the authorities dismissed Nauen from his job, and he spent the summer months at Hegau, near Lake Constance. His landscape drawings of this period, which were composed of small-scale elements, were very different from the large-surface works of previous years.

BIBLIOGRAPHY
E. Suermondt: *Heinrich Nauen* (Leipzig, 1922)
E. Marx: *Heinrich Nauen* (Recklinghausen, 1966)
G. Aust: 'Heinrich Nauen', *Die rheinischen Expressionisten* (exh. cat., Bonn, Städt. Kstmus., 1979), pp. 335–52
Heinrich Nauen (exh. cat., Krefeld, Kaiser Wilhelm Mus., 1980)

BARBARA LANGE

Naukratis [now Kawm al-Gi'cif]. City in ancient Egypt that flourished during the 26th Dynasty (664–525 BC) in the north-western Delta. Discussions about the links between the Aegean and Egypt during the late orientalizing and Archaic periods of Greece focus erroneously on Naukratis, which was not occupied by the Egyptians before the 7th century BC. Tradition maintains that Psammetichus I (*reg* 664–610 BC) introduced the eastern Greeks into Egypt as a resident class of foreign mercenaries in the service of the pharaoh. Before Amasis (*reg* 570–526 BC), Naukratis was allegedly the only trading post in the whole of Egypt in which an alien merchant might conduct business. It is best regarded as an Egyptian establishment of no earlier than the 26th Dynasty (rather than as a Greek foundation in the literal sense) in which alien merchants from eastern Greece were obliged to reside. During the course of the 4th century BC Naukratis became a true city state and survived into the 7th century AD.

The northern part of the site is earlier than the rest. Excavations have revealed a Milesian temple to Apollo, a Samian temple to Hera, a temple to the Dioskouroi, a temple to Aphrodite, fronted by a stepped altar, and a factory that produced scarabs, small portable amulets and figurines in faience. Numerous fragments of limestone statuettes, apparently in an Archaic Greek style, found scattered about the site of the Temple of Aphrodite, are most closely paralleled by a group of sculptures excavated on Cyprus. The Egyptian fragments are inadequately published, but some of the more complete examples are now in the British Museum, London (see fig.). The Greek pottery recovered from Naukratis provides little evidence of the site's supposed connections with the eastern Greeks, since it appears to derive mainly from the Corinth and Attica of the late 7th century BC. Moreover, it is unlikely that the Naukratis sanctuary to the Dioskouroi would have arisen in an eastern Greek context, since these deities were

Naukratis, alabaster statuette, h. 533 mm, 6th century BC (London, British Museum)

not particularly associated with Asia Minor (the homeland of the eastern Greeks). The archaeological record and the literary tradition are therefore not in accord, and sweeping generalizations about Naukratis' key role in Egyptian influence on emerging Greek art should be avoided. The city's relations with the Carians and the island of Cyprus during this same period are also open to discussion.

LÄ

BIBLIOGRAPHY

F. W. von Bissing: 'Naukratis, Studies in the Age of Greece and Egyptian Settlements at Naukratis', *Bull. Soc. Royale Archéol., Alexandrie*, xxxix (1951), pp. 33–82

W. M. Davis: 'Ancient Naukratis and the Cypriotes in Egypt', *Götting. Misz.*, xxxv (1979), pp. 13–23

G. P. Schaus: 'A Foreign Vase Painter in Sparta', *Amer. J. Archaeol.*, lxxxiii (1979), pp. 102–6

W. D. E. Coulson and A. Leonard jr: *Naukratis: Preliminary Report on the 1977–1978 and 1980 Seasons*, i of *Cities of the Delta* (Malibu, 1981)

W. M. Davis: 'Egypt, Samos and the Archaic Style in Greek Sculpture', *J. Egyp. Archaeol.*, lxvii (1981), pp. 61–81

ROBERT S. BIANCHI

Naukratis Painter. *See* VASE PAINTERS, §II.

Naukydes (*fl c.* 420–*c.* 390 BC). Greek sculptor. He was born in Argos and during the Classical period produced works in bronze, which are mentioned in ancient sources but no longer survive. Pliny (XXIV.xix.50) dated his floruit to 400–397 BC. His statue of *Cheimon* at Olympia (Pausanias: VI.ix.3) celebrated a victory of 448 BC but may have been made later. A statue of the boxer *Eukles*, also at Olympia (Pausanias: VI.vi.2), belongs to the late 5th century BC or early 4th, and his gold and ivory *Hebe* (Pausanias: II.xvii.5), which stood beside the cult statue, attributed to Polykleitos, in the Temple of Hera at Argos, must date after 423 BC, probably near the end of the century. Pausanias stated that Naukydes was the brother of Polykleitos (II.xxii.7) and that he was the teacher of a different, probably younger Polykleitos (VI.vi.2). The statue base of *Eukles*, however, names Naukydes' father as Patrokles, who was also the father of the sculptor Daidalos of Sikyon.

Naukydes seems to have specialized in statues of athletes, though his *Hermes*, *Hebe* and a *Hekate* at Argos show an interest in divine figures. Whether a pupil of Polykleitos or not, Naukydes seems to have been a follower and probably continued and experimented with the ideas of the master (*see* POLYKLEITOS, §2). Pliny stated that Naukydes made a *Diskobolos* (*Natural History* XXXIV.xix.80). This statue has long been associated with Roman copies representing an athlete preparing to throw a discus (e.g. Rome, Mus. Nuo.). The stance, with right foot advanced, can be compared to the position of the sockets for feet on the *Eukles* base. Similarly, the Roman *Hermes of Troizen* (Athens, N. Archaeol. Mus.) may copy Naukydes' *Hermes* (Pliny: XXXIV.xix.80). The connection between Naukydes' group of a man sacrificing a ram (Pliny: XXXIV.xix.80) and the statue of *Phrixos* seen by Pausanias on the Athenian Acropolis (I.xxxiv.2) is more problematical.

BIBLIOGRAPHY

Pauly–Wissowa

Pliny: *Natural History*

Pausanias: *Guide to Greece*

A. M. U. Linfert: *Von Polyklet zu Lysipp* (Giessen, 1966)

D. Arnold: *Die Polykletnachfolge* (Berlin, 1969)

G. Despinis: 'Zum Hermes von Troizen', *Mitt. Dt. Archäol. Inst.: Athen. Abt.*, xcvi (1981), pp. 237–44

CHARLES M. EDWARDS

Nauman, Bruce (*b* Fort Wayne, IN, 6 Dec 1941). American sculptor, photographer and performance artist working with video. He studied mathematics and later art with Italo Scanga (*b* 1932) at the University of Wisconsin (1960–64). At the University of California at Davis (1965–6) his teachers included William T. Wiley (*b* 1937) and Robert Arneson (*b* 1930). Upon graduation (MFA, 1966) he exhibited enigmatic, fibreglass sculpture. Nauman himself was already the subject of his art. Although he was a formidable draughtsman, Nauman's neon works, films, videotapes, performances, installations, sculpted body parts and word plays at first seemed frustratingly art-less. His was an art of exploration: he used himself, his person and his witty brand of inquiry to examine the parameters of art and the role of the artist. This questioning elicited strong emotional, physical and intellectual responses, and it often resulted in objects of formal beauty. *Neon Templates of the Left Half of my Body, Taken at Ten Inch Intervals* (1966; priv. col., see 1972 exh. cat., no. 17) and the colour photograph *Self Portrait as a Fountain* (1966; New York, Whitney) show him first extracting strangely compelling neon forms from the contours of his body and, in the latter, whimsically challenging preconceived notions of the 'fountain'.

Interested in new forms of music and literature, Nauman used the evocative power of language (in drawings, video scripts and neon installations), dismantling linguistic structure, creating puns and oxymorons, and linking contradictory words in alliterative sequences, as in *Violins Violence Silence* (neon tubing, 1.58×1.66×0.15 m, 1981–2; Baltimore, MD, Mus. A.). Using flashing neon signs, he stripped words and, later, actions of their conventional meanings, as in *Welcome Shaking Hands* (1985; see Silverthorne and others, pp. 52–3), leaving disquieting ironies and moral dilemmas.

BIBLIOGRAPHY
Bruce Nauman: Work from 1965 to 1972 (exh. cat. by J. Livingston and M. Tucker, Los Angeles, CA, Co. Mus. A.; New York, Whitney; 1972)
Bruce Nauman (exh. cat. by K. Schmidt, E. Joosten and S. Holsten, Otterlo, Kröller-Müller; Baden-Baden, Staatl. Ksthalle; 1981)
Bruce Nauman (exh. cat. by B. Richardson, Baltimore, MD, Mus. A., 1982)
P. Schjeldahl: *Art of our Time: The Saatchi Collection*, i (London, 1984)
J. Silverthorne and others: 'Collaboration Bruce Nauman', *Parkett*, 10 (1986) [issue devoted to Nauman]
Bruce Nauman (exh. cat. by J. Simon and J. C. Ammann, London, Whitechapel A.G., 1987)
C. van Bruggen: *Bruce Nauman* (New York, 1988)
Bruce Nauman: Prints, 1970–89 (exh. cat., ed. C. Cordes; New York, Castelli Graphics; Chicago, Donald Young Gal.; 1989) [cat. rai.]
Bruce Nauman (exh. cat., ed. J. Simon; Minneapolis, Walker A. Cent., 1994) [cat. rai.]

CONSTANCE W. GLENN

Naumburg. German town in Saxony-Anhalt on the River Saale, with a population of *c.* 34,000 (1988). The bishop of Naumburg was a suffragan of the archbishop of Magdeburg.

1. CATHEDRAL. Situated to the north-west of the old town on the site of the former Vorburg, the cathedral is dedicated to SS Peter and Paul. It is famed in particular for its sculptures.

(i) Architecture. A provostry at the settlement (recorded in 1021) was raised to cathedral status in 1028 when the bishopric of Zeitz was transferred there. The early Romanesque cathedral was a cruciform aisled basilica with three bays in the nave and six in each side aisle, a Saxon alternating system of piers and a flat ceiling. It had a transept with side apses rather than a crossing sectioned off by arches, a square east chancel with a shorter apse, two west towers and between them a west apse with a small crypt. The present building was begun before 1213 by Bishop Engelhard (*reg* 1207–42) with the replacement of the nave and aisles. After a change of plan, the cathedral

was completely rebuilt from east to west up to the mid-13th century. A preliminary consecration in 1242 is recorded, indicating that the nave and aisles were complete. The older Marienstiftskirche, the burial church of the Eckehardians on the axis of the cathedral, was at first to be retained beside the cathedral but was later incorporated into the rebuilt west chancel (complete by *c.* 1260). The east chancel, in the middle axis of which stands a polygonal pillar (a feature that became common only after the mid-14th century), replaced the Late Romanesque apse *c.* 1330. The west towers, the southern one of which was completed only in 1894, have their models in Laon and Bamberg.

The cathedral, like its Romanesque predecessor, is a cruciform aisled basilica (total length *c.* 100 m) and has a double chancel, an east crypt and two pairs of towers on either side of the chancels. The nave and aisles form a *Gebundenes System* based on the dimensions of the crossing square, with three nave bays corresponding to six bays in the side aisles. The square of the eastern chancel is extended by an extra bay and a $\frac{6}{10}$ polygonal apse and is flanked by rectangular side chancels (beneath the east towers) with apses. The west towers project beyond the side aisles and enclose between them the square west chancel with a sexpartite rib vault and ending with a $\frac{5}{8}$ apse. The whole building is vaulted, mostly with groin vaulting. The central part of the high, tripartite hall crypt under the east chancel originates from the previous building (*c.* 1160–70) and has a nave and two aisles in three bays, with fine ornamental capitals of *c.* 1170 (see §(ii) below). Around 1210–20 a two-bay extension was added under the crossing and a three-bay extension under the apse, also with very high-quality ornamental capitals. The architecture of the east rood screen forms the west wall of the crypt; the three-bay, groin-vaulted hall screen rises above a socle with three steps and is the oldest surviving example of its type. The Early Gothic west chancel is articulated by clustered responds. Above the socle in the polygonal part runs a gallery, at the level of which are 12 founder figures, and at the nave end of the chancel is a fine rood screen (see §(ii) below).

To the south of the cathedral extensive parts of the old cloister survive. The Dreikönigskapelle (*c.* 1420) and the parish church, the Marienkirche, form a continuation of the south and east sides of the cloister, the High Gothic part of which was roofed in 1343. The former baptismal chapel of St John the Baptist in the chancel of the Marienkirche was transferred to the cathedral cemetery in 1866. After 1945 the cathedral underwent a thorough restoration.

BIBLIOGRAPHY
W. Pinder: *Der Naumburger Dom und seine Bildwerke* (Berlin, 1925)
H. Küas: *Die Naumburger Werkstatt*, Forschungen zur deutschen Kunstgeschichte, xxvi (Berlin, 1937)
E. Schubert: *Der Naumburger Dom* (Berlin, 1968)
G. Leopold and E. Schubert: *Die frühromanischen Vorgängerbauten des Naumburger Doms*, Corpus der romanischen Kunst im thüringisch-sächsischen Gebiet, series A (Architektur), iv (Berlin, 1972)
G. Dehio: *Bezirk Halle*, ed. E. Lehmann, Hb. Dt. Kstdkml. (Berlin, 1976)
J.-H. Mrusek: *Drei sächsische Kathedralen: Merseburg–Naumburg–Meissen* (Dresden, 1976)
E. Schubert: *Der Dom zu Naumburg* (Munich and Berlin, 1990)

BETTINA GEORGI, ERNST ULLMANN

(ii) Sculpture and furnishings. The most important works in the cathedral are those of the NAUMBURG MASTER (*see* MASTERS, ANONYMOUS, AND MONOGRAMMISTS, §I). These include not only the figural sculpture of the west rood screen (reliefs showing scenes from the Passion and a monumental *Crucifixion* group) and the west chancel (12 life-size founders' statues) but also the natural ornamentation (identifiable plants) on the capitals, friezes and keystones. They attain a realism unique in the Middle Ages and are among the finest works of medieval German sculpture. A dependence on the sculptures of Bamberg Cathedral (*see* BAMBERG, §2(ii)) has been recognized.

At the time of the construction of the world-famous west chancel (*c.* 1250–60), the so-called west rood screen was erected to serve as an entrance façade to the chancel. The outstanding architecture and sculpture of the rood screen and chancel are middle German Early Gothic and are attributed to the Naumburg Master. Their dependence on French models is evident, but no less clear is the recasting of French High Gothic into middle German Early Gothic. The Passion reliefs depicting the *Last Supper*, the *Betrayal of Christ*, the *Arrest of Christ*, the *Denial of Peter* in two scenes and *Christ before Pilate* (the *Flagellation* and *Christ Carrying the Cross* were added in wood in 1737) bring the dramatic events of the Passion into the perspective of human destiny. Despite the dependence on earlier models, these expressive works with their delicate ornamentation adopt a new approach: a humanistic and realistic interpretation of the Gospel texts, telling the story in thoughtful, psychological terms. The statues in the portal of the west rood screen depict a Crucifix flanked by the *Virgin*, *St John* and two *Censing Angels*. The moment of Christ's death and the deep shock of his mother and of the apostle John are expressed in a natural, portrait-like manner that is deeply moving in its precise yet grandiose rendering of suffering and grief (*see* CRUCIFIX, §3(i) and fig. 4).

The 12 founder figures in the west apse stand in front of the responds between the windows and are carved out of the same blocks of stone as the responds themselves. With a profound expressive power comparable to that of the rood-screen sculptures, these life-size statues depict individuals shaped by their fates and characters. From south to north the founders portrayed are: *Gerburg, Konrad, Hermann* and *Reglindis* (*see* DRESS, §IV, 3 and fig. 15), *Dietmar, Syzzo, Wilhelm, Thimo, Eckehard II* and his wife *Uta* (see fig. 1), *Gepa* (or *Berchta* or *Adelheid*) and *Dietrich*. Since they all lived in the 11th century and thus were long dead by 1250, the only basis for the artist's inventions was sparse historical information on their lives and their donations to the cathedral. The document of 1249 that names these 12 '*primi fundatores*' asks others to support the building as they did and promises to such benefactors prayers for the salvation of their souls. The practice of saying intercessions for the founders was probably the main reason for their prominent position far above eye-level yet within the context of the decorative programme of the west chancel. The stained-glass windows of the west chancel show the *ecclesia triumphans*, in which the founders take their place at the lowest level of the hierarchy beside the Naumburg bishops. The statues are so vivid and natural, yet at the same time of such

1. Naumburg Cathedral, west chancel, statues of *Eckehard II* and his wife *Uta* by the Naumburg Master, stone, life-size, early 1240s or *c.* 1250–60

artistic excellence, that scholars still have difficulty in seeing them as part of a process of development within the history of 13th-century European sculpture, and their dating still varies between the early 1240s and the decade *c.* 1250–60 (*see also* GOTHIC, §III, 1(iii)(b)). The only sculpture by the Naumburg Master in Naumburg that can indeed be dated with any certainty is the tombstone of the patron who built the west chancel, *Bishop Dietrich II*, who died in 1272. This is clearly the sculptor's latest work in Naumburg. The life-size statue of a deacon holding a lectern was undoubtedly made some years before the tombstone.

Apart from its figural sculptures, Naumburg Cathedral is also remarkable for its architectural carving. The Late Romanesque ornamentation exhibits a Lower Rhenish influence and is closely related to that of St Andreas in Cologne. The artistic quality of the capitals is high, as, for example, in the stylized Late Romanesque capitals of the east crypt: although the earlier capitals (*c.* 1170) show a Saxon influence, the later ones (*c.* 1210–20) are Rhenish in inspiration. Like the figure sculptures discussed above, the plants on the Early Gothic capitals, corbels, friezes and keystones are reproduced with lifelike fidelity and are all identifiable. These works are among the finest of medieval German sculpture, and their realism was unparalleled for centuries before or after (see fig. 2). In the west crypt the realistic treatment of the flowers, leaves and fruit suggests that they were taken from the flora of the cathedral hill. The composition is strict and harmonious, the shapes taut and clearly cut.

The painting of all the Early Gothic Naumburg sculptures has been renewed or restored several times. Originally it would have been much brighter, conveying the same sense of vitality as the stone statues themselves. The workshop that produced the sculptures and the Early Gothic architectural ornamentation has been shown to have been active in Reims, Amiens, Noyon, Metz, Strasbourg and especially Mainz before Naumburg, after which it was active in Meissen.

Among the other high-quality furnishings of Naumburg Cathedral that survived the iconoclasm of the Reformation and the purifying restoration of 1874–8 are retables, sculptured tombs of stone and bronze, stalls from the 13th to the 16th century, including the west choir-stalls with very richly carved back rests, and medieval stained glass. Three of the five slender windows in the west chancel have stained glass dating from the time of construction (*c*. 1250–60). Like the architecture and sculpture of the chancel, these glass paintings are works of the highest rank by European standards (*see* GOTHIC, §VIII, 5). In the east chancel four medieval stained-glass windows (*c*. 1330–40 and 15th century) of high artistic quality have been preserved.

2. Naumburg Cathedral, vault boss in the apse of the west chancel, *c*. 1250–60

BIBLIOGRAPHY

C. P. Lepsius: *Über das Alterthum und die Stifter des Domes zu Naumburg und deren Statuen im westlichen Chor desselben* (1822), i of *Mitteilungen aus dem Gebiet historisch-antiquarischer Forschungen*, ed. K. E. Förssemann (Halle, 1822)

H. Bergner: *Die Stadt Naumburg*, Beschreibende Darstellung der älteren Bau- und Kunstdenkmäler der Provinz Sachsen und angrenzender Gebiete, xxiv (Halle, 1903)

H. Küas: *Die Naumburger Werkstatt*, Forschungen zur deutschen Kunstgeschichte, xxvi (Berlin, 1937)

J. Jahn: *Die Schmuckformen des Naumburger Domes* (Leipzig, 1944)

W. Schlesinger: *Meissner Dom und Naumburger Westchor: Ihre Bildwerke in geschichtlicher Betrachtung* (Münster and Cologne, 1952)

E. Schubert: *Der Westchor des Naumburger Doms: Ein Beitrag zur Datierung und zum Verständnis der Standbilder* (Berlin, 1964, 2/1965)

G. Leopold and E. Schubert: *Die frühromanischen Vorgängerbauten des Naumburger Doms*, Corpus der romanischen Kunst im thüringisch-sächsischen Gebiet, series A (Architektur), iv (Berlin, 1972)

E. Schubert: *Naumburg: Dom und Altstadt* (Leipzig, 1983) [photographs by F. Hege]

ERNST SCHUBERT,
with BETTINA GEORGI, ERNST ULLMANN

Nauru, Republic of. Isolated raised coral atoll of *c*. 21 sq. km with a population of *c*. 9000 (UN estimate, 1989), lying just south of the Equator in the central Pacific Ocean, 305 km west of Banaba. Nauru is usually classified as part of Micronesia. It has been an independent state since 1968. Traditional Nauruan culture was most thoroughly recorded by Paul Hambruch in 1910 (published 1914–15), by which time it had already changed greatly due to the influence of whalers, traders and some European settlers. When the island's rich phosphate mines began to be worked in 1907 the pace of change increased further, and since 1920 the island's traditional material culture has been largely supplanted by imported goods

and practices. The distinctive Nauruan language, however, has survived, as has an oral culture rich in songs and myths. There has also been a revival of traditional dancing and weaving, stimulated in part by participation in festivals of South Pacific arts. Studies of historic collections in German museums (e.g. Berlin, Mus. Vlkerknd.; Hamburg, Mus. Vlkerknd.) would enable scholars to provide a fuller picture of pre-1920 Nauruan material culture.

Traditionally economic life was based on the exploitation of coconut and pandanus and on fishing. Coconut was an important source of food and drink, especially during droughts, providing also the raw materials for the manufacture of house thatch, clothing, baskets and many other artefacts. Pandanus was only slightly less significant as a source of food and raw material. A third tree of importance was the *tomano* (*Calophyllum*), boards from which were sewn together to make canoes. Nauruan aesthetic life focused on sports and games, singing and dancing, and particularly on string figure competitions, where the Nauruans attained a level of creative excellence unequalled elsewhere in the records of this art form. More than 100 different designs have been documented (Maude, 1971). Decorative arts were generally restricted in range. There was no loom, no figure carving and little tattoo. As often throughout Micronesia (the parallels with Kiribati being especially close), there was a high standard of woven-fibre objects, particularly baskets, mats and nets. There were also carefully finished objects of personal adornment, including braided girdles, caps and headbands, and necklaces, armlets and anklets made from shells, feathers, flowers and teeth. One form of headband, exclusive to Nauru, incorporated the spiked bodies of butterflies. A visitor's description of 1895 catches the prevailing aesthetic (Senfft in Fabricius, 1992, pp. 271–2):

The female dancers take the greatest care with their toilet. They spend hours combing their hair, rubbing their bodies with coconut oil and adjusting their small mats, girdles and flowers. Other ornaments which they like to wear are delicately coloured fish, which are worn in their hair or on their bosoms, or fishtails strung together to make a girdle and scarves made of long women's hair.

The most remarkable examples of Nauruan plaiting are the mats once worn by pregnant women. These incorporated designs indicating clan membership (Hambruch, 1914–15, p. 243). The distinctive plaiting included wefts that ran parallel to the sides, rather than diagonally. Plain check with double wefts were the most common, although a few mats included twill. The natural colour of the pandanus contrasted with the black, red or brown colour of the dyed hibiscus fibre in chequerwork and interlocking diamond designs.

BIBLIOGRAPHY

EWA: 'Micronesian Cultures'
P. Hambruch: *Nauru*, 2 vols (1914–15), II/B/1-2 of *Ergebnisse der Südsee-Expedition, 1908–1910*, ed. G. Thilenius (Hamburg, 1913–36)
C. H. Wedgwood: 'Report on Research Work in Nauru Island, Central Pacific', *Oceania*, vi/4 (1936), pp. 359–91; vii/1 (1936), pp. 1–33
H. Maude: *The String Figures of Nauru Island* (Adelaide, 1971)
S. Petit-Skinner: *The Nauruans* (San Francisco, 1981)
L. Hanson and F. A. Hanson: *The Art of Oceania: A Bibliography*, Ref. Pubns A. Hist. (Boston, MA, 1984)
The Art of Micronesia (exh. cat. by J. Feldman and R. Rubinstein, Honolulu, Hawaii A. G., 1986)
W. Fabricius: *Nauru, 1888–1900: An Account in German and English Based on Official Records of the Colonial Section of the German Foreign Office Held by the Deutsches Zentralarchiv in Potsdam*, ed. and trans. D. Clark and S. Firth (Canberra, 1992)

PETER GATHERCOLE

Nautilus cup. Standing-cup of carved and polished nautilus shell mounted in gold or silver set with gemstones. Its principal function was decorative, although in some examples the lip of the shell was cut away to facilitate its use as a drinking vessel. The finest examples were made in Germany between 1550 and 1650, and later examples are rare. The cup was sometimes conceived as a grotesque or marine creature, of which the nautilus shell, often later replaced in silver, formed the body. Representations of Poseidon, mermaids, mermen, seahorses and griffins were favoured motifs, their figures often forming the stem. Nautilus shells were also incorporated into nefs (for example the Burghley Nef, *c.* 1527; London, V&A; *see* FRANCE, fig. 74).

Nauwjncx, Herman. *See* NAIWINCX, HERMAN.

Navajo. Indigenous people of the Southwest region of North America (*see under* NATIVE NORTH AMERICAN ART). Navajo culture developed relatively recently (*c.* 15th century AD), although by the late 20th century the Navajo people had become the largest indigenous group in the USA.

Navan Fort [anc. Emain Macha]. Hilltop enclosure and ritual site at Navan, Co. Armagh, Ireland. It was constructed *c.* 95 BC, and it is recorded in the Ulster Cycle and other Irish legends as the capital of the northern Irish province of Ulster. Navan Fort is recognized archaeologically as one of a group of Irish 'royal sites', including Tara

and Dun Ailinne, whose most unusual architectural feature is an enclosure bank placed outside a ditch, in contrast to the normal defensive arrangement of bank within a ditch. The site was excavated by Dudley Waterman between 1963 and 1971.

Evidence was recovered of Neolithic occupation, and one of two earthworks in the enclosure, known as Site A, was used in both the Bronze Age and the early medieval period. The second, more substantial mound comprising Site B measured 45 m in diameter, standing 5–6 m high; this was the focus of the most interesting activity on the hill. A Bronze Age settlement under this mound, dating to *c.* 700 BC, comprised an enclosure containing a circular house and an outer stockade. The house was rebuilt several times on the same spot, and it produced an amount of important Bronze Age and Iron Age material, including such high-status objects as part of a scabbard. The most extraordinary find was the skull of a Barbary ape, which must have come from Spain or North Africa and might well have been seen as a suitable gift for a king. Around 100 BC the house was dismantled and replaced by an enormous circular structure 40 m across and composed of 5 concentric rings of wooden posts. At the centre, a massive post, shown by dendrochronological analysis to have been felled in 95 or 94 BC and measuring perhaps 12 m high, was the focus of a passageway between the timbers. The structure may have been roofed, but it is unlikely to have been residential in nature. Not long after its construction the building was filled in with stone, the protruding timbers destroyed by fire and the whole mound covered with several metres of earth and turves. This action appears to have been the deliberate ending of a ritual site rather than the result of attack.

The immediate surroundings of the site are strongly associated with power and ritual; they include the ritual pool at King's Stables and four decorated trumpets found below a hill at Loughnashade. The great earthwork known as the Dorsey, 27 km south of Navan Fort, was constructed at the same time as the central post and may mark the territorial boundary of Ulster.

BIBLIOGRAPHY

'Navan Fort', *Current Archaeol.*, xxii (1970), pp. 304–8
J. P. Mallory: *Navan Fort* (Belfast, 1985)

SARA CHAMPION

Navarrete, Juan Fernández de [Mudo, El] (*b* Logroño, *c.* 1538; *d* Toledo, 28 March 1579). Spanish painter and draughtsman. He was a deaf mute, and the principal sources for his life and work are writings by Fray José de Sigüenza and Ceán Bermúdez. He received his early training in the Hieronymite monastery of La Estrella in Logroño, and as a young man he travelled in Italy, visiting Milan, Rome, Naples and Venice. The majority of Navarrete's paintings were commissioned for the royal monastery church of S Lorenzo at the Escorial near Madrid, which was then being built by Philip II. In 1566 he was first mentioned there when he was engaged in repairing paintings in the collection. On 6 March 1568 he was named a court painter at an annual salary of 200 ducats, in addition to which he was to receive payment for commissioned work. Although he was required to live at the Escorial, he obtained royal permission to spend long periods in Madrid and Logroño, where he painted for the monastery. The small panel depicting the *Baptism* (*c.* 1568; Madrid, Prado) was the sample piece or '*prueba*' that he presented to Philip II. It is painted in clear, vivid colours with meticulous detail, and in both style and technique it is reminiscent of Roman and Flemish Mannerist works. He soon abandoned this style for the Venetian manner of painting, probably in response to the preference of his royal patron for that school, and he practised it so successfully that he came to be known as 'the Spanish Titian'.

Between 1569 and 1575 Navarrete painted eight canvases for the two sacristies of the Escorial, in which his art reached maturity. In the *Adoration of the Shepherds* (Madrid, Escorial) the darkness of the night is penetrated by three sources of light emanating from the Christ Child, the heavens and a candle, demonstrating that Navarrete had absorbed the techniques of Correggio and Jacopo Bassano. In the *Martyrdom of St James* (1571; Madrid, Escorial) the saint is shown at the instant of martyrdom, the pallor of death already on his face; the naturalism with which he is portrayed heightens the immediacy of the scene. In the large canvas *Abraham and the Three Angels* (1576; Dublin, N.G.; see fig.), which he painted for the guest-room or *recibimiento* of the monastery, the extent to which Navarrete assimilated Titian's technique can be seen in his use of light and shade, in his rich, glowing palette and in certain passages of the brushwork, such as Abraham's robe, where the paint is applied with fluidity and thickness, and where the brushstrokes are clearly visible. His outlines are more clearly defined than those of Titian's later style, and the figures are monumental and dignified. Navarrete's work as a whole is imbued with piety and devotion, which accorded well with contemporary religious sentiment, and his paintings are 'truly images of devotion that inspire prayer' (Sigüenza).

The *Abraham and the Three Angels* so pleased the King that he entrusted Navarrete with the formidable task of painting 32 canvases for the minor altars of the basilica, for which the contract was signed on 21 August 1576. This was followed in January 1579 by the prestigious commission for the paintings of the high altarpiece. This should have been the crowning glory of Navarrete's career, but he died just three months later in the house of his friend, the architect and sculptor Nicolás de Vergara (ii), and was buried in S Juan de los Reyes, Toledo. At the time of his death, Navarrete had only finished eight canvases of *Apostles* for the basilica altars (the series was completed by Alonso Sánchez Coello, Luis de Carvajal and Diego de Urbina).

Navarrete's *Apostles* in the basilica are heroically life-size and appear somewhat larger by the painter taking a chest-high point of view, thereby throwing the head and shoulders into dramatic relief against the sky. An outstanding feature is the variety of very beautiful skyscapes indicating different times of day and weather conditions. In spite of his disabilities and poor health, Navarrete not only achieved recognition, but of all the painters, both Spanish and Italian, who worked at the Escorial he was the most successful in pleasing his patron. He expressed those qualities of piety and decorum on which Philip II insisted in religious art. He combined a Venetian style of painting with strong naturalistic tendencies and an interest in tenebrism.

Navarrete also painted portraits, though none has been identified. He made drawings for vestments, and of the preparatory drawings that he undoubtedly made for his paintings only a *Lion Drinking* (Madrid, Prado) is universally accepted as autograph. He probably portrayed himself as St Luke holding his portrait of the Virgin in the *St Mark and St Luke* (1578; Madrid, Escorial).

BIBLIOGRAPHY

Ceán Bermúdez

J. de Sigüenza: *La fundación del monasterio de el Escorial* (Madrid, 1605/*R*1963)

J. Zarco Cuevas: *Pintores españoles en San Lorenzo el Real de el Escorial* (Madrid, 1931) [illus. and doc.]

J. Yarza Luaces: 'Navarrete 'El Mudo' y el monasterio de la Estrella', *Bol. Semin. Estud. A. & Arqueol.*, xxxviii (1972), pp. 323–6

R. Mulcahy: '*Abraham and the Three Angels* by Juan Fernández de Navarrete "El Mudo"', *Apollo*, cvii (1978), pp. 118–23

——: 'The High Altarpiece of the Basilica of San Lorenzo de el Escorial: An unpublished document', *Burl. Mag.*, cxxii (1980), pp. 188–92

J. Yarza Luaces: ' "El Mudo": El pintor de El Escorial?', *Fragmentos*, iv–v (1985), pp. 75–95

T. de Antonio Sáenz: *Pintura española del ultimo tercio del siglo XVI en Madrid: Juan Fernández de Navarrete, Luis de Carvajal y Diego de Urbina*, 3 vols (diss., Madrid, U. Complutense, 1987)

B. Davidson: 'Navarrete in Rome', *Burl. Mag.*, cxxxv (1993), pp. 93–6

Juan Fernández de Navarrete 'el Mudo': Pintor de Felipe II (exh. cat., Logroño, 1995)

ROSEMARIE MULCAHY

Navarro, Luis Díez. *See* DÍEZ NAVARRO, LUIS.

Nave. Main western space in a church, the area used by the congregation.

Juan Fernández de Navarrete: *Abraham and the Three Angels*, oil on canvas, 2.86×2.38 m, 1576 (Dublin, National Gallery of Ireland)

Nave, Bartolomeo della (*fl* Venice, early 17th century). Italian merchant and collector. Little is known of his life, but he had one of the most outstanding collections of the early 17th century in Venice. Many contemporaries praised it: Vincenzo Scamozzi wrote that della Nave had acquired some of Cardinal Pietro Bembo's antiquities and that he also possessed 100 paintings, among them 20 works by Titian, of great quality; the anonymous author of a life of Titian (1622) numbered him among the most important collectors of works by that master; Giambattista Marino, in his *La galleria*, described many works that belonged to him. According to Moschetti, he was admired by the Aldobrandini, the Ludovisi, the Bevilacqua, the princes of Poland, Condé, Mantua and others. Simon Vouet admired his 'studio di bellissime pitture'. Ridolfi pointed out that della Nave had bought works from the collection of Alessandro Vittoria and that he was connected with Palma Giovane. Mason-Rinaldi has proposed that the *Portrait of a Collector* by Palma Giovane (Birmingham, Mus. & A.G.) represents della Nave.

In 1636 della Nave's collection was put up for sale, perhaps following his death, and became the object of lively competition between James, 3rd Marquess of Hamilton (1606–49) (represented by his brother-in-law, the English ambassador in Venice, Lord Basil Feilding), Thomas Howard, 14th Earl of Arundel, and King Charles I. At first, it seems, they agreed to divide the paintings between them, but in the event all were acquired (in 1638) by Lord Feilding for the Marquess of Hamilton. After Hamilton's execution (1649), the greatest part of the collection went to the Netherlands, where it was acquired *c.* 1650 by the Habsburg Archduke of Austria Leopold-William, Governor of the Spanish Netherlands. About 200 of the Venetian paintings subsequently went to Vienna, where *c.* 50 still remain, as the heart of the Venetian collections of the Kunsthistorisches Museum. Among these are the *Three Philosophers* (*see* GIORGIONE, fig. 4) and the *Adoration of the Shepherds*, both by Giorgione, fragments of the S Cassiano altarpiece by Antonello da Messina and several works by Titian, for example the *Nymph and Shepherd*. Della Nave also owned Giorgione's *Finding of Paris* (untraced), which Marcantonio Michiel had seen when it was in Taddeo Contarini's collection and had described as an early work.

BIBLIOGRAPHY

V. Scamozzi: *L'idea dell'architettura universale* (Venice, 1615), p. 306
G. Marino: *La galleria* (Venice, 1620)
G. A. Moschetti: *Il pulice* (Venice, 1625), p. 2
C. Ridolfi: *Meraviglie* (1648); ed. D. von Hadeln (1914–24)
E. K. Waterhouse: 'Paintings from Venice from Seventeenth-century England', *It. Stud.*, vii (1952), pp. 1–23
S. Savini-Branca: *Il collezionismo veneziano nel '600* (Padua, 1964), pp. 251–4
K. Garas: 'Die Entstehung der Galerie des Erzherzogs Leopold-Wilhelm', *Jb. Ksthist. Samml. Wien*, xxvii (1967), pp. 39–80
S. Mason-Rinaldi: *Palma il Giovane: L'opera completa* (Milan, 1984), p. 76
P. Shakeshaft: ' "To much bewiched with thoes intysing things": The Letters of James, Third Marquis of Hamilton, and Basil, Viscount Feilding, Concerning Collecting in Venice 1635–1639', *Burl. Mag.*, cxxviii (1986), pp. 114–32

MICHEL HOCHMANN

Navez, François-Joseph (*b* Charleroi, 16 Nov 1787; *d* Brussels, 11 Oct 1869). Belgian painter. He studied from 1803 to 1808 under Joseph François at the Brussels Académie. While still a student, he won several prizes; the Brussels Société des Beaux-Arts, impressed by his *Virgil Reading the Aeneid* (untraced), which won first prize at the 1812 Ghent Salon, offered him a grant to continue his studies in Paris. From 1813 to 1816 he made rapid progress in the studio of David, with whom he returned to Brussels when the latter was exiled in 1816. The two artists became particularly close, and Navez's works from this time, such as the *De Hemptinne Family* (1816; Brussels, Mus. A. Anc.) and *St Veronica* (1816; priv. col., see 1985–6 exh. cat., pl. xxii), strongly reflect David's influence in their technical accomplishment and naturalism. In 1817, with the backing of David and others, Navez obtained a grant to go to Italy, where he remained until 1821. He was initially at a loss without David but found encouragement among the group of French artists based at the Villa Medici in Rome: Victor Schnetz, Léopold Robert and François-Marius Granet were among his closest friends there. He became a fervent admirer of Ingres and took an interest in the Nazarenes. His painting accordingly developed a purist streak, although he held fast to the tenets of naturalism learnt from David. Typical of Navez's Roman work are his *Hagar and Ishmael* (1820; Brussels, Mus. A. Anc.; see fig.) and his first great biblical subject, *Elisha Resurrecting the Son of the Shunamite Woman* (1821; Amsterdam, Rijksmus.), an imposing and austere work of undeniable monumentality. In Navez's portraits such as *Man with a Guitar* (1821; Charleroi, Mus. Com. B.-A.) a Romantic sensibility emerges, which is traceable to Ingres, although in others, such as *Henri Voordecker* (1816;

François-Joseph Navez: *Hagar and Ishmael*, oil on canvas, 2.21×1.71 m, 1820 (Brussels, Musée d'Art Ancien)

Brussels, Mus. A. Anc.), he was far more vigorous in his handling than Ingres.

Returning to Brussels in January 1822, Navez was disappointed to find himself generally regarded as a portrait and genre painter: his ambition remained to be a history painter. Fortunately, patrons from the Netherlands commissioned him to produce religious works such as the *Incredulity of St Thomas* (1823; Amsterdam, St Franciscus-Xaverkerk) and *St Cecilia* (1824; Mons, Mus. B.-A.). Navez also found that his association with David, whose successor he was considered, put him out of step with the new artistic climate in Brussels, where Romanticism in the manner of Gustaf Wappers was in vogue. Navez's *Athaliah Questioning Joash* (Brussels, Mus. A. Anc.) was badly received at the Brussels Salon of 1830, and Navez considered moving to Paris. He stayed in Brussels, however, on being offered the directorship of the Académie des Beaux-Arts, but sent *Athaliah* to the Paris Salon of 1834, where its strongly theatrical character and Orientalist overtones won him a gold medal.

Navez himself subsequently adopted a sugary and sentimental brand of Romanticism. *Brother Philippe's Geese* (exh. Brussels Salon, 1833; untraced) and *Vert-Vert Landing at Nantes* (exh. 1836; destr.) brought him success and showed how he could adapt to prevailing tastes. His star pupils—J. B. van Eycken (1809–53), Jean-François Portaels, Léopold Robert and J. Stallaert (1825–1903)—to whom he passed on his academic principles, also met with considerable success in the 1845 Salon. However, the paintings shown by the Belgian Realists at the 1851 Salon established a vogue that was beyond even Navez's powers of assimilation. (Ironically, the most talented of his many pupils went on to become well-known exponents of Realism, notably Constantin Meunier, Eugène Smits and Alfred Stevens (i).) Navez ceased exhibiting after 1851 but was nonetheless highly productive. Religious pictures of this period include the *Rich Young Man* (1854), the *Judgement of Solomon* (1855; both Brussels, Mus. A. Anc.) and the *Raising of the Son of the Widow of Nain* (1857; Brussels, Saint-Joseph). He also continued to paint portraits. Navez resigned from the directorship of the Académie des Beaux-Arts in 1859. Hard of hearing and blind, he devoted his last years to lengthy correspondence, for the most part with French and Belgian artists. His letters are a rich source of information on the artistic life of his period.

UNPUBLISHED SOURCES

Brussels, Bib. Royale Albert 1er [letters]

BIBLIOGRAPHY

L. Alvin: *François-Joseph Navez: Sa vie, son oeuvre et sa correspondance* (Brussels, 1870)

D. Coekelberghs: *Les Peintres belges à Rome de 1700 à 1830* (Brussels, 1976), pp. 251–76

D. Coekelberghs and P. Loze, eds: *Un Ensemble néo-classique à Bruxelles: Le Grand Hospice et le quartier du Béguinage* (Brussels, 1983), pp. 322, 329–37

1770–1830: Autour du néo-classicisme en Belgique (exh. cat. by S. Valcke, R. Kerremans and D. Coekelberghs, Brussels, Mus. Ixelles, 1985–6), pp. 230–39, 426–9

S. Valcke: 'De Heilige Cecilia van Fr. J. Navez', *De wagenmenner en andere verhalen Album Discipulorum Prof. Dr. M. de Mayer* (Ghent, 1986)

DOMINIQUE VAUTIER

Navrátil, Josef Matěj (*b* Slané, 17 Feb 1798; *d* Prague, 21 April 1865). Bohemian painter. He learnt decorative wall painting from his father and also studied at the Prague Academy of Fine Arts from 1819 to 1823. With his skill and academic prestige he was much in demand as a restorer of wall paintings and a creator of new ones. From the late 1830s to the early 1860s he and his assistants maintained a leading position in this sphere. Of particular importance was his decoration of Liběchov Castle (1838–43) for the patron of Czech art, Count Antonín Veith. One of his largest undertakings was the decoration (early 1850s) of the imperial possessions at Zákupy and Ploskovice. Other assignments included painting shop-signs.

His exhibits in both oil and gouache at the Prague annual art exhibitions suggest that he started with portraiture, then moved on to landscapes (e.g. *Large Mountain Landscape*, early 1850s; Prague, N.G., Convent of St Agnes) and finally genre paintings (e.g. *In Chlumecký's Cellar*, 1850s; Prague, N.G., Convent of St Agnes). His extensive oeuvre includes sketches and studies, sometimes virtuoso, of character types from urban and village life, and also scenes set in a theatrical environment. His still-life studies, which often received their final form as wall decorations rather than free-standing pictures, are also notable. This range had its own logic, generating a totality from both Romantic and realistic viewpoints and also from a hedonistic and critical attitude towards the reality expressed in central European Biedermeier.

Navrátil's work often juxtaposed folk elements and intellectualism, sensuousness and an ironic paraphrase of conventional landscape or figural style. Unlike the Munich painter, Carl Spitzweg, with whom he became acquainted, he rarely aimed at genre painting in the strict sense of the word. For Navrátil the painter's fantasy and treatment of history, as cultivated in the 1850s by the Rococo Revival, were a means of counterbalancing critical realism and the exaggeration of caricature. This trend was not confined to ornament and fashion but also left its mark on painting, as in his amatory scenes, which are redolent of the work of Constantine Guys and other French painters (e.g. *Lady with Officer*, c. 1850; Prague, N.G., Convent of St Agnes). Although Navrátil travelled widely, he visited France only once, in 1858.

Navrátil's treatment of colour and light lay in revivifying or 'modernizing' the local, predominantly Baroque tradition of wall painting. Classed as a colourist, he stands in Bohemia as the antithesis of his contemporary Josef Hellich, who represented the newer academic, draughtsman tradition. Both of them were active in the movement of Czech artists seeking their rights from the 1830s. Navrátil represented the practical artists, closely connected to urban circles, and he became president of the association of Czech artists in 1850.

BIBLIOGRAPHY

J. Pečírka: *Josef Navrátil* (Prague, 1940)

O. Macková: 'Nové poznatky o obrazech Josefa Navrátila' [New findings regarding the paintings of Josef Navrátil], *Umění*, xiv (1966), pp. 231–46 [Ger. summary]

Die tschechische Malerei des xix. Jahrhunderts (exh. cat., ed. J. Kotalík; Vienna, Belvedere, 1984), pp. 48–50 [entry by M. Nováková]

ROMAN PRAHL

Naxos. Greek island at the centre of the Aegean Cyclades. It is the largest and most fertile of that island group and has been an important centre since prehistoric times. As well as agricultural wealth, the island also possesses extensive marble deposits and is a rare source of the abrasive mineral emery, which was used for working marble objects.

1. Bronze Age. 2. Greek. 3. Early Christian and Byzantine.

1. BRONZE AGE. By the 1990s the most significant prehistoric finds on Naxos had been from Early (EC) and Late Cycladic (LC) contexts (*c.* 3500–*c.* 2000 BC and *c.* 1600–*c.* 1050 BC respectively). The earliest excavations, mainly of EC cemetery sites, were conducted by C. Tsountas in the late 19th century, his work being augmented by that of C. Doumas in the 1960s. The most important Bronze Age settlement, Grotta (the northern and north-western coastal area of modern Naxos town), as well as the neighbouring EC and LC cemetery on the hill of Aplomata, were investigated from 1949 onwards by N. Kondoleon and, after his death, by V. Lambrinoudakis. Grotta poses exceptional problems for the excavator, since much of the deposit is now below sea-level. Finds from the early work of Tsountas are in the National Archaeological Museum in Athens; the remainder is in the Archaeological Museum in Naxos and in a collection in the village of Apeiranthos.

Early Cycladic cemeteries are widely scattered over the island. At one important cemetery (Ayioi Anargyroi) the graves may have been grouped into those that were richer and those that were poorer, suggesting some kind of social distinction. In general, the richer burials may have marble figurines and vases, and occasionally bronze jewellery, tools or weapons; the poorer may have only pottery, perhaps together with a few beads or other modest offerings. Ayioi Anargyroi also had an interesting structural feature in the form of a stone-built platform, apparently for ceremonial purposes. Other EC architectural remains are the simple houses of the Grotta settlement and the tiny fort at Panormos in the south-west of the island, where the rooms are squeezed into a walled circuit with

towers. Unique stone slabs, apparently EC, with scenes showing hunting, fighting and boating, have been found at Korfi t'Aroniou. The figures are depicted with a sort of pointillé technique (Apeiranthos, Archaeol. Col.). Folded-arm figurines from the cemetery of Spedos constitute one of the most important types of EC stone figurine (*see* CYCLADIC, fig. 10).

The Middle Cycladic (MC) period (*c.* 2000–*c.* 1600 BC) is not well known, although there are clear signs (at Grotta and Mikre Vigla) of occupation. A group of cist graves at Aila, which span the transition from MC to LC, produced, as well as characteristic pottery, an important group of bronze tools and weapons.

Like other major Cycaldic centres, Naxos seems to have succumbed to Minoan influence at the beginning of the LC period. There is some evidence of this in the Aila pottery, as well as at other sites on the island, and an earlier view that Naxos might have escaped this otherwise universal trend must now be discarded. Many of the discoveries from Grotta belong to LC III (*c.* 1390–*c.* 1050 BC) and are predictably Mycenaean in character. The settlement itself was extensive, although the precise limits have not yet been determined. The best-preserved finds of this period come from three chamber tombs on the hill of Aplomata and the nearby site of Kamini, which was probably part of the same cemetery. Most striking are the series of 'stirrup jars' decorated with stylized octopuses and other pictorial schemes (*see* CYCLADIC, fig. 7c). Some ritual vases have clay snakes attached to them. Also of interest is a cylinder seal of Near Eastern type, some gold-leaf rosettes (*see also* CYCLADIC, §VII, 1), pierced probably for attachment to garments, bronze swords and iron dress pins (from Kamini; all Naxos, Archaeol. Mus.). Iron occurred only at the very end of the Bronze Age in the Aegean, and its appearance at Kamini supports the conclusions of excavations at Grotta that the area was occupied continuously during the transition from Bronze to Iron Age.

BIBLIOGRAPHY
C. Tsountas: 'Kykladika', *Archaiol. Ephemeris* (1898), cols 137–212; (1899), cols 73–134
K. Scholes: 'The Cyclades in the Later Bronze Age: A Synopsis', *Annu. Brit. Sch. Athens*, li (1956), pp. 9–40
N. Kondoleon: 'Mykenaike Naxos' [Mycenaean Naxox], *Epeteris Etaireias Kykladikon Meleton*, i (1961), pp. 600–08
C. Doumas: *Early Bronze Age Burial Habits in the Cyclades* (Göteborg, 1977)
C. P. Kardara: *Aplomata Naxou: Kineta euremata taphon A kai B* [Aplomata on Naxos: movable finds from Tombs A and B] (Athens, 1977)
V. Fotou: 'Les Sites de l'époque néolithique et de l'âge du bronze à Naxos', *Les Cyclades*, Centre National de la Recherche Scientifique (Paris, 1983), pp. 15–57

2. GREEK. Naxos has relatively few architectural remains from the Classical and Roman periods, although there are two important Archaic buildings. The island was an early centre of monumental sculpture, and the known quarry sites (especially that at Apollona) probably produced stone for building as well as for sculpture.

(*i*) *Architecture*. A temple, probably dedicated to Apollo and of the time of the tyrant Lygdamis (*c.* 530 BC), stood on the islet of Palati, now a promontory, opposite Naxos town. Apart from the reconstructed doorway to the cella

1. Naxos, partial reconstruction of the Temple of Demeter and Kore, Yiroulas, *c.* 530 BC; the Early Christian basilica is in the background

nothing survives beyond the foundations, although it is clear that the temple was in the Ionic order and to some extent followed the grandiose tendencies of Archaic Ionic architecture, with double colonnades at its front and rear. Like other buildings on the island it was converted into a church in Early Christian times. At Naxos town the site of the ancient acropolis is presumably marked by the impressive Venetian fortifications. Architectural remains on the lower ground around the citadel are chiefly Hellenistic and Roman and include the colonnades of an agora. Just outside Naxos town, at Iria, are the remains of a large granite and marble temple probably dedicated to Dionysos. It was first erected in more modest materials in the 8th century BC but was rebuilt in the 6th century BC and survived into Roman times.

At Yiroulas, near the village of Sangri, another Archaic temple (*c*. 530 BC) underlies a three-aisled Early Christian basilica (see fig. 1). It was dedicated to Demeter and Kore and had an unusual square plan, like the Archaic telesterion at Eleusis, the chief sanctuary of these divinities. From a porch, with five columns *in antis*, two doors led into the cella, where five further columns of unequal height supported the pitched roof. The whole structure, including the roof tiles, was of marble. The variety of architectural fragments found have allowed a complete reconstruction on paper. The style was Ionic, although the column capitals were Aiolic with leaf decoration. Parts of the masonry are crudely finished, perhaps to suggest a cave, and the interior decoration included painted plaster. In front of the temple, to its south-west, was a repository within a setting of columns. A precinct wall was added (or rebuilt) in the 4th century BC and inscribed boundary stones set up. A secular village seems to have grown up around the sanctuary at the time of its conversion into a basilica (?6th century AD). Some architectural features of the temples at Yiroulas and

Palati can be related to those of Naxian buildings in the Sanctuary of Apollo on DELOS.

In an elevated position in the interior of Naxos and commanding impressive views of the south of the island is the remarkable Pirgos Cheimarrou, a Hellenistic tower (probably 3rd or 2nd century BC) preserved to about 20 m in height (the third floor). The masonry is of excellent quality, and the internal cantilevered spiral staircase is partly preserved.

BIBLIOGRAPHY
N. M. Kondoleon: 'Anaskaphe en Naxo' [Excavation on Naxos], *Praktika Athen. Archaiol. Etaireias* (1954), pp. 330–38
G. Gruben and W. Koenigs: 'Der "Hekatompedos" von Naxos', *Archäol. Anz.* (1968), pp. 693–717
V. K. Lambrinoudakis, G. Gruben and M. Korres: 'Anaskaphes Naxou' [Excavations of Naxos], *Praktika Athen. Archaiol. Etaireias* (1977), pp. 378–86; (1979), pp. 249–58; (1981), pp. 293–7; (1983), pp. 297–8
A. W. Lawrence: *Greek Aims in Fortification* (Oxford, 1979), pp. 192–3, 470
H. W. Catling: 'Archaeology in Greece', *Archaeol. Rep.: Council Soc. Promotion Hell. Stud. & Managing Cttee Brit. Sch. Archaeol. Athens*, xxxiii (1986–7), p. 47

(ii) Sculpture. Naxos was the first major centre of monumental marble sculpture production in Greece. This was due partly to its marble sources, from which raw material for the majority of early Archaic sculptures came and partly to its proximity to the Sanctuary of Apollo on Delos, for which dedications were commissioned (*see* GREECE, ANCIENT, §IV, 2(ii)(b)). Occupying a geographical position between two key areas of sculpture production, Ionia and Attica, work from the island sometimes displays characteristics of both. Its influence, however, seems to have declined before the end of the Archaic period. Of outstanding interest for the development of both style and technique of Archaic sculpture are the kouroi, broken and/or unfinished, found still lying in quarries near Melanes and Apollona. The original block of stone was

2. Naxos, unfinished kouros lying in a quarry, *c.* 600–*c.* 560 BC

drilled round and then detached from its quarry bed by the insertion of damped wedges beneath. The figures were worked, at least in part, before they left the quarry (see fig. 2), which explains why sculpture workshops tended to be located near by. A number of finished kouroi have also been found on the island, for example in the Sanctuary of Demeter at Yiroulas, near Sangri (Naxos, Archaeol. Mus.). However, the best-known early works are mainly from Delos: they include the Naxian *Colossos* (*c.* 600 BC; Delos, Archaeol. Mus. and London, BM) and the Nikandre Kore (*c.* 650 BC; Athens, N. Archaeol. Mus.), as well as a base signed by Euthykartides (*c.* 600 BC; Delos, Archaeol. Mus.). The row of monumental lions (early 6th century BC; *in situ*) along the approach to the Temple of Leto at Delos may also be Naxian, as certainly is the famous sphinx (*c.* 560 BC; Delphi, Archaeol. Mus.; *see* DELPHI, fig. 4) from Delphi. The latter's similarity to two korai (*c.* 560–*c.* 550 BC; Athens, Acropolis Mus., 619 and 677) from the Athenian Acropolis suggests that they too are Naxian. Some of the kouroi from the Ptoion Sanctuary in Boiotia are of Naxian marble and probably of Naxian workmanship: a late Archaic grave stele (*c.* 490 BC; Athens, N. Archaeol. Mus.) from the same area signed by Alxenor of Naxos further attests to the peripatetic activities of Naxian sculptors at this time.

BIBLIOGRAPHY

J. G. Pedley: *Greek Sculpture of the Archaic Period: The Island Workshops* (Mainz, 1976)

W. Fuchs and J. Florens: *Die geometrische und archaische Plastik* (1987), i of *Die griechische Plastik* (Munich, 1987–), pp. 150–60

R. L. N. BARBER

3. EARLY CHRISTIAN AND BYZANTINE. More churches from this period (*c.* 4th–14th century AD) survive on Naxos than on any other island of the archipelago. They are an important record of the island's political and economic development, particularly since written sources are silent. That Naxos seems to have occupied a special place in the Cyclades is suggested not only by the monuments but also by an inscription (1052) in the church of the Virgin Protothronos at Chalki, which mentions the 'bishop Leon' and 'the Protospatharios and Tourmarches of the territory of Naxos Nicetas'. The island's importance is further suggested by the fact that the Venetian Marco I Sanudo (*reg* 1207–27) settled on Naxos in 1207, when he created his Aegean dukedom.

The earliest surviving churches include five Early Christian basilicas and the centrally planned chuch of the Virgin Drossiani, near Moni, decorated with wall paintings dating from the first half of the 7th century. Some wall paintings in the semicircular wall of the apse of the Virgin Protothronos also date from this period. Their fine quality is comparable with that of mosaics in the great centres of the Byzantine Empire (Rome, Ravenna, Thessaloniki), indicating a local artistic flowering. Aniconic decoration, probably of the early 9th century, survives in single- or two-aisled domed churches (e.g. Hagios Artemios, nr Sagri; Hagia Kyriake, nr Apeiranthos; Hagios Ioannis 'stou Adissarou'; and in a complex of two free-cross churches near Apeiranthos). Fourteen examples of aniconic layers are known, and their number reflects the island's prosperity during the Iconoclastic period (726–843).

Numerous Middle Byzantine churches also survive. Their walls are generally made of undecorated rubble masonry, with cylindrical domes and apses. The wall paintings (second quarter of the 10th century) that decorate the apse of the rock-cut church of the Nativity in the monastery of Kaloritsa are of particular interest, since wall paintings of this period are rare in Greece. In the first half of the 9th century the three-aisled basilica of the Virgin Protothronos at Chalki was transformed into a cross-in-square church ('transitional type'), with aniconic decoration depicting crosses on the semicircular wall of the apse. The dome and upper parts of the church were decorated with frescoes towards the end of the 10th century; the dome was repainted in 1052. Other cross-in-square churches include Hagios Mamas, near Kato Potamia, which is probably contemporary with or slightly later than the Virgin Protothronos; the Virgin Damiotissa (11th century), with 13th-century wall paintings; and Hagios Georgios Diassoritis, with wall paintings (third quarter of the 11th century) in an expressive style similar to those in the south-west chapel and crypt of HOSIOS LOUKAS, Phokis. Few wall paintings survive from the Komnenian period apart from a layer (early 12th century) in the church of Hagios Nikolaos at Sagri and a few fragments in Hagios Georgios Diassoritis.

Despite the Latin occupation of the island from 1207, Orthodox churches continued to be constructed and decorated until the beginning of the 14th century. As in most parts of Greece, there are numerous 13th-century monuments: simple, single-aisled churches, usually barrel-vaulted or surmounted with a dome, and using construction methods similar to those of the earlier period. The wall paintings are of good quality and follow contemporary stylistic trends. Of particular interest are those in Hagios Ioannis at Kerami, which can be dated to the 1260s; some representations (1260–80) in the rock-cut church of Kaloritsa; and the last layer of wall paintings (1270) at Hagios Nikolaos, Sagri. In some monuments the volume of the figures is more accentuated, as in the twin church of Hagios Nikolaos (1260–80; paintings now Athens, Byz. Mus.) and Hagios Georgios near Lathrino (late 13th century). The wall paintings in the churches of the Virgin at Archatos (1285) and the neighbouring Virgin 'stis Giallous' (1288–9) were probably from the same workshop. The presence on Naxos until at least the end of the 13th century of wealthy, educated patrons ensured the existence of local workshops and brought artists from elsewhere, who introduced new stylistic trends in wall painting. The 14th-century examples, however, are fewer in number and of inferior quality; most date from the first two decades and were probably decorated by local artists with Constantinopolitan connections.

BIBLIOGRAPHY

G. Dimitrokaleis: *Symbolai eis tin meletin ton byzantinon mnimeion tis Naxou* [Contributions to the study of Byzantine monuments in Naxos] (Athens, 1972)

N. Drandakis: *Oi palaiochristianikes toichographies sti Drosiani tis Naxou* [The Early Christian wall paintings at Drosiani in Naxos] (Athens, 1988)

M. Chadzidakis, ed.: *Byzantine Art in Greece: Naxos* (Athens, 1989)

M. Panayotidi: 'Les Peintures murales de Naxos', *Corsi Cult. A. Ravenn. & Byz.*, xxxviii (1991), pp. 281–303

MARIA PANAYOTIDI

Nay, Ernst Wilhelm (*b* Berlin, 11 June 1902; *d* Cologne, 8 April 1968). German painter. After completing his schooling at Thüringen in 1915, he returned to Berlin, where, with no formal tuition, he produced his first paintings: landscapes and portraits of his friends and family, for example *Franz Reuter* (1925; Hamburg, Ksthalle). On the basis of these he was accepted as a scholarship student at the Berlin Akademie by Karl Hofer in 1925; the tonal painting being practised there, however, had little relevance to him. In 1928 he went to Paris, where he became especially interested in the work of Nicolas Poussin. In 1931, after showing works in various exhibitions, Nay was awarded the Staatspreis of the Preussische Akademie, which involved a nine-month stay at the Villa Massimo in Rome. His small-scale animal pictures, verging between Surrealism and abstraction, gave way in the succeeding years, during which he spent the summer months in Pomerania on the Baltic coast, to pictures of Baltic fishermen such as the *Departure of the Fisherman* (1936; Hannover, Sprengel Mus.). The formal basis of his art first took shape in these works, with primeval forms arranged in rhythmic movement. In the 1930s and 1940s these were always coupled with mythical settings, in which, according to Nay, a deeper reality could be discerned.

In summer 1937 Nay visited Norway, financed by Edvard Munch, whom he met again there in the following summer. The series of brilliantly coloured *Lofoten Pictures*, named after the Norwegian area in which they were painted, give form to the elemental forces of this lonely mountain landscape. In the same year two of Nay's paintings were included in the exhibition of 'degenerate' art (*see* ENTARTETE KUNST) toured through Germany by the Nazis, and ten of his paintings were seized from public exhibitions. He was called up for military service in 1940, and as a soldier in France he managed to find time to paint and draw in the studio of the French sculptor Pierre Térouanne in Le Mans. He later asserted that the traumatic events of the period gave birth to new developments in European painting.

On his release from imprisonment by the Americans in 1945, Nay settled in Hofheim, near Frankfurt. There, from 1945 to 1948, he painted a series entitled *Hecate Pictures* after the Greek goddess of the moon; each represents a single figure or amorous couples with brightly coloured bodies interwoven like fans into an equally vivid background. *Girl's Head* (1947; Cologne, Mus. Ludwig) is characteristic of his style at this time. The detailed, dynamically organized formal structure makes it possible for the human figure to be perceived only in fragmentary form as a part of nature. The references to Classical mythology and Christianity, combined with idealistic humanitarian themes, bear comparison with the work of Picasso, although it would be misleading to speak of a direct influence. Nay exhibited his work widely during this period and also began setting down his artistic theories in written form, leading to the publication of his treatise on colour in 1955.

Nay adopted abstraction in his painting *Shepherd I* (1948; priv. col), turning the archaic figure into a self-sufficient structure of colour. In the early 1950s he painted two series, *Fugal Pictures* and *Rhythmic Pictures*, in which

Ernst Wilhelm Nay: *In Blazing Colours*, oil on canvas, 1.25×2.0 m, 1955 (Bloomington, IN, Indiana University Art Museum)

colours and forms became simpler, flatter and more clearly defined in relation to each other. He generally relied in these pictures, such as a *Garden* (1952; Essen, Mus. Flkwang), painted after he moved to Cologne in 1951, on a freedom of handling and translucency of colour that betray a familiarity with the early work of Vasily Kandinsky. They led, moreover, to the *Disc Pictures*, which he painted from 1955 to 1963 and with which he first gained international recognition.

In the first *Disc Pictures*, such as *In Blazing Colours* (1955; Bloomington, IN U. A. Mus.; see fig.), he wished to convey the impression that the circles appeared as a result of the movement of the brush, that invention, that is to say, sprang directly from the act of painting. In Nay's view such simple forms served both as spiritual symbols, because of their arithmetical basis, and as expressions of elemental forces. The largest and most important work in the series, *Freiburg Picture* (2.55×6.55 m, 1956), was commissioned for the vestibule of the new building for the Chemisches Institut at Freiburg University. Nay was at the height of his international fame during this period, representing Germany at the Venice Biennale in 1956, participating in the São Paulo Biennale in 1960 and in the same year receiving a major award from the Solomon R. Guggenheim Foundation.

Nay embarked on a new phase with his *Eye Pictures* (1964–5), in which he used an anthropomorphic symbol related to motifs in his *Fugal Pictures* and directly derived from his *Discs*. All the pictures in this group, which were the subject of great controversy when they were exhibited at *Documenta III* (Kassel, 1964), where they were displayed on the ceiling in a special room, are characterized by pronounced tonal contrasts and a vibrant sense of depth. In 1965 he began to eliminate the personal touch, on which he had previously relied, and to stress the flatness of the surface in simple compositions, in which he balanced positive and negative shapes, in a manner somewhat reminiscent of the late paper cut-outs by Henri Matisse. In spite of his international reputation, Nay was increasingly marginalized as an artist during the last years of his life, often because of the assumption that work such as his was impersonal and decorative. His reputation was not properly resuscitated until the 1980s.

WRITINGS
Vom Gestaltwert der Farbe: Fläche, Zahl, Rhythmus (Munich, 1955)

BIBLIOGRAPHY
E. W. Nay (exh. cat., Hannover, Kestner-Ges., 1950)
W. Haftmann: *E. W. Nay* (Cologne, 1960)
E. W. Nay: Retrospektive (exh. cat., Stuttgart, Württemberg. Kstver., 1966–7)
E. W. Nay 1902–1968: Bilder und Dokumente (exh. cat., Nuremberg, German. Nmus., 1980–81)
E. W. Nay 1902–1968, Bilder kommen aus Bildern. Gemälde und unveröffentlichte Schriften aus vier Jahrzehnten (exh. cat., Krefeld, Mus. Haus Lange; Münster, Westfäl. Kstver.; Hamburg, Kstver.; 1985)
E. W. Nay (exh. cat., Cologne, Mus. Ludwig, 1990)

ANGELA SCHNEIDER

Naya, Carlo (*b* Tronzano Vercellese, nr Vercelli, 2 Aug 1816; *d* Venice, 30 May 1882). Italian photographer. His interest in photography began after he completed his degree in law at the University of Pisa (1840). In 1857 he settled in Venice and opened a laboratory and studio in the Piazza San Marco. He concentrated on architectural views and on reproductions of works of art. At first he relied commercially on the photographic market that Carlo Ponti had created in Venice. He first received international recognition at the Troisième Exposition de la Société Française de Photographie, in Paris in 1859, where he exhibited a series of photographs, for which he used the dry collodion process. In 1862 he won a medal at the Great Exhibition of London.

Among Naya's most important photographs are the series of Giotto's frescoes in the Cappella degli Scrovegni in Padua, taken in 1865 before their restoration. In Venice he expanded his business and had several employees, with whom he carried out an exhaustive photographic documentation of the city, producing images suitable for both the tourist and the art historian. Many of these were collected into albums of various sizes. Naya also composed charming genre scenes of local folklore; although he staged some of the scenes in the studio, he achieved others by means of photomontage. These were very popular as souvenirs (see Zannier, pl. 22).

Naya was involved in a copyright dispute in 1882, one of the first of its kind in Europe, but in February he won the court case that he had brought against several of his colleagues, including Ponti. The Naya business continued after his death under the direction of his wife, Ida Lessjak, and another photographer, Tommaso Filippi. In 1918 Osvaldo Boehm took over the business, including the photographic plates, which are still conserved there, and part of the Naya archive.

BIBLIOGRAPHY
I. Zannier: *Venezia, archivio Naya* (Venice, 1981)
P. Constantini and I. Zannier: *Venezia nella fotografia dell'ottocento* (Venice, 1986)

ITALO ZANNIER

Nayaka. Dynasties in south India that were established in the 16th century by governors (Skt *nāyaka*: 'leader') of the VIJAYANAGARA kingdom. Nayaka Nagama was the first governor, appointed to MADURAI, the furthest centre from Vijayanagara. Vaiyappa Nayaka was appointed to GINGEE in 1526 and Sevappa Nayaka to THANJAVUR in 1532. Another governor was appointed to VELLORE. These positions became hereditary, and the governors were meant to check each other's power in case their loyalty became questionable. Given the climate of suspicion in which the governorships were formed, it is not surprising that they declared independence with the collapse of Vijayanagara in 1565 and that they were constantly engaged in war with each other. A particular hostility existed between Madurai and Thanjavur, especially as the latter under Acyutappa Nayaka (*reg* 1560–1600) remained loyal to Vijayanagara. Tension was not eased when the Madurai Nayakas moved their government to Tiruchirapalli, only 60 km from Thanjavur. The Nayakas did much to beautify temples. For example, Acyutappa was responsible for the main entrance tower (*see* GOPURA) of the Shiva Temple at Tiruvannamalai, and Tirumalai Nayaka (*reg* 1623–59) undertook substantial reconstruction of the Minakshi Temple, Madurai. Nayaka rule at Thanjavur was brought to an end in 1674 with the establishment of the

Mahratta Bhonsle lineage. At Madurai, Nayaka rule ended in 1739 after Safdar 'Ali and Chanda Sahib attacked the city and the regent Minakshi, wife of Vijayaranga Cokkanatha (*reg* 1706–31), was imprisoned in her palace, where she took poison.

BIBLIOGRAPHY

S. L. Huntington: *The Art of Ancient India: Buddhist, Hindu, Jain* (New York and Tokyo, 1985)

J. MARR

Nayin. *See* NA'IN.

Nayshābūr. *See* NISHAPUR.

Nay-ta-hut. *See* YAHUDIYA, TELL EL-.

Naywinck, Harman. *See* NAIWINCX, HERMAN.

Nazarenes. Group of artists working in Rome and later northern Europe from 1818 to the 1840s, several of whom, including FRIEDRICH OVERBECK, FRANZ PFORR and PETER CORNELIUS, had been part of the Lukasbrüder, a small fraternity of young artists originally based in Vienna. The terms 'Nazarene' and Lukasbrüder have often been used interchangeably. Strictly speaking, the Lukasbrüder were a formally organized group whose span of activity, in both Vienna and Rome, lasted from 1809 to 1818; the Nazarene group embraces the members of the Lukasbrüder and dozens of other artists who shared a leaning toward spiritually ponderous subjects, a commitment to crystalline linearity and local colour and a fascination with Renaissance art of the 15th and early 16th centuries, including the work of Dürer and Raphael. By *c.* 1817 the Lukasbrüder were beginning to be called *Die Nazarener.* The name was mockingly applied, probably first by Johann Christian Reinhart, because of the group's heavy concentration on biblical subjects, the strict monastic life they lived at S Isidoro, a 16th-century Irish Franciscan monastery in Rome, and their costume of wide, trailing cloaks and long flowing hair. The term 'Nazarene' later came to be applied to younger artists, including Julius Schnorr von Carolsfeld (*see* SCHNORR VON CAROLSFELD, (2)), who were followers of the Lukasbrüder and worked in Italy and northern Europe until *c.* 1850.

1. THE LUKASBRÜDER, 1809–18. The founders of the Lukasbrüder were six young German, Swiss and Austrian students associated with the Akademie der Bildenden Künste in Vienna, who in July 1809 formed an artistic fraternity, the Lukasbund. Its original members were Overbeck, Pforr, Ludwig Vogel, Joseph Wintergerst, Joseph Sutter (1781–1866) and Franz Hottinger (1788–1828). Although originating in Vienna, in 1810 the group shifted the centre of its activity to Rome, where it expanded slowly until its dissolution in 1818. Its later members included Cornelius, Wilhelm Schadow, JOHANN SCHEFFER VON LEONHARDSHOFF and PHILIPP VEIT. Rejecting Late Baroque classicism, the Lukasbrüder drew inspiration from early German and Italian Renaissance painting as well as from folk imagery, which they developed into an intense, linear style adequate to their naive, albeit impassioned, commitment to nature.

The original group of six held regular drawing sessions and discussion groups in Overbeck's lodgings in Vienna in 1808–9. They had been attracted to one another by their common commitment to artistic and spiritual sincerity as an antidote to facile eclecticism. Sceptical of academic models of mechanical competence, they looked to the earlier art displayed in the Imperial Picture Gallery, the Belvedere in Vienna, to the writings of Goethe, Schiller, Wilhelm Wackenroder, Ludwig Tieck and Friedrich von Schlegel, as well as to the example of Eberhard Wächter, as they evolved new expectations for artistic behaviour and production. It was their conviction that art must be 'characteristic', thereby reflecting the individuality of the artist and society rather than catering to the taste of a cosmopolitan aristocracy. The works of such early Renaissance masters as Masaccio and Fra Angelico were particularly admired by the Lukasbrüder for their emotional sincerity, their allegiance to observed nature and their reflection of a society that had been more spiritually integrated than was that of Napoleonic Europe.

The closing of the Akademie early in 1809 forced the young artists to turn to one another for support, and, drawing on the inspiration of Enlightenment literary associations, they created their own *Bund* on 10 July of that year. When in October Wintergerst moved to Bavaria as the *Bund*'s 'first apostle', diplomas were created for each member. These carried the signatures and symbols of each member, as well as a stamp depicting St Luke at work, and they became the formal symbol of the group's spiritual solidarity. When the Akademie reopened in February 1810, financial constraints prevented the readmission of all but Sutter. As a result, Overbeck, Pforr, Vogel and Hottinger left for Italy in May, arriving in Rome on 3 July 1810. They entered the city's active community of artists from Germany, Austria, Switzerland and Scandinavia, establishing friendships with Bertel Thorvaldsen and Joseph Anton Koch. They also devoted themselves to the study of antique sites and the frescoes of Raphael and Michelangelo in the Vatican. In October 1810 Vogel secured inexpensive lodgings in the monastery of S Isidoro a Copelecase, later Via degli Artisti, where they revived their life drawing sessions and discussions, and resumed work on the paintings that they had brought from Vienna. These were Pforr's *Entry of Rudolf von Habsburg into Basle in 1273* (1808–9/10; Frankfurt am Main, Städel. Kstinst.; for illustration *see* PFORR, FRANZ), Vogel's *Return of the Soldiers to Morgarten* (1809–15; untraced) and Overbeck's *Entry into Jerusalem* (1809–24; destr.).

From 1809 to 1812 significant changes occurred within the Lukasbund. Hottinger severed his ties with the group and left Rome in September 1811, while Wintergerst arrived in April 1811. Giovanni Colombo (*c.* 1784–1853) became a new member of the group in November 1810, as did Cornelius in February 1812. In June 1812 Pforr died, and in December Vogel and Colombo left for Switzerland and Austria respectively. The lease on S Isidoro also expired, and Overbeck, Cornelius and Wintergerst, the remaining members, dispersed and found separate lodgings elsewhere in Rome. Two paintings characteristic of these early years are Overbeck's portrait of *Franz Pforr* (1810; Berlin, Neue N.G.) and Pforr's *Sulamith and Maria* (1810; Schweinfurt, Samml. Schäfer). By the end of 1812 the first phase was over. The *Bund* had become far less cohesive, with Overbeck, Cornelius and Wintergerst working in Rome, Sutter and Colombo in Vienna and Vogel in Zurich.

The second Roman phase of the Lukasbund, from 1813 to 1816, was characterized by new, diverse initiates and by an increased interest in a heroic nationalism espoused by Cornelius. During these years, several members were converted to Catholicism, and there was an increased religiosity within their work as is evident in Overbeck's painting *Christ with Mary and Martha* (1815; Berlin, Tiergarten N.G.; *see* OVERBECK, FRIEDRICH, fig. 2). Wintergerst departed for Ellwangen in February 1813. Shortly thereafter, Wilhelm Schadow was admitted to the group, along with the poet Zacharias Werner (1768–1823), who was the only member who was not an artist. Scheffer von Leonhardshoff was admitted in October 1815 and Johannes Veit (1790–1854) and Philipp Veit early in 1816. Finally, in July 1816 Sutter and Colombo arrived in Rome, ending their years of relative isolation in Austria. In this second phase the Lukasbund also developed a circle of associates who were not actually members. Konrad Eberhard, Ridolfo Schadow, Ernst Platner (1773–1855) and Johannes Schaller (1777–1842) took part in the group's drawing sessions or the readings and discussions held on Saturday evenings as did Karl Leybold (1786–1844) and Johann Karl Eggers (1787–1863). None, though, was issued diplomas or formally admitted to the Lukasbund.

By 1816 the Lukasbund had lost most of its vitality. In May of that year Overbeck, Cornelius, Schadow and Philipp Veit began work on a major commission, the Casa Bartholdy frescoes (1816–19; Berlin, Alte N.G.) for one of the rooms in the Palazzo Zuccari (now the Biblioteca Hertziana), the home of Salomon Bartholdy, the Prussian consul general in Rome. Overbeck instigated the project, and the four artists each painted two frescoes illustrating the *Story of Joseph*. These works, which are set in landscapes and architectural frameworks reminiscent of the Italian Renaissance, constituted their first joint commission and brought them prominence as painters of monumental frescoes. Following the completion of this project Cornelius and Overbeck were commissioned by the Marchese Carlo Massimo to fresco three rooms of his Roman villa, work that continued after the dissolution of the Lukasbund and later involved other Nazarene artists also. The early optimism that followed the restoration (1814) of the monarchy in France, as well as the increased maturity of the Lukasbrüder, diminished the need for the group's supportive insularity. There is no formal record of their dissolution, but the reported admission of Ferdinand Olivier (*see* OLIVIER, (2)) and Julius Schnorr von Carolsfeld (*see* SCHNORR VON CAROLSFELD, (2)) in September 1817 could have had little real significance.

2. THE NAZARENES AND THEIR INFLUENCE, AFTER 1818. By 1818 the Lukasbrüder no longer constituted a fraternity and had been effectively absorbed into what came to be known as the Nazarene movement, a larger and more loosely constituted group of artists, including Olivier, Schnorr von Carolsfeld, FERENC SZOLDATITS and JOHANN ANTON RAMBOUX. The Lukasbrüder's radical emphases on individual character, simplicity and sincerity were now subsumed in the Nazarenes' more monumental, revivalist style suitable to the celebration of traditional social or religious institutions or values throughout central and western Europe. Schnorr von Carolsfeld was a particularly active member of the Nazarenes in Rome. His painting *Angelica, Medoro and Orlando* (1821–7; for illustration *see* SCHNORR VON CAROLSFELD, (2)) for the Casa Massimo in Rome (*in situ*), exemplifies the group's interest in the revival of monumental art.

By the 1840s the art of the Nazarenes was beginning to be eclipsed by that of Realism, although their work was to have a strong influence on historical and religious painting in Europe well into the 1850s. Though frequently religious in orientation, it embraced themes from classical mythology, folk-tales, the landscape and contemporary literature, as it spread northward from Rome to Düsseldorf, Frankfurt am Main, Munich, Dresden and Vienna. Various artists took up teaching posts in Germany (*see* GERMANY, §III, 4), thereby imparting their knowledge of Nazarene principles to a younger generation of German artists. Ingres, who was in Rome from 1806, was influenced by it, as were such British artists as WILLIAM DYCE and A. W. N. Pugin. FORD MADOX BROWN also admired their work after his arrival in Rome in 1845.

BIBLIOGRAPHY
H. Riegel: *Geschichte des Wiederauflebens der deutschen Kunst zu Ende des 18. und Angang des 19. Jahrhunderts* (Hannover, 1876)
Overbeck und sein Kreis (exh. cat., Lübeck, Mus. Behnhaus, 1926)
A. Neumeyer: 'Beiträge zur Kunst der Nazarener in Rom', *Repert. Kstwiss.*, I (1929), pp. 64–80
R. Benz and A. von Schneider: *Die Kunst der deutschen Romantik* (Munich, 1939)
J. C. Jensen: 'Über die Gründung des Lukasbundes', *Wagen* (1958), pp. 105–22
K. Andrews: *The Nazarenes: A Brotherhood of German Painters in Rome* (Oxford, 1964)
J. C. Jensen: 'I Nazareni: Das Wort, der Stil', *Klassizismus und Romantik in Deutschland: Gemälde und Zeichnungen aus der Sammlung Georg Schäfer, Schweinfurt* (exh. cat., ed. K. Kaiser; Nuremberg, Ger. Nmus., 1966), pp. 46–52
R. Bachleitner: *Die Nazarener* (Munich, 1976)
H. von Einem: *Deutsche Malerei des Klassizismus und der Romantik, 1760–1840* (Munich, 1978)
Die Nazarener (exh. cat. by H. Dorre and others, Frankfurt am Main, Städel Kstinst., 1978)
U. Krenzlin: 'Zu einigen Problemen nazarenischer Kunst: Goethe und die nazarenische Kunst', *Städel-Jb.*, n. s., vii (1979), pp. 231–50
W. Vaughan: *German Romantic Painting* (New Haven, 1980)
I Nazareni a Roma (exh. cat. by G. Piantoni and S. Susinno, Rome, G.N.A. Mod., 1981)
W. Geismeier: *Die Malerei der deutschen Romantik* (Dresden, 1984)
A. Schmidt: 'Hainbündler und Lukasbrüder: Eine vergleichende Studie', *Niederdt. Beitr. Kstgesch.*, xxiii (1984), pp. 163–74
B. Rittinger: 'Zur Entwicklung der nazarenischen Wandmalerei', *Wien. Jb. Kstgesch.*, xli (1988), 97–138
ROBERT E. McVAUGH

Nazareth [Heb. Nazerat; Arab. al-Nāṣira]. Town in Israel, associated with the Annunciation to the Virgin Mary and the early life of Christ. A centre of Christian pilgrimage from the early 4th century AD, it survived the Arab conquest in AD 636 but was in ruins when it was conquered by the Crusaders at the end of the 11th century. It became the seat of a Latin archbishopric, and Crusader churches included a new basilica over the Grotto of the Annunciation and a church dedicated to St Joseph on the alleged site of the carpenter's shop. After the Battle of Hattin (1187), it was alternately under Ayyubid and Crusader control, but the Christian monuments were razed in 1263 on the orders of the Mamluk sultan Baybars I (*reg* 1260–

77). It was only after 1620, when the Druze amir Fakhr al-Din II (*reg* 1590–1635) allowed the Franciscans to settle there, that Nazareth slowly revived as a centre of pilgrimage.

1. CATHEDRAL OF THE ANNUNCIATION. Tancred (*reg* 1111–12), ruler of the Crusader principality of Galilee, repaired an ancient basilica that he found standing over the Grotto of the Annunciation, a church recorded in 1103 by the pilgrim Saewulf. Archbishop Letard, elected 1158, replaced this church with a new cathedral, which was well advanced in 1183 but razed in 1263. Its Baroque successor, built by the Franciscans in 1730, has been replaced by a third church, begun in the mid-20th century.

Archbishop Letard's church, the plan of which has been recovered in excavation, was 75 m long and 30 m wide, with three eastern apses in echelon, rectangular on the outside. A non-projecting transept preceded the choir bay, and there was an aisled nave of six bays. The Grotto of the Annunciation formed the crypt, under the nave. Five capitals of outstanding quality, carved in local white sandstone, were found in 1908 (see fig. and JERUSALEM, LATIN KINGDOM OF, fig. 4). Many other fragments, but no more complete capitals, have been discovered in the course of subsequent excavations beneath the modern basilica. As these excavations have not been fully published, vital archaeological evidence is missing. Scholarly debate has centred on three issues: the purpose and location of the sculptures in the church, the date of the work and the origin of the studio.

It has been suggested that the main west door of the church had a *Christ in Majesty* flanked by angels on the tympanum and column statues on the jambs, surmounted by the capitals. A figure of *St Peter* has been located on the trumeau. The evidence for some of this reconstruction is slight, but it provides a possible context for all the sculpture that has been found. An alternative location for the capitals is in a ciborium-aedicula above the Grotto of the Annunciation. Although it has been suggested that this provides an interior setting, which could explain the near perfect condition of the capitals, there is little evidence for the existence of such a structure.

The capitals were found buried, in pristine condition but with the background left rough and apparently unfinished. This led to suggestions that they were never installed in the church but were hidden away when the Latin Kingdom fell in 1187 and were never recovered. The stylistic parallels normally proposed for the sculpture suggest a date nearer *c.* 1150, however, and it is possible that the roughened background may have been intentional, either for decorative reasons or as a ground for plaster.

The figure style reveals a fluid handling of drapery and, through the elongation and distortion of the figures, achieves a rare sense of spirituality. The fragments of larger figures demonstrate a comparable command of technique and expression. Stylistic parallels have been traced in western Europe: a single capital in the church at Plaimpied, Berry, France, is clearly by one of the Nazareth sculptors, but it is unique in the church and stylistically quite out of place in Berry. Clear but less close links can be drawn between the Nazareth work and sculpture from Vienne, in the middle Rhône Valley, and Jonzy and Charlieu Abbey in Burgundy. Connections also exist with the Early Gothic sculpture of Chartres Cathedral and Notre-Dame, Etampes; these would help to explain the proposed column statue portal at Nazareth. Other work in the region has been connected with the Rhône Valley school centred on Vienne, notably the capitals in the north transept of the Holy Sepulchre Church, Jerusalem, but the connection between these and Nazareth is disputed. The work of the Nazareth studio has not been traced with certainty elsewhere, but a torso at Chatsworth, Derbys, recorded as coming from the region, is part of the same group. It is carved from a different, harder stone and might represent the work of the studio at another location. It would indeed be surprising if sculpture of the Nazareth standard were limited to a single site.

Nazareth, Cathedral of the Annunciation, detail from a capital perhaps representing a scene from the *Life of St James the Great*, sandstone, *c.* 1150

BIBLIOGRAPHY

P. Viaud: *Nazareth et ses deux églises de l'Annonciation et de St Joseph* (Paris, 1910)

P. Deschamps: *Terre sainte romane*, Nuit Temps (La Pierre-qui-vire, 1964), pp. 249–55

B. Bagatti: *Excavations at Nazareth*, i (Jerusalem, 1969)

M. Barasch: *Crusader Figural Sculpture in the Holy Land* (New Brunswick, NJ, 1971)

Z. Jacoby: 'Le Portail de l'église de l'Annonciation de Nazareth au XIIe siècle', *Mnmts Piot*, lxiv (1981), pp. 141–94

A. Borg: 'Romanesque Sculpture from the Rhône Valley to the Jordan Valley', *Crusader Art in the 12th Century*, ed. J. Folda, British Archaeological Research Reports (Oxford, 1982), pp. 97–120

J. Folda: *The Nazareth Capitals and the Crusader Shrine of the Annunciation* (University Park and London, 1986)

Z. Jacoby: 'The Composition of the Nazareth Workshop and Recruitment of Sculptors for the Holy Land in the 12th Century', *The Meeting of Two Worlds*, ed. V. Goss (Kalamazoo, 1986), pp. 145–59

ALAN BORG

Nazca [Nasca]. Pre-Columbian culture and art style of the south Peruvian coastal area, named after the modern town of Nazca. The culture flourished between *c.* 400 BC and *c.* AD 800 and appears to have been the dominant influence in the area during the Early Intermediate period (*c.* 300 BC–*c.* 600 AD; *see also* SOUTH AMERICA, PRE-CO-LUMBIAN, §III, 1(i)). Nazca art is best known through its pottery and the large-scale markings (termed Nazca lines) etched on the desert floor.

1. Introduction. 2. Pottery. 3. Nazca lines.

1. INTRODUCTION.

(i) Geography. The Nazca culture area comprises the valleys of the Chincha, Pisco, Ica, Nazca and Acari rivers in the narrow strip of the western coastal desert of South America that runs from Ecuador to northern Chile. Between the rich, narrow valleys lie segments of elevated desert known as the pampa. The Nazca valley had been inhabited more or less continually for 3000 years before European contacts. During the period of Nazca culture, as still today, the economy was agricultural, based principally on cotton but also including maize, grapes, tobacco, barley, squash, melons and tubers; it had a strong dependence on irrigation and the control of water in general. The mountains, which reach a height of over 1000 m within 5 km of the eastern edge of the coastal strip, are the sole source of water, since annual rainfall in the Nazca region is less than 6 mm, making it one of the driest places on earth. However, about four or five times a century an erratic weather pattern called 'El Niño' transports an equatorial precipitation system down from Ecuador and Colombia, producing more than a hundred times the normal amount of rainfall, often resulting in disastrous floods. Although palaeoclimatological studies (Craig and Psuty, 1968) suggest that no significant long-term climatic changes have occurred in the region since the Early Intermediate period, such micro-fluctuations in climate as 'El Niño' may have profoundly affected settlement patterns and agricultural practices.

Unlike the other pampas to the south and north, the Nazca pampa is strewn with sharp volcanic fragments of an average size about that of a fist. These are coated with 'desert varnish', a surface layer composed of the oxides of manganese and iron deposited by aerobic micro-organisms. When the dark surface stones are scraped away, the pinkish, unoxidized underlying surface is revealed, and this contrast was exploited in the creation of the famous Nazca lines (*see* §3 below).

(ii) Chronology. The chronology of Nazca culture is based on pottery finds (*see* §2 below); different systems divide it into either four periods or nine phases. These are: Period I (equivalent to the Proto-Nazca period and Phase 1; *c.* 400–250 BC), Period II (equivalent to the Monumental Nazca period and phases 2–4; *c.* 250 BC–*c.* AD 100), Period III (equivalent to the Proliferous Nazca period and phases 5 and 6; *c.* AD 100–*c.* 300) and Period IV (equivalent to the Disjunctive Nazca period and phases 7–9; *c.* 300–*c.* 600).

(iii) Settlement patterns. Studies of settlement patterns in the Nazca valley (Strong, 1957; Rowe, 1963) suggest that sites were widespread, the largest being CAHUACHI (Kawachi) on the Nazca River. It consists of several colossal adobe pyramid–plaza complexes and an adjacent burial ground, and it was occupied during all four Nazca periods. It may have been the capital of a small state created during Period II, as the public administrative and ceremonial buildings and most burials date from that time. The largest structure there (h. 20 m) is the Great Temple, built against a natural rise that fronts the valley below and the pampa beyond. Plazas and adobe apartments, probably élite residences, flank its base, some as large as 50×75 m. Other Period II sites in adjacent river valleys, and the sheer size of Cahuachi, suggest that it may have been an incipient city state. There is evidence for site abandonment in the Nazca area during Period III, when the valley apparently became decentralized in general. Excavations at Cahuachi, however, suggest that towards the end of this period it may have been a pilgrimage centre (Silverman, 1990).

La Estaquería, the second largest site, lies a few kilometres downstream and dates from Period III. Also surrounded by a massive burial ground, its principal component is an adobe platform that was probably crowned by a large, rectangular temple, of which the only remains are 12 rows of wooden posts at 2 m intervals, each *c.* 2 m high and notched at the top, which possibly supported a roof. La Estaquería may have been a religious centre tied closely to Cahuachi.

Period IV is characterized by scattered, relatively populous centres along the Nazca River and its tributaries, for example HUACA DEL LORO on the Tunga River. This has one of the few circular structures found on the south Peruvian coast; it is built of thick stone- and rubble-walls, rather than the usual adobe, and was apparently plastered and painted a bright red.

2. POTTERY. Nazca pottery includes brightly coloured bottles, plates and single- and double-spouted vessels with bridge handles. These wares were pre-fired and decorated with painted figures, usually outlined in black, including anthropomorphic felines, falcons and porpoises. Such representations on ceremonial vessels suggest an appreciation of the powers of these animals and a desire to incorporate their attributes into human behaviour. Most such finds are from tombs, some of which include gold nose-rings, earrings and diadems, indicative of a highly stratified society.

(i) Period I (c. 400–c. 250 BC). During this period the Nazca style emerged from that of the earlier PARACAS culture to the north. Period I pottery is pre-fired, painted and finely incised. Principal colours are red, white and black; orange, grey and brown also occur. Vessel shapes are often modelled on human figures, and a bridge handle and spout may adorn the top.

(ii) Period II (c. 250 BC–c. AD 100). Emergent styles became established and clearly defined in this period. Vessels include bottles with two spouts on top connected by a

bridge handle, shallow bowls, bowls with curved sides and plates with rounded bottoms. The designs are outlined in black on a red-slipped surface and utilize at least eight different colours. Of the realistic plant–animal decorative motifs, most seem to represent items that were either a part of the food chain or that might have been revered for their exotic nature, for example the jaguar and monkey, both indigenous to the jungles far beyond the Andes. Other forms include: chilli peppers, beans, maize; the deer, fox, monkey, llama, spider, snake, fish and various birds, especially the condor and humming-bird. Many of these creatures also occur among the etched figures of the Nazca pampa (*see* §3 below). Few imaginary animals are depicted, but a mustachioed feline, conceivably a deity, is represented.

(iii) Period III (c. AD *100–c. 300).* The number and variety of shapes increased in this period, with vessels becoming taller and more angular. Designs are highly embellished and less naturalistic, for example a little amoeba-like monster adorns some vessels (see fig. 1). A proliferation of depictions of trophy heads with eyes sealed shut and lips fastened with thorns suggests that during Period III a theocratic–military social structure may have dominated the Nazca area; the marked changes in the pottery possibly indicate HUARI influence from the north-east.

(iv) Period IV (c. 300–c. 600). This period is marked by a more decadent style, with designs degenerating to random, abstract convolutions and the range of vessel shapes increasing even further. The colour of the background surface is more often red than white, and new design elements include crude erotic representations, providing evidence of contact with distant cultures to the north and south.

1. Nazca pottery, ceremonial vessel, h. 135 mm, from the Nazca valley, Period III, *c.* AD 100–*c.* 300 (Lima, Museo Nacional de Antropología y Arqueología)

3. NAZCA LINES.

(i) Introduction. These features cover more than 9 million sq. m of pampa surface and range in width from 200 m to a few centimetres. They appear as light markings on a dark background and were first termed 'lines' by outsiders who rediscovered them from the air in the late 1930s, although they were already well known to the local inhabitants. Variously classified as 'geoglyphs', 'markings' and 'figural drawings', the lines are strictly etchings, made by removing overlying darker matter. The forms they take include abstract geometric figures, long straight lines and biomorphic drawings. There are *c.* 300 geometric figures, consisting principally of triangles and trapezoids (specifically truncated trapezoidal figures; see fig. 2), to which are appended long, thin triangles. Zigzag lines, labyrinthine spirals and unicursal designs that a person on foot can walk into and out of without crossing a given area more than once (see fig. 2) also occur, although long, straight lines of kilometric dimensions, together with trapezoids, constitute most of the figures. Aveni (1990) catalogued the dimensions and directions of more than 700 of these, totalling 1300 km in combined length.

Practically all the straight lines radiate from 62 or more interconnected focal-points. The biomorphic figural drawings are much smaller and are therefore more difficult to recognize, except from low altitudes. They are confined largely to the north-east corner of the pampa, on the south bank of the Ingenio River. Subjects include the monkey, fish, spider, flower and many birds, including a hummingbird, condor and cormorant, most of which also occur on Nazca pottery (*see* §2 above). Associated pottery finds indicate that the straight lines may date from approximately the same period as the biomorphic designs, although the two phenomena do not appear to be linked physically. While the dimensions of the Nazca lines and figures are impressive, their construction is not a spectacular feat of engineering, nor was advanced technology necessary.

(ii) Origins and function. At least five main hypotheses have been advanced in this connection.

(a) Calendars and astronomy. Kosok (1965) first suggested that the lines point to astronomical events taking place at the local visible horizon, which were used to mark the course of the agricultural year. Reiche (1949, 1968) noted coincidences between the directions of lines and the position of sunrise and sunset on the solstices and also suggested a pairing of certain animal figures with stellar groupings; thus, the spider was said to resemble Orion, the long-necked cormorant to point to the solstice direction and the monkey to indicate the polar motion of stars. These 'zodiacal animals' were supposedly identified with times of the year when a distinct episode of their life cycle took place. This hypothesis, based on the need for an agrarian people in an arid climate to predict and reckon mnemonically the rise and fall of the river for irrigation purposes, has a close precedent in Nilotic Egypt.

Although both Kosok's and Reiche's arguments lacked systematic collection and analysis of data, Hawkins (1969) tested the astronomical hypothesis by conducting a photogrammetric survey of alignments on 21 trapezoids and

2. Nazca lines, aerial view of the northern end of the pampa showing etched figures

72 lines at the north-east corner of the pampa. Using a computer, he attempted to match the directions with orientations to astronomical events, concluding that there was no overall evidence that the lines point to astronomical objects. However, his perspective was largely that of a northern, high-latitude observer (he excluded, for example, the rising and setting positions of the sun on the day of its passage through zenith, a major celestial event in the tropical sky); and neither Hawkins, Kosok nor Reiche considered ethnographic and ethnohistorical information on astronomical practices among South American cultures.

In fact, in other systems of linear organization in the Andes, astronomical alignments were included in complex, multi-functional systems that must be viewed holistically. For example, the *ceque* system of Cuzco (Zuidema, 1977) was a radial, mnemonic scheme overlying the Inca capital; it served to organize social space, kinship, irrigation and water rights, and the calendar.

(b) Geometry. This hypothesis states that, although this was not their sole function, the lines convey a knowledge of precise geometry. Reiche (1949, 1968) considered that the contours of certain figures could have been drawn only through the use of quantized units of length. However, the idea of a modular unit of measurement (e.g. the distance between the nose and the fingers of an extended arm) has yet to be systematically argued.

(c) Water and irrigation. There seems little doubt that the straight lines relate to water—specifically, that they served as a ritual device upon which worshippers walked or danced to induce rain from the mountain gods, and that they functioned as a ritually based map to indicate the path of underground water (a sophisticated underground irrigation system exists in the valley areas adjacent to the pampa). Urton's (1990) study of Nazca documents of early Spanish colonial date indicates that a temporal division of water rights according to the Andean *mi'ta* system of shared labour existed at this time, if not earlier, suggesting a motive for local people to trek across the pampa in an organized and prescribed manner.

The points at which water occurs on the pampa, together with the direction in which it moves, correlate strongly with the radial line centres. Nearly all such networks are located either on the last of a descending series of hills or on the high dunes flanking the borders of the Ingenio and Nazca rivers and their tributaries. The axes of trapezoids, often joined to the ends of the lines, are usually oriented along watercourses; about two-thirds have the apex pointing upstream. Viewed from the radial centres, of those lines that intersect the horizon in the range through which the sun passes during the year, the slightly higher proportion are positioned around the place where the sun rises on the day, in late October, that it passes the zenith. This is the time when water begins to run in the rivers and their underground canals. The irrigation and astronomical hypotheses may therefore be related.

(d) Pathways. The lines evidently functioned as pathways; remains of footpaths can still be seen in some, and

there are many resemblances between the lines and South American Pre-Columbian roads. Hyslop (1984) discovered several characteristics common to both Inca roads and Nazca lines: long, straight segments varying less than 3° over distances of 10 km; kinks and sharp bends rather than slow curves; edging of low rubble piles; stone cairns, usually in pairs, at points where the road either narrows or widens; parallel edges sometimes widening abruptly into antiparallel or trapezoidal segments; and the existence of parallel roadways that often run side by side for some distance.

Other 'pathway' hypotheses variously propose that: the trapezoids were places of assembly for cults of the dead, with different kin groups meeting on different trapezoids; the lines passing into the trapezoids were genealogical links, providing information about relationships among the various cults that met on the large plaza-like trapezoids; the biomorphic figures were floors for sacred dances relating to the worship of the dead.

The myriad lines that have been mapped do, indeed, reveal a pattern that could take a traveller via hundreds of possible routes across the pampa. Just as at Cuzco the specific *huacas* (sacred places) of particular *ceque* lines (*see* §(a) above) were associated with worshippers linked by kinship, so a particular Nazca line may have been assigned to its ritual walkers.

(e) Art form. This interpretation has been applied mainly to the biomorphic figures, which echo decorative designs on Nazca pottery. Modern observers tend to view these figures as images projected on a flat surface, but they may never have been intended to be seen from above, by either gods or people. However, the creation process on the pampa does resemble that involved in certain sculpted palaeolithic forms, where artists did not so much apply decoration to a given space or material but rather liberated a pre-existing form from the medium surrounding it. Thus, Nazca artists may have recognized images in the spaces between the capillary-like dry tributaries (*quebradas*) that cross the pampa and articulated them by carefully removing portions of the desert pavement. For example, some of the etched figures seem to fit perfectly into the space that contains them. Morris (1975) likened some figures, particularly the monkey, to forms of haptic art, which is intended to be experienced not by viewing but by moving over and through it.

BIBLIOGRAPHY

B. Cobo: *Historia del Nuevo Mundo* (1633); Biblioteca de Autores Españoles, xci–xcii (Madrid, 1956)
M. Reiche: *Mystery on the Desert: A Study of the Ancient Figures and Strange Delineated Surfaces Seen from the Air near Nazca, Peru* (Nazca, 1949)
W. D. Strong: 'Paracas, Nazca and Tihuanacoid Cultural Relationships in Southern Peru', *Mem. Soc. Amer. Archaeol.*, xiii (1957) [whole issue]
J. H. Rowe: 'Urban Settlements in Ancient Peru', *Ñawpa Pacha*, i (1963), pp. 1–27
P. Kosok: *Life, Land and Water in Ancient Peru* (New York, 1965)
J. H. Rowe: 'Urban Settlement in Ancient Peru', *Peruvian Archaeology: Selected Readings*, ed. J. H. Rowe and D. Menzel (Palo Alto, 1967), pp. 293–320
A. Craig and N. Psuty: *Marine Desert Ecology of Southern Peru: Final Report* (Boca Raton, 1968)
T. Patterson: 'Late Pre-ceramic and Early Ceramic Cultures of the Central Coast of Peru', *Ñawpa Pacha*, vi (1968), pp. 115–33
M. Reiche: *Mystery on the Desert* (Stuttgart, 1968)
G. Hawkins: 'Ancient Lines in the Peruvian Desert: Final Scientific Report for the National Geographic Society', *Smithsonian Astrophysical Observatory Report No. 906–4* (Cambridge, MA, 1969)
L. G. Lumbreras: *De los pueblos, las culturas y las artes del antiguo Perú* (Lima, 1969; Eng. trans. by B. J. Meggers, Washington, DC, 1974)
R. Morris: 'Aligned with Nazca', *Artforum*, xiv (1975), pp. 26–39
D. Menzel: *Pottery Style and Society in Ancient Peru: Art as a Mirror of History in the Inca Valley, 1350–1570* (Berkeley, 1976)
R. T. Zuidema: 'The Inca Calendar', *Native American Astronomy*, ed. A. Aveni (Austin, 1977), pp. 219–59
W. Isbell: 'Prehistoric Ground Drawings of Peru', *Sci. Amer.*, ccxxxix (1978), pp. 140–53
T. Morrison: *Pathways to the Gods: The Mystery of the Andes Lines* (Lima, 1978)
G. Urton: 'Animals and Astronomy in the Quechua Universe', *Proc. Amer. Philos. Soc.*, cxxv (1981), pp. 110–27
J. Hyslop: *The Inka Road System* (New York, 1984)
A. Aveni: 'The Nazca Lines: Patterns in the Desert', *Archaeology*, xxxix/4 (1986), pp. 32–40
J. Reinhard: *The Nazca Lines: A New Perspective on their Origin and Meaning* (Lima, 1986)
A. Aveni: 'Order in the Nazca Lines', *The Lines of Nazca*, ed. A. Aveni (Philadelphia, 1990), pp. 41–114
H. Silverman: 'The Early Nazca Pilgrimage Centre of Cahuachi and the Nazca Lines', *The Lines of Nazca*, ed. A. Aveni (Philadelphia, 1990), pp. 207–44
G. Urton: 'Andean Social Organization and the Maintenance of the Nazca Lines', *The Lines of Nazca*, ed. A. Aveni (Philadelphia, 1990), pp. 173–206

ANTHONY AVENI

Nazism [National Socialism]. German political ideology and movement founded by Adolf Hitler (1889–1945) and promoted through his Nazi Party (Nationalsozialistische Deutsche Arbeiterpartei) from 1921 to 1945.

1. Introduction. 2. Art and architecture.

1. INTRODUCTION. The Nazis took power in Germany in 1933, when Hitler became Chancellor and Dictator, and began the ruthless application of their totalitarian policies, based in particular on anti-Semitism, extreme nationalism and militarism. Their expansionist ambitions led in 1939 to World War II. With the imminent defeat of Germany in 1945, Hitler committed suicide in Berlin. During their regime the Nazis imposed strict controls on all aspects of culture, including art and architecture. Similar stylistic features, especially in architecture, were also to be found in Austria, Switzerland, France, Spain, Portugal, Eastern Europe and, in particular, Fascist Italy. However, compared with other extreme right-wing governments in Europe, the Nazis were particularly rigorous in their intolerance towards any tendencies in art guided by criteria other than craftsmanship and nationalist content.

The Nazi definition of what was to be considered as art was rooted in the 19th century, as regards both style and subject-matter, and idealized the values of the *Volk*. As early as 1902 there was a debate in the Reichstag on the allegedly excessive foreign influence on German art through the 'partisans of French Impressionism'. Subsequent nationalist attacks included the measures taken against the Bauhaus by the Thüringen government in 1925. Such activities opposed the internationalism of the avant-garde and promoted those who expressed German expansionist aspirations in their works. After the world economic crisis of 1923–9 extreme conservative circles asserted that Germany was suffering from a 'cultural crisis' for which

Semitic or 'Mongol–Bolshevist' (i.e. Communist) subversion was responsible. National culture was seen as founded solely on racial factors.

The mouthpiece for such ideas was the Kampfbund für Deutsche Kultur, founded by Alfred Rosenberg (1893–1946) in 1927, the original members of which came predominantly from Richard Wagner's circle in Munich, including university teachers, publishers, theatre managers, writers, clergymen, teachers and artists. The Kampfbund instigated political actions in the cultural field, such as the dismissal of museum directors who had promoted avant-garde art or the closing of exhibitions showing allegedly 'corrupt' art, declaring these acts to be the expressions of 'healthy popular outrage'. Attacks were also directed against certain styles of architecture, in particular the Functionalist style of the Bauhaus, which the Kampfbund saw as reflecting Bolshevist–Jewish thinking.

2. ART AND ARCHITECTURE. The campaign against avant-garde art intensified after the Nazi seizure of power in 1933, which inaugurated a fanatical bringing-into-line (*Gleichschaltung*) in the political, social and cultural spheres: books were burned, newspapers and periodicals banned, institutions closed and artists and writers dismissed or forbidden to work. The Reichsministerium für Volksaufklärung und Propaganda and the Reichskulturkammer, both directed by Josef Goebbels (1897–1945), the Minister of Propaganda, were the main instruments of Nazi cultural politics. One of the subsidiary organizations was the Reichskammer der Bildenden Künste, the body responsible for fine arts (the first president was the architect Eugen Hönig (*b* 1873), and from 1937 the painter Adolf Ziegler (*b* 1892)).

There were initially differences of opinion between Goebbels and Rosenberg as to what was to be considered 'German' art, especially as regards Expressionism. Goebbels wanted to evaluate Expressionism as 'German' and integrate it into a nationalist art concept as Benito Mussolini had done with Futurism in Italy. Rosenberg rejected Expressionism as 'degenerate'. Hitler decided the issue personally in favour of Rosenberg. In 1937 the action against ENTARTETE KUNST was put into effect, causing mainly Expressionist works to be confiscated from museums and largely destroyed. Most of the artists branded as 'degenerate' went into exile.

Munich became the 'capital' of Nazism and Nazi art. Between 1933 and 1937 the Haus der Deutschen Kunst (now the Haus der Kunst; see fig.) by PAUL LUDWIG TROOST was built there; it was completed after his death in 1934 by his wife Gerdy Troost and the architect Leonhard Gall. The Haus der Deutschen Kunst was inaugurated in 1937 with an elaborate ceremony and an exhibition of what was intended to be regarded as true German art. Its most important publication was the periodical *Kunst im dritten Reich* (later *Kunst im deutschen Reich*), edited by Rosenberg. Art criticism was replaced by the 'art report', used to disseminate judgements pronounced at the centre. Whereas National Socialism had

Paul Ludwig Troost: Haus der Deutschen Kunst (now Haus der Kunst), Munich, 1933–7

clearly defined its aesthetic antagonist, *entartete Kunst*, from the outset, as was displayed in a spectacular exhibition in 1937, it had a somewhat vague vision of a 'German art'. Over two million Germans saw the Nazis' judgement on modernism, whereas the first *Grosse deutsche Kunstausstellung* of 1937 in the Haus der Deutschen Kunst attracted at most a third of that number. It was followed by seven further exhibitions of official Nazi art in the same building. The ideology of their content is summed up by the catchphrase 'Blood and Soil'.

Architecture was considered an especially suitable means for influencing the masses and demonstrating power. Building was initially intended to create jobs and meet military needs, with factories by such architects as HERBERT RIMPL, together with youth hostels, motorways, airports and barracks. The projects soon included prestigious buildings for the Nazi Party and the State. These were integrated into large-scale urban programmes (e.g. in Munich and Linz) and were of hardly any practical use to the population. On the death of Troost in 1934, ALBERT SPEER became the principal Nazi architect. For Berlin, which was to be renamed 'Germania', a grid system made up of military routes and ceremonial streets was planned, as well as an unexecuted project for a Grosse Volkshalle (versions, 1938; Berlin, Landesarchv; Munich, Bayer. Haupstaatsarchv)—a domed structure 300 m high; other buildings were designed by Emil Fahrenkamp, Wilhelm Kreis and Cäsar Pinnau. In Nuremberg Speer laid out a ground for party rallies on an area of 16.5 sq. km. The Reichsstelle für Raumordnung not only erected monumental party, military and cultural buildings but also put up memorials throughout Germany to the German dead of the Franco-Prussian War (1870–71) and World War I, including examples by Kreis and Clemens Klotz.

Such modern structural materials as steel and concrete were rejected or, where they could not be avoided, were faced with natural stone, to reinforce the desired effect of monumentality. For private houses a timbered construction was favoured, to signal homeliness (e.g. work by Paul Schultze-Naumburg and Paul Schmitthenner). Public buildings made use of Roman and other classical features: Speer and Troost sought the authority of Palladio, Leo von Klenze and Karl Friedrich Schinkel and the exponents of French Revolutionary architecture, Claude-Nicolas Ledoux and Etienne-Louis Boullée, for their intimidatory, megalomaniac architecture. Characteristic of this style is a neo-classicism of especial severity and harshness, aiming primarily at colossal effects to demonstrate the Nazi notion of a 'Thousand-Year Reich'. Such structural elements as pilasters and cornices were cultivated, and applied ornamentation eschewed, since it might, in betraying the changing styles of different eras, point to its own transitoriness. The monumental classicism of Nazi architecture can be compared with that of STALINIST ARCHITECTURE developing at the same time in the USSR.

Drawing stylistically and thematically on the 19th century, National Socialist pictorial art placed genre painting at the forefront. Long since discarded by modernism, this mode had survived among provincial artists preoccupied with the values of the 'homeland' (*Heimat*), who lacked the innovative originality of the art termed 'degenerate'. The old thematic canon of the 19th-century art schools and academies, regarded as utterly exhausted by the beginning of the 20th century, was resurrected under the aegis of nationalism. Such traditional subjects as landscapes, studies of peasants and craftsmen, individual and group portraits, animal pictures, still-lifes, nudes and allegories were supplemented by pictures of sport and sportsmen, industrial work and landscapes, merchant and military ships and, above all, war itself.

Although industrial production was highly developed, Nazi art mainly presented a state of production, especially in depicting farm and craft work, that was archaic, or at least pre-industrial. By the depiction of idyllic scenes or individuals in heroic, monumental poses, while systematically obscuring the existence of workers in industrial mass production, such problems as unemployment and proletarianization were meant to be screened off. The paintings of craftsmen represented German industriousness in keeping with the idea that 'work ennobles'; the peasants, mostly shown ploughing, were meant to suggest the earthiness and strength of the 'people without space' who needed to occupy land to the east. An art that claimed to be realistic because it was figurative depicted a social reality that already belonged to the past.

Stylistically, Nazi art drew on the examples of German Renaissance and Romantic art. Such artists as Adolf Wissel (1894–1973) and Willy Jäckel (1888–1944) painted in this eclectic manner, in which the monumental heroic pose was reserved for the male figure. Such imagery reflected the Nazis' anti-proletarian contempt for the masses, while it was also intended to symbolize the 'German people's will to resist'. This was made particularly clear in the many paintings of war and the soldier, shown as a muscular warrior fixing the enemy with a level gaze. Destruction, death and suffering were not depicted and wounding only to emphasize heroism. War themes are to be found especially in the work of Elk Eber, Werner Peiner (*b* 1897) and Franz Eichhorst (1885–1948), for example *Anti-tank Defence* (1938), part of a mural for the Schöneberg Rathaus, Berlin.

Images of women were dominated by the nude, which quantitatively far surpassed other female subjects such as the mother–child motif, which played an important role in propaganda and portraits. Here the salon painting of the 19th century (e.g. by Hans Makart) was continued. Women were presented as affectionate, soft, lascivious and healthy, often in an impressionistic–naturalistic manner, for example by Ivo Saliger (1894–1986), Karl Truppe (1887–1959) and Raffael Schuster-Woldan (1864–1933). Other versions of the theme showed a coolly classical, photographic style, for example work by Paul M. Padua (1903–81), Ziegler and Peiner.

In sculpture of the nude, physical characterizations of man and woman with such qualities as masculine hardness and feminine pliancy emerge still more strongly, above all in the work of Josef Thorak (1889–1952) and ARNO BREKER (e.g. the female figure *Grace*, plaster, h. 2.1 m; see 1983 exh. cat., p. 32). Such sculptures decorated squares, parade grounds, ceremonial sites, and state and party buildings, performing the same public tasks as architecture: for example Thorak's *Comradeship* (plaster, h. *c.* 5 m, 1937; destr.) for the German Pavilion at the Exposition Internationale des Arts et Techniques dans la

Vie Moderne in Paris in 1937 (see 1983 exh. cat., p. 81). Such works were modelled on those by such 19th-century classical sculptors as Bertel Thorvaldsen and Adolf von Hildebrand, though without regard for their humanist aims. The work of such sculptors as Richard Scheibe and Fritz Klimsch, who had helped to shape modern sculpture, became slick, cool and bombastic during the Third Reich. However, while these artists still generally respected the human measure, Breker, Thorak, Adolf Wamper (*b* 1901) and Fritz Koelle (1895–1953) pushed their figures to outlandish, cyclopean proportions. These monumental nudes were meant to intimidate the onlooker and demonstrate pure power with their triumphant expressions and highly schematized, depersonalized muscular physiques. Their aggressive titles made no secret of the ideological preparation for war.

While the painting of the Nazi era disappeared into the stores of museums and state buildings after its demise, its architecture, in so far as it survived destruction in World War II, continued to be used, restored and cared for. Some of the large stone sculptures, integrated into other architectural contexts, but still accessible to the public, also survived.

BIBLIOGRAPHY

EARLY SOURCES

C. Vinnen: *Protest deutscher Künstler* (Jena, 1911)
A. Hitler: *Mein Kampf* (Munich, 1925)
A. Rosenberg: *Der Mythos des 20. Jahrhunderts: Eine Wertung der seelisch-geistigen Gestaltenkämpfe unserer Zeit* (Munich, 1930)
A. Hitler: *Die deutsche Kunst als stolzeste Verteidigung des deutschen Volkes* (Munich, 1934)
A. Rosenberg: *Revolution in der bildenden Kunst?* (Munich, 1934)
P. Schultze-Naumburg: *Kunst aus Blut und Boden* (Leipzig, 1934)
W. Rittich: *Architektur und Bauplastik der Gegenwart* (Berlin, 1936)
H. Schrade: *Bauten des Dritten Reiches* (Leipzig, 1937)
Kst Dritten Reich, i–ii (1937–8); cont. as *Kst Dt. Reich*, iii–viii (1939–44)
Grosse deutschen Kunstausstellung (exh. cats, Munich, Haus Dt. Kst., 1937–44) [cats of annual exh.]
B. Feistel-Rohmeder: *Im Terror des Kunstbolschewismus: Urkundensammlung des 'Deutschen Kunstberichtes' aus den Jahren 1927–33* (Karlsruhe, 1938)
J. Goebbels: *Signale der neuen Zeit: 25 ausgewählte Reden von Dr. Joseph Goebbels* (Munich, 1938)
G. Troost: *Das Bauen im neuen Reich*, 2 vols (Bayreuth, 1938)
W. Willrich: *Säuberung des Kunsttempels: Eine kunstpolitische Kampfschrift zur Gesundung deutscher Kunst im Geiste nordischer Art* (Munich and Berlin, 2/1938)

GENERAL

H. Brenner: *Die Kunst des Nationalsozialismus* (Reinbek, 1963)
J. Wulf, ed.: *Die bildenden Künste im Dritten Reich* (Gütersloh, 1963)
A. Teut: *Architektur im Dritten Reich, 1933–1945* (Berlin, Frankfurt am Main and Vienna, 1967)
B. Miller-Lane: *Architecture and Politics in Germany, 1918–1945* (Cambridge, MA, 1968)
G. Kratsch: *Kunstwart und Dürerbund* (Göttingen, 1969)
B. Hinz: *Die Malerei im deutschen Faschismus: Kunst und Konterrevolution* (Munich and Vienna, 1974)
P. Liska: *Nationalsozialistische Kunstpolitik* (Berlin, 1974)
Katalog Kunst im Dritten Reich: Dokumente der Unterwerfung (Frankfurt am Main, 1974)
K. Herding and H.-E. Mittig: *Kunst und Alltag im NS-System: Albert Speers Berliner Strassenlaternen* (Giessen, 1975)
H. Hinkel: *Zur Funktion des Bildes im deutschen Faschismus* (Giessen, 1975)
R. Steinberg, ed.: *Nazi-Kitsch* (Darmstadt, 1975)
J. Petsch: *Baukunst und Stadtplanung im Dritten Reich: Herleitung, Bestandsaufnahme, Entwicklung, Nachfolge* (Munich, 1976)
A. Rabinbach: 'Beauty of Labour: The Aesthetics of Production in the Third Reich', *J. Contemp. Hist.*, xi/4 (Dec 1976), pp. 43–76
O. Thomae: *Die Propaganda-Maschinerie: Bildende Kunst und Öffentlichkeitsarbeit im Dritten Reich* (Berlin, 1978)
B. Hinz, ed.: *Die Dekoration der Gewalt: Kunst und Medien im Faschismus* (Giessen, 1979)
K. Wolbert: *Die Nackten und die Toten des 'Dritten Reiches': Folgen einer politischen Geschichte des Körpers in der Plastik des deutschen Faschismus* (Giessen, 1982)
R. Merker: *Die bildenden Künste im Nationalsozialismus: Kulturideologie, Kulturpolitik, Kulturproduktion* (Cologne, 1983)
Skulptur und Macht: Figurative Plastik in Deutschland der 30er und 40er Jahre (exh. cat, ed. R. Szymanski; Berlin, Akad. Kst, 1983)
Katalog Inszenierung der Macht: Ästhetische Faszination im Faschismus (Berlin, 1987)
M. G. Davidson: *Kunst in Deutschland, 1933–1945: Eine wissenschaftliche Enzyklopädie der Kunst im Dritten Reich*, 4 vols (Tübingen, 1988–)
B. Hinz, ed.: *NS-Kunst: 50 Jahre danach: Neue Beiträge* (Marburg, 1989)
For further bibliography *see* ENTARTETE KUNST.

SIGRUN PAAS

Nazzoni, Niccolò. *See* NASONI, NICOLAU.

Ndebele. Nguni-speaking people of Southern Africa. Historically they are divided into two distinct groups: one, living in Zimbabwe, has been mostly amalgamated into the North Sotho; the other, with a population of *c.* 330,000, lives on the high plains of Transvaal Province, South Africa, surrounded by such South Sotho people as the Pedi and Tswana. This second group comprises two chiefdoms: Ndzundza (also referred to as the people of Chief Mapoch or Mahlangu) and Manala. In the mid-19th century the Ndzundza were one of the major forces in the eastern Transvaal, but they were defeated by the Boers during the war of 1882–3. Their land was confiscated, and they were dispersed throughout the Transvaal and forced into service as indentured labourers. In 1923 they were able to purchase some land and began to regroup. In the mid-1970s the South African government established the 'homeland' of Kwa-Ndebele. Both the southern groups produce the beadwork for which Ndebele are famous, but it is only the Ndzundza who are noted for their elaborate wall painting. Ndebele arts have been quite widely illustrated, especially the wall paintings (see bibliography).

A great variety of beadwork designs are used to decorate traditional Ndebele women's dress, worn for rituals or gala occasions such as celebrations following men's or women's initiation, weddings or feasts given to honour the ancestors. The main items of apparel include hide aprons, breastplates, wedding trains and gala blankets (formerly capes). White beads are combined with a range of other colours. For ritual occasions they also carry elaborately beaded dance staffs. Unmarried women wear bead-covered grass coils around the waist, neck, arms and legs. After marrying they shave their heads and wear a small crocheted cap or a scarf wrapped around the head to make it look small, thus accentuating the long neck that has brass and copper rings stacked from chin to clavicle (see fig.). Their arms and lower legs also usually have a great many copper and brass rings, in the late 20th century often simulated by aluminium or plastic car trim. The overall visual effect is of a magnificent, colourful pyramid.

The elaborate Ndebele homestead decorations, consisting of complex geometric forms painted in a wide variety of colours, dates from *c.* 1945. Commercially produced oxide pigments or various earths found in the area are used. The earlier style was a simple outlining of doors and windows, but it became more elaborate with the proliferation of the rectangular 'highveld house' (Frescura), whose

Ndebele traditional dress worn by artist Elizabeth Masilela in front of her thatched-roof mud house, Roosenekal, Transvaal Province, South Africa; from a photograph by Elizabeth Ann Schneider, 1978

expanse of flat, mud-plastered walls provided further scope for expression (*see* AFRICA, fig. 66). It has proved a highly visible means of group identification, both internally and in the midst of Sotho speakers. The importance of the wall paintings to the Ndzundza probably relates to their turbulent history, which has created a strong sense of deprivation and self-awareness among their descendants and a need for group recognition.

House decoration relates directly to beadwork, and in both the style is characterized by outlined, complex design-units of angular rather than curvilinear elements. Although most motifs are non-representational, even the occasional figurative images are usually adapted to this style. The geometric aspect is undoubtedly influenced by beadwork techniques. The most immediately noticeable aspect of the designs is their symmetry (bilateral, rotational or translational), although symmetry in colour is less often found (Schneider, 1985). Designs are adapted from many sources including blankets, yardage and linoleum floors, or even vehicle number plates. Houses or buildings with chimneys, windows and stairs are sometimes rendered in triangles, rectangles and arrows; other designs are embellished with versions of Victorian architectural decorations found in nearby urban areas; occasionally imagery includes representations of cars, buses or aeroplanes.

There is evidence that variations in style and colour indicate different geographical locations and chiefdoms. Most Ndebele living under the paramount chief in south-central Transvaal use commercial colour pigments or bright acrylic paints purchased from the trading store. The Ndebele villagers living in Nebo magisterial district in eastern Transvaal under a rival chief use black river-soil and whitewash to create their distinctive decorations, while the wives of Ndebele tenant labourers on farms owned by Whites usually decorate in the earth colours found in their particular area. The finer texture of commercial colours permits more elaborate and complex designs, while coarse and sandy earth materials limit the artists to broader and simpler configurations.

After the establishment of Kwa-Ndebele, there was a sharp drop in the number of decorated homesteads. In this barren, dusty area the overcrowded shelters are improvised from metal sheets, cardboard sections and hessian and do not provide a painting surface, which leads to disruption of wall decoration. However, this Ndebele art form began to receive much international attention in the 1980s and early 1990s with the publication of large-format illustrated books on the subject (e.g. Courtney-Clarke) and the promotion of the work of such individual Ndebele artists as Esther Mahlangu (*b* 1935). Her versions of wall paintings produced on canvas have been included in a number of international exhibitions (e.g. 1991–2, exh. cat).

BIBLIOGRAPHY
J. Walton: *African Village* (Pretoria, 1956)
R. Rasmussen: *Ndebele Wars and Migrations, c. 1821–1839* (diss., Los Angeles, UCLA, 1975)
F. Frescura: *Rural Shelters in South Africa* (Johannesburg, 1981)
Ndebele Images (exh. cat. by S. Priebatsch and N. Knight, Johannesburg, 1983) [useful colour pls]
E. Schneider: 'Ndebele Mural Art', *Afr. A.*, xviii/3 (1985), pp. 60–67, 100
M. Courtney-Clarke: *Ndebele: The Art of an African Tribe* (New York, 1986) [excellent pls]
E. Schneider: *Paint, Pride and Politics: Aesthetic and Meaning in Transvaal Ndebele Wall Art* (diss., Johannesburg, U. Witwatersrand, 1986)
Africa Now (exh. cat., Las Palmas de Gran Canaria, Cent. Atlantic. A. Mod.; Groningen, Groniger Mus.; Mexico City, Cent. Cult. A. Contemp.; 1991–2)

ELIZABETH ANN SCHNEIDER

Nea Anchialos [anc. Pyrasos; formerly Phthiotic Thebes]. Greek town on the Pagasitic Gulf, 17 km south of Volos in the nome of Magnesia. It was built in 1907/8 to accommodate Greek refugees from Anchialos (now Pomorie) in Bulgaria. Excavations by the Greek Archaeological Service have confirmed the existence of a settlement at this site from as early as the 2nd millennium BC. It was destroyed in 1200 BC and rebuilt after 900 BC. From the 5th century BC it developed as a trading centre and became the port of the inland city of Thebes, gradually absorbing the population of the latter. In 196 BC it was conquered by the Romans, and it became part of the Thessalian League. From the 2nd century AD Pyrasos was known as Phthiotic Thebes, and the city enjoyed a period of particular prosperity from the 4th century to the early 7th. In the second half of the 7th century its fortunes declined, but it continued to be mentioned in inscriptions until the 9th century.

The town preserves a wall from the Roman period, which was repaired under Justinian I. It was fortified with towers, and it stretched from the ancient acropolis of Pyrasos down to the sea. A group of buildings, probably an agora or hospital, with eight phases of construction from the Roman and Early Christian periods, lies in the southern foothills of the acropolis hill. The remains of other secular buildings include those of a paved avenue with arcades and shops, and from the 5th century AD a hypocaust and a private villa. The Roman cemetery was situated on the east side of Pyrasos at a place known as Ta Dodeka ('the twelve'); many tombs from various periods and of all types have been found inside and outside the walls.

The town's importance as a religious centre is demonstrated by the wealth of Christian monuments that have been uncovered. To the west of the paved avenue and to the south-east of the hypocaust and villa is Basilica A, also known as the Basilica of Hagios Demetrios (mid-5th century; see EARLY CHRISTIAN AND BYZANTINE ART, fig. 12). It has three aisles, a narthex, a baptistery with a mosaic floor, a service room, probably a *skeuophylakeion* (sacristy), and an atrium with a fountain. Its elaborate sculptural decoration is comparable mainly with work from Constantinople and Thessaloniki. The basilica was destroyed by fire in the 7th century or first half of the 8th. To the west of Hagios Demetrios are the remains of a two-storey building with important sculptural decoration that dates to the late Roman period, but which continued in use probably as the bishop's palace until the 7th century. The basilica of Bishop Elpidios or Basilica B (second half of the 5th century) takes its name from the local bishop commemorated in an inscription. It was a three-aisled basilica with galleries, a narthex, atrium, *skeuophylakeion* and baptistery. Basilica C (*c.* 532; destr. late 7th century), which was part of a larger complex, is the biggest and most elaborate building of the town. It was a three-aisled basilica with a narthex and atrium; an inscription records restoration work by Archpriest Peter. Excavations have shown that it was built on the site of two earlier basilicas (mid- or second half of the 4th century and mid- or second half of the 5th century); these had replaced Mycenean and Roman buildings. Basilica C had rich sculptural decoration and mosaic floors with geometric designs and animal motifs. A mosaic workshop was found to the south of the basilica, while to the south of the atrium are the remains of a monumental 4th-century baptistery. It consisted of a square open-air structure (10.5×10.5 m), enclosing an octagonal font and surrounded by a three-aisled ambulatory. The interior walls of the square structure were clad with marble revetment and the floor with polychrome *opus sectile*. Of the two churches (5th–6th century) found outside the city walls, Basilica D was probably a cemetery church. It had three-aisles, a narthex, atrium and square grave chambers on the north, south and east sides touching the main body of the church. Its original mosaic decoration represented a wide variety of subject-matter. The second extramural church, known as the Basilica of Martyrios (431), also had three aisles and a narthex, with marble and mosaic floors. Martyrios was probably a donor and is mentioned in an inscription on a closure slab at the entrance to the sanctuary.

BIBLIOGRAPHY

G. Soteriou: 'Ai christianikai Thebai tis Thessalias' [Christian Thebes of Thessaly], *Archaiol. Ephimeris* (1929), pp. 1–158
A. Avramea: *I byzantini Thessalia mechri tou 1204* [Byzantine Thessaly until 1204] (Athens, 1974), pp. 150–56
J. Koder and Fr. Hild: *Hellas und Thessalia* (1976), i of *Tabula imperii byzantini* (Vienna, 1976–), pp. 271–2
P. E. Lazarides: 'Phthiotides Thebai' [Phthiotic Thebes], *Archaiol. Ephimeris* (1987), pp. 313–35

JENNY ALBANI

Neagle, John (*b* Boston, MA, 4 Nov 1796; *d* Philadelphia, PA, 17 Sept 1865). American painter. He spent most of his life in Philadelphia, where he received his first art instruction from his schoolfriend Edward F. Peticolas and more formal training from the drawing-master Pietro Ancora. About 1813 Neagle was apprenticed to the sign and coach decorator Thomas Wilson who introduced him to the painters Bass Otis (1784–1861) and Thomas Sully, both of whom encouraged the young artist.

In 1818 Neagle set up as a portrait painter in Philadelphia. After brief spells in Lexington, KY (where he was awed by the quality of Matthew Harris Jouett's work), and in New Orleans he returned to Philadelphia where he remained for the rest of his career. In July 1825 Neagle and the engraver James Barton Longacre (1794–1869) travelled to Boston to visit Gilbert Stuart, who offered criticism of one of Neagle's portraits, also sitting for his likeness (1825; Boston, MA, Athenaeum, on dep. Boston, MA, Mus. F.A.). Stuart's portrait style influenced Neagle throughout his career.

In the autumn of 1825 Neagle received a commission for his most famous painting, *Pat Lyon at the Forge* (1825–6; Boston, MA, Athenaeum). It was extraordinary for its time, as it showed the subject at work in his blacksmith's shop, in leather apron with shirt sleeves rolled above the elbows.

Early in 1826 Neagle received a commission for a series of portraits, depicting actors and actresses in costume, which were used as models for engravers. The engravings appeared as frontispieces in a series of stories, based on popular plays, entitled the *Acting American Theatre*. Upon satisfactory completion of the first eight portraits, Neagle was asked to paint more in New York. On 28 May 1826, in Philadelphia, he married Mary Chester Sully, niece and stepdaughter of Thomas Sully. During their honeymoon in New York, Neagle painted 24 portraits (most of the surviving canvases are at the Players' Club, New York), of which 16 were engraved and issued. Neagle and Sully dominated the art of portraiture in Philadelphia. When Sully increased his prices, he always informed Neagle, who then adjusted his, but never higher than those of his mentor.

Neagle was a founder-member of the Artists' Fund Society of Philadelphia and its president from 1835 to 1843. In 1830–31 he was a director of the Pennsylvania Academy of the Fine Arts. About 1853 Neagle suffered an attack of paralysis, which severely affected his technique. Much of his autograph material, including his daybook, is in the manuscript collection of the Historical Society of Pennsylvania, Philadelphia.

BIBLIOGRAPHY
Exhibition of Portraits by John Neagle (exh. cat., ed. M. Fielding; Philadelphia, PA Acad. F.A., 1925)
M. Lynch: 'John Neagle's Diary', *A. America*, xxxvii (1929), pp. 79–99

MONROE H. FABIAN

Nea Nikomedia. Site of Neolithic settlement of the 7th millennium BC, on the Macedonian plain west of the River Vardar-Axios, Greece. The site comprises a low settlement mound that yielded a wide range of craft products (including painted pottery and anthropomorphic figurines) and timber-framed buildings, including a shrine. It was partially excavated from 1961–3 by Robert Rodden, and the material recovered is in the Archaeological Museum, Veria. The low but extensive mound had two main levels from early in the north Greek Neolithic sequence, and a much later Neolithic phase; of these, the early phases, equivalent to the 'Proto-Sesklo' phase of Thessaly to the south, are the most significant.

The hand-formed pottery included simple bowls, ring-footed bowls, globular vessels and *askoi* (spouted pouring vessels); some examples were decorated with red paint on a white slip, or occasionally with white paint on a red ground or slip. The accomplished, mainly geometric, designs employed included zigzags, chevrons, triangles and lozenges. Fired clay anthropomorphic figurines were in the general Balkan tradition of the time. One notable complete female figurine, 175 mm high, has bulbous legs, a narrow waist and broad shoulders, with raised, folded arms and the hands resting on small breasts. The head is a tall, rod-like cylinder with a pinched nose and eyes delineated by incised slits; the legs, torso and head were modelled separately and then pegged together before drying. Other cylindrical forms are pierced at the top and have an encircling incised line; these have been interpreted as phallic representations. Stamps with individual geometric designs were also made from fired clay. Stone was skilfully worked into small axes, studs and plugs, which may have been decorative; a few stylized creatures, probably frogs or toads, were made from serpentine. Simple square and rectangular timber-framed buildings were constructed; clay house models from other northern Greek sites suggest that these would have had pitched roofs (*see* PREHISTORIC EUROPE, fig. 15). In one phase six smaller buildings surrounded a structure measuring *c.* 10 m square, with two internal partitions. Since this building also contained five female figurines of the type described above and three serpentine toads, it has been interpreted as a special structure, possibly a shrine.

BIBLIOGRAPHY
R. Rodden: 'Excavations at the Early Neolithic site of Nea Nikomedeia, Greek Macedonia', *Proc. Prehist. Soc.*, xxviii (1962), pp. 267–88
——: 'An Early Neolithic Village in Greece', *Sci. Amer.*, ccxii (1965), pp. 82–92
J. Nandris: 'The Development and Relationships of the Earlier Greek Neolithic', *Man*, v (1970), pp. 191–213
D. Theocharis: *Neolithic Greece* (Athens, 1973)
M. Gimbutas: *The Goddesses and Gods of Old Europe* (London, 1982)

ALASDAIR WHITTLE

Nea Paphos. See PAPHOS, NEW.

Neapolis (i). Site of the capital of the Scythian kingdom in the Crimea on a plateau on the outskirts of modern Symferopol' in Ukraine. Archaeological investigations began in the 19th century, but they were conducted intensively from the 1940s to 1960s. The city was founded in the late 4th century BC, reaching its zenith in the 2nd century BC under the rulers Skiluros and Palakos. Neapolis maintained close contact with the Greeks in the cities on the north coast of the Black Sea whose culture strongly influenced the Scythians; Greeks also formed part of the city's population. In the 3rd century AD Neapolis was destroyed by the Goths. Excavations have uncovered underground dwellings, grain storage pits, large houses with three chambers, public and religious buildings, the city square with a grand porticoed building, and a massive defensive wall with towers and gateways. Other finds are reliefs in stone of King Skiluros and Palakos (a joint portrait) and of the young Palakos on horseback, fragments of sculpture, Greek inscriptions and a variety of household objects of both Greek and local provenance. Outside the town walls lay a necropolis. Noteworthy are the rock-cut burial vaults with wall paintings, one of which (1st–2nd century AD) portrays a Scythian with a lyre, a horseman, a boar hunt and a carpet with a chequered pattern of yellow, black and red squares. There is also a stone mausoleum with 72 richly furnished tombs (2nd century BC–2nd century AD) probably belonging to members of the royal dynasty. Horse skeletons, weapons and a mass of ornaments, including gold rings and earrings, were found in the burial chamber.

BIBLIOGRAPHY
P. N. Schul'ts: *Mavzolei Neapolya skifskogo* (Moscow, 1953)

YA. V. DOMANSKY

Neapolis (ii). *See under* NAPLES, §I, 1.

Nearchos Painter. *See* VASE PAINTERS, §II.

Nebbia, Cesare (*b* Orvieto, *c.* 1536; *d* Orvieto, 1614). Italian painter and draughtsman. He was a pupil of GIROLAMO MUZIANO and much influenced by Federico Zuccaro, and Vasari cited him as a promising painter. Between 1562 and 1575 Nebbia was continuously employed in Orvieto, producing altarpieces and frescoes in the cathedral, for example the *Marriage at Cana* (1569), the *Crucifixion* (1574) and the *Crowning with Thorns* (1575; all Orvieto, Mus. Opera Duomo). In Rome, where from 1579 his name appeared in the register of the Accademia di S Luca, he executed an *Ecce homo* and another *Crowning with Thorns* (1576; oratory of the Gonfalone), a *Noli me tangere* (1579; S Maria degli Angeli), decorations in the Sforza Chapel, S Maria Maggiore (1582), *Heraclius Taking the Cross* (1582–4; Santissimo Crocifisso), the *Martyrdom of St Lawrence* (1589; S Susanna) and decorations in the Borghese Chapel, Trinità dei Monti (*c.* 1590). Under Pope Sixtus V he was responsible, with Giovanni Guerra, for the decorations in the Sistine Library, and he also worked on the Scala Santa, in the Vatican Palace and in the Lateran Palace. In 1597 he was principal of the Accademia di S Luca. Two years later he received payment for the cartoons of *St Matthew* and *St Mark* for the mosaics in the cupola of St Peter's. The following year he painted the *Dream of Constantine* (S Giovanni in Laterano). In 1603–4 he decorated, with Zuccaro, the hall in the Collegio Borromeo, Pavia. He retired to Orvieto in 1609. His works are executed in pale colours, and the Mannerist compositions, complex, but unoriginal and filled with stiff, heavy draperies, show the influence of Muziano and Zuccaro, the former at the beginning and again towards the end of his career. A prolific artist, Nebbia was a typical interpreter of the age of the Counter-Reformation in Rome.

BIBLIOGRAPHY

Thieme–Becker

G. Baglione: *Le vite de' pittori, scultori et architetti* (1642); ed. V. Mariani (1925), pp. 116–17

U. Procacci: 'Una *Vita* inedita del Muziano', *A. Ven.*, viii (1954), pp. 249–64

A. Peroni: 'Il Collegio Borromeo: Architettura e decorazione', *I quattro secoli del Collegio Borromeo di Pavia* (Pavia, 1961)

J. Hess: 'Some Notes on Paintings in the Vatican Library', *Kunstgeschichtliche Studien zu Renaissance und Barock* (1967), pp. 163–79

R. E. Mack: 'Girolamo Muziano and Cesare Nebbia at Orvieto', *A. Bull.*, lvi/3 (1974), pp. 410–13

A. Satolli: 'La pittura dell'eccellenza: Prolegomeni ad uno studio su Cesare Nebbia nel suo tempo', *Boll. Ist. Stor. A. Orviet.*, xxxvi (1980), pp. 17–222

M. C. Abromson: *Painting in Rome during the Papacy of Clement VIII (1592–1605): A Documented Study* (New York, 1981)

Oltre Raffaello: Aspetti della cultura figurativa del '500 romano (exh. cat., ed. L. Cassanelli and S. Rossi; Rome, Villa Giula; and elsewhere; 1984), pp. 162–4 [entries by A. Vannugli]

A. Zuccari: *I pittori di Sisto V* (Rome, 1992)

Roma di Sisto V (exh. cat., ed. M. L. Madonna; Rome, Pal. Venezia, 1993) [exh. pamphlet & subsequent book]

R. Eitel Porter and A. Satolli: 'Cesare Nebbia's Work for the Palazzo Simoncelli: Drawings and Frescoes', *Burl. Mag.*, cxxxvi (1994), pp. 433–8

R. Eitel Porter: 'Cesare Nebbia at the Vatican, the "Sale dei Foconi" ', *Apollo* (Nov. 1995), pp. 19–24 [bibliog.]

——: *Das graphische Oeuvre des Cesare Nebbia* (diss., U. Vienna, in preparation)

ANTONIO VANNUGLI

Nebmaatre. *See* AMENOPHIS III.

Nebot, Balthasar (*fl* 1730–65). English painter, possibly of Spanish origin. Apart from his marriage in London in the late 1720s, no details of his life are known, although a number of signed and dated works survive. He is best known for two remarkable series of garden views, the earlier being a set of eight of the *Gardens of Hartwell House, Bucks*, one of them dated 1732 and another dated 1738 (all Aylesbury, Bucks Co. Mus.). The later series exists in more than one set and depicts the *Gardens of Studley Royal* and *Fountains Abbey, Yorks* (e.g. four sold at Christie's, 11 April 1980, lot 92, one signed and dated 1762). There are also several signed and dated examples of his *Covent Garden Market* (version, 1735; Woburn Abbey, Beds; version, 1737; London, Tate). Nebot also painted small genre scenes on copper and one signed and dated portrait of *Thomas Coram* (1741; London, Foundling Hosp.).

BIBLIOGRAPHY

Waterhouse: *18th C.*

C. H. Collins Baker: 'Nebot and Boitard: Notes on Two Early Topographical Painters', *Connoisseur*, lxxv (1926), pp. 3–6

E. K. Waterhouse: *Painting in Britain, 1530 to 1790*, Pelican Hist. A. (London, 1953, rev.4/1978), p. 162

J. Harris: *The Artist and the Country House* (London, 1979)

Manners and Morals: Hogarth and British Painting, 1700–1760 (exh. cat. by E. Einberg, London, Tate, 1988), pp. 106–7, 116, 245

RICHARD JEFFREE

Nebridio da Cremona, Frate (*fl* 1463; *d* before 1503). Italian illuminator and painter. In 1463 he wrote to the Duke of Milan's agent in Cremona requesting consideration for a commission to paint an altarpiece for a memorial altar erected in S Agostino, Cremona; this would suggest that he was a painter as well as an illuminator. In 1503, in a payment made to his nephew Marchino for the illumination of a Gradual, Nebridio is referred to as deceased. Two signed illuminations survive: a cutting in Bologna with a representation of *St Augustine* (Bologna, Mus. Civ., Palagi, no. 130) and another showing the *Resurrection* (Cambridge, MA, Fogg, MS. 1916.28). On the Bolognese cutting, Nebridio identifies himself on a scroll as a 'son of the saint', that is, an Augustinian. His style displays a density of decoration characterized by courtliness and elegance and shows the survival of Late Gothic influences in Cremonese art. Levi d'Ancona detected a reflection of the style of Bonifacio Bembo and of the later work of Belbello da Pavia in Nebridio's illuminations and suggested a Venetian connection between Nebridio and Belbello, an idea that was rejected by Bandera. A number of works have been attributed to Nebridio, including a Breviary dated 1467 (Rome, Bib. Casanatense, B.VI.5, MS. 1182), another in Oxford (Oxford, Bodleian Lib., MS. Can.Lit.368), an Antiphonal completed before 1480 (Cremona, Mus. Civ. Ponzone, Cod. IX) and the Mainardi Missal, illuminated after 1491 (Cremona, Bib. Stat. & Lib. Civ., MS. 188).

BIBLIOGRAPHY

M. Levi d'Ancona: 'Frate Nebridio: Il maestro del messale Mainardi', *A. Lombarda*, vii/2 (1963), pp. 87–92

S. Bandera: 'Persistenze tardogotiche a Cremona: Frate Nebridio e altri episodi', *Paragone*, 323 (1977), pp. 34–72

CHARLES M. ROSENBERG

Neck amphora. Ancient pottery form, used as a storage jar (*see* GREECE, ANCIENT, figs 71(i)d, 95 and 98).

Necker, Jost de. *See* NEGKER, JOST DE.

Necking. *See under* CINCTURE.

Necropolis [Gr. *nekropolis*: 'city of the dead']. Type of large cemetery. Although the term is used loosely of concentrations of burials, especially in the ancient world, in its strictest sense the tombs are architectural structures laid out in streets. Such arrangements were especially prevalent in ancient Egypt, owing to the importance there of providing a suitable setting for eternal life after death; they were laid out to the west of every settlement (i.e. the direction of the setting sun) and away from the Nile flood plain (as dry conditions were required to preserve the bodies). Royal tombs were located in separate areas away from the tombs of the general populace. Major necropoleis were at ABYDOS and near the cities of HERMOPOLIS MAGNA, MEMPHIS and THEBES (i). The Etruscan civilization is also characterized by necropoleis, such as the Banditaccia necropolis (7th–5th century BC; for illustration *see* CERVETERI) and the Crocefisso del Tufo necropolis (*see* ORVIETO, fig. 1).

For further information and bibliography *see* EGYPT, ANCIENT, §VIII, 2(ii) and ETRUSCAN, §II, 1.

Nedeham [Nedam], **James** (*fl* 1514; *d* Boulogne-sur-Mer, 22 Sept 1544). English architect. A carpenter by training, he was made a freeman of the London Carpenters Company in 1514 and was engaged in military works in Calais in 1522–3. Subsequently he worked for Cardinal Wolsey before entering the service of Henry VIII. In 1531 he was appointed Master Carpenter of the King's Works but in the following year was promoted to Surveyor of the Works. He was the first building craftsman to hold the post, all his predecessors having been administrative clerks. Unlike them Nedeham had a technical knowledge of architecture, and the records show that he drew 'platts' (plans) and made moulds for the direction of the masons. The royal works for which he was responsible included the roof of the Great Hall (1532–4; *see* HAMPTON COURT PALACE, fig. 2) at Hampton Court Palace, the Jewel House in the Tower of London (1535–6), the fitting up of St Augustine's Abbey, Canterbury, for the accommodation of Anne of Cleves (1539; destr.) and the conversion of monastic buildings at Dartford and Rochester in Kent into royal houses (1539–42; destr.). The great hammer-beam roof at Hampton Court, Gothic in structure but with Italianate embellishments, is his principal surviving work. In 1544 he took part in the King's French campaign and died at Boulogne-sur-Mer.

See also LONDON, §V, 4.

BIBLIOGRAPHY
Harvey
H. M. Colvin, ed.: *History of the King's Works*, iii–iv (London, 1975–82)

HOWARD COLVIN

Needham, (Noel) Joseph (Terence Montgomery) (*b* London, 9 Dec 1900; *d* Cambridge, 24 March 1995). English historian and scientist. He is best known for his magisterial work, *Science and Civilisation in China* (1954–), left incomplete at his death. He was the only child of a physician and was educated at Oundle School and Caius College, Cambridge, where he studied physiology and biochemistry, gaining his degree in 1922. He was elected a fellow of Caius College in 1924, and in 1933 he was named Sir William Dunn Reader in biochemistry, specializing in embryology. His interests, however, soon extended beyond the laboratory to the history and philosophy of science, politics and economics. During the 1930s he became interested in the civilization of China, teaching himself Chinese. In 1942 he led a scientific mission to China and remained for four years as scientific adviser to the British Embassy. In 1943 he became a foreign member of the Academia Sinica and received the Chinese Order of the Brilliant Star (Jing xing da yuan zhang). After World War II he was named the first Director of the Natural Sciences Department of UNESCO. He resigned in 1948 to return to Cambridge and resume his post in biochemistry, although his attention was largely devoted to *Science and Civilisation in China*, a systematic and comprehensive survey of traditional Chinese culture and its contributions to science. The six volumes published in his lifetime covered such diverse topics as astronomy and the instruments used in observing the heavens, civil and military engineering, the invention of paper and printing, textile technology and the working of gold. In 1971 he was elected a Fellow of the British Academy, an unusual

honour for a scientist, and in 1972 he became president of the International Union of the History and Philosophy of Science. His first wife, Dorothy Moyle (*d* 1987), was also a scientist, as was his second, Lu Gwei-Djen (*d* 1991).

WRITINGS
with others: *Science and Civilisation in China* (Cambridge, 1954–)
The Development of Iron and Steel Technology in China (London, 1958/R Cambridge, 1964)
with Wang Ling and D. J. de Solla Price: *Heavenly Clockwork: The Great Astronomical Clocks of Medieval China* (Cambridge, 1960, rev. 2/1986)
C. A. Ronan, ed.: *The Shorter Science and Civilisation in China* (Cambridge, 1978)
Science in Traditional China: A Historical Perspective (Cambridge, MA, 1981)
The Hall of Heavenly Records: Korean Astronomical Instruments and Clocks, 1380–1780 (Cambridge, 1986)

BIBLIOGRAPHY
Obituary, *The Times* (27 March 1995)

□

Neef, Sebastien de. *See* NEVE, SEBASTIEN DE.

Neeffs [Neefs], **Jacob** [Jacques] (*b* Antwerp, 3 June 1610; *d* Antwerp, after 1660). Flemish etcher and engraver. He may have been apprenticed to Marinus Robyn van der Goes. In 1632–3 Neeffs became a master; in 1644 he took on Jacob van de Velde (*fl* 1632–44) as a pupil and in 1660 Emmanuel van Winghen (*fl* 1674–97). Neeffs was a follower of Rubens, one of the last to work under the master himself. He made an engraving (Hollstein, no. 20) after Rubens's *Martyrdom of St Thomas* (1637; Prague, N. Mus., Šternberk Pal.) and an etching (Hollstein, no. 29) after the *Farm of Laken* (*c*. 1618; London, Buckingham Pal., Royal Col.). Neeffs contributed to van Dyck's *Iconography* (*c*. 1632–44); he etched the title-page, finished van Dyck's *Self-portrait* (Hollstein, no. 76), added burin-work to the portrait of *Frans Snyders* (Hollstein, no. 91), whose face had been etched by van Dyck himself, and engraved the portrait of *Antonius de Tassis*. Neeffs's oeuvre includes many reproductive prints after Gerard Seghers and Philip Fruytiers, as well as Annibale Carracci, Abraham van Diepenbeeck, van Dyck, Jacob Jordaens and Theodoor van Thulden.

Between 1635 and 1659 Jacob Neeffs illustrated some ten books, mainly published in Antwerp and Leuven (e.g. Guilielmus Becanus's *Serenissimi Principis Ferdinandi Hispaniarum Infantis S.R.E. Cardinalis triumphalis introitus in Flandriae metropolium Gandavum* (Antwerp, Johannes Meursius, 1636); Jan Ciermans's *Disciplinae mathematicae traditae anno institutae Societatis Jesu seculari* (Leuven, Evrard de Witte, 1640). Neeffs was also co-publisher of the *Studium seraphicum Sacri Ordinis Franciscani* (Antwerp, Willem Lesteens, 1643), for which he made engravings after van Thulden. For the *Marques d'honneur de la maison de Tassis* (Antwerp, Officina Plantiniana, 1643) Neeffs collaborated with Matheus Borrekens (*c*. 1615–70), Cornelis Galle (ii), Wenceslaus Hollar, Pieter de Jode, Theodor van Merlen, Michel Natalis and Paulus Pontius.

BIBLIOGRAPHY
BNB; Hollstein: *Dut. & Flem.*
Rubens in der Grafik (exh. cat., ed. K. Renger and G. Unverfehrt; U. Göttingen, Kunstsamml., 1977), p. 71

CHRISTIAN COPPENS

Neefs [Neeffs]. Flemish family of artists. All three members of the family, (1) Pieter Neefs (i) and his sons (2) Ludovicus Neefs and (3) Pieter Neefs (ii), specialized in paintings of architectural interiors. Their most frequent subject was the interior of Antwerp Cathedral; the details of sculpture, altars and paintings vary in accuracy, and sometimes the subject seems to be very freely interpreted. The Neefs also liked to depict the effects of artificial illumination in crypt-like spaces (in the manner of Hendrick van Steenwijck the younger). Iconographic and stylistic similarities make the works of Pieter (i) and Pieter (ii) often difficult to distinguish. On a few occasions the father signed his works DEN AUDEN NEEFS. Generally speaking, those works dated before c. 1640 (when Pieter (ii) would have become involved in the workshop) are superior in quality. It is also possible that works attributed to either Pieter (i) or Pieter (ii) are, in fact, by Ludovicus, the least-known member of the family. The figures in the architectural views by the various Neefs were painted by such artists as Frans Francken II and Frans Francken III, Jan Breughel I, Sebastiaen Vrancx, Adriaen van Stalbemt, David Teniers (ii), Gonzales Coques and Bonaventura Peeters.

(1) Pieter Neefs (i) (*b* Antwerp, ?1578; *d* Antwerp, 1656–61). Painter and draughtsman. It has been suggested that he was born just after his elder brothers, who were born in 1576 and 1577 in Antwerp, where the family lived. Pieter was probably taught by Hendrick van Steenwijk the elder or younger; the latter's influence is evident in his work. The earliest record of Pieter Neefs (i) is a signed and dated painting of the *Interior of a Gothic Church* (1605; Dresden, Gemäldegal. Alte Meister). In 1609–10 Pieter was enrolled as a master in the Guild of St Luke in Antwerp, and on 30 April 1612 he married Maria Lauterbeens (*d* 1655–6), with whom he had five children. In 1636 he painted an *Interior of St Paul's, Antwerp* (Amsterdam, Rijksmus.). His paintings have a delicate tonality with a softness in the transitions between light and shade. He is known to have been alive on 26 February 1656, but, in the *Gulden cabinet* of 1661, Cornelis de Bie wrote about Pieter in the past tense.

(2) Ludovicus Neefs (*b* Antwerp, 22 Jan 1617; *d* Antwerp, ?1649). Painter, son of (1) Pieter Neefs (i). Of the few known paintings by him, one (Madrid, Prado) is signed and dated *F. L. Neefs 1646* and another (Dresden, Gemäldegal. Alte Meister) *Frater Ludovicus Neefs An. 1649*. The word *Frater* before the artist's name suggests that he was a monk. In the monastery of St Augustine in Antwerp a monk of this name was recorded as having died on 17 November 1649 'at the age of 26'. Since the son of Pieter Neefs (i) would have been 32 years old in 1649, it is not certain whether he can be identified with that Augustine friar (though it is possible that an error was made in the record).

(3) Pieter Neefs (ii) (*b* Antwerp, 23 May 1620; *d* Antwerp, after 1675). Painter, son of (1) Pieter Neefs (i). By 1640 he was collaborating with his father and was never apparently enrolled as an independent master in the Guild of St Luke. He was still active in 1675, the year that

appears on his last known dated painting (Vaduz, Samml. Liechtenstein).

BIBLIOGRAPHY

Verzameling der Graf- en Gedenkschriften van de Provincie Antwerpen, Arrond. Antwerpen, IV: Antwerpen—Abdijen en Kloosters [Collection of epitaphs and memoirs from the Province of Antwerp, District of Antwerp, IV: Antwerp—Abbeys and Monasteries], i (Antwerp, 1859), pp. 257, 275

F. J. Van den Branden: *Geschiedenis der Antwerpsche schilderschool*, ii (Antwerp, 1883), pp. 126–32

H. Jantzen: *Das niederländische Architekturbild* (Leipzig, 1910)

W. Stechow: 'The *Cathedral at Bonn*: A Drawing by Pieter Neefs the Elder', *A.Q.* [Detroit], xvii (1954), pp. 286–90

G. Martin: *The Flemish School*, London, N.G. cat. (London, 1970), pp. 98–103

Flemish Drawings of the Seventeenth Century from the Collection of Frits Lugt, Institut Néerlandais, Paris (exh. cat., London, V&A; Paris, Fond. Custodia, Inst. Néer.; Bonn, Stadt. Kstmus.; Brussels, Bib. Royale Albert Ier; 1972), pp. 76–7, no. 57

C. Lawrence: '*Interior of Antwerp Cathedral* by Pieter Neeffs I', *Perceptions*, ii (1982), pp. 17–21

FRANS BAUDOUIN

Neel, Alice (Hartley) (*b* Merion Square, PA, 28 Jan 1900; *d* New York, 13 Oct 1984). American painter and printmaker. She graduated from the Philadelphia School of Design for Women in 1925 and settled in New York with her husband, the Cuban artist Carlos Enríquez. After the death of their first daughter from diphtheria and the break-up of the marriage, Neel suffered a nervous breakdown, and her career was not fully launched until the 1930s. She was supported by the Public Works of Art Project (PWAP) (*see* UNITED STATES OF AMERICA, §XII) in 1933 and from 1935 until the early 1940s by the Works Progress Administration (WPA), but there was little critical or financial support for her work until the 1960s. Although she never remarried, she had two sons by different fathers; she often painted them and, eventually, their wives and children.

Alice Neel stubbornly pursued a career as a figurative painter when trends and tastes favoured abstraction. She painted still-lifes, landscapes and genre scenes, but her favourite subject-matter was people—members of her own family, friends, acquaintances and even those strangers whose appearance and character intrigued her. Working directly on the canvas and rarely giving her surfaces a completely finished look, Neel used expressive distortion, a brilliant colour sense and inventive compositions to record the physiognomy and body language of her subjects. Because they were not commissioned portraits, Neel was free to express her own views about the sitter, many of whom were poor or in situations of stress, for example *T. B. Harlem* (1940; Washington, DC, N. Mus. Women A.), which shows a man recovering from an operation.

Neel's vividly characterized portraits of New York artists and intellectuals such as *Robert Smithson* (1962; priv. col., see 1979 exh. cat., no. 6), *Andy Warhol* (1970; New York, Whitney) and *Henry Geldzahler* (1967; New York, MOMA) finally brought her fiercely idiosyncratic style to the attention of a wider public. The success of Pop art and Photorealism in the 1960s and 1970s also made Neel's work more acceptable. A small retrospective at the Whitney Museum in 1974 led to other exhibitions and national awards in the last decade of her life. She was a marvellous public speaker, as unconventional and pungent with words as she was with paint, and spoke more eloquently about her paintings than most of her critics.

Neel sold little of her work because her sitters could rarely afford to buy their own portraits, and few collectors found her strongly characterized images of unknown people appealing. Thus she still owned most of her work at her death. It constitutes both the personal biography of an artist with a voracious curiosity about people and a moving record of American character in the 20th century.

BIBLIOGRAPHY
Alice Neel (exh. cat. by E. Solomon, New York, Whitney, 1974)
Alice Neel: The Woman and her Work (exh. cat., essay by C. Nemser; Athens, U. GA Mus. A., 1975)
A. Sutherland Harris and L. Nochlin: *Women Artists, 1550–1950* (New York, 1977), pp. 323–4
Alice Neel (exh. cat. by H. Hope, Fort Lauderdale, FL, Mus. A., 1978)
E. Munro: *Originals: American Women Artists* (New York, 1979)
P. Hills, ed.: *Alice Neel* (New York, 1983) [extensive transcripts of the artist's own comments on her life and work]
Alice Neel (exh. cat. by A. Sutherland Harris, Los Angeles, CA, Loyola Marymount U., A.G., 1983)

ANN SUTHERLAND HARRIS

Neel, (George) Edric (*b* 20 April 1914; *d* Bournemouth, 8 April 1952). English architect. He studied at the Cambridge School of Architecture (BA, 1931; MA, 1938), before working with Wells Coates and then with Denys Lasdun and Patrick Gwynne before World War II. In the early war years he experimented for the Cement and Concrete Association, chiefly in Coventry, on designs for rational, practicable prototypes for housing. In 1943 Neel formed the Arcon Group with Rodney Thomas and Raglan Squire (*b* 1912). A new kind of research unit sponsored by a few manufacturers, Arcon aimed to improve the poor links between British industry and architecture. A. M. Gear joined in 1948, and the group continued in existence until 1967. Its greatest success was the Arcon Mark V temporary prefabricated house, containing *c.* 2500 components. This modest-looking dwelling, assiduously developed and refined by Neel and his colleagues, made other British prefabricated house-types of the time seem amateurish and inept. Between 1945 and 1948, 41,000 examples were erected. The group continued with its research and development projects on materials and techniques, producing many designs for building-types, especially for tropical countries, but it never designed buildings to individual commissions. After Neel's death the group never recaptured the high reputation it had enjoyed under his leadership. He was one of the most dedicated and consistently rational of the British designers who endeavoured to reconcile architecture with industrial production during and after World War II.

BIBLIOGRAPHY
Obituary, *Builder*, clxxxii/5696 (1952), p. 584
The Arcon Group, 1943–67 (London, 1967) [A. M. Gear and Associates' rep.]
R. Squire: *Portrait of an Architect* (London, 1984)

Neeld, Joseph (*b* 13 Jan 1789; *d* London, 24 March 1856). English politician, collector and patron. He was educated at Harrow School and had a long parliamentary career. He embodied the traditional patrician virtues of landowning patrons. On inheriting £900,000 from his maternal great uncle, Phillip Rundell, a goldsmith, he bought Grittleton House in Wiltshire, which he had designed in a Romanesque style by James Thomson (1800–83). Thomson also designed other buildings for Neeld in Wiltshire at Leigh Delamere, Alderton and Chippenham. Neeld bought numerous paintings, particularly to decorate the great staircase hall at Grittleton. He was chiefly interested in British painting and sculpture and owned works by such artists as Constable, William Etty, Gainsborough, John Gibson (i), Benjamin West, Richard Wilson and others.

BIBLIOGRAPHY
Obituary, *Gent. Mag.*, i (1856), pp. 527–8
Obituary, *The Times* (26 March 1856)
T. S. R. Boase: *English Art, 1800–1870*, Oxford Hist. Eng. A., x (Oxford, 1959), p. 5

JULIAN SHEATHER

Neer, van der. Dutch family of painters. The artists include (1) Aert van der Neer, a landscape painter, and his two eldest sons, (2) Eglon (Hendrick) van der Neer, known for his Dutch genres and Johannes [Jan] van der Neer (1637/8–65), a landscape painter who appears to have imitated his father's work. Johannes was also listed in Amsterdam, along with Aert van der Neer, as a *wyntapper* (tavernkeeper). None of his paintings is known for certain.

(1) Aert [Aernout] **van der Neer** (*b* Amsterdam, ?1603–4; *d* Amsterdam, 9 Nov 1677). Although generally known by the name of Aert, he usually signed himself Aernout. According to Houbraken, van der Neer spent his youth in Arkel near Gorinchem (Gorkum), a town on the river Waal, east of Dordrecht, where he worked as a *majoor* (steward) for the lords of Arkel. He became an amateur painter, possibly as a result of his contact with the Camphuyzen brothers Rafael Govertsz. (1597/8–1657) and Jochem Govertsz. (1601/2–59). Aert married Lysbeth Govertsdr (Liedtke) who was almost certainly Rafael and Jochem's sister. Rafael acted as witness at the baptism of their daughter Cornelia in 1642. Around 1632 van der Neer and his wife moved to Amsterdam where, in about 1634, their eldest son, (2) Eglon, was born.

Aert's earliest-known painting is a genre scene dated 1632 (Prague, N.G. Šternberk Pal.) in the style of Pieter Quast. Dated the following year is a landscape (Amsterdam, P. de Boer; see Bachmann, 1982, fig. 2), signed jointly by van der Neer and Jochem Camphuyzen. Aert's earliest independent landscapes, exemplified by *River Landscape with Riders* (1635; Cologne, Gal. Edel), have a strong stylistic link with the Camphuyzens, particularly Rafael, and also show the influence of Alexander Keirincx, Gillis d'Hondecoeter (for example the *Country Road*, Amsterdam, Rijksmus.) and Roelandt Savery, all artists from the Frankenthal school who took the idiom of Flemish landscape painting, particularly the tradition of Gillis van Coninxloo, to the Netherlands. This is evident in van der Neer's representation of trees with thick gnarled trunks and heavy foliation, particularly close to those in Hondecoeter's oeuvre. Even in some of his later paintings, such as *Winter Landscape* (1643; Great Britain, priv. col.; see 1986 exh. cat., no. 110) and *View of a River in Winter* (Amsterdam, Rijksmus.), van der Neer continued to use a number of Flemish devices, among them the placement of isolated figures on meandering paths or frozen rivers and the use of trees to close off one side of the composition. His views of skaters on frozen waterways are also Flemish in origin, reminiscent of Hendrick Avercamp's renderings of the same subject, painted some 50 years earlier in the tradition of Pieter Bruegel the elder. The restricted palette of earthy colours in some of van der Neer's paintings of the early 1640s suggests another source of inspiration: that of the Haarlem 'tonal' phase of landscape painting, developed during the 1620s and 1630s by Jan van Goyen, Salomon van Ruysdael and Pieter de Molijn (for example *Landscape with Duck Shooting*, 1642; Frankfurt am Main, Städel. Kstinst.).

By the mid-1640s Aert had established his own style and begun to specialize in a small number of subjects: winter scenes, exemplified by *Frozen Canal* (Worcester, MA, A. Mus.) and a *Frozen River by a Town at Evening* (London, N.G., 969); snow storms, typified by *Winter Scene* (London, Wallace); and nocturnes, especially moonlit river views, represented by *Landscape in Moonlight* (The Hague, Mauritshuis). He also produced many sunrises and sunsets, particularly the latter, including *Landscape with a River at Evening* (London, N.G., 2283). His landscapes have certain characteristic features: they are viewed from a slightly raised vantage-point and often incorporate a river or path that stretches (often to a small bank) right across the composition before receding into the background. Frequently small figures animate the foreground and middle distance; the far bank of the river is often broken by the irregular silhouette of a townscape, and trees typically frame one side of the picture. Although most of van der Neer's landscapes are imaginary, a few contain recognizable buildings or topographical details, which suggest his familiarity with a particular location; for example, the ruins of Kostverloren, a castle on the bank of the Amstel, feature in *Moonlit Landscape with Castle* (1646; Jerusalem, Israel Mus.).

Perhaps van der Neer's greatest contribution to Dutch landscape painting was his ability to represent light, often subdued by heavy cloud formations or by the descending darkness of evening, through the use of subtle tonal changes, creating a sense of space and atmosphere. In his *Views of a River in Winter* (1655–60; Amsterdam, Rijksmus.), for example, he accurately captured the nature of northern light in winter. There is an emphasis on cool blue hues, alleviated in places by warmer touches of reds describing clothing and buildings. A bleaker winter atmosphere is conveyed in a *Frozen River by a Town at Evening* (London, N.G., 969), where grey and brown tones prevail. His nocturnes of the 1640s and 1650s provide further examples of this ability to capture the quality of light. In a *River near a Town by Moonlight* (London, N.G., 239) local colour is almost totally eliminated and replaced by a monochromatic build-up of browns, dull greens and pale greys, with touches of silver to represent the moonlight illuminating the clouds and reflecting on the water.

It is generally agreed that van der Neer's greatest work was produced from the mid-1640s until *c.* 1660. In 1659 and 1662 he is documented as having been the keeper of a tavern on the Kalverstraat (Bachmann, 1982, p. 10) with his son Johannes. On 12 December 1662 he was declared bankrupt; his property, including his paintings, was appraised and the latter considered to be of little value. Aert, however, continued to paint, residing in a state of extreme poverty on the Kerkstraat, near the Leidsegracht, until his death.

BIBLIOGRAPHY
A. Houbraken: *De groote schouburgh* (1718–21/*R* 1976), iii, p. 172
C. Hofstede de Groot: *Holländischen Maler* (1907–28), vii, pp. 283–8
A. Bredius: 'Waar is Aermont van de Neer begraven?', *Oud-Holland*, xxxix (1921), p. 114
N. Maclaren: *The Dutch School*, London, N.G. cat. (London, 1960), pp. 260–65
F. Bachmann: *Die Landschaften des Aert van der Neer* (Neustadt, 1966)
W. Stechow: *Dutch Landscape Painting of the Seventeenth Century* (London, 1966/*R* New York, 1980), pp. 96–8, 176–82
F. Bachmann: 'Die Brüder Rafael und Jochem Camphuysen und ihr Verhältnis zu Aert van der Neer', *Oud-Holland*, lxxxv (1970), pp. 243–50
——: *Art van der Neer als Zeichner* (Neustadt, 1972)
——: 'Die Herkunft der Frühwerke des Aert van der Neer', *Oud-Holland*, lxxxix (1975), pp. 213–22
F. Duparc: *Mauritshuis Hollandse schilderkunst: Landschappen in de 17de eeuw* (The Hague, 1980), pp. 60–64
G. Bachmann: *Aert van der Neer, 1603/4–1677* (Bremen, 1982)
M. Zeldenrust: 'Aert van der Neer's *Rivier landschap bij maanlicht opgheldered*', *Bull. Rijksmus.*, xxxi (1983), pp. 99–104
W. Liedtke: 'Aert van der Neer: *A Canal with a Footbridge by Moonlight*', *Liechtenstein: The Princely Collections* (exh. cat., ed. J. O'Neill; New York, Met., 1985), pp. 255–6
Dutch Landscape: The Early Years (exh. cat., ed. C. Brown; London, N.G., 1986), pp. 222–3
Masters of 17th-century Dutch Landscape Painting (exh. cat., ed. P. Sutton; Amsterdam, Rijksmus.; Boston, MA, Mus. F.A.; Philadelphia, PA, Mus. A.; 1987), pp. 39–41, 381–6

L. B. L. HARWOOD

(2) Eglon (Hendrick) van der Neer (*b* Amsterdam, *c.* 1634; *d* Düsseldorf, 3 May 1703). Son of (1) Aert van der Neer. His birth date is based on Houbraken's statement that the artist was 70 years old when he died. He apparently studied first with his father and then with the genre and history painter Jacob van Loo. According to Houbraken, van der Neer was in France *c.* 1654, where he served as painter to the Counts of Dona, Dutch governors of the principality of Orange. He returned to Holland by 1659 and is recorded as a resident of Amsterdam at the time of his marriage to Maria van Wagensvelt in Rotterdam on 20 February 1659. The couple had 16 children.

By 1664 van der Neer had moved to Rotterdam, where he remained until 1679. During that time he made numerous trips to Amsterdam and to The Hague, where he joined the painters' confraternity Pictura in 1670. Adriaen van der Werff became his apprentice in Rotterdam *c.* 1671–6. Van der Neer's wife died in 1677, and two years later he moved to Brussels where he remained until 1689. In 1681 he married the miniature painter Marie du Chatel (*d* 1697), daughter of the Flemish genre painter François du Chatel (1625–94); this second marriage produced nine children.

After *c.* 1685 van der Neer's career was dominated by his service as painter to various noble courts. Possibly because of the esteem accorded an earlier portrait of *Marie Anne, Wife of Charles II of Spain* (Speyer, Hist. Mus. Pfalz), van der Neer was offered a position as court painter to Charles II in 1687. Apparently he never went to Spain (he is recorded in Amsterdam in 1689), but in 1696 and again in 1699 John William, the Elector Palatine, interceded on the artist's behalf in an attempt to obtain overdue payments from the Spanish court. In 1690 van der Neer accepted a position as court painter to John William and moved to the court at Düsseldorf in that year. After his second wife's death in 1697, he married Adriana Spilberg (*b* 1652), an accomplished portrait painter and daughter of Johann Spilberg II, his predecessor at the Düsseldorf court.

Van der Neer's mature works consistently display the smooth, seemingly brushless technique characteristic of the school of LEIDEN 'FINE' PAINTERS. An early series of single three-quarter-length female figures, such as *Girl Holding a Letter* (*c.* 1650; Amsterdam, Rijksmus.), is thematically indebted to works by Gerard ter Borch (ii), but the precise, shimmering execution is derived from Gerrit Dou and more importantly Frans van Mieris (i), who painted a similar series of female figures in about 1663 (*Woman with a Parrot*; London, N.G.). Van der Neer's elegant ladies are shown reading (1665; New York, Met.), drawing (London, Wallace), proffering food (1665; Vaduz, Samml. Liechtenstein) or playing musical instruments (*Woman Playing the Mandolin*; Copenhagen, Stat. Mus. Kst.); all activities are performed with polite gentility. Van der Neer revived this compositional type in a series of lute players from the 1670s (e.g. *Woman Tuning a Lute*; 1678; Munich, Alte Pin.), though these later paintings place greater emphasis on the figure's sculptural qualities.

Van der Neer is one of the few artists of the late 17th century who continued to incorporate symbolic meaning into his genre paintings. They are, however, updated and given a sophisticated veneer with the introduction of stylish 'French' costume and architecture. For example, a moralizing message has been proposed for the *Lady Washing her Hands* (1675; The Hague, Mauritshuis; see fig.), in which an elegant lady washes her hands in the basin held for her by a page. The ewer and basin, long interpreted as symbols of purity, signify the lady's virtuous detachment from the brothel scene in the background. The expression of a moralizing theme through the juxta-position of virtue and vice is traditional, but the fashionable dress of the lady and her page, as well as the elegant classical architecture of the interior, clearly reflect the decorative and material preferences of the late 17th-century northern Netherlands.

Similarly, van der Neer's portraits correspond to the material aspirations of his sitters. The soberly dressed pair in *Couple in an Interior* (*c.* 1665–70; Boston, Mus. F.A.) smugly complement the understated elegance of the interior. An unusual feature of this portrait is the resplendent life-sized painting of a nude Venus over the chimneypiece.

Van der Neer began working on history paintings in the 1670s. *Judith* (London, N.G.) is related to his lute players, which also focus on a single figure set close to the picture plane; the resemblance is heightened by the fact that Judith is clothed in contemporary 'allegorical' dress. His depiction of the unusual biblical subject of *Gyges and the Wife of Candaules* (*c.* 1675–80; Düsseldorf, Kstmus.) is also set in an elegant contemporary interior.

The first of van der Neer's numerous representations of *Tobias and the Angel* (1685; Berlin, Gemäldegal.), which places large-scale figures in a landscape setting, marks the beginning of his gradual shift towards landscape painting.

Eglon van der Neer: *Lady Washing her Hands*, oil on panel, 490×395 mm, 1675 (The Hague, Koninklijk Kabinet van Schilderijen 'Mauritshuis')

A later version of the same subject (1690; Amsterdam, Rijksmus.) shows the figures much reduced in scale, and the primary focus of the composition is transferred to the landscape itself. Curiously, van der Neer's landscapes show little evidence of his early training with his father and instead signal a nostalgic return to landscape styles of nearly a century earlier. With their densely wooded hills and lush, meticulously sculpted foliage, they are personal interpretations of the extraordinarily detailed and highly prized landscapes of Adam Elsheimer. Van der Neer's exacting and refined technique enabled him to re-create the exquisite enamel-like character of Elsheimer's landscapes, and these works only enhanced the reputation he had originally established as a figure painter. Cosimo III de' Medici, Grand Duke of Tuscany, commissioned a *Self-portrait* of van der Neer late in the artist's career (Florence, Uffizi), which was to show him working on or holding 'some small work with figures'. It is significant that van der Neer chose a landscape rather than a genre painting for this honoured setting.

BIBLIOGRAPHY
A. Houbraken: *De groote schouburgh* (1718–21/*R* 1976), iii, pp. 172–5
C. Hofstede de Groot: *Holländischen Maler* (1907–28), v, pp. 505–62
H. Gerson: *Ausbreitung und Nachwirkung der holländischen Malerei des 17. Jahrhunderts* (Haarlem, 1942/*R* 1983)
Masters of Seventeenth-century Dutch Genre Painting (exh. cat., ed. P. Sutton; Philadelphia, Mus. A.; W. Berlin, Gemäldegal.; London, RA; 1984), pp. 269–71
De Hollandse fijnschilders: Van Gerard Don tot Adriaen van der Werff (exh. cat. by Peter Hecht, Amsterdam, Rijksmus., 1989), pp. 130–54

MARJORIE E. WIESEMAN

Nef. Vessel in the form of a ship used at the dining-table. Its earliest-known use, recorded in 12th-century France, was probably as a drinking vessel. By the 15th century it was performing several functions: as a receptacle for salt, goblets, napkins, eating utensils or perhaps meat. It became an elaborate, sometimes mechanical, table ornament, with the early simple boat shape superseded in the 16th century by fully and accurately rigged ships, often peopled with tiny figures (e.g. the Burghley Nef, *c.* 1527; London, V&A; *see* FRANCE, fig. 74).

Nefs were executed in gold, silver or silver gilt enriched with enamel and gemstones. The hulls were made of rock crystal, hardstones or nautilus shell. Nefs were, therefore, valued and precious objects that were paraded at feasts in most of the courts of Europe and were given as presents by royalty and aristocracy. They were popular throughout the 16th century, but by the 17th century their artistic importance had declined. They were, however, still produced in Germany, where they enjoyed a brief period of popularity in the 19th century.

BIBLIOGRAPHY
C. Oman: *Medieval Silver Nefs* (London, 1963)
F. Robin: 'Le Luxe de la table dans les cours princières', *Gaz. B.-A.*, 6th ser., lxxxvi (1975), pp. 1–16

Nefertari (*fl c.* 1270 BC). Egyptian queen of the 19th Dynasty. Nefertari was the Great Royal Wife of Ramesses II (*reg c.* 1279–*c.* 1213 BC) during at least the first half of his reign. By far the most prominent of the royal spouses of this king, she is well attested in both Egyptian and cuneiform texts and is represented on numerous royal monuments throughout Egypt and Nubia. At ABU SIMBEL, her slim figure, clad in flowing linen garments and crowned with tall plumes flanked by graceful bovine horns, is ubiquitous in both the Great Temple and the Small Temple—which was dedicated to her in association with the Goddess Hathor of Ibshek (Abu Simbel). She was only the second royal spouse to be so honoured. Her predecessor in this respect, Queen Tiye, was a Great Wife of Amenophis III (*reg c.* 1390–*c.* 1353 BC), whom Ramesses II often emulated in other contexts. The bovine horns, in the sculptures of Nefertari at Abu Simbel, are probably associated with the Goddess Isis-Sothis. Nefertari is depicted with an almost identical crown in her tomb at Thebes, but the horns are conspicuously absent, since she is shown in the guise of Osiris. Her sumptuously decorated tomb (QV 66) is the largest and best known in the Valley of the Queens. Virtually the entire complex, composed of two major chambers (each with subsidiary apartments) linked by a north–south descending corridor, was embellished with painted reliefs carved into a thick plaster coating, which masked the poor quality of the native rock. Despite the precarious state of its preservation (already evident at its discovery in 1904) the tomb decoration is distinguished by a lavish (but not garish) use of colour, fine quality of linework and extensive use of shading effects—the last seen most clearly on the face of the queen, her pleated garments and flowing sashes. The iconography includes extracts from the Egyptian Book of the Dead and scenes of the Queen offering to numerous divinities. The tomb exhibits stylistic affinities with monuments of

Sethos I (*reg c.* 1290–*c.* 1279 BC) in addition to those of Ramesses II.

BIBLIOGRAPHY
LÄ: 'Nofretere'
E. Schiaparelli: *Relazione sui lavori della missione archeologica italiana in Egitto (anni 1903–1920): Esplorazione della 'Valle delle Regine'* (Turin, 1924)
C. Desroches Noblecourt and C. Kuentz: *Le Petit Temple d'Abu Simbel*, 2 vols (Cairo, 1968)
G. Thausing and H. Goedicke: *Nofretari: Eine Dokumentation der Wandgemälde ihres Grabes* (Graz, 1971)

C. A. KELLER

Nefertiti (*reg c.* 1353–*c.* 1336 BC). Egyptian queen, principal wife of AKHENATEN. Throughout Akhenaten's reign only Nefertiti was afforded the status of Great Royal Wife, enjoying privileges never bestowed on the spouse of any other Egyptian king before or since. She was the mother of six daughters. The date of her death and the location of her tomb are unknown.

Reliefs, paintings and statuary depict Nefertiti as often as her husband, and during the first years of his reign she was shown with the same physiognomy, characterized by enormous swelling thighs. Later, a distinctive portrait type was created for her, different from Akhenaten's but, like his, subject to stylistic evolution. The famous painted limestone bust of Nefertiti (Berlin, Ägyp. Mus., 21300; see fig.), which typifies the Queen's portrait type, retains some elements of the early style, while an unfinished brown quartzite head (Cairo, Egyp. Mus., JE 59286) is rendered in the later softened, 'idealizing' style. In early representations she wears either a tripartite or a 'Nubian' wig, crowned with an elaborate headdress, but in later images this is replaced by the tall, cylindrical blue crown seen in the Berlin bust.

The painted reliefs, mainly sandstone, of Akhenaten's first five regnal years are almost exlusively from Thebes (e.g. Luxor Mus., J. 205-211). In them, Nefertiti is shown worshipping the sun god Aten with her husband, riding with him in a chariot between their palace and the temple or attending on him in domestic scenes, all themes that became more prominent in monuments at the later capital of Akhetaten (el-Amarna). Yet another tableau first documented at Thebes, showing the King and Queen bestowing rewards on loyal followers (see RAMOSE, TOMB OF), later became ubiquitous at Akhetaten. However, representations of Nefertiti officiating in the sun cult alone, known from the decoration of monumental piers, are unique to Thebes. A life-size statue head (Hamburg, Mus. Kst & Gew., 1966.96) that shows Nefertiti wearing a characteristic double uraeus probably dates from this Theban phase, when she was also sometimes depicted as a sphinx.

At el-Amarna, alabaster and painted limestone reliefs of Nefertiti were found on the walls of temples, palaces and private dwellings, on royal and private stelae and in the tombs of courtiers, as well as in the royal tomb. In addition to the iconography established during the Theban years, further domestic themes are shown, such as the royal family at table. The representations in a suite of rooms in the royal tomb depicting Akhenaten and Nefertiti mourning the death of their second daughter Meketaten are unique. Nefertiti is also the only Egyptian queen shown in the pose of dispatching an enemy, a motif otherwise

Queen Nefertiti, painted limestone, h. 500 mm, from the studio of the sculptor Thutmose at Tell el-Amarna, h. 0.50 m, 18th Dynasty, c. 1340 BC (Berlin, Ägyptisches Museum)

C. Traunecker: 'Aménophis IV et Néfertiti: Le Couple royal d'après les talatates du IXe pylône de Karnak', *Bull. Soc. Fr. Egyp.*, cvii (1986), pp. 17–44
R. Krauss: '1913–1988: 75 Jahre der Büste der Nofretete/Nefertiti in Berlin I', *Jb. Preuss. Kulthes.*, xxiv (1987), pp. 87–124
C. Aldred: *Akhenaten: King of Egypt* (London, 1988)
M. Muller: *Die Kunst Amenophis' III und Echnatons* (Basle, 1988)
R. Krauss: 'Nofretete: Eine Schönheit vom Reissbrett?', *Mus. J.: Ber. Mus.*, v/2 (3 April 1989), pp. 25–7
E. R. Russmann: *Egyptian Sculpture in the Cairo and Luxor Museums* (Austin, TX, 1989), pp. 112–23

R. KRAUSS

Negker [Denecker; Dienecker; Necker], **Jost** [Jobst] **de** (*b* Antwerp, *c.* 1485; *d* Augsburg, *c.* 1544). Flemish draughtsman, designer of woodcuts and engraver, active in Germany. His earliest dated print was published in 1508 in Leiden, where he seems to have had ties, since he was later involved in the production of book illustrations there. The same year, he appears to have established himself in Augsburg, where he produced many outstanding woodcuts for the workshop of Emperor Maximilian I; several of his woodblocks survive (e.g. the *Triumph of Emperor Maximilian I*, 1508; B. 32, after Hans Burgkmair I). According to Bénézit, de Negker invented the chiaroscuro woodcut technique (*see* WOODCUT, CHIAROSCURO, §2). He also contributed to the development of multicolour printing. De Negker also executed engravings after Dürer, Holbein, Lucas van Leyden and others.

BIBLIOGRAPHY
Bénézit; Hollstein: *Dut. & Flem.*; Hollstein: *Ger.*; Thieme–Becker
A. von Bartsch: *Le Peintre-graveur* (1803–21) [B.]

JETTY E. VAN DER STERRE

Nègre, Charles (*b* Grasse, 9 May 1820; *d* Grasse, 16 Jan 1880). French photographer and painter. He trained as a painter with Paul Delaroche, Michel-Martin Drolling and Ingres, and he began an honourable career exhibiting regularly at the Salon from 1843 to 1853 with genre and historical scenes such as the *Death of Abel* (exh. 1852; untraced). He took up photography in 1844, initially as an aid to painting. In 1852 he set off to photograph the monuments of southern France. He brought back 100 calotypes (architecture, landscape and genre scenes), some of which were published by Goupil with a text as *Le Midi de la France* (1854–5), and he then took photographs of Notre-Dame in Paris (1853) and Chartres Cathedral (1854–5). These were printed by heliogravure, a technique he perfected for the Duc de Luynes competition for a photographic printing technology (1856), for which he won second prize and was much praised. In 1858 Nègre was commissioned by Napoleon III to report on the home for convalescent workers in Vincennes. He produced glass negatives of architectural views and scenes from the inmates' daily lives.

In these series and in many other works Nègre experimented with a variety of genres. As an architectural photographer he developed a way of seeing that combined the objective and the picturesque. In his uncluttered approach he played with relief and texture to animate a surface, as in *Postern of the Abbey of Montmajour* (1852), with contrasts of form and with shadow throwing into relief the geometry of a building. The modernity of his vision also derives from his framing: he cut the façade of

exclusively reserved for the king. Statuary depicting Nefertiti was set up in association with the boundary stelae that defined the limits of Akhetaten and in the precinct of the Great Temple there. The house of the sculptor THUTMOSE yielded several representations of the Queen, among them a virtually intact statue, one quarter life-size (Berlin, Ägyp. Mus., 21263), which may show her pregnant. Several heads intended for composite statues of Nefertiti are also known, and two plaster masks from the same house have been assigned to her. Small-scale works include a painted limestone dyad of the royal couple (Paris, Louvre) and a triad that adds a daughter to the group (London, U. Coll. Petrie Mus.). Like those of her husband, images of Nefertiti were attacked as part of the *damnatio memoriae* in the post-Amarna period.

BIBLIOGRAPHY
L. Borchardt: *Porträts der Königin Nofret-ete* (Leipzig, 1923)
Akhenaten and Nefertiti (exh. cat. by C. Aldred, New York, Brooklyn Mus., 1973)
R. W. Smith and D. B. Redford: *The Akhenaten Temple Project I: Initial Discoveries* (Warminster, 1976)
M. Eaton-Krauss: 'Miscellanea amarnensia', *Chron. Egypte*, lvi (1981), pp. 245–64

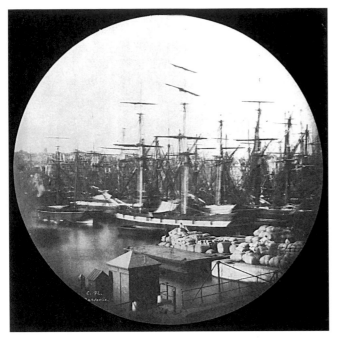

Charles Nègre: *Entrance to the Port of Marseille*, salted paper print on paper, diam. 160 mm, 1852 (Ottawa, National Gallery of Canada)

Chartres Cathedral, for example, in order to include the steps in the image of the *South Portico*. Sometimes he used light in order to create a lyrical atmosphere, as in *East Gallery of the Cloister of St Trophime d'Arles* (1852).

In Nègre's landscapes the geometric rigour of certain compositions sometimes comes close to Synthetism, as in *Entrance to the Port of Marseille* (1852; see fig.), even bordering on abstraction. Like Gustave Le Gray and Henri le Secq, Nègre was also interested in the vibrations of light through foliage (e.g. *Forest of Le Muy*, 1852). In numerous genre scenes he conveyed the animation of Paris by capturing people in the middle of their work under an intense light. He tried to fix movement by a combination of lenses or a subtly studied pose, as in his *Chimneysweeps Walking* (?1851; A. Jammes priv. col., see 1976 exh. cat., no. 29), aiming for the 'instantaneous' at a time of technical difficulty. Elsewhere, he focused on the picturesque qualities of the motif, on contrasts of light or on adventurous compositions.

As a portraitist Nègre created some astonishing images, in which the figure stands out against a rigorously constructed background (as in that of *Auguste Préault*, c. 1856; Paris, priv. col.). The intimist vision of the genre scenes recurs in certain images (such as a series of images of children in a park). Nègre also undertook commissioned portraits, in which he managed to remain personally engaged, concentrating on the model's psychology (as in the portrait of the actress *Rachel*, 1853; A. Jammes priv. col., see 1976 exh. cat., fig. 6) or on compositional effects (e.g. *Lord Brougham and his Family on the Terrace of the Villa Leader at Cannes*, 1862, see 1976 exh. cat., no. 185). Nègre always worked in a craftsmanlike way and produced some prints of a very high quality. In 1863 he went back

to live in the Midi for health reasons, practising only as a commercial seaside photographer.

PHOTOGRAPHIC PUBLICATIONS

Le Midi de la France: Sites et monuments historiques photographiés par Charles Nègre, peintre (Paris, 1854–5)

BIBLIOGRAPHY

A. Jammes: *Charles Nègre* (Paris, 1963)
Charles Nègre (exh. cat., text J. Borcoman; Ottawa, N.G., 1976)
Charles Nègre: Photographe (exh. cat., text F. Heilbrun; Arles, Mus. Réattu; Paris, Mus. Luxembourg; 1980–81)

HÉLÈNE BOCARD

Negreiros, Almada. *See* ALMADA NEGREIROS.

Negret, Edgar (*b* Popayán, 1920). Colombian sculptor. He studied at the Escuela de Bellas Artes in Cali (1938–43), with Jorge Oteiza in Popayán (1944–6) and at the Clay Club Sculpture Center in New York (1948–50). He began exhibiting his work during the 1940s, when it still showed traces of academicism and the influence of Rodin. He began to experiment with a variety of materials, including plaster, ceramics, iron and steel, and to investigate the possibility of developing an abstract sculptural language while maintaining clear links with reality. Such is the case with *Glass with a Flower* (steel, 350×200×200 mm, 1949; Popayán, Mus. Negret), in which the object identified by the title is 'drawn' in space as a metal line. After living in Paris (1950–52), then in Spain and from 1955 to 1963 in New York, he finally settled on aluminium as the most appropriate material. At first he cut out shapes from aluminium sheets, assembling them as interlocked forms in a single plane, as in *Equinox* (wood and polychromed aluminium, 1000×700×200 mm, 1957; Popayán, Mus. Negret). Soon he moved from such wall-hanging reliefs to free-standing sculptures made from modular elements; although these works are self-sufficient as abstract sculptures, they maintained links with identifiable subject-matter through the clues provided by their titles, such as *Kachina* (polychromed aluminium, 1300×220×220 mm, 1957; Popayán, Mus. Negret).

Negret made acute reference in his sculpture to both technology and nature, using a strict and measured sense of order. By painting the aluminium in red, blue, white or matt black, he toned down its metallic quality and gave the sculptures an illusion of lightness, so that they sometimes seem about to rise from the ground. The elements are fastened down, however, with clearly visible screws that draw attention to their structure and to the processes and tools used in their fabrication, as in *Coupling* (painted aluminium, 600×900×700 mm, 1972; Popayán, Mus. Negret), one of a later group of sculptures in which he curved the aluminium sheets into arched forms. Negret's sculptures, among the most innovative in post-war Latin American art, could be described as hybrids of natural forms and machinery, conveying the artist's view of existence as based at once on nature and on technology as a human product. The Museo Negret was established in Popayán in 1986 by the Colombian government as a permanent collection surveying Negret's development as a sculptor.

BIBLIOGRAPHY

Negret: Las etapas creativas (exh. cat. by G. Carbonell, Bogotá, Fond. Cult. Cafetero, 1976)

Edgar Negret (exh. cat., intro. A. Caicedo; Madrid, Mus. A. Contemp., 1983) [retro.]

J. H. Aguilar: 'Negret: La cultura del aislamiento', *Arte* [Bogotá], ii/3 (1987), pp. 40–53

EDUARDO SERRANO

Negretti. *See* PALMA.

Negroponte, Antonio da. *See* FALIER, ANTONIO.

Nehshāpūr. *See* NISHAPUR.

Neidhardt, Juraj (*b* Zagreb, 15 Oct 1901; *d* Sarajevo, 13 July 1979). Croatian architect, teacher, urban planner and writer. He studied architecture at the Akademie der Bildenden Künste, Vienna, under Peter Behrens and gained a diploma in 1924. From 1930 to 1932 he worked for Behrens in Berlin and between 1932 and 1936 was the only paid assistant in Le Corbusier's studio in Paris. During this time Neidhardt was involved in several major projects, including a department store in Alexanderplatz, Berlin. He also won second prize in a competition for the Yugoslav Pavilion at the Exposition Internationale des Arts et Techniques dans la Vie Moderne, Paris (1937). In 1937 he returned to Zagreb, where he designed and built the Theological School for the Zagreb Diocese. He then moved to Sarajevo and became a professor (1953) in the Architectural Faculty at the University of Sarajevo. Bosnian architecture and its regional characteristics preoccupied Neidhardt for the rest of his life. His principal works included low-cost housing estates, for example at Vares, Zenica and Ljubija, and, more prominently, the Philosophy Faculty (1955–9), the Institute of Physics and Chemistry (1959–64; both heavily damaged 1994) and the urban plan (1954) for the centre of Marindvor, all in Sarajevo. His buildings and major urban schemes were all concerned with the synthesis of traditional building elements and modern technological and artistic developments, with a strong emphasis on the integration of architecture with landscape.

WRITINGS

with D. Grabrijan: *Arhitektura Bosne i put u savremeno* [Architecture of Bosnia and towards the modern movement], intro. Le Corbusier (Sarajevo, 1957) [priv. edn]

BIBLIOGRAPHY

P. Tvrtković: 'Yugoslav Architecture Today', *Archit. Des.*, xxviii (1958), pp. 199–203

PAUL TVRTKOVIĆ

Neidhart, Wolfgang, II (*b* Ulm, *bapt* 18 Jan 1575; *d* Augsburg, 1632). German bronze-founder. He came of an old-established family of gun-founders. From 1596 to 1632 he was bronze-, gun- and bell-founder to the city of Augsburg, which in the years around 1600 was being splendidly decorated with monumental fountains and other urban ornaments in bronze. Most of these were executed while Neidhart was in charge of the foundry. Between 1597 and 1600 he cast the *Hercules* fountain and probably also the *Mercury* fountain by Adriaen de Vries. In 1603 the city commissioned from Hans Reichle a monumental group of the *Archangel Michael Vanquishing Satan* for the façade of the Zeughaus (*in situ*). Neidhart cast the main section in 1605/6 and the remaining figures between then and 1607. He undoubtedly also cast the figures for the rood altar attributed to Reichle in the church of SS Ulrich and Afra (erected 1605; *in situ*), while the eagle that Reichle sculpted for the Siegelhaus was cast in 1606. In 1620 Neidhart cast the city's coat of arms by Christoph Murmann (*c.* 1564–1630) over the entrance to the new Rathaus of Augsburg. Between 1620 and 1626 he cast 13 busts of emperors (by unknown sculptors) for the Lower Hall of the building.

In the case of the bronze works of Georg Petel, the only work of his that Neidhart is known to have cast is a coat of arms for Ottheinrich Fugger dating from 1630 (Kirchheim im Schwaben, Schloss Fugger). He is believed to have also cast the large Crucifix with a kneeling figure of *Mary Magdalene* in the Niedermünster in Regensburg and the executioners in a *Crucifixion* group (Berlin, Skulpgal.). Neidhart's work was continued by his sons, Wolfgang III (1597–1653) and Christoph.

BIBLIOGRAPHY

RDK; Thieme–Becker

A. Nägele: 'Fünf Generation einer schwäbischen Erzgiesserfamilie Neidhart', *Württemberg. Jb. Statistik & Landeskd.* (1914), pp. 112–37

——: 'Ein Augsburger Erzgiesser und seine Werke', *Christ. Kst.*, xi (1914–15), pp. 135–53, 168–82

K. Feuchtmayr and A. Schädler: *Georg Petel (1601/2–1634)* (Berlin, 1973), pp. 90, 111, 115–16, 140, 145, 199

H. Friedel: *Bronzebildmonumente in Augsburg, 1589–1606* (Augsburg, 1974), pp. 59, 72, 81, 88, 124

Elias Holl und das Augsburger Rathaus (exh. cat., ed. W. Baer, H. W. Kruft and B. Roeck; Augsburg, Rathaus, 1985), pp. 144–7, 262–4

DOROTHEA DIEMER

Neilson, Jacques (*b* London, 1714; *d* Paris, 3 March 1788). French weaver of English birth. He was the son of Jacques Neilson, a sea merchant of Scottish origin domiciled in London, and of Marie Maguiel. He moved to France at an early age and initially resided with his uncle Gilbert Neilson, a Paris surgeon, in the Rue Dauphine, later inheriting his estate (1761).

With the support of Louis-Antoine de Pardaillon de Gondrin, Duc d'Antin, Directeur of the Bâtiments du Roi, Neilson joined the Gobelins (*see* GOBELINS, §2) in April 1728, where he concentrated on the high-warp weaving technique in the workshop of Jean Jans the younger. In 1743 he left the Gobelins to devote himself to painting, and he worked in the studios of Charles-Antoine Coypel, Charles Parrocel and Maurice-Quentin de La Tour. In August 1749 Neilson returned to the Gobelins as director of one of the two low-warp workshops. In 1751 the two low-warp workshops were amalgamated under the sole direction of Neilson, who then applied himself to perfecting the low-warp technique (for further discussion of high-warp and low-warp techniques *see* TAPESTRY, §I). From 1750 he had begun to practise a technique in which the outlines of the designs were traced on to strips of wax-paper that were then placed underneath the warp, enabling tapestries to be produced from the original designs. This was a method of avoiding the inversion of design that normally occurred in the low-warp technique. The technique was perfected by Neilson by 1756 and introduced to the Louvre in Coypel's studio and, notably, in the presence of Jean-Baptiste Oudry. Another highly significant advantage resulting from this technique was the lack of deterioration of the design cartoons, which had previously been cut into strips and placed underneath the warp. Henceforth the cartoons remained intact and could be kept alongside the weaver during the entire weaving process, thus allowing constant verification of the design.

Thanks to these improvements, which were officially recognized by Abel-François Poisson de Vandières, Marquis de Marigny, in a certificate dated 23 December 1760, citing the progress made in Neilson's workshop, Marigny authorized in 1761 the execution, in the low-warp technique, of four works from the *Story of Esther* series of wall hangings, completed in 1765, after Jean-François de Troy, for the London residence of Lord Foley. Neilson, an entrepreneur, had succeeded in developing the sale of tapestries to England and wished to establish trade in France. There were objections to this, and the undeniable success of Neilson gave rise to a certain envy on the part of high-warp weavers who went to the extent of reproaching him for what they called his 'British haughtiness'.

Towards the end of his life, Neilson took pleasure in recalling that tapestries produced in his low-warp workshop, as perfect as those woven in the high-warp workshops, had been presented to the kings of Denmark and Sweden, to the Emperor Joseph II and to the Comte and Comtesse du Nord (Paul Petrovich and Maria Feodorovna, the son and daughter-in-law of Catherine the Great) among others. Marigny himself had commissioned four sections of the *Loves of the Gods* series of wall hangings after Boucher (e.g. *Eros and Psyche*, *c.* 1770; Paris, Louvre), Carle van Loo, Jean-Baptiste Pierre and Joseph-Marie Vien, the production of which was successfully entrusted to both the high-warp and low-warp workshops. Neilson also produced tapestries for upholstered armchairs, sofas and screens. Some of these were woven from designs by Maurice Jacques and were highly successful.

Although Neilson claimed to have invented a 'new loom operated by a bascule mechanism', which facilitated weaving by enabling the loom to be placed in a vertical position, Jacques-Germain Soufflot, who was in charge of the Gobelins from 1756 to 1776, maintained that the idea had been perfected by Neilson with the collaboration of Jacques Vaucanson (1709–82) in 1756. Nevertheless, Neilson was the inventor of the *vautoir*, a type of comb that guaranteed an even distribution of the warp over the rollers. In 1767 Neilson secured the reopening of the Séminaire des Gobelins for training purposes.

In 1769 the dye workshop at the Gobelins was placed under the authority of Audran, Pierre-François Cozette and Neilson. Audran and Cozette, specialists in the high-warp weaving technique, resigned in 1773, and as Neilson had studied the problems connected with dyeing since 1736, he remained the sole director until 1783. In June 1773 Neilson had managed to obtain the post of low-warp weaver for his son Daniel-Marie Neilson (*d* 1799), who was an efficient assistant and had carried out research in the dye workshop in collaboration with his father. Jacques Neilson carried out significant experiments with dyes, which were recorded from 1773 to 1779.

BIBLIOGRAPHY
A. Curmer: *Notice sur Jacques Neilson entrepreneur et directeur des teintures de la Manufacture royale des tapisseries des Gobelins au XVIIIe siècle* (Paris, 1878)
M. Fenaille: *Etat général des tapisseries de la Manufacture des Gobelins depuis son origine jusqu'à nos jours 1600–1900*, 4 vols (Paris, 1903–23)
J. Mondain-Monval: *Correspondance de Soufflot avec les directeurs des Bâtiments concernant la Manufacture des Gobelins 1756–1780* (Paris, 1918)

CHANTAL GASTINEL-COURAL

Neithardt, Matthis Gothardt-. *See* GRÜNEWALD, MATTHIAS.

Neizvestny, Ernst (*b* Sverdlovsk [now Yekaterinburg], 9 April 1925). Russian sculptor. After serving as a volunteer in World War II, he enrolled at the Art Institute in Riga before studying sculpture at the Surikov Institute in Moscow, graduating in 1954. Often regarded as one of the first dissidents in the culture of the post-Stalinist period (a contemporary of Yevgeny Yevtushenko and Andrey Voznesensky), Neizvestny achieved immediate notoriety at the exhibition held at the Manezh, Central Exhibition Hall in Moscow in 1962 to mark the 30th anniversary of the Moscow section of the Artists' Union. It was here that Neizvestny argued with Nikita Khrushchov over the 'ugliness' of his sculptures—a confrontation that, paradoxically, later evolved into a friendship (Neizvestny's design for Khrushchov's tomb was erected in the Novodevichy Cemetery in 1974).

Partly as a result of this protection, Neizvestny received a number of official commissions beginning in the mid-1960s, such as the monument to the children of the world at the Artek Pioneer Camp in the Crimea (1966), illustrations to an edition of Dostoyevsky's *Prestupleniye i nakazanie* (Crime and Punishment; 1971) and the large decorative relief for the Institute of Electronics in Moscow in 1974. Even so, the intense, tormented images of Neizvestny's sculptures often evoked official displeasure. Refusing to abide by the canons of academic art and Socialist Realism, Neizvestny experimented with many styles—Cubism, abstract art and Expressionism—and sent works to Western exhibitions (e.g. drawings and sculptures to the Grosvenor Gallery, London, in 1964, 1965 and 1968; and to the Galerie Gmurzynska, Cologne, in 1970). In 1976 he emigrated, settling in New York in 1977.

Neizvestny achieved an international reputation as a sculptor who both continued the traditions of the Russian monumental style (Sergey Konyonkov was one of his teachers in Moscow) and reacted against it, often imbuing his works with metaphysical and occult dimensions. He assimilated many influences, including Michelangelo, Egyptian art (Neizvestny designed a monument for the Aswan Dam in 1969), Picasso and the philosophy of Dostoevsky. From the 1950s Neizvestny concentrated on preparatory work for the *Tree of Life*, a monumental mixed-media work that would incorporate sculpture, painting, light and ritual, which would rise above the skyline of a city. Many of Neizvestny's sculptures of heads and groups in marble and other stone, together with his acrylic sketches, can be regarded as studies for this work.

PUBLISHED WRITINGS
O sinteze v iskusstve [On synthesis in art] (Ann Arbor, 1982)
Govorit Neizvestny [Neizvestny speaks] (Frankfurt, 1984)

BIBLIOGRAPHY
J. Berger: *Art and Revolution: Ernst Neizvestny and the Role of the Artist in the USSR* (London, 1969)
M. De Micheli: *Ernst Neizvestny* (Milan, 1978)
E. Egeland: *Ernst Neizvestny* (Oakville, Ont., 1984)

JOHN E. BOWLT

Nejeloff. *See* NEYELOV.

Nekheb. *See* KAB, EL-.

Nekhen. *See* HIERAKONPOLIS.

Nel Gómez, Pedro (*b* Anori, Antioquia, 1899; *d* Medellín, 1984). Colombian painter, watercolourist, draughtsman, sculptor and printmaker. He studied engineering and architecture, both of which later influenced the conception of space in his paintings. From 1925 he travelled around Europe, settling until 1931 in Florence, where he was influenced in his choice of medium and style by Renaissance frescoes. The ascendancy at that time of the Mexican muralist movement also affected his decision to work on a large scale and to concentrate on subjects related to Colombian traditions. The murals that he produced on public buildings on his return to Colombia represented aspects of the daily life of his fellow countrymen.

In spite of the fact that there was a general move in Latin American painting to affirm national cultural values, Nel Gómez, because of his links with Mexican muralism, was criticized in some quarters for not giving priority to pictorial values. Nevertheless as a teacher he exerted a considerable influence on the nationalist spirit of younger artists such as Carlos Correa and Débora Arango. He also produced oil paintings, sculptures, drawings, prints and especially watercolours; these generally depicted still-lifes, landscapes and nudes, executed in bright colours and powerful brushstrokes.

BIBLIOGRAPHY
C. Jiménez Gómez: *Pedro Nel Gómez* (Bogotá, 1981)
Cien años de arte colombiano (exh. cat. by E. Serrano, Bogotá, Mus. A. Mod., 1985)

EDUARDO SERRANO

Nelli (di Nello), Ottaviano (di Martino) (*b* Gubbio, *c.* 1370; *d* Gubbio, ?1444). Italian painter. His brother Tommaso and his father, Martino Nelli (or Melli), are both documented as painters. His grandfather Mello di Gubbio is undocumented but signed the *Virgin and Child in Glory* (Gubbio, Mus. Duomo), a panel previously attributed to Guiduccio Palmerucci (*fl* 1315–49). In 1403 Nelli signed a polyptych of the *Virgin and Child with Saints* (ex-S Agostino, Pietralunga; Perugia, G.N. Umbria), a work that shows the influence both of local stylistic traditions and of Orvietan painting. Later, Nelli was influenced by Sienese and Bolognese painters and, more importantly, by Lombard and Burgundian styles. He interpreted the decorative, Late Gothic style in a humorous and homely way, showing lively narrative treatment. His rustic figures are painted in bright colours but also have a certain elegance of line. These characteristics are evident in the fresco cycle of the *Life of the Virgin* (1410–20; Gubbio, S Francesco). He also painted a polyptych (dispersed) of a later date, probably for the same church. This once comprised the *Adoration of the Magi* (Worcester, MA, A. Mus.), *St Jerome* (Avignon, Mus. Petit Pal.), the *Circumcision* and the *Mystic Marriage of St Francis* (both Rome, Pin. Vaticana). As well as the important fresco cycle of the *Life of the Virgin*, dated 1424 and influenced by Gentile da Fabriano, in the chapel of the Palazzo Trinci at Foligno, Nelli executed fresco cycles in Gubbio for S

Agostino and S Domenico, while in the Palazzo Beni, Gubbio, he frescoed a secular cycle, including personifications of the Virtues and Vices. Nelli is also recorded in the Romagna, at Assisi and Fano, and at Urbino, where he is first documented in 1417 and was evidently influenced by the Salimbeni brothers' frescoes in the oratory of S Giovanni Battista (completed 1416).

Fewer of Nelli's panel paintings survive. Two paintings of the *Madonna of Humility* (Hannover, Niedersächs. Landesmus.; Avignon, Mus. Petit Pal.) are both datable to the 1420s, and there are four panels in a private collection in Florence. A small panel of *St John the Baptist Rebuking Herod* (Florence, Fond. Longhi) is close in style to the Foligno frescoes.

BIBLIOGRAPHY
Bolaffi; Thieme–Becker
L. Bonfatti: *Memorie storiche di Ottaviano Nelli* (Gubbio, 1843)
F. Santi: 'Un capolavoro giovanile di Ottaviano Nelli', *A. Ant. & Mod.*, iii/12 (1960), pp. 373–84
R. Roli: 'Considerazioni sull'opera di Ottaviano Nelli', *A. Ant. & Mod.*, iv/13 (1961), pp. 114–24
L. Castelfranchi Vegas: *Il gotico internazionale in Italia* (Rome, 1966), p. 43
F. Rossi: 'Un ciclo d'affreschi allegorici di Ottaviano Nelli', *A. Ant. & Mod.*, ix/34 (1966), pp. 197–208
B. Berenson: *Central and North Italian Schools* (London, 1968), i, pp. 289–91; ii, pl. 511
B. Toscano: 'La pittura umbra del quattrocento', *La pittura italiana del quattrocento* (Milan, 1986), pp. 322–4
M. R. Silvestrelli: 'Nelli Ottaviano', *La pittura in Italia: Il quattrocento*, ii (Milan, 1987), p. 715
F. Todimi: *Le pitture umbre*, 2 vols (Milan, 1989)
A. De Marchi: *Gentile da Fabriano* (Milan, 1992), pp. 11–12, 116–17, 122–3, 130–33, 217

ENRICA NERI LUSANNA

Nelli, Suor Plautilla [Pulisena] (*b* Florence, 1523; *d* Florence, 7 May 1588). Italian painter. Daughter of a painter, Luca Nelli, she entered the convent of S Caterina di Siena in Florence in 1537. She studied painting with Fra Paolino, a pupil of Fra Bartolommeo, and executed works, including altarpieces, for her convent and outside patrons. In the *Last Supper* (Florence, S Maria Novella), executed from a cartoon by Agnolo Bronzino and reminiscent of Fra Bartolommeo's restrained early style, the still-life and the starched tablecloth are carefully observed. For the *Deposition* (Florence, Mus. S Marco), probably executed after a design by Andrea del Sarto, she was reputed to have used the corpse of a nun for the figure of Christ. The *Adoration of the Magi* (Parma, Gal. N.), her own composition, is again reminiscent of del Sarto with its graceful drapery and harmony of light and shade. Nelli's solemn and undramatic compositions had gone out of fashion by the mid-16th century. She inherited Fra Paolino's important collection of drawings by Fra Bartolommeo and is said to have trained other nuns in painting, including Agata Traballesi and Maria Ruggieri.

BIBLIOGRAPHY
Thieme–Becker
G. Vasari: *Vite* (1550, rev. 2/1568); ed. G. Milanesi (1878–85), v, pp. 79–80
G. Greer: *The Obstacle Race: The Fortunes of Women Painters and their Work* (London, 1979), pp. 185, 228

Nelme, Anthony (*fl* London, 1672–1722). English goldsmith. In 1672 he became an apprentice to Richard Rowley and in 1679 a freeman of the Goldsmiths' Company, London. In 1685 Nelme was recorded as a goldsmith at the Golden Bottle, Amen Corner, London, and in 1691 he opened another shop in Foster Lane. He was one of the most successful native English goldsmiths of the late 17th century and the early 18th and evidently ran a large workshop, producing a great variety of silverware ranging from such elaborate, ceremonial pieces as maces and pilgrim bottles to domestic and ecclesiastical wares. His earliest works are in the Restoration style prevalent from the 1660s (e.g. altar candlesticks, 1694; Windsor Castle, Berks, Royal Col.). Although his signature appears on a petition (1697; London, Goldsmiths' Co.) against admitting foreign goldsmiths to the freedom of the Goldsmiths' Company, much of his work from the beginning of the 18th century reflects Huguenot influence (e.g. pilgrim bottles, 1715; Chatsworth, Derbys). This indicates that he may have employed immigrant journeymen or purchased their work and overstruck it with his own mark. His best-known works, however, are the domestic wares in the austere Queen Anne style, characterized by simple, geometric forms often devoid of decoration, except for an engraved coat of arms (e.g. octagonal hot-water jug, 1713; Oxford, Ashmolean). His son Francis Nelme (*fl* 1719–39) became his partner in 1721 and took over the business in 1722.

BIBLIOGRAPHY

J. F. Hayward: *Huguenot Silver in England, 1688–1727* (London, 1959)

A. G. Grimwade: *London Goldsmiths, 1697–1837: Their Marks and Lives* (London, 1976, rev. 3/1990)

T. Schroder: *English Domestic Silver, 1500–1900* (London, 1988)

SARAH YATES

Nelson, George (*b* Hartford, CT, 29 May 1908; *d* New York, 5 March 1986). American designer, writer and architect. He studied at Yale University, New Haven, CT (BA, 1928; BFA, 1931), and at the Catholic University of America in Washington, DC (1932). Winning the Rome Prize in 1932, he was named a Fellow of the American Academy in Rome in 1934; while there he wrote 'Architects of Europe Today', published as 12 articles in *Pencil Points* in 1936–7, an early introduction of European architects to a wide American audience. From 1934 to 1949 he held a succession of editorial and management posts at *Architectural Forum* and had a major influence on the magazine's progressive point of view and its success with readers. From 1948 to 1975 he was editor of *Interiors* magazine. He also wrote *Industrial Architecture of Albert Kahn Inc.*, which in 1939 was an early recognition of Kahn's factories as architecture, and *Tomorrow's House* (1945), a plea for rationality and simplicity in domestic design. His later books include *How to See* (1977) and *George Nelson on Design* (1979).

As a designer, Nelson had a series of offices under various partnership names in New York from 1936. Their work included the Storagewall (1944–5), the prototype of the room dividers of the 1950s, as well as many other familiar furniture designs. He was also active as an exhibition designer, and, although not primarily an architect-builder, he designed some houses including the Fairchild house, New York (1940–41), with William Hamby (*b* 1902) and the Holiday house in Quoque, Long Island (1950), with Gordon Chadwick. In 1946 Nelson became design director for the Herman Miller furniture company,

and his own designs and his employment of other designers such as Charles Eames expanded a regional furniture manufacturer into an interiors firm of international influence. He was also an active lecturer as well as an organizer of the International Design Conference at Aspen, CO, from 1965.

WRITINGS

'Architects of Europe Today', *Pencil Points*, xvi (1935), pp. 4–12 [Marcello Piacentini]; pp. 54–62 [Helweg-Mœller]; pp. 129–36 [Wassili and Hans Luckhardt]; pp. 214–22 [Gio Ponti]; pp. 368–74 [Le Corbusier]; pp. 453–60 [Ludwig Mies van der Rohe]; pp. 556–66 [Ivar Tengbom]; xvii (1936), pp. 7–14 [Giuseppe Vaccaro]; pp. 128–36 [Eugène Beaudouin]; pp. 288–98 [Raymond McGrath]; pp. 422–32 [Walter Gropius]; pp. 527–40 [Tecton]

'Notes on the Monotype', *Pencil Points*, xviii (1937), pp. 785–92

Industrial Architecture of Albert Kahn Inc. (New York, 1939)

with Henry Wright: *Tomorrow's House* (New York, 1945)

How to See (Boston, 1977)

George Nelson on Design (New York, 1979)

BIBLIOGRAPHY

Contemp. Architects

P. Blake: 'Remembering George Nelson', *Interior Des.*, lvii (June 1986), pp. 302–3

R. Caplan: 'Circumstantial Evidence (What we Have Learned from George Nelson)', *Indust. Des.*, xxxiii (May–June 1986), pp. 15–16

JAMES D. KORNWOLF

Nelson, James. *See under* HOPKINS, LAWFORD & NELSON.

Nelson, Paul (Daniel) (*b* Chicago, IL, 8 Nov 1895; *d* Marseille, 30 Aug 1979). French architect of American birth. After studying literature at Princeton University, NJ, he joined the US Air Force in 1917. He fought in France, in Meuse and Argonne. He studied architecture at the Ecole des Beaux-Arts, Paris, in Emmanuel Pontrémoli's (1865–1956) studio in 1920, and then in 1924 in Auguste Perret's studio. Graduating in 1927, he opened a firm in Paris. His first project, the Brooks house at 80 Boulevard Arago, was greatly influenced by Perret. In 1929 in Hollywood he designed the modernist décor for the film *What a Widow* in which he showed the work of his friends Georges Braque, André Derain, Henri Laurens and Pablo Picasso. From 1930 he focused on the requirements of hospital architecture, in which he became a specialist of international renown. In unexecuted projects such as the 'Maison de Santé Minimum' (1930), 'Cité Hospitalière de Lille' (1932) and 'Pavillon de Chirurgie d'Ismailia' (1934) he developed a rationalist methodology that attempted to define form through a minute analysis of the building's needs. This culminated in such projects as the 'Maison Suspendue' (1936–8) and the 'Palais de la Découverte' (1938), which he designed in collaboration with Oscar Nitzchké (1900–91). The 'Maison Suspendue' comprised prefabricated units suspended in a steel cage. Nelson's primary concerns were with the changing functions of the building and the users' needs. From 1946 to 1956 Nelson built the hospital at Saint-Lô, Normandy, in which for the first time he used the oval operating theatres designed for Ismailia. From 1957 to 1960 he taught in the USA at various institutions. Back in France in 1960 he built various projects, among which were the compact hospital in Dinan, Brittany, built in tower form, with departments grouped round the lift shafts (1963) and the hospital complex at Arles (1965). He was appointed Professor at the Franco-American Studio of the Ecole des Beaux-Arts, Paris, in 1963 and at the International Studio of Luminy, Marseille, in 1967.

WRITINGS

La Cité hospitalière de Lille (Paris, 1932)
Deux études hospitalières (Paris, 1936)
La Maison suspendue (Paris, 1937)

BIBLIOGRAPHY

J. Abram: 'Paul Nelson 1895–1979', *Archit. Movt. Cont.*, xv (1987), pp. 81–95
J. Abram, K. Frampton, T. Riley: 'Paul Nelson', *Bull. Inst. Fr.-Amer..* (April 1989) [special issue]
J. Abram, T. Riley: *The Filter of Reason: The Work of Paul Nelson* (New York, 1990)

JOSEPH ABRAM

Nelson Tjakamarra [Jagamara; Jakamarra], **Michael** (*b* Pikilyi, N. Territory, ?1947–9). Australian Aboriginal painter. He was an initiated man of the Warlpiri tribe and one of the most articulate spokesmen of the Papunya Tula artists. Nelson studied at Yuendumu mission school, leaving at 13 after tribal initiation to work across the Territory in the cattle industry. After a period in the army he returned to his family at Yuendumu, then in 1976 married and moved to neighbouring Papunya. For seven years he observed the work of the older artists while working for the Papunya Council and occasionally assisting his uncle Jack Tjupurrula (*b c.* 1925) on his paintings before beginning to paint for himself in 1983. Nelson's bold designs, often incorporating several Dreaming stories on one canvas, with subtle infilling of multicoloured dots and with delicate brushwork, earned immediate attention. He won the National Aboriginal Art Award in 1984 and in 1985 produced the painting *Five Dreamings* (Melbourne, priv. col., see 1988–90 exh. cat., p. 103), which became one of the most reproduced works of Australian art of the 1980s. He exhibited in the Sydney Biennale of 1986. Two solo exhibitions in Melbourne followed, and he gained wider recognition when his design was selected for the mosaic (196 m×196 m) in the forecourt of Australia's new Parliament House in Canberra, and when he hand-painted an M3 race car (1989) in the BMW Art Car Project. He was custodian of the country around Mt Singleton, which accounts for the Possum, Snake, Two Kangaroos, Flying Ant and Yam Dreamings depicted in his paintings. In 1993 he was awarded the Australia Medal for services to Aboriginal art.

BIBLIOGRAPHY

Origins, Originality + Beyond (exh. cat., ed. N. Waterlow; Sydney, A.G. NSW, 1986), pp. 272–3
S. Nairne: *The State of the Art: Ideas & Images in the 1980s* (London, 1987), pp. 217–19
Dreamings: The Art of Aboriginal Australia (exh. cat., ed. P. Sutton; New York, Asia Soc. Gals; U. Chicago, Smart Mus.; Melbourne, Mus. Victoria; Adelaide, S. Austral. Mus.; 1988–90), pp. 102–5, 127–8, 139, 142, 239
Kunst am Automobil/Automobile Art, BMW Art Car Collection (Munich, 1991) [Eng. and Ger. text]
V. Johnson: *The Art of Michael Jagamara Nelson* (Sydney, 1995)

VIVIEN JOHNSON

Nemea. Site of the ancient Greek Nemean Games, 5 km from the modern village of Nemea and 30 km south-west of Corinth, Greece. The remains of the Temple of Zeus (*c.* 340–*c.* 320 BC) stand on the east bank of the River Nemea. Its architect is unknown, but Skopas has been suggested because of similarities between the temple and that of Athena Alea at Tegea, known to have been built by Skopas. Local marly limestone was the principal construction material while the sima was of marble, and there is evidence that marble tiles were used for the roof, with acroteria at the corners. This gleaming roof surmounted a peristyle coated with stucco to look like marble. It has six columns on the east and west façades and twelve along each flank; the Doric columns are extremely attenuated, like those of Pergamene architecture a century later. A ramp at the front leads to an altar 41 m long. The cella, on a raised stylobate, had a free-standing Corinthian colonnade along both side walls and across its west end. This was surmounted by Ionic half-columns attached to piers, with quarter-columns at the two ends. A sunken crypt that may have been used for oracular purposes lies in the adyton (inner chamber) behind the cella. There is no opisthodomos. Painted decoration, including a Doric frieze in red and blue, has been discovered. Enough of the pediment floor is preserved to show that it never had statuary. To the south-west are the foundations of other buildings of the 4th century BC: one (l. 85 m) probably served as a *xenon* (guest house) and another as a bathhouse. A Christian basilica was built over the west end of the *xenon* in the 5th century AD, using blocks from the temple.

BIBLIOGRAPHY

B. W. Hill, L. T. Lands and C. K. Williams: *The Temple of Zeus at Nemea* (Princeton, 1966)
F. A. Cooper, S. G. Miller and S. G. Miller: *The Temple of Zeus at Nemea: Perspectives and Prospects* (Athens, 1983)
A. Abraldes: 'The Temple of Zeus', *Nemea: A Guide to the Site and Museum*, ed. S. Miller (Berkeley, 1989)

FREDERICK COOPER

Nemerov, Diane. *See* ARBUS, DIANE.

Nemes [Nágel], **Endre** (*b* Pécsvárad, nr Pécs, 1909; *d* Stockholm, 22 Sept 1985). Swedish painter of Czech birth and Hungarian origin. He changed his surname from Nágel in 1928. Following his education in Slovakia and Budapest, he became a pupil of Willi Nowak (1886–1977) at the Academy of Fine Arts, Prague, from 1930 to 1935. He first exhibited in Prague in 1936, and he was a member of the avant-garde ARTISTIC FORUM. Forced to emigrate in 1938 he went to Helsinki, where he worked as a teacher for two years. In 1940 he moved to Norway, from where he soon fled to Sweden because of his involvement in the anti-Fascist resistance. In 1941 he was among the founder-members of the Surrealist MINOTAURGRUPPEN, and in 1948 he became a Swedish citizen. He exhibited regularly in Sweden and worldwide from 1941.

Nemes's early works show the influence of late Cubism and Czech Surrealism and exploit the Surrealist technique of associative montage, which he continued to use throughout his career. His later works as a whole derive their style from Pittura Metafisica and Surrealist painting and are composed from historical and art-historical fragments of memory, rearranged and endowed with new, often ambivalent meanings. As a result, however, of his intellectual rigour, his work, which is dominated by the experience of Central Europe, in particular the history-laden atmosphere of Prague, displays Kafkaesque anxiety and avoids the compositional automatism inherent in the

Surrealist method. Nemes executed a number of murals in Sweden (e.g. Skövde, 1955) and was an important teacher. In 1983 the Endre Nemes Museum was founded in Pécs with a donation by the artist of 250 works. Many of his paintings are also held by the Konstmuseum, Göteborg.

BIBLIOGRAPHY

J. Kotalik: 'Endre Nemes', *Opus Int.*, ix (1968)
R. v. Holten: 'Un Kafka de la peinture: Endre Nemes', *L'Oeil*, 8–9 (1973), pp. 217–18
Endre Nemes (exh. cat. by L. Németh, P. Weiss and E. Nemes, Budapest, N.G., 1982)
T. Millroth: *Endre Nemes* (Stockholm, 1985)
F. Romvary and others: *Endre Nemes Muzeum*, cat. (Pécs, 1985)

LAJOS NÉMETH

Nemes Lampérth, József (*b* Budapest, 13 Sept 1891; *d* Sátoraljaújhely, nr Miskolc, 24 May 1924). Hungarian painter and draughtsman. He was among the most outstanding figures of Hungarian avant-garde painting. He studied at the School for Industrial Drawing (1909–11) and the Academy of Fine Arts (1911–12) in Budapest. In the summer of 1911 he worked at the painters' school of Nagybánya. He began exhibiting in 1910, but his career was curtailed by psychiatric illness. His training had little effect on his work, which is characterized by closed forms and an expressive tonality in the manner of Fauvism or Die Brücke, although there is no evidence of direct influence. Throughout his life his work became more condensed and essential in form. The rather intense composition of Nemes Lampérth's earliest still-lifes is formed by violent brushstrokes and a relatively thick application of oil paint, as in *Kitchen Still-life* (1910; priv. col., see Molnár, no. 2) and *Plant Still-life* (1910–11; Budapest, N.G.). One of his most important paintings is *Lying in State* (1912; Budapest, N.G.), which depicts his deceased father surrounded by enormous candles. The space in this picture is created by the dynamic intercession of bands of paint broken up into horizontal and vertical planes. Mainly due to breaks at the edges this expansive form of shaping tends to pull apart the space within the picture, and is of moving intensity.

Nemes Lampérth went to Paris for one year in 1913. He fought in World War I, but he was wounded and discharged in 1916. In the same year, suffering increasingly from fits of depression, he was admitted to a closed psychiatric ward for the first time. Nevertheless, he painted two of his most successful oil paintings that year: *Standing Female Nude Facing the Painter* and *Standing Female Nude with her Back to the Painter* (both Budapest, N.G.). The nudes, formed with a strong sculptural plasticity stand in front of a torn background of amorphous black and green areas; the light falling on the figures is transformed into planes. His still-lifes of 1916, for example *Still-life with a Lamp* (Pécs, Pannonius Mus.), are also characteristically tightly and economically composed with relatively few colours and a small number of simple objects. In these and the preceding works Nemes Lampérth concentrated on problems of form.

Throughout his career Nemes Lampérth produced equally valuable pen or brush drawings on paper in black, brown or coloured ink, as studies for his oil paintings or large-scale compositions. The majority are landscapes, frequently drawn in Indian ink. These are characterized by dynamic lines of force, with strong contrasts, and they strike a tragic note, as in the *Pont Neuf* (1913) and *Fence-Palings* (1918; both Budapest, N.G.). Nemes Lampérth also attempted the representation of movement with nudes in red chalk.

Nemes Lampérth associated with the Activists, who, organized by Lajos Kassák, grouped around such avant-garde magazines as *Tett* in 1915 and *Ma* in 1916. Nemes Lampérth's expressive portrait of *Lajos Kassák* appeared in *Ma* in October 1917 and Kassák was the earliest and most understanding supporter and critic of his art. During the 1919 Hungarian Council Republic, Nemes Lampérth accepted a professorship at the Proletarian Fine Arts Workshop. After the Revolution was suppressed he emigrated to Berlin in 1920. He took part in a group exhibition at the Galerie Gurlitt in Berlin with 19 large-scale wash drawings. Gustav Ekström, a Swedish collector, bought his pictures and invited him to live in his house in Stockholm. It was here that Nemes Lampérth's schizophrenia manifested itself. He returned to Hungary, where he spent the rest of his life in mental hospitals and painted using softer tones. He died of tuberculosis.

BIBLIOGRAPHY

R. Pertorini and B. Szij: 'Adatok Nemes Lampérth József patográfiájához' [Some data relating to the medical history of József Nemes Lampérth], *Pszichológiai Szemle*, ix (1966), pp. 383–413
Z. Molnár: *Nemes Lampérth József* (Budapest, 1967)
Magyar Aktivizmus [Hungarian activism] (exh. cat., ed. J. Szabó; Pécs, Pannonius Mus., 1973)
O. Mezei and K. Mezey: 'Nemes Lampérth ismeretlen képei és levelei' [Unknown pictures and letters of Nemes Lampérth], *Művészet*, xv/12 (1974), pp. 8–9
O. Mezei: 'József Nemes Lampérth unbekannte Berliner Bilder und deren Platz in einem Lebenswerk', *Acta Hist. A. Acad. Sci. Hung.*, xxi (1975), pp. 151–65
J. Szabó: 'József Nemes Lampérth', *Magyar Művészet, 1890–1919* [Hungarian art, 1890-1919], ed. L. Németh (Budapest, 1981), pp. 600–04

MÁRIA SZOBOR-BERNÁTH

Nemi. Site with sanctuary of the goddess Diana beside the lake of the same name that fills a volcanic crater in the Alban hills 25 km south-east of Rome, Italy. Both lake and town take their name from the *nemus* (Lat.: 'sacred wood'). The sanctuary originated before the 6th century BC as the centre for a local cult in the territory of the Latin town of Aricia; it continued to flourish under Roman rule until the 4th century AD. The peculiar slave priesthood of Diana Nemorensis was the inspiration for Sir James Frazer's *The Golden Bough* (London, 1890–1915), while the picturesque scenery of the area attracted English landscape artists in the late 18th and 19th centuries, notably J. M. W. Turner, who painted several views of the lake.

The main remains of the sanctuary now visible to the north-east of the lake are of a large rectangular terraced precinct (*c.* 44,000 sq. m), with retaining walls constructed as a series of arched niches faced in pseudo-reticulate masonry. Archaeological discoveries made there are recorded from the mid-17th century onwards, but the first systematic excavations were by Sir John Savile Lumley (later Lord Savile) in 1885. He identified a large masonry podium in the western half of the precinct as the Temple of Diana itself, but this does not correspond with Vitruvius' description of that temple (*On Architecture*, IV.viii.4), which is probably the still unexcavated building shown on a plan of 1856 as standing further up the hillside. Lumley also explored several rooms on the north side of the precinct and selected areas within it, finding numerous votive and architectural terracottas, coins and some sculpture. His own share of the finds, presented to the Castle Museum at Nottingham, England, is now the main archaeological collection from the sanctuary. Much of what was found in further digging after 1885 on behalf of the landowner, Prince Orsini, is now untraceable, but the Ny Carlsberg Glyptotek in Copenhagen acquired most of the best sculpture as well as material from earlier antiquarian collections, while the bronzes and terracottas went elsewhere (e.g. Rome, Villa Giulia).

On the basis of these finds a broad chronology of the site can be defined. Initially the sanctuary consisted merely of a triple image of Diana in bronze (c. 500 BC), standing in a clearing in the sacred wood, an image shown on coins issued in 43 BC (e.g. Oxford, Ashmolean). In the late 4th century BC to the early 3rd, however, the site began to receive buildings decorated with architectural terracottas, and it became a focus for votive offerings made for health and fertility. The third phase (c. 100 BC) consisted of the large-scale landscaping of the sanctuary, with a terraced precinct and new temples. Finally, in the early Roman Empire, the sanctuary was eclipsed by the summer villas of emperors and aristocrats attracted by Nemi's scenic beauty. A theatre adjoining the sanctuary, excavated by Morpurgo in 1928, was rebuilt early in the 1st century AD by Volusia Cornelia, the proprietor of the luxurious villa near by. The emperor Caligula (reg AD 37–41) had a sumptuous floating palace on a ship moored in the lake, one of two vessels uncovered in spectacular excavations between 1928 and 1931, during which the lake was partially drained. The ships were preserved in a specially built museum near the lake (Nemi, Mus. Navi), but they were largely destroyed during hostilities in 1944.

BIBLIOGRAPHY

G. Ucelli: *Le navi di Nemi* (Rome, 1940)

F. Poulsen: 'Nemi Studies', *Acta Archaeol.* [Copenhagen], xii (1941), pp. 1–52

Mysteries of Diana: The Antiquities from Nemi in Nottingham Museums (Nottingham, 1983)

F. Coarelli: *I santuari del Lazio in età repubblicana* (Rome, 1987), pp. 165–85

T. F. C. BLAGG

Nemours, Jacques d'Armagnac, Duc de. *See* JACQUES D'ARMAGNAC.

Nemrik. *See under* ESKI MOSUL REGION.

Nemrut Dağ. Site in the southern Anatolian kingdom of Commagene, eastern Turkey, west of the River Euphrates. Nemrut Dağ was one of a series of dynastic shrines built by local monarchs in the first half of the 1st century BC. The shrine was initially investigated by Karl Humann and Otto Puchstein in 1890 and later by Friedrich-Karl Dörner from 1939 to 1963.

From the 6th century BC to the 2nd, Commagene was a province under the Achaemenid Persians, Alexander the Great and the Seleucid Hellenistic Greeks, but it became an independent monarchy under Ptolemaios (originally its governor; reg c. 163–c. 130 BC) and Samos (reg c. 130–c. 100

BC). However, Mithradates I Kallinikos (reg c. 100–c. 70 BC) and his son Antiochus I Theos (reg c. 69–c. 36 BC) transformed Commagene, which was then, like neighbouring Armenia, poised politically between the western empire of Rome and the eastern empire of Parthia. Coins that had hitherto appeared sporadically were minted in quantity at this time, with the customary obverse profile portrait head (right-facing, like Seleucid Greek examples) and the name in Greek on the reverse. These coins have a generally Armenian character.

Mithradates I initiated, and Antiochus I completed, a lavish architectural and artistic programme of political and religious intent, claiming their divinity and descent from combined Persian and Greek ancestry. Unusually long Greek inscriptions illuminate their intentions. They evolved a distinctive form of the practice, fairly widespread in the east, of blending together originally different deities (syncretism). By Antiochus' time such deities included Zeus–Oromasdes (Greek Zeus and Iranian Ahura Mazda), Apollo–Mithra–Helios–Hermes (three Greek gods with the Iranian Mithra) and Artagnes-Herakles-Ares (the Iranian Verethragna with the Greek Herakles and Ares). Zeus' consort Hera and Tyche, the female personification of Commagene, were important goddesses.

Two types of sanctuary arose in significant places: the precinct (Gr. *temenos*) and the sacred monument (Gr.

Nemrut Dağ, head of statue from the west terrace of the sanctuary of King Antiochus I Theos, h. over 2 m, c. 69–c. 36 BC

hierothesion) devoted to the dynastic cult. Both types included explanatory Greek texts and architectural forms of mixed Greek, Anatolian and Iranian derivation. Their sculptures incorporated Greek, Iranian, Armenian and Commagenian costumes and motifs in an unrealistic, Greco–Persian style characteristic of PARTHIAN art. A fragmentary inscribed basalt stele from Adıyaman, with a figure of Helios and the legs and feet of a king (possibly Mithradates I or Antiochus I), was perhaps originally in a precinct at neighbouring Samosata on the Euphrates. Mithradates I built a dynastic shrine at a site by modern Karakuş (near the ancient capital, Arsameia) for his mother, Isias. This was a circular mound, surrounded by three groups of three limestone Doric columns, surmounted by sculptures including animals (Zeus' eagle, Hera's cow and Herakles' lion) and relief stelae showing a king in a farewell handshake (Gr. *dexiosis*) with a woman. A similar *hierothesion* at Sesönk, with a mound and three pairs of Doric limestone columns surmounted by sculptures, including pairs of seated figures, may have been built by Mithradates, perhaps for his wife Laodice.

A fragmentary Greek text may indicate that Mithradates I began the greatest Commagenian *hierothesion*, Nemrut Dağ, high above Arsameia (now Gerger), perhaps with stelae of gods (Mithra–Apollo and Helios–Hermes) and ancestors. Antiochus I Theos vastly extended his father's programme and spectacularly transformed the mountaintop Nemrut Dağ precinct, 2150 m above sea-level. Antiochus' burial tumulus of limestone gravel (50 m high) was flanked by terraces east and west with similar limestone installations. A central platform bears a row of colossal divine statues (see fig.) originally 8 m high (from left to right, Herakles' lion, Zeus' eagle, Antiochus I, Commagene personified, Zeus–Oromasdes, Apollo–Mithra–Helios–Hermes, Artagnes–Herakles–Ares, Zeus' eagle and Herakles' lion), with Greek texts behind. There are further platforms bearing more sculptures of eagles and lions as well as stelae depicting Antiochus clasping hands with Zeus, Herakles, Mithra and Commagene. Antiochus' investiture with the ring (diadem) of office is also depicted, and one relief, dated 7 July 62 BC, legitimizes his claims through astral theology.

Each terrace contained rows of reliefs portraying the ancestors of Antiochus and his wife Selene back to Alexander the Great (*reg* 332–323 BC) and the Achaemenid Persian Darius I (*reg* 521–486 BC). The east terrace had a great rectangular altar for ceremonies, and it may once have been decorated by a relief head, possibly of Antiochus I. Antiochus' sanctuary may recall earlier Anatolian (perhaps Hittite) precedents. A temenos was constructed at Direk Kale and another at Ancoz on the Euphrates. The latter included a fragmentary handclasp relief (possibly of Mithradates I), and a third temenos at Kesun has yielded the top of a stele showing Herakles clasping the hand of a king who may be Mithradates I. At Kılafık Hüyük the temenos included an inscribed basalt stele bearing a depiction of Antiochus I.

Antiochus I later built two further *hierothesia*. At Arsameia, a processional way with rock-cut tomb (perhaps for Mithradates I) was decorated with three more platforms (described by the excavators as Socles I–III) with limestone relief stelae. Socle III included a scene of Mithradates I clasping Herakles' hand, and Socle II was decorated with two fragmentary reliefs of father and son clasping Mithra's hand. Finally Socle I incorporated smaller reliefs portraying father and son. Cult rooms contained provincial Hellenistic Greek geometric mosaics. Limestone heads of Antiochus I and a queen (perhaps Selene or Laodice) were also discovered. Antiochus' last *hierothesion*, at Arsameia, comprised a gated precinct before a rock tomb and rock relief (4 m high) of his grandfather Samos. At Haydaran, a nonroyal rock-tomb relief of a married couple reflects royal style. Little is known of Antiochus' successors, Mithradates II (*reg c.* 36–20 BC), who erected a small, last *hierothesion* below Nemrut Dağ to his mother, sister and niece; Antiochus II (*d* 29 BC) and Antiochus III (*reg* 20 BC–AD 17). Thereafter the Romans occupied Commagene, the kings became titular, and, on the death of Antiochus IV Epiphanes (*reg* AD 38–72), it became a Roman province. A last monument overlooks Athens: the ruined hilltop mausoleum of a descendant, Philopappos, with reliefs dated to *c.* AD 114–16.

BIBLIOGRAPHY

K. Humann and O. Puchstein: *Reisen in Kleinasien und Nordsyrien* (Berlin, 1890)
J. Waldis: *Sprache und Stil der grossen griechischen Inschrift von Nemrud Dağ* (Heidelberg, 1920)
F. K. Dörner and R. Naumann: *Forschungen in Kommagene* (Berlin, 1939)
H. Dorrie: *Der Königskult des Antiochos von Kommagene im Lichte neuer Inschriften-Funde* (Göttingen, 1964)
J. H. Young: 'Commagenian Tiaras, Royal and Divine', *Amer. J. Archaeol.*, lxviii (1964), pp. 29–34
H. Waldmann: *Die kommagenischen Kultreformen unter König Mithradates I Kallinikos und seinem Sohne Antiochos I*, Etudes préliminaires aux Religions orientales dans l'Empire Romain, 34 (Leiden, 1973) [with bibliog., pp. xvi–xviii]
M. A. R. Colledge: *Parthian Art* (London, 1977)
W. Höpfner: *Arsameia am Nymphaios II: Das Hierothesion des Königs Mithradates I Kallinikos von Kommagene nach den Ausgrabungen von 1963 bis 1967*, Istanbuler Forsch., 33 (Berlin, 1983)
R. D. Sullivan: *Near Eastern Royalty and Rome* (Toronto, 1990)

MALCOLM A. R. COLLEDGE

Nénot, Henri-Paul [Paul-Henri] (*b* Paris, 1853; *d* Geneva, 1934). French architect. He was a pupil of Charles-Auguste Questel and Jean-Louis Pascal at the Ecole des Beaux-Arts, Paris. He won the Grand Prix in 1877 and during his period of study in Rome, in 1882, entered the competition for the monument to Victor-Emmanuel II. He was awarded first prize, but this was a purely honorary award as foreigners were excluded from the competition. Soon after his return from Rome to Paris in 1884 Nénot won the competition for the enlargement of the Sorbonne University. When doubts were raised concerning Nénot's youth and lack of experience, Charles Garnier testified to his ability when he worked for him on the Paris Opéra. The New Sorbonne (completed 1901) consisted of faculty buildings extending the courtyard plan of the original site and including a new auditorium. Nénot demonstrated skill in planning and scale while using traditional French styles in an eclectic manner. His other principal works include the Institut Océanographique (1910) and the Banque Dreyfus (1912), Paris, and the Casino at Evians-les-Bains. In 1927 he entered the competition for the League of Nations Building, Geneva, in partnership with the Swiss architect Julien Flegenheimer. Their conservative but practical design was awarded first prize and formed the basis for the building completed after Nénot's death by an international team of architects.

WRITINGS

La Nouvelle Sorbonne (Paris, 1895)
Monographie de la nouvelle Sorbonne (Paris, 1903) [intr. C. Gréard]

BIBLIOGRAPHY

A. de Menoît: 'Les Maîtres de l'architecture française', *Constr. Mod.*, xi (1895), pp. 325–8
A. Louvet: 'Paul-Henri Nénot (1853–1934)', *Architecture* [Paris], xlviii (1935), pp. 241–4
J. Favier: 'Le Palais de la Société des Nations à Genève, par M. Nénot, Broggi, Flegenheimer, LeFèvre et Vago, architectes', *Constr. Mod.*, lii (1937), pp. 26–8
——: 'Salon 1938: La Rétrospective Paul-Henri Nénot (1853–1934)', *Constr. Mod.*, liii (1938), pp. 527–30

□

Nenov, Ivan (*b* Sofia, 17 May 1902). Bulgarian painter, ceramicist, sculptor, mosaicist and designer. In 1925 he graduated in painting from the National Academy of Arts (Natsionalna Hudozhestvena Academia) in Sofia. During the 1930s he declared his support for progressive tendencies in Bulgarian art by joining the NEW ARTISTS' SOCIETY, meanwhile working in his preferred media of oils and tempera. His compositions of monumental figures are painted in a style that stresses classical purity and decorative details (e.g. *Morning*, 1936; Sofia, N.A.G.). In 1932 and during 1936–8 he worked in a design studio in Italy and during that time experimented with a post-Cubist style (e.g. *Dolphinarium*, 1938; Sofia, N.A.G.). Paintings such as *By the Sea* (1943), *Girl with Fish* (1946) and *Sozopol's Window* (1958; all Sofia, N.A.G.) have vivid colour and strongly synthesized forms. From the 1930s he also produced ceramic objects and sculpture and worked in mosaic. He received an award for his work at the Triennale of Applied Arts in Milan in 1936. By the 1950s he was principally a ceramicist, exhibiting decorative pots with zoomorphic and anthropomorphic designs and small figurines, all made of terracotta or glazed chamotte, and having the female form as their principal subject. He regularly participated in the Venice Biennale, the Concórso Internazionale della Ceramica d'Arte in Faenza and in exhibitions in New York.

BIBLIOGRAPHY

B. Ivanov: 'Khudozhnikit Ivan Nenov na 60 godini', *Izkustvo*, 6 (1962), pp. 19–23
E. Klincharov: *Ivan Nenov* (Sofia, 1962)
D. Avramov: 'Zhivopista na Ivan Nenov: Po sluchai 70 godini' [The painting of Ivan Nenov], *Prob. Izkustvoto*, 3 (1972), pp. 25–37
Ivan Nenov: Painting, Graphics, Ceramics (exh. cat. by S. Russev, 1975)

JULIANA NEDEVA-WEGENER

Neo-Attic. Term coined by Heinrich Brunn in his *Geschichte der griechischen Künstler* (Stuttgart, 1853) to designate sculptors of the 1st century BC to the 2nd century AD who added the epithet *Athenaios* ('the Athenian') after their signatures. The sculptors produced copies and adaptations of earlier statues, such as the bronze herm of *Apollonios*, son of Archias, based on the head of the *Doryphoros* by Polykleitos (?2nd half of the 1st century BC; Naples, Mus. Archeol., 4885), and marble reliefs on kraters, candelabra etc also derived from earlier works (see fig.). The style arose from the Attic neo-Classical movement of the mid- to late 2nd century BC (*see* GREECE, ANCIENT, §IV, 2(iv)),

Neo-Attic krater depicting *Dionysus, Satyr and Hermaphrodite*, marble, h. 940 mm (excluding foot), *c.* AD 110 (Pisa, Camposanto)

and Neo-Attic workshops served rich patrons in Pergamon, Alexandria and above all Rome and Italy, as well as in Greece itself. Important Neo-Attic works include those from the MAHDIA SHIPWRECK near Tunis (*c.* 100 BC; Tunis, Mus. Alaoui), and various reliefs found at Peiraeus, including those based on the shield of the *Athena Parthenos* by Pheidias (2nd century AD; Peiraeus, Archaeol. Mus.). Typical of the Neo-Attic style are a volute krater by Sosibios (mid-1st century BC; Paris, Louvre), which combines disparate figures (maenads, dancers with weapons, nymphs etc), modelled on prototypes of different dates into a unified decorative scheme, and a marble rhyton by Pontios (late 1st century BC; Rome, Mus. Conserv.) with three maenads around its neck, perhaps based on a series by KALLIMACHOS. Although Neo-Attic art with its eclectic formalism and artificiality was the antithesis of the realism of Roman art, the style was extremely important, as it helped to transmit Classical Greek forms to Roman, and thus to western European, art.

BIBLIOGRAPHY

F. Hauser: *Die neuattischen Reliefs* (Stuttgart, 1889)
E. Loewy: *Neuattische Kunst* (Leipzig, 1922)
W. Fuchs: *Die Vorbilder der neuattischen Reliefs* (Berlin, 1959)
——: *Der Schiffsfund von Mahdia* (Tübingen, 1963)
——: 'Paralipomena', *Kotinos: Festschrift für Erika Simon*, ed. H. Froning, T. Hölscher and H. Mielsch (Mainz, 1992), pp. 199–203

WERNER FUCHS

Neo-classicism. Term coined in the 1880s to denote the last stage of the classical tradition in architecture, sculpture, painting and the decorative arts. Neo-classicism was the successor to Rococo in the second half of the 18th century and was itself superseded by various historicist styles in the first half of the 19th century. It formed an integral part of THE ENLIGHTENMENT in its radical questioning of received notions of human endeavour. It was also deeply involved with the emergence of new historical attitudes towards the past—non-Classical as well as Classical—that were stimulated by an unprecedented range of archaeological discoveries, extending from southern Italy and the eastern Mediterranean to Egypt and the Near East, during the second half of the 18th century. The new awareness of the plurality of historical styles prompted the search for consciously new and contemporary forms of expression. This concept of modernity set Neo-classicism apart from past revivals of antiquity, to which it was, nevertheless, closely related. Almost paradoxically, the quest for a timeless mode of expression (the 'true style', as it was then called) involved strongly divergent approaches towards design that were strikingly focused on the Greco-Roman debate. On the one hand, there was a commitment to a radical severity of expression, associated with the Platonic Ideal, as well as to such criteria as the functional and the primitive, which were particularly identified with early Greek art and architecture. On the other hand, there were highly innovative exercises in eclecticism, inspired by late Imperial Rome, as well as subsequent periods of stylistic experiment with Mannerism and the Italian Baroque.

However rationally dictated, these fresh interpretations of the Classical evoked powerful emotional responses to the past that require Neo-classicism to be understood within the broader movement of Romanticism, rather than as its opposite. Arguably, the most original phase of Neo-classicism anticipated the political revolution in France with which it is inevitably associated, providing visible expressions of ideology in buildings and images. By the early 19th century an increasing concern with archaeological fidelity, together with the daunting range of newly explored cultures and alternative styles (including the medieval, Gothic and Oriental), began to inhibit imaginative experiment and originality of vision within the Classical tradition for all but a few outstanding artists and designers. Moreover, what had originated as a style inspired, in part, by principles of republicanism was transformed under Napoleon I into a fashionable and international language of imperial opulence.

1. Archaeology and the rise of historicism. 2. The search for a contemporary style. 3. Education and society. 4. Nature and classicism. 5. The late phase.

1. ARCHAEOLOGY AND THE RISE OF HISTORICISM. From the mid-18th century antiquity could no longer be regarded as finite, either in time or place. The remarkable burst of archaeological activity during the latter half of the 18th century served to encourage a growing awareness of historical change and of the almost limitless fund of inspiration offered by the diverse cultures that comprised antiquity. In this pluralistic revaluation of the past, aesthetics swiftly emerged as a necessary discipline to assess the relative values of art. The striking discoveries in Roman

domestic life, gradually uncovered at Herculaneum (from 1738; *see* HERCULANEUM, §VI) and Pompeii (from 1748; *see* POMPEII, §VI), were disseminated through the plates of the official publication *Le antichità di Ercolano esposte* (1755–92). The full impact of these finds on the visual arts was slow to take effect, but literal transpositions from engravings of wall paintings can already be seen in such modish works as Joseph-Marie Vien's the *Cupid Seller*, exhibited at the 1763 Salon (Fontainebleau, Château; *see* VIEN, JOSEPH-MARIE, fig. 1). Among the objects uncovered were bronze tripods, such as that found in the Temple of Isis, Pompeii, in the early 1760s; these spawned a type of furniture derived from what became known as the *Athénienne* (after the object's appearance in Vien's *Virtuous Athenian Girl*, 1763; Strasbourg, Mus. B.-A.; for further discussion *see* POMPEIAN REVIVAL).

Rome, which by the mid-century had become the main focus of the GRAND TOUR, brought together not only influential patrons and collectors (notably the *milordi inglesi*) but also the most progressive young artists and designers in Europe. The record of decisive encounters with the cultural palimpsest of Rome before 1800 constitutes a roll-call of such influential figures in the arts as Robert Adam, James Adam, Antonio Canova, Jacques-Louis David, John Flaxman, Jacques Gondoin, Joshua Reynolds, Charles Percier, Pierre-François-Léonard Fontaine, James Stuart and Bertel Thorvaldsen. In the city that Wilhelm Tischbein described as 'the true centre of the arts', a major reassessment of antiquity and the achievements of later flowerings of classicism, such as the Renaissance and the Baroque, began to inspire fresh visionary and poetic compositions, which replaced the traditional, laborious studies of antique exemplars. The distinction of the period between 'imitation' and 'copying'—that is, following the creative spirit rather than the letter of antiquity—was vividly demonstrated in the works and influence of Giovanni Battista Piranesi, in his lifelong crusade to improve contemporary design through a formidable output of engraved images. At the forefront of this shift from the interpretative towards the speculative and experimental was a significant group of students at the Académie de France in Rome during the 1740s and early 1750s. It included Charles-Michel-Ange Challe, Charles-Louis Clérisseau, Charles de Wailly, Pierre-Martin Dumont, Jean-Laurent Legeay, Louis-Joseph Le Lorrain, Ennemond-Alexandre Petitot and Marie-Joseph Peyre. Their innovative ideas, which derived from a radical reappraisal of antique forms and structures and were mainly developed in temporary festival structures, were subsequently to have a far-reaching influence after the artists had dispersed to work throughout Europe, as far as Russia.

Although Rome continued to be a centre for cultural interchange throughout the most productive phases of Neo-classicism, many challenging new discoveries were being made elsewhere in an increasing number and range of archaeological expeditions throughout the Mediterranean and the Near East. While recognition of the reforming potential of Greek antiquity can be traced back to Jean-Louis de Cordemoy earlier in the century, a fresh interest was awakened by the radical questioning of Roman design in favour of Greece in Marc-Antoine Laugier's

Essai sur l'architecture (Paris, 1753). Like Rousseau's quest for fundamentals in human nature and social conduct, the cult of the Primitive, signified by the rustic 'Vitruvian hut' of rough-hewn trees that was illustrated in Laugier's frontispiece, emphasized the functional and almost ethical principles of truthful construction. Similar ideas were then being advocated independently in Venice through the Socratic teachings of Carlo Lodoli. Far more significant and persuasive, however, was the highly emotive advocacy of Greek art as a cultural phenomenon by JOHANN JOACHIM WINCKELMANN, initiated through his manifesto *Gedanken über die Nachahmung der griechischen Werke in der Malerei und Bildhauerkunst* (Dresden, 1755; Eng. trans., London, 1765), followed by his equally influential *Geschichte der Kunst des Alterthums* (Dresden, 1764). His poetic and highly persuasive writing, evoking the nobility of Hellenic life and achievements, was largely based on a deep knowledge of Classical authors and Roman copies of Greek original works of art. In lyrical passages of empathetic analysis, he created an awareness of Greek art and civilization on a par with Piranesi's potent imagery of Rome (*see also* GREEK REVIVAL, §2). Understandably, his ideas had a less immediate influence on architecture, which features less in his writings than sculpture or painting. This is perhaps reflected in the brittle decorative pastiches of Greek temples that Carlo Marchionni added during the

early 1760s to the villa (now Villa Torlonia) of Winckelmann's patron, Cardinal Alessandro Albani, in Rome (*see* ROME, §V, 27). Within the main *salone* of the villa, Anton Raphael Mengs's acclaimed ceiling painting *Parnassus with Apollo and the Muses* (1760–61; *in situ*) provided a pictorial equivalent that owed far more to Raphael than to Greek antiquity, despite its featuring of a baseless Doric column and its relief-like composition. The first true Greek Revival building was, in fact, James Stuart's Doric temple (1758) in the park at Hagley Hall, Hereford & Worcs (*see* GREEK REVIVAL, §1). Also in 1758, Julien-David Le Roy's publication in Paris of the first reliable illustrations of the principal monuments in Athens, *Les Ruines des plus beaux monuments de la Grèce*, anticipated Stuart's and Nicholas Revett's more carefully considered *Antiquities of Athens* (3 vols, London, 1762–95; *see* GREEK REVIVAL, fig. 1). Following the 'discovery' (*c.* 1746) of the gaunt Doric temples at Paestum in southern Italy, a sequence of publications, which ironically culminated in sublime etchings (*Différentes vues . . . de Pesto*, 1778) by Piranesi, helped, by the end of the century, to transform the Greek Revival in architecture from an archaeological interest into an emotional understanding.

Predictably, the extravagant claims advanced for Greek architecture and design provoked a fierce polemical battle, led, on the Roman side, by Piranesi with his magisterial

1. Jacques-Louis David: *Lictors Bringing Brutus the Bodies of his Sons*, oil on canvas, 3.25×4.25 m, 1789 (Paris, Musée du Louvre)

survey *Le antichità romane* (Rome, 1756), followed during the 1760s by his series of ambitious archaeological folios, with themes ranging from Rome's achievements in architectural composition and ornament to Roman engineering and urban planning. In certain of these works Piranesi championed the Etruscans as the sole mentors of Rome's creative genius; in fact, Etruscanology had already begun to develop as an important field of enquiry in its own right, with the establishment of the Accademia Etrusca at Cortona in 1726 and the Museo Etrusco Guarnacci at Volterra in 1727. Demonstrations of Roman achievement further afield appeared in Robert Wood's folios on *The Ruins of Palmyra* (London, 1753) and *The Ruins of Baalbec* (London, 1757), as well as in Robert Adam's *Ruins of the Palace of the Emperor Diocletian at Spalatro in Dalmatia* (London, 1764). Other expeditions and books, such as James Dawkins's and Richard Chandler's *Ionian Antiquities* (London, 1769; additions 1797), were subsequently sponsored by the SOCIETY OF DILETTANTI, an extremely influential dining club of leading British patrons and *cognoscenti*.

2. THE SEARCH FOR A CONTEMPORARY STYLE. Winckelmann's assertion in 1755 that 'there is only one way for the moderns to become great and, perhaps, unequalled: by imitating the Ancients' encapsulated Neo-classicism's concern with fostering contemporary art and values. During the 1750s the new theories and practice in art and design were impelled by a deliberate aim to replace what was seen as the frivolity and superficiality of the Rococo by an art with greater seriousness and moral commitment. In their different ways, theorists and teachers such as Winckelmann, Joshua Reynolds and Francesco Milizia emphasized the reforming power of antiquity, while Denis Diderot's regular critiques of the annual Salons in Paris praised the moral values of paintings by Jean-Baptiste Greuze at the expense of those by François Boucher. By the mid-1750s the Scottish artist Gavin Hamilton was pioneering in Rome a new type of history painting that featured morally uplifting themes from antiquity; this was perfected by Jacques-Louis David with such heroic exhibition pieces as *Andromache Mourning Hector* (exh. Salon 1783; Paris, Ecole N. Sup. B.-A., on dep. Paris, Louvre), *Oath of the Horatii* (exh. Salon 1785; Paris, Louvre; *see* DAVID, JACQUES-LOUIS, fig. 1) and the *Lictors Bringing Brutus the Bodies of his Sons* (1789; Paris, Louvre; see fig. 1); these drew, thematically as well as formally, on authentic sources and came close to paralleling David's active involvement with Revolutionary politics. Likewise, the *Death of Marat* (1793; Brussels, Mus. A. Anc.; *see* FRANCE, fig. 25) provided a new kind of political icon in the manner of a secular Pietà, complementing David's designs for Revolutionary festivals of Liberty and of the Supreme Being, which similarly exploited the heritage of Classical symbolism. During the same period, the semicircular plans and tiered seating of Greek theatres and Roman *curiae* were being adapted for political assemblies, passing later into building patterns for legislative halls, such as Benjamin Henry Latrobe's House of Representatives (1803–7; destr. 1812–15) for the US Capitol in Washington, DC.

Contemporary sculpture, following Winckelmann's precepts of 'noble simplicity and calm grandeur', likewise showed a new seriousness of purpose, as well as formal restraint. In the work of Canova, Neo-classicism's greatest sculptor, complex energies and powerful emotions were confined within relief-like compositions and governed by geometrical settings, as, for example, in works as varied as *Hercules and Lichas* (1795–1815; Rome, G.N.A. Mod.) and the funerary monument to *Clement XIV* (1783–7; Rome, SS Apostoli; see fig. 2). Among the most eloquent examples of the uses of funerary geometry is Canova's poignant tomb of *Maria Christina of Austria* (1798–1805; Vienna, Augustinerkirche; *see* CANOVA, ANTONIO, fig. 3), where a stark pyramid frames a dramatic tableau of personifications, including Death, Mourning, Piety and Beneficence. Likewise, Jean-Antoine Houdon, Joseph Nollekens and Johann Gottfried Schadow attempted in their portrait sculpture to reconcile the incidences of likeness and psychological character within the timeless properties of the Ideal, as derived from ancient prototypes. In Houdon's words, 'one of the finest attributes of the difficult art of sculpture is truthfully to preserve the form and render the image of men who have achieved glory or good for their country'. The same dilemma between the

2. Antonio Canova: funerary monument to *Clement XIV*, marble, 1783–7 (Rome, SS Apostoli)

3. James Stuart: Painted Room (from 1759), Spencer House, London

universal and the particular, recognized by Reynolds in his *Discourses on Art* (London, 1769–90), was one that he attempted to resolve in his portraits by the use of such Classical prototypes as the *Apollo Belvedere* (Rome, Vatican, Mus. Pio-Clementino) for *Commodore Keppel* (*c.* 1753–4; London, N. Mar. Mus.; *see* REYNOLDS, JOSHUA, fig. 1). The tension between the Ideal and the three-dimensional conventions of pictorial composition were, however, avoided in the stark simplicity of such line engravings as Flaxman's illustrations to the Homeric epics (published 1793 and 1795) and Dante (published 1807), effectively demonstrating Winckelmann's 'noble simplicity' or, as William Blake put it in another context, 'the wiry line of rectitude'.

In the applied and decorative arts, theorists such as Charles-Nicolas Cochin *le fils* similarly advocated an emphasis on austerity and geometric restraint; their sharp reaction against the curvilinear and sensuous forms of such Rococo designers as Germain Boffrand and Juste-Aurèle Meissonnier was expressed in Cochin's celebrated article *Supplication aux orfèvres, ciseleurs, sculpteurs en bois pour les appartements et autres*, published in *Mercure de France* (Dec 1754). In France this was to launch a fashion for the so-called GOÛT GREC, as pioneered by Le Lorrain's furnished interiors (1756–8; now Chantilly, Mus. Condé) for the Parisian financier Ange-Laurent de La Live de Jully.

The new style was taken to a greater pitch of refinement by such outstanding *menuisiers* and *ébénistes* of the Louis XVI era as Georges Jacob (ii) and Jean-Henri Riesener, and its influence spread through the production of the copious plates of Jean-François de Neufforge's *Recueil élémentaire d'architecture* (10 vols, Paris, 1757–68 and 1772–80), in which the author claimed to imitate 'the masculine, simple, and majestic manner of the ancient architects of Greece and of the best modern architects'. These reactions to the *goût pompadour* also display a considerable element of revival of the arts of the Grand Siècle of Louis XIV, as found in Anges-Jacques Gabriel's masterpiece of geometric harmony and restraint, the Petit Trianon (1762–8) at Versailles (*see* VERSAILLES, fig. 4).

In England the PALLADIANISM of the early 18th century, led by William Kent, Richard Boyle, 3rd Earl of Burlington and 4th Earl of Cork, and Thomas Coke, 1st Earl of Leicester, had anticipated continental Neo-classicism by several decades, in creating architecture and interiors from direct archaeological sources. Kent had been among the first designers in Europe to reintroduce the antique style of grotesque painting in such works as the Presence Chamber (1724) in Kensington Palace, London, inspired by Raphael's decorations in the Vatican loggias and the Villa Madama, Rome (*see* RAPHAEL, fig. 9). However, a major new phase of experiments, involving radical and imaginative styles of design *all'antica*, took place between 1760 and 1780. These included James Stuart's Painted Room (from 1759) in Spencer House, London (see fig. 3), the first convincingly Neo-classical interior with integrated furnishings in Europe. This scheme, combining Greek and Roman decorative and architectural sources within a framework of painted Raphaelesque grotesques, contained a suite of carved and gilt seat furniture. Particularly notable were four sofas incorporating winged lions and a pair of ormolu tripod candelabra–perfume burners supported by stands richly decorated in keeping with the surrounding walls. Equally remarkable was the first Pompeian interior, complete with classicizing Klismos chairs, in the gallery at Packington Hall, Warwicks (1785–8), designed by the Adams' assistant Joseph Bonomi in collaboration with the owner, Heneage Finch, 4th Earl of Aylesford (for illustration *see* POMPEIAN REVIVAL). With its dominant colour scheme of deep reds and lustrous blacks, shared in common by the walls, ceilings, hangings and upholstery, this interior preceded by many years the main Pompeian Revival schemes on the Continent.

Under Neo-classicism, the search for a new or 'true style'—one that would be peculiar to the late 18th century and responsive to fresh social needs—took a variety of forms. In architectural design, eclectic solutions included Jacques-Germain Soufflot's Ste Geneviève (begun 1755; now the Panthéon), Paris (*see* SOUFFLOT, JACQUES-GERMAIN, fig. 3), whose design combined Greek and Roman forms with Gothic principles of vaulting, while at the same time observing Laugier's advocacy of columnar functionalism (*see also* RATIONALISM (i)). Piranesi's modest reconstructed church of S Maria del Priorato (1754–5; Rome; *see* PIRANESI, GIOVANNI BATTISTA, fig. 2) incorporates motifs drawn from Etruscan, late Imperial Roman and Mannerist sources in accordance with the bold philosophy of design advocated in his treatise *Parere su l'architettura* (Rome, 1765), which defended an extreme eclecticism. This broadly based system of composition found its most accomplished and original application in the architecture and furniture designs of Piranesi's associate Robert Adam. The consummate mastery with which Adam exploited an awkward series of given spaces and changes of level at Syon House (1760–69), London, is displayed in the Anteroom, where rich colours and textures are combined with Greek and Roman decorative sources to create an effect of patrician opulence. The highly self-conscious and consumer-led Adam Style (defended and illustrated in *The Works in Architecture of Robert and James Adam*, i–ii (London, 1773–9)), reached its most experimental form in a series of Etruscan rooms. In the most complete surviving example, the Etruscan Dressing-room (*c.* 1775–6; for illustration *see* ETRUSCAN STYLE) at Osterley Park, London, the unifying system of ornament combined ingredients from Pompeian wall decoration with motifs and colours from antique vase paintings, then believed to be Etruscan.

Stylistic solutions involving extremes in geometric simplification and surface austerity were predictably limited to paper projects, such as Friedrich Gilly's design for a Schauspielhaus in Berlin (pen and ink with wash, *c.* 1798; ex-Tech. Hochsch., Berlin, 1945); Etienne-Louis Boullée's design for a gigantic spherical cenotaph to Isaac Newton (pen and ink with wash, 1784; Paris, Bib. N.; for illustration *see* BOULLÉE, ETIENNE-LOUIS); and Claude-Nicolas Ledoux's engravings of visionary designs for the Saline de Chaux at Arc-et-Senans, near Besançon, later published in his *L'Architecture considérée sous le rapport de l'art, des moeurs et de la législation* (vol. i, Paris, 1804). Works of a more practicable nature that were actually executed included such public buildings as Jacques Gondoin's anatomy lecture theatre (1780; see fig. 4) at the Ecole de Chirurgie (now Faculté de Médecine), Paris, its interior displaying a remarkable fusion of the Pantheon in Rome and a Greek theatre.

Thomas Jefferson and Clérisseau had recourse to a celebrated Roman exemplar, the Maison Carrée, Nîmes (*see* NÎMES, fig. 2) for the basic form, albeit considerably enlarged, of the State Capitol (1785–99), Richmond, VA (*see* UNITED STATES OF AMERICA, fig. 5). Other striking solutions included Ledoux's ingenious series of toll-houses or *barrières* (1785–9) erected around Paris, and Leo von Klenze's Walhalla (1830–42) near Regensburg, which consisted of a peripteral Doric temple sited on the crest of a hill and containing busts of celebrated Germans (for an illustration of the interior *see* GREEK REVIVAL, fig. 3). In all these works, classic restraint was to be seen as expressive of civic and national virtues.

3. EDUCATION AND SOCIETY. In the applied arts the new mass-production processes of the early years of the Industrial Revolution, often allied to the use of new synthetic materials, were swiftly adapted to the simplified forms and abstracted ornaments characteristic of astringent Neo-classical design. Britain came to fulfil a pioneering role with the foundation in 1754 of the Royal Society for the Encouragement of Arts, Manufactures and Commerce, the first organization established to promote industrial design. Its founder-members included the potter Josiah Wedgwood, who in his new factory, the Etruria works, opened in 1769 near Burslem, Staffs, exploited the vase forms, colours and decorative vocabulary of Pierre François Hugues d'Hancarville's *Collection of Etruscan, Greek and Roman Antiquities from the Cabinet of the Honble Wm Hamilton* (4 vols, Naples, 1766–76). Wedgwood's new materials, also inspired by the ancient world, were black basalts imitating Etruscan bronzes, and jasperware inspired by Roman cameo glass (for illustration *see* WEDGWOOD). A comparable entrepreneurial spirit was shown by Matthew Boulton, a fellow member of the Royal Society of Arts. At his Soho factory in Birmingham Boulton produced abstracted classicizing forms in a wide range of ornamental metalwork, from ormolu, Sheffield plate and silver (*see* ENGLAND, fig. 79) to cast-iron architectural fittings. Both men also belonged to the Lunar Society, an influential discussion group of industrialists, scientists and avant-garde designers in the English Midlands, who met on evenings when they could travel by moonlight. This pioneering concern with the control of design and manufacture in industry bore fruit internationally early in the next century, through such outstanding architects as Schinkel, who in 1819 helped found the influential Technische Deputation in Prussia.

The role of the Royal Society of Arts highlights the central importance given to education in the theoretical and practical concerns of Neo-classicism. The very nature of the Enlightenment and the objective of Diderot's and d'Alembert's *Encyclopédie* (Paris, 1751–72) was to promote enquiry into the broadest range of activities; the arts were seen to have an important responsibility in spreading knowledge, as well as serving the interests of an ever-widening public. Consequently numerous art academies were established during the later 18th century to improve the intellectual training of artists and architects (*see* ACADEMY, §4). Moreover, the subject-matter of art and the range of specialized building types extended accordingly to meet the needs of a wider social clientele. Accompanying this concern with education was the rise of professional organizations for artists and architects (often providing qualifications and diplomas) to enhance their social status, as exemplified in Reynolds's programme for the Royal Academy (established 1768) in London. Within this institution, the status of women artists was recognized with the inclusion of Angelica Kauffman and Mary Moser among the 40 founder-academicians, and the social significance of the institution was signalled by the Academy's

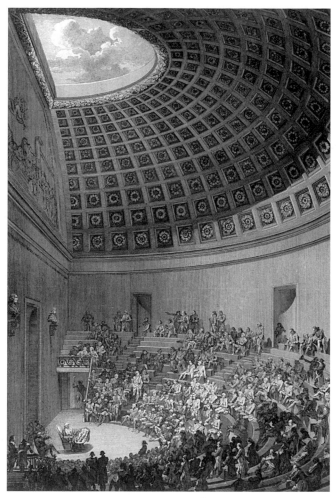

4. Jacques Gondoin: interior of the anatomy lecture theatre, Ecole de Chirurgie (now Faculté de Médecine), Paris, 1780; engraving from Poulleau: *Description des écoles de chirurgie* (Paris, 1780)

impressive headquarters in Sir William Chambers's Somerset House (from 1776; moved to Burlington House by 1869), London.

In response to the didactic role of art as a moral and intellectual force in society, public museums and art galleries also began to be established, involving educationally motivated programmes of display and housed in some of the earliest custom-built structures. Such private galleries as the Uffizi in Florence and the Antiquarium at the Residenz in Munich (*see* MUNICH, fig. 5) had been in existence since the Renaissance, while cabinets of curiosities and *Kunstkammern* (*see* KUNSTKAMMER) had been developed in the 17th century. In 1753 the British government founded the British Museum in London from the collection of Sir Hans Sloane, while in Paris the Musée Central des Arts in the Palais du Louvre was designated a public museum in 1792. In the last quarter of the 18th century, in the reigns of Clement XIV (*reg* 1769–75) and Pius VI (*reg* 1775–1800), the Vatican's unrivalled collection of antiquities was arranged within a sequence of sophisticated displays, and in the early 19th century several important new museums and galleries were constructed in Europe (*see* MUSEUM, §§I and II; *see also* FRANCE, §XIV; GERMANY, §XIV; ITALY, §XIV; and ENGLAND, §XIV).

The attention paid to the developing social commitments of artists, architects and designers, as well as new areas of patronage and widening audiences, posed new problems over the definition of 'art'. Creating forms of universal significance with eternal validity related uneasily at times to the search for fresh modes of contemporary expression and demands for new subject-matter. This dilemma is vividly illustrated by such works as Benjamin West's *Death of General Wolfe* (1770; Ottawa, N.G.; *see* WEST, BENJAMIN, fig. 1), where the event is controversially depicted in modern dress despite the use of historical formulae. Particularly challenging was Jean-Baptiste Pigalle's *Voltaire Nude* (1770–76; Paris, Inst. France), an uncompromising marble statue of the elderly writer reminiscent of the antique ('Borghese') *Dying Seneca* (Paris, Louvre). A revaluation of Nature and its associated phenomena, in which the emotions were seen to play an increasingly dominant role, is expressed in such paintings as Joseph Wright of Derby's *Experiment on a Bird in the Air Pump* (1768; London, N.G.; for illustration *see* ENLIGHTENMENT, THE) portraying human reactions of excitement and apprehension to scientific enquiry. In George Stubbs's *Horse Devoured by a Lion* (exh. ?1763; London, Tate), the wild character of the enveloping landscape amplifies an epic subject, later to be a favourite theme of such 19th-century Romantic artists as Géricault.

4. NATURE AND CLASSICISM. The conception of landscape as Nature perfected by mankind's intervention, characteristic of art and landscape design in the previous 200 years, was now replaced by one in which sentiment and idealized forms demanded a deeper act of involvement by the spectator. This is reflected in works as diverse as the imaginary landscape paintings of Richard Wilson or Joseph Anton Koch and such portraits as Gainsborough's *Mrs Richard Brinsley Sheridan* (1785; Washington, DC, N.G.A.) or Wilhelm Tischbein's *Goethe in the Roman Campagna* (1787; Frankfurt am Main, Städel. Kstinst. & Städt. Gal.; for illustration *see* GOETHE, JOHANN WOLFGANG VON). Ideas first explored in the early 18th century by Alexander Pope and Kent attained new levels of significance in such poetic landscape gardens as Stourhead, Wilts, developed from 1743 by its owner, Henry Hoare the younger (for illustration *see* STOURHEAD), and ERMENONVILLE, near Senlis, created between 1766 and 1776 by Louis-René de Girardin and to be, appropriately, a temporary resting-place for Jean-Jacques Rousseau's remains in a tomb designed by the ruin painter Hubert Robert. In this type of garden a calculated sequence of symbolic structures—intact or ruined classical temples, rough-hewn grottoes and rustic structures—was carefully sited to arouse a variety of responses from the perambulating visitor (a person of SENSIBILITÉ), as characterized by Girardin's *Promenade ou itinéraire des jardins d'Ermenonville* (1788). Marie-Antoinette's severely classical dairy at Rambouillet, designed by Hubert Robert and constructed in 1785–8 by Jacques-Jean Thévenin (*fl* 1770–90), opens into a rocky grotto framing a marble statue of the nymph Amalthea and provided a setting for the Queen

and her retinue to act out pastoral pursuits in harmony with Arcadian Nature (*see* DAIRY).

Edmund Burke's essay *A Philosophical Enquiry into the Origin of our Ideas of the Sublime and the Beautiful* appeared in 1756 during the long evolution of literary-inspired gardening in Britain and marked a new critical stage in its analysis of the psychological roots of aesthetic perception (*see* SUBLIME, THE). This discussion culminated in the Picturesque debate of the 1790s led by Richard Payne Knight and Uvedale Price, which involved a conflict between the regular, geometric forms of the Classical ideal and the consciously asymmetrical, pictorial forms associated with the emerging GOTHIC REVIVAL (for illustration *see* PICTURESQUE). Architectural solutions to this dilemma, whereby buildings were carefully integrated with the surrounding landscape, included Knight's own house Downton Castle (1772–8), Hereford & Worcs, with its medieval castellar exterior and a classical dining rotunda among the principal rooms within. Robert Adam's exceptional sequence of Scottish castles of the 1780s and 1790s, such as Culzean Castle (1777–92), Strathclyde, and Seton Castle (1789–91), Lothian, while retaining an uncompromising classical symmetry and simplicity of volume, was effectively sited to bring out the full scenic potential through oblique views and dramatic settings. Similarly, the pioneering villa (*c.* 1802) in the Italianate style at Cronkhill, Salop, by John Nash (*see* NASH, JOHN, fig. 1) involved a scenic composition that deployed classical forms in a skilfully asymmetrical plan (for further discussion of gardens *see* GARDEN, §VIII, 4(ii) and (iv)).

By the early 19th century the newly awakened forces of the emotional and pictorial in art were beginning to undermine the dominance of certain aesthetic and cultural principles associated with the classical tradition over past centuries. Moreover, an increasing search for archaeological truth served to impair imaginative processes and to weaken the character of the Neo-classical movement to a point where, according to Honour, it was 'drained of the force of conviction' and replaced by an international style of great decorative finesse and fashionable appeal.

5. THE LATE PHASE. The adoption of Neo-classicism as an official style by the Jacobins of the French Revolution (*see* FRANCE, fig. 47), accompanied by secular cults of Republican imagery, was succeeded during the Napoleonic age by the spread throughout Europe, by means of Bonapartist regimes, of a propagandist language of absolutism. Greek austerity was exchanged for the florid rhetoric of Imperial Roman art, extending from the creation of large urban-planning projects and public monuments down to schemes of interior decoration and furnishing (*see* DIRECTOIRE STYLE and CONSULATE STYLE). At its highest level, the applied arts of the First Empire (1804–15) involved such outstanding designers as Charles Percier and Pierre-François-Léonard Fontaine, whose *Recueil de décorations intérieures comprenant tout ce qui a rapport à l'ameublement* (Paris, 1801) served as a manifesto for this politically motivated classicism. Defining the official Napoleonic style, works ranged from the Arc de Triomphe du Carrousel (1806–7), Paris, with its polychromatic programme of imperial imagery, to interiors for the châteaux of Saint-Cloud and Malmaison (for

illustration *see* FONTAINE, PIERRE-FRANÇOIS-LÉONARD) and for the Palais des Tuileries in Paris, and such ceremonial settings as that depicted by David in the *Coronation of Napoleon in Notre-Dame* (1805–7; Paris, Louvre; version Versailles, Château). With the spread of the empire and its needs for an appropriate political image, the new classicism was developed by able practitioners: in Italy, for example, by such architects as Luigi Cagnola, Giovanni Antonio Selva and Giuseppe Valadier, and such designers as Antonio Basoli (1774–1843), Luigi Canonica and Pelagio Palagi. Meanwhile, the sculptural identity of Napoleon and his family was provided by Canova, who produced several monumental images between 1803 and 1809, including a bronze equestrian statue of the Emperor (later completed as *Charles III of Naples and Spain*, 1807–19; Naples, Piazza Plebiscito), a colossal standing nude figure depicting *Napoleon as Mars the Pacifier* (marble, 1803–6; London, Apsley House; bronze replica, 1809; Milan, Brera) and *Paolina Borghese Bonaparte as Venus Victorious* (marble, 1804–8; Rome, Gal. Borghese), which is strangely reminiscent of Etruscan burial effigies while being the best-known, if unconventional, portrait of Napoleon's sister. Like the Roman Empire, its principal source of inspiration, the Napoleonic era converted for its use the decorative language of invaded cultures, notably that of ancient Egypt following the North African campaign in 1798. The resulting researches made by Vivant Denon, the future director of the Musée Napoléon (formerly the Musée Central des Arts), were published in the form of two influential source-books, *Voyage dans la basse et la haute Egypte pendant les campagnes du général Bonaparte* (2 vols, Paris, 1802) and *Description de l'Egypte* (24 vols, Paris, 1809–22), and often converted into designs for the imperial court. Examples of this new taste in the decorative arts are Martin-Guillaume Biennais's coin-cabinet (*c.* 1800–14; New York, Met.) based on the pylon at Qus (Apollinopolis Parva) in Upper Egypt and a lavish Egyptian service in Sèvres porcelain (1809–12; London, Apsley House; for further discussion *see* EGYPTIAN REVIVAL and EMPIRE STYLE).

In Britain the contemporary REGENCY STYLE, despite strong affinities in its formal language and decorative values to the French Empire style, was largely saved from a similar stereotyped character by the originality of a number of artists, architects and designers working within the classical tradition. Soane's exceptional and complex system of interlocking interiors for the Bank of England (1788–1833), London, with an ingenious use of toplighting and daring abstractions of classical structure and ornament, made it the most original public building of late Neo-classicism anywhere in Europe (*see* SOANE, JOHN, §2). Flaxman, apart from various funerary monuments (e.g. *Lord Nelson*, 1808–18; London, St Paul's Cathedral) and book illustrations to the Homeric epics and the works of Dante (*see* §2 above), was a highly versatile designer in the applied arts. In addition to his early work for Wedgwood (e.g. the jasperware vase with the *Apotheosis of Homer*, 1786; London, BM), he served the royal goldsmiths Rundell, Bridge & Rundell (*see* ENGLAND, §IX, 1(v)). Thomas Hope, a discerning patron of such artists as Canova and Flaxman, exerted a considerable influence as a designer himself, transforming the interior of his own

house (1799–1801; destr. 1850) in Duchess Street, London, and publishing the designs in his *Household Furniture and Interior Design* (London, 1807; for illustration *see* HOPE, (1)). Inspired by Piranesi and familiar with the contemporary work of Percier, Fontaine and Denon, he created a sequence of highly personal rooms, complete with furniture according to stylistic themes, and incorporating material from Greek, Roman, Egyptian, Indian and Turkish sources (for illustration *see* EGYPTIAN REVIVAL). In 1818–19 and 1823 he remodelled and extended his country house, The Deepdene (destr. 1967), Surrey, with skilful Picturesque planning, incorporating similar ideas.

In its most original and productive aspects, the period of late Neo-classicism covering the first quarter of the 19th century was a time of considerable achievements in urban design, involving a large number of major public buildings and civic works. Almost in contrast to the art of the Napoleonic age, the later GREEK REVIVAL—ideologically associated with both liberal and nationalist movements—became the preferred style for significant monuments. Outstanding among these were buildings and structures in Berlin by Carl Gotthard Langhans and Schinkel, in Edinburgh by Thomas Hamilton and William Henry Playfair, in Philadelphia by Benjamin Latrobe and Pierre-Charles L'Enfant and in St Petersburg by Thomas-Jean de Thomon (e.g. the Stock Exchange, 1805–10; now the Central Naval Museum; *see* RUSSIA, fig. 11) and Andreyan Zakharov (e.g. the Admiralty Building, 1806–12; for illustration *see* ZAKHAROV, ANDREYAN). The most significant innovations in planning as such, however, were in England, where between 1754 and 1775 John Wood I and John Wood II pioneered highly original and flexible housing patterns in Bath, Avon, in response to the natural contours of the site (e.g. the King's Circus, 1754–*c.* 1766, and the Royal Crescent, 1767–*c.* 1775; *see* BATH (i), fig. 3). Many of these ideas were exploited in London from 1813 on a metropolitan scale by John Nash (i), with the active encouragement of the Prince Regent (later George IV, *reg* 1820–30) in the innovative scheme for Regent's Park with its related royal processional route (*see* NASH, JOHN, fig. 2; *see also* LONDON, fig. 7). Nash's ingenious blend of 'natural' landscape in the current Picturesque mode, placed within the heart of a monumental scheme of formal classical terraces and individual villas in the parkland, together with a satellite village and water-borne services by canal, was to provide key concepts for the GARDEN CITY movement 100 years later.

The fact that Nash's design for Regent's Park can be interpreted as either Neo-classical or Romantic (or even considered within the context of the hybrid term ROMANTIC CLASSICISM) indicates the degree of ambiguity of works of art and design within the classical tradition in the early 19th century. As Honour has pointed out (p. 186–7), early Romantic artists such as Anne-Louis Girodet had trained in David's studio and had emerged to develop a style that exploited rhapsodic and supernatural effects and themes found in contemporary nationalist literature in northern Europe (e.g. Girodet's *Ossian and the French Generals*, 1800–02; Malmaison, Château N.; *see* GIRODET, ANNE-LOUIS, fig. 2). Meanwhile, LES PRIMITIFS—artists who had taken the cult of Primitivism and simplicity to puritan extremes—left few works of any significance but disturbed the careful balance and ambiguity that had made the Neo-classical style so effective a force in its early development. Even the conventional polarity so often devised between Ingres, the ostensibly archetypal Neo-classicist, and Delacroix, the Romantic, appears more complex when the subject-matter and strong degree of sentiment are examined, even in Ingres's most classicizing works.

Like the social forces that condition their origins, maturation and development, stylistic movements have a lifespan that determines their relevance and effectiveness as well as, ultimately, their replacement by fresh intellectual climates. Neo-classicism, while still traced as an identifiable mode of classicism well into the 19th century in, for example, Alexander Thomson's churches in Glasgow or Thomas Couture's Salon paintings and James Pradier's sculptures in France, had ceased to be a commanding idea. In the 20th century it reappeared, most significantly in architecture, as an influence on designers with strong classical sympathies as sharply contrasting as Mies van der Rohe and Albert Speer, and it has made a questionable 'come-back' in certain aspects of the Post-modern movement (*see* POST-MODERNISM, §1).

See also CLASSICISM, §§5 and 6.

BIBLIOGRAPHY

SOURCES

M.-A. Laugier: *Essai sur l'architecture* (Paris, 1753, rev. 1755/*R* 1972; Eng. trans., 1755)
D. Diderot: *Salons* (1759–81); ed. J. Adhémar and J. Seznec, 4 vols (Oxford, 1957–67, rev. 1983)
J. Reynolds: *Discourses on Art* (London, 1778); ed. R. R. Wark (San Marino, CA, 1959/*R* New Haven and London, 1975)
L. Eitner, ed.: *Neo-classicism and Romanticism, 1750–1850*, Sources & Doc. Hist. A., i (Englewood Cliffs, NJ, 1970)
G. B. Piranesi: *The Polemical Works*; ed. and trans. by J. Wilton-Ely (Farnborough, 1972) [contains *Della magnificenza ed architettura de' Romani* (Rome, 1761), *Parere su l'architettura* (Rome, 1765) and *Diverse maniere* (Rome, 1769) among other works]
J. Winckelmann: *Writings on Art*, ed. D. Irwin (London, 1972)

GENERAL

H. T. Parker: *The Cult of Antiquity and the French Revolutionaries* (Chicago, 1937)
N. Pevsner: *Academies of Art* (Cambridge, 1940)
M. Praz: *Gusto neoclassico* (Florence, 1940); Eng. trans. as *On Neo-classicism* (London, 1972)
F. D. Klingender: *Art and the Industrial Revolution* (London, 1947, rev. 1967)
D. Irwin: *English Neo-classical Art* (London, 1966)
R. Rosenblum: *Transformations in Late 18th-century Art* (Princeton, 1967)
H. Honour: *Neo-classicism*, Style & Civiliz. (Harmondsworth, 1968, rev. 1977)
P. Gay: *The Enlightenment, an Interpretation: The Science of Freedom* (New York, 1970)
J. M. Crook: *The Greek Revival* (London, 1972)
Age of Neo-classicism (exh. cat., ACGB, 1972)
J. Rykwert: *The First Moderns* (Cambridge, MA, 1980)

MONOGRAPHS

C. Justi: *Winckelmann und seine Zeitgenossen*, 3 vols (Leipzig, 1923)
J. Fleming: *Robert Adam and his Circle* (London, 1962, rev. 1978)
W. Herrmann: *Laugier and 18th-century French Theory* (London, 1962)
R. Rosenblum: *Jean-Auguste-Dominique Ingres* (London, 1967)
D. Watkin: *Thomas Hope (1769–1831) and the Neo-classical Idea* (London, 1968)
N. Goodison: *Ormolu: The Work of Matthew Boulton* (London, 1974)
G. Pavanello: *L'opera completa del Canova* (Milan, 1976)
J. Wilton-Ely: *The Mind and Art of Piranesi* (London, 1978)
D. Irwin: *John Flaxman (1755–1826): Sculptor, Illustrator, Designer* (London, 1979)
A. Brookner: *Jacques-Louis David* (London, 1980)
M. Snodin, ed.: *Karl Friedrich Schinkel: A Universal Man* (London, 1991)

A. Potts: *Flesh and the Ideal: Winckelmann and the Origins of Art History* (London, 1994)

ARCHITECTURE

T. F. Hamlin: *Greek Revival Architecture in America* (New York, 1944)
J. Summerson: *Architecture in Britain, 1530–1830*, Pelican Hist. A. (Harmondsworth, 1953, rev. 7/1983)
H. R. Hitchcock: *Architecture: Nineteenth and Twentieth Centuries*, Pelican Hist. A. (Harmondsworth, 1958, rev. 1977)
J. Harris: 'Le Geay, Piranesi and International Neo-classicism in Rome, 1740–1750', *Essays in the History of Art Presented to Rudolf Wittkower* (London, 1967), pp. 189–996
D. Wiebenson: *Sources of Greek Revival Architecture* (London, 1969)
K. Woodbridge: *Landscape and Antiquity: Aspects of English Culture at Stourhead, 1718–1835* (Oxford, 1970)
N. Pevsner: *A History of Building Types* (London, 1976)
A. Braham: *The Architecture of the French Enlightenment* (London, 1980)
R. Middleton and D. Watkin: *Neo-classical and 19th-century Architecture* (London, 1980)
D. Watkin and T. Mellinghoff: *German Architects and the Classical Ideal, 1740–1840* (London, 1987)
D. Stillman: *English Neo-classical Architecture*, 2 vols (London, 1988)
J. Wilton-Ely: *Piranesi as Architect and Designer* (New Haven, 1993)

PAINTING AND SCULPTURE

W. Friedlaender: *From David to Delacroix* (Cambridge, MA, 1950)
E. K. Waterhouse: *Painting in Britain, 1530–1790*, Pelican Hist. A. (Harmondsworth, 1953)
F. Novotny: *Painting and Sculpture in Europe, 1780–1880*, Pelican Hist. A. (Harmondsworth, 1960)
M. Whinney: *Sculpture in Britain, 1530–1830*, Pelican Hist. A. (Harmondsworth, 1964)
M. Levey: *Painting and Sculpture in France, 1700–89*, Pelican Hist. A. (Harmondsworth, 1992)

APPLIED AND DECORATIVE ARTS

F. J. B. Watson: *Louis XVI Furniture* (London, 1960)
E. Harris: *The Furniture of Robert Adam* (London, 1963)
M. Gallet: *Demeures parisiennes: L'Epoque de Louis XVI* (Paris, 1964)
S. Eriksen: *Early French Neo-classicism* (London, 1974)
A. González-Palacios: *Il tempio del gusto: Le arti decorative in Italia fra classicismi e barocco: Roma e il regno delle due Sicilie*, 2 vols (Milan, 1984)
J. Wilton-Ely: 'Pompeian and Etruscan Tastes in the Neo-classical Country House Interior', *Conference Proceedings. The Fashioning and Functioning of the British Country House: Washington, 1985*, pp 51–77
A. González-Palacios: *Il granducato di Toscana e gli stati settentrionali*, 2 vols (Milan, 1986)
G. Worsley: 'Antique Assumptions', *Country Life*, clxxxvi (6 Aug 1992), pp. 48–50

JOHN WILTON-ELY

Neo-Dadaism Organizers. Group of Japanese artists who showed at the Yomiuri Independent exhibitions of the late 1950s and developed 'anti-art' activities modelled on those of the DADA movement. There were frequent dissolutions and reformings, but the group that formed in March 1960 included Masunobu Yoshimura (*b* 1932), Genpei Akasegawa (*b* 1937), Shūsaku Arakawa, Shō Kazakura, Ushio Shinohara (*b* 1933) and Sōroku Toyoshima (and later Shintarō Tanaka (*b* 1940) and Shin Kinoshita); with the exception of Tetsumi Kudō and Tomio Miki, who associated with the group but never joined, it seemed then to comprise all the major 'anti-art' artists in Japan.

In 1960 three exhibitions were held, the first in April at the Ginza Art Gallery in Tokyo. These included performances, such as that by Yoshimura to mark the opening of a show (see 1985 exh. cat., p. 66), as well as the works, which often incorporated *objets trouvés*. It can be said that the Neo-Dadaism Organizers were, rather than a group or movement, a symbol of rejection, centred on the young generation who opposed the tendency to progress once again on the model of Western art (such as *Art informel*) during the period of recovery after the shock of defeat in

World War II. After the group's dissolution, the individual artists returned to their own courses of development.

WRITINGS
Neo dadaizumu oruganaizāzu dai'ichikaiten densensho [The first Neo-Dadaism Organizers exhibition: a declaration] (Tokyo, 1960)

BIBLIOGRAPHY
U. Shinohara: *Zen'ei no michi* [The way of the avant-garde] (Tokyo, 1968)
Reconstructions: Avant-garde Art in Japan, 1945–1965 (exh. cat., intro. D. Elliott and K. Kaido; Oxford, MOMA, 1985)

SHIGEO CHIBA

Neofiguración. Paraguayan movement, active in the second half of the 1960s. It developed in Asunción as the Paraguayan equivalent of the Nueva Figuración movement in Argentina. However, it formulated its own guidelines and aims, and had a considerable influence on later developments in the visual arts in Paraguay. It represented an approach to figurative art halfway between *Art informel* and Expressionism, between a preoccupation with the physical material of the painting and the intention of distorting the figure. It was used by a group of Paraguayan artists to loosen the rigid pictorial image that had become accepted in the 1950s and to assimilate aspects of historical experience that had not until then played a part in artistic development. Social criticism was approached from two different angles within Neofiguración. The first, represented primarily by Carlos Colombino and Olga Blinder, had a sense of drama and a strong political message; the second, represented by William Riquelme (*b* 1944) and Ricardo Migliorisi, had a more satirical perspective and a playful and irresponsible spirit that to some extent was characteristic of the time.

See also PARAGUAY, §IV, 2.

BIBLIOGRAPHY
M. A. Fernández: *Art in Latin America Today: Paraguay* (Washington, DC, 1969)
O. Blinder and others: *Art actual en el Paraguay* (Asunción, 1983)
T. Escobar: *Una interpretación de las artes visuales en el Paraguay* (Asunción, 1984)

TICIO ESCOBAR

Neo-Georgian. Stylistic term applied to the revival in the UK in the late 19th century and the 20th of the classical GEORGIAN STYLE of domestic architecture and interior and furniture design from the period 1714–1830. Similar, contemporary revivals of late 18th- and early 19th-century Georgian colonial styles also took place in such countries as the USA and Australia (*see* COLONIAL REVIVAL). Neo-Georgian was one of the most popular architectural styles in the UK between 1900 and 1930; it continued to be employed despite the advent of Modernism, and in the 1980s a new phase of popularity began, stimulated by the anti-modernist, eclectic and pluralist trends of POST-MODERNISM.

1. ARCHITECTURE. The origins of the Neo-Georgian style can be found in the 1860s. The house (1860–62; destr.) at 2 Palace Green, Kensington, London, designed for William Makepeace Thackeray by Frederick Hering (1800–69), who drew on Thackeray's sketches, was an early, isolated example reflecting a literary interest in the 18th century. Another precursor is Crabbet Park (1872–3), E. Sussex, designed for their own use by the poet Wilfred Scawen Blunt and his wife Lady Anne Blunt; its

bilateral symmetry and central emphasis distinguish it from contemporary work in the prevalent Queen Anne Revival style, for example by Richard Norman Shaw and W. E. Nesfield. For such architects, schooled in the Gothic Revival, this symmetry was uncomfortable and was generally avoided even in buildings that reproduced Georgian decorative details. Symmetry can be taken as a defining characteristic of Neo-Georgian, although plans were frequently asymmetrical behind regular façades, partly to accommodate the more complicated social requirements of the age.

Neo-Georgian themes were later developed by Shaw (e.g. 170 Queens Gate, Kensington, 1887–8) and his pupils, including Ernest Newton and Mervyn Macartney (1853–1932), as well as by his admirers, for example Reginald Blomfield. They were also used by architects involved with the Arts and Crafts Movement. Shaw's work subsequently influenced Edwin Lutyens, who became the most celebrated of the many Neo-Georgian architects active before 1914. Lutyens found compositional devices to extend Neo-Georgian designs for large country houses; he also introduced the style for large urban buildings, in which Neo-Georgian can be distinguished from the contemporaneous Baroque Revival by the use of red brick with stone dressings, pitched roofs and general avoidance of large-scale architectural orders. Most architects worked in both styles, selecting according to building type and tradition, but after the succession of King George V in 1910 the idea of a Georgian revival was considered highly appropriate. Neo-Georgian was thereafter preferred for public housing, and it achieved an almost universal popularity with the London County Council Architects' Department until 1930. A more severe aesthetic was developed, relying solely on proportion and materials and virtually without ornament. Neo-Georgian was also used in the design of new towns; Welwyn Garden City (begun 1924), for example, was designed almost entirely in the style, used for houses and public buildings alike.

Neo-Georgian thus preceded Modernism as an architecture of anonymous public service, but its use began to be challenged in the 1930s. At the same time, Neo-Georgian architects working in that decade began to prefer a more accurate reproduction of the later Georgian period, paralleled in the Regency revival in interior decoration. After 1945 the style was often discouraged and denigrated by influential critics, but it remained popular with institutions and individual clients, and some fine buildings by such architects as E. Vincent Harris and Albert E. Richardson employed the style with an individual character that had been lacking in the 1920s and 1930s. After 1950 younger architects, including Raymond Erith, Donald MacMorran (1904–65) and Francis Johnson (*b* 1910), developed personal styles based on classical precedent, although Erith, the most prominent, dissociated himself from pre-World War II Neo-Georgian. The resurgence of Neo-Georgian in the 1980s, led by Erith's partner Quinlan Terry, who preferred 17th-century sources and Baroque detail (e.g. Richmond riverside development, near London, 1983–8), achieved an unprecedented degree of critical and commercial acceptance, and many practices without a firm attachment to classicism were willing to adopt the style when required by clients.

BIBLIOGRAPHY
L. Weaver: *Smaller Country Houses of Today*, 2 vols (London, 1910–19)
R. Gradidge: *Dream Houses: The Edwardian Ideal* (London, 1980)
D. Calabi: *Architettura domestica in Gran Bretagna, 1890–1939* (Milan, 1982)
J. M. Robinson: *The Latest Country Houses* (London, 1984)
A. Powers, ed.: *Real Architecture* (London, 1987)
A. Powers: 'Larkhall', *Architects' J.* (1989), Sept, pp. 50–56
G. Stamp: 'MacMorran and Whitby—A Progressive Classicism', *Mod. Painters*, iv/4 (1991), pp. 56–60

ALAN POWERS

2. DECORATIVE ARTS AND PAINTING. The revival of 18th-century models in architecture was paralleled in the decorative arts. Crucially, however, what tended to be revived were elements of classical design rather than literal copies of original items of furniture, glass, silver or ceramics. Robert Adam (i) was a much quarried source of design ideas, often reduced to a Neo-classical shorthand of paterae, swags and drops applied to unmistakably modern objects such as grand pianos, coffee tables and gas fires.

In furniture, the most popular sources of design were the pattern books published by Adam, Thomas Chippendale, George Hepplewhite and Thomas Sheraton, all of which were republished in facsimile several times during the 19th and early 20th centuries. Although the quality of workmanship was often excellent, the designs were adapted to allow for machine manufacture and a more economic use of materials. The result was invariably a dilution of the design, resulting in a spindly effect that instantly differentiated revival versions from period originals. Particularly popular between 1890 and 1910 was satinwood furniture with painted decoration in the manner of Sheraton, produced by firms such as Edwards & Roberts, Maples and Hampton & Sons, all of London. The domestic effect of this revivalism is best demonstrated by the interiors of Manderston, Borders Region, which was built in 1903–5 and furnished by the London firm of Mellier & Co. Manderston has a 'Chippendale' dining room and an 'Adam' morning room. Some of the finer interiors were designed by architects, such as the furniture, carpets and decoration of the White House (1907–10), Shiplake, Oxon, by George Walton. The popularity of this type of interior lasted a long time. Stanford Hall (remodelled 1928 by White Allom), Leics, had a 'Georgian' mahogany dining room and 'Adam' bedrooms. The style persisted into the 1930s for the first-class reception rooms of transatlantic liners.

In silver, ceramics and textiles, the muscularity and careful proportions of the Georgian models were similarly diluted to produce etiolated yet often fussier versions for a mass market. A number of pottery manufacturers founded in the 18th century, such as Adams & Co. and Wedgwood, turned to reproductions of their earlier wares or new designs in the old manner. One of the most successful examples of the latter was Wedgwood's 'Edme' pattern, designed by John Goodwin in 1908 for the French market and made in Queen's Ware (the body designed by the firm's founder Josiah Wedgwood). It was in continuous production from 1913. In art, the 18th century came to represent an ideal pre-industrial elysium, from which ideas were garnered by such artists as the illustrator Kate Greenaway. Genre pictures in vaguely Regency settings were particularly popular and both fed off and encouraged Georgian revivalism in interior decoration through the ready availability of engravings made from successful Royal Academy paintings by William Quiller Orchardson, Marcus Stone (ii) and others.

BIBLIOGRAPHY
C. Aslet: *The Last Country Houses* (New Haven and London, 1982)
R. Reilly: *Wedgwood*, ii (London, 1989)

Neo-Gothic. *See* GOTHIC REVIVAL.

Néo-Grec. Term used for a manifestation of the Neo-classical style initiated in the decorative arts of France during the Second Empire (1852–71) of Napoleon III and his wife, the Empress Eugénie. Based on the standard repertory of Greco-Roman ornament, it combined elements from the Adam, Louis XVI and Egyptian styles with a range of motifs inspired by discoveries at Pompeii, where excavations had begun in 1848; it can be identified by the frequent use of Classical heads and figures, masks, winged griffins, sea-serpents, urns, medallions, arabesques, lotus buds and borders of anthemion, guilloche and Greek fret pattern. Néo-Grec was eclectic, abstracted, polychromatic and sometimes bizarre; it enjoyed popularity as one of the many revival styles of the second half of the 19th century.

In Paris, the Néo-Grec style was best exemplified in the famous 'Maison Pompéienne' (1856–8; destr. 1891) designed for Prince Napoléon Bonaparte (*see* BONAPARTE, (10)) by Alfred Nicolas Normand; the style of this colourfully decorated house was derived from the 'third style' of Pompeii *c.* 82–79 BC, as may be seen in Normand's design for the atrium (pencil, ink, watercolour and gouache, Paris, 1860; Paris, Mus. A. Déc.). Some of the painted room decorations were the work of Jean-Léon Gérôme. In furniture, the Empress Eugénie's passion for the 18th century resulted in a vogue for the styles of Louis XV and Louis XVI, recreated either in direct imitation or in the more fanciful Néo-Grec manner; the latter pieces were often painted, ebonized and gilded, with shallow carving or incised decoration and crossed or tripod, hocked and hoofed legs. Rooms of this period were crowded with seating of all kinds, upholstered in button-tufted velvet, damask or corded silk with fringes, tassels and bobbles, a treatment echoed in the window curtains; this style is depicted in a plate (London, V&A) from *Le Magasin de Meubles* (Paris, 1865–7) illustrating Néo-Grec window treatment. Tripod stands, often dangling chains with pendant balls, and classical figures of bronze supporting candelabra were favoured items.

In the USA, Néo-Grec coincided with an interest in Egyptian artefacts, which sometimes led to an exotic fusion of themes, as in the painted and gilded beech-wood stool (*c.* 1865; New York, Met.) designed by Alexandre Roux (*fl* 1837–81). More typical was the solid, rectilinear parlour furniture manufactured by such companies as M. & H. Schrenkeisen and George Hunzinger (*fl* 1861–80), both of New York, where the heightened chair crests were carved with such Néo-Grec devices as scrolled volutes, foliate forms, palmettes and roundels, topped by enlarged acroteria and miniature pediments (e.g. parlour suite no. 95 from the M. & H. Schrenkeisen catalogue,

New York, 1879; Winterthur, DE, Mus. & Gdns. Lib.). This fashionable furniture was frequently categorized with the American Eastlake style, which also featured angular forms and incised decoration.

The ceramics, silver and glass produced at this time commonly exhibited ancient Greek pottery forms; the shapes included the amphora and the kylix (a shallow, footed bowl). Both silver and glass manufacturers preferred slender, elegant vessels engraved or applied with Classical designs and frequently resting on tripod bases with hoofed feet, an example being a vase of wheel-engraved glass set in cast bronze feet (Toronto, Royal Ont. Mus.), made in the 1870s, possibly in France. The many diverse objects that are now accepted as Néo-Grec are appreciated as a lively, disciplined embellishment of Classical traditions.

A group of painters in Paris, active from the mid-1840s and led by Gérôme, were dubbed the Néo-Grecs, for their popular renderings of antiquity. They lived and worked together in a house on the Rue de Fleurus, which their friend and champion, the writer Théophile Gautier, called 'little Athens'. Besides Gérôme, the original members included Jean-Louis Hamon and Henri-Pierre Picou (1824–95). The group painted intimate scenes, drawn from Classical literature, of everyday life in Greece of the 5th century BC. Their nude or gauzily draped maidens and youths in short tunics were depicted with photographic realism and an underlying homoeroticism, typified by Gérôme's well-known painting *The Cockfight* (oil, 1846; Paris, Louvre). Although highly fashionable for a while, the Néo-Grec painters' work attracted criticism for its preciousness and pseudo-intellectualism.

BIBLIOGRAPHY

C. H. Stranahan: *A History of French Painting* (London, 1889), pp. 329–35

K. L. Ames: 'Sitting in (Néo-Grec) Style', *19th C.* [New York], ii (1976), pp. 51–8

G. M. Ackerman: *The Life and Work of Jean-Léon Gérôme* (London, 1986) [with cat. rais.]

□

Neo-Impressionism. Term applied to an avant-garde, European art movement that flourished from 1886 to 1906. The term Neo-Impressionism was coined by the art critic Félix Fénéon in a review, 'Les Impressionistes' (in *La Vogue*; Paris, 1886), of the eighth and last Impressionist exhibition. Camille Pissarro had convinced his Impressionist colleagues to allow paintings by himself, his son Lucien Pissaro, Paul Signac and GEORGES SEURAT to be shown together in a single room, asserting a shared vision and inviting comparison. Fénéon considered Albert Dubois to be one of the 'new Impressionists'; the group soon included Charles Angrand, Louis Hayet, Henri Edmond Cross, Léo Gausson, Hippolyte Petitjean and Maximilien Luce.

Fénéon paid homage with the term Neo-Impressionism to the group's rebellious precursors, Monet, Auguste Renoir and Alfred Sisley, while distinguishing the new group's innovations. Impressionism, for Fénéon, was synonymous with instinct and spontaneity, whereas Neo-Impressionism was based on reflection and permanence. Although the Impressionists obeyed rules of colour contrast, they did so pragmatically and not according to the codified, scientific principles that were adopted by the Neo-Impressionists, who believed that painting could be based on rules that would make it possible to replicate the luminosity of nature on canvas. These rules would enable the artist to perfect his individual vision but were not intended to be used as a formula. The techniques associated with Neo-Impressionism were initiated by Seurat and were distinguished by the application of discrete units of paint, combined according to various theories of colour. This gave rise to the terms Pointillism, which refers to the application of dots of paint, and Divisionism, which involves the separation of colour through individual strokes of pigment (*see* DIVISIONISM).

1. ORIGINS AND THEORETICAL BACKGROUND. In the mid-1880s Seurat had become interested in several newly published studies of light and colour, including the experiments of the American physicist Ogden Rood, discussed in *Students' Text-book of Colour: or, Modern Chromatics, with Applications to Art and Industry* (New York, 1881), as well as the colour discs of James Maxwell and the theories of Heinrich-Wilhelm Dove. Seurat adopted Rood's belief that 'optical mixture' was preferable to the 'palette mixture' employed by Delacroix and the Impressionists. The goal of optical mixture was luminosity, which was aided by the adoption of separate dots of colour. These small dots also permitted the artists to paint on dry areas of canvas, in contrast to the Impressionists, who painted wet strokes upon wet to capture changing conditions of light and atmosphere. Neo-Impressionists made use of the laws of simultaneous and successive contrast gleaned from Michel-Eugène Chevreul's *De la loi du contraste simultané des couleurs et ses applications* (Paris, 1839), in which he explained that simultaneous contrast occurs when two complementaries are juxtaposed to create an effect of great intensity and vibrancy; successive contrast is the appearance around a passage of one colour of a halo of its complement.

This interest in colour extended to the borders around the canvases. At first, Seurat favoured white frames, believing that gold competed with the orange hues in his paintings. After a brief period of experimentation with dots applied directly to the frame, he settled on adding a dotted inner border of complementary colours on the canvas, between the image and the white frame.

As well as a desire to replicate natural light and colour, the Neo-Impressionists sought scientific mastery of composition. Seurat was particularly influenced by Charles Henry's *L'Esthétique scientifique* (Paris, 1855), an exploration of physiological responses to line and colour. According to Henry, upward lines and warm colours produced a 'dynamogenous' or uplifting effect, and downward lines and cold colours an 'inhibitory' one. Seurat's *The Parade* (1887–8; New York, Met.; see fig.) is composed on a balance of such diagonal lines arranged according to the golden section, a ratio recommended by Henry for determining the placement of horizontals and verticals in a composition. However, the work of Seurat and his circle attempted more than the sum of the scientific systems derived from Chevreul, Rood and Henry. Like the contemporary Symbolist writers, the Neo-Impressionists wished to evoke a mood and to go beyond the mere appearance

Neo-Impressionist painting by Georges Seurat: *The Parade*, oil on canvas, 0.98×1.50 m, 1887–8 (New York, Metropolitan Museum of Art)

of nature to an underlying structure and meaning. At regular gatherings at Signac's studio Cross and Dubois met the Symbolist writers Gustave Kahn, Fénéon and Henri de Régnier. These writers saw in Seurat's work a search for a timeless monumentality that evoked the art of Ancient Egypt and Greece.

Both the Neo-Impressionists and Symbolists were acquainted with anarchist beliefs, including the writings of the Russian aristocrat Prince Pyotr Kropotkin, whose *Paroles d'un Révolté* (Paris, 1885) popularized the socialist views of William Morris. Kropotkin's emphasis upon the importance of art in everyday life, his belief that art should be in the service of revolution and his support for the individuality of the artist were all attractive to the group. Although they contributed illustrations and subscribed to, and at times financially supported, anarchist publications such as Jean Grave's *La Révolte* and *Les Temps nouveaux*, the Neo-Impressionists were not militant anarchists. They held that their radicalism lay in the very nature of their innovative art, which would help bring about the downfall of the status quo and all that was conservative; the style itself was helping to create a new society. Moreover, a painting's content could contribute to this end: factories, peasants, and industrial suburbs were depicted to show the meanness of daily life.

2. DIFFUSION OF NEO-IMPRESSIONISM IN EUROPE. Seurat's entries for the Impressionist exhibition of 1886, most notably the *Grande Jatte*, led to an invitation to show in Brussels at the avant-garde exhibition society, Les XX,

with Camille Pissarro in February 1887. Octave Maus, secretary of the group, welcomed the opportunity to show the controversial painting in Brussels and in an article, 'Les Vingtistes Parisiens' (in *Art moderne*, 1886), proclaimed Seurat 'the Messiah of a new art'. Seurat attended the opening in Brussels accompanied by Signac. In 1888 French Neo-Impressionism was represented at Les XX with 12 paintings by Signac and 13 by Dubois. The presence of these works in Brussels created a new group of Belgian Neo-Impressionists within Les XX. In summer 1887 Alfred William Finch had become the first Belgian to adopt Neo-Impressionist techniques, and by 1889 he was joined by fellow Vingtistes Anna Boch, Henry Van de Velde, Théo Van Rysselberghe and Jan Toorop. In 1890 Georges Lemmen adopted the style, creating some of his most successful portraits, such as *Julie* (1891; Chicago, IL, A. Inst.), and marine paintings in the Neo-Impressionist manner. Seurat exhibited at Les XX in 1889 and 1891; in 1892 the Vingtistes sponsored a memorial exhibition in his honour.

The Belgians came close to dominating the movement by 1892. Neo-Impressionism was introduced to the Netherlands by the exhibition by Les XX held at The Hague in 1892, in which Van de Velde and Toorop played major roles. Dutch artists who adopted Neo-Impressionism included Joseph Aarts, Hendricus Peter Bremmer and Jan Vijlbrief (1868–95). Neo-Impressionism had little influence outside France, Belgium and the Netherlands. The German artists, Paul Baum (1859–1932) and Christian Rohlfs, experimented with divided colour; and the Italians

Angelo Morbelli and Plinio Nomellini were also briefly attracted to the technique of Divisionism, but there was no real sympathy for the French style.

3. THE DECLINE OF NEO-IMPRESSIONISM AND THE 'SECOND PHASE' OF INFLUENCE. Major shows of Neo-Impressionist works continued to be held in Paris, including an exhibition in early 1893 at the Hôtel Brébant and four shows during 1893 and 1894 at the Galerie Rue Laffitte. However, Neo-Impressionism suffered a severe blow with Seurat's death in 1891. In 1890 Dubois had died, and Angrand had become disenchanted with the Neo-Impressionist technique. Lucien Pissarro and Camille Pissarro also grew weary of what they came to think of as a tedious formula. After several seasons, the Vingtistes abandoned the style: Toorop rejected Neo-Impressionism for Symbolism, Van de Velde turned first to the decorative arts and then to architecture, and after 1895 Lemmen became increasingly involved in the decorative arts and the creation of *intimiste* paintings.

In 1896 Neo-Impressionism experienced a revival created by PAUL SIGNAC, whose book, *D'Eugène Delacroix au Néo-Impressionnisme* (Paris, 1899), which first appeared as a series of articles in the *Revue Blanche*, attracted a new generation of converts. Attracted by this book and by the bold, later work of Signac and Cross, younger artists of the Fauve group, including Henri Matisse and André Derain, were drawn to Neo-Impressionist colour theories, as, for example, in Matisse's *Luxe, Calme et Volupté* (1904–5; Paris, Pompidou). Robert Delaunay, Jean Metzinger and Gino Severini all experimented with Pointillism as a means to produce dynamic and vibrant colour.

BIBLIOGRAPHY

P. Signac: *D'Eugène Delacroix au Néo-Impressionnisme* (Paris, 1899); ed. F. Cachin (Paris, 1964)
J. Rewald: *Post-Impressionism: From van Gogh to Gauguin* (New York, 1956, rev. 1978)
W. I. Homer: *Seurat and the Science of Painting* (Cambridge, MA, 1964/R 1978)
Neo-Impressionism (exh. cat. by R. L. Herbert, New York, Guggenheim, 1968)
J. U. Halperin: *Félix Fénéon: Oeuvres plus que complètes*, 2 vols (Geneva, 1970)
J. Sutter: *The Neo-Impressionists* (London, 1970)
Post-Impressionism: Cross Currents in European Painting (exh. cat., London, RA, 1979)
The Aura of Neo-Impressionism: The W. J. Holliday Collection (exh. cat. by E. Lee, Indianapolis, Mus. A., 1983)
R. Thompson: *Seurat* (Oxford, 1985)
Exposition du Pointillisme (exh. cat., Tokyo, N. Mus. W.A., 1985)
Georges Seurat, 1859–1891 (exh. cat. by R. L. Herbert, New York, Met., 1991)

JANE BLOCK

Neo-Liberty. Italian architectural movement that developed in the second half of the 1950s as a reaction to the widespread diffusion of the International Style, especially in relation to the sensitive historic environment of many Italian cities. Its name was originally coined by detractors of the movement to imply that it was simply a revival of the Italian *Stile Liberty* or Art Nouveau. The initiators of the movement were the Turin architects Roberto Gabetti (*b* 1925) and Aimaro d'Isola (*b* 1928), who were both pupils of Carlo Mollino at the Politecnico, Turin. In 1957 the architectural journal *Casabella Continuità*, edited by Ernesto Nathan Rogers and Vittorio Gregotti, published a number of works by Gabetti and d'Isola, including the influential Borsa Valori (1953) and Bottega d'Erasmo residential block (1953–6), both in Turin. In presenting their work, the architects declared their rejection of the idealist and doctrinaire theories of the Modern Movement, preferring instead to immerse themselves in the continuation of a local building tradition in the interests of an educated and bourgeois clientele. This sparked off an international debate that polarized on the one hand the defenders of the orthodoxy of the Modern Movement, led by the British critic Reyner Banham (1922–88), and on the other a group of architects from Turin, Novara and Milan who supported the views expressed in *Casabella*. While having their own differences, Vittorio Gregotti from Novara, Aldo Rossi, Guido Canella and Gai Aulenti from Milan, together with Gabetti, d'Isola and Giorgio and Giuseppe Raineri from Turin, were united in their wish to heal the rupture they perceived in the history of architecture through a reappraisal of the sources of the Modern Movement. The ideas expressed by Gabetti and d'Isola were part of a general move away from the purist principles of the Modern Movement at that time, and, like many other architects, they continued to develop new approaches in their architecture in the 1960s and after.

BIBLIOGRAPHY

R. Gabetti, A. d'Isola and V. Gregotti: 'L'impegno della tradizione', *Casabella*, 215 (1957), pp. 62–75
R. Banham: 'Neo-Liberty: The Italian Retreat from Modern Architecture', *Archit. Rev.* [London], cxxv/747 (1959), pp. 231–5
Controspazio, 4–5 (1977), pp. 84–93 [corr. on the debate repr. from *Casabella*]
F. Cellini and C. d'Amato: *Gabetti e Isola: Progetti e architettura, 1950–1985* (Milan, 1985)

ANDREA NULLI

Neon. Term used in its widest meaning to refer to luminous devices containing neon, mercury vapour, argon or other inert gases and their combinations used in electric signs or lamps generally tubular in shape. This extended definition is also applied in an artistic context. In its narrower, more technical sense, neon (from Gr. *neos*: 'new') is a rare inert gas that was discovered in 1898 and that was immediately recognized as a new element by its unique glow when electrically stimulated. The vapour-tube device filled with neon gas was invented by Georges Claude in Boulogne-Billancourt near Paris in 1910. When a high voltage was applied to the two electrodes at either end of the tube, it emitted a deep red light. With other gases, mercury vapour and their mixtures, a small range of colours was obtained in the following years in tubes that could be cut to any length, bent and formed by skilled craftsmen into almost any shape and used for signs that had, however, a very limited lighting capacity. When industrially produced, low-tension fluorescent straight tubing of white (and occasionally coloured) light in standardized sizes came into use in the 1930s, results approaching natural lighting were obtained.

Artists have incorporated both straight and curved 'neon' devices in pieces of sculpture or in interior or exterior environmental statements. Although neon tubes were widely used in the 1930s for decorative and advertising purposes, only very few artists employed them in their works during that period, for example the Czech artist and architect Zdeněk Pešánek (1896–1965) in a sculpture entitled *Man and Wife* (1935–6; Louny, Benedikt Rejt Gal.). The first attempt to use neon light as the principal material of a sculpture can be ascribed to Gyula Košice in Buenos Aires in 1946. His constructivist, dynamic *Luminous Structures* were conceived in the spirit of Lucio Fontana's *Manifiesto blanco*; Fontana in turn created an elaborate, elegant neon ceiling called *Spatial Concept* for the Triennale in Milan in 1951.

In the works of American artist Stephen Antonakos (*b* 1926), chromatic high-tension neon, available in a large spectrum, takes a prominent part in both his interior and exterior environmental pieces. Of the latter such permanent installations as *Incomplete Neon Circles* (1978) at the Federal Building, Dayton, OH, *Neon for 42nd Street* (1981), New York, or *Neons for the Tacoma Dome* (1984), Tacoma, WA, display a formal language of circles and squares; their fragmented versions, composed of arcs and right angles are rather different from the preceding Minimalist artistic statements and in particular Dan Flavin's works, whose fluorescent light systems with standardized tubes were put to their most effective use in large-scale interior installations, exploring the phenomenon of coloured perception in space (e.g. *Untitled (To Donna)*, 1971; Paris, Pompidou). The conceptual artists Joseph Kosuth and Bruce Nauman had introduced neon light both for the purpose of a critical commentary on language mechanisms (e.g. Kosuth's *Five Words in Orange Neon*, 1965; Paris, L. & M. Durand-Dessert) and for a graphic demonstration in de-forming real space (e.g. Nauman's *My Name as Written at the Surface of the Moon*, 1968; Bordeaux, Mus. A. Contemp.). Nauman sometimes also tested the capacities of apprehension of the spectator in such fluorescent lamp installations as *Dream Passage with Four Corridors* (1983–4; Paris, Pompidou). Neon is present in some works by the Arte Povera artist Mario Merz (e.g. *Giap's Igloo*, 1968; Paris, Pompidou), principally in order to stimulate the perception of materials such as stone, concrete, wax, textiles or paper in their daily usage, or in the works of Keith Sonnier in order to test the perception of hardness, colour and light (*Sel VII*, 1978; artist's col., see 1989 exh. cat.; *Sel Piece*, 1981; Paris, Gal. Fabre).

Martial Raysse also attempted to challenge the perceptual capacities of the spectator in pieces in which he outlined human faces, hearts and palm trees with multicoloured neon tubing, thereby alluding simultaneously to the artificiality of modern times, and to the purity and innocence of a new way of life (e.g. *America, America*, 1964; Paris, Pompidou; see fig.). Brilliantly coloured neon tubing is also the principal building material in Chryssa's sculptures, which contain mysterious symbols and alphabetical elements in an attempt to bridge the gap between Classical Greek and Byzantine civilization and the modern electrically dominated environment (*Clytemnestra*, 1968; Washington, DC, Corcoran Gal. A.; *Gates to Times Square*, 1966; Buffalo, NY, Albright–Knox A.G.).

Piotr Kowalski (*b* 1927) and François Morellet used neon devices in their sculptural works and installations with the intention of implicating the public in the apperception of basic physical and technological facts. Kowalski's *Manipulator No. 3* (1967; Paris, Pompidou) placed the spectator into an active situation, whereas his *Pyramid*

Neon light sculpture by Martial Raysse: *America, America*, 2.40×1.65×0.45 m, 1964 (Paris, Pompidou, Musée National d'Art Moderne)

(1973) in Bordeaux tested his architectural awareness. Morellet used neon light conspicuously in his early programmed installations in museums, galleries and in the street, and more subtly in later geometrical works or in outside installations such as *Neons with Two Rhythms of Interference* (1986) at the Grande Halle de la Villette, Paris.

The various uses of neon in art correspond to the need for creating coloured dynamic light effects, for modelling interior and exterior spaces and for modifying existing architecture. Although it can be maintained that neon light, from Las Vegas to Tokyo, symbolizes the energy and vitality of modern life, its presence in works conceived by artists operates rather as an antidote to hectic agitation and invites quiet contemplation and meditation.

BIBLIOGRAPHY

Kunst–Licht–Kunst (exh. cat., Eindhoven, Stedel. Van Abbemus., 1966)
W. Ellenbass: *Fluorescent Lamps* (London, 1971)
——: *Light Sources* (London, 1972)
R. Stern: *Let There Be Neon* (New York, 1979)
Luminous Art for the Urban Landscape (exh. cat. by O. Giorgia, Washington, DC, Project A., 1981)
M. Webb: *The Magic of Neon* (Salt Lake City, 1983)
Electra: L'Electricité et l'électronique dans l'art au XXe siècle (exh. cat. by F. Popper, Paris, Mus. A. Mod. Ville Paris, 1983)
A. Bodet: 'Néon: De L'Electricité dans l'art', *Beaux-A.*, viii (1983), pp. 52–7, 96–8
G. Breerette: 'Espace, lumière, repos', *Le Monde* (16 Dec 1983)
Néon, fluor et cie (exh. cat., Brussels, Inst. Sup. Etud. Lang. Plast., 1984)
Directions: Keith Sonnier: Neon (exh. cat., Washington, DC, Hirshhorn, 1989)
D. Elger: *Neon Stücke: Joseph Kosuth, Mario Merz, François Morellet, Maurizio Nannucci, Bruce Nauman, Richard Serra, Keith Sonnier* (Stuttgart, 1990)
F. Popper: *Art of the Electronic Age* (London, 1993)

FRANK POPPER

Neo-Palladianism. *See* PALLADIANISM.

Neo-plasticism. Term coined by PIET MONDRIAN and first used in 1919 as the title of a collection of his writings published by the dealer Léonce Rosenberg. It gained currency as a descriptive term applied to Mondrian's theories of art and to his style of painting, in which a grid, delineated by black lines, was filled with blocks of primary colour (see fig.). The original term applied to some of his principles was *nieuwe beelding* (new imagery); he also used *abstract-reële schilderkunst* (abstract-real painting) and Neo-Cubism. Neo-plasticism applied to all aspects of design that were part of daily life. The evanescence of natural shapes was reduced to a few essential expressive means: horizontal and vertical lines, areas of primary colour and black and white. For Mondrian a composition had to present a dynamic balance, in which the internal was externalized and the external internalized. Mondrian published *Le Néo-plasticisme* while in Paris, having become convinced that his theories, published in DE STIJL, were almost unknown beyond his native country. A collection of his articles was translated into German and published in 1925 as *Neue Gestaltung* as the fifth in the series of Bauhausbücher. His theories were published in English for the first time in 1937 under the title of 'Plastic Art and Pure Plastic Art' in *Circle: An International Survey of Constructivism.*

No distinct school of Neo-plasticists ever existed, although some works by artists including Jean Gorin, César Domela, Jean Helion and Burgoyne Diller may be described as Neo-plasticist. Mondrian's theories were to a large extent disseminated by verbal communication through numerous discussions with other painters, sculptors, architects and writers. Neo-plasticism was promoted from 1929 by the movement CERCLE ET CARRÉ, founded by Michel Seuphor, and three issues of its eponymous journal (1930). Mondrian and other artists exhibited in an exhibition of Neo-plasticism in 1930 at the Galerie 23 in Paris. The style spread to the USA when Mondrian visited in 1940 and became a member of AMERICAN ABSTRACT ARTISTS, many of whom experimented with Neo-plasticism.

Piet Mondrian: *Composition in Yellow and Blue*, oil on canvas, 520×520 mm, 1929 (Rotterdam, Museum Boymans–van)

WRITINGS

P. Mondrian: *Le Néo-plasticisme: Principe général de l'équivalence plastique* (Paris, 1919)

BIBLIOGRAPHY

J. R. Lane and S. C. Larsen, eds: *Abstract Painting and Sculpture in America, 1927–1944* (Pittsburgh, 1983)
J. Holtzman: *The New Art, the New Life: The Collected Writings of Mondrian* (Boston, MA, and London, 1986)
P. Overy: *De Stijl* (London, 1991)
I. Rike: *Mondriaan's 'Nieuwe Beelding' in English* (Amsterdam, 1991)

H. HENKELS

Neo-Platonism. Philosophical movement that developed in the 3rd century AD and reinterpreted the ideas of PLATO. It was inaugurated by Plotinus (AD 204/5–70) and continued by Porphyry (232–*c.* 305), Iamblichus (*c.* 250–*c.* 325), Proclus (410 or 412–85) and others, flourishing first in Rome, then at Apamea in Syria and later in both Athens and Alexandria. Pagan Neo-Platonism died out during the 6th century, but Neo-Platonic thought continued to be influential in Byzantium and the medieval West as well as in medieval Islamic and Jewish philosophy. Many Neo-Platonic ideas were taken over by Christian thinkers, in particular by St Augustine (354–430) in the West and Pseudo-Dionysius (*c.* 500) in the East. In the 15th century Neo-Platonism was studied at the 'Platonic Academy' of MARSILIO FICINO, and it became a major source for several influential humanists (*see* HUMANISM).

Whereas for Plato the world as it was perceived in sense-experience was only a copy of the world of abstract forms, the Neo-Platonists developed a more complex metaphysics. Plotinus held that there were three further levels of reality beyond the material world: first Soul, then Mind and finally the One. He regarded the One as transcendent and ultimately beyond the grasp of philosophy; it could be reached only through mystical experience. The One was also the source of all things. It did not actively create the lower levels of being but, like an overflowing fountain, gave rise to them without itself experiencing any change. On the other hand, philosophical questioning could help in comprehending the levels of Mind and Soul, and much of Plotinus' work examines philosophical problems concerning these levels and their relations both to the One and to the material world. Plotinus' successors elaborated this metaphysical picture still further, subdividing the levels of reality and filling out his account of them. In particular, there is in Proclus the notion that between the One and Mind there are divine 'henads', which mediate the transition from the One to the rest of reality. Proclus identified the henads with the traditional Greek gods, holding that each god, while primarily a henad, was also manifested in different forms at each of the lower levels. So, for example, as well as the henad that was Zeus, there was an intelligible Zeus on the level of Mind and another Zeus on the level of Soul.

Despite these developments, the Neo-Platonists regarded themselves not as independent philosophers but as interpreters of Plato and of the whole previous philosophical and cultural tradition. Many Neo-Platonists wrote lengthy commentaries on Aristotle, and some also offered interpretations of Homer, Hesiod and other works of Greek literature and mythology. As interpreters, the Neo-Platonists were concerned to explain away contradictions and inconsistencies in Plato and Aristotle. In their attempts to demonstrate the essential unity of all Greek thought they made extensive use of allegorical interpretation, which they applied, for example, to Plato's myths and to episodes in Homer (*see also* MYTHOLOGICAL PAINTING AND SCULPTURE, §§1–3).

The Neo-Platonists' views on art were based on their metaphysics. Plotinus (*Ennead* I.vi) follows Plato's account in the *Symposium* of the ascent to the Form of Beauty, stressing that things perceived by the senses are beautiful only because they imitate the Form. He further argues (*Ennead* V.viii.1) that an artist in creating his work imitates the Form directly. This implicitly contradicts Plato's argument (*Republic* X) that the artist can only imitate sensible particulars; it thus opens the way to a higher evaluation of art than in Plato. Ultimately, however, art cannot reveal the highest reality but must be superseded by philosophical understanding and mystical experience. Plotinus mentions Pheidias' statue of *Zeus* (*see* PHEIDIAS, §2) as an example of a sculpture whose model is in the intelligible, not the sensible, world (V.viii.1). This example, already traditional when Plotinus used it, is used again by Proclus (Diehl, i, p. 265, lines 18ff). Proclus' point, however, is not quite the same. He declares that Pheidias' model was Zeus as described by Homer; if Pheidias had succeeded in imitating the Zeus of the intelligible world, the result would have been even finer. Proclus was more interested in poetry, especially Homer, than visual art. He offered extensive allegorical interpretations of Homeric myths in an attempt to answer Plato's attack on poetry (Kroll, i, pp. 69–205). His underlying theory, that art can imitate what lies beyond the sensible world, is the same as that of Plotinus, and like Plotinus he holds that art, revealing as it is, cannot penetrate the very highest metaphysical level. For Proclus, Homeric poetry is inspired and so able to present some metaphysical realities in symbolic terms. It can even go beyond the intelligible world to impart truths about the divine henads. Nevertheless, such poetic symbols must ultimately be discarded if full union with the One is to be achieved.

BIBLIOGRAPHY

Plotinus: *Enneads* (MS.; *c.* AD 260); Eng. trans., ed. A. H. Armstrong, Loeb Class. Lib., 7 vols (Cambridge, MA, 1966–88)

Proclus: *Commentary on Plato's 'Republic'* (MS.; mid-5th century AD); ed. W. Kroll, 2 vols (Leipzig, 1899–1901); Fr. trans. by A. J. Festugière, 3 vols (Paris, 1970)

——: *Commentary on Plato's 'Timaeus'* (MS.; mid-5th century AD); ed. E. Diehl, 3 vols (Leipzig, 1903–6); Fr. trans. by A. J. Festugière, 5 vols (Paris, 1966–8)

A. Chastel: *Art et humanisme à Florence au temps de Laurent le Magnifique: Etudes sur la Renaissance et l'humanisme platonicien* (Paris, 1959)

A. H. Armstrong, ed.: *The Cambridge History of Later Greek and Early Medieval Philosophy* (Cambridge, 1967)

J. M. Rist: *Plotinus: The Road to Reality* (Cambridge, 1967)

R. T. Wallis: *Neoplatonism* (London, 1972)

A. D. R. Sheppard: *Studies on the 5th and 6th Essays of Proclus' Commentary on the Republic*, Hypomnemata 61 (Göttingen, 1980)

D. J. O'Meara: *Plotinus: An Introduction to the Enneads* (Oxford, 1993)

ANNE SHEPPARD

Neo-primitivism. Russian movement that took its name from Aleksandr Shevchenko's *Neo-primitivizm* (1913). This book describes a crude style of painting practised by members of the DONKEY'S TAIL group. Mikhail Larionov, Natal'ya Goncharova, Kazimir Malevich and Shevchenko himself all adopted the style, which was based on the conventions of traditional Russian art forms such as the *lubok*, the icon and peasant arts and crafts. The term Neo-primitivism is now used to describe a general aspiration towards primitivism in the work of the wider Russian avant-garde during the period 1910–14. It embraces the work of such disparate painters as Chagall, David Burlyuk and Pavel Filonov, and poets such as Velimir Khlebnikov and Aleksey Kruchonykh.

Neo-primitivism was to a certain extent inspired by the impact of Expressionism; adherents of both movements shared an admiration for the expressive power of naive art forms and a desire to rediscover a national artistic style. However, in its most extreme form Neo-primitivism was more daring and flamboyant. The surprising colours and gross distortions of Malevich's painting *Floor Polishers* (1911; Amsterdam, Stedel. Mus.) and the simplistic bravado of Larionov's *Soldier on a Horse* (1912; London, Tate), for example, were decisive developments on Western examples and sprang from a more rigorously defined theoretical basis. Members of Donkey's Tail held that traditional Russian culture had lost its distinctive character and identity following the introduction of elegant European standards by Peter the Great. They wished to return to their national artistic origins and to express them anew in painterly form. Consequently they looked back to traditional art forms for inspiration and spurned European fine art traditions of representation.

The old Russian print or LUBOK played a crucial role in the elaboration of Neo-primitivism. Larionov, Goncharova and Chagall were all to some extent influenced by its subject-matter and stylistic devices. In their own works, words and texts decorate brightly coloured compositions, people and objects float arbitrarily one above the other in the flattened and indeterminate picture space, and the same characters that animate the hilarious topsy-turvy world of the Russian *lubok* are delineated in a flat and distorted figurative style. The beauty of ancient icons inspired artists such as Goncharova, Malevich and Vladimir Tatlin to give way to subtle colouring, inverted perspective and bold simplicity. Goncharova's *Four Evangelists* (1911; St Petersburg, Rus. Mus.) are particularly notable in this respect. Signboards, painted trays, embroideries, the work of children and naive artists, prehistoric and Siberian tribal art also offered inspiration to the avant-garde, who built up magnificent collections of such artefacts and proudly showed them alongside their own Neo-primitive works in exhibitions such as *Target* (1913).

Neo-primitivism profoundly influenced the work of the Russian poets. Mayakovsky wrote a poem about shop signboards, Khlebnikov chose prehistoric and pagan themes in such poems as *Shaman and Venus, Vila and*

Wood Goblin and *The Maiden's God*, while Kruchonykh based some of his poems on the example of the *lubok* and chose the coarser aspects of peasant life with which to offend the refined and cultured tastes of society. Moreover these poems are filled with deliberate archaisms, naiveties, lapses, incorrect spellings and wrong word transfers, which find their counterpart in the Neo-primitive style of Donkey's Tail. Neo-primitivism was not only a vibrant and instinctive style of painting. In its attempt to re-evaluate in painterly terms the visual traditions of the Russian nation and to revitalize art by adopting a more spontaneous and expressive approach, it left its stamp on an entire generation of Russian artists.

WRITINGS

A. Shevchenko: *Neo-Primitivizm: Yego teoriya, yego vozmozhnosti, yego dostizheniya* [Neo-primitivism: its theory, its potentials, its achievements] (Moscow, 1913); Eng. trans. in J. Bowlt: *Russian Art of the Avant-garde* (New York, 1976), pp. 41–54
V. Markov: *Russian Futurism* (London, 1969)

BIBLIOGRAPHY

I. Davies: 'Primitivism in the First Wave of the Twentieth Century Avant-garde in Russia', *Studio Int.*, clxxxvi (1973), pp. 80–84
J. E. Bowlt: 'Neo-Primitivism and Russian Painting', *Burl. Mag.*, cxvi (1974), pp. 132–40
M. Betz: 'The Icon and Russian Modernism', *Artforum*, xv/10 (1977), pp. 3–45
A. Parton: *Mikhail Larionov and the Russian Avant-garde* (Princeton and London, 1993)

ANTHONY PARTON

Néo-Réalisme. Term used to describe a movement among certain French painters in the 1920s and 1930s, resulting in works of a poetic naturalist style. Among the main exponents were Maurice Asselin, Jean-Louis Boussingault, Maurice Brianchon, Charles Dufresne, André Dunoyer de Segonzac, Raymond-Jean Legueult (*b* 1898), Robert Lotiron (*b* 1886) and Luc-Albert Moreau; Dunoyer de Segonzac was the unofficial leader. Though there was no conscious grouping, various of these artists were associated in an informal way. *Néo-Réalisme* arose in reaction to modern movements such as Cubism and Surrealism, which were seen as breaking with the French tradition. Essentially it was a manifestation of the postwar 'rappel à l'ordre', and the artists concerned attempted to steer a path between modernism and academicism. It placed primary emphasis on the study of reality and nature as ordinarily perceived, and its aesthetic was well summed up by Dunoyer de Segonzac's statement (Jamot, p. 102):

> The search for originality at any price has led only to a terrible monotony. The world of illegibility, the lecture-picture and the puzzle-picture, which are a result of a decadent symbolism, is going to become dated. . .In actual fact the French tradition has been carried on quietly by Vuillard, Bonnard, Matisse and many others. . .There has been no break with the magnificent school which stretches from Jean Fouquet to Cézanne.

Typical of the style is Dunoyer de Segonzac's *Church of Chaville (Winter)* (1934–7; Paris, Mus. A. Mod. Ville Paris). *Néo-Réalisme* is not connected with the later movement Nouveau Réalisme.

BIBLIOGRAPHY

P. Jamot: *André Dunoyer de Segonzac* (Paris, 1929)
R. Nacenta: *School of Paris* (London, 1960), pp. 35–6

Neo-Romanticism. British movement of the 1930s to early 1950s in painting, illustration, literature, film and theatre. Neo-Romantic artists focused on a personal, poetic vision of the landscape and on the vulnerable human body, in part as an insular response to the threat of invasion during World War II. Essentially Arcadian and with an emphasis on the individual, the Neo-Romantic vision fused the modernist idioms of Pablo Picasso, André Masson and Pavel Tchelitchew with Arthurian legend, the poetry of William Wordsworth (1770–1850) and the prints of William Blake and Samuel Palmer. Celebrated as modern yet essentially traditional, its linear, lyrical and poetic characteristics were thought to epitomize the northern spirit. Neo-Romanticism flourished in response to the wartime strictures, threat of aerial bombardment and postwar austerity of the 1940s, in an attempt to demonstrate the survival and freedom of expression of the nation's spiritual life.

Neo-Romanticism was first used as a term by Raymond Mortimer in the *New Statesman and Nation* (March 1942) and was widely applied during the 1940s as a tentative, all-embracing category, notably to the work of Paul Nash, John Piper, Henry Moore, Ivon Hitchens and Graham Sutherland, who by 1946 was regarded as the leading Neo-Romantic; his Wordsworthian paraphrasing of the Pembrokeshire landscape, for example in *Entrance to a Lane* (1939; London, Tate), was a seminal work for the development of an emergent generation that included John Minton, Michael Ayrton, John Craxton, Keith Vaughan, Robert Colquhoun and Robert MacBryde. Sutherland's rendering of landscape for symbolic purposes was emulated by other artists, as in John Minton's *Recollections of Wales* (1944; Brit. Council Col.; see fig.).

After the mid-1940s the Arts Council of Great Britain and the British Council promoted Neo-Romantic artists at home and abroad, but hopes of leading the European avant-garde were gradually eroded by an indigenous pop culture and the arrival of American Abstract Expressionism. The hothouse atmosphere of the blockade disappeared, and many artists migrated south, as can be seen in John Minton's *Road to Valencia* (1949; AC Eng). Kenneth Clark, Peter Watson, John Lehmann and Colin Anderson were major patrons and advocates of the movement, and Herbert Read, Geoffrey Grigson and Wyndham Lewis were among the writers influential in its promotion. Many of the artists were themselves active writers, with John Piper's *British Romantic Artists* (London, 1942) and Michael Ayrton's art criticism for *The Spectator* (1946–8), in particular, contributing to the acceptance of the movement. Between 1942 and 1946 young Neo-Romantic painters and writers gathered in London: in Bedford Gardens at the studio of Minton, Colquhoun and MacBryde and at Peter Watson's flat in Palace Gate; however, there was never an official group. What united most of these young men, apart from aesthetic interests and wartime hardship, was their outsider status as homosexuals. As the Neo-Romantic spirit declined in the 1950s, so did the reputations of this lost generation of artists.

The term is sometimes also applied, especially in the USA, to the dream-like landscapes and figures painted in the 1930s by a group of artists based in Paris, including

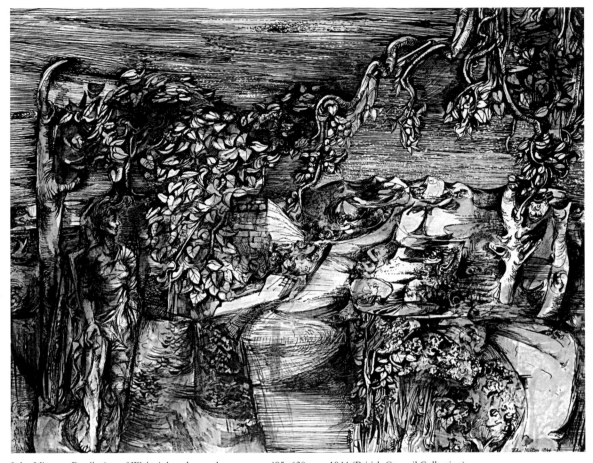

John Minton: *Recollections of Wales*, ink and gouache on paper, 495×630 mm, 1944 (British Council Collection)

Tchelitchew, Eugene Berman and his brother Leonid Berman (*b* 1896) and Christian Bérard.

BIBLIOGRAPHY
R. Ironside: *Painting Since 1939* (London, 1947)
A Paradise Lost: The Neo-Romantic Imagination in Britain 1935–55 (exh. cat., ed. D. Mellor; London, Barbican A.G., 1987)
M. Yorke: *The Spirit of the Place: Nine Neo-Romantic Artists and their Times* (London, 1988)
V. Button: *British Neo-Romanticism* (diss., U. London, in preparation)

VIRGINIA BUTTON

Neo-Tudor. Architectural style originally associated with the English Domestic Revival and employed by architects of the ARTS AND CRAFTS MOVEMENT. As early as the 1860s Richard Norman Shaw and W. E. Nesfield produced designs in the OLD ENGLISH style after sketching tours in the south-eastern counties, inspired by such architects as George Devey. Characteristic building features were tile-hanging, hipped gables and applied half-timbering, for example in Shaw's design of Cragside (1869–85), near Rothbury, Northumb. (*see* ENGLAND, fig. 10). At the same time the search for a national style identified the domestic architecture of the Elizabethan and Jacobean eras as the most appropriate models. The Royal Jubilee Exhibition (1887) in Manchester featured a reconstruction of 'Old Manchester and Salford', a model village in 16th-century style half-timbering. Used for houses and cottages at Port Sunlight (from 1888), as well as at Bedford Park (from 1875) and later Hampstead Garden Suburb (from 1905), both in London, the style's picturesque quality came to dominate modern house design. After World War I speculative builders adopted it wholeheartedly for the extensive suburban developments growing around British cities, as an antidote to the Neo-Georgian municipal estates. Semi-detached houses, with half-timbering and roughcast gables, leaded lights and decorative brickwork, embodied security and stability in the brand new suburbs and gave home owners a feeling of continuity. A parallel style also influenced interior decoration, with vernacular-orientated furnishings being devised in a mass-produced format. Heavily criticized by contemporary architects and critics, Neo-Tudor nevertheless determined the appearance of most inter-war suburban developments.

BIBLIOGRAPHY
A. Saint: *Richard Norman Shaw* (Yale, 1976)
P. Davey: *Arts and Crafts Architecture* (London, 1980)
A. M. Edwards: *The Design of Suburbia: A Critical Study in Environmental History* (London, 1981)
P. Oliver, I. Davis and I. Bentley: *Dunroamin: The Suburban Semi and its Enemies* (London, 1981)

Nepal. Country in the central Himalayas bordering the Tibetan Autonomous Region of China on the north and India on the south. Roughly rectangular in shape (some 1650 km in length and 160 km in width at its widest point), Nepal is inhabited by approximately 17 million people.

I. Introduction. II. Art of the prehistoric and protohistoric periods. III. Architecture. IV. Sculpture. V. Painting. VI. Other arts. VII. Ethnic arts. VIII. Museums.

I. Introduction.

In both geographic and cultural senses, Nepal (see fig. 1) is a contact zone where diverse features, climates and traditions meet. Trade routes passing through the Kathmandu Valley brought wealth and contact with India, Tibet and China. However, the isolation imposed by the surrounding mountains fostered a strong and confident cultural identity. The art of Nepal reflects both this intermixing and individuality. Most works are religious, created in the context of Nepal's two main (and intermingling) religions: Hinduism and Buddhism.

1. Geography and climate. 2. History and civilization. 3. Religion and iconography.

1. GEOGRAPHY AND CLIMATE. Nepal's diverse features and climates range from the arctic conditions of the Himalayan Mountains in the north to the jungles and tropical climate of the Terai or southern plains. The Himalayan foothills, or middle hills, which are such an important part of Nepal's geography, are rent north to south by several great Himalayan river systems. These carve deep valleys and gorges as they rush to the plains, where they join the great rivers of northern India. The elevated plain of the Kathmandu Valley, the political, cultural and economic centre of the country, is situated at an altitude of about 1400 m and occupies some 650 sq km. Located in the midst of the hill region, the Kathmandu Valley is roughly equidistant from Tibet to the north and India to the south. The major Nepalese river systems bypass the valley; it is drained by a small local system, consisting of several tributaries that coalesce in the Bagmati river, which eventually finds its way to the sacred Ganga.

The climate of the Kathmandu Valley is mild and pleasant; for the farmers, the cycle of seasons is focused on the monsoon, the precious rains that, when plentiful and timely, ensure a generous rice crop, but when skimpy bring hunger and hardship. Legends assert that the Kathmandu Valley was once a lake, and this tradition has been confirmed by modern investigations that reveal lake-bed sediments on the valley floor. The extraordinary fertility of these ancient soils, combined with the skills of local farmers, have resulted in bounteous rice harvests, and

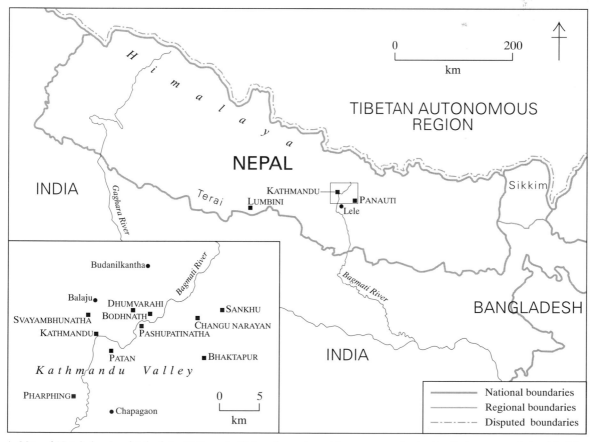

1. Map of Nepal showing detail of the Kathmandu Valley; those sites with separate entries in this dictionary are distinguished by CROSS-REFERENCE TYPE

from ancient times the Kathmandu Valley's agricultural riches have contributed to an economic environment that encourages both trade and the arts, two occupations for which its inhabitants have long been famed.

BIBLIOGRAPHY

P. P. Karan: *Nepal: A Cultural and Physical Geography* (Lexington, KY, 1960)

N. B. Thapa and D. P. Thapa: *Geography of Nepal (Physical, Economic, Cultural and Regional)* (Bombay, 1969)

2. HISTORY AND CIVILIZATION. Although modern Nepal encompasses thousands of sq. km of territory, the Nepal of most of recorded history was a small nation state centred on the Kathmandu Valley and its immediate environs, the *Nepāla maṇḍala* of medieval inscriptions and documents. For nearly 2000 years this tiny area has been the focus of an extraordinary cultural efflorescence, where achievements in the fine arts were brought to heights hardly to be expected in a valley so small and so isolated from other centres of culture.

The civilization of Nepal was built by a process of gradual accretion and mingling. The population of the Kathmandu Valley has long been subject to succeeding waves of immigration, largely from the Indian states to the south, which brought Indian cultural influence into the life of the valley dwellers. The denizens of the valley, the Newars, who speak a Tibeto-Burman language, are most likely a mixture of original settlers from the north, perhaps combined with some autochthonous peoples, who later merged with settlers from India. The hypothetical northern origins of the population explain the Tibeto-Burman language and the Mongoloid cast of the features of so many Newars, while Indian immigration accounts for the largely Indian framework of Newar culture and the Indian inspiration found everywhere in art and religion.

Several intriguing sculptures provide evidence of an art-producing state by the time of the first centuries of the Christian era (see Pal, 1974–8, i, figs 54, 62), but recorded history in Nepal begins only with an inscribed pillar dated Shaka year 386 (AD 464) at CHANGU NARAYAN, the most important Vaishnava temple in the valley. This inscription provides the first documentary evidence of the Lichchhavi rulers (*c.* 300–800) who oversaw a golden age in Nepalese art and culture. The origins of the Nepalese Lichchhavis, contemporaries of the Gupta rulers in India, are problematic, but their important role as bringers of Indian culture makes likely the southern origins that tradition assigns them. Under Lichchhavi rule many important Indian governmental institutions were imported and established, while the two great Indian religions of the time, Buddhism and Hinduism, flourished under Lichchhavi patronage. But, while the documents of Lichchhavi rule in Nepal amply attest the great and overriding influence of Indian culture in the development of Nepalese civilization, inscriptions also provide evidence of the more obscure northern origins of the local populace, in the form of numerous non-Sanskrit, Tibeto-Burman or proto-Newari names for places and offices.

The Lichchhavi line eventually weakened and lost the reins of power, and by the 9th century AD Nepal entered a time of political instability and historical obscurity from which it did not emerge until well into the medieval period. Historians variously term the period from *c.* 800 to *c.* 1200

the Transitional period or the Thakuri period (after an epithet used by some of the kings). The year 879 marks the establishment of the *Nepāla Saṃvat*, which stood as the national era until the 18th century, but there is no solid documentation to clarify why the new era was begun. The few and precious medieval chronicles that survive establish lines of kings for the Transitional period whose names and regnal dates have been painstakingly corroborated by historians working with scattered manuscripts and inscriptions. These documents, however, convey little of the political, social or cultural life of Nepal during these long centuries. Nonetheless, throughout this period the culture of Nepal remained continuous, unbroken by any major upheaval or invasion that would destroy traditions and bring a totally new civilization into place. Despite its historical obscurity, this was a time when the arts flourished and many of the finest Nepalese sculptures were produced, while some of the most important of the many Buddhist monasteries in the Kathmandu Valley were established at the end of this period during the 10th to 12th centuries. These monasteries served as a refuge for distinguished monks fleeing the Islamic destruction of the great monastic centres of northern India.

The Malla kings, after whom the Malla period of Nepalese history is named, first appear in *c.* 1200 with an obscure ruler known as Ari Malla. The political confusion of the Transitional period continued, despite an apparent change in dynastic rule, until the 14th century, when Sthiti Malla (*reg c.* 1382–95), an ambitious young prince of uncertain origins, took the reins of power and subdued the battling chieftains of the Kathmandu Valley to found a unified kingdom. His grandson Yaksha Malla (*reg c.* 1428–82) was perhaps the most powerful of the Malla kings, claiming conquests far beyond the traditional confines of the *Nepāla maṇḍala*. His kingdom, however, was divided among his inheritors, and within several years the pattern of later Malla Nepal was established, with kings eventually ruling in separate kingdoms in KATHMANDU, BHAKTAPUR and PATAN (ii), the three towns that remain the most important of the valley.

Under the later Malla kings the architectural marvels of the Kathmandu Valley took shape. Enriched by the trade with Tibet that formed an important part of Nepal's revenues and vying amongst themselves for cultural supremacy, the kings of the three city states covered their dominions with gilt-roofed temples, gleaming stupas and spacious squares studded with sculpture; they instituted dramas and religious celebrations, and organized their subjects into a tightly knit hierarchical society on the Brahmanical model. Among these kings several names stand out: the braggart 'poet-king' of Kathmandu, Pratapa Malla (*reg* 1641–74); Sri Nivasa (*reg* 1661–84), builder of much of Patan's glorious Darbar Square; his son Yoganarendra (*reg* 1684–1705), a musician who, legend recounts, disappeared and is still expected to return; and Bhupatindra Malla (*reg* 1696–1722), whose statue (see fig. 2) crowns a pillar near Darbar Square, Bhaktapur.

The wealth of the Kathmandu Valley and the weakness of the contentious, later Malla kings attracted the attention of an ambitious young prince from the hills, Prithvi Narayan of the Shah dynasty of Gorkha, a family that claimed descent from the kings of Rajasthan. In 1768–9

2. Portrait statue of King Bhupatindra Malla, copper repoussé with gilt, early to mid-18th century, Bhaktapur

Prithvi Narayan brought a 20-year campaign for the valley to a climax by conquering first Kathmandu, then Patan and Bhaktapur, and the Malla period drew to a close. Modern Nepal was born.

Uninterested in the arts, the Gorkha kings were true members of the Kshatriya, or warrior class, absorbed in conquest and government. They were the first group of immigrants into the valley to resist acculturation, and they consciously stayed apart from the Newars, who had absorbed all previous conquerors and immigrants into their complicated and colourful social fabric. Although royal patronage for building and cultural pursuits dwindled, the new administrators proved vigorous defenders of Nepal's sovereignty. Under successive Shah kings, the borders of Nepal were expanded until they eventually reached the boundaries of the present state. In the 19th century the rightful kings were usurped by a minister, Jang Bahadur Rana (reg 1846–56; 1857–77), who established his family as de facto rulers for a century and neutralized the British threat to Nepalese sovereignty by a policy of military strength combined with friendly gestures to the giant to the south. In 1951 the Rana regime was overthrown by a popular rebellion, and after a period of political instability the Shah dynasty returned to the throne, making the country one of the last true monarchies in the world and the only one with a Hindu king. In the late 20th century the transition to a democratically elected government had become an important political issue, and in 1991

King Birendra agreed to relinquish much of his traditional power to a democratically elected government.

BIBLIOGRAPHY

G. Tucci: *Preliminary Report of Two Scientific Expeditions in Nepal* (Rome, 1956)
L. Petech: *Medieval History of Nepal* (Rome, 1958, rev. 1984)
D. Regmi: *Ancient Nepal* (Calcutta, 1960)
The Art of Nepal (exh. cat. by S. Kramrisch, New York, Asia Soc. Gals, 1964)
D. Regmi: *Medieval Nepal*, 3 vols (Calcutta, 1965–6)
P. R. Sharma: *Preliminary Study of the Art and Architecture of the Karnali Basi, West Nepal* (Paris, 1972)
P. Pal: *Sculpture* and *Painting*, i and ii of *The Arts of Nepal*, 2 vols (Leiden, 1974–8)
Nepal: Where the Gods Are Young (exh. cat. by P. Pal, New York, Asia Soc. Gals; Seattle, A. Mus.; Los Angeles, Co. Mus. A.; 1975)
M. Slusser: *Nepal Mandala: A Cultural Study of the Kathmandu Valley*, 2 vols (Princeton, 1982)
P. Pal: *Art of Nepal: A Catalogue of the Los Angeles County Museum of Art Collection* (Los Angeles, 1985)
G. Béguin: *Les Arts du Népal et du Tibet* (Paris, 1987)

IAN ALSOP

3. RELIGION AND ICONOGRAPHY. HINDUISM, the state religion, and Buddhism (mainly Mahayana and Vajrayana, *see* BUDDHISM, §§I; III, 1 and 5) have been practised side by side in Nepal for centuries. A further strain of religious life consists of indigenous ideas and practices. These have penetrated both Hinduism and Buddhism, which have evolved so closely that they are hardly two separate religious systems. The institution of caste is important in both, the Newar Buddhist caste of Vajracharya fulfilling the priestly function of the Brahmans of Hinduism. The distinctive Buddhist practice of monasticism was given up from the 14th century. Both Hindus and Buddhists venerate ancestors and perform similar rites of passage. Although their pantheons are for the most part distinct, the gods and goddesses are conceptually and iconographically similar, and there is extensive overlap. For example, the deity known as Red Matsyendranatha, worshipped in a temple in Patan, is regarded by both Hindus and Buddhists as the patron of the Kathmandu Valley. The deity's complex character seems to incorporate an indigenous Newar deity and a Master of Yoga of the Natha sect who lived perhaps in the 10th century. Worshippers identify the god as an aspect of Shiva or Vishnu or as the *bodhisattva* Avalokiteshvara, and members from all communities participate in the celebration of his festivals.

Both Hinduism and Buddhism have been influenced by the system of ideas known as Tantra, named for a vast body of texts. Tantra prescribes an esoteric system of mental and physical practices aimed at breaking psychic barriers, attaining power to manipulate the forces of the universe and providing a shorter path to the traditional Buddhist goal of liberation. The Tantric symbol, the *vajra*, originally an attribute of the rain and war god Indra, is a ubiquitous motif in Nepalese art, featuring in sculpture, wood-carving and painting. It is identified *inter alia* as the thunderbolt, symbolizing the intuitive flash of insight, and as the diamond, representing the indestructible quality of the doctrine. It is held as an attribute by such deities of Tantric Buddhism as Vajrapani (see fig. 13 below) and is sometimes anthropomorphized as Vajrapurusha.

In both Hindu and Buddhist Tantric practice the female principle is emphasized. Merging with the indigenous cult of the Mother Goddess, worship of Hindu and Buddhist goddesses forms an important part of popular religion. The term *śakti* is generally applied to all goddesses. The Hindu understanding of *śakti* is energy, the female often conceived as the dominant force in the cosmogonical process. In Buddhist theory, the male symbolizes means or method (*upāya*), while the female is the more passive wisdom (*prajñā*). In both systems the union of opposites symbolizing non-duality is represented by sexually joined divine couples. This imagery is common both in Hindu and Buddhist sculpture and painting. Most Nepalese deities have gentle and terrifying sides. The pacific form of the deity is worshipped with offerings of flowers, lighted lamps, fruits and sweets. In their fierce manifestations the deities demand blood and alcohol. Thus, cocks, goats and buffaloes are offered to Shiva in his fierce form of Bhairava and the goddess in her form as Durga. The meat is eaten by donors unless this is proscribed by caste rules.

Sacred places in the Kathmandu Valley revered and honoured by most Nepalese reflect the varied religious strains. The long list includes the temple of the Red Matsyendranatha in Patan and its counterpart the temple of the White Matsyendranatha in Kathmandu; the great stupa of SVAYAMBHUNATHA and the stupa at BODHNATH, the latter associated especially with Tibetan forms of Buddhism from about the 13th century, the great temple of PASHUPATINATHA on the Bagmati River and the sacred tank with the fine image of the Sleeping Vishnu at BUDHANILKANTHA.

(i) Hindu iconography. (ii) Buddhist iconography. (iii) Indigenous traditions.

(i) Hindu iconography. Most of the wide range of iconographic forms developed in India (*see* INDIAN SUBCONTINENT, §II, 1) are known in Nepal, but certain representations were favoured. The most prominent among the many Hindu deities are Shiva, Vishnu and Durga, who is known more popularly as Bhagavati. As in India, Shiva is usually worshipped in the aniconic form of the *linga*, sometimes represented with one or four faces. In the latter case, Shiva's female aspect is represented in the north, his terrifying aspect in the south, his royal and ascetic forms in the west and east (e.g. Pal, 1974–8, i, figs 123–7). A favoured form is the Uma-Maheshvara image, in which Shiva is represented in his benign form embracing his wife Uma. They are shown sitting with their entourage often including their sons, the gods Ganesha and Karttikeya, in their lofty residence on Mount Kailasa (e.g. Pal, 1974–8, i, figs 128–38). Shiva is also widely worshipped in his terrifying form, Bhairava. Representations may consist of only a masklike head with bulging eyes, fangs and wildly flying hair. Alternatively, the god stands in a menacing and militant posture, often on recumbent figures. He usually has many arms holding in his hands such attributes as the shield, bell, *vajra*, trident, severed head, cup and sword. He may have five heads, four facing in the cardinal directions with one above (e.g. Pal, 1985, nos S56, S58–60). Such representations are similar to images of the Tantric Buddhist deity Mahakala.

Favoured Vaishnava images include Vishnu lying on the serpent Shesha in the cosmic ocean. Seemingly unique to Nepal is the placement of such images in large tanks as at Budhanilkantha and Balaju. The images refer to the period between the destruction of the universe and its creation anew, when Vishnu sleeps on the primordial waters. The setting also probably relates to an indigenous tradition of sacred springs. Vishnu is frequently represented seated on his part-bird, part-human mount, Garuda; alternatively a standard surmounted by Garuda or a kneeling image of Garuda was placed before the doors of Vaishnava temples (see Pal, 1974–8, i, figs 98–105). Other frequent representations include Vishnu Vishvarupa, from whom the whole universe emanates (see fig. 18 below). Particularly powerful is the ten-headed image at Changu Narayan (see Slusser, 1982, pl. 372f). Vishnu Vikranta, representing the myth of the dwarf *avatāra* (incarnation), is a further important theme in Nepal (see fig. 14 below). Vishnu's ten *avatāra*s are often carved on wooden roof struts embellishing temples (see Gail, 1984, pls xi and xxii).

Durga (or Bhagavati) is often shown in her triumphant aspect killing the buffalo demon Mahisha. During the Dasain festival, usually in October, this feat is re-enacted by the ritual slaughter of hundreds of buffaloes. The mother deities, considered emanations of Bhagavati, are important in Nepalese temple embellishment (e.g. see Gail, 1984, pls xlvi and xlvii). The eight mothers are responsible for the cardinal and intermediate directions: Brahmani (east), Maheshvari (south-east), Kaumari (south), Vaishnavi (south-west), Varahi (west), Indrani (north-west), Chamunda (north), Mahalakshmi (north-east). They are often depicted in the appropriate positions on the struts of pyramidal temples (*degas*; *see* §III, 2 (i) below).

The guardians of the world (*lokapāla*) or regents of the directions of space (*dikpāla*) are usually represented in wood carvings on both sides of the four doors of a pyramidal temple. The planet deities (the same as those of ancient India but excluding Rahu, associated with eclipses) are carved on both sides of the extended door lintels (see Gail, 1980).

(ii) Buddhist iconography. Buddhist iconography is dominated by the historical Buddha Shakyamuni and the *bodhisattva* of compassion, Avalokiteshvara (e.g. Pal, 1974–8, i, figs. 8, 166–8). Among the many aspects of Avalokiteshvara, Lokanatha images are most prominent in Nepal. Lokanatha is represented with two arms, the right hand making the gesture of munificence (*varada mudrā*), the left holding a red lotus (see Pal, 1974–8, i, figs 187–97). Maitreya, the Buddha of the future, often appears in the garb of the Buddha without attributes characteristic in India. In the few surviving early depictions the main distinguishing feature seems to be the rendering of the robe: while the Buddha's garment falls smoothly over his body, as in Indian images produced at Sarnath, Maitreya's robe is characterized by striated folds, following the sculpture of Gandhara and Mathura (see Gail, 1990). Less common is the *bodhisattva* of wisdom, Manjushri, who in legend is said to have cleft the mountains to drain the water of a vast lake covering the Kathmandu Valley. As in

India, his distinctive attribute is the sword. However, the oldest known image, a relief on a Buddhist stele, shows him as Siddhaikavira ('Perfect Hero'), making the gesture of munificence and holding the blue lotus (see Gail, 1987).

An important iconographic subject inside monasteries of the *bahal* type (*see* §III, 2(ii) below) is the five metaphysical Buddhas, represented in metal sculpture and wood-carvings. They are differentiated by their gestures: Vairochana, preaching (*dharmacakra mudrā*); Akshobhya, earth-touching (*bhūmisparśa mudrā*); Ratnasambhava, munificence (*varada mudrā*); Amitabha, meditating (*dhyāna mudrā*); Amoghasiddhi, blessing or protection (*abhaya mudrā*). Vajrasattva appears as the Adibuddha holding a *vajra* and bell (*ghaṇṭā*).

Vajrayana or Tantric Buddhism adds a set of Mahabuddhas, similarly named (e.g. Mahavairochana) and represented with three heads and a multitude of arms (see Gail, 1991). Buddhas and Mahabuddhas form part of painted *maṇḍala*s (diagrams symbolizing the universe), where they are associated with the cardinal directions (see Pal, 1974–8, ii, figs 203–18). Also important in the embellishment of Newar monasteries are the five *bodhisattva*s emanating from the five Buddhas (see Getty, 1914, p. 45). From the 12th century onward, the Buddhas and *bodhisattva*s were represented with their respective mounts (*vāhana*). Further, wooden struts and decorative gables are often carved with the five protective goddesses (*pañcarakṣā*; see Gail, 1991).

An even greater variety of Buddhist deities is depicted on cloth hangings (*see* §V, 1(ii) below) and in illustrated manuscripts (*see* §V, 1(i) below). *Pañcarakṣā* manuscripts, for example, contain miniature paintings of the five goddesses following iconographical formulae set down in the *Sādhanamālā*, a collection of texts setting forth methods of evoking a given deity. Both cloth hangings and illustrated manuscripts abound with embracing pairs of Buddhist deities.

Also common in Nepalese iconography are the eight auspicious signs (*aṣṭamaṅgala*): endless knot (*śrīvatsa*), lotus (*paṅkaja*), standard (*dhvaja*), pot (*kalaśa*), pair of whisks (*camara yugma*), pair of fish (*matsya yugma*) and conch (*śaṅkha*).

BIBLIOGRAPHY

A. Getty: *The Gods of Northern Buddhism* (Oxford, 1914)

P. Pal and D. C. Bhattacharyya: *The Astral Divinities of Nepal* (Varanasi, 1969)

P. Pal: *Vaiṣṇava Iconology in Nepal: A Study of Art and Religion* (Calcutta, 1970)

W. Donner: *Nepal: Raum, Mensch und Wirtschaft* (Wiesbaden, 1972)

S. Greenwold: 'Monkhood Versus Priesthood in Newar Buddhism', *The Anthropology of Nepal*, ed. C. von Fürer-Haimendorf (Warminster, 1973)

P. Pal: *Sculpture* and *Painting*, i and ii of *The Arts of Nepal*, 2 vols (Leiden, 1974–8)

M. R. Allen: *The Cult of Kumari: Virgin Worship in Nepal* (Kathmandu, 1975)

S. Gupta, D. J. Hoens and T. Goudriaan: *Hindu Tantrism* (Leiden, 1979)

A. Gail: 'Planets and Pseudoplanets in Indian Literature and Art with Special Reference to Nepal', *E. & W.*, n. s., xxx/1–4 (1980), pp. 133–46

L. Bangdel: *The Early Sculptures of Nepal* (New Delhi, 1982)

M. Slusser: *Nepal Mandala: A Cultural Study of the Kathmandu Valley*, 2 vols (Princeton, 1982)

A. Gail: *Ikonographie hinduistischer Pagoden in Patan Kathmandutal* (1984), i of *Tempel in Nepal* (Graz, 1984–8)

G. Toffin: *Société et religion chez les Néwar du Népal* (Paris, 1984)

P. Pal: *Art of Nepal: A Catalogue of the Los Angeles County Museum of Art Collection* (Los Angeles, 1985)

A. Gail: 'A Licchavi Manjushri Recently Discovered in Tapahiti, Patan, Nepal', *Berlin. Indol. Stud.*, iii (1987), pp. 279–81

——: 'The Newly Discovered Maitreya from Sankhamul', *Makaranda: Essays in Honour of Dr. James C. Harle*, ed. C. Bautze-Picron (Delhi, 1990), pp. 91–3

R. Levy with Kedar Raj Rajopadhyaya: *Mesocosm: Hinduism and the Organization of a Traditional Newar City in Nepal* (Berkeley, 1990)

A. Gail: *Klöster in Nepal: Ikonographie buddhistischer Klöster im Kathmandutal* (Graz, 1991)

ADALBERT J. GAIL

(iii) Indigenous traditions. Newar traditions, integrated to some extent with Hinduism and Buddhism, include the cult of sacred places, especially springs, and the worship of unhewn stones, still carried out in the countryside, in temples and monasteries and in city streets. The stones have in some cases become identified with Hindu or Buddhist deities.

In mountain villages ethnic groups such as the Gurung, Magar, Tamang and Rai turn to shamans for treatment of the sick or the warding off of evil spirits and in other situations where mediators between people and supernatural beings are required. The ritual objects of the shaman, often made of wood, are usually carved. They include a knife (*phurbu*) with wooden handle and triangular blade, a double-faced drum (*dhyangro*) made of wood and skin and mounted on a handle similar to that of the knife and a ritual vase (*bumba*). The wood used in making the knife and drum is determined by the tree that appears to the shaman in a dream or trance. Cosmologies and symbolism associated with their form and decoration have been influenced by the great Asiatic religions; the sculpture of knife and drum handles frequently includes such elements as the *vajra* and endless knot.

In eastern Nepal fountains are sometimes flanked by wooden figures, standing or seated in prayer. Originating from animistic traditions, such sculptures are offered on the death of a relative or in fulfilment of a vow. Being in the open air and near water they develop a wrinkled patina that marries harmoniously with their archaic style. Similar sculptures are placed in proximity to temples or on bridges. Some houses contain large figures of people praying or playing the tambour, intended for protection and good luck.

In the Himalayan region, as milk is an important element in ritual, the vessels and utensils used for handling it are carved with decorative and symbolic designs. The wooden milk pots of the Rai and Sherpa of eastern Nepal are carved with complex compositions and have handles reminiscent of a lizard's body. Wooden spoons used to decant milk have long pendulum-shaped handles. Axial bars of the churn are carved with geometric motifs. The Kham-Magar (Magar of the west) decorated the bars of churns with human and animal figures. Such carved and decorated ritualistic instruments and tools for everyday life are scarcely known by ethnologists and hardly studied by art historians.

BIBLIOGRAPHY

J. Hitchcock and R. Jones, eds: *Spirit Possession in the Nepal Himalayas* (Warminster, 1976)

S. R. Mumford: *Himalayan Dialogue: Tibetan Lamas and Gurung Shamans in Nepal* (Madison, 1989)

ERIC CHAZOT

II. Art of the prehistoric and protohistoric periods.

Nepal's prehistory is best discussed in terms of two of the country's three main zones: the Terai, the narrow strip of flat land in the south contiguous to the Indian plains, and the Pahar, dominated by the central range of mountains surrounding the Kathmandu Valley. Almost nothing is known of the prehistory of the third zone, the Himal, the stretch of snow-covered ranges along the Tibetan frontier.

The prehistory of the Terai is associated closely with that of the adjoining plains of north India, and its chronology is similar to the chronology of that area. The few scientific excavations undertaken in the region, however, provide only a fragmented picture. Stone tools, mainly Neolithic celts, have been found reportedly in various locations, including Kottarni, a village in Navalparasi District, and in Jhapa-Baijnathpur in Morang. Their dating is uncertain, but they are similar to finds in north India. Deposits of Northern Black Polished ware, found in north India at Hastinapura and other sites, have been discovered through excavation and are dated to *c.* 600 BC.

Almost all archaeological investigation in this area had as its chief aim the discovery and identification of sites associated with the life of the Buddha (*c.* 563–483 BC) and the history of Buddhism. Hence the area that came under scrutiny was relatively small. LUMBINI, the Buddha's birthplace, is clearly identified by the inscription of the Maurya-dynasty Indian emperor Ashoka (*reg c.* 269–232 BC) on a pillar found at the site. The pillar, bearing the characteristic Mauryan polish, is itself one of the most beautiful objects of antiquity found in the Terai. Excavations at Lumbini, Kodan and Tilaurakot, considered by many to be the site of at least part of the ancient settlement of Kapilavastu, and explorations at nearby towns such as Sasaniya, have unearthed the remains of various architectural structures, including the foundations of several stupas and a large number of terracotta and stone sculptures. Notable among the latter for their artistic merit are a terracotta figure of a woman with a parrot and a terracotta plaque of Sri Lakshmi standing on a lotus plant, both from Tilaurakot and datable to the 2nd century BC.

In the Pahar, the Kathmandu Valley appears to have an artistic tradition that dates to the ancient period. A thorough archaeological survey of the valley has yet to be carried out, but surface finds, such as Palaeolithic and highly polished Neolithic tools, indicate early settlement. No reliably datable remains have yet been excavated for the period before the 5th century AD, and no generally accepted chronology has been established for the valley before that date. It is only in the 5th century that the earliest inscription (AD 464) in Sanskrit and the earliest dated sculpture (AD 467) appear.

There is as yet no hard evidence that any architectural monument dates to the period before AD 300. This restriction includes the stupas of Patan, often attributed to Ashoka, and the *vihāra* at Cha-bahil, often attributed to his daughter, Charumati. There are, however, some 30–40 pieces of stone sculpture that may date from the 1st to 3rd centuries AD (see fig. 3; *see also* §IV, 1(i) and fig. 11 below). This dating is based on the fact that they differ markedly in artistic conception from the sculpture of subsequent periods and that some of them bear characteristics similar to sculptures of the Kushana period of India and may have been influenced by the Mathura school (*see* INDIAN SUBCONTINENT, §V, 5(i)). Some of these pieces remain *in situ*, scattered throughout the valley. All of them are severely damaged, and many appear to be worn by centuries of worship. Their identification is therefore difficult, and their dating is perilously uncertain because of the conservative nature of the Nepalese artistic tradition and the tendency for iconic formulae to survive for long periods of time, and because copies of ancient works were made at later times. Of these pieces, the most well known, and often considered to be the oldest, is the male torso found in Hadigaon (see fig. 3) and variously dated from the 1st or 2nd century AD to the 3rd and identified as either a *yakṣa* (male nature spirit) or a *bodhisattva*. Other sculptures include a head of Shiva and a head in grey schist, supposedly of Virupaksha, both of which have been dated to the 2nd or 3rd century AD. Several of the remaining figures are of female deities, particularly

3. *Yakṣa* or *bodhisattva*, stone, from Hadigaon, Protohistoric period, *c.* 1st–3rd centuries AD (Kathmandu, National Museum of Nepal)

Lakshmi, Hariti and the *aṣṭamātṛkā* (Skt: 'eight mothers'). These are all small figures, but in their solidity the artists have created the impression of intense elemental power. Among the most notable are the Kumari of the Bhagavati temple of Jayabageshvari, the Hadigaon Mother Goddess at Kotal-Tol, the Mother Goddess at Balkhu and the Gajalakshmi figure at Chyasalhiti, Patan. Others include the early Mahishamardini figure from the Ganesha temple of Hadigaon, the Brahmani from the Bagalamukhi temple of Patan, the Maheshvari and Vaishnavi figures at Changu Narayan, the Mother Goddess of Haugal-bahal, Patan, the Vaishnavi figure from Subalhiti, Patan, and finally the powerful Hariti figure of Balaju. Among early Vaishnava sculptures are the standing Vishnu at the Satya Narayana temple and the standing Vishnu (badly damaged) in the Ganesha temple, both in Hadigaon. Also important is the *caturmūrti* (four-form representation), dated to the 3rd century AD, that stands in the courtyard of the Rastriya Nachghar in Kathmandu, which contains standing figures of Brahma, Vishnu, Shiva and Devi.

BIBLIOGRAPHY

R. V. Joshi: 'Pre-historic Exploration in Kathmandu Valley, Nepal', *Anc. India*, xxii (1966), pp. 75–82

N. R. Banerjee and B. K. Rijal: 'Three Early Sculptures in the National Museum of Nepal', *Anc. Nepal*, iv (1968), pp. 37–43

S. B. Deo: *Archaeological Excavations at Kathmandu, 1965* (Kathmandu, 1968)

——: *Archaeological Excavations in Nepal Terai, 1964* (Kathmandu, 1968)

N. R. Banerjee and J. L. Sharma: 'Neolithic Tools from Nepal and Sikkim', *Anc. Nepal*, ix (1969), pp. 53–8

D. Mitra: *Excavations at Tilaura-kot and Kodan and Explorations in the Nepalese Tarai* (Kathmandu, 1972)

P. Pal: *Sculpture*, i of *The Arts of Nepal*, 2 vols (Leiden, 1974–8)

L. Bangdel: *The Early Sculptures of Nepal* (New Delhi, 1982)

M. Slusser: *Nepal Mandala: A Cultural Study of the Kathmandu Valley*, 2 vols (Princeton, 1982)

J. L. Sharma: 'Neolithic Tools from Nepal', *Anc. Nepal*, lxxv (1983), pp. 1–12

L. Bangdel: *Nepal: Zweitausend fünfhundert Jahre nepalesischer Kunst* (Leipzig, 1987)

THEODORE RICCARDI JR

III. Architecture.

The Kathmandu Valley's most conspicuous buildings are its graceful brick and wood temples with two or more stacked tile roofs. These are part of a regional tradition, in which the same materials (with the addition of metalwork decoration for more elaborate structures) are used for varied building types: domestic, civic and religious. Cities such as Kathmandu, Bhaktapur and Patan are characterized by streets lined with joined brick buildings, two or three storeys high, with intricately carved wooden balconies, windows and doors; rooms are arranged around inner courtyards. Palaces, also built around paved courtyards, line great darbar squares. Fountains, stupas and stone temples with north Indian-style *śikharas* (towers) add variety to a harmonious and impressive architectural setting.

1. Lichchhavi and Transitional periods, *c.* AD 300–*c.* 1200. 2. Malla period, *c.* 1200–1769. 3. After 1769.

1. Lichchhavi and Transitional periods, *c.* AD 300–*c.* 1200.

Except for stupas, pillars and other remains at places near Nepal's border with India that are associated with the birth and youth of Buddha Shakyamuni, surviving examples of early Nepalese architecture are largely confined to the Kathmandu Valley. Even in this basin extant ancient structures are limited to a few fountains, votive pillars, simple shrines and certain other structures erected during the period of the Lichchhavi occupation, *c.* AD 300–800, and the subsequent Transitional period that ended in *c.* 1200 with the emergence of the various local dynasties named 'Malla'. Since there are so few authenticated ancient structures, and archaeology was unwelcome within the sacred confines of the Kathmandu Valley, knowledge of early Nepalese architecture rests largely on other sources: the records of those who erected, used or saw such buildings in use, fragmentary architectural remains above ground (foundation courses, stone columns and pillars, doorjambs, lintels, sills, steps, fountain spouts, decorative fragments and more) and comparative art-historical research. Together these critical indices demonstrate a long architectural continuum rooted in north India of the earliest centuries AD and culminating in the late medieval architecture that characterizes the architectural milieu of the Kathmandu Valley today.

The inscribed stelae of the Lichchhavis, who apparently came with a rich cultural baggage to Nepal from north India *c.* AD 300, are studded with references to temples and monasteries, palaces and community buildings, stupas, fountains, reservoirs, canals, pillars and platforms that attest to a varied architectural environment but rarely provide clues to its appearance. Such references, if far less copious, continue in the inscriptions and manuscripts of the Transitional period, where they are supplemented with an occasional miniature painting that illustrates, if schematically, such architectural features as a stupa, monastery or pillar. But of what must have been a vast concourse of structures erected over nearly a millennium, only a few survivals can be identified.

One of these, a type only recently recognized, is a simple shrine for sheltering a *liṅga*, the emblem of Shiva. Named *āvaraṇa* (Skt: 'cover') in Lichchhavi inscriptions, the shrine consists of a massive monolithic roof supported on four short columns that are sometimes decorated with guardian figures and other ornament. One of these Lichchhavi shrines stands near the Pashupatinatha temple (see fig. 4), and a sizable cluster stood near Lele village on the southern rim of the valley until destroyed by a flood in 1982. Such shrines also survive as separated parts, often put to other uses, two of which bear inscriptions that date them to the 7th century AD. There is also at least one *liṅga* shrine, in Banepa, which is far more elaborate and can most likely be assigned to the Transitional period.

Other survivals from the Lichchhavi and Transitional periods are stone votive pillars, which were erected in front of shrine portals. They were usually inscribed and typically bore aloft a portrait image of the donor in the guise of a humanized Garuda, the vehicle and companion of Vishnu. (By the 17th century the avian features of such pillar emblems were abandoned in favour of frankly human royal portraits.) More common ancient survivals are the step fountains, known as *praṇālī*s in the inscriptions, which take the form of extensive terraced pits giving access to waterspouts far below. Some of these can be identified as Lichchhavi works by inscriptions and art objects within

4. Shiva *liṅga* shrine, Rajarajeshvari-ghat, Pashupatinatha, Lichchhavi period, *c.* AD 300–*c.* 800

them. Although no step fountain can be verified by associated materials to the Transitional period, such structures probably continued to be built, as they are mentioned in inscriptions and were constructed throughout the Malla period and even later.

In both periods (and in Malla times as well) it was the custom to erect 'spigot fountains' (called *jaladroṇī* by the Lichchhavis), small water reservoirs raised on supports whose spigots could be unstoppered by the thirsty passer-by. Many are inscribed and dated, leaving no doubt that, like the *praṇālī*s and the *khāṭaka*s (ponds, reservoirs) so frequently mentioned in the stelae and used into modern times, they were a ubiquitous feature of the architectural landscape of ancient Nepal.

Except for the four or five so-called 'Ashokan' stupas in Patan city that probably predate the Lichchhavi arrival, most monumental stupas in the Kathmandu Valley are historically certified foundations of early Lichchhavi rulers. They have been so renovated and enlarged over the years, however, that only sectioning would reveal the original core monument and clarify what it looked like. By the 7th century AD many must have been adorned with decorative relief plaques, a number of which have survived, some even apparently *in situ*. The engaged chapels and soaring finials that the stupas now exhibit correspond to doctrinal evolution and were not part of the original design.

Thousands of miniature stupas, usually referred to as *caitya*s, have also survived from the Lichchhavi and Transitional periods. These small stone *caitya*s, rarely taller than a metre, seem more sculptural than architectural in nature, but they are important to Nepalese architectural history because they are often conceived as miniature temples embellished with architectural and ornamental motifs that give some indication of the appearance of the larger buildings they stood among. Some of these buildings, it seems, belonged to the Newar-style canon of post-and-lintel construction that characterizes the well-known corpus of the Malla period, the architectural glory of the

Kathmandu Valley still. Fragmentary remains above ground suggest that the older examples depended more on stone than on the brick and wood typically preferred by the Mallas, but inscriptional and physical evidence leaves no doubt that brick and wood were also used.

All avenues of research indicate that this particular canon was widely employed before the Malla period in the construction not only of temples but also of palace (and perhaps domestic) compounds, of monastic quadrangles and of various kinds of community buildings. Many palaces are named—and occasionally partly described—in local and foreign records pertaining to the Lichchhavis and their immediate successors. Although the evidence is admittedly in part conjectural, it appears that in essential ways such early palaces resembled successor Malla-period palace compounds composed of accretionary dwelling quadrangles interspersed with various temples, shrines and spouting fountains. Documentation of Buddhist monastic architecture is surer because—no matter how recent the elevations of these quadrangles may be (they often replace earlier ones destroyed by fire, earthquake and time)—many rise on stone foundation courses that stylistically can have been created only in the Lichchhavi period. Of the many monasteries mentioned in the records, only a handful have been identified with specific sites and of these only one elevation, Rudravarna-mahavihara in Patan, reconstructed or renovated in the last quarter of the 12th century, can be said with some certainty to pre-date the Malla period. Records indicate that *dharmaśālā*s (community buildings, public shelters) existed in abundance before AD 1200, and the *caitya*s tell something of specific forms, such as the 'sohra kuṭṭa' or 16-columned *maṇḍapa* (a common form in the Malla period). Further, one example survives from the Transitional period. This is Kashtha-mandapa (1143), the famous monumental *dharmaśālā* of brick and wood, from which the Nepalese capital city, Kathmandu, takes its name.

Nepalese written records from between AD 464 and 1200 provide the same inventory of structures known in the succeeding period, down to such minor features as ritual platforms and ambulatory temple carts and palanquins. Further, some, like the fountains and pillars, can be physically shown as forms continuing into modern times. It therefore seems probable that companion structures, if still above ground, would reveal a like continuum. Such 12th-century buildings as Rudravarna-mahavihara and Kasthamandapa, or the Indreshvara Mahadeva temple (1294) at PANAUTI, the oldest dated Newar-style temple, did not come into being without long antecedents. The inescapable conclusion is that the Nepalese who occupied the Kathmandu Valley before the Malla period would have dwelt in an architectural milieu similar to that of their successors.

Art-historical research has shown that the basic inspiration of the Newar-style canon, labelled for its practitioners not its originators, is Kushana, a power in northern India during the first three centuries AD. About the 6th century, towards the end of the succeeding Gupta period, the style had become largely outmoded, surviving only in such provincial outposts as Kerala, for example, and Nepal. Even so, it did not remain rigidly static but embraced new ideas from time to time (for example the elaboration of the number of superimposed roofs); these, while superficially affecting the canon, did not alter the basic type, which remains intact. The builders in Nepal did not work in isolation from India and used the same architectural manuals (*vāstu-śāstras*) as did their Indian counterparts. They knew about and were able to build the newly fashionable *śikhara* of the Guptas, as is attested by at least one survival from the late Lichchhavi period or early Transitional period in the compound of the Pashupatinatha temple. But to judge by the *śikhara*'s relative infrequency in the architectural scene today, Nepalis have always preferred the earlier style, legacy of the distant Kushanas.

BIBLIOGRAPHY
U. Wiesner: *Nepalese Temple Architecture: Its Characteristics and its Relations to Indian Development*, Studies in South Asian Culture, viii (Leiden, 1978)
——: 'Nepalese Votive Stupas of the Licchavi Period: The Empty Niche', *The Stupa, its Religious, Historical and Architectural Significance*, ed. A. L. Dallapiccola and S. Zingel-Avé Lallemant (Wiesbaden, 1980), pp. 166–74
M. Slusser: 'Nepalese *Caityas* as Mirrors of Medieval Architecture', ibid., pp. 157–65
——: *Nepal Mandala: A Cultural Study of the Kathmandu Valley*, 2 vols (Princeton, NJ, 1982), i, pp. 127–87

MARY SHEPHERD SLUSSER

2. MALLA PERIOD, *c.* 1200–1769. Three main types of religious buildings were constructed during the Malla period. The most distinctive are brick-and-wood pyramidal temples with two or more roofs stacked one upon the other. Buddhist monasteries, now mostly used for other purposes, make up a second group. These two types were built using similar materials and techniques, and, as they represent more traditional Nepalese building practices, they are discussed first. The third type of structure, the *śikhara* temple, is distinguished by a curvilinear tower derived from Indian models.

(i) Pyramidal temples (*dega*s). (ii) Buddhist monasteries. (iii) *Śikhara* temples.

*(i) Pyramidal temples (*degas*).* The Newari word '*dega*', originating from the Sanskrit *devagṛha* ('god's house') and meaning temple, is often used to denote pyramidal temples in preference to 'pagoda', which is not of Nepalese origin. Consisting of a simple sanctum with its two or three superimposed slanting roofs, the *dega* was built at a variety of sites in the Kathmandu Valley—on city squares, at crossroads, near rivers and on hillsides. Monumental in form, it was often founded by royal families; the *dega* characterizes the palace areas of the Malla capitals of Kathmandu, Patan and Bhaktapur, and represents the epitome of Newar architecture.

Square in plan, the *dega* stands on a brick socle (unless it crowns a palace wing). It may have two, three or five roofs, the two-roof type being the most ancient. Two of the most renowned examples are the Changu Narayan Dega and Pashupatinatha Dega, both Hindu centres of national importance. Both are mentioned as early as the 3rd to 5th century (that at Changu Narayan has sculpture dating from the 5th to 7th century) but were destroyed by fire and rebuilt, the Changu Narayan Dega in 1698 and the Pashupatinatha Dega in 1702. Both structures are two-roofed and in this respect seem to preserve their original form.

The body of the temple (see fig. 5) consists of inner and outer walls made of wood and bricks. The inner enclosure, demarcating the sanctum, supersedes the outer one in height. Both are covered by slanting roofs. The area between the inner and outer walls forms a circumambulation path (*pradakṣiṇa-patha*). From the 17th century onwards, the lower part of the outer brick wall was sometimes replaced by wooden pillars. In this case the arcades transformed the closed circumambulation path into an open one. As in Indian temples, the highest point of the superstructure rises above the sanctum, and the tower is thus used as an architectural means of emphasizing the sanctum's ritual importance. Free-standing, square pyramidal temples with only one roof are not original structures (they do not properly emphasize the sanctum) but are instead two or three-roofed pyramidal temples rebuilt at a reduced height after their destruction or damage by earthquakes, fire or other causes.

The origin of the two-roofed *dega*, built, it appears, from an early date in Nepal, is one of the most frequently debated questions of Nepalese architecture. Both Indian (Wiesner, 1978) and Chinese influence have been suggested. In discussing the problem it is useful to view the pyramidal temple in the context of traditional secular architecture in Nepal. The same materials, brick and wood, are used for secular and sacred buildings. Features such as lattice windows occur in both and are characterized by extended lintels and sills. Both types of building have slanting roofs protruding over the walls supported by wooden struts. Secular buildings, such as the Kashthaman-dapa (*see* §1 above), have the same type of superimposed roofs as the pyramidal temple. There is, in fact, not a single architectural element in traditional temple building that

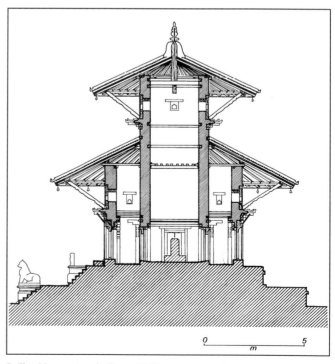

5. Char Narayan temple, Patan, 1565; east–west section

6. Jagannātha *dega*, Kathmandu, 17th century

could not be sufficiently explained by general building methods in Nepal or the general Hindu practice developed in India of pointing out the position of the sanctum. Establishing a convincing historical link with the slanted-roofed buildings of Kerala, Gujarat, Kashmir or China remains difficult.

Decorative embellishment offered a means of individualizing the *dega* (see figs 6 and 7). While some forms of decoration are rooted in religious significance, others reflect changes in style or taste. Carved wooden doors and windows are a main decorative element (*see also* §VI, 7, below). Doors consist of one or three openings (7a). Above the single entrance, or central entrance if there are three, is a richly carved semicircular disc (*toraṇa*; 7b). The door lintel (7c) is elongated and lavishly decorated with carvings. There is a dentil-shaped cornice (7d) above the lintel, and above the cornice is a central wooden window with one or two windows on each side (7e), depending on the size of the temple. Curved, carved brackets, embedded in the wall (7f), connect the outer door posts and the extended lintel. At the base of the doorframe on either side are rhomboid-shaped flaps (7g) carved with figural motifs. Set into the wall on each side of the door are small niches with decorative gables (7h). The *dega*'s slanting roof is supported by slim, beautifully carved struts (7i) resting on the cornice. The oldest preserved struts, from the 13th–14th century, are carved with graceful female figures entwined in the branches of trees (*śālabhañjikās*). Each strut is made from a single piece of wood, and the figures, though deeply carved, retain the outline of the beam. In later centuries the large figures carved in the middle of the struts were usually related to the main deity worshipped in the temple. The incarnations of Vishnu might be carved on a Vishnu temple or aspects of Shiva on a Shiva temple. Mother goddesses, fierce Bhairava figures and epic heroes are also depicted. From the 16th to 18th centuries additional pieces were added to strut figures. These included the arms of many-armed Tantric deities, emblems and garments, which were pegged on the figures. To enhance their visual impact, the main struts were often framed with smaller ones.

The focus of temple ceremony and ritual is the cult figure housed in the sanctum, usually a stone or metal

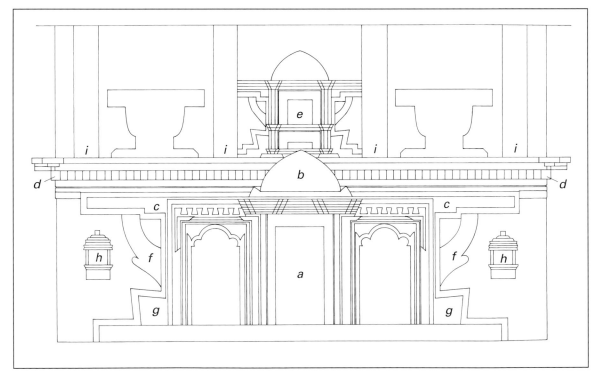

7. Areas of embellishment of a Nepalese temple façade: (a) door consisting of one or three parts (including panels and frames); (b) *toraṇa*, a semicircular disc above the (middle) door; (c) extended lintel; (d) dentil-shaped cornice above the lintel carrying the roof struts; (e) windows; (f) curved brackets set into the wall; (g) rhomboid flaps carved with figural motifs; (h) small niches with decorative gables; (i) carved struts

image of the temple deity. The Newars, however, are also inclined towards aniconic images, and the deity may, for example, be represented in the sanctum by unhewn stones. Such old, popular traditions persist in the Valley alongside the general Hinduization of the pantheon and of ritual practices.

The iconographic programme of a pyramidal temple essentially follows a universal ideal: each temple is a manmade microcosm reflecting the god-penetrated macrocosm. Each temple is, at the same time, by way of its underlying geometric pattern (*maṇḍala*), an image of the universe.

(ii) Buddhist monasteries. The Newar Buddhist monastery essentially follows the Indian model, with rooms arranged around an open inner courtyard. The room opposite the entrance serves as the monastery's shrine. Earlier Indian examples built on similar plans include the structural monasteries of Gandhara and Bihar and the rock-cut monasteries of western India at sites such as Ajanta. Nepalese monasteries are usually two-storey brick-and-wood structures with a single sloping roof. The exterior has few windows (or in some cases blind windows).

This historical type of structure survives in two variants, known in Nepali as *bahil* and *bahal* (and in Newari as *bahī* and *bāhā*). The *bahil* complex, which may have served as a residence for celibate monks, seems to represent the more traditional type. In the Vajrayana Buddhism of Nepal monks were allowed to marry, and the *bahal* served as a residence for married monks and their families. Perhaps the most striking difference between the two is the way in which the sanctuary is emphasized. In the *bahil* the shrine opposite the entrance differs only slightly from the general structure. The sanctuary is marked out only by its doors, the window of a Tantric (non-orthodox) sanctum on the upper floor and a turret on top of the roof (see fig. 8). In some cases the lower sanctum is surrounded by a circumambulation path. The struts are simple, with no figural or floral carvings, and the space around the courtyard has no dividing walls. The whole structure usually stands on a plinth, broken by only one staircase, leading to the main sanctum.

In contrast, the *bahal* is built at street-level. The lower and upper floors have dividing walls creating separate living-quarters for married monks and their families. The shrine opposite the entrance has two or three superimposed roofs, similar to those of the pyramidal temple, rising above the rest of the structure. The façade of the *bahal* shrine is more lavishly embellished than that of the *bahil*. Main areas of decoration include the semicircular disc (*toraṇa*) above the door, the roof struts and the windows of the first upper floor. *Toraṇa* decorations are varied. The historical Buddha Shakyamuni is often depicted flanked by his disciples Shariputra and Maudgalyayana (see fig. 9). A symbolic representation of the three jewels (*triratna*) is created when the Buddha is flanked by Prajnaparamita, representing the law (*dharma*), and Lokeshvara, representing the community of monks (*saṃgha*). The carvings of the roof struts frequently represent the five metaphysical Buddhas (*tathāgatas*), the five *bodhisattvas* emanating from them and the five protective goddesses. The windows of the first upper storey are often

8. Chikan-bahil, Patan, 15th century or earlier, monastery courtyard facing sanctuary

designed as niches, in which the five metaphysical Buddhas are placed.

From the 15th century or earlier the *bahal* sometimes took the form of a residential quarter (Joseph, 1971). The individual houses of the monks' families and the temple were grouped around a spacious courtyard. All of the residences faced the courtyard, a shared area for work and gatherings. These three types of monasteries demonstrate the historical transition from ancient monastic Buddhism to the Hinduized Buddhism of the Kathmandu Valley. The *bahal* forming a residential quarter reflects most clearly the dissolution of celibate Buddhism in Nepal.

In all three types of monastery the courtyard is crowded with such donations as votive stupas, stone *maṇḍalas* and religious sculpture. The best-preserved *bahils* are Chikan-bahil (see fig. 8 above) and Pintu-bahil in Patan. A particularly well-endowed historical *bahal* is Uku-bahal in Patan. Other outstanding examples are Itum-bahal in Kathmandu and Chaturbrahma-mahavihara in Bhaktapur. Interesting examples of residential-quarter *bahals* are Bu-bahal in Patan and Dhvaka-bahal in Kathmandu.

(iii) Śikhara temples. The most important non-traditional building type in the Kathmandu Valley is the temple with a curvilinear tower, derived from the Indian *śikhara*. Historical records offer no indication of when such temples were first built in Nepal. The earliest dated example appears to be the small Narasimha temple (dedicated to Vishnu in the form of the man-lion) on the palace square in Patan. An inscribed foundation stone states that the temple was consecrated by King Purandarasimha in 1589. The exterior walls of the square sanctum are divided into five faces or vertical salients (creating the *pañcaratha* form common in India). The temple has four entrances (unusual in India), one in the central section of each side, which are entered through porticos (*mukhamaṇḍapas*). The crowning element is a wheel (*cakra*), an emblem of Vishnu. The building is constructed of bricks coated with plaster. Stone was used for the eight portico pillars, wood for the pilasters and beams. The Jagatnarayana temple (1860) in Patan is similar. In both cases *nāgas*

9. Kva-bahal, Patan, 17th century, *toraṇa* with Buddha and disciples

(serpent deities) are the only decoration on the external walls of the sanctum.

Several *sikhara* temples were built of grey stone. The most prominent of these is the Krishna temple on the palace square in Patan, constructed by order of King Siddhinarasimha in 1637. The temple is built in three storeys and is surrounded by arcades. The *sikhara* is crowned by a golden vase-shaped element (*kalaśa*). The temple's sixteen pavilions and four miniature shrines shine with similar golden pinnacles. A frieze illustrating scenes from the *Rāmāyaṇa* decorates the façade of the ground-floor and a frieze of scenes from the *Mahābhārata* the first floor. In some temples a *sikhara*-like tower was added above a lower floor built in the style of the traditional *dega*. Such structures can be termed 'mixed *sikhara*' temples. Examples include the Shiva temple at Nuga-Tol, Patan.

BIBLIOGRAPHY

M. B. Jospeh: 'The Viharas of the Kathmandu Valley' *Orient. A.*, n. s., xvii/2 (1971), pp. 121–43
W. Donner: *Nepal: Raum, Mensch und Wirtschaft* (Wiesbaden, 1972)
M. Slusser and G. Vajracharya: 'Two Medieval Nepalese Buildings: An Architectural and Cultural Study', *Artibus Asiae*, xxxvi/3 (1974), pp. 169–218
W. Korn: *The Traditional Architecture of the Kathmandu Valley* (Kathmandu, 1977)
U. Wiesner: *Nepalese Temple Architecture: Its Characteristics and its Relations to Indian Development*, Studies in South Asian Culture, viii (Leiden, 1978)
M. Slusser: *Nepal Mandala: A Cultural Study of the Kathmandu Valley*, 2 vols (Princeton, 1982)
A. Gail: *Ikonographie hinduistischer Pagoden in Patan Kathmandutal* and *Ikonographische Untersuchungen zur späten Pagode und zum Sikhara-Tempel*, i and ii of *Tempel in Nepal* (Graz, 1984–8)
J. K. Locke: *Buddhist Monasteries of Nepal: A Survey of the Bahas and Bahis of the Kathmandu Valley* (Kathmandu, 1985)
A. Gail: *Klöster in Nepal: Ikonographie buddhistischer Klöster im Kathmandutal* (Graz, 1991)

ADALBERT J. GAIL

3. AFTER 1769. The history of Nepal took a dramatic new course as a result of the unification of the country in 1768–9 by Prithvi Narayan Shah, who captured the Kathmandu Valley from his outpost in Gorkha. At the time there appears to have been little major building beyond the Kathmandu Valley other than King Prithvi's palaces at Gorkha, which were strongly influenced by the Newar craftsmen of the Malla dynasties (*see* §I, 2, above).

Between the mid-18th century and the mid-19th the Shah dynasty, whose interests, unlike their predecessors', lay in politics and development rather than architecture, followed the traditional style of architecture created in the Malla period with modifications to the proportions of rooms and openings to allow more light into buildings; however, these traditional modes of construction were later superseded by designs imported by the Rana regime, which sought inspiration from farther afield. During the early 19th century there was a brief interest in the application of Arabian motifs. The use of the plastic medium of stucco allowed exotic façades to be created, as can be seen in the former Bagh Durbar, built in 1805 by Prime Minister Bhimsen Thapa, and his landmark, the Bhimsen Stambha (Tower), erected in 1825. This interest in non-indigenous forms heralded the arrival of a new approach, generally referred to later as the Rana style, which was imported direct from the distant West.

Jang Bahadur Rana, the country's first hereditary prime minister (*reg* 1846–56; 1857–77), was also the first Nepalese dignitary to travel to Europe. Visiting England and

France, he was especially struck by the architecture and became one of those responsible for introducing the Neo-classical style to Nepal at the same time that it was coming into prominence in Great Britain (*see* NEO-CLASSICISM). Inspired by frequent voyages to Europe, later Rana prime ministers constructed, in the space of a hundred years, well over 50 large palace estates as private dwellings for their growing families and retinues. Many of these palaces had well-known European models. For example, the Kaiser Mahal (1895) took its inspiration from the 17th-century château of Versailles, outside Paris, while an addition (1905) to the Hanuman Dhoka palace was modelled on the National Gallery (1834–7), London (*see* VERSAILLES, §1; and ENGLAND, §II, 5). Perhaps the most remarkable palace of this period is the Singha Durbar in Kathmandu, which was built by Chandra Shumsher for his family in 1903 (see fig. 10). With a work force of two engineers and three thousand men, this palace, which contained about seventeen hundred rooms set around seven large courtyards, was completed in just eleven months. At the time it was considered to be the largest private dwelling in Asia. The palace was full of period interiors shipped direct from London, with crystal chandeliers from Belgium and a replica of a Victorian theatre complete with stage machinery fit for British music-hall performances. The Singha Durbar was later given by

Chandra Shumsher to the State as the official seat of the prime minister. In the 1950s it became the government secretariat of the king, but in 1973 it was ravaged by a fire that left only the main west wing standing.

Outside the Kathmandu Valley, architectural development occurred mostly as a result of influences from neighbouring areas. In the lowlands of Nepal—the Terai, which borders Bihar in India—architectural styles are reminiscent of the brick and stucco structures across the border. The Janaki Mandir, built about the beginning of the 20th century, is a typical southern Nepalese copy of 17th-century Mughal religious architecture. The structures are solid brick and stucco with wide verandahs, high ceilings and flat, brick-vaulted roofs. Of necessity walls are protected from the weather by wide, arcaded verandahs running around the perimeter. Openings are small, and the white stucco decoration is simple. These characteristics contrast greatly with the traditional local dwellings of mud plaster on a bamboo frame with straw or leaf thatch.

A distinctive style of monumental architecture is found at high altitudes in the northern regions of Nepal: the Buddhist monastic complexes of the Solu Khumbu and Helambu regions. Many existing buildings have only been constructed or reconstructed within the last century; those of Tengboche in Khumbu and of Chiwong in Solu were both founded in 1923. Stylistically, these buildings borrow

10. West wing of the Singha Durbar, Kathmandu, 1903; rest of the palace destroyed 1973

the formalized layout of Tibetan monasteries, catering for the damper climates of the southern slopes of the Himalayas with sloping roofs originally of shingle or stone slabs. The monasteries are solid structures of rough-hewn stone, crudely plastered with mud and washed with a distinctive red clay. The windows are of pine-wood with composite decorated lintels. Often in front of the temple (*lhakang*) there is a courtyard enclosed by a timber arcade, within which rituals and traditional dances take place.

Traditional domestic architecture adds enormously to the quality of the built environment in Nepal. Over 30 ethnic groups have contributed to the mosaic of architectural styles built to suit the varied climate and environment. These range from the strong rectilinear format of the rough-dressed stone rubble houses capped with geometric slates of the Gurung to the more ethereal style of the lowland Tharu long-houses. The latter, often over 50 m long, are of wattle and daub with sombre interiors and small windows to keep out the heat and rain during the summer months. Exteriors and interiors are often highly decorated with primitive low reliefs moulded in clay and stencilled with patterns to relieve the darkness.

Western influence on the modern architecture of Nepal has done little to encourage the continuation of the built environment for which the Kathmandu Valley was so renowned. The expanding population and the influx of people from the mountains and fields of a country that formerly had an agrarian-based economy has put enormous pressures on the cities and towns. The lack of planning legislation has allowed the uncontrolled expansion of poorly constructed concrete-framed brick boxes in a way that takes no account of earlier clearly defined town plans and fails to restrict building to non-arable land.

BIBLIOGRAPHY

D. Snellgrove: *Buddhist Himalaya* (Oxford, 1957)
D. R. Regmi: *Modern Nepal. Rise and Growth in the Eighteenth Century* (Calcutta, 1961)
The Physical Development Plan for the Kathmandu Valley, Government of Nepal, Department of Physical Planning (Kathmandu, 1969)
L. F. Stiller: *Rise of the House of Gorkha* (Delhi, 1973)
C. Pruscha: *Kathmandu Valley: The Preservation of Physical Environment and Cultural Heritage: A Protective Inventory*, 2 vols (Vienna, 1975)
W. Korn: *The Traditional Architecture of the Kathmandu Valley* (Kathmandu, 1977)
J. Sanday: *Monuments of the Kathmandu Valley* (Paris, 1979)
C. Jest: *Monuments of Northern Nepal* (Paris, 1981)

JOHN SANDAY

IV. Sculpture.

Nepal is particularly renowned for its fluid and graceful sculpture in stone, metal and wood. The subject-matter is mainly religious, the gods and goddesses of the Hindu and Buddhist pantheons predominating. Works show a unity of style across the range of materials and themes. However, within this strong overall continuity, broad stylistic trends are discernible. Names and biographies of artists are rare before the modern period.

1. Before *c.* AD 800. 2. Transitional period, *c.* 800–*c.* 1200. 3. Malla period, *c.* 1200–1769. 4. After 1769.

1. BEFORE *c.* AD 800. It appears that by the beginning of the 1st century AD the Kathmandu Valley was the domain of a non-Aryan ethnic group variously called Nipas, Abhiras or Gopalas. Nepalese chronicles state that the Gopalas were suppressed by the Kiratas. Any sculpture produced by Gopalas or Kiratas at this early date remains to be discovered.

Nepal's earliest-known sculpture (in stone) can be dated on the basis of style to *c.* 300 AD, roughly the time when the Lichchhavis (*reg c.* 300–800), one of several Sanskritized peoples who migrated to Nepal from eastern India, gained prominence. From the 4th to the 6th centuries the Lichchhavi kings of Nepal ruled contemporaneously with India's Gupta dynasty, so it is not surprising that the Lichchhavis were influenced by Gupta culture. However, some similarities between Lichchhavis and Guptas may be due to common Kushana-period origins. This view is supported by numismatic and linguistic evidence. For example, Lichchhavi coins resemble Kushana rather than Gupta coins; and certain terms, for example *viśvāsika*, denoting a governor, are known from Kushana-period and Lichchhavi inscriptions but are unknown in Gupta-period sources.

Lichchhavi rule can be divided into the undocumented period preceding the pillar inscription of AD 464 (the earliest written record of Nepalese history) and the documented Lichchhavi period. A small group of stone figures (some 30–40 pieces, most of them badly damaged; *see also* §II above) can be assigned to the former; a larger body of exceptionally fine work is known from the latter. A number of metal images from the late Lichchhavi period have been identified, though most surviving metal sculpture dates from after the 6th century. These few surviving examples document an early fine tradition of metal craftsmanship. No examples of wood sculpture survive from this early period.

(i) Stone. (ii) Metal.

(i) *Stone.* The three main characteristics of stone sculpture produced before AD 800 are: the appearance of flatter, non-Aryan native facial features, a close relationship to the Kushana-period Mathura style of eastern India and stylistic idioms of Gupta-period art. Although these elements dominate Nepalese sculpture chronologically, in the art of the later Lichchhavi period all may appear simultaneously, due to the conservative nature of the Nepalese tradition.

The Kushana-period Mathura style is evident, for example, in the broken torso of a standing figure, variously identified as a *bodhisattva* or a *yakṣa*, found at Hadigaon and stylistically datable to the undocumented Lichchhavi period (Kathmandu, N. Mus.; see fig. 3 above). Like Mathura images, the figure has a fleshy stomach and deep navel and wears a sash tied with a large knot (now damaged) above the left leg. Shared features also include the 'wet-look' of the pleats of the *dhotī* hanging between the legs, the style of wearing the garment over the left shoulder and the thick gathering of folds along the left shoulder and arm. The semicircular curve of the sash hanging at knee length is particularly characteristic of the early Mathura style of eastern India; in the art of Mathura itself the sash hangs diagonally from waist to knee. A close relationship with eastern India is also suggested by an iconographic feature of all early Nepalese Vishnu images:

the god is depicted holding the mace in his left hand, a variation that does not occur in works from Mathura itself. In the conservative Nepalese tradition such features persist in later times.

A seated image of the Mother Goddess, Hariti (*c.* 3rd century AD; see fig. 11), in a sunken shrine close to Darbar Square in Patan, is rendered with knees apart and legs hanging down (in a posture known as *pralamba pādāsana*), a pose similar to that of the portrait statues of the Kushana kings of Mathura (Mathura, Archaeol. Mus.). Her arms, spread out from her body, rest on her thighs, the left hand holds a fish, and the right hand displays the boon-giving gesture (*varada mudrā*), with palm wide open and fingers slightly curved. Interestingly, this gesture appears frequently in early Nepalese sculpture but is rare in Kushana-period works from Mathura and Gandhara, gaining popularity in India only in the Gupta period. The goddess's erect, slender torso seems to be bare; she wears a sari-like lower garment, the pleats in the middle falling in a distinctive pattern of folds on the vertical face of the bench. A characteristic of early Nepalese sculpture, this fold pattern gradually disappears in the documented Lichchhavi period. Though the image is badly damaged, it still conveys the vigorous, active personality of the goddess skilfully endowed by the artist.

11. *Hariti* (*c.* 3rd century AD), stone, Kva-bahal, Patan

A gradual stylistic development is apparent in a standing male figure, often considered a royal portrait (*c.* early 4th century AD; Kathmandu, N. Mus.). The face of the figure is framed by a plain halo; the arms are spread wide, the left hand holding a lotus bud and the right grasping the folds of a sash. The torso is bare, with neither the sacred thread nor necklace seen in later Lichchhavi images. The figure wears a trilobe crown (compared with later examples, it is lower, with the emphasis on horizontality), an unusual belt, two simple bracelets and heavy earrings, designed after the *āmalaka* fruit. Only one other representation of such earrings is known, on a statue of Shiva in a shrine near Pashupatinatha. An important feature of the statue is its native physiognomy: round face, almond-shaped eyes with the mere suggestion of eyebrows and non-Aryan flat nose. The semicircular curve of the sash hanging across the thighs is in accordance with the Kushana-period style of eastern India, but the flatter stomach and tiny navel are more characteristic of later work. Further, the early open palm gesture has become a cupped one more like 5th-century sculptures. This continuity with the early tradition, combined with the emergence of new stylistic elements, makes a 4th-century date convincing.

The earliest date occurring on Nepalese sculpture is AD 467. Two images of Vishnu Vikranta (representing the story of the dwarf incarnation), with identical inscriptions providing King Manadeva's name as the reigning monarch, were once considered to be contemporary, a view now questioned on the basis of stylistic differences (see Pal, 1974, figs 1 and 2). The date is likely to be correct for the work still *in situ* on the bank of the rivulet Tilaganga. Its figures are rendered with the somewhat dwarfish proportions characteristic of early sculpture; the arms of the main figure are raised as if lifting a heavy weight, a feature that gradually disappears after the early 6th century. In the second work (Kathmandu, N. Mus.), from Lajimpat, figures are more elongated, and an increased naturalism (characteristic of 7th-century sculpture) is evident in their relaxed postures. The palaeography of the inscription from Lajimpat also supports a later date, as does the use of different spelling rules of Sanskrit grammar.

Closer to the sophisticated style of India's Gupta-period images (evident in Nepalese works from about the 6th century, due to the time-lag in transmission) is a head of Shiva emerging from the smoothly polished column of a *linga* (see fig. 12). The image stood beneath a tree in Mrigasthali and was in worship until its disappearance in 1986. The hair, adorned with crescent moon, is elegantly tied with a rosary of tiny pearl-like beads. Facial features—large eyes, long nose and sensitive, full lower lip—closely follow the Gupta idiom.

A group of monumental works was created under the patronage of kings probably of Nipa or Abhira lineage, who by the 7th century were so Sanskritized that they changed their last name to Gupta, presumably to elevate their social status. A reclining figure of Vishnu (dated AD 641–2) remains in worship at BUDHANILKANTHA, some 24 km north of Kathmandu. The image, some 6 m in length, rests in the middle of a pond, the water representing the cosmic ocean, where the god sleeps on the cushion-like coils of the serpent Ananta. A masterpiece

12. Ekamukha ('single-faced') *liṅga* (*c.* 6th century AD), stone, formerly Mrigasthali

of Nepalese art, it shares a number of stylistic features with Gupta-period sculpture: a sensitive lower lip, broad chest, massive shoulders and slim waist. Perhaps the most admirable quality is its sense of tranquility. Belonging to the same group of works are a second image of the reclining Vishnu at Balaju and a sculpture of Krishna subduing the serpent Kaliya in the Hanuman Dhoka palace, Kathmandu.

(ii) Metal. India's ancient Sanskrit literature refers to Nepal as a source of superior-quality copper, and 7th-century Lichchhavi inscriptions indicate that finished metal products were exported to India as well. A Chinese ambassador visiting Nepal in about the 7th century described the impressive metalwork of Nepalese palaces, including golden dragon-like waterspouts. Little of this early work has survived; until recently a number of scholars argued that metalwork appeared only after the 12th century in Nepal and that its style was derived from that of Pala-period Bengal. The earliest-surviving object is now considered to be a gilt sheath (about half a metre high) executed in the repoussé technique probably in the undocumented Lichchhavi period (*c.* 3rd–5th century AD). Depicting Vishnu mounted on his vehicle Garuda, the sheath served

as a metal protective cover (*kavaca* or *kośa*) for a stone image still in worship at CHANGU NARAYAN, about 6 km north of Bhaktapur. Inscriptions state that the sheath was repaired in AD 607 during the reign of King Amsuvarma and again in 1694 by a Malla king. It is unknown how much of the original remains, as the sheath is almost always covered by piles of flowers offered to the god, and priests for religious reasons do not allow photographs (a few of poor quality have been published). A stylistic analysis is thus difficult, and little is known about the stylistic impact of such early works on later metal sculpture.

A statue of the Buddha Shakyamuni (Cleveland, OH, Mus. A.), originally from the Yangvala monastery (now known as Yengu-bahal), near Darbar Square, Patan, bears an inscription with a date equivalent to AD 591. This elegant figure stands barefoot on a lotus, its diaphanous robe, blown by a breeze, revealing the form of the eternally youthful divine body. The work shares many features of India's Gupta-period style: hair rendered in tiny curls, a full, sensitive lower lip, half-closed eyes shaped like lotus buds, straight nose and, above all, a calm and contemplative inner serenity. It was assumed to be of Indian origin until the inscription was read.

A standing Buddha figure (Heller priv. col.), in some ways similar, bears a short inscription palaeographically of the 7th century AD, a date in keeping with the style of the statue. While the example in the Cleveland Museum exhibits the fleshy yet tight body inherited from Kushana-period sculpture of Mathura, the Buddha in the Heller collection has lost this quality. Further, the face is less naturalistically treated, and the *uṣṇīṣa* (cranial protuberance) is beginning to take on the pointed shape favoured in later periods.

Stylistic developments are interestingly displayed in three images of Vajrapani, considered an attendant of the Buddha and a counterpart of the Hindu god Indra (New York, Met.; ex-Humann priv. col.; and Los Angeles, CA, Co. Mus. A.; see fig. 13). His attribute, the thunderbolt, is carried in the left hand in the image in the Metropolitan Museum and anthropomorphized in the other two examples; in both cases a dwarf-like figure stands to the left of the god, who holds the upper part of the weapon protruding above the figure's head. Iconographically similar, the three images can be assigned a chronology on the basis of style.

The Vajrapani in the Metropolitan Museum wears a thin *dhotī* with a simple knotted belt; a sash falls diagonally over the hips, its folds and those of the *dhotī*'s pleats creating rhythmic curves. Though he wears earrings and a mitre-shaped crown, usually associated with the god Indra, standard ornaments seen from the 7th century AD onward are absent. The waist is fleshy but tight, a quality shared with the Buddha in the Cleveland Museum. A date of *c.* 6th–7th century is likely.

In comparison the Vajrapani once in the Humann collection has gentler facial features, his half-closed eyes looking down with compassion on all living beings. Other features related to those of Gupta-period works include the diaphanous *dhotī* that falls in graceful waves between the legs and the sash loosely tied around the hips. The fine proportions of the figure are accentuated by the sacred thread hanging from the left shoulder to the knee and by the placement of the dwarf next to the tall figure of the god. These features might suggest an early date, but the work shows a tendency towards ornateness. The figure wears earrings, necklace, armbands, bracelets and an extraordinary and elegant crown. It is likely to date to the 7th century.

The Vajrapani in the Los Angeles County Museum is simpler in appearance: the crown unpretentious, ornaments fewer and the folds of the *dhotī* less stylish. The artist has emphasized sturdy masculine features rather than compassionate ones; the overall effect is of physical solidity and simplicity, which might suggest an early date. Several features, however, make this impossible: the halo is pointed, a design never seen before the 7th century but regularly employed after that date; the flat two-dimensional quality created by the halo is inconsistent with early metal

13. Vajrapani, bronze alloy with traces of gilt, h. 132 mm, 8th century AD (Los Angeles, CA, County Museum of Art)

sculptures; and a gentle facial expression, a hallmark of the Gupta-period style, is absent. The 8th-century date usually attributed is probably correct.

Perhaps the only female figure attributable to this early period is an image of a goddess, with ornaments including a beautiful tiara, armlets and bracelets (Cleveland, Bickford priv. col.; see Pal, 1974, fig. 218). Despite its diminutive size, the work conveys a sense of monumentality. The facial expression is gentle; the vibrancy of youth and health flow from face and body. Her ample breasts, narrow waist and broad hips are a representation of the ideal female form continued in works of later centuries.

BIBLIOGRAPHY

G. Vajracharya: 'Pracina murtikalako visayama' [On the subject of ancient sculpture], *Purnima*, i/3 (1964), pp. 14–18

The Art of Nepal (exh. cat. by S. Kramrisch, New York, Asia Soc. Gals, 1964)

N. R. Banerjee and B. K. Rijal: 'Three Early Sculptures in the National Museum of Nepal', *Anc. Nepal*, iv (1968), pp. 37–43

S. Czuma: 'A Gupta Style Bronze Buddha', *Bull. Cleveland Mus. A.*, lvii/2 (1970), pp. 55–67

M. Slusser and G. Vajracharya: 'Early Nepalese Sculptures', *Illus. London News*, cclx/6893 (1972), pp. 68–73

——: 'Some Nepalese Stone Sculptures: A Reappraisal within their Cultural and Historical Context', *Artibus Asiae*, xxxv/1–2 (1973), pp. 79–138

P. Pal: *Sculpture*, i of *The Arts of Nepal* (Leiden, 1974)

M. Slusser: 'On the Antiquity of Nepalese Metalcraft', *Archvs Asian A.*, xxix (1976), pp. 80–95

G. Vajracharya: 'Licchavi Inscriptions on Two Bronze Buddha Images', *Archvs Asian A.*, xxix (1976), p. 93

F. Asher: *The Art of Eastern India, 300–800* (Minneapolis, 1980)

L. Bangdel: *The Early Sculptures of Nepal* (New Delhi, 1982)

M. Khanal: *Changu nārayanakā aitihāsika sāmagri* [Historical materials of Changu Narayan] (Kathmandu, 1983)

L. Bangdel: *Nepal: Zweitausend fünf hundert Jahre nepalesischer Kunst* (Leipzig, 1987)

2. TRANSITIONAL PERIOD, c. 800–c. 1200. The post-Lichchhavi period was characterized by political instability. Forceful royal edicts like those of the Lichchhavi kings were no longer carved in stone. Among surviving monuments, not a single royal commission is known; all were provided by members of the public. Succession, it appears, was intended to alternate between the eldest members of two royal families. Power sometimes passed smoothly but more often with bloodshed. The continual struggle for political survival from one generation to the next seems to have so occupied royal personages that they had little time for visual pleasure.

The arts, however, were surprisingly undisturbed. Socio-religious institutions known as *gūṭhī*s remained active. Some organized seasonal festivals, while others were responsible for the creation of new images and the annual repair of temples. Most *gūṭhī*s were supported by profits from land donated by pious people; financially independent, they could remain aloof from palace politics. Led by the elders of the community, the *gūṭhī*s played a vital role in protecting and promoting culture and the arts.

Further, throughout the period trade flourished along the India–Tibet trade route passing through the Kathmandu Valley, bringing prosperity to merchants, who patronized artistic activity—commissioning illustrated manuscripts or establishing temples or monasteries. The trade route facilitated the exchange of ideas as well as merchandise. Tibetan and Nepalese scholars studied and practised Mahayana and Tantric Buddhism in the valley's many monasteries. Before the destruction of Indian monasteries by raids in the 12th century, Tibetan scholars also had direct contact with these famed institutions. After the 12th century they turned mainly to Nepal for religious and aesthetic inspiration. Sculpture survives in stone and metal, but few examples in wood have withstood the ravages of time.

(i) Stone. (ii) Metal.

(i) Stone. Perhaps the most remarkable example of stone sculpture from the early Transitional period is a high relief of Vishnu Vikranta standing in the courtyard of the Changu Narayan temple (see fig. 14). Illustrating the story of Vishnu and the demon king Bali, it is one of the few examples in Nepalese sculpture employing continuous narration. In the middle of the lower section of the relief Vishnu is depicted in the guise of a dwarf Brahman asking the demon king for land equal in measurement to three of his steps. On the viewer's right on the lower level, Bali, who prided himself on his generosity, and his queen are shown engaged in the ritual of giving the donation to the dwarf. In the story, as Vishnu takes the first two steps he grows so enormously tall that he stretches from the nether world to the heavens leaving no space for the third step. In the centre of the relief the multi-armed cosmic Vishnu stands firmly with legs apart.

The popularity of this theme as early as the Lichchhavi period is attested by the reliefs from Tilaganga and

Lajimpat (*see* §IV, 1(i) above). However, despite general similarities in theme and style, the example at Changu Narayan exhibits many features of later development. For example, the main figure of Vishnu is adorned with a beautiful halo with a bead and flame decoration along the border. Lichchhavi artists were familiar with this motif but seldom used it, while in later periods it became a common feature. Another addition in the Changu relief is the flying figures hovering in the stylized clouds on either side of the main figure. In Nepal such flying figures make their first appearance in the Transitional period. The inclusion of solar and lunar discs in the upper section of the relief is also an element not found in earlier works.

The most remarkable achievement of the artists of the Transitional period is the convincing arrangement of multiple arms so that their attachment to the god's shoulders seems realistically possible. A comparison of the image at Changu Narayan with those of previous centuries makes evident the artists' struggle in the earlier period. Few Lichchhavi images have more than four arms. The artist of the Vishnu from Lajimpat achieved some success by hiding the upper part of the two additional arms behind the shoulders, but unlike the arms of the image at Changu they protrude unnaturally. Thus in the early Transitional period artists continued to improve their techniques, producing outstanding work. This high quality does not, however, characterize all examples. It appears that, while some centres or schools of Nepalese sculpture flourished in the early Transitional period, others began a gradual decline.

This view of sculptural development is supported by a comparison of three images from the Transitional period: a statue of the Buddhist child god Manjunatha (Manjushri) at Manjushri-Tol in Kathmandu (see fig. 15) with two images of the sun god, Surya (*in situ* at Thapahiti and Patan, Mus. Excav. Archaeol. Ant., from Saugal; see Pal, 1974, figs 28–9). On the basis of an inscription, the image of Manjunatha is dated *c.* AD 920. The Surya images, at Thapahiti and from Saugal, are dated 1065 and 1083 respectively. An outstanding feature of the Manjunatha figure is a sense of volume so pronounced that although the image is not carved in the round (as one writer has suggested), it looks as though it might be. This appealing roundness is a characteristic inherited from Lichchhavi-period sculptors who produced, for example, the Varaha image at Dhumbarahi and the Brahma image at Chapagaon. After the Transitional period this degree of modelling reappears only in the 17th century, when an artist attempted to revive the Lichchhavi style. It is absent from the Surya images, in which the artists seem more concerned with iconographic details of dress and attributes than with aesthetic quality. The legs of the gods are shown as disproportionately thin and flat; the boldness of earlier, highly modelled works gives way to a feeling of exhaustion.

A further remarkable feature in the image of Manjunatha is a sense of natural grace, which is absent in the Surya images. The innocent boyish face and body of Manjunatha are so alive that the figure appears about to move. In the single known Lichchhavi work depicting boyhood, the image that shows Krishna subduing the serpent Kaliya at the Hanuman Dhoka palace in Kathmandu, the face and

14. Vishnu Vikranta (*c.* 9th century AD), stone, 622×495 mm, Changu Narayan

15. Manjunatha (*c.* AD 920), stone, h. 887 mm, Manjushri-Tol, Kathmandu

huge parasol symbolizing the heavens is shown at the top of the relief. A flying figure (*apsarās*) hovers above Uma, who, like a queen in an ancient palace, is attended by two female servants, one holding a *caurī* ('whisk'), the other massaging her right foot.

Unlike earlier representations of this time-honoured theme, the Uma-Maheshvara in Kva-bahal is crowded with figures placed close together. Earlier works on this theme omit the descending Ganga, the *apsarās* and other figures as well as the parasol—the artists preferring simple compositions with effective focus. Artists of the Transitional period, on the other hand, preferred crowded scenes in which they could convey their complete knowledge of a theme and exercise a love of detail. Both characteristics were passed on to later generations of artists.

Towards the end of the Transitional period a predilection for frontality becomes evident—and this, too, is even more favoured in later centuries. During the Lichchhavi period and early Transitional period figures in a narrative work were depicted as if on stage: they looked at each other and talked to each other but never looked at the audience. At the end of the 12th century or the beginning of the 13th, sculpture loses this quality of frozen dramatic action. For example, a relief at Pharphing, thematically a copy of earlier Vishnu Vikranta depictions (see Pal, 1974, fig. 4), shows no concern for lively interaction; all the figures stand frontally as if posing for a group picture.

Thus, the elegant artistic tradition of the Lichchhavi period continued to develop in some centres in the early Transitional period. Fine examples other than those already discussed include two images from about the 9th century: an Avalokiteshvara at Kathesimbhu, Kathmandu, and a Kartikeya at Hadigaon; and two Uma-Maheshvara images (New York, Rockefeller priv. col.; Los Angeles, Ullman priv. col.) from about the 10th century. By the 11th century stone sculpture was characterized by reduced three-dimensionality, increased ornateness and a preference for frontality. Further examples of important later works include two images from about the 11th century— a Lakshmi (Kathmandu, N. Mus.) and a Garudasena Vishnu at Deopatan, Kathmandu—as well as a Surya image from Naksal dated 1159 (Kathmandu, N. Mus.) and a Narasimha image (*c.* 12th century) at Changu Narayan.

(ii) Metal. The Lichchhavi-period style was gradually modified in metal sculpture of the Transitional period, allowing an increasing emergence of national characteristics. In this period Nepalese style became more clearly distinguishable from other south Asian styles, though fine early work retains Lichchhavi-period features. A remarkable example from early in the Transitional period is a graceful image of the Buddha meditating peacefully in the cross-legged position, hands folded in his lap (Los Angeles, CA, Co. Mus. A.). A 9th-century date can be assigned in the light of the palaeographical evidence of a short text inscribed on the base. The Buddha wears a thin robe with the upper edge gathered around his chest and shoulders. Inherited from Lichchhavi-period style are the sensitively delineated youthful body, half-closed eyes, full lips and sense of serenity conveyed by the image. The Buddha has a flame halo indicating divinity. His ears are elongated, and his well-proportioned head—displaying the protrusion

figure are not really boyish. The Manjunatha image surpasses the Lichchhavi work in this respect and is by any standard a great achievement. The Surya images, however, reveal no naturalism; they are mannered, static and without expression. The main concern is iconographical completeness, a tendency that foreshadows developments of later periods. The stylistic difference between the Manjunatha image and the Surya images is greater than might be expected from the time difference in their execution. This variance does not seem to result from an abrupt change in a short timespan within a tradition that was characteristically conservative. Rather it seems to indicate the co-existence of different schools or centres progressing or declining at different rates.

An image illustrating other developments characteristic of the Transitional period is the relief at Kva-bahal, in Patan, dated AD 987 and depicting the divine family of Shiva and Uma (Uma-Maheshvara; see Pal, 1974, fig. 27). The couple relax on a low bench watching a dance performance by the *gaṇa*s (their dwarflike attendants), who are represented on the lower level of the relief. Uma is leaning against her husband with her arm on his thigh, while he embraces her lovingly. Behind Shiva stands his mount, the bull Nandi. Near the bull, Kumara, the young son of the divine couple, rides playfully on a peacock. Just above the bull's head, the heavenly river Ganga, represented anthropomorphically, descends toward earth. A

(*uṣṇīṣa*) that symbolizes his supernatural wisdom—is covered with curly hair. The simplicity and naturalism of this image, characteristic of Lichchhavi-period work and inspired by India's Gupta-period style, began to recede towards the end of the 10th century. It appears that variant styles co-existed as some artists departed from the traditional aesthetic vision and adopted innovations more readily. Developments in metal sculpture are, in this respect, similar to developments in stone sculpture.

Ornateness is characteristic of metal sculpture of the later Transitional period. That some artists were already working in this style early in the period is evident from a repoussé metal image of the god Vishnu (see fig. 16), made as a protective cover for a stone image, dated AD 983. The god is depicted with four arms, standing frontally on a base decorated with stylized flowers and leaves and is surrounded by an elaborate aureole. His ornaments include heavy earrings, two different necklaces of pearls and precious stones, armlets, bracelets and anklets. Such profuse ornamentation, expected at a later period, is unusual at this date. Although haloes with a bead-and-flame motif are ubiquitous by the 10th century, the flame combined with a triple row of beads and vegetal motif is unusual so early. If the image did not bear a dated inscription, it would be difficult to believe that it is a work of the 10th century.

16. Vishnu, repoussé copper alloy with gilt, h. 473 mm, AD 983 (Los Angeles, CA, County Museum of Art)

It is interesting to compare this image with another depicting Vishnu carried on his mount Garuda (Garudasana Vishnu) dated 1004 (New York, Zimmerman priv. col.; see Pal, 1974, fig. 30). Since the time difference between these two images is only 21 years, a close stylistic similarity might be expected, especially as both are executed in the repoussé technique. Instead, they differ widely in style. Compared to the Vishnu in the Los Angeles County Museum of Art, the Vishnu in the Zimmerman collection is simpler and wears fewer ornaments. There is no attempt at overall ornateness, no elaborate aureole with vegetation or bead-and-flame motif. The stylistic differences between these two contemporary repoussé works indicate the simultaneous existence of two schools.

However, while the image depicting Vishnu carried by Garuda in the Zimmerman collection appears conservative in comparison with the Vishnu image produced 21 years earlier, when it is compared with Lichchhavi-period examples of the same theme, iconographic and stylistic developments characteristic of the Transitional period are evident. For example, in two Lichchhavi-period stone sculptures, the image of Vishnu carried by Garuda (*c.* 7th–8th century; Los Angeles, CA, Co. Mus. A.) and the 9th-century image on the same theme in the courtyard of the Changu Narayan temple (for illustration *see* CHANGU NARAYAN), the god is presented without his consort. In the example in the Zimmerman collection, Vishnu is flanked by two diminutive wives. When consorts of the gods were depicted in Lichchhavi-period sculpture, they were usually rendered in naturalistic proportions, while in later periods they are often smaller than their spouses. The Vishnu image in the Zimmerman collection appears to be the earliest dated Nepalese work to exhibit this feature, which became increasingly common in the Malla period.

Further, in the example in the Zimmerman collection, Garuda is larger than Vishnu, while in Lichchhavi examples the bird is either the same size or slightly smaller. Perhaps the artist of the work in the Zimmerman collection made Garuda larger in order to show his ability to carry the god through the sky. However, though the bird is in a flying position, he does not really look as if he is flying. In the Changu courtyard image, the artist has successfully conveyed the action of flying by emphasizing the powerful, wind-blown, aerodynamically spread wings and horizontally projecting chest. This admirable quality of motion is absent in the depiction of Vishnu carried by Garuda in the Zimmerman collection.

A further difference is a modification in the usual earlier round or oval shape of the wheel held by the god. Instead, flames erupting from the wheel in the example in the Zimmerman collection give it a pointed shape. Though a pointed wheel of this type occurs in a stone carving dated AD 640 at Yangal-hiti, Kathmandu, it was rarely used by Lichchhavi-period artists. The pointed wheel, however, became increasingly popular in the Transitional period, when the round wheel virtually disappeared.

A particularly successful work showing stylistic developments typical of the Transitional period is a representation of Durga subduing the Buffalo Demon dated 1090 (Los Angeles, CA, Co. Mus. A.). Also a repoussé metal cover for a stone image, it has holes worn through it from daily ritual bathing and anointment. The goddess has eight arms. Except for the lowermost left hand, which holds the tail of the buffalo, each of her other hands carries a weapon or armour: a shield, bow, trident, wheel, sword, arrow and thunderbolt—the multitude of arms and weapons signifying her militant power. While the goddess is usually shown fighting the demon emerging from the animal's body, in this example the artist has successfully captured the calm moment following the fierce battle. Durga stands victorious, placing her right foot on the head of the buffalo, submissively positioned on the stylized rocks. The representation of the goddess's smooth, slender, elongated youthful body with its slightly swollen lower abdomen and firm breasts—visible through her diaphanous garment—testifies to the artist's ability to portray the beauty of the female anatomy in accordance with prevailing conventions. In addition to such usual ornaments as necklaces, earrings and armlets, the goddess wears a tripartite diadem.

Two fine images of the goddess Vasudhara, dated 1088 and 1162 (Bennet priv. col.; Chicago, Alsdorf priv. col.), provide interesting insights into the process of change. Produced nearly a hundred years apart, they share many common features and show that innovation sometimes appeared first in relatively insignificant parts of a work. Vasudhara is the goddess of wealth and of new crops; fresh unhusked rice is always offered to her during her autumnal worship. Many metal images and paintings of Vasudhara survive but few stone sculptures, perhaps because she is worshipped as a personal household goddess inside the family chapel, not in public temples, where stone sculpture is more typical. The metal images in the Bennet and Alsdorf collections are iconographically similar. In both statues the goddess is seated in the *lalitāsana* (posture of relaxation) with the right foot on a lotus. Both images have six arms performing the same functions. Each goddess makes the gesture of adoring the Buddha and the gesture of charity and holds a jewel, the *Prajñāpāramitā* text, a sheaf of grain and a water jar. The Vasudhara in the Bennet collection wears a crown with the figures of the directional Buddhas, but the Vasudhara in the Alsdorf collection wears a tripartite tiara decorated with precious stones. While this variation may or may not be the result of the time difference between the images, other differences clearly show later developments. The Vasudhara in the Alsdorf collection wears a long necklace not seen in earlier datable sculpture but often encountered in later works. While both figures stand on lotus pedestals, the arrangement of the leaves differs. In the example in the Bennet collection the two rows of petals are arranged so that each petal in the upper row is placed between two petals in the lower one. This style, which gives the flower a naturalistic look, goes back to the Lichchhavi period. In the example in the Alsdorf collection each upper petal is placed exactly on top of the lower petal. This vertically symmetrical lotus design, which is never seen in earlier-dated Nepalese art, became a ubiquitous feature in later periods. Given the conservative nature of Nepalese art, artists probably felt reluctant to introduce new elements in important and highly visible parts of the work. Instead, they restricted new developments to insignificant units such as these. This principle also applies to painting, where

a new style often makes its first appearance unpretentiously at the bottom of a *paubhā* or canvas.

Thus, though stylistic developments in metal sculpture in the Transitional period may at first appear confusing, they can be coherently explained. Lichchhavi artists handed down a tradition of simplicity and naturalism. From the 10th century some artists developed an interest in a more ornate style. Consequently, two different schools flourished side by side, the one adhering to the traditional style, the other showing a greater interest in new developments. The repetition of themes, which is a characteristic of Nepalese art, allows for a study of step-by-step development and shows that the evolution of style in the Transitional period is the result of local development. Stylistic similarities between these Nepalese metal images and those of other parts of the Indian subcontinent result more from their derivation from the same sources of the Gupta period than from the influence of contemporary Indian sources.

BIBLIOGRAPHY

G. Vajracharya: 'Pracina murtikalako visayama' [On the subject of ancient sculpture], *Purnima*, i/3 (1964), pp. 14–18
The Art of Nepal (exh. cat. by S. Kramrisch, New York, Asia Soc. Gals, 1964)
P. Pal: *Sculpture*, i of *The Arts of Nepal* (Leiden, 1974)
Nepal: Where the Gods Are Young (exh. cat. by P. Pal, New York, Asia Soc. Gals; Seattle, WA, A. Mus.; Los Angeles, CA, Co. Mus. A.; 1975)
M. Slusser: 'On the Antiquity of Nepalese Metalcraft', *Archvs Asian A.*, xxix (1976), pp. 80–95
K. Khandalavala: 'The Chronology of the Arts of Nepal and Kashmir', *Lalit Kala*, xix (1979), pp. 32–44
A. Macdonald and A. Vergati Stahl: *Newar Art: Nepalese Art during the Malla Period* (Warminster, 1979)
U. von Schroeder: *Indo-Tibetan Bronzes* (Hong Kong, 1981)
M. Slusser: *Nepal Mandala: A Cultural Study of the Kathmandu Valley*, 2 vols (Princeton, 1982)
I. Alsop: 'Five Dated Nepalese Metal Sculptures', *Artibus Asiae*, xlv/2–3 (1984), pp. 207–16
P. Pal: *Art of Nepal: A Catalogue of the Los Angeles County Museum of Art Collection* (Los Angeles, 1985)

GAUTAM VAJRACHARYA

3. MALLA PERIOD, *c.* 1200–1769. During the Malla period there was a gradual falling off in the quality of work in the medium of stone and a corresponding increase in the importance of metal in sculpture. The greatest period of Nepali wood sculpture spanned the Transitional (*c.* 800–1200) and Malla periods, though few securely datable examples survive from before *c.* 1200. Some of the most beautiful examples date from the 12th–14th centuries. An increasingly decorative approach was applied to sculpture in all media, with ever greater attention to surface detail. In early Malla-period works this increasingly decorative aspect did not reflect a decline of the formal skills of the sculptors, but in later years decoration tended to cover weak sculptural forms.

(i) Stone. A weariness is already evident in stone sculpture of the early Malla period (1200–1482). When the same themes are treated as in previous centuries, they are executed on a less ambitious scale and with less authority and finesse. For instance, of the many images depicting Shiva and his consort Uma (Uma-Maheshvara) that dot the Kathmandu Valley, post-1200 examples are inferior in liveliness, technique and size (see Pal, 1974, figs 132, 136 and 144). No longer did sculptors attempt the great and

complicated monolithic sculptures in stone at which their Lichchhavi predecessors excelled. There are no Malla-period equivalents to the great image of the reclining Vishnu at Budhanilkantha nor to the masterful depiction of Krishna subduing the serpent Kaliya of the Hanuman Dhoka palace in Kathmandu. Those Malla-period stone sculptures of monumental size that do exist, such as the great Garuda (see Pal, 1974, fig. 103) of 1690 in Darbar Square, Kathmandu, or the huge Buddhas lining the approach to Svayambhu stupa, tend to be tired renditions of themes mastered in earlier centuries and are often almost architectural in nature, consisting—as in the case of the Svayambhu Buddha figures—of several carved pieces fitted together.

(ii) Wood. Perhaps the finest works of the great period of Nepalese sculpture in wood, straddling the Transitional and early Malla periods, are the carved roof-supporting struts of the temples and monasteries of the Kathmandu Valley (*see also* §VI, 7 below and fig. 30). Stylistic developments are evident within the period. The languid and elongated forms of *yakṣis* (female nature spirits) on the 12th-century struts of the shrine at Uku-bahal in Patan (see Slusser, 1982, ii, fig. 162), for example, developed into the more compact and vigorous figures on 13th- to 14th-century struts such as those (see Slusser, 1982, ii, fig. 192) of the Shiva temple at Sulimha-Tol, Patan, or those of the complexes at Itum-bahal and Yatkha-bahal, Kathmandu. From the 16th century onwards, however, strut figures became increasingly stereotyped and conventional. Typical examples include those (see Slusser, 1982, ii, fig. 193) of the Taleju temple, Kathmandu.

Although wood was used most widely in Nepalese art as an element of architectural support (as in the case of struts) or decoration, it was also used in the Transitional and Malla periods as a medium for free-standing sculpture. Such sculptures were usually carved almost entirely in the round, although the back was often only sketchily completed and then painted; in some cases further embellishments were added in repoussé gilt copper. The best examples could once be seen in the annual 'exhibition of the gods' (Newari *bahidyaḥ bvāyegu*), a celebration now held only rarely in the Buddhist monasteries of the valley. Examples in European collections include large, standing 15th-century *boddhisattva* figures (Paris, Mus. Guimet). Carved struts and free-standing sculptures continued to be produced for temple embellishment up to and after the end of the Malla period, but the later production is ever weaker and less sculptural in quality. Though the apogee and decline of wood sculpture came later than that of stone, the same gradual process of deterioration is evident in the later Malla period.

(iii) Metal. What Malla-period Nepal lost in sculpture in stone and eventually in wood, it gained in sculpture in metal (*see also* §VI, 4 below). The early Malla period (*c.* 1200–1482) was a golden age of Nepalese metal sculpture, during which an array of work dazzling in its quantity and quality was produced, much of which survives. Metal sculptors used two techniques: lost-wax casting and repoussé. Works produced by the lost-wax process are marked both by unusual materials and virtuoso finishing. Sacred statuary was almost always cast in pure copper and,

17. Tara, copper and gilt, h. 515 mm, 13th–14th centuries (New York, Metropolitan Museum of Art)

once cast, was almost always gilt by the mercury gilding process. Not until the end of the Malla period is there evidence of frequent use of any other material for statuary casting. These techniques set the Nepalese tradition apart from all of the surrounding traditions, where the preferred metals were brass or bronze alloys, and where gilding was comparatively rare. The use of pure copper and subsequent gilding, often highlighted by inset gems, resulted in a lovely glowing finish that still imbues Nepalese images with a seductive charm. A sinuous figure of Tara (13th or 14th century; see fig. 17) is an excellent example. This commanding image shows a development from the simpler figures of previous centuries (see, for example, 1975 exh. cat., no. 14) in the increased use of decoration and abundant use of inlaid stones. It was part of the genius of the 13th- and 14th-century Nepalese metal sculptors that their love for luscious decoration in no way detracted from the elegance and nobility of form developed by earlier generations.

In the technique of repoussé the artist works by hammering and chiselling a sheet of metal into the desired shape. Malla-period repoussé craftsmen produced enormous quantities of work of a quality that has never been seen before or since in South Asia. Examples can be found covering temple and palace façades (largely from the later Malla period) throughout the Kathmandu Valley, notably at the Harati temple near the Svayambhu stupa and at the gilt Taleju gate to the royal palace in Bhaktapur. The technique was also used to produce the stunning Buddhist priests' crowns from the Transitional and early Malla periods, the gilt copper sheaths used to embellish important stone icons during major ceremonies and, occasionally, free-standing sculptures such as the image of the Vishvarupa (universal) form of Vishnu (see fig. 18) standing near Darbar Square, Kathmandu. Commissioned by Pratapa Malla, King of Kathmandu, in 1657, it is one of the most remarkable examples of Nepal's repoussé sculpture.

To both techniques Newar artists brought a degree of skill that earned for their makers the reputation for the finest work in the Himalayan region and led to these artists being eagerly sought by patrons all over the north. The departure of many Newar metal sculptors for the courts and monasteries of surrounding states and their influence on the artistic development of areas such as Tibet (*see* TIBET, §III) and China was one of the most striking phenomena of the Malla period. The most important of these emigré artists was ARNIKO (Anige), who in the latter half of the 13th century worked in both Tibet and China, where he was eventually put in charge of the imperial workshops at the capital Dadu, now Beijing (Peking). Most of the treasures of the great Tibetan monasteries of Shalu, Sakya and Gyantse reflect the importance of the Newar workers who must have thrived around these sites. The repoussé marvels of Sakya show especially clearly the hands of emigrant Newar metalworkers.

In the later Malla period (1482–1769) there is an increased interest on the part of patrons in multi-limbed figures of Tantric deities from both the Buddhist and the Hindu pantheons, reflecting the prevalence of Tantric cults in these religions (*see* HINDUISM, §I and BUDDHISM, §III, 1 and 5). Although complicated Tantric imagery occurred in Nepalese art from the 12th century, in the later Malla period the classically balanced figures of the earlier centuries, such as the standing Buddha or standing Tara or Lakshmi, almost entirely disappear, to be replaced by the exotic figures of multi-limbed deities, such as Chakra Samvara or Hevajra, two important Buddhist Tantric gods, or the Vishvarupa form of Vishnu.

The reliance of the early Malla sculptors on dazzling techniques of surface decoration continued during the later Malla period, when many sculptures were encrusted with cabochon-cut hardstones. However, from the 15th century onwards sculptural forms were weaker, becoming repetitive and conventional.

Although most metal sculpture of the Malla period was produced in the Kathmandu Valley, an interesting if derivative style developed under the Khasa Malla rulers, whose kingdom encompassed parts of western Nepal and the neighbouring region of Tibet. Perhaps the most interesting single image of certifiably Khasa origins is a perplexing figure of Prajnaparamita (see fig. 19). This plump goddess bears two inscriptions: one, in Tibetan, identifies the image as 'yum', a popular Tibetan epithet for Prajnaparamita, while another, in the Devanagari script common to western Nepal long before it gained currency in the Kathmandu Valley, states that the image was a donation of a wife of Prithvi Malla (*reg c.* 1338–58), the last of the great Khasa Malla chiefs. The figure is a fascinating study in multiple artistic influences. The technique and metallurgy of the solidly cast and thickly gilded copper image immediately identify the Newar influence, which is predominant, while the peculiar base and elements of the fleshy modelling indicate some contact with northern Indian, and specifically with Pala, styles.

Other Khasa Malla bronzes reinforce the impression of Newar influence and suggest that the kings of this once powerful state followed a Himalayan norm in inviting Newar artists to their court. Production after the mid-14th century fell off in quality, and the Newar artists (and their descendants) called to serve the Mallas in western Nepal may well have migrated to Tibet when the Malla kings lost their grip on their far-flung state. Eventually the southern part of the kingdom disintegrated into the many small

18. Vishnu Vishvarupa (1657), cast and repoussé copper and gilt, 1657, near Darbar Square, Kathmandu

19. Prajnaparamita, copper and gilt, 14th century, Khasa Malla tradition (Washington, DC, Freer Gallery of Art)

principalities later conquered by the kings of Gorkha in their drive to unify what is now the kingdom of Nepal.

BIBLIOGRAPHY

G. Tucci: *Preliminary Report of Two Scientific Expeditions in Nepal* (Rome, 1956)
The Art of Nepal (exh. cat. by S. Kramrisch, New York, Asia Soc. Gals, 1964)
P. R. Sharma: *Preliminary Study of the Art and Architecture of the Karnali Basi, West Nepal* (Paris, 1972)
P. Pal: *Sculpture,* i of *The Arts of Nepal* (Leiden, 1974)
Nepal: Where the Gods Are Young (exh. cat. by P. Pal, New York, Asia Soc. Gals; Seattle, WA, A. Mus.; Los Angeles, CA, Co. Mus. A.; 1975)
M. Slusser: 'On the Antiquity of Nepalese Metalcraft', *Archvs Asian A.,* xxix (1976), pp. 80–95
U. von Schroeder: *Indo-Tibetan Bronzes* (Hong Kong, 1981)
M. Slusser: *Nepal Mandala: A Cultural Study of the Kathmandu Valley,* 2 vols (Princeton, 1982)
P. Pal: *Art of Nepal: A Catalogue of the Los Angeles County Museum of Art Collection* (Los Angeles, 1985)
G. Béguin: *Les Arts du Nepal et du Tibet* (Paris, 1987)

IAN ALSOP

4. AFTER 1769. Received opinion marks 1769—the year Prithivi Narayan Shah of Gorkha forged the Malla kingdoms and diverse Himalayan hill tribes and petty fiefdoms into a single state—as a watershed in the history of Nepalese sculpture. According to this view, that is the year when the creative spark of the Newars was extinguished. The 'catastrophe' theory of Nepalese art history is, inevitably, oversimplified. There was a nadir, but this was not reached until the 20th century (following a slow decline that steepened under the suzerainty of the hereditary Rana premiers). Furthermore, there was a considerable revival in Newar art after 1950, and in the 1990s many hundreds of sculptors were flourishing.

The indigenous sculptors of the Kathmandu Valley suffered a reduction of both patronage and self-esteem after the conquests of 1769. The Rana dynasty, established in 1846, combined a vigorous commitment to the Hindu faith with a delight in the grandiose style and imagery of the British Raj, both of which further undermined the work of the Buddhist artists of Kathmandu, Patan and Bhaktapur. Several sculptures from the Rana period bear witness to the conflict that developed between the regime and artistic community. For instance, one bronze statue installed in the courtyard of the Uku-bahal in Patan was meant to represent a disciple of the Buddha, but the Prime Minister (Juddha Shamsher Rana) compelled the artist to shape the figure in his image, and there he stands, resplendent in the uniform of State. Generally, during the Rana years, metalworkers from clans that had formerly specialized in producing images of gods (from both the Buddhist and the Hindu pantheons) were reduced to casting only bells, bowls, pots and other domestic utensils. But a few craftsmen were able to preserve and carry forward the lost-wax techniques and the sculptural traditions into the 20th century. During the 1920s, for instance, a school for sculptors was established by the master craftsman Yog Man Shakya, in the Mahabuddha-bahal, Patan.

The decline in artistic activity occurred during a period when reports of the excellence of Nepalese art were spreading through the Western world: foreign interest was instigated by visits to Europe made by Jung Bahadur Rana, and this interest contributed to the revival of Nepalese sculpture once Nepal's era of isolation came to an end. When the monarchy was restored to power in 1951 by a popular revolution that overthrew the Ranas, new channels opened to the outside world. Two events in particular introduced new opportunities for indigenous sculptors: an exhibition of Nepalese arts and crafts was held in Patan, which attracted the attention of the small expatriate community in the country; and Boris Lissanovich (a former dancer in the Diaghilev ballet) opened the first hotel in Kathmandu, the Royal Palace, and installed a shop there that served as an outlet for traditionally fashioned statues produced by local artists.

From the 1950s the market for 'curios' expanded with Nepal's burgeoning tourist industry. With hundreds of thousands of overseas visitors travelling to the Kathmandu Valley annually, thriving communities of sculptors were occupied in the production of lost-wax images: figures termed 'business gods' by the artists, to distinguish them from those that are enshrined and worshipped. At worst, the 'business god' is cheap and gimcrack; many mass-produced images of Shakyamuni Buddha or Ganesh, or figurines based upon the erotic carvings of temple eaves, are sold for a few rupees. (Even these images, however, are produced using traditional methods: each cast in an individual clay mould.) At its best, the image is endowed with a fine sense of form and balance and will have been produced with careful attention to detail by a gifted artist; additionally, the Newar artist is beginning to experiment with both form and content. The subject-matter for the Nepalese sculptor was traditionally religious and remains so, but the contemporary artist, working for the curio shop, has been liberated from the strictures that bound his ancestors. The Western patron is rarely concerned with iconographic niceties and demands none of the exactitude expected by the worshipper. As a consequence, new 'gods' are being invented that bear no precise resemblance to any deity in the indigenous pantheon, or old gods are represented in new ways. Furthermore, in a departure from past practice, statues are often ornately decorated with elaborate chasing across the surface; in the process, orthodox tenets may be flouted: Buddha can now be seen wearing a robe depicting birds and flowers instead of the prescribed plain cloth (see fig. 20); and a figure of the goddess Tara can provide the ground for an engraved landscape.

Notwithstanding these innovations, Newar sculpture remains firmly embedded within the cultural traditions of the past. Wood-carving is also beginning to flourish again for the tourist market. Traditions are being explored, reworked and reassessed, but they provide an enduring well-spring from which the artist draws his inspiration and motivation. The term tourist art often evokes denigration, yet in the late 20th century tourism in Nepal has engendered a vitality and integrity in the indigenous artist that was scarce, if not absent, from work produced in the previous 150 years.

BIBLIOGRAPHY
I. Alsop and J. Charlton: 'Image Casting in Oku Bahal', *Contrib. Nep. Stud.*, i (1973), pp. 22–48
E. Lo Bue: 'Buddhist Himalayan Art in the XXth Century', *Himalayan Cult.*, i (1978)
——: 'Himalayan Sacred Art in the XXth Century', *A. Int.*, xxiv (1981), pp. 114–28
——: *Himalayan Sculpture in the XXth Century* (diss., U. London, SOAS, 1981)
T. Riley-Smith: *Buddhist God-Makers of the Kathmandu Valley* (diss., Cambridge U., 1982)
——: 'The Idol as Art: Western Tourism and Newar Aesthetics', *Cambridge Anthropol.*, viii/1 (1983), pp. 53–73

T. P. B. RILEY-SMITH

V. Painting.

The delicacy of the painter's materials and the vicissitudes of time have conspired to leave only clues to the earliest Nepalese painting. Although a 5th-century Lichchhavi inscription mentions wall paintings, no examples of this date survive. The earliest-known Nepalese paintings occur in palm-leaf manuscripts, dating possibly to the 10th century. Numerous examples, both delightful to the eye and uniquely Nepalese, are known from the following centuries. When in the 17th century and early 18th the style began to stagnate, it was revived by influences from Tibet and from the Indian Rajput and Pahari schools. In

20. Shakyamuni Buddha (1979), copper and silver, *h* 300 mm, from Patan (Cambridge, Tristram and Louisa Riley-Smith private collection)

the 20th-century traditional and international styles have been practised side by side.

1. Traditional painting. 2. External influences.

1. TRADITIONAL PAINTING. Traditional paintings are preserved on palm leaf, paper and cloth in the form of illuminated manuscripts, banners or hangings (Newari *paubhā*) and painted scrolls (*vilampu*).

(i) Manuscripts. (ii) *Paubhā*s. (iii) Painted scrolls.

(i) Manuscripts. The most important evidence of the earliest stages of the Nepalese painting tradition is contained in illuminated manuscripts. The earliest dated examples are from the 11th century; some undated manuscripts may be as early as the 10th century. Several factors have contributed to the preservation of the beautiful calligraphy and paintings of these early manuscripts in a condition that sometimes approaches the miraculous. One is the essential conservatism of Nepalese culture, which has survived for some 1400 years with no major revolutions in religious thought to incite people to cast off one set of religious customs and beliefs—and accompanying artefacts—for another. A second is the way manuscripts are stored. The palm-leaf manuscripts of the early periods were protected by wooden slat covers, often themselves beautifully decorated with paintings (see figs 21–2 below), sometimes encased in gilded copper and then usually wrapped in cloth for further protection. Ironically, the ignorance of later Newar lay folk of both Buddhist and Hindu persuasions also conserved the early manuscripts: as scripts changed and knowledge of Sanskrit became confined to an ever-narrowing circle of literati and sages, the books in lay households were opened less and less, and often came to be regarded in illiterate households as objects of reverence in and of themselves. There are magnificent manuscripts lying in the homes of devout Buddhists and Hindus that are never opened and read, and may not have been opened for centuries. They are laid upon the family altar, where they are revered along with the other family icons.

(a) Before *c.* 1300. (b) *c.* 1300–1600.

(a) Before c. *1300.* Early manuscripts in Nepal were almost exclusively made of palm leaves, cut in narrow strips, with lengths varying from 250 mm to 600 mm. The longer format is found more often in earlier manuscripts, while the shorter formats tend to appear in manuscripts from the 13th century and later, although they are occasionally found in earlier manuscripts. The text was written in one of the many scripts developed by Newar scribes over the centuries, using an ink made from lampblack; the paintings were applied in pigments made from various mineral and vegetable sources with a glue or gum binder.

The social aspects of the production of Nepalese manuscript illuminations remain unclear. It is uncertain whether the illuminations were applied by the same artist who provided the calligraphy of the text, or whether the task of illuminating the manuscript was the preserve of a specialized group of painters, or even of a specialized group of the priestly caste to whom the reading and reciting of most of these texts was entrusted. The high level of artistic achievement found in many of the ancient palm-leaf manuscripts and their wooden covers would suggest that this was the work of professionals devoted solely to their art. Evidence from inscriptions suggests that from at least the 14th century onwards the task of painting *paubhā*s or banner paintings was entirely the preserve of the *citrakāra* (Skt: 'picture-maker') group, a caste with relatively low status that exists to the present day, many members still following the traditional calling. It may well be that the tradition of the *citrakāra* has an older history than available evidence has so far documented.

Another puzzling aspect of the early Nepalese manuscript illumination tradition is its precise connection with related yet distinct traditions from India. Many scholars convinced of the cultural superiority of India have attempted to consider all of Nepalese art of the early medieval and later periods as an offshoot of the Pala tradition of northern India. In fact, the two art traditions are better compared as parallel but separate offshoots of the great Indian traditions of the Gupta period. By and large, this dictum can be applied to a comparison of the early Nepalese and Pala manuscript painting traditions. An examination of manuscript paintings from approximately the same period—for example the 12th century and early 13th—reveals important differences between the two styles. The Nepalese style (see fig. 21) is elegant, suave and soft. Outlines are delicate, facial features and hands are rendered with a supple finesse; the faces are usually round, with small and delicately drawn features and similarly proportioned hands and feet. In the best examples

21. Cover of a *Prajñāpāramitā* manuscript (detail), wood with copper gilt, 1207 (Chicago, private collection)

there is a fineness in the line, colouring and shading that makes these early illuminations the apogee of Nepalese painting. The palette is strong and lively, in many cases dominated by the strong red favoured by Nepalese painters of all periods. The contemporary style in Pala India offers many contrasts. The drawing is quick and vigorous, suggesting a rapid execution. The features of the deities are all more exaggerated than in the calm Nepalese drawings; jutting chins and eyes, an angular disposition of arms and legs and heavy breasts on the goddesses all create an impression of deities invading the space they occupy. The palette, too, is different, balanced more towards yellows than the Nepalese red (see Pal and Meech-Pekarik, 1988, pls 8–13).

Almost all examples of Nepalese and Pala painting exhibit these stylistic differences. However, cultural contacts, particularly in the Buddhist world, between the great Pala centres and the Kathmandu Valley during the period of early palm-leaf manuscript paintings resulted in some anomalies. These include manuscripts that appear to have been written in northern India and then illuminated in Nepal, or by a Nepalese artist in northern India, and at least one example that appears to be in a Nepalese script but is illustrated by intriguingly Pala-like illuminations (see Losty, 1989). But even in these cases the anomaly is proved by the distinctness of the two styles; where the script would dictate painting in the Pala style, it is surprising to find the very different Nepalese and vice versa.

The brief description above of Nepalese style holds for the entire period from the beginning of the tradition in the 10th century or the 11th until the 13th. Nonetheless, definite trends can also be noted over time. Many of the earliest covers and illuminations exhibit a somewhat tentative and awkward quality, with a hesitancy and heavy-handedness in the line and shading that bear witness to a tradition at its beginnings or in the process of new developments (see Pal and Meech-Pekarik, 1988, pl. 22). In the 12th century and early 13th the Nepalese style in manuscript illumination reached a peak of perfection. The best of these paintings exhibits an elegance and nobility that harks back to the great cave paintings of Ajanta; more than one art historian has noted the remarkable spiritual and aesthetic closeness of the great Gupta murals and the tiny illuminations of Nepal in the 12th century and the early 13th (see fig. 21 and also Pal and Meech-Pekarik, 1988, pls 23–5). Towards the end of the 13th century the style thickens and becomes more abstract, as the colourful and highly stylized painting that might be termed 'Newar' style began to develop (see Pal and Meech-Pekarik, 1988, pls 27–8).

The subject-matter of early Nepalese manuscript illuminations tends to fall into several easily defined categories. Although the majority of surviving early palm-leaf paintings are Buddhist, there are several striking examples of Shaivite and other Brahmanical paintings. Almost all are covers; Brahmanical page-illuminations are rare. Shaivite covers depict well-known Shaivite themes, such as the adoration of the *liṅga* or the divine family of Shiva and Uma (Uma-Maheshvara); other Brahmanical subjects depicted on early covers include such themes as the ten incarnations (*daśāvatāra*) of Vishnu.

A relatively small number of themes is treated in the more plentiful Buddhist material. By far the most popular Buddhist text in early Nepal, and the one most frequently illuminated, is the *Aṣṭasāhasrikā Prajñāpāramitā* ('Perfection of wisdom in eight thousand verses'). The illumination of this text followed several formats of varying complexity. In cases where the covers as well as several pages are illuminated, one cover is usually painted with scenes from the life of the Buddha, while the other has a portrayal of the four-armed form of the goddess Prajnaparamita. The goddess is often surrounded by further scenes from the life of the Buddha, continued from the first cover, or by depictions of other Mahayana goddesses, such as Vasudhara and Tara. The illuminations on the pages of such a manuscript can vary in number from six to many more; the simplest scheme consists of three pairs of figures, placed face to face on *verso* and *recto* pages, at the beginning, middle and end of the manuscript. The first pair almost always portray Amitabha Buddha on folio 1 *verso* and Prajnaparamita on folio 2 *recto*, while the other illuminations portray male and female *bodhisattva*s. More elaborate illumination schemes for the *Aṣṭasāhasrikā Prajñāpāramitā* include other figures from the Buddhist pantheon, sometimes including many-armed Tantric figures. Two extraordinary 11th-century manuscripts of this text, one dated 1015 (Cambridge, U. Lib.) and another dated 1071 (Calcutta, Asiat. Soc.), are richly illustrated with numerous illuminated pages, each with three figures to a page (see Pal and Meech-Pekarik, 1988, figs 31–2, 34–5, pls 20–21). Another popular and often illustrated Buddhist text is the *Pañcarakṣā*, which usually features simple illuminations of the five Buddhas and their corresponding Pancharaksha goddesses, placed in the text at the beginning of the chapter devoted to each of the goddesses. Another important Mahayana text, the *Kāraṇḍavyūha*, was also occasionally illuminated with scenes from the career of the great *bodhisattva* Avalokiteshvara.

(b) c. *1300–1600.* Around 1300 the art of illuminating manuscripts began to go through a process of change. In the 14th century the widespread use of paper in the production of manuscripts was introduced. This eventually resulted in a flexibility in format and page size and the development of entirely new book types, such as the folding book (Newari *thyāsaphū*), which was to become one of the most popular formats from the 15th century onwards (*see also* §2, (ii) below). No definite break occurred between the use of palm leaf and paper: there are very old paper manuscripts, particularly of the type known as '*nīlapatra*' or 'blue leaf', manufactured of layered handmade paper dyed with indigo to a deep blue-black hue; conversely, palm leaf was used for books until the middle of the 17th century and beyond.

The development of a new style is evident towards the end of the 14th century. Gradually, the slim and elegant figures of the 12th century begin to thicken and become more robust. Shoulders and chests are wider, features become more dense and thickly drawn. There is still a grace in line, and the colouring and shading is skilfully done; but the attraction in these paintings is their earthiness and stolidity. The setting gradually changes, becoming more elaborate and stylized; by the beginning of the 15th

22. Covers of a *Pañcarakṣā* manuscript with goddesses and Buddhas, wood with painted figures, each cover 57×352 mm, Nepal, 15th century (New York, private collection)

century the plain single-coloured backgrounds, occasionally splashed with diminutive flowers, that characterized manuscript illuminations of the 12th century have given way to the elaborate arabesques and swirls that are a feature of the 'Newar' style as seen, for example, on the painted wooden covers of a 15th-century *Pañcarakṣā* manuscript (see fig. 22). Figures previously portrayed against an open space begin to find themselves confined to cartoon-like boxes bordered either by elaborate columns or candy-cane coloured palm trees (a device particularly favoured during the 16th century). Busier and perhaps less classical than the settings of the earlier paintings, these backgrounds have an energy and movement. Such uniquely Newar devices lend works of the 14th–16th centuries an exuberance that is an important aspect of Newar medieval painting.

The later medieval periods abound with material of both Buddhist and Hindu inspiration, and there are some manuscripts that cannot be categorized exclusively under either religious heading, such as the illustrated medical or astrological treatises or the astrologers' 'dreambooks'. All of these usually take the form of the folding book. Art historians tended to be interested in the banner paintings, or *paubhā*s (*see* §(ii) below), that survive in some quantities from the mid-14th century. This was at the expense of the fascinating variety and stylistic diversity of manuscripts from the same time onwards. The finest 14th-century *paubhā*s and manuscript illuminations bring the finely honed draughtsmanship and sensibility of the 12th-century manuscript illuminations into the service of the newly developed and more visually complex Newar style. Works of this period are stunning not only because of their fine drawing and shading but also because of the daring coloration and psychedelic patterning, perhaps best exemplified by the almost startling depiction of a Tantric

deity, such as the Buddhist god Samvara, deep red in colour, against a vibrantly coloured red flame background. The best manuscript illuminations from the 14th century exhibit the combination of fine and precise drawing, complex and stylized patterning and bright coloration that characterizes the best of medieval Newar painting.

As styles developed and changed there was at the same time a gradual decline in the artistic sensibility and craftsmanship exhibited by paintings. In later periods the patterns began to be repeated in generation after generation until the style eventually became stagnant, not to be revived until infused with influences from Tibet and from Indian Pahari and Rajput miniature painting styles in the 17th and 18th centuries (*see* §2, (i) and (ii) below). While still attractive, the manuscript illuminations from the 16th century onwards often seem to be repetitions of earlier developments, and they lack the virtuoso drawing that makes the 14th-century examples so compelling.

BIBLIOGRAPHY

The Art of Nepal (exh. cat. by S. Kramrisch, New York, Asia Soc. Gals, 1964)
Nepal: Where the Gods Are Young (exh. cat. by P. Pal, New York, Asia Soc. Gals; Seattle, WA, A. Mus.; Los Angeles, CA, Co. Mus. A.; 1975)
P. Pal: *Painting*, ii of *The Arts of Nepal* (Leiden, 1978)
M. Slusser: *Nepal Mandala: A Cultural Study of the Kathmandu Valley*, 2 vols (Princeton, NJ, 1982)
P. Pal: *Art of Nepal: A Catalogue of the Los Angeles County Museum of Art Collection* (Los Angeles, 1985)
G. Béguin: *Les Arts du Nepal et du Tibet* (Paris, 1987)
P. Pal and J. Meech-Pekarik: *Buddhist Book Illuminations* (Hurstpierpoint, 1988)
J. Losty: 'Bengal, Bihar, Nepal? Problems of Provenance in 12th-century Illuminated Buddhist Manuscripts', pts 1 & 2, *Orient. A.*, xxxv/2 & 3 (1989), pp. 86–96, 140–9

IAN ALSOP

*(ii) Paubhā*s. No known Nepalese painted cloth banner (Newari *paubhā*) predates the early 13th century, but a

much longer history is suggested by the finished perfection of extant examples (see fig. 23), their close stylistic relationship to Nepalese manuscript illuminations of the 11th and 12th centuries and their stylistic affinities with more ancient Indian mural painting. Notwithstanding the unmistakable national distinctiveness of these early *paubhā*s, their style is related to those of Bengal and Bihar (loosely, Pala) and is ultimately rooted in the painting of Gupta-period India, a rich tradition that to some extent survived even into the 17th century.

All *paubhā*s were inspired by religion, Buddhism accounting for most surviving examples and Hinduism for the remaining few, a disparity yet to be explained. Traditionally, they were used as meditational devices and as icons displayed permanently in domestic chapels or intermittently inside and outside temples and shrines. Inscriptions and the content of paintings show that *paubhā*s sometimes served to commemorate a variety of socio-religious events, such as a ritual concerning the principal deity pictured, a rite of passage related to advancing human age (*bhīmaratha*), ceremonies for the family dead, or the meritorious restoration of a renowned shrine or an offering to it. Further, whatever the specific purpose, the commissioning of such a painting was thought to confer material and spiritual benefit not only on the donor and his immediate family, but also on all mankind.

The principal themes of the paintings are provided by the major deities of the Buddhist and Hindu pantheons. The earliest Buddhist paintings favoured transcendental aspects of the Buddha (*tathāgata*), such as Ratnasambhava and Amitabha, depicted as benign and majestic figures on a pair of 13th-century *paubhā*s (Los Angeles, CA, Co. Mus. A., see fig. 23; and Boston, MA, Mus. F.A.), or the goddess of wisdom Prajnaparamita (dated 1379; Paris, Mus. Guimet). By at least the mid-14th century *paubhā*s also depicted the wrathful divinities of Vajrayana Buddhism, such as the goddess Vajravarahi (see Pal, 1985, pl. 45).

Also featured were Samvara, Hevajra and Chandamaharoshana, shown as awesome standing or kneeling figures usually in frenzied sexual union with their equally awesome consorts (see Pal, 1978, pl. 109). The entwined deities, often described as 'erotic', are simply a spectacular form of Vajrayana Buddhist imagery, symbolizing the union of forces whence comes the supreme state of enlightenment. These wrathful deities were joined by the fearful god Mahakala as well as others—but perhaps somewhat later, since no surviving representations pre-date the mid-16th century.

Also frequently depicted is the goddess of abundance, Vasudhara. She is usually presented as the sovereign of a whole family of related divinities disposed in a *mandala*, a complex geometric arrangement that compresses the cosmos into visual, two-dimensional order. The earliest known dated Nepalese *paubhā* is a Vasudhara *mandala* of 1367 (priv. col., see 1975 exh. cat., pl. 43). The moon god Chandra and, infrequently, the sun god Surya, borrowed from the Hindu pantheon, also became favourite subjects for Buddhist *mandala* paintings (see Pal, 1985, pl. P12).

The few known Hindu *paubhā*s, stylistically one with Buddhist examples, depict a limited number of important deities, especially Vishnu and sometimes Durga, usually incorporated in elaborate *mandala*s (see Pal, 1985, pl. P11). The only known painting with a Shaivite theme, dated 1480 by its inscription, depicts the ascetic Agastya (Baltimore, MD, Mr & Mrs J. G. Ford priv. col., see 1975 exh. cat., pl. 57, where the *paubhā* is dated *c*. 1450 and the main figure identified as Shiva in his form as the Supreme Teacher, whom Agastya closely resembles).

The depiction of the central deity on a *paubhā* was often supplemented by diverse subjects drawn from an enormous body of sacred literature such as the Buddhist *jātaka*s (stories of the Buddha's previous lives) and *avadāna*s (moral fables) or the Hindu epics and Puranas (compendia of legends and religious instructions). Such edificatory tales were usually illustrated in comic-strip fashion, with framed cartouches organized symmetrically around the principal deity.

On the Vasudhara *mandala* of 1367, the Suchandra *avadāna*, a tale of the conversion of a non-believer emphasizing worship of the goddess, is visually narrated in such fashion. From at least the time of this painting Nepalese *paubhā*s are usually characterized by the inclusion of several other framed scenes along the lower edge. They depict a ceremony conducted by a crowned Buddhist priest, possibly representing the consecration of the *paubhā* and including the donors, one or more groups of pious spectators and, frequently, dancers and musicians. When they are present, Newari inscriptions parallel these scenes of consecration and may date the painting, state its purpose, identify the donor and provide supplementary information.

Judging by contemporary practice, which in the conservative Nepali milieu is so often similar to that of the past, there were no ateliers; painters worked alone or in kinship groups amidst the domestic activity of the home. They were largely domiciled in the Kathmandu Valley, the heartland of Nepal, but a number were active in the bazaars and the Buddhist monasteries of Tibet. With one known exception, a Vaishnava painting dated 1420 (Los Angeles, CA, Co. Mus. A.), the painters of the early *paubhā*s are anonymous. The single known inscription naming the painter and 20th-century practice suggest that all probably belonged to the *citrakāra* (painter) caste of the Newars.

All *paubhā*s are painted on cotton fabric, sized and burnished. They vary in size according to the wishes or wealth of the commissioner and are usually somewhat longer than they are wide, though some, as governed by subject–matter, may be square; for example, the Mahaganapati *mandala* of *c*. 1450 (priv. col., see Pal, 1978, pl. 89). To begin a painting the desired composition was first carefully drawn on the prepared fabric in black or red, and the outlines were then developed with colours. These consisted of a restricted palette of water-soluble pigments of vegetable and mineral origin, chiefly a variety of exceptional and distinctive reds, the hallmark of the Nepalese *paubhā*s, blue, yellow, green and white. These pigments are occasionally supplemented with gold, and, rarely, a fragment of solid gold is found to underlie the paint over the centre of the principal deity's chest.

In the absence of any technical study, the binding medium for the pigments is unknown. It may be a gum resin or more likely, as suggested by contemporary *citrakāra*

23. *Paubhā* depicting the Buddha Ratnasambhava and acolytes, opaque colours on cotton, 410×329 mm, early 13th century (Los Angeles, CA, County Museum of Art)

practice, animal-skin glue, a factor doubtless affecting the traditionally low status of this marvellously skilled caste. The technique, which has been variously described as opaque watercolour, gouache or tempera, produced exquisite paintings of uncommon brilliance, warmth and richness that are endowed with a subtle sheen and, when properly preserved, capable of enduring in pristine condition for centuries.

The several hundred known Nepalese *paubhā*s painted between 1200 and 1600 are distinguished as a group by a number of common characteristics. Whatever idiosyncratic elements were introduced by the individual painter, or whatever broader changes occurred from century to century, the fundamental aspect of any *paubhā*, the representation of the central deity, was moulded by immutable canonical and iconographic regulations, long established and codified in sacred Indian texts such as the *vāstu-śāstra*s (containing rules for art and architecture) and Puranas. The proportions of the divine body were rigidly prescribed, and the figure was drawn to an exact scale before colour was applied—a technique observable, for example, in the Vishnu *maṇḍala* of 1420, the painted surface of which has flaked from the god's chest (Los Angeles, CA, Co. Mus. A.). Colours, postures, gestures and the range of cognizances displayed by the individual deities were also predetermined, and any deviation rendered the work inauspicious and therefore useless.

The overall composition of early Nepalese *paubhā*s was also prescribed and formulaic. Symmetry and order were paramount. From the earliest known paintings of the transcendental aspects of the Buddha to the end of the period, benign deities were consistently represented as immortal sovereigns, hieratically seated on elaborate thrones positioned at centre stage and harmoniously surrounded in an ordered way with lesser divinities. Similarly, once introduced, wrathful deities were universally pictured against a field of symbolic fire, painted in brilliant reds, covered with intricate scrollwork and encircled with stylized tongues of flame. Though the *maṇḍala* pattern could be individually manipulated, it, too, had to conform in terms of prescribed colours; the number, kind and arrangement of the divine occupants; and wellestablished patterns that visually expounded notions of cosmic order.

The primacy of the selected principal deity, or deity and consort, is guaranteed by placement and size in relation to the surrounding company. This is usually true even in *maṇḍala* configurations, where the principals are markedly smaller than in other formats. Although frontality is characteristic (see fig. 23), the hieratic quality is softened in many paintings by rendering the principal figure in a more relaxed posture with inclined head. Full profile is reserved for consorts of the copulating gods; three-quarter profile is common for subsidiary figures (e.g. the acolytes who turn towards Ratnasambhava in fig. 23). It is occasionally used when representing principal figures, for example the discoursing Shakyamuni and Nagarjuna depicted in an early 15th-century work (priv. col., see Pal, 1978, pl. 78). Subtle changes were introduced over time to modify the idealized faces inherited from Gupta-period India.

Though the posture of the principal figures, benign or wrathful, was largely ordained by textual recommendations, convention governed other aspects. It is convention, for example, that dictates the curiously forward thrust hips of Ratnasambhava's acolytes in works of *c.* 1200 (see fig. 23). This stance is employed some two centuries later in more exaggerated form in a depiction of four Taras approaching Avalokiteshvara (Los Angeles, CA, Co. Mus.

A.). Nonetheless, artists managed at times to draw convincing figures relatively free of these restrictions. In later paintings representations of the human form became more linear, as ties with the inherited volumetric forms that characterize the earlier works became more distant.

Unabashedly figurative, the *paubhā*s are without landscapes. Trees, flowers, water and rocks are introduced for their symbolic or decorative value, and in conceptualized rather than imitative forms. Thus, in a *paubhā* representing Mara's assault (Boston, MA, Mus. F.A.), the tree overhanging Shakyamuni meditating at Bodhgaya is introduced only to symbolize the locale. The scattered blossoms throughout many paintings only indicate the divine presence. Similarly, the highly stylized rock formations, a *sine qua non* of Nepalese art, are used in the painting of Agastya both to symbolize the ascetic's rocky cave and as colourful and pervasive ornament. Animals are an exception to the painters' preference for conceptualizing nature; such creatures as monkeys and gazelles, in particular, are rendered with faultless fidelity. Inexplicably, the horse uniformly results in caricature.

*Paubhā*s make limited use of perspective and shadows or shading. Light is evenly spread throughout, as befits the notion of the divine world eternally suffused with radiance; volume is achieved through highlighting or by varying the colour intensities. *Paubhā*s are further characterized by precise yet fluid drawing, the use of bold and vivid colours harmoniously juxtaposed, the judicious balance of line against mass and an obvious delight in detail. Indeed, it is the embellishments of the ornate thrones, the sumptuous jewellery, patterned textiles, intricate scrollwork and related ornament that in the end make of these paintings not only icons for worship but objects of art that are an enduring delight to behold.

Nepalese *paubhā*s, bound by canonical and iconographic conformity, preserve styles that were extinguished elsewhere. But, although artists were constrained by an inheritance from which they could not fully depart, they were not stifled. Their individualism is apparent in many ways. For example, while adhering to the strict rules of symmetry evident in all *paubhā*s, the 16th-century painter of Mara's assault on the meditating Buddha at Bodhgaya contrived to assemble the turbulent company in a manner seen in no other painting. Likewise, there is no known precedent for a painting commemorating a restoration of the prestigious Svayambhu stupa, which, icon though it may be, is also a cartographic *tour de force* (Washington, DC, A. P. Burleigh priv. col., see Slusser, 1987, Pls I and II). Other paintings, such as that depicting Shakyamuni and Nagarjuna, because they were executed in Tibet or commissioned by Tibetan patrons in Nepal, embrace uncommon aspects that further individualize them.

BIBLIOGRAPHY

Nepal Where the Gods are Young (exh. cat. by P. Pal, New York, Asia Soc. Gals; Seattle, WA, A. Mus.; Los Angeles, CA, Co. Mus. A.; 1975)

P. Pal: *Painting*, ii of *The Arts of Nepal* (Leiden, 1978)

M. Slusser: *Nepal Mandala: A Cultural Study of the Kathmandu Valley*, 2 vols (Princeton, 1982)

P. Pal: *Art of Nepal: A Catalogue of the Los Angeles County Museum of Art Collection* (Los Angeles, 1985)

M. Slusser: 'On a Sixteenth Century Pictorial Pilgrim's Guide from Nepal', *Archvs Asian A.*, xxxviii (1985), pp. 6–36

——: 'The Cultural Aspects of Newar Painting', *Heritage of the Kathmandu Valley, Proceedings of an International Conference: Lubeck, 1985*, pp. 1–15

G. Béguin: *Art ésotérique de l'Himâlaya: Catalogue de la donation Lionel Fournier*, Paris, Mus. Guimet cat. (Paris, 1990)

S. Huntington and J. Huntington: *Leaves from the Bodhi Tree: The Art of Pâla India (8th–12th Centuries) and its International Legacy* (Seattle and London, 1990)

MARY SHEPHERD SLUSSER

(iii) Painted scrolls. It is impossible to know when the earliest painted scrolls (Newari: *vilampu*) were produced in Nepal. Most surviving examples date from *c.* 1600 to *c.* 1900. Usually 2.2 to 3 m in length (though sometimes longer), the scrolls are executed on rough cotton cloth. They are narrative in character, the story divided into a sequence of scenes progressing from the viewer's left to right in one or more horizontal registers. Occasionally the painted area may be nearly square, the scroll thus resembling a painted hanging (*paubhā*; see §(ii) above). However, *paubhā*s usually exhibit a large central divinity surrounded by smaller scenes illustrating relevant mythology, while painted scrolls are divided into horizontal sections of nearly equal dimensions. Each section in the sequence is usually separated from the next by floral motifs. In some examples a caption in Newari identifies the personages in each section, and a colophon may give the date of painting, the name of the patron and other information.

Didactic in purpose, scrolls were used mainly by priests and monks in instructing the faithful. Among surviving examples Buddhist subjects are more numerous than Hindu. An outstanding 19th-century example illustrates the *Svayambhu purāṇa*, the sacred legend of Nepal (Paris, Mus. Guimet). Other common themes include stories of the Buddha's previous lives (*avadāna* and *jātaka*), the legendary history of a Buddhist monastery, or a Kathmandu Valley festival such as that of Red Avalokiteshvara (Matsyendranatha) in Patan (see fig. 24). Popular Hindu religious rituals illustrated include the Ekadashi-vrata, the worship of Vishnu on the 11th day of each month. Numerous scrolls illustrate scenes from the life of Krishna, especially from the *Viṣṇu purāṇa* and *Bhāgavata purāṇa*. Generally, painted scrolls were kept in temples or monasteries, often stored rolled up and displayed only on certain occasions. These included, for instance, the July–August Newar Buddhist festival of 'viewing the gods in the monastery' (Newari *bahi-dyo boyegu*), when statues and paintings normally concealed were displayed. Scrolls were often hung on the walls of inner courtyards.

Stylistically, painted scrolls show Indian, particularly Rajput, influence. Kings and aristocrats wear costumes similar to those represented in Rajput paintings, while farmers, when depicted, wear local dress. Kings and their courtiers (but not always divinities) are depicted in profile. Temples, monasteries and domestic buildings are typically Newar, with the architectural details carefully rendered. Rajasthani influence is apparent, however, in the treatment

24. Painted scroll illustrating the festival of Red Avalokiteshvara (Matsyendranatha) at Patan (detail, depicting the ritual of Amophasa Lokesvara performed by the king), opaque colour on cloth, 0.60×2.20 m, 1712 (Paris, private collection)

of trees, mountains and landscapes. Dominant colours are dark and strong greens and reds, with blue-grey used for mountains and skies. Stylistic developments from the 17th century to the 19th are in keeping with those evident in other types of painting, with earlier work more linear and more spare.

Horizontal strip-paintings reminiscent of scrolls were used for murals in royal palaces, for instance the Hanuman Dhoka in Kathmandu and the palace in Bhaktapur. Such horizontal strip-paintings are also known elsewhere in the Himalayas, for instance in 17th–19th-century murals at Sujanpur Tira in the Kangra Valley.

BIBLIOGRAPHY
M. Chandra: 'A Painted Scroll from Nepal', *Prince of Wales Mus. Bull.*, i (1955), pp. 6–14
J. Eracle: 'La Tentation du roi Rukmangada', *Bull. Annu., Mus. Ethnog.*, xiii (1970), pp. 15–33
P. Pal: *Painting*, ii of *The Arts of Nepal* (Leiden, 1978)
S. Lienhard: *Die Legende vom Prinzen Viśvantara: Eine nepalesische Bilderrolle aus der Sammlung des Museums für indische Kunst* (Berlin, 1980)
A. Vergati: 'Le Roi faiseur de pluie: Une Nouvelle Version de la légende d'Avalokiteśvara Rouge au Népal', *Bull. Ecole Fr. Extrême-Orient*, lxxiv (1985), pp. 287–303

ANNE VERGATI

2. EXTERNAL INFLUENCES. The two main stylistic influences during the 17th to the 19th centuries were Tibetan painting and contemporary Indian schools of painting in Rajasthan and the Punjab Hills. Tibetan influence is exhibited particularly in painted hangings (Newari *paubhā*; Tibetan *thang-ka, thanka*), while stylistic features of Rajasthan and the Punjab Hills are more evident in illustrated manuscripts, folding books and albums. In the mid-19th century Newar artists were for the first time influenced by European taste, mainly as a result of the foreign travels of the Ranas, who gained political power in 1846. The Ranas visited Europe and returned to Nepal to commission palaces in a Neo-classical style (*see* §III, 3 above) and portraits conforming to 19th-century European aesthetics. While occasionally following European models for portraits, artists continued to produce statues and ritual objects for their Tibetan clients, as well as paintings to meet local demand.

The fall of the Ranas in 1951 meant the end of Nepal's isolationist policy and the opening of the valley to foreigners. In 1965 the Nepal Association of Fine Arts was founded with the aim of encouraging modern Nepalese painting as well as traditional Newar art. Various trends in European painting, from Impressionism to Expressionism, from naive to abstract art, found followers in Nepal. Some Newar painters, however, continued to produce high-quality traditional work, commissioned by local temples or dealers. Some of these paintings have entered the Western market as antiques. The most outstanding representative of traditional Newar painting is probably Siddhi Muni Shakya (*b* 1932), the son of another great master, Ananda Muni Shakya (1903–44), whose acquaintance with ancient and modern European art enriched native inspiration. Siddhi Muni's painted hangings and drawings are mostly rendered in a decorative and florid style influenced by Tibetan painting, especially when illustrating Buddhist subjects. His Hindu themes are influenced by the contemporary style of much Indian religious painting rather than

by European taste. Some talented younger artists, such as Roshan Shakya (*b* 1960), though generally influenced by the Tibetan style, occasionally work in the ancient Newar painting tradition.

BIBLIOGRAPHY
T. P. Mainali, ed.: *Contemporary Art and Artists of Nepal* (Kathmandu, 1975)

(i) Tibetan influence. With the continued decline of Buddhism in the Nepal Valley in the 17th century, Newars looked increasingly to Tibet as a cultural model. At this time Tibet was enjoying a unique period of political power and artistic activity under the fifth Dalai Lama. Newar artists continued to be invited to Tibet to decorate monasteries, especially those belonging to the Dalai Lamas' religious order, but few painters are mentioned among the artists who worked in central and western Tibet during the first half of the 17th century. By *c*. 1500 Tibetan painters had developed a distinct tradition of their own, and the influence of Newar painting in Tibet from that time onwards was slight. On the contrary, some elements, such as the treatment of landscape in Newar *paubhā*s of that period are clearly derived from Tibetan painting. In Newar painting before the 17th century there is no clear indication of the sky, and trees are merely employed as symbols to denote outdoor scenes or as devices to divide the events in a narrative sequence. By the mid-17th century Newar painters, following a formula derived from Tibetan painting, attempted to create a natural setting with trees, swirling clouds and snowy peaks at the horizon. Elements of Tibetan style found in Newar painting of this period include fleecy cloud patterns, jagged snowy peaks, Chinese dragons, Tibetan snow-lions, peonies instead of lotuses in the decoration of thrones, flying scarves, swirling garments and probably the serpentine golden rays radiating in the haloes of some Buddhist deities.

Whereas in several examples of Newar painting of the 17th century such elements appear ill digested, in some 19th-century illuminations and *paubhā*s they are so well assimilated that attribution to Newar or Tibetan painting may raise problems. Although the Newar hand is generally betrayed by iconographic preferences and certain graphic and decorative elements, the attribution to Newar or Tibetan painting remains difficult for a group of hangings (*thang-ka*s) painted in Tibet, particularly at Tashilhunpo, near Shigatse, on the main trade route from the Kathmandu Valley to Lhasa. Cultural ties between Tibet and the Kathmandu Valley were strengthened by trading agreements, especially during the 17th century. While Tibetan monks began taking over the most important Buddhist sites in the valley, namely Svayambhu hill and Bodhnath stupa, Newar communities prospered in various parts of Tibet, particularly in the central and southern towns. Newars in Tibet were all high-caste Buddhist traders and artists, who generally married Tibetan women and whose sons were regarded as Nepalese citizens. They respected and admired Tibetan Buddhist institutions even more than their own, since Buddhism in the Kathmandu Valley had developed into a caste system where even priesthood and monkhood had become hereditary preserves, and monasteries were no longer great centres of learning. Some Newars joined Tibetan monasteries, particularly Tashilhunpo, as scribes and possibly painters. Newar traders who halted there commissioned an ever-increasing number of painted hangings and took these back to the Kathmandu Valley. Although the style of these paintings is distinctly Tibetan, the inscriptions are in Newari, and the deities portrayed are those particularly cherished by Newar Buddhists: besides the Buddha Shakyamuni, the *bodhisattva* Amoghapasha Lokeshvara, the *pañcaraksā* goddesses, Tara, Ushnishavijaya in her stupa and the *maṇḍala* of Vasudhara. At the bottom of some of these paintings there are figures of donors dressed in Newar style, sometimes arranged in rows; conversely, traders are dressed in the Tibetan fashion in an early 18th-century Newar horizontal narrative scroll (Newari *vilampo*; New Delhi, N. Mus.), illustrating the story of Shronakotikarna. After the Chinese military invasion and subsequent Cultural Revolution, this particular style of painting disappeared. Nonetheless, Tibetan influences were still detectable in the traditional Newar painting of the late 20th century (*see* §3 below).

(ii) Influence of Indian miniatures. Both Shaivism and Vaishnavism were supported by the Malla dynasties from the 13th century and by the Gorkhas from 1769. As India was a model for Hindu Newar culture, by the mid-17th century manuscript painting by Newar artists came under the influence of contemporary Indian schools of painting, while Buddhist art in particular was influenced by the painting tradition of Tibet (*see* §(i) above). The painters' palette consequently shows a wider variety, and, along with bright red backgrounds, there are strong blues and greens and muted colours after *c.* 1700. Paper had by then almost entirely replaced palm leaf, although texts continued to be copied in the oblong format characterizing palm-leaf manuscripts. In the 17th century album painting was introduced from India along with square and vertical formats, which were used in addition to the more traditional horizontal one. But the Newar style continued to be original both in iconography and in the use of colours, which have little in common with those of 17th-century north Indian painting, and no single school may be regarded as the source of Indian influence.

In manuscript illustration the same styles were followed for both religious and secular themes but, whereas deities continued to be painted in the traditional manner, following iconographic and iconometric conventions, the figures of devotees were adapted from Indian painting. Idealized and stereotyped in posture and conventional in arrangement, they are clearly drawn against striking monochromatic backgrounds. Occasionally faces were drawn from life, particularly in the case of portraits of kings. The landscape, with rolling green hills, bulbous trees and sometimes jagged peaks covered in snow, with fleecy clouds above, borrowed elements from both India and Tibet. The foliage and placement of architectural elements are related to Pahari painting, but mountains and buildings are local in form, and the style is typically Newar. The landscape and buildings are integrated in a single composition, according to strict symmetry. When sequential narration is employed, various events are separated by trees rather than by the pillars that are found in early

25. *Amoghapasha Lokeshvara*, opaque colour on paper, 320×250 mm, late 18th century (ex-Aniko collection, Geneva); elements drawn from Indian miniature painting include the white railing lined with flowering trees

manuscript illustration. The larger size of folios in the 19th century allowed the introduction of more figures and landscape elements, but painters continued to follow their graphic tradition of decorative design characterized by bright, contrasting colours, in the 19th century and later.

Narrative subjects predominate in picture books (Skt *kalāpustaka*; Newari *thyāsāpu*), rather than in manuscript form. Oblong folios of small dimensions are glued to one another lengthwise, so that the entire manuscript can be folded up. The text is limited to captions, each folio being entirely devoted to the painting. Narrative paintings were also produced as sets of loose folios kept together as albums, measuring as much as 350×550 mm. The subject matter of such albums is similar to that of Indian painting: *Rāgamāla* sets, Hindu mythological texts such as the *Bhāgavata purāṇa*, erotica and portraits.

In the first quarter of the 17th century folding book illustrations were marked by a particular style characterized by a flamboyant and intricate vegetal ornamentation pervading the background, with meandering tendrils forming medallions; by unnaturally slim and thin-waisted figures with disproportionately large faces, hands and feet; and by landscape elements in which painters seem to be unconcerned with naturalistic representation: slender trees with stripes of various hues rise from multicoloured rock formations, while birds and animals are far from lifelike. Around 1700 the repetitive rolling-hill motif characterizing much narrative painting of the previous century was occasionally reduced to an undulating line dividing the surface of the painting into two registers. The propensity to divide the composition into two bands led in the last quarter of the 19th century to attempts to camouflage the separation with thickets rather than ridges. In some royal portraits and depictions of deities of *c.* 1800 and later the background is provided by a uniform pattern of flowering trees set against the railing of a terrace (see fig. 25), a characteristic of 18th-century Indian miniature painting.

BIBLIOGRAPHY

P. Pal: *Painting*, ii of *The Arts of Nepal* (Leiden, 1978)
A. Macdonald and A. Vergati Stahl: *Newar Art: Nepalese Art during the Malla Period* (Warminster, 1979)
E. Lo Bue: 'The Artists of the Nepal Valley—II', *Orient. A.*, n. s., xxxi/4 (1985–6), pp. 409–19

ERBERTO F. LO BUE

VI. Other arts.

While most Nepalese art is religious, personal adornment has provided an additional motivation for a range of arts, including textiles, dress and jewellery. Both religious and secular works are made in metal, terracotta and wood, with tourism providing an important new market in modern Nepal.

1. Dress. 2. Jewellery. 3. Masks. 4. Metalwork. 5. Terracotta. 6. Textiles. 7. Wood-carving.

1. DRESS. Styles of dress altered greatly after Nepal was opened to the world following the end of the Rana regime in 1951; imported clothing has made some impact, but traditional garments, expressing ethnic identity, continue to be woven locally and worn. Examples include the black wraparound cloth (Newari *parsi*) with red borders worn by Newar women of the farmer (*jyapu*) caste, the white shawl with red and green embroidered motifs of the Atpare Rai women and the white draped cotton garments of Dangaura Tharu women. Most urban women, predominantly Brahman, Chetri and Newar, still wear the *sārī* and blouse, together with a shawl in winter. Women in rural areas—Limbu, Rai, Gurung, Magar and Tamang—commonly wear a short, cross-over blouse with either a wrapped and pleated length of handwoven cloth of *sārī* length or a tubular skirt, held in place by a wraparound sash (Nepali *paṭukā*), which gives support and also provides pockets. A headcloth, sometimes intricately embroidered, may also be worn. Shawls or woollen open-fronted waistcoats (*lukunī*) give protection from the cold. In the mountain areas women wear a blouse under a Tibetan-style sleeveless, long wrapover dress made of wool as well as multicoloured aprons front and back.

The traditional national dress for men comprises a mid-thigh-length, cross-over long-sleeved cotton garment (*labedā*), with matching jodhpur-shaped trousers (*suruwāl*). A western-style jacket, sometimes with waistcoat, is added on formal occasions, together with a traditional cap (*topī*). Rural men often wear a sash, which provides pockets and can hold a *kukrī*. In warmer areas the trousers may be replaced by a cotton, wraparound garment. In the mountains, men wear woollen trousers, waistcoats and capes, jackets or full-length coats.

BIBLIOGRAPHY
D. B. Bista: *People of Nepal* (Kathmandu, 1967, rev. 4/1980)

SUSI DUNSMORE

2. JEWELLERY. In this country of extreme ethnic diversity, jewellery is a conspicuous part of the system of signs by which people distinguish themselves from and identify themselves with one another. Because the categories of distinction expressed by jewellery both follow and cut across classifications according to geographic locale, religion, linguistic affinity and economic status, it is not possible to draw up a concise and definitive typology of styles and ethnicity. For example, the Newars of the Kathmandu Valley are like the Sherpa and Tibetans, to whom they are linguistically related (Tibeto-Burman speakers), in that women of these groups never pierce their noses; in this they distinguish themselves clearly from the politically dominant and linguistically Indo-Aryan Hindus (e.g. Thakur, Brahman, Chetri), who invariably do so. Among Newars, those of the Hindu faith are like caste Hindus in the tradition of giving a particular necklace of many strands of fine glass beads with one large segmented cylindrical bead of gold, called *tilhari*, at marriage. Buddhist Newars have a distinctive counterpart in the *thayo* necklace (see fig. 26). This uniquely Nepalese necklace, featuring a golden pendant of faceted ovoid shape, is invariably worn by female donor figures in painting and sculpture from the time of the late Malla kings (16th–18th century). The

26. *Thayo* necklace, gold and copper alloy with inlaid turquoise and ?coral, l. 343 mm, 19th century (Los Angeles, CA, County Museum of Art)

thayo necklace is also worn by Kathmandu's famed Living Goddess, Kumari, a virgin girl who embodies the Tantric divinity known to Hindus as an aspect of Durga and to Buddhists as a form of Tara. Fine specimens from the 17th century to the 19th, with characteristic repoussé motifs on velvet mountings, are included in many Western collections.

The jewellery appreciated most universally in Nepal by the late 20th century was of high-carat gold, worked to traditional or modern design. Because gold is considered a safe investment, and craftsmen's fees are slight in comparison to the metal's intrinsic value, jewellery is quite frequently melted down for reconversion to cash or for refashioning according to taste. Frustrating as this may be for students of design, it is the continuing proof of an ancient axiom of Hindu philosophy: only the metal of a golden ring is real, i.e. imperishable; its 'ring-ness' is illusory, being subject to infinite modification.

The most highly developed and best-documented tradition of Nepali jewellery-making is that of the Newars, superb craftsmen in many materials. Fine metalwork is the particular speciality of the Buddhist Shakya and Vajracharya castes. Curiously, the lost-wax technique of casting religious images and ritual paraphernalia is seldom used for jewellery production. Surface decoration by insetting small pieces of gems and hardstones is, however, common to both image-making and classical jewellery. The most typical technique of Newar jewellery fabrication is repoussé finished with chasing. Old pieces that survive are usually in gilded copper or brass, often with individual motifs sewn to shaped and padded backings of red velvet. Motifs reflect Hindu and Buddhist as well as generically 'auspicious' and decorative traditions.

Jewellery is also part of a system of body markings that protect the wearer from supernatural forces and inauspicious influences. Styles of ornamentation both signal and further the wearer's progress through the stages of life. For example, silver anklets of solid cuff or dangling charm design are often given to toddlers 'to make the legs grow straight' and 'to light the child's path'.

Further complexes of body adornment both mark and fulfil the constitution of auspicious womanhood at marriage. Apart from the jewellery of dowry settlements, a gift of substance that remains the woman's inalienable property for life, ritual acceptance of prescribed ornaments is integral to the lengthy proceedings of both Hindu and Buddhist marriages. Widows give up wearing jewellery altogether. Women are richly adorned at all other life-cycle rites as well, most particularly in the concluding phases of puberty rituals, which themselves are seen as marriages to divinity. On these occasions especially, and to a lesser extent at all times, women are considered to be goddesses, and jewellery for each of the body's divisions is the *lakṣaṇa* (Skt: sign, mark, token) of such divinity. This wide range of jewellery, worn especially by women but also by men, has been continually admired by visitors from the time of the 7th-century pilgrim Xuanzang. It has, however, received little systematic study. There is still much work to be done on the documentation of its design diversity and historical development.

BIBLIOGRAPHY

P. H. Bajracarya: 'Newar Marriage Customs', *Anc. Nepal*, xx–xxi (1954), pp. 53–5, 62ff
A. Höfer: 'Gold- und Silberschmuck aus Nepal', *Archv Vlkerknd.*, xxvii (Vienna, 1973), pp. 5–13
M. Allen: *The Cult of Kumari: Virgin Worship in Nepal* (Kathmandu, 1975)
M. Schmidt-Thomé and Tsering Tashi Thingo: *Materielle Kultur und Kunst der Sherpa*, Khumbu Himal, x (Innsbruck and Munich, 1975)
Nepal: Where the Gods are Young (exh. cat. by P. Pal, New York, Asia Soc. Gals; Seattle, WA, A. Mus.; Los Angeles, CA, Co. Mus. A.; 1975), pl. 95 and p. 125
A. Macdonald and A. Vergati Stahl: *Newar Art: Nepalese Art during the Malla Period* (Warminster, 1979)
H. Gabriel: 'The Tilhari, Nepalese Married Woman's Necklace', *Ornament*, v/4 (1982)
M. Slusser: *Nepal Mandala: A Cultural Study of the Kathmandu Valley*, 2 vols (Princeton, 1982)
P. Pal: *Art of Nepal: A Catalogue of the Los Angeles County Museum of Art Collection* (Los Angeles, 1985)
L. S. Dubin: *History of Beads: From 30,000 B.C. to the Present* (1987), pp. 211–12

BRONWEN BLEDSOE

3. MASKS. Dance, theatre and other rituals and performances have involved the wearing of masks since ancient times. These have been carried out within the context of Hinduism, Buddhism or indigenous religious systems such as shamanism. Although in decline, such rites and performances still occur, and masks are worn by shamans, monks and groups of amateurs and professionals. The characters represented may be mythological or historical, divine or demonic, human or animal. Styles vary according to region and use, ranging from a bare shadow of a face simply evoked by a few strokes of the adze to

27. Magar mask, wood decorated with white clay, h. 290 mm, from west Nepal (Paris, private collection)

sophisticated portraits. Materials employed include metal, wood, papier-mâché, textiles, animal skins (goat, elephant, monkey, fox), bone and tortoise-shell.

Three main regional groups can be identified. In the Terai, near the Indian border, masks are related to those of India, ranging from examples close to those of central Indian tribes to styles inspired by the art of north India and Bengal. In the Himalayan foothills a great variety of styles and characters is represented in the masks of diverse ethnic groups. Carved wooden masks used by the Magar in village dances during religious festivals, for example, often have a glossy black patina adorned with white clay (see fig. 27). Such works, so far rarely studied, have great power and intrinsic beauty. The Buddhism of the Himalayan highlands has inspired an art of mask-making close to that of Tibet, but retaining certain national and regional characteristics. The features of Buddhist heroes and gods are adjusted to local tastes, and the shapes of masks are borrowed from pre-Buddhist forms. In all these regions the mask is more than an object of entertainment or disguise. It serves a religious function in ritual and initiation ceremonies. Cults of possession favour the idea that the gods and spirits are incarnated in the mask-wearers, the masks representing their living faces.

BIBLIOGRAPHY
D. Frank: *Dreamland Nepal* (New Delhi, 1978), pls 19, 102
M. Slusser: *Nepal Mandala: A Cultural Study of the Kathmandu Valley*, 2 vols (Princeton, 1982), pp. 236–7, 304, 324, 347–8
P. Pal: *Art of Nepal: A Catalogue of the Los Angeles County Museum of Art Collection* (Los Angeles, 1985), p. 181

ERIC CHAZOT

4. METALWORK. The earliest dated Nepalese metal image (AD 591; Cleveland, OH, Mus. A.; *see* §IV, 2(ii), above) confirms the skill of Nepalese craftsmen at an early date; the esteem in which they continued to be held in the 13th century is well illustrated by the career of the master craftsman ARNIKO. Summoned to Tibet with a team of assistants in 1260 by the abbot Phags-pa, he eventually reached the Mongol court in Beijing, where he became 'director general of all workers in bronze'.

Copper was the favourite medium for Nepalese sculptors over the centuries. It is a material that promotes artistry: soft enough to allow its surface to be deeply chased, it is also well suited to fire-gilding, a traditional technique still practised in the Kathmandu Valley. The hills around the valley contained veins of copper ore, the high quality of which is noted in medieval Sanskrit texts. It appears that brass replaced copper as the most commonly used alloy in the last century; the East India Company provided a source of brass and zinc, and, with the wealth of traditional patrons curtailed, the cheaper material came into favour. Today some 70% of the images produced for the tourist market are brass and some 25% copper; although popular references are made to 'Nepalese bronzes', this alloy has rarely been used by Newar craftsmen.

Metal-casting in Nepal remains essentially a cottage industry. Hundreds of households are engaged in the business of producing metal images by the lost-wax method, with the majority centred in the ancient city of Patan (particularly in the south-western quarter of the city). The metal casters belong to an exclusive Buddhist caste, the *bare* (the word is reputedly a corruption of a Sanskrit honorific term for monk) or *shakya* (the family name of Lord Buddha, used by the most numerous sub-caste of the *bare*). The *bare* have their own distinctive culture. They occupy networks of courtyards that are readily distinguishable from the domestic buildings of other Newar castes: they are related architecturally and functionally to the medieval monasteries of northern India. Each court contains a chapel dedicated to Buddha (within which, typically, a large metal statue of the deity resides), where the daily round of worship is conducted. There is a closed guild of craftsmen—few sculptors who work in the valley were not born into the *bare* caste. In similar fashion, monopolies exist for the coppersmith and blacksmith castes: the former are particularly renowned for the large metal pots and cauldrons produced by repoussé work; the latter have extended their services to automobile and motor-cycle maintenance.

The sculptors refer to themselves as 'god-makers', and almost all their work remains religious in content. The workshop is typically centred on the home, where parents and children work at modelling wax figures and building clay moulds in a well-lit upper room. Perhaps once a fortnight the focus shifts to a backyard where the family pursues the tense, difficult and dangerous occupation of metal-casting. The basic raw material used in the first stage of god-making is a mixture of beeswax and tree resin, collected in the mountains and traded in the valley by the Tamang and others. The mixture varies according to the season (additional resin stiffens the wax in the hot summer months), and some craftsmen incorporate clarified oil as well. The wax, warmed over a charcoal fire-pot, is usually shaped with a solid clay template carrying the impression of a torso, an arm, a face and so on; in this way, the modelling skills of one artist (perhaps long dead) can be preserved and exploited by less gifted members of his family. Once the repertory of parts has been established, the craftsman assembles them into his chosen model, using a sharp trimming knife and a shaping tool of horn or wood. The quality of the finished product at least partly depends on the amount of time taken in assembling the image; Newar craftsmen place great store on balance and the 'cleanness' of line and appearance. A complex Tantric deity may demand many hours of attention before it meets with the craftsman's satisfaction.

The investment of the wax model takes place in two stages. In the first a liquid slip composed of fine clay, water and cow-dung is painted on with a cloth, a brush or (traditionally) a feather. This same sanctifying and purifying mixture is applied to the earthen floors of a Newar home prior to religious festivals and domestic ceremonies. The wax receives several such applications: the thin consistency of the slip ensures that every detail etched in wax will be preserved in the mould when the wax is melted out and, subsequently, in the metal image itself. On each occasion, the figure is placed to dry in a draught, away from direct sunlight; the craftsmen are always concerned that the wax may blister in the heat, causing a blemish on the metal's surface after casting. After the first stage, a thicker mixture of rice husk and clay is smeared over and applied inside the hollow figure (see fig. 28). The god-maker also drives a number of small nails through the wax into the core: these will serve as chaplets, buttressing the inner and outer sections of clay moulding after dewaxing. By now, he will also have attached wax pipes (or sprues) to the base of the image, providing the matrix for channels down which molten metal will eventually flow; a clay 'mouth' will be formed over these.

Most sculptors do their own casting but, whereas modelling and moulding is a relaxed and harmonious pursuit, Newar craftsmen rarely enjoy the work of metal-casting itself. The coal-fired furnace, now usually driven by an electric fan directed into the flames, is regarded—like all of the artist's tools—as an incarnation of Vishvakarma, the architect of the universe who shaped the earth and the sky with his hands. Respect is shown to the furnace, which presents a physical threat to the artisans; white-hot flames shoot out from the crude covering of bricks and clay, and no protective clothing is worn against the intense heat other than sacking wrapped about the hands. The retort containing hammered scraps of metal is lifted to and from the furnace with the help of long cross-armed tongs. Not infrequently the hours of hard labour at the kiln may prove to be in vain. If, for instance, air has not entirely escaped during casting, the image may be damaged beyond repair; it is probably in recognition of this risk that medium-sized and larger images, and especially complex Tantric ones, are cast in separate parts, to be assembled later. More often than not, however, the enterprise is successful. Once the figure has cooled, and the excess metal has been sawn off, it is polished with

28. Newar craftsman applying a thick clay coating to a wax model for a metal image, Patan, 1980

hand-files. Finally, the statue is passed to a chaser or gilder for further embellishment. With the exception of the electric fan and the blow-torch, replacing buffalo-skin bellows and coal embers, the techniques of lost-wax casting and fire-gilding employed by Newar craftsmen have hardly changed from those of their predecessors.

BIBLIOGRAPHY
R. Reeves: *Cire-Perdue Casting in India* (Delhi, 1962)
P. Pal: *Vaiṣṇava Iconology in Nepal: A Study of Art and Religion* (Calcutta, 1970)
I. Alsop and J. Charlton: 'Image Casting in Oku Bahal', *Contributions Nep. Stud.*, i (1973), pp. 22–48
M.-L. de Labriffe: 'Etude de la fabrication d'une statue au Nepal', *Kailash*, i/3 (1973)
P. Pal: 'Bronzes in Nepal', *A. Asia*, iv/5 (1974), pp. 31–7
M. Shepherd Slusser: 'On the Antiquity of Nepalese Metalcraft', *Archvs Asian A.*, xxix (1976), pp. 80–95
E. Lo Bue: 'Himalayan Sculpture in the XXth Century' (PhD diss., SOAS, U. London, 1981)
——: 'Statuary Metals in Tibet and the Himalayas: History, Tradition and Modern Use', BM Occas. Pap. No. 15, ed. W. A. Oddy and W. Zwalf (London, 1981), pp. 33–67
——: 'Casting of Devotional Images in the Himalayas: History, Tradition and Modern Techniques', ibid., pp. 69–86
U. von Schroeder: *Indo-Tibetan Bronzes* (Hong Kong, 1981)
T. P. B. Riley-Smith: 'Buddhist God-Makers of the Kathmandu Valley', (PhD diss., Cambridge U., 1982)

T. P. B. RILEY-SMITH

5. TERRACOTTA. The earliest-known Nepalese terracottas, figures of humans and animals probably dating from the 3rd century BC (Kathmandu, Dept Archaeol.), were found at sites near the southern border with India and resemble contemporary Indian artefacts. Figures probably representing a universal Mother Goddess are characterized by an elaborate coiffure or headdress, large circular ear ornaments, jewellery, draped clothing, protruding eyes, prominent nose and a large mouth; female figures with more naturalistic features may represent tree spirits or dancers. Animal figurines—including rams, horses, bulls and elephants—have a red slip and are further decorated with impressed motifs of leaves, arrow-heads, dots and lines. The earliest surviving terracottas from the Kathmandu Valley (c. 7th–8th centuries AD, Los Angeles, CA, Co. Mus. A.) are from Dumvarahi. They include bejewelled riders wearing the sacred thread, humped bulls, horses, elephants and camels. The animals, modelled by hand in two halves joined medially, are hollow and decorated with a red pigment.

Nepalese art appears to have been stimulated by Buddhist monks fleeing the Muslim invasions of India in the 11th and 12th centuries. The elegant, statuesque figures of Nepalese art changed into a more sinicized style under growing Tibetan influence from the 16th century. A 17th-century plaque (Los Angeles, CA, Co. Mus. A.) of Luyipa, a Mahasiddha, was probably modelled from a sketch of a Tibetan work. Artists used a variety of pattern books to depict basic iconography, adding details of changing fashions in dress, hairstyles and jewellery. Terracottas of Hindu deities from the Transitional period (c. 800–1200) depict Bhairava and Chamunda, ferocious aspects of Shiva and Durga, and Ganesha. By the late 20th century specialist craftsmen were making Bhairava heads and masks for festivals, and for sale in the tourist market.

BIBLIOGRAPHY
A. K. Coomaraswamy: *History of Indian and Indonesian Art* (New York, 1927)
Nepalese Art, Dept Archaeol. (Kathmandu, 1966)
E. Waldschmidt and R. Waldschmidt: *Nepal: Art Treasures from the Himalayas* (London, 1969)
M. Slusser: *Nepal Mandala: A Cultural Study of the Kathmandu Valley*, 2 vols (Princeton, 1982)
P. Pal: *Art of Nepal: A Catalogue of the Los Angeles County Museum of Art Collection* (Los Angeles, 1985)

KEN TEAGUE

6. TEXTILES. Kautilya's *Arthaśāstra*, a Sanskrit text on statecraft originating in the 3rd century BC, records trade in woollen blankets from Nepal, attesting the antiquity of Nepal's textile production. Writing in 1836, Alan Campbell described 17 different types of textile. The range continues to be considerable, a result of the ethnic, geographic and climatic diversity in the country, the different functions—utilitarian, decorative, ceremonial—and, in some degree, cross-border influences. Women are the principal producers, although some spinning and weaving is done by men. The work is not caste-related, except for tailoring, which is undertaken largely by the Damai caste.

In the cold high mountain region yak hair and sheep wool are the major raw materials. The yak hair is used for weaving tents and hard-wearing blankets and rugs, and the local Baruwal or imported Tibetan wool for clothing. Woollen textiles are produced mainly on three types of loom: the back-strap or body-tension loom, the four-shaft horizontal frame loom with treadles and the stout vertical frame loom, on which knotted-pile carpets, used as saddle-blankets and sitting rugs, are produced. Among the colourful designs are floral, medallion, dragon, tiger and phoenix motifs. Sources of natural dyes include walnut, madder, rhubarb, berberis and pine cones. The arrival of many skilled carpet-weavers among Tibetan refugees led, in the 1960s, to increased carpet production and its spread to other parts of Nepal to meet demand for home and export markets.

In the milder foothills, the raw materials include cotton, hemp, nettle and wool. Woollen clothing, worn in winter, is woven mainly on back-strap looms from the wool of Baruwal sheep by Gurung women. They also weave *radī*—white, brown and black natural-colour tapestry-patterned felted rugs—used widely throughout Nepal as floor or sleeping mats.

Textiles woven from nettle fibre are among the most remarkable in Nepal. Fibre has been extracted from the nettle (Rai *allo*, Latin *Girardinia diversifolia*) for centuries, particularly by Rai, Sherpa, Gurung and Tamang, living at or near an altitude of 1500 m, where the plant thrives in deciduous forest. The stem bark is stripped, boiled, washed, beaten and scraped to extract the fibre, which is then spun with hand spindles and knotted into fish-nets or woven on back-strap looms into sacks, mats, jackets and waistcoats. From the 1980s improved fibre processing and weaving techniques widened the range of products to include a tweed-like combination of *allo* and wool.

Among the best-known cotton textiles are the strips of white, black, orange and red cloth, intricately patterned, from which the traditional men's caps (*topī*) are made. The cloth, locally called *ḍhākā* cloth, is woven on bamboo-and-wood two-shaft treadle looms, mainly by Limbu and Rai women, using the inlay technique—a plain, white ground weave with supplementary coloured weft laid alongside the ground weft in areas selected by the weaver, without charts or counting threads, to create a pattern. Some weavers employ a tapestry method: the coloured weft threads are not supplementary but are woven back and forth in their own pattern area to form the structure of the fabric. Among the infinite variety of patterns, applied also to shawls and blouse pieces, are diamonds, zigzag, flower shapes and the temple and elephant-trunk motifs (see fig. 29). With the introduction in the 1980s of a wide range of colours and yarns, including local silk, the multicoloured textiles gained international recognition. By the late 20th century cotton cloth for garments was still woven by some ethnic groups, using the same type of treadle loom, often with four instead of two shafts, to obtain twill, diamond and pigeon-eye patterns. Large wooden-frame looms with fly shuttle attachment have been introduced in most areas and are also used to weave *ḍhākā* cloth in western Nepal (Palpa).

In the hot, southern plains (Terai) most textiles are made from cotton, although the locally grown jute is widely used for colourful, striped mats woven on back-strap looms. In some areas, where electricity is available, power-driven looms are employed to produce a wide range of textiles for clothing and home furnishing.

Textile decoration applied after weaving includes block-printing, tie-dyeing, batik, embroidery, appliqué and quilting. Textile-related activities practised in most rural areas include knitting, crochet, braiding, plaiting and interlacing.

29. Cotton *ḍhākā* cloth for a *ṭopī* from the middle mountain region of Nepal (detail), 700×180 mm, 1980 (private collection); traditional inlay-weaving technique, elephant-trunk and temple pattern

Examples of a range of Nepalese textiles are held in the British Museum, Museum of Mankind, and the Horniman Museum and Library, both London, the Musée de l'Homme, Paris, and the National Museum of Nepal, Kathmandu.

BIBLIOGRAPHY

Arthaśāstra (*c.* 500 BC–AD 300, ascribed to Kautilya); Eng. trans. by R. Shamasastri (Mysore, 1923), p. 90

A. Campbell: 'Notes on the States of the Arts of Cotton Spinning, Weaving, Printing and Dyeing in Nepal', *J. Asiat. Soc. Bengal*, v (1836), pp. 219–27

C. Jest: *Dolpo* (Paris, 1975)

M. Schmidt-Thomé and Tsering Tashi Thingo: *Materielle Kunst und Kultur der Sherpa* (Innsbruck and Munich, 1975)

C. L. Gajurel and K. K. Vaidya: *Traditional Arts and Crafts of Nepal* (Delhi, 1984)

S. Dunsmore: *Nepalese Textiles* (London, 1993)

SUSI DUNSMORE

7. WOOD-CARVING. As practised in the Kathmandu Valley, wood-carving qualifies as a major art form. It is the domain of a Newar caste known as *sthapit*, a name derived from *sthapati* (Skt: 'builder') and ultimately from Sthapati, the designer-painter-carpenter son of Vishvakarma, one of the four heavenly architects of Vedic and later mythology. Its most distinctive use is in architecture, serving both tectonic and ornamental purposes, but it was also used to create independent sculptures. Although, like many of the companion Nepalese arts, wood-carving is essentially a thing of the past, there are still a few families who carry on the tradition and, besides carving for the tourist trade, have done creditable restoration work on many of the decaying public buildings.

(i) Architectural uses. Most buildings in the Kathmandu Valley conform to an architectural canon developed over millennia in which plain brick walls contrast with elaborate wood-carving, sometimes known as 'Newar style' (*see also* §III, 2 and figs 6–7 above). In the traditional three-storey dwellings in villages and towns such carving is usually limited to doorframes and windows. Window openings are without glass and filled with intricately joined lattices, fixed or movable. Window lattices and frames are modest on the lower floors and, according to means, elaborate on the upper floors. Varied and complex in design and execution, windows are designated by a number of special names and provide some of the most spectacular examples of the wood-carver's art in the Kathmandu Valley. As the traditional style of house gives way to concrete and glass, carved windows are no longer made, and the old ones are left unrepaired and even destroyed.

It is inside the Buddhist monastery quadrangles (*vihāra*s) and on the temple exteriors, Hindu and Buddhist, that the art of the Nepali wood-carver is seen in its most highly developed form (*see* §III, 2(i) above), an elaboration sometimes equalled in palace structures and *dharmaśālā*s (community buildings, public shelters). The principal ground-floor façade of the temple—and in those of square plan, all the façades—is dominated by an extensive tripartite portal that conceals or replaces most of the brickwork. The latter is further diminished by inset blind windows and other carved plaques. The central doorway (or doorways) is surmounted by the canted, free-standing tympanum, known as *toraṇa*, an elaborate relief filled with images and ornament. The ends of rafters supporting the upper

storeys are carved into a continuous encircling frieze of human, animal or bird heads, above and below which run parallel bands of varied ornament. Although there are some single-storey temples, two or three storeys are more common, the brick walling of the upper storeys interrupted with windows of varying sizes, intricately carved and usually blind. The *vihāra* quadrangle maintains a sober exterior in which carved wood plays a minor role, although the entrance may be surmounted by an elaborately carved *toraṇa*. In the interior wood-carving is used extensively, especially in the wing housing the shrine, and it is here that some of the finest Nepalese wood-carving occurs.

The massive overhanging roofs of the traditional brick-and-wood buildings are partly supported by wooden brackets braced against the walls and carved into high-relief images, often of superhuman size. When the roofs are multiple the brackets become progressively fewer and smaller in accordance with the diminishing size of the roof they help to support. On all levels the corner brackets are the largest, and they are usually carved alternately in the forms of fantastic guardian animals, rampant lion (*śārdūla*) and griffin. The intervening brackets, depicting various gods and demigods, surmount a small panel carved with accessory images.

The most beautifully carved brackets are the earliest surviving examples, dating between about the 12th and 14th centuries. Probably fewer than a hundred remain, distributed among some dozen sites in the Kathmandu Valley and its nearby extensions, and of these many are in a state of decay. The only ones that can be dated with reasonable exactitude are on the Indreshvara Mahadeva Temple at PANAUTI constructed in 1294. They appear to be the originals, since there is no indication of restoration or replacement. Nine brackets on the *vihāra* known as Uku-bahal were probably carved between 1167 and 1174, the date of the restoration of the building. The remaining examples can be dated only roughly on the basis of style or historical evidence respecting the buildings to which they are attached. Such early brackets typically depict *yakṣi*s (female nature spirits), provocative goddesses of fertility with firm breasts, delicate waists and ample hips (see fig. 30). Posed in elegant triple curve (*tribhaṅga*), they are canopied by the tree they symbolically fertilize and into whose luxurious foliage they reach. Sometimes they are accompanied by a bird or child. On the Indreshvara Mahadeva Temple at Panauti the *yakṣi*s are largely displaced by other deities and by characters from the Indian epics.

Most brackets created from about the 16th century on, though functionally important, do not compare favourably with earlier examples. For the most part they are folkish works with awkwardly pieced-on parts and strident colours, whose allure derives mainly from erotica displayed on the lowermost panels. In all earlier cases, the lowermost panels contain minor figures, single or paired, who act as atlantids for the larger images. Any rare erotica are remote from the crude representations of the later brackets. Also, unlike the latter, the early brackets are not pieced. The sides of the beam were also carved, so that essentially the images qualify as sculpture in the round. Further, although the bracket's primary function is support, this did not inhibit the artists from daringly chiselling out large areas

30. Wooden bracket figure of a *yakṣi* with a parrot (*c.* 1294), over life-size, Indreshvara Mahadeva Temple, Panauti

The architects and artists of Nepal, however they might personalize their works over the centuries, owed their basic inspiration to the artists of India, especially during the Kushana and Gupta periods (*c.* AD 1st–6th centuries). It is directly from India that such motifs as the *yakṣi* and atlantids proceed, as do the magnificent temple doorways in all their myriad detail. Although the existing elevations of the majority of Newar-style buildings in the Kathmandu Valley—and the carving on them—were realized between the 16th and 18th centuries, they replace antecedent structures, some of whose foundations go back to at least the 5th century. In wood-carving, as in all Nepalese arts, there has been a continuum spanning a millennium and more.

(ii) Free-standing sculptures. When the wood-carvers of medieval Nepal turned their considerable skills to the carving of independent images, the carpenter often triumphed over the sculptor. Some examples, however, are superb carvings that compete with the best work in bronze and stone. Independent sculptures mainly depict gods and demigods, but there are also various attendant figures, portrait images of donors, devotees and historic or mythological persons and animals, notably the vehicles assigned to the gods. Some images are carved in one piece, often even large ones, but most exhibit some piecing, particularly respecting arms and legs. Further, the wood-carver often teamed with the metallurgist, the latter providing gilded head and hands, the former the wooden torso. Jewellery was also frequently provided by the metallurgist, although on most images it is fully carved and faithfully replicates in minute detail the crowns and other lavish ornaments that were, and sometimes still are, in actual use. Most of the images were painted, often over a thin layer of gesso. Skin was given symbolic colours appropriate to the particular representation, and the garments painted in even when already rendered by carving.

Large independent sculptures in the round were customarily employed as the principal cult object in shrines that did not enjoy ones of bronze or stone, and smaller examples served as accessories or for worship in domestic chapels. They sit or stand on lotus bases and are surrounded with mandorlas carved as one with the image. They are often provided with a separate, ingeniously carved, shrine-like throne—intricately ornamented with human, animal, plant and fantasy creatures—which is itself a splendid example of the wood-carver's art. A remarkable image type that has neither base nor mandorla is the head, or mask, of the god Bhairava. Carved in infinite detail, these images provide some of the most stunning independent wood-carvings in Nepal.

Although there are exceptions, few wooden sculptures have survived *in situ*, but a number are preserved in local and foreign collections. One of the most impressive collections is in Nepal, at Bhaktapur, where a museum devoted solely to this art has been established. That even these few have escaped centuries of neglect, and in the case of exterior carvings the rigours of the monsoon climate, is in part due to the almost exclusive use of sal (Skt *śāla*; Lat. *Vatica robusta*), a tropical hardwood extremely resistant to termites and decay.

of the beam to free limbs and achieve exquisite detail. A few bracket images appear to be stylistically intermediate between the early and late groups. In them the *yakṣi* and atlantid motif is preserved but the carving is less finely executed.

Wood is, and has been, carved in many parts of Nepal outside the Kathmandu Valley—resulting in some remarkable works including masks—but in such contexts wood-carving is largely a folk art (*see also* §§I, 3(iii) and VI, 3 above). An exception is among the Thakali, Sherpa and other traditionally Buddhist communities who live near the northern border contiguous with Tibet. Although politically Nepalese, these communities are culturally more akin to their northern neighbours and construct their monasteries in the same fashion and embellish them with carved wood whose inspiration belongs to a non-Nepali tradition.

BIBLIOGRAPHY
S. Deo: 'Glimpses of Nepal Woodwork', *J. Ind. Soc. Orient. A.*, n. s., iii (1968–9)
E. Waldschmidt and R. Waldschmidt: *Nepal: Art Treasures from the Himalayas* (London, 1969), pp. 138–44, pl. 46–64
M. Slusser: 'The Wooden Sculptures of Nepal', *A. Asia*, iv/5 (1974), pp. 51–7
U. Wiesner: *Nepalese Temple Architecture: Its Characteristics and its Relations to Indian Development*, Stud. S. Asian Cult., viii (Leiden, 1978)
M. Slusser: 'Indreśvara Mahādeva: A Thirteenth-century Nepalese Shrine', *Artibus Asiae*, xli/2–3 (1979), pp. 185–225
——: *Nepal Mandala: A Cultural Study of the Kathmandu Valley* (Princeton, 1982), i, pp. 127–47; ii, pls 112–207
P. Pal: *Art of Nepal: A Catalogue of the Los Angeles County Museum of Art Collection* (Los Angeles, 1985), pls S11, S34–6, S57, S58 and S67

MARY SHEPHERD SLUSSER

VII. Ethnic arts.

Within the kingdom of Nepal approximately 15 major ethnic groups and many minor ones, relatively isolated from each other by cultural and geographical barriers, continue their traditional ways. The lands they inhabit can be divided into three broad areas: the high mountain region, the middle hills region and the Terai. Environment dictates the kinds of food, clothing and shelter necessary and possible within each region, as well as providing the raw materials of art. Art is not made as personal expression, but for utilitarian purposes, both ordinary and sacred. Creative energy is associated with the gods of learning and skill, not with individual talent.

1. HIGH MOUNTAIN REGION. Most of the people living in the high mountain areas of the northern border region have migrated from Tibet over centuries, still observing many of the customs and practices of their native land. Much of their material culture and trade is related to the raising of yaks. Dairy products are traded for many of their necessary goods. The hair and wool of the yak and its crossbreeds are woven into a number of possessions, including tents and ropes, blankets and spreads, carpets and finely woven and colourful clothing. Both men and women spin, weave and sew. Their household wealth—brass and copper vessels, carpets and carved tables—is a colourful and extravagant contrast to the severity of the land. Much of their household material culture, ranging from the simplest wooden teabowl to utensils of gold and silver, turquoise and coral, is related to the process of preparing and serving a brothlike 'tea'.

2. MIDDLE HILLS REGION. Below these mountain heights is the area known as the middle hills. Dominated by north–south ranges diminishing towards the distant flatlands of the Terai, the land is a complicated area of rugged side canyons and steep ridges. Different hill groups—Gurung, Magar, Rai, Limbu, Tamang—speak different languages and observe somewhat varied customs and traditions, but all work with the same native raw materials.

The hill people are primarily farmers, cultivating crops of maize, rice, wheat and millet, and keeping herds of sheep and goats and some water buffalo. The rough wool and hair of sheep and goats is woven into simple capelike jackets and blankets. A mountain variety of stinging nettle also provides a tough, durable fibre. All such weaving is done by the women. The men of these same households use bamboo to make varied forms of baskets and mats. The hill men also carve local woods for household and ritual tools. Satellite communities of caste-specific workers, including musician–tailors, cobblers, goldsmith–blacksmiths, occasional potters and Chunaro, a caste group whose work is lathe-turning wooden pots (see fig. 31), supply the village's needs.

The Kathmandu Valley occupies a special position within this middle hills region. Blessed with a subtropical monsoon climate and fertile land, the valley has produced great surpluses of grains and developed into a major entrepôt. Successive waves of immigrants have been assimilated to create the valley's diverse Newar society (*see* §I, 2 above). A complex hierarchy of caste groups maintains its stability, order and form. The material culture reflects the complexity of the Newar heritage. Intricate carved windows adorn façades and courtyards of brick. Ornate gold necklaces and headbands contribute to the richness of the bride. Complex elaborations of simple vase and pitcher forms enhance Newar feasts.

With the exception of only a few artistic processes, most of the art of the valley is created by professional artists assigned by their caste position to work with a particular material and process. The copper workers pound great vessels for brewing liquor and cooking feasts. Goldsmiths and silversmiths sit together in family workshops, hammering teardrop earrings or linking chains. Other families use the lost-wax process to convert images in wax to images in brass or copper. Potters throw thick clay forms, which they paddle into simple pots for carrying and storing water, for brewing and serving beer. Some of

31. Chunaro lathe-turners making a wooden pot, near the village of Gandrung, west Nepal, *c.* 1980

these simple forms are elaborated with faces of deities such as Bhairava (a fierce form of Shiva) or Varahi (a mother goddess represented with a boar's head) to use for ceremonial beer or brew. Woodworkers carve intricate windows and doorways for temple and home. All of these artists and artisans are trained within their extended family to continue a family heritage.

3. THE TERAI. An extension of the Gangetic plain of India, the Terai has a semi-tropical climate that supports dense jungles, as well as producing significant surpluses of grains. Two of the major ethnic groups of the Terai are the Tharu and Maithil. The Maithil have a highly developed literary and philosophical tradition based on Sanskrit forms and an elaborate social hierarchy ranging from priests to sweepers. Much of the artistic creation is done by caste-professional artists. The Maithili women continue an artistic tradition of ritual painting on the clay walls and floors of their homes.

In comparison with the Maithil, the Tharu live more simply and freely, by farming and fishing. Tharu women weave a variety of colourful baskets, sew appliqué clothing and hand-build pottery. Tharu potters make ritual horses and beer pitchers. Both Tharu and Maithili women create granaries in sun-baked clay, arranged within the interior of homes to function as space definers as well.

BIBLIOGRAPHY
C. L. Gajurel and K. K. Vaidya: *Traditional Arts and Crafts of Nepal* (Delhi, 1984)
J. Chase: *Not Art Apart: Ethnic Cultures and Arts of Nepal* (in preparation)

JUDITH CHASE

VIII. Museums.

The Kathmandu Valley has one of the highest densities of monuments and Nepalese art works in the world; only a small fraction of Nepal's artistic wealth is housed in museums. Institutional and private collections in the West are growing, however. Widespread Western interest in Newar art followed the opening of Nepal to tourism in the 1960s and was boosted by a number of exhibitions, including *The Art of Nepal*, held at the Asia Society Galleries in New York in 1964, and *Tantra*, held at the Hayward Gallery in London in 1971. Important collections have been assembled in the USA and Europe, as well as in India and Nepal itself.

1. COLLECTIONS OUTSIDE NEPAL. Western scholarly interest in Newar culture and art began in 1824, when Brian Houghton Hodgson, one of the first British residents in Kathmandu, started collecting texts in Sanskrit and Newari with a view to discovering the main features of Buddhism. Hodgson sent to Calcutta a number of manuscripts, many of which were illuminated, as well as vertical banners painted on cotton (Newari *paubhā*). These were eventually divided between collections in Calcutta, London, Oxford and Paris.

The most representative collection of Newar illustrated manuscripts of Buddhist and Hindu texts is held by the University Library, Cambridge. The earliest palm-leaf manuscripts date to the 11th century; some examples retain their original carved and painted wood covers. The same library holds 'picture books' (Newari *thyāsāpu*) of a

horizontal format as well as illustrated albums of a vertical format. Early illuminated manuscripts and manuscript covers are also found in the India Office Library and British Library in London, the Los Angeles County Museum (mostly from the Nasli and Alice Heeramaneck Collection), the Cleveland Museum of Art, the Museum of Fine Arts in Boston and the Musée Guimet in Paris.

The most important collections of Newar painting, including both *paubhā*s and long horizontal narrative scrolls (Newari *vilampu*), are held by the Los Angeles County Museum (chiefly from the Heeramaneck Collection), the Museum of Fine Arts in Boston, the Musée Guimet (from the collection donated by Hodgson to the Institut de France in 1866 and, more recently, from the collection of Lionel Fournier) in Paris, the Victoria and Albert Museum and British Museum, both in London, the Prince of Wales Museum in Bombay and the Bharat Kala Bhavan in Varanasi. Individual paintings, drawings and sketchbooks for artists worth attention are also in the Newark Museum, the Rijksmuseum voor Volkenkunde in Leiden and the Royal Library in Copenhagen. The most remarkable private collection of Newar painting is that of Jack Zimmermann in New York, which also includes important examples of sculpture. Notable individual pieces are in the Neotia Collection in Calcutta. Several interesting works collected by Edward Binney III are in the San Diego Museum of Art.

The most representative collections of Newar sculpture, chiefly in copper (generally mercury-gilded) and brass but also in stone and carved and painted wood, are found in the Los Angeles County Museum, the Museum of Fine Arts in Boston, the Musée Guimet, the Asian Art Museum in San Francisco, the Cleveland Museum of Art, the Newark Museum, the Brooklyn Museum and the Victoria and Albert Museum, where in addition an interesting collection of 20th-century metal images is held on loan. The most important private collections of Newar statuary are those of John F. Ford in Baltimore, Doris Wiener and Samuel Eilenberg in New York, Philip Goldman in London, H. K. Swali in Bombay, Norton Simon in New York and Los Angeles and Michael Scratton at the Ashmolean Museum in Oxford.

Interesting ritual and domestic objects, as well as illuminated manuscripts, paintings and statues, are held by the National Museum in New Delhi, the Indian Museum and the Asiatic Society in Calcutta, the Museum für Indische Kunst in Berlin, the Musée d'Ethnographie in Geneva, the Denver Art Museum, the Seattle Art Museum, the Merseyside County Museum in Liverpool, the Royal Asiatic Society in London, the Museum van Aziatische Kunst in Amsterdam, the Musées Nationaux d'Art et d'Histoire in Brussels and the Gerd-Wolfgang Essen Collection in Hamburg.

BIBLIOGRAPHY
The Art of Nepal (exh. cat. by S. Kramrisch, Asia Soc. Gals, New York, 1964)
Tantra (exh. cat., intro. P. Rawson; London, Hayward Gal., 1971)
P. Pal: *Sculpture* and *Painting*, i and ii of *The Arts of Nepal*, 2 vols (Leiden, 1974–8)
Les Mandalas himalayens du Musée Guimet (exh. cat. by G. Béguin, Paris, Mus. Guimet, 1981)
P. Pal: *Art of Nepal: A Catalogue of the Los Angeles County Museum of Art Collection* (Los Angeles, 1985)

Art ésotérique de l'Himalaya: Catalogue de la donation Lionel Fournier (exh. cat. by G. Béguin, Paris, Mus. Guimet, 1990)

Die Götter des Himalaya: Buddhistische Kunst Tibets: Die Sammlung Gerd-Wolfgang Essen, 2 vols (exh. cat. by G.-W. Essen and Tsering Tashi Thingo, Cologne, Josef-Haubrich-Ksthalle; Munich, Haus Kst.; Berlin, Staatl. Museen Preuss. Kultbes.; 1990)

2. MUSEUMS IN NEPAL. The most important collection of sculpture is held by the National Museum in Kathmandu. Outstanding early works in stone include the torso from Hadigaon dating perhaps to the 3rd century AD, the male figure often identified as a royal portrait (*c.* 4th century AD) and the stele from Lajimpat portraying Vishnu Vikranta (AD 467). Among later masterpieces are a Lakshmi (*c.* 10th–11th century), a scene of the birth of the Buddha (*c.* 10th–13th century) from Deopatan, a 13th-century relief depicting Brahma and a 14th-century relief depicting Vishnu. The most important metal images housed in the National Museum are a 9th-century copper standing Buddha, a 10th-century copper standing Vishnu, 14th-century gilt copper images of the *bodhisattva* Namasamgiti and of the transcendent Buddha Amoghasiddhi, a 15th-century gilt copper image of the *boddhisattva* Padmapani, a 15th–16th-century gilt copper image of the transcendent Buddha Akshobhya, a 17th-century gilt copper image of the previous Buddha Dipankara, a 17th-century image of the Hindu goddess Varahi and an 18th-century image of the future Buddha Maitreya made of silver. Other exceptional sculptures include a 15th-century polychrome wood-carving of a dancing girl and a 17th-century terracotta stele devoted to the goddess Mahagauri. Ivory items include a statue of the *ṛṣi* Bhringin and an elaborately carved mirror handle. The National Museum also holds a few scrolls painted on cotton (Newari *paubhā*).

An important collection of wooden statuary is kept at the National Art Gallery located in the Royal Palace at Bhaktapur. It includes a 15th-century female donor, a Vasudhara (*c.* 15th–16th century), a 16th-century Hayagriva covered with plaster and painted in red, a 17th-century dancing Shiva in his aspect as the embodiment of all things (*viśvarūpa*) and a 17th-century dancing Ganesha. Noteworthy paintings in this museum include a *paubhā* depicting Shiva as 'lord of the dance' (*Nṛtyeśvara*) and dated to the equivalent of AD 1659, a few illuminated manuscripts and manuscript covers, 'picture books' and paintings on paper. Illuminated manuscripts and manuscript covers are also kept at the National Library in Kathmandu.

A representative collection of stone images is housed in the small museum near the stupa on Svayambhu Hill. Several of them bear inscriptions with dates in the 16th and 17th centuries. Two important 7th- and 8th-century stone friezes are kept at the Police Club in Kathmandu, and other art objects can be found at the small museum located in the Royal Palace of Patan.

BIBLIOGRAPHY

E. Waldschmidt and R. Waldschmidt: *Nepal: Art Treasures from the Himalayas* (London, 1969)

P. Pal: *Sculpture* and *Painting*, i and ii of *The Arts of Nepal* (Leiden, 1974–8)

B. P. Khanal: *A Glimpse of Nepalese Arts*, Kathmandu N. Mus. cat. (Kathmandu, 1977)

ERBERTO F. LO BUE

Neresheim Abbey. Benedictine abbey, 16 km from Nördlingen, in the Swabian Alps, Baden-Württemberg, Germany. It was founded in 1095 by Graf Hartmann I von Dillingen. Its first church was built in the 12th century, but in 1695, to mark the 600th anniversary of the monastery, the façade and interior were remodelled in the Baroque style, although the tower, built in 1617–26 by Peter Schwarz (*d* 1626) in a Romanesque style, was left unaltered. At the same time new service buildings were constructed, and in 1699–1726 new monastic quarters, designed by Michael Weidemann, were built. The final phase of building was the construction of a new church. A site on the northern edge of the monastic complex was prepared in 1745, before an architect had been selected.

In 1747 the abbot Aurelius Braisch engaged Balthasar Neumann to design the church, having been impressed by his Benedictine monastery church of Münsterschwarzach, begun in 1727 and then nearing completion. Although Neumann's first proposals for Neresheim used a Latin cross plan, as at Münsterschwarzach, his revised designs had a symmetrical arrangement of nave and choir with a domed crossing. This change enabled the 17th-century tower to be retained, as specified, and provided entrances into the church from the east and west wings of the monastery.

The west front of the church, articulated with two orders of pilasters, swells forwards in its three central bays, which indicate the width of the nave. The side bays, however, mask the true width of the aisles, which are reduced to narrow passages by Neumann's use of an 'inner membrane', where a sequence of curvilinear forms is created by a succession of massive piers, faced by diagonally set pilasters and placed in front of the straight walls of the nave and chancel. These support oval domes, while at the crossing four pairs of free-standing columns, also placed diagonally, uphold a central rotunda, the dominating feature of the composition (*see* NEUMANN, BALTHASAR, fig. 3).

The vaulting was executed, after Neumann's death, in timber, shallower than he intended; Martin Knoller carried out a series of frescoes (1770–75) in *trompe l'oeil* on the saucer domes. They depict, at the entrance, *Christ Driving the Money-changers from the Temple*; at the crossing, the *Trinity Presiding over the Heavenly Host*; at the north transept, the *Baptism*; at the south transept, the *Presentation of Christ*; above the monks' choir, the *Resurrection*; above the chancel, *Christ among the Doctors*; and at the high altar, the *Last Supper*. In 1776 Thomas Schaidhauf began the stuccowork for the interior, then turned to the liturgical furniture, finally finishing the altars in 1801. Twelve months later, when church holdings were annexed by Napoleon, the property and buildings of Neresheim were sold to the house of Thurn and Taxis, which used them for commercial purposes. The church was returned to the Benedictines in the 20th century and was magnificently restored in the 1970s.

BIBLIOGRAPHY

P. Weissenberger: *Baugeschichte der Abtei Neresheim* (Stuttgart, 1934)

G. Neumann: *Neresheim* (Munich, 1947)

J. Gamer: 'Die Benediktinerabteikirche Neresheim', *Balthasar Neumann in Baden-Württemberg* (exh. cat., ed. G. Thiem; Stuttgart, Staatsgal., 1975), pp. 93–119

D. Booth: *Art and Geometry: The Church Designs of Balthasar Neumann* (diss., U. Toronto, 1990) [bk in preparation]

CHRISTIAN F. OTTO

Nerezi, St Panteleimon. Byzantine monastery in the Republic of Macedonia, 5 km south-west of Skopje. It was founded by the imperial prince Alexios Komnenos, the grandson of Alexios I Komnenos (*reg* 1081–1112), and the date 1164 is given on the lintel of the church's main door. Little remains of the conventual buildings, but the church, which was restored in the 1960s, contains some of the finest frescoes in Macedonia, executed by a 12th-century artist from Constantinople. It is cross-in-square in plan, with a domed octagonal drum and four smaller square drums rising from the centre and corner bays respectively. The eastern bays serve as forechoirs of the main apse and are accessible from both the altar and nave, while the western pair of bays form separate chapels accessible only from the narthex. These architectural features are similar to those found in other churches of the Komnenian period. The exterior of the Nerezi church is built in cloisonné masonry with colonnettes and carved capitals decorating the recessed windows. The sculptural decoration inside the church includes an elaborately carved iconostasis and a plaster frame around the fresco-icon of the church's patron, St Panteleimon, depicting peacocks drinking from a kantharos.

Several of the church's original frescoes survive. The middle zone preserves several scenes from the lives of Christ (the *Presentation in the Temple*, the *Transfiguration*, the *Raising of Lazarus*, the *Entry into Jerusalem*, the *Deposition* and the *Lamentation*) and the Virgin (the *Birth of the Virgin* and the *Presentation of the Virgin*) as well as one scene from a liturgical cycle of the *Communion of the Apostles*. The lower zone is filled with full-length and medallion portraits of Church Fathers around the altar, poets and monks in the lateral bays, military saints in the western bay and deacons, bishops, physicians and martyrs in the prothesis, diaconicon and western pair of chapels. The sophisticated style of these paintings is characterized by the refined Classical facial features of such figures as SS Tryphon and Panteleimon, the elegant poses of the figures in the festive cycle, the extensive use of bold highlights and the rhythmical integration of the figures into the landscape backgrounds. Despite working within the confines of traditional iconographic conventions, the Nerezi artist has nevertheless heightened the emotional impact of certain scenes by emphasizing the gestures and facial expressions of the participants.

The frescoes in the walls' upper zone and in the vaults were donated by a certain Stojko, whose name is inscribed on the image of the Archangel Michael, possibly from 1491–2. The same donor may also have been responsible for the restoration of several Christological scenes and medallion portraits dated to the 12th century, thus disrupting the original decorative programme.

BIBLIOGRAPHY

N. Okunev: 'La Découverte des anciennes fresques du monastère de Nerèz', *Slavia*, vi/2–3 (1927), pp. 603–9

M. Rajković: 'Slikarstvo Nereza' [The painting of Nerezi], *Zborn. Radova Vizant. Inst.*, iii (1955), pp. 195–206

P. Miljković-Pepek: *Nerezi* (Belgrade, 1966)

V. J. Djurić: *Vizantijske freske u Jugoslaviji* [Byzantine frescoes in Yugoslavia] (Belgrade, 1974; Ger. trans., Belgrade, 1976), pp. 15–17, 236–7

SRDJAN DJURIĆ

Neri, Filippo [Philip]. *See* FILIPPO NERI.

Neri da Rimini (*fl* Bologna, 1300–?1322). Italian illuminator. He signed and dated a series of works of great stylistic coherence: the folio with *Christ in Majesty* (Venice, Fond. Cini) dating from 1300, and the Gradual of 1303 from S Silvestro, Larciano (Pistoia); the page from an Antiphonal of 1308 (Cleveland, OH, Mus. A., Wade Fund 53.365) and the choir-book written in 1314 (Bologna, Mus. Civ., MS. 540). A document records his presence in Rimini in 1306, and the signed nocturnal Antiphonal in Faenza Cathedral was commissioned in 1309. Variations within this group and related works (further fragments: Venice, Fond. Cini; a choir-book, London, Amati priv. col.; choir-books, Venice, S Maria della Fava), can best be explained by the presence of collaborators. Neri, moving from his familiarity with Giottesque painting in Rimini, developed a series of light and luminous chromatic experiments that tend to dematerialize the figures (which often possess an almost humorous vivacity); the application of paint is free, and stain-like areas accompany more intense zones of colour and strokes of white lead applied extremely freely and thickly, almost like calligraphy. The decoration accompanying the figures is for the most part sombre.

The only manuscript illuminated by Neri that is not a choir-book is a Commentary on the Gospels (1322; Rome, Vatican, Bib. Apostolica, MS. Urb. lat. 11), commonly accepted as by him, although unsigned. Here the small framed scenes are closer to larger-scale painting, and reveal contacts with Pietro da Rimini. This suggests that Neri's career can be interpreted in the context of local painting.

BIBLIOGRAPHY

P. Toesca: *Monumenti e studi per la storia della miniatura: La collezione U. Hoepli* (Milan, 1930), pp. 31–4

A. Corbara: 'Due antifonari miniati del riminese Neri', *La Bibliofilia*, ccxvii (1935), pp. 317–31

P. Toesca: *Il trecento* (Turin, 1951/*R* 1971), pp. 718, 834

C. Volpe: *La pittura riminese del trecento* (Milan, 1965), pp. 10–11, 70

G. Mariani Canova: *Miniature dell'Italia settentrionale nella fondazione Giorgio Cini* (Vicenza, 1978), pp. 16–22

A. Conti: *La miniatura bolognese: Scuole e botteghe* (Bologna, 1981), pp. 55–7

ALESSANDRO CONTI

Neri di Bicci (*b* Florence, 1418; *d* Florence, 4 Jan 1492). Italian painter, son of BICCI DI LORENZO. He was the last artist member of the family, whose workshop can be traced back to his grandfather LORENZO DI BICCI. Under Neri's direction, the workshop was extremely successful and catered to a wide variety of patrons. The details of its activity, including the names of the many pupils and assistants that passed through it, are recorded between 1453 and 1475 in the workshop diary, the *Ricordanze*, the most extensive surviving document relating to a 15th-century painter.

1. Life and work. 2. Style and patronage. 3. The *Ricordanze*.

1. LIFE AND WORK.

(i) To 1452. (ii) After 1452.

(i) To 1452. He was enrolled in 1434 in the Compagnia di S Luca and began to make his way as a painter in the

thriving family workshop. Vasari described Neri as the second son of Lorenzo, to whom he attributed works now given to Neri's father Bicci. The confusion was first pointed out by Domenico M. Manni in his edition (1768) of Baldinucci's *Notizie dei professori del disegno* and then by Gaetano Milanesi in his commentary to Vasari's *Vite* (1878). Milanesi's analysis restored the real relationships between the three painters and reconstructed the pictorial production of Bicci di Lorenzo and his son Neri. In June 1438 Neri is named along with Bicci as a witness in a dispute between Bastiano di Giovanni, a gold-beater, and Domenico di Giovanni Lapi. On 15 December of the same year he delivered to his father a payment of 15 florins on account, for a panel painting commissioned by Donato Barbadori for the chapel of S Frediano in S Felicita, Florence. In 1439–40 Neri worked with his father on the

trompe-l'oeil funerary monument to *Luigi Marsili* (1342–94) frescoed in Florence Cathedral and in 1440 he painted and dated an *Annunciation* in S Angelo a Legnaia. In these early works his style was virtually indistinguishable from that of Bicci and the other painters of the workshop. Documents indicate that in 1444 he painted a triptych (untraced) depicting the *Virgin and Child Enthroned with Six Saints* for the chapel of S Giacomo in SS Annunziata, Florence (reconstructed by Zeri: central panel, sold before 1980, London, Colnaghi's; side panels, Florence, Accad. and Oberlin Coll., OH, Allen Mem. A. Mus.). In these panels the style is more developed, showing similarities of detail with the painting of Fra Filippo Lippi and Paolo Schiavo.

In this period Neri not only began to achieve an autonomy of form in his painting, but also probably took

1. Neri di Bicci: *Assumption of the Virgin*, tempera on panel, 2.43×2.23 m, 1455 (Ottawa, National Gallery of Canada)

2. Neri di Bicci: *Coronation of the Virgin with Eleven Saints*, tempera on panel, 1459 (Florence, Galleria dell'Accademia)

over the management of the workshop. In April 1447 he painted a predella (untraced) for S Martino, Maiano, paid for on 27 August 1460. In 1452, the year of his father's death, Neri dated a painting of the *Virgin Enthroned with Four Saints* (San Miniato, Mus. Dioc. A. Sacra), commissioned by Nicoluccio d'Antonio from Canneto in Valdelsa, near Empoli, for the church of S Giorgio there. In the same year Neri was entrusted with an important project for one of the most eminent Florentine families: a fresco cycle illustrating scenes from the *Life of St Giovanni Gualberto*, commissioned by Giovanni Spini and Salvestro Spini for the family chapel in Santa Trìnita. Only the *Annunciation* over the entrance arch survives.

(ii) After 1452. From the *Ricordanze* the most important events of Neri's life and his most important works can be reconstructed. The first information regarding the presence of a pupil in the workshop, Cosimo Rosselli, dates from 4 May 1453. The first work mentioned is a frescoed tabernacle at Ponte di Stagno near Florence depicting the *Virgin and Four Saints* (Santa Maria a Castagnolo, nr Lastra a Signa) painted for Luca da San Colombano at

Settimo on 15 June 1453. The most prestigious commission of this period was a tabernacle depicting *Moses and the Four Evangelists* (destr.) for the Sala dell'Udienza, in the Palazzo della Signoria. This tabernacle was to house a copy of Justinian's *Digest* in Greek. The commission, from the Gonfaloniere Tommaso di Lorenzo Soderini, was begun on 15 August 1454. In another project for the Republic, commissioned on 24 January 1455, Neri collaborated with Vittorio di Lorenzo Ghiberti, Piero del Massaio and four other painters on the decoration of a model for a tapestry *spalliera* (untraced) for the Palazzo della Signoria.

The workshop's activity in the Spini Chapel of Santa Trìnita, Florence, resumed with the execution of the altarpiece depicting the *Assumption of the Virgin* (begun 28 February 1455; Ottawa, N.G.; see fig. 1). On 1 March 1455 Neri started work in the Vallombrosan monastery of Pancrazio on the fresco commissioned by the abbot Benedetto Toschi and now considered his masterpiece; the large lunette, depicting *St Giovanni Gualberto Enthroned with Saints and Blessed Persons of his Order* (Florence, Santa Trìnita), contains curious echoes of Piero della

3. Neri di Bicci: *Annunciation*, tempera on panel, 1464 (Florence, Galleria dell'Accademia)

Francesca, Fra Filippo Lippi and Domenico Veneziano. On 1 March 1456 a new contract with Cosimo Rosselli was drawn up. On 5 March 1457 Michele Agnolo di Papi of Arezzo commissioned an altarpiece depicting the *Madonna of Mercy* for S Maria delle Grazie, Arezzo (Arezzo, Gal. & Mus. Med. & Mod.). In this painting Neri returned to traditional schemes. The frames and other carpentry work were provided by Giuliano da Maiano. On 5 June 1457 Neri settled a few financial matters with Stefano d'Antonio Vanni that went back to his father's partnership with him (1426–34). On 8 November 1457 he was commissioned by Giovanni Spinellini, at the suggestion of the Florentine Cathedral authorities, to produce a *Virgin and Saints* for S Sisto, Viterbo (*in situ*). The finished altarpiece was delivered on 28 July 1459.

On 3 June 1458, commissioned by Antonio di Berto Cardini, Neri began to fresco a chapel in S Francesco, Pescia (*in situ*). He painted four saints on the wall, an epigraph and a wooden crucifix carved by Giuliano da Maiano. This is considered one of the most interesting and noteworthy of the painter's works, precisely because of its composite nature. On 19 October 1458 Giusto d'Andrea arrived in the workshop and remained intermittently until 6 February 1461. Francesco Botticini was taken on as a pupil on 22 October 1459 and left the workshop on 24 July 1460. The workload continued to increase and on 22 November 1458 Neri rented a second workshop at the Porta Rossa in the centre of Florence. A further important project was the fresco depicting scenes from the *Passion* (untraced) in the refectory of the Florentine monastery of S Onofrio, known as di Fuligno. These pictorial cycles were finished on 20 March 1462.

On 25 November 1459 Neri received the commission for an altarpiece depicting the *Coronation of the Virgin with*

Eleven Saints (Florence, Accad.; see fig. 2) for the church of the monastery of S Felice, Piacenza. This work is notable for its monumental composition and for the unusually large number of figures, though it shows very few changes of style. Against the old medieval background Neri placed modern elements, decorative and architectural, borrowed from Fra Filippo Lippi and Domenico Veneziano. Neri's faces are typically immobile, harsh and wooden and the images of the Infant Christ are most often doll-like. Nonetheless, he never lacked commissions. On 6 June 1460 he began an altarpiece, commissioned by Bartolommeo Lenzi, for the church of the Innocenti, depicting the *Coronation of the Virgin with Saints* (Florence, Gal. Osp. Innocenti). In this panel the poses of the figures are freer and there are stylistic references to Andrea del Castagno. On 29 October 1460 Giovanni d'Antonio was taken on as a *garzone* (shop boy) in the workshop, where he remained until 1469. On 4 November 1460 Bernardo di Stefano Rosselli began collaborating with Neri.

The workshop's activity continued at a lively rate. An important *Assumption of the Virgin* (untraced), dated 25 August 1462, was painted for the sacristy of the church of the Hermit, Camáldoli (nr Arezzo), commissioned by the general of the Camaldolensians, Mariotto Allegri. On 19 November Neri painted a wooden crucifix carved by Romualdo di Candeli for the church of S Cristoforo, Strada (*in situ*). On 8 October 1463 Benedetto di Domenico d'Andrea entered the workshop as a pupil, to remain until 1 January 1470. On 10 December 1463 Neri painted an altarpiece depicting the *Virgin and Saints* for Antonio, parish priest of San Miniato, to be sent to the parish church of San Verano, Pèccioli, near Pisa (*in situ*). On 9 January 1464 he began for Agnolo di Neri Vettori an *Annunciation* (Florence, Accad.; see fig. 3) for the church of the monastery of the Càmpora (destr.). On 30 May 1464 he painted for Tanai de' Nerli, a prominent Florentine citizen, an altarpiece depicting *St Felicity and her Seven Sons* (Florence, S Felicita). A fresco with scenes from the *Life of St Benedict* (untraced), painted for the abbot Jacopo in the upper cloister of the Camaldolese Monastery in Florence, was begun on 10 April 1465.

Commissions from important Florentine families continued with, on 17 May 1465, the painting of stone coats of arms in the convent of S Maria del Carmine for Tommaso di Lorenzo Soderini. These are still *in situ*, although the colours have disappeared. On 19 June 1465 Neri and Baldovinetti gave an assessment of the panel depicting *Dante Alighieri Holding a Volume of the 'Divine Comedy'* painted by Domenico di Michelino for Florence Cathedral (*in situ*). On 5 November the contract of another pupil terminated: Giosuè di Santi (1427–84), who had apparently been working with Neri for some time, though the date of his arrival is not known. On 20 January 1466 Neri's nephew Dionigi d'Andrea di Bernardo di Lottino (*b* 1455), the son of his wife Costanza's brother, came to work in the shop. On 10 July Neri was commissioned by a devout lady who lived in the monastery at Candeli to paint a *Coronation of the Virgin* (Cintoia, near Florence, S Bartolo). This was a favourite subject, which he repeated over many years without noticeable variations in composition.

On 6 March 1467 Neri recorded the final episode of a complicated affair. An altarpiece (untraced) was valued for him by Strozzi and Baldovinetti. The panel, begun much earlier in 1438 by Bicci di Lorenzo for Bartolommeo Lapacci, formerly bishop of Cortona and prior of S Romolo, Florence, had been completed by Neri. When the prelate's heirs had difficulty paying for the work, it was deposited with the painter Giovanni d'Antonio and valued again on 17 November by Strozzi and Domenico di Michelino. On 24 November Neri finally received payment from Amedeo, the new prior of S Romolo, and the panel was placed on the altar of the church.

On 7 May 1471 a monumental altarpiece was begun, another *Coronation of the Virgin*, the only one still preserved with its predella and the original frame made by Giuliano da Maiano, for the Camaldolese abbey of S Pietro a Ruoti, in Valdambra near Arezzo. It was finished on 14 October 1472 and placed on the altar on 25 October. On 31 October 1471, commissioned by Tommaso di Lorenzo Soderini, Neri repaired and repainted an earlier polyptych for S Maria del Carmine. Only one section of this remains, a *St Margaret* painted over a *St Frediano* (Cambridge, MA, Fogg). On 27 September 1474 Neri recorded the last surviving painting mentioned in the *Ricordanze*: an altarpiece depicting the *Virgin and Child with Saints* (Radda in Chianti, S Maria al Prato), painted for Mariotto Gondi and Niccolò di Goro di Radda. The carpentry and the frame (untraced) were executed by Zanobi di Domenico. Two other works (untraced) are mentioned in a contract dated 30 January 1475 with Ser Amedeo, procurator of the convent of S Niccolò di Cafaggio (destr.) in the former Via del Cocomero in Florence. One of these two panels was completed on 31 October, the other on 3 November 1475.

The diary ends on 24 April 1475, with a note on the purchase of a piece of cloth for a cloak for Neri's son Bicci. But the latest date, written in the margin, is 18 February 1484, when the painter appointed the notary Ser Domenico Bonsi to act for him in the purchase of a house. An altarpiece with *St Sebastian with SS Bartholomew and Nicholas* (Volterra, Pin. Com.), commissioned by the *contrada* (district) of Prato Marzio, Volterra, and painted for the church of S Marco there, is dated 1478. Another panel depicting the *Virgin and Child with Four Saints* (Siena, Pin. N., formerly at Casole, Valdelsa) is dated 1482.

In 1488 Neri was active in the convent of S Maria, Monticelli, near Florence, where he received (1 April) 8 bushels of grain for painting done there; on 10 May he was paid for a frontal (untraced) depicting the *Legend of St Francis* and the *Building of S Maria degli Angeli*; on 1 November he painted a door panel for Suor Cecilia, the mother superior of the convent. The last information on Neri, then over 70 years old, is dated 14 May 1491 and concerns a valuation he carried out, together with Domenico Ghirlandaio, Filippo di Giuliano (*fl* 1480–91) and Baldovinetti, of the altarpiece painted by his old pupil Botticini for the Compagnia di S Andrea dalla Veste Bianca of the Collegiata of Empoli (*in situ*).

Though active throughout most of the 15th century, Neri remained faithful, at least in content, to the tradition established by his father and grandfather and with his death on 4 January 1492 came also the demise of a workshop that had stood out for over a century for the wealth of its production. He was buried in S Maria del Carmine. Of his four sons and two daughters, none were artists: Neri's mercantile aspirations probably induced his sons to abandon the vocation of their father, grandfather and great-grandfather.

2. STYLE AND PATRONAGE. Neri's work was decorative, two-dimensional and technically accomplished but entirely devoid of inspiration. The compositions, for example his countless *Annunciations* and *Coronations*, are inexpressive and repetitive, and the figure drawing is awkward. Until the 1450s Neri's paintings had a rather unsophisticated but carefully worked freshness. A typical example is the Pisa *Coronation* (Pisa, Mus. N. S Matteo) painted between 1444 and 1452, which teems with figures and lively ornamental motifs. After the 1450s he adopted forms learnt from the artists associated with Renaissance painting, from Fra Filippo Lippi (but with results more obviously reminiscent of Paolo Schiavo) to Fra Angelico and Domenico Veneziano. A certain dryness of outline has been compared with the harsh style of Andrea del Castagno, but this is probably due rather to their shared taste for incisive drawing. Neri's later works were, however, rather tired and repetitive.

Despite shortcomings, Neri's paintings, with their simple and clearly identifiable style, lavishly adorned with gold, azurite and lakes, were keenly sought after throughout his career by the most varied clientele, representing every stratum of society from the ruling class of Florence to the artisans of the Chianti region; from noble families like the Spini, Soderini and Rucellai to small Florentine shopkeepers; from the abbots of powerful religious orders like the Vallombrosans of Santa Trinita and S Pancrazio to ordinary parish priests from the surrounding countryside. This capacity to satisfy the demands and tastes of the most varied patrons is the most outstanding characteristic of Neri as an artist. With the preservation of his *Ricordanze*, it has made him one of the best-known painters of 15th-century Florence, notwithstanding his clearly rather modest artistic talents.

3. THE 'RICORDANZE'. On 10 March 1453 Neri began his *Ricordanze* (Florence, Uffizi, MS. 2), a workshop diary, which is the most extensive surviving original document to record the activity of a 15th-century painter. The 189 sheet volume is almost certainly the fourth such diary kept in the workshop (the MS. is marked with the letter D, and there is reference to a C volume for 1452). Until 24 April 1475 Neri recorded both workshop and family affairs: commissions for paintings, the names and often the profession and social status of patrons, descriptions and dimensions of works, techniques and colours used, the type of carpentry, the style of frames, the scenes depicted in predella panels, and prices. The whole provides an exhaustive account of the activity of a medieval painter's workshop.

While commissions for altarpieces were the most prestigious, the workshop also produced or coloured small panels for private patrons. These were made of wood, gesso, stucco or even marble carved in relief, and some were the work of renowned artists such as Desiderio da Settignano or Luca della Robbia. The diary also mentions the gilding of wooden or metal articles such as chandeliers, torch holders and various items for religious use. They also painted fabrics, frontals and shop signs, relief sculpture in stone, terracotta and gesso, coats of arms, portrait busts and statues. They painted wooden statues carved by artists such as Giuliano da Maiano (who as a carpenter also provided the workshop, between 1455 and 1472, with picture frames) or by the Camaldolese monk Romualdo di Candeli, an obscure sculptor who produced wooden crucifixes of various sizes and other religious articles. Another area of activity was the restoration, adaptation and modernization of paintings from earlier periods.

The diary lists the workshop's paint suppliers by name; usually they were apothecaries, with occasionally a religious organization such as the Compagnia degli Gesuati. Neri also recorded the names of painters and artists with whom he came into contact through his work. These included Fra Filippo Lippi, Desiderio da Settignano, Giuliano da Maiano, Benedetto da Maiano, Maso Finiguerra, Masaccio's brother, known as Scheggia, Domenico di Michelino, Zanobi Strozzi and Alesso Baldovinetti.

The business was carried on in two different locations—the diary mentions one shop in Via S Salvadore in the Oltrarno district and another, more central, at the Porta Rossa, near Piazza della Signoria. The intense, varied work of the organization must have required a considerable number of assistants. 22 pupils were registered by Neri during the period of the *Ricordanze*, but only three of these are well known: Cosimo Rosselli, Giusto d'Andrea and Francesco Botticini. Others, who came and went rather quickly, are mentioned only by their baptismal names. Neri noted the dates when they entered the workshop, the time they remained there, the day they left and the wages they received. He also recorded family affairs: the birth of his children, marriages of relatives, illnesses and epidemics, rentals of houses and lands, harvests of crops and production of wine, oil and firewood. His business transactions, disputes with insolvent customers, investments and loans of money and goods are also documented in the *Ricordanze*, which thus provide a complete and detailed record of a full personal and professional life, diligently registered in the author's laconic lines. An active, versatile personality is revealed; artistic life was only one aspect of Neri's numerous, mainly commercial, interests.

Furthermore, from the minute detail of the painter's day-to-day activity over more than 20 years, a picture emerges of the social environment in which a 16th century Florentine painter worked and the transformations in style and taste that took place in that century. Notwithstanding his failure to keep abreast of artistic developments, the large capacity and high technical standards of the workshop kept Neri's paintings in demand both from the less cultivated classes and the influential ruling groups in the city.

WRITINGS

Ricordanze (1453–75; Florence, Uffizi, MS. 2); ed. B. Santi (Pisa, 1976)

BIBLIOGRAPHY

EARLY SOURCES

G. Vasari: *Vite* (1550; rev. 2/1568); ed. G. Milanesi (1878–85), ii, pp. 58–60 [also contains G. Milanesi: 'Commentario alla vita di Lorenzo Bicci' (1878), pp. 63–8]

F. Baldinucci: *Notizie* (1681–1728); ed. D. M. Manni (1768), iii, pp. 110–21

J. W. Gaye: *Careggio* (1839–40), ii, p. vi

GENERAL

Colnaghi; Thieme–Becker

A. Venturi: *Storia* (1901–40), i, pp. 431–2

R. van Marle: *Italian Schools* (1923–38), x, pp. 523–46

M. Wackernagel: *Der Lebensraum des Künstlers in der florentinischen Renaissance* (Leipzig, 1938)

A. Chastel: *L'arte italiana*, i (Florence, 1962), p. 341

B. Berenson: *Florentine School* (1963), i, pp. 152–8

P. Dal Poggeto: *Arte in Valdelsa dal sec. XII al sec. XVII* (Certaldo, 1963), pp. 54–5

A. Chastel: *I centri del rinascimento: Arte italiana, 1460–1500* (Milan, 1965), p. 72

SPECIALIST STUDIES
'Ricordanze'

G. Poggi: 'Le Ricordanze di Neri di Bicci (1453–1475)', *Il Vasari*, i (1928), pp. 317–38

——: 'Le Ricordanze di Neri di Bicci (1453–1475), *Il Vasari*, iii (1930), pp. 133–53, 222–34

——: 'Le Ricordanze di Neri di Bicci (1453–1475)', *Il Vasari*, iv (1931), pp. 189–202

B. Santi: 'Dalle Ricordanze di Neri di Bicci', *An. Scu. Norm. Sup. Pisa*, n. s. 2, iii/1 (1973), pp. 169–88

Specific works

G. Poggi: 'Della tavola di Francesco di Giovanni Botticini per la Compagnia di S Andrea di Empoli', *Riv. A.*, iii (1905), pp. 258–64

G. Carocci: 'Un dipinto di Neri di Bicci nella chiesa di S Verano a Péccioli (Pisa)', *Illus. Fiorentino*, iii (1906), pp. 31–2

——: 'Un quadro di Neri di Bicci nella chiesa di S Lucia al Borghetto (Tavarnelle)', *Illus. Fiorentino*, iii (1907), pp. 46–7

A. Del Vita: 'La Pinacoteca d'Arezzo', *Rass. A.*, xv (1915), pp. 75–88 (87)

I. Vavasour Elder: 'Alcuni dipinti e oggetti d'arte nei dintorni di Firenze', *Rass. A.*, xvi (1916), pp. 257–64 (259)

F. Tarani: *La Badia di S Pancrazio a Firenze* (Pescia, 1923), p. 54

W. R. V.: 'The Three Archangels by Neri di Bicci', *Bull. Detroit Inst. A.*, viii (1926), pp. 13–16

L. Pescetti: 'La Pinacoteca di Volterra', *Emporium*, lxxi (1930), pp. 208–20 (219)

G. Gronau: 'Das Erzengebild des Neri di Bicci aus der Kirche S Spirito: Kleine wissenschaftliche Beiträge', *Mitt. Ksthist. Inst. Florenz*, iii (1931), pp. 430–34

P. Torriti: *La Pinacoteca nazionale di Siena: I dipinti dal XII al XV secolo* (Genoa, 1977), p. 418

E. Carli: *La Pinacoteca di Volterra* (Pisa, 1980), pp. 42–3

B. Santi: 'Due dipinti recuperati di Neri di Bicci', *Scritti di storia dell'arte in onore di Roberto Salvini* (Florence, 1984), pp. 329–34

A. Paolucci: *La Pinacoteca di Volterra* (Florence, 1989), pp. 131–2

Other

L. Manzoni: *Statuti e matricole dell'arte dei pittori della città di Firenze, Perugia e Siena* (Rome, 1904), p. 130

G. Poggi: 'Neri di Bicci e Giuliano da Maiano', *Riv. A.*, iii (1905), pp. 128–9

A. Colasanti: 'Opere d'arte ignote o poco note', *Boll. A.*, iv (1910), pp. 184–92 (188–9)

R. Longhi: 'Ricerche su Giovanni di Francesco', *Pinacotheca*, i (1928), pp. 34–48 (36., n. 1)

Catalogo della mostra del tesoro di Firenze sacra (Florence, 1933), pp. 73, 121

R. Graves Mather: 'Documents Mostly New Relating to Florentine Painters and Sculptors of the Fifteenth Century', *A. Bull.*, xxx (1948), pp. 20–65 (43–44)

Mostra d'arte sacra della diocesi e della provincia dal sec. XI al XVIII (Arezzo, 1950)

R. Longhi: 'Il Maestro di Pratovecchio', *Paragone*, iii/35 (1952), pp. 10–37 (22, 35)

L. Bartolini Campetti: 'Opere d'arte toscane ignote o poco note', *An. Scu. Norm. Sup. Pisa*, n. s. 1, xxii (1954)

W. Cohn: 'Notizie storiche intorno ad alcune tavole fiorentine del '300 e del '400', *Riv. A.*, xxxi (1956), pp. 41–72

A. M. Maetzke: *Arte nell'Aretino: Recuperi e restauri dal 1968 al 1974* (Florence, 1974), pp. 92–4

——: *Arte nell'Aretino: Dipinti e sculture restaurati dal XIII al XVIII secolo* (Florence, 1979), pp. 48–9

B. Santi: *Tesori d'arte antica a San Miniato* (Genoa, 1979), pp. 79–83

C. Frosinini: 'Il passaggio di gestione in una bottega fiorentina del primo '400: Bicci di Lorenzo e Neri di Bicci', *Ant. Viva*, xxvi/1 (1987), pp. 5–14

——: 'Neri di Bicci', *La pittura in Italia nel quattrocento*, ii (Milan, 1987), pp. 715–16

F. Petrucci: 'La pittura a Firenze nel quattrocento', *La pittura in Italia nel quattrocento*, i (Milan, 1987), p. 291

BRUNO SANTI

Nering, Johann Arnold (*b* Wesel, *bapt* 17 March 1659; *d* Berlin, 21 Oct 1695). German architect and engineer. He first trained as a fortifications engineer at Elector Frederick William of Brandenburg's court in Berlin in 1676 before making a study trip to Italy (1677–9). In 1678 he became an engineer, rising to engineer-colonel in the Brandenburg general staff (1685) and then electoral Director of Works (1691), a position from which he dominated architecture in Berlin until his death. He first worked on waterway locks and fortifications, and then from 1679 he worked continuously at the Berlin Stadtschloss (destr. World War II, ruins removed *c.* 1950). There he completed the Alabastersaal (1681–5), the Orangery (1684) in the pleasure garden, a multi-storey arcaded gallery (1685–90) between the apartments of the Elector and those of his wife, and a two-storey arcade in the palace courtyard. This was fronted by a giant order of half columns in the manner of an ancient peristyle modelled on Bernini's third design (1665) for the Louvre, Paris, and Francesco Borromini's courtyard (begun 1637) of the oratory of S Filippo Neri in Rome. In the 1680s Elector Frederick III of Brandenburg (later Frederick I, King of Prussia) engaged Nering to work on his country palaces, and he built a chapel (1684–5) in Schloss Köpenick, near Berlin, and enlarged (1689–95) Schloss Oranienburg to a three-winged structure with open arcaded gallery. Nering also provided plans (1688) for the construction of Friedrichstadt in Berlin (*see* BERLIN, §I, 2), comprising 300 two-storey houses for the Huguenots on a rectilinear street grid. Other works in Berlin included a number of nobles' palaces in a simple Palladian style, such as the Palais Danckelmann (1689–90; destr. 1886); the first stone bridge, the Lange Brücke (1692–4), linking the old city with the palace district and intended as the site for an equestrian statue of the Great Elector; and the French merchants' hall (1689–90; destr. 1707). At his death Nering was involved with several projects, including a plan for the Arsenal; a country residence in Lietzenburg for the Electress Sophie Charlotte (later Schloss Charlottenburg; *see* BERLIN, §IV, 2); and designs for the Parochialkirche, erected from 1696 by Martin Grünberg (1655–1706) to reduced and altered plans. Nering was overshadowed, however, by Andreas Schlüter and often underrated. He combined French, Palladian and Roman Baroque elements to form his own style. His training enabled him, despite a moderate talent, to create a monumental architecture in a sober classical Baroque style matching the Elector's royal aspirations.

BIBLIOGRAPHY

R. Borrmann: *Die Bau- und Kunstdenkmäler von Berlin* (Berlin, 1893, rev. 1982)

G. Fritsch: *Die Burgkirche zu Königsberg in Preussen und ihre Beziehung zu Holland: Ein Beitrag zur Neringforschung* (Königsberg, 1930)

G. Nehring: *Johann Arnold Nering: Ein preussischer Baumeister* (Essen, 1985)

H. Engel: 'Johann Arnold Nering', *Baumeister, Architekten, Stadtplaner: Biographien zur baulichen Entwicklung Berlins*, ed. W. Ribbe and W. Schäche (Berlin, 1987), pp. 35–46

FRITZ-EUGEN KELLER

Nerio (*fl* Bologna, *c.* 1310–25). Italian illuminator. His signature appears in a Codex of Justinian (Paris, Bib. N., MS. lat. 8491, fol. 4*r*), but he cannot be certainly identified in documents. He was nonetheless the strongest artistic personality of Bolognese illuminators active in the second and early third decades of the 14th century. His work in the choir books of S Domenico, Bologna (detached leaf, Venice, Fond. Cini, 2158.28), places his activity around 1320.

Nerio's style gradually diverged from that of the Master of 1311, named from the *Statuto dei merciai* (Bologna, Mus. Civ. Med., MS. 631) of that year, an illuminator who collaborated with Jacopino da Reggio on a copy of Gratian's *Decretals* (Rome, Vatican, Bib. Apostolica, MS. lat. 1375). Nerio's earliest works were also copies of this text (Florence, Bib. N. Cent., MS. Magliabechiano XXXI.22; and another in the Regional Library, České Budějovice, Krajská Knihovna). He used the same designs, painted with sharply outlined zones of colour, as the Master of 1311, but he increasingly accentuated the three-dimensional rendering of the figures. Such a development inevitably suggests acquaintance with the work of Giotto, although this is often elusive, as if Nerio's art developed in parallel with that of Giotto rather than being derived from it. His use of pale colours suggests, however, that he was familiar with Giotto's frescoes in the Arena Chapel, Padua, especially the *Story of Joachim and Anna* (cf. the detached miniature in London, BL, Add. MS. 32058, fol. 2*r*; and, if it can be attributed to Nerio, the *Libro di multi belli miraculi e de li vicii*, London, BL, Add. MS. 22557).

Many of the small illuminations of the Paris Justinian show an interest in the Antique, seen in the costumes, possibly derived from Byzantine sources, and in such subjects as *Venus and Cupid* (fol. 170*v*). The iconography of some of the Gospel scenes also suggests that Nerio was a cultured artist. A few detached miniatures (London, V&A, MSS 876–8: 9024 C, D, F; MS. 883: 9035 E) can be dated *c.* 1320, while those in Munich (Staatl. Graph. Samml., 40093–6) appear to be slightly earlier.

BIBLIOGRAPHY

A. Conti: *La miniatura bolognese: Scuole e botteghe* (Bologna, 1981), pp. 58–60, 63–5, 73

F. Avril and M.-T. Gousset: *Manuscrits enluminés d'origine italienne*, ii, Paris, Bib. N. cat. (Paris, 1984), pp. 114–15

Die italienische Miniaturen des 13.–16. Jahrhunderts (exh. cat. by U. Bauer-Eberhardt, Munich, Staatl. Graph. Samml., 1984), pp. 69–72

ALESSANDRO CONTI

Nerio, Andrea di. See ANDREA DI NERIO.

Nerio, Ugolino di. See UGOLINO DI NERIO.

Nerli, G(irolamo) P(ieri) B(allati), Marchese (*b* Siena, 21 Feb 1860; *d* Nervi, 24 June 1926 or Siena, 11 March 1947). Italian painter, active in Australia and New Zealand. He studied in Florence at the Accademia di Belle Arti under Antonio Ciseri and Giovanni Muzziolo (1854–94). He also responded to the art of the Scapigliati group and the Macchiaioli. In 1885 he travelled to Australia, where he worked and exhibited in Melbourne and Sydney. He met leading Australian artists including Charles Conder, whose early paintings share affinities with his style. Nerli exhibited portraits and figure compositions, though his reputation rests on small-scale sketches of contemporary subjects in and around Sydney and Melbourne; these are painted in a fluid impressionistic manner, such as the *Beach at Port Melbourne from the Foreshore, St Kilda* (*c.* 1888; Melbourne, N.G. Victoria). In 1892 Nerli visited Samoa, where he painted several portraits of the Scottish writer Robert Louis Stevenson (e.g. Edinburgh, N.G.; New Haven, CT, Yale U., Beinecke Lib.). Nerli went to New Zealand in 1889 to exhibit works at the Dunedin *South Seas Exhibition*. He returned to Dunedin in 1893, setting up a studio and taking private pupils. In 1895 he was appointed teacher of painting at the Dunedin School of Art. Among his pupils was Frances Hodgkins. Nerli had an important influence on Australian and New Zealand art through the introduction of modern subjects, *plein-air* figure and landscape painting and Impressionist technique. He moved to London in 1904 and spent his last years at the Villa Durallo at Nervi, where he died according to one of the two death certificates that exist. His work is represented in the major public collections in Australia and New Zealand.

BIBLIOGRAPHY
B. Currie: 'Signor Nerli', *A. & Australia*, xvi (1978), pp. 55–60
Nerli: An Exhibition of Paintings and Drawings (exh. cat. by M. Dunn, R. Collins and P. Entwisle, Dunedin, NZ, Pub. A.G., 1988), p. 185

MICHAEL DUNN

Nero [Nero Claudius Drusus Germanicus Caesar] (*b* Antium [now Anzio], 15 Dec AD 37; *reg* AD 54–68; *d* Rome, 9 June AD 68). Roman emperor and patron. His influence on Roman architecture was profound, despite his premature death from suicide. In AD 59 he completed the Circus of Caligula in the valley of the Vatican, in which he introduced Greek games (the Ludi Juvenales) to Rome. The Baths of Nero (AD 62–4), built to the west of Agrippa's Pantheon, stunned his contemporaries by their splendour. As restored by Alexander Severus (AD 227), the baths comprised a symmetrical building with an adjoining gymnasium, but it is impossible to say whether its Neronian form anticipated the great Imperial *thermae* (*see* ROME, ANCIENT, §II, 1(i)(d)). The Emperor was blamed for a fire that broke out during the night of 18 July AD 64 and destroyed many parts of the city, not only because of the many crimes he had committed, but also because of the grandiose works he had undertaken for the renewal of the city. Although Nero's direct responsibility for the fire remains doubtful, the city was in fact rebuilt to his taste. New building standards were adopted to prevent the repetition of such vast fires, including the restriction of the height of buildings to 70 feet (*c.* 21.35 m), and the replacement of the narrow, winding alleys of the old town by regular, broad streets.

To replace the imperial palace on the Palatine—the Domus Transitoria which the fire had destroyed when it was still incomplete—Nero began the Domus Aurea, an enormous complex of buildings that was to extend from the Caelian to the Esquiline (*see* ROME, §V, 5 and ROME,

ANCIENT, fig. 27). It was designed on the lines of a country villa, with thermal baths, porticos, nymphaea, tempietti and other purely scenographic architectural features. The palace incorporated ingenious mechanical arrangements worked out by the architects SEVERUS AND CELER, including ceilings that scattered perfumes and flowers, and a great banqueting hall with a revolving vault or ceiling. The building was not yet finished when Vespasian (*reg* AD 69–79) drained the lake that lay at the centre of the complex and built the Colosseum in its place. Most of the palace was destroyed by fire (AD 104), although the Baths of Trajan (AD 109) incorporated some decorative elements in its foundations.

BIBLIOGRAPHY
N. Dacos: *La Découverte de la Domus Aurea et la formation des grotesques à la Renaissance* (London, 1969)
M. T. Griffin: *Nero: The End of a Dynasty* (London, 1984)

LUCA LEONCINI

Neroccio de' Landi. *See* LANDI, NEROCCIO DE'.

Neroni, Bartolommeo (di Sebastiano) [il Riccio] (*b* ?Siena, 1505–15; *d* before 12 July 1571). Italian painter, illuminator, architect, stage designer and engineer. His earliest surviving documented works, illuminations for an Antiphonal, signed and dated 1531–2 (ex-Olivetan convent, Finalpia; Genoa, Bib. Berio), suggest training with Sodoma, but he seems to have been drawn relatively quickly into the orbit of other influential painters in Siena, such as Domenico Beccafumi and Baldassare Peruzzi, the latter having returned there after the Sack of Rome (1527). Although he shows an affinity with all three at one time or another, the breadth of Neroni's activities, from painting to engineering and especially his architectural work, most closely resembles Peruzzi's career, and Vasari describes him as a follower of Peruzzi.

Neroni's first independent large-scale commission, in which he was strongly influenced by Sodoma, is the fresco depicting the *Departure of SS Maurus and Placid*, executed in 1534 for the cloister of the convent of Monte Oliveto Maggiore. In the same year he was also commissioned to decorate the chapel of the master masons in the cathedral, Siena. Fragments of the fresco survive, notably scenes depicting the *Martyrdom of the Four Crowned Martyrs* (Siena, Mus. Opera Duomo). The design of the chapel is based on Peruzzi's frescoes (1516) in the Ponzetti Chapel, S Maria della Pace, Rome, and the figure style reflects aspects of Sodoma, Beccafumi and Peruzzi. The figures have the sharp-nosed features of those of Beccafumi, the eyes are soft and limpid as in Sodoma's figures, and the bodies and full, monumental spatial composition recall Peruzzi's work. In later works the links with Sodoma are strengthened. In the *Lamentation at the Cross* (Siena, Col. Chigi–Saraceni), executed (1537–9) for the Compagnia di S Giovanni Battista della Morte, the dark tonalities and fleshy, solid figures mark a turning away from Peruzzi's style. The *Coronation of the Virgin* (Siena, Pin. N.), possibly dating from the mid-1540s, also strongly reveals the influence of Sodoma in the twisting figures and the dark tonality. Another example of Sodoma's influence can be seen in the *Dead Christ* (1554–6; Siena, Col. Monte dei Paschi). Neroni's artistic relationship to Sodoma was probably reinforced by his marriage to Sodoma's daughter in 1542. He is also cited as Sodoma's heir. Nonetheless, elements emerge to recall the work of Beccafumi, as in the Fondi tomb frescoes (1547–8) in the Capella Azzoni for the church of S Agostino, Siena.

Neroni is recorded as providing *apparati* (temporary architectural decorations) for the entry of Pope Paul III into Siena (1538, 1540). His name is associated with several buildings in Siena. He may have been responsible for designing the Palazzo Chigi alla Postierla (?1548), with its rusticated quoining, and for completing the Palazzo Tantucci alla Dogana (1548–9). In 1554–6 he built the Conservatorio delle Derelitte. The relatively plain, brick panelled façade with stark pilasters recalls Peruzzi. The garden façade of the Palazzo Guglielmi nel Casato, Siena, its storeys linked by giant pilasters, recalls Peruzzi's façade for the Villa Farnesina, Rome. In 1560 he designed a stage set (untraced) for the Teatro degli Intronati, Siena. From the end of 1552 until the surrender of Siena to Florence in 1555, Neroni was active building fortifications and making military models and drawings (destr.). He is documented working at Sinalunga, Chiusi and Massa Marittima (1552) and Monterotondo Marittima and Chiusdino (1553). In January 1555 he was forced to move from his workshop so that a guard house could be built there. After the fall of the Republic he went to Lucca, where he taught drawing and perspective and military architecture. He returned to Siena definitively in 1568.

A collection of drawings by Neroni (Siena, Bib. Com. Intronati, S. IV. 6), consisting largely of machines, mills, pumps and siphons, are largely copied from the earlier Sienese engineers Mariano Taccola and Francesco di Giorgio Martini. Copies after military drawings by Francesco di Giorgio (Turin, Bib. Reale, MS. Ser. Mil. 238) have been attributed to Neroni. Whether his interest in these matters was spontaneous or the result of a commission is not known. Neroni's last years were relatively difficult. Designs for the lectern and choir-stalls to be executed in wood in the cathedral, Siena, date from 1567, but Neroni had to take his claim for salary to court. He was responsible for the bishop's chair (1567), and a wooden lectern behind the main altar was designed by him. Designs for these works are in the Museo dell'Opera del Duomo, Siena. Through ill-health he was forced to renounce commissions as early as 1567. Among the artists who worked for him at various times are Girolamo Mazzei, Crescenzio Gambarelli, Tiberio Billo (*fl* 1574), Michelangelo d'Antonio Anselmi and, possibly, Bartolommeo di Francesco Almi. Almost all his work is located in Siena and on Sienese territory.

UNPUBLISHED SOURCES

Siena, Bib. Com. Intronati, MS. L.II.6 [E. Romagnoli: *Biografia cronologica de' bellartisti senesi dal secolo XII a tutto il XVIII*, vii [before 1835]], pp. 711–805

BIBLIOGRAPHY

Thieme–Becker

P. Torriti: *Le miniature antifonali di Finalpia* (Genoa, 1953)

F. Secchi-Tarugi: 'Aspetti del manierismo nell'architettura senese del cinquecento', *Palladio*, xvi (1966), pp. 103–30

A. Cornice: *Indagine per un catalogo dell'opera di Riccio* (diss., U. Genoa, 1973–4)

P. A. Riedl: *Das Fondi-Grabmal in S Agostino zu Siena* (Heidelberg, 1979)

A. Cornice: 'Bartolommeo Neroni', *L'arte a Siena sotto i Medici, 1555–1609* (Rome, 1980), pp. 27–47

F. S. Santoro, ed.: *Da Sodoma a Marco Pino* (Siena, 1988), pp. 147–69

G. Scaglia: *Francesco di Giorgio: Checklist and History of Manuscripts and Drawings in Autographs and Copies from c. 1470 to 1687 and Renewed Copies, 1764–1839* (Bethlehem, PA, 1992)

NICHOLAS ADAMS

Nervi, Pier Luigi (*b* Sondrio, 21 June 1891; *d* Rome, 9 Jan 1979). Italian architect and engineer. He graduated in civil engineering from the University of Bologna in 1913. Before and after serving in World War I, he worked for the Società per Construzione Cimentizia (SCC) in Bologna, subsequently going into practice in Rome, as a partner initially in Nervi and Nebbiosi (1923–32) and then with Nervi and Bartolia, until 1960, when with his three sons, Antonio, Vittorio and Mario, he set up Studio Nervi. He first achieved wide acclaim for the Berta Municipal Stadium (won in competition, 1929; completed 1932) in Florence. It was praised internationally not only as a feat of engineering but also for its design and economy, and the building demonstrated his ability to integrate function with abstract sculptural form, for example in the elegant interlaced helical supports of the external staircases. Between 1935 and 1942, again through winning a competition, Nervi designed a series of aircraft hangars for the Italian air force, the first of which at Orvieto (1938) determined their form: long pointed barrel vaults, constructed on latticed grids of light crossing members, rising from complex triangulated edge-beams. The various sized ribs were prefabricated from reinforced concrete rather than pouring them in place. In these hangars Nervi produced the first version of his diamond-patterned lamella vault. When the German army destroyed the hangars (1944) during their retreat in World War II, most of the joints where the ribs crossed remained intact.

During the early 1940s Nervi invented *ferro-cimento*, a fine cement mix on meshes of small-section steel, to enable him to precast thin (and therefore light) bent or folded membranes, thus providing intrinsic strength through shape rather than mass. Prefabricated in the factory or on the ground, such units could be made to a high level of accuracy. This is the principle on which the two exhibition halls (1947–9) in Valentino Park, Turin, often considered his finest work, were executed. For Salon B with a span of 100 m, bent shells with window-openings and stiffeners were precast and laid on shuttering along the lines of great segment arches, which together formed the corrugated vault, their ends joined *in situ*. Once set, the *ferro-cimento* arches themselves were used as shuttering for concrete ribs in the troughs and peaks of the corrugations formed by the units. The arched shells of the vault were collected into triple fan-shaped groups (using tapered, as opposed to parallel-sided precast units) on to buttress columns, which transmit the load (following the line of the vault) to the ground. Despite a misunderstanding during construction that limits the spatial effect of the apse between the two halls (for the second of which, Salon C, Nervi used the diamond grid pattern of the aircraft hangars), they remain a major engineering achievement. The methods were applied to circular as well as rectangular buildings such as the Kursaal Casino Restaurant (1950; with Attilio la Padula) at Ostia and the main hall of Chianciano Terme (1952; with Mario Loreti and Mario Marchi).

Pier Luigi Nervi (with Annibale Vitellozzi): Palazzetto dello Sport, Rome, 1957

It was during the period 1953 to 1955 that Nervi developed reusable moulds for ferroconcrete to speed up construction of buildings in which repetitive units could be easily cast *in situ*. Examples include the GATTI Wool Factory (1953) in Rome, whose ceiling was cast one bay at a time with the moulds poured, then lowered, moved on and reused, and the Fiat Factory (1955), Turin. Also in the 1950s he developed the technique of hydraulic pre-stressing, used to lighten the supports for many of the major buildings that followed. These include two sports halls for the Olympics of the 1960s in Rome, which became international prototypes. The saucer dome of the Palazzetto dello Sport (1957; with Annibale Vitellozzi; see fig.), *c.* 60 m in diameter, is supported by an interlaced lattice of beams, precast to form a filigree overlapping petal pattern, apparently growing from the central compression ring. The points of the petals are collected into a series of fans like folded paper at the perimeter. The dome, in the shape of an upturned shell, appears to be floating, secured to the ground only by the 'guy-ropes' of its struts. The saucer dome of the larger Palazzo dello Sport (1959; with Marcello Piacentini), 100 m in diameter, has radial ribs but is less impressive externally, surrounded as it is by a glazed walkway supported by conventional though slender columns.

Among many examples of Nervi's designs for other buildings the Pirelli Tower (1956–8; with Gio Ponti and others; for illustration *see* PONTI, GIO), Milan, is outstanding. Massive treelike columns reach through the building, reducing in diameter in proportion to the superimposed load, supporting wholly cantilevered floors to free the perimeter and displaying the insubstantial curtain of the external walls.

He collaborated with Marcel Breuer and Bernard Zehrfuss from 1953 to 1958 on the UNESCO headquarters in Paris. Nervi's structural ideas are at once evident in the folded slab roof of reinforced concrete in the auditorium building, the entrance canopy and the piloti on which the main block is supported. In the 1960s Nervi contributed to the design of the floor system of Australia Square (1961–7) in Sydney by Harry Seidler. With his son Antonio Nervi, he designed the fan-shaped Papal Audience Hall (completed 1971) for the Vatican. It is independent of columns, emphasizing the sculptural plastic quality of poured concrete and developing further the technique used in the exhibition halls in Turin.

WRITINGS

Aesthetics and Technology in Building: The Charles Eliot Norton Lectures, 1961–1962 (Cambridge, MA, 1965)

BIBLIOGRAPHY

G. C. Argan: *Pier Luigi Nervi* (Milan, 1955)
The Works of Pier Luigi Nervi (London, 1957)
A. L. Huxtable: *Pier Luigi Nervi* (New York, 1960)
A. Pico: *Pier Luigi Nervi* (Rome, 1969)
S. Musmeci: 'Pier Luigi Nervi's Legacy', *The Architect*, iv/4 (1980), pp. 13–17
A. Kato and others: 'Pier Luigi Nervi', *Process: Archit.*, xxxiii (1981) [special issue]
F. Z. L. de Irizarry: *Work and Life of Pier Luigi Nervi: Architect* (Monticello, IL, 1984)

ELIZABETH MITCHELL WALTER

Nervo, Roberto Montenegro. *See* MONTENEGRO, ROBERTO.

Nery, Ismael (*b* Belém do Pará, 9 Oct 1900; *d* Rio de Janeiro, 6 April 1934). Brazilian draughtsman and painter. He went to Rio de Janeiro in 1909 and enrolled in the Escola Nacional de Belas Artes in 1915. In 1920 he made his first trip to Europe, completing his studies at the Académie Julian in Paris. On his return to Brazil in 1921 he worked as a technical draughtsman in the Patrimônio

Nacional architecture and topography section of the Treasury. In 1922 he married Adalgisa Noel Ferreira, who was to become known as the poet and novelist Adalgisa Nery. On his second trip to Europe between 1927 and 1928 he discovered the work of the Surrealists and of Chagall. Nery was already steeped in his own Thomist-based philosophical-religious doctrine, which his close friend the poet Murilo Mendes called *essencialismo*. He used that and Surrealist themes such as dream and nightmare, spirit and flesh to create an artistic vocabulary that he expressed in painting, poetry and, more freely, in drawing. His images centre on the human body, especially that of the artist himself (e.g. *Self-portrait*, U. São Paulo, Inst. Estud. Bras.), in an obsessive play of masks and mirrors, revealing a search for identity. Recurrent themes in works such as *Standing Figure* (*c.* 1927–8; U. São Paulo, Mus. A. Contemp.) are a fusion of I and the Other, the attraction of the Double, a joining of masculine and feminine, and Adam and Eve united in love and death. He also painted portraits such as that of *Adalgisa* (Campos do Jordão, Pal. Boa Vista). He died from tuberculosis and received recognition only with the 1966 retrospective organized by the Petite Galerie, Rio de Janeiro.

BIBLIOGRAPHY
M. de Andrade: 'Ismael Nery', *Diário nacional* [São Paulo] (10 April 1928)
M. Mendes: 'Recordação de Ismael Nery', *O estado de São Paulo* (1 July 1948–22 Jan 1949) [series of articles]
A. Nery: *A imaginária* (Rio de Janeiro, 1959)
Ismael Nery (exh. cat., intro. A. Bento; Rio de Janeiro, Petite Gal., 1966)
A. Bento: *Ismael Nery* (São Paulo, 1973)
J. Klintowitz: *Mestres do desenho brasileiro* (São Paulo, 1983)
Ismael Nery: 50 anos depois (exh. cat., ed. A. Amaral; U. São Paulo, Mus. A. Contemp., 1984)

ROBERTO PONTUAL

Nesch, (Emil) Rolf [Rudolf] (*b* Ober-Esslingen, Württemberg, 7 Jan 1893; *d* Oslo, 27 Oct 1975). Norwegian painter and graphic artist of German birth. He studied with the decorative painter, Hagenmeyer, in Heidenheim in 1907 and attended the Kunst- und Gewerbeschule in Stuttgart between 1908 and 1912. He decided to become a painter in 1912 and went to Dresden, where he came into contact with works by members of Die Brücke and studied at the Kunstakademi for two periods (1912–14 and 1920–23). He was sent to the front before finishing his studies. After World War I he travelled and visited Ernst Ludwig Kirchner in Davos in 1924. Kirchner's influence on him resulted in appreciably more expressive paintings, drawings and prints at that time. As early as 1925 Nesch began experimenting with odd juxtapositions of unconventionally handled printing techniques, as in *Café Vaterland* (1926; Oslo, N.G.), which he later developed, notably, into his *Metallgrafikk*—COLLAGRAPH prints produced by laying different objects, including metal pieces, on to the plate (see below). Nesch moved to Hamburg, where he became one of the leading figures in the Secession. At this time Nesch developed, together with Karl Ballmer, a painting technique (*pulverteknikk*) that involved sprinkling dry pigment in several layers on to a lacquered surface with fixative between each layer, into which the image was scratched. In these paintings there is a tension between the hazy colouring of the dry planes and the signlike forms. Like most of his colleagues, Nesch was also inspired by Edvard Munch and late

Expressionism in Hamburg. With the series of 24 etchings of *Karl Muck and his Orchestra* (1931; Oslo, N.G.) he was established as an unusually gifted printmaker. These black-and-white prints, for which he used drypoint and etching techniques, among others, present compositions in which music and musicians are united rhythmically (for further illustration *see* ETCHING, fig. 7).

When the political situation in Germany became intolerable, Nesch decided to move to Norway in 1933, mainly attracted by the association with Edvard Munch. Initially, as a German and a non-traditional artist, he was met with reserve in Oslo. Living in poverty, he was able to remain in Norway only with support from the patron Rolf Stenersen (1899–1978). During the German occupation of Norway he became permanently disabled, the result of an injury that was probably self-inflicted in order to avoid German military service. Nesch continued to experiment in his new homeland and also produced a number of sculptures: fetish-like figures in different materials, such as *Attila* (1939–40; Oslo, N.G.). His first *Materialbilder* ('material pictures'), such as *Music* (1934–5; Oslo, Konserthuset), were related to the earlier printing plates from the beginning of the 1930s. They were also evidently inspired by *Jugendstil*, African masks and, later on, by Norwegian folk art. He welded or glued to the picture surface anything he came across, including metal netting, pieces of wood and coloured glass. Most of the subjects were allegorical stories, impressions of nature or romantic themes developed through a partly abstracted figuration, for example *Girl with a Bird* (1939; Oslo, N.G.) and the autobiographical and symbolic *St Sebastian* (1941–3; Stuttgart, Gal. Stadt). Nesch's use of *objets trouvés* is reminiscent of Kurt Schwitters's *Merzbilder*: Schwitters was also an exile in Norway, between 1937 and 1940.

Nesch did not paint in Norway but experimented in printmaking techniques. Two series of prints record his experiences in the fishing grounds off the Lofoten Islands in northern Norway (1936; 11 out of 20 prints in Oslo, Kommunes Kstsaml.) and off western Norway, in 1936 and 1938; they re-create the arduousness and intensity of life at sea. Both series were made from collage-like accretions on the plate of etched, drilled, punched and some loose and colour-coated metal pieces, which produced relief-embossed 'monotypes' or collagraphs. This particular technique had been developed in 1932 for the series of the *Bridges of Hamburg* (12 of 20 in Oslo, N.G.). The variety of textures, the economically delineated but striking figures and the emotive use of colour in these collagraphs increase their decorative effect. The fishing theme again emerged in the enormous *Materialbilder* depicting the *Herring Fishery* (33 sq. m, begun 1939, installed 1956; Oslo, Indust. & Eksportens Hus).

Nesch's marriage to the actress Ragnhild Hald in 1949, an entrée into the theatrical world, provided further stimulus: Nesch's sense of humour and love of experiment can be seen in, for example, the coloured collagraph *Come In!* (1949; Oslo, N.G.) and the *Ringgrafikk* entitled *Vikings* (1953; Oslo, N.G.), made using concentrically grooved plates. His reputation continued to spread in Norway and abroad as he experimented more widely in prints and mixed-media works. He represented Norway at two Biennales, in Venice (1962) and in São Paulo

(1973). His last works were decorative, free reflections on the themes of fish and birds, his handling of these subjects showing a certain similarity to the drawings he had made in Hagenbeck's zoological garden in Hamburg 40 years earlier, with an emphasis on recognizable form and movement (e.g. from the series *To Fly, Bird*, 1969; Oslo, N.G.). He had an appreciable influence on his Norwegian contemporaries, notably on Sigurd Winge (*b* 1909) and Olav Strømme, artists who were close friends, with whom he had travelled and worked from his first years in Norway. To mark the centenary of his birth, a gallery was opened in Kulturhuset in Ål, where Nesch lived from 1951 until his death. The gallery has his name and shows works from his estate. At the same time exhibitions were held both in Norway (Oslo, N. Gal.; Svolvær, Faste Gal.) and in Germany (Schleswig, Schleswig-Holstein. Landesmus.; Esslingen, Gal. Stadt; Heidenheim, Kstmus.).

See also ETCHING, fig. 7.

WRITINGS
Zeugnisse eines ungewöhnlichen Künstlerlebens in turbulenter Zeit, ed. M. Bruhns (Gifkendorf, 1993) [incl. corr. with German friends after 1922]

BIBLIOGRAPHY
NKL
A. Hentzen: *Rolf Nesch: Graphik, Materialbilder, Plastik* (Stuttgart, 1960)
J. Askeland: *Rolf Nesch: Alkymisten* (Oslo, 1969)
The Graphic Art of Rolf Nesch (exh. cat. by J. Askeland and others, Detroit, MI, Inst. A., 1969)
J. Askeland: *Lofot-serien av Rolf Nesch* (Oslo, 1976)
S. Helliesen: *Med Rolf Nesch på teaterturné til Finnmark* [With Rolf Nesch on a theatrical tour to Finnmark] (Oslo, 1976)
E. H. Hjelle, ed.: *Rolf Nesch: Karl Muck og hans orkester* (Oslo, 1977)
S. Helliesen: *R. Nesch's grafiske verker*, Oslo, N.G. cat. (Oslo, in preparation)

SUSANNE RAJKA

Nesebŭr [Nesebŭr; anc. Mesembria]. Town situated on a peninsula on the Bulgarian Black Sea coast. It was founded by Greek colonists from Megara in the late 6th century BC, and it remained an important city and naval base until the Turkish conquest in the 15th century AD. Its ancient name of Mesembria suggests that it had originally been a Thracian fortification (*bria*) of a local king called Mesa, but after the foundation of the Greek colony it developed, particularly in the 3rd and 2nd centuries BC, into a major port and trading centre. As early as the 4th century BC Mesembria's coins were circulating widely throughout the Thracian interior and even beyond the Danube in Dacia. The city was at war with its neighbour Apollonia Pontica (now Sozopol in Bulgaria) during the first half of the 2nd century BC, was briefly captured by the Dacians in the second half of the 1st century BC and was included in the Roman province of Thrace from AD 46. It flourished during the 2nd century AD and was able to survive the Gothic invasions of the 4th and 5th centuries thanks to its naturally strong defensive location. Unlike the coastal cities further north, Mesembria survived the Slav and Avar invasions of the 6th and 7th centuries and was retained as a naval base by the Byzantines until the 14th century apart from brief occupations by the Bulgarians in 812–c. 864, 1308–23, 1328–31 and 1333–66.

The Roman and Byzantine fortifications, which command the narrow approach to the main peninsula, replaced earlier Hellenistic defences and survive, in part, to a height of 6 m. Although the museum contains some architectural and sculptural fragments of Hellenistic and Roman date, Nesebŭr's historic past is largely represented by its fine collection of early Christian and Byzantine churches. Among the earlier of these is the 'Old Metropolis', which was probably built in the late 5th century; its plan closely resembles that of St John Stoudios in Constantinople (*see* ISTANBUL, §III, 6) and like that basilica probably originally had colonnades separating nave and aisles and a gallery over narthex and aisles. Although now roofless, the church still stands to its full height. Its surviving internal arrangements probably date to the early 6th century: massive *opus mixtum* piers divide the nave from the aisles, which have galleries above them with arches almost as large as those below. Little of the atrium survives, but the single apse at the east end retains its *synthronon*. The 'Sea Basilica' on the northern edge of the peninsula is built of ashlar blocks with a three-sided apse and a tripartite narthex; its marble architectural decoration contains bricks stamped with the name of Justinian. The Byzantine churches include the cross-in-square church of St John the Baptist (10th or 11th century) and the 14th-century churches of St John Aleitourgetos, the Pantokrator, St Theodore, St Paraskeva and SS Michael and Gabriel, whose exterior brick-patterned decorations are related to the Palaiologan monuments of Constantinople (now Istanbul) and Thessaloniki. As a 'museum town' Nesebŭr also boasts numerous restored timber houses of the 19th century and early 20th.

BIBLIOGRAPHY
T. Ivanov and V. Velkov, eds: *Nessèbre*, 2 vols (Sofia, 1969–80) [Ivanov (i); Velkov (ii)]
R. Hoddinott: *Bulgaria in Antiquity* (London, 1975)

ANDREW POULTER

Nesfield. English family of artists. (1) William Andrews Nesfield was a prominent garden designer in the mid-19th century, specializing in decorative parterre gardens for country-house terraces and lawns. One of his sons, (2) William Eden Nesfield, trained as an architect and was largely responsible for developing the Queen Anne Revival style in the late 1860s. Another son, Markham Nesfield (*b c.* 1842; *d* London, 1874), followed his father's profession; during his brief career he laid out the Italian garden at Regent's Park, London, as well as gardens at Doddington Place (Kent), Glanusk Park (Powys) and elsewhere.

(1) William Andrews Nesfield (*b* Chester-le-Street, Co. Durham, 19 Feb 1794; *d* London, 2 March 1881). Painter and garden designer. Educated at Trinity College, Cambridge University, he served in the army from 1809 to 1816, both in Spain during the Peninsular War and in Canada during the War of 1812, retiring as a lieutenant. He then took up watercolour painting with some success, exhibiting at the Old Water-Colour Society, London, between 1823 and 1851. His works, mainly landscapes (examples London, BM, V&A, and elsewhere), were the result of numerous tours, particularly in Wales, Scotland and Yorkshire. John Ruskin was among his admirers. Following the marriage of a sister in 1826 to the architect Anthony Salvin, Nesfield turned to garden design, establishing himself as one of the most influential practitioners of the mid-Victorian era. For his collaborative work with Salvin at several country houses, as well as with various other architects, including Edward Blore and Charles

Barry, Nesfield revived the fashion for *parterres de broderie*, a principal feature of 16th- and 17th-century gardening. Formed out of low box hedging and coloured gravels, they were seen as particularly appropriate for new houses built in the style of the Elizabethan or Jacobean Revival, such as Blore's Worsley Hall (1837–43, destr.), Lancs, for which Nesfield borrowed from early 17th-century French Baroque patterns. He also used such schemes for the garden terraces of houses built at other times and in different styles, including William Kent's Palladian-style Holkham Hall (begun 1734), Norfolk, where in the 1850s matching parterres were laid out around the newly acquired St George and the Dragon fountain by Charles R. Smith (1798–1888). Massive sculptural groups provided the central focus for several of Nesfield's other gardens, particularly in the 1860s, including the Atlas fountain at Castle Howard, N. Yorks—originally made by John Thomas for the Great Exhibition, London, in 1851—and *Perseus Saving Andromeda* by James Forsyth (1827–1910) in the gardens at Witley Court, Hereford & Worcs (house destr.). Nesfield's greatest undertaking, the arcaded and canalized gardens (*c.* 1861, destr.) at the Royal Horticultural Society's premises in South Kensington, London, was compromised and unpopular. Successful surviving examples of his work on a more modest scale include the maze he laid out at Somerleyton Hall (late 1840s), Suffolk, and the diminutive garden, terrace and sculpted basin at Broughton Hall (late 1850s), N. Yorks.

BIBLIOGRAPHY
B. Elliott: *Victorian Gardens* (London, 1986)
I. C. Laurie: 'Nesfield in Cheshire', *Gdn Hist.*, xv (1987), pp. 145–56
C. Ridgway: 'William Andrews Nesfield: Between Uvedale Price and Isambard Kingdom Brunel', *J. Gdn. Hist.*, xiii (1993), pp. 69–89

ROBERT WILLIAMS

(2) W(illiam) E(den) Nesfield (*b* Bath, 2 April 1835; *d* Brighton, 25 March 1888). Architect, designer and painter, son of (1) William Andrews Nesfield. He was educated at Eton College but left to enter the office of William Burn in London in 1851. He worked in turn for J. K. Colling (1815–1905), who may have introduced him to Gothic, and for his uncle, Anthony Salvin. With RICHARD NORMAN SHAW, whom he had met in Burn's office, he studied A. W. N. Pugin's decorative work at the Palace of Westminster and became an enthusiastic supporter of the Gothic Revival. He made a long continental tour in 1857–8, during which he showed eclectic interests and drew the Parthenon in Athens as well as Chartres Cathedral in France. Other trips to France and Italy in 1859–61 provided the material for his illustrated book *Specimens of Medieval Architecture* (1862).

In 1859 Nesfield set up his office in Bedford Row, London. One of his first projects was an unsuccessful entry for the competition for the Manchester Assize Courts, submitted jointly with Shaw in 1859. Otherwise, like many country-house architects, Nesfield was mistrustful of self-advertisement, and family connections made it scarcely necessary to the launching of his career. His first commission, for a canopied tomb in an exaggerated Gothic Revival style to one of Lord Crewe's ancestors in St Bertoline's Barthomley (1856), Cheshire, followed his father's design of the great parterre at Crewe Hall, Cheshire. Most of Nesfield's work before 1865 was for garden

and estate buildings. In 1861 he was commissioned to enlarge Combe Abbey (destr.), Warwicks, for Lord Craven, adding a large exuberant wing, which involved the destruction of part of the old house. This started his career as a specialist in designing country houses. His background and education gave him the assurance to feel at ease with landed clients.

From 1863 until 1876 Nesfield shared offices with Shaw, entering a loose arrangement that was only a formal parnership between 1866 and 1869, though they did not undertake joint commissions. They developed a style of domestic architecture, the OLD ENGLISH STYLE, deriving from their study of old pubs and cottages in Kent and Sussex. This style combined elements of English rural vernacular with Japanese motifs and a striking use of ornament. It was a more flamboyant development of the estate architecture of GEORGE DEVEY. Nesfield was an inventive designer of ornament, sometimes taking a hand in the execution itself, personally incising plasterwork and even sticking in the stumps of green bottles. (Perhaps influenced by Japonisme, he also made highly mannered designs for screens.) Through his brother Markham, Nesfield obtained the commission to design a lodge (1865, destr.) at the end of the long walk in Regent's Park, London. He used the Old English style for lodges and cottages for country houses but did not consider it appropriate for a gentleman's country house. Cloverley Hall, Salop, a large house built in 1865–70 (main block destr.), which has more in common with Nesfield's work at Combe Abbey, has fine detailing in the ironwork, carved stone panels and bricks only 57 mm high, which were laid with razor-sharp mortar joints.

In the late 1860s and during the early 1870s Nesfield's work contributed to the development of the QUEEN ANNE REVIVAL. In 1863 he had drawn plans (not executed) for remodelling Croxteth Hall, near Liverpool, in which the new north front would have continued the style of the existing west front of 1702. This may have alerted him to the possibility of adapting elements of Queen Anne domestic architecture. His aim was to emulate the spirit of the old work rather than to copy it. In 1866 he designed the lodge at Kew Gardens, London, built in red brick in sympathy with the 17th-century Kew Palace, with a steeply pitched roof, dormer windows with segmental pediments and a tall moulded chimney-stack. The building was highly influential in the development of the Queen Anne Revival. Nesfield's first mature exercise in Queen Anne Revival was the lodge (1868) to Kinmel Park, near Abergele, Clwyd, better proportioned and more lavishly decorated than the lodge at Kew, with an incrustation of Japanese discs, which Nesfield and Shaw called pies, probably derived from motifs used in Japanese porcelain and engravings. He had already designed the Kinmel home farm (1866, now Plas Kinmel), and in 1871–4 he remodelled and enlarged the main house (see fig.). The remodelling was inspired by Christopher Wren's work at Hampton Court, which Nesfield visited with the client, H. R. Hughes, in 1868. Kinmel is built of red brick with stone quoins, great sash windows and prominent glazing bars but has a tall slate roof that clearly derives from French 17th-century châteaux. It was devastated by fire in

W. E. Nesfield: Kinmel, Clwyd, 1871–4; remodelling of the earlier house

1976 but has been restored, though with the loss of much of the fine plasterwork inside.

In 1872–4 Nesfield remodelled Bodrhyddan Hall, Clwyd, replacing the original Queen Anne façade with a new façade that has a projecting centre bay, a tall Dutch gable and prominent corbels. In 1872–5 he was commissioned by Murray Tuke to design a bank in Saffron Walden, Essex, in which, as in most of his work, he combines elements of different styles. In a letter to Tuke, he wrote, 'I have tried to imitate that quaint beautiful old house, called, I believe, Nell Gwyn's.' This building, the Nell Gwynne House, Newport, Essex, however, is half-timbered with an overhanging first storey, quite unlike Nesfield's brick bank, with its mullioned windows and frieze of sunflowers.

Nesfield was prone to melancholy, which was exacerbated by overwork, illness and the closely spaced deaths of his father and Salvin. In the second half of the 1870s he undertook fewer commissions. He retired to Brighton, made a late marriage and occupied the few remaining years before his death in 1888 with painting, 'a form of artistic expression for which he believed he was best fitted', according to his obituary in the *Builder*. His effervescent personality of happier years is clear from his letters to his friend Rev. J. F. W. Bullock, for whom he restored and enlarged (1871) the church at Radwinter, near Saffron Walden, Essex, and rebuilt much of the village in 1873–7.

WRITINGS
Specimens of Medieval Architecture (London, 1862)
Letters (Radwinter, 1989) [facs. edn of Nesfield's letters to J. F. W. Bullock]

BIBLIOGRAPHY
Obituary, *Builder*, liv (1888), pp. 225, 229, 244, 269
H. B. Cresswell: 'William Eden Nesfield, 1835–1888: An Impression and a Contrast', *Archit. Rev.*, ii (1897), pp. 23–32
J. Hebb: 'William Eden Nesfield', *RIBA J.*, n. s. 3, x (1903), pp. 396–400
M. Girouard: *The Victorian Country House* (Oxford, 1971)
A. Service, ed.: *Edwardian Architecture and its Origins* (London, 1975)
A. Saint: *Richard Norman Shaw* (New Haven, 1976)
M. Girouard: *Sweetness and Light: The Queen Anne Movement, 1860–1900* (Oxford, 1977)
C. Aslet: 'The Country Houses of W. E. Nesfield', *Country Life*, clxiii (1978), pp. 678–81, 766–9

CLIVE ASLET

Nesiotes. *See under* KRITIOS AND NESIOTES.

Ness, Rupert (*b* Wangen, Allgäu, 24 Nov 1670; *d* Ottobeuren, 20 Oct 1740). German churchman, writer and patron. He entered the Order of St Benedict in 1688 and studied philosophy and theology at Ottobeuren and at the Benedictine university at Salzburg. He was ordained a priest in 1694 and began pastoral work in Tisis, Vorarlberg. His first theological writings date from 1702. Having served as agriculturalist (1703–10) to the abbey of Ottobeuren, he was elected the 52nd abbot of Ottobeuren on 8 May 1710. In 1711 he became regional governor, in 1712 imperial councillor and hereditary chaplain and in 1718 *praeses* (president) of the Benedictine congregation at Salzburg. He is regarded as the second founder of Ottobeuren through his commissioning (1711) of an extensive building programme (*see* OTTOBEUREN), in which the architecture mirrors the mind and faith of its builder, being a synthesis of Benedictine order and freedom, severity and serenity, individual and community, nature and art, worldliness and spirituality. The building marks the flowering of German late Baroque monastery architecture in the prestigious, imperial style. The exact progress of the building of the monastery and its new church can be reconstructed from the 14 surviving volumes of the Abbot's diaries (Ottobeuren, Benedictine abbey; Munich, Bayer. Haupstaatsarchv), which are divided into political, ecclesiastical and economic sections. Portraits of *Rupert Ness* (1723, 1735; both Ottobeuren, Benedictine abbey) were painted by Jakob Karl Stauder.

WRITINGS
Ottobeuren, Benedictine abbey [diaries (13 vols)]
Munich, Bayer. Haupstaatsarchv [diary (one vol., 1740)]

BIBLIOGRAPHY
N. Lieb: 'Abt Rupert Ness von Ottobeuren', *Lebensbilder aus dem Bayerischen Schwaben* (Munich, 1952), pp. 284–321 [bibliog.]
A. Kolb OSB: 'Abt Rupert II. Ness von Ottobeuren und sein Wappen', *Stud. & Mitt. Gesch. Benediktiner-Ordens & Zweige*, lxix (1958), pp. 236–9 [bibliog.]
A. M. Miller: *Abt Rupert Ness: Der Herr mit den drei Ringen* (Freiburg im Breisgau, 1959, Kempten, 4/1977) [novel]
L. Schrott, ed.: *Bayerische Kirchenfürsten* (Munich, 1964), pp. 213–30
R. Raffalt: 'Reichsabtei Ottobeuren', *Europäische Barockklöster*, ed. H. Schindler (Munich, 1972), pp. 159–77
A. Kolb OSB: *Im Einen und Dreieinigen* (Donauwörth, 1978)
K. Bosl: *Bosls Bayerische Biographie: 8000 Persönlichkeiten aus 15 Jahrhunderten* (Regensburg, 1983), p. 547 [bibliog.]
G. M. Lechner OSB: *Das geistliche Porträt: Graphisches Kabinett Göttweig* (Krems, 1986), p. 34, no. 26
H. Pörnbacher: *Die Literatur des Barock*, ii, Bayerische Bibliothek (Munich, 1986), pp. 944–7, 1276

GREGOR M. LECHNER

Nessa. *See* NISA.

Nesterov, Mikhail (Vasil'yevich) (*b* Ufa [now in Bashkirskaya Republic of Russia], 31 May 1862; *d* Moscow, 18 Oct 1942). Russian painter. From 1877 to 1881 and again from 1884 to 1886 he studied at the Moscow School of Painting, Sculpture and Architecture under the Realist painters Vasily Perov and Illarion Pryanishnikov. Between 1881 and 1884 he worked under Pavel Chistyakov (1832–1919) at the Academy of Arts, St Petersburg. At the estate of Savva Mamontov at Abramtsevo he met the most influential painters of the period, then at the epicentre of the development of Russian Art Nouveau. Nesterov sought to combine this style with a deep Orthodox belief; however, in his desire to revive religious art he was influenced more by French Symbolism, particularly by Bastien-Lepage, than by old Russian icon painting. All of Nesterov's canvases are marked by a lyrical synthesis between the figures and their landscape surroundings, as in *Hermit* (1888–9; Moscow, Tret'yakov Gal.), which shows the stooped figure of an old man against a northern landscape of stunted trees and still water. The large oil painting *Vision of Young Bartholomew* (1889–90; Moscow, Tret'yakov Gal.) depicts the legend of the childhood of the Russian saint Sergey of Radonezh. A monk appears to the young Bartholomew (the future St Sergius) and prophesies a glorious future for him. The simplified outlines and muted colours of the Abramtsevo landscape recall the works of the French artist Puvis de Chavannes, which Nesterov saw on a trip to Paris in 1889.

In the 1880s–90s Nesterov executed many wall paintings for churches, for example those that decorated the new church of St Vladimir in Kiev, which had been built in the old Byzantine style in 1882. After 1900 he painted many of the famous figures of his day including the writer *Lev Tolstoy* (1907; Moscow, Tolstoy Mus.) and the physiologist *Ivan Pavlov* (1935; Moscow, Tret'yakov Gal.). Nesterov continued to paint portraits of prominent figures, including the sculptor *Vera Mukhina* (1940; Moscow, Tret'yakov Gal.). Nesterov shows the sculptor at work on a plaster model, which she moulds through her sheer physical energy. The composition, on a diagonal, reinforces the effect of energy and is quite different from that of the portrait of the scientist Pavlov, who is shown in profile in a horizontal format that emphasizes the quiet processes of contemplation. Nesterov's most ambitious and large-scale pre-revolutionary painting was *In Rus'* [The Heart of the People] (1916; Moscow, Tret'yakov Gal.), an attempt to present a generalized image of Russia on the eve of threatening and irreversible changes.

WRITINGS
A. A. Rusakova, ed.: *M. V. Nesterov: Vospominaniya* [M. V. Nesterov: memoirs] (Moscow, 1985)

BIBLIOGRAPHY
A. Mikhaylov: *Mikhail Vasil'yevich Nesterov: Zhizn' i tvorchestvo* [Mikhail Vasil'yevich Nesterov: life and work] (Moscow, 1958)
I. I. Nikonova: *Mikhail Vasil'yevich Nesterov* (Moscow, 1972)
A. Rousakova: *Mikhail Nesterov* (Leningrad, 1990); Eng. and Fr. trans. by A. Bromfield and N. Rogovskaya (Leningrad, 1990)

MARIAN BURLEIGH-MOTLEY

Nestor, Palace of. *See under* PYLOS.

Nestora. *See* KAKOVATOS.

Nestorianism. Doctrinal position on the nature of Jesus Christ followed by the Nestorian or Assyrian Church, more properly known as the Ancient Church of the East. The name is derived from Nestorius (*c.* AD 381–*c.* 451), who was Patriarch of Constantinople (now Istanbul) between 428 and 431. The theological views that came to be associated with him had arisen in the late 4th century among Christian thinkers of the Antioch school, who rejected the Orthodox dogma as established at the Council of Nicaea in 325. The Antiochenes taught that Christ had two distinct natures, human and divine, whereas the Nicene formula maintained that these two natures were perfectly united in Christ. The Christological debate intensified when Nestorius, a follower of the Antioch school, succeeded to the patriarchate. After he was deposed, the doctrine he represented was declared heretical. By the mid-5th century the Nestorians had split away from the Orthodox Church and controlled the see of Seleucia-Ctesiphon in Iraq, later spreading into Iran. For the next 800 years the Nestorian Church flourished, establishing important missionary communities in Central Asia, India and China, where inscribed stelae commemorating its expansion have been found (see fig.). Converts were also made among the Turks and Mongols. From the 11th century the Nestorian Church began to decline under the attacks of the Mongols (now converted to Islam), until in the 14th century it was forced to remove itself into Kurdistan, where it survived into the 20th century.

Cast of a stele commemorating the introduction and spread of Nestorianism in China, h. *c.* 2 m, from near Chang'an (now Xi'an, Shaanxi Province), AD 781 (Paris, Musée Guimet)

Although little evidence survives of the great period of Nestorian expansion, it is known that images were not only displayed and venerated in Nestorian churches but that they also played an important role in the liturgy. Up to the 11th century, Nestorian church architecture reflects the increasingly elaborate symbolism of the liturgy, which was centred around the sanctuary and the ambo. The icon of Christ, the cross and the Gospels were all incorporated into this symbolic ritual. After the 11th century elements of the liturgy fell into disuse, and the churches were correspondingly simplified.

Icons were taken to missionary countries and workshops were set up in the new communities that blended local and Nestorian artistic traditions. The cult of the cross was widespread: the Nestorians worshipped the plain Parousia cross (symbol of Christ's second coming) and rejected the Crucifix, which was adopted by the West after the 6th century, considering it blasphemous to dwell upon the historical moment of Christ's suffering and death. The lack of images in Nestorian churches in Kurdistan may suggest that the cult of images was prohibited in modern times, although it is equally likely that this may be explained by poverty and the loss of artistic traditions.

The art and architecture of the Nestorian Church developed in isolation from the Orthodox Church. The basic rectangular plan of their churches was inherited from ancient Mesopotamian architecture (e.g. Ctesiphon and Hira, Iraq), and this type was widespread, although between the 11th and 13th centuries architects began to abandon the traditional plan in favour of a domed basilical church inspired by Islamic architecture, such as the church of the convent of St Eugenia at Mosul in Iraq. As the Nestorian missionaries moved east they both helped to spread influences from western Asia and Persia and absorbed the artistic influences of the civilizations they encountered. In Sino-Central Asia, to the west of the Gobi Desert, frescoes of the late 9th century (Berlin, Mus. Ind. Kst) have been found in the church at the ancient city of Khocho, near Karakhoja. In China churches were apparently built in the traditional architectural style, as is suggested by the inscribed stele found at Chang'an (now Xi'an, Shaanxi Prov.), which Emperor Taizong (*reg* 627–50) erected to commemorate his foundation of a church and monastery in 635. Both Sino-Central Asia and China have also yielded carved stone crosses that combine elements of Chinese, Near Eastern and Persian artistic traditions, for example the cross from Dunhuang, Gansu Province, dated after 1035 (Paris, Bib. N.) and one found in the Shizi (Cross) Temple (*in situ*) near Fangshan County, *c.* 64 km south-west of Beijing.

BIBLIOGRAPHY
A. C. Moule: *Christians in China before the Year 1550* (London, 1930)
A. R. Vine: *The Nestorian Churches* (London, 1937)
A. C. Moule: *Nestorians in China: Some Corrections and Additions* (London, 1940)
L. Abramowski and A. E. Goodman, eds: *A Nestorian Collection of Christological Texts*, 2 vols (Cambridge, 1972)
J. Dauvillier: *Histoire et institutions des églises orientales au moyen âge* (London, 1983)

SARAH MORGAN

Netherlands, Kingdom of **the.** European country bordered by the North Sea to the west and north, by Belgium to the south and by Germany to the east (see fig. 1). It is often erroneously called Holland, after one of its provinces. It covers an area of 41,159 sq. kms, including the West Frisian Islands to the north and islands in the Caribbean. The country's population is *c.* 15 million; the capital and largest city, AMSTERDAM, has a population of over 700,000. Politically a parliamentary democracy with a constitutional monarchy, the country is divided administratively into 12 provinces and 633 municipalities.

1. Map of the Kingdom of the Netherlands; those sites with separate entries in this dictionary are distinguished by CROSS-REFERENCE TYPE.

I. Introduction. II. Architecture. III. Painting and graphic arts. IV. Sculpture. V. Interior decoration. VI. Furniture. VII. Ceramics. VIII. Glass. IX. Metalwork. X. Objects of vertu. XI. Textiles. XII. Patronage. XIII. Collecting and dealing. XIV. Museums. XV. Art education. XVI. Art libraries and photographic collections. XVII. Historiography. XVIII. Periodicals.

DETAILED TABLE OF CONTENTS

I. *Introduction.*

1. HISTORY. The area was occupied in pre-Roman times by Germanic tribes; following Roman occupation (12 BC–AD 300) the Franks and Saxons settled there, the former becoming dominant and incorporating the Netherlands into their European empire. Frankish decline was followed from the 10th century by the development of various semi-autonomous states, later mostly reintegrated under the Dukes of Burgundy and Philip the Bold (*reg* 1363–1404) in the 14th century. The Seventeen Provinces of the Habsburg Netherlands, corresponding roughly with the present-day Benelux countries, resulted from the marriage of Mary of Burgundy to the Holy Roman Emperor Maximilian I in 1477; Spanish rule followed when Philip II of Spain inherited the Habsburg Netherlands in 1555–6. Opposition in the northern Netherlands, however, in particular from Protestants and the nobility, led to the Dutch Revolt in 1568 and the Eighty Years War (1568–1648); the United Provinces (Holland, Zeeland, Utrecht, Gelderland, Groningen, Friesland and Overijssel,

all in the north) came together in 1579 claiming independence. In the following decade the form of a republic was chosen, which was not recognized by Spain until 1648 with the Peace of Westphalia. The southern Netherlands remained Spanish and Catholic, eventually becoming the Austrian Netherlands following the War of the Spanish Succession (1701–14). The 17th century was a golden age for the Dutch Republic, when colonial territories (e.g. in Indonesia, Ceylon, South Africa and Brazil) brought new wealth and encouraged a corresponding boom in architecture and the arts. Subsequent stagnation in the 18th century was followed after the Batavian Revolution (1795) by a brief period of French rule (1810–14). The north and south were then reunited in 1815 as the Kingdom of the Netherlands under William I, with the south finally splitting to become the independent Kingdom of BELGIUM in 1830. The Dutch economy was weak during and after World War I, and German occupation during World War II cost 240,000 lives and ruined much of the country. In the second half of the 20th century the country surrendered its colonies and assumed a leading role in the European community.

2. CULTURAL IDENTITY. The fact that the Netherlands, despite its relative stability compared to other European nation states, was not constituted in its present boundaries until the 1830s has resulted in a certain ambiguity concerning its cultural identity. Historians and politicians hold varying views on this issue. Some feel that the Netherlands belongs naturally to the Seventeen Provinces of the Habsburg Netherlands. Others argue that the secession of the seven northern provinces in 1579 and the founding of the Dutch Republic, the territory of which covered much of today's Kingdom of the Netherlands, created a historical fact that cannot be undone. Proponents of this theory tend to attach great worth in those attainments of the Republic, especially political independence and religious tolerance, that were lacking in the southern provinces. A third concept of the Netherlands draws a line around the community of Dutch and Flemish speakers, as an organic cultural unit. A country built on this foundation would include the northern Netherlands (with or without Friesland, which has its own language) and Flemish Belgium.

No single vision of the Netherlands can evoke a nation whose historical or ethnic identity speaks for itself. The southern boundary between a Netherlandish realm and a French one is historically unstable; the eastern division between the Netherlands and Germany breaches a linguistic continuum. The northern and western borders with the sea are equally dynamic. In the 20th century, the coastline was halved by the construction of sea dykes, while an entire new province (Flevoland) was reclaimed from the waters of the former Zuider Zee. The inland waterways, fed by and connected to the Rhine and Meuse rivers and their tributaries, form a delta covering most of the provinces of Zeeland and South Holland and parts of Utrecht and Gelderland. Nearly half the population lives in this area, which lies largely below sea-level and requires constant maintenance.

These regional historical and geographical factors have combined to produce a strongly local sense of loyalty in the population, with nationalism having long been a weaker force. Personal allegiance is paid not to an abstract nation but to the individual's clan, city, religion, social or professional group or political party. Such a unit knows itself to be a minority incapable of establishing a lasting hegemony in any major sphere; at most, it can claim to command the moral high ground, the fight for which is characteristic of Dutch public discourse. This has unquestionably influenced the character of Dutch society: in a spirit of grudging cooperation, competing groups and interests have manoeuvred at close quarters, in the most densely populated country of Europe, with phenomenally little civil warfare. The same ability to compromise may also have helped keep the northern Netherlands relatively free of invasion.

3. ECONOMY. The ambiguities of the Dutch cultural identity are less apparent in the economy of the Netherlands. Since the Middle Ages, the country has been a leading agricultural, maritime and commercial nation. Following the transformation of much land from bog to pasture from the 12th to 14th centuries, farmers concentrated on high-value crops. Produce was brought in from the Baltic on Dutch ships to be sold by Dutch merchants in wealthy markets abroad. Agricultural exports, together with cod and herring, were a major source of national income. The resultant capital inflow stimulated urbanization: by 1500, an exceptionally high 44% of the population of the province of Holland lived in towns of more than 2500 inhabitants. Between 1580 and 1680, a period when the urbanization of western Europe as a whole was not higher than 15%, this figure leapt to 60%. During those hundred years Amsterdam attained world leadership as a centre for finance, while the Dutch East India Company, in its time the largest commercial enterprise in the world, dominated trade from the Cape of Good Hope to Japan.

Like other Europeans, the Dutch spent much of their wealth on luxury goods, including art. The production of art was commensurately high. In the 16th century the northern Netherlands was a leading centre for sculpture, printmaking and painting, a position it retained, for the latter two arts, throughout much of the 17th century. The northern Netherlands had the highest concentration of artists in Europe between 1400 and 1800, with the so-called Golden Age stimulating interest in a broad range of subject-matter. The visual arts—especially painting, with such celebrated exponents as Rembrandt and van Gogh—became an essential element in the national image. In this respect, the Netherlands can be compared only to Italy among the countries of Europe.

BIBLIOGRAPHY
J. A. van Houtte and others, eds: *Algemene geschiedenis der Nederlanden*, 13 vols (Utrecht, 1949–58)
J. L. Price: *Culture and Society in the Dutch Republic during the 17th Century* (London, 1974)
D. P. Blok and others, eds: *Algemene geschiedenis der Nederlanden*, 15 vols (Haarlem, 1977–83)
A. M. van der Woude: *Nederland over de schouder gekeken* (Utrecht, 1986)
S. Schama: *The Embarrassment of Riches: An Interpretation of Dutch Culture in the Golden Age* (London, 1987/R 1988)
GARY SCHWARTZ

II. Architecture.

Dutch architecture is strongly grafted on to that of the surrounding regions, all the more because the Netherlands is poorly off for stone. Only in south-west Limburg are several types available (marl, Kunrader sandstone, carboniferous sandstone and Nivelstein sandstone); elsewhere, builders were dependent on imports. The principal import routes for stone were the major rivers. Tufa, Drachenfels trachyte and red Mainz sandstone were brought in via the Rhine and its tributaries. In the east, yellow and red sandstone were brought in from Germany, from Bentheim and Bremen respectively. Brick was reintroduced around the middle of the 12th century, at first as a filler for hollow walls, but soon as the building material for smaller churches. It is not clear exactly where the revival in brick production first occurred or if the Cistercian and Premonstratensian monasteries played a role. The earliest bricks, also known as *kloostermoppen*, or monastery bricks, were unusually large, but the format gradually decreased. Natural stone continued to be used for large buildings and such ornamental elements as columns, capitals and window-frames. However, imports from the Rhine area eventually lost out to a rising stone trade with Belgium. From 1200 Tournai stone was brought to the coastal areas via the River Scheldt, and from 1400 the trade with Brabant (Gobertange stone for walls) and Flanders (Lede stone for ornamental work) gained the upper hand. At the end of the 14th century, Bentheim stone was being used at Kampen and, *c.* 1450, at Utrecht. From then on Bentheim stone gained in popularity and was used all over the western Netherlands.

BIBLIOGRAPHY

J. Hollestelle: *De steenbakkerij in de Nederlanden tot omstreeks 1560* [Brickmaking in the Netherlands up to 1560] (Assen, 1961)

A. Slinger, H. Janse and G. Berends: *Natuursteen in monumenten* (Zeist, 1980)

G. Berends: 'Baksteen in Nederland in de Middeleeuwen', *Rijksdienst voor de Monumentenzorg, Restauratie Vademecum*, ii (1989), pp. 1–19

2. Maastricht, Onze-Lieve-Vrouwekerk, aerial view from the south-west showing the westwork (*c.* 1000) and the nave with pseudo-transepts, transept and choir (*c.* 1150)

1. Before *c.* 1200. 2. *c.* 1200–*c.* 1500. 3. *c.* 1500–*c.* 1795. 4. *c.* 1795–*c.* 1890. 5. *c.* 1890–1945. 6. After 1945.

1. BEFORE *c.* 1200.

(i) The earliest buildings, AD 400–800. (ii) Romanesque.

(i) The earliest buildings, AD *400–800.* Christian architecture began in the southern region of the Netherlands. However, little is known about the earliest buildings. In Maastricht the Onze-Lieve-Vrouwekerk stood in the centre of the old Roman town from the 4th century AD. Near it, traces have been found of a three-aisled wooden building, on a rectangular foundation, with, in the east, an internal apse, but it is not certain whether this was a religious building. Outside the Roman city walls, there was a wooden sanctuary dedicated to St Servatius, replaced in the 6th century by a rectangular stone church without aisles and with a recessed choir. This church was in turn replaced in the 8th century by a basilican church, which had rectangular subordinate compartments instead of transepts.

Christian conversion of the northern region began systematically only in the late 7th century AD. In 695 the Anglo-Saxon missionary Willibrord acquired the Roman castellum at Utrecht as the principal seat for his Frisian archbishopric, later the diocese of Utrecht, which comprised most of the northern Netherlands. There he maintained a Frankish church, dedicated to St Martin (*c.* 600), and added a second church immediately next to it, dedicated to St Salvator. This complex probably served as a double cathedral. The foundations of the chapel of the Holy Cross (pulled down in 1826; foundations re-excavated 1929, 1993) appear to be those of one of these two churches. These foundations consisted of a rectangular nave and a recessed square choir. On both the south and north side of the nave there was a small, almost square annexe.

(ii) Romanesque.

(a) Southern region. Romanesque architecture in the Netherlands is related to that elsewhere in the German empire. Although in the past the buildings in the south of the Netherlands have been classified as Meuse valley or Mosan architecture (mainly because a substantial part of this region of the Netherlands belonged to the diocese of Liège), there is no evidence of a regional style.

Among the earliest remnants of Romanesque architecture is the westwork (*c.* 1000) of the Onze-Lieve-Vrouwekerk in Maastricht, a rectangular tower block without a western entrance, flanked by slightly taller round stair-turrets (see fig. 2). The interior of this westwork contains a crypt, a choir and several floors, the function of which is not clear. (The westwork was raised in height in the 12th century.) The lower parts of a similar westwork also survive in Thorn. In Susteren the westwork (third quarter of the 11th century) has square rather than round stair-turrets, and originally these were lower than the central tower. The three-aisled basilican nave at Susteren has an arcade of alternating piers and columns, with the piers connected by large blind arches. The nave is thus, as it were, divided into three bays. East of the nave is the transept, followed by a choir bay terminating in an apse that is flanked by two square side chapels with apsidal niches in the thickness of the wall, situated respectively left and right of a doorway. The side walls of the choir bay have a rudimentary three-storey elevation, consisting of a bipartite arch, three blind niches and a clerestory, as at St Lucius in Werden (Germany, 1063). The eastern doorways lead into a five-aisled outer crypt, set to the east of the choir, that is reminiscent of the earlier one in Essen (Germany, 1051). The architecture of the church in Wessem too was related to that in Essen and Werden. It had a crossing supported by Ionic capitals, rounded transept ends and a tripartite choir *in echelon*, consisting of an apse preceded by a choir bay, flanked by a chapel on each side with an apsidal interior and a rectangular exterior.

The most important church in the south was St Servatius in Maastricht (*see* MAASTRICHT, §3). At the beginning of the 11th century, or a little earlier, it was rebuilt from the ground up and was consecrated in 1039 in the presence of the German emperor. The new church had a choir terminating in an apse, polygonal transept arms with aisles, a basilican nave and a very large westwork, the lower parts of which are preserved in the current west end. The rounded-off transept ends are the earliest examples known in both the Rhine and Meuse valleys and Flanders. The church of St Servatius was rebuilt again under Provost Humbert (*reg* 1051–86) and at this time acquired a rectangular transept, a crypt under the crossing and, at the east end, flanking the apse, square chapels and entrances. The westwork was raised and its interior adapted. Finally, around the mid-12th century the west and east ends of the church were once again rebuilt. The westwork now consists of a large western choir. About halfway up the walls are galleries with beautifully carved capitals. On the first storey there is a large domed hall—flanked by smaller spaces to the north, south and west—that once overlooked the nave. This hall is known as the 'Keizerzaal'. The nave was given two new portals on the north side. A presumably 11th-century south-west portal was replaced by the Gothic Berg portal (built in two phases, 1170–80/*c.* 1215). The capitals of the choir and west end, like the nave portals, show north-Italian influence. The 12th-century westwork (*see* WESTWORK, fig. 3) was of great importance for architecture in the Rhine–Meuse region, where it was much imitated. The choir was no less important. The 11th-century apse was given a dwarf gallery and flanking towers after the example of the imperial cathedral at Speyer (Germany) and became the model for many 12th-century choirs in the Rhine–Meuse region.

North Italian influence is also apparent in the nave of the Onze-Lieve-Vrouwekerk in Maastricht (*c.* 1150) and that (1138–43) of the church in Rolduc. Both naves have pseudo-transepts, as did the lost cathedrals of Novara and Pavia (both *c.* 1120–30). Furthermore, in Rolduc there is also a trefoil crypt (1130s) and choir (*c.* 1130). Like the cathedral of Liège, on which it was dependent, the Onze-Lieve-Vrouwekerk has a rounded-off choir with an ambulatory to the east of a T-transept. On the east side of each transept arm there is an apsidal chapel. The nave aisles are covered by rising barrel vaulting, as are the northern- and southernmost side compartments of the Keizerzaal in St Servatius. This vaulting was derived from that in the gallery of the Palatine chapel in Aachen. At the

end of the 12th century Mosan economic and cultural significance began to decline, and architecture began to be more influenced by that in Cologne and its surroundings. For example, the architecture of the minster of Roermond, a former Cistercian nunnery founded in *c.* 1220, is narrowly related to that of St Quirin in Neuss in Germany.

(*b*) *Northern region.* After the Viking invasions the churches of Utrecht were restored in the 10th century, with large-scale reconstruction taking place during the episcopacy of Bishop Adelbold (*reg* 1010–27), who had a new cathedral built, dedicated to St Maarten. This church was the predecessor of the present cathedral. It had a westwork, a three-aisled nave, a transept with an east chapel on each arm and a choir without a crypt. The church of St Salvator (also named Oudmunster, i.e. former minster) was also rebuilt at this time, acquiring a large crypt and a rectangular tower block at the west end. There were now three churches in the cathedral complex: the cathedral of St Maarten, the church of St Salvator and in between them the rededicated church of the Holy Cross. In addition, an interesting group of churches was built around the cathedral, consciously forming a cross, as in Paderborn and Bamberg in Germany. The St Pieterskerk (consecrated 1048) was to the east, exactly on the cathedral's axis; to the south was the Benedictine abbey of St Paul; to the north the St Janskerk; and to the west the Mariakerk. Of these four churches only the St Pieterskerk survives in fairly good condition, although its double-towered west façade was lost, while the choir and south choir chapel were rebuilt. However, the crypt, with its handsome decorated columns of Nivelstein sandstone, the transept—except for the vaults—and the nave, which has an arcade of monolithic red sandstone columns with cushion capitals, all date from the 11th century. The choir and flanking chapels ended in apses that were semicircular on the interior but polygonal on the exterior. Only the northern chapel survives. It is barrel-vaulted and once had two storeys: the upper chapel gave access to the choir, the lower one to the crypt. The exterior of the church was enlivened by blind round-headed niches around the windows, a motif first used at Ravenna. The abbey of St Paul and the St Janskerk were similar to the St Pieterskerk, although the abbey church had no crypt but a more extensive choir, with two chapels on either side of the apse. The St Janskerk later acquired a westwork with an apse between the two towers. In view of their similarities, these three churches have all been ascribed to a single patron, Bishop Bernold (*reg* 1027–54), who probably co-operated closely with the emperor, Henry III (*reg* 1046–56). The same Bernold is also regarded as the patron of the church of St Maarten in Emmerich, Germany, and the Grote Kerk, dedicated to St Lebuïnus, in Deventer (see fig. 3). Another building erected by Bernold and Henry III is the imperial palace of Lofen, built in the north-west corner of the cathedral complex at Utrecht and in use until the mid-13th century. Only parts of the ground floor remain, incorporated in cellars of buildings at present on the site.

The Mariakerk, Utrecht, was founded by Bishop Koenraad (*reg* 1076–99) and was the most interesting of the 12th-century churches in the northern region. Although

3. Deventer, Grote Kerk, interior view of the crypt, mid-11th century

destroyed in the 19th century, it is well known through its depiction in the extremely meticulous drawings and paintings of Pieter Saenredam. The choir and transept were consecrated in 1099, but the remainder of the building was not completed until after 1134, following a different plan that clearly exhibited north Italian influences. A quadripartite vault with broad, flat ribs was introduced, and galleries were inserted above the aisles, interrupted by pseudo-transepts. The façade also recalled Italian examples. The style of this church was imitated in the Klaaskerk in Utrecht, and in Hochelten and Wissel in Germany.

For the rest, architecture in the Utrecht diocese hardly shows any cohesion. To the east, the basilica of St Plechelmus in Oldenzaal, built of Bentheim sandstone, is related to 12th-century Westphalian architecture. This church is a completely (groin-)vaulted-over basilica with a transept, with an absidiole at the east end of each arm. Between the absidioles and choir bay (the original termination has been lost) there were two small rectangular compartments that had passages to choir and transept. Only the southern one survives. The nave has a two-storey elevation, with one nave bay corresponding to two bays in the side aisles. This implies an alternating system for the arcade. The church makes a somewhat heavy impression, particularly since the building is low and the windows and arches unprofiled and not recessed.

Along the coast were the two abbey churches of Egmond Binnen and Rijnsburg, the most important foundations of the Counts of Holland. The church in Rijnsburg had an imposing two-towered front, and a trefoil east end, a layout that was found more frequently in coastal districts (Aardenburg, Antwerp and Kortrijk) and that was also used in Kampen. The two-towered front was also a feature at Egmond, Arnhem (the St Janskerk) and Deventer (the Bergkerk). Parish churches were generally built of tufa. Usually these were small, single-aisled, unvaulted churches, without transepts; only in Friesland do annexes sometimes take the place of transepts. There is also frequently a west

tower or, as sometimes occurs in Groningen and Friesland, a reduced westwork.

See also VERNACULAR ARCHITECTURE, §II, 1(iv).

BIBLIOGRAPHY

M. D. Ozinga: *De romaanse Kerkelijke bouwkunst* (Amsterdam, 1949)
J. J. F. W. van Agt: 'Gereduceerde westwerken in het Oude Friesland', *Ned. Ksthist. Jb.* (1950–51), pp. 57–82
E. H. Ter Kuile: 'De architectuur', *Duizend jaar bouwen in Nederland: De bouwkunst van de middeleeuwen* (1958), i, pp. 131–90
H. A. van den Berg: 'Plattegrondsvormen van middeleeuwse kerken in Groningen en Friesland', *Kon. Ned. Oudhdknd. Bond: Bull. KNOB* (1970), pp. 14–27
Ned. Mnmt. Gesch. & Kst. (Amsterdam, 1975) [whole vol.]
H. E. Kubach and A. Verbeek: *Katalog der vorromanischen und romanischen Denkmäler* (1976), i–iii of *Romanische Baukunst an Rhein und Maas* (Berlin, 1976–89)
E. H. ter Kuile: *De romaanse kerkbouwkunst in de Nederlanden* (Zutphen, 1982)
H. M. Haverkate and C. J. van der Peet: *Een kerk van papier: De geschiedenis van de voormalige Mariakerk te Utrecht* (Utrecht and Zutphen, 1985)
H. A. van den Berg: 'In pago cui nomen Ostrache: Zum Typus der einschiffigen Kirche mit Annexen in Friesland', *Baukunst des Mittelalters in Europa: H. E. Kubach zum 75. Geburtstag* (Stuttgart, 1986)
A. J. J. Mekking: *De Sint-Servaaskerk te Maastricht* (Utrecht and Zutphen, 1986)
——: 'Een kruis van kerken rond Koenraads hart', *Utrecht: Kruispunt van de middeleeuwse kerk*, Clavis Kunsthistorische Monografieën, 7 (Utrecht and Zutphen, 1988), pp. 21–55
B. Koopmans: *Een elfde-eeuws keizerlijk paleis in Utrecht: Lofen* (Utrecht and Zutphen, 1989)
H. E. Kubach and A. Verbeek: *Architekturgeschichte und Kunstlandschaft* (1989), iv of *Romanische Baukunst an Rhein und Maas* (Berlin, 1976–89)
A. F. W. Bosman: *De Onze Lieve Vrouwekerk te Maastricht* (Utrecht and Zutphen, 1990)
A. J. J. Mekking: 'De zogenoemde Bernold-kerken in het sticht Utrecht: Herkomst en betekenis van hun architectuur', *Utrecht tussen kerk en staat*, Utrechtse Bijdragen tot de Mediëvistiek, 10, ed. R. E. V. Stuip and C. Vellekoop (Hilversum, 1991), pp. 103–51
T. A. S. M. Panhuysen: 'De Sint-Servaaskerk te Maastricht in de vroege middeleeuwen', *Kon. Ned. Oudhdknd. Bond: Bull. KNOB*, xc/1 (1991), pp. 15–24
E. den Hartog: *Romanesque Architecture and Sculpture in the Meuse Valley* (Leeuwarden and Mechelen, 1992)
A. J. J. Mekking: *De Grote of Lebuïnuskerk te Deventer: De 'dom' van het oversticht veelzijdig bekeken* (Utrecht and Zutphen, 1992)
Kon. Ned. Oudhdknd. Bond: Bull. KNOB, xciii/4–5 (1994), pp. 133–96 [discussion of the oldest churches in Utrecht]
A. van Deijk: *Romaans Nederland* (Amsterdam, 1994)
E. den Hartog: 'Provincie-gotiek of vroeg-gotiek? Een herwaardering van het Bergportaal van de St Servaaskerk te Maastricht naar aanleiding van de restauratie van 1992', *Kon. Ned. Oudhdknd. Bond: Bull. KNOB*, xciii/6 (1994), pp. 197–213

2. *c.* 1200–*c.* 1500.

(i) Religious. (ii) Secular.

(i) Religious. Since architectural style was frequently imported along with the stone, architecture in the Netherlands during the 13th century exhibits great diversity. For instance, in Zeeland there are offshoots of the Flemish Scheldt Gothic, a style that flourished *c.* 1200 to 1250 in the southern Netherlands (*see* BELGIUM, §II, 1). The sexpartite rib vaults of the churches dedicated to St Walpurgis in Zutphen and St Lebuïnus in Deventer, both of which are known as the Grote Kerk, indicate the influence of contemporary churches in Cologne. Even the rebuilt cathedral of Utrecht was characterized by an overwhelmingly foreign influence, by that of Cologne Cathedral in particular. The nave (*c.* 1230) of Ootmarsum is an example of an entirely Westphalian type of hall

church, with its thick walls (owing to the absence of buttresses), alternating arcade system, octopartite domical rib vaults in the central nave and quadripartite rib vaults in the aisles is an example of an entirely Westphalian type of hall church. Only in Groningen and Friesland, from the late 12th century onwards, did a native brick-built style develop with its own characteristics.

(a) Romano-Gothic. (b) Gothic.

(a) Romano-Gothic. The earliest brick churches in Groningen and Friesland were Romanesque and unvaulted (e.g. Marsum), but gradually they became increasingly Gothic, hence the descriptive term 'Romano-Gothic'. Typical Romano-Gothic churches of the first half of the 13th century were on a rectangular plan (without aisles) and often covered with domical vaults with a variable number of ribs, sometimes ending in a pendant boss (e.g. the choir of the Dutch Reformed church at Bozum, see fig. 4; the Martinikerk, Groningen; and the church at Eestrum). The interiors were whitewashed. From 1250 onwards another type of church predominated: the interior, with octopartite domical vaults over square bays, is painted red (e.g. the churches at Huizinge, 't Zandt and Zeerijp). The ribs usually have an ornamental, semicircular profile. Where no ribs were constructed, they were probably painted in (e.g. at Hantumhuizen). Exteriors are relieved by blind niches with ornamental masonry. Below the roof Lombard arches could be added, sometimes supported by decorated corbels (e.g. at Stedum). Owing to the weakness of the underlying ground, many towers in the region are lopsided (e.g. at Bierum). As sagging towers could seriously damage the actual church building, they are often detached (as at Zeerijp, Noordwolde and Garmerwolde). Between 1200 and 1250 a particular type of church architecture, the so-called Scheldt Gothic, was developed in Tournai and surroundings. A particularly good example of this in the Netherlands is the church of St Bavo in Aardenburg (first quarter of the 13th century), of which the nave and transept remain intact. The trefoil choir was replaced by a hall choir, a type that is more often found along the Flemish coast. The nave is characterized by the use of grey Tournai stone and a lack of vertical emphasis. The elevation consists of a pointed arcade carried by columns with volute capitals, a triforium with round arches and a small clerestory. The nave is covered by a wooden ceiling. The exterior is enlivened by groups of three lancet windows lighting the aisles, by wall passages in front of the clerestory windows and by round stair-turrets flanking the west and transept façades. More to the north, Tournai stone was often replaced by brick. This Dutch brick variant can be seen at Brouwershaven, Kloosterzande, the Koorkerk in Middelburg and at Loosduinen and remained popular well into the 14th century.

(b) Gothic.

Utrecht Cathedral. The most classically Gothic example of Dutch architecture is the elevation of the choir of Utrecht Cathedral (see fig. 5 and UTRECHT, §1). Rebuilding of the cathedral started after a fire in 1253 but did not get under way until 1288. The project lasted for centuries. Both the long period of construction and the troublesome

4. Bozum, Dutch Reformed church, interior detail of the choir vault, before 1250

relationship with the chapter of the neighbouring church of St Salvator contributed to design changes: in the choir alone, at least four campaigns can be distinguished. The choir ambulatory (completed 1295) has five shallow radiating chapels, as did the choir (1243–55) of Tournai Cathedral. The detailing, on the other hand, reveals more similarities with the choir (begun 1248) of Cologne Cathedral. The influence of Cologne is also dominant in the richly executed south aisle of Utrecht Cathedral (completed c. 1320). The more sober north aisle was erected at the same time as the west tower, itself the showpiece of the Bishop of Utrecht. The central aisle of the choir was finished at the end of the 14th century and consists of arcade, triforium and clerestory, with quadripartite rib vaults over single bays. The 112.5 m tower, with its characteristic three-storey elevation, comprises a base of two rectangular blocks, one above the other, and an airy octagonal superstructure. Constructed relatively rapidly, it was imitated many times, in Amersfoort, Rhenen and Wijk-bij-Duurstede, and in such churches as the St Janskerk, Maastricht, and the St Martinikerk, Groningen. The Utrecht tower was also reflected in the design of the towers of Eemnes, Soest and Amerongen.

The transept, monastery buildings and chapter of Utrecht Cathedral were built after the choir, and the nave was not completed until 1517, without stone vaulting or flying buttresses. (The west tower, connected to the nave only by an elevated bridge, provided no support whatsoever, and so the unstable nave collapsed like a house of cards in 1674 during a violent hurricane; the ruins were cleared in the course of the 19th century. Several other churches in Utrecht lost their towers during this storm.)

Other major town churches and workshops. The Gothic elevation of the Utrecht choir had virtually no influence, certainly none from the point of view of style. However, it may have stimulated the rebuilding of churches in larger towns that began in the second half of the 14th century. The choirs built from 1350 to 1450 do not form a coherent

5. Utrecht Cathedral, interior view of the choir, showing crossing, and lost south wall of the nave, late 13th century–late 14th; drawing by Pieter Saenredam (Utrecht, Gemeente Archief)

group. The Nieuwe Kerk in Delft, the churches in Zaltbommel and Tiel, and the St Jacobskerk in The Hague (*see* THE HAGUE, §V, 1) have deep aisle-less choirs with a transept. Other choirs lack a transept (e.g. at Hasselt, Hattem and Steenwijk), perhaps in imitation of mendicant churches. The choir flanked by two smaller subsidiary choirs was also widespread (e.g. at the St Jacobikerk, Utrecht, and the Onze-Lieve-Vrouwekerk in Kampen). In the larger churches, there are sometimes hall choirs, vaulted as in the Grote Kerk (dedicated to St Michael) in Zwolle and the St Joriskerk, Amersfoort; or with wooden barrel vaults as in the western Netherlands (e.g. Schoonhoven, Schiedam and Oudewater). The choir with aisles but no ambulatory developed in Breda and survives in the Oude Kerk in Delft and at Geertruidenberg. At the end of the 14th century the most important urban parish churches were given a choir with ambulatory, the earliest examples being the choirs of the Bovenkerk in Kampen and the St Janskerk in 's Hertogenbosch (*see* 'S HERTOGENBOSCH, §2). They were followed by such churches as St Bavo in Haarlem (*see* HAARLEM, §3), the St Walburgiskerk in Zutphen, the Nieuwe Kerk (1385–1408) and the Oude Kerk in Amsterdam (*see* AMSTERDAM, §V, 1), the Bergkerk in Deventer, the Pieterskerk in Leiden and the Grote Kerk (c. 1400–20) in Harderwijk.

Such building demanded considerable expertise and may have been done by masters from the large workshops in Utrecht, 's Hertogenbosch (c. 1380–1529) and Kampen. In 1369 a Master Rutger was appointed master mason of the Kampen workshop. He was a son of Michael van

Savoye, the head of the Cologne lodge (*see* SAVOYE). Rutger's brothers worked on Prague Cathedral, and Rutger too may well have worked there. This would explain the influence of Prague Cathedral on the choir lantern of the Bovenkerk in Kampen. The net vaults, window tracery and wall passage at clerestory level are all derived from Prague (*see* PRAGUE, §IV, 2(i)). From documents Master Rutger is also known to have worked in the St Pieterskerk (c. 1390–1412) in Leiden, and on the evidence of style he has been connected to the building of the choirs of the Nieuwe Kerk (1385–1408) in Amsterdam and of the Grote Kerk (c. 1400–20) in Harderwijk. When Master Rutger died (?1402), the Kampen workshop lost much of its prestige and the Utrecht and Brabant workshops came to dominate Dutch church building.

The so-called Brabant Gothic style, based on French Rayonnant architecture (*see* BELGIUM, §II, 1), left traces in the northern Netherlands, for example at the St Janskerk, 's Hertogenbosch, the Onze-Lieve-Vrouwekerk, Dordrecht, and St Gertrudis, Bergen-op-Zoom. The Brabant-style churches are richly decorated, and their elevations comprise an arcade, a triforium faced with tracery (or an open passage with a balustrade) and a clerestory. The arcade is usually columnar, with capitals in the form of frilly leaves; the larger churches have clustered piers without capitals. Main vessels normally have quadripartite rib vaults; after 1500 smaller spaces are often provided with star or net vaults. Choirs generally have an ambulatory with radiating chapels. Enormous west towers were popular, but many of them remained incomplete, as at Dordrecht, Veere and Zierikzee. A print after a design of the Zierikzee tower (1529) by Rombout Keldermans II shows that the present tower should have received four more storeys and was intended to be 130 m high. From 1400 Brabant Gothic penetrated the western Netherlands, and columns, capitals and complete façades were brought in ready-made from the southern Netherlands, so that the same scheme could be ordered in different places. For example, the transept gables (late 15th century) of the Hooglandse Kerk in Leiden (*see* LEIDEN, fig. 1) and the church of Mary Magdalen in Goes are almost identical.

One of the earliest master masons with an extensive practice in the western Netherlands was Everaert Spoorwater (*d* 1474), who from c. 1439 was simultaneously Master of the Works at the main churches in Antwerp and Dordrecht. He was also involved in the construction of the choir of the church at Bergen-op-Zoom and the transept of St Bavo, Haarlem. He probably also played a part in rebuilding churches at Hulst, Brielle, Veere and Tholen. His churches are typified by their generous layout, a simple but somewhat ponderous design and the use of as many prefabricated elements as possible. In the large Brabant Gothic churches the components of the building flow over into one another with remarkable smoothness. In Everaert's work they are strictly divided: the arcade is purely columnar, and in the elevation each small column is differentiated. The accounts of the building of the Haarlem transept provide a glimpse of Everaert's efficient working methods. He made his original designs on the site and then returned to Antwerp, where he had these worked up into three models: one for himself, one for the quarry and one for the patron, who could thus check the goods delivered to him. In this way, when the stone was delivered, only a few masons were needed to construct the building. The KELDERMANS family, a dynasty of stonecutters and masons who can be traced over seven generations, also had a widespread practice in both the southern and northern Netherlands, for example at Breda, Bergen-op-Zoom, Veere, Middelburg, Wouw, Haarlem, Delft and Alkmaar.

Regional variations. As in other countries, Dutch scholars have tried to define several schools of architecture—Lower Rhine Gothic, Mosan Gothic, Kempen Gothic and Hollands Gothic. It should be noted, however, that not all these churches in a particular area correspond to the established 'regional type' and that more often than not this 'regional type' recurs in other areas.

Brabant Gothic was not adopted throughout the Netherlands. From the end of the 14th century various churches in the lower Rhine region were rebuilt in the style of Xanten Cathedral in Germany. Examples of this style, known as Lower Rhine Gothic, include the St Stevenskerk, Nijmegen, the St Eusebiuskerk, Arnhem, and the St Maartenskerk in both Doesburg and Zaltbommel. These churches have no transept, the three aisles in the nave are of approximately the same width, and the star and net vaults are very flat. In addition to the basilica type, the pseudo-basilica also occurs, in, for example, the St Petruskerk in Venray. Gisbert Schairt (*c.* 1380–1452) of Bommel, who was trained in the Xanten workshop, is known to have worked (mid–15th century) at Zaltbommel and (from *c.* 1425) at Nijmegen. In Zaltbommel, the side aisles of the nave terminate in a square bay with a rounded-off outer corner, a feature that first occurs (from *c.* 1412) in Gisbert's work in Kranenburg, Germany.

In the Meuse region the earliest examples of the Gothic style were mendicant churches, including, at Maastricht, both the Dominican church (consecrated 1294) and the Franciscan church (nave, late 13th century; choir, 15th century). These probably influenced the late 14th-century programmes of (re)building of the St Janskerk and the St Mathiaskerk in Maastricht, as well as the churches of Meerssen, Thorn and Sittard. The choirs are usually aisleless, but—since they are the same height as the nave—they appear lofty. The transept, if present, does not extend far beyond the side aisles. The elevation generally consists of a columnar arcade—with each column surrounded by four colonettes—a false triforium and a clerestory. Although Mosan Gothic, as the style is known, is not a homogeneous style, there is a standard type of calyx capital, decorated with perpendicular, very angular leaves.

After 1450 a Gothic style in brick developed in the sandy terrain of the Kempen. This style, known as Kempen Gothic, flourished in the first half of the 16th century, when virtually all the village churches in the area were rebuilt. (Unfortunately, most were replaced by Gothic Revival buildings, so that they are now known only from the sketchbooks (*c.* 1800) of H. Verhees.) Stone was used only for decoration, the 'streaky bacon' effect produced by alternating layers of stone and red brick being especially picturesque. Massive and generously proportioned towers are said to be typical of the style (e.g. at Alphen, Chaam, Vught and Oirschot), as are wooden barrel vaulting and a

preference for the pseudo-basilica plan. The hall church type is rarely found in this region. The transept is usually narrower and lower than the nave and sometimes has polygonal terminations; the choir is simple. The windows are not large and are flanked on the exterior by simple, blind niches. Sometimes small gables were built above the aisles, raising the windows in order to improve interior lighting. An added pitched roof connected these gables with the low saddleback roof. Series of transverse saddleback roofs also occur.

Around 1500 an indigenous brick style developed in Holland, characterized by lofty wooden barrel vaults. Among the largest examples of this style, known as Hollands Gothic, are the hall churches at Monnikendam and Edam and the Westerkerk in Enkhuizen. The columns are widely spaced, and the wall surface is reduced to a minimum to accommodate the large, broad windows. Cruciform churches without aisles are found in West Friesland (e.g. at Oosthuizen, Oosterblokker, Venhuizen) and in Zeeland (e.g. Nisse). The gable ends of the West Frisian churches are ornamented with blind niches. The Oude Kerk in Amsterdam acquired its present shape after the original hall church was rebuilt as a basilica with a series of chapels along the nave, each with a transverse roof. Despite the use of very simple materials—triforium balustrade and small wall columns are executed in wood—the interior appears lofty and spacious. The former Nieuwezijdskapel in Amsterdam was modelled on the Oude Kerk. Outside Amsterdam the pseudo-basilica with small transverse gables and pitched roofs over the aisles was frequent (e.g. at Poortugaal, Rijswijk and Koudekerk aan de Rijn). Another notable type of church is the so-called Hague hall type, which takes its name from its oldest example, the St Jacobskerk in The Hague. Examples of this type can be seen at Voorburg, Vianen and Aalsmeer. Typical are the contiguous pitched roofs over the aisles of these churches, so deep, broad and high that they almost transform the interior into a series of transverse naves and the central nave into a series of crossing compartments.

BIBLIOGRAPHY

F. Gorissen: *Ein Heiligtum des Niederrheins* (Kranenburg, 1953)

M. D. Ozinga: *De gotische Kerkelijke bouwkunst* (Amsterdam, 1953)

L. Devliegher: 'De St Bavokerk te Aardenburg', *Kon. Ned. Oudhdknd. Bond: Bull. KNOB*, 6th ser., ix (1956), pp. 197–214

E. H. ter Kuile: 'De architectuur', *Duizend jaarbouwen in Nederland: De bouwkunst van de middeleeuwen*, i (1958), pp. 191–365

R. Meischke: 'Het kleurenschema van de middeleeuwse kerkinterieurs van Groningen', *Kon. Ned. Oudhdknd. Bond: Bull. KNOB*, lxv/3–4 (1966), pp. 57–91

T. H. Haakma Wagenaar: 'Het voltooiingsontwerp voor de St Lievensmonstertoren te Zierikzee', *Kon. Ned. Oudhdknd. Bond: Bull. KNOB*, lxx (1971), pp. 31–6

J. J. M. Timmers: *De kunst van het Maasland, ii: De gotiek en de renaissance* (Assen, 1980) pp. 1–107

W. H. Vroom: *De financiering van de kathedraalbouw in de middeleeuwen en in het bijzonder van de dom van Utrecht* (Maarssen, 1981)

C. Peeters: *De Sint Janskathedraal te 's Hertogenbosch* (The Hague, 1985)

J. H. van Mosselveld, ed.: *Keldermans: Een architectonisch netwerk in de Nederlanden* (The Hague and Bergen-op-Zoom, 1987)

R. Meischke: *De gotische bouwtraditie: Studies over opdrachtgevers en bouwmeesters in de Nederlanden* (Amersfoort, 1988)

A. J. J. Mekking: *Het spel met toren en kapel: Bouwen pro en contra Bourgondië van Groningen tot Maastricht* (Utrecht and Zutphen, 1992)

L. Helten: *Kathedralen für Bürger: Die St Nikolauskirche in Kampen und der Wandel architektonischer Leitbilder städtischer Repräsentationen im 14. Jahrhundert* (Utrecht and Amsterdam, 1994)

(ii) Secular. The earliest fortifications in the Netherlands took the form of moated sites and motte-and-bailey castles (e.g. Montferland and Mergelpe near Nijmegen). Stone castles first appeared in the 11th century, and until well into the 13th century many castles, especially in the coastal areas (e.g. at Leiden, Oostvoorne, Teylingen), were built on a circular plan. Donjons were not very popular, although the Reuzentoren that was added to Valkhof Castle in Nijmegen by Emperor Frederick I (Barbarossa) was an impressive exception: it measured 9×18 m and was approximately 48 m high. From the 12th to the 14th century smaller towers were erected throughout the country in several forms: more or less rectangular (the Schierstins in Veenwouden, and Nijenbeek); D-shaped (Dever near Lisse); and rectangular with angle turrets (Heenvliet). An interesting series of 'town castles' built in the 13th and 14th centuries as residences for the city's aristocracy lined the fashionable canals in Utrecht. In spite of their crenellations and massive style, the large windows on the front and back clearly show that the function of these castles was mainly that of appearance.

An important castle builder was Count Floris V of Holland (*reg* 1256–96). To control the Frisians in the north he built castles at Medemblik, Alkmaar and Rekerdam (between 1282 and *c.* 1290), apparently modelling these on the castles of Edward I of England. Of these, only the one at Medemblik remains. It has a more or less square plan with round towers on the angles; in the middle of three of the sides is a square tower, the fourth side being dominated by the gate-house. Another castle of this type was built by Floris at Muiden (destr. *c.* 1300); in the 14th century it was rebuilt on its old foundations. Other examples of the square castle with angle towers exist at Ammersoyen and Brederode (with square angle turrets). The type remained popular into the 15th century (e.g. Helmond, Woerden, Wijk-bij-Duurstede and Doorwerth). Castles such as those at Loevestein, Doornenburg, and Middachten, built in the 14th century, have a more residential character.

Apart from building castles, Floris added extensively to the residence of the Counts of Holland in The Hague. His father, William II, following his coronation as King of the Holy Roman Empire in 1248, had started the building of a royal palace (*see also* THE HAGUE, §I, 1). Of this palace a two-storey rectangular building remains, with angle turrets like those of the Gravensteen in Ghent. At right angles to this, and over the foundations of a smaller wing that may never have been completed, Floris added an important ceremonial hall, the present Ridderzaal, which is more or less free-standing and may well reflect the architecture of Westminster Hall, London, especially as Floris entertained close ties with the English court. The main façade of the Ridderzaal, with its flanking round stair turrets and its elaborate decoration, has been compared to the west façade of Salisbury Cathedral. Another important residential complex is the Markiezenhof in Bergen-op-Zoom, dating to the 15th and 16th centuries.

Most Dutch castles did not have particularly thick walls. A wide moat usually offered sufficient protection. With the introduction of fire-arms this situation altered, and castellans had to make sure an enemy was kept well away from the walls. For this purpose moats were broadened.

Earthen or stone walls offered further protection, and bastions were added (e.g. at Loevestein, Montfort, Wildenborch). Other castles received more up-to-date towers (e.g. Rozendaal and Wijk-bij-Duurstede). Probably one of the most impressive artillery castles was that of Vredenburg in Utrecht, built in 1528 by Rombout Keldermans II for Charles V in order to keep the city of Utrecht under control. Apart from the fortifications and palaces, medieval secular building in the Netherlands includes a great number of city walls (e.g. Maastricht, Nijmegen and Zutphen) and gates, city halls (e.g. Haarlem, Sluis, Middelburg, Veere, Gouda, Schoonhoven and Hulst), guild halls and other such civic buildings. There are also numerous medieval houses, most of which are barely recognizable as such, since they were often extensively rebuilt and given new façades, for instance the Huis de Rode Poort at Utrecht, the former residence of the provost of Utrecht Cathedral.

BIBLIOGRAPHY
C. L. Temminck-Groll: *Middeleeuwse huizen te Utrecht en hun relatie met die van andere noordwesteuropese steden* (The Hague, 1963)
P. E. van Reyen: *Middeleeuwse kastelen in Nederland* (Bussum, 1965, rev. 1976)
J. Hoekstra, ed.: *Liber castellorum* (Zutphen, 1981)
M. van Vlierden: *Het Utrechtse huis de Rode Poort en zijn piscina* (Utrecht and Zutphen, 1989)
A. J. J. Mekking: 'De Grote Zaal van Floris V te Den Haag: Een onderzoek naar de betekenis van het concept', *Holland in wording. Vijfde Muiderberg-symposium: Muiderberg, 1990* (Hilversum, 1991), pp. 65–90

E. DEN HARTOG

3. *c.* 1500–*c.* 1795.

(i) Early Renaissance. (ii) Dutch Mannerism. (iii) Dutch classicism. (iv) French influence: Louis XIV and Louis XV. (v) Louis XVI and Neoclassicism.

(i) Early Renaissance. In the first half of the 16th century, when the Renaissance was at its peak in Italy and its achievements had also become manifest in Italian architecture, the dominant style north of the Alps, including the Netherlands, was still Gothic (*see* §2(ii) above). The first signs of Renaissance architecture in these regions emerge in the buildings that can be seen painted in the background of some pictures from *c.* 1500. The first true Renaissance structures that were constructed were temporary triumphal arches made of wood and cloth to add lustre to the festive welcoming ceremonies on the occasion of royal visits to towns, for example the triumphal arches built to honour the entry of Charles V in a number of Netherlandish cities such as Ghent in 1515 and 1520.

There were three channels through which the new Italian forms were introduced into the north. Published ornament prints, by Raphael and his pupils among others, found their way into the Netherlands as early as the first decades of the 16th century and were used by painters, cabinetmakers and architects. In architecture these Renaissance ornaments were initially combined with Late Gothic styles of building, without any obvious understanding of the essence and background of the style to which they originally belonged. One example of this is the Huis van Marten van Rossum (*c.* 1535) in Zaltbommel. This stone gate-house is built entirely in the Gothic tradition but has large candelabra on either side of the central gateway that seem directly copied from the ornament prints of Raphael and his followers.

During the first half of the 16th century there were also several Italians staying in the region at the invitation of prominent Netherlandish noblemen, and they introduced the language of Italian Renaissance forms directly into the Netherlands. For example, TOMASSO VINCIDOR was involved in the rebuilding (from 1529) of BREDA CASTLE for Henry III of Nassau, with the addition of a square courtyard surrounded by an arcade of Classical Doric columns. Alexander Pasqualini, a military engineer, came to the Netherlands at the invitation of the Counts of Buren, and he designed the tower (1532) of the Gothic church in IJsselstein, for which he used a beautiful accumulation of three triumphal arches with Doric, Ionic and Corinthian pilasters, exactly as in Italian examples.

Perhaps most important, however, for the spread of the new Italian style in the Netherlands were architectural treatises. Elaborate illustrations provided sculptors and architects with direct examples, while the accompanying texts offered general background information and explained the ideas of absolute harmony and the use in design of purely mathematical proportions. A Dutch translation of Serlio's treatise on the correct use of orders was published by Pieter Coecke van Aelst in Antwerp in 1539, just two years after its appearance in Venice. This made the Classical orders accessible to any carpenter who could read. Such books flowed out of Antwerp, bringing the Renaissance to the remotest parts of the northern Netherlands. In the introduction to his own architectural pattern books, Hans Vredeman de Vries later wrote that he had first been introduced to the work of Serlio when working as an apprentice in a cabinetmakers' workshop in Kollum in remote Friesland. Although Serlio's work was never entirely forgotten, Dutch architects of the late 16th century and the 17th used more contemporary Italian treatises, such as those by Vignola (1562), Palladio (1570) and Scamozzi (1615). Scamozzi's book in particular became very popular in Holland, and the Dutch translation was reprinted many times.

(ii) Dutch Mannerism. In the second half of the 16th century and the first quarter of the 17th domestic architecture became much more important, for after the revolt against Spain in 1568 both the court and the Church ceased to provide architects with commissions, thus leaving only civic and urban architecture. By the end of the 16th century Dutch towns had generally adopted the use of stone façades. The ridge of the roof mostly ran perpendicular to the street façade, finished by a progressively narrower top section that connected with the wooden roof construction behind. Because the architectural forms of the Italian Renaissance were intended to function on a monumental width, it was not possible to apply them in a straightforward manner to these façades. However, Dutch Mannerism did use the orders on a monumental scale, by crowning the central section of the façade with a rather grand and highly un-Italian gable in place of the traditional bell-tower. An early example of this composition was the Stadhuis (1564–5) of The Hague, greatly influenced by the Stadhuis (1561–5) in Antwerp, attributed to Cornelis Floris (*see* ANTWERP, fig. 9). Only a few carefully chosen Classical elements decorate the ground floor, with a series of very modest frontons over the windows. Above that, however, follows a row of powerful Doric pilasters, finished with a projecting entablature decorated entirely according to Serlio. Above this line towers a gable in which Ionic and Corinthian orders are set one above the other. The style associated with Floris was influential in the development of Dutch Mannerism. His ideas were spread by the pattern books of Hans Vredeman de Vries, who also produced edited versions of the works of Vitruvius and Serlio. Vredeman de Vries here offered a whole range of variations on the possible proportions of the orders, thereby emphasizing the importance of decorative and inventive aspects. He also added his own examples, such as ornaments that could be used to decorate the front of traditional narrow houses.

About 1600 important Dutch houses and town buildings were elaborately decorated with a wide variety of sculptural ornament. This proliferation of ornament unified the façade, which was divided into bays by the windows, becoming a network of ornament, with local accents sometimes provided by the doorway and the gable. The majority of city houses were built on narrow plots, and nearly all were finished with a gable. By 1600 gables were commonly used as the setting for inventive and playful ornament compositions with pilasters, herms, scrolls, strapwork, obelisks or cartouches. The DECORATIVE GABLE became so popular that it was also employed on broader-fronted houses and civic buildings. The style of town houses also influenced the various monumental civic buildings that were begun at the very end of the 16th century, such as gateways, weigh-houses and town halls, as can be seen in the new façade (1593–8) of the Stadhuis in Leiden (see fig. 6). Its final design was the result of collaboration between the Leiden builder Claes Cornelisz. and the Haarlem city architect Lieven de Key; the stones were supplied by Luder van Bentheim from Bremen. The façade is elongated with a separate entrance that is finished with a richly decorated gable only three bays wide. The central section, with staircase, shows an accumulation of strictly architectonic and some fanciful elements, such as austere pilasters and columns on the ground floor, followed by sumptuous scrollwork, herms and obelisks on the upper floor. During the extension of 1604 an extra gable was added on either side so that the façade seems to be divided into a series of individual, narrower façades.

The two most important architects of the late 16th century and early decades of the 17th were Lieven de Key in Haarlem and Hendrick de Keyser in Amsterdam. The work of these architects shows the transition from the playful Mannerist forms of the 16th century to the more rigid, classicizing architecture of the 17th century. At first sight the many houses built by de Keyser on the new ring of canals in Amsterdam, for example the Huis met de Hoofden (House of the Heads; 1622) on the Keizersgracht (*see* AMSTERDAM, fig. 2), give the impression that the busy decorative style of the 16th century was simply continued. However, behind the profusion of decorative elements there is a very carefully proportioned façade. In 1631, ten years after de Keyser's death, a book about his work was published, *Architectura moderna*. In it de Keyser is described as the most important innovator of Dutch architecture because he was the first to return to the old

6. Claes Cornelisz. and Lieven de Key: central façade of the Stadhuis, Leiden, 1593–8

principles of 'ingenious building', meaning that he reintroduced the mathematical regularity of antiquity as the basis of architecture. As the city architect of Amsterdam, de Keyser was the head of the city building company known as the Stadsfabryck (town factory). In this role (*see* KEYSER, DE, (1), §2) he designed a number of important public buildings in Amsterdam, such as the city's first Exchange (1608–11; destr. 1838), and at least two Protestant churches in the new city extensions, the Zuiderkerk (1603) and the Westerkerk (1620). The Noorderkerk (1620) is also attributed to him. He introduced new types of floor-plan into these churches, which were designed specially for the Protestant service. The plan of the Noorderkerk is based on the Greek cross, while those of the Zuiderkerk and the Westerkerk (especially that of the latter) are based on two joined Greek crosses. These churches with their strictly mathematical floor-plans were much imitated in Holland in the course of the 17th century.

(iii) Dutch classicism. While elsewhere the dominant style in architecture remained that of de Keyser and his followers, a group of architects in Haarlem, including Jacob van Campen, developed a different style in the 1620s, which lasted until *c.* 1700. The ornamental element was reduced to Classical orders of pilasters incorporated into a rigid mathematical plan. This also determined the position of the walls and the windows. Unlike de Keyser's designs, the decoration in those of van Campen was more harmonious with the structure of the rest of the building and

was no longer treated as a separate element. Pilasters served to accentuate the division into bays and were made exactly according to the description in the Italian treatises instead of being variants of one kind or another or completely new inventions. The main sources of inspiration for this new style were the north Italian buildings of Palladio and Scamozzi. In France at the time a similar kind of classicizing architecture was popular, and there were developments there that were also of importance to Dutch architecture. In the Dutch Republic this style is known as classicizing Baroque or Dutch Classicism. It was more austere and less picturesque than that of the previous decades, and its popularity is thought to be related to the growing wealth of certain groups in the Netherlands. This growth in wealth was accompanied by a new, more modish lifestyle adopted by the more prominent members of the bourgeoisie. The new classicism was more restrained and impersonal—and for that reason more imposing—than the exuberant and playful architecture of the beginning of the 17th century. With this combination of sobriety and massiveness, the classicizing Baroque provided the perfect setting for fashionable life in the 'Golden Age'.

At the centre of these developments was the court in The Hague of Stadholder Frederick Henry (*see* ORANGE NASSAU, (3)), who had been brought up in France and was keen to add refinement and embellishments to court life. He was in this way a powerful influence on cultural matters in the Dutch Republic. The most important promoter of classicism at the court was Constantijn Huygens (i), who was secretary to Frederick Henry as well as a diplomat, poet and composer (*see* HUYGENS, (1)). He was also the Stadholder's cultural adviser, charged with finding suitable painters and architects, and it was through Huygens that Jacob van Campen and soon afterwards Pieter Post, also from Haarlem, were introduced to the court. While van Campen had designed his first buildings in Amsterdam in the 1620s, it was in The Hague in the 1630s that he was given the opportunity of building in a mature classicizing style: with Post as his assistant, he designed the Mauritshuis (now a museum) for Johan Maurits van Nassau-Siegen in 1633, and the following year work was begun on Huygens's house (both buildings on the Plein). With the building of the Mauritshuis (for illustration *see* CAMPEN, JACOB VAN), the classicizing Baroque was established as the style chosen by the nobility, the status-conscious members of the ruling class, wealthy merchants and governing bodies. Its plan is purely symmetrical, with a clear division of the façade by means of correct pilasters and a central projection crowned by a fronton. It is not a direct borrowing from Italian architecture but a close following of Italian academic theory. A French influence is also noticeable, especially in the way the interior is divided into two identical apartments.

Jacob van Campen's most important design, also the most important example of Dutch classicism, was the new Stadhuis (1648–55) in Amsterdam (now the Royal Palace; *see* AMSTERDAM, §V, 2 and TOWN HALL, fig. 3). This monumental building is divided into a number of blocks, with corner pavilions and projecting central sections. The outer walls are decorated all the way around with rows of Composite and Corinthian pilasters, in accordance with Scamozzi. Inside, the rooms of the various governing bodies are arranged in hierarchical order on the main floor. The projecting central section was used by the burgomasters, that at the back of the building by the bailiff and aldermen responsible for justice. The four corner pavilions were used by the four financial 'corner stones' of the city council: the treasury, the treasury extraordinary, the governors of the orphanages and the audit office. Each room is decorated with allegorical figures and scenes from Classical mythology and legends reflecting its specific function.

The spread of Dutch classicism was brought about primarily through the work of two of Jacob van Campen's ex-assistants, Pieter Post (*see* POST, (1)) and PHILIPS VINGBOONS. In 1646 Post became architect to the Stadholder, soon becoming the most sought-after designer in court circles in The Hague. Besides palaces and stately homes, he also designed conference rooms and other types of buildings such as a gun foundry and a powder magazine. In all these he adhered to the principles of pure symmetry and balanced proportions. In the case of monumental and public buildings he would, if so required, include more decoration in the form of Classical pilasters or sculptural cartouches. In strict accordance with classicist principles, however, these decorative elements were considered to be of secondary importance, for the real beauty of the architecture lay in the harmony of its proportions. Post's most famous building for Frederick Henry is the

Huis ten Bosch in The Hague (*see* THE HAGUE, §V, 3). The Stadholder died during its construction, but his widow, Amalia von Solms, ordered the completion of the building as a monument to her late husband. This becomes clear from the cross-shaped central hall, the Oranjezaal. Its iconographical programme, composed with the help of Jacob van Campen and others, idealizes the deeds of Frederick Henry.

At the same time, Vingboons was working for a completely different circle. He received commissions, not from prominent figures at The Hague court but from wealthy merchants and the ruling classes in Amsterdam who built their houses on the new ring of canals surrounding the old city centre. The land on these canals was usually sold in plots c. 8 or 9 m wide, and the houses built on these plots all had traditional gables because their narrow façades did not allow a gable with eaves perpendicular to the façade, as required by Classical theory. This required a completely different type of roof construction, with a ridge parallel to the façade of the house. These narrow Amsterdam façades did not lend themselves to the rigorous form of classicism applied by Post, and it was the inventive mind of Vingboons that solved the problem. He replaced the old-fashioned stepped gable with a neckgable, so that the central bay would be extended right up to the ridge of the roof. The neck was then decorated on both sides with scrollwork that followed the sloping roof

7. Jacob Roman: façade (1693) of the Stadhuis, Deventer

behind. Sometimes people bought two adjoining plots and built houses of twice the normal width. The façades of these houses extended over a width of *c.* 15 m so that they could easily be finished off with a roof parallel to the façade, sometimes topped by a fronton.

From the beginning, façades with and without pilasters were equally prevalent. In the case of the latter, the rhythm of the proportions could be deduced only from the positioning of the windows. In the late 1660s the use of fully pilastered walls became less popular. The late works of both Post and Vingboons show a growing simplification, with a drastic reduction of Classical ornamentation, even in buildings with an obvious public function. This simplification and increasing austerity can be seen as a further consequence of the mentality that had introduced classicism at the beginning of the 17th century. The more prominent citizens adopted a more withdrawn lifestyle, which in architecture led to houses with more serene exteriors and richer interiors. As the exterior walls became simpler, the middle bay became the focus for extra decoration, around the main entrance and the window above it. The final phase of Dutch classicism, in the last three decades of the 17th century, has therefore come to be known as the Austere style. The essence of the Austere style is an aesthetic in which there is less sculptural work on the façade, but monumentality is achieved by the austere rhythm of the angular entrance and sharp, precise windows with no decorative frames. The new façade (1693) of the Stadhuis in Deventer (see fig. 7) by Jacob Roman, architect to the stadholder from 1689, shows this new ideal with an extreme austerity and distinction. In the country houses built at this time by King–Stadholder William III and his nobles, the mathematical ground-plan became an even more important part of the design. Examples of these brick buildings with a cubiform simplicity include the castles at Amerongen (1673–8), Zeist (1677–86) by Jacob Roman and Middachten (1695) by Jacob Roman and Steven Vennekool.

(iv) French influence: Louis XIV and Louis XV. In 1686 the expelled French Huguenot Daniel Marot I arrived in the Netherlands, where he introduced new styles of decoration that had developed in France with the circle of artists at the court of Louis XIV. They believed that the unity of architecture, interior and garden was of special importance and that this unity could occur only when one person controlled all the different tasks. In this period, then, a new kind of artist came to prominence, known as the *dessinateur* or designer, who, independently of skilled craftsmen, made designs for furniture-makers, blacksmiths, carpet-weavers, carpenters and stone masons. When Marot arrived in the Netherlands, his talents were quickly noticed by William III and his circle, who very much needed somebody familiar with the newest developments in French art and style and who had also made a deep impression on the Dutch nobles. For William III and his circle, Marot worked mainly as an interior and garden designer, on such projects as the castle at Zeist and HET LOO (for illustration *see* MAROT, (2)). In this way he was involved in the luxurious interiors (*see* §V, 2 below) in the country houses mentioned above, which, from the outside, seemed so austere and unapproachable.

After the death of William III in 1702, Marot was forced to concentrate more on works in Amsterdam and The Hague. Besides reworking a number of interiors in The Hague, he produced designs for façades, including the Huis Schuylenburch (1715), the Huis Wassenaer–Obdam (1717) and the new ceremonial entrance (1736) for the Huis ten Bosch. The Huis Schuylenburch is one of the first examples of the use of Louis XIV ornament for gable decoration. The façade wall remained flat and sober as in the earlier period, but over the middle bay and above the roof-line was a conglomeration of festive ornaments derived from interior decoration. After this style was established in 1715, Marot and such followers as Jan van Logteren and Frans Blancard spent the following decades working along these lines without essentially acquainting themselves with more recent developments in France, where first the new lighter Regency style and then, towards 1730, the elegant and asymmetrical Rococo had overtaken the pompous style associated with the reign of Louis XIV. In the 1730s the Fleming Jan Pieter van Baurscheit (ii) introduced a lighter and more sculptural style in such projects as the Beeldenhuis (1730; façade reconstr.) in the Hendrikstraat and the façade (1733; destr.) of the van-Dishoeck-huis (later the Stadhuis), both in Vlissingen (see fig. 8). The façade became less architectonic and more sculptural in construction, sometimes with Baroque curves around the central balcony. The canal house gables in Amsterdam of that time also show that ornamentation was becoming increasingly sculptural and organic in appearance.

8. Jan Pieter van Baurscheit (ii): façade (1733; destr.) of the van-Dishoeck-huis (later the Stadhuis), Vlissingen

9. Henry Triquetti and J. B. Dubois: Paviljoen Welgelegen (1785–9), Haarlem

Ornamentation of the asymmetrical Rococo kind did not come into general use for exterior work on any scale until after 1750, in the form of a modest door- or window-frame or, on a monumental scale, sculptural decoration for the façade. Pieter de Swart studied architecture in Paris, and on his return to the Netherlands he became architect to the stadholder. He was responsible for the introduction of the true Louis XV architecture from France, a style that limits the use of rocaille ornament to the interior, leaving the exterior stark and almost free of ornament. His most important works are the Huis Patras (1760) and the former Paleis Nassau–Weilburg (1767; now the Royal Theatre), both in The Hague.

(v) Louis XVI and Neo-classicism. The great importance enjoyed internationally by the art of Classical antiquity in the second half of the 18th century, stimulated by the excavations at Pompeii, the writings of Winckelmann and various publications about the monuments of Greece, was also felt in the Netherlands. Dutch architects were aware of the work of their foreign counterparts, not least those of Robert Adam and François de Neufforge, and knew of their publications containing new insights and ideas. Some well-travelled gentlemen who actually went to Italy were also influential. It is likely that people knew the most important examples of this new style in Ghent and Brussels. The three most important architects in Holland were Leendert Viervant in Haarlem and his brother-in-law Jacob Otten-Husly and Abraham van der Hart in Amsterdam. One of Viervant's projects in Haarlem was the gallery–library (1779) of the Teylers Foundation, an oval cupola that is lit by the windows that ring the roof. At ground-level, cases for instruments line the walls and are integrated with the panelling, surmounted by built-in bookcases on the gallery above. Otten Husly's most important work is the Felix Meritis building (1787), on the Keizersgracht in Amsterdam, for the Felix Meritis Society. Built to house the various departments of the Society, it has a monumental façade with Corinthian pilasters. Abraham van der Hart was city architect of Amsterdam and was professionally responsible for many public buildings, including the Maagdenhuis (1784), the Catholic girls' orphanage on the Spui. His commission here was to produce a monumental but very sober building, and its austerity links it with the Austere style of the late 17th century (see also fig. 35 below).

One of the best examples of Neo-classical architecture in the Netherlands is the Paviljoen Welgelegen (1785–9; see fig. 9) in Haarlem, built as a country home for the Amsterdam banker Henry Hope. The monumental main section of the building, with a raised central section, houses three large rooms that served as a gallery for Hope's collection of pictures. In the less formal wings were the guest rooms and accommodation for domestic staff, with Hope's own living-quarters situated at the far end of the art gallery. This unusual building was originally designed by Henry Triquetti (1704–74), the Sardinian consul and a friend of Hope. The design was later carried out under the supervision of J. B. Dubois (1762–1851), a young architect from the southern Netherlands who had probably gained experience of this use of plaster in architecture, as it was fairly commonly used in Ghent and Brussels from 1775 onwards.

BIBLIOGRAPHY

E. Neurdenburg: *Hendrick de Keyser: Beeldhouwer en bouwmeester van Amsterdam* (Amsterdam, 1930)

M. D. Ozinga: *Daniel Marot: De schepper van den Hollandschen Lodewijk XIV-stijl* (Amsterdam, 1938)

F. A. J. Vermeulen: *Handboek tot de geschiedenis der Nederlandsche bouwkunst,* iii (The Hague, 1941)

P. T. A. Swillens: *Jacob van Campen: Schilder en bouwmeester, 1595–1657* (Arnhem, 1961, 2/1979)

C. A. van Swigchem: *Abraham van der Hart (1747-1820), architect: Stadsbouwmeester van Amsterdam* (Amsterdam, 1965)

K. A. Ottenheym: *Philips Vingboons, 1607–1678: Architect* (Zutphen, 1969)

H. Zantkuijl: *Bouwen in Amsterdam* (Amsterdam, 1975)

R. Vos and F. Leeman: *Het nieuwe ornament: Gids voor de renaissancearchitectuur en -decoratie in Nederland in de 16de eeuw* (The Hague, 1986)

F. Grijzenhout and C. van Tuyll van Serooskerken, eds: *Edele eenvoud: Neo-classicisme in Nederland, 1765–1800* (Zwolle, 1989)

L. H. M. Quant and others, eds: *Paviljoen Welgelegen, 1789–1989* (Haarlem, 1989)

J. J. Terwen and K. A. Ottenheym: *Pieter Post, 1608–1669* (Zutphen, 1993)

R. Meischke and others: *Huizen in Nederland: Amsterdam* (Zwolle and Amsterdam, 1995)

K. A. OTTENHEYM

4. *c.* 1795–*c.* 1890. From 1795 to 1813 the French Revolution and subsequent period of Napoleonic rule had a detrimental influence on the Netherlands. Trade links were broken, colonies were lost to foreign powers, and the country was annexed by the French empire (1810–14). The few buildings constructed in this period were mostly executed in an uninspired Louis XVI Neo-classical style (*see* §3(v) above). The only short-lived improvement was due to Louis Napoleon, who, as King of Holland (*reg* 1806–10), favoured a sober form of Neo-classicism. In practice, however, he had too little money for this and, as it turned out, too little time. In Utrecht, therefore, he had some large houses joined together to create a palace, of which the ballroom and large entrance are incorporated in the present-day Universiteitsbibliotheek on the Wittevrouwenstraat. For this, he employed the French architect Jean-Thomas Thibault, who was assisted by the German Jan David Zocher the elder (1763–1817).

Of greater significance was the encouragement given by Louis Napoleon to talented young Dutch architects, by financing their study in Paris or Rome. They included Jan de Greef, Zeger Reijers (1790–1857) and JAN DAVID ZOCHER the younger, who became the most important architects in the Netherlands following the fall of Louis Napoleon (1814) and the restoration of the monarchy. They put into effect the architectural schemes of King William I. De Greef and Reijers turned the former huntinglodge of Soestdijk, near Amersfoort, into a robust Empire-style country house with Palladian design elements. The 17th-century Paleis Noordeinde in The Hague (*see* THE HAGUE, fig. 1) was decorated (1816–22) in a classical style by Bartholomeus Ziesenis (1768–1820) and de Greef.

After 1820 Dutch architecture was also influenced by the Greek Revival style, for example the St Willebrorduskerk (1827) in The Hague, by Adrianus Tollus (1783–1847); the pavilion (1826) for William I in Scheveningen, by Adriaan Noordendorp; and the former Accijnhuisje (Customs House; 1827) in The Hague, by Zeger Reijers. In Utrecht and Rotterdam, Pieter Adams (1778–1846) practised the classicism of this period in an unorthodox and monumental manner; sadly, however, the Rotterdam work was destroyed in the bombing of 1940. Best known is his Winkel van Sinkel (Sinkel's Shop; 1836) in Utrecht,

an early department store with large cast-iron caryatids. He gave the Stadhuis in Utrecht a Doric façade (1828). Also in Utrecht, Christiaan Kramm (1797–1875) built the Paleis van Justitie (1834–7), which is in a sober Doric style compared with the work of Adams. Closer to Adams's robust classicism was the Haarlemmerpoort (1838) in Amsterdam, by Cornelis Alewijn (*fl* 1840–50), and the Paleis van Justitie (1846) in Leeuwarden, by Thomas Romein. Amsterdam's second Koopmansbeurs (Merchants' Exchange; 1840–45) attracted most public attention: it was designed by Jan David Zocher the younger, who sought a practical simplicity and applied only sparing classical decoration. The Belgian architect Tieleman-Frans Suys adopted a conspicuously headstrong classicism, for example in the Mozes en Aaron Kerk (1837–41) in Amsterdam, which incorporates a porticoed façade with twin towers, and Neo-classical details in juxtaposition with Mannerist elements.

The simple Dutch Neo-classical style was followed in the mid-19th century by a generally less inventive use of pattern books, which stimulated the need for a revival of early 17th-century Dutch Mannerism. This style, called Dutch Renaissance Revival, was adopted until the early 20th century. The work of Cornelis Outshoorn is a forceful expression of this. He was a practical classicist with a sense of function and space. He gained great renown with his Paleis voor Volksvlijt (Palace of National Industry; 1857–64; destr. 1929), an iron and glass structure that was inspired by Joseph Paxton's Crystal Palace (1851; destr.) designed for the Great Exhibition in London. Outshoorn also designed the Amstel Hotel (1863–7; for illustration *see* OUTSHOORN, CORNELIS), situated on the right bank of the Amstel River in Amsterdam. While several of his earlier buildings had been constructed of brick stuccoed over to resemble stone, the hotel suggests his interest in Dutch Renaissance architecture in the use of exposed brickwork, blended, nevertheless, with elements of Empire-style architecture, such as the French-inspired mansard roofs.

The Gothic Revival style developed in the Netherlands as well and was originally intended to be a freer form of expression in contrast to classicism, except, perhaps, in the Catholic south of the country, where church architecture still adhered to an older Gothic tradition. Numerous country houses were decorated in the Gothic Revival style, influenced by buildings in England and Germany. King William II (*reg* 1840–49) introduced an English 'Perpendicular' style to the Netherlands, exemplified by the Gothische Zaal (Gothic Hall), opposite the Paleis Noordeinde, and by the Willemskerk and adjacent houses, all in The Hague. The writings of A. W. N. Pugin, Sulpiz and Melchior Boisserée and Jean-Baptiste-Antoine Lassus were also known in the Netherlands, chiefly through the efforts of Joseph A. Alberdingk Thijm, who was the most important leader of the Catholic emancipation movement. He and the architect P. J. H. CUYPERS helped to spread the Gothic Revival style in the Netherlands, which was supported by the restoration of the episcopal hierarchy (1853). Cuypers worked in Roermond, his home town, as an architect and designer of furniture, interiors and applied arts. His ideas on this and on the 'honest' use of materials were in accord with those of William Morris. In the

10. P. J. H. Cuypers: Rijksmuseum (1876–85), Amsterdam

practice of architecture he aligned himself with the French architect Viollet-le-Duc, often quoting the latter's pronouncement that every form not indicated by the structure has to be rejected. Cuypers built and decorated many churches in a free Gothic style, rather sober in grammar, but with the spiritual exuberance of the Counter-Reformation. His houses and large public buildings include formal elements of the French and Dutch Renaissance. Cuypers made his fame in particular with the Rijksmuseum (1876–85; see fig. 10) and the Centraal Station (1885–9), both in Amsterdam. He also worked on the restoration of the Munsterkerk in Roermond, and undertook a rather free re-creation of the castle of De Haar at Haarzuilens, near Utrecht. In 1865 he moved to Amsterdam, where he founded the Rijksmuseumschool (later the Quellinusschool) and where he taught applied arts and art history. Many young architects started practice in his Amsterdam office, including K. P. C. de Bazel, J. L. M. Lauweriks and Hendrik T. Wijdeveld. There they learnt about architecture and the applied arts, mastering a new grammar of form that they gradually began to apply during the second half of the 19th century.

BIBLIOGRAPHY

J. J. Vriend: *De bouwkunst van ons land*, 3 vols (Amsterdam, 1938–50), i, *De steden* (2/1942)
R. C. Hekker: 'De Nederlandse bouwkunst in het begin van de negentiende eeuw', *Kon. Ned. Oudhdknd. Bond: Bull. KNOB*, 6th ser., iv (1951), pp. 1–28
E. H. ter Kuile: *Duizend jaar bouwen in Nederland*, ii (Amsterdam, 1957), pp. 184–94
H. P. R. Rosenberg: *De 19de-eeuwse kerkelijke bouwkunst in Nederland* (The Hague, 1972)
J. van Laarhoven, ed.: *Naar gothieken kunstzin, kerkelijke kunst en cultuur in Noord-Brabant in de negentiende eeuw* ('s-Hertogenbosch, 1979)

5. *c*. 1890–1945. The changes that occurred in the late 19th century, when the Netherlands shifted from a predominantly agricultural country into a modern capitalist state, called for new building types, including government buildings, offices, banks, schools, hospitals, shops and houses. Throughout the third quarter of the 19th century this typological development had been concealed behind historicizing forms, but after 1880 this practice was increasingly attacked by, among others, H. P. Berlage, who sought a new style for a new age. However, he believed that until such a style had been developed, copying was preferable: otherwise, monstrosities would be created. Berlage's office building for the insurance company De Algemeene (1892–4; destr. 1963) on the Damrak, Amsterdam, was the herald of this innovation in the Netherlands. Here he used materials in a sober manner and applied distinct and mostly allegorical decoration and primary colours. This Dutch Nieuwe Kunst movement, the equivalent of the early Modernism also emerging elsewhere in Europe and in the USA, was applied in the architectural sphere chiefly by Berlage, K. P. C. de Bazel and Willem Kromhout. Its key work is Berlage's Koopmansbeurs (Merchants' Exchange, *c*. 1898–1903; see fig. 11) on the Damrak, Amsterdam. Here he strove for a practical architecture, in which primary attention was paid to function while the external treatment was generally sufficient to serve as a basis for further development by subsequent generations. Although this viewpoint showed

11. H. P. Berlage: Koopmansbeurs (*c.* 1898–1903), Amsterdam

a great deal of idealism, it is nevertheless true that Berlage's Koopmansbeurs represents a brave attempt to move away from the age-old, traditional grammar of form.

Berlage's influence was far-reaching, extending not only to the expressionists of the AMSTERDAM SCHOOL but also to the elementarists of the De Stijl and Nieuwe Zakelijkheid (New Objectivity) groups, who variously developed his ideas about space, materials, form and function (*see* ELEMENTARISM, DE STIJL and NEUE SACHLICHKEIT). De Bazel was less of a radical and showed a more easy-going, lyrical temperament. Kromhout began as Berlage did, as his American Hotel (1899–1902) on the Leidesplein in Amsterdam reveals, but later he associated himself with the Amsterdam school's individualistic expressionism. The decorative Art Nouveau of France and Belgium and Germany's *Jugendstil* were given few opportunities, except as attractive possibilities for office buildings and shops.

After 1915 the Amsterdam school arose out of this controversy between general and individual objectives. Its architects wanted to give their buildings a clear aesthetic value once more, which in their opinion was lacking in the architecture of their great predecessor Berlage. Their personal wish for form sometimes led to a strong lyricism ('painting in brick'), which characterized much of the public housing built between 1915 and 1930. This occurred throughout the Netherlands but chiefly at Amsterdam-Zuid, which was planned by Berlage and executed (1917–30) by Amsterdam school architects. It enjoyed international fame as a commendable example of urban planning and housing design. Michel de Klerk and P. L. Kramer designed the most noteworthy parts, namely P. L. Takstraat (for illustration *see* AMSTERDAM SCHOOL), Tellegenstraat, Henriëtte Ronnerplein, Thérèse Schwartzeplein and Vrijheidslaan. Kramer's many bridges in Amsterdam are also typical of the Amsterdam school. (For an illustration of Kramer's De Bijenkorf department store in

The Hague *see* KRAMER, P. L.; for an illustration of de Klerk's 'Het Scheep' housing complex in Amsterdam *see* KLERK, MICHEL DE.)

The impact on architecture from *De Stijl*, a periodical published by Theo van Doesburg, occurred around the same time (1917). *De Stijl* propagated the beginnings of absolute abstraction, which banned each relation to nature. Ultimate harmony was expected from this, in which life and work would coincide, resulting in a new evaluation of life for the age. New shapes and colours were the formal means for achieving this. Gerrit Rietveld best expressed these intentions with a new spatial awareness, which first led to great freedom and second established a clear relationship between external and internal spaces. He expressed this with extreme vehemence in the Schröder House (1924), Utrecht, but light, air and space continued to play a large part in his later work. After beginning in Berlage's manner, J. J. P. Oud followed the tenets of De Stijl, as in his façade (1924–5; destr. 1940) for the Café De Unie on Coolsingel in Rotterdam (rebuilt at Mauritsweg 35 in 1986). These forceful expressions of Elementarism and abstract intentions were largely over by 1926, and the achievements mainly incorporated into the international modernism of Nieuwe Zakelijkheid. In this the concern was only with the optimal elaboration of function, out of which it was believed good architecture would be self-generating. Hence, in the Hook of Holland, Oud built housing blocks (1925–9) with ingenious ground-plans, which also achieved a great feeling of openness and quiet in an urban environment (for an illustration of one housing estate *see* OUD, J. J. P.). Brinkman & van der Vlugt designed the well-known Van Nelle Factory (1925–31; for illustration *see* BRINKMAN, (2)), Rotterdam, in close collaboration with the patron C. H. van der Leeuw (1890–1973). Johannes Duiker (*see* BIJVOET & DUIKER) built the Zonnestraal Sanatorium (1924–5) in Hilversum at the same time and the Openluchtschool voor het Gezonde Kind (Open-air School for the Healthy Child; 1929–30) in Cliostraat, Amsterdam. His conspicuous experiments with high-rise buildings found a partial realization in the 'Nirwana' block of flats (1927–30), with Jan Gerko Wiebenga (1886–1974), on Willem Witsenplein, The Hague. Van der Vlugt and Duiker represent severe Functionalism (Dut. Nieuwe Bouwen) in its most striking aspect.

Rietveld occupied a unique position in this milieu, not only because of his lyrical avowal of the primacy of space but also through his far-reaching efforts to make minimal use of building materials. The three residential blocks (1930–34) that he built on Erasmuslaan and Robert Schumannstraat (see fig. 12), Utrecht, and the residential block (1932) in Vienna for the Wiener Werkbundsiedlung, are entirely consistent with this. Another prominent contemporary was W. M. Dudok, who applied ideas influenced by Frank Lloyd Wright about space and materials in an elegant Functional architecture, for example the Raadhuis (1924–31; for illustration see DUDOK, W. M.), Hilversum. As Hilversum's municipal architect, Dudok made an extensive contribution to the creation of spacious and well-lit public housing. Jan Buijs, who had similar aims, built De Volharding (1927–8), a department store and offices in The Hague, for the cooperative of the same name. Functionalism gradually weakened at the end of the 1930s. In his Shell Building (1938–42), Wassenaarseweg, The Hague, Oud showed clearly that he no longer gave

preference to intellectual abstraction. This provoked vehement discussions, which eventually became ideological and, like architectual activity itself, were interrupted for a considerable time by the German occupation of the Netherlands.

Apart from these movements, the achievements of which led to a high level of international recognition for Dutch architecture, there were other ideas current in the inter-war years. These were most clearly formulated by Groep '32, who sought to modify strict Functionalism with the introduction of ornament. Members included Albert Boeken and Arthur Staal. Alongside these related trends, an entirely different movement came into existence in the 1920s, the Delft school (see DELFT SCHOOL (ii)), led by the neo-Thomist Martinus Jan Granpré Molière, who, notwithstanding his insight into the problems of architecture and urban planning, wanted to avoid severing contact with 'age-old' values. He called for a trustworthy tradition, because as a modern Catholic he stood apart from Functionalism, which generally expressed Socialist opinions. His building of the garden suburb of Vreewijk (1916–19), Rotterdam, various council houses at Naaldwijk (1930) and Zwijndrecht (1931–4) and the chapel of the Groot-Seminarie (1938–9) in Haaren demonstrated an enlightened tradition. His numerous large and small houses were valued for their simplicity and practicality. This architecture also came to an end in 1940.

For a discussion of parallel developments in interior design during this period see §V, 4 below.

12. Gerrit Rietveld: residential block (1932), Robert Schumannstraat, Utrecht

6. AFTER 1945. At the beginning of the post-war period the Netherlands lost its leading position in architecture, and five years passed before reconstruction and the alleviation of the housing shortage were tackled. The building trades were largely pre-industrial. Architecture was partly traditional and partly practical–functional. Functionalism's light, air and space soon became common property, but the use of white stucco to achieve maximum abstraction was regarded as too impractical. Furthermore, such a refined aesthetic met with scant approval, while the need for a material connection with nature became a greater concern. Pronounced social change meant that new building types were needed to accommodate health, culture and recreation. This also applied to services for trade, traffic and industry, which increased in number and complexity. The architect was often the director of an office, in which several disciplines had to be practised. Middle-of-the-road Functionalists who were largely responsible for determining the appearance of Dutch architecture after 1945 include M. F. Duintjer (1908–83), Auke Komter, G. H. M. Holt, Arthur Staal and Jan Piet Kloos. Of greater significance were Gerrit Rietveld (still), J. H. van den Broek, Jacob B. Bakema (see VAN DEN BROEK & BAKEMA), Hugh Aart Maaskant and Willem van Tijen. Almost all of them belong to the second generation of innovators born early in the 20th century. They gave post-war reconstruction architecture its overwhelmingly Functional character.

These architects were not looking for a new style but for new solutions to the problem of public housing. Bakema, in Rietveld's footsteps, saw architecture as an instrument of human self-awareness. He and Aldo van Eyck were editors of the periodical Forum and used it as their mouthpiece. In it, and through the architectural group TEAM TEN, they proclaimed the end of CIAM and the International Style that emanated from it. They believed that architecture that preserved the distinct spheres of living, working and traffic had in the meantime become impossible. They put forward new ideas based on the study of 'natural' urban milieux in Africa, Asia and the USA that had not yet been 'interfered' with. In 1959 they defended their point of view at the CIAM congress in Otterlo, which subsequently turned out to be the last. The idea that architecture and urban planning should fundamentally not be separated had been explored in the Lijnbaan shopping centre (1949–53), Rotterdam, where Bakema and van den Broek demonstrated the 'function of the form', which expresses this totality, unlike the Functionalism of the 1920s and 1930s, where the notion of separate functions persisted. Van Eyck achieved international recognition with his Burgerweeshuis (City Orphanage, 1957–60; for illustration see EYCK, ALDO VAN), IJsbaanpad, Amsterdam, which acquired the configuration of a village through the use of simple materials: concrete, brick and glass. Also in Amsterdam he organized c. 500 public play areas.

Meanwhile the young Herman Hertzberger came to the fore as co-editor of Forum (1959–63) and as the architect of buildings in which he did not emphasize any particular shape. He wished purely to stimulate new possibilities, as a result of which his work is varied and has the appearance of being anonymous. The best known is his Centraal

Beheer (1968–72), an office building in Apeldoorn, organized as separate pavilions, each with individual open-plan offices. This period was characterized by a great deal of theoretical discussion about architecture between architects. Writings by Alexander Tzonis, Robert Venturi, Reyner Banham, Charles Jencks and M. Tafuri were also much read in the Netherlands. In the 1970s Dutch architects continued to be increasingly opposed to prevailing norms. Some withdrew by espousing conceptual attitudes so far removed from practicality that in all respects Dutch architecture regressed. This period of Postmodernism ended c. 1980, when a measure of reality began to prevail. Rem Koolhaas and his Office for Metropolitan Architecture (OMA) returned to the Netherlands because of important commissions. In collaboration with H. van Meer (b 1928), housing was built in Amsterdam on the north side of the IJ. Van Eyck had built the Hubertushuis (1973–8), Amsterdam, a home for single mothers and their children, and c. 1980 Piet Blom was able to realize his 'homes on the city's roof' on a spacious scale and with many variants, round the mouth of the River Rotte. In De Peperklip (1982), Rotterdam, Carel Weeber (b 1937) returned to an emphatic total concept for this extensive public housing. In the 1980s numerous office towers were built, faced with dark reflecting glass that gave an impression of inaccessibility. This apparent self-assurance provided little opportunity for self-fulfilment, which led to expectations of a definite reaction in the next century.

BIBLIOGRAPHY
H. P. Berlage and others: Moderne bouwkunst in Nederland, 20 vols (Rotterdam, 1932–5)
J. J. Vriend: De bouwkunst van ons land, 3 vols (Amsterdam, 1938–50), i, De steden (2/1942)
G. Fanelli: Architettura moderna in Olanda (Florence, 1968; Dut. trans., The Hague, 1981)
I. L. Szénássy: Architectuur in Nederland, 1960–1967 (Amsterdam, 1969)
E. Bergvelt and others: De Amsterdamse school, 1910–1930 (Amsterdam, 1975, 2/1979)
M. Bock: Architectura, 1893–1918 (Amsterdam, 1975)
A. van der Woud, T. van Leeuwen and P. Hefting: Americana, 1880–1930 (Amsterdam, 1975)
D. I. Grinberg: Housing in the Netherlands, 1900–1940 (Delft, 1977)
G. Fanelli: Architettura edilizia urbanistica Olanda, 1917–1940 (Florence, 1978)
Het Nieuwe Bouwen: Previous History (exh. cat., Amsterdam, Ned. Doc. Bouwkunst, 1982)
Het Nieuwe Bouwen Rotterdam, 1920–1960 (exh. cat., Rotterdam, Mus. Boymans–van Beuningen, 1982)
M. Bock and others: Van het Nieuwe Bouwen naar een nieuwe architectuur: Groep '32 (The Hague, 1983)
B. Rebel: Het Nieuwe Bouwen: Het Functionalisme in Nederland, 1918–1945 (Assen, 1983)
Het Nieuwe Bouwen Amsterdam, 1920–1960 (exh. cat., Amsterdam, Stedel. Mus., 1983)
Het Nieuwe Bouwen De Stijl: Neo-Plasticism in Architecture (exh. cat., The Hague, Gemeentemus., 1983)
Het Nieuwe Bouwen International: CIAM Housing Town Planning (exh. cat., Otterlo, Rijksmus. Kröller-Müller, 1983)
The Amsterdam School: Dutch Expressionist Architecture, 1915–1930 (exh. cat., ed. W. de Wit; New York, Cooper-Hewitt Mus., 1983)
PIETER SINGELENBERG

III. Painting and graphic arts.

1. Before c. 1400. 2. c. 1400–c. 1525. 3. c. 1525–c. 1550. 4. c. 1550–c. 1680. 5. c. 1680–c. 1800. 6. c. 1800–c. 1900. 7. After c. 1900.

1. BEFORE c. 1400. The survival of paintings from the northern Netherlands in the period preceding the 15th

century is exceptionally rare. The few known works provide insufficient evidence to trace either a school or any possible early north Netherlandish tradition. A number of early accounts of paintings have been corrected or doubted in recent art-historical literature, and the number of early pictures assumed to be north Netherlandish has consequently been reduced. A continuing and distinct tradition can be detected only in late 14th-century manuscript painting.

What were previously regarded as the oldest products of north Netherlandish painting, the two dedication miniatures from the Evangeliary of Egmond (The Hague, Kon. Bib., MS. 76 F 1; see Hoogewerf), were probably, in fact, made in Ghent or the Lower Rhine area *c*. AD 975. The script originated at Reims at the end of the 9th century, and the illumination, comprising images of the four Evangelists and canon tables, is associated with the former so-called Franco-Saxon style of monastic workshops in northern France. The Utrecht Sacramentary (Berlin, Staatsbib. Preuss. Kultbes., MS. 691), dated on stylistic grounds to the second half of the 10th century, can be localized with even less certainty owing to a lack of comparable material. The only figurative illumination consists of the depiction on fol. 1*r* of a priest holding out a chalice and eucharistic scale to the hand of God, which appears to come out of the enlarged initial letter T (*Te igitur*). This initial is filled in with characteristic interlace motifs of the Franco-Saxon style.

North Netherlandish illumination during the Romanesque period was clearly restricted to the provision of decorated initials in red or green, with tendrils into which animals are sometimes introduced. Interlace decoration is again often found, as well as penwork infill. A typical example is the illumination of an early 12th-century *Moralia in Job* (Rijksuniv. Utrecht, Bib., MS. 86). These modest decorations are also found in a *Martinellum* (Rijksuniv. Utrecht, Bib., MS. 124), a collection of texts about St Martin, patron saint of Utrecht Cathedral, dating to the end of the 12th century. The initial I of *Igitur* is done in red on an alternating blue and green background and constructed from interlace. Leaves sprout from the stem.

In the course of the 14th century illuminated examples of the works of Jacob van Maerlant were available in the northern Netherlands. They were presumably also produced and illuminated there, although that is not absolutely certain. Typical of this problem is the abundantly decorated Rijm Bible of 1332 (The Hague, Rijksmus. Meermanno-Westreenianum, MS. 10 B 21). The full-page miniature on fol. 152*v*, depicting the *Destruction of Jerusalem by the Romans under Titus*, is dated and signed by Michiel van der Borch. Nothing more is known about this artist or where he worked. This picture, as well as the numerous small-scale miniatures, suggests an unmistakably French influence in the decorative treatment of faces and clothes, individuals in mannered poses, absence of depth and a predominantly graphic style, which is sometimes virtually sketchy.

An example of van Maerlant's *Der naturen bloeme* (Leiden, Bib. Rijksuniv., MS. BPL/14A) departs in some

13. North Netherlandish school: *Virgin and Child with Kneeling Donor*; miniature from the Hours of Margaret of Cleves, 96×133 mm, *c*. 1395–1400 (Lisbon, Museu Calouste Gulbenkian, MS. LA 148, fols 19*v*–20*r*)

respects from these features owing to a tendency towards greater realism, in particular with the figure of the kneeling donor, whose lifelike portrait has been attempted on the inserted full-page miniature. Below are the coats of arms of the IJsselstein family of Utrecht. Nevertheless, the illuminations of the whole manuscript obviously display many connections with those in a Flemish *Romance of Alexander* completed in 1343 (Oxford, Bodleian Lib., MS. Bodl. 264). In connection with this tendency towards realism there is an exceptional miniature from the *Armorial of Gelderland* (before 1378; Brussels, Bib. Royale Albert 1er, MSS 15652–6, fol. 26*r*). It consists of a coloured pen drawing of the enthroned Holy Roman Emperor Charles IV surrounded by the seven Electors. Unusual tension is achieved through each individual's facial features, sketched naturalistically, resulting in a unique, expressive gallery of portraits. Influenced by the court of the Counts of Holland, which moved from Henegouwen to The Hague in the second half of the 14th century, and by the *Devotio moderna*, indigenous production of illuminated books with characteristic illumination gradually increased. This started with the Hours of Margaret of Cleves (*c.* 1395–1400; Lisbon, Mus. Gulbenkian, MS. LA 148; see fig. 13).

Evidence of monumental painting of this period is, if anything, scarcer. In the Bergkerk at Deventer there is a wall painting (*c.* 1198–1200) of a bishop. In the St Pieterskerk in Utrecht various remains of wall paintings partly dating from the Romanesque period were uncovered following restoration. The oldest, a figure of *Christ* within a double mandorla, flanked by two other figures, occurs in the apse of the north chapel. On the vaults, around the keystones, there are 13th-century representations of angels, abbots and prophets. Around 1300 a painting of the *Crucifixion* was done on the crossing pillar. Also probably from that period are some surviving fragments of tomb decorations. These and other finds can be classed as the work of local craftsmen, lacking any particular quality or individuality. Whether belonging to the Romanesque or Gothic styles, their significance is mainly of an archaeological and documentary nature.

The two oldest and, for this period, only panel paintings date from the second half of the 14th century. The *Crucifixion with Hendrik van Rijn* (Antwerp, Kon. Mus. S. Kst.) was painted *c.* 1363 by an anonymous north Netherlandish master, probably from Utrecht. The figures are set against a gold background consisting of a methodically repeated relief ornament of gilded tiles with a lion motif. The figures of the Virgin and St John wear garments notable for their broad and supple drapery folds. The painting of the surrounding frame is striking for its imitation of precious stones. The memorial picture of the *Virgin and Child and St George with the Knights of Montfoort* (Amsterdam, Rijksmus.) is also from Utrecht. Four knights from the Montfoort family—the fourth introduced by his patron saint, St George—kneel in prayer in front of the Virgin. This last figure certainly reveals French influence. The very vigorous restoration of the panel makes it harder to trace further or more precise points of comparison.

BIBLIOGRAPHY

G. J. Hoogewerff: *De Noord-Nederlandsche schilderkunst*, i (The Hague, 1936)
A. W. Byvanck: *La Miniature dans les Pays-Bas septentrionaux* (Paris, 1937)
Verluchte handschriften uit de Nederlanden tot 1550 (exh. cat., Amsterdam, Mus. Willet–Holthuijsen, 1954)
R. Meischke: 'Het kleurenschema van de middeleeuwse kerkinterieurs van Groningen', *Kon. Ned. Oudhdkn. Bond: Bull. KNOB*, lxv (1966), pp. 57–91
L. M. J. Delaissé: *A Century of Dutch Manuscript Illumination* (Berkeley and Los Angeles, 1968)
Middelnederlandse handschriften uit Europese en Amerikaanse bibliotheken (exh. cat. by J. Deschamps, Brussels, Bib. Royale Albert 1er, 1970)
La Miniature hollandaise: Le Grand Siècle de l'enluminure du livre dans les Pays-Bas septentrionaux (exh. cat., Brussels, Bib. Royale Albert 1er, 1971)
O. Pächt and U. Jenni: *Die illuminierten Handschriften und Inkunabeln der Österreichischen Nationalbibliothek, iii: Holländische Schule*, 2 vols (Vienna, 1975)
G. de Werd: 'Von Utrecht bis Maastricht', *Die Parler und der schöne Stil, 1350–1400: Europäische Kunst unter den Luxemburgern*, (exh. cat., ed. A. Legner; Cologne, Ksthalle, 1978), pp. 109–11
A. Châtelet: *Les Primitifs hollandais: La Peinture dans les Pays-Bas du Nord au XVe siècle* (Paris, 1980)
Schatten van de Koninklijke Bibliotheek: Acht eeuwen verluchte handschriften (exh. cat., The Hague, Rijksmus. Meermanno–Westreenianum, 1980)
C. L. Temminck Groll: 'De St-Pieterskerk te Utrecht', *Kon. Ned. Oudhdknd. Bond: Bull. KNOB*, lxxxi (1982), pp. 75–117
Liturgische handschriften uit de Koninklijke Bibliotheek (exh. cat., The Hague, 1983)
P. Vandenbroeck: *Catalogus schilderkunst 14e en 15e eeuw: Koninklijk Museum voor Schone Kunsten* (Antwerp, 1985)
P. C. Boeren: *Catalogus van de liturgische handschriften van de Koninklijke Bibliotheek* (The Hague, 1988)
K. van der Horst: *Illuminated and Decorated Medieval Manuscripts in the University Library* (Utrecht, 1989)
The Golden Age of Dutch Manuscript Painting (exh. cat., Utrecht, Catharijneconvent; New York, Pierpont Morgan Lib.; 1989)

CYRIEL STROO

2. *c.* 1400–*c.* 1525. In the 15th century three main areas above the Maas and Rhine rivers can be identified as constituting the northern Netherlands: Holland, Utrecht and Gelderland. In the west, the county of Holland was ruled by the Dukes of Bavaria (*reg* 1349–1433) and formed a political unit with Zeeland and Hainaut [Henegouwen], with The Hague as the capital from the second half of the 14th century. Holland reached as far north as the Zuiderzee and included West Friesland. East of Holland was the bishopric of Utrecht, which also included Overijssel, Drenthe and the town of Groningen. Utrecht was not only the seat of the bishopric but also the cultural and artistic centre of the north in the 15th century. The Duchy of Gelderland was ruled by the house of Jülich until 1423, followed by the Counts of Egmont until 1473. The Dukes of Burgundy gained control over Holland and Zeeland in 1433; over Utrecht in 1455, though it remained officially independent; and over Gelderland in 1473. From then onwards, Holland, Utrecht and Gelderland were integrated into the Burgundian Netherlands, an area roughly covering present-day Belgium, the Netherlands and northwestern France. In 1477 Mary of Burgundy married Archduke Maximilian of Austria, and the Burgundian territories thus passed to the Habsburgs, which underscores the problematic nature of framing the northern Netherlands (Holland, Utrecht and Gelderland) as an autonomous cultural unit.

North Netherlandish painting matured first in manuscripts (*see* §1 above), produced under the active patronage of the ruling courts and the church. Among the early patrons were the counts of Holland, Zeeland and Hainaut:

Albert, Duke of Bavaria (*reg* 1389–1404), his second wife, Margaret of Cleves (*d* 1411), and his later successors William VI of Bavaria (*reg* 1404–17), Jacqueline of Bavaria (*reg* 1417–33) and her husband, John III of Bavaria (*reg* 1417–25). The arts also flourished in the episcopal city of Utrecht and in a lesser degree in Gelderland under Count Arnold van Egmont (1423–73). Though many early north Netherlandish painters are documented, their oeuvre cannot always be identified. However, the pioneering research of James Marrow and others (see 1989–90 exh. cat.) has dramatically increased knowledge of the two most neglected and problematic periods in north Netherlandish visual culture: 1395–1415 and 1490–1520. Leading painters such as the Master of Margaret of Cleves (*fl c.* 1395–1400), whose works include the *Biblia pauperum* (*c.* 1395–1400; London, BL, MS. Kings 5) and the Hours of Margaret of Cleves (*c.* 1395–1400; Lisbon, Mus. Gulbenkian, MS. LA 148; see fig. 13 above), and the Master of Dirc van Delft (*fl c.* 1405–10), best known for his *Table of the Christian Faith* (*c.* 1405–10; New York, Pierpont Morgan Lib., MS. M. 691), introduced a variety of pictorial innovations inspired by the new religious *Devotio moderna* movement. The teachings of Geert Groote, with their emphasis on a new spirituality based on emotionalism, the imitation of Christ and the Passion, were disseminated in panel, manuscript, wall and canvas paintings throughout the northern Netherlands and beyond, via newly founded convents of the Windesheim congregation (1386–7) and the Brethren and Sisters of the Common Life in Deventer (1391). By the end of the 14th century the nature of manuscript decoration had begun to change from small illustrations accompanying the text to full-page images that acted almost as independent paintings. As the textual demands began to loosen, the artists enjoyed a new freedom to explore broader aesthetic interests.

Between 1415 and 1425 masters of the second generation of manuscript painters familiar with the *Devotio moderna*, as well as with the south Netherlandish illuminations of Jan Malouel and the Limbourg brothers, began to experiment with movement, individuality, new spatial compositions (through the use of atmospheric and linear perspective), narrative details, 'realistic' depictions of landscape and new, often more naturalistic, border decorations. They include the Master of the Morgan Infancy Cycle (*fl* 1415–20), the Master of Marie de Gueldre (*fl* 1415) and the Passion Master of Marie de Gueldre (*fl* 1415–20), the Master of Otto van Moerdrecht and the Master of Zweder van Culemborg. New directions were taken by the Master of Catherine of Cleves in the Book of Hours of Catherine of Cleves (New York, Pierpont Morgan Lib., MSS M. 917 and 945), painted for the Duchess of Gelders (1417–76). Often considered the most sophisticated manuscript produced in the northern Netherlands in the 15th century (*see* MASTERS, ANONYMOUS, AND MONOGRAMMISTS, §I: MASTER OF CATHERINE OF CLEVES, figs 1 and 2), it shows extensive borrowing from the Master of Flémalle and also from Jan van Eyck, who worked between 1422 and 1424 for John of Bavaria as court painter in The Hague, where he may have collaborated on the Turin–Milan Book of Hours (Turin, Mus. Civ.; for illustration

see TURIN-MILAN HOURS), begun *c.* 1380, with new decoration commissioned after 1417.

Karel van Mander, writing in 1604, neglected the art of manuscript illumination and situated the beginnings of Dutch painting in Haarlem at the end of the third quarter of the 15th century, with the work of the panel painters Albert van Ouwater, 'Dieric van Haarlem', perhaps identical to Dieric Bouts (later active in Leuven), and Geertgen tot Sint Jans. The last resided with the Knights of St John in Haarlem, for whom he painted a large altarpiece (dismembered Oct 1573), to which a *Lamentation* (Vienna, Ksthist. Mus.; *see* GEERTGEN TOT SINT JANS, fig. 1) originally belonged. A free interpretation of Geertgen's altarpiece, painted in the 16th century (Aachen Domschatzkam.), suggests that the original consisted of an *Ecce homo* on the left wing, a *Crucifixion* at the centre and the *Lamentation* on the right. Compared to that of these panel painters, the work of Haarlem illuminators active between 1445 and 1520, including the Master of the Haarlem Bible (*fl c.* 1450–75), the Master of the London Jason (*fl c.* 1475–80) and Jan Spierinck (*fl* 1485–1519), who left a substantial oeuvre, is modest. There is a strong but little studied pictorial connection between the work of Dieric Bouts and many Haarlem painters, including the Master of the Tiburtine Sibyl, who may have trained with Bouts in Leuven; the Master of the Taking of Christ (*fl* 1463–1505), who painted the organ-shutters of St Bavo's in Haarlem in 1465; and Jan Arentsz. (*fl* 1465–95). The Master of the Gathering of Manna is perhaps identical with Jacob Clementsz. (*fl* 1460–67) or Simon Jansz. (*fl* 1435–75). The second Haarlem generation includes Jan Willemsz. (*fl* 1470–90), the brothers Mouwerijn Simonsz. van Waterlandt (*fl* before 1473; *d* 1509) and Claes Simonsz. van Waterlandt (*fl* 1485–90), both of whom have been associated with the Master of the Figdor Deposition, Cornelis Willemsz. (*fl* 1481–1523) and Jacob Jansz. van Haarlem (*fl* 1483–1509), possibly the Master of the Brunswick Diptych. Confusion still exists between Jacob Jansz.'s work and that of his pupil, Jan Mostaert, a Haarlem follower of Geertgen, who painted portraits, such as that of *Abel van de Coulster* (*c.* 1510–16; Brussels, Mus. A. Anc.); but his work also shows a new sense of curiosity, revealing his interest in landscape, in the history of man (e.g. the *First Family*, 1520–25; Williamstown, MA, Clark A. Inst.) and in the then newly discovered continent of North America (e.g. the '*West Indies Landscape*', 1545; Haarlem, Frans Halsmus.).

After Haarlem, Delft was the most important centre for panel painting in the northern Netherlands, and it was a close second after Utrecht for manuscript painting. A comparison of the paintings of the Master of the Virgo inter Virgines (for illustration *see* MASTERS AND MONOGRAMMISTS, §I: MASTER OF THE VIRGO INTER VIRGINES) with book illustrations produced at Delft between 1483 and 1498 suggests that he should be identified with either Dirc Jansz. (*fl* 1474–95) or Pieter de Maelre (*fl* 1450–95). He was a narrator, who accompanied his main themes with secondary scenes from everyday life. Manuscript painters active in Delft between 1475 and 1500 produced less lavish manuscripts than their fellow artists of the Ghent–Bruges school, but they did use the visual vocabulary of painters active in the southern Netherlands, such as Dieric Bouts (Leuven), Hans Memling and Gerard David (both Bruges) and Hugo van der Goes (Ghent). Although very few panel paintings made in Utrecht between 1460 and 1500 have survived, manuscripts produced there provide some impression of its visual culture of the period, especially the Hours of Mary van Vronenstein (or Hours of Jan van Amerongen; Brussels, Bib. Royale Albert 1er, MS. II. 7619) by the Master of Evert van Soudenbalch and his circle or the Book of Hours of Gijsbrecht van Brederode (U. Liège, Bib. Gén., MS. Wittert 13) by the Master of Gijsbrecht van Brederode (*fl* 1460–70).

In Amsterdam, still a small city with limited possibilities in the early 16th century, painters had to be multitalented to survive, let alone thrive. One who did was Jacob Cornelisz. van Oostsanen, who designed embroideries, stained glass and woodcuts, and painted portraits, frescoes and altarpieces, such as the *Nativity* (1512; Naples, Capodimonte), originally placed in the Boelens family chapel in the Carthusian monastery of St Andries in Amsterdam. Jacob was the brother of Cornelis Buys I (*fl* 1490–1524), who is usually identified as the Master of Alkmaar, after the *Seven Acts of Mercy* (1504; Amsterdam, Rijksmus.) for the St Laurenskerk (Grote Kerk) in Alkmaar; although painted in a somewhat provincial style, this work is important for having shifted the emphasis from scenes of an apocalyptic vision to one of everyday life.

The first Leiden painter whom van Mander mentioned was Cornelis Engebrechtsz., who painted in an agitated, dynamic manner, with numerous figures in various contorted stances, as shown in a *Lamentation* (*c.* 1508) and a *Crucifixion* (*c.* 1517–22; both Leiden, Stedel. Mus. Lakenhal; for illustration *see* ENGEBRECHTSZ., CORNELIS), both for the Augustinian convent of Marienpoel, near Leiden. Engebrechtsz. was the second teacher of Lucas van Leyden, who was first taught in Leiden by his father Hugo Jacobsz. Lucas is best known for the artistic dialogue he developed with Albrecht Dürer and for the range of new themes and techniques he introduced to the graphic arts. His engravings are refined, with subtle tonal effects, often rivalling the effects that could be obtained in chiaroscuro woodcuts and through the use of atmospheric perspective in painting. Lucas's prints influenced Marcantonio Raimondi, Andrea del Sarto and Jacopo da Pontormo, and they were later adapted by Hendrick Goltzius, Jacques de Gheyn II and Rembrandt. Although Lucas's fame rests more on his prints and drawings, he was also an excellent painter. Among his most influential pictures are a *Last Judgement* (1526–7; Leiden, Stedel. Mus. Lakenhal; *see* LUCAS VAN LEYDEN, fig. 4), commissioned by the children of Claes Dircksz. van Swieten for the St Pieterskerk in Leiden, and *Moses and the Worship of the Golden Calf* (*c.* 1530; Amsterdam, Rijksmus.). In his pictures technical mastery is combined with a vigorous realism to produce works often characterized by unusual narratives, such as the latter, dealing with the theme of intemperance and its consequences.

Many early north Netherlandish artists cannot be linked with a particular town and led a more transient existence. Lucas van Leyden's father, Hugo Jacobsz., is known to have been active at Leiden, Ghent and Gouda. His now-dismembered altarpiece of *St John the Baptist* was probably painted for the new church in Gouda between 1485 and 1493. There was also considerable movement between the north and the south: Willem Vrelant moved from Utrecht to Bruges in 1454, Gerard David from Oudewater to Bruges in 1484 and to Antwerp in 1515, and Marinus van Reymerswaele from Romerswael (Walcheren) to Antwerp in 1509, though he later returned to Middelburg.

BIBLIOGRAPHY

M. J. Friedländer: *Die altniederländische Malerei*, 14 vols (Berlin, 1924–37); Eng. trans. as *Early Netherlandish Painting*, 16 vols (Leiden, 1967–76)

E. Panofsky: *Early Netherlandish Painting: Its Origins and Character* (Cambridge, 1953/R New York, 1978)

Middeleeuwse kunst der Noordelijke Nederlanden (exh. cat., ed. R. van Luttervelt; Amsterdam, Rijksmus., 1958)

J. Snyder: 'The Early Haarlem School of Painting', *A. Bull.*, xlii (1960), pp. 113–32

W. Stechow: *Northern Renaissance Art, 1400–1600: Sources and Documents* (Englewood Cliffs, NJ, 1966)

C. D. Cuttler: *Northern Painting from Pucelle to Bruegel* (New York, 1968)

L. M. J. Delaissé: *A Century of Dutch Manuscript Illumination* (Berkeley and Los Angeles, 1968)

J. Snyder: 'The Early Haarlem School of Painting', *A. Bull.*, liii (1971), pp. 48–55

W. Gibson: *The Paintings of Cornelis Engebrechtsz* (New York and London, 1977)

'Lucas van Leyden', *Ned. Ksthist. Jb.*, xxix (1978) [whole issue]

Lucas van Leyden: Grafiek (exh. cat. by J. P. Filedt Kok, Amsterdam, Rijksmus., 1978)

J. D. Bangs: *Cornelis Engebrechtsz.'s Leiden* (Assen, 1979)

A. Châtelet: *Early Dutch Painting* (Fribourg, 1980; rev. New York, 1981)

J. Snyder: *Northern Renaissance Art: Painting, Sculpture and the Graphic Arts from 1350 to 1575* (Englewood Cliffs, NJ, 1985)

The Golden Age of Dutch Manuscript Painting (exh. cat. by J. H. Marrow, H. L. M. Defoer, A. S. Korteweg and W. C. M. Wüsstefeld, Utrecht, Catharijneconvent; New York, Pierpont Morgan Lib.; 1989–90)

3. *c.* 1525–*c.* 1550. North Netherlandish painters began creating a new style in painting from about the second quarter of the 16th century. Though guided by many of the same new interests in naturalism and humanism as contemporary Italian Renaissance artists, the northerners built their new art on different traditions. Whereas the Italians aimed to revive the Classical style still visible in the ancient Roman remains around them, the northern artists had no such tradition on which to draw. Their glorious past centred on the Gothic period, with its emphasis on light, colour, delicate detail and symbolism. Netherlandish artists were thus faced with a particularly fascinating challenge: to reconcile a world of medieval symbolism with that of contemporary humanism. By the early 16th century the strong emphasis on regional styles that had marked both north and south Netherlandish art of the 15th century gave way to an increasingly international outlook and receptiveness to outside influences, especially from Italy. Whereas south Netherlandish artists tried to balance the new influences from the Italian High Renaissance with a respect for Netherlandish traditions, their colleagues in the north, especially the group of artists known as the Romanists (*see* ROMANISM), were much more aggressive in shedding their heritage. An important pioneer of this movement had been Jan Gossart, who, although south Netherlandish, played a significant role in introducing an Italianate style to the north through his work in the service of Philip of Burgundy, later Bishop of Utrecht. After a visit to Italy in 1508–9, in the retinue of Philip (then still a sea admiral), Gossart abandoned his early style in favour of an inflated classicism derived from

Michelangelo and Dürer. Gossart's *St Luke Drawing the Virgin* (1513–14; Prague, N.G., Šternberk Pal.; *see* GOSSART, JAN, fig. 2) is a textbook study of Italian interests in linear perspective, classicizing architecture, ancient sculptural traditions and robust anatomy, but in his emphatic treatment of each of these he failed to capture the harmony of the Italian Renaissance style. Towards the end of 1515 Philip of Burgundy commissioned Gossart, who seems to have settled in Zeeland on his return from Italy, to decorate his Castle of Suytburg (now Souburg, Walcheren Island), which he intended to make a Renaissance centre in the north. The only surviving picture that seems likely to have formed part of this decoration is Gossart's *Neptune and Amphitrite* (1516; Berlin, Bodemus.; *see* GOSSART, JAN, fig. 3), which, with its inflated forms, seems more like a parody of Michelangelo's style than the homage that he surely intended it to be.

Although unprecedented in Netherlandish art, Gossart's two secular, life-size nude figures were never copied or imitated. The real turning-point in the development of north Netherlandish art came a decade later, after the return from Italy in 1524 of Jan van Scorel, a native of Alkmaar who had studied with Jacob Cornelisz. van Oostsanen in Haarlem (1512–17). While in Rome, where he studied the works of Michelangelo and Raphael, van Scorel had been appointed curator of the papal collections under Pope Adrian VI (*reg* 1522–3). On his return to Utrecht, following the premature death of the Pope, van Scorel introduced Italian and antique vocabulary to his fellow northerners, along with a more painterly Venetian approach to the rendering of landscape. His first important altarpiece executed after his return, the triptych with the *Entry of Christ into Jerusalem* (c. 1526; Utrecht, Cent. Mus.; *see* SCOREL, JAN VAN, fig. 1), was commissioned by Herman Lokhorst (*d* 1527), canon of Utrecht Cathedral. Van Scorel's attempt to imitate Raphael can be seen in the *Baptism of Christ* (c. 1527–9; Haarlem, Frans Halsmus.; *see* SCOREL, JAN VAN, fig. 2), which was painted for the Knights of St John during his stay in Haarlem (1527–30), as was the *Mary Magdalene* (c. 1530; Amsterdam, Rijksmus.). Also carried out about the same time was his group portrait of the *Twelve Members of the Haarlem Brotherhood of Jerusalem Pilgrims* (c. 1528; Haarlem, Frans Halsmus.), showing a number of half-length figures looking out of the picture, with three-quarter-profile heads arranged in rows. This composition scheme was popular in the beginning of the 16th century and was used by Dirck Jacobsz. in his group portrait of the *Seventeen Guardsmen of the Arquebusiers' Guild* (1529; Amsterdam, Rijksmus.) and again by van Scorel in his group portrait of the *Five Leaders of the Jerusalem Order* (1541; Utrecht, Cent. Mus.). In 1530 van Scorel settled permanently in Utrecht, having two years earlier been made Canon of the St Mariakerk. He travelled to France in 1540–42 to deliver altarpieces ordered by the abbey of Marchiennes (fragments, Douai, Mus. Mun.), he and his workshop painted the triptych with the *Finding of the True Cross* (1541; Breda, Grote Kerk; *in situ*) and he was called to Ghent in 1550 to restore the Ghent Altarpiece (Ghent, St Bavo) by Hubert and Jan van Eyck.

Van Scorel had two pupils of renown: Maarten van Heemskerck and Anthonis Mor. While van Heemskerck

14. Maarten van Heemskerck: *Family Portrait*, oil on panel, 1.19×1.41 m, c. 1530 (Kassel, Schloss Wilhelmshöhe, Gemäldegalerie Alte Meister)

thrived in Haarlem, Mor moved south and registered in Antwerp in 1547, after his apprenticeship with van Scorel in Utrecht. Before working with van Scorel in Haarlem between 1527 and 1529, van Heemskerck had first studied with Cornelis Willemsz. (*fl* 1481–?1552) of Haarlem and Jan Lucas van Delft (*fl* 1515–20). Van Heemskerck also went to Italy, but before his departure for Rome, where he remained between 1532 and 1536, he painted a *Rest on the Flight into Egypt* (1532; Washington, DC, N.G.A.), sometimes attributed to van Scorel, and donated a *St Luke Painting the Virgin* (1532; Haarlem, Frans Halsmus.) to his fellow artists for the chapel of the painters' guild in St Bavo's, Haarlem. Van Heemskerck is known not only for his ability to assimilate ancient and Italian art in his paintings but also for his numerous designs for engravings (over 600), which negotiated the humanistic and religious culture of his day. He made a fascinating series of drawings of Roman monuments when he visited Rome in the 1530s (*see* HEEMSKERCK, MAARTEN VAN, fig. 1), and these are among the best surviving documents of the condition of the Roman Forum, the construction of St Peter's and the general appearance of the Eternal City at that time. Besides subject pictures, which show the influence of Michelangelesque forms and classicizing poses, van Heemskerck's oeuvre also includes portraits, such as those of *Anna Codde* and *Pieter Bicker* (both 1529; Amsterdam, Rijksmus.), the *Self-portrait before the Colosseum* (1533; Cambridge, Fitzwilliam) and the *Family Portrait* (c. 1530; Kassel, Schloss Wilhelmshöhe; see fig. 14), now known to represent Pieter Jan Foppesz. and his family. The altarpiece of the *Passion* and the *Martyrdom of St Lawrence* (1538–42; Linköping Cathedral), originally placed on the highly visible altar of the St Laurenskerk in Alkmaar, shows van Heemskerck in an agitated, dynamic mode. It is a representative example of his vigorous appropriation and transformation of the Italian and *all'antica* manner in the northern Netherlands in the first half of the 16th century, the largest of its kind produced in the country.

15. Pieter Aertsen: *Butcher's Stall*, oil on panel, 1.24×1.69 m, 1551 (Uppsala, Universitet Konstsamling)

However, it was dismembered during the iconoclastic riots and finally ended up in Sweden, which profoundly disturbed subsequent understanding of the impact of Renaissance sources on the visual culture in the northern Netherlands in the 16th century.

Some north Netherlandish artists rejected the Italian interests of their countrymen and developed new regional interests that would help shape the styles of the following centuries. Religious and secular subjects alike were increasingly treated as scenes from everyday life. One artist who played an important role in this development was Pieter Aertsen, a native of Amsterdam, who spent the years 1535 to *c.* 1555 in Antwerp. The contribution he made to the development of still-life and the depiction of peasant life on his return to his native Amsterdam can best be seen in examples painted during his absence from the northern Netherlands. In the *Butcher's Stall* (1551; Uppsala, U. Kstsaml.; see fig. 15) Aertsen provided a vivid rendering of a market stall complete with cuts of beef, pork and poultry. In the background landscape, glimpsed through the open doorway, are a woman and child mounted on a donkey led by an older man. It is only on examining this detail that the true subject of the painting, the Flight into Egypt, and the symbolic role of the foodstuffs become apparent. Such a fresh approach to naturalism would have a profound influence on the evolution of Dutch painting during the second half of the 16th century and throughout much of the 17th.

BIBLIOGRAPHY

EARLY SOURCES

D. Lampsonius: *Lamberti Lombardi apud Eburones pictoris celeberrimi vita* (Bruges, 1566)

K. van Mander: *Schilder-boeck* (Haarlem, [1603]–1604)

C. de Bie: *Het gulden cabinet* (1661)

J. von Sandrart: *Teutsche Academie* (1675–9); ed. A. R. Peltzer (1925)

A. van Houbraken: *De groote schouburgh* (1718–21)

J. Campo Weyerman: *De levens-beschryvingen der Nederlandsche kontschilders en schilderesen*, 4 vols (The Hague, 1729–69)

J. van Gool: *De nieuwe schouburgh* (1750–51)

J.-B. Descamps: *La Vie des peintres flamands, allemands et hollandais*, 4 vols (Paris, 1753–64)

J. Immerseel jr: *De levens en werken der Hollandsche en Vlaamsche kunstschilders, graveurs en bouwmeesters*, 3 vols (Amsterdam, 1842–3)

C. Kramm: *De levens en werken der Hollandsche en Vlaamsche kunstschilders, beeldhouwers, graveurs en bouwmeesters, van den vroegsten tot op onzen tijd*, 4 vols (Amsterdam, 1857–64)

A. Nijstad: *Nederlandse schilders in publikaties voor 1700: Een register* (The Hague, 1978)

GENERAL

Tentoonstelling van Noord-Nederlandsche Schilder- en beeldhouwkunst vóór 1575, 2 vols (exh. cat., Utrecht, Geb. Kst. & Wetenschappen, 1913)

C. L. van Balen: *De blijde inkomst der renaissance in de Nederlanden* (Leiden, 1930)

B. Cnattingius and A. L. Romdahl: *Maerten Heemskercks Laurentiusaltare i Linköpings Domkyrka* (Stockholm, 1953)

Jan van Scorel (exh. cat., Utrecht, Cent. Mus., 1955)

R. van Luttervelt: 'Renaissancekunst in Breda: Vijf studies', *Ned. Ksthist. Jb.*, xxv (1962), pp. 55–104

G. von der Osten and H. Vey: *Painting and Sculpture in Germany and the Netherlands, 1500 to 1600*, Pelican Hist. A. (Harmondsworth, 1969)

M. A. Faries: *Jan van Scorel: His Style and its Historical Context* (diss., Bryn Mawr Coll., PA, 1972)

M. Braman Buchan: *The Paintings of Pieter Aertsen* (diss., New York U., Inst. F.A., 1975)

K. P. F. Moxey: *Pieter Aertsen, Joachim Beuckelaer and the Rise of Secular Painting in the Context of the Reformation* (New York and London, 1977)

I. M. Veldman: *Maarten van Heemskerck and Dutch Humanism of the Sixteenth Century* (Amsterdam, 1977)

Jan van Scorel in Utrecht: Altaarstukken en schilderijen omstreeks 1540, documenten, technisch onderzoek (exh. cat.; Utrecht, Cent. Mus.; Douai, Mus. Mun.; 1977)

J. A. Levenson: *Jacopo de' Barbari and Northern Art of the Early Sixteenth Century* (diss., New York U., Inst. F.A., 1978)

R. Grosshaus: *Maerten van Heemskerck: Die Gemälde* (Berlin, 1980)

J. A. L. de Meyere: *Jan van Scorel (1495–1562): Schilder voor prinsen en prelaten* (Utrecht, 1981)

H. Malecki: *Die Familie des Pieter Jan Foppesz.: Genese und Bedentung des Kasseler Familienbildes des Maerten van Heemskerck* (Kassel, 1983)

E. K. J. Reznicek: 'A Survey of Recent Discoveries and of Bibliography concerning Dutch Art, 1500–1600', *Netherlandish Mannerism: Papers Given at a Symposium in Nationalmuseum, Stockholm, September 21–22, 1984* (Stockholm, 1985), pp. 6–13

Kunst voor de beeldenstorm, 2 vols (exh. cat., ed. W. T. Kloek, W. Halsema-Kubes and R. J. Baarsen; Amsterdam, Rijksmus., 1986)

4. *c*. 1550–*c*. 1680. By the mid-16th century, Dutch painting and graphic arts show a wide range of contrasting influences and eclectic modes of representation, including local variants in figure, portrait and landscape painting, as well as local adaptations of styles of Italian Mannerism, the school of Fontainebleau and the style formulated at the court of Rudolf II in Prague. The formative role of the Antwerp school, especially Pieter Bruegel the elder and Frans Floris, in the evolution of Dutch art is now also generally recognized. After the Spanish siege and subsequent fall of Antwerp in 1585, many Flemish artists migrated north. This thwarted Antwerp's leading cultural and economic position and split the Netherlands. It also accelerated the economic and artistic growth of Amsterdam, Dordrecht, Haarlem, Leiden, Delft and Gouda (the six so-called major towns of Holland), as well as Middelburg, Utrecht, The Hague and Rotterdam, each of which became an important centre of artistic activity. Because these centres were relatively close to one another, however, and travel was easy, the regional distinctions are not as pronounced as, for instance, in Italy. Dutch artists frequently moved from one centre to another. With the official recognition of the Dutch Republic in 1648, a new brand of mercantilism in the wealthy provinces of Holland and Zeeland led to unprecedented economic and cultural expansion, resulting in one of the most intensely creative periods of artistic production: the so-called 'Golden Age' attracted bankers, merchants, skilled labourers and, above all, artists, as well as diverse new industries and enterprises. In this dynamic climate, new directions were taken, for instance, in genre painting, landscape, townscape, architectural interiors and still-life, at the expense of biblical and history subjects, which still formed the mainstay of painted themes elsewhere in Europe. Much of Dutch art is devoted to domestic and domesticating subject-matter; it may look realistic, but it is not always truthful.

(i) Middelburg. (ii) Haarlem. (iii) Leiden. (iv) Amsterdam. (v) Utrecht. (vi) Delft. (vii) The Hague. (viii) Other centres.

(i) Middelburg. As early as 1523 Flemish exiles sought refuge in Middelburg, the capital of Zeeland and the official staple for French wine for the entire Netherlands. Among the émigré artists was Ambrosius Bosschaert (i), whose family was from Antwerp; he established a local tradition in Middelburg of painting still-lifes with flowers, fruit and exotic shells, often with *vanitas* overtones (*see* VANITAS). (In 1615 he was in Bergen-op-Zoom and the following year became a citizen of Utrecht.) His three sons, Ambrosius Bosschaert (ii), Johannes Bosschaert (1610/11–1628 or later) and Abraham Bosschaert (*c*. 1612/13–1643), followed his example, as did his brother-in-law, the still-life painter Balthasar van der Ast. In contrast Adriaen van de Venne painted figure subjects, such as the *Allegory of the Twelve Years' Truce* (1616; Paris, Louvre). Van de Venne also left Middelburg, moving to The Hague in 1625, followed by the landscape painter Jan Frans van Geel the following year. The enigmatic Salomon Mestdach (*fl* 1617–after 1628) pursued a rigid and more conservative portrait style in Middelburg, reminiscent of Antonis Mor, Frans Francken the elder, Willem Key and Frans Pourbus the elder.

(ii) Haarlem. The formative experience of Flemish migration shaped the first authentically north Netherlandish school, in Haarlem, between *c*. 1580 and *c*. 1620. A group of Dutch Mannerist painters, draughtsmen and engravers gathered around Hendrick Goltzius, Cornelis Cornelisz. van Haarlem and the Fleming Karel van Mander I. They were all interested in studies of anatomy and proportion. Cornelisz. van Haarlem's *Massacre of the Innocents* (1591; Haarlem, Frans Halsmus.), with its violent contortions, foreshortenings, Herculean nudes and forced perspective, illustrates the late 16th-century style in Haarlem. Fundamental to the evolution of this exaggerated manner was the influence of the Rudolfine court style as practised by Bartholomäus Spranger, whose drawings were brought back to Haarlem by van Mander, who showed them to Goltzius. Spranger's visual rhetoric was further propagated in the northern Netherlands *c*. 1600 by two Germans, Hans von Aachen and Joseph Heintz (i). Like Spranger, Goltzius eagerly adopted the ornamental contrapposto and *figura serpentinata*, effective devices of visual rhetoric that increased movement and emotion of the figure (see fig. 16). After a trip to Italy in 1590–91, however, Goltzius redefined his style in a less agitated, more classicizing direction. His work was influential, not in the least because his ideas were widely disseminated through his own publishing house and through reproductive prints after his works by engravers such as his son-in-law Jacob Matham, the Antwerp-born Jacques de Gheyn II and Jan Saenredam.

During the first decades of the 17th century only Goltzius and Cornelisz. van Haarlem of the older generation were still active in Haarlem. The city nonetheless established itself as a centre for innovations in history, portrait, landscape, marine and still-life painting, though it lost its artistic lead to Amsterdam *c*. 1625. The aspiring history painters in the first half of the century were Frans de Grebber (1573–1649), Pieter de Grebber and Pieter Soutman. In the second half of the 17th century a classicizing and Flemish-influenced style of history painting was practised by Salomon de Bray, his son Jan de Bray and Caesar van Everdingen of Alkmaar, who temporarily worked in Haarlem and Amsterdam. Many of the artists of both generations of Haarlem history painters were

16. Hendrick Goltzius: *Standing Female Nude with Money Pouch*, pen and dark brown ink, brown wash, 228×147 mm, *c.* 1588 (Amsterdam, Rijksmuseum)

de Velde arrived in Haarlem, where they forged a homogeneous school of naturalistic landscape painting. Another immigrant was Willem Buytewech, whose drawings and prints are often considered more important than his paintings. The term 'tonal phase' has been applied to the landscapes painted in Haarlem in the 1620s and 1630s by such artists as Pieter Molyn, Salomon van Ruysdael and the Haarlem-trained Jan van Goyen: their work was deliberately restricted in colour, and the figures occupied a steadily diminishing place in the composition. This stylistic trend and limited palette were also adopted by contemporary still-life and marine painters. Salomon van Ruysdael's nephew, Jacob van Ruisdael, often considered the most influential 17th-century Dutch landscape artist, painted mostly dune landscapes and forest views around Haarlem. After his arrival in Amsterdam in *c.* 1656, he produced a wider range of often more expressive landscapes as well as occasional marines and townscapes.

Haarlem-born Nicolaes Berchem, who was influenced by Pieter van Laer and Utrecht Italianists such as Jan Both and Jan Baptist Weenix, produced Italianate landscapes in paintings, drawings and prints. This landscape tradition (*see* DUTCH ITALIANATES) was continued by his pupils Hendrick Mommers (1623–93/7) and Willem Romeijn, while Jan Wijnants and the highly successful Philips Wouwerman reached a greater technical perfection in their landscapes. More unusual in subject-matter were the Brazilian views of Frans Post, brother of the leading architect Pieter Post; Frans travelled to the Dutch colony in the retinue of John Maurice of Nassau-Siegen, the newly appointed governor-general. These were the first landscapes of South America ever painted by a European artist.

Architectural painting also flourished in Haarlem, where Jan Saenredam's son, Pieter Saenredam, specialized in the depiction of important buildings and church interiors. The genre of TOWNSCAPE painting was further developed by the brothers Job and Gerrit Berckheyde, as in the latter's *Grote Markt and the Grote Kerk, Haarlem* (1674; London, N.G.; for illustration *see* BERCKHEYDE, (2)). Although Hendrick Vroom's equally new and realistic approach to the painting of ships and naval encounters inspired Cornelis Vroom and Pieter Mulier (*c.* 1615–1670), there was no significant development of marine painting in Haarlem after the first generation of the 17th century.

An innovative style of still-life painting emerged in Haarlem, influenced by the Antwerp-based prototypes of Osias Beert and Clara Peeters. The sober still-lifes of the first-generation artists Floris van Dyck, Floris van Schooten and Nicolas Gillis (*fl* ?1620–30) were transformed by the second generation of Pieter Claesz and Willem Heda into more balanced, unified compositions, with lower viewpoints and the use of a lighter palette, as well as more tactile effects. It is argued that many still-lifes contain *vanitas* or allegorical connotations culled from folk sayings, proverbs and contemporary emblematic literature. Willem Heda's pupils included his son Gerrit Heda (1620–before 1701) and the Frisian-born Maerten Boelema (*c.* 1600–after 1664). The third generation of Haarlem still-life painters specialized in ornate, possibly less moralistic and more ostentatious still-lifes (*pronkstilleven*) in vertical format, a form that developed mainly outside Haarlem.

invited by Jacob van Campen to decorate Prince Frederick Henry's palaces in and around The Hague.

Portrait painting in Haarlem in the first half of the 17th century was dominated by Frans Hals, van Mander's former pupil. Jan Verspronck and Hendrik Pot were Haarlem's other leading portraitists. Besides swiftly executed individual portraits, genre scenes, and the odd religious picture with a portrait character, Hals painted nine major group portraits, including three of the *Officers of the St George Civic Guard Company, Haarlem* (1616, 1627, *c.* 1639; all Haarlem, Frans Halsmus.; *see* HAARLEM, fig. 2). In addition to his five sons and his brother Dirck, Frans Hals's only documented pupils were Pieter van Roestraten and Vincent Laurensz. van der Vinne. The writer Houbraken claimed that he also taught Dirck van Delen, Adriaen van Ostade, Philips Wouwerman and Adriaen Brouwer, but did not mention Judith Leyster, or her spouse, Jan Miense Molenaer, who concentrated on pictures of peasants, inspired by Brouwer and van Ostade. The latter's pupils Cornelis Bega and Cornelis Dusart worked in their master's idiom. Probably also active in Haarlem was the enigmatic Jacobus Vrel, whose domestic interiors are sometimes attributed to Isaak Koedijck.

After the death of Gillis van Coninxloo III in Amsterdam, his talented pupils Hercules Segers and Esaias van

(iii) Leiden. Leiden was less culturally diverse and spiritually heterodox than Haarlem, in spite of the founding of its university in 1575. It more than doubled its population between 1581 and 1600, and by 1626 it had become the second city of the northern Netherlands. A local artistic tradition was established by Isaac Claesz. van Swanenburgh, who painted history subjects and portraits and also made designs for stained-glass windows. He is perhaps best known for his series of six paintings of the *Old and the New Trade* (all Leiden, Stedel. Mus. Lakenhal). His son Jacob van Swanenburgh, who was Rembrandt's first teacher, laid the basis for a school of painting that became prominent only towards the mid-17th century.

Both Rembrandt and Jan Lievens began their careers in Leiden. Nearly everything known about Rembrandt's early youth in the town is derived from a short biography in the *Beschryvinghe der stadt Leyden* ('Description of the city of Leiden') by Jan Jansz. Orlers (1570–1646). Rembrandt was enrolled briefly at Leiden University in May 1620, was apprenticed to van Swanenburgh and then worked for six months with Pieter Lastman in Amsterdam. Rembrandt probably shared a studio in Leiden with Jan Lievens, who had trained with Joris van Schooten (1587–1651), as well as with Lastman. Rembrandt's early, Leiden-period paintings are often intense and harshly coloured, such as the *Clemency of Emperor Titus* (1626; Leiden, Stedel. Mus. Lakenhal). In 1625 and 1626 he painted his first large histories for PETRUS SCRIVERIUS as well as moralizing paintings for the citizens of Leiden. By 1628 he had also gained some experience in portrait painting, the genre for which he established such a considerable reputation after his move to Amsterdam in 1631. Lievens also produced a considerable oeuvre of history and figure paintings as well as portraits. His early work in Leiden is closely related to that of Rembrandt, although the exact nature of their relationship is hard to establish. Lievens seems to have left Leiden for England in 1632, the year after Rembrandt's departure for Amsterdam.

It was not until 1648 that a painters' guild was founded in Leiden and that a distinctive pictorial style emerged. Characterized by minute attention to surface and detail, this kind of painting, now known as Leiden 'Fine' painting, had been practised successfully for some time by Gerrit Dou. His paintings were expensive, the cost often being calculated according to finish and the time devoted to execution. His influence became manifest in the works of younger masters, LEIDEN 'FINE' PAINTERS such as Abraham van den Tempel, Quiringh van Brekelenkam, Pieter van Slingeland, Gabriel Metsu and especially Frans van Mieris (i). After Dou, van Mieris was the principal representative of the Leiden 'Fine' painters. As with the paintings by his teacher, Gerrit Dou, the work of van Mieris, well-documented only after 1657, was extremely popular with collectors at the time, including Cosimo III de' Medici, Grand Duke of Tuscany, and Archduke Leopold William in Vienna. Van Mieris's colours are stronger than those of his contemporaries. Paintings by his son Jan van Mieris (1660–90) are rare, while those by Willem are similar to his father's, but often more detailed. Willem's son Frans van Mieris (ii) continued his grandfather's style. Another likely pupil of Dou was Metsu, most of whose career was spent in Leiden, though he later

settled in Amsterdam in 1657. The chronology of Metsu's oeuvre is still problematic. He painted mostly domestic genre scenes, such as the *Sick Child* (*c.* 1662; Amsterdam, Rijksmus.; *see* METSU, GABRIEL, fig. 1), which was influenced by Vermeer and Pieter de Hooch. Jan Steen is not associated with a single Dutch town, yet the influence of the Leiden painters on his work was decisive. He was closer in style to Frans van Mieris (i) than to Dou, as shown in his *Woman Eating Oysters* (late 1650s; The Hague, Mauritshuis). His paintings, more than those of his colleagues, contain numerous moralizing allusions to contemporary sayings, popular folklore, proverbs, aphorisms, emblems, literature and even theatre.

Abraham van den Tempel was a prominent Leiden portrait painter who left for Amsterdam in 1660. His pupil Arie de Vois painted small-format portraits—typical of the Leiden school—as well as arcadian landscapes and genre scenes. Apart from *vanitas* paintings, still-lifes were not popular in Leiden. David Bailly is often called the father of *vanitas* painting, despite the fact that only three works of his in this genre are known: a *vanitas* drawing in the *album amicorum* of Cornelis de Montigny de Clarges (1624; The Hague, Kon. Bib.), a still-life he added in his portrait by Thomas de Keyser (Paris, priv. col.) and the *Vanitas Still-life with a Portrait of a Young Painter* (1651; Leiden, Stedel. Mus. Lakenhal; for illustration *see* BAILLY, DAVID). Bailly also painted conservative portraits and conversation pieces. His pupils included his nephews, the Delft-born Harmen van Steenwijck (1612–after 1655) and Pieter van Steenwijck (*c.* 1615–after 1654), and Pieter Potter, all of whom specialized in *vanitas* still-lifes. During his stay in Leiden from 1625 to the early 1630s, Jan Davidsz. de Heem produced so-called *vanitas–studium* still-lifes, which were small-size pictures of books painted in grey and brown tones. De Heem also left Leiden for Antwerp, where he more or less remained, though in 1636 he established a workshop in Utrecht, which produced numerous freely composed but lavish flower-pieces (for illustration *see* STILL-LIFE, fig. 2).

(iv) Amsterdam. In the late 16th century many Flemings settled in the economically expanding Amsterdam, including Hans Bol and David Vinckboons from Mechelen, via Middelburg; Jacob Savery I and Roelandt Savery from Kortrijk; and Paul Vredeman de Vries (1567–after 1630), Willem and Adriaen van Nieulandt and Gillis van Coninxloo III from Antwerp. The last, who arrived in Amsterdam, via Frankenthal, in 1595, had a profound influence on the formation of the Antwerp and Amsterdam schools of landscape painting. Also active at the turn of the century in Amsterdam were Cornelis Ketel from Gouda and native Amsterdammers Gerrit Pietersz. Sweelinck, brother of the composer Jan Pietersz. Sweelinck, and the draughtsman, printmaker and publisher Claes Jansz. Visscher.

In the first decades of the 17th century Amsterdam became the commercial capital of the Netherlands, stimulated by the newly imported skills as well as industries and such supporting financial institutions as the Chamber of Insurance (1598), the United East India Company (Verenigde Oostindische Compagnie or VOC; 1602), the Commodities Exchange (1608), the Exchange Bank (1609), the Lending Bank (1614) and the Grain Exchange

17. Rembrandt: *Conspiracy of Claudius Civilis*, oil on canvas, 1.96×3.09 m, 1661–2 (Stockholm, Nationalmuseum)

(1616). With business expanding, a school of painting flourished in Amsterdam as never before, but showed stylistic coherence only for a brief period. In the early part of the century Pieter Lastman, Jan Pynas, Jacob Pynas, Claes Moeyaert and Jan Tengnagel, a group of artists usually referred to as the PRE-REMBRANDTISTS, forged an Italianate style of history painting. An Italian influence was also strong in the history paintings of Werner van den Valckert.

After Rembrandt left Leiden for Amsterdam in 1631, he joined forces with the influential art dealer Hendrick van Uylenburgh (1587–1661), later marrying his niece Saskia in 1633. The portrait of *Nicolaes Ruts* (1631; New York, Frick) is one of a series of *c.* 50 portraits Rembrandt painted in Amsterdam from November 1631 to December 1635 (*see* OIL PAINTING, colour pl. I). Although kept busy with portrait commissions, Rembrandt was nonetheless able to pursue his main interests as a history painter. Through Constantijn Huygens the elder, he was commissioned to paint for the Stadholder Frederick Henry adaptations (both Munich, Alte Pin.) of Rubens's *Raising of the Cross* (*see* BAROQUE, fig. 2) and *Descent of the Cross* (both Antwerp Cathedral; *see* RUBENS, PETER PAUL, fig. 3); a subsequent order for the Stadholder comprised the *Entombment*, the *Resurrection* and the *Ascension* (all Munich, Alte Pin.). Rembrandt frequently painted Old Testament subjects such as the unprecedented *Samson Threatening his Father-in-Law* (*c.* 1635; Berlin, Gemäldegal.), the *Blinding of Samson* (*c.* 1635; Frankfurt am Main, Städel. Kstinst. & Städt. Gal.), the *Happy Story of Tobias* (1637; Stuttgart, Staatsgal.) and the *Angel Leaving Tobit and his Family*

(1637; Paris, Louvre; *see also* OIL PAINTING, colour pl. II). He also painted four major group portraits: two of members of the surgeons' guild, the *Anatomy Lesson of Dr Nicolaes Tulp* (1632; The Hague, Mauritshuis) and the *Anatomy Lesson of Dr Deyman* (1656; Amsterdam, Rijksmus.), and one of a civic guard, the *Militia Company of Capt. Frans Banning Cocq and Lt Willem van Ruytenburch*, known as the '*Night Watch*' (1642; Amsterdam, Rijksmus.; *see* AMSTERDAM, fig. 4), which was one of the eight paintings by various artists that were ordered for the hall of the Arquebusiers (the Kloveniersdoelen) between 1639 and 1645.

Rembrandt's financial collapse on 8 January 1653 caused complications that were to plague him for the rest of his life. About 125 documents relate to this crisis, which was precipitated by Rembrandt's obstinate refusal to pay for the expensive house he had bought in 1639. In December 1655 he held a voluntary sale and on 10 July 1656 applied for insolvency (*cessio bonorum*). It was in that period that he painted the portrait of *Jan Six* (1654; Amsterdam, Col. Six) and a depiction of his common-law wife Hendrickje Stoffels as a *Woman Bathing in a Stream* (1655; London, N.G.; *see* REMBRANDT VAN RIJN, figs 7 and 8). Among Rembrandt's late works was the so-called '*Jewish Bride*' (*c.* 1665; Amsterdam, Rijksmus.), possibly a scene from the play *The Royal Shepherdess Aspasia* (1656) by Jacob Cats (i). Perhaps Rembrandt's most notable late achievement was the *Conspiracy of Claudius Civilis* (1661–2; Stockholm, Nmus.; *see* fig. 17) for the Amsterdam Stadhuis, designed by Jacob van Campen and officially opened in 1655. Initially, the artists chosen to decorate the new town hall were Ferdinand Bol, Govaert Flinck, Thomas de Keyser, Jan Lievens, Nicolaes van Helt Stockade (1614–99) and Willem Strijcker (?1606/7–?1673/7). In 1659 the burgomasters awarded Flinck the commission of 12 huge paintings depicting the uprisings of the Batavians against the Roman invaders, based on Tacitus' *Histories*. After Flinck's death in 1660, the commission was divided between Jacob Jordaens, Lievens and Rembrandt. The last delivered his painting in 1661, but in the following year it was removed and never returned. Jürgen Ovens was hastily commissioned to paint a mediocre substitute. In 1697 a painter known as Le Grand from Antwerp painted two further large scenes and the ceiling frescoes, but four other spaces remain empty to this day.

Rembrandt was also a prolific draughtsman and etcher and left more than 80 self-portraits in various media (*see* REMBRANDT VAN RIJN, fig. 5). His many pupils included Dou, Jan Joris van Vliet, Isack Jouderville, Willem de Poorter, Jacob Backer, Ferdinand Bol, Govaert Flinck, Jan Victors, Abraham van der Hecken (*d* after 1655), Reynier van der Gherwen (*d* 1662), Gerrit van der Horst (*c.* 1612–?1652), J. van Dorsten, Gerbrand van den Eeckhout, Leendert Cornelisz. van Beyeren (*c.* 1600–49), Abraham Furnerius, Christoph Paudiss, Lambert Doomer, Carel Fabritius, Samuel van Hoogstraten, Jürgen Ovens, Bernhardt Keil, Barent Fabritius, Karel van der Pluym, Nicolaes Maes, Johann Ulrich Mayr, Constantijn van Renesse, Willem Drost, H. Dullaert (1636–84), Jan van Glabbeeck (before 1634–after 1686), Arent de Gelder, Johannes Leupenius and his own son Titus van Rijn.

The landscape tradition imported from Flanders to Amsterdam was maintained by Alexander Keirinckx, though it lacks the same coherence as that of Haarlem. The Haarlem style influenced the next generation of Amsterdam landscape artists with the arrival of Jacob van Ruisdael in Amsterdam *c.* 1656. They included Ruisdael's most talented pupil Meindert Hobbema; Allart van Everdingen; Jan van Kessel, whose best work is still hidden under the names of Ruisdael and Hobbema; Aert van der Neer, the most celebrated Dutch specialist in nocturnal and sunset landscapes; and Philips Koninck, whose canvases are among the largest of all Dutch painted landscapes.

The Italianate landscape was represented by Bartholomeus Breenbergh and Cornelis van Poelenburch, and later by Jan Asselijn, Jan Both and Jan Baptist Weenix. Their work is usually basked in the golden sunlight and transparent shadows of the Roman Campagna, often with antique ruins; this is no doubt the result of their prolonged stay in Rome, where as members of the SCHILDERSBENT they were known as *Bentveughels* ('Birds of a feather'). After 1650 Italianate landscape painters began to settle increasingly in Amsterdam, with Berchem moving there after 1670. His most important pupil, Karel Du Jardin, is often considered the most Italianate of all Dutch painters. Adam Pynacker produced large decorative hangings for patrician houses in Amsterdam. Jan Hackaert was the youngest notable Italianate painter of his generation.

The Haarlem marine painting tradition was developed further in Amsterdam, above all by Simon de Vlieger and Willem van de Velde II. The latter occupied a central position in Dutch MARINE PAINTING. He made studies and paintings of a wide variety of vessels in very balanced compositions. His father, Willem van de Velde I, is best known for his pen-and-ink drawings of ships. Jan van de Cappelle represented ships at anchor in quiet river inlets and harbours, while Reinier Nooms specialized in views of Mediterranean harbours, towns and coastlines. Ludolf Bakhuizen adopted a more dynamic mode of marine painting, and he became the leading marine artist in Amsterdam after the van de Veldes moved to England in 1672. Adriaen van de Velde, younger brother of Willem van de Velde II and the only non-marine artist in the family, remained in Amsterdam and often painted the staffage figures in landscape paintings of Wijnants, van Ruisdael and Hobbema (*see* HOBBEMA, MEINDERT, fig. 1), as well as in the townscapes of Jan van der Heyden, whose career as an inventor is better documented than his activities as a painter. Emanuel de Witte was among the few artists in Amsterdam to paint church interiors, but he also executed history paintings, portraits, harbour views and genre scenes.

Willem Kalf, who came to Amsterdam from Rotterdam, was one of the few still-life painters recognized by his contemporaries as a great master. His large, ornate still-lifes show an exquisite tactile rendering of various ornamental objects, often with a sophisticated play of reflections. Amsterdam still-life paintings were usually executed in a vertical format. Willem van Aelst also painted sumptuous still-lifes and introduced the asymmetrical flower-piece with strong diagonals, a new composition type that was widely followed and refined in the 18th century by one of his outstanding pupils, Rachel Ruysch (see fig. 20 below). The most representative of the Amsterdam painters of reptiles and insects in imaginative settings was Otto Marseus van Schrick.

The truly important developments in small-scale figure painting took place outside Amsterdam: in Delft, with Pieter de Hooch and Vermeer; in Deventer, with Gerard ter Borch; and in Leiden with Dou, Frans van Mieris (i) and the young Metsu, who arrived in Amsterdam in 1657 and entered the most fruitful decade of his career. De Hooch also settled in Amsterdam (by 1661), but his work slowly declined, falling far below the level of his production in Delft.

(v) Utrecht. It was not until 1611 that the painters in Utrecht formed a guild of St Luke, with a college of painters following in 1639. In fact the Utrecht school of painting was at its height between those two dates. The artists of this school introduced an Italianate representational approach based on works by Caravaggio, as well as Ludovico and Annibale Carracci, Orazio Gentileschi and Bartolomeo Manfredi. Leading the UTRECHT CARAVAGGISTI (as they were known) for much of that period were Abraham Bloemaert and his pupils Hendrick ter Brugghen, Gerrit van Honthorst and Jan van Bijlert, as well as Paulus Moreelse and his pupil Dirck van Baburen.

Ambrosius Bosschaert (i), Balthasar van der Ast and the Flemish landscape painter Roelandt Savery settled in Utrecht in 1619. The Flemish element was further strengthened by the arrival of two Antwerp immigrants, Gillis de Hondecoutre and the marine painter Adam Willaerts. The Flemish-oriented classicizing style of history painting continued to flourish under Bloemaert and Joachim Wtewael until the middle of the century. Jan van Bronchorst painted ceiling decorations and designed the windows (destr.) for the Nieuwe Kerk in Amsterdam (1647). The Italian experience permeated the landscapes of Cornelis van Poelenburch and Jan Both. Jan Davidsz. de Heem's activity in Utrecht between 1667 and 1672 influenced Abraham Mignon (1640–78) and many other Dutch flower painters of his generation.

(vi) Delft. In the first half of the century, the artistic climate in Delft was revitalized by such immigrants as Frans Spierincx (1551–1630) of Antwerp. He established tapestry manufactories, employing weavers and cartoon designers who were mainly of Flemish descent. Other Flemish immigrants included Hans Jordaens I, who painted intimate history and mythological scenes, and the architectural painter Bartholomeus van Bassen, both from Antwerp, the landscape painter Willem van den Bundel (1575–after 1653) from Brussels, and the Delft-born Anthonie Palamedesz., son of Flemish parents, who was famous for his guardroom and genre scenes, while his brother Palamedes Palamedesz. (1607–38) specialized in battle scenes.

The leading Delft history painters were Leonard Bramer and Christiaen van Couwenberg (1604–67). Bramer received many official commissions, from among others the Dutch stadholder and the Delft municipality. He was one of the few artists in the northern Netherlands involved in

painting large-scale frescoes and decorated the Nieuwe Doelen in Delft. Van Couwenbergh, the son of a silversmith in Mechelen, was closely linked to Haarlem and Utrecht history painters and was involved in the decorations of the hunting-lodge at Honselaarsdijk, the Huis ter Nieuburch at Rijswijk, the Oude Hof in The Hague and the Oranjezaal of the Huis ten Bosch, outside of The Hague.

Delft became important as an artistic centre towards the middle of the 17th century with the work of the architectural painters Gerrit Houckgeest, Hendrik Cornelisz. van Vliet and Emanuel de Witte, and with the arrival of Paulus Potter and Carel Fabritius from Amsterdam and of the Rotterdam-born Pieter de Hooch from Haarlem. Before his departure to Amsterdam, de Hooch created his finest domestic scenes, such as the *Domestic Interior* (*c.* 1659–60; Berlin, Gemäldegal.). Fabritius's experiments in wide-angle perspective such as his *View of Delft* (1652; London, N.G.) or the *Goldfinch* (1654; The Hague, Mauritshuis; for illustration *see* FABRITIUS, (1)) reveal an artist interested in optical and illusionistic effects. His promising career was cut short by the explosion of the arsenal of the States of Holland and West Friesland in 1654.

The chronology of the work of Johannes Vermeer, arguably Delft's most well-known painter, is still somewhat problematic. Although he aspired initially to be a history painter, as his early *Christ in the House of Mary and Martha* (*c.* 1655; Edinburgh, N.G.) suggests, the majority of his small oeuvre consists of domestic interior scenes, such as *Woman Reading a Letter* (*c.* 1662–5; Amsterdam, Rijksmus.; *see* VERMEER, JOHANNES, fig. 5), exterior scenes such as the *'Little Street'* (*c.* 1658–60; Amsterdam, Rijksmus.; *see* fig. 18) and the magnificent *View of Delft* (*c.* 1661; The Hague, Mauritshuis; *see* DELFT, fig. 2). By 1671 the only artists of significance active in Delft were Vermeer and Cornelis de Man (1621–1706), who painted portraits, figure paintings, the occasional church interior and possibly some marine paintings.

(vii) The Hague. A number of artists worked in the administrative centre of the Dutch Republic, including Daniel Mijtens I, who was there between 1610 and 1618, Bartholomeus van Bassen between 1622 and 1652, and Esaias van de Velde. In 1625 Adriaen van de Venne moved from Middelburg to The Hague to paint allegorical, moralistic and biblical scenes. The presence of the stadholder and his entourage, as well as many foreign diplomats and aristocrats, attracted prominent portrait painters, including Jan van Ravesteyn, Evert Crijnsz. van der Maes (1577–1656), Jan Mijtens and Adriaen Hanneman. Particularly important was the arrival in 1637 of Gerrit van Honthorst, who emulated van Dyck's portrait style, although not as successfully as Hanneman. However, van Honthorst was appointed as court painter to the stadholders Frederick Henry and later William II and participated in the decorations of Honselaarsdijk, Rijswijk and the Huis ten Bosch. Landscape painters such as Moses van Uyttenbroeck and Jan van Goyen worked there, as did Karel Du Jardin, between 1656 and 1658. Caspar Netscher settled in The Hague in 1662. He painted elegant portraits in a French-oriented manner, while his sober domestic scenes,

18. Johannes Vermeer: *'Little Street'*, oil on canvas, 543×440 mm, *c.* 1658–60 (Amsterdam, Rijksmuseum)

such as the *Lace-maker* (1664; London, Wallace), show the influence of both Dou and Frans van Mieris (i). Abraham van Beyeren was the most representative still-life painter active in The Hague during the second half of the 17th century.

(viii) Other centres. Smaller centres produced prominent Rembrandt pupils, for example Samuel van Hoogstraten, Nicolaes Maes and Arent de Gelder, all from Dordrecht. Among other significant masters active there was the history and portrait painter Godfried Schalcken, a pupil of van Hoogstraten, and Jacob Cuyp. The latter's son Aelbert Cuyp is famous for his golden landscapes and river scenes, many of which feature animals. Aelbert's work had a significant influence on Dutch landscape painting in the 17th and 18th centuries.

Gerard ter Borch of Zwolle was the most prominent artist from the eastern area of the Dutch Republic, which produced few significant artists. He travelled extensively abroad and worked in Amsterdam, Haarlem, The Hague, Deventer, Zwolle and Kampen. Ter Borch produced mainly portraits, usually full-length against a neutral background. He also painted genre scenes, with a few figures against a vaguely defined background, and a unique eye-witness record of the *Ratification of the Treaty of Münster* (1648; London, N.G.). His most famous pupil was Caspar Netscher.

For further discussion of the development of Dutch genre painting *see* SPECIALIZATION.

Wurzbach

BIBLIOGRAPHY

EARLY SOURCES

D. Lampsonius: *Lamberti Lombardi apud Eburones pictoris celeberrimi vita* (Bruges, 1565)

K. van Mander: *Schilder-boeck* (Haarlem, [1603]–1604)

G. de Bie: *Het gulden cabinet* (1661)

J. von Sandrart: *Teutsche Academie* (1675–9); ed. A. R. Peltzer (1925)

A. van Houbraken: *Groote schouburgh der Nederlandsche konstschilders en schilderessen* (Amsterdam, 1718–21)

J. C. Weyerman: *De levens-beschryvingen der Nederlandsche konstschilders en schilderessen*, 4 vols (The Hague, 1729–69)

J. van Gool: *De nieuwe schouburgh* (1750–51)

J.-B. Descamps: *La Vie des peintres flamands, allemands et hollandais*, 4 vols (Paris, 1753–64)

J. Smith: *A Catalogue Raisonné of the Works of the Most Eminent Dutch, Flemish and French Painters*, 9 vols (London, 1829–42)

J. Immerseel jr: *De levens en werken der Hollandsche en Vlaamsche kunstschilders, graveurs en bouwmeesters*, 3 vols (Amsterdam, 1842–3)

C. Kramm: *De levens en werken der Hollandsche en Vlaamsche kunstschilders, beeldhouwers, graveurs en bouwmeesters, van den vroegsten tot op onzen tijd*, 4 vols (Amsterdam, 1857–64)

C. Hofstede de Groot: *Holländischen Maler* (1907–28)

A. Bredius: *Künstler-Inventare: Urkunden zur Geschichte der holländischen Kunst des XVIten, XVIIten und XVIIIten Jahrhunderts*, 7 vols (The Hague, 1915–21)

A. Nijstad: *Nederlandse schilders in publikaties voor 1700: Een register* (The Hague, 1978)

CONTEMPORARY ART THEORY

F. Junius: *De pictura veterum* (Amsterdam, 1637; Eng. trans., London, 1638; Dut. trans., Middelburg, 1641)

P. Angel: *Lof der schilder-kunst* (Leiden, 1642)

W. Goeree: *Inleydingh tot de practijck der algemeene schilderconst* (Middelburg, 1670) [a blend of mainly Italian Renaissance writers]

S. van Hoogstraeten: *Inleyding tot de hooge schoole der schilderkonst: anders de zichtbare wereld* (Rotterdam, 1678) [essentially an update of van Mander's *Schilder-boeck*, containing many paraphrases of his work]

W. Goeree: *Natuurlyck en schilderkonstig ontwerp der menschkunde* (Amsterdam, 1682) [a free version after Leonardo's *Trattato della pittura*]

G. de Lairesse: *Het groot schilderboeck* (Amsterdam, 1701)

R. de Piles: *Cours de peinture par principes* (Paris, 1708)

A. Houbraken: *De groote schouburgh* (1718–21)

GENERAL

W. Martin: *De Hollandse schilderkunst in de zeventiende eeuw*, 2 vols (Amsterdam, 1935–6)

G. J. Hoogewerff: *Nederlandsche kunstenaars te Rome, 1600–1725* (The Hague, 1942)

W. Bernt: *Die niederländischen Maler des 17. Jahrhunderts*, 4 vols (Munich, 1948–62); Eng. trans., 3 vols (London and New York, 1970)

G. J. Hoogewerff: *De Bentvueghels* (The Hague, 1952)

W. Bernt: *Die niederländischen Zeichner des 17. Jahrhunderts*, 2 vols (Munich, 1957–8)

E. Plietzsch: *Holländische und flämische Maler des XVII. Jahrhunderts* (Leipzig, 1960)

J. Rosenberg, S. Slive and E. H. ter Kuile: *Dutch Art and Architecture, 1600–1800*, Pelican Hist. A. (Harmondsworth, 1966, rev. 3/1977)

E. de Jongh: *Zinne- en minnebeelden in de schilderkunst van de zeventiende eeuw* ([Amsterdam, 1967])

K. D. H. Haley: *The Dutch in the Seventeenth Century* (London, 1972)

R. H. Fuchs: *Dutch Painting* (London and New York, 1978)

S. Alpers: *The Art of Describing: Dutch Art in the Seventeenth Century* (Chicago, 1983)

B. Haak: *The Golden Age: Dutch Painters of the Seventeenth Century* (New York, 1984) [with extensive bibliog. on Dutch painters, grouped systematically according to genre and individual artists]

The Dutch World of Painting (ex. cat. by G. Schwartz, Vancouver, A.G., 1986)

S. Schama: *The Embarrassment of Riches: An Interpretation of Dutch Culture in the Golden Age* (New York, 1987)

J. I. Israel: *Dutch Primacy in World Trade, 1585–1740* (Oxford, 1989)

Dawn of the Golden Age: Northern Netherlandish Art, 1580–1620 (exh. cat., ed. G. Luijten and others; Amsterdam, Rijksmus., 1993–4)

THEMATIC

H. Jantzen: *Das niederländische Architekturbild* (Leipzig, 1910)

R. Warner: *Dutch and Flemish Flower and Fruit Painters of the XVIIth and XVIIIth Centuries* (Amsterdam, 1928, 2/1975)

A. Riegl: *Das holländische Gruppenporträt*, 2 vols (Vienna, 1931)

A. B. de Vries: *Het Noord-Nederlandsch portret in de tweede helft van de 16e eeuw* (Amsterdam, 1934)

L. Preston: *Sea and River Painters of the Netherlands in the Seventeenth Century* (London, 1937)

Caravaggio en de Nederlanden (exh. cat. by J. G. van Gelder, Utrecht, Cent. Mus.; Antwerp, Kon. Mus. S. Kst.; 1952)

I. Bergström: *Dutch Still-life Painting in the Seventeenth Century* (New York, 1956)

W. Stechow: *Dutch Landscape Painting of the Seventeenth Century* (London, 1966)

H. G. Franz: *Niederländische Landschaftsmalerei im Zeitalter des Manierismus*, 2 vols (Graz, 1969)

Regenten en regentessen, overlieden en chirurgijns: Amsterdamse groepsportretten van 1600 tot 1835 (exh. cat. by B. Haak, Amsterdam, Hist. Mus., 1972)

L. J. Bol: *Die holländische Marinemalerei des 17. Jahrhunderts* (Brunswick, 1973)

H. Gerson: *Hollandse portretschilders van de zeventiende eeuw* (Maarssen, 1975)

Tot lering en vermaak: Betekenissen van Hollandse genrevoorstellingen uit de zeventiende eeuw (exh. cat. by E. de Jongh, Amsterdam, Rijksmus., 1976)

A. Blankert: *Nederlandse 17e-eeuwse italianiserende landschapschilders / Dutch 17th-century Italianate Landscape Painters* (Soest, 1978) [rev. and enlarged edn of exh. cat., Utrecht, Cent. Mus., 1965]

Gods, Saints and Heroes: Dutch Painting in the Age of Rembrandt (exh. cat. by A. Blankert and others, Washington, DC, N.G.A.; Detroit, MI, Inst. A.; 1980–81)

W. A. Liedtke: *Architectural Painting in Delft: Gerard Houckgeest, Hendrik van Vliet, Emanuel de Witte* (Doornspijk, 1982)

C. S. Schloss: *Travel, Trade and Temptation: The Dutch Italianate Harbor Scene, 1640–1680* (Ann Arbor, 1982)

A. Kettering: *The Dutch Arcadia: Pastoral Art and its Audience in the Golden Age* (Montclair, NJ, 1983)

Masters of Seventeenth-century Dutch Genre Painting (exh. cat., ed. P. C. Sutton; Philadelphia, PA, Mus. A.; W. Berlin, Gemäldegal.; London, RA; 1984)

Masters of 17th-century Dutch Landscape Painting (exh. cat., ed. P. C. Sutton; Amsterdam, Rijksmus.; Boston, MA, Mus. F.A.; Philadelphia, PA, Mus. A.; 1987–8)

Mirror of Empire: Dutch Marine Art of the Seventeenth Century (exh. cat. by G. S. Keyes, Minneapolis, MN, Inst. A.; Toledo, OH, Mus. A.; Los Angeles, CA, Co. Mus. A.; 1990–91)

5. *c.* 1680–*c.* 1800. The artistic production of the 18th century is often considered derivative of that of previous generations and has received considerably less scholarly attention than that paid to the 17th century. In the last quarter of the 17th century the upper middle class began to adopt a more ostentatious and luxurious lifestyle, essentially patterned on French fashion. Art and architecture, as well as the increased class conscience, reflect this fundamental change towards a French-oriented style. In 1672 a substantial part of the Dutch Republic was occupied by the French, and in 1678 Louis XIV agreed to relinquish these territories after signing the Peace of Nijmegen, followed by the Peace of Rijswijk in 1698. After the death of King William III, a second period without stadholder rule lasted from 1702 to 1747, during which the Republic was involved in several wars of succession. From 1766 onwards the frictions between pro- and contra-Orange factions became more apparent. This already precarious situation was further aggravated by the catastrophic aftermath of the fourth Anglo–Dutch war in 1780–84, the armed Prussian intervention in 1787 and the French invasion in 1793–4. The combined effects of these events sealed the fate of the Dutch Republic.

The writer Houbraken probably expressed a widely held contemporary opinion that Adriaen van der Werff was the greatest Dutch painter of this period. Together with Arent de Gelder and the Liège-born Gérard de Lairesse, he marked the transition from the 17th century to the 18th.

19. Adriaen van der Werff: *Self-portrait with a Portrait of his Wife, Margaretha Rees, and their Daughter Maria*, oil on canvas, 810×655 mm, 1699 (Amsterdam, Rijksmuseum)

Van der Werff, who specialized in biblical and mythological scenes, received many commissions from courts all over Europe. In his *Self-portrait with a Portrait of his Wife, Margaretha Rees, and their Daughter Maria* (1699; Amsterdam, Rijksmus.; see fig. 19), he is shown with a medal with the effigy of John William, the Elector Palatine, who in 1697 gave him a contract that made him the highest paid court painter. The Elector also provided commissions for Eglon van der Neer and, between 1710 and 1713, for Rachel Ruysch (see fig. 20; *see also* STILL-LIFE, fig. 4), who did so much to continue the still-life tradition of Willem van Aelst.

Rembrandt's mature style continued to exert influence in the early 18th century, especially in the art of de Gelder. Gérard de Lairesse, another self-confessed Rembrandt admirer, followed French classicizing theory both in his paintings and in his influential writings. Principally a history painter, he decorated the princely dwellings of King William III at Soesdijk and Het Loo, also designing a series of seven large canvases with scenes from Roman history (*c.* 1688) for the Council Room of the Binnenhof in The Hague. His ideas were adopted and developed by Jacob de Wit, who lived for a while in Antwerp and who may have played an instigating role in popularizing the decorative grisaille and bas-relief painting (*trompe l'oeil* sculpture) that was placed above windows and doors in burgher dwellings. De Wit also studied the works of Rubens and van Dyck, as did Theodoor van der Schuur (1670–1707) and Augustinius Terwesten. As a Catholic, de Wit received major commissions to execute paintings for Catholic churches and chapels in the Dutch Republic. He influenced Aert Schouman, Dirk van der Aa (1731–1809), Abraham van Strij I and his brother Jacob van Strij.

Cornelis Troost was a typical 18th-century portrait painter, whose style is sometimes compared to that of Hogarth. He painted life-size group portraits, but his small-scale family portraits in the vein of ter Borch, de Hooch and Thomas de Keyser became very fashionable. Like Jean-Etienne Liotard and Jean-Baptiste Perronneau, foreigners who visited the Netherlands, Troost used pastel, a medium that gained in popularity in the 18th century. Heroman van der Mijn and his sons Frans and George painted conversation pieces for the English market. Some English painters such as Charles Howard Hodges even settled in Amsterdam. Portraiture continued to flourish with Jan Maurits Quinkhard, Tibout Regters, Hendrik Pothoven, Wybrand Hendriks, Adriaan de Lelie and Jan Ekels II.

After 1689 the Leiden legacy of Dou and Frans van Mieris (i) was perpetuated by the latter's sons Jan (1660–90) and Willem, and his grandson Frans van Mieris (ii). In Dordrecht Gerrit Dou was imitated by Godfried Schalcken, who in his turn was followed by Karel de Moor. The ter Borch and Metsu tradition was continued by Eglon van der Neer in Amsterdam and by Jan Verkolje I in Delft. After the death of Cornelis Dusart, Adriaen van Ostade's pupil, figure painting with peasant subjects lost importance.

Church interiors were no longer in demand, while townscapes, painted by such artists as Isaak Ouwater, Reinier Vinkeles and Dirk Langendijk, became more fashionable, as did topographical drawings and watercolours. Isaac de Moucheron was a major figure of the decorative landscape tradition in the 18th century, while the arcadian landscape was refined by Jan van Huysum. Other prominent landscape painters were Jan ten Compe and Paulus La Fargue. Van Huysum painted decorative hunting still-lifes and flower-pieces, highly decorative and ornate genres that had replaced the traditional 17th-century still-lifes. Another 18th-century development was painted wallpaper, which often contained references to Aelbert Cuyp's compositions. Artists involved in this speciality, especially towards the end of the century, were Jurriaan Andriessen, Wouter Johannes van Troostwijk and Jacob van Strij, an imitator of Cuyp.

BIBLIOGRAPHY

Scheen

Dutch Conversation Pieces of the 18th and 19th Centuries (exh. cat. by A. Staring, London, Anglo-Netherlands Soc., 1947)

A. Staring: *De Hollanders thuis: Gezelschapsstukken uit drie eeuwen* (The Hague, 1956)

Dutch Masterpieces of the Eighteenth Century (exh. cat. by E. R. Mandle, Minneapolis, MN, Inst. A.; Toledo, OH, Mus. A.; Philadelphia, PA., Mus. A.; 1971–2)

Age of Elegance: Eighteenth-century Dutch Painting from the Rijksmuseum (exh. cat. by W. Kloek, W. Loos and G. Jansen, London, N.G., 1995)

HANS J. VAN MIEGROET

6. c. 1800–c. 1900. Throughout the 19th century, Dutch painting was strongly dominated by the influence of 17th-century painting, which functioned as a touchstone of quality. Around 1800, artists and art lovers generally felt that, after the 'Golden Age' of the 17th century, there had followed a period of artistic decline in the 18th century, as easel painting had been marginalized by the popularity of hanging interiors with painted wall decorations (mostly on canvas): as a result, towards the end of the 18th century there were few distinguished painters left. However, with the beginning of a new century, after the French Revolution and the consequent political changes throughout Europe, it seemed that a new era was developing, in which the arts (in particular painting) might again flourish. The methods and ideas of c. 1800 were to dominate Dutch painting until well into the third quarter of the 19th century and to remain popular, alongside new trends, with a more conservative public long after that. However, after 1850, new ideas, in particular those of the Barbizon school, gradually entered the Netherlands, introducing a gentle but distinct break with the existing tradition.

(i) c. 1800–c. 1850. (ii) c. 1850–c. 1900.

(i) c. 1800–c. 1850. As in the 17th century, most painters specialized in one particular genre. Innovations first became noticeable in landscape painting. By about 1800, such painters as Egbert van Drielst, Jacob van Strij, Pieter Gerardus van Os and Wouter Johannes van Troostwijk had developed a way of rendering nature that was strongly influenced by the work of such 17th-century predecessors as Jacob van Ruisdael, Meindert Hobbema and Aelbert Cuyp. However, their peaceful scenes of forests and open fields with figures and cattle also had a distinctive character of their own, the neat brushwork and restrained colour revealing the influence of Neo-classicism. Van Troostwijk was least directly influenced by examples from the past: his unpretentious scenes (e.g. *Landscape in Gelderland*,

20. Rachel Ruysch: *Still-life with Flowers and Plums*, oil on canvas, 840×640 mm, 1703 (Vienna, Gemäldegalerie der Akademie der Bildenden Künste)

c. 1808; Amsterdam, Rijksmus.; see fig. 21) seem to anticipate the later developments of the Hague school.

After 1813 the ideas of these artists were taken further by the slightly younger generation of landscape painters that included Andreas Schelfhout, who specialized in scenes on ice, and Barend Cornelis Koekkoek, who depicted mostly forests. Such artists sometimes distanced themselves more than the previous generation had from the work of past masters. The choice of motifs in their rather stereotyped scenes often evokes a romantic atmosphere, although their well-balanced composition schemes and delicate technique place their work far apart from the true Romantic movement in Germany and France. Such artists as Johannes Waruardus Builders (1811–90), Jacob Jan van der Maaten (1820–79), Lambertus Hardenberg (1822–1900) and Hendrik Kruseman van Elten (1829–1904) followed, departing still further from traditional schemes in favour of a freer, less detailed style, based on more direct observation of nature. In his early years Johan Barthold Jongkind, who was a pupil of Schelfhout, also belonged to this group; he developed his mature style in France, however, as a precursor of the Impressionists.

A comparable development can be seen in maritime painting, beginning with Nicolaas Baur (1767–1820) and Martinus Schouman (1770–1848), continuing in the work of Johannes Christiaan Schotel and ending with Louis Meijer and Hermanus Koekkoek (1815–82), brother of Barend Cornelis. However, maritime artists long continued to limit themselves to a small number of more or less fixed

21. Wouter Johannes van Troostwijk: *Landscape in Gelderland*, oil on canvas laid down on panel, 450×400 mm, *c.* 1808 (Amsterdam, Rijksmuseum)

composition schemes, more so than did landscape painters. Stylistically, the work of Meijer and Koekkoek fits in with examples of townscapes, a genre that did not become popular again until after *c.* 1830. It was practised by such artists as Kasparus Karsen, who specialized in paintings of old buildings; Cornelis Springer, who liked to fill his scenes with figures dressed in 17th-century costume; and Jan Weissenbruch, whose static scenes are remarkable especially for their striking effects of light.

Both landscapes and seascapes with figures were practised by Wijnand Nuyen, one of the few artists whose paintings were genuinely Romantic in their expression of feeling. Nuyen worked in France in the early 1830s, where he was much impressed by the work of Delacroix, Eugène Isabey and Richard Parkes Bonington. His relatively free handling of the brush and fresh colours influenced many other painters, in particular Johannes Bosboom, who later became highly successful through his depictions of church interiors.

In genre painting there was also some development of traditional idioms. The work of Abraham van Strij I still depends heavily on the 17th century, especially in the way his scenes are structured. This was already less clearly the case in the paintings of Willem Bartel van der Kooi and Pieter Christoffel Wonder. Younger artists used the traditional 17th-century subject categories to develop new themes, which they rendered in a lively, but very precise manner. Such artists included Petrus van Schendel, whose speciality was scenes by candlelight; David Joseph Bles, who favoured scenes with figures in 18th-century costume; and Herman Frederik Carel ten Kate, who painted waiting-room scenes with 17th-century soldiers (see also fig. 36

below). Two other painters that can be placed in this tradition are August Allebé, who painted primarily interiors with figures and became a highly influential professor and director at the Rijksacademie van Beeldende Kunsten in Amsterdam during the 1880s, and Lawrence Alma-Tadema, whose paintings of Classical Roman scenes became famous after his emigration to England in 1870.

Portrait painting was an important sideline for most genre painters, but there were also a number of true specialists in this field. The most important were Charles Howard Hodges, who brought with him some of the flamboyance of English 18th-century portrait painting when he moved to the Netherlands in 1792, and Jan Adam Kruseman, who worked in a more finished manner. In the northern and eastern provinces there were various travelling portrait painters, in particular Berend Kunst (1794–1881) from Groningen. These mostly anonymous artists worked mostly in pastel, using a rather primitive, but occasionally charming, style.

A genre that occupied a somewhat isolated position, being more derivative of 17th- and 18th-century painting (especially the work of Jan van Huysum) than any other genre, was that of the floral still-life. The most important practitioners were the van Spaendonck brothers, Gerard and Cornelis, who worked for a long time at the French court; Anthony Oberman (1781–1845); and Georgius van Os, brother of Pieter Gerardus. Later on floral still-lifes became the special domain of such female painters as Maria Vos (1824–1906) and Margaretha Roosenboom (1843–96), who also worked in a freer style in watercolour.

The only genre that did not become popular in the Netherlands in the 19th century was history painting. According to the academic hierarchy of subjects, this was the top category, which made many theoreticians and critics worried about the situation in the Netherlands. Because the Dutch state, unlike many foreign governments, was unwilling to give substantial financial support to the visual arts, there were only a few artists who applied themselves to this genre. Most of the painters who regularly produced historical scenes earned a living primarily by painting genre scenes and portraits or by teaching. The best-known history painter was Jan Willem Pieneman, Director of the Koninklijke Academie in Amsterdam from 1820, whose enormous *Battle of Waterloo* (1824; Amsterdam, Rijksmus.; see fig. 22) is one of the few large battle scenes in 19th-century Dutch painting. His son Nicolaas Pieneman and Charles Rochussen are among the few true history painters of the younger generation. Rochussen was also important as an illustrator of historical literature.

Other artists who regularly showed history paintings of interest include Simon Opzoomer (1819–78), Johannes Egenberger (1822–97) and Hendrik Albert van Trigt (1829–99). Their work was inspired by both Dutch and French art. In Paris, Egenberger and van Trigt received training from, among others, Ary Scheffer, who originally came from Dordrecht but had established himself in Paris in 1811 to become a world-famous painter of religious and literary themes. It should be noted that in the 19th century the concept of history painting still, as in previous centuries, extended beyond historical scenes and also included religious themes. Scheffer's overwhelming success gave Dutch critics the hope that this genre might also

22. Jan Willem Pieneman: *Battle of Waterloo*, oil on canvas, 5.76×8.36 m, 1824 (Amsterdam, Rijksmuseum)

become popular in the Netherlands, but, with the exception of Cornelis Kruseman, a cousin of Jan Adam, who produced a number of more or less successful works in the style of the Nazarenes, no developments of significance seem to have taken place. Stylistically, Scheffer himself belonged primarily to the French tradition, although he always maintained contact with colleagues and collectors in Holland, where his work was also periodically exhibited.

(ii) c. *1850–*c. *1900.* After *c.* 1850 a distinctive break with the existing tradition manifested itself first in landscape painting under the influence of the Barbizon school. The most important innovators were Willem Roelofs, who himself worked in Barbizon in the early 1850s, and Gerard Bilders. Both spent much time painting in the village of Oosterbeek near Arnhem, where between 1855 and 1865 they were joined by various other young artists who wished to free themselves from their academic training by working in the open air. Apart from Roelofs and Bilders, the group, which towards 1870 was to develop into the famous HAGUE SCHOOL, included the Maris brothers (Jacob, Matthijs and Willem), Paul Joseph Constantin Gabriël and Anton Mauve.

The Hague school, named after the city where most of its followers lived and worked for a shorter or longer period, is known for the loose, at times almost sketchy, technique and the dominant use of green-greyish colours, without local effects of light. Subjects were no longer chosen primarily for their anecdotal value but increasingly for their pictorial possibilities. The Hague school painters

were not so dependent on the past as the previous generation: they were more confident, which may be related to the strengthening economy of the 1870s and the Netherlands' more important international role. After *c.* 1880 the Hague school also became known outside Holland, in particular in England, the USA and Canada, where much of the work was exported. The principles of the movement continued to appeal to many artists until after World War I (among them Piet Mondrian in his early years).

Besides landscapes—with or without cattle (for illustrations *see* MARIS, (1) and (3))—the Hague school tended to paint scenes from the lives of peasants and fishermen. From 1855 Jozef Israëls, who had begun his career as a history painter, concentrated on scenes of fishermen (e.g. *Passing Mother's Grave*, 1856; Amsterdam, Stedel. Mus.; for illustration *see* ISRAËLS (1)). Later he became known internationally for his bleak, boldly painted interiors with poor people. H. W. Mesdag confined himself to painting imposing beach views and seascapes, a genre in which he became enormously successful. Stylistically the later church interiors by Bosboom can also be categorized as of the Hague school (for illustration *see* BOSBOOM, JOHANNES). Matthijs Maris, on the other hand, was to break away from the Hague school tradition after moving to London in 1877, where he produced dark fairy-tale scenes and dream landscapes in a highly individual style anticipating Symbolism. The Hague school also provided the background for the early work of Vincent van Gogh. Van

23. George Hendrik Breitner: *Three Women Standing on a Bridge*, oil on canvas, 620×1020 mm, 1887 (Amsterdam, Stedelijk Museum)

Gogh was related to Mauve, who for a short while helped his painting. His work occupies a unique position in 19th-century Dutch painting, although his characteristic style did not develop until he moved to France in 1886, where he came into contact with the Post-Impressionists.

Over the years, various other Hague school painters left The Hague. Some moved to Laren, a picturesque village in the Gooi region, which had been discovered by Israëls and Mauve in the 1870s. Several younger artists followed, and this led, in the course of the 1890s, to the creation of a true artists' colony with many prominent members. One of the best known, after Mauve (Israëls never properly established himself in Laren) is Albert Neuhuys, who had much success internationally with his sombre, but elegantly painted peasant interiors. He is sometimes regarded as the 'founder' of the 'Laren school', a stylistic variant of the Hague school, characterized by close attention to colour effects, even though a general tonal effect remained popular. The favourite subject of these artists was the bleak peasant interior, which in some cases had an almost mass-produced character.

In addition, numerous representatives of other movements also moved to Laren, which by 1900 became the most important Dutch artistic centre after Amsterdam and The Hague. Many of these artists had trained at the Rijksacademie in Amsterdam, which was headed by Allebé from 1885. It was here that the so-called Amsterdam Impressionist movement began, which flourished from the second half of the 1880s and remained in vogue until the 1920s. Its main representatives were Jacobus van Looy; George Hendrik Breitner; Maurits van der Valk (1857–1935), who became known especially for his etchings; Floris Verster, the only one who did not train at the

Rijksacademie; and Isaac Israëls, the son of Jozef. The Amsterdam Impressionists concentrated, to a much greater degree than the Laren school painters, on effects of colour and light; another characteristic is the elegant, virtuoso brushwork, with particularly striking results in the work of Israëls and Breitner (e.g. Breitner's *Three Women Standing on a Bridge*, 1887; Amsterdam, Stedel. Mus.; see fig. 23). Their choice of subject-matter was also more varied than that of the Laren painters: besides landscapes, townscapes became a favourite subject, and they, particularly Verster, frequently produced still-lifes and portraits. Although the work of Willem Witsen and Jan Pieter Veth, who is known primarily as a portrait painter, cannot really be described as impressionistic, it is nevertheless included in this movement. Their search for a greater sense of form reveals especially the influence of Allebé.

After *c.* 1890 Dutch painting divided into two main tendencies. The first can—with some caution—be labelled the Impressionist mainstream. It includes the work of any followers of the Hague and Laren schools, the Amsterdam Impressionists or a combination of these schools. Until World War I, and still after, this group included by far the majority of Dutch painters. The second main current, which emerged *c.* 1890, can be best described as Symbolist. This movement includes all those artists who were trying to find a way of expressing the hidden world behind the visible reality. A number of such artists, among them Jan Toorop, Simon Mentijn (1866–1948), Hendricus Jansen, Johan Thorn Prikker and Antoon Molkenboer (1872–1960), were in contact with various international Symbolist movements, especially in France and Belgium. As well as oil, they often favoured pastel, watercolour, pen and ink, pencil and printmaking techniques. A more specifically Dutch trend was what is known as Community art (*Gemeenschapskunst*): its main representatives were Antoon Derkinderen, Richard Roland Holst and Willem Adriaan van Konijnenburg. They encouraged the making of mural paintings and other monumental decorations in public buildings (hence the movement's name) and developed a formula strongly based on the use of geometrical shapes and greyish colours, without actually abandoning the figurative element. For many Symbolists (especially those who were in touch with international movements) the work of van Gogh—which was introduced to Holland partly through their activities—formed an important source of inspiration.

BIBLIOGRAPHY
G. H. Marius: *De Hollandsche schilderkunst in de negentiende eeuw* (The Hague, 1903); Eng. trans. by A. Teixeira de Mattos as *Dutch Painting in the Nineteenth Century* (London, 1908)
A. M. Hammacher: *Amsterdamse impressionisten en hun kring* (Amsterdam, 1941)
J. Knoef: *Een eeuw Nederlandse schilderkunst* (Amsterdam, 1948)
150 jaar Nederlandse kunst (exh. cat. by H. L. C. Jaffé and others, Amsterdam, Stedel. Mus., 1963)
J. de Gruyter: *De Haagse school*, 2 vols (Amsterdam, 1968)
'Het vaderlandsch gevoel': Vergeten negentiende-eeuwse schilderijen over onze geschiedenis ['The patriotic sentiment': forgotten 19th-century paintings about our history] (exh. cat. by W. H. Vroom and others, Amsterdam, Rijksmus., 1978)
Kunstenaren der idee: Symbolistische tendenzen in Nederland, c. 1880–1930 [Ideological artists: symbolist tendencies in the Netherlands, *c.* 1880–1930] (exh. cat. by C. Blotkamp and others, The Hague, Gemeentemus., 1978)
De Haagse school: Hollandse meesters van de 19e eeuw (exh. cat. by R. de Leeuw, J. Sillevis and C. Dumas, The Hague, Gemeentemus., 1983)
J. P. Koenraads: *Laren en zijn schilders* (Laren, 1985)
Op zoek naar de Gouden eeuw: Nederlandse schilderkunst, 1800–1850 [In search of the Golden Age: Dutch painting, 1800–1850] (exh. cat. by L. van Tilborgh and G. Jansen, Haarlem, Frans Halsmus., 1986)
R. Bionda and C. Blotkamp, eds: *De schilders van tachtig: Nederlandse schilderkunst, 1880–1895* (Zwolle, 1991)

JAN JAAP HEIJ

7. AFTER *c.* 1900. In the 20th century, Dutch painting achieved international importance, particularly through the art movements DE STIJL (1917–32) with Piet Mondrian and COBRA (1948–51) with Karel Appel. These two movements revealed the extremes in Dutch art, between a rigid impersonal aesthetic and a direct discharge of emotion. The influence of Vincent van Gogh affected the early work of many painters at both extremes long after World War II.

(i) Painting, video film and photography. (ii) Prints.

(i) Painting, video film and photography. Around the turn of the century the battle between order and spontaneity in Dutch painting had not yet manifested itself. The style of the Hague school was flourishing, and Amsterdam Impressionism was practised by such painters as George Hendrik Breitner and Isaac Israëls. Their sketchlike painting style and especially Breitner's persistent dark colours influenced the work of many Dutch painters up to the 1940s. They gave impetus to a form of Expressionism exemplified by Suze Robertson. Jan Toorop used Pointillism in his work up to *c.* 1910 in predominantly realistic subject-matter. He then developed a personal linear Symbolism in drawings in which the influence of his youth in

the Dutch East Indies found expression. His contemporary Johan Thorn Prikker also used Pointillism after Symbolism. From the end of the 19th century the Socialist form of Symbolism called Community art (*Gemeenschapskunst*), in particular the work of Richard Roland Holst up to *c.* 1940, was of great significance for the development of monumental art.

The vivid colouring of French art really penetrated the Netherlands through a younger generation, initially via the elegant works that Jan Sluijters began in 1906 to send to the Netherlands from Paris. These works caused a great stir. Another pioneer was KEES VAN DONGEN (see fig. 24), who emigrated to France and joined the Fauves. Meanwhile, between 1907 and 1914, as van Gogh's works became influential, Sluijters and his circle, including Leo Gestel and Piet Mondrian, absorbed various aspects of Pointillism, Fauvism, Cubism and Futurism. Light played such a role in their style that it was called 'Luminism'.

Sluijters, who was regarded as the greatest living Dutch painter until after World War II, became a fashionable portrait painter in Amsterdam in the period between the wars, just as van Dongen did in Paris. Both relied on a more traditional Expressionism. Gestel also moved away from his Luminist manner. He became 'father' of the Bergen school that existed from 1914 around the village of Bergen in North Holland and that was characterized by a form of Cubist Expressionism in subdued shades. The influence of the French Cubist Henri Le Fauconnier, who stayed in the Netherlands in those years and proclaimed Cézanne's teaching, applied strongly here.

Mondrian held on tightly to the thread of experimentation. His work developed from the Hague Impressionist

24. Kees van Dongen: *Finger on the Cheek*, oil on canvas, 650×540 mm, *c.* 1905–10 (Rotterdam, Museum Boymans–van Beuningen)

style towards 'Luminism': he combined this with his own form of Cubism, in which a symbolic vision emerged *c.* 1910 (*see* MONDRIAN, PIET, fig. 1), supported by his theosophical philosophy. In the later phase of this Cubism, form became further reduced, leading in 1920 to his well-known compositions in vertical and horizontal lines combined with square areas in the three primary colours (for illustration *see* NEO-PLASTICISM). His work and theories made him the most important exponent of De Stijl, of which THEO VAN DOESBURG was the instigator and great propagandist. This movement, which initially published a journal, counted among its members not only painters, including Bart van der Leck and the Hungarian Vilmos Huszár, but also architects. Internationally it exercised great influence over future developments in 20th-century art, in particular geometric abstraction in painting. Van Doesburg was also involved with Dada activities, under the pseudonym I. K. Bonset. The collages of Thijs Rinsema, Otto van Rees and Paul Citroen, who was mainly known for portrait drawings, also demonstrated the Dada spirit.

Various forms of Expressionism gained prominence, firstly in the work of Jacoba van Heemskerk, who was strongly orientated towards Germany. The Expressionism of Die Brücke spread from 1921 through the Groningen group De Ploeg (The Plough), the leader of which was Jan Wiegers. Hendrik Chabot emerged in Rotterdam with his heavily exaggerated earthy style. He was indirectly involved with the group De Branding (The Breaker) that formed in his town (1917–26) and was committed to a combination of Expressionism and Symbolism. The same

25. Pyke Koch: *Shooting Gallery*, oil on canvas, 1.7×1.3 m, 1931 (Rotterdam, Museum Boymans–van Beuningen)

combination arose in the work of Jacob Bendien, Janus de Winter and Erich Wichman. Herman Kruyder, a painter active in Heemstede and elsewhere, was an exceptional loner, with his mysterious poetic Cubist compositions.

The 'return to tradition' so dominant in the years between the wars brought out a number of important Magic or neo-Realists. The Magic Realists included Pyke Koch (see fig. 25) and Albert Carel Willink, and the Realists more strictly speaking, included Charley Toorop, Wim Schuhmacher, Dick Ket and Raoul Hynckes (1893–1973). Constructivist work was done by Chris Beekman and Lou Loeber. Utrecht was the centre of a modest form of Surrealism, with Johannes Moesman its foremost representative.

In 1945 various artists tried to take up the threads of experiments started before World War I, with the support of Willem Sandberg, the new director of the Stedelijk Museum in Amsterdam. Members of the Vrij Beelden (Free Images) group (1947–53) led this move, including the originally Surrealist and subsequently abstract Expressionist Piet Ouborg (see fig. 26) and the abstract painter Willem Hussem. The Experimentele Groep in Holland (1948–9) produced Expressionist work inspired by 'primitive art' and children's drawings: its members included KAREL APPEL, Constant (e.g. the *Burnt Earth*, 1951; Amsterdam, Stedel. Mus.) and Corneille, who were also co-founders of the international movement Cobra. Lucebert, a poet member of that group, later threw himself into painting as a sharply socially critical Expressionist. Appel acquired a great international reputation with his violent, emotive style of painting, inclined to abstraction, which he developed from the mid-1950s, using strong colours straight from the tube on to canvases of ever-increasing size. Various other artists developed a form of Expressionism, some in a more figurative direction, such as Gerrit Benner and Jaap Nanninga, and others predominantly abstract, such as Ger Lataster. Willem de Kooning, who was born in Rotterdam and who in 1926 moved to the USA, became one of the greatest of the American Abstract Expressionists. At the same time the brothers Bram and Geer van Velde from the Netherlands were absorbed into the Ecole de Paris, the former as a solitary Expressionist and the latter as a lyrical Cubist. Such artists as Bram Bogart and Jaap Wagemaker created matter painting characterized by a rough material in which, for example, sand was mixed in with the paint. Starting with *Art informel*, Kees van Bohemen (1928–85) developed into a lyrical Expressionist, interpreting consumer society, and Jan Cremer (*b* 1940) into a 'barbaric' Expressionist. The mysterious element of Magic Realism appeared meanwhile in the work of Co Westerik.

In the 1960s a reaction to Primitivism and the discharge of emotion of the 1950s came with the NUL group (1960–62) and the short lived attempt to make a very impersonal art out of industrial materials and products. However, the work of Nul's best-known members, Jan Schoonhoven and Armando, was characterized primarily by a poetic tone. The same is true of the abstracted landscape images of Ben Akkerman, who belonged to no particular movement. Detached composition was much more emphatic in Ad Dekkers's subtle reliefs and Peter Struycken's geometric, computer-generated work: De Stijl was their point of

26. Pict Ouborg: *The Sign*, oil on canvas, 510×650 mm, 1947 (The Hague, Gemeentemuseum)

departure, and they belonged to the circle around the international journal *Structure* (1958–64). Compositions with cliché images from consumer society, in the manner of American Pop art, occurred in the collage paintings of Gustave Asselbergs (1938–67). This was continued in a more concealed way in the work of Reinier Lucassen and Alfons Freymuth (*b* 1940). They combined quotations from widely known modern art works on one canvas, making them into an individual Expressionist style; J. C. J. van der Heyden compressed geometric shapes and fragments, for example of photographs, into an individual hermetic symbolism. In the turbulent 1960s, happenings with a partly political, partly artistic character took place. The ideal of removing the distinction between the artist and public was fostered by, for example, the international Fluxus movement, which was very successful in Holland. Playing with elements from consumer society and culture began at the end of the 1960s in conceptual art: for example, Jan Dibbets manipulated observed reality through photographs, and Ger van Elk repeatedly made new discoveries in a range of techniques.

In the 1970s artists concentrated firmly on their individuality, and performance art arose. Then the new medium of video took on an important role both as a means of recording performances and conceptual works, and as a self-contained means of expression. Livinus van der Bundt (1909–79) was a pioneer of Dutch video. Further developments of this medium followed a more poetic, contemplative direction. The work of Michel Cardena (*b* 1934) was outspokenly narrative, while Lydia Schouten (*b* 1948), in her performances and videos, was often concerned ironically with consumer society.

Photography, increasingly regarded as part of the visual arts, was included in art in various ways (most notably in the later part of the century), for example in installations. Sigurður Guðmundsson from Iceland and Bas Jan Ader (1942–75) used it in conceptual work. Ed van der Elsken and Oscar van Alphen (*b* 1923) gained reputations for their documentary photography. Daan van Golden, obsessed with the clichés of daily reality and culture, combined it with painting and drawing. One other form of conceptual art was 'fundamental painting', which arose in the 1970s. Edgar Fernhout, originally a neo-Realist painter, came to be regarded as a leader of this tendency in the Netherlands in his later development. Painting, regarded in the 1970s as generally a spent art form, broke loose in all aspects *c*. 1980 under the influence of the German Neue Wilden and the Young Italians with figurative work by such artists as René Daniels and Marlene Dumas. Rob Scholte (*b* 1958) reverted to Pop art to a limited degree with his compositions made of elements from consumer society.

BIBLIOGRAPHY

F. M. Huebner: *Die neue Malerei in Holland* (Leipzig and Arnhem, 1921)

P. Fierens: *L'Art hollandais contemporain* (Paris, 1933)

A. M. Hammacher: *Stromingen en persoonlijkheden, een halve eeuw schilderkunst in Nederland, 1900-1950* (Amsterdam, 1955)

A. B. Loosjes-Terpstra: *Moderne Kunst in Nederland, 1900-1914* (Utrecht, 1959/*R* 1987)

C. Wentinck: *Die Nederlandse schilderkunst sinds Van Gogh* (Nijmegen, 1959)

150 jaar Nederlandse Kunst, schilderijen, beelden, tekeningen, grafiek, 1813-1963 (exh. cat. by H. L. C. Jaffé and others, Amsterdam, Stedel. Mus., 1963)

C. Wintinck: 'Die Nederlandse Schilderkunst in de twintigste eeuw', in *Kunstgeschiedenis der Nederlanden, XI, Twintigste eeuw I* (Antwerp, 1965)

K. Schippers: *Holland Dada* (Amsterdam, 1974)

A. Venema: *De Bergense School* (Baarn, 1976)

Kunstenaren der idee, Symbolistische tendenzen in Nederland, c. 1800–1930 (exh. cat. by C. Blotkcamp and others, The Hague, Gemeentemus., 1978)

A. Vienna: *De Ploeg, 1918–1930* (Baarn, 1978)

G. Imanse, ed.: *Van Goph tot Cobra, Nederlandse schilderkunst van 1880–1950* (Amsterdam, 1981)

——: *De Nederlandse identiteit in de kunst na 1945* (Amsterdam, 1984)

W. Stokvis, ed.: *De doorbraak van de moderne kunst in Nederland, de jaren 1945–1951* (Amsterdam, 1984/*R* 1990)

J. Fritz-Jobse and F. Burkom, eds: *Een nieuwe synthese: Geometrisch-abstracte kunst in Nederland, 1945–1960* (The Hague, 1988)

A. Grondman and others, eds: *De automatische verbeelding: Nederlandse surrealisten* (Amsterdam, 1989)

J. Wesseling: *Alles was mooi, een geschiedenis van de Nul-beweging* (Amsterdam, 1989)

R. Kuipers: *Kunstgreep: Overzicht van kunst en cultuur in Nederland na 1945* (Groningen, 1991)

W. Stokvis and K. Zijlmans, eds: *Vrij spel: Nederlandse kunst in de jaren 1970–1990* (Amsterdam, 1993)

P. Boyens and J. Boyens: *Expressionisme in Nederland 1910–1930* (Zwolle and Laren, 1994)

(ii) Prints. In printmaking too the influence of the Hague school was notable until far into the 20th century. Etchings first came into fashion again within the Amsterdam Impressionist circle, which heralded the new century with Willem Witsen's town views and East Asian scenes by Marius Bauer. Graphic art was important for such Symbolists as Jan Toorop and Richard Roland Holst. Around the turn of the century the woodcut mainly attracted the attention of architects and, through their love of ornament, interior and book designers. Graphic artists were stimulated by such teachers as Pieter Dupont, a master of engraving, Antoon Derkzen van Angeren, a strongly emotive etcher, and Jessurum de Mesquita, known for his stylized animal figures.

M. C. Escher earned international fame through his mathematical games with figurative motifs in lithographs and woodcuts. Naturalism was interpreted by Dirk van Gelder (1907–90) and in an extremely refined way by Jan Mankes. The etchings and lithographs of Jeanne Bieruma Oosting (*b* 1898) offer a more romantic version. Dirk Nijland returned to very simple images in his woodcuts. Willem van Leusden was a Surrealist in his graphic works and, like many of his contemporaries, was inspired by the great Dutch 17th-century etcher Hercules Segers. Expressionism found powerful interpretation in the woodcuts of Jacoba van Heemskerk and Jan Wiegers. The group De Ploeg (The Plough) supported Hendrik Nicolaas Werkman, whose poetic, experimental prints in many respects formed the basis of the development of graphic art and

typography after World War II. Another De Ploeg member was the geometric abstract artist Wobbe Alkema. The woodcuts of Petrus Alma are examples of Neue Sachlichkeit.

After World War II the painter Harry van Kruiningen (*b* 1906) emerged as a talented graphic artist. He made his name chiefly by his experimental approach to etching. The Cobra artists Karel Appel, Constant, Corneille and Lucebert each took an individual route with graphic art, as did such abstract Expressionists as Ger Lataster. Anton Heyboer made influential Primitivist etchings that incorporate texts. Co Westerik produced Magic Realist graphic art. Aad Veldhoen (*b* 1934) was an accomplished realist etcher, while Marte Röling (*b* 1935) used a form of Pop art in her prints. A poetic geometric abstraction is found in the graphic art of sculptor Carel Visser and, in an exceedingly cool manner, in screenprints by Peter Struycken.

BIBLIOGRAPHY

Wendigen, ii/7 (Sept–Oct 1919) [issue dedicated to woodcuts]

L. Bosch: *Nederlandse prentkunst sedert 1900, etsen en gravures* (Utrecht, 1927)

J. A. van der Boom: *De moderne houtsnede in Nederland* (Amsterdam, 1928)

C. de Moor: *Postzegelkunst: De vormgeving van de Nederlandse postzegel* (The Hague, 1960)

J. Schwencke: *Het beeld van het Nederlandse exlibris, 1880–1960* (Amsterdam, 1960)

J. J. van Wessem: *Nederlandse grafiek na 1945* (Hilversum, 1964)

Hedendaagse Nederlandse grafiek (exh. cat., intro. W. F. Lash; Leiden, Stedel. Mus. Lakenhal, 1967)

Grafiek na 1945 (uit eigen bezit) (exh. cat., Utrecht, Cent. Mus., 1972)

Grafiekmanifestatie 1978: Een overzicht van de Nederlandse grafiek sinds 1975 (exh. cat. by J. E. Bokhoven, Schiedam, Stedel. Mus., 1978)

A. J. Vervoorn: *Nedenlandse prentkunst, 1840–1940* (Lochem, 1983)

H. Redeker: *Hedendaagse prentkunst in Nederland* (Amsterdam, 1984)

WILLEMIJN STOKVIS

IV. Sculpture.

1. Before *c.* 1568. 2. *c.* 1568–*c.* 1800. 3. *c.* 1800–1900. 4. After 1900.

1. BEFORE *c.* 1568. It has become traditional to divide medieval Dutch sculpture into two periods: the early 12th century to the late 14th and the late 14th century to the mid-16th. The earlier period is represented mainly by stone sculpture, of which there are only a few surviving examples. In the later Middle Ages wood sculpture predominates, of which a larger number of works have survived. The scarcity of surviving sculpture in the northern Netherlands is due mainly to the iconoclastic outbreak of the later 16th century. Many of the medieval sculptural works found within the present boundaries of the Netherlands are not indigenous, yet a few series of stone sculptures and quite a number of wood-carvings were produced by distinctively Dutch workshops.

(i) Before c. 1380. The earliest example of this period is a tympanum depicting in low relief *St Peter with Count Dirk VI and his Mother Petronilla* (Amsterdam, Rijksmus.), originally decorating the entrance portal to the great abbey of Egmond Binnen in Holland and dating from the second quarter of the 12th century. Its red sandstone suggests a German origin, but as the relief is carved from a sarcophagus lid, the work may have been done locally. Yet it is an isolated piece. Most sculptural works from this period are imported products from regions lying outside the present

Dutch borders, such as Westphalia to the east and Tournai and the Meuse area to the south. Thus the tympanum relief depicting *Abraham with Souls on his Lap* (late 12th century) preserved at the Grote Kerk at Zwolle is a Westphalian piece of work, as are some coffin slabs of yellow Bentheim sandstone, with effigies in very low relief, found in the provinces of Friesland, Groningen and Drenthe and apparently belonging to a larger series in Germany.

In the second half of the 12th century there was great sculptural activity in and around Maastricht (*see* MAAS-TRICHT, §3(ii)). Although the sculptural works here are embedded in the larger Meuse style of the area, for the greater part beyond the present boundaries of the Neth-erlands, Maastricht seems to have been a centre of its own, in no way inferior to such other towns as Liège. There is a large series of decorated and historiated capitals, dating from the mid-12th century to *c.* 1200 (at Rolduc, the earliest showing Lombard influence, and at Maastricht in the church of St Servatius and the basilica of Onze-Lieve-Vrouwe). Among the several reliefs preserved in Maas-tricht are a very fine tympanum depicting *Christ in Majesty* (*see* ROMANESQUE, fig. 41) in the cloisters of St Servatius and a relief depicting an *Oath on the Relics* in Onze-Lieve-Vrouwekerk. They are similar in style to four important reliefs (*c.* 1170) from the choir enclosure in the St Pieter-skerk at Utrecht, which were found in 1965 during restoration works. They depict the *Crucifixion, Pilate,* the *Empty Tomb* and the *Three Marys at the Tomb* (see fig. 27). Large parts of the original polychromy have been pre-served, and the style comes close to that of the *Oath on the Relics* in Maastricht.

At a later date, in the second quarter of the 13th century, a rich south-eastern entrance porch was added to St Servatius. Though heavily restored in the 16th century and especially in the 19th, it is one of the very few monumental portals found in the Netherlands or indeed in the Meuse area. It is clearly of French inspiration, made by French sculptors perhaps with the help of local craftsmen on the decorative parts. The few funerary monuments with effigies found in the Netherlands at this period are all imported products, starting with the heavily restored monument to *Count Gerard of Gelder and his Wife Margaretha* (after *c.* 1231) in the Munsterkerk at Roer-mond. Made of stone from Baumberg, Germany, it was the first great double tomb in Europe. There are great tombs of Tournai stone with episcopal effigies in Utrecht Cathedral and at Westbroek, and of Namur or Tournai stone with effigies of ladies and knights at Gorinchem, Geervliet, IJsselstein and Utrecht. All are old-fashioned in style, especially when compared with the contemporary freestone effigies of England and France. They must have been made at the south Netherlandish centres of Tournai and Namur–Liège, on the evidence of similar effigies preserved in present-day Belgium. The only noteworthy examples of wood-carved figures from this period are a few statues of the Virgin as *Sedes sapientiae* (Throne of Wisdom). Stylistic analysis suggests that the better ones (e.g. Utrecht, Catharijneconvent) are works from the Meuse area, influenced by the well-known Meuse metal-working tradition. Other, more rustic works may have been imported from Westphalia.

27. North Netherlandish school: *Three Marys at the Tomb*, sandstone relief with traces of polychromy, 800×800 mm, *c.* 1170 (Utrecht, St Pieterskerk)

(ii) c. 1380–c. 1490. Claus Sluter inaugurated a new sculptural style in Europe with his works for the charter-house of Champmol near Dijon (from 1389 onwards; *see* SLUTER, CLAUS, §1). Yet although he was born and bred in Holland, nothing is found there that points to his sources. Stone sculpture of *c.* 1400 and of the Late Gothic period in the Netherlands is largely architectural, except for some isolated pieces imported from elsewhere. These include three great late medieval tombs commemorating the Lords of Breda in the Grote Kerk at Breda. The material of the tombs came from abroad, and the tombs were either shipped to Breda or made on the spot by foreign sculptors. The same is true of the medieval funerary slabs found in the Netherlands: it is not until later in the 16th century that local regional workshops can be discerned.

The first examples of local architectural sculpture in this period were executed for the St Janskerk (*see* 'S HERTOGENBOSCH, §2) at 's Hertogenbosch, and were made in a lodge on the site. Inside the church there is a large series of bosses (*c.* 1380–1425), and outside are the remains of straddling figures on the flying buttresses, buttress statues, spandrel reliefs and portal sculpture (15th century and early 16th). Though more than three quarters of the exterior sculpture has been lost through wear and 19th-century restoration, what is left is impressive and was in 1989 collected in a new church museum. A second centre of activity was Utrecht. At the end of the 15th century and the beginning of the 16th sculptural works of high quality were produced here, especially for the cathe-dral, by the anonymous master of the spandrel reliefs in the Van Diepholt chapel, by Jan Nude (statues for either the rood screen or the sacrament-house) and by Jan van Schayck (bosses and corbels). Several stone epitaphs for canons, mostly figuring a bust of the Virgin with the donor

28. Adriaen van Wesel: *Virgin and Child*, oak, h. 550 mm, *c.* 1480 (Amsterdam, Rijksmuseum)

and his patron saint, also testify to the fact that Utrecht was a centre of sculptural activity.

Wood sculpture flourished in the Netherlands in the last quarter of the 15th century and the first half of the 16th (just as it did in the neighbouring region of the Lower Rhine and in the Flemish towns of Brussels and Antwerp). Individual carvers and centres can even be identified. For

example, at Utrecht, seat of a bishopric and the cultural centre of the northern Netherlands, ADRIAEN VAN WESEL worked from *c.* 1470–90 (see fig. 28). He was the head of an important workshop that produced altar retables for several towns, among them 's Hertogenbosch (the Confraternity of Our Lady). At Utrecht he was followed by the anonymous Master of the Stone Head of the Virgin (named after a sandstone head of the Virgin in the Rijksmuseum Het Catharijneconvent, Utrecht). This workshop also made several retables, some of which were even exported to Norway (the only ones to have survived). Also active in Holland was the anonymous Master of Joachim and Anna, named after a group of the *Meeting of Joachim and Anna* (Amsterdam, Rijksmus.). Though it has not been possible to find out in which Dutch town he worked, he was a contemporary of Adriaen van Wesel, his work showing the same intimacy in the representation of figures, but with less artistic virtuosity.

Another distinct personality, active at 's Hertogenbosch *c.* 1460–70, was the Master of the Statues of Coudewater. His statues of saints are characterized by a static, pillar-like form imposed by the block of wood. He influenced sculptors working in the present-day province of North Brabant far into the 16th century (e.g. the Master of Soeterbeeck, the Master of Leende). The carver of the stalls with misericords (*c.* 1430–60) in the great church at 's Hertogenbosch is anonymous; but a known craftsman, Jan Borchmans, made the stalls with misericords (burnt in 1944) at Oirschot, which were based on those at 's Hertogenbosch. Similar stalls are found at Breda and Zaltbommel (St Maartenskerk) and, outside the province of North Brabant, at Alkmaar, Bolsward, Haarlem and Sittard. A few sculptors' workshops are also known in the duchy of Gelre, comprising roughly the present-day provinces of Limburg, North Brabant (the eastern part), Gelderland and Overijssel and forming an artistic unity with the region of the Lower Rhine. They produced large numbers of altar retables and statues of saints, several of which survive in parish churches of the region and in museums. The most important sculptor was Arnt van Kalkar, also known as Arnt van Zwolle (*b* Kalkar; *fl* 1484; *d* Zwolle, 1491–2), who worked at Zwolle from 1484 until his death. His style was carried on into the beginning of the 16th century by Driess Holthuys (*fl* 1496) and Jan van Halderen (his most famous successors in the Lower Rhenish region being Henrik Douvermann (*fl c* 1480, *d* 1530) and Arnt van Tricht).

See also ROMANESQUE, §III, 1(viii).

BIBLIOGRAPHY

M. Coppens: *Gothic Choir-stalls in the Netherlands*, 2 vols (Amsterdam, 1945)
D. P. R. A. Bouvy: *Middeleeuwse beeldhouwkunst in de Noordelijke Nederlanden* (Amsterdam, 1947)
——: *Beeldhouwkunst van de middeleeuwen tot heden uit het Aartsbisschoppelijk Museum te Utrecht* (Amsterdam, 1962)
T. Müller: *Sculpture in the Netherlands, Germany, France and Spain, 1400–1500*, Pelican Hist. A. (Harmondsworth, 1966)
G. von der Osten and H. Vey: *Painting and Sculpture in Germany and the Netherlands, 1500–1600*, Pelican Hist. A. (Harmondsworth, 1969)
H. Meurer: *Das Klever Chorgestühl und Arnt Beeldesnider* (Düsseldorf, 1970)
Beelden uit Brabant: Laatgotische kunst uit het oude hertogdom, 1400–1520 (exh. cat., 's Hertogenbosch, Noordbrabants Mus., 1971)
J. J. M. Timmers: *De kunst van het Maasland*, 2 vols (Assen, 1971–80)

J. Leeuwenberg and W. Halsema-Kubes: *Beeldhouwkunst in het Rijksmuseum* (The Hague, 1973)

Adriaen van Wesel (ca. 1417/ca. 1490): Een Utrechtse beeldhouwer uit de late middeleeuwen (exh. cat., ed. W. Halsema-Kubes, G. Lemmens and G. de Werd; Amsterdam, Rijksmus., 1980)

C. Peeters: 'De Sint Janskathedraal te 's Hertogenbosch', *De Nederlandse monumenten van geschiedenis en kunst* (The Hague, 1985)

——: *De bouwloods van de St.-Janskathedraal te 's Hertogenbosch* ('s-Hertogenbosch, 1989)

Laat-gotische beeldsnijkunst uit Limburg en Grensland (exh. cat., Sint-Truiden, Prov. Mus. Relig. Kst, 1990)

P. Williamson: 'Roof Bosses from Utrecht and Jan van Schayck, Beeldensnijder', *Oud Holland*, 105 (1991), pp. 140–51

H. Tummers: 'Medieval Effigial Monuments in the Netherlands', *J. Ch. Mnmts Soc.*, 7 (1992), pp. 19–33

——: 'Recente vondsten betreffende vroege grafscuptuur in Nederland: Dertiende en veertiende eeuw', *Kon. Ned. Oudhdknd. Bond: Bull. KNOB*, 92 (1993), pp. 34–40

R. Falkenburg and others, eds: *Beelden in de late middeleeuwen en renaissance* (Zwolle, 1994)

(iii) *c. 1490–c. 1568.*

(a) The Elsloo school and related early developments. Probably at Roermond there existed a large workshop with several sculptors, comprising two generations from *c.* 1490 until 1550. The workshop, which produced hundreds of statues, is named after the anonymous Master of Elsloo. Influenced by the sculpture of Gelderland and the Lower Rhine, the artist went even further than Arnt van Kalkar in the modelling of sharply gesturing figures in a rather graphic style.

Somewhat different from the wood-carvers of the Elsloo workshop, though active at the same time, was Jan van Steffeswert, who worked in Maastricht in the south of the province of Limburg at the beginning of the 16th century. Several signed works by him are now known (his total oeuvre comprising some 40 works), and these show the influence of the graphic style of such printmakers as Israhel van Meckenem (ii). With the Renaissance-like details and decoration in his statues, he stands on the threshold of a new era.

H. A. TUMMERS

(b) Other later developments. The formal vocabulary of the Renaissance had completely established itself in the Netherlands by *c.* 1550: inspiration for decorative work initially came primarily from the southern Netherlands. Woodwork was the special province of Renaissance ornament, for example the church pews (1538–40) by Jan Terwen Aertsz. (1511–89) in the Grote Kerk of Dordrecht; such rood screens as those of the Westerkerk of Enkhuizen and the St Pieterskerk of Leiden (both *c.* 1542); and the pulpit (1548) of the Oude Kerk of Delft. Richly ornamented rood lofts in wood or stone appeared (1543) in the Mariakerk (destr.) of Utrecht, designed by Jan van Scorel and executed by Jan van Oey, and in the churches of Rhenen (*c.* 1550–60; *in situ*). Notable works also included the canons' bench (from 1563–8; parts preserved in the cathedral, Centraal Museum and the Rijksmuseum Het Catharijneconvent, Utrecht) of Utrecht Cathedral by Anthonis Petersz. and the organ gallery (from 1567–8; now in Utrecht, Cent. Mus.) in the Buurkerk of Utrecht. Colijn de Nole came to Utrecht from Kamerrijk *c.* 1530 and died there between 1555 and 1558. He worked primarily in stone and made gravestones and large-scale tombs, frequently in cooperation with the sculptor Willem van Noort (*b* before 1524; *d* 1556), who had also become the city architect of Utrecht in 1540: their work includes the tomb (1538–9; destr.) of *Jo de Wit* in the Mariakerk (destr.), Utrecht; the mausoleum of Reynout van Brederode and Philippote van der Marck in the church of Vianen (*c.* 1542); and the mausoleum (*c.* 1535) of Engelbert van Nassau in the Grote Kerk in Breda. De Nole also produced the large-scale and richly ornamented chimney-piece (1543–5; *in situ*) in the Oude Raadhuis of Kampen. De Nole's son, Jacob Colijn de Nole, continued the work of his father (including the tomb of *Goert van Reede and Geertruyt van Nijenrode* in the church of Amerongen, *c.* 1585; partly destr.).

BIBLIOGRAPHY

J. S. Witsen Elias: *Koorbanken, koorhekken en kansels* (Amsterdam, 1946)

——: *Het snijwerk aan Nederlandse koorbanken en preekstoelen tot het einde van de XVIe eeuw* (Utrecht and Brussels, 1949)

M. Casteels: *De beeldhouwers De Nole te Kamerrijk, te Utrecht en te Antwerpen* (Brussels, 1961)

W. T. Kloek, W. Halsema-Kubes and R. J. Baarson: *Kunst voor de beeldenstorm: Noordnederlandse kunst, 1525–1580* (The Hague, 1986)

R. Vos and F. Leeman: *Het nieuwe ornament: Gids voor de renaissance-architectuur en -decoratie inde 16de eeuw in Nederland* (The Hague, 1986)

Kunst voor de beeldenstorm: Noordnederlandse kunst, 1525–1580 (exh. cat., ed. J. P. Filedt Kok, W. Halsema-Kubes and W. T. Kloek; Amsterdam, Rijksmus., 1986)

A. de Groot: 'Beelden in de Dom van Utrecht in de zestiende eeuw', *Ned. Ksthist. Jb.*, xxxxv (1994), pp. 39–97

2. *c.* 1568–*c.* 1800. In the second half of the 16th century the Netherlands produced several sculptors who studied in Italy: owing to lack of demand for their work at home, they were active for the most part abroad. After a 20-year sojourn in Italy, Willem Daniëlsz. van Tetrode returned to Delft and worked there from 1568 on a greatly admired high altar in the Oude Kerk: ornamented with tens of marble and alabaster figures, it was destroyed as early as 1573 during an iconoclastic riot. His three figures (1568–70) in the guild chapel of the Oude Kerk have also been lost. In 1574 van Tetrode settled in Cologne, where he must have died before 1588. Only a few smaller bronze and marble figures by him survive. They exhibit an Italianate style and great attention to musculature, for example *Hercules and Cacus* (see fig. 29). Part of his oeuvre was copied in prints in Cologne by Adriaen de Weerdt and Isaac Duchemin (*fl c.* 1573–after 1590). Jan Gregor van der Schardt (*c.* 1530–after 1581), born in Nijmegen, left the Netherlands early, never to return. He was active *c.* 1560 in Bologna (at the same time as Giambologna, who had a decisive influence on his style) and in Rome, Florence and Venice. From 1570 until his death he was employed by Maximilian II at Nuremberg, where his works included polychrome terracotta portrait busts and medallions, remarkable for their realism, which can be seen as prototypes of the portrait busts by Hendrick de Keyser I. Four versions of his bronze *Mercury* survive. Adriaen de Vries, from The Hague, also worked in the style of Giambologna. Although he signed his work as *Adrianus Fries Hagiensis Batavus*, he can be considered a Dutch sculptor only by courtesy: because he received no commissions in his native land, he produced all his work abroad, in Rome, Augsburg and Prague. He also made bronze figures (now Stockholm, Drottningholm Slott and Nmus.) for the Neptune Fountain (1615–17) in Frederiksborg Castle for Christian IV (*reg* 1588–1648) of Denmark.

29. Willem Daniëlsz. van Tetrode: *Hercules and Cacus*, alabaster, h. 355 mm, *c.* 1570–80 (Hamburg, Museum für Kunst und Gewerbe)

Hendrick de Keyser I was the most important sculptor of the first quarter of the 17th century; he was also an architect. His sculptures were produced after he settled in Amsterdam in 1591. They consist for the most part of psychologically realistic portrait busts (see fig. 30) and also include a bronze statue of *Erasmus* in Rotterdam (commissioned 1618) and his masterpiece, William the Silent of Nassau's mausoleum (1614–21) in the Nieuwe Kerk of Delft (for illustration *see* KEYSER, (1)), decorated with the Virtues in bronze and inspired by Francesco Primaticcio's tomb of Henry II in Saint-Denis Abbey, Paris. In 1613 de Keyser also made the figure of *St John the Evangelist* for the rood loft of the Onze-Lieve-Vrouwekerk in 's Hertogenbosch. His son-in-law and student, Nicholas Stone I, who returned to England shortly afterwards, made the *SS Peter and Paul* and *Justice* for this rood loft. Another student was Gerard Lambertsz., to whom the extremely realistic *Madness* (now Amsterdam, Rijksmus.) for the Amsterdam madhouse is attributed, and who executed de Keyser's designs in Frederiksborg Castle. After Hendrick de Keyser's death, his son Pieter took over the studio. Pieter's works include the tomb of *Piet Heyn* (*c.* 1636) in the Oude Kerk of Delft and the tomb of *Eric Soop* in Skara Cathedral in Sweden. His younger brother Willem took his place as city stone mason of Amsterdam in 1647. Willem specialized in relief work, including the battle scenes on the tombs of *Admiral Maarten Harpertsz. Tromp* (Delft, Oude Kerk) and *Commander Jan van Galen* (1654; Amsterdam, Nieuwe Kerk).

Although various Dutch sculptors of lesser importance were involved in commissions, mostly decorative, for various cities in the Netherlands, it was primarily the Flemish who in the course of the 17th century set the standard for taste and artistic development. François Dieussart, trained in Italy, came to the Netherlands from Flanders in 1641 and made a number of portraits of members of the House of Orange. The most influential by far, however, were Artus Quellinus (i) from Antwerp and Rombout Verhulst from Mechelen. Their classical Baroque style was a favourite of Frederick Henry (*reg* 1625–47) and was also the best suited to the classicizing Baroque style of architecture that had come to the Netherlands *c.* 1630. Together with François Du Quesnoy, Quellinus had been educated in Rome and—after earlier commissions from Frederick Henry—was brought to Amsterdam to execute the decoration of the Amsterdam Stadhuis (now the Royal Palace) on the Dam, built by Jacob van Campen. He set up a large studio for this purpose and remained in Amsterdam until 1664/5. In addition to Verhulst, who had followed him in 1646 on his journey to the north, Quellinus employed Artus Quellinus (ii), Willem de Keyser and Bartholomeus Eggers. Work on the Stadhuis was done, primarily from 1650–60, in the following order: the court room, with its famous caryatids and reliefs of historic scenes; the great gallery; the burghers' chamber; the friezes for chimney-pieces; and the two gable tympana. Numerous terracotta studies have survived. In addition to the Baroque style of the figures, the work is typified by the ornamental plasticity of the festoons, garlands and cornucopias. Quellinus (i) also made portraits (e.g. the busts of burgomaster *Andries de Graaf*, 1665; Amsterdam, Rijksmus., and *Johan de Wit*, 1665; Dordrecht, Dordrechts Mus.; and portrait medallions) and mausolea (e.g. for the princely pair Engelbert van Immerzeel and Hélène de Montmorency in the church at Bokhoven, 1649). Like other sculptors in the 17th and 18th centuries, he also worked in ivory (*see* §X, 1 below).

Verhulst established himself independently in Leiden in 1658, where he executed the decorative sculpture for buildings by Pieter Post as well as gravestones and tombs. At the end of 1663 he moved to The Hague, where he received tomb commissions for famous people throughout the country. Verhulst's work is characterized specifically by his sensitive handling of texture and physiognomy and his use of black and white marble. One of his students was Johannes Blommendael, whose commissions included work for William III. Pieter Xavery, from Antwerp, specialized in Leiden in small-scale figures in terracotta, as did Albert Jansz. Vinckenbrinck in Amsterdam, who worked mainly in boxwood. Eggers also concentrated on small-scale work after 1680, following a vain attempt at competition with Verhulst.

Decorative and garden sculpture pieces were particularly popular, but exceptionally little has survived. In general its quality is rather mediocre, and once again almost all the genuinely talented sculptors came from the South Netherlands: many pieces were also ordered directly from the south. Jan Baptist Xavery settled in The Hague, specializing in tombs, chimney-pieces, garden vases and garden figures. His principal work is the marble *Allegory of Faith* (1735) under the organ of the Grote Kerk of St Bavo in Haarlem. Jacob Cressant, from Abbeville, settled in Utrecht in 1728, moving to Amsterdam in 1742, and is best known for his marble busts of professors. His son, Jacob Mattheus Cressant (1734–94), was also a competent sculptor. Etienne-Maurice Falconet came to The Hague in 1778 with his daughter-in-law, Marie Anne Falconet-Collot (1748–1821), whose portrait busts of William V and his consort have survived. Sculptors of Dutch origin were Ignatius van Logteren and his son Jan, active in Amsterdam. Willem Hendrik van der Wall worked in Utrecht in a purely decorative style, also carving in wood. Anthonie Ziesenis (1731–1801), from Hannover, became city sculptor of Amsterdam and sculptor for the East India Company.

BIBLIOGRAPHY
M. van Notten: *Rombout Verhulst, sculpteur, 1624–98* (The Hague, 1907)
E. Neurdenburg: *Hendrick de Keyser* (Amsterdam, 1930)
——: *De zeventiende-eeuwse beeldhouwkunst in de Noordelijke Nederlanden* (Amsterdam, 1948)
K. D. H. Freemantle: *The Baroque Town-Hall of Amsterdam* (Utrecht, 1959)
C. H. de Jonge: 'Noordnederlandse beeldhouwkunst in de zeventiende eeuw', *Kstgesch. Nederlanden*, v (1964), pp. 937–60
A. Staring: 'De beeldende kunst der Republiek in de achttiende eeuw', *Kstgesch. Nederlanden*, viii (1964), pp. 1494–1546
J. Rosenberg, S. Slive and E. H. ter Kuile: *Dutch Art and Architecture, 1600–1800*, Pelican Hist. A. (Harmondsworth, 1966), pp. 419–27
L. O. Larsson: *Adrian de Vries: Adrianus Fries Hagiensis Batavus, 1545–1626* (Vienna and Munich, 1967)
L. J. van der Klooster: 'Jan Baptist Xavery (1697–1742): Documentie over enkele van zijn werken', *Ned. Kst. Jb.*, xxi (1970), pp. 99–138
C. H. F. Avery: 'Hendrick de Keyser as a Sculptor of Small Bronzes', *Bull. Rijkmus.*, xxi (1973), pp. 3–24
J. Leeuwenberg and W. Halsema-Kubes: *Beeldhouwkunst in het Rijksmuseum* (The Hague and Amsterdam, 1973)
F. T. Scholten: *Rombout Verhulst in Groningen: Zeventiende-eeuwse praalgraven in Midwolde en Stedum* (Utrecht, 1983)
A. Radcliffe: 'Schardt, Tetrode, and Some Possible Sculptural Sources for Goltzius', *Netherlandish Mannerism: Stockholm, 1984*, pp. 97–108
W. T. Kloek, W. Halsema-Kubes and R. J. Baarson: *Kunst voor de beeldenstorm: Noordnederlandse kunst, 1525–1580* (The Hague, 1986)
J. Nijstadt: 'Willem Danielsz. van Tetrode', *Ned. Ksthist. Jb.*, xxxvii (1986), pp. 259–79
Kunst voor de beeldenstorm: Noordnederlandse kunst, 1525–1580 (exh. cat., ed. J. P. Filedt Kok, W. Halsema-Kubes and W. T. Kloek; Amsterdam, Rijksmus., 1986)
W. Halsema-Kubes: 'Bartholomeus Eggers' keizers- en keizerinnenbusten voor keurvorst Friedrich Wilhelm van Brandenburg', *Bull. Rijksmus.*, xxxvi (1988), pp. 44–53
——: 'Kleinplastiek van Albert Jansz. Vinchenbrinck', *Bull. Rijksmus.*, xxxix (1991), pp. 414–25
H. Honnens de Lichtenberg: *Johan Gregor van der Schardt: Bildhauer bei Kaiser Maximilian II, am Dänischen Hof und bei Tycho Brahe* (Copenhagen, 1991)
J. Becker: *Hendrick de Keyser: Standbeeld van Desiderius Erasmus in Rotterdam* (Bloemendaal, 1993)
Dawn of the Golden Age: Northern Netherlandish Art, 1580–1620 (exh. cat., ed. G. Luijten and others; Amsterdam, Rijksmus., 1993), pp. 401–12, 501–4
M. Westermann: 'A Monument for Roma Belgica: Functions of the *oxaal* at 's Hertogenbosch', *Ned. Ksthist. Jb.*, xxxxv (1994), pp. 383–446

ILJA M. VELDMAN

30. Hendrick de Keyser I: *Vincent Jacobsz. Coster*, marble, h. 750 mm, 1608 (Amsterdam, Rijksmuseum)

3. *c.* 1800–1900. Most important early 19th-century sculptors in the Netherlands came from the southern provinces and most stayed in the newly established Belgian kingdom after the separation of 1830. Later in the 19th century many sculptors underwent their training abroad. The Dutch academies were, furthermore, dominated by foreigners. Lodewijk Royer, born in Mechelen and from 1837 director of the sculpture department at the Koninklijke Academie in Amsterdam, long held a kind of monopoly in the production of statues of historical figures in a realistic style (see fig. 31). Although this production was not as prolific as in neighbouring countries, there was a growing sense of nationalism after the end of the French regime that led to statues of national heroes recalling the country's past greatness. Those artists inclined towards Romanticism, especially after 1840, were again dominated by foreign, notably Belgian, influences. Besides a basic knowledge of the human figure, the classical rules of beauty remained nevertheless a vital part of the teaching of sculpture.

Shortly after 1850 there was a revival of the Gothic style in sculpture, influenced by the architect P. J. H. Cuypers. A related contemporary idea was that of community art, based on the notion that architecture combines all the other arts. Although the sculptural elements of Cuypers's Catholic church buildings were inspired above all by Gothic prototypes, the architechural sculpture for his secular public buildings were influenced primarily by the 17th-century Baroque tradition of the sculptors Artus Quellinus (i) and François Du Quesnoy.

31. Lodewijk Royer: *Michiel de Ruyter*, cast iron, 1841, The Rotunda, Koopmanshaven, Vlissingen

Because there was no real search for a new language of forms, these developments did not directly yield distinctive results in sculpture.

Cuypers's numerous commissions for buildings made it clear that Holland had also a shortage of qualified masons and cabinetmakers. To overcome this problem Cuypers opened artists' workshops in Roermond (1853) and Amsterdam, the latter for decorative work for the Rijksmuseum (1876–85). The underlying thought was that practical training of this kind would help to popularize stone masonry and woodcutting and bring about a revival of the sculpture-as-craft tradition. Neither of these subjects was taught at the academies, where the emphasis lay on modelling in clay and wax. The results were so impressive that the Amsterdam workshop was given permission in 1879 to move from the building-shed of the Rijksmuseum to the Quellinus School, an art and craft school. Although the more prominent sculptural elements of Cuypers's buildings were executed by the workshop in the Quellinus School, they were designed elsewhere, by such artists as François Vermeylen (1824–88), a Leuven professor, and the Moravian Ludwig Jünger (*b* 1856). The designs for the Rijksmuseum involved one Dutch sculptor: Bartholomeus Johannes van Hove, who, like Vermeylen and Jünger, was a typical representative of 19th-century academicism. During the last decades of the 19th century van Hove concentrated on making portraits.

In the mid-1890s the courses given at the Quellinus School began to bear fruit. Several of the then famous sculptors, such as Joseph Mendes da Costa and Lambertus Zijl, had begun their careers at the workshop. They became known primarily for their decorative sculpture for buildings and for furniture in the so-called Nieuwe Kunst style, the Dutch variant of Art Nouveau. Mendes da Costa's work can be distinguished by its Eastern-inspired forms, while Zijl often worked in collaboration with the architect H. P. Berlage, using an abstracted medieval style with enlarged shapes and simplified contours. Zijl's free-standing sculptures are angular and broadly modelled in an Impressionist manner that is quite similar to that of the Belgian sculptor George Minne.

Towards the end of the century the architects J. L. M. Lauweriks and K. P. C. de Bazel initiated an anti-naturalistic trend, based on the aesthetic principles of sculpture of ancient cultures from the Near East, India and China. This was related to their interest in occult, Theosophical and masonic doctrines. Although never active as a sculptor himself, Lauweriks, especially, was an important supporter of new thinking in sculpture, for example concerning truth to materials. Among the sculptors working for Lauweriks and de Bazel were Rien Hack (1871–1939) and Kees Oosschot (1870–1945). Although their sculptural work was carefully designed on the drawing-table and was primarily decorative in function, their importance lies in the fact that they trained sculptors who were later to become well known for their collaboration with architects of the Amsterdam school. Mendes da Costa and Zijl were also influential in this respect. At the end of the century, however, the majority of Dutch sculptors, for example Pier Pander, still adhered to academic standards.

4. AFTER 1900. Surveys of 20th-century Dutch sculpture often begin with a description of the Koopmansbeurs (*c*. 1898–1903) in Amsterdam, for which the architect H. P. Berlage asked the assistance of several young artists, including the sculptors Lambertus Zijl and Joseph Mendes da Costa. Their contributions—characterized by the incorporation of features of both early medieval sculpture and the decorative arts of ancient cultures from the Near East—were a continuation of a development that had begun in the last decade of the 19th century. However, it was through discussions and publications involving the Koopmansbeurs that Dutch architectural sculpture became known to a wider public and gained the popularity it was to enjoy for a long period.

A decade later it was clear that architects of the Amsterdam school viewed architecture as the mother of the arts, within which a union of the arts could be achieved. Unlike Berlage, they thought that a certain amount of freedom should be allowed within the structural limits of a building: this gave rise to a more sensual, expressive style in architectural sculpture. Influenced, for example, by Theosophy, they used archaic and exotic elements in their decorative sculpture. This was also connected with technical requirements. Collaboration with architects forced sculptors to work with rough types of stone and tropical woods not previously used in sculpture. The hardness of these materials dictated a language of compressed form, for which the sculpture of ancient Egypt and Assyria provided ideal examples. Such building materials as granite and basalt were also introduced in freestanding sculpture, as was concrete, from 1920. Many sculptors had their first experience of these materials abroad. Because of massive unemployment, many sculptors went to work in workshops in Germany. As a result, German monumental sculpture was introduced in the Netherlands, together with the direct carving of the school of Adolf von Hildebrand. In the period between the World Wars especially, working *en taille directe* or following related aesthetic concepts was thought to be progressive in the Netherlands. Apart from John Raedecker, who was the leading sculptor of the 1920s and 1930s, sculptors associated with the Amsterdam school include Hendrik van den Eijnde (1869–1939) and Hildo Krop (1884–1970), who ran the highly influential sculpture workshop of the Scheepvaarthuis (1913–16).

During the years between the World Wars influence from German Expressionism and Die Brücke was noticeable in wood sculptures by artists of the De Ploeg (The Plough) group in Groningen and, especially, in the work of such Rotterdam sculptors as Hendrik Chabot. Leendert Bolle (1879–1942) worked in a hybrid style combining Cubism and Expressionism. Cubist and Constructivist tendencies were secondary to other styles. The sculptor Johan Uiterwaal (1897–1972), for example, earned a living in Utrecht with neo-Baroque work. In addition, from the 1920s he made Constructivist sculptures of dancing figures, which did not meet with any interest until after World War II. In the 1930s the relationship between sculpture and architecture became less important. Many sculptors turned to the new interpretation of classicism introduced by such artists as Aristide Maillol or to a form of expressive realism. This traditionalist tendency, with

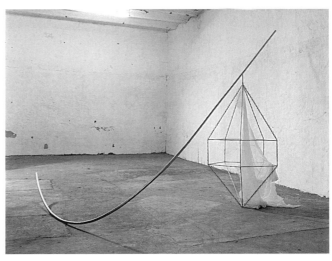

32. Henk Visch: *Adjusting the Sails of Reason to the Breeze of my Longings*, aluminium and net curtain, 3.8×2.5 m, 1987 (artist's collection)

much emphasis on the anatomy of the human figure, was to characterize many war memorials, some erected as long as 40 years after World War II. A leading figure in this development was Mari Andriessen (1897–1979).

Among the first sculptors to make non-figurative work immediately after World War II was Toon Kelder (1894–1973), who from 1947 made linear wire sculptures. Around 1950 a number of artists gained prominence who had trained partly or entirely abroad and had been influenced by Jacques Lipchitz and, in particular, Ossip Zadkine. They included Willem Reyers (1910–58) and Wessel Couzijn. Their designs for the merchant navy war memorial (1951) in Rotterdam are regarded as milestones in Dutch sculpture. Following his entry for the first Cobra exhibition at the Stedelijk Museum in Amsterdam in 1949, Shinkichi Tajiri became for a while highly influential, for example with his 'Junk' sculptures (1950–51). Other sculptors associated with Cobra were Karel Appel and Lotti van der Gaag (*b* 1923). Abstract Expressionist tendencies emerged in the work of Tajiri and, in the late 1950s, in that of Couzijn and his wife Pearl Perlmuter (*b* 1915).

After World War II several sculptors were influenced by De Stijl in three-dimensional abstract geometrical constructions. These artists included Joost Baljeu, André Volten (*b* 1925) and Carel Visser. While De Stijl always remained a spiritual background for Baljeu and Volten, Visser took a more independent stand, being also significantly influenced by Brancusi. Since the 1960s Peter Struycken also followed the ideals of De Stijl. Struycken's work is primarily two-dimensional, although he was involved in various sculptural projects as part of the allocation of a percentage of sculptural monuments for public buildings and areas. From the mid-1960s interest in traditional sculpture waned. Because of this, the influential sculpture departments of, for example, the academies at Arnhem and The Hague were closed, and, under the guidance of Struycken and Joop Beljon (*b* 1922) respectively, the emphasis there was shifted to site specificity and monumental form.

Most objects after *c.* 1970 were made with the idea that the combination of materials and form expressed the concept of either an action or the object itself. During these years Jan Dibbets—inspired by the example of Richard Long—incorporated natural materials in his sculptural projects. Carel Visser, as well as creating serial metal sculptures, began from the mid-1970s to use such random objects as tyres and cardboard boxes in combination with natural materials. Later most younger sculptors were led by their intuition and associations, with less emphasis on the nature of the materials used. Many of them, including Sigurdur Guðmundsson and Henk Visch, went through a period in which they explored other fields of art and design before taking up sculpture in the 1980s. Such sculpture frequently expressed a mysterious inner power, in particular the work of Visch, who seemed to hover between abstraction and an other-worldly figurative sense. Visch worked with various materials, including aluminium, sometimes combined with horsehair, velvet draperies or net curtains (see fig. 32).

BIBLIOGRAPHY

J. A. Alberdingk Thijm: *Over nieuwere beeldhouwkunst, vooral in Nederland* (Rotterdam, 1886)

F. M. Huebner: *Niederländische Plastik der Gegenwart* (Dresden, 1924)

A. M. Hammacher: *Beeldhouwkunst van deze eeuw en een schets van haar ontwikkeling in de negentiende eeuw* (Amsterdam, 1955)

P. K. van Daalen: *Nederlandse beeldhouwers in de negentiende eeuw* (The Hague, 1957)

R. W. A. Bionda, E. de Jong and J. de Vries, eds: 'Monumentale beeldhouwkunst in Nederland', *Ned. Ksthist. Jb.*, xxxiv (1983) [whole issue]

P. Hefting: *De eigen ruimte: Beeldhouwkunst in Nederland na 1945* (Amsterdam, 1987)

Y. Koopmans: *Muurvast & gebeiteld: Beeldhouwkunst in de bouw, 1840–1940/Fixed & Chiselled: Sculpture in Architecture, 1840–1940* (Rotterdam, 1994)

E. Langedijk and others: *Louis Royce, 1793–1868: Een Vlaamse beeldhouwer in Amsterdam* (Amsterdam, 1994)

YPE KOOPMANS

V. Interior decoration.

1. Before 1600. 2. 1600–*c.* 1745. 3. *c.* 1745–1850. 4. After 1850.

1. BEFORE 1600. Much information about the interiors of upper-class houses can be deduced from 14th- and 15th-century Flemish paintings. Throughout the Middle Ages life was defined by great mobility, resulting in a considerable need for furniture and textiles that could be moved easily. The room depicted in Rogier van der Weyden's *Annunciation* (*c.* 1430–35; Paris, Louvre; see fig. 33), used for living as well as sleeping, has a completely upholstered bed; other pieces of furniture had no fixed places and were moved according to need. The decoration is plain, the focus of attention being the fireplace and the geometric pattern of the tile floor.

The most important room in each palace, castle or house of any size was the great hall. Here sentence was passed, important guests were received and the whole household gathered at mealtimes. The most prominent feature was the fireplace, decorated with architectural carvings and ornaments. The remaining decoration was adapted to the nature of the activities carried out; for example, for important celebrations, series of tapestries were hung up. From the 14th century, tapestries were widely used. Many important households ordered several series from which to choose. As well as figured tapestries there were those woven with decorative and heraldic motifs. The arrangement of furniture was not permanent, with tables made of loose planks and trestles erected only at mealtimes.

From the beginning of the 15th century domestic life shifted towards the use of private rooms, laid out and decorated luxuriously and comfortably. Wooden ceilings were painted with coats of arms and allegories. Windows were partly covered with leaded glass in cross-shaped divisions and could be partly closed with shutters. The luxurious character of these rooms was due mainly to the soft furnishings. In one of the private rooms a bed placed on a low podium was surrounded by curtains and was sometimes provided with a cloth canopy.

Less is known about the interiors of middle-class houses, although some details can be deduced from estate inventories and archaeological finds. Access to a typical town house was through an entrance hall, which was used as a shop or for business or living. Behind the entrance hall was the kitchen, for sleeping, cooking, eating and washing. Some houses also had a separate living-room. Originally the fireplace was in the middle of the kitchen; fireplaces against the wall were introduced in imitation of the aristocratic town house. In smaller dwellings there was usually only one fireplace, which, apart from heating, was used for the preparation of food and drink. Large houses had two or more fireplaces and in some cases an oven made of earthenware tiles. The arrangement of the kitchen included chairs and a trestle table for dining. After the meal the table was folded up and leant against or hung on the wall or stored away. In the living-room, apart from chairs, there were chests and other storage furniture, for example the sideboard, which could equally be placed against a wall or in the middle of the room; pewter plates and other pewterware were placed on it, in imitation of the displays of plate on buffets in grander houses. There were no individual bedrooms. The bedstead of the man and woman of the house was in the kitchen or in one of the heated living-rooms. Beds for children and servants were placed in various other rooms. Most houses had a cellar below and possessed a spacious attic used for the storage of firewood, peat and provisions.

Stone walls were plastered and hung with damp-proof panelling. Chests were often built into the walls and could be closed with wooden doors. The floor was made of wooden boards often strewn with sand, or of brick or unglazed tiles. In most houses the floor remained uncovered. Woven mats were used in a few houses, floor carpets were almost never used. The late medieval house of the well-to-do burgher was lit by means of a brass chandelier hung from the beamed ceiling. Candlesticks, sconces, oil lamps and lanterns were also used, made of brass, iron and wood, but also of pewter and earthenware.

In comparison with architecture, the Renaissance had little influence on the interior. Although motifs were often borrowed from Classical Antiquity, for example to decorate furniture, the layout and decoration of the late medieval house described above stayed broadly unaltered until the beginning of the 17th century.

MAARTEN BROEKEMA

33. Rogier van der Weyden: *Annunciation*, oil on panel, 860×920 mm, *c.* 1430–35 (Paris, Musée du Louvre)

2. 1600–*c.* 1745. During the first quarter of the 17th century the interior decoration of grand houses was characterized by a Mannerist style that combined grotesque ornament with a pastiche of Classical elements. Such architectural features as fireplaces and door-surrounds as well as buffets and cupboards were enriched with virtuoso displays of carving. Termes and masks juxtaposed with brackets, columns, broken pediments and panelling inlaid with ebony often contrasted dramatically in their proportions. Motifs were derived from such 16th-century pattern books as Hans Vredeman de Vries's *Differents pourtraicts de menuiserie* (Antwerp, 1565). Important pieces of furniture, such as heavy draw-tables with bulbous cup and cover legs, had similar ornament and were rarely moved, but chairs were of lighter construction and were arranged as the occasion required. With beamed or coffered ceilings and floors patterned with tiles or parquet, rooms in this style were often more agitated in effect than harmonious.

By the 1630s French ideas about planning, furniture arrangement and the disposition of ornament were increasingly understood and followed. The organization of rooms *en enfilade*, opening off each other with the doorways aligned to provide lengthy vistas, was an application of the axial planning developed at Versailles. Classical ornament was used with greater restraint, regularity and correctness and with greater harmony of proportion. Textiles assumed a more important role in furnishings; wall hangings, table-covers and the upholstery of seat furniture were coordinated throughout the room, producing a unified effect much admired in the engravings of Parisian interiors by Abraham Bosse, which were available from print-sellers in Amsterdam. These innovations are recorded in contemporary Dutch paintings of interiors; in *The Visit* (*c.* 1630; Geneva, Mus. A. & Hist.; see fig. 34), by Gonzales Coques, the hangings of the built-in box-bed, the chair and bench cushions and the fireplace valance are all *en suite*. The

34. Gonzales Coques: *The Visit*, oil on panel, 0.86×1.18 m, *c.* 1630 (Geneva, Musée d'Art et d'Histoire)

projecting chimney-hood, a typically Dutch feature, is supported by out-sized caryatids, although marble columns were also popular. The fireplace surround is faced with Delftware tiles, and above the panelling costly Chinese export porcelain is displayed; both uses illustrate the importance of ceramics in 17th-century Dutch interiors. In many prosperous homes sumptuous materials were combined with great simplicity; walls were hung with tooled and gilt leather and tables covered with Turkish or Persian carpets, but wooden floors were still often left bare. Window curtains, where used, were of thin material and strictly utilitarian; interior shutters arranged in tiers were more common.

Towards the end of the 17th century a stronger contrast developed between the increasing richness of interior decoration and the sober restraint of Dutch architecture. After the Revocation of the Edict of Nantes in 1685, the spread of the French court style of furnishing was greatly accelerated by the emigration to the Netherlands of many talented Huguenot craftsmen in search of greater religious tolerance. The Parisian architect and designer Daniel Marot the elder (*see* MAROT, (2)), who had been employed as a draughtsman at the court of Louis XIV, was immediately appointed chief architect of William, Prince of Orange, who, despite his political rivalry with France, wanted his palace and gardens at HET LOO transformed by the latest French decorative schemes. When William married Mary Stuart and became King of England in 1689,

Marot followed him to work at Hampton Court and Kensington Palace in London between 1694 and 1697 but returned to the Netherlands some time between 1697 and 1700. The style of Daniel Marot, which later became known as the WILLIAM AND MARY STYLE, quickly assumed an international character as an expression of the growing confidence of monarchy. Interiors in this style could be found in the Netherlands, in some of the German courts, in the country houses of the English aristocracy (*see* ENGLAND, fig. 38) and in such remote seats of provincial governors as WILLIAMSBURG in Virginia. In the Netherlands the spread of the William and Mary style was due in part to its adaptability to a wide range of circumstances. No major architectural features were required, and an appearance of great luxury could be created in spaces either grand or intimate. In The Hague, the seat of the stadholder, the influence of the court style was the strongest; it was adopted gradually in the north. Because of its aristocratic associations the style was accepted more slowly, and less systematically, by the merchant families of Amsterdam.

The unity of the interiors at Het Loo was ensured by Marot's supervision of the smallest details, and his influential designs were published in numerous suites of engravings. In lesser houses this superintendence was provided by an upholsterer, who supplied and coordinated all the textiles and advised about the acquisition of other furnishing items. Textiles were a crucial component, and the walls of rooms of any pretension were hung with panels of silk, damask, wool or linen, often in contrasting colours or trimmed with braid or fringe in a different shade. Such strong colours as crimson, bright yellow or deep green were favoured. Tapestries were still in use, although they were fitted flat to the wall rather than allowed to hang loosely. For the first time window curtains, topped by elaborate pelmets, became important elements in the overall appearance of a room; in bedrooms these could be coordinated with bed-hangings and valances to provide further unity.

In a state apartment the bedroom was the culmination of an *enfilade* of reception rooms that might consist of several antechambers and a salon for dining preceding the bedchamber, with private garderobes and closets beyond. As the focus of this carefully controlled approach, the state bed was a triumph of the upholsterer's art and was often set apart by means of a raised platform or a balustrade. At Menkemaborg, in Uithuizen, the bed has a tall canopy with scrolled cresting and valances, an elaborate headboard and scrolled base valances, all upholstered in yellow silk with hangings to match. Ordered in 1710, it was undoubtedly the most expensive single item of furniture in the house. Derived from Marot's designs for the beds of Louis XIV's several mistresses, such a complex design was a departure from the general French preference for simpler, box-shaped beds.

In grand reception rooms furniture was characterized by rich surface treatments. Japanning and marquetry were fashionable, as was the use of lacquer panels from China or Japan, which were set into the walls as panelling, or cut up and used for cabinet doors, table-tops or mirror-frames. Such small case pieces as clocks were made of ebony or ebonized wood and enriched with mounts of chased silver or silver gilt. In general, proportions tended to be tall and narrow. The tall cabinet with large paired doors, supported on a stand with four legs linked by stretchers, was an important piece of display furniture. Tall, caned chairs, derived from imported Chinese prototypes, were very popular, as were chairs with narrow, intricately carved backs; these were normally arranged in a row against the walls and brought into the centre of the room only when required. Triads of furniture, consisting of a table and a mirror flanked by a pair of candle stands, all decorated *en suite*, made an impressive ensemble that was widely adopted. The group was often placed between two windows to take advantage of the light. The grandest examples were made of silver, as was the set (untraced) made by Adam Loofs (*fl* 1660–1710) and given by William to Mary as a New Year's present in 1680; but the fact that examples in less costly materials survive attests to the popularity of the triad further down the social scale.

Massed arrays of ceramics—on top of case furniture, beneath chests raised on stands, as garnitures on top of overdoors or on mantelpieces, or in fireplaces during the summer months—were a distinctive feature of the William and Mary interior. Collections of imported Chinese porcelain and imitation chinoiserie Delftware had been displayed in prosperous Dutch homes throughout the 17th century, but in Marot's designs these assumed a more architectural role; for example, larger pieces were grouped

into pyramids above corner fireplaces. Enormous blue-and-white urns or jardinières (see fig. 48 below) held orange trees, and a tall tulip vase for cut flowers, standing over a metre in height, might have filled a corner (e.g. *c.* 1700; London, V&A). Silver also played a vital role in the interior, especially after dark when candle- or fire-light was reflected by the richly worked surfaces of silver sconces, mirror-frames or fire-dogs; these were often deeply embossed with flowers or the more formal motifs of the French classical style that became fashionable after 1690. The influence of the William and Mary style was so persistent that the succeeding French styles, especially the Rococo, developed in the Netherlands somewhat later than elsewhere in Europe.

JUDITH A. NEISWANDER

3. *c.* 1745–1850. Around 1745 the earliest Rococo interiors were created in light and cheerful colours. This elegant, French-inspired style was promoted principally by the architect Pieter de Swart, who had trained in Paris. These interiors were less dictated by formality than in the Baroque: strict etiquette was replaced by a more relaxed lifestyle, one governed by comfort and luxury. The Baroque custom that an architect or upholsterer was responsible for the total interior design now found general acceptance. Such elements as ceilings, walls, panelling, furnishings and upholstery were thus assembled into a harmonious whole.

The hierarchy and function of the various rooms changed as a result of the new lifestyle. As well as the *appartement de parade*, intended for official receptions, and the private apartment, there was the so-called *appartement de société*, for receiving friends and family. Such an apartment was created out of a number of connected existing rooms that were used for such social activities as concerts

35. Drawing-room of Nieuwe Gracht 74, Haarlem, designed by Abraham van der Hart for Willem Philip Kops, 1793 (Amsterdam, Rijksmuseum)

36. Herman Frederik Carel ten Kate: *Mon Salon, Plein*, watercolour, 318×488 mm, 1849; from the Album of Queen Sophia (The Hague, Oranje-Nassau-Museum, on loan to Apeldoorn, Rijksmuseum Paleis Het Loo)

or card-playing evenings. The most important room in both the official and private apartments was the bedroom. The most striking piece of furniture in this room continued to be the richly upholstered bed, which was often placed in an alcove. Just as in the Baroque, the rooms associated with the bedroom—the garderobe, cabinet or boudoir— were decorated with valuable materials.

The use of stuccowork expanded enormously during this period; stuccoed white ceilings gave a lightness to the interior (*see also* STUCCO AND PLASTERWORK, §III, 10(i)(d)). This effect was strengthened by the use of high sash windows, which allowed in much more daylight than the small leaded glass panels of the previous period. Next to the architect, the upholsterer played an important role in creating the Rococo interior. He could choose from such materials as Chinese silk and printed or painted cottons from India, as well as the textiles used during the Baroque. These exotic fabrics were generally used in rooms of a more private character. Floors were carpeted more often, with oriental as well as locally produced carpets. In simpler interiors the number of textiles remained limited, and reed mats were used instead of carpets.

Between 1770 and 1820 interior decoration was determined by Neo-classicism, which developed from an arbitrary application of classical ornament to a more rigid and sober version of the formal language derived from Classical Antiquity. This style seemed to lend itself well to interior decoration (see fig. 35); for example, sections of very low wall panelling could serve as the base for a row of pilasters or columns. The use of pilasters made it possible to divide

the walls vertically and symmetrically. The ornament, often derived from Roman wall paintings and Greek vases, was also distributed symmetrically over the walls and the stuccoed ceilings.

After 1800 classical ornament was employed less eclectically. The Empire style interior developed in the Netherlands *c.* 1806–10, when Louis Bonaparte commissioned the redecoration of a number of palaces, including the Royal Place on Dam Square in Amsterdam. Dutch furniture-makers and upholsterers engaged on these projects took their inspiration principally from illustrations in journals and such books as *Recueil des décorations intérieurs* (Paris, 1801) by Charles Percier and Pierre-François Léonard. Hangings and carpets displayed the same colour scheme as used in chair and wall coverings. Furniture was organized symmetrically around the room, its first function being an element of the decoration of the room, its practical function of secondary importance. Furniture was deployed in a less formal manner in private rooms. Chairs were no longer placed against the walls but in a circle around the fireplace.

The middle-class lifestyle characteristic of the period after 1815 is well expressed in the Biedermeier interior, which reflected the demands of everyday domestic life. In contrast to the 18th century, the need was now for modest homes with appropriate divisions into a limited number of rooms. Each room had a function that corresponded to a specific activity of daily life. Formality and the display of prosperity played a subordinate role. A uniform colour scheme and symmetrical division of space, points of departure of the Empire interior, were no longer important. The primary concern was to create a homely atmosphere, and for the first time it was possible to accommodate inherited furniture or objects of sentimental value. As a result of the use of older furniture and a liking for knicknacks, an interior was established that appeared to grow naturally and that reflected the personal taste of its occupants.

The living-room as the central locus of family life was undoubtedly the most important room of the house. By studying contemporary watercolours of interiors, a number of striking characteristics can be discerned (see fig. 36). The frequent use of bold and bright colours is evident. Walls were either painted or covered with wallpaper that was often printed with a floral pattern or with a simple stripe. The horizontal lines of the room were emphasized by separate handling of the ceiling and walls. Hanging paintings at the same height further enhanced this effect. The floor was covered entirely with a single carpet with a repeating pattern or was made of bare wooden boards or parquet. Windows had simple curtains in light materials. Symmetry was no longer important, and furniture could be rearranged according to the taste and needs of the occupants. The living-room was designed so that different activities could be housed simultaneously. This was achieved by informal groupings of furniture. In a corner of the room or along the wall was a corner settee or sofa, in front of which was a round or square table surrounded by a number of chairs. The whole family gathered here daily to drink tea, to play games or to read. A second furniture group could exist around the writing-table with an easy-chair. In the course of the century the informality of the interior increased; not only were further groupings of furniture established, but the variety of the furnishings also expanded. In contrast to early Biedermeier furniture, pieces of the late Biedermeier became heavier once more.

MAARTEN BROEKEMA

4. AFTER 1850. The large cities of the Netherlands expanded rapidly in the second half of the 19th century, and new residential areas were built for different segments of the population. The furnishing of the middle-class house at the end of the 19th century was, if possible, even more crowded and cluttered than in the preceding years, and the dark upholstery, elaborate curtain treatments and profusion of knicknacks created a dimly lit, richly ornamented environment. Gradually there arose a demand, at first only in limited artistic and intellectual circles, for unity of style and a simpler type of interior decoration. Several craft schools were established, and in the 1870s and 1880s attention focused on the revival of the 16th-century Dutch interior. Leaders in this movement included Eduard A. von Saher (*b* 1849), who was the Director of the Kunstnijverheidsschool (Craft School) of Haarlem from 1880 to 1918.

During the last decade of the 19th century the first generation of graduates from the craft schools tried to achieve a new style in interior decoration that would suit modern times, characterized by new trends such as socialism and women's emancipation. Closely related to the ideas of William Morris and the Arts and Crafts Movement, the central concepts in the development of Nieuwe Kunst,

or Rationalism, were honesty and logic. Construction techniques were to be expressed in the finished product, and the materials used were to be exposed, not concealed. The ideal was a design that united architecture, interior and furnishings, right down to the eating utensils, in a coherent whole based on a modular system. These innovators favoured the English country house style, with rooms grouped around a central hall, and some suburban villas and larger town houses were built in the new style. The interior design was calm and spacious, and furniture was frequently set in a squared-off, symmetrical pattern. Walls were usually panelled with oak, and sometimes cupboards or benches were built into the panelling. Rugs with geometrically stylized designs or Persian carpets were spread on the parquet floor. Curtains, in quiet colours like the rest of the soft furnishings, were hung in straight vertical folds. Ceilings frequently had exposed oak beams.

The most important leader in the new trend was H. P. Berlage; an example of his work is the interior of the St Hubertus Hunting Lodge (1915; Otterlo, Hoge Veluwe National Park). A typical feature of his Rationalist interiors was the exposed, unornamented brick wall. Other Rationalist interior designers include K. P. C. de Bazel and Jacob van den Bosch (1868–1948). Willem Penaat, who was especially interested in low-cost housing, is particularly noteworthy. His Rationalist working-class interiors, with basic furniture, were simplified versions of more expensive types produced on commission. Because of the materials employed and the refined construction techniques, interiors of this type, made and sold by van Wisselingh & Co. of Amsterdam, were extremely expensive. An innovation was the use of the batik technique for upholstery fabrics, tablecloths and wall coverings made locally or imported.

After 1910 several younger architects and furniture-designers turned away from the dogmatic simplicity of Rationalism. They developed an expressive formal language in which construction played a subordinate role. The Amsterdam school shared with Rationalism a striving for harmony of style and a synthesis of the different arts, but objective simplicity was replaced by more expressive forms and the decorative aspect was paramount. However, interior design commissions in this style were relatively rare in practice because of their high cost and radical nature. The best-known examples are found in such public buildings as theatres (e.g. interior of the Tuschinski Theatre, Amsterdam, by Jaap Gidding, 1920–21) or offices (e.g. interior of the administrative rooms of the Scheepvaarthuis, Amsterdam, 1915). The Amsterdam school domestic interior is characterized by an intimate spatial character achieved with low ceilings and broad, low windows, the upper panes in stained glass to moderate the light. Dark panelling also contributed a strongly horizontal effect. In contrast to the Rationalist interior, the furnishings were more informal. A low sideboard replaced the tall china-cabinet, and wallpaper, carpets and such upholstery fabrics as rep and cretonne were chosen in Amsterdam school colours: warm shades of red, green and brown, as well as purple and orange with black. Decorative motifs were abstract and lively and sometimes evoked oriental themes. Wrought-iron fireplaces and light fixtures completed the décor. The most important representative of this style was Michel de Klerk; other designers include P. L. Kramer and Hildo Krop (1884–1970).

The architects and designers who assembled around the art periodical *De stijl* (1917–31) favoured a completely different concept of design. They envisioned an abstract language of forms, intended as a reflection of a new or future society, that had much in common with Constructivism. Only a few projects in interior design are considered to belong to De Stijl, but the movement exercised considerable influence. The interior was seen as an abstract composition, with the furnishings characterized by tones of grey or bright colours (later, exclusively primary colours); fabrics and carpets of a solid colour or original design; a squared-off, frequently asymmetrical placement of furniture; and the use of colour to interrupt the plane of the wall, floor or ceiling, producing another perception of space. Expensive materials were not used; wood was usually painted. The best-known and most extreme De Stijl interior is that of the Schröder house (1924) in Utrecht by Gerrit Rietveld, where the movable walls permit a flexible division of space. Theo van Doesburg was another important De Stijl designer, as was Vilmos Huszár, whose *Spatial Colour Composition in Grey, Brugmanhuis, The Hague* (1924; see fig. 37) was executed as the music-room in the home of the Dada poet and essayist Til Brugman.

37. *Spatial Colour Composition in Grey, Brugmanhuis, The Hague* by Vilmos Huszár, 1924; the interior of the music-room; chair and table by Gerrit Rietveld

Rationalist, Amsterdam school and De Stijl domestic interiors in their pure forms were created for a few wealthy clients; during the 1920s the more popular type of interior decoration incorporated elements of all these styles and was called the Nieuwe Zakelijkheid (New Objectivity) or the Hague school. This style is characterized by balance, asymmetry and spaciousness, with rectilinear, machine-made furniture and built-in cupboards and benches designed to save space. Wood was usually kept to natural finishes, sometimes set off by colour accents. Fabrics were of one colour or with a simple design, and carpets had simple, linear motifs. This modern and practical style of decoration was promoted by popular periodicals devoted to interior design. Some of the designers who worked in the Nieuwe Zakelijkheid style were Paul Bromberg, HENDRIK WOUDA, Cor Alons (1892–1967), Cornelis van der Sluys (1881–1944), Frits Spanjaard (1889–1978) and Willem Penaat. Modern working-class interiors were produced by LOV (Labor omnia vincit), a factory in Oosterbeek founded on socialist principles. Although not yet accredited, the profession of interior designer became a specialized discipline during the 1920s and was taught as a separate subject in craft-school curricula.

Functionalism, which made its breakthrough in the Netherlands in the 1920s in such progressive architectural circles as De 8 in Amsterdam and Opbouw (Buildup) in Rotterdam, went much further in the stripping down of the interior and had a more aggressively politicized character. Interiors and furniture were to be shorn of all aesthetic traits and reduced to pure function; key concepts were machine production, standardization and light, air and sun in the house. Tubular-steel furniture gave an optical effect of spaciousness because of its light, shiny construction. Walls and ceilings were painted white. The floor was covered by linoleum, rush matting or carpets in solid colours or with simple geometric motifs. Curtains and fabrics with a coarse weave, frequently in primary colours, were preferred. The chimney-piece disappeared or was greatly reduced. Important Functionalist interior designers included Rietveld, Mart Stam, J. J. P. Oud and Willem H. Gispen (1890–1981). This style was popular with the left-leaning cultural élite, although many people found an interior of this type cold and underfurnished. An example is the house of Van der Leeuw in Rotterdam by Brinkman & van der Vlugt (1929; see 1982 exh. cat., p. 58). After 1935 the excessively clinical character of Functionalism was already on the wane. Wooden furniture reappeared, curved lines were once again permitted in the interior, and fabrics with large floral prints became popular. METZ & Co., in Amsterdam and The Hague, supplied high-quality furniture and furnishing materials and was the sole agent in the Netherlands for the London firm of Liberty & Co.

After World War II many houses had to be completely refurnished during the period of widespread reconstruction, and the austere norms for interior decoration promoted by the Stichting Goed Wonen (Good living foundation) were not much different from those of Functionalism (see 1987 exh. cat.). In the 1950s such influences from Scandinavia as bentwood furniture made their appearance, and the Italian style, with its organic and attenuated forms, also influenced the Dutch interior after the late 1950s. Such interior designers as Johan Niegeman (1902–77), Hein Salomonson (*b* 1919), LIANG IE KHO (see fig. 38), Jaap J. Penraat (*b* 1918), Cora Nicolaï-Chaillet (1919–75) and Benno Premsela (*b* 1920) remained faithful to the principles of Functionalism while introducing such innovations as multi-purpose wall systems.

In the 1960s and 1970s increasing prosperity was reflected in the Dutch interior. Relaxed societal norms and greater leisure resulted in a more informal approach to the house. A broader spectrum of furnishings was on offer, and decorating magazines introduced new international fashions. Open fireplaces became popular, as well as wall-to-wall carpeting, L-shaped sofa combinations, open kitchens, colour televisions, rectangular leather sofas and swivel chairs. Plastic household objects in such bright colours as red, orange, purple and apple green became fashionable, as were new seating possibilities like the cube, beanbag and inflatable chair. At the end of the 1960s there was a revolt against urban growth and the anonymous uniformity of blocks of flats. Builders abandoned the high-rise for lower buildings set around a courtyard and houses with bay windows, smaller window-panes and peaked roofs. Furnishings were characterized by a return to more natural materials: rush matting on the floor, large house-plants, furniture from flea markets, Indian textiles and cushions on the floor. The new colour was brown. More conservative middle-class households had heavy oak furniture with leather upholstery. Houses were once again filled with knicknacks, just as they had been in the late 19th century. At the end of the 1970s a malaise crept into the interior design trade as a result of the declining economy. To remedy this the Beroepsvereniging van Nederlandse Interieurarchitecten (Professional organization of interior architects) was founded in 1975.

Around 1980 the light, modern interior returned to favour; whatever had been painted brown was repainted white. Cotton carpeting was a much loved fashionable floor covering. The all-white interior designs of Jan des Bouvrie (*b* 1942) became fashionable. Interest in De Stijl, Rietveld furniture and Functionalist interiors with tubular-steel chairs and linoleum floors revived, especially among better-educated young people. 'Design' was in vogue, and there was renewed interest in industrial design as a career, especially as exemplified by the Italian Post-modernist design teams of Memphis and Alchymia. Such Dutch designers and architects as Rob Eckhardt (*b* 1953) began to design very imaginative interiors. Also during the 1980s and 1990s the country cottage interior became widely popular, a trend that originated in England. Old pine furniture was treated or imported ready-to-use from Britain, and colour returned to the interior with uphol-stered furniture, draped curtains in floral fabrics and flat-woven Indian rugs on wooden floors. More formal variants included antique furniture or such French touches as white or coloured iron garden-chairs and terracotta flowerpots.

See also TILE, §II, 2.

BIBLIOGRAPHY

P. Clarijs: *Een eeuw Nederlandse woning* (Amsterdam, 1941)
W. van der Pluym: *Vijf eeuwen binnenhuis en meubels in Nederland, 1450–1950* (Amsterdam, 1954)
S. W. A. Drossaers and T. H. Lunsingh Scheurleer: *Inventarissen van de inboedels in de verblijven van de Oranjes, 1567–1795* (The Hague, 1974)

38. 'Aquila' kitchen designed by Liang Ie Kho, manufactured by Bruynzeel, 1966

T. H. Lunsingh Scheurleer: 'The Dutch and their Homes in the Seven-teenth Century', *Winterthur Conference Report. Arts of the Anglo-American Community in the Seventeenth Century: Winterthur, 1974*
F. van Burkom: 'Kunstvormgeving in Nederland', *De Amsterdamse school, 1910–1930* (exh. cat., Amsterdam, Stedel. Mus., 1975), pp. 71–108
P. Thornton: *Seventeenth-century Interior Decoration in England, France & Holland* (New Haven and London, 1978/R 1981)
P. Fuhring and R. Eggink: *Binnenhuisarchitektuur in Nederland, 1900–1981* (The Hague, 1981)
Het Nieuwe Bouwen in Rotterdam, 1920–1960 (exh. cat., Rotterdam, Mus. Boymans–van Beuningen, 1982)
N. Troy: *The De Stijl Environment* (Cambridge, MA, and London, 1983)
E. Bergvelt and others: 'Het Nieuwe Bouwen en het interieur/Nieuwe Bouwen and the interior', *Het Nieuwe Bouwen Amsterdam, 1920–1960* (exh. cat., Amsterdam, Stedel. Mus., 1983), pp. 112–41
P. Timmer: 'The Amsterdam School and Interior Design: Architects and Craftsmen against the Rationalists', *The Amsterdam School: Dutch Expressionist Architecture, 1915–1930* (exh. cat., New York, Cooper-Hewitt Mus., 1983), pp. 121–44
P. Thornton: *Authentic Decor: The Domestic Interior, 1620–1920* (London, 1984/R 1985)
M. Boot, T. Asselbergs and B. Vreeken: 'Ontworpen voor de woning', *Holland in vorm, 1945–1987* (exh. cat., The Hague, 1987), pp. 139–79 [Dut. and Eng. edns]
R. Baarsen and others: *Courts and Colonies: The William and Mary Style in Holland, England and America* (New York, 1988)

PETRA DUPUITS, JUDITH A. NEISWANDER

VI. Furniture.

1. Before 1600. 2. 1600–1630. 3. 1631–1715. 4. 1716–1850. 5. After 1850.

1. BEFORE 1600. The earliest surviving Dutch furni-ture dates from the Late Middle Ages, when the Gothic style dominated. The most common method of construc-tion was frame and panel, with letter inlay as one of the most distinctive decorative motifs; such popular orna-ments as Gothic arches, tracery, buttresses and pinnacles were derived from architecture. In the Middle Ages the woodworking trades were organized in the Guild of St Joseph; specialist carving, however, was executed by a sculptor, who was a member of the Guild of St Luke, the painters' guild. Guild regulations concerning apprentice-ships and masterpieces safeguarded the quality of work.

A simple and commonly used medieval chair was the *driestal*, with or without a back, sometimes with a triangular seat and with turned legs connected by rails and stretchers. The most important pieces of late medieval seat furniture were settles and armchairs, which were often boxed in and also served as storage chests. Settles normally stood along the wall or in front of the hearth and could be drawn up to the table at mealtimes. Simple plank benches with stick legs were found in the homes of the lowest classes, whereas finer forms had slab-end supports. This type was also made as a single seater, called a *scabelle* or *schemel*. A special type of bench, the *strijcsitten*, had a turned back. High-backed settles with profiled armrests were often built into the wall panelling or wainscot. Many 15th-century Flemish paintings depict furnished interiors in which an imposing armchair with a high back, featuring letter inlay or carving, stands next to a bed.

By far the most common type of table in the Middle Ages was of trestle form, consisting of free-standing supports on which a loose board rested. They were erected only at mealtimes; the top and trestles were normally leant against or hung on the wall. In exceptional cases the table-top was painted. An extremely rare painted example is preserved in the Norbertine monastery of Berne at Hees-wijk-Dinther; the painting includes medallions with biblical scenes, the central one of which depicts the *Last Supper*. The top can be folded up by means of hinges.

The chest was the most important piece of storage furniture. It was usually placed against the wall or by the bed. Important documents and valuables were kept in small chests, while linen, blankets, cushions, clothes, food etc were stored in larger ones. Those with a flat top could also be used as seats, tables and even beds. The homes of richer citizens often contained one or more dressers intended for storage and display. The dresser is among the most characteristic pieces of 15th-century furniture, and in the guild regulations of such towns as Amsterdam, Utrecht and Deventer a dresser was one of the master-pieces required from chestmakers or joiners. A well-preserved and very fine dresser, in the Rijksmuseum, Amsterdam (see fig. 39), is decorated on four sides and thus was intended as a free-standing piece, possibly for the display of plate. The emblem of a firebrand with crossed arrows indicates that it was commissioned by one of the archers' companies in Alkmaar, probably around 1525. Other types of storage chest were rare, with the exception of shallow, built-in wall chests called *spinde*. Four fine oak pantry doors with carving, wrought-iron hinges and lock plates are in the Stadhuis at Zwolle. They were made in 1449 by the chestmaker Johan Lubeke, wood-carver Berend and blacksmith Herman van Campen.

Beds were an important feature of medieval interiors. The bedstead of the master of the house and his wife generally stood in the kitchen or living-room; this type of bed, frequently depicted in 15th-century paintings, consisted of a plain wooden framework hung with curtains that were tied back during the day and drawn at night. The bedding and drapery were always much more costly than the woodwork.

It was not until the first years of the 16th century that the Renaissance influenced the northern Netherlands. The

39. Wooden dresser, 1035×1470×745 mm, *c.* 1525 (Amsterdam, Rijksmuseum)

structural form of furniture remained Gothic, while Renaissance decorative motifs began to appear. Such naturalistic ornaments as flowers, leaves and tendrils became increasingly important, and the distinction between the trades of furniture-making and carving became sharper. Ornamental prints were of great significance in the dissemination of such Renaissance ornament as grotesques, arabesques and candelabra. From the mid-16th century elaborately scrolling strapwork designs were popular. Although the fashion originated in France, it was such Dutchmen as Cornelis Bos and Cornelis Floris who combined strapwork with classical grotesques and developed the new idiom. The design language of the High Renaissance reached a high point in the engravings of Hans Vredeman de Vries and his son Paul (1567–after 1630), whose work remained the most important source for furniture-makers into the 17th century.

2. 1600–1630. In the first half of the 17th century furniture in the northern Netherlands took on a national character, although the Late Renaissance design language of the 16th century continued to dominate for some time. At the beginning of the 17th century, under the influence of 16th-century Italian and Spanish examples, a classic type of chair evolved. The so-called Spanish chair has a square seat and back and stands on four legs connected by stretchers that are often carved or profiled. The legs are in the form of balusters or Tuscan columns; the seat and back support nailed upholstery; the back posts are

headed by small lions; and the armrests end in leafwork or lions' masks. In contrast to Late Gothic pieces, oak was no longer used exclusively. Most 17th-century chair-frames are of walnut or occasionally of ebony or rose-wood. Tables also achieved a specifically Dutch form in the first half of the 17th century, comprising a board on four vase-shaped legs, such as those in the 16th-century prints of Hans Vredeman de Vries. These tables are called turned, bulbous, ball or cup and cover tables. They were made of oak enlivened with bands of ebony.

Although the chest remained an important piece of storage furniture, its function was largely taken over by the cupboard. Chestmakers now called themselves cup-board-makers. Various types of cupboard emerged, and it is possible to distinguish regional differences. The Zeeland cupboard is almost as high as it is wide and has a lower and an upper stage, each with two (or below sometimes three) doors. The uprights are headed by Zeeland's characteristic hermaphrodite caryatids, often capped by consoles with lions' masks. The doors are decorated with simple mouldings, and many Zeeland cupboards sport decorative inlay, for which such special woods as ebony, rose-wood and satin-wood were employed. A chest partic-ularly richly decorated with inlay (Rotterdam, Mus. Boy-mans–van Beuningen) has perspectival architectural scenes in the intarsia, called *doorkijkjes* ('see-throughs'), in the square panels of the upper stage and in the doors of the lower cupboard. The intarsia technique in the Netherlands seems to have been employed chiefly in Zeeland, concen-trated in various workshops in Middelburg, the capital of the province. Intarsia was, however, also frequently used in the southern Netherlands, and it is not always possible to distinguish between the various workshops.

In Holland, the most important province of the Dutch Republic, there were several types of cupboard. With the *toogkast* both the doors and the sides are bow-shaped over the full height. This design has also mistakenly been called the Utrecht cupboard; research has demonstrated that the type originated in Holland. These oak cupboards are often decorated with bands of ebony.

One of the most expensive types of cupboard from Holland is the *beeldenkast*, a carved cupboard comprising an upper and a lower section, each with two doors and separated by a frieze. The uprights of the upper and sometimes also the lower cupboard are styled as carved figures, from which the cupboard takes its name. These are often caryatids with symbolic significance, such as the virtues Faith, Hope and Charity. On the doors and elsewhere there are reliefs, often after prints by the Mannerist painter Maarten van Heemskerck of Haarlem; this is probably true of a *beeldenkast* in the Rijksmuseum, Amsterdam. The reliefs on the door panels tell the story of Susanna. It is a very richly carved example of oak decorated with ebony. In the carvings on the upper cupboard Faith can be recognized with a cross, Hope with a dove and anchor and Charity with two children. The iconography of the carvings and relief is connected to the original purpose of the cupboard, because many *beelden-kasten* accompanied the bride on marriage and were used for storing linen. The detailed ornamental and sculptural carving of such cupboards was executed by specialist tradesmen. The simpler fretwork and the manufacture of

the piece itself were the cabinetmaker's job. Guild rules concerning the division of labour between both trades was very specific, so these *beeldenkasten* had to be the collab-orative work of cabinetmaker and wood-carver. Column and pilaster cupboards were simpler and cheaper. Half-columns or pilasters were used for corner or centre supports. The carving is much rougher than on the *beeldenkasten*. The same motifs were repeated time and time again, such as the foliated frieze with vase in the cornice, from which these cupboards became known as *vaaskasten* ('vase cupboards').

Beds from the first half of the 17th century are known chiefly from paintings. They remained an important item of furniture, as in the Middle Ages. One example (Am-sterdam, Rijksmus.) that also appears in the prints of Hans Vredeman de Vries is built of rose-wood decorated with ivory, has a canopy supported by posts and can be closed with luxurious curtains. Some bedsteads were built into a corner of the room and were often integrated with the wall panelling. One ensemble comprising panelling with fireplace, pieces of wainscoting and a built-in bed (Am-sterdam, Rijksmus.) comes from a house in Dordrecht and is dated 1626 on the mantelpiece. It is a masterpiece of joinery with polished outlines and perfect pen-and-dart joints. Carving is restricted to consoles on the cornice and pilasters. The square intarsia decorations are attractively placed in the centre of the panels. The whole ensemble, in oak, ebony, rose-wood, satin-wood and palm-wood, is by a Dordrecht master who must have been strongly influenced by the use of the intarsia technique in Zeeland.

3. 1631–1715. After 1630 a classicizing Baroque style held sway in both architecture and furniture, which became identified with Dutch classicism. This style is distinguished by the adoption of the Classical orders and a repertory of ornament favouring flower and fruit garlands. It is ex-pressed in all its glory in the Stadhuis (begun 1648, now the Royal Palace) on Dam Square in Amsterdam, the masterpiece of the architect Jacob van Campen. The style was highly suitable for Amsterdam merchants, whose recently acquired wealth could be demonstrated in the decoration of their newly built houses on the canals. Exotic woods, imported in large quantities by the Dutch merchant fleet, were widely used as veneers on oak foundations. There was a pronounced influence from Chinese and particularly Japanese lacquerwork. As a result of Baroque influence furniture acquired a greater plasticity. The hallmarks of the style were more national: fewer regional variations are distinguishable.

The love of plasticity is evident in the shape of chair legs, particularly the spiral leg, which was used well into the 17th century. Many tables also had turned legs, while those with bulbous legs akin to supports popular in the early 17th century were now mostly made of rose-wood or ebony. The positioning of console tables gave walls a greater three-dimensionality, entirely in the spirit of the Baroque. A special group of tables made by wood-carvers had large diagonally placed S-shaped legs; made in the Auricular style, the fanciful mollusc-like shapes sometimes completely dominate the structure of the piece. The Dutch silversmiths Paulus and Adam van Vianen and Johannes Lutma (i), and the painter Gerbrand van den Eeckhout, a

40. *Kussenkast*, rose-wood veneer on oak with ebony, 2.49×2.27×0.86 m, second half of the 17th century (Amsterdam, Rijksmuseum)

son and brother of goldsmiths, played an important part in the creation and development of this style (*see* §IX, 1(ii) below).

For cupboards the two-door type, articulated through pilasters and columns, predominated. They acquired a highly three-dimensional aura from the angled corner columns with their bases and the swellings on raised panels, from which they are also called *kussenkasten* (bombé cupboards). The name *rankenkast* ('foliated cupboard') is taken from the decoration of acanthus tendrils and flower and fruit garlands on pilaster shafts, which served to emphasize the architectural countenance of the cupboard. The openwork carving is generally of the same type of wood (rose-wood or ebony) as the veneer on the carcass. Heads and cartouches on the capitals and the cornice were carved out of solid wood. In very luxurious examples, such as a *kussenkast* (see fig. 40) in the Rijksmuseum, Amsterdam, the spiral pillars are made from turned solid ebony.

In the final quarter of the 17th century furniture in the northern Netherlands was decorated with marquetry in various woods (*see* WOOD, colour pl. IV, fig. 2). Two-door cupboards were usually raised on legs. Cupboards with marquetry decoration in the form of eight-pointed stars and circles are called *sterkasten* ('star cupboards'). In *bloemkasten* ('flower cupboards') flower trails represented in marquetry flowed over the doorposts, frieze, legs and X-frame stretchers. The sides sport marquetry flower vases, and the doors present a monumental appearance by depicting large vases placed on the ends of a table, as seen in a cabinet attributed to Jan van Mekeren (*c.* 1700; Amsterdam, Rijksmus.; *see* MARQUETRY, fig. 1). This type,

with its shallow cornice and flat panels, deviates markedly from the plastic *kussenkast*. *Sterkasten* were traditionally made in Zeeland but were probably also found in other centres. That is certainly so for *bloemkasten*, which continued to be made into the 18th century. The names of several makers are known. An inventory of the property of Philippus van Santwijk of The Hague dated 1700 mentions many cabinets as well as tables, candle stands and mirrors, usually described as being inlaid with flowers. At Twickel Castle near Delden in the province of Overijssel there are two cupboards made by him with exceptionally fine marquetry, and a closely related example is in the Rijksmuseum in Amsterdam. An inventory of his workshop made after his death lists, among other things, 14 cabinets and 2 writing-cabinets with mirrors, 24 walnut tables, 20 of oak and 25 candle stands (examples in Amsterdam, Rijksmus.; Amerongen, Casteel). The journal of a journey through the Netherlands in 1711 by the German Zacharias von Uffenbach reveals that furniture with floral marquetry was also made in Rotterdam, where he saw examples in the workshop of Balten Gessingh; no works by this craftsman, however, have been identified.

In the last quarter of the 17th century there was a decline in inventiveness and originality in furniture; the same tendril friezes and fruit-and-flower garlands were repeated time and again. An innovative impulse came from France when, after the Revocation of the Edict of Nantes in 1685, many French Protestant craftsmen fled to the Netherlands. The architect and designer Daniel Marot I introduced the Louis XIV style into the Netherlands through his designs for architecture, gardens, interiors (*see* §V, 2, above) and furniture. His published designs for mantelpieces, carved tables with accompanying candle stands and mirrors, wall- and table-clocks, and chairs and state beds with such decorative motifs as symmetrically grouped C-curves, broken S-curves, palms, shells, masks and lambrequins, give a good picture of the William and Mary style. In general the furniture conveys a stronger sculptural feeling than in the previous period. A good example is a boldly carved table (The Hague, Mauritshuis), which was probably made after Marot's design. The initials AA on this table belong to Amalia van Anhalt, for whom Marot built Schloss Oranienstein near Diez an der Lahn (Germany) in 1707.

4. 1716–1850. In the first half of the 18th century Dutch furniture was strongly influenced by English forms. English Queen Anne chairs were popular, with a plain curved back, vase-shaped splat and cabriole front legs. Chair-frames were generally made of walnut faced with richly figured walnut veneers, and the finer pieces are enlivened with marquetry. Writing-cabinets, also influenced by English examples, were often made in the Netherlands during this period. The lower stage incorporates drawers and a writing-flap that could be folded down, while the upper cupboard often has two doors framing plates of looking-glass.

A version of the late Louis XIV style was employed in the Netherlands well into the second quarter of the century, when the influence of the Rococo was already noticeable. The contours of furniture began to curve, and symmetry in ornamentation was abandoned. In the 18th century

Dutch furniture never went as far as French pieces in allowing the elements to flow into each other; thus the back posts remained separate, and the legs never lack a division at the seat-rail level. In Amsterdam the furniture-maker Andries Bonge worked in the Rococo style; many pieces by him are known, including a signed commode (Amsterdam, Hist. Mus.).

The principal piece of storage furniture in this period was the cabinet, one of the most characteristic Dutch pieces of the 18th century. The cabinet was constructed from a lower stage with drawers across the full width and an upper cupboard enclosed by double doors. The strict rectangularity of design gave way in the early 18th century to cabinets with corner trusses set diagonally; the cornice was shaped, and eventually the front and sides were of bombé form. Rococo shell motifs were frequently incorporated in the cresting. Cabinets were veneered with either walnut or mahogany, and sometimes the doors were fronted by mirrors, as in a very rich Rococo example (Amsterdam, Rijksmus.; see fig. 41) where the mirror panels are back-painted in the Chinese manner. Veneered with walnut and rose-wood and with silver fittings, it must have been vastly expensive. A variation on such closed cabinets was the china-cabinet, in which porcelain could be displayed on shelves behind glazed doors.

Around 1770 the first influence of Neo-classicism, another style that originated in France, began to be felt. Curved lines disappeared, and such decorative motifs as laurel crowns, rosettes, acanthus leaves and strapwork were derived from ancient Greece and Rome. This style must have had a greater attraction for the sober Dutchman than the playful Rococo. A greater liking for mahogany and satin-wood, in both veneer and the solid, developed in this period.

The cabinet remained the principal piece of furniture for storage and retained the same division with drawers below and doors above. The shape became strictly rectangular again, but the severity was softened by chamfered corner trusses. The upper stage was sometimes divided by pilasters and headed by an arch; plain door panels with a small central medallion suspended from a ribbon executed in marquetry are typical. During the last quarter of the 18th century the low buffet or sideboard-cabinet developed into a piece of characteristically Dutch furniture. It is fronted by two doors, and the top is fitted with a hinged leaf that opens to reveal glassware and porcelain; under the leaf there is usually a pewter washing-up bowl.

After 1800 the preference for designs from Classical antiquity was continued in the Empire style, which found a great following in the Netherlands under Louis Bonaparte, King of Holland. In Amsterdam the German-born furniture-maker Carel Breytspraak (d 1810) worked in this style; various pieces by him are preserved in the Royal Palace in Amsterdam (see fig. 42). Antiquity was also an important source of inspiration for the late Empire and Biedermeier styles, although the furniture is generally simpler and less monumental. By 1850 a preference for various revival styles gained the upper hand. A new age was heralded with the disappearance of the guilds and the introduction of woodworking machinery.

BIBLIOGRAPHY

A. Berendsen: *Het Nederlandse interieur* (Utrecht, 1950)

T. H. Lunsingh Scheurleer: *Catalogus van meubelen en betimmeringen in het Rijksmuseum* (Amsterdam, 1952)

W. van der Pluym: *Vijf eeuwen binnenhuis en meubels in Nederland, 1450–1950* (Amsterdam, 1954)

T. H. Lunsingh Scheurleer: *Van haardvuur tot beeldscherm: Vijf eeuwen interieur- en meubelkunst in Nederland* [From hearth to television screen: five centuries of interior design and furniture-making in the Netherlands] (Leiden, 1961)

U. W. Schneede: 'Interieurs von Hans und Paul Vredeman', *Ned. Ksthist. Jb.*, xviii (1967), pp. 125–66

T. H. Lunsingh Scheurleer: 'The Dutch and their Homes in the Seventeenth Century', *Winterthur Conference Report. Arts of the Anglo-American Community in the Seventeenth Century: Winterthur, 1974*

P. Eames: *Medieval Furniture: Furniture in England, France and the Netherlands from the Twelfth to the Fifteenth Century* (London, 1977)

J. M. W. van Voorst tot Voorst: *Meubels in Nederland, 1840–1900*, 2 vols (Lochem, 1979)

Thuis in de late middeleeuwen: Het Nederlands burgerinterieur, 1400–1535 [At home in the Middle Ages: the Dutch bourgeois interior, 1400–1535] (exh. cat., Zwolle, Prov. Overijssels Mus., 1980)

R. Baarsen and others: *Courts and Colonies: The William and Mary Style in Holland, England and America* (New York, 1988)

NICOLINE A. ZEMERING

5. AFTER 1850. Around 1850 there was little demand for high-quality furniture, except in The Hague, where the aristocracy, as well as colonials and civil servants returned from Indonesia, provided a better market. Several furniture factories appeared in the city, the largest being the Anna Paulowna Meubelenfabriek founded by the brothers Horrix; the Koninklijke Nederlandsche Meubelenfabriek, owned by H. P. Mutters, and H. PANDER & Zonen were

41. Cabinet, veneers of walnut, rose-wood and other woods on oak, 1.79×2.37×0.63 m, c. 1750 (Amsterdam, Rijksmuseum)

42. Commode with mahogany veneer and gilt-bronze mounts, by Carel Breytspraak, 1809 (Amsterdam, Stichting Koninklijk Paleis)

also well known. The period of revival styles began around 1850, although Gothic Revival furniture had already become fashionable as an alternative to Empire and Biedermeier types; elements of the latter disappeared after 1850 and were replaced by a mania for ornament drawn from a wide range of international sources. Many furniture-makers used such model books as *Le Garde-meuble*, published in 1867 and between 1887 and 1895, as a reference for designs or details. The revival of Baroque and Rococo idioms was particularly strong during this phase, combined with elements from other stylistic periods; the result was a medley of styles in an interior or even in a single article of furniture. French polishing,

staining and veneering were popular, as well as ebonizing (the use of black lacquer on furniture). Dutch lacquer-workers were internationally famous, the best known being Gerrit van der Lugt (*b* 1827). Some cabinets were decorated with paintings in *vernis Martin*, frequently of mildly risqué scenes, or with ornaments of composition or cut-out paste. Gilding of details or entire pieces of furniture was carried out by mirror- and framemakers and became especially popular after 1870, when the Louis XVI style was introduced for salons and music-rooms.

From the second half of the 19th century, chairs with curved lines were preferred: side chairs with cabriole front legs and pear-shaped backs finished with a crest ornament were fashionable until 1870. The most common ladies' armchair was of 'crinoline' form, the Dutch version of the voltaire; the seat was generally low, sprung and upholstered. The upholsterer's role became increasingly important as overstuffed chairs and sofas were widely popular. The best known was the 'crapaud', a model that dominated the market.

In the opinion of furniture-makers, ornament turned a piece of furniture into something closer to a work of art. Naturalistic imitations of still-lifes, hunting scenes or historical tableaux were greatly admired; sideboards, in particular, were considered suitable for these richly carved decorations, although considerably greater restraint was exercised after 1870. Naturalism was replaced by stylized ornament, a shift spearheaded by architects. The Dutch Renaissance provided sources for their attempts at a new degree of unity and purity of style, particularly for dining-room and library furniture. The imitation of traditional historic styles was not the only trend during this period, as can be seen in the fashion for rustic furniture intended to give the appearance of having been constructed from branches. Another innovation was the development of rattan and cast-iron furniture in response to the growing popularity of the verandah, the conservatory and the winter garden.

Negative reactions to the artistic quality of Dutch furniture were already widespread in the 1860s, although furniture design declined further towards the end of the century due to increased mass production. Factories installed power machinery that could rapidly produce frames, joints and ornamental-work. This degradation of craftsmanship provoked much criticism, particularly from architects and artists who, in contrast to most furniture manufacturers, were far more articulate in matters of artistic theory and design. The architect P. J. H. Cuypers taught style and ornamental technique for about ten years at the Rijksschool voor Kunstnijverheid, which was founded in 1881 at the Rijksmuseum in Amsterdam. Most of the artists who were later responsible for the reform of Dutch furniture design were taught by Cuypers. They designed and produced furniture in their own studios and workshops or commissioned well-known furniture-makers to execute their designs. Around the turn of the century a number of workshops appeared in rapid succession, including the Atelier voor Architectuur, Kunstnijverheid en Versieringskunst (Atelier for architecture, crafts and ornament) of K. P. C. de Bazel and J. L. Mathieu Lauweriks in 1895, the Kunstwerkplaats Amstelhoek, with a

43. Furniture in the Nieuwe Kunst style by Gerrit Willem Dijsselhof, 1896 (The Hague, Gemeentemuseum)

furniture workshop supervised by Willem Penaat, in 1898, the Kunstwerkplaats of VAN WISSELINGH & Co. in 1898, 'T BINNENHUIS in 1900, DE WONING in 1902 and De Ploeg in 1904, all in Amsterdam; in The Hague there were Arts and Crafts (owned by JOHN UITERWIJK & Co.) in 1898 and Die Haghe in 1902.

An energetic effort was made to create forms determined by function and unrelated to previous historical styles. Gilding and veneering went out of fashion in progressive furniture, although Empire and Biedermeier elements persisted. After 1890 the 'honest' Gothic technique of wood construction—pegged mortice-and-tenon joints emphasized by large-headed nails or ebony or ivory caps—was an example of reformed principles in practice. Ornament remained, but far less attention was paid to it: stylized plant motifs, geometric patterns or oriental elements were preferred. The earliest furniture in this Nieuwe Kunst (or Rationalist) style was designed in 1896 by Gerrit Willem Dijsselhof as part of a unified interior for the Amsterdam physician W. van Hoorn (The Hague, Gemeentemus.; see fig. 43).

Although Art Nouveau influences are apparent, two main branches can be distinguished within the Nieuwe Kunst style. The first is a decorative tradition, with design as the end product. Furniture of this type was extremely expensive and included work by Dijsselhof, as well as by C. A. Lion Cachet, T. W. Nieuwenhuis and Johan Thorn Prikker. The second strand was Rationalist, in which construction was the central issue for both form and ornament, as exemplified by the work of H. P. Berlage, Lauweriks, de Bazel, Penaat, Jacob van den Bosch (1868–1948) and others of their circle. The Rationalist style was particularly prominent in Amsterdam, but its stern austerity did not find favour with working- and lower middle-class customers who preferred the more showy mass-produced products. For this reason modern Rationalist furniture remained costly and was bought mainly by well-to-do intellectuals from such stores as 't Binnenhuis. It was gradually realized that the public needed to be educated, and that a craft revival would make sense only if a link were made between the arts and industry; to this end, various organizations and societies were formed. Unfortunately, the furniture industry paid little attention to these enthusiastic initiatives, and the Nieuwe Kunst style faded from fashion around 1910.

The new generation of professional designers preferred a more expressive approach. Two principal movements appeared around the beginning of World War I: one originated with the architects and furniture designers of the Amsterdam school and lasted from 1910 until 1930; the other, Nieuwe Beelding (New Image), originated with the artists and architects associated with the periodical De stijl. While the former was interested primarily in the individual formal language of each piece, frequently executed in costly materials, the DE STIJL movement tried to achieve universal, abstract solutions.

The designs of Michel de Klerk, P. L. Kramer, Hildo Krop (1884–1970) and other representatives of the Amsterdam school can be seen as a reaction to Rationalism. Using heavily sculpted three-dimensional forms, a wide spectrum of textile colours (green, purple, red, yellow,

44. Chair, chromed metal tubing, by Mart Stam, 1926 (Amsterdam, Stedelijk Museum)

black and gold) and luxurious and exotic woods (mahogany, ebony, coromandel, oak, rose-wood), they created furniture in a sober Dutch version of the Art Deco style. The majority of these pieces were one-of-a-kind, many of them executed by 't Woonhuys of Amsterdam.

The chairs by the only furniture-maker of the De Stijl group, GERRIT RIETVELD, were a logical result of his experiments with the concept of space and his analysis of the verb 'to sit'. In contrast to the Amsterdam school designers, Rietveld wanted to design as functional a piece of furniture as possible; his best-known example is the Red-Blue chair of 1918 (e.g. Amsterdam, Stedel. Mus.). Rationalist principles are also evident in the designs by such members of the De Stijl circle as Vilmos Huszár, Theo van Doesburg and Jan Wils: all inessential detail has been left out in order to arrive at the greatest possible simplicity.

In concert with Russian concepts of Constructivism, De Stijl prepared the way for the Nieuwe Zakelijkheid (New Objectivity) or Hague school movement, which dominated design from c. 1925 into the 1930s (see §V, 4 above). Its functional designs and largely geometric forms were conceived for simple mechanized production; native woods in a neutral finish, stained or painted were preferred, although sometimes part of the furniture was coloured to contrast with the visible wooden construction. The work of HENDRIK WOUDA, head of the Modern Interiors department of H. Pander & Zonen, is distinguished by its refined lines and expressive contrast between colours and surfaces. His seating designs, in particular, are characterized by uncluttered, cubic forms, with Frank Lloyd Wright's influence evident in chairs with high spoked backs (e.g. The Hague, Gemeentemus.). Other influential figures included Cor Alons, Frits Spanjaard and Cornelis van der Sluys. The furniture industry made full use of the straightforward designs of this style for its own mass production. Such companies as METZ & Co., Pander and LOV (Labor omnia vincit), famous for their high-quality furniture, were members of the BKI (Bond voor Kunst en Industrie) and usually recorded the name of the designer on the products they sold.

Within the international Modern Movement there was constant experimentation to find a contemporary style of design. Various designers focused their sights on metal tubing, which had already found its place in the bicycle, bed and office furniture industries. After experiments at the Bauhaus in Germany and elsewhere, it was the Dutch architect Mart Stam who in 1926 designed the first chair without back legs, made of bent chromed metal tubing (e.g. Amsterdam, Stedel. Mus.; see fig. 44). The Fabriek voor Metaalbewerking of Rotterdam, headed from 1916 by the designer W. H. Gispen (1890–1981), was one of the first factories in the Netherlands to experiment with the production of Nieuwe Zakelijkheid tubular-steel furniture in 1929, but genuine mass production was never fully achieved because the public continued to prefer wood for domestic furniture; thus, tubular furniture retained an élitist character.

After World War II major technological changes, the development of new materials and increased consumer demand (particularly after 1955) resulted in increased production. Dutch designers established themselves independently and began to experiment with new technologies. Through the Stichting Goed Wonen (Good living foundation) they tried to stimulate the market and educate the public, but only a few Dutch factories responded, among them Artifort with LIANG IE KHO (see also fig. 38 above), De Cirkel with FRISO KRAMER, Gispen with Wim Rietveld (1924–85) and 't Spectrum with Martin Visser (b 1922). The high-frequency press, invented by Charles and Ray Eames, increased laminating capability; Cor Alons (1892–1967), J. C. Jansen (b 1897) and Han Pieck (b 1923) were the first to use the new technique for chairs in the late 1940s.

Standardization offered commercial advantages and was particularly applicable for wall systems (e.g. 'Pas-Toe' designed by Cees Braakman (b 1917) for UMS). Wood remained the preferred material, particularly oak and birch. Designs were generally simple and unadorned, sometimes bordering on the dull; often the influence of Scandinavian design was strongly apparent. Nevertheless it was this type of unit that awakened the public to the possibilities of contemporary furniture, providing traditional styles with a genuine competitor. Dirk van Sliedrecht (b 1920) produced successful designs for chairs combining rattan seats with metal supporting parts, resulting in a functional, light and inexpensive product. In 1967 the first plastic bucket seat was produced in the Netherlands, a design by Theo Tempelman (b 1931) produced by AP Originals. Artifort retained a strong position in the purpose-built furniture market, both domestically and internationally, in the 1960s;

45. 'Amsterdammer' storage unit, wood and plastic, designed by Aldo van den Nieuwelaar, made by UMS-Pastoe, Utrecht, 1978 (Utrecht, Centraal Museum)

but most other Dutch companies were too timid to invest in specialized machinery that might have offered greater design possibilities, and the daring and inventiveness characteristic of Italian and Scandinavian furniture were missing from their products.

During the 1970s some designers began to produce small quantities of work in their own studios. One of the first to break away from the corporate system was the goldsmith and furniture designer Gijs Bakker (*b* 1942). Through his designs (e.g. laminated wooden chairs produced for Castelijn and Artifort) and his exhibitions of work by young designers, he demonstrated the rich store of unappreciated talent in the country. In general furniture retained its factory-style, Functionalist character; the chrome and steel tube made a comeback influenced by Italian design, and various designers continued to explore the possibilities of laminated wood. Occasionally, the industry would take up the challenge and batch-produce one of these designs. Examples are the chairs designed by Bruno Ninaber van Eyben (*b* 1950), Fons Kooymans (*b* 1953), Radboud van Beekum (*b* 1950) and Bakker. In 1978 Aldo van den Nieuwelaar (*b* 1944) designed the distinctive 'Amsterdammer' storage unit (see fig. 45), made from a combination of wood and plastic. Marketed in the late 1970s, it enjoyed unprecedented popularity. Gradually, through a growing demand by the younger public for contemporary furniture, the concept of 'design' became synonymous with quality, and the names of designers were increasingly featured. Designers who were able to develop a successful range included Jan des Bouvrie (*b* 1942), Gerard van den Berg (*b* 1947) and the team of Pierre Mazairac (*b* 1943) and Karel Boonzaaijer (*b* 1948).

Technical innovation, which in the past had influenced form and use, was no longer appreciated for itself alone. The new generation of designers considered Functionalist principles increasingly inhibiting. In addition, the Italian studios Alchymia and Memphis played an influential role. Ornament returned as a trademark of style, and designers once again saw themselves as artists, making conscious use of the connotations and significance of form, colour and material. Mass production was rejected completely, with some furniture available only as unique objects sold in art galleries. This trend is best exemplified by the work of such designers as Ed Annink (*b* 1957), Peer de Bruyn (*b* 1960), Rob Eckhardt (*b* 1953), Bob Verheyden (*b* 1964) and Niek Zwartjes (*b* 1960).

BIBLIOGRAPHY

L. Gans: *Nieuwe Kunst: De Nederlandse bijdrage tot de Art Nouveau* [New art: the Dutch contribution to Art Nouveau] (Utrecht, 1960)

J. van Voorst tot Voorst: *Meubels in Nederland, 1840–1900*, ii (Lochem, 1979)

F. Leidelmeier and D. van der Cingel: *Art Nouveau en Art Deco in Nederland* (Amsterdam, 1983)

H. Martens and M. Teunissen: 'Meubels-Geschiedenis', *Industrie & Vormgeving in Nederland, 1850–1950* (exh. cat., Amsterdam, Stedel. Mus., 1985), pp. 249–59

P. Vöge and B. Westerveld: *Stoelen: Nederlandse ontwerpen, 1945–1985* [Chairs: Dutch designs, 1945–1985] (Amsterdam, 1986)

M. Boot, T. Asselbergs and B. Vreeken: 'Ontworpen voor de woning' [Design for the interior], *Holland in vorm, 1945–1987* (exh. cat., The Hague, 1987), pp. 139–79 [Dut. and Eng. edns]

MONIQUE D. J. M. TEUNISSEN

VII. Ceramics.

1. Before 1650. 2. 1650–1750. 3. 1751–1830. 4. After 1830.

1. BEFORE 1650. Young, alluvial sea clay is found in the west and north of the Netherlands and elsewhere old clay from the Tertiary period and the beginning of the Quaternary period. These clays were used for such ceramic products as bricks and roof- and floor-tiles, for which simple preparation of the extracted clay was sufficient. The results, however, were porous and unsuitable for household use. To make the pieces water-resistant they were, in time, glazed, before firing, with a slip made from a mixture of clay and lead sulphide (galena). During firing (*c.* 950°) it formed a transparent glaze. The pots were decorated with *sgrafitto* or before glazing with a layer of white slip. During the early Middle Ages indigenous production was supplemented by imports of better or more richly decorated earthenwares; until *c.* 1200 the so-called Pingsdorf ware was imported from the area between Cologne and Bonn and from Andenne. More important, however, were the imported stonewares from Cologne, Siegburg, Frechen and Raeren, which were used extensively in the Netherlands after *c.* 1400 and comprised mainly drinking vessels, cups and jugs. Local and imported earthenwares consisted of pots and pans for household use in a variety of shapes; at this time dishes and plates were generally made of wood or metal (brass or pewter). Earthenwares had a functional design and were provided with a transparent lead glaze, occasionally coloured green in part or all over by the addition of copper-oxide. Utrecht and Bergen-op-Zoom were important centres for the production of lead-glazed earthenwares, especially after

46. Maiolica jug, h. 200 mm, made in Utrecht, *c.* 1560 (Leeuwarden, Gemeentelijk Museum Het Princessehof)

1400. During the 16th century the use of white slips became increasingly widespread. Ornaments and figures were also introduced using the sliptrailing technique.

Around 1560 the range of ceramics was expanded with local production of tin-glazed earthenwares. Until then these wares had been known only through occasional imports from Spain, Italy and Antwerp. Maiolica (earthenware covered with a tin glaze on the front and transparent lead glaze on the back), which was fired in the kiln on triangular trivets, had been introduced c. 1500 by Italians in Antwerp (see ANTWERP, §III, 2). These methods of manufacture and tilemaking techniques were introduced to Utrecht and Haarlem by settlers from Antwerp. This development accelerated after 1585, and c. 1600 maiolica wares and tin-glazed tiles were produced in the economically flourishing northern Netherlands, in Haarlem, Amsterdam, Rotterdam and Delft. At first, output comprised plates, dishes, drug jars (albarelli) and syrup jugs, while the manufacture of tiles was generally kept separate. Around 1600, to satisfy new consumer demand, all the workshops produced large quantities of plates, dishes and tiles, and to a lesser degree apothecaries' wares and drinking vessels. Maiolica was decorated in the 'Italian-Antwerp' manner, with stylized leaf motifs, ornamental patterns (see fig. 46) or, rarely, a figurative decoration taken from an engraved print.

The tin-glazed wall-tile originated in the Netherlands c. 1580 (see TILE, §II, 2). First introduced in Antwerp by the Italians as a glazed floor-tile and intended for the wealthy, it developed into a wall-tile in the north and was intended for the urban, middle-class population in the west of the Netherlands. This had far-reaching consequences for tile decoration; medieval ornamentation, partly originating from the inlaid lead-glazed floor-tile, was abandoned in favour of an expanded figurative portion. This development culminated c. 1650 in decoration that comprised one single figured scene per tile with small, corner decoration.

Until 1620 decoration consisted mainly of stylized leaf motifs with pomegranates, grapes and stylized flowers (e.g. four polychrome tiles; Rotterdam, Hist. Mus.; see also TILE, colour pl. XIII, fig. 2); later there were also various series depicting animals. Between 1625 and 1650 tiles were decorated with people carrying out daily activities and trades, but after 1640 flowers and birds became popular. Until c. 1625 the tiles were painted in polychrome and later chiefly in blue, with the exception of tiles decorated with birds and flowers, which were intended for the residences of rich rural people.

The manufacture of slipware pots and pans, in addition to plates and dishes, also continued. Decoration became richer, and trailed decoration was mainly used. The important centres of production were Bergen-op-Zoom, Gouda and the northern part of the provinces of Holland and Friesland. Local production was complemented by imports of fine decorated pieces from Wanfried an der Werra, the area north of Krefeld and Ochtrup (both just in German territory). Stoneware drinking vessels were partly replaced after 1600 by glass jugs mostly from the Westerwald, and the latter remained in general use in the Netherlands until the end of the 19th century.

47. Blue-and-white Delftware lidded jug, h. 260 mm, possibly made at the Porceleynen Schotel, Delft, c. 1625–40 (Amsterdam, Rijksmuseum)

The development of the ceramics industry was, however, disrupted shortly after 1600. From 1602, at first on a small scale but after 1610 more extensively, the Dutch East India Company imported Chinese porcelain, known as 'Kraak' porcelain, into the Netherlands (see CHINA, §VII, 4(v)). Until 1620 the arrival of c. 100,000 pieces of porcelain per year forced the hand of the maiolica- and tile-makers: a number of maiolica firms went into liquidation c. 1620. Another group of manufacturers concentrated on tile production, which was not threatened by porcelain, while a third group ensured their output was appreciably cheaper by making coarser wares with less refined decoration. These were aimed at the Dutch lower classes and were made for export to northern Germany, Flanders, northern France, the coast of France down to Bordeaux, and perhaps England. These somewhat coarser but boldly painted dishes comprised a separate group in the period up to 1675, and their decoration was often similar to that used on tiles. Dishes remained a small category of wares, which were increasingly coarsely and primitively painted.

Another option for the maiolica producers was to refine production so that the quality of goods could imitate Chinese porcelain as closely as possible and thus seize the adjacent market. There were, however, numerous technical difficulties to overcome: for example, if a dish was made thinner it warped during drying and firing. To improve the composition of the body, marl, either from Tournai in the southern Netherlands or from Norwich in England, had to be added to the mixture. This new product had a better clay mixture and was glazed all over with a very white tin glaze. Firing was now done in cylindrical ceramic saggars, and the trivet marks found on earlier wares no longer appeared. Developed in Delft between 1618 and 1624, it was called faience or Dutch Delftware (*see* DELFT, §3). During the 17th century the term *Hollands porceleyn* was used. The developments occurred in two factories: the Porceleynen Schotel owned by Elizabeth Cornelisdr. Suycker and the Porceleynen Lampetkan of Cornelis Harmansz. Valckenhoven (*d* 1637). Arguably the most important individual was Willem Jansz. Verstraeten, technical director at the Porceleynen Schotel between 1615 and 1625, who set up his own factory in Haarlem in 1625. At this time wares were almost always decorated with European ornaments and motifs. Only a few objects, such as small jugs, salt-cellars, mustard-pots and altar vases, the forms of which did not come from China, were deliberately decorated in the Chinese style (see fig. 47).

All the plate and dish manufacturers, whether they continued to produce the increasingly coarse maiolica or changed to the technically improved Delftware, marked all their wares before 1620 with a round, flowing mark on the reverse of the item, which originated in Italy. During the 1650s popular shapes included the scalloped dish derived from metalwork forms. Output from the Porceleynen Schotel and Porceleynen Lampetkan consisted mainly of small plates (from *c.* 200 mm in diameter) with a border and decoration featuring a wide range of landscapes and figures, which were often related to contemporary tile designs.

Friesland in particular had a flourishing ceramics industry due to its system of good waterways and the high quality of the clay in its soil. One of the most important factories there was Schritsen, established in 1598 in Harlingen; it continued operation until 1803. The two main products of the Frisian factories were wall-tiles and Maiolica dishes, the latter either painted in blue or multicoloured.

2. 1650–1750. Chinese porcelain production was severely curtailed between *c.* 1645 and 1650 due to the war between the ruling Ming dynasty and the invading Manchus, when the kilns at Jingdezhen were badly damaged. Porcelain imports into the Netherlands, which had increased to 250,000 pieces annually, were reduced to

nothing in five years. The owners of the Porceleynen Schotel and the Porceleynen Lampetkan seized the opportunity to fill the gap in the market. They began making large volumes of faience decorated with Chinese-style painting; others, however, quickly followed, and before 1665 there were more than 20 faience factories in Delft mass-producing imitation porcelain. Much of the faience with decoration derived from Chinese Transitional ware, attributed from *c.* 1920 to producers in Frankfurt am Main, was in fact made in Delft, partly for export to German courts. In addition a significant quantity of pieces was also decorated with finely painted Dutch landscapes and biblical subjects. The best producer of this type of ware was the painter Frederik van Frytom (1632–1702), who decorated plates, dishes and plaques with fine blue-and-white Dutch and Italianate landscapes (e.g. blue-and-white plaque, 1659; Amsterdam, Rijksmus.).

Changes occurred in the industry *c.* 1680, when the saturation of the market caused the most inventive Delftware producers to seek new directions. In addition to the blue-and-white pieces they also experimented with colour: gilding and a garnet-red enamel were introduced by Jacob Wemmersz. Hoppesteyn, the owner of the faience factory Het Jonge Moriaenshoofd in Delft. It is very likely that Hoppesteyn gleaned the idea from the decoration on Japanese Kakiemon porcelain, which had been exported to the Netherlands on a modest scale from 1670. As well as the new polychrome wares, South Chinese Yixing wares (red stonewares) were also imitated, especially by Ary de Milde. Makers of red stoneware teapots were the first to register marks in order to protect their work from competition; this concept was quickly adopted by other makers.

Chinese porcelain was once again imported into Europe in large quantities from 1683. The porcelain, decorated with an attractive blue, presented formidable competition to blue-and-white Delftware. Polychrome porcelain decorated with *famille verte* colours (green, red, blue, yellow and aubergine purple) was also imported. As a reaction to these two types of porcelain blue-painted wares were accordingly adapted both in form and decoration, and there is evidence of a greater refinement in production. Polychrome-painted faience, however, was also made on a large scale. In contrast to the subtle efforts of Hoppesteyn, who worked in both high-fired colours and enamels, production was generally restricted to the high-fired colours green, yellow, purple and blue. A high-firing red and black were also developed, which placed high-fired polychrome Delftware of this period among the most technically advanced ceramics in history.

The most important faience-makers between 1660 and 1720 were members of the van Eenhoorn family: the Grieksche A factory was founded in Delft by Wouter van Eenhoorn (*d* 1679) in 1658 (no marked pieces by him are known); he was replaced by his son Samuel van Eenhoorn (1655–86) in 1678, who was in turn succeeded in 1686 by his brother-in-law Adriaensz. Kocks (*d* 1701). The factory remained in the family until 1722. Lambertus van Eenhoorn, one of Samuel's brothers, owned the Metalen Pot factory in Delft from 1691 to 1721. This factory was of great significance under Wouter and Samuel for the distinct improvement and refinement of blue-and-white faience mainly in the style of porcelain made in China during the

48. Pair of Delftware jardinières, h. 385 mm each, made at the Metalen Pot, Delft, *c.* 1690–1720 (Amsterdam, Rijksmuseum)

Wanli period (1573–1620) and Transitional style (1620–44). Their interpretations of these styles can be considered the first true chinoiserie decoration. Under Kocks, the most important supplier to the court of William III and Mary II, wares were chiefly decorated in the style of Chinese Kangxi wares (1662–1722) but also in the Louis XIV style; the latter was introduced into the Netherlands by the Huguenot Daniel Marot I, whose designs also influenced other factories (see fig. 48). Lambertus van Eenhorn and Kocks also produced very fine polychrome faience between 1690 and 1720. Decoration was often derived from imported goods or was, during periods of high import, deliberately different.

Around 1680 Japanese porcelain-makers vigorously increased their output of polychrome wares, incorporated other styles of decoration and began, at first on a small scale but after 1700 more extensively, to export Kakiemon and Imari porcelain made in Arita, Hizen Province (now Saga and Nagasaki prefectures), to Europe. This Japanese porcelain, which was quite different from Chinese porcelain decorated with the *famille verte* palette, was imitated in Delft just before 1700. The Grieksche A Factory was particularly successful at interpreting these designs (e.g. polychrome inkwell, 1701–22; Brussels, Musées Royaux A. & Hist.). During this second period of Delftware production (1685–1725) three categories of faience were made: a fine bright-blue painted faience, produced in numerous forms decorated with Chinese motifs, chinoiseries or European designs (e.g. tulip vase, late 17th century; Amsterdam, Rijksmus.); fine polychrome faience painted with high-fired colours on a black, dark-brown, olive-green or deep-blue ground (large and small decorative pieces were made in this style as well as household wares, e.g. black coffeepot, *c.* 1700; Delft, Stedel. Mus. Prinsenhof); and polychrome wares decorated with enamels, mainly imitating Japanese Imari porcelain (e.g. two

small polychrome flowerpots, 1721; Rotterdam, Mus. Boymans–van Beuningen).

From 1710 the Chinese exported Imari-style porcelain, known as Chinese Imari, into Europe. This porcelain and the Chinese porcelain painted in *famille rose* colours, which was introduced into the Netherlands from *c.* 1725, presented further competition to polychrome Delftware. This, however, was not the only reason for a 25-year decline in the Delftware industry that lasted until 1750, during which time several manufacturers ceased production. The economic depression, which had been apparent in Europe since *c.* 1650 (apart from a brief economic upturn between 1685 and 1700), reached its nadir in the Netherlands between 1725 and 1750. It was chiefly an agricultural crisis, but it affected the whole economy. In addition many faience factories and works were founded in Germany, France and England after 1700; they produced wares for their indigenous markets and so limited the export opportunities for the Delft factories. Eventually hard-paste European porcelain—produced from *c.* 1708–9 at Meissen—provided the uppermost social group, mainly in Germany, with luxury services and decorative wares so that this market was also lost to the Delftware producers. Between 1725 and 1755 the industry in Delft was reorganized and continued to develop earlier innovations. In addition to this production a great deal of coarsely decorated household wares was also produced, probably replacing to some degree the use of pewter.

The use of wall-tiles as a fashionable product in urban, middle-class houses in the western Netherlands had already ceased before 1650. Fully decorated tiles were used after *c.* 1640 chiefly in the prosperous country areas in the provinces of Holland, Zeeland and Friesland. In the last quarter of the 17th century tiles were exported in large amounts to Germany, Denmark, the southern Netherlands (Flanders), France and the Iberian Peninsula. In urban kitchens undecorated tiles or tiles featuring children's games or landscapes were used. In rural areas flowers and birds were popular, complemented after 1650 by ships and sea monsters. This remained unchanged until the end of the 17th century, and thereafter most tiles were decorated with landscapes and biblical subjects. After 1650 the most important centres of tile production were Rotterdam and Harlingen and Makkum in the province of Friesland. The tile pictures of seascapes and harbour scenes by Cornelis Boumeester (1652–1733) of Rotterdam, who often signed his work, are quite exceptional. In the 18th century the Aelmis family were very influential in the production of tiles in Rotterdam (see TILE, fig. 7). Other centres of production included Utrecht, Alkmaar and Amsterdam; large-scale tile pictures were exported to Portugal from Amsterdam by the van der Kloet and van Oort families. Factories in Harlingen (e.g. Schritsen, Zoutsloot (c. 1660–1910) and Kerkpoort (c. 1660–1910)), Makkum and briefly in Bolsward (1737–1810) in Friesland produced two main products: blue-and-white or purple-and-white wall-tiles and heavy, multicoloured maiolica dishes.

3. 1751–1830. Shortly after 1750 the European economy revived. Delft faience factories obtained additional opportunities after 1755 due to the stagnation of imports of German porcelain as a result of the Seven Years War (1756–63). After 30 years of limited production there was a positive upturn from 1755 to 1765. As well as the coarsely decorated household wares—by then already in production for 30 to 40 years and intended after 1750 for the increasingly prosperous rural population—many small polychrome figures, groups and tureens in the shape of animals and fruit were made in the style of German porcelain (e.g. lidded tureen, 1750–75; Brussels, Musées

Royaux A. & Hist.). Many luxury wares were also produced, some well painted in blue but for the most part decorated with high-temperature colours. In line with German porcelain, pieces decorated with enamels, principally in imitation of Meissen porcelain, were also made (e.g. tureen and dish from the Grieksche A Factory, 1750–75; The Hague, Gemeentemus.). Many pieces from this period were dated, and it seems that at least some of them were made for special occasions.

In 1764 it was once again stated that all faience objects had to be stamped with a mark; pieces were evidently marked only in periods of limited production. At such times there was a reversion to the former guild conditions. There were still about eight faience factories in Delft, all of which produced wares of an adequate standard; no single factory, however, was outstandingly innovative. The best-known names from this period are Zacharias Dextra, owner of the 3 Vergulden Astonnekens, and Johannes van Duin (d 1777), owner of the Porceleynen Schotel.

After 1775, as well as making everyday Delftwares, manufacturers supplied their Orangist customers with portraits of William V, Stadholder of the Netherlands, and his wife Wilhelmina of Prussia. A huge quantity of garnitures were made in a simple, Louis XV style, but designs were no longer adapted to new fashions. The invasion of the French armies in 1795 and the ensuing period of war (until 1815) curbed production once again. There were careful attempts to make creamware (cream-coloured earthenware with a lead glaze) in Delft; little, however, is known about the output and the factories involved. The pieces known to have been made in Delft are marked PICCARDT DELFT, for Henricus A. Piccardt, who from 1800 was the owner of the Porceleyne Fles Faience Factory.

49. Faience ewer, h. 190 mm, and basin, diam. 370 mm, decorated in enamels, made in the factory of Johan van Kerckhoff, Arnhem, c. 1760–70 (Amsterdam, Rijksmuseum)

50. Hard-paste porcelain tureen, h. 205 mm, made in Weesp, decorated in enamels at the factory of Joannes de Mol, Oud Loosdrecht, 1770–74 (Amsterdam, Rijksmuseum)

The decline in imported porcelain from Germany in 1756 encouraged the establishment of new faience factories. In 1759 Johan van Kerckhoff (*d* 1773) started a faience factory in Arnhem staffed partly with German workers. In 1767, however, the first marketing problems arose, and after van Kerckhoff's death the business folded. The best Arnhem pieces in blue, purple and polychrome (using both high-fired colours and enamels) were decorated with fairly large-scale flowers, figures and landscapes with ornamental borders (see fig. 49). The scale of the decoration in relation to the size of the object attracted attention, as Delft faience painters were accustomed to filling completely the surface with small figures surrounded by overlapping motifs.

In Friesland decorative ware of high quality was produced in the second half of the 18th century, as were high-quality *tegeltableaux* ('tile-panels'). These two products can be distinguished from Delftware by a lesser degree of refinement of both the materials and the painting. However, they have a surprising charm because of their unique style and character.

In 1757 the first Dutch porcelain factory was founded in Weesp, near Amsterdam. It flourished briefly between 1760 and 1765 under the direction of the owner, Count Bertram Gronsveld Diepenbroick-Impel. The factory produced high-quality, hard-paste porcelain tea-services, statues and parts of services, particularly large and small tureens, decorated with enamels in a restrained Louis XV style (see fig. 50). Some of the workers were German and French, including the French–German painter Louis Gerverot (1747–1829), who before his arrival in Weesp had also worked in Niderviller and Fürstenberg. The factory was already encountering problems by 1767, and production ceased in 1771.

In 1774 Joannes de Mol, minister of the village of Oud Loosdrecht, founded a porcelain factory to take over the stock and some undecorated wares from Weesp. The factory at Oud Loosdrecht was intended to provide work for the impoverished local people, but again they relied on German designers and painters. Until 1784 a variety of table-services, tea- and coffee-services, pierced wares and all kinds of small household items were made. Wares were well designed and decorated with floral sprays, birds and scenes, partly in underglaze blue but mostly in polychrome enamels. During the early period wares were made in a restrained Louis XV style, while later they adopted the Louix XVI style (e.g. ewer and basin, *c.* 1780; Stockholm, Nmus.). In 1786 the Oud Loosdrecht Factory closed, but the existing stock and a large quantity of undecorated porcelain was moved to a factory in Ouder Amstel, close to Amsterdam. There, large quantities of services and household items decorated with pastoral scenes, animals, birds and flowers were made. In 1800 the factory was run by the firm of George Dommer, who in 1809 moved the whole enterprise to Nieuwer Amstel. It is not certain in which year production ceased.

In 1776 Anton Lyncker (*d* 1781) founded a factory for the production of hard-paste porcelain in The Hague. Soft-paste porcelain from Doornik and hard-paste porcelain from Ansbach and other places, was also decorated there. The designs were mainly in Louis XV and Neoclassical styles and were very delicately painted (e.g. ewer and basin, 1775–80; The Hague, Gemeentemus.). After Lyncker's death, his widow and son continued the business, but production finally ceased in 1790.

After 1760 the Dutch ceramics industry suffered from strong foreign competition. In 1765 German porcelain was once again imported into the Netherlands in addition to soft-paste services from Tournai and porcelain from the factory of Sèvres. For the producers of Delftware, however, the continuing popularity of English creamware from the factory of Josiah Wedgwood finally crushed the once ubiquitous Delftware industry.

4. AFTER 1830. In 1836 Petrus Regout (1801–78) set up the Sphinx Factory in Maastricht, where, from 1845, with English technical help and assistance from English workers, transfer-printed earthenwares were made. As a result of this initiative, Maastricht became a centre for the production of table-services, and *c.* 1860 another factory, the Société Céramique, was founded. The services from these factories are very English in style and decoration and are distinguishable only by their mark. Numerous services were exported, especially from the Sphinx Factory, to Asia, South America and the USA.

In 1876 Joost Thooft of the Piccardt family assumed control of the Porceleyne Fles, the only surviving Delftware factory, where production was confined to creamware decorated partly with transfer-printing. Thooft wanted to revive the industry, using similar processes to those developed by Wedgwood. Under the direction of Adolf Le Comte (1850–1921), who came to the works as artistic adviser, a new product was created: tin glazes were no longer employed, and instead mostly blue decoration was applied straight on to the body under a transparent glaze. The design and decoration for some of these wares were partly exact copies of 17th- and 18th-century Delft-ware; the majority, however, were original designs by Le Comte.

After 1850 the Tichelaar Factory in Friesland, which had been producing tin-glazed earthenware since the end of the 17th century, switched to decorative earthenware and, to a lesser extent, tiles. Initially this earthenware consisted of large-scale plaques, but after some time the factory began to produce large quantities of blue or multicoloured faience, following the examples of earlier Delftware. (In the 20th century the factory was successfully to develop its own idiom.)

In 1883 Wilhelm Wolff von Gudenberg (1855–1930) founded the Rozenburg Factory (1886–1914) in The Hague for the production of artwares. From 1880 he had been employed at the Porceleyne Fles as a technical and artistic expert. An innovative style of wares was introduced in 1884, which coincided with the arrival of T. C. A. COLENBRANDER: bold, abstract underglaze patterns designed by Colenbrander were introduced (e.g. dish, 1887; The Hague, Gemeentemus.). Colenbrander left the factory in 1889 and was succeeded by J. JURRIAAN KOK, who in 1899 developed a soft-paste porcelain. This so-called 'eggshell' porcelain produced in Art Nouveau shapes was decorated by such artists as Sam Schellink with naturalistic motifs including birds, flowers and insects (see fig. 51). These wares were particularly successful at the Exposition Universelle of 1900 in Paris. Earthenwares designed in the style of Rozenburg wares were also made in Purmerend (1894–1904) by Wed. N. S. A. Brandjes & Co., by the firm Holland (1893–1920) in Utrecht and in Gouda after 1898 by such factories as the Plateelbakkerij Zuid Holland. After c. 1910 the Plateelbakkerij Zuid Holland developed its own style, including a form of matt decoration.

The influence of William Morris, the Dutch translation (1894) of Walter Crane's *The Claims of Decorative Art* (1892) and ideas relating to the role of art in a new, socialist society were very strong in the Netherlands. In 1898 the jeweller Willem Hoeker founded the earthenware factory Amstelhoek, near Amsterdam. In 1900 it was enlarged with a workshop for metalwork directed by Jan Eisenlöffel and a furniture workshop under Willem Penaat. The ceramics were designed until c. 1900–01 by the sculptor Lambertus Zijl and thereafter under his direction by Christiaan J. van der Hoef (1875–1933); they were made from red- or yellow-firing clays partly inlaid with white-fired clay. Decoration was geometric or based on abstract plant and/or animal motifs. The factory was under the technical direction of Govert M. Augustijn, from a family of potters in Bergen-op-Zoom. In 1902 Augustijn returned to Bergen-op-Zoom, where he ran the earthenware factory De Kat, which made wares in the Amstelhoek style.

In 1895 J. M. Lob founded the Distel Delftware Factory in Amsterdam, where at first earthenwares in the Rozenburg style were made; after 1902, however, BERT NIENHUIS was appointed head of the decorative department, and wares were then decorated with matt glazes and geometric designs. All these factories, however, existed only for a short time: Amstelhoek went bankrupt in 1903 and in a scaled-down form merged with Distel in 1910 (closed 1923). De Kat ceased production in 1914. Related

51. Soft-paste 'eggshell' porcelain vase, decorated by Sam Schellink, h. 277 mm, made at the Rozenburg Factory, The Hague, 1902 (Amsterdam, Rijksmuseum)

to the production of these factories was the work of the firm Amphora (1908–33) in Oegstgeest, where, under van der Hoef, decorative wares were made. After 1915 imitations of Rozenburg wares were also made. At the Arnhemsche Fayencefabriek (1907–36) wares with matt glaze were made, which were strongly influenced by those of Nienhuis for Distel. The work of the potter Willem C. Brouwer was more traditional than earthenwares produced at Amstelhoek; after a period of study and experimentation in Gouda, he ran a pottery in Leiderdorp from 1901 where fine modern decorative and household items were made in a crafts tradition.

After World War I independent art potters set up in business: Chris Lannooy learnt the profession as a painter at Rozenburg (1895) and at a workshop in Gouda, which made simple flowerpots (1899). From c. 1910, after a series of experiments, he concentrated on the production of vases and dishes decorated with fluid glazes; only his early work was seldom painted. After working as a designer at Distel, Nienhuis taught at the Haarlem School voor Kunstnijverheid (1906–12), the Handfertigkeitsseminar in Hagen, Germany (1911–17), and the Quellinus Kunstnijverheidsschool in Amsterdam (until 1938). Through these posts he influenced a generation of potters who became active after World War II. Also worthy of note during this period is the art potter Johannes H. Andrée, who first worked in his father's pottery factory in Apeldoorn but after *c.* 1920 began to work independently, making refined decorative wares with monochrome glazes. Important factories included the firm Eskaf of Steenwijk, where, from 1919, well-designed decorative and household wares with monochrome glazes were made under the direction of the sculptor Hildo Krop (1884–1970), and the Ram Pottery founded in Arnhem in 1920, which made wares to designs by T. C. A. Colenbrander. All these ventures were short-lived due to the economic crisis of 1929.

After World War II table-services were made in Maastricht by the factories Sphinx and Société Céramique (merged 1958). A third factory, Mosa, founded by one of Petrus Regout's sons, made porcelain services. The Delftware factories Zuid-Holland (1898–1965) and Goedewaagen (1779–1961) in Gouda and the Fris Factory in Edam (1947–69) produced services with modern designs in pastel shades. Small establishments made vases and flowerpots in the craft manner, and after 1960 there was a growing number of art potters.

In 1956 the Porceleyne Fles in Delft began an experimental department under Theo Dobbelman. Such young and later very successful studio potters as Lies Cosijn and Adriek Westenenk were invited to experiment with materials, designs and decorative techniques. The venture proved to be very successful. Another group of self-taught potters, including Jan van der Vaart (*b* 1931), Johan van Loon (*b* 1934) and Sonja Landweer, worked in Amsterdam shortly before 1960. Van de Vaart taught at the Rietveldacademie in Amsterdam (1968–); van Loon, who had trained as a textile designer, worked for the Kongelige Porcelænsfabrik in Copenhagen producing individual wares and in 1971 became a lecturer at the art school in Enschede. The younger generation of studio potters was internationally orientated, and influences from England (Hans Coper and Lucie Rie), Germany and Denmark were evident. Technical advances in kilns and improved porcelain pastes made increasingly high-fired products possible. After 1970 mainly stoneware and porcelain were produced, and such potters as Geert Lap (*b* 1951), Leen Quist and Babs Haenen (*b* 1948) won international acclaim.

BIBLIOGRAPHY

B. Rackham: *Early Netherlands Maiolica* (London, 1926)
F. W. Hudig: *Delfter Fayence* (Berlin, 1929)
C. H. Jonge: *Oud-Nederlandsche maiolica en Delftsch aardewerk* (Amsterdam, 1947)
W. J. Rust: *Nederlands porselein* (Amsterdam, 1952)
A. J. de Lorm: *Catalogus van Arnhems aardewerk* (Arnhem, 1961)
M. G. Spruit-Ledeboer: *Nederlandse keramiek, 1900–1975* (Assen, 1976)
W. M. Zappey: 'Amstelporselein', *Vrienden Ned. Cer.: Mededbl.*, lxxxvi–lxxxvii/2–3 (1977)
E. J. van Straaten: *Dubbelgebakken aardewerknijverheid in Nederland, 1876–1940* (The Hague, 1979); also in *Mededbl., Ned. Ver. Vrienden Cer.*, liv–lv/2–3 (1979)
D. Korf: *Nederlandse majolica* (Bussum, 1981)
J. D. van Dam: 'Geleyersgoet en Hollants porceleyn', *Mededbl., Ned. Ver. Vrienden Cer.*, cviii/4 (1982), pp. 3–93 [with Eng. summary]
P. J. Tichelaar: *Fries tinglazuuraardewerk* (Leeuwarden, 1982)
T. Martin and others: *Rozenburg, 1883–1917* (The Hague, 1983)
E. Schaap, J. D. van Dam and P. J. Tichelaar: *Dutch Tiles in the Philadelphia Museum of Art* (Philadelphia, 1984)
P. J. Tichelaar: *Catalogus tinglazuur-aardewerk en tegels*, Makkum, Fries. Aardewerkmus. De Waag cat. (Makkum, 1984)
M. G. Spruit-Ledeboer: *Nederlandse keramiek, 1975–1985* (Amsterdam, 1985)
M. R. Bogaers, K. Gaillard and M. L. Ten Horn-van Nispen: *De Porceleyne Fles* (Utrecht, 1986)
J. de Kleyn: *Volksaardewerk in Nederland sedert de late middeleeuwen* (Lochem, 1986)
Amstelhoek, 1897–1910 (exh. cat., ed. J. D. van Dam and A. Hidding; Leeuwarden, Gemeentelijk Mus. Het Princessehof, 1986)
J. D. van Dam: *Nederlands tegels* (Utrecht, 1988) [with Eng. summary]
W. M. Zappey, A. L. den Blaauwen and A. W. A. van der Goes: *Loosdrechts porselein, 1774–1784* (Zwolle, 1988)
J. D. van Dam: *Gedateerd Delfts aardewerk* (Amsterdam and Zwolle, 1991)
M. R. Bogaers: *Drukdecors op Maastrichts aardewerk, 1850–1900* (Lochem, 1992)
J. D. van Dam and G. J. van der Hoek: *Index op Mededelingenblad Vrienden van de Nederlandse Ceramiek* [i–lii], *Mededbl. Ned. Ver. Vrienden Cer.* [liii–cxliii] and *Vorman uit Vuur* [cxliv–cl] (in preparation)

J. D. VAN DAM

VIII. Glass.

The Romans had introduced glass to the Netherlands, either importing it or actually making it there, but it was not until the 10th or 11th century that glass production began to prosper again, specifically in the wooded parts of the southern Netherlands. Window-glass, drinking glasses, bottles and beakers were presumably imported to the north from the southern Netherlands, France and Germany.

In the 16th century crystal glass was brought to the Netherlands by skilled Venetian glassblowers. After the fall of Antwerp in 1585, many glass workshops moved to the northern Netherlands. The rise of the United Netherlands and the emergence of a wealthy merchant class with refined artistic tastes provided a strong impetus to the glass industry in the 17th century. Amsterdam, in particular, attracted many Italian glassblowers despite the potential fire risk of locating furnaces in an urban area; The Hague, Rotterdam and Haarlem also became important glassmaking centres, and there were glass workshops in Hoorn, Muiden, Dordrecht, Delft, Utrecht, Amersfoort, Zutphen, Nijmegen, Zwolle, 's Hertogenbosch, Maastricht and Middelburg. Most of these workshops survived until the late 18th century, and some—including those in Delft and 's Hertogenbosch—continued into the 19th century. The mass-produced drinking glasses *à la façon de Venise* were of good quality, richly patterned with such fanciful decoration as *latticinio* and *reticello*, which commonly consists of white, blue and green glass threads combined with enamel and gilding. Among the most popular items were winged glasses, with delicately and sinuously curled wings on either side of the stem. In the 17th century some glass forms were developed in the Netherlands: the large mug with a metal lid, the tall, fluted glass and the onion-shaped bottle with a long neck. *Pasglazen* (tall beakers), bell beakers and mill glasses were intended for less formal occasions, when the drinking was likely to be particularly heavy.

In the Netherlands it was a favoured pastime to decorate glass with cold-colour painting or with diamond-point engraving. The latter was introduced by Venetian glassblowers and was a highly popular technique from the early 17th century until the late 18th, especially among amateurs practising a distinctively Dutch style. They worked mostly on commemorative glasses, engraved for special occasions, and many examples are both signed and dated. One

52. Glass roemer, engraved with flowers and insects by Anna Roemer Visscher, h. 160 mm, 1621 (Amsterdam, Rijksmuseum)

particularly competent glass-engraver was Anna Roemer Visscher (1583–1651), who engraved simple mottoes as well as images of plants, fruits and insects, which she copied from prints on to *Waldglas* beakers and roemers (e.g. of 1621; Amsterdam, Rijksmus.; see fig. 52). Her sister Maria Tesselschade (1594–1649) was also a talented diamond-point engraver, as was Anna Maria van Schurman (1607–78). These women were in addition accomplished embroiderers (*see* §XI, 2 below). Willem Mooleyser (*fl* 1660–97) was the first Dutch engraver to fill in the figures that he used in decoration, whereas only outlines had been engraved previously. Mooleyser worked on glasses *à la façon de Venise* and often took his images from prints of peasant scenes. Willem Jacob van Heemskerk (1613–92) of Leiden specialized in adding edifying sayings and short poems to bottles, plates and drinking glasses; his graceful and fluent lines are unparalleled achievements in the field of glass calligraphy (e.g. beaker, 1679; Amsterdam, Rijksmus.).

Towards the end of the 17th century Bohemian crystal and English lead glass, both suited to engraving and cutting, were imitated in the Netherlands. The quality of glass, however, remained slightly inferior, so that the import of foreign glass, in particular from England, soon adversely affected the Dutch glass industry. In the 18th century the more solid types of glass were used for wheel-engraving, a technique much practised in Germany. The most accomplished Dutch wheel-engraver was Jacob Sang (*d* 1783) from Amsterdam. In the 1720s the diamond-point engraver Frans Greenwood (1680–1763) of Dordrecht invented the technique known as stippling, in which the image on the glass is built up out of a mass of dots showing a variety of densities; the effects achieved rivalled those found in mezzotint prints. Greenwood worked after prints, whereas AERT SCHOUMAN worked from his own designs and was, moreover, a professional artist rather than an amateur. The stipple technique was particularly fashionable in Dordrecht and The Hague during the 18th century.

In the 18th century German and English glassware influenced not only the composition of Dutch glass but also its design: forms became simpler, goblets tended to be straight instead of curved, stems became heavier and the base would often be massive and straight. Twist-stemmed glasses, with white and coloured glass threads intertwined in the stem, came to the Netherlands from England. In the Netherlands fragile pipe-stemmed glasses were developed; these usually remained undecorated.

In the 19th century the glass industry in the Netherlands was not of great importance. Early in the 20th century an attempt was made to improve the situation: the Kristalunie in Maastricht and the Royal Leerdam Glassworks, near Utrecht, commissioned artists to make new glass designs, which, they hoped, would revive the Dutch industry. Designs by the architects K. P. C. de Bazel and H. P. Berlage resulted from this initiative. In the late 20th century such experimental artists and designers as A. D. COPIER and Floris Meydam (*b* 1919) succeeded in gaining an international reputation for Leerdam.

BIBLIOGRAPHY
E. Schrijver: *Glas en kristal* (Haarlem, 1980)
J. R. Liefkes: *Museum Mr Simon van Gijn: Catalogus van de glasverzameling* (Dordrecht, 1987)
HILLIE SMIT

IX. Metalwork.

1. Gold and silver. 2. Base metals.

1. GOLD AND SILVER.

(i) Before 1600. (ii) 1600–1813. (iii) 1814–1900. (iv) After 1900.

(i) Before 1600. Most silverware made before the 16th century in the Low Countries was produced in the more prosperous southern areas (now Belgium), and consequently silver made in the northern regions before the mid-16th century is indistinguishable from that made in the south. It was only after independence in 1579 that Dutch silversmiths began to use distinctly Dutch forms and styles, which were largely a synthesis of the styles of the southern Low Countries and the Rhineland. The main centres of 16th-century Dutch goldsmiths' work were Amsterdam (*see* AMSTERDAM, §IV, 2), Utrecht and Delft,

and those of lesser importance Zwolle, Deventer and 's Hertogenbosch.

To a large extent the main characteristics of 16th-century Dutch silver reflect the social and political structures of the region. As in Germany (but unlike England) plate was made and marked in a large number of towns, reflecting the absence of central government. There was no powerful aristocracy in the Netherlands, and the considerable quantity of domestic plate made for private use is indicative of the more democratic nature of society, a tendency that continued throughout the 17th and 18th centuries (see §(ii) below). There was, for example, little demand for either the *Schatzkammer* objects made by goldsmiths for the leading courts of Europe or the more expensive silver-gilt objects. In the Netherlands most plate was left in the white, although it was generally made to a high technical standard.

Knowledge of the evolution of styles and forms of early Dutch silver is limited, as only a tiny percentage of plate survives. Documentary evidence and sporadic survivals, however, make it possible to identify the principal trends. As early as 1517 the Renaissance style was accepted in Utrecht, where a contract for the manufacture of a set of sanctuary gates in that year specified that they should be in the 'Antique' (i.e. Renaissance) style rather than the 'Modern' (i.e. Gothic). It is difficult to ascertain the prevalence of the Renaissance style in early Dutch silver, as conservative taste continued to prevail in certain sections of society, notably the guilds. The earliest surviving plate with Renaissance features dates from the 1530s and includes a coconut-cup (c. 1530; Amsterdam, Rijksmus.) and a chalice of 1535 made in 's Hertogenbosch.

In place of a strong aristocratic clientele, the most important patrons of goldsmiths were civic bodies and guilds. Large quantities of plate were commissioned for civic banquets, such as that illustrated in Anthuenis Claeissins's *Banquet of Magistrates* (1574; Bruges, Groeningemus.). A particular form of civic patronage initiated by the town councils of Deventer, Zwolle and Kampen in the 1530s consisted of ordering commemorative cups in memory of former council members. These are usually engraved with the names and coats of arms of the deceased (examples in Zwolle, Prov. Overijssels Mus.). The somewhat conservative character of guild commissions is illustrated by two of the most important surviving 16th-century silver pieces, both of which are drinking horns: one made in 1547 for the arquebusiers' guild of Amsterdam and the other in 1566 for the St George's guild (both Amsterdam, Hist. Mus.). The decoration of the former is in the Gothic style, and this type of object was itself somewhat unfashionable by the mid-16th century. The early Mannerist style, which is occasionally evident in Dutch plate (e.g. an Amsterdam beadle's badge; 1548), failed to evolve into a distinct style in the Netherlands, as it did in Antwerp (see ANTWERP, §III, 4), probably also a result of conservative taste.

For both civic and private patrons the most prestigious type of object was, as elsewhere, the standing-cup and cover (e.g. of 1569; Amsterdam, Rijksmus.; see fig. 53). These were generally made for display rather than practical use. Other vessel forms fashionable in the Netherlands included large, tall beakers and shallow-bowled tazzas.

53. Silver standing-cup and cover with the crest of the van Beresteyn family, h. 260 mm, Amsterdam, 1569 (Amsterdam, Rijksmuseum)

Beakers were particularly common as they were used not only for domestic purposes but also as the standard form of communion-cup in the Protestant Reformed Church. These objects are often superbly decorated, illustrating the high level of technical accomplishment of goldsmiths during this period. Beakers are often finely engraved, and the centres of the dishes on tazzas are finely embossed with pictorial scenes.

Another type of object associated with the Netherlands is the silver glass holder. Made to support *Waldglas* roemers, these highly elaborate objects are generally in the form of a baluster stem surmounted by three brackets, the angles of which could be adjusted to grip the base of a glass by means of a screw mechanism contained within the body. It is likely that these luxurious objects were made principally for display, although some 17th-century paintings show them in use. However, the skills of goldsmiths were not generally matched by the development of original forms.

The maritime basis of the Dutch economy led to a considerable interest in the natural exotica that arrived on returning ships. These items were often elaborately mounted in silver or silver gilt, and coconut- and nautilus-cups in particular are often found with Dutch marks. The production of outstanding nautilus-cups is especially associated with Delft and Utrecht, although little survives from Delft that dates from before *c.* 1580. The greatest 16th-century Dutch goldsmith, JACQUES BYLIVERT, was born and trained in Delft before leaving in 1578 to seek employment in the Medici court workshop in Florence. Many nautilus-cups are depicted in late 16th- and 17th-century Dutch still-lifes. A nautilus-cup (1596; Toledo, OH, Mus. A.) made by Jan van Royesteyn of Utrecht and decorated with figures of satyrs, sea monsters and dolphins appears in a still-life by Pieter Claesz (1634; Münster, Westfäl. Landesmus.).

BIBLIOGRAPHY

J. W. Fredericks: *Dutch Silver*, 4 vols (The Hague, 1952–61)
K. A. Citroen: *Amsterdam Silversmiths and their Marks* (New York, 1975)
J. F. Hayward: *Virtuoso Goldsmiths and the Triumph of Mannerism, 1540–1620* (London, 1976)
Kunst voor de beeldenst orm [Art before the iconoclasm] (exh. cat. by T. W. Kloek and others, Amsterdam, Rijksmus., 1986)

(ii) *1600–1813*. The political circumstances of the United Provinces during the 17th and 18th centuries affected the character of Dutch silver in several respects. Firstly, the absence of strong central government due to the federation of largely autonomous states meant that the goldsmiths' craft continued to flourish in many towns, despite the gradually increasing domination of Amsterdam (*see* AMSTERDAM, §IV, 2). Secondly, the existence of a large and prosperous middle class ensured a more widespread market for plate than existed in other countries, while at the same time suppressing demand for some of the more ostentatious types of plate. Whereas the most important patrons in England and in France were the court and aristocracy, a major role in patronage and the determination of style in the Netherlands was played by wealthy merchants and civic bodies, for example guilds and town councils.

Throughout the 17th and 18th centuries wares were stamped with a maker's mark, date letter and the coat of arms of the town. In 1663 a fourth mark, the lion of Holland, was introduced and was gradually adopted by other provinces. Plate was marked in over 50 towns, although their relative importance as centres of production fluctuated. In the early 17th century the most important centres were Utrecht, Delft, Haarlem and Amsterdam.

Towns that had been major centres during the medieval period, for example Deventer, Breda, Bergen-op-Zoom and Nijmegen, were in decline, while Groningen, Leeuwarden, Rotterdam and Dordrecht became more important, although all were eclipsed by Amsterdam and The Hague. Goldsmiths in The Hague, the seat of government, attracted patronage from both the court of the House of Orange and resident foreigners, while the manufacture of gold and silver in Amsterdam, the commercial capital, grew faster than anywhere else. In 1614 Amsterdam had about 300 goldsmiths, compared with 80 in The Hague and 60 in Haarlem. By the mid-18th century the disparity had increased dramatically, with between 400 and 500 goldsmiths working in Amsterdam alone, more than the total in the rest of the country.

(a) Style and decoration. The first distinctly Dutch style to emerge from Mannerism was the AURICULAR STYLE, largely created by the VAN VIANEN family of Utrecht. Plate in this style is characterized by embossed fleshy scrolls and abstract forms that emphasize the malleability of silver. The evolution of the style may partly reflect the popular interest in anatomical and botanical studies in the Netherlands. At their most extreme the works of Paulus van Vianen and his brother, Adam van Vianen, are highly sculptural. Such objects as Paulus van Vianen's 'Diana and Acteon' ewer and dish (1613; Amsterdam, Rijksmus.; for illustration *see* VIANEN, VAN, (2)) or a series of figural salt-cellars (*c.* 1620; Amsterdam, Rijksmus.) by Adam van Vianen were conceived more as works of art for the collectors' cabinet than as utilitarian plate.

During the second quarter of the 17th century the style was promoted by Dutch goldsmiths working in other cities, for example Christiaen van Vianen in London, Johannes Lutma (i) (e.g. gilt covered cup, 1639; Baltimore, MD, Walters A.G.) in Amsterdam and Andries Grill (1604–65) in The Hague. The first two, in particular, produced works in a fully matured interpretation of the Auricular style. Other goldsmiths throughout the Netherlands in the mid-17th century worked in a simplified version of the style that used less intricate relief and was better suited to the requirements of practical plate. It evolved into a separate style, characterized by the use of embossing, that placed equal emphasis on the malleable qualities of the metal and on its attractive reflective qualities. Large, plain candlesticks and other plate (e.g. dish, 1646; Culemborg, SS Barbara and Antony), of impressive size but thin gauge, continued to be made in this style until the last quarter of the 17th century.

An equally popular decorative technique was engraving, especially in Friesland and the north-east Netherlands, where embossing seems to have been less popular. The styles of engraved decoration generally followed that of contemporary embossed plate, often combining abstract Auricular ornament or conventional cartouches of fruit and foliage with pictorial scenes; the last were frequently derived from printed sources, for example a beaker (1648; Rotterdam, Boymans–van Beuningen) engraved with a map showing the siege of Breda in 1637 from a print by Claes Jansz. Visscher I.

54. Silver tureen by Adam Loofs, w. 238 mm, The Hague, 1701 (The Hague, Gemeentemuseum)

After the mid-17th century the Auricular style was replaced by a fashion for botanically accurate floral decoration that was paralleled by both marquetry decoration on furniture and the contemporary vogue for flower paintings. This new style evolved from a transitional phase characterized by the use of fleshy, botanical ornament. Among the best-known examples is a set of sconces (1647; Rotterdam, Mus. Boymans–van Beuningen) by MICHIEL DE BRUYN VAN BERENDRECHT of Utrecht. The floral style seems to have evolved contemporaneously in the Netherlands and France and to have been introduced later in England.

The technique that was most suitable for the style was embossing, of which CLAES FRANSEN BAERDT was a notable exponent, although attractive examples with engraved decoration or cagework are also extant. The most important centres for the production of embossed silver in the second half of the 17th century were The Hague and Amsterdam. In these towns, the richest in the country, the greatest demand was for large-scale, display silver (e.g. covered cup, 1660; Deventer, Mus. De Waag), to which the embossed, floral style was well suited. Among its leading practitioners were Hans Brechtel (1608–75) and Adriaen van Hoecke (1635–1716) in The Hague and Johannes Lutma (ii) and Michiel Esselbeck (1611–71) in Amsterdam.

In the late 17th century a new style, strongly French in character, was introduced by Huguenot craftsmen, for example Richard Musseau (fl 1694–1702), who moved to the Netherlands after their expulsion from France during the 1680s. Many settled in Amsterdam and The Hague, and the style flourished more in these cities than elsewhere.

In The Hague the development of the style reflected the taste of William, Prince of Orange (later William III of England), whose patronage of Daniel Marot I did much to promote the style.

The Huguenot style in Dutch silver is characterized by carefully considered proportions, a subtle balance of plain and decorated surfaces and a greater use of cast components. A new repertory of ornament, for example classical motifs, cut-card decoration, lambrequins, husks and gadroons, was introduced, creating a more formal effect than the preceding floral style (e.g. silver tureen by Adam Loofs (fl 1660–1710), 1701; The Hague, Gemeentemus.; see fig. 54). Dutch silversmiths who were working outside court circles retained their predilection for embossed decoration on wares of relatively thin gauge, but the essential features of the Huguenot style appeared on ordinary domestic silver in the form of more restrained ornament. Examples of teaware and coffeeware from the second quarter of the 18th century, for example, survive in large quantities and are generally decorated with broad bands of flutes between narrower bands of embossed, formal foliage (e.g. coffee-urn, 1729; Amsterdam, Rijksmus.).

There is little evidence of the Rococo style in Dutch silver until the mid-18th century, and even then the forms, rather than the decorative features, of the style were favoured by silversmiths and patrons. The most notable exponents of the style operated outside the mainstream of the Dutch silversmiths' trade. The Huguenot brothers Louis Metayer and Philippe Metayer were born in Rouen and worked in the Netherlands during the mid-18th century. They made gold boxes as well as plate and specialized in finely chased relief decoration. Their finest surviving work is an embossed gold covered cup (1754; Amsterdam, Rijksmus.; see fig. 55). The survival of such unusual works, however, emphasizes the lack of demand in the Netherlands for elaborate goldsmiths' work in comparison with that of other northern European countries.

Broad, smooth flutes and undulating surfaces were popular on silverware during the 1750s and 1760s, as were

55. Gold covered cup by Louis Metayer and Philippe Metayer, h. 240 mm, Amsterdam, 1754 (Amsterdam, Rijksmuseum)

forms inspired by fruits, for example a teapot and milk jug in the form of melons (1765; Arnhem, Gemeentemus.). In comparison with silverware produced elsewhere, chased or applied Rococo ornament and engraved heraldic decoration were relatively uncommon. Two other successful practitioners of the Rococo style were REYNIER BRANDT and Johannes Schiotling (1730–99), both of whom ran large workshops in Amsterdam during the 1760s and early 1770s.

The Neo-classical movement also failed to become popular until the 1770s. The leading goldsmiths in Amsterdam during the early phase of Neo-classicism continued to be Brandt and Schiotling (e.g. tureen, 1780; Amsterdam, Hist. Mus.). As with the Rococo style, the Dutch response to Neo-classicism was distinctly muted when compared with contemporary French and English silver. Dutch silver from the last quarter of the 18th century is characterized by the use of thin gauge metal and austere forms and decoration. There is little evidence of the embossed and applied cast ornament that distinguishes silver made in London.

During the French occupation (1795–1814) the use of gilding, for example, that was so fashionable in France during the Empire period, was never widely popular in the Netherlands; Dutch silver continued to be characterized by geometric forms, plain surfaces and restrained ornament (e.g. oval box decorated with piercing and beading, 1800; Amsterdam, Rijksmus.). The massive and ostentatious products of the leading manufacturers in London and Paris in the early 19th century, for example Rundell, Bridge & Rundell or Jean Baptiste Claude Odiot, are generally absent from Dutch silver.

(b) Forms. The range of forms favoured by Dutch silversmiths and their patrons was never as extensive as that of countries with more aristocratic patronage. Throughout the 17th and 18th centuries, however, specific types of plate and decorative techniques were associated with certain regions. At the end of the 16th century and the beginning of the 17th the dominant centres of production of elaborate goldsmiths' work were Utrecht, Delft and Amsterdam. Such objects as nautilus-cups, tankards and drinking-horns made for the guilds are in the Mannerist style and do not display any distinctively Dutch features. During this period the tazza, or standing-dish, was popular in the Netherlands. The broad, shallow centre of the dish was ideally suited to pictorial embossing or engraving.

Other objects of a ceremonial or decorative nature that are typically Dutch include pairs of standing-cups and covers (often commissioned for use at guild banquets), silver glass holders and the so-called 'windmill-cups'. Glass holders were conceived as elaborate stems designed to be attached to the feet of glass roemers, the standard Dutch drinking vessels of the period (e.g. set of 1609; Amsterdam, Hist. Mus. and Rijksmus.; *see* AMSTERDAM, fig. 6). Windmill-cups are a Dutch version of the wager-cup and take the form of a miniature windmill surmounting an inverted cup (e.g. in Amsterdam, Rijksmus.). The sails of the windmill were turned by blowing through a tube mounted to the side of the cup, and the wager involved drinking the contents of the cup before the sails stopped.

56. Silver wedding casket, 88×73×53 mm, Bolsward, 1650 (Leeuwarden, Fries Museum)

The most characteristic Dutch vessel of the 17th century was the beaker, which performed the same function in the Netherlands as the tankard in Germany and, to an extent, the standing-cup and cover in England: it was not only a large, domestic vessel suitable for beer but also a symbol of wealth and as such was frequently decorated with sophisticated engraved ornament. Engraved beakers from Bolsward, Leeuwarden and Zwolle are among the finest surviving examples of this type. Regional variations in decoration occur—a spiked wreath usually appears around the base of beakers made in Friesland and Groningen (e.g. of 1619–20; Groningen, Groninger Mus.)—but the same basic, tapering, cylindrical form was used for beakers made throughout the Netherlands.

Forms generally made only in the northern Netherlands during the 17th century include wedding caskets (*knottekistje*) and brandy bowls (*brandewijnskom*). The former were used to hold coins that were presented by a man to his prospective bride (e.g. of 1650 made in Bolsward; Leeuwarden, Fries Mus.; see fig. 56), while the latter were associated with ceremonies of childbirth and are usually octagonal or oval with two flat, cast handles. The bowls are decorated either with engraved or embossed ornament (e.g. of 1651; Leeuwarden, Fries Mus.).

The most prestigious type of plate in the first half of the 17th century continued to be the ewer and basin, which was used as a vehicle for all styles of decoration from the Mannerist and Auricular to the embossed floral. The importance of the ewer and basin in the second half of the 17th century, however, began to decline with the increasing popularity of such other large-scale forms as the toilet service (e.g. of 1665; The Hague, Gemeentemus.), display pieces for the sideboard and the layette basket. The silver layette basket is a form particularly associated with the Netherlands and was designed to contain the linen needed for new-born children. These shallow, oblong baskets are generally embossed in the floral style and fitted with large, flat handles. Few examples are extant. One of the finest was made by Hans Brechtel of The Hague (1652; Dutch Royal Col.). Few appear to have been made after the 17th century. Sets of large covered jars and beakers, known as garnitures, inspired by imported Chinese porcelain and made to decorate mantelpieces, were also popular.

The range of Dutch domestic silver expanded considerably in the late 17th century and the early 18th. The most dramatic developments were associated with the fashion for drinking tea and coffee. Large urns with one or three taps (*kraantjeskannen*) were used to dispense coffee mixed with milk and sometimes cinnamon. Large numbers of teapots, -kettles and -caddies were produced in The Hague, Amsterdam and towns in the north. Most pots and kettles are pear-shaped and usually embossed with flutes or foliage. Tea-caddies were made either in an inverted vase shape imitating Chinese porcelain or are of a simple, oblong form. Cream jugs are not common in Dutch silver, presumably due to a different way of taking tea than in England.

There were few formal innovations during the mid- and late 18th century. Stock-in-trade items included candlesticks, tureens, sauceboats, teaware and baskets. Such items as dinner plates do not appear to have been made as frequently in the Netherlands as in England or France, presumably indicating a preference for imported Chinese porcelain plates.

The most elaborate types of plate usually follow the forms of contemporary French silver. An example is a soup tureen made in Amsterdam by Valentijn Casper Boemke (1764; Gilbert priv. col., on loan to Los Angeles, CA, Co. Mus. A.), the form of which is derived from a design of the 1750s by Thomas Germain but is smaller, lighter and with simplified ornament. Cake-baskets, however, became a showpiece of Dutch silversmithing in the mid- and late 18th century. The form differs from that generally made in England in its oval shape and two handles. Dutch baskets in both the Rococo and Neoclassical styles are characterized by a profuse use of pierced and engraved ornament with applied decoration to the borders.

BIBLIOGRAPHY

J. W. Fredericks: *Dutch Silver*, 4 vols (The Hague, 1952–61)

T. M. Duyvené de Wit-Klinkhamer and M. H. Gans: *Geschiedenis van het Nederlands zilver* (Amsterdam, 1958); Eng. trans. as *Dutch Silver* (London, 1961)

Nederlands zilver, 1580–1830/Dutch Silver, 1580–1830 (exh. cat., ed. A. L. den Blaauwen; Amsterdam, Rijksmus., 1979) [bilingual text]

TIMOTHY SCHRODER

(iii) 1814–1900. In 1814 new hallmarking regulations for gold and silver were established. Quality symbols for 22, 20, 18 and 14 carat gold, two standards—934 (i.e. 93.4% pure metal) and 833 (i.e. 83.3% pure metal)—and annual date letters were introduced. The assay office mark consists of a head of Minerva, with a letter on the helmet to indicate the regional office.

Neo-classical forms with beaded edges and openwork or engraved decoration disappeared after 1820. From the 1820s to the 1840s heavy-looking rounded forms in the Biedermeier style were decorated with filet- or corded edging and fluted ornament, for example on a teapot with a matching stand (1835; priv. col.; see fig. 57a) by Johannes Adrianus van der Toorn (1775–1845). Until the 1840s, however, undecorated pieces remained popular. During this period most silversmiths worked in Amsterdam, where Theodorus Gerardus Bentveld (1782–1853), Diederik Lodewijk Bennewitz (1764–1826), Jacobus Carrenhof (1771–1848) and Hendrik Smits (1772–1841), and later Pieter Pieterse, were active. It was the only town where specialist spoonmakers operated, such as the Hellweg family, who were active between 1753 and 1965, Hendrik Adolph Schuss (1802–83) and his family, and the Tarner family. The leading gold- and silversmiths in The Hague included François Marcus Simons (1750–1828), van der Toorn and Daniel Pijzel (1773–1836), whose son Albertus Daniel Pijzel was a co-founder of the firm Pijzel & Carbentus.

Around 1850 there was increased interest in 18th-century styles, particularly the Queen Anne, Louis XV and Louis XVI, for silverware. Johannes Mattheus van Kempen (1814–77) of Utrecht observed in a pamphlet of 1851, *Over de vormen van gouden en zilveren werken* (On the forms of wrought gold and silver objects), that there was no original contemporary style. He made definite distinctions between Greek, Gothic, Renaissance, Louis XIV and Louis XV ornaments and rejected eclecticism. His interpretations of these styles appeared on the objects that he submitted to the Great Exhibition of the Industry of All Nations of 1851 in London. The silversmiths Johannes George Grebe and M. Lucardi of Rotterdam also submitted a naturalistic beaker and a Rococo chased tea-kettle respectively to the Great Exhibition.

In the second half of the 19th century a significant amount of silver was still made by hand. Van Kempen was the first to install a steam-driven machine in his workshop in Utrecht in 1852. The German engraver and designer Hermann Bauer made dies for him. In 1858 van Kempen moved to Voorschoten, near The Hague, where his business rapidly expanded and became the largest

factory in the country. By that time such other manufacturers as Carel Joseph Begeer (1840–79) used steam-driven presses to manufacture simple shapes in different sizes. Objects were engraved or chased by hand before being passed to the assembly department for the addition of cast and die-stamped finials, bases, handles and spouts. By this method a large variety of products could be manufactured. Spherical, pear- and melon-shaped vessels, richly decorated with flower and leaf motifs, are typical of this period (e.g. coffeepot, 1858; Zoetermeer, Van Kempen & Begeer Mus.; see fig. 57c).

After 1865 the popularity of heavily decorated silver declined, and completely plain silver was revived, but in spherical shapes that were specially designed to be produced by machine. The pieces are frequently entirely or partly decorated with guilloche engravings and beaded edges (e.g. coffeepot, 1879; Zoetermeer, Van Kempen & Begeer Mus.; see fig. 57b). During this period a wide variety of presentation pieces, particularly statues, centrepieces, goblets and inkstands, were also produced. These pieces are often decorated with a profusion of machine-made components, for example bunches of flowers and grapes, figurines, trees and animals. Simple cups, stems and bases were assembled to individual specifications so that each piece was different. The best-known designer in this field was the painter Gerardus Wilhelmus van Dokkum (1828–1903), who designed numerous display pieces for the firm of Van Kempen between 1845 and 1898 (Schoonhoven, Ned. Goud-, Zilver- & Klokkenmus.).

Simple domestic objects, for example trays, coffee- and tea-services, candlesticks, baskets, dishes, cruet sets, casters and cutlery, similar to those used in other European countries, were designed by anonymous draughtsmen for the numerous Dutch silverware manufacturers. There are only two typical Dutch forms: spoon vases (*lepelvazen*) and biscuit boxes (*koektrommels*) (examples in Schoonhoven, Ned. Goud-, Zilver- & Klokkenmus.). The latter were always made in pairs—round for rusks and square

57. Dutch silverware of the 19th century (from left to right): (a) teapot, with stand and heater, by Johannes Adrianus van der Toorn, silver and ebony, h. 265 mm, The Hague, 1835 (private collection); (b) silver coffeepot by Van Kempen workshop, h. 190 mm, Voorschoten, 1879 (Zoetermeer, Van Kempen en Begeer Museum); (c) silver coffeepot by Van Kempen workshop, h. 235 mm, Utrecht, 1858 (Zoetermeer, Van Kempen en Begeer Museum)

for rolled wafers. Until 1880 all these objects were made in the fashionable styles of the 19th century. Thereafter a lack of genuine 17th- and 18th-century silver, which was widely admired, stimulated the production of copies in old styles and even fakes.

After 1895 the influence of the English Arts and Crafts Movement appeared in Dutch silver. In 1897 Frans Zwollo (1872–1945) began to give classes in Haarlem in the production of handmade silver. His work and that of his pupils (including his son Frans Zwollo jr (1896–1989) and George Henri Lantman) is characterized by hammered surfaces with spiral ornaments and radiating lines. Wares in this style were made until the 1930s (*see* §(iv) below).

BIBLIOGRAPHY

Nederlands zilver, 1815–1916 (exh. cat., ed. B. Jansen; The Hague, Gemeentemus., 1960)
Fries zilver (exh. cat., Leeuwarden, Fries Mus., 1968)
Mensen en zilver [People and silver] (exh. cat. by S. A. C. Begeer, Rotterdam, Mus. Boymans–van Beuningen, 1975–6)
Leids zilver [Leiden silver] (exh. cat., Leiden, Stedel. Mus. Lakenhal, 1977)
Nederlands zilver, 1580–1830/Dutch silver, 1580–1830 (exh. cat., ed. A. L. den Blaauwen; Amsterdam, Rijksmus., 1979) [bilingual text]
E. Voet: *Nederlandse goud- en zilvermerken* (Leiden, 1982)
Frans Zwollo en zijn tijd (exh. cat., Rotterdam, Mus. Boymans–van Beuningen, 1982)
Nijmeegs zilver, 1400–1900 [Nijmegen silver, 1400–1900] (exh. cat., Nijmegen, Mus. Commanderie St Jan, 1983)
N. I. Schadee: *Zilverschatten* [Silver treasures] (Rotterdam, 1991–2)
A. Krekel-Aalberse: 'On the Forms of Wrought Gold and Silver Objects: A Word of Introduction for the Specimens of the Art Sent to the Great Exhibition by J. M. van Kempen', *Dec. A. Soc. J.*, xvi (1992), pp. 42–3

(iv) After 1900. During the early 20th century traditional, historical styles for silver remained popular. Tea-services and other large silver wares in the Art Nouveau style, with naturalistic or curvilinear ornament, were seldom made in the Netherlands. One exception is a large coffee- and tea-service decorated with a border of ferns (examples in Rotterdam, Mus. Boymans–van Beuningen), made by the firm of C. J. Begeer after a design by Professor A. F. Gips (1861–1943), which was displayed at the Exposition Universelle of 1900 in Paris.

58. Tea-service and tray designed by Jan Eisenlöffel, silver and ebony, h. of teapot with stand 215 mm, diam. of tray 280 mm, made by Stoffels & Co., Amsterdam, 1903 (private collection)

Improvements in traditional handicraft were only one aspect of the renaissance in Dutch gold- and silverwork during this period. There were also attempts by a number of artists *c.* 1900, including JAN EISENLÖFFEL, Cornelis Begeer and Willem Hoeker, to adapt the design of silverware to machine production. These designs emphasize the construction of the pieces. Eisenlöffel was the first silversmith in the Netherlands to work in this 'constructive' style. For the Exposition Universelle of 1900 in Paris he designed plain silver that was intended to be mass-produced (Darmstadt, Hess. Landesmus.). These pieces are assembled from separate parts that are rivetted. Simple shapes are accentuated by the sparse application of such geometric ornaments as squares, circles and triangles, which were engraved along edges, enamelled or openworked (e.g. tea-service and tray designed by Eisenlöffel, 1903; priv. col.; see fig. 58).

Eisenlöffel did not realize his aim of limited mass production of silver in modern designs until 1905, when he was contracted to design for Carel Joseph Anton Begeer (1883–1956). A number of Eisenlöffel's designs were executed at the workshop that Begeer ran in the factory of his father, C. J. Begeer, in Utrecht. Silver in this 'constructive' style was also made at the factory established by Johannes Matthews van Kempen (1814–77) in Voorschoten, but its designer is unidentified. At the same time silver in the Arts and Crafts style continued to be produced. The two most striking examples of this style, a vase (1917; Amsterdam, Rijksmus.) by Carel J. A. Begeer and a three-piece tea-service (The Hague, Gemeentemus.) that Johannes Steltman (1891–1961) designed for the 1925 Exposition Internationale des Arts Décoratifs et Industriels Modernes in Paris, were inspired by the work of the 17th-century Dutch goldsmiths Adam van Vianen, Paulus van Vianen and Johannes Lutma (i) and are the antithesis of the angular forms and straight lines of the international Art Deco.

In the 1920s and 1930s the 'constructive' style evolved into Functionalism. Christa Ehrlich (*b* 1903), a pupil of Josef Hoffmann in Vienna, made cylinder-shaped designs (e.g. tea-set, 1931–41; Schoonhoven, Ned. Goud-, Zilver- & Klokkenmus.) for Van Kempen, Begeer & Vos (the three firms had amalgamated in 1919); these were made using the deep-drawing press. As these pieces were finished by machine, they are undecorated.

After World War II the demand for mass-produced silverware in modern designs was replaced by that for stainless steel wares, but fine, handmade silver pieces continued to be made. Heavy-looking asymmetrical shapes with rounded contours are characteristic of the post-war, so-called 'New Streamline' style. The most important designer of that period was Gustav Beran (*b* 1912; e.g. candelabra, 1957; Schoonhoven, Ned. Goud-, Zilver- & Klokkenmus.). In 1991 a number of gold- and silversmiths formed a group, led by Jan van Nouhuys (*b* 1949), to produce and promote fine contemporary art objects.

BIBLIOGRAPHY

Klokken, Zilveren, Sieraden, 1900–1930 [Clocks, silver, jewellery, 1900–1930] (exh. cat. by H. Dommisse, P. Schipper and A. Krekel-Aalberse, Schoonhoven, Ned. Goud-, Zilver- & Klokkenmus., 1976)
Amstelhoek, 1897–1910 (exh. cat., ed. J. D. van Dam and A. Hidding; Leeuwarden, Gemeentelijk Mus. Het Princessehof, 1986)

Christa Ehrlich: Weens ontwerpster in Nederland[Christa Ehrlich: Viennese designer in the Netherlands] (exh. cat. by A. Krekel-Aalberse, Schoonhoven, Ned. Goud-, Zilver- & Klokkenmus., 1988)
Legaat N. F. Havermans, 1909–1987 (exh. cat. by A. Krekel-Aalberse, Ghent, Mus. Sierkst, 1988)
A. Krekel-Aalberse: *Art Nouveau and Art Deco Silver* (London, 1989)
J. van Nouhuys: *Zilver in beweging* [Silver in motion] (Schoonhoven, 1991)
Silver of a New Era: International Highlights of Precious Metalware, 1880–1940 (exh. cat., Rotterdam, Mus. Boymans–van Beuningen, 1992)
ANNELIES KREKEL-AALBERSE

2. BASE METALS.

(i) Pewter. Pewter objects were manufactured in many parts of the Netherlands from the 13th century. The principal raw material, tin, was imported from England or Saxony. Among the earliest items made in pewter are flagons, to which there are documentary references in Deventer as early as 1284–5. Dishes, jugs, tankards and town flagons were also made during the 13th and 14th centuries, and the bulk of the pewter produced was for corporations, town councils, guilds and the Church. In the 16th century the pewtering industry expanded steadily. Demand extended into the domestic market, and the number of pewterers rose considerably, although substantial amounts of finished pewter were imported from England during the 17th century. Dutch pewterers tended to serve only their own immediate locality. Amsterdam was the exception, as its produce was distributed throughout the Netherlands (*see* AMSTERDAM, §IV, 2).

Towards the end of the 16th century a separation of the traditional multi-trade guild into specialized guilds took place in Amsterdam, and there and in Haarlem autonomous pewterers' guilds were established. During the 17th century pewterers' guilds were also created in Delft (1632), Rotterdam (1635) and Amersfoort (1680). These guilds controlled the composition of the alloy and the training of pewterers through an apprenticeship system. Each guild established its own rules for the composition of pewter, although these varied only marginally. Two basic standards were set: one termed 'fine' tended to have a tin content of more than 94% and was used for flatware, while the other, *keurtin*, a lower standard with over 90% tin, was used for hollow-ware.

In the 17th century vast quantities of plates and dishes, drinking vessels, flagons, candlesticks, spoons and other household items were made. Elaborate decoration does not usually appear on pewter made in the Netherlands and is restricted to engraved coats of arms, garlands, inscriptions and dates. Various types of drinking vessels appeared in the 16th and 17th centuries, for example ''s Hertogenbosch' tankards, which are small, squat vessels, often engraved with the coat of arms of a town and with a medallion inserted in the bottom. Guild flagons inscribed with the name of the guild or its masters also survive, although they are less elaborate than contemporary German examples. The Dutch pewter wine flagon (*pijpkan*) usually has a long spout closed with a lid (e.g. early 17th century; Rotterdam, Mus. Boymans–van Beuningen; see fig. 59). Pewter items are frequently depicted in 17th-century Dutch paintings. Flagons and dishes can be seen in a *Peasant Interior with Hurdy-gurdy Player* (1653; London, N.G.) by Adriaen van Ostade (*see* OSTADE, VAN,

59. Pewter *pijpkan* (also known as the '*Jan Steen*' *kan*), h. 201 mm, Amsterdam, early 17th century (Rotterdam, Museum Boymans–van Beuningen)

(1), fig. 2). An analysis of 78 contemporary Rotterdam inventories produced over 10,500 items of pewter, of which 57% were plates and dishes of various styles. In Rotterdam, in particular, pewterers received large commissions from the city governors and such local wealthy families as the Bisschop family.

Several categories of marks were used. Each pewterer was required to place his stamp or maker's mark on a touch plate, but only the plate from Haarlem (Haarlem, Frans Halsmus.) survives. A quality mark, which varied from guild to guild, was also usually required. The quality marks used included the town coat of arms, a pewterer's hammer, a crown, a crowned rose and an angel mark. The crowned rose indicated that the tin was from Cornwall. During the late 17th century tin from South-east Asia began to augment supplies from European sources. An analysis of all identified pewterers after 1520 shows that the main centres of pewter production were Amsterdam, Rotterdam, Deventer and Leiden. Such other towns as Dordrecht, Leeuwarden, Utrecht, Zwolle, The Hague, Delft and Nijmegen were important centres in the 17th and 18th centuries. Pewterers are recorded in 38 other towns.

The early 18th century was a period of consolidation, but decline set in because of the increasing popularity of such other materials as silver, brass, earthenware and porcelain. Rotterdam, for example, had at least 26 pewterers in 1650 and 30 by the 1750s, but the number had fallen to 12 by 1800. Pewterers in Rotterdam exported their goods to France, particularly to Rouen and Bordeaux. Jan Boogaert (1682–1760) and Hendrik Jongeling (1678–1727) are known to have produced teapots, dishes and candlesticks for French clients. In Amsterdam, the most important centre of pewter production, 87 masters were operating in 1688, 51 in 1751 but only 25 in 1809. By 1819 there were only about 150 pewterers at work in the Netherlands. In some areas the guilds were disbanded in

1812, while in Amsterdam the guild had fallen into disuse before 1820.

In the 19th century there was a further decline, although there was still some demand from rural areas for plates, spoons, hot-water bottles, coffeepots, urns and liquid measures. Efforts were made to modernize methods of production, and pewter was spun by machine rather than cast, but the range of goods produced was limited. By 1900 there were only a handful of pewter firms operating, one of the last being that of Kamhof of Zwolle, which operated for most of the 19th century and whose last active member retired in 1939. The appearance of the Art Nouveau style stimulated the production of pewter, but the market was dominated by the German firm of J. P. Kayser & Sohn. The Gerofabriek in Zeist manufactured pewter articles in the early 20th century. These were initially hammered by hand but were later machine-made. In the 1920s and 1930s the factory produced pewter tableware, characterized by austere forms designed by Christiaan J. van der Hoef (1875–1933) and Georg Nilssen.

(ii) Brass, bronze, copper and iron. During the early medieval period the brass and copper industries in the Low Countries were based along the River Meuse and centred at Dinant. During the 13th century the region was beset with conflict, which encouraged craftsmen to move to Middelburg and Maastricht and later to other parts of Flanders and the southern Netherlands. Copper was imported from Germany, while tin came from either Cornwall or Saxony and the calamine from the area around the River Meuse.

A substantial part of the production of both brass and bronze was devoted to such ecclesiastical objects as candlesticks (see 1986 Rijksmus. cat., p. 75), crucifixes and reliquaries. Some domestic wares were also manufactured, in particular cooking pots, lavabos, jugs and aquamaniles. Much of the production was exported to France and England through Antwerp. Iron was widely worked in the Netherlands before 1520. Most blacksmiths produced tools, but a few manufactured wrought-iron gates, doors, cast cooking pots and fire-backs.

From the 16th century the brass and bronze industry prospered. There were substantial exports of raw brass and finished goods in brass, bronze and copper to England and southern Europe. Following the Spanish occupations of Antwerp in 1576 and 1585, the centres of the industry, initially in the southern Netherlands, shifted to Rotterdam, Amsterdam and northern Holland. A system of guilds, similar to that found among pewterers, evolved with the two principal trades being the founders and brasiers. Few examples of brass or copper were marked by their makers, but it was usual for bronze-founders to sign their mortars and bells. It is difficult to distinguish brass, copper and bronze wares made elsewhere in the Low Countries from items that are Dutch, because the methods of construction, styles and alloys are similar. Many items are therefore catalogued as 'Flemish'.

The principal towns associated with bronze-founding and -casting were Deventer, Amsterdam, Utrecht, The Hague, Breda, Kampen, Groningen, Rotterdam and Enkhuizen. Bells, mortars and weights, often decorated, and cooking pots of various forms were commonly produced. Prolific founders included Willem Wegewart (*d* 1620) and Hendrick ter Horst (*fl* 1620–60; e.g. bronze mortar, 1641; London, V&A), both from Groningen, and François Hemony (1609–67) and Pieter Hemony (1619–80) from Amsterdam. The last two specialized in bell-founding. Examples of their work can be seen in the Oude Kerk, Amsterdam, and the Nieuwe Kerk, Delft.

A wide range of domestic brass and copper wares was made in the Netherlands in the 17th and 18th centuries, including cooking vessels, plates, dishes, tankards, cups, candlesticks, warming-pans, foot-warmers, sconces, lanterns and lamps. Many paintings of this period depict the use of domestic brass vessels. *Mother beside a Cradle* (*c.* 1659–60; Berlin, Gemäldegal.) by Pieter de Hooch shows a brass warming-pan hanging by the bed and a chamber candlestick on the table. Many brass gates and screens were also made during this period. The brass screen (1649) in the Nieuwe Kerk, Amsterdam, by Johannes Lutma (i) is one of the best examples of metalwork in the Auricular style fashionable in the first half of the 17th century. Some items are typically Dutch, for example the type of candlestick known as the *Heemskirk*, and finely engraved copper and brass tobacco-boxes (e.g. early 18th century; London, V&A; see fig. 60). Brass and copper curfews, known as *vursherm*, were also popular during the 17th and 18th centuries (examples in London, V&A).

Several processes developed in England in the 18th century led to the mass production of iron that could be easily cast. These benefits eventually reached the Netherlands. The range of domestic goods made was limited; mostly stoves, fire-backs and cooking pots were produced. Iron continued to be used for tools, gates and other decorative work.

The brass industry faced competition from manufacturers in Birmingham and from Sweden and Germany during the 19th century, and consequently production declined. Wares in such materials as earthenware, silver and Britannia metal began to replace those in copper and brass. The range of goods produced in copper and brass

60. Brass tobacco-box, diam. 108 mm, early 18th century (London, Victoria and Albert Museum)

was still considerable, but the emphasis changed towards coffeepots, urns, milk cans, jugs and jardinières.

Brasiers continued to operate in Amsterdam, Rotterdam, Groningen, Zwolle, Utrecht and The Hague. Manufacturers in the 19th century included Frans Zwollo (1872–1945) in The Hague, Louis van Voorst (1800–79) in Utrecht, and Jacob van den Bosch (1868–1948), H. P. Berlage and G. Lautman (1875–1937), all in Amsterdam. The development of the Art Nouveau style towards the end of the 19th century stimulated demand for copper and brass ware, and several makers specialized in Art Nouveau pieces (e.g. copper wine-cooler, after 1900; Prague, Mus. Dec. A.).

From *c.* 1830 ornamental objects in iron were produced by the Nering Bögel factory in Deventer and the Schutz factory in Zeist. Railings, wrought-iron gates and doors were popular in the 19th century. In the late 19th century ornamental wrought iron was made by the forge of Vincent & Co. in Schiedam and the factory of F. W. Braat in Delft. Many decorative items, particularly street and garden furniture, were made in the Art Nouveau style. By *c.* 1930 the industrial manufacture of cast iron and wrought-iron had virtually ceased, as production was labour-intensive. A few small firms continue to operate.

BIBLIOGRAPHY
A. J. G. Verster: *Tin door de eeuwen* (Amsterdam, 1954)
——: *Brons in den tijd* (Amsterdam, 1956)
H. U. Haedeke: *Metalwork* (London, 1970)
B. Dubbe: *Tin en tinnegieters in Nederland* (Lockem, 1976)
Keur van tin uit de havensteden Amsterdam, Antwerpen en Rotterdam (exh. cat., Amsterdam, Mus. Willet-Holthuysen, 1979)
A. L. de Blaauwen: *Koper & brons*, Amsterdam, Rijksmus. cat. (The Hague, 1986)

PETER HORNSBY

X. Objects of vertu.

1. IVORY. In contrast to the South Netherlands, France and Germany, where ivory-carving flourished, this art seems to have been little practised in the northern Netherlands. A number of northern Netherlandish carvers worked in ivory, but few pieces by them are extant. Those ivories that are preserved are chiefly by southern Netherlandish carvers who settled in the northern Netherlands. The earliest surviving Netherlandish ivories, a *Virgin and Child* and *St Anne and the Holy Trinity* (both Utrecht, Catharijneconvent), date from the end of the 15th century and the beginning of the 16th. Both are heavily influenced by contemporary wood-carving.

The 17th-century sculptor Albert Jansz. Vinckenbrinck from Amsterdam probably carved miniatures in ivory, as well as in box-wood and fruit-wood, as many ivories are attributed to him in catalogues of 18th-century collections. The Flemish sculptor Artus Quellinus (i), who worked in the northern Netherlands *c.* 1648–64, was also an ivory-carver. The *Mercury* and *Venus* (both St Petersburg, Hermitage) attributed to him and the signed and dated *Sleeping Child* (1641; Baltimore, MD, Walters A.G.) date from before his move to the North. No ivories are extant from his time in Amsterdam (1650–64/5). His pupil, Rombout Verhulst from Mechelen, is associated with two high-quality ivory portrait medallions (mid-17th century; Amsterdam, Rijksmus.; see fig. 61) and a *Venus and Amor*

61. Ivory portrait medallions attributed to Rombout Verhulst, each 122×87 mm, mid-17th century (Amsterdam, Rijksmuseum)

(Berlin, Bodemus.), a group that possesses the realism characteristic of his work.

A number of ivory portrait medallions of Dutch statesmen, for example those of *Johan van Oldenbarneveldt* and *The de Witt Brothers* (both Amsterdam, Rijksmus.), were made in the northern Netherlands but cannot be ascribed to a specific artist. The sculptor Pieter Xavery, born in Antwerp and active in Leiden, made an *Adam and Eve* (Amsterdam, Rijksmus.) in ivory. It is his only work in this medium. The ivory-carver Frans van Bossuit moved from Brussels to Amsterdam *c.* 1680 after a long stay in Rome. His figures and reliefs of biblical and classical subjects found a ready market with the Dutch collectors of his time, and many of his works are listed in 18th-century sale catalogues. Many of his ivories are preserved, including a fine relief of *Venus and Adonis* (Amsterdam, Rijksmus.).

Jean Mansel (*fl* 1681–1717), a Huguenot ivory-carver from Dieppe, was registered in 1681 as a citizen of Amsterdam, where he made two medallions with mythological subjects (both Amsterdam, Hist. Mus.). He moved to Maastricht in 1687/8 and there made ivory medallion portraits (examples in Maastricht, Bonnefantenmus.) and was probably also active in Maastricht's arms industry. The sculptor Jan Ebbelaar (*c.* 1666–1706), active in The Hague and later in Amsterdam, also worked in ivory. In his will he left all his ivory and tools to his pupil Petrus Allard. No work by either artist in this medium is extant. Ivory-carvers working in Amsterdam at the end of the 17th century also made domestic items, for example knife-handles on two sets of knives and forks (1698; Baltimore, MD, Walters A.G.; Brunswick, Herzog Anton Ulrich-Mus.) with blades bearing Amsterdam marks.

No ivory pieces by the Amsterdam silversmith and ivory-carver Jan Lankhorst (*fl* 1704–33) are extant, although Lambert ten Kate, an 18th-century collector, is known to have owned plaster casts of Lankhorst's work. The sculptor Jan Baptist Xavery from Antwerp entered the service of William IV in 1729 and settled in The Hague. He carved a variety of works in ivory, for example free-standing pieces (e.g. *Satyr* and *Female Satyr*, 1729; Amsterdam, Rijksmus.), portrait medallions, including one of the stadholder (1733; Heino, Stichting Hannema–de Stuers Fund.), and two female heads representing *Cleopatra* (1732) and *Lucretia* (1734; both Amsterdam, Rijksmus.). He was influenced by the work of Frans van Bossuit. A sculptor in the same circle to which Xavery belonged is Nicolaas Seunties (*fl* 2nd half of the 18th century), who often worked from the designs of Daniel Marot I. He made five oval ivory relief portraits: two self-portraits and three of family members. Only the *Self-portrait 'en face'* (Amsterdam, Rijksmus.) survives. It is not known whether 19th-century Dutch sculptors carved in ivory. In the early 20th century the material was again used by artists. The sculptor Johan Coenraad Altdorf (1876–1955) carved some ivory figures of animals (e.g. Otterlo, Rijksmus. Kröller-Müller) in the Art Deco style.

BIBLIOGRAPHY

E. Neurdenburg: *De zeventiende eeuwsche beeldhouwkunst in de Noordelijke Nederlanden* (Amsterdam, 1947)
J. Leeuwenberg and W. Halsema-Kubes: *Beeldhouwkunst in het Rijksmuseum* (The Hague and Amsterdam, 1973)
C. Theuerkauff: 'Zu Francis van Bossuit (1635–1692), "Beeldsnyder in yvoor"', *Wallraf-Richartz-Jb.*, 37 (1975), pp. 119–82
R. H. Randall jr: *Masterpieces of Ivory from the Walters Art Gallery* (New York, 1985)
C. Theuerkauff: *Die Bildwerke in Elfenbein des 16.–19. Jahrhunderts*, Berlin, Skulpgal. cat., ii (Berlin, 1986)
R. Koekkoek: *Gotische ivoren in het Catharijneconvent* (Utrecht, 1987)

WILHELMINA HALSEMA-KUBES

2. JEWELLERY. Little research into the history of Dutch jewellery has been undertaken; what is known has been gleaned from inventories and portraits. There was no distinctive Dutch tradition in design until the late 20th century: the nobility followed the fashions of other European courts, and the conservatism of the Dutch people led to the introduction of new trends only slowly

and with moderation. In the 16th and 17th centuries a number of prominent Dutch goldsmiths seem also to have designed jewellery. They migrated to the major courts elsewhere in Europe, including that of Rudolf II in Prague, where Paulus van Vianen and Hans Vermeyen (*d* 1606 settled; that of Henry VIII in London, where Hans van Antwerpen, John Crispijn, Alexander van Brussel and John van Utrecht worked; and the Medici court in Florence, where Jacques Bylivert was active during the last quarter of the 16th century.

There is, however, a strong tradition of provincial costume jewellery in the Netherlands. From the 16th century it was fashionable to wear caps with small side clips, from which the *casque* (a small, square metal plate that is attached to each side of a headdress) originates. Among the ornaments worn by both men and women were earrings, clasps, chains, waistcoat buttons, cap-drops, *stukken* (men's buttons) and rings. They were made of gold and silver and adorned with such precious materials as diamond (used in the provinces of Friesland, Holland and Zeeland), pearl and, particularly on necklaces, garnet and coral. Both the type of jewellery worn and the materials used advertised the status and religion of the wearer; for example, a forehead-clasp worn on the right showed that the wearer was married. Most of the jewellery uses one or two materials, worked in an elaborate design; filigree is a common technique on such items as forehead-clasps (examples in Staphorst, Boerderij). Regional folk ornaments have influenced the design of mainstream jewellery in the Netherlands. A gold parure (*c*. 1824–38; Amsterdam, Rijksmus.), produced by Guillaume Louis Ploem (1786–1869) and C. Charles Colsoul in collaboration with Johan Lorenz Holzapfel (*c*. 1794–1844), is heavily worked in filigree and is unadorned with precious gemstones, both of which lend it a distinctively Dutch character.

The jewellery produced *c*. 1900 by the goldsmith L. W. van Kooten, after designs by Bert Nienhuis, may be regarded as characteristic Dutch examples of the Art Nouveau style. It also evinces a Rationalist, functional tendency: simple in form and abstract in design, with only an occasional hint of natural motifs (examples of *c*. 1908–11; Amsterdam, Rijksmus.).

In the 1960s Emmy van Leersum (1930–84) and Gijs Bakker (*b* 1942) introduced simple, abstract forms using such common materials as stainless steel, plastic and aluminium (e.g. bracelet, 1970; see fig. 62) to eliminate the status element of jewellery. In their minimalist, geometric designs they emphasized the specific qualities of the material and concentrated on the relation between the object and the body (e.g. shoulder-piece by Gijs Bakker, aluminium, 1967; priv. col., see Staal and Wolters, pl. 350). A number of craftsmen, including Otto Boekhoudt (*b* 1944) and Robert Smit (*b* 1941), produced jewellery that is abstract and geometric in form but made from more traditional materials and techniques (e.g. silver necklace by Boekhoudt, 1968; priv. col., see Staal and Wolters, pl. 333). Anneke Schat (*b* 1942) also used traditional techniques and such materials as gold, silver and precious gems but produced work that, in its expressiveness of form, contrasted with the prevailing constructivist approach. Likewise, Marion Herbst (*b* 1944) attained an

62. Aluminium bracelet by Emmy van Leersum, 1970 (Amsterdam, private collection)

immense critical popularity with her colourful, playful work that was freer in form.

In the 1980s designers experimented with such materials as titanium, perspex, wood, paper and textiles. LAM de Wolf (*b* 1944), for example, produced work that blurred the boundaries between clothing, jewellery and sculpture (e.g. object in textile and wood, 1986; priv. col., see Staal and Wolters, pl. 339). In the 1990s artists once again began to work with precious metals; for example, Annelies Planteydt (*b* 1956) and Peggy Bannenberg (*b* 1959) produced ornaments in silver and gold, while Philip Sajet (*b* 1953) mixed pebbles and pieces of uncut glass with gold in his jewellery.

BIBLIOGRAPHY
W. Koonings and B. W. Buenk: *Smeedkunst en sieraad: Historie in heden* [Metalwork and jewellery: past and present] (Lelystad, 1967)
R. Turner: *Contemporary Jewellery: A Critical Assessment, 1945–1975* (London, 1976)
D. G. Bakker-Stijkel: *Wie 't breed heeft, laat het breed hangen* [Those who are well off also show off] (Arnhem, 1982)
W. Diepraam, C. Nieuwhoff and C. Oorthuys: *Klederdrachten* [Traditional costume] (Amsterdam, 1984)
Images, Sieraden, Schmuck, Jewellery (exh. cat., Laren, Singer Mus., 1986)
G. Staal and H. Wolters, eds: *Holland in Vorm, 1945–1987* (The Hague, 1987) [Dut. and Eng. edns]

MONIQUE MOKVELD

3. GOLD BOXES. The earliest gold boxes produced in Amsterdam were the work of Huguenot goldsmiths from Paris and Blois who settled there *c.* 1684. They lived in the environs of the Kalverstraat and produced watchcases. The little scarlet enamelled gold box set with diamonds, known as Queen Mary II's patch-box (Brit. Royal Col.), previously thought to be English, is Dutch. It was made *c.* 1690 by Adam Loofs (*fl* 1660–1710). Dutch gold boxes generally follow the form of the English Georgian 'shaped' snuff-box (*see* ENGLAND, §X, 3); usually in chased gold, early 18th-century Dutch examples are characterized by their solidity and decorative themes culled from the Scriptures. The earliest extant gold box (1735; Holland, priv. col.) known to have been made in Amsterdam is the work of a watchmaker. The most distinguished maker of snuff-boxes in the Netherlands in the 18th century was Jean Saint (*fl* 1730–*c.* 1750). A gold snuff-box (Amsterdam, Rijksmus.) by him in the Louis XV style is dated 1739. He and his circle continued producing gold boxes until *c.* 1750. The initials I.S. stamped on his boxes, long undeciphered, have been identified as those of Saint. Louis Metayer was another Amsterdam goldsmith who made gold boxes in the 1740s, sometimes with a carved mother-of-pearl relief panel set in the lid.

BIBLIOGRAPHY
K. A. Citroen: *Nederlands goud* (Utrecht, 1963)
——: *Amsterdam Silversmiths and their Marks* (Amsterdam and Oxford, 1975)
A. K. Snowman: *18th-century Gold Boxes of Europe* (London, 1990)

A. KENNETH SNOWMAN

XI. Textiles.

1. Tapestry. 2. Embroidery. 3. Woven and printed. 4. Carpets.

1. TAPESTRY. It used to be assumed that in the mid-16th century the art of tapestry in the northern Netherlands, unlike that of the southern Netherlands, was of little importance. Since the 1970s, however, research has shown

that such workshops as that of Willem Andriesz. de Raedt (*d c.* 1568) in Leiden were of major importance and supplied products of high quality. Towards the end of the century the arrival of large numbers of Flemish refugees considerably improved the tapestry industry. The main centres were Delft, Gouda, Schoonhoven and Amsterdam. Most of the workshops were limited in size and produced smaller items (e.g. table-covers, firescreens and cushion-covers). The Dutch frequently made tapestries with naturalistic flower patterns, which were used as table-covers. This practice, frequent in the 17th century, has been connected with the strong interest in botany at that time and with the custom of strewing flowers on a laid table.

The most famous workshop for large narrative tapestries was that of Frans Spiering (*c.* 1550–1630) in Delft. Spiering had previously run a flourishing workshop and a business dealing in tapestries in Antwerp. In 1591 he established himself in Delft, in the old Agnietenklooster, and he immediately received a number of major commissions, among them orders from the States-General and from Henry Howard, 1st Earl of Northampton (1540–1614), in England. Several beautiful tapestries from Spiering's workshop have survived, including three pieces from the famous *Diana* series (Amsterdam, Rijksmus.). The designs for this series were probably made before 1591, and the tapestries were supplied over a period of years by various contractors. They are made of wool and silk and are rich in detail, with a great variety of rather pale colours. The style can be described as Mannerist. From 1607 Karel van Mander II (1579–1623), son of Karel van Mander I, became the leading designer in Spiering's workshop. He was responsible for a number of designs, including the histories of *Scipio* and *Alexander the Great* (both Amsterdam, Rijksmus.). In 1615 van Mander started his own workshop in Delft, to the great dissatisfaction of Spiering, and the following year he succeeded in winning a major commission from Christian IV of Denmark to weave a series of 26 tapestries (1617–19; destr. 1859) for Frederiksborg Castle in Copenhagen. In 1622 his workshop was forced to close because of financial difficulties. Meanwhile, in 1620 Spiering's workshop had been taken over by his sons Aert Spiering and Pieter Spiering; in 1641 they sold it to Maximiliaan van der Gught (1603–89), who already owned a workshop in Gouda.

BIBLIOGRAPHY
H. Göbel: *Die Niederlande*, 2 vols (1923), i of *Wandteppiche* (Leipzig, 1923–34); Eng. trans. as *Tapestries of the Lowlands* (New York, 1974)
G. T. van Ysselsteyn: *Geschiedenis der tapijtweverijen in de Noordelijke Nederlanden*, 2 vols (Leiden, 1935)
A. M. L. E. Mulder-Erkelens: *Facetten van de verzameling*, ii of *Wandtapijten* (Amsterdam, 1971) [tapestries in the Rijksmuseum]
Geweven boeket [Woven bouquet] (exh. cat. by V. Woldbye, Amsterdam, Rijksmus., 1971–2)
J. M. Bangs: *Documentary Studies in Leiden Art and Crafts, 1475–1575* (diss., U. Leiden, 1976)

M. W. F. SIMON THOMAS

2. EMBROIDERY. In the late Middle Ages there was a flourishing tradition of ecclesiastical embroidery in the northern Netherlands. Technically, this work inevitably had much in common with that of the more affluent southern Netherlands, but it is quite distinctive in style. A

few orphreys with figures of saints (Utrecht, Catharijne-convent) can be associated with a documented embroiderer's workshop in Utrecht, that of Jacob van Malborch (*fl* 1500–25), and many other pieces can be grouped around such contemporary artists as Lucas van Leyden, Jacob Cornelisz. van Oostsanen of Amsterdam, the Master of Alkmaar and Cornelis Engebrechtsz. of Leiden on the basis of the style of the scenes depicted. The repetition of scenes or figures in very expensive techniques (e.g. *or nué*) or in less costly silk embroidery without metal thread offers a valuable insight into the workshop practice of the period. While links have been posited between the above-mentioned groups and workshops in Amsterdam, Utrecht and possibly Leiden, records also reveal the presence of embroiderers in many more towns. They belonged to the Guild of St Luke, together with painters, sculptors and stained-glassmakers, and in at least one instance there is a record of a glassmaker being commissioned to design an embroidery.

After the Reformation there was a drastic reduction in church commissions, but they by no means disappeared altogether. The Catholics retained their hidden churches, and fine vestments and chalice veils decorated with the coiling stems of Baroque floral ornament were produced in the 17th century and later, as were antependiums in various types of raised work. Women members of lay religious communities, for example the 'Maagden van den Hoek' in Haarlem, are also credited with much ecclesiastical needlework.

In the 17th century professional embroiderers in some towns began to have guilds of their own. Their numbers had been considerably reinforced by colleagues from the southern Netherlands, who had fled to the north after the fall of Antwerp in 1585. Their talents were now expended on secular work (e.g. fine bookbindings, sword-belts, comb-cases, gloves, bags, knife-cases, stomachers and even wall hangings for the aristocracy and the wealthy merchant class). Needle-painting of the most refined type was used for exquisite flowers and fruit on these objects, as well as for flower-pieces done in coloured silks in emulation of those by contemporary painters (*see* §III, 4 above). A fine example of 1650 (Amsterdam, Rijksmus.; see fig. 63) is signed by the Amsterdam embroiderer and painter Wynant Haelwech (1617/18–*c*. 1650). Needle-painting was also taught as an accomplishment at fashionable French schools, and poets rhapsodized about the skills in pictorial needlework of such young ladies as Anna Maria van Schurman (1607–78), Anna Roemer Visscher (1583–1651), Maria Tesselschade (1594–1649) and Margareta Godewijk (1627–77). (The first three were also skilled glass-engravers; *see* §VIII above.)

Meanwhile, since the 16th century there had grown up a tradition of fine white linen embroidery. Bed-linen embroidered with large letters and insertions in fine cut and drawn threadwork was particularly popular in Friesland and Groningen. This whitework lingered on in peasant embroidery on the island of Marken until the 1950s or 1960s. Marken also inherited a tradition of coloured silk embroidery from the 17th century (Arnhem, Rijksmus. Vlksknd. Ned. Openluchtmus.). At that period blackwork was much in favour among peasant women for caps and shifts; upper-class women in the towns also often

63. Embroidered picture by Wynant Haelwech, silk needle-painting on satin in long and short stitch, 510×365 mm, 1650 (Amsterdam, Rijksmuseum)

wore blackwork caps, and handkerchiefs with fine black embroidery formed part of Friesian betrothal rituals. Another notable form of 17th-century embroidery in North Holland is coloured applied work in wool, often with armorial designs. Coats of arms also figured prominently on the wool-embroidered cushions commissioned for the use of town councillors, polder board officials and suchlike in the 17th and 18th centuries (e.g. cushion made for the Delft Polder Board, mid-17th century; Amsterdam, Rijksmus.). Dutch embroidery of the 18th century also includes a refined type of corded quilting, known as *Zaans stikwerk*, and gaily coloured crewelwork skirts (e.g. The Hague, Gemeentemus.). Otherwise French fashions were followed for the most part, though the thrifty Dutch often substituted yellow silk for the gold and silver thread so popular elsewhere.

In the 19th century the Netherlands participated in the general decline of embroidery into 'fancywork' and Berlin woolwork, a situation blamed in the 1870s on the predominance of amateurs. The architect P. J. H. Cuypers led the way in a revival of church embroidery, and, in emulation of English reformers, old techniques were assiduously studied and art needlework classes were instituted at applied art schools and elsewhere. Pioneers of modern design included GERRIT WILLEM DIJSSELHOF, his wife (1865–1960) and Margaretha Verwey (1867–1947), and many leading designers in other fields also created embroidery patterns. In the 1920s and 1930s many innovative embroidery artists, including Nita Homberg-Hannema and Christina van Zeegen, broke away from traditional ideas. After World War II the Netherlands followed various international trends in the development of embroidery as an art form in its own right.

BIBLIOGRAPHY

P. Wardle: 'The Netherlands', *Needlework: An Illustrated History*, ed. H. Bridgeman and E. Drury (New York and London, 1978), pp. 175–84 [extensive bibliog.]

——: 'Needle and Bobbin in Seventeenth-century Holland', *Bull. Needle & Bobbin Club*, cxvi (1983), pp. 3–28

M. Simon Thomas: 'Gottfried Semper en de Nederlandse kunstnaaldbeweging in de negentiende eeuw: "per ardua ad astra"' [Gottfried Semper and the Dutch art needlework movement in the 19th century: 'per ardua ad astra'], *Jong Holland*, ii (1986), pp. 40–54

P. Wardle: '"Embroidery Most Sumptuously Wrought": Dutch Embroidery Designs in the Metropolitan Museum of Art, New York', *Bull. Needle & Bobbin Club*, cxix (1986), pp. 2–44

S. de Bodt: *. . . op de raempte off mette brodse: Nederlands borduurwerk uit de zeventiende eeuw* [. . . on the loom or embroidered: Dutch embroidery of the 17th century] (Haarlem, 1987)

P. Wardle: '"A Resurgent Technique": Art Needlework in the Netherlands', *J. Dec. A. Soc.*, xi (1987), pp. 10–15

Schilderen met gouddraad en zijde [Painting with gold thread and silk] (exh. cat. by S. de Bodt and others, Utrecht, Catharijneconvent, 1987)

K. Stolleis: 'Ein spätgotisches Kaselbesatz aus dem Umkreis des Meisters van Alkmaar', *Opera textilia variorum temporum* (Stockholm, 1988), pp. 77–92

S. de Bodt: 'Borduurwerkers te 's Hertogenbosch' [Embroiderers at 's Hertogenbosch], *In Buscoducis: Kunst uit de Bourgondische tijd te 's Hertogenbosch, Bijdragen* (Maarssen and The Hague, 1990), pp. 482–6

——: 'Borduurwerkers aan het werk voor de Utrechtse kapittel- en parochiekerken, 1500–1570', *Oud-Holland*, cv (1991), pp. 1–31

PATRICIA WARDLE

3. WOVEN AND PRINTED. In the 17th century a flourishing silk industry developed in Haarlem. The material was known as 'narrow weave' because of the narrowness of the strips of fabric produced (only some 400 mm). The patterns were generally fairly simple. Towards the end of the 17th century Amsterdam grew in importance as a centre for silk-weaving, partly due to the stream of French Huguenots entering the city after the Revocation of the Edict of Nantes in 1685. The industry reached its peak *c.* 1730, after which it gradually declined, mainly as a result of competition from England and France. Nothing of the Amsterdam and Haarlem silk production survives in Dutch collections, yet the quality of these fabrics, especially those produced in Amsterdam, was apparently so high that at the beginning of the 18th century they were even exported to France. Several beautiful designs of outstanding quality have been preserved in the collection of the Duc de Richelieu (1730–37; Paris, Bib. Assemblée N.).

In the 18th century a new fabric was developed, known as 'mock velvet' or *velours d'Utrecht*. It had a short goat-hair pile on a linen warp and weft and at first was probably intended to imitate expensive silk velvet. Patterns could be imposed by flattening the pile in certain places with a heated copper roller. The origin of the fabric remains a matter of dispute, but it is believed to have been woven not only in Utrecht but also, for instance, in Amsterdam and Kampen. It had a good reputation in many countries, mainly because of its lustrous surface. At the beginning of the 20th century the production of mock-velvet was revived in a number of places in the Netherlands. Using the original rollers, the Trijpweverij in Hengelo was able

to bring the traditional patterns back on to the market, while at the same time such designers as T. W. NIEUWENHUIS were commissioned to make new designs.

At the end of the 16th century and throughout the 17th Haarlem was the centre of a world-famous linen damask industry (*see* LINEN DIAPER AND DAMASK). As with the production of tapestries, the industry flourished after the arrival of large numbers of Flemish refugees *c.* 1585. At that time the linen trade was already prospering in Haarlem; the surrounding area, with its clear streams full of iron and magnesium and its ready supplies of potash from Amsterdam, was considered the ideal place for bleaching the fabric. The most famous workshops were those of Passchier Lamertijn (1563–1620), from the Flemish town of Kortrijk, and the Haarlem-born Quirijn Jansz. Damast (*d* 1650). Both carried out work for the government as well as for prominent families in the Netherlands and abroad; the Frisian nobility, in particular, often commissioned work. The finest surviving examples are those that were woven earliest. The patterns were rather narrow and were repeated (sometimes in mirror image) several times across the width of the fabric. Methods were developed later that allowed the weaving of broader patterns; in 1601 Lamertijn made a broad design for the Stadholder Maurits van Nassau and became the first weaver to apply for a patent. Broad-woven linen was decorated with hunting parties, mythological and biblical stories and even sea battles. A typically Dutch decoration was the *banquet op tafel*, a detailed image of a table with food and tableware.

With the introduction of the Jacquard loom the images became increasingly uniform and less interesting. Only in the 20th century did the weaving of linen damask show signs of revival, this time in a number of factories in the province of North Brabant. The best-known was J. P. F. van Dissel's linen mill in Eindhoven, which produced designs by the industrial artist CHRIS LEBEAU from 1905. His patterns, based on plants and animals (Assen, Prov. Mus. Drenthe; and Amsterdam, Rijksmus.), are considered to be among the best examples of Art Nouveau in the Netherlands. During the first quarter of the century there was also a brief upsurge of cotton damask, which was popular with interior decorators for wall coverings and upholstery. It was woven after designs by Nieuwenhuis in the factory of W. G. J. Ramaer & Co. in Helmond. These cotton damask fabrics were made in one or two colours and depict stylized images of plants and flowers (see fig. 64).

The development of textile printing was greatly stimulated during the 17th century by trade with Asia. Chintz was imported from India by the Dutch East India Company and in the second half of the 17th century became so popular that the Dutch inevitably began to imitate it (*see* COTTON). Within a few decades this led to a great expansion of the textile industry, particularly in the area around Amsterdam, where wooden printing blocks were used to print in the 'Indian way', that is with stain dyes to ensure the washability of the fabrics (*see* TEXTILE, §III, 1(ii)(f)). The patterns, mainly floral designs, were strongly influenced by Indian chintzes, which, along with the Dutch imitations, played an important role in the clothing and interior decoration of the 18th century. Towards the end

64. Woven damask fabric with sunflower motif designed by T. W. Nieuwenhuis, made by W. G. J. Ramaer & Co., Helmond, 1909 (Amsterdam, Rijksmuseum)

of the 18th century Dutch textile printing declined owing to fierce competition from abroad. A second period of growth began halfway through the 19th century when a number of factories in Haarlem, Leiden and Helmond developed a cheap wax-printing method by which they could reproduce Indonesian batiks mechanically. Towards 1900, industrial artists became interested in the traditional batik method. Johan Thorn Prikker was one of the first artists who managed to use the technique satisfactorily, developing new designs rather than imitating Indonesian patterns. These modern batiks were much sought after in the early 20th century and were sold by the Arts and Crafts art gallery in The Hague, of which Thorn Prikker was artistic director. Later, many very fine designs were made by Chris Lebeau, whose batik work is strongly reminiscent of his early damask patterns.

BIBLIOGRAPHY
G. T. van Ysselsteyn: 'Het Haarlemse smalweversgilde' [The Haarlem guild of narrow-weavers], Jversl. Sticht. Textielgesch. (1957), pp. 28–41
——: White Figurated Linen Damask from the 15th to the Beginning of the 19th Century (The Hague, 1962)
N. Rothstein: 'Dutch Silks: An Important but Forgotten Industry of the 18th Century or a Hypothesis', Oud-Holland, lxxix (1964), pp. 152–71
P. Thornton: Baroque and Rococo Silks (London, 1965)
J. M. Joosten: 'De batik en de vernieuwing van de nijverheidskunst in Nederland, 1892–1905' [Batik and the revival of Dutch industrial art, 1892–1905], Ned. Ksthist. Jb., xxiii (1972), pp. 407–29
M. Prinet: Le Damas de lin historié du XVI au XIX siècle (Berne, 1982)
L. Oei, ed.: Indigo: Leven in een kleur [Indigo: life in one colour] (Weesp, 1985)
M. Simon Thomas: 'Textiel', Industrie & Vormgeving in Nederland, 1850–1950 (exh. cat., Amsterdam, Stedel. Mus., 1985), pp. 79–121
S. de Bodt: . . . op de raempte off mette brodse . . . Nederlands borduurwerk uit de zeventiende eeuw [. . . on the loom or embroidered . . . Dutch embroidery of the 17th century] (Haarlem, 1987)
E. Hartkamp-Jonxis, ed.: Sits: Oost-west relaties in textiel [Chintz: East-west relations in textiles] (Zwolle, 1987)
Schilderen met gouddraad en zijde [Painting with gold thread and silk] (exh. cat. by S. de Bodt and others, Utrecht, Catharijneconvent, 1987)

4. CARPETS. Well-established trade links with Turkey guaranteed a regular supply of oriental carpets from an early date, and their popularity can be seen from the interiors depicted in 17th-century paintings. At this period, and also in the 18th and 19th centuries, the carpets manufactured in the Netherlands itself were simply woven in tapestry and double-cloth techniques. The centre of production was Hilversum, and the carpets woven there were cheap and soft, although from the 18th century they began to include coarser materials such as cow-hair. The first attempts to imitate the technique used in the much admired oriental carpets were made c. 1820 at the Koninklijke Deventer Tapijtweverij. These 'Smyrna' or 'Deventer' carpets soon became a success, and in the 19th century they won numerous prizes at national and international industrial exhibitions. Following the oriental technique, the carpets were entirely knotted by hand on a vertical loom, using loose lengths of thick wool that could be dyed to almost any colour. Thus, in principle, the patterns of individual carpets could vary. They were often based on oriental examples, but there were also carpets with patterns in various fashionable period styles.

Towards the end of the 19th century more factories began to produce 'Smyrna' carpets. In 1896 the Amersfoort Tapijtweverij hired the decorative artist T. C. A. Colenbrander. His designs were an important source of innovation in the industry; only the wealth of colour in some of his carpets and the typically flat character of the patterns recall oriental models. In 1901 the Amersfoort factory, still under the artistic direction of Colenbrander, was taken over by the much larger Deventer factory, and subsequently more and more industrial artists began to design carpets. Among the best known is Jaap Gidding (1887–1955), who designed the carpets for the Tuchinsky Theatre in Amsterdam c. 1920.

BIBLIOGRAPHY
G. Doorman: 'De Koninklijke Deventer-Tapijtfabriek en de invoering der fabricage van smyrnatapijten in Nederland' [The Royal Deventer Tapestry Factory and the origins of the Smyrna carpet industry in Holland], Het Nederlandsch octrooiwezen en de techniek der 19de eeuw [The Dutch patent system and technical progress in the 19th century] (The Hague, 1947), pp. 86–91
M. Simon Thomas: 'K.V.T.', Industrie & Vormgeving in Nederland, 1850–1950 (exh. cat., Amsterdam, Stedel. Mus., 1985), pp. 94–7

M. W. F. SIMON THOMAS

XII. Patronage.

From the later Middle Ages on, patronage of the arts in the northern Netherlands was a characteristic feature of the culture of the Church, the courts, the aristocracy, the cities, corporate groups, burgher families and, in later centuries, of cultural organizations and individuals. The earliest court of the northern Netherlands now known to have distinguished itself strikingly through art patronage was that of Duke Albert I of Bavaria (reg 1358–1404), who ruled over Holland, Zeeland and Hainault. The splendour and extent of his commissions are known thanks to the preservation of his treasury—alas not the treasury of his precious belongings themselves, but the paper treasury of his account-books, which include many commissions for artistic luxury goods. The Bavarian court in The Hague had international dynastic connections, and many of Albert's purchases were made outside his own territories, in Flanders and France. Nonetheless, the impact of his patronage on the level of artistry in Holland and Utrecht is undoubted. Some of the manuscripts made locally for him and for his second wife, Margaret of Cleves, vie with the most accomplished work of the period anywhere in Europe. A later regent of the realm, John of Bavaria, brought Jan van Eyck to The Hague (1422–4). Had John's rule been more stable, this signal act of patronage could have established the northern Netherlands as the leading transalpine art centre of the 15th century. In 1425 John met an art lover's death when assassins smeared poison on his prayerbook—no doubt a splendid manuscript made to his order— which he was often seen to kiss.

Shortly thereafter, rule over Holland devolved to the Dukes of BURGUNDY. Their patronage of the arts, from their seats in Dijon and Brussels, had the opposite effect to that of the Holland–Bavaria line: it drained talent away from the country rather than attracting it. In the neighbouring Duchy of Guelders, ruled by an ally of the king of France, leading patrons were equally unwilling to settle for second best. The French-born Mary of Guelders, who corresponded with her relative Jean, Duc de Berry, ordered manuscripts, including a splendid prayerbook in the vernacular (Berlin, Staatsbib. Preuss. Kultbes., MS. Germ. qu. 42) from the scriptorium of a monastery near Arnhem. These examples reveal an underestimated aspect of court patronage in the Netherlands: it was often practised by women. It is no coincidence that the book considered the high-point of Dutch manuscript art was made for the niece of Margaret of Cleves and the successor of Mary of Guelders: Catherine of Cleves (1417–76), wife of the Duke of Guelders. The two dispersed parts of her famous Book of Hours (c. 1440) are now reunited (New York, Pierpont Morgan Lib., MSS M. 917; M. 945). Manuscripts such as these were undoubtedly made to order, but the records speak of lesser acquisitions that were bought ready-made. Patronage of the arts also played a significant role at the (southern Netherlandish) court of Mary of Habsburg, regent of the Netherlands from 1531 to 1555 and was characteristic of the Mechelen-based courts of Margaret of Austria (reg 1507–30) and Mary of Hungary.

The third and most important seat of power in the northern Netherlands in this period, alongside the courts of Holland and Guelders, was the Bishopric of Utrecht. From the 13th to the early 16th century, the construction of the cathedral involved expenditure on furnishings and liturgical objects, which provided the stimulus for the emergence of Utrecht as a centre for the production of sculpture, metalwork and needlework. This, in turn, facilitated the development of patronage at dozens of smaller ecclesiastical establishments—parish and collegiate churches, convents and monasteries—as well as at local courts, by lay orders such as the Teutonic Knights, by civic governments and by individuals.

In addition to their obligatory disbursements on behalf of the *fabrica*, two of the bishops of Utrecht, the half-brothers David (1455–96) and Philip of Burgundy, illegitimate sons of Philip the Good, bestowed private patronage of a high order. Their now long-forgotten courts in Souburg and Wijk bij Duurstede were focal points of humanistic scholarship, literature and art. Philip of Burgundy kept Jan Gossart in his employ for 16 years but also patronized such diverse painters as Hieronymus Bosch and Jacopo de' Barbari. The last bishop of Utrecht with secular power, Philip died in debt and with eroded authority. Nonetheless, the Church and its prelates remained significant patrons of the arts throughout most of the 16th century before fading from the scene as city after city became Protestantized.

Some of the lost initiative was taken up by the growing towns themselves. This is illustrated in the greatest surviving relic of large-scale patronage in the 16th century, the stained-glass windows of the St Janskerk in Gouda. After a fire gutted the building in 1552, the township canvassed likely sponsors all over the country. The earliest donors were royalty, aristocrats, princes of the Church and the most powerful burghers and guilds of Gouda. After the Reformation, the remaining windows were paid for by the other cities of Holland and the Rijnland Water Board.

Stained glass was a popular object of patronage for those deemed worthy of perpetual association with a fixture of a church. It was relatively inexpensive and provided maximum public exposure for the donor, complete with coat of arms and sometimes a portrait. Lesser mortals and institutions were more likely to donate carved and painted altarpieces or precious liturgical objects for one of the many altars that filled pre-Reformation churches. The donor's personal involvement ranged from initiating and supervising a commission to pledging funds towards the purchase of a finished product on the open market, with or without the addition of donors' portraits.

In the course of the 16th century the patterns of patronage following the transnational lines of Church and court gave way in the northern Netherlands to the more parochial inter- and intracity networks formed by the emerging patrician class. One result was that the social worlds of artists and their patrons grew closer and sometimes overlapped. This occurred in Leiden when the painter Isaac van Swanenburgh, as a member of the town council from 1576 until his death in 1614, stimulated municipal art patronage, while seeing to it that he was its foremost beneficiary.

This rather extreme example demonstrates the more general truth that patronage of the arts in the Dutch Republic is often inextricable from political patronage. The Amsterdam magistrate Joan Huydecoper I used his position as captain in the civic guard to glorify his clan through art and poetry. Huydecoper had a poem praising his late father and himself painted on to Govaert Flinck's group portrait of a civic-guard corps celebrating the Treaty of Westphalia (1648; Amsterdam, His. Mus.). The regent patronized Flinck and the poet Jan Vos, both in his public offices and privately. As burgomaster, Huydecoper assumed special responsibility in the 1650s for the construction of the Stadhuis, a great vehicle for the patronage of all the arts, and it was Jan Vos who owned the glass factory that delivered the windows for the building. The burgo-master's influence is suspected in the humiliating ousting of Jacob van Campen as chief architect and his replacement by the town carpenter Daniel Stalpaert, a member of Huydecoper's extended family.

A more selfless art lover from the Amsterdam patriciate was Jan Six, who was immortalized through his patronage of Rembrandt. Yet, even the relationship between these two leading figures was not guided entirely by shared taste. Six owed his political position to his father-in-law, Nicolaes Tulp, whose portrait by Rembrandt in the *Anatomy Lesson of Dr Nicolaes Tulp* (The Hague, Mauritshuis) established the painter's reputation in Amsterdam. Had Six been as influential in city politics as Huydecoper, the history of painting in mid-17th-century Amsterdam would no doubt have been very different. But his secondary status made him dependent on men such as Huydecoper, limiting his effectiveness as patron of as difficult a client as Rembrandt (for Rembrandt's virtuoso etched portrait of Jan Six *see* REMBRANDT VAN RIJN, fig. 7).

Dutch government and society, while emanating an image of a certain coherence to the outside world, was to its participants more like a kaleidoscope of clashing and tumbling allegiances. At many levels, embattled groups sought to shore up their identity with symbols, images and works of art. The States General, which did not consider patronage of the arts to be part of its responsibility, nonetheless purchased 12 paintings of the Batavian Uprising by Otto van Veen (Amsterdam, Rijksmus.) at a key juncture in the Eighty Years War (1568–1648), by which the Republic won its independence from Spain. This story and its depiction provided the States with a sense of legitimacy in revolt.

Moved by similar considerations, many other bodies in the country served as *ad hoc* patrons of the arts. Paintings and other artistic objects were ordered and purchased, for their new owners' use and as gifts, by the provincial states, the admiralties, the townships and their offices, charities, civic guard companies, guilds, water boards, commercial enterprises, brotherhoods, orders and other groups. The Dutch East India Company and the West India Company sent artists to their overseas territories to create visual records of their holdings. Glorious entries and public celebrations were often the occasion for spurts of high-powered patronage, in which the visual arts were joined with architecture and poetry. Despite the moderate sup-pression of Catholicism and the opposition of the Calvin-ists to ecclesiastical art, the churches never ceased to order art, though obviously on a smaller scale than in the southern Netherlands.

Other important forms of individual patronage existed. The discovery that one patron, Pieter Claesz. van Ruyven, 'may have bought half of Vermeer's production in the years 1657 to 1675' (Montias) alters the prevalent image of the Dutch art market being open and anonymous. The relative invisibility of this form of patronage may be due to a reluctance on the part of Dutch burghers to flaunt their wealth due to a sense of embarrassment at being so rich (Schama). Public spending on the arts was likewise inhibited by sumptuary laws and the profession (or pose) of Republican simplicity by office-holders.

The largest single source of patronage was the court of the stadholder in The Hague. The Princes of Orange and Counts of Nassau (*see* ORANGE NASSAU), owners of the greatest art collection in the country, continued to add to it and, starting with Prince Frederick Henry, to build and furnish palaces on a grand-seigneurial scale. Their ambi-tions were stimulated by the earlier example of Henry III of Nassau-Dillenburg (1483–1538), whose palaces at Breda and Brussels were major artistic centres in their time, and by the extended stay in the Netherlands, from 1621 onwards, of the Winter King and Queen, Frederick V of the Palatinate (*reg* 1610–23) and his wife Elizabeth Stuart.

Frederick Henry and his wife, Amalia von Solms, worked closely with the Prince's secretary Constantijn Huygens the elder (*see* HUYGENS, (1)) in all matters pertaining to art. The conscientious and well-informed Huygens, himself a brilliant poet, musician and amateur medallist, wrote critical judgements of a kind no one else committed to paper. He displayed sensitivity to the aes-thetic qualities and innovations of the artists he discussed—foremost among them Rembrandt—but he also had a sharp eye for the interests of his employer and an instinct for what art could do for him at court. His contacts and knowledge rendered his princely patrons dependent on him in an area of immense importance to them—their posthumous glory. After the death of Frederick Henry, Huygens helped Amalia von Solms build and decorate a memorial to him at the palace of Huis ten Bosch outside The Hague (*see* THE HAGUE, §V, 3). (The choice of Huis ten Bosch for replication in Japan Holland Village in Nagasaki, a theme park opened in March 1992, is a tribute to Huygens's success as an engineer of posterity.)

The relations between the members of the House of Orange, Huygens and the artists he hired for them reveal a patron–broker–client system in full operation in the arts. It illuminates the patterns of behaviour into which the various parties tend to fall, thereby making it possible to recognize these functions even when the historical evi-dence is more fragmentary. However, it must be admitted that no one else in the history of the northern Netherlands fulfilled the role of the broker with the dedication and expertise brought to it by Huygens.

Following the death of Frederick Henry, court patron-age began to metamorphose from networking to favourit-ism, and it declined to a level that could be matched by a self-made man such as Gerrit Braamcamp. At the same time the best career opportunities for Dutch artists once more crossed the border and were concentrated in the German courts of Berlin, Munich and Kassel. In his book of 1750–51 on Dutch painters, Johan van Gool sketched an art world dominated by the relatively few people of means with an interest in the arts.

With the emergence in the mid-18th century of cultural societies, a new form of patronage evolved, which put public money to work for the good of the commonweal. In the Netherlands this tendency began late and produced few institutions of importance. The great exception is the still-extant Teylers Foundation in Haarlem (founded 1778), in which the collecting and the commissioning of art took their place alongside the study of theology and science. Initially, furtherance of the visual arts was very much subordinate, but in the course of time it has risen to be the main concern of the Foundation.

The efforts of such societies seem pathetically inadequate next to the spending on art by Louis Napoleon, the French Emperor's brother, in his brief tenure as king of Holland (*reg* 1806–10). His purchase of two major private collections for the new national museum was in itself an act of unequalled decisiveness. The patronage of King William I, who has often been cited as a great promoter of the arts in his new Kingdom of the Netherlands, is revealed under close scrutiny to have been relatively insignificant. His son William II put together a great collection of Old Masters, which the nation was, however, unwilling to buy after his unexpected death. Around mid-century, a statement by the Liberal Minister of the Interior, J. R. Thorbecke, lifted from its context, became a slogan for both champions and critics of public patronage: 'Art is no concern of the government's.'

This attitude could not be maintained for long. The conscience of the public with regard to the preservation of monuments was appealed to with great success by the aristocratic bureaucrat Victor de Stuers, in a pamphlet entitled *Holland op z'n smalst* ('How narrow[-minded] Holland can be', 1873). The unstaunched flow of artistic treasures out of the country led a group of private art lovers to found the Vereeniging Rembrandt (Rembrandt Society) in 1883 to support museum acquisitions. These and other initiatives eventually led to programmes covering a vast range of artistic activities, from art education to art publishing. In many cases the body involved had a religious, nationalistic, political or cultural colouring, or a social aim with a place for art. The patronage of art academies and museums often therefore served sectarian purposes. With the progressive evisceration of religious groups and social classes, these functions, which came to be perceived as a public responsibility, were abandoned on the doorstep of the government.

The most prominent present-day patrons of the arts in the Netherlands are the Ministry of Education, Science and Culture, whose operations vitally affect all functions of the art world, including the art market, and the government-licensed Prince Bernhard Foundation, which transfers considerable amounts of money from legalized gambling to the arts. A national Arts Council advises the Ministry and monitors its artistic decisions. Until it was discontinued in 1987, an artist-support programme, run by the Ministry of Social Affairs, attracted international attention. The artists on this programme, numbering over 2000 at its height, produced more than 200,000 works of art for their patron. Since then, the National Service for the Visual Arts (Rijksdienst Beeldende Kunst) was given responsibility for finding an elegant way to dispose of these holdings.

Below those centralized institutions, patronage of the arts is diffused throughout society. Local bylaws reserve certain percentages of urban renewal or public building projects for artistic enrichment. These schemes are run by unconnected bureaucratic committees and citizen councils throughout the country. By the 1990s the functioning of the archipelago of art patronage had come into question, and the government had undertaken efforts to diminish its custodianship of such a large part of the art world. In 1991 the first national museum was disengaged from the Ministry, as part of a larger effort. Museums were increasingly encouraged to seek sponsors to help finance their activities.

BIBLIOGRAPHY

M. Tóth-Ubbens: 'Van goude, zelver, juellen ende andere saken: Twintig jaaren Haagse tresorie-rekeningen betreffende beeldende kunst en kunstnijverheid ten tijde van Albrecht van Beieren, 1358–1378', *Oud-Holland*, lxxviii (1963), pp. 87–134

S. W. H. Drossaers and T. H. Lunsingh Scheurleer: *Inventarissen van de inboedels in de verblijven van de Oranjes en daarmee gelijk te stellen stukken, 1567–1795*, 3 vols (The Hague, 1974–6)

D. P. Snoep: *Praal en propaganda: Triumfalia in de noordelijke Nederlanden in de 16de en 17de eeuw* (Alphen aan den Rijn, 1975)

C. W. Fock: 'The Princes of Orange as Patrons of Art in the Seventeenth Century', *Apollo*, 110 (1979), pp. 466–75

J. Sterk: *Philips van Bourgondië (1465–1524), bisschop van Utrecht, als protagonist van de renaissance: Zijn leven en mecenaat* (Zutphen, 1980)

W. H. Vroom: *De financiering van de kathedraalbouw in de middeleeuwen, in het bijzonder de dom van Utrecht* (Maarssen, 1981)

G. Schwartz: *Rembrandt, his Life, his Paintings: A New Biography* (Harmondsworth, 1985)

B. Dubbe and W. H. Vroom: 'Mecenaat en kunstmarkt in de Nederlanden gedurende de zestiende eeuw', *Kunst voor de beeldenstorm: Noordnederlandse kunst, 1525–1580*, 2 vols (exh. cat., Amsterdam, Rijksmus., 1986)

The Dutch World of Painting (exh. cat. by G. Schwartz, Vancouver, A.G., 1986)

S. Schama: *The Embarrassment of Riches: An Interpretation of Dutch Culture in the Golden Age* (New York, 1987)

F. P. van Oostrom: *Het woord van eer: Literatuur aan het Hollandse hof omstreeks 1400* (Amsterdam, 1987); rev. and trans. as *Court and Culture: Dutch Literature, 1350–1450* (Berkeley, CA, 1992)

E. Hinterding and F. Horsch: '"A Small but Choice Collection": The Art Gallery of King Willem II of the Netherlands (1792–1849)', *Simiolus*, xix (1989), pp. 5–122

L. F. Jacobs: 'The Marketing and Standardization of South Netherlandish Carved Altarpieces: Limits on the Role of the Patron', *A. Bull.*, lxxi (1989), pp. 208–29

J. M. Montias: *Vermeer and his Milieu: A Web of Social History* (Princeton, 1989)

The Golden Age of Dutch Manuscript Painting (exh. cat. by J. H. Marrow and others, Utrecht, Catharijneconvent; New York, Pierpont Morgan Lib.; 1989)

W. Oosterbaan Martinius: *Schoonheid, welzijn, kwaliteit: Kunstbeleid en verantwoording na 1945* (The Hague, 1990)

C. B. Smithuijsen: *De hulpbehoevende mecenas: Particulier initiatief, overheid en cultuur, 1940–1990* (Zutphen, 1990)

J. Verheul and J. Dankers: *Tot stand gekomen met steun van . . .: Vijftig jaar Prins Bernhard Fonds, 1940–1990* (Zutphen, 1990)

M. J. Bok and G. Schwartz: 'Schilderen in opdracht in Holland in de 17e eeuw', *Holland: Reg.–Hist. Tijdschr.*, xxiii (1991), pp. 183–95 [and other articles in that issue]

J. C. Dagevos and others, eds: *Kunst-zaken: Particulier initiatief en overheidsbeleid in de wereld van de beeldende kunst* [The business of art: private initiatives and government policy in the world of the visual arts] (Kampen, 1991)

D. Freedberg and J. de Vries, eds: *Art in History, History in Art: Studies in Seventeenth-century Dutch Culture* (Santa Monica, CA, 1991)

B. Kempers: 'Opdrachtgevers, verzamelaars en kopers: Visies op kunst in Holland tijdens de Republiek', *Holland: Reg.–Hist. Tijdschr.*, xxiii (1991), pp. 196–209

E. Bergvelt: 'Koning Willem I als verzamelaar, opdrachtgever en weldoener van de Noordnederlandse musea', *Staats- en natievorming in Willem I's Koninkrijk (1815–1830)*, ed. C. A. Tamse and W. Witte (Brussels, 1992), pp. 261–85

G. Nijsten: *Het hof van Gelre* (Kampen, 1992)

F. van Oostrom: *Aanvaard dit werk: Over Middelnederlandse auteurs en hun publiek* [Accept this work: on Middle Dutch authors and their public] (Amsterdam, 1992)

A. M. E. L. Hoogenboom: *'de stand des kunstenaars': De positie van kunstschilders in Nederland in de eerste helft van de negentiende eeuw* (Leiden, 1993)

Maria van Hongarije, 1505–1558: Koningen tussen keizers en kunstenaars (exh. cat. by B. van den Boogert and others, Utrecht, Catharijneconvent; 's Hertogenbosch, Noordbrabants Mus.; 1993)

D. Eichberger and L. Bearen: 'Family Members and Political Allies: The Portrait Collection of Margaret of Austria', *A. Bull.*, lxxvii (1995), pp. 225–48

GARY SCHWARTZ

XIII. Collecting and dealing.

Although there have always been collectors who specialized, until the 19th century most collections generally comprised to some degree both natural curiosities and art. In the 19th century a firmer distinction evolved between the creations of nature and art works. In the northern Netherlands three types of collection were distinguished in terms of ownership: those of the stadholders, those of burghers and those that were public collections.

Leaving aside the reliquaries, plate, valuable precious metals and natural objects kept in church treasuries during the Middle Ages, the first collections in the Netherlands were formed in the early 16th century. At first their focus was coins; collections of Classical coins were often complemented by a series of portraits of Roman emperors. In the second half of the 16th century there was growing interest in archaeological finds from the Roman period and the Middle Ages and simultaneously, on account of the first Dutch expeditions to the East Indies, in such exotic items as porcelain, lacquerwork, ethnographica and natural objects. Among the first important collectors was the physician Berent ten Broecke (known as Bernardus Paludanus; 1550–1633). His collection at Enkhuizen comprised principally Egyptian and Roman antiquities that he had brought back from his travels. He also owned precious metals (both worked and unworked), coins and medals, ceramics (Chinese porcelain, Italian maiolica and earthenware from various countries) and ethnographica from East Asia. It is not known whether he also collected paintings or works on paper.

Prince Frederick Henry (*see* ORANGE NASSAU, (3)) was the first stadholder to assemble a collection of any magnitude. His quarters in the Paleis Noordeinde, The Hague, were fitted out with expensive tapestries and furnishings. In the 1630s the collection of paintings consisted of works by Rubens, by Anthony van Dyck and also by painters of the Dutch and particularly Utrecht schools, including Cornelis van Poelenburch and Gerrit van Honthorst. The other palaces were also hung with many works of art. Rembrandt painted the *Passion* series (Munich, Alte Pin.) between 1634 and 1639 for the court. Frederick Henry's wife, Amalia von Solms (*see* ORANGE NASSAU, (4)), had an early collection of porcelain and lacquerwork. Constantijn Huygens the elder (*see* HUYGENS, (1)), secretary to Frederick Henry, exerted great influence on the formation of the Stadholder's collection, as he was closely involved with the acquisition of works of art for the court, as well as supervising commissions (*see* §XII above). He also had his own collection. For some years too Johan Maurits, Count of Nassau-Siegen (*see* NASSAU, (1)), had a collection in The Hague. His country house was fitted out with paintings, drawings, natural objects and ethnographica accumulated during his period of office in Brazil.

After the daughters of Frederick Henry and Amalia von Solms married German princes, there was an exodus of paintings from the House of Orange collection. The remainder was formed into a collection by William III, which was assembled in a gallery in the palace of Het Loo. It did not remain intact for long: some of the paintings were sold at public auction in Amsterdam in 1713.

Outside the court at The Hague the most important collections were those of well-to-do regents and merchants in the main towns of Holland and Zeeland. By far the greatest number were in the trading metropolis of Amsterdam. The collection of the brothers Jan and Gerard REYNST in Amsterdam was particularly rich in Italian paintings and antique sculpture, which gave it international appeal. Jan Reynst operated as a merchant in Venice, where he actively collected art works; he was able to acquire the complete collection of the Venetian nobleman Andrea Vendramin. Jan's cabinet was brought to Amsterdam and put together with that of Gerard, a councillor and alderman of Amsterdam. His house on the Keizersgracht in Amsterdam was, according to a contemporary, decorated like 'a royal palace'. As well as paintings, he owned antique marble sculpture, Egyptian antiquities and natural objects. He had the most important paintings and sculptures in his collection reproduced as prints. His widow sold 24 paintings and 12 sculptures to the States of Holland and West-Friesland for 80,000 guilders. These works were part of the 'Dutch gift', a present to Charles II when he acceded to the English throne in 1660, which was intended to foster cordial political relations with the Dutch Republic. (Some of the paintings (Brit. Royal Col.) are still at Hampton Court Palace, near London.) The Reynst cabinet was one of many to be found in the Republic in the 17th and 18th centuries; in Amsterdam alone there must have been tens of collections of diverse scope and quality. JAN SIX, GERRIT BRAAMCAMP, CORNELIS PLOOS VAN AMSTEL, JAN GILDEMEESTER and Adriaan van der Hoop (1778–1854) in Amsterdam, the brothers Pieter and Jan de BISSCHOP in Rotterdam and Hendrick van Heteren (1672–1749) and his son Adriaan Leonard (1724–1800) in The Hague were among the most important collectors. Some artists were also collectors, of whom Rembrandt is the best known; the paintings, works on paper, antiquities and exotic objects in his collection also served as studio props.

Dutch bourgeois collections were not usually installed in monumental halls but in relatively small rooms. When documents mention a *raritey [en] camer* this mostly comprised a collection of natural and exotic objects, although this did not necessarily exclude art. In such a space, which might also be a study, the objects were hung on the walls, laid out on tables or kept in cupboards with drawers. Collections of paintings were usually hung throughout the house until the early 18th century. Some collectors had already set aside a separate room for their collection in the 17th century. Around 1700 it was increasingly the practice to concentrate the most important part of the collection in one room or hall. A number of collectors in the main Dutch towns had such *schilderijenkamers* in the 18th century.

Growing demand for art works created much work for dealers in paintings and for book- and print-sellers. Around 1700 JAN PIETERSZ. ZOOMER was one of the leading dealers in Amsterdam. Those with the greatest buying power imported art from abroad; the Rotterdam ship-owner and paintings dealer Jacques Meyers (*d* 1721), for example, offered for sale 20 masterpieces by Nicolas Poussin that he had acquired at high prices from French collections. Some art dealers were also collectors, and the distinction between collector and dealer is not easy to trace.

Until the 18th century the only public collections were those in the anatomy theatres of various Dutch universities and schools, such as those in Leiden, Amsterdam, Rotterdam and Delft. In such a *theatrum anatomicum*, where lectures were presented to students and anatomy was taught, there was often a display of anatomical specimens and other natural, ethnographic and archaeological objects. The *theatrum* of the university at Leiden was particularly famous, and the botanical garden there had a covered gallery hung with maps, other art works and natural objects. Some towns, such as 's Hertogenbosch, had municipal collections of rarities, housing both artistic and natural objects. As many objects had direct connections with local history, these collections can be regarded as precursors of antiquities rooms.

There was a sharp increase in the number of collections in the 18th century, and increasing specialization is detectable, either in dedicated collections of scientific interest or exclusively in setting up a cabinet of paintings. The art that was collected in the 18th century was mainly 'old' art, in other words 17th-century Dutch paintings. Italian and French art was relatively rare and expensive and was well-represented in only a few collections. Some kept their collections intentionally small, such as the Commissioner General GOVERT VAN SLINGELANDT in The Hague, who aimed to have an exquisite collection restricted to 40 works. Whenever he acquired a new item he disposed of one that was of lesser quality according to his taste. A contemporary of van Slingelandt, the official Pieter Lyonet (1706–89), also from The Hague, had a famous collection of shells; he also owned important paintings, including Johannes Vermeer's *Woman Reading a Letter* (Amsterdam, Rijksmus.).

Under the influence of the Enlightenment, many associations existed in the 18th century that were responsible for maintaining a collection. The collector PIETER TEYLER of Haarlem directed in his will that his possessions should be administered by two foundations, one to promote Christianity, and the other to promote the study of nature, history, numismatics, drawing and poetry. Teyler's collection remains intact at the Teylers Museum, Haarlem.

Much of the stadholders' collection was dispersed through inheritance and sale in the 17th and 18th centuries, but at various points the collection was built up again. Stadholder William IV (*see* ORANGE NASSAU, (7)) and his wife, Anna of Hannover, augmented the remainder of William III's collection through a number of important purchases. There was an increased level of collecting under their son, William V (*see* ORANGE NASSAU, (8)), who had a special gallery built in the Buitenhof in The Hague. It was filled with paintings from country houses elsewhere, and in 1768 he bought the entire van Slingelandt collection for 50,000 guilders, intended for this gallery. In 1774 the paintings room was opened to the public on three days of the week. The collection was supervised by the painter

Tetar Philip Christiaan Haag (1737–1812), who had also taught the Prince drawing. The French seized the collection as booty in 1795 and took it to Paris, where the paintings remained until 1815. They were returned to the Netherlands and in 1822 a home was found for the collection in the Mauritshuis, The Hague; in the late 1970s the original picture gallery was restored and reopened as the Schilderijenzaal Prins Willem V. Although King William I stimulated artists by expanding patronage, he never kept a personal collection. William II (*see* ORANGE NASSAU, (10)) did have a collection, housed in his palace in Brussels. After the outbreak of the Belgian Uprising the paintings were moved to The Hague. A significant part of them was put in a specially built room; the rest were hung in rooms in the palace. In 1850 and after, about 350 paintings, a number of drawings and some 30 sculptures were sold at auction.

The number of private collections rose in the 19th century. Further specialization is evident, influenced by scientific developments. The highly diverse collections that united natural and art objects were divided up. There was also differentiation within these two main categories. Natural objects were categorized according to new scientific ideas. Collectors sometimes concentrated on just one of these subdivisions. Art collectors also specialized, for example in Japanese porcelain or 17th-century Dutch history prints. Many private collections now formed the basis of museums (*see* §XIV below). Examples include the Museum Bredius in The Hague, derived from the collection of Abraham Bredius, and the Museum Boymans–van Beuningen in Rotterdam. The latter owes its existence to the collector F. J. O. BOYMANS, who left his possessions to the city of Rotterdam, and it was subsequently expanded through legacies, gifts and purchases, notably, in 1959, of the collection of DANIEL GEORGE VAN BEUNINGEN.

From the last decades of the 19th century the Dutch art market played an important role in the dissemination of modern art. J. H. de Bois (1878–1946) was one of the leading dealers. At first he was employed by the firm Van Wisselingh & Co. in Amsterdam, a company headed by Vincent van Gogh (1866–1911), a cousin of the painter. A specialist in modern art, de Bois later became head of a filial in The Hague, where he organized several sales exhibitions and sold works by such artists as Odilon Redon, Herman Kruyder, Matthijs Maris and Vincent van Gogh, for whose family he sold countless paintings and drawings (e.g. *Flowering Chestnut Tree*; now Otterlo, Rijksmus. Kröller-Müller). In 1913 de Bois, who was also a print and book publisher and publicist, established himself as an independant art dealer in Haarlem.

Collectors were often guided by advisers in the choice of objects they acquired; the critic H. P. Bremmer, for example, was particularly influential in the formation of a collection of van Gogh paintings for HÉLÈNE KRÖLLER-MÜLLER. In the first half of the 20th century the collector was usually assisted by a particular art dealer who was well informed about market prices and the values of works. Although the art trade and auction system have expanded enormously, in the Netherlands there is now rarely such a direct relationship between collector and dealer. After World War II mainly modern, particularly contemporary, art was collected, and only a few collectors were concerned with earlier art.

BIBLIOGRAPHY

H. Enno van Gelder, C. Reedijk and A. B. de Vries, eds: *150 jaar Koninklijk Kabinet van Schilderijen, Koninklijke Bibliotheek, Koninklijk Penningkabinet* (The Hague, [1967])

R. W. Scheller: 'Rembrandt en de encyclopedische kunstkamer', *Oud-Holland*, lxxxiv (1969), pp. 81–147

A.-M. S. Logan: *The 'Cabinet' of the Brothers Gerard and Jan Reynst* (Amsterdam, Oxford and New York, 1979)

T. Laurentius, J. W. Niemeijer and G. Ploos van Amstel: *Cornelis Ploos van Amstel: Kunstverzamelaar en prentuitgever* (Assen, 1980)

O. Impey and A. MacGregor, eds: *The Origins of Museums: The Cabinet of Curiosities in Sixteenth- and Seventeenth-century Europe* (Oxford, 1985)

E. Bergvelt and R. Kistemaker, eds: *De wereld binnen handbereik: Nederlandse kunst- en rariteitenverzamelingen, 1585–1735* (Zwolle, 1992)

J. F. Heijbroek and E. L. Wouthuysen: *Kunst, Kennis en commercie: De kunsthandelaar J. H. de Bois (1878–1946)* [Art, knowledge and commerce: the art dealer J. H. de Bois (1878–1946)] (Amsterdam and Antwerp, 1993)

J. A. VAN DER VEEN

XIV. Museums.

The Dutch have traditionally been modest collectors; none of the museum collections (with the exception of the Teylers Museum in Haarlem, founded in 1778) dates from before the 19th century, by which time much of the country's cultural inheritance was no longer available. Nevertheless there are more than 700 museums in the Netherlands, and frequent and varied exhibitions are held. Dutch museums are financed partly by central government and partly by local authorities, although increasingly they are being encouraged to seek sponsorship from elsewhere; some are subsidized by private foundations. The Vereeniging Rembrandt (Rembrandt Society), a private institution founded in 1883, provides museums with annual subsidies for purchasing works of art.

The core of the large national collections of earlier art at the Rijksmuseum, Amsterdam, and the Mauritshuis, The Hague, is formed by the collections assembled by the stadholders and the Princes of Orange during the 17th and 18th centuries (*see* §XIII above). In the late 1970s the picture gallery of William V, the last Dutch stadholder, was reopened in The Hague as the Schilderijenzaal Prins Willem V, with the pictures hanging according to their original arrangement of 1774. The national collections are also indebted to the efforts of King Louis Napoleon (*reg* 1806–10), the founder of the Rijksmuseum, and to William I (*reg* 1813–40). Donations from private individuals have also contributed to the growth of both museums and have led to the foundation of several new national museums during the 20th century. The Rijksmuseum Kröller-Müller in Otterlo, which houses a collection of 19th- and 20th-century art (including works by van Gogh), was founded in 1938 when HÉLÈNE KRÖLLER-MÜLLER presented her collection to the State; in the 1960s an important collection of sculpture was installed in the museum gardens. The Rijksmuseum Twenthe in Enschede, which includes a collection of early paintings, was donated by the van Heek family, and the Rijksmuseum Vincent van Gogh in Amsterdam was established in 1973 with the help of a generous loan from the van Gogh Foundation.

The three largest cities (Amsterdam, Rotterdam and The Hague) all have a wide variety of museums. The Rijksmuseum in Amsterdam houses decorative arts and crafts in addition to its collection of Old Masters. It is also the home of the Rijksprentenkabinet. Also in Amsterdam are the Historisch Museum, the Joods Historisch Museum, the Rembrandthuis (with a collection of etchings by Rembrandt), the Museum Overholland (which houses 20th-century drawings) and the Stedelijk Museum, the largest museum of modern art in the Netherlands.

The Museum Boymans–van Beuningen in Rotterdam houses one of the country's finest collections of paintings and applied art (both early and modern). Also in Rotterdam is the Historisch Museum, and the Nederlands Architectuurinstituut, designed by Jo Coenen.

The Haags Gemeentemuseum in The Hague has the largest collection in the world of works by Piet Mondrian, together with paintings by artists of the Hague school and an important collection of applied art. In addition, it is the home of the Nederlands Kostuummuseum and a significant collection of musical instruments. Other museums in The Hague include the Haags Historisch Museum, the Rijksmuseum Hendrik Willem Mesdag (with a collection of works by H. W. Mesdag of the Hague school), the Panorama Mesdag (showing Mesdag's circular panorama of Scheveningen) and the Koninklijk Kabinet van Schilderijen 'Mauritshuis'.

The provincial capitals also have considerable collections of cultural and art-historical importance, mostly based on local 19th-century collections. The Frans Halsmuseum, Haarlem, has early paintings, including civic guard portraits and portraits of regents by Frans Hals. The Centraal Museum, Utrecht, houses paintings by, among others, Jan van Scorel, the Utrecht Caravaggisti and the Dutch Italianate painters. The Gemeentemuseum, Arnhem, has 20th-century works by Magic Realist painters and by women. In Assen the Provinciaal Museum van Drenthe houses a collection of *Jugendstil* and Art Deco works, and the Fries Museum in Leeuwarden has a collection of Frisian silver. The Groninger Museum in Groningen includes works by members of the 20th-century group De Ploeg and other contemporary art.

Important collections are also held in museums in some of the smaller towns, such as the Dordrechts Museum, which has a collection of paintings by Aelbert Cuyp, and the Museum Mr Simon van Gijn (Arts and Crafts), also in Dordrecht; the Stedelijk Van Abbemuseum in Eindhoven has a collection of contemporary art, and the Stedelijk Museum Het Catharina Gasthuis in Gouda houses photography and 16th- and 17th-century paintings. Examples of 19th- and 20th-century art are held by the Singer Museum in Laren, and the Stedelijk Museum De Lakenhal in Leiden has early paintings, including works by Lucas van Leyden. Asian art is also found in a number of museums, including the Rijksmuseum voor Volkenkunde in Leiden. The Gemeentemuseum in Schiedam has a collection of paintings by the Cobra group.

Museums specializing in decorative arts include the Museum Huis Lambert van Meerten in Delft (tiles), the Gemeentelijk Museum Het Princessehof in Leeuwarden (ceramic objects and tiles) and the Nederlands Goud-, Zilver- en Klokkenmuseum in Schoonhoven. Many houses and castles are also open to the public, among them the Rijksmuseum Paleis Het Loo in Apeldoorn, which is devoted exclusively to displaying the lifestyles of the kings and stadholders of the Orange Nassau family.

BIBLIOGRAPHY

Amsterdam (1957–81); continued as *Kunstschrift* (from 1982) (various articles)
Museumjournaal (various articles)
Museumvisie (various articles)
R. van Luttervelt: *The Rijksmuseum and other Dutch Museums* (London, 1967)
F. J. Dupare: *Een eeuw strijd voor Nederlands cultureel erfgoed* [One hundred years of fighting for the Netherlands' cultural heritage] (The Hague, 1974)
R. Molegraaf: *Nederlandse Museumgids: Musea, oudheidkamers, bezoekers-centra, planten- en dierentuinen, officiële instanties* (The Hague, 1980, rev. 3/1986)
Het groot museumboek (Amsterdam, 1980, rev. 5/1987)
Honderd jaar Rijksmuseum, 1885–1985 (Weesp, 1985)
P. Hecht and G. Luyten: 'Nederland verzamelt oude meesters: Tien jaar aankopen en achtergronden', *Kunstschrift*, xxx/6 (1986), pp. 191–217
Kröller-Müller: Honderd jaar bouwen en verzamelen (Haarlem, 1988)

ANNEMARIE VELS HEIJN

XV. Art education.

Little is known about professional training in the Netherlands before the 18th century; it is also difficult to distinguish between true vocational training and drawing instruction for amateurs. The principal source of information on this period is van Mander's *Schilder-boeck*. In the 15th and 16th centuries artists were organized in various guilds (e.g. the Guild of St Luke for painters) that laid down the rules for their education. According to guild rules, a master had to accept between two and four pupils per year and the training period lasted from two to five years. There were thus presumably pupils at different stages of development in one studio. Pupils began their training aged 12–14 years, going on to serve their master as assistants. The precise content of the education is unknown, but it probably involved copying and collaborating on the master's paintings. Drawing exercises constituted an important technical component and aided the study of composition. A pupil made studies from life as well as from the Antique and after famous works, for example, by Raphael and Michelangelo; theory was learnt from books. There was a great difference in the education provided by different masters, probably dependent to some degree on the payment of fees for training.

In the late 17th century and the early 18th several drawing academies (*tekenacademies*) were set up: the first was that of the artists' society Pictura in The Hague (1682), which was followed by examples in Leiden (1694), Utrecht (1696) and Amsterdam (1718). Also known as drawing colleges or drawing schools, these were not academies in the Italian or French sense; rather, they provided opportunities for artists and dilettanti to draw from the nude model alongside their studio practice. Gradually, more emphasis was placed on didactic matters, and pupils were accepted for study. According to the treatises by Willem Goeree (1668), Samuel van Hoogstraten (1678), Gérard de Lairesse (1701) and Arnold Houbraken (1718–21), the ideal teaching method for drawing was based on three stages, namely the study of prints, of sculpture and of the model. This method originated in the more classicist art theories of Charles Le Brun, among others. The human figure was the normal subject for a good drawing, with

emphasis on musculature and outline. In practice various approaches were worked on at the same time in the academies, so that there was no reference to the ideal hierarchy.

Theoretical subjects, mainly perspective and anatomy, were also studied in the academies, through the influence of dilettanti and possibly in order to raise artists' status. A number of artists provided an informal forum for drawing from the naked model in their studios. The so-called Rembrandt Academy, with about 25 pupils, probably comprised advanced artists who finished their training period by studying with the master. (For further discussion *see* ACADEMY, §3.)

In the 18th century the establishment of drawing academies continued, although their character changed. The new academies and combinations of drawing academies and social clubs were comparable to the many societies that were founded during the same period. Besides the familiar drawing evenings, viewings and discussions of works of art were organized. Originally organized by and intended for wealthy amateurs, the number of artists who participated in drawing academies began to increase. At the end of the century almost every main centre had its own drawing society, club or academy, for example Haarlem (1796), Rotterdam (1773) and Dordrecht (1774). The number of pupils increased to the point where gradually the academy became a place of formal training. This contributed to the official demise of the guilds (1798). Although the training at an academy was comparable with that received in the 17th century, there was less emphasis on studying the Antique for the purpose of history painting, and more attention was paid to Dutch landscape and genre painting.

For example, the Stadstekenacademie in Amsterdam (founded 1718) languished as a drawing college until 1767 but thereafter revived as a recognized society–academy. In 1773 the academy members set up a drawing college to provide general instruction in draughtsmanship for young people. Lectures on theory were given at the Stadsteken-academie by dilettanti members such as Cornelis Ploos van Amstel, Jacob Otten-Husly and Jacobus Buys. These dealt with drawing methods, the history of the academy or more polemical subjects such as the status of Dutch landscape painting.

After *c.* 1820 the drawing academies had to make way for the government's hierarchical system of art education. With the establishment of the new Kingdom of the Netherlands in 1815, a central government came into being, which took the opportunity to set up a national academy after the French model. A vain attempt to do this had already been made under Louis Napoleon (*reg* 1806–10). In 1817 William I introduced a law that divided art education into three levels: drawing schools for the general education of children and future craftsmen; drawing academies in the large towns, which would offer training in building construction, surveying and perspective alongside regular training in draughtsmanship; and two royal academies, in Amsterdam and Antwerp, for training artists and architects. An important impetus behind this law was the stimulation of the applied arts by means of better training in draughtsmanship.

In theory the studio system should have been partly replaced by daytime education at the royal academies, but in practice the Amsterdam academy, the Koninklijke Academie van Beeldende Kunsten (KAvBK), could not offer this. Prospective artists therefore still visited studios where in addition they could learn painting. A number of large studios of this kind existed in The Hague and Amsterdam in the first half of the 19th century, including those of Cornelis Kruseman and Jan Adam Kruseman, Louis Meyer (1810–66) and Hendrik van de Sande Bakhuijzen (1795–1864). The French academic doctrine employed by the KAvBK (continual drawing after the Antique and emphasis on history painting) was not in line with pupils' learning in the studios of landscape and genre painters; nor was the art market in the northern Netherlands interested in history painting. This situation was made even worse by the merging of the Amsterdam drawing academy (second level) with the KAvBK. The other subjects at the KAvBK—architecture, engraving and sculpture—prospered even less, also aggravated by the economic malaise in the northern Netherlands, which continued at least until 1860. As in France, a Prix de Rome (*Grote Prijs*) was presented in the Netherlands from 1825, but the poor results and obscure prizewinners demonstrated the KAvBK's shortcomings, and in 1853 the government abolished the competition.

There were a number of changes in art education between 1860 and 1870. The KAvBK was closed down; a new diploma for teachers of drawing was introduced in 1863, when drawing was introduced as a subject in the primary schools; the number of specialized trade schools increased, and the Hogere Burgerschool (HBS) was established. The latter high school included a number of technical subjects in its curriculum that until then had been taught in the academies. The preparations for the drawing teacher's diploma generated considerable interest, particularly at the academy in The Hague. Women were admitted to the academies for the first time in 1870. Schools of applied art were established, influenced by the growing movement in the applied arts, with such subjects as drawing and the theory of ornamentation. The drawing academy in The Hague, formerly the academy of the Pictura, successfully embraced applied art c. 1860; the Kunstnijverheid, Haarlem, was founded in 1879; and the Rijksschool voor Kunstnijverheid, Amsterdam, was founded in 1881.

The successor to the KAvBK, the Rijksacademie van Beeldende Kunsten in Amsterdam (RAvBK; founded 1870), expressly taught fine art. Architecture had disappeared from the academy's curriculum, having been taken over by the Polytechnische School (later the Technische Hogeschool) at Delft in 1863. The RAvBK profited from renewed interest in art and the economic upturn, particularly marked in Amsterdam. It set aside the KAvBK's dogmatism and offered daytime classes, with more attention paid to practical exercises in painting, sculpting and engraving, although drawing and theory still dominated. The 'box' system (providing studios for advanced students at the academy) and the Prix de Rome were successfully reintroduced, the latter in 1884. Tuition in the studio of a renowned master was also largely replaced by daytime classes in The Hague and Rotterdam; although studio painting still took place, it was on a voluntary basis and often followed completion of academy training. The RAvBK expanded under the artist August Allebé, director from 1880 to 1907. Such notable artists as Jan Pieter Veth, Jan Toorop, Antoon Derkinderen, Willem Witsen and Jacobus van Looy studied there; together with artists and designers from the Kunstnijverheidsschool in Haarlem and the Rijksnormaalschool in Amsterdam (e.g. Gerrit Willem Dijsselhof) they gave an important stimulus to Dutch art at the turn of the 20th century.

A new constitution in the 1920s abolished many applied art schools and brought the rest under technical education. Several colleges were merged, including the Instituut voor Kunstnijverheidsonderwijs (1924), later the Rietveldacademie, in Amsterdam, where, under the leadership of the designer Mart Stam, director from 1939 to 1948, experiments in industrial design in the Bauhaus tradition were tried. New directions were also taken at the RAvBK in 1920–30, under Richard Roland Holst, director from 1926 to 1934. Committed to Community art, he also set up a department for monumental art, but the RAvBK remained conservative and focused on the traditional fine arts. Beyond the realm of the established schools, the Nieuwe Kunstschool was set up in Amsterdam in 1933 by Paul Citroen, according to the concept of Johannes Itten. After World War II the two approaches to art education, Bauhaus and the traditional nature observation methods, were used alongside each other. Gradually the Bauhaus method gave way to the *Vrije Expressie* approach, with its emphasis on individual growth influenced by developments in art (e.g. Cobra) and the ideas of Herbert Read.

Evidence of a lack of structured coherence between the various component disciplines and in their content led to protests and debates about reform that lasted throughout the 1960s and 1970s. In 1963 Haarlem Ateliers was established by a number of artists reacting to traditional art education, with the intention of developing pupils' initiative through practical guidance from professionals in the studio. The Mammoth Act, passed in 1968, divided all Dutch education into three levels, but the place of art subjects was a continuing source of debate because of the danger of adapting the special character of this education. Eventually it was decided to bring all art education within the scope of Hoger Beroepsonderwijs (Higher Vocational Training), with the exception of the RAvBK, the Jan van Eijckacademie in Maastricht, Ateliers '63 and the Keramisch Centrum in Heusden, all four of which in 1984 obtained the status of postgraduate institute. The RAvKB became an institute of practical study for art students, following the model of Ateliers '63. The remaining schools of applied art gained academy status, whereby an element of the historic distinction between fine and applied art was removed. In the 1990s most of the 15 academies ran courses in both free and applied art. The number of subjects steadily increased after World War II to encompass graphic art, photography, film and television design, industrial design, ceramics and fashion, as well as teacher training courses.

BIBLIOGRAPHY

K. van Mander: *Schilder-boeck* ([1603]–1604)

W. Goeree: *Inleydinge tot de algemeene teyken-konst* (Amsterdam, 1668)

S. van Hoogstraten: *Hoogeschoole der schilderkonst* (Amsterdam, 1678)

G. de Lairesse: *Grondlegginge ter teekenkonst* (Amsterdam, 1701)

A. Houbraken: *De groote schouburgh* (1718–21)

A. Derkinderen: *De Rijksacademie van Beeldende Kunsten te Amsterdam* (Amsterdam, 1908)

P. Citroen: *Een tekenles, de stip* [A drawing lesson, the dot] (Rotterdam, 1960/*R* 1992)

P. Knolle: 'De Amsterdamse stadstekenacademie, een 18de-eeuwse "oefenschool" voor modeltekenaars', *Ned. Ksthist. Jb.*, xxx (1979), pp. 1–41 [Eng. summary]

J. Willink: *De Rijksakademie en de ideologie van de 'vrije kunst'* (Amsterdam, 1979) [Eng. summary]

M. van de Kamp and others, eds: *De Lucaskrater: Historie en analyse van meningen over het beeldende-kunstonderwijs aan de kunstacademies in Nederland* (Assen, 1984)

E. A. de Klerk: ' "Academy-beelden" and "teeken-schoolen" in Dutch 17th-century Treatises on Art', *Leids Ksthist. Jb.* (1989), pp. 283–8

H. Miedema: 'Over vakonderwijs aan kunstschilders in de Nederlanden tot de zeventiende eeuw', *Leids Ksthist. Jb.* (1989), pp. 268–83 [Eng. summary]

H. van Rheeden: *Om de vorm: Een eeuw teken-, handarbeid- en kunstnijverheidsonderwijs in Nederland* (Amsterdam, 1989)

A. Martis: *Voor de kunst en voor de nijverheid: Het ontstaan van het kunstnijverheidsonderwijs in Nederland* (diss., U. Amsterdam, 1990)

J. Reynaerts: 'Van atelier naar academie: Schilders in opleiding, 1850–1900', *De schilders van tachtig: Nederlandse schilderkunst, 1880–1895* (exh. cat., Amsterdam, Rijksmus. van Gogh, 1991)

H. van Rheeden and others: *Nog een tekenles: Drie bijdragen naar aanleiding van 'Een tekenles, de stip' van Paul Citroen* [Another drawing lesson: three contributions occasioned by 'A drawing lesson, the dot' by Paul Citroen] (The Hague, 1992)

E. van Odijk, J. Reynaerts and E. van Uitert, eds: *Er is eene Rijks-Akademie...: Over ruimte voor kunstenaars* (Bussum, 1995) [Dut. and Eng. text]

J. A. H. REYNAERTS

XVI. Art libraries and photographic collections.

A fairly large proportion of libraries in the Netherlands possess important collections on the history of art. Among these are several of the largest older libraries, where a collection of art-historical literature was systematically assembled during the late 19th century and the 20th around an existing core of older literature. Important examples are the Koninklijke Bibliotheek, The Hague, and the libraries of the universities of Leiden, Utrecht and Amsterdam, each of which has an art history department; these libraries each hold between 70,000 and 100,000 volumes. Of the various museum libraries the oldest and most significant is in the Rijksmuseum, Amsterdam, with *c.* 100,000 books and 30,000 auction catalogues. The libraries of the Museum Boymans–van Beuningen, Rotterdam, the Gemeentemuseum, The Hague, and the Stedelijk Museum, Amsterdam, include material on art after 1930, the last specializing in contemporary art. The most important library covering Western visual arts is the Rijksbureau voor Kunsthistorische Dokumentatie (RKD) in The Hague, which contains *c.* 380,000 volumes, including more than 100,000 auction catalogues. Several libraries are devoted to architectural literature, including those of the Rijksdienst voor de Monumentenzorg in Zeist, the Technische Universiteit in Delft and the Nederlands Architectuurinstituut in Rotterdam.

Numerous Dutch museums contain photographic libraries, some of which are specialized; their contents are usually related to the collections of the museum to which they belong, and they are generally accessible only to the museum staff. The art history institutes of various universities also possess collections of photographs, reproductions and slides, which, although intended primarily for the use of their own staff and students, are frequently accessible to outside researchers. The most important photographic library for Western visual art from the late Middle Ages onwards is at the RKD, which, with more than three million photographs and reproductions, is also the largest collection of its kind in the world. Some 1,700,000 photographs and reproductions are of non-Dutch art, while the rest are concerned with contemporary Dutch and Belgian art. Documentation also includes colour slides, but only in the field of contemporary Dutch art. As a supplement to the collection there are also microfiches, including the *Marburg Index*, and the entire collection of the Witt Library and of the sculpture department of the Conway Library, both in London. The RKD was founded in 1932, initially based on the documentation collected by the art historian Cornelis Hofstede de Groot. It was subsequently enlarged by the systematic addition of photographs and reproductions; the documentation collected by numerous art historians, including Max Jacob Friedländer, as well as that belonging to various other institutions, was also incorporated. The principal part of the collection is organized by individual artists, but there are also smaller segments that are ordered iconographically, including the *DIAL* (*Decimal Index of the Art of the Low Countries*), published from 1950 to 1982 by the RKD. The collection of the Iconographisch Bureau, also in The Hague, is an important complement to the RKD. It is devoted to Dutch portraiture and is organized according to the subjects of the portraits. The most important collection of photographs of Dutch architecture is held by the Rijksdienst voor de Monumentenzorg.

BIBLIOGRAPHY

E. J. Duparc: *Een eeuw strijd voor nederlands cultureel erfgoed* (The Hague, 1975), pp. 233–4, 352–6

I. van Hamelsveld: 'Information Services in the Fields of Art and Architecture', *A. Libs J.*, xii/1 (1987), pp. 8–11

RUDOLF EKKART

XVII. Historiography.

Early forms of the historiography of art in the Netherlands are to be found in literary and general historical works, including chronicles (e.g. M. van Vaernewijk: *Den spieghel der Nederlandscher audheydt*, Ghent, 1568), accounts of travels (e.g. L. Guicciardini: *Descrittione di . . . tutti i Paesi Bassi*, Antwerp, 1567) and diaries. Dutch writers on art history were influenced by direct knowledge of Classical works on the subject (e.g. Pliny) and humanistic digests of those works, particularly in Italy; they also extolled the fame of Dutch art since the time of Jan van Eyck, who was credited with the 'invention' of painting in oils. Such an important innovation played a role in Dutch nationalism similar to that of the alleged invention of book-printing by Laurens Coster of Haarlem: the young Dutch nation pointed to its cultural achievements to assert its position amid its older European neighbours. A comparison was regularly drawn with classical antiquity and with states in the forefront of European civilization, most elaborately in Hugo de Groot's *Parallelon* (written in 1602; published in Haarlem, 1801–3). Apart from nationalistic works of this kind, descriptions of particular cities are important sources since they record, with local pride, information about famous citizens (e.g. Ampzing on Haarlem).

As in art history, so in art historiography Italy was the model for forms and motifs. The humanist Dominique Lampson (1532–99) of Liège compiled a biography of Lambert Lombard, *Lamberti Lombardi apud Eburones pictoris celeberrimi vita* (Bruges, 1565), as a model for the young art of the Netherlands, for which he sought to find a system of rules in the scientific analysis of Plinian motifs. He took as his direct model the life of Michelangelo by Vasari, to whom he supplied information about Dutch painters for the second edition of the *Vite* (1568). The illustrations to that edition, and Giovio's illustrated *Vite*, doubtless prompted Lampson to compile his *Pictorum aliquot celebrium Germaniae inferioris effigies* (Antwerp, 1572), a collection of 22 portraits of Netherlandish painters with laudatory verses in Latin and with a brief account of their work and personal characteristics. A sequel was compiled by Hendrik Hondius, *Pictorum aliquot celebrium praecipue Germaniae inferioris effigies* (The Hague, *c.* 1610). At about the same time the poet and painter LUCAS DE HEERE wrote some picture-poems (*Den hof en boomgaerd der poësien*, Ghent, 1565), after the style of the French Pléiade, including a defence of the Violieren (the Antwerp rhetoricians' guild) and an ode to the van Eyck brothers' Ghent altarpiece; these show a thorough knowledge of ancient and humanistic writings on art and founded a genre that flourished in the northern Netherlands in the 17th century, notably in the picture-poems of Joost van den Vondel (1587–1679) and Jan Vos (1593–1649).

Dutch literature on the subject of art really began with the *Schilder-boeck* (Haarlem, [1603]–1604) by de Heere's pupil Karel van Mander I (*see* VAN MANDER, (1)). In addition to lives of Classical and Italian artists, van Mander collected information about nearly 200 Netherlandish painters. He combined earlier sources with his own research and opinions and applied Vasari's threefold division of history to Netherlandish art: its beginning, after the Gothic style, with van Eyck; the new efflorescence with Jan van Scorel's Italian experience; and its perfection in the work of the Mannerists and especially Hendrick Goltzius. Together with a didactic poem (*De Grondt der edel vry schilderkonst*), a commentary on Ovid and an iconographical lexicon (*Wtbeeldinghe*), van Mander's biographies were part of a grandiose effort to secure for Netherlandish painting a social and intellectual place among the liberal arts; their intention and composition formed a model for succeeding generations. In the tradition of illustrated lives of painters and under the influence of van Mander and van Dyck's *Iconography*, Joannes Meyssens (1612–70) composed his *Images de divers hommes d'esprit* (Antwerp, 1649); the illustrations from this work, together with the portraits from Lampson, were published in London as late as 1705 as *The True Effigies of the Most Eminent Painters*. Meyssen's portraits also formed the basis of *Het gulden cabinet* (Antwerp, 1661), for which the poet and lawyer CORNELIS DE BIE composed extensive laudatory texts, many in verse.

The fullest biographies of the painters of the Golden Age in the Netherlands were given by the painter ARNOLD HOUBRAKEN in *De groote schouburgh* (Amsterdam, 1718–21). Influenced by his teacher Samuel van Hoogstraten's *Inleyding tot de hooge schoole der schilderkonst* (1678) and the theories of Gérard de Lairesse (*Groot schilderboek*,

1707), Houbraken relied for his biographies, to a greater extent than van Mander, on poems, portraits and descriptions of towns; he saw them in the light of Neo-classical theory, which he found exemplified in the work of Adriaen van der Werff. *De nieuwe schouburg* (1750–51) by the animal painter JAN VAN GOOL was intended as a continuation of Houbraken. His interest in contemporary painters and the numerous art collections outweighed the didactic and theoretical bias that characterized earlier biographies. In the *Levensbeschrijvingen der Nederlandsche konstschilders en konstschilderessen* (3 vols, The Hague, 1729–69) the painter and writer Jacob Campo Weyerman made use of Houbraken's material together with a seasoning of piquant anecdotes. The shift of main interest from art theory and art production to art collecting is also seen in Gerard Hoet's *Catalogus of naamlyst der schilderyen, met derzelven pryzen* (2 vols, The Hague, 1752; a third volume by Pieter Terwesten (1714–98), 1770).

From the last quarter of the 18th century increased interest in national art history was shown by learned societies of a nationalist and philosophical character. In opposition to the cultural dominance of France (which affected *inter alia* artistic biography and theory through translations of de Piles etc), the influence of these societies became decisive after the defeat of Napoleon and the recovery of plundered art treasures from Paris. The Kingdom of the United Netherlands, set up in 1814, and the independent Kingdom of Belgium that arose from the revolution of 1830 to a large extent based their claims to historical recognition on their internationally acknowledged artistic record. This led to all manner of rhetorical nationalistic interpretations of history, the defence of the non-academic art of the northern Netherlands and the Belgian cult of Rubens. The collective biography by Roeland van Eynden (1747–1819) and Adriaan van der Willigen (1766–1841), *Geschiedenis der vaderlandsche schilderkunst* (Haarlem, 1816–20; supplement 1840), which was still chronologically arranged, also belongs to the apologetic and nationalist tradition.

Interest in 'typically' Dutch, anti-academic art revived again after 1830 and 1848 under French influence, this time that of the bourgeois-democratic art historians Hippolyte Taine, Théophile Thoré and Eugène Fromentin. In each case basically political motives led to a suspension of the cult of monuments and a historico-critical examination of archives (e.g. Paul Scheltema with the first modern biography of Rembrandt, *Rembrandt: Redevoering over hef leven en de verdiensten van Rembrandt van Rijn*, Amsterdam, 1853). The combination of artistic and historical interests led in 1883 to the foundation of the periodical *Oud-Holland*. Order was brought into the artistic heritage *c.* 1900 by means of historical research and scholarship, largely on the German model. Abraham Bredius summarized the results of his work in archives and museums in eight volumes of the *Künstler-Inventaren* (The Hague, 1915–22). A basis for the classification of the works of numerous 17th-century artists was provided by CORNELIS HOFSTEDE DE GROOT in his *Beschreibendes und kritisches Verzeichnis der Werke der hervorragendsten holländischen Maler des 17. Jahrhunderts* (10 volumes; Esslingen and Paris, 1907–28). In the next generation FRITS LUGT produced *Les Marques des collections de dessins et d'estampes*

(Amsterdam, 1921; suppl., 1956) and *Répertoire des catalogues de ventes publiques . . .* (3 vols, The Hague, 1938–64), standard works of collector's history. The papers bequeathed by these three scholars form the basis of the Rijksbureau voor Kunsthistorische Documentatie (*see* §XVI above).

To a notable extent Dutch art history is concentrated on the great national masters; the Rembrandt-Corpus, for example, developed spectacular methods of identifying the master's works. On the whole, Dutch research has not taken much interest in the art of other countries. As regards classical art, Franciscus Junius's *De pictura veterum* (1637) appeared in Dutch versions from 1641, the best edition being that of Rotterdam (1694). It contains a collection of classical texts on the fine arts but is of more interest from the point of view of philology and art theory than of practical use. Modern Dutch art history received a powerful impulse from iconography with RAYMOND VAN MARLE's pioneering work *Iconographie de l'art profane au moyen âge et à la renaissance* (2 vols, The Hague, 1931), in the tradition of French iconography. New methods were suggested by G. J. HOOGEWERFF, who held the chair of iconology at the Utrecht Institute from 1950 to 1955. The Institute later established a centre for Dutch iconography, art theory and emblematology. Professor Hans van de Waal of Leiden discussed ideas and forms of presentation of history in *Drie eeuwen vaderlandsche geschieduitbeelding, 1500–1800: Een iconologische studie* (2 vols, The Hague, 1952) and laid the basis for a systematic iconography in the photo-project *DIAL* (*Decimal Index of the Art of the Low Countries*, 1950–82) and the iconographic classification system *Iconoclass* (1973–85).

BIBLIOGRAPHY

BWN

K. van Mander: *Schilder-boeck* ([1603]–1604)
C. de Bie: *Het gulden cabinet* (1661)
A. Houbraken: *De groote schouburgh* (1718–21)
F. Lugt: 'History of art', *The Contribution of Holland to the Sciences: A Symposium*, ed. A. J. Barnouw and B. Landheer (New York, 1943), pp. 179–211
J. Hubaux and J. Puraye: 'Dominique Lampson: Lamberti Lombardi. . .vita', *Rev. Belge Archéol. & Hist. A.*, xviii (1949), pp. 53–77
J. Becker: 'Zur niederländischen Kunstliteratur des 16. Jahrhunderts: Lucas de Heere', *Simiolus*, vi (1972–3), pp. 113–27
——: 'Zur niederländischen Kunstliteratur des 16. Jahrhunderts: Domenicus Lampsonius', *Ned. Ksthist. Jb.*, xxiv (1973), pp. 45–61
J. A. Emmens with S. H. Levie: 'The History of Dutch Art History', *Kunsthistorische opstellen*, ii (Amsterdam, 1981), pp. 35–50
P. P. Fehl and others: 'Franciscus Junius and the Defence of Art', *Artibus & Hist.*, iii (1981), pp. 9–55
H. Miedema: *Kunst, kunstenaar en kunstwerk bij Karel van Mander: Een analyse van zijn levensbeschrijvingen* (Alphen aan den Rijn, 1981)
T. J. Broos: *Tussen zwaart en ultramarijn: De levens van schilders beschreven door Jacob Campo Weyerman (1677–1747)* (Amsterdam, 1990)
A. W. Reinink: 'The Continuing Future of the Present in the Visual Arts', *The Humanities in the Nineties: A View from the Netherlands*, ed. E. Zürcher and T. Legendorff (Amsterdam, 1990), pp. 207–26
L. de Vries: *Diamante gedenkzuilen en leerzaeme voorbeelden: Een bespreking van Johan van Gools 'Nieuwe Schouburg'* (Groningen, 1990)
Aspecten van vijftig jaar kunsthistorisch onderzoek, 1938–1988: Colloquium georganiseerd ter gelegenheid van vijftig jaar zelfstandigheid der Koninklijke academie van wetenschappen, letteren en schone kunsten van België: Brussel, 1990
F. Grijzenhout and H. van Veen, eds: *De gouden eeuw in perspectief: Het beeld van de Nederlandse zeventiende-eeuwse schilderkunst in later tijd* (Nijmegen, 1992) [extensive bibliog.]
E. de Jongh: 'Seventeenth-century Dutch Painting: Multi-faceted Research', *Historical Research in the Low Countries*, ed. N. C. F. van Sas and E. Witte (The Hague, 1992), pp. 35–46
J. de Man, ed.: *Kunst op schrift: Een inventarisatie van Nederlandstalige publikaties op het gebied van kunsttheorie en esthetica, 1670–1820* (Leiden, 1993)

JOCHEN BECKER

XVIII. Periodicals.

This article provides a list, arranged chronologically by first date of publication, of the most important art periodicals published in the Netherlands and includes all those with 50% or more of their articles devoted to art. For the history of periodicals in the Netherlands, *see* PERIODICALS, §III, 5(viii). The frequency of publication is given by the following abbreviations: W—weekly, F—fortnightly, M—monthly, B—bi-monthly, Q—quarterly, H—half-yearly, Y—yearly, O—occasionally or irregularly. Other frequencies are given by formulae such as '5 nos, Y', meaning 5 issues per year. With regard to continuations or incorporations under another title, the periodicals are referred to by the year and letter under which they are listed (e.g. '1846a' means *De Nederlandsche teekenportefeuille*, 1846–7). Where appropriate the publishing body is given after the title.

1828 *Magazijn voor schilder- en toonkunst* (Dordrecht, 1828–9), 2 vols, O
1832 *Euphrosyne: Tijdschrift voor de Hollandsche kleeding* (Amsterdam, 1832), 12 nos in 1 vol., M
1834 *Nederlandsch bouwkundig magazijn* (Amsterdam, 1834–8), 11 nos, intended freq. M
1837 *Pictura: Verzameling van uitgezochte studiën voor eerstbeginnenden en gevorderden in de teekenkunst* (The Hague, 1837–42), 6 vols, M
1840a *De beeldende kunsten* (The Hague, 1840–42), 3 vols, Q
1840b *De kunstkronijk* (from 1878 *De kunstkroniek*), Nederlandsche Maatschappij voor Schoone Kunsten (The Hague, 1840–59), 20 vols, M; new ser. (The Hague and Leiden, 1860–76), 18 vols, M; new ser. (The Hague and Leiden, 1878–1906; 1910), 15 vols, M [incorp. 1848b in 1850; cont. as 1879]
1843a *Bouwkundige bijdragen*, Maatschappij tot Bevordering der Bouwkunst (Amsterdam, 1843–81), 26 vols [cont. as 1881a]
1843b *Bouwkundig magazijn of Schetsen voor handwerkslieden* (Gorinchem, 1843–51), 9 vols, O; new ser. (Gorinchem, 1852–6), 5 vols, O
1844 *De Nederlandsche kunst-spiegel* (The Hague, 1844/5–6/7), 2 vols, M
1846a *De Nederlandsche teekenportefeuille* (The Hague, 1846–7), 2 vols, Q
1846b *Nederlandsch kunst- en letterblad* (Utrecht, 1846), 1 vol. [suppl. to *Nederlandsch muzikaal tijdschrift*]
1846c *Teekenkundig magazijn* (Gorinchem, 1846–51), 6 vols, M
1847 *De Hollandsche schilderschool* (The Hague, ?1847) [cont. as 1848]
1848 *Hollandsch schilder- en letterkundig album* (The Hague, 1848–9), 2 vols, B [cont. from 1847; incorp. into 1840b]
1849 *Pictura: Een blad voor beoefenaars en voorstanders der schilderkunst* (Arnhem, 1849), 24 nos in 1 vol., F
1850 *Album der schoone kunsten, romantisch, kritiesch en historiesch tijdschrift voor Hollandsche en Vlaamsche letterkunde en kunst* (Haarlem, 1850–54), 5 vols, ?M
1855 *De Dietsche warande: Tijdschrift voor Nederlandsche oudheden en nieuwere kunst en letteren*, subtitle varies with each ser. (Amsterdam, 1855–74), 10 vols; new ser. (Amsterdam, 1876–86), 5 vols; new ser. (Ghent, later The Hague, 1887–99), 12 vols
1864 *Tijdschrift voor photographie* (Arnhem, 1864–6, 1868–97), 25 vols, M
1866 *De opmerker: Weekblad voor beeldende kunst en technische wetenschap*, Genootschap Architectura et Amicitia (Arnhem, 1866–1918), 53 vols, W
1870 *Kunst en industrie* (Amsterdam, 1870–83), 14 vols, M
1873a *Het gildeboek: Tijdschrift voor kerkelijke kunst en oudheidkunde*, from 1956 *Kunst en religie*, St Bernulphus-Gilde (Utrecht, 1873–81), 3 vols, Q; new ser. (Utrecht, 1886–99), 4 vols, Q; new ser. (Utrecht, 1918–62), 43 vols, 3 nos, Y
1873b *De kunstbode* (Zaltbommel, 1873), 1 vol., W [cont. as 1874]
1874 *De Nederlandsche kunstbode tot opwekking: Aankweeking en veredeling van den Nederlandschen kunstsmaak en schoonheidszin* (Haarlem, 1874–6), 3 vols, W [cont. from 1873b; cont. as 1879]

1876 *Mededeelingen van de rijksadviseurs voor de monumenten van geschiedenis en kunst*, Departement van Onderwijs, Kunsten en Wetenschap (The Hague, 1876–8), 2 nos

1877 *Archief voor Nederlandsche kunstgeschiedenis* (Rotterdam, 1877–90), 7 vols, O

1878 *Verslagen omtrent 's rijks verzamelingen van geschiedenis en kunst*, Ministerie van Onderwijs, Kunsten en Wetenschap, from 1968 *De Nederlandsche Rijksmusea*, Ministerie van Cultuur, Recreatie en Maatschappelijk Werk (The Hague, 1878–1987), 109 vols, Y

1879 *Nederlandsche kunstbode* (Haarlem, 1879–81), 3 vols, W [cont. from 1874]

1881a *Bouwkundig tijdschrift*, Maatschappij tot Bevordering van de Bouwkunst (Amsterdam, 1881–1908), 24 vols, B [cont. from 1843a; cont. as 1909a]

1881b *Bouwkundig weekblad* [incorp. 1893 in 1927 to form *Bouwkundig weekblad Architectura*, Maatschappij tot Bevordering der Bouwkunst] (Amsterdam, 1881–1941; 1943–1969), 87 vols, W [cont. as 1970c]

1883 *Oud-Holland: Nieuwe bijdragen voor de geschiedenis der Nederlandse kunst, letterkunde, nijverheid, enz.*, from 1923 subtitle varies, Netherlands Institute for Art History (Amsterdam, 1883–1971; The Hague, 1973–), O, from 1893 Q, from 1923 O, from 1926 B, from 1951 Q; from 1950 suppl. 1946g [Dut., Fr., Eng. and Ger.; from 1973 with Eng. summaries]

1884a *Kunstbode* (Amsterdam, 1884–5), 1 vol., W

1884b *Maandblad gewijd aan de belangen van het teekenonderwijs en de kunstnijverheid in Nederland*, from 1912 *Maandblad voor het teekenonderwijs in Nederland*, Nederlandsche Vereeniging voor het Teekenonderwijs (Amsterdam, 1884/5–1930/31), 47 vols, M

1885a *De ambachtsman* (Maassluis, 1885–93), 8 vols, W; from 1901 2 nos, M [cont. as 1893]

1885b *De bouwmeester*, Genootschap Architectura et Amicitia (Arnhem, 1885–95), 7 vols, B [incorp. into 1890]

1885c *Navorscher op het gebied der photographie* (Nijmegen, 1885–), 11 vols

1885d *Verslag: Vereeniging Rembrandt Nationaal fonds kunstbehoud* (Amsterdam, 1885–), Y

1886 *Vademecum der bouwvakken* (Amsterdam, 1886–1928), 43 vols, 1886 M; later B

1889 *Lux* (Amsterdam, 1889–1927), 39 vols [incorp. 1894a; incorp. 1915a; incorp. into 1908] [photography], M

1890 *De architect*, Genootschap Architectura et Amicitia (Arnhem, 1890–1915), 22 vols, B [incorp. 1885b]

1891a *Arti et industriae* (The Hague, 1891–2), 2 vols, Q

1891b *Photographisch jaarboek*, from 1893/4 *Fotografisch jaarboek* (Amsterdam, 1891–5), 4 vols, Y

1893 *Architectura*, Genootschap Architectura et Amicitia (Maassluis, 1893–1917; 1921–6), 30 vols, W. [cont. from 1885a; incorp. into 1881b]; suppl.: *Architectura technisch gedeelte* (1893–8), 6 vols [incorp. into main periodical]

1894a *Geïllustreerd weekblad voor fotografie* (Zutphen, 1894–1910), 17 vols, W [incorp. into 1889]

1894b *De kunstwereld* (Amsterdam, 1894–9), 6 vols, W

1898a *Bouw en sierkunst: Revue bimestrielle de l'art antique et moderne* (Haarlem, 1898–1904), 4 vols, B [Dut. and Fr.]

1898b *Hollandsche prentkunst* (Amsterdam, 1898), 1 vol.

1899a *Bulletin KNOB*, Koninklijke Nederlandse Oudheidkundige Bond, 1st ser. (Amsterdam, 1899–1907), 8 vols, Y; 2nd ser. (Leiden, 1908–20), 13 vols, Y; 3rd ser. *Oudheidkundig jaarboek* (Utrecht, 1921–31), 11 vols, Y; 4th ser. (Leiden, 1932–46), 13 vols, Y except 1944–5; 5th ser. *Bulletin van den Nederlandschen oudheidkundigen bond* (Leiden, 1947), 1 vol., Y; 6th ser. *Bulletin & nieuws-bulletin van de Nederlandse*, from 1949 *Koninklijke Nederlandse oudheidkundige Bond* (Leiden, 1948–64), 17 vols, Y; *Bulletin van de Koninklijke Nederlandse oudheidkundige bond* (Leiden, 1965–), starts with vol. lxiv

1899b *Camera obscura* (Amsterdam, 1899/1900–1900/01), 2 vols, M [Eng., Ger., Dut. and Fr.]

1899c *Maandblad der Vereeniging voor verbetering van vrouwenkleeding*, from 1910 *Onze Kleeding: Maandblad van de Vereeniging vakschool voor verbetering van vrouwen- en kinderkleeding* (The Hague, 1899–1918), 19 vols, M

1902 *De bouwwereld* (Amsterdam, 1902–24), 23 vols, W

1903a *Het huis*, from 1928 *Het Nederlandsche en Nederlandsch-Indische huis* (Amsterdam, 1903–31), 20 vols, M

1903b *Moderne kunstwerken* (Amsterdam, 1903–10), 8 vols, M

1904 *Kritiek van beeldende kunsten en kunstnijverheid* (Amsterdam, 1904–6), 3 vols, M

1905a *Fotografisch maandschrift* (Bolsward, 1905/6–1913/14), 9 vols, M

1905b *Jonge kunst*, Nederlandsche Vereeniging voor Ambachts- en Nijverheidskunst (Haarlem, 1905/6), 18 nos in 2 vols, M [incorp. into *Onze kunst* (Antwerp)]

1907 *Bulletin van de Maatschappij voor beeldende kunsten* (Amsterdam, 1907–21), 15 vols

1908 *De camera*, from 1927 *Lux – De Camera* (The Hague, 1908–33), 44 vols, Q [incorp. 1889]

1909a *Bouwkunst*, Maatschappij tot Bevordering van de Bouwkunst (The Hague, 1909–14), 6 vols, B

1909b *Klei*, Vereeniging van Nederlandsche Baksteenfabricanten, from 1962 *Klei en keramiek*, Nederlandse Keramische Vereeniging (Amsterdam, 1909–44), 36 vols, M; new ser. (Rijswijk, 1951–79), 29 vols, M [cont. as 1980e]

1909c *Kunst* (Amsterdam, 1909–42), 42 vols, W

1911a *De ark: Tijdschrift voor algemene reclamekunst* (Amsterdam, 1911), 4 nos in 1 vol., Q

1911b *Kunst aan het volk* (Amsterdam, 1911–13)

1911c *Kunst en kunstleven* (The Hague, 1911–12), 2 vols, M

1912a *Binnenhuiskunst* (Amsterdam, 1912/13), 1 vol., B

1912b *Gewapend beton* (Amsterdam, 1912–36), 24 vols, M

1913 *Beeldende kunst* (Utrecht, 1913–42), 30 vols, M

1914 *Jaarboekje van de Vereeniging tot bevordering der grafische kunst* (Rotterdam, 1914–24), 11 vols, Y

1915 *Oude kunst* (Haarlem, 1915–21; 1929–30), 8 vols, M; suppl.: *Veilingskroniek* (1917–18), 52 nos in 2 vols, W

1916a *Het journaal van den modernen kunstkring* (Amsterdam, 1916–17), 2 vols

1916b *De Nederlandsche musea* (Utrecht, 1916–17), 4 nos

1916c *Het signaal*, Kunstgroep Het signaal (Bussum, 1916–17), 2 vols, Y

1917 *De stijl: Maandblad voor de moderne beeldende vakken*, founding ed. Theo van Doesburg (Leiden, 1917–28; 1932/R 1968), 89 nos in 16 vols, 1 no. in 1932, M

1918a *De Cicerone: Algemeen maandschrift over kunst* (The Hague, 1918–19), 2 vols, M

1918b *Jaarverslag Vereeniging Hendrick de Keyser* (Amsterdam, 1918–), Y [historical buildings and monuments]

1918c *Levende kunst* (The Hague, 1918–20), 3 vols, M

1918d *Vaevo: Aesthetische vorming door beeldende expressie en beeldende voorstelling*, Vereeniging tot bevordering van het Aesthetisch element in het Voortgezet onderwijs (The Hague, 1918–58), 45 vols

1918e *Wendingen*, Genootschap Architectura et Amicitia (Amsterdam, 1918–31), 12 vols, O

1919a *Binnenhuis en buitenwereld* (The Hague, 1919–39), 21 vols, M

1919b *Jaarboek Nederlandsche ambachts- en nijverheidskunst* (Rotterdam, 1919–31), 10 vols, Y

1919c *Kunst in Arnhem*, Arnhemsche Kunstkring (Arnhem, 1919), 1 vol., M

1919d *Mededelingen van de Dienst voor schone kunsten der gemeente 's Gravenhage*, from 1955 *Mededelingen Gemeentemuseum Den Haag* (The Hague, 1919–60), 14 vols, B

1919e *Het orgaan der Federatie van Nederlandsche beeldende kunstenaars vereenigingen* (Renkum, 1919–21), 3 vols, M

1920a *Tampon: Orgaan voor de leerlingen en oud-leerlingen der School voor de grafische Vakken* (Utrecht, 1920–72), 47 vols, Q

1920b *Tijdschrift voor volkshuisvesting en stedebouw*, from 1958 *Stedebouw en volkshuisvesting*, Nederlands Instituut voor Volkshuisvesting en Stedebouw (Amsterdam, 1920–) M, later B

1921 *Mededelingen van het Nederlands Instituut te Rome* (The Hague, 1921–), Y

1922a *Maandblad kunst aan het volk*, Vereeniging kunst aan het volk (Delft, 1922–30), 9 vols, M

1922b *Maandblad van den Amsterdamschen kunstkring 'Voor Allen'* (Amsterdam, 1922–9), 8 vols, M

1922c *Mecano* (Leiden, 1922–3/R 1980), 5 nos [Dada]

1923 *Bouwen*, Betonbond (Haarlem, 1923–6), 4 vols, F

1924a *Heemschut: Voor behoud van stedelijke en landschappelijke schoonheid* (Amsterdam, 1924–), B

1924b *Maandblad voor beeldende kunsten* (Amsterdam, 1924–50), 26 vols, M; suppl. 1929a

1927a *De delver*, Vereeniging Kunstkring Delft (Delft, 1927/8–1940/41), 14 vols, M

1927b *Internationale revue i 10* (Amsterdam, 1927–9), 22 nos in 2 vols, M [architecture, design]

1929a *Bulletin van de Vereeniging van vrienden der Aziatische kunst* (Amsterdam, 1929–82); 1929–44 suppl. in 1924b, M; 1946–9 suppl. in 1946i, M; from 1950 Q

1929b *Het roomsch-katholieke bouwblad*, from 1940 *Het (from 1946 Katholiek) bouwblad*, from 1960 *Tijdschrift voor architectuur en beeldende kunsten*, from 1971 *TA/BK* (1929–39; Voorburg, 1940–41; The Hague, 1946–59; Heerlen, 1960–72), 39 vols, F [incorp. 1930e in 1934; incorp. into 1970g]

1930a *Balans* (Maastricht, 1930/31), 1 vol., Y

1930b *Bouw en techniek*, from 1932 *de 8 en Opbouw*, from 1932 Architectenkern 'de 8', Amsterdam, and Opbouw, Rotterdam (Rotterdam, 1930–43/R 1985), 14 vols, F

1930c *Het grafisch museum*, Museum voor de Grafische Vakken en het Verbond van Boekenvrienden (Utrecht, 1930/31–8), 8 vols, Q

1930d *De kunst der Nederlanden* (Amsterdam and Brussels, 1930–31), 1 vol., M

1930e *Van bouwen en sieren*, Algemeene rooms katholieke Kunstenaarsvereeniging (Den Bosch, 1930–33), 4 vols [incorp. into 1929b]

1931a *Forum: Maandschrift voor letteren en kunst* (Rotterdam, 1931–5), 4 vols, M

1931b *Maandbericht van de Vereeniging Tempelbouw* (Rotterdam, 1931–6), 6 vols, M

1932 *Boekcier*, Nederlandschen Ex-Libris Kring (Maastricht, 1932–40), 7 vols, M; (Wassenaar, later The Hague, 1946–63), 18 vols, M [cont. as 1964]

1934 *Cosmorama: Maandblad voor internationale fotokunst* (Meppel, 1934–43), 9 vols, 8 nos Y, from 1937 M

1935 *Kroniek van hedendaagsche kunst en kultuur*, from 1940 *Kroniek van kunst en kultuur* (Bussum, 1935/6–65), 24 vols, B

1936 *Prisma der kunsten*, Nederlandsche kunstenaarsvereenigingen, Nederlandsche Vereeniging voor Ambachts- en Nijverheidskunst (Zeist, 1936–7), 2 vols, M

1937 *Bulletin Museum Boymans* (from 1958 *Boymans–van Beuningen*) (Rotterdam, 1937–71), 21 vols, Q; new ser. (1972–8), 33 nos, B

1938 *Bulletin van de Vereeniging voor Japansche grafiek en kleinkunst*, 1st ser. (Bovenkerk, later Wassenaar, 1938–42), 12 nos, O; 2nd ser. (Wassenaar, 1942–9), 12 nos, O; 3rd ser. (Wassenaar, 1955–9), 4 nos, O

1940 *Halcyon: Driemaandelijks tijdschrift voor boek-, druk- en prentkunst* (The Hague, 1940–42), 3 vols, Q

1941a *Nederlandsch jaarboek voor fotokunst* (Hengelo, 1941–9), 6 nos, Y

1941b *Orgaan der Nederlandsch-Duitsche kultuurgemeenschap/Monatschrift der Niederländisch-Deutschen Kulturgemeinschaft* (The Hague, 1941–4), 4 vols, M [Dut. and Ger.]

1941c *De vrije kunstenaar* (1941–5/R 1970), 33 nos, O

1942 *De schoow. Tijdschrift gewijd aan het kulturele leven in Nederland*, Nederlandsche Kultuurkamer (?The Hague, 1942–5), 4 vols, F

1943 *De stijl: Maandschrift der officieuze societeit gewijd aan kunst en wetenschap* (1943), 4 nos, M [cont. as 1944b]

1944a *Kunst van Nederland* (Naarden, 1944–7), 3 vols, O

1944b *Maecenas* (Voorburg, 1944–5), 7 nos, O [cont. from 1943; cont. as *En passant*]

1946a *Ambacht* (Amsterdam, 1946–8), 2 vols, M

1946b *Bouw*, Stichting Bouw (The Hague, 1946–), F

1946c *Constgbesellen*, Nederlandsche Vereeniging van Kunsthandelaren (Delft, 1946–8), 3 vols, M

1946d *Forum: Maandschrift voor architectuur en gebonden kunsten*, from 1984/5 subtitle in Eng., Genootschap Arti et Amicitia (Amsterdam, 1946/7–), M, from 1960 B, from 1980 Q [from 1984/5 in Dut. and Eng.]

1946e *Jaarboekje Nederlandsche kastelenstichting* (The Hague, 1946–), Y

1946f *Kroniek van de Vriendenkring van het Rembrandthuis*, from 1969 *Kroniek van het Rembrandthuis*, Stichting Het Rembrandthuis (Amsterdam, 1946–), H

1946g *Kunsthistorische mededeelingen van het Rijksbureau voor kunsthistorische documentatie*, from 1950 *Mededelingen van het Rijksbureau voor kunsthistorische documentatie*, from 1950 suppl. of 1883 (The Hague, 1946–60), 15 vols, Q

1946h *Open oog: Avandgardecahier voor visuele vormgeving* (Amsterdam, 1946–?), 2 nos, O

1946i *Phoenix: Maandblad voor beeldende kunsten* (Amsterdam, 1946–9), 4 vols, M; suppl. 1929a

1947a *Nederlandsch* (from 1954 *Nederlands*) *kunsthistorisch jaarboek*, from 1954 with alternate title *Netherlands Yearbook for History of Art*, from 1972 Foundation for Dutch Art-Historical Publications (Bussum and Weesp, 1954–86; Houten, 1987; Haarlem, 1988; The Hague, 1989; Zwolle, 1990–), M, from 1960 B, from 1980 Q [from 1984/5 in Dut. and Eng.]

1947b *Rotterdam bouwt*, incorp. 1953b in 1957 to form *Stedebouw*, title change in 1966 *Stedenbouw* [incl. architecture in Belgium] (Rotterdam, 1947–), M

1948a *Goed wonen*, Stichting Goed Wonen (Rotterdam, 1948–68), 21 vols, M [cont. as 1969c]

1948b *Kunst en kunstleven*, Kunstenaarsvereniging De Onafhankelijken (The Hague, 1948–50), 2 vols, M

1948c *Reflex*, Experimentele Groep in Holland (Amsterdam, 1948–9), 2 vols, Y

1949a *Cement*, Nederlandse Betonvereniging (Amsterdam, 1949–), M

1949b *Het onafhankelijk schetsblad*, Beeldende Kunstenaarsvereniging De Onafhankelijken (Amsterdam, 1949/50), 14 nos in 1 vol., B [cont. as 1955b] [drawing]

1950 *K & B*, Stichting Kunst en Bedrijf (Amsterdam, 1950–82), Q [cont. as 1982d]

1951a *Bulletin internationales Burgenforschungs-Institut* (Rosendaal, 1951–), Y [Eng., Fr., Ger.]

1951b *Creatie*, Vereniging tot bevordering van absolute kunst (Amsterdam, 1951), 1 vol., O

1951c *Zwart en wit* (Amsterdam, 1951–65), 7 vols, Q, from 1955 2 nos, Y [cont. as 1980k] [drawing]

1953a *Bulletin van het Rijksmuseum* (The Hague, 1953–), Q

1953b *Nieuwbouw Nederland* (Rotterdam, 1953–6), 3 vols [incorp. into 1947b]

1953c *Wikor: Algemeen tijdschrift voor de rijpere jeugd over kunst en haar verschijningsvormen*, from 1968 *A.k.t., algemeen kunsttijdschrift*, Stichting Werk- en Informatiecentrum voor Kunst ten Dienste van het Onderwijs aan de Rijpere Jeugd (The Hague, later Groningen, 1953–70), 18 vols, 10 nos, Y

1954 *Mededelingenblad Vrienden van de Nederlandsche ceramiek*, from 1979 *Mededelingenblad Nederlandsche Vereeniging van Vrienden van de ceramiek*, from 1992 *Vormen uit vuur* (Amsterdam, 1954–91; Zwolle, 1992–), Q

1955a *Museumjournaal* (Amsterdam, 1955–88), 23 vols, B [combined with 1977g to form 1988c]

1955b *Onafhankelijke schetsen* (Amsterdam, 1955/6), 1 vol., B [cont. from 1949b] [drawing]

1957 *Openbaar kunstbezit*, from 1982 *Kunstschrift*, Stichting Openbaar Kunstbezit (Amsterdam, 1957–), B

1958 *Exlibris-wereld*, Ex-Libris Kring (Amsterdam, 1958–), Q

1959a *Baksteen* (Arnhem, 1959–82), 24 vols, B

1959b *Tentoonstellingsagenda*, Rijksbureau voor Kunsthistorische Documentatie (The Hague, 1959–86), 28 vols, 17 nos, Y [cont. as 1987h]

1959c *Textielhistorische bijdragen*, Stichting Textielgeschiedenis (Hengelo, 1959–), Y

1960 *Zien*, Stichting Architectuur (Utrecht, 1960–67), 8 vols, M [cont. as 1968j]

1963 *Kunst van nu* (Amsterdam, 1963–), M

1964 *Exlibris 64*, Nederlandse Ex-Libris Kring (Muiderberg, 1964), 1 vol., Y [cont. from 1932]

1966a *Antiek* (Lochem, 1966–), 10 nos, Y [Eng. summaries through 1984]

1966b *Simiolus: Kunsthistorisch tijdschrift*, in 1971 subtitle *A Quarterly for the History of Art*, from 1972 subtitle *Netherlands Quarterly for the History of Art*, Foundation for Dutch Art-Historical Publications (Amsterdam, 1966/7–69; Nijmegen, 1970/71; Maarsen, 1980–83; Utrecht, 1984–), 3 nos, Y, from 1971 Q [from 1971 in Dut. and Eng.]

1967 *De lamp: Voorlichtings en opinieblad met betrekking tot het behoud en het herstel van de Amsterdamse binnenstad*, from 1988 *Binnenstad*, Vereniging Vrienden van de Amsterdamse binnenstad Diogenes (Amsterdam, 1967–), B

1968a *Bijvoorbeeld: Vormgeving en kunst* (Mijdrecht, 1968–), Q

1968b *Futura: Visies ter visie, informatie- en kommunikatieblad van het Nederlands Architectengenootschap* (The Hague, 1968–84), 17 vols, M [cont. from 1960]

1969a *Feniks*, Stichting Kroniek van Kunst en Kultuur (Amsterdam, 1969), 3 nos, O

1969b *Kunsthistorische studien van het Nederlands historisch instituut te Rome* (The Hague, 1969–76), 4 vols, O

1969c *Wonen: Maandblad voor wonen en woonkultuur*, Stichting Wonen (Amsterdam, 1969), 1 vol., M [cont. from 1948a; cont. as 1970g]

1969d *De woonstede door de eeuwen heen/Maisons d'hier et d'aujourd'hui*, Nederlandse Kastelen Stichting and Association Royale des Demeures Historiques de Belgique (Doorn and Ayeneux, 1969–), Q [Dut. and Fr.]

1970a *De architect* (The Hague, 1970–), M

1970b *Bulletin Beroepsvereniging van beeldende kunstenaars BBK '69* (Amsterdam, 1970–75), 23 nos, Q

1970c *Plan: Onafhankelijk tijdschrift voor ontwerp en omgeving* (The Hague, 1970–), B [cont. from 1881b]

1970d *Stichting Alde Fryske kerken* (Leeuwarden, 1970–), B

1970e *Verenigingsblad musea restaurateurs en technici*, from 1972 *Conserveren – restaureren*, Vereniging van restauratoren en technici (Amsterdam, 1970–79), 10 vols

1970f *Vincent*, Rijksmuseum Vincent van Gogh (Amsterdam, 1970–76), 4 vols, Q

1970g *Wonen*, from 1973 *Wonen—TA/BK*, Stichting Wonen (Amsterdam, 1970–72; Deventer, 1973–85), 16 vols, M, from 1973 F [cont. from 1969c; incorp. 1929b in 1973; cont. as 1986a]

1971a *Mededelingenblad van de Vereniging van Vrienden der Aziatische kunst*, from 1987 *Aziatische Kunst* (Amsterdam, 1971–), Q

1971b *Museummemo*, Gemeente 's-Gravenhage, Dienst Schone Kunsten (The Hague, 1971–), Y

1971c *Tegel*, Stichting Vrienden van het Tegelmuseum It Noflik Sté (Otterlo, 1971–), Y

1972 *Bulletin van het Stedelijk Museum* (Amsterdam, 1972–), M

1973a *Fandangos* (Maastricht, 1973–8), 11 nos, O

1973b *Jaarboek en verslag Stichting Menno van Coehoorn*, from 1975 *Jaarboek Stichting Menno van Coehoorn* (The Hague, 1973–), Y

1973c *Pulchri*, Schilderkundig Genootschap Pulchri Studio (The Hague, 1973–), 5 nos, Y

1973d *Het vijf kerken restauratieplan*, Publiciteitscommissie Binnenstadskerken (Utrecht, 1973–), Q

1975a *Antiekrevue*, from 1978 *Kunst en antiekrevue* (The Hague, 1975–), M

1975b *Bulletin van de Stichting oude Hollandse kerken* (Leiden, 1975–), B

1975c *KunstWERK*, Kunsthistorisch Instituut of the Katholieke Universiteit Nijmegen (Nijmegen, 1975–81), 24 nos, O

1975d *Stichting oude gelderse kerken* (Velp, 1975–), B

1976a *Bulletin van het Dordrechts Museum* (Dordrecht, 1976–), B

1976b *Kunstbeeld* (Alphen aan den Rijn, 1976–), M

1976c *Open house: Housing and the Built Environment*, Stichting Architecten Research (Eindhoven, 1976–), Q [Eng.]

1976d *Op weg naar de heilstaat*, from 1979 *De heilstaat*, Kunsthistorisch Instituut of the Universiteit van Amsterdam (Amsterdam, 1976–83), 8 vols, Q

1977a *Akt: Aktueel kunsttijdschrift*, Instituut voor Kunstgeschiedenis of the Rijksuniversiteit Groningen (Groningen, 1977–), Q

1977b *Bulletin Stichting oude Zeeuwse kerken* (Middelburg, 1977–), B

1977c *Bulletin van het Centraal Laboratorium voor onderzoek van voorwerpen van kunst en wetenschap* (Amsterdam, 1977), 1 no.

1977d *Bulletin van het Rijksmuseum Twenthe* (Enschede, 1977–), Q

1977e *Bulletin Vereniging van edelsmeden en sieraadontwerpers* (Amsterdam, 1977–94), B [incorp. into 1968a]

1977f *Camera Oldtimer Club*, from 1982 *Photohistorisch tijdschrift*, Vereniging Fotografica (Haarlem, 1977–)

1977g *Dutch Art + Architecture Today*, Netherlands Office for Fine Arts (The Hague, 1977–88), 10 vols, B [combined with 1955a to form 1988c] [Dut. and Eng.]

1977h *Ephemera* (Amsterdam, 1977–8), 9 nos, M

1977i *Reflexions*, Canon Photo Gallery (Amsterdam, 1977–80), 4 vols, M; (Amsterdam, 1982–7), 34 nos, B

1978a *Artzien* (Amsterdam, 1978–82), O

1978b *Modern Brabant* (Den Bosch, 1978), 2 nos, O

1978c *Het prachtige blad glamoer* (Nijmegen, 1978–9), 6 nos, M

1978d *Tableau: Fine Arts Magazine* (Amsterdam, 1978–), B [Eng. summaries]

1979a *Hard werken* (Rotterdam, 1979–82), 10 nos, Q

1979b *Kunst laaft*, Vereniging van Verzamelaars van Grafiek (Amsterdam, 1979–85), 10 nos, O

1979c *Magazijn* (1979), 2 nos, O

1979d *Metropolis M: Tweemaandelijks tijdschrift over hedendaagse kunst* (Amsterdam, 1979–), B

1979e *Pomflet*, Provinciaal Overijssels Museum (Zwolle, 1979–), Q

1980a *Het bestaan* (Leeuwarden, 1980–84), 4 nos, O

1980b *Dossier* (Amsterdam, 1980), 1 no., O

1980c *De Enschedese school* (Enschede, 1980–82), 10 nos, O

1980d *De hant* (Amsterdam, 1980), 2 nos, O

1980e *Klei, glas, keramiek*, from 1992 *KGK: Tijdschrift voor klei, glas en keramiek*, Nederlandse Keramische Federatie (Tiel, 1980–91; Heemskerk, 1992–), M [cont. from 1909c]

1980f *Kunstlicht*, Vakgroep Kunstgeschiedenis of the Vrije Universiteit (Amsterdam, 1980–), Q

1980g *Modern denken*, Stichting Vrouwen in de Beeldende Kunst (Amsterdam, 1980–84), 8 nos, O

1980h *Monumenten*, Stichting Monumenten and the Monumentenwacht (Cuyk, 1980–), B

1980i *Perspektief: Quarterly Photography Magazine*, Stichting Perspektief (Rotterdam, 1980–), B, from 1981 Q [Dut. and Eng.]

1980j *ZIEN: The Precious Picture Magazine*, Stichting Pretentieus (Rotterdam, 1980–86), 9 nos, O [cont. as 1988a] [contemporary photography; Eng.]

1980k *Zwart en wit* (Oosterbeek, 1980–82), 7 nos, Q [cont. from 1951c] [drawing]

1981a *Drukwerk de zaak* (Groningen, 1981–9), 40 nos, B

1981b *Fodor*, Museum Fodor (Amsterdam, 1981–8), 7 vols, B

1981c *Industriële archeologie*, Stichting Industriële Archeologie in Nederland (Tilburg, 1981–92), 11 vols, Q [cont. as 1992b]

1981d *Items: Tijdschrift voor vormgeving*, Stichting Openbaar Kunstbezit (Amsterdam, 1981–), Q

1981e *OASE: Ontwerp, onderzoek, onderwijs*, Stichting OASE (Delft, 1981–), Q

1981f *Regout: Tijdschrift voor liefhebbers en kenners van aardewerk. Petrus Regout & Co 'De Sphinx' te Maastricht* (Leeuwarden, 1981–2), 2 vols, 10 nos, Y

1982a *Catharijnebrief: Mededelingen van de Vereniging van Vrienden van het Museum Het Catharijneconvent* (Utrecht, 1982–), Q

1982b *Decorum*, Kunsthistorisch Instituut & Prentenkabinet der Rijksuniversiteit Leiden (Leiden, 1982–), Q

1982c *Ja* (Amsterdam, 1982), 1 no., O

1982d *Kunst en omgeving*, Stichting Kunst en Bedrijf (Amsterdam, 1982–7), 6 vols [cont. from 1950; cont. as 1987e]

1982e *Leids kunsthistorisch jaarboek*, from 1994 *Leidse kunsthistorische reeks* (Leiden, 1982–), Y

1983a *Amsterdamse monumenten*, Gemeentelijk Bureau Monumentenzorg (Amsterdam, 1983–8), 6 vols, Q

1983b *Artillerie*, Kunsthistorisch Instituut of the Katholieke Universiteit van Nijmegen (Nijmegen, 1983–8), 6 vols, O

1983c *Castellogica*, Nederlandse Kastelen Stichting (Doorn, 1983–), O

1983d *Code* (Amsterdam, 1983–9), 1 no., O

1983e *Industriële vormgeving* (Delft, 1983–), B

1983f *Newski Prospekt* (Amsterdam, 1983), 1 no., O

1983g *Plaatwerk* (Amsterdam, 1983–7), 24 nos, O [photography]

1983h *Teylers Museum magazijn*, Teylers Museum (Haarlem, 1983–), Q

1984a *De angst* (Amsterdam, 1983–4), 2 nos, O

1984b *Beeld*, Stichting Beeld, Kunsthistorisch Instituut of the Universiteit van Amsterdam (Amsterdam, 1984–9), 4 vols, Q [cont. as 1990d]

1984c *Geschiedenis van de Nederlandse fotografie in monografieën en thema-artikelen*, Prentenkabinet, Rijksuniversiteit Leiden (Alphen aan den Rijn, 1984–), 3 nos, Y

1984d *Groninger kerken*, Stichting Oude Groninger Kerken (Groningen, 1984–), Q

1984e *Jong Holland* (The Hague, 1984–), Q [post-1850 art in the Netherlands]

1984f *Kaag: Schotschrift* (Amsterdam, 1984–6), 6 nos, O

1984g *Kostuum*, Nederlandse Kostuumvereniging voor mode en streekdracht (Amersfoort, 1984–), Y

1984h *Pares, Interpares* (Amsterdam, 1984–5), 7 nos, M

1984i *Ruimte*, Foundation Women in the Visual Arts (Amsterdam, 1984–), Q

1984j *Textuur*, Nederlands Textielmuseum (Tilburg, 1984–), Q

1985a *d'Arts* (Groningen, 1985–), O [management]

1985b *Het bassin* (Maastricht, 1985–7), 7 nos, 0

1985c *Hoogsteder-Naumann Mercury* (Zwolle, 1985–92), 14 vols, O

1985d *Kunst en beleid in Nederland*, Boekmanstichting (Amsterdam, 1985–), Y

1985e *Mediamatic: European Media Art Magazine* (Amsterdam, 1985–), Q [Eng.]

1985f *De sluitsteen*, Cuypers Genootschap (Ohè en Laak, 1985–), 3 nos, Y [19th-century Dutch architecture]

1986a *Archis: Tijdschrift voor architectuur, stedebouw en beeldende kunst*, Stichting Wonen (Deventer, 1986–), M [cont. from 1970g]

1986b *Het moment: Kwartaalboek voor nieuwe literatuur en kunst* (Amsterdam, 1986–), Q

1986c *Traces: Sporen in literatuur en kunsten* (Amsterdam, 1986/7), 2 nos, O

1986d *Van Gogh bulletin*, Rijksmuseum Vincent van Gogh (Amsterdam, 1986–), Q

1986e *Wiederhall* (Amsterdam, 1986–), 10 nos, Y [contemporary architecture]

1987a *Avant garde: Revue interdisciplinaire et internationale, arts et littérature au XX siècle* (Amsterdam, 1987–), 3 nos, Y

1987b *Beelding*, Stichting Beeldspraak (The Hague, 1987–), 10 nos, Y [fine arts, architecture]

1987c *Dutch Heights: Art and Culture of the Netherlands*, Ministerie van Welzijn, Volksgezondheid en Cultuur (Rijswijk, 1987–), Q [Eng.]

1987d *Gezond bouwen & wonen* (The Hague, 1987–), Q

1987e *Kwartaalblad K & B, tijdschrift voor kunst en omgeving*, Stichting Kunst en Bedrijf (Amsterdam, 1987–91), 5 vols, Q [cont. from 1982d]

1987f *PRO – Pro Art and Architecture: International Magazine for Constructivism*, Foundation PRO (Dordrecht, 1987–), 3 nos, Y [Dut. and Eng.]

1987g *De Rijksakademie*, Rijksakademie van Beeldende Kunsten (Amsterdam, 1987–90), 4 vols, 3 nos, Y

1987h *Tentoonstellingsboekje* (The Hague, 1987–91), 5 vols, 8 nos, Y [cont. as suppl. of 1987i]

1987i *Vitrine* (The Hague, 1987–), 8 nos, Y [from 1992 suppl. *De Nederlandse tenoonstlingsagenda*]

1987j *De witte raaf* (Arnhem, 1987–), O

1988a *Blind*, Blind Trust (Amsterdam, 1988–9) 1 no., O [cont. from 1980j] [contemporary photography]

1988b *Glas en keramiek* (Asperen, 1988–), B

1988c *Kunst & museumjournaal* (Gilze, 1988–), B

1988d *Kunstwerk* (Amsterdam, 1988–), B

1988e *Nieuwsbrief Mauritshuis*, from 1993 *Mauritshuis in focus*, Rijksmuseum het Mauritshuis (The Hague, 1988–), Q

1988f *Polysemisch tijdschrift POSE*, Polysemisch Instituut (Den Bosch, 1988–93), 9 nos, O [contemporary art]

1989a *Boekman cahier: Kwartaalschrift over kunst, onderzoek en beleid*, Boekmanstichting (Amsterdam, 1989–), Q

1989b *Delineavit et sculpsit*, Vrienden van het Prentenkabinet der Rijksuniversiteit Leiden (Leiden, 1989–), Q [pre-1850 graphic art]

1989c *Toonbeeld*, Vakgroep Kunstgeschiedenis of the Rijksuniversiteit Utrecht (Utrecht, 1989–), Q

1990a *Jaarboek Monumentenzorg*, Rijksdienst voor de Monumentenzorg (Zwolle, 1990–), Y

1990b *Kunsthistorici*, Vereniging van Nederlandse Kunsthistorici (Utrecht, 1990–), Q

1990c *Polis*, Vereniging Polis, Podium voor Stedebouwkunde (Delft, 1990–), 2 nos Y

1990d *R.E.M.: Lees & kijktijdschrift*, Stichting Beeld (Amsterdam, 1990–), Q [cont. from 1984b]

1990e *Zeezucht*, Theatre Zeebelt (The Hague, 1990–), O [performance art]

1991a *Boris & Conny* (Amsterdam, 1991), 1 no., O

1991b *Jaarboek Haags Gemeentemuseum* (The Hague, 1991–), Y

1991c *Keramika*, Museum het Princessehof (Leeuwarden, 1991–), Q

1991d *Nieuwsbrief Nederlands Fotoarchief* (Rotterdam, 1991–), Q

1991e *Origine: Tijdschrift over kunst, antiek en interieur* (Haarlem, 1991–), Q

1991f *Vereniging Rembrandt Nationaal Fonds kunstbehoud* (Amsterdam, 1991–), 2 nos, Y

1992a *Affiche* (Arnhem, 1992–), Q

1992b *Erfgoed van industrie en techniek* (Delft, 1992–), Q [cont. from 1981c]

1992c *kM: Vakblad voor beeldende kunstenaars en restauratoren* (Maastricht, 1992–), Q

1992d *Simulacrum*, Stichting Simulacrum, Kunsthistorisch Instituut Amsterdam (Amsterdam, 1992–), Q

1993a *Art & Value* (Amsterdam, 1993/4–), Q

1993b *Nieuwsbrief Nederlands Fotogenootschap* (Amsterdam, 1993–), Q

1993c *Nieuwsbrief Stedelijk Museum Bureau Amsterdam* (Amsterdam, 1993/4–), O

1993d *De tinkoerier* (Amsterdam, 1993–), O

1993e *ZAPP magazine* (Amsterdam, 1993–), Q [video magazine]

1994a *Artkitchen* (Amsterdam, 1994), 1 no., O

1994b *Streams* (Amsterdam, 1994–), M

GEERT-JAN KOOT

Netherlands Antilles. *See under* ANTILLES, LESSER.

Netsch, Walter (Andrew). *See under* SKIDMORE, OWINGS & MERRILL.

Netscher, Caspar (*b* ?Heidelberg, 1639; *d* The Hague, 15 Jan 1684). Dutch painter of German origin. His father was the German sculptor Johann Netscher (*d c.* 1641) and his mother the daughter of Vetter, Mayor of Heidelberg.

At an early age Caspar came to Arnhem, where he was apprenticed to Hendrik Coster, a little-known still-life and portrait painter (*fl* 1638–59). About 1654 Netscher moved to Deventer, where he completed his training in the workshop of Gerard ter Borch (ii). A number of signed and, occasionally, dated copies by Netscher after ter Borch survive from this period, such as the copy (1655; Gotha, Schloss Friedenstein) after ter Borch's *Parental Admonition* (*c.* 1654; Amsterdam, Rijksmus.) and a freely handled version (1659; untraced) of ter Borch's *Doctor's Visit* (1635; Berlin, Gemäldegal.). Netscher's first independent compositions, for example the small pendants *Portrait of a Man* and *Portrait of a Woman* (both 1656; Utrecht, Cent. Mus.), were strongly influenced by ter Borch. That these works are all fully signed suggests that Netscher held a special position in his master's workshop.

After completing his training *c.* 1658–9, he set off for Italy but got no further than Bordeaux, where on 25 November 1659 he married Margaretha Godijn, the daughter of a Walloon Protestant émigré. The young family moved to The Hague, where Netscher joined the painters' society Pictura on 25 October 1662. During his early years in The Hague he painted mostly small genre scenes, for example the *Chaff Cutter with a Woman Spinning and a Young Boy* (Philadelphia, PA, Mus. A.) and *The Kitchen* (Berlin, Gemäldegal.), which still show the dominant influence of ter Borch, noticeable in the use of rather dark colours and a preference for low-life subjects such as stable and kitchen interiors. However, *c.* 1664–5 Netscher's manner of painting became looser, his palette brighter and his choice of subjects more pretentious. During this period he painted sumptuous interiors with elegantly dressed young men and women (e.g. *Gathering of Musicians*, 1666; Dresden, Gemäldegal. Alte Meister; see fig.). Important elements in the paintings of this period are the fine rendering of silk and brocade and an arched format, which indicates that Netscher was also influenced by Leiden 'fine painters' such as Gerrit Dou and Frans van Mieris (i). In imitation of Dou, Netscher also began to paint genre scenes with half-length figures in a niche or window over a sculpted frieze (e.g. *Two Boys Blowing Bubbles*; London, N.G.). Another clearly recognizable source of inspiration for Netscher at this time was the masters of the Delft school. Netscher's masterpiece *The Lace-maker* (1664; London, Wallace) seems inconceivable without the examples of Pieter de Hooch and, above all, Johannes Vermeer.

After *c.* 1667 portraits gradually became Netscher's main interest, and the number of genre pieces decreased. In his portraits he followed the elegant, aristocratic court style of The Hague followers of Anthony van Dyck: Adriaen Hanneman, Jan Mijtens and Jan de Baen. However, he hardly ever worked on the life-size scale so popular among these painters. Netscher's portraits tend to have the same small format as his genre pictures. In the background he often added luxurious elements such as parks, fountains and sculptures, motifs that are not always merely decorative but sometimes contain some symbolic reference to the sitter. From the 1670s until his death Netscher was the most sought-after portrait painter in The Hague and able to ask good prices for his work. In order to meet the enormous demand he resorted to workshop

Caspar Netscher: *Gathering of Musicians*, oil on panel, 595×460 mm, 1666 (Dresden, Gemäldegalerie Alte Meister)

executed the design in oil and how much money he had received for it. An example of such an inscription appears on the *verso* of the *Letter Writer* (1664; London, BM), which is a preparatory study for the painting of the same subject (1665; Dresden, Gemäldegal. Alte Meister). Similar notes can be found on the backs of some quickly sketched studies for portraits in pen or chalk, which he probably used to give prospective clients an idea of his range as an artist.

BIBLIOGRAPHY

C. Hofstede de Groot: *Holländischen Maler* (1907–28), v, pp. 146–308

D. Angulo Iniguez: 'La Reina Dona Mariana recibe al embaja por holandés Beverninck, cuadro atribuido a G. Netscher', *Arch. Esp. A.*, xlvi (1974), pp. 351–2

P. H. J. Goldman: 'Two Rediscovered Portraits by Caspar Netscher', *Connoisseur*, clxxxix/761 (1975), pp. 264–5

J. G. van Gelder: 'Caspar Netscher's portret van Abraham van Lennep uit 1672', *Jb. Amstelodanum*, lxx (1978), pp. 227–38

E. Benkö: 'The Archetype of Netscher's *Portrait of Mary II Stuart* in Brussels and its Use', *Mus. Royaux B.-A. Belgique: Bull.*, xxx–xxxiii (1981–4), pp. 123–33

Masters of Seventeenth-century Dutch Genre Painting (exh. cat., ed. P. C. Sutton; Philadelphia, PA, Mus. A.; Berlin, Gemäldegal.; London, RA; 1984)

Portretten van echt en trouw [Portraits of matrimony and betrothal] (exh. cat., ed. E. de Jongh; Haarlem, Frans Halsmus., 1986)

De Hollandse fijnschilders van Gerard Dou tot Adriaen van der Werff (exh. cat. by P. Hecht, Amsterdam, Rijksmus., 1989–90), pp. 156–80

F. Simons: *Theodoor Netscher, 1661–1728: Ein vergeten schilder* (Voorburg, 1990)

G. JANSEN

Netti, Francesco (*b* Santeramo in Colle, nr Bari, 24 Dec 1832; *d* Naples, 28 Aug 1894). Italian painter and critic. He was taught privately by Giuseppe Bonolis but first studied law. After taking his degree, however, he enrolled in 1855 at the Accademia di Belle Arti in Naples and also attended the independent art school run by the painters Tommaso De Vivo (1787/90–1884) and Michele De Napoli (1808–92). In 1856 Netti went to Rome where he remained for three years studying Ancient art. On his return to Naples he came to know the artist Domenico Morelli and from 1862 to 1864 attended the life-drawing classes of Filippo Palizzi. His first officially exhibited work was the *Death of St Joseph Calasanzio* (1859; Naples, Scu. Media Stat. Vittorio Emanuele II), which adopts the style of De Napoli's religious works. He then painted the *Madness of Haidée* (1860; untraced) and the dramatic scene of revolutionary activity, *An Event of 15 May 1848* (exh. 1862; Naples, Mus. N. S Martino). In contrast to many records of the turbulence of this period, Netti's picture shows a historical subject in domestic terms, with a family barricaded inside their house while shooting from a window. Having achieved a certain renown in Naples, he went to France in order to distance himself from the influence of Morelli and to find his own individual style. He worked in both Paris and the artists' colony at Grez-sur-Loing, producing such works as *Festival at Grez* (1869–70; Bari, Pin. Prov.) and *After the Ball* (1872; Naples, Capodimonte), clearly inspired by contemporary French Realist paintings.

In 1871 Netti returned to Italy with a renewed interest in rural subject-matter and a painting style that had a sketchy, almost unfinished appearance. At exhibitions in Naples (1877) and Turin (1880) he showed paintings with

methods such as the in-filling of portrait heads, a method commonly used by popular portrait painters since the late 16th century. He also left a large part of the portrait production to his sons Theodorus (*b* Bordeaux, 1661; *d* Hontenisse, 1728) and Constantijn (*b* The Hague, *bapt* 16 Dec 1668; *d* The Hague, 27 March 1723), a process that did not always add to the quality of the work. A number of portraits were engraved by Abraham Blooteling and Wallerant Vaillant almost immediately after their completion.

From 1667 Netscher also made history paintings, which, like his portraits and genre pieces, were of a small format (e.g. *Bathsheba*; Munich, Alte Pin.); most of the historical and religious works date from the 1670s. Some of these were also immediately published as prints, for example *Lucretia* by Cornelis van Meurs (*fl* ?Paris, 1676–8). In the 1680s Netscher also painted a number of pastoral landscape scenes (e.g. *Shepherd and Shepherdess*, 1683; Brunswick, Herzog Anton Ulrich-Mus.). Besides several hundred paintings, Netscher left a considerable number of excellent drawings, many of which can be directly related to his paintings. The drawings include intimate genre scenes (e.g. *Girl with a Top*; Amsterdam, Hist. Mus.) and individual studies of hands and arms in black or red chalk (Amsterdam, Rijksmus.). Netscher apparently kept his drawings as a record of his painted work. In a few cases he wrote on the *verso* when and for whom he had

themes from antiquity in the manner of Jean-Léon Gérôme, Lawrence Alma-Tadema and Morelli, for example *Gladiators Fighting during a Dinner at Pompei* (1880; Naples, Capodimonte). Netti's most accomplished work is *At the Court of Assizes* (1882; Bari, Pin. Prov.), in which he borrowed from the stylistic devices of both photography and Japanese woodcuts. In 1884 he travelled to the eastern Mediterranean, bringing back sketches of the Bosphorus and the memory of clear, bright light, both influences on subsequent paintings including *The Siesta* (1884; Bari, Pin. Prov.). The last years of life were devoted to *The Harvesters* (1890–94), a realistic cycle of three paintings, *Riposo in mietitura* (priv. col.; see exh. cat., p. 120), *Il parto dei mietitori* (ex-Rome, G.N.A. Mod.; see exh. cat., p. 121) and *La messe* (unfinished; Naples, Gall. Accad. B.A.; see 1980 exh. cat., p. 122), in the preparation of which, for the first time, he made equal use of photographs and sketches. Netti also established a notable reputation as an art critic, championing the cause of Realism in both literature and art. His critical approach to art was similar to that of Francesco de Sanctis in literature, founded upon 'intrinsic analysis' and seeking to evaluate the work of art's moment of creation.

WRITINGS
Per l'arte italiana (Trani, 1895)
Scritti vari (Trani, 1895)
A. De Rinaldis, ed.: *Critica d'arte* (Bari, 1938)
L. Galante, ed.: *Francesco Netti: Scritti critici* (Rome, 1980)

BIBLIOGRAPHY
Thieme–Becker
Francesco Netti (1832–1894): Un intellettuale del Sud (exh. cat., ed. C. Farese Sperken; Bari, Pin. Prov., 1980)
L. Galante: 'Francesco Netti, il critico e il pittore', *An. U. Lecce*, ii (1981), pp. 103–36

MARIANTONIETTA PICONE PETRUSA

Nettos Painter. *See* VASE PAINTERS, §II.

Netzer, Hubert (*b* Isny, Allgau, 5 Oct 1865; *d* Munich, 15 Oct 1939). German sculptor. He trained first with the German sculptor Johannes Hoffart (*b* 1851) in Munich and then from 1891 under Wilhelm von Rümann at the Akademie der Bildenden Künste, Munich. After working independently for a number of years he taught at the Kunstakademie in Düsseldorf from 1911 to 1930, though he retained his studio in Munich throughout that time. In 1931 he moved back to Munich. In the works created during his early years in Munich, Netzer, as a product of the naturalist, neo-Baroque school centred on Rümann, fluctuated between Neo-classicism as preached by Adolf von Hildebrand and the stylizations of Jugendstil. While both the Triton Fountain (inaugurated in 1893) in Herzog-Wilhelm-Strasse in Munich, with the god of the sea resting on a projecting rock, and the picturesquely animated Prometheus Group (1896), on the gable of Würzburg University, have features suggestive of the Baroque, the Narcissus Fountain (1896–7; Munich, Bayer. Nmus.), with its more concisely controlled forms, clearly reveals Netzer's familiarity with Hildebrand. On the other hand the effects of Jugendstil can be observed in the Fountain of the Norns in Munich, completed in 1907 and originally intended for Karlsplatz but now standing on Maximiliansplatz, with the sweeping curves of the pool of water, the

ornamentation of twining plants and the block-like silhouettes of the three Fates. In the choice of theme there is also nostalgia for the Germany of the past, which was then very widespread and later came to be tinged with nationalism.

Based on the last monumental work executed for Munich, the Jonas Fountain (1910) with its Baroque inspiration, and commissions for tombstones and designs for medallions, Netzer's figural works on the eve of World War I gradually adopted the heroic–pathetic stance that helped to prepare the groundwork for art in the Third Reich. This is exemplified in the *Throwers of Thunderbolts*, begun in 1913–14 and completed in 1926 in the Rheinstadion in Düsseldorf, a war memorial panel (also for Düsseldorf) and in the *Boxer* exhibited in 1939.

BIBLIOGRAPHY
R. Klapheck: 'Hubert Netzer', *Kst Alle: Mal., Plast., Graph., Archit.*, xxxiii (1917–18), pp. 348–61
H. D. Hofmann: *Kleinplastik und figürliches Kunsthandwerk aus den Beständen des Münchner Stadtmuseums, 1880–1930* (Munich, 1974), pp. 11, 62, 67
M. G. Davidson: *Kunst in Deutschland, 1935–1945* (Tübingen, 1988), p. 478

CLEMENTINE SCHACK VON WITTENAU

Neuberger, Roy R. (*b* Bridgeport, CT, 21 July 1903). American museum founder, collector and patron. He lived in Paris from 1924 to 1929 where he became friendly with writers and artists and began to collect the work of living artists. He collected 19th- and early 20th-century American paintings as well as some pieces from other periods but became best known as a patron and friend of Milton Avery, from whom he eventually purchased about 120 paintings.

As Neuberger became more successful with his investment firm of Neuberger & Berman, he began to donate pieces from his collection to the Metropolitan Museum of Art and Whitney Museum of American Art in New York, Yale University, New Haven, CT, Smith College, Northampton, MA, and over 60 other institutions. Donations began in 1948 and continued during the 1960s and 1970s. In 1974, at the suggestion of Governor Nelson Rockefeller, he donated the bulk of his collection to the recently founded branch of the State University of New York at Purchase; 30 paintings by Avery formed the core of the Neuberger Museum there. He subsequently remained active in New York as a collector, as a contributor to several museums, and on the boards of various cultural and educational organizations.

BIBLIOGRAPHY
The Neuberger Collection: An American Collection: Paintings, Drawings and Sculpture (exh. cat., foreword D. Robbins and D. W. Scott; Providence, RI Sch. Des., Mus. A.; Washington, DC, Smithsonian Inst.; 1968)

DAVID M. SOKOL

Neuburg an der Donau. German town in Bavaria with a population of 26,000. It lies on high Jurassic rock cut by the River Danube. The settlement developed as a fortified crossing-point, and the town's origins are Roman. In the 8th and 9th centuries it was the site of the court of the Bavarian dukes (remains of whose fortress survive in the Münz in the Schloss) and then of the Frankish kings. Around 1002 Emperor Henry II founded a Benedictine convent in the town. Its church (destr.) was a vaulted

Gothic basilica with columns. Neuburg was a fiefdom of the Pappenheims between 1150 and 1256. Its oldest church is the parish church of St Peter, first mentioned in 1214–17 (rest. and altered 1641–71). From 1247 the town belonged to the Wittelsbachs, and it was granted a town charter in 1332. In 1392 it came under the control of Ingolstadt, and from 1447 under that of Landshut. From 1502 Neuburg was the official residence of the junior Palatinate branch, and Elector Palatine Otto Henry lived there (1522–44, 1552–5). The upper gate (*c.* 1540) remains from the town's 16th-century fortifications.

From 1569 to 1685 the town was the residence of the Pfalz-Neuburg dynasty. Remarkable houses dating from the 16th to the 18th centuries survive. Joseph Heintz I and Alexander Pasqualini (ii) drew up plans (1603–6) for the Rathaus (1609; rest. 1640–42; interior rebuilt), which was executed by Gilg Vältin. The walls (1607; now Hohe Schanze esplanade) were designed by Elias Holl I. The Jesuits built a college (1617–20; rest. 1692), and since 1617 the former Spitalkirche zum Heiligen Geist has been a parish church. Johann Serro (*fl* 1640–70) built the latter's tower before 1656 on an earlier base, and the flat-roofed, richly furnished body of the church dates from 1723–6. The Ursuline convent was founded by Count Palatine John William (*reg* 1690–1716) in 1699, Valentin Brenner building its church (1700); the convent was disestablished

in 1811. The Jesuit grammar school was rebuilt (1711) after a fire, and in 1722 the Mariensäule on the market square was made. The Baroque library of Kaisheim monastery was transferred to a prayer-room (1731) in 1804. In 1777 Neuburg reverted to Bavaria.

1. SCHLOSS. The Schloss has four large wings around an irregular courtyard. Parts of the oldest section (1368–92) are preserved in the five-storey building above the north gate, the Nadelöhrbau. In the 16th century Hans Knotz (*fl*1527–38), Paul Beham from Nuremberg (1532–6) and Jeremias Wagner (after 1536) worked on the building. The gate-house that faces the town is articulated by four Corinthian columns and two blind arches, with three pairs of pilasters framing the windows above. The cast-iron railing (1543) on the balcony is by Leonhard Schmelcher from Augsburg. The narrow ends of the north (altered 1534–8), south and west (both 1531–45) wings have scalloped gables (see fig.), and there is Italianate, two-storey arcading in the courtyard. The Schlosskapelle (1538–41) in the west wing has a gallery running around it on columns or brackets with stuccoed parapets, and the painted ceiling consists of a flat-topped cloister vault with curved undersurfaces above lunettes. In 1542 Otto Henry commissioned a *Crucifixion* relief from Martin Hering for the Schlosskapelle (now cemetery chapel). Hans Bocksberger I painted the interior (1542–3). The gateway (1545) has coffered barrel vaulting with heads in relief and animals. The courtyard loggias of the west wing have coffered stellar vaulting (see Hitchcock, fig. 76), and some *sgraffito* wall paintings survive. The armoury (west wing) has groin vaulting supported on squat, red marble columns, and the Rittersaal (north wing) has a heavy, coffered ceiling. Painted grotesques adorn the walls of the straight stair-well.

After the castle had been plundered in the Schmalkaldic War (1546–7), there was a flurry of building and decorative work executed by craftsmen from Munich, Freising and Braunau. A fountain (*c.* 1535; untraced) was cast for the bathroom by Pankraz Labenwolf and Sebald Hirder (*d*1563) in Nuremberg. The wall paintings that have been partly uncovered were probably the work of Jörg Breu (ii), Hans Bocksberger I and Melchior Feselen (Dehio and Gall, p. 37). From 1665 Philipp William (later Count Palatine, *reg* 1685–90) built the four-storey east wing with fifteen bays between two round towers, which stand impressively above the town. A grotto with shell decoration and artificial fountains was described in 1661 and 1667 and restored in 1747.

Neuburg an der Donau, view of the north wing of the Schloss from the south-west, mostly 1534–8

2. ST MARIA. Built on the site of the Benedictine convent church, the present building is a hall church with a gallery and four bays, a square choir, royal boxes above the choir aisles and a semicircular apse. The nave and aisles have rib vaulting with round arches. Count Palatine Frederick IV's court architect, Siegmund Doctor, produced the first design (1605), which was revised by Joseph Heintz (i) (1606) and was executed (1607–18) by Gilg Vältin from Grisons. It began as a Protestant court church, but, after a political and religious change, the Jesuits were installed there in 1617. The unusually pure stuccowork (1616–19) by Michele Castelli, Antonio Castelli and Pietro

Castelli follows the geometric lines of the architecture. The façade successfully incorporates the one-storey tower with a domed roof and a lantern completed *c*. 1630 by Hans Alberthal and Johann Matthias Kager (1575–1634). The system of powerful pillars and cornices in the apse and nave is also applied to the façade.

There are statues of the *Apostles*, *St Ignatius* and another Jesuit saint on the walls of the aisles, and the west wall is decorated with high reliefs of the *Birth of the Virgin* and *Assumption of the Virgin*. In the vestibule there are portraits of *Emperor Henry II*, his wife *Kunigunde*, the *Archangel Michael*, *Count Palatine Wolfgang William*, his first wife, *Magdalena*, and a picture of the town. Beside the high altar are the tombs of *Magdalena* (*d* 1628) and *Wolfgang William* (*d* 1653). Masters from Wessobrunn stuccoed the west gallery *c*. 1700 and the choir *c*. 1725. The church contains the high altar and two side altars (1752–6) by Joseph Anton Breitenauer, altarpieces by Domenico Zanetti (*d* after 1712) from Bologna, and a Rococo pulpit (1756).

BIBLIOGRAPHY

J. Heider: *Neuburg an der Donau* (Neuburg, 1867)

H. Stierhof: *Wand- und Deckenmalereien des Neuburger Schlosses im 16. Jahrhundert* (Munich, 1872)

G. Dehio and F. Gall: *Handbuch der deutschen Kunstdenkmaler: Östliches Schwaben* (Munich and Berlin, 1954), pp. 37–41

H.-R. Hitchcock: *German Renaissance Architecture* (Princeton, 1981)

ERNST ULLMANN

Neuchâtel [Lat. Novum Castellum; Ger. Neuenburg]. Capital city of the French speaking canton of Neuchâtel, western Switzerland. It is on the north shore of Lac de Neuchâtel at the foot of the Jura Mountains and at the head of the Val de Ruz. The first written record of the city—a donation charter (Grenoble, Archvs Dépt. Isère) drawn up by Rodolphe III, King of Burgundy and dating from AD 1011 that mentions a 'Novum Castellum' described as a 'most royal scat'—was undoubtedly set down long after the first occupation of its earliest site. This early record notes that Neuchâtel served as a bridgehead for the Kingdom of Burgundy, which lay on the far side of the Jura Mountains, and it was not long afterwards that the dynasty of the future Comtes de Neuchâtel was established. The family was responsible for a number of foundations, and until 1373 they set their mark on the development of the region. By 1707 there was a considerable number of pretenders to the title of Prince de Neuchâtel, and a sovereign court was set up to decide among them who should rightfully claim the title.

Initially, Neuchâtel consisted of a four-cornered enceinte protected to the west by a great dry ditch cut into the rock. After the middle of the 12th century, a collegiate church and a new château were built. In 1450 a fire destroyed most of the buildings, necessitating major reconstruction of the château and the Collegiate Church of Notre-Dame, although the rib vaults of the latter survived relatively unscathed. The church contains the medieval cenotaph of the *Comtes de Neuchâtel* (see fig.). Restored in 1840, it is a veritable 'family portrait' and one of the most important polychromed secular monuments in southern Europe. Gradually, a town was established below the church and château as a result of the craft activities centred around the Rue des Moulins and the commercial activities based either on the shores of the

Neuchâtel, Collegiate Church of Notre-Dame, the tomb of the *Comtes de Neuchâtel*, stone (rest. 1840), from 1372

lake (in the area of the Croix-du-Marché) or at the foot of the tower built to protect the eastern gate of the original defensive wall. From the eastern gate a bridge led into a new quarter of the city, the Neubourg, which was fortified as early as the 13th century.

After the Reformation of the 16th century (during which time Neuchâtel became one of the first French-speaking centres in Switzerland), the city developed by spreading further out into the lake. In 1570 the sovereign Léonor d'Orléans (1540–73) was responsible for the building of the Renaissance Maison des Halles, which set the standard for a style particular to the area of Lac de Neuchâtel, Bieler See and Murtensee. Laurent Perroud (*fl* *c*. 1545–81) may have been the architect. He did, however, erect several fountains, among them the Justice Fountain (1545–7) and the Banneret Fountain (1581), the figures of which are comparable to those adorning fountains in other Swiss towns. The Hôtel de Ville (planned 1455) was rebuilt between 1579–1582 (dem. 1860) by the stonemasons François Racine and Pierre Roulet and served once more— as it had done for more than a century—as a type of bridge linking the two banks of the River Seyon. At the beginning of the 17th century the Catholic sovereign Henri d'Orléans-Longueville (1595–1663), during a period of conflict with his subjects, decided to transfer the seat of government to a nearby town that was to be built for the purpose and to be called Henripolis. Although the plan proved to be a failure, the fact that it had been proposed influenced Neuchâtel's future development and that of the region as a whole during the following centuries.

During the Enlightenment of the 18th century several sumptuous private residences were built, and a new suburb was established in the vineyards to the east of the city. Erasmus Ritter (1726–1805) from Berne built a hôtel (1768) for Pierre-Alexandre DuPeyrou, a friend of Jean-Jacques Rousseau. DuPeyrou supported the establishment of a theatre, which was built by the stonemasons Jean-Jacques and Jacob Rosselet between 1766 and 1769 alongside the medieval city wall. Due to the munificence of the merchant David de Pury, Neuchâtel acquired a hospital (1779–83), by Jonas-Louis Reymond (1742–1814) and his brother Abraham-Louis Reymond (1740–1813), and, facing it, a monumental new Hôtel de Ville (1783–90) by PIERRE-ADRIEN PÂRIS. The latter building became a symbol of the triumphant hegemony of the great trading aristocracy, encouraged in their rise to power by the Kings of Prussia, who from 1707 also had the title of Prince de Neuchâtel. By the early 19th century Neuchâtel had a population of 4600. During the reign of Alexandre Berthier (whom Napoleon I made Prince de Neuchâtel in 1806), the city was endowed by Jacques-Louis de Pourtalès with a new hospital (1808; after plans by Ludwig-Samuel Stürler: 1768–1840); the construction of its chapel enabled him to reintroduce Catholicism, which had been suppressed since 1530. In 1815 Neuchâtel and its canton became part of the Swiss Confederation.

During the 19th century the city gates were gradually demolished, and a plan was proposed to reclaim land along the entire lakeshore for development in accordance with an urban-planning project of 1826 that called for the diversion of the River Seyon, until that time dividing the city. The Collège de la Promenade (1868), the Musée d'Art et d'Histoire (1880), the Académie (1886), the Ecole de Commerce (1901) and buildings of the Université de Neuchâtel were scattered throughout the newly created neighbourhoods on the lakefront, and further construction in the 20th century of similar types of buildings confirmed the essentially public nature of these artificially created areas. The Institut de Physique (by Maurice Billeter, b 1913), the Winterthur Assurance headquarters and the Réunies tobacco factory illustrate the principal trends of the architecture that, after World War II, dominated almost the whole urban area and new riverbanks. In 1870 the Collegiate Church of Notre-Dame underwent major restoration by Léo Châtelain (1839–1913), who built a second tower, reconstructed the portal and the west front and completely stripped the interior of all its stonework, which had lost all of its original colour and had since the Reformation been covered with successive layers of whitewash. As a result of the restoration, the church appeared coherent visually, and it became a romantic and triumphant symbol of the Protestant faith. From 1884 the painter Paul Robert (1851–1923) and the English decorator CLEMENT J. HEATON, inspired by the Arts and Crafts Movement in Britain, executed designs for the staircase and hall of the Musée d'Art et d'Histoire. The popularity of this movement in Neuchâtel and nearby La Chaux-de-Fonds provided a basis for the early training of LE CORBUSIER. In 1906 the engineer Guillaume Ritter (1835–1912) completed the design for the new church of Notre-Dame. Instead of the yellow sandstone of the region, it was built in artificial stone in imitation of the pink sandstone of

Alsace. Its Gothic Revival style invited comparison with the original Collegiate Church. Several important painters have worked in Neuchâtel, among them MAXIMILIEN DE MEURON in the first half of the 19th century.

BIBLIOGRAPHY
A. Lombard: *L'Eglise collégiale de Neuchâtel* (Neuchâtel, 1931, 2/1961)
J. Courvoisier: *La Ville de Neuchâtel*, Les Monuments d'art et d'histoire du canton de Neuchâtel, i (Basle, 1955)
A. Schaller-Aeschlimann: *Das Kenotaph der Grafen von Neuenburg* (Basle, 1974)
P. von Allmen, ed.: *Léo Châtelain, architecte, 1839–1913* (Neuchâtel, 1985) [collected works]
J. P. Jelmini: *Neuchâtel, l'esprit, la pierre, l'histoire* (Hauterive, 1986)
L.-E. Roulet: 'La Raison d'être du monument des comtes de Neuchâtel en Suisse', *Procès-verbaux & Mém. Acad. Sci., B.-Lett. & A. Besançon & Franche-Comté*, clxxxviii (1988–9)

MARC EMERY

Neudörfer, Johann (*b* ?Nuremberg, 1497; *d* ?Nuremberg, 1563). German writer, calligrapher and mathematician. He was renowned as a strict teacher of arithmetic and geometry. His calligraphic talents were recognized early. Albrecht Dürer, who lived on the same street until 1509, probably used his designs for the scripts in his woodcuts of the *Map of the Eastern Hemisphere* (1515) and of the portrait of *Ulrich Varnbüler* (1522), his painting of the *Four Apostles* (1526; Munich, Alte Pin.) and possibly in the woodcuts of the *Triumphal Arch of Emperor Maximilian I* (1515) and those illustrating his *Etliche Underricht, zu Befestigung der Stett, Schloss und Flecken* (Nuremberg, 1527). In 1519 Neudörfer published his *Fundament . . . seinen Schulern zu einer Unterweysung gemacht* (Nuremberg), the first writing manual printed in Germany, and in 1538 he completed his finest treatise, *Eine gute Ordnung*, a catalogue of styles of script, ways of holding a pen and the correct manner of forming letters. He published two other treatises on writing in Nuremberg in 1544 and 1549. Neudörfer periodically participated in other artistic projects, for example he designed the inscription on the reverse of the medal (1538; Nuremberg, Ger. Nmus.) commemorating the new fortifications around Nuremberg Castle, by Peter Flötner.

Neudörfer's close relationship with many of Nuremberg's artists is evident in his *Nachrichten von Künstlern und Werkleuten* (Nuremberg, 1547). He was the first German biographer of artists, and his text predates by three years first edition of Vasari's *Vite*, providing valuable information about the city's important artists and their work.

Numerous portraits of Neudörfer exist, the earliest being medals by the Master of the Stabius Group (1520 and 1523), followed by those by Hans Schwarz (1532; see Kapr, p. 17), Mathes Gebel (1531; Nuremberg, Ger. Nmus.), Joachim Deschler (1554; Santa Barbara, U. CA, A. Mus.) and Jakob Binck (see Kapr, p. 17). The so-called Master of the Neudörfer Portraits painted Johann and his wife in 1527 (Kassel, Schloss Wilhelmshöhe). In 1561 the Nuremberg City Council acknowledged Neudörfer's international fame when it paid 32 florins for his portrait for the Rathaus (now Nuremberg, Ger. Nmus.; for illustration *see* NEUFCHATEL, NICOLAS). The artist Nicolas Neufchatel represented Neudörfer explaining a dodecahedron to his son; a copy that Neufchatel made for Neudörfer is in Lille (Mus. B.-A.).

BIBLIOGRAPHY

G. W. K. Lochner, ed.: *Des Johann Neudörfer Nachrichten von Künstlern und Werkleuten daselbst aus dem Jahre 1547* (Vienna, 1875)

G. Habich: *Die deutschen Schaumünzen des 16. Jahrhunderts* (Munich, 1929–35), I, i, nos 320–21; I, ii, nos 1068, 1617

A. Kapr, ed.: *Johann Neudörfer d. Ä.: Der grosse Schreibmeister der deutschen Renaissance* (Leipzig, 1956)

Albrecht Dürer, 1471–1971 (exh. cat., Nuremberg, Ger. Nmus., 1971)

Nuremberg: A Renaissance City, 1500–1618 (exh. cat. by J. C. Smith, Austin, U. TX, Huntington A.G., 1983)

J. C. Smith: *German Sculpture of the Later Renaissance, c. 1520–1580: Art in an Age of Uncertainty* (Princeton, 1994)

JEFFREY CHIPPS SMITH

Neue Künstlervereinigung München [NKVM; Ger.: 'New Artists Association of Munich']. Organization founded as an independent exhibiting group to counteract the inability of both official outlets and the Munich Secession to accommodate avant-garde practice. It was established at the home of Marianne Werefkin, and was subsequently entered in the Munich Association's Register on 22 March 1909. Vasily Kandinsky was elected president and Alexei Jawlenski vice-president; Alexander Kanoldt (1881–1939) was appointed secretary and Adolph Erbslöh (1881–1947) chairperson of the association's exhibition committee. Gabriele Münter and Alfred Kubin offered their allegiance; other dedicated supporters included Heinrich Schnabel, Oscar Wittenstein and the Russian dancer Aleksandr Sakharov.

Kandinsky designed the membership card and publicly proclaimed the aims of the association by means of a circular. He promoted the Symbolist idea of 'artistic synthesis', and his colour woodcut poster for the first NKVM exhibition accordingly reduced literary allusion and focused on simplified planes of colour. On the recommendation of Hugo von Tschudi, the NKVM was permitted to use the privately owned Moderne Galerie Thannhauser for this exhibition (1–15 December 1909). Other artists who exhibited included Paul Baum (1859–1932), Erma Bossi, Karl Hofer, Vladimir Bekhteyev (1878–1971), Moisey Kogan and Pierre-Paul Girieud. Landscape predominated in the 128 works exhibited, with still-life, portraiture and figural compositions in evidence. The range of stylistic treatment was likewise varied and embraced the media of graphics and sculpture. Critical and public reception of this exhibition was hostile.

The second exhibition (1–14 September 1910) provoked further controversy owing to Kandinsky's decision to invite a large contingent of young artists from Paris and Russia. The exhibition catalogue, which included texts by Henri le Fauconnier, David Burlyuk and Vladimir Burlyuk, Kandinsky and Odilon Redon, emphasized universalist aims. G. J. Wolf railed in *Die Kunst für Alle*: 'The beautiful and culturally renowned name of Munich is being used as a roost for an artists' association of mixed Slavic and Latin elements.... There is not one Munich painter amongst them.' The vivid colouration and abstraction of Kandinsky's *Composition II* and *Improvization X* elicited much press criticism. Franz Marc felt the need to publish a defence of the NKVM. A controversy within the association arose between the more conservative group centred around Erbslöh and Kanoldt and the more radical painters under Kandinsky's leadership. A final break occurred on 2 December 1911 when the NKVM jury considered arrangements for its next exhibition, scheduled to open at Thannhauser's gallery on 18 December. Kandinsky was obliged to submit his large-scale painting *Composition V* for approval. Its rejection led to the resignation of Kandinsky, Münter, Marc and Kubin from the association, and to their planning of the exhibition Der Blaue Reiter.

The number of artists who participated in the third NKVM exhibition was drastically reduced. Otto Fischer (1870–1947), an art historian who joined the association in 1911, attempted to justify the motives of the conservative element in the group in his book *Das Neue Bild* (1912). Stressing the role of the object in the work of art, he declared: 'A painting is not solely expression, but also representation.' This publication caused the withdrawal of Bekhteyev, Jawlenski and Werefkin from the NKVM, and no further exhibitions were held.

WRITINGS

F. Marc: *Zur Ausstellungen der Neuen Künstlervereinigung bei Thannhauser* (Munich, 1911)

BIBLIOGRAPHY

H. Uhde-Bernays: 'Ausstellungen', *Der Cicerone*, ii/1 (1910), p. 30

G. J. Wolf: 'Von Ausstellungen', *Kst Alle: Mal., Plast., Graph., Archit.*, xxvi/3 (1910), pp. 68–70

O. Fischer: *Das Neue Bild* (Munich, 1912)

J. Eichner: *Kandinsky und Gabriele Münter: Von Ursprüngen moderner Kunst* (Munich, 1957)

P. Selz: *German Expressionist Painting* (Los Angeles, 1957)

L. Buchheim: *Der Blaue Reiter und die 'Neue Künstlervereinigung München'* (Feldafing, 1959)

Auguste Macke–Franz Marc: Briefwechsel (Cologne, 1964)

P. Vogt: *Geschichte der deutscher Malerei im 20. Jahrhundert* (Cologne, 1972)

R. Gollek: *Der Blaue Reiter im Lenbachhaus München* (Munich, 1974)

B. Herbert: *German Expressionism: Die Brücke and Der Blaue Reiter* (London, 1983)

S. Behr: *Women Expressionists* (Oxford, 1988)

SHULAMITH BEHR

Neue Leben [Ger.: 'new life']. Swiss group of artists active from 1918 to 1920. It was founded in Basle in 1918 and came to prominence primarily through four exhibitions of its members' work: at the Kunsthalle in Basle (1918 and 1920), the Kunsthaus in Zurich (1919) and the Kunsthalle in Berne (1920). The driving force behind it was Fritz Baumann (1886–1942), a painter and teacher from Basle who before World War I returned to his native city having studied in Munich, Karlsruhe, Paris and Berlin (where he was a member of the circle associated with the magazine *Der Sturm*). With Arnold Brügger (1888–1975), Otto Morach (1887–1973), Niklaus Stoecklin (1896–1982) and Alexander Zschokke (1894–1981), he initiated a loose association of 44 known artists, women and men, of whom a considerable number worked in the arts and crafts. Lively contacts were established between Neue Leben and avant-garde artists living in exile in Switzerland, particularly the Dada group in Zurich, and also artists in Geneva and Ticino. Other prominent members were Hans Arp, Alice Bailly, Augusto Giacometti, Marcel Janco, Oscar Lüthi (1882–1945), Francis Picabia and Sophie Taeuber-Arp.

Neue Leben exposed the Swiss public to such international art movements as Cubism, Futurism and Expressionism, typical of the heterogeneity of the period. Baumann's manifesto, written in 1918, was consequently less concerned with formulating maxims relating to a current style than with the expectation of a radical shift and a 'really new comprehensive style'. Similar hopes with a greater political emphasis were voiced in the *Manifest radikaler Künstler* (Zurich, 1919). Its main themes were the uncompromising wish to remove the boundaries between 'applied' and 'fine' art, to be guided by the power of originality and to redefine the role of the artist both aesthetically and socially.

BIBLIOGRAPHY

F. Baumann: *Das Neue Leben: Für die neue Bewegung in der Kunst* (Basle, 1918)

M. Heller and L. Windhöfel: 'Das Neue Leben', *Künstlergruppen in der Schweiz, 1910–1936* (exh. cat., ed. B. Stutzer; Aarau, Aargau. Ksthaus, 1980), pp. 60–93

C. Geelhaar and M. Stucky: *Expressionistische Malerei in Basel um den ersten Weltkrieg* (Basle, 1983)

MARTIN HELLER

Neue Sachlichkeit [Ger.: 'new objectivity']. Term applied to the representative art that was developed in Germany in the 1920s by artists including MAX BECKMANN, OTTO DIX and GEORGE GROSZ. The term MAGIC REALISM is associated but not directly related to it. The use of 'Neue Sachlichkeit' may derive from the Dutch word *zakelijkheid*, which was used from *c*. 1900 to describe the work of such Dutch architects as H. P. Berlage; this was followed by *nieuwe zakelijkheid* used from 1923 to indicate the reaction against Expressionism in architecture. The political events in Europe and the general mood to which they gave rise influenced painting, design and photography (e.g. the work of ALBERT RENGER-PATSCH), as well as architecture. Despite the wide significance of objectivity at this time, the term applies primarily to a movement in German painting, and it is this with which this article is primarily concerned.

Neue Sachlichkeit was 'new' in so far as it was in contradistinction to 19th-century Naturalism and the work of the Nazarenes, and it was frequently characterized by a satirical social realism. The general mood in Germany in the 1920s was conditioned by the experience of World War I. The war fever that artists had depicted, mainly in an Expressionist style, subsided after the first months in the battlefields: the cruelty and senselessness of war was to become a recurrent theme in the work of Neue Sachlichkeit artists. Moreover, the sobering effect of both the war and the failure of the revolutionary events in Germany in 1918–19 gave rise to an unsentimental, coolly factual view of reality. As an attitude and style, Neue Sachlichkeit was a reaction to the past, to patriotism and to grand gestures. As Wilhelm Michel wrote: 'We are dealing with a *new* objectivity . . . We are dealing with a discovery of *things* after the crisis of the *ego*' (*Dt. Kst & Dek.*, 1925). Neue Sachlichkeit in Germany was closely linked to wider European developments: throughout Europe the period following the war was characterized by a *rappel à l'ordre* and to more traditional figurative styles.

The principal centres of the movement in Germany were the cities of Berlin, Dresden, Karlsruhe, Cologne, Düsseldorf, Hannover and Munich. However, the various exponents of Neue Sachlichkeit never joined into groups or formed a school, and they were scattered throughout Germany. The term was first applied to these various artists by Gustav F. Hartlaub, Director of the Städtische Kunsthalle Mannheim, for an exhibition of paintings that

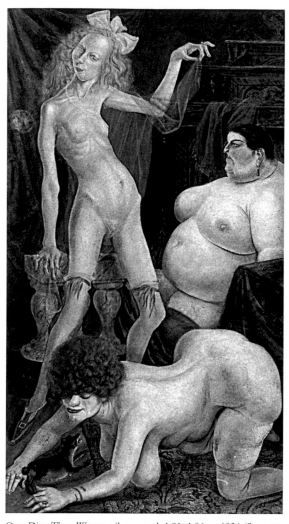

Otto Dix: *Three Women*, oil on panel, 1.81×1.06 m, 1926 (Stuttgart, Galerie der Stadt Stuttgart)

he organized in Mannheim in 1925. The title of the exhibition, which was originally to be Post-Expressionism, became a synonym for diverse tendencies in figurative art. Hartlaub exhibited the artists whom he saw as the successors of the waning Expressionism, and who, in his opinion, pointed towards the future of German art in the 1920s. He exhibited 124 works by 32 artists, including Beckmann, Grosz, Dix, Alexander Kanoldt (1881–1939) and Georg Schrimpf.

The original, historical meaning of Neue Sachlichkeit differs widely, however, from the present understanding of the term. The artists of this tendency came from very different social classes and thus pursued quite opposite ideas regarding both subject-matter and politics. Although Hartlaub distinguished between right and left, between 'verists' and 'classicists', over the decades totally contradictory definitions of Neue Sachlichkeit were made. It was not until the 1970s that art scholarship distinguished clearly between the different tendencies of Neue Sachlichkeit. Accordingly, the verists (Beckmann, Dix, Grosz,

Emperor Maximilian II and his daughter *Anne of Austria*, several copies of which survive.

While none of Neufchatel's known portraits postdates 1573, his influence on Nuremberg's painters lasted until the end of the 16th century. Nicolas Juvenel I, a Netherlander who also settled in the city in 1561, skilfully emulated his style, as did Andreas Herneisen (*fl* 1564), Hans Strauch and Hans Hoffmann. Neufchatel's art also affected the character of the stunning terracotta portrait busts and reliefs by Johann Gregor van der Schardt.

BIBLIOGRAPHY

Joachim von Sandrart: *Teutsche Academie* (1675–9); ed. A. R. Peltzer (1925), pp. 135, 318

R. A. Peltzer: 'Nicholas Neufchatel und seine Nürnberger Bildnisse', *Münchn. Jb. Bild. Kst*, n. s. 1, iii (1926), pp. 187–231

H. Delanney: *Nicolas de Neufchâtel: Sa vie et ses oeuvres* (Mons, 1927)

M. Davies: *National Gallery Catalogues: Early Netherlandish School* (London, 1945, rev. 3/1968), pp. 155–8

K. Pilz: 'Nürnberg und die Niederlande', *Mitt. Ver. Gesch. Stadt Nürnberg*, xliii (1952), esp. pp. 72–6

P. Strieder: 'Zur Nürnberger Bildniskunst des 16. Jahrhunderts', *Münch. Jb. Bild. Kst*, n. s. 2, vii (1956), esp. pp. 122–3, 132–3

A. Pigler: *Szépmüvészeti Múzeum Budapest: Katalog der Galerie Alter Meister*, i (Tübingen, 1968), pp. 481–3

H. Geissler: *Zeichnung in Deutschland: Deutsche Zeichner, 1540–1640*, i (Stuttgart, 1979), no. E 5

Nuremberg: A Renaissance City, 1500–1618 (exh. cat. by J. C. Smith, Austin, U. TX, Huntington A. G., 1983), pp. 69–71, 75, 78, 81, 86, 304

Wenzel Jamnitzer und die Nürnberger Goldschmiedekunst, 1500–1700 (exh. cat., Nuremberg, Ger. Nmus., 1985), pp. 87, 92–3, 103, 128, 174–6, 192–3; nos 758, 772, 776

J. C. Smith: 'Netherlandish Artists and Art in Renaissance Nuremberg', *Simiolus*, xx (1990/91), esp. pp. 153–6

H. Honnens de Lichtenberg: *Johan Gregor van der Schardt* (Copenhagen, 1991), pp. 11, 15–16, 20, 26–7, 68–9, 137, 139, 175, 210, 240

JEFFREY CHIPPS SMITH

Neufforge, Jean-François de (*b* Comblain-au-Pont, nr Liège, 1 April 1714; *d* Paris, 19 Dec 1791). Flemish architect and engraver. He arrived in Paris *c.* 1738 and studied engraving with Pierre Edmé Babel and architecture with Jacques-François Blondel. His style was formed while engraving plates for Julien-David Le Roy's book *Les Ruines des plus beaux monuments de la Grèce* (Paris, 1758). Neufforge's importance rests on his *Recueil élémentaire d'architecture* (1757–68, 1772–80), an immense publication containing some 900 architectural engravings, nearly all of which were not only designed but also engraved by Neufforge himself. It is a traditional architect's pattern-book but is of unprecedented scope, containing virtually every type of civic and domestic building then known, including such structures as prisons and lighthouses that had only recently been considered worthy of an architect's attention. In addition, it covers such topics as interior decoration, gardens and methods of construction. In his designs for domestic architecture, Neufforge included models to suit every level of patron, from the most modest to the most aristocratic. The designs draw both on antiquity and the High Renaissance, and the *Recueil* was extensively used as a source-book throughout the late 18th century.

In the plates of his later volumes, however, especially those illustrating public buildings, Neufforge strove for increasingly novel compositions in a way that anticipates the visionary designs of Etienne-Louis Boullée and Claude-Nicolas Ledoux. In the organization of façades he was governed by 'visions of contrasting masses' (Kaufmann, p. 152). Like Jean-Charles Delafosse, with whom he is often compared, he subverted established practice and challenged expectation, allowing discordant juxtapositions of forms and contradictions of weight and balance: a tiny, pin-like steeple crowns a town house that also features an aggressive frontispiece of giant Corinthian columns, while in other designs, over-heavy elements such as obelisks and pyramids weigh down the supporting structures. In some façades tensions are set up between the central and peripheral elements through a transference of emphasis to the latter. In others the forms are used in a piecemeal and independent fashion: a country retreat is constructed of three distinct elements that look as if they could be pulled apart like a child's building blocks.

Some of the structures to which Neufforge and other architects were turning their attention for the first time, including prisons, lighthouses and funerary monuments of all kinds, brought with them an inherent sense of the emblematic; their symbolic forms now entered fully into the vocabulary of the age. Neufforge added to the emblematic embellishment of these structures, decorating a prison with heavy bands of restraining rustication and a cemetery entrance, crowned by an obelisk, with applied obelisks framing the portal. The same search for novelty affects Neufforge's plans, which are governed by practical, decorative or symbolic considerations. In particular, he developed a square plan divided into nine smaller units, a composition that was to be much used by Ledoux. Other novel plans include a triangular Temple de la Guerre and a 'Bâtiment à représenter les quatre saisons ou les quatre éléments', in which four circular units are grouped around a circle, which does not contain a principal room but rather a spiral staircase.

WRITINGS

Recueil élémentaire d'architecture, 10 vols (Paris, 1757–68 and 1772–80)

BIBLIOGRAPHY

E. Kaufmann: *Architecture in the Age of Reason* (New York, 1968), pp. 151–4

S. Eriksen: *Early Neoclassicism in France* (London, 1974), pp. 47, 57, 207, 295

A. Braham: *The Architecture of the French Enlightenment* (London, 1980, 2/1989), pp. 60–61, 64, 235

R. Middleton and D. Watkin: *Neoclassical and Nineteenth Century Architecture*, 2 vols, Hist. World Archit. (London, 1987), i, p. 70

C. Baines and D. Wiebenson: 'Jean-François de Neufforge: the *Recueil élémentaire d'architecture*', *Catalogue of French Books in the Millard Collection*, Washington, DC, N.G.A. (in preparation)

CLAIRE BAINES

Illustration Acknowledgements

We are grateful to those listed below for permission to reproduce copyright illustrative material and to those contributors who supplied photographs or helped us to obtain them. The word 'Photo:' precedes the names of large commercial or archival sources who have provided us with photographs, as well as the names of individual photographers (where known). It has generally not been used before the names of owners of works of art, such as museums and civic bodies. Every effort has been made to contact copyright holders and to credit them appropriately; we apologize to anyone who may have been omitted from the acknowledgements or cited incorrectly. Any error brought to our attention will be corrected in subsequent editions. Where illustrations have been taken from books, publication details are provided in the acknowledgements below.

Line drawings, maps, plans, chronological tables and family trees commissioned by the *Dictionary of Art* are not included in the list below. All of the maps in the dictionary were produced by Oxford Illustrators Ltd, who were also responsible for some of the line drawings. Most of the line drawings and plans, however, were drawn by one of the following artists: Diane Fortenberry, Lorraine Hodghton, Chris Miners, Amanda Patton, Mike Pringle, Jo Richards, Miranda Schofield, John Tiernan, John Wilson and Philip Winton. The chronological tables and family trees were prepared initially by Kate Boatfield and finalized by John Johnson.

Montañés, Juan Martínez *1, 3* Photo: J.J. Martín González; *2* Photo: Conway Library, Courtauld Institute of Art, London

Monte Albán Prof. Michael Coe, Harvard University, Cambridge, MA

Montecassino *2* Vatican Museums, Vatican City, Rome

Montenegro *2* Leksikografski Zavod 'Miroslav Krleza', Zagreb; *3* Musée National d'Art Moderne, Paris

Montevideo Photo: Testoni Studios, Montevideo

Monti, Raffaelle Board of Trustees of the Victoria and Albert Museum, London

Monticelli, Adolphe Photo: © RMN, Paris

Montorsoli, Giovanni Angelo Photo: Archivi Alinari, Florence

Montpellier Photo: Giraudon, Paris

Montreal *1* Photo: Jean-Claude Marsan; *2* National Gallery of Canada, Ottawa

Mont-Saint-Michel Abbey Photo: Arch. Phot. Paris/© DACS, 1996

Monument, public *1* Photo: Arch. Phot. Paris/© DACS, 1996; *2* Photo: Archivi Alinari, Florence; *3* Photo: RCHME/© Crown Copyright; *4* Photo: Conway Library, Courtauld Institute of Art, London

Moore: (1) Albert Joseph Moore City Art Gallery, York

Moore, Charles W. © Esto, Marmaroneck, NY/Photo: Wayne Andrews

Moore, Henry *1* Photo: Beedle and Cooper; *2* Tate Gallery, London

Moorish style Photo: RCHME/© Crown Copyright

Moosbrugger, Caspar Kloster Einsiedeln

Mopope, Stephen Photo: Native American Painting Reference Library, Oklahoma City, OK

Mor, Antonis *1* Museo del Prado, Madrid; *2* Photo: © RMN, Paris

Morales, Luis de Real Academia de San Fernando, Madrid

Moran, Thomas National Museum of American Art, Washington, DC/ Photo: Art Resource, New York/Lent by the US State Department of the Interior, Office of the Secretary

Morandi, Giorgio © DACS, 1996

Morava Republic Institute for Protection of Cultural Monuments, Belgrade/Photo: K. Denic

Morazzone *1* Photo: Alberto Bertoni; *2* Museo d'Arte Antica, Castello Sforzesco, Milan

Morbelli, Angelo Photo: Courtauld Institute of Art, London

Moreau: (1) Louis-Gabriel Moreau Musée des Beaux-Arts, Rouen

Moreau, Gustave *1* Armand Hammer Collection, UCLA, at the Armand Hammer Museum of Art and Cultural Center, Los Angeles, CA; *2* Photo: © RMN, Paris

Moreelse, Paulus Rijksdienst Beeldende Kunsten, Amsterdam (on loan to the Centraal Museum, Utrecht)

Morelli, Domenico *1–2* Photo: Archivi Alinari, Florence

Morelli, Giovanni Photo: Dr Willi Zavaritt, Bergamo

Moretto *1* Pinacoteca Civica Tosio–Martinengo, Brescia; *2* Trustees of the National Gallery, London

Morienval, Notre-Dame Photo: Zodiaque, St-Léger-Vauban

Morinck, Hans Landesdenkmalamt Baden-Württemberg, Karlsruhe

Mori Sosen Itsuo Art Museum, Osaka

Morisot, Berthe Trustees of the National Gallery, London

Morland: (2) George Morland Syndics of the Fitzwilliam Museum, Cambridge

Mormons Press Office of the Church of Jesus Christ of the Latter-Day Saints, Birmingham

Morocco Photo: Nadia Erzini

Moroni, Andrea Museo Civico, Padua

Moroni, Giovanni Battista *1* Trustees of the National Gallery, London; *2* Photo: Bridgeman Art Library, London

Morrice, James Wilson National Gallery of Canada, Ottawa

Morris, William *1–2, 4* William Morris Gallery, London; *3* Board of Trustees of the Victoria and Albert Museum, London

Morse, Samuel F. B. Photo: Terra Foundation for the Arts (Daniel J. Terra Collection)

Mortensen, Richard Statens Museum for Kunst, Copenhagen

Mortimer, John Hamilton Board of Trustees of the Victoria and Albert Museum, London

Mosaic *1* Photo: Gabinetto Fotografico Nazionale, Istituto Centrale per il Catalogo e la Documentazione, Rome; *2* Photo: Hirmer Fotoarchiv, Munich; *3* Photo: Scala, Florence; *4, 8* Photo: Ampliaciones y Reproducciones MAS, Barcelona; *5* Vatican Museums, Vatican City, Rome; *6* Soprintendenza per i Beni Ambientali e Architettonici di Ravenna; *7* Photo: Anthony Kersting, London

Mosca Padovano, Giovanni Maria Institute for Art PAN, Prague (neg. 154085)/Photo: Jerzy Langda

Moscow *1–2, 10–11, 13* Photo: Vsevolod Vygolov; *3–4, 7–8* Photo: NOVOSTI Photo Library, London; *5–6, 9* David King Collection, London; *12* Photo: VAAP, Moscow

Moser (ii): (2) Karl Moser *3* Photo: Heidi Naef

Moser, Lukas Photo: Bildarchiv Foto Marburg

Mosque *1* Photo: Anthony Kersting, London; *2* Photo: Bernard O'Kane; *3* Photo: W. Denny

Mossi *1–2* Photo: Christopher D. Roy

Mostaert: (1) Jan Mostaert Photo: © ACL Brussels

Mother-of-pearl Metropolitan Museum of Art, New York (Gift of Mr and Mrs Leopold Blumka, 1969; no. 69.226)

Motherwell, Robert National Gallery of Art, Washington, DC (Gift of the Collectors' Committee)/© ARS, New York, and DACS, London, 1996

Moucheron, de: (2) Isaac de Moucheron Historisch Museum, Amsterdam/Stedelijk Museum, Amsterdam

Mount, William Sidney New-York Historical Society, New York

Mt Athos *1–2* Photo: Alexandria Press, London

Mt Fuji Trustees of the British Museum, London

Mounting *1–2, 4* Trustees of the British Museum, London; *3* Bildarchiv, Österreichische Nationalbibliothek, Vienna

Mozambique Photo: Centro de Formacão Fotografica, Maputo

Boulder, CO (no. 10342); *47* University of Colorado Museum, Boulder, CO (no. 23487); *48* Photo: Rick Riewe; *49* Canadian Museum of Civilization, Hull, Québec (no. 74-19035); *50* Wheelwright Museum of the American Indian, Santa Fe, NM (no. 60/802); *51* British Library, London (no. YV1989.b.2564); *52* McCord Museum, Montreal; *56* School of American Research, Santa Fe, NM (cat. no. M.431); *57* Manitoba Museum of Man and Nature, Winnipeg; *58* Maryhill Museum of Art, Goldendale, WA/Photo: Mrs Fanny van Duyn, Tygh Valley, OR; *59* Canadian Museum of Civilization, Hull, Québec (no. 74-121); *60* Canadian Museum of Civilization, Hull, Québec (no. 74-7048); *62* Dean and Chapter of Canterbury; *63* British Library, London (no. 1785.b.18); *64* Rochester Museum and Science Centre, Rochester, NY; *65* Field Museum of Natural History, Chicago, IL (neg. no. 16319); *66* Phoebe A. Hearst Museum of Anthropology, University of California, Berkeley, CA; *67* Photo: Marvin Cohodas; *68* Peabody Museum, Harvard University, Cambridge, MA/Photo: David Deharport; *69* Staatliche Schlösser und Gärten, Wörlitz; *70* Fowler Museum of Cultural History, UCLA, Los Angeles, CA; *71* Collection of Indian Art Centre, Department of Indian Affairs and Northern Development, Canada/Photo: Lawrence Cook; *72* Natural History Museum of Los Angeles County, Los Angeles, CA (Lost and Found Traditions Collection)/Photo: Bobby Hansson; *73* St Louis Art Museum, St Louis, MO (Purchase: Eliza McMillan Fund)

Nativity group Bayerisches Nationalmuseum, Munich

Natoire, Charles-Joseph Archives Nationales, Paris

Nattier: (2) Jean-Marc Nattier Photo: © RMN, Paris

Naturalism Museum of Art, Columbus, OH (Bequest of Janet French Houston)

Naukratis Trustees of the British Museum, London

Naumburg *1* Domstift Naumburg; *2* Photo: Bildarchiv Foto Marburg

Navarrete, Juan Fernández de National Gallery of Ireland, Dublin

Navez, François-Joseph Musées Royaux des Beaux-Arts de Belgique, Brussels

Naxos *1* Athens Archaeological Society, Athens; *2* Deutsches Archäologisches Institut, Athens

Nay, Ernst Wilhelm Indiana University Art Museum, Bloomington, IN (Gift of James S. Adams)/Photo: Dr Salchow

Nazareth Photo: Conway Library, Courtauld Institute of Art, London

Nazca *1* Museo Nacional de Antropología y Arqueología, Lima/Photo: R.T. Zuidema; *2* Servicio Aerofotográfico Nacional, Lima

Nazism Photo: AKG Ltd, London

Ndebele Photo: Dr Elizabeth Ann Schneider

Neer: (2) Eglon van der Neer Mauritshuis, The Hague

Nefertiti Staatliche Museen zu Berlin, Preussischer Kulturbesitz

Nègre, Charles National Gallery of Canada, Ottawa

Nemrut Dağ Werner Forman Archive, London/Photo: Edgar Knobloch

Neo-Attic Photo: Archivi Alinari, Florence

Neo-classicism *1* Photo: Giraudon, Paris; *2* Photo: Archivi Alinari, Florence; *3* Photo: RCHME/© Crown Copyright; *4* Photo: Conway Library, Courtauld Institute of Art, London

Neo-Impressionism Metropolitan Museum of Art, New York (Bequest of Stephen C. Clark, 1960; no. 61.101.17)

Neon Musée National d'Art Moderne, Paris/© ADAGP, Paris, and DACS, London, 1996

Neo-plasticism Museum Boymans–van Beuningen, Rotterdam

Neo-Romanticism British Council, London

Nepal *2, 4, 11–12, 14–15, 18, 30* Photo: Mary Shepherd Slusser; *3* Photo: Prof. Theodore Riccardi jr; *6* Hutchison Library, London; *8–9* Photo: Adalbert J. Gail; *10* Photo: Robert Harding Picture Library, London; *13* Los Angeles County Museum of Art, Los Angeles, CA (Nasli and Alice Heeramaneck Collection, Museum Associates Purchase); *16* Los Angeles County Museum of Art, Los Angeles, CA (Gift of the Ahmanson Foundation); *17* Metropolitan Museum of Art, New York (Louis V. Bell Fund, 1966; no. 66.179); *19* Freer Gallery of Art, Smithsonian Institution, Washington, DC; *20, 28* Photo: T.P.B. Riley-Smith; *21* Photo: Thomas J. Pritzker, Chicago; *22* Photo: Doris Viennaer, Inc.; *23* Los Angeles County Museum of Art, Los Angeles, CA (Nasli and Alice Heeramaneck Collection, purchased with funds provided by the Jane and Justin Dart Foundation); *24* Photo: Anne Vergati; *25* Photo: Erberto F. Lo Bue; *26* Los Angeles County Museum of Art, Los Angeles, CA (Gift of Mrs F. Daniel Frost); *27* Photo: Eric Chazot; *29* Photo: Susi Dunsmore; *31* Photo: Judith Chase

Neri di Bicci *1* National Gallery of Canada, Ottawa; *2* Photo: Archivi Alinari, Florence; *3* Photo: Scala, Florence

Nervi, Pier Luigi Photo: Archivi Alinari, Florence

Nesfield: (2) W. E. Nesfield Photo: Anthony Kersting, London

Nestorianism Photo: © RMN, Paris

Netherlands, the *2* Photo: Guy Van Grinsven; *3–4, 6–9* Rijksdienst voor de Monumentenzorg, Zeist; *5, 27* Gemeente Archiefdienst, Utrecht; *10, 16, 18–19, 21–2, 28, 30, 35, 39–41, 48–53, 55, 61, 63–4* Rijksmuseum, Amsterdam; *11* Photo: Dienst Publieke Werkes, Amsterdam; *12* Kunsthistorisch Institute, Rijksuniversiteit, Groningen; *13* Art Archive of the Calouste Gulbenkian Foundation, Lisbon; *14* Photo: Bridgeman Art Library, London; *15* Uppsala University; *17* Statens Konstmuseer, Stockholm; *20* Gemäldegalerie der Akademie der Bildenden Künste, Vienna; *23, 37, 44* Stedelijk Museum, Amsterdam; *24* Museum Boymans–van Beuningen, Rotterdam/© ADAGP, Paris, and DACS, London, 1996; *25* Museum Boymans–van Beuningen, Rotterdam/© DACS, 1996; *26* Haags Gemeentemuseum, The Hague/© DACS, 1996; *29* Photo: Museum für Kunst und Gewerbe, Hamburg; *31* Photo: Dr Y. Koopmans; *32* Photo: Peter Cox/© DACS, 1996; *33* Photo: © RMN, Paris; *34* Musée d'Art et d'Histoire de la Ville de Genève, Geneva; *36* Rijksmuseum Paleis Het Loo, Apeldoorn; *38, 43, 54* Haags Gemeentemuseum, The Hague; *42* Vrije Universiteit, Amsterdam; *45* Photo: PASTOE, Utrecht; *46–7* Museum Het Princessehof, Leeuwarden; *56* Photo: Foto Dikken and Hulsinga; *57–8* Photo: Annelies Krekel-Aalberse; *59* Museum Boymans–van Beuningen, Rotterdam; *60* Board of Trustees of the Victoria and Albert Museum, London; *62* © Stichting Beeldrecht, Amsterdam/Photo: Rien Basen

Netscher, Caspar Photo: Staatliche Kunstsammlungen Dresden

Neuburg an der Donau Photo: Bildarchiv Foto Marburg

Neuchâtel Service Cantonal des Monuments et des Sites, Neuchâtel

Neue Sachlichkeit Galerie der Stadt Stuttgart/© DACS, 1996

Neufchatel, Nicolas Bayerische Staatsgemäldesammlungen, Munich